TEACHER'S EDITION

# myPerspectives™

## AMERICAN LITERATURE

Pearson

NEW YORK, NEW YORK • BOSTON, MASSACHUSETTS
CHANDLER, ARIZONA • GLENVIEW, ILLINOIS

Photo locators denoted as follows: Top (T), Center (C), Bottom (B), Left (L), Right (R), Background (Bkgd)

COVER: © niroworld/Fotolia, (Bkgd) ©Brandon Bourdages/123RF T3: londoneye/Getty Images; T5B: PathDoc/Shutterstock; T5B: Franck Boston/Shutterstock; T19: Victoria Kisel/Shutterstock; T20: karandaev/fotolia; T23: Jojje/Shutterstock; T25: Nikada/Getty Images; T26B: Creativa Images/Shutterstock; T32: Monkey Business Images/Shutterstock; T33B: Hocus Focus Studio/Getty Images; T34: artagent/Fotolia; T4: Artishok/Shutterstock; T5B: Derek Latta/E+/Getty Images; T5B: OJO Images Ltd/Alamy

Acknowledgments of third-party content appear on page R81, which constitutes an extension of this copyright page.

---



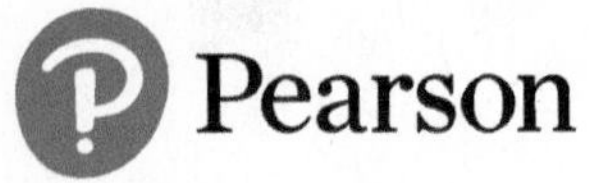


ISBN-13: 978-0-13-333870-6
ISBN-10: 0-13-333870-3
7 17

# Welcome!

*my*Perspectives™ *English Language Arts* is a student-centered learning environment where you will analyze text, cite evidence, and respond critically about your learning. You will take ownership of your learning through goal-setting, reflection, independent text selection, and activities that allow you to collaborate with your peers.

Each unit of study includes selections of different genres—including multimedia—all related to a relevant and meaningful Essential Question. As you read, you will engage in activities that inspire thoughtful discussion and debate with your peers allowing you to formulate, and defend, your own perspectives.

*my*Perspectives *ELA* offers a variety of ways to interact directly with the text. You can annotate by writing in your print consumable, or you can annotate in your digital Student Edition. In addition, exciting technology allows you to access multimedia directly from your mobile device and communicate using an online discussion board!

We hope you enjoy using *my*Perspectives *ELA* as you develop the skills required to be successful throughout college and career.

# Authors' Perspectives

*my*Perspectives is informed by a team of respected experts whose experiences working with students and study of instructional best practices have positively impacted education. From the evolving role of the teacher to how students learn in a digital age, our authors bring new ideas, innovations, and strategies that transform teaching and learning in today's competitive and interconnected world.

"The teaching of English needs to focus on engaging a new generation of learners. How do we get them excited about reading and writing? How do we help them to envision themselves as readers and writers? And, how can we make the teaching of English more culturally, socially, and technologically relevant? Throughout the curriculum, we've created spaces that enhance youth voice and participation and that connect the teaching of literature and writing to technological transformations of the digital age."

## Ernest Morrell, Ph.D.

is the Macy professor of English Education at Teachers College, Columbia University, a class of 2014 Fellow of the American Educational Research Association, and the Past-President of the National Council of Teachers of English (NCTE). He is also the Director of Teachers College's Institute for Urban and Minority Education (IUME). He is an award-winning author and in his spare time he coaches youth sports and writes poems and plays. Dr. Morrell has influenced the development of *my*Perspectives in Assessment, Writing & Research, Student Engagement, and Collaborative Learning.

## Elfrieda Hiebert, Ph.D.

is President and CEO of TextProject, a nonprofit that provides resources to support higher reading levels. She is also a research associate at the University of California, Santa Cruz. Dr. Hiebert has worked in the field of early reading acquisition for 45 years, first as a teacher's aide and teacher of primary-level students in California and, subsequently, as a teacher and researcher. Her research addresses how fluency, vocabulary, and knowledge can be fostered through appropriate texts. Dr. Hiebert has influenced the development of *my*Perspectives in Vocabulary, Text Complexity, and Assessment.

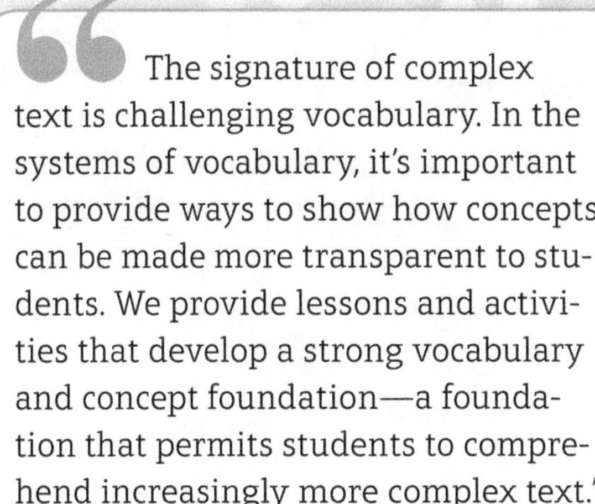

"The signature of complex text is challenging vocabulary. In the systems of vocabulary, it's important to provide ways to show how concepts can be made more transparent to students. We provide lessons and activities that develop a strong vocabulary and concept foundation—a foundation that permits students to comprehend increasingly more complex text."

## Kelly Gallagher, M.Ed.

teaches at Magnolia High School in Anaheim, California, where he is in his thirty-first year. He is the former co-director of the South Basin Writing Project at California State University, Long Beach. Mr. Gallagher has influenced the development of *my*Perspectives in Writing, Close Reading, and the Role of Teachers.

"The *my*Perspectives classroom is dynamic. The teacher inspires, models, instructs, facilitates, and advises students as they evolve and grow. When teachers guide students through meaningful learning tasks and then pass them ownership of their own learning, students become engaged and work harder. This is how we make a difference in student achievement—by putting students at the center of their learning and giving them the opportunities to choose, explore, collaborate, and work independently."

"It's critical to give students the opportunity to read a wide range of highly engaging texts and to immerse themselves in exploring powerful ideas and how these ideas are expressed. In *my*Perspectives, we focus on building up students' awareness of how academic language works, which is especially important for English language learners."

## Jim Cummins, Ph.D.

is a Professor Emeritus in the Department of Curriculum, Teaching and Learning of the University of Toronto. His research focuses on literacy development in multilingual school contexts as well as on the potential roles of technology in promoting language and literacy development. In recent years, he has been working actively with teachers to identify ways of increasing the literacy engagement of learners in multilingual school contexts. Dr. Cummins has influenced the development of *my*Perspectives in English Language Learner and English Language Development support.

Each unit focuses on an engaging topic related to the Essential Question.

VOLUME ONE

# UNIT 1 Writing Freedom

## Words That Shaped a Nation



### UNIT INTRODUCTION



Teachers lead the shared reading experience, providing modeling and support, as students begin exploring perspectives on the unit topic.

###  WHOLE-CLASS LEARNING



### SMALL-GROUP LEARNING

An Essential Question frames all unit activities and discussions.

ESSENTIAL QUESTION: What is the meaning of freedom?

## INDEPENDENT LEARNING



These selections can be accessed via the Interactive Student Edition.

## PERFORMANCE-BASED ASSESSMENT



All unit activities are backwards-designed to the Performance-Based Assessment.

## UNIT REFLECTION



## DIGITAL PERSPECTIVES

SCAN FOR MULTIMEDIA

Use the BouncePage app whenever you see "Scan for Multimedia" to access:

- Unit Introduction Videos
- Media Selections/Media Enrichment
- Modeling Videos
- Selection Audio Recordings

Additional digital resources can be found in:

- Interactive Student Edition
- *my*Perspectives+

VOLUME ONE

# UNIT 2 The Individual and Society

## Fitting In, or Standing Out?

The Launch Text introduces a perspective on the unit topic.

Teachers lead the shared reading experience, providing modeling and support, as students begin exploring perspectives on the unit topic.

Students encounter diverse perspectives on the unit topic, working in collaborative teams.

### UNIT INTRODUCTION



### WHOLE-CLASS LEARNING



### SMALL-GROUP LEARNING

ESSENTIAL QUESTION: What role does individualism play in American society?

Students self-select a text to explore an aspect of the unit topic and share their learning with the class.

## INDEPENDENT LEARNING



These selections can be accessed via the Interactive Student Edition.



## PERFORMANCE-BASED ASSESSMENT



## UNIT REFLECTION



## DIGITAL PERSPECTIVES

SCAN FOR MULTIMEDIA

Use the BouncePage app whenever you see "Scan for Multimedia" to access:

- Unit Introduction Videos
- Media Selections/Media Enrichments
- Modeling Videos
- Selection Audio Recordings

Additional digital resources can be found in:

- Interactive Student Edition
- *my*Perspectives+

VOLUME ONE

# UNIT  Power, Protest, and Change

## A Spirit of Reform

The Launch Text models the mode of writing that will be at the core of the Performance-Based Assessment.

Performance Tasks build toward and prepare students for the Unit Performance-Based Assessment.

### UNIT INTRODUCTION



### WHOLE-CLASS LEARNING



### SMALL-GROUP LEARNING

ESSENTIAL QUESTION: In what ways does the struggle for freedom change with history?

## INDEPENDENT LEARNING

POETRY COLLECTION 1

I, Too | The Negro Speaks of Rivers | Refugee in America | Dream Variations
*Langston Hughes*

POETRY COLLECTION 2

Douglass *Paul Laurence Dunbar*
The Fifth Fact *Sarah Browning*
Who Burns for the Perfection of Paper
*Martín Espada*

HISTORY

*from* The Warmth of Other Suns
*Isabel Wilkerson*

ESSAY

What a Factory Can Teach a Housewife
*Ida Tarbell*

PERSUASIVE ESSAY

*from* Books as Bombs *Louis Menand*

MEDIA: PODCAST

A Balance Between Nature and Nurture
*Gloria Steinem*

These selections can be accessed via the Interactive Student Edition.

PERFORMANCE-BASED ASSESSMENT PREP



## PERFORMANCE-BASED ASSESSMENT



## UNIT REFLECTION



## DIGITAL PERSPECTIVES

SCAN FOR MULTIMEDIA

Use the BouncePage app whenever you see "Scan for Multimedia" to access:

- Unit Introduction Videos
- Media Selections/Media Enrichment
- Modeling Videos
- Selection Audio Recordings

Additional digital resources can be found in:

- Interactive Student Edition
- *my*Perspectives+

Students pull together their notes, evidence, completed activities, and Performance Tasks to prepare for the Performance-Based Assessment.

VOLUME TWO

# UNIT  Grit and Grandeur

## The Importance of Place

### UNIT INTRODUCTION



### WHOLE-CLASS LEARNING



Comparing a text and media version of classic literature deepens the learning experience and develops critical skills.

### SMALL-GROUP LEARNING

ESSENTIAL QUESTION: What is the relationship between literature and place?

## INDEPENDENT LEARNING

SHORT STORY
**The Rockpile**
*James Baldwin*

POETRY
**The Latin Deli: An Ars Poetica**
*Judith Ortiz Cofer*

ESSAY
**Untying the Knot**
*Annie Dillard*

POETRY COLLECTION 3
**The Wood-Pile | Birches**
*Robert Frost*

These selections can be accessed via the Interactive Student Edition.

PERFORMANCE-BASED ASSESSMENT PREP



## PERFORMANCE-BASED ASSESSMENT



## UNIT REFLECTION



A rich array of media selections engage students in multi-modal learning.

## DIGITAL PERSPECTIVES

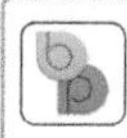


Use the BouncePage app whenever you see "Scan for Multimedia" to access:

- Unit Introduction Videos
- Media Selections/Media Enrichment
- Modeling Videos
- Selection Audio Recordings

Additional digital resources can be found in:

- Interactive Student Edition
- *my*Perspectives+

Access multimedia resources directly from print by using your mobile or tablet device.

Digital resources, including editable worksheets, can be found in *my*Perspectives+.

VOLUME TWO

# UNIT 5 Facing Our Fears

## Victims and Victors

Comparing classic literature to other media brings relevance and engagement to the classroom.

### UNIT INTRODUCTION



### WHOLE-CLASS LEARNING



### SMALL-GROUP LEARNING

ESSENTIAL QUESTION: How do we respond when challenged by fear?

## INDEPENDENT LEARNING



These selections can be accessed via the Interactive Student Edition.

PERFORMANCE-BASED ASSESSMENT PREP



## PERFORMANCE-BASED ASSESSMENT



## UNIT REFLECTION



Unit Reflection allows students to revisit learning goals and review skills and content learned.

## DIGITAL PERSPECTIVES

SCAN FOR MULTIMEDIA

Use the BouncePage app whenever you see "Scan for Multimedia" to access:

- Unit Introduction Videos
- Media Selections/Media Enrichment
- Modeling Videos
- Selection Audio Recordings

Additional digital resources can be found in:

- Interactive Student Edition
- *my*Perspectives+

VOLUME TWO

# UNIT  Ordinary Lives, Extraordinary Tales

## The American Short Story

### UNIT INTRODUCTION



### WHOLE-CLASS LEARNING



### SMALL-GROUP LEARNING

ESSENTIAL QUESTION: What do stories reveal about the human condition?

## INDEPENDENT LEARNING



These selections can be accessed via the Interactive Student Edition.

PERFORMANCE-BASED ASSESSMENT PREP

## PERFORMANCE-BASED ASSESSMENT



## UNIT REFLECTION



## DIGITAL PERSPECTIVES

Use the BouncePage app whenever you see "Scan for Multimedia" to access:

- Unit Introduction Videos
- Media Selections/Media Enrichment
- Modeling Videos
- Selection Audio Recordings

Additional digital resources can be found in:

- Interactive Student Edition
- *my*Perspectives+

# Student-Centered Learning

*my*Perspectives promotes student-centered learning through a unit organization that:

- gives students increasing responsibility for the learning process as they understand expectations, set goals, use self-assessment measures, and monitor and reflect on their learning.
- supports active learning in which students annotate texts, answer questions, pose questions of their own, and construct knowledge as they search for meaning.
- promotes social collaboration and interaction among learners in ways that strengthen positive interdependence and individual accountability.
- engages students in making choices in their learning and work they are producing.
- provides flexibility for teachers to manage resources to match learner needs.

## UNIT INTRODUCTION

- An open-ended Essential Question is posed to stimulate thoughtful student inquiry into the richness of a topic.
- The Launch Text, unit opener video, and discussion board engage students by provoking and generating interest in the unit topic.
- Unit goals link directly to the demands of the Performance-Based Assessment.

## WHOLE-CLASS LEARNING

- Teachers model, instruct, and support with anchor texts as the class broadens its perspective of the unit topic.
- Activities focus on making meaning, language development, and effective expression.
- Students develop and share their perspectives on the unit topic through writing in a targeted mode.

## SMALL-GROUP LEARNING

- Students work collaboratively to broaden their perspectives on the unit topic.
- Teachers facilitate and encourage collaboration as students work in groups.
- Students develop presentations, participate in group discussions and debates, and share their learning with the class in an array of speaking and listening activities.

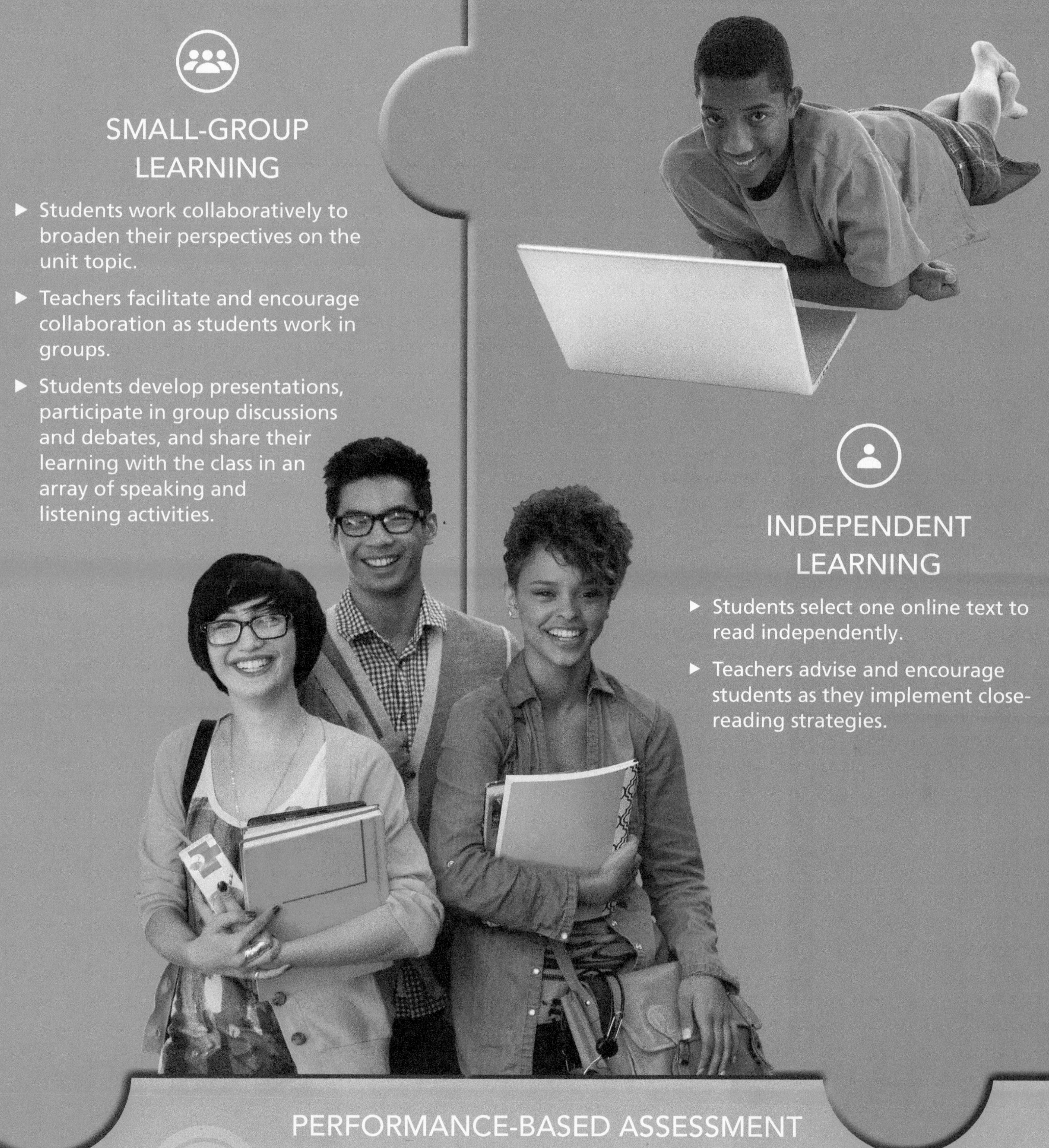

## INDEPENDENT LEARNING

- Students select one online text to read independently.
- Teachers advise and encourage students as they implement close-reading strategies.

## PERFORMANCE-BASED ASSESSMENT

Students are required to demonstrate their learning by pulling together the content knowledge, process skills, and learning habits they acquired, practiced, and engaged in throughout the unit.

# Interactive Student Edition

Whether your students use the print or digital version, the Student Edition is interactive!

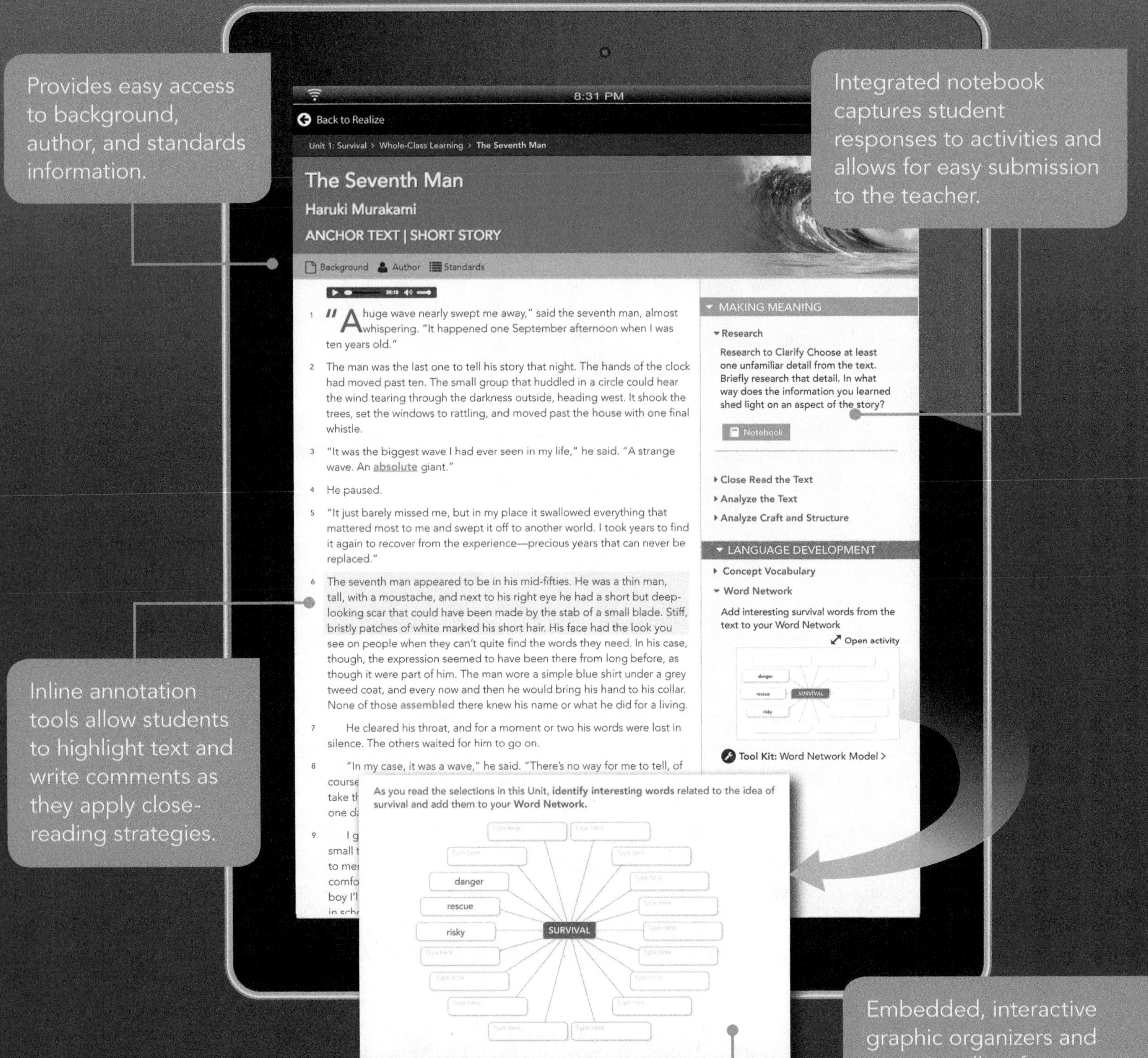


Provides easy access to background, author, and standards information.

Integrated notebook captures student responses to activities and allows for easy submission to the teacher.

Inline annotation tools allow students to highlight text and write comments as they apply close-reading strategies.

Embedded, interactive graphic organizers and activities allow for interaction at point-of-use.

Download the Pearson BouncePages App to access audio, video, and multimedia selections through your mobile device!

MAKING MEANING

**About the Author**

In 1978, **Haruki Murakami** (b. 1949) was attending a baseball game in Japan where the American player Dave Hilton hit a double. In that moment, Murakami had a flash of inspiration during which he decided he could write a novel. He began writing that evening. Since then, his numerous novels and short stories have been translated more than the works of any other Japanese writer of his generation.

**Tool Kit**
First-Read Guide and Model Annotation

**STANDARDS**
Reading Literature
By the end of grade 9, read and comprehend literature, including stories, dramas, and poems, in the grades 9–10 text complexity band proficiently, with scaffolding as needed at the high end of the range.

## The Seventh Man

### Concept Vocabulary

You will encounter the following words as you read "The Seventh Man." Before reading, note how familiar you are with each word. Then, rank the words in order from most familiar (1) to least familiar (6).

| WORD | YOUR RANKING |
|---|---|
| desperate | 1 |
| entranced | 4 |
| hallucination | 2 |
| premonition | 3 |
| profound | 5 |
| meditative | 6 |

After completing the first read, come back to the concept vocabulary and review your rankings. Mark changes to your original rankings as needed.

### First Read FICTION

Apply these strategies as you conduct your first read. You will have an opportunity to complete the close-read notes after your first read.

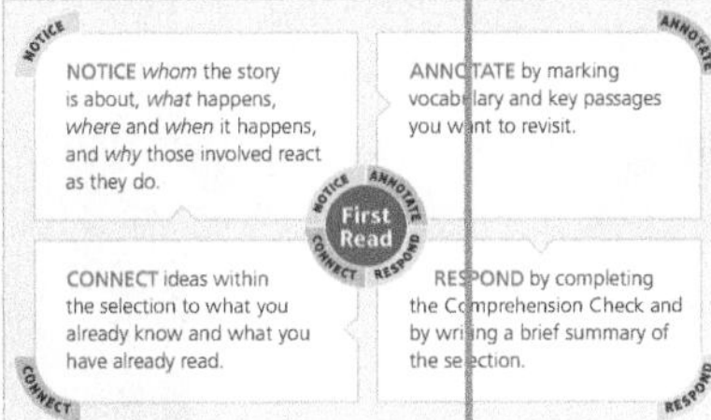

NOTICE
NOTICE *whom* the story is about, *what* happens, *where* and *when* it happens, and *why* those involved react as they do.
ANNOTATE
ANNOTATE by marking vocabulary and key passages you want to revisit.
First Read
CONNECT ideas within the selection to what you already know and what you have already read.
CONNECT
RESPOND by completing the Comprehension Check and by writing a brief summary of the selection.
RESPOND








ANCHOR TEXT | SHORT STORY

# The Seventh Man

Haruki Murakami

BACKGROUND
Hurricanes that originate in the northwest Pacific Ocean are called typhoons. They can stretch up to 500 miles in diameter and produce high winds, heavy rains, enormous waves, and severe flooding. On average, Japan is hit by three severe typhoons each year due to its location and climatic conditions.

SCAN FOR MULTIMEDIA

1 "A huge wave nearly swept me away," said the seventh man, almost whispering. "It happened one September afternoon when I was ten years old."

2 The man was the last one to tell his story that night. The hands of the clock had moved past ten. The small group that huddled in a circle could hear the wind tearing through the darkness outside, heading west. It shook the trees, set the windows to rattling, and moved past the house with one final whistle.

3 "It was the biggest wave I had ever seen in my life," he said. "A strange wave. An absolute giant."

4 He paused.

5 "It just barely missed me, but in my place it swallowed everything that mattered most to me and swept it off to another world. I took years to find it again and to recover from the experience—precious years that can never be replaced."

6 The seventh man appeared to be in his mid-fifties. He was a thin man, tall, with a moustache, and next to his right eye he had a short but deep-looking scar that could have been made by the stab of a small blade. Stiff, bristly patches of white marked his short hair. His face had the look you see on people when they can't quite find the words they need. In his case, though, the expression seemed to have

NOTES

**CLOSE READ**
ANNOTATE: Mark details in paragraph 2 that describe where the action takes place.

QUESTION: What can you tell about the story's setting?

The mood was very dark and dreary. There was a sense of doom.



A write-in Student Edition allows students to annotate the text and respond to questions.

# Close-Reading Routine

*myPerspectives* motivates students to read a text thoughtfully, apply strategies as they read, and critically examine the text.

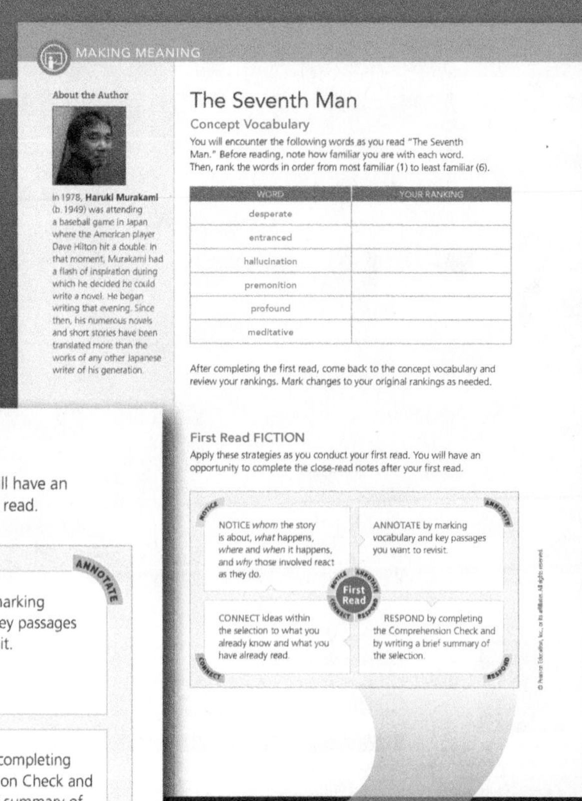


Students apply first-read routines as they independently read and annotate texts.

MAKING MEANING

THE SEVENTH MAN

## Close Read the Text

1. The model, from paragraph 5 of the story, shows two sample annotations, along with questions and conclusions. Close read the passage, and find another detail to annotate. Then, write a question and your conclusion.

Close Read — ANNOTATE · QUESTION · CONCLUDE

ANNOTATE: This phrase describes the wave in almost human terms.

QUESTION: What effect does this word choice create?

CONCLUDE: This description makes the wave seem alive and evil.

"It just barely missed me, but in my place it swallowed everything that mattered most to me and swept it off to another world. I took years to find it again and to recover from the experience—precious years that can never be replaced."

ANNOTATE: This word is repeated.

QUESTION: Why does the author repeat the word *years*?

CONCLUDE: The repetition emphasizes how long it takes the man to recover from the experience.

Models show students how to close read the text.

Students close read complex and rich text passages, studying structures, diction, and other elements of author's craft.

not seem to have reached him. He might have been so absorbed in whatever it was he had found that my call made no impression on him. K. was like that. He would get involved with things to the point of forgetting everything else. Or possibly I had not yelled as loudly as I had thought. I do recall that my voice sounded strange to me, as though it belonged to someone else.

29 Then I heard a deep rumbling sound. It seemed to shake the earth.

NOTES

CLOSE READ

**ANNOTATE:** In paragraph 27, mark the details the author uses to describe the waves.

**QUESTION:** Why does the author include so many contrasting descriptions?

**CONCLUDE:** In what ways is the author preparing you for what comes next?

Closer Look notes, found only in the Teacher's Edition, provide additional close-reading opportunities.

Digital Annotation Highlights focus on passages in the Interactive Teacher's Edition.

## TEACHING

### CLOSER LOOK

#### Analyze Character

Students may have marked paragraph 10 during their first read. Use this paragraph to help students understand the seventh man's friendship with K.

**ANNOTATE:** Have students mark details in the paragraph that describe K.'s appearance and personality.

**QUESTION:** What overall impression does the author create of K.? How does the author characterize the relationship between K. and the seventh man?

**Possible response:** K. is an artistic, sensitive boy who is often picked on because he is physically different from most boys his age. His speech impediment and difficulty with academics lead most people to think something is wrong with him. K. and the seventh man are best friends. The seventh man feels protective of K., and often stands up for him when he is picked on by others.

**CONCLUDE:** How does the author's characterization of K. and his friendship with the seventh man help you understand the impact of K.'s death?

**Possible response:** The seventh man viewed himself as K.'s protector. When K. was lost to the wave the seventh man lost his best friend, and he blamed himself for failing to protect K., carrying that guilt with him for most of his life.

Remind students that there are two types of characterization. In **direct characterization**, ... a character's traits. ...**ion**, an author ...racter by describing ...e, does, and says, as ...ers react to him or ...o draw conclusions

NOTES

Unit 2: Survival > **Whole-Class Learning: The Seventh Man**

36:18

1 "A huge wave nearly swept me away," said the seventh man, almost whispering. "It happened one September afternoon when I was ten years old."

2 The man was the last one to tell his story that night. ***The hands of the clock had moved past ten.*** The small group that huddled in a circle could hear ***the wind tearing through the darkness outside***, heading west. It shook the trees, set the windows to rattling, and moved past the house with one final whistle.

3 "It was the biggest wave I had ever seen in my life," he said. "A strange wave. An absolute giant."

4 He paused.

5 "It just barely missed me, but in my place it swallowed everything that mattered most to me and swept it off to another world. I took years to find it again and to recover from the experience–precious years that can never be replaced."

6 The seventh man appeared to be in his mid-fifties. He was a thin man, tall, with a moustache, and next to his right eye he had a short but deep-looking scar that could have been made by the stab of a small blade. Stiff, bristly patches of white marked his short

looks like, feels like, or sounds like. You may wish to model the close read using the following think-aloud format. Possible responses to questions on the student page are included. You may also want to print copies of the Close-Read Guide for students to use.

**ANNOTATE:** As I read paragraph 2, I notice and highlight the details *the hands of the clock had moved past ten* and *the wind tearing through the darkness outside*. These details suggest to me that the story is set at night during a storm.

Hide Annotation Highlights

# Building Literacy

For each selection, students **Make Meaning** through first- and close-read routines and by analyzing author's craft and structure. Students also complete **Language Development** activities with concept vocabulary and conventions practice tasks. **Effective Expression** activities provide students with opportunities to share their learning through written and oral projects.

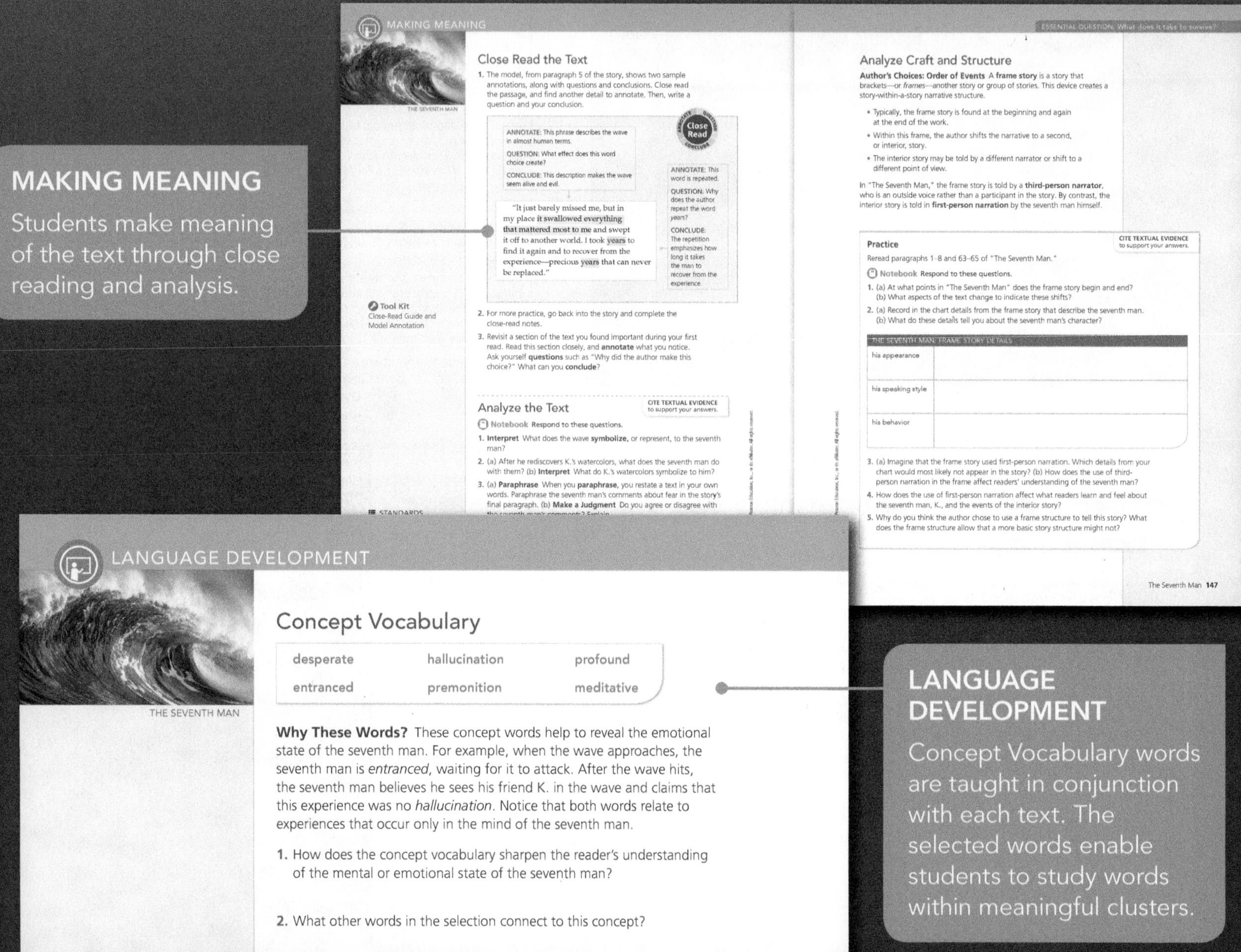

MAKING MEANING

THE SEVENTH MAN

## Close Read the Text

1. The model, from paragraph 5 of the story, shows two sample annotations, along with questions and conclusions. Close read the passage, and find another detail to annotate. Then, write a question and your conclusion.

ANNOTATE: This phrase describes the wave in almost human terms.

QUESTION: What effect does this word choice create?

CONCLUDE: This description makes the wave seem alive and evil.

"It just barely missed me, but in my place **it swallowed everything that mattered most to me** and swept it off to another world. I took **years** to find it again and to recover from the experience—precious **years** that can never be replaced."

ANNOTATE: This word is repeated.

QUESTION: Why does the author repeat the word *years*?

CONCLUDE: The repetition emphasizes how long it takes the man to recover from the experience.

Tool Kit
Close-Read Guide and Model Annotation

2. For more practice, go back into the story and complete the close-read notes.
3. Revisit a section of the text you found important during your first read. Read this section closely, and **annotate** what you notice. Ask yourself **questions** such as "Why did the author make this choice?" What can you **conclude**?

## Analyze the Text

CITE TEXTUAL EVIDENCE to support your answers.

Notebook Respond to these questions.

1. **Interpret** What does the wave **symbolize,** or represent, to the seventh man?
2. (a) After he rediscovers K.'s watercolors, what does the seventh man do with them? (b) **Interpret** What do K.'s watercolors symbolize to him?
3. (a) **Paraphrase** When you **paraphrase,** you restate a text in your own words. Paraphrase the seventh man's comments about fear in the story's final paragraph. (b) **Make a Judgment** Do you agree or disagree with the seventh man's comments? Explain.

STANDARDS

ESSENTIAL QUESTION: What does it take to survive?

## Analyze Craft and Structure

**Author's Choices: Order of Events** A **frame story** is a story that brackets—or *frames*—another story or group of stories. This device creates a story-within-a-story narrative structure.

- Typically, the frame story is found at the beginning and again at the end of the work.
- Within this frame, the author shifts the narrative to a second, or interior, story.
- The interior story may be told by a different narrator or shift to a different point of view.

In "The Seventh Man," the frame story is told by a **third-person narrator**, who is an outside voice rather than a participant in the story. By contrast, the interior story is told in **first-person narration** by the seventh man himself.

### Practice

CITE TEXTUAL EVIDENCE to support your answers.

Reread paragraphs 1–8 and 63–65 of "The Seventh Man."

Notebook Respond to these questions.

1. (a) At what points in "The Seventh Man" does the frame story begin and end? (b) What aspects of the text change to indicate these shifts?
2. (a) Record in the chart details from the frame story that describe the seventh man. (b) What do these details tell you about the seventh man's character?

| THE SEVENTH MAN: FRAME STORY DETAILS | |
|---|---|
| his appearance | |
| his speaking style | |
| his behavior | |

3. (a) Imagine that the frame story used first-person narration. Which details from your chart would most likely not appear in the story? (b) How does the use of third-person narration in the frame affect readers' understanding of the seventh man?
4. How does the use of first-person narration affect what readers learn and feel about the seventh man, K., and the events of the interior story?
5. Why do you think the author chose to use a frame structure to tell this story? What does the frame structure allow that a more basic story structure might not?

The Seventh Man 147

LANGUAGE DEVELOPMENT

THE SEVENTH MAN

## Concept Vocabulary

| desperate | hallucination | profound |
|---|---|---|
| entranced | premonition | meditative |

**Why These Words?** These concept words help to reveal the emotional state of the seventh man. For example, when the wave approaches, the seventh man is *entranced*, waiting for it to attack. After the wave hits, the seventh man believes he sees his friend K. in the wave and claims that this experience was no *hallucination*. Notice that both words relate to experiences that occur only in the mind of the seventh man.

1. How does the concept vocabulary sharpen the reader's understanding of the mental or emotional state of the seventh man?
2. What other words in the selection connect to this concept?

**MAKING MEANING**

Students make meaning of the text through close reading and analysis.

**LANGUAGE DEVELOPMENT**

Concept Vocabulary words are taught in conjunction with each text. The selected words enable students to study words within meaningful clusters.

EFFECTIVE EXPRESSION
THE SEVENTH MAN
Writing to Sources
Critical writing is a type of argumentation in which you explain your insights about a literary work and persuade others to share your point of view. Like any argument, critical writing requires you to state a claim, or position, and to support it with strong evidence.
Assignment
Write a critical review of "The Seventh Man" that could appear in your school paper or website. State specific reasons why you either recommend or do not recommend the story to other readers.
Your review should include:
Title and author of the work being reviewed
A brief summary of the work
STANDARDS
150 UNIT 2 • SURVIVAL
ESSENTIAL QUESTION: What does it take to survive?
Speaking and Listening
Assignment
With a partner, prepare a retelling of "The Seventh Man" from another point of view. For example, you may choose to retell the story from K.'s parents' point of view, or from that of a hidden onlooker. Refresh your memory by rereading the selection. Then, follow these steps to complete the assignment.
1. Identify Your Character Choose your character and determine how he or she fits into the original story. Decide what important information you will need to tell your audience to clarify the character's background and motivations.
2. Plan Your Retelling Once you've identified your character, think about his or her perspective on the events in the story. As you plan your retelling, keep the following in mind:
How does your character see the story differently from the seventh man? What fresh perspective does he or she offer?
Make a list of the story events, as experienced by your character. Then, weave those events into a coherent retelling.
Choose language that is appropriate to the character you chose. For example, a child would choose simple words and sentences and may not fully understand what is he or she is observing.
3. Prepare Your Delivery Practice your retelling with your partner. Include the following performance techniques to help you achieve the desired effect.
Vary your intonation to reflect the emotions of your character. Avoid speaking in a flat, monotone style.
As you speak, use facial expressions and gestures that help convey your character's personality.
Make eye contact with your audience to engage them in the story.
4. Evaluate Retellings As your classmates deliver their retellings, listen attentively. Use an evaluation guide like the one shown to analyze their delivery.
EVALUATION GUIDE
EVIDENCE LOG


## EFFECTIVE EXPRESSION

Students are provided with frequent opportunities to practice writing within the unit's focus mode.

Throughout the unit, students participate in speaking and listening, writing, and research activities that enable them to share learning.

# Assessments to Inform Instruction

## YEAR-LONG ASSESSMENT

### Beginning-of-Year Test

- Tests all standards that will be taught in the school year.
- Allows you to use test data to plan which standards need focus.

### Mid-Year Test

- Tests mastery of standards taught in the first half of the year.
- Provides an opportunity to remediate; if administered online, remediation is assigned automatically.

### End-of-Year Test

- Allows you to use results to determine mastery of standards, place students in classes for the following school year, and to capture final assessment data.

## UNIT-LEVEL ASSESSMENT

### Selection Activities

- Instructional activities can be used to assess students' grasp of critical concepts.

### Formative Assessments

- Selection activities can be used as formative checks.
- Notes in the Teacher's Edition offer suggestions for reteaching.

### Selection Tests

- Test items track student progress toward mastering standards taught with the selection.

### Performance Tasks

- Each unit includes both a writing and a speaking and listening performance task.
- Performance Tasks prepare students for success on the end-of-unit Performance-Based Assessment.

### Unit Tests

- Students apply standards taught in the unit with new texts.
- These tests provide an opportunity to remediate; if administered online, remediation is assigned automatically.

### Performance-Based Assessments

- All unit activities are backwards-mapped to the end-of-unit Performance-Based Assessment.
- Students use their notes, knowledge, and skills learned to complete a project.

Technology-enhanced items allow students to experience next-generation assessment formats.

# Personalize for Learning

The Teacher's Edition provides support before, during, and after each selection to help you personalize learning for your students.

A continuous improvement loop is built in to help teachers perform formative assessment and remediation.

A full range of reading supports is provided for each text, based on text complexity rubrics.

PERSONALIZE FOR LEARNING WHOL

## Reading Support

| Text Complexity Rubric: The Seventh Man | |
|---|---|
| **Quantitative Measures** | |
| **Lexile:** 910 **Text Length:** 5,860 words | |
| **Qualitative Measures** | |
| Knowledge Demands ①—❷—③—④—⑤ | Life experience demands: The situations may be unfamiliar to some readers (experiencing a typhoon, tragedy of losing someone in a natural disaster), but the situations and emotions are clearly explained. |
| Structure ①—❷—③—④—⑤ | Use of flash-back, flash-forward (transitions from narration in third person and the seventh man's story told in first person) |
| Language Conventionality and Clarity ①—②—❸—④—⑤ | Figurative language; complex descriptions |
| Levels of Meaning/Purpose ①—②—❸—④—⑤ | Multiple levels of meaning (events are described that also signify emotions of guilt or of self-forgiveness); concepts and meanings are mostly explained and easy to grasp. |

DECIDE AND PLAN

### English Language Support

Provide English Learners with support for context and vocabulary as they read the selection. **PI.8; PI.12**

**Knowledge Demands** Tell students that this short story is about an event that occurred during a typhoon. They should expect to see language that describes weather and the sea. (high tide, low tide,...)

**Language Conventiality and Clarity** Students may find the use of sensory language difficult to grasp. Explain that the author often uses words in a figurative way to create feelings or sensations. Figurative language is language that is used imaginatively rather than literally. Such expressions can be difficult for second-language learners.

### Strategic Support

Provide students with strategic support to ensure that they can successfully read the text.

**Knowledge Demands** Use the background information to discuss typhoons. Determine students' prior knowledge and experience with natural disasters. Provide additional background if needed.

**Structure** Discuss what it means to flash-back or flash-forward in a text. Point out that a story might switch back and forth to different time periods. If students continue to have difficulty with the time sequence, point out clues to transitions between past and present; for example, sentences that say that the man is telling a story, or use of first and third person. When students reread, have them note each transition from past to present.

### Challenge

Provide students who need to be challenged with ideas for how they can go beyond a simple interpretation of the text.

**Text Analysis** For students that grasp the time transitions, have them identify the use of first person when the seventh man is speaking, and descriptions in third person when the story moves to the present.

**Written Response** Ask students to speculate on what might have happened if the seventh man had made different choices in his life. Have them analyze each choice he made and determine how his life might have differed if he had chosen differently. Have them rewrite the story with reflection the choices.

TEACH

### Read and Respond

Have the class do their first read of the selection. Then have them complete their close read. Finally, work with them on the Making Meaning, Language Development, and Effective Expression activities.

98C

Text complexity rubrics provide targeted suggestions for learner levels, including English Language supports that are based on the demands of the text.

## Standards Support Through Te

**IDENTIFY NEEDS**

Analyze results of the Beginning-of-Year Assessment, focusing on the items relating to Unit 2. Also take into consideration student performance to this point and your observations of where particular students struggle.

**ANALYZE AND REVISE**

- Analyze student work for evidence of student learning.
- Identify whether or not students have met the expectations in the standards.
- Identify implications for future instruction.

**TEACH**

Implement the planned lesson, and gather evidence of student learning.

- If students have perfo scaffolds before assigr
- If students have done keep progressing and
- Use the Selection Resc students continually ir

| Instructional Standar | |
|---|---|
| | Catching Up |
| Reading | Review conte students to e understand t have differen different con<br>You may wish the Order of to help stude the basic seq narrative. |
| Writing | You may wish the Reteach a Anecdotes w students und anecdote can an argument. |
| Speaking and Listening | You may wish the Reteach a worksheet or help students to plan and r excerpt. |
| Language | You may wish the Clauses v help students function of c<br>Review conte students to e understand t have differen different con |

PERSONALIZE FOR LEARNING

**Challenge**
Encourage interested students to expand the Research to Explore activity by learning about the motto of other branches of the U.S. military, including the Air Force, Army, Coast Guard, and Navy, in addition to the Marines. Students can also branch and present their results in a poster

PERSONALIZE FOR LEARNING

**English Language Support**
**Idioms** Explain to students that *eye of the storm* in paragraph 15 is an idiomatic expression—the words used are not meant literally. If students struggle to understand idioms, encourage them to look for context clues. Instruct students to keep reading to get clues about the meaning of this expression (*No such "eye" existed, of course: we were just in that momentary quiet spot at the center of the pool of whirling air*). Make sure students understand that eye of the storm means "a calm in the middle of a turbulent situation. **ALL LEVELS**

English Language Support notes provide support for skills and concepts such as idioms, figurative language, and multiple-meaning words.

Practical and easy-to-implement supports ensure that all students' needs are met as they practice and apply standards with each text.

## and Learning Cycle

DE AND PLAN

ems matching these standards, then provide selection -level lesson provided in the Student Edition.

ning-of-Year Assessment, then challenge them to g them opportunities to practice the skills in depth.

he Planning Pages for The Seventh Man to help y to master the standards.

**Man**

| This Year | Looking Forward |
|---|---|
| **RL.9-10.4** Determine the meaning of words and phrases as they are used in the text. | Have students analyze the subtleties and nuances of various word choices. |
| **RL.9-10.5** Analyze how an author's choices concerning how to structure a text, order events within it, and manipulate time create such effects as mystery, tension, or surprise. | Have students recast the beginning of the story without the frame and analyze the impact on the story as a whole. |
| **W.9-10.3.a-e** Write narratives to develop real or imagined experiences or events using effective technique, well-chosen details, and well-structured event sequences. | Encourage students to incorporate both real and fictional anecdotes in their writing. |
| **SL.9-10.4.b** Plan, memorize and present a recitation that: conveys the meaning of the selection and includes appropriate performance techniques (e.g., tone, rate, voice modulation) to achieve the desired aesthetic effect. | You may wish to challenge students to memorize and recite increasingly longer or more complex selections. |
| **L.9-10.1.B** Use various types of phrases to convey specific meanings and add variety and interest to writing or presentations. | You may wish to challenge students to use increasingly complex phrases and clauses in their writing. |
| **L.9-10.4a** Use context as a clue to the meaning of a word or phrase. | Have students analyze the subtleties and nuances of various word choices in different contexts. |

Whole-Class Learning 98D

# Customize and Enrich

DIGITAL PERSPECTIVES

**Enriching the Text** In 2013, the environmental scientist Tim Jarvis re-created Shackleton's voyage from Elephant Island to South Georgia in a replica of the *James Caird*. Jarvis and his crew used the same clothing, food, and navigational equipment that Shackleton had. The documentary *Shackleton: Death or Glory* chronicles the journey. Find a clip from the documentary online and show students (after previewing it yourself). Then, have students write a paragraph explaining how the clip enhances their understanding of the selection "The Voyage of the *James Caird*." For example, students might gain a better understanding of the size of the boat and the harsh conditions Shackleton and his men endured.

Digital Perspectives offers suggestions for using digital resources to strengthen concepts being taught.

AUTHOR'S PERSPECTIVE **Jim Cummins**

**Importance of Background Knowledge** It is important for all students, and especially English Language Learners, to tap into background knowledge when they read a text. It is incumbent on teachers to help students access this knowledge and integrate it with new textual information. One way to do this is to encourage groups to share what they know about the topic of the text before they begin reading. For example, on a superficial level, some students may have prior knowledge about sailing, which can help to scaffold understanding of "The Voyage of the *James Caird*." On a deeper level, more students may be able to relate to the idea of forcing oneself to go to extremes or taking risks in order to help others. After students have completed their first read, have them discuss how their background knowledge helped them understand the text.

Author's Perspective notes offer expert insights on topics, including incorporating first-language knowledge, building background knowledge, and academic and conversational vocabulary.

**FORMATIVE ASSESSMENT**

**Analyze Craft and Structure**

- **If** students fail to identify the frame, **then** have them look for clues that indicate the point of view. For example, the person narrating the frame may not be involved in the interior story.
- **If** students are unable to identify the point of view, **then** remind them to pay close attention to pronoun usage.

A formative assessment opportunity with recommended prescriptive activities is provided with each skill lesson.

# English Language Support

*myPerspectives* provides supports for English Language Learners at the Emerging, Expanding, and Bridging levels. Various resources can be used flexibly in print and online to meet your students' individual needs.

Selection audio can be found in the Interactive Student Edition and via BouncePages in the print Student Edition.

## The Moral Logic of Survivor Guilt

Nancy Sherman

ANCHOR TEXT | OPINION PIECE

Background  Author  Standards

1 If there is one thing we have learned from returning war veterans—especially those of the last decade—it's that the emotional reality of the soldier at home is often at odds with that of the civilian public they left behind. And while friends and families of returning service members may be experiencing gratefulness or relief this holiday,[1] many of those they've welcomed home are likely struggling with other emotions.

Is the sense of responsibility soldiers feel toward each other irrational?

2 High on that list of emotions is guilt. Soldiers often carry this burden home—survivor guilt being perhaps the kind most familiar to us. In war, standing here rather than there can save your life but cost a buddy his. It's flukish luck, but you feel responsible. The guilt begins an endless loop of counterfactuals—thoughts that you could have or should have done otherwise, though in fact you did nothing wrong. The feelings are, of course, not restricted to the battlefield. But given the magnitude[2] of loss in war, they hang

Glossary terms are defined at point of use and include English and Spanish audio.

BACKGROUND

Traumatic events take a toll on the physical and mental well-being of the individuals who must endure them. Survivors of the Holocaust, rescue workers, and war veterans, for example, might wonder how they were able to make it out alive when others did not. The term "survivor guilt" is used to describe these feelings.

SCAN FOR MULTIMEDIA

1 If there is one thing we have learned from returning war veterans—especially those of the last decade—it's that the emotional reality of the soldier at home is often at odds with that of the civilian public they left behind. And while friends and families of returning service members may be experiencing gratefulness or relief this holiday,[1] many of those they've welcomed home are likely struggling with other emotions.

Is the sense of responsibility soldiers feel toward each other irrational?

2 High on that list of emotions is guilt. Soldiers often carry this burden home—survivor guilt being perhaps the kind most familiar to us. In war, standing here rather than there can save your life but cost a buddy his. It's flukish luck, but you feel responsible. The guilt begins an endless loop of counterfactuals—thoughts that you could have or should have done otherwise, though in fact you did nothing wrong. The feelings are, of course, not restricted to the battlefield. But given the magnitude[2] of loss in war, they hang heavy there and are pervasive. And they raise the question of just how irrational those feelings are, and if they aren't, of what is the basis of their reasonableness.

NOTES

**burden** (BURD n) *n.* something that is carried with difficulty or obligation

CLOSE READ

ANNOTATE: Mark words in paragraph 1 that show opposites.

QUESTION: What groups of people are being contrasted by using these opposites?

CONCLUDE: What does this contrast suggest about the two groups?

1. **this holiday** This essay was originally published the day before the 4th of July (Independence Day).
2. **magnitude** *n.* great size or extent.



The Moral Logic of Survivor Guilt **33**

GLOSARIO: VOCABULARIO ACADÉMICOS / VOCABULARIO

## VOCABULARIO ACADÉMICOS/ VOCABULARIO DE CONCEPTOS

El vocabulario académico está en letra azul.

### Pronunciation Key

| Symbol | Sample Words | Symbol | Sample Words |
|---|---|---|---|
| a | at, catapult, Alabama | ihr | |
| a | father, charms, argue | o | |
| ahr | far, archaic, argument | oh | |
| ar | marry, various, arrogant | oo [lig] | |
| aw | law, maraud, caution | oo | boot, soup, crucial |
| awr | pour, organism, forewarn | ow | now, stout, flounder |
| ay | ape, sails, implication | oy | boy, toil, oyster |
| ayr | Mary, compare, hair | u | us, disrupt, understand |
| ee | even, teeth, really | uh | ago, focus, contemplation |
| eer | sneer, veneer, sincere | uhr | under, guttural, discolor |
| eh | ten, repel, elephant | ur | bird, urgent, perforation |
| ehr | merry, verify, terribly | y | by, delight, identify |
| ih | is, continue, fugitive | | |

Concept and Academic Vocabulary words are defined in Spanish.

**A**

**abash / avergonzar** *v.* apenar

accentuate / acentuar *v.* enfatizar una característica particular de algo o hacer que una cosa sea más notable

**accentuated / acentuó** *v.* enfatizó; realzó el efecto de

accept / aceptar *v.* recibir algo que se da

**accrued / acumulado** *v.* agregado o incrementado regularmente

ambiguity / ambigüedad *s.* estado o cualidad de ser indefinido; vago

ambiguous / ambiguo *adj.* que tiene más de un significado

amicably / amigablemente *adv.* de manera amigable o amistosa

analyze / analizar *v.* examinar o estudiar en detalle para aprender más

# El Septimo Hombre

Haruki Murakami

CUENTO | RESUMEN AUDIO

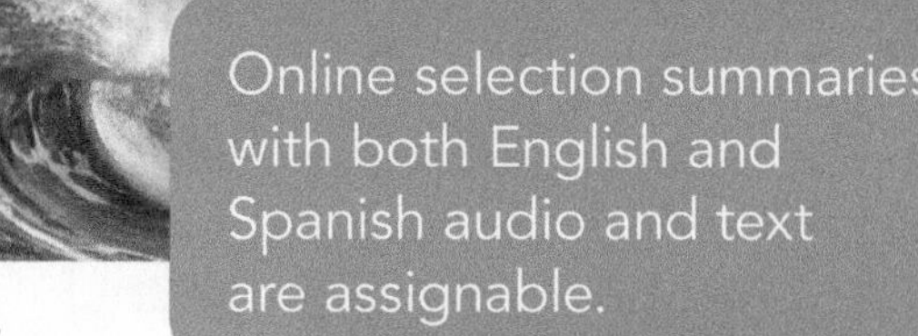

00:00/04:27

English / Inglés

*El séptimo* hombre de Haruki Murakami empieza con una introducción del narrador y protagonista, llamado el "séptimo hombre", puesto que es el último de un grupo de siete en contar su historia. No hay explicación sobre este grupo. Su objetivo sólo se puede adivinar por el tipo de historia que cuenta el séptimo hombre y por el entorno.

La historia en sí misma empieza en la infancia del séptimo hombre, en una población costera de Japón, y se centra en la relación de amistad con un niño al que se refiere como K. K es algo más joven que el narrador, y frágil, necesitado del apoyo y la protección del narrador. K tiene un gran talento artístico que el narrador admira

Online selection summaries with both English and Spanish audio and text are assignable.

Unit 2: Survival > Whole-Class Learning: The Seventh Man

1 "A huge wave nearly swept me away," said the seventh man, almost whispering. "It happened one September afternoon when I was ten years old."

2 The man was the last one to tell his story that night. *The hands of the clock had moved past ten.* The small group that huddled in a circle could hear *the wind tearing through the darkness outside*, heading west. It shook the trees, set the windows to rattling, and moved past the house with one final whistle.

3 "It was the biggest wave I had ever seen in my life," he said. "A strange wave. An absolute giant."

4 He paused.

5 "It just barely missed me, but in my place it swallowed everything that mattered most to me and swept it off to another world. I took years to find it again and to recover from the experience–precious years that can never be replaced."

6 The seventh man appeared to be in his mid-fifties. He was a thin

short but deep-looking scar that could have been made by the stab of a small blade. Stiff, bristly patches of white marked his short

You may wish to model the close read using the following think-aloud format. Possible responses to questions on the student page are included. You may also want to print copies of the Close-Read Guide for students to use.

**ANNOTATE:** As I read paragraph 2, I notice and highlight the details *the hands of the clock had moved past ten* and *the wind tearing through the darkness outside*. These details suggest to me that the story is set at night during a storm.

Hide Annotation Highlights

Highlighted passages in the Interactive Teacher's Edition focus on a key element of the text type or illustrate how language choices develop cohesion and link ideas, events, and concepts within a text.

## ENGLISH LANGUAGE SUPPORT LESSON

The Seventh Man

### Analyze Craft and Structure

Author's Choices: Order of Events

**Objective** Students will learn to describe a sequence of events using a variety of words and sentence structures.

### JUMP START

Tell students to listen as you describe the following order of events. *My friend Julio came to my house. Then we walked to the pizza shop. Then we played soccer. Then we went home.*

Ask students for their evaluation of the sentences. Point out that your description used the word *then* many times to describe sequence. Ask: *How can we put more variety into our language when we're talking about sequence of events?*

### TEACH

Display this sample sentence:

*First, the sky began to change. Next, the wind began to howl and the rain began to beat against the house.*

Ask students which words indicate the order of events.

Next, display the second sample sentence. Point out that it's a variation of the first sentence.

*After the sky began to change, the wind began to howl and the rain began to beat against the house.*

Ask students which word tells about the order of events.

Introduce these other words that show time order: *last, afterward, subsequently, when, before, before long, as soon as, later, finally.*

To challenge students, have them rewrite the sentence one more time to show a different sequence.

**Possible response:** *When the sky began to change, the wind began to howl and the rain began to beat against the house.*

Remind students that when they read, it's important to pay attention to the order of events. The order of events presented in the story may not be the order in which the events actually happened. Stories can flash back and flash forward.

For example, read aloud the following events from "The Seventh Man."

a. The Seventh Man is telling his story.

b. K. was swept off by a wave.

c. The Seventh Man got past his guilt.

Ask students in what order the events are told in the story. (*a, b, c*) Then ask in what order the events happened. (*b, c, a*) Point out that the events are told in that order because "The Seventh Man" is a frame story—a story within a story. In "The Seventh Man," the narrator is telling his story, which occurred at an

Printable English Language Support Lessons provide additional instructional opportunities.

# Personalize for Teaching

Lesson planning is easy and efficient with clearly labeled support at point of use in the Teacher's Edition.

A trade book alignment with suggestions for integrating longer works within the unit is provided. Lesson plans for recommended titles are available online.

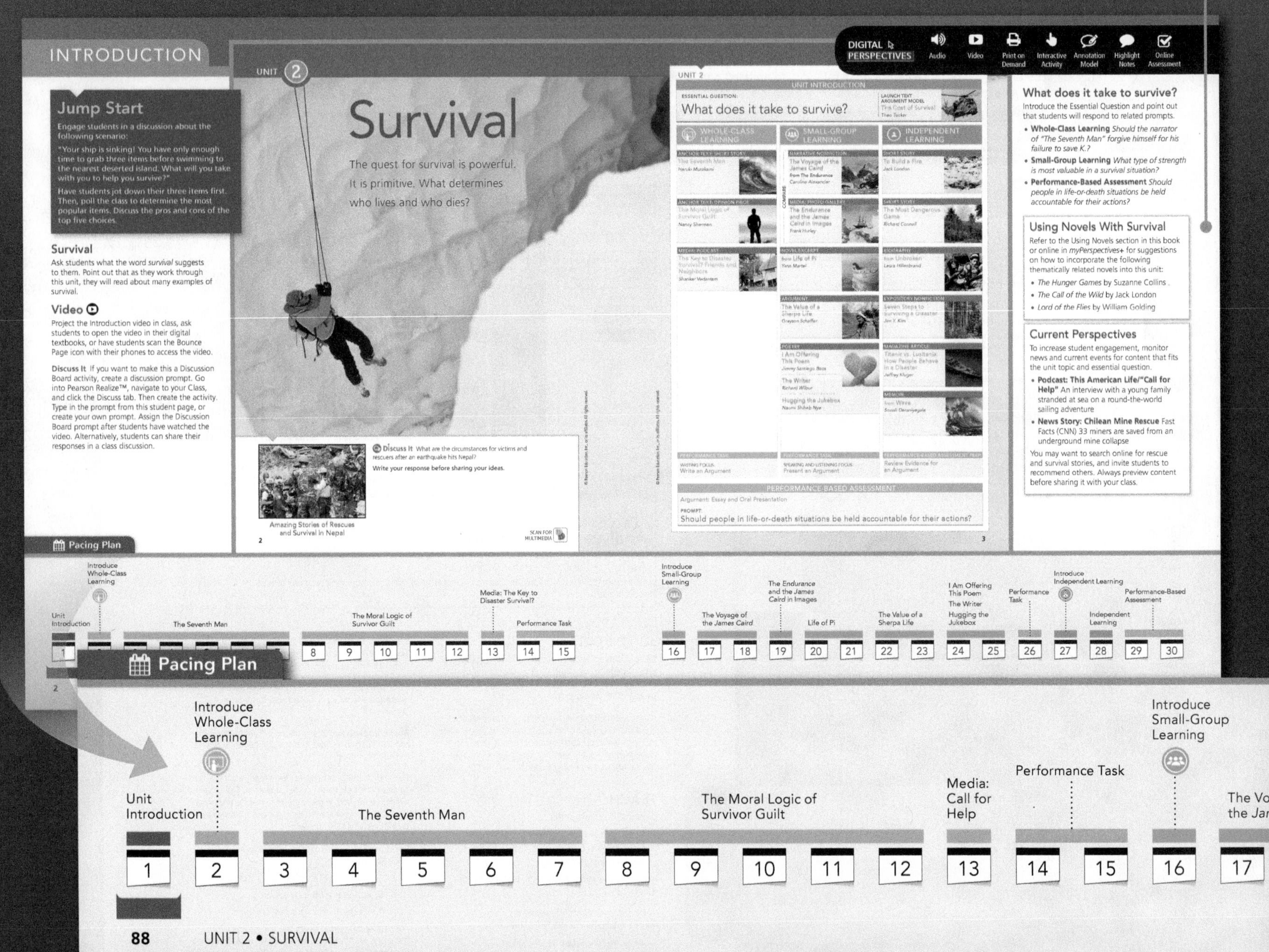

PLANNING WHOLE-CLASS LEARNING • THE SEVENTH MAN

## The Seventh Man

**AUDIO SUMMARIES** Audio summaries of "The Seventh Man" are available in both English and Spanish and can be assigned to students in Pearson Realize™. Assigning these summaries prior to reading the selection may help students build additional background knowledge and set a context for their first read.

### Summary

"The Seventh Man" begins on a stormy night in a house where a group of people is sharing stories. The unnamed seventh man tells his story last and describes a huge wave that changed his life forever. He explains that he grew up in a seaside town in Japan, where he and his best friend, described only as K., were as close as brothers. A typhoon strikes and when the eye of the storm passes over, the seventh man's father allows the boys to go outside. They go down to the beach to play. When the a tsunami strikes, the seventh man runs for his life, leaving K. behind. He struggles with guilt for into his adult life. Forty years later, the seventh man makes an important realization.

### Insight

The choices survivors make are not always easy or clear. Reading "The Seventh Man" will help students begin their reflections on how complicated survival can be. Although a survivor may have escaped with his or her life, that life may never be the same.

Some students may find "The Seventh Man" disturbing. The realization that a childhood decision might color someone's whole life is sobering and may require support.

Planning pages provide essential information, including selection summaries, insights, and links to the Essential Question.

Digital Perspectives identifies online resources.

DIGITAL PERSPECTIVES

Audio

Video

Print on Demand

Interactive Activity

Annotation Model

Highlight Notes

Online Assessment

Lesson Resources provides at-a-glance listings of standards, student-facing resources, on-level and reteaching support, and even a place for you to write in your own resources!

### LESSON RESOURCES

| | Making Meaning | Language Development | Effective Expression |
|---|---|---|---|
| Lesson | First Read<br>Close Read<br>Analyze the Text<br>Analyze Craft and Structure | Concept Vocabulary<br>Word Study<br>Conventions | Writing to Sources<br>Speaking and Listening |
| Instructional Standards | RL.9–10.4<br>RL.9–10.5<br>PI.5<br>PI.6a | L.9–10.1b<br>L.9–10.4a<br>PII.3, PII.4, PII.5 | W.9–10.3.a–e<br>SL.9–10.4.b<br>PI.1, PI.5, PI.11 |
| **STUDENT RESOURCES** | Search for these resources in myPerspectives Digital Student Edition or myPerspectives+ | | |
| Selection Resources | Audio Selection<br>Student Modeling Video<br>Close-Read Guide<br>First-Read Guide | Word Network | Evidence Log |
| **TEACHER RESOURCES** | Search for these resources in myPerspectives Digital Teacher's Edition or myPerspectives+ | | |
| Selection Resources | Annotation Model<br>Audio Summaries<br>Additional English Language Support<br>Analyze Text<br>Frame Story Graphic Organizer<br>Order of Events | Dependent Clause Tree<br>Concept Vocabulary<br>Suffixes<br>Clauses | Anecdotes<br>Recitations |
| Reteach and Practice | Analyze the Text<br>Frame Story | Concept Vocabulary<br>Suffixes<br>Clauses | Anecdotes<br>Recitations |
| Assessment | | | Selection Test |
| My Resources* | • Map of Japan<br>• ___<br>• ___<br>• ___ | • Sentence Strips<br>• Tree diagram for dependent clauses<br>• ___<br>• ___ | • ___<br>• ___<br>• ___ |

* These resources are suggested at point of use in this lesson.

Whole-Class Learning 98B

The *Endurance* and the *James Caird* in Images — 19

*from* Life of Pi — 20, 21

The Value of a Sherpa Life — 22, 23

I Am Offering This Poem; The Writer; Hugging the Jukebox — 24, 25

Performance Task — 26

Introduce Independent Learning — 27

Independent Learning — 28

Performance-Based Assessment — 29, 30

Unit Introduction 89

A Pacing Plan provides recommended pacing.

# Resources for Flexibility

*myPerspectives+* includes hundreds of additional teacher resources you can use to customize your lessons. Interactive lessons, grammar tutorials, digital novels, and more are student-facing to allow students to work independently.

interactive lessons

grammar tutorials

graphic organizers and rubrics

trade book lesson plans digital novels

myPerspectives™

- Digital novels, including classics such as *Great Expectations, Pride and Prejudice, The Adventures of Tom Sawyer, Alice in Wonderland, The Scarlet Letter,* and *Romeo and Juliet*
- Novel lesson plans for over 100 titles, including those aligned to each unit
- Interactive lessons to help students develop critical writing, speaking, and listening skills
- High-interest readings and resources for struggling students
- Engaging grammar and academic vocabulary tutorials
- Writing Whiteboard Activities for an interactive and engaging classroom experience
- Editable grammar worksheets for extra practice with this crucial skill
- Generic graphic organizers and rubrics that can be used with any lesson

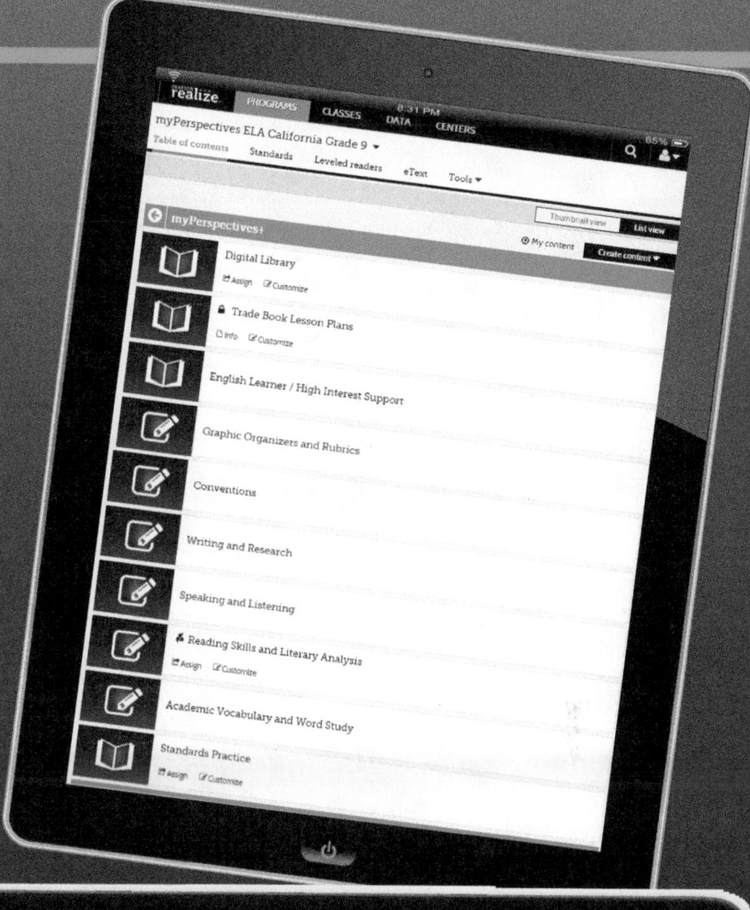


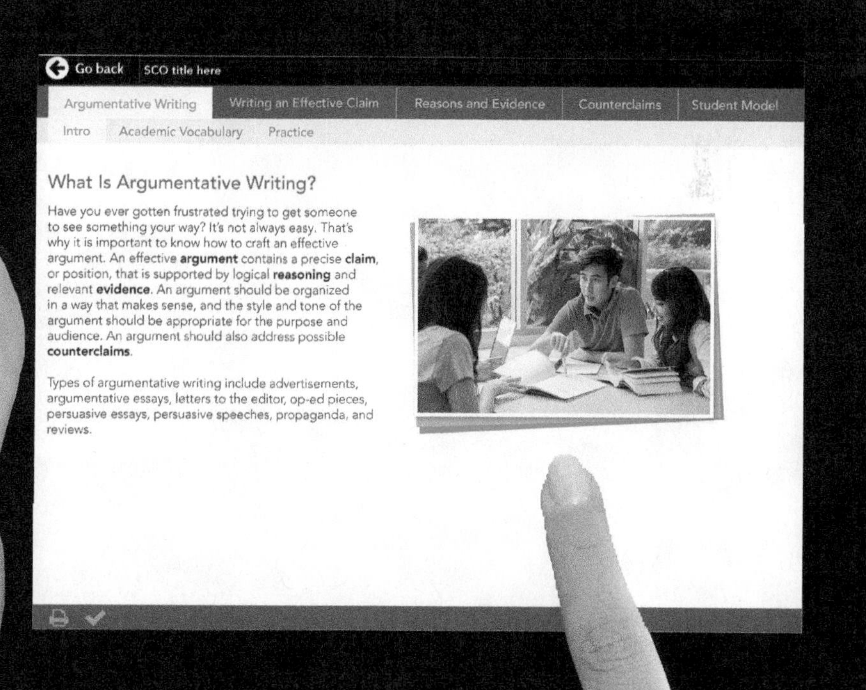

# PEARSON realize™

Pearson Realize™ is your online destination for digital resources, assessments, and data. Flexible classroom management tools give you an amazing amount of freedom and control.

Easily manage your classes and data.

**YOU HAVE THE POWER**

**Customize** the program to make it your own.

- Rearrange content
- Upload your own content
- Add links to online media
- Edit resources and assessment

All program-specific resources, flexible agnostic resources, and assessments are available in one location for easy lesson planning and presentation.

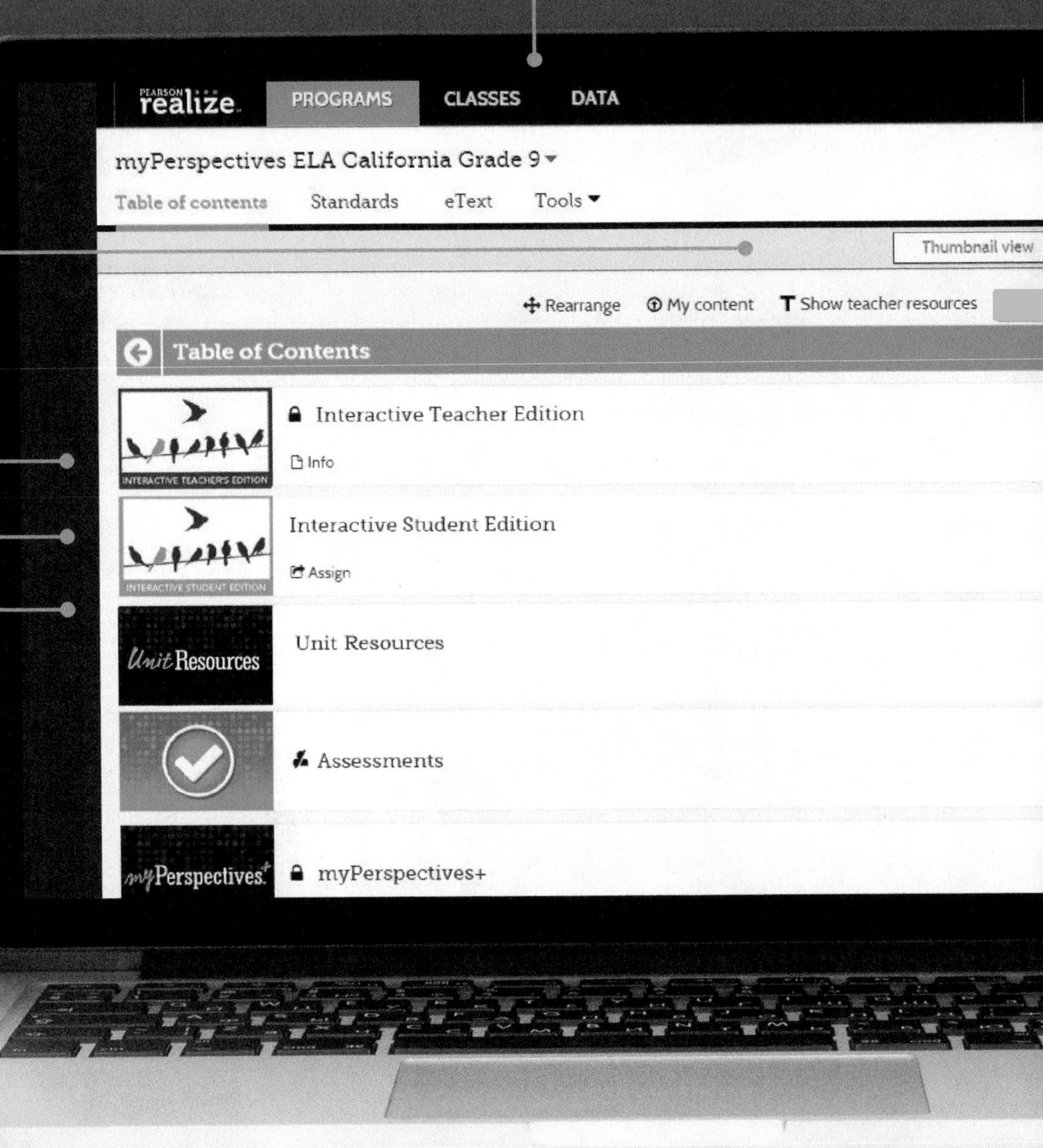

realize.
PROGRAMS
CLASSES
DATA
CENTERS
myPerspectives Grade 9
Table of Contents
Standards
eText
Tools
Assign
Info
Customize
Unit 2 : Survival
UNIT INTRODUCTION
The Cost of Survival
WHOLE-CLASS LEARNING
Unit 2 Whole-Class Learning Overview
The Seventh Man
Teacher Resources
The Moral Logic of Survivor Guilt
Unit 2 Whole-Class Learning Performance Task
SMALL-GROUP LEARNING
Unit 2 Small-Group Learning Overview
The Voyage of the James Caird
The Seventh Man
Audio Summary
Frame Story
Frame Story Reteach
Concept Vocabulary
Suffixes
Selection resources are available at point of use!
DIGITAL PERSPECTIVES
Audio
Video
Document
Annotation Highlights
EL Highlights
Online Assessment
Digital Perspectives in the Teacher's Edition identifies digital resources available for each lesson.

# UNIT 1: Words That Shaped a Nation

## Integrating Trade Books with *my*Perspectives

These titles provide students with another perspective on the topic of words that shaped a nation, touching upon many of the ideas found within the unit selections.

Depending on your objectives for the unit, as well as your students' needs, you may choose to integrate the trade book into the unit in several ways, including:

- **Supplement the unit** Form literature circles and have the students read one of the trade books throughout the course of the unit as a supplement to the selections and activities.
- **Substitute for unit selections** If you replace unit selections with a trade book, review the standards taught with those selections. Teacher Resources that provide practice with all standards are available.
- **Extend Independent Learning** Extend the unit by replacing independent reading selections with one of these trade books.
- **Pacing** However you choose to integrate trade books, the Pacing Guide below offers suggestions for aligning the trade books with this unit.

## Trade Book Lesson Plans

Trade book lesson plans for *Uncle Tom's Cabin, The Federalist Papers,* and *The Legend of Sleepy Hollow and Other Stories* are available online in *my*Perspectives+.

### Pacing Guide: Unit Supplement

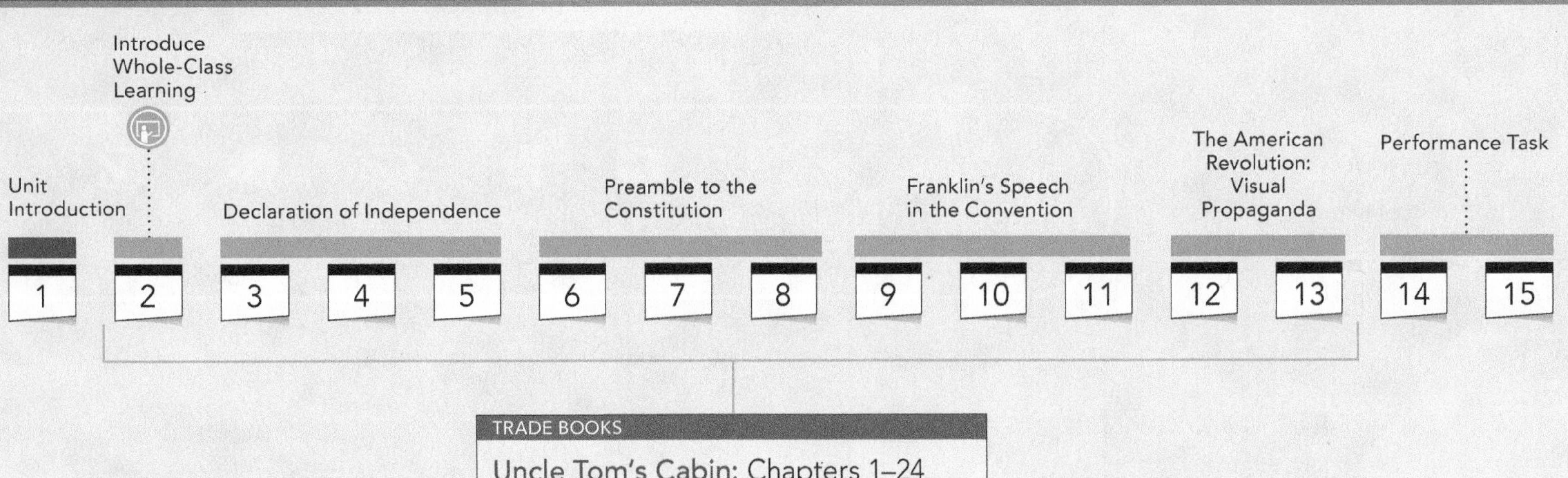

## Suggested Trade Books

### Uncle Tom's Cabin

Harriet Beecher Stowe

Lexile: 1050

Among the best-selling books of the 19th century, this novel portrays the hardships of slavery in America. It is often cited as one of the reasons for the rise of the Abolitionist movement leading up to the Civil War.

**Connection to Essential Question**

Stowe finds good not only in freedom, but also in the kindness and faith that allow people to endure until they are free. As freedom is a goal for many characters throughout the novel, the Essential Question: *What is the difference between seeing and knowing?* is central to the text.

### The Federalist Papers

James Madison

Lexile: 1450

A series of essays by three Founding Fathers argues for the ratification of the Constitution.

**Connection to Essential Question**

These documents are foundational to our democracy; some of the most influential concern how to make a government "free" rather than tyrannical. The writers directly grapple with the Essential Question: *What is the difference between seeing and knowing?*

### The Legend of Sleepy Hollow and Other Stories

Washington Irving

Lexile: 1380

This classic and imaginative short story collection is set during colonial times.

**Connection to Essential Question**

A number of Irving's stories concern supernatural events rooted in the American Revolutionary War, a period in which the Essential Question: *What is the difference between seeing and knowing?* came to the fore.

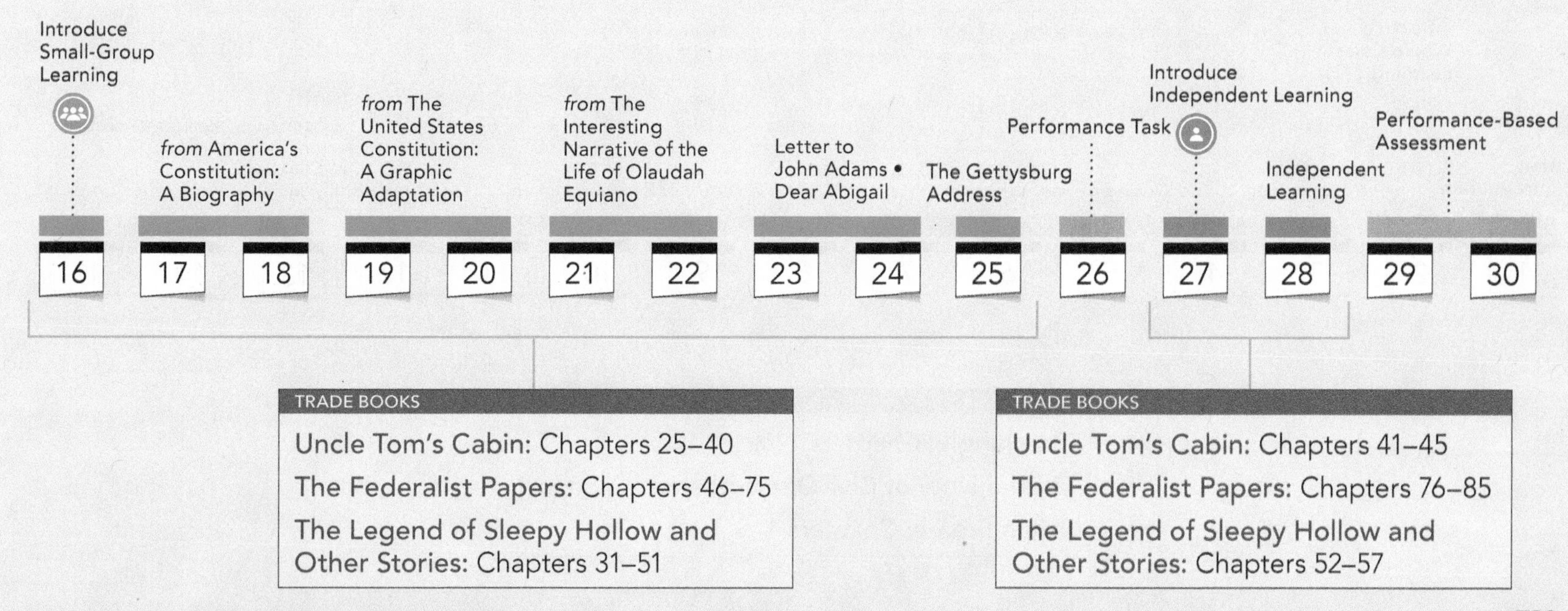

# UNIT 2: The Individual and Society

## Integrating Trade Books with *my*Perspectives

These titles provide students with another perspective on the topics of the individual and society, touching upon many of the ideas found within the unit selections.

Depending on your objectives for the unit, as well as your students' needs, you may choose to integrate the trade book into the unit in several ways, including:

- **Supplement the unit** Form literature circles and have the students read one of the trade books throughout the course of the unit as a supplement to the selections and activities.
- **Substitute for unit selections** If you replace unit selections with a trade book, review the standards taught with those selections. Teacher Resources that provide practice with all standards are available.
- **Extend Independent Learning** Extend the unit by replacing independent reading selections with one of these trade books.
- **Pacing** However you choose to integrate trade books, the Pacing Guide below offers suggestions for aligning the trade books with this unit.

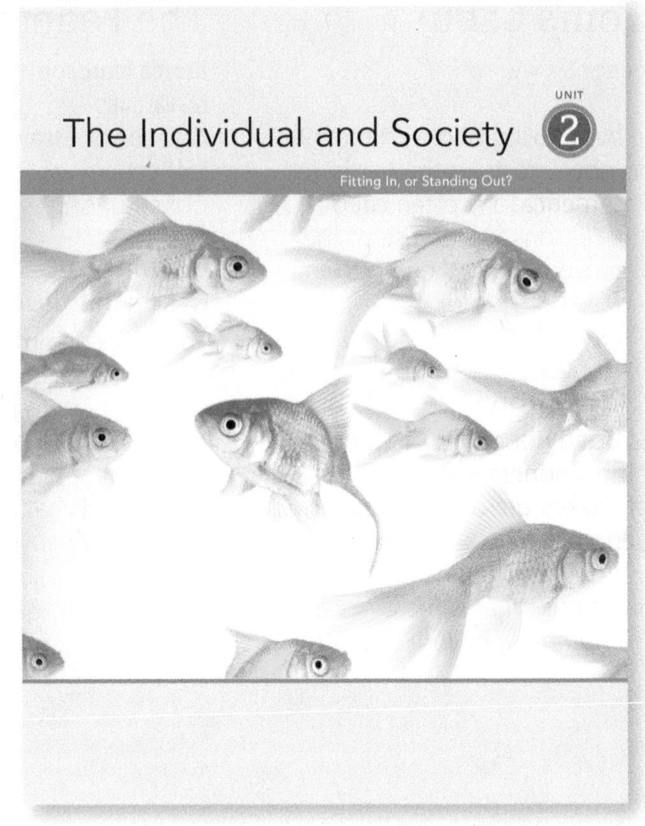

UNIT
The Individual and Society 2
Fitting In, or Standing Out?


## Trade Book Lesson Plans

Trade book lesson plans for *The Jungle, On the Duty of Civil Disobedience*, and *Ethan Frome* are available online in *my*Perspectives+.

### Pacing Guide: Unit Supplement

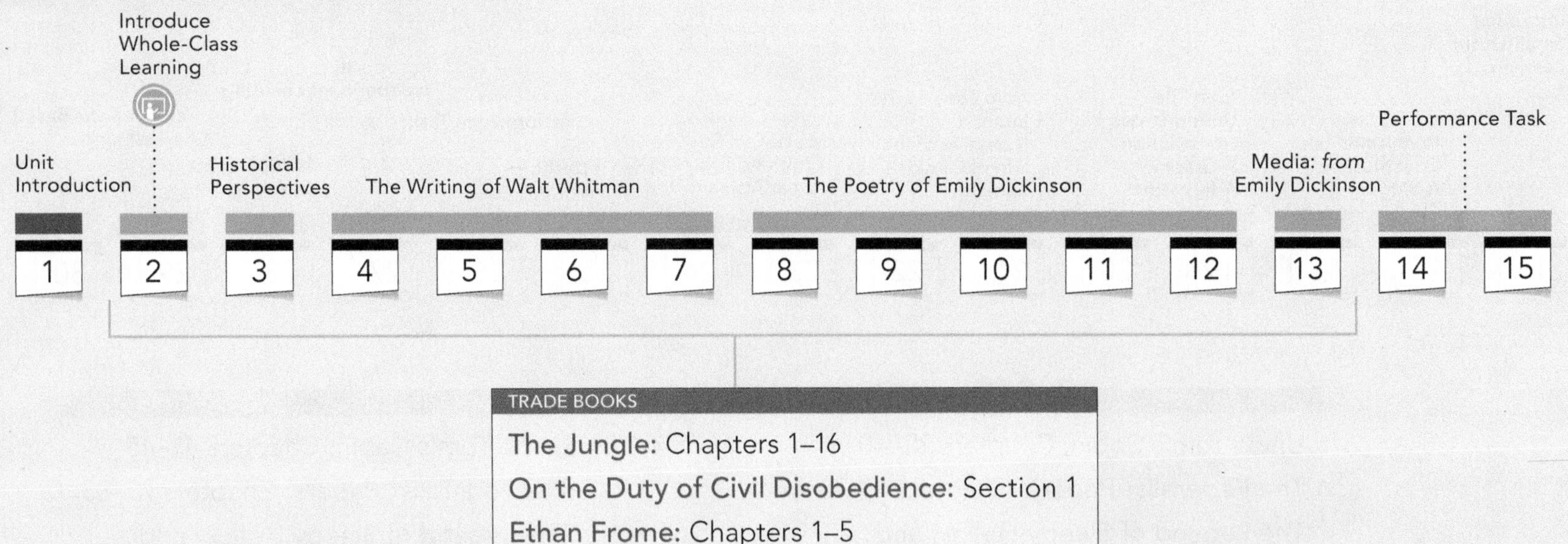

# Suggested Trade Books

## The Jungle

Upton Sinclair

Lexile: 1170

This text tells the story of an immigrant family in Chicago and the terrible abuses of labor in the meatpacking industry at the time.

### Connection to Essential Question

*The Jungle* is a call for more socialist policies as a counterbalance to the suffering caused by factory owners' greed and corruption. In this way, the novel perhaps takes a more negative perspective on the Essential Question: *What role does individualism play in American society?*

## On the Duty of Civil Disobedience

Henry David Thoreau

Lexile: 1340

Thoreau argues that citizens have a moral responsibility not to cooperate with the government, on the grounds that doing so would make them complicit in the spread of slavery.

### Connection to Essential Question

This essay is famous for laying the underpinnings of the civil rights movement's tactics. Thoreau argued for individual resistance, not just group resistance, and went to jail for it. As a major text in American culture, it offers insight into the roots of the Essential Question: *What role does individualism play in American society?*

## Ethan Frome

Edith Wharton

Lexile: 820–1200

A man and his wife's cousin fall in love with each other; both are torn between their desires and their responsibilities.

### Connection to Essential Question

The plot of *Ethan Frome* focuses on conflicts between individualism and social obligations, directly attempting to answer the Essential Question: *What role does individualism play in American society?*

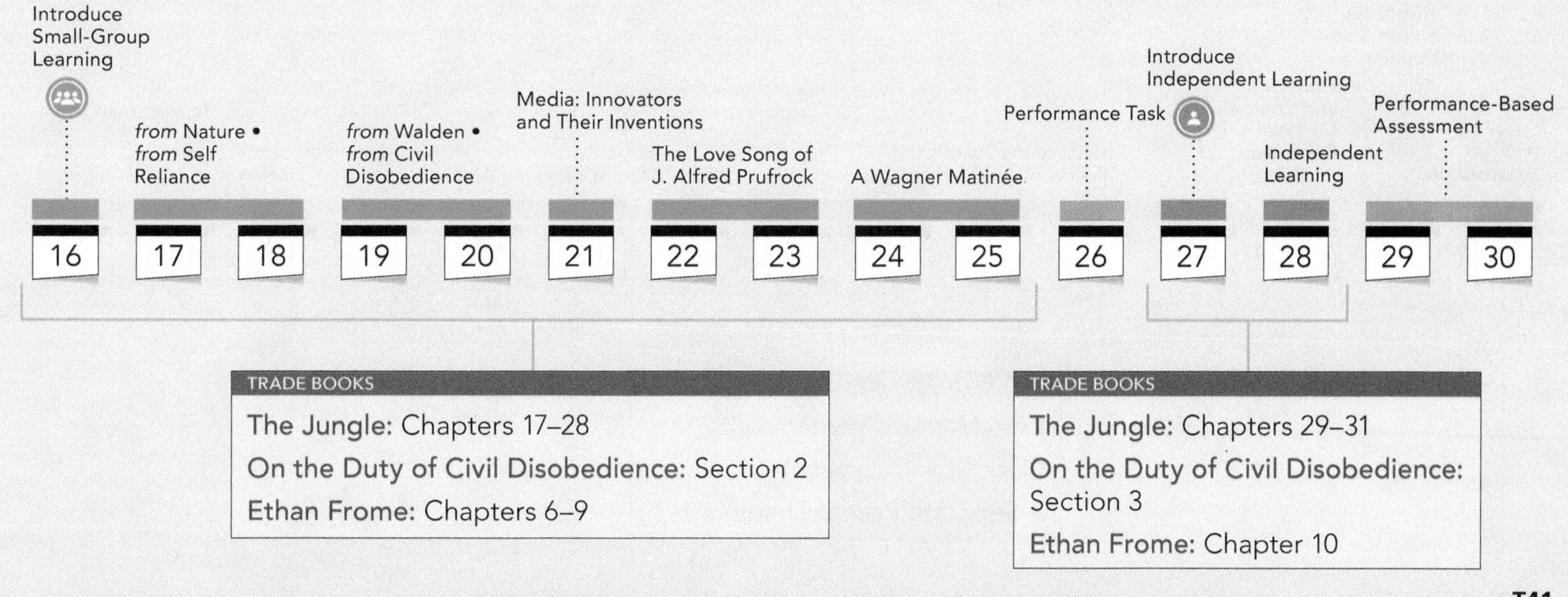

# UNIT 3: Power, Protest, and Change

## Integrating Trade Books with *my*Perspectives

These titles provide students with another perspective on the topics of power, protest, and change. They touch upon many of the ideas found within the unit selections.

Depending on your objectives for the unit, as well as your students' needs, you may choose to integrate the trade book into the unit in several ways, including:

- **Supplement the unit** Form literature circles and have the students read one of the trade books throughout the course of the unit as a supplement to the selections and activities.
- **Substitute for unit selections** If you replace unit selections with a trade book, review the standards taught with those selections. Teacher Resources that provide practice with all standards are available.
- **Extend Independent Learning** Extend the unit by replacing independent reading selections with one of these trade books.
- **Pacing** However you choose to integrate trade books, the Pacing Guide below offers suggestions for aligning the trade books with this unit.

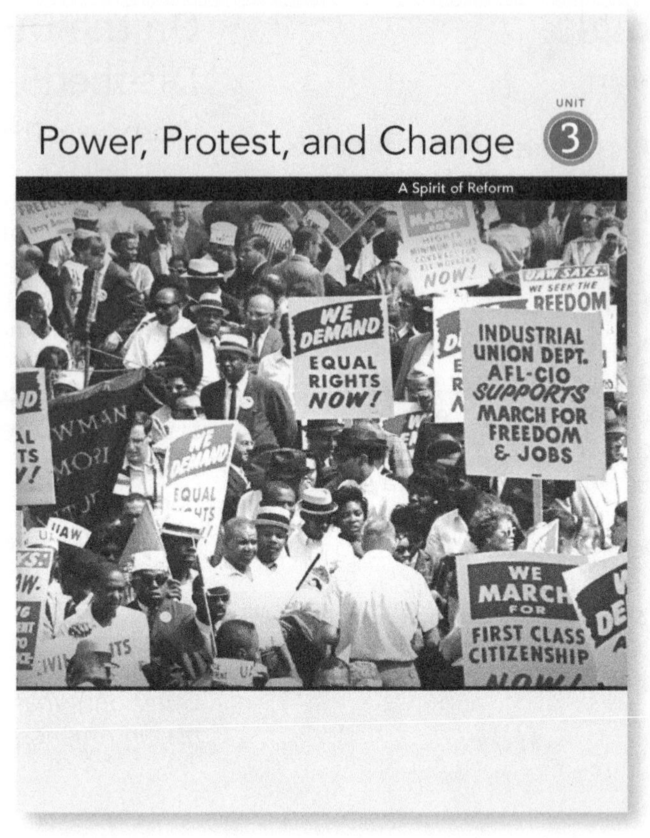


## Trade Book Lesson Plans

Trade book lesson plans for *I Am Malala, Black Boy,* and *A Separate Peace* are available online in *my*Perspectives+.

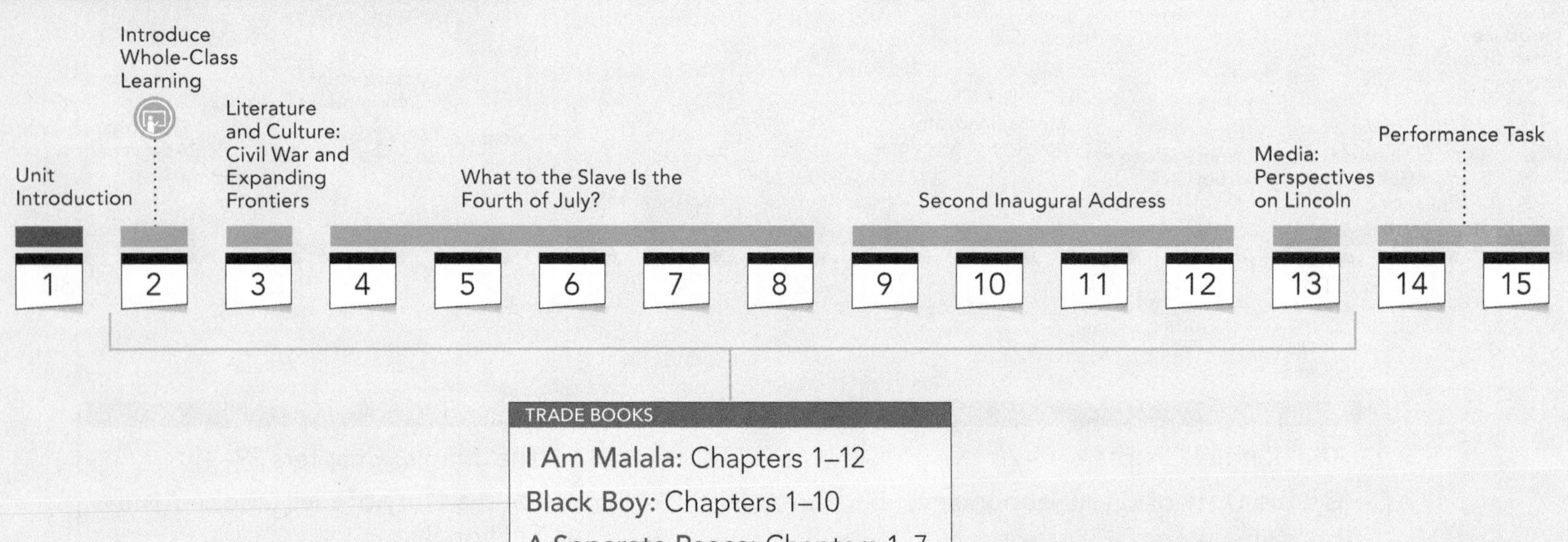

## Suggested Trade Books

### I Am Malala

Malala Yousafzai

Lexile: 1000

A girl who campaigns for education faces intimidation and then attempted murder. She miraculously survives and recovers to continue her advocacy.

#### Connection to Essential Question

Equal access to education in Pakistan has been an issue for decades. But the recent tension and violence was unprecedented, giving rise to the Essential Question: *In what ways does the struggle for freedom change with history?*

### Black Boy

Richard Wright

Lexile: 950

A boy grows up, becomes a man, and follows his conscience amid violence and dishonesty.

#### Connection to Essential Question

Wright looks for freedom in different ways, including education, moving north, and getting involved in politics. He is initially enamored with communism, but decides the Communist Party is harmful despite its good intentions. Wright's experience is relevant to the Essential Question: *In what ways does the struggle for freedom change with history?*

### A Separate Peace

John Knowles

Lexile: 1110

Rivalry and a serious injury test two young men's friendship.

#### Connection to Essential Question

The teenagers have a lot of freedom during the summer, but this is a temporary respite from the war that they may have to fight. Time constrains freedom here—as the young men get older, they get closer and closer to enlisting. Their experience provides another angle on the Essential Question: *In what ways does the struggle for freedom change with history?*

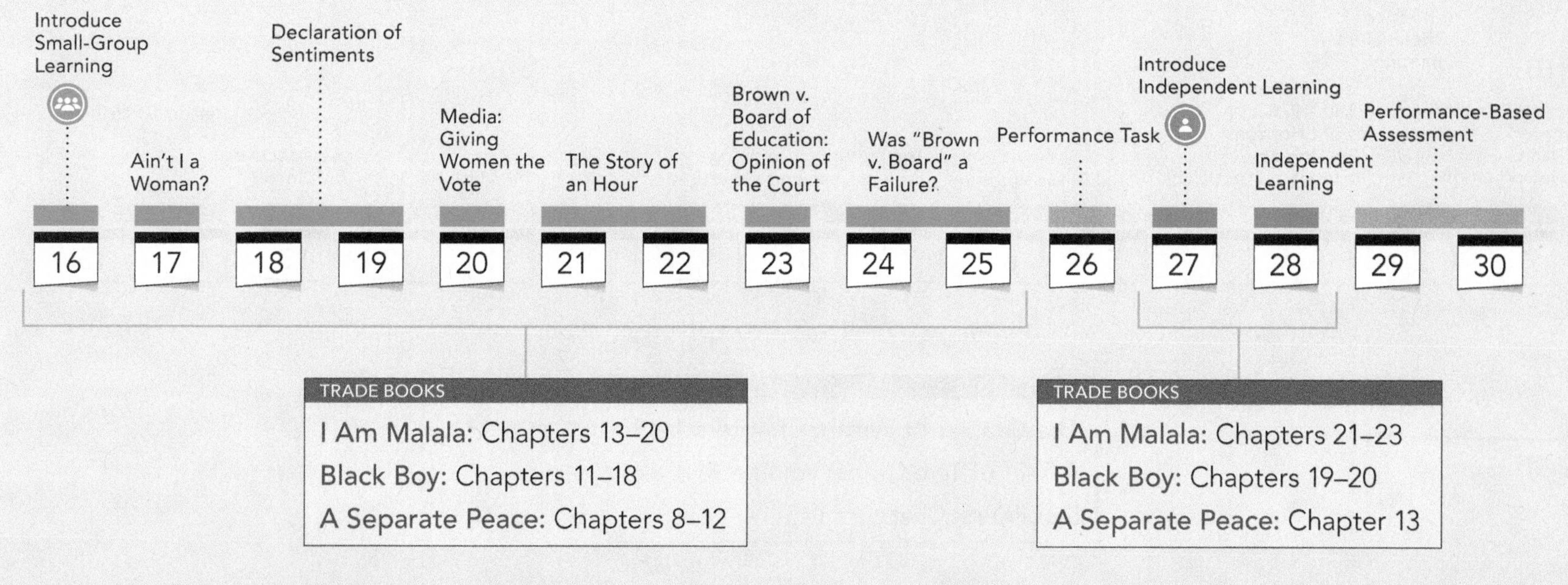

# UNIT 4: Grit and Grandeur

## Integrating Trade Books with *my*Perspectives

These titles provide students with another perspective on the topics of grit and grandeur, touching upon many of the ideas found within the unit selections.

Depending on your objectives for the unit, as well as your students' needs, you may choose to integrate the trade book into the unit in several ways, including:

- **Supplement the unit** Form literature circles and have the students read one of the trade books throughout the course of the unit as a supplement to the selections and activities.
- **Substitute for unit selections** If you replace unit selections with a trade book, review the standards taught with those selections. Teacher Resources that provide practice with all standards are available.
- **Extend Independent Learning** Extend the unit by replacing independent reading selections with one of these trade books.
- **Pacing** However you choose to integrate trade books, the Pacing Guide below offers suggestions for aligning the trade books with this unit.

## Trade Book Lesson Plans

Trade book lesson plans for *The Grapes of Wrath, A Tale of Two Cities,* and *Dubliners* are available online in *my*Perspectives+.

### Pacing Guide: Unit Supplement

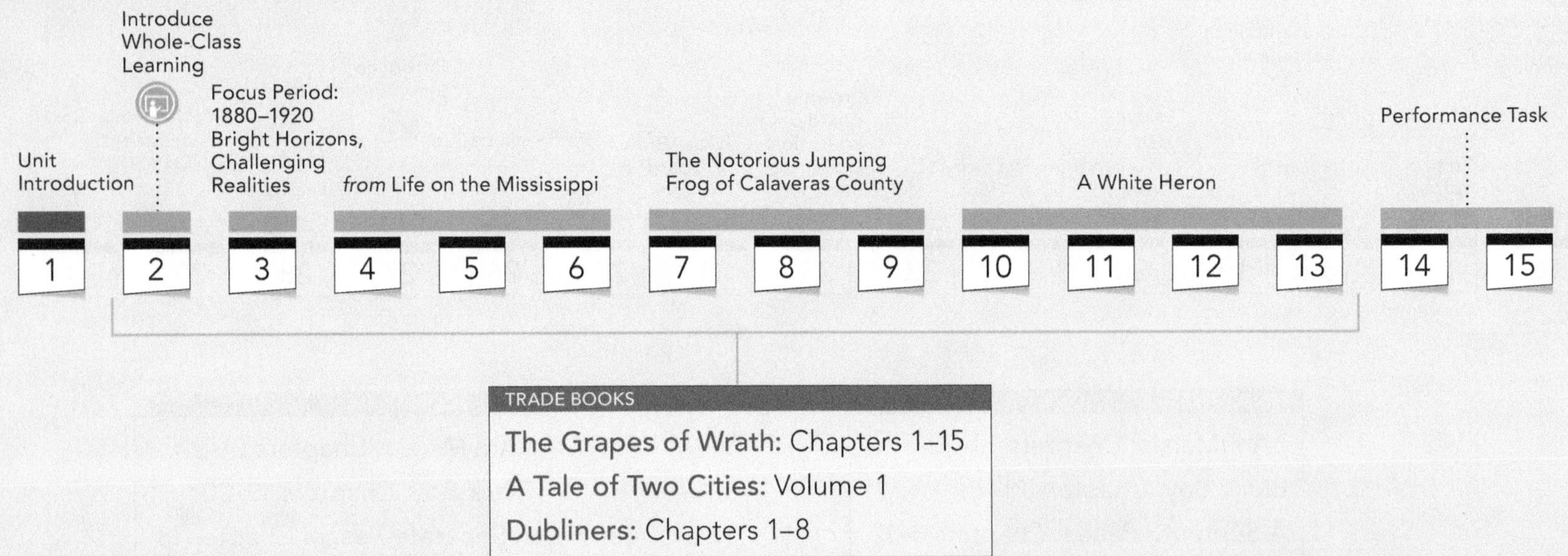

## Suggested Trade Books

### The Grapes of Wrath

John Steinbeck

Lexile: 680

Drought forces a farm family from their home during the Great Depression, and they travel seeking work.

**Connection to Essential Question**

Steinbeck vividly portrays the conditions of the Dust Bowl, from devastated crops to the migrant labor camps of California. The novel shows the effects of these conditions on his characters, giving insight into the Essential Question: *What is the relationship between literature and place?*

### A Tale of Two Cities

Charles Dickens

Lexile: 460–1130

Dickens follows a colorful cast of characters in Paris and London in the lead-up to the French Revolution.

**Connection to Essential Question**

The novel famously opens with a set of dualistic images to set the "best of times....worst of times" contrast. The dualism at the heart of the book reveals how different the conditions for the aristocrats are compared to those of the poor. Geography and time are key to the plot and this novel sheds important light on the Essential Question: *What is the relationship between literature and place?*

### Dubliners

James Joyce

Lexile: 900

This series of stories features residents of Dublin across social classes who experience life-changing revelations.

**Connection to Essential Question**

The city of Dublin is as much a character as any of the speaking roles, raising the Essential Question: *What is the relationship between literature and place?* Joyce illustrates the spirit of change and revolution during the most optimistic years of Irish nationalism.

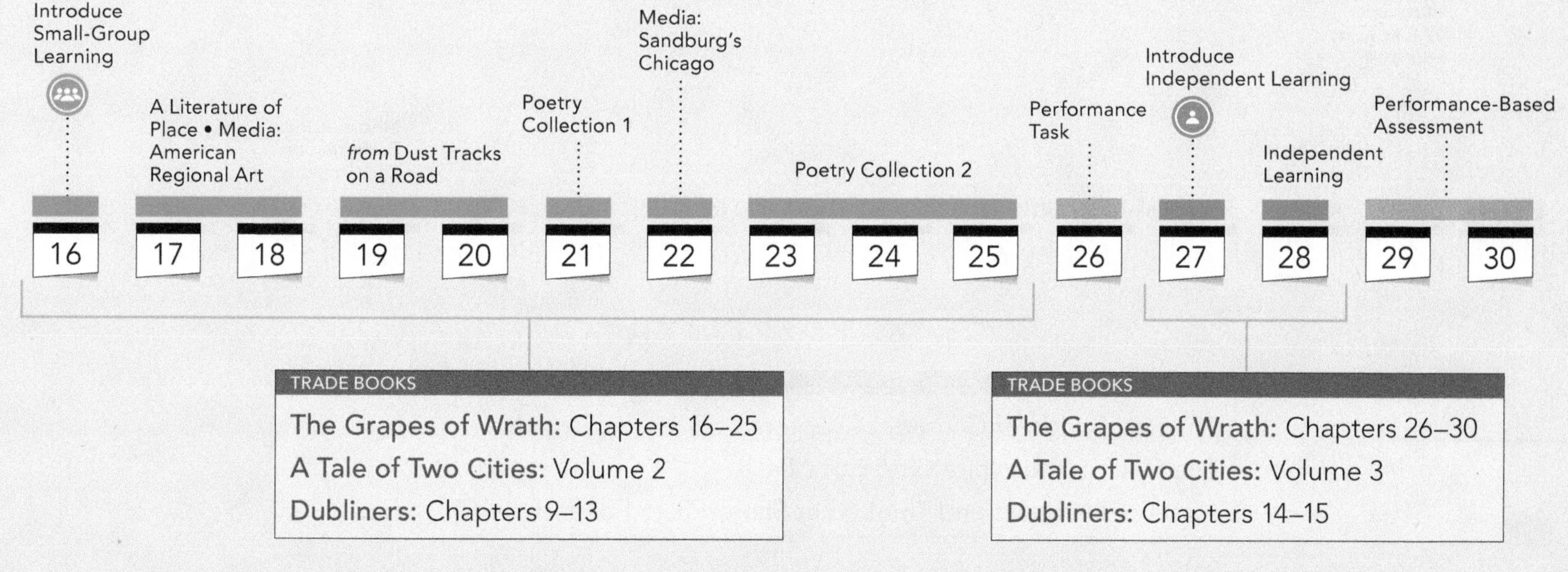

# UNIT 5: Facing Our Fears

## Integrating Trade Books with *my*Perspectives

These titles provide students with another perspective on the topic of facing our fears, touching upon many of the ideas found within the unit selections.

Depending on your objectives for the unit, as well as your students' needs, you may choose to integrate the trade book into the unit in several ways, including:

- **Supplement the unit** Form literature circles and have the students read one of the trade books throughout the course of the unit as a supplement to the selections and activities.
- **Substitute for unit selections** If you replace unit selections with a trade book, review the standards taught with those selections. Teacher Resources that provide practice with all standards are available.
- **Extend Independent Learning** Extend the unit by replacing independent reading selections with one of these trade books.
- **Pacing** However you choose to integrate trade books, the Pacing Guide below offers suggestions for aligning the trade books with this unit.

## Trade Book Lesson Plans

Trade book lesson plans for *The Red Badge of Courage, The Devil in the White City, and Heart of Darkness and the Secret Sharer* are available online in *my*Perspectives+.

### Pacing Guide: Unit Supplement

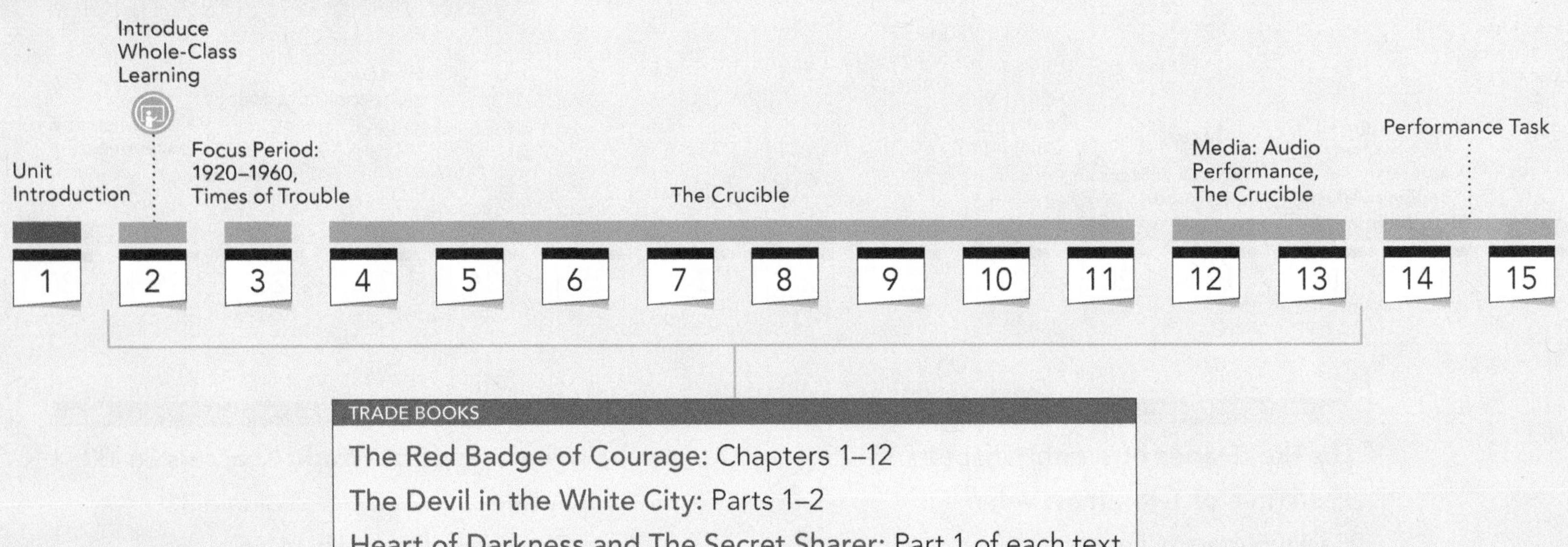

## Suggested Trade Books

### The Red Badge of Courage

Stephen Crane

Lexile: 660–900

A soldier in the Civil War runs in fear from battle, then tries to make his way back to the front.

#### Connection to Essential Question

Unlike most earlier war stories, the protagonist's emotions in this text receive more attention than what happens around him, making it provide special insight into the Essential Question: *How do we respond when challenged by fear?* The story revolves around Henry's shame and efforts to make up for his earlier cowardice.

### The Devil in the White City

Erik Larson

Lexile: 1170

At the 1893 World's Fair, two men have recently completed great projects: the architect behind most of the Fair's buildings—and a serial murderer who built a hotel nearby.

#### Connection to Essential Question

Fear comes in two forms in this book: the mundane, everyday fear of failure that Burnham fought as he organized the massive fair, and the horror evoked by Holmes's ghoulish crimes. Both relate to the Essential Question: *How do we respond when challenged by fear?*

### Heart of Darkness and The Secret Sharer

Joseph Conrad

Lexile: 1020–1320

A man voyages downriver to meet an ivory trader in the heart of the Belgian Congo, and encounters the full horrors of colonialism.

#### Connection to Essential Question

The brutality of imperialism caused Kurtz to descend into wild cruelty, and causes Marlow to flee back to Europe—the horrors of the Belgian Congo create extreme reactions in answer to the Essential Question: *How do we respond when challenged by fear?*

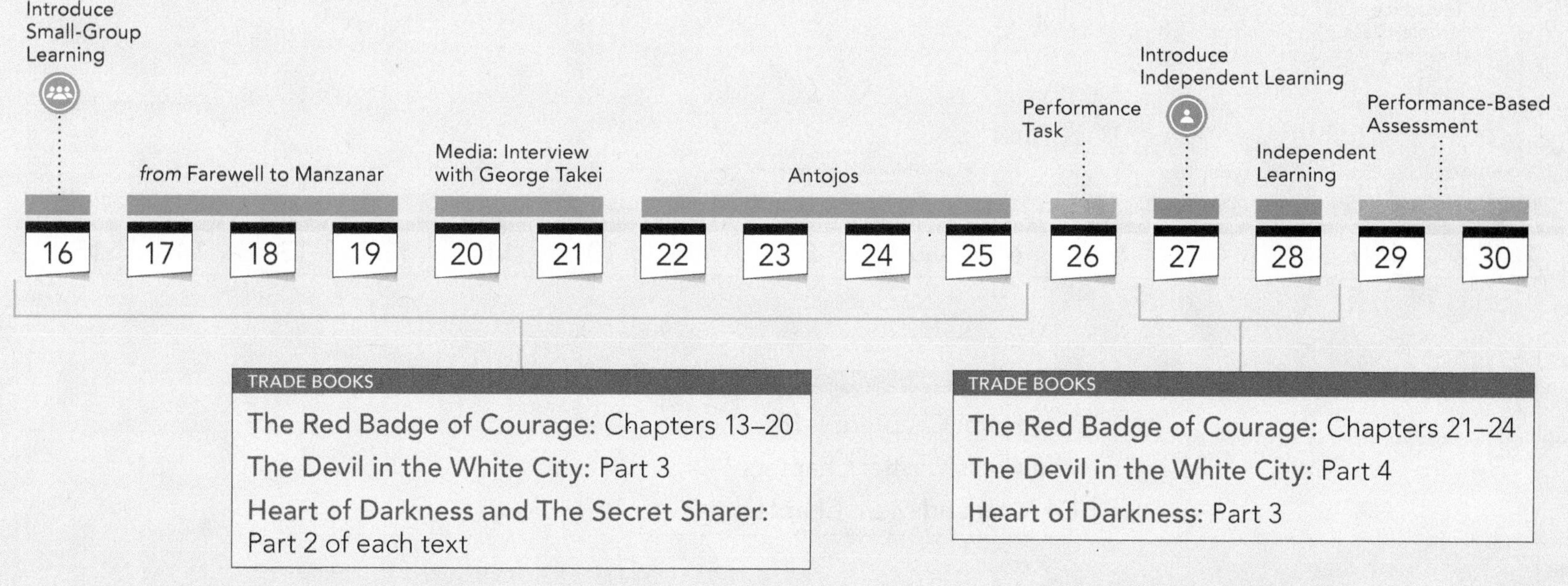

# UNIT 6: Ordinary Lives: Extraordinary Tales

## Integrating Trade Books with *my*Perspectives

These titles provide students with another perspective on the topic of ordinary lives and extraordinary tales, touching upon many of the ideas found within the unit selections.

Depending on your objectives for the unit, as well as your students' needs, you may choose to integrate the trade book into the unit in several ways, including:

- **Supplement the unit** Form literature circles and have the students read one of the trade books throughout the course of the unit as a supplement to the selections and activities.
- **Substitute for unit selections** If you replace unit selections with a trade book, review the standards taught with those selections. Teacher Resources that provide practice with all standards are available.
- **Extend Independent Learning** Extend the unit by replacing independent reading selections with one of these trade books.
- **Pacing** However you choose to integrate trade books, the Pacing Guide below offers suggestions for aligning the trade books with this unit.

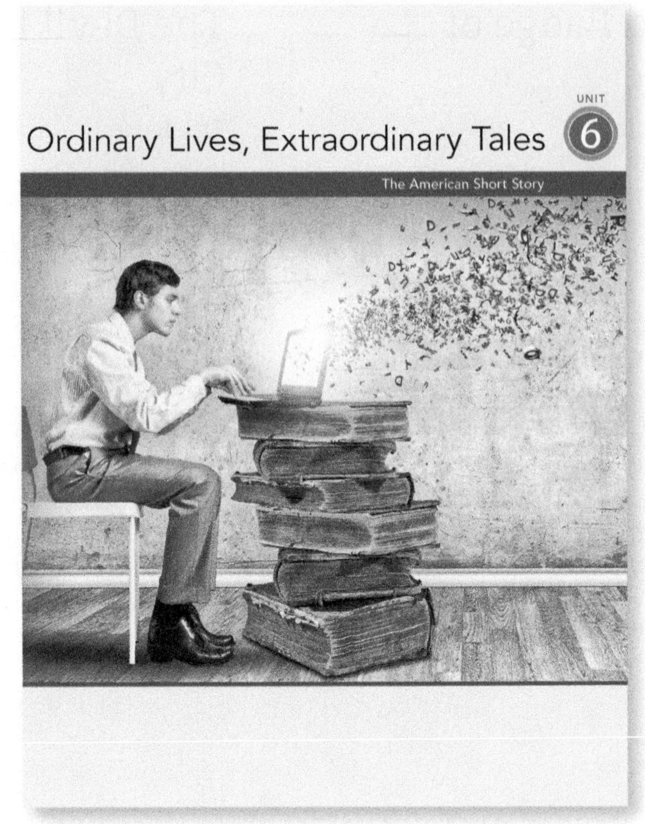

UNIT
Ordinary Lives, Extraordinary Tales 6
The American Short Story


## Trade Book Lesson Plans

Trade book lesson plans for *The Help, The Glass Castle,* and *Of Mice and Men* are available online in *my*Perspectives+.

### Pacing Guide: Unit Supplement

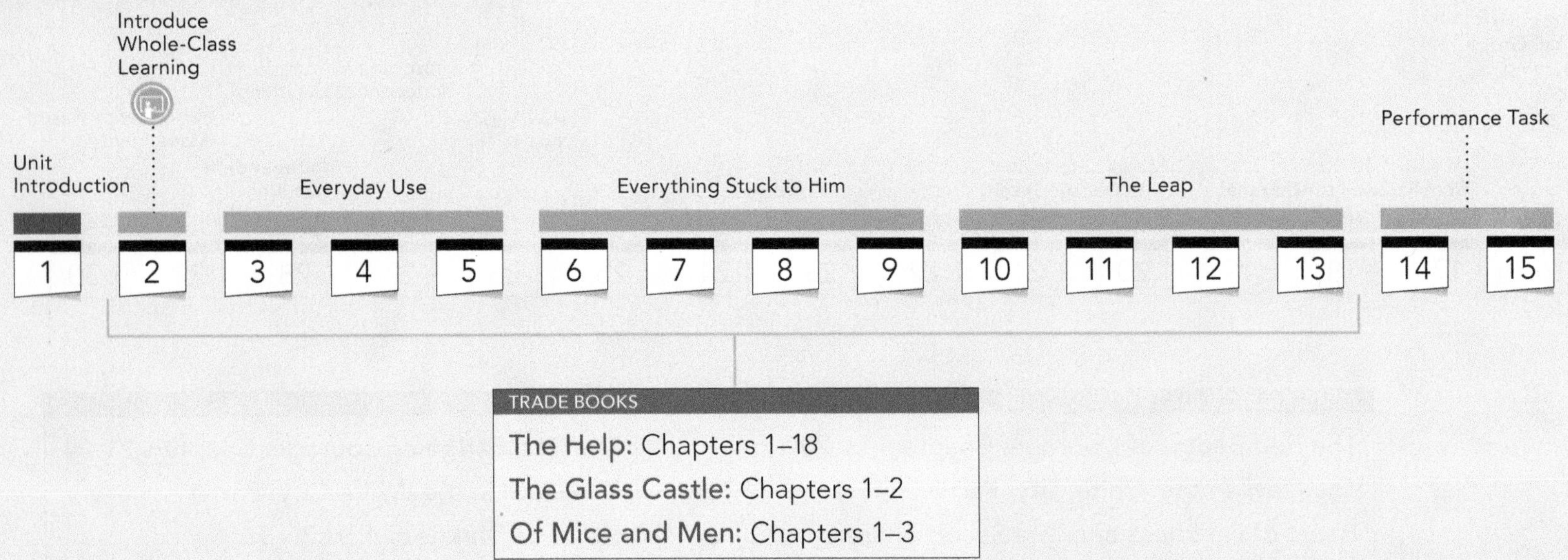

## Suggested Trade Books

### The Help

Kathryn Stockett

Lexile: 730

A group of women in 1960s Mississippi become friends and write a book exposing terrible labor conditions among African American housekeepers.

#### Connection to Essential Question

This novel focuses on a friendship forged to help reveal the indignity that housekeepers endured. The work required to gather details for the groundbreaking, dangerous book and the friendships that develop in this challenging work combine to provide an angle on the Essential Question: *What do stories reveal about the human condition?*

### The Glass Castle

Jeannette Walls

Lexile: 1010

A memoir describes a young woman's unconventional childhood.

#### Connection to Essential Question

Walls portrays her family life movingly, notably in how she and her siblings saw nothing wrong until later in life. In attempting to portray her life's story, Walls provides insight into the Essential Question: *What do stories reveal about the human condition?*

### Of Mice and Men

John Steinbeck

Lexile: 630

Two migrant workers in the Great Depression try to make a better life and run into trouble.

#### Connection to Essential Question

Characters with good and kind intent cause tragedy through misunderstandings. This classic fable sheds light on the Essential Question: *What do stories reveal about the human condition?*

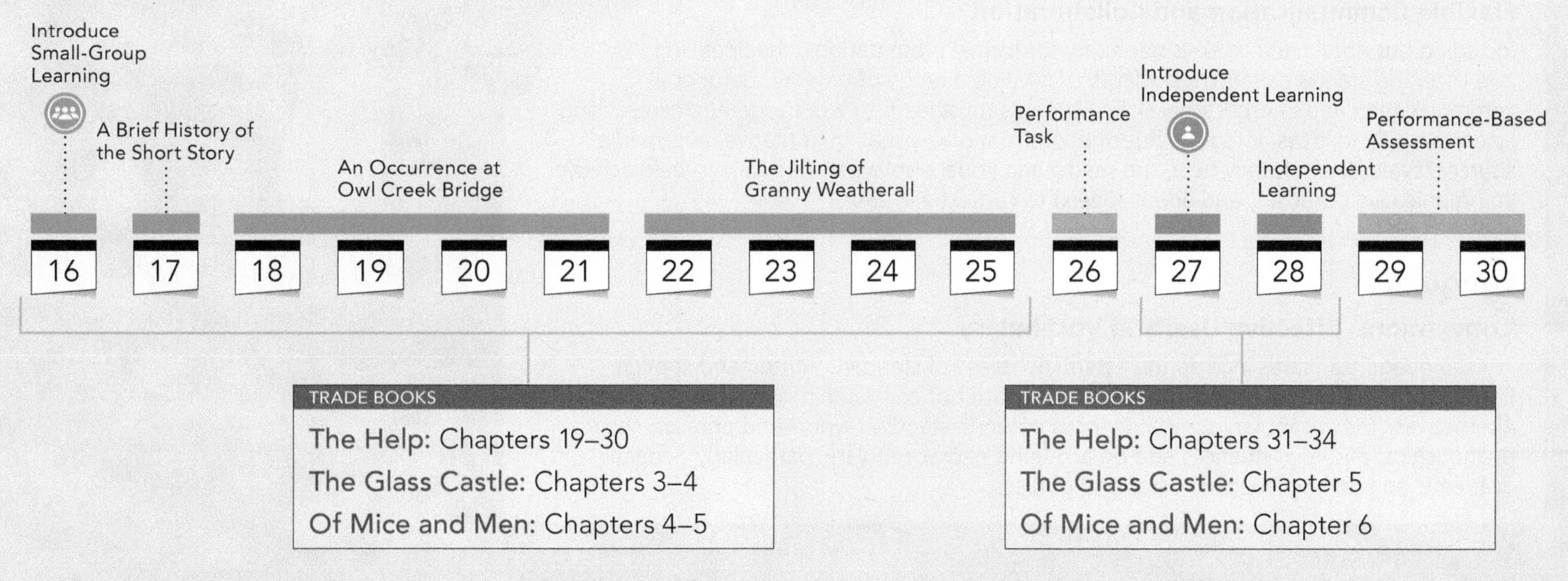

# Standards Correlation

## Key Features of the Standards



### Reading

**Text Complexity and the Growth of Comprehension**

The Reading standards place equal emphasis on the sophistication of what students read and the skill with which they read. Standard 10 defines a grade-by-grade "staircase" of increasing text complexity that rises from beginning reading to the college and career readiness level. Whatever they are reading, students must also show a steadily growing ability to discern more from and make fuller use of text. This process should include making an increasing number of connections among ideas and between texts, considering a wider range of textual evidence, and becoming more sensitive to inconsistencies, ambiguities, and poor reasoning in texts.

### Writing

**Text Types, Responding to Reading, and Research**

The Standards acknowledge the fact that whereas some writing skills, such as the ability to plan, revise, edit, and publish, are applicable to many types of writing, other skills are more properly defined in terms of specific writing types: arguments, informative/explanatory texts, and narratives. Standard 9 stresses the importance of the writing-reading connection by requiring students to draw upon and write about evidence from literary and informational texts. Because of the centrality of writing to most forms of inquiry, research standards are prominently included in this strand, though skills important to research are infused throughout the document.

### Speaking and Listening

**Flexible Communication and Collaboration**

Including but not limited to skills necessary for formal presentations, the Speaking and Listening standards require students to develop a range of broadly useful oral communication and interpersonal skills. Students must learn to work together, express and listen carefully to ideas, integrate information from oral, visual, quantitative, and media sources, evaluate what they hear, use media and visual displays strategically to help achieve communicative purposes, and adapt speech to context and task.

### Language

**Conventions, Effective Use, and Vocabulary**

The Language standards include the essential "rules" of standard written and spoken English, but they also approach language as a matter of craft and informed choice among alternatives. The vocabulary standards focus on understanding words and phrases, their relationships, and their nuances and on acquiring new vocabulary, particularly general academic and domain-specific words and phrases.

## Correlation to *myPerspectives*™ *English Language Arts*

The following correlation shows points at which focused standards instruction is provided in the Student Edition. The Teacher's Edition provides further opportunity to address standards through Personalize for Learning notes and additional resources available only in the Interactive Teacher's Edition.

| Grade 11 Standards for Literature | | |
|---|---|---|
| **STANDARD CODE** | **Standard** | **Print and Interactive Edition** |
| **Key Ideas and Details** | | |
| **RL.11.1** | Cite strong and thorough textual evidence to support analysis of what the text says explicitly as well as inferences drawn from the text, including determining where the text leaves matters uncertain. | **SE/TE:** The Writing of Walt Whitman, 164; "The Notorious Jumping Frog of Calaveras County," 426; "A White Heron," 444; *The Crucible* (audio), 689; "Everyday Use," 774; "Everything Stuck to Him," 788; "The Leap," 802; Students will address this standard in *Analyze the Text* features which appear with every literature selection. |
| **RL.11.2** | Determine two or more themes or central ideas of a text and analyze their development over the course of the text, including how they interact and build on one another to produce a complex account; provide an objective summary of the text. | **SE/TE:** "The Story of an Hour," 356; "A White Heron," 444; *The Crucible,* Act IV, 680 |
| **RL.11.3** | Analyze the impact of the author's choices regarding how to develop and relate elements of a story or drama (e.g., where a story is set, how the action is ordered, how the characters are introduced and developed). | **SE/TE:** "A Wagner Matinée," 258; "The Story of an Hour," 356; *The Crucible,* Act I, 598; *The Crucible,* Act II, 626; *The Crucible,* Act III, 658; "Antojos," 734; "Everyday Use," 774; "Everything Stuck to Him," 792; "The Leap," 802 |
| **Craft and Structure** | | |
| **RL.11.4** | Determine the meaning of words and phrases as they are used in the text, including figurative and connotative meanings; analyze the impact of specific word choices on meaning and tone, including words with multiple meanings or language that is particularly fresh, engaging, or beautiful. | **SE/TE:** The Writing of Walt Whitman, 166; The Poetry of Emily Dickinson, 180; "A Wagner Matinée," 260; "The Notorious Jumping Frog of Calaveras County," 428; "Chicago" / "Wilderness," 500; *The Crucible,* Act IV, 682; "The Leap," 804; "The Jilting of Granny Weatherall," 855 |
| **RL.11.5** | Analyze how an author's choices concerning how to structure specific parts of a text (e.g., the choice of where to begin or end a story, the choice to provide a comedic or tragic resolution) contribute to its overall structure and meaning as well as its aesthetic impact. | **SE/TE:** The Writing of Walt Whitman, 164; The Poetry of Emily Dickinson, 180; "The Love Song of J. Alfred Prufrock," 244; "A White Heron," 448; "Chicago" / "Wilderness," 500; "In the Longhouse, Oneida Museum" / "Cloudy Day," 518; *The Crucible,* Act I, 598; *The Crucible,* Act II, 626; "Antojos," 734; "Everything Stuck to Him," 788; "An Occurrence at Owl Creek Bridge," 840; "The Jilting of Granny Weatherall," 854; "An Occurrence at Owl Creek Bridge" / "The Jilting of Granny Weatherall," 856 |
| **RL.11.6** | Analyze a case in which grasping a point of view requires distinguishing what is directly stated in a text from what is really meant (e.g., satire, sarcasm, irony, or understatement). | **SE/TE:** "The Love Song of J. Alfred Prufrock," 244; "The Story of an Hour," 358; "The Notorious Jumping Frog of Calaveras County," 426; *The Crucible,* Act III, 658 |
| **Integration of Knowledge and Ideas** | | |
| **RL.11.7** | Analyze multiple interpretations of a story, drama, or poem (e.g., recorded or live production of a play or recorded novel or poetry), evaluating how each version interprets the source text. | **SE/TE:** The Poetry of Emily Dickinson, 184; "Great Lives: Emily Dickinson," 189; The Poetry of Emily Dickinson / "Great Lives: Emily Dickinson," 190; *The Crucible, / The Crucible,* (audio)," 690 |
| **RL.11.8** | (Not applicable to literature) | |
| **RL.11.9** | Demonstrate knowledge of eighteenth-, nineteenth- and early-twentieth-century foundational works of American literature, including how two or more texts from the same period treat similar themes or topics. | **SE/TE:** The Writing of Walt Whitman, 164; The Poetry of Emily Dickinson, 180; "The Notorious Jumping Frog of Calaveras County," 430 |

# Standards Correlation

| Grade 11 Standards for Literature (continued) | | |
|---|---|---|
| **STANDARD CODE** | **Standard** | **Print and Interactive Edition** |
| **Range of Reading and Level of Text Complexity** | | |
| **RL.11.10** | By the end of grade 11, read and comprehend literature, including stories, dramas, and poems, in the grades 11–CCR text complexity band proficiently, with scaffolding as needed at the high end of the range. | **SE/TE:** First-Read Guide, Unit 1: 130, Unit 2: 266, Unit 3: 384, Unit 4: 536, Unit 5: 742, Unit 6: 862; Close-Read Guide, Unit 1: 131, Unit 2: 267, Unit 3: 385, Unit 4: 537, Unit 5: 743, Unit 6: 863; The Writing of Walt Whitman, 152; The Poetry of Emily Dickinson, 170; "The Love Song of J. Alfred Prufrock," 236; "A Wagner Matinée," 248; "The Story of an Hour," 352; "The Notorious Jumping Frog of Calaveras County," 418; "A White Heron," 432; "Chicago" / "Wilderness," 492; "In the Longhouse, Oneida Museum" / "Cloudy Day," 510; *The Crucible,* Act I, 560; *The Crucible,* Act II, 600; *The Crucible,* Act III, 628; *The Crucible,* Act IV, 660; *The Crucible,* (audio), 686; "Antojos," 722; "Everyday Use," 764; "Everything Stuck to Him," 780; "The Leap," 794; "An Occurrence at Owl Creek Bridge," 828; "The Jilting of Granny Weatherall," 842 |

| Grade 11 Standards for Informational Text | | |
|---|---|---|
| **STANDARD CODE** | **Standard** | **Print and Interactive Edition** |
| **Key Ideas and Details** | | |
| **RI.11.1** | Cite strong and thorough textual evidence to support analysis of what the text says explicitly as well as inferences drawn from the text, including determining where the text leaves matters uncertain. | **SE/TE:** *Declaration of Independence,* 24; *Speech in the Convention,* 46; *Walden* / "Civil Disobedience," 226; *What to the Slave Is the Fourth of July?,* 294; *Life on the Mississippi,* 414; *Farewell to Manzanar,* 715; Students will address this standard in Analyze the Text features which appear with every informational text selection. |
| **RI.11.2** | Determine two or more central ideas of a text and analyze their development over the course of the text, including how they interact and build on one another to provide a complex analysis; provide an objective summary of the text. | **SE/TE:** "Nature" / "Self-Reliance," 210; *Second Inaugural Address,* 304; *Ain't I a Woman?,* 334; "A Literature of Place," 470 |
| **RI.11.3** | Analyze a complex set of ideas or sequence of events and explain how specific individuals, ideas, or events interact and develop over the course of the text. | **SE/TE:** *America's Constitution: A Biography,* 81; *The United States Constitution: A Graphic Adaptation,* 89; "A Literature of Place," 470; *Farewell to Manzanar,* 715; "A Brief History of the Short Story," 824 |
| **Craft and Structure** | | |
| **RI.11.4** | Determine the meaning of words and phrases as they are used in a text, including figurative, connotative, and technical meanings; analyze how an author uses and refines the meaning of a key term or terms over the course of a text (e.g., how Madison defines faction in Federalist No. 10). | **SE/TE:** *Brown v. Board of Education: Opinion of the Court,* 367; *Life on the Mississippi,* 416; *Dust Tracks on a Road,* 490; *The Way to Rainy Mountain,* 528 |
| **RI.11.5** | Analyze and evaluate the effectiveness of the structure an author uses in his or her exposition or argument, including whether the structure makes points clear, convincing, and engaging. | **SE/TE:** *Preamble to the Constitution / Bill of Rights,* 34; "The American Revolution: Visual Propaganda," 58; *America's Constitution: A Biography,* 81; *The United States Constitution: A Graphic Adaptation,* 89; "Nature" / "Self-Reliance," 210; *What to the Slave Is the Fourth of July?,* 294; *Second Inaugural Address,* 304; *Declaration of Sentiments* / "Giving Women the Vote," 350; *Brown v. Board of Education: Opinion of the Court,* 369; "Was 'Brown v. Board' a Failure?", 377; *Brown v. Board of Education: Opinion of the Court,* 78; "A Brief History of the Short Story," 824 |
| **RI.11.6** | Determine an author's point of view or purpose in a text in which the rhetoric is particularly effective, analyzing how style and content contribute to the power, persuasiveness, or beauty of the text. | **SE/TE:** *Speech in the Convention,* 46; *America's Constitution: A Biography,* 80; *The Interesting Narrative of the Life of Olaudah Equiano,* 98; *Letter to John Adams / Dear Abigail,*116; *Gettysburg Address,* 122, 124; *Walden* / "Civil Disobedience," 226, 228; *Second Inaugural Address,* 304; *Ain't I a Woman?,* 334; *Declaration of Sentiments* / "Giving Women the Vote," 350; *Life on the Mississippi,* 414; *Dust Tracks on a Road,* 488, 490; *The Way to Rainy Mountain,* 528; *Farewell to Manzanar,* 715 |

| Grade 11 Standards for Informational Text (continued) | | |
|---|---|---|
| **STANDARD CODE** | **Standard** | **Print and Interactive Edition** |
| **Integration of Knowledge and Ideas** | | |
| **RI.11.7** | Integrate and evaluate multiple sources of information presented in different media or formats (e.g., visually, quantitatively) as well as in words in order to address a question or solve a problem. | **SE/TE:** "The American Revolution: Visual Propaganda," 58; *America's Constitution: A Biography / The United States Constitution: A Graphic Adaptation,* 90; "Perspectives on Lincoln," 316; *Declaration of Sentiments /* "Giving Women the Vote," 350; "Chicago" / "Wilderness" / "Sandburg's Chicago," 508; *Farewell to Manzanar /* "Interview with George Takei," 720 |
| **RI.11.8** | Delineate and evaluate the reasoning in seminal U.S. texts, including the application of constitutional principles and use of legal reasoning (e.g., in U.S. Supreme Court majority opinions and dissents) and the premises, purposes, and arguments in works of public advocacy (e.g., *The Federalist*, presidential addresses). | **SE/TE:** *Declaration of Independence,* 24; *What to the Slave Is the Fourth of July?,* 294; *Brown v. Board of Education: Opinion of the Court /* "Was 'Brown v. Board' a Failure?", 378 |
| **RI.11.9** | Analyze seventeenth-, eighteenth-, and nineteenth-century foundational U.S. documents of historical and literary significance (including The Declaration of Independence, the Preamble to the Constitution, the Bill of Rights, and Lincoln's Second Inaugural Address) for their themes, purposes, and rhetorical features. | **SE/TE:** *Declaration of Independence,* 24; *Preamble to the Constitution / Bill of Rights,* 34; *Letter to John Adams / Dear Abigail,* 114; *Gettysburg Address,* 122; "Nature" / "Self-Reliance," 210; *Second Inaugural Address,* 304; *Declaration of Sentiments,* 345 |
| **Range of Reading and Level of Text Complexity** | | |
| **RI.11.10** | By the end of grade 11, read and comprehend literary nonfiction in the grades 11–CCR text complexity band proficiently, with scaffolding as needed at the high end of the range. | **SE/TE:** *Declaration of Independence,* 16; *Preamble to the Constitution / Bill of Rights,* 30; *Speech in the Convention,* 40; "The American Revolution: Visual Propaganda," 52; *America's Constitution: A Biography,* 72; *The United States Constitution: A Graphic Adaptation,* 82; *The Interesting Narrative of the Life of Olaudah Equiano,* 92; *Letter to John Adams / Dear Abigail,* 102; *Gettysburg Address,* 118; First-Read Guide, Unit 1: 130, Unit 2: 266, Unit 3: 384, Unit 4, Unit 5: 742: 536, Unit 6: 862; Close-Read Guide, Unit 1: 131, Unit 2: 267, Unit 3: 385, Unit 4: 537, Unit 5: 743, Unit 6: 863; The Writing of Walt Whitman, 152; "Great Lives: Emily Dickinson,"186; "Nature" / "Self-Reliance," 204; *Walden /* "Civil Disobedience," 214; "Innovators and Their Inventions," 230; *What to the Slave Is the Fourth of July?,* 288; *Second Inaugural Address,* 300; "Perspectives on Lincoln," 310; *Ain't I a Woman?,* 330; *Declaration of Sentiments,* 338; "Giving Women the Vote," 346; *Brown v. Board of Education: Opinion of the Court,* 360; "Was 'Brown v. Board' a Failure?", 370; *Life on the Mississippi,* 406; "A Literature of Place," 462; *Dust Tracks on a Road,* 480; "Sandburg's Chicago," 502; *The Way to Rainy Mountain,* 520; *Farewell to Manzanar,* 704; "Interview with George Takei," 716; "A Brief History of the Short Story," 820 |

| Grade 11 Writing Standards | | |
|---|---|---|
| **STANDARD CODE** | **Standard** | **Print and Interactive Edition** |
| **Text Types and Purposes** | | |
| **W.11.1** | Write arguments to support claims in an analysis of substantive topics or texts, using valid reasoning and relevant and sufficient evidence. | **SE/TE:** *Declaration of Independence,* 28; *Speech in the Convention,* 50; Whole-Class Performance Task, Unit 1: 60, Unit 5: 692; *The Interesting Narrative of the Life of Olaudah Equiano,* 101; Performance-Based Assessment, Unit 1: 134, Unit 5: 746; *The Crucible,* Act IV, 684 |
| **W.11.1.a** | Introduce precise, knowledgeable claim(s), establish the significance of the claim(s), distinguish the claim(s) from alternate or opposing claims, and create an organization that logically sequences claim(s), counterclaims, reasons, and evidence. | **SE/TE:** *Declaration of Independence,* 28; *Speech in the Convention,* 50; Whole-Class Performance Task, Unit 1: 61, 64, Unit 5: 693, 696; *America's Constitution: A Biography,* 81; *The Interesting Narrative of the Life of Olaudah Equiano,* 101; Performance-Based Assessment, Unit 1: 133, Unit 5: 745; *The Crucible,* Act IV, 684 |

# Standards Correlation

| Grade 11 Writing Standards (continued) | | |
|---|---|---|
| STANDARD CODE | Standard | Print and Interactive Edition |
| **W.11.1.b** | Develop claim(s) and counterclaims fairly and thoroughly, supplying the most relevant evidence for each while pointing out the strengths and limitations of both in a manner that anticipates the audience's knowledge level, concerns, values, and possible biases. | **SE/TE:** *Declaration of Independence,* 28; *Speech in the Convention,* 50; Whole-Class Performance Task, Unit 1: 61, 63, Unit 5: 694; *The Interesting Narrative of the Life of Olaudah Equiano,* 101; *The Crucible,* Act IV, 684 |
| **W.11.1.c** | Use words, phrases, and clauses as well as varied syntax to link the major sections of the text, create cohesion, and clarify the relationships between claim(s) and reasons, between reasons and evidence, and between claim(s) and counterclaims. | **SE/TE:** *Declaration of Independence,* 28; *Speech in the Convention,*50; Whole-Class Performance Task, Unit 1: 65, Unit 5: 698; *The Interesting Narrative of the Life of Olaudah Equiano,* 101; *The Crucible,* Act IV, 684 |
| **W.11.1.d** | Establish and maintain a formal style and objective tone while attending to the norms and conventions of the discipline in which they are writing. | **SE/TE:** *Declaration of Independence,* 28; *Speech in the Convention,* 50; Whole-Class Performance Task, Unit 1: 66, Unit 5: 698; *The Interesting Narrative of the Life of Olaudah Equiano,* 101; *The Crucible,* Act IV, 684 |
| **W.11.1.e** | Provide a concluding statement or section that follows from and supports the argument presented. | **SE/TE:** *Declaration of Independence,* 28; *Speech in the Convention,* 50; Whole-Class Performance Task, Unit 1: 64, Unit 5, 696; *The Interesting Narrative of the Life of Olaudah Equiano,* 101; *The Crucible,* Act IV, 684 |
| **W.11.2** | Write informative/explanatory texts to examine and convey complex ideas, concepts, and information clearly and accurately through the effective selection, organization, and analysis of content. | **SE/TE:** *America's Constitution: A Biography / The United States Constitution: A Graphic Adaptation,* 90; *Gettysburg Address,* 125; "A Wagner Matinée," 261; *What to the Slave Is the Fourth of July?,* 298; *Second Inaugural Address,* 308; Whole-Class Performance Task, Unit 3: 318, Unit 4: 450; *Ain't I a Woman?,* 337; Performance-Based Assessment, Unit 3: 388, Unit 4: 540; *Life on the Mississippi* / "The Notorious Jumping Frog of Calaveras County," 430; "A Literature of Place" / "American Regional Art," 478; "In the Longhouse, Oneida Museum" / "Cloudy Day" / *The Way to Rainy Mountain,* 531; *Farewell to Manzanar* / "Interview with George Takei," 720; "An Occurrence at Owl Creek Bridge" / "The Jilting of Granny Weatherall," 856 |
| **W.11.2.a** | Introduce a topic; organize complex ideas, concepts, and information so that each new element builds on that which precedes it to create a unified whole; include formatting (e.g., headings), graphics (e.g., figures, tables), and multimedia when useful to aiding comprehension. | **SE/TE:** Whole-Class Performance Task, Unit 3: 319, Unit 4: 451, 454; Performance-Based Assessment, Unit 3: 387, Unit 4: 539; *Life on the Mississippi* / "The Notorious Jumping Frog of Calaveras County," 430 |
| **W.11.2.b** | Develop the topic thoroughly by selecting the most significant and relevant facts, extended definitions, concrete details, quotations, or other information and examples appropriate to the audience's knowledge of the topic. | **SE/TE:** *Preamble to the Constitution / Bill of Rights,* 38; Whole-Class Performance Task, Unit 3: 319, 322, Unit 4: 452; *Life on the Mississippi* / "The Notorious Jumping Frog of Calaveras County," 430 |
| **W.11.2.c** | Use appropriate and varied transitions and syntax to link the major sections of the text, create cohesion, and clarify the relationships among complex ideas and concepts. | **SE/TE:** Whole-Class Performance Task, Unit 3: 323, Unit 4: 454–456; "Perspectives on Lincoln," 317; Performance-Based Assessment: Unit 4: 540-541; "The Love Song of J. Alfred Prufrock," 247 |
| **W.11.2.d** | Use precise language, domain-specific vocabulary, and techniques such as metaphor, simile, and analogy to manage the complexity of the topic. | **SE/TE:** Whole-Class Performance Task, Unit 3: 324; *Declaration of Sentiments* / "Giving Women the Vote," 350; *America's Constitution: A Biography,* 80; *Walden* / "Civil Disobedience," 228; "A Wagner Matinée," 260 |
| **W.11.2.e** | Establish and maintain a formal style and objective tone while attending to the norms and conventions of the discipline in which they are writing. | **SE/TE:** *The Interesting Narrative of the Life of Olaudah Equiano,*100; *What to the Slave Is the Fourth of July?,* 298; Whole-Class Performance Task, Unit 4: 456 |
| **W.11.2.f** | Provide a concluding statement or section that follows from and supports the information or explanation presented (e.g., articulating implications or the significance of the topic). | **SE/TE:** Whole-Class Performance Task, Unit 3: 318, 322, 324, Unit 4: 450, 454; *Ain't I a Woman?,* 337; Performance-Based Assessment, Unit 3: 389, Unit 4: 540-541; *Life on the Mississippi* / "The Notorious Jumping Frog of Calaveras County," 431 |
| **W.11.3** | Write narratives to develop real or imagined experiences or events using effective technique, well-chosen details, and well-structured event sequences. | **SE/TE:** The Writing of Walt Whitman, 168; The Poetry of Emily Dickinson, 184; Whole-Class Performance Task, Unit 2: 192, Unit 6: 808; *"Nature" / "Self-Reliance,"* 213; Performance-Based Assessment, Unit 2: 270, Unit 6: 866; *Second Inaugural Address,* 308; "Everyday Use," 778; "Everything Stuck to Him," 792; "The Leap," 806; Small-Group Performance Task, Unit 6: 859 |

| Grade 11 Writing Standards (continued) | | |
|---|---|---|
| STANDARD CODE | Standard | Print and Interactive Edition |
| **W.11.3.a** | Engage and orient the reader by setting out a problem, situation, or observation and its significance, establishing one or multiple point(s) of view, and introducing a narrator and/or characters; create a smooth progression of experiences or events. | **SE/TE:** The Writing of Walt Whitman, 168; The Poetry of Emily Dickinson, 184; "Everyday Use," 778; "Everything Stuck to Him," 792; "The Leap," 806; Whole-Class Performance Task, Unit 2: 193-194, Unit 6: 809-810; Performance-Based Assessment, Unit 2: 269 |
| **W.11.3.b** | Use narrative techniques, such as dialogue, pacing, description, reflection, and multiple plot lines, to develop experiences, events, and/or characters. | **SE/TE:** The Writing of Walt Whitman, 168; The Poetry of Emily Dickinson, 184; "Nature" / "Self-Reliance," 213; "Everyday Use," 778; "Everything Stuck to Him," 792; "The Leap," 806; Whole-Class Performance Task, Unit 2: 197, Unit 6: 810, 814; Small-Group Performance Task, Unit 6: 859 |
| **W.11.3.c** | Use a variety of techniques to sequence events so that they build on one another to create a coherent whole and build toward a particular tone and outcome (e.g., a sense of mystery, suspense, growth, or resolution). | **SE/TE:** The Writing of Walt Whitman, 168; The Poetry of Emily Dickinson, 184; "Everything Stuck to Him," 792; "The Leap," 806; Whole-Class Performance Task, Unit 2: 192-199, Unit 6: 808-810, 814; Performance-Based Assessment, Unit 2: 370-372, Unit 6: 866-867 |
| **W.11.3.d** | Use precise words and phrases, telling details, and sensory language to convey a vivid picture of the experiences, events, setting, and/or characters. | **SE/TE:** The Writing of Walt Whitman, 168; The Poetry of Emily Dickinson, 184; "Nature" / "Self-Reliance," 213; "Everyday Use," 778; "Everything Stuck to Him," 792; "The Leap," 806; Whole-Class Performance Task, Unit 2: 195, 198, Unit 6: 813 |
| **W.11.3.e** | Provide a conclusion that follows from and reflects on what is experienced, observed, or resolved over the course of the narrative. | **SE/TE:** The Writing of Walt Whitman, 168; The Poetry of Emily Dickinson, 184; "Everything Stuck to Him," 792; "The Leap," 806; Whole-Class Performance Task, Unit 2: 194, 197, Unit 6: 810, 814 |
| Production and Distribution of Writing | | |
| **W.11.4** | Produce clear and coherent writing in which the development, organization, and style are appropriate to task, purpose, and audience. | **SE/TE:** *Declaration of Independence,* 28; *Preamble to the Constitution / Bill of Rights,* 38; *Speech in the Convention,* 50; The Writing of Walt Whitman, 168; The Poetry of Emily Dickinson, 184; *What to the Slave Is the Fourth of July?,* 298; *Second Inaugural Address,* 308; "A White Heron," 448; *The Crucible,* Act IV, 684; "Everyday Use," 778; "Everything Stuck to Him," 792; "The Leap," 806; Whole Class Performance Task, Unit 1, Unit 2, Unit 3, Unit 4, Unit 5, Unit 6 |
| **W.11.5** | Develop and strengthen writing as needed by planning, revising, editing, rewriting, or trying a new approach, focusing on addressing what is most significant for a specific purpose and audience. | **SE/TE:** *Life on the Mississippi* / "The Notorious Jumping Frog of Calaveras County," 430; Whole Class Performance Task, Unit 1, Unit 2, Unit 3, Unit 4, Unit 5, Unit 6 |
| **W.11.6** | Use technology, including the Internet, to produce, publish, and update individual or shared writing products in response to ongoing feedback, including new arguments or information. | **SE/TE:** "The American Revolution: Visual Propaganda," 59; "The Love Song of J. Alfred Prufrock," 247; "Perspectives on Lincoln," 317; Whole-Class Performance Task, Unit 1: 67, Unit 2: 199; Performance-Based Assessment, Unit 1: 136 |
| Research to Build and Present Knowledge | | |
| **W.11.7** | Conduct short as well as more sustained research projects to answer a question (including a self-generated question) or solve a problem; narrow or broaden the inquiry when appropriate; synthesize multiple sources on the subject, demonstrating understanding of the subject under investigation. | **SE/TE:** *Gettysburg Address,* 125; "A Wagner Matinée," 261; Whole-Class Performance Task, Unit 3: 318; "Antojos," 737; "A Brief History of the Short Story," 826 |
| **W.11.8** | Gather relevant information from multiple authoritative print and digital sources, using advanced searches effectively; assess the strengths and limitations of each source in terms of the task, purpose, and audience; integrate information into the text selectively to maintain the flow of ideas, avoiding plagiarism and overreliance on any one source and following a standard format for citation. | **SE/TE:** Whole-Class Performance Task, Unit 1: 61, 63, Unit 3: 318, 320-321, Unit 4: 452, Unit 5: 694; *Gettysburg Address,* 125; Performance-Based Assessment, Unit 1: 133-134, Unit 3: 380-381; *Walden* / "Civil Disobedience," 229; "A Wagner Matinée," 261; *What to the Slave Is the Fourth of July?,* 298; "Perspectives on Lincoln," 317 |
| **W.11.9** | Draw evidence from literary or informational texts to support analysis, reflection, and research. | **SE/TE:** The Poetry of Emily Dickinson / "Great Lives: Emily Dickinson," 190; Performance-Based Assessment, Unit 3: 388; "A Literature of Place" / "American Regional Art," 478; "In the Longhouse, Oneida Museum" / "Cloudy Day" / *The Way to Rainy Mountain,* 531; *The Crucible,* Act IV, 682 |

# Standards Correlation

| Grade 11 Writing Standards (continued) | | |
|---|---|---|
| STANDARD CODE | Standard | Print and Interactive Edition |
| W.11.9.a | Apply *grades 11–12 Reading standards* to literature (e.g., "Demonstrate knowledge of eighteenth-, nineteenth- and early-twentieth-century foundational works of American literature, including how two or more texts from the same period treat similar themes or topics"). | **SE/TE:** The Poetry of Emily Dickinson / "Great Lives: Emily Dickinson," 190; *The Crucible,* Act IV, 684; *The Crucible / The Crucible* (audio), 690 |
| W.11.9.b | Apply *grades 11–12 Reading standards* to literary nonfiction (e.g., "Delineate and evaluate the reasoning in seminal U.S. texts, including the application of constitutional principles and use of legal reasoning [e.g., in U.S. Supreme Court Case majority opinions and dissents] and the premises, purposes, and arguments in works of public advocacy [e.g., *The Federalist*, presidential addresses]"). | **SE/TE:** *America's Constitution: A Biography / The United States Constitution: A Graphic Adaptation,* 90; *Brown v. Board of Education: Opinion of the Court* / "Was 'Brown v. Board' a Failure?" *378; Farewell to Manzanar* / "Interview with George Takei," 720 |
| Range of Writing | | |
| W.11.10 | Write routinely over extended time frames (time for research, reflection, and revision) and shorter time frames (a single sitting or a day or two) for a range of tasks, purposes, and audiences. | **SE/TE:** Whole-Class Performance Task, Unit 1: 60, Unit 2: 192, Unit 3: 318, Unit 4: 450, Unit 5: 692, Unit 6: 808; Performance-Based Assessment, Unit 1: 134, Unit 2: 270, Unit 3: 388, Unit 4: 540, Unit 5: 746, Unit 6: 866 |

| Grade 11 Speaking and Listening Standards | | |
|---|---|---|
| STANDARD CODE | Standard | Print and Interactive Teacher's Edition |
| Comprehension and Collaboration | | |
| SL.11.1 | Initiate and participate effectively in a range of collaborative discussions (one-on-one, in groups, and teacher-led) with diverse partners *on grades 11–12 topics, texts, and issues,* building on others' ideas and expressing their own clearly and persuasively. | **SE/TE:** Share Your Independent Learning, Unit 1: 132, Unit 2: 268, Unit 3: 386, Unit 4: 538, Unit 5: 744, Unit 6: 864; Unit Reflection, Unit 2: 273; "Everyday Use," 778 |
| SL.11.1.a | Come to discussions prepared, having read and researched material under study; explicitly draw on that preparation by referring to evidence from texts and other research on the topic or issue to stimulate a thoughtful, well-reasoned exchange of ideas. | **SE/TE:** Unit Reflection, Unit 2: 273, Unit 3: 391, Unit 5: 749, Unit 6: 869; Small-Group Performance Task, Unit 3: 380; *The Crucible,* Act II, 627; "Everyday Use," 778 |
| SL.11.1.b | Work with peers to promote civil, democratic discussions and decision-making, set clear goals and deadlines, and establish individual roles as needed. | **SE/TE:** Small-Group Performance Task, Unit 1: 126, Unit 2: 262, Unit 4: 532; *Walden* / "Civil Disobedience," 229; Students will address this standard in *Working as a Team* features which appear in the Small Group Learning Overview lessons. |
| SL.11.1.c | Propel conversations by posing and responding to questions that probe reasoning and evidence; ensure a hearing for a full range of positions on a topic or issue; clarify, verify, or challenge ideas and conclusions; and promote divergent and creative perspectives. | **SE/TE:** *Declaration of Independence,* 28; The Poetry of Emily Dickinson, 184; *Walden* / "Civil Disobedience," 229; "The Story of an Hour," 358; "A White Heron," 448; Small-Group Performance Task, Unit 5: 738, Unit 6: 858; Students will address this standard in *Launch Activity* features which appear in the Unit Introduction and in *Working as a Team* features which appear in the Small Group Learning Overview lessons. |
| SL.11.1.d | Respond thoughtfully to diverse perspectives; synthesize comments, claims, and evidence made on all sides of an issue; resolve contradictions when possible; and determine what additional information or research is required to deepen the investigation or complete the task. | **SE/TE:** *Walden* / "Civil Disobedience," 229; "The Story of an Hour," 358; Students will address this standard in *Launch Activity* features which appear in the Unit Introduction, in *Working as a Team* features which appear in the Small Group Learning Overview lessons, and *Group Discussion Tips* which appear throughout the program. |
| SL.11.2 | Integrate multiple sources of information presented in diverse formats and media (e.g., visually, quantitatively, orally) in order to make informed decisions and solve problems, evaluating the credibility and accuracy of each source and noting any discrepancies among the data. | **SE/TE:** "The American Revolution: Visual Propaganda," 59; *The United States Constitution: A Graphic Adaptation,* 89; "Perspectives on Lincoln," 316; "American Regional Art," 477; "Chicago" / "Wilderness" / "Sandburg's Chicago," 508–509; "Interview with George Takei," 719 |
| SL.11.3 | Evaluate a speaker's point of view, reasoning, and use of evidence and rhetoric, assessing the stance, premises, links among ideas, word choice, points of emphasis, and tone used. | **SE/TE:** *Speech in the Convention,* 50; *Gettysburg Address,* 124; "Great Lives: Emily Dickinson," 189; The Poetry of Emily Dickinson / "Great Lives: Emily Dickinson," 190; Small-Group Performance Task, Unit 2: 263; *What to the Slave Is the Fourth of July?*, 298; *Second Inaugural Address,* 308; "Giving Women the Vote," 349; "Interview with George Takei," 719 |

## Grade 11 Speaking and Listening Standards (continued)

| STANDARD CODE | Standard | Print and Interactive Teacher's Edition |
|---|---|---|
| **Presentation of Knowledge and Ideas** | | |
| **SL.11.4** | Present information, findings, and supporting evidence, conveying a clear and distinct perspective, such that listeners can follow the line of reasoning, alternative or opposing perspectives are addressed, and the organization, development, substance, and style are appropriate to purpose, audience, and a range of formal and informal tasks. | **SE/TE:** *Preamble to the Constitution / Bill of Rights,* 38; *Letter to John Adams / Dear Abigail,* 117; Small-Group Performance Task, Unit 1: 127, Unit 2: 263, Unit 3: 381, Unit 4: 533, Unit 5: 739; "Innovators and Their Inventions," 234, Performance-Based Assessment, Unit 2: 272, Unit 4: 542, Unit 5: 748; Unit Reflection, Unit 4: 543; *The Crucible,* Act IV, 684; "The Leap," 806 |
| **SL.11.5** | Make strategic use of digital media (e.g., textual, graphical, audio, visual, and interactive elements) in presentations to enhance understanding of findings, reasoning, and evidence and to add interest. | **SE/TE:** *Speech in the Convention*, 50; "The American Revolution: Visual Propaganda," 59; "The Love Song of J. Alfred Prufrock," 246; "Perspectives on Lincoln," 316; "Chicago" / "Wilderness" / "Sandburg's Chicago," 508; Performance-Based Assessment, Unit 6: 868 |
| **SL.11.6** | Adapt speech to a variety of contexts and tasks, demonstrating a command of formal English when indicated or appropriate. | **SE/TE:** The Writing of Walt Whitman, 168; The Poetry of Emily Dickinson, 184; Performance-Based Assessment, Unit 2: 272; Small-Group Performance Task, Unit 3: 381; *Dust Tracks on a Road,* 491; "Everything Stuck to Him," 792; "An Occurrence at Owl Creek Bridge" / "The Jilting of Granny Weatherall," 856 |

## Grade 11 Language Standards

| STANDARD CODE | Standard | Print and Interactive Edition |
|---|---|---|
| **Conventions of Standard English** | | |
| **L.11.1** | Demonstrate command of the conventions of standard English grammar and usage when writing or speaking. | **SE/TE: SE/TE:** Whole-Class Performance Task, Unit 1: 65, Unit 2: 198, Unit 5: 697; *The Interesting Narrative of the Life of Olaudah Equiano,* 100; "The Love Song of J. Alfred Prufrock," 246; *What to the Slave Is the Fourth of July?*, 296; *Second Inaugural Address,* 306; *Declaration of Sentiments,* 345; *Brown v. Board of Education: Opinion of the Court,* 369; "Was 'Brown v. Board' a Failure?", 377; *The Crucible,* Act I, 599; "Antojos," 736; "Everything Stuck to Him," 790 |
| **L.11.1.a** | Apply the understanding that usage is a matter of convention, can change over time, and is sometimes contested. | **SE/TE:** *Declaration of Independence,* 26; *Preamble to the Constitution / Bill of Rights,* 36; *The Interesting Narrative of the Life of Olaudah Equiano,* 100; *Ain't I a Woman?,* 336; *The Crucible,* Act I, 599; "Everyday Use," 776; "A Brief History of the Short Story," 826; "An Occurrence at Owl Creek Bridge," 841 |
| **L.11.1.b** | Resolve issues of complex or contested usage, consulting references (e.g., *Merriam-Webster's Dictionary of English Usage, Garner's Modern American Usage*) as needed. | **SE/TE:** *Declaration of Independence,* 26; "Everyday Use," 776 |
| **L.11.2** | Demonstrate command of the conventions of standard English capitalization, punctuation, and spelling when writing. | **SE/TE:** *Speech in the Convention,* 48; "A Literature of Place," 471; Whole-Class Performance Task, Unit 6: 811 |
| **L.11.2.a** | Observe hyphenation conventions. | **SE/TE:** "The Love Song of J. Alfred Prufrock," 246; "A Literature of Place," 471 |
| **L.11.2.b** | Spell correctly. | **SE/TE:** Whole-Class Performance Task, Unit 1: 67, Unit 2: 199, Unit 3: 324–325, Unit 4: 457, Unit 5: 699, Unit 6: 815; *America's Constitution: A Biography / The United States Constitution: A Graphic Adaptation,* 91; The Poetry of Emily Dickinson / "Great Lives: Emily Dickinson," 191; "In the Longhouse, Oneida Museum" / "Cloudy Day" / *The Way to Rainy Mountain,* 531; *The Crucible / The Crucible* (audio), 691; *Farewell to Manzanar* "Interview with George Takei," 721 |

# Standards Correlation

| Grade 11 Language Standards (continued) | | |
|---|---|---|
| **STANDARD CODE** | **Standard** | **Print and Interactive Teacher's Edition** |
| **Knowledge of Language** | | |
| **L.11.3** | Apply knowledge of language to understand how language functions in different contexts, to make effective choices for meaning or style, and to comprehend more fully when reading or listening. | **SE/TE:** "Nature" / "Self-Reliance," 212; *What to the Slave Is the Fourth of July?,* 296; *Second Inaugural Address,* 306; *Ain't I a Woman?,* 336; *Brown v. Board of Education: Opinion of the Court,* 369; "Was 'Brown v. Board' a Failure?", 377; "A White Heron," 446; *The Crucible*, Act I, 599; "Everything Stuck to Him," 790 |
| **L.11.3.a** | Vary syntax for effect, consulting references (e.g., Tufte's *Artful Sentences*) for guidance as needed; apply an understanding of syntax to the study of complex texts when reading. | **SE/TE:** *Declaration of Independence,* 26; *Speech in the Convention,* 48; "Nature" / "Self-Reliance," 212; Whole-Class Performance Task, Unit 3: 323, Unit 4: 455; "Everyday Use," 776; "An Occurrence at Owl Creek Bridge," 841 |
| **Vocabulary Acquisition and Use** | | |
| **L.11.4** | Determine or clarify the meaning of unknown and multiple-meaning words and phrases based on *grades 11–12 reading and content*, choosing flexibly from a range of strategies. | **SE/TE:** *Preamble to the Constitution / Bill of Rights,* 36; *The Interesting Narrative of the Life of Olaudah Equiano,* 92; *Gettysburg Address,* 118; "A Literature of Place," 462; *Dust Tracks on a Road,* 488; "Chicago" / "Wilderness," 492; "In the Longhouse, Oneida Museum" / "Cloudy Day," 510; *The Way to Rainy Mountain,* 520; *Farewell to Manzanar,* 704; "Antojos," 722; "An Occurrence at Owl Creek Bridge," 839 |
| **L.11.4.a** | Use context (e.g., the overall meaning of a sentence, paragraph, or text; a word's position or function in a sentence) as a clue to the meaning of a word or phrase. | **SE/TE:** *America's Constitution: A Biography,* 72; *Letter to John Adams / Dear Abigail,* 102; "Nature" / "Self-Reliance," 204; "The Love Song of J. Alfred Prufrock," 236; *Ain't I a Woman?,* 330; *Declaration of Sentiments,* 338; "Was 'Brown v. Board' a Failure?", 370; "A Literature of Place," 462; "Chicago" / "Wilderness," 492; "In the Longhouse, Oneida Museum" / "Cloudy Day," 510; *The Way to Rainy Mountain,* 520; "Antojos," 722; "A Brief History of the Short Story," 820; "An Occurrence at Owl Creek Bridge," 828 |
| **L.11.4.b** | Identify and correctly use patterns of word changes that indicate different meanings or parts of speech (e.g., *conceive, conception, conceivable*). | **SE/TE:** *Declaration of Independence,* 26; *Letter to John Adams / Dear Abigail,* 114; The Writing of Walt Whitman, 166; The Poetry of Emily Dickinson, 182; *Walden* / "Civil Disobedience," 214, 226; "The Love Song of J. Alfred Prufrock," 244; "A Wagner Matinée," 248; "The Story of an Hour," 352; *Brown v. Board of Education: Opinion of the Court,* 360; *Life on the Mississippi,* 416; "A Literature of Place," 469; *Dust Tracks on a Road,* 480; "Chicago" / "Wilderness," 499; *The Way to Rainy Mountain,* 527; *Farewell to Manzanar,* 704, 713; "The Leap," 804; "A Brief History of the Short Story," 824; "An Occurrence at Owl Creek Bridge," 839; "The Jilting of Granny Weatherall," 842, 853 |
| **L.11.4.c** | Consult general and specialized reference materials (e.g., dictionaries, glossaries, thesauruses), both print and digital, to find the pronunciation of a word or determine or clarify its precise meaning, its part of speech, its etymology, or its standard usage. | **SE/TE:** *Declaration of Independence,* 26; *Preamble to the Constitution / Bill of Rights,* 36; *Speech in the Convention,* 48; *America's Constitution: A Biography,* 79; *The Interesting Narrative of the Life of Olaudah Equiano,* 98; The Poetry of Emily Dickinson, 182; "Nature" / "Self-Reliance," 210; "A Wagner Matinée," 258; *What to the Slave Is the Fourth of July?,* 296; *Declaration of Sentiments,* 343; "Was 'Brown v. Board' a Failure?", 375; "A White Heron," 446; "In the Longhouse, Oneida Museum" / "Cloudy Day," 517; *The Crucible,* Act II, 625; The Crucible, Act IV, 680; "Antojos," 734; Whole-Class Performance Task, Unit 6: 813 |
| **L.11.4.d** | Verify the preliminary determination of the meaning of a word or phrase (e.g., by checking the inferred meaning in context or in a dictionary). | **SE/TE:** *Gettysburg Address,* 118; The Writing of Walt Whitman, 166; *Ain't I a Woman?,* 330; *Declaration of Sentiments,* 338; *Life on the Mississippi,* 416; "A White Heron," 446; *Farewell to Manzanar,* 713 |

| Grade 11 Language Standards (continued) | | |
|---|---|---|
| STANDARD CODE | Standard | Print and Interactive Teacher's Edition |
| **L.11.5** | Demonstrate understanding of figurative language, word relationships, and nuances in word meanings. | **SE/TE:** The Poetry of Emily Dickinson, 182; "The Notorious Jumping Frog of Calaveras County," 428; *Dust Tracks on a Road,* 488; "In the Longhouse, Oneida Museum" / "Cloudy Day," 518; *The Way to Rainy Mountain,* 529; *The Crucible,* Act I, 597; *The Crucible*, Act III, 657; "The Jilting of Granny Weatherall," 855 |
| **L.11.5.a** | Interpret figures of speech (e.g., hyperbole, paradox) in context and analyze their role in the text. | **SE/TE:** "A Wagner Matinée," 260; "The Notorious Jumping Frog of Calaveras County," 426; *Dust Tracks on a Road,* 490; "Chicago" / "Wilderness," 500 |
| **L.11.5.b** | Analyze nuances in the meaning of words with similar denotations. | **SE/TE:** *Gettysburg Address,* 122; *Second Inaugural Address,* 306; "The Story of an Hour," 356; "The Notorious Jumping Frog of Calaveras County," 428; *The Crucible,* Act III, 657 |
| **L.11.6** | Acquire and use accurately general academic and domain-specific words and phrases, sufficient for reading, writing, speaking, and listening at the college and career readiness level; demonstrate independence in gathering vocabulary knowledge when considering a word or phrase important to comprehension or expression. | **SE/TE:** Unit Goals, Unit 1: 4, Unit 2: 140, Unit 3: 276, Unit 4: 394, Unit 5: 546, Unit 6: 752; *The United States Constitution: A Graphic Adaptation*, 82; "Innovators and Their Inventions," 230; *Second Inaugural Address*, 306; *Brown v. Board of Education: Opinion of the Court,* 367; "American Regional Art," 472, 477; "Sandburg's Chicago," 502, 507; Small-Group Performance Task, Unit 4: 533; *The Crucible,* Act II, 625; "Interview with George Takei," 716, 719 |

Bill of Rights
Congress of the United
OIN, or DIE.
People

UNIT

# Writing Freedom

## Words That Shaped a Nation

INTRODUCTION

## Jump Start

Engage students in discussion based on the following questions:

Why do we interpret language differently today than at the time of the Founding Fathers? Will you be teaching students twenty years from now about the Constitution, using even more changed language?

Ask students to write three reasons why it will most likely be valid to speak about the Constitution using conventions that have changed even more over time.

## Words That Shaped a Nation

Ask students what the term *words that shaped a nation* suggests to them. Point out that as they work through this unit, they will read many examples showing how powerful words can alter people's lives.

## Video

Project the introduction video in class, ask students to open the video in their digital textbooks, or have students scan the Bounce Page icon with their phones to access the video.

**Discuss It** If you want to make this a digital activity, go online and navigate to the Discussion Board. Alternatively, students can share their responses in a class discussion.

### Block Scheduling

Each day in this pacing calendar represents a 40–50 minute class period. Teachers using block scheduling may combine days to reflect their class schedule. In addition, teachers may revise pacing to differentiate and support core instruction by integrating components and resources as students require.

UNIT 1

# Writing Freedom

## Words That Shaped a Nation

Boston Tea Party

**Discuss It** In what ways is the concept of "no taxation without representation" central to America's identity as a nation?

Write your response before sharing your ideas.

SCAN FOR MULTIMEDIA

2



### Pacing Plan

| Unit Introduction | Introduce Whole-Class Learning | Historical Perspectives | Declaration of Independence | | Preamble to the U.S. Constitution • Bill of Rights | | | Speech in the Convention | | | The American Revolution: Visual Propaganda | | Performance Task | |
|---|---|---|---|---|---|---|---|---|---|---|---|---|---|---|
| 1 | 2 | 3 | 4 | 5 | 6 | 7 | 8 | 9 | 10 | 11 | 12 | 13 | 14 | 15 |

DIGITAL PERSPECTIVES

 Audio  Video  Document  Annotation Highlights  EL Highlights Online Assessment

UNIT 1

## UNIT INTRODUCTION

ESSENTIAL QUESTION:

What is the meaning of freedom?

LAUNCH TEXT
ARGUMENT MODEL
Totally Free?

### WHOLE-CLASS LEARNING

HISTORICAL PERSPECTIVES

*Focus Period: 1750–1800*
A New Nation

ANCHOR TEXT: FOUNDATIONAL DOCUMENT

Declaration of Independence
*Thomas Jefferson*

▸ MEDIA CONNECTION: John F. Kennedy Reads the Declaration of Independence

ANCHOR TEXT: FOUNDATIONAL DOCUMENTS

Preamble to the Constitution
*Gouverneur Morris*

Bill of Rights
*James Madison*

ANCHOR TEXT: SPEECH

Speech in the Convention
*Benjamin Franklin*

▸ MEDIA CONNECTION: The U. S. Constitution

MEDIA: IMAGE GALLERY

The American Revolution: Visual Propaganda

PERFORMANCE TASK

WRITING FOCUS:
Write an Argument

### SMALL-GROUP LEARNING

COMPARE

EXPOSITORY NONFICTION

*from* America's Constitution: A Biography
*Akhil Reed Amar*

GRAPHIC NOVEL

*from* The United States Constitution: A Graphic Adaptation
*Jonathan Hennessey and Aaron McConnell*

AUTOBIOGRAPHY

*from* The Interesting Narrative of the Life of Olaudah Equiano
*Olaudah Equiano*

LETTER | BIOGRAPHY

Letter to John Adams
*Abigail Adams*

*from* Dear Abigail: The Intimate Lives and Revolutionary Ideas of Abigail Adams and Her Two Remarkable Sisters
*Diane Jacobs*

SPEECH

Gettysburg Address
*Abraham Lincoln*

PERFORMANCE TASK

SPEAKING AND LISTENING FOCUS:
Present an Argument

### INDEPENDENT LEARNING

ESSAY

*from* Democracy Is Not a Spectator Sport
*Arthur Blaustein with Helen Matatov*

SPEECH

Reflections on the Bicentennial of the United States Constitution
*Thurgood Marshall*

POETRY

Speech to the Young Speech to the Progress-Toward
*Gwendolyn Brooks*

The Fish
*Elizabeth Bishop*

SHORT STORY

The Pedestrian
*Ray Bradbury*

POLITICAL DOCUMENT

*from the* Iroquois Constitution
*Dekanawidah, translated by Arthur C. Parker*

ARGUMENT

*from* Common Sense
*Thomas Paine*

PERFORMANCE-BASED ASSESSMENT PREP

Review Evidence for an Argument

### PERFORMANCE-BASED ASSESSMENT

Argument: Essay and Video Commentary

PROMPT:
What are the most effective tools for establishing and preserving freedom?



## What is the meaning of freedom?

Introduce the Essential Question and point out that students will respond to related prompts.

- **Whole-Class Learning** *Which statement do you find most compelling for Americans today: the Preamble to the Constitution or the first sentence of paragraph three of the Declaration of Independence?*
- **Small-Group Learning** *Do narratives provide strong evidence to support arguments about American freedoms?*
- **Performance-Based Assessment** *What are the most effective tools for establishing and preserving freedom?*

### Using Trade Books

Refer to the Teaching With Trade Books section for suggestions on how to incorporate the following thematically related titles into this unit:

- *Uncle Tom's Cabin* by Harriet Beecher Stowe
- *The Federalist Papers* by James Madison
- *The Legend of Sleepy Hollow and Other Stories* by Washington Irving

### Current Perspectives

To increase student engagement, search online for speeches or stories about freedom. Invite your students to recommend stories they find. Always preview content before sharing it with your class.

- **News Story: To Achieve Sustainable Development Goals, Leaders Must Focus on Human Rights (Huffington Post)** What are the tenets of the UN's Declaration on Human Rights?
- **Video: Is the United States falling behind in women's rights? (CNN)** How do some other countries have greater protections for women's rights than the United States?

Introduce Small-Group Learning

*from* America's Constitution: A Biography

Media: *from* The United States Constitution: A Graphic Adaptation

*from* The Interesting Narrative of the Life of Olaudah Equiano

Letter to John Adams • *from* Dear Abigail: The Intimate Lives and Revolutionary Ideas of Abigail Adams and Her Two Remarkable Sisters

Gettysburg Address

Performance Task

Introduce Independent Learning

Independent Learning

Performance-Based Assessment

16 17 18 19 20 21 22 23 24 25 26 27 28 29 30

### About the Unit Goals

These unit goals were backward designed from the Performance-Based Assessment at the end of the unit and the Whole-Class and Small-Group Performance Tasks. Students will practice and become proficient in many more standards over the course of this unit.

## Unit Goals

Review the goals with students and explain that as they read and discuss the selections, they will improve their skills in reading, writing, research, language, and speaking and listening.

- Have students watch the video on Goal Setting.
- A video on this topic is available online in the Professional Development Center.

**Reading Goals** Tell students they will read and evaluate arguments and nonfiction narratives, as well as informative essays, to better understand the ways writers express ideas.

**Writing and Research Goals** Tell students that they will learn the elements of argumentative writing. They will also write their own arguments. Students will write for a number of reasons, including organizing and sharing ideas. They will conduct research to clarify and explore ideas.

**Language Goals** Tell students that they will develop a deeper understanding of differences in language style in various contexts. They will then practice using a "voice" in their own writing.

**Speaking and Listening Goals** Students will work together to build on one another's ideas, develop consensus, and communicate with one another.

### HOME Connection

A Home Connection letter to students' parents or guardians is available in myPerspectives+. The letter explains what students will be learning in this unit and how they will be assessed.



## Unit Goals

Throughout this unit, you will deepen your perspective of American freedoms by reading, writing, speaking, listening, and presenting. These goals will help you succeed on the Unit Performance-Based Assessment.

Rate how well you meet these goals right now. You will revisit your ratings later when you reflect on your growth during this unit.

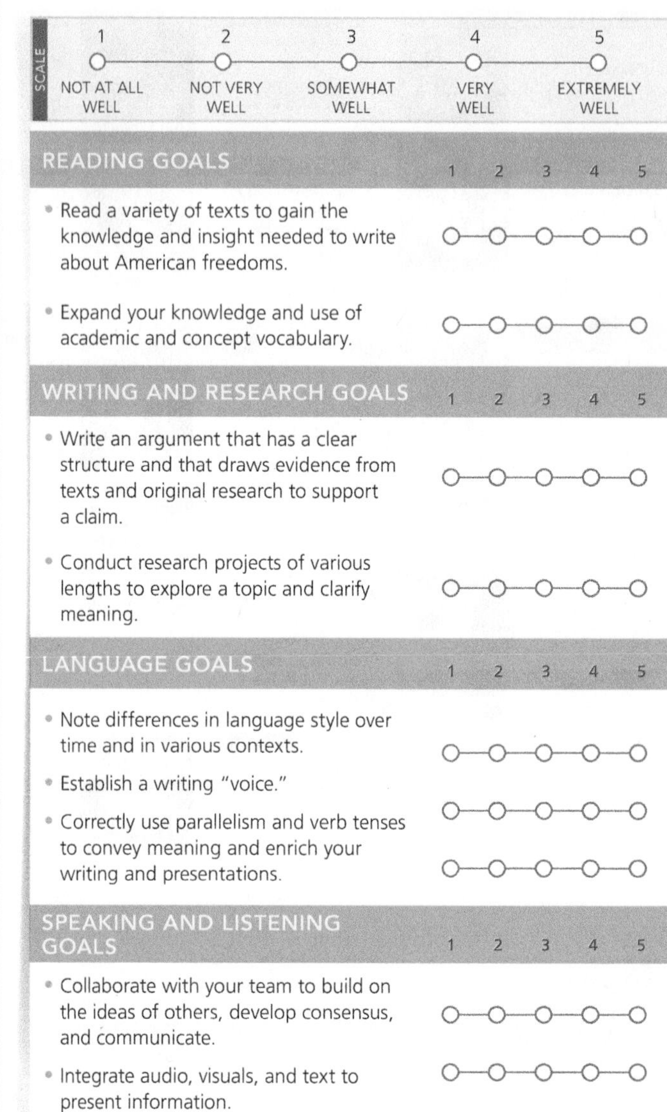

| SCALE | 1 | 2 | 3 | 4 | 5 |
|---|---|---|---|---|---|
| | NOT AT ALL WELL | NOT VERY WELL | SOMEWHAT WELL | VERY WELL | EXTREMELY WELL |

| READING GOALS | 1 | 2 | 3 | 4 | 5 |
|---|---|---|---|---|---|
| • Read a variety of texts to gain the knowledge and insight needed to write about American freedoms. | | | | | |
| • Expand your knowledge and use of academic and concept vocabulary. | | | | | |

| WRITING AND RESEARCH GOALS | 1 | 2 | 3 | 4 | 5 |
|---|---|---|---|---|---|
| • Write an argument that has a clear structure and that draws evidence from texts and original research to support a claim. | | | | | |
| • Conduct research projects of various lengths to explore a topic and clarify meaning. | | | | | |

| LANGUAGE GOALS | 1 | 2 | 3 | 4 | 5 |
|---|---|---|---|---|---|
| • Note differences in language style over time and in various contexts. | | | | | |
| • Establish a writing "voice." | | | | | |
| • Correctly use parallelism and verb tenses to convey meaning and enrich your writing and presentations. | | | | | |

| SPEAKING AND LISTENING GOALS | 1 | 2 | 3 | 4 | 5 |
|---|---|---|---|---|---|
| • Collaborate with your team to build on the ideas of others, develop consensus, and communicate. | | | | | |
| • Integrate audio, visuals, and text to present information. | | | | | |

**STANDARDS**

**Language**

Acquire and use accurately general academic and domain-specific words and phrases, sufficient for reading, writing, speaking, and listening at the college and career readiness level; demonstrate independence in gathering vocabulary knowledge when considering a word or phrase important to comprehension or expression.



SCAN FOR MULTIMEDIA 

### AUTHOR'S PERSPECTIVE Ernest Morrell, Ph.D.

**Why Goal Setting Matters** Establishing goals helps students take responsibility for their own learning and become independent scholars and thinkers. One way to encourage students to set, follow, and achieve goals is to have them write their goals down. Students can use the following process for crafting well-defined and measurable goals:

- *Decide What You Want:* Have students skim the Unit 1 Table of Contents and decide what they most want to learn from the unit. Guide students to set specific, realistic goals, such as "learn and correctly use five new concept words from the unit."
- *Write the Goals Down:* Have students draft the goals in clear, precise language. Students should also include a way to measure results so they can assess their progress.
- *Set a Time Frame:* Have students include a realistic schedule for completion, using the length of the selections in Unit 1 as a guide. As necessary, have students break large goals into smaller ones to make the goal more likely to be completed. When students take more responsibility for their learning, they may learn to rely more on themselves and take more interest in their success.

DIGITAL PERSPECTIVES

## Academic Vocabulary: Argument

Understanding and using academic terms can help you to read, write, and speak with precision and clarity. Here are five academic words that will be useful to you in this unit as you analyze and write arguments.

**Complete the chart.**

1. Review each word, its root, and the mentor sentences.
2. Use the information and your own knowledge to predict the meaning of each word.
3. For each word, list at least two related words.
4. Refer to a dictionary or other resources if needed.

TIP

FOLLOW THROUGH
Study the words in this chart, and mark them or their forms wherever they appear in the unit.

| WORD | MENTOR SENTENCES | PREDICT MEANING | RELATED WORDS |
|---|---|---|---|
| **confirm**<br><br>ROOT:<br>***-firm-***<br>"strong"; "steadfast" | 1. We could *confirm* the bird's species by its unusual song.<br>2. Please *confirm* your position on this topic; right now, I am unsure where you stand. | | confirmation; unconfirmed |
| **demonstrate**<br><br>ROOT:<br>***-mon-***<br>"show"; "point out" | 1. In today's art class, Justin will *demonstrate* his use of pastels.<br>2. Like humans, some apes use facial expressions to *demonstrate* feelings. | | |
| **supplement**<br><br>ROOT:<br>***-ple-***<br>"fill" | 1. Some people *supplement* their diet with a daily multivitamin.<br>2. Camila will *supplement* her income by taking a second, part-time job. | | |
| **establish**<br><br>ROOT:<br>***-sta-***<br>"stand" | 1. That observant witness was able to *establish* the suspect's alibi.<br>2. Max reports that he is second in his class, but his grades *establish* that he is actually first. | | |
| **conviction**<br><br>ROOT:<br>***-vict-/-vinc-***<br>"conquer" | 1. A speaker is far more effective if she speaks with confidence and *conviction.*<br>2. During the debate, the candidate's *conviction* about the rightness of his policies seemed to weaken. | | |





## Academic Vocabulary: Argument

Introduce the academic vocabulary words in the chart. Point out that the root of each word provides a clue to its meaning. Discuss the mentor sentences to ensure students understand each word's usage. Students should also use the mentor sentences as context to help them predict the meaning of each word. Check that students are able to fill the chart in correctly. Complete pronunciations, parts of speech, and definitions are provided for you. Students are only expected to provide the definition.

Possible responses:

**confirm** *v.* (kuhn FURM)
**Meaning:** to make firm; establish
**Related words:** confirmation, confirmed
**Additional words related to the root *-firm-*:** affirm, affirmation

**demonstrate** *v.* (DEHM uhn strayt)
**Meaning:** to show; to explain
**Related words:** demonstrable, demonstration
**Additional words related to the root *-mon-*:** remonstrance, remonstrate

**supplement** *v.* (SUHP luh mehnt)
**Meaning:** to add to
**Related words:** supplemental, supplementary
**Additional words related to the root *-plere-*:** complement, implement

**establish** *v.* (ehs TAB lihsh)
**Meaning:** to prove; to demonstrate
**Related words:** establishing, establishment
**Additional words related to the root *-sta-*:** stability, stabilize

**conviction** *n.* (kuhn VIHK shuhn)
**Meaning:** the state or appearance of being convinced
**Related words:** convict, convictive
**Additional words related to the root *-vict- / -vinc-*:** victim, victory, invincible

### PERSONALIZE FOR LEARNING

**English Language Support**

**Cognates** Many of the academic words have Spanish cognates. Use these cognates with students whose home language is Spanish.

identify – identificar | supplement – suplemento
demonstrate – demostrar | confirm – confirmar

Not all English learners will recognize and use these cognates automatically. Help students build their cognate awareness by pointing out that these cognates share the same root in both English and Spanish. **ALL LEVELS**

## Purpose of the Launch Text

The Launch Text provides a common introduction to the unit theme for all students. After they read the Launch Text, all students will be able to participate in discussions about freedom.

**Lexile 1140L** The easier reading level of this selection makes it perfect to assign for homework. Students will need little or no support to understand it. Additionally, "Totally Free?" provides a writing model for the Performance-Based Assessment students will complete at the end of the unit.

## Launch Text: Argument Model

Remind students to determine the author's central claim in the argument and to figure out how she organizes evidence and reasons that support her claim. Have students also identify the writer's audience—to whom is she speaking (writing)? Whom does she want to convince that her argument is valid? How does she tailor her essay to fit that particular group of readers?

Encourage students to read this text on their own and annotate unfamiliar words and sections of text they think are particularly important.

### AUDIO SUMMARIES

Audio summaries of "Totally Free?" are available online in both English and Spanish in the Interactive Teacher's Edition or Unit Resources. Assigning these summaries before students read the Launch Text may help them build additional background knowledge and set a context for their reading.



LAUNCH TEXT | ARGUMENT MODEL

This selection is an example of an **argument**, a type of writing in which the author presents a claim and organizes evidence and reasons to support that claim. This is the type of writing you will develop in the Performance-Based Assessment at the end of the unit.

**As you read,** look closely at the writer's argument, including the consideration of various viewpoints. Mark facts and examples that provide strong evidence to support the main claim.

# Totally Free?

NOTES

1 If you ask a dozen high school students to define *freedom*, odds are that ten of them will answer, "Freedom means that I can do anything I want." For many people, freedom is an absolute. It implies the right to think, speak, or act however one wishes. Because we live in a civil society, however, we need to consider other people's rights as we exercise our own freedoms. A better world would combine essential human freedoms with the understanding that my freedoms should not conflict with your right to lead a safe and happy life.

2 Suppose that those ten high school students had the total freedom they describe. They might drive a car without a license, because they were free to do so. They might even drive *your* car, because total freedom means that they can have anything they want and do anything they like. They would be free to attend school or not, to run screaming down the hallways if they chose, or even to treat other people cruelly without fear of reprisal. Total freedom could result in lawless mayhem.

3 Despite their desperate desire to be free from England's rule, our nation's early leaders carefully defined freedoms in the Bill of Rights. They did not say, "Everyone is free to do as he or she chooses." They said, "Congress shall make no law respecting an establishment of religion, or prohibiting the free exercise thereof; or abridging the freedom of speech, or of the press; or the right of the people peaceably to assemble, and to petition the Government for a redress





SCAN FOR MULTIMEDIA 

## PERSONALIZE FOR LEARNING

### English Language Support

**Idioms** Note the expression *odds are* in the first sentence. Remind students that this is an **idiom**, an expression that means something more than or different from the literal meaning of the words. Here, "odds are" refers to mathematical odds (likelihood). In this context, the expression means "probably" or "it is very likely that." Provide more examples of idioms and expressions, such as *think outside the box* and *time flies*. Work with students to determine their meanings. **EMERGING/EXPANDING**

of grievances." They established a delicate line between the rights of individuals and the power of the government.

4 In his 1941 State of the Union address, President Franklin Roosevelt identified four key freedoms as being basic human rights: freedom of speech and expression, freedom of worship, freedom from want, and freedom from fear. Those are not freedoms that one finds in a dictatorship. Nor are they freedoms that we grant to each other without the oversight and protection of government institutions. With the government's help, and the writing of laws, my freedom from want does not allow me to steal your food, and your freedom of speech does not let you publish lies about me. We are free, but only up to the point at which our freedoms clash.

5 Is it even possible to be "totally free"? A person living "off the grid," far away from civilization, might achieve that kind of liberation. Such a person could live as he or she pleased without ever imposing on the freedoms of others.

6 Most of us, however, live in a community. We are bound by laws that both restrict and protect us. If we live in a dictatorship, we may be more restricted and less protected. If we live in a democracy, we may be more protected and less restricted. Human history is a balancing act between the desire for individual freedom and the need to protect everyone's freedoms.

7 *Freedom* implies a lack of restraint, but we are all better off if our freedoms are preserved and protected. At the same time, as members of a society, we must be sure that our freedoms do not conflict. "Life, liberty, and the pursuit of happiness" are powerful goals, but we must never allow one person's liberty to impose on another's happiness. ❧

NOTES

### WORD NETWORK FOR WRITING FREEDOM

**Vocabulary** A word network is a collection of words related to a topic. As you read the unit selections, identify words related to freedom, and add them to your Word Network. For example, you might begin by adding words from the Launch Text, such as *restricted* and *liberty*. For each word you add, note a related word, such as a synonym or an antonym. Continue to add words as you complete this unit.

**Tool Kit**
Word Network Model

FREEDOM
restricted | curtailed
liberty | liberation





DIGITAL PERSPECTIVES   

## Word Network for Writing Freedom

Tell students that they can fill in the Word Network as they read the texts in the unit, or they can record the words elsewhere and add them later. Point out to students that people may have personal associations with some words. A word that one student thinks is related to the concept of freedom might not be a word another student would pick. However, students should feel free to add any word they personally think is relevant to their Word Network. Each person's Word Network will be unique. If you choose to print the Word Network, distribute it to students at this point so they can use it throughout the rest of the unit.

### AUTHOR'S PERSPECTIVE Elfrieda Hiebert, Ph.D.

**Word Networks** Vocabulary word networks enable students to learn, use, and retain a large number of useful words related to a particular concept. In addition, generating vocabulary in this way can help students appreciate the subtleties of an author's word choice and evaluate the effectiveness of an author's style. Using vocabulary word networks also helps students choose more precise words when they write and edit. Finally, forging connections among related words, as opposed to teaching the words individually, allows students to approach new words with confidence and knowledge.

When students discuss the unit's theme, they can choose from a wide variety of related words, each with its own connotation, to create a word network. While students may not know more complex words at first, they do know common conversation words and words that get at the big idea. These words can serve as a gateway to the more complex words they will encounter in these selections.

# INTRODUCTION

## Summary

Have students read the introductory paragraph. Provide them with tips for writing a summary:

- Write in the present tense.
- Make sure to include the author and title of the work.
- Be concise: a summary should not be equal in length to the original text.
- If you need to quote the words of the author, use quotation marks.
- Don't put your own opinions, ideas, or interpretations into the summary. The purpose of writing a summary is to accurately represent what the author says, not to provide a critique.

If necessary, students can refer to the Tool Kit for help in understanding the elements of a good summary.

**See possible Summary on student page.**

## Launch Activity

Tell students that they will have many opportunities to discuss the topic of freedom as they work their way through this unit. After students each perform their task individually, give them time to meet with others who performed the same task. Remind them to combine and refine their responses. Then each group can present their response to the class.



## Summary

Write a summary of "Totally Free?" Remember that a **summary** is a concise, complete, and accurate overview of a text. It should not include a statement of your opinion or an analysis.

**Possible response:** The author of this argument makes the case that freedom should not conflict with safety and happiness. If anyone could do whatever he or she wanted, people could hurt each other or take each other's possessions. Absolute freedom would be chaotic. Instead, our laws are arranged so that one person's freedom does not impinge on another's. There is a balance between getting to do what we want and keeping the community safe. We need restrictions for protection; a good government is one that can give us lots of protection with relatively little restriction.

## Launch Activity

**Define and Explain** Roll a six-sided die, and use your result to perform one of these tasks.

1. Write a definition of the word *freedom*.
2. Describe a historical example of freedom.
3. Describe a current example of freedom.
4. Explain why freedom is important to you.
5. Explain why freedom is important to a society.
6. Explain how freedom might be protected or preserved.

Find other classmates who performed the same task. Share your responses, and consider how best to convey your thinking to the rest of the class. For example, you may combine your answers, or you may revise them to write a new answer. Then, share your work with the class.





## PERSONALIZE FOR LEARNING

### Strategic Support

Make sure students can distinguish between the terms *evidence* and *reason(s)*. Before students write their summary of "Totally Free?" they may wish to complete a chart such as the following. They can base their summary on the text in their chart.

| **Author's central claim:** "Human history is a balancing act between individual freedom and the need to protect the community." (paragraph 6) |
|---|
| **Evidence that shows it is necessary to protect the community:** If a high school student had total freedom, and she wanted to drive someone else's car without asking, she could steal the car with no penalty. |
| **Reasons why we need to balance different people's rights and freedoms:** One person's freedom might conflict with another person's right to be safe and happy. It's necessary to compromise so that people have a reasonable amount of freedom that doesn't take away others' rights. |

## QuickWrite

Consider class discussions, the video, and the Launch Text as you think about the prompt. Record your first thoughts here.

PROMPT: **What are the most effective tools for establishing and preserving freedom?**

**Possible response:** The article suggests that someone would have to live far away from civilization to be "totally free." I agree with this. Isolation is a very effective tool for establishing and preserving freedom. If people can't find you or reach you, they can't control you. There's a reason why people who don't want to be found so often go into the wilderness to hide.

Of course, that level of isolation would keep people from doing what they want. People congregate in places where useful things are, and most people want to spend time with friends and family. There is a compromise to strike.

### EVIDENCE LOG FOR WRITING FREEDOM

Review your QuickWrite. Summarize your initial position in one sentence to record in your Evidence Log. Then, record evidence from "Totally Free?" that supports your position.

After each selection, you will continue to use your Evidence Log to record the evidence you gather and the connections you make. The graphic shows what your Evidence Log looks like.

**Tool Kit**
Evidence Log Model

Title of Text: ____________ Date: ______

| CONNECTION TO PROMPT | TEXT EVIDENCE/DETAILS | ADDITIONAL NOTES/IDEAS |
|---|---|---|
| | | |

How does this text change or add to my thinking? Date: ______

SCAN FOR MULTIMEDIA



DIGITAL PERSPECTIVES  

## QuickWrite

In this QuickWrite, students should present their own response to the prompt based on the material they have read and viewed in the Unit Overview and Introduction. This initial response will help inform their work when they complete the Performance-Based Assessment at the end of the unit. Students should make sure they present their position clearly and support it with well-reasoned evidence and accurate details.

**See possible QuickWrite on student page.**

## Evidence Log for Writing Freedom

Students should record their initial position in their Evidence Logs along with evidence from "Totally Free?" that supports this position.

If you choose to print the Evidence Log, distribute it to students at this point so they can use it throughout the rest of the unit.

### Performance-Based Assessment: Refining Your Thinking

- Have students watch the video on Refining Your Thinking.
- A video on this topic is available online in the Professional Development Center.

### PERSONALIZE FOR LEARNING

**English Language Support**

**Vocabulary for QuickWrite** Before students write their answers to the prompt, you may wish to supply a list of relevant words and go over their meanings with students. Useful words/terms might include *effective, effectively, preservation, protect, protection, liberty, lawful, unlawful, civil rights, society, ensure, guarantee, safety measures,* and *respect.* **EXPANDING/BRIDGING**

# OVERVIEW

## WHOLE-CLASS LEARNING

### What is the meaning of freedom?

Engage students in a conversation about the meaning of freedom. Point out that freedom can be interpreted in different ways, and that the freedom Americans enjoy today has not always been without struggle. During Whole-Class Learning, students will read selections about how the Founding Fathers established documents to safeguard the rights of American citizens.

### Whole-Class Learning Strategies

Review the Learning Strategies with students and explain that as they work through Whole-Class Learning they will develop strategies to work in large-group environments.

- Have students watch the video on Whole-Class Learning Strategies.
- A video on this topic is available online in the Professional Development Center.

You may wish to discuss some action items to add to the chart as a class before students complete it on their own. For example for "Listen actively," you might solicit the following from students:

- If you don't understand someone's point, ask for further clarification.
- Take notes to help you retain information.

### Block Scheduling

Each day in this Pacing Plan represents a 40–50 minute class period. Teachers using block scheduling may combine days to reflect their class schedule. In addition, teachers may revise pacing to differentiate and support core instruction by integrating components and resources as students require.

## OVERVIEW: WHOLE-CLASS LEARNING

ESSENTIAL QUESTION:

# What is the meaning of freedom?

As you read these selections, work with your whole class to explore the meaning of freedom.

**From Text to Topic** For Thomas Jefferson and the other founders, freedom meant breaking away from Great Britain and establishing a nation based on democratic principles and individual liberties. Convincing the colonial majority of that idea would take persuasive words and images. For James Madison and Benjamin Franklin, after independence, freedom needed to be codified in a constitution—again, not an easy task. Issues relating to independence gripped Americans in the mid-eighteenth century. As you read, consider what the selections show about the meaning of American freedom during the country's formative years, and how they continue to shape our ideas about freedom today.

## Whole-Class Learning Strategies

Throughout your life, in school, in your community, and in your career, you will continue to learn and work in large-group environments.

Review these strategies and the actions you can take to practice them as you work with your whole class. Add ideas of your own for each step. Get ready to use these strategies during Whole-Class Learning.

| STRATEGY | ACTION PLAN |
|---|---|
| Listen actively | • Eliminate distractions. For example, put your cellphone away.<br>• Jot down brief notes on main ideas and points of confusion.<br>• |
| Clarify by asking questions | • If you're confused, other people probably are, too. Ask a question to help your whole class.<br>• Ask follow-up questions as needed—for example, if you do not understand the clarification or if you want to make an additional connection.<br>• |
| Monitor understanding | • Notice what information you already know and be ready to build on it.<br>• Ask for help if you are struggling.<br>• |
| Interact and share ideas | • Share your ideas and answer questions, even if you are unsure.<br>• Build on the ideas of others by adding details or making a connection.<br>• |



SCAN FOR MULTIMEDIA



### Pacing Plan

| 1 | 2 | 3 | 4 | 5 | 6 | 7 | 8 | 9 | 10 | 11 | 12 | 13 | 14 | 15 |
|---|---|---|---|---|---|---|---|---|---|---|---|---|---|---|
| Unit Introduction | Introduce Whole-Class Learning | Historical Perspectives | Declaration of Independence | | Preamble to the U.S. Constitution • Bill of Rights | | | Speech in the Convention | | | The American Revolution: Visual Propaganda | | Performance Task | |

WHOLE-CLASS LEARNING

DIGITAL PERSPECTIVES

CONTENTS

HISTORICAL PERSPECTIVES

Focus Period: 1750–1800

## A New Nation

The second half of the eighteenth century was a dramatic period of deep social engagement, as Americans wrestled with the possibility of independence—and the challenges of governing the country that resulted from it.

ANCHOR TEXT: FOUNDATIONAL DOCUMENT

## Declaration of Independence

*Thomas Jefferson*

When is a colony justified in seeking freedom from the country that governs it?

▸ MEDIA CONNECTION: John F. Kennedy Reads the Declaration of Independence

ANCHOR TEXT: FOUNDATIONAL DOCUMENTS

## Preamble to the Constitution *Gouverneur Morris*

## Bill of Rights *James Madison*

Why do Americans need a governing document, and what rights should it guarantee?

ANCHOR TEXT: SPEECH

## Speech in the Convention

*Benjamin Franklin*

How do you persuade people to support a document with which they do not completely agree?

▸ MEDIA CONNECTION: The U. S. Constitution

MEDIA: IMAGE GALLERY

## The American Revolution: Visual Propaganda

A picture is worth a thousand words—especially when it comes to propaganda.

PERFORMANCE TASK

WRITING FOCUS

## Write an Argument

The Whole-Class readings were born during a time when conflicts between Great Britain and its American colonies were about to change history. After reading, you will write an argument about the continuing relevance of these foundational documents.





## Contents

**Anchor Texts** Preview the anchor texts and image gallery with students to generate interest. Encourage students to discuss other texts they have read or movies or television shows they have seen that deal with the pursuit of freedom. Promote students' discussion in this topic by raising thoughtful questions on events involving freedom struggles that students know about in current news.

You may wish to conduct a poll to determine which selection students think looks most interesting. Discuss the reasons for their preference. Students can return to this poll after they have read the selections to see if their preference changed.

## Performance Task

**Write an Argument** Explain to students that after they have finished reading the selections, they will write an argument about the Founders' decision to declare independence. To help them prepare, encourage students to think about the topic as they progress through the selections and as they participate in the Whole-Class Learning experience.

Introduce Small-Group Learning

- 16–17: *from* America's Constitution: A Biography
- 18–19: Media: *from* The United States Constitution: A Graphic Adaptation
- 20–21: *from* The Interesting Narrative of the Life of Olaudah Equiano
- 22–24: Letter to John Adams • *from* Dear Abigail: The Intimate Lives and Revolutionary Ideas of Abigail Adams and Her Two Remarkable Sisters
- 25: Gettysburg Address
- 26: Performance Task
- 27: Introduce Independent Learning
- 28: Independent Learning
- 29–30: Performance-Based Assessment

16 17 18 19 20 21 22 23 24 25 26 27 28 29 30

TEACHING

## HISTORICAL PERSPECTIVES

# A New Nation

## Voices of the Period

This section analyzes word meaning and usage. After students read each quotation, ask questions like these to spark discussion:

- What does Samuel Adams mean by the phrases "our contest" and "an asylum"? **Possible responses:** By "our contest" he means the colonists' struggle with Great Britain. By "an asylum," he means a shelter or haven.
- Which words does George Washington capitalize that we would not capitalize today? Why do you think he capitalizes each one? **Possible responses:** *Enemy, Honor, Success, Country, Soldiers, Freemen, Liberty*—he capitalizes each word to emphasize its importance to what he is saying.
- Which context clues in the third quotation tell you the meaning of the word *manumission*? **Possible responses**: Clues such as "signed," "I who had been a slave" and "became my own master, and completely free" show that a manumission document must be one that legally frees an enslaved African from bondage.

## History of the Period

Freedom was a central concern during the period 1750–1800. Religious groups such as the Pilgrims, Puritans, Quakers, and Catholics had settled in North America in order to achieve religious freedom. Over time, the American colonists came to expect more freedom than they would have in England. When the "mother country" began to rescind freedoms and impose unfair taxes rather than allow Americans more liberty to govern themselves, the colonists rebelled. Ask students to discuss how limited freedom made the colonists angry enough to begin a war with people to whom they were related through ancestry, as well as through ties of family, friendship, business, language, and culture.



# A New Nation

## Voices of the Period

*"Courage, then, my countrymen; our contest is not only whether we ourselves shall be free, but whether there shall be left to mankind an asylum on earth for civil and religious liberty."*

—Samuel Adams,
advocate for colonial rights and
signer of the Declaration of Independence

*"The Enemy have now landed on Long Island, and the hour is fast approaching, on which the Honor and Success of this army, and the safety of our bleeding Country depend. Remember officers and Soldiers, that you are Freemen, fighting for the blessings of Liberty—that slavery will be your portion, and that of your posterity, if you do not acquit yourselves like men."*

—George Washington,
then- Commander-in-Chief
of the Continental Army

*"Accordingly he signed the manumission that day; so that, before night, I who had been a slave in the morning, trembling at the will of another, . . . became my own master, and completely free. I thought this was the happiest day I had ever experienced. . . ."*

—Olaudah Equiano,
abolitionist and formerly
enslaved African

## History of the Period

**Founded on Freedom** The quest for freedom drove the establishment of the colonies. The Pilgrims and Puritans settled Massachusetts so that they could practice their religion freely. The Quakers, who settled Pennsylvania, and the Catholics, who settled Maryland, also brought their religious convictions with them as they fled from England's restrictions.

**An "American" Society** By the mid-eighteenth century, the thirteen disparate colonies had created a new society. Each colony was fiercely independent, but together they viewed themselves as different from societies across the Atlantic. "American" society generally valued equality and opportunity. It was much more homogenous than what was commonplace in Europe, without either nobility or a class of paupers who had no chance of bettering their lives. (Enslaved African Americans were the notable exception. Indentured servants also had limits on their freedom.) Furthermore, most of the colonial governments had two-house legislatures, elected by voters. The colonial governments may not have been fully democratic by modern standards, but colonists had—and expected—far more rights and freedoms than their counterparts in England did.

**Tightening Controls** By the mid-1700s, most Americans took pride in being in charge of their colonial governments, so the demands that Great Britain began to make after winning the French



TIMELINE

1700

**1754:** The Albany Congress discusses Benjamin Franklin's Plan of Union for the Colonies.

DICTIONARY OF THE ENGLISH LANGUAGE

**1755: England** Samuel Johnson's *Dictionary of the English Language* is published.

**1765:** The British Parliament taxes the Colonies with the Stamp Act.

**1768:** British troops occupy rebellious Boston.



## PERSONALIZE FOR LEARNING

**Strategic Support**
Help students use the text headings and the timeline labels to summarize what they learn from this section. Students might work in pairs or small groups to complete a chart with information like that suggested in the chart.

| Heading or Timeline Time and Place | Key Words and Phrases | Main Ideas and Events Covered |
|---|---|---|
| Founded on Freedom | quest, "practice their religion freely," Pilgrims, Puritans, Massachusetts, Quakers, Pennsylvania, Catholics, Maryland | Most colonies are founded on religious freedom. |
| An "American" Society | | |

## Integration of Knowledge and Ideas

**Notebook** How was each of the causes resolved as a result of the American Revolution? Which effect do you think may have been most on the minds of the Americans when they rebelled? Which may have been least?

### Causes and Effects of the American Revolution

| CAUSES | | EFFECTS |
|---|---|---|
| • Britain imposes taxes without providing for colonial representation in Parliament.<br>• Britain issues the Intolerable Acts to punish the American "rebels."<br>• A growing number of colonial leaders see themselves more as American than as British. | The American Revolution → | • The thirteen British colonies become the independent United States of America.<br>• The United States becomes an example for other peoples seeking freedom and self-government.<br>• American trade becomes free of British restrictions.<br>• Westward expansion becomes possible, extending to the Mississippi River. |

and Indian War (known in Britain as the Seven Years' War) led inevitably to trouble. Colonists who were eager to move west were stymied by the Proclamation of 1763, which forbade settlement beyond the Appalachian Mountains. Furthermore, the taxes that Britain imposed to pay the cost of securing victory grew more and more onerous to the colonists. Quickly, "no taxation without representation" became a colonial rallying cry.

In response, England tightened its grip. In 1774, Parliament cracked down on American freedoms even more, with laws that the colonists called the Intolerable Acts. Then, in April 1775, the conflict turned from words and laws to bullets and deaths when the first shots were fired at Lexington and Concord in Massachusetts, the hotbed of rebellion.

**Declaring Independence** Six months before patriots and redcoats clashed in Massachusetts, colonial delegates had gathered to consider their complaints at the First Continental Congress. A few weeks after the events at Lexington and Concord, the Second Continental Congress convened in Philadelphia. By June, the colonies were on the road to a real break from Britain.



**1770:** Colonists and British soldiers clash in the Boston Massacre.

**1773:** Parliament's Tea Act prompts the Boston Tea Party.

**1774:** Colonial representatives meet for the First Continental Congress.

**1775:** The American Revolution begins.

**1776:** The Second Continental Congress adopts the Declaration of Independence.

1776

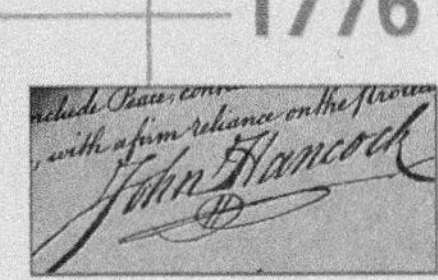




## Integration of Knowledge and Ideas

**Possible responses:**

The Revolution resolved the first two causes because the former colonies no longer had to pay British taxes or obey British laws. It resolved the third cause because, after the war, the former colonists were officially no longer British—they were full-fledged Americans.

Some students may say that independence, freedom from British trade restrictions, and/or freedom to expand westward were most on Americans' minds, depending upon their particular needs and attitudes. Some students will say that probably only a few Americans were thinking about becoming an example to other peoples who yearned for freedom and self-government.

## Timeline

Tell students to examine the 1700-1800 Timeline. Encourage pairs or small groups of students to use text headings and timeline labels to summarize what they learn. Each portion identifies major events in American history.

## PERSONALIZE FOR LEARNING

**English Language Support**

**Unfamiliar Language/ Figurative Language** Work with students to develop a chart that provides definitions or explanations for words and phrases they do not understand.

**EXPANDING/BRIDGING**

| Phrase from the Text | Definition or Explanation |
|---|---|
| "no taxation without representation" | It is unfair for the English lawmaking group, Parliament, to tax us when we aren't allowed to elect and send our own lawmakers to speak and vote for us in Parliament. |
| "England tightened its grip." | English leaders treated the colonists more and more unfairly. |
| "hotbed of rebellion" | a place where many rebels live and often meet to complain about their bad treatment and discuss reasons and ways to rebel against unfair leaders |

## History of the Period (cont'd)

Have students focus on the section of the text labeled "Defining Freedoms." Point out that independence from Great Britain was only the first step in building the nation. Encourage a discussion by asking students the following question: *Why were there many different approaches to building a nation, and why did the Founders have to try several before finding one that seemed successful?*

HISTORICAL PERSPECTIVES • FOCUS PERIOD: 1750–1800

When the delegates officially declared the colonies' independence, they made freedom a central factor in their rationale. It is "self-evident," they stated, that all people have "unalienable rights, that among these are life, liberty, and the pursuit of happiness." In concluding, they pronounced the colonies to be "free and independent states."

**Breaking the Bonds** The new United States battled for independence for the next seven years. The British had a clear goal: to keep the rebellious colonies within the British Empire. The Americans were more divided, however. Although probably no more than 20 percent of the American people were loyal to Great Britain, many others were uncertain about this radical venture of independence. Undeterred, the patriots fought on.

The colonies had a population of about 2.5 million and no standing military forces. By contrast, Great Britain boasted a population of about 7.5 million as well as the world's most powerful army and navy. However, the colonists were fighting on home territory, whereas the British were 3,000 miles away from home and lacked easy access to supplies.

Then, in 1778, France entered the war on the side of the Americans. It was French aid that enabled the Americans to win the decisive battle at Yorktown. Tradition says that as the British surrendered, their band played "The World Turn'd Upside Down," a fitting tune for what had happened. The new nation that had demanded and won its independence would be unique in the world of its day: a self-governing democracy. In 1783, the Treaty of Paris officially brought the American Revolution to an end.

**Defining Freedoms** Having fought for freedom, the new nation had to structure a government that would preserve it. The Articles of Confederation, approved in 1777 and formally ratified in 1781, confirmed the union of the thirteen states as one nation. However, the agreement largely left each state free to function on its own—an arrangement that created an often dysfunctional union. Correcting the problems led to a complete re-creation of the governmental structure and triggered the writing of the Constitution of the United States.

Not satisfied with the guarantees of freedom embedded in the Constitution, however, many leaders urged the creation of what became the Bill of Rights. These first ten amendments to the Constitution focus on guarantees of individual liberties, including freedom of speech, freedom of the press, and the right to legal counsel and trial by jury.

These rights did not extend to all Americans, however. For all of the focus on freedom and individual rights in the founding of the United States, enslaved African Americans—about 20 percent of the population—were left out of this discussion. In addition, even though property requirements were abolished for male voters in the new nation, 125 years would pass before suffrage was extended to American women.

**A Motivating Force** Freedom has been a defining goal throughout American history. The literature in this unit explores how freedom has shaped the United States, and how authors of both the past and present have applied visions of freedom to an ever-changing world.



TIMELINE

1777

**1777:** The thirteen original states adopt the Articles of Confederation.

**1781:** American forces defeat the British at Yorktown.

**1783:** The Treaty of Paris ends the American Revolution.

**1787:** Delegates meet in Philadelphia to create a new constitution.

**1788:** The United States Constitution is ratified.



PERSONALIZE FOR LEARNING

**Strategic Support**

Depending on your students' needs, encourage pairs or small groups of students to continue using text headings and timeline labels, as in the chart below, to summarize what they learn.

Other headings you may use might be:
A Motivating Force
1777: United States
1781: Yorktown

| Text Heading | Unfamiliar Words and Phrases | Main Ideas and Events Covered |
|---|---|---|
| Breaking the Bonds | "radical venture," *undeterred, patriots, undeniable, access, decisive* | With indispensable help from France, American patriots fight and win the Revolutionary War. |
| Defining Freedoms | "Articles of Confederation," *ratified, confirmed, dysfunctional,* "the Constitution of the United States," *guarantees, embedded, amendments* | The Articles of Confederation lead to a dysfunctional central government. The Constitution is an effective document. |

## Literature Selections

**Literature of the Focus Period** Several of the selections in this unit were written during the focus period and pertain to the establishment of a free United States and the rights granted to some, but not all, of its people:

- Declaration of Independence, Thomas Jefferson
- Preamble to the Constitution, Gouverneur Morris
- Bill of Rights, James Madison
- Speech in the Convention, Benjamin Franklin
- from *The Interesting Narrative of the Life of Olaudah Equiano*, Olaudah Equiano
- Letter to John Adams, Abigail Adams
- from *Common Sense*, Thomas Paine

**Connections Across Time** A consideration of the importance of freedom both preceded and continued past the focus period. Indeed, it has influenced writers and commentators in many times and places.

- from *America's Constitution: A Biography*, Akhil Reed Amar
- from *Dear Abigail: The Intimate Lives and Revolutionary Ideas of Abigail Adams and Her Two Remarkable Sisters*, Diane Jacobs
- Gettysburg Address, Abraham Lincoln
- from *Democracy Is Not a Spectator Sport*, Arthur Blaustein with Helen Matatov
- Reflections on the Bicentennial of the United States Constitution, Thurgood Marshall
- "Speech to the Young | Speech to the Progress-Toward," Gwendolyn Brooks
- "The Fish," Elizabeth Bishop
- "The Pedestrian," Ray Bradbury
- *from the* Iroquois Constitution, Dekanawidah, translated by Arthur C. Parker



**1789:** George Washington is elected the first President of the United States.

**1791:** Ten amendments—the Bill of Rights—are added to the Constitution.

**1789: France** The French Revolution begins.

**1796:** John Adams is elected the second U.S. president.

**1800:** Thomas Jefferson is elected the third U.S. president.

1800



### PERSONALIZE FOR LEARNING

**Challenge**
Invite students to choose one of the famous people, events or documents mentioned in this section. Ask them to research their topic and use what they have learned to write a short newspaper article from the point of view of a writer living during the Revolutionary War.

DIGITAL PERSPECTIVES

## Literature Selections

Preview the selection titles and have students compare and contrast ways that the unit selections might explore the idea of freedom. Also point out the additional Focus Period Literature found in myPerspectives. Encourage students to utilize these selections for additional evidence as they complete the Whole-Class Performance Task.

## Comprehension Check

Ask students to discuss answers to these questions in a group.

1. How did some immigrants' desire for religious freedom lead colonists to rebel against British rule?

**Possible response:** Once the colonists gained some degree of religious freedom in their new home, they enjoyed it. When King George III began to threaten their liberty, many colonists rebelled.

2. In the mid-1700s, how did "American society" compare to British society in terms of the rights and freedoms ordinary people enjoyed?

**Possible response:** The colonists had more freedom than ordinary people had in England. There was no upper class of nobles in America, and no one was hopelessly poor, either. In England, the lower classes did not have as much freedom or as many opportunities to improve their lives.

3. In what ways did Great Britain "tighten controls" on the colonists following the end of the French and Indian War (or Seven Years' War)?

**Possible response:** Colonists were not allowed to settle beyond the Appalachian Mountains. To pay for the war, Britain imposed high taxes on the colonies, even though they had no representatives in Parliament.

4. In what way was freedom a central idea in the Declaration of Independence?

**Possible response:** One was that people are born with a set of rights. King George was doing the opposite: he was taking rights away from the colonists.

5. What were two important differences between the Articles of Confederation and the Constitution?

**Possible response:** One was that the Articles of Confederation led to a failed central government. Another was that the people who wrote the Constitution did want one.

# Declaration of Independence

**AUDIO SUMMARIES**
Audio summaries of the Declaration of Independence are available online in both English and Spanish in the Interactive Teacher's Edition or Unit Resources. Assigning these summaries prior to reading the selection may help students build additional background knowledge and set a context for their first read.


## Summary

In the Declaration of Independence, written by Thomas Jefferson and adopted on July 4,1776, the British colonies in North America declared their independence from Great Britain and explained their reasons for doing so. The introduction asserts that the "Laws of Nature and of Nature's God" entitle all people to equality. The preamble declares, "that all men are created equal" and they have certain rights that cannot be taken away—"among these are Life, Liberty, and the pursuit of Happiness." In addition, the Declaration of Independence states that when a government fails to protect these rights, the people have the right to overthrow that government. The Declaration then lists twenty-seven specific abuses of power by King George III. It concludes, "these united Colonies are, and … ought to be Free and Independent States" without "… allegiance to the British king."


### Insight

The words from the preamble to the Declaration of Independence are famous worldwide. Similar ideas can be found in the *Declaration of the Rights of Man and Citizen* drafted at the time of the French Revolution. A list of natural rights also appears in *The Universal Declaration of Human Rights* adopted by the United Nations in 1948.

ESSENTIAL QUESTION:
What is the meaning of freedom?

## Connection to the Essential Question

The Declaration of Independence is a founding document in American history and connects to the Essential Question. The document explains reasons why the American colonists sought political freedom and asserts their right to personal freedoms including "Life, Liberty and the pursuit of Happiness."

WHOLE-CLASS LEARNING PERFORMANCE TASK
Which statement do you find most compelling for Americans today: the Preamble to the Constitution or the first sentence of paragraph three of the Declaration of Independence?

## Connection to Performance Tasks

**Whole-Class Learning Performance Task** As students examine this document, they will consider the prompt and how these lines express American freedom.

UNIT PERFORMANCE-BASED ASSESSMENT
What are the most effective tools for establishing and preserving freedom?

**Unit Performance-Based Assessment** This selection mentions two important tools for establishing and preserving freedom: overthrowing an oppressive government and establishing a new democratic government.

DIGITAL PERSPECTIVES

Audio

Video

Document

Annotation Highlights

EL Highlights

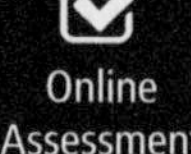
Online Assessment

## LESSON RESOURCES

| | Making Meaning | Language Development | Effective Expression |
|---|---|---|---|
| Lesson | **First Read**<br>**Close Read**<br>**Analyze the Text**<br>**Analyze Craft and Structure** | **Concept Vocabulary**<br>**Word Study**<br>**Conventions and Style** | **Writing to Sources**<br>**Speaking and Listening** |
| **Instructional Standards** | **RI.1** Cite strong and thorough textual evidence . . .<br>**RI.8** Delineate and evaluate the reasoning in seminal U.S. texts . . .<br>**RI.9** Analyze seventeenth-, eighteenth-, and nineteenth-century foundational U.S. documents . . .<br>**RI.10** By the end of grade 11, read and comprehend literary nonfiction . . . | **L.1.a** Apply the understanding that usage is a matter of convention . . .<br>**L.1.b** Resolve issues of complex or contested usage . . .<br>**L.3.a** Vary syntax for effect . . .<br>**L.4.b** Identify and correctly use patterns of word changes . . .<br>**L.4.c** Consult general and specialized reference materials . . . | **W.1** Write arguments . . .<br>**SL.1.c** Propel conversations . . . |
| **STUDENT RESOURCES** | | | |
| Available online in the Interactive Student Edition or Unit Resources | Selection Audio<br>First-Read Guide: Nonfiction<br>Close-Read Guide: Nonfiction | Word Network | Evidence Log |
| **TEACHER RESOURCES** | | | |
| **Selection Resources** Available online in the Interactive Teacher's Edition or Unit Resources | Audio Summaries<br>Annotation Highlights<br>EL Highlights<br>English Language Support Lesson: Persuasive Techniques<br>Analyze Craft and Structure: Argumentation | Concept Vocabulary and Word Study<br>Conventions and Style: Changes in Syntax and Usage | Writing to Sources: Editorial<br>Speaking and Listening: Class Discussion |
| **Reteach/Practice (RP)** Available online in the Interactive Teacher's Edition or Unit Resources | Analyze Craft and Structure: Argumentation (RP) | Word Study: Latin Root *-rect-* (RP)<br>Conventions and Style: Changes in Syntax and Usage (RP) | Writing to Sources: Editorial (RP)<br>Speaking and Listening: Class Discussion (RP) |
| **Assessment** Available online in Assessments | Selection Test | | |
| **My Resources** | A Unit 1 Answer Key is available online and in the Interactive Teacher's Edition. | | |

# Reading Support

| Text Complexity Rubric: Declaration of Independence | |
|---|---|
| **Qualitative Measures** | |
| Lexile 1390 Text Length 1,322 words | |
| **Qualitative Measures** | |
| Knowledge Demands ①—②—③—❹—⑤ | Historical knowledge demands; students will need to be familiar with events leading up to the creation of the Declaration of Independence in order to grasp the ideas. |
| Structure ①—②—❸—④—⑤ | The selection begins with explanatory paragraphs followed by a list of grievances and final declaration. |
| Language Conventionality and Clarity ①—②—③—④—❺ | The selection contains many lengthy, dense sentences written with highly formal language and some nonstandard capitalization and spelling. |
| Levels of Meaning/Purpose ①—②—❸—④—⑤ | The meaning/purpose is straightforward, but the concepts may be hard for some to grasp because of sophisticated language and supporting concepts that are complex. |

DECIDE AND PLAN

## English Language Support

Provide English Learners with support for knowledge demands and language as they read the selection.

**Knowledge Demands** Before reading the text, make sure students have sufficient background information about what led to the Declaration of Independence; for example, the frustration the colonists had about British tax policies in America. Making notes of what they know so far will help them as they read the text.

**Language** Work with students to reword long and complex sentences. Using the language from the selection, suggest simpler sentences. For example, in paragraph 1: *There comes a time when a certain group feels the need to dissolve, or split up, the political ties that have connected them with another.* Ask students to read the new sentences and discuss.

## Strategic Support

Provide students with strategic support to ensure that they can successfully read the text.

**Background Knowledge** Make sure students understand the grievances that are the focus of the Declaration of Independence. Ask students to name some of the reasons the colonists wanted to be independent from British rule.

**Language/Clarity** For students who may have difficulty with difficult and complex sentences, encourage them to break the sentences down into smaller chunks and identify the meaning of unfamiliar words or phrases. It may help to work in pairs and go through the text line by line, paraphrasing as they read aloud.

## Challenge

Provide students who need to be challenged with ideas for how they can go beyond a simple interpretation of the text.

**Text Analysis** Have students choose a grievance from the Declaration of Independence and retell it to a partner. Encourage them to include details and descriptive language. They may refer to the text as needed to remember details, but should use their own words.

**Written Response** Have students write a letter from the King of Great Britain addressed to the colonists responding to the Declaration of Independence.

TEACH

## Read and Respond

Have the class do their first read of the selection. Then, have them complete their close read. Finally, work with them on the Making Meaning, Language Development, and Effective Expression activities.

# Standards Support Through Teaching and Learning Cycle

## IDENTIFY NEEDS

Analyze results of the Beginning-of-Year Assessment, focusing on the items relating to Unit 1. Also take into consideration student performance to this point and your observations of where particular students struggle.

## DECIDE AND PLAN

- If students have performed poorly on items matching these standards, then provide selection scaffolds before assigning them the on-level lesson provided in the Student Edition.
- If students have done well on the Beginning-of-Year Assessment, then challenge them to keep progressing and learning by giving them opportunities to practice the skills in depth.
- Use the Selection Resources listed on the Planning pages for Declaration of Independence to help students continually improve their ability to master the standards.

**Instructional Standards: Declaration of Independence**

| | Catching Up | This Year | Looking Forward |
|---|---|---|---|
| **Reading** | You may wish to administer the **Analyze Craft and Structure: Argumentation (RP)** worksheet to help students identify the central ideas of a text, how they are developed, and how they build on one another. | **RI.8** Delineate and evaluate the reasoning in seminal U.S. texts, including the application of constitutional principles and use of legal reasoning and the premises, purposes, and arguments in works of public advocacy. | You may wish to challenge students to read an argumentative essay and identify the claim and counterclaim and then analyze how the evidence supports each point of view. |
| **Writing** | You may wish to administer the **Writing to Sources: Editorial (RP)** worksheet to help students understand how to clearly state a claim and support it with evidence. | **W.1** Write arguments to support claims in an analysis of substantive topics or texts, using valid reasoning and relevant and sufficient evidence. | Have students identify the claims that are made in the text of the Declaration of Independence and then determine how those claims are supported. |
| **Speaking and Listening** | You may wish to administer the **Speaking and Listening: Class Discussion (RP)** worksheet to help students understand how to hold a group discussion by asking and answering questions in order to promote divergent perspectives. | **SL.1.c** Propel conversations by posing and responding to questions that probe reasoning and evidence; ensure a hearing for a full range of positions on a topic or issue; clarify, verify, or challenge ideas and conclusions; and promote divergent and creative perspectives. | Have students engage in a classroom discussion about how the Declaration of Independence still affects everyday life so long after being written. |
| **Language** | You may wish to administer the **Conventions and Style: Changes in Syntax and Usage (RP)** worksheet to help students understand how language style and usage can change over time. | **L.1.a** Apply the understanding that usage is a matter of convention, can change over time, and is sometimes contested. | Challenge students to research how language has changed from when the Declaration of Independence was written and today. |

## ANALYZE AND REVISE

- Analyze student work for evidence of student learning.
- Identify whether or not students have met the expectations in the standards.
- Identify implications for future instruction.

## TEACH

Implement the planned lesson, and gather evidence of student learning.

## Jump Start

FIRST READ Set the following scene for students: "Imagine that you are soldiers dressed in ragged clothes. It's winter. Snow and ice surround you. A few of you have light jackets; some are barefoot. All are hungry, huddled in tents without floors. Badly defeated in the last battle, all you can think of is home. What spoken words might inspire you to keep fighting?"

Have students discuss this question. Then explain that they are about to read a document that gave those soldiers courage to fight on.

### Concept Vocabulary

Circulate among students as they rank their words. Remind them that they will find the definitions as they read them in the text.

FIRST READ

As they read, students should perform the steps of the first read:

NOTICE: Encourage students to notice how Jefferson organized the document in order to make it as persuasive as possible.

ANNOTATE: Remind students to mark unfamiliar words as well as parts of the text that surprise or confuse them, and language that they find especially expressive.

CONNECT: Encourage students to go beyond the selection to make connections between the Declaration of Independence and other historical documents or historical events they are familiar with.

RESPOND: Students will demonstrate their understanding of the text by answering questions and writing a summary.

Point out to students that while they will always compete the Respond step at the end of the first read, the other steps will probably happen somewhat concurrently. You may wish to print copies of the **First Read Guide: Nonfiction** for students to use.

**Remind students that during their first read they should not answer the close-read questions that appear in the selection.**

# Declaration of Independence

## Concept Vocabulary

You will encounter the following words as you read the Declaration of Independence. Before reading, note how familiar you are with each word. Then, rank the words in order from most familiar (1) to least familiar (6).

| WORD | YOUR RANKING |
|---|---|
| unalienable | |
| constrains | |
| tyranny | |
| assent | |
| acquiesce | |
| rectitude | |

After completing the first read, come back to the concept vocabulary and review your rankings. Mark changes to your original rankings as needed.

## First Read NONFICTION

Apply these strategies as you conduct your first read. You will have an opportunity to complete the close-read notes after your first read.

NOTICE the general ideas of the text. *What* is it about? *Who* is involved?

ANNOTATE by marking vocabulary and key passages you want to revisit.

CONNECT ideas within the selection to what you already know and what you have already read.

RESPOND by completing the Comprehension Check and by writing a brief summary of the selection.



**Tool Kit**
First-Read Guide and Model Annotation

STANDARDS
**Reading Informational Text**
By the end of grade 11, read and comprehend literary nonfiction in the grades 11–CCR text complexity band proficiently, with scaffolding as needed at the high end of the range.

About the Author

# Thomas Jefferson (1743–1826)

**Author of the Declaration of Independence**

When you look at all of Thomas Jefferson's achievements, it seems almost nothing was beyond his reach. Not only did he help our nation win its independence and serve as its third president, but he also founded the University of Virginia, helped establish the public school system, designed his own home, invented a type of elevator for sending food from floor to floor, and created the decimal system for American money. He was a skilled violinist, an art enthusiast, and a brilliant writer.

**Revolutionary Leader** Born into a wealthy Virginia family, Jefferson attended the College of William and Mary and went on to earn a law degree. While serving in the Virginia House of Burgesses, he became an outspoken defender of American rights. When conflict between the colonists and the British erupted into revolution, Jefferson emerged as a leader in the effort to win independence.

**Valued Statesman** When the war ended, Jefferson served as the American minister to France for several years. He then served as the nation's first secretary of state and second vice president before becoming president in 1801.

**Building the Nation** While in office, Jefferson negotiated with France to buy a tract of land extending from the southern coast of Louisiana north into what is now Canada. This vast expanse of land included all of present-day Arkansas, Missouri, Iowa, Oklahoma, Kansas, and Nebraska. It also included most of North and South Dakota, northeastern New Mexico, northern Texas, and portions of Minnesota, Colorado, Montana, and Wyoming. This enormous real-estate deal became known as the Louisiana Purchase, and it was one of the defining achievements of Jefferson's presidency. In a single treaty, Jefferson added more than 800,000 uncharted square miles to the holdings of the nation, effectively doubling its size.

**The Lewis and Clark Expedition** Jefferson had long wanted to pursue exploration of the Pacific Northwest. The completion of the Louisiana Purchase strengthened his resolve. He convinced Congress to allocate $2,500 to fund an expedition, writing:

> *The river Missouri, and Indians inhabiting it, are not as well known as rendered desirable by their connection with the Mississippi, and consequently with us. . . . An intelligent officer, with ten or twelve chosen men . . . might explore the whole line, even to the Western Ocean. . . .*

The "intelligent officer" he had in mind was his secretary, Captain Meriwether Lewis (1774–1809). Captain William Clark became co-leader of the group, which became known as the Corps of Discovery. Between 1804 and 1806, the team completed an 8,000-mile trek from St. Louis to the source of the Missouri River, across the Rocky Mountains to the Pacific coast, and back to Missouri.

**A Patriotic Departure** On the morning of July 4, 1826, the fiftieth anniversary of the Declaration of Independence, Jefferson died at the age of 83. John Adams, Jefferson's fellow contributor to the Declaration of Independence, died several hours later, after his longtime friend. Adams's last words were "Thomas Jefferson still survives."





AUTHOR'S PERSPECTIVE **Kelly Gallagher, M.Ed.**

**Teacher as the Best Reader in the Class** Rather than being the wizard behind the curtain, use modeling to do the work of reading in front of students. When students see that even good readers wrestle with difficult text, they gain confidence. Use these methods:

- **Using think-alouds.** Choose a passage from this unit and model read alouds/think alouds to show students what effective readers do when they are confused. The *Annotate Question Conclude* feature and the teacher edition support highlight the importance of this work.
- **Marking the text.** If students say they don't understand, have them use a yellow highlighter (or sticky notes) for parts they understand and a pink highlighter for those they don't.
- **Using sentence starters.** To identify where students are having comprehension problems, have them complete this sentence starter: "I don't understand..." Then, as a class, work to resolve the issues. Use these additional sentence starters: *I noticed...; I wonder...; I think...; I'm surprised that...; I realized...; I'm not sure...*
- It is also important for students to know that applying tools like these doesn't always work: sometimes, readers have to live with ambiguity.

## CLOSER LOOK

### Analyze Syntax

Students may have marked paragraphs 1–2 and the first sentence of paragraph 3 during their first read. Use these paragraphs to help students identify Jefferson's syntax. Encourage them to talk about the annotations that they marked. You may want to model a close read with the class based on the highlights shown in the text.

**ANNOTATE:** Have students mark details in the paragraphs that show Jefferson's sentence length and structure as he introduces his argument, or have students participate while you highlight them. For example, the author first states where he is—in Congress—and when he is writing—July 4, 1776. Next, Jefferson begins to outline why he and his fellow representatives feel compelled to explain their decision to the world.

**QUESTION:** How might the nature of the document dictate the syntax Jefferson uses to open the Declaration of Independence?

**Possible response:** Jefferson's sentence length and structure seem typical of a formal or legal document.

**CONCLUDE:** Help students to formulate conclusions about Jefferson's syntax, including the period in which he was writing and the nature of the document.

**Possible response:** The time period and the nature of an author's work have a strong influence on the **syntax** he or she employs.

Remind students that **syntax** is the arrangement of words in sentences. Syntax can have an effect on the formality and tone of a piece of writing.

Additional **English Language Support** is available in the Interactive Teacher's Edition.

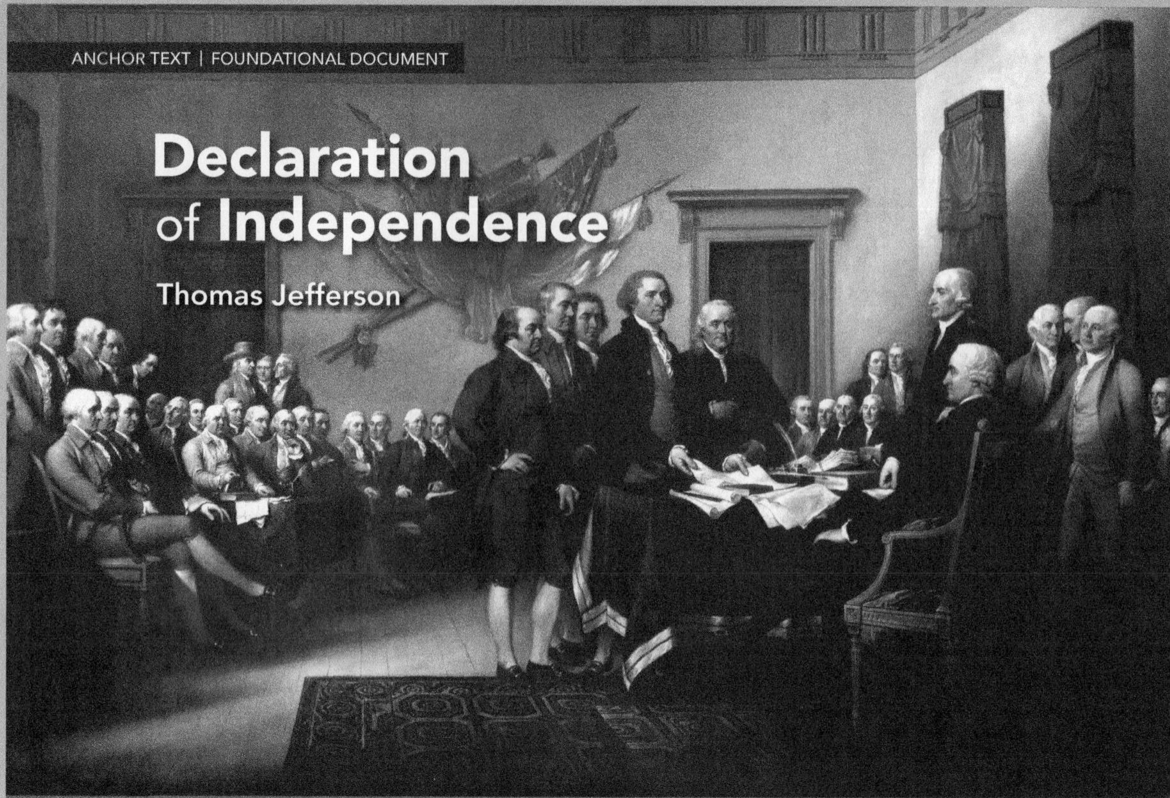

ANCHOR TEXT | FOUNDATIONAL DOCUMENT

# Declaration of Independence

**Thomas Jefferson**

SCAN FOR MULTIMEDIA

BACKGROUND

The Continental Congress was formed in 1774 by the American colonies to coordinate resistance to British laws considered by most colonists to be unfair. In the summer of 1776, after about a year of war against Britain, representatives met to consider an official break with Britain.

NOTES

**unalienable** (uhn AYL yuh nuh buhl) *adj.* impossible to take away or give up

## IN CONGRESS, July 4, 1776.

1 *The unanimous declaration of the thirteen united states of America,*

2 When in the course of human events, it becomes necessary for one people to dissolve the political bands which have connected them with another, and to assume among the powers of the earth, the separate and equal station to which the laws of nature and of nature's God entitle them, a decent respect to the opinions of mankind requires that they should declare the causes which impel them to the separation.

3 We hold these truths to be self-evident: that all men are created equal; that they are endowed by their creator with certain unalienable rights, that among these are life, liberty and the pursuit of happiness; that to secure these rights, governments are instituted among men, deriving their just powers from the consent





## DIGITAL PERSPECTIVES

**Illuminating the Text** Find and show a video that highlights one or more of the historical events leading up to July 4, 1776. Examples might include the Stamp Act, the Boston Tea Party, the Intolerable Acts, the Siege of Boston, and battles at Lexington and Concord and at Bunker Hill. Have students take brief notes on the video.

As students read the Declaration of Independence, they can look for references Jefferson may have made to the event or events in the video. Always preview videos before sharing them with the class. **(Research to Clarify)**

of the governed; that whenever any form of government becomes destructive of these ends, it is the right of the people to alter or to abolish it, and to institute new government, laying its foundation on such principles and organizing its powers in such form, as to them shall seem most likely to effect their safety and happiness. Prudence, indeed, will dictate that governments long established should not be changed for light and transient causes; and accordingly all experience hath shown, that mankind are more disposed to suffer, while evils are sufferable, than to right themselves by abolishing the forms to which they are accustomed. But when a long train of abuses and usurpations,[1] pursuing invariably the same object evinces a design to reduce them under absolute despotism, it is their right, it is their duty, to throw off such government, and to provide new guards for their future security. Such has been the patient sufferance of these colonies; and such is now the necessity which **constrains** them to alter their former systems of government. The history of the present King of Great Britain is a history of repeated injuries and usurpations,[1] all having in direct object the establishment of an absolute **tyranny** over these states. To prove this, let facts be submitted to a candid world.

4 He has refused his **assent** to laws the most wholesome and necessary for the public good.

5 He has forbidden his governors to pass laws of immediate and pressing importance, unless suspended in their operation till his assent should be obtained; and when so suspended, he has utterly neglected to attend to them.

6 He has refused to pass other laws for the accommodation of large districts of people, unless those people would relinquish the right of representation in the legislature, a right inestimable to them and formidable to tyrants only.

7 He has called together legislative bodies at places unusual, uncomfortable, and distant from the depository of their public records, for the sole purpose of fatiguing them into compliance with his measures.

8 He has dissolved representative houses repeatedly, for opposing with manly firmness his invasions on the rights of the people.

9 He has refused for a long time, after such dissolutions, to cause others to be elected, whereby the legislative powers, incapable of annihilation, have returned to the people at large for their exercise, the state remaining in the mean time exposed to all the dangers of invasion from without, and convulsions within.

10 He has endeavored to prevent the population of these states; for that purpose obstructing the laws for naturalization of foreigners, refusing to pass others to encourage their migrations hither, and raising the conditions of new appropriations of lands.

1. **usurpations** (yoo zuhr PAY shuhnz) *n.* unlawful or violent seizures of power or possessions.

NOTES

**CLOSE READ**

ANNOTATE: Mark words in the last two sentences of paragraph 3 that seem especially strong or extreme.

QUESTION: Why would Jefferson employ such strong language?

CONCLUDE: What effect might this language have had on the American colonists? The British officials?

**constrains** (kuhn STRAYNZ) *v.* requires or forces

**tyranny** (TIHR uh nee) *n.* oppressive power

**assent** (uh SEHNT) *n.* approval or agreement





DIGITAL PERSPECTIVES

## CLOSE READ

Remind students to focus on strong language—words and phrases that connote strongly negative emotions. If necessary, point out that "strong language" can refer to swear words, but here it does not—obviously, Jefferson uses no swear words in the Declaration. You may wish to model the Close Read using the following think-aloud format. Possible responses to questions on the student page are included. You may also want to print copies of the **Close-Read Guide: Nonfiction** for students to use.

**ANNOTATE:** As I read the last two sentences in paragraph 3, I notice and annotate the phrases "repeated injuries" and "absolute tyranny." This seems like strong language to me—both phrases connote strongly negative emotions.

**QUESTION:** These are strong, descriptive phrases that Jefferson uses to make his point that the colonists' treatment by the King of Great Britain has always been extreme, punitive, and unjust.

**CONCLUDE:** I can conclude that the American colonists would agree with Jefferson and that his language would stir up their own anger at the king. I can conclude that British officials (since they are loyal to the king) would feel highly insulted by words like *injuries, usurpations,* and *tyranny*. They would probably think that using such language makes Jefferson a traitor.

## PERSONALIZE FOR LEARNING

### English Language Support

**Unfamiliar Words** Review paragraphs 6–8 with students. Note that the Declaration is densely written and contains many words and phrases with which students may be unfamiliar. You may wish to closely read the text with them in small groups. Work together with students to shorten and rephrase sentences in simpler language.

For example, the sentence *He has dissolved representative houses repeatedly, for opposing with manly firmness his invasions on the rights of the people* (paragraph 8) might be rephrased as *The king has dissolved organized groups that oppose him.* **EXPANDING/BRIDGING**

## CLOSE READ

Remind students to look for Jefferson's use of harsh language that connotes intense and negative emotions. You may wish to model the Close Read using the following think-aloud format.

**ANNOTATE:** In paragraph 27, I find and annotate the verbs *plundered, ravaged, burnt,* and *destroyed*. Grouping these verbs together in a list shows that Jefferson thinks the king is a cruel, violent person.

**QUESTION:** Probably Jefferson uses these verbs because they are frightening and violent-sounding. He wants to draw attention to the king's repeatedly malicious behavior and how it is negatively affecting and harming colonists.

**CONCLUDE:** I can conclude that in 1776, these violent-sounding verbs demonstrate the resentment that colonists feel toward the hostile and violent actions of the king.

NOTES

11 He has obstructed the administration of justice, by refusing his assent to laws for establishing judiciary powers.

12 He has made judges dependent on his will alone, for the tenure of their offices, and the amount and payment of their salaries.

13 He has erected a multitude of new offices, and sent hither swarms of officers to harass our people, and eat out their substance.

14 He has kept among us in times of peace standing armies without the consent of our legislatures.

15 He has affected to render the military independent of, and superior to, the civil power.

16 He has combined with others to subject us to a jurisdiction foreign to our constitution, and unacknowledged by our laws; giving his assent to their acts of pretended legislation:

17 For quartering[2] large bodies of armed troops among us:

18 For protecting them, by a mock trial, from punishment for any murders which they should commit on the inhabitants of these states:

19 For cutting off our trade with all parts of the world:

20 For imposing taxes on us without our consent:

21 For depriving us in many cases, of the benefits of trial by jury:

22 For transporting us beyond seas to be tried for pretended offenses:

23 For abolishing the free system of English laws in a neighboring province, establishing therein an arbitrary government, and enlarging its boundaries so as to render it at once an example and fit instrument for introducing the same absolute rule into these colonies:

24 For taking away our charters, abolishing our most valuable laws, and altering fundamentally the forms of our governments:

25 For suspending our own legislatures, and declaring themselves invested with power to legislate for us in all cases whatsoever.

26 He has abdicated government here, by declaring us out of his protection and waging war against us.

**CLOSE READ**

**ANNOTATE:** Mark the verbs in paragraph 27 that describe what the king has done to the colonists.

**QUESTION:** Why do you think Jefferson chose these verbs?

**CONCLUDE:** What is the effect of this language?

27 He has plundered our seas, ravaged our coasts, burned our towns, and destroyed the lives of our people.

28 He is at this time transporting large armies of foreign mercenaries to complete the works of death, desolation and tyranny, already begun with circumstances of cruelty and perfidy scarcely paralleled in the most barbarous ages, and totally unworthy the head of a civilized nation.

29 He has constrained our fellow citizens taken captive on the high seas to bear arms against their country, to become the executioners of their friends and brethren, or to fall themselves by their hands.

30 He has excited domestic insurrections amongst us, and has endeavored to bring on the inhabitants of our frontiers, the merciless Indian savages, whose known rule of warfare, is an undistinguished destruction of all ages, sexes, and conditions.

31 In every stage of these oppressions we have petitioned for redress in the most humble terms: Our repeated petitions have been

2. **quartering** *v.* housing.





## PERSONALIZE FOR LEARNING

### Strategic Support

**Paraphrasing** Review paragraphs 4–31 with students. For students to fully appreciate the impact of the Declaration of Independence, they need to be able to understand each "abuse" that Jefferson lists in paragraphs 4–31. As they closely read this section, students might complete a chart such as the following to help them list and explain some of the abuses:

| Paragraph number | Quotation from the text | My notes on this quotation's meaning |
|---|---|---|
| 13 | "He has erected a multitude of new offices, and sent hither swarms of officers to harass our people, and eat out their substance." | "Offices" means jobs, not buildings—the king has invented a bunch of useless or harmful jobs for his officers to do, and then made the colonists pay the officers. |
| 17 | "For quartering large bodies of armed troops among us" | The king forces the colonists to provide housing for English soldiers (who are the colonists' enemies). |

answered only by repeated injury. A prince whose character is thus marked by every act which may define a tyrant, is unfit to be the ruler of a free people.

32 Nor have we been wanting in attentions to our British brethren. We have warned them from time to time of attempts by their legislature to extend an unwarrantable jurisdiction over us. We have reminded them of the circumstances of our emigration and settlement here. We have appealed to their native justice and magnanimity, and we have conjured them by the ties of our common kindred to disavow these usurpations, which, would inevitably interrupt our connections and correspondence. They too have been deaf to the voice of justice and of consanguinity.[3] We must, therefore, **acquiesce** in the necessity, which denounces our separation, and hold them, as we hold the rest of mankind, enemies in war, in peace friends.

33 We, therefore, the representatives of the United States of America, in General Congress assembled appealing to the Supreme Judge of the world for the **rectitude** of our intentions, do in the name and by authority of the good people of these colonies, solemnly publish and declare that these united colonies are and of right ought to be free and independent states; that they are absolved from all allegiance to the British Crown, and that all political connection between them and the state of Great Britain is and ought to be totally dissolved; and that as free and independent states, they have full power to levy war,

NOTES

**acquiesce** (ak wee EHS) *v.* accept something reluctantly but without protest

**rectitude** (REHK tuh tood) *n.* morally correct behavior or thinking; uprightness

3. **consanguinity** (kon sang GWIHN uh tee) *n.* blood relationship.

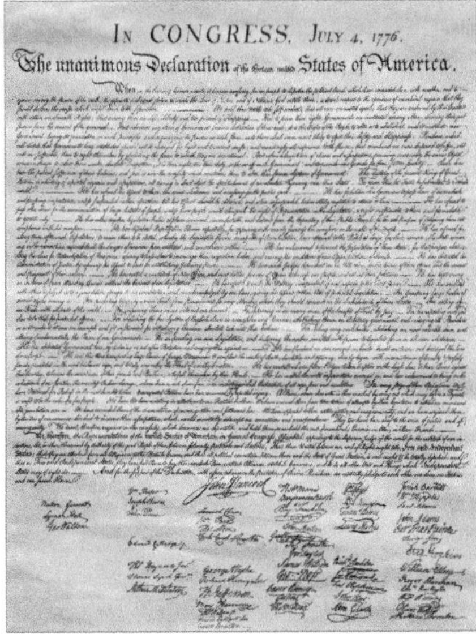


Image of the final, signed version of the Declaration of Independence





## PERSONALIZE FOR LEARNING

### English Language Support

**Antiquated Language** Note the first sentence in paragraph 32: "Nor have we been wanting in attentions to our British brethren." Tell students that today's English speakers and writers rarely use language like this. Unpack the sentence for students by first rephrasing it as follows: "We have not been wanting in attentions to our British brethren, either." Point out that, in this context, the word *wanting* means "neglectful." Thus, a more modern way to express this thought might be: "We have not neglected to keep in close contact with the British people, either." Help students identify and rephrase other antiquated language such as "we have conjured them by the ties of our common kindred"; "Supreme Judge of the world"; and "of right ought to be." **EXPANDING/BRIDGING**

CLOSER LOOK

## Identify Mood

Students may have marked the last sentence in the Declaration. Use the last sentence to help students identify Jefferson's shift toward using words with a positive connotation in this paragraph.

**ANNOTATE:** Have students mark words and phrases in the last sentence of paragraph 33 that help them identify words and phrases with a positive emotional appeal.

**QUESTION:** Guide students to consider what these phrases might tell them. Ask them to identify why Jefferson might choose to use words that have a positive connotation.

**Possible responses:** Jefferson wants to end on a hopeful and positive note and includes language that helps emphasize this. He also wants to acknowledge the gratitude he feels for the support of his fellow colonists and the steps they are taking toward independence.

**CONCLUDE:** Help students to formulate conclusions about the impact the Declaration had.

**Possible responses:** It probably gave the colonial army courage and made the other colonists feel more hopeful about the war they were fighting. It no doubt angered the king and his supporters. It inspired freedom fighters in other countries and at other points in history.

Remind students that a shift in **mood** can be an effective tool in writing that sets forth an argument or tries to persuade an audience.

NOTES

war, conclude peace, contract alliances, establish commerce, and to do all other acts and things which independent states may of right do. And for the support of this declaration, with a firm reliance on the protection of divine providence, we mutually pledge to each other our lives, our fortunes and our sacred honor.

*The 56 signatures on the Declaration appear in the positions indicated:*

Column 1

Georgia:
*Button Gwinnett*
*Lyman Hall*
*George Walton*

Column 2

North Carolina:
*William Hooper*
*Joseph Hewes*
*John Penn*

South Carolina:
*Edward Rutledge*
*Thomas Heyward, Jr.*
*Thomas Lynch, Jr.*
*Arthur Middleton*

Column 3

Massachusetts:
*John Hancock*

Maryland:
*Samuel Chase*
*William Paca*
*Thomas Stone*
*Charles Carroll of Carrollton*

Virginia:
*George Wythe*
*Richard Henry Lee*
*Thomas Jefferson*
*Benjamin Harrison*
*Thomas Nelson, Jr.*
*Francis Lightfoot Lee*
*Carter Braxton*

Column 4

Pennsylvania:
*Robert Morris*
*Benjamin Rush*
*Benjamin Franklin*
*John Morton*
*George Clymer*
*James Smith*
*George Taylor*
*James Wilson*
*George Ross*

Delaware:
*Caesar Rodney*
*George Read*
*Thomas McKean*

Column 5

New York:
*William Floyd*
*Philip Livingston*
*Francis Lewis*
*Lewis Morris*

New Jersey:
*Richard Stockton*
*John Witherspoon*
*Francis Hopkinson*
*John Hart*
*Abraham Clark*

Column 6

New Hampshire:
*Josiah Bartlett*
*William Whipple*

Massachusetts:
*Samuel Adams*
*John Adams*
*Robert Treat Paine*
*Elbridge Gerry*

Rhode Island:
*Stephen Hopkins*
*William Ellery*

Connecticut:
*Roger Sherman*
*Samuel Huntington*
*William Williams*
*Oliver Wolcott*

New Hampshire:
*Matthew Thornton*





PERSONALIZE FOR LEARNING

### English Language Support

**Choral Reading** Call students' attention to paragraph 33. Encourage students to stand up and chorally read the last sentence of the Declaration of Independence after discussing its meaning. Before they read, make sure students understand the meanings of words and phrases in the last sentence. Ask students to go through the text and find words and phrases that need further clarification. Practice these words as a class.

| Word or Phrase | Meaning |
|---|---|
| *reliance* | the ability to count on someone or something |
| "divine providence" | a loving God or higher power |
| "mutually pledge" | promise together |
| "our fortunes" | our fates; what will happen to us in the future |
| "sacred honor" | very important ability to be as good as possible at all times so that you and others can be proud of you |

**EMERGING/EXPANDING**

DIGITAL PERSPECTIVES

MEDIA CONNECTION

John F. Kennedy Reads the Declaration of Independence

**Discuss It** In 1957, then-Senator John F. Kennedy read the Declaration of Independence as part of an Independence Day radio broadcast. What do you think the reading would have meant to radio listeners?

**Write your response before sharing your ideas.**

SCAN FOR MULTIMEDIA 

## Comprehension Check

**Complete the following items after you finish your first read.**

1. What does Jefferson state directly as the reason this declaration had to be written?

2. According to Jefferson, what is a people's duty when their government is abusive?

3. What new relationship between Great Britain and the United States is announced in this document?

4. **Notebook** Write a summary of the Declaration of Independence to confirm your understanding of the text.

### RESEARCH

**Research to Clarify** Choose at least one unfamiliar detail from the text. Briefly research that detail. In what way does the information you learned shed light on an aspect of the document?

**Research to Explore** Conduct research to find out how some signers of the Declaration of Independence expressed their convictions about the document.





### PERSONALIZE FOR LEARNING

**Challenge**
Challenge students to create a detailed graphic organizer like the one shown that shows how the Declaration of Independence is organized and why Jefferson organized it as he did.

| Paragraph number(s) | Summary of this section | Purpose of this section |
|---|---|---|
| 1–3 | All men are equal and have rights that the King is denying the people of the colonies. | to introduce the Declaration and the reasons for it |
| | | |

## Media Connection

Play the Media Connection audio in class, ask students to open the audio in their interactive textbooks, or have students scan the Bounce Page icon with their phones to access the audio.

**Possible response:** Hearing the historic document read, especially by Senator Kennedy of Massachusetts, who was already a popular public figure, probably would have been a powerful reminder of the meaning of freedom. This would have been especially relevant in 1957. At that time, African Americans were still struggling to obtain civil rights and freedom from cruel discriminatory treatment despite the fact that the Civil War had been over and slavery had been illegal for almost a hundred years.

## Comprehension Check

**Possible responses:**

1. The purpose is to give the reasons why it has become necessary for the United States to dissolve a political bond and become a separate nation.
2. It is their duty to "throw off" (or overthrow) the government and put safeguards in place to keep this from happening again.
3. If the two countries can repair their relationship, peace may be restored—but if not, they will continue to engage in war, as enemies.
4. Answers will vary. Sample response: All people are created equal and entitled to certain inalienable rights, for the protection of which governments are created. For people in the American colonies, the king has not protected these rights. He has committed numerous offences against the colonies and ignored their attempts to seek redress of grievances. The colonists have appealed to the British people, too, but they have not helped their "brethren" obtain fair treatment from the king. For these reasons, the colonies declare themselves independent of Great Britain and have created a new government with the full powers of independent states.

## Research

**Research to Clarify** If students struggle to come up with an unfamiliar detail to research, suggest that they focus on one of the following: 1) reasons why the colonists did not formally declare themselves independent until 1776 (when the war had already been raging for a year); 2) Enlightenment philosophers (such as John Locke) whom Jefferson read and admired to the extent that he included their ideas in the Declaration.

**Research to Explore** Encourage students to choose a famous signer of the Declaration of Independence from the list below the document. They can use search terms such as "John Adams's opinion of the Declaration of Independence."

## Jump Start

**CLOSE READ** Ask students how they think different groups of people might have reacted to the Declaration of Independence. Have students consider the soldiers in the colonial army, the British soldiers whom King George had sent to subdue the colonies, and the loyalists (those colonists who remained loyal to the king). Lead a discussion on these three groups' probable reactions.

## Close Read the Text

Work with students on the annotation model, and then have them complete items 2 and 3 on their own. When they have finished, review and discuss the sections students marked. If needed, continue to model close reading by using the Annotation Highlights in the Interactive Teacher's Edition.

## Analyze the Text

Possible responses:

1. Jefferson is preparing to contrast the rights that the colonists claim with the king's behavior. **DOK 3**
2. (a) People do not decide to change governments because of minor irritations. **DOK 2**
   (b) People may be unwilling to face upheaval and bloodshed at the change in government. **DOK 3**
3. (a) The king has been contemptuous of the colonists' efforts to establish their own laws. **DOK 2**
   (b) Since the king has ignored the colonists' efforts to make their own laws, they were tempted to declare independence. **DOK 3**
4. The purpose of the document is to explain why the colonies feel that they have been left with no other choice but to declare their independence. **DOK 3**
5. Jefferson declares that freedom is based upon having certain basic "inalienable" human rights. If a ruler or leader does not protect these rights, people are not free. **DOK 3**

MAKING MEANING

DECLARATION OF INDEPENDENCE

## Close Read the Text

1. This model, from paragraph 2 of the text, shows two sample annotations, along with questions and conclusions. Close read the passage, and find another detail to annotate. Then, write a question and your conclusion.

ANNOTATE: This is very grand language, referring to all of human history.

QUESTION: Why does Jefferson present this argument in the context of the entirety of human history?

CONCLUDE: Jefferson is saying that the severing of political ties between nations is of momentous importance.

When in the course of human events, it becomes necessary for one people to dissolve the political bands which have connected them with another, . . . a decent respect to the opinions of mankind requires that they should declare the causes which impel them to the separation.

ANNOTATE: These words seem to be gentle.

QUESTION: Why might Jefferson have chosen such language?

CONCLUDE: Perhaps he wanted to make his argument sound reasoned and logical, and not angry.

2. For more practice, go back into the text and complete the close-read notes.
3. Revisit a section of the text you found important during your first read. **Annotate** what you notice. Ask yourself **questions** such as "Why did the author make this choice?" What can you **conclude**?

**Tool Kit**
Close-Read Guide and Model Annotation

## Analyze the Text

CITE TEXTUAL EVIDENCE to support your answers.

Notebook Respond to these questions.

1. **Make Inferences** Why does Jefferson begin with points about human rights before discussing the colonists' specific grievances?
2. (a) **Interpret** What does Jefferson mean by saying that people do not change governments for "light reasons"? (b) **Speculate** Why might people be more inclined to put up with a government that is less than satisfactory rather than change it?
3. (a) **Generalize** According to Jefferson, what has been the king's attitude toward the laws of the colonies? (b) **Analyze** Why is that attitude an important factor in the decision to declare independence?
4. **Historical Perspectives** The signers of the Declaration of Independence knew that their announcement could mean war with powerful, well-equipped Britain. In your opinion, why isn't that idea more prominent in the document?
5. **Essential Question:** ***What is the meaning of freedom?*** What have you learned about American freedoms from reading this text? How does Jefferson connect the meaning of freedom to the idea of human rights?

STANDARDS

**Reading Informational Text**
- Cite strong and thorough textual evidence to support analysis of what the text says explicitly as well as inferences drawn from the text, including determining where the text leaves matters uncertain.
- Delineate and evaluate the reasoning in seminal U.S. texts, including the application of constitutional principles and use of legal reasoning and the premises, purposes, and arguments in works of public advocacy.
- Analyze seventeenth-, eighteenth-, and nineteenth-century foundational U.S. documents of historical and literary significance for their themes, purposes, and rhetorical features.





### FORMATIVE ASSESSMENT

### Analyze the Text

- **If** students fail to cite evidence, **then** remind them to support their ideas with specific information from the text.
- **If** students struggle to make a generalization about the king's attitude toward the colonists' efforts to make their own laws, **then** define a *generalization*, and provide examples.

### PERSONALIZE FOR LEARNING

**English Language Support**
**Identifying Persuasion in an Argument**
Preview several commercials using online sources and select one. Have students watch the commercial to look for persuasive techniques at work.

Ask students to identify the persuasive technique and write a few sentences explaining why they think the argument is or is not convincing.
**EMERGING**

Ask students to write a few sentences explaining the persuasive technique, giving examples of the persuasive language used. Then ask students to add a few sentences in which they evaluate how well the commercial used the specific persuasive technique to present and support the idea.
**EXPANDING**

## Analyze Craft and Structure

**Author's Purpose: Argumentation** An **argument** is writing that is meant to get readers to think in a certain way or take a particular action. In an effective argument, the writer presents reasons and supports them with convincing evidence. He or she also uses a variety of **persuasive appeals**, or ways of framing ideas for specific effect:

- **Appeals to Emotion:** ideas or language that attempts to influence readers' feelings; appeals to emotion may include **charged language**—strong words with powerful connotations—as well as references to the divine, references to concepts like justice or fairness, and stories or anecdotes.
- **Appeals to Logic:** ideas or language that connects to readers' rationality or reason; appeals to logic emphasize relationships between evidence, such as facts, and consequences or outcomes.
- **Appeals to Authority:** ideas or language that suggests the writer has special expertise or demonstrates character in a way that merits readers' attention on the subject.

### Practice

**CITE TEXTUAL EVIDENCE** to support your answers.

**Notebook** Respond to these questions.

1. (a) What appeal to emotion does Jefferson use in paragraph 1? (b) Why is this an important technique for him to use as he begins his argument?
2. (a) Mark examples of appeals to emotion in this excerpt from paragraph 2.

   *But when a long train of abuses and usurpations, pursuing invariably the same object, evinces a design to reduce them under absolute despotism, it is their right, it is their duty, to throw off such government, and to provide new guards for their future security. Such has been the patient sufferance of these colonies; and such is now the necessity which constrains them to alter their former systems of government. The history of the present king of Great Britain is a history of repeated injuries and usurpations, all having in direct object the establishment of an absolute tyranny over these states.*

   (b) How does the description of Great Britain and its king constitute charged language? Explain, citing specific words.
3. (a) Which kind of appeal is represented by Jefferson's organized list of grievances? (b) How does the evidence he provides add to his argument?
4. Jefferson wrote this document during the Age of Reason, an era characterized by logic and scientific methodology. How does the Declaration of Independence reflect Jefferson's faith in reason?





Ask students to write a paragraph explaining the persuasive technique used, giving examples and adding additional techniques and examples that the commercial writer could have used to support the argument. Have pairs of students discuss the techniques and examples they added and how successful they were in supporting the argument. **BRIDGING**

An expanded **English Language Support Lesson** on Persuasive Techniques is available in the Interactive Teacher's Edition.

DIGITAL PERSPECTIVES

## Analyze Craft and Structure

Expand on the techniques with more detail for students:

- *Appeals to emotion* can include highly charged negative connotations, but effective persuasive writing does not go so far as to lie or maliciously defame the opposing side. For example, Jefferson calls King George a "tyrant," but he also spells out why the colonists believe this is so. He does not engage in pointless name-calling.
- *Appeals to logic* succeed if the arguments are built on *verifiable* evidence rather than claims that cannot be proven. For example, a car commercial might point out safety equipment that other brands do not have; these are facts that a consumer can easily verify.
- *Appeals to authority* are based on the credibility and stature of the author or speaker. They emphasize the author's position as a person with special knowledge or experience of a topic.

For more support, see **Analyze Craft and Structure: Argumentation**

### Practice

**Possible responses:**

1. (a) Inclusion of the word *unanimous*

   (b) Unanimity suggests that the decision is correct.
2. (a) Students might mark "abuses and usurpations."

   (b) Jefferson contrasts the king's "abuses," with the colonists' "rights."
3. (a) The list of grievances is based on evidence, reasoning, and ethical judgments.

   (b) The evidence ensures that the argument will not be discounted as just an emotional appeal.
4. Jefferson's Declaration is a demonstration of the logical thinking valued during the Age of Reason.

### FORMATIVE ASSESSMENT

### Analyze Craft and Structure

- **If** students are unable to contrast Jefferson's attitude toward the king with his attitude toward the colonists, **then** display in one column charged words Jefferson uses to describe the king, and in a second column words to describe the colonists.
- **If** students fail to identify types of persuasive techniques used in the Declaration, **then** provide an example of each type. For more Reteach and Practice, see **Analyze Craft and Structure: Argumentation (RP)**.

## Concept Vocabulary

**Why These Words?** Discuss with students some differences between the words *acquiesce* and *assent*. The first is a verb that means "to accept [something]." This word connotes reluctance: when you acquiesce you give in with some degree of reluctance to something you do not necessarily want to do or accept. The second is a verb (which can be used as a noun, as well) that means "give approval or agreement." *Assent* connotes authority over others—someone who gives his or her assent gives something a "stamp of approval."

Possible responses:

1. The vocabulary words show the seriousness of the colonists' concerns about their rights.
2. Choices include *abuses, despotism, neglected, invasions,* and *convulsions*.

### Practice

Possible responses:

1. Responses will vary but should accurately reflect the meaning of each word.
2. Responses will vary, but students should be able to demonstrate their understanding of the nuances of their word choices.

### Word Network

Possible words: *endowed, liberty, consent, usurpations, independent, justice*

## Word Study

For more support, see **Concept Vocabulary and Word Study**.

Possible responses:

1. "rightness or correctness"
2. In chemistry, *rectify* means "to use distillation to refine or purify a solution." In electronics, *rectify* means "to change alternating current (AC) to direct current (DC)."

### FORMATIVE ASSESSMENT

**Concept Vocabulary**

**If** students fail to see connections among the words, **then** have them see the words in context.

**Word Study**

**If** students fail to define *rectitude*, **then** use the word in two context sentences. For Reteach and Practice, see **Word Study: Latin Root -*rect*- (RP).**



LANGUAGE DEVELOPMENT

DECLARATION OF INDEPENDENCE

## Concept Vocabulary

| unalienable | tyranny | acquiesce |
|---|---|---|
| constrains | assent | rectitude |

**Why These Words?** These concept vocabulary words convey ideas about power and rights. For example, Jefferson refers to life, liberty, and the pursuit of happiness as *unalienable* rights. He states that the king's actions established absolute *tyranny* over the colonies.

1. How does the concept vocabulary help readers grasp the issues leading to the Declaration of Independence?
2. What other words in the selection connect to these concepts?

**WORD NETWORK**

Add words related to freedom from the text to your Word Network.

### Practice

**Notebook** Complete these activities.

1. Use each concept vocabulary word in a sentence that demonstrates your understanding of the word's meaning.
2. In two of your sentences, replace the concept vocabulary word with a synonym. What is the effect? For example, which sentence is stronger? Which one makes the sentence seem more positive or more negative?

## Word Study

**Latin Root: -*rect*-** The Latin root -*rect*- means "right" or "straight." It is the basis for many English words, including such mathematical terms as *rectangular* (having right angles) and *rectilinear* (formed by straight lines).

1. Write a definition of *rectitude* that demonstrates your understanding of its Latin root.
2. Use a print or online college-level dictionary to find the meanings of *rectify* as the word relates to chemistry and as it relates to electronics.

**STANDARDS**

Language

- Apply the understanding that usage is a matter of convention, can change over time, and is sometimes contested.
- Resolve issues of complex or contested usage, consulting references as needed.
- Vary syntax for effect, consulting references for guidance as needed; apply an understanding of syntax to the study of complex texts when reading.
- Identify and correctly use patterns of word changes that indicate different meanings or parts of speech.
- Consult general and specialized reference materials, find the pronunciation of a word or determine or clarify its precise meaning, its part of speech, its etymology, or its standard usage.





### AUTHOR'S PERSPECTIVE Elfrieda Hiebert, Ph.D.

**Author's Word Choice** In a text, authors may or may not explicitly state the underlying theme. When the theme is left unstated, readers will have to put together clues in the text to infer the author's overarching message about life. Among the most useful clues are the author's choice of words, and understanding how vocabulary functions in this way can help students identify the selection's theme.

Teachers can convey the power of vocabulary to convey theme by selecting a narrative from Unit 1 and guiding students to find words and phrases that are part of a network. The words should be related because of their denotations, connotations, or imagery, for example. Model for students how to choose words that belong in a network. For example, if a passage describes cooking, students can select words from the passage such as *warm, clean, fragrant*, and *sweetness*. Be sure the list is narrowly focused and students can explain the relationship among the words and why they chose each word. Then have students explore the effect of the words and explain how they convey the author's theme and make the story richer.

## Conventions and Style

**Changes in Syntax and Usage** Language changes over time. During the eighteenth century, when Jefferson wrote the Declaration of Independence, English spelling was almost identical to that of today's English. However, there are elements of Jefferson's style—the style of his era—that may seem old-fashioned to today's readers.

- **Syntax:** the structure of sentences. Some of Jefferson's sentences are very long by today's standards; in fact, the second paragraph of the Declaration is a lengthy single sentence.
- **Usage:** the way in which a word or phrase is used. Jefferson uses some words that would rarely be used—and might even be contested—today. For example, the word *consanguinity* in paragraph 32 is a term that few modern writers would use.
- **Formality:** the level of familiarity with which writers address the reader. While there are still ceremonial and public forums that require formal language, American culture is more casual now than it was in the eighteenth century. Both the purpose of the document and the style of the era are reflected in the Declaration's high level of formality.

### Read It

1. Reread paragraphs 1–2 of the Declaration of Independence. Identify four words or phrases that represent an earlier style of English.
2. Locate Jefferson's use of *conjured* in paragraph 32. What does the word mean to Jefferson in this context? What does the word often mean today? Use an etymological dictionary or other source to explain how the two meanings are connected by word origin and word history.
3. **Connect to Style** What qualities of eighteenth-century style do you find in paragraphs 28–29? Consider syntax, usage, and level of formality.

### Write It

**Notebook** Rewrite this excerpt from the Declaration of Independence. Use modern English usage and syntax to express the same meaning. Then, compare the two versions and take note of ways in which each version would likely appeal to different audiences.

> He has refused his assent to laws, the most wholesome and necessary for the public good.
>
> He has forbidden his governors to pass laws of immediate and pressing importance, unless suspended in their operation till his assent should be obtained; and when so suspended, he has utterly neglected to attend to them.





## PERSONALIZE FOR LEARNING

### English Language Support

**Antiquated Language** Emphasize that many of the words and phrases that Jefferson uses in the Declaration are rarely, if ever, used by today's English speakers and writers. Work with students to develop a chart that provides modern definitions or equivalents for antiquated words and phrases. **EXPANDING/BRIDGING**

**DIGITAL PERSPECTIVES**

## Conventions and Style

**Changes in Syntax and Usage** Encourage students to search the Declaration's text for more long sentences. For example, the first sentence in paragraph 33 ("We, therefore...publish and declare, that...and to do all other acts and things which independent states may of right do.") contains 127 words. Its subject is *We* and its main verbs are *publish and declare*. It has four direct objects, each of which begins with *that* (meaning "the fact that..." or "the idea that..."). For more support, see **Conventions and Style: Changes in Syntax and Usage**.

### Read It

Possible responses:

1. Examples include *hath shown, usurpations,* and *sufferance*.
2. By *conjured*, Jefferson means "pleaded with." Today, the verb to *conjure* usually means "to create or imagine something." The two meanings are connected through the Latin word root *jurare*, which means "to swear."
3. Each paragraph consists of one long, complicated sentence. Jefferson uses dramatic, antiquated-sounding phrases such as "works of death, desolation and tyranny" and "cruelty & perfidy scarcely paralleled in the most barbarous ages." Jefferson's writing is highly structured according to the style of his time, befitting a formal argument presented to government officials.

### Write It

Possible responses:

The king has refused to agree to laws that are important to the welfare of the colonists. The king has forbidden his governors to pass laws of importance without first getting his agreement, yet he neglects giving any agreement.

**FORMATIVE ASSESSMENT**

### Conventions and Style

**If** students struggle to identify antiquated language in paragraphs 28 and 29, **then** read aloud an excerpt such as the following and provide replacements for words rarely used today: "circumstances of cruelty & perfidy scarcely paralleled in the most barbarous ages, and totally unworthy the head of a civilized nation." For Reteach and Practice, see **Conventions and Style: Changes in Syntax and Usage (RP).**

## Writing to Sources

Help students clarify Jefferson's central claim: declaring independence is the only thing that the colonists can do—given their circumstances. Point out to students that Jefferson is appealing for independence on ethical and logical grounds. Ask students to give examples of evidence Jefferson offers to support this claim, such as his list of accusations against King George III.

Then ask students to sum up Jefferson's reasons why the colonists have decided to declare independence. For more support, see **Writing to Sources: Editorial.**

### Reflect on Your Writing

1. If students need support, point out that, like the Declaration of Independence, their editorial includes a claim, evidence, and reasons. It should also include appeals to ethics, logic, authority, and/or emotion.
2. Responses will vary. Students should be able to give reasons to justify their choice.
3. Responses will vary. Have students list specific examples of words and phrases they have chosen to clearly express their ideas and make their editorial memorable to readers.

### FORMATIVE ASSESSMENT

### Writing to Sources

**If** students are having difficulty thinking of reasons why they and their classmates deserve more independence at school, **then** ask them whether they think some high school students deserve more independence than others deserve, and why. For Reteach and Practice, see **Writing to Sources: Editorial (RP).**

DECLARATION OF INDEPENDENCE

## Writing to Sources

The Declaration of Independence represents the position of one side in a conflict. There were numerous other colonial writings, including speeches, pamphlets, and essays, that centered on the same conflict. Together, these multiple writings are a record of the ongoing debate over the colonies' relationship with Britain. Today, debates over public issues often take place in the media—in newspaper articles and editorials.

**Assignment**

An editorial is a brief argumentative essay that appears in a newspaper or on a news site and expresses a position on an issue. Write an **editorial** for a local or school newspaper in which you argue your side of an issue that affects your school or community. Use modern syntax and usage, but apply some of Jefferson's persuasive techniques. For example, present a list of reasons just as Jefferson does in the Declaration of Independence.

Your editorial should include:

- a clear statement of your claim, or position
- a list of reasons that support and clarify your claim
- appeals to emotion, logic, and—if warranted—authority
- a concluding statement that follows from the argument

**Vocabulary and Conventions Connection** Consider including several of the concept vocabulary words. Also, remember to use appropriate word choices, grammar, syntax, and a style that makes your ideas clear.

| unalienable | tyranny | acquiesce |
|---|---|---|
| constrains | assent | rectitude |

### Reflect on Your Writing

After you have drafted your editorial, answer the following questions.

1. How did writing your editorial help you understand Jefferson's writing process?
2. Which of the reasons that you listed do you think offers the strongest evidence in support of your argument?
3. **Why These Words?** The words you choose can greatly increase the effect of your writing. Which words helped you create a clear and memorable argument?

**STANDARDS**

**Writing**

Write arguments to support claims in an analysis of substantive topics or texts, using valid reasoning and relevant and sufficient evidence.

**Speaking and Listening**

Propel conversations by posing and responding to questions that probe reasoning and evidence; ensure a hearing for a full range of positions on a topic or issue; clarify, verify, or challenge ideas and conclusions; and promote divergent and creative perspectives.





### PERSONALIZE FOR LEARNING

**Strategic Support**

For students to correctly complete the writing assignment, they need to follow the guidelines in the Assignment box. If necessary, before they write, go over with them the bulleted list of elements that their editorial needs to include.

Make sure they understand the following terms:

- claim, or position
- evidence for claim's validity
- reasons to support and clarify
- appeals to emotion, logic, and authority

## Speaking and Listening

**Assignment**

You may have listened to the 1957 recording of Senator John F. Kennedy reading the Declaration of Independence. Listen to that recording again and think about his presentation. Then, participate in a **class discussion** about these questions:

- Would you find it meaningful to hear a modern politician of your choice reading this historical document today? Why or why not?
- Would it be just as meaningful to hear the document read by a classmate or a neighbor? Explain.

1. **Think About the Question** Before the discussion, consider the meaning of the Declaration of Independence.
   - Does Kennedy's reading enhance your understanding of the document?
   - Which aspects of the Declaration would a modern politician most likely consider important?
2. **Prepare Your Contribution** Make some notes for the discussion.
   - Which modern politician would you choose as a reader? Why?
   - In what ways would a reading from a classmate or a neighbor be more or less meaningful?
3. **Discuss the Questions** Keep these principles in mind.
   - Speak clearly so that your listeners can follow what you are saying.
   - Respond respectfully to the opinions of others.
   - Be prepared to answer questions that your teacher or classmates ask about your positions.
4. **Listen and Evaluate** As your classmates speak, listen attentively. Decide whether you agree or disagree with their ideas, and why. Contribute your responses with care, and support them with specific examples. In addition, take brief notes that will help as you complete a presentation evaluation guide.



**PRESENTATION EVALUATION GUIDE**

**Rate each statement on a scale of 1 (not demonstrated) to 5 (demonstrated).**

☐ Classmates made meaningful contributions to the discussion.

☐ All of the details in the assignment were discussed.

☐ Each person spoke clearly and in an appropriate tone of voice.

☐ Speakers supported their positions with specific examples.

**EVIDENCE LOG**

Before moving on to a new selection, go to your Evidence Log and record what you learned from the Declaration of Independence.



**PERSONALIZE FOR LEARNING**

### English Language Support

**Choral Reading** Encourage students to form small groups and choose one long paragraph or a few shorter ones from the Declaration of Independence to read chorally after listening two or more times to Kennedy's 1957 reading of that portion of the document. Ask students to model their reading on Kennedy's pronunciation, diction, and tone. After they rehearse their readings, give groups an opportunity to perform for the class. **EMERGING/ EXPANDING**

DIGITAL PERSPECTIVES

## Speaking and Listening

**1. Think About the Question**

- Responses will vary. Hearing a (relatively) modern reading of the document by an accomplished speaker may help some students to better understand the dense, archaic language in the document.
- Responses will vary. Some modern politicians (depending on their views) might consider all mentions of freedom important. Politicians who are keenly interested in Revolutionary War history might consider aspects of the document that refer to specific historical events (such as the Stamp Act and the Intolerable Acts) important.

**2. Prepare Your Contribution**

- Responses will vary. Students will probably choose politicians whom they and/or their families and friends admire. Encourage them to give reasons for their choices.
- Responses will vary. Some students may assume that since politicians are used to public speaking, they might be able to give more meaningful readings of the Declaration. Other students may find more meaning in a reading by someone they know.

**3. Discuss the Questions** If necessary, go over the guidelines for discussion with students.

**4. Listen and Evaluate** If necessary, ask students what it means to listen attentively and respond respectfully. Encourage them to take notes and use these as they complete the presentation evaluation guide. For more support, see **Speaking and Listening: Class Discussion.**

Evidence Log Support students in completing their Evidence Log. This paced activity will help prepare them for the Performance-Based Assessment at the end of the unit.

### FORMATIVE ASSESSMENT

### Speaking and Listening

**If** students have difficulty choosing a politician who might do a good job of reading the Declaration, **then** play for them a few short audio recordings of politicians from different backgrounds and political parties. For Reteach and Practice, see **Speaking and Listening: Class Discussion (RP).**

### Selection Test

Administer the Declaration of Independence Selection Test, which is available in both print and digital formats online in Assessments.

# Preamble to the Constitution • Bill of Rights

**AUDIO SUMMARIES**
Audio summaries of the Preamble to the United States Constitution and the Bill of Rights are available online in both English and Spanish in the Interactive Teacher's Edition or Unit Resources. Assigning these summaries prior to reading the selection may help students build additional background knowledge and set a context for their first read.

## Summary

The Preamble to the United States Constitution summarizes the framers' goals in establishing the Constitution, which include establishing justice and promoting peace and safety.

The Bill of Rights comprises the first ten amendments to the U.S. Constitution. These amendments guarantee individual freedoms and rights by placing specific limits on government power. Among the rights specified are freedom of religion, speech, press, and assembly.

### Insight

Most of the Founders of our country came from the elite class of educated landowners, but they realized that they were trying to build a nation of citizens who were working people. With the opening words of the Constitution—"We the People of the United States"—the Founders make it obvious that it is the *people* who are responsible for the creation of the Constitution.

ESSENTIAL QUESTION
What is the meaning of freedom?

## Connection to the Essential Question

The United States Constitution is a founding document in American history and connects to the Essential Question, "What is the meaning of freedom?" The Preamble explains the reasons for creating the Constitution, the various sections describe the set-up of the government, and the Bill of Rights lists the rights and freedoms guaranteed to all citizens.

WHOLE CLASS LEARNING PERFORMANCE TASK
Which statement do you find most compelling for Americans today: the Preamble to the Constitution or the first sentence of paragraph three of the Declaration of Independence?

UNIT PERFORMANCE-BASED ASSESSMENT
What are the most effective tools for establishing and preserving freedom?

## Connection to Performance Tasks

**Whole-Class Learning Performance Task** As students examine this document, they will consider the prompt and how lines from this important text express American freedom.

**Unit Performance-Based Assessment** The Preamble to the United States Constitution and the Bill of Rights demonstrate the importance of establishing a system of laws that explicitly describes the branches of government, their powers, and the rights and freedoms of its citizens.

DIGITAL PERSPECTIVES

 Audio  Video  Document  Annotation Highlights 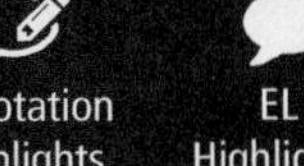 EL Highlights 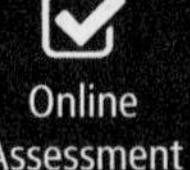 Online Assessment

## LESSON RESOURCES

| | Making Meaning | Language Development | Effective Expression |
|---|---|---|---|
| **Lesson** | **First Read**<br>**Close Read**<br>**Analyze the Text**<br>**Analyze Craft and Structure** | **Concept Vocabulary**<br>**Word Study**<br>**Conventions and Style** | **Writing to Sources**<br>**Speaking and Listening** |
| **Instructional Standards** | **RI.10** By the end of grade 11, read and comprehend literary nonfiction . . .<br>**RI.5** Analyze and evaluate the effectiveness of the structure an author uses . . .<br>**RI.9** Analyze seventeenth-, eighteenth-, and nineteenth-century foundational U.S. documents . . . | **L.1.a** Apply the understanding that usage is a matter of convention . . .<br>**L.4** Determine or clarify the meaning of unknown and multiple-meaning words and phrases . . .<br>**L.4.c** Consult general and specialized reference materials . . . | **W.2.b** Develop the topic thoroughly . . .<br>**SL.4** Present information, findings, and supporting evidence . . . |
| **STUDENT RESOURCES** | | | |
| Available online in the Interactive Student Edition or Unit Resources | Selection Audio Summaries<br>First-Read Guide: Nonfiction<br>Close-Read Guide: Nonfiction | Word Network | Evidence Log |
| **TEACHER RESOURCES** | | | |
| **Selection Resources** Available online in the Interactive Teacher's Edition or Unit Resources | Audio Summaries<br>Annotation Highlights<br>EL Highlights<br>English Language Support Lesson: Word Study: Multiple-Meaning Words<br>Analyze Craft and Structure: Structure | Concept Vocabulary and Word Study<br>Conventions and Style: Punctuation for Enumeration | Writing to Sources: Extended Definition<br>Speaking and Listening: Speech |
| **Reteach/Practice (RP)** Available online in the Interactive Teacher's Edition or Unit Resources | Analyze Craft and Structure: Structure (RP) | Word Study: Multiple-Meaning Words (RP)<br>Conventions and Style: Punctuation for Enumeration (RP) | Writing to Sources: Extended Definition (RP)<br>Speaking and Listening: Speech (RP) |
| **Assessment** Available online in Assessments | Selection Test | | |
| **My Resources** | A Unit 1 Answer Key is available online and in the Interactive Teacher's Edition. | | |

# Reading Support

| Text Complexity Rubric: Preamble to the Constitution • Bill of Rights | |
|---|---|
| **Quantitative Measures** | |
| **Lexile** 1930; 1580 **Text Length** 52 words; 693 words | |
| **Qualitative Measures** | |
| Knowledge Demands ①—②—❸—④—⑤ | Historical knowledge demands; students should be familiar with historical events leading up to the creation of the Bill of Rights in order to grasp the ideas. |
| Structure ①—❷—③—④—⑤ | The selection is clearly organized with introductory paragraphs (Preamble) followed by numbered list of amendments. |
| Language Conventionality and Clarity ①—②—③—❹—⑤ | The selection contains many lengthy, dense sentences written with highly formal language and some nonstandard capitalization and spelling. |
| Levels of Meaning/Purpose ①—②—❸—④—⑤ | The meaning/purpose is straightforward, but the concepts may be hard for some to grasp because of sophisticated language and supporting concepts that are complex. |

DECIDE AND PLAN

## English Language Support

Provide English Learners with support for knowledge demands and language as they read the selection. **PI.8; PI.12**

**Knowledge Demands** Before reading the text, make sure students have sufficient background information about what led to the creation of the Bill of Rights. Point out that most of the amendments are aimed at limiting what the government can do. Making notes of what they know so far will help them as they read the text.

**Language** Help students reword long and complex sentences. Using the language from the selection, suggest simpler sentences that convey the same meaning. For example, for Amendment III: *Congress may not force people to keep soldiers in their homes.* Ask students to read the new sentences and discuss.

## Strategic Support

Provide students with strategic support to ensure that they can successfully read the text.

**Language / Clarity** If students have difficulty with the complex sentences and language in the selection, encourage them to break the sentences down into smaller chunks and identify the meaning of unfamiliar words or phrases. It may help to work in pairs and go through the selection line by line.

**Levels of Meaning / Purpose** As students read, ask them to stop and summarize the main ideas and rights granted by each amendment. If students have trouble finding the main ideas, ask them to read more than once and ask questions to direct them to the main ideas.

## Challenge

Provide students who need to be challenged with ideas for how they can go beyond a simple interpretation of the text.

**Text Analysis** Have students discuss the Preamble to the United States Constitution. Have students explain what each of these parts means: *establish justice, insure domestic tranquility, provide for the common defense, promote the general welfare, and secure the blessings of liberty to ourselves and our posterity.*

**Written Response** Have students choose the amendment from the Bill of Rights that they believe is most important. Ask them to write an essay explaining their choice.

TEACH

## Read and Respond

Have students do their first read of the selection. Then, have them complete their close read. Finally, work with them on the Making Meaning, Language Development, and Effective Expression activities.

# Standards Support Through Teaching and Learning Cycle

## IDENTIFY NEEDS

Analyze results of the Beginning-of-Year Assessment, focusing on the items relating to Unit 1. Also take into consideration student performance to this point and your observations of where particular students struggle.

## DECIDE AND PLAN

- If students have performed poorly on items matching these standards, then provide selection scaffolds before assigning them the on-level lesson provided in the Student Edition.
- If students have done well on the Beginning-of-Year Assessment, then challenge them to keep progressing and learning by giving them opportunities to practice the skills in depth.
- Use the Selection Resources listed on the Planning pages for Preamble to the Constitution | Bill of Rights to help students continually improve their ability to master the standards.

**Instructional Standards: Preamble to the Constitution | Bill of Rights**

| | Catching Up | This Year | Looking Forward |
|---|---|---|---|
| **Reading** | You may wish to administer the **Analyze Craft and Structure: Structure (RP)** worksheet to teach students how text features make documents easier to read and understand. | **RI.5** Analyze and evaluate the effectiveness of the structure an author uses in his or her exposition or argument, including whether the structure makes points clear, convincing, and engaging. | Have students look at an explanatory essay with text features and analyze how they affect the text. |
| **Writing** | You may wish to administer the **Writing to Sources: Extended Definition (RP)** worksheet to help students understand how good writers comprehensively explore their topic by supplying readers with relevant facts and details, definitions, and quotations. | **W.2.b** Develop the topic thoroughly by selecting the most significant and relevant facts, extended definitions, concrete details, quotations, or other information and examples appropriate to the audience's knowledge of the topic. | Have students read the selection and then analyze and evaluate how the authors used facts, definitions, details and quotations to present their point of view. |
| **Speaking and Listening** | You may wish to administer the **Speaking and Listening: Speech (RP)** worksheet to help students understand how good speakers present their research in a clear and coherent manner with their audience in mind. | **SL.4** Present information, findings, and supporting evidence, conveying a clear and distinct perspective, such that listeners can follow the line of reasoning, alternative or opposing perspectives are addressed, and the organization, development, substance, and style are appropriate to purpose, audience, and a range of formal and informal tasks. Use appropriate eye contact, adequate volume, and clear pronunciation. | Challenge students to plan a mock debate. Pairs of students should choose a topic and each student should be prepared to discuss and defend his or her point of view in a clear and logical way. |
| **Language** | You may wish to administer the **Conventions and Style: Punctuation for Enumeration (RP)** worksheet to help students understand how clauses are used. | **L.1.a** Apply the understanding that usage is a matter of convention, can change over time, and is sometimes contested. | Challenge students to use increasingly varied sentence structures in their writing. |

## ANALYZE AND REVISE

- Analyze student work for evidence of student learning.
- Identify whether or not students have met the expectations in the standards.
- Identify implications for future instruction.

## TEACH

Implement the planned lesson, and gather evidence of student learning.

TEACHING

## Jump Start

FIRST READ Prior to students' first read, ask them what they know about the political controversy in this country between people who believe in a strong federal government and those who would rather the federal government not have too much control.

Point out to students that the people who wrote the documents they are about to read had to think about this very same controversy more than two hundred years ago.

## Preamble to the Constitution | Bill of Rights

What is the purpose of the Preamble to the Constitution? What does the Preamble to the Bill of Rights explain about these first ten amendments? Modeling these questions will bring the selections to life and connect them to the Performance Task question. Selection audio and print capability for the selection are available in the Interactive Teacher's Edition.

## Concept Vocabulary

Circulate among students as they rank their words. Remind them that they will find the definitions in the side column beside each word.

### FIRST READ

As they read, students should perform the steps of the first read.

NOTICE: Encourage students to notice how the Preamble to the Constitution and the Bill of Rights include many important rules for the U.S. government to follow.

ANNOTATE: Remind students to mark unfamiliar words, parts of the text that confuse them, and parts that contain topics they know about.

CONNECT: Encourage students to go beyond the selection to make connections between the text and information they know about civil rights, law enforcement, and court cases in the United States.

RESPOND: Students will demonstrate their understanding of the text by answering questions and writing a summary. You may wish to print copies of the **First-Read Guide: Nonfiction** for students to use.

**Remind students that during their first read, they should not answer the close-read questions that appear in the selection.**

MAKING MEANING

About the Authors

**Gouverneur Morris** (1752–1816), a distinguished scholar, represented Pennsylvania at the Constitutional Convention. He made some 173 speeches during the proceedings of the Convention, many of them in opposition to slavery. His work on the Preamble to the Constitution earned him the title "Penman of the Constitution."

**James Madison** (1751–1836) grew up in Virginia and later served in the state's legislature. The youngest member of the Continental Congress, he was skilled at working with delegates who held opposing views. He is often called "Father of the Constitution" for his role in drafting that document and the Bill of Rights, which followed it. Madison later served as the United States's fourth president.

**Tool Kit**
First-Read Guide and Model Annotation

STANDARDS
**Reading Informational Text**
By the end of grade 11, read and comprehend literary nonfiction in the grades 11–CCR text complexity band proficiently, with scaffolding as needed at the high end of the range.

# Preamble to the Constitution
# Bill of Rights

## Concept Vocabulary

You will encounter the following words as you read the Preamble to the Constitution and the Bill of Rights. Before reading, note how familiar you are with each word. Then, rank the words in order from most familiar (1) to least familiar (6).

| WORD | YOUR RANKING |
|---|---|
| exercise | |
| abridging | |
| petition | |
| redress | |
| infringed | |
| prescribed | |

After completing the first read, come back to the concept vocabulary and review your ratings. Mark changes to your original rankings as needed.

## First Read NONFICTION

Apply these strategies as you conduct your first read. You will have an opportunity to complete the close-read notes after your first read.

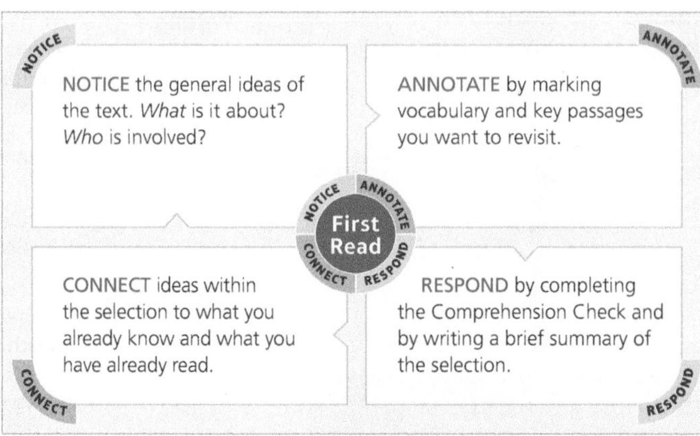

NOTICE
NOTICE the general ideas of the text. *What* is it about? *Who* is involved?
ANNOTATE
ANNOTATE by marking vocabulary and key passages you want to revisit.
First Read
CONNECT ideas within the selection to what you already know and what you have already read.
RESPOND by completing the Comprehension Check and by writing a brief summary of the selection.
CONNECT
RESPOND






PERSONALIZE FOR LEARNING

**English Language Support**
**Unfamiliar Words and Expressions** The Constitution (including the Bill of Rights) is densely written in formal, sometimes antiquated, language. The text contains many words and phrases with which students may be unfamiliar. Depending upon your students' needs, you may wish to closely read the text with them in small groups. Model rephrasing parts of the text in simpler, clearer language. For example, the phrase "Congress shall make no law respecting an establishment of religion, or prohibiting the free exercise thereof" might be rephrased as: "Congress may not make any laws that establish a national religion or take away people's right to freedom of religion." **EXPANDING/BRIDGING**

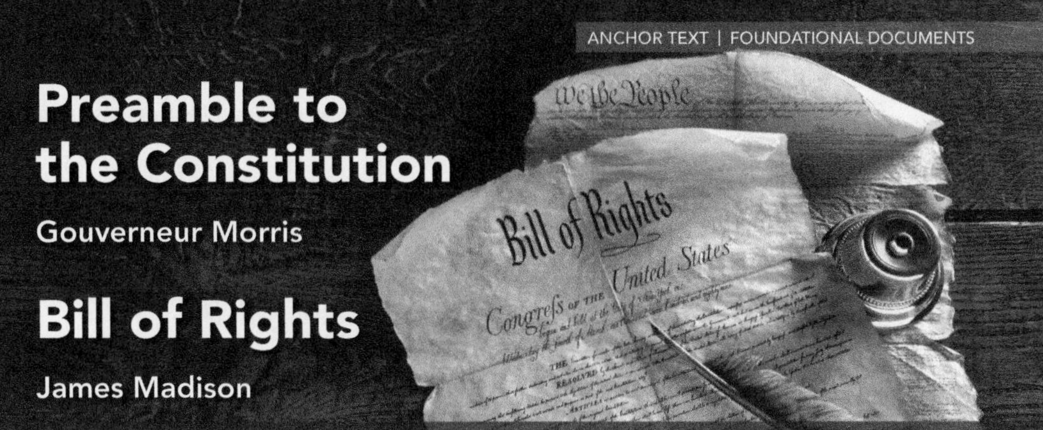

# Preamble to the Constitution

Gouverneur Morris

# Bill of Rights

James Madison

BACKGROUND

After the Framers approved the Constitution, several of them called for the addition of more protections for individual liberties. James Madison wrote up a list of amendments. Congress passed them, and the states ratified ten of them. These ten amendments are now known as the Bill of Rights.

SCAN FOR MULTIMEDIA 

### Preamble to the United States Constitution

1 We the people of the United States, in order to form a more perfect union, establish justice, insure domestic tranquility, provide for the common defense, promote the general welfare, and secure the blessings of liberty to ourselves and our posterity, do ordain and establish this Constitution for the United States of America.

* * *

### Bill of Rights

**Preamble**

2 Congress of the United States begun and held at the City of New York, on Wednesday the fourth of March, one thousand seven hundred and eighty-nine.

3 THE Conventions of a number of the States, having at the time of their adopting the Constitution, expressed a desire, in order to prevent misconstruction or abuse of its powers, that further declaratory and restrictive clauses should be added: And as extending the ground of public confidence in the Government, will best ensure the beneficent ends of its institution.

4 RESOLVED by the Senate and House of Representatives of the United States of America, in Congress assembled, two thirds of both Houses concurring, that the following Articles be proposed to the Legislatures of the several States, as amendments to the Constitution of the United States, all, or any of which Articles, when ratified by three fourths of the said Legislatures, to be valid to all intents and purposes, as part of the said Constitution; viz.[1]

1. **viz** *abbr.* that is; namely.

NOTES

CLOSE READ

ANNOTATE: Mark the nouns in paragraph 1, which is the Preamble to the Constitution.

QUESTION: Why does the author list this particular series of nouns?

CONCLUDE: What do these nouns establish as the purpose of this document?

**CLOSE READ**

As they close read paragraph 1, remind students to focus on nouns that are meant to show the purpose of the Constitution. Possible responses to questions on the student page are included. You may also want to print copies of the **Close-Read Guide: Nonfiction** for students to use.

**ANNOTATE:** As I read the Preamble to the United States Constitution, I annotate every noun I can find. Some of these are *union, justice,* and *tranquility*.

**QUESTION:** Most of these nouns have to do with goals—positive outcomes the author hopes the Constitution will achieve if it becomes law.

**CONCLUDE:** The purpose of the Constitution was to achieve a strong union of states with stated rights and protections for its citizens.

Additional **English Language Support** is available in the Interactive Teacher's Edition.

**PERSONALIZE FOR LEARNING**

**English Language Support**

**Choral Reading** Review the Preamble. Encourage students to stand up and chorally read the Preamble to the Constitution after discussing what the authors want this paragraph to express: "We the people of the United States, in order to form a more perfect union, establish justice, insure domestic tranquility, provide for the common defense, promote the general welfare, and secure the blessings of liberty to ourselves and our posterity, do ordain and establish this Constitution for the United States of America."

**EMERGING/EXPANDING**

# TEACHING

## CLOSE READ 

Remind students to look for adjectives in Amendment VI and figure out the significance of those adjectives. You may wish to model the Close Read using the following think-aloud format. Possible responses to questions on the student page are included.

**ANNOTATE:** I know that adjectives describe or give information about nouns. In looking through paragraph 11, I see right away that the noun *prosecutions* is described by the adjective *criminal*. Both *speedy* and *public* describe *trial*, so I'll mark them, too. I also see the adjective *impartial*. It takes a while before I come to the next adjective, *compulsory*. It describes the process. What process? The process "for obtaining witnesses." That phrase gives information about the noun *process*, but it's a phrase, not a word, so I'm not going to mark it.

**QUESTION:** There are only five adjectives in this paragraph, but each one is very important because it helps define the rights of those accused of crimes. Every trial is supposed to be speedy and public. Every jury is supposed to be impartial, and so on.

**CONCLUDE:** The language might help people accused of crimes understand that they have protected rights. This amendment helps establish a judicial system that considers individuals fairly.

NOTES

**exercise** (EHK suhr syz) *n.* implementation; state of putting something into action

**abridging** (uh BRIHJ ihng) *adj.* limiting

**petition** (puh TIHSH uhn) *v.* formally request; seek help from

**redress** (rih DREHS) *n.* correction; setting right of some wrong

**infringed** (ihn FRIHNJD) *v.* violated

**prescribed** (prih SKRYBD) *v.* stated in writing; set down as a rule

5 ARTICLES in addition to, and Amendment of the Constitution of the United States of America, proposed by Congress, and ratified by the Legislatures of the several States, pursuant to the fifth Article of the original Constitution.

**Amendment I**

6 Congress shall make no law respecting an establishment of religion, or prohibiting the free **exercise** thereof; or **abridging** the freedom of speech, or of the press; or the right of the people peaceably to assemble, and to **petition** the Government for a **redress** of grievances.

**Amendment II**

7 A well regulated militia, being necessary to the security of a free State, the right of the people to keep and bear arms, shall not be **infringed**.

**Amendment III**

8 No soldier shall, in time of peace be quartered in any house, without the consent of the owner, nor in time of war, but in a manner to be **prescribed** by law.

**Amendment IV**

9 The right of the people to be secure in their persons, houses, papers, and effects, against unreasonable searches and seizures, shall not be violated, and no warrants shall issue, but upon probable cause, supported by oath or affirmation, and particularly describing the place to be searched, and the persons or things to be seized.

**Amendment V**

10 No person shall be held to answer for a capital,[2] or otherwise infamous crime, unless on a presentment or indictment of a Grand Jury, except in cases arising in the land or naval forces, or in the militia, when in actual service in time of war or public danger; nor shall any person be subject for the same offence to be twice put in jeopardy of life or limb; nor shall be compelled in any criminal case to be a witness against himself, nor be deprived of life, liberty, or property, without due process of law; nor shall private property be taken for public use, without just compensation.

CLOSE READ

**ANNOTATE:** Mark the adjectives that appear in Amendment VI.

**QUESTION:** Why are the few adjectives used in this section important?

**CONCLUDE:** What effect might this language have on someone accused of a crime?

**Amendment VI**

11 In all criminal prosecutions, the accused shall enjoy the right to a speedy and public trial, by an impartial jury of the State and district wherein the crime shall have been committed, which district shall have been previously ascertained by law, and to be informed of the nature and cause of the accusation; to be confronted with the witnesses against him; to have compulsory process for obtaining witnesses in his favor, and to have the Assistance of Counsel[3] for his defense.

2. **capital** *adj.* punishable by execution.
3. **Counsel** *n.* lawyer or group of lawyers giving advice about legal matters and representing clients in court.





### CROSS-CURRICULAR PERSPECTIVES

**Social Studies** Point out that in paragraph 11, Amendment VI states that defendants are supposed to be judged by "an impartial jury of the State and district wherein the crime shall have been committed." Ask whether this is always the case today. If necessary, inform students that sometimes a defendant's lawyer asks for what is called a "change of venue" (a change of location for the trial). Have students research when changes of venue are warranted. **Possible response:** Press leaks surrounding a case may make it likely that jury members in the area will become biased, hostile, or prejudiced against the defendant. Other factors might include travel costs and locations of witnesses and evidence.

**Amendment VII**

12 In suits[4] at common law, where the value in controversy shall exceed twenty dollars, the right of trial by jury shall be preserved, and no fact tried by a jury, shall be otherwise re-examined in any Court of the United States, than according to the rules of the common law.

**Amendment VIII**

13 Excessive bail[5] shall not be required, nor excessive fines imposed, nor cruel and unusual punishments inflicted.

**Amendment IX**

14 The enumeration in the Constitution, of certain rights, shall not be construed to deny or disparage others retained by the people.

**Amendment X**

15 The powers not delegated to the United States by the Constitution, nor prohibited by it to the States, are reserved to the States respectively, or to the people. ❧

NOTES

4. **suits** *n.* lawsuits, or legal actions brought by one party against another.
5. **bail** *n.* property or money given to the court to ensure that an arrested person released from custody will return at a certain time.

## Comprehension Check

**Complete the following items after you finish your first read.**

1. According to its Preamble, who is responsible for establishing the Constitution?

2. What laws are forbidden in Amendment I of the Bill of Rights?

3. Which amendments cover legal proceedings?

4. **Notebook** Write a summary of the Preamble to the Constitution and a summary of the Bill of Rights to confirm your understanding of the texts.

### RESEARCH

**Research to Clarify** Choose at least one unfamiliar detail from these texts. Briefly research that detail. In what way does the information you learned shed light on an aspect of these documents?





DIGITAL PERSPECTIVES 

## Comprehension Check

**Possible responses:**

1. "We the people" are responsible for establishing it.
2. The following are forbidden: laws that establish a national religion or that deny Americans the freedom to worship as they choose; laws that limit freedom of speech, freedom of the press, freedom to assemble peaceably, or freedom to seek the government's help in correcting a wrong that seems illegal or unjust.
3. Amendments V–VIII cover legal proceedings.
4. Answers will vary. Sample response: The Preamble to the Constitution presents the purpose of the Constitution. The Bill of Rights guarantees the federal government's protection of a variety of rights and freedoms, including freedom of religion, speech, the press, and assembly; the right to petition and the right to a fair trial. The Bill of Rights also declares that any powers not assigned to the federal government, nor prohibited to the states, are under the states' control.

## Research

**Research to Clarify** If students struggle to come up with an unfamiliar detail to research, suggest that they focus on one of the following: 1) what it means in Amendment I to "petition the government for a redress of grievances"; 2) what the following phrase means in Amendment II: "A well regulated militia, being necessary to the security of a free State"; or 3) what the term "probable cause" means in Amendment IV.

## PERSONALIZE FOR LEARNING

### Challenge

Point out that most of the first ten Amendments to the Constitution are about individual people's rights and freedoms. Ask students to find out how the subjects of the 17 Amendments that follow relate to those of the first ten. Challenge students to create a detailed graphic organizer that shows what they learn from their research. An example of a partially completed chart is shown on this page.

| Amendment Number | Text of the Amendment | Main Topic |
| --- | --- | --- |
| 11 | "The Judicial power of the United States shall not be construed to extend to any suit in law or equity, commenced or prosecuted against one of the United States by Citizens of another State, or by Citizens or Subjects of any Foreign State." | a limit on the powers of U.S. courts |

# TEACHING

## Jump Start

**CLOSE READ** Ask students to think of all the things they are free to do now that they weren't allowed to do when they were younger.

Ask them which one of these freedoms they could easily give up. Which one would they really not want to give up? Have students share their responses to see if they agreed on either of their choices.

## Close Read the Text

Work with students on the annotation model, and then have them complete items 2 and 3 on their own. When they have finished, review and discuss the sections students marked. If needed, continue to model close reading by using the Annotation Highlights in the Interactive Teacher's Edition.

## Analyze the Text

Possible responses:

1. The phrase "to ourselves and our posterity" (our descendants) shows that the Constitution is intended to guide the U.S. government for many generations. **DOK 2**
2. Amendment II provides for the enforcement of Americans' rights by force, if necessary. **DOK 3**
3. (a) People charged with crimes will not need to pay overly high bail or fines, nor will punishments be inhumane. **DOK 2**
   (b) Even people who break laws have rights that the government guarantees. **DOK 3**
4. Enslaved African Americans were not granted these rights and freedoms. Women's rights were not specifically mentioned in the Constitution. In reality, women had fewer rights than men had. **DOK 3**
5. Responses will vary. Possible response: Freedom (or lack of freedom) affects many different aspects of a society. **DOK 4**

### FORMATIVE ASSESSMENT

### Analyze the Text

- **If** students fail to cite evidence, **then** remind them to support their ideas with specific information from the text.
- **If** students struggle to infer that the Constitution was meant to last for generations, **then** point out and define the word *posterity* in the Preamble.



MAKING MEANING

PREAMBLE TO THE CONSTITUTION | BILL OF RIGHTS

## Close Read the Text

1. This model—Amendment III of the Bill of Rights—shows two sample annotations, along with questions and conclusions. Close read the passage, and find another detail to annotate. Then, write a question and your conclusion.

Close Read (ANNOTATE, QUESTION, CONCLUDE)

ANNOTATE: These parallel phrases speak to both peace and wartime situations.

QUESTION: What do these details say about early American attitudes toward the military?

CONCLUDE: They suggest that early Americans wanted to limit military power unless it was needed.

No soldier, shall in time of peace be quartered in any house, without the consent of the owner, nor in time of war, but in a manner to be prescribed by law.

ANNOTATE: The paragraph presents contrasting ideas—"consent of the owner" and "prescribed by law."

QUESTION: What balance of power do these terms suggest?

CONCLUDE: In peacetime, personal choice overrides government concerns; the opposite may be true during wartime.

**Tool Kit**
Close-Read Guide and Model Annotation

2. For more practice, go back into the text and complete the close-read notes.
3. Revisit a section of the text you found important during your first read. **Annotate** what you notice. Ask yourself **questions** such as "Why did the author make this choice?" What can you **conclude**?

## Analyze the Text

CITE TEXTUAL EVIDENCE to support your answers.

**Notebook** Respond to these questions.

1. **Analyze** How can you tell from the Preamble that the Constitution is meant to do more than merely resolve the country's issues at that time?
2. **Connect** How does Amendment II of the Bill of Rights reinforce Amendment I?
3. (a) **Paraphrase** When you **paraphrase**, you restate a text in your own words. Paraphrase Amendment VIII. (b) **Analyze** How does this amendment relate to the theme of freedom? Explain.
4. **Historical Perspectives** Which Americans were not granted the freedoms and rights set forth in the Constitution and the Bill of Rights?
5. **Essential Question:** ***What is the meaning of freedom?*** What have you learned about American freedoms by reading these documents?

STANDARDS

**Reading Informational Text**

- Analyze and evaluate the effectiveness of the structure an author uses in his or her exposition or argument, including whether the structure makes points clear, convincing, and engaging.
- Analyze seventeenth-, eighteenth-, and nineteenth-century foundational U.S. documents of historical and literary significance for their themes, purposes, and rhetorical features.





PERSONALIZE FOR LEARNING

### English Language Support

**Antiquated Language** Explain that some of the words and phrases used in the Constitution are rarely used by today's English speakers and writers. Work with students to develop a two-column chart providing modern definitions for antiquated language. For example, the phrase "domestic tranquility" might be translated "peace at home." **EXPANDING/BRIDGING**

## Analyze Craft and Structure

**Author's Choices: Structure** Both the Constitution and the Bill of Rights are **resolutions**, or legal foundational statements that explain a set of decisions approved by a governing body. Likewise, both begin with a **preamble**, a statement that explains who is issuing the document and for what purpose. The text that follows the Preamble to the Bill of Rights illustrates a simple structure called **enumeration**, in which the major ideas (the first ten amendments) are listed in numerical order. Each of the amendments follows a regular structure, beginning with a **heading**, or label.

### Practice

**CITE TEXTUAL EVIDENCE** to support your answers.

Answer these questions.

1. What does the preamble to the Bill of Rights tell readers about the reasons the document was created?
2. Why is "RESOLVED" used to begin the second paragraph of the Preamble?
3. Explain why enumeration is an effective organizational pattern for the Bill of Rights.
4. (a) In the chart, record the major idea of each amendment listed—specifically, what rights or related set of rights does each amendment protect? (b) How is Amendment IX different from the other amendments? Explain.

| AMENDMENT | MAJOR IDEA |
|---|---|
| II | In the U.S., people have the right to bear arms (carry weapons). |
| III | Government can't force people to provide shelter for soldiers in the people's own homes. |
| IV | Except under very specific circumstances, government officials can't arrest people or search their homes for evidence. |
| VI | People accused of crimes have certain rights, including the right to a speedy public trial and an impartial jury. |
| VII | In civil cases, complainants have the right to a jury trial; these cases cannot be tried more than once. |
| X | If the Constitution doesn't give the U.S. government a certain power, then that power goes to individual states and/or people. |





DIGITAL PERSPECTIVES 

## Analyze Craft and Structure

**Author's Choices: Structure** Review with students the following structures in nonfiction text: chronological order, problem-and-solution, cause-and-effect, main idea and supporting details, and compare-and-contrast. Point out that an author chooses a text's structure based on the text's genre and purpose. For example, authors of biographies and autobiographies often write them in chronological order. Manual writers often organize information in a series of step-by-step instructions. Since the Bill of Rights is a legal document, it makes sense to organize the amendments in numerical order. People who use the Bill of Rights as a reference are likely to associate each amendment with its number. Arranging the amendments by number makes them easy to locate. For more support, see **Analyze Craft and Structure: Structure.**

### Practice

Possible responses:

1. The Preamble states that the Bill of Rights was written to avoid any confusion about the Constitution and also to avoid any abuses of power.
2. The word *resolved* in all capital letters means that members of Congress have officially agreed upon these ten amendments to the Constitution—these matters have been resolved or settled, so it is no longer necessary to argue about them.
3. When many items are presented, enumeration helps readers to distinguish them and locate them again if necessary.
4. (a) See possible responses in chart on student page. (b) Amendment IX does not spell out a specific right. Instead, it states that individuals may have other rights not specifically stated in the Constitution.

## FORMATIVE ASSESSMENT

### Analyze Craft and Structure

- **If** students are unable to identify the purpose of the use of *resolved*, **then** ensure students have an understanding of the definition of the word by providing a list of other words with the root *-solv-* (e.g., *solve, solvent, dissolve*).
- **If** students are unable to state why enumeration is an effective organizational pattern, **then** challenge students to imagine what other organizational patterns might have been used. For example, if the amendments have been grouped according to subject matter, what types of structural elements (headings) might have been used? For Reteach and Practice, **see Analyze Craft and Structure: Structure (RP).**

## Concept Vocabulary

**Why These Words?** Point out that three of the words—*exercise, petition,* and *redress*—can function as verbs or nouns. The other three verbs—*infringed, abridging,* and *prescribed*—have closely related words that are nouns: *infringement, abridgement,* and *prescription.*

Possible responses

1. The vocabulary words suggest legal limitations and remedies. They allow writers to spell out in an official, precise manner the people's rights and to ensure that those rights are not compromised.
2. Other such words include *justice*, *warrants*, *indictment*, *prosecutions*, *jury*, and *witnesses*.

### Practice

Possible responses:

1. Sample sentences:
   - By unfairly taxing the colonies, Britain *infringed* on the colonists' rights.
   - The colonists *petitioned* the king and Parliament for relief from unfair legislation.
   - The First Amendment forbids *abridging* freedom of the press.
2. Synonyms include *use* (for *exercise*), *limiting* (for *abridging*), *appeal to* (for *petition*), *compensation* (for *redress*), *violated* (for *infringed on*), and *established* (for *prescribed*). Students' analyses of their synonym pairs will vary.

### Word Network

Possible words: *warrants, seized, deprived*

## Word Study

For more support, see **Concept Vocabulary and Word Study.**

Possible responses

1. Sample sentences:
   - By performing this *exercise* faithfully, you will strengthen your stomach muscles.
2. Responses will vary.

### FORMATIVE ASSESSMENT

#### Concept Vocabulary

**If** students fail to see connections among the words, **then** have them use four or more of the words in a strong-context paragraph.

#### Word Study

**If** students fail to distinguish among multiple meanings for *exercise,* **then** display phrases such as *aerobic exercise* or *completing a grammar exercise.* For Reteach and Practice, see **Word Study: Multiple-Meaning Words (RP).**



LANGUAGE DEVELOPMENT

PREAMBLE TO THE CONSTITUTION | BILL OF RIGHTS

## Concept Vocabulary

| exercise | petition | infringed |
|---|---|---|
| abridging | redress | prescribed |

**Why These Words?** These concept vocabulary words suggest legal limitations or remedies. For example, the Bill of Rights was written to ensure that nothing *infringed* upon citizens' rights. The document outlines basic rights but does not explain certain points in detail—for example, exactly what *redress* will be available when a wrong is committed. Both *infringed* and *redress* refer to legal matters.

1. How does the concept vocabulary allow the writers to present ideas with both formality and precision?
2. What other words in these documents connect to the concept of legal limitations or remedies?

### Practice

Notebook Complete these activities.

1. Use each concept vocabulary word in a sentence that demonstrates your understanding of the word's meaning.
2. Replace each concept word with a synonym. Use a thesaurus, if you wish. Then, consider which word best expresses your meaning. Which is the clearer, more precise word?

WORD NETWORK

Add words related to freedom from the text to your Word Network.

## Word Study

**Multiple-Meaning Words** The concept vocabulary word *exercise* has more than one meaning. As a noun, *exercise* can refer to physical exertion that maintains or improves health. It also can refer to an activity that tests or displays a particular skill. As a verb, it can refer to the action of physical training or the action of implementing one's right to do something.

1. Write four sentences using the word *exercise*. Each sentence should demonstrate one of the four meanings of the word noted above.
2. The concept words *abridging*, *petition*, and *prescribed* are also multiple-meaning words. For each word, write its meaning as it is used in the Bill of Rights. Then, write a second meaning for each word. Use a college-level dictionary to verify your work.

STANDARDS

Language

- Apply the understanding that usage is a matter of convention, can change over time, and is sometimes contested.
- Determine or clarify the meaning of unknown and multiple-meaning words and phrases based on *grades 11–12 reading and content,* choosing flexibly from a range of strategies.
- Consult general and specialized reference materials, both print and digital, to find the pronunciation of a word or determine or clarify its precise meaning, its part of speech, its etymology, or its standard usage.





### PERSONALIZE FOR LEARNING

#### English Language Support

**Understanding Multiple-Meaning Words** Provide students a list of multiple-meaning words found in the selection.

Have pairs of students choose one of the multiple-meaning words and write its possible parts of speech and meanings. Then ask students to select which meaning the word has in the selection.

**EMERGING**

Have pairs of students choose one of of the multiple-meaning words and write its parts of speech and meanings. Then ask students to write a sentence for each of the meanings of the word.

**EXPANDING**

Have students work independently to find a multiple-meaning word in the selection. Have each student write the word's possible meanings

## Conventions and Style

**Punctuation for Enumeration** Listing, or enumeration, is an important characteristic of the style used in these documents. When enumerating ideas, place a comma between each item in the series. The choice to use the **serial comma** in a list of three or more enumerated items is a matter of style. If it is used, the serial comma is placed immediately before the coordinating conjunction (usually *and, or,* or *nor*). In addition, enumerated text must demonstrate **parallel structure.** For instance, if two items in the list are prepositional phrases, then the remaining items should also be prepositional phrases.

| TYPE OF ITEM | EXAMPLE OF PARALLEL STRUCTURE |
|---|---|
| single words | *nor be deprived of life, liberty, or property* (*nouns, from Amendment V*) |
| phrases | *in order to form a more perfect union, [to] establish justice, [to] insure domestic tranquility, [to] provide for the common defense, [to] promote the general welfare, and [to] secure the blessings of liberty to ourselves and our posterity* (*infinitive phrases, from the Preamble to the Constitution*) |
| clauses | *Excessive bail shall not be required, nor [shall] excessive fines [be] imposed, nor [shall] cruel and unusual punishments [be] inflicted* (*independent clauses, from Amendment VIII*) |

### Read It

1. Add commas to each sentence about these documents. Then, identify what type of item has been enumerated in each sentence.
   a. The Preamble to the Constitution secures "the blessings of liberty" to the American people to their descendants and to every generation.
   b. These brief historic and comprehensive amendments shape many aspects of American life.
   c. Today, Americans can read the text of the Bill of Rights online they can purchase printed copies or they can see one of the original documents on display.
2. Notebook **Connect to Style** Reread the Preamble to the Constitution. Explain how enumeration helps Madison convey a great deal of information in a compact space.

### Write It

Notebook Use enumeration to revise and expand upon these sentences. Use commas to make the enumeration clear.

EXAMPLE

**Original Sentence:** Amendment VI identifies rights of defendants.

**Sentence with Enumeration:** According to Amendment VI, defendants **will have a speedy and public trial, will face witnesses,** and **will be represented by a lawyer.**

1. James Madison included several freedoms in Amendment I.
2. Today, the Bill of Rights does many things for Americans.

TIP

CLARIFICATION

Serial commas can increase the clarity of your writing. Consider this sentence without a serial comma: "The actress plays Marina, a mermaid and a comedian." Did the actress play one person, Marina, who is a mermaid and a comedian? Or did she play three separate characters? Use of the serial comma eliminates this ambiguity.





and parts of speech. Then ask each student to write a sentence for each of the meanings of the word. **BRIDGING**

An expanded **English Language Support Lesson** on Multiple-Meaning Words is available in the Interactive Teacher's Edition.

DIGITAL PERSPECTIVES

## Conventions and Style

**Punctuation for Enumeration** Point out that speech writers and authors of persuasive texts often use parallelism to emphasize and balance related ideas. Punctuation is a key element of the enumeration style. Ask students to look closely at the second row in the table, which shows the example of parallel phrases. Have students identify the active verb and the noun in each phrase: (form/union; establish/justice; insure/tranquility; provide/defense; promote/welfare; secure/blessings). Point out that some of the phrases contain an article and an adjective or adjective phrase. Explain that this does not affect the parallelism of the phrases.

For more support, see **Conventions and Style: Punctuation for Enumeration.**

### Read It

Possible responses:

1. **a.** A comma should appear after *people* and after *descendants.* Prepositional phrases beginning with the word *to* are enumerated.
   **b.** A comma should appear after *brief* and *historic.* Adjectives are enumerated.
   **c.** A comma should appear after *online* and after *copies.* Independent clauses are enumerated.
2. **Connect to Style** Students should identify the enumerated phrases in Amendment I that begin with the gerunds *respecting, prohibiting,* and *abridging.*
   The Preamble lists many complex purposes; serial commas help readers identify each one separately.

### Write It

Possible responses:

1. James Madison included the freedoms of religion, speech, the press, peaceful assembly, and petition in Amendment I.
2. Today, the Bill of Rights outlines rights, protects liberties, and provides a foundation for citizen action.

**FORMATIVE ASSESSMENT**

### Conventions and Style

- **If** students have difficulty identifying parallel structure, **then** display a sentence such as the following: *In the morning I eat breakfast, brush my teeth, and say goodbye to my parents before I leave for the bus stop.* Circle the serial commas in the sentence.

For Reteach and Practice, see **Conventions and Style: Punctuation for Enumeration (RP).**

## Writing to Sources

Point out to students that writing an extended definition requires that they elaborate upon the amendment. Depending upon the strategies students choose to use, they may add a considerable amount of information. Remind them not to lose sight of the key concept of the amendment. The point of an extended definition is to clarify the key concept, not to make it obscure to their audience. For more support, see **Writing to Sources: Extended Definition.**

### Reflect on Your Writing

Responses will vary. Tips follow:

1. If students need support, give examples of the techniques listed in the Assignment box. An example of an extended definition of Amendment II might be: During the Revolutionary War, the United States needed militias (armies made up of local people who owned their own weapons) to fight their oppressors, the British. This might be why the Constitution authors thought it was important for individual citizens to be able to "bear arms."
2. Responses will vary. If students struggle, have them give an example of how their writing might be unclear if they had not used one of the techniques.
3. Have students list examples of phrases they have chosen to express their extended definitions.

### FORMATIVE ASSESSMENT

### Writing to Sources

**If** students have difficulty using the techniques listed in the Assignment box, **then** give examples of ways to use each technique in an extended definition of one of the ten amendments. Alternatively, you may wish to match each technique to one of the amendments and give an example of a way to use each technique to clarify that particular amendment. For Reteach and Practice, see **Writing to Sources: Extended Definition (RP).**





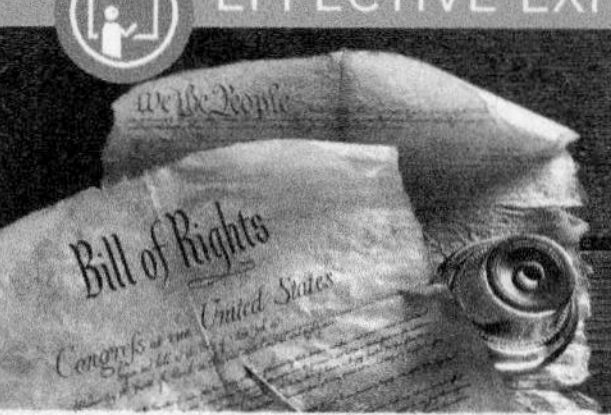


PREAMBLE TO THE CONSTITUTION | BILL OF RIGHTS

## Writing to Sources

The Preamble to the Constitution and the Bill of Rights are examples of informative writing. Like other kinds of informative writing, they were written primarily to convey facts. The facts are organized and presented in a way that best suits the writer's purpose and the audience's needs.

**Assignment**

An extended definition is an informative text—usually one or two paragraphs—that explains a key concept. Choose and reread one amendment from the Bill of Rights. Then, write an **extended definition** of a key word or concept presented in that amendment. Your extended definition should explain both the dictionary meaning of the word or concept and any shades of meaning reflected in the amendment. Use at least two of these techniques to clarify your information and engage readers.

- Compare and contrast the word or concept with more familiar words or concepts.
- Discuss what the word or concept does *not* mean.
- Identify meanings that people often assign to the word or concept.
- Provide examples of ways in which the word or concept is used today.
- Share a personal experience that helped you understand the word or concept.

**Vocabulary and Conventions Connection** Consider including several of the concept vocabulary words. Also, remember to use commas correctly if you include enumeration.

| exercise | petition | infringed |
|---|---|---|
| abridging | redress | prescribed |

**STANDARDS**

**Writing**
Develop the topic thoroughly by selecting the most significant and relevant facts, extended definitions, concrete details, quotations, or other information and examples appropriate to the audience's knowledge of the topic.

**Speaking and Listening**
Present information, findings, and supporting evidence, conveying a clear and distinct perspective such that listeners can follow the line of reasoning, alternative or opposing perspectives are addressed, and the organization, development, substance, and style are appropriate to purpose, audience, and a range of formal and informal tasks.

### Reflect on Your Writing

After you have drafted your extended definition, answer these questions.

1. Which techniques did you use to develop your extended definition?
2. In what ways did those techniques strengthen your writing?
3. **Why These Words?** The words you choose make a difference in your writing. Which words made your text more powerful or precise?





### DIGITAL PERSPECTIVES

**Illuminating the Standard** For students to correctly complete the writing assignment, they need to understand what "extended definition" means. Point out that they will need to understand and explain every word of the Amendment they are defining. To do so, they should pick and use at least two of the techniques described in the Assignment box. First and foremost, students should make sure that they themselves understand exactly what the Amendment is saying *before* they try to explain it to others in an extended definition.

## Speaking and Listening

**Assignment**
Write and deliver a **speech** about the Bill of Rights, in which you explain how the document as a whole, or a particular amendment, applies to your life. If you wish, work as a class to share these speeches as part of a lecture series called "It's My Right!"

1. **Write the Speech** Think about the Bill of Rights. How does it relate to your life? Which amendments are especially significant to you? Why?
   - Have you had any experiences involving freedom of religion, freedom of speech, or freedom of the press? If so, think about the protections offered by Amendment I.
   - How do you expect the Bill of Rights to affect your life in the future?
   - Draft your speech, using facts and examples to illustrate your personal response to the document.
2. **Deliver the Speech** To prepare to deliver your speech, review your text and practice presenting it. Mark the words you will emphasize, points at which to pause or stop for effect, and so on.
   - As you deliver the speech, make eye contact with your audience. Don't stare; rather, look at audience members for a few seconds to make sure they understand your message.
   - Use appropriate volume so everyone can hear you, even in the back rows. Carry yourself proudly, and hold your head up so that your voice carries.
   - Avoid rushing. Remember that your audience has not heard your speech before. Give them time to absorb your words and meaning.
3. **Evaluate Your Presentation** After your speech, use the evaluation guide to assess how well you presented your ideas. Did you fulfill the assignment by showing how the Bill of Rights applies to your life? Were your ideas logical, clear, and appropriate to your audience and subject? Use your self-evaluation to establish several goals for your next oral presentation.

PRESENTATION EVALUATION GUIDE

**Rate each statement on a scale of 1 (not demonstrated) to 5 (demonstrated).**

☐ I conveyed a personal understanding of the Bill of Rights.

☐ I held the audience's attention.

☐ I used appropriate eye contact to convey meaning and sufficient volume to be heard.

☐ I did not rush and pronounced words correctly and clearly.

EVIDENCE LOG

Before moving on to a new selection, go to your Evidence Log and record what you learned from the Preamble to the Constitution and from the Bill of Rights.





PERSONALIZE FOR LEARNING

**English Language Support**

**Writing and Delivering a Speech** Depending on your students' needs, go over their written speeches with them to be sure they have used correct grammar and natural-sounding language, and that they have a clear understanding of what they have to say. Provide extra rehearsal time and feedback before students deliver their speeches to classmates. **EMERGING/ EXPANDING**

DIGITAL PERSPECTIVES

## Speaking and Listening

1. **Write the Speech** Responses will vary. If students have difficulty thinking of ways that the Bill of Rights is relevant to their lives, ask questions such as the following: Have you ever written something (such as a speech, a blog post, or a news article) that was censored by your school or by a website? Has anyone you know experienced discrimination of any kind? Have you ever been to court, or has anyone you know? Do you think people are usually treated fairly in court? Do you know any lawyers who defend people accused of crimes? What have these lawyers told you about their experiences?
2. **Deliver the Speech** If necessary, go over with students the guidelines for giving a speech.
3. **Evaluate Your Presentation** If necessary, ask students what "appropriate eye contact" and "appropriate volume" mean. Before they complete the presentation evaluation guide, remind them that they will be evaluating their own performance, not someone else's. As they complete the guide, they should rephrase each item in their mind. For example, the first item should be rephrased as "I clearly conveyed a personal understanding of the Bill of Rights." For more support, see **Speaking and Listening: Speech.**

Evidence Log Support students in completing their Evidence Log. This paced activity will help prepare them for the Performance-Based Assessment at the end of the unit.

### FORMATIVE ASSESSMENT

**Speaking and Listening**

**If** students have difficulty speaking in front of a group, **then** remind them that the audience members, their classmates, are on their side. Their classmates want them to write an interesting speech and do a good job of delivering it. For Reteach and Practice, see **Speaking and Listening: Speech (RP).**

**Selection Test**

Administer the "Preamble to the Constitution and The Bill of Rights" Selection Test, which is available in both print and digital formats online in **Assessments.** 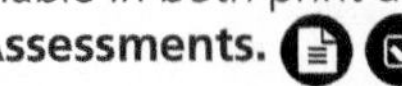

# Speech in the Convention

**AUDIO SUMMARIES**
Audio summaries of "Speech in the Convention" are available online in both English and Spanish in the Interactive Teacher's Edition or Unit Resources. Assigning these summaries prior to reading the selection may help students build additional background knowledge and set a context for their first read.


## Summary

On September 17, 1787, the last day of the Constitutional Convention, Benjamin Franklin delivered his famous speech. Franklin urged all the delegates to sign the document, although he did not approve of everything the document contained. Franklin argued that whenever a group of men assembled to create something as complicated as the proposed document, no one could expect "a perfect solution." Franklin said he believed that the Constitution, as drafted, "even with its faults," was better than anything likely to emerge from future debate. Franklin also advised delegates to avoid discussing their objections with their constituents, because doing so might prevent the public from accepting it. Franklin ended the speech by urging all delegates to sign the document and turn their attention to carrying out its ideals.


### Insight

Benjamin Franklin's views on important subjects of the day were respected. At the time of the convention, Franklin was still in discussion with various groups of young scholars. Reading this speech can help students to understand how Franklin sought out many voices to produce a constitution that represented all citizens. The fact that he urged the convention delegates to vote for a unanimous acceptance of the Constitution indicates how concerned he was that the objections of a few might sabotage the work of many at this convention.

ESSENTIAL QUESTION:
**What is the meaning of freedom?**

## Connection to the Essential Question

Benjamin Franklin's speech in the Convention provides a political perspective on the Essential Question, "What is the meaning of freedom?" The speech makes it clear that in a representative republic the beliefs or points of view of one group of people cannot be wholly satisfied. Democracies, no matter their exact structure, must reflect the views of most of the people, thus implying that compromise is essential.

WHOLE-CLASS LEARNING PERFORMANCE TASK
**Which statement do you find most compelling for Americans today: the Preamble to the Constitution or the first sentence of paragraph three of the Declaration of Independence?**

UNIT PERFORMANCE-BASED ASSESSMENT
**What are the most effective tools for establishing and preserving freedom?**

## Connection to Performance Tasks

**Whole-Class Learning Performance Task** Franklin struggles to consider the Constitution as it is written. His ideas about compromise suggest that the earlier foundational documents leave some questions open. Students may consider Franklin's attitude as they address the prompt.

**Unit Performance-Based Assessment** Franklin's speech in the Convention addresses the central question of the Unit Performance-Based Assessment. The text makes it clear that having a formal document that explains the structure of government and the rights of its citizens, even if not perfect, is essential for establishing and preserving freedom.

DIGITAL PERSPECTIVES

 Audio  Video  Document  Annotation Highlights  EL Highlights 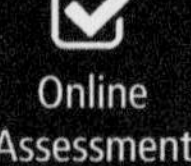 Online Assessment

## LESSON RESOURCES

| | Making Meaning | Language Development | Effective Expression |
|---|---|---|---|
| **Lesson** | **First Read**<br>**Close Read**<br>**Analyze the Text**<br>**Analyze Craft and Structure** | **Concept Vocabulary**<br>**Word Study**<br>**Conventions and Style** | **Writing to Sources**<br>**Speaking and Listening** |
| **Instructional Standards** | **RI.10** By the end of grade 11, read and comprehend literary nonfiction . . .<br>**RI.1** Cite strong and thorough textual evidence . . .<br>**RI.6** Determine an author's point of view . . . | **L.2** Demonstrate command of the conventions . . .<br>**L.3.a** Vary syntax for effect . . .<br>**L.4.c** Consult general and specialized reference materials . . . | **W.1** Write arguments . . .<br>**SL.3** Evaluate a speaker's point of view . . .<br>**SL.5** Make strategic use of digital media . . . |
| **STUDENT RESOURCES** | | | |
| Available online in the Interactive Student Edition or Unit Resources | Selection Audio<br>First-Read Guide: Nonfiction<br>Close-Read Guide: Nonfiction | Word Network | Evidence Log |
| **TEACHER RESOURCES** | | | |
| **Selection Resources** Available online in the Interactive Teacher's Edition or Unit Resources | Audio Summaries<br>Annotation Highlights<br>EL Highlights<br>English Language Support Lesson: Rhetorical Devices<br>Analyze Craft and Structure: Rhetoric | Concept Vocabulary and Word Study<br>Conventions and Style: Syntax and Rhetoric | Writing to Sources: Evaluation<br>Speaking and Listening: Video Recording |
| **Reteach/Practice (RP)** Available online in the Interactive Teacher's Edition or Unit Resources | Analyze Craft and Structure: Rhetoric (RP) | Word Study: Latin Suffix: *-ity* (RP)<br>Conventions and Style: Syntax and Rhetoric (RP) | Writing to Sources: Evaluation (RP)<br>Speaking and Listening: Video Recording (RP) |
| **Assessment** Available online in Assessments | Selection Test | | |
| **My Resources** | A Unit 1 Answer Key is available online and in the Interactive Teacher's Edition. | | |

# Reading Support

| Text Complexity Rubric: Speech in the Convention | |
|---|---|
| **Quantitative Measures** | |
| **Lexile:** 1500 **Text Length:** 668 words | |
| **Qualitative Measures** | |
| Knowledge Demands ①—②—③—❹—⑤ | Historical knowledge of events leading up to the Constitutional Convention, as well as background information about Benjamin Franklin, will be helpful. |
| Structure ①—❷—③—④—⑤ | The selection is in standard letter format. |
| Language Conventionality and Clarity ①—②—③—④—❺ | The selection contains many lengthy, dense sentences written with highly formal language and some nonstandard capitalization and spelling. |
| Levels of Meaning/Purpose ①—②—③—❹—⑤ | The meaning/purpose is straightforward, but the concept may be hard for some to grasp because of sophisticated language and supporting concepts that are complex. |

DECIDE AND PLAN

## English Language Support

Provide English Learners with support for knowledge demands and language as they read the selection.

**Knowledge Demands** Before reading the text, help students summarize the background information. For example, *Representatives from the states drafted a new Constitution, which was very difficult because there were so many competing ideas and views.* Making notes of what they know will help them as they read the text.

**Language** Help students read dense text. Suggest simpler sentences that convey the same meaning. For example for sentence 1: *Even though I don't agree with everything in this Constitution right now, I know that my opinion may change when I have more information and experience.* Ask students to discuss the new sentences.

## Strategic Support

Provide students with strategic support to ensure that they can successfully read the text.

**Knowledge Demands** Determine students' prior knowledge about the events leading up to the Constitutional Convention, as well as Benjamin Franklin's role. Provide additional background if needed.

**Language** Have students work in pairs to break down sentences into smaller chunks in order to understand their meaning. Ask students to highlight words or phrases that they don't understand. As a group, help to define some of the terms they find difficult.

## Challenge

Provide students who need to be challenged with ideas for how they can go beyond a simple interpretation of the text.

**Text Analysis** Ask students to discuss the reasons Benjamin Franklin believes the delegates should support the Constitution. Ask them to comment on why he does not believe they should share any doubts they have with their constituents. Ask students if they agree or disagree with his opinion.

**Written Response** Ask students to identify expressions that are not ones we hear in modern speech. Have them each write how we might say the same thing today. For example, *most sects in religion, think themselves in possession of all truth…* Ask partners to read their sentences aloud to compare the different ways they said the same thing.

TEACH

## Read and Respond

Have students do their first read of the selection. Then, have them complete their close read. Finally, work with them on the Making Meaning, Language Development, and Effective Expression activities.

# Standards Support Through Teaching and Learning Cycle

## IDENTIFY NEEDS

Analyze results of the Beginning-of-Year Assessment, focusing on the items relating to Unit 1. Also take into consideration student performance to this point and your observations of where particular students struggle.

## DECIDE AND PLAN

- If students have performed poorly on items matching these standards, then provide selection scaffolds before assigning them the on-level lesson provided in the Student Edition.
- If students have done well on the Beginning-of-Year Assessment, then challenge them to keep progressing and learning by giving them opportunities to practice the skills in depth.
- Use the Selection Resources listed on the Planning pages for **Speech in the Convention** to help students continually improve their ability to master the standards.

**Instructional Standards: Speech in the Convention**

| | Catching Up | This Year | Looking Forward |
|---|---|---|---|
| **Reading** | You may wish to administer the **Analyze Craft and Structure: Rhetoric (RP)** worksheet to help students understand how authors can use language strategically to make a point. | **RI.1** Cite strong and thorough textual evidence to support analysis of what the text says explicitly as well as inferences drawn from the text, including determining where the text leaves matters uncertain. | Challenge students to read the text of political speech and point out the rhetorical devices that are used. |
| **Writing** | You may wish to administer the **Writing to Sources: Evaluation (RP)** worksheet to teach students how to analyze the parts of an argument and evaluate its use of rhetoric. | **W.1** Write arguments to support claims in an analysis of substantive topics or texts, using valid reasoning and relevant and sufficient evidence. | Challenge students to choose a point of view on a topic, such as how Ben Franklin affected support for the Constitution, and write a brief argument to support their claims. Partners should critique and evaluate each other's argument and use of rhetoric. |
| **Speaking and Listening** | You may wish to administer the **Speaking and Listening: Video Recording (RP**) worksheet to help students understand how to evaluate a speaker's point of view as well as use of evidence and rhetoric. | **SL.5** Make strategic use of digital media in presentations to enhance understanding of findings, reasoning, and evidence and to add interest. | Challenge small groups of students to work together to write a mock political speech that uses rhetorical devices, and then record the speech. The group should agree on content as well as the intended tone of the speech. |
| **Language** | You may wish to administer the **Conventions and Style: Syntax and Rhetoric (RP)** worksheet to help students understand how these devices can contribute to the clarity and persuasiveness of writing. | **L.2** Demonstrate command of the conventions of standard English capitalization, punctuation, and spelling when writing.<br>**L.3.a** Vary syntax for effect, consulting references for guidance as needed; apply an understanding of syntax to the study of complex texts when reading. | Challenge students to find examples of rhetoric and syntax in a text and discuss how the text would be different if the devices were not used. |

## ANALYZE AND REVISE

- Analyze student work for evidence of student learning.
- Identify whether or not students have met the expectations in the standards.
- Identify implications for future instruction.

## TEACH

Implement the planned lesson, and gather evidence of student learning.

## Jump Start

FIRST READ Before students' first read, discuss an aphorism by Ben Franklin: "There are no gains without pains" or "Diligence is the mother of good luck." Ask students what qualities Franklin seems to admire most. What advice is he suggesting?

### Concept Vocabulary

Provide support to students as they rank their words. Remind them that the definitions of these words appear in the side column next to the text.

### FIRST READ

The first time they go through the selection, students should perform the steps of the first read:

NOTICE: Encourage students to pay attention to the way Franklin builds arguments to persuade detractors to support the Constitution, despite their reservations.

ANNOTATE: Ask students to mark passages that might help them track Franklin's main points in favor of the Constitution.

CONNECT: Encourage students to go beyond the selection to make connections with their own experiences. What strategies have they used to convince their friends or family members about a plan or idea of their own?

RESPOND: Students will demonstrate their understanding of the text by answering questions and writing a summary.

Point out to students that they will perform the first three steps concurrently as they are doing their first read. They will complete the Respond step after they have finished the first read. You may wish to print copies of the **First-Read Guide: Nonfiction** for students to use.

**Remind students that during their first read, they should not answer the close-read questions that appear in the selection.**

MAKING MEANING

# Speech in the Convention

## Concept Vocabulary

You will encounter the following words as you read the speech Benjamin Franklin gave at the Constitutional Convention in 1787. Before reading, note how familiar you are with each word. Then, rank the words in order from most familiar (1) to least familiar (6).

| WORD | YOUR RANKING |
|---|---|
| infallibility | |
| despotism | |
| corrupted | |
| prejudices | |
| salutary | |
| integrity | |

After completing the first read, come back to the concept vocabulary and review your rankings. Mark changes to your original rankings as needed.

## First Read NONFICTION

Apply these strategies as you conduct your first read. You will have an opportunity to complete the close-read notes after your first read.

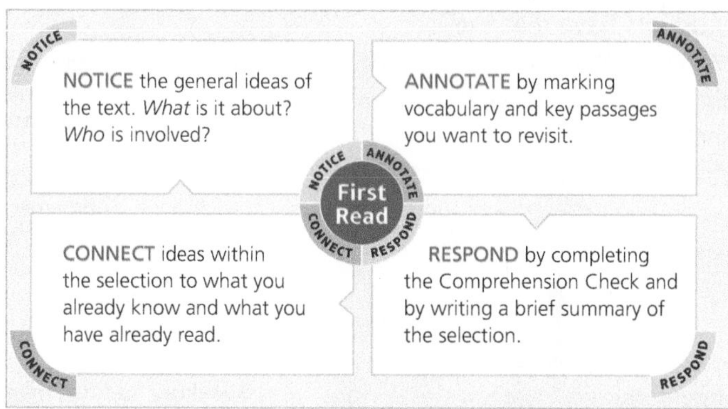
NOTICE the general ideas of the text. *What* is it about? *Who* is involved?
ANNOTATE by marking vocabulary and key passages you want to revisit.
First Read
CONNECT ideas within the selection to what you already know and what you have already read.
RESPOND by completing the Comprehension Check and by writing a brief summary of the selection.

**Tool Kit**
First-Read Guide and Model Annotation

STANDARDS
**Reading Informational Text**
By the end of grade 11, read and comprehend literary nonfiction in the grades 11–CCR text complexity band proficiently, with scaffolding as needed at the high end of the range.

### VOCABULARY DEVELOPMENT

**Word Forms** Model other forms of the word *despotism* in sentences.

Our citizens do not want *despotism*.
Their ruler is *despotic*.
Hitler was a *despot*.

| Word | Part of Speech | Meaning |
|---|---|---|
| despotism | noun | cruel government with total power |
| despotic | adjective | cruel, and having total power |
| despot | noun | a cruel ruler having total power |

DIGITAL PERSPECTIVES

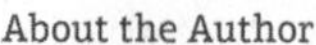

About the Author

## Benjamin Franklin

From his teen years until his retirement at age forty-two, Benjamin Franklin (1706–1790) worked as a printer. He got his start as an apprentice to his brother James Franklin, a Boston printer. By the time he was sixteen, Ben was not only printing, but writing parts of his brother's newspaper. Using the name "Silence Dogood," he wrote letters satirizing daily life and politics in Boston. When he was seventeen, Franklin moved to Philadelphia to open his own print shop. This move gave birth to one of his most enduring contributions to American culture, *Poor Richard's Almanack*. This annual publication, which was published from 1732 to 1752, contained information, observations, and advice and was a colonial bestseller.

**The "Write" Reputation** Just as he had signed "Silence Dogood" to the letters he wrote for his brother's paper, Franklin created a fictitious author/editor for the *Almanack*. The chatty Richard Saunders, or Poor Richard, first appeared as a dull and foolish astronomer. However, over the years his character developed, becoming more thoughtful, pious, and funny.

Like most almanacs, *Poor Richard's Almanack* contained practical information about the calendar, the sun and moon, and the weather. It also featured a wealth of homespun sayings and observations, or aphorisms, many of which are still quoted today. It was these aphorisms that made the *Almanack* so popular. Franklin included an aphorism at the top or bottom of most of the Almanack's pages. The wit and brevity of these sayings allowed him to weave in many moral messages, while also entertaining his readers.

**Inventor and Scientist** When Franklin was forty-two, he retired from the printing business to devote himself to science. He proved to be as successful a scientist as he had been a printer. Over the course of his life, Franklin was responsible for inventing the lightning rod, bifocals, and a new type of stove. He confirmed the laws of electricity, charted the Gulf Stream, and contributed to the scientific understanding of earthquakes and ocean currents. In spite of all these achievements, Franklin is best remembered for his career in politics.

**Statesman and Diplomat** Franklin played an important role in drafting the Declaration of Independence, enlisting French support during the Revolutionary War, negotiating a peace treaty with Britain, and drafting the United States Constitution. In his later years, he was the United States ambassador to England and then to France. Even before George Washington earned the title, Franklin was considered to be "the father of his country."

**American Success Story** Perhaps it is no surprise that a person of Franklin's accomplishments, longevity, and historic importance would write the story of his life. Franklin's *The Autobiography* remains a classic of the genre as well as a prototype for the American success story. Franklin wrote the first section of the work in 1771, when he was sixty-five years old. At the urging of friends, he wrote three more sections—the last shortly before his death—but succeeded in bringing the account of his life only to the year 1759. Though never completed, his autobiography, filled with his opinions and advice, provides not only a record of his achievements, but also an understanding of his extraordinary character.





## Speech in the Convention

Why does Franklin start out his speech with a humorous anecdote? What value might humor have at such a serious convention? Modeling these and other questions readers might ask will bring "Speech in the Convention" to life and connect it to the Performance Task question. Selection audio and print capability for the selection are available in the Interactive Teacher's Edition.

### PERSONALIZE FOR LEARNING

**English Language Support**

**Unfamiliar Words** The last paragraph of About the Author discusses Franklin's autobiography. Students may not know the meaning of *autobiography*, "a life story written by the person himself or herself." Point out that About the Author is an example of a biography, a life story. Students may find it helpful to see the breakdown of the prefix and roots for these two words: *biography— bio* (life) + *graph* (writing); and *autobiography—auto* (self) + *bio* (life) + *graph* (writing). Help them to list and define other words with the same prefix and roots, such as *automobile, autograph, biology, and graph.* **ALL LEVELS**

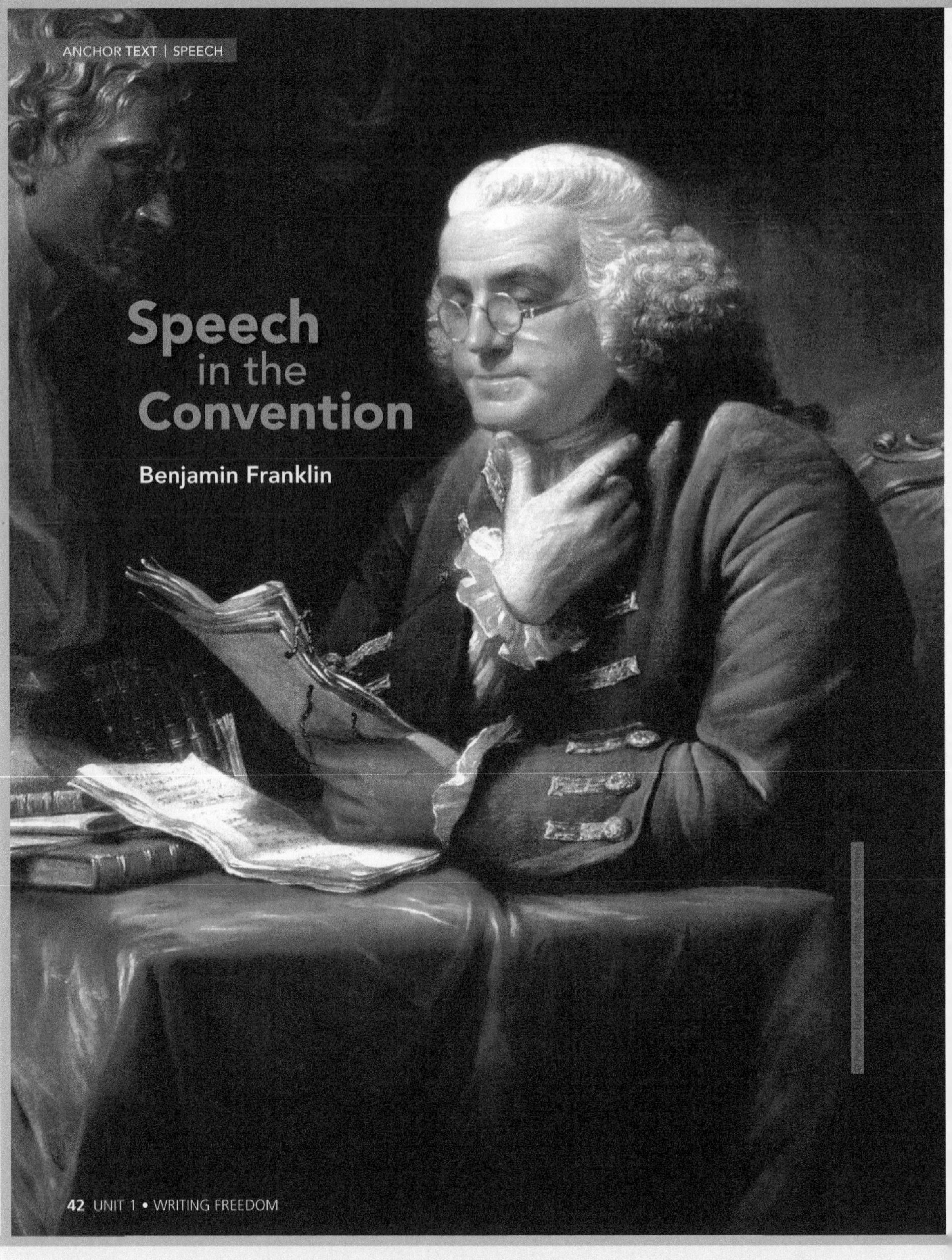


## CROSS-CURRICULAR PERSPECTIVES

**Social Studies** Have students research and write a brief report about the Constitutional Convention of 1787 to help them understand the context of Franklin's speech. They should find out why a new constitution was needed. Propose that students pursue the answers to these questions or others that they develop on their own:

- How many states were involved in the convention?
- Who were the important "framers" of the Constitution?
- What plans for a constitution were suggested?
- What compromises were made? **(Research to Explore)**

DIGITAL PERSPECTIVES

BACKGROUND

After the American Revolution, each of the newly independent states created its own constitution. While Congress was able to pass limited laws, it had no power to tax the states or regulate issues, such as trade, that were affected by state boundaries. These problems led to the Constitutional Convention in 1787. Representatives from twelve states met to approve a national constitution. The argument was lively and often contentious. At the age of eighty-one, Benjamin Franklin—representing Pennsylvania—brought his diplomatic skills to the debate.

SCAN FOR MULTIMEDIA

*Mr. President,*

1 I confess, that I do not entirely approve of this Constitution at present; but, Sir, I am not sure I shall never approve it; for, having lived long, I have experienced many instances of being obliged, by better information or fuller consideration, to change my opinions even on important subjects, which I once thought right, but found to be otherwise. It is therefore that, the older I grow, the more apt I am to doubt my own judgment of others. Most men, indeed, as well as most sects in religion, think themselves in possession of all truth, and that wherever others differ from them, it is so far error. . . . Though many private persons think almost as highly of their own **infallibility** as of that of their sect, few express it so naturally as a certain French lady, who, in a little dispute with her sister, said, "But I meet with nobody but myself that is *always* in the right." *"Je ne trouve que moi qui aie toujours raison."*

2 In these sentiments, Sir, I agree to this Constitution, with all its faults,—if they are such; because I think a general government necessary for us, and there is no form of government but what may be a blessing to the people, if well administered; and I believe, farther, that this is likely to be well administered for a course of years, and can only end in **despotism**, as other forms have done before it, when the people shall become so **corrupted** as to need despotic government, being incapable of any other. I doubt, too, whether any other convention we can obtain, may be able to make a better constitution; for, when you assemble a number of men, to have the advantage of their joint wisdom, you inevitably assemble with those men all their **prejudices**, their passions, their errors of opinion, their local interests, and their selfish views. From such an assembly can a *perfect* production be expected? It therefore astonishes me, Sir, to find this system approaching so near to perfection as it does; and I think it will astonish our enemies, who are waiting with confidence to hear, that our councils are confounded like those of the builders of Babel, and that our states are on the point of separation, only to meet hereafter for the purpose of cutting one another's throats. Thus I consent, Sir, to this Constitution, because I expect no better, and because I am not sure that it is not the best. The opinions I have had

NOTES

**infallibility** (ihn fal uh BIHL uh tee) *n.* inability to be in error

CLOSE READ

ANNOTATE: Franklin refers humorously to "a certain French lady." Mark her words and their English translation in paragraph 1.

QUESTION: Why does Franklin choose to illustrate his point in this way?

CONCLUDE: What is the effect of this quotation?

**despotism** (DEHS puh tihz uhm) *n.* absolute rule; tyranny

**corrupted** (kuh RUHPT ihd) *adj.* dishonest

**prejudices** (PREHJ uh dihs ihz) *n.* unfavorable opinions or feelings formed beforehand or without factual support





## CLOSE READ

Ask students to focus on Franklin's humorous anecdote in paragraph 1. Encourage them to talk about the annotations that they marked. You may wish to model the Close Read using the following think-aloud format. Possible responses to questions on the student page are included. You may also want to print copies of the **Close-Read Guide: Nonfiction** for students to use.

**ANNOTATE:** As I read the first paragraph, I see that the words of "a certain French lady" are in italics, with an English translation of her statement just before the French. Those are the words that I annotate.

**QUESTION:** Franklin is telling his audience that people often feel strongly that their opinion is right. His anecdote shows despite that feeling, everyone is wrong some of the time. Nobody is infallible.

**CONCLUDE:** Franklin's humorous story about a frivolous fight probably made his audience laugh. He likely intended for this humor to relieve some of the stress of the moment and to make his audience more open to his ideas. Also, the story made a serious point that may have made his audience think about holding too zealously to their opinions, specifically their reservations about the Constitution.

Additional **English Language Support** is available in the Interactive Teacher's Edition.

## PERSONALIZE FOR LEARNING

### English Language Support

**Paraphrasing for Comprehension** Focus on this sentence from paragraph 2: *I think it will astonish our enemies, who are waiting with confidence to hear, that our councils are confounded like those of the builders of Babel, and that our states are on the point of separation, only to meet hereafter for the purpose of cutting one another's throats.*

Help students to parse the sentence by recognizing that (1) *astonish* means "surprise"; (2) that the enemies are, above all, the British; (3) the comparison with Babel means the enemy expects the government will collapse for lack of communication; (4) that the states will separate and fight bitterly. Then help students paraphrase the sentence. **ALL LEVELS**

CLOSER LOOK

## Analyzing Author's Viewpoint

Students may have marked paragraph 2 during their first read. Use this paragraph to help students understand Franklin's summation. Encourage them to talk about the annotations that they marked.

**ANNOTATE:** Have students mark a sentence in paragraph 2 that states Franklin's view about the harm of publically voicing their objections to the Constitution, or have students participate while you highlight the sentence.

**QUESTION:** What is Franklin's view about the positive value of "real or apparent unanimity"? He says that presenting a united front will be good on the international stage.

**Possible response:** He views such unanimity as sending a positive message that will strengthen the government.

**CONCLUDE:** How does Franklin connect unanimity in his final statement with his initial points about fallibility?

**Possible response:** He suggests that they put aside their objections, recognizing that their objections may be wrong, and join together.

Remind students that an **author's viewpoint** is his or her thoughts and perspective on a topic. Understanding an author's viewpoint can help them to determine his or her purpose. In this speech, Franklin's clear purpose is to persuade the convention to vote—unanimously—for the Constitution. The details help explain why he feels this way.

NOTES

**salutary** (SAL yuh tehr ee) *adj.* beneficial; promoting a positive purpose

**integrity** (ihn TEHG ruh tee) *n.* virtue; commitment to moral or ethical principles

of its *errors* I sacrifice to the public good. I have never whispered a syllable of them abroad. Within these walls they were born, and here they shall die. If every one of us, in returning to our constituents, were to report the objections he has had to it, and endeavor to gain partisans in support of them, we might prevent its being generally received, and thereby lose all the **salutary** effects and great advantages resulting naturally in our favor among foreign nations, as well as among ourselves, from our real or apparent unanimity. Much of the strength and efficiency of any government, in procuring and securing happiness to the people, depends on *opinion,* on the general opinion of the goodness of that government, as well as of the wisdom and **integrity** of its governors. I hope, therefore, for our own sakes, as a part of the people, and for the sake of our posterity, that we shall act heartily and unanimously in recommending this Constitution, wherever our influence may extend, and turn our future thoughts and endeavors to the means of having it *well administered.*

3 On the whole, Sir, I cannot help expressing a wish, that every member of the convention who may still have objections to it, would with me on this occasion doubt a little of his own infallibility, and, to make manifest our *unanimity,* put his name to this instrument. ❧

MEDIA CONNECTION

The U. S. Constitution

**Discuss It** How does this video help you understand the challenges that Franklin faced in persuading the delegates to approve the Constitution?

**Write your response before sharing your ideas.**

SCAN FOR MULTIMEDIA 

**WriteNow** Express and Reflect

**Modern Paraphrase** Ask students to review paragraph 1 and prepare to rewrite it in contemporary language. Benjamin Franklin delivered his speech more than 225 years ago, so it reflects the way people spoke during the colonial era. Have students rewrite his ideas in their own language, keeping in mind the serious circumstances and impressive group Franklin was addressing.

## Comprehension Check

Complete the following items after you finish your first read.

1. What does Franklin admit has caused him to change his mind in the past?

2. Why does Franklin believe that any constitution the Convention approves will be an imperfect document?

3. Why does Franklin want the delegates to keep their divided opinions to themselves once the Constitution is approved?

4. Whose "opinion" does Franklin believe is key to a government's strength and efficiency?

5. **Notebook** Write a summary of Franklin's speech to confirm your understanding of the text.

## RESEARCH

**Research to Clarify** Choose at least one unfamiliar detail from the text. Briefly research that detail. In what way does the information you learned shed light on an aspect of the speech?

**Research to Explore** Conduct research on an aspect of the text you find interesting. For example, you might research why Franklin was one of the most popular authors and public figures of his time.





DIGITAL PERSPECTIVES

## Comprehension Check

Possible Responses:

1. Franklin has changed his mind when he has had "better information" or has given a matter "fuller consideration."
2. Franklin believes that any document created by a group of people will be subject to the participants' "prejudices," "passions," "errors of opinion," "local interests," and "selfish views."
3. Revealing the objections might keep people from supporting the Constitution and might make the United States lose the favor of other countries.
4. He believes that the people must have an opinion of the goodness of that government and of its leaders' wisdom and integrity.
5. Franklin uses his years of experience to urge his fellow delegates to accept the Constitution. He admits that any legal document created by a committee will be imperfect, but he argues that it is strong overall and that it will benefit the people and the nation.

## Research

**Research to Clarify** If students have difficulty coming up with a detail to research, suggest that they focus on one of the following topics: another member of the Constitutional Convention or the relationship of the United States to England at the time of the convention.

**Research to Explore** If students find the topic is too broad, suggest that they focus on Franklin's public works or scientific efforts, keeping in mind how these efforts benefited people and contributed to his popularity.

### PERSONALIZE FOR LEARNING

**Challenge**

Have students research the fight to ratify the Constitution. Ask students to consider these questions, or one that they develop on their own.

- Who were the Federalists and Anti-Federalists?
- In which states was the battle close?
- What were *The Federalist Papers*?
- What was the ratification timeline, by state?

## Jump Start

CLOSE READ Ask students for their impressions of Ben Franklin. Do they think of him as serious, self-important, funny, or down-to-earth? Encourage them to give their reasons. Invite them to tell what they'd like to ask him about his speech to the convention.

## Close Read the Text

Work with students on the annotation model, and then have them complete items 2 and 3 on their own. When they have finished, review and discuss the sections students marked. If needed, continue to model close reading by using the Annotation Highlights in the Interactive Teacher's Edition.

## Analyze the Text

Possible responses:

1. Franklin's main point is that the delegates should approve the Constitution, even if they have doubts about it. He may speak directly to Washington, but his words are for every delegate to hear. **DOK 2**
2. (a) Franklin admits that he sometimes doubts his own judgment, especially when it comes to believing that his opinions are right. **DOK 2** (b) If Franklin, perhaps the most revered delegate, could doubt his own judgment, then the delegates who do not plan to approve the Constitution ought to consider doubting their own judgment. **DOK 3**
3. (a) Because of God's judgment, the builders went their separate ways, and the Tower of Babel was never completed. Franklin's purpose is to warn the delegates that their disputes may cause the Constitution never to be established. **DOK 2** (b) It is effective because it compares their work in building a nation to another very large task that failed. **DOK 3**
4. They would want a list of individual rights to be added—the Bill of Rights. **DOK 2**
5. Responses will vary.

### FORMATIVE ASSESSMENT

### Analyze the Text

- **If** students fail to cite evidence, **then** remind them to support their ideas with specific information from the text.
- **If** students have difficulty interpreting/criticizing the allusion to Babel, **then** discuss it in more detail, explaining that Babel became a metaphor for lack of communication and strife.

MAKING MEANING

SPEECH IN THE CONVENTION

## Close Read the Text

1. This model, from paragraph 1 of the speech, shows two sample annotations, along with questions and conclusions. Close read the passage, and find another detail to annotate. Then, write a question and your conclusion.

ANNOTATE: The word "confess" is a startling beginning to a speech.

QUESTION: Why does Franklin say this?

CONCLUDE: By confessing to his own struggle, Franklin shows that compromise is not a sign of weakness.

I confess, that I do not entirely approve of this Constitution at present; but, Sir, I am not sure I shall never approve it; for, having lived long, I have experienced many instances of being obliged, by better information or fuller consideration, to change my opinions. . . .

ANNOTATE: Franklin reminds listeners of his old age.

QUESTION: Why does he make this point?

CONCLUDE: He is reminding them of his age and experience—he has authority his listeners lack.

2. For more practice, go back into the text and complete the close-read notes.
3. Revisit a section of the text you found important during your first read. Read this section closely, and **annotate** what you notice. Ask yourself **questions** such as "Why did the author make this choice?" What can you **conclude**?

**Tool Kit**
Close-Read Guide and Model Annotation

## Analyze the Text

CITE TEXTUAL EVIDENCE to support your answers.

**Notebook** Respond to these questions.

1. **Draw Conclusions** Franklin addresses his remarks to "Mr. President"—George Washington, who led the proceedings. How can you tell that his remarks do not concern Washington alone?
2. (a) Early in the speech, what does Franklin admit that he sometimes doubts? (b) **Connect** How does this admission relate to his overall argument?
3. An **allusion** is a passing or unexplained reference to something from history or culture. (a) **Interpret** In paragraph 2, what is the purpose of Franklin's allusion to the builders of Babel? (b) **Criticize** Do you consider this allusion to be effective? Explain.
4. **Historical Perspectives** In what ways does Franklin fear the delegates may undermine the Constitution even after they sign it? Explain.
5. **Essential Question:** *What is the meaning of freedom?* What have you learned about the nature of freedom by reading this speech?

**STANDARDS**

**Reading Informational Text**

- Cite strong and thorough textual evidence to support analysis of what the text says explicitly as well as inferences drawn from the text, including determining where the text leaves matters uncertain.
- Determine an author's point of view or purpose in a text in which the rhetoric is particularly effective, analyzing how style and content contribute to the power, persuasiveness or beauty of the text.





### PERSONALIZE FOR LEARNING

**Strategic Support**

Students may have difficulty understanding that Franklin used his own "shortcomings," specifically his inability to always count on the correctness of his judgments, as a way of getting members of the convention to reconsider their positions/judgments. Use a "personal" example to help them understand: I never liked eating sushi until my friend let me try hers. It was delicious, and now I try lots of new foods. So, why don't you try this dish?

## Analyze Craft and Structure

**Author's Purpose: Rhetoric** Franklin's speech was successful: The Constitution was approved and sent to the states for ratification. Franklin's text provides examples of several **rhetorical devices**, or ways of using language for effect, that appeal to an audience and produce a successful oratory.

- **Paradox** is a statement or idea that seems contradictory but actually presents a truth. For example, in Shakespeare's *Hamlet*, the statement "I must be cruel to be kind" seems illogical. On reflection, however, it demonstrates a deeper truth: Sometimes, one must face a painful reality in order to rise above or learn from it.
- **Concession** is the acknowledgment of an opponent's arguments.
- **Rhetorical questions** are questions asked for effect—to make a point, or introduce a topic. The speaker does not expect the audience to answer, because the answer is obvious.

While not strictly an example of a rhetorical device, a speaker's **tone,** or attitude toward the subject and audience, can also sway listeners. Phrasing and word choice combine to convey tone, which may be ironic, serious, humorous, friendly, distant, cynical, earnest, and so on.

### Practice

**CITE TEXTUAL EVIDENCE** to support your answers.

**Notebook** Complete these activities.

1. Use the chart to identify examples from Franklin's speech of each rhetorical device noted. Explain how each device serves to strengthen Franklin's argument or influence his audience.

| RHETORICAL DEVICE | EFFECT |
|---|---|
| paradox: | Franklin expresses doubt about the document. Identifying with those who doubt makes them willing to listen. |
| concession: | |
| rhetorical question: | Franklin emphasizes realistic expectations of the delegates. "From such an assembly can a perfect production be expected?" |

2. (a) Choose the set of adjectives that best describes the tone of the first paragraph of this speech.
   - ☐ slyly humorous and self-deprecating
   - ☐ deeply earnest, concerned, and frustrated
   - ☐ serious, witty, and informal

   (b) Explain your choice, citing specific words and phrases that support your answer.

3. During his long political career, Franklin had extensive experience as a diplomat. In what ways does this speech reflect a diplomatic approach to conflict? Explain.





DIGITAL PERSPECTIVES 

## Analyze Craft and Structure

**Author's Purpose: Rhetoric** Ask students whether they prefer to listen to a speaker who is serious or humorous. Discuss the effect of approaches different from Franklin's. What impact would a demanding or negative tone have on an audience? What if a speaker insisted that he or she was always right or wouldn't admit the possibility that critics could make a good point? Point out that the rhetorical devices listed here provide specific strategies to persuade listeners. **Analyze Craft and Structure: Rhetoric.**

### Practice

Possible responses:

1. See possible responses in chart on student page.
2. slyly humorous and self-deprecating
3. Responses will vary. Student responses should demonstrate an understanding of the role of a diplomat and how it is related to Franklin's role as a representative at the Constitutional Convention. Responses should also state similar rhetorical strategies Franklin would have used in the two roles.

### FORMATIVE ASSESSMENT

#### Analyze the Text

- **If** students have difficulty completing the chart, **then** provide an example of each device and ask students to explain its appeal.

For Reteach and practice, see **Analyze Craft and Structure: Rhetoric (RP).**

## PERSONALIZE FOR LEARNING

### English Language Support

**Rhetorical Devices** Have students think of a topic for a speech. Ask them to identify the audience the speech is intended for and the rhetorical devices they would use in their speech. **EMERGING**

Have students outline a short speech that they might deliver. Ask them to identify the audience their speech is intended for and the rhetorical devices they will use in their speech. **EXPANDING**

Have students prepare a short speech. Ask them to start by selecting their audience and the rhetorical devices they will use in their speech. Have volunteers deliver their speeches for the class. After the speech is over, ask the class to identify some of the rhetorical devices used in the speech. **BRIDGING**

An expanded **English Language Support Lesson** on Rhetorical Devices is available in the **Interactive Teacher's Edition.**

# TEACHING

## Concept Vocabulary

**Why These Words?** Point out *integrity* and *corrupted/corruption* are antonyms. Pairing words with antonyms can help with understanding and remembering difficult vocabulary.

Possible responses:

1. *Integrity* and *salutary* convey goals; *despotism, prejudice,* and *corrupted* suggest potential roadblocks in the way of achieving those goals.
2. Other such words include *right, error, dispute, faults, wisdom, passions, selfish,* and *perfection*.

### Practice

Possible responses:

1. The people might be unwilling to compromise.
2. The government would become a dictatorship, and citizens would likely fight.
3. The Constitution could include a system of checks and balances.
4. Prejudice tends to cause people to view another group in a narrow-minded way and then to use their judgment to treat them unfairly.
5. a peaceful society, progress, growth
6. A person with a good moral character would be likely to act in a moral way while in office.

### Word Network

Possible words: *obliged, despotic, constitution, opinions, objections*

## Word Study

For more support, see **Concept Vocabulary and Word Study.**

Possible responses:

1. *Posterity* means "future descendants."
2. Possible example: *authority*, "the right or power to enforce compliance."

### FORMATIVE ASSESSMENT

### Concept Vocabulary

**If** students struggle to identify the concept, create two simple word webs, and put *vice* in the middle of one, *virtue* in the middle of the other **then** have students place in one of the webs each concept vocabulary word, its antonyms, and the Word Network vocabulary.

### Word Study

**If** students struggle to define words with the *-ity* ending, **then** suggest that they start with easier vocabulary, such as *ability, creativity, diversity, majority, possibility* then have them underline the base words and give their meaning before moving on to more difficult words with the *-ity* ending. For Reteach and Practice, see **Word Study: Latin Suffix: *-ity* (RP).**



LANGUAGE DEVELOPMENT

SPEECH IN THE CONVENTION

## Concept Vocabulary

| infallibility | corrupted | salutary |
|---|---|---|
| despotism | prejudices | integrity |

**Why These Words?** These concept vocabulary words are used to describe human vices and virtues, especially when it comes to the power governments can wield over citizens. Franklin believes any government can be *corrupted*, and that those in positions of leadership should have *integrity*.

1. How does the concept vocabulary suggest human goals—and the human failings that make the achievement of those goals difficult?
2. What other words in the speech connect to this concept?

**WORD NETWORK** Add words related to freedom from the text to your Word Network.

### Practice

**Notebook** Respond to these questions.

1. Why might it be difficult to deal with people who never doubt their own *infallibility*?
2. What are two negative effects that might result from a government ruled by *despotism*?
3. What safeguards could a constitution include to minimize the chance that a government will be *corrupted*?
4. Name two ways in which *prejudices* can affect human behavior.
5. What *salutary* effects can result from cooperation?
6. Would you vote for a candidate who displayed *integrity*? Why or why not?

## Word Study

**Latin Suffix: *-ity*** The suffix *-ity* means "state or quality of." When this suffix is added to an adjective, the resulting word is a noun. For example, in the word *infallibility*, the suffix is added to the adjective *infallible*, which means "incapable of failing." The resulting noun means "the state of being incapable of failing."

1. Find and define two other words near the end of Franklin's speech that end with the suffix *-ity*. Check your definitions in a print or digital college-level dictionary.
2. Identify and define two other words that end with the suffix *-ity*. Use a dictionary to verify your definitions.

**STANDARDS**

Language

- Demonstrate command of the conventions of standard English capitalization, punctuation, and spelling when writing.
- Vary syntax for effect, consulting references for guidance as needed; apply an understanding of syntax to the study of complex texts when reading.
- Consult general and specialized reference materials, both print and digital, to find the pronunciation of a word or determine or clarify its precise meaning, its part of speech, its etymology, or its standard usage.





### DIGITAL PERSPECTIVES

**Enriching the Text** Direct students to find and listen to the Colonial Williamsburg podcast that contains an interview with actor John Hamant. Hamant provides insight into Franklin, his wit, and his methods when appearing before an audience.

The interview also includes an interpretive reading of part of Franklin's speech. Have students discuss what Hamant says concerning Franklin's methods. Ask them to tell what they learned about how Franklin's methods relate to his purpose/viewpoint.

## Conventions and Style

**Syntax and Rhetoric Parallelism** is the use of similar grammatical forms or patterns to express similar ideas. Effective use of parallelism adds rhythm and balance to writing and strengthens connections among ideas. Faulty parallelism presents equal ideas in a distracting and potentially confusing mix of grammatical forms.

EXAMPLE

**Nonparallel:** Franklin **was supportive of** the Constitution, **went to express** his feelings, and **was writing** emphatically about the document.

**Parallel:** Franklin **supported** the Constitution, **expressed** his feelings to others, and **wrote** emphatically about the document.

The parallel sentence states three similar ideas as phrases that begin with an action verb in the simple past tense.

### Read It

1. Underline the parallel elements in these sentences.
   a. The sensible, brilliant, and influential James Wilson was among the delegates from Pennsylvania.
   b. Franklin was too weak to deliver the speech himself—but was the weakness due to his unremitting pain, his unceasing work for compromise, or his exhaustion after days of argument?
   c. Wilson read the speech, which came at a critical moment in the proceedings, addressed the need for compromise, and swayed several delegates.
2. **Connect to Style** Reread paragraph 2 of Franklin's speech. Identify two examples of parallelism. Explain the ideas the parallel items express.

### Write It

**Notebook** Rewrite each sentence so that it uses parallelism. Be sure to place commas to separate the ideas or details.

EXAMPLE

**Incorrect:** *Fueled by love for liberty, eager to form an effective government,* and *with personal determination,* several political leaders founded the Society for Political Inquiries in 1787.

**Correct:** *Fueled by love for liberty, eagerness to form an effective government,* and *personal determination*, several political leaders founded the Society for Political Inquiries in 1787.

1. The society's members considered issues of government, wrote essays on political topics, and there were discussions about how governments can serve people.
2. At the Constitutional Convention, throughout the fight for state ratification, and when Washington was president, this group continued to function.

TIP

USAGE

When you use correlative conjunctions (which appear in pairs) to achieve parallelism, make sure that the words are in the correct order.

*Incorrect*: Franklin **not only** wanted unanimity **but also** civility.

*Correct*: Franklin wanted **not only** unanimity **but also** civility.





DIGITAL PERSPECTIVES

## Conventions and Style

**Syntax and Rhetoric** Give students some simple examples of parallelism from Franklin's own aphorisms:

*Industry gives comfort and plenty and respect.*
*To be humble to superiors is duty, to equals courtesy, to inferiors nobleness.*

Then ask them to underline or read each separate grammatical structure. For more support, see **Conventions and Style: Syntax and Rhetoric.** 

### Read It

Possible responses:

1. a. sensible, brilliant, and influential.
   b. his unremitting pain, his unceasing work for compromise, or his exhaustion after days of argument
   c. came at a critical moment in the proceedings, addressed the need for compromise, and swayed several delegates.
2. their prejudices, their passions their errors of opinion, their local interests, and their selfish views. Franklin's parallelism helps the audience remember certain ideas. The rhythm that it establishes helps to hold the audience's attention.

### Write It

Possible responses:

1. The society's members considered issues of government, wrote essays on political topics, and discussed how governments can serve people.
2. At the Constitutional Convention, throughout the fight for state ratification, and during Washington's presidency, this group continued to function.

CROSS-CURRICULAR PERSPECTIVES

**Humanities** Connect students with a familiar, modern example of a speech that famously uses parallelism: Martin Luther King Jr.'s "I Have a Dream" speech. The speech, which is available online, contains numerous examples of parallelism that students should be able to identify without great difficulty.

FORMATIVE ASSESSMENT

### Analyze the Text

**If** students have difficulty rewriting the sentences, **then** remind them that with parallel construction, each phrase should have the same grammatical structure; help them to parse the uncorrected example, showing how the sentence begins with a noun phrase (love for liberty); an adjective phrase (personally determined), and another adjective phrase (personally determined). For Reteach and Practice, see **Conventions and Style: Syntax and Rhetoric (RP).**

# TEACHING

## Writing to Sources

Remind students that Franklin's goal, or purpose, was central to his speech to the convention. First, encourage them to write a brief statement of Franklin's central purpose. Ask students to remember what he was trying to convince his audience to do. Next they might list Franklin's basic arguments that supported this purpose. As they write their evaluations, they should consider whether his arguments provided strong support for this central purpose. For more support, see **Writing to Sources: Evaluation.**

### Reflect on Your Writing

1. If students need support, encourage them to focus first on their general opinion of Franklin's speech, and then to check their evaluation to be sure that they supported this central opinion with evidence. They should follow the same procedure with each subsequent opinion and its supporting evidence.
2. Students may want to review the rhetorical devices lesson in Analyze Craft and Structure and try to use one or more devices to promote their own evaluation/opinions. Encourage them to discuss which devices are most helpful and which are easiest to use.
3. **Why These Words?** Responses will vary. Have the students list specific examples of the useful, expressive words that they included in their evaluation.

### FORMATIVE ASSESSMENT: Writing to Sources

**If** students experience difficulty with the assignment, **then** have them begin with a simple opinion: e.g., Franklin's speech is a masterpiece, or Franklin's speech is not a masterpiece. Then have them try to respond to only one of the bullets in the Assignment box before continuing with additional bullets. For Reteach and Practice, see **Writing to Sources: Evaluation (RP).**

EFFECTIVE EXPRESSION

SPEECH IN THE CONVENTION

## Writing to Sources

When you evaluate a text—whether you do so in writing, in discussions with other readers, or just in your own thinking process—you consider what an author sought to achieve in a piece of writing and whether he or she was successful.

**Assignment**

Franklin's speech in the Convention has been called a masterpiece. Do you agree? Write an **evaluation** of the speech. Consider Franklin's goal and the techniques he used to accomplish it. Be sure to include these elements in your evaluation:

- an introduction that includes a statement of your position
- at least one reference to Franklin's goal
- valid reasoning, supported by textual evidence that clearly relates to each point
- specific references to the ideas Franklin conveyed and to his use of rhetorical devices
- original rhetorical devices that help you make your points
- a conclusion that reasserts your opinion in a memorable way

**Vocabulary and Conventions Connection** Consider including several of the concept vocabulary words in your evaluation. Also, remember to use parallelism to emphasize related ideas and create rhythm in your writing.

| infallibility | corrupted | salutary |
|---|---|---|
| despotism | prejudices | integrity |

### Reflect on Your Writing

After you have drafted your evaluation, answer the following questions.

1. What evidence did you provide in your evaluation?
2. What rhetorical devices did you use in your evaluation?
3. **Why These Words?** The words you choose make a difference in your writing. Which words helped you express your ideas?

STANDARDS

**Writing**
- Write arguments to support claims in an analysis of substantive topics or texts, using valid reasoning and relevant and sufficient evidence.
- Provide a concluding statement or section that follows from and supports the argument presented.

**Speaking and Listening**
- Evaluate a speaker's point of view, reasoning, and use of evidence and rhetoric, assessing the stance, premises, links among ideas, word choice, points of emphasis, and tone used.
- Make strategic use of digital media in presentations to enhance understanding of findings, reasoning, and evidence and to add interest.





### PERSONALIZE FOR LEARNING

**English Language Support**

**Fact and Opinion** Work with students to master the distinction between facts and opinions. Make sure they understand that their opinions are their judgments or beliefs about something. In writing, opinions should be supported with facts and details. Facts can be checked to prove whether they are true or false. Ask for examples of opinions about Franklin — (Franklin wrote interesting aphorisms. Franklin was a great scientist.) and facts (Ben Franklin was born in 1706. Franklin's first job was as a printer's apprentice.).

Encourage students to create pre-writing outlines; each opinion should be followed by several facts, arguments, reasoning, and/or evidence. **ALL LEVELS**

## Speaking and Listening

**Assignment**
As a class, prepare to make a **video recording** of a dramatic delivery of Franklin's speech. Follow these steps to complete the assignment.

1. **Discuss the Speech** Use a class discussion to clarify your thoughts about the speech. Be prepared to share notes you made while reading the text as you and your classmates respond to these questions.
   - What is Franklin's opinion of the Constitution in its draft form?
   - How does he use concession and paradox as he argues his position?
   - What is his tone? How does Franklin's tone appeal to his audience and help persuade them of the validity of his opinion?
   - What are some of the ways in which Franklin's tone could be expressed in a dramatic reading?
2. **Practice and Present** Work together to decide who will read various parts of the speech. Have classmates take a few minutes to practice their parts individually, using Franklin's punctuation to help with phrasing and checking the pronunciation of challenging words. Next, practice together so that the reading moves smoothly from one speaker to the next. Then, present the speech as your teacher makes a video recording. Remember these points:
   - Be quiet and attentive while others are presenting their parts.
   - Use the tone and emphasis that you think Franklin might have used if he had delivered the speech himself.
   - Use appropriate gestures to convey key points.
3. **Evaluate the Video** Schedule sufficient time to watch the video. Allow about ten minutes for the follow-up discussion. Then, use the evaluation guide to analyze what you saw and heard. Encourage everyone to contribute. If possible, add the video to the class website or digital portfolio.

**EVALUATION GUIDE**

**Rate each statement on a scale of 1 (not demonstrated) to 5 (demonstrated). Be prepared to defend your rating, using examples.**

- [ ] Speakers clearly conveyed the text's meaning.
- [ ] Speakers held the audience's attention.
- [ ] Speakers used the tone and emphasis that Franklin likely intended when he wrote the speech.
- [ ] Speakers used appropriate gestures and body language.

**EVIDENCE LOG**

Before moving on to a new selection, go to your Evidence Log and record what you learned from Franklin's speech in the Convention.





## Speaking and Listening

1. **Discuss the Speech** Work with students to review what they have learned about the content and presentation of the speech.
2. **Practice and Present** You may want to review key elements of an effective speech with students.
   - **Posture** Sit or stand in a natural pose, without moving nervously.
   - **Gestures** Think about gestures and movements that may be appropriate to the speech and to Franklin's purpose.
   - **Voice** Speak in a natural voice, not too soft or too loud. Stress important words and phrases, never falling into a monotone or sing-song. Keep in mind Franklin's purpose and tone in the speech.

   Have partners work together to practice their parts of the speech. Encourage them to offer kind and helpful criticism. If time allows, have them take an additional practice together. Then instruct students to use the Presentation Evaluation Guide to provide feedback before presenting to the class.
3. **Evaluate the Video** Invite students to give positive criticism about their classmates' speeches and to offer useful comments. For more support, see **Speaking and Listening: Video Recording.**

Evidence Log Support students in completing their Evidence Log. This paced activity will help prepare them for the Performance-Based Assessment at the end of the unit.

### PERSONALIZE FOR LEARNING

**Strategic Support**

**Choral Reading** As an alternative to individual performances, students might practice their reading as a group effort, learning from each other about posture, gestures, and voice. Then they could also record the speech—with or without video—as a choral reading.

### FORMATIVE ASSESSMENT

**Speaking and Listening**

**If** students struggle with their initial speaking effort, **then** encourage them to study their partner's evaluation, and to practice another time, alone. For Reteach and Practice, see **Speaking and Listening: Video Recording (RP).**

**Selection Test** 

Administer the "Speech in the Convention" Selection Test, which is available in both print and digital formats online in Assessments.

# The American Revolution: Visual Propaganda

**AUDIO SUMMARIES**
Audio summaries of "The American Revolution: Visual Propaganda" are available online in both English and Spanish and can be assigned to students in the Interactive Teacher's Editon or Unit Resources. Assigning these summaries prior to reviewing the selection may help students build additional background knowledge and set a context for their first review.

## Summary

"The American Revolution: Visual Propaganda" is a selection of historical political cartoons and propaganda images drawn during the leadup to the Revolution. Image 1 includes a title, "JOIN, or DIE," and shows a snake cut into multiple pieces. Each piece is labeled with the abbreviation for one of the colonies.

Image 2 is an engraving that shows the Boston Massacre. In the image, British soldiers are shown shooting at colonists at close range. Image 3 is a cartoon that shows Americans in a cage hung from the liberty tree. They are being fed fish by British soldiers who seem to be laughing at them. Image 4 is a colonist's flag picturing a fully-coiled snake. The caption "Dont tred on me" explains that the snake is ready to strike. Image 5, "Poor Old England," is a political cartoon showing King George attempting to control the colonies.

### Insight

Viewing these images will help students understand how the colonists decided to rise up against England. It was neither overnight nor unanimous; people who supported revolution had to convince others that England's actions were intolerable.

ESSENTIAL QUESTION:
What is the meaning of freedom?

## Connection to Essential Question

"The American Revolution: Visual Propaganda" will help students gain insight into the Essential Question, "What is the meaning of freedom?" Emotionally compelling images that may misrepresent real events (as in the image of the Boston Massacre) may seem coercive to some students. This may lead to valuable discussions around questions such as *Does propaganda interfere with freedom? If so, is that interference justified in the name of a cause that will increase freedom more?*

WHOLE-CLASS LEARNING PERFORMANCE TASK
*Which statement do you find most compelling for Americans today: the Preamble to the Constitution or the first sentence of paragraph three of the Declaration of Independence?*

UNIT PERFORMANCE-BASED ASSESSMENT
*What are the most effective tools for establishing and preserving freedom?*

## Connection to Performance Tasks

**Whole-Class Learning Performance Task** As students consider the prompt, these images may help them decide which lines from the foundational documents are most important to their own generation.

**Unit Performance-Based Assessment** In this Performance Task, students will make an argument to answer the question: "What are the most effective tools for establishing and preserving freedom?" These images, and their topic, are a good source for them to draw on as they consider the question.

DIGITAL PERSPECTIVES

 Audio  Video  Document  Annotation Highlights  EL Highlights  Online Assessment

## LESSON RESOURCES

| | Making Meaning | Effective Expression |
|---|---|---|
| Lesson | **First Review**<br>**Close Review**<br>**Analyze the Media**<br>**Media Vocabulary** | **Speaking and Listening** |
| Instructional Standards | **RI.10** By the end of grade 11, read and comprehend literary nonfiction . . .<br>**RI.7** Integrate and evaluate multiple sources of information . . . | **SL.5** Make strategic use of digital media . . . |
| **STUDENT RESOURCES** | | |
| Available online in the Interactive Student Edition or Unit Resources | Selection Audio<br>First-Review Guide: Media: Art and Photography<br>Close-Review Guide: Media: Art and Photography | Evidence Log |
| **TEACHER RESOURCES** | | |
| **Selection Resources**<br>Available online in the Interactive Teacher's Edition or Unit Resources | Audio Summaries<br>Media Vocabulary | Speaking and Listening: Multimedia Presentation |
| **My Resources** | A Unit 1 Answer Key is available online and in the Interactive Teacher's Edition. | |

## Media Complexity Rubric: The American Revolution: Visual Propaganda

| Quantitative Measures | |
|---|---|
| Format and Length | 5 political cartoons with captions |
| **Qualitative Measures** | |
| Knowledge Demands<br>① ② ❸ ④ ⑤ | To fully understand cartoons, prior knowledge is needed about American Revolution (colonial protest against Great Britain, Boston Massacre, British blockade). |
| Structure<br>① ❷ ③ ④ ⑤ | Each visual is labeled with extended caption, making it easy to find information to explain visuals. |
| Language Conventionality and Clarity<br>① ② ❸ ④ ⑤ | Some of the cartoons contain slogans, abbreviations of colonies, and one engraving with archaic language (not all legible). Captions have explicit language with some complex sentences. |
| Levels of Meaning/Purpose<br>① ② ③ ❹ ⑤ | Cartoons use symbolism, humor, and irony, some of which are explained in captions; viewer needs to study details of cartoons and analyze explanations in order to interpret meaning. |

## Jump Start

FIRST REVIEW Read the following text from a fictional newspaper ad: IN QUICKSTER SHOES, YOU'LL FLY LIKE THE WIND. Then invite students to offer a picture that might accompany this text and encourage potential buyers. **Possible responses:** A handsome athlete flying across a finish line in Quickster shoes. A comic cheetah racing above a plain in Quickster shoes.

## The American Revolution: Visual Propaganda

Does a picture have a different effect from that of an article on the same topic? Is the picture's effect stronger or weaker? Why? Modeling these and other questions readers might ask will bring "The American Revolution: Visual Propaganda" to life and connect it to the Performance Task question. Selection audio and print capability for the selection is available in the Interactive Teacher's Edition.

## Media Vocabulary

Encourage students to discuss the media vocabulary. Have they seen the terms in texts before? Review the three terms and discuss how they are related. What is visual propaganda? How are "appeal" and "symbolism" alike? How are they different?

### FIRST REVIEW

The first time they go through the selection, students should perform the steps of the first review:

LOOK: Students should examine each image and read the accompanying information about each piece of propaganda.

NOTE: Ask students to note their observations about details that catch their attention.

CONNECT: Encourage students to connect to political propaganda that they have seen on television or in newspapers.

RESPOND: Students will demonstrate their understanding by answering questions and writing a description.

Point out to students that they will perform the first three steps concurrently as they are doing their first review. They will complete the Respond step after they have finished the first review. You may wish to print copies of the **First-Review Guide: Media: Art and Photography** for students to use.

MAKING MEANING

**About Visual Propaganda**

Whether printed on posters or in newspapers, sewn into the design of a flag, broadcast in television commercials, or presented in other forms, **visual propaganda** uses striking images (and sometimes simple slogans) to convey a persuasive message, especially during times of turmoil, such as war. One of the earliest examples can be seen in Mesopotamian carvings announcing a military victory in 2250 B.C.The Bayeux Tapestry provided woven visual propaganda about the Norman Conquest in A.D.1066. Visual propaganda was especially critical during the Russian Revolution in 1917, and during World War I, when the political poster was created to rouse patriotic fervor.

# The American Revolution: Visual Propaganda

## Media Vocabulary

These words or concepts will be useful to you as you analyze, discuss, and write about visual propaganda.

| | |
|---|---|
| **propaganda:** information, ideas, or rumors spread widely and deliberately to help or harm a person, group, movement, cause, or nation | • Creators of propaganda attempt to persuade people by presenting images and words that strongly suggest a particular *slant*, or viewpoint.<br>• Propaganda encourages people to react emotionally rather than logically—for example, to vote a certain way out of fear or to oppose a cause out of anger. |
| **appeal:** the ability to attract and engage an audience's mind or emotions | • A logical appeal (called *logos*) influences reason.<br>• An emotional appeal (called *pathos*) targets or manipulates people's feelings.<br>• Propaganda depends much more heavily upon pathos than upon logos. |
| **symbolism:** the use of images or objects to represent ideas or qualities | • Symbolism uses images and objects that many people associate with certain concepts, such as a flag to represent a country, a rose to represent love, or the color red to represent danger.<br>• In propaganda, symbolism appears primarily in visuals because it provides a quick way to convey meaning.<br>• An image or object can have more than one symbolic meaning. The meaning can vary from one culture to another. |

## First Review MEDIA: ART AND PHOTOGRAPHY

Apply these strategies as you conduct your first review.

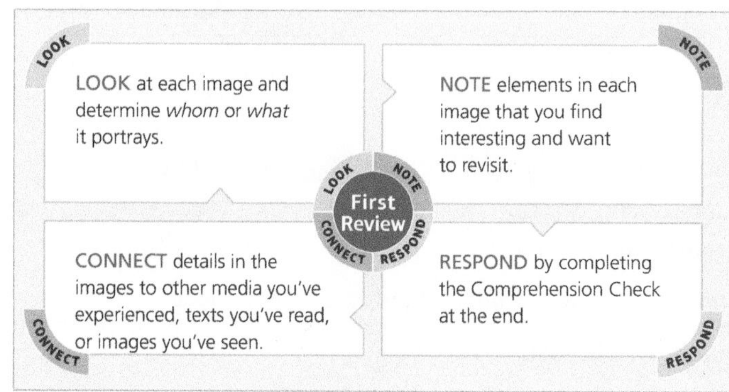


STANDARDS

**Reading Informational Text**
By the end of grade 11, read and comprehend literary nonfiction in the grades 11–CCR text complexity band proficiently, with scaffolding as needed at the high end of the range.





### PERSONALIZE FOR LEARNING

**English Language Support**

**Multiple-Meaning Words** Help students to understand the multiple meanings of *appeal* and *symbol*.

- *Appeal:* beg, attract.
- *Symbol*: a sign or mark, something that stands for something else.

Ask them to draw or act out each of these basic meanings. Finally, review the vocabulary chart showing the meaning of each word in relationship to propaganda. Connect these meanings to the basic meaning of each word. **ALL LEVELS**

DIGITAL PERSPECTIVES   

# The American Revolution: Visual Propaganda

BACKGROUND

The practice of persuading people with paintings, drawings, and other kinds of images has a long history in the United States, dating back to the colonial period. The images that follow are examples of visual propaganda published by both the colonists and the British in support of their respective causes.

SCAN FOR MULTIMEDIA 

**IMAGE 1: Join or Die** This political cartoon was published by Benjamin Franklin in 1754. The segments of the snake are labeled with the initials of American colonies. The purpose of the cartoon was to urge the colonies to unite against the French in the French and Indian War. During the American Revolution, it took on new meaning as a symbol of colonial protest against Great Britain.

NOTES





CLOSER REVIEW

## Analyze Impact of Images 

Students may have noted the vivid "Join, or Die" title in image 1 during their first review. Use this part of the image to help students understand how the powerful picture of the dismembered snake affected the colonists and led to their joining the British against the French in the French and Indian War. Encourage them to talk about what they noted. You may want to model a close review.

**NOTE:** Have students note details in the image that show the meaning of the snake as a symbol of the colonies, or have students participate while you note them.

**Possible response:** Students should note the abbreviations for the colonies on each section of the snake.

**QUESTION:** Guide students to consider what these details might tell them. Ask what a viewer can infer from the title of the image, the broken segments of the snake, and the open mouth of the snake. What impact do these details have? Accept student responses.

**Possible responses:** Students should note that the snake represents the colonies. Students can infer from these details that the snake will die if its individual parts are separated/not united. It will lose its power and authority.

**CONCLUDE:** Help students to formulate conclusions about the importance of these details in the image. Ask students why the artist chose a snake, rather than another animal such as a hawk.

**Possible response:** The snake is a creature that symbolizes power, cleverness, and even respect. Also, snakes produce fear in many people. The image would immediately convey the idea that a powerful creature had been rendered helpless and impotent because it was no longer whole.

Remind students that a graphic designer chooses **images** deliberately for impact. The designer's decisions determine whether the image has a strong effect on viewers or a weak one.

PERSONALIZE FOR LEARNING

**Strategic Support** Invite students to each write a word that comes to mind when they think of "snake." Then gather student responses and discuss why people are often fearful of snakes, their forked tongues, and their venom. Encourage students to share their opinions about whether or not a snake is an effective choice for this image.

## CLOSER REVIEW

### Analyze One-Sided Presentation

Review Image 2. The note points out that the details of the Boston Massacre differ between the image and what actually happened. Discuss with students how this one-sided presentation supported the colonial view that the British government and its soldiers were oppressive. Encourage students to talk about what they noted on their own. You may want to model a close review with the class.

**NOTE:** Have students note details in the print that show how the event differed from what is presented. Or have students participate while you note them. You might also want to point out that the engraver, Paul Revere, was a patriot who knew what had actually happened and was trying to make propaganda.

**QUESTION:** Guide students to consider what these details tell them about how propaganda may slant the truth. Ask what a viewer can infer from these slanted details, and accept student responses.

**Possible responses:** A slanted response shows only one side of the story. This print, for instance, does not take into account the British side of the story. This one-sidedness reflects the colonial viewpoint that the British were oppressive.

**CONCLUDE:** Help students to develop conclusions about the importance of each detail that deviates from the actual events of the Boston Massacre. Ask students why Paul Revere might have included details that he knew were not accurate.

**Possible response:** Paul Revere was creating propaganda, and so his concern was to make a point about the British—that they were cruel and unconcerned about the lives of Americans—and not to let the facts or the truth undermine his point.

Remind groups that the point of **propaganda** is to convey a viewpoint as effectively as possible, even if that means utilizing a **one-sided viewpoint** or a distortion of facts.

**IMAGE 2: The Boston Massacre**
Paul Revere engraved this image in 1770 after the Boston Massacre, in which several colonists were shot to death by British soldiers. Revere's depiction does not show the events exactly as they happened. For example, the Americans had been rioting against the British authorities when the shots were fired. Also, the British did not have a clear firing line. Rather, they had been surrounded and were struggling with the crowd.

NOTES





## DIGITAL PERSPECTIVES

**Enriching the Media** This print in Image 2 has been widely studied and discussed. Search online for a video of an analysis of Revere's print, such as those by the Discovery Channel or the American Antiquarian Society. Be sure to preview any video before showing it to the class. After the video has ended, lead a class discussion on why Revere may have included the inaccuracies that he did in the engraving.

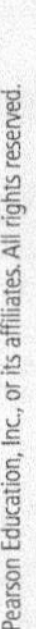

**IMAGE 3: The Bostonians in Distress** This print was published in a London newspaper during the British blockade of Boston in 1774. In the image, colonists feed caged Bostonians as the British navy continues to keep Boston Harbor closed. The image may have amused the British—but it may have provoked very different feelings among Americans who saw it.

NOTES



DIGITAL PERSPECTIVES

CLOSER REVIEW

## Analyze the Point of View of an Image

The caption of Image 3 explains that the print appeared in a British newspaper. Discuss with students how the print suggests the negative viewpoint of the artist about the Americans. Encourage students to talk about what they noted. You may want to model a close review with the class.

**NOTE:** Have students note details in the print that show the British view of the Americans, or have students participate while you note them.

**Possible Response:** Students may notice powerless Americans in a cage being fed.

**QUESTION:** Guide students to consider what these details tell them about the British view of Americans. Ask students to identify the artist's purpose in including such an image of the Americans. Do you agree that the image may have amused the British?

**Possible responses:** The artist was making a point, crudely, that Americans were beasts.

**CONCLUDE:** Help students to develop conclusions about the importance of each detail that shows the British viewpoint. Ask students why the artist might have included details that would likely insult Americans. In addition to amusing the British, what might have been another purpose of the artist?

**Possible response:** The artist was directing his propaganda to the English citizens, not the Americans. He likely didn't care how the Americans reacted, and may have even wanted to insult them. In addition to amusing the British, the artist probably wanted to use humor to enlist support for British actions in the colonies.

Remind students that **viewpoint** describes the way a writer or artist sees a person or situation. The viewpoint often directs the kinds of details the writer or artist includes.

PERSONALIZE FOR LEARNING

### English Language Support

**Background** Review Image 3 and consider offering students some additional background about the initial struggle between the colonies and England. Post the following timeline and discuss each entry: **1765:** Stamp Act (colonial tax on printed materials); **1766:** repeal of the Stamp Act; **1767:** Towns end Acts (taxes on goods, including tea); **1770:** Boston Massacre; **1773:** Boston Tea Party; **1773-1774:** British closing of Boston Harbor. **ALL LEVELS**

CLOSER REVIEW

## Analyze the Purpose of an Image

Students may have made a connection between Image 4 and Image 5. Both prints show a change in viewpoint and purpose from the earlier, related prints. Use Image 4 to help students understand that the colonies were now engaged in fighting for independence from the British. Its purpose was to show defiance and to issue a warning. Image 5 shows that British criticism was now turning from the colonies toward their king, who had not been able to win the war quickly. Encourage students to talk about what they noted. You may want to model a close review with the class.

**NOTE:** Have students note details in the prints that show the purpose of each one, or have students participate while you note them.

**QUESTION:** Guide students to consider what details, such as the coiled snake and the words "Don't tread on me," suggest in Image 4. What can they tell from the way the characters are drawn in Image 5? What details suggest that the character on the right is weak?

**Possible response:** The coiled snake looks dangerous, ready to attack, and the words are a warning. In Image 5, the king on the right may have control over the colonists, but they are pulling away, and the strings look like they might break. Because he has a crutch, he appears weak.

**CONCLUDE:** Help students to formulate conclusions about the importance of these details in the prints. Why might the artist have included these details?

**Possible response:** In Image 4, the coiled snake and the words "Don't tread on me" suggest that the colonies are strong and unafraid of confronting the British, that they won't tolerate their oppressive measures any longer. The artist was signaling the pride and confidence of the colonies. In Image 5, the details about the king and the posture of the colonists suggest the king is vulnerable even though he still holds power.

Remind students that a common **purpose of an image** as propaganda is to persuade an audience about a particular view.

**IMAGE 4: The Gadsden Flag** Colonist Christopher Gadsden created this flag during the American Revolution. Referencing Franklin's "Join or Die" cartoon, the flag is expressly directed at the English, showing a whole snake ready to strike.

NOTES

**IMAGE 5: Poor Old England** The caption for this cartoon reads, "Poor Old England, Endeavoring to Reclaim His Wicked American Children." The scene represents efforts by King George III to harness and control the colonists, who show no signs of either respecting or submitting to the king's wishes. This cartoon was published in London in 1777, fourteen months after the signing of the Declaration of Independence.

NOTES





PERSONALIZE FOR LEARNING

### Strategic Support

**Connect to Known Information** Review Image 5 with students and encourage them to make connections to information they already know. Post these topics at the top of a three-column chart: Subject Matter, Details, Purpose. Then have students focus on each topic as they study this image. You may want to use the same approach with other images here so students can compare and contrast the subject matter in each image.

## Comprehension Check

Use the chart to note details about each image. Identify the main people and/or objects in the image and the activity depicted. Use the captions where helpful. In the final column, express your idea about the overall purpose of the image as a piece of propaganda.

| IMAGE | PEOPLE AND/OR OBJECTS | ACTIVITY IN THE IMAGE | PURPOSE OF THE IMAGE |
|---|---|---|---|
| IMAGE 1  JOIN, or DIE. | a. See possible responses in Teacher's Edition. | b. | c. |
| IMAGE 2  | d. | e. | f. |
| IMAGE 3  | g. | h. | i. |
| IMAGE 4  DONT TREAD ON ME | j. | k. | l. |
| IMAGE 5  | m. | n. | o. |





DIGITAL PERSPECTIVES

## Comprehension Check

Possible responses:

a. A snake is cut into eight parts, each part labeled with the initials of a colony or region.

b. The snake appears to be dying because it has been cut apart.

c. The image seems meant to encourage colonial unity.

d. Colonists and British soldiers confront each other.

e. The British soldiers are firing into the crowd at close range, killing colonists.

f. The image seems meant to depict British authority as oppressive, cruel, and uncaring about the colonists.

g. Some Bostonians are in a cage. British cannons line the shore, pointing at ships in the distance.

h. Three men in a boat are trying to feed fish to the caged Bostonians.

i. The image is meant to mock the colonists who are being mistreated by the British.

j. A coiled rattlesnake looks ready to strike.

k. The snake warns, "Don't tred on me."

l. The image seems meant to encourage patriotic feeling and to warn Britain that by abusing the people in its American colonies, Britain will wind up being hurt.

m. The king is on the right, and the colonists are on the left.

n. The king is holding the strings that control the colonists, but they are leaning away from him. The king is also hobbled with a peg leg and a crutch.

o. The image expresses that the king's control over the colonies may be at a breaking point, given his weakness and the colonists' ability to pull away.

### CROSS-CURRICULAR PERSPECTIVES

**Art** After students review the propaganda prints, encourage them to draw their own political cartoon. Ask them to start with an idea related to politics, such as a law they might like to see changed or a local or state election. Next, have them jot down ideas for an image. Finally have them make a sketch and then a drawing.

TEACHING

MAKING MEANING

J O I N, or D I E.

THE AMERICAN REVOLUTION: VISUAL PROPAGANDA

## Jump Start

CLOSE REVIEW Ask students to consider what they learn about the American Revolution from studying the propaganda. Were they surprised to learn that Paul Revere slanted his image to fit his viewpoint about British oppression? What else did they find surprising?

## Close Review the Media

Remind students to look for elements and details they did not at first observe. You may wish to print copies of the **First-Review Guide: Media: Art and Photography** for students to use.

## Analyze the Media

Possible responses:

1. (a) The snake, an example of symbolism, represents the colonies. **DOK 2** (b) The flag stands for the colonists' courage and their defiance of British rule. **DOK 2**
2. (a) From the colonial point of view, both show that Great Britain is cruel. **DOK 2** (b) Britain is shown treating Americans with cruelty by firing on them, seemingly unprovoked (Image 2), and by treating them as animals and starving them (Image 3). **DOK 2**
3. The images suggest an American identity of underdogs and righteous fighters, while the British identity is characterized by unfairness and power. **DOK 3**
4. Responses will vary. Possible response: The inspiration for the American sense of freedom derived from a desperate and violent armed struggle, yet the struggle was based on principles and ideas about liberty. **DOK 3**

## Media Vocabulary

Ask the following questions to make sure students incorporate the vocabulary: How does each print/image represent propaganda? Does the print include any symbols/symbolism? For more support, see **Media Vocabulary**.

Possible responses:

1. Students may choose Images 2 or 3 and will comment on the violence portrayed in the British soldiers' actions.
2. Responses should express an understanding of the meaning of *resolve* and how it is expressed in the images.
3. (a) The image does not show that Americans had been rioting and does not show the Americans surrounding the British. (b) Answers should address the untrustworthy nature and the purpose of propaganda.

## Close Review

Revisit the images and your first-review notes. Write down any new observations that seem important. What **questions** do you have? What can you **conclude**?

## Analyze the Media

**CITE TEXTUAL EVIDENCE** to support your answers.

**Notebook** Respond to these questions.

1. (a) In Image 1, what does the snake represent? (b) **Connect** How does that representation shed light on the meaning of Image 4?
2. (a) **Compare and Contrast** From the colonial point of view, how do Images 2 and 3 have a similar slant? (b) **Analyze** Which details in the two images suggest that slant? Explain.
3. **Historical Perspectives** What do these images suggest about the colonists' growing sense of an American versus a British sense of identity? Explain.
4. **Essential Question:** *What is the meaning of freedom?* What have you learned about American freedoms from analyzing these images?

LANGUAGE DEVELOPMENT

## Media Vocabulary

Use these words as you discuss and write about the images.

propaganda appeal symbolism

1. Which image most clearly presents the British as aggressors in the conflict with the colonies? Explain your choice, citing details from the image.
2. Which image most clearly expresses the colonists' resolve in their fight against Britain? Explain your choice, citing details from the image.
3. **(a)** In what ways does Image 2 distort facts in order to present a story that is favorable to one side? **(b)** What does this image suggest about propaganda as a source of reliable information? Explain.

STANDARDS

Reading Informational Text

- Analyze and evaluate the effectiveness of the structure an author uses in his or her exposition or argument, including whether the structure makes points clear, convincing, and engaging.
- Integrate and evaluate multiple sources of information presented in different media or formats as well as in words in order to address a question or solve a problem.





**FORMATIVE ASSESSMENT**

### Analyze the Media

- **If** students fail to cite evidence from the notes or prints, **then** remind them to support their ideas with specific details from these sources.

### Media Vocabulary

- **If** students struggle to use the vocabulary words in their discussion or writing, **then** have them review the definitions again and repeat these questions: How does each image represent propaganda? Does the image include symbols/symbolism?

## Speaking and Listening

**Assignment**

With a partner, create an imaginary candidate who is campaigning for a major office, and develop a **political infomercial,** or extended, informative advertisement. Design and write the script for a presentation, including images that take a particular slant. Include a campaign slogan and a logo. As you work, take into account aspects of propaganda, appeal, and symbolism. Record and present the infomercial to the class.

TIP

PROCESS

Make sure that you and your partner agree to and understand the slant that your infomercial will present. Doing so will help you choose images and decide what to say about them.

**1. Plan the Project** To help you prepare your infomercial, consider these questions.

- What ideas does the candidate represent? What is his or her stance on issues such as education, the economy, and national defense?
- What facts from real life will you include? Which sources will you research for that information? Which visuals will best present that information in a way that helps the candidate's cause?
- How will you display your ideas and images? For example, you might create a video, use presentation software, or project on a whiteboard.

**2. Consider Image Choices** As you select or create images, consider the appeal that each one will have. For example, decide whether it adds emotional impact, symbolism, information, or serves another purpose.

EVIDENCE LOG

Before moving on to a new selection, go to your Evidence Log and record what you learned from "The American Revolution: Visual Propaganda."

| ELEMENT | PURPOSE |
|---|---|
| | |
| | |
| | |
| | |
| | |

**3. Prepare the Script** Once you have a final set of images and ideas, decide how you will weave them together to create your infomercial.

- Decide on the order of presentation. Add transitions to link related ideas.
- Create a pacing guide to determine the amount of time you will spend on each image.
- Choose which partner will narrate, and allow time to practice.

**4. Present and Discuss** Record the infomercial and share it with the class. After all of the infomercials have been presented, discuss how the types of techniques and images students used compare to that of American Revolutionary War propaganda.

STANDARDS

Speaking and Listening

Make strategic use of digital media in presentations to enhance understanding of findings, reasoning, and evidence and to add interest.





PERSONALIZE FOR LEARNING

### Challenge

**Research** Encourage students to research additional political cartoons from the Revolutionary War era, such as "The Repeal, Or The Funeral of Miss Americ-Stamp," "A Society of Patriotic Ladies, at Edenton in North Carolina," or "The American Rattlesnake." Ask them to provide background, a note/caption, and an explanation of the significance of each piece of propaganda.

DIGITAL PERSPECTIVES

## Speaking and Listening

If partners have trouble developing a candidate, suggest that they base their candidate on a real-life politician. For a slogan, they could brainstorm words that describe their candidate, and use one or more words to create a slogan and a logo.

1. **Plan the Project** Encourage partners to write out answers to each question, so that they can better prepare their infomercial. After they have answered each question, they can develop a step-by-step plan for moving forward. The chart should help them with creating images for their project.
2. **Consider Image Choices** Encourage students to be creative in searching for images, which can use humor or juxtaposition to convey ideas. Guide them to use appropriate images.
3. **Prepare the Script** Partners might put each image on an index card, so that they can reorder or remove images as they progress. Once they have determined the order in which images will be presented, they can decide on pacing and choosing a narrator.
4. **Present and Discuss** Invite students to offer reflections on how the propaganda gallery influenced their own infomercial. Did their work on the infomercial help them better understand and appreciate the colonial-era images? For more support, see **Speaking and Listening: Multimedia Presentation.**

MAKE IT INTERACTIVE

Using the Interactive Teacher's Edition, project one image at a time from "The American Revolution: Visual Propaganda." Read each of the following cartoon-style captions. Ask students how such a caption would change the impact of each image.

- Say it ain't so!
- End British tyranny NOW!
- Free America today!
- You asked for it!
- I've got a hold on you!

Evidence Log Support students in completing their Evidence Logs. This paced activity will help prepare them for the Performance-Based Assessment at the end of the unit.

### FORMATIVE ASSESSMENT

### Speaking and Listening

- **If** students struggle with creating images for their infomercial, **then** have them go online and see a few campaign commercials of real-life candidates.

## Jump Start

Should the Founding Fathers have declared independence from Great Britain? Ask students to write two sentences about their first reaction to the question. Do they feel inclined to say "Yes" or "No"? What is the main reason for their first reaction? Have students share what they wrote.

## Write an Argument

Make sure students understand what they are being asked to do in the Assignment. Point out that there had been attempts at reconciliation with Great Britain before the colonies declared their independence.

Students should complete the assignment using word processing software to take advantage of editing tools and features.

## Elements of an Argument

Remind students that an effective argument, such as "Totally Free?" contains the listed required elements, is organized in a logical manner, and uses word choice and tone to create a sense of seriousness and authority.

**MAKE IT INTERACTIVE**

Project "Totally Free?" from the Interactive Teacher's Edition and have students identify the elements of an argument in this essay. Tell them to find the author's claim, a counterclaim, reasons, evidence, and the author's concluding statement.

PERFORMANCE TASK: WRITING FOCUS

WRITING TO SOURCES

- DECLARATION OF INDEPENDENCE
- PREAMBLE TO THE CONSTITUTION
- BILL OF RIGHTS
- SPEECH IN THE CONVENTION
- THE AMERICAN REVOLUTION: VISUAL PROPAGANDA

# Write an Argument

You have just read a variety of documents from the early years of our nation. Each text reveals, in its own way, the principles that guided the nation's founders and other Americans of that era.

**Assignment**

Write a brief **argumentative essay** in which you address this question:

> **Which statement do you find most compelling for Americans today: the Preamble to the Constitution or the first sentence of paragraph three of the Declaration of Independence?**

Begin by choosing a position and stating a claim. Then, use specific details from the texts, historical examples, and your observations of our society today to support your claim. Make sure that your reasons link directly to your claim.

**Tool Kit**
Student Model of an Argument

### Elements of an Argument

In an **argument** a writer articulates a position, viewpoint, belief, or stand on an issue. Well-written arguments may convince readers to change their minds about an issue or to take a certain action.

An effective argument contains these elements:

- a precise claim
- consideration of counterclaims, or opposing positions, and a discussion of their strengths and weaknesses
- logical organization that makes clear connections among claim, counterclaims, reasons, and evidence
- word choices that are appropriate for a given audience
- clear reasoning and well-chosen evidence
- a concluding statement or section that logically completes the argument
- formal and objective language and tone
- error-free grammar, including correct and consistent use of verbs

ACADEMIC VOCABULARY

As you craft your argument, consider using some of the academic vocabulary you learned in the beginning of the unit.

confirm
demonstrate
supplement
establish
conviction

**Model Argument** For a model of a well-crafted argument see the Launch Text, "Totally Free?" Review the Launch Text for examples of the elements of an effective argument. You will look more closely at these elements as you prepare to write your own argument.

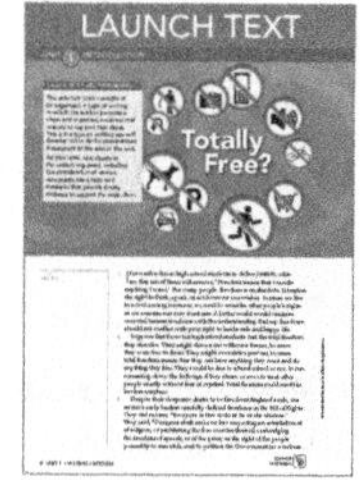


STANDARDS

Writing

- Write arguments to support claims in an analysis of substantive topics or texts, using valid reasoning and relevant and sufficient evidence.
- Write routinely over extended time frames and shorter time frames for a range of tasks, purposes, and audiences.

## Prewriting / Planning

**Break Down the Prompt** Reading the prompt carefully and thoroughly can assist you in your planning. Complete these sentences to ensure that you understand the task that you are being asked to accomplish.

1. I am supposed to write a(n) an argumentive essay.
2. In my own words, the question I must answer is which of the two statements is more compelling.
3. My writing must include a claim, a counterclaim, reasoning, evidence, and a conclusion.
4. I need to use examples from from websites and from the texts in Unit 1 as evidence and connect my ideas to connect my claim, counterclaim, reasons, and evidence in an organized way that makes sense to my readers.

**Develop a Claim** Start by deciding on a basic response to the question in the prompt. Then, develop your response into a claim. Use the sentence frame below to do so. Then, as you gather details and clarify your ideas, adjust your claim to reflect your new thinking.

I believe that ______________________________

______________________________

because ______________________________

______________________________.

**Gather Evidence** The assignment asks you to use a variety of evidence, including examples from history, to support your position. In what sorts of resources might you find the types of historical information you need? Write some possibilities here.

______ ______ ______

______ ______ ______

______ ______ ______

Always confirm your evidence by using more than one source.

**Connect Across Texts** The prompt asks you to connect your ideas to the texts you have read. The Launch Text shows you two means of doing this:

- You may **paraphrase**, or restate ideas in your own words. The Launch Text presents a paraphrase in the discussion of Roosevelt's "Four Freedoms" speech (his 1941 State of the Union address).
- You may also use **direct quotations**, as happens when the Launch Text quotes from the Declaration of Independence.

### EVIDENCE LOG

Review your Evidence Log and identify key details you may want to cite in your argument.

### STANDARDS

Writing
- Introduce precise, knowledgeable claim(s), establish the significance of the claim(s), distinguish the claim(s) from alternate or opposing claims, and create an organization that logically sequences claim(s), counterclaims, reasons, and evidence.
- Develop claim(s) and counterclaims fairly and thoroughly, supplying the most relevant evidence for each while pointing out the strengths and limitations of both in a manner that anticipates the audience's knowledge level, concerns, values, and possible biases.





DIGITAL PERSPECTIVES

## Prewriting/Planning

**Develop a Claim** Remind students that the first step in writing an argument is to take a position on the question. Explain that for this assignment, their claim will stem from whether they think the Founders should have tried harder to reconcile with Great Britain instead of declaring independence.

**Gather Evidence** Have students review their Evidence Log to find possible support for their claim. Remind them to go back and review the selections in Unit 1 to identify additional or stronger evidence for their argument (or—possibly—evidence that seems to refute their claim). Students should also make a plan for identifying and citing evidence from other sources.

**Connect Across Texts** Make sure students understand the difference between paraphrasing and using direct quotations. If you want students to include footnotes that cite their sources, give them a format model for quoting from books (including the Student Edition), magazines, and websites.

### AUTHOR'S PERSPECTIVE Kelly Gallagher, M.Ed.

**Pump up the Volume of Writing** Spend some time talking to kids about why they should write—not just how. Students should write more than the teacher can grade. To help students get the most from their writing, teachers can use techniques such as these:

- **Confer** Teachers can achieve more in a two-minute conference than they can by spending five-to-seven minutes writing comments on a paper. Developing writers need face time with the most experienced writer in the class—the teacher.
- **Model** Teachers can model how they write by frequently writing in front of students. Show students that effective writing extends far past correctness. Teachers can do this in short bursts, and model authentic writing, whether brainstorming a topic, working to add details, or revising to find the right word. Note: other times the teacher can bring a model to class that has already been written for the students to study.
- **Share models of excellent writing.** Show students models from professional writers and from other students. As they study mentor texts, students begin to see the moves a writer has made, and they can work to emulate those moves.
- **Use a rubric.** Experiment with changing the rubric. Encourage students to help you build it. This creates buy-in when the students see that each rubric is personalized to some degree to their needs.

## Enriching Writing With Research

**Using Research** Encourage students to consult websites that contain reliable content on this period in U.S. history. Remind them that sites with addresses ending with *.gov, .edu,* and *.org.* are often more reliable that those ending with *.com*. Students can use their local library's online catalog to find print materials that relate to their topic. Tell students that, besides nonfiction books (including biographies), well-researched works of historical fiction can be good sources.

### Read It

Point out that World War II was already raging in early 1941, when FDR gave his State of the Union speech. (However, the United States did not enter the war until December of that year.) Ask students how FDR's "four freedoms" might have been related to the war.

**Using a Search Engine** Direct students' attention to the third box down in the flowchart. Ask why the author of "Totally Free?" might have chosen to focus on FDR's "Four Freedoms" speech rather than on options 1 or 3.

PERFORMANCE TASK: WRITING FOCUS

### ENRICHING WRITING WITH RESEARCH

**Using Research** A strong argument is always based on sound evidence and thoughtful, logical support. You may find support for your ideas in online or library resources.

### Read It

This excerpt from the Launch Text provides an example of the use of researched evidence. After doing some reading, the writer decided to use Franklin D. Roosevelt's "Four Freedoms" speech to support the contention that freedoms should not clash.

The writer located a specific speech from American history to support the claim that we need to consider other people's rights and needs as we exercise our own freedoms.

LAUNCH TEXT EXCERPT

In his 1941 State of the Union address, President Franklin Roosevelt identified four key freedoms as being basic human rights: freedom of speech and expression, freedom of worship, freedom from want, and freedom from fear. Those are not freedoms that one finds in a dictatorship. Nor are they freedoms that we grant to each other without the oversight and protection of government institutions. With the government's help, and the writing of laws, my freedom from want does not allow me to steal your food, and your freedom of speech does not let you publish lies about me. We are free, but only up to the point at which our freedoms clash.

**Using a Search Engine** As you develop an argument, you may not have specific examples and reasons in mind. You may need to use a search engine wisely to develop your argument's support. The writer of the Launch Text may have used a path like this.

To narrow the search, the writer used a phrase rather than just the word *freedom*.

Search: Freedom in American History

Result: A website on different meanings of freedom over time in America

Action: Skim article to locate interesting and relevant examples.
1. Civil War: A new birth of freedom
2. World War II: The Four Freedoms
3. Cold War: The Free World

Search: The Four Freedoms

Notice how one search led to a second, more specific search, and so on until the writer found the best possible support for the claim.

Result: An article about the "Four Freedoms" speech from the FDR Presidential Library

Actions: Skim article to learn about the Four Freedoms. Decide whether they apply to the original argument—and, if so, how.



AUTHOR'S PERSPECTIVE **Jim Cummins, Ph.D.**

**Writing Enhances Student Identity** Writing is an expression of oneself, and writing projects that self into the new social spheres. However, students learning English are often defined by what they are missing rather than by what they possess. While teaching writing through the Performance Tasks in *myPerspectives*, you may want to supplement the writing instruction and practice for English learners by using *identity texts*. These texts allow students to invest their identities into their writing. The results hold a mirror up to students and reflect their identities in a positive light. Teachers can use this process:

1. Encourage students to have a hand in picking the topic to ensure they are writing about something that reflects themselves or their identities. Have students write their drafts in English, illustrate them, and work with various sources, such as parents and older students fluent in their home language, to translate the drafts into their home language.
2. Publish these texts. Help students share identity texts with multiple audiences including peers, teachers, parents, grandparents, sister classes, and the media. It is critical that students share their writing with broad audiences to build this positive experience. Students are likely to receive

College and Career Readiness

### Write It

Review the facts and evidence that you have gathered. Use this flowchart to organize your materials.

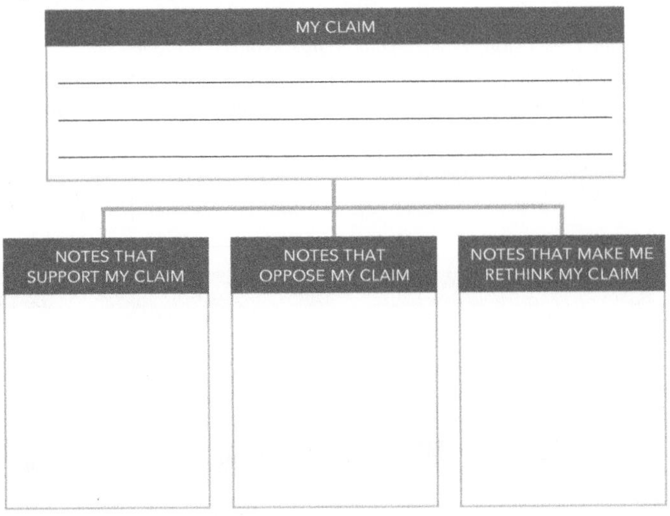


**Notes That Support My Claim** Some information you find may offer direct and fairly obvious support for your claim. Other information may require some interpretation or explanation on your part. For example, in the excerpt from the Launch Text, the writer analyzed the researched information about Roosevelt's speech and demonstrated how it supports the claim.

**Notes That Oppose My Claim** As you read and review sources, you may find some material that contradicts your claim. Consider working that material into the discussion of a counterclaim. You might start in one of these ways:

- Although [research source] states that ________, I believe that ________.
- [Research source] claims that ________. Nevertheless, it is clear that ________.
- Despite [research source]'s assertion that ________, it seems more likely that ________.

Remember to supply evidence that supports your rejection of any counterclaim that you mention.

**Notes That Make Me Rethink My Claim** Sometimes, your research will send you in a new direction. It may change your original ideas and make you rethink your claim. Do not be afraid to scrap your original plan if new evidence changes your mind. Just as architects or engineers do, good writers frequently discard a flawed plan and start over.

TIP

CONVENTIONS
Be sure to quote sources correctly.

- Run a short quotation from a source into the text and enclose it in quotation marks.
- Set off a long quotation in a block with all lines indented from the left. Such block quotations do not use quotation marks.

STANDARDS

Writing

- Develop claim(s) and counterclaims fairly and thoroughly, supplying the most relevant evidence for each while pointing out the strengths and limitations of both in a manner that anticipates the audience's knowledge level, concerns, values, and possible biases.
- Gather relevant information from multiple authoritative print and digital sources, using advanced searches effectively; assess the strengths and limitations of each source in terms of the task, purpose, and audience; integrate information into the text selectively to maintain the flow of ideas, avoiding plagiarism and overreliance on any one source and following a standard format for citation.



DIGITAL PERSPECTIVES

## Write It

**Notes That Support My Claim** If necessary, have students reread the Launch Text excerpt that appears on the student page. Ask students to judge how successfully the author uses FDR's "four freedoms" to explain what she means by "the point at which our freedoms clash."

**Notes That Oppose My Claim** Ask students what the Launch Text author uses as a counterclaim in "Totally Free?" If necessary, direct them to paragraph 2 of her essay:

> Suppose that those ten high-school students had the total freedom they describe. They might drive a car without a license, because they were free to do so. They might even drive *your* car, because total freedom must mean that they can have anything they want and do anything they like. They would be free to attend school or not, to run screaming down the hallways if they chose, or even to treat other people cruelly without fear of reprisal. Total freedom could result in lawless mayhem.

The author claims that "human history is a balancing act between individual freedom and the need to protect the community." The author then contends that "total freedom" is not an advisable option. Paragraph 2 refers to a counterclaim (by ten students) that "Freedom means that I do anything I want." The Launch Text author says in paragraph 2 that allowing teenagers free rein "could result in lawless mayhem."

positive feedback and affirmation of self by providing true audiences with which to share their work.

Writing and publishing identity texts helps ELL students take active control and ownership of the learning process and invest their identities in their drafts.

## Drafting

**Organize Your Text** Ask volunteers to distinguish the *elements* of an argument (claim, counterclaims, valid reasoning, evidence, and concluding statement) from the organization of an argument (introduction, a body, and a conclusion.)

Ask how an argumentative essay might benefit from having a formal style without slang, contractions, or personal anecdotes.

**Write a First Draft** As students write their first draft, they should focus on getting their ideas on paper and on incorporating all of the elements of an argument. Tell students to assume that their readers have only basic prior knowledge of the topic. Encourage students to grab their readers' attention in the introduction by including an interesting and relevant quotation from one of the texts in Unit 1, or a brief, compelling historical anecdote that helps to usher in their claim.

PERFORMANCE TASK: WRITING FOCUS

## Drafting

**Organize Your Text** Your text should include three parts:

- the **introduction**, in which you state your claim
- the **body**, in which you provide analysis, supporting reasons, and evidence. Each paragraph of your body should focus on one idea and evidence that directly supports it.
- the **conclusion**, in which you summarize or restate your claim

Use a formal style to get your points across. Avoid slang, contractions, and personal ("I") statements. The following chart will help you organize your thoughts.

Topic: ____________________

Question: ____________________

| CLAIM | COUNTERCLAIM |
|---|---|
| | |
| **EVIDENCE** | **EVIDENCE** |
| 1. ______ | 1. ______ |
| 2. ______ | 2. ______ |
| 3. ______ | 3. ______ |
| **REASONS/SUPPORT FOR EVIDENCE** | **REASONS/SUPPORT FOR EVIDENCE** |
| 1. ______ | 1. ______ |
| 2. ______ | 2. ______ |
| 3. ______ | 3. ______ |

**Write a First Draft** Refer to your chart as you write your first draft. Make sure to include a precise claim and to address counterclaims where possible. Write a conclusion that follows logically from your argument, supports your claim, and adds interest to your writing.

**Use Rhetorical Devices** **Rhetorical devices** are patterns of language that create emphasis and build emotion. While they do not replace sound reasoning and evidence, they can help to present your ideas in a memorable way. Consider using one or more of the following rhetorical devices in your essay:

- **Repetition:** Repeat key words to focus your argument.
- **Parallelism:** Repeat related ideas in the same grammatical structures.
- **Analogy:** Use comparisons to help readers grasp ideas.

STANDARDS

Writing

- Introduce precise, knowledgeable claim(s), establish the significance of the claim(s), distinguish the claim(s) from alternate or opposing claims, and create an organization that logically sequences claim(s), counterclaims, reasons, and evidence.
- Provide a concluding statement or section that follows from and supports the argument presented.





PERSONALIZE FOR LEARNING

### English Language Support

**Organizing Text** Support students as they complete the chart on the student page. Tell them that they do not need to write complete sentences in their chart—they should just write words and phrases that will help them remember what to include in their first draft. Give examples to help students distinguish between the terms *evidence* and *reason(s)*. For example, you might point out that muddy paw prints on a kitchen floor are *evidence* (clues or proof) that an animal has been there. Then point out that some people don't want to live with pets. Ask, "What might their *reasons* be?" **Possible responses:** They might be afraid of animals. They might not like cleaning up after animals. They might not have enough money to pay for food, cat litter, visits to the vet, and so on. **EMERGING/EXPANDING**

LANGUAGE DEVELOPMENT: CONVENTIONS

## Create Cohesion: Tense Sequence

A **sequence of tenses** means that there is agreement among the tenses of verbs in related sentences or clauses. In formal writing, it is important to maintain **consistency of tense** from one sentence to the next unless the time frame of the action changes.

### Read It

The Launch Text uses verbs correctly to point to both past and current situations.

*President Franklin Roosevelt **identified** four key freedoms… (past)*

*These **are** not freedoms that one **finds** in a dictatorship. (present)*

Within a sentence, verbs are consistent in tense if the actions are consistent in time.

*Because we **live** in a society, we **need** to consider other people's rights and needs as we **exercise** our own freedoms. (all present tense)*

When actions vary in time, the writer applies logic to sequence the verbs. In this example, the action of developing laws took place in the past but still applies today, and those laws restrict and protect us in the present.

*Our government **has developed** laws that both **restrict** us and **protect** us. (present perfect; present; present)*

### Write It

As you draft your essay, use logic to sequence verbs. Use the tense of the independent clause plus any key transitional words to determine the tense of dependent clauses. In most compound sentences, keep the tense consistent. Here are some examples.

| | |
|---|---|
| **present + past** | I **am** eager to read the biography that you **recommended.** |
| **present perfect + present** | Now that she **has mastered** French, Alice **enjoys** Quebec. |
| **present + future** | Until the senator **returns,** I **will wait** patiently in her office. |
| **present + present** | Actors **recite** the Bill of Rights, and the audience **listens** raptly. |
| **past perfect + past perfect** | The colonists **had complained,** but the king **had ignored** them. |
| **future + future** | We **will follow** the law, or we **will face** the consequences. |
| **past + past perfect** | We **arrived** in plenty of time, but the tour guide **had left.** |

TIP

USAGE

Change tense only when the timing of an action changes. In general:

- Use the present tense when writing about your own ideas and opinions, factual topics that are widely known, or actions in a written work.
- Use the past tense when writing about past events or completed studies or analyses.

STANDARDS

**Writing**
Use words, phrases, and clauses as well as varied syntax to link the major sections of the text, create cohesion, and clarify the relationships between claim(s) and reasons, between reasons and evidence, and between claim(s) and counterclaims.

**Language**
Demonstrate command of the conventions of standard English grammar and usage when writing or speaking.





DIGITAL PERSPECTIVES

## Create Cohesion: Tense Sequence

### Read It

Emphasize that when you are writing about historical events, verb tenses are very important—they signal the time frame you are writing about. Display the following examples and have students identify the underlined verbs' tenses:

- I love historical fiction novels, but my sister prefers biographies. (two present-tense verbs)
- Do you know that King Henry VIII married six different wives? (one present-tense and one past-tense verb)
- He beheaded two of them and divorced another two. One died during her marriage to Henry, and one survived when Henry died. (five past-tense verbs)

**MAKE IT INTERACTIVE**

Project "Totally Free?" from the Interactive Teacher's Edition and ask students to identify additional examples of verb tenses. Here is an example from paragraph 3:

- ...our nation's early leaders carefully **defined** freedoms in the Bill of Rights. (past tense)
- They **did not say**, "Everyone **is** free to do as he or she **chooses**." (past tense, present tense, present tense)
- They **said**, "Congress **shall make** no law respecting an establishment of religion...." (past tense, future tense)

HOW LANGUAGE WORKS

**Create Cohesion: Tense Sequence** Ask students to look closely at excerpts from various works of literature and identify verb tenses in related sentences. Here is an example from Jane Austen's novel *Persuasion,* Chapter 1:

Vanity was the beginning and the end of Sir Walter Elliot's character; vanity of person and of situation. (past tense) He had been remarkably handsome in his youth; and, at fifty-four, was still a very fine man. (pluperfect tense and past tense) Few women could think more of their personal appearance than he did, nor could the valet of any new made lord be more delighted with the place he held in society. (present conditional tense, past tense, present conditional tense) He considered the blessing of beauty as inferior only to the blessing of a baronetcy; and the Sir Walter Elliot, who united these gifts, was the constant object of his warmest respect and devotion. (past tense, past tense, past tense)

## Revising

### Evaluating Your Draft

Before students begin revising their writing, they should first evaluate their draft to make sure it contains all of the required elements, is organized in a logical manner, and adheres to the norms and conventions of argumentative writing.

### Revising for Focus and Organization

**Strong, Logical Connections** Students should also ensure that their argument flows smoothly, and that they used correct verb tenses and transitions to link ideas together and create cohesion. You might suggest that students read their arguments aloud to a partner or record themselves reading as a strategy for identifying necessary revisions.

### Revising for Evidence and Elaboration

**Word Choice and Style** Remind students as they revise their argument that using precise language and maintaining a formal tone is an important part of argumentative writing. Remind students that the purpose of an argument is to convince readers of a claim, so the word choices and tone they use should match that of a formal conversation with a teacher—not that of an informal conversation with a friend.

PERFORMANCE TASK: WRITING FOCUS

## Revising

### Evaluating Your Draft

Use this checklist to evaluate the effectiveness of your first draft. Then, use your evaluation and the instructions on this page to guide your revision.

| FOCUS AND ORGANIZATION | EVIDENCE AND ELABORATION | CONVENTIONS |
|---|---|---|
| ☐ Provides an introduction that establishes a precise claim. | ☐ Develops the claim and responds to counterclaims by using facts and details that provide relevant evidence and reasons. | ☐ Attends to the norms and conventions of the discipline, especially regarding sequence and consistency of verb tenses. |
| ☐ Distinguishes the claim from opposing claims. | ☐ Provides adequate examples for each major idea. | |
| ☐ Provides a conclusion that follows from the argument. | ☐ Uses word choices and rhetorical devices effectively. | |
| ☐ Establishes a logical organization and develops a progression throughout the argument. | ☐ Establishes and maintains a formal style and an objective tone. | |
| ☐ Uses words, phrases, and clauses to clarify the relationships between and among ideas. | | |

**WORD NETWORK**

Include interesting words from your Word Network in your argument.

### Revising for Focus and Organization

**Strong, Logical Connections** An argument should be built on sound logic that includes strong reasons, definitive evidence, and clear connections. Consider these strong and weak reasons for a pay increase. Connecting words that clarify relationships between ideas are underlined.

- Strong Reasoning: I deserve a raise, as shown by the fact that clients consistently ask to work with me.
- Strong Reasoning: I deserve a raise because my contract calls for an increase after six months.
- Weak Reasoning: Since my brother makes more than I do, I deserve a raise.
- Weak Reasoning: I deserve a raise because I want one.

### Revising for Evidence and Elaboration

**Word Choice and Style** As you work to create an objective, formal tone, consider replacing informal words and phrases with more formal choices. Here are some examples of informal and formal transitional words and phrases.

| INSTEAD OF . . . | USE . . . |
|---|---|
| also | in addition |
| anyway | nevertheless |
| basically | in summary |
| plus | furthermore |
| so | therefore |

**STANDARDS**

**Writing**

Establish and maintain a formal style and objective tone while attending to the norms and conventions of the discipline in which they are writing.





### HOW LANGUAGE WORKS

**Verb Tenses** As students revise their arguments, remind them to use correct verb tenses and transitions to connect and show relationships among people and events and to create cohesion in their writing. You may want to show a few examples of sentences in which verb tenses are used first incorrectly, then correctly. For example:

**Incorrect:** Even today we admire Thomas Jefferson because he stands up for his beliefs and would support them strongly in writing.

**Correct:** Even today we admire Thomas Jefferson because he stood up for his beliefs and did a fine job of supporting them strongly in writing.

PEER REVIEW

Exchange arguments with a classmate. Use the checklist to evaluate your classmate's argument and provide supportive feedback.

1. Is the claim clear?
   ☐ yes ☐ no If no, explain what confused you.
2. Do you find the argument convincing?
   ☐ yes ☐ no If no, tell what you think might be missing.
3. Does the essay conclude in a logical way?
   ☐ yes ☐ no If no, indicate what you might change.
4. What is the strongest part of your classmate's argument? Why?

## Editing and Proofreading

**Edit for Conventions** Reread your draft for accuracy and consistency. Correct errors in grammar and word usage. Check for consistency of verb tense in related sentences and clauses.

**Proofread for Accuracy** Read your draft carefully, looking for errors in spelling and punctuation. Be sure to capitalize place names and names of documents correctly.

## Publishing and Presenting

Post your claim and your strongest reason or piece of evidence on your class's online discussion board. Ask classmates to comment on your post. Review others' posts and point out what you like best about what you read.

## Reflecting

Consider what you learned by writing your text. Did you use research effectively to find support for your claim? What did you find to be the most difficult part of this assignment? Why? Think about what you might do differently the next time you write an argument.

STANDARDS

**Writing**

Develop and strengthen writing as needed by planning, revising, editing, rewriting, or trying a new approach, focusing on addressing what is most significant for a specific purpose and audience.





DIGITAL PERSPECTIVES

## Peer Review

Remind students to review their classmate's work for clarity and completeness—they do not need to agree with the writer's position. However, they might suggest a counterclaim that could strengthen their classmate's argument.

## Editing and Proofreading

As students proofread, they should check for correct grammar, spelling, and punctuation as well as the items listed on the Student Edition page. Remind them that although many word processing programs catch grammar and spelling errors, they are not foolproof. Students should still review their work manually.

## Publishing and Presenting

Before students post their claims and evidence, and review their classmates' posts, remind them to:

- Include in their post only their claim and their strongest piece of evidence.
- Keep comments positive.
- Use correct grammar, capitalization, and punctuation. (This isn't texting with friends—it's a written conversation with classmates about an academic topic.)
- Avoid using all capitals—it reads as if you're yelling.
- Don't just agree; move the discussion forward by building on classmates' ideas.
- Be brief and clear. Carefully read your post before you press "Enter."

## Reflecting

Students should reflect not only on their argument and the process of writing it, but also on the comments received from their peers.

PERSONALIZE FOR LEARNING

| **Strategic Support**<br>**Using Online Discussion Boards**<br>Monitor the discussion on the class's online discussion board. If the discussion seems stalled at any point, post your own questions and comments to move the discussion along. Model how to build on other posters' ideas. For example: | **Pablo:** My claim is that the excerpt from the Declaration of Independence is more compelling to us today because it expresses ideas that are more relevant to today's society: we are all created equal and have equal rights. The Preamble to the Constitution is more about the issues of that time in history. | **Ana:** I pretty much agree with Pablo, but I don't think we should overlook how the Preamble is relevant. We still have to be aware and fight for justice, domestic tranquility, and all the other purposes it lists. |
|---|---|---|

# OVERVIEW

## SMALL-GROUP LEARNING

### What is the meaning of freedom?

In the Constitution, "freedom"encompasses many ideas about the intentions of the United States as a developing nation. It is "We the people," that do ordain and establish the Constitution. The words show that the Constitution is a deed—an action, not just words. During Small-Group Learning, students will read selections that explore both the ideals and the compromises that were needed to form a union called the United States.

### Small-Group Learning Strategies

Review the Learning Strategies with students and explain that they will develop strategies to work in small-group environments.

- Have students watch the video on Small-Group Learning Strategies.
- A video on this topic is available online in the Professional Development Center.

You may wish to discuss some action items to add to the chart as a class before students complete it on their own. For example, for "Clarify," you might solicit the following from students:

- Take thorough notes, so that you are able to contribute specific ideas in your groups.
- Ask questions of your classmates to make sure you understand important details.

**Block Scheduling**

Each day in this Pacing Plan represents a 40-50 minute class period. Teachers using block scheduling may combine days to reflect their class schedule. In addition, teachers may revise pacing to differentiate and support core instruction by integrating components and resources as students require.

OVERVIEW: SMALL-GROUP LEARNING

ESSENTIAL QUESTION:

## What is the meaning of freedom?

As you read these selections, work with your group to explore the meaning of freedom.

**From Text to Topic** The colonies had gained their independence and created a free nation, but freedom had not come to all. The Constitution had not settled the issue of slavery—and by 1790, when the first census in the United States was taken, approximately 700,000 African Americans were enslaved. The issue of slavery laid the foundation for the Civil War, arguably the most tragic time in the history of the United States. As you read, consider what these selections show about the nation's continuing efforts to define freedom.

### Small-Group Learning Strategies

Throughout your life, in school, in your community, and in your career, you will continue to learn and work with others. Use these strategies during Small-Group Learning. Add ideas of your own at each step.

| STRATEGY | ACTION PLAN |
|---|---|
| Prepare | • Complete your assignments so you are prepared for group work.<br>• Take notes on your reading so you can contribute to your group's discussions.<br>• |
| Participate fully | • Make eye contact to signal that you are listening and taking in what is being said.<br>• Use text evidence when making a point.<br>• |
| Support others | • Build on ideas from others in your group.<br>• State the relationship of your points to those of others—whether you are supporting someone's point, refuting it, or taking the conversation in a new direction.<br>• |
| Clarify | • Paraphrase the ideas of others to ensure that your understanding is correct.<br>• Ask follow-up questions.<br>• |



SCAN FOR MULTIMEDIA



### Pacing Plan

Introduce Whole-Class Learning

Unit Introduction | Historical Perspectives | Declaration of Independence | Preamble to the U.S. Constitution • Bill of Rights | Speech in the Convention | The American Revolution: Visual Propaganda | Performance Task

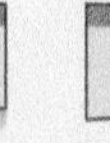

1 2 3 4 5 6 7 8 9 10 11 12 13 14 15

## CONTENTS

COMPARE







DIGITAL PERSPECTIVES

## Contents

**Selections** Circulate among groups as they preview the selections. You might encourage groups to discuss any knowledge they already have about any of the selection or the situations and settings shown in the images. Students may wish to take a poll within their group to determine which selections look the most interesting.

Remind students that communicating and collaborating in groups is an important skill that they will use throughout their lives—in school, in their careers, and in their community.

## Performance Task

**Present an Argument** Give groups time to read about and briefly discuss the panel discussion they will create after reading. Encourage students to do some preliminary thinking about what a panel discussion is and how they might organize theirs. This may help focus their subsequent reading and group discussion.

Introduce Small-Group Learning

*from* America's Constitution: A Biography

Media: *from* The United States Constitution: A Graphic Adaptation

*from* The Interesting Narrative of the Life of Olaudah Equiano

Letter to John Adams • *from* Dear Abigail: The Intimate Lives and Revolutionary Ideas of Abigail Adams and Her Two Remarkable Sisters

Gettysburg Address

Performance Task

Introduce Independent Learning

Independent Learning

Performance-Based Assessment

16 17 18 19 20 21 22 23 24 25 26 27 28 29 30

SMALL-GROUP LEARNING

# OVERVIEW

## SMALL-GROUP LEARNING

### Working as a Team

1. **Take a Position** Remind groups to let all members share their responses. You may wish to set a time limit for this discussion.
2. **List Your Rules** You may want to have groups share their lists of rules and consolidate them into a master list to be displayed and followed by all groups.
3. **Apply the Rules** As you circulate among the groups, ensure that students are staying on task. Consider a short time limit for this step.
4. **Name Your Group** This task can be creative and fun. If students have trouble coming up with a name, suggest that they think of something related to the unit topic. Encourage groups to share their names with the class.
5. **Create a Communication Plan** Encourage groups to agreed-upon times during the day to share ideas and include the times in their plans. They should also devise a method for recording and saving their communications.

### Accountable Talk

Remind students that groups should communicate politely. You can post these Accountable Talk suggestions and encourage students to add their own. Students should:

**Remember to . . .**
Ask clarifying questions.

**Which sounds like . . .**
Can you say that again?
Would you give me an example?
I think you said _____. Did I understand you correctly?

**Remember to . . .**
Explain your thinking

**Which sounds like . . .**
I believe this is true because _____.

**Remember to . . .**
Build on the ideas of others.

**Which sounds like . . .**
When _____ said _____ it made me think of _____.



## OVERVIEW: SMALL-GROUP LEARNING

### Working as a Team

1. **Take a Position** In your group, discuss the following question:

   **Do you think teenagers today should have more freedom—or less—than they do now?**

   As you take turns sharing your positions, be sure to provide reasons for your choice. After all group members have shared, discuss the convictions that students expressed and the arguments they proposed to support their views.

2. **List Your Rules** As a group, decide on the rules that you will follow as you work together. Two samples are provided. Add two more of your own. As you work together, you may add or revise rules based on your experience.
   - Everyone should have a chance to speak.
   - Group members should not interrupt each other.
   - ______________________________
   - ______________________________

3. **Apply the Rules** Share what you have learned about the meaning of freedom. Make sure each person in the group contributes. Take notes and be prepared to share with the class something you learned from another member of your group.

4. **Name Your Group** Choose a name that reflects the unit topic.

   Our group's name: ______________________________

5. **Create a Communication Plan** Decide how you want to communicate with one another. For example, you might use email, an online bulletin board, or a collaborative annotation tool.

   Our group's decision: ______________________________





## FACILITATING SMALL-GROUP LEARNING

### Forming Groups

You may wish to form groups for Small-Group Learning so that each consists of students with different learning abilities. Some students may be adept at organizing main points, others may better see points of comparison and connection. Others speak to the points easily, and some take notes well, synthesize, and share the information. A good mix of abilities can make the experience of Small-Group Learning dynamic and productive.

## Making a Schedule

First, find out the due dates for the small-group activities. Then, preview the texts and activities with your group, and make a schedule for completing the tasks.

| SELECTION | ACTIVITIES | DUE DATE |
|---|---|---|
| *from* America's Constitution: A Biography | | |
| *from* The United States Constitution: A Graphic Adaptation | | |
| *from* The Interesting Narrative of the Life of Olaudah Equiano | | |
| Letter to John Adams<br>*from* Dear Abigail: The Intimate Lives and Revolutionary Ideas of Abigail Adams and Her Two Remarkable Sisters | | |
| Gettysburg Address | | |

## Working on Group Projects

As your group works together, you'll find it more effective if each person has a specific role. Different projects require different roles. Before beginning a project, discuss the necessary roles, and choose one for each group member. Some possible roles are listed here. Add your ideas to the list.

**Project Manager:** monitors the schedule and keeps everyone on task
**Researcher:** organizes research activities
**Recorder:** takes notes during group meetings

________________________________________

________________________________________

________________________________________

________________________________________

SCAN FOR MULTIMEDIA



DIGITAL PERSPECTIVES

## Making a Schedule

Encourage groups to preview the reading selections and to consider how long it will take them to complete the activities accompanying each selection. Point out that they can adjust the due dates for particular selections as needed as they work on their small-group projects, however, they must complete all assigned tasks before the group Performance Task is due. Encourage groups to review their schedules upon completing the activities for each selection to make sure they are on track to meet the final due date.

## Working on Group Projects

Point out to groups that the roles they assign can also be changed later. Students might have to make changes based on the skills of particular students. Try to make sure that there is no favoritism, cliquishness, or stereotyping by gender or other means in the assignment of roles.

Also, review the roles in each group. Based on your understanding of students' individual strengths, you might find it necessary to suggest some changes within the group or among groups.

AUTHOR'S PERSPECTIVE **Kelly Gallagher, M.Ed.**

**Meaningful Talk** Instead of asking teacher-directed questions that lead students to see specific elements, give the power back to the students. Help them find their own big ideas and support them by building in talk opportunities. Use these two strategies to help students achieve deeper comprehension.

- *See the Relevance in Reading:* Teachers have students read great works of literature to give students an opportunity to think deeply about issues that will affect their lives. Asking students "What is worth talking about here?" helps them find themes and interpretations and get to the heart of the unit theme.
- *One Question; One Comment Strategy:* To get students to revisit a chapter or passage they find particularly challenging and generate an in-depth discussion of the text, teachers can ask students to come to class with one question and one comment generated from their reading assignment. During the class discussion, have the first student share one comment or question. The next student can answer the question, respond to the comment, or build on the discussion with his or her own question or comment. Continue the process until everyone in class has participated.

Using these strategies will lessen student dependence on the teacher and so help to build independence.

# *from* America's Constitution: A Biography

**AUDIO SUMMARIES**
Audio summaries of "*from* America's Constitution: A Biography" are available online in both English and Spanish in the Interactive Teacher's Edition or Unit Resources. Assigning these summaries prior to reading the selection may help students build additional background knowledge and set a context for their first read.

## Summary

In "*from* America's Constitution: A Biography," Akhil Reed Amar explains how the United States Constitution came to be written and eventually ratified. Amar describes the conflicts that arose among the delegates at the Constitutional Convention in Philadelphia in 1787. Once the Constitution was written and approved by the delegates, at least nine of the thirteen states had to agree in order for the document to go into effect. Most states held special elections or set up commissions to decide on ratification. The Constitution was not ratified until June 1788, and it took another two years for all the states to approve it. Amar makes it clear why the Constitution and its ratification remain a significant achievement. For the first time in history, ordinary people were acknowledged as the source of power in their government, with the right to approve the laws that would govern them.

### Insight

Reading "*from* America's Constitution: A Biography" will help students understand that the freedoms Americans take for granted are the result of the early leaders and citizens of the United States engaging in careful consideration, conflict, and compromise. The War for Independence resulted in the new country's freedom to determine its own course. After the war, determining that course required the resolution of many internal conflicts before the nation would be on a safe footing and its citizens assured of the rights they desired.

ESSENTIAL QUESTION:
What is the meaning of freedom?

## Connection to the Essential Question

The selection "*from* America's Constitution: A Biography" connects to the Essential Question, "What is the meaning of freedom?" This nonfiction text explains the democratic processes by which the American people were able to consider, create, examine, and approve the essential document under which their government would function and they would be ruled.

SMALL-GROUP LEARNING PERFORMANCE TASK
Do narratives provide strong evidence to support arguments about American freedoms?

UNIT PERFORMANCE-BASED ASSESSMENT
What are the most effective tools for establishing and preserving freedom?

## Connection to Performance Tasks

**Small-Group Learning Performance Task** In this Performance Task, students will consider whether narratives provide strong evidence to support arguments about American freedoms. Students will identify key points in Akhil Amar's narrative that demonstrate the role of the people in establishing and preserving freedoms.

**Unit Performance-Based Assessment** This selection mentions two important tools for establishing and preserving freedom: selecting representatives to participate in the writing of the Constitution and holding special state elections or convening special state committees to approve its ratification.

DIGITAL PERSPECTIVES

Audio

Video

Document

Annotation Highlights

EL Highlights

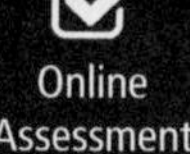
Online Assessment

## LESSON RESOURCES

| | Making Meaning | Language Development |
|---|---|---|
| Lesson | **First Read**<br>**Close Read**<br>**Analyze the Text**<br>**Analyze Craft and Structure** | **Concept Vocabulary**<br>**Word Study**<br>**Author's Style** |
| Instructional Standards | **RI.10** By the end of grade 11, read and comprehend literary nonfiction . . .<br>**RI.6** Determine an author's point of view . . .<br>**L.4.a** Use context as a clue . . . | **L.4.c** Consult general and specialized reference materials . . .<br>**RI.3** Analyze a complex set of ideas . . .<br>**RI.5** Analyze and evaluate the effectiveness of the structure an author uses . . . |
| **STUDENT RESOURCES** | | |
| Available online in the Interactive Student Edition or Unit Resources | Selection Audio<br>First-Read Guide: Nonfiction<br>Close-Read Guide: Nonfiction | Word Network |
| **TEACHER RESOURCES** | | |
| **Selection Resources**<br>Available online in the Interactive Teacher's Edition or Unit Resources | Audio Summaries<br>Annotation Highlights<br>EL Highlights<br>English Language Support Lesson: Latin Suffix *-ist*<br>*from* America's Constitution: A Biography: Text Questions<br>Analyze Craft and Structure: Rhetoric | Concept Vocabulary and Word Study<br>Author's Style: Historical Narrative as Argument |
| **Reteach/Practice (RP)**<br>Available online in the Interactive Teacher's Edition or Unit Resources | Analyze Craft and Structure: Rhetoric (RP) | Word Study: Latin Suffix *–ist* (RP)<br>Author's Style: Historical Narrative as Argument (RP) |
| **Assessment**<br>Available online in Assessments | Selection Test | |
| **My Resources** | A Unit 1 Answer Key is available online and in the Interactive Teacher's Edition. | |

# Reading Support

| Text Complexity Rubric: *from* America's Constitution: A Biography | |
|---|---|
| **Quantitative Measures** | |
| **Lexile:** 1360 **Text Length:** 2,322 words | |
| **Qualitative Measures** | |
| Knowledge Demands ①—②—③—❹—⑤ | Explores the complex history of the Constitution. Explanation is provided for some of the complex ideas, but some understanding of American history is assumed. |
| Structure ①—②—❸—④—⑤ | The selection includes many digressions that make connecting ideas somewhat difficult. There are no headings to help organize ideas. |
| Language Conventionality and Clarity ①—②—❸—④—⑤ | Some sentences in the selection are complex, with multiple clauses and difficult vocabulary. The selection also contains some figurative language. |
| Levels of Meaning/Purpose ①—②—❸—④—⑤ | The purpose is clear (to explain how the Constitution came to be), but may be hard for some to grasp because of sophisticated language and supporting concepts that are complex. |

DECIDE AND PLAN

## English Language Support

Provide English Learners with support for knowledge demands and meaning/purpose as they read the selection.

**Knowledge Demands** Make sure students understand the terms they need to know in order to grasp larger concepts. For example, before they read the lengthy paragraph 9, be sure they understand the terms *ratification, Preamble, Articles of Confederation, Federalist/Anti-Federalist, approbation/disapprobation.*

**Meaning/Purpose** Once students have defined difficult words, have them reread each paragraph, stopping to summarize the main points every few sentences. Ask them to write sentences restating the information they understood. For example, this sentence could summarize paragraph 5: *The Constitution was created when representatives from twelve states met in order to revise the Articles of Confederation.*

## Strategic Support

Provide students with strategic support to ensure that they can successfully read the text.

**Knowledge Demands** Have students work in pairs to review terms they will need to know in order to grasp the meaning of the selection. For example, *ratification, Preamble, Articles of Confederation, Federalist/Anti-Federalist, approbation/ disapprobation.*

**Language/Clarity** For students who may have difficulty with complex sentences, encourage them to break the sentences down into smaller chunks and rephrase the main ideas in their own words. Then have them reread the whole sentences.

## Challenge

Provide students who need to be challenged with ideas for how they can go beyond a simple interpretation of the text.

**Text Analysis** Ask students to read aloud paragraph 5 about how "the people" were represented in the ratification process. What was unusual about the process?

**Written Response** In the selection, the author personifies the Constitution as a living thing:...*the Constitution was still struggling to be born...*

Have students write an essay that explores the idea that the Constitution is a living document. How is it alive? What are some examples of its living nature?

TEACH

## Read and Respond

Have the groups read the selection and complete the Making Meaning and Language Development activities.

# Standards Support Through Teaching and Learning Cycle

## IDENTIFY NEEDS

Analyze results of the Beginning-of-Year Assessment, focusing on the items relating to Unit 1. Also take into consideration student performance to this point and your observations of where particular students struggle.

## DECIDE AND PLAN

- If students have performed poorly on items matching these standards, then provide selection scaffolds before assigning them the on-level lesson provided in the Student Edition.
- If students have done well on the Beginning-of-Year Assessment, then challenge them to keep progressing and learning by giving them opportunities to practice the skills in depth.
- Use the Selection Resources listed on the Planning pages from ***from* America's Constitution: A Biography** to help students continually improve their ability to master the standards.

**Instructional Standards: *from* America's Constitution: A Biography**

| | Catching Up | This Year | Looking Forward |
|---|---|---|---|
| **Reading** | You may wish to administer the **Analyze Craft and Structure: Rhetoric (RP)** worksheet to help students understand how analogies can make a complex set of ideas easier to understand. | **RI.6** Determine an author's point of view or purpose in a text in which the rhetoric is particularly effective, analyzing how style and content contribute to the power, persuasiveness, or beauty of the text. | Challenge students to read a text that employs rhetorical devices and evaluate how the rhetoric adds to the persuasiveness of the text. |
| **Language** | You may wish to administer the **Author's Style: Historical Narrative as Argument (RP)** worksheet to help students understand how authors can use the structure of a text to support their point of view. | **RI.3** Analyze a complex set of ideas or sequence of events and explain how specific individuals , ideas, or events interact and develop over the course of the text.<br>**RI.5** Analyze and evaluate the effectiveness of the structure an author uses in his or her exposition or argument, including whether the structure makes points clear, convincing, and engaging. | You may wish to challenge students to think about how they would use specific text structures to support a point of view. For example, cause and effect might be used to persuade readers to take action to prevent a particular problem. |

## ANALYZE AND REVISE

- Analyze student work for evidence of student learning.
- Identify whether or not students have met the expectations in the standards.
- Identify implications for future instruction.

## TEACH

Implement the planned lesson, and gather evidence of student learning.

# FACILITATING

## Jump Start

FIRST READ Ask students to think of their favorite game. Have students imagine what the game would be like if there were no rules. Ask groups to draw some conclusions about the value of rules. Point out that the U.S. Constitution is, in effect, a rulebook for our government.

## *from* America's Constitution: A Biography

What information would you expect to find in a biography of the U.S. Constitution? Modeling this and other questions readers might ask will bring "*from* America's Constitution: A Biography" to life and connect it to the Performance Task question. Selection audio and print capability for the selection are available in the Interactive Teacher's Edition.

## Concept Vocabulary

Have groups briefly discuss the three concept vocabulary words. Have they encountered any of the words before? Do they recognize the prefix, suffix, or base word of any of the concept vocabulary words? Have groups consider the strategy of identifying synonym and antonym context clues and discuss its advantages and disadvantages.

## FIRST READ

Have students perform the steps of the first read independently:

NOTICE: Encourage students to notice which Founders of the Constitution are mentioned and what their roles in the process were.

ANNOTATE: Remind students to mark passages that describe the innovations the Founders employed in creating the Constitution and in developing the process of ratification.

CONNECT: Encourage students to make connections between what they already know about the Constitution and new information they are reading about here.

RESPOND: Students will demonstrate their understanding of the text by answering questions and writing a summary.

Point out to students that they will perform the first three steps concurrently as they are doing their first read. They will complete the Respond step after they have finished the first read. You may wish to print copies of the **First-Read Guide: Nonfiction** for students to use.



MAKING MEANING

AMERICA'S CONSTITUTION: A BIOGRAPHY

## Comparing Text to Media

You will read and compare an excerpt from *America's Constitution: A Biography* and an excerpt from the graphic novel *The United States Constitution: A Graphic Adaptation*. First, complete the first-read and close-read activities for *America's Constitution: A Biography.*

THE UNITED STATES CONSTITUTION: A GRAPHIC ADAPTATION

About the Author

**Akhil Reed Amar** (b. 1958), an expert on constitutional law, has been called one of the nation's top legal thinkers. Amar graduated from Yale Law School, where he was an editor for the *Yale Law Journal*. He has written several books and articles about the law—works important enough to have been referenced in a number of Supreme Court cases.

# *from* America's Constitution: A Biography

### Concept Vocabulary

As you perform your first read, you will encounter these words.

conclave eminent populist

**Context Clues** An unfamiliar word may become clearer if you use **context clues**—that is, helpful words and phrases in the surrounding text. Here are two types of context clues.

**Synonyms:** New Hampshire became the ninth state to **ratify** the Constitution, approving the document by a margin of 57 to 47.

**Antonyms:** Opponents of the new Constitution were relatively **rigid**, but proponents such as Madison and Franklin were resourceful and flexible.

Apply your knowledge of context clues and other vocabulary strategies to determine the meanings of unfamiliar words you encounter during your first read.

### First Read NONFICTION

Apply these strategies as you conduct your first read. You will have an opportunity to complete a close read after your first read.

NOTICE the general ideas of the text. *What* it is about? *Who* is involved?

ANNOTATE by marking vocabulary and key passages you want to revisit.

CONNECT ideas within the selection to what you already know and what you have already read.

RESPOND by completing the Comprehension Check and by writing a brief summary of the selection.

First Read: NOTICE, ANNOTATE, CONNECT, RESPOND

STANDARDS

**Reading Informational Text**
By the end of grade 11, read and comprehend literary nonfiction in the grades 11–CCR text complexity band proficiently, with scaffolding as needed at the high end of the range.

**Language**
Use context as a clue to the meaning of a word or phrase.





AUTHOR'S PERSPECTIVE **Jim Cummins, Ph.D.**

**Literacy Engagements** Academic language is found primarily in printed text rather than in everyday conversation. Thus, when students have abundant access to printed texts and engage actively with these texts, they have far greater opportunities to broaden their vocabulary knowledge and develop strong reading comprehension skills. Students' engagement will be enhanced when they discuss in small groups the texts they have read in *myPerspectives* as well as other selections of their choice. Teachers can help make texts more meaningful to students in the following ways:

- **Scaffold Meaning:** Visuals such as illustrations and graphic organizers in the text enhance students' understanding. Students who are learning English can also use electronic translators and bilingual dictionaries to gain access to the meaning of words or phrases.

EXPOSITORY NONFICTION

# *from* America's Constitution: A Biography

Akhil Reed Amar

BACKGROUND
Between 1777 and 1787, the United States used a constitution called the Articles of Confederation rather than the Constitution we use today. The Articles of Confederation created a very weak federal government. It soon became apparent that a document demonstrating more clarity would be helpful. There was great debate about whether to simply change the Articles of Confederation or replace them, as well as what this replacement might look like.

SCAN FOR MULTIMEDIA

1 It started with a bang. Ordinary citizens would govern themselves across a continent and over the centuries, under rules that the populace would ratify and could revise. By uniting previously independent states into a vast and indivisible nation, New World republicans would keep Old World monarchs at a distance and thus make democracy work on a scale never before dreamed possible.

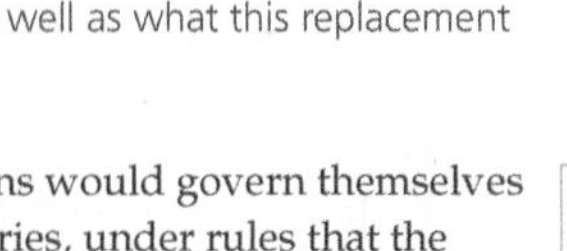

"We . . . do"

With simple words placed in the document's most prominent location, the Preamble laid the foundation for all that followed. "We the People of the United States, . . . do ordain[1] and establish this Constitution . . ."

2 These words did more than promise popular self-government. They also embodied and enacted it. Like the phrases "I do" in an exchange of wedding vows and "I accept" in a contract, the Preamble's words actually performed the very thing they described. Thus the Founders' "Constitution" was not merely a text but a deed—a *constituting*. We the People *do* ordain. In the late 1780s, this was the most democratic deed the world had ever seen.

3 Behind this act of ordainment and establishment stood countless ordinary American voters who gave their consent to the Constitution via specially elected ratifying conventions held in the thirteen states beginning in late 1787. Until these ratifications took place, the Constitution's words were a mere proposal—the text of a contract yet to be accepted, the script of a wedding still to be performed.

4 The proposal itself had emerged from a special conclave held in Philadelphia during the summer of 1787. Twelve state governments—all except Rhode Island's—had tapped several dozen leading public

NOTES

Mark context clues or indicate another strategy you used that helped you determine meaning.

**conclave** (KON klayv) *n.*

MEANING:

1. **ordain** *v.* officially order or decree.





DIGITAL PERSPECTIVES

## Concept Vocabulary

**CONCLAVE** If groups are struggling to define *conclave* in paragraph 4, point out that surrounding words and phrases refer to the nature of the gathering. These include *tapped several dozen . . . in Philadelphia, the Philadelphia conferees,* and *thirty-nine*. These details should lead students to infer that a conclave is a private meeting of some importance.

**Possible response:** A *conclave* must be "a gathering or meeting."

Additional **English Language Support** is available in the Interactive Teacher's Edition.

- **Connect to Students' Lives:** It is important to activate students' pre-existing knowledge so that they can relate new information to what they already know. English learners can use their first language as a resource to help them extend their English academic skills (e.g., by brainstorming in groups, writing in the first language as a stepping stone to writing in English, and carrying out Internet research in their first language).
- **Extend Language:** Teachers can extend students' academic language skills by consistently and explicitly drawing attention to new words, unusual syntax, and other textual features that are not found in everyday conversation.

## Concept Vocabulary

**EMINENT** If groups are struggling to define *eminent* in paragraph 4, refer to its part of speech. *Eminent* modifies *man* and is an adjective. Have groups look at the list of men following the word. Ask which names they recognize. Highlight *leading public servants*, *George Washington*, *Benjamin Franklin*, and *James Madison*, *Alexander Hamilton*. Then have groups identify another word from the last sentence of the paragraph that describes these men (*notables*). These steps should lead students to infer that someone who is *eminent* is successful, well-known, and respected.

**Possible response: *Eminent*** must mean "famous, respected, important."

NOTES

Mark context clues or indicate another strategy you used that helped you determine meaning.

**eminent** (EHM uh nuhnt) *adj.*

MEANING:

servants and private citizens to meet in Philadelphia and ponder possible revisions of the Articles of Confederation, the interstate compact that Americans had formed during the Revolutionary War. After deliberating behind closed doors for months, the Philadelphia conferees unveiled their joint proposal in mid-September in a document signed by thirty-nine of the continent's most **eminent** men, including George Washington, Benjamin Franklin, James Wilson, Roger Sherman, James Madison, Alexander Hamilton, Gouverneur Morris, John Rutledge, and Nathaniel Gorham. When these notables put their names on the page, they put their reputations on the line.

5 An enormous task of political persuasion lay ahead. Several of the leaders who had come to Philadelphia had quit the conclave in disgust, and others who had stayed to the end had refused to endorse the final script. Such men—John Lansing, Robert Yates, Luther Martin, John Francis Mercer, Edmund Randolph, George Mason, and Elbridge Gerry—could be expected to oppose ratification and to urge their political allies to do the same. No one could be certain how the American people would ultimately respond to the competing appeals. Prior to 1787, only two states, Massachusetts and New Hampshire, had ever brought proposed state constitutions before the people to be voted up or down in some special way. The combined track record from this pair of states was sobering: two successful popular ratifications out of six total attempts.

6 In the end, the federal Constitution proposed by Washington and company would barely squeak through. By its own terms, the document would go into effect only if ratified by specially elected conventions in at least nine states, and even then only states that said yes would be bound. In late 1787 and early 1788, supporters of the Constitution won relatively easy ratifications in Delaware, Pennsylvania, New Jersey, Georgia, and Connecticut. Massachusetts joined their ranks in February 1788, saying "we do" only after weeks of debate and by a close vote, 187 to 168. Then came lopsided yes votes in Maryland and South Carolina, bringing the total to eight ratifications, one shy of the mark. Even so, in mid-June 1788, a full nine months after the publication of the Philadelphia proposal, the Constitution was still struggling to be born, and its fate remained uncertain. Organized opposition ran strong in all the places that had yet to say yes, which included three of America's largest and most influential states. At last, on June 21, tiny New Hampshire became the decisive ninth state by the margin of 57 to 47. A few days later, before news from the North had arrived, Virginia voted her approval, 89 to 79.

7 All eyes then turned to New York, where Anti-Federalists initially held a commanding lead inside the convention. Without the acquiescence of this key state, could the new Constitution really work as planned? On the other hand, was New York truly willing to say no and go it alone now that her neighbors had agreed to form a new, more perfect union among themselves? In late July, the state





### FACILITATING SMALL-GROUP CLOSE LEARNING

**CLOSE READ: Expository Nonfiction** As groups perform their close read, you should circulate and offer assistance as required.

- Point out the dramatic way the author begins the selection. Have groups evaluate the effect of this beginning.
- Remind students that informative and explanatory texts usually have a sentence that clearly identifies the topic. The topic sentence does not always appear at the beginning of a paragraph in a nonfiction selection. Have readers locate the topic sentence of the passage, noting that it is not the first sentence of a paragraph.
- Have groups indicate how they determined what the topic sentence was. Methods may include a close reading that compares sentences to see which is the broadest.

ultimately said yes by a vote of 30 to 27. A switch of only a couple of votes would have reversed the outcome. Meanwhile, the last two states, North Carolina and Rhode Island, refused to ratify in 1788. They would ultimately join the new union in late 1789 and mid-1790, respectively—well after George Washington took office as president of the new (eleven!) United States.

8 Although the ratification votes in the several states did not occur by direct statewide referenda,[2] the various ratifying conventions did aim to represent "the People" in a particularly emphatic way—more directly than ordinary legislatures. Taking their cue from the Preamble's bold "We the People" language, several states waived standard voting restrictions and allowed a uniquely broad class of citizens to vote for ratification-convention delegates. For instance, New York temporarily set aside its usual property qualifications and, for the first time in its history, invited all free adult male citizens to vote. Also, states generally allowed an especially broad group of Americans to serve as ratifying-convention delegates. Among the many states that ordinarily required upper-house lawmakers to meet higher property qualifications than lower-house members, none held convention delegates to the higher standard, and most exempted delegates even from the lower. All told, eight states elected convention delegates under special rules that were more **populist** and less property-focused than normal, and two others followed standing rules that let virtually all taxpaying adult male citizens vote. No state employed special election rules that were more property-based or less populist than normal.

9 In the extraordinarily extended and inclusive ratification process envisioned by the Preamble, Americans regularly found themselves discussing the Preamble itself. At Philadelphia, the earliest draft of the Preamble had come from the quill of Pennsylvania's James Wilson, and it was Wilson who took the lead in explaining the Preamble's principles in a series of early and influential ratification speeches. Pennsylvania Anti-Federalists complained that the Philadelphia notables had overreached in proposing an entirely new Constitution rather than a mere modification of the existing Articles of Confederation. In response, Wilson—America's leading lawyer and one of only six men to have signed both the Declaration of Independence and the Constitution—stressed the significance of popular ratification. "This Constitution, proposed by [the Philadelphia draftsmen], claims no more than a production of the same nature would claim, flowing from a private pen. It is laid before the citizens of the United States, unfettered by restraint. . . . By their *fiat*,[3] it will become of value and authority; without it, it will never receive the character of authenticity and power." James Madison agreed, as he made clear in a mid-January 1788 New York newspaper essay today known as *The Federalist* No. 40—one of a long series

NOTES

Mark context clues or indicate another strategy you used that helped you determine meaning.

**populist** (POP yuh lihst) *adj.*

MEANING:

2. **referenda** *n.* public votes on particular issues.
3. **fiat** (FEE uht) *n.* command that creates something.





DIGITAL PERSPECTIVES

## Concept Vocabulary

**POPULIST** If groups are struggling to define *populist* in paragraph 8, point out that surrounding words and phrases give clues to the word's meaning. These words and phrases include *less property-focused than normal* and *rules that let all taxpaying male citizens vote*. Have groups think of synonyms and antonyms for *populist*. Synonyms include *free*, *common*, and *autonomous*. An antonym might be *elitist*.

**Possible response:** ***Populist*** must mean "having to do with ordinary people."

## VOCABULARY DEVELOPMENT

**Word Anaylsis** Ask groups to focus on *referenda* (paragraph 8), the plural of *referendum*. Point out the unusual endings of both the singular and plural forms of the word. Explain that the word is derived from Latin, which determines its irregular plural ending. Have groups think of other words that follow this pattern. Examples include *millennia*, *curricula*, and *memoranda*.

CLOSER LOOK

## Analyze Analogies 

Circulate among groups as students conduct their close read. Suggest that groups close read paragraph 10. Encourage them to talk about the annotations that they mark. If needed, provide the following support.

**ANNOTATE:** Have students mark details in the paragraph that make analogies between the American people and God, or work with small groups to have students participate while you highlight them together.

**QUESTION:** Guide students to consider what these details might tell them. Ask what a reader can infer from what or whom the author is comparing the American people to, and accept student responses.

**Possible response:** The author is trying to show the similarity between God as the creator of the world and the American people as the creators of the Constitution.

**CONCLUDE:** Help students formulate conclusions about the importance of these details in the text.

**Possible response:** *Publius* describes the American people as the supreme authority, which is also a way of describing God. The author talks about the "ultimate sovereign" (God) and juxtaposes that reference immediately with the "temporal sovereign," the American people. The phrase "constitution in their own image" calls to mind the phrase from Genesis about God making man in his image. The effect of all this is to elevate the concept of the Constitution as a document created by a higher being.

Remind students that writers often use **analogies** or comparisons to help readers see their ideas in a fresh way.

NOTES

of columns that he wrote in partnership with Alexander Hamilton and John Jay under the shared pen name "Publius." According to Madison/Publius, the Philadelphia draftsmen had merely "proposed a Constitution which is to be of no more consequence than the paper on which it is written, unless it be stamped with the approbation[4] of those to whom it is addressed. [The proposal] was to be submitted *to the people themselves*, [and] the disapprobation of this supreme authority would destroy it forever; its approbation blot out antecedent errors and irregularities." Leading Federalists across the continent reiterated the point in similar language.

10 With the word *fiat*, Wilson gently called to mind the opening lines of Genesis. In the beginning, God said, *fiat lux*, and—behold!—there was light. So, too, when the American people (Publius's "supreme authority") said, "We do ordain and establish," that very statement would do the deed. "Let there be a Constitution"—and there would be one. As the ultimate sovereign of all had once made man in his own image, so now the temporal sovereign of America, the people themselves, would make a constitution in their own image.

11 All this was breathtakingly novel. In 1787, democratic self-government existed almost nowhere on earth. Kings, emperors, czars, princes, sultans, moguls, feudal lords, and tribal chiefs held sway across the globe. Even England featured a limited monarchy and an entrenched aristocracy alongside a House of Commons that rested on a restricted and uneven electoral base. The vaunted English Constitution that American colonists had grown up admiring prior to the struggle for independence was an imprecise hodgepodge of institutions, enactments, cases, usages, maxims, procedures, and principles that had accreted[5] and evolved over many centuries. This Constitution had never been reduced to a single composite writing and voted on by the British people or even by Parliament.

12 The ancient world had seen small-scale democracies in various Greek city-states and pre-imperial Rome, but none of these had been founded in fully democratic fashion. In the most famous cases, one man—a celebrated lawgiver such as Athens's Solon or Sparta's Lycurgus—had unilaterally ordained his countrymen's constitution. Before the American Revolution, no people had ever explicitly voted on their own written constitution.

13 Nor did the Revolution itself immediately inaugurate popular ordainments and establishments. True, the 1776 Declaration of Independence proclaimed the "self-evident" truth that "Governments are instituted among Men, deriving their just Powers from the Consent of the Governed." The document went on to assert that "whenever any Form of Government becomes destructive of [its legitimate] Ends, it is the Right of the People to alter and abolish it, and to institute new Government." Yet the Declaration only

4. **approbation** *n.* praise or approval.
5. **accreted** *v.* grown or accumulated gradually.





PERSONALIZE FOR LEARNING

### Strategic Support

**Central Ideas** Have several groups of students analyze the first half of the selection, while an equal number of groups analyzes the second half. Instruct each group to discuss the main idea in its half, and then agree on one sentence that sums up that central idea. When the groups have finished, pair first halves with second halves, and have them share their central ideas. Then have each larger group work together to combine their ideas into one sentence that states the selection's central idea.

imperfectly acted out its bold script. Its fifty-six acclaimed signers never put the document to any sort of popular vote.

NOTES

14 Between April and July 1776, countless similar declarations issued from assorted towns, counties, parishes, informal assemblies, grand juries, militia units, and legislatures across America. By then, however, the colonies were already under military attack, and conditions often made it impossible to achieve inclusive deliberation or scrupulous tabulation. Many patriots saw Crown loyalists in their midst not as fellow citizens free to vote their honest judgment with impunity, but rather as traitors deserving tar and feathers, or worse. (Virtually no arch-loyalist went on to become a particularly noteworthy political leader in independent America. By contrast, many who would vigorously oppose the Constitution in 1787–88—such as Maryland's Samuel Chase and Luther Martin, Virginia's Patrick Henry and James Monroe, and New York's George Clinton and John Lansing—moved on to illustrious post-ratification careers.)

America could boast a breakthrough in political science.

15 Shortly before and after the Declaration of Independence, new state governments began to take shape, filling the void created by the ouster of George III. None of the state constitutions ordained in the first months of the Revolution was voted on by the electorate or by a specially elected ratifying convention of the people. In many states, sitting legislatures or closely analogous Revolutionary entities declared themselves solons[6] and promulgated or revised constitutions on their own authority, sometimes without even waiting for new elections that might have given their constituents more say in the matter, or at least advance notice of their specific constitutional intentions.

16 In late 1777, patriot leaders in the Continental Congress proposed a set of Articles of Confederation to govern relations among the thirteen states. This document was then sent out to be ratified by the thirteen state legislatures, none of which asked the citizens themselves to vote in any special way on the matter.

17 Things began to change as the Revolution wore on. In 1780, Massachusetts enacted a new state constitution that had come directly before the voters assembled in their respective townships and won their approval. In 1784, New Hampshire did the same. These local dress rehearsals (for so they seem in retrospect) set the stage for the Preamble's great act of continental popular sovereignty in the late 1780s.

18 As Benjamin Franklin and other Americans had achieved famous advances in the natural sciences—in Franklin's case, the invention of bifocals, the lightning rod, and the Franklin stove—so with the Constitution America could boast a breakthrough in political science. Never before had so many ordinary people been invited to

6. **solons** (SOH luhnz) *n.* lawmakers, especially wise ones. Refers to Solon, the statesman who framed the democratic laws of Athens.





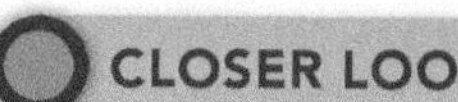

## Compare Attitudes 

Circulate among groups as students conduct their close read. Suggest that groups close read paragraphs 15–17. Encourage them to talk about the annotations that they mark. If needed, provide the following support.

**ANNOTATE:** Have students mark details in these paragraphs that show how Americans' attitudes were changing with regard to the people's input in government, or work with small groups to have students participate while you highlight them together.

**QUESTION:** Guide students to consider what these details might tell them. Ask what a reader can infer about the evolution of people's attitudes in regard to their participation in government.

**Possible response:** The American people wanted more of a participatory role in government matters.

**CONCLUDE:** Help students formulate conclusions about the importance of these details in the text. Ask students why the author might have included these details.

**Possible responses:** A dress rehearsal is a final practice that mimics a real performance. By the early 1780s, some states were including the voters in the decisions about their state constitutions. By calling these "local dress rehearsals," the author acknowledges them as precedents for participatory democracy, which came to fruition in the ratification of the Constitution.

Remind students that authors use exposition to present information or explain something. In this case, the author explains how the role of the citizen changed as governmental structures in America evolved and changed.

## CROSS-CURRICULAR PERSPECTIVES

**Humanities** Although the idea of democracy seemed highly innovative in the 1780s, it was actually the product of an ancient civilization. In about 500 B.C., a Greek ruler introduced the idea of *demokratia*, or "rule by the people." The system lasted for only about 200 years. The concept of democracy lived on, however, and continues to influence today's world. Have groups research more about the first democracies of ancient Greece. Then have them make a Venn diagram to compare and contrast ancient democracies with elements of our own American system.

## Comprehension Check

Possible responses:

1. It was drafted in Philadelphia in the summer of 1787.
2. Nine states had to ratify the Constitution before it could take effect.
3. *The Federalist* was a series of newspaper essays, published in New York in 1788, which presented arguments in favor of adopting the new Constitution. "Publius" was the pen name under which James Madison, Alexander Hamilton, and John Jay wrote the essays.
4. Summaries will vary. Possible response: Amar celebrates the Constitution as a remarkable, democratic achievement. He describes the differing viewpoints and the compromise that led to the document's approval by a majority of delegates. He explores the extensive ratification process, especially the ways in which the states included ordinary Americans. He then emphasizes what made the Constitution—and the democracy that it represented—unique in the world at that time.

## Research

**Research to Explore** If groups struggle to come up with a research topic, you may want to suggest that they focus on one of the following topics: absolute monarchy, constitutional monarchy, or the Ottoman or Mogul Empire.

NOTES

deliberate and vote on the supreme law under which they and their posterity would be governed. James Wilson fairly burst with pride in an oration delivered in Philadelphia to some twenty thousand merrymakers gathered for a grand parade on July 4, 1788. By that date, enough Americans had said "We do" so as to guarantee that the Constitution would go into effect (at least in ten states—the document was still pending in the other three). The "spectacle, which we are assembled to celebrate," Wilson declared, was "the most dignified one that has yet appeared on our globe," namely, a

> people free and enlightened, establishing and ratifying a system of government, which they have previously considered, examined, and approved! . . .
>
> . . . You have heard of Sparta, of Athens, and of Rome; you have heard of their admired constitutions, and of their high-prized freedom. . . . But did they, in all their pomp and pride of liberty, ever furnish, to the astonished world, an exhibition similar to that which we now contemplate? Were their constitutions framed by those, who were appointed for that purpose, by the people? After they were framed, were they submitted to the consideration of the people? Had the people an opportunity of expressing their sentiments concerning them? Were they to stand or fall by the people's approving or rejecting vote?

19 The great deed was done. The people had taken center stage and enacted their own supreme law. ❧

## Comprehension Check

**Complete the following items after you finish your first read. Review and clarify details with your group.**

1. When and where was the Constitution drafted?
2. Once the Constitution was approved, what more had to happen before it could go into effect?
3. What was *The Federalist*, and who was "Publius"?
4. **Notebook** Confirm your understanding of the text by writing a summary.

## RESEARCH

**Research to Explore** Choose something that interested you from the text, and formulate a research question.





## PERSONALIZE FOR LEARNING

### English Language Support

**Understanding the Latin Suffix *-ist*** Display the following words: *optimist, perfectionist, pessimist, dentist, artist, physicist.*

Ask students to choose three of the words and write their definitions. If students are having difficulty, have them use a dictionary. **EMERGING**

Ask students to write a definition of these words. Then ask volunteers to explain how the use of the suffix relates to the meaning of the word. **EXPANDING**

Have students think of three other *–ist* suffix words. Have them write their possible meanings and parts of speech. Then ask them to write a sentence for each of the meanings of the word. **BRIDGING**

An expanded **English Language Support Lesson** on Latin Suffix *-ist* is available in the Interactive Teacher's Edition.

MAKING MEANING

## Close Read the Text

With your group, revisit sections of the text you marked during your first read. **Annotate** details that you notice. What **questions** do you have? What can you **conclude**?

AMERICA'S CONSTITUTION: A BIOGRAPHY

## Analyze the Text

**CITE TEXTUAL EVIDENCE** to support your answers.

**Notebook** Complete the activities.

1. **Review and Clarify** With your group, reread paragraphs 4 and 5 of the selection. What kind of document was the Constitution in the summer of 1787? What does this fact indicate about the power of "We the People"?
2. **Present and Discuss** Now, work with your group to share the passages from the selection that you found especially important. Take turns presenting your passages. Discuss what you noticed in the selection, what questions you asked, and what conclusions you reached.
3. **Essential Question:** ***What is the meaning of freedom?*** What has this text taught you about American freedoms? Discuss with your group.

**TIP**

**GROUP DISCUSSION**
Keep in mind that readers often have differing interpretations of a text. Use the varying perspectives to encourage group members to learn from one another and to clarify their own views.

LANGUAGE DEVELOPMENT

## Concept Vocabulary

conclave eminent populist

**Why These Words?** The three concept vocabulary words from the text are related. With your group, determine what the words have in common. How do these word choices contribute to the meaning of the text?

### Practice

**Notebook** Confirm your understanding of these words by writing a two- or three-sentence paragraph that includes all three words. Make their meaning clear from the context.

**WORD NETWORK**
Add words related to freedom from the text to your Word Network.

## Word Study

**Notebook** **Latin Suffix: *-ist*** The Latin suffix *-ist* identifies a word as an adjective or a noun. It often appears in words that relate to attitudes or philosophies. For example, the word *realist* means "a person who sees thing as they really are."

1. Write two definitions for the concept vocabulary word *populist*—one for the word's meaning as a noun and the other for the word's meaning as an adjective.
2. Use a dictionary to find definitions for *naturist, feminist,* and *idealist.* Then, choose one of the words and write two sentences—one using the word as a noun and the other using it as an adjective.

**STANDARDS**
**Language**
Consult general and specialized reference materials, both print and digital, to find the pronunciation of a word or determine or clarify its precise meaning, its part of speech, its etymology, or its standard usage.





DIGITAL PERSPECTIVES

## Jump Start

CLOSE READ Ask students to think about how the Constitution might affect their lives. Does their family pay taxes? Do they enjoy freedom of speech? Tell students that if their answers to any of these questions are yes, then they are affected by the Constitution.

## Close Read the Text 

Model close reading as needed by using the Annotation Highlights in the Interactive Teacher's Edition.
Remind groups to use Accountable Talk in their discussions and to support one another as they complete the close read.

## Analyze the Text

**Possible response:**

1. The Constitution is like a contract in that it created a binding promise between the American people and the U.S. government. Also, the document would be valid only when the people approved it. These facts indicate that the power of "We the people" is great.
2. **Passages will vary by group.** Remind students to explain why they chose their passage.
3. **Responses will vary by group.**

## Concept Vocabulary

**Why These Words? Possible response:** The three words relate to groups and individuals. They affect the text by reflecting the delegates' differing opinions and the importance of the Constitution as a document of "the People."

### Practice

**Possible response:** Late one night, the board of directors met in a **conclave** to choose a new company president. The directors reviewed **eminent** leaders with successful careers. The **populist** leader appeals to many in the city.

### Word Network

Possible words: *ratify, delegate, sovereign*

## Word Study

For more support, see **Concept Vocabulary and Word Study.**

**Possible responses: (1)** noun: a person who believes in the rights of ordinary people; adjective: representing the opinions and rights of ordinary people **(2)** She is a feminist who has challenged laws that are unfair to working women. Because of her feminist agenda, I intend to vote for her.

**FORMATIVE ASSESSMENT**

### Analyze the Text

**If** the students struggle to close-read the text, **then** provide the ***from*** **America's Constitution: A Biography: Text Questions** available online in the Interactive Teacher's Edition or Unit Resources. Answers and DOK levels are also available.

### Concept Vocabulary

**If** the students struggle to identify the concepts of inclusiveness and exclusiveness, **then** have them look online for the meanings of these words.

### Word Study

**If** students fail to understand the effect of the Latin suffix *–ist,* **then** suggest they write the definitions on pieces of paper and review them with a partner.
For Reteach and Practice, see **Word Study: Latin Suffix *-ist* (RP).**

## Analyze Craft and Structure

**Author's Choices: Rhetoric** Point out to students that Amar uses analogies to create strong, almost jolting, images. In this respect, he is like a poet in his writing. For more support, see **Analyze Craft and Structure: Rhetoric.**

### Practice

See possible responses in chart on student page.

### FORMATIVE ASSESSMENT

### Analyze Craft and Structure

**If** students struggle to understand the analogies in the selection, **then** have them reread the selected paragraphs with one question in mind: What is being compared to what? For Reteach and Practice, see **Analyze Craft and Structure: Rhetoric (RP).**

AMERICA'S CONSTITUTION: A BIOGRAPHY

## Analyze Craft and Structure

**Author's Choices: Rhetoric** An **analogy** is an extended comparison. It is based on the idea that the relationship between one pair of things is like the relationship between another pair. The use of an analogy can clarify complex ideas by explaining an unfamiliar notion in terms of a familiar one. For example, in paragraph 4, Amar introduces the idea that the Preamble to the Constitution is like the words "I accept" in a contract:

> Like the phrases "I do" in an exchange of wedding vows and "I accept" in a contract, the Preamble's words actually performed the very thing they described.

Using this analogy, Amar makes the point that the Constitution represented a binding commitment that affected how people live their lives.

### Practice

**CITE TEXTUAL EVIDENCE** to support your answers.

Reread the passages noted in the chart. For each analogy, identify the two things being compared. Then, explain the idea the analogy helps to clarify. Work independently. Then, share your analysis with your group.

| TEXTUAL DETAILS | TWO THINGS BEING COMPARED | MEANING |
|---|---|---|
| "I do" / "we do" (paragraphs 1, 2, 3, 6, 18) | couple being married and the American people | The analogy suggests that agreeing to the Constitution was a total commitment and perhaps even a sacred act. |
| *fiat lux* (paragraph 10) | God's commandment for light in Genesis and the American people | The people's accepting of the Constitution would put it into action, as God's proclamation of "Let there be light" began Creation. |
| invention of bifocals, the lightning rod, and the Franklin stove (paragraph 18) | advances in the natural sciences and a breakthrough in political science | The Constitution was as important a discovery as Franklin's discoveries in the natural sciences. |

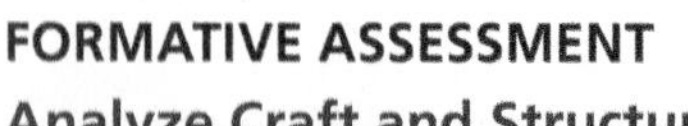

STANDARDS

**Reading Informational Text**
Determine an author's point of view or purpose in a text in which the rhetoric is particularly effective, analyzing how style and content contribute to the power, persuasiveness, or beauty of the text.





PERSONALIZE FOR LEARNING

### Strategic Support

**Analyzing Analogies** Remind students that an analogy uses a familiar idea to understand an unfamiliar one. Reinforce students' analytical skills by having them examine the comparisons in the chart and deciding, for each comparison, which is the familiar idea or thing and which is the unfamiliar one. Establishing these comparisons will aid students in interpreting the analogies.

LANGUAGE DEVELOPMENT

## Author's Style

**Historical Narrative as Argument** A **biography** is a type of narrative nonfiction that tells the story of someone's life. By calling his book a "biography" of the Constitution, Amar indicates that he is telling a story. However, it is not the story of a life, but of a document. Within that story, Amar presents his point of view or position on the Constitution's significance. The story he tells, then, is not just a historical narrative—it is also an argument. Amar states his main idea or principal claim at the end of paragraph 2:

> In the late 1780s, this [the drafting of the U. S. Constitution] was the most democratic deed the world had ever seen.

Amar goes on to present an in-depth description of the conflicts and drama that arose around the ratification of the Constitution, using varied techniques and evidence to tell the story and develop his claim.

- **Historical Details:** Amar is writing for an audience of general readers, not scholars. He includes historical details that provide important background information for such readers. For example, in paragraph 8, he shows how the rules of the ratifying conventions were based on groundbreaking democratic principles.
- **Numerical Data:** Amar presents numerical facts to support his interpretation of events.
- **Quotations:** Amar interweaves quotations from historical figures. These passages add drama to the story he is telling and reinforce the argument he is presenting.

### Read It

Work on your own to identify examples of Amar's use of historical details, numerical data, and quotations. Explain how each example helps to tell the story of the Constitution and build Amar's argument. Share and discuss your responses with your group.

| TYPE OF EVIDENCE | EFFECT |
|---|---|
| Historical Details | Amar uses a quotation by James Wilson to refute arguments by Anti-Federalists. |
| Numerical Data | Amar uses states' ratification election results to demonstrate the level of support for ratification. |
| Quotations | Amar again uses a quotation by James Wilson, this time to extol the virtues of the Constitution over those of Athens, Sparta, and Rome. |

### Write It

**Notebook** Choose a favorite song, graphic novel or comic book, movie, game, or other text. Write a "biography" of the work in which you both tell the story of its development and defend a claim about its importance. Weave in historical details, facts, and quotations.

EVIDENCE LOG

Before moving on to a new selection, go to your Evidence Log and record what you have learned from the excerpt from *America's Constitution: A Biography*.

STANDARDS

**Reading Informational Text**

- Analyze a complex set of ideas or sequence of events and explain how specific individuals, ideas, or events interact and develop over the course of the text.
- Analyze and evaluate the effectiveness of the structure an author uses in his or her exposition or argument, including whether the structure makes points clear, convincing, and engaging.





DIGITAL PERSPECTIVES

## Author's Style

**Historical Narrative as Argument** Point out that a biography is usually about a human being, but in this selection, it is about a document. Ask students to consider the author's attitude toward the Constitution. Amar celebrates the document almost as if it were a human being. For more support, see **Author's Style: Historical Narrative as Argument.**

### Read It

See possible responses in chart on student page.

### Write It

Responses will vary, but all student responses should be written in the style of a biography and include quotations and factual evidence.

Evidence Log Support students in completing their Evidence Log. This paced activity will help prepare them for the Performance-Based Assessment at the end of the unit.

## FORMATIVE ASSESSMENT

### Author's Style

**If** students struggle to understand how the use of different types of factual evidence helps the author build a compelling narrative, **then** have them reread the selected paragraphs and for each statement ask themselves, How does this help me better understand the topic? For Reteach and Practice, see **Author's Style: Historical Narrative as Argument (RP).**

### Selection Test

Administer the "*from* America's Constitution: A Biography (*with an excerpt from* The United States Constitution: A Graphic Adaptation)" Selection Test, which is available in both print and digital formats online in Assessments.

HOW LANGUAGE WORKS

**Descriptors** Amar often uses adjectives and adverbs to emphasize the extraordinary nature of the Constitution and its relationship to "the people." Point out the use of these parts of speech in the following paragraphs:

- use of *most* in paragraphs 1, 2, and 18
- use of *barely, lopsided, uncertain*, and *decisive* in paragraph 6

Have groups evaluate and discuss the effects of these words in the selection.

# *from* The United States Constitution: A Graphic Adaptation

**AUDIO SUMMARIES**
Audio summaries of "*from* The United States Constitution: A Graphic Adaptation" are available online in both English and Spanish in the Interactive Teacher's Edition or Unit Resources. Assigning these summaries prior to reviewing the selection may help students build additional background knowledge and set a context for their first review.

## Summary

*The United States Constitution: A Graphic Adaptation* is a graphic novel written by Jonathan Hennessey and illustrated by Aaron McConnell. This excerpt explores the ratification process of the Constitution, including both the opposing views of the Federalists, those who believed in states' sovereignty, and the Anti-Federalists, those who favored a strong central government. The author includes excerpts from *The Federalist Papers*, anonymously written documents intended to promote the ratification of the Constitution. The excerpt also explores the development of the Bill of Rights, the first ten amendments to the Constitution, designed to protect the rights of the individual and ensure that government remains in the hands of the people.

### Insight

Reading this excerpt from *The United States Constitution: A Graphic Adaptation* will help students understand how the Founders envisioned the Constitution. Checks and balances are a key theme—both between the branches of government and between different factions seeking election.

ESSENTIAL QUESTION:
What is the meaning of freedom?

## Connection to Essential Question

"*from* The United States Constitution: A Graphic Adaptation" will help students gain insight into the Essential Question, "What is the meaning of freedom?" The Constitution is intended to dynamically balance competing influences, preventing any one group from overwhelming the others.

SMALL-GROUP LEARNING PERFORMANCE TASK
Should the Founding Fathers have tried harder to reconcile with Great Britain instead of declaring independence?

UNIT PERFORMANCE-BASED ASSESSMENT
What are the most effective tools for establishing and preserving freedom?

## Connection to Performance Tasks

**Small-Group Learning Performance Task** The excerpt from *The United States Constitution: A Graphic Adaptation* will provide students with additional, vivid examples of the difficulty and the successes the Founders faced in formulating the Constitution and Bill of Rights—both of which can be used as points in the Performance Task.

**Unit Performance-Based Assessment** In this Performance Task, students will make an argument to answer the question: "What are the most effective tools for establishing and preserving freedom?" They can draw on themes from these images to answer this question.

DIGITAL PERSPECTIVES

 Audio  Video  Document  Annotation Highlights | EL Highlights | Online Assessment

## LESSON RESOURCES

| | Making Meaning | Effective Expression |
|---|---|---|
| **Lesson** | **First Review**<br>**Close Review**<br>**Analyze the Media**<br>**Media Vocabulary** | **Writing to Compare** |
| **Instructional Standards** | **RI.10** By the end of grade 11, read and comprehend literary nonfiction . . .<br>**L.6** Acquire and use accurately general academic and domain-specific words and phrases . . .<br>**RI.3** Analyze a complex set of ideas . . .<br>**RI.5** Analyze and evaluate the effectiveness of the structure an author uses . . . | **RI.7** Integrate and evaluate multiple sources of information . . .<br>**W.2** Write informative/explanatory texts . . .<br>**W.9.b** Apply *grades 11–12 reading standards* . . . |
| **STUDENT RESOURCES** | | |
| Available online in the Interactive Student Edition or Unit Resources | Selection Audio<br>First-Review Guide: Media: Art and Photography<br>Close- Review Guide: Media: Art and Photography | Evidence Log |
| **TEACHER RESOURCES** | | |
| **Selection Resources**<br>Available online in the Interactive Teacher's Edition or Unit Resources | Audio Summaries<br>Media Vocabulary<br>*from* The U.S. Constitution: A Graphic Adaptation: Media Questions | Writing to Compare: Informative Essay |
| **Assessment**<br>Available online in Assessments | Selection Test | |
| **My Resources** | A Unit 1 Answer Key is available online and in the Interactive Teacher's Edition. | |

## Media Complexity Rubric: *from* The United States Constitution: A Graphic Adaptation

| Qualitative Measures | |
|---|---|
| Format and Length: 4 graphic novel pages | |
| **Qualitative Measures** | |
| Knowledge Demands<br>1—2—**3**—4—5 | Covers discipline-specific content (U.S. Constitution, Bill of Rights). Content is explained, but prior knowledge of the subject is necessary for full understanding. |
| Structure<br>1—2—**3**—4—5 | Ideas are organized chronologically. Correspondence of text to graphics makes structure easy to navigate, but also presents a challenge of interpreting meaning from both text and illustrations. |
| Language Conventionality and Clarity<br>1—2—**3**—4—5 | Language is formal and academic; many sentences are complex, with multiple clauses; original language from *The Federalist Papers* is included (archaic late 18th-century language) |
| Levels of Meaning/Purpose<br>1—2—3—**4**—5 | Overall purpose is explicit and narrowly focused (exploring Federalists and Bill of Rights), but many supporting concepts are sophisticated and complex; illustrations contain symbolism. |

# FACILITATING

## Jump Start

FIRST REVIEW Ask students what they think the saying "A picture is worth a thousand words" means. Engage students in a discussion of the value of images. Ask students to consider when images are better than words.

## *from* The United States Constitution: A Graphic Adaptation

How can an artist create a graphic adaptation of the U.S. Constitution's development? How could such an adaptation be engrossing? Modeling these and other questions readers might ask will bring this excerpt from *The United States Constitution: A Graphic Adaptation* to life and connect it to the Performance Task question. Selection audio and print capability for the selection are available in the Interactive Teacher's Edition.

## Media Vocabulary

Have groups briefly discuss the media vocabulary. Have they encountered any of these terms before?

Ask students to identify the layout, a speech balloon, and a caption on the first page of the selection. Point out that the layout contains both speech balloons and captions. Remind students that each frame in the layout is called a panel.

## FIRST REVIEW

Have students perform the steps of the first review independently:

LOOK: Have students look at the images and read the accompanying captions and speech balloons.

NOTE: Remind students to focus on images that stand out to them. It might be the representation of the three branches of government or the side-by-side images of "human" cutouts at the end of the selection.

CONNECT: Encourage students to connect the drawings to other images they have seen.

RESPOND: Students will demonstrate their understanding by answering questions and writing a description.

Point out to students that they will perform the first three steps concurrently as they are doing their first review. They will complete the Respond step after they have finished the first review. You may wish to print copies of the **First-Review Guide: Media: Art and Photography** for students to use.



## MAKING MEANING

### Comparing Text to Media

This graphic adaptation focuses on the ratification process of the Constitution and the creation of the Bill of Rights. After reviewing this selection, you will look for similarities and differences between the selections.

About the Author

As an adult, **Jonathan Hennessey** gained a new appreciation for his childhood in historic New England, and he notes that "I often find nothing more entertaining than some scrupulously researched historical account." *The United States Constitution: A Graphic Adaptation* is his first published work.

## *from* The United States Constitution: A Graphic Adaptation

### Media Vocabulary

These words or concepts will be useful to you as you analyze, discuss, and write about graphic novels.

| | |
|---|---|
| **Layout:** overall design and look of a graphic presentation | • Layout deals with the arrangement of graphic panels on a page and with the relationship of text and images within each panel. |
| **Speech Balloon:** shape used in graphic novels and comic books to show what a character says | • A "tail" points from the balloon to the person speaking. If the tail is a series of small bubbles, the balloon expresses a thought.<br>• An artist may use a dotted balloon outline to indicate whispered words or jagged "spikes" in the outline to indicate shouting or screaming. |
| **Caption:** separate text that presents information that cannot be expressed quickly and easily in dialogue | • A caption may appear anywhere inside or outside a panel. It may be broken into several boxes for a panel. |

### First Review MEDIA: ART AND PHOTOGRAPHY

Apply these strategies as you conduct your first review.

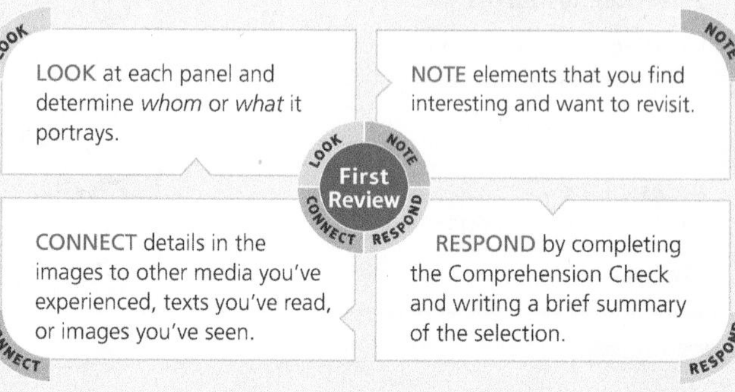

LOOK
LOOK at each panel and determine *whom* or *what* it portrays.
NOTE
NOTE elements that you find interesting and want to revisit.
First Review
CONNECT
CONNECT details in the images to other media you've experienced, texts you've read, or images you've seen.
RESPOND
RESPOND by completing the Comprehension Check and writing a brief summary of the selection.


**Notebook** As you study the graphic novel, record your observations and questions, noting which panel they refer to for later reference.

STANDARDS

**Reading Informational Text**
By the end of grade 11, read and comprehend literary nonfiction in the grades 11–CCR text complexity band proficiently, with scaffolding as needed at the high end of the range.

**Language**
Acquire and use accurately general academic and domain-specific words and phrases, sufficient for reading, writing, speaking, and listening at the college and career readiness level; demonstrate independence in gathering vocabulary knowledge when considering a word or phrase important to comprehension or expression.





## FACILITATING SMALL-GROUP CLOSE READING

**CLOSE READ: Organizing Groups** You may wish to form groups for Small-Group Learning so that each consists of a mix of students with artistic ability and those with other talents. Those with artistic abilities may excel at interpreting the images, but other students may be more adept at synthesizing information or grasping relationships between images and text.

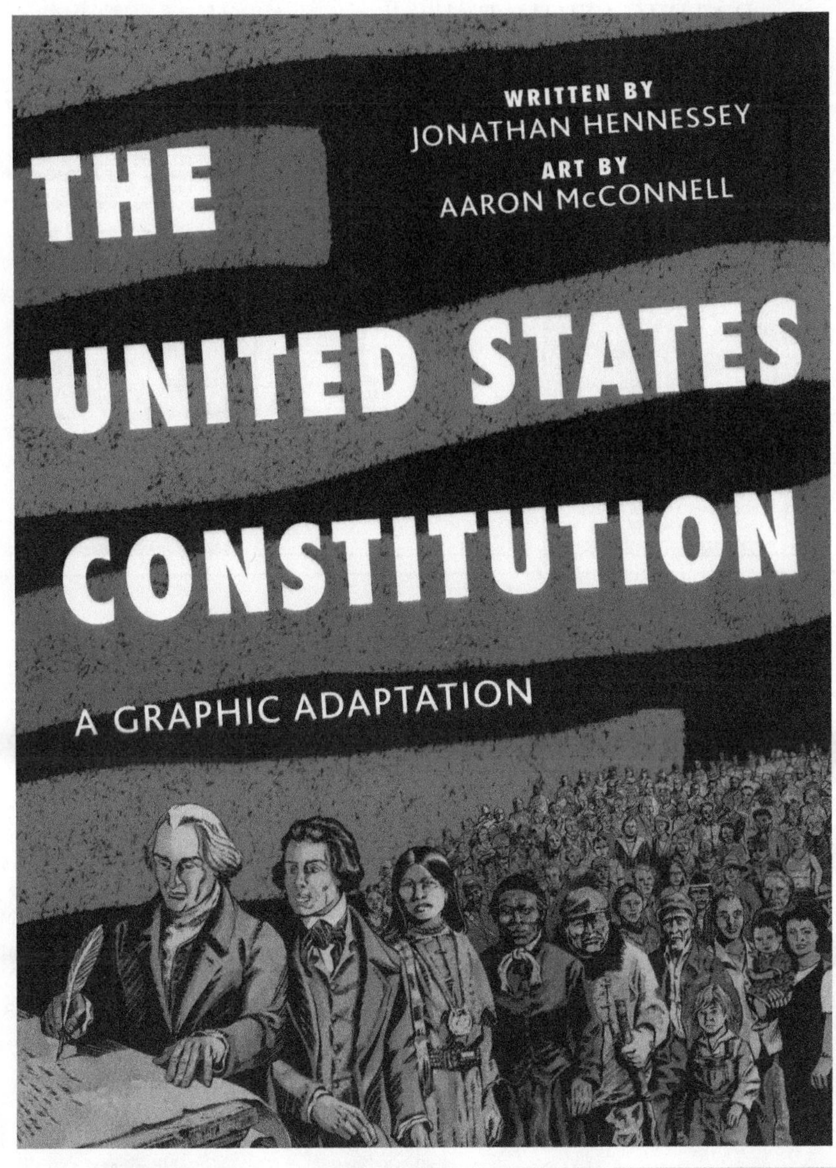


BACKGROUND

While the Articles of Confederation created Congress, it did not create a capable national government. Individual states continued to conduct foreign diplomacy, and Georgia was threatening its own war with Spain. Furthermore, Congress failed to deal effectively with Shays's Rebellion in Massachusetts. These and other weaknesses convinced leaders that revisions to the Articles were necessary to form a stronger national government.

SCAN FOR MULTIMEDIA 

DIGITAL PERSPECTIVES  

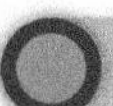 CLOSER REVIEW

## Analyze Composition

Circulate among groups as students conduct their close review. As groups review the cover panel, encourage them to talk about what they note. If needed, provide the following support.

**NOTE:** Have students note details in the panel that explain the arrangement, or work with small groups to have students participate while you note them together.

**QUESTION:** Guide students to consider what these details might tell them. Ask what a viewer can infer from the people in the panel, and accept student responses.
**Possible responses:** The man in the foreground is probably a framer of the Constitution, but he is followed by a large and diverse group of people, indicating that the Constitution is supported by the American people as a whole.

**CONCLUDE:** Help students to formulate conclusions about the importance of these details in the panel. Ask students why the artist might have included these details.
**Possible responses:** These details show that although only a few men framed the Constitution, the document protects the rights of all the people.

Remind students that **composition** refers to the placement or arrangement of visual elements in a piece of art or visual media. Image placement conveys meaning. In the cover panel, the framers of the Constitution are closest to the reader, in the foreground. This helps show their leadership of a diverse nation, which is represented by the people shown in the background.

PERSONALIZE FOR LEARNING

### English Language Support

**Significant Symbols** Support students in a discussion about the cultural significance of the symbols in the cover image. Help them identify elements such as the red, white, and blue colors and the stripe shapes, which are reminiscent of the American flag. Discuss the elements of diversity reflected in the crowd standing behind the Founding Fathers. Have students discuss why the illustrator might have chosen these typical American symbols as a cover image for the graphic novel about the Constitution. **ALL LEVELS**

## CLOSER REVIEW

### Interpret Images

Circulate among groups as students conduct their close review. Suggest that groups review panels 2 and 4. Encourage them to talk about what they note. If needed, provide the following support.

**NOTE:** Have students note details in the panels that illustrate Anti-Federalist concerns, or work with small groups to have students participate while you note them together.

**QUESTION:** Guide students to consider what these details might tell them. Ask what a viewer can infer from panel 4, in which the three branches of government are represented as bodies with buildings as heads, and accept student responses.

**Possible responses:** The government is not just a group of offices; it is the real people who work in them.

**CONCLUDE:** Help students formulate conclusions about the importance of these details in the drawing. Ask students why the author might have included these details.

**Possible responses:** People were worried that the new government was not expressly Christian, was too powerful, and was not interested in the voice of the people.

Remind students that when **interpreting images** in a graphic presentation, the reader is decoding the author and illustrator's intentions in their use of strong imagery to convey meaning. It is important to note that not all comics are created to be funny. Some emphasize drama, politics, or adventure.

## RATIFICATION: Federalists vs. Anti-Federalists

1

IN THE VOTE TO SEND DELEGATES TO RATIFY THE CONSTITUTION, MORE PEOPLE WOULD HAVE A SAY ON THEIR LAWS—AND THE SHAPE OF THEIR FUTURE—THAN EVER BEFORE.

AND FOR THIS VOTE, MOST STATES REDUCED OR ABOLISHED THEIR RULES ABOUT OWNING PROPERTY.

2

UP TO THAT TIME A *FEDERALIST* WAS SOMEONE WHO BELIEVED FIRST AND FOREMOST IN THE SOVEREIGNTY OF THE STATES, WHILE AN *ANTI-FEDERALIST* WANTED A STRONG, CENTRAL GOVERNMENT TO RULE OVER THEM, JUST AS THE CONSTITUTION WOULD ESTABLISH...

...BUT IN WHAT TODAY WOULD BE CALLED POLITICAL SPIN, THE ONES PUSHING HARDEST TO RATIFY THE CONSTITUTION TOOK THE FEDERALIST NAME FOR THEIR OWN PURPOSE, TO HELP WIN OVER THE COMMON PEOPLE.

3

UNDER THE PEN NAME PUBLIUS, HAMILTON, MADISON, AND JOHN JAY WROTE 85 ESSAYS NOW KNOWN AS *THE FEDERALIST PAPERS* TO EXPLAIN AND CHAMPION THEIR CAUSE.

To the people of the state of New York: you are called upon to deliberate on a new Constitution for the United States of America ...

4

84 UNIT 1 • WRITING FREEDOM

### VOCABULARY DEVELOPMENT

**Word Analysis** Tell students that *Publius* (panel 3) was a common given name in ancient Rome. Ask students to suggest its meaning. Point out that it looks like the word *public*. In fact, *Publius* means "the people." Have groups discuss why Jay, Madison, and Hamilton adopted the name as their pen name in *The Federalist Papers.*

5

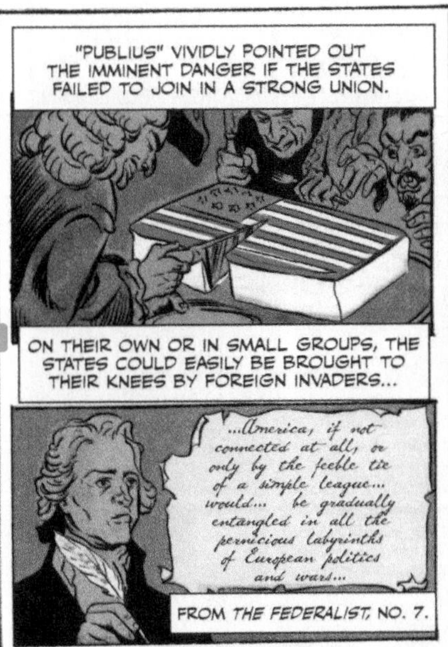


6

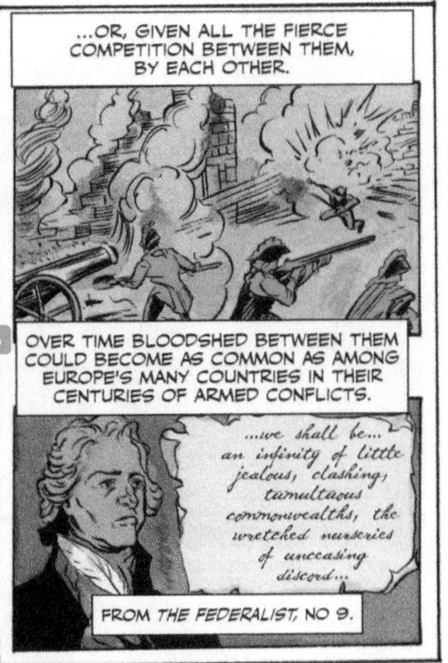


7

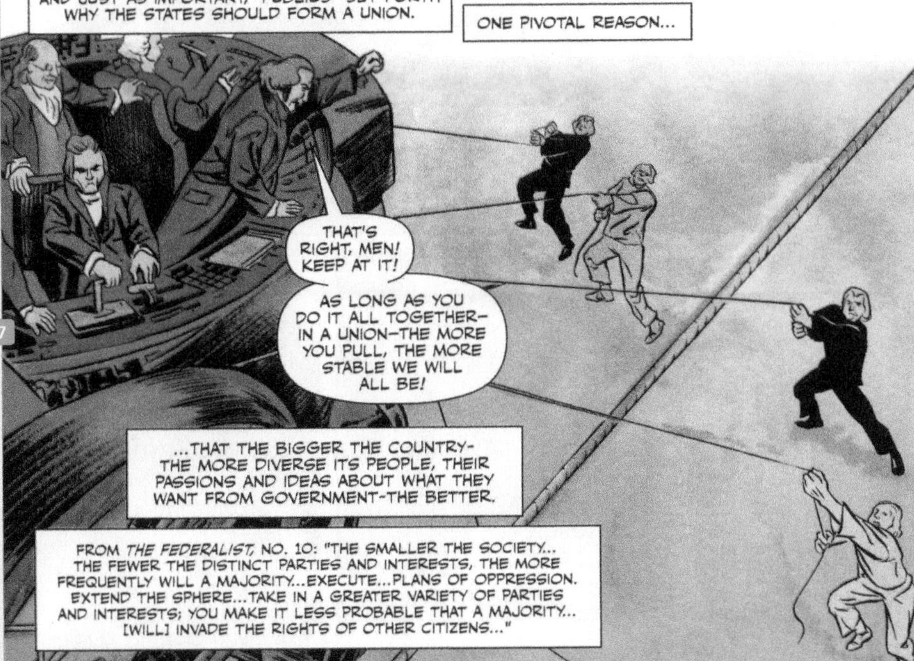


*from* The United States Constitution: A Graphic Adaptation **85**

## DIGITAL PERSPECTIVES

**Enriching the Media** Panels 5–7 include direct quotations from *The Federalist Papers.* Explain to students that beginning in 1787, John Jay, Alexander Hamilton, and James Madison published 85 articles and essays making the case for a stronger government under the Constitution. Have students use the Internet to collect links to several of *The Federalist Papers.* Have students select a paper to read and then write a summary of its argument. Have students read their summaries to the class. Then, have the class summarize the intent of the Papers in general. **(Research to Explore)**

DIGITAL PERSPECTIVES

## CLOSER REVIEW

### Interpret Images 

Circulate among groups as students conduct their close review. Suggest that groups close review panels 5–7, which illustrate the danger of no union and the value of a strong union. Encourage them to talk about what they note. If needed, provide the following support.

**NOTE:** Have students note details in the panels that show the dangers of a weak union and the advantages of a strong union, or work with small groups to have students participate while you note them together.

**QUESTION:** Guide students to consider what these details might tell them. Ask what a viewer can infer from what is happening in the upper images in panels 5 and 6, as opposed to what is happening in the lower image, and accept student responses.

**Possible responses:** In the upper images, foreign powers are cutting the United States into pieces and countrymen are fighting against each other. The lower image shows everybody pulling together to maintain the strength of the nation.

**CONCLUDE:** Help students to formulate conclusions about the importance of these details in the images. Ask students why the author might have included these details.

**Possible responses:** These details illustrate the dangers that the country faced at that time, and then proposes a way to solve those problems.

Explain that the **images** in a graphic adaptation are set apart by panels. A panel refers to a framed image. It offers the reader a perspective, or point of view. For example, panels 5 and 6 are divided in half.

The top part of the panel displays a visual representation of a weak union. The bottom part of the panel provides the perspective that this is what the Founders were envisioning when writing the particular section of *The Federalist Papers.*

Remind students that **interpreting images** includes analyzing the design and organization of the images, not just the content of the pictures.

## CLOSER REVIEW

### Analyze Text Boxes

Circulate among the groups as students conduct their close review. Suggest that groups close review panels 8–11. Encourage them to talk about what they note. If needed, provide the following support.

**NOTE:** Have students note details in these panels that help to analyze the text, or work with small groups to have students participate while you note them together.

**QUESTION:** Guide students to consider what these details might tell them. Ask what the states were worried about, and accept student responses.

**Possible responses:** These states were worried about the enormous power given to the government. They wanted "one thing." That thing is mentioned in the script in the last panel—a Bill of Rights.

**CONCLUDE:** Help students formulate conclusions about the importance of these details in the panels. Ask students why the author might have included these details.

**Possible responses:** The whole page is leading up to the Bill of Rights. But the author saves its mention for panel 13, the tension of the story.

Point out that there are no speech balloons on this page, just **text boxes.** Explain that the author chose to use direct narration in order to tell what is happening instead of indirect dialogue that expresses ideas through the speech of the characters.

## PERSONALIZE FOR LEARNING

### Strategic Support

**Clarifying the Elements of an Argument** Call student attention to panel 11. If students struggle to comprehend the elements of the argument for ratification, have them find the text box in panel 11 that summarizes people's fears (". . . that the government would simply be too powerful"). Ask students to identify the caption that tells how the Federalists responded to these fears (". . . by promising to quickly add one thing to the Constitution"). Point out that this "give and take" between groups with different perspectives is an essential means of governing.

# The Bill of Rights: AMENDMENTS 1–10

DIGITAL  PERSPECTIVES 

## CLOSER REVIEW

### Compare Images

Circulate among groups as students conduct the close review. Suggest that groups review panels 18 and 19. Encourage them to talk about what they note. If needed, provide the following support.

**NOTE:** Have students note details in the panels that lend themselves to a comparison, or work with small groups to have students participate while you note them together.

**QUESTION:** Guide students to consider what these details might tell them. Ask what a viewer can infer from what was noted, and accept student responses.

**Possible responses:** The images are almost the same, except in the first panel, the individual in the center is a different color from the rest. This difference highlights the focus on the rights of the individual.

**CONCLUDE:** Help students formulate conclusions about the importance of these details in the panel. Ask students why the author might have included these details.

**Possible responses:** The author wanted to show that in addition to protecting the rights of the individual against the majority, the Bill of Rights also protects groups of people from the possible excesses of government.

When readers **compare images** they see that the artist used both color and graphic weight to show contrast in the images of the last two panels. Guide students to note that the individual was highlighted by a brighter, lighter color making it stand out in the panel on the bottom left. The less vivid color of the other people causes them to fade into the background. The panel on the right shows all the shapes with the same graphic weight.

## PERSONALIZE FOR LEARNING

### English Language Support

**Analyze the Panels** Use the following activities to support students in interpreting panels 14–19.

Have students explain the action in each panel, using phrases and short sentences. Have them identify which panel or panels show people being protected from a government that is oppressive. **EMERGING**

Have students explain how the panels are related to each other, using increasingly detailed sentences. Have them identify which panels mention rights that are in the Bill of Rights, and tell what these rights are. **EXPANDING**

Have students use detailed sentences to describe the action in each panel and explain how the panels relate to each other. Have them evaluate whether the panels make a strong case for their argument. **BRIDGING**

## Comprehension Check

Possible responses:

1. Before the ratification process, a *federalist* was a person who believed in the sovereignty of the states. During that process, the word *federalist* was adopted by those who promoted the Constitution, which established a strong central government.
2. The three branches of government are depicted as the buildings in which the branches now operate replacing the heads of men. This gives the impression that the branches are representing people.
3. The reasons included the dangers faced by the states: an inability to defend against foreign invasion, war breaking out within the union, and a smaller majority seizing control of government and depriving other citizens of their rights.
4. The Bill of Rights contains the assumption that people have certain rights by birth.
5. **Possible response:** The process of ratifying the Constitution switched the meanings of the terms *Federalist* and *Anti-Federalist.* Federalists now campaigned for the Constitution while Anti-Federalists argued against it. Essays known today as *The Federalist Papers* helped explain the Constitution and warned of the problems that might result if it were not ratified. Eight states ratified the document over a period of nine months. Massachusetts submitted changes and capitulated only under the threat of another convention. Its vote made the Constitution the law of the land, but New York and Virginia would not ratify it without the promise of a Bill of Rights.

## Research

**Research to Clarify** If students struggle to select an unfamiliar detail from the graphic adaptation images, have them look through the selection, panel by panel, being prepared to explain the action in or meaning of each panel. Tell them that when they reach a panel where they hesitate or are confused, they may have hit the unfamiliar detail that they can research.

**Research to Explore** If students struggle to identify something from the graphic adaptation that interests them, ask them what they remember from the selection. Which image was the most memorable? Their responses should lead them to what interests them the most.

## Comprehension Check

Complete the following items after you finish your first review. Review and clarify details with your group.

1. As the fight for ratification began, how did the meaning of the word *federalist* change? Refer to panels 1–4.
2. How does the artist visually depict the three branches of government? Refer to panels 4 and 11.
3. Identify three reasons "Publius" gave in support of a strong federal government. Refer to panels 5–7.
4. According to the author, what assumption about human rights does the Bill of Rights reflect?
5. **Notebook** Write a summary to confirm your understanding of the ratification of the Constitution, as presented in the graphic adaptation.

### RESEARCH

**Research to Clarify** Choose at least one unfamiliar detail from the graphic adaptation. Briefly research that detail. In what way does the information you found shed light on your understanding of the Constitution or the Bill of Rights?

**Research to Explore** Choose something that interested you from the graphic adaptation, and formulate a research question about it.





### CROSS-CURRICULAR PERSPECTIVES

**Art** Discuss with students the impact that a carefully chosen visual has. Make available to students a full listing of the Bill of Rights, the first ten amendments to the Constitution. Have them choose an amendment in the Bill of Rights and draw a page that illustrates it, using a layout with panels, captions, and speech balloons. They may wish to follow the style in the graphic adaptation they have just read, or they may choose their own style.

MAKING MEANING

## Close Review

With your group, review your notes and, if necessary, revisit the graphic adaptation. Record any new observations that seem important. What **questions** do you have? What can you **conclude**?

THE UNITED STATES CONSTITUTION: A GRAPHIC ADAPTATION

## Analyze the Media

CITE TEXTUAL EVIDENCE to support your answers.

Complete the activities.

1. **Present and Discuss** Choose the part of the graphic adaptation you find most interesting or powerful. Share your choice with the group and discuss why you chose it. Explain what you noticed about that part, what questions it raised for you, and what conclusions you reached about it.
2. **Synthesize** With your group, review the entire graphic adaptation. How do the images, speech balloons, and captions work together to reveal the difficult moments in this part of the Constitution's "story"? Do they inform, entertain, or both? Explain.
3. **Notebook** **Essential Question:** ***What is the meaning of freedom?*** How did the Constitution and the Bill of Rights clarify the meaning of freedom for Americans? Support your response with evidence from the graphic adaptation.

LANGUAGE DEVELOPMENT

## Media Vocabulary

layout speech balloon caption

Use these vocabulary words in your responses to the following questions.

1. **(a)** Which panel presents a caption with no image? **(b)** What do readers learn from that panel? **(c)** How does the arrangement of the caption text reflect its content?
2. **(a)** Which appears more often in this excerpt—speech balloons or captions? **(b)** Why do you think that Hennessey and McConnell chose to present so much information in one way instead of the other?
3. Choose the series of panels that you think most clearly conveys a large amount of information. Explain the visual choices that make those panels effective.

STANDARDS

**Reading Informational Text**

- Analyze a complex set of ideas or sequence of events and explain how specific individuals, ideas, or events interact and develop over the course of the text.
- Analyze and evaluate the effectiveness of the structure an author uses in his or her exposition or argument, including whether the structure makes points clear, convincing, and engaging.





DIGITAL PERSPECTIVES

## Jump Start

CLOSE REVIEW Have students imagine that they are living in 1788. The Constitution has been written but it has yet to be ratified. Have them consider how people of that time thought of this document, which would deeply impact their lives. How might students have felt if they lived in 1788?

## Close Review

If needed, model close reviewing by using the Closer Review notes in the Interactive Teacher's Edition.

Remind groups to use Accountable Talk in their discussions and to support one another as they complete the close review.

## Analyze the Media

**Possible responses:**

1. Answers will vary but should address parts of the graphic adaptation that are especially dramatic (such as the panel depicting the angry crowd of opponents) or intriguing (such as the image of Americans "pulling together").
2. Responses will vary, but students should cite specific examples from the graphic adaptation to support their assertions.
3. **Notebook** Responses will vary, but students should discuss the concerns that people had about a government that was too powerful, as well as the protections afforded by the Bill of Rights. Some students might also point out that a strong government can provide stability for its people and that the Constitution tried to strike a balance.

## Media Vocabulary

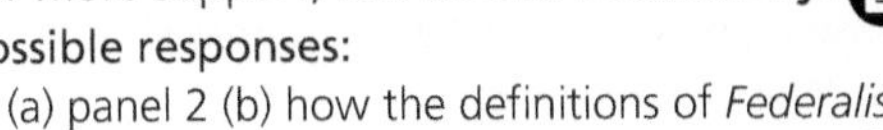

For more support, see **Media Vocabulary.**

**Possible responses:**

1. (a) panel 2 (b) how the definitions of *Federalist* and *Anti-Federalist* switched (c) The *layout* of the text helps convey meaning. Text is displayed on opposite sides of the panel, showing disagreement
2. (a) *captions* (b) It would take many images and many *speech balloons* to express that information. In addition, it would be difficult to identify a speaker for much of the information.
3. Panels 5–7 convey a lot of ideas and information. Panels 5–6 show disagreement by splitting the panels and showing opposing images. Panel 7 uses the metaphor of a ship to explain ideas.

### FORMATIVE ASSESSMENT

### Analyze the Media

**If** the students struggle to close review the graphic adaptation, **then** provide the ***from* The U.S. Constitution: A Graphic Adaptation: Media Questions** available online in the Interactive Teacher's Edition or Unit Resources.

### Media Vocabulary

**If** students struggle to identify the difference between speech balloons and captions, **then** stage a brief choral reading of several panels of the graphic adaptation. Assign a narrator to read captions, and have several speakers read the speech balloons. Since there is no main character as a speaker, these roles will be small. If the groups still fail to recognize the difference, you should intervene with hints and tips.

# FACILITATING

## Writing to Compare

As students prepare to compare information they've gathered about ratifying the U.S. Constitution from a text and a graphic adaptation, they will consider the strengths of each medium in conveying the information.

**Analyze the Texts** Encourage groups to divide up the work, with members focusing on one text or the other. Suggest that more members work on the excerpt from "America's Constitution," since there is more information there. Make sure each group comes up with an original topic for the last row of the chart.

Possible responses:

a. selection of delegates for ratification votes

b. The opening of the text mentions the need for states to unify and "keep Old World monarchs at a distance." Quotations from James Wilson emphasize that the people had the opportunity to revise the proposed Constitution as they best saw fit.

c. Arguments listed include the idea that the Constitution should have been only a revision of the Articles of Confederation, not a completely new document.

d. Details of the process include creation of the Constitution.

e. The text explains that, unlike other elections, elections for ratification delegates in several states would not require voters to own property.

f. Quotations from the *Federalist Papers* show needs filled by Constitution.

g. Three individuals voice complaints in one of the illustrations: there is no religious test, there is not enough focus on the states, and the men who drafted the Constitution are aristocrats.

h. A diagram of architectural columns shows the order in which the states ratified the Constitution.

i. An illustration of a globe emphasizes how unusual it was to allow so many people to have a say in how their government is organized.

Possible responses

1. Direct quotations support ideas. Illustrations emphasize key points.
2. Answers will vary; most students may choose "America's Constitution."
3. The graphic adaptation gives a more memorable account because the illustrations create a stronger impression in the reader's mind. Answers will vary.

### FORMATIVE ASSESSMENT

### Prepare to Compare

**If** students are unable to compare the graphic adaptation with the text, **then** for each content element have them ask: From which source did I learn the most about the topic?

EFFECTIVE EXPRESSION

AMERICA'S CONSTITUTION: A BIOGRAPHY

THE UNITED STATES CONSTITUTION: A GRAPHIC ADAPTATION

## Writing to Compare

You have read two works that provide historical information about the ratification of the U.S. Constitution. Now, deepen your understanding by comparing and writing about the two works.

**Assignment**

An informative text explains how or why something is true. Write an **informative essay** in which you explain how reading both *America's Constitution: A Biography* and *The United States Constitution: A Graphic Adaptation* helps a person more fully understand the ratification of the U.S. Constitution. Your essay should address these questions:

- What are the strengths of each medium?
- What unique kinds of information does each text present, and how?

To support your central idea, cite evidence from both texts. Support may take the form of quotations, paraphrases, summaries, or descriptions.

### Planning and Prewriting

**Analyze the Texts** With your group, discuss how each text presents different types of information about the Constitution. Use the chart to gather your notes. Generate your own topic for the last row.

| TOPIC | AMERICA'S CONSTITUTION: A BIOGRAPHY | THE UNITED STATES CONSTITUTION: A GRAPHIC ADAPTATION |
|---|---|---|
| the need for a Constitution | b. | f. |
| objections to the Constitution | c. | g. |
| the ratification process | d. | h. |
| a. See answers in Teacher's Edition. | e. | i. |

**Notebook** Respond to these questions.

1. What strategies or techniques are used to communicate key ideas in each text?
2. Which gives a more thorough account of the Constitution's origins? How?
3. Which gives a more memorable account? How so?

STANDARDS

**Reading Informational Text**
Integrate and evaluate multiple sources of information presented in different media or formats as well as in words in order to address a question or solve a problem.

**Writing**
- Write informative/explanatory texts to examine and convey complex ideas, concepts, and information clearly and accurately through the effective selection, organization, and analysis of content.
- Apply *grades 11–12 Reading standards* to literary nonfiction.





### PERSONALIZE FOR LEARNING

**Strategic Support**

**Research and Order of Events** To help students organize events sequentially, have pairs of students research to determine the years that the following took place.

- Declaration of Independence
- American Revolution
- Articles of Confederation
- Constitutional Convention
- ratification of Constitution
- Bill of Rights added to Constitution

## Drafting

**Develop a Main Idea** Review your Prewriting notes. With your group, draw some conclusions about the main strengths of each text. Then, work independently to draft a main idea for your essay by completing the following frame.

> **Main Idea:** Reading both the historical narrative and the graphic novel can help a person better understand the origins of the Constitution. This is because the historical narrative ______________________, whereas the graphic novel ______________________.

Take turns sharing your completed main idea with the group. Discuss which versions are stronger, and why. Use group members' feedback to revise your main idea.

**Choose Evidence** Your main idea contains a general statement about each text. In your essay, you must support each general statement with evidence—quotations, descriptions, summaries, or paraphrases. One possible general statement and two pieces of supporting evidence are shown here.

EXAMPLE

**General Statement:** The graphic novel communicates key ideas in memorable ways.

- **Evidence:** Panel 8 showing shaded stamps of states that had ratified the Constitution and unshaded stamps of those that had not
- **Evidence:** vivid image in panel 5 of the U.S. flag being sliced like a cake

Work with your group to identify strong pieces of evidence for each of your general statements. Take notes in a chart like this one.

| GENERAL STATEMENT | EVIDENCE | PAGE/PANEL NUMBER |
|---|---|---|
| | | |
| | | |

**Write a Draft** Draft your essay independently. Include your main idea in the introduction. Include each general statement and your evidence for it in a separate body section. In your conclusion, make an observation about one or both texts that leaves your reader with some food for thought.

### Review, Revise, and Edit

When you are finished drafting, exchange papers with a group member. Ask your peer to comment on both the content and organization of your essay. Use the feedback to guide your revisions. Finally, edit and proofread your work. Replace vague language with more specific words and phrases. Correct any errors in grammar, spelling, or punctuation that you discover.

EVIDENCE LOG

Before moving on to a new selection, go to your Evidence Log and record what you learned from the excerpts from *America's Constitution: A Biography* and *The United States Constitution: A Graphic Adaptation.*





DIGITAL PERSPECTIVES

## Drafting

**Develop a Main Idea** Remind students that it is at this stage of the assignment that they will switch from working in groups to working independently. Once the groups are done discussing the strengths of each text, students will begin working individually on their essays, beginning with completing the sentence frames.

**Choose Evidence** Encourage students to use their prewriting charts as a starting point for gathering evidence. Note that they will probably need to return to the texts to gather additional evidence that directly supports their main idea.

**Write a Draft** Remind students that their essays need to indicate the strengths of each medium and identify the unique kinds of information each text presents.

## Review and Revise

As students revise, encourage them to review their draft to be sure they have explained their thinking clearly. Ask them to review their word choice. Finally, remind students to check for grammar, usage, and mechanics.

For more support, see **Writing to Compare: Informative Essay.**

Evidence Log Support students in completing their Evidence Log. This paced activity will help prepare them for the Performance-Based Assessment at the end of the unit.

## FORMATIVE ASSESSMENT

### Writing to Compare

**If** students struggle to support their general statements, **then** ask them to review each text for more support.

### Selection Test

Administer the "*from* America's Constitution: A Biography (*with an excerpt from* The United States Constitution: A Graphic Adaptation)" Selection Test, which is available in both print and digital formats online in Assessments.

PERSONALIZE FOR LEARNING

### Challenge

**Building Understanding** Have groups discuss how the genres and/or media of the first two selections in the Small-Group Learning section affected students' understandings of and receptiveness to the lessons presented throughout the unit. Encourage students to share which genre or medium they found more understandable or thought-provoking. Remind students that no one genre is better than another, and that a genre or format they find easy to understand may be challenging for another student.

# *from* The Interesting Narrative of the Life of Olaudah Equiano

**AUDIO SUMMARIES**
Audio summaries of this excerpt from *The Interesting Narrative of the Life of Olaudah Equiano* are available online in both English and Spanish in the Interactive Teacher's Edition or Unit Resources. Assigning these summaries prior to reading the selection may help students build additional background knowledge and set a context for their first read.

## Summary

In this excerpt from the autobiography *The Interesting Narrative of the Life of Olaudah Equiano,* the author describes his journey as a captured slave aboard a ship traveling from his native Africa to the Caribbean. Equiano, like the other captives, endures terrible conditions onboard. The slaves are packed into the cargo hold, where they suffer from intolerable heat, foul smells, and quickly spreading illness. Upon their arrival in the Caribbean, Equiano fears that the white men who come aboard to examine the slaves are cannibals about to eat them. Local Africans explain to Equiano that he and the others are to be sold as workers.

### Insight

Reading the excerpt from *The Interesting Narrative of the Life of Olaudah Equiano* will help students understand the cruelty, suffering, and fears of those African captives who were brought to America as slaves. While the Constitution safeguarded the rights for most white males to participate in their government, it denied any rights to slaves, all of whom were considered property.

ESSENTIAL QUESTION:
What is the meaning of freedom?

## Connection to Essential Question

*The Interesting Narrative of the Life of Olaudah Equiano* presents an enslaved African's experience as an angle to the question "What is the meaning of freedom?" This biographical text makes clear that many who lived at the time of the founding of the United States were denied of the freedoms provided by the new Constitution.

SMALL-GROUP LEARNING PERFORMANCE TASK
Do narratives provide strong evidence to support arguments about American freedoms?

UNIT PERFORMANCE-BASED ASSESSMENT
What are the most effective tools for establishing and preserving freedom?

## Connection to Performance Tasks

**Small-Group Learning Performance Task** In this Performance Task, students will consider whether narratives provide strong evidence to support arguments about American freedoms. Students will note that in this narrative, a man is destined for the United States not to claim the freedoms promised to all men in the Constitution, but rather to serve as a slave to the people who enjoyed those freedoms.

**Unit Performance-Based Assessment** This selection offers a counterpoint to the unit performance-based assessment by providing evidence of how the Constitution initially did not establish and preserve freedom for those brought to the country as slaves. However, the fact that the people could participate in government and make changes in the Constitution eventually led the people to end slavery by granting full citizenship to former African-American slaves and their heirs. Unfortunately, this process took more than one hundred and fifty years to achieve. Still, that formal process becomes a tool that the Constitution can use to implement change and establish, expand, and preserve freedom.

DIGITAL PERSPECTIVES

 Audio  Video  Document  Annotation Highlights  EL Highlights Online Assessment

## LESSON RESOURCES

| *From* The Interesting Narrative of the Life of Olaudah Equiano | Making Meaning | Language Development | Effective Expression |
|---|---|---|---|
| Lesson | **First Read**<br>**Close Read the Text**<br>**Analyze the Text**<br>**Analyze Craft and Structure** | **Concept Vocabulary**<br>**Word Study**<br>**Conventions and Style** | **Writing to Sources** |
| Instructional Standards | **RI.10** By the end of grade 11, read and comprehend literary nonfiction . . .<br>**RI.6** Determine an author's point of view . . .<br>**L.4** Determine or clarify the meaning of unknown and multiple-meaning words and phrases . . . | **L.4.c** Consult general and specialized reference materials . . .<br>**L.1** Demonstrate command of the conventions . . .<br>**L.1.a** Apply the understanding that usage is a matter of convention . . . | **W.2.f** Provide a concluding statement . . . |
| **STUDENT RESOURCES** | | | |
| Available online in the Interactive Student Edition or Unit Resources | Selection Audio<br>First-Read Guide: Nonfiction<br>Close-Read Guide: Nonfiction | Word Network | Evidence Log |
| **TEACHER RESOURCES** | | | |
| **Selection Resources** Available online in the Interactive Teacher's Edition or Unit Resources | Audio Summaries<br>Annotation Highlights<br>EL Highlights<br>English Language Support Lesson: Eighteenth-Century Narrative Style<br>*from* The Interesting Narrative of the Life: Text Questions<br>Analyze Craft and Structure: Literary Nonfiction | Concept Vocabulary and Word Study<br>Conventions and Style: Eighteenth-Century Narrative Style | Writing to Sources: Argument |
| **Reteach/Practice (RP)** Available online in the Interactive Teacher's Edition or Unit Resources | Analyze Craft and Structure: Literary Nonfiction (RP) | Word Study: Latin Root *-ject-* (RP)<br>Conventions and Style: Eighteenth-Century Narrative Style (RP) | Writing to Sources: Argument (RP) |
| **Assessment** My Resources Available online in Assessments | Selection Test | | |
| **My Resources** | A Unit 1 Answer Key is available online and in the Interactive Teacher's Edition. | | |

# Reading Support

| Text Complexity Rubric: *from* The Interesting Narrative of the Life of Olaudah Equiano | |
|---|---|
| **Quantitative Measures** | |
| **Lexile:** 1240 **Text Length:** 1,146 words | |
| **Qualitative Measures** | |
| Knowledge Demands ① ❷ ③ ④ ⑤ | The situation will be unfamiliar to readers (an enslaved African's account of his harrowing journey aboard a slave ship), but the situations and emotions are clearly explained. |
| Structure ① ❷ ③ ④ ⑤ | Organization of the first-person narrative is mostly straightforward and sequential. |
| Language Conventionality and Clarity ① ② ❸ ④ ⑤ | Sentences are long and descriptive with nested clauses, some use of passive voice, and some unfamiliar vocabulary. For example, the writer references necessary tubs (toilets) and galling of the chains (chafing/soreness). |
| Levels of Meaning/Purpose ① ❷ ③ ④ ⑤ | Meaning and concepts are straightforward. The main purpose of the selection is to convey the details of a harrowing journey on a slave ship. |

DECIDE AND PLAN

## English Language Support

Provide English Learners with support for knowledge demands and language as they read the selection.

**Knowledge Demands** Before reading the text, have students summarize the background information. Making notes of what they know so far will help them as they read the text. Clarify unfamiliar words—*necessary tubs (toilets), galling of the chains (chafing/soreness).*

**Language** Students will likely have difficulty with some of the unfamiliar vocabulary. Instead of trying to understand every word, encourage students to scan for events in each paragraph that they understand. Ask them to write sentences restating the information they understood.

## Strategic Support

Provide students with strategic support to ensure that they can successfully read the text.

**Knowledge Demands** After reading the background information, make sure students understand the situation that is the focus of the selection—a harrowing journey on a slave ship. Ask students what they know about slave ships.

**Language** Help students reword long and complex sentences. Using the language from the selection, suggest simpler sentences that convey the same meaning. For example, for paragraph 1: *When the ship was ready, we were forced below the deck. The stench and crowded conditions were unbearable.* Ask students to read the new sentences and discuss.

## Challenge

Provide students who need to be challenged with ideas for how they can go beyond a simple interpretation of the text.

**Text Analysis** Have students discuss one of the anecdotes the writer includes in his narrative—for example, when the ship's crew throws away their extra fish instead of sharing it with the slaves. How do these anecdotes make the narrative more compelling?

**Written Response** The writer uses vivid descriptions to describe the horror of his journey. Have students select a part of the narrative they found to be most powerful. Then have students discuss what about that particular section was so powerful.

TEACH

## Read and Respond

Have the groups read the selection and complete the Making Meaning and Language Development activities.

# Standards Support Through Teaching and Learning Cycle

## IDENTIFY NEEDS

Analyze results of the Beginning-of-Year Assessment, focusing on the items relating to Unit 1. Also take into consideration student performance to this point and your observations of where particular students struggle.

## DECIDE AND PLAN

- If students have performed poorly on items matching these standards, then provide selection scaffolds before assigning them the on-level lesson provided in the Student Edition.
- If students have done well on the Beginning-of-Year Assessment, then challenge them to keep progressing and learning by giving them opportunities to practice the skills in depth.
- Use the Selection Resources listed on the Planning pages for *The Interesting Narrative of Olaudah Equiano* to help students continually improve their ability to master the standards.

**Instructional Standards: *from* The Interesting Narrative of Olaudah Equiano**

| | Catching Up | This Year | Looking Forward |
|---|---|---|---|
| **Reading** | You may wish to administer the **Analyze Craft and Structure: Literary Nonfiction (RP)** worksheet to help students understand how rhetoric and other literary devices are used in order to have an impact on the reader. | **RI.6** Determine an author's point of view or purpose in a text in which the rhetoric is particularly effective, analyzing how style and content contribute to the power, persuasiveness, or beauty of the text. | Challenge students to have a discussion about how the rhetorical devices used in this narrative affect the reader. |
| **Writing** | You may wish to administer the **Writing to Sources: Argument (RP)** worksheet to help students understand how to support the claims that they make using rhetoric, clear reasoning and evidence. | **W.2.f** Provide a concluding statement or section that follows from and supports the information or explanation presented. | Have students write an argumentative essay based on the selection and then trade with partners. Students will critique how well the claim is supported and whether counterclaims are adequately addressed. |
| **Language** | You may wish to administer the **Conventions: Eighteenth-Century Narrative Style (RP)** worksheet to help students understand how punctuation can affect a text and the reader's reaction to it.<br><br>Have students revist the Latin root *-ject*. Ask them to offer a few sentences with words that use the root, such as *reject* and *eject*. | **L.1** Demonstrate command of the conventions of standard English grammar and usage when writing or speaking.<br><br>**L.1.a** Apply the understanding that usage is a matter of convention, can change over time, and is sometimes contested. | You may wish to challenge students to experiment with using punctuation in a way that creates tension, suspense, or a feeling of anticipation. |

## ANALYZE AND REVISE

- Analyze student work for evidence of student learning.
- Identify whether or not students have met the expectations in the standards.
- Identify implications for future instruction.

## TEACH

Implement the planned lesson, and gather evidence of student learning.

# FACILITATING

## Jump Start

FIRST READ Ask students to discuss what they know about the practice of slavery in the United States before the Civil War. Ask them what they think the idea of freedom might have meant to an enslaved person.

### *from* The Interesting Narrative of the Life of Olaudah Equiano

What would the daily life of a slave be like? What activities are slaves barred from doing? What *must* they do? Modeling these and other questions readers might ask will bring "*from* The Interesting Narrative of the Life of Olaudah Equiano" to life and connect it to the Performance Task question. Selection audio and print capability for the selection are available in the Interactive Teacher's Edition.

### Concept Vocabulary

Ask students whether they have encountered any of the concept words before. Do they recognize the prefix, suffix, or base word of any of the concept vocabulary words?
Have groups consider the strategy of finding base words and discuss its advantages.

### FIRST READ

Have students perform the steps of the first read independently:

NOTICE: Encourage students to notice who the narrator is and what is happening to him.

ANNOTATE: Remind students to focus on particularly rich passages that include certain literary elements. In this narrative, the setting is particularly important.

CONNECT: Encourage students to go beyond the text to make connections. They may have seen recent movies that deal with slavery, for example.

RESPOND: Students will demonstrate their understanding of the text by answering questions and writing a summary.

Point out to students that while they will always complete the Respond step at the end of the first read, the others steps will probably happen somewhat concurrently. You may wish to print out the **First-Read Guide: Nonfiction** for students to use.

MAKING MEANING

About the Author

The son of a West African tribal elder, **Olaudah Equiano** (1745–1797) might have followed in his father's footsteps had he not been sold into slavery. He was taken first to the West Indies and later brought to Virginia, where he was purchased by a British captain and employed at sea. Renamed Gustavus Vassa, Equiano was enslaved for nearly ten years. After managing his master's finances and making his own money in the process, he amassed enough to buy his own freedom. In later years, he settled in England and devoted himself to the abolition of slavery. In addition to writing his two-volume autobiography to publicize the plight of slaves, he lectured and rallied public sympathy against the cruelties of slavery.

## *from* The Interesting Narrative of the Life of Olaudah Equiano

### Concept Vocabulary

As you perform your first read of this excerpt from *The Interesting Narrative of the Life of Olaudah Equiano*, you will encounter these words.

loathsome wretched dejected

**Base Words** Words that seem unfamiliar may actually contain words you know. Try looking for such familiar base words "inside" unfamiliar words. The word *insupportable*, for example, contains the base word *support*. You know that *support* means "to bear" or "to hold up." In this word, the prefix *in-* means "not," and the suffix *-able* means "capable of being." *Insupportable* means "not capable of being borne or held up."

Note how the addition of prefixes or suffixes affects the meaning of the base word in these words.

| | |
|---|---|
| un**merci**fully | in a manner without mercy |
| **height**ened | made higher or more intense |
| **marine**rs | sailors |

Apply your knowledge of base words and other vocabulary strategies to determine the meanings of unfamiliar words you encounter during your first read.

### First Read NONFICTION

Apply these strategies as you conduct your first read. You will have an opportunity to complete a close read after your first read.

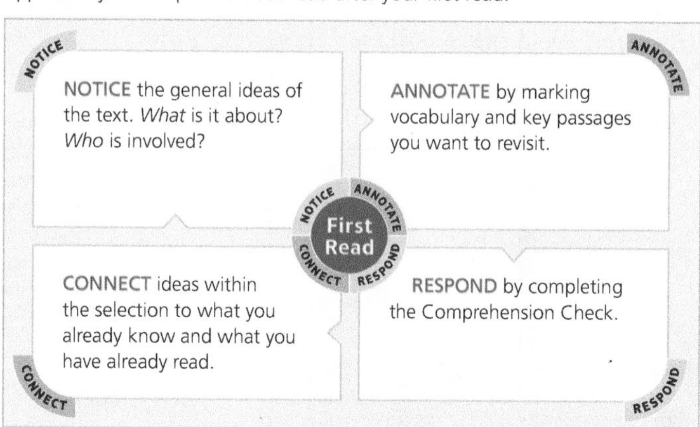

NOTICE the general ideas of the text. *What* is it about? *Who* is involved?
ANNOTATE by marking vocabulary and key passages you want to revisit.
CONNECT ideas within the selection to what you already know and what you have already read.
RESPOND by completing the Comprehension Check.
First Read
NOTICE
ANNOTATE
CONNECT
RESPOND


STANDARDS

Reading Informational Text
By the end of grade 11, read and comprehend literary nonfiction in the grades 11–CCR text complexity band proficiently, with scaffolding as needed at the high end of the range.

Language
Determine or clarify the meaning of unknown and multiple-meaning words and phrases based on *grades 11–12 reading and content*, choosing flexibly from a range of strategies.





### FACILITATING SMALL-GROUP CLOSE LEARNING

**CLOSE READ: Memoir** As groups perform the close read, circulate and offer support as needed.

- Remind students that a memoir is a type of autobiographical writing that tells about a person's own life, usually focusing on the writer's involvement in historically or culturally significant events—either as a participant or an eyewitness.
- A memoir differs from an autobiography in that it focuses more on the world in which the writer has lived, rather than on the writer's introspections.
- Challenge students to determine the main idea of the text and the specific details that refine the main idea.

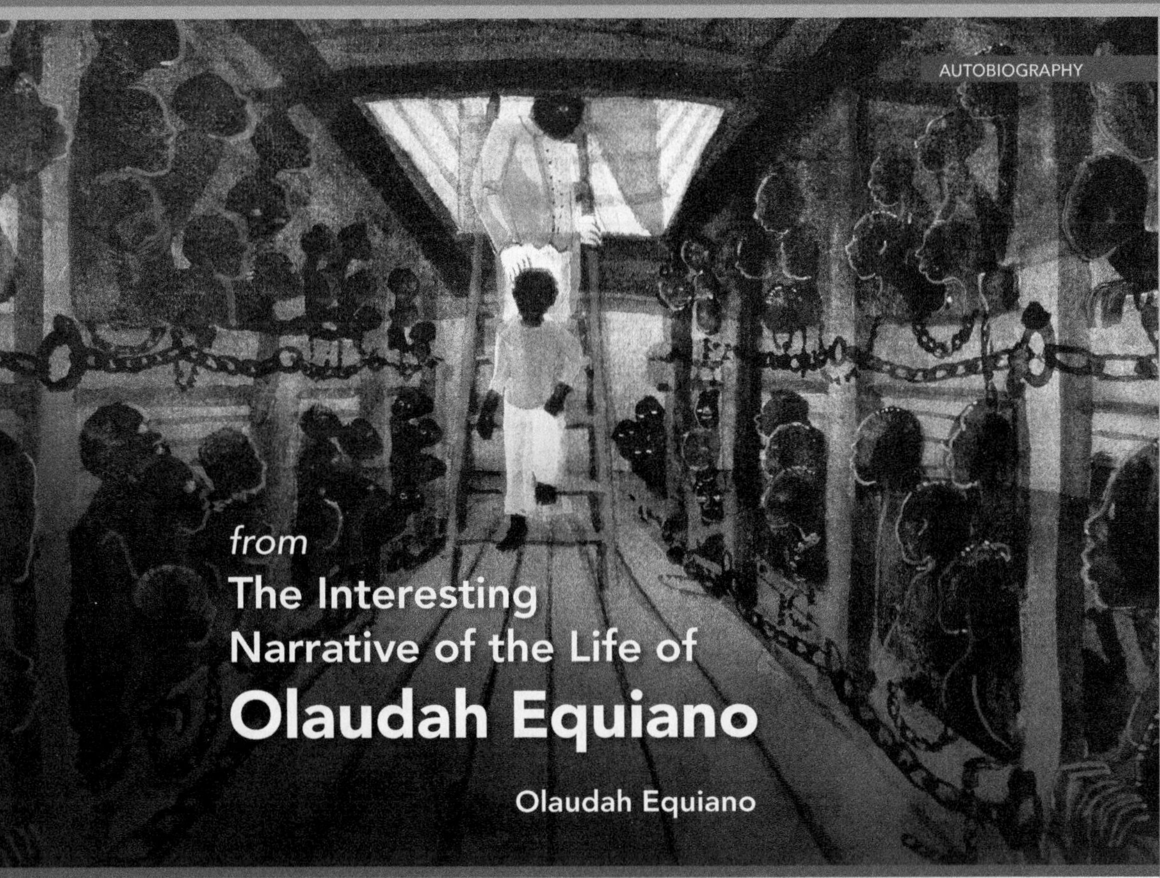


# *from* The Interesting Narrative of the Life of Olaudah Equiano

Olaudah Equiano

DIGITAL PERSPECTIVES   

## Concept Vocabulary

**LOATHSOME** If groups are struggling to define *loathsome* in paragraph 1, point out that the word has a base word and a suffix. The suffix *–some*, when used to form an adjective, means "characterized by a certain state or action." So *loathsome* would mean "characterized by loathing." *Loath* is the base word of *loathsome*. By using the context in the selection as well, students may be able to infer the meaning of *loathsome*. Some context clues are "stench" and "intolerably."

**Possible response:** ***Loathsome*** must mean "disgusting or revolting."

BACKGROUND

In the first several chapters of his autobiography, Olaudah Equiano describes how slave traders kidnapped him and his sister from their home in West Africa and transported them to the African coast. During this six- or seven-month journey, Equiano was separated from his sister and held at a series of way stations. After reaching the coast, Equiano was shipped with other captives to North America. The following account describes this horrifying journey.

SCAN FOR MULTIMEDIA 

1 At last when the ship we were in, had got in all her cargo, they made ready with many fearful noises, and we were all put under deck, so that we could not see how they managed the vessel. But this disappointment was the least of my sorrow. The stench of the hold while we were on the coast was so intolerably **loathsome**, that it was dangerous to remain there for any time, and some of us had been permitted to stay on the deck for the fresh air; but now that the whole ship's cargo were confined together, it became absolutely pestilential. The closeness of the place, and the heat of the climate, added to the number in the ship, which was so crowded that each had scarcely room to turn himself, almost suffocated us.

NOTES

Mark base words or indicate another strategy you used that helped you determine meaning.

**loathsome** (LOHTH suhm) *adj.*

MEANING:

 Additional **English Language Support** is available in the Interactive Teacher's Edition.





DIGITAL PERSPECTIVES

**Illuminating the Text** Point out that the selection students are reading is only a brief part of the beginning of Equiano's story. Have students use the Internet to find a biography of Olaudah Equiano. Have them find out what Equiano did after he purchased his way out of slavery. Encourage students to discuss what kind of person Equaino must have been. **(Research to Clarify)**

## Concept Vocabulary

**WRETCHED** If students are struggling to define *wretched* in paragraph 2, point out that the base word of *wretched* is *wretch*. Students may be familiar with the word from the song "Amazing Grace": ". . . That saved a wretch like me." In addition to being a verb ending, the ending *–ed* is a suffix and means "characterized by." In describing the "wretched situation," Equiano uses words such as *aggravated, galling, filth, suffocated, shrieks,* and *groans of the dying.* Work with students to infer the meaning of *wretched* based on these clues.

**Possible response:** *Wretched* must mean "miserable or unhappy."

**DEJECTED** If students are struggling to define *dejected* in paragraph 4, point out that the base word of *dejected* is *deject*. The suffix *–ed* means "characterized by." In the context of paragraph 4 of the selection, the "dejected fellow" decides to drown himself after two other slaves jump off the ship, "preferring death to such a life of misery." From this context, the meaning of *dejected* can be inferred.

**Possible response:** *Dejected* must mean "depressed or unhappy."

NOTES

Mark base words or indicate another strategy you used that helped you determine meaning.

**wretched** (REHCH ihd) *adj.*

MEANING:

Mark base words or indicate another strategy you used that helped you determine meaning.

**dejected** (dee JEHK tihd) *adj.*

MEANING:

2 This produced copious perspirations, so that the air soon became unfit for respiration, from a variety of loathsome smells, and brought on a sickness among the slaves, of which many died—thus falling victims to the improvident avarice, as I may call it, of their purchasers. This **wretched** situation was again aggravated by the galling of the chains, now become insupportable, and the filth of the necessary tubs, into which the children often fell, and were almost suffocated. The shrieks of the women, and the groans of the dying, rendered the whole a scene of horror almost inconceivable. Happily perhaps, for myself, I was soon reduced so low here that it was thought necessary to keep me almost always on deck; and from my extreme youth I was not put in fetters.[1] In this situation I expected every hour to share the fate of my companions, some of whom were almost daily brought upon deck at the point of death, which I began to hope would soon put an end to my miseries. Often did I think many of the inhabitants of the deep much more happy than myself.

3 I envied them the freedom they enjoyed, and as often wished I could change my condition for theirs. Every circumstance I met with, served only to render my state more painful, and heightened my apprehensions, and my opinion of the cruelty of the whites.

4 One day they had taken a number of fishes; and when they had killed and satisfied themselves with as many as they thought fit, to our astonishment who were on deck, rather than give any of them to us to eat, as we expected, they tossed the remaining fish into the sea again, although we begged and prayed for some as well as we could, but in vain; and some of my countrymen, being pressed by hunger, took an opportunity, when they thought no one saw them, of trying to get a little privately; but they were discovered, and the attempt procured them some very severe floggings. One day, when we had a smooth sea and moderate wind, two of my wearied countrymen who were chained together (I was near them at the time), preferring death to such a life of misery, somehow made through the nettings and jumped into the sea; immediately, another quite **dejected** fellow, who, on account of his illness, was suffered to be out of irons, also followed their example; and I believe many more would very soon have done the same, if they had not been prevented by the ship's crew, who were instantly alarmed. Those of us that were the most active, were in a moment put down under the deck; and there was such a noise and confusion amongst the people of the ship as I never heard before, to stop her, and get the boat out to go after the slaves. However, two of the wretches were drowned, but they got the other, and afterwards flogged him unmercifully, for thus attempting to prefer death to slavery. In this manner we continued to undergo more hardships than I can now relate, hardships which are inseparable from this accursed trade. Many a time we were near suffocation from the want of fresh

1. **fetters** (FEHT uhrz) *n.* chains.





VOCABULARY DEVELOPMENT

**Word Analysis** Read paragraph 2. Remind students that Equiano's memoir was published in 1789 and was a bestseller in its time. Today, however, some of the language is archaic. Archaic words are words that were used in the past but are no longer commonplace. Have students scan the text for archaic words. Some examples include *improvident*, *avarice*, and *galling*. Have students use context clues, word parts, or reference materials to define these words. Ask if they can think of related words that are more common today.

DIGITAL PERSPECTIVES  

air, which we were often without for whole days together. This, and the stench of the necessary tubs, carried off many.

5 During our passage, I first saw flying fishes, which surprised me very much; they used frequently to fly across the ship, and many of them fell on the deck. I also now first saw the use of the quadrant;[2] I had often with astonishment seen the mariners make observations with it, and I could not think what it meant. They at last took notice of my surprise; and one of them, willing to increase it, as well as to gratify my curiosity, made me one day look through it. The clouds appeared to me to be land, which disappeared as they passed along. This heightened my wonder; and I was now more persuaded than ever, that I was in another world, and that every thing about me was magic. At last, we came in sight of the island of Barbados, at which the whites on board gave a great shout, and made many signs of joy to us. We did not know what to think of this; but as the vessel drew nearer, we plainly saw the harbor, and other ships of different kinds and sizes, and we soon anchored amongst them, off Bridgetown.[3] Many merchants and planters now came on board, though it was in the evening. They put us in separate parcels,[4] and examined us attentively. They also made us jump, and pointed to the land, signifying we were to go there.

NOTES

2. **quadrant** (KWOD ruhnt) *n.* instrument used by navigators to determine the position of a ship.
3. **Bridgetown** capital of Barbados.
4. **parcels** (PAHR suhlz) *n.* groups.



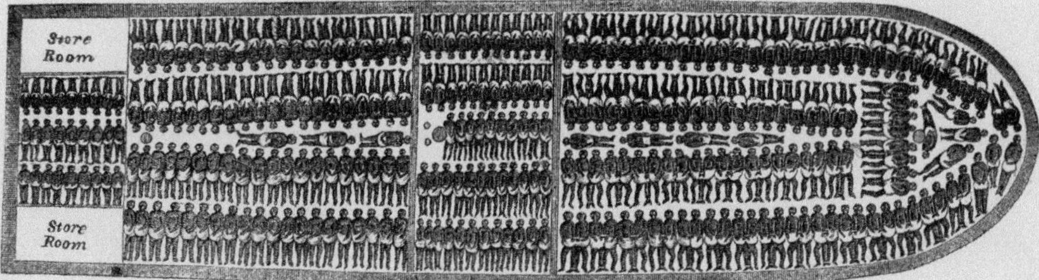


This portion of a 1788 British abolitionist poster depicts the *Brookes*, a slave ship, and the maximum number of slaves that it could transport legally. Slave traders carried as many slaves as the law allowed, knowing that many would die during the journey.



CLOSER LOOK

## Finding the Main Idea

Circulate among the groups as students conduct their close read. Suggest that groups read paragraph 5. Encourage them to talk about the annotations that they mark. If needed, provide the following support.

**ANNOTATE:** Have students mark details in the paragraph that point to the main idea, or work with small groups to have students participate while you highlight them together.

**QUESTION:** Guide students to consider what these details might tell them. Ask what a reader can infer from what was marked, and accept student responses.

**Possible response:** Olaudah was in a completely new environment that contained many things he had not heard of or did not understand.

**CONCLUDE:** Help students formulate conclusions about the importance of these details in the text. Ask students why the author might have included these details.

**Possible response:** The author wanted to express how completely his life had been changed when he was sold into slavery.

Remind students that the **main idea** is not always directly stated at the beginning of a paragraph. In some cases, it is necessary to read through the entire paragraph and determine what the details in large part support.

PERSONALIZE FOR LEARNING

### English Language Support

**Draw Conclusions** Review paragraph 5 and discuss the situation onboard. Have students point to a series of details about the conditions slaves endured, crossing from Africa to the Caribbean. Have students use familiar verbs to draw conclusions about slavery and the slaveowners. **EMERGING**

Have students use a variety of verbs and adverbials to explain the conditions that slaves endured crossing the Atlantic Ocean. Have students draw conclusions based on their observations. **EXPANDING**

Have students explain conclusions about the slaves and slaveowners drawn from a close reading of the text. Have students use a variety of verbs and adverbials in their explanations. **BRIDGING**

NOTES

6 We thought by this, we should be eaten by these ugly men, as they appeared to us; and, when soon after we were all put down under the deck again, there was much dread and trembling among us, and nothing but bitter cries to be heard all the night from these apprehensions, insomuch, that at last the white people got some old slaves from the land to pacify us. They told us we were not to be eaten, but to work, and were soon to go on land, where we should see many of our country people. This report eased us much. And sure enough, soon after we were landed, there came to us Africans of all languages.

7 We were conducted immediately to the merchant's yard, where we were all pent up together, like so many sheep in a fold, without regard to sex or age. . . . We were not many days in the merchant's custody, before we were sold after their usual manner, which is this: On a signal given (as the beat of a drum), the buyers rush at once into the yard where the slaves are confined, and make choice of that parcel they like best. . . . ❧





96 UNIT 1 • WRITING FREEDOM

## Comprehension Check

Complete the following items after you finish your first read. Review and clarify details with your group.

1. According to Equiano, what physical hardships do the captives suffer during their passage across the Atlantic Ocean?

2. What do some captives do to escape the misery of the Atlantic crossing?

3. Why does Equiano blame the illness aboard ship on the "improvident avarice" of the slave traders?

4. How does Equiano's youth affect his treatment during the voyage?

5. What happens to the captives when the ship reaches Barbados?

6. **Notebook** Confirm your understanding of the text by creating a timeline of the narrative's events.

### RESEARCH

**Research to Clarify** Choose at least one unfamiliar detail from the text. Briefly research that detail. In what way does the information you learned shed light on an aspect of the narrative?

**Research to Explore** This autobiographical account may spark your curiosity to learn more about the author, the era, or the topic. You may want to share what you discover with your group.





DIGITAL PERSPECTIVES

## Comprehension Check

Possible responses:

1. The captives are half-starved and chained in the crowded, hot, suffocating hold of the ship.
2. Some choose death as a better fate than the conditions on the ship.
3. He is pointing out that although the traders intend to make a profit by selling the slaves, the traders' cruelty leads to the illness and death of those same slaves.
4. He expresses a youthful wonder about navigation, and one of the mariners let him look through the quadrant.
5. They are penned up in the merchant's yard and sold into slavery.
6. Timeline events: (1) Equiano and the other captives are confined to the suffocating heat below deck. (2) Some die, and Equiano envies them their "freedom." (3) A few who try to steal some fish are caught and flogged. (4) When two captives commit suicide by jumping overboard, and a third survives the attempt, the beatings become worse. (5) The ship arrives in Bridgetown, where the captives meet some slaves who already are working there. (6) The captives prepare to be sold into slavery.

## Research

**Research to Clarify** If students struggle to come up with an unfamiliar detail, you may want to suggest they focus on one of the following topics: What did a quadrant look like, and how did it function? What economic role did Barbados play in the transport of slaves to the United States? How did Equiano's memoir change people's perceptions about slavery?

**Research to Explore** If students struggle to find accounts of other slaves, you may want to suggest narratives by the following: Solomon Northup, Frederick Douglass, and Harriet Ann Jacobs.

PERSONALIZE FOR LEARNING

### Challenge

**Comparing Memoir to Film** Tell students that Olaudah Equiano was a character in the 2007 movie *Amazing Grace*, a story about the abolition of the slave trade in Great Britain. Have students watch the movie and then analyze how Equiano's voice in the written text compares to the character's voice in the movie.

# FACILITATING

## Jump Start

**CLOSE READ** Ask students to imagine a slave's life and the freedoms they think would be most difficult to live without. Why would a slave risk the consequences of running away from captivity?

As students discuss these questions in their groups, ask them what they might have done if they had lived in Equiano's time. Would they have become abolitionists?

## Close Read the Text

Model close reading as needed by using the Annotation Highlights in the Interactive Teacher's Edition.

Remind groups to use Accountable Talk in their discussions and to support one another as they complete the close read.

## Analyze the Text

**Possible responses:**

1. Students should refer to the lack of room, sanitation, and ventilation. The crowding was the result of greed: the more captives transported, the more money made.
2. Students may focus on details in paragraph 4, in which Equiano tells of three fellow captives who attempted suicide rather than live in slavery.
3. Those who have had freedom taken away can offer a special interpretation of its meaning.

## Concept Vocabulary

**Why These Words? Possible response:** The words reflect the horrific situation in which the captives found themselves and evoke an emotional response from readers.

### Practice

**Possible responses:**

- The foul, unclean food given to the captives was *loathsome*.
- Without any personal privacy, the captives felt *wretched*.

### Word Network

**Possible words:** *confined, slavery, irons*

## Word Study

For more support, see **Concept Vocabulary and Word Study.**

Responses will vary and should each show how the definition of the root contributes to the definition of the word.

MAKING MEANING

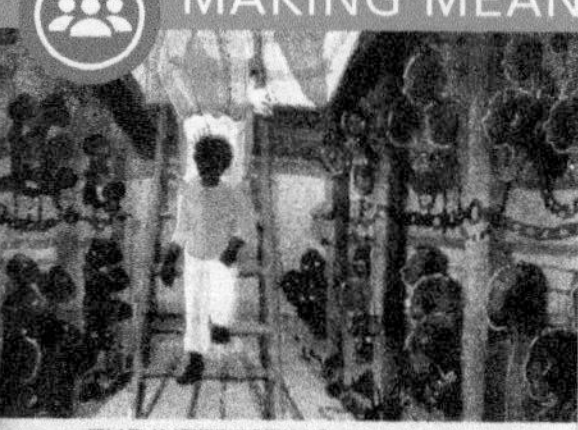

THE INTERESTING NARRATIVE OF THE LIFE OF OLAUDAH EQUIANO

## Close Read the Text

With your group, revisit sections of the text you marked during your first read. **Annotate** details that you notice. What **questions** do you have? What can you **conclude**?

## Analyze the Text

**CITE TEXTUAL EVIDENCE** to support your answers.

**Complete the activities.**

1. **Review and Clarify** With your group, reread paragraph 1 of the selection. Discuss the conditions that the African captives endured aboard the ship. Why were so many people crowded below deck?
2. **Present and Discuss** Now, work with your group to share the passages from the selection that you found especially important. Take turns presenting your passages. Discuss what you noticed in the selection, what questions you asked, and what conclusions you reached.
3. **Essential Question:** ***What is the meaning of freedom?*** What have you learned about American freedoms from reading this text? Discuss with your group.

**TIP**

**GROUP DISCUSSION**
In order to have a successful discussion, everyone should participate. Encourage group members to take turns offering their ideas and opinions.

LANGUAGE DEVELOPMENT

## Concept Vocabulary

| loathsome | wretched | dejected |
|---|---|---|

**Why These Words?** The three concept vocabulary words from the text are related. With your group, discuss the words and determine what they have in common. How do these word choices enhance the impact of the text?

**WORD NETWORK**
Add words related to freedom from the text to your Word Network.

### Practice

**Notebook** Confirm your understanding of these words from the text by using them in sentences. Be sure to include context clues that hint at each word's meaning.

## Word Study

**Notebook** **Latin Root: *-ject-*** The Latin root *-ject-* means "to throw." It contributes to the meaning of the concept vocabulary word *dejected*, as well as many other words in English.

1. Explain how the meaning of the root *-ject-* is evident in the meaning of the word *dejected.*
2. Look up each of these words in a dictionary: *conjecture, trajectory,* and *projection*. Explain how the root *-ject-* contributes to the meaning of each of the words.

**STANDARDS**

**Reading Informational Text**
Determine an author's point of view or purpose in a text in which the rhetoric is particularly effective, analyzing how style and content contribute to the power, persuasiveness, or beauty of the text.

**Language**
Consult general and specialized reference materials, both print and digital, to find the pronunciation of a word or determine or clarify its precise meaning, its part of speech, its etymology, or its standard usage.



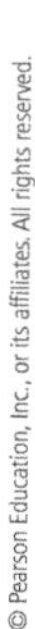


## FORMATIVE ASSESSMENT

### Analyze the Text

**If** students struggle to close read the text, **then** provide the ***from* The Interesting Narrative of the Life: Text Questions** available in the Interactive Teacher's Edition or Unit Resources. Answers and DOK levels are also available.

### Concept Vocabulary

**If** students struggle to identify the concept, **then** have them suggest synonyms for each word and decide what they have in common.

### Word Study

**If** students fail to come up with words with the root *-ject*, **then** provide them with a list of prefixes and suggest they plug in each prefix and see if it is a word they recognize. For Reteach and Practice, see **Word Study: Latin Root: *-ject-* (RP).**

## Analyze Craft and Structure

**Literary Nonfiction: Persuasive Purpose** *The Interesting Narrative of the Life of Olaudah Equiano* is an example of a **slave narrative**, or an autobiographical account of a person's life as a slave. Most slave narratives, written when slavery was a legal practice, have an implicit, or unstated, persuasive purpose: to expose the evils of slavery and, in so doing, turn the public against the practice. Equiano's account combines factual details and personal reflections with powerful descriptive language that constitute **emotional appeals** to his readers. Notice, for example, how words such as *shrieks* and *groans* evoke readers' sympathy and outrage in this depiction of the ship that brought Equiano from Africa:

> The shrieks of the women, and the groans of the dying, rendered the whole a scene of horror almost inconceivable.

The abolitionist movement in the United States owed much to the revelations of former slaves. Only the hardest of hearts could fail to be moved by Equiano's narrative.

**CITE TEXTUAL EVIDENCE** to support your answers.

### Practice

As a group, complete this chart. Identify passages from the autobiography that give factual details, passages that convey personal reflections, and passages that feature strong descriptive language. Then, explain the persuasive impact of each passage.

| ELEMENT OF SLAVE NARRATIVE | EXAMPLES FROM TEXT | PERSUASIVE IMPACT |
|---|---|---|
| Factual details | "the heat of the climate, added to the number in the ship, . . . so crowded that each had scarcely room to turn himself, almost suffocated us." "... rather than give any of them [fish] to us to eat, as we expected, they tossed the remaining fish into the sea. . . ." | Readers see the awful conditions on the ship and the cruelty of the white sailors. |
| Personal reflections | "I envied them [inhabitants of the sea] the freedom they enjoyed, and as often wished I could change my condition for theirs." "I was now more persuaded than ever that I was in another world, and that everything about me was magic." | Evokes deep sympathy for Equiano; reader is also able to see Equiano's world from his perspective |
| Strong descriptive language | "Many a time we were near suffocation from the want of fresh air, which we were often without for whole days together. This, and the stench of the necessary tubs, carried off many." | Makes readers feel as if they are there with Equiano; also gives credibility to Equiano's account |





**DIGITAL PERSPECTIVES**

## Analyze Craft and Structure

**Literary Nonfiction: Persuasive Response** Explain to students that slave narratives are just one of many forms that literary nonfiction can take. Biographies, essays, travel writing, and creative nonfiction are additional subcategories of this genre. For more support, see **Analyze Craft and Stucture: Literary Nonfiction.**

### Practice

See possible responses in chart on student page.

**FORMATIVE ASSESSMENT**

### Analyze Craft and Structure

**If** students struggle to complete the chart, **then** provide practice in differentiating among factual details, personal reflection, and strong descriptive language. For Reteach and Practice, see **Analyze Craft and Stucture: Literary Nonfiction (RP).**

**PERSONALIZE FOR LEARNING**

### Strategic Support

**Drawing Conclusions** Students may have difficulty drawing conclusions for the Persuasive Impact column of the group chart. Help them reach this next level of thinking by asking, after each example from the text is offered, "How did that make you feel? If you had been there, what would you be feeling?"

# FACILITATING

## Conventions and Style

**Eighteenth-Century Narrative Style** Remind students that style is embodied in how a writer uses language. Style is related to voice—a writer's distinctive "sound" or way of "speaking" on the page. So, even though Equiano's writing displays the style of the eighteenth century, it also is an exhibit of his individual voice. For more support, see **Conventions and Style: Eighteenth-Century Narrative Style.**

### Read It

Possible responses:

- The passage is expressed as one sentence.
- The plural *fishes* is an eighteenth-century usage.
- Instead of periods, the author uses semicolons and commas to make a lengthy sentence that conveys the captives' misery.

### Write It

Possible response:

One day they caught a number of fish. They killed and satisfied themselves with as many as they thought were sufficient. To the astonishment of those of us who were on deck, who thought that they would give us some of the catch, they tossed the remaining fish into the sea again. We begged and prayed for some as well as we could, but we were denied. Some of my countrymen were very hungry. When they thought that no one would see them, they took the chance of trying to get a few fish secretly. They were discovered, however, and the attempt caused them to be flogged severely.

### FORMATIVE ASSESSMENT

### Conventions and Style

**If** students have difficulty determining when a sentence should end, **then** remind them that a sentence expresses a complete thought and must have a subject and a predicate. Practice with several of the sentences from the selection. For Reteach and Practice, see **Conventions and Style: Eighteenth-Century Narrative Style (RP).**

LANGUAGE DEVELOPMENT

THE INTERESTING NARRATIVE OF THE LIFE OF OLAUDAH EQUIANO

## Conventions and Style

**Eighteenth-Century Narrative Style** Equiano's account is an example of eighteenth-century narrative style. The formal language of the period has several characteristics that distinguish it from modern style.

| CHARACTERISTIC | EIGHTEENTH-CENTURY STYLE | MODERN STYLE |
|---|---|---|
| **Sentence Length:** the number of words, phrases, and clauses in a sentence | Sentences are long and contain multiple clauses and phrases. | Sentences vary in length, and most have fewer than three clauses. |
| **Usage:** the ways in which words are commonly used | Word meanings change over time, as do word forms, including formation of singular and plural nouns. Modern readers may contest usage or need to confirm archaic meanings. | Word meanings and forms continue to change over time. In addition, new words continue to enter the English language from other languages or are coined to refer to new situations, ideas, or objects. |
| **Mechanics:** punctuation and spelling | Eighteenth-century writers punctuated text however they chose. | Punctuation marks are used according to established conventions. |

### Read It

**Notebook** Work individually. Read the passage from Equiano's narrative carefully, and then answer the questions that follow.

> One day they had taken a number of fishes; and when they had killed and satisfied themselves with as many as they thought fit, to our astonishment who were on deck, rather than give any of them to us to eat, as we expected, they tossed the remaining fish into the sea again, although we begged and prayed for some as well as we could, but in vain; and some of my countrymen, being pressed by hunger, took an opportunity, when they thought no one saw them, of trying to get a little privately; but they were discovered, and the attempt procured them some very severe floggings.

- How many sentences does the passage contain?
- Identify an example of eighteenth-century usage.
- What punctuation marks does the author use to separate details regarding the plight of the captives?

### Write It

**Notebook** Rewrite the passage in modern style. Then, share passages with your group and discuss whether or not the change in style lessened the persuasive impact of the original passage.

**STANDARDS**

**Writing**

- Write arguments to support claims in an analysis of substantive topics or texts, using valid reasoning and relevant and sufficient evidence.
- Establish and maintain a formal style and objective tone while attending to the norms and conventions of the discipline in which they are writing.

**Language**

- Demonstrate command of the conventions of standard English grammar and usage when writing or speaking.
- Apply the understanding that usage is a matter of convention, can change over time, and is sometimes contested.





### PERSONALIZE FOR LEARNING

**English Language Support**

**Eighteenth-Century Narrative Style** Provide students with a long sentence from the text in eighteenth-century style.

Have students paraphrase the ideas in the sentence in modern English. **EMERGING**

Have students rewrite the sentence in modern English, and ask them to explain any differences. **EXPANDING**

Have students rewrite the ideas of the sentence in modern English. Then ask them to write a brief paragraph explaining the differences between the two. **BRIDGING**

An expanded **English Language Support Lesson** on Eighteenth-Century Narrative Style is available in the Interactive Teacher's Edition.

EFFECTIVE EXPRESSION

## Writing to Sources

**Assignment**

With your group, prepare an **argument** related to the abolitionist cause. Choose from the following options.

- ☐ a **literary review** of Equiano's autobiography, arguing that the events he describes, and the manner in which he describes them, provide powerful support for the abolitionist movement
- ☐ a **letter** to the British Parliament, using evidence from the selection to urge its members to abolish the slave trade
- ☐ an **advertisement** for the British abolitionist movement that uses graphics and text, inspired by specific details from the autobiography, to make a strong point about the need for change

**Project Plan** Work with your group to divide the option that you chose into manageable sections or parts. Discuss your ideas and consider the types of supporting evidence you will use, including those that appeal to readers' emotions. Then, assign each member one part of the writing.

Working Title: ______________________

| SECTION OR PART | ASSIGNED GROUP MEMBER |
|---|---|
| Claim | |
| Reason 1 | |
| Supporting details from the selection | |
| Reason 2 | |
| Supporting details from the selection | |
| Reason 3 | |
| Supporting details from the selection | |

**Tying It Together** Work together to draft an introduction that touches on all the sections that you plan to write. Once everyone has written his or her section, work together to draft a logical and memorable conclusion.

TIP

COLLABORATION

Group members responsible for preparing the reasons that support the claim should work together to decide the order in which to list the reasons.

EVIDENCE LOG

Before moving on to a new selection, go to your Evidence Log and record what you learned from *The Interesting Narrative of the Life of Olaudah Equiano.*





DIGITAL PERSPECTIVES

## Writing to Sources

Students may struggle to select which writing assignment they should pursue. Have group members discuss what they know about each literary form. Have the groups decide upon the form with which they feel most comfortable. One or two students in each group should focus on research that includes the British abolitionist movement and Equiano's role in that cause.

**Project Plan** Remind groups to make sure everyone is assigned a specific task as they create their Project Plan. Check the Project Plan to ensure that each group member bears a responsibility for the group's progress and has the resources and support to fulfill that responsibility.

**Tying It Together** As groups compile the work of individual members, make sure that there are transitions in the final product to keep the piece from sounding choppy. **For more support,** see **Writing to Sources: Argument.**

Evidence Log Support students in completing the Evidence Log. This paced activity will help prepare them for the Performance-Based Assessment at the end of the unit.

### FORMATIVE ASSESSMENT

### Writing to Sources

**If** students struggle to decide which kind of source to write to, **then** provide them with examples of each literary form. For Reteach and Practice, see **Writing to Sources: Argument (RP).**

### Selection Test

Administer "*from* The Interesting Narrative of the Life of Olaudah Equiano" Selection Test, which is available in both print and digital formats online in Assessments.

PERSONALIZE FOR LEARNING

### English Language Support

**Summaries** Have students write brief summaries of their experience in writing to a source, using complete sentences and key words. **EMERGING**

Have students write increasingly concise summaries of their experience in writing to a source, using complete sentences and key words. **EXPANDING**

Have students write clear and coherent summaries of their experience in writing to a source, using complete and concise sentences and key words. **BRIDGING**

# Letter to John Adams • *from* Dear Abigail

**AUDIO SUMMARIES** of "Letter to John Adams" and "*from* Dear Abigail" are available online in both English and Spanish in the Interactive Teacher's Edition or Unit Resources. Assigning these summaries prior to reading the selection may help students build additional background knowledge and set a context for their first read.

## Summary

In a letter to John Adams dated March 31, 1776, Abigail Adams describes the conditions she found in Boston shortly after the British had left the city. She expresses her hopefulness now that she is able to return home. She asks her husband to "remember the women" as he works with other men on the issue of independence. She urges John not to put all power in the hands of the men.

In *Dear Abigail*, historian Diane Jacobs describes John Adams's view of the people and events that led to the approval of the Declaration of Independence. John's mood changes from unhappiness with the convention's slow progress to delight at its final achievement. The excerpt describes the public reading of the document in Boston and the joyous celebrations that followed. The text ends with a quotation from a later letter in which Abigail once again raises questions about the role of women, especially the education of young girls.

### Insight

Reading "Letter to John Adams" and the excerpt from *Dear Abigail* will help students think about the hard work and sacrifices of the people involved in drafting the Declaration of Independence. They will come to appreciate how some colonial women, although supportive of the actions taken by the men at the Continental Convention, nonetheless felt that their rights and freedoms were ignored.

ESSENTIAL QUESTION:
What is the meaning of freedom?

## Connection to the Essential Question

"Letter to John Adams" and the excerpt from *Dear Abigail* have multiple connections to the Essential Question, "What is the meaning of freedom?" The letter relates to the central idea expressed in the Declaration of Independence that "all men are created equal." In fact, colonists who were not landowners and those who were slaves or women were not included in this famous phrase. Yet, despite the restrictive language of the document, many colonial women such as Abigail Adams felt that "all the people" rejoiced at their newly declared independence.

SMALL-GROUP LEARNING PERFORMANCE TASK
Do narratives provide strong evidence to support arguments about American freedoms?

UNIT PERFORMANCE-BASED ASSESSMENT
What are the most effective tools for establishing and preserving freedom?

## Connection to Performance Tasks

**Small-Class Learning Performance Task** In this Performance Task, students will consider whether narratives provide strong evidence to support arguments about American freedoms. In these selections, students will find strong primary-source evidence of the convictions about freedom by both John Adams and Abigail Adams, who pleads for the freedom of women.

**Unit Performance-Based Assessment** This selection raises an important issue that students must consider as they respond to the Performance-Based Assessment. Students must evaluate whether colonial leaders were reasonable in ignoring the rights of women as they considered independence and the subsequent establishment of government.

DIGITAL PERSPECTIVES

 Audio  Video  Document  Annotation Highlights  EL Highlights  Online Assessment

## LESSON RESOURCES

| | Making Meaning | Language Development | Effective Expression |
|---|---|---|---|
| Lesson | **First Read**<br>**Close Read**<br>**Analyze the Text**<br>**Analyze Craft and Structure** | **Concept Vocabulary**<br>**Word Study**<br>**Author's Style** | **Speaking and Listening** |
| Instructional Standards | **RI.10** By the end of grade 11, read and comprehend literary nonfiction . . .<br>**RI.9** Analyze seventeenth-, eighteenth-, and nineteenth-century foundational U.S. documents . . .<br>**L.4.a** Use context as a clue . . . | **L.4.b** Identify and correctly use patterns of word changes . . .<br>**RI.6** Determine an author's point of view . . . | **SL.4** Present information, findings, and supporting evidence . . . |
| **STUDENT RESOURCES** | | | |
| Available online in the Interactive Student Edition or Unit Resources | Selection Audio<br>First-Read Guide: Nonfiction<br>Close-Read Guide: Nonfiction | Word Network | Evidence Log |
| **TEACHER RESOURCES** | | | |
| **Selection Resources** Available online in the Interactive Teacher's Edition or Unit Resources | Audio Summaries<br>Annotation Highlights<br>EL Highlights<br>English Language Support Lesson: Oral Presentation<br>Letter to John Adams • *from* Dear Abigail: Text Questions<br>Analyze Craft and Structure: Primary and Secondary Sources | Concept Vocabulary and Word Study<br>Author's Style: Voice | Speaking and Listening: Oral Presentation |
| **Reteach/Practice (RP)** Available online in the Interactive Teacher's Edition or Unit Resources | Analyze Craft and Structure: Primary and Secondary Sources (RP) | Word Study: Word Families (RP)<br>Author's Style: Voice (RP) | Speaking and Listening: Oral Presentation (RP) |
| **Assessment** Available online in Assessments | Selection Test | | |
| **My Resources** | A Unit 1 Answer Key is available online and in the Interactive Teacher's Edition. | | |

# Reading Support

| Text Complexity Rubric: Letter to John Adams • *from* Dear Abigail | |
|---|---|
| **Quantitative Measures** | |
| Lexile 1230; 1300 Text Length 1,210 words; 1,908 words | |
| **Quantitative Measures** | |
| Knowledge Demands ①—②—③—❹—⑤ | Historical knowledge demands; selections deal with documents written toward the end of the Revolutionary War and contain references to events at that time. |
| Structure ①—②—❸—④—⑤ | The first selection is in the form of letters from Abigail Adams to her husband, John. The second selection is a contemporary narrative excerpt about the life of Abigail Adams. Both selections have conventional structure and contain numerous digressions. |
| Language Conventionality and Clarity ①—②—③—❹—⑤ | The letters were written during the Revolutionary War period and contain difficult and unfamiliar spelling, grammar and sentence structure. |
| Levels of Meaning/Purpose ①—②—❸—④—⑤ | The main ideas are not difficult, but the concepts may be hard for some to grasp because of difficult language and supporting concepts that are complex. |

DECIDE AND PLAN

## English Language Support

Provide English Learners with support for knowledge demands and language as they read the selection.

**Knowledge Demands** Make sure students understand the context of Abigail Adams's letters to her husband. Determine students' prior knowledge and provide additional background if needed.

**Language** Help students reword long and complex sentences. Using the language from the selection, suggest simpler sentences that convey the same meaning. For example, the last sentence of "Letter to John Adams," paragraph 1: *I hope the soldiers (from the Southern states) are not representative of the rest of the people in the South.* Ask students to read the new sentences and discuss.

## Strategic Support

Provide students with strategic support to ensure that they can successfully read the text.

**Knowledge Demands** After reading the background information, make sure students understand the historical context of the selection. Ask students to share what they know and help them fill in important contextual information.

**Language / Clarity** For students who may have difficulty with challenging and complex sentences, encourage them to break the sentences down into smaller chunks or identify the meaning of unfamiliar words or phrases. Then have them reread the whole sentences.

## Challenge

Provide students who need to be challenged with ideas for how they can go beyond a simple interpretation of the text.

**Text Analysis** Have students reread Abigail Adams's letters. How does she compare the treatment of women by men to the treatment of the colonists by the king?

**Written Response** Remind students that Abigail Adams's letters were written more than 200 years ago. Have students imagine Abigail Adams as a modern-day woman writing a letter to her husband. Ask students to write as Abigail, raising the important modern issues that might concern her today.

TEACH

## Read and Respond

Have groups read the selection and complete the Making Meaning and Language Development activities.

# Standards Support Through Teaching and Learning Cycle

## IDENTIFY NEEDS

Analyze results of the Beginning-of-Year Assessment, focusing on the items relating to Unit 1. Also take into consideration student performance to this point and your observations of where particular students struggle.

## DECIDE AND PLAN

- If students have performed poorly on items matching these standards, then provide selection scaffolds before assigning them the on-level lesson provided in the Student Edition.
- If students have done well on the Beginning-of-Year Assessment, then challenge them to keep progressing and learning by giving them opportunities to practice the skills in depth.
- Use the Selection Resources listed on the Planning pages to help students continually improve their ability to master the standards.

**Instructional Standards: Letter to John Adams • *from* Dear Abigail**

| | Catching Up | This Year | Looking Forward |
|---|---|---|---|
| **Reading** | You may wish to administer the **Analyze Craft and Structure: Primary and Secondary Sources (RP)** worksheet to help students understand how primary sources add interest, depth and context to writing. | **RI.9** Analyze seventeenth-, eighteenth-, and nineteenth-century foundational U.S. documents of historical and literary significance for their themes, purposes, and rhetorical features. | Challenge students to discuss how Abigail Adams's letters to John Adams are different in content, tone, and style from *Dear Abigail*, which is a secondary source. |
| **Speaking and Listening** | You may wish to administer the **Speaking and Listening: Oral Presentation (RP)** worksheet to teach students how to think critically about different forms of media and the point of view that they represent. | **SL.4** Present information, findings, and supporting evidence, conveying a clear and distinct perspective and a logical argument, such that listeners can follow the line of reasoning, alternative or opposing perspectives are addressed, and the organization, development, substance, and style are appropriate to purpose, audience, and a range of formal and informal tasks. Use appropriate eye contact, adequate volume, and clear pronunciation. | Challenge pairs of students to consider the same piece of media and analyze its point of view, tone, word choice, etc. Then have the partners compare and discuss their analysis. |
| **Language** | You may wish to administer the **Author's Style: Voice (RP)** worksheet to help students understand how the style, purpose, and point of view come through in the voice of a text. | **RI.6** Determine an author's point of view or purpose in a text in which the rhetoric is particularly effective, analyzing how style and content contribute to the power, persuasiveness, or beauty of the text. | Challenge students to determine the kind of voice being used in the informational, biographical, and autobiographical texts that they read. Remind them to think about how the information that an author chooses to include helps an audience understand the purpose for the text. |

## ANALYZE AND REVISE

- Analyze student work for evidence of student learning.
- Identify whether or not students have met the expectations in the standards.
- Identify implications for future instruction.

## TEACH

Implement the planned lesson, and gather evidence of student learning.

# FACILITATING

## Jump Start

**FIRST READ** Before groups begin their first read, ask them to think about what ideas might be considered revolutionary during the late 18th century. How might these ideas differ from revolutionary ideas in today's world?

### Concept Vocabulary

Have groups briefly discuss the three concept vocabulary words. Have they encountered any of the words before? Do they recognize the prefix, suffix, or base word of any of the concept vocabulary words?

Have groups consider the strategy of context clues and discuss its advantages and disadvantages.

### FIRST READ

Have students perform the steps of the first read independently:

NOTICE: Encourage students to notice the point of view of the writers of the different letters.

ANNOTATE: Remind students to focus on paragraphs of key revolutionary ideas or of particular interest.

CONNECT: Encourage students to make connections between the revolutionary ideas in the selection and ideas they may have encountered in other readings or in their own lives.

RESPOND: Students will demonstrate their understanding of the text by answering questions and writing a summary.

Point out to students that they will perform the first three steps concurrently as they are doing their first read. They will complete the Respond step after they have finished the first read. You may wish to print copies of the **First-Read Guide: Nonfiction** for students to use.

MAKING MEANING

LETTER | BIOGRAPHY

## Letter to John Adams

## *from* Dear Abigail: The Intimate Lives and Revolutionary Ideas of Abigail Adams and Her Two Remarkable Sisters

### Concept Vocabulary

As you perform your first read of these two texts, you will encounter the following words.

vassals foment dissented

**Context Clues** When you come to an unfamiliar word in a text, you can often determine its meaning by using **context clues**—nearby words and phrases that provide hints to a word's meaning. Such hints may come in the form of descriptions.

**Description as Context Clue:**
**Passage:** "Others have committed abominable **ravages** . . . both the house and furniture of the Solicitor General have fallen prey to their own merciless party."

**Explanation:** The description of a person's house and furniture as "prey" to a "merciless party" suggests that ravages means something like "destruction."

Apply your knowledge of context clues and other vocabulary strategies to determine the meanings of unfamiliar words you encounter during your first read.

### First Read NONFICTION

Apply these strategies as you conduct your first read. You will have an opportunity to complete a close read after your first read.

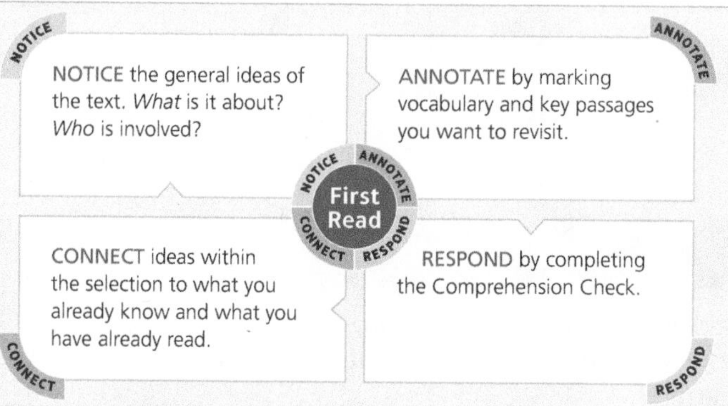

NOTICE
NOTICE the general ideas of the text. *What* is it about? *Who* is involved?
ANNOTATE
ANNOTATE by marking vocabulary and key passages you want to revisit.
First Read
CONNECT
CONNECT ideas within the selection to what you already know and what you have already read.
RESPOND
RESPOND by completing the Comprehension Check.


STANDARDS
**Reading Informational Text**
By the end of grade 11, read and comprehend literary nonfiction in the grades 11–CCR text complexity band proficiently, with scaffolding as needed at the high end of the range.
**Language**
Use context as a clue to the meaning of a word or phrase.





### FACILITATING SMALL-GROUP CLOSE READ

**CLOSE READ: Letters** Remind students that letters are considered primary sources—original documents from a particular time period, either historical or in modern times. Letters offer a view of the writer's opinions and perspectives on issues of the time, and personalized accounts of events taking place at that time. Have groups consider as they read which parts of the letters give insight to the events of the time, and which passages illustrate Abigail's and John's points of view about events or social issues.

## About the Authors

**Abigail Adams** (1744–1818) was the wife of John Adams, the second president of the United States, and the mother of John Quincy Adams, the sixth president. She was also one of the most important and influential women of her time. A dedicated supporter of women's rights and the American Revolutionary movement, Adams wrote many letters to her husband and others expressing her opinions. In these letters, she included vivid descriptions that capture the essence of life in early America.

Adams was born Abigail Smith in Weymouth, Massachusetts. At the age of nineteen, she married John Adams. The couple had three sons and two daugthers. Abigail, who had not been educated as a child, made sure all of her children—including a daughter—received a thorough education. This was something few American girls enjoyed at the time.

Abigail died in 1818, after spending the last seventeen years of her life at the Adams family home in Massachusetts. In 1840, a first volume of her letters was published. In the ensuing decades, other collections, biographies, and histories have followed. Today, Abigail Adams is widely recognized as a writer and a pioneer of the American women's movement.

**Diane Jacobs,** who lives in New York City, is the author of several acclaimed biographies. In addition to *Dear Abigail*, Jacobs has written about the contemporary filmmaker Woody Allen and about Mary Wollstonecraft, the eighteenth-century British author of *A Vindication of the Rights of Woman*.

## Backgrounds

### Letter to John Adams

Throughout their courtship and marriage, John and Abigail Adams wrote more than one thousand letters to one another. Although their letters are often affectionate and even playful, they also reflect the couple's underlying awareness that they were key players in the unfolding of history. Abigail wrote this and several other letters to her husband while he attended the Second Continental Congress in Philadelphia.

### *From* Dear Abigail: The Intimate Lives and Revolutionary Ideas of Abigail Adams and Her Two Remarkable Sisters

The correspondence between Abigail and John Adams sheds light on Revolutionary-era America. This selection by a modern historian sets their letters within the context of the work of the Continental Congress and the adoption of the Declaration of Independence.





DIGITAL PERSPECTIVES

## Letter to John Adams • *from* Dear Abigail: The Intimate Lives and Revolutionary Ideas of Abigail Adams and Her Two Remarkable Sisters

What are some of the challenges women faced during the time of the American Revolution? How might Abigail's ideas differ from those of her husband, John? Modeling these and other questions readers might ask will bring "Letter to John Adams" and "*from* Dear Abigail" to life and connect them to the Performance Task question. Selection audio and print capability for the selection are available in the Interactive Teacher's Edition.

## VOCABULARY DEVELOPMENT

**Graphic Organizers** Have students analyze the word *foment*, using a four-square diagram. Guide students as they complete the diagram.

| | |
|---|---|
| **Definition:** to instigate or stir up trouble | **Synonyms:** provoke, incite, agitate |
| **Example Sentence:** Abigail Adams and her friends believed it was necessary to foment a rebellion for women's rights. | **Other forms in different tenses:** fomented, fomenter |

FACILITATING

## CLOSER LOOK

### Making Inferences 

Circulate among groups as students conduct their close read. Suggest that groups close read paragraphs 1–3. Encourage them to talk about the annotations that they mark. If needed, provide the following support.

**ANNOTATE:** Have students mark details in these paragraphs that describe how Abigail feels about the British, or have students participate while you highlight them together.

**QUESTION:** Guide students to consider what these details might tell them. Ask what a reader can infer from how Abigail feels about the British, and accept student responses.

**Possible response:** She states that the British are a common enemy and that the British feel that the people of the Colony are uncivilized. She also feels that the British are depriving the people of the Colony of their liberty. Based on these statements, one could infer she does not like the British.

**CONCLUDE:** Help students to formulate conclusions about the importance of these details in the text. Ask students why the author might have included these details.

**Possible responses:** Abigail may have wanted to confirm that her revolutionary ideas were similar to those of her husband, John, who was attending the Second Continental Congress at the time.

**Making inferences** about Abigail's intentions for expressing her feelings about the British is helpful in understanding her purpose for writing the letter to her husband.

## Concept Vocabulary

**VASSALS** If groups are struggling to define the word *vassals* in paragraph 1, point out that context clues will help them understand the word. Point out the phrases *gentry lords; common people; uncivilized natives.* Guide students to the definition of *gentry*. Students should be able to infer that *vassals* are people subordinate to another group. In Medieval times, a *vassal* was a person who gave his loyalty to a feudal lord. The vassal lived on the lord's land and was protected by him.

**Possible response:** "*Vassals* are people who are subservient to others."

Additional **English Language Support** is available in the Interactive Teacher's Edition.

SCAN FOR MULTIMEDIA

NOTES

Mark context clues or indicate another strategy you used that helped you determine meaning.

**vassals** (VAS uhlz) *n.*

MEANING:

*Braintree*[1] *March 31, 1776*

1 I wish you would ever write me a letter half as long as I write you; and tell me if you may where your fleet are gone? What sort of defense Virginia can make against our common enemy? Whether it is so situated as to make an able defense? Are not the gentry[2] lords and the common people **vassals**, are they not like the uncivilized natives Britain represents us to be? I hope their rifle men who have shown themselves very savage and even blood thirsty; are not a specimen of the generality of the people.

2 I am willing to allow the Colony great merit for having produced a Washington but they have been shamefully duped by a Dunmore.[3]

3 I have sometimes been ready to think that the passion for liberty cannot be equally strong in the breasts of those who have been accustomed to deprive their fellow creatures of theirs. Of this I am certain that it is not founded upon that generous and Christian principal of doing to others as we would that others should do unto us.

4 Do not you want to see Boston; I am fearful of the small pox, or I should have been in before this time. I got Mr. Crane to go to our

1. **Braintree** town in eastern Massachusetts that was the home of John and Abigail Adams.
2. **gentry** (JEHN tree) *n.* people of high social standing.
3. **Dunmore** John Murray, 4th earl of Dunmore, was the British colonial governor of Virginia. He provoked strong feelings among Virginians when he dissolved the legislature and later used troops loyal to the British throne to attack the colony's troops in late 1775 and early 1776.





## PERSONALIZE FOR LEARNING

### Challenge

**Research** To support the reference to Dunmore in paragraph 2, have students research Dunmore's Proclamation, which was in response to the belief that Virginia colonists were forming armies to incite rebellion against the British. Dunmore wanted to put an end to activities by Virginia colonists whom he considered traitors. He also offered emancipation to slaves who volunteered to leave their owners and fight on the side of the British. Students should present a summary of the proclamation and the effects it had on the Virginia colonists.

house and see what state it was in. I find it has been occupied by one of the doctors of a regiment, very dirty, but no other damage has been done to it. The few things which were left in it are all gone. Cranch has the key which he never delivered up. I have wrote to him for it and am determined to get it cleaned as soon as possible and shut it up. I look upon it a new acquisition of property, a property which one month ago I did not value at a single shilling,[4] and could with pleasure have seen it in flames.

5 The town in general is left in a better state than we expected, more owing to a percipitate[5] flight than any regard to the inhabitants, though some individuals discovered a sense of honor and justice and have left the rent of the houses in which they were, for the owners and the furniture unhurt, or if damaged sufficient to make it good.

6 Others have committed abominable ravages. The mansion house of your President [John Hancock] is safe and the furniture unhurt whilst both the house and furniture of the Solicitor General [Samuel Quincy] have fallen a prey to their own merciless party. Surely the very fiends feel a reverential awe for virtue and patriotism, whilst they detest the paricide[6] and traitor.

7 I feel very differently at the approach of spring to what I did a month ago. We knew not then whether we could plant or sow with safety, whether when we had toiled we could reap the fruits of our own industry, whether we could rest in our own cottages, or whether we should not be driven from the sea coasts to seek shelter in the wilderness, but now we feel as if we might sit under our own vine and eat the good of the land.

8 I feel a gaieti de Coar[7] to which before I was a stranger. I think the sun looks brighter, the birds sing more melodiously, and nature puts on a more cheerful countenance. We feel a temporary peace, and the poor fugitives are returning to their deserted habitations.

*I desire you would remember the ladies, and be more generous and favourable to them than your ancestors.*

9 Though we felicitate[8] ourselves, we sympathize with those who are trembling least the lot of Boston should be theirs. But they cannot be in similar circumstances unless pusillanimity and cowardice should take possession of them. They have time and warning given them to see the evil and shun it.—I long to hear that you have declared an independency—and by the way in the new code of laws which I suppose it will be necessary for you to make I desire you would remember the ladies, and be more generous and favorable to them than your ancestors. Do not put such unlimited power into the hands of the husbands. Remember all men would be tyrants if they could. If particuliar care and attention is not paid

NOTES

4. **shilling** *n.* former British coin worth one twentieth of a pound.
5. **percipitate** *adj.* precipitate; done very hastily or rashly.
6. **paricide** *n.* parricide; person who kills a parent or other relative.
7. **gaieti de Coar** *gaieté de coeur;* French for "joy of heart."
8. **felicitate** *v.* wish happiness; to congratulate.





DIGITAL PERSPECTIVES  

## CLOSER LOOK

### Infer Author's Beliefs

Circulate among groups as students conduct their close read. Suggest that groups close read paragraph 9. Encourage them to talk about the annotations that they mark. If needed, provide the following support.

**ANNOTATE:** Have students mark details in this paragraph that describes how Abigail advocates for women's rights, or have students participate while you highlight them.

**QUESTION:** Guide students to consider what these details might tell them. Ask what a reader can infer from what Abigail suggests to her husband, and accept student responses.

**Possible response:** She states that the new code of laws should remember the ladies and be more generous to them than his ancestors were. By this she must mean that the old laws do not favor women and that she wants the new laws to be more inclusive of women.

**CONCLUDE:** Help students to formulate conclusions about the importance of these details in the text. Ask students why the author might have included these details.

**Possible response:** Abigail was an advocate of women's rights in the early days of the colonies. She wants to make sure that when the Second Continental Congress declares independence and forms a new code of laws that women will be equally represented.

Remind students that a *letter* is a written message addressed to a specific reader or readers and contains varying contents of the **author's beliefs**. A *personal letter* is not intended for publication. When Abigail Adams sent these messages to her husband, she likely intended to influence him, but it is unlikely she considered her ideas would be read by a general audience.

## DIGITAL PERSPECTIVES

**Illuminating the Text** Point out that Abigail's letter was written on March 31, 1776. To help students understand how Boston changed from British to American control in March of 1776, have them search online for information in the form of video clips from movies, works of art, or other forms of media. Suggest students search for "General William Howe" and the battle of "Dorchester Heights." Ask students how viewing these images gives them a deeper understanding of how Boston changed during Abigail Adams's time. **(Research to Clarify)**

FACILITATING

## Concept Vocabulary

**FOMENT** If students are struggling to define the word *foment* in paragraph 9, have them use context clues in the paragraph to help them determine meaning. Prior to using this word, Abigail has asked John not to "put such unlimited power in the hands of husbands" and "that all men would be tyrants if they could." This suggests that women do not have the rights and privileges that men do. Abigail states that "if particular care and attention is not paid to the ladies we are determined to *foment* a rebellion." Here, the word *rebellion* gives a clue to the meaning of the word *foment*. When someone foments a rebellion, it most likely means the person will cause, incite, provoke, or encourage a rebellion. Have students use a Thesaurus to find other synonyms for *foment*.

**Possible response:** "*Foment* is to stir up or provoke."

NOTES

Mark context clues or indicate another strategy that you used helped you determine meaning.

**foment** (foh MEHNT) *v.*

MEANING:

to the ladies we are determined to foment a rebellion, and will not hold ourselves bound by any laws in which we have no voice, or representation.

10 That your sex are naturally tyrannical is a truth so thoroughly established as to admit of no dispute, but such of you as wish to be happy willingly give up the harsh title of master for the more tender and endearing one of friend. Why then, not put it out of the power of the vicious and the lawless to use us with cruelty and indignity with impunity. Men of sense in all ages abhor those customs which treat us only as the vassals of your sex. Regard us then as beings placed by providence under your protection and in imitation of the supreme being make use of that power only for our happiness.

### *April 5*

11 Not having an opportunity of sending this I shall add a few lines more; though not with a heart so gay. I have been attending the sick chamber of our neighbor Trot whose affliction I most sensibly feel but cannot describe, stripped of two lovely children in one week. George the eldest died on Wednesday and Billy the youngest on Friday, with the canker fever, a terrible disorder so much like the throat distemper, that it differs but little from it. Betsy Cranch has been very bad, but upon the recovery. Becky Peck they do not expect will live out the day. Many grown persons, are now sick with it, in this street. It rages much in other towns. The mumps too are very frequent. Isaac is now confined with it. Our own little flock are yet well. My heart trembles with anxiety for them. God preserve them.

12 I want to hear much oftener from you than I do. March 8 was the last date of any that I have yet had.—You inquire of whether I am making salt peter.[9] I have not yet attempted it, but after soap making believe I shall make the experiment. I find as much as I can do to manufacture clothing for my family which would otherwise be naked. I know of but one person in this part of the town who has made any, that is Mr. Tertias Bass as he is called who has got very near a hundred weight which has been found to be very good. I have heard of some others in the other parishes. Mr. Reed of Weymouth has been applied to, to go to Andover to the mills which are now at work, and has gone. I have lately seen a small manuscript describing the proportions for the various sorts of powder, fit for cannon, small arms and pistols. If it would be of any service your way I will get it transcribed and send it to you.—Every one of your friends send their regards, and all the little ones. Your brother's youngest child lies bad with convulsion fits. Adieu. I need not say how much I am your ever faithful friend.

9. **salt peter** *n.* saltpeter; a form of potassium nitrate used to make gunpowder.





CROSS-CURRICULAR PERSPECTIVES

**Science** In paragraph 12, Abigail discusses some of the items the colonists need that they make themselves, including saltpeter, which is another term for potassium nitrate. It was made from things the colonists could find in nature: cow manure, wood ash, green plants, and burned thistles. Have students research the process used to make saltpeter and determine what it was used for. Then have them write a short explanation as to why John Adams might want Abigail to begin making it.

**106** UNIT 1 • WRITING FREEDOM

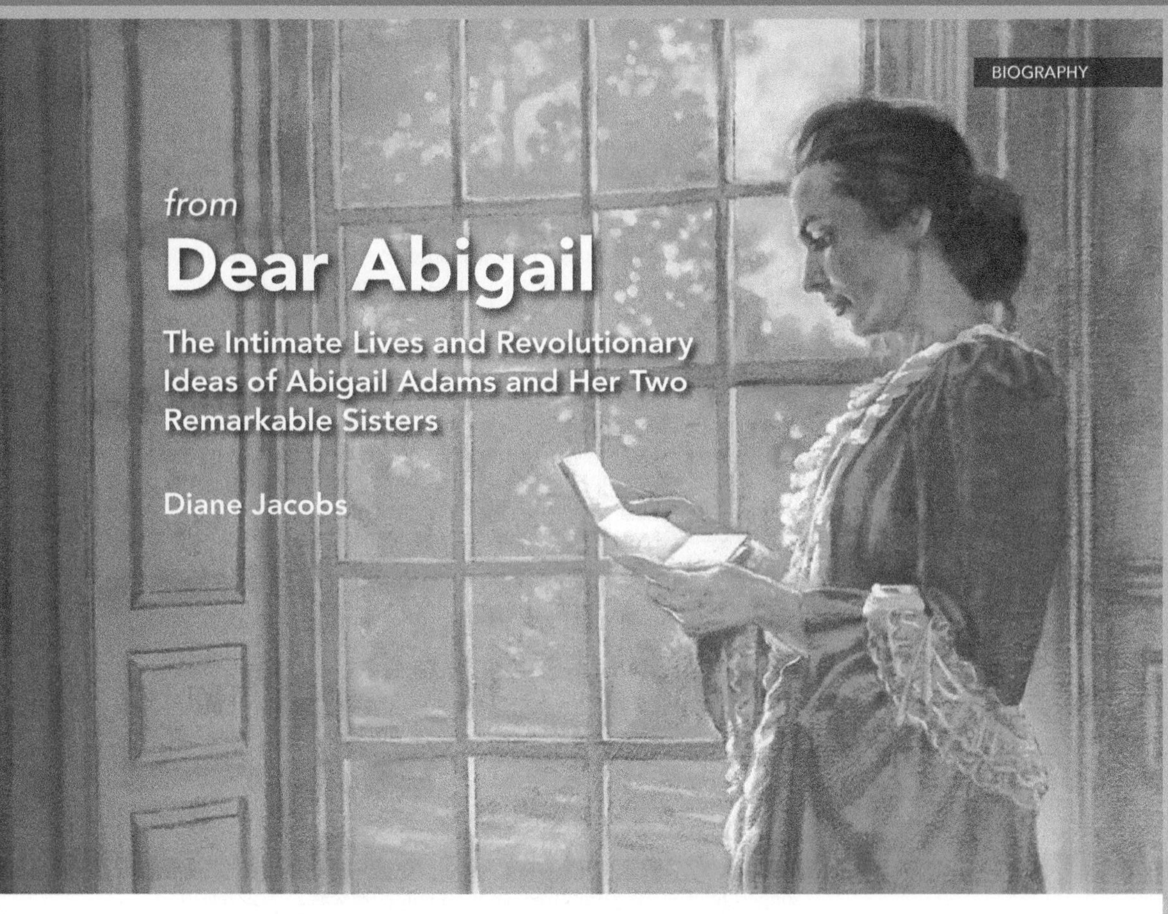


from

# Dear Abigail

## The Intimate Lives and Revolutionary Ideas of Abigail Adams and Her Two Remarkable Sisters

Diane Jacobs

DIGITAL PERSPECTIVES

SCAN FOR MULTIMEDIA

NOTES

1 Writing to Abigail about the fierce effort it took him to compose *Thoughts on Government*[1] at the same time that he was working day and night at Congress, John lamented that none of his present endeavors would bring them an easier life. "I shall get nothing [for writing this pamphlet], I believe, because I never get any thing by any thing that I do," he complained, while assuring her he was not above commiserating her lack of help on the farm or writing paper for all his preoccupation with posterity and the greater good. Strawberries and an early spring in the dirty city did little to console him. He longed, he said, to walk in their garden and to the cornfields, the orchards, and the Common.[2] "Instead of domestic felicity, I am destined to public contentions," he brooded. "Instead of rural felicity, I must reconcile myself to the smoke and noise of a city."

2 So he wished to be home. And yet his overriding desire at the moment was for Congress to make a declaration of independence

1. ***Thoughts on Government*** document written by John Adams in 1776, notable for proposing the three branches of American government, including a system of checks and balances.
2. **the Common** large public park in Boston, Massachusetts.





## PERSONALIZE FOR LEARNING

### English Language Support

**Unpacking a Complex Sentence** The second sentence in paragraph 1 is a complex sentence that may contain some unfamiliar vocabulary words. Remind students that when they come across complex sentences, they can "unpack" the sentence by breaking it into smaller parts. Work with students to unpack the information in the sentence and give meaning to unfamiliar words such as *commiserating*, *preoccupation*, *posterity*, and the idiom the *greater good*. 1. John writes that he will get nothing for writing the pamphlet because he thinks he never gets anything for what he does. 2. He declares to Abigail that he has sympathy for the lack of help on their farm and writing paper. 3. He has sympathy for her even though he is very concerned with the good of future generations. **ALL LEVELS**

## CLOSER LOOK

### Make Inferences

Circulate among groups as students conduct their close read. Suggest that groups close read paragraph 4. Encourage them to talk about the annotations that they mark. If needed, provide the following support.

**ANNOTATE:** Have students mark details in this paragraph that describes Jefferson's qualifications to draft the Declaration of Independence, or have students participate while you highlight them.

**QUESTION:** Guide students to consider what these details might tell them. Ask what a reader can infer from Jefferson's beliefs and experience, and accept student responses.

**Possible response:** Jefferson is smart, well educated, and moral. He should be able to make fair and just decisions.

**CONCLUDE:** Help students to formulate conclusions about the importance of these details in the text. Ask students why the author might have included these details.

**Possible responses:** The author may have wanted to show why Jefferson was the right person to draft a declaration. His beliefs and knowledge qualified him because he believed in goodness, fairness, and virtue. His knowledge of history and philosophy guided the principles of the declaration. His experience as a scientist and inventor shows he had a keen, creative mind.

Point out that the author guides the reader to **make inferences** by using Adams's own words to support points in the text. The second to last sentence in paragraph 4 is supported by a direct quotation.

NOTES

from Great Britain. It had to be sooner rather than later because without it there was no hope for the foreign assistance—from France in particular—which was crucial to winning the war. On June 7, the Virginia delegate Richard Henry Lee of Virginia raised a motion for independence in Congress; it was supported by Massachusetts and six other colonies, while another six—Pennsylvania, Delaware, Maryland, South Carolina, New Jersey, and New York—remained unsure.

3 With everyone hoping for a unanimous verdict, the vote was set three weeks in the future, while a committee to consider the tone and nature of the prospective document immediately convened. It consisted of five members: the most prominent being John, Benjamin Franklin, and the redheaded Virginian who shared Thomas Paine's[3] veneration for the passions: Thomas Jefferson. Considered to be even more eloquent than the far better-known authors of *Poor Richard* and *Thoughts on Government*, 33-year-old Jefferson was chosen to write the text.

4 Like Franklin, Jefferson was a scientist and inventor. He had created a retractable bed and a tilt-top table as well as an indoor weather vane and his own Palladian estate, Monticello. Educated at William and Mary, he was as steeped in history and philosophy as Adams and also adored his wife, a wealthy widow, who was currently pregnant and in poor health. He was a slaveholder who professed to dislike slavery, a statesman ambitious to succeed on the large stage who hated leaving home. As he began drafting the American declaration—in the middle state of Pennsylvania, on a desk of his own design—he longed for southern Monticello as Adams longed for northern Braintree. Though Jefferson was a deist, rejecting Christ and original sin, he shared Adams's obsession with goodness. "Everything is useful which contributes to fix in the mind principles and practices of virtue," he believed.

5 Jefferson was gangly, fidgety, six-foot-two-and-a-half, and as quiet as Franklin in Congress. But he rode his horse elegantly, spoke up regularly in committees, and, despite his aversion to arguing, proved impregnable to opposing views. For better and for worse, no one and nothing swayed him. He had little use for either the vagaries[4] of individuals or venerated ideals.

6 "We are hastening rapidly to great events," John had written Abigail at the end of April, adding that "It requires . . . serenity of temper, a deep . . . understanding and . . . courage . . . to ride in this whirlwind" of Congressional discord. By the end of May, he was telling her that affairs were in a critical state. Then, in the middle of June, exultant after Henry Lee raised a motion for separation from England, he wrote, "These throes will usher in the birth of a fine boy."

3. **Thomas Paine's** Thomas Paine was a highly influential writer who argued passionately for American independence from England.
4. **vagaries** (VAY guh reez) *n.* unpredictable actions or ideas.





## WriteNow Express and Reflect

**Letter** Call student attention to paragraph 2. During the time of the American Revolution, the colonists looked to France to help them with their cause. In paragraph 2, the author states that there would be no hope of help from France without a written declaration of independence.

Ask students to write a letter to the ambassador of France, asking him to ask King Louis XVI of France to help with the American cause. Students should state and describe specific reasons why the colonists need their help.

7 On July 1, twenty days after that initial motion, Congress resumed its debate on independence with John Dickinson of Pennsylvania arguing against and John Adams for an immediate break from both Parliament and King George III. John spoke fervidly for two hours to a rapt audience. A clear majority of nine colonies sided with him, but in a preliminary vote the delegates from Pennsylvania (out of respect for Dickinson, though most of its citizens favored independence), South Carolina, and Delaware **dissented**, while New York, with its high percentage of loyalists, abstained. Still hoping for unanimity, Congress agreed to delay the formal vote until the following morning.

8 That night word arrived that a flotilla of British boats had sailed into New York Harbor, panicking George Washington's unprepared Army and adding pressure for some buoying news. The next day John Dickinson, for the sake of unity, announced he would abstain from the voting, throwing Pennsylvania to the majority. South Carolina and Delaware joined Pennsylvania, while New York continued to abstain. The motion was called to the floor and carried.

9 July 3 was spent amending Jefferson's declaration—much to the proprietary writer's chagrin. The most significant change, insisted on by South Carolina and Georgia, was the elimination of a passage implicitly condemning slavery. Jefferson had accused the King of waging "cruel war against human nature" by capturing and transporting innocent Africans "into slavery in another hemisphere, or to incur miserable death in their transportation thither." This was a daring, if bewildering, opinion from a southern slaveholder. Jefferson claimed to be proud of it and to rue its loss. Other of his favorite passages were also cut or tightened during the nearly twelve-hour debate over wording, but Jefferson's voice remained, and on the afternoon of July 4, all of Congress endorsed it.

*"We are hastening rapidly to great events"*

10 John Adams could hardly contain his exuberance. "Yesterday the greatest question was decided, which ever was debated in America, and a greater, perhaps, never was or will be decided among men," he wrote Abigail. What felt hopelessly slow just a month ago now seemed remarkably expeditious. Looking back to the first arguments with England in the early 1760s, "and recollect[ing] the series of political events, the chain of causes and effects, I am surprised at the suddenness as well as the greatness of this Revolution," he exulted. And, of course, "calamities" and "distresses" might lie in the future; surely the threat of tyranny by the majority, which he had warned against in *Thoughts on Government*, would pose a threat in the coming years. And, yes, it would be far better for the war if independence had been declared seven months before and foreign alliances were set in place. And yet: "July [of] 1776, will be the most memorable

NOTES

Mark context clues or indicate another strategy you used that helped you determine meaning.

**dissented** (dih SEHNT ihd) *v.*

MEANING:





DIGITAL PERSPECTIVES

## Concept Vocabulary

**DISSENTED** If students are struggling to define the word *dissented*, point out that the base word, *dissent,* in paragraph 7, may help them determine meaning. Students may also look for context clues in paragraph 7, which discusses a vote for an immediate break from Parliament and England's King George III. Point out the clause "A clear majority of nine colonies *sided with* him." Students should understand that *sided with* means "agreed with." Point out the clause "but in a preliminary vote the delegates from Pennsylvania, . . . South Carolina, and Delaware dissented." Students should infer that these states were in opposition to the nine states that voted to side with Adams, so the term *dissented* means "opposed" or "disagreed."

**Possible response:** "***Dissented*** can mean "disagreed; took an opposing view."

PERSONALIZE FOR LEARNING

### Strategic Support

**Sequence of Events** Point out the references to specific dates in paragraphs 7 and 9. To help students understand the sequence of events in the entire selection, have pairs work together to build a timeline. Students should go back to the beginning of the selection, and note or annotate events, including dates if applicable. Students can then organize the basic information on a timeline to show sequence.

# FACILITATING

## CLOSER LOOK

### Make Inferences

Circulate among groups as students conduct their close read. Suggest that groups close read paragraph 10. Encourage them to talk about the annotations that they mark. If needed, provide the following support.

**ANNOTATE:** Have students mark details in this paragraph that show how John Adams feels the events of July 1776 will be celebrated, or have students participate while you highlight them.

**QUESTION:** Guide students to consider what these details might tell them. Ask what a reader can infer from Adam's description of future events, and accept student responses.

**Possible response:** Adams feels that the events of July 1776 will be the most memorable epoch in the history of America. He seems to believe that its significance will continue to be an important event in the lives of Americans well into the future.

**CONCLUDE:** Help students to formulate conclusions about the importance of these details in the text. Ask students why the author might have included these details.

**Possible responses:** The author wanted to illustrate the importance of the events of July 1776 by showing Adams's enthusiasm and prediction of how the Declaration of Independence would be celebrated for years to come.

Point out the language John Adams uses to describe the celebrations he anticipates: "pomp and parade, with shews, sports, guns, bells, bonfires, and illuminations." Guide students to see that this type of language helps readers to **make inferences** about how significant John Adams felt this historical event would be.

NOTES

**Drafting the Declaration of Independence in 1776** This 1859 painting by Alonzo Chappel depicts the work of the "Committee of Five": (*right to left*) Roger Sherman, Robert Livingston, John Adams, Thomas Jefferson, and Benjamin Franklin.

epocha,[5] in the history of America.—I am apt to believe that it will be celebrated, by succeeding generations, as the great anniversary." It ought, John declared, to be commemorated and "solemnized with pomp and parade, with shews,[6] sports, guns, bells, bonfires and illuminations from one end of this continent to the other from this time forward forever."

11 On July 18, a week after they were inoculated for smallpox, and with no one yet showing symptoms of the disease, Mary and Richard, Abigail, and Betsy joined masses of patriots lining King Street in front of the Boston State House, the seat of the first elected legislature in the New World. The ragtag troops who had chased the British out of Boston four months earlier stood before them, respectably armed at least for the moment. An officer, Colonel Crafts, appeared on the balcony and began to read:

5. **epocha** (EHP uh kuh) *n.* archaic form of "epoch," a distinct and significant era in history.
6. **shews** *n.* archaic form of "shows."





## PERSONALIZE FOR LEARNING

### English Language Support

**Nominalization** Tell students that some verbs can be transformed into nouns with similar meanings. Point out the words, *celebrated*, *declared*, and *commemorated* in paragraph 10. Note that all of these words are written in the past tense. Write the present tense of each word: *celebrate*, *declare*, *commemorate*. Tell students that by dropping the final *-e* and adding the suffix *–tion*, the words can be transformed from verbs into nouns: *celebration*, *declaration*, and *commemoration*. Encourage students to use both verb and noun forms in a sentence that illustrates their meanings. **EMERGING**

DIGITAL PERSPECTIVES

12 When in the course of human events, it becomes necessary for one people to dissolve the political bonds which have connected them with another, and to assume among the powers of the earth a separate and equal station to which the Laws of Nature and of Nature's God entitle them, a decent respect to the opinions of mankind requires that they should declare the causes which impel them to the separation.

13 The Smith sisters'[7] lives spoke volumes on the causes for separation, and the spirit of the declaration was familiar, for they had avidly read the great thinkers of the Enlightenment[8] who so informed Jefferson's view. Yet, if his concepts were not original, the occasion was a first in history, and Richard Cranch as well as Mary, Abigail, and Betsy stood spellbound at the beautiful expression of what they felt and knew. "We hold these truths to be self-evident, that all men are created equal, that they are endowed by their Creator with certain unalienable Rights, that among these are Life, Liberty, and the pursuit of Happiness." And on it went.

14 "God Save the King" was already a memory. When Colonel Crafts finished reading the Declaration of Independence, he shouted, "God Save our American States." The people picked up this chant and ran with it, as Richard Cranch reported to John in a letter the following week. There were three cheers that "rended the air," Abigail wrote in her own description, and they were followed by an elated ringing of bells; the cannons roared, and rifles' shots rang in the air. "After dinner the king's arms were taken down from the State House and every vestige of him from every place in which it appeared and burnt in King Street. Thus ends royal authority in this State," she concluded, "and all the people shall say Amen."

15 By July 22, Abigail was ill with the "excruciating pain in my head and every limb" that was said to "portend[9] a speedy eruption," which occurred a few days later, and though she produced only one pox, her symptoms were sufficiently grueling for the doctor to declare her immune. John Quincy's case too was mild but conclusive, while Mary's eldest daughter, Betsy Cranch, the frailest of them all, fainted and lay listless in bed. Her mother and brothers, on the other hand, produced no symptoms. By the end of July, Mary had been inoculated four times and was still healthy as the day she left Braintree, as were Charles and Tommy Adams, who had been inoculated twice. It seemed fitting when Nabby, the calmest of them all, came through with almost no suffering. The doctor, however, insisted that she be inoculated a second time, on the odd chance that her symptoms were "false."

16 Even after her single pox dissipated, Abigail felt light-headed from the disease. "The smallpox is a great confuser of the mind, I am really

NOTES

7. **Smith sisters** Abigail Adams and her sisters; Smith was their family surname.
8. **the Enlightenment** European intellectual movement in the seventeenth and eighteenth centuries that emphasized the power of reason.
9. **portend** (pawr TEHND) *v.* foreshadow; indicate.





CLOSER LOOK

## Make Inferences

Circulate among groups as students conduct their close read. Suggest that groups close read paragraphs 13 and 14. Encourage them to talk about the annotations that they mark. If needed, provide the following support.

**ANNOTATE:** Have students mark details in these paragraphs that describe how Abigail felt during the July 18th reading of the Declaration of Independence on King Street, or have students participate while you highlight them.

**QUESTION:** Guide students to consider what these details might tell them. Ask what a reader can infer from Abigail's feelings and responses, and accept student responses.

**Possible response:** Abigail and her sisters were spellbound by the reading of the beautiful words. They felt the meaning of the words and knew them well. After burning the vestiges of the King, Abigail states that "all people shall say Amen." It is clear that Abigail and the others felt the weight of oppression lifted and were overjoyed at the prospect of liberty.

**CONCLUDE:** Help students to formulate conclusions about the importance of these details in the text. Ask students why the author might have included these details.

**Possible response:** The author most likely included these details to show Abigail's joy at the reading of the declaration and her happiness and approval that the vestiges of the king were burned. The ending statement that "all people shall say Amen" lifts her joy to the level of prayer.

Remind students that including details, evidence, and quotations provides readers with information from which they can **make inferences** about the facts and the people in the text.

CROSS-CURRICULAR PERSPECTIVES

**Science** Review paragraph 16 with students. Smallpox was a deadly disease that had been brought to the colonies by settlers. Survivors were often badly scarred with pockmarks or they became blind. In the late 1790s, a doctor named Edward Jenner noticed that people who caught cowpox, a mild viral infection in cows, became immune to the disease. After some experimenting, Jenner concluded that the cowpox infection caused people to become immune from smallpox. Jenner went on to perform further studies and experiments, leading to the development of a smallpox vaccination. Encourage students to find out more about smallpox during Colonial times and its deadly effects on both colonists and Native Americans.

CLOSER LOOK

## Make Inferences

Circulate among groups as students conduct their close read. Suggest that groups close read paragraphs 16–17. Encourage them to talk about the annotations that they mark. If needed, provide the following support.

**ANNOTATE:** Have students mark details in these paragraphs that demonstrate how Abigail advocates women's rights, or have students participate while you highlight them.

**QUESTION:** Guide students to consider what these details might tell them. Ask what a reader can infer from Abigail's support for women, and accept student responses.

**Possible response:** Abigail suggests that women want to be educated and that a more liberal plan be made for future generations that will include education and development of learned women and that women will benefit greatly from these changes. It seems that Abigail has great hope and belief in the abilities of women to do great things.

**CONCLUDE:** Help students to formulate conclusions about the importance of these details in the text. Ask students why the author might have included these details.

**Possible responses:** The author most likely included these details to show Abigail's support of women's rights and how she foresaw a better future for women in the newly formed country.

Remind students to use what they read in the text and what they already know when **making inferences**. As students read these paragraphs about Abigail Adams's feelings on the rights of women, have them recall what they learned in the previous selection, "Letter to John Adams."

NOTES

put to it to spell the commonest word," she told John. Yet when John gave her an opening, she had no trouble expounding on her favorite topic of women in the new nation. "If you complain of neglect of education in sons, What shall I say with regard to daughters, who every day experience the want of it," she began. And continued:

17 I most sincerely wish that some more liberal plan might be laid and executed for the benefit of the rising generation, and that our new constitution may be distinguished for learning and virtue. If we mean to have heroes, statesmen, and philosophers, we should have learned women. The world perhaps will laugh at me, and accuse me of vanity, but you know I have a mind too enlarged and liberal [to be vain]. If much depends as is allowed upon the early education of youth and the first principals which are instilled take deepest root, great benefit must arise from literary accomplishments in women.

18 This time John assured Abigail "Your sentiments of the importance of education in women are exactly agreeable to my own," though women who displayed their wits were contemptible, he felt impelled to add. ❧





PERSONALIZE FOR LEARNING

### English Language Support

**Multiple Meanings** Read aloud paragraph 18 to students. Point out the word *wit* and ask students to determine its meaning. Point out that *wit* is a noun that can describe a person who has humor. In this case, however, the word *wit* is a noun that describes a person with intelligence. Ask students why they think that John Adams felt the need to add that "women who displayed their wits were contemptible." **ALL LEVELS**

## Comprehension Check

Complete the following items after you finish your first read. Review and clarify details with your group.

LETTER TO JOHN ADAMS

1. In her letter of March 31, 1776, what does Abigail Adams ask that John provide?

2. What does Abigail report to John about the state of homes in Boston?

3. What advice does Abigail Adams give her husband regarding women's rights?

4. **Notebook** Confirm your understanding of the text by writing a summary.

*from* DEAR ABIGAIL

1. Cite two reasons for John Adams's unhappiness in the late spring of 1776.

2. Name two contradictions regarding Thomas Jefferson that the text explores.

3. What document does Colonel Crafts, an army officer, read to a crowd assembled in front of the Boston State House?

4. **Notebook** Confirm your understanding of the text by drawing a storyboard of events.

### RESEARCH

**Research to Clarify** Choose at least one unfamiliar detail from one of the texts. Briefly research that detail. In what way does the information you found shed light on an aspect of that text?





DIGITAL PERSPECTIVES

## Comprehension Check

### Letter to John Adams

Possible responses:

1. She wants news of the war with Great Britain, especially what is happening in Virginia.
2. She reports that their home had been occupied and was left filthy. Other homes were damaged and ransacked by the soldiers.
3. Abigail Adams urges John to allow women greater freedom from their husbands and a voice and representation in making laws.
4. **Notebook** Possible response: Abigail Adams wants news of the fighting in Virginia. She reports that their house is in good shape, but that other homes have been ravaged by the occupying soldiers. She urges her husband to ensure that the new government will give women greater rights. Finally, she reports that there is much sickness in town and that she has information about how to make saltpeter, or cannon powder.

### *from* Dear Abigail

1. He knows his work will not benefit his family financially and wishes that he could be with Abigail at their country home.
2. Jefferson is a slaveholder who claims that he dislikes slavery; a statesman who yearns for a larger audience but doesn't like to leave home; a deist who rejects traditional teachings about Christ and original sin but shares Adams's obsession with goodness.
3. The Declaration of Independence
4. **Notebook** Storyboards should trace the main events in this text: John's feelings of being unappreciated, the issue of ratification of the Declaration of Independence, the elation of the people in Boston over its passage, and Abigail Adams's concern for provisions in the new constitution for women's education.

## Research

**Research to Clarify** If groups struggle to identify an unfamiliar detail, suggest that they focus on one of the following from the "Letter to John Adams":

- the reference to being "shamefully duped by a Dunmore" (paragraph 3)
- the roles of John Hancock and Solicitor General Samuel Quincy (paragraph 6)

Or you may suggest these items from *Dear Abigail*:

- John Adams's *Thoughts on Government* (paragraph 1)
- a detail about Thomas Jefferson (paragraph 4) such as the drafting of the declaration
- the position of Parliament and King George III on the colonies (paragraph 7)

## Jump Start

CLOSE READ Ask students to think about how women's rights have changed since the time of Abigail Adams. What rights do women have now that Abigail did not in her time? What might Abigail think if she were alive today? Would she advocate for further change for women? What might those changes involve?

## Close Read the Text

Model close reading as needed by using the Annotation Highlights in the Interactive Teacher's Edition.

Remind groups to use Accountable Talk in their discussions and to support one another as they complete the close read.

## Analyze the Text

**Possible responses**

1. Students may mention the subsequent removal of the images of the King of England as evidence that the Bostonians were thrilled to hear that there had been a decision to make a formal break with the mother country.
2. Responses will vary by group. Students may focus on Adams's discussion of the tyranny of men in her letter or on Jacobs's characterization of Jefferson.
3. Responses will vary by group. Achieving freedom can be a long and difficult process, and not all citizens may achieve freedom.

## Concept Vocabulary

**Why These Words?** Possible response: The words are about oppression and rebellion.

### Practice

**Possible responses:**

- In ancient feudal societies, ***vassals*** had to fight in a lord's army and pay him tribute in return for being allowed to farm his land.
- Unhappy with poor working conditions, union members began to ***foment*** revolution in the form of a strike.
- Because some students ***dissented***, we could not achieve a unanimous vote.

### Word Network

**Possible words:** *tyrants, rebellion, unalienable, representation, patriotism, unlimited*

## Word Study

**Possible responses:**

(1) dissenter (noun), dissension (noun), dissentingly (adverb); (2) Answers will vary based on word chosen.

For more support, see **Concept Vocabulary and Word Study.**

MAKING MEANING

LETTER TO JOHN ADAMS
*from* DEAR ABIGAIL

## Close Read the Text

With your group, revisit sections of the text you marked during your first read. **Annotate** details that you notice. What **questions** do you have? What can you **conclude**?

## Analyze the Text

CITE TEXTUAL EVIDENCE to support your answers.

**Complete the activities.**

1. **Review and Clarify** With your group, reread paragraph 14 from *Dear Abigail*, in which the author discusses the public reading of the Declaration of Independence. Why do you think the Bostonians reacted as they did?
2. **Present and Discuss** Now, work with your group to share the passages from the two selections that you found especially important. Take turns presenting your passages. Discuss what you noticed in the selections, what questions you asked, and what conclusions you reached.
3. **Essential Question:** *What is the meaning of freedom?* What have you learned about American freedoms from reading these texts? Discuss with your group.

TIP

GROUP DISCUSSION
Encourage group members to be positive, encouraging, and open to divergent viewpoints and opinions.

LANGUAGE DEVELOPMENT

## Concept Vocabulary

vassals foment dissented

**Why These Words?** The three concept words from the texts are related. With your group, discuss the words and determine what they have in common. How do these word choices enhance the impact of the texts?

### Practice

**Notebook** Confirm your understanding of these words by using each one in a sentence. Include context clues that help readers figure out what each word means.

WORD NETWORK
Add words related to freedom from the text to your Word Network.

## Word Study

**Notebook** **Word Families** Groups of words that share a common base but have different prefixes, suffixes, or both, are called **word families**. The concept word *dissented*, for instance, is built upon the base word *dissent*.

**Complete the following activities.**

1. Use an online dictionary or other source to identify other members of the word family that includes *dissented*. Write three of those related words, and identify their parts of speech.
2. Choose a word from one of these texts that you think is part of a word family. Research the word and verify your choice. Write the original word and two related words. Identify each word's part of speech.

STANDARDS
**Reading Informational Text**
Analyze seventeenth-, eighteenth-, and nineteenth-century foundational U.S. documents of historical and literary significance for their themes, purposes, and rhetorical features.
**Language**
Identify and correctly use patterns of word changes that indicate different meanings or parts of speech.

## FORMATIVE ASSESSMENT

### Analyze the Text

**If** students struggle to close read the text, **then** provide the **Letter to John Adams • *from* Dear Abigail: Text Questions** available online in the Interactive Teacher's Edition or Unit Resources. Answers and DOK levels are also available.

### Concept Vocabulary

**If** students struggle to identify the concept, **then** have them look online for synonyms for these words. Students can use the synonyms to construct a word map for each word.

### Word Study

**If** students fail to identify word families, **then** provide a list of potential words from the text to pairs. Ask students which words do they think could be part of a word family. Then have pairs write two words that are part of the word family.

For Reteach and Practice, see **Word Study: Word Families (RP).**

## Analyze Craft and Structure

**Primary and Secondary Sources** Research sources can be classified into one of two categories—primary sources or secondary sources.

- **Primary sources**, created by people who directly participated in or observed an event, give readers first-hand information about a topic. They include diaries, journals, letters, newspaper articles, and speeches. They may also include functional texts, such as government forms, schedules, or blueprints.
- **Secondary sources**, written by people with indirect knowledge, rely on primary sources or other secondary sources for information. Secondary sources include biographies, encyclopedias, and book reviews.

These classifications into primary and secondary categories are not absolutely set, but depend largely on how a text is used by a researcher.

TIP

CLARIFICATION

Original drawings, paintings, news footage, pottery, and photographs are some non-text items that are categorized as primary sources. These can be excellent research sources, and they should be documented with citations.

### Practice

**CITE TEXTUAL EVIDENCE** to support your answers.

Analyze and evaluate how Jacobs uses primary sources to add interest, clarity, and legitimacy to the points she is making. For example, ask: "What does this quotation from a primary source do? Does it make the point clearer?" Work individually to gather your notes in this chart. Then, share your observations with your group.

| *DEAR ABIGAIL* | PRIMARY SOURCE INFORMATION | EFFECT |
|---|---|---|
| Paragraph 1 | "I shall get nothing [for writing this pamphlet], I believe, for I never get anything by any thing that I do." | John's character—namely, his feelings of being unappreciated and overworked—is clarified. |
| Paragraph 6 | "We are hastening rapidly to great events." | The quotation creates interest because it builds tension and suspense in the narrative. |
| Paragraph 10 | "July [of] 1776, will be the most memorable epocha, in the history of America. . . . the great anniversary." | Readers get caught up in the excitement and appreciate John's understanding of the importance of the events. |
| Paragraph 17 | "If much depends as is allowed upon the early education of youth and the first principals which are instilled take deepest root, great benefit must arise from literary accomplishments in women." | Readers get a clearer understanding of Abigail's fight for equal education for women and her efforts to pressure her husband to support it. |

**Notebook** Respond to these questions.

1. Which use of a primary source in the excerpt from *Dear Abigail* did you find most effective? Why?
2. Review or scan the two secondary sources related to Abigail Adams in this text—the brief biography and the excerpt from *Dear Abigail*. Identify one trait each secondary source attributes to Abigail Adams. Then, cite a passage from Adams's letter that either supports that interpretation of her character or challenges it. Explain your choices.





DIGITAL PERSPECTIVES 

## Analyze Craft and Structure

**Primary and Secondary Sources** Remind students that Abigail Adams's letters to John are primary sources. The biography of John and Abigail is a secondary source, but supported with quotations that are primary sources.

For more support, see **Analyze Craft and Structure: Primary and Secondary Sources.**

### Practice

See possible responses in chart on student page.

### Notebook

Possible responses:

1. "I am apt to believe that it will be celebrated, by succeeding generations, as the great anniversary." It ought, John declared, to be commemorated and "solemnized with pomp and parade, with shews, sports, guns, bells, bonfires and illuminations from one end of this continent to the other from this time forward forever." This is effective because it shows Adams's excitement about the declaration and hope for the future.
2. Abigail Adams is described as being intent on promoting women's rights. In her letter to John Adams, she implores: "If particular care and attention is not paid to the ladies we are determined to foment a rebellion..." This and other quotations exhibit how strongly she felt about the issue, and how surprisingly bold and forceful she was with her husband. Her plea could almost be viewed as a threat.

**FORMATIVE ASSESSMENT**

### Analyze Craft and Structure

**If** students have difficulty completing the chart, **then** demonstrate identifying primary sources and their effects by working through paragraph 1 together. For Reteach and Practice, see **Analyze Craft and Structure: Primary and Secondary Sources (RP).**

FACILITATING

## Author's Style

**Voice** Remind students that authors often use voice to persuade a reader about a certain topic, or they use voice to describe things or events around them. An author might use a different tone, diction, or syntax when trying to persuade a reader about something than when describing a thing or an event. For more support, **see Author's Style: Voice.**

### Read It

See possible responses in chart on student page.

### Write It

**Possible responses:** As a writer, Abigail Adams is interested in reporting on daily life, eager to express her opinions, and willing to share her personal life and thoughts. For example, in her letter to her husband, she writes of her feelings regarding the coming of spring. Quoted in *Dear Abigail,* she writes of her illness. In both cases, Abigail Adams's frank, personal voice enlivens the text and helps describe a brilliant and determined woman.

**FORMATIVE ASSESSMENT**

### Author's Style

**If** students fail to identify aspects of Abigail Adams's voice as a writer, review the meaning of the terms *diction, syntax,* and *tone.* **Then** find examples that illustrate each in the selection and read them aloud. Ask students to determine the types of words used, sentence structure and length, and the attitude of the writer. For Reteach and Practice, see **Author's Style: Voice (RP).**

LANGUAGE DEVELOPMENT

LETTER TO JOHN ADAMS
*from* DEAR ABIGAIL

## Author's Style

**Voice** A writer's **voice** is the way in which his or her personality is revealed on the page. It is the sense the reader gains of the person behind the words. Voice is created through a combination of elements:

- **diction:** the types of words a writer uses
- **syntax:** the types of sentences a writer uses, including structure, length, and variety
- **tone:** the writer's attitude toward the topic or audience

Voice is also influenced by the writer's consideration of his or her **audience**, or readers, and **purpose**, or reason for writing. Since writers adapt their diction, syntax, and tone to suit specific audiences and purposes, a writer's voice can vary from one text to another. For example, John Adams's voice is warm and personal in letters to his wife, but impersonal and formal in public documents.

### Read It

Work individually. Use this chart to explore aspects of Abigail Adams's voice as a writer. Cite examples from both texts, and briefly explain how her combination of diction, syntax, and tone creates a sense of her personal qualities. Discuss your findings with your group.

| PASSAGES FROM LETTER TO JOHN ADAMS | TYPE(S) OF DICTION, SYNTAX, AND TONE | PERSONALITY TRAIT(S) OF ADAMS |
|---|---|---|
| "I wish you would ever write me a letter half as long as I write you; and tell me if you may where your fleet are gone?" | tone of wanting and concern. | firmness and forthrightness |
| "I need not say how much I am your ever faithful friend."<br>"I desire you would remember the ladies, and be more generous and favorable to them than your ancestors." | formal syntax | personableness and cheerfulness<br>strength and seriousness |
| PASSAGES QUOTED IN *DEAR ABIGAIL* | | |
| "'Thus ends royal authority in this State,' she concluded, 'and all the people shall say Amen.'" | celebratory tone | personableness and elatedness |
| "...Abigail was ill with the 'excruciating pain in my head and every limb...'"<br>"If we mean to have heroes, statesmen, and philosophers, we should have learned women." | diction includes descriptive details declarative tone | honesty and some self pity (fort)<br>strength and seriousness |

STANDARDS
**Reading Informational Text**
Determine an author's point of view or purpose in a text in which the rhetoric is particularly effective, analyzing how style and content contribute to the power, persuasiveness or beauty of the text.

### Write It

**Notebook** Review your notes from the chart. Then, write a paragraph in which you describe Abigail Adams's voice as a writer. Use textual examples to support your view. Share your paragraph with your group, and discuss.





HOW LANGUAGE WORKS

**Eighteenth-Century Narrative Style**
Remind students that the eighteenth-century formal language style that Abigail Adams uses is very different from our modern style. Have students go back through the text and find examples of sentences that have 1) multiple clauses and prepositional phrases, 2) word meanings that have changed in modern times, or words that are no longer used (archaic), and 3) punctuation marks that do not follow established conventions of modern writing. Have students discuss how these examples are different from modern language.

EFFECTIVE EXPRESSION

## Speaking and Listening

**Assignment**

Create an **oral presentation** based on the selections and present it to the whole class. Choose from the following options.

- ☐ **Dialogue** Write and present a dramatization of a conversation between John and Abigail Adams in which the two discuss the colonies' struggle for freedom from Great Britain. Base the conversation on the information provided in the texts. Strive to capture each speaker's unique opinions and point of view.
- ☐ **Dramatic Reading** Present a reading of the March 31st portion of Abigail Adams's letter to John Adams. Decide how you will divide the text among members of your group so that everyone participates. Then, discuss your interpretation of the text, and consider how you will use your voices and gestures to capture its distinct qualities.
- ☐ **Public Announcement** Both Abigail Adams's letter and the excerpt from *Dear Abigail* mention the threat that smallpox posed in Revolutionary-era America. Research the symptoms of smallpox; the types of people who are especially vulnerable; its progression, treatment, and potential outcomes. Then, write and deliver the announcement that might have been read to citizens of Boston in 1776 warning them of the presence of the disease in their community. Refer to Adams's letter for ideas about diction and tone.

EVIDENCE LOG

Before moving on to the next selection, go to your Evidence Log and record what you learned from Abigail Adams's letter to John Adams and the excerpt from *Dear Abigail*.

**Project Plan** First, identify the information, details, or passages you will use from the texts. Use the chart to determine which details you will include, why they are important, and how you will use them in the presentation. If you feel that you need additional material, decide which group members will do the research.

| Detail from Text(s) | Reason to Use Detail | How Group Will Present Detail |
|---|---|---|
| | | |
| | | |
| | | |
| | | |

**Presentation Plan** Decide which members of the group will produce the writing required for the assignment, and which members will deliver the presentation. Make sure that all members have an equal role, and allow all members to contribute their ideas before finalizing the presentation.

STANDARDS

**Speaking and Listening**

Present information, findings, and supporting evidence, conveying a clear and distinct perspective and a logical argument, such that listeners can follow the line of reasoning, alternative or opposing perspectives are addressed, and the organization, development, substance, and style are appropriate to purpose, audience, and a range of formal and informal tasks.





DIGITAL PERSPECTIVES 

## Speaking and Listening

**Assignment** If students are struggling with which assignment to choose, guide them by giving a brief description of role-play, reader's theater, and public service announcements. Students who enjoy acting out roles on stage may be comfortable with role-play. Encourage students to have a basic idea as to their role-play without writing actual scripts. They may enjoy ad-libbing their parts. Students who enjoy reading might be better suited for Reader's Theater. Allow students time to practice their parts, giving feedback as necessary. Demonstrate tone of voice, projection, and other aspects of oral interpretation of literature to guide them. For more support, **Speaking and Listening: Oral Presentation.**

**Project Plan** Allow time for students to do any additional research they may need to support their assignment.

**Presentation Plan** The chart will help students organize their presentations and think through how they will use words and phrases from the selection. Tell students to practice in front of a mirror or their peers to improve speaking skills.

**Evidence Log** Support students in completing their Evidence Log. This paced activity will help prepare them for the Performance-Based Assessment at the end of the unit.

### FORMATIVE ASSESSMENT

### Speaking and Listening

**If** students struggle with creating an oral presentation, **then** have them search the Internet for videos of students giving oral presentations as suggested here. For Reteach and Practice, see **Speaking and Listening: Oral Presentation (RP).**

### Selection Test

Administer the "Letter to John Adams • Dear Abigail" Selection Test, which is available in both print and digital formats online in Assessments.

PERSONALIZE FOR LEARNING

### English Language Support

**Oral Presentation** Have students choose a topic for an oral presentation. Tell them it should be a topic they know well.

Ask students to write their position on the topic, the audience, and what tone they will use. Have them practice with a partner. **EMERGING**

Ask students to write a short outline of their presentation. Remind them that they should make sure their position on the topic comes across, and that they should keep in mind the right tone and register, according to their topic and their audience. Ask students to share their ideas with a small group. **EXPANDING**

Have students write a paragraph summarizing their presentation. The paragraph should include their point of view on the topic, and use the same language and tone they would use for their intended audience. Ask students to use their paragraph to help them present their ideas. **BRIDGING**

An expanded **English Language Support Lesson** on Oral Presentation is available in the Interactive Teacher's Edition.

# Gettysburg Address

**AUDIO SUMMARIES**
Audio summaries of "Gettysburg Address" are available online in both English and Spanish in the Interactive Teacher's Edition or Unit Resources. Assigning these summaries prior to reading the selection may help students build additional background knowledge and set a context for their first read.

## Summary

President Lincoln delivered the Gettysburg Address on November 19, 1863, at a ceremony dedicating the Soldiers' National Cemetery at Gettysburg, Pennsylvania. There, 7,500 Union soldiers had died in battle a few months earlier. Lincoln begins his speech by noting that 87 years earlier, in 1776, the country's founding fathers created a new nation dedicated to the idea that "all men are created equal." Lincoln then notes that the country is fighting a civil war to determine whether this nation "can long endure." He states that those who died in battle had fought to preserve the Union. Lincoln asserts that the work of these soldiers was not finished. He believes it is the living who must continue fighting for the nation's survival so as to assure the survival of a "government of the people, by the people and for the people."

### Insight

Reading the Gettysburg Address will help students think about how important it is to safeguard people's rights, as stated in the Constitution. He urges our country's citizens to endure sacrifices in order to expand these rights to a new group of people who had been denied them.

ESSENTIAL QUESTION:
What is the meaning of freedom?

## Connection to the Essential Question

The Gettysburg Address has a two-part connection to the Essential Question, "What is the meaning of freedom?" This speech alludes to the central idea expressed in the Declaration of Independence that "all men are created equal." It also connects the Essential Question to the Constitution, which does not address the issue of slavery but which allows for change over time through the amendment process.

SMALL-GROUP LEARNING PERFORMANCE TASK
Do narratives provide strong evidence to support arguments about American freedoms?

UNIT PERFORMANCE-BASED ASSESSMENT
What are the most effective tools for establishing and preserving freedom?

## Connection to Performance Tasks

**Small-Group Learning Performance Task** In this Performance Task, students will consider whether narratives provide strong evidence to support arguments about American freedoms. In the Gettysburg Address, students will read one of the most inspiring and enduring calls to action for an end to war, national unity, and principles of freedom and liberty.

**Unit Performance-Based Assessment** This selection provides challenging insight into the Performance-Based Assessment question on the establishment and preservation of freedom. Students must evaluate whether the deaths of thousands of citizens is justified when trying to establish new freedoms not explicitly mentioned in founding documents such as the Constitution.

DIGITAL PERSPECTIVES

 Audio  Video  Document  Annotation Highlights  EL Highlights 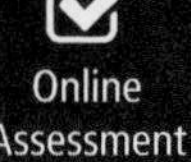 Online Assessment

## LESSON RESOURCES

| | Making Meaning | Language Development | Effective Expression |
|---|---|---|---|
| **Lesson** | **First Read**<br>**Close Read**<br>**Analyze the Text**<br>**Analyze Craft and Structure** | **Concept Vocabulary**<br>**Word Study**<br>**Author's Style** | **Research** |
| **Instructional Standards** | **RI.10** By the end of grade 11, read and comprehend literary nonfiction . . .<br>**RI.6** Determine an author's point of view . . .<br>**RI.9** Analyze seventeenth-, eighteenth-, and nineteenth-century foundational U.S. documents . . .<br>**L.4** Determine or clarify the meaning of unknown and multiple-meaning words and phrases . . .<br>**L.4.d** Verify the preliminary determination . . . | **L.5.b** Analyze nuances in the meanings of words . . .<br>**RI.6** Determine an author's point of view . . .<br>**SL.3** Evaluate a speaker's point of view . . . | **W.2** Write informative/explanatory texts . . .<br>**W.7** Conduct short as well as more sustained research projects . . . |
| **STUDENT RESOURCES** | | | |
| Available online in the Interactive Student Edition or Unit Resources | Selection Audio<br>First-Read Guide: Nonfiction<br>Close-Read Guide: Nonfiction | Word Network | Evidence Log |
| **TEACHER RESOURCES** | | | |
| **Selection Resources** Available online in the Interactive Teacher's Edition or Unit Resources | Audio Summaries<br>Annotation Highlights<br>EL Highlights<br>English Language Support Lesson: Verb Tense Consistency<br>Gettysburg Address: Text Questions<br>Analyze Craft and Structure: Rhetoric | Concept Vocabulary and Word Study<br>Conventions and Style: Antithesis | Research: Report |
| **Reteach/Practice (RP)** Available online in the Interactive Teacher's Edition or Unit Resources | Analyze Craft and Structure: Rhetoric (RP) | Word Study: Denotation and Connotation (RP)<br>Author's Style: Antithesis (RP) | Research: Report (RP) |
| **Assessment** Available online in Assessments | Selection Test | | |
| **My Resources** | A Unit 1 Answer Key is available online and in the Interactive Teacher's Edition. | | |

# Reading Support

| Text Complexity Rubric: Gettysburg Address | |
|---|---|
| **Quantitative Measures** | |
| **Lexile** 1490 **Text Length** 264 words | |
| **Qualitative Measures** | |
| Knowledge Demands<br>① ② ③ **❹** ⑤ | Historical knowledge demands; selection is a speech given at the dedication of the cemetery at Gettysburg after a battle that marked a turning point in the Civil War. |
| Structure<br>① **❷** ③ ④ ⑤ | The selection is a short, straightforward speech. |
| Language Conventionality and Clarity<br>① ② **❸** ④ ⑤ | The selection contains some complex sentences. Vocabulary is mostly on-level. There is some unfamiliar language (four score and seven years ago). |
| Levels of Meaning/Purpose<br>① ② ③ **❹** ⑤ | The meaning and purpose are straightforward, though some of the language may be difficult to grasp. |

DECIDE AND PLAN

## English Language Support

Provide English Learners with support for knowledge demands and language as they read the selection.

**Knowledge Demands** Before students read, make a list of some of the terms and phrases they will need to understand: *four score, conceived, proposition, dedicated, consecrate, hallow, in vain,* and *perish*. Discuss and define each term as needed.

**Language** Students may have difficulty with some of the complex sentences. Instead of trying to understand every word, encourage students to scan for ideas in each paragraph that they understand. Ask them to write sentences restating the information they understood.

## Strategic Support

Provide students with strategic support to ensure that they can successfully read the text.

**Knowledge Demands** Use the background information to review what students know about the Civil War and the Battle of Gettysburg. Remind students that Union soldiers won the battle against Confederate soldiers, which was a turning point in the war.

**Levels of Meaning / Purpose** As students read, have them note that the address is separated into three parts. The first paragraph talks about the past, the second paragraph addresses the present, and the last paragraph is about the future. Have students restate the main ideas from each paragraph in their own words.

## Challenge

Provide students who need to be challenged with ideas for how they can go beyond a simple interpretation of the text.

**Text Analysis** Have students reread the selection, taking note of words that are repeated (*dedicate, we, cannot, here*). Ask students why they think Lincoln chose to repeat these words. What effect does the use of repetition have on Lincoln's address?

**Written Response** Remind students that the Gettysburg Address remains one of the most read speeches in history. Have students write an essay about why the speech is still relevant today.

TEACH

## Read and Respond

Have the groups read the selection and complete the Making Meaning, Language Development, and Effective Expression activities.

# Standards Support Through Teaching and Learning Cycle

## IDENTIFY NEEDS

Analyze results of the Beginning-of-Year Assessment, focusing on the items relating to Unit 1. Also take into consideration student performance to this point and your observations of where particular students struggle.

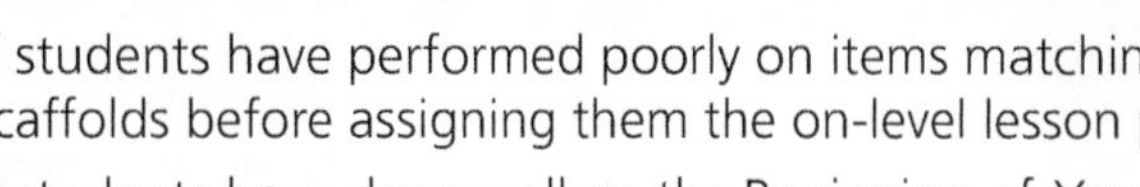

## DECIDE AND PLAN

- If students have performed poorly on items matching these standards, then provide selection scaffolds before assigning them the on-level lesson provided in the Student Edition.
- If students have done well on the Beginning-of-Year Assessment, then challenge them to keep progressing and learning by giving them opportunities to practice the skills in depth.
- Use the Selection Resources listed on the Planning pages for the Gettysburg Address to help students continually improve their ability to master the standards.

**Instructional Standards: Gettysburg Address**

| | Catching Up | This Year | Looking Forward |
|---|---|---|---|
| **Reading** | You may wish to administer the **Analyze Craft and Structure: Rhetoric (RP)** worksheet to help students understand the difference between formal and informal diction. | **RI.6** Determine an author's point of view or purpose in a text in which the rhetoric is particularly effective, analyzing how style and content contribute to the power, persuasiveness, or beauty of the text. | Challenge students to recognize whether other political texts are written in formal or informal diction as they read. Have them also consider the effect that a certain kind of diction has on a text. |
| **Speaking and Listening** | You may wish to administer the **Author's Style: Antithesis (RP)** worksheet to help students understand opposites and parellelism. | **SL.3** Evaluate a speaker's point of view, reasoning, and use of evidence and rhetoric, assessing the stance, premises, links among ideas, word choice, points of emphasis, and tone used. | You may wish to challenge students to use a variety of verb tenses in their writing. |

## ANALYZE AND REVISE

- Analyze student work for evidence of student learning.
- Identify whether or not students have met the expectations in the standards.
- Identify implications for future instruction.

## TEACH

Implement the planned lesson, and gather evidence of student learning.

# FACILITATING

## Jump Start

**FIRST READ** Ask students to imagine they have the responsibility of President Abraham Lincoln during the Civil War. The war, the bloodiest in the history of the United States, has raged on for more than two years. What words of encouragement would they give the troops? What would they say to convince the Union soldiers to continue to fight to keep the United States a united nation?

## Concept Vocabulary

Have groups briefly discuss the three concept vocabulary words. Have they encountered any of the words before? Do they recognize the prefix, suffix, or base word of any of the concept vocabulary words?

Have groups consider the strategy of familiar word parts and discuss its advantages and disadvantages.

### FIRST READ

Have students perform the steps of the first read independently:

NOTICE: Encourage students to notice the general ideas contained in the speech. What are some of the points Abraham Lincoln is making?

ANNOTATE: Remind students to highlight any confusing or difficult vocabulary or ideas so they can revisit these areas.

CONNECT: Students should increase their understanding by connecting what they've read to other texts and their knowledge of historical events of the Civil War.

RESPOND: Students will demonstrate their understanding of the text by answering questions and writing a summary.

Point out to students that they will perform the first three steps concurrently as they are doing their first read. They will complete the Respond step after they have finished the first read. You may wish to print copies of the **First-Read Guide: Nonfiction** for students to use.

# Gettysburg Address

## Concept Vocabulary

As you perform your first read of the Gettysburg Address, you will encounter these words.

| dedicated | consecrate | hallow |
|---|---|---|

**Familiar Word Parts** When determining the meaning of an unfamiliar word, look for word parts, such as roots or affixes, that you know. Doing so may help you unlock word meanings.

**Unfamiliar Word:** *prologue*

**Familiar Word Parts:** You may recognize the prefix *pro-*, which means "forward" or "forth." Likewise, you may recognize the root *-log-*, which means "word" or "reason" and appears in the words *dialogue*, *logic*, and *eulogy*.

**Possible Meaning:** When you combine your knowledge of the two word parts, you can figure out that *prologue* means something like "words that come first."

**Confirm Meaning:** Use a dictionary or other language resource to check your analysis of a word's meaning. One dictionary definition of *prologue* is "an introductory part of a text; a preface."

Apply your knowledge of familiar word parts and other vocabulary strategies to determine the meanings of unfamiliar words you encounter during your first read.

## First Read NONFICTION

Apply these strategies as you conduct your first read. You will have an opportunity to complete a close read after your first read.

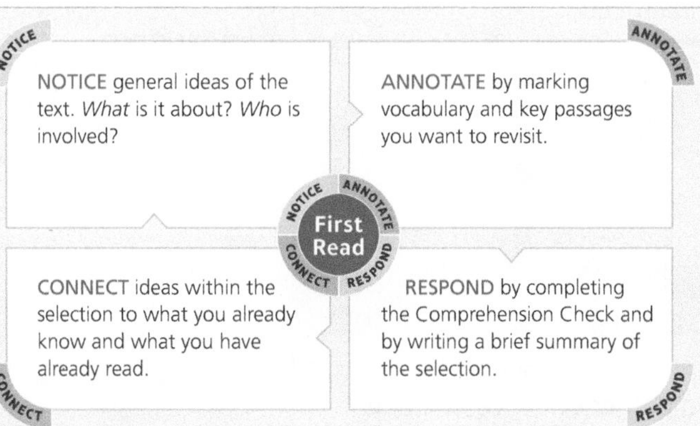

NOTICE
NOTICE general ideas of the text. *What* is it about? *Who* is involved?
ANNOTATE
ANNOTATE by marking vocabulary and key passages you want to revisit.
First Read
NOTICE ANNOTATE CONNECT RESPOND
CONNECT ideas within the selection to what you already know and what you have already read.
RESPOND by completing the Comprehension Check and by writing a brief summary of the selection.
CONNECT
RESPOND


**STANDARDS**

**Reading Informational Text**
By the end of grade 11, read and comprehend literary nonfiction in the grades 11–CCR text complexity band proficiently, with scaffolding as needed at the high end of the range.

**Language**
- Determine or clarify the meaning of unknown and multiple meaning words and phrases based on *grades 11–12 reading and content*, choosing flexibly from a range of strategies.
- Verify the preliminary determination of the meaning of a word or phrase.





### FACILITATING SMALL-GROUP CLOSE READING

**CLOSE READ: Speech** As groups perform the close read, circulate and offer support as needed.

- Remind students that a speech is a primary source and can give understanding of a historical period.
- Encourage groups to look for the speaker's main ideas and consider the purpose and timing of the speech.
- Ask groups to look at the way Lincoln expresses his ideas. Students should look for rhythm, repetition, and imagery. Students should be aware of the impact of these artistic choices on Lincoln's ability to convey his ideas.

About the Author

## Abraham Lincoln

Serving as president during one of the most tragic periods in American history, Abraham Lincoln (1809–1865) fought to reunite a nation torn apart by war. His courage, strength, and dedication in the face of an overwhelming national crisis made him one of the most admired and respected American presidents.

Lincoln was born into a family of humble means. As a child, his duties on his parents' farm limited his opportunities to receive a formal education. Still, he was an avid reader and developed an early interest in politics. He served in the Illinois state legislature and ran for the United States Senate against Stephen Douglas. Lincoln lost the election, but his heated debates with Douglas brought him national recognition and helped him win the presidency in 1860.

**Troubled Times** Shortly after his election, the Civil War erupted. Throughout the war, Lincoln showed great strength and courage. He also demonstrated his gift for oratory. He was invited to make "a few appropriate remarks" in November 1863 for a dedication of the Gettysburg battlefield as a national cemetery. The world has long remembered what he said there.

Lincoln's great care as a writer shows in the Gettysburg Address, as it does in many of his other speeches. He worked diligently and thoughtfully to prepare messages that would have the effect he desired. Two important aspects of the Gettysburg speech are its brevity—just 272 words—and its reaffirmation of the democratic principles at the heart of American government.

Stories abound regarding Lincoln's drafting of the speech: He wrote it the week before; he wrote it the night before; he wrote it on the train while traveling to the event; he wrote it on a scrap of paper. Certainly, he was still revising as he spoke, adding key words, such as "under God," that he knew would stir his listeners.

**A Life Cut Short** While the Civil War continued to rage, Lincoln was elected to a second term as President. He was killed by an assassin's bullet in 1865 while attending the theater with his wife.





DIGITAL PERSPECTIVES  

## Gettysburg Address

What challenges did Lincoln face during the time of the Civil War? How might Lincoln encourage people to endure and to keep up their spirits after one of the bloodiest battles that took place on United States soil?

Modeling these and other questions readers might ask will bring the Gettysburg Address to life and connect it to the Performance Task question. Selection audio and print capability for the selection are available in the Interactive Teacher's Edition.

### VOCABULARY DEVELOPMENT

**Word Forms** Tell students that the word *dedicate* can appear in other, related word forms.

| Word | Part of Speech | Meaning |
|---|---|---|
| dedicate | verb | |
| dedicator | noun | |
| dedicatory | adjective | |

Model sentences using other forms of *dedicate*.

This *dedicatory* plaque celebrates the anniversary of the end of the Civil War.

The *dedicator* placed the plaque at the entrance of the Gettysburg cemetery.

# FACILITATING

## Concept Vocabulary

**DEDICATED, CONSECRATE, HALLOW** If students are struggling to define the words *dedicated, consecrate,* and *hallow* in paragraphs 1 and 3, have them look for context clues in the later part of the speech. The phrase "from these honored dead" and the clause "that we here highly resolve that these dead shall not have died in vain" should give students clues to determine word meanings. Point out that the words are used as verbs. In this case, the word *dedicated* means "committed to doing something." Lincoln is asking for people to be dedicated to "the unfinished work" and the "great task remaining before us." Point out that all three words have definitions that are similar but meanings that are subtly different. Encourage students to use a thesaurus to find synonyms for each.

**Possible responses:**

*Dedicated:* "committed to doing something"
*Consecrate:* "to cause to be revered or honored"
*Hallow:* "to honor as holy"

Additional **English Language Support** is available in the Interactive Teacher's Edition.

SPEECH

# Gettysburg Address

Abraham Lincoln

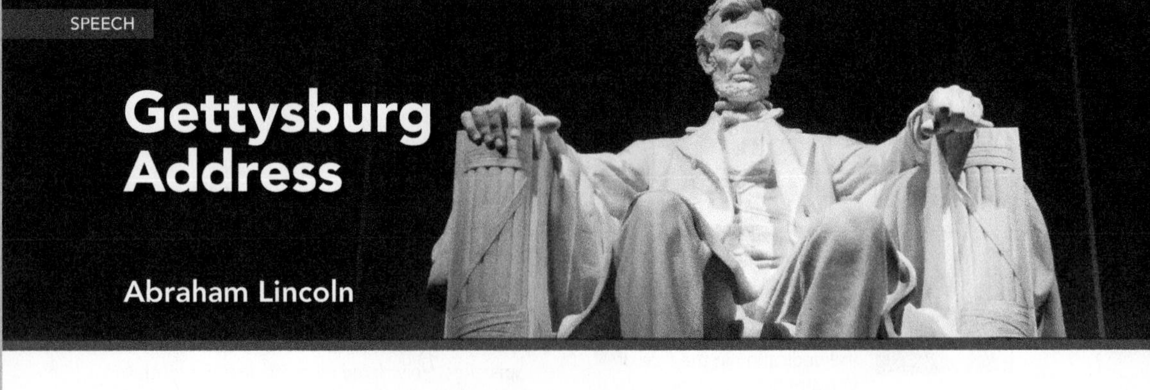

SCAN FOR MULTIMEDIA

BACKGROUND

Abraham Lincoln gave this speech to 15,000 people at the consecration of a new military cemetery in the town of Gettysburg, Pennsylvania—the site of the bloodiest battle ever fought on American soil, and the turning point of the Civil War. At the time of this speech, the war had been raging for more than two years. Lincoln needed to gain continuing support for a bloody conflict that was far from over.

NOTES

Mark familiar word parts or indicate another strategy you used that helped you determine meaning.

**dedicated** (DEHD uh kayt ihd) *adj.*

MEANING:

**consecrate** (KON suh krayt) *v.*

MEANING:

**hallow** (HAL oh) *v.*

MEANING:

## November 19, 1863

1 Four score and seven years ago our fathers brought forth on this continent a new nation, conceived in Liberty, and **dedicated** to the proposition that all men are created equal.

2 Now we are engaged in a great civil war, testing whether that nation, or any nation so conceived and so dedicated, can long endure. We are met on a great battle-field of that war. We have come to dedicate a portion of that field, as a final resting place for those who here gave their lives that that nation might live. It is altogether fitting and proper that we should do this.

3 But, in a larger sense, we cannot dedicate—we cannot **consecrate**—we cannot **hallow**—this ground. The brave men, living and dead, who struggled here, have consecrated it, far above our poor power to add or detract. The world will little note, nor long remember what we say here, but it can never forget what they did here. It is for us the living, rather, to be dedicated here to the unfinished work which they who fought here have thus far so nobly advanced. It is rather for us to be here dedicated to the great task remaining before us—that from these honored dead we take increased devotion to that cause for which they gave the last full measure of devotion—that we here highly resolve that these dead shall not have died in vain—that this nation, under God, shall have a new birth of freedom—and that government of the people, by the people, for the people, shall not perish from the earth.





**WriteNow** Inform and Explain

**Speech** Review paragraphs 1 and 2 of this important speech. Lincoln's Gettysburg Address was written in 1863 and reflected the style of speech-writing language at the time. Invite students to rewrite the speech, using modern but formal language. You may wish to get them started by pointing out that four score and seven years (paragraph 1) means 87 years. Have groups share their rewritten speeches.

## Comprehension Check

Complete the following items after you finish your first read. Review and clarify details with your group.

1. According to Lincoln, what did "our fathers" create eighty-seven years ago?

2. According to Lincoln, the Civil War is a test of what idea?

3. Why have the speaker and the audience met on the battlefield at Gettysburg?

4. According to Lincoln, why are they unable to "dedicate," "consecrate," or "hallow" the battlefield?

5. At the end of the speech, how does Lincoln characterize the American system of government?

6. **Notebook** Confirm your understanding of the text by writing a summary.

### RESEARCH

**Research to Clarify** Choose at least one unfamiliar detail from the text. Briefly research that detail. In what way does the information you learned shed light on an aspect of the speech?

**Research to Explore** Ask one focused question you would like answered about the Battle of Gettysburg. Then, do some research to find the answer.





DIGITAL PERSPECTIVES

## Comprehension Check

Possible responses:

1. "Our fathers" created a new nation.
2. The war is testing whether a nation that was founded on America's principles can endure, or survive.
3. They have met to dedicate a portion of the battlefield to the men that died in battle.
4. The ground already has been dedicated, consecrated, and hallowed by those who took part in the battle, especially those who died.
5. It is a government "of the people, by the people, for the people" and will continue forever.
6. Lincoln begins by recalling the nation's founding on principles of liberty and equality. He says that the current struggle is a test to see whether the United States now can survive. He and his audience have gathered to dedicate a portion of the Gettysburg battlefield to those who died there. In a larger sense, however, the ground already has been hallowed by those who perished there. Lincoln urges his listeners to resolve that the dead will be remembered, that the nation will have a new birth of freedom, and that its government will continue forever.

## Research

**Research to Clarify** If students struggle to choose a detail to research, suggest they look for a particular word whose meaning is unclear or unfamiliar.

**Research to Explore** If students have trouble formulating a question, you may want to suggest that they learn more about the Battle of Gettysburg or the national park at Gettysburg now.

### DIGITAL PERSPECTIVES

**Illuminating the Text** Point out to students that Lincoln's address is noted for its conciseness. On that same day, Edward Everett, a politician and orator from Massachusetts, delivered a two-hour speech prior to Lincoln's address. Go online to find documentary footage discussing the power of the Gettysburg Address in relation to Edward Everett's much lengthier speech from the same day. Ask students to share how these videos helped them understand the differences between the two speeches.

## Jump Start

**CLOSE READ** Ask students to think about any speeches they have heard from our president or other political leaders. How is Lincoln's speech different from those of present-day national leaders?

## Close Read the Text 

Model close reading as needed by using the Annotation Highlights in the Interactive Teacher's Edition. Remind groups to use Accountable Talk in their discussions and to support one another as they complete the close read.

## Analyze the Text

1. **Responses will vary by group.** Students should note how Lincoln moves from describing the principles for which the colonists fought to describing the conflict that is being fought in his own time for much the same reason. He sets the scene for his next points.
2. **Responses will vary by group.** Remind students to explain why they chose the passage they presented to group members.
3. **Responses will vary by group.**

## Concept Vocabulary

**Why These Words? Possible response:** The words reflect the idea of showing honor—in this case, honor for the fallen in battle and their ideals.

### Practice

**Possible responses:** The author *dedicated* her latest novel to her mother.
The gravestones in a cemetery are usually considered *consecrated* monuments.
The president *hallows* the Tomb of the Unknowns with a floral wreath.

### Word Network

**Possible words:** *liberty, equal, battlefield, cause, nobly*

## Word Study

For more support, see **Concept Vocabulary and Word Study.**

Possible responses:
(1) *dedicated:* reserved for special use/honor; *consecrate:* to make something honored/sacred; *hallow:* to honor/holy
(2) committed, sworn

---

MAKING MEANING

GETTYSBURG ADDRESS

## Close Read the Text

With your group, revisit sections of the text you marked during your first read. **Annotate** details that you notice. What **questions** do you have? What can you **conclude**?

## Analyze the Text

**CITE TEXTUAL EVIDENCE** to support your answers.

**Complete the activities.**

1. **Review and Clarify** With your group, reread paragraph 2. How does Lincoln build upon his introduction and prepare the audience for his main points in paragraph 3?
2. **Present and Discuss** Now, work with your group to share the passages from the selection that you found especially important. Take turns presenting your passages. Discuss what you noticed in the selection, what questions you asked, and what conclusions you reached.
3. **Essential Question:** ***What is the meaning of freedom?*** What has this text revealed about American freedoms? Discuss with your group.

**TIP**

CLARIFICATION
The Gettysburg Address is short, but it is by no means a group of random comments. As a group, discuss the purpose of each paragraph and the main idea it expresses. How would an outline of the speech look?

LANGUAGE DEVELOPMENT

## Concept Vocabulary

dedicate　consecrate　hallow

**Why These Words?** The three concept vocabulary words are related. With your group, discuss the words and determine what they have in common. How do these word choices enhance the impact of the text?

### Practice

**Notebook** Confirm your understanding of the vocabulary words by using them in sentences. Use context clues that hint at each word's meaning.

## Word Study

**Notebook** **Denotation and Connotation** In his address, Lincoln says that he cannot *dedicate, consecrate*, or *hallow* the battlefield ground. The three concept vocabulary words have similar **denotations**, or definitions, but different **connotations**, or nuances in meaning.

1. Write the denotations of the three words. Then, explain the connotations each one conveys. Note that connotations may involve slightly different meanings, or simply intensity of meaning.
2. Use a thesaurus to find two other words that share denotations with *dedicate*. Then, explain how their connotations differ.

**WORD NETWORK**

Add words related to freedom from the text to your Word Network.

**STANDARDS**

**Reading Informational Text**
• Determine an author's point of view or purpose in a text in which the rhetoric is particularly effective, analyzing how style and content contribute to the power, persuasiveness, or beauty of the text.
• Analyze seventeenth-, eighteenth-, and nineteenth-century foundational U.S. documents of historical and literary significance for their themes, purposes, and rhetorical features.

**Language**
Analyze nuances in the meaning of words with similar denotations.





---

## FORMATIVE ASSESSMENT

### Analyze the Text

**If** students struggle to close read the text, **then** provide the **Gettysburg Address: Text Questions** available in the Interactive Teacher's Edition or Unit Resources. Answers and DOK levels are also available.

### Concept Vocabulary

**If** students struggle to identify the concept, **then** have them look online for other synonyms for these words. Students can use the synonyms to construct a word map for each word.

### Word Study

**If** students fail to explain word connotations, **then** have them review the denotations. Read aloud the word to students and ask students to play a word association game by writing down the first thing they think of when they hear the word. For Reteach and Practice, see **Word Study: Denotation and Connotation (RP).**

## Analyze Craft and Structure

**Author's Choices: Diction** A writer's choice and arrangement of words, known as **diction**, helps to express the writer's ideas clearly and precisely and to give the writing a unique quality. Diction may be formal or informal, technical or plain, elevated or simple. A speaker's choice of diction is intimately connected to his or her purpose for writing, as well as to considerations of the audience and the occasion.

Consider the solemn, serious formality of Lincoln's diction at the beginning of his address at Gettysburg—and imagine how he might have expressed the same ideas more informally.

FORMAL: Four score and seven years ago, our fathers brought forth on this continent a new nation. . . .

INFORMAL: Eighty-seven years ago, our early leaders created a new nation, right here. . . .

### Practice

**CITE TEXTUAL EVIDENCE** to support your answers.

Identify passages in the Gettysburg Address that include diction you find powerful or beautiful. Consider how the passage might sound with less formality by rewriting it. Then, explain the impact of Lincoln's diction. One example has been done for you. Complete the chart independently, and then share with your group.

| PASSAGE WITH POWERFUL DICTION | REWRITTEN PASSAGE | IMPACT OF LINCOLN'S DICTION |
|---|---|---|
| Four score and seven years ago, our fathers brought forth on this continent a new nation. | Eighty-seven years ago, our early leaders created a new nation, right here. | adds power, grandeur to the speech |
| conceived in Liberty, and dedicated to the proposition that all men are created equal. | This nation was founded on freedom and committed to the idea that all people are equal. | Reminds people of the lofty principles of human rights. |
| Now we are engaged in a great civil war, testing whether that nation, or any nation so conceived and so dedicated, can long endure. | We're fighting a great war right now, and it's a test to see whether a nation like ours can keep going. | Sets a significant challenge for people to keep fighting for the nation. |
| The world will little note, nor long remember what we say here, but it can never forget what they did here. | Today's ceremony is insignificant; what's important is . . . that we respect these dead soldiers and use their example to inspire us to care more about the ideal for which they died. | Adds a sense of solemnity to the great battle at Gettysburg. |

DIGITAL PERSPECTIVES 

## Analyze Craft and Structure

**Author's Choices: Diction** Remind students that diction is the special attention an author pays to word choice and sentence style, intended to communicate a point to a reader or listener.

As students complete the chart, encourage them to consider other choices Lincoln had and the power of the words he decided to use. For more support, see **Analyze Craft and Structure: Diction.**

### Practice

See possible responses in chart on student page.

### FORMATIVE ASSESSMENT

### Analyze Craft and Structure

**If** students are unable to identify passages that represent diction that is powerful or beautiful, **then** read the speech aloud to students. Instruct students to close their eyes as they listen to how Lincoln expresses his ideas. Remind students that formal diction gives a greater sense of importance to an occasion. For Reteach and Practice, see **Analyze Craft and Structure: Diction (RP).**

### CROSS-CURRICULAR PERSPECTIVES

**Social Studies** The Battle of Gettysburg, fought in Pennsylvania in July 1863, was an important Union victory and marked a turning point in the war. The Union's victory effectively stopped the Confederate Army from gaining a stronghold in Union territory. General Robert E. Lee was forced to retreat his army to Virginia. The Confederate Army never regained its military strength after this battle. Encourage students to find out more about the battle at Gettysburg and share their findings with their group.

# FACILITATING

## Author's Style

**Rhetorical Devices: Antithesis** Remind students that rhetorical devices are the tools used by writers to choose words and phrasing in order to create meaning. Some rhetorical devices play on the sounds or structure of words, such as onomatopoeia (words that imitate the sounds they describe) or alliteration (repetition of initial consonants in words). Other rhetorical devices are based on word meanings, such as simile and metaphor (which compare things). Parallelism and antithesis are rhetorical devices that can utilize both word or phrase sounds and meanings. For more support, see **Author's Style: Rhetorical Devices: Antithesis.**

### Read It

Possible responses:

1. *gave their lives/nation might live;* It is antithesis because it compares those who died with those who live.
2. *living/dead;* It is not formal antithesis because it is simply describing two categories of men and not making a larger point.
3. *nor long remember what we say here/never forget what they did here;* It is antithesis because it emphasizes the great sacrifice of the dead as being more important and more enduring than the people dedicating the battlefield.
4. *shall not have died in vain/shall have a new birth of freedom;* It is antithesis because it connects the soldiers' death and sacrifice with a higher cause, the survival of the nation.

### Write It

**Notebook** Answers will vary.

---

### FORMATIVE ASSESSMENT

### Author's Style

**If** students struggle to identify opposites in parallelism examples, **then** have them focus on finding words in the sentences that are either identical or synonyms, or that are antonyms. Then have students explain the larger meaning for the choice of words. For Reteach and Practice, see **Author's Style: Rhetorical Devices: Antithesis (RP).**

## LANGUAGE DEVELOPMENT

GETTYSBURG ADDRESS

## Author's Style

**Rhetorical Devices: Antithesis** Lincoln was both a master writer and a master orator. In the Gettysburg Address, he makes insightful use of **contrast,** or the juxtaposition of opposing ideas. In some cases, he uses the rhetorical device of **antithesis,** which is a type of parallelism. Antithesis presents contrasting ideas in similar grammatical structures, such as the same types of phrases or clauses. Thus, antithesis allows a speaker to make use of the rhythmic effects of parallelism, while drawing readers' or listeners' attention to powerful oppositions.

EXAMPLES

**Parallelism:** I stand here today humbled by the task before us, grateful for the trust you have bestowed, mindful of the sacrifices borne by our ancestors. —Barack Obama

**Antithesis:** My fellow Americans, ask not what your country can do for you, ask what you can do for your country. —John F. Kennedy

### Read It

Mark the contrasting or opposing elements in each passage from the address. Then, note whether or not each is an example of formal antithesis. Share your work with your group, and discuss and clarify any points of confusion.

1. We have come to dedicate a portion of that field, as a final resting place for those who here gave their lives that the nation might live.
2. The brave men, living and dead, who struggled here…
3. The world will little note, nor long remember what we say here, but it can never forget what they did here.
4. …we here highly resolve that these dead shall not have died in vain—that this nation, under God, shall have a new birth of freedom…

### Write It

Write a paragraph in which you describe a speech, performance, artwork, concert, or other cultural work that you saw live, on television, or online. Use at least two examples of antithesis in your paragraph.

STANDARDS

**Reading Informational Text**
Determine an author's point of view or purpose in a text in which the rhetoric is particularly effective, analyzing how style and content contribute to the power, persuasiveness, or beauty of the text.

**Speaking and Listening**
Evaluate a speaker's point of view, reasoning, and use of evidence and rhetoric, assessing the stance, premises, links among ideas, word choice, points of emphasis, and tone used.





## PERSONALIZE FOR LEARNING

### English Language Support

**Understanding Antithesis** Display the following words: *antisocial, misfortune, submerge.*

Ask students to choose one word, identify its prefix, and determine the meaning of its prefix. Then have students identify a prefix that has the opposite meaning. If students are having difficulty, have them use a dictionary or thesaurus. **EMERGING PI.12**

Ask students to identify the prefixes for all three words and determine the meaning of the prefixes. Then have them identify prefixes with the opposite meaning for each. **EXPANDING PI.12**

Have students chose one of the words and identify the meaning of its prefix. Then have them identify a prefix with the opposite meaning. Then ask students to come up with two new words using the prefix and its opposite and use both words in a sentence. **BRIDGING PI.12**

An expanded **English Language Support Lesson** on Antithesis is available in the Interactive Teacher's Edition.

EFFECTIVE EXPRESSION

## Research

**Assignment**

With your group, prepare a **research report** that focuses on an aspect of Lincoln's speech. Choose from the following options.

- ☐ a **comparison-and-contrast presentation** about the five different known versions of the Gettysburg Address, showing the changes that Lincoln made each time and evaluating their effectiveness
- ☐ a **review** of three eyewitness accounts of the ceremony at Gettysburg that day, summarizing each account and noting details that shed light upon the address itself
- ☐ an **analysis of the historical context** of the address, sharing information about the Battle of Gettysburg (July 1863) and considering how that context shaped the content of Lincoln's address

**Project Plan** Before you begin, identify the tasks you will need to accomplish in order to complete your report. Start with the tasks noted in the chart, and add others that you consider important. Then, assign individual group members to each task. Finally, determine how you will present the report. For example, will you include historical images—and, if so, where will you find them, and how will you show them?

Working Title: ______________________

| TASK | ASSIGNED TO |
|---|---|
| researching texts for factual information | |
| researching images (if used) | |
| | |
| | |

**Tying It Together** Work together to organize the information all group members collect. Write paragraphs incorporating this information. Then, write an introduction and a conclusion for the report. Read the report aloud within the group, and decide together on revisions. Then, share your finished product with the whole class.



EVIDENCE LOG

Before moving on to a new selection, go to your Evidence Log and record what you learned from the Gettysburg Address.

STANDARDS

Writing

- Write informative/explanatory texts to examine and convey complex ideas, concepts, and information clearly and accurately through the effective selection, organization, and analysis of content.
- Conduct short as well as more sustained research projects to answer a question or solve a problem; narrow or broaden the inquiry when appropriate; synthesize multiple sources on the subject, demonstrating understanding of the subject under investigation.



DIGITAL PERSPECTIVES

## Research

Students may struggle to select which assignment for their group to research. Have group members discuss their strengths and interests and encourage them to choose the assignment that best allows them to demonstrate their strengths. Groups with strengths in language skills may be best suited for the first option. If a group has a particular interest in the historical aspect of the assignment and members are apt at doing research, they may choose the third option. For more support, see **Research: Report.**

**Project Plan** Make sure everyone in each group has been assigned a specific task. Students may work as researchers of text and facts, researchers of supporting visuals, organizers of data and information, writers, and editors of the final research report.

**Tying It Together** Remind students that research reports should contain a main idea or premise and supporting facts and details. Remind students to use reliable sources and to annotate their reports with a bibliography and footnotes.

**Evidence Log** Support students in completing their Evidence Log. This paced activity will help prepare them for the Performance-Based Assessment at the end of the unit.

### FORMATIVE ASSESSMENT

**Research**

**If** students struggle with developing a research report, **then** suggest they work together to create an outline for their presentation, detailing the main ideas and supporting facts. For Reteach and Practice, see **Research: Report (RP).**

**Selection Test**

Administer the "Gettysburg Address" Selection Test, which is available in both print and digital formats online in Assessments.

### PERSONALIZE FOR LEARNING

**Challenge**

**Speculate** Ask students to speculate what might have happened if the Confederacy had won the Battle of Gettysburg. Have them write an account predicting how the course of history might have changed. Encourage students to include key historical figures in their account, such as Abraham Lincoln, General Robert E. Lee, and Ulysses S. Grant. Invite students to share and debate their accounts. Remind students to support their predictions with historical facts.

# FACILITATING

## Present an Argument

Before groups begin work on their projects, have them clearly differentiate the role each group member will play. Remind groups to consult the schedule for Small-Group Learning to guide their work during the Performance Task.

Students should complete the assignment using presentation software to take advantage of text, graphics, and sound features.

## Plan with Your Group

**Analyze the Texts** Remind students that the selections take place in different time periods in history and that the changing Constitution reflected the political climate and events of the time. Students should include quotations from the text to support their argument.

**Gather Evidence** As students gather evidence, have them begin thinking about the positions they might take in their panel discussion.

PERFORMANCE TASK: SPEAKING AND LISTENING FOCUS

SOURCES

- *from* AMERICA'S CONSTITUTION: A BIOGRAPHY
- *from* THE UNITED STATES CONSTITUTION: A GRAPHIC ADAPTATION
- *from* THE INTERESTING NARRATIVE OF THE LIFE OF OLAUDAH EQUIANO
- LETTER TO JOHN ADAMS
- *from* DEAR ABIGAIL: THE INTIMATE LIVES AND REVOLUTIONARY IDEAS OF ABIGAIL ADAMS AND HER TWO REMARKABLE SISTERS
- GETTYSBURG ADDRESS

## Present an Argument

**Assignment**

You have read a variety of texts, both historic and contemporary, in a range of different genres. Several of these texts are narratives that the writers use to support or imply positions on questions of American freedom. Work with your group to present a **panel discussion** that addresses this question:

**Do narratives provide strong evidence to support arguments about American freedoms?**

Use examples from the texts in this section to support your positions.

## Plan With Your Group

**Analyze the Texts** With your group, identify the texts in this section that are either fully narratives or include narrative elements. Consider the arguments about freedom that are either directly stated or that readers can infer from the narrative details. Use the chart to gather your observations.

| NARRATIVE DETAILS | RELATED ARGUMENT |
|---|---|
| | |
| | |
| | |
| | |
| | |
| | |

**Make a Generalization** Using your analysis, write a generalization about the use of narrative as evidence to support an argument.

**Generalization:** Narratives do/do not provide strong evidence to support an argument because ______________________________

______________________________

**Gather Evidence** Prepare for the discussion by identifying additional examples from the texts that you might use to illustrate your ideas during the panel discussion.

STANDARDS

**Speaking and Listening**
Work with peers to promote civil, democratic discussions and decision-making, set clear goals and deadlines, and establish individual roles as needed.





AUTHOR'S PERSPECTIVE **Ernest Morrell, Ph.D.**

**How to Package a Speech/Oral Presentation** The small-group speaking and listening activity will help students learn how to engage an audience during a presentation. This is important for students as they prepare for careers, public service and higher education. Help students learn to become better speakers by reminding them to ask themselves these questions as they practice and rehearse their speeches and oral presentation:

- *Posture:* Does my posture convey authority and ease? Do I look relaxed and comfortable as I'm presenting?
- *Body language:* How do I connect physically with my audience? For instance, do I make eye contact, lean forward at key point to show emphasis, and use appropriate gestures?
- *Voice:* Am I changing my voice by varying my pitch and volume to show emotion and convey meaning? Does my voice project to the back rows?
- *Humor:* How do I add humor when it suits my audience and purpose? Do I tell jokes or anecdotes, for instance?
- *Tone:* Do I speak with passion to engage my audience?

Remind students that the way they present their information is often just as important as what they are saying.

**Organize Your Discussion** Assign roles, including a role for a moderator who will keep panelists on point and ask questions if there is a lull in the conversation. Have each person in your group use the evidence you gathered to write his or her own talking points for the presentation. Then, meet to decide how you will begin the discussion, the amount of time each speaker will talk, how you will deal with follow-up questions, and how you will end the discussion.

## Rehearse With Your Group

**Practice With Your Group** Once you have established the rules for your discussion, try a run-through. Use this checklist to evaluate how well your process works and whether your ideas and evidence are sound. Then, use your evaluation and these instructions to make changes before you present your discussion to the class.

| CONTENT | COLLABORATION | PRESENTATION TECHNIQUES |
|---|---|---|
| ☐ The discussion responds to the question in the assignment.<br>☐ Speakers present a position and supporting evidence.<br>☐ Speakers support their observations with evidence from the texts. | ☐ The discussion flows smoothly and seems well-planned.<br>☐ Speakers interact with each other naturally.<br>☐ The moderator introduces the speakers and keeps the conversation on track. | ☐ Panelists have equal opportunities to speak, and respond appropriately to one another's insights or questions.<br>☐ Speakers speak clearly and at an appropriate volume.<br>☐ Speakers use gestures and eye contact effectively. |

**Fine-Tune the Content** Does one panelist dominate the conversation? Make sure that every group member has a chance to present his or her views. If necessary, go back to the texts to gather additional details that will help balance the presentation.

**Brush Up on Your Presentation Techniques** Remember that you are holding a conversation that is also, to some extent, a performance. Modify your tone and volume so that your audience understands your ideas and evidence. Explain your observations clearly, using language that is appropriate for an academic setting.

## Present and Evaluate

As you present your panel discussion, consider your audience's response. Do listeners seem convinced by your argument? Are they interested in the ideas? Watch the presentations by other groups and discuss how yours is similar to or different from theirs.

**STANDARDS**

**Speaking and Listening**
Present information, findings, and supporting evidence, conveying a clear and distinct perspective, such that listeners can follow the line of reasoning, alternative or opposing perspectives are addressed, and the organization, development, substance, and style are appropriate to purpose, audience, and a range of formal and informal tasks.





**DIGITAL PERSPECTIVES**

**Organize Your Discussion** Make sure that each student has a role for the discussion. Remind students that in a discussion, each participant should have a firm idea of the points he or she wishes to make (the "talking points") but must also be familiar enough with the content to be able to respond to questions and the flow of the discussion.

## Rehearse With Your Group

**Practice With Your Group** Allow students plenty of time to practice their parts. Students may practice their parts individually, in pairs, or in small groups.

**Fine-Tune the Content** As students rehearse, give support regarding their pacing, volume, intonation, and eye contact with the audience. Encourage group members to give constructive feedback.

**Brush-Up on Your Presentation Techniques** Encourage students to have a "dress-rehearsal" for their presentation. Students may sit on stools in a semi-circle, or they may sit behind a table. Remind students that in a discussion, they can refer to their notes, but they should be comfortable enough with the content that they are only infrequently reading verbatim from notes.

## Present and Evaluate

Before presenting the panel discussion, set expectations for the audience. Have students consider these questions as groups perform.

- How well did each panel member present his or her argument?
- What was the result of the discussion in regards to the prompt?

Encourage students to offer constructive criticism as well as praise for student presentations.

**PERSONALIZE FOR LEARNING**

### English Language Support

**Panel Discussion** When choosing roles for the discussion, keep students' language proficiency level in mind. Pair English language learners with strong readers for additional practice. Model students' parts to help them convey meaning through voice, tempo patterns, facial expressions, and gestures. If possible, videotape rehearsals, or have students practice on a recorder. Allow students time to view the recordings and work out any issues with pronunciation and pauses after periods or commas in sentences. **ALL LEVELS**

# OVERVIEW

## INDEPENDENT LEARNING

### What is the meaning of freedom?

Encourage students to think carefully about what they have already learned about how the Founders' writing and speeches shaped Americans' concept of freedom. Suggest they decide what more they want to know about the unit topic of the meaning of freedom. This is a key first step to previewing and selecting the text they will read in Independent Learning.

### Independent Learning Strategies

Review the Learning Strategies with students and explain that as they work through Independent Learning they will develop strategies to work on their own.

- Have students watch the video on Independent Learning Strategies.
- A video on this topic is available online in the Professional Development Center.

Students should include any favorite strategies that they might have devised on their own during Whole-Class and Small-Group Learning. For example, for the strategy "Take notes," students might include:

- Review the notes and questions the readings raised for you about specific ideas you thought you may want to explore.
- Compare your notes with classmates, to clarify and to broaden your thinking.

**Block Scheduling**

Each day in this Pacing Plan represents a 40–50 minute class period. Teachers using block scheduling may combine days to reflect their class schedule. In addition, teachers may revise pacing to differentiate and support core instruction by integrating components and resources as students require.

OVERVIEW: INDEPENDENT LEARNING

ESSENTIAL QUESTION:

## What is the meaning of freedom?

Ideas about what freedom means, and who is or is not free, may depend on time, place, and the person telling the story. In this section, you will complete your study of writings about American freedom by exploring an additional selection related to the topic. You'll then share what you learn with classmates. To choose a text, follow these steps.

**Look Back** Think about the selections you have already studied. Which aspects of the meaning of freedom do you wish to explore further?

**Look Ahead** Preview the texts by reading the descriptions. Which one seems most interesting and appealing to you?

**Look Inside** Take a few minutes to scan the text you chose. Choose a different one if this text doesn't meet your needs.

### Independent Learning Strategies

Throughout your life, in school, in your community, and in your career, you will need to rely on yourself to learn and work on your own. Review these strategies and the actions you can take to practice them during Independent Learning. Add ideas of your own for each category.

| STRATEGY | ACTION PLAN |
|---|---|
| Create a schedule | • Understand your goals and deadlines.<br>• Make a plan for what to do each day.<br>• |
| Practice what you have learned | • Use first-read and close-read strategies to deepen your understanding.<br>• After reading, evaluate the usefulness of the evidence to help you understand the topic.<br>• After reading, consult reference sources for background information that can help you clarify meaning.<br>• |
| Take notes | • Record important ideas and information.<br>• Review your notes before preparing to share with a group.<br>• |



SCAN FOR MULTIMEDIA



**Pacing Plan**

| Day | Activity |
|---|---|
| 1 | Unit Introduction |
| 2 | Introduce Whole-Class Learning |
| 3 | Historical Perspectives |
| 4–5 | Declaration of Independence |
| 6–8 | Preamble to the U.S. Constitution • Bill of Rights |
| 9–11 | Franklin's Speech in the Convention |
| 12–13 | The American Revolution: Visual Propaganda |
| 14–15 | Performance Task |

**DIGITAL PERSPECTIVES**    

## CONTENTS

Choose one selection. Selections are available online only.

ESSAY

*from* Democracy Is Not a Spectator Sport
*Arthur Blaustein with Helen Matatov*

How much does freedom depend on civic engagement?

SPEECH

Reflections on the Bicentennial of the United States Constitution
*Thurgood Marshall*

Supreme Court Justice Marshall observes that the U.S. Constitution is a living document.

POETRY

Speech to the Young
Speech to the Progress-Toward *Gwendolyn Brooks*

The Fish *Elizabeth Bishop*

Is freedom physical, psychological, or perhaps both?

SHORT STORY

The Pedestrian *Ray Bradbury*

In a highly restrictive society, what acts of freedom become acts of crime?

POLITICAL DOCUMENT

*from the* Iroquois Constitution
*Dekanawidah, translated by Arthur C. Parker*

Before the arrival of Europeans, the Iroquois Nations developed a constitution of their own.

ARGUMENT

*from* Common Sense *Thomas Paine*

British-born American patriot Thomas Paine wrote that "the sun never shined on a cause of greater worth" than America's independence.

PERFORMANCE-BASED ASSESSMENT PREP

Review Evidence for an Argument
Complete your Evidence Log for the unit by evaluating what you've learned and synthesizing the information you have recorded.

SCAN FOR MULTIMEDIA





## Contents

**Selections** Encourage students to scan and preview the selections before choosing the one they would like to read. Suggest that they consider the genre and subject matter of each one before making their decision. You can use the information on the following Planning pages to advise students in making their choice.

Remind students that the selections for Independent Learning are only available in the interactive edition of *my*Perspectives. Allow students who do not have digital access at home to preview the selections using classroom or computer lab technology. Then either have students print the selection they choose or provide a printout for them.

### Performance-Based Assessment Prep

**Review Evidence for an Argument** Point out to students that collecting evidence during Independent Learning is the last step in completing their Evidence Log. After they finish their independent reading, they will synthesize all the evidence they have compiled in the unit.

The evidence students collect will serve as the primary source of information they will use to complete the writing and oral presentation for the Performance-Based Assessment at the end of the unit.

Introduce Small-Group Learning 

- 16–17: *from* America's Constitution: A Biography
- 18–19: Media: *from* The United States Constitution: A Graphic Adaptation
- 20–21: *from* The Interesting Narrative of the Life of Olaudah Equiano
- 22–24: Letter to John Adams • *from* Dear Abigail: The Intimate Lives and Revolutionary Ideas of Abigail Adams and Her Two Remarkable Sisters
- 25: Gettysburg Address
- 26: Performance Task
- 27: Introduce Independent Learning
- 28: Independent Learning
- 29–30: Performance-Based Assessment

  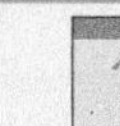       

16 17 18 19 20 21 22 23 24 25 26 27 28 29 30

INDEPENDENT LEARNING

# *from* Democracy Is Not a Spectator Sport

## Summary

In this essay from *Democracy Is Not a Spectator Sport,* Arthur Blaustein and Helen Matatoz argue that America was founded on an agreement that a fair society could be formed based on the idea of freedom and equal economic opportunity for all. While these principles worked for much of our history, they no longer do. The shift from local economic communities to a national economy along with the shift from individual or small group work to corporate employment has produced a new level of destructive social inequality. The authors say that government plays an important role in protecting basic freedoms in our democracy. However, they believe that new intervening economic structures such as volunteerism, civic engagement, nonprofit corporations, and nongovernmental organizations are important to restoring freedoms in our democracy.

## Insight

Reading this text will help students understand how political and economic factors are deeply intertwined in our nation's history. They will see that economic freedom plays an important role in establishing and maintaining political and personal freedoms and in ensuring the benefits promised by our Founders.

### SELECTION RESOURCES

- First-Read Guide: Nonfiction
- Close-Read Guide: Nonfiction
- *from* Democracy Is Not a Spectator Sport: Text Questions
- Audio Summaries
- Selection Audio
- Selection Test

## Connection to the Essential Question

The essay offers a unique perspective on the question, "What is the meaning of freedom?" It explores the idea that economic freedoms are an essential part of the foundation, growth, and maintenance of our political system, as it guarantees personal freedoms.

## Connection to Performance-Based Assessment

This selection provides a contemporary economic perspective on the question, "What are the most effective tools for establishing and preserving freedom?" The essay stresses the importance of adjusting existing social structures and finding new ones as a means of achieving a nation based on personal freedom and equal economic opportunity.

### Text Complexity Rubric: *from* Democracy Is Not a Spectator Sport

| Quantitative Measures | |
|---|---|
| **Lexile:** 1480 **Text Length:** 6,131 words | |
| **Qualitative Measures** | |
| Knowledge Demands<br>① ② ③ **❹** ⑤ | Explores complex themes that will be challenging (history of economic and political theory as it relates to the individual and community); explanation is provided for many ideas, but is complicated. |
| Structure<br>① **❷** ③ ④ ⑤ | Organization is logical and headings help provide structure. |
| Language Conventionality and Clarity<br>① ② ③ **❹** ⑤ | The selection contains a significant amount of subject-specific vocabulary and many lengthy, complex sentences. |
| Levels of Meaning/Purpose<br>① ② ③ **❹** ⑤ | The main idea is evident, but the concept may be hard for some to grasp because of sophisticated language and supporting concepts that are complex. |

SELECTION RESOURCES

- First-Read Guide: Nonfiction
- Close-Read Guide: Nonfiction
- Reflections on The Bicentennial of the United States Constitution: Text Questions
- Audio Summaries
- Selection Audio
- Selection Test

# Reflections on The Bicentennial of The United States Constitution

## Summary

In his speech, Supreme Court Justice Thurgood Marshall argues that the celebrations marking the writing of the Constitution are misguided. He asserts that the document was defective from its start and did not produce the "more perfect Union" Americans now enjoy. For example, the phrase, "We the People," intentionally did not include slaves and women, but only "the Whole Number of Free Persons." Marshall points out that the compromises made by the delegates at the Constitutional Convention were, in fact, based on commercial and financial considerations. He believes that the true value of our framework of government results from the judiciary's interpretation of the Constitution's meaning and the changes made through the amendments.

## Insight

Reading "Reflections On The Bicentennial Of The United States Constitution" will help students understand that the meaning of "freedom" within a democratic republic is not a fixed idea. Rather, Thurgood Marshall suggests that the idea changes over time.

## Connection to the Essential Question

The speech "Reflections On The Bicentennial Of The United States Constitution" connects to the Essential Question, "What is the meaning of freedom?" This speech explores the idea that the freedoms guaranteed to Americans under the Constitution evolved over time and are much broader today than the Founding Fathers originally envisioned.

## Connection to Performance-Based Assessment

This selection provides an historical perspective on the question "What are the most effective tools for establishing and preserving freedom?" It introduces and clarifies the idea that at different times our nation held different views about the freedoms guaranteed by the Constitution. The selection also demonstrates that the Constitution has helped to broaden the number of freedoms Americans enjoy today.

## Text Complexity Rubric: Reflections on the Bicentennial of the United States Constitution

| Quantitative Measures | |
|---|---|
| **Lexile:** 1330 **Text Length:** 1,789 words | |
| **Qualitative Measures** | |
| Knowledge Demands<br>① ② ③ **❹** ⑤ | Selection contains many historical references about events leading up to and following the creation of the U.S. Constitution, not all of which are explained. |
| Structure<br>① ② **❸** ④ ⑤ | The selection is written in conventional essay format with many digressions to provide evidence. There are many lengthy quotes interspersed throughout the essay. |
| Language Conventionality and Clarity<br>① ② ③ **❹** ⑤ | The selection contains many lengthy, complex sentences with embedded clauses. There are many quotes and above level vocabulary. |
| Levels of Meaning/Purpose<br>① ② **❸** ④ ⑤ | The meaning/purpose is straightforward, but the concept may be hard for some to grasp because of sophisticated language and supporting concepts that are complex. |

SELECTION RESOURCES

- First-Read Guide: Poetry
- Close-Read Guide: Poetry
- Speech to the Young / Speech to the Progress-Toward • The Fish: Text Questions
- Audio Summaries
- Selection Audio
- Selection Test

# Speech to the Young / Speech to the Progress-Toward • The Fish

## Summary

In Gwendolyn Brooks's poem, "Speech to the Young / Speech to the Progress-Toward," the speaker gives advice to young people, telling them not to let others put them down or take away their happiness. The speaker advises young people to respond to the naysayers in their lives by not dwelling on the past or yearning for the future, but by living in the present.

In Elizabeth Bishop's poem, "The Fish," the speaker describes catching a large fish, noting that it does not fight to get away. The speaker uses sensory language to describe in extreme detail how the fish looked. At the end of the poem, the speaker notices that the fish has other pieces of fishing line in its mouth, indicating that it has been caught many times before. In the end, the speaker notices rainbows in the water caused by spilled oil and lets the fish go.

## Insight

Reading these poems will help students begin to think about other aspects of freedom they may encounter in their daily lives. For example, they may consider how they deal with others who attempt to diminish their self-value, as well as how they relate to creatures in the wild.

## Connection to the Essential Question

These poems—"Speech to the Young / Speech to the Progress Toward" and "The Fish"—will help students answer the Essential Question, "What is the meaning of freedom?" The first poem stresses the importance of self-esteem in living life freely. The second poem stresses the importance of recognizing the significance of freedom in dealing with nature's creatures.

## Connection to Performance-Based Assessment

Students may wish to use the poems in this collection as a source for personal anecdotes when writing their arguments in response to the question posed in the Performance-Based Assessment, "What are the most effective tools for establishing and preserving freedom?"

### Text Complexity Rubric: Speech to the Young / Speech to the Progress-Toward • The Fish

| Quantitative Measures | |
|---|---|
| Lexile: NP; NP Text Length: 12 lines, 76 lines | |
| **Qualitative Measures** | |
| Knowledge Demands ①—②—❸—④—⑤ | Some life-experience demands. The poems explore themes that are not complex, but are written with a great deal of symbolism and abstraction. (freedom/overcoming adversity). |
| Structure ①—❷—③—④—⑤ | Both poems are written in free verse form with varied rhyme and meter. |
| Language Conventionality and Clarity ①—②—❸—④—⑤ | Both poems contain figurative language. Vocabulary is on level. "Speech to the Young / Speech to the Progress-Toward" has several epithets that may be confusing (down-keeper, sun-slappers, self-soilers, harmony-hushers). |
| Levels of Meaning/Purpose ①—②—❸—④—⑤ | Both poems have multiple levels of meaning, but the concepts are relatively easy to grasp. |

DIGITAL PERSPECTIVES: Audio | Video | Document | Annotation Highlights | EL Highlights | Online Assessment

# The Pedestrian

## Summary

In Ray Bradbury's short story, "The Pedestrian," Leonard Mead leaves his house early one evening in 2053 to take a walk. The streets are empty, for everyone else is at home watching TV. As Mead walks, he observes the flicker of TV lights and occasional shadows behind curtains. On his return walk home, the only police car in the city flashes a bright light on him. A metallic voice from the driverless car tells him to stop. The police car asks Mead questions about his identity, his occupation, his address, and what he is doing. He explains that he is out "for air, and to see, and just to walk." Mead is told to get into the backseat, which is like a small prison with bars. When he asks where he is going, the police car tells Mead he is going to a psychiatric hospital. On the way, Mead points out his own house, but there is no response and the police car just proceeds.

## Insight

Reading "The Pedestrian" will help students reflect on the relationship between personal freedom and technological control in the future. Some students may require support with the idea that the personal freedoms of nonconforming citizens may not survive in highly technological societies. In fact, these individuals may be imprisoned as a result of their need to express their humanity.

SELECTION RESOURCES

- First-Read Guide: Fiction
- Close-Read Guide: Fiction
- The Pedestrian: Text Questions
- Audio Summaries
- Selection Audio
- Selection Test

## Connection to the Essential Question

The science fiction short story "The Pedestrian" connects to the Essential Question, "What is the meaning of freedom?" This short story text explores the idea of freedom in a dysfunctional future society in which technology has become predominant. The story raises the question of whether an individual can express and maintain freedom in a society where technology seeks to control all human behavior.

## Connection to Performance-Based Assessment

This selection provides an unusual perspective on the question, "What are the most effective tools for establishing and preserving freedom?" It is the first selection in the unit in which students must consider how the idea of personal freedoms may evolve in future societies and if they will be valued in the same way that they have been in the past.

### Text Complexity Rubric: The Pedestrian

| **Quantitative Measures** | |
|---|---|
| **Lexile:** 1080 **Text Length:** 1,443 words | |
| **Qualitative Measures** | |
| Knowledge Demands (1 – **2** – 3 – 4 – 5) | Futuristic situation dealing with humanity and technology; while the story is set in the future, the selection contains clues to help with meaning. |
| Structure (1 – **2** – 3 – 4 – 5) | The story is organized sequentially with some dialogue. |
| Language Conventionality and Clarity (1 – 2 – **3** – 4 – 5) | The selection contains some long, complex sentences with significant use of metaphor and simile. |
| Levels of Meaning/Purpose (1 – 2 – **3** – 4 – 5) | Multiple levels of meaning; description of events are interspersed with dialogue. Some sophisticated concepts about individuality, groups and technology. |

# *from* the Iroquois Constitution

**SELECTION RESOURCES**

- First-Read Guide: Nonfiction
- Close-Read Guide: Nonfiction
- *from* the Iroquois Constitution: Text Questions
- Audio Summaries
- Selection Audio
- Selection Test


## Summary

In this excerpt from the political document The Iroquois Constitution, the prophet Dekanawidah speaks of the Tree of Great Peace that gives shelter and protection to the Iroquois nations. He explains why and how the Five Nations, a group of five Iroquois tribes, should come together to form a union, or confederacy, for their common good. He describes the ceremonies that will be performed when a new confederate lord is to be installed. He explains how the lord must always speak the truth, deal with conflict with endless patience and good will, treat his people with tenderness, and act selflessly on their behalf.


## Insight

Reading "*from* The Iroquois Constitution" will help students understand how a political system formed by five Native American tribes predates the American experiment. They will see the importance of rituals, discussion, and consensus in defining and maintaining democratic ideas.

## Connection to the Essential Question

The political document "*from* The Iroquois Constitution" explores the question, "What is the meaning of freedom?" It presents the idea of diverse groups of people uniting to form a political system that guarantees safety and freedoms to participating groups. Students should note the basic similarity between the intent of this document and the United States Constitution.

## Connection to Performance-Based Assessment

This political document provides a nontraditional and historical perspective on the question, "What are the most effective tools for establishing and preserving freedom?" The selection stresses how both rituals and discussions address key concerns of a political system. Such concerns include the election of leaders, the protection of people through mutual defense, the resolution of social conflict, and the care of participating members.

### Text Complexity Rubric: *from* The Iroquois Constitution

| **Quantitative Measures** | |
|---|---|
| **Lexile:** 1510 **Text Length:** 907 words | |
| **Qualitative Measures** | |
| Knowledge Demands ①—②—③—**❹**—⑤ | Historical knowledge demands; the selection is an historical agreement created to promote peace within five Native American tribes. |
| Structure ①—②—**❸**—④—⑤ | Selection is a speech that presents the requirements for joining the Iroquois Confederacy. There are many descriptive passages that may be challenging. |
| Language Conventionality and Clarity ①—②—③—**❹**—⑤ | Selection is written in formal language with extensive use of symbolism involving the natural world. |
| Levels of Meaning/Purpose ①—②—③—**❹**—⑤ | The main idea is clear, but the concept may be hard for some to grasp because of sophisticated language and supporting concepts that are complex. |

DIGITAL PERSPECTIVES | Audio | Video | Document | Annotation Highlights | EL Highlights | Online Assessment

# *from* Common Sense

## Summary

In Thoughts On The Present State of American Affairs—a chapter from *Common Sense*—Thomas Paine provides a powerful argument in 1775–76 against the idea that reconciliation with Britain is a better course of action than seeking independence. Paine counters the argument that Britain has protected the colonies by pointing out that these actions were for Britain's own financial gain. He believes that with reconciliation, the British monarchy would only repeat the same injustices and war would be inevitable. Paine provides a rough sketch of what a representative government might look like, including a congress and President. He calls for a Continental Conference to draw up laws to establish such a union.

## Insight

Reading "Thoughts On The Present State of American Affairs" will help students understand the grievances that colonists suffered under Great Britain's rule. They will learn about the great debate that occurred between loyalists to the British monarchy and those colonists who sought independence as a means of achieving political and economic freedom and self-determination.

SELECTION RESOURCES

- First-Read Guide: Nonfiction
- Close-Read Guide: Nonfiction
- *from* Common Sense: Text Questions
- Audio Summaries
- Selection Audio
- Selection Test

## Connection to the Essential Question

The essay "Thoughts On The Present State of American Affairs" connects to the Essential Question, "What is the meaning of freedom?" by exploring the important relationships between economic and political freedom and self-determination.

## Connection to Performance-Based Assessment

This essay provides important historical background on the question, "What are the most effective tools for establishing and preserving freedom?" The selection stresses the need to fight against tyrannical oppression in order to achieve political and economic freedom. It also touches upon the need for formal governmental structures and procedures to preserve freedom.

### Text Complexity Rubric: *from* Common Sense

| Quantitative Measures | |
|---|---|
| **Lexile:** 1300L **Text Length:** 6,266 words | |
| **Qualitative Measures** | |
| Knowledge Demands ①—②—③—④—❺ | Historical knowledge demands; selection presents reasons America should be independent from Britain. Background knowledge is assumed. |
| Structure ①—②—③—❹—⑤ | The selection is a first-person opinion that contains many lengthy, dense paragraphs with no headings to break up the text. |
| Language Conventionality and Clarity ①—②—③—④—❺ | Sentences are long with embedded clauses and use of archaic language. |
| Levels of Meaning/Purpose ①—②—③—❹—⑤ | The purpose is clear (an argument for American independence from Britain), but the concepts may be hard for some to grasp because of difficult language and supporting concepts that are complex. |

# ADVISING

You may wish to direct students to use the generic **First-Read** and **Close-Read Guides** in the Print Student Edition. Alternatively, you may wish to print copies of the genre-specific **First-Read** and **Close-Read Guides** for students. These are available online in the Interactive Student Edition or Unit Resources.

## FIRST READ

Students should perform the steps of the first read independently.

NOTICE: Students should focus on the basic elements of the text to ensure they understand what is happening.

ANNOTATE: Students should mark any passages they wish to revisit during their close read.

CONNECT: Students should increase their understanding by connecting what they've read to other texts or personal experiences.

RESPOND: Students will write a summary to demonstrate their understanding.

Point out to students that while they will always complete the Respond step at the end of the first read, the other steps will probably happen somewhat concurrently. Remind students that they will revisit their first-read annotations during the close read.

After students have completed the First-Read Guide, you may wish to assign the Text Questions for the selection that are available in the Interactive Teacher's Edition.

### Anchor Standards

In the first two sections of the unit, students worked with the whole class and in small groups to gain topical knowledge and greater understanding of the skills required by the anchor standards. In this section, they are asked to work independently, applying what they have learned and demonstrating increased readiness for college and career.



## INDEPENDENT LEARNING

### First-Read Guide

**Tool Kit**
First-Read Guide and Model Annotation

Use this page to record your first-read ideas.

Selection Title: ______

NOTICE

**NOTICE** new information or ideas you learned about the unit topic as you first read this text.

ANNOTATE

**ANNOTATE** by marking vocabulary and key passages you want to revisit.

NOTICE ANNOTATE First Read CONNECT RESPOND

**CONNECT** ideas within the selection to other knowledge and the selections you have read.

**RESPOND** by writing a brief summary of the selection.

CONNECT

RESPOND



STANDARD

**Reading** Read and comprehend complex literary and informational texts independently and proficiently.

DIGITAL PERSPECTIVES

## Close-Read Guide

Use this page to record your close-read ideas.

**Tool Kit**
Close-Read Guide and Model Annotation

Selection Title: ______________________________

### Close Read the Text

Revisit sections of the text you marked during your first read. Read these sections closely and **annotate** what you notice. Ask yourself **questions** about the text. What can you **conclude**? Write down your ideas.



### Analyze the Text

Think about the author's choices of patterns, structure, techniques, and ideas included in the text. Select one and record your thoughts about what this choice conveys.

### QuickWrite

Pick a paragraph from the text that grabbed your interest. Explain the power of this passage.

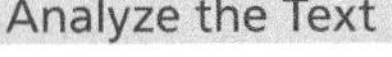

STANDARD
**Reading** Read and comprehend complex literary and informational texts independently and proficiently.





## CLOSE READ

Students should begin their close read by revisiting the annotations they made during their first read. Then, students should analyze one of the author's choices regarding the following elements:

- **patterns,** such as repetition or parallelism
- **structure,** such as enumeration or problem-solution
- **techniques,** such as appeal to ethics or appeal to logic
- **ideas,** such as the author's main idea or claim

**MAKE IT INTERACTIVE**
Group students according to the selection they have chosen. Then, have students meet to discuss the selection in depth. Their discussions should be guided by their insights and questions.

## PERSONALIZE FOR LEARNING

### English Language Support

**Read Aloud, Confirm Predictions, and Complete KWL Chart** Pair students or put them in groups so they can take turns reading aloud to one another. Each student can read one paragraph, or you can split up the text in any other way that makes sense. For example, for a short story, you may wish to assign different characters and the role of the narrator to individual students to take turns reading aloud.

Have students make predictions as they listen, and then have partners or groups discuss, compare, and confirm the predictions they made. Ask: *Did anything surprise you? Were any predictions correct? Which ones?* Finally, have partners or groups work together to add more details about what they learned to the Close Read the Text box on their Close-Read Guide.
**ALL LEVELS**

# ADVISING

## Share Your Independent Learning

### Prepare to Share

Explain to students that sharing what they learned from their Independent Learning selection provides classmates who read a different selection with an opportunity to consider the text as a source of evidence during the Performance-Based Assessment. As students prepare to share, remind them to highlight how their selection contributed to their knowledge of the concept of freedom as well as how the selection connects to the question *What is the meaning of freedom?*

### Learn From Your Classmates

As students discuss the Independent Learning selections, direct them to take particular note of how their classmates' chosen selections align with their current position on the Performance-Based Assessment question.

**MAKE IT INTERACTIVE**

Pair each student with another who read a different Independent Learning selection. Have pairs work together to outline the similarities and differences in the way the two selections addressed or related to the subject of freedom.

### Reflect

Students may want to add their reflection to their Evidence Log, particularly if their insight relates to a specific selection from the unit.

**Evidence Log** Support students in completing their Evidence Log. This paced activity will help prepare them for the Performance-Based Assessment at the end of the unit.

INDEPENDENT LEARNING

EVIDENCE LOG

Go to your Evidence Log and record what you learned from the text you read.

## Share Your Independent Learning

### Prepare to Share

What is the meaning of freedom?

Even when you read something independently, your understanding continues to grow when you share what you have learned with others. Reflect on the text you explored independently and write notes about its connection to the unit. In your notes, consider why this text belongs in this unit.

### Learn From Your Classmates

**Discuss It** Share your ideas about the text you explored on your own. As you talk with your classmates, jot down ideas that you learn from them.

### Reflect

Review your notes, and mark the most important insight you gained from these writing and discussion activities. Explain how this idea adds to your understanding of the meaning of freedom.

STANDARDS

**Speaking and Listening**

Initiate and participate effectively in a range of collaborative discussions (one-on-one, in groups, and teacher-led) with diverse partners on *grades 11–12 topics, texts, and issues,* building on others' ideas and expressing their own clearly and persuasively.





AUTHOR'S PERSPECTIVE **Ernest Morrell, Ph.D.**

**Learning From Others** Independent Learning helps students build vocabulary, background knowledge, and fluency. Teach students how learn from each other by modeling how to ask clarifying questions when other students are sharing their experiences. Questions like these can guide the discussion:

- Why did you choose this text? For example, did the topic interest you? Have you heard of the author or read anything else by the author?
- For narrative text: What is the problem in the story? When and where does the story take place? Why?
- For nonfiction text: How is the information organized? What is the most interesting thing you've learned so far?
- What parts of the text do you think were most important? Why?
- Did the text meet your expectations? Why or why not? Would you recommend this text to a classmate? Explain your answer.
- How does the text relate to other texts you have read on this subject? How does it relate to your life?

PERFORMANCE-BASED ASSESSMENT PREP

## Review Evidence for an Argument

At the beginning of this unit, you took a position on the following question:

**What are the most effective tools for establishing and preserving freedom?**

EVIDENCE LOG

Review your Evidence Log and your QuickWrite from the beginning of the unit. Have your ideas changed?

| ☐ YES | ☐ NO |
|---|---|
| Identify at least three pieces of evidence that have caused you to reevaluate your ideas. | Identify at least three pieces of evidence that have reinforced your initial position. |
| 1. | 1. |
| 2. | 2. |
| 3. | 3. |

State your position now: ______________________

______________________

Identify a possible counterclaim: ______________________

______________________

**Evaluate the Strength of Your Evidence** Consider your argument. Do you have enough evidence to support your claim? Do you have enough evidence to refute a counterclaim? If not, make a plan.

☐ Do online research. ☐ Skim a textbook.

☐ Reread a selection. ☐ Speak with an expert.

☐ Other: ______________________

STANDARDS

Writing

Introduce precise, knowledgeable claim(s), establish the significance of the claim(s), distinguish the claim(s) from alternate or opposing claims, and create an organization that logically sequences claim(s), counterclaims, reasons, and evidence.





DIGITAL PERSPECTIVES

## Review Evidence for an Argument

**Evidence Log** Make sure students understand that their opinions on an issue can change as they learn more about it and as they encounter other points of view. Remind students that their Evidence Log tracked the growth of their thinking during the unit. As they carefully consider what they've learned and the evidence they've found, the initial position they took on the question *"What are the most effective tools for establishing and preserving freedom?"* might continue to change.

**Evaluate the Strength of Your Evidence** Students have the choice of many different sources when looking for information about the topic, including:

- political philosophy textbooks
- mass-market political philosophy books
- history books that describe a society's movement toward or away from freedom
- magazine articles
- websites about people or organizations dedicated to establishing and preserving freedom

Students need to judge not just the quantity of the evidence they gather about their topic, but also the reliability of that evidence. Discuss what might make evidence more credible, and suggest these questions:

- Did the evidence come from a reliable source, such as governmental, educational, and professional organizations?
- Has it been reviewed by experts for accuracy?
- Does it include references to other sources?

## Writing to Sources: Argument

Students should complete the Performance-Based Assessment independently, with little to no input or feedback during the process. Students should use word processing software to take advantage of editing tools and features.

Prior to beginning the Assessment, ask students to consider what lessons about freedom have been learned over the course of our nation's history. What decisions and actions led to positive outcomes and which were problematic?

### Review the Elements of Effective Argument

Students can review the work they did earlier in the unit as they complete the Performance-Based Assessment. They may also consult other resources such as:

- the elements of an effective argument, including language, tone, and grammar, as well as how to organize an argument, available in Whole-Class Learning
- their Evidence Log
- their Word Network

Although students will use evidence from the unit selections for their argument, they may need to collect additional evidence, including facts, quotations, anecdotes, or other examples that support their argument.

PERFORMANCE-BASED ASSESSMENT

SOURCES

- WHOLE-CLASS SELECTIONS
- SMALL-GROUP SELECTIONS
- INDEPENDENT-LEARNING SELECTION

PART 1

## Writing to Sources: Argument

In this unit, you read a variety of texts that considered the meaning of American freedom. You saw the Founders' concerns about how to establish a nation that offered freedom to at least some of its citizens, and you read other texts that demonstrated how a nation "conceived in liberty" was tested over time.

**Assignment**

Write an **argumentative essay** in which you respond to this question:

**What are the most effective tools for establishing and preserving freedom?**

Use the Anchor Texts to identify some of the most successful tools (processes, government institutions, value systems, documents, and so on) that the Founders established. Use other texts from the unit to demonstrate how well those tools have stood the test of time. Supplement your ideas with examples from your own research that confirm your argument. Consider and address possible counterclaims.

**Reread the Assignment** Review the assignment to be sure you fully understand it. The task may reference some of the academic words presented at the beginning of the unit. Be sure you understand each of the words given below in order to complete the assignment correctly.

**Academic Vocabulary**

| confirm | supplement | conviction |
|---|---|---|
| demonstrate | establish | |

WORD NETWORK

As you write and revise your argument, use your Word Network to help vary your word choices.

**Review the Elements of Effective Argument** Before you begin writing, read the Argument Rubric. Once you have completed your first draft, check it against the rubric. If one or more of the elements are missing or not as strong as they could be, revise your essay to add or strengthen those components.

STANDARDS

Writing

- Write arguments to support claims in an analysis of substantive topics or texts, using valid reasoning and relevant and sufficient evidence.
- Write routinely over extended time frames and shorter time frames for a range of tasks, purposes, and audiences.





AUTHOR'S PERSPECTIVE Kelly Gallagher, M.Ed.

**Building a Writing Portfolio with Students**

Teachers can create a portfolio that enables students to demonstrate the variety of writing they complete over the year. There are three elements of keeping a portfolio—collection of all the writing a student has done, selection of the best pieces, and reflection to evaluate growth.

Teachers can set the criteria using such categories as *Best Argument, Best Narrative Piece, Best Informative Piece, Best On-Demand Writing, Best Poetry, Best Blended Genre, Best Writing from Another Class, Best Model of Revision,* and *Best Single Line You Wrote this Year*. Students should also include a reflective letter at the end of the year. To help them learn to reflect, use questions like these throughout the year.

- Where does your writing still need improvement? How will you improve?
- Reflect on a struggle you faced during this unit. How did you overcome it?
- Discuss a specific writing strategy you used and how it worked for you.
- What strengths have you developed as a writer? Where are those strengths found in this portfolio?

At the end of the year, students can review these pieces to see their growth as writers.

## Argument Rubric

| | Focus and Organization | Evidence and Elaboration | Language Conventions |
|---|---|---|---|
| 4 | The introduction is engaging and establishes the claim in a compelling way.<br>Valid reasons and evidence address and support the claim. Counterclaims are clearly acknowledged.<br>The ideas progress logically, connected by a variety of sentence transitions.<br>The conclusion offers fresh insight into the claim. | The sources of evidence are comprehensive and specific and contain relevant information.<br>The tone of the argument is formal and objective.<br>Vocabulary is used strategically and appropriately for the audience and purpose. | The argument consistently uses standard English conventions of usage and mechanics. |
| 3 | The introduction is engaging and establishes the claim in a way that grabs readers' attention.<br>Reasons and evidence address and support the claim. Counterclaims are acknowledged.<br>The ideas progress logically, and sentence transitions connect readers to the argument.<br>The conclusion restates important information. | The sources of evidence contain relevant information.<br>The tone of the argument is mostly formal and objective.<br>Vocabulary is generally appropriate for the audience and purpose. | The argument demonstrates accuracy in standard English conventions of usage and mechanics. |
| 2 | The introduction establishes the claim.<br>Some reasons and evidence address and support the claim. Counterclaims are briefly acknowledged.<br>The ideas progress somewhat logically. A few sentence transitions connect readers to the argument.<br>The conclusion offers some insight into the claim and restates information. | The sources of evidence contain some relevant information.<br>The tone of the argument is occasionally formal and objective.<br>Vocabulary is somewhat appropriate for the audience and purpose. | The argument demonstrates some accuracy in standard English conventions of usage and mechanics. |
| 1 | The claim is not clearly stated.<br>No reasons or evidence for the claim are included, and counterclaims are not acknowledged.<br>The ideas do not progress logically. The sentences are often short and choppy and do not connect readers to the argument.<br>The conclusion does not restate any information that is important. | No reliable or relevant evidence is included.<br>The tone of the argument is informal.<br>The vocabulary is limited or ineffective. | The argument contains mistakes in standard English conventions of usage and mechanics. |





DIGITAL PERSPECTIVES

## Argument Rubric

As you review the Argument Rubric with students, remind them that the rubric is a resource that can guide their revisions. Students should pay particular attention to the differences between an argument that contains all of the required elements (a score of 3) and one that is comprehensive, engaging, and progresses in a logical and thoughtful manner (a score of 4).

PERSONALIZE FOR LEARNING

**English Language Support**

Review the definitions for the academic vocabulary for this assignment. Encourage students to use each word in a short sentence to show its meaning. Then review the definition of argument and of writing claims to support their argument. You may give students sentence frames to help them build their claim. For example: *It is my conviction that* ____. **ALL LEVELS**

## Speaking and Listening: Video Commentary

Students should annotate their writing mode in preparation for the videorecorded commentary, marking the important elements. Remind students to include in their commentary a claim, reasons, evidence, as well as quotations that support their claim.

Remind students that the effectiveness of an oral writing mode relies on how the speaker establishes credibility with his or her audience. If a speaker comes across as confident and authoritative, it will be easier for the audience to give credence to the speaker's presentation.

**Review the Rubric** As you review the Oral Presentation Rubric with students, remind them that it is a valuable tool that can help them plan their presentation. They should strive to include all of the criteria required to achieve a score of 3. Draw their attention to some of the subtle differences between scores of 2 and 3.

PERFORMANCE-BASED ASSESSMENT

PART 2

## Speaking and Listening: Video Commentary

**Assignment**

Imagine that representatives of a television station have called on you to be their expert on the concept of freedom. Present a **video commentary,** based on the final draft of your argument, to be used during coverage of a presidential debate.

Follow these steps to make your presentation lively and engaging.

- Read your text aloud, keeping the television audience in mind. Highlight the material you most want to emphasize for that audience.
- Practice your delivery. Remember to look up at the camera regularly instead of staring down at your paper.
- Have a classmate operate the camera as you deliver your commentary.

**Review the Rubric** The criteria by which your commentary will be evaluated appear in the rubric below. Review the criteria before delivering your commentary to ensure that you are prepared.

| | Content | Use of Media | Presentation Techniques |
|---|---|---|---|
| 3 | The content and delivery are appropriate for a television audience.<br>The commentary is clearly organized and easy to follow. | The voice on the recording is consistent and audible.<br>The camera holds steady, and facial expressions are clearly visible. | Speech is clear and at an appropriate volume.<br>Tone and pace vary to maintain interest.<br>The speaker looks regularly at the camera to engage the audience. |
| 2 | The content and delivery are consistent, although some content may not be clearly meant for a television audience.<br>The commentary is organized and fairly easy to follow. | The voice on the recording may vary but is mostly audible.<br>The camera generally holds steady, so most facial expressions are visible. | Speech is clear most of the time and usually has an appropriate volume.<br>Tone and pace are inconsistent.<br>The speaker looks occasionally at the camera. |
| 1 | The content and delivery are generic, with no specific audience in mind.<br>The commentary is disorganized and may be difficult to follow. | The voice on the recording sometimes fades in and out.<br>The camera does not hold steady or is not focused on the face, so the expressions are rarely visible. | The speaker mumbles occasionally, speaks too quickly, and/or does not speak loudly enough.<br>The speaker fails to look at the camera. |





### DIGITAL PERSPECTIVES

**Preparing for the Assignment** To help students understand how to effectively deliver commentary, find examples on the Internet of speakers such as presidential candidates or news commentators. Show examples to the class, encouraging discussion as to what makes each speaker effective (e.g., voice modulation, gestures, tone, and so on). Engage students in critical evaluation as to what each individual speaker may do to improve his or her delivery. Prior to their video recording, suggest students practice in front of a mirror, incorporating some of the speaking behaviors they viewed.

## Reflect on the Unit

Now that you've completed the unit, take a few moments to reflect on your learning.

### Reflect on the Unit Goals

Look back at the goals at the beginning of the unit. Use a different colored pen to rate yourself again. Think about readings and activities that contributed the most to the growth of your understanding. Record your thoughts.

### Reflect on the Learning Strategies

**Discuss It** Write a reflection on whether you were able to improve your learning based on your Action Plans. Think about what worked, what didn't, and what you might do to keep working on these strategies. Record your ideas before joining a class discussion.

### Reflect on the Text

Choose a selection that you found challenging, and explain what made it difficult.

Explain something that surprised you about a text in the unit.

Which activity taught you the most about the meaning of American freedoms? What did you learn?

SCAN FOR MULTIMEDIA



DIGITAL PERSPECTIVES

## Reflect on the Unit

- Have students watch the video on Reflecting on Your Learning.
- You may choose to watch the video on this topic that is available online in the Professional Development Center.

### Reflect on the Unit Goals

Students should re-evaluate how well they met the Unit Goals now that they have completed the unit. You might ask them to provide a written commentary on the goal they made the most progress with as well as the goal they feel warrants continued focus.

### Reflect on the Learning Strategies

**Discuss It** If you want to make this a digital activity, go online and navigate to the Discussion Board. Alternatively, students can share their learning strategies reflections in a class discussion.

### Reflect on the Text

Consider having students share their text reflections with one another.

MAKE IT INTERACTIVE

Have students prepare a slide that summarizes their Reflections on the Text by addressing a challenging text, something surprising, or an activity that taught the most about freedom.

Divide students into groups according to their choice and have them collate their slides into a presentation. Groups can then share presentations with the class.

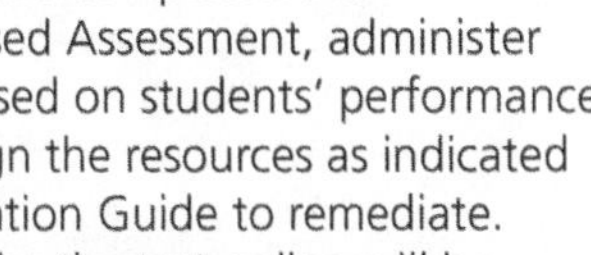

**Unit Test and Remediation**
After students have completed the Performance-Based Assessment, administer the Unit Test. Based on students' performance on the test, assign the resources as indicated on the Interpretation Guide to remediate. Students who take the test online will be automatically assigned remediation, as warranted by test results.

PERSONALIZE FOR LEARNING

**Strategic Support**
**Evaluate and Reflect** If students struggle while reflecting on unit goals, project the unit goals for the class to view as they write their reflections. Review the goals with students. Be prepared to assist students as they evaluate their Action Plan. Review each point in the Action Plan, turning the statements into questions as students evaluate and reflect.

# The Individual and Society

UNIT

Fitting In, or Standing Out?

## Jump Start

**The Individual and Society: Fitting In, or Standing Out?**

Engage students in a discussion about what it feels like to be a new kid at school or the only one who doesn't know anybody at a party. Have students jot down three things to do when you get that feeling of being the "odd one out." Discuss the students' items and decide on the top five suggestions. Poll the class for the two most difficult items to put into action.

## Video

Project the introduction video in class, ask students to open the video in their digital textbooks, or have students scan the BouncePage icon with their phones to access the video.

**Discuss It** If you want to make this a Discussion Board activity, create a discuss prompt. Go into Pearson Realize™, navigate to your Class, and click the Discuss tab. Then create the activity, and type in the prompt from this student page, or create your own prompt. Assign the Discussion Board prompt after students have watched the video. Alternatively, students can share their responses in a class discussion.

## Block Scheduling

Each day in this pacing calendar represents a 40–50 minute class period. Teachers using block scheduling may combine days to reflect their class schedule. In addition, teachers may revise pacing to differentiate and support core instruction by integrating components and resources as students require.

UNIT 2

# The Individual and Society

## Fitting In, or Standing Out?

Richard Blanco Reads "One Today"

**Discuss It** This poem, read by its author at President Barack Obama's 2013 inaugural, praises America as a society of individuals. How do the details of the poem present individual Americans? What connections among individuals does Blanco see?

Write your response before sharing your ideas.

SCAN FOR MULTIMEDIA

138



## Pacing Plan

Introduce Whole-Class Learning

| Day | Activity |
|---|---|
| 1 | Unit Introduction |
| 2 | Introduce Whole-Class Learning |
| 3 | Historical Perspectives |
| 4–7 | The Writing of Walt Whitman |
| 8–12 | The Poetry of Emily Dickinson |
| 13 | Media: *from* Emily Dickinson |
| 14–15 | Performance Task |

DIGITAL PERSPECTIVES

 Audio  Video Document  Annotation Highlights  EL Highlights  Online Assessment

UNIT 2

UNIT INTRODUCTION

ESSENTIAL QUESTION: What role does individualism play in American society?

LAUNCH TEXT NARRATIVE MODEL
from Up from Slavery
Booker T. Washington

 WHOLE-CLASS LEARNING

HISTORICAL PERSPECTIVES
Focus Period: 1800–1870
An American Identity

ANCHOR TEXT: ESSAY | POETRY
The Writing of Walt Whitman
Walt Whitman

COMPARE

ANCHOR TEXT: POETRY COLLECTION
The Poetry of Emily Dickinson
Emily Dickinson

MEDIA: RADIO BROADCAST
from Emily Dickinson
from Great Lives
BBC Radio 4

PERFORMANCE TASK
WRITING FOCUS:
Write a Personal Narrative

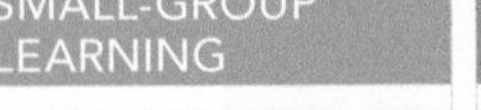 SMALL-GROUP LEARNING

PHILOSOPHICAL WRITING
from Nature
from Self-Reliance
Ralph Waldo Emerson

PHILOSOPHICAL WRITING
from Walden
from Civil Disobedience
Henry David Thoreau

MEDIA: PUBLIC DOCUMENTS
Innovators and Their Inventions

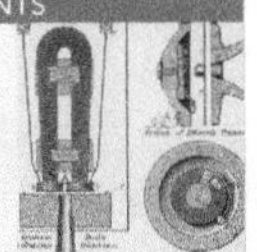

POETRY
The Love Song of J. Alfred Prufrock
T. S. Eliot

SHORT STORY
A Wagner Matinée
Willa Cather

PERFORMANCE TASK
SPEAKING AND LISTENING FOCUS:
Present a Personal Narrative

 INDEPENDENT LEARNING

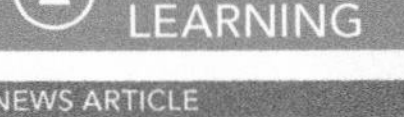

NEWS ARTICLE
Sweet Land of . . . Conformity?
Claude Fischer

LITERARY CRITICISM
Reckless Genius
Galway Kinnell

SHORT STORY
Hamadi
Naomi Shihab Nye

SHORT STORY
Young Goodman Brown
Nathaniel Hawthorne

PERFORMANCE-BASED ASSESSMENT PREP
Review Evidence for a Personal Narrative

PERFORMANCE-BASED ASSESSMENT

Narrative: Personal Narrative and Storytelling Session

PROMPT:
What significant incident helped me realize that I am a unique individual?





## What role does individualism play in American society?

Introduce the Essential Question and point out that students will respond to related prompts.

- **Whole-Class Learning** *How has my personal experience shaped my view of individualism? Do I see it as a guiding principle, something to be avoided, or both?*
- **Small-Group Learning** *When is it difficult to march to the beat of a "different drummer" and stand on your own as an individual? What are the risks and rewards of nonconformity?*
- **Performance-Based Assessment** *What significant incident helped me realize that I am a unique individual?*

### Using Novels About the Individual and Society

Refer to the Teaching with Novels section for some thematically-related novels to use in this unit.

- *The Jungle* by Upton Sinclair
- *On the Duty of Civil Disobedience* by Henry David Thoreau
- *Ethan Frome* by Edith Wharton

### Current Perspectives

Search online for stories of persons whose willingness to be different led to societal change.

- **Article: Revealed: Elon Musk's Plan to Build a Space Internet (Bloomberg)** Musk, an innovator, pursues ideas others might not.
- **Video: My Daughter Malala (TED Talks)** The father of the famous young champion of girls' education tells why his daughter is so strong.

| Day | Activity |
|---|---|
| 16 | Introduce Small-Group Learning |
| 17–18 | from Nature • from Self-Reliance |
| 19–20 | from Walden • from Civil Disobedience |
| 21 | Media: Innovators and Their Inventions |
| 22–23 | The Love Song of J. Alfred Prufrock |
| 24–25 | A Wagner Matinée |
| 26 | Performance Task |
| 27 | Introduce Independent Learning |
| 28 | Independent Learning |
| 29–30 | Performance-Based Assessment |

## About the Unit Goals

These unit goals were backward designed from the Performance-Based Assessment at the end of the unit and the Whole-Class and Small-Group Performance Tasks. Students will practice and become proficient in many more standards over the course of this unit.

## Unit Goals

Review the goals with students and explain that as they read and discuss the selections in this unit, they will improve their skills in reading, writing, research, language, and speaking and listening.

**Reading Goals** Tell students they will read and evaluate nonfiction narratives. They will also read arguments and informative essays to better understand the ways writers express ideas.

**Writing and Research Goals** Tell students that they will learn the elements of writing a nonfiction narrative. They will also write their own nonfiction narratives. Students will write for a number of reasons, including organizing and sharing ideas, reflecting on experiences, and gathering evidence. They will conduct research to clarify and explore ideas.

**Language Goals** Tell students that they will develop a deeper understanding of effective style choices regarding diction and sentence variety. They will practice correct usage of concrete, abstract, and compound nouns in their own writing.

**Speaking and Listening** Explain that students will work together to build on one another's ideas, develop consensus, and communicate with one another. They will also incorporate audio, visuals, and text in presentations.

### HOME Connection

A Home Connection letter to students' parents or guardians is available in the Interactive Teacher's Edition. The letter explains what students will be learning in this unit and how they will be assessed.



## Unit Goals

Throughout this unit, you will deepen your perspective on the concept of individualism by reading, writing, speaking, listening, and presenting. These goals will help you succeed on the Unit Performance-Based Assessment.

Rate how well you meet these goals right now. You will revisit your ratings later when you reflect on your growth during this unit.

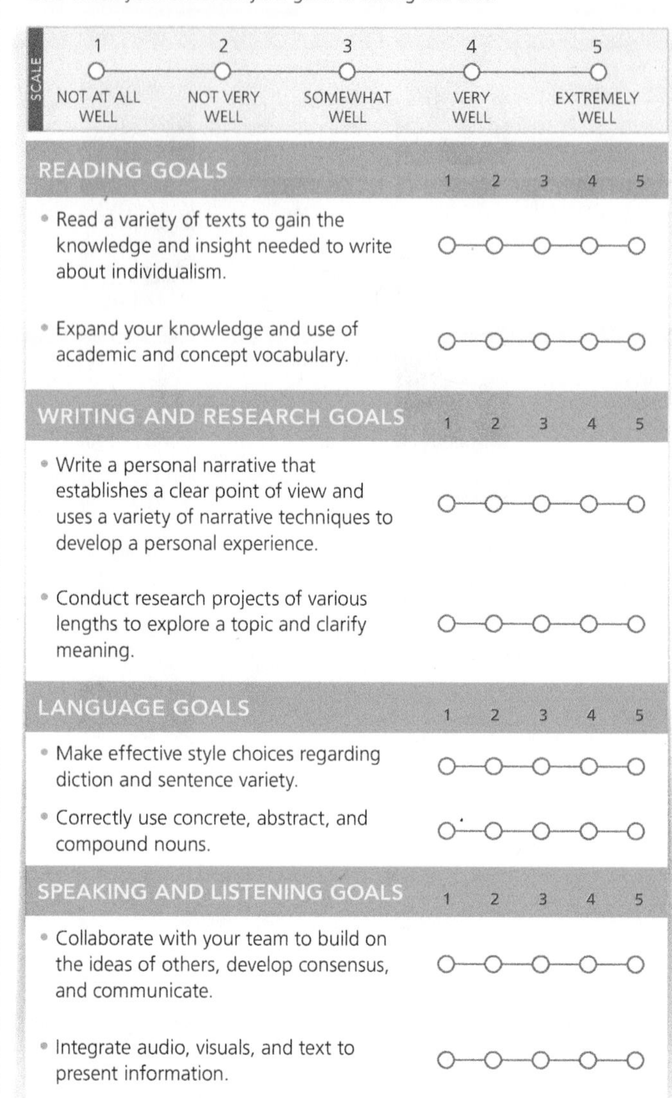

SCALE

| 1 | 2 | 3 | 4 | 5 |
|---|---|---|---|---|
| NOT AT ALL WELL | NOT VERY WELL | SOMEWHAT WELL | VERY WELL | EXTREMELY WELL |

| READING GOALS | 1 | 2 | 3 | 4 | 5 |
|---|---|---|---|---|---|
| • Read a variety of texts to gain the knowledge and insight needed to write about individualism. | ○ | ○ | ○ | ○ | ○ |
| • Expand your knowledge and use of academic and concept vocabulary. | ○ | ○ | ○ | ○ | ○ |
| **WRITING AND RESEARCH GOALS** | **1** | **2** | **3** | **4** | **5** |
| • Write a personal narrative that establishes a clear point of view and uses a variety of narrative techniques to develop a personal experience. | ○ | ○ | ○ | ○ | ○ |
| • Conduct research projects of various lengths to explore a topic and clarify meaning. | ○ | ○ | ○ | ○ | ○ |
| **LANGUAGE GOALS** | **1** | **2** | **3** | **4** | **5** |
| • Make effective style choices regarding diction and sentence variety. | ○ | ○ | ○ | ○ | ○ |
| • Correctly use concrete, abstract, and compound nouns. | ○ | ○ | ○ | ○ | ○ |
| **SPEAKING AND LISTENING GOALS** | **1** | **2** | **3** | **4** | **5** |
| • Collaborate with your team to build on the ideas of others, develop consensus, and communicate. | ○ | ○ | ○ | ○ | ○ |
| • Integrate audio, visuals, and text to present information. | ○ | ○ | ○ | ○ | ○ |

**STANDARDS**

**Language**

Acquire and use accurately general academic and domain-specific words and phrases, sufficient for reading, writing, speaking, and listening at the college and career readiness level; demonstrate independence in gathering vocabulary knowledge when considering a word or phrase important to comprehension or expression.



SCAN FOR MULTIMEDIA

### AUTHOR'S PERSPECTIVE Ernest Morrell, Ph. D.

**Self-Assessing Progress** The Unit Goals will help students share responsibility for their learning. This taking ownership of their own learning is an important step for students as they prepare for life in higher education, in their professional career, and as leaders in their families and communities. One way to encourage students to practice monitoring their own learning is to give them guiding questions like these to help them assess their progress as they work through the unit. Remind students to ask themselves such questions as they complete each selection or activity in the unit so they can track their progress.

- Do I have a better understanding of the parts of an argument and how to recognize them when reading and using them when writing?
- Do I have a better understanding of the differences between academic and concept vocabulary?
- Am I recognizing different types of phrases and clauses?
- Am I effective when I collaborate with others?

## Academic Vocabulary: Personal Narrative

Academic terms appear in all subjects and can help you read, write, and discuss with more precision. Here are five academic words that will be useful to you in this unit as you analyze and write personal narratives.

**Complete the chart.**

1. Review each word, its root, and the mentor sentences.
2. Use the information and your own knowledge to predict the meaning of each word.
3. For each word, list at least two related words.
4. Refer to a dictionary or other resources if needed.

TIP

FOLLOW THROUGH
Study the words in this chart, and mark them or their forms wherever they appear in the unit.

| WORD | MENTOR SENTENCES | PREDICT MEANING | RELATED WORDS |
|---|---|---|---|
| **significant**<br><br>ROOT:<br>***-sign-***<br>"sign" | 1. The fire was a *significant* event in our town's history.<br>2. Ms. Barnes made no *significant* changes to my report. | | signify; significance |
| **incident**<br><br>ROOT:<br>***-cid-***<br>"fall" | 1. Myron described the *incident* in great detail to the reporter.<br>2. We avoided an embarrassing *incident* by leaving the room. | | |
| **unique**<br><br>ROOT:<br>***-uni-***<br>"one" | 1. Each of these tables is a *unique*, handmade item.<br>2. My hairstyle is *unique*; no one would dare to copy it. | | |
| **sequence**<br><br>ROOT:<br>***-sequ-***<br>"follow" | 1. A first-grader should be able to recite numbers in *sequence* to 100.<br>2. Follow the *sequence* of directions, and the recipe will turn out well. | | |
| **impact**<br><br>ROOT:<br>***-pact-***<br>"press";<br>"fasten" | 1. His books had a strong *impact* on my beliefs and interests.<br>2. The *impact* of vaccines on public health has been considerable, and has lead to a healthier population. | | |





## PERSONALIZE FOR LEARNING

**English Language Support**

**Cognates** Many of the academic vocabulary words have Spanish cognates:

evidence – evidencia valid – válido

formulate – formular logical –lógico

Not all English learners will recognize and use these cognates automatically. Help students build their cognate awareness by pointing out that these cognates share the same root in both English and Spanish. **ALL LEVELS**

DIGITAL PERSPECTIVES  

## Academic Vocabulary: Personal Narrative

Introduce the blue academic vocabulary words in the chart on the student page. Point out that the root of each word provides a clue to its meaning. Discuss the mentor sentences to ensure students understand each word's usage. Students should also use the mentor sentences as context to help them predict the meaning of each word. Check that students are able to fill the chart in correctly. Complete pronunciations, parts of speech, and definitions are provided for you. Students are only expected to provide the definition.

**Possible responses:**
**significant** *n.* (sihg NIHF uh kuhnt)
**Meaning:** having or expressing a meaning
**Related Words:** *signify, significance*
**Additional words related to the root *-sign-*:** *signal, designate*
**incident** *n.* (IHN suh duhnt)
**Meaning:** something that happens; happening; occurence
**Related Words:** *incidents, incidental*
**Additional words related to the root *-cide-*:** *accident, coincide*
**unique** *adj.* (yoo NEEK)
**Meaning:** one and only; single; sole
**Related Words:** *uniquely, uniqueness*
**Additional words related to the root *-uni-*:** *universal, unicycle*
**sequence** *n.* (SEE kwuhns)
**Meaning:** the following of one thing after another in chronological, causal, or logical order
**Related Words:** *sequenced, sequential*
**Additional words related to the root *-sequ-*:** *consequence, sequel*
**impact** *n.* (IHM pakt)
**Meaning:** a striking together; violent contact; collision
**Related Words:** *impacts, impacted*
**Additional words related to the root *-pact-*:** *compact, compactly*

## Purpose of the Launch Text

The Launch Text provides students with a common starting point to address the unit topic. After they read the Launch Text, all students will be able to participate in discussions about the individual and society.

**Lexile: 1090** The easier reading level of this selection makes it perfect to assign for homework. Students will need little or no support to understand it.

Additionally, this excerpt from *Up From Slavery* provides a writing model for the Performance-Based Assessment students will complete at the end of the unit.

## Launch Text: Narrative Model

Remind students that this excerpt from *Up From Slavery* is an example of a personal narrative. Have them pay attention to the details that the author includes; explain that these details help the reader imagine what it was like to be Booker T. Washington arriving at Hampton for the first time. Ask students to think about what it is that makes this story compelling to any audience. How does the author make the story feel meaningful to readers, given that they have not shared the author's experience?

Encourage students to read this text on their own and annotate unfamiliar words and sections they think are particularly important.

AUDIO SUMMARIES

Audio summaries of *Up From Slavery* are available online in both English and Spanish in the Interactive Teacher's Edition or Unit Resources. Assigning these summaries before students read the Launch Text may help them build additional background knowledge and set a context for their reading.



LAUNCH TEXT | NARRATIVE MODEL

This selection is an example of a **narrative text.** It is a **personal narrative**—the author tells a story about himself, using a first-person point of view. This is the type of writing you will develop in the Performance-Based Assessment at the end of the unit.

**As you read,** notice the author's use of specific details. Mark words and phrases that convey his experiences and feelings with vividness and clarity.

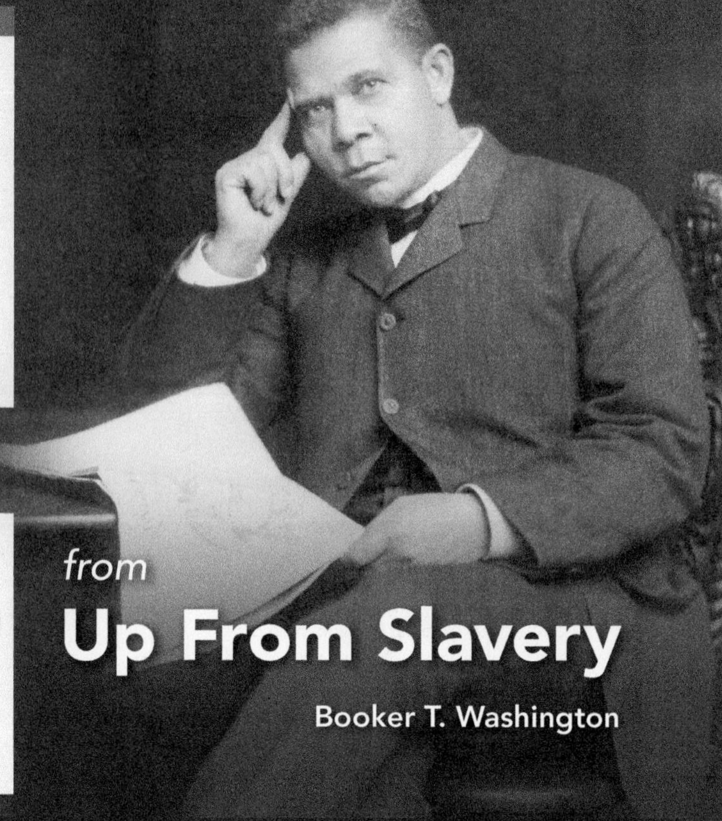

About the Author

**Booker T. Washington** (1856–1915) was born into slavery and overcame enormous obstacles to become a noted author, educator, and advisor to two American presidents. This excerpt is from chapter 3 of his autobiography *Up From Slavery,* in which Washington describes his experiences at Hampton Institute in the early 1870s.

*from*

# Up From Slavery

Booker T. Washington

NOTES

1 When I had saved what I considered enough money with which to reach Hampton, I thanked the captain of the vessel for his kindness, and started again. Without any unusual occurrence I reached Hampton, with a surplus of exactly fifty cents with which to begin my education. To me it had been a long, eventful journey; but the first sight of the large, three-story, brick school building seemed to have rewarded me for all that I had undergone in order to reach the place. . . .

2 As soon as possible after reaching the grounds of the Hampton Institute, I presented myself before the head teacher for assignment to a class. Having been so long without proper food, a bath, and change of clothing, I did not, of course, make a very favorable impression upon her, and I could see at once that there were doubts in her mind about the wisdom of admitting me as a student. I felt that I could hardly blame her if she got the idea that I was a worthless loafer or tramp. For some time she did not refuse to admit me, neither did she decide in my favor, and I continued to linger about her, and





SCAN FOR MULTIMEDIA 

PERSONALIZE FOR LEARNING

### Strategic Support

**Background** Provide students with some historical context to help them understand *Up From Slavery.* Booker T. Washington was born into slavery in 1856. After the Civil War, he worked in coal furnaces and coal mines before making his way to Hampton Institute in Virginia, where this excerpt from *Up From Slavery* takes place. Washington worked his way through school and went on to become the founding leader of Tuskeegee Normal and Industrial Institute in Alabama. Under his stewardship, Tuskeegee became a well-funded vocational school for African Americans. Washington was a famous and controversial figure. He believed that African Americans' best path out of the subordination of sharecropping was vocational education, not fighting for civil rights. His views clashed with other African American leaders of the time, such as W.E.B. DuBois, but Washington was extremely influential among both African Americans and white Americans.

DIGITAL PERSPECTIVES  

to impress her in all the ways I could with my worthiness. In the meantime I saw her admitting other students, and that added greatly to my discomfort, for I felt, deep down in my heart, that I could do as well as they, if I could only get a chance to show what was in me.

3 After some hours had passed, the head teacher said to me: "The adjoining recitation-room needs sweeping. Take the broom and sweep it."

4 It occurred to me at once that here was my chance. Never did I receive an order with more delight. I knew that I could sweep, for Mrs. Ruffner had thoroughly taught me how to do that when I lived with her.

5 I swept the recitation-room three times. Then I got a dusting-cloth and I dusted it four times. All the woodwork around the walls, every bench, table, and desk, I went over four times with my dusting-cloth. Besides, every piece of furniture had been moved and every closet and corner in the room had been thoroughly cleaned. I had the feeling that in a large measure my future depended upon the impression I made upon the teacher in the cleaning of that room. When I was through, I reported to the head teacher. She was a "Yankee" woman who knew just where to look for dirt. She went into the room and inspected the floor and closets; then she took her handkerchief and rubbed it on the woodwork about the walls, and over the table and benches. When she was unable to find one bit of dirt on the floor, or a particle of dust on any of the furniture, she quietly remarked, "I guess you will do to enter this institution."

6 I was one of the happiest souls on earth. The sweeping of that room was my college examination, and never did any youth pass an examination for entrance into Harvard or Yale that gave him more genuine satisfaction. I have passed several examinations since then, but I have always felt that this was the best one I ever passed.

NOTES

WORD NETWORK FOR THE INDIVIDUAL AND SOCIETY

**Vocabulary** A word network is a collection of words related to a topic. As you read the unit selections, identify words related to *individualism* and add them to your Word Network. For example, you might begin by adding words from the Launch Text, such as *worthiness*. For each word you add, note a related word, such as a synonym or an antonym. Continue to add words as you complete this unit.

**Tool Kit**
Word Network Model

worthiness | value

INDIVIDUALISM





## Word Network for The Individual and Society

Students may fill in the Word Network as they read the texts in the unit, or they may choose to just jot down words as they read and complete the Word Network when they are done.

Explain to students that many word associations are subjective; one student might think a word relates to the individual and society, while another student does not. Tell students to fill in the Word Network with any words they think are relevant. Each student's Word Network will be unique. If you choose to print the Word Network, distribute it to students at this point so they can use it throughout the rest of the unit.

AUTHOR'S PERSPECTIVE **Elfrieda Hiebert, Ph.D.**

**Generative Vocabulary** Rare words are the words that typically account for only 10 percent or less of all the words in a text, compared to the more common vocabulary words that students know better. Generative vocabulary strategies can help students build their rare vocabulary.

Generative refers to the way students can apply knowledge of how words work—morphologically and conceptually—when encountering new words. Building off of a big idea like this unit's unit topic, words can be taught as networks of ideas rather than as single, unrelated but grade-appropriate words. Studying words in conceptual groupings enables students to learn more words while reading.

Although some "unit topic" words may be unfamiliar to students, the overarching concept will not be. Students may not know every word related to the idea of "unit topic," but the concept of connections between "something about the unit topic" should be familiar to them. Word networks help students build vocabulary as they see a wide variety of words can relate to one concept.

# INTRODUCTION

## Summary

Have students read the introductory paragraph. Provide them with tips for writing a summary:

- Write in the present tense.
- Make sure to include the title of the work.
- Be concise: a summary should not be equal in length to the original text.
- If you need to quote the words of the author, use quotation marks.
- Don't put your own opinions, ideas, or interpretations into the summary. The purpose of writing a summary is to accurately represent what the author says, not to provide a critique.

If necessary, students can refer to the Tool Kit for help in understanding the elements of a good summary.

**See possible summary on Student page.**

## Launch Activity

Tell students that they will have many opportunities to discuss the individual and society as they work their way through this unit. Explain that in this activity, all students will have a chance to tell a story about an experience they have had, and to listen to their peers tell stories about their own experiences. Encourage students to keep an open mind and really listen to their classmates. Have students share any experiences they have had with the various objects.



## Summary

Write a summary of the excerpt from *Up From Slavery*. A **summary** is a concise, complete, and accurate overview of a text. It should not include a statement of your opinion or an analysis.

Possible response: Booker T. Washington wrote this personal narrative to describe how he became a student at the Hampton Institute. In the narrative, when Washington reaches the institute, he rushes to speak to the head teacher and doesn't make a great first impression. Washington is worried when he sees her admit other students before him. The next chance he gets to make a good impression is when the head teacher asks him to clean a room. He does so as thoroughly as he can—and for his success, she lets him in. Washington explains that he has taken many more conventional exams since that point, but he has never been more satisfied than he was about this one that got him into college.

## Launch Activity

**Tell a Story** Form a talk circle. One by one, take an object from a bag of assorted everyday objects. Then, return to your seat in the circle.

- If you like, trade objects with the person to your left or right.
- Think about a time when you used the object you are holding, or think about what a similar object meant to you at some point in your life. What story could you tell that springs from that incident or moment?
- When your turn comes, tell a one-minute story triggered by the object you chose.
- As you listen to classmates' stories, consider whether your own story about each object would be similar or different. Once everyone has had a turn, discuss what those similarities and differences mean about each person's uniqueness and about the connections among people.





### PERSONALIZE FOR LEARNING

**English Language Support**

**Active Listening** Students may think that listening is passive since they are not required to speak. Explain that listening simply requires them to participate in a different way. Listeners aim, first, to understand fully what the speaker says. Some students may find that taking notes helps them to stay focused while they listen and to remember ideas or questions that come up for them. Listeners also aim to engage with what the speaker says. When the speaker is finished speaking, listeners may want to pose questions, either to get clarification of something they do not understand, or to have the speaker expand on the content of something he or she said. **ALL LEVELS**

## QuickWrite

Consider class discussions, the video, and the Launch Text as you think about the prompt. Record your first thoughts here.

PROMPT: **What significant incident helped me realize that I am a unique individual?**

Possible response: My sister was a star student, and she is a year older than me. Because of that, many of the teachers I had compared me to her. In eighth grade, I started teaching myself to program, using lessons I found online for a programming language called Python. Later that year, I showed my science teacher a game I'd made. He was impressed! Then it hit me—my sister never studied anything that wasn't for school. She spent all her time making her class work perfect, but she wasn't learning any other skills that were useful. For the first time, I realized that I didn't need to be like her. I liked programming, and it made me feel like I had my own special talents.

### EVIDENCE LOG FOR THE INDIVIDUAL AND SOCIETY

Review your QuickWrite and summarize your initial idea in one sentence to record in your Evidence Log. Then, record evidence from the excerpt from *Up From Slavery* that connects to your idea.

After each selection, you will continue to use your Evidence Log to record the evidence you gather and the connections you make. The graphic shows what your Evidence Log looks like.

**Tool Kit**
Evidence Log Model

Title of Text: ____________ Date: ______

| CONNECTION TO PROMPT | TEXT EVIDENCE/DETAILS | ADDITIONAL NOTES/IDEAS |
|---|---|---|
| | | |

How does this text change or add to my thinking? Date: ______

SCAN FOR MULTIMEDIA



DIGITAL PERSPECTIVES

## QuickWrite

In this QuickWrite, students should present their own answer to the question based on the material in the Unit Opener. This initial response will help inform their work when they complete the Performance-Based Assessment at the end of the unit.

Students should make sure they describe an incident and explain what it was about the experience that helped them realize they were unique.

**See possible QuickWrite on Student page.**

## Evidence Log for The Individual and Society

Students should record their initial thinking and include evidence from *Up From Slavery* that supports it.

If you have decided to print the Evidence Log, distribute the copies now. Students will be able to use it throughout the unit.

### Performance-Based Assessment: Refining Your Thinking

- Have students watch the video on Refining Your Thinking
- A video on this topic is available online in the Professional Development Center.

## PERSONALIZE FOR LEARNING

### Strategic Support

**Breaking Down the Text** For some readers, an essay can seem long and intimidating. Explain to students that they can break the text down into smaller chunks to make it more manageable. Guide students through the process with the excerpt from *Up From Slavery*. Tell them to read the first paragraph and then stop. When everyone has finished reading, ask students to state the main idea of the paragraph. Write the idea on the board or on chart paper. Then use the same procedure for each of the subsequent paragraphs. Then, have a student read aloud the six summary sentences, which should provide a summary of the entire text.

# OVERVIEW

## WHOLE-CLASS LEARNING

### What role does individualism play in American society?

Throughout America's history, individuals have sought opportunity, success, and prosperity. In the nineteenth century, Americans worked to make a better life—often it is the person who stood out from society who is remembered for his or her willingness to try something original. During Whole-Class Learning, students will read selections about some of the individuals whose unique actions and ideas helped to shape a fledgling nation.

### Whole-Class Learning Strategies

Review the Learning Strategies with students and explain that as they work through Whole-Class Learning, they will develop strategies to work in large-group environments.

- Have students watch the video on Whole-Class Learning Strategies
- A video on this topic is available in the Professional Development Center.

You may wish to discuss some action items to add to the chart as a class before students complete it on their own. For example, for "Interact and share ideas," you might solicit the following from students:

- Ask and answer questions with your classmates as your share your ideas and understanding.
- Compare notes with classmates.

**Block Scheduling**

Each day in this Pacing Plan represents a 40–50 minute class period. Teachers using block scheduling may combine days to reflect their class schedule. In addition, teachers may revise pacing to differentiate and support core instruction by integrating components and resources as students require.

## OVERVIEW: WHOLE-CLASS LEARNING

ESSENTIAL QUESTION:

# What role does individualism play in American society?

As you read these selections, work with your whole class to explore the meaning of individualism.

**From Text to Topic** For Walt Whitman, individualism formed the cornerstone of life in America. His writing celebrates the promise of America, in which all people can make an impact by developing their unique abilities. For Emily Dickinson, individualism meant looking inward to express the deepest musings of the soul. As you read, consider what the selections show about perceptions of individualism in American society in the nineteenth century. Also, consider how these works influence American attitudes toward individualism today.

## Whole-Class Learning Strategies

Throughout your life, in school, in your community, and in your career, you will continue to learn and work in large-group environments.

Review these strategies and the actions you can take to practice them. Add ideas of your own for each step. Get ready to use these strategies during Whole-Class Learning.

| STRATEGY | ACTION PLAN |
|---|---|
| Listen actively | • Eliminate distractions. For example, put your cellphone away.<br>• Record brief notes on main ideas and points of confusion.<br>• |
| Clarify by asking questions | • If you're confused, other people probably are, too. Ask a question to help your whole class.<br>• Ask follow-up questions as needed—for example, if you do not understand the clarification or if you want to make an additional connection.<br>• |
| Monitor understanding | • Notice what information you already know and be ready to build on it.<br>• Ask for help if you are struggling.<br>• |
| Interact and share ideas | • Share your ideas and answer questions, even if you are unsure.<br>• Build on the ideas of others by adding details or making a connection.<br>• |



SCAN FOR MULTIMEDIA



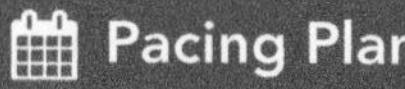

Pacing Plan

Introduce Whole-Class Learning

Unit Introduction | Historical Perspectives | The Writing of Walt Whitman | The Poetry of Emily Dickinson | Media: *from* Emily Dickinson | Performance Task

1

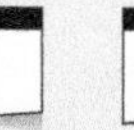

2 3 4 5 6 7 8 9 10 11 12 13 14 15

WHOLE-CLASS LEARNING

CONTENTS

HISTORICAL PERSPECTIVES

Focus Period: 1800–1870

An American Identity

During the early to mid-nineteenth century, Americans looked both inward and outward, determining their identity and shaping a distinctly "American" character.

ANCHOR TEXT: ESSAY | POETRY

The Writing of Walt Whitman

*Walt Whitman*

With its bold, energetic language and embracing vision, Whitman's work is for many readers America's epic poem.

COMPARE

ANCHOR TEXT: POETRY COLLECTION

The Poetry of Emily Dickinson

*Emily Dickinson*

In brief, precise poems, this great American writer describes sweeping vistas of thought and feeling.

MEDIA: RADIO BROADCAST

*from* Emily Dickinson

*from Great Lives*

*BBC Radio 4*

A poem written in the mid-1860s remains fresh and meaningful for contemporary readers.

PERFORMANCE TASK

WRITING FOCUS

Write a Personal Narrative

The Whole-Class readings were written during a time when American literature celebrated the individual. After reading, you will write a personal narrative that shows how a life experience has shaped your understanding of individuality.





DIGITAL PERSPECTIVES

## Contents

**Anchor Texts** Preview the anchor texts and media with students to generate interest. Ask students what they know about Walt Whitman as America's poet. Encourage students to discuss other texts they may have read, as well as movies or television shows they may have seen that deal with Americans who are known for their individualism.

Emily Dickinson is another notable American individual. She was most often called a loner, yet many find her poems strong and haunting. Ask students which of these two poets seems more interesting to them, then have them discuss the reasons for their choices.

### Performance Task

**Write a Personal Narrative** Explain to students that after they have finished reading the selections, they will write a nonfiction narrative about how their personal experiences have shaped whether they view individualism as a guiding principle, something to be avoided, or both. To help them prepare, encourage students to think about the topic as they progress through the selections and as they participate in the Whole-Class Learning experience.

Introduce Small-Group Learning

*from* Nature • *from* Self-Reliance

*from* Walden • *from* Civil Disobedience

Media: Innovators and Their Inventions

The Love Song of J. Alfred Prufrock

A Wagner Matinée

Performance Task

Introduce Independent Learning

Independent Learning

Performance-Based Assessment

16 17 18 19 20 21 22 23 24 25 26 27 28 29 30

## HISTORICAL PERSPECTIVES

### An American Identity

This section analyzes the key ideas and events of the Focus Period: America's independence and growth; the birth of individualism, "manifest destiny" and the settlers' mistreatment of Native Americans, improved travel and the Industrial Revolution, and the rise of abolitionists who worked to free the slaves. Have students connect these key events with the unit topic.

### Voices of the Period

Explain that the idea of individualism was unique to America. Ask students what alternative ideology may exist that would be in conflict with individualism. Have groups discuss these questions: *How did the idea of individualism influence events that occurred between 1800 and 1870? How might another ideology have altered the course of history?*

### History of the Period

With improved transportation, floods of arriving immigrants, and the industrial revolution, the United States grew tremendously during the period between 1800–1870. Ask students whether they think growth would have been as dramatic without the concept of individualism as a driving force.



# An American Identity

## Voices of the Period

*"I have always supported measures and principles and not men. I have acted fearless and independent and I never will regret my course."*

—Davy Crockett,
frontiersman, folk hero, and statesman

*"I have an almost complete disregard of precedent, and a faith in the possibility of something better. It irritates me to be told how things have always been done. I defy the tyranny of precedent. I go for anything new that might improve the past."*

—Clara Barton,
founder of the American Red Cross

*"There will never be a really free and enlightened State until the State comes to recognize the individual as a higher and independent power, from which all its own power and authority are derived, and treats him accordingly."*

—Henry David Thoreau,
author of "Civil Disobedience" and *Walden*

## History of the Period

**What Is an American?** French writer Alexis de Tocqueville came to America in the early 1830s with a colleague to study and write about American prisons. Instead, they ended up traveling extensively and studying American democracy. In his book *Democracy in America,* de Tocqueville coined the word *individualism* as a way of describing the attitudes he found in America, where people are "always considering themselves as standing alone, [imagining] that their whole destiny is in their own hands."

**Jefferson's Bargain** In 1803, President Thomas Jefferson purchased from France 828,000 square miles of North America for $15 million—about three cents per acre—and in the process, more than doubled the size of the United States. Jefferson sent explorers Meriwether Lewis and William Clark, with their Corps of Discovery, to investigate the land, people, and plants and animals of the new territory. They crossed the continent, reached the Pacific Ocean, and led the way for decades of westward-bound settlers.

**The War of 1812** In the War of 1812, the United States once again defeated Great Britain, asserting its independence from European control. However, the most important effect of the war may have been the sense of solidarity it fostered within the young nation.

**The People's President** The 1828 election of Andrew Jackson, "the People's President," ushered in the era of the "common man." The center of power began to shift west, even as a two-party system was emerging.

### TIMELINE

1800

**1803:** The Louisiana Purchase nearly doubles the size of the United States.

**1804–1806:** Lewis and Clark lead an exploration of the Louisiana Purchase, reaching the Pacific Ocean.

**1804: France** Napoleon Bonaparte declares himself emperor.

**1807:** Robert Fulton's steamboat makes its first trip, from New York City to Albany.

**1808–1833: Latin America** Independence movements result in wars and the creation of new governments.





### PERSONALIZE FOR LEARNING

**Strategic Support**

**Individualism** Discuss the "Voices of the Period" quotes with students. Ask students to consider their school or community experience in terms of individualism. Direct students to consider rules and policies at school or within their community to determine which are made for the benefit of the individual and which are made for the benefit of the group or community. Ask students to share opinions about whether some of these rules would be improved if they shifted focus.

DIGITAL PERSPECTIVES

## Integration of Knowledge and Ideas

**Notebook** From which countries did the United States acquire land during this era? How do you think these acquisitions influenced the way that Americans viewed themselves and their nation's future by the 1850s?

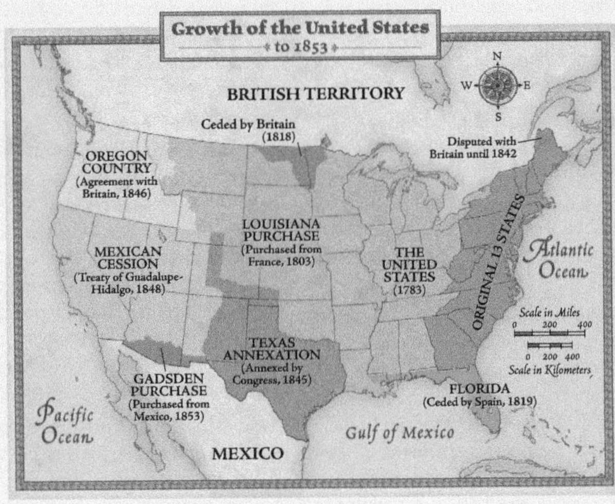


**Manifest Destiny** Many Americans believed in Manifest Destiny, the idea that it was their right to settle America's lands across the continent. By 1840, about 40 percent of the U.S. population lived west of the Appalachian Mountains. By 1860, following the great pioneer migrations to Oregon, California, and Texas, only about half of the population lived in the eastern part of the United States. Westward expansion inspired an upsurge of national pride and self-awareness.

**Trail of Tears** The tragic policy of "Indian removal," a result of westward expansion, resulted in the confiscation of tribal lands and the relocation of more than 100,000 Native Americans. On the 1838 Trail of Tears, for example, thousands of Cherokee perished on the trek from Georgia to Oklahoma, where the promise of freedom from white settlement would last for only about 15 years.



**1812:** The United States declares war on Great Britain; a treaty ends the war in 1814.

**1813: England** Jane Austen's *Pride and Prejudice* is published.

**1825:** The Erie Canal is completed, spurring canal building across the nation.

**1831:** Cyrus McCormick invents the mechanical reaper.

**1838:** Cherokees are forced from Georgia to Oklahoma Territory on the "Trail of Tears."

1840



## Integration of Knowledge and Ideas

Have students analyze the map and draw conclusions to answer the two questions.

**Possible responses:** The United States acquired land from France, Britain, Mexico, and Spain. The acquisition of land shows that Americans were intent on growing and becoming powerful and independent.

## Timeline

Tell students to examine the 1800–1870 Timeline, and to reflect on the key events.

Encourage a discussion by asking students how one event may have led to or influenced another. Ask students to discuss how improved transportation and communication may have influenced other events.

PERSONALIZE FOR LEARNING

### English Language Support

Help students to better understand the concept of *manifest destiny* by discussing the literal meaning of the phrase. Explain that *manifest* means clear or obvious and *destiny* refers to something fated or certain to occur. Guide students to understand that this phrase implies an indisputable right. Ask students how the literal meanings of the words may have influenced behavior associated with the concept. **ALL LEVELS**

## History of the Period (cont.)

Have students focus on the paragraph titled "A Flood of New Ideas." Point out that the concept of individualism led to the growth of democracy, and improvements in public education, women's rights, and the work of abolitionists. Encourage a discussion by asking students the following question: *How does the idea of individualism continue to make the United States a unique place to live?*

### HISTORICAL PERSPECTIVES • FOCUS PERIOD: 1800–1870

**On the Move** Travel was transformed in the nineteenth century by new methods and routes of transportation. The National Road, begun in 1811, reached St. Louis and the Mississippi River by mid-century. In 1860, nearly 1,000 steamboats were plying the Mississippi, and some 30,000 miles of railroad track had been spread across the nation. The lure of the West motivated this revolution in transportation, which created a bond between existing and new states.

**Coming to America** In the first half of the nineteenth century, hundreds of thousands of immigrants—mostly European—were arriving on American shores. By the 1850s, the number was in the millions. Pushed from home by hardships and revolutions, these people were lured by a land of opportunity.

**The Industrial Revolution** A machine called the cotton gin, which separated cotton fibers from seeds, invented in 1793, revolutionized American industry. By 1860, more than 1,000 factories, mainly in New England, were turning more than 400 million pounds of Southern cotton into cloth, which was then sold around the world. However, while factories boomed in the North, enlarging the job market for women and immigrants, slavery grew stronger in the South.

**A Flood of New Ideas** Buoyed by a sense of their power to improve society, Americans set out to reform what they saw as problems or failures. Voters demanded better schools and public education slowly began to expand. Reform movements sprang up in religion, in temperance, and in women's rights. All brought important changes, but the most revolutionary movement was the drive to end slavery.

**Slavery and the Civil War** States in the North had declared slavery illegal by 1804 and had begun the gradual emancipation of enslaved African Americans within their borders. By 1860, however, slavery was more entrenched than ever in the South. Out of a population of 31.5 million, there were four million enslaved African Americans and about 500,000 free blacks. In six states in the Deep South, the slave population accounted for approximately half of the total population.

Abolitionists—people who worked to end slavery—were black and white, Northern and sometimes Southern. They organized, preached, spoke, published newspapers, and wrote books. They also helped fugitives flee slavery via a network of secret escape routes into the North and into Canada, known as the Underground Railroad. As their actions intensified, they helped push the nation to the breaking point—the eruption of the Civil War. The war lasted for four years and remains to date the deadliest conflict in American history.

**Individualism in the Reconstruction Era** America emerged from the Civil War with many questions unresolved. Chief among these was how to guarantee the rights of millions whom law and tradition had previously treated as property rather than people. The Reconstruction Era that followed the war was a tumultuous period in which former slaves capitalized on their newfound freedoms, including sending a record number of African Americans into government. The period did not last long, however, as a backlash ensued that included widespread violence. Freedoms for African Americans were rolled back and the rights of individuals were quashed, as the gains of Reconstruction evaporated and the Jim Crow system became firmly established throughout the South.



### TIMELINE

1836

**1837:** Samuel F. B. Morse patents the telegraph.

**1845: Ireland** Potato famine begins, leading to massive immigration to North America.

**1849:** The Gold Rush begins in California.

**1850:** Nathaniel Hawthorne's *The Scarlet Letter* is published.

**1851:** Herman Melville's *Moby-Dick* is published.

### PERSONALIZE FOR LEARNING

**Strategic Support**

**Historical Timelines** Help students understand that the timeline's developer decides what events to include based on relevance to the topic being examined. Ask students: *Why do you think the developer of this timeline included certain international events?* Accept all reasonable answers. Students may suggest that these events put history in perspective and they show how international events affected the situation in the United States.

Divide students into groups, with students of different abilities working together. Ask each group to analyze the international events in the timeline and draw conclusions about their relevance to the U.S. events. Then, have a discussion to compare conclusions.

## Literature Selections

**Literature of the Focus Period** A number of the selections in this unit were written during the Focus Period and pertain to the expansion of the United States, the reforms of American society, and the actions of individuals who influenced its history and culture:

The Writing of Walt Whitman

The Poetry of Emily Dickinson

from "Nature" • from "Self-Reliance," Ralph Waldo Emerson

from *Walden* • from "Civil Disobedience," Henry David Thoreau

"Young Goodman Brown," Nathaniel Hawthorne

**Connections Across Time** A consideration of the importance of American individualism both preceded and continued past the Focus Period. Indeed, it has influenced writers and commentators in many times and places.

"The Love Song of J. Alfred Prufrock," T. S. Eliot

"A Wagner Matinée," Willa Cather

"Sweet Land of . . . Conformity?" Claude Fischer

"Reckless Genius," Galway Kinnell

"Hamadi," Naomi Shihab Nye

ADDITIONAL FOCUS PERIOD LITERATURE

**UNIT 1**
The Gettysburg Address, Abraham Lincoln

**UNIT 3**
"What to the Slave Is the Fourth of July?," Frederick Douglass

Second Inaugural Address, Abraham Lincoln

"Ain't I a Woman?," Sojourner Truth

Declaration of Sentiments, Elizabeth Cady Stanton

**UNIT 4**
"The Notorious Jumping Frog of Calaveras County," Mark Twain

**UNIT 6**
"The Tell-Tale Heart," Edgar Allan Poe



**1854: Japan** The Treaty of Kanagawa opens Japan to trade with the United States.

**1860:** Abraham Lincoln is elected the sixteenth U.S. President.

**1861–1865:** The Union and the Confederacy fight the Civil War.

**1865:** The Reconstruction Era begins in the South.

1870



DIGITAL PERSPECTIVES

## Literature Selections

Have students compare and contrast the genres of poetry and persuasive essay. Students may point out that poetry is rich with sensory images whereas persuasive essays often focus on abstract ideas or principles. Point out that these genres can effectively borrow from one another. For example, Walt Whitman's poetry contains rich imagery but also sets forth principles. Have students discuss how they might use elements of poetry in a persuasive essay and vice versa.

Have students review the selections in this unit organized under *Literature of the Focus Period* and *Connections Across Time*. Also point out the additional Focus Period Literature found in the Interactive Student Edition. Encourage them to utilize these selections for additional evidence as they complete the Performance-Based Assessment in this unit.

## Comprehension Check

Ask students to answer these questions independently and then to discuss them in a group.

1. How did the United States grow between 1800 and 1870?

**Possible responses:** The Louisiana Purchase from France added 828,000 square miles to the U.S.; Settlers expanded their settlements, taking over tribal lands and relocating Native Americans; Hundreds of thousands of immigrants arrived, mostly from Europe.

2. What factors led to increased immigration to the United States?

**Possible responses:** Westward expansion and the development of railroads, as well as the California Gold Rush and the Irish Potato Famine led to increased immigration to the United States.

3. What beliefs did Americans hold about themselves and their country between 1800 and 1870?

**Possible responses:** That they were entitled to settle America's lands (manifest destiny); that the rights of the individual were essential.

PERSONALIZE FOR LEARNING

### English Language Support

Ask students to identify unfamiliar idioms and phrases in the text. For example: *Trail of Tears, promise of freedom, lure of the West, land of opportunity,* and *face of labor.* Encourage students to use internet tools to find the meanings of these words and phrases, then use context to define each phrase. Have students keep a list of phrases and their meanings. **ALL LEVELS**

# The Writing of Walt Whitman

**AUDIO SUMMARIES**
Audio summaries of "The Writing of Walt Whitman" are available in both English and Spanish and can be assigned to students in the Interactive Teacher's Edition or Unit Resources. Assigning these summaries prior to reading the selection may help students build additional background knowledge and set a context for their first read.

## Summary

In "Preface to the 1855 Edition of *Leaves of Grass*," Whitman asserts that America "does not repel the past" but rather accepts that its greatest strength is its diversity. He believes the nation is "the greatest poem" in history because it is a welcoming, "teeming nation of nations." In "Song of Myself," the speaker celebrates himself and invites his soul and others to join him as he enjoys nature as one "well-built house." In "I Hear America Singing," the speaker hears the various songs of the workers who contribute to America's culture and rejoices in them. In "On a Beach at Night Alone," the speaker describes a mother and a daughter as they realize that all things in the universe are connected to them and to each other. In "America," the speaker describes the nation as a mother whose life is centered on nurturing her children.

### Insight

Individualism runs deep in the American character. Many writers from the early days of the nation through to the present have commented on the special contributions that individualism has made in the development of the nation. Much of Whitman's writing celebrates the role of the individual in our culture.

ESSENTIAL QUESTION:
What role does individualism play in American society?

## Connection to Essential Question

The preface to *Leaves of Grass* and poems of Walt Whitman presented here connect to the Essential Question, "What role does individualism play in American society?" All these writings glorify the importance of individualism in creating and shaping the uniqueness of American culture.

WHOLE-CLASS LEARNING PERFORMANCE TASK
How has my personal experience shaped my view of individualism? Do I see it as a guiding principle, something to be avoided, or a combination of both?

UNIT PERFORMANCE-BASED ASSESSMENT
What significant incident helped me realize that I am a unique individual?

## Connection to Performance Tasks

**Whole-Class Learning Performance Task** In this Performance Task, students will consider the question, "How has my personal experience shaped my view of individualism? Do I see it as a guiding principle, something to be avoided, or both?" The personal experiences that Whitman describes and praises serve as models for similar personal experiences that may have shaped students' attitudes toward individualism in their own lives.

**Unit Performance-Based Assessment** These selections from the writing of Walt Whitman offer numerous examples of experiences that relate to the idea that everyone is a unique individual with significant incidents that have shaped his or her character.

DIGITAL PERSPECTIVES

Audio

Video

Document

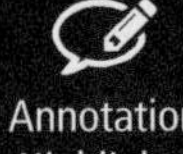
Annotation Highlights

EL Highlights

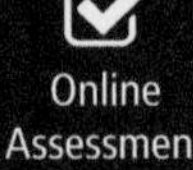
Online Assessment

## LESSON RESOURCES

| | Making Meaning | Language Development | Effective Expression |
|---|---|---|---|
| **Lesson** | **First Read**<br>**Close Read**<br>**Analyze the Text**<br>**Analyze Craft and Structure** | **Concept Vocabulary**<br>**Word Study**<br>**Conventions and Style** | **Writing to Sources**<br>**Speaking and Listening** |
| **Instructional Standards** | **RL.10** By the end of grade 11, read and comprehend literature . . .<br>**RL.1** Cite strong and thorough textual evidence . . .<br>**RI.10** By the end of grade 11, read and comprehend literary nonfiction . . .<br>**RL.5** Analyze how an author's choices . . .<br>**RL.9** Demonstrate knowledge of eighteenth-, nineteenth-, and early twentieth-century foundational works of American literature . . . | **RL.4** Determine the meaning of words and phrases . . .<br>**L.4.b** Identify and correctly use patterns of word changes . . .<br>**L.4.d** Verify the preliminary determination . . . | **W.3.d** Use precise words and phrases . . .<br>**SL.6** Adapt speech to a variety of contexts and tasks . . .<br>**W.3** Write narratives . . .<br>**W.3.e** Provide a conclusion . . . |
| **STUDENT RESOURCES** | | | |
| Available online in the Interactive Student Edition or Unit Resources | Selection Audio<br>First-Read Guide: Poetry<br>Close-Read Guide: Poetry | Word Network | Evidence Log |
| **TEACHER RESOURCES** | | | |
| **Selection Resources** Available online in the Interactive Teacher's Edition or Unit Resources | Audio Summaries<br>Annotation Highlights<br>EL Highlights<br>English Language Support Lesson: Oral Interpretation<br>Analyze Craft and Structure: Poetic Structures | Concept Vocabulary and Word Study<br>Conventions and Style: Diction | Writing to Sources: Narrative Account<br>Speaking and Listening: Oral Interpretation |
| **Reteach/Practice (RP)** Available online in the Interactive Teacher's Edition or Unit Resources | Analyze Craft and Structure: Poetic Structures (RP) | Word Study: Latin Combining Form *multi-* (RP)<br>Conventions and Style: Diction (RP) | Writing to Sources: Narrative Account (RP)<br>Speaking and Listening: Oral Interpretation (RP) |
| **Assessment** Available online in Assessments | Selection Test | | |
| **My Resources** | A Unit 2 Answer Key is available online and in the Interactive Teacher's Edition | | |

# Reading Support

| Text Complexity Rubric: The Writing of Walt Whitman | |
|---|---|
| **Quantitative Measures** | |
| **Lexile:** 1900; N/P; N/P; N/P; N/P **Text Length:** 322 words; 88 lines; 11 lines; 14 lines; 6 lines | |
| **Qualitative Measures** | |
| Knowledge Demands ①—❷—③—④—⑤ | Some historical knowledge demands. Students should be familiar with the historical period of the poems and essay. |
| Structure ①—②—❸—④—⑤ | Poems are written in free verse. "Song of Myself" has unconventional narration. The essay, "Preface to the 1855 Edition of *Leaves of Grass*" contains the use of ellipses instead of full sentences. |
| Language Conventionality and Clarity ①—②—❸—④—⑤ | Language is largely explicit and easy to understand with some occasions for more complex meaning. The selections contain mostly on-level vocabulary with a moderate amount of figurative language. |
| Levels of Meaning/Purpose ①—②—❸—④—⑤ | Meaning and concepts are mostly straightforward. The main purpose of the selections is to convey Whitman's celebration of freedom and individuality. "Preface to the 1855 Edition of *Leaves of Grass*" and "Song of Myself" are more complex and contain multiple levels of meaning. |

DECIDE AND PLAN

## English Language Support

Provide English Learners with support for structure and language as they read the selection.

**Structure** If students have difficulty following the narration in "Song of Myself" draw their attention to the use of *I*, *me*, and *myself*. Discuss Whitman's use of "Me" in section 14. Explain that he is referring to a deeper part of himself.

**Language** Students may get confused reading passages with figurative language, for example in Section 51, *The past and present wilt—I have fill'd them, emptied them. And proceed to fill my next fold of the future.* Ask questions to guide students to understand that these are figurative rather than literal phrases.

## Strategic Support

Provide students with strategic support to ensure that they can successfully read the text.

**Language** Discuss the meaning and use of the words *I, my, me, myself,* and *soul.* Ask students to read sentences in the first section with these words. Point out the use of the words as different parts of the speaker.

**Levels of Meaning/Purpose** If students have difficulty understanding the multiple levels of meaning in "Song of Myself," focus on individual paragraphs. Ask students to first state the events that happen. Then ask them to reread the section to determine what feelings or ideas are conveyed by the speaker's words.

## Challenge

Provide students who need to be challenged with ideas for how they can go beyond a simple interpretation of the text.

**Text Analysis** Ask students to explain the meaning of the selection "On The Beach At Night Alone." How does the speaker feel about his place in the world? How does his repetition of the word *all* help to emphasize the feeling that everything is connected? Ask volunteers to describe a time they felt connected with everything.

**Written Response** Have students add several lines to the poem "I Hear America Singing" in the style of Whitman. Encourage them to think of modern day professions or craftspeople to celebrate.

TEACH

## Read and Respond

Have students do their first read of the selection. Then have them complete their close read. Finally, work with them on the Making Meaning, Language Development, and Effective Expression activities.

# Standards Support Through Teaching and Learning Cycle

## IDENTIFY NEEDS

Analyze results of the Beginning-of-Year Assessment, focusing on the items relating to Unit 2. Also take into consideration student performance to this point and your observations of where particular students struggle.

## DECIDE AND PLAN

- If students have performed poorly on items matching these standards, then provide selection scaffolds before assigning them the on-level lesson provided in the Student Edition.
- If students have done well on the Beginning-of-Year Assessment, then challenge them to keep progressing and learning by giving them opportunities to practice the skills in depth.
- Use the Selection Resources listed on the Planning pages for "The Writing of Walt Whitman" to help students continually improve their ability to master the standards.

**Instructional Standards: The Writing of Walt Whitman**

| | Catching Up | This Year | Looking Forward |
|---|---|---|---|
| **Reading** | You may wish to administer the **Analyze Craft and Structure: Poetic Structures (RP)** worksheet to help students understand the epic sweep of the theme. | **RL.5** Analyze how an author's choices concerning how to structure specific parts of a text contribute to its overall structure and meaning as well as its aesthetic impact.<br>**RL.9** Demonstrate knowledge of eighteenth-, nineteenth-, and early twentieth-century foundational works of American literature, including how two or more texts from the same period treat similar themes or topics. | Ask students to list Whitman's poems, labeling each with the kind of poetic structure each poem reflects. Suggest they show how the structure influences the poet's meaning. |
| **Writing** | You may wish to administer the **Writing to Sources: Narrative Account (RP)** worksheet to help students write narrative text with vivid language. | **W.3.d** Use precise words and phrases, telling details, and sensory language to convey a vivid picture of the experiences, events, setting, and/or characters. | You may wish to challenge students to write a short poem in which they use sensory language to reflect on their feelings about a topic of their choice. |
| **Speaking and Listening** | You may wish to administer the **Speaking and Listening: Oral Interpretation (RP)** worksheet to prepare for class oral readings. | **SL.6** Adapt speech to a variety of contexts and tasks, demonstrating a command of formal English when indicated or appropriate. | Challenge students to add background music or photos to their presentations. |
| **Language** | You may wish to administer the **Word Study: Latin Combining Form *multi-* (RP)** worksheet to help students use *multi-* and create words that use this form.<br>Give students the **Conventions and Style: Diction (RP)** worksheet to understand how the poet projects his earthy tone. | **L.4.b** Identify and correctly use patterns of word changes that indicate different meanings or parts of speech.<br>**L.4.d** Verify the preliminary determination of the meaning of a word or phrase. | Suggest partners review each other's writing. Challenge students to use sensory language, as well as make use of onomatopoeia. |

## ANALYZE AND REVISE

- Analyze student work for evidence of student learning.
- Identify whether or not students have met the expectations in the standards.
- Identify implications for future instruction.

## TEACH

Implement the planned lesson, and gather evidence of student learning.

# TEACHING

## Jump Start

**FIRST READ** Prior to students' first read, ask them to share their thoughts about what diversity means in the United States.

## The Writing of Walt Whitman

How did Walt Whitman see the United States? How did he see his relationships with other people and his surroundings? Modeling these and other questions readers might ask will bring "The Writing of Walt Whitman" to life and connect it to the Performance Task question. Selection audio and print capability for the selection are available in the Interactive Teacher's Edition.

## Concept Vocabulary

Circulate among students as they rank their words. Remind them that they will find the definitions of these words in the side column beside each word's location in the text.

### FIRST READ

As they read, students should perform the steps of the first read:

NOTICE: Encourage students to use Whitman's comments and observations to help them understand his perspective on the concept of individualism.

ANNOTATE: Remind students to mark vocabulary and key passages. For example, in the author's biography, students will find several key points about his beliefs and the themes expressed in his work.

CONNECT: Encourage students to go beyond the texts and think about how the ideas about people, nature, and the world expressed in the texts connect with their own experiences and ideas.

RESPOND: Students will demonstrate their understanding of the text by answering questions.

Point out to students that they will perform the first three steps concurrently as they are doing their first read. They will complete the Respond step after they have finished the first read. You may wish to print copies of the **First-Read Guide: Nonfiction** and the **First-Read Guide: Poetry** for students to use.

**Remind students that during their first read, they should not answer the close-read questions that appear in the selection.**

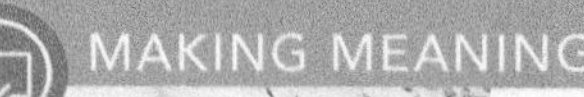


ESSAY | POETRY COLLECTION

## The Writing of Walt Whitman

- *from* the Preface to the 1855 Edition of *Leaves of Grass*
- *from* Song of Myself
- I Hear America Singing
- On the Beach at Night Alone
- America

### Concept Vocabulary

You will encounter the following words as you read part of an essay and a number of poems by Walt Whitman. Before reading, note how familiar you are with each word. Then, rank the words in order from most familiar (1) to least familiar (6).

| WORD | YOUR RANKING |
|---|---|
| ampler | |
| teeming | |
| vast | |
| breadth | |
| prolific | |
| multitudes | |

After completing the first read, come back to the concept vocabulary and review your rankings. Mark changes to your original rankings as needed.

### First Read NONFICTION and POETRY

Apply these strategies as you conduct your first read. You will have an opportunity to complete the close-read notes after your first read.

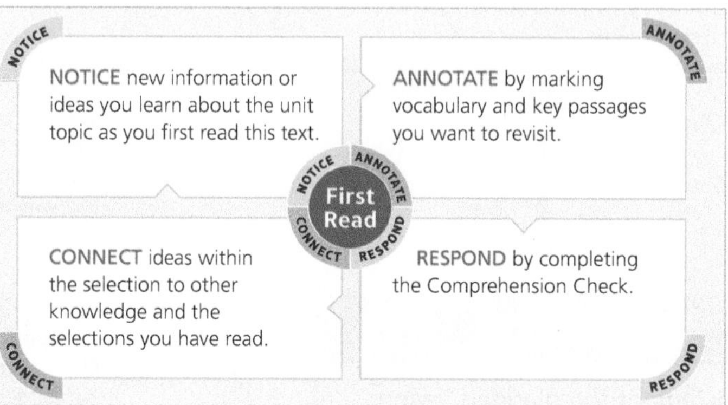

NOTICE
NOTICE new information or ideas you learn about the unit topic as you first read this text.
ANNOTATE
ANNOTATE by marking vocabulary and key passages you want to revisit.
First Read
CONNECT ideas within the selection to other knowledge and the selections you have read.
CONNECT
RESPOND by completing the Comprehension Check.
RESPOND


**Tool Kit**
First-Read Guide and Model Annotation

**STANDARDS**

**Reading Literature**
By the end of grade 11, read and comprehend literature, including stories, dramas, and poems, in the grades 11–CCR text complexity band proficiently, with scaffolding as needed at the high end of the range.

**Reading Informational Text**
By the end of grade 11, read and comprehend literary nonfiction in the grades 11–CCR text complexity band proficiently, with scaffolding as needed at the high end of the range.





AUTHOR'S PERSPECTIVE **Kelly Gallagher, M.Ed.**

**First Read Strategies** As students encounter unfamiliar and challenging text for the first time, some may hit a frustration point early. Students often think that if they don't understand something on the first try, then they will never understand. Comprehension when reading is not an all-or-nothing situation. Share these strategies for getting through the gray areas:

- ***Read on With Uncertainty*** Students who are "a little bit lost" may be able to read a little further to resolve confusion. Model this mindset with the opening paragraphs of a novel or long work. Read the text and show students what questions you already have. Demonstrate that many questions arise at the beginning as readers place themselves in the world the writer has created. Good readers can live with

DIGITAL PERSPECTIVES

About the Author

## Walt Whitman

Walt Whitman (1819–1892) was born on Long Island and raised in Brooklyn, New York. His education was not formal, but he read widely, including the works of Sir Walter Scott, Shakespeare, Homer, and Dante. Trained to be a printer, Whitman spent his early years working at times as a printer and at other times as a journalist. When he was twenty-seven, he became the editor of the *Brooklyn Eagle*, a respected newspaper, but the paper fired him in 1848 because of his opposition to slavery. After accepting a job at a newspaper in New Orleans, Whitman traveled across the country for the first time, observing the diversity of America's landscapes and people.

**A New Vocation** Whitman soon returned to New York City, however, and in 1850, he quit journalism to devote his energy to writing poetry. Impressed by Ralph Waldo Emerson's prophetic description of a new kind of American poet, Whitman had been jotting down ideas and fragments of verse in a notebook for years. His work broke every poetic tradition of rhyme and meter as it celebrated America and the common person. When the first edition of *Leaves of Grass* was published in 1855, critics attacked Whitman's subject matter and abandonment of traditional poetic devices and forms. Noted poet John Greenleaf Whittier hated Whitman's poems so much that he hurled his copy of *Leaves of Grass* into the fireplace. Emerson, on the other hand, responded with great enthusiasm, remarking that the collection was "the most extraordinary piece of wit and wisdom that America has yet contributed."

**His Life's Work** Though Whitman did publish other works in the course of his career, his life's work proved to be *Leaves of Grass*, which he continually revised, reshaped, and expanded until his death in 1892. The poems in later editions became less confusing, repetitious, and raucous, and more symbolic, expressive, and universal. He viewed the volume as a single long poem that expressed his evolving vision of the world, and in its poems he captured the diversity of the American people and conveyed the energy and intensity of all forms of life. Today, *Leaves of Grass* is regarded as one of the most important and influential collections of poetry ever written.

## Background

### The Writing of Walt Whitman

During the nineteenth century, American writers found their own voices and began to produce literature that no longer looked to Europe. Emerson, Thoreau, Poe, Dickinson—each contributed to a recognizably American style, but no one sounded as utterly American as Whitman. His style incorporates the plain and the elegant, the high and the low, the foreign and the native. It mixes grand opera, political oratory, journalistic punch, everyday conversation, and biblical cadences. Whitman's sound is the American sound. From its first appearance as twelve unsigned and untitled poems, *Leaves of Grass* grew to include 383 poems in its final, "death-bed" edition (1892). In the preface to the 1855 edition, Whitman wrote: "The proof of a poet is that his country absorbs him as affectionately as he absorbed it." There is little doubt that, according to his own definition, Whitman proved himself a poet.





this confusion because within a few paragraphs or pages, key ideas often become clearer.

- ***Monitor Comprehension*** To make their comprehension more concrete for students, have them use two different colors to mark the text: one color for text they understand and another color to highlight the text that is challenging to them. This will help pinpoint areas of confusion and show how much of the text they understand.
- ***Apply Fix-It Strategies*** Students who are struggling with comprehension may use fix-it strategies to start by rereading at the word level and decoding words they don't know. They can then move to the sentence level to make sure that they are following the text.

When students have the tools to monitor their comprehension, they may feel more empowered to get through their first read. Once they can get past the literal interpretation of text, they can then move toward uncovering deeper meaning.

ANCHOR TEXT | ESSAY

# *from* the Preface to the 1855 Edition of Leaves of Grass

Walt Whitman

## CROSS-CURRICULAR PERSPECTIVES

**Humanities** Have students each write a poem in blank verse expressing his or her concept of humanity, of civilization, or of the human race. Explain or remind students that blank verse does not rhyme and is written in iambic pentameter. This means that each line has ten syllables, one unstressed syllable followed by a stressed syllable. Encourage volunteers to read their completed blank verse poems to the class.

SCAN FOR MULTIMEDIA

1 America does not repel the past or what it has produced under its forms or amid other politics or the idea of castes or the old religions . . . accepts the lesson with calmness . . . is not so impatient as has been supposed that the slough still sticks to opinions and manners and literature while the life which served its requirements has passed into the new life of the new forms . . . perceives that the corpse is slowly borne from the eating and sleeping rooms of the house . . . perceives that it waits a little while in the door . . . that it was fittest for its days . . . that its action has descended to the stalwart and well-shaped heir who approaches . . . and that he shall be fittest for his days.

2 The Americans of all nations at any time upon the earth have probably the fullest poetical nature. The United States themselves are essentially the greatest poem. In the history of the earth hitherto the largest and most stirring appear tame and orderly to their ampler largeness and stir. Here at last is something in the doings of man that corresponds with the broadcast doings of the day and night. Here is not merely a nation but a teeming nation of nations. Here is action untied from strings necessarily blind to particulars and details magnificently moving in vast masses. Here is the hospitality that forever indicates heroes. . . . Here are the roughs and beards and space and ruggedness and nonchalance that the soul loves. Here the performance disdaining the trivial unapproached in the tremendous audacity of its crowds and groupings and the push of its perspective spreads with crampless and flowing breadth and showers its prolific and splendid extravagance. One sees it must indeed own the riches of the summer and winter, and need never be bankrupt while corn grows from the ground or the orchards drop apples or the bays contain fish or men beget children upon women. . . . ❧

NOTES

**CLOSE READ**

ANNOTATE: Mark details in paragraph 1 that relate to death and other details that relate to new life or rebirth.

QUESTION: Why does Whitman include these details? What is dying and what is being born?

CONCLUDE: What impression of America do these references create?

**ampler** (AM pluhr) *adj.* more abundant

**teeming** (TEE mihng) *adj.* full

**vast** (vast) *adj.* very great in size

**breadth** (brehdth) *n.* wide range; expansive extent

**prolific** (pruh LIHF ihk) *adj.* fruitful; abundant

## CLOSE READ 

Point out that although *Leaves of Grass* is a poetry collection, Whitman begins the collection with a prose preface. In it, he describes the essence of the United States, as he observed it during his travels. You may wish to model the Close Read using the following think-aloud format. Possible responses to questions on the Student page are included. You might also print copies of the **Close-Read Guide: Nonfiction** for students to use.

**ANNOTATE:** As I read the first paragraph, I notice and mark words that relate to death and rebirth. I can see that when Whitman uses the word "life" there is usually something about death in the same sentence or the following sentence.

**QUESTION:** I think Whitman includes these details to emphasize change, specifically the transformation from life to death to new life, and new forms of life. He seems to be describing the death of traditions and old ideas, the end of how things were done in the past, before America was established.

**CONCLUDE:** I can infer from these references that Whitman sees America as a new nation, free of past traditions. Instead of mourning what is passing away, he celebrates a new day.

## WriteNow Analyze and Interpret

**Essay** Review paragraph 1 with students. Have students each write a brief essay about why Whitman punctuated the first paragraph in such an unusual way. What positive and negative effects does this have on the reader? How would this preface change if Whitman had used more conventional punctuation?

ANCHOR TEXT | POETRY

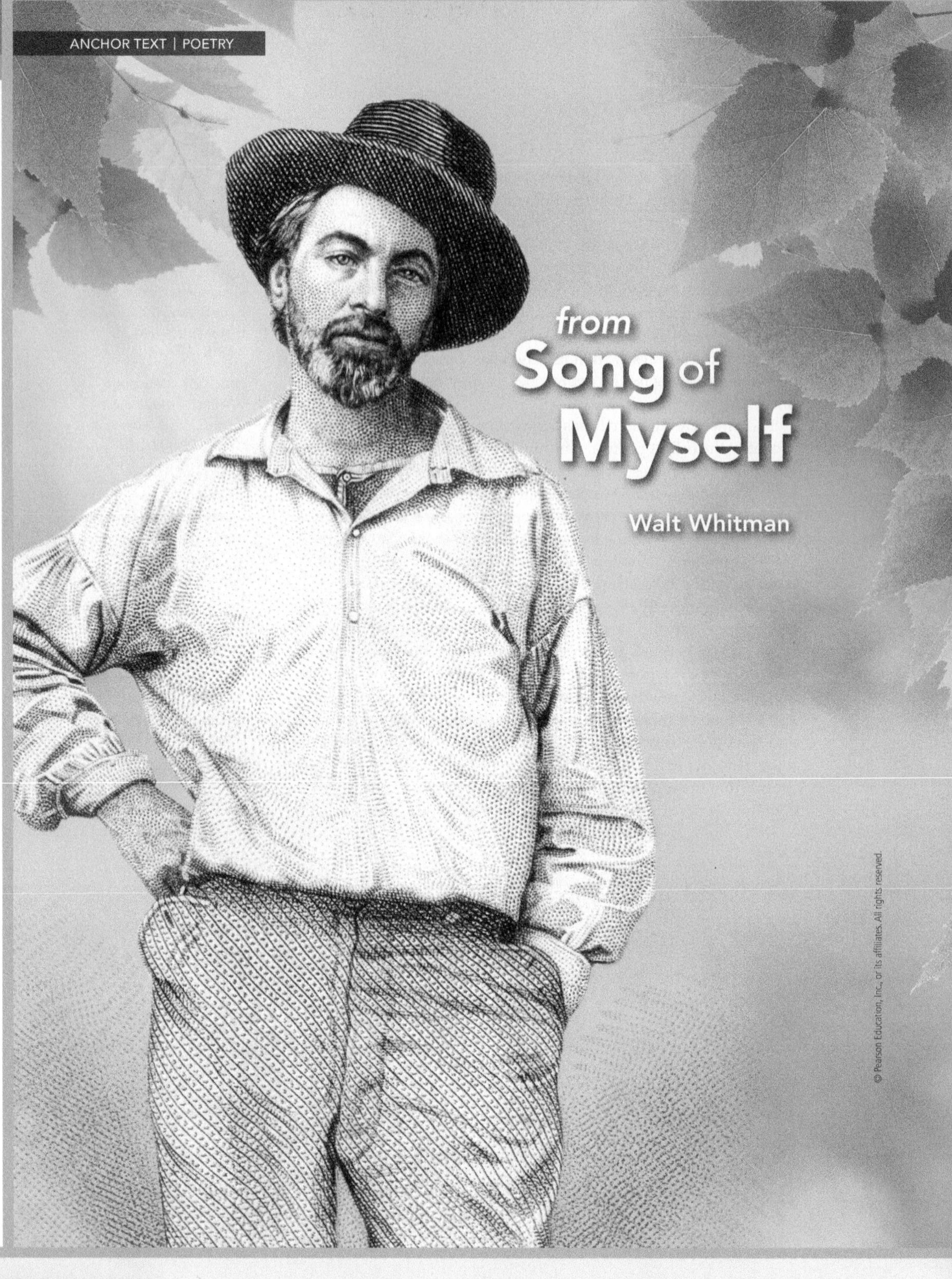

# from Song of Myself

Walt Whitman



## PERSONALIZE FOR LEARNING

### Strategic Support

**Vocabulary** Review section 1 with students. Invite students to skim the sections of "Song of Myself" and identify words and phrases that might challenge some readers, especially those who are building their English language skills. For example, in section 1, what does the phrase "Creeds and schools in abeyance" mean? The footnote defines *abeyance*, but not the entire line. (Possible response: "temporarily ignoring what one has learned in school and other places")

Students might work with partners or in small groups to identify unfamiliar terms and phrases, and discuss their possible meanings. Have them share their terms and discussion with the class. Gently correct any misinterpretations, or suggest that students check the definitions in a dictionary.

*1*

I celebrate myself, and sing myself,
And what I assume you shall assume,
For every atom belonging to me as good belongs to you.

I loaf and invite my soul,
I lean and loaf at my ease observing a spear of summer grass.

My tongue, every atom of my blood, formed from this soil, this air.
Born here of parents born here from parents the same, and
their parents the same,
I, now thirty-seven years old in perfect health begin,
Hoping to cease not till death.

Creeds and schools in abeyance,[1]
Retiring back a while sufficed at what they are, but never forgotten,
I harbor for good or bad, I permit to speak at every hazard,
Nature without check with original energy.

*6*

A child said *What is the grass?* fetching it to me with full hands,
How could I answer the child? I do not know what it is any
more than he.

I guess it must be the flag of my disposition, out of hopeful
green stuff woven.

Or I guess it is the handkerchief of the Lord,
A scented gift and remembrancer[2] designedly dropped,
Bearing the owner's name someway in the corners, that we may see
and remark, and say *Whose?*

. . .

What do you think has become of the young and old men?
And what do you think has become of the women and children?

They are alive and well somewhere,
The smallest sprout shows there is really no death,
And if ever there was it led forward life, and does not wait at the
end to arrest it,
And ceas'd the moment life appear'd.

All goes onward and outward, nothing collapses,
And to die is different from what anyone supposed, and luckier.

1. **abeyance** (uh BAY uhns) *n.* temporary suspension.
2. **remembrancer** *n.* reminder.

NOTES

**CLOSE READ**

**ANNOTATE:** In Section 6, mark the questions.

**QUESTION:** Why does Whitman choose to present these ideas as questions?

**CONCLUDE:** What is the effect of these questions?

## CLOSE READ

Remind students to focus on how Whitman uses words and sentence structure to convey meaning and mood. You may wish to model the close read using the following think-aloud format. Possible responses to questions on the Student page are included. You might also print copies of the **Close-Read Guide: Poetry** for students to use.

**ANNOTATE:** As I read section 6, I look for sentences that end with a question mark.

**QUESTION:** The questions seem to mark a transition in the poem, and they may cause the reader to pause and take notice. It could be the author's intent to make this part of the poem sound more like a conversation.

**CONCLUDE:** These questions help show how Whitman reached his conclusions and they also help him explain his beliefs. Combining statements with questions creates free verse that sounds like dialogue. The conversation is a thoughtful discussion that the speaker is having with himself.

## VOCABULARY DEVELOPMENT

**Word Analysis** Have students identify the words in sections 1 and 6 that contain the suffix *-ance*: *abeyance* and *remembrancer*. Remind them that the suffix *-ance* means "state or quality of." Thus, *resistance* is "the state of resisting." *Annoyance* is "the quality of being annoying." How might this help them determine the meanings of *abeyance* and *remembrancer?*

## TEACHING

NOTES

*9*

The big doors of the country barn stand open and ready,
The dried grass of the harvest-time loads the slow-drawn wagon.
The clear light plays on the brown gray and green intertinged,
The armfuls are pack'd to the sagging mow.

I am there, I help, I came stretch'd atop of the load,
I felt its soft jolts, one leg reclined on the other,
I jump from the crossbeams and seize the clover and timothy,
And roll head over heels and tangle my hair full of wisps.

*14*

The wild gander leads his flock through the cool night,
*Ya-honk* he says, and sounds it down to me like an invitation,
The pert may suppose it meaningless, but I listening close,
Find its purpose and place up there toward the wintry sky.

The sharp-hoof'd moose of the north, the cat on the house-sill,
  the chickadee, the prairie dog,
The litter of the grunting sow as they tug at her teats,
The brood of the turkey hen and she with her half-spread wings,
I see in them and myself the same old law.

The press of my foot to the earth springs a hundred affections,
They scorn the best I can do to relate them.

I am enamor'd of growing outdoors,
Of men that live among cattle or taste of the ocean or woods,
Of the builders and steerers of ships and the wielders of axes and
  mauls, and the drivers of horses,
I can eat and sleep with them week in and week out.

What is commonest, cheapest, nearest, easiest, is Me,
Me going in for my chances, spending for vast returns,
Adorning myself to bestow myself on the first that will take me,
Not asking the sky to come down to my good will,
Scattering it freely forever.

*17*

These are really the thoughts of all men in all ages and lands,
  they are not original with me,
If they are not yours as much as mine they are nothing, or next
  to nothing,
If they are not the riddle and the untying of the riddle they are nothing,
If they are not just as close as they are distant they are nothing.

This is the grass that grows wherever the land is and the water is,
This is the common air that bathes the globe.

Additional **English Language Support** is available in the Interactive Teacher's Edition.

### PERSONALIZE FOR LEARNING

**English Language Support**

**Comprehension** Review section 14 with students. Remind students that they do not have to understand every word or phrase in a poem in order to understand its main point. For example, read the last stanza in section 14 with them. Discuss what the narrator is saying about himself: He is common (ordinary) and cheap, takes chances, spends freely, adorns himself to try to be attractive to others, and wastes resources. He is not comparing himself favorably with others. Then encourage students to share what they think lines 18 and 19 mean: "Not asking the sky to come down to my good will, / Scattering it freely forever." Students probably will have several different interpretations, but poetry is meant to be interpreted in different ways by different readers. **ALL LEVELS**

### 51

The past and present wilt—I have fill'd them, emptied them,
And proceed to fill my next fold of the future.

Listener up there! what have you to confide to me?
Look in my face while I snuff the sidle of evening,[3]
(Talk honestly, no one else hears you, and I stay only a minute longer.)

Do I contradict myself?
Very well then I contradict myself,
(I am large, I contain **multitudes**.)

I concentrate toward them that are nigh,[4] I wait on the door-slab.

Who has done his day's work? who will soonest be through with his supper?
Who wishes to walk with me?

Will you speak before I am gone? will you prove already too late?

### 52

The spotted hawk swoops by and accuses me, he complains of my gab and my loitering.

I too am not a bit tamed, I too am untranslatable,
I sound my barbaric yawp[5] over the roofs of the world.

The last scud[6] of day holds back for me,
It flings my likeness after the rest and true as any on the shadow'd wilds,
It coaxes me to the vapor and the dusk.

I depart as air, I shake my white locks at the runaway sun,
I effuse[7] my flesh in eddies, and drift it in lacy jags.

I bequeath[8] myself to the dirt to grow from the grass I love,
If you want me again look for me under your boot soles.

You will hardly know who I am or what I mean,
But I shall be good health to you nevertheless,
And filter and fiber your blood.

Failing to fetch me at first keep encouraged,
Missing me one place search another,
I stop somewhere waiting for you.

3. **snuff . . . evening** put out the last light of day, which moves sideways across the sky.
4. **nigh** *adj.* near.
5. **yawp** *n.* hoarse cry or shout.
6. **scud** *n.* low, dark, wind-driven clouds.
7. **effuse** (ih FYOOZ) *v.* pour out.
8. **bequeath** (bih KWEETH) *v.* hand down or pass on.

NOTES

**CLOSE READ**

**ANNOTATE:** In Section 51, mark details that suggest the speaker is talking to a specific person or group of people.

**QUESTION:** Why does the speaker include these references? Whom is the speaker addressing?

**CONCLUDE:** What is the effect of this approach?

**multitudes** (MUHL tuh toodz) *n.* large number of people or things; masses





## CLOSE READ

Remind students to notice how Whitman uses language to focus the reader's attention. You may wish to model the Close Read using the following Think-Aloud format. Possible responses to questions on the student page are included.

**ANNOTATE:** I will look for details in section 51 that indicate the speaker is using direct address.

**QUESTION:** The speaker has reached his own revelation and is now addressing the reader directly.

**CONCLUDE:** The effect is that the reader is being urged forward with the speaker to heed his advice.

## DIGITAL PERSPECTIVES

**Enriching the Text** Challenge students to compare this version of "Song of Myself" with an earlier version, perhaps the 1855 original text. Have them locate similar passages in the two poems and examine the changes that Whitman made in the later version. Discuss whether these revisions change the meaning of the poem. Is the passage clearer in one of the versions? Can students feel a better connection to the poet and his ideas in one version? Why?

TEACHING

## CLOSE READ

Remind students to focus on the workers Whitman mentions in lines 2–8. Ask students how they think Whitman decided which workers to include in the poem. You may wish to model the Close Read using the following think-aloud format. Possible responses to questions on the Student page are included.

**ANNOTATE:** As I read lines 2–8, I notice that most of the lines name a type of work or worker. So, I will review each line to find all the kinds of workers that Whitman mentions.

**QUESTION:** The speaker is acknowledging a wide array of American workers. He is not speaking about jobs of wealth or prestige, but those of average Americans.

**CONCLUDE:** I think the speaker is acknowledging and praising these workers. He understands and appreciates their important contributions to the building of America.

Additional **English Language Support** is available in the Interactive Teacher's Edition.

ANCHOR TEXT | POETRY

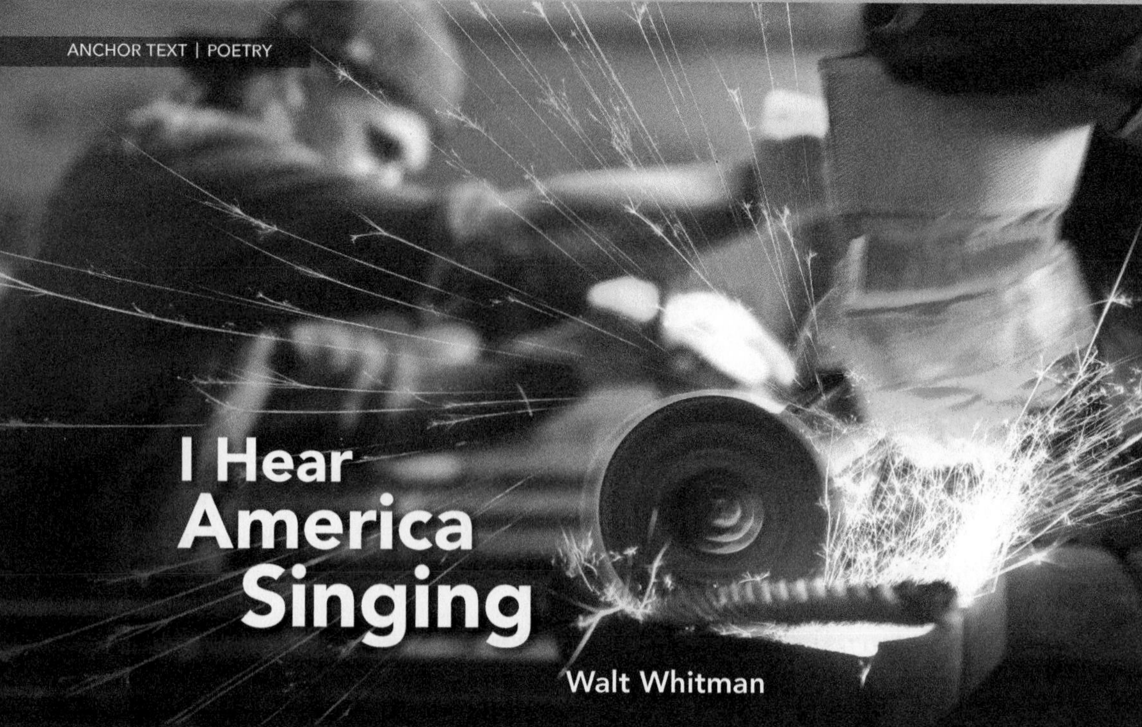

# I Hear America Singing

Walt Whitman

SCAN FOR MULTIMEDIA

NOTES

**CLOSE READ**

**ANNOTATE:** Mark the various kinds of workers mentioned in lines 2–8.

**QUESTION:** Why does the speaker name so many kinds of workers?

**CONCLUDE:** What is the effect of these references?

I hear America singing, the varied carols I hear,
Those of mechanics, each one singing his as it should be blithe and strong,
The carpenter singing his as he measures his plank or beam,
The mason singing his as he makes ready for work, or leaves off work.
The boatman singing what belongs to him in his boat, the deckhand singing on the steamboat deck,
The shoemaker singing as he sits on his bench, the hatter[1] singing as he stands,
The woodcutter's song, the plowboy's on his way in the morning, or at noon intermission or at sundown,
The delicious singing of the mother, or of the young wife at work, or of the girl sewing or washing,
Each singing what belongs to him or her and to none else,
The day what belongs to the day—at night the party of young fellows, robust, friendly,
Singing with open mouths their strong melodious songs.

1. **hatter** *n.* person who makes, sells, or cleans hats.





## WriteNow Express and Reflect

**Poem** Review lines 1–7 with students to discuss the types of jobs Whitman celebrates in this poem. Ask students to write a short poem related to one of the jobs mentioned in "I Hear America Singing." Poems might focus on any aspect of that job. Tell students they can write in free verse, as Whitman does, or use another poetic form. Provide time for volunteers to share their poetry.

ANCHOR TEXT | POETRY

# On the Beach at Night Alone

Walt Whitman

SCAN FOR MULTIMEDIA

On the beach at night alone,
As the old mother sways her to and fro singing her husky song,
As I watch the bright stars shining, I think a thought of the clef[1]
of the universes and of the future.

A vast similitude[2] interlocks all,
All spheres, grown, ungrown, small, large, suns, moons, planets,
All distances of place however wide,
All distances of time, all inanimate forms,
All souls, all living bodies though they be ever so different, or in
different worlds,
All gaseous, watery, vegetable, mineral processes, the fishes, the
brutes,
All nations, colors, barbarisms, civilizations, languages,
All identities that have existed or may exist on this globe, or any
globe,
All lives and deaths, all of the past, present, future,
This vast similitude spans them, and always has spann'd,
And shall forever span them and compactly hold and enclose them.

NOTES

1. **clef** *n.* symbol that is placed at the beginning of a line of written music to indicate the pitch of the notes.
2. **similitude** (suh MIHL uh tood) *n.* similarity or likeness.





DIGITAL PERSPECTIVES  

## CLOSER LOOK

### Identify the Theme

Students may have marked lines 1–12 during their first read. You may want to model a close read with the class based on the highlights shown in the text.

**ANNOTATE:** Have students mark the word repeated in lines 1–12 that helps them to identify the theme of this poem, or have students participate while you highlight it.

**QUESTION:** Guide students to consider what a reader can infer from the repetition of the word *all*. Accept student responses.
**Possible response:** The poet is stressing that everything—all planets, all distances of place and time, all living bodies—is connected.

**CONCLUDE:** Help students form conclusions about the importance of this repetition in the poem. What does it tell them about the theme?
**Possible response:** Whitman believed that everything, living or not, large or small, is connected. We are all one.

Remind students that Whitman often writes about this **theme** of interconnectedness. As he writes in "Song of Myself," "For every atom belonging to me as good belongs to you." Stress that identifying an author's perspective on life can help readers better understand and appreciate his or her work.

Additional **English Language Support** is available in the Interactive Teacher's Edition.

## PERSONALIZE FOR LEARNING

### Strategic Support

**Theme** Students may require support to identify the theme of a poem because it is often implied rather than explicitly stated. Remind students that a poem's theme is not its topic, but rather the "big idea" about life that the author is trying to convey. Have students create and complete T-charts. In one column, students should record any themes, and in the other column, they should record details that demonstrate or indicate the theme.

## CLOSER LOOK

### Using Punctuation 

Remind students to notice how Whitman uses punctuation, especially commas, to change the rhythm of his poetry and set off his ideas. You may want to model a close read with the class based on the highlights shown in the text.

**ANNOTATE:** Have students mark the punctuation in this poem, or have them participate while you highlight it.

**QUESTION:** Guide students to consider how the punctuation affects the tone and impact of the poem. Ask what a reader can infer from Whitman's use of commas, and accept student responses.

**Possible responses:** The commas give the poem a choppy feel, but also make it sound more thoughtful and passionate, like a stream of consciousness.

**CONCLUDE:** Help students to form conclusions about the importance of punctuation in "America." Ask why the author might have written these lines as a series of single words and short phrases.

**Possible response:** Perhaps Whitman used this series of words and short phrases to suggest his message instead of stating it explicitly.

Remind students that authors can use both words and **punctuation** to communicate. Whitman did not follow the usual rules for writing poetry—or nonfiction—but he used and presented words in new ways to create unique connections with his readers.

ANCHOR TEXT | POETRY

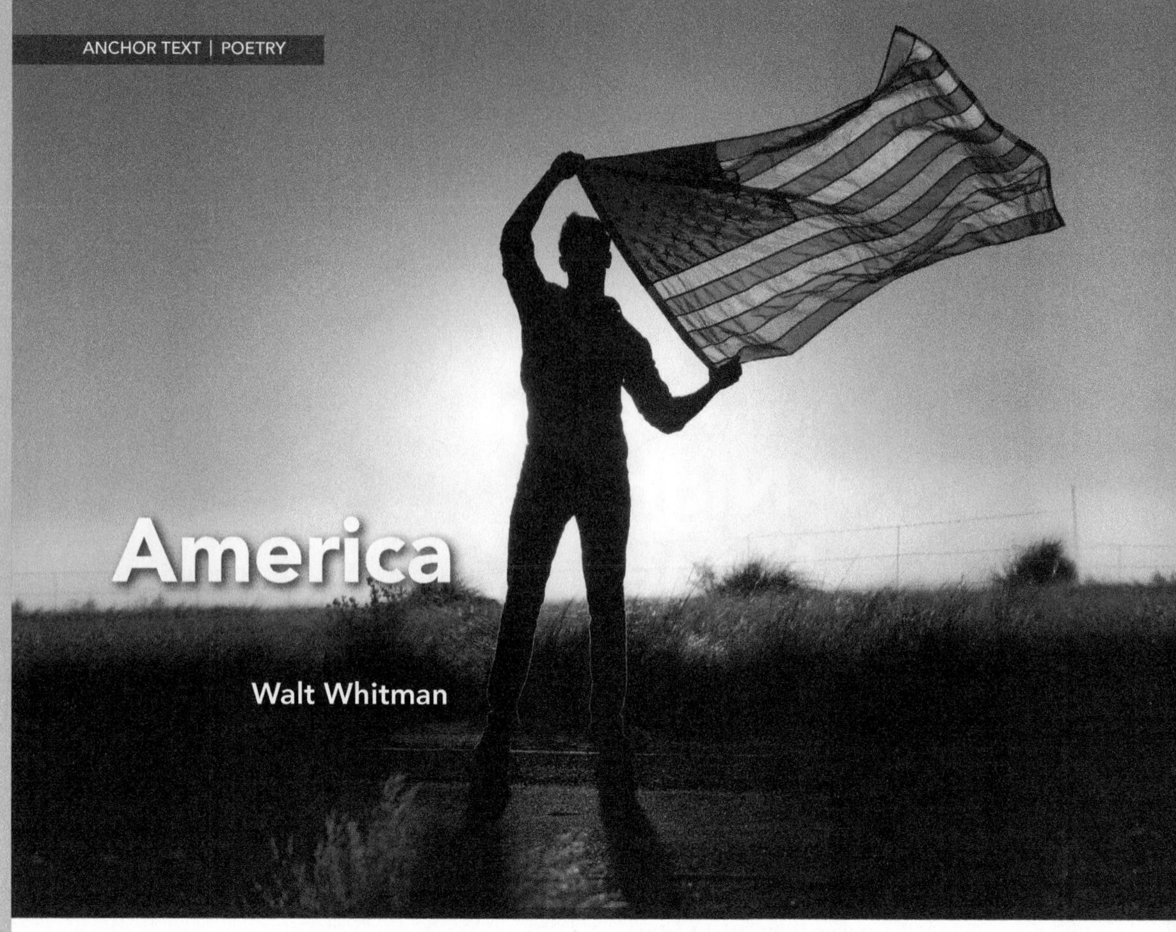

# America

Walt Whitman

SCAN FOR MULTIMEDIA

NOTES

Center of equal daughters, equal sons,
All, all alike endear'd, grown, ungrown, young or old,
Strong, ample, fair, enduring, capable, rich,
Perennial[1] with the Earth, with Freedom, Law and Love,
A grand, sane, towering, seated Mother,
Chair'd in the adamant[2] of Time.

1. **perennial** *adj.* enduring; consistently recurring or returning.
2. **adamant** *n.* legendary rock of impenetrable hardness.





## PERSONALIZE FOR LEARNING

### English Language Support

**Unusual Spelling, Punctuation, and Capitalization** Review lines 1–6 with students. Remind English Learners that poets and other writers often bend the rules of spelling, punctuation, and capitalization. For example, Whitman begins the poem "America" with the word *centre* which is the British spelling of the American English word *center*. Whitman also substitutes apostrophes for the letter *e* in the words *endear'd* and *Chair'd*. American English uses apostrophes to show missing letters, too, but this practice is restricted mostly to contractions, such as *don't*. Whitman sometimes also capitalizes words that do not begin a sentence and are not proper nouns. Ask students to point out some of these atypically capitalized words. (*Freedom, Law, Love, Mother, Time*) **ALL LEVELS**

## Comprehension Check

Complete the following items after you finish your first read.

1. In his Preface to *Leaves of Grass*, how does Whitman define America's attitude toward the past?

2. In Section 1 of "Song of Myself," what does the speaker celebrate and sing?

3. In Section 52 of "Song of Myself," what does the speaker "bequeath" to the dirt?

4. Cite three types of songs the speaker hears in "I Hear America Singing."

5. According to the speaker in "On the Beach at Night Alone," what connects all things?

6. In the opening line of "America," how does the speaker describe the nation?

### RESEARCH

**Research to Clarify** Choose at least one unfamiliar detail from the text. Briefly research that detail. In what way does the information you learned shed light on an aspect of Walt Whitman's work?

**Research to Explore** Conduct research to find out why Whitman was regarded as a revolutionary writer in his time.





DIGITAL PERSPECTIVES 

## Comprehension Check

**Possible responses:**

1. In Whitman's definition, America does not repel the past or what it has produced. It accepts the lessons of the past with calmness.
2. Himself
3. He bequeathes himself to the dirt.
4. Any three: mechanics, the carpenter, the mason, the boatman, the deckhand, the shoemaker, the hatter, the woodcutter, the plowboy, the mother, the young wife, the girl
5. A vast similitude, or similarity
6. The nation is described as a center of equal daughters and equal sons.

**Research to Clarify** If students struggle to identify a detail to research, you might suggest that they focus on free verse or one of the kinds of work mentioned in "I Hear America Singing."

**Research to Explore** If students have difficulty getting started, have them use this search term on the Web: *Walt Whitman revolutionary*. They will find extensive information.

### CROSS-CURRICULAR PERSPECTIVES

**Art/Music** Invite each student to choose one of Whitman's poems and either illustrate it or set it to music. If students choose a longer poem, they might focus on just one section of it. Encourage creativity! Provide time for students to share their work with the class and explain why they illustrated a poem the way they did or why their selection of music made sense.

## Jump Start

CLOSE READ Ask students to consider the following prompt: *How would you describe America? What is the essence of our nation?* As students discuss this prompt in their groups, ask them to compare their ideas with Whitman's description of America.

## Close Read the Text

Work with students on the annotation model and then have them complete items 2 and 3 on their own. When they have finished, review and discuss the sections that students marked. If needed, continue to model close reading by using the Annotation Highlights in the Interactive Teacher's Edition.

## Analyze the Text

Possible responses:

1. (a) Whitman means that the American people are very diverse. **DOK 2** (b) "Here," he notes, "are the roughs and beards and space and ruggedness and nonchalance that the soul loves." In "I Hear America Singing," he celebrates the diversity of American workers. **DOK 2**
2. (a) The speaker focuses on the urgency of the moment; details that relate to time include: "the past and the present wilt;" "fill my next fold of the future"; "I stay only a minute longer"; "I wait"; "before I am I gone"; "prove already too late" **DOK 2** (b) The speaker seems to want the listener to share the same sense of urgency, and in the face of time passing, express ideas with bold honesty, unafraid of contradictions. **DOK 4**
3. I won't be tamed or made to follow rules in expressing my ideas. **DOK 2**
4. (a) The "clef of the universes and of the future" is rephrased in the line "A vast similitude interlocks all." It is further developed by the other lines of the stanza, which provide examples of this connection across universe and time. **DOK 3**
5. Although Whitman celebrates himself as a strong individual, he also sees a cosmic connection between himself and all other Americans. **DOK 3**
6. Answers will vary, but should include references to Whitman's work.

### FORMATIVE ASSESSMENT

### Analyze the Text

- **If** students fail to cite evidence, **then** remind them to support their ideas with specific information from the text.
- **If** students struggle to analyze the poems, **then** discuss how to interpret or summarize a poem with them and illustrate with examples.



MAKING MEANING

THE WRITING OF WALT WHITMAN

## Close Read the Text

1. This model, from paragraph 2 of the Preface to *Leaves of Grass*, shows two sample annotations, along with questions and conclusions. Close read the passage and find another detail to annotate. Then, write a question and your conclusion.

ANNOTATE: The passage contains some repeated words.
QUESTION: What idea does the repetition emphasize?
CONCLUDE: Whitman emphasizes a "right now" picture of America.

Here at last is something in the doings of man that corresponds with the broadcast doings of the day and night. Here is not merely a nation but a teeming nation of nations. . . . Here are the roughs and beards and space and ruggedness and nonchalance that the soul loves.

Close Read (ANNOTATE, QUESTION, CONCLUDE)

ANNOTATE: This list juxtaposes concrete and abstract nouns.
QUESTION: Why does Whitman include these particular nouns?
CONCLUDE: He is painting a diverse and exuberant picture of America.

2. For more practice, go back into the text and complete the close-read notes.
3. Revisit a section of the text you found important during your first read. Read this section closely and **annotate** what you notice. Ask yourself **questions** such as "Why did the author make this choice?" What can you **conclude**?

**Tool Kit**
Close-Read Guide and Model Annotation

## Analyze the Text

CITE TEXTUAL EVIDENCE to support your answers.

Notebook Respond to these questions.

1. (a) **Interpret** In the Preface to *Leaves of Grass*, what does Whitman mean when he calls America a "nation of nations"? (b) **Connect** How does he develop that idea in "I Hear America Singing"?
2. (a) In Section 51 of "Song of Myself," what attitude toward time does the speaker express? Cite time-related details to support your answer. (b) **Analyze** What does the speaker seem to want of the listener? Explain.
3. **Summarize** What main idea does the speaker express in lines 2–3 of Section 52 of "Song of Myself"?
4. **Interpret** In "On the Beach at Night Alone," how does the second stanza state and develop the "thought" the speaker has in the third line of the poem? Explain.
5. **Historical Perspectives** The French political thinker Alexis de Tocqueville wrote that Americans are "always considering themselves as standing alone, [imagining] that their whole destiny is in their own hands." To what extent do you think Walt Whitman's writing illustrates that idea?
6. **Essential Question: *What role does individualism play in American society?*** What have you learned about American individualism from reading Whitman's writings?

**STANDARDS**
Reading Literature
- Cite strong and thorough textual evidence to support analysis of what the text says explicitly as well as inferences drawn from the text, including determining where the text leaves matters uncertain.
- Analyze how an author's choices concerning how to structure specific parts of a text contribute to its overall structure and meaning as well as its aesthetic impact.
- Demonstrate knowledge of eighteenth-, nineteenth-, and early-twentieth-century foundational works of American literature, including how two or more texts from the same period treat similar themes or topics.





PERSONALIZE FOR LEARNING

### English Language Support

**Main Idea** Explain that finding the main idea in a text means deciding what the author is trying to tell readers. Students must separate details and examples from the main thought. Have a volunteer read lines 2 and 3 from Section 52 of "Song of Myself" aloud, or read them yourself:

I too am not a bit tamed. I too am untranslatable,
I sound my barbaric yawp over the roofs of the world.

Review with students, if necessary, the meanings of unfamiliar words in these lines. Point out that the prefix *un-* gives them a clue that *untranslatable* means "not translatable." Help them understand that these lines are not about shouting from rooftops. They are about expressing your ideas freely without worrying about what others think. **ALL LEVELS**

## Analyze Craft and Structure

**Poetic Structures** Traditional epic poetry tells a long story about a hero whose adventures embody the values of a nation. Today, many readers consider *Leaves of Grass* an American epic because it expresses national ideals. Underlying the poem's diverse subjects is the constant echo of an **epic theme**—that all people are inherently equal and connected by the shared experience of being alive. Whitman uses specific poetic structures to establish a sense of epic sweep suitable for this theme.

- **Free Verse:** Unlike formal verse, which has strict rules, free verse has irregular meter, no rhyme scheme, and varying line lengths. It simulates natural speech. Free verse allows Whitman to shape every line and stanza to suit his meaning, rather than fitting his message to a form:

  *Do I contradict myself?*

  *Very well then I contradict myself, . . .*

- **Anaphora:** A type of rhetorical device, anaphora is the repetition of a word or group of words at the beginnings of successive sentences or sections of text. It creates a majestic tone and rhythm.

  *If they are not yours as much as mine . . .*

  *If they are not the riddle and the untying of the riddle . . .*

  *If they are not just as close as they are distant . . .*

- **Catalogue:** Whitman's use of catalogues, or lists, of people, objects, or situations evokes the infinite range of elements that make up human experience. "I am enamor'd," he writes,

  *Of the builders and steerers of ships and the wielders of axes and mauls, and the drivers of horses . . .*

### Practice

**CITE TEXTUAL EVIDENCE** to support your answers.

**Notebook** Answer the questions, and complete the activity.

1. (a) How does line 1 of Section 17 of "Song of Myself" express Whitman's epic theme? (b) How does "On the Beach at Night Alone" relate to this theme?
2. (a) Cite specific lines from Section 51 of "Song of Myself" that sound like natural speech. Explain your choices. (b) What does this speech-like quality suggest about the speaker's attitudes toward the listener and the topic?
3. (a) Identify at least one example of each poetic structure as it appears in the Preface or poems. (b) For each example, explain how it contributes to the expansive, epic-like quality of the work.

| POETIC STRUCTURE | EFFECT |
| --- | --- |
| free verse: The first three lines of "Song of Myself" | Each line alludes to the interconnectedness of all people. |
| anaphora: Who has done his day's work? Who will soonest be through with his supper? Who wishes to walk with me? | Repeating the word *who* emphasizes that the poet is seeking answers. |
| catalogues: The delicious singing of the mother, or of the young wife. . .or of the girl . . . | Listing many types of people and their songs emphasizes common experiences. |





## PERSONALIZE FOR LEARNING

**Strategic Support**

**Anaphora** Tell students that *anaphora* is from a Greek word that means "repetition." *Anaphora* simply means "the repetition of a phrase at the beginning of two or more lines of poetry in a row." Have students each write a simple poem, rhyming or not, using the same phrase to begin at least two lines. For example:

In the morning, . . .
In the morning, . . .
In the morning, . . .

**DIGITAL PERSPECTIVES** 

## Analyze Craft and Structure

**Poetic Structures** Discuss with students why a poet might choose to use free verse instead of meter and rhyming. What advantages and disadvantages does free verse offer? Help students recognize that while free verse offers many choices of expression, some readers expect poetry to have a more traditional poetic structure. For more support, see **Analyze Craft and Structure: Poetic Structures.**

**MAKE IT INTERACTIVE**

Have students write a description of their classroom, school, or community in free verse. Encourage volunteers to share their poems with the class. Then compare these poems with an expository paragraph on the same topic. How are they the same, and how are they different? **Possible response:** The poems and an expository paragraph would both describe the same topic, but the poem might include anaphora or cataloguing. Both forms could use figurative language. The poem will be written in stanzas instead of paragraphs.

### Practice

Possible responses:

1. (a) Whitman connects his own thoughts with those of all men in all ages and lands, emphasizing his epic theme that the experience of life links all human beings. (b) By constructing most of the poem as a catalogue, Whitman is able to be all-inclusive and universal in his statement in line five that a "vast similitude interlocks all."
2. (a) "Listener up there! what have you to confide to me?" / "Do I contradict myself?/Very well then I contradict myself." These lines sound almost like a conversation. (b) This quality suggests that the speaker is comfortable with both the reader and the topic.
3. See possible responses in chart on student page.

**FORMATIVE ASSESSMENT**

### Analyze Craft and Structure

- **If** students fail to identify an example of free verse, **then** have them look for any two consecutive lines in Whitman's poems. Remind them that free verse does not rhyme or have a regular meter, or beat.
- **If** students are unable to identify an example of anaphora, **then** direct them to section 17 of "Song of Myself." Lines 2, 3, and 4 begin with parallel structure, or anaphora.

For Reteach and Practice, see **Analyze Craft and Structure: Poetic Structures (RP).**

TEACHING

## Concept Vocabulary

### Why These Words?

Possible responses:

1. The ideas of abundance emphasizes Whitman's preoccupation with America's plenitude, variety, diversity, and vast potential for growth.
2. Other words include *masses, crowds, extravagance, riches, varied, all,* and *perennial.*

### Practice

Possible responses:

1. A pint is the ampler; it is double the measure of a cup.
2. Travel might be slow due to the large volume of traffic. Housing might be hard to find.
3. You would probably feel fearful because a raft is small and an ocean is so big.
4. He or she would want to point out his or her qualifications.
5. The person would need to write many songs.
6. Large numbers of people enjoy watching sports.

### Word Network

**Possible words:** *audacity, stalwart, ruggedness, opinions, untied*

## Word Study

For more support, see **Concept Vocabulary and Word Study**

Possible responses:

1. *Multiply* means "to find the product of."
2. Examples include *multiple*, *multiplication*.

### FORMATIVE ASSESSMENT

**Concept Vocabulary**

**If** students fail to see the connection, **then** have them use each word in a sentence and think about their similarities.

**Word Study**

**If** students misspell the root words, **then** have them check spellings in a dictionary. For Reteach and Practice, see **Word Study: Latin Combining Form *multi-* (RP).**

LANGUAGE DEVELOPMENT

THE WRITING OF WALT WHITMAN

## Concept Vocabulary

| ampler | vast | prolific |
|---|---|---|
| teeming | breadth | multitudes |

**Why These Words?** These concept words are used to describe abundance, even overabundance. Whitman believes that all people of all times are connected. As he writes in "On the Beach at Night Alone," a "*vast* similitude interlocks all." America is a "*teeming* nation of nations," Whitman declares, that "showers its *prolific* and splendid extravagance."

1. How does the concept vocabulary clarify the reader's understanding of Whitman's worldview?
2. What other words in these selections connect to this concept?

### Practice

**Notebook** Answer these questions.

1. Which is the *ampler* unit of measure: a pint or a cup? Explain.
2. Why might life in a *teeming* urban area be challenging?
3. How would you feel if you were set adrift on a raft in a *vast* ocean? Why?
4. Why might a job candidate emphasize his or her *breadth* of experience?
5. What would a songwriter need to do to be considered *prolific*?
6. Why do *multitudes* of people sometimes gather in sports stadiums?

**WORD NETWORK**

Add words related to individualism from the text to your Word Network.

## Word Study

**Latin Combining Form: *multi-*** A **combining form** is a word part that can be added to a word or to another word part—such as a root or an affix—to create a new word. The Latin combining form *multi-* means "many" or "much." In the word *multitudes*, it combines with *-tude*, another word-forming element that means "state or quality of." *Multitudes*, thus, means "the state or quality of being multiple or many."

1. *Multi-* is part of some words that relate to math or science. Write a definition of *multiply* that demonstrates your understanding of the combining form *multi-*. Check your answer in a college-level dictionary.
2. Identify and define two other words that include *multi-* and relate to math or science. Consult etymological references in a dictionary to verify your choices.

**STANDARDS**

**Reading Literature**
Determine the meaning of words and phrases as they are used in the text, including figurative and connotative meanings; analyze the impact of specific word choices on meaning and tone, including words with multiple meanings or language that is particularly fresh, engaging, or beautiful.

**Language**
- Identify and correctly use patterns of word changes that indicate different meanings or parts of speech.
- Verify the preliminary determination of the meaning of a word or phrase.





AUTHOR'S PERSPECTIVE **Elfrieda Hiebert, Ph.D.**

**Collecting Sentences** To help students become more adept with words, give them the experience of working with them. By studying sentences that use new vocabulary well, students can build their vocabulary strength. Encourage students to collect model sentences using two strategies:

- **Find sentences in the text.** Help students locate sentences that use new vocabulary, or have students identify sentences where word choice truly packs power into the text. Discuss how the words are used and have students emulate the writer by writing similar sentences.
- **Find sentences in online vocabulary resources** When students are learning new words, it is useful to see the word used correctly in a variety of contexts. Many online dictionaries provide contemporary and cross-curricular examples to help learners see the words in action.

There are several benefits of this approach. First, a study of words and the way they are used can help students appreciate and understand writers. Second, looking closely at vocabulary and the spectrum of related words can help students improve their own writing.

## Conventions and Style

**Author's Choices: Diction** Whitman's style is as individual and as revolutionary as his use of poetic structure. His **diction,** or word choice, features the following elements:

- **Variety of Types of Words:** Whitman's poetry features an exuberant blend of different types of diction.

| Simple: *wherever the land is and the water is* | Intellectual: *Creeds and schools in abeyance* |
|---|---|
| Sensory: *I shake my white locks at the runaway sun.* | Abstract: *Nature without check with original energy.* |
| Specific: *I loaf and invite my soul* | General: *I am large, I contain multitudes* |

- **Onomatopoeia:** Whitman sometimes uses sensory words that mimic the sounds they name.
  EXAMPLE: *I sound my barbaric yawp over the roofs of the world.*
- **Words in Pairs:** One of Whitman's favorite tactics is to use words in pairs joined by *and*. These pairings create a biblical cadence, assert the sacred quality of everyday things, and suggest a higher unity behind the diversity of life Whitman describes.
  EXAMPLE: *If they are not the riddle and the untying of the riddle they are nothing*

In the end, even Whitman's simple and specific words, such as *grass,* come to represent larger ideas, while his more intellectual or abstract words, such as *atom* and *multitudes,* come to take on an almost sensory weight.

### Read It

1. In these lines of Whitman's, mark specific or sensory words. Then, mark abstract or general words. Finally, identify words paired by *and.*
   a. All goes onward and outward, nothing collapses.
   b. The old mother sways while she sings her husky song.
   c. I roll head over heels and tangle my hair full of wisps.
2. Reread Section 14 of "Song of Myself." Identify two instances of onomatopoeia, two sensory words or phrases, and two abstract or general words.
3. Notebook **Connect to Style** In a brief paragraph, explain how Whitman's diction in "I Hear America Singing" makes his portrait of America seem comprehensive and fundamental, like a passage in scripture or an epic. Then, identify the shift in diction in the final line and explain its effect.

### Write It

Notebook Write three sentences in which you imitate Whitman's style of pairing words, using pairs of words from the list.

| sneakers | ocean | malls | stream | expand | data |
|---|---|---|---|---|---|
| sky | laboratories | pixels | laces | farms | channel surf |





DIGITAL PERSPECTIVES 

## Author's Style

**Author's Choices: Diction** As you review these examples of Whitman's diction with students, consider providing additional examples. For more support, see **Author's Choices: Diction.**

**MAKE IT INTERACTIVE**

Project line 1 of section 1 and line 13 of section 52 of "Song of Myself" from the Interactive Teacher's Edition and ask students to identify examples of words in pairs.

**Possible responses:**

- words in pairs: "I celebrate myself, and sing myself" (section 1, line 1); "And filter and fiber your blood." (section 52, line 13)

### Read It

**Possible responses:**

1. specific or sensory words: *sways, sings, husky, song*
   abstract or general words: *all, nothing, onward, outward*
   words connected by *and*: *head over heels / tangle my hair*
2. **Possible responses:**
   onomatopoeia: *Ya-honk, grunting*; sensory words/phrases: *taste the ocean or woods, sharp-hoof'd*; abstract or general words: *nearest, easiest*
3. **Connect to Style**
   **Possible responses:**
   Whitman formats each line and sentence similarly, and the structure gives the lines a quick and rhythmic pace. He celebrates the workers of America and their songs. The diction of the poem changes in the last line as the workers move from day to night.

### Write It

**Possible responses:**

I swim in the streams and in the ocean; Creation occurs on the farms and in the laboratories; I see the pixels, the data, as I channel surf.

## HOW LANGUAGE WORKS

**Word Choice** Explain that authors choose their words very carefully to convey a precise meaning and tone. Have students analyze the effect of the author's word choice in these lines from "Song of Myself."

| Phrases | Effect of the Word (possible responses) |
|---|---|
| section 9, line 3: the brown gray and green intertinged | creates an image of the interplay of colors in dried grass |
| section 9, line 6: one leg reclined on the other | suggests a person who is at ease |
| section 14: line 12: taste of the ocean or woods, | reminds readers of the scent and taste of saltwater and growing plants |
| section 14, line 13: wielders of axes and mauls | creates an image of a big, strong person |

**FORMATIVE ASSESSMENT**

### Author's Style

**If** students struggle with finding examples of onomatopoeia, **then** ask them to read several stanzas of "Song of Myself" aloud and listen for words that sound like what they name.
For Reteach and Practice, see **Author's Style: Diction. (RP).**

## Writing to Sources

Explain to students that when they write about an event that happened while they were working, they need to begin by providing background so readers can picture the scene and understand their attitude toward the event. This might include specific details about their surroundings and people involved in the event. Remind students to use sensory language, describing what they saw, heard, felt, smelled, or tasted. Encourage them to go beyond clichés, such as "dark as night" and "sing like a bird."

**Vocabulary and Style Connection** As students write their narratives, they should include several of the concept vocabulary words, as well as onomatopoeic words and sensory language. For more support, see **Writing to Sources: Narrative Account.**

### Reflect on Your Writing

1. Responses will vary. If students need support, discuss the difference between telling a story and sharing a reflection on the event.
2. Responses will vary. Invite volunteers to share some of the precise details and sensory language they used.
3. Responses will vary. Challenge students to offer examples of the varying diction they included in their accounts.
4. **Why These Words?** Responses will vary. Have students list specific words they have chosen to add clarity and interest to their narratives.

### FORMATIVE ASSESSMENT

### Writing to Sources

**If** students struggle to include specific details or sensory language in their narratives, **then** ask them to picture the scene in their minds and jot down what they see, hear, feel, smell, or taste. For Reteach and Practice, see **Writing to Sources: Narrative Account (RP).**

THE WRITING OF WALT WHITMAN

## Writing to Sources

In "I Hear America Singing," Walt Whitman vividly describes the work that various Americans do. His descriptions are full of **sensory language**—words and phrases that appeal to one or more of the five senses. Sight and hearing are the chief senses engaged in "I Hear America Singing." However, Whitman also appeals to touch, as when he refers to the carpenter who is measuring "his plank or beam."

**Assignment**

Using Section 9 of "Song of Myself" as a model, write a brief **narrative account** about something that happened to you while you were working. You may narrate an event related to household chores, homework, or an after-school job. Use precise details and sensory language to make your account vivid and interesting for readers. Be sure to include your reactions to the event and also your reflections on what the event revealed to you about yourself.

**Vocabulary Connection** Consider using several of the concept vocabulary words in your narrative account.

| ampler | vast | prolific |
|---|---|---|
| teeming | breadth | multitudes |

### Reflect on Your Writing

After you have drafted your narrative account, answer the following questions.

1. Does your narrative account both tell a story and share a reflection?
2. What sensory language did you use?
3. How much did you vary your diction?
4. **Why These Words?** The words you choose make a difference in your writing. Which words helped you make your narrative vivid and engaging?

STANDARDS

**Writing**

- Write narratives to develop real or imagined experiences or events using effective technique, well-chosen details, and well-structured event sequences.
- Use precise words and phrases, telling details, and sensory language to convey a vivid picture of the experiences, events, setting, and/or characters.
- Provide a conclusion that follows from and reflects on what is experienced, observed, or resolved over the course of the narrative.

**Speaking and Listening**

Adapt speech to a variety of contexts and tasks, demonstrating a command of formal English when indicated or appropriate.





### PERSONALIZE FOR LEARNING

**English Language Support**

**Oral Interpretation** Have partners choose a line or two from one of Whitman's poems that conveys an idea which is important to him—nature, the common man, America, and so on.

Ask partners to list any repetition or wording that helped them with meaning. Then have them work together to decide on Whitman's tone, or attitude toward his subject, and to select words and sounds they will emphasize. Have them practice reading aloud to each other. **EMERGING**

Ask small groups to identify repetition or other poetic devices or language that helped them determine meaning in lines from two of Whitman's poems. Then have them compare their choices: Are they similar? Different? How? Have them identify the poet's tone and decide how they will read the lines, including words or sounds they'll emphasize, gestures they'll use, and any other techniques to convey meaning to their audience. Then have students take turns reading the lines aloud. **EXPANDING**

## Speaking and Listening

**Assignment**
With a partner, prepare and deliver an **oral interpretation** of one of the poems by Whitman. As you prepare, discuss how to read the poem to preserve the flow of the lines and the excitement and expansiveness of the verse. Then, deliver your oral interpretation to the class as a whole.

1. **Choose a Poem** Together, review the poems by Walt Whitman in this section. Choose the one that appeals to you the most, whether for its themes or language.
2. **Analyze the Poem** Once you and your partner have chosen a poem, reread it carefully to analyze its structure and meaning. Decide whether you will present the text together in a choral reading or will divide it into parts for individual interpretation. Take a few minutes to discuss the level of formality and tone, or emotional attitude, you want to convey. In addition, consider how you will use your voices and gestures to emphasize meaning and demonstrate your interpretation of the poem. Together, mark up the text with notes that you can follow as you read for the class. Keep in mind that you should work together to build a single overall impression of the poem.
3. **Rehearse Your Presentation** Read the poem aloud, following the notes and presentation cues you have drawn up together. Pay special attention to the ways in which your reading can enhance Whitman's meaning. Consider how body language, including gestures, can contribute to the impact of your reading. Likewise, vary your volume and pace to make your reading as expressive as possible.
4. **Evaluate Partner Readings** After you have presented your oral interpretation and listened to those of your classmates, use a presentation evaluation guide like the one shown to assess what you heard.

PRESENTATION EVALUATION GUIDE

**Rate each statement on a scale of 1 (not demonstrated) to 5 (demonstrated). Be prepared to defend your ratings, using examples.**

☐ The speakers held the audience's attention.

☐ The speakers clearly conveyed the poem's main idea.

☐ The speakers used effective pacing and employed suitable volume, emphasis, and tone.

☐ The speakers used appropriate gestures and body language to emphasize aspects of the poem.

EVIDENCE LOG

Before moving on to a new selection, go to your Evidence Log and record what you learned from the writing of Walt Whitman.





PERSONALIZE FOR LEARNING

Have partners choose one of Whitman's ideas that appeals to them, find examples of it in his poetry, and then prepare to read their selected lines aloud. Tell them to prepare a short introduction to their presentation and practice their delivery, offering each other suggestions about tone, pacing, appropriateness of gestures, and so on. **BRIDGING**

An expanded **English Language Support Lesson** on Oral Interpretation is available in the Interactive Teacher's Edition. 

DIGITAL PERSPECTIVES

## Speaking and Listening

1. **Choose a Poem** If partners decide to base their presentation on "Song of Myself," encourage them to focus on only one or two sections of this poem.
2. **Analyze the Poem** Remind partners, if necessary, that if they decide to use choral reading, they will read their poem together. Have partners agree on and mark words and phrases to emphasize, where to pause, facial expressions that will complement the formality and tone, and so on. Point out that different partners might interpret a poem in somewhat different ways.
3. **Rehearse Your Presentation** Encourage partners to make changes as they seek to strengthen their presentation. They might also video record themselves and look for possible improvements. Have them use the Evaluation Guide to provide feedback to their partners prior to presenting to the class.
4. **Evaluate Partner Readings** Encourage students to make one supportive comment about each presentation.

For more support, see **Speaking and Listening: Oral Interpretation.**

Evidence Log Support students in completing their Evidence Log. This paced activity will help prepare them for the Performance-Based Assessment at the end of the unit.

### FORMATIVE ASSESSMENT

### Speaking and Listening

- **If** students struggle to decide how to interpret their poem, **then** have them list several possible interpretations and choose the one that appeals to them.
- **If** students struggle to add body language or gestures to their interpretation, **then** have them experiment (or watch other pairs) until they find gestures that feel comfortable to them.

For Reteach and Practice, see **Speaking and Listening: Oral Interpretation (RP).**

### Selection Test

Administer "The Writing of Walt Whitman" Selection Test, which is available in both print and digital formats online in Assessments.

# The Poetry of Emily Dickinson

**AUDIO SUMMARIES**
Assigning these summaries prior to reading the selection may help students build additional background knowledge and set a context for their first read.

## Summary

In "The Soul selects her own Society—" the speaker describes choosing a friend, rejecting others, and finally turning one's attention away from the world. In "The Soul unto itself," the speaker sees the soul as a person's deepest feelings, perhaps the subconscious. In "Fame is a fickle food," the speaker refers to fame as food, here today and gone tomorrow. In "They shut me up in Prose—" the speaker compares attempts to force her to write prose to a time when, as a child, she was locked in a closet to keep her quiet. In "There is a solitude of space," the speaker lists different forms of solitude, but concludes that the solitude offered by the immortal soul is the greatest of all. In "I heard a Fly buzz—when I died—" the speaker describes details she experiences at the moment of her death. In "I'm Nobody! Who are you?" the speaker asserts that fame is an inferior way of life.

### Insight

Dickinson's unique individuality found expression not only in the subject of her poems but also in their structure and form. Dickinson stresses the joys of being oneself while fighting the stifling conventions of society.

ESSENTIAL QUESTION:
What role does individualism play in American society?

## Connection to Essential Question

The poems of Emily Dickinson presented here connect to the Essential Question, "What role does individualism play in American society?" All these poems celebrate the value of the self as a means of achieving personal satisfaction and reflect the notion that individualism is an essential characteristic of American culture.

WHOLE-CLASS LEARNING PERFORMANCE TASK
How has my personal experience shaped my view of individualism? Do I see it as a guiding principle, something to be avoided, or a combination of both?

UNIT PERFORMANCE-BASED ASSESSMENT
What significant incident helped me realize that I am a unique individual?

## Connection to Performance Tasks

**Whole-Class Learning Performance Task** In this Performance Task, students will consider the question, "How has my personal experience shaped my view of individualism? Do I see it as a guiding principle, something to be avoided, or both?" The personal experiences that Dickinson describes result from introspection about the meaning of her life and observations about how society often is a confining and oppressive force. Dickinson's insights may help students identify and evaluate their own attitudes toward individualism.

**Unit Performance-Based Assessment** These poems by Emily Dickinson offer a range of examples that demonstrate how small incidents and observations may, upon reflection, help shape a person's view of his or her own uniqueness as an individual.

DIGITAL PERSPECTIVES

 Audio  Video  Document  Annotation Highlights  EL Highlights 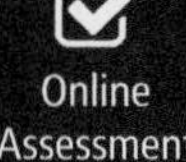 Online Assessment

## LESSON RESOURCES

| | Making Meaning | Language Development | Effective Expression |
|---|---|---|---|
| Lesson | **First Read**<br>**Close Read**<br>**Analyze the Text**<br>**Analyze Craft and Structure** | **Concept Vocabulary**<br>**Word Study**<br>**Conventions and Style** | **Writing to Sources**<br>**Speaking and Listening** |
| Instructional Standards | **RL.10** By the end of grade 11, read and comprehend literature . . .<br>**RL.5** Analyze how an author's choices . . .<br>**RL.4** Determine the meaning of words and phrases . . . | **L.4.b** Identify and correctly use patterns of word changes . . .<br>**L.4.c** Consult general and specialized reference materials . . .<br>**L.5** Demonstrate understanding of figurative language . . . | **RL.7** Analyze multiple interpretations of a story . . .<br>**W.3** Write narratives . . .<br>**W.3.d** Use precise words and phrases . . .<br>**SL.1.c** Propel conversations . . .<br>**SL.6** Adapt speech to a variety of contexts and tasks . . . |
| **STUDENT RESOURCES** | | | |
| Available online in the Interactive Student Edition or Unit Resources | Selection Audio<br>First-Read Guide: Poetry<br>Close-Read Guide: Poetry | Word Network | Evidence Log |
| **TEACHER RESOURCES** | | | |
| **Selection Resources**<br>Available online in the Interactive Teacher's Edition or Unit Resources | Audio Summaries<br>Annotation Highlights<br>EL Highlights<br>English Language Support Lesson: Text Messages<br>Analyze Craft and Structure: Poetic Structure and Style | Concept Vocabulary and Word Study<br>Conventions and Style: Parts of Speech | Writing to Sources: Blog Post<br>Speaking and Listening: Readings |
| **Reteach/Practice (RP)**<br>Available online in the Interactive Teacher's Edition or Unit Resources | Analyze Craft and Structure: Poetic Structure and Style (RP) | Word Study: Word Derivations (RP)<br>Conventions and Style: Parts of Speech (RP) | Writing to Sources: Blog Post (RP)<br>Speaking and Listening: Readings (RP) |
| **Assessment**<br>Available online in Assessments | Selection Test | | |
| **My Resources** | A Unit 2 Answer Key is available online and in the Interactive Teacher's Edition | | |

# Reading Support

| Text Complexity Rubric: The Poetry of Emily Dickinson | |
|---|---|
| **Quantitative Measures** | |
| **Lexile:** NP; NP; NP; NP; NP; NP; NP **Text Length:** 12 lines; 8 lines; 10 lines; 12 lines; 8 lines; 16 lines; 8 lines | |
| **Qualitative Measures** | |
| Knowledge Demands<br>1—2—**3**—4—5 | Poems explore complex themes of the self and death. Concepts are often obscure and may be difficult to grasp. |
| Structure<br>1—**2**—3—4—5 | Most poems are written in conventional iambic meter with heavy use of dashes to interrupt flow and force reader to pause. |
| Language Conventionality and Clarity<br>1—2—**3**—4—5 | The poems contain mostly on-level vocabulary with significant use of figurative language including simile, metaphor, personification, and heavy use of imagery. |
| Levels of Meaning/Purpose<br>1—2—3—**4**—5 | Ideas are complex but relate to universal experiences. |

DECIDE AND PLAN

## English Language Support

Provide English Learners with support for language and meaning as they read the selection.

**Language** Students may need help not only with the metaphors and similes, but with the structure of the language and the vocabulary. For example, in "Fame is a fickle food," make sure students know that the word *fickle* means "likely to change."

**Meaning** Work with students to help them understand the meaning of metaphors. For example, explain that in "They shut me up in Prose—," the speaker is comparing her brain to a caged bird. *Still! Could themself have peeped—and seen my Brain—go round—They might as wise have lodged a Bird For Treason—in the Pound—*

## Strategic Support

Provide students with strategic support to ensure that they can successfully read the text.

**Language** Remind students that, they may find that the metaphors and similes in the poems that do not have clear meanings. Give an example and work through together any difficult language.

**Meaning** Have students who have difficulty understanding metaphors and similes, mark phrases they don't understand. Then have them work with a partner to try to figure out the comparison the poet is making.

## Challenge

Provide students who need to be challenged with ideas for how they can go beyond a simple interpretation of the text.

**Text Analysis** Ask students to make a list of all the metaphors and similes they find in one of the poems. Pair students and have one say a simile or metaphor and the other describe the image conveyed by these words.

**Written Response** In the poem "They shut me up in Prose—," the speaker repeatedly refers to "they." Ask students to write an essay about who "they" is and why "they" want to control the speaker.

TEACH

## Read and Respond

Have students do their first read of the selection. Then have them complete their close read. Finally, work with them on the Making Meaning, Language Development, and Effective Expression activities.

# Standards Support Through Teaching and Learning Cycle

## IDENTIFY NEEDS

Analyze results of the Beginning-of-Year Assessment, focusing on the items relating to Unit 2. Also take into consideration student performance to this point and your observations of where particular students struggle.

## DECIDE AND PLAN

- If students have performed poorly on items matching these standards, then provide selection scaffolds before assigning them the on-level lesson provided in the Student Edition.
- If students have done well on the Beginning-of-Year Assessment, then challenge them to keep progressing and learning by giving them opportunities to practice the skills in depth.
- Use the Selection Resources listed on the Planning pages for "The Poetry of Emily Dickinson" to help students continually improve their ability to master the standards.

**Instructional Standards: "The Poetry of Emily Dickinson"**

| | Catching Up | This Year | Looking Forward |
|---|---|---|---|
| **Reading** | You may wish to administer the **Analyze Craft and Structure: Poetic Structure and Style (RP)** worksheet to help students understand how all the elements work together to create a surprise or unexpected emotion at the end of a poem. | **RL.5** Analyze how an author's choices concerning how to structure specific parts of a text contribute to its overall structure and meaning as well as its aesthetic impact. | Suggest that students find at least two examples of paradox in Dickinson's poems—such as "finite infinity." Then create paradoxes with other nouns that connote deep feeling. |
| **Writing** | You may wish to administer the **Writing to Sources: Blog Post (RP)** worksheet to help students describe personal events that communicate deep feelings. | **W.3.d** Use precise words and phrases, telling details, and sensory language to convey a vivid picture of the experiences, events, setting, and/or characters. | Challenge students to consider the blog and a Dickinson poem. Have them write a review in which they explain which form—the blog or poem—best achieves its purpose. |
| **Speaking and Listening** | You may wish to administer the **Speaking and Listening: Readings (RP)** worksheet to help students express how oral presentations evoke aesthetic responses. | **SL.6** Adapt speech to a variety of contexts and tasks, demonstrating a command of formal English when indicated or appropriate. | Ask students to identify the speaker's tone in one of the Dickinson poems, and be prepared to discuss the tone in small groups. |
| **Language** | You may wish to administer the **Conventions and Style: Parts of Speech (RP)** worksheet to help students understand the poet's use of concrete nouns to describe an abstract concept. | **RL.5** Identify and correctly use patterns of word changes that indicate different meanings or parts of speech. | Challenge students to write a paragraph that connects unlike nouns to a common theme such as<br>• things are not always as they appear<br>• time flies<br>• look before you leap<br>• treat others as you want to be treated |

## ANALYZE AND REVISE

- Analyze student work for evidence of student learning.
- Identify whether or not students have met the expectations in the standards.
- Identify implications for future instruction.

## TEACH

Implement the planned lesson, and gather evidence of student learning.

## Jump Start

**FIRST READ** Why does a good metaphor stick with us? Ask students to recall any metaphors they are familiar with. Suggest that they think about popular songs, books, poems, and even dialogue in films. Engage students in a discussion about why some metaphors are memorable. Suggest that metaphors get at "truth" in a new way and ask students to discuss whether this rings true to them.

## Concept Vocabulary

Circulate among students as they rank their words. Remind them that they will find the definitions of these words in the side column beside each word's location in the text.

### FIRST READ

The first time they go through the selection, students should perform the steps of the first read:

NOTICE: You may want to encourage students to notice which of Dickinson's poems tell a story or crystalize a moment in the speaker's life and which cannot be categorized in this way.

ANNOTATE: Remind students to mark passages that contain figurative language that may require analysis for better comprehension.

CONNECT: Encourage students to go beyond the text to make connections between how Dickinson writes about concepts such as the soul, fame, and captivity and how they usually think about these concepts.

RESPOND: Students will demonstrate their understanding of the text by answering questions.

Point out to students that they will perform the first three steps concurrently as they are doing their first read. They will complete the Respond step after they have finished the first read. You may wish to print copies of the **First-Read Guide: Poetry** for students to use.

**Remind students that during their first read, they should not answer the close-read questions that appear in the selection.**

MAKING MEANING

POETRY COLLECTION

# The Poetry of Emily Dickinson

- The Soul selects her own Society –
- The Soul unto itself
- Fame is a fickle food
- They shut me up in Prose –
- There is a solitude of space
- I heard a Fly buzz – when I died –
- I'm Nobody! Who are you?

## Concept Vocabulary

You will encounter the following words as you read these poems by Emily Dickinson. Before reading, note how familiar you are with each word. Then, rank the words in order, from most familiar (1) to least familiar (5).

| WORD | YOUR RANKING |
|---|---|
| emperor | |
| imperial | |
| treason | |
| sovereign | |
| captivity | |

After completing the first read, come back to the concept vocabulary and review your rankings. Mark changes to your original rankings as needed.

## First Read POETRY

Apply these strategies as you conduct your first read. You will have an opportunity to complete the close-read notes after your first read.

**Tool Kit**
First-Read Guide and Model Annotation

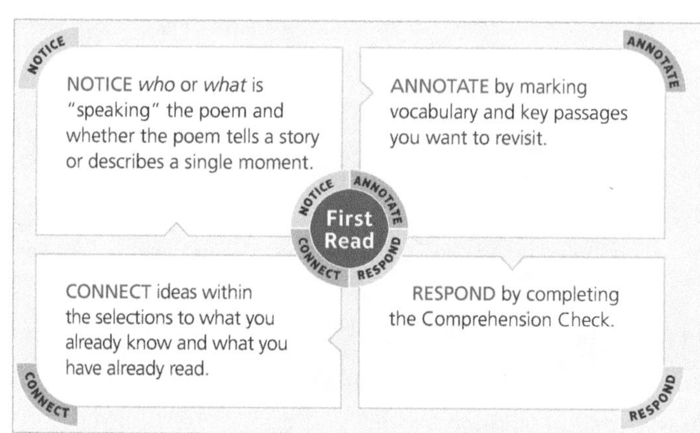

NOTICE
NOTICE *who* or *what* is "speaking" the poem and whether the poem tells a story or describes a single moment.
ANNOTATE
ANNOTATE by marking vocabulary and key passages you want to revisit.
First Read
CONNECT ideas within the selections to what you already know and what you have already read.
RESPOND by completing the Comprehension Check.
CONNECT
RESPOND


STANDARDS
**Reading Literature**
By the end of grade 11, read and comprehend literature, including stories, dramas, and poems, in the grades 11–CCR text complexity band proficiently, with scaffolding as needed at the high end of the range.





### PERSONALIZE FOR LEARNING

**English Language Support**

**Figurative Language** Help students comprehend figurative language by proposing the following strategy. Have students note lines that contain metaphors, similes, and/or personification that they do not understand. Then, have students identify and look up definitions of any unfamiliar words used in this figurative language. Finally, have students use the definitions and context to help them figure out the meanings of the metaphors, providing support where needed.
**ALL LEVELS**

About the Poet

## Emily Dickinson

Emily Dickinson (1830–1886) wrote nearly two thousand poems with a unique voice of lyrical intensity. Dickinson is invariably named as one of our nation's greatest poets. Yet in her own lifetime, only a small circle of friends and relatives knew of Dickinson's poetic genius.

**A Life Apart** Born into a prominent family in Amherst, Massachusetts, Dickinson attended Amherst Academy and nearby Mount Holyoke Female Seminary. As a teenager she had an active social life, but over time she became increasingly reclusive, rarely venturing from her home after she was thirty. Devoting most of her time to writing poetry, she saw only the occasional visitor and communicated with friends and family mainly through letters.

**Insecure Genius** Uncertain about her abilities, in 1862 Dickinson sent four poems to the influential literary critic Thomas Wentworth Higginson. With the poems she enclosed a card in which she asked, "Are you too deeply occupied to say if my verse is alive?" Higginson recognized her talent and encouraged her to keep writing.

**Dickinson's Legacy** Although she sometimes enclosed poetry in letters, Dickinson published only a handful of her poems in her lifetime. When she died, her sister Lavinia found more than one thousand poems in the drawers of Dickinson's dresser, neatly tied in bundles known as fascicles. Dickinson left instructions that the poems be destroyed, but her family overrode that wish, recognizing that such a valuable legacy should be shared.

**The Belle of Amherst** In the years since the publication of her work, Dickinson has become the subject of plays, novels, and poems that have romanticized her life and celebrated her genius with varying levels of sentimentality and accuracy. In these works, Dickinson has been given a public personality that may or may not resemble the truth of who she was. However, in her poems, the writers who have followed her find no peer.



## Background

### The Poetry of Emily Dickinson

Unfortunately, Dickinson's early editors, including Thomas Wentworth Higginson, diminished the power of Dickinson's verse by changing it to be more conventional in language and style. Higginson was especially concerned by Dickinson's unorthodox use of dashes and capitalization. He failed to recognize that Dickinson crafted her poems with great precision and that eccentric capitalization and punctuation were important elements in her poetry.

When Thomas H. Johnson came out with his edition of Emily Dickinson's poetry in 1955, he restored original elements, including the dashes and capital letters, so that today we can read the poems as Dickinson meant them to be read. With the appearance of the Johnson edition, appreciation for Dickinson's poetic genius blossomed, and she is now acknowledged as a visionary who was far ahead of her time.

## The Poetry of Emily Dickinson

What societal pressures may make people feel stifled? What is freedom? What does it take for a person's spirit to feel free? Modeling these and other questions readers might ask will bring Emily Dickinson's poems to life and connect them to the Performance Task question. Selection audio and print capability for the selection are available in the Interactive Teacher's Edition.

## PERSONALIZE FOR LEARNING

### Strategic Support

**Theme** If students struggle to see common or related themes in the poems, have students pair up to discuss their interpretations of the poems, agreeing upon and noting one or more themes for each poem. Then, have students determine the relationship between the poems. **EXPANDING**

# TEACHING

## CLOSER LOOK

### Interpret Personification

Students may have marked lines 1–4 during their first read. Use this first stanza to help students understand Dickinson's use of personification to give the "soul" human attributes and to make a larger point about human nature. Encourage them to talk about the annotations that they marked. You may want to model a close read with the class based on the highlights shown in the text.

**ANNOTATE:** Have students mark details in the first stanza that demonstrate personification, or have students participate while you highlight them.

**QUESTION:** Guide students to consider what these details might tell them. Ask what a reader can infer from the soul's actions of selecting a society, closing a door, and no longer being present, and accept student responses.
**Possible response:** These details imply a lack of concern for, or interest in, the opinions and cares of society as a whole.

**CONCLUDE:** Help students to formulate conclusions about the importance of these details in the text. Ask students why the author might have included these details, and accept student responses.
**Possible response:** The author uses personification to portray a certain detachment in the choices the Soul makes.

Remind students that **personification** is a figure of speech in which a thing, an idea, or an animal is given human attributes. Personification can make descriptions of nonhuman things or ideas more vivid, or can help readers better relate to the thing or idea being described.

Additional **English Language Support** is available in the Interactive Teacher's Edition.

SCAN FOR MULTIMEDIA

NOTES

**emperor** (EHM puhr uhr) *n.* ruler of highest rank and authority, especially of an empire

The Soul selects her own Society –
Then – shuts the Door –
To her divine Majority –
Present no more –

Unmoved – she notes the Chariots – pausing –
At her low Gate –
Unmoved – an **Emperor** be kneeling
Upon her Mat –

I've known her – from an ample nation –
Choose One –
Then – close the Valves of her attention –
Like Stone –





## DIGITAL PERSPECTIVES

**Enriching the Text** Have students find reliable sources to get additional insight into the biography of Emily Dickinson, including any details that discuss her reclusiveness. Divide students into small groups to share the information that they found and and to reflect upon "The Soul selects her own Society—" in light of these facts. Then, have a group representative present each group's conclusions to the class. **(Research to Clarify)**

DIGITAL PERSPECTIVES

# The Soul unto itself

Emily Dickinson

SCAN FOR MULTIMEDIA

The Soul unto itself
Is an imperial friend –
Or the most agonizing Spy –
An Enemy – could send –

Secure against its own –
No treason it can fear –
Itself – it's Sovereign – Of itself
The Soul should stand in Awe –

NOTES

**imperial** (ihm PEER ee uhl) *adj.* like something associated with an empire; magnificent or majestic

**treason** (TREE zuhn) *n.* betrayal of trust or faith, especially against one's country

**sovereign** (SOV ruhn) *n.* monarch or ruler





CLOSER LOOK

## Understand Theme

Students may have marked lines 1–4 during their first read. Use this stanza to help students understand the theme of this poem. Encourage them to talk about the annotations that they marked. You may want to model a close read with the class based on the highlights shown in the text.

**ANNOTATE:** Have students mark details in lines 1–4 that describe the nature of the "soul," or have students participate while you highlight them.

**QUESTION:** Guide students to consider what these details might tell them. Ask what a reader can infer from the paradoxical descriptions: first the soul is described as an imperial friend and then as a spy and an enemy, and accept student responses.
**Possible response:** Dickinson seems to be saying that the soul can betray us or be our best help.

**CONCLUDE:** Help students to formulate conclusions about the importance of these details in the text. Ask students why the author might have included these details.
**Possible response:** Dickinson is reflecting upon the deepest feelings of human beings, which she says will have their way, regardless of what our more superficial selves decide.

Point out that this poem has a **universal theme**, a message about life that is expressed regularly in different cultures and across time periods. Remind students there is no single correct statement of theme for a literary work. Clarify that it is, however, possible to come up with an incorrect theme if a reader misunderstands the central idea of a work.

PERSONALIZE FOR LEARNING

### Strategic Support

**Universal Theme** If students struggle to see how the theme of this poem written in the 1800s might be relevant to people today, assign small groups to relate the theme to something in their own lives or to a story that they read about or saw in a film. Remind students to come up with stories that show how people can be their own best friend or their own worst enemy.

# TEACHING

## CLOSE READD

As students look for words with *f, t,* and *c* sounds, you may wish to model the Close Read using the following think-aloud format. Possible responses to questions on the Student page are included. You may also want to print copies of the **Close-Read Guide: Poetry** for students to use. 

**ANNOTATE:** I notice and mark multiple words that have *f, t,* and *c* sounds.

**QUESTION:** The author repeats these sounds to emphasize words and ideas in the poem.

**CONCLUDE:** The repeated sounds contribute to the cadence and rhythm of the poem, but they also add a harshness to the tone of the poem.

SCAN FOR MULTIMEDIA

NOTES

**CLOSE READ**

**ANNOTATE:** Mark the repeated use of *f, t,* and *c* sounds throughout the poem.

**QUESTION:** Why does the author repeat these consonant sounds?

**CONCLUDE:** What quality do these repeated sounds create?

Fame is a fickle food
Upon a shifting plate
Whose table once a
Guest but not
The second time is set
Whose crumbs the crows inspect
And with ironic caw*
Flap past it to the
Farmer's corn
Men eat of it and die

* **caw** *n.* piercing cry of a crow or raven.





## PERSONALIZE FOR LEARNING

### English Language Support

**Figurative Language** Review lines 5–9 in this poem. Help students decode the figurative language of the poem by asking them to identify and look up unfamiliar words. Then, ask a volunteer to describe in his or her own words the image the poet sets out in these lines. Once students can clearly "see" the image, guide them in a discussion about how the image relates to the idea of fame in the poem. **ALL LEVELS**

ANCHOR TEXT | POETRY

# They shut me up in Prose –

Emily Dickinson

SCAN FOR MULTIMEDIA

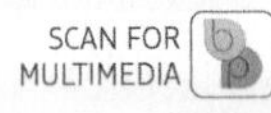

They shut me up in Prose –
As when a little Girl
They put me in the Closet –
Because they liked me "still" –

Still! Could themself have peeped –
And seen my Brain – go round –
They might as wise have lodged a Bird
For Treason – in the Pound –

Himself has but to will
And easy as a Star
Look down upon Captivity –
And laugh – No more have I –

NOTES

**captivity** (kap TIHV ih tee) *n.* condition of being held prisoner





CLOSER LOOK

## Interpret Metaphors

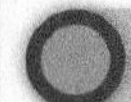

Students may have marked lines 1–4 during their first read. Use this stanza to help students understand how to interpret metaphors. Encourage them to talk about the annotations that they marked. You may want to model a close read with the class based on the highlights shown in the text.

**ANNOTATE:** Have students mark details in lines 1–4 that expand upon the metaphor "they shut me up in prose," or have students participate while you highlight them.

**QUESTION:** Guide students to consider what these details might tell them. Ask what a reader can infer from the speaker's assertion that she was in a closet and made to be "still" and accept student responses.
**Possible response:** She felt stifled or imprisoned. She felt unable to move freely.

**CONCLUDE:** Help students to formulate conclusions about the importance of these details in the text. Ask students why the author might have included these details.
**Possible response:** The combination of the details surrounding imprisonment with the metaphor "shut me up in prose" implies that the speaker felt silenced—her words were locked up—when she had to write prose because poetry is her only form of true or free expression.

Explain to students that this poem contains an **extended metaphor** that runs through the entire poem.

CROSS-CURRICULAR PERSPECTIVES

**Humanities** Have students find and select a poem written by one of Dickinson's contemporaries, such as Whitman, Longfellow, or Browning. Ask students to prepare a short presentation for the class that compares and contrasts one of Dickinson's poems to the poem they have selected.

## CLOSE READ 

Remind students that in this short poem, Dickinson has described solitude in several ways. You may wish to model the Close Read using the following think-aloud format. Possible responses to questions on the Student page are included.

**ANNOTATE:** As I read the poem I notice and highlight the details that describe different types of solitude in lines 1–3.

**QUESTION:** The speaker names these forms of solitude as a comparison to the solitude of the soul.

**CONCLUDE:** These details provide images of isolation, but the speaker uses them as examples that pale in comparison to the "polar privacy" of the soul.

ANCHOR TEXT | POETRY

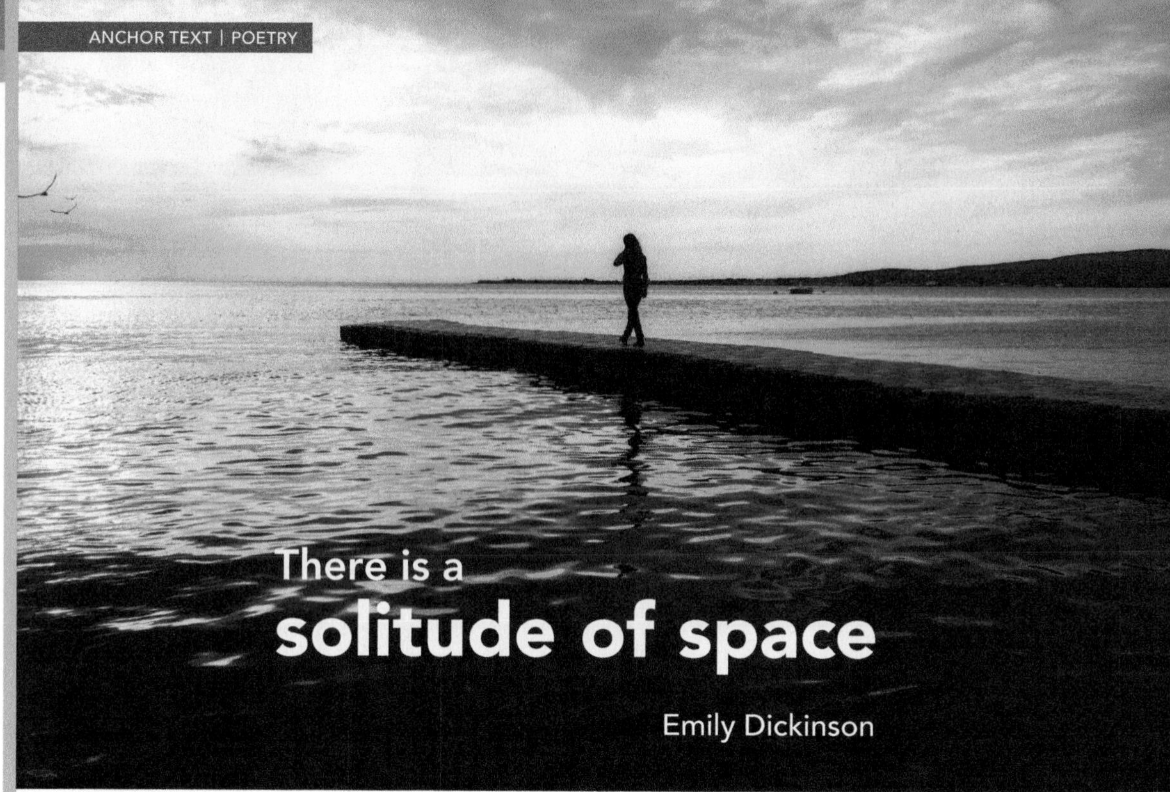

# There is a solitude of space

Emily Dickinson

 SCAN FOR MULTIMEDIA

NOTES

**CLOSE READ**

**ANNOTATE:** Mark the types of solitude the speaker identifies in the first three lines.

**QUESTION:** Why does the speaker make a point of identifying different types of solitude?

**CONCLUDE:** What is the effect of these details?

There is a solitude of space
A solitude of sea
A solitude of Death, but these
Society shall be
Compared with that profounder site
That polar privacy
A soul admitted to itself –
Finite Infinity.





### VOCABULARY DEVELOPMENT

**Word Use** Ask students to consider Dickinson's uses of the word *society* to mean "the situation of being in the company of other people." Discuss with students alternative meanings of the word, including: a social class; a superior or elegant class of people. Ask students to consider which meaning Dickinson uses in "The Soul selects her own Society—."

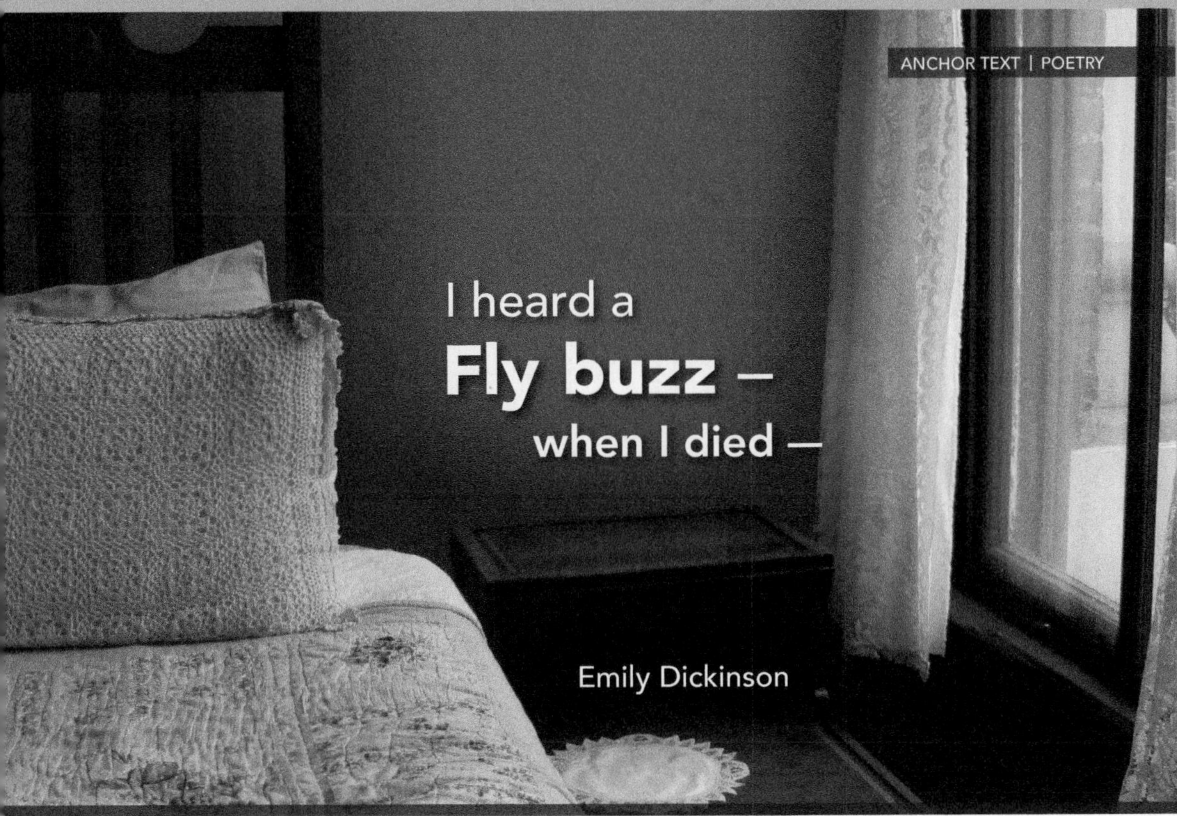

I heard a Fly buzz – when I died –
The Stillness in the Room
Was like the Stillness in the Air –
Between the Heaves of Storm –

The Eyes around – had wrung them dry –
And Breaths were gathering firm
For that last Onset – when the King
Be witnessed – in the Room –

I willed my Keepsakes – Signed away
What portion of me be
Assignable – and then it was
There interposed a Fly –

With Blue – uncertain – stumbling Buzz –
Between the light – and me –
And then the Windows failed – and then
I could not see to see –

NOTES





DIGITAL PERSPECTIVES

CLOSER LOOK

## Analyze Sensory Details

Students may have marked lines 13–16 during their first read. Use these lines to help students understand how the speaker describes sensory details. Encourage them to talk about the annotations that they marked. You may want to model a close read with the class based on the highlights shown in the text.

**ANNOTATE:** Have students mark sensory details in lines 13–16, or have students participate while you highlight them.

**QUESTION:** Guide students to consider what these sensory details might tell them about the speaker.

**Possible response:** The sound of the stumbling buzz "Between the light—and me" are the last things the speaker senses. "The Windows failed" and "I could not see to see" describe the moment of death.

**CONCLUDE:** Help students to formulate conclusions about the importance of these details in the text.

**Possible response:** The fly may represent the speaker's soul at the moment of death.

Remind students that in poetry, **sensory details** are used to help readers experience a scene more fully.

ANCHOR TEXT | POETRY

# I'm Nobody! Who are you?

Emily Dickinson

SCAN FOR MULTIMEDIA

NOTES

I'm Nobody! Who are you?
Are you – Nobody – too?
Then there's a pair of us!
Don't tell! they'd advertise – you know!

How dreary – to be – Somebody!
How public – like a Frog –
To tell one's name – the livelong June –
To an admiring Bog!



Additional **English Language Support** is available in the Interactive Teacher's Edition.



## WriteNow Express and Reflect

**Poetry** Review lines 1–4. Have students work on their own poems using the title "Who Are You?" Encourage students to delve into their creativity for this assignment. Explain that though Dickinson's title will serve as inspiration, their poems do not have to emulate or resemble the poetry they have read. Ask volunteers to read their completed poems to the class.

## Comprehension Check

Complete the following items after you finish your first read.

1. In "The Soul selects her own Society –," what leaves the soul "unmoved"?

2. In "The Soul unto itself," of what does the speaker say the Soul should stand in awe?

3. In "Fame is a fickle food," what food do the crows prefer to the crumbs left by fame?

4. In "They shut me up in Prose –," why do "they" put the little girl in the closet?

5. According to the speaker in "There is a solitude of space," is death the deepest type of solitude?

6. In "I heard a Fly buzz – when I died –," what do the speaker and those in attendance expect to experience when "the last Onset" occurs?

7. According to the speaker in "I'm Nobody! Who are you?," what would be "dreary"?

### RESEARCH

**Research to Clarify** Choose at least one unfamiliar detail from the poems. Briefly research that detail. In what way does the information you learned shed light on an aspect of Emily Dickinson's poetry?

**Research to Explore** Conduct research to find out what happened to Dickinson's writing after her death.





DIGITAL PERSPECTIVES

## Comprehension Check

Possible responses:

1. "Her divine majority" leaves the soul unmoved.
2. It should stand in awe of itself.
3. They prefer the farmer's corn.
4. "They" want the girl to be "still."
5. No, the deepest type of solitude is the solitude of the soul.
6. The death of the speaker.
7. To be "Somebody" would be dreary.

## Research

**Research to Clarify** If students struggle to come up with a detail to research, you may want to suggest that they focus on one of the following topics: the soul; society; fame.

**Research to Explore** If students are unsure about how to approach the research question, direct students to reread Meet the Author at the beginning of the selection. Tell students that they can focus on one of the following topics: Information about Dickinson's family's decision to publish her poetry after her death, against the poet's wishes; Specific details about what editors changed in Dickinson's poetry to reflect conventional ideas.

PERSONALIZE FOR LEARNING

### Challenge

**Poetry Research** Encourage interested students to research more of Dickinson's poetry. Advise students to look for unedited versions of Dickinson's poetry, which are not yet in the public domain. Explain that some of Dickinson's poems that can be found online are likely to be edited versions. Students may want to analyze common themes in Dickinson's poems and/or take notes on Dickinson's use of figurative language.

TEACHING

## Jump Start

CLOSE READ Explain to students that Dickinson's poems read like lyrics from a song and are short, with a single speaker, identified as "I." Point out that Dickinson went to lengths to let readers know that the "I" in the poems was not she, but rather the person she had in her mind while writing the poem. Help them understand her uncanny ability to use concrete images to describe abstract concepts.

## Close Read the Text

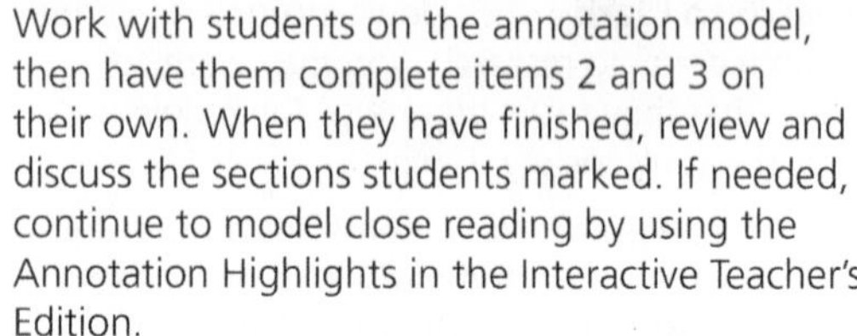

Work with students on the annotation model, then have them complete items 2 and 3 on their own. When they have finished, review and discuss the sections students marked. If needed, continue to model close reading by using the Annotation Highlights in the Interactive Teacher's Edition.

## Analyze the Text

Possible responses:

1. (a) She decides whom to include in her own society. **DOK 1** (b) She shuts the door to the rest. **DOK 1**
2. Both souls are selective about whom they accept. In the first poem, the soul stands alone; in the second, it admits only a select few. **DOK 2**
3. (a) blue, uncertain, stumbling **DOK 1** (b) Dickinson seems to be using these adjectives to describe the act of dying itself. **DOK 3**
4. (a) The speaker does not want attention. **DOK 2** (b) "The Soul selects her own Society" and "Fame is a fickle food" both express similar tension. In the first, the soul selects her society and shuts the door to the rest; in the second, men eat the "food" of fame and die. **DOK 2**
5. Individualism doesn't always mean standing out. People who are private and introspective can show individualism, too. **DOK 3**

### FORMATIVE ASSESSMENT

### Analyze the Text

- **If** students fail to cite evidence, **then** remind them to support their ideas with specific information from the text.
- **If** students struggle to identify a theme or message about life in "I'm Nobody, Who are you?" **then** help them look for clues in a text that reveal the writers meaning.



MAKING MEANING

THE POETRY OF EMILY DICKINSON

## Close Read the Text

1. This model, from lines 1-4 of "I heard a Fly buzz – when I died –," shows two sample annotations, along with questions and conclusions. Close read the passage, and find another detail to annotate. Then, write a question and your conclusion.

Close Read: ANNOTATE, QUESTION, CONCLUDE

ANNOTATE: The speaker repeats the word *Stillness.*

QUESTION: Why is this word important enough to repeat?

CONCLUDE: The word suggests the intensity of the atmosphere and the sense of waiting.

I heard a Fly buzz – when I died –
The Stillness in the Room
Was like the Stillness in the Air –
Between the Heaves of Storm –

ANNOTATE: Both *Stillness* and *Storm* begin with *s.*

QUESTION: Why does the poet use words with this sound pattern?

CONCLUDE: The sound connects *Stillness* and *Storm,* and suggests that the room only seems still; dramatic events are taking place under the surface.

2. For more practice, go back into the poems and complete the close-read notes.
3. Revisit a section of a poem you found important during your first read. **Annotate** what you notice. Ask yourself **questions** such as "Why did the poet make this choice?" What can you **conclude?**

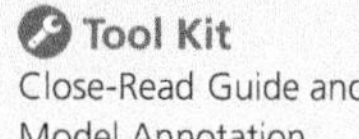

**Tool Kit**
Close-Read Guide and Model Annotation

## Analyze the Text

CITE TEXTUAL EVIDENCE to support your answers.

Notebook Respond to these questions.

1. (a) In "The Soul selects her own Society –," what choice does the Soul make? (b) **Interpret** What happens after the soul makes her choice? (c) **Generalize** What is the soul's attitude toward the world's attractions?
2. **Compare and Contrast** How are the souls in "The Soul selects her own Society –" and "The Soul unto itself" alike and different? Explain.
3. (a) In the final stanza of "I heard a Fly buzz – when I died –," what adjectives does the speaker use to describe the buzzing of the fly? (b) **Draw Conclusions** What statement about dying is Dickinson making in this poem?
4. (a) **Interpret** In "I'm Nobody! Who are you?," how does the speaker feel about receiving attention? (b) **Connect** Identify two other poems in this grouping that express a similar tension between the private self and a social, or public, self. Explain your choices.
5. **Essential Question:** ***What role does individualism play in American society?*** What have you learned about the nature of individualism from reading these poems?

STANDARDS

**Reading Literature**

- Determine the meaning of words and phrases as they are used in the text, including figurative and connotative meanings; analyze the impact of specific word choices on meaning and tone, including words with multiple meanings or language that is particularly fresh, engaging, or beautiful.
- Analyze how an author's choices concerning how to structure specific parts of a text contribute to its overall structure and meaning as well as its aesthetic impact.





PERSONALIZE FOR LEARNING

### English Language Support

**Getting the Message** Provide the first two columns of the chart and have partners complete the third about three of Dickinson's poems:

| Poem | Poem's focus | Message |
|---|---|---|
| The Soul selects her own Society | the Soul | |
| Fame is a fickle food | fame | |
| I'm Nobody! Who are you? | nobody versus somebody | |

## Analyze Craft and Structure

**Poetic Structure and Style** Poets use rhyme to emphasize ideas, convey mood, and unify groups of lines. With **exact rhyme,** two or more words have identical sounds in their final stressed syllables, as in *one/begun.* With **slant rhyme,** the final sounds are similar but not identical, as in *one/stone* or *firm/room.* Dickinson's frequent use of slant rhyme where readers expect exact rhyme makes her poetry surprising and thought-provoking.

*I've known her – from an ample nation –*
*Choose One –*
*Then – close the Valves of her attention –*
*Like Stone –*

Another hallmark of Dickinson's style is her fondness for paradox. A **paradox** is a statement that seems contradictory but actually presents a truth. For example, the statement "You must sometimes be cruel to be kind" is a paradox. It sounds contradictory, but it makes sense when you consider that there are times when seemingly unkind words or actions may actually help someone. Dickinson often explores paradoxes about the nature of solitude, selfhood, society, the mind, nature, and many other abstract concepts.

### Practice

CITE TEXTUAL EVIDENCE to support your answers.

Notebook Respond to these questions.

1. (a) Examine the use of slant and exact rhyme in "I heard a Fly buzz – when I died –." Use the chart to identify rhyming words, and note the lines on which they appear. (b) What is the effect of the exact rhyme after so many slant rhymes?

| LINES | RHYMING WORDS | TYPE OF RHYME |
|---|---|---|
| 2, 4 | Room, Storm | slant rhyme |
| 6, 8 | firm, room | slant rhyme |
| 14, 16 | me, see | exact rhyme |
| | | |
| | | |

2. (a) Which two words create a slant rhyme in the second stanza of "The Soul selects her own Society –"? (b) How does Dickinson's avoidance of exact rhyme in this poem fit with her characterization of the "Soul"?
3. (a) Explain how the first line of "I heard a Fly buzz – when I died –" is a paradox. (b) A two-word paradox, such as *cruel kindness*, is called an *oxymoron*. Identify an oxymoron in "There is a solitude of space," and explain the apparent contradiction. (c) For both poems, what explanation makes the situation possible, even though it seems impossible?
4. (a) Which of these poems present human understanding as something boundless or unlimited? (b) Which present it as something small and limited? (c) How would you define Dickinson's view of the individual self?





DIGITAL PERSPECTIVES  

## Analyze Craft and Structure

**Poetic Structure and Style** Discuss with students why they think Dickinson makes unconventional choices such as slant rhyme and paradox. Ask students to express whether they enjoy the elements of Dickinson's style and to give reasons for their responses. For more support, see **Analyze Craft and Structure: Poetic Structure and Style.**

**MAKE IT INTERACTIVE**

Have students select one of the poems and note examples of slant rhyme and exact rhyme. Then, have students write poems on a similar theme using these techniques. Ask volunteers to read their poems aloud.

### Practice

Possible responses:

1. See possible responses on the student page.
2. (a) *gate, mat;* (b) She is selecting her own way of "rhyming," just as the soul selects its own society.
3. (a) The first line is a paradox because you cannot hear when you are dead. (b) Finite infinity; Something that ends cannot be endless. (c) Both are theoretical. They are used to explain a feeling or moment and are not literal.
4. (a) "There is a solitude of space"; (b) "They shut me up in Prose—" (c) Answers will vary but should be supported with examples.

**FORMATIVE ASSESSMENT**

### Analyze Craft and Structure

- **If** students fail to cite evidence, **then** remind them to support their ideas with specific information from the text.
- **If** students struggle to analyze Dickinson's poetic style, **then** discuss rhyme and phrasing, and illustrate with examples. For more support, see **Analyze Craft and Structure: Poetic Structure and Style (RP).**

Have partners complete the chart, and provide examples, if needed. Then have one student write a text message from the speaker of one of the poems, and have the other student write a text message in response. Continue until partners have each written several messages. Then bring all together and have them share. **ALL LEVELS**

An expanded **English Language Support Lesson** on Text Messages, which will help students write blog posts, is available in the Interactive Teacher's Edition.

## Concept Vocabulary

**Why These Words?** The words *imperial, sovereign,* and *emperor* connote domination and authority, while *treason* and *captivity* suggest a counterpoint to authority. Without the *majority,* there is no dominance. Individuality could be seen as a contrast to majority and these poems portray individuality.

Possible responses:

1. The words convey strength and domination.
2. Other words include *secure, heaves, storm, king.*

### Practice

Possible responses:

1. Last year's budget passed easily because the majority of voters supported it.
   The emperor is the supreme ruler in the land.
   Our queen and king are the heads of our imperial court.
   The double agent was convicted of treason for betraying his country.
   The sovereign preferred to be called "Supreme Leader," rather than "Your Majesty."
   Some wild animals seem happier in captivity than free in the jungle.
2. majority: minority; emperor: peasant, serf, slave; imperial: low-level, subordinate, inferior; treason: loyalty, faithfulness, devotion, constancy, allegiance; sovereign: laborer, servant; captivity: freedom, liberty, autonomy, independence

### Word Network

Possible words: *sovereign, privacy, solitude*

## Word Study

For more support, see **Concept Vocabulary and Word Study.**

Possible responses:

1. Examples include *empire* (noun), "an aggregate of nations" and *imperialism* (noun), "the policy of extending the authority of a nation."
2. A *czar* is a Russian emperor; a *kaiser* is a German emperor; a *caesar* is a Roman emperor.

### FORMATIVE ASSESSMENT

#### Concept Vocabulary

**If** students fail to see the connection between the words, **then** have them use each word in a sentence.

#### Word Study

**If** students fail to understand word derivations, **then** have them use resources such as an online dictionary to look up word meanings and word origins. For Reteach and Practice, see **Word Study: Word Derivations (RP).**

LANGUAGE DEVELOPMENT

THE POETRY OF EMILY DICKINSON

## Concept Vocabulary

| emperor | treason | captivity |
|---|---|---|
| imperial | sovereign | |

**Why These Words?** These concept words are used to discuss the power of nations. An *emperor* is a supreme ruler who oversees an *imperial* state. *Treason* is a crime against a nation, and *captivity* is a punishment a state can impose.

1. How does the concept vocabulary emphasize Dickinson's ideas about the supreme power of the soul?
2. What other words in the poems connect to this concept?

**WORD NETWORK**

Add words related to individualism from the text to your Word Network.

### Practice

**Notebook** Respond to the following.

1. Use each concept word in a sentence that demonstrates your understanding of the word's meaning.
2. Identify as many antonyms for each concept word as you can. Then, ask classmates about each antonym—for example, "True or false: *Monarch* is an antonym for *emperor.*"

## Word Study

**Word Derivations** In "The Soul selects her own Society –," Dickinson uses the word *emperor*. In "The Soul unto itself," she uses the word *imperial*. These words have similar derivations. *Emperor* is derived from the Latin noun *imperator. Imperial* is derived from the Latin adjective *imperialis*. Both Latin words can ultimately be traced back to the same root word, the Latin verb *imperare*, meaning "to command." As you would expect, the English words *emperor* and *imperial* have related meanings.

1. Find, define, and identify the parts of speech of two other words that have the same derivation as *imperial* and *emperor*.
2. Use a dictionary or online source to compare the precise meanings and derivations of these related words: *czar, kaiser, caesar*.

**STANDARDS**

**Language**

- Identify and correctly use patterns of word changes that indicate different meanings or parts of speech.
- Consult general and specialized reference materials, both print and digital, to find the pronunciation of a word or determine or clarify its precise meaning, its part of speech, its etymology, or its standard usage.
- Demonstrate understanding of figurative language, word relationships, and nuances in word meanings.





### VOCABULARY DEVELOPMENT

**Concept Vocabulary Reinforcement** Students will benefit from additional examples and practice with the concept vocabulary. Reinforce their comprehension with "show-you-know" sentences. The first part of the sentence uses the vocabulary word in an appropriate context. The second part of the sentence—the show-you-know part—clarifies the first. Model the strategy with this example for *captivity.* Lisa couldn't believe that she would be in *captivity* until her family got home, and yet, here she was, trapped in the attic, with no way to open the locked door. Ask students to create their own "show you know" sentences with each concept vocabulary word.

## Conventions and Style

**Parts of Speech** Every English word, depending on its meaning and its use in a sentence, can be identified as one of the eight parts of speech: noun, pronoun, verb, adjective, adverb, preposition, conjunction, or interjection. A **noun** names any one of a class of people, places, things, or ideas.

- An **abstract noun** refers to an idea, quality, or concept rather than to a specific object.
- A **concrete noun** names something that you can experience through your five senses.

TIP

USAGE

There is no grammatical difference between concrete and abstract nouns. Both can be subjects, direct objects, or objects of prepositions. The difference is solely in the nature of the things they name.

| ABSTRACT NOUNS | | CONCRETE NOUNS | |
|---|---|---|---|
| individualism | requirement | door | chariot |
| eloquence | outrage | stone | windowsill |
| discovery | loneliness | sea | sky |

Emily Dickinson uses concrete nouns to describe abstract concepts. This approach allows her to explore large abstract ideas—such as death, individuality, or fame—in ways that make them tangible and immediate.

### Read It

1. Identify each underlined word as an abstract noun or a concrete noun.
   a. Fame is a fickle food / Upon a shifting plate
   b. They shut me up in Prose – / As when a little Girl
   c. A solitude of Death, but these / Society shall be
2. **Connect to Style** Reread the first stanza of "I heard a Fly buzz – when I died –." Identify two concrete nouns. How do those nouns suggest the speaker's view of death?
3. **Notebook** Choose another poem from this collection, and explain how Dickinson uses a concrete noun to describe an abstract idea.

### Write It

**Notebook** Choose one of these abstract nouns. Then, write a passage in which you use concrete nouns and images to describe the abstract noun.

| charity | compassion | courage | determination |
|---|---|---|---|
| enthusiasm | fear | generosity | hope |





## PERSONALIZE FOR LEARNING

### English Language Support

**Nouns** Have students come up with a list of ten concrete nouns and ten abstract nouns. Then, have students write five sentences, choosing from words on their lists. Their sentences should use concrete nouns to describe abstract nouns. Explain that this is a creative exercise and that, like Dickinson, they will be creating metaphors with these sentences. Have students read their favorite sentences aloud. **ALL LEVELS**

## Conventions and Style

**Parts of Speech** Discuss the definition of a concrete noun with students. As you review the examples of abstract and concrete nouns, discuss the effect of Dickinson's use of concrete nouns to convert ideas into images. For more support, see **Conventions and Style: Parts of Speech.**

**MAKE IT INTERACTIVE**

Have students select one of the poems and identify all of its nouns. Then, have them list abstract and concrete nouns in a T-chart. Finally, have students link the concrete nouns to the ideas they illustrate.

### Read It

Possible responses:

1. **a.** *fame*: abstract; *plate*: concrete
   **b.** *prose:* abstract; *girl:* concrete
   **c.** *solitude:* abstract; *Death:* concrete; *Society:* abstract
2. concrete nouns: fly, room ; Readers can picture a person who is about to die, laying on a bed in a room. The active fly is in her awareness until her awareness is no more and the reader understands death because the "window" of her awareness closes.
3. Responses will vary, but should include a concrete noun that describes an abstract idea, and an explanation for how it does so.

### Write It

Possible responses:

Fear, a monster with huge claws, lives under the bed. Six feet tall and hairy, Fear growls and snarls—but only at night. It casts a terrifying shadow that shakes in the wind.

## FORMATIVE ASSESSMENT

### Conventions and Style

**If** students are having trouble distinguishing abstract nouns from concrete nouns, **then** tell them to imagine drawing a picture of the noun. If the noun cannot be rendered in a drawing, it is likely an abstract noun. For Reteach and Practice, see **Conventions and Style: Parts of Speech (RP).**

## Writing to Sources

Explain to students that while they will be using information from the poems to create the voice of their blogger, the voice is their own creation. Encourage them to select poems that they enjoyed the most. Explain that they should spend some time rereading the poems and gathering evidence about the speaker's experiences. For more support, see **Writing to Sources: Blog Post.**

### Reflect on Your Writing

1. Responses will vary. If students need support, ask them to describe the lines or images that attracted them to the poems they chose.
2. Responses will vary. Encourage students to share their thoughts about the era in which the blogger lived, the blogger's gender, and the blogger's age.
3. **Why These Words?** Responses will vary. If students need support ask them to pick out concrete nouns—nouns that describe things that can be drawn or photographed.

### FORMATIVE ASSESSMENT

### Writing to Sources

**If** students struggle to write their blogs based on several poems, **then** have them work with one or two poems that they understand well. For Reteach and Practice, see **Writing to Sources: Blog Post (RP).**

EFFECTIVE EXPRESSION

THE POETRY OF EMILY DICKINSON

## Writing to Sources

A blog, short for *web log*, is a site on which a writer presents separate entries, or posts, in reverse chronological order. Blogs can focus on any topic and can be written for many different purposes. Perhaps you have read blog posts that recount events in the writer's life, revealing his or her personality and worldview. In some respects, Emily Dickinson's poems are like blog posts: They are serial expressions of her observations on fundamental aspects of life, including identity, love, nature, death, and immortality.

**Assignment**

Write a **blog post** as if you were the first-person speaker in Dickinson's poems. Give an account of a day in your life, using your interpretation of words, lines, and images from at least two of Dickinson's poems to describe your experiences and observations. Consider what the poetic details suggest about the speaker's character. Include elements such as these:

- precise words and sensory language
- words and phrases that suggest a specific tone, or emotional attitude, such as excitement, tranquility, or reflectiveness.
- a conclusion that sums up the speaker's worldview or opinion

**Vocabulary and Conventions Connection** Consider including several of the concept vocabulary words. Also, try to use concrete nouns to characterize abstract ideas and make them tangible and vivid for readers.

| emperor | treason | captivity |
|---|---|---|
| imperial | sovereign | |

### Reflect on Your Writing

After you have drafted your blog post, answer the following questions.

1. Which poems contributed the most details to your blog post? Why did you choose those poems?
2. How would you describe the speaker that you created?
3. **Why These Words?** The words you choose make a difference in your writing. Which words helped you make your account descriptive and interesting?

STANDARDS

**Reading Literature**
Analyze multiple interpretations of a story, drama, or poem, evaluating how each version interprets the source text.

**Writing**
- Write narratives to develop real or imagined experiences or events using effective technique, well-chosen details, and well-structured event sequences.
- Use precise words and phrases, telling details, and sensory language to convey a vivid picture of the experiences, events, setting, and/or characters.

**Speaking and Listening**
- Propel conversations by posing and responding to questions that probe reasoning and evidence; ensure a hearing for a full range of positions on a topic or issue; clarify, verify, or challenge ideas and conclusions; and promote divergent and creative perspectives.
- Adapt speech to a variety of contexts and tasks, demonstrating a command of formal English when indicated or appropriate





PERSONALIZE FOR LEARNING

### Strategic Support

**Voice** For students who struggle to create a voice for their blogger, have them outline their blogger's character before they begin writing. They should decide on the following for their characters: Name, age, gender, occupation, hobbies, description of a typical day, place of residence. Once the students have determined these facts about their blogger, have them select one poem with an idea or experience that they would like their blogger to blog about. Support and guide the students through the process.

## Speaking and Listening

**Assignment**
Participate in a **class discussion** about "The Soul selects her own Society –." Either volunteer to read the poem aloud or simply listen as others do so. As you listen, consider how each reader's choices to emphasize certain words or phrases, indicate line breaks, and reflect the poem's distinctive punctuation affect how you hear and understand the poem. Then, discuss your observations.

1. **Listen to the Readings** Focus on the interpretive choices each reader makes.
   - As you listen, read along in the text.
   - Jot down points at which the reader's pace or emphasis surprises you. Consider whether this surprise illuminates an aspect of the poem, or—perhaps—misrepresents the poem in some way.
   - Share your responses, citing specific examples.
2. **Analyze the Readings** Now, take time to think more deeply about the effects of each reader's interpretive choices.
   - What words or phrases did different readings emphasize? Did these choices clarify or obscure the poem's meaning?
   - What emotional tone or attitude did different readers bring to the poem? Were some choices of tone more appropriate than others? Did some tonal choices reveal nuances in the poem's meaning?
   - Did the reader deliver his or her reading with conviction, speaking at an effective rate and volume? How did the speaker's delivery affect what you heard and appreciated in the poem?
   - Summarize your analysis in two or three sentences. Then, continue to participate in the discussion. As you share ideas and observations with classmates, ask questions and strive to understand one another's ideas and observations.
3. **Evaluate the Readings** Use a presentation evaluation guide like the one shown to assess each speaker's reading.

PRESENTATION EVALUATION GUIDE

**Rate each statement on a scale of 1 (not demonstrated) to 5 (demonstrated). Be prepared to defend your rating, using examples.**

☐ The reader's interpretation effectively communicated the poem's point of view, meaning, and tone.

☐ The reader's speaking rate and volume reflected the thoughts, feelings, and ideas expressed in the poem in an appropriate way.

☐ The reading held the audience's attention.

EVIDENCE LOG

Before moving on to a new selection, go to your Evidence Log and record what you learned from the poetry of Emily Dickinson.





PERSONALIZE FOR LEARNING

**English Language Support**
**Pronunciation** To support students who struggle with pronunciation, ask for a volunteer to make a recording of the poem for them. Then, provide the recording to the struggling students. Have students work with the recordings to improve their pronunciation and prepare their own reading. **ALL LEVELS**

DIGITAL PERSPECTIVES

## Speaking and Listening

Explain to students that oral interpretations of a poem are very personal. They express the reader's personality as well as their perspective and ideas. Differences from one interpretation to another may be subtle and not entirely planned.

1. **Listen to the Readings** Guide students to have a pen and paper prepared for notes and to give readers their undivided attention. Suggest that listeners try following along in the text during the first two or three readings. Then, have students put away the poem and just listen. Ask students how the listening experience is different with and without the text in front of them.
2. **Analyze the Readings** Explain to students that there is no single correct way to read a poem. As with any work of art, each person will have his or her own interpretation and that interpretation will be reflected in the reading.
3. **Evaluate the Readings** Tell students to express at least one thing they enjoyed about the presentation.

For more support, see **Speaking and Listening: Readings.**

Evidence Log Support students in completing their Evidence Log. This paced activity will help prepare them for the Performance-Based Assessment at the end of the unit.

### FORMATIVE ASSESSMENT

**Speaking and Listening**

- **If** students struggle with reading the poem aloud, **then** suggest that they practice their reading skills at home before their classroom reading.
- **If** students have trouble coming up with something they enjoyed about each reading, **then** suggest that they notice the reader's body language, posture, tone of voice, rate, volume and expression.

For Reteach and Practice, see **Speaking and Listening: Readings (RP)**

**Selection Test**
Administer the "The Poetry of Emily Dickinson" Selection Test, which is available in both print and digital formats online in Assessments.

# *from* Emily Dickinson

**AUDIO SUMMARIES**
Audio summaries of "Great Lives: Emily Dickinson" are available in both English and Spanish and can be assigned to students in the Interactive Teacher's Edition or Unit Resources. Assigning these summaries prior to reviewing the selection may help students build additional background knowledge and set a context for their first review.

## Summary

This BBC podcast features an interview with the Welsh poet Gywneth Lewis. First, there is a reading of "I'm Nobody! Who are You?" by Emily Dickinson. Then, in the interview, Lewis discusses her views on the 19th century American poet. Lewis points out that the poet lived a life of solitude and says that Dickinson was famous for not being famous. However, Lewis also says that Dickinson's poems are deeply powerful. Lewis has come to enjoy and understand the poems after years of frustration with them. Lewis says that Dickinson was a category buster whose greatest strength was her ability to live according to her belief that "mere sense of living is joy enough."

### Insight

This selection delves into an enigmatic poet. Her work is strange and compelling, and it delves into questions of selfhood and identity.

ESSENTIAL QUESTION:
What role does individualism play in American society?

## Connection to Essential Question

This radio broadcast provides an interesting perspective on the Essential Question. Dickinson stayed away from society at large, and yet her work has greatly influenced society. Her poetry, and the conversation and analysis in the podcast, may lead students to consider how society can benefit from people who live as recluses.

WHOLE-CLASS LEARNING PERFORMANCE TASK
How has my personal experience shaped my view of individualism? Do I see it as a guiding principle, something to be avoided, or a combination of both?

UNIT PERFORMANCE-BASED ASSESSMEN
What significant incident helped me realize that I am a unique individual?

## Connection to Performance Tasks

**Whole-Class Learning Performance Task** Dickinson's seclusion went against social norms of the time, suggesting that she viewed individualism as a guiding principle. Her decision provides a model for students to evaluate as they complete the Performance Task.

**Unit Performance-Based Assessment** Gwyneth Lewis's analysis of the poetry of Emily Dickinson may help students see how life experiences shape people as they grow. Dickinson wanted to live "an undistracted life," and that was a bold and unique choice. In addition, "I'm Nobody! Who are You?," the Dickinson poem read at the beginning of the podcast suggests that, paradoxically, lack of identity can itself be a unique identity.

DIGITAL PERSPECTIVES

 Audio  Video  Document  Annotation Highlights  EL Highlights 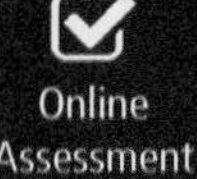 Online Assessment

## LESSON RESOURCES

| | Making Meaning | Language Development | Language Development Effective Expression |
|---|---|---|---|
| Lesson | **First Review**<br>**Close Review**<br>**Analyze the Media** | **Media Vocabulary** | **Writing to Compare** |
| Instructional Standards | **RI.10** By the end of grade 11, read and comprehend literary nonfiction . . .<br>**RL.7** Analyze multiple interpretations of a story . . .<br>**SL.3** Evaluate a speaker's point of view . . . | | **RL.7** Analyze multiple interpretations of a story . . .<br>**W.9** Draw evidence from literary or informational texts . . .<br>**W.9.a** Apply *grades 11–12 Reading standards. . .*<br>**SL.3** Evaluate a speaker's point of view . . . |
| **STUDENT RESOURCES** | | | |
| Available online in the Interactive Student Edition or Unit Resources | Selection Audio<br>First-Review Guide: Media Audio<br>Close-Review Guide: Media Audio | Word Network | Evidence Log |
| **TEACHER RESOURCES** | | | |
| **Selection Resources**<br>Available online in the Interactive Teacher's Edition or Unit Resources | Audio Summaries | Media Vocabulary | Writing to Compare: Compare-and-Contrast Essay |
| **My Resources** | A Unit 2 Answer Key is available online and in the Interactive Teacher's Edition | | |

## Media Complexity Rubric: *from* Emily Dickinson

| **Quantitative Measures** | |
|---|---|
| **Format and Length** | Approximately 4-minute excerpt of a podcast about Emily Dickinson |
| **Qualitative Measures** | |
| Knowledge Demands<br>① ② ❸ ④ ⑤ | To fully appreciate the podcast, prior knowledge of Emily Dickinson and her poems will be helpful. |
| Structure<br>① ❷ ③ ④ ⑤ | The clip includes the reading of "I'm Nobody! Who are You?" followed by an interview/discussion with a modern day poet, Gwyneth Lewis, about Dickinson. |
| Language Conventionality and Clarity<br>① ② ❸ ④ ⑤ | The dialogue in the clip contains some sophisticated analysis and some challenging vocabulary and idiomatic language. |
| Levels of Meaning/Purpose<br>① ② ❸ ④ ⑤ | Meaning and concepts are relatively straightforward but may be difficult to grasp due to sophisticated language. |

## Jump Start

**FIRST REVIEW** It isn't hard to find people who look for fame and notoriety in today's world. Why do people try to stand out? Is it simply for attention, or because they have some important message that needs to be shared? What are some of the ways you get the attention of your friends, teachers, or parents?

### *from* Emily Dickinson  

What do some people do to become well-known or famous? What role does technology play in the quest to become famous? Modeling these and other questions readers might ask will bring the excerpt from the radio program about Emily Dickinson to life and connect it to the Performance Task question.

### Media Vocabulary

Encourage students to discuss the media vocabulary. Have they seen these terms before? Do they use any of them in their speech or writing?

### FIRST REVIEW

The first time they listen to the audio, students should perform the steps of the first review:

LISTEN: Remind students to pay attention to the reading of Dickinson's poem "I'm Nobody! Who are you?" especially noticing when the reader inserts pauses or emphasizes words and phrases.

NOTE: Encourage students to note details that give them insight into Dickinson's life and work.

CONNECT: Encourage students to make connections between Dickinson's eccentricities and reclusiveness and other artists' lifestyles and relationships with the world.

RESPOND: Students will demonstrate their understanding by answering questions and writing a summary.

Point out to students that they will perform the first three steps concurrently as they are doing their first review. They will complete the Respond step after they have finished the first review. You may wish to print copies of the **First-Review Guide: Media Audio** for students to use.

MAKING MEANING

THE POETRY OF EMILY DICKINSON

## Comparing Text to Media

The radio broadcast presented here offers another view of Emily Dickinson and her poetry. In this section, you will compare the ways in which a written text and a radio broadcast can provide information.

from EMILY DICKINSON

About the Poet

**Gwyneth Lewis** (b. 1959), the poet interviewed in this broadcast, was born and raised in Wales and grew up speaking both Welsh and English. After earning degrees from both Cambridge and Oxford, she moved to the United States, where she studied creative writing at Columbia and Harvard. Lewis returned to Wales to work as a producer and director of documentaries at BBC Wales. In 2005, she became the first National Poet of Wales, a post similar to that of Poet Laureate in the United States.

# *from* Emily Dickinson

### Media Vocabulary

These words will be useful to you as you analyze, discuss, and write about radio broadcasts.

| | |
|---|---|
| **Host:** master of ceremonies, moderator, or interviewer on a broadcast | • An effective host puts the guests at ease so that the broadcast flows smoothly.<br>• The host guides the conversation so that the guests stay on topic and provide useful or interesting information to the audience. |
| **Interview:** conversation in which a host asks questions of one or more guests | • Formal interviews are often prepared in advance with a script and rehearsal.<br>• Informal interviews are unrehearsed and have a more free-flowing format. |
| **Commentary:** remarks that illustrate a point, prompt a realization, or explain something | • Commentary can come not only from guests but also from the host.<br>• Authorities on a topic provide *expert commentary*. |

### First Review MEDIA: AUDIO

Apply these strategies as you conduct your first review. You will have an opportunity to complete a close review after your first review.

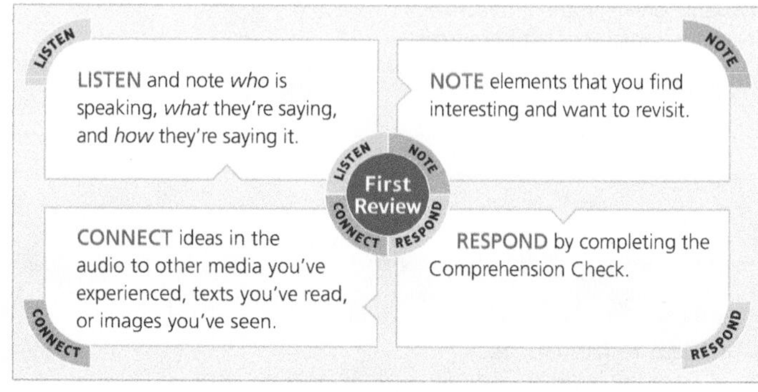

LISTEN
LISTEN and note *who* is speaking, *what* they're saying, and *how* they're saying it.
NOTE
NOTE elements that you find interesting and want to revisit.
First Review
CONNECT ideas in the audio to other media you've experienced, texts you've read, or images you've seen.
RESPOND by completing the Comprehension Check.
CONNECT
RESPOND


**Notebook** As you listen, record your observations and questions, making sure to note time codes for later reference.

STANDARDS

Reading Informational Text

By the end of grade 11, read and comprehend literary nonfiction in the grades 11–CCR text complexity band proficiently, with scaffolding as needed at the high end of the range.



### CROSS-CURRICULAR PERSPECTIVES

**Humanities** Have students research and select a poem by another early 20th century female poet. Tell students to create a presentation of their selected poem, using whatever media they choose. Suggest the following options: a recorded reading of the poem; a live reading of the poem; a visual presentation (either video or on poster board) that includes drawings or photographs. Spend a class period on the presentations.

DIGITAL PERSPECTIVES   

MEDIA | RADIO BROADCAST

# *from* Emily Dickinson

## *from* Great Lives

BBC Radio 4

BACKGROUND

Emily Dickinson's poems are generally quite short and filled with everyday words. Those characteristics do not make them "easy," however. They are open to interpretation—indeed, much literary criticism over the years has been devoted to analyzing them and their author. In this 2011 episode of *Great Lives*, a biographical series produced by the British Broadcasting Company's Radio 4, Welsh poet Gwyneth Lewis is asked for her assessment of Dickinson's work.

SCAN FOR MULTIMEDIA 

NOTES





CLOSER REVIEW

## Analyze Evidence

Students may have noted details in 1:42 to 2:15 in the audio during their first review. Use this part of the audio to help students analyze the reading of "I'm Nobody! Who are you?" Encourage them to talk about what they noted. You may want to model a close review with the class.

**NOTE:** Have students note in the audio when Parris states "Or blog, these days" (2:12) or have students participate while you note this detail.

**QUESTION:** Guide students to consider what this detail might tell them. Ask what a listener can infer from this comment, and accept student responses.

**Possible response:** Readers can infer that Parris was being clever, comparing Dickinson's use of "bog" to a blog.

**CONCLUDE:** Help students to formulate conclusions about the importance of this detail in the audio. Ask students why Parris might have included this comment.

**Possible response:** In Dickinson's poem, the frog in the bog is used as a metaphor for the "somebodies" who keep announcing their names. Parris's comment brings to light that today, many people use social media to try to make themselves into "somebodies." This clever comment brings out the relevance of this poem to today.

Explain to students that for literature or poetry to remain relevant, it must contain a **universal theme**, a message about life that is expressed regularly in many different cultures and time periods.

PERSONALIZE FOR LEARNING

### English Language Support

**Group Discussion** Have English Language Learners listen to the audio once again, noting what they consider to be three to five important ideas in the broadcast. Then, lead a group discussion in which students share their ideas. After discussion, ask the group to arrive at a consensus of the 5 key ideas. Support the discussion where needed by helping students with comprehension of detailed and complex concepts. **ALL LEVELS**

# TEACHING

## Comprehension Check

Possible responses:

1. She reads Dickinson's "I'm Nobody! Who are you?"
2. Lewis says Dickinson was so adept at being a nobody that she became a somebody.
3. Lewis says that she has a "tortured relationship" with Dickinson.
4. She calls Dickinson an "existential pioneer."
5. Lewis describes Dickinson as very eccentric. She lived in her father's house and was a recluse.
6. She made it part of her vocation to find ecstasy in living.

## Comprehension Check

Complete the following items after you finish your first review.

**1.** Which poem does Gwyneth Lewis read at the beginning of the radio broadcast?

**2.** According to Lewis, what was Dickinson "adept" at doing?

**3.** What phrase does Lewis use to describe her relationship to Dickinson?

**4.** What type of pioneer does Lewis call Dickinson?

**5.** How does Lewis describe Dickinson's life?

**6.** What ability of Dickinson's does Lewis find encouraging?





### PERSONALIZE FOR LEARNING

**Challenge**

**Quotation Interpretation** According to Lewis, Dickinson said: "I find ecstasy in living. The mere sense of living is joy enough." Have students consider Dickinson's poetry in light of this quote and note whether they can see Dickinson's philosophy reflected in some or all of her poems. Then, lead a class discussion to share student insights.

## Close Review

Review your notes and, if necessary, listen to the broadcast again. Record any new observations that seem important. What **questions** do you have? What can you **conclude?**

from EMILY DICKINSON

## Analyze the Media

CITE TEXTUAL EVIDENCE to support your answers.

Notebook Respond to these questions.

1. **(a)** What did you notice about Gwyneth Lewis's reading of "I'm Nobody! Who Are You?" **(b) Connect** In what ways does her reading resemble or differ from the way you would read the poem?
2. **(a) Analyze** Lewis thinks that Dickinson speaks through her poetry about her vocation. What does she mean? **(b) Assess** Do you agree with Lewis's statement? Why or why not?
3. **Synthesize** Does Lewis's commentary change your own perception of Dickinson's work? Why or why not?
4. **Historical Perspectives** Lewis mentions that Dickinson was "able to live a life undistracted by many of the things that distract us." How do you think American life in the nineteenth century enabled Dickinson to live a less distracted life?
5. **Essential Question:** ***What role does individualism play in American society?*** What have you learned about American individualism from listening to this broadcast?

LANGUAGE DEVELOPMENT

## Media Vocabulary

host interview commentary

Use the vocabulary words in your responses to the questions.

1. What role does Matthew Parris play in the broadcast? How can you tell?
2. What does Matthew Parris add to the information that listeners get from Gwyneth Lewis?
3. Explain why you think the broadcast begins with Lewis's reading of "I'm Nobody! Who Are You?"

WORD NETWORK

Add words related to individualism from the broadcast to your Word Network.

STANDARDS

**Reading Literature**
Analyze multiple interpretations of a story, drama, or poem, evaluating how each version interprets the source text.

**Speaking and Listening**
Evaluate a speaker's point of view, reasoning, and use of evidence and rhetoric, assessing the stance, premises, links among ideas, word choice, points of emphasis, and tone used.





PERSONALIZE FOR LEARNING

**English Language Support**

**Compare Text and Audio** Have emerging language learners pair up to explain their ideas about comparisons between the text and audio versions of the poem, "I'm Nobody! Who are you?" using phrases and short sentences and general academic words. **ALL LEVELS**

DIGITAL PERSPECTIVES

## Jump Start

CLOSE REVIEW Ask students to consider the following: What would it be like to be a poet, artist, or musician? As students discuss the prompt in their groups, ask them to consider whether they see the advantages that withdrawing from society might have in living life as a poet, artist, or musician.

## Close Review

Remind students to clarify anything they did not understand during their first review. You may wish to print the **Close-Review Guide: Media Audio** for students to use.

## Analyze the Media

Possible responses:

1. (a) She makes the poem's questions sound like challenges. (b) Answers will vary, but should be supported. **DOK 3**
2. (a) Dickinson talks about her life itself as her vocation. (b) Yes. Dickinson's poetry is about the basics of living. **DOK 3**
3. Yes. Reading with the idea of "busting" categories sheds new light on the poems. **DOK 2**
4. The lack of technology made life simpler but even so, she chose a reclusive life to be less distracted. **DOK 2**
5. Answers will vary, but should be supported with information from the broadcast.

## Media Vocabulary

Possible responses:

1. Matthew Parris is the host of the broadcast. He leads the interview.
2. He guides the interview to elicit revealing commentary from Lewis about Dickinson.
3. Answers will vary, but should be supported.

For more support, see **Media Vocabulary.**

## Word Network

Possible words: *somebody, vocation, pioneer*

**FORMATIVE ASSESSMENT**

**Analyze the Media**

**If** students struggle to synthesize Lewis's comments with their own understanding of the Dickinson's poems, **then** discuss individual poems with the idea of Dickinson being a "category buster," and illustrate with examples.

## Writing to Compare

As students prepare to compare Gwenyth Lewis's interpretation of the Emily Dickinson poem "I'm Nobody! Who are you?" with their own interpretations, they will consider various elements of the poem.

### Prewriting

**Analyze the Texts** Allow students to listen to the podcast multiple times so that they can take detailed notes. If your classroom has access to individual computers and headphones, allow students to listen to the podcast individually, in shifts if necessary.

**See possible responses in chart on student page.**

Possible responses:

a. • The reader uses a flat, unemotional vocal tone.
 • There are frequent short pauses
 • The reader increases her reading rate at times to produce short bursts of words.

b. • "The words are simple, but she's a category buster of a poet."
 • "The poem can be read in a sentimental way, but . . . underneath there's a toughness."
 • Finds Dickinson to be an "existential pioneer"; for her "the mere sense of living is joy enough"

c. • The reading is done in an intense way that seems to challenge the listener. The reading could also be done in a slower, more thoughtful way, as if the speaker were mulling something over.
 • The reading rate should be more even.
 • Frequent short pauses are appropriate, because the poems contain dashes.

d. • Lewis is correct. Dickinson is able to compress a great deal of meaning into relatively few words. Her poetry was revolutionary.
 • The poem should not be read in a sentimental way.
 • Lewis seems knowledgeable about Dickinson's life.

Possible responses:

1. Lewis is correct about Dickinson being a pioneer. Dickinson's work is indeed difficult, and Lewis is right to focus on Dickinson's themes of living and nature.
2. Lewis speaks of a "toughness" lying underneath the simple words of Dickinson's poem. The mood is more one of isolation than toughness.



EFFECTIVE EXPRESSION

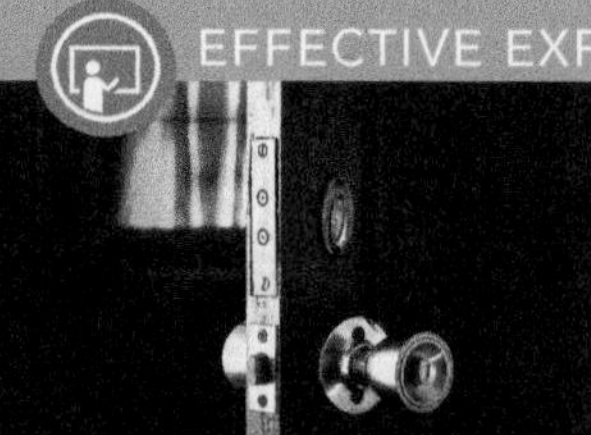

THE POETRY OF EMILY DICKINSON

*from* EMILY DICKINSON

STANDARDS

**Reading Literature**
Analyze multiple interpretations of a story, drama, or poem, evaluating how each version interprets the source text.

**Writing**
• Apply *grades 11–12 Reading standards* to literature.
• Draw evidence from literary or informational texts to support analysis, reflection, and research.

**Speaking and Listening**
Evaluate a speaker's point of view, reasoning, and use of evidence and rhetoric, assessing the stance, premises, links among ideas, word choice, points of emphasis, and tone used.

## Writing to Compare

You have read several of Emily Dickinson's poems, including "I'm Nobody! Who are you?" You have also listened to a radio broadcast in which the Welsh poet Gwenyth Lewis gives both a reading and an analysis of "I'm Nobody! Who are you?" Now, deepen your understanding of the poem by comparing Lewis's interpretation of it with your own, in writing.

**Assignment**

Write a **compare-and-contrast essay** in which you describe Lewis's interpretations of "I'm Nobody! Who are you?" and then present your own interpretation. How are your interpretations similar? How are they different? Support your ideas with details from Dickinson's poem, from the BBC broadcast, and from your own prior knowledge.

### Prewriting

**Analyze the Texts** An **interpretation** can be a new version of a text, such as an oral reading, or a commentary on a text's meaning or importance. Listen again to the broadcast. Use the chart to record your observations and evaluation.

- First, record notes about Lewis's reading of "I'm Nobody! Who are you?" What is her tone of voice? What pace and volume does she use? What words does she emphasize? How would you describe the personality of the speaker she creates?
- Next, record notes about Lewis's understanding of both the poem and Dickinson. Include key quotations from both poets.
- Finally, decide whether you agree with each point you noted in the first column. Would you have made similar choices in an oral reading of the poem? Do you share Lewis's understanding of the poem and poet, or do you have different ideas?

| LEWIS'S INTERPRETATION | AGREE OR DISAGREE? WHY? |
|---|---|
| Her reading of "I'm Nobody! Who are you?"<br>• a. See possible responses in Teacher's Edition.<br>•<br>•<br>• | c.<br>•<br>•<br>•<br>• |
| Her understanding of the poem and poet<br>• b.<br>•<br>•<br>• | d.<br>•<br>•<br>•<br>• |

**Notebook** Respond to these questions.

1. Where does your interpretation of Dickinson align with Lewis's?
2. Where does your interpretation of Dickinson depart from Lewis's?

## Drafting

**Draw Conclusions** Review your Prewriting notes. Use one color to mark points of agreement between Lewis's interpretation(s) of Dickinson and your own. Use a second color to mark points of difference. Are your interpretations mostly similar, or mostly different? How so? Express your conclusions in the form of a thesis statement.

**Thesis Statement:** ______________________________

______________________________

______________________________

**Organize Ideas** In this essay, you will compare and contrast Lewis's interpretation of Dickinson and your own. Consider using one of the following two formats.

**Block Organization**

I. **Lewis's interpretations**
   A. her oral reading of the poem
   B. her understanding of the poem
   C. her understanding of Dickinson

II. **My interpretation**
   A. how I would read the poem
   B. how I understand the poem
   C. my understanding of Dickinson

**Point-by-Point Organization**

I. **Oral readings of the poem**
   A. Lewis's choices
   B. what I would do similarly or differently

II. **Understandings of the poem**
   A. Lewis's
   B. my own

III. **Understandings of Dickinson herself**
   A. Lewis's
   B. my own

**Express an Evaluation** As you draft your essay, do the following:

- Include your thesis statement in the introduction.
- Write one paragraph for each major heading or subheading in your outline. Include evidence from both Dickinson's poem and the broadcast to support your ideas.
- Develop a conclusion in which you evaluate Lewis's interpretations of Dickinson in general terms. In your view, does she capture the spirit of both the poem and the poet? Does she help readers understand this poet in a new way? Or are her interpretations in some way "off the mark"?

### Review, Revise, and Edit

When you are done drafting, reread your essay. Bracket your thesis statement. Mark sections about Lewis's interpretation in one color and sections about your own interpretation in another color. Are they generally balanced? If not, revise to emphasize both equally. After revising, edit for word choice and sentence structure. Proofread to eliminate errors in spelling, grammar, and punctuation.

EVIDENCE LOG

Before moving on to a new selection, go to your Evidence Log and record what you've learned from the BBC radio broadcast featuring Gwenyth Lewis.





DIGITAL PERSPECTIVES 

## Drafting

**Draw Conclusions** Encourage students to go beyond the evidence they compiled in the prereading and gather additional evidence on which to base their conclusions.

**Organize Your Ideas** Remind students to provide support for all the interpretations they present in their essay.

**Express an Evaluation** After students have completed their drafts, have them check their content against whichever of the two outlines they used to make sure they covered all the points listed.

## Review, Revise, and Edit

As students revise, encourage them to review their draft to be sure they have explained their thinking clearly. Ask them to make sure their conclusions are supported by evidence from the podcast. Finally, remind students to check for grammar, usage, and mechanics.

For more support, see **Writing to Compare: Compare-and-Contrast Essay.**

**Evidence Log** Support students in completing their Evidence Log. This paced activity will help prepare them for the Performance-Based Assessment at the end of the unit.

### FORMATIVE ASSESSMENT

### Writing to Compare

**If** students struggle to analyze the oral reading of the poem, **then** review key elements of poetry, such as rhythm and tone.

## Jump Start

What makes a person embrace or reject individualism?

Ask students to think about two things they learned about individualism after reading the poetry selections. As students share, ask them to cite specific examples from the texts to support their ideas. Ask students to picture someone who stands out from the crowd. What makes that person distinctive? Then have students turn the spotlight on themselves and consider the same question about their own uniqueness.

## Write a Personal Narrative

Ask students whether they value independence and self-reliance. Make sure they understand that their answer to this question should guide them in choosing experiences for their personal narrative. Students should complete the assignment using word processing software to take advantage of editing tools and features.

### Elements of a Personal Narrative

Remind students that a well-crafted personal narrative, such as *Up From Slavery,* contains all of the listed required elements, is organized in a logical manner, and contains descriptive and vivid language that reflects on personal experience.

**MAKE IT INTERACTIVE**

Project *Up From Slavery* from the Interactive Teacher's Edition and have students identify the elements of a personal narrative, such as a clear point of view, use of dialogue and description, and a conclusion that reflects the events in the narrative.

## Academic Vocabulary

Encourage students to connect the academic vocabulary to each experience they choose by answering questions like these for each word. Was this a **significant** experience in my life? Did this experience have a strong **impact** on me?

PERFORMANCE TASK: WRITING FOCUS

WRITING TO SOURCES

- THE WRITING OF WALT WHITMAN
- THE POETRY OF EMILY DICKINSON
- *from* EMILY DICKINSON

**Tool Kit**
Student Model of a Personal Narrative

## Write a Personal Narrative

Individualism usually refers to a belief in the value of self-reliance and personal independence. You have just read several poems by writers who embrace the importance of the individual as a unique soul or as a critical part of a community.

**Assignment**

Write a brief **personal narrative** in which you address this question:

> How has my personal experience shaped my view of individualism? Do I see it as a guiding principle, something to be avoided, or a combination of both?

Begin by choosing an incident from your life that has shaped your view of individualism. Develop that memory into a narrative, sequencing events so that they reveal how you acquired the view you now hold. Connect your ideas to details from the texts you have just read.

ACADEMIC VOCABULARY

As you craft your personal narrative, consider using some of the academic vocabulary you learned in the beginning of the unit.

significant
incident
unique
sequence
impact

### Elements of a Personal Narrative

A **personal narrative** is a first-person story about a real-life experience. In a personal narrative, the author is the narrator. In additional, a well-written personal narrative contains these elements:

- a clear and consistent point of view
- a smooth sequence of events or experiences
- effective use of dialogue and/or description to develop the events and characterize the people in the narrative
- precise words and sensory language to clarify experiences
- a conclusion that follows from and reflects on the events presented in the narrative
- error-free grammar and spelling

### Analyze the Writing Model

**Model Personal Narrative** For a model of a well-crafted personal narrative, see the Launch Text excerpt from *Up From Slavery*. Review the Launch Text for examples of the elements of a well-crafted personal narrative. You will look more closely at these elements as you prepare to write your own personal narrative.

STANDARDS
**Writing**
- Write narratives to develop real or imagined experiences or events using effective technique, well-chosen details, and well–structured event sequences.
- Write routinely over extended time frames and shorter time frames for a range of tasks, purposes, and audiences.





AUTHOR'S PERSPECTIVE **Kelly Gallagher, M.Ed.**

**The Best Writer in the Room** Intensive modeling is one of the most effective ways to improve writing instruction. When teachers model at every stage of the writing process, they stop *assigning* writing and start *teaching* it. While you are teaching writing through this Performance Task, show your students how you attack these parts of the assignment:

**Prewriting** Brainstorm topics that elicit experiences, such as trips, drives, or unusual people or places. Ask students to add their own ideas to your list.

**Drafting** Outline an experience and draft alongside students.

## Prewriting / Planning

**Establish the Situation** Reread the questions in the prompt and think about the poems you have read and your own experiences. Then, think about a situation that influenced your views on individualism, whether in a positive or a negative way. Break down the situation into consecutive events, and tell how you felt then—and how you feel now. Remember that individualism involves how you weigh the needs of an individual against the sometimes competing needs of a larger group.

| EVENT | HOW I FELT THEN | HOW I FEEL NOW |
|---|---|---|
| First, | | |
| Next, | | |
| Then, | | |
| Finally, | | |

**Gather Evidence** Your evidence for a personal narrative often springs from your own memories. However, many things can spur those memories. Return to the reading selections in Whole-Class Learning, and find examples of the writers' views on individualism. Think about how their experiences reflect or contradict your own.

| TITLE OF SELECTION | INDIVIDUALISM MEANS . . . |
|---|---|
| | |
| | |
| | |
| | |

**Connect Across Texts** The prompt asks you to connect details from poems by Whitman or Dickinson to your own experience. Begin by skimming the texts and considering which of your chart entries might provide evidence. Note which text or texts come closest to your own views on individualism. Choose a comment from the text that you might quote within your narrative.

EVIDENCE LOG

Review your Evidence Log and identify key details you may want to use in your personal narrative.

STANDARDS

Writing

Engage and orient the reader by setting out a problem, situation, or observation and its significance, establishing one or multiple point(s) of view, and introducing a narrator and/or characters; create a smooth progression of experiences or events.





DIGITAL PERSPECTIVES

## Prewriting / Planning

**Establish the Situation** *Individualism* is an abstract term. Some students may find it easier to focus on the qualities of independence and self-reliance that are at the heart of individualism. Then they can think concretely about an experience and the way it shaped their views on individualism.

**Gather Evidence** As a starting point, students might try to remember any strong reactions they experienced while reading the poetry. Did a specific poem—or even a line from a poem—particularly impress them? Did a specific poem resonate in a personal way? Did any evoke strong emotions, either positive or negative?

**Connect Across Texts** Encourage students to write a brief paragraph in response to the following: What is your view of individualism? Are your feelings positive, negative, or a mix of both? Give your reasons. Then have students find a line from one of the poems that connects with their view.

**Revising** Use your model or a student model as an example.

Do this work in front of students each time. While it may seem more efficient to follow the same steps with each class or show a perfectly polished narrative, don't take this path. If you authentically model the work of writing, students may be more open to the work of writing.

## Drafting

**Developing Conflict** Discuss with students examples of books or movies that include internal struggle and examples that include external struggle. Tell students that one work may include both types.

**Following Story Structure** Discuss story structure in greater detail with students. Consider drawing the story arc so students can visualize the rise and fall of action. Encourage students to incorporate this structure into their narrative.

PERFORMANCE TASK: WRITING FOCUS

## Drafting

**Developing Conflict** All narratives are driven by a **conflict**—a struggle between opposing forces. The conflict may be **internal**, or occurring within the thoughts and feelings of a narrator or person in the story. Alternatively, the struggle may be **external**, or occurring between two people, or between a person and an outside force. A story is more engaging for readers when the conflict is clearly developed using precise, exciting language.

**Following Story Structure** All narratives follow a basic progression in which the conflict is introduced, developed, and resolved. As you write, decide which details of your narrative belong in each section of the plot.

- In the **exposition,** set the scene and introduce the conflict. For this assignment, you may also choose to begin the discussion about individualism.
- In the **rising action, climax,** and **falling action,** present events in chronological order, build the conflict to its point of greatest tension, and then resolve it.
- In the **conclusion,** reflect on the events described in the narrative. For this assignment, you may choose to summarize how the events shaped your views of individualism.

STANDARDS

**Writing**

- Engage and orient the reader by setting out a problem, situation, or observation and its significance, establishing one or multiple point(s) of view, and introducing a narrator and/or characters; create a smooth progression of experiences or events.
- Use a variety of techniques to sequence events so that they build on one another to create a coherent whole and build toward a particular tone and outcome.
- Provide a conclusion that follows from and reflects on what is experienced, observed, or resolved over the course of the narrative.

LAUNCH TEXT EXAMPLE

**Model:** ***from*** **Up From Slavery**

| EXPOSITION |
|---|
| Narrator arrives at Hampton, looking shabby after his travels. Head teacher fails to see him as an individual worthy of Hampton, her school. |

| MAIN PART OF NARRATIVE |
|---|
| *Rising Action:* Head teacher orders narrator to sweep. He cleans the room thoroughly. |
| *Climax:* Teacher evaluates the room. |
| *Falling Action:* Teacher accepts the narrator. |

| CONCLUSION |
|---|
| Adult narrator reflects on the incident and explains its importance. |

**Personal Narrative Organizer**

| EXPOSITION |
|---|
| |

| MAIN PART OF NARRATIVE |
|---|
| *Rising Action:* |
| *Climax:* |
| *Falling Action:* |

| CONCLUSION |
|---|
| |





AUTHOR'S PERSPECTIVE **Jim Cummins, Ph.D.**

**Scaffolding Text Patterns** Students learning English may be challenged by a blank page. Support them with scaffolding to help them organize their narrative and flesh out their outlines. They may benefit from using sentence frames like the following to help them map out their writing.

**Introduction:** Based on my personal experiences, I see individualism as ________.

**Evidence from your own memories of events:** My point of view is based on my personal experiences, including ________.

**Reflection:** Looking back, it seems that ________.

Remind students that the writing process is recursive, and they will be able to refine their outlines and sentence frames as they draft. These are simply tools to help them organize their thoughts before they begin writing.

LANGUAGE DEVELOPMENT: STYLE

## Add Variety: Precise Words and Phrases

The English language contains more than one million words. Nevertheless, as you write, you may find that only one word best fits your meaning for a certain detail. Narrowing down language to choose precise words and phrases means finding the word or words that say exactly what you mean.

### Read It

Consider these examples from the Launch Text. Booker T. Washington chose precise words and phrases to help his readers understand his experience.

- *To me it had been a long, eventful journey; but the first sight of the large, three-story, brick school building seemed to have rewarded me for all that I had undergone in order to reach the place.* **(*Undergone* means "experienced," but it has a connotation of suffering. It suggests that the author had a journey that was long and difficult.)**
- *I felt that I could hardly blame her if she got the idea that I was a worthless loafer or tramp.* **(The precise nouns *loafer* and *tramp*, combined with the adjective *worthless*, reveal Washington's fears about how the head teacher sees him.)**

### Write It

As you draft your personal narrative, carefully choose words that exactly express your feelings, actions, and observations. Here are a few examples that show the power of precise language.

| INSTEAD OF... | TRY THIS... |
|---|---|
| The meal was **good.** | The meal was *mouthwatering, well-seasoned, substantial...* |
| I wore a red **top.** | I wore a *beet-colored polo,* a *burgundy turtleneck,* a *ruby t-shirt...* |
| We all felt **sad.** | We all felt *somber, regretful, sick at heart...* |
| They **walked** up the road. | They *sauntered, staggered, toddled like children...* |
| "Be careful," I **said.** | "Be careful," I *warned, whispered, muttered to myself...* |

TIP

USAGE

Some words share denotations, or dictionary meanings, but have subtly different connotations. Some connotations are positive, whereas others are negative. For example, *clever* has a positive connotation, but *wily* has a negative one. Likewise, *cozy* has a positive connotation, but *cramped* has a negative one. Be careful to choose words that fit your meaning exactly.

STANDARDS

**Writing**

Use precise words and phrases, telling details, and sensory language to convey a vivid picture of the experiences, events, setting, and/or characters.





DIGITAL PERSPECTIVES

## Add Variety: Precise Words and Phrases

### Read It

Brainstorm with students a list of synonyms for the highlighted words, *undergone, worthless, loafer.* Allow them to use a thesaurus. Discuss whether any of these synonyms might have been reasonable alternatives for the highlighted words. Have them give reasons why or why not.

### Write It

As students write their drafts, they should think about their word choice, making sure to select words that best exemplify the given situation. Remind them that strong sensory words are an element of good narrative writing.

Consider providing additional practice in word choice by expanding on the examples in the chart. For each vague word under INSTEAD OF, ask students to offer an additional alternative that might be added to the chart, under the TRY THIS. For example, "The meal was *scrumptious, hearty,* and *zesty.*"

PERSONALIZE FOR LEARNING

### Strategic Support

**Noticing Vague Words** Help students brainstorm a list of overused words that are vague and imprecise, such as *nice* (The outfit is nice.), *thing/things* (He threw things on the floor.), or *stuff* (She put some stuff in the bag.) Then have students work with a partner to list more precise words to substitute for each vague word they identify. Provide time for pairs to share some of their examples with others in class.

## Making Writing Sophisticated

**Reflecting on Events** Point out to students that a reflection describes the personal meaning of an event, situation, or moment. As students consider the personal meaning of the events described in their own narratives, they might try to recall why they chose that particular experience. What made it significant? Why was it so memorable? This line of questioning may lead them to a new reflection on the personal meaning of the event.

### Read It

**Connecting the Past to the Present** In connecting a past event to the present, students might think about its impact. Did the event change their life in any way? How did it cause a change? What does that change mean to them?

**MAKE IT INTERACTIVE**

Project *Up From Slavery* from the Interactive Teacher's Edition and ask students to identify the transitional words and phrases used to show the connection between the past and present.

Then remind students to use transitional words and phrases to help show a smooth sequence of events and experiences.

## MAKING WRITING SOPHISTICATED

**Reflecting on Events** The difference between a compelling personal narrative and a simple anecdote is that in a personal narrative, the narrator usually reflects on and comments on events from the past. Nonfiction narrative writers relate events in sequence—but they also describe their feelings about those events and explain why and how those events were painful, instructive, or inspiring.

### Read It

These examples from the Launch Text show how the writer moves back and forth between actions and thoughts, feelings and reflections.

LAUNCH TEXT EXCERPT

After some hours had passed, the head teacher said to me: "The adjoining recitation-room needs sweeping. Take the broom and sweep it."

It occurred to me at once that here was my chance. Never did I receive an order with more delight. I knew that I could sweep, for Mrs. Ruffner had thoroughly taught me how to do that when I lived with her.

I swept the recitation-room three times.

...

When she was unable to find one bit of dirt on the floor, or a particle of dust on any of the furniture, she quietly remarked, "I guess you will do to enter this institution."

I was one of the happiest souls on earth. The sweeping of that room was my college examination, and never did any youth pass an examination for entrance into Harvard or Yale that gave him more genuine satisfaction. I have passed several examinations since then, but I have always felt that this was the best one I ever passed.

The writer turns from the head teacher's command to his own thoughts and feelings at the time. This detail helps the reader understand how the incident affected him.

Again, the writer turns from narrating the events to sharing his thoughts about the experience.

Here, the writer records a reflection from his present vantage point—the time in which he is actually writing, as opposed to the time he is writing about.

**Connecting the Past to the Present** Writers of strong personal narratives reflect on the importance of the stories they tell by connecting the past to the present. In any personal narrative, a reader must understand the importance of the memory being recalled.

Booker T. Washington connects his present self to his past self. He points out that although he has passed many exams in his life, the sweeping test was the most important because it allowed him to start his education at Hampton. This led, in turn, to his life as a teacher, an author, and an orator. If Washington had omitted the sentence that connects the past to the present, the reader might not understand why he recounted this incident in his autobiography.





**PERSONALIZE FOR LEARNING**

### English Language Support

**Difficult Concepts** Help students understand the concept of reflecting on past experience. Encourage them to recall their first day in a new school. Ask: What was it like? How did you feel? What did it mean to you? Record their responses, and then point out that these are their reflections on a past experience. Then have students practice using the language by telling a partner more about some of their past experiences and how those experiences impacted them. **ALL LEVELS**

College and Career Readiness

## Write It

Return to the "How I Felt Then/How I Feel Now" chart you completed in Prewriting. Use the following steps to integrate your feelings into your narrative.

- Find each event from the chart in your narrative.
- Have you mentioned your "then" feeling from the chart in your essay? If not, decide how you might work it into the narrative. Here are some basic examples:

  [Event happened], making me feel ______________________________.

  I was never more [feeling] than when [event happened]. ______________________________.

- Remember that you may also show how you felt through dialogue, or by describing actions or appearance. Here are some more sophisticated examples:

  "I can't believe my luck," I moaned as [event happened]. ______________________________.

  As [event happened], my face got hot, and my hands felt sweaty. ______________________________.

- Consider how to include your "now" feeling. This might appear near the event in question, or it might appear in your conclusion. Here are examples of both:

  I felt ______________ when [event happened], although now it just seems funny. ______________________________.

  Although the [events] were traumatic at the time, looking back, I realize that they taught me a valuable lesson: ______________________________.

**TIP**

PUNCTUATION
Make sure to punctuate dialogue correctly.

- Use quotation marks before and after a character's exact words.
- Use a comma to set off a quotation from the speaker's tag (e.g., *I said*).
- If the quotation is a question or exclamation, keep the question mark or exclamation point inside the quotation marks.

**Use Precise Words** Readers will better understand your feelings and ideas if you use powerful, precise words. Use this graphic to replace some of your "feelings" words with stronger, more precise choices. Write a feeling word from your text in the first box in each pair. Then, write a more precise word in the second box.

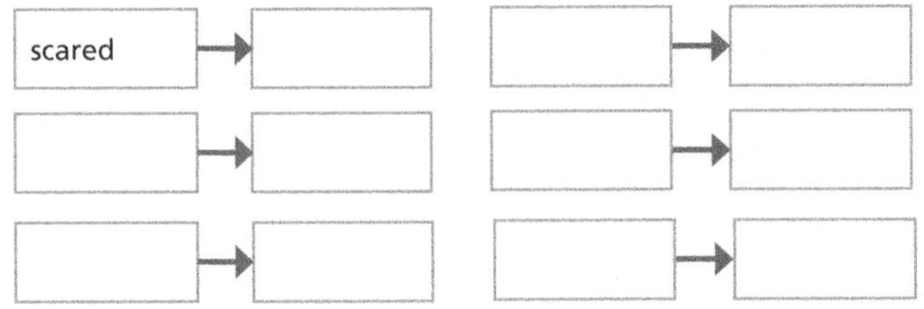


STANDARDS
Writing
- Use narrative techniques, such as dialogue, pacing, description, reflection, and multiple plot lines, to develop experiences, events, and/or characters.
- Provide a conclusion that follows from and reflects on what is experienced, observed, or resolved over the course of the narrative.





DIGITAL PERSPECTIVES

## Write It

Encourage students to read through their narrative paragraph by paragraph. As they finish each paragraph, they should consider whether to include a reflection about their feelings at that point in the narrative.

**Use Precise Words** Help students brainstorm a list of precise words related to feelings that might be appropriate for their writing. Possible examples include: *ecstatic, contented; miserable, melancholy; alarmed, terrified; frustrated, discouraged; peaceful, calm.* Encourage students to take advantage of a print or digital thesaurus as they make final improvements to their narrative.

PERSONALIZE FOR LEARNING

### Strategic Support

**Graphic Organizers** Help students create word webs for a variety of words related to feelings, including those discussed in Write It. For example:

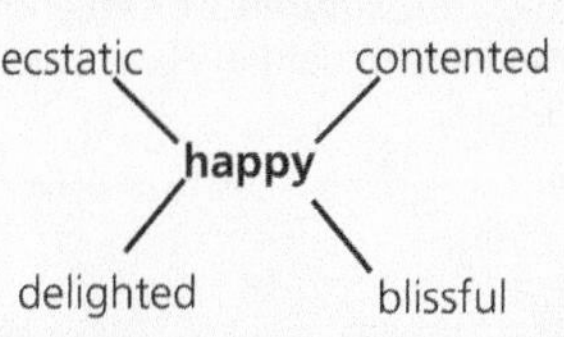

## Revising

### Evaluating Your Draft

Before students begin revising their writing, they should first evaluate their draft to determine whether it contains the necessary elements, is organized well, and adheres to the conventions of personal narratives.

### Revising for Focus and Organization

**First-Person Narration** As students revise their personal narratives, they might imagine themselves speaking to a friend about the personal experience of which they are writing. Does their narrative sound natural? Are they including all information necessary for a reader to be able to understand the events of the narrative?

### Revising for Evidence and Elaboration

**Sensory Language** Remind students that sensory language often contains comparisons that describe an action or event in terms of other things. For example, *The ball banged the garage door like a sledge hammer.* Encourage students to try using sensory comparisons to strengthen their writing.

PERFORMANCE TASK: WRITING FOCUS

## Revising

### Evaluating Your Draft

Use this checklist to evaluate the effectiveness of your first draft. Then, use your evaluation and the instruction on this page to guide your revision.

| FOCUS AND ORGANIZATION | EVIDENCE AND ELABORATION | CONVENTIONS |
|---|---|---|
| ☐ Provides an exposition that sets the scene, introduces the conflict, and establishes a point of view.<br>☐ Establishes a sequence of events that unfolds smoothly and logically.<br>☐ Includes a conclusion that resolves the narrative in a satisfying way. | ☐ Uses techniques such as dialogue, description, and reflection to develop the experience being narrated.<br>☐ Uses precise words and phrases, specific details, and sensory language to clarify events for the reader.<br>☐ Uses vocabulary and word choice that is appropriate for the audience and purpose. | ☐ Attends to the norms and conventions of the discipline, especially regarding sequence of events and appropriate attention to connotative meanings. |

### Revising for Focus and Organization

**First-Person Narration** As the narrator of your own story, you can describe what you saw, experienced, thought, and felt. You can also describe what others did or said, as well as what you imagine they may have thought or felt. However, you cannot with authority say exactly what others felt or thought. Reread your narrative and make sure you have presented a first-person point of view consistently, and that you have not included information that steps outside the limits of that perspective.

**Conclusion** A satisfying, effective conclusion connects to the story being told and explores the significance of those events. Review your conclusion, and make sure it succeeds in doing both.

### Revising for Evidence and Elaboration

**Sensory Language** Return to your narrative, and imagine that you are a stranger encountering your story for the first time. Decide whether any sections feel flat or uninteresting. Then, consider adding sensory details to show what you as the narrator saw, heard, smelled, tasted, and felt. This might involve simple additions or changes to certain words. Consider these examples:

**Lacking Sensory Details:** I *walked slowly* along the path.
**Using Sensory Details:** I *scuffed my way* along the *gravel* path.

**Lacking Sensory Details:** A *bird called* from a tree.
**Using Sensory Details:** An *owl screeched* from a *shadowy tree*.

WORD NETWORK

Include interesting words from your Word Network in your personal narrative.

STANDARDS

**Writing**
Use precise words and phrases, telling details, and sensory language to convey a vivid picture of the experiences, events, setting, and/or characters.

**Language**
Demonstrate command of the conventions of standard English grammar and usage when writing or speaking.





HOW LANGUAGE WORKS

**Precise Words and Language** Help students to create a chart of precise words and phrases related to the five senses—and focused on their narrative. Later, they might use this chart in their writing. For example: **sight/**dazzling autumn sunset; enormous turquoise balloon; tiny short-haired Chihuahua. Have students continue the chart using all five senses.

PEER REVIEW

Exchange narratives with a classmate. Use the checklist to evaluate your classmate's personal narrative and provide supportive feedback.

1. Did the narrative explain how the experience shaped the writer's views about individualism?
   ☐ yes ☐ no If no, explain what might be added.
2. Did the sequence of events lead naturally to the writer's views on individualism?
   ☐ yes ☐ no If no, tell what needs clarifying.
3. Are the writer's views on individualism clear to you now?
   ☐ yes ☐ no If no, suggest what you might change.
4. What is the strongest part of your classmate's narrative? Why?

## Editing and Proofreading

**Edit for Conventions** Reread your draft for accuracy and consistency. Correct errors in grammar and word usage. Be sure that any shifts in time between past and present are clear.

**Proofread for Accuracy** Reread your draft carefully, looking for errors in spelling and punctuation. Be sure to punctuate dialogue correctly.

## Publishing and Presenting

Use an app of your choice to save your personal narrative as an ebook. Depending on the app, you may include illustrations, and you may have a choice of preserving it in print or as a vocal recording. Share your ebook with others in your class. Ask your classmates to leave comments on a comment sheet that you provide. As you read classmates' ebooks, remember to keep your comments positive and helpful.

## Reflecting

Consider what you learned by writing your personal narrative. Would a different incident from your life have provided a stronger response to the prompt? Does your narrative accurately reflect what happened to you and explain its importance in shaping your view about individualism? Think about what you might do differently the next time you write a personal narrative.

STANDARDS

Writing

- Develop and strengthen writing as needed by planning, revising, editing, rewriting, or trying a new approach, focusing on addressing what is most significant for a specific purpose and audience.
- Use technology, including the Internet, to produce, publish, and update individual or shared writing products in response to ongoing feedback, including new arguments or information.





DIGITAL PERSPECTIVES

## Editing and Proofreading

Offer some words and phrases that might help students show a shift to the past. Examples include *at that time/moment, back then, on that occasion.* Words or phrases that show a return to the present might include *now, at present, presently, today, as of now.* Remind students that as they proofread, they should check their writing carefully for grammar, spelling, and punctuation errors.

## Publishing and Presenting

Given that their narratives are based on personal experience, students may wish to use photographs to illustrate their work. Photographs might include images of people, places, or objects described in their narratives.

## Reflecting

Suggest students use the Peer Review form to evaluate their own work. The next time they write a narrative, they might try to revise and edit their writing in that same objective manner, as if critiquing another person's work.

PERSONALIZE FOR LEARNING

**English Language Support**

**Speaking and Listening** Have partners take turns reading their narratives aloud to each other in a natural speaking voice. Then ask them each tell their partner what they liked best about the narrative and to explain why. **ALL LEVELS**

# OVERVIEW

## SMALL-GROUP LEARNING

### What role does individualism play in American society?

Throughout American history, those who are unique enough to stand out in society often have been the very ones who do things that have a long-lasting impact on our culture. During Small-Group Learning, students will read selections that feature some of this country's boldest thinkers and innovators.

### Small-Group Learning Strategies

Review the Learning Strategies with students and explain that as they work through Small-Group Learning they will develop strategies to work in small-group environments.

- Have students watch the video on Small-Group Learning Strategies.
- A video on this topic is available online in the Professional Development Center.

You may wish to discuss some action items to add to the chart as a class before students complete it on their own. For example, for "Participate fully," you might solicit the following contributions from students by:

- Sharing questions or experiences in your group's discussion
- Asking others for their experiences and comparing notes with others in your group

**Block Scheduling**

Each day in this Pacing Plan represents a 40-50 minute class period. Teachers using block scheduling may combine days to reflect their class schedule. In addition, teachers may revise pacing to differentiate and support core instruction by integrating components and resources as students require.

OVERVIEW: SMALL-GROUP LEARNING

ESSENTIAL QUESTION:

## What role does individualism play in American society?

As you read these selections, work with your group to explore the meaning of individualism.

**From Text to Topic** In the nineteenth century, America's spirit of individualism was evident in every sphere of activity, from the arts to exploration to the development of new technologies. For instance, the completion of the Erie Canal in 1825—the first transportation system between New York City and the Great Lakes that did not require carrying cargo over land—helped open the West to settlers. In 1844, Samuel Morse sent the first telegraph message, pioneering the first near-instant means of communication between cities. As you read, consider how these selections show individualism in all realms of American life.

## Small-Group Learning Strategies

Throughout your life, in school, in your community, and in your career, you will continue to develop strategies when you work in teams. Use these strategies during Small-Group Learning. Add ideas of your own for each step.

| STRATEGY | ACTION PLAN |
|---|---|
| Prepare | • Complete your assignment so that you are prepared for group work.<br>• Organize your thinking so you can contribute to your group's discussions. |
| Participate fully | • Make eye contact to signal that you are listening and taking in what is being said.<br>• Use text evidence when making a point. |
| Support others | • Build on ideas from others in your group.<br>• Invite others who have not yet spoken to join the discussion. |
| Clarify | • Paraphrase the ideas of others to ensure that your understanding is correct.<br>• Ask follow-up questions. |





SCAN FOR MULTIMEDIA

### Pacing Plan

| Day | Activity |
|---|---|
| 1 | Unit Introduction |
| 2 | Introduce Whole-Class Learning |
| 3 | Historical Perspectives |
| 4–7 | The Writing of Walt Whitman |
| 8–12 | The Poetry of Emily Dickinson |
| 13 | Media: *from* Emily Dickinson |
| 14–15 | Performance Task |

DIGITAL PERSPECTIVES

CONTENTS







## Contents

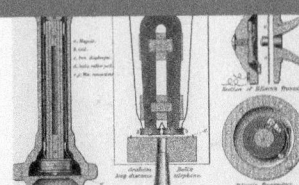

**Selections** Circulate among groups as they preview the selections. You might encourage groups to discuss ideas they already have about any of the selections or the situations and settings shown in the photographs. Students may wish to take a poll within their groups to determine which selections look the most interesting.

Remind students that communicating and collaborating in groups is an important skill that they will use throughout their lives—in school, in their careers, and in their community.

## Performance Task

**Present a Personal Narrative** Give groups time to read about and briefly discuss the oral presentation they will create after reading. Encourage students to do some preliminary thinking about the types of text selections they may want to use. This may help them focus their reading and group discussions to shed light on their performance tasks.

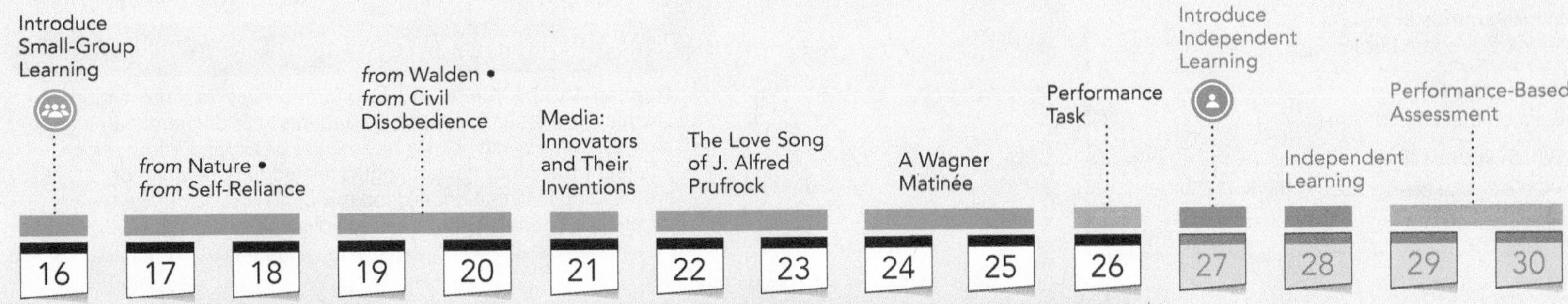

# OVERVIEW

## SMALL-GROUP LEARNING

### Working as a Team

1. **Take a Position** Remind groups to let all members share their responses. You may wish to set a time limit for this discussion. Encourage students to use specific texts to strengthen the ways in which they express their own ideas.
2. **List Your Rules** You may want to have groups share their lists of rules and consolidate them into a master list to be displayed and followed by all groups. Suggest students add to the lists as they go through the selections.
3. **Apply the Rules** As you circulate among the groups, ensure that students are staying on task. Consider a short time limit for this step.
4. **Name Your Group** This task can be creative and fun. If students have trouble coming up with a name, suggest that they think of something related to the unit topic. Or, suggest they draw on selection or theme that especially interests them. Encourage groups to share their names with the class.
5. **Create a Communication Plan** Encourage groups to include in their plans agreed-upon times during the day to share ideas. They should also devise a method for recording, saving their communications, and making it accessible to all the group members.

### Accountable Talk

Remind students that groups should communicate politely. You can post these Accountable Talk suggestions and encourage students to add their own. Students should:

**Remember to . . .**
Ask clarifying questions.

**Which sounds like . . .**
Could you repeat that please?

Can you give me a specific example?

I think you said ______. Is that correct?

**Remember to . . .**
Explain your thinking.

**Which sounds like . . .**
I think this is true because ______.

**Remember to . . .**
Build on the ideas of others.

**Which sounds like . . .**
When ______ said ______, it made me think of ______.

## OVERVIEW: SMALL-GROUP LEARNING

### Working as a Team

1. **Take a Position** In your group, discuss the following question:

   **Do you think American teenagers today would rather fit in than stand out? Explain.**

   As you take turns sharing your positions, provide reasons for your choice. After all group members have shared, discuss connections among the ideas that were presented.

2. **List Your Rules** As a group, decide on the rules that you will follow as you work together. Two samples are provided. Add two more of your own. As you work together, you may add or revise rules based on your experience together.
   - Be open to multiple perspectives and creative responses.
   - Give reasons for your opinions and encourage others to do so as well.
   - ______________________________
   - ______________________________

3. **Apply the Rules** Share what you have learned about individualism in America. Make sure each person in the group contributes. Take notes as you listen to others and be prepared to share with the class one thing that you heard from another member of your group.

4. **Name Your Group** Choose a name that reflects the unit topic.

   Our group's name: ______________________________

5. **Create a Communication Plan** Decide how you want to communicate with one another. For example, you might text, set up an online chat, or use the private messaging feature on a social media website.

   Our group's decision: ______________________________

### FACILITATING SMALL-GROUP LEARNING

**Forming Groups** You may wish to form groups for Small-Group Learning so that each consists of students with different learning abilities. Some students may be adept at organizing information whereas others may have strengths related to generating or synthesizing information. A good mix of abilities can make the experience of Small-Group Learning dynamic and productive.

## Making a Schedule

First, find out the due dates for the Small-Group activities. Then, preview the texts and activities with your group and make a schedule for completing the tasks.

| SELECTION | ACTIVITIES | DUE DATE |
|---|---|---|
| *from* Nature<br>*from* Self-Reliance | | |
| *from* Walden<br>*from* Civil Disobedience | | |
| Innovators and Their Inventions | | |
| The Love Song of J. Alfred Prufrock | | |
| A Wagner Matinée | | |

## Working on Group Projects

As your group works together, you'll find it more effective if each person has a specific role. Different projects require different roles. Before beginning a project, discuss the necessary roles and choose one for each group member. Some possible roles are listed here. Add your ideas to the list.

**Project Manager:** monitors the schedule and keeps everyone on task
**Researcher:** organizes research activities
**Recorder:** takes notes during group meetings

________________________________________

________________________________________

________________________________________

________________________________________

SCAN FOR MULTIMEDIA



DIGITAL PERSPECTIVES

## Making a Schedule

Encourage groups to preview the reading selections and to consider how long it will take them to complete the activities accompanying each selection. Point out that they can adjust the due dates for particular selections as needed as they work on their small-group projects, however, they must complete all assigned tasks before the group Performance Task is due. Encourage groups to review their schedules upon completing the activities for each selection to make sure they are on track to meet the final due date. Suggest that they come up with ways to help one another meet the interim dates their group sets up. This will encourage accountability for meeting deadlines for all members of the group.

## Working on Group Projects

Point out to groups that the roles they assign can also be changed later. Students might have to make changes based on who is most adept at, or interested in, doing a particular task. Try to make sure that there is no favoritism, cliquishness, or stereotyping by gender or other means in the assignment of roles.

Also, you should review the roles each group assigns to its members. Based on your understanding of students' individual strengths, you might find it necessary to suggest some changes.

AUTHOR'S PERSPECTIVE **Ernest Morrell, Ph.D.**

**Supporting Small-Group Learning**
Because the dominant mode of discourse in classrooms has historically been teacher-led, many students may not be immediately comfortable discussing and collaborating in groups. The first few times students meet in their groups, you may need to provide additional support by setting expectations for collaborative behavior and discussions. Remind students that it is important for all group members to contribute to discussion, but that no one member of the group should monopolize discussion. Whether students are speaking or listening, they should be active participants. Visit groups to explain that even when students aren't speaking, they should be listening to other group members and noting important points that they would like to build upon when it is their turn to speak.

# *from* Nature • *from* Self-Reliance

**AUDIO SUMMARIES** of "Nature" and "Self-Reliance are available in both English and Spanish and can be assigned to students in the Interactive Teacher's Edition or Unit Resources. Assigning these summaries prior to reading the selection may help students build additional background knowledge and set a context for their first read.

## Summary

In "Nature," Ralph Waldo Emerson describes his feelings of exhilaration, as he stands alone in the woods, feeling God, the Universal Being, as it flows through him. He is acutely aware of everything around him as it lifts his spirits. He claims, "I am nothing. I see all," thereby suggesting that a person can only experience personal discovery by losing oneself in the totality of existence. He claims that this power to transcend oneself "does not reside in nature, but in man, or in a harmony of both." In "Self-Reliance," Emerson explores the idea that in order to fulfill their potential, individuals must be willing to think for themselves and resist pressures to conform to society's rules and customs. Those who choose to rely on others' opinions cannot achieve true individuality or greatness.

### Insight

Reading the excerpts from "Nature" and "Self-Reliance" will help students understand that individualism often involves learning to identify and accept one's unique qualities in a society that stresses conformity to social norms. Students will explore the importance of individuality, independence, and an appreciation for nature as it relates to their own position in society.

ESSENTIAL QUESTION:
What role does individualism play in American society?

## Connection to Essential Question

The excerpts from "Nature" and "Self-Reliance" connect to the Essential Question, "What role does individualism play in American society?" Both essays celebrate the importance of individualism to the formation of the American character.

SMALL-GROUP LEARNING PERFORMANCE TASK
When is it difficult to march to the beat of a "different drummer" and stand on your own as an individual? What are the risks and rewards of nonconformity?

UNIT PERFORMANCE-BASED ASSESSMENT
What significant incident from my past helped me to realize that I am a unique individual?

## Connection to Performance Tasks

**Small-Class Learning Performance Task** In this Performance Task, students will draw on the ways in which the texts in the unit approach the concept of nonconformity and use them to write a speech on the subject.

**Unit Performance-Based Assessment** These excerpts from two essays by Ralph Waldo Emerson offer numerous examples of incidents that helped the author to shape his belief in the importance of individualism in American life and culture.

DIGITAL PERSPECTIVES

Audio

Video

Document

Annotation Highlights

EL Highlights

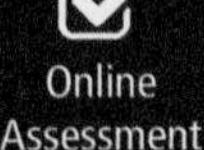
Online Assessment

## LESSON RESOURCES

| | Making Meaning | Language Development | Effective Expression |
|---|---|---|---|
| Lesson | **First Read**<br>**Close Read**<br>**Analyze the Text**<br>**Analyze Craft and Structure** | **Concept Vocabulary**<br>**Word Study**<br>**Conventions and Style** | **Writing to Sources** |
| **Instructional Standards** | **RI.10** By the end of grade 11, read and comprehend literary nonfiction . . .<br>**L.4.a** Use context as a clue . . .<br>**RI.2** Determine two or more central ideas of a text . . .<br>**RI.5** Analyze and evaluate the effectiveness of the structure . . .<br>**RI.7** Analyze seventeenth-, eighteenth-, and nineteenth-century foundational U.S. documents . . . | **L.4.c** Consult general and specialized reference materials . . .<br>**L.3** Apply knowledge of language . . .<br>**L.3.a** Vary syntax for effect . . . | **W.3** Write narratives . . . |
| **STUDENT RESOURCES** | | | |
| Available online in the Interactive Student Edition or Unit Resources | Selection Audio<br>First-Read Guide: Nonfiction<br>Close-Read Guide: Nonfiction<br>Word Network | Word Network | Evidence Log |
| **TEACHER RESOURCES** | | | |
| **Selection Resources** Available online in the Interactive Teacher's Edition or Unit Resources | Audio Summaries<br>Annotation Highlights<br>EL Highlights<br>English Language Support Lesson: Using *Wh-* Questions<br>*from* Nature • *from* Self-Reliance: Text Questions<br>Analyze Craft and Structure: Development of Ideas | Concept Vocabulary and Word Study<br>Conventions and Style: Sentence Variety | Writing to Sources: Story Element |
| **Reteach/Practice (RP)** Available online in the Interactive Teacher's Edition or Unit Resources | Analyze Craft and Structure: Development of Ideas (RP) | Word Study: Latin Root *-sanct-* (RP)<br>Conventions and Style: Sentence Variety (RP) | Writing to Sources: Story Element (RP) |
| **My Resources** | A Unit 2 Answer Key is available online and in the Interactive Teacher's Edition | | |

# Reading Support

| Text Complexity Rubric: *from* Nature • *from* Self-Reliance | |
|---|---|
| **Quantitative Measures** | |
| **Lexile:** 960; 980 Text Length: 487 words; 579 words | |
| **Qualitative Measures** | |
| Knowledge Demands ①—②—❸—④—⑤ | Contains references to transcendental ideas ("occult relation between man and vegetable," Universal Being), not all of which are explained. Students may need more background about these terms and transcendentalism in general. |
| Structure ①—②—❸—④—⑤ | The selections are first-person essays. Information is logically organized, but connections between ideas are not always explicit. |
| Language Conventionality and Clarity ①—②—❸—④—⑤ | The selections contain clear, direct prose and some above-level vocabulary. In "Nature," nature is personified and the writer uses some figurative language. |
| Levels of Meaning/Purpose ①—②—❸—④—⑤ | The meaning is mostly straightforward. Elements of mysticism/union with the universe may be challenging. |

DECIDE AND PLAN

## English Language Support

Provide English Learners with support for knowledge demands and language as they read the selection.

**Knowledge Demands** Before students read, review background information on Transcendentalism and its idea that individuals can look to nature to understand themselves and a higher being. Then review parts of the selection that may be confusing, for example: *I become a transparent eyeball; I am nothing; I see all; the currents of the Universal Being circulate through me; I am part or parcel of God.*

**Language** Discuss the meaning and use of personification in the following line: *The greatest delight which the fields and woods minister is the suggestion of an occult relation between man and the vegetable. I am not alone and unacknowledged. They nod to me, and I to them.* Explain that *occult*, means "supernatural or otherworldly."

## Strategic Support

Provide students with strategic support to ensure that they can successfully read the text.

**Knowledge Demands** Make sure students understand the role of nature and the individual in Transcendentalism. Have students work with a partner to identify key details in the selections that convey the connection between people and nature.

**Language** If students have difficulty with complex sentences, work together to break down sentences into smaller chunks in order to understand their meanings. Ask students to highlight words or phrases that they don't understand. As a group, help clarify some of the sentences they find difficult.

## Challenge

Provide students who need to be challenged with ideas for how they can go beyond a simple interpretation of the text.

**Text Analysis** Have students discuss the last paragraph of "from Nature." Point out the fourth line: *Nature always wears the colors of the spirit.* What is the relationship between a person's mood and nature? Ask students if they agree with this idea.

**Written Response** Ask students to write a description of an experience they have had in nature. Ask them to describe the setting and how they felt. Did they feel comforted? connected?

TEACH

## Read and Respond

Have the groups read the selection and complete the Making Meaning, Language Development, and Effective Expression activities.

# Standards Support Through Teaching and Learning Cycle

## IDENTIFY NEEDS

Analyze results of the Beginning-of-Year Assessment, focusing on the items relating to Unit 2. Also take into consideration student performance to this point and your observations of where particular students struggle.

## DECIDE AND PLAN

- If students have performed poorly on items matching these standards, then provide selection scaffolds before assigning them the on-level lesson provided in the Student Edition.
- If students have done well on the Beginning-of-Year Assessment, then challenge them to keep progressing and learning by giving them opportunities to practice the skills in depth.
- Use the Selection Resources listed on the Planning pages for "Nature" and "Self-Reliance" to help students continually improve their ability to master the standards.

**Instructional Standards: *from* Nature • *from* Self-Reliance**

| | Catching Up | This Year | Looking Forward |
|---|---|---|---|
| **Reading** | You may wish to administer the **Analyze Craft and Structure: Development of Ideas (RP)** worksheet to help students see how many forms of writing often follow the narrative form of beginning, middle, and end.<br><br>You may wish to connect Emerson's ideas to the way he describes them. Give students the **Conventions and Style: Sentence Variety (RP)** worksheet so they can see how the variety helps hold audience attention. | **RI.2** Determine two or more central ideas of a text and analyze their development over the course of the text, including how they interact and build on one another to produce a complex analysis; provide an objective summary of the text.<br><br>**RI.5** Analyze and evaluate the effectiveness of the structure an author uses in his or her exposition or argument, including whether the structure makes points clear, convincing, and engaging. | Ask students to reflect on places they may want to preserve—in their cities, towns, neighborhood, or even at home. In small groups, they can discuss how they could lay out their argument for keeping a place they believe is under a threat of being destroyed. |
| **Writing** | You may wish to administer the **Writing to Sources: Story Element (RP)** worksheet to help students plan their presentations from beginning to end. | **W.3** Write narratives to develop real or imagined experiences or events using effective technique, well-chosen details, and well-structured event sequences. | Suggest that students may wish to write a short narrative of an event that is important to them. |
| **Language** | You may wish to administer the **Word Study: Latin Root *-sanct-*** worksheet to help students with their use of adjectives with common roots. | **L.4.c** Consult general and specialized reference materials, both print and digital, to find the pronunciation of a word or determine or clarify its precise meaning, its part of speech, its etymology, or its standard usage. | Challenge students to use increasingly more varied sentences in their writing. |

## ANALYZE AND REVISE

- Analyze student work for evidence of student learning.
- Identify whether or not students have met the expectations in the standards.
- Identify implications for future instruction.

## TEACH

Implement the planned lesson, and gather evidence of student learning.

## Jump Start

FIRST READ Ask students how it feels to be out in a natural setting, such as a park or wilderness area. How does it differ from being inside or on a city street? Have them think of the contrast between what they see, hear, and smell in the two settings.

## *from* Nature • *from* Self-Reliance

What can we learn from the titles Emerson gives to the two essays? Modeling this and other questions readers might ask will bring the excerpts from "Nature" and "Self-Reliance" to life and connect them to the Performance Task question. Selection audio and print capability for the selection are available in the Interactive Teacher's Edition.

## Concept Vocabulary

Have groups briefly discuss the three concept vocabulary words. Have they encountered any of the words before? Have groups consider the strategy of using context clues and discuss its advantages and disadvantages.

## FIRST READ

Have students perform the steps of the first read independently:

NOTICE: Encourage students to notice the general ideas in the text. What is the topic of the first excerpt? The second?

ANNOTATE: Remind students to focus on particularly rich passages that contain ideas that students find intriguing or perhaps puzzling.

CONNECT: Encourage students to make connections to their own lives. How would they describe their relationship to nature? Do they consider themselves to be self-reliant?

RESPOND: Students will demonstrate their understanding of the text by answering questions and writing a summary.

Point out to students that they will perform the first three steps concurrently as they are doing their first read. They will complete the Respond step after they have finished the first read. You may wish to print copies of the **First-Read Guide: Nonfiction** for students to use.

MAKING MEANING

About the Author

**Ralph Waldo Emerson** (1803–1882) was born in Boston, the son of a Unitarian minister. He entered Harvard at the age of fourteen. After postgraduate studies at Harvard Divinity School, he became pastor of the Second Church of Boston. Emerson's career as a minister, however, was short-lived. Grief-stricken at his wife's death, and dissatisfied with his faith, Emerson resigned after three years and went to Europe. There, he met many of the leading thinkers of the day. Upon his return to the United States, Emerson settled in Concord, Massachusetts, and began to write seriously. His ideas helped forge the Transcendentalist movement, which celebrated the individual and the power of the human mind. Using material from his lectures and journals, Emerson published *Essays* in 1841. The collection brought him international fame. Even today, Emerson is one of the most quoted writers in American literature.

STANDARDS

**Reading Informational Text**
By the end of grade 11, read and comprehend literary nonfiction in the grades 11–CCR text complexity band proficiently, with scaffolding as needed at the high end of the range.
**Language**
Use context as a clue to the meaning of a word or phrase.

## *from* Nature
## *from* Self-Reliance

### Concept Vocabulary

As you perform your first read of these excerpts from "Nature" and "Self-Reliance," you will encounter these words:

sanctity    transcendent    redeemers

**Context Clues** To find the meaning of an unfamiliar word, look for **context clues.** Words and phrases that appear in the same sentence or in nearby sentences may help you determine the meaning of the unfamiliar word.

**Example:** At all times she acts with respectful *decorum*, even when others try to anger her.

**Context clues:** According to the sentence, *decorum* is a respectful way to behave—something that would be difficult for most people to maintain when angered.

**Possible meaning:** *Decorum* means "dignity or control appropriate to an occasion."

Apply your knowledge of context clues and other vocabulary strategies to determine the meanings of unfamiliar words you encounter during your first read.

### First Read NONFICTION

Apply these strategies as you conduct your first read. You will have an opportunity to complete a close read after your first read.

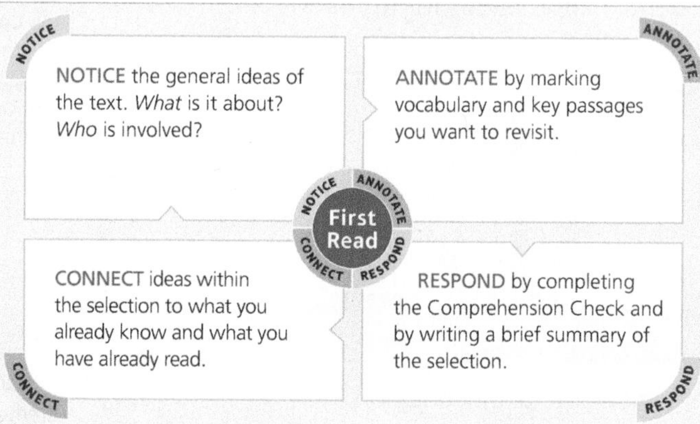

NOTICE
NOTICE the general ideas of the text. *What* is it about? *Who* is involved?
ANNOTATE
ANNOTATE by marking vocabulary and key passages you want to revisit.
First Read
CONNECT
CONNECT ideas within the selection to what you already know and what you have already read.
RESPOND
RESPOND by completing the Comprehension Check and by writing a brief summary of the selection.






AUTHOR'S PERSPECTIVE **Jim Cummins, PhD.**

**Importance of Background Knowledge** It is important for all students, and especially for English learners, to learn to tap into their background knowledge when they read a text. Teachers can help students access this knowledge and integrate it with new textual information. One way to do this is to encourage groups to share what they know about the topic of the text before they begin reading. For example, some students may have prior knowledge about nature, which can help to scaffold understanding of the excerpts "Nature" and "Self-Reliance." On a deeper level, more students may be able to relate to the idea of their being responsible for the development of their minds. After students have completed their first read, have them discuss how their background knowledge helped them understand the text.

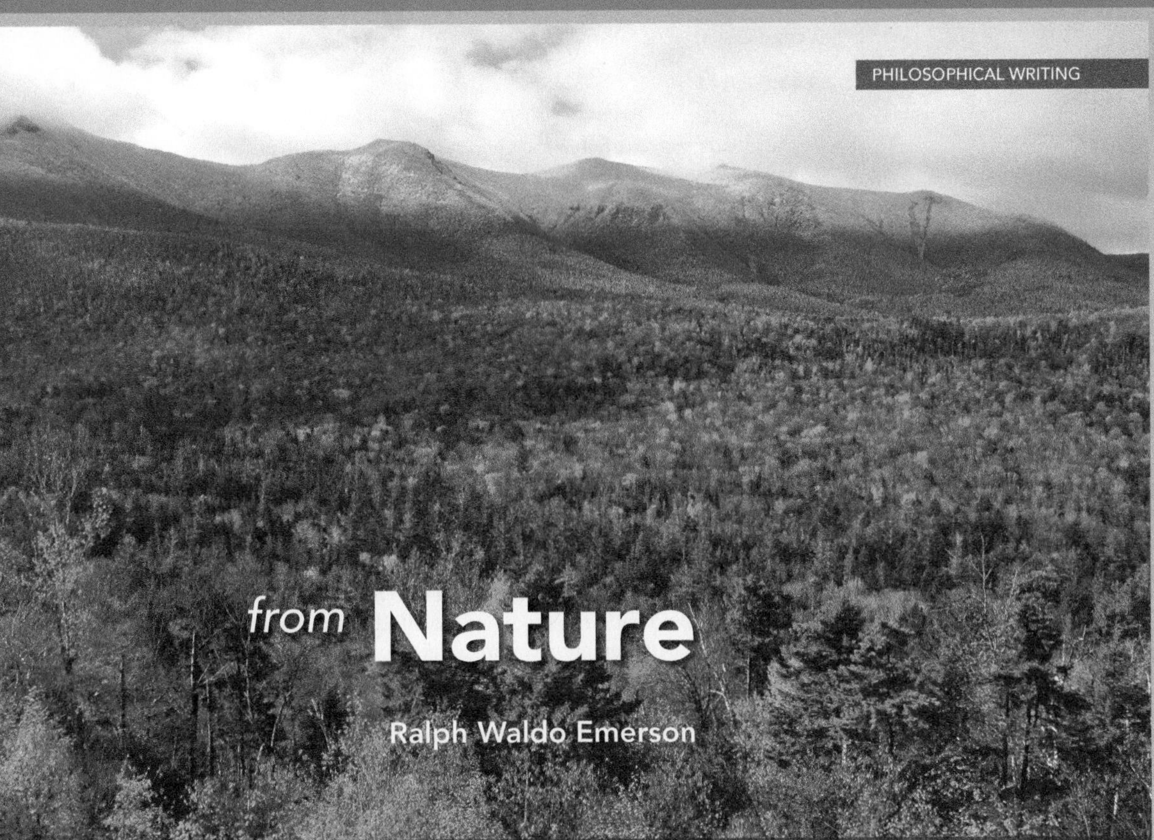


# from Nature

Ralph Waldo Emerson

## Concept Vocabulary

**SANCTITY** If groups are struggling to define *sanctity* in paragraph 1, point out that surrounding words and phrases refer to this word. These include the phrase "plantation of God." Discuss this phrase's meaning. Students probably know that at a plantation, a certain crop is planted; for example, a cotton plantation. Lead students to conclude that a forest is a plantation of trees, and the trees grow by God's design. Now, when students consider the meaning of *sanctity*, they will bring to their analysis an understanding that God, or a higher being, is involved.

**Possible responses:** *Sanctity* must mean "holiness, purity, blessedness."

BACKGROUND

During the 1830s and 1840s, Emerson and a small group of like-minded friends gathered regularly in his study to discuss philosophy, religion, and literature. The Transcendental Club developed a philosophical system that stressed intuition, individuality, and self-reliance. In 1836, Emerson published "Nature," the Transcendental Club's unofficial statement of belief.

SCAN FOR MULTIMEDIA 

1 Nature is a setting that fits equally well a comic or a mourning piece. In good health, the air is a cordial[1] of incredible virtue. Crossing a bare common,[2] in snow puddles, at twilight, under a clouded sky, without having in my thoughts any occurrence of special good fortune, I have enjoyed a perfect exhilaration. I am glad to the brink of fear. In the woods, too, a man casts off his years, as the snake his slough, and at what period soever of life is always a child. In the woods is perpetual youth. Within these plantations of God, a decorum and sanctity reign, a perennial festival is dressed, and the guest sees not how he should tire of them in a thousand years. In

NOTES

Mark context clues or indicate another strategy you used that helped you determine meaning.

**sanctity** (SANGK tuh tee) *n.*

MEANING:

1. **cordial** (KAWR juhl) *n.* a strong, sweet liquor.
2. **common** *n.* piece of open public land.



## FACILITATING SMALL-GROUP CLOSE LEARNING

**CLOSE READ: Philosophical Writing** As groups perform the close read, circulate and offer support as needed.

- Tell groups that the word *philosophy* can have many meanings. In the context of this selection, it is a search for an understanding of values and reality.
- Philosophical writing can seem dense and difficult to understand. Readers of philosophy usually have to read and think about the writing a number of times. Students should not be discouraged if they don't understand Emerson's work at first glance. If they reread the selection, they will see that it becomes clearer.
- Students should stop after each paragraph and summarize what they think Emerson is saying.

CLOSER LOOK

## Analyze Descriptions

Circulate among groups as students conduct their close read. Suggest that groups read paragraph 1. Encourage them to talk about the annotations that they mark. If needed, provide the following support.

**ANNOTATE:** Have students mark details in the paragraph that describe human beings in relationship to the woods, or work with small groups to have students participate while you highlight them together.

**QUESTION:** Guide students to consider what these details might tell them. Ask what a reader can infer from the impression the author creates, and accept student responses.
**Possible responses:** Emerson suggests that nature has the ability to make people feel that they are young again. They are rejuvenated and return to the stability of reason and faith.

**CONCLUDE:** Help students formulate conclusions about the importance of these details in the text. Ask students why the author might have included these details.
**Possible responses:** When Emerson says that he becomes a transparent eyeball, he means that nature shows him his essence, and he becomes part of a divine experience.

Remind students that in this form of nonfiction writing, the author is often the **subject** of the selection. Emerson uses a natural scene to reveal an ideal view of man's relationship to nature.

Additional **English Language Support** is available in the Interactive Teacher's Edition.

NOTES

the woods, we return to reason and faith. There I feel that nothing can befall me in life—no disgrace, no calamity (leaving me my eyes), which nature cannot repair. Standing on the bare ground—my head bathed by the blithe air and uplifted into infinite space—all mean egotism vanishes. I become a transparent eyeball; I am nothing; I see all; the currents of the Universal Being circulate through me; I am part or parcel of God. The name of the nearest friend sounds then foreign and accidental: to be brothers, to be acquaintances, master or servant, is then a trifle and a disturbance. I am the lover of uncontained and immortal beauty. In the wilderness, I find something more dear and connate[3] than in the streets or villages. In the tranquil landscape, and especially in the distant line of the horizon, man beholds somewhat as beautiful as his own nature.

2 The greatest delight which the fields and woods minister is the suggestion of an occult relation between man and the vegetable. I am not alone and unacknowledged. They nod to me, and I to them. The waving of the boughs in the storm is new to me and old. It takes me by surprise, and yet is not unknown. Its effect is like that of a higher thought or a better emotion coming over me, when I deemed I was thinking justly or doing right.

3 Yet it is certain that the power to produce this delight does not reside in nature, but in man, or in a harmony of both. It is necessary to use these pleasures with great temperance. For nature is not always tricked[4] in holiday attire, but the same scene which yesterday breathed perfume and glittered as for the frolic of the nymphs is overspread with melancholy today. Nature always wears the colors of the spirit. To a man laboring under calamity, the heat of his own fire hath sadness in it. Then there is a kind of contempt of the landscape felt by him who has just lost by death a dear friend. The sky is less grand as it shuts down over less worth in the population. ❧

3. **connate** (KON ayt) *adj.* existing within someone since birth; inborn.
4. **tricked** *v.* dressed.





DIGITAL PERSPECTIVES

**Illuminating the Text** Find and show students a video about the Transcendentalist movement. Explain that Transcendentalism, which flourished between 1830 and 1855 and was centered in Massachusetts, represented the emergence of a new national culture. Before this, Americans imitated the culture of Great Britain, to a large extent. Some Transcendentalist tenets include the unity of all beings, the goodness of human beings, and the superiority of insight over logic and experience. Have students discuss the importance of Transcendentalism to Americans' embrace of individualism. **(Research to Clarify)**

PHILOSOPHICAL WRITING

# *from* Self-Reliance

Ralph Waldo Emerson

BACKGROUND

Individuality, independence, and an appreciation for the wonders of nature are just a few of the principles that Ralph Waldo Emerson helped to instill in our nation's identity. His essay "Self-Reliance" grew out of a series of lectures that he conducted in the 1830s.

SCAN FOR MULTIMEDIA 

1 There is a time in every man's education when he arrives at the conviction that envy is ignorance; that imitation is suicide; that he must take himself for better, for worse, as his portion; that though the wide universe is full of good, no kernel of nourishing corn can come to him but through his toil bestowed on that plot of ground which is given to him to till. The power which resides in him is new in nature, and none but he knows what that is which he can do, nor does he know until he has tried. Not for nothing one face, one character, one fact makes much impression on him, and another none. This sculpture in the memory is not without preestablished harmony. The eye was placed where one ray should fall, that it might testify of that particular ray. We but half express ourselves, and are ashamed of that divine idea which each of us represents. It may be safely trusted as proportionate and of good issues, so it be faithfully imparted, but God will not have his work made manifest by cowards. A man is relieved and gay when he has put his heart into his work and done his best; but what he has said or done otherwise, shall give him no peace. It is a deliverance which does not deliver. In the attempt his genius deserts him; no muse befriends; no invention, no hope.

NOTES





**WriteNow** Analyze and Interpret

**Essay** Direct students' attention to the following statements from paragraph 1: "There comes a time in every man's education when he arrives at the conviction that . . . imitation is suicide." "A man is relieved and gay when he has put his heart into his work and done his best; but what he has said or done otherwise, shall give him no peace." Have students consider these statements in their groups. Then have them write a brief essay telling whether or not they agree that these statements apply to all people.

# FACILITATING

## Concept Vocabulary

**TRANSCENDENT** If groups are struggling to define *transcendent* in paragraph 2, point out that they can use context clues to infer the meaning. Ask them to identify what Emerson is referring to in the phrase "the same transcendent destiny." How are great men ". . . advancing on chaos and the Dark"?

**Possible response:** They are going beyond the highest mind. *Transcendent* must mean "beyond the limits of the material world; divine."

**REDEEMERS** If groups are struggling to define *redeemers* in paragraph 2, direct students' attention to the phrases "not minors and invalids," "guides," "benefactors," "obeying the Almighty effort" and "advancing on the chaos and the Dark." Discuss how these context clues point to the meaning of *redeemers*.

**Possible response:** *Redeemers* must mean "saviors; people who rescue others from spiritual difficulties."

**CLOSER LOOK**

### Determine Main Ideas

Circulate among groups as students conduct their close read. Suggest that groups close read and annotate paragraphs 3–5. If needed, provide the following support.

**ANNOTATE:** Have students mark details in these paragraphs that show the main idea of the excerpt, or work with small groups to have students participate while you highlight them together.

**QUESTION:** Ask what a reader can infer from what was annotated, and accept student responses.

**Possible response:** People should think for themselves, as great men did.

**CONCLUDE:** Ask students why the author might have included these details.

**Possible response:** By being self-reliant, one fulfills one's true nature.

Remind students that Emerson's writing supports a **main idea.**

Point out Emerson's ability to shock his readers by using phrases such as "the hobgoblin of little minds." Students may suggest that this language opens the reader's mind and causes the reader to question accepted norms.

Additional **English Language Support** is available in the Interactive Teacher's Edition.

NOTES

Mark context clues or indicate another strategy you used that helped you determine meaning.

**transcendent** (tran SEHN duhnt) *adj.*

MEANING:

**redeemers** (rih DEE muhrz) *n.*

MEANING:

2 Trust thyself: every heart vibrates to that iron string. Accept the place the divine providence has found for you; the society of your contemporaries, the connection of events. Great men have always done so and confided themselves childlike to the genius of their age, betraying their perception that the absolutely trustworthy was stirring at their heart, working through their hands, predominating in all their being. And we are now men, and must accept in the highest mind the same transcendent destiny; and not minors and invalids in a protected corner, but guides, redeemers, and benefactors. Obeying the Almighty effort and advancing on chaos and the Dark. . . .

3 Society everywhere is in conspiracy against the manhood of every one of its members. Society is a joint-stock company[1] in which the members agree for the better securing of his bread to each shareholder, to surrender the liberty and culture of the eater. The virtue in most request is conformity. Self-reliance is its aversion. It loves not realities and creators, but names and customs.

4 Whoso[2] would be a man must be a nonconformist. He who would gather immortal palms must not be hindered by the name of goodness, but must explore if it be goodness. Nothing is at last sacred but the integrity of your own mind. Absolve you to yourself, and you shall have the suffrage of the world. . . .

5 A foolish consistency is the hobgoblin of little minds, adored by little statesmen and philosophers and divines. With consistency a great soul has simply nothing to do. He may as well concern himself with his shadow on the wall. Speak what you think now in hard words and tomorrow speak what tomorrow thinks in hard words again, though it contradict everything you said today. "Ah, so you shall be sure to be misunderstood?"—is it so bad, then, to be misunderstood? Pythagoras was misunderstood, and Socrates, and Jesus, and Luther, and Copernicus, and Galileo, and Newton,[3] and every pure and wise spirit that ever took flesh. To be great is to be misunderstood. . . . ❧

1. **joint-stock company** similar to a publicly owned corporation, in which risk is spread among numerous investors.
2. **Whoso** *pr.* archaic term for "whoever."
3. **Pythagoras ... Newton** individuals who made major contributions to scientific, philosophical, or religious thinking.





VOCABULARY DEVELOPMENT

**Multiple Meanings** Tell students that the word *transcendent* in paragraph 2 has multiple, albeit related, meanings. Discuss the following sentences with students:

1. The quarterback's transcendent performance was key in the team's surprise victory.
2. My parents believe strongly in angels and other transcendent beings.
3. The antislavery movement understood the transcendent importance of emancipation.

Have students reread the following sentence from paragraph 2: "And we are now men, and must accept in the highest mind the same transcendent destiny; . . ." Guide students to decide which meaning is used in the quotation—sentence 1, 2, or 3. Discuss how to use context clues to define a word with multiple meanings.

# Comprehension Check

Complete the following items after you finish your first read. Review and clarify details with your group.

*from* NATURE

1. Under what circumstances, according to Emerson, does "mean egotism" vanish?

2. What does Emerson say is "the greatest delight" of being in contact with nature?

3. Under what circumstances, according to Emerson, does nature appear to be melancholy and sad?

4. **Notebook** Confirm your understanding of the text by writing a summary.

*from* SELF-RELIANCE

1. According to Emerson, what idea makes "every heart" vibrate?

2. What virtue does society demand, and what does Emerson recommend in its place?

3. According to Emerson, what is the "hobgoblin of little minds"?

4. **Notebook** Confirm your understanding of the excerpt by writing two sentences that summarize its key content.

## RESEARCH

**Research to Clarify** Choose at least one unfamiliar detail from one of these texts. Briefly research that detail. In what way does the information you learned shed light on an aspect of the text?

**Research to Explore** Conduct research on an aspect of the text you find interesting. For example, you may want to learn more about Emerson's abolitionist politics. Share what you discover with your group.





## CROSS-CURRICULAR PERSPECTIVES

**Humanities** Tell students that other American schools of philosophy followed transcendentalism. These included pragmatism, realism, and process philosophy. Have interested students do research to find out more about these movements and report back to the class. Have the class ask whether Transcendentalism influenced any of these later schools of thought.

DIGITAL PERSPECTIVES  

# Comprehension Check

Nature

**Possible responses:**

1. Mean egotism vanishes when one is in nature.
2. "The greatest delight" is "the suggestion of an occult relation," or feeling a spiritual connection, between people and the natural world.
3. Nature can have such a look when the person viewing nature is feeling melancholy and sad.
4. Emerson expresses his belief that the meaning of existence can be found by exploring the natural world. He describes how, through his exploration of nature, he has discovered that he is spiritually connected with the universe, with God, and with every living thing. He includes all of humanity in this connection.

Self-Reliance

**Possible responses:**

1. Trusting thyself make every heart vibrate.
2. Society demands conformity, but Emerson recommends self-reliance and nonconformity.
3. A foolish consistency is the hobgoblin of little minds.
4. Emerson encourages readers to avoid blindly conforming to the ideas or behaviors dictated by society or peers. He urges readers, instead, to think and act independently.

## Research

**Research to Clarify** If students struggle to find or decide upon a research topic, you may want to suggest that they focus on one of the following: Emerson's visits to the woods or wilderness areas; the relation of Pythagoras, Socrates, Jesus, Martin Luther, Copernicus, Galileo, or Isaac Newton with the society in which each man lived.

**Research to Explore** If students struggle to identify a topic for their research, you may want to suggest that they focus on one of the following: another essay by Emerson, such as "The American Scholar;" another famous Transcendentalist, such as Margaret Fuller or Amos Bronson Alcott; or Emerson's influence on another writer, such as Walt Whitman.

# FACILITATING

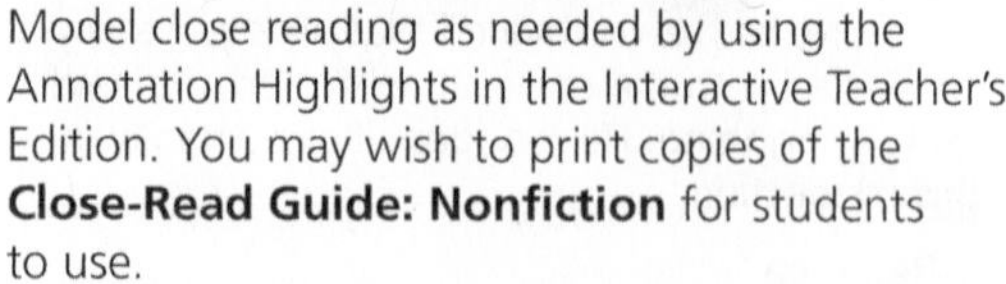

## Jump Start

CLOSE READ Ask students to consider the following prompt: *What values are formed through a relationship with nature?* As students discuss the prompt, have them consider the question from the points of view of a farmer, a city dweller, and someone who lives in the suburbs.

## Close Read the Text

Model close reading as needed by using the Annotation Highlights in the Interactive Teacher's Edition. You may wish to print copies of the **Close-Read Guide: Nonfiction** for students to use.

Remind groups to use Accountable Talk in their discussions and to support one another as they complete the close read.

## Analyze the Text

Possible responses:

1. Whether students feel Emerson's reaction is universal or extreme, they should describe Emerson's "perfect exhilaration" in nature and his sense of a divine connection with the world.
2. Answers will vary but should relate directly to details in the passage.
3. Answers will vary widely but should refer directly to the texts.

## Concept Vocabulary

**Why These Words?** Possible response: The words relate to the concept of faith and emphasize the importance of developing a personal sense of spirituality.

### Practice

Possible responses:

1. To preserve the *sanctity* people might observe silence, pray, or follow a ritual.
2. A person might experience a *transcendent* moment when recognizing some greater power.
3. *Redeemers* might help others by stopping them from committing a crime or sin.

### Word Network

**Possible words:** *nonconformist, egotism, conviction, misunderstood*

## Word Study

For more support, see **Concept Vocabulary and Word Study.**

Possible responses:

*sanctify:* to make holy; *sanctum:* holy or sacred inner place; *sanctimonious:* making an exaggerated show of holiness or moral superiority; *sanctuary:* holy place or refuge

MAKING MEANING

*from* NATURE
*from* SELF-RELIANCE

TIP

GROUP DISCUSSION
Reading aloud from the text can help all group members focus on the writer's ideas and style. Take turns reading interesting, confusing, or thought-provoking passages. After each reading, discuss the meaning and then dig deeper with thorough analysis.

WORD NETWORK
Add words related to individualism from the texts to your Word Network.

STANDARDS
**Reading Informational Text**
- Determine two or more central ideas of a text and analyze their development over the course of the text, including how they interact and build on one another to produce a complex analysis; provide an objective summary of the text.
- Analyze and evaluate the effectiveness of the structure an author uses in his or her exposition or argument, including whether the structure makes points clear, convincing, and engaging.
- Analyze seventeenth-, eighteenth-, and nineteenth-century foundational U.S. documents of historical and literary significance for their themes, purposes, and rhetorical features.

**Language**
Consult general and specialized reference materials, both print and digital, to find the pronunciation of a word or determine or clarify its precise meaning, its part of speech, its etymology, or its standard usage.

## Close Read the Text

With your group, revisit sections of the texts you marked during your first read. **Annotate** details that you notice. What **questions** do you have? What can you **conclude?**

## Analyze the Text

CITE TEXTUAL EVIDENCE to support your answers.

**Notebook** Complete the activities.

1. **Review and Clarify** With your group, reread paragraph 1 of the excerpt from "Nature." Describe how Emerson is affected by nature. Is his experience in nature universal to all people, or is it unique to him?
2. **Present and Discuss** Now, work with your group to share the passages from the selections that you found especially important. Take turns presenting your passages. Discuss what you noticed in the selection, what questions you asked, and what conclusions you reached.
3. **Essential Question:** *What role does individualism play in American society?* What have these texts taught you about the individual and society? Discuss with your group.

LANGUAGE DEVELOPMENT

## Concept Vocabulary

sanctity transcendent redeemers

**Why These Words?** The three concept vocabulary words are related. With your group, determine what the words have in common. How do these word choices enhance the impact of the essays?

### Practice

**Notebook** Confirm your understanding of these words by answering the questions. Use the vocabulary word in your answer.

1. What might people do to preserve the *sanctity* of a special place?
2. When might a person experience a *transcendent* moment?
3. How might *redeemers* help other people?

## Word Study

**Notebook Latin Root: *-sanct-*** The word *sanctity* contains the Latin root *-sanct-*, which means "holy," and the suffix *-ity*, which turns adjectives into abstract nouns. Write several other words that you suspect contain the Latin root *-sanct-*. Use etymological information in a college-level dictionary to verify your choices. Record the words and their meanings.

## FORMATIVE ASSESSMENT

### Analyze the Text

**If** students struggle to close read the text, **then** provide the ***from* Nature • *from* Self-Reliance: Text Questions** available online in the Interactive Teacher's Edition and Unit Resources. Answers and DOK levels are also available.

### Concept Vocabulary

**If** students struggle to identify the concept, **then** have them review the definitions and decide what the words have in common.

### Word Study

**If** students fail to find other words with the Latin root *–sanct-*, **then** suggest they work with a partner to consult a dictionary or online source. Have partners review each definition and check the etymological information to see if there are similarities. For Reteach and Practice, see **Word Study: Latin Root *-sanct-* (RP).**

## Analyze Craft and Structure

**Development of Ideas** An **essay** is a short work of nonfiction in which an author presents ideas on a specific topic. Often, an essay involves an open-ended exploration of ideas. Reading Emerson's essays, you may feel as if you are walking beside him as he converses, continually discovering new connections. Through his explorations, Emerson elaborates a **philosophical vision,** or interpretation of humanity's situation in the world. To help readers see life from his perspective, he employs strategies such as these:

- **Setting the Scene:** Emerson grounds his discussion in a shared experience—a walk in the woods, or a moment when one takes charge of one's life.
- **Re-envisioning the Ordinary:** Starting from shared experience, Emerson transforms it, showing its larger implications. In "Nature," for example, he finds that a walk in the woods restores youth and connects him more deeply to the world. He re-envisions this walk as a journey into the infinite.
- **Re-defining Words:** Emerson develops specific associations for key terms. In "Nature," for example, the term *nature* grows from a reference to fields and woods to include associations with the spirit.
- **Finding Limits:** Emerson may reflect on how far his vision should extend. In "Nature," for example, he concludes that the power of nature to delight is not unlimited.

### Practice

**CITE TEXTUAL EVIDENCE** to support your answers.

**Notebook** Work on your own to analyze Emerson's presentation of his vision in these two essays. Complete a chart like this one. Then, share and discuss your findings with your group.

| *from* NATURE | *from* SELF-RELIANCE |
|---|---|
| Summary of Vision<br>humanity's relationship to nature: | Summary of Vision<br>significance of being an individual: |
| References to Shared Experience | References to Shared Experience |
| How the Shared Experience Reflects the Vision | How the Shared Experience Reflects the Vision |
| Meanings and Associations of Key Terms<br>nature:<br>harmony: | Meanings and Associations of Key Terms<br>self-reliance:<br>great men:<br>manhood:<br>society:<br>conformity:<br>consistency: |
| Limits/Lack of Limits | Limits/Lack of Limits |





DIGITAL PERSPECTIVES

## Analyze Craft and Structure

**Development of Ideas** Remind students that writers go through preliminary stages in which they generate ideas. Then they eliminate some and work with others that seem to fit. This process can happen over and over again, and with it, each writer develops his or her own voice, style, and vision. For more support, see **Analyze Craft and Structure: Development of Ideas**

### FORMATIVE ASSESSMENT

### Analyze Craft and Structure

**If** students fail to analyze Emerson's presentation of his vision, **then** revisit key passages to identify which are claims of the argument, central ideas, or part of the development. For Reteach and Practice, see **Analyze Craft and Structure: Development of Ideas (RP).**

## PERSONALIZE FOR LEARNING

### English Language Support

**Using *Wh-* Questions** Arrange students in groups for each writing type on the chart.

Have groups answer *Wh-* questions about the text. **EMERGING**

Have groups ask and answer *Wh-* questions about the text. **EXPANDING**

| | |
|---|---|
| **Description of a Place** | Where can you find perpetual youth? Paragraph 1<br>What comparison does he make about it? Paragraph 1 |
| **Personality Profile** | What is a nonconformist? Paragraph 7<br>Why does he value this trait? Paragraphs 7–8 |
| **Memoir** | What kind of person speaks with hard words? Paragraph 8<br>Why does Emerson recommend this? Paragraph 8 |

Have partners use the text to ask and answer *Wh-* questions and share their questions with their groups. **BRIDGING**

An expanded **English Language Support Lesson** on Using *Wh-* Questions is available in the Interactive Teacher's Edition.

# FACILITATING

## Conventions and Style

**Sentence Variety** Discuss how a variety of sentence choices makes for interesting, and sometimes dramatic, prose. For example, have students imagine a paragraph with long, complex sentences that ends with a very terse, simple sentence. Ask students to consider the effect of such a choice. For more support, see **Conventions and Style: Sentence Variety.**

### Read It

1. complex; 1 subordinate clause, 1 independent clause
2. compound; 3 independent clauses
3. complex; 1 subordinate clause, 1 independent clause
4. simple; 1 independent clause
5. compound; 2 independent clauses

### Write It

Possible response:

Emerson's ideal of nature is appealing, but his experience is not universal. Although some people have transcendent responses to a walk in the woods, others remain unimpressed. When a friend and I take a nature hike, my friend might "become a transparent eyeball," but I might simply be annoyed by the bugs. There is no single correct way to respond to nature.

### FORMATIVE ASSESSMENT

## Conventions and Style

**If** students are unable to distinguish compound sentences, **then** point out that the clauses of the compound sentence are connected by a part of speech called a conjunction. Have students identify the conjunctions in the compound sentences in this section.

For Reteach and Practice, see **Conventions and Style: Sentence Variety (RP).**

LANGUAGE DEVELOPMENT

from NATURE
from SELF-RELIANCE

## Conventions and Style

**Sentence Variety** One way in which writers hold the attention of their readers is by varying the types of sentences they use. There are four kinds of sentences, categorized by the number and types of clauses they contain. **Independent clauses** have a subject and verb and can stand alone as complete thoughts. **Subordinate** (or **dependent**) **clauses** also have a subject and verb but cannot stand alone as complete thoughts. This chart shows the components of the four kinds of sentences. (Independent clauses are underlined once; dependent clauses are underlined twice.)

| KIND OF SENTENCE | COMPONENTS | EXAMPLES |
| --- | --- | --- |
| simple | a single independent clause | I have enjoyed a perfect exhilaration.<br>In the woods is perpetual youth. |
| compound | two or more independent clauses | They nod to me, and I [nod] to them.<br>It takes me by surprise, and yet [it] is not unknown. |
| complex | one independent clause + at least one subordinate clause | The sky is less grand as it shuts down over less worth in the population. |
| compound-complex | two or more independent clauses + at least one subordinate clause | Within these plantations of God, a decorum and sanctity reign, a perennial festival is dressed, and the guest sees not how he should tire of them in a thousand years. |

Emerson often uses the complex, compound, and compound-complex sentences typical of formal nineteenth-century prose. However, he also includes shorter, simple sentences to vary the flow of the text. The result is a text that is more conversational—and, therefore, more engaging.

### Read It

**Notebook** Identify each sentence in this paragraph as simple, compound, complex, or compound-complex. Explain each choice.

(1) Although society thrives on conformity, progress depends on individuality. (2) Emerson may celebrate individuality, but he does not address progress, and we should not ignore it. (3) While we need strong leaders, those leaders would be ineffective without loyal followers. (4) Every person must assume both roles. (5) No one can lead all the time, so we should become leaders in our areas of strength and follow others when they have greater experience and knowledge.

### Write It

**Notebook** Write a paragraph consisting of at least four sentences. Include at least one example of each kind of sentence: simple, compound, complex, and compound-complex.

STANDARDS

**Writing**

Write narratives to develop real or imagined experiences or events using effective technique, well-chosen details, and well-structured event sequences.

**Language**

- Apply knowledge of language to understand how language functions in different contexts, to make effective choices for meaning or style, and to comprehend more fully when reading or listening.
- Vary syntax for effect, consulting references for guidance as needed; apply an understanding of syntax to the study of complex texts when reading.





HOW LANGUAGE WORKS

**Kinds of Sentences** Provide students with additional practice in identifying sentence types. Ask students to review these sentences from Emerson's essay "The American Scholar" to determine which are simple, compound, and complex.

- Our anniversary is one of hope, and, perhaps, not enough of labor. (simple)
- Man is not a farmer, or a professor, or an engineer, but he is all. (compound)
- The chemist finds proportions and intelligible method throughout matter, and science is nothing but the finding of analogy, identity, in the most remote parts. (compound)
- The theory of books is noble. (simple)
- When he can read God directly, the hour is too precious to be wasted in other men's transcripts of their readings. (complex)

EFFECTIVE EXPRESSION

## Writing to Sources

**Assignment**

Respond to one of Emerson's essays by writing a **story element** for a first-person narrative related to Emerson's ideas. Work initially with other group members to use them as a sounding board for your ideas, but then write individually. The narrative can be either fiction or nonfiction. Choose from the following options. Check the box of the one you chose.

☐ **Setting:** Write a vivid description of a place in which a character feels the "perpetual youth" that Emerson describes in "Nature." For your narrative, choose a setting that is different from the forest that Emerson describes.

☐ **Character:** Create a personality profile of someone who fits Emerson's idea of a nonconformist in today's society. Describe in detail the types of things he or she eats, loves, writes, listens to, says, and so on. Make explicit connections to ideas in Emerson's essays where you can.

☐ **Dialogue:** Write a dialogue for a scene including two or more characters in which you capture what it means to "speak what you think now in hard words." Include a brief introduction explaining who the characters are and what the situation is.

**Narrative Plan** Work with your group to plan the narrative element that you chose. Discuss how your story element connects to Emerson's ideas, and consider integrating some quotations from his essays into your writing.

Working Title: ______________________________

EVIDENCE LOG

Before moving on to a new selection, go to your Evidence Log and record what you learned from the excerpts from "Nature" and "Self-Reliance."

| NARRATIVE ELEMENT |
|---|
| Details to include: |
| Ideas to express: |
| Quotation(s) from Emerson's writing to use: |

**Tying It Together** Work individually to draft your writing. Then, read your work aloud to a partner or your group and discuss revisions. Look for ways to make your writing stronger. Also, consider additional ideas or quotations from Emerson's essays that support the idea you are developing.





PERSONALIZE FOR LEARNING

### Challenge

**Interview** Encourage interested students to create a brief video in which they imagine that they are a news crew interviewing Ralph Waldo Emerson about his philosophy and the Transcendentalist Movement in general. What questions should they ask Emerson? Students can write scripts on which to base their interviews.

DIGITAL PERSPECTIVES

## Writing to Sources

Remind students that a narrative is a kind of writing that tells a story. Narratives are often told in chronological order. Help students differentiate among the three story elements to help them determine which they will choose to respond to. For more support, see **Writing to Sources: Story Element.**

**Narrative Plan** Have groups work together to select one of the story elements to respond to in their narrative. Make sure that each group is able to connect their written work to Emerson's thoughts. Check to make each group has made assignments, and that the work is divided evenly among group members.

**Tying It Together** As students write their narrative texts, have them make sure that any quotations from Emerson's writing are accurate and well-placed. You may want to ask students to write a brief reflection about the process they adhered to. Is there anything they would do differently if they were starting again?

**Evidence Log** Support students in completing the Evidence Log. This paced activity will help prepare them for the Performance-Based Assessment at the end of the unit.

### FORMATIVE ASSESSMENT

### Writing to Sources

**If** students are unable to choose among the three story elements, **then** provide them with examples of each kind so that they can decide with a more complete understanding. For Reteach and Practice, see **Writing to Sources: Story Element (RP).**

### Selection Test

Administer the "*from* Nature / *from* Self-Reliance" Selection Test, which is available in both print and digital formats online in Assessments.

# *from* Walden • *from* Civil Disobedience

**AUDIO SUMMARIES** of the excerpts from *Walden* and from *Civil Disobedience* are available in both English and Spanish and can be assigned to students in the Interactive Teacher's Edition or Unit Resources. Assigning these summaries prior to reading the selection may help students build additional background knowledge and set a context for their first read.

## Summary

In the excerpt from *Walden*, Henry David Thoreau recounts several places he considered living before settling on Walden Pond, where he has decided to "live free and uncommitted." Thoreau considers his cabin, though incomplete, to be a paradise in which he is free of time and social constraints. After living there for several seasons, Thoreau decides to leave Walden, having realized that he has other lives to live. In the excerpt from "Civil Disobedience," Thoreau agrees with the motto "That government is best which governs least." He believes that his government is rarely useful or efficient and no longer represents the real will of the people. According to Thoreau, government is best when it steps aside and lets its citizens act in their own interests.

### Insight

Reading the excerpts from *Walden* and from "Civil Disobedience" will help students understand that individualism often involves taking a stand against the accepted views of society. Students will note the importance of exploring one's personal beliefs and determining a course of action that allows for individual growth and self-determination.

ESSENTIAL QUESTION:
What role does individualism play in American society?

## Connection to Essential Question

The excerpts from *Walden* and from "Civil Disobedience" connect to the Essential Question, "What role does individualism play in American society?" Both essays celebrate the importance of fighting against the constraints of society in order to establish one's own individuality as well as an essential characteristic of the American character.

SMALL-GROUP LEARNING PERFORMANCE TASK
When is it difficult to march to the beat of a "different drummer" and stand on your own as an individual? What are the risks and rewards of nonconformity?

UNIT PERFORMANCE-BASED ASSESSMENT
What significant incident helped me to realize that I am a unique individual?

## Connection to Performance Tasks

**Small-Class Learning Performance Task** In this Performance Task, students will draw on the ways in which the texts in the unit approach the concept of nonconformity and use them to write a speech on the subject.

**Unit Performance-Based Assessment** These excerpts from two writings by Ralph Waldo Emerson offer numerous examples of incidents that helped the author to shape his belief in the importance of individualism in American life and culture.

DIGITAL PERSPECTIVES

 Audio  Video  Document  Annotation Highlights  EL Highlights 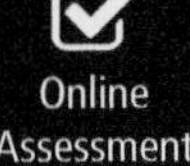 Online Assessment

## LESSON RESOURCES

| | Making Meaning | Language Development | Effective Expression |
|---|---|---|---|
| Lesson | **First Read**<br>**Close Read**<br>**Analyze the Text**<br>**Analyze Craft and Structure** | **Concept Vocabulary**<br>**Word Study**<br>**Conventions and Style** | **Speaking and Listening** |
| Instructional Standards | **RI.10** By the end of grade 11, read and comprehend literary nonfiction . . .<br>**RI.1** Cite strong and thorough textual evidence . . .<br>**RI.6** Determine an author's point of view . . .<br>**L.4.b** Identify and correctly use patterns of word changes . . . | **L.4.b** Identify and correctly use patterns of word changes . . .<br>**RI.6** Determine an author's point of view . . . | **SL.1.b** Work with peers to promote civil, democratic discussions . . .<br>**SL.1.c** Propel conversations . . .<br>**SL.1.d** Respond thoughtfully to diverse perspectives . . . |
| **STUDENT RESOURCES** | | | |
| Available online in the Interactive Student Edition or Unit Resources | Selection Audio<br>First-Read Guide: Nonfiction<br>Close-Read Guide: Nonfiction | Word Network | Evidence Log |
| **TEACHER RESOURCES** | | | |
| **Selection Resources** Available online in the Interactive Teacher's Edition or Unit Resources | Audio Summaries<br>Annotation Highlights<br>EL Highlights<br>English Language Support Lesson: Discussion<br>*from* Walden • *from* Civil Disobedience: Text Questions<br>Analyze Craft and Structure: Author's Point of View | Concept Vocabulary and Word Study<br>Conventions and Style: Author's Style | Speaking and Listening: Discussion |
| **Reteach/Practice (RP)** Available online in the Interactive Teacher's Edition or Unit Resources | Analyze Craft and Structure: Author's Point of View (RP) | Word Study: Latin Prefix *super-* (RP)<br>Conventions and Style: Author's Style (RP) | Speaking and Listening: Discussion (RP) |
| **Assessment** | Selection Test | | |
| **My Resources** | A Unit 2 Answer Key is available online and in the Interactive Teacher's Edition. | | |

# Reading Support

| Text Complexity Rubric: *from* Walden • *from* Civil Disobedience | |
|---|---|
| **Quantitative Measures** | |
| **Lexile** 1200; 980 **Text Length** 3,518 words; 545 words | |
| **Qualitative Measures** | |
| Knowledge Demands ①—②—❸—④—⑤ | *Walden* explores complex themes (the meaning of life, existential questions); "Civil Disobedience" explores the role of government. Background information about the historical period of American history and Transcendental movement will be helpful. |
| Structure ①—②—❸—④—⑤ | The selections are first-person essays that are logically organized, but connections between ideas are not always completely explicit or in a predictable sequence. |
| Language Conventionality and Clarity ①—②—③—❹—⑤ | Selections are dense with metaphor and complex vocabulary and sentence structure. |
| Levels of Meaning/Purpose ①—②—③—❹—⑤ | Concepts have multiple meanings; meaning is not always explicit; the main idea is clear, but some of the supporting concepts are complicated. |

DECIDE AND PLAN

## English Language Support

Provide English Learners with support for language and levels of meaning/purpose as they read the selection.

**Language** Students will likely have difficulty with the numerous complex sentences and above-level vocabulary. Instead of trying to understand every word, encourage students to scan for ideas in each paragraph that they understand. Ask them to write sentences restating the information they understood.

**Levels of Meaning/Purpose** Help students rephrase main ideas by pulling sentences from the reading. For example, on page 2 of the excerpt from *Walden*, *I do not propose to write an ode to dejection, but to brag as lustily as chanticleer in the morning, standing on his roost, if only to wake my neighbors up.* Define difficult words and help students restate the sentence. *I want to wake up the reader as a rooster wakes up the neighborhood.*

## Strategic Support

Provide students with strategic support to ensure that they can successfully read the text.

**Language** If students have difficulty with some of the complex or figurative language, have them break down the sentences into smaller chunks. Then have them highlight any words that are confusing because they are used figuratively, for example *Time is but the stream I go a-fishing in. I drink at it; but while I drink I see the sandy bottom and detect how shallow it is.*

**Levels of Meaning/Purpose** As students read, ask them to make notes of the main ideas. For example, *yet this government never of itself furthered any enterprise, but by the alacrity with which it got out of its way.* They may write the line *government works best when it stays out of the way.* If students have trouble finding the main ideas, ask them to read or listen more than once and ask questions to direct them to the main ideas.

## Challenge

Provide students who need to be challenged with ideas for how they can go beyond a simple interpretation of the text.

**Text Analysis** Ask students to read aloud the last paragraph on page 3 of the excerpt from *Walden*. Ask students to discuss Thoreau's opinions on simplicity. Do they agree or disagree? Why?

**Written Response** Have students consider Thoreau's view of the railroads on page 4 of the excerpt from *Walden*. Then ask students to write a commentary on the effects of modern technology on society in Thoreau's style.

TEACH

## Read and Respond

Have the groups read the selection and complete the Making Meaning, Language Development, and Effective Expression.

# Standards Support Through Teaching and Learning Cycle

## IDENTIFY NEEDS

Analyze results of the Beginning-of-Year Assessment, focusing on the items relating to Unit 2. Also take into consideration student performance to this point and your observations of where particular students struggle.

## DECIDE AND PLAN

- If students have performed poorly on items matching these standards, then provide selection scaffolds before assigning them the on-level lesson provided in the Student Edition.
- If students have done well on the Beginning-of-Year Assessment, then challenge them to keep progressing and learning by giving them opportunities to practice the skills in depth.
- Use the Selection Resources listed on the Planning pages for the excerpts from *Walden* and "Civil Disobedience" to help students continually improve their ability to master the standards.

**Instructional Standards: *from* Walden • *from* "Civil Disobedience"**

| | Catching Up | This Year | Looking Forward |
|---|---|---|---|
| **Reading** | You may wish to administer the **Analyze Craft and Structure: Author's Point of View (RP)** worksheet to help students understand that what they are reading is totally based on the author's point of view. | **RI.1** Cite strong and thorough textual evidence to support analysis of what the text says explicitly as well as inferences drawn from the text, including determining where the text leaves matters uncertain. | You may want to encourage students to write a critique of the style of writing Thoreau used in his writings in order to communicate his point of view. |
| **Speaking and Listening** | You may wish to administer the **Speaking and Listening: Discussion (RP)** worksheet to show students their need to share ideas with others in order to learn new ideas and perspectives. | **SL.1.d** Respond thoughtfully to diverse perspectives; synthesize comments, claims, and evidence made on all sides of an issue; resolve contradictions when possible; and determine what additional information or research is required to deepen the investigation or complete the task. | Ask students to chart out how they might look for evidence on a project in another class. |
| **Language** | You may wish to administer the **Conventions and Style: Author's Style (RP)** worksheet to help students see more clearly the elements Thoreau used to create an informal style. | **RI.6** Determine an author's point of view or purpose in a text in which the rhetoric is particularly effective, analyzing how style and content contribute to the power, persuasiveness, or beauty of the text. | Challenge students to compare Emerson and Thoreau's style of writing and the effect each writer had on readers. |

## ANALYZE AND REVISE

- Analyze student work for evidence of student learning.
- Identify whether or not students have met the expectations in the standards.
- Identify implications for future instruction.

## TEACH

Implement the planned lesson, and gather evidence of student learning.

# FACILITATING

## Jump Start

**FIRST READ** Why might a person live alone and away from the world? What are the advantages or disadvantages of this choice? Engage students in a discussion about choosing to live very simply, which sets the context for reading *Walden* and "Civil Disobedience."

### *from* Walden • *from* Civil Disobedience

Is it possible to earn a living today by working only one or two days a week? If so, how? Modeling questions readers might ask will bring *Walden* and "Civil Disobedience" to life and connect them to the Performance Task question. Selection audio and print capability for the selection are available in the Interactive Teacher's Edition.

### Concept Vocabulary

Have groups briefly discuss the three concept vocabulary words. Have they encountered any of the words before? Do they recognize the suffix or base word of any of the concept vocabulary words? Have groups consider the strategy of using familiar word parts and discuss its advantages and disadvantages.

### FIRST READ

Have students perform the steps of the first read independently:

NOTICE: Encourage students to notice the different themes of *Walden* and "Civil Disobedience."

ANNOTATE: Remind students to mark any passages that explain why Thoreau went to the woods and what he found there. In "Civil Disobedience," have students consider Thoreau's opinion of government.

CONNECT: Have students think about a place they go to find peace. In "Civil Disobedience," have them consider the reasons for government.

RESPOND: Students will demonstrate their understanding of the text by answering questions and writing a summary.

Point out to students that they will perform the first three steps concurrently as they are doing their first read. They will complete the Respond step after they have finished the first read. You may wish to print copies of the **First-Read Guide: Nonfiction** for students to use.

MAKING MEANING

About the Author

**Henry David Thoreau** (1817–1862) was born in Concord, Massachusetts, where he spent most of his life. After graduating from Harvard, he became a teacher. In 1841, Thoreau moved into the home of another famous Concord resident, Ralph Waldo Emerson, where he lived for two years. Fascinated by Emerson's Transcendentalist ideas, Thoreau became Emerson's friend and disciple. Rather than return to teaching, he decided to devote his energies to living by his beliefs. The literary results of that decision include his masterwork, *Walden* (1854). When Thoreau died at the age of forty-four, he had published little and received no public recognition. Emerson, however, knew that future generations would cherish his friend. Speaking at Thoreau's funeral, Emerson said: "The country knows not yet, or in the least part, how great a son it has lost. . . . [W]herever there is knowledge, wherever there is virtue, wherever there is beauty, he will find a home."

STANDARDS

**Reading Informational Text**
By the end of grade 11, read and comprehend literary nonfiction in the grades 11–CCR text complexity band proficiently, with scaffolding as needed at the high end of the range.

**Language**
Identify and correctly use patterns of word changes that indicate different meanings or parts of speech.

## *from* Walden

## *from* Civil Disobedience

### Concept Vocabulary

As you perform your first read of the excerpts from *Walden* and "Civil Disobedience," you will encounter these words.

sufficed superfluous vital

**Familiar Word Parts** Words that seem unfamiliar may contain **familiar word parts,** such as roots, prefixes, or suffixes, that you already know. When you encounter an unfamiliar word, identify any familiar word parts, and consider how they might contribute to the meaning of the unfamiliar word. Then, draw a conclusion about the word's likely meaning.

**Unfamiliar Word:** *insensibly*

**Word in Context:** It is remarkable how easily and *insensibly* we fall into a particular route, . . .

**Familiar Word Parts:** the prefix *in-*, which often means "not"; the root *-sens-*, which means "sense"; and the suffix *-ly*, which often appears in adverbs that tell how something is done

**Conclusion:** *Insensibly* has a meaning related to *sense*. The word probably means "in a way that is not connected to the senses" or possibly "in a way that does not make sense."

Apply your knowledge of familiar word parts and other vocabulary strategies to determine the meanings of unfamiliar words you encounter during your first read.

### First Read NONFICTION

Apply these strategies as you conduct your first read. You will have an opportunity to complete a close read after your first read.

NOTICE the general ideas of the text. *What* is it about? *Who* is involved?

ANNOTATE by marking vocabulary and key passages you want to revisit.

CONNECT ideas within the selection to what you already know and what you've already read.

RESPOND by completing the Comprehension Check and by writing a brief summary of the selection.





### FACILITATING SMALL-GROUP CLOSE READING: NONFICTION

**CLOSE READ: Philosophical Writing** As groups perform the close read, circulate and offer support as needed.

- Remind students that philosophical writing can be hard to follow at first glance. An additional close read may be beneficial in determining Thoreau's intent.
- Point out that even though Thoreau's works are classified as philosophical writing, Thoreau had a subtle sense of humor. Challenge students to find examples of humor, including puns, in Thoreau's writing.
- Examples from two of Thoreau's works are presented in this selection. Ask students to think about how the ideas in the excerpts share commonalities, yet are also very different.

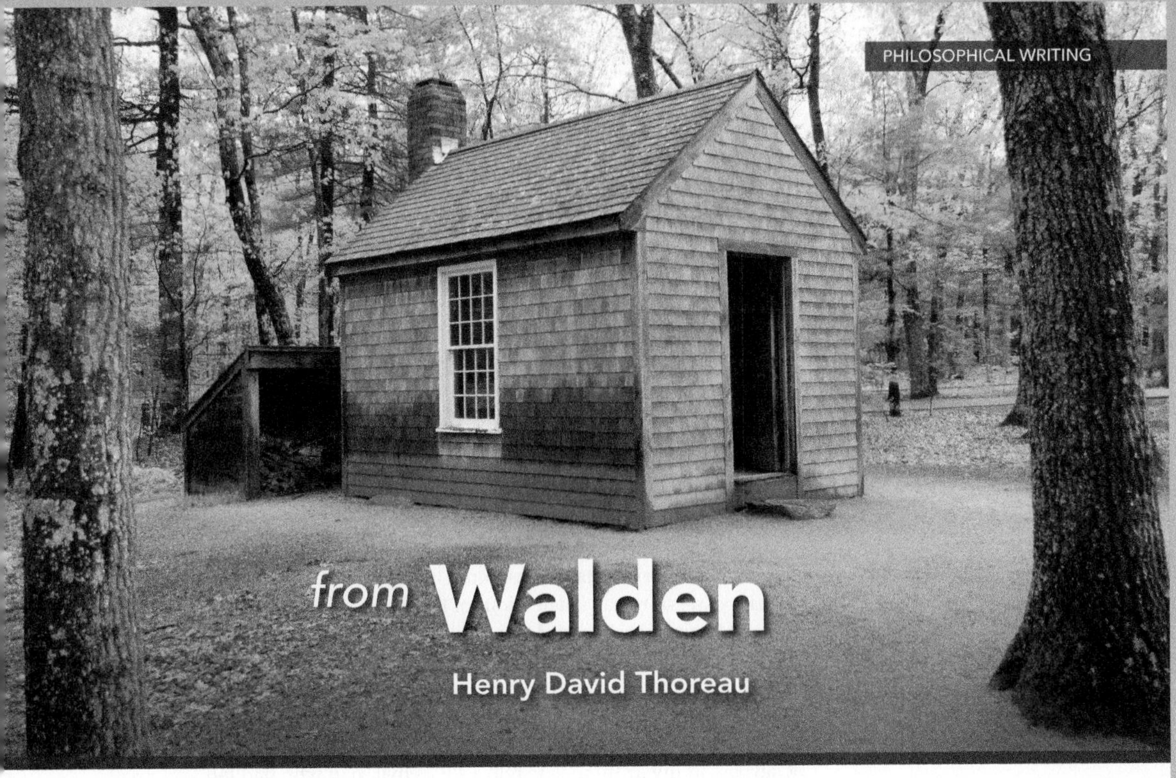


# *from* Walden

Henry David Thoreau

DIGITAL PERSPECTIVES

BACKGROUND

From 1845 to 1847, Henry David Thoreau lived alone in a one-room cabin he built at Walden Pond near Concord, Massachusetts. This experience led him to write *Walden*, a blend of natural observation, social criticism, and philosophical insight. It remains one of the greatest examples of nature writing in American literature.

SCAN FOR MULTIMEDIA

## *from* Where I Lived, and What I Lived For

1 At a certain season of our life we are accustomed to consider every spot as the possible site of a house. I have thus surveyed the country on every side within a dozen miles of where I live. In imagination I have bought all the farms in succession, for all were to be bought, and I knew their price. I walked over each farmer's premises, tasted his wild apples, discoursed on husbandry[1] with him, took his farm at his price, at any price, mortgaging it to him in my mind; even put a higher price on it—took everything but a deed of it—took his word for his deed, for I dearly love to talk—cultivated it, and him too to some extent, I trust, and withdrew when I had enjoyed it long enough, leaving him to carry it on. This experience entitled me to be regarded as a sort of real-estate broker by my friends. Wherever I sat, there I might live, and the landscape radiated

NOTES

1. **husbandry** (HUHZ buhn dree) *n.* farming.





VOCABULARY DEVELOPMENT

**Archaic Meanings** Direct students' attention to the word *husbandry* in paragraph 1. Although the word now relates to farming, in earlier times it meant "prudent and economic management of a household." Tell students that the word comes from the Old Norse words *hus*, meaning "house," and *bondi*, meaning "dweller." Ask students to suggest reasons why the word is now used only in reference to farming.

## FACILITATING

### Concept Vocabulary

**Sufficed** If groups are struggling to define *sufficed* in paragraph 1, point out its word parts. *Suffice* derives from the Latin *sufficere* meaning "put a foundation under; be enough." *Sufficed* is the past tense form of *suffice* that means "was enough or adequate."

**Possible response:** *Sufficed* must mean "was adequate."

Additional **English Language Support** is available in the Interactive Teacher's Edition.

NOTES

Mark familiar word parts or indicate another strategy you used that helped you determine meaning.

**sufficed** (suh FYST) *v.*

MEANING:

from me accordingly. What is a house but a sedes, a seat?—better if a country seat. I discovered many a site for a house not likely to be soon improved, which some might have thought too far from the village, but to my eyes the village was too far from it. Well, there might I live, I said; and there I did live, for an hour, a summer and a winter life; saw how I could let the years run off, buffet the winter through, and see the spring come in. The future inhabitants of this region, wherever they may place their houses, may be sure that they have been anticipated. An afternoon **sufficed** to lay out the land into orchard woodlot and pasture, and to decide what fine oaks or pines should be left to stand before the door, and whence each blasted tree could be seen to the best advantage; and then I let it lie, fallow[2] perchance, for a man is rich in proportion to the number of things which he can afford to let alone.

2 My imagination carried me so far that I even had the refusal of several farms—the refusal was all I wanted—but I never got my fingers burned by actual possession. The nearest that I came to actual possession was when I bought the Hollowell Place, and had begun to sort my seeds, and collected materials with which to make a wheelbarrow to carry it on or off with; but before the owner gave me a deed of it, his wife—every man has such a wife—changed her mind and wished to keep it, and he offered me ten dollars to release him. Now, to speak the truth, I had but ten cents in the world, and it surpassed my arithmetic to tell, if I was that man who had ten cents, or who had a farm, or ten dollars, or all together. However, I let him keep the ten dollars and the farm too, for I had carried it far enough; or rather, to be generous, I sold him the farm for just what I gave for it, and, as he was not a rich man, made him a present of ten dollars, and still had my ten cents, and seeds, and materials for a wheelbarrow left. I found thus that I had been a rich man without any damage to my poverty. But I retained the landscape, and I have since annually carried off what it yielded without a wheelbarrow. With respect to landscapes:

3 "I am monarch of all I *survey*,
My right there is none to dispute."[3]

4 I have frequently seen a poet withdraw, having enjoyed the most valuable part of a farm, while the crusty farmer supposed that he had got a few wild apples only. Why, the owner does not know it for many years when a poet has put his farm in rhyme, the most admirable kind of invisible fence, has fairly impounded it, milked it, skimmed it, and got all the cream, and left the farmer only the skimmed milk.

5 The real attractions of the Hollowell farm, to me, were: its complete retirement, being about two miles from the village, half a mile from the nearest neighbor, and separated from the highway by a broad field; its bounding on the river, which the owner said protected

2. **fallow** (FAL oh) *adj.* left uncultivated or unplanted.
3. **"I ... dispute"** from William Cowper's *Verses Supposed to Be Written by Alexander Selkirk.*





### WriteNow Analyze and Interpret

**Essay** Refer students to paragraph 4, specifically the phrase "the most valuable part of a farm." Discuss what Thoreau meant by this phrase. Have students write a brief essay explaining this phrase from Thoreau's point of view. Have them answer this question: How does a poet get more from a farm than a farmer does?

it by its fogs from frosts in the spring, though that was nothing to me; the gray color and ruinous state of the house and barn, and the dilapidated fences, which put such an interval between me and the last occupant; the hollow and lichen-covered apple trees, gnawed by rabbits, showing what kind of neighbors I should have; but above all, the recollection I had of it from my earliest voyages up the river, when the house was concealed behind a dense grove of red maples, through which I heard the house-dog bark. I was in haste to buy it, before the proprietor finished getting out some rocks, cutting down the hollow apple trees, and grubbing up some young birches which had sprung up in the pasture, or, in short, had made any more of his improvements. To enjoy these advantages I was ready to carry it on; like Atlas,[4] to take the world on my shoulders—I never heard what compensation he received for that—and do all those things which had no other motive or excuse but that I might pay for it and be unmolested in my possession of it; for I knew all the while that it would yield the most abundant crop of the kind I wanted if I could only afford to let it alone. But it turned out as I have said.

6 All that I could say, then, with respect to farming on a large scale (I have always cultivated a garden) was that I had had my seeds ready. Many think that seeds improve with age. I have no doubt that time discriminates between the good and the bad; and when at last I shall plant, I shall be less likely to be disappointed. But I would say to my fellows, once for all, As long as possible live free and uncommitted. It makes but little difference whether you are committed to a farm or the county jail.

7 Old Cato,[5] whose "De Re Rustica" is my "Cultivator," says, and the only translation I have seen makes sheer nonsense of the passage, "When you think of getting a farm, turn it thus in your mind, not to buy greedily; nor spare your pains to look at it, and do not think it enough to go round it once. The oftener you go there the more it will please you, if it is good." I think I shall not buy greedily, but go round and round it as long as I live, and be buried in it first, that it may please me the more at last. . . .

8 I do not propose to write an ode to dejection, but to brag as lustily as chanticleer[6] in the morning, standing on his roost, if only to wake my neighbors up.

9 When first I took up my abode in the woods, that is, began to spend my nights as well as days there, which, by accident, was on Independence Day, or the fourth of July, 1845, my house was not finished for winter, but was merely a defense against the rain, without plastering or chimney, the walls being of rough weatherstained boards, with wide chinks, which made it cool at night. The upright white hewn studs and freshly planed door

NOTES

4. **Atlas** (AT luhs) from Greek mythology, a Titan who supported the heavens on his shoulders.
5. **Old Cato** (KAY toh) Roman statesman (234–149 B.C.). "De Re Rustica" is Latin for "Of Things Rustic."
6. **chanticleer** (CHAN tuh klihr) *n.* rooster.





## CLOSER LOOK

### Infer Key Ideas 

Circulate among groups as students conduct their close read. Suggest that groups read paragraphs 6 and 7. Encourage them to talk about the annotations that they mark. If needed, provide the following support.

**ANNOTATE:** Have students mark details in the paragraphs that address Thoreau's belief in less ownership in favor of a higher, nonmaterial value. You may also work with small groups to have students participate while you highlight them together.

**QUESTION:** Guide students to consider what these details might tell them. Ask them why it makes "little difference" whether a person is on a farm or in a jail.

**Possible response:** Real freedom is a state of mind, and it can be accessed anywhere.

**CONCLUDE:** Help students formulate conclusions about the importance of these ideas in the text. Ask students what the author meant in the paragraph about Cato.

**Possible response:** If it is pleasing to visit a farm before buying it, then why buy it? Thoreau says that just visiting is more pleasing than ownership.

Remind students that authors often include information to help readers **infer key ideas**. Thoreau does this by juxtaposing seemingly contradictory concepts. This forces the reader to focus more closely on the meaning behind the apparent contradiction.

## CROSS-CURRICULAR PERSPECTIVES

**Social Studies** Thoreau references the Roman statesman Cato in paragraph 7. Tell students that Marcus Portius Cato was an ancient Roman statesman and orator. Have students find out more about Cato and write a brief report of their findings, including a description of his writing about agriculture. Would Thoreau have liked Cato's policies if he had lived at that time?

FACILITATING

## Concept Vocabulary

**SUPERFLUOUS** If groups are struggling to define *superfluous* in paragraph 11, point out its familiar word parts. *Super-* is a prefix meaning "over" or "above," and *fluous* is from the Latin root word *fluere*, meaning "to flow." *Superfluous* means "overflowing," or "more than what is needed."

**Possible response:** *Superfluous* must mean "excessive."

NOTES

and window casings gave it a clean and airy look, especially in the morning, when its timbers were saturated with dew, so that I fancied that by noon some sweet gum would exude from them. To my imagination it retained throughout the day more or less of this auroral[7] character, reminding me of a certain house on a mountain which I had visited the year before. This was an airy and unplastered cabin, fit to entertain a traveling god, and where a goddess might trail her garments. The winds which passed over my dwelling were such as sweep over the ridges of mountains, bearing the broken strains, or celestial parts only, of terrestrial music. The morning wind forever blows, the poem of creation is uninterrupted; but few are the ears that hear it. Olympus is but the outside of the earth everywhere. . . .

10 I went to the woods because I wished to live deliberately, to front only the essential facts of life, and see if I could not learn what it had to teach, and not, when I came to die, discover that I had not lived. I did not wish to live what was not life, living is so dear; nor did I wish to practice resignation, unless it was quite necessary. I wanted to live deep and suck out all the marrow of life, to live so sturdily and Spartanlike[8] as to put to rout all that was not life, to cut a broad swath and shave close, to drive life into a corner, and reduce it to its lowest terms, and, if it proved to be mean, why then to get the whole and genuine meanness of it, and publish its meanness to the world; or if it were sublime, to know it by experience, and be able to give a true account of it in my next excursion. For most men, it appears to me, are in a strange uncertainty about it, whether it is of the devil or of God, and have *somewhat hastily* concluded that it is the chief end of man here to "glorify God and enjoy him forever."[9]

Mark familiar word parts or indicate another strategy you used that helped you determine meaning.

**superfluous** (suh PUR floo uhs) *adj.*

MEANING:

11 Still we live meanly, like ants; though the fable tells us that we were long ago changed into men; like pygmies we fight with cranes:[10] it is error upon error, and clout upon clout, and our best virtue has for its occasion a **superfluous** and evitable wretchedness. Our life is frittered away by detail. An honest man has hardly need to count more than his ten fingers, or in extreme cases he may add his ten toes, and lump the rest. Simplicity, simplicity, simplicity! I say, let your affairs be as two or three, and not a hundred or a thousand; instead of a million count half a dozen, and keep your accounts on your thumbnail. In the midst of this chopping sea of civilized life, such are the clouds and storms and quicksands and thousand-and-one items to be allowed for, that a man has to live, if he would not founder and go to the bottom and not make his port at all, by dead reckoning,[11] and he must be a great calculator indeed who succeeds. Simplify, simplify. Instead of three meals

7. **auroral** (aw RAWR uhl) *adj.* resembling the dawn.
8. **Spartanlike** *adj.* like the people of Sparta, an ancient Greek state whose citizens were known to be hardy, stoical, simple, and highly disciplined.
9. **"glorify ... forever"** the answer to the question "What is the chief end of man?" in the Westminster catechism.
10. **like ... cranes** In the *Iliad*, the Trojans are compared to cranes fighting against pygmies.
11. **dead reckoning** navigating without the assistance of stars.





### VOCABULARY DEVELOPMENT

**Inferring Meaning** Direct students' attention to the adverbs *deliberately* and *meanly*, in paragraphs 10 and 11. Point out that both words describe the verb *live*. Have students discuss what it means to live deliberately versus meanly.

Which phrase explains *deliberately* in paragraph 10? ("to front only the essential facts of life") Which phrase explains *meanly* in paragraph 11? ("like ants") Help students conclude that although the adverbs are not antonyms, they are in opposition to each other in Thoreau's writing.

a day, if it be necessary eat but one; instead of a hundred dishes, five; and reduce other things in proportion. Our life is like a German Confederacy,[12] made up of petty states, with its boundary forever fluctuating, so that even a German cannot tell you how it is bounded at any moment. The nation itself, with all its so-called internal improvements, which, by the way, are all external and superficial, is just such an unwieldy and overgrown establishment, cluttered with furniture and tripped up by its own traps, ruined by luxury and heedless expense, by want of calculation and a worthy aim, as the million households in the land; and the only cure for it as for them is in a rigid economy, a stern and more than Spartan simplicity of life and elevation of purpose. It lives too fast. Men think that it is essential that the *Nation* have commerce, and export ice, and talk through a telegraph, and ride thirty miles an hour, without a doubt, whether *they* do or not; but whether we should live like baboons or like men, is a little uncertain. If we do not get out sleepers,[13] and forge rails, and devote days and nights to the work, but go to tinkering upon our *lives* to improve *them*, who will build railroads? And if railroads are not built, how shall we get to heaven in season? But if we stay at home and mind our business, who will want railroads? We do not ride on the railroad; it rides upon us. . . .

NOTES

> I have always been regretting that I was not as wise as the day I was born.

12 Time is but the stream I go a-fishing in. I drink at it; but while I drink I see the sandy bottom and detect how shallow it is. Its thin current slides away, but eternity remains. I would drink deeper; fish in the sky, whose bottom is pebbly with stars. I cannot count one. I know not the first letter of the alphabet. I have always been regretting that I was not as wise as the day I was born. The intellect is a cleaver; it discerns and rifts its way into the secret of things. I do not wish to be any more busy with my hands than is necessary. My head is hands and feet. I feel all my best faculties concentrated in it. My instinct tells me that my head is an organ for burrowing, as some creatures use their snout and forepaws, and with it I would mine and burrow my way through these hills. I think that the richest vein is somewhere here-abouts; so by the divining rod[14] and thin rising vapors I judge; and here I will begin to mine. . . .

### *from* The Conclusion

13 I left the woods for as good a reason as I went there. Perhaps it seemed to me that I had several more lives to live, and could not spare any more time for that one. It is remarkable how easily and

12. **German Confederacy** At the time, Germany was a loose union of thirty-nine independent states with no common government.
13. **sleepers** *n.* ties supporting railroad tracks.
14. **divining rod** a forked branch or stick alleged to reveal underground water or minerals.





## CLOSER LOOK

### Analyze Figurative Language 

Circulate among groups as students conduct their close read. Suggest that groups read paragraph 12. Encourage them to talk about the annotations that they mark. If needed, provide the following support.

**ANNOTATE:** Have students locate examples of figurative language in paragraph 12. Have students mark details in this paragraph that utilize figurative language, or work with small groups to have students participate while you highlight them together.

**QUESTION:** What effect does Thoreau create with this instance of figurative language?

**Possible responses:** Thoreau equates time with a stream he is fishing in.

**CONCLUDE:** Help students formulate conclusions about the importance of figurative language in the text. Ask students why the author might have included these instances of figurative language to describe life and time?

**Possible responses:** Life and time are all around us, yet a description of their relationship to our existence might be vague and unsatisfying. By using figurative language, Thoreau makes comparisons of unlikely things, which brings the larger topics of life and time into focus.

Remind students that authors may use **figurative language**, words and expressions whose meanings are not literal, to portray philosophical beliefs.

## DIGITAL PERSPECTIVES

**Enriching the Text** Review paragraph 13. To help students understand what Thoreau's life on Walden Pond was like, show them a film that portrays this experience. Ask students to compare the common image of Thoreau's life at Walden—isolated, alone, ascetic—with the actuality: He frequently had guests over, and he went into town nearly every day.

NOTES

insensibly we fall into a particular route, and make a beaten track for ourselves. I had not lived there a week before my feet wore a path from my door to the pondside; and though it is five or six years since I trod it, it is still quite distinct. It is true, I fear that others may have fallen into it, and so helped to keep it open. The surface of the earth is soft and impressible by the feet of men; and so with the paths which the mind travels. How worn and dusty, then, must be the highways of the world, how deep the ruts of tradition and conformity! I did not wish to take a cabin passage, but rather to go before the mast and on the deck of the world, for there I could best see the moonlight amid the mountains. I do not wish to go below now.

14 I learned this, at least, by my experiment; that if one advances confidently in the direction of his dreams, and endeavors to live the life which he has imagined, he will meet with a success unexpected in common hours. He will put some things behind, will pass an invisible boundary; new, universal, and more liberal laws will begin to establish themselves around and within him; or the old laws be expanded, and interpreted in his favor in a more liberal sense, and he will live with the license of a higher order of beings. In proportion as he simplifies his life, the laws of the universe will appear less complex, and solitude will not be solitude, nor poverty poverty, nor weakness weakness. If you have built castles in the air, your

## PERSONALIZE FOR LEARNING

### English Language Support

**Close Read** Review paragraphs 13 and 14 with students. Students who need English language support will benefit from particularly close readings of Thoreau's prose.

Discuss these paragraphs of the excerpt from *Walden*. Have students use phrases and short sentences to explain the ideas in Thoreau's writing, based on an additional close reading of the text. **EMERGING**

Discuss these paragraphs of the excerpt from *Walden*. Have students use increasingly detailed sentences to explain the ideas and processes in Thoreau's writing, based on an additional close reading of the text. **EXPANDING**

Discuss these paragraphs of the excerpt from *Walden*. Have students use a variety of detailed sentences to explain the ideas and processes in Thoreau's writing, based on an additional close reading of the text. **BRIDGING** work need not be lost; that is where they should be. Now put the foundations under them. . . .

NOTES

15 Why should we be in such desperate haste to succeed, and in such desperate enterprises? If a man does not keep pace with his companions, perhaps it is because he hears a different drummer. Let him step to the music which he hears, however measured or far away. It is not important that he should mature as soon as an apple tree or an oak. Shall he turn his spring into summer? If the condition of things which we were made for is not yet, what were any reality which we can substitute? We will not be shipwrecked on a vain reality. Shall we with pains erect a heaven of blue glass over ourselves, though when it is done we shall be sure to gaze still at the true ethereal heaven far above, as if the former were not? . . .

16 However mean your life is, meet it and live it; do not shun it and call it hard names. It is not so bad as you are. It looks poorest when you are richest. The faultfinder will find faults even in paradise. Love your life, poor as it is. You may perhaps have some pleasant, thrilling, glorious hours, even in a poorhouse. The setting sun is reflected from the windows of the almshouse[15] as brightly as from the rich man's abode; the snow melts before its door as early in the spring. I do not see but a quiet mind may live as contentedly there, and have as cheering thoughts, as in a palace. The town's poor seem to me often to live the most independent lives of any. Maybe they are simply great enough to receive without misgiving. Most think that they are above being supported by the town; but it oftener happens that they are not above supporting themselves by dishonest means, which should be more disreputable. Cultivate poverty like a garden herb, like sage. Do not trouble yourself much to get new things, whether clothes or friends. Turn the old; return to them. Things do not change; we change. Sell your clothes and keep your thoughts. God will see that you do not want society. If I were confined to a corner of a garret[16] all my days, like a spider, the world would be just as large to me while I had my thoughts about me. The philosopher said: "From an army of three divisions one can take away its general, and put it in disorder; from the man the most abject and vulgar one cannot take away his thought." Do not seek so anxiously to be developed, to subject yourself to many influences to be played on; it is all dissipation. Humility like darkness reveals the heavenly lights. The shadows of poverty and meanness gather around us, "and lo! creation widens to our view."[17] We are often reminded that if there were bestowed on us the wealth of Croesus,[18] our aims must still be the same, and our means essentially the same. Moreover, if you are restricted in your range by poverty, if you cannot buy books and

15. **almshouse** (OMZ hows) *n.* government-run home for people too poor to support themselves.
16. **garret** (GAR iht) *n.* attic.
17. **"and ... view"** from the sonnet "To Night" by the British poet Joseph Blanco White (1775–1841).
18. **Croesus** (KREE suhs) King of Lydia (d. 546 B.C.), believed to be the wealthiest person of his time.





## PERSONALIZE FOR LEARNING

### Strategic Support

**Theme** Review paragraph 15 with students. Remind students that the theme is the central idea, message, or insight that a literary work reveals. When the theme is implied, the reader must analyze different elements in the text for clues to the word's meaning.

Ask students to apply this understanding of theme to paragraph 15 of the excerpt from *Walden*. Have groups work together to decide what Thoreau is saying in this paragraph. Students may be familiar with the phrase "different drummer." Have them explain what Thoreau means in the first three sentences of the paragraph.

## Concept Vocabulary

**VITAL** If groups are struggling to define *vital* in paragraph 16, point out its familiar word parts. *Vital* derives from the Latin *vitalis* meaning "life" or "esssential to life."

**Possible response:** *Vital* must mean "necessary or important."

NOTES

Mark familiar word parts or indicate another strategy you used that helped you determine meaning.

**vital** (VY tuhl) *adj.*

newspapers, for instance, you are but confined to the most significant and vital experiences; you are compelled to deal with the material which yields the most sugar and the most starch. It is life near the bone where it is sweetest. You are defended from being a trifler. No man loses ever on a lower level by magnanimity[19] on a higher. Superfluous wealth can buy superfluities only. Money is not required to buy one necessary of the soul. . . .

17 The life in us is like the water in the river. It may rise this year higher than man has ever known it, and flood the parched uplands; even this may be the eventful year, which will drown out all our muskrats. It was not always dry land where we dwell. I see far inland the banks which the stream anciently washed, before science began to record its freshets.[20] Everyone has heard the story which has gone the rounds of New England, of a strong and beautiful bug which came out of the dry leaf of an old table of apple-tree wood, which had stood in a farmer's kitchen for sixty years, first in Connecticut, and afterward in Massachusetts—from an egg deposited in the living tree many years earlier still, as appeared by counting the annual layers beyond it; which was heard gnawing out for several weeks, hatched perchance by the heat of an urn. Who does not feel his faith in a resurrection and immortality strengthened by hearing of this? Who knows what beautiful and winged life, whose egg has been buried for ages under many concentric layers of woodenness in the dead dry life of society, deposited at first in the alburnum[21] of the green and living tree, which has been gradually converted into the semblance of its well-seasoned tomb—heard perchance gnawing out now for years by the astonished family of man, as they sat round the festive board—may unexpectedly come forth from amidst society's most trivial and handselled furniture, to enjoy its perfect summer life at last!

18 I do not say that John or Jonathan[22] will realize all this; but such is the character of that morrow[23] which mere lapse of time can never make to dawn. The light which puts out our eyes is darkness to us. Only that day dawns to which we are awake. There is more day to dawn. The sun is but a morning star. ❧

19. **magnanimity** (mag nuh NIHM uh tee) *n.* generosity.
20. **freshets** (FREHSH its) *n.* river floods resulting from heavy rain or melted snow.
21. **alburnum** (al BUR nuhm) *n.* soft wood between the bark and the heartwood, where water is conducted.
22. **John or Jonathan** average person.
23. **morrow** *n.* literary term for "tomorrow;" archaic term for "morning."





### WriteNow Express and Reflect

**Essay** In paragraph 16, Thoreau basically says that life can be as enjoyable and enriching for a poor person as for a rich person. Many students will find this an unusual and perhaps surprising claim. Ask students to write a brief essay about this paragraph. The first part of the essay should explain what Thoreau is saying in the paragraph. In the second part of the essay, have students agree or disagree with Thoreau's point of view. Have them provide reasons for their preference.

DIGITAL PERSPECTIVES

PHILOSOPHICAL WRITING

# *from* Civil Disobedience

Henry David Thoreau

BACKGROUND

The Mexican War was a conflict between Mexico and the United States that took place from 1846 to 1848. The war was caused by a dispute over the boundary between Texas and Mexico, as well as by Mexico's refusal to discuss selling California and New Mexico to the United States. Believing that President Polk had intentionally provoked the conflict before gaining congressional approval, Thoreau and many other Americans strongly objected to the war. In protest, Thoreau refused to pay his taxes and was forced to spend a night in jail. Afterward, he wrote "Civil Disobedience," urging people to resist governmental policies with which they disagree.

SCAN FOR MULTIMEDIA 

1 I heartily accept the motto, "That government is best which governs least";[1] and I should like to see it acted up to more rapidly and systematically. Carried out, it finally amounts to this, which also I believe: "That government is best which governs not at all"; and when men are prepared for it, that will be the kind of government which they will have. Government is at best but an expedient; but most governments are usually, and all governments are sometimes, inexpedient. The objections which have been brought against a standing army, and they are many and weighty, and deserve to prevail, may also at last be brought against a standing government.

NOTES

1. **"That ... least"** the motto of the *United States Magazine and Democratic Review,* a literary-political journal.





CLOSER LOOK

## Examine an Argument

Circulate among groups as students conduct their close read. Suggest that groups close read paragraph 1 of "Civil Disobedience." Encourage them to talk about the annotations that they mark. If needed, provide the following support.

**ANNOTATE:** Have students mark phrases or sentences in the paragraph that set forth the argument against the power of government, or work with small groups to have students participate while you highlight these phrases and sentences together.

**QUESTION:** Guide students to consider what these details might tell them. What is wrong with a standing government? When will there be no government?

**Possible responses:** A standing government does not express the will of the people. There will be no government when people are prepared for it.

**CONCLUDE:** Help students formulate conclusions about the importance of these details in text. Ask students why the author might have included these statements.

**Possible response:** Maybe he included the statements to shock the reader and force the reader to really ponder the purpose of government and whether the present government is fulfilling its purpose.

Remind students that an **argument** is the position that a writer presents, supported by evidence. Tell them that Thoreau used deductive reasoning in his argument because he begins with a general statement and then he supports it with reason.

## CROSS-CURRICULAR PERSPECTIVES

**Social Studies** Have students research and write a brief report about the Mexican-American War. Have them focus on these points:

- What events led to the war?
- Did President Polk intentionally start the war?
- What were the war's outcomes?

Have small groups apply what they learned about the Mexican-American War to Thoreau's opinion of government in "Civil Disobedience." Discuss how the government's action led Thoreau to his conclusions about government in general. **(Research to Explore)**

# FACILITATING

## CLOSER LOOK

### Connect to Essential Question

Circulate among groups as students conduct their close read. Suggest that groups read paragraphs 1 and 2. Encourage them to talk about the annotations that they mark. If needed, provide the following support.

**ANNOTATE:** Have students mark details in these paragraphs that connect to the Essential Question, *What role does individualism play in American society?*, or work with small groups to have students participate while you highlight them together.

**QUESTION:** Guide students to consider what these details might tell them. Ask what happened during the Mexican-American War that troubled Thoreau deeply. Ask what a reader can infer from what was marked, and accept student responses.

**Possible response:** A few people twisted the government to suit their own purposes. Government gets in the way of the accomplishments of Americans.

**CONCLUDE:** Help students formulate conclusions about the importance of these details in the text. Ask students how the details relate to the Essential Question.

**Possible response:** Government as it was in the late 1840s stood in contrast to the ideal of individualism. Thoreau believed that the government stood in the way of individualism.

Explain to students that the Essential Question for Unit 2 has to do with political and philosophical theories. These theories lend themselves to comparison with Thoreau's philosophical writings.

Additional **English Language Support** is available in the Interactive Teacher's Edition.

NOTES

The standing army is only an arm of the standing government. The government itself, which is only the mode which the people have chosen to execute their will, is equally liable to be abused and perverted before the people can act through it. Witness the present Mexican war, the work of comparatively a few individuals using the standing government as their tool; for in the outset, the people would not have consented to this measure.

2 This American government—what is it but a tradition, though a recent one, endeavoring to transmit itself unimpaired to posterity, but each instant losing some of its integrity? It has not the vitality and force of a single living man; for a single man can bend it to his will. It is a sort of wooden gun to the people themselves; and, if ever they should use it in earnest as a real one against each other, it will surely split. But it is not the less necessary for this; for the people must have some complicated machinery or other, and hear its din, to satisfy that idea of government which they have. Governments show thus how successfully men can be imposed on, even impose on themselves, for their own advantage. It is excellent, we must all allow; yet this government never of itself furthered any enterprise, but by the alacrity with which it got out of its way. *It* does not keep the country free. *It* does not settle the West. *It* does not educate. The character inherent in the American people has done all that has been accomplished; and it would have done somewhat more, if the government had not sometimes got in its way. For government is an expedient by which men would fain[2] succeed in letting one another alone; and, as has been said, when it is most expedient, the governed are most let alone by it. Trade and commerce, if they were not made of India rubber,[3] would never manage to bounce over the obstacles which legislators are continually putting in their way; and, if one were to judge these men wholly by the effects of their actions, and not partly by their intentions, they would deserve to be classed and punished with those mischievous persons who put obstructions on the railroads.

3 But, to speak practically and as a citizen, unlike those who call themselves no government men, I ask for, not at once no government, but *at once* a better government. Let every man make known what kind of government would command his respect, and that will be one step toward obtaining it. . . . ❧

2. **fain** *adv.* gladly.
3. **India rubber** form of crude rubber.





## PERSONALIZE FOR LEARNING

### Strategic Support

**Government and Ideas** Review the conclusion in paragraph 3. Some students may express surprise, even dismay, at the vehemence of Thoreau's argument against government. Point out that the United States is a democracy, where free speech is a protected right. Discuss the irony of the government protecting the rights of those who speak out against it. Ask students what kind of government Thoreau might find acceptable.

## Comprehension Check

Complete the following items after you finish your first read. Review and clarify details with your group.

*from* WALDEN

1. What advice does Thoreau offer to his "fellows" about ownership of land or property?

2. What did Thoreau hope to discover by living in the woods?

3. What advice does Thoreau give to those living in poverty?

4. **Notebook** Confirm your understanding of the text by writing a summary.

*from* CIVIL DISOBEDIENCE

1. What motto does Thoreau endorse at the beginning of this selection?

2. How does Thoreau define the best possible kind of government?

3. At the end of the text, what does Thoreau ask his readers to do?

4. **Notebook** Confirm your understanding of the text by writing two sentences that summarize its key content.

## RESEARCH

**Research to Clarify** Choose at least one unfamiliar detail from one of the texts. Briefly research that detail. In what way does the information you learned shed light on an aspect of the text?

**Research to Explore** The excerpt from *Walden* may have sparked your curiosity to learn more. For example, you may want to know what Walden Pond is like today. Share what you discover with your group.





## PERSONALIZE FOR LEARNING

### Challenge

**Text-to-World Connection** Explain to students that civil disobedience is the refusal to obey some of the laws of government in order to influence government policy or lawmaking. Civil disobedience uses only nonviolent techniques.

Tell students that Thoreau's essay on civil disobedience has had a far-reaching effect around the world. Mahatma Gandhi was influenced by the essay, and his tactics, in turn, affected Martin Luther King, Jr., in his work for civil rights.

Ask students to do some research on a place, person, or movement that was influenced by Thoreau's essay. Have students share their findings in small groups.

DIGITAL PERSPECTIVES

## Comprehension Check

*from* Walden

**Possible responses:**

1. Thoreau advises his "fellows" to avoid the commitments of ownership.
2. He hoped to discover the essential facts of life.
3. He advises impoverished people to live life and find the best in it.
4. Thoreau reflects on his inspection of potential properties for his home and concludes that it is wise to avoid the commitments of ownership. He confides that he took up an abode in the woods in order to discover the essential features of life. People would do well, he says, to simplify their lives and to live at a slower pace. They should not allow themselves to be caught up in a desperate race for success. Indeed, being true to oneself may mean living in a way that is like marching to a different drummer. Living in poverty, in fact, may be a key to independence.

*from* Civil Disobedience

**Possible responses:**

1. Thoreau accepts the motto "That government is best which governs least."
2. Thoreau claims that government is best which governs not at all.
3. He asks them to stand up and declare what kind of government would command their respect.
4. The best government is that which governs least. If people declare openly what kind of government they want, government will improve.

## Research

**Research to Clarify** If groups struggle to identify an unfamiliar detail, you may want to suggest that they focus on one of the following [from *Walden*]: whether or not seeds improve with age, reference to Olympus (end of paragraph 9), the German Confederacy in the 1840s, or the status of the railroad industry in the late 1840s.

**Research to Explore** If groups struggle to find information about Walden Pond, have them look online on the National Park Service website. Discuss the irony of Walden Pond being administered by the National Park Service, given Thoreau's dim view of government. And yet, if the pond had remained private property, it might not have remained in its pristine state.

# FACILITATING

## Jump Start

CLOSE READ **Ask students if they have ever thought of doing something that would identify them as a nonconformist. As students discuss these actions in their groups, ask them to consider whether they think it is better to be a conformist or a nonconformist, and why.**

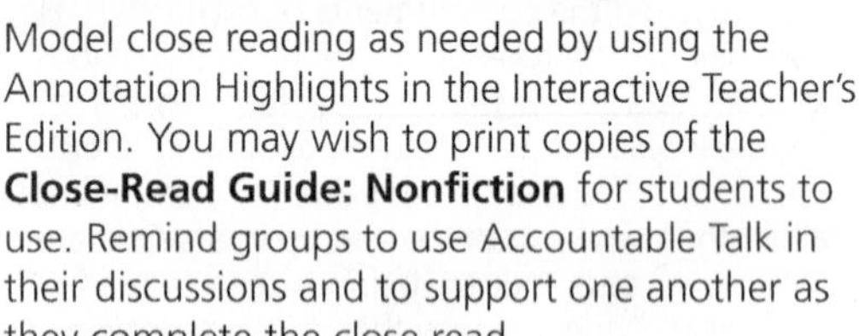

## Close Read the Text

Model close reading as needed by using the Annotation Highlights in the Interactive Teacher's Edition. You may wish to print copies of the **Close-Read Guide: Nonfiction** for students to use. Remind groups to use Accountable Talk in their discussions and to support one another as they complete the close read.

## Analyze the Text

Possible responses:

1. To Thoreau, it's best just to imagine ownership because he believes in simplifying life.
2. Answers will vary, but should include passages and specific details noticed, questions, and conclusions.
3. Answers will vary, but should include ideas about the individual and society and text references.

## Concept Vocabulary

**Why These Words? Possible response:** The words enhance Thoreau's messages about simplicity vs. complexity and nonconformity vs. conformity.

### Practice

Possible responses:

1. If everything sufficed, he or she would likely be content.
2. Purchasing superfluous, or unnecessary, items results in needless expense.
3. Technology is vital to many people's lives but perhaps not necessary for survival.

### Word Network

Possible words: independent, unmolested, conformity, retirement, withdraw

## Word Study

Possible responses:

*Superfluous* comes from the prefix *super-* and the root *fluere,* meaning "to flow." Together they mean "overflowing" or "more than enough."
*superhuman:* exceptional human abilities
*supernatural:* mysterious, unearthly
*superficial:* shallow, cursory
*superhighway* a large, wide highway

For more support, see **Concept Vocabulary and Word Study.**

MAKING MEANING

from WALDEN
from CIVIL DISOBEDIENCE

## Close Read the Text

With your group, revisit sections of the texts you marked during your first read. **Annotate** what you notice. What **questions** do you have? What can you **conclude?**

TIP

GROUP DISCUSSION
Be sure to follow rules for participating in group discussions, speaking in turn, and addressing each participant with respect. In a discussion, it is often unlikely that all group members will agree, but everyone deserves to be heard and to receive thoughtful consideration.

## Analyze the Text

**CITE TEXTUAL EVIDENCE** to support your answers.

**Notebook** Complete the activities.

1. **Review and Clarify** With your group, reread paragraph 1 of the excerpt from *Walden*. Describe Thoreau's attitude toward home ownership. How does this outlook relate to his experience in the woods and to his overall view of how life should be lived?
2. **Present and Discuss** Now, work with your group to share the passages from the selections that you found especially important. Take turns presenting your passages. Discuss what you noticed in the selections, what questions you asked, and what conclusions you reached.
3. **Essential Question:** *What role does individualism play in American society?* What have these texts taught you about the relationship between the individual and society? Discuss with your group.

WORD NETWORK
Add words related to individualism from the texts to your Word Network.

LANGUAGE DEVELOPMENT

## Concept Vocabulary

sufficed superfluous vital

**Why These Words?** The concept vocabulary words from these texts are related. With your group, determine what the words have in common. How do these word choices enhance the impact of the texts?

### Practice

**Notebook** Confirm your understanding of these words by answering these questions. Use the vocabulary word from each question in your answer.

1. If everything in someone's life *sufficed,* would he or she most likely be content? Explain.
2. How would refusing to purchase *superfluous* items help your budget?
3. In the modern world, is technology *vital* to survival?

STANDARDS
**Reading Informational Text**
• Cite strong and thorough textual evidence to support analysis of what the text says explicitly as well as inferences drawn from the text, including determining where the text leaves matters uncertain.
• Determine an author's point of view or purpose in a text in which the rhetoric is particularly effective, analyzing how style and content contribute to the power, persuasiveness, or beauty of the text.
**Language**
Identify and correctly use patterns of word changes that indicate different meanings or parts of speech.

## Word Study

**Notebook Latin Prefix: *super-*** The Latin prefix *super-* means "above" or "over." Explain how the meaning of the prefix contributes to the meaning of *superfluous.* Then, find four other words that have this same prefix. Record the words and their meanings.





### FORMATIVE ASSESSMENT

**Analyze the Text**
• **If** students struggle to close read the text, then provide the ***from* Walden • *from* Civil Disobedience: Text Questions** available online in the Interactive Teacher's Edition and Unit Resources. Answers and DOK levels are also available.

**Concept Vocabulary**
**If** students struggle to identify the concept, **then** have them use each word in a sentence and think about what is similar about the sentences.

**Word Study**
**If** students fail to find four other words with the prefix *super-,* **then** suggest they consult a dictionary to develop a list of words.

For Reteach and Practice, see **Word Study: Latin Prefix *super-* (RP).**

## Analyze Craft and Structure

**Author's Point of View** An author's **point of view** is the perspective the writer adopts toward a situation or set of issues. In both *Walden* and "Civil Disobedience," Thoreau presents arguments that build on **philosophical assumptions,** or principles and beliefs that he takes for granted and that form a foundation for his ideas. Some assumptions are **explicit,** or directly stated. Other assumptions, however, are **implicit,** or not stated outright.

For example, a writer might hold certain beliefs about human nature, divine or spiritual matters, the nature of society, or another aspect of life. A writer may not explain these fundamental beliefs; nevertheless, they may be the basis for his or her ideas. In order to identify and consider these implicit assumptions, the reader must tease them out from details the writer does supply. Then, the reader must consider how these assumptions contribute to the author's overall position or ideas.

### Practice

**CITE TEXTUAL EVIDENCE** to support your answers.

**Notebook** Respond to these questions.

1. (a) What implicit assumption does Thoreau rely on when he discusses the relationship of money and the soul in *Walden*? (b) Do you believe Thoreau's assumption is valid? Why or why not?
2. (a) Identify the explicit assumption with which Thoreau begins his discussion in "Civil Disobedience." (b) What counterarguments, or opposing views, to this assumption might someone present?
3. (a) In *Walden*, how does Thoreau support his point that "It makes but little difference whether you are committed to a farm or the county jail"? (b) What implicit assumption does this statement suggest? (c) Do you agree? Explain.
4. Record Thoreau's implicit assumptions on a variety of issues as they are revealed in *Walden*. List specific details that allow you to identify each assumption.

| ISSUE | IMPLICIT ASSUMPTION | DETAILS |
|---|---|---|
| Desire for freedom | Possible response: Commitments limit a person's independence. | Possible response: As long as possible live free and uncommitted. |
| Simplicity of life | Possible response: Simplicity enhances clarity and happiness. | Possible response: In proportion as he simplifies his life, the laws of the universe will appear less complex . . . |
| Nonconformity | Possible response: Nonconformity may be required for independence and truth to self. | Possible response: Let him step to the music which he hears, however measured or far away. |





**DIGITAL PERSPECTIVES**

## Analyze Craft and Structure

**Author's Point of View** Explain to students that Thoreau uses the first-person point of view in his writing. Using the pronoun *I*, he speaks from his unique perspective. Help students see that this point of view lends a directness and authenticity to his writing that might not otherwise be there. For more support, see **Analyze Craft and Structure: Author's Point of View.**

### Practice

Possible responses:

1. (a) Thoreau implicitly assumes that money is unrelated to the requirements of the soul. (b) Students should present a reasonable defense of their evaluation.
2. (a) Thoreau begins with the explicit assumption that government is best when it operates least. (b) Counterarguments may include the objection that government is required to ensure the rights of a minority and that it is necessary for the administration of complex tasks such as foreign relations, product regulation in commerce, and transportation networks.
3. (a) Thoreau explains the work and responsibility that goes into a farm. (b) It implies that both are difficult and burdensome. (c) I don't agree. A farm is something that a person chooses and from which he or she reaps rewards for hard work and commitment. Jail is forced punishment against your will.

**FORMATIVE ASSESSMENT**

### Analyze Craft and Structure

**If** students are unable to identify implicit assumptions in Thoreau's text, **then** have them focus on only one paragraph (for example, paragraph 1 in "Civil Disobedience") and analyze each sentence to determine which statements have implicit assumptions. For Reteach and Practice, see **Analyze Craft and Structure: Author's Point of View (RP).**

### HOW LANGUAGE WORKS

**Point of View** Remind students that an author who writes in the first-person point of view uses the pronouns *I* and *we* to present the perspective from which the work is written. An author who writes from the third-person point of view uses a narrator who may or may not be a character in the story or nonfiction piece. The narrator uses the pronouns *he, she, they,* and so on to describe the action. A story can also be told from the omniscient point of view, where an all-knowing observer can describe everything that happens and can express the thoughts of all the characters. Like third-person point of view, the omniscient point of view also uses third-person pronouns. Have the class discuss the advantages and disadvantages of each point of view.

FACILITATING

## Conventions and Style

**Author's Style** As you review Thoreau's style with students, consider providing additional examples to reinforce aspects of conversational style:

- "I left the woods for as good a reason as I went there." (diction)
- "...to brag as lustily as chanticleer in the morning. . . ." (figure of speech)
- "Time is but the stream I go a-fishing in. I drink at it; but while I drink I see the sandy bottom and see how shallow it is." (analogy)

For more support, see **Conventions and Style: Author's Style.**

### Read It

Possible responses:

1. The underlined portions exhibit direct address of the reader, figurative language, and concise statement, respectively.
2. Paragraph 13: I had not lived there more than a week before my feet wore a path from my door to the pondside. . . . (anecdote); I did not wish to take a cabin passage , but rather to go before the mast and on the deck of the world. . . . (analogy).
3. A conversational style enables a philosophical writer to avoid the impression of lecturing to or preaching at readers. It also allows the writer to include anecdotes and sensory images to describe feelings and impressions.

### Write It

Reviews should focus on an evaluation of the excerpt and should exhibit at least two of the techniques discussed for a conversational style.

### FORMATIVE ASSESSMENT

### Conventions and Style

**If** students are struggling to discriminate between figures of speech and analogies, **then** remind them that analogies are usually extended comparisons. A figure of speech might appear in a single sentence, but if the comparison is longer than a sentence, it is probably an analogy.

For Reteach and Practice, see **Conventions and Style: Author's Style (RP).**

LANGUAGE DEVELOPMENT

from WALDEN
from CIVIL DISOBEDIENCE

## Conventions and Style

**Author's Style** A writer's **style** is the unique manner in which he or she puts thoughts into words. In his philosophical writing, Thoreau uses a broad range of devices to establish a **conversational style,** as if he were talking informally to a friend.

- Typically, Thoreau's **diction,** or **word choice,** is simple and direct:
  *I went to the woods because I wished to live deliberately . . .*
- Thoreau often combines plain statements with **figures of speech**—imaginative comparisons that engage the thinking of his readers:
  *In the midst of this chopping sea of civilized life, such are the clouds and storms and quicksands . . .*
- By using **analogy,** or extended comparison, Thoreau highlights related ideas or explains the unfamiliar in terms of the familiar:
  *Our life is like a German Confederacy, made up of petty states, with its boundary forever fluctuating . . .*

Other devices that contribute to Thoreau's conversational style include **direct address of the reader** *(Let your affairs be as two or three)*, **brief anecdotes** (short, illustrative stories, like that of the Hollowell Place), and **pithy statements** (wise and concise statements—*we do not ride upon the railroad; it rides upon us*).

### Read It

1. Work individually. In a sentence or two, explain how each underlined part of this passage from *Walden* contributes to Thoreau's conversational style and to his overall point. Then, meet with your group to compare your responses.

> Moreover, if you are restricted in your range by poverty, if you cannot buy books and newspapers, for instance, you are but confined to the most significant and vital experiences; you are compelled to deal with the material which yields the most sugar and the most starch. It is life near the bone where it is sweetest.

2. **Connect to Style** Reread paragraph 13 of the excerpt from *Walden*. Mark and then label two words or phrases that contribute to Thoreau's conversational style.
3. **Notebook** In a sentence or two, explain why a conversational style might be especially useful for a philosophical writer such as Thoreau.

### Write It

**Notebook** Write a paragraph-long review of the excerpt from "Civil Disobedience." Create a conversational style in your review by using some of the techniques discussed above.

STANDARDS

**Reading Informational Text**
Determine an author's point of view or purpose in a text in which the rhetoric is particularly effective, analyzing how style and content contribute to the power, persuasiveness, or beauty of the text.





PERSONALIZE FOR LEARNING

### English Language Support

**Taking Part in Discussion** Have student pairs list ideas for discussion based on the ideas in Thoreau's "Civil Disobedience." Then have students discuss one of the topics from their list in a group discussion with other pairs. Encourage all students to take turns, listen to others respectfully, and politely state their opinions when it is their turn to speak. **ALL LEVELS**

An expanded **English Language Support Lesson** on Discussion is available in the Interactive Teacher's Edition.

EFFECTIVE EXPRESSION

## Speaking and Listening

**Assignment**

With your group, hold a **discussion** in which you respond to these excerpts from Thoreau's philosophical writings. Choose from the following options:

- ☐ Brainstorm for a **list** of current or past events in which citizens have followed Thoreau's advice in "Civil Disobedience" to stand up and *make known what kind of government would command [their] respect.* Explain your reasons for including each example.
- ☐ Prepare a **response** to this statement adapted from Thoreau: *It is always better to march to the beat of one's own drummer.* Take turns offering and supporting your opinions.
- ☐ Formulate a **prosecution** or a **defense** of Thoreau's decision to withhold payment of his taxes. Marshal evidence and reasons to support your perspective, making sure that you deal directly with Thoreau's rationale for civil disobedience.

**Finding Evidence** Most of the evidence you will use during this discussion should come from Thoreau's writings. However, you may need additional information to have a lively conversation. This decision will depend on the topic you have chosen to discuss. For example, you may need to conduct some research about American or world history, or U.S. tax laws.

**Holding the Discussion** Make sure that everyone has a chance to speak and to express opinions that are supported with evidence from the text or from related research. If questions emerge from your discussion, decide together how you will locate the answers.

**Considering All Responses** Philosophical ideas can generate a wide variety of responses—and that can make a discussion exciting. Be open to the idea that many interpretations can be valid.

**Asking Questions** Get in the habit of asking questions to clarify your understanding of another reader's ideas. You can also use questions to call attention to areas of confusion, debatable points, or errors. In addition, offer elaboration on the points that others make by providing examples. To move a discussion forward, summarize and evaluate tentative conclusions reached by the group members.

**Notes:**

EVIDENCE LOG

Before moving on to a new selection, go to your Evidence Log and record what you learned from the excerpts from *Walden* and "Civil Disobedience."

STANDARDS

**Speaking and Listening**

- Work with peers to promote civil and democratic discussions and decision-making, set clear goals and deadlines, and establish individual roles as needed.
- Propel conversations by posing and responding to questions that probe reasoning and evidence; ensure a hearing for a full range of positions on a topic or issue; clarify, verify, or challenge ideas and conclusions; and promote divergent and creative perspectives.
- Respond thoughtfully to diverse perspectives; synthesize comments, claims, and evidence made on all sides of an issue; resolve contradictions when possible; and determine what additional information or research is required to deepen the investigation or complete the task.





PERSONALIZE FOR LEARNING

### Strategic Support

**Presenting an Argument** Point out that all three discussion options are based on students' ability to present a full and focused argument. Make sure that students understand what an argument is in this context: the position, or claim, that a speaker presents, which is supported by evidence. At each stage of their process, have groups evaluate the quality of their arguments. Remind them that a good argument is clearly presented and strongly supported.

DIGITAL PERSPECTIVES

## Speaking and Listening

If groups have trouble deciding upon which assignment option to choose, encourage them to consider which option plays to the group's strengths the most. For example, if one or more group members are familiar with debate strategies, formulating a defense could be a good option. If the group feels more comfortable with a focus on research, then brainstorming a list of current or past events would work well.

**Finding Evidence** If students are doing research online, have them determine effective key words for their search; for example, "civil disobedience historical events" for the first possible assignment.

**Holding the Discussion** Have each group deliver its presentation to the other class groups. Have the listeners ask questions of the presenters. If two groups have chosen the same topic, have students note differences in each presentation.

**Considering All Responses** Encourage students to keep an open mind and give thought to the viewpoints that other students bring.

**Asking Questions** Remind students to be respectful during discussions by allowing everyone an opportunity to speak and by not interrupting when others are speaking.

For more support, see **Speaking and Listening: Discussion.**

Evidence Log Support students in completing their Evidence Log. This paced activity will help prepare them for the Performance-Based Assessment at the end of the unit.

### FORMATIVE ASSESSMENT

### Speaking and Listening

**If** students struggle with their online research, **then** have them refine their key words until they yield helpful results. For Reteach and Practice, see **Speaking and Listening: Discussion (RP).**

### Selection Test

Administer the "*from* Walden | *from* Civil Disobedience" Selection Test, which is available in both print and digital formats online in Assessments. 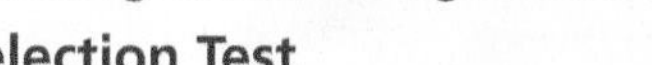

# Innovators and Their Inventions

**AUDIO SUMMARIES**
Audio summaries of "Innovators and Their Inventions" are available in both English and Spanish and can be assigned to students in the Interactive Teacher's Edition or Unit Resources. Assigning these summaries prior to reviewing the selection may help students build additional background knowledge and set a context for their first review.

## Summary

This selection includes patent documents, which give proof that someone has invented something. The first is from the invention of the telephone, by Alexander Graham Bell. Bell was born in Scotland, but did his most famous work in the United States. Another inventor claimed to have invented the telephone on the same day, leading to a dispute that Bell ultimately won.

The second is from the invention of the windshield wiper, by Mary Anderson. Before this invention, driving was more dangerous. Drivers who couldn't see because of obstructions on the windshield would have to stop and clean off the window by hand. Or, worse, try to clean them off while still driving!

### Insight

These papers show how creative individuals can make an enormous impact on the world. On the other hand, a patent document also shows that great ideas aren't necessarily unique. Elisha Gray may well have invented the telephone at the same time as Bell, but he didn't end up getting the patent.

ESSENTIAL QUESTION:
What role does individualism play in American society?

## Connection to Essential Question

"Innovators and Their Inventions" provides a visual representation related to the Essential Question. Individualism in the process of invention is often critical.

SMALL-GROUP LEARNING PERFORMANCE TASK
When is it difficult to march to the beat of a "different drummer" and stand on your own as an individual? What are the risks and rewards of nonconformity?

UNIT PERFORMANCE-BASED ASSESSMENT
What significant incident from my past helped me realize that I am a unique individual?

## Connection to Performance Tasks

**Small-Group Learning Performance Task** In this performance task, students will draw on the ways in which the texts and features in the unit approach the concept of nonconformity and use them to write a speech on the subject.

**Unit Performance-Based Assessment** This selection will contribute to the students' understanding of how they are unique individuals by showing a few of the accomplishments of historical individuals.

**DIGITAL PERSPECTIVES**

 Audio  Video  Document  Annotation Highlights  EL Highlights  Online Assessment

## LESSON RESOURCES

| | Making Meaning | Effective Expression |
|---|---|---|
| Lesson | **First Review**<br>**Close Review**<br>**Analyze the Media**<br>**Media Vocabulary** | **Speaking and Listening** |
| Instructional Standards | **RI.10** By the end of grade 11, read and comprehend literary nonfiction . . .<br>**L.6** Acquire and use accurately general academic and domain-specific words and phrases . . . | **SL.4** Present information, findings, and supporting evidence . . . |
| **STUDENT RESOURCES** | | |
| Available online in the Interactive Student Edition or Unit Resources | Selection Audio<br>First-Review Guide: Media Art/Photography<br>Close- Review Guide: Media Art/Photography | Evidence Log |
| **TEACHER RESOURCES** | | |
| Selection Resources Available online in the Interactive Teacher's Edition or Unit Resources | Audio Summaries<br>Media Vocabulary<br>Innovators and Their Inventions: Media Questions | Speaking and Listening: Speech |
| My Resources | A Unit 2 Answer Key is available online and in the Interactive Teacher's Edition | |

## Media Complexity Rubric: Innovators and Their Inventions

**Quantitative Measures**

**Format and Length** 2 images of drawings with captions

| Qualitative Measures | |
|---|---|
| Knowledge Demands<br>① ❷ ③ ④ ⑤ | To fully understand drawings, prior knowledge about patents and how they work will be helpful. Some explanation is given. |
| Structure<br>① ❷ ③ ④ ⑤ | Each image is explained with an extended caption, making it easy to find information to explain visuals. The drawings themselves also contain labels. |
| Language Conventionality and Clarity<br>① ② ❸ ④ ⑤ | Some of the captions and labels contain technical terms that may need further explanation. Captions have some complex sentences. |
| Levels of Meaning/Purpose<br>① ❷ ③ ④ ⑤ | The images depict drawings of early American inventions. Ideas and concepts are straightforward and easily accessible. |

# FACILITATING

## Jump Start

FIRST REVIEW Have you ever thought up an invention? Did you make a drawing or write an explanation of your invention? Encourage students to describe their inventions. Then engage students in a discussion about how inventors of today are different from inventors who lived in the 1800s. Explain that these differences will help prepare them for viewing inventions from the past, such as the telephone.

## Innovators and Their Inventions

What methods might inventors today use to illustrate their inventions? How are these methods different from innovators of long ago? As you model these and other questions, connect them to the Performance Task question. Audio for the selection is available in the Interactive Teacher's Edition.

## Media Vocabulary

Encourage groups to discuss the media vocabulary. Ask groups to look at the terms to see what they have in common. Students should notice that the term "specifications" refers to both written information and illustrations whereas "cross-section" and "figure" are terms for components of a diagram specifically. Point out that in this context, the term "figure" refers to an illustration. A *figure* can also refer to an amount expressed in numbers or the shape of a human body.

### FIRST REVIEW

Have students perform the steps of the first review independently:

LOOK: Remind students to focus on the visual elements of the diagrams and the labels to understand the information about the invention.

NOTE: Encourage students to mark any parts of the diagram they find interesting.

CONNECT: Encourage students to make connections between the diagrams they see here and other diagrams they may have had experience with.

RESPOND: Students will demonstrate their understanding by answering questions and writing a description.
Point out to students that they will complete the Respond step after they have finished the first review. You may wish to print copies of the **First-Review Guide: Media: Art/Photography.**

MAKING MEANING

**About Technical Drawings**

Some public documents include **technical drawings,** which are scale diagrams that show how something is constructed or how it functions. Individual inventors often create technical drawings to explain their innovations to a wider audience. Multiple views, including close-up details of key parts, are usually required to fully illustrate a new invention. When applying for a **patent**—the exclusive right to sell a product—inventors include technical drawings that show each important part in detail.

# Innovators and Their Inventions

## Media Vocabulary

These words will be useful to you as you analyze, discuss, and write about visual public documents and the text features that they contain.

| | |
|---|---|
| **Specifications:** section of a patent application in which the inventor fully describes the invention | • Specifications include both verbal descriptions and detailed diagrams that illustrate the invention's parts and functions.<br>• Patent specifications come before the claims, in which the applicant defines the scope of protection being requested (such as the right to prevent others from selling the invention). |
| **Cross-section:** view of a three-dimensional object that shows the interior as if a cut has been made across the object | • A cross-section shows the parts inside a solid shape, revealing details that are not visible from the outside.<br>• Labels or callouts may identify parts revealed within.<br>• Details are shown using an exact scale, or ratio that compares the size of the illustration with the actual size of the invention. |
| **Figure:** one of a set of drawings or illustrations | • Figures are usually given consecutive numbers or letters so they can be referred to in accompanying text.<br>• The term is often abbreviated as *fig.* |

## First Review MEDIA: PUBLIC DOCUMENT

Apply these strategies as you conduct your first review. You will have an opportunity to complete a close review after your first review.

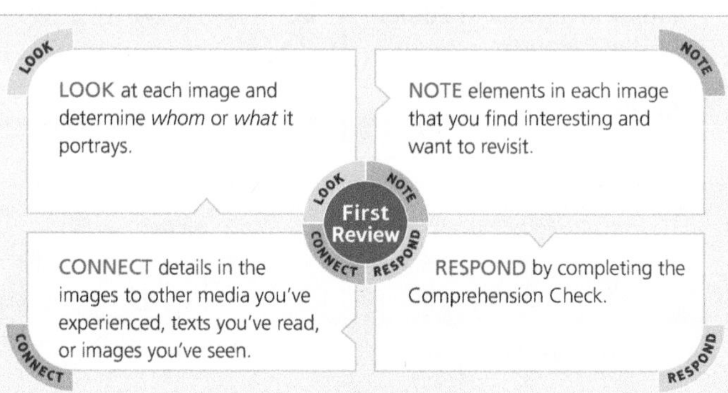
LOOK
NOTE
LOOK at each image and determine *whom* or *what* it portrays.
NOTE elements in each image that you find interesting and want to revisit.
First Review
CONNECT details in the images to other media you've experienced, texts you've read, or images you've seen.
RESPOND by completing the Comprehension Check.
CONNECT
RESPOND

**STANDARDS**

**Reading Informational Text**
By the end of grade 11, read and comprehend literary nonfiction in the grades 11–CCR text complexity band proficiently, with scaffolding as needed at the high end of the range.

**Language**
Acquire and use accurately general academic and domain-specific words and phrases, sufficient for reading, writing, speaking, and listening at the college and career readiness level; demonstrate independence in gathering vocabulary knowledge when considering a word or phrase important to comprehension or expression.

### PERSONALIZE FOR LEARNING

**English Language Support**

**Nominalization** Write the word *specification*. Tell students that this word is from the verb, "specify," which means "to state something in detail." The root word "specific" is an adjective meaning "precise." The word *specific* is changed to a noun by adding the suffix, "-ation." "Specification" is a noun meaning a "detailed description." "Specifications" is the plural form of the word.
**ALL LEVELS**

MEDIA | PUBLIC DOCUMENT

# Innovators and Their Inventions

BACKGROUND

A patent documents the government's recognition that a person has invented something. Nobody else is allowed to make, use, or sell that invention without the inventor's permission until the patent expires. The federal government has been issuing patents, including those for the inventions discussed here, since George Washington signed the Patent Act of 1790.

SCAN FOR MULTIMEDIA

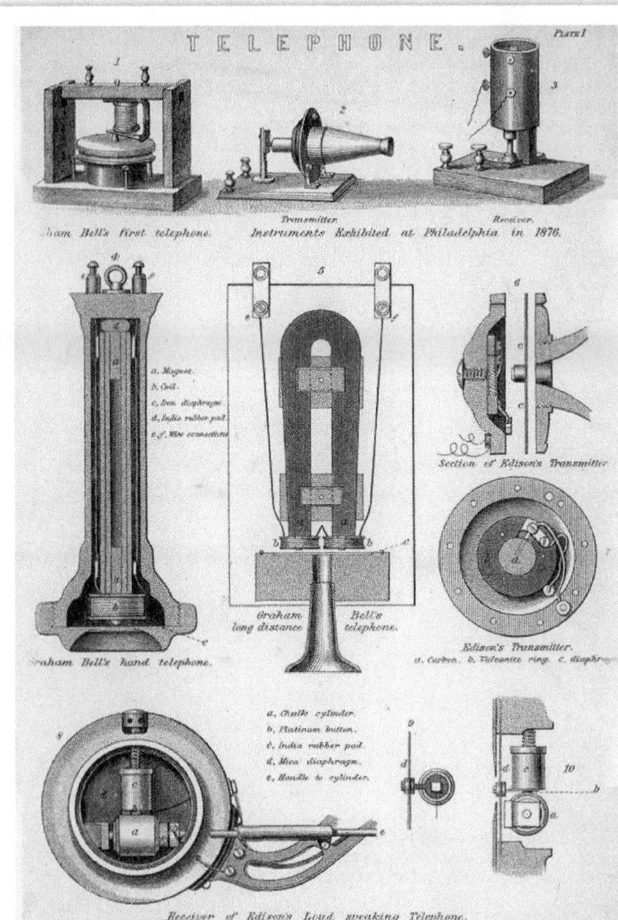


**IMAGE 1: Diagram of Telephone Components** Alexander Graham Bell was born in Scotland, but he did his most famous work as a scientist and inventor in the United States. After many years of experimenting with sound—specifically, how sound could be transmitted electrically—Bell filed a patent for the telephone on February 14, 1876. On the same day, another inventor, Elisha Gray, also submitted a claim that he had invented the telephone. The controversy was settled when Bell received the patent for the telephone, now considered one of the most valuable patents in the world.

NOTES





CLOSER REVIEW

## Analyze Public Documents

Circulate among groups as students conduct their close review. Suggest that groups review Image 1. Encourage them to talk about what they note. If needed, provide the following support.

**NOTE:** Have students note details in the telephone diagram that show cross-sections of Bell's hand telephone (4), and Edison's transmitter (6), or have students participate while you note them. Point out that each figure in the diagram is numbered and lettered labels specify parts in some of the figures.

**QUESTION:** Guide students to consider what these details might tell them. Ask what a viewer can infer from the details and labels in the figures of the telephone diagram, and accept student responses.

**Possible response:** The diagram shows Bell's first telephone and instruments exhibited at Philadelphia in 1878. The diagram also shows detailed parts of the telephone transmitter and receiver, including cross-sections of various parts.

**CONCLUDE:** Help students formulate conclusions about the importance of these details in the diagram. Ask students why the artist might have included these details.

**Possible response:** The artist wants to show the parts of the telephone and details of how these parts are put together to make up the invention. Remind students that **public documents** are legal records and other information preserved by the government and available to the public.

## DIGITAL PERSPECTIVES

**Enriching the Text** Have students go online to conduct research on Elisha Gray. Gray Gray was an American inventor who was said to have filed a patent for his invention of the telephone two hours after Bell submitted his own patent. Gray actually filed an *announcement* of an invention (the telephone) he expected to patent. Bell was awarded the patent, but soon became involved in a legal battle over who was the true inventor of the telephone. Bell eventually won the lawsuit and was legally named the inventor of the telephone. It was determined later that the device described in Gray's announcement would have worked.

# FACILITATING

## CLOSER REVIEW

### Analyzing Public Documents

Circulate among groups as students conduct their close review of Image 2, Mary Anderson's Window Cleaning Device. Encourage students to talk about what they note. If needed, provide the following support.

**NOTE:** Have students note details in the diagram of the window cleaning device that show the detailed components of the invention, or have students participate while you note them. Point out the numbered figures and lettered labels that specify parts of the figures.

**QUESTION:** Guide students to consider what these details might tell them. Ask what a viewer can infer from the details and labels in the figures, and accept student responses.

**Possible response:** The diagram shows them how the windshield wiper works at the top right. Figures label the parts of the invention and show how they are put together.

**CONCLUDE:** Help students formulate conclusions about the importance of these details in the diagram. Ask students why the artist might have included these details.

**Possible response:** The artist wants to show the parts of the windshield wiper device and details that outline how these parts are put together to make up the invention.

Remind students that the purpose of **public documents** related to patents is to secure an idea and prove its rightful owner.

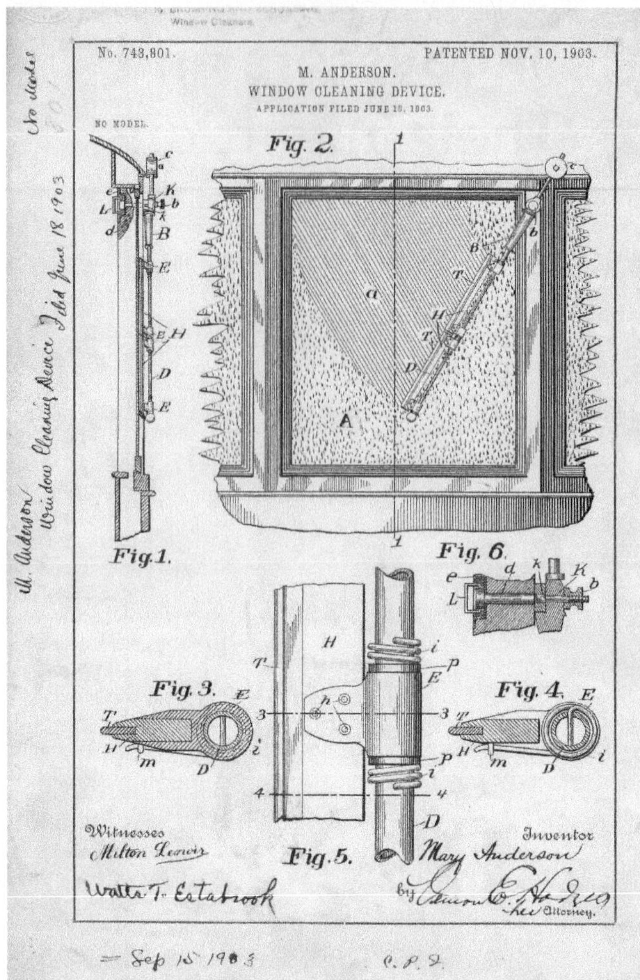


**IMAGE 2: Mary Anderson's Window-Cleaning Device** Patent applications often include detailed images to clarify the design and use of the device in the application. This image is a diagram of the first windshield wiper, patented by Mary Anderson. It is operated by pulling a lever inside of the vehicle. Before her invention, drivers would reach out and wipe down windshields by hand—sometimes stopping the vehicle to do so, and sometimes doing so while driving.

NOTES





## PERSONALIZE FOR LEARNING

### Strategic Support

**Viewing Details** To help students see the details in Image 2 and interpret the illustrations and script in the diagrams, project the diagrams on a screen to enlarge the images and enhance the labeling. Or, you may wish to provide a magnifying lens for students to use as they view the fine details of the drawings in their small groups.

## Comprehension Check

**Complete the following items after you finish your first review. Review and clarify details with your group.**

**1.** In the technical drawings of Bell's telephone, which components are labeled 2 and 3?

**2.** In Figure 4 of the telephone components, what do the labels lettered *a* to *e* name?

**3.** According to information included on the diagrams of the window-cleaning device, when did Anderson apply for this patent, and when was it awarded?

**4.** In Figure 2 of the diagrams for the window-cleaning device, what is part A?

### RESEARCH

**Research to Clarify** Choose at least one unfamiliar element in the technical drawings. Briefly research that element. In what way does the information you learned shed light on an aspect of the drawings or on the work of inventing a new technology?

**Research to Explore** These technical drawings might make you curious about the patent application process. Find out what a patent application includes, where it is filed, who determines whether the patent is granted, and how that decision is made. You may want to share what you discover with your group.





DIGITAL PERSPECTIVES 

## Comprehension Check

Possible responses:

1. Figure 2 shows the transmitter, and Figure 3 shows the receiver.
2. The lettered labels name five important internal parts of Bell's hand telephone.
3. The application was filed on September 18, 1903. It was awarded on November 10 of the same year.
4. Part A is the pane of glass being cleaned by the device.

## Research

**Research to Clarify** If students struggle to come up with an unfamiliar element of the drawings, suggest that they focus on the cross-section view of a technical illustration. Students may wish to find additional examples of cross-section illustrations, perhaps from a science text or an instructional manual for a vehicle, appliance, or other device. Students may want to explain how the cross-section views offer an internal view of parts, a view that other types of illustrations do not provide.

**Research to Explore** Encourage students to explore the U.S. patent and trademark office website, using the patent process overview as the starting point for learning more about the patent application process. Alternatively, students may want to find a literary nonfiction text, or other reliable source, that describes a well-known inventor's experience with the patent process.

### PERSONALIZE FOR LEARNING

**Challenge**

**Inventions of the 1800s** Challenge student groups to search the Internet for patents of inventions of the 1800s. Have students write a brief history of the patent and the inventor and present their information on a slide show using presentation software.

# FACILITATING

## Jump Start

CLOSE REVIEW Ask students to consider the following prompt: *What invention do you think would make life easier in today's modern world?* Have them consider the ways in which the invention of the telephone improved communication and the windshield wiper improved travel.

## Close Review

Model close reviewing by using the Closer Review note in the Interactive Teacher's Edition. Remind students to look for elements and details they did not observe during their first review.

Remind groups to use Accountable Talk in their discussions and to support one another as they complete the close review.

## Analyze the Media

Possible responses:

1. Figure 2 of Anderson's patent drawing is the most informative figure because this view gives the clearest image of the parts.
2. The technical drawings give accurate visual information about the external and internal parts of each invention. A detailed explanation of how the parts function probably would accompany text.
3. Answers will vary, but should reflect a connection to the invention documents.

## Media Vocabulary

Possible responses:

1. The multiple **figures** of the telephone help viewers understand the need for both a transmitter and a receiver. The views include both the outside appearance, as well as **cross-sections,** which clarify internal parts.
2. In addition to the detailed, labeled diagrams, Mary Anderson's complete **specifications** probably included a technical description of the new invention so its purpose and function could be clearly understood.
3. To understand a complex device, you need to understand both its external and internal parts. External views show what the device looks like from the outside, including any parts with which the user directly interacts. **Cross-sections** show parts that are hidden but are essential for the device to function.

For more support, see **Media Vocabulary.**

MAKING MEANING

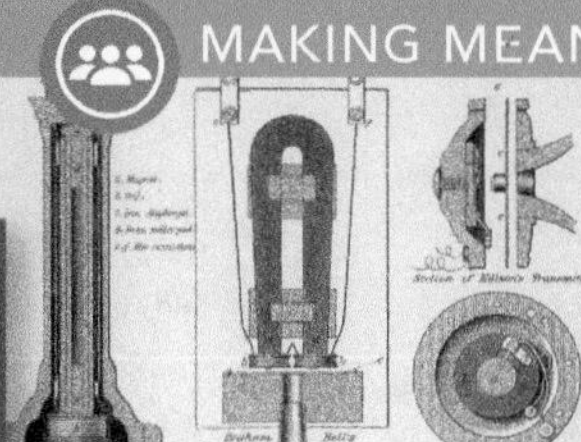

INNOVATORS AND THEIR INVENTIONS

## Close Review

With your group, revisit the technical drawings and your first-review notes. Write down any new observations that seem important. What **questions** do you have? What can you **conclude?**

## Analyze the Media

**CITE TEXTUAL EVIDENCE** to support your answers.

Notebook **Complete the activities.**

1. **Present and Discuss** Choose the drawing you find more interesting or informative. Share your choice with the group and discuss why you chose it. Explain what you noticed in the drawing, what questions it raised for you, and what conclusions you reached about it.
2. **Review and Synthesize** With your group, review both technical drawings. How do they provide information about the inventions they illustrate? What do the drawings alone tell you about how these inventions work? What information might accompanying text provide that would help you understand each device's function?
3. **Essential Question:** ***What role does individualism play in American society?*** What have these public documents taught you about the role that innovative individuals play in society? Discuss with your group.

TIP

**GROUP DISCUSSION**

Begin your discussion of the technical drawings by reviewing all titles, captions, and labels as a group. Refer to the labels to make sure each group member is looking at the same image or part during the discussion.

LANGUAGE DEVELOPMENT

## Media Vocabulary

specifications cross-section figure

Use these words as you discuss and write about the technical drawings.

1. Why is it useful to have more than one technical drawing of an early telephone to understand the parts of this invention, as well as its origins?
2. In addition to the drawings shown here, what information did Anderson probably include in her patent application for a window-cleaning device? Explain.
3. Both drawings include multiple views of the invention. Why are multiple views needed to show how something works?

STANDARDS

**Speaking and Listening**

Present information, findings, and supporting evidence, conveying a clear and distinct perspective, such that listeners can follow the line of reasoning, alternative or opposing perspectives are addressed, and the organization, development, substance, and style are appropriate to purpose, audience, and a range of formal and informal tasks.





## FORMATIVE ASSESSMENT

### Analyze the Media

**If** students struggle to cite evidence to support their answers, **then** discuss how to select appropriate information from the technical drawings and illustrate with examples. You may also want to provide the **Innovators and Their Inventions: Media Questions** available online in the Interactive Teacher's Edition or Unit Resources. Answers and DOK levels are also available.

### Media Vocabulary

**If** students struggle to use the three terms as they discuss and write about the technical drawings, **then** have them review the definitions of *figures* and *cross-section.*

EFFECTIVE EXPRESSION

## Speaking and Listening

**Assignment**

Consider this question with your group: How have each of the two inventions pictured in these public documents affected people's lives in different ways? Then, discuss other inventions that have changed people's lives. Consider surprising inventions, such as sticky notes, as well as more obvious ones. Decide which invention of all the ones you discussed has had the greatest impact on society. Then, write a one-minute **speech** in which you state and support your position. Deliver your speech to the class.

**Choose a Position** Begin to answer the question by considering as many impacts as possible. Ask yourselves how life would be different without each invention. Collect your thoughts in a chart.

| | INVENTION | INVENTION | INVENTION |
|---|---|---|---|
| Use and function | | | |
| Importance | | | |

**Plan Your Argument** After you have determined your position, plan your speech. Begin with a strong statement of your claim about the impact of the invention you chose, and then provide support. Aim to include at least three ideas that support your position. Finally, end your speech with a conclusion that restates your claim.

| PLAN YOUR ARGUMENT |
|---|
| Claim: |
| Support:<br>1.<br>2.<br>3. |
| Conclusion: |

**Present Your Speech and Debate** Deliver your speeches, and have your classmates score them. After the initial speeches, allow time for discussion, in which students compare their positions and make some generalizations about the impact of technical innovation on society.

EVIDENCE LOG

Before moving on to a new selection, go to your Evidence Log and record what you learned from "Innovators and Their Inventions."





## PERSONALIZE FOR LEARNING

### English Language Support

**Sentence Starters** Help students justify their opinions by giving them sentence starters, for example:

- In my opinion (statement of opinion or claim) _____.
- Evidence that supports my claim is _____.
- A statistic that supports my opinion is _____.
- An example that supports my statement is _____.

**EMERGING**

DIGITAL PERSPECTIVES   

## Speaking and Listening

**Choose a Position** Remind students that when presenting an opinion, they must first make a claim that expresses their position. Then they should support their claim with evidence. Students should also keep in mind that they must present evidence to show that any counterclaims made are not founded.

**Plan Your Argument** Encourage students to include different kinds of evidence that support their claims, such as facts, examples, and statistics. Students should note their sources.

**Present Your Speech and Debate** Suggest that students score the presentations based on whether they strongly agree (1), agree (2), disagree (3), or strongly disagree (4). Once students have had the opportunity to present a rebuttal, allow students time to change their scores. Allow students the opportunity to give a rationale for their scores. For more support, see **Speaking and Listening: Speech.**

**Evidence Log** Support students in completing their Evidence Log. This paced activity will help prepare them for the Performance-Based Assessment at the end of the unit.

### FORMATIVE ASSESSMENT

### Speaking and Listening

**If** students are unable to effectively present an opinion with effective support, **then** have students go back and reread the Assignment question. Suggest they brainstorm their ideas using the chart on the student page. For Reteach and Practice, see **Speaking and Listening: Speech (RP).**

# The Love Song of J. Alfred Prufrock

**AUDIO SUMMARIES**
Audio summaries of "The Love Song of J. Alfred Prufrock" are available in both English and Spanish and can be assigned to students in the Interactive Teacher's Edition or Unit Resources. Assigning these summaries prior to reading the selection may help students build additional background knowledge and set a context for their first read.

## Summary

In T. S. Eliot's poem "The Love Song of J. Alfred Prufrock," the speaker is a middle-aged man. The speaker invites us to join him in a walk through the foggy streets of a cityscape, as he describes his feelings of inadequacy. The speaker discusses his inability to make decisions—especially with respect to a woman he cares for—and complains about the repetitive boredom of his days as an emotional nobody. At the end, the speaker is at the beach, listening to mermaids sing—but not to him. Still, he seems to be comforted by the sea, which provides an escape from other humans in society.

### Insight

Reading "The Love Song of J. Alfred Prufrock" will help students understand the difficulty that men and women experience in maintaining their individualism and finding a fulfilling place in the modern world.

ESSENTIAL QUESTION:
What role does individualism play in American society?

## Connection to Essential Question

"The Love Song of J. Alfred Prufrock" connects to the Essential Question, "What role does individualism play in American society?" by expressing the frustrations and disillusionments of trying to live a meaningful individualistic existence.

SMALL-GROUP LEARNING PERFORMANCE TASK
When is it difficult to "march to the beat of a different drummer" and stand on your own as an individual? What are the risks and rewards of nonconformity?

UNIT PERFORMANCE-BASED ASSESSMENT
What significant incident from my past helped me to realize that I am a unique individual?

## Connection to Performance Tasks

**Small-Group Learning Performance Task** In this Performance Task, students will draw on the ways in which this poem and the other selections in the unit approach the concept of nonconformity and then write a speech on the subject.

**Unit Performance-Based Assessment** This poem offers a description of an individual who reflects on his experiences. The incidents he reflects on lead the individual to some emotional comfort. Prufrock's experiences may help students consider what is important in life and transfer any realizations to their own experiences.

DIGITAL PERSPECTIVES

 Audio  Video  Document  Annotation Highlights  EL Highlights 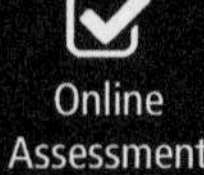 Online Assessment

## LESSON RESOURCES

| | Making Meaning | Language Development | Effective Expression |
|---|---|---|---|
| **Lesson** | **First Read**<br>**Close Read**<br>**Analyze the Text**<br>**Analyze Craft and Structure** | **Concept Vocabulary**<br>**Word Study**<br>**Conventions and Style** | **Writing to Sources** |
| **Instructional Standards** | **RL.10** By the end of grade 11, read and comprehend literature . . .<br>**RL.5** Analyze how an author's choices . . .<br>**RL.6** Analyze a case in which grasping point of view . . .<br>**L.4.a** Use context as a clue . . . | **L.4.b** Identify and correctly use patterns of word changes . . .<br>**L.1** Demonstrate command of the conventions . . .<br>**L.2.a** Observe hyphenation conventions . . . | **SL.5** Make strategic use of digital media . . . |
| **STUDENT RESOURCES** | | | |
| Available online in the Interactive Student Edition or Unit Resources | Selection Audio<br>First-Read Guide: Poetry<br>Close-Read Guide: Poetry | Word Network | Evidence Log |
| **TEACHER RESOURCES** | | | |
| **Selection Resources** Available online in the Interactive Teacher's Edition or Unit Resources | Audio Summaries<br>Annotation Highlights<br>EL Highlights<br>English Language Support Lesson: Creating a Character Sketch<br>The Love Song of J. Alfred Prufrock: Text Questions<br>Analyze Craft and Structure: Poetic Structure | Concept Vocabulary and Word Study<br>Conventions and Style: Compound Nouns | Writing to Sources: Digital Presentation |
| **Reteach/Practice (RP)** Available online in the Interactive Teacher's Edition or Unit Resources | Analyze Craft and Structure: Poetic Structure (RP) | Word Study: Latin prefixes *di-* and *dis-* (RP)<br>Conventions and Style: Compound Nouns (RP) | Writing to Sources: Digital Presentation (RP) |
| **Assessment** Available online in Assessments | Selection Test | | |
| **My Resources** | A Unit 2 Answer Key is available online and in the Interactive Teacher's Edition. | | |

# Reading Support

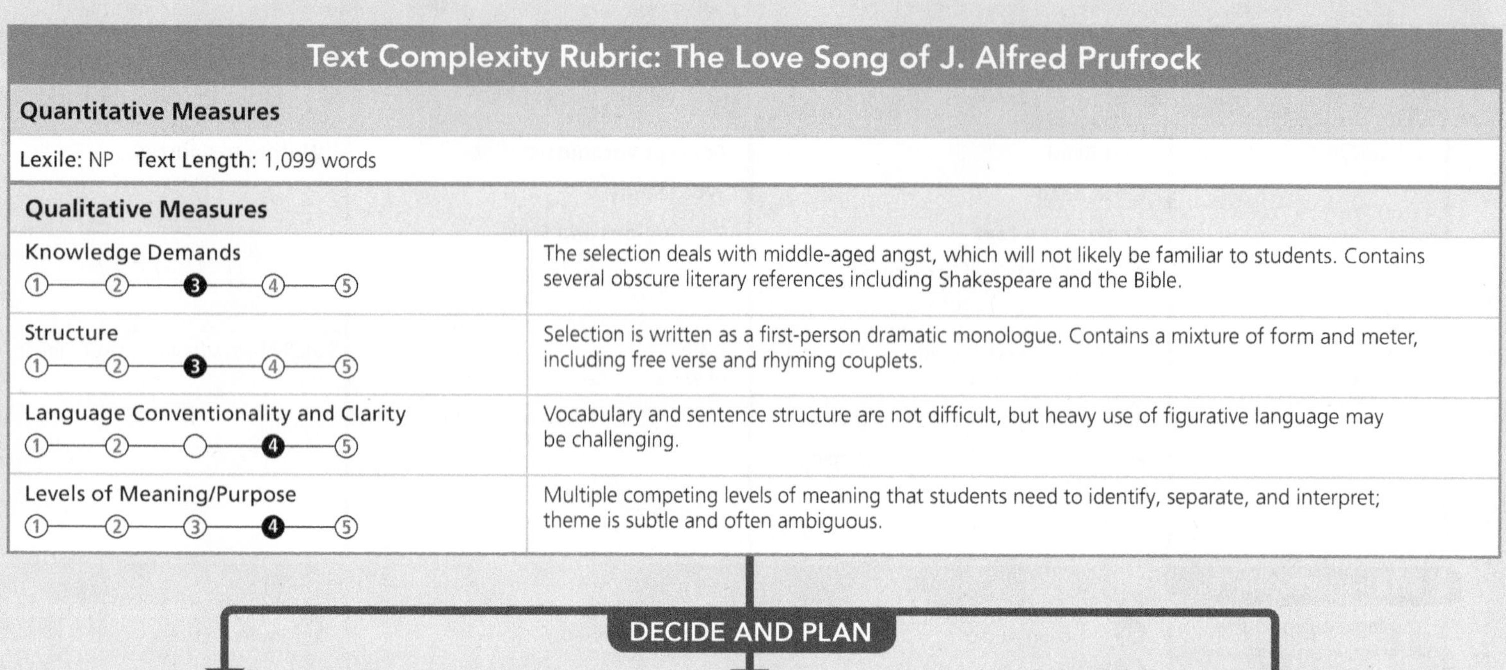

| Text Complexity Rubric: The Love Song of J. Alfred Prufrock | |
|---|---|
| **Quantitative Measures** | |
| **Lexile:** NP **Text Length:** 1,099 words | |
| **Qualitative Measures** | |
| Knowledge Demands<br>1—2—**3**—4—5 | The selection deals with middle-aged angst, which will not likely be familiar to students. Contains several obscure literary references including Shakespeare and the Bible. |
| Structure<br>1—2—**3**—4—5 | Selection is written as a first-person dramatic monologue. Contains a mixture of form and meter, including free verse and rhyming couplets. |
| Language Conventionality and Clarity<br>1—2—○—**4**—5 | Vocabulary and sentence structure are not difficult, but heavy use of figurative language may be challenging. |
| Levels of Meaning/Purpose<br>1—2—3—**4**—5 | Multiple competing levels of meaning that students need to identify, separate, and interpret; theme is subtle and often ambiguous. |

DECIDE AND PLAN

## English Language Support

Provide English Learners with support for language and levels of meaning/purpose as they read the selection.

**Language** Students may get confused reading passages with figurative language. For example in interpreting the metaphor in lines 15–22. Ask questions to guide students to understand that the writer is comparing the fog to a cat. Have students list words that are cat-like *(muzzle, licked, leap, curled.)*

**Levels of Meaning/Purpose** To help students to track the ideas in the poem, suggest that they keep a log of lines that are repeated. For example, *There will be time; Do I dare; Should I presume; Would it have been worth it.* Discuss how these repetitive phrases affect the meaning of the poem.

## Strategic Support

Provide students with strategic support to ensure that they can successfully read the text.

**Knowledge Demands** Using the selection background information, discuss the feeling of regret in the poem. Have students find specific lines in the poem that reflect these feelings. For example, *And indeed there will be time To wonder, "Do I dare?'' and, "Do I dare?"* What does the narrator wish to do?

**Levels of Meaning/Purpose** Students will likely have difficulty with the ambiguity of the poem. Ask students to first state what is literally happening in each stanza. Then ask them to reread the paragraph to determine what feelings or ideas are conveyed.

## Challenge

Provide students who need to be challenged with ideas for how they can go beyond a simple interpretation of the text.

**Text Analysis** Ask students to describe the conflict the narrator feels. What is he longing to say to someone? Why is he afraid? Have students work in pairs to find lines to support their opinions.

**Written Response** The speaker in the poem seems to be very worried about what people think. Have students write a letter of advice to a young Alfred Prufrock, telling him how to live a life without regret.

TEACH

## Read and Respond

Have the groups read the selection and complete the Making Meaning, Language Development, and Effective Expression activities.

# Standards Support Through Teaching and Learning Cycle

## IDENTIFY NEEDS

Analyze results of the Beginning-of-Year Assessment, focusing on the items relating to Unit 2. Also take into consideration student performance to this point and your observations of where particular students struggle.

## DECIDE AND PLAN

- If students have performed poorly on items matching these standards, then provide selection scaffolds before assigning them the on-level lesson provided in the Student Edition.
- If students have done well on the Beginning-of-Year Assessment, then challenge them to keep progressing and learning by giving them opportunities to practice the skills in depth.
- Use the Selection Resources listed on the Planning pages for "The Love Song of J. Alfred Prufrock" to help students continually improve their ability to master the standards.

**Instructional Standards: The Love Song of J. Alfred Prufrock**

| | Catching Up | This Year | Looking Forward |
|---|---|---|---|
| **Reading** | You may wish to administer the **Analyze Craft and Structure: Poetic Structure (RP)** worksheet to help students understand the structure of the poem, as the structure identifies both speaker and listener. | **RL.5** Analyze how an author's choices concerning how to structure specific parts of a text contribute to its overall structure and meaning as well as its aesthetic impact.<br>**RL.6** Analyze a case in which grasping point of view requires distinguishing what is directly stated in a text from what is really meant. | Challenge students to discuss topics from which they could create dramatic monologues. |
| **Writing** | You may want to administer the **Writing to Sources: Digital Presentation (RP)** worksheet to help students extend the message of the poem. | **SL.5** Make strategic use of digital media in presentations to enhance understanding of findings, reasoning, and evidence and to add interest. | Ask partners to draw on parts of the digital presentations to write a brief dramatic monologue. |
| **Language** | Review the **Word Study: Latin prefix *di-* and *dis-* (RP)** worksheet to better familiarize students with the prefixes.<br>You may wish to administer the **Conventions and Style: Compound Nouns (RP)** worksheets to help students see how the poet hyphenated words to say exactly what he wanted. | **L.4.b** Identify and correctly use patterns of word changes that indicate different meanings or parts of speech.<br>**L.2.a** Observe hyphenation conventions. | Have students locate other Latin prefixes they recognize in the selection.<br>Suggest that partners trade drafts of their dramatic monologues and do peer reviews with constructive feedback. |

## ANALYZE AND REVISE

- Analyze student work for evidence of student learning.
- Identify whether or not students have met the expectations in the standards.
- Identify implications for future instruction.

## TEACH

Implement the planned lesson, and gather evidence of student learning.

## Jump Start

FIRST READ Ask students to think about what happens when they "talk to themselves" in a verbal stream of consciousness. These thoughts might include self-analysis, imagined dialogue, or even half-thoughts, impressions, and free associations. Encourage groups to discuss how this interior "talk" affects their everyday lives. When is it helpful and when is it not?

## Concept Vocabulary

Have groups briefly discuss the three concept vocabulary words. Have they encountered any of the words before? Have groups consider the strategy of using context clues to identify meaning, and discuss the advantages and disadvantages of this strategy.

## FIRST READ

Have students perform the steps of the first read independently:

NOTICE: Encourage students to determine who the speaker and which details help them decide if the poem tells a story or expresses an emotion influence the meaning of the poem.

ANNOTATE: Remind students that they should also annotate the poetic devices that stand out on the first read so they can return later to analyze them.

CONNECT: Encourage students to go beyond the poem to think about how the text connects either to their own experience or with other poems they have encountered.

RESPOND: Students will demonstrate their understanding of the text by answering questions and writing a summary.

Point out to students that they will perform the first three steps concurrently as they are doing their first read. They will complete the Respond step after they have finished the first read. You may wish to print copies of the **First-Read Guide: Poetry** for students to use.

MAKING MEANING

# The Love Song of J. Alfred Prufrock

## Concept Vocabulary

As you perform your first read of "The Love Song of J. Alfred Prufrock," you will encounter these words.

tedious indecisions digress

**Context Clues** Use **context clues** to find the meanings of unfamiliar words in a text. Context clues include the words, punctuation, and images that surround an unknown word.

**Example:** "the evening, sleeps so peacefully! / Smoothed by long, fingers. / Asleep . . . tired . . . or it *malingers,* / Stretched on the floor, here beside you and me."

**Context clues:** The word *malingers* appears to be related to "asleep," "tired," and "stretched on the floor," but the word *or* suggests that it's not quite sleep.

**Possible meaning:** *Malingers* may mean "lazes about, sleepily."

Apply your knowledge of context clues and other vocabulary strategies to determine the meanings of unfamiliar words you encounter during your first read.

## First Read POETRY

Apply these strategies as you conduct your first read. You will have an opportunity to complete a close read after your first read.

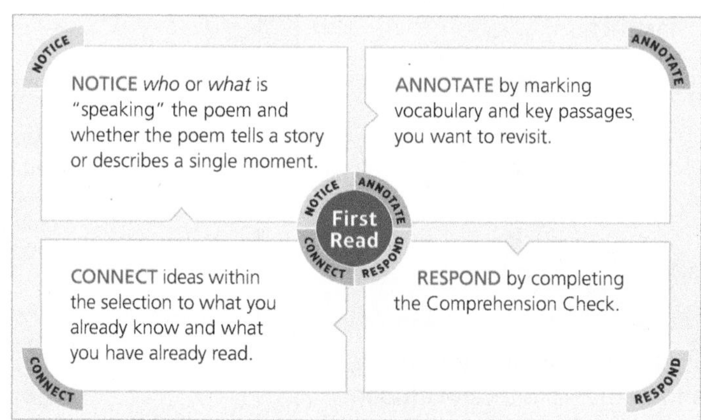

NOTICE
NOTICE *who* or *what* is "speaking" the poem and whether the poem tells a story or describes a single moment.
ANNOTATE
ANNOTATE by marking vocabulary and key passages you want to revisit.
First Read
CONNECT
CONNECT ideas within the selection to what you already know and what you have already read.
RESPOND
RESPOND by completing the Comprehension Check.


STANDARDS

**Reading Literature**
By the end of grade 11, read and comprehend literature, including stories, dramas, and poems, in the grades 11–CCR text complexity band proficiently, with scaffolding as needed at the high end of the range.

**Language**
Use context as a clue to the meaning of a word or phrase.





## FACILITATING SMALL-GROUP CLOSE READING

**CLOSE READ: Poetry** As groups perform the close read, circulate and offer support as needed. Students may benefit from more context.

- Beginning with the first line, this poem takes the reader on a walk with a man through the narrow winding streets of a big, foggy city. As the man walks, readers are privy to his most intimate thoughts, wishes, fears, and regrets.
- Encourage students to read the lines of the poem aloud so that they can hear this famous voice, the way he weaves in and out of rhyme and meter, past and present, allusion and imagery, statements and questions.
- Encourage students to read each stanza as a new breath, a new thought, and accept that the connections among the stanzas are not always apparent.

About the Poet

## T. S. Eliot

T. S. Eliot (1888–1965) was born into a wealthy family in St. Louis and grew up in an environment that promoted intellectual development. He attended Harvard University, where he published a number of poems in the school's literary magazine. In 1910, the year Eliot received his master's degree in philosophy, he completed "The Love Song of J. Alfred Prufrock."

**A Literary Sensation** Just before the outbreak of World War I, Eliot moved to England, where he became acquainted with Ezra Pound, another young American poet. Pound convinced Harriet Monroe, the editor of *Poetry* magazine, to publish "Prufrock." Shortly thereafter, Eliot published a collection entitled *Prufrock and Other Observations* (1917). Eliot's use of innovative poetic techniques and his focus on the despair of modern urban life caused a sensation in the literary world.

**Facing a New World** Eliot made his literary mark against the backdrop of a rapidly changing society. Disillusioned with the ideologies that produced the devastation of World War I, many people were searching for new ideas and values. Eliot was among a group of such writers and visual artists who called themselves Modernists. Modernist poets believed that poetry had to reflect the genuine, fractured experience of life in the twentieth century, not a romanticized idea of what life was once like.

In 1922, Eliot published *The Waste Land*, a profound critique of the spiritual barrenness of the modern world. Filled with allusions to classics of world literature and to Eastern culture and religion, it was widely read and greatly affected writers and critics.

**A Return to Tradition** In his search for something beyond the "waste land" of modern society, Eliot became a member of the Church of England in 1927. He began to explore religious themes in poems such as "Ash Wednesday" (1930) and *Four Quartets* (1943)—works that suggest a belief that religion can heal the wounds inflicted by society. In later years, Eliot wrote several plays and a sizable body of literary criticism. In 1948, he received the Nobel Prize in Literature.



## Background

### The Love Song of J. Alfred Prufrock

In this poem, J. Alfred Prufrock, a stuffy and inhibited man who is pained by his own passivity, invites the reader, or some unnamed visitor, to join him on a journey. Where Prufrock is and where he is going are open to debate. The most important part of this journey takes place within the inner landscape of Prufrock's emotions, memory, and intellect as he meditates on his life.



DIGITAL PERSPECTIVES

## The Love Song of J. Alfred Prufrock

What does Prufrock worry about? What are the things that concern him? Modeling these and other questions readers might ask will bring "The Love Song of J. Alfred Prufrock" to life and connect them to both the unit's Essential Question and the Performance Task question. Selection audio for the selection is available in the Interactive Teacher's Edition.

PERSONALIZE FOR LEARNING

### English Language Support

**Analyzing Diction** This poem was written in 1910, and much of its diction is elevated, so students may discover many unfamiliar words and others that are familiar but used in unfamiliar and/or figurative ways. Encourage students to mark these words as they read and discuss their meanings in their groups.

For example, invite students to discuss *muttering* (line 5), *insidious* (line 9), *muzzle* (line 16), and *terrace* (line 20). Ask: *How does each word contribute to the literal meaning and the emotion of the poem?* **ALL LEVELS**

POETRY

# The Love Song of J. Alfred Prufrock

T. S. Eliot

## CROSS-CURRICULAR PERSPECTIVES: ART

The painting that accompanies this poem is *Victorian Man in the City* by Eugene Ivanov, a contemporary Russian-Czech artist, painter, and illustrator who lives and works in Prague. His work features imagery from dreams and the collective unconscious. It combines elements of three different artistic styles: cubism, surrealism, and expressionism. Born in 1966, Ivanov has illustrated more than one hundred books. Discuss with students whether this illustration is an appropriate choice to accompany "The Love Song of J. Alfred Prufrock." Ask groups how a person from the Victorian Age might have perceived a modern city.

SCAN FOR MULTIMEDIA 

*S'io credessi che mia risposta fosse*
*a persona che mai tornasse al mondo,*
*questa fiamma staria senza più scosse.*
*Ma per ciò che giammai di questo fondo*
*non tornò vivo alcun, s'i'odo il vero,*
*senza tema d'infamia ti rispondo.*[1]

Let us go then, you and I,
When the evening is spread out against the sky
Like a patient etherized[2] upon a table;
Let us go, through certain half-deserted streets,
The muttering retreats
Of restless nights in one-night cheap hotels
And sawdust restaurants with oyster-shells:
Streets that follow like a **tedious** argument
Of insidious intent
To lead you to an overwhelming question . . .
Oh, do not ask, "What is it?"
Let us go and make our visit.

In the room the women come and go
Talking of Michelangelo.[3]

The yellow fog that rubs its back upon the window-panes,
The yellow smoke that rubs its muzzle on the window-panes,
Licked its tongue into the corners of the evening,
Lingered upon the pools that stand in drains,
Let fall upon its back the soot that falls from chimneys,
Slipped by the terrace, made a sudden leap,
And seeing that it was a soft October night,
Curled once about the house, and fell asleep.

And indeed there will be time[4]
For the yellow smoke that slides along the street
Rubbing its back upon the window-panes;
There will be time, there will be time
To prepare a face to meet the faces that you meet;
There will be time to murder and create,
And time for all the works and days[5] of hands

NOTES

Mark context clues or indicate another strategy you used that helped you determine meaning.

**tedious** (TEE dee uhs) *adj.*

MEANING:

1. ***S'io credessi . . . ti rispondo*** This epigraph is a passage from Dante's *Inferno,* in which one of the damned, upon being asked to tell his story, says, "If I believed my answer were being given to someone who could ever return to the world, this flame [his voice] would shake no more. But since no one has ever returned alive from this depth, if what I hear is true, I will answer you without fear of disgrace."
2. **etherized** (EE thuh ryzd) *adj.* anesthetized with ether.
3. **Michelangelo** (my kuhl AN juh loh) famous Italian artist and sculptor (1475–1564).
4. **there will be time** These words echo the speaker's plea in the English poet Andrew Marvell's "To His Coy Mistress": "Had we but world enough and time . . . "
5. **works and days** The ancient Greek poet Hesiod wrote a poem about farming called "Works and Days."





DIGITAL PERSPECTIVES 

## Concept Vocabulary

**TEDIOUS** If groups are struggling to define *tedious* in line 8, point out the context clues of "restless nights" in line 6 and "insidious intent" in line 9. Also point out that poetry, by its nature, offers less context, and therefore fewer context clues, than prose, so they may need to refer to a dictionary or thesaurus.

**Possible response:** In this context, *tedious* means "tiresome, dull, boring. "

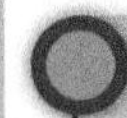

CLOSER LOOK

## Analyze an Internal Monologue

Circulate among groups as students conduct their close read. Suggest that groups close read lines 1–12 for clues about what Prufrock is doing. Encourage them to talk about the annotations that they marked. If needed, provide the following support:

**ANNOTATE:** Have students mark details in the first 12 lines that reveal Prufrock's qualities or actions, or work with small groups to have students participate while you highlight them together.

**QUESTION:** Guide students to consider what these observations might tell them. Ask what a reader can infer from these poetic choices and accept student responses.

**Possible response:** The speaker in "The Love Song of J. Alfred Prufrock" expresses what appear to be random thoughts and irregular musings by an aging man who is practically paralyzed by his lack of confidence.

**CONCLUDE:** Help students to formulate conclusions about the importance of the internal monologue. Ask students why the poet might have made this choice.

**Possible response:** Prufrock is walking through a deserted city. He seems distant from any action in the places he describes. He is inviting the reader to join him.

Remind students that a **dramatic monologue** is a poem in which the speaker addresses a silent listener. In the process, the speaker reveals his or her character. In this poem, the speaker seems sad and lonely.

### VOCABULARY DEVELOPMENT: WORD ANALYSIS

**Suffix *-ize*** Use the word *etherized* (line 3) to teach the meaning of the suffix *-ize*, which means "to cause to be, conform to, or resemble something" or, in this case, "to treat with a method." Offer examples of other words with the suffix, such as *Americanize, plagiarize, idolize, hypothesize, hospitalize, winterize,* and *economize.* Challenge students to find more examples and to use the words in a sentence to show that they understand their meanings. Ask, *Why is* etherized *perfect in the simile in line 3?*

# FACILITATING

## Concept Vocabulary

**INDECISIONS** If groups are struggling to define *indecisions* in line 32, point out the phrase on the next line: "a hundred visions and revisions." Here, the poet provides another example of the way Prufrock makes up his mind, or not. By using this context clue, students can infer the meaning of *indecisions*.

**Possible responses:** *Indecisions* must mean "hesitation or doubt."

**DIGRESS** If groups are struggling to define *digress* in line 66, point to the questions that follow in lines 68 and 69 and to the general rambling tone of this section of the poem. Prufrock is distracted by the "arms that are braceleted" and the "perfume from a dress," thoughts that give a context clue about the meaning of *digress*.

**Possible responses:** *Digress* must mean "wander, meander, or drift."

Additional **English Language Support** is available in the Interactive Teacher's Edition.

NOTES

Mark context clues or indicate another strategy you used that helped you determine meaning.

**indecisions** (ihn dee SIHZH uhnz) *n.*

MEANING:

That lift and drop a question on your plate;
Time for you and time for me,
And time yet for a hundred **indecisions**,
And for a hundred visions and revisions.
Before the taking of a toast and tea.

In the room the women come and go
Talking of Michelangelo.

And indeed there will be time
To wonder, "Do I dare?" and, "Do I dare?"
Time to turn back and descend the stair,
With a bald spot in the middle of my hair—
(They will say: "How his hair is growing thin!")
My morning coat, my collar mounting firmly to the chin,
My necktie rich and modest, but asserted by a simple pin—
(They will say: "But how his arms and legs are thin!")
Do I dare
Disturb the universe?
In a minute there is time
For decisions and revisions which a minute will reverse.

For I have known them all already, known them all—
Have known the evenings, mornings, afternoons,
I have measured out my life with coffee spoons;
I know the voices dying with a dying fall
Beneath the music from a farther room.
So how should I presume?

And I have known the eyes already, known them all—
The eyes that fix you in a formulated phrase,
And when I am formulated, sprawling on a pin,
When I am pinned and wriggling on the wall,
Then how should I begin
To spit out all the butt-ends of my days and ways?
And how should I presume?

And I have known the arms already, known them all—
Arms that are braceleted and white and bare
(But in the lamplight, downed with light brown hair!)
Is it perfume from a dress
That makes me so **digress**?
Arms that lie along a table, or wrap about a shawl.
And should I then presume?
And how should I begin?

Mark context clues or indicate another strategy you used that helped you determine meaning.

**digress** (dih GREHS) *v.*

MEANING:

⌘ ⌘ ⌘





## PERSONALIZE FOR LEARNING

### Strategic Support

**Relating Description to Character** Review lines 37–60. Open a discussion about self-consciousness in the poem. Discuss what it means to be *self-conscious*, and point to examples of this quality exhibited by the speaker. Students may be confused by references to the speaker's bald spot (line 40), thinning hair (line 41), and thinning arms and legs (line 44), all qualities of his middle-aged physique. Ask to cite other lines that suggest heightened self-consciousness. For example, students may notice his reference to his mode of dress (lines 42–43) or the feeling that he is "pinned and wriggling on the wall" (line 58). Suggest that self-consciousness is not only a theme of this poem, it is also a prevalent theme of modernism.

Shall I say, I have gone at dusk through narrow streets
And watched the smoke that rises from the pipes
Of lonely men in shirt-sleeves, leaning out of windows? . . .

I should have been a pair of ragged claws
Scuttling across the floors of silent seas.[6]

⌘ ⌘ ⌘

And the afternoon, the evening, sleeps so peacefully!
Smoothed by long fingers,
Asleep . . . tired . . . or it malingers,
Stretched on the floor, here beside you and me.
Should I, after tea and cakes and ices,
Have the strength to force the moment to its crisis?
But though I have wept and fasted, wept and prayed,
Though I have seen my head (grown slightly bald) brought in
    upon a platter,[7]
I am no prophet—and here's no great matter;
I have seen the moment of my greatness flicker,
And I have seen the eternal Footman[8] hold my coat, and snicker.
And in short, I was afraid.

And would it have been worth it, after all,
After the cups, the marmalade, the tea,
Among the porcelain, among some talk of you and me,
Would it have been worth while,
To have bitten off the matter with a smile,
To have squeezed the universe into a ball
To roll it towards some overwhelming question.
To say: "I am Lazarus,[9] come from the dead,
Come back to tell you all. I shall tell you all"—
If one, settling a pillow by her head,
    Should say: "That is not what I meant at all.
    That is not it, at all."

And would it have been worth it, after all,
Would it have been worth while,
After the sunsets and the dooryards and the sprinkled streets,
After the novels, after the teacups, after the skirts that trail
    along the floor—
And this, and so much more?—

6. **I should . . . seas** In Shakespeare's *Hamlet,* the hero, Hamlet, mocks the aging Lord Chamberlain, Polonius, saying, "You yourself, sir, should be old as I am, if like a crab you could go backward" (II. ii. 205–206).
7. **head . . . platter** a reference to the prophet John the Baptist, whose head was delivered on a platter to Salome as a reward for her dancing (Matthew 14:1–11).
8. **eternal Footman** death.
9. **Lazarus** (LAZ uh ruhs) Lazarus is resurrected from the dead by Jesus in John 11:1–44.

NOTES





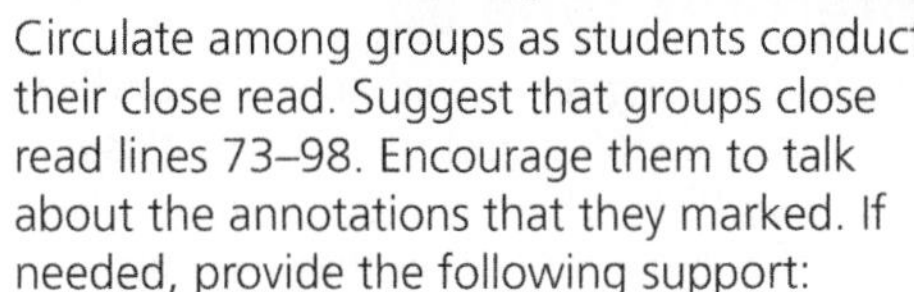


CLOSER LOOK

## Examine Literary Allusions

Circulate among groups as students conduct their close read. Suggest that groups close read lines 73–98. Encourage them to talk about the annotations that they marked. If needed, provide the following support:

**ANNOTATE:** Have students mark details in lines 73–98 that are allusions. Point out that these are explained by footnotes. You may also choose to have students participate while you highlight the allusions together.

**QUESTION:** Guide students to consider what these allusions might tell them. Ask what a reader can infer from their abundance and critical importance in the poem, and accept student responses.

**Possible response:** Although "The Love Song of J. Alfred Prufrock" is about one man on a walk one night, it feels much bigger, partly because the many allusions connect it to a larger cultural heritage.

**CONCLUDE:** Help students to formulate conclusions about the importance of the allusions. Ask students why the poet might have made these choices.

**Possible response:** The poet wants his readers to think about the modern experience as it is informed and created by the past, so evoking familiar images and words gives readers a broader context and makes connections between the speaker and literary giants.

Remind students that an **allusion** is a literary reference to a well-known person, event, place, piece of writing, or work of art. Allusions are a form of figurative language; they are a literary shortcut that packs a lot of meaning into a few words.

PERSONALIZE FOR LEARNING

### English Language Support

**Understanding Idioms** Review lines 87–105. Point out to groups how Prufrock repeatedly asks, Would it have been worth it? Explore the origin and meaning of the idiomatic adjective phrase *worth it* with students. Its denotation is "useful and important," but even more, it connotes that something is rewarding despite difficulties involved. Being "worth it" implies *meaning*, an elusive goal that the modernists both question and pursue. Ask students, *What is "worth it" for you?* You may also introduce related idioms such as "for what it's worth," "to be worth your while," or "worth one's salt." **ALL LEVELS**

## CLOSER LOOK

### Interpret Tone 

Circulate among groups as students conduct their close read. Suggest that groups close read lines 108–125. Encourage them to talk about the annotations that they marked. If needed, provide the following support:

**ANNOTATE:** Have students mark the lines in which the words have the most emotional power, or work with small groups to have students participate while you highlight them together.

**QUESTION:** Guide students to consider what emotions these words evoke and accept student responses.

**Possible response:** The tone of this poem is one of regret and despair. Prufrock sees himself as a supporting character, not the central hero. He sees himself as a fool rather than a tragic hero. The beauties and pleasures of the word are denied to him.

**CONCLUDE:** Help students formulate conclusions about the tone. Ask students why the poet might have made this choice.

**Possible response:** The poet wants his readers to feel the despair of the modern era, the sad, oppressive feeling of having wasted one's life in the pursuit of people and things that are inconsequential at best, meaningless at worst.

Remind students that the **tone** of a piece of literature is the writer's attitude toward his or her subject. Tone is greatly influenced by the connotations of the writer's words. Tone is closely related to **mood**, the overall feeling that the literary work evokes in its readers.

NOTES

It is impossible to say just what I mean!
But as if a magic lantern[10] threw the nerves in patterns
on a screen:
Would it have been worth while
If one, settling a pillow or throwing off a shawl,
And turning toward the window, should say:
"That is not it at all,
That is not what I meant, at all."

⌘ ⌘ ⌘

No! I am not Prince Hamlet, nor was meant to be;
Am an attendant lord, one that will do
To swell a progress,[11] start a scene or two,
Advise the prince; no doubt, an easy tool,
Deferential, glad to be of use,
Politic, cautious, and meticulous;
Full of high sentence,[12] but a bit obtuse;
At times, indeed, almost ridiculous—
Almost, at times, the Fool.

I grow old . . . I grow old . . .
I shall wear the bottoms of my trousers rolled.

Shall I part my hair behind? Do I dare to eat a peach?
I shall wear white flannel trousers, and walk upon the beach.
I have heard the mermaids singing, each to each.

I do not think that they will sing to me.

I have seen them riding seaward on the waves
Combing the white hair of the waves blown back
When the wind blows the water white and black.

We have lingered in the chambers of the sea
By sea-girls wreathed with seaweed red and brown
Till human voices wake us, and we drown.

10. **magic lantern** early device used to project images on a screen.
11. **To swell a progress** to add to the number of people in a parade or scene from a play.
12. **Full of high sentence** speaking in a very ornate manner, often offering advice.





## DIGITAL PERSPECTIVES

### Illuminating the Text

**Interpreting a Single Line** Direct students' attention to line 121: "I shall wear the bottoms of my trousers rolled." Tell them that this is one of the most interpreted lines of poetry in English literature. Challenge students to search online for at least three interpretations of the meaning of the line. Ask them to decide which one, if any, they agree with, or to come up with an original interpretation of their own. **(Research to Clarify)**

## Comprehension Check

**Complete the following items after you finish your first read. Review and clarify details with your group.**

1. At what time of day are the opening lines of the poem set?

2. In the opening stanza, Prufrock invites someone to go with him. Describe the place he plans to visit.

3. What atmospheric condition does Prufrock describe in lines 15–25?

4. Name three questions that Prufrock asks himself.

5. Whom does Prufrock say he has heard singing "each to each"?

6. **Notebook** Confirm your understanding by drawing an illustration of one or more key moments from the poem.

## RESEARCH

**Research to Clarify** Choose at least one unfamiliar detail from the text. Briefly research that detail. In what way does the information you learned shed light on an aspect of the poem?

**Research to Explore** Find out more about Modernism, the artistic movement embraced by Eliot and other early-twentieth-century writers and artists. Find out how this movement broke with the past—and how the work of its pioneers was received at the time.





DIGITAL PERSPECTIVES

## Comprehension Check

Possible responses:

1. The poem is set in the early evening, at teatime.
2. Prufrock plans to visit a "half-deserted" and seedy part of town, where there are "cheap hotels" and restaurants with sawdust on the floor.
3. Prufrock describes a "yellow fog" of dusk, which he compares to the movements of a cat.
4. Any three are acceptable: "Do I dare?" (line 38), "Do I dare/Disturb the universe?" (lines 45–46); "So how should I presume?" (line 54); "And how should I presume?" (line 61); "And should I then presume?/And how should I begin?" (lines 68– 69); "And this, and so much more?—"
5. He has heard the mermaids singing.
6. Storyboards should include key moments from the poem, such as the following: Prufrock walking along streets in a seedy neighborhood; women discussing Michelangelo; Prufrock on a foggy evening; Prufrock dressed for work, having tea; Prufrock confessing his love, only to be told that "That is not it at all"; Prufrock growing older, walking along a beach while mermaids sing to each other.

## Research

**Research to Clarify If** groups struggle to come up with a research topic, **then** you may want to suggest that they focus on one of these topics: morning coats, bottom-dwelling sea crabs, marmalade, magic lanterns, John the Baptist, the Fool, or mermaids.

**Research to Explore If** groups want a different way to explore this topic, **then** direct them to research famous literary modernists such as Charles Baudelaire, Gustave Flaubert, Arthur Rimbaud, Paul Verlaine, Franz Kafka, or Ezra Pound, and visual modernist such as Édouard Manet, Henri Matisse, Pablo Picasso, Paul Cézanne, Wassily Kandinsky, or Edvard Munch. Ask: *What makes this writer or artist a modernist?*

## PERSONALIZE FOR LEARNING

### Challenge

**Ezra Pound** Challenge students to find out more about Ezra Pound and his relationship with T.S. Eliot. Pound (1885–1972), also an American expatriate who lived in London, France, and later in Italy, is credited with developing the Imagist movement in poetry, stressing precision and economy of language that harkens to Chinese and Japanese forms. Pound helped shape the careers of James Joyce, Robert Frost, and Ernest Hemingway in addition to Eliot. His biography is full of twists and turns, including prison, treason, love affairs, and psychosis.

## Jump Start

**CLOSE READ** Engage students in a discussion of the poet in society as the "prophet"—the person who shines a spotlight on society's ills. Ask students if Eliot fits this category, and if so, how. In addition, you may want to ask students why the poem's title includes the words "Love Song." What makes it a love song, and who is the intended audience?

## Close Read the Text

Model close reading as needed by using the notes in the Interactive Teacher's Edition.

Remind groups to use Accountable Talk in their discussions and to support one another's ideas.

## Analyze the Text

**Possible responses:**

1. Prufrock's invitation to visit "sawdust restaurants" is far from the romantic ideal of a first date. Students may say the invitation is unlikely to be accepted as it is unrewarding.
2. Students may focus on details that reflect alienation or isolation.
3. Answers will vary, but should be supported.

## Concept Vocabulary

**Why These Words? Possible response:** The words relate to negative traits, emphasizing Prufrock's anxious, bleak view of the world.

### Practice

Possible responses:

1. A *tedious* conversation would be boring and, therefore, not desirable.
2. *Indecisions* can make people less efficient because they cause people to spend too much time making up their minds.
3. Signs that someone is beginning to *digress* include rambling, talking about things that are only slightly related to the original topic, or losing his or her train of thought.

### Word Network

**Possible words:** visions, revisions, decisions

## Word Study

For more support, see **Concept Vocabulary and Word Study.**

**Possible responses:** *diverge:* to separate or move in different directions; *dilate:* to expand or become wider or larger

MAKING MEANING

THE LOVE SONG OF J. ALFRED PRUFROCK

## Close Read the Text

With your group, revisit sections of the text you marked during your first read. **Annotate** details that you notice. What **questions** do you have? What can you **conclude?**

## Analyze the Text

**CITE TEXTUAL EVIDENCE** to support your answers.

**Complete the activities.**

1. **Review and Clarify** With your group, reread lines 1–12 of the poem. The speaker of the poem, J. Alfred Prufrock, invites someone to join him on a journey. What is unusual about his invitation? Is it likely to be accepted? Why or why not?
2. **Present and Discuss** Now, work with your group to share the passages from the poem that you found especially important. Take turns presenting your passages. Discuss what you noticed in the selection, what questions you asked, and what conclusions you reached.
3. **Essential Question:** ***What role does individualism play in American society?*** What has this poem taught you about the individual and society? Discuss with your group.

**TIP**

GROUP DISCUSSION

When discussing poetry, begin by reading a passage for sense. Follow the sentence structure and identify the subject and verb, if necessary. After your group understands the basic meaning, continue your analysis by looking at the poetic techniques, such as rhythm and rhyme, imagery, and figurative language.

LANGUAGE DEVELOPMENT

## Concept Vocabulary

tedious    indecisions    digress

**Why These Words?** The three concept vocabulary words from the text are related. With your group, discuss the words and determine what they have in common. How do these word choices enhance the impact of the poem?

### Practice

**Notebook** Confirm your understanding of the concept vocabulary words by answering these questions. Use the vocabulary word in your answer.

1. Would you like to have a *tedious* conversation? Explain.
2. How can *indecisions* affect someone's efficiency?
3. What are some signs that a speaker is beginning to *digress*?

**WORD NETWORK**

Add words related to individualism from the text to your Word Network.

## Word Study

**Latin Prefix: *di-* / *dis-*** The Latin prefix *di-* or *dis-* means "not" or "away." This prefix (not to be confused with the Greek prefix *di-*, meaning "two") occurs in many common English words, as well as in some mathematical and scientific terms.

1. Write the meaning of the mathematical term *diverge.*
2. Write the meaning of the scientific term *dilate.*

Use a dictionary to confirm your definitions for both words.

**STANDARDS**

Reading Literature

- Analyze how an author's choices concerning how to structure specific parts of a text contribute to its overall structure and meaning as well as its aesthetic impact.
- Analyze a case in which grasping point of view requires distinguishing what is directly stated in a text from what is really meant.

Language

Identify and correctly use patterns of word changes that indicate different meanings or parts of speech.





## FORMATIVE ASSESSMENT

### Analyze the Text

**If** students struggle to close read the text, **then** provide the **The Love Song of J. Alfred Prufrock: Text Questions** available in the Interactive Teacher's Edition.

### Concept Vocabulary

**If** students struggle to identify the concept, **then** ask groups to act out the meaning of each word and decide if a word is negative or positive.

### Word Study

**If** students fail to find several other words with the prefix *di-* / *dis-*, **then** have them use online dictionary resources to locate words beginning with *di- or dis-* for words belonging in this group.

For Reteach and Practice, see **Word Study: Latin Prefixes *di-* and *dis-* (RP).**

## Analyze Craft and Structure

**Poetic Structure** A troubled J. Alfred Prufrock invites an unidentified companion, perhaps a part of his own personality, to walk with him as he considers how life and love are passing him by. His so-called love song is a **dramatic monologue,** a poem or speech in which a character addresses a silent listener. Images, dialogue, and other details reveal Prufrock's inner conflicts as he continues through his evening.

Prufrock is the **speaker,** or voice of the poem. Details reflect his **point of view,** the perspective or vantage point from which the monologue is told. To understand the speaker's point of view, consider details that describe the following elements:

- *Physical Traits:* What words does Prufrock use to describe his own appearance? How do others perceive him—or how does Prufrock feel he is perceived?
- *Emotional Traits:* What is Prufrock's overall mood? Which details reveal that mood?
- *Verbal Traits:* What is the speaker's unique way of talking? When Prufrock repeats himself, what kinds of things does he say? How does this reflect his values or preoccupations?

### Practice

**CITE TEXTUAL EVIDENCE** to support your answers.

1. (a) Work together to complete the chart. Identify details that reveal Prufrock's personal qualities. (b) What do these details suggest about Prufrock's view of himself and life as a whole?

| PHYSICAL TRAITS | EMOTIONAL TRAITS | VERBAL TRAITS |
|---|---|---|
| | | |

2. (a) How can the first line of the poem be interpreted to suggest that Prufrock sees himself as divided, both seeking and fearing action? (b) At what other points does he express a deeply conflicted sense of self?
3. (a) In lines 49–54, what image does Prufrock use to describe how he has "measured out" his life? (b) In your own words, explain how Prufrock has lived.





DIGITAL PERSPECTIVES

## Analyze Craft and Structure

**Poetic Structure** Remind students that when reading poetry, they should never confuse the speaker with the poet. Prufrock is a fictional character conceived by the poet to convey meaning. In fact, Eliot was only in his twenties when he wrote this poem. For more support, see **Analyze Craft and Structure: Poetic Structure**

### Practice

Possible responses:

1. *Physical Traits*: thinning hair, bald spot; thin arms and legs; wears formal coat and tie with "a simple pin"; Others make comments about his inadequacies.
   *Emotional Traits*: loneliness; self-consciousness, intimidation; lack of confidence, anxiety; regretful, resentful, constrained; indecisive, tentative; He seems anxious, resigned, and self-critical.
   *Verbal Traits*: He asks a lot of questions; He frequently repeats himself, and his repetition seems to speak to his preoccupation with his own perceived inadequacies.
2. (a) Prufrock refers to himself as "you and I."
   (b) He refers to himself as divided in line 31 when he says, "Time for you and time for me." Also, his vacillation between the desire to speak and his inability to do so suggests deep internal conflict.
3. (a) He uses the image of coffee spoons.
   (b) Possible response: He has lived a careful life, with little risk, and he has lived a life filled with trivial but well-mannered social occasions.

### FORMATIVE ASSESSMENT

### Analyze Craft and Structure

**If** students are unable to identify the specific textual examples, **then** have them skim the selection to look for descriptions of Prufrock's appearance, words that describe what he is feeling, and what he says when he repeats himself. For Reteach and Practice, see **Analyze Craft and Structure: Poetic Structure (RP).**

## PERSONALIZE FOR LEARNING

### English Language Support

**Creating a Character "Sketch"** Tell students they will make an illustration of Prufrock (physical traits) with a speech balloon (verbal traits) and caption (emotional traits). Explain they can draw and paint, use computer drawing tools, or make a collage.

Remind students that the author's use of figurative language allows him to compare items while creating imagery. Arrange students in groups.

Have them find and list details for one category of the chart.

1. What he looks like
2. What he says
3. How he feels

Have students share their ideas. Guide students to write a caption, such as:

Prufrock feels he's getting close to death and is afraid. (Lines 84–86)

An expanded **English Language Support Lesson** on Creating a Character Sketch is available in the Interactive Teacher's Edition.

# FACILITATING

## Conventions and Style

**Compound Nouns** There is a third kind of compound nouns called **open compounds**. These are pairs of words that appear to be two words, but since neither word functions independently to convey the meaning of the whole, they are compound nouns. Examples are *bus stop, washing machine,* and *science fiction*. In open compounds, the words function together as one noun to name a single person, place, thing, or idea. The first word is not an adjective in the normal sense because if it were deleted or replaced with another adjective, the noun would lose its referential meaning. For more support, see **Conventions and Style: Compound Nouns.**

### Read It

Possible responses:

1. *partygoers*: closed
2. *lifetime*: closed
3. *walk-through, passers-by*: both hyphenated; *nighttime*: closed
4. *daydreaming, woolgathering, makeup:* all closed

### Write It

Possible responses:

Prufrock's monologue is modernism in a *nutshell*. His *viewpoint* condenses the anxieties about daily routines that concerned many modernist artists. The *grab-bag* of allusions reflects Prufrock's *self-consciousness* about past literary traditions. By the end of the poem, readers sense the passions and fears that boil within this *wind-mouth*.

The new compound noun, *wind-mouth*, is hyphenated because it is an original term. The hyphen helps reader understand that it is one word that combines two words.

### FORMATIVE ASSESSMENT

### Conventions and Style

**If** students are unable to identify compound nouns, **then** have them look for pairs of words that name one person, place, or thing. For Reteach and Practice, see **Conventions and Style: Compound Nouns (RP).**



LANGUAGE DEVELOPMENT

THE LOVE SONG OF J. ALFRED PRUFROCK

## Conventions and Style

**Compound Nouns** Eliot uses many compound nouns in "The Love Song of J. Alfred Prufrock," including some that he invented just for use in this poem. A **compound noun** is a noun that is made with two or more words. In a **closed compound,** there is no space between the words. In a **hyphenated compound,** a hyphen separates the words.

| CLOSED COMPOUNDS | HYPHENATED COMPOUNDS |
|---|---|
| **From "Prufrock":** | **From "Prufrock":** |
| necktie | oyster-shells |
| afternoons | window-panes |
| lamplight | shirt-sleeves |
| **Other examples:** | **Other examples:** |
| basketball | brother-in-law |
| sunrise | house-builder |
| keyboard | six-year-old |

Closed compounds are words that have been long accepted as single nouns. Hyphenated compounds often are newer forms, or words that are used less frequently.

Hyphens may be used to join words and avoid ambiguity. In some cases, hyphens are not required but are a matter of style. For example, Prufrock describes mermaids as "sea-girls." Eliot could have presented the phrase without a hyphen: "sea girls." By creating an original, hyphenated noun, Eliot may be suggesting Prufrock's skill with words, his need to categorize and classify, or his precise nature.

### Read It

Mark the compound nouns in these sentences. Identify each one as closed or hyphenated.

1. Prufrock hears a conversation among women who seem to be partygoers.
2. He worries that he has spent his lifetime focused on trivial, unimportant matters.
3. The speaker's walk-through at nighttime seems to take place in isolation, without passers-by or companions other than the unnamed listener.
4. Prufrock's digressions might suggest daydreaming or woolgathering, but the precise way he presents his word-pictures makes that unlikely.

### Write It

**Notebook** Write four sentences that include compound nouns. Include at least one compound noun that is not commonly used. Decide whether your new compound noun will be closed or hyphenated, and explain your reasoning.

STANDARDS

**Speaking and Listening**
Make strategic use of digital media in presentations to enhance understanding of findings, reasoning, and evidence and to add interest.

**Language**
- Demonstrate command of the conventions of standard English grammar and usage when writing or speaking.
- Observe hyphenation conventions.





## WriteNow Express and Reflect

**Poem** Encourage students to write original poems in the style of "The Love Song of J. Alfred Prufrock," in which they develop a dramatic monologue of a character other than themselves. Suggest that they consider using a historic personality that they are interested in or an ancestor.

Encourage them to use dialogue, extended metaphors, repetition, and questions as Eliot does. Give them an opportunity to share their poems either by reading them aloud, printing copies for others, or posting on a digital platform.

EFFECTIVE EXPRESSION

## Writing to Sources

**Assignment**

With your group, create a **digital presentation** that explains, amplifies, or extends key ideas about J. Alfred Prufrock's worldview. Choose from these options:

- ☐ a **slide show** that presents images reflecting phrases from the poem or your mental picture of Prufrock, accompanied by appropriate music
- ☐ an **oral recitation and discussion** in which readers recite important lines from the poem and then discuss how those lines reflect Prufrock's character and concerns
- ☐ a **filmed oral response** in which group members share their reactions to the poem by citing specific lines and explaining their meaning and effect

**Project Plan** Work with your group to plan your digital presentation. Use this chart to determine how you will integrate content and media elements, including audio and visual materials. Also, consider how you will organize your presentation to include a strong introduction, a complete body, and an effective conclusion. Choose transitions that will make the organization of your presentation clear.

| PART | CONTENT | | MEDIA | |
|---|---|---|---|---|
| | Ideas | Related lines from Eliot's poem | Visual | Audio |
| Introduction | | | | |
| Transition | | | | |
| Body | | | | |
| Transition | | | | |
| Conclusion | | | | |

EVIDENCE LOG

Before moving on to a new selection, go to your Evidence Log and record what you learned from "The Love Song of J. Alfred Prufrock."





PERSONALIZE FOR LEARNING

### Strategic Support

**Choosing Audio Tracks** Suggest that groups choose audio tracks that do not include words so that they can more easily fade in and out at the beginning, the end, and during transitions. Also, suggest that they find music that reflects the content of their presentations, perhaps a piece of haunting classical music that suggests alienation to support the content of Eliot's poem. They also may want to choose music from the same historical period as the poem, by searching "1910 music." Thanks to the vast stores of recorded music now available digitally, students may have access to many choices.

DIGITAL PERSPECTIVES

## Writing to Sources

The presentation suggestions include audio recording, video recording, or both. First, members of the group must choose, by consensus, which assignment they will complete. Encourage groups to choose their assignment based on group members' individual strengths. For example, if a group member has experience in video recording, the filmed oral response might work well.

**Project Plan** As students refine their presentations, suggest that "less is more." Presentations might be limited to about five minutes. Encourage groups to rehearse several times before they record their final presentations. Give groups ample opportunities to share their products with the whole group or online. For more support, see **Writing to Sources: Digital Presentation.**

**Evidence Log** Support students in completing their Evidence Log. This paced activity will help prepare them for the Performance-Based Assessment at the end of the unit.

### FORMATIVE ASSESSMENT

### Writing to Sources

**If** students are unable to create digital plans, **then** have them create story boards that show their intentions and goals. For Reteach and Practice, see **Writing to Sources: Digital Presentation (RP).**

### Selection Test

Administer the "The Love Song of J.Alfred Prufrock" Selection Test, which is available in both print and digital formats online in Assessments.

# A Wagner Matinée

**AUDIO SUMMARIES** of "A Wagner Matinée" are available in both English and Spanish and can be assigned to students in Pearson Realize™. Assigning these summaries prior to reading the selection may help students build additional background knowledge and set a context for their first read.

## Summary

In Willa Cather's short story "A Wagner Matinée," the narrator, Clark, receives a letter from his Uncle Howard in Nebraska saying that his Aunt Georgiana is coming to Boston to settle an estate. The letter sparks Clark's boyhood memories of the time he spent on his uncle's farm and how his aunt helped him with his studies and taught him to play the piano. Georgiana was a talented music teacher at the Boston Conservatory, but she left her position when she met Howard, married him, and moved to the farm. Clark decides to entertain his aunt by taking her to a concert of works by Richard Wagner, one of her favorite composers. After the concert, Georgiana begins to cry and tells Clark that she does not want to leave. Clark understands that Georgiana's refusal to leave is based on her realization that she faces a more difficult, less beautiful life when she returns to the farm.

### Insight

Reading "A Wagner Matinée" will help students understand that the pressure of society to conform—in this case by marrying and raising a family—may destroy an individual's unique talents and dreams of success. Students might explore the importance of holding on to one's dreams despite pressures to conform.

ESSENTIAL QUESTION:
What role does individualism play in American society?

## Connection to Essential Question

Willa Cather's short story "A Wagner Matinée" connects to the Essential Question "What role does individualism play in American society?" by exploring the consequences of one woman's life choices. Aunt Georgiana's life does not allow her to pursue her unique interests.

SMALL-GROUP LEARNING PERFORMANCE TASK
When is it difficult to march to the beat of a "different drummer" and stand on your own as an individual? What are the risks and rewards of nonconformity?

UNIT PERFORMANCE-BASED ASSESSMENT
What significant incident from my past helped me to realize that I am a unique individual?

## Connection to Performance Tasks

**Small-Group Learning Performance Task** In this Performance Task, students will draw on the ways in which "A Wagner Matinée" and the other selections in the unit approach the concept of nonconformity and then write a speech on the subject.

**Unit Performance-Based Assessment** Aunt Georgiana's contrasting experiences on the farm and in the concert hall may help students begin to consider the writing prompt for the Performance-Based Assessment.

DIGITAL PERSPECTIVES

 Audio  Video  Document  Annotation Highlights 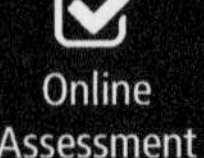 EL Highlights Online Assessment

| | Making Meaning | Language Development | Effective Expression |
|---|---|---|---|
| Lesson | **First Read**<br>**Close Read**<br>**Analyze the Text**<br>**Analyze Craft and Structure** | **Concept Vocabulary**<br>**Word Study**<br>**Conventions and Style** | **Writing to Sources** |
| Instructional Standards | **RL.10** By the end of grade 11, read and comprehend literature . . .<br>**RL.3** Analyze the impact of the author's choices . . .<br>**L.4.b** Identify and correctly use patterns of word changes . . . | **L.4.c** Consult general and specialized reference materials . . .<br>**RL.4** Determine the meaning of words and phrases . . .<br>**L.5.a** Interpret figures of speech . . . | **W.2** Write informative/explanatory texts . . .<br>**W.7** Conduct short as well as more sustained research projects . . . |
| **STUDENT RESOURCES** | | | |
| Available online in the Interactive Student Edition or Unit Resources | Selection Audio<br>First-Read Guide: Fiction<br>Close-Read Guide: Fiction | Word Network | Evidence Log |
| **TEACHER RESOURCES** | | | |
| **Selection Resources** Available online in the Interactive Teacher's Edition or Unit Resources | Audio Summaries<br>Annotation Highlights<br>EL Highlights<br>A Wagner Matinée: Text Questions<br>English Language Support Lesson: Choosing Topics and Key Words<br>Analyze Craft and Structure: Character Development | Concept Vocabulary and Word Study<br>Conventions and Style: Figurative Language | Writing to Sources: Research Report |
| **Reteach/Practice (RP)** Available online in the Interactive Teacher's Edition or Unit Resources | Analyze Craft and Structure: Character Development (RP) | Word Study: Word Derivations (RP)<br>Conventions and Style: Figurative Language (RP) | Writing to Sources: Research Report (RP) |
| **Assessment** Available online in Assessments | Selection Test | | |
| **My Resources** | A Unit 2 Answer Key is available online and in the Interactive Teacher's Edition | | |

# Reading Support

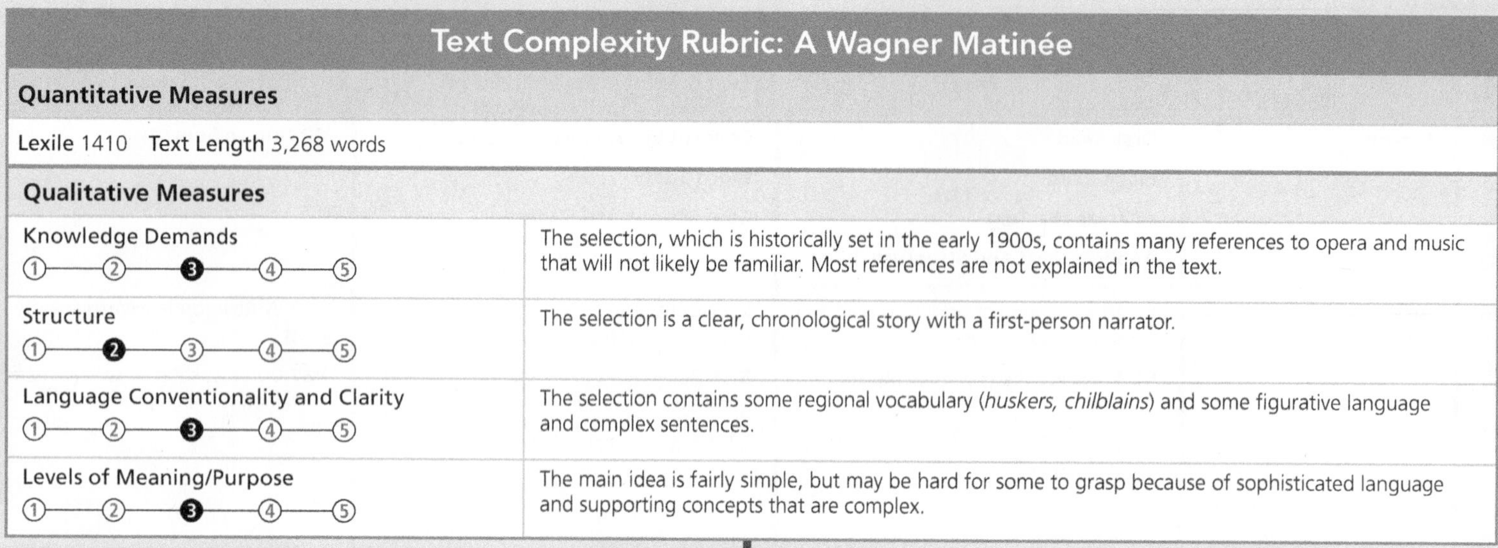

| Text Complexity Rubric: A Wagner Matinée | |
|---|---|
| **Quantitative Measures** | |
| **Lexile** 1410 **Text Length** 3,268 words | |
| **Qualitative Measures** | |
| Knowledge Demands<br>① ② **❸** ④ ⑤ | The selection, which is historically set in the early 1900s, contains many references to opera and music that will not likely be familiar. Most references are not explained in the text. |
| Structure<br>① **❷** ③ ④ ⑤ | The selection is a clear, chronological story with a first-person narrator. |
| Language Conventionality and Clarity<br>① ② **❸** ④ ⑤ | The selection contains some regional vocabulary (*huskers, chilblains*) and some figurative language and complex sentences. |
| Levels of Meaning/Purpose<br>① ② **❸** ④ ⑤ | The main idea is fairly simple, but may be hard for some to grasp because of sophisticated language and supporting concepts that are complex. |

DECIDE AND PLAN

## English Language Support

Provide English Learners with support for language and levels of meaning/purpose as they read the selection.

**Language** Students may get confused reading passages with figurative language. For example, from paragraph 15: *It never really dies, then, the soul? It withers to the outward eye only, like that strange moss which can lie on a dusty shelf half a century and yet, if placed in water, grows green again.* Ask questions to guide students to understand that these are figurative rather than literal phrases.

**Levels of Meaning/Purpose** To help students sort out the events and ideas in the story, suggest that they keep a log of the main events, stating them in their own words. For example, from paragraph 1: *The narrator learns his aunt will be visiting the very next day.*

## Strategic Support

Provide students with strategic support to ensure that they can successfully read the text.

**Knowledge Demands** Students may find the many musical references confusing. Have students work in pairs to research the musical references throughout the story.

**Language/Clarity** For students that may have difficulty with complex sentences, encourage them to break the sentences down into smaller chunks and identify the meaning of unfamiliar words or phrases. Then have students reread the sentences.

## Challenge

Provide students who need to be challenged with ideas for how they can go beyond a simple interpretation of the text.

**Text Analysis** Ask students to describe the effect music has on Clark's Aunt Georgiana. Why is Clark surprised by her reaction during the concert? What did he expect might happen? Have students comment on Aunt Georgiana's feelings at the end of the story.

**Written Response** After discussing what Aunt Georgiana has given up all of the years she has lived in Nebraska, have students write an argument for or against her decision.

TEACH

## Read and Respond

Have the groups read the selection and complete the Making Meaning, Language Development, and Effective Expression activities.

# Standards Support Through Teaching and Learning Cycle

## IDENTIFY NEEDS

Analyze results of the Beginning-of-Year Assessment, focusing on the items relating to Unit 2. Also take into consideration student performance to this point and your observations of where particular students struggle.

## DECIDE AND PLAN

- If students have performed poorly on items matching these standards, then provide selection scaffolds before assigning them the on-level lesson provided in the Student Edition.
- If students have done well on the Beginning-of-Year Assessment, then challenge them to keep progressing and learning by giving them opportunities to practice the skills in depth.
- Use the Selection Resources listed on the Planning pages for "A Wagner Matinée" to help students continually improve their ability to master the standards.

**Instructional Standards: "A Wagner Matinée"**

| | Catching Up | This Year | Looking Forward |
|---|---|---|---|
| **Reading** | You may wish to administer the **Analyze Craft and Structure: Character Development (RP)** worksheet to familiarize students with how an author develops characters. | **RL.3** Analyze the impact of the author's choices regarding how to develop and relate elements of a story or drama. | Ask students to identify which parts of the story were most revealing of Aunt Georgiana's character and discuss their thoughts. |
| **Writing** | You may wish to administer the **Writing to Sources: Research Report (RP)** worksheet to help students refine a topic that has to do with the issues surrounding Aunt Georgiana's locale. | **W.7** Conduct short as well as more sustained research projects to answer a question or solve a problem; narrow or broaden the inquiry when appropriate; synthesize multiple sources on the subject, demonstrating understanding of the subject under investigation. | Challenge students to imagine being Clark, and write a thank-you letter to Aunt Giorgiana from his perspective as an adult. |
| **Language** | You may wish to administer the **Conventions and Style: Figurative Language (RP)** worksheet to help students read the selection with more awareness of the writer's precise choice of words.<br>You may wish to administer the **Word Study: Word Derivations (RP)** worksheet to help students understand various derivations of the word *movere*, meaning "to move." | **RL.4** Determine the meaning of words and phrases as they are used in the text, including figurative and connotative meanings; analyze the impact of specific word choices on meaning and tone, including words with multiple meanings or language that is particularly fresh, engaging, or beautiful.<br>**L.4.c** Consult general and specialized reference materials, both print and digital, to find the pronunciation of a word or determine or clarify its precise meaning, its part of speech, its etymology, or its standard usage. | Challenge students to find uses for the derivations of *movere*, showing especially how "to move" relates to many aspects of Aunt Georgiana's experience (her move from Boston to Nebraska; she was "moved" by the music, etc.). |

## ANALYZE AND REVISE

- Analyze student work for evidence of student learning.
- Identify whether or not students have met the expectations in the standards.
- Identify implications for future instruction.

## TEACH

Implement the planned lesson, and gather evidence of student learning.

## Jump Start

**FIRST READ** To set the context for reading "A Wagner Matinée," engage students in a discussion about the effect of music in their lives. What music do they enjoy most?

### A Wagner Matinée  

What are some possible reasons that people make long moves across hundreds of miles? What might be the hardest part of leaving your home behind and moving to a new place? Modeling these and other questions readers might ask will bring "A Wagner Matinée" to life and connect students to the Performance Task prompt. Selection audio and print capability for the selection are available in the Interactive Teacher's Edition.

### Concept Vocabulary

Have groups briefly discuss the three vocabulary words. Do they recognize the prefix or base word of any of the concept vocabulary words?

Have groups consider the strategy of familiar word parts and discuss its advantages or disadvantages.

### FIRST READ

Have students perform the steps of the first read independently:

NOTICE: Encourage students to determine the main characters, the key events, and the setting as they read.

ANNOTATE: Remind students that they should annotate unfamiliar vocabulary and take special note of rich dialogue, vivid imagery, and the most important events as they read.

CONNECT: Encourage students to go beyond the narrative to think about how the text connects to their own experience.

RESPOND: Students will demonstrate their understanding of the text by answering questions and writing a summary.

Point out to students that they will perform the first three steps concurrently as they are doing their first read. They will complete the Respond step after they have finished the first read. You may wish to print copies of the **First-Read Guide: Fiction** for students to use.

MAKING MEANING

**About the Author**

As a child, **Willa Cather** (1873–1947) moved from her birthplace in Virginia to the Nebraska frontier, where many of her neighbors were immigrant farmers. Cather went on to receive a college degree, work as an editor at a Pittsburgh newspaper, and become a full-time writer in New York City. Still, it was prairie life that inspired many of her best-known works, including *O! Pioneers, My Ántonia,* and *One of Ours,* which won the Pulitzer Prize in 1923.

# A Wagner Matinée

## Concept Vocabulary

As you perform your first read of "A Wagner Matinée," you will encounter these words.

overture　　motifs　　prelude

**Familiar Word Parts** When you come to an unfamiliar word in a text, see whether the word contains any familiar word parts you can use to determine the word's meaning. A familiar word part may be a prefix, a suffix, a base word, or a root. Consider this example of the strategy:

**Unfamiliar Word:** *physiognomy*

**Word in Context:** The most striking thing about her *physiognomy,* however, was an incessant twitching of the mouth and eyebrows, . . .

**Familiar Word Part:** the root *-phys-,* which appears in words such as *physical* and *physician*

**Conclusion:** *Physiognomy* has a meaning related to a person's body. Context clues, such as "incessant twitching," support that assumption. You can then verify the meaning in a reliable dictionary.

Apply your knowledge of familiar word parts and other vocabulary strategies to determine the meanings of unfamiliar words you encounter during your first read.

## First Read FICTION

Apply these strategies as you conduct your first read. You will have an opportunity to complete a close read after your first read.

NOTICE *whom* the story is about, *what* happens, *where* and *when* it happens, and *why* those involved react as they do.

ANNOTATE by marking vocabulary and key passages you want to revisit.

CONNECT ideas within the selection to what you already know and what you have already read.

RESPOND by completing the Comprehension Check and by writing a brief summary of the selection.

**STANDARDS**

**Reading Literature**
By the end of grade 11, read and comprehend literature, including stories, dramas, and poems, in the grades 11–CCR text complexity band proficiently, with scaffolding as needed at the high end of the range.

**Language**
Identify and correctly use patterns of word changes that indicate different meanings or parts of speech.





### FACILITATING SMALL-GROUP CLOSE READING

**CLOSE READ: Short Story** As groups perform the close read, circulate and offer support as needed.

- Remind groups that as they read a narrative, they should work to identify the main characters and conflict.
- This story includes a narrator and his aunt. Encourage students to look for details that describe their relationship. Groups should also work together to discuss the details that help readers see the similarities and differences between the characters.

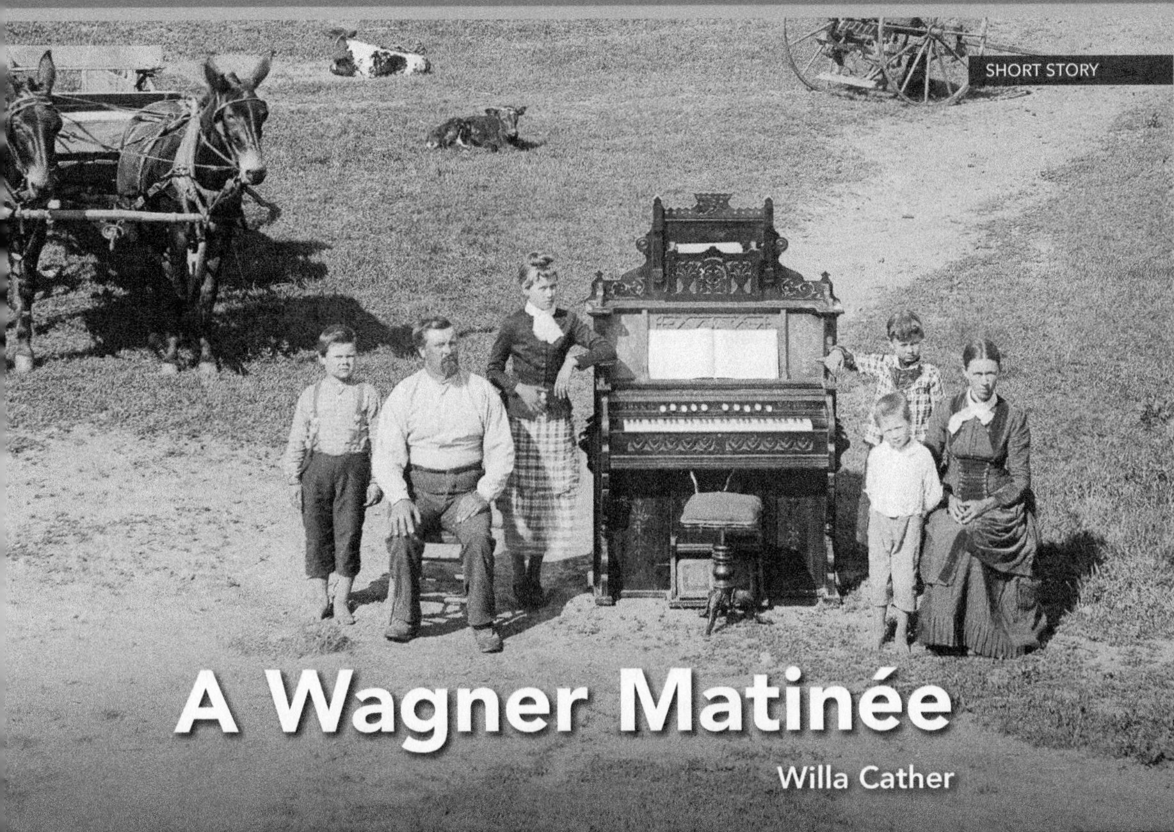

SHORT STORY

# A Wagner Matinée

Willa Cather

BACKGROUND

Richard Wagner was one of the nineteenth century's great composers. His operas are characterized by adventurous harmonies and an innovative blend of music and drama. To many, Wagner's music represents the idea of high culture. In this story, Cather contrasts the stark realities of frontier life with life in a more cultured world.

SCAN FOR MULTIMEDIA



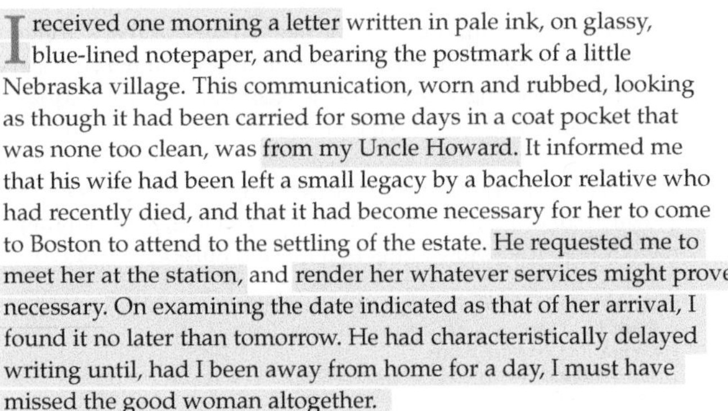

1 I received one morning a letter written in pale ink, on glassy, blue-lined notepaper, and bearing the postmark of a little Nebraska village. This communication, worn and rubbed, looking as though it had been carried for some days in a coat pocket that was none too clean, was from my Uncle Howard. It informed me that his wife had been left a small legacy by a bachelor relative who had recently died, and that it had become necessary for her to come to Boston to attend to the settling of the estate. He requested me to meet her at the station, and render her whatever services might prove necessary. On examining the date indicated as that of her arrival, I found it no later than tomorrow. He had characteristically delayed writing until, had I been away from home for a day, I must have missed the good woman altogether.

NOTES



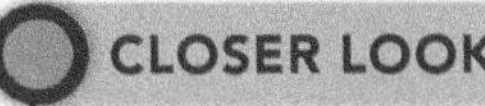

DIGITAL PERSPECTIVES

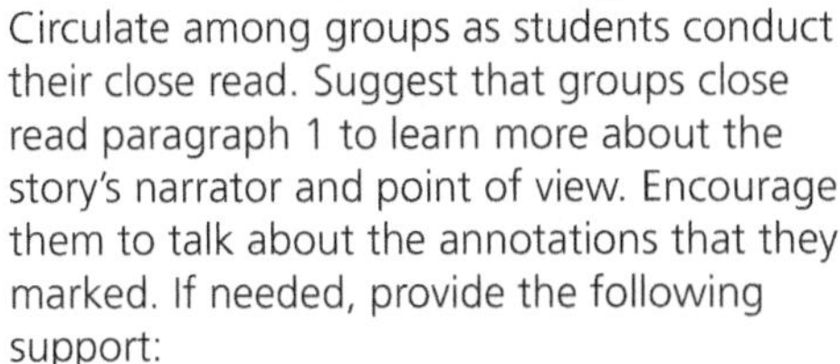

CLOSER LOOK

## Analyze a Narrator

Circulate among groups as students conduct their close read. Suggest that groups close read paragraph 1 to learn more about the story's narrator and point of view. Encourage them to talk about the annotations that they marked. If needed, provide the following support:

**ANNOTATE:** Have students mark details in the first paragraph that show them something about the narrator, the "I" who is telling the story, or work with small groups to have students participate while you highlight them together.

**QUESTION:** Guide students to consider what these details might tell them. Ask what a reader can infer from these choices and accept student responses.

**Possible response:** The narrator of "A Wagner Matinée" is the nephew of Uncle Henry, and his wife is the "good woman" who is coming to Boston. The narrator seems kind and dutiful. He writes in a formal tone and observes details carefully.

**CONCLUDE:** Ask students if they have enough evidence to conclude whether the narrator is also the protagonist or main character. Ask students to support their answers with reasons.

**Possible response:** There is not enough evidence in the first paragraph to determine whether the narrator will be the protagonist. The aunt who is coming to visit may be the main character, but we will only "see" her through the eyes of her nephew, who is telling the story. Encourage students to be open to a "wait and see" approach as they delve deeper into their analysis.

Remind students that the **narrator** is the voice that tells a story. The writer's choice of a narrator determines a fictional work's point of view, which, in turn, determines the type and amount of information that is revealed to the reader.

PERSONALIZE FOR LEARNING

### English Language Support

**Specialized Vocabulary** Review the exposition of the story, presented in paragraph 1. This story was first published in a magazine in 1904, so the diction and syntax may seem stilted, formal, complex, or even verbose to modern readers. Make sure that readers understand the meaning of the vocabulary used. For example, ensure comprehension of the legal terms *legacy, bachelor,* and *estate* that set up the reason for the aunt's return to Boston. Ask: *What does "legacy" mean here? What does it mean to call someone a "bachelor," and how does it affect this situation? What is an "estate," and why does it need to be "settled"?* **ALL LEVELS,**

NOTES

2 The name of my Aunt Georgiana called up not alone her own figure, at once pathetic and grotesque, but opened before my feet a gulf of recollections so wide and deep that, as the letter dropped from my hand, I felt suddenly a stranger to all the present conditions of my existence, wholly ill at ease and out of place amid the surroundings of my study. I became, in short, the gangling farmer boy my aunt had known, scourged with chilblains and bashfulness, my hands cracked and raw from the corn husking. I felt the knuckles of my thumb tentatively, as though they were raw again. I sat again before her parlor organ, thumbing the scales with my stiff, red hands, while she beside me made canvas mittens for the huskers.

3 The next morning, after preparing my landlady somewhat, I set out for the station. When the train arrived I had some difficulty in finding my aunt. She was the last of the passengers to alight, and when I got her into the carriage she looked not unlike one of those charred, smoked bodies that firemen lift from the *débris* of a burned building. She had come all the way in a day coach; her linen duster[1] had become black with soot and her black bonnet gray with dust during the journey. When we arrived at my boardinghouse the landlady put her to bed at once, and I did not see her again until the next morning.

4 Whatever shock Mrs. Springer experienced at my aunt's appearance she considerately concealed. Myself, I saw my aunt's misshapen figure with that feeling of awe and respect with which we behold explorers who have left their ears and fingers north of Franz Josef Land,[2] or their health somewhere along the upper Congo.[3] My Aunt Georgiana had been a music teacher at the Boston Conservatory, somewhere back in the latter sixties. One summer, which she had spent in the little village in the Green Mountains[4] where her ancestors had dwelt for generations, she had kindled the callow[5] fancy of the most idle and shiftless of all the village lads, and had conceived for this Howard Carpenter one of those absurd and extravagant passions which a handsome country boy of twenty-one sometimes inspires in a plain, angular, spectacled woman of thirty. When she returned to her duties in Boston, Howard followed her; and the upshot of this inexplicable infatuation was that she eloped with him, eluding the reproaches of her family and the criticism of her friends by going with him to the Nebraska frontier. Carpenter, who of course had no money, took a homestead in Red Willow County,[6] fifty miles from the railroad. There they measured off their eighty acres by driving across the prairie in a wagon, to the wheel of which they had tied a red cotton handkerchief, and counting its revolutions. They built a dugout in the red hillside, one of those

1. **duster** *n.* short, loose smock worn while traveling to protect clothing from dust.
2. **Franz Josef Land** group of islands in the Arctic Ocean.
3. **Congo** river in central Africa.
4. **Green Mountains** mountains in Vermont.
5. **callow** (KAL oh) *adj.* immature; inexperienced.
6. **Red Willow County** county in southwestern Nebraska that borders on Kansas.





## VOCABULARY DEVELOPMENT

**Graphic Organizer** Call student attention to the vocabulary opportunities in paragraph 2. Cather's prose offers many opportunities for vocabulary development. Rich, vivid words such as *gangling, scourged, chilblain, debris, angular, infatuation,* and *elude* can provide students with new understandings and additions to their personal lexicons. Have students choose two or three of these unfamiliar words to use as the center of word webs in which they explore both the word's denotation and connotations. Then, have them use the words in new sentences that they write themselves.

cave dwellings whose inmates usually reverted to the conditions of primitive savagery. Their water they got from the lagoons where the buffalo drank, and their slender stock of provisions was always at the mercy of bands of roving Indians. For thirty years my aunt had not been farther than fifty miles from the homestead.

5 But Mrs. Springer knew nothing of all this, and must have been considerably shocked at what was left of my kinswoman. Beneath the soiled linen duster, which on her arrival was the most conspicuous feature of her costume, she wore a black stuff dress whose ornamentation showed that she had surrendered herself unquestioningly into the hands of a country dressmaker. My poor aunt's figure, however, would have presented astonishing difficulties to any dressmaker. Her skin was yellow from constant exposure to a pitiless wind, and to the alkaline water which transforms the most transparent cuticle into a sort of flexible leather. She wore ill-fitting false teeth. The most striking thing about her physiognomy, however, was an incessant twitching of the mouth and eyebrows, a form of nervous disorder resulting from isolation and monotony, and from frequent physical suffering.

6 In my boyhood this affliction had possessed a sort of horrible fascination for me, of which I was secretly very much ashamed, for in those days I owed to this woman most of the good that ever came my way, and had a reverential affection for her. During the three winters when I was riding herd for my uncle, my aunt, after cooking three meals for half a dozen farmhands, and putting the six children to bed, would often stand until midnight at her ironing board, hearing me at the kitchen table beside her recite Latin declensions and conjugations, and gently shaking me when my drowsy head sank down over a page of irregular verbs. It was to her, at her ironing or mending, that I read my first Shakespeare; and her old textbook of mythology was the first that ever came into my empty hands. She taught me my scales and exercises, too, on the little parlor organ which her husband had bought her after fifteen years, during which she had not so much as seen any instrument except an accordion, that belonged to one of the Norwegian farmhands. She would sit beside me by the hour, darning and counting, while I struggled with the "Harmonious Blacksmith"; but she seldom talked to me about music, and I understood why. She was a pious woman; she had the consolation of religion; and to her at least her martyrdom was not wholly sordid. Once when I had been doggedly beating out some passages from an old score of "Euryanthe" I had found among her music books, she came up to me and, putting her hands over my eyes, gently drew my head back upon her shoulder, saying tremulously, "Don't love it so well, Clark, or it may be taken from you. Oh! dear boy, pray that whatever your sacrifice be it is not that."

7 When my aunt appeared on the morning after her arrival, she was still in a semi-somnambulant[7] state. She seemed not to realize that

NOTES

7. **semi-somnambulant** (SEHM ee som NAM byuh luhnt) *adj.* resembling a sleepwalker.





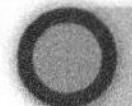

CLOSER LOOK

## Analyze Descriptive Details

Circulate among groups as students conduct their close read. Suggest that groups close read paragraph 5 and annotate the descriptive details they find. Encourage them to talk about the annotations that they marked. If needed, provide the following support:

**ANNOTATE:** Have students mark the descriptive details they find most interesting or significant, or work with small groups to have students participate while you highlight them together.

**QUESTION:** Guide students to consider what these descriptive details might tell them. Remind them to consider all five senses, not only the sense of sight.

**Possible response:** We can imagine what Georgiana looks like: her plain black dress, her yellow skin, her false teeth, and her incessant twitch.

**CONCLUDE:** Help students to formulate conclusions about using these descriptive details to further their understanding of Georgiana's character and ultimately, the story's theme.

**Possible response:** Georgiana's life in Nebraska has been extremely harsh, isolating, and physically difficult.

Remind students that **description** is a portrait in words of a person, place, or thing. Descriptive writing uses imagery that appeals to sight, hearing, taste, smell, and touch. Writers use description to help develop character or theme in a text.

## DIGITAL PERSPECTIVES

**Illuminating the Text** Suggest that students find and share photographs of life on the prairie during the 1880s and 1890s, when this story takes place. They might search terms such as *dugout, sod house,* or *homesteader*. They will see that this life was challenging and tedious, the land was flat and treeless, and the temperatures were extreme in both summer and winter. Have students speculate about what life must have been like for homesteaders such as Georgiana and Howard. Based on the photographs, ask: *What would it have been like to live here day after day and year after year?* Have students write short descriptive paragraphs on this topic. **(Research to Explore)**

NOTES

she was in the city where she had spent her youth, the place longed for hungrily for half a lifetime. She had been so wretchedly trainsick throughout the journey that she had no recollection of anything but her discomfort, and, to all intents and purposes, there were but a few hours of nightmare between the farm in Red Willow County and my study on Newbury Street. I had planned a little pleasure for her that afternoon, to repay her for some of the glorious moments she had given me when we used to milk together in the straw-thatched cowshed, and she, because I was more than usually tired, or because her husband had spoken sharply to me, would tell me of the splendid performance of Meyerbeer's *Les Huguenots*[8] she had seen in Paris in her youth. At two o'clock the Boston Symphony Orchestra was to give a Wagner program, and I intended to take my aunt, though as I conversed with her I grew doubtful about her enjoyment of it. Indeed, for her own sake, I could only wish her taste for such things quite dead, and the long struggle mercifully ended at last. I suggested our visiting the Conservatory and the Common[9] before lunch, but she seemed altogether too timid to wish to venture out. She questioned me absently about various changes in the city, but she was chiefly concerned that she had forgotten to leave instructions about feeding half-skimmed milk to a certain weakling calf, "Old Maggie's calf, you know, Clark," she explained, evidently having forgotten how long I had been away. She was further troubled because she had neglected to tell her daughter about the freshly opened kit of mackerel in the cellar, that would spoil if it were not used directly.

8 I asked her whether she had ever heard any of the Wagnerian operas, and found that she had not, though she was perfectly familiar with their respective situations and had once possessed the piano score of *The Flying Dutchman*. I began to think it would have been best to get her back to Red Willow County without waking her, and regretted having suggested the concert.

9 From the time we entered the concert hall, however, she was a trifle less passive and inert, and seemed to begin to perceive her surroundings. I had felt some trepidation[10] lest one might become aware of the absurdities of her attire, or might experience some painful embarrassment at stepping suddenly into the world to which she had been dead for a quarter of a century. But again I found how superficially I had judged her. She sat looking about her with eyes as impersonal, almost as stony, as those with which the granite Ramses[11] in a museum watches the froth and fret that ebbs and flows about his pedestal, separated from it by the lonely stretch of centuries. I have seen this same aloofness in old miners who drift into the Brown Hotel at Denver, their pockets full of bullion, their linen soiled, their

8. ***Les Huguenots*** (lay oo guh NOH) opera written in 1836 by Giacomo Meyerbeer (1791–1864).
9. **Common** Boston Common, a small park in Boston.
10. **trepidation** (trehp uh DAY shuhn) *n.* fearful anxiety; apprehension.
11. **Ramses** (RAM seez) one of the eleven Egyptian kings by that name who ruled from c. 1292 B.C. to 1075 B.C.





## PERSONALIZE FOR LEARNING

### English Language Support

**Similes** Review paragraph 9 and help students explore the figurative comparison between Aunt Georgiana and the statue of Ramses in a museum. The narrator claims that "aloofness" is one quality that the two have in common, but suggests that it is more than that. He also uses the words *stony* and *impersonal* to describe both his aunt and the statue.

Support understanding by drawing a Venn diagram with "Aunt Georgiana" on one side, "Statue of Ramses" on the other, and have students list their similarities in the middle area of overlap. Based on this discussion, have them write sentences about what the simile tells them about the main character. **ALL LEVELS,**

DIGITAL PERSPECTIVES

haggard faces unshorn, and who stand in the thronged corridors as solitary as though they were still in a frozen camp on the Yukon, or in the yellow blaze of the Arizona desert, conscious that certain experiences have isolated them from their fellows by a gulf no haberdasher could conceal.

10 The audience was made up chiefly of women. One lost the contour of faces and figures, indeed any effect of line whatever, and there was only the color contrast of bodices past counting, the shimmer and shading of fabrics soft and firm, silky and sheer, resisting and yielding: red, mauve, pink, blue, lilac, purple, ecru, rose, yellow, cream, and white, all the colors that an impressionist finds in a sunlit landscape, with here and there the dead black shadow of a frock coat. My Aunt Georgiana regarded them as though they had been so many daubs of tube paint on a palette.

11 When the musicians came out and took their places, she gave a little stir of anticipation, and looked with quickening interest down over the rail at that invariable grouping; perhaps the first wholly familiar thing that had greeted her eye since she had left old Maggie and her weakling calf. I could feel how all those details sank into her soul, for I had not forgotten how they had sunk into mine when I came fresh from plowing forever and forever between green aisles of corn, where, as in a treadmill, one might walk from daybreak to dusk without perceiving a shadow of change in one's environment. I reminded myself of the impression made on me by the clean profiles of the musicians, the gloss of their linen; the dull black of their coats, the beloved shapes of the instruments, the patches of yellow light thrown by the green-shaded stand-lamps on the smooth, varnished bellies of the cellos and the bass viols in the rear, the restless, wind-tossed forest of fiddle necks and bows; I recalled how, in the first orchestra I had ever heard, those long bow strokes seemed to draw the soul out of me, as a conjuror's stick reels out paper ribbon from a hat.

I could feel how all those details sank into her soul, . . .

12 The first number was the Tannhäuser **overture**. When the violins drew out the first strain of the Pilgrims' chorus, my Aunt Georgiana clutched my coat sleeve. Then it was that I first realized that for her this singing of basses and stinging frenzy of lighter strings broke a silence of thirty years, the inconceivable silence of the plains. With the battle between the two **motifs**, with the bitter frenzy of the Venusberg[12] theme and its ripping of strings, came to me an overwhelming sense of the waste and wear we are so powerless to combat. I saw again the tall, naked house on the prairie, black and grim as a wooden fortress; the black pond where I had learned to swim, the rain-gullied clay about the naked house; the four dwarf ash seedlings on which the dishcloths were always hung to dry before

12. **Venusberg** (VEE nuhs buhrg) legendary mountain in Germany where Venus, the Roman goddess of love, held court.

NOTES

Mark familiar word parts or indicate another strategy you used that helped you determine meaning.

**overture** (OH vuhr chuhr) *n.*

MEANING:

**motifs** (moh TEEFS) *n.*

MEANING:





## Concept Vocabulary

**OVERTURE** If groups are struggling to define *overture* in paragraph 12, point out that the context makes it clear that it is a musical "number" that happens at the beginning of a longer performance. Explain that the prefix *over-*, which means "excessive" in words such as *overcooked* and "above" in words such as *overcoat*, is not helpful here, but the context clues are significant, and enough to make the meaning clear. Have students define the word.

**Possible response:** an orchestral composition that introduces an opera

**MOTIFS** If groups are struggling to define *motifs* in paragraph 12, point out that the word is similar to *motive*, which pertains to motion or movement. Suggest that a *motif* might refer to a theme within a piece of music. Have students use familiar word parts to define the word.

**Possible response:** a musical theme or feature

Additional **English Language Support** is available in the Interactive Teacher's Edition.

## PERSONALIZE FOR LEARNING

### Strategic Support

**Motifs** Point out that in paragraph 12, beginning with "I reminded myself," the narrator again weaves past with present as he both vividly describes what he sees in the present moment and allows it to trigger a fond memory of "the first orchestra I had ever heard." This is one of the motifs of the story: the past informs the present, which, in turn, informs the past in a recurring cycle.

Have students find other examples of this in the story and discuss how this pattern contributes to the story's meaning and theme.

CLOSER LOOK

## Analyze Flashback

Circulate among groups as students conduct their close read. Suggest that groups close read paragraph 13, and annotate the sentences that reflect events that do not happen in the concert hall. If needed, provide the following support:

**ANNOTATE:** Have students annotate the sentences in the paragraph that reflect action in the past, or work with small groups to have students participate while you highlight them together.

**QUESTION:** Guide students to consider what these details tell them about earlier events in the characters' lives, and accept student responses.

**Possible response:** These people know each other and have spent time together. Aunt Georgiana has musical talent that has not been revealed in the story until now.

**CONCLUDE:** Help students to formulate conclusions about the flashback in this paragraph and about all of the flashbacks in the story.

**Possible response:** This flashback is especially powerful because it allows us to understand more fully how Georgiana had loved and cared for the narrator and how music connected them long ago and does again.

Remind students that a **flashback** is a scene within a narrative that interrupts the sequence of events to relate an event that occurred in the past.

NOTES

the kitchen door. The world there is the flat world of the ancients; to the east, a cornfield that stretched to daybreak; to the west, a corral that stretched to sunset; between, the sordid conquests of peace, more merciless than those of war.

13 The overture closed. My aunt released my coat sleeve, but she said nothing. She sat staring at the orchestra through a dullness of thirty years, through the films made, little by little, by each of the three hundred and sixty-five days in every one of them. What, I wondered, did she get from it? She had been a good pianist in her day, I knew, and her musical education had been broader than that of most music teachers of a quarter of a century ago. She had often told me of Mozart's operas and Meyerbeer's, and I could remember hearing her sing, years ago, certain melodies of Verdi. When I had fallen ill with a fever she used to sit by my cot in the evening, while the cool night wind blew in through the faded mosquito netting tacked over the window, and I lay watching a bright star that burned red above the cornfield, and sing "Home to our mountains, oh, let us return!" In a way fit to break the heart of a Vermont boy near dead of homesickness already.

CROSS-CURRICULAR PERSPECTIVES

**Music** Review paragraph 13 and draw student attention to the importance of music to this story. Locate recordings of several of the musical pieces by Richard Wagner referred to in the text, such as the Tannhäuser Overture, the prelude to *Tristan and Isolde*, or the "Prize Song" from *Die Meistersinger von Nürnberg*. As you play the music for students, have them freewrite about what the music makes them picture, think about, or feel. Ask: *What emotions does this music evoke? How does it do so?* Encourage students to imagine hearing these compositions in a concert hall played by a full orchestra in real time.

14 I watched her closely through the **prelude** to *Tristan and Isolde,* trying vainly to conjecture what that warfare of motifs, that seething turmoil of strings and winds, might mean to her. Had this music any message for her? Did or did not a new planet swim into her ken? Wagner had been a sealed book to Americans before the sixties. Had she anything left with which to comprehend this glory that had flashed around the world since she had gone from it? I was in a fever of curiosity, but Aunt Georgiana sat silent upon her peak in Darien.[13] She preserved this utter immobility throughout the numbers from the *Flying Dutchman,* though her fingers worked mechanically upon her black dress, as though of themselves they were recalling the piano score they had once played. Poor old hands! They were stretched and pulled and twisted into mere tentacles to hold, and lift, and knead with; the palms unduly swollen, the fingers bent and knotted, on one of them a thin worn band that had once been a wedding ring. As I pressed and gently quieted one of those groping hands, I remembered, with quivering eyelids, their services for me in other days.

15 Soon after the tenor began the "Prize Song," I heard a quick-drawn breath, and turned to my aunt. Her eyes were closed, but the tears were glistening on her cheeks, and I think in a moment more they were in my eyes as well. It never really dies, then, the soul? It withers to the outward eye only, like that strange moss which can lie on a dusty shelf half a century and yet, if placed in water, grows green again. My aunt wept gently throughout the development and elaboration of the melody.

16 During the intermission before the second half of the concert, I questioned my aunt and found that the "Prize Song" was not new to her. Some years before there had drifted to the farm in Red Willow County a young German, a tramp cow puncher who had sung in the chorus at Bayreuth,[14] when he was a boy, along with the other peasant boys and girls. On a Sunday morning he used to sit on his blue gingham-sheeted bed in the hands' bedroom, which opened off the kitchen, cleaning the leather of his boots and saddle, and singing the "Prize Song," while my aunt went about her work in the kitchen. She had hovered about him until she had prevailed upon him to join the country church, though his sole fitness for this step, so far as I could gather, lay in his boyish face and his possession of this divine melody. Shortly afterward he had gone to town on the Fourth of July, lost his money at a faro[15] table, ridden a saddled Texas steer on a bet, and disappeared with a fractured collarbone.

17 "Well, we have come to better things than the old *Trovatore* at any rate. Aunt Georgie?" I queried, with well-meant jocularity.

NOTES

Mark familiar word parts or indicate another strategy you used that helped you determine meaning.

**prelude** (PRAY lood) *n.*

MEANING:

13. **peak in Darien** mountain on the Isthmus of Panama; from "On First Looking Into Chapman's Homer," by English poet John Keats (1795–1821).
14. **Bayreuth** (by ROYT) city in Germany known for its annual festivals of Wagner's music.
15. **faro** (FAR oh) *n.* gambling game in which players bet on the cards to be turned up from the top of the dealer's deck.

## Concept Vocabulary

**PRELUDE** If groups are struggling to define *prelude* in paragraph 14, point out that the context makes it clear that it is another type of musical composition. Explain that knowing that the prefix *pre-* means "happening before" can help them determine the word's exact meaning. Have students use familiar word parts to define the word.

**Possible response:** A *prelude* is "a piece of music that comes before the main part of the work."

## PERSONALIZE FOR LEARNING

### English Language Support

**Connotation** Focus students' attention on the sentence in paragraph 15, "It never really dies, then, the soul?" and the subsequent comparison of the soul to a "strange moss." Earlier in the story, in paragraph 11, the narrator says he "could feel how all those details sank into her soul," and then he recalls that the "low bow strokes seemed to draw the soul out of me."

Lead a discussion of the word *soul.* Explore both the denotation ("the spiritual part of a human being, in contrast to the body") and the connotations of the word *soul* with students by creating a group word web. *Soul* is clearly an abstract noun and one that nearly defies definition. Students will likely bring a variety of prior knowledge and experience to this discussion. **ALL LEVELS,**

CLOSER LOOK

## Analyze Imagery

Circulate among groups as students conduct their close read of paragraphs 18 to 24. Suggest that groups annotate the part of these paragraphs that most directly addresses or expresses the story's theme. If needed, provide the following support:

**ANNOTATE:** Have students highlight the sentence or sentences in paragraph 22 that develop an image, or work with small groups to have students participate while you highlight them together.

**QUESTION:** Guide students to consider what the water image suggests, and accept student responses.

**Possible response:** The writer includes language that develops an image of a powerful river that takes Aunt Georgiana to a different place that is either more beautiful or more peaceful than where she is. The story suggests that music has the potential to be a "shining current" that can carry a person into a completely different reality. The narrator explicitly states this in paragraph 22 in the sentence that begins, "From the trembling of her face . . ." This is a beautiful, long sentence that is both the climax of the story and a statement of its theme.

**CONCLUDE:** Help students to formulate conclusions about why the writer may have included these details.

**Possible response:** The image reveals the power of the music. The music transports Georgiana. It carries readers back into the past and also into a timeless place that defies words. Georgiana does not want to leave this "place" once she arrives.

Remind students that **imagery** is the use of figurative language to create a picture that represents an idea for readers. Writers often use images to help them convey a message.

NOTES

18 Her lip quivered and she hastily put her handkerchief up to her mouth. From behind it she murmured, "And you've been hearing this ever since you left me, Clark?" Her question was the gentlest and saddest of reproaches.

19 "But do you get it, Aunt Georgiana, the astonishing structure of it all?" I persisted.

20 "Who could?" she said, absently; "why should one?"

21 The second half of the program consisted of four numbers from the *Ring*. This was followed by the forest music from *Siegfried*[16] and the program closed with Siegfried's funeral march. My aunt wept quietly, but almost continuously. I was perplexed as to what measure of musical comprehension was left to her, to her who had heard nothing for so many years but the singing of gospel hymns in Methodist services at the square frame schoolhouse on Section Thirteen. I was unable to gauge how much of it had been dissolved in soapsuds, or worked into bread, or milked into the bottom of a pail.

22 The deluge of sound poured on and on; I never knew what she found in the shining current of it; I never knew how far it bore her, or past what happy islands, or under what skies. From the trembling of her face I could well believe that the *Siegfried* march, at least, carried her out where the myriad graves are, out into the gray, burying grounds of the sea; or into some world of death vaster yet, where, from the beginning of the world, hope has lain down with hope, and dream with dream and, renouncing, slept.

23 The concert was over; the people filed out of the hall chattering and laughing, glad to relax and find the living level again, but my kinswoman made no effort to rise. I spoke gently to her. She burst into tears and sobbed pleadingly, "I don't want to go, Clark, I don't want to go!"

24 I understood. For her, just outside the door of the concert hall, lay the black pond with the cattle-tracked bluffs, the tall, unpainted house, naked as a tower, with weather-curled boards; the crookbacked ash seedlings where the dishcloths hung to dry, the gaunt, moulting turkeys picking up refuse about the kitchen door. ❧

16. ***Siegfried*** (SEEG freed) opera based on the adventures of Siegfried, a legendary hero in medieval German literature.





### WriteNow Analyze and Interpret

**Write a Letter** Review paragraph 24 and ask students whether the narrator could truly understand his aunt. Challenge students to write a letter from Aunt Georgiana to Uncle Howard in which she tells what happened on the day of the concert, mixing imagery and details from the text with those from their own imaginations.

As students take on the voice of the narrator's aunt, encourage them not to be timid or shy, but to express themselves as openly and honestly as possible. Give students the opportunity to share their letters by reading them aloud or posting them in the classroom.

## Comprehension Check

Complete the following items after you finish your first read. Review and clarify details with your group.

1. Why does Aunt Georgiana travel to Boston?

2. When Clark was a boy, what subjects did he learn from Aunt Georgiana?

3. What is Clark's initial feeling about being in public with his aunt?

4. What does Aunt Georgiana do when the violins start playing the Pilgrims' chorus?

5. What does Aunt Georgiana do and say at the end of the concert?

6. **Notebook** Confirm your understanding of the story by writing a summary.

## RESEARCH

**Research to Clarify** Choose at least one unfamiliar detail from the text. Briefly research that detail. In what way does the information you learned shed light on an aspect of the story?

**Research to Explore** Conduct research on an aspect of the text you find interesting. For example, you may want to learn more about the operas by Richard Wagner that Cather mentions in the story. You may want to share what you discover with your group.





DIGITAL PERSPECTIVES

## Comprehension Check

Possible responses:

1. She needs to be present for the settling of the estate of a recently deceased relative.
2. He learned Latin, Shakespeare, mythology, and music.
3. He feels anxious and embarrassed about how out of place and ill at ease she seems.
4. She clutches Clark's coat sleeve.
5. She bursts into tears and says, "I don't want to go, Clark, I don't want to go!"
6. Clark, the narrator, has received a note from his Uncle Howard stating that his Aunt Georgiana is coming to Boston from their home in Nebraska to be present at the settling of a relative's estate. Clark remembers his aunt with love because she had been good to him while she raised him for three years alongside her own six children. To show his gratitude, he takes her to a concert. He thinks she will enjoy it because she had been trained in classical music. The music stirs her soul, awakening all the love of beauty the desolate, brutal prairie had nearly extinguished.

## Research

**Research to Clarify** If groups struggle to come up with a research topic, you may want to suggest that they focus on one of these topics: the Boston Conservatory, Richard Wagner, Ramses, Venusberg, Mozart, Meyerbeer, Verdi, *The Flying Dutchman*, or the *Siegfried* march.

**Research to Explore** If groups want to explore a different area of research, suggest that they learn more about sod houses or dugouts, which were common on the Great Plains of the United States after the federal government passed the Homestead Act. Encourage students to share photographs or illustrations of these homes.

PERSONALIZE FOR LEARNING

### Challenge

**The Homestead Acts** The detail in paragraph 21 about "the square frame schoolhouse on Section Thirteen" is a reflection of the way Homestead Acts created land grants for farmers during the years following the Civil War. A full "section" was 640 acres, and various acts granted a quarter-section, a half-section, or even a full section. The Kinkaid Amendment of 1904 granted full sections to homesteaders in western Nebraska, perhaps an inspiration for Cather's tale.

Encourage students to learn more about the various Homestead Acts and their effects on United States history and society, both positive and negative.

## Jump Start

CLOSE READ Ask groups to think about the powerful effect that music can have on individuals or on society. First, ask them to think of a piece of music that holds great meaning for them as individuals. Then, ask them to generalize about the role of music in a society. What pieces of music might be important to the majority of people in the United States?

## Close Read the Text 

Model close reading as needed by using the Annotation Highlights in the Interactive Teacher's Edition. Remind groups to use Accountable Talk in their discussions and to support one another as they complete the close read.

## Analyze the Text

**Possible responses:**

1. Siegfried's funeral march might also suggest Georgiana's because she will return to her life of endless toil and no beauty—a metaphorical grave.
2. Chosen passages will likely include those that show Georgiana's reaction to the music because they show how culture is vital to the soul.
3. The story suggests that music and the arts are ways to affirm individuality and express emotions.

## Concept Vocabulary

**Why These Words? Possible response:** The words are all related to music. They increase understanding by clarifying musical forms.

### Practice

**Possible responses:**

The loud and lively *overture* set the stage for the excitement of the show to follow.
The gentle *prelude* sounded like a waterfall.
The repetition of four notes was as a unifying *motif*.

### Word Network

**Possible words:** *recollections*, *appearance*, *sacrifice*, *aloofness*, *existence*, *venture*, *solitary*, *conscious*

## Word Study

For more support, see **Concept Vocabulary and Word Study.**

**Possible responses:**

1. The Latin word *motivus* means "moving, impelling." *Motif,* meaning "will, drive, motivation," derives from *motivus.*
2. *motive:* causing or being the reason for something; *locomotive:* a powered rail vehicle used to pull trains

MAKING MEANING

A WAGNER MATINÉE

## Close Read the Text

With your group, revisit sections of the text you marked during your first read. **Annotate** details that you notice. What **questions** do you have? What can you **conclude?**

## Analyze the Text

**CITE TEXTUAL EVIDENCE** to support your answers.

**Complete the activities.**

1. **Review and Clarify** With your group, reread paragraph 22. In what sense might Siegfried's funeral march be thought of as Georgiana's funeral march, too? Discuss with your group.
2. **Present and Discuss** Now, work with your group to share the passages from the selection that you found especially significant. Take turns presenting your passages. Discuss what you noticed in the selection, what questions you asked, and what conclusions you reached.
3. **Essential Question:** ***What role does individualism play in American society?*** What has this text taught you about individualism? Discuss with your group.

**WORD NETWORK**

Add words related to individualism from the text to your Word Network.

LANGUAGE DEVELOPMENT

## Concept Vocabulary

| overture | motifs | prelude |
|---|---|---|

**Why These Words?** The three concept vocabulary words are related. With your group, discuss the words and determine which concept they share. How do these words contribute to your understanding of the text?

### Practice

**Notebook** Confirm your understanding of the concept vocabulary words by using them in sentences. Consult reference materials, such as print or online dictionaries, to check the accuracy of your work.

## Word Study

**Notebook** **Word Derivations** In "A Wagner Matinée," Clark refers to the *motifs* in an opera. The word *motif* descended from the Latin word *motivus*, meaning "moving; impelling."

1. Explain how the meaning of the Latin root word *motivus* contributes to the meaning of *motifs.*
2. Identify two other words that descend from *motivus.* Write their definitions.

**STANDARDS**

**Reading Literature**
Analyze the impact of the author's choices regarding how to develop and relate elements of a story or drama.

**Language**
Consult general and specialized reference materials, both print and digital, to find the pronunciation of a word or determine or clarify its precise meaning, its part of speech, its etymology, or its standard usage.





## FORMATIVE ASSESSMENT

### Analyze the Text

**If** students struggle to close read the text, **then** provide the **A Wagner Matinée: Text Questions** available on online in the Interactive Teacher's Edition or Unit Resources. Answer and DOK levels are also available.

### Concept Vocabulary

**If** students struggle to identify the concept, **then** share music to model these terms.

### Word Study

**If** students fail to identify three words related to *motor*, **then** suggest that they use an online resource to find them.
For Reteach and Practice, see **Word Study: Word Derivations (RP).**

## Analyze Craft and Structure

**Author's Choices: Character Development** The term **characterization** refers to the art of revealing characters' personalities. In **direct characterization,** a writer simply states what a character is like, as in "She was a pious woman." In **indirect characterization,** a writer uses one or more of the following methods to provide clues about a character:

- describing a character's appearance and mannerisms
- presenting a character's words, thoughts, and actions
- showing ways in which other characters react to a character
- including comments that other characters make about a character

The point of view in which a story is told also affects how readers learn about characters. For example, this story uses **first-person point of view**—Clark, the narrator, is part of the action and uses the pronouns *I, me,* and *we.* As a result, readers' impressions filter through Clark's eyes.

### Practice

**CITE TEXTUAL EVIDENCE** to support your answers.

1. Complete this chart independently to analyze Cather's use of Clark to characterize Aunt Georgiana indirectly. Record one example for each method. Then, share with your group.

| METHOD OF CHARACTERIZATION | EXAMPLES FROM TEXT |
|---|---|
| physical description given by Clark | twitches nervously, yellow skin, ill-fitting false teeth, hands like tentacles, thin wedding ring |
| other comments made by Clark | "For thirty years my aunt had not been farther than fifty miles from the homestead." |
| Aunt Georgiana's words and actions | She "wept quietly" during the funeral march. She says, "Don't love it so well, Clark, or it may be taken from you." |

**Notebook** Answer the questions.

2. What do Clark's thoughts and feelings about his aunt indirectly reveal about his personality? Explain.
3. **(a)** How do Clark's feelings toward his aunt change during the story? **(b)** How do his feelings affect your response to Georgiana? **(c)** How do Clark's feelings about his aunt affect your attitude toward him as a character?





DIGITAL PERSPECTIVES

## Analyze Craft and Structure

**Character Development** Review the four techniques of indirect characterization. To further develop the concept, ask students to consider ways they might show specific traits. For example, to show assertiveness, a writer could show the character arguing with a sales clerk. To show kindness, a writer could show that the character interacting with pets. For more support, see **Analyze Craft and Structure: Character Development.**

### Practice

Possible responses:

1. See possible responses in the chart on the student page.
2. They reveal that he is both very fond of his aunt and judgmental of her as well.
3. (a) He becomes more empathic toward her. (b) His shift makes me feel more sympathetic toward Georgiana. Through his description, we gain a better idea of what she has given up. (c) Clark's softening toward and newfound understanding of his aunt makes me more sympathetic to him.

### FORMATIVE ASSESSMENT

### Analyze Craft and Structure

**If** students struggle to understand the four methods of indirect characterization, **then** have them reread the story with these questions in mind: *How do you learn about Aunt Georgiana? How do you learn about Clark?* For Reteach and Practice, see **Analyze Craft and Structure: Character Development (RP).**

### HOW LANGUAGE WORKS

**More Figures of Speech** Explain that while we may associate figurative language with poetry, good writers borrow this tool to build rich evocative sentences into their prose. In addition to the three types of figurative language defined and explained in the Conventions and Style section, offer four more:

- **Synecdote:** using a part of something, or something related to it, to represent a larger and usually more abstract idea. Example: In the statement, "The pen is mightier than the *sword*," the *pen* represents speech and diplomacy and the *sword* represents war and violence.
- **Oxymoron:** juxtaposing two opposite or contradictory words for effect. Examples: "a wise fool" or "I wake to sleep."
- **Personification:** giving human qualities to an inanimate object. Example: The rain kissed my cheek.
- **Allusion:** referring to a well-known person, event, place, or work of art. Example: My brother is a genuine Romeo with the ladies.

# FACILITATING

## Conventions and Style

**Figurative Language** Impress upon students how figurative language helps achieve language economy because it adheres to the principle that "Less is more." A good writer can pack a lot of meaning into a figure of speech because it implicitly suggests many meanings. For example, comparing the soul to the "strange moss" is an evocative way to express deep meaning about such an abstract idea. This density of meaning that offers infinite interpretational possibility is what makes figurative language so enjoyable and satisfying to read and write. For more support, see **Conventions and Style: Figurative Language.**

### Read It

See possible responses in chart on student page.

### Write It

Possible responses:

Aunt Georgiana was as frail and brittle as an autumn leaf. (simile)

During the concert, Aunt Georgiana's eyes were fireflies shimmering in the dark of the concert hall. (metaphor)

Aunt Georgiana felt that her heart would explode. (hyperbole)

### FORMATIVE ASSESSMENT

### Conventions and Style

**If** students are unable to understand figurative language, **then** offer a more common example such as "My love is like a red, red rose," Robert Burns's famous simile, and ask: *How is love like a rose?* For Reteach and Practice, see **Conventions and Style: Figurative Language (RP).**

LANGUAGE DEVELOPMENT

A WAGNER MATINÉE

STANDARDS

**Reading Literature**
Determine the meaning of words and phrases as they are used in the text, including figurative and connotative meanings; analyze the impact of specific word choices on meaning and tone, including words with multiple meanings or language that is particularly fresh, engaging, or beautiful.

**Language**
Interpret figures of speech in context and analyze their role in the text.

## Conventions and Style

**Figurative Language** Language that is used imaginatively rather than literally is called **figurative language.** Most fiction writers and poets—and many nonfiction writers, as well—use figurative language to convey ideas and emotions in a more nuanced and expressive way than plain statements would allow. Simile, metaphor, and hyperbole are three common types of figurative language.

- A **simile** is a comparison between two dissimilar things using an explicit word of comparison, such as *like, as,* or *resemble.* (Note that some writers may use the expression "not unlike," which actually means "like.") For example, Cather compares the soul to moss in this simile: "It withers to the outward eye only, like that strange moss which can lie on a dusty shelf half a century and yet, if placed in water, grows green again."
- A **metaphor** is a comparison that does not use an explicit word of comparison. Instead, the comparison is either implied or directly stated, often using a form of the verb *to be*, as in this example: "Wagner had been a sealed book to Americans before the sixties." Wagner is a composer, not a book. Cather's metaphor shows that no orchestra played Wagner's music before the 1860s.
- **Hyperbole** is exaggeration for effect. For example, Cather uses hyperbole when Clark comments, "there were but a few hours of nightmare between the farm in Red Willow County and my study on Newbury Street." Georgiana had traveled from Nebraska to Boston, so clearly more than "a few hours" had passed.

### Read It

Work individually. Identify each example as a simile, a metaphor, or hyperbole, and explain your response. Then, share and discuss your responses with your group.

| EXAMPLE | TYPE OF FIGURATIVE LANGUAGE | EXPLANATION |
|---|---|---|
| The deluge of sound poured on and on; I never knew what she found in the shining current of it . . . | metaphor | It compares the flow of the music to a watery current without using *like* or *as*. |
| . . . when I came fresh from ploughing forever and forever between green aisles of corn . . . | hyperbole | It exaggerates the amount of time that has passed. |
| . . . she looked not unlike one of those charred, smoked bodies that firemen lift from the *débris* of a burned building | simile | It compares Georgiana's appearance to a charred body using the phrase *not unlike*. |

### Write It

**Notebook** Write a simile, a metaphor, and an example of hyperbole to describe Aunt Georgiana. Label each type of figurative language you use.





PERSONALIZE FOR LEARNING

**Strategic Support**

**Adding Headings** Each of the reports in the Writing to Sources assignment can be enhanced by well-written headings that indicate the focus of the information that follows. Headings should be short, informative, concrete, and parallel in structure. Headings are like mini-titles and should

EFFECTIVE EXPRESSION

## Writing to Sources

**Assignment**

Prepare an informative **research report** that will help readers understand the historical context of Cather's story. Choose from the following project options:

- ☐ a **comparison and contrast** of rural Nebraska and Boston in the early 1900s, in which you include information about population density, living situations, transportation, jobs, clothing, and culture
- ☐ a **how-to essay** with a diagram that explains in detail how cornhuskers in the early twentieth century husked corn, including what parts of the process were difficult or laborious
- ☐ a **problem-solution letter** that gives helpful information to someone considering moving far away to a very different locale in the late 1800s, and that includes topics such as ways to maintain communication with friends and relatives, ways to make a living, and possible lifestyle changes

**Project Plan** As a group, discuss the types of information you will need to find. Then, develop a research plan that assigns responsibilities to individual group members and establishes deadlines for everyone to meet. Consult a variety of sources, including primary, secondary, print, and digital. Use the chart to organize your efforts.

| TYPE OF INFORMATION | PRIMARY SOURCES | SECONDARY SOURCES | ASSIGNED TO | DEADLINE |
|---|---|---|---|---|
| | | | | |
| | | | | |
| | | | | |
| | | | | |

**Tying It Together** Your research goal is to gather information that will allow you to create a complete picture of the topic. Once you have gathered information, review it as a group. Make sure that the sources are reliable and that all of the information is sufficient, credible, and relevant. Then, organize the writing tasks and complete your report.

EVIDENCE LOG

Before moving on to the next selection, go to your Evidence Log and record what you learned from "A Wagner Matinée."

STANDARDS

Writing

- Write informative/explanatory texts to examine and convey complex ideas, concepts, and information clearly and accurately through the effective selection, organization, and analysis of content.
- Conduct short as well as more sustained research projects to answer a question or solve a problem; narrow or broaden the inquiry when appropriate; synthesize multiple sources on the subject, demonstrating understanding of the subject under investigation.





DIGITAL PERSPECTIVES 

## Writing to Sources

As students conduct research, remind them to use dependable sources. Suggest that they limit their search to sources published in the last five years that come from reputable writers (not students or blogs). Also remind them that online sources ending in .gov or .edu, or reputable sources such as Britannica or National Geographic are preferable to sources ending in .com or .net.

**Project Plan** Remind students to align information from Cather's story with the information found through research.

**Tying It Together** Remind students that drafts are the framework of their writing, they are not final. Explain that as they revise, students will add appropriate transitions and resolve inconsistencies in style, tone, diction, and syntax as they make revisions. For more support, see **Writing to Sources: Research Report**

**Evidence Log** Support students in completing their Evidence Log. This paced activity will help prepare them for the Performance-Based Assessment at the end of the unit.

### FORMATIVE ASSESSMENT

### Writing to Sources

**If** students are struggling to make their group's writing cohesive and smooth, **then** encourage them to read their parts aloud to each other to hear the places in the writing that need revision. For Reteach and Practice, see **Writing to Sources: Research Report (RP).**

### Selection Test

Administer the "A Wagner Matinée" Selection Test, which is available in both print and digital formats online in Assessments.

## PERSONALIZE FOR LEARNING

### English Language Support

**Choosing Topics and Key Words** Have partners choose a topic for a comparison/contrast essay about an aspect of life in rural Nebraska as compared to Boston in the early 1900s. Tell them to use the paragraph numbers to help them locate details: details. Students may choose to select topics such as *clothing; culture, homes,* and *jobs*. Encourage students to create a chart and then gather details from the selection, noting paragraph numbers. **EMERGING**

Have students provide a blank chart for the appropriate topic. Have groups complete the chart and then list key words. **EXPANDING**

Have students work independently to complete a chart for their topic. Then have partners with the same topic compare their charts and list key words to research. **BRIDGING**

An expanded **English Language Support lesson** on Choosing Topics and Key Words is available in the Interactive Teacher's Edition

## Present a Personal Narrative

Before groups begin work on their projects, have them clearly differentiate the role each group member will play. Remind groups to consult the schedule for Small-Group Learning to guide their work during the Performance Task.

Students should complete the assignment using presentation software to take advantage of text, graphics, and sound features.

## Plan With Your Group

**Analyze the Text** Students should analyze the ways in which each of the unit's texts approach the subject of nonconformity. Look for similarities and differences in approach, and the advantages and disadvantages of each approach.

**Connect Evidence to Experience** As students look for evidence from their text, remind them that actions, thoughts, and feelings can all be considered evidence. They may want to use a T-chart as they gather their evidence, placing the details from the selection in one column and the details about themselves in the other.

PERFORMANCE TASK: SPEAKING AND LISTENING FOCUS

SOURCES

- *from* NATURE
- *from* SELF-RELIANCE
- *from* WALDEN
- *from* CIVIL DISOBEDIENCE
- INNOVATORS AND THEIR INVENTIONS
- THE LOVE SONG OF J. ALFRED PRUFROCK
- A WAGNER MATINÉE

# Present a Personal Narrative

**Assignment**

Plan and deliver a **group speech** that uses evidence from the texts in Small-Group Learning, as well as your own experiences and observations, to explore the challenges of nonconformity. Use the following prompt to guide your work:

> **When is it difficult to march to the beat of a "different drummer" and stand on your own as an individual? What are the risks and rewards of nonconformity?**

Draw on both Emerson's and Thoreau's ideas about nonconformity as starting points. Use precise language and quotations from the texts, as well as individual experiences and observations to support your ideas.

## Plan With Your Group

**Analyze the Texts** Discuss the ways in which the texts you have read approach the topic of nonconformity. For example, consider Emerson's experiences in nature, the creativity of inventors who find new solutions to old problems, or Aunt Georgiana's bravery and independence in setting a different course for her life, regardless of the results. Use the chart to record your group's ideas about nonconformity as expressed in these selections.

| TEXT | WHAT IT SHOWS ABOUT NONCONFORMITY |
|---|---|
| *from* Nature / *from* Self-Reliance | |
| *from* Walden / *from* Civil Disobedience | |
| Innovators and Their Inventions | |
| The Love Song of J. Alfred Prufrock | |
| A Wagner Matinée | |

**Connect Evidence to Experiences** Combine textual evidence with your own real-life examples and experiences that support your group's views. Then, complete this statement:

Nonconformity is difficult when ____________________. Nonconformity is risky because ____________________. It can be rewarding when ____________________.

**STANDARDS**

**Speaking and Listening**

Work with peers to promote civil, democratic discussions and decision-making, set clear goals and deadlines, and establish individual roles as needed.





AUTHOR'S PERSPECTIVE **Ernest Morrell, Ph.D.**

**Strategic Use of Media** Media is becoming more important as a communication tool, but teachers need to guide students to understand media's value. As groups plan their presentation, remind them that it is important to use media and visuals strategically so that they support the presentation but don't dominate it. Share these suggestions:

- Students should ensure that each piece of media has a specific purpose and is not mere "filler."
- Encourage students to let the content of their **personal narrative** drive their decisions about which media support to include, rather than finding appealing media and trying to force fit it into a presentation where it might not work.
- Remind groups that although media and visuals can enhance a presentation, the content of what students say during the presentation is what is most important.
- Ultimately, the presentation should be able to stand alone without media support and still make sense.

**Organize Your Presentation** Work individually to write a three-minute informal speech. Remember to include references to the texts, quotations from the texts, and your own experiences to support your ideas. Then, review each group member's speech. Decide how you will introduce the speeches, provide transitions between them, and conclude your presentation.

## Rehearse With Your Group

**Practice With Your Group** Use this checklist to evaluate the effectiveness of your group's first run-through. Then, use your evaluation and these instructions to guide your revision.

| CONTENT | PRESENTATION TECHNIQUES |
|---|---|
| ☐ The speeches respond to the prompt thoroughly and coherently. | ☐ Speakers enunciate clearly and use gestures and eye contact effectively. |
| ☐ The speeches are presented in a logical sequence. | ☐ Speakers vary pitch and volume to add interest to their words. |
| ☐ Speakers draw on evidence from both the texts and individual experiences and observations. | ☐ Speakers speak fluently, without hesitations or repetitions. |

**Fine-Tune the Content** If a speech is too long, too short, off-topic, or incomplete, work together to revise it.

**Brush Up on Your Presentation Techniques** Although an informal speech may be relaxed and friendly in tone, it should not be sloppy. Make sure that your speech is expressive and articulate, both in its content and in your presentation. Your words should help your audience to understand your ideas and to appreciate the textual evidence and personal experiences you use to support them.

## Present and Evaluate

As you present your series of speeches, consider your audience's response. Use questions such as these to evaluate the presentation:

- Does the speech offer clear reasoning and provide enough evidence to support the group's overall position on nonconformity?
- Does the speech bring together real-life experiences with examples from the texts in this section?

Once all the speeches have been delivered, you may wish to select two or three favorite parts. Be ready to explain what you like about each one.



**STANDARDS**

**Speaking and Listening**

- Evaluate a speaker's point of view, reasoning, and use of evidence and rhetoric, assessing the stance, premises, links among ideas, word choice, points of emphasis, and tone used.
- Present information, findings, and supporting evidence, conveying a clear and distinct perspective, such that listeners can follow the line of reasoning, alternative or opposing perspectives are addressed, and the organization, development, substance, and style are appropriate to purpose, audience, and a range of formal and informal tasks.



## DIGITAL PERSPECTIVES

**Organize Your Presentation** Each group will need to decide on a logical order for their presentation. Groups might follow the order in which the selections appear in the book, or they may decide to organize the speakers based on the content of the speeches.

## Rehearse With Your Group

**Practice With Your Group** Remind students that group members should practice in advance. Some students may be uncomfortable speaking before the class. Tell these students that the more they practice, the easier it will be for them to deliver their speech.

**Fine-Tune the Content** As groups practice their speeches, have group members suggest places where information might be added or deleted.

**Brush Up on Your Presentation Techniques** Group members may want to watch speeches on TV or the Internet. Have them pay attention to how the volume of the speaker's voice changes when he or she wants to make a point. Have students pay attention to body language, too. Remind them to use good posture, make eye contact with their audience, and integrate appropriate gestures.

**MAKE IT INTERACTIVE**

Suggest that groups video record their rehearsal and watch together as a strategy for refining their presentation.

## Present and Evaluate

Before beginning each group's presentation, set the expectations for the audience. You may wish to have students consider these questions as groups present.

- Were the experiences presented in a logical sequence?
- Did the personal and selection examples support the thesis statement regarding nonconformity?
- Which presentation techniques did this group excel at?

## PERSONALIZE FOR LEARNING

**English Language Support**

**Delivering a Speech** You may want to modify the length of the speeches of those for whom English is a second language.

Help students plan and deliver a brief speech, in which they use evidence to support their ideas and feelings, using short sentences and phrases. Provide extra time for them to practice delivering their speeches. **EMERGING**

Make sure students use evidence and facts to support their ideas, and ensure that they use a variety of sentence structures. **EXPANDING**

Have students plan and deliver their speech, expressing complex and abstract ideas. Make sure the speeches are well-supported by evidence and reason, and that they are informal in tone. **BRIDGING**

# OVERVIEW

## INDEPENDENT LEARNING

### What role does individualism play in American society?

Encourage students to think carefully about what they have already learned and what more they want to know about individualism in American society. This is a key first step to previewing and selecting the text they will read in Independent Learning.

### Independent Learning Strategies

Review the Learning Strategies with students and explain that as they work through Independent Learning, they will develop strategies to work on their own.

- Have students watch the video on Independent Learning Strategies.
- A video on this topic is available online in the Professional Development Center.

Students should include any favorite strategies that they might have devised on their own during Whole-Class and Small-Group Learning. For example, for the strategy "Create a schedule," students might include:

- Make outlines for topics that you want to cover.
- Allocate a set amount of time for each major point, to ensure that you'll be able to finish your presentation in time.

### Block Scheduling

Each day in this Pacing Plan represents a 40-50 minute class period. Teachers using block scheduling may combine days to reflect their class schedule. In addition, teachers may revise pacing to differentiate and support core instruction by integrating components and resources as students require.

OVERVIEW: INDEPENDENT LEARNING

ESSENTIAL QUESTION:

## What role does individualism play in American society?

In this section, you will complete your study of the role of individualism in American life by exploring an additional selection related to the topic. You'll then share what you learn with classmates. To choose a text, follow these steps.

**Look Back** Think about the selections you have already studied. Which aspects of individualism do you wish to explore further? Which time period interests you the most?

**Look Ahead** Preview the texts by reading the descriptions. Which one seems most interesting and appealing to you?

**Look Inside** Take a few minutes to scan the text you chose. Choose a different one if this text doesn't meet your needs.

## Independent Learning Strategies

Throughout your life, in school, in your community, and in your career, you will need to rely on yourself to learn and work on your own. Review these strategies and the actions you can take to practice them during Independent Learning. Add ideas of your own for each category.

| STRATEGY | ACTION PLAN |
|---|---|
| Create a schedule | • Understand your goals and deadlines.<br>• Make a plan for what to do each day.<br>• |
| Practice what you have learned | • Use first-read and close-read strategies to deepen your understanding.<br>• After you read, evaluate the usefulness of the evidence to help you understand the topic.<br>• Consider the quality and reliability of the source.<br>• |
| Take notes | • Record important ideas and information.<br>• Review your notes before preparing to share with a group.<br>• |



SCAN FOR MULTIMEDIA



### Pacing Plan

| Day | Activity |
|---|---|
| 1 | Unit Introduction |
| 2 | Introduce Whole-Class Learning |
| 3 | Historical Perspectives |
| 4–7 | The Writing of Walt Whitman |
| 8–12 | The Poetry of Emily Dickinson |
| 13 | Media: *from* Emily Dickinson |
| 14–15 | Performance Task |

DIGITAL PERSPECTIVES

CONTENTS

Choose one selection. Selections are available online only.

NEWS ARTICLE

**Sweet Land of . . . Conformity?**
*Claude Fischer*

Are we Americans really as individualistic as we like to think?

LITERARY CRITICISM

**Reckless Genius**
*Galway Kinnell*

A great contemporary poet explains why the reclusive, private Emily Dickinson is one of America's most intelligent and fearless poets.

SHORT STORY

**Hamadi**
*Naomi Shihab Nye*

What makes Hamadi such a remarkable individual?

SHORT STORY

**Young Goodman Brown**
*Nathaniel Hawthorne*

A Puritan discovers the dark side of individualism.

PERFORMANCE-BASED ASSESSMENT PREP

**Review Evidence for a Personal Narrative**

Complete your Evidence Log for the unit by evaluating what you have learned and synthesizing the information you have recorded.

SCAN FOR MULTIMEDIA





## Contents

**Selections** Encourage students to scan and preview the selections before choosing the one they would like to read. Suggest that they consider the genre and subject matter of each one before making their decision. You can use the information on the following Planning pages to advise students in making their choice.

Remind students that the selections for Independent Learning are only available in the Interactive Student Edition. Allow students who do not have digital access at home to preview the selections using classroom or computer lab technology. Then either have students print the selection they choose or provide a printout for them.

### Performance Based-Assessment Prep

**Review Evidence for a Personal Narrative**
Point out to students that collecting evidence during Independent Learning is the last step in completing their Evidence Log. After they finish their independent reading, they will synthesize all the evidence they have compiled in the unit.

The evidence students collect will serve as the primary source of information they will use to complete the writing and oral presentation for the Performance-Based Assessment at the end of the unit.

Introduce Small-Group Learning — 16
*from* Nature • *from* Self-Reliance — 17, 18
*from* Walden • *from* Civil Disobedience — 19, 20
Media: Innovators and Their Inventions — 21
The Love Song of J. Alfred Prufrock — 22, 23
A Wagner Matinée — 24, 25
Performance Task — 26
Introduce Independent Learning — 27
Independent Learning — 28
Performance-Based Assessment — 29, 30

INDEPENDENT LEARNING

# Sweet Land of . . . Conformity?


## Summary

In this selection, Claude Fischer argues that Americans are not as individualistic as many citizens of European nations. He cites research showing that American individualism is far more complex than it seems. For example, most Americans believe that regardless of the circumstances, people should follow the law and support their country, right or wrong. American individualism shows itself in the belief of some that Americans determine their own fates and that the government should stay out of citizens' personal and economic concerns. Fischer concludes that Americans believe in the freedom of an individual to commit to a group, or not. However, once they do commit, Americans tend to remain loyal even when the group's goals contradict individualistic goals.


## Insight

Reading "Sweet Land of . . . Conformity?" will help students realize that belief in American individuality is a complex matter that often contradicts the ideals and actions of everyday Americans.

SELECTION RESOURCES

- First-Read Guide: Nonfiction
- Close-Read Guide: Nonfiction
- Sweet Land of . . . Conformity?: Text Questions
- Audio Summaries
- Selection Audio
- Selection Test

## Connection to the Essential Question

This selection connects to the Essential Question, "What role does individualism play in American society?" by exploring how the ideal of individualism in American culture may not align with many of the beliefs and practices of its citizens.

## Connection to Performance-Based Assessment

This selection connects to the Performance-Based Assessment prompt, "What significant incident from my past helped me to realize that I am a unique individual?" Students should consider the role individualism and conformity play in their own lives and in the lives of those they know.

### Text Complexity Rubric: Sweet Land of . . . Conformity?

| Quantitative Measures | |
|---|---|
| **Lexile:** 1310 **Text Length:** 1,837 words | |
| **Qualitative Measures** | |
| Knowledge Demands ① ② ③ ❹ ⑤ | Selection deals with the flawed idea of America as individualistic. Contains many subject-specific references (communal voluntarism, collectivism), not all of which are explained. |
| Structure ① ② ❸ ④ ⑤ | The selection is a straightforward third-person essay, which is logically organized, but some connections may be difficult to follow. |
| Language Conventionality and Clarity ① ② ❸ ④ ⑤ | Some sentences in the essay are complex, with quotations and difficult vocabulary. The selection contains references that may need clarification, including *laissez faire* and *soap-box rhetoric*. |
| Levels of Meaning/Purpose ① ② ❸ ④ ⑤ | Selection has only one level of meaning. The main concept and supporting ideas are clearly stated, but the concept may be hard to grasp because of sophisticated language and complex supporting concepts. |

DIGITAL PERSPECTIVES

Audio | Video | Document | Annotation Highlights | EL Highlights | Online Assessment

SELECTION RESOURCES

- First-Read Guide: Nonfiction
- Close-Read Guide: Nonfiction
- Reckless Genius: Text Questions
- Audio Summaries
- Selection Audio
- Selection Test

# Reckless Genius

## Summary

In his essay, "Reckless Genius," Galway Kinnell explains why he considers Emily Dickinson "one of the most intelligent of poets and also one of the most fearless." The poets who wrote at the same time as Dickinson were more conventional, and they did not think that she was an important poet. However, Kinnell says that she was brave and innovative. He says these qualities, along with her reckless abandon of poetic conventions, made her a unique American genius. Kinnell points out that Dickinson's poems offer deep insights into the most valued aspects of life, especially when they are read as a group focused on a particular theme. He argues that Dickinson could not have achieved her greatness without breaking rules in two categories. He says she made new rules for rhyme and rhythm.

## Insight

Reading "Reckless Genius" will help students realize that finding one's individuality often involves breaking conventions of traditional society and accepting the lack of approval these actions may bring.

## Connection to the Essential Question

Galway Kinnell's essay, "Reckless Genius," connects to the Essential Question, "What role does individualism play in American society?" by defending one of America's most famous poets. The text explores how Emily Dickinson's genius resulted, in large part, from her willingness to depart from the poetic conventions of her day.

## Connection to Performance-Based Assessment

This selection connects to the Performance-Based Assessment prompt, "What significant incident from my past helped me to realize that I am a unique individual?" Students may reflect on the role that courage and fearlessness play in creating true originality and individualism.

### Text Complexity Rubric: Reckless Genius

| **Quantitative Measures** | |
|---|---|
| **Lexile:** 1400 **Text Length:** 599 words | |
| **Qualitative Measures** | |
| Knowledge Demands (1–2–**3**–4–5) | The selection will require knowledge of Emily Dickinson's work and includes many poetic references as well as technical terms that are not always explained. |
| Structure (1–2–**3**–4–5) | The selection is a critical analysis and defense of Emily Dickinson's work. The organization is mostly straightforward and conventional. |
| Language Conventionality and Clarity (1–2–**3**–4–5) | The selection has a lot of subject-specific vocabulary, not all of which is defined. Language is often used with figurative power and some sentences are unconventional. |
| Levels of Meaning/Purpose (1–2–**3**–4–5) | The main purpose is clear, but may be hard for some to grasp because of sophisticated language and supporting concepts that are complex. |

# Hamadi

## Summary

In Naomi Shihab Nye's short story, "Hamadi," Susan, a Palestinian teenage girl living in America, discovers her individuality and heritage with the aid of a wise older Arab family friend. Susan feels especially close to the man named Hamadi who lives simply and enjoys books and ideas. Susan invites Hamadi to join her, her friends, and her family as they go out caroling one Christmas holiday to raise money for a charity. While caroling, Susan's friend, Tracy, becomes upset and starts crying over a boy she has a crush on but who is dating another girl. Hamadi, although a stranger to Tracy, offers her comfort and tells her that people find meaning in life by moving on. He advises, "We don't stop where it hurts. We turn a corner. It is the reason why we are living. To turn a corner."

### Insight

Reading "Hamadi" will show students that finding one's individuality involves embracing cultural heritage and seeking knowledge from unexpected sources.

**SELECTION RESOURCES**

- First-Read Guide: Fiction
- Close-Read Guide: Fiction
- Hamadi: Text Questions
- Audio Summaries
- Selection Audio
- Selection Test

## Connection to the Essential Question

Naomi Shahib Nye's short story, connects to the Essential Question, "What role does individualism play in American society?" The story shows how individualism can come from painful, personal experiences.

## Connection to Performance-Based Assessment

This selection connects to the Performance-Based Assessment prompt, "What significant incident from my past helped me to realize that I am a unique individual?" Susan's desire to explore her personal connection with Hamadi enables her to see how caring and wisdom can help a friend transcend a difficult situation and grow as an individual.

### Text Complexity Rubric: Hamadi

| Quantitative Measures | |
|---|---|
| **Lexile:** 790 **Text Length:** 3,128 words | |
| **Qualitative Measures** | |
| Knowledge Demands ①—②—**3**—④—⑤ | Explores complex themes that may be unfamiliar to some (the immigrant experience); explanation is provided for only some of the complex ideas. Background information about Kahlil Gibran may be helpful. |
| Structure ①—②—**3**—④—⑤ | Organization is mostly evident and sequential. |
| Language Conventionality and Clarity ①—②—**3**—④—⑤ | Selection contains figurative language. The syntax includes many complex sentences that have several subordinate clauses or phrases. |
| Levels of Meaning/Purpose ①—②—③—**4**—⑤ | Multiple levels of meaning (events are described that also signify emotions of belonging and alienation); concepts and meanings are not always explained and may be difficult to grasp. |

DIGITAL PERSPECTIVES — Audio | Video | Document | Annotation Highlights | EL Highlights | Online Assessment

SELECTION RESOURCES

- First-Read Guide: Fiction
- Close-Read Guide: Fiction
- Young Goodman Brown: Text Questions
- Audio Summaries
- Selection Audio
- Selection Test

# Young Goodman Brown


## Summary

In Nathaniel Hawthorne's short story, "Young Goodman Brown," the hero says goodbye to his wife Faith before embarking on a mysterious overnight trip. He meets his traveling companion, an older man carrying a walking stick in the form of a black snake. Brown insists that he must return home, but the stranger tells Brown that he has traveled with many of the townspeople over the years. Brown soon realizes that his companion looks like the devil. Upon arriving at a ceremony in the woods, Brown and a cloaked woman are led to the altar. Brown recognizes the woman as Faith and warns her to look to heaven. Immediately, Brown finds himself alone in the woods. When he returns home the next morning, Brown is forever changed.


## Insight

Reading "Young Goodman Brown" may help students understand that ability to stand firm in one's beliefs brings with it personal challenges that may negatively affect one's life on a daily basis.

## Connection to the Essential Question

Nathaniel Hawthorne's short story "Young Goodman Brown" connects to the Essential Question, "What role does individualism play in American society?" by exploring the consequences that rejecting community norms can have on a person's happiness.

## Connection to Performance-Based Assessment

This selection connects to the Performance-Based Assessment prompt, "What significant incident from my past helped me to realize that I am a unique individual?" Goodman Brown's experience has a profoundly negative impact on the way he views the world following the incident described. In the Performance Task, students are free to explore the effects that an important incident had in their life and its relationship to their own sense of individualism.

### Text Complexity Rubric: Young Goodman Brown

| **Quantitative Measures** | |
|---|---|
| **Lexile:** 1210 **Text Length:** 5,240 words | |
| **Qualitative Measures** | |
| Knowledge Demands ①—②—❸—④—⑤ | Unfamiliar and fantastical situation involving a young man's confrontation with evil and subsequent distrust of his family and community. Though students will not be able to relate to their own experiences, the situation and feelings are explained. |
| Structure ①—②—❸—④—⑤ | The selection is a linear story with third-person narrator. |
| Language Conventionality and Clarity ①—②—③—❹—⑤ | Selection contains many long, complex sentences. Selection is written in archaic language style of early-American Puritans, which will be challenging. |
| Levels of Meaning/Purpose ①—②—③—❹—⑤ | The selection is allegorical with complex moral and philosophical themes that are not explicit. |

# ADVISING

You may wish to direct students to use the generic **First-Read** and **Close-Read Guides** in the Print Student Edition. Alternatively, you may wish to print copies of the genre-specific **First-Read** and **Close-Read Guides** for students. These are available online in the Interactive Student Edition or Unit Resources.

## FIRST READ

Students should perform the steps of the first read independently.

NOTICE: Students should focus on the basic elements of the text to ensure they understand what is happening.

ANNOTATE: Students should mark any passages they wish to revisit during their close read.

CONNECT: Students should increase their understanding by connecting what they've read to other texts or personal experiences.

RESPOND: Students will write a summary to demonstrate their understanding.

Point out to students that while they will always complete the Respond step at the end of the first read, the other steps will probably happen somewhat concurrently. Remind students that they will revisit their first-read annotations during the close read.

After students have completed the First-Read Guide, you may wish to assign the Text questions for the selection that are available in the Interactive Teacher's Edition.

### Anchor Standards

In the first two sections of the unit, students worked with the whole class and in small groups to gain topical knowledge and greater understanding of the skills required by the anchor standards. In this section, they are asked to work independently, applying what they have learned and demonstrating increased readiness for college and career.

INDEPENDENT LEARNING

## First-Read Guide

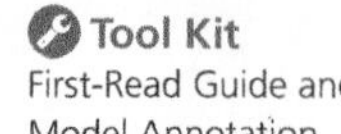


First-Read Guide and Model Annotation

**Use this page to record your first-read ideas.**

**Selection Title:** ______________________________

**NOTICE** new information or ideas you learn about the unit topic as you first read this text.

**ANNOTATE** by marking vocabulary and key passages you want to revisit.

First Read

**CONNECT** ideas within the selection to other knowledge and the selections you have read.

**RESPOND** by writing a brief summary of the selection.



STANDARD

**Reading** Read and comprehend complex literary and informational texts independently and proficiently.



## PERSONALIZE FOR LEARNING

**Strategic Support**

**Text Preview** To help students who struggle to read independently to notice words, passages, and other items that might unlock the meaning of a text, have them first conduct a text preview. Ask them to notice the text's title, visuals, captions, headings, or other text features (including text enclosed in quotation marks, words shown in all capital letters, or the use of different type treatments such as italic or bold). Based on their observations, remind students to speculate on the topic or genre of the text and the author's purpose for writing. Have students meet in small groups to share their preview observations and speculations about the text they will read. After their first read, encourage groups to meet again to discuss how their speculations actually fit the content of the text.

## Close-Read Guide

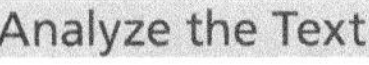
**Tool Kit**
Close-Read Guide and Model Annotation

Use this page to record your close-read ideas.

Selection Title: ____________________

### Close Read the Text

Revisit sections of the text you marked during your first read. Read these sections closely and **annotate** what you notice. Ask yourself **questions** about the text. What can you **conclude?** Write down your ideas.

Close Read — ANNOTATE · QUESTION · CONCLUDE

### Analyze the Text

Think about the author's choices of patterns, structure, techniques, and ideas included in the text. Select one, and record your thoughts about what this choice conveys.

### QuickWrite

Pick a paragraph from the text that grabbed your interest. Explain the power of this passage.



STANDARD
**Reading** Read and comprehend complex literary and informational texts independently and proficiently.



DIGITAL PERSPECTIVES

Students should begin their close read by revisiting the annotations they made during their first read. Then, students should analyze one of the author's choices regarding the following elements:

- **patterns,** such as repetition or parallelism
- **structure,** such as cause-and-effect or problem-solution
- **techniques,** such as description or dialogue
- **ideas,** such as the author's main idea or claim

You may wish to print copies of the Close-Read Guide for students to use.

**MAKE IT INTERACTIVE**
Group students according to the selection they have chosen. Then, have students meet to discuss the selection in depth. Their discussions should be guided by their insights and questions.

## PERSONALIZE FOR LEARNING

### Strategic Support

**Annotations** Reinforce the strategies of close reading for students who struggle with its benefits. After they complete the Close-Read Guide, review the experience. Have students choose a first-read annotation that helped them understand the text more deeply during the close read. Discuss the following questions with students:

- How did a revisit of the first-read annotation help you better understand the text during your close read?
- What did you learn about that passage during the close read? What strategies did you use to study the passage you marked?
- What can you conclude about the text, based on the passage you selected?

Ask for volunteers to discuss how using the First-Read and Close-Read Guides helped them understand the text better.

# ADVISING

## Share Your Independent Learning

### Prepare to Share

Explain to students that sharing what they learned from their Independent Learning selection provides classmates who read a different selection with an opportunity to consider the text as a source of evidence during the Performance-Based Assessment. As students prepare to share, remind them to highlight how their selection contributed to their knowledge of the concept of the individual and society as well as how the selection connects to the question *What role does individualism play in American society?*

### Learn From Your Classmates

As students discuss the Independent Learning selections, direct them to take particular note of how their classmates' chosen selections align with their current position on the Performance-Based Assessment question.

### Reflect

Students may want to add their reflection to their Evidence Log, particularly if their insight relates to a specific selection from the unit.

**Evidence Log** Support students in completing their Evidence Log. This paced activity will help prepare them for the Performance-Based Assessment at the end of the unit.

INDEPENDENT LEARNING

## Share Your Independent Learning

**Prepare to Share**

What role does individualism play in American society?

Even when you read something independently, your understanding continues to grow when you share what you have learned with others. Reflect on the text you explored independently and write notes about its connection to the unit. In your notes, consider why this text belongs in this unit.

EVIDENCE LOG

Go to your Evidence Log and record what you learned from the text you read.

**Learn From Your Classmates**

**Discuss It** Share your ideas about the text you explored on your own. As you talk with your classmates, jot down a few ideas that you learn from them.

**Reflect**

Review your notes, and mark the most important insight you gained from these writing and discussion activities. Explain how this idea adds to your understanding of the concept of individualism.

STANDARDS

**Speaking and Listening**
Initiate and participate effectively in a range of collaborative discussions with diverse partners on grades 11–12 topics, texts, and issues, building on others' ideas and expressing their own clearly and persuasively.





AUTHOR'S PERSPECTIVE **Ernest Morrell, Ph.D.**

**Active Listening and Learning** It's important to support students as they learn and develop the skills of participating in small-group discussions. As students discuss their Independent Learning selection with classmates, remind them that it is important to be an active, but not dominant, participant. Explain that an active participant is one who speaks confidently but also listens carefully to others, while a dominant participant is one who takes over and does not allow others to contribute. Remind students that being an active listener involves these strategies:

PERFORMANCE-BASED ASSESSMENT PREP

## Review Evidence for a Personal Narrative

At the beginning of this unit, you responded to the following question:

**What significant incident helped me realize that I am a unique individual?**

EVIDENCE LOG

Review your Evidence Log and your QuickWrite from the beginning of the unit. Have the texts you read altered your original thoughts about the incident?

| ☐ YES | ☐ NO |
| --- | --- |
| Identify at least three ideas from the texts that have caused you to reevaluate your original idea. | Identify at least three ideas from the texts that reinforced your original idea. |
| 1. | 1. |
| 2. | 2. |
| 3. | 3. |

Develop your thoughts into a topic sentence: *I first became aware of myself as a unique human being when:*

________________________________________

________________________________________

________________________________________

The incident took place:

| WHEN | WHERE | WITH WHOM |
| --- | --- | --- |
| | | |

STANDARDS

**Writing**

Engage and orient the reader by setting out a problem, situation, or observation and its significance, establishing one or multiple point(s) of view, and introducing a narrator and/or characters; create a smooth progression of experiences or events.





DIGITAL PERSPECTIVES

## Review Evidence for a Personal Narrative

**Evidence Log** Students should understand that their ideas about a topic could evolve as they learn more about the subject and are exposed to additional points of view. Point out that just because they took an initial position on the question *What significant incident from my past helped me to realize that I am a unique individual?* doesn't mean that their position can't change after careful consideration of their learning and evidence.

- **Taking notes:** Students who take useful notes capture the speaker's main points and note ideas to contribute once the speaker is done talking.
- **Restating others' ideas to show understanding:** Encourage students to use such language as "This is what I heard you saying . . ." and "I think this is what you meant when you said . . . "
- **Asking clarifying questions:** When they don't understand, or if they want to move the conversation forward, students might ask peers questions like, "Could you explain what you meant when you said . . . ?"

## Writing to Sources: Personal Narrative

Students should complete the Performance-Based Assessment independently, with little to no input or feedback during the process. Students should use word processing software to take advantage of editing tools and features.

Prior to beginning the Assessment, ask students to think about what makes a person unique. Is it a special talent or ability to do something? It is the way a person thinks or relates to others? Or is it something special that a person may contribute to family, friends, or the community in which he or she lives?

**Review the Elements of a Personal Narrative** Students can review the work they did earlier in the unit as they complete the Performance-Based Assessment. They may also consult other resources such as:

- the elements of an effective personal narrative, including a clear point of view, well-developed characters, a smooth sequence of events or experiences, dialogue and description, sensory language, and a reflective conclusion, available in Whole-Class Learning
- their Evidence Log
- their Word Network

Although students will use ideas from unit selections for their personal narrative, they will need to embellish their own experience with precise details of the event and sensory language.

SOURCES

- WHOLE-CLASS SELECTIONS
- SMALL-GROUP SELECTIONS
- INDEPENDENT-LEARNING SELECTION

PART 1

## Writing to Sources: Personal Narrative

In this unit, you read a variety of texts that explore ideas about individuality. Each text, in its own way, sings the praises of nonconformity, independence, and a life of awareness and contemplation.

**Assignment**

Write a **personal narrative** in which you describe an event from your life that answers this question:

> **What significant incident helped me realize that I am a unique individual?**

Choose an incident that you are comfortable describing and sharing with others. Connect your personal experience to ideas expressed in the texts from this unit. Show how your experience illustrates or departs from the ideas these texts express. End with a conclusion about the ways in which the understanding you gained from the incident affects your life today.

**WORD NETWORK**

As you write and revise your personal narrative, use your Word Network to help vary your word choices.

**Reread the Assignment** Review the writing prompt to be sure you fully understand it. The assignment may reference some of the academic words presented at the beginning of the unit. Be sure you understand each of the words in order to complete the assignment correctly.

**Academic Vocabulary**

| | | |
|---|---|---|
| significant | unique | impact |
| incident | sequence | |

**Review the Elements of a Personal Narrative** Before you begin writing, read the Narrative Rubric. Once you have completed your first draft, check it against the rubric. If one or more of the elements is missing or is not as strong as it could be, revise your narrative to add to or strengthen that component.

**STANDARDS**

**Writing**

Write narratives to develop real or imagined experiences or events using effective technique, well-chosen details, and well-structured event sequences.

- Write routinely over extended time frames and shorter time frames for a range of tasks, purposes, and audiences.

## Narrative Rubric

| | Focus and Organization | Evidence and Elaboration | Language Conventions |
|---|---|---|---|
| 4 | The introduction engages the reader and sets the scene for a specific situation.<br>A unique point of view is clearly established and maintained.<br>The events appear in a clear sequence and build toward a particular outcome.<br>The conclusion follows from and reflects on the rest of the narrative. | Dialogue, pacing, reflection, and description adeptly move the narrative forward.<br>Precise details and vivid sensory language give readers a clear picture of events. | The text employs standard English conventions of usage and mechanics consistently and accurately. |
| 3 | The introduction is somewhat engaging and sets the scene for a specific situation.<br>A clear point of view is established and maintained.<br>The events appear in a clear sequence and mostly combine to build toward a particular outcome.<br>The conclusion follows from the rest of the narrative. | Dialogue, reflection, and description move the narrative forward.<br>Precise details and some sensory language give readers a clear picture of events. | The text generally employs standard English conventions of usage and mechanics. |
| 2 | The introduction sets the scene for a specific situation.<br>A point of view is established and maintained, with occasional lapses.<br>The events appear mostly in sequence, although some events may not belong, and some events that would clarify the narrative do not appear.<br>The conclusion follows from the narrative. | Some dialogue, reflection, or description is used in the narrative.<br>Some details and one or two examples of sensory language are included. | The text inconsisently employs standard English conventions of usage and mechanics. |
| 1 | The introduction fails to set a scene or is omitted altogether.<br>The point of view is not always clear.<br>The events do not appear in a clear sequence, and events that would clarify the narrative may not appear.<br>The conclusion does not follow from the narrative or is omitted altogether. | Appropriate narrative techniques such as dialogue, pacing, or reflection, are not used.<br>Details are vague or missing. No sensory language is included. | The text does not employ standard English conventions of usage and mechanics. |





DIGITAL PERSPECTIVES

## Narrative Rubric

As you review the Narrative Rubric with students, remind them that the rubric is a resource that can guide their revisions. Students should pay particular attention to the differences between a narrative that contains all of the required elements (a score of 3) and one that is comprehensive, engaging, and progresses in a logical and thoughtful manner (a score of 4).

PERSONALIZE FOR LEARNING

### Strategic Support

**Sequence** Suggest that students first organize a sequence of events in their narrative. Have them use a timeline to place events in a logical chronological order. As students begin to write their first draft, have them use their outline as a guide. Stress the importance of using transitions to add clarity and cohesion.

## Speaking and Listening: Storytelling

Students should annotate their written narrative in preparation for the oral presentation, marking the important elements (anecdotes, dialogue, and sensory language) as well as details that describe why they are unique individuals.

Remind students that the effectiveness of an oral narrative relies on how the speaker establishes credibility with his or her audience. If a speaker comes across as confident and authoritative, it will be easier for the audience to give credence to the speaker's presentation.

**Review the Storytelling Rubric** As you review the Storytelling Rubric with students, remind them that it is a valuable tool that can help them plan their presentation. They should strive to include all of the criteria required to achieve a score of 3. Draw their attention to some of the subtle differences between scores of 2 and 3.

PERFORMANCE-BASED ASSESSMENT

PART 2

## Speaking and Listening: Storytelling Session

**Assignment**

Even if you have never seen a professional storyteller, you have probably witnessed great storytelling. Stand-up comedians, lecturers, teachers, and other public speakers tell stories that engage, amuse, and instruct listeners. Use the personal narrative you wrote as the basis for an oral **storytelling session.**

Follow these steps to make your storytelling presentation active and interesting.

- Read your personal narrative aloud, and consider ways to make it stronger as an oral piece. You may want to shorten some sections, or add dramatic detail to others. Make those revisions, and then memorize the story.
- Practice your delivery in front of a mirror. Modulate your voice, adding highs and lows, and use gestures that add meaningful emphasis. If you find yourself stumbling over some words, change them. You do not need to stick to the story exactly as it appears on the page.
- As you deliver your story, relax, avoid rushing, and speak with expression.

**Review the Rubric** The criteria by which your storytelling will be evaluated appear in the rubric below. Review the criteria before telling your story to ensure that you are prepared.

STANDARDS

Speaking and Listening

- Present information, findings, and supporting evidence, conveying a clear and distinct perspective, such that listeners can follow the line of reasoning, alternative or opposing perspectives are addressed, and the organization, development, substance, and style are appropriate to purpose, audience, and a range of formal and informal tasks.
- Adapt speech to a variety of contexts and tasks, demonstrating a command of formal English when indicated or appropriate.

| | Content | Presentation Techniques |
|---|---|---|
| 3 | The story has a clear beginning, middle, and end, and the sequence is easy to follow.<br>The story expresses a significant insight in an engaging, entertaining way. | The speaker enunciates clearly and uses an appropriate volume throughout the story.<br>The speaker varies the tone and pace to maintain interest.<br>The speaker uses movement and expression to enliven the performance. |
| 2 | The story has a beginning, middle, and end, and the sequence is mostly easy to follow.<br>The story expresses an insight and is somewhat entertaining or engaging. | The speaker enunciates clearly most of the time and usually uses appropriate volume.<br>The speaker varies the tone and pace to some extent.<br>The speaker uses some movement and expression. |
| 1 | The story does not have a clear beginning, middle, and end, and the sequence is hard to follow.<br>The story does not express an insight and is not engaging. | The speaker does not enunciate clearly and does not use an appropriate volume.<br>The speaker does not vary tone and pace at all.<br>The speaker does not use movement or expression. |



272 UNIT 2 • THE INDIVIDUAL AND SOCIETY

DIGITAL PERSPECTIVES

**Preparing for the Assignment** To help students understand what an effective narrative presentation looks and sounds like, find examples on the Internet of students or adults telling narrative stories about their own personal experiences. Project the examples and have students note the techniques of the speaker (gestures, pacing, tone, and so on). Have students incorporate some of the effective techniques they observe in the clips, for example, humor, tension, drama, and starting with a leading question when telling their own personal story.

## Reflect on the Unit

Now that you've completed the unit, take a few moments to reflect on your learning.

### Reflect on the Unit Goals

Look back at the goals at the beginning of the unit. Use a different colored pen to rate yourself again. Think about readings and activities that contributed the most to the growth of your understanding. Record your thoughts.

### Reflect on the Learning Strategies

**Discuss It** Write a reflection on whether you were able to improve your learning based on your Action Plans. Think about what worked, what didn't, and what you might do to keep working on these strategies. Record your ideas before a class discussion.

### Reflect on the Text

Choose a selection that you found challenging and explain what made it difficult.

Explain something that surprised you about a text in the unit.

Which activity taught you the most about the concept of individualism? What did you learn?

SCAN FOR MULTIMEDIA

**STANDARDS**

**Speaking and Listening**

- Initiate and participate effectively in a range of collaborative discussions with diverse partners on *grades 11–12 topics, texts, and issues,* building on others' ideas and expressing their own clearly and persuasively.
- Come to discussions prepared, having read and researched material under study; explicitly draw on that preparation by referring to evidence from texts and other research on the topic or issue to stimulate a thoughtful, well-reasoned exchange of ideas.



DIGITAL PERSPECTIVES  

## Reflect on the Unit

- Have students watch the video on Reflecting on Your Learning.
- A video on this topic is available online in the Professional Development Center.

### Reflect on the Unit Goals

Students should re-evaluate how well they met the Unit Goals now that they have completed the unit. You might ask them to provide a written commentary on the goal they made the most progress with as well as the goal they feel warrants continued focus.

### Reflect on the Learning Strategies

**Discuss It** If you want to make this a digital activity, go online and navigate to the Discussion Board. Alternatively, students can share their learning strategies reflections in a class discussion.

### Reflect on the Text

Consider having students share their text reflections with one another.

**MAKE IT INTERACTIVE**

Have students prepare a one-minute narrative that summarizes their reflection. Video record group narratives. Then present the videos to the class. Encourage students to ask questions and discuss what they learned about the concept of individualism.

**Unit Test and Remediation** 

After students have completed the Performance-Based Assessment, administer the Unit Test. Based on students' performance on the test, assign the resources as indicated on the Interpretation Guide to remediate. Students who take the test online will be automatically assigned remediation, as warranted by test results.

## PERSONALIZE FOR LEARNING

### English Language Support

**Exchanging Information** Support English Language Learners in exchanging information and ideas by encouraging them to participate in discussions. Give students time to think about how they are going to answer the Reflect on the Text question. Then pair students with a more proficient English speaker. Have students share their answers. To check understanding, ask students to share what their partner said. Have pairs return to their groups and share their ideas. **ALL LEVELS**

VOTES
FOR
WOMEN
MEETING
WE PROTEST
SCHOOL
SEGREGATION
WE PROTEST
SCHOOL
SEGREGATION

UNIT

# Power, Protest, and Change

## A Spirit of Reform

## Jump Start

Start a classroom discussion by presenting this scenario:

"A friend of yours is forming a group that will try to change the rules to give students more of a say in how the school is run. Would you join this group? Why or why not? What kinds of changes might it make? What could the group do to make its position known?"

Have students write down their answers. Then, have volunteers read their responses aloud. Discuss the pros, cons, and feasibility of each of the suggestions.

## Power, Protest, and Change

Ask students what the word *protest* means to them. Tell students that as they work through this unit, they will encounter people, real and fictional, who are protesting various injustices.

## Video

Project the Introduction video in class; ask students to open the video in their interactive textbooks; or have students scan the Bounce Page icon with their phones to access the video.

**Discuss** to make this a digital activity, go online and navigate to the Discussion Board. Alternatively, students can share their responses in class.

### Block Scheduling

Each day in this Pacing Plan represents a 40–50 minute class period. Teachers using block scheduling may combine days to reflect their class schedule. In addition, teachers may revise pacing to differentiate and support core instruction by integrating components and resources as students require.

# Power, Protest, and Change

## A Spirit of Reform

Civil Rights Marches

**Discuss It** Perhaps more than any other country, the United States was founded on dreams people had of shaping the society in which they lived. What were some of those dreams?

**Write your response before sharing your ideas.**

274

SCAN FOR MULTIMEDIA

### Pacing Plan

| Day | Activity |
|---|---|
| 1 | Unit Introduction |
| 2 | Introduce Whole-Class Learning |
| 3 | Historical Perspectives |
| 4–8 | *from* What to the Slave Is the Fourth of July? |
| 9–12 | Second Inaugural Address |
| 13 | Media: Perspectives on Lincoln |
| 14–15 | Performance Task |

WHOLE-CLASS LEARNING (Days 2–15)

DIGITAL PERSPECTIVES

 Audio  Video  Document  Annotation Highlights  EL Highlights | Online Assessment

UNIT 3

## UNIT INTRODUCTION

ESSENTIAL QUESTION: In what ways does the struggle for freedom change with history?

LAUNCH TEXT
INFORMATIVE MODEL
The Zigzag Road to Rights

### WHOLE-CLASS LEARNING

HISTORICAL PERSPECTIVES
*Focus Period: 1850–1890*
Civil War and Social Change

ANCHOR TEXT: SPEECH
*from* What to the Slave Is the Fourth of July?
*Frederick Douglass*

ANCHOR TEXT: SPEECH
Second Inaugural Address
*Abraham Lincoln*

MEDIA: IMAGE GALLERY
Perspectives on Lincoln

PERFORMANCE TASK
WRITING FOCUS:
Write an Informative Essay

### SMALL-GROUP LEARNING

SPEECH
Ain't I a Woman?
*Sojourner Truth*

COMPARE

PUBLIC DOCUMENT
Declaration of Sentiments
*Elizabeth Cady Stanton*

MEDIA: PODCAST
Giving Women the Vote
*Sandra Sleight-Brennan*

SHORT STORY
The Story of an Hour
*Kate Chopin*

COMPARE

LEGAL OPINION
Brown v. Board of Education: Opinion of the Court
*Earl Warren*

MAGAZINE ARTICLE
Was Brown v. Board a Failure?
*Sarah Garland*

PERFORMANCE TASK
SPEAKING AND LISTENING FOCUS:
Hold a Panel Discussion

### INDEPENDENT LEARNING

POETRY COLLECTION 1
The Poetry of Langston Hughes
*Langston Hughes*

POETRY COLLECTION 2
Douglass
*Paul Laurence Dunbar*

The Fifth Fact
*Sarah Browning*

Who Burns for the Perfection of Paper *Martín Espada*

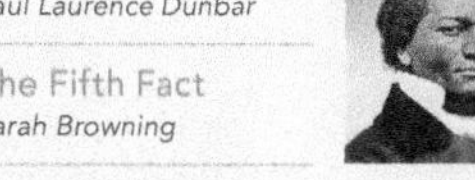

HISTORY
*from* The Warmth of Other Suns
*Isabel Wilkerson*

ESSAY
What a Factory Can Teach a Housewife
*Ida Tarbell*

PERSUASIVE ESSAY
*from* Books as Bombs
*Louis Menand*

MEDIA: PODCAST
A Balance Between Nature and Nurture
*Gloria Steinem*

PERFORMANCE-BASED ASSESSMENT PREP
Review Evidence for an Informative Essay

## PERFORMANCE-BASED ASSESSMENT

Informative Text: Essay and Podcast

PROMPT:
What motivates people to struggle for change?



275

## In what ways does the struggle for freedom change with history?

Introduce the Essential Question and point out that students will respond to related prompts.

- **Whole-Class Learning** *Did the nation achieve the goals that Douglass and Lincoln desired?*
- **Small-Group Learning** *What were the goals of these reformers? Why did they want to achieve those goals?*
- **Performance-Based Assessment** *What motivates people to respond to the need for change?*

### Using Novels With Power, Protest, and Change

Refer to the Using Novels section in this book or online in myPerspectives+ for suggestions on how to incorporate the following thematically related novels into the unit.

- *The Jungle* by Upton Sinclair
- *Invisible Man* by Ralph Ellison
- *Mockingjay* by Suzanne Collins

### Current Perspectives

To increase student engagement, search online for stories related to protests, and invite your students to recommend stories they find. Always preview content before sharing it with your class.

- **Podcast: Weekend Edition Sunday/"Berkeley's Fight for Free Speech Fired Up Student Protest Movement" (NPR)** A look back at the Free Speech Movement at the University of California, Berkeley, on its 50th anniversary
- **News Story: "Top 10 American Protest Movements" (*Time* Magazine)** A history of ten important protest movements

Introduce Small-Group Learning

| 16 | 17 | 18 | 19 | 20 | 21 | 22 | 23 | 24 | 25 | 26 | 27 | 28 | 29 | 30 |
|---|---|---|---|---|---|---|---|---|---|---|---|---|---|---|
| Introduce Small-Group Learning | Ain't I a Woman? | Declaration of Sentiments | | Media: Giving Women the Vote | The Story of an Hour | | Brown v. Board of Education: Opinion of the Court | Was "Brown v. Board" a Failure? | | Performance Task | Introduce Independent Learning | Independent Learning | Performance-Based Assessment | |

## About the Unit Goals

These unit goals were backward designed from the Performance-Based Assessment at the end of the unit and the Whole-Class and Small-Group Performance Tasks. Students will practice and become proficient in many more standards over the course of this unit.

## Unit Goals

Review the goals with students and explain that as they read and discuss the selections in this unit, they will improve their skills in reading, writing, research, language, and speaking and listening.

- Have students watch the video on Goal Setting.
- A video on this topic is available online in the Professional Development Center.

**Reading Goals** Students will examine and evaluate informative texts. They will also read speeches, public documents, fiction, articles, and poems to gain understanding of and insight into the ways writers express ideas.

**Writing and Research Goals** Students will learn the elements of an explanation and then write their own informative essays. They will clarify and explore ideas by conducting research.

**Language Goals** Students will examine how writers use phrases and clauses. They will demonstrate their deeper understanding of these elements in their own writing.

**Speaking and Listening Goals** Explain to students that they will work together to build on one another's ideas, develop consensus, and communicate with one another. They will also learn to incorporate audio, visuals, and text in presentations.

### HOME Connection

A Home Connection letter to students' parents or guardians is available in myPerspectives+. The letter explains what students will be learning in this unit and how they will be assessed.



## Unit Goals

Throughout this unit, you will deepen your perspective on power, protest, and change by reading, writing, speaking, listening, and presenting. These goals will help you succeed on the Unit Performance-Based Assessment.

Rate how well you meet these goals right now. You will revisit your ratings later when you reflect on your growth during this unit.

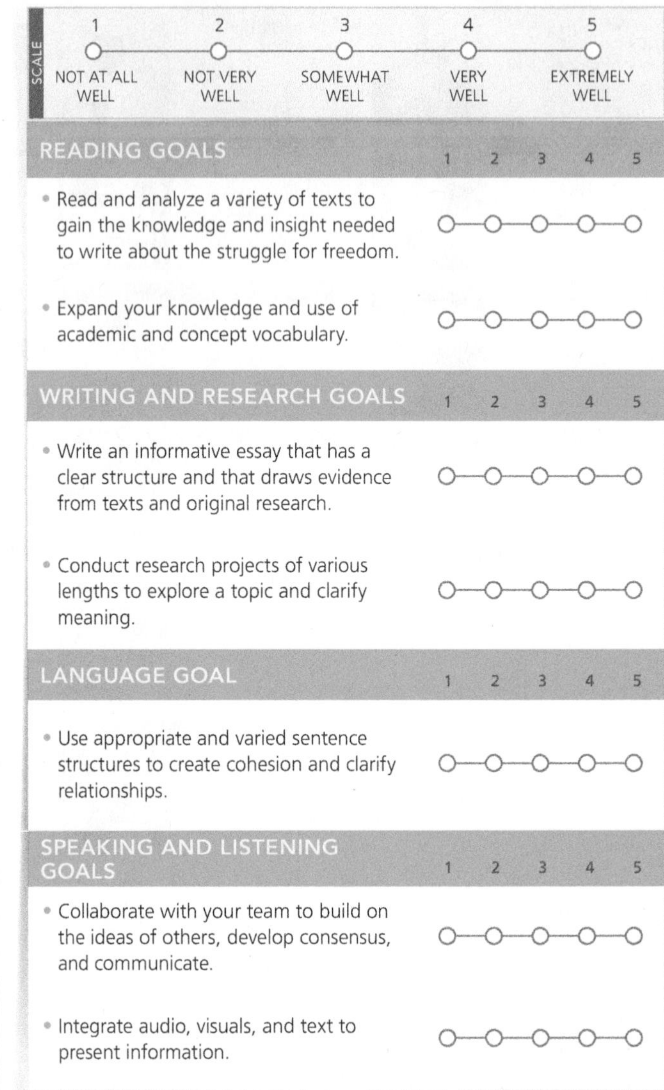

SCALE

| 1 | 2 | 3 | 4 | 5 |
|---|---|---|---|---|
| NOT AT ALL WELL | NOT VERY WELL | SOMEWHAT WELL | VERY WELL | EXTREMELY WELL |

| READING GOALS | 1 | 2 | 3 | 4 | 5 |
|---|---|---|---|---|---|
| • Read and analyze a variety of texts to gain the knowledge and insight needed to write about the struggle for freedom. | O | O | O | O | O |
| • Expand your knowledge and use of academic and concept vocabulary. | O | O | O | O | O |

| WRITING AND RESEARCH GOALS | 1 | 2 | 3 | 4 | 5 |
|---|---|---|---|---|---|
| • Write an informative essay that has a clear structure and that draws evidence from texts and original research. | O | O | O | O | O |
| • Conduct research projects of various lengths to explore a topic and clarify meaning. | O | O | O | O | O |

| LANGUAGE GOAL | 1 | 2 | 3 | 4 | 5 |
|---|---|---|---|---|---|
| • Use appropriate and varied sentence structures to create cohesion and clarify relationships. | O | O | O | O | O |

| SPEAKING AND LISTENING GOALS | 1 | 2 | 3 | 4 | 5 |
|---|---|---|---|---|---|
| • Collaborate with your team to build on the ideas of others, develop consensus, and communicate. | O | O | O | O | O |
| • Integrate audio, visuals, and text to present information. | O | O | O | O | O |

**STANDARDS**

**Language**

Acquire and use accurately general academic and domain-specific words and phrases, sufficient for reading, writing, speaking, and listening at the college and career readiness level; demonstrate independence in gathering vocabulary knowledge when considering a word or phrase important to comprehension or expression.



SCAN FOR MULTIMEDIA 

### AUTHOR'S PERSPECTIVE Ernest Morrell, Ph.D.

**Goal Setting and Identity** Teachers can help to build student responsibility and ownership for their learning, and this work will develop student recognition of the value of setting goals. When students think about their own identity and the future, they need to understand the difference between hoping and planning. They need a strategy for setting goals that will help them become the person they want to be. To support these developing identities, ask students these questions in discussion:

- What does it mean to think of yourself as a powerful speaker and presenter? What would that look like?
- What goals can you set to develop these skills?
- These skills are critical to your success in the next stage of your life, whether that is college or the workplace. What steps can you take to develop these skills as you finish high school?

## Academic Vocabulary: Informative Text

Academic terms appear in all subjects and can help you read, write, and discuss with precision and clarity. Here are five academic words that will be useful to you in this unit as you analyze and write informative texts.

**Complete the chart.**

1. Review each word, its root, and the mentor sentences.
2. Use the information and your own knowledge to predict the meaning of each word.
3. For each word, list at least two related words.
4. Refer to a dictionary or other resources if needed.

TIP

FOLLOW THROUGH
Study the words in this chart, and mark them or their forms wherever they appear in the unit.

| WORD | MENTOR SENTENCES | PREDICT MEANING | RELATED WORDS |
|---|---|---|---|
| informational<br><br>ROOT:<br>***-form-***<br>"shape"; "image" | 1. This *informational* pamphlet tells about the history of the village.<br>2. The students found the remarks both *informational* and inspirational. | | inform; informative; uninformed; misinformed |
| inquire<br><br>ROOT:<br>***-quir-/-quer-***<br>"ask" | 1. If you want to find out why your application was denied, you must *inquire.*<br>2. In my research, I *inquire* about the reasons for certain social customs. | | |
| verbatim<br><br>ROOT:<br>***-verb-***<br>"word" | 1. The actor knew the script so well that he could quote it *verbatim.*<br>2. The witness's ability to give a *verbatim* account persuaded the jury that her memory was reliable. | | |
| deduction<br><br>ROOT:<br>***-duc-***<br>"lead" | 1. The astronomer's *deduction* was based on years of observation.<br>2. The writer presented the objective facts and then shared his *deduction* from them. | | |
| specific<br><br>ROOT:<br>***-spec-***<br>"sort"; "kind" | 1. Your report topic is too broad; find one that is more *specific.*<br>2. Was there one *specific* event that caused the war, or were there many? | | |





DIGITAL PERSPECTIVES 

## Academic Vocabulary: Informative Essay

Direct students' attention to the academic vocabulary words in the chart. Remind them that clues to a word's meaning can be found in its root. Discuss the mentor sentences and ensure that students grasp each word's usage. Mentor sentences also provide context to help students predict the meaning of each word. Check students' charts to be sure they are complete and correct. Complete pronunciations, parts of speech, and definitions are provided for you. Students are expected to provide only the definitions.

**Possible responses:**

**informational** *adj.* (ihn furhr MAY shuhn uhl)
**Meaning:** providing facts, details, or knowledge
**Related words:** inform, informative
**Additional words related to the root *-form-*:** uninformed, misinformed

**inquire** *v.* (ihn KWYR)
**Meaning:** to ask for information
**Related words:** inquirer, inquiringly
**Additional words related to the roots *-quir-* or *-quer-*:** inquiry, inquisition

**verbatim** *adv.* (vuhr BAY tihm)
**Meaning:** in the exact words; exactly
**Related words:** verbal, verbally
**Additional words related to the root *-verb-*:** verbalism, verbalize

**deduction** *n.* (dih DUK shuhn)
**Meaning:** the process of using reason or logic to come to a conclusion or form an opinion
**Related words:** deduct, deductively
**Additional words related to the root *-duc-*:** induction, reduction

**specific** *adj.* (spuh SIHF ihk)
**Meaning:** detailed; clearly defined
**Related words:** specifics, specifically
**Additional words related to the root *-spec-*:** specify, species

### PERSONALIZE FOR LEARNING

**English Language Support**
**Provide Context** Students may not have experience with all of the Academic Vocabulary words or their related forms. If needed, provide additional examples of related words. Work with students to construct context sentences for these words. Point out the parts of speech of the related words. For example, *inform* is a verb, *information* is a noun, and *informational* is an adjective related to that noun. **ALL LEVELS**

# INTRODUCTION

## Purpose of the Launch Text

The Launch Text provides students with a common starting point to address the unit topic. After reading the Launch Text, all students will be able to participate in discussions about power, protest, and change.

**Lexile: 1160L** The easier reading level of this selection makes it perfect to assign for homework. Students will need little or no support to understand it.

Additionally, "The Zigzag Road to Rights" provides a writing model for the Performance-Based Assessment students will complete at the end of the unit.

## Launch Text: Informative Essay Model

Remind students that they will be writing an informative essay. While its topic will be different from that of "The Zigzag Road to Rights," this model gives students insight into this type of writing.

Tell students to notice the structure of the text. They will see that, except for in the introductory and summary paragraphs, the author discusses events in the order in which they occurred, from 1776 to 1965.

Encourage students to read this text on their own and annotate unfamiliar words and sections of text they think are particularly important.

### AUDIO SUMMARIES

Audio summaries of "The Zigzag Road to Rights" are available online in both English and Spanish in the Interactive Teacher's Edition or Unit Resources. Assigning these summaries before students read the Launch Text may help them build additional background knowledge and set a context for their reading.



LAUNCH TEXT | INFORMATIVE MODEL

This selection is an example of an **informative text,** a type of writing in which an author examines concepts through the careful selection, organization, and analysis of information. This is the type of writing you will develop in the Performance-Based Assessment at the end of the unit.

**As you read,** think about how the information is shared. Mark the text to help you answer this question: How does the writer help readers understand the main point of the essay?

# The Zigzag Road to Rights

NOTES

1 When we look back at history, we often like to identify trends. Viewing the big picture, we may see a steady push toward progress. However, every fight for rights involves a series of advances and setbacks. The struggle for equal recognition of African Americans demonstrates a zigzag road to rights.

2 The push-and-pull of this struggle was evident at the birth of the nation. In his original draft of the Declaration of Independence, Thomas Jefferson included a strong condemnation of slavery, protesting this "cruel war against human nature." Jefferson wanted the Declaration of Independence to grant freedom to all men. However, at the Continental Congress in 1776, both northern and southern slaveholders objected to any mention of African American rights. Powerful indeed was their pressure. Any mention of slavery was deleted from the Declaration.

3 Although the removal of Jefferson's antislavery paragraph was a severe setback, reformers did not give up hope. With the ratification of the Constitution, they gained an important tool for change. Article V describes the conditions required for amending the Constitution. Laws can be changed, and rights can be gained.

4 The struggle took another crucial step forward in 1863, when President Abraham Lincoln issued the Emancipation Proclamation. It asserted that "all persons held as slaves" within states that had seceded from the Union "are, and henceforward shall be, free." Still, freedom for slaves depended upon a Union victory. Slavery remained legal in border states loyal to the Union, as well as in Confederate areas under Northern control.



SCAN FOR MULTIMEDIA 

## PERSONALIZE FOR LEARNING

### Strategic Support

**Create a Timeline** Have students create a timeline that includes both the progress made toward equal recognition of African Americans and the challenges and setbacks they faced. Direct students to place events that supported the struggle above the timeline. Setbacks should be placed below the timeline. This will help create a visual representation of "The Zigzag Road to Rights."

5 The hope of change promised by Article V paid off in 1865. Congress passed the Thirteenth Amendment, abolishing slavery in the United States. "Neither slavery nor involuntary servitude . . . shall exist within the United States, or any place subject to their jurisdiction." The next two amendments, adopted in 1868 and 1870, made African Americans citizens and gave them the right to vote. The expanded Constitution reflects a nation willing to change.

6 Yet these significant advances did not guarantee full rights for black Americans, as evidenced by a landmark decision by the Supreme Court in 1896. In the case of *Plessy v. Ferguson*, seven of eight Supreme Court justices voted in support of Louisiana's Separate Car Act, which made it illegal for blacks to travel in trains reserved for white passengers. This decision set an important legal precedent: "Separate, but equal" facilities were constitutional.

7 That decision was eventually reversed in 1954, when the Supreme Court issued a unanimous decision in the case of *Brown v. Board of Education*. Finding that "separate educational facilities are inherently unequal," the decision promised an end to segregation. Once again, progress toward equal rights surged forward.

8 Nonetheless, no single case, law, or amendment could instantly erase the long tradition of prejudice and inequality. For example, even though the Fifteenth Amendment guaranteed African Americans the right to vote, state and local laws and policies often kept black Americans from voting through tactics such as poll taxes, voter registration exams, and intimidation. These strategies were outlawed by the Voting Rights Act of 1965.

9 The history of African American rights features many crucial victories, from the Emancipation Proclamation through the Voting Rights Act. However, the record of the struggle also includes the difficult stumbling blocks that have had to be overcome. While the path to progress is not smooth, one thing is certain: The zigzag will continue into the future. History teaches us that rights gained can be lost, curtailed, or ignored—and perhaps gained once more. ❧

NOTES

### WORD NETWORK FOR POWER, PROTEST, AND CHANGE

**Vocabulary** A Word Network is a collection of words related to a topic. As you read the unit selections, identify words related to the idea of struggle, and add them to your Word Network. You might begin with words from the Launch Text, such as *setbacks*. For each word you identify, add a related word. Continue to add words as you complete this unit.

**Tool Kit**
Word Network Model

STRUGGLE

setbacks | impediments





DIGITAL PERSPECTIVES 

## Word Network for Power, Protest, and Change

Tell students that they can fill in the Word Network as they read the texts in the unit, or they can record the words elsewhere and add them later. Point out to students that people may have personal associations with some words. A word that one student thinks is related to the concept of power, protest, and change might not be a word another student would pick. However, students should feel free to add any word they personally think is relevant to their Word Network. Each person's Word Network will be unique. If you choose to print the Word Network, distribute it to students at this point so they can use it throughout the rest of the unit.

AUTHOR'S PERSPECTIVE **Elfrieda Hiebert, Ph.D.**

**Using a Digital Thesaurus** As students work to develop and expand their Word Networks about the concept of struggle, introduce them to the Digital Vocabulary Tools available to them. In addition to providing synonyms that will help students grow their vocabulary, many online thesauruses also allow the user to sort the words by complexity. For example, synonyms for the word *resistance* include *fight, battle, refusal, struggle, contention, hindrance,* and *impediment.* When the words are sorted to reveal the most complex synonyms, however, only *impediment* remains. This feature can enable students to learn more complex words that they may not be exposed to regularly. Help students to see the limits of a thesaurus by reminding them that although the words in a Word Network may be linked by the concept, they have subtle differences in meaning and cannot necessarily be substituted for one another in a sentence.

# INTRODUCTION

## Summary

Have students read the introductory paragraph. Provide them with tips for writing a summary:

- Write in the present tense.
- Make sure to include the title of the work.
- Be concise: A summary should not be equal in length to the original text.
- If you need to quote the words of the author, use quotation marks.
- Don't put your own opinions, ideas, or interpretations into the summary. The purpose of writing a summary is to accurately represent what the author says, not to provide a critique. If necessary, students can refer to the Tool Kit for help in understanding the elements of a good summary.

**See possible summary on the Student page.**

## Launch Activity

Tell students that they will have many opportunities to discuss power, protest, and change as they work their way through this unit.

Explain that there are no right or wrong answers in this activity. The goal is to arrive at a consensus that reflects, as much as possible, the views of everyone in the class. Encourage students to express their opinions clearly and to respect the opinions of others.

Note that the process suggested in the Launch Activity builds toward actually composing a focus statement together with selected and precise words.



## Summary

Write a summary of "The Zigzag Road to Rights." Remember that a **summary** is a concise, complete, and accurate overview of a text. It should contain neither opinion nor analysis.

**Possible response:** In the informative text "The Zigzag Road to Rights," the author presents the highs and lows of the struggle for equal recognition of African Americans. She presents, in chronological order, both the triumphs and the setbacks of the movement.

In the 1700s, Thomas Jefferson condemned slavery, but other members of the Constitutional Convention didn't allow his protest into the Declaration of Independence.

The Emancipation Proclamation freed slaves only in states that had joined the Confederacy. Even the passage of the Thirteenth Amendment did not give African Americans full rights.

It was still constitutional to have "separate but equal" facilities. This was reversed in 1954, but the struggle isn't over. There may be many obstacles to overcome in the future.

## Launch Activity

**Draft a Focus Statement** Complete this focus statement: The struggle for freedom is __________, __________, and __________.

- Working individually, choose three words or phrases to complete the statement. Write each one on a separate sticky note.
- Place everyone's sticky notes on a board where they can be seen. Then, work together to group words or phrases that are synonyms or that are otherwise closely related.
- Again working individually, decide which three words or phrases you think best complete the focus statement. Place a tally mark on each sticky note that lists one of your choices.
- As a class, use the tally results to create a single focus statement. Identify the words or phrases that received the most votes. Then, discuss whether those three words or phrases create the strongest statement.
- Once the class has selected three words or phrases, discuss how the order in which they are placed affects the meaning of the focus statement. Choose the best order, and finish the statement.





PERSONALIZE FOR LEARNING

**English Language Support**

**Adjectives** Students may need support to understand the focus question, *What characterizes any struggle for freedom?* Rephrase the question to clarify its meaning. For example, *What words describe a struggle for freedom? Is it difficult or easy to fight for freedom? (difficult)* Guide students to use the adjectives to complete the focus statement. For example, *The struggle for freedom is ____ (difficult). What other adjectives can we use?* **ALL LEVELS**

## QuickWrite

Consider class discussions, the video, and the Launch Text as you think about the prompt. Record your first thoughts here.

PROMPT: **What motivates people to struggle for change?**

**Possible response:** I think that people want to be treated fairly. In addition, many people are made uncomfortable when they see other people treated unfairly. People seem to be motivated to struggle for change by this uncomfortable feeling. People can also be motivated to struggle for change by a desire to be safe. When people feel as if they and their families are at risk, they are willing to do almost anything to protect those that they love.

### EVIDENCE LOG FOR POWER, PROTEST, AND CHANGE

Review your QuickWrite. Summarize your initial position in one sentence in your Evidence Log. Then, record evidence from "The Zigzag Road to Rights" that supports your position.

After each selection, you will continue to use your Evidence Log to record the evidence you gather and the connections you make. The graphic shows what your Evidence Log looks like.

Title of Text: ______ Date: ______

| CONNECTION TO PROMPT | TEXT EVIDENCE/DETAILS | ADDITIONAL NOTES/IDEAS |
|---|---|---|
| | | |

How does this text change or add to my thinking? Date: ______

**Tool Kit**
Evidence Log Model

SCAN FOR MULTIMEDIA



DIGITAL PERSPECTIVES  

## QuickWrite

In this QuickWrite, students should present their own response to the prompt based on the material they have read and viewed in the Unit Overview and Introduction. This initial response will help inform their work when they complete the Performance-Based Assessment at the end of the unit. Students should make sure they present their position clearly and support it with well-reasoned evidence and accurate details.

**See possible QuickWrite on the Student page.**

## Evidence Log for The Power, Protest, and Change

Students should record their initial position in their Evidence Logs along with evidence from "The Zigzag Road to Rights" that supports this position.

If you choose to print the Evidence Log, distribute it to students at this point so they can use it throughout the rest of the unit.

### Performance-Based Assessment: Refining Your Thinking

- Have students watch the video on Refining Your Thinking.
- A video on this topic is available online in the Professional Development Center.

### PERSONALIZE FOR LEARNING

**Strategic Support**

**Breaking Down the Assignment** Help students deconstruct the QuickWrite prompt into smaller prompts. For example, ask them to think about what motivated the civil rights marchers. (See paragraph 8 as an example.) How did the lack of equality affect their day-to-day lives?

# OVERVIEW

## WHOLE-CLASS LEARNING

### In what ways does the struggle for freedom change with history?

Lead students in a brief discussion about freedom, including physical freedom, political freedom, and economic freedom. Use specific examples from today to make these needs real to students. Be sure to touch on times in the history of the United States when some or all of its people were not free.

### Whole-Class Learning Strategies

Review the Learning Strategies with students.

- Have students watch the video on Whole-Class Learning Strategies.
- A video on this topic is available online in the Professional Development Center.

You may wish to discuss some action items to add to the chart as a class. For example, for "Monitor understanding," suggest that students:

- Ask clarifying questions.
- Take notes and jot down interesting or thought-provoking points.

OVERVIEW: WHOLE-CLASS LEARNING

ESSENTIAL QUESTION:

## In what ways does the struggle for freedom change with history?

As you read these selections, work with your whole class to explore the struggle for freedom.

**From Text to Topic** For Frederick Douglass, the struggle for freedom meant a perilous escape from slavery. For Abraham Lincoln, it meant waging war against his fellow citizens. The issue of slavery polarized the country before the Civil War. As you read, consider what the selections show about the struggle for freedom during the Focus Period—and its relationship to our ideas of freedom today.

### Whole-Class Learning Strategies

Throughout your life, in school, in your community, and in your career, you will continue to learn and work in large-group environments.

Review these strategies and the actions you can take to practice them as you work with your whole class. Add ideas of your own for each step. Get ready to use these strategies during Whole-Class Learning.

| STRATEGY | ACTION PLAN |
|---|---|
| Listen actively | • Eliminate distractions. For example, put your cellphone away.<br>• Record brief notes on main ideas and points of confusion.<br>• |
| Clarify by asking questions | • If you're confused, other people probably are, too. Ask a question to help your whole class.<br>• Ask follow-up questions as needed; for example, if you do not understand the clarification or if you want to make an additional connection.<br>• |
| Monitor understanding | • Notice what information you already know and be ready to build on it.<br>• Ask for help if you are struggling.<br>• |
| Interact and share ideas | • Share your ideas and offer answers, even if you are unsure of them.<br>• Build on the ideas of others by adding details or making a connection.<br>• |



SCAN FOR MULTIMEDIA



### Block Scheduling

Each day in this Pacing Plan represents a 40–50 minute class period. Teachers using block scheduling may combine days to reflect their class schedule. In addition, teachers may revise pacing to differentiate and support core instruction by integrating components and resources as students require.

### Pacing Plan

| Day | Activity |
|---|---|
| 1 | Unit Introduction |
| 2 | Introduce Whole-Class Learning |
| 3 | Historical Perspectives |
| 4–8 | *from* What to the Slave Is the Fourth of July? |
| 9–12 | Second Inaugural Address |
| 13 | Media: Perspectives on Lincoln |
| 14–15 | Performance Task |

WHOLE-CLASS LEARNING (Days 2–15)

DIGITAL PERSPECTIVES

CONTENTS



Overview: Whole-Class Learning 283



## Contents

**Anchor Texts** Generate interest in the upcoming selections by previewing the anchor texts. Ask students to describe any movies, television shows, videos, or songs they know of that deal with the struggle for freedom.

Ask student volunteers to say which selection they think seems most interesting and to explain why. After students have completed the readings, you may want to ask them if their earlier assessments still hold true.

## Performance Task

**Write an Informative Essay** Tell students that when they finish reading the selections, they will write an informative essay about the goals that Frederick Douglass and Abraham Lincoln had for their country. Encourage them to keep that topic in mind as they read the selections, jot down their ideas, and participate in the Whole-Class Learning experience.

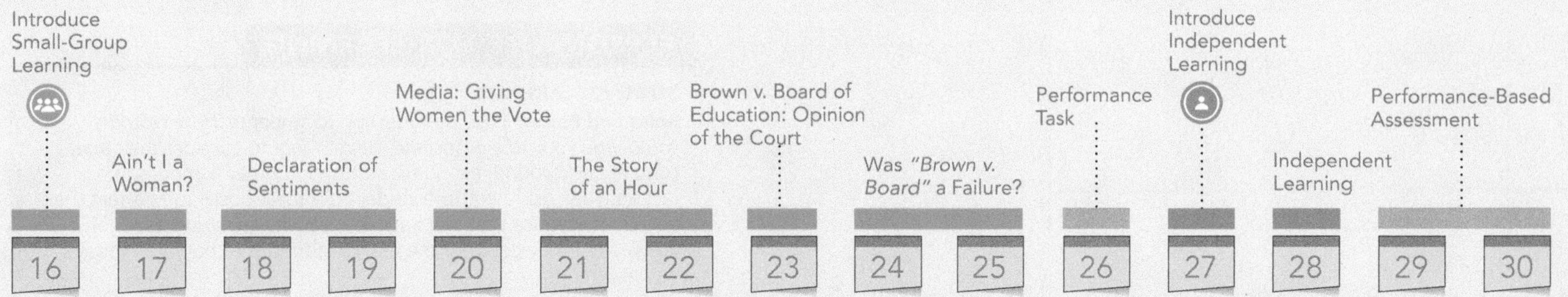

# TEACHING

## Historical Perspectives

This section analyzes the events of the Focus Period: the words of key people during slavery and the Civil War, expansion into the frontier, the Seneca Falls Convention on women's rights, reforms in public education and the justice system, and industrialization. Have students connect these key events with the unit topic.

## History of the Period

Explain what is meant by the observation that as experience shapes individuals, experience also shapes nations. Ask students if they agree, and ask them to support their opinion with examples. Events between 1850 and 1890 changed the laws, the government, and the American people. Have groups discuss this question: How did events such as the Civil War and the expansion into the frontier make it possible for the United States and its people to grow and mature?

Social justice was a highly contentious issue during the period 1850–1890. Slavery was debated without resolution; the union of the country broke down, North against South; and discord devolved into Civil War. Ask students to discuss why they think resolving the question of slavery was of ultimate importance to the future of the United States and its people.

The voices include an author, a president, and an abolitionist. Ask students what common goal these leaders shared. How did their roles for implementing these goals differ? Discuss what students believe are the lasting influences of these three people.



# Civil War and Social Change

## Voices of the Period

"*. . . I would write something that would make this whole nation feel what an accursed thing slavery is.*"

—Harriet Beecher Stowe, author of *Uncle Tom's Cabin*

"*In your hands, my dissatisfied fellow countrymen, and not in mine, is the momentous issue of civil war. The government will not assail you. . . . You have no oath registered in heaven to destroy the government, while I shall have the most solemn one to 'preserve, protect, and defend' it.*"

—Abraham Lincoln, President of the United States from 1861 to 1865

"*Those who profess to favor freedom, and yet deprecate agitation, are men who want crops without plowing up the ground. They want rain without thunder and lightning. They want the ocean without the awful roar of its many waters. This struggle may be a moral one, or it may be a physical one, or it may be both moral and physical, but it must be a struggle. Power concedes nothing without a demand. It never did and it never will.*"

—Frederick Douglass, abolitionist

## History of the Period

**Dreams of Shaping Society** More than any other nation, the United States was founded on dreams people had of shaping the society in which they lived. The Puritans who colonized New England came to build a new society, a society in which they could freely practice their religion. Some 150 years later, the American revolutionaries wrote a constitution that gave citizens powerful tools to continue reshaping society—tools such as freedom of speech and an elected, representative government. With these tools, citizens could change the course of the country.

**The Crisis of Slavery** By 1850, though, the question of whether those tools were enough became grave. About 88 percent of the African Americans in the country—approximately 14 percent of the nation's total population—were enslaved: treated as property, forced to work for others, torn in many cases from their own families, and subject to various other abuses and cruelties. Many in the nation cried out for change, but the economy of the South depended on the use of enslaved African Americans for labor. When challenged, many in the South rallied to the defense of the institution.

In the North, industry was replacing agriculture as the motor of the economy. Northern states had begun passing antislavery laws in the eighteenth century, and by 1850 slavery had all but vanished in the North. Critics of slavery were becoming

### TIMELINE

1850

**1850: China** Taiping Rebellion begins.

**1852:** Harriet Beecher Stowe's *Uncle Tom's Cabin* is published.

**1857:** In the *Dred Scott* decision, the U.S. Supreme Court rules that people of African descent cannot become U.S. citizens.

**1859:** John Brown, an abolitionist, leads a raid on the federal arsenal at Harpers Ferry, Virginia.

**1860:** Abraham Lincoln is elected president.

**1861:** The Civil War begins with Confederate forces firing on Fort Sumter, South Carolina.





### PERSONALIZE FOR LEARNING

**Strategic Support**

**Roles and Power** Pose this question to students: *How would you define your role in society?* Guide them to consider their age, cultural background, economic status, and other demographic factors. Then ask them to consider how these social roles affect their power to advance their own agenda. Finally, ask students to jot down what they consider the main institutions of power in today's world.

## Integration of Knowledge and Ideas

**Notebook** What does the information shown in these charts help you understand about differences between the North and South in their economies, population densities, and overall lifestyles? How do you think these differences affected the outcome of the Civil War?

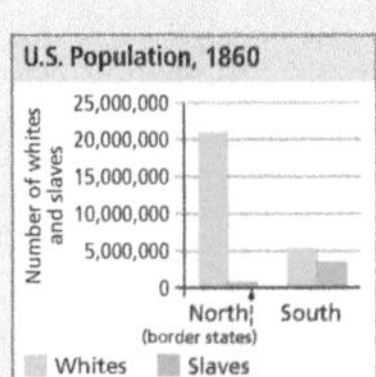


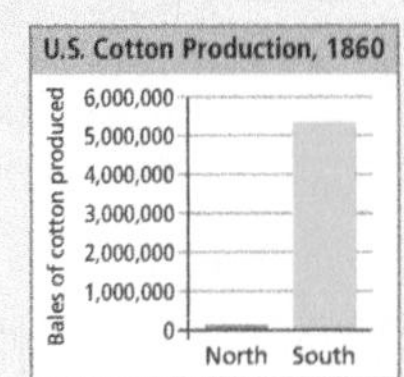


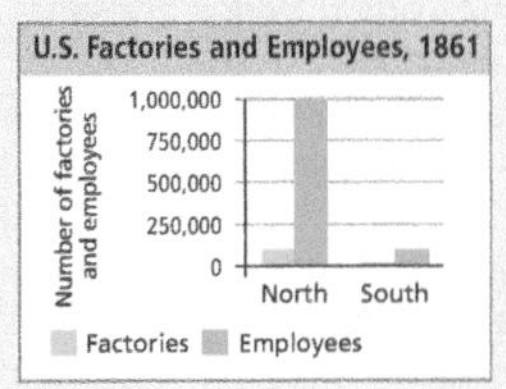


vocal in their opposition, with abolitionists campaigning against slavery and assisting runaway slaves.

**Civil War** When Abraham Lincoln was elected president in 1860, the divisions between North and South only sharpened. Beginning with South Carolina in 1860, 11 Southern states seceded (separated) from the United States. In 1861, the Civil War began, pitting North against South. After years of suffering and devastation, the North won the war in 1865. This victory set the nation's future course, for it decided the issue of slavery: No longer would anyone be enslaved in the United States. In addition, it made clear the fact that the centers of economic influence in the country had shifted from the agricultural South to the industrial North. Finally, it confirmed the strength of the country's central government in relation to the states.

**Expansion and Progress** Before the Civil War, the country had been busily expanding, adding new territories and states as settlers pushed west, seeking land. After the war, the country continued to grow at a furious pace. Settlers continued to move west, forcing Native Americans from their lands. Immigrants flooded the nation's cities, providing labor. For the first time, electricity was being used on a large scale for everything from city lights to factory machines. The nation began linking frontiers to cities with railway tracks and telegraph wires.

**Reform Movements** While forces such as westward expansion and immigration were reshaping the nation, reformers were attempting to transform society. Pioneers such as Horace



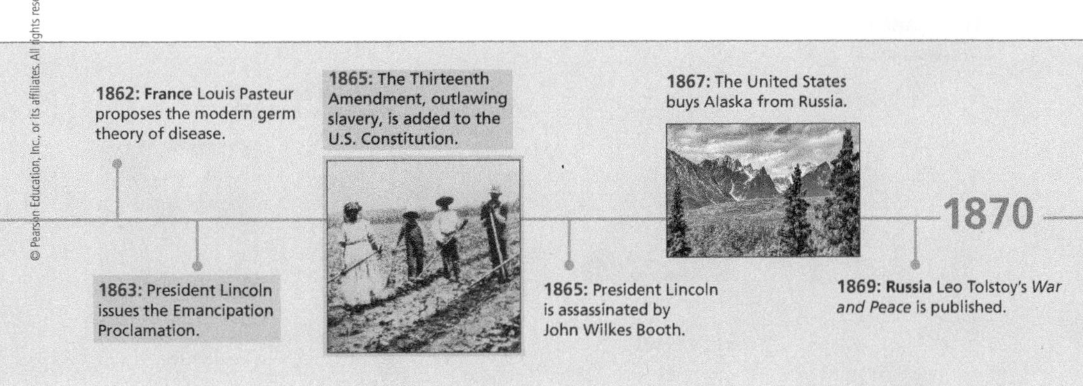

1862: France Louis Pasteur proposes the modern germ theory of disease.
1863: President Lincoln issues the Emancipation Proclamation.
1865: The Thirteenth Amendment, outlawing slavery, is added to the U.S. Constitution.
1865: President Lincoln is assassinated by John Wilkes Booth.
1867: The United States buys Alaska from Russia.
1869: Russia Leo Tolstoy's War and Peace is published.
1870




DIGITAL PERSPECTIVES

## Integration of Knowledge and Ideas

Have students analyze the data in each chart and draw conclusions to answer the two questions.

**Possible response:** The North had many more people than the South—with many more white people and far fewer slaves than the South. This gave the North the advantage of having more non-slave-owning white people from which to form and maintain an army to fight against slave-owners and other white Southerners who were in favor of slavery. More people worked in factories in the North than in the South, so the standard of living was probably better for more Northerners than Southerners because so many Northerners were regular wage earners. The larger number of factories in the North would also have helped the North manufacture and maintain equipment and weapons needed to fight the war. These factors, among many others, helped the North win the war over the South.

## Timeline

Tell students to examine the 1850–1890 Timeline, and to reflect on the key events. Encourage a discussion by asking students how and why similar events might have taken place in different parts of the world over the same period. Ask students if this might suggest any similarities or differences among the lives people may have led in the United States, China, France, and Russia.

PERSONALIZE FOR LEARNING

### English Language Support

**Verb Tense** Have students examine the verbs in the timeline: are these verbs in the past or the present tense? Identify them as present tense. Point out that for timeline entries, verbs can be in the present tense even though they are about events in the past. For each event on the timeline, have students change the tense of the verb from present to past, helping them as needed with irregular verb forms. Then ask students to make statements in the past tense for each entry. For example: In 1867, the United States bought Alaska from Russia.

# TEACHING

## History of the Period

Have students focus on the last paragraph of the text, "A Legacy of Protest," and remind them that history is an unfolding story. Point out that the triumphs and failures of the past are connected to both the present and the future. Encourage a discussion by asking students the following question: *How did the fight for justice and freedom, especially for African Americans and women, lay the groundwork for the lives you and the people you know live today?*

Ask students to choose to be in one of three groups: African Americans, women, or workers. Translate how each group might address the general term "social justice" in their specific group's fight for equal rights in history and today.

## HISTORICAL PERSPECTIVES • FOCUS PERIOD: 1850–1890

Mann championed public education. Other activists pushed forward reforms of the justice system, leading to the development of the modern prison. During this period, women also began pursuing political and economic rights equal to men's.

**A Historic Convention** In the years around 1850, women were discouraged from playing most major roles in public life. Their rights to property were limited. In addition, women did not yet have the right to vote. In 1848, Elizabeth Cady Stanton and Lucretia Mott helped organize the Seneca Falls Convention, which met to discuss women's rights. There, Stanton introduced a resolution to pursue the right to vote for women. With the support of Frederick Douglass, a former slave and an active abolitionist, the resolution passed.

**The Movement for Women's Rights** Reformers such as Stanton, Mott, and Susan B. Anthony campaigned vigorously for women's rights. Their tactics included lobbying politicians, holding public lectures, publishing newspapers, picketing, and marching.

**Social Progress** Some reforms were seen at the time. Even before the Seneca Falls Convention, some states had passed laws giving women the right to their own property, although their husbands still had the right to manage shared property.

Some states, including ones newly added to the Union, passed laws allowing women to vote. The right to vote was not granted to women nationwide, however, until the ratification of the Nineteenth Amendment to the Constitution in 1920.

**A Nation Comes of Age** In the decades from 1850 to 1914, the United States grew from a largely agricultural society into a modern industrial giant. During this time, important issues such as the freedom of African Americans, the rights of women, and the rights of workers were discussed and argued. In the end, the society of the United States was reshaped, not just by reformers, but by forces such as war, technological progress, and economic development. These forces laid the foundations of the nation we know today.

**A Legacy of Protest** The issues of power and change raised during the period were not resolved once and for all, however. Even though slavery had been abolished, injustices against African Americans continued. New eras of protest were born in the effort to end racial discrimination. Women's lives had generally improved but voting equality was still an unachieved goal, and other forms of inequality continued to reign. Protests continued. The literature in this unit tells of the ongoing struggle for social justice.

### TIMELINE

1870

**1872:** Susan B. Anthony is arrested for trying to vote in a presidential election.

**1874: France** Claude Monet gathers Impressionist painters for their first exhibit.

**1876:** Baseball's National League is founded.

**1876:** Alexander Graham Bell patents the telephone.

**1877:** The Reconstruction Era ends in the South.

**1879:** Thomas Edison invents a practical electric light.





## PERSONALIZE FOR LEARNING

### Strategic Support

**Historical Timelines** Using the timeline for reference, open a discussion about historical timelines with a prompt that sparks discussion. *Timelines do much more than show a sequence of events. Can anyone name some of the other things they show?* Accept all reasonable answers that point to an understanding of patterns. Examples should include telling a story (progression of events), showing how events influence future events (cause and effect), and showing how prevailing themes and struggles play out simultaneously across cultures (recognition of trends).

Have learners of different abilities work in pairs to analyze the timeline. Ask the partners to identify some of the patterns on the timeline. Remind them that they should focus on the relationships between the events.

## Literature Selections

**Literature of the Focus Period** Several of the selections in this unit were written during the Focus Period and pertain to the deep conflicts of the era over power and change:

from "What to the Slave Is the Fourth of July?" Frederick Douglass

Second Inaugural Address, Abraham Lincoln

"Ain't I a Woman?" Sojourner Truth

Declaration of Sentiments, Elizabeth Cady Stanton

"The Story of an Hour," Kate Chopin

"Douglass," Paul Laurence Dunbar

**Connections Across Time** The struggle against social injustice and for the expansion of rights continued past the Focus Period. In addition, the struggles of the Focus Period have influenced contemporary writers and commentators.

*Brown v. Board of Education*: Opinion of the Court, Earl Warren

"Was *Brown v. Board* a Failure?" Sarah Garland

"The Fifth Fact," Sarah Browning

"Who Burns for the Perfection of Paper," Martín Espada

from *The Warmth of Other Suns,* Isabel Wilkerson

"What a Factory Can Teach a Housewife," Ida Tarbell

from *Books as Bombs*, Louis Menand

"A Balance Between Nature and Nurture," Gloria Steinem

ADDITIONAL FOCUS PERIOD LITERATURE

**Student Edition**

UNIT 2

The Writing of Walt Whitman

- *from* The Preface to the 1885 edition of *Leaves of Grass*
- *from* Song of Myself
- "I Hear America Singing"
- "On the Beach at Night Alone"
- "America"

The Poetry of Emily Dickinson

- "The Soul selects her own Society —"
- "The Soul unto itself"
- "Fame is a fickle food"
- "They shut me up in Prose —"
- "There is a solitude of space"
- "I heard a fly buzz — when I died —"
- "I'm Nobody! Who are you?"



**1882: Europe** The Triple Alliance (Germany, Austria-Hungary, and Italy) is formed.

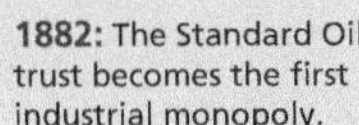

**1882:** The Standard Oil trust becomes the first industrial monopoly.

**1883:** The Brooklyn Bridge is opened.

**1884:** Mark Twain's *The Adventures of Huckleberry Finn* is published.

**1886:** The Statue of Liberty is dedicated in New York Harbor.

1890

**1890:** The U.S. Census Bureau declares the frontier closed.



PERSONALIZE FOR LEARNING

### English Language Support

**Time Sequence Words** Ask students what time sequence words they can think of to compare events on the timeline *(before, after, during)*. Model phrases using these words, such as, *two years before, a year after,* or *during the years.* Ask questions about the sequence of events in the timeline, and encourage students to answer using time sequence words. For example, you might ask, *Did Alexander Graham Bell patent the telephone before or after Edison invented the electric light?* (Alexander Graham Bell patented the telephone three years *before* Edison invented the electric light.)

DIGITAL PERSPECTIVES

## Literature Selections

Have groups explore the different ways that fiction and nonfiction present events. For example, writers of fiction create imaginary characters, events, and dialogue that nonetheless capture the reality of a specific era. This is true in "The Story of an Hour," which reveals the frustration and entrapment many women felt in the late nineteenth century because they were denied basic rights. Have students compare and contrast how each genre reveals basic ideas and themes of the era and the struggle for power, protest, and change.

Have students review the selections in this unit organized under *Literature of the Focus Period* and *Connections Across Time*. Also point out the additional Focus Period Literature found in myPerspectives. Encourage them to use these selections for additional evidence as they complete this unit.

## Comprehension Check

Ask students to answer these questions independently and to then discuss them in a group.

1. Why is the U.S. Constitution an important influence during the period from 1850 to 1890?

   **Possible response:** The Constitution detailed the rights and responsibilities of people and government. If the people were going to be able to demand and secure new rights, the government had to agree to change, or amend, the Constitution.

2. How did the economy of the United States change during this period?

   **Possible response:** The economy changed from one dominated by agriculture, especially in the South, to one dominated by industry and manufacturing, especially in the North.

3. What did the Civil War decide about the relationship between state governments and the central government?

   **Possible response:** With the North victorious and governed by the central government, the central government gained greater authority over state governments—including governments of states that left the Union and formed the confederate South.

4. How did the expansion of the frontier affect Native Americans?

   **Possible response:** Settlers seeking land and opportunities forced Native American from their lands.

5. What are three causes that reformers fought for during this period?

   **Possible response:** Horace Mann supported public education. Reformers also supported changes in the justice system, especially to reform prisons. Elizabeth Cady Stanton, Lucretia Mott, and Susan B. Anthony fought for women's rights.

# *from* What to the Slave Is the Fourth of July?

**AUDIO SUMMARIES**
Audio summaries of the excerpt from "What to the Slave Is the Fourth of July?" are available online in both English and Spanish in the Interactive Teacher's Edition or Unit Resources. Assigning these summaries prior to reading the selection may help students build additional background knowledge and set a context for their first read.

## Summary

In his speech "What to the Slave Is the Fourth of July?" Frederick Douglass honors the principles of liberty and justice embodied in the Declaration of Independence, but refuses to celebrate Independence Day. In this excerpt, Douglass asks why he and his people should celebrate America's freedom from tyranny, while they continue to suffer the tyranny of slavery. He condemns slavery as "the great sin and shame of America." Replying to critics who wish abolitionists would argue their case rationally instead of denouncing all opposition as false, Douglass asserts that there is no case to argue. Justice doesn't require proof—everyone knows what justice demands, but millions are denied it. Douglass looks into the darkness and sees hope.

### Insight

Reading the excerpt from "What to the Slave Is the Fourth of July?" provides students with an authentic voice from the past—a voice that reveals the hypocrisy of those in power and expresses the fury necessary to affect change in a country convinced of its righteousness. Given the strain on race relations in America, the selection may evoke some strong feelings from students, and class discussions may need to be carefully monitored to keep students on topic.

ESSENTIAL QUESTION:
**In what ways does the struggle for freedom change with history?**

## Connection to Essential Question

This excerpt from "What to the Slave Is the Fourth of July?" has a direct connection to the Essential Question—*In what ways does the struggle for freedom change with history?* Frederick Douglass recalls the struggle fought and the freedoms won when America gained independence from England, and he contrasts that struggle and those freedoms with the bondage still suffered by American slaves.

WHOLE-CLASS LEARNING PERFORMANCE TASK
**Did the nation achieve the goals that Douglass and Lincoln desired?**

UNIT PERFORMANCE-BASED ASSESSMENT
**What motivates people to struggle for change?**

## Connection to Performance Tasks

**Whole-Class Learning Performance Task** In this Performance Task, students will research and report on whether the nation achieved the goals that Douglass and Lincoln desired. In the excerpt from "What to the Slave Is the Fourth of July?" Douglass states quite explicitly what some of his goals for the nation are. Students will consider those goals as they work on their essays.

**Unit Performance-Based Assessment** This selection provides insight into the mind of someone who worked tirelessly for change throughout his lifetime.

DIGITAL PERSPECTIVES

Audio

Video

Document

Annotation Highlights

EL Highlights

Online Assessment

## LESSON RESOURCES

| | Making Meaning | Language Development | Effective Expression |
|---|---|---|---|
| Lesson | **First Read**<br>**Close Read**<br>**Analyze the Text**<br>**Analyze Craft and Structure** | **Concept Vocabulary**<br>**Word Study**<br>**Conventions and Style** | **Writing to Sources**<br>**Speaking and Listening** |
| Instructional Standards | **RI.10** By the end of grade 11, read and comprehend literary nonfiction . . .<br>**RI.1** Cite strong and thorough textual evidence . . .<br>**RI.5** Analyze and evaluate the effectiveness of the structure an author uses . . .<br>**RI.8** Delineate and evaluate the reasoning in seminal U.S. texts . . . | **L.1** Demonstrate command of the conventions . . .<br>**L.3** Apply knowledge of language . . .<br>**L.4.c** Consult general and specialized reference materials . . . | **W.2** Write informative/explanatory texts . . .<br>**W.2.e** Establish and maintain a formal style . . .<br>**SL.3** Evaluate a speaker's point of view . . . |
| **STUDENT RESOURCES** | | | |
| Available online in the Interactive Student Edition or Unit Resources | Selection Audio<br>First-Read Guide: Nonfiction<br>Close-Read Guide: Nonfiction | Word Network | Evidence Log |
| **TEACHER RESOURCES** | | | |
| **Selection Resources**<br>Available online in the Interactive Teacher's Edition or Unit Resources | Audio Summaries<br>Annotation Highlights<br>EL Highlights<br>English Language Support Lesson: Argumentative Structure<br>Analyze Craft and Structure: Argumentative Structure | Concept Vocabulary and Word Study<br>Conventions and Style: Types of Phrases | Writing to Sources: Informative Paragraph<br>Speaking and Listening: Dramatic Reading |
| **Reteach/Practice (RP)**<br>Available online in the Interactive Teacher's Edition or Unit Resources | Analyze Craft and Structure: Argumentative Structure (RP) | Word Study: Latin Prefix: *ob-* (RP)<br>Conventions and Style: Types of Phrases (RP) | Writing to Sources: Informative Paragraph (RP)<br>Speaking and Listening: Dramatic Reading (RP) |
| **Assessment**<br>Available online in Assessments | Selection Test | | |
| **My Resources** | A Unit 3 Answer Key is available online and in the Interactive Teacher's Edition. | | |

# Reading Support

| Text Complexity Rubric: What to the Slave Is the Fourth of July? | |
|---|---|
| **Quantitative Measures** | |
| **Lexile:** 1220 **Text Length:** 1,809 words | |
| **Qualitative Measures** | |
| Knowledge Demands ①—②—③—❹—⑤ | Understanding of the speech requires basic knowledge of the Declaration of Independence and the history of the Fourth of July, slavery, and abolition. This context is not provided by the text. |
| Structure ①—②—③—❹—⑤ | The selection is a written version of a speech that was delivered orally; therefore, the structure may be difficult. Long passages have no sub-sections, and multiple rhetorical questions are posed before any conclusions are suggested. |
| Language Conventionality and Clarity ①—②—③—❹—⑤ | Speech uses formal rhetoric characteristic of writing and speech from the pre-Civil War era. Students may not be familiar with the style, syntax, and above-level vocabulary. |
| Levels of Meaning/Purpose ①—②—❸—④—⑤ | The main concept (that slavery is wrong) is strongly stated, but phrased in rhetorical language and not stated at first. Supporting concepts are explained in complex ways. |

DECIDE AND PLAN

## English Language Support

Provide English Learners with support for knowledge demands and language as they read the selection.

**Knowledge Demands** Before students read, determine what they understand of the background information. Ask *What's the name of the person speaking? Is he white or African American? What is his background?* (He was a slave.)

**Language** Present specific phrases and help students unravel the meaning. For example, write *those I represent* (paragraph 1) and ask *What group of people could Frederick Douglass represent?* (African Americans) *What is he asking when he says* Are the great principles of freedom and justice extended to us? (Are African Americans treated fairly?)

After helping students understand the language, have them practice reading sections of the speech aloud to a partner.

## Strategic Support

Provide students with strategic support to ensure that they can successfully read the text.

**Knowledge Demands** Use the background information to review what students know about slavery. Discuss that the speech was written in 1852, prior to the abolition of slavery in 1865.

**Language and Meaning** As students read, ask them to look for some of the phrases about slavery that make Douglass's viewpoint clear (for example, *denounce . . . everything that serves to perpetuate slavery; the conduct of the nation seems equally hideous and revolting*). If students have trouble locating these phrases, direct their attention to lines about the main point (*My subject . . . is American slavery*). Have them reread the section, looking for clarifying words.

## Challenge

Provide students who need to be challenged with ideas for how they can go beyond a simple interpretation of the text.

**Text Analysis** Ask students to explain why Douglass hears "the mournful wail of millions" when people celebrate the 4th of July. Have students practice reading sections of the speech aloud to one another or to the class.

**Written Response** Ask students to speculate about what Frederick Douglass might think about freedom in the United States today, without slavery. Would he think there are still reasons to be mournful about equality in this country? Why or why not? Have them write a paragraph stating their ideas.

TEACH

## Read and Respond

Have students do their first read of the selection. Then, have them complete their close read. Finally, work with them on the Making Meaning, Language Development, and Effective Expression activities.

# Standards Support Through Teaching and Learning Cycle

## IDENTIFY NEEDS

Analyze results of the Beginning-of-Year Assessment, focusing on the items relating to Unit 3. Also take into consideration student performance to this point and your observations of where particular students struggle.

## DECIDE AND PLAN

- If students have performed poorly on items matching these standards, then provide selection scaffolds before assigning them the on-level lesson provided in the Student Edition.
- If students have done well on the Beginning-of-Year Assessment, then challenge them to keep progressing and learning by giving them opportunities to practice the skills in depth.
- Use the Selection Resources listed on the Planning pages for " What to a Slave Is the Fourth of July?" to help students continually improve their ability to master the standards.

**Instructional Standards: What to the Slave Is the Fourth of July?**

| | Catching Up | This Year | Looking Forward |
|---|---|---|---|
| **Reading** | You may wish to administer the **Analyze Craft and Structure: Argumentative Structure (RP)** worksheet to help students understand the basic structure of argumentative writing. | **RI.5** Analyze and evaluate the effectiveness of the structure an author uses in his or her exposition or argument, including whether the structure makes points clear, convincing, and engaging. | Have students identify the claim, reasons, and evidence to support the reasons. |
| **Writing** | You may wish to administer the **Writing to Sources: Informative Paragraph (RP)** worksheet to help students understand how to connect research to historical texts. | **W.2** Write informative/explanatory texts to examine and convey complex ideas, concepts, and information clearly and accurately through the effective selection, organization, and analysis of content. | Encourage students to write an analysis of another of Douglass's speeches. |
| **Speaking and Listening** | You may wish to administer the **Speaking and Listening: Dramatic Reading (RP)** worksheet to help students understand how to identify examples of tone. | **SL.3** Evaluate a speaker's point of view, reasoning, and use of evidence and rhetoric, assessing the stance, premises, links among ideas, word choice, points of emphasis, and tone used. | You may wish to challenge students to identify additional examples in Douglass's speech where he is emphasizing his ideas. |
| **Language** | You may wish to administer the **Conventions and Style: Types of Phrases (RP)** worksheet to help students identify all the words included in a noun phrase or verb phrase. | **L.1** Demonstrate command of the conventions of standard English grammar and usage when writing or speaking. | Have students identify several noun and verb phrases in the selection and determine each noun or verb as well as the other words in the phrase. |

## ANALYZE AND REVISE

- Analyze student work for evidence of student learning.
- Identify whether or not students have met the expectations in the standards.
- Identify implications for future instruction.

## TEACH

Implement the planned lesson, and gather evidence of student learning.

## Jump Start

FIRST READ Before students undertake their first read, challenge them to name states that had no slaves in 1840. The answers are Maine, Vermont, Massachusetts, and Wisconsin. The remaining Northern states had anywhere from fewer than 10 to more than 100 slaves. When Douglass gave this speech just 12 years later, slavery affected many lives in all parts of the country.

## What to the Slave Is the Fourth of July?

How does Douglass feel about Independence Day? Does America's independence from Britain mean much to a person who was born a slave? Modeling questions readers might ask as they read the excerpt from "What to the Slave Is the Fourth of July?" for the first time brings the text alive and connects it to the Whole-Class Performance Task assignment. Selection audio and print capability for the selection are available in the Interactive Teacher's Edition.

## Concept Vocabulary

Ask students if they've ever heard, read or used the words. Reassure them that the definitions for these words are listed in the selection.

### FIRST READ

As they read, students should perform the steps of the first read:

NOTICE: Students should ask *who, what, where, when*, and *why* questions about Douglass's speech.

ANNOTATE: Students should mark any unfamiliar words or confusing sentences they will revisit during their close read.

CONNECT: Students should connect what they're reading to other protest works they have read.

RESPOND: Students will demonstrate their understanding by answering questions and writing a summary. Point out to students that while they will always complete the Respond step at the end of the first read, the other steps will probably happen concurrently. You may wish to print copies of the **First-Read Guide: Nonfiction** for students to use.

**Remind students that during their first read, they should not answer the close-read questions that appear in the selection.**

MAKING MEANING

About the Speaker

**Frederick Douglass** (1818–1895) was born into slavery in Maryland. He nevertheless learned to read and write, and at the age of 21 he escaped to Massachusetts. There, he joined the abolitionist cause and quickly became one of its most powerful public speakers, lecturing against slavery and campaigning for civil rights for all people. He published his autobiography, established a newspaper for African Americans, and went on to hold several governmental positions.

**Tool Kit**
First-Read Guide and Model Annotation

STANDARDS
**Reading Informational Text**
By the end of grade 11, read and comprehend literary nonfiction in the grades 11–CCR text complexity band proficiently, with scaffolding as needed at the high end of the range.

# *from* What to the Slave Is the Fourth of July?

## Concept Vocabulary

You will encounter the following words as you read this excerpt from "What to the Slave Is the Fourth of July?" Before reading, note how familiar you are with each word. Then, rank the words in order from most familiar (1) to least familiar (6).

| WORD | YOUR RANKING |
|---|---|
| obdurate | |
| stolid | |
| disparity | |
| denounce | |
| equivocate | |
| conceded | |

After completing the first read, come back to the concept vocabulary and review your rankings. Mark changes to your original rankings as needed.

## First Read NONFICTION

Apply these these strategies as you conduct your first read. You will have an opportunity to complete the close-read notes after your first read.

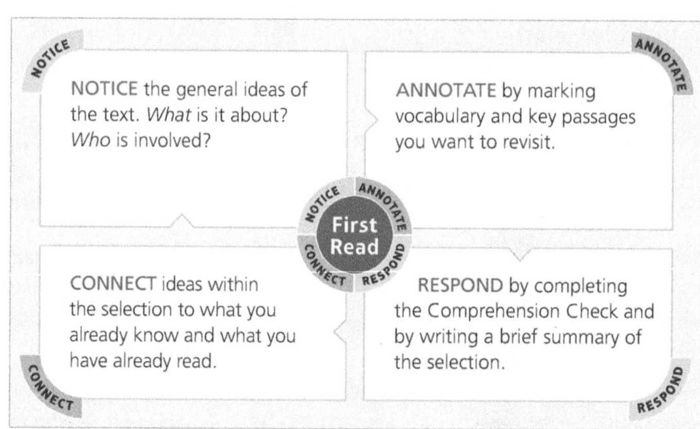
NOTICE the general ideas of the text. *What* is it about? *Who* is involved?
ANNOTATE by marking vocabulary and key passages you want to revisit.
First Read
CONNECT ideas within the selection to what you already know and what you have already read.
RESPOND by completing the Comprehension Check and by writing a brief summary of the selection.

AUTHOR'S PERSPECTIVE **Jim Cummins, Ph.D.**

**Bringing in Multi-Literacies** If students have the opportunity to integrate text with other modalities such as art, performance, audio, and video, their writing will benefit.

New forms of technology have brought in new methods for effective communication. Devices such as smartphones and tablets allow students to express themselves easily, and students are well-versed in these new communication methods. Building these new modes of communication into classroom practices can increase student engagement while providing language production opportunities.

As students consider questions about power, protest, and change, bring in new media. Have groups create a mini-drama that they script, perform, and film to share with other students in the class. This hands-on activity will tap into student energies and interests that writing may not. Student confidence and engagement can transfer to later activities in the unit.

# *from* What to the Slave Is the Fourth of July?

Frederick Douglass

BACKGROUND

On July 5, 1852, Frederick Douglass addressed an audience at the Rochester (New York) Ladies' Anti-Slavery Society. At a time when many people—some who were against slavery in principle—viewed the total abolition of slavery as a radical cause, Douglass pulled no punches in pleading his case.

SCAN FOR MULTIMEDIA

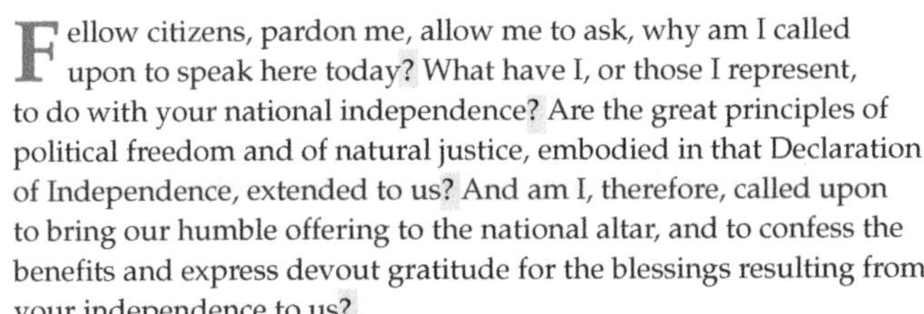

1 Fellow citizens, pardon me, allow me to ask, why am I called upon to speak here today? What have I, or those I represent, to do with your national independence? Are the great principles of political freedom and of natural justice, embodied in that Declaration of Independence, extended to us? And am I, therefore, called upon to bring our humble offering to the national altar, and to confess the benefits and express devout gratitude for the blessings resulting from your independence to us?

2 Would to God, both for your sakes and ours, that an affirmative answer could be truthfully returned to these questions! Then would my task be light, and my burden easy and delightful. For who is there so cold that a nation's sympathy could not warm him? Who so **obdurate** and dead to the claims of gratitude that would not thankfully acknowledge such priceless benefits? Who so **stolid** and selfish that would not give his voice to swell the hallelujahs of a nation's jubilee,[1] when the chains of servitude had been torn from

NOTES

**obdurate** (OB dur iht) *adj.* resistant to persuasion

**stolid** (STOL ihd) *adj.* feeling little or no emotion

1. **hallelujahs of a nation's jubilee** praises to God at the time of celebrating a national anniversary.

DIGITAL PERSPECTIVES

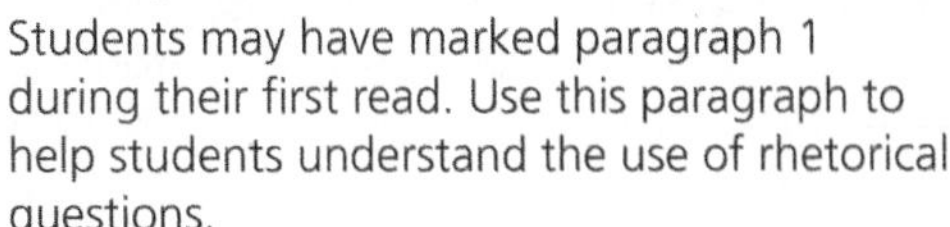

CLOSER LOOK

## Analyze Rhetorical Devices

Students may have marked paragraph 1 during their first read. Use this paragraph to help students understand the use of rhetorical questions.

**ANNOTATE:** Have students highlight the punctuation marks at the ends of the sentences.

**QUESTION:** What type of sentence is this paragraph composed of? Does Douglass expect his audience to answer these questions? Why does he ask them? How would the opening of the speech be different if the last two sentences were statements instead of questions?

**Possible responses:** They are all questions. No, he does not. Opening with a series of questions draws the audience into his speech; it also softens the impact of the harsh point he is making: that blacks do not share the freedom of other Americans. The opening of the speech would be more argumentative, more negative.

**CONCLUDE:** Why might a speaker use rhetorical questions such as these in a speech?

**Possible response:** Questions usually require an answer, so asking your audience a question makes them think about what you are saying. Also, a question is softer than a statement, so asking about an unpleasant truth is easier for your audience to consider than stating the unpleasant truth.

Point out to students that rhetorical questions occur in everyday speech as well as in oratory and literature. Any question that is asked without expecting an actual answer is a **rhetorical question**. Everyday examples include "Are you kidding me?" and "Why is this happening?"

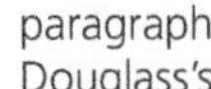

DIGITAL PERSPECTIVES

**Illuminating the Text** Refer to the background paragraph, and play a video of an actor delivering Douglass's speech and have groups discuss how hearing the speech enhanced their understanding of it. Then, have groups share with the class how the video provided insight into the text. Encourage them to consider how or if their view of Douglass's effectiveness as a public orator changed based on hearing the speech. Especially effective readings by James Earl Jones and Danny Glover are available online. **(Research to Clarify)**

# TEACHING

Remind students that speech writers use various devices to provoke reactions in their listeners. One such rhetorical device is parallelism. You may wish to model the Close Read using the following think-aloud format. Possible responses to questions on the student page are included. You may also want to print copies of the **Close-Read Guide: Nonfiction** for students to use.

ANNOTATE: As I read paragraph 4, I notice and mark two examples of parallelism.

QUESTION: The first example connects "humanity," "liberty," and "the constitution and the Bible." The second example connects two things Douglass says he will not do and one thing he says he will do.

CONCLUDE: The use of parallelism enables listeners to sense connections among ideas and to understand Douglass's key points. The repeated use of "in the name of" makes the point that Douglass is not just arguing for his own benefit, but also for all people who are opposed to slavery. The repetition of "I will" speaks of Douglass's individual ability and determination to protest and seek change.

NOTES

**disparity** (dih SPAR uh tee) *n.* great difference or inequality

his limbs? I am not that man. In a case like that, the dumb might eloquently speak, and the "lame man leap as an hart."[2]

3 But such is not the state of the case. I say it with a sad sense of the **disparity** between us. I am not included within the pale of glorious anniversary! Your high independence only reveals the immeasurable distance between us. The blessings in which you, this day, rejoice are not enjoyed in common. The rich inheritance of justice, liberty, prosperity, and independence, bequeathed[3] by your fathers, is shared by you, not by me. The sunlight that brought light and healing to you has brought stripes and death to me. This Fourth of July is yours, not mine. You may rejoice; I must mourn. To drag a man in fetters[4] into the grand illuminated temple of liberty, and call upon him to join you in joyous anthems, were inhuman mockery and sacrilegious irony. Do you mean, citizens, to mock me, by asking me to speak today? . . .

4 Fellow citizens, above your national, tumultuous joy, I hear the mournful wail of millions! whose chains, heavy and grievous yesterday, are, today, rendered more intolerable by the jubilee shouts that reach them. If I do forget, if I do not faithfully remember those bleeding children of sorrow this day, "may my right hand forget her cunning, and may my tongue cleave to the roof of my mouth!"[5] To forget them, to pass lightly over their wrongs, and to chime in with the popular theme would be treason most scandalous and shocking, and would make me a reproach before God and the world. My subject, then, fellow citizens, is American slavery. I shall see this day and its popular characteristics from the slave's point of view. Standing there identified with the American bondman, making his wrongs mine, I do not hesitate to declare, with all my soul, that the character and conduct of this nation never looked blacker to me than on this Fourth of July! Whether we turn to the declarations of the past or to the professions of the present, the conduct of the nation seems equally hideous and revolting. America is false to the past, false to the present, and solemnly binds herself to be false to the future. Standing with God and the crushed and bleeding slave on this occasion, I will, in the name of humanity which is outraged, in the name of liberty which is fettered, in the name of the Constitution and the Bible, which are disregarded and trampled upon, dare to call into question and to **denounce**, with all the emphasis I can command, everything that serves to perpetuate slavery—the great sin and shame of America! "I will not **equivocate**; I will not excuse;" I will use the severest language I can command; and yet not one word shall escape me that any man, whose judgment is not blinded by prejudice, or who is not at heart a slaveholder, shall not confess to be right and just.

CLOSE READ

ANNOTATE: **Parallelism** is the repetition of words or phrases that have similar grammatical structures. In the last two sentences of paragraph 4, mark two examples of parallelism.

QUESTION: What ideas do these examples of parallelism connect?

CONCLUDE: How does the use of parallelism add to the power and meaning of this section of the speech?

**denounce** (dih NOWNS) *v.* criticize harshly

**equivocate** (ih KWIHV uh kayt) *v.* use unclear language to avoid committing oneself to something

2. **"lame man leap as an hart"** reference to the biblical passage Isaiah 35:6, promising God's rescue of the weak and fearful. (A *hart* is a male deer.)
3. **bequeathed** (bih KWEETHT) *adj.* handed down.
4. **fetters** *n.* chains.
5. **"may . . . mouth"** reference to the biblical passage Psalm 137, referencing the grief of Jews who had been taken as captives to Babylon (c. 600 B.C.).





## CROSS-CURRICULAR PERSPECTIVE

**Social Studies** The "liberty" that Douglass refers to in paragraph 4 was a much-debated topic in the early nineteenth century. In fact, abolitionism and women's suffrage were closely entwined. In the early nineteenth century, women agitated for the abolition of slavery by writing articles, pamphlets, and petitions. Several women, most notably the Grimke sisters, delivered fiery anti-slavery speeches to audiences around the country. The clergy denounced the women for addressing "mixed" audiences—both men and women in attendance. The Grimkes, along with other women, began to fight for women's rights, as well, seeing strong parallels between their situation and that of the slaves. When Elizabeth Cady Stanton and Lucretia Mott were denied seats at the 1840 World Anti-Slavery Convention, they held a landmark convention for women's rights. Have students discuss how entwining the issue of slavery with women's rights both helped and harmed each issue.

DIGITAL PERSPECTIVES

5 But I fancy I hear some one of my audience say, "It is just in this circumstance that you and your brother abolitionists fail to make a favorable impression on the public mind. Would you argue more, and denounce less; would you persuade more, and rebuke[6] less; your cause would be much more likely to succeed." But, I submit, where all is plain, there is nothing to be argued. What point in the antislavery creed would you have me argue? On what branch of the subject do the people of this country need light? Must I undertake to prove that the slave is a man? That point is conceded already. Nobody doubts it. The slaveholders themselves acknowledge it in the enactment of laws for their government. They acknowledge it when they punish disobedience on the part of the slave. There are seventy-two crimes in the State of Virginia which, if committed by a black man (no matter how ignorant he be), subject him to the punishment of death; while only two of the same crimes will subject a white man to the like punishment. What is this but the acknowledgment that the slave is a moral, intellectual, and responsible being? The manhood of the slave is conceded. It is admitted in the fact that Southern statute books are covered with enactments forbidding, under severe fines and penalties, the teaching of the slave to read or to write. When you can point to any such laws in reference to the beasts of the field, then I may consent to argue the manhood of the slave. When the dogs in your streets, when the fowls of the air, when the cattle on your hills, when the fish of the sea, and the reptiles that crawl, shall be unable to distinguish the slave from a brute, then will I argue with you that the slave is a man!

> Must I undertake to prove that the slave is a man?

6 For the present, it is enough to affirm the equal manhood of the Negro race. Is it not astonishing that, while we are plowing, planting, and reaping, using all kinds of mechanical tools, erecting houses, constructing bridges, building ships, working in metals of brass, iron, copper, silver and gold; that, while we are reading, writing and ciphering,[7] acting as clerks, merchants, and secretaries, having among us lawyers, doctors, ministers, poets, authors, editors, orators, and teachers; that, while we are engaged in all manner of enterprises common to other men, digging gold in California, capturing the whale in the Pacific, feeding sheep and cattle on the hillside, living, moving, acting, thinking, planning, living in families as husbands, wives, and children, and, above all, confessing and worshipping the Christian's God, and looking hopefully for life and immortality beyond the grave, we are called upon to prove that we are men!

7 Would you have me argue that man is entitled to liberty? That he is the rightful owner of his own body? You have already declared it. Must I argue the wrongfulness of slavery? Is that a question for Republicans? Is it to be settled by the rules of logic and

NOTES

**conceded** (kuhn SEED ihd) *v.* admitted

6. **rebuke** (rih BYOOK) *v.* criticize.
7. **ciphering** (SY fuhr ihng) *v.* computing using arithmetic.

CLOSER LOOK

## Analyze Arguments

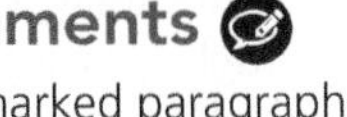

Students may have marked paragraph 5 during their first read. Use this paragraph to help students understand the part of Douglass's argument that he advances in this paragraph.

**ANNOTATE:** Have students mark facts that Douglass cites to support his thesis that slaves are human.

**QUESTION:** What do the facts Douglass cites have in common?

**Possible response:** They are all related to laws that restrict the rights and freedom of slaves.

**CONCLUDE:** What does Douglass mean when he says, ". . . then I may consent to argue the manhood of the slave"?

**Possible response:** Douglass is saying that he won't even bother to argue about whether slaves are people until someone can cite laws forbidding the teaching of animals to read or write, or crimes for which animals may be put to death.

Remind students that when they **analyze an argument**, they need to think about why specific facts are included. How do these facts strengthen the speaker's position? Do these facts elicit an emotional reaction in the listener?

Additional **English Language Support** is available in the Digital Teacher's Edition.

## PERSONALIZE FOR LEARNING

**Strategic Support**

**Argument** Review Douglass' argument in paragraph 5. Point out to students that although Douglass gives an anti-slavery speech to an abolitionist group, he does it as if debating a political opponent. Ask, "Why might an argument help people who already agree with you?" (Elicit that the argument's claim and logic, as in an editorial, help supporters clarify their thinking and better argue for a cause.) After students grasp the purpose of an editorial, open a discussion about logic. Ask students to provide examples of logical thought. Then help assemble small groups of varied learners. Have each group find three instances of Douglass's application of logic. They should label his claim, the implied counterclaim by those who support slavery, and the evidence that refutes that counterclaim. For each of their three examples, groups should write a sentence that summarizes the example's logic. Example: Paragraph 5: "Must I undertake to prove that the slave is a man?" (Evidence follows through the paragraph.) Logic: Douglass uses the ideas of legal punishment and achievement to prove that African Americans are human beings.

# TEACHING

## CLOSE READ 

Point out that this speech began in a cool, logical way, with Douglass asking why he was invited to speak and using rational arguments to convey the evil of slavery. Now, however, the emotional content of the speech increases as Douglass builds to a passionate conclusion. You may wish to model the Close Read using the following think-aloud format. Possible responses to questions on the student page are included.

**ANNOTATE:** As I read paragraph 10, I note and mark words that suggest how strongly Douglass feels.

**QUESTION:** The phenomena Douglass uses in his comparison—fire, thunder, storm, whirlwind, and earthquake—are destructive. He may be referring to such destructive forces to describe attitudes that he wants to destroy.

**CONCLUDE:** The language shows Douglass's passion for the issue. He wants the institution of slavery to be destroyed, so he uses words that connote destruction.

Additional **English Language Support** is available in the Interactive Teacher's Edition.

NOTES

argumentation, as a matter beset with great difficulty, involving a doubtful application of the principle of justice, hard to be understood? How should I look today, in the presence of Americans, dividing and subdividing a discourse, to show that men have a natural right to freedom—speaking of it relatively and positively, negatively and affirmatively? To do so would be to make myself ridiculous, and to offer an insult to your understanding. There is not a man beneath the canopy of heaven that does not know that slavery is wrong for him.

8 What, am I to argue that it is wrong to make men brutes, to rob them of their liberty, to work them without wages, to keep them ignorant of their relations to their fellow men, to beat them with sticks, to flay their flesh with the lash, to load their limbs with irons, to hunt them with dogs, to sell them at auction, to sunder their families, to knock out their teeth, to burn their flesh, to starve them into obedience and submission to their masters? Must I argue that a system thus marked with blood, and stained with pollution, is wrong? No! I will not. I have better employment for my time and strength than such arguments would imply.

9 What, then, remains to be argued? Is it that slavery is not divine; that God did not establish it; that our doctors of divinity are mistaken? There is blasphemy in the thought. That which is inhuman cannot be divine! Who can reason on such a proposition? They that can, may; I cannot. The time for such argument is passed.

**CLOSE READ**

**ANNOTATE:** In paragraph 10, mark words that suggest how strongly Douglass feels. Mark adjectives, nouns that name forms of expression, and nouns that name natural phenomena.

**QUESTION:** Why does Douglass compare certain forms of expression to natural phenomena?

**CONCLUDE:** What is the effect of this language?

10 At a time like this, scorching irony, not convincing argument, is needed. O! had I the ability, and could I reach the nation's ear, I would, today, pour out a fiery stream of biting ridicule, blasting reproach, withering sarcasm, and stern rebuke. For it is not light that is needed, but fire; it is not the gentle shower, but thunder. We need the storm, the whirlwind, and the earthquake. The feeling of the nation must be quickened; the conscience of the nation must be roused; the propriety[8] of the nation must be startled; the hypocrisy of the nation must be exposed; and its crimes against God and man must be proclaimed and denounced.

11 What, to the American slave, is your Fourth of July? I answer: a day that reveals to him, more than all other days of the year, the gross injustice and cruelty to which he is the constant victim. To him, your celebration is a sham; your boasted liberty, an unholy license; your national greatness, swelling vanity; your sounds of rejoicing are empty and heartless; your denunciation of tyrants, brass-fronted impudence; your shouts of liberty and equality, hollow mockery; your prayers and hymns, your sermons and thanksgivings, with all your religious parade and solemnity, are, to Him, mere bombast, fraud, deception, impiety,[9] and hypocrisy—a thin veil to cover up crimes which would disgrace a nation of savages. There is not a nation on the earth guilty of practices more shocking and bloody than are the people of these United States, at this very hour. . . .

8. **propriety** (pruh PRY uh tee) *n.* behavior that is accepted as socially correct or proper.
9. **impiety** (ihm PY uh tee) *n.* lack of respect for God.





## PERSONALIZE FOR LEARNING

### English Language Support

**Related Words** Review paragraphs 7–9. Point out that some words that may be unfamiliar might be related to words students know. Ask students to look at the word *argumentation* in paragraph 7. This may seem like an unfamiliar word, but students may know a related word they can find in paragraph 8 *(argue)*. Have students scan paragraphs 8 and 9 for other related forms (*arguments*, paragraph 8; *argued,* paragraph 9). Ask them to say the meaning of the forms they know and to figure out the meaning of the related words.
**ALL LEVELS PI.6C**

12 Allow me to say, in conclusion, notwithstanding the dark picture I have this day presented, of the state of the nation, I do not despair of this country. There are forces in operation which must inevitably work the downfall of slavery. "The arm of the Lord is not shortened,"[10] and the doom of slavery is certain. I, therefore, leave off where I began, with hope. While drawing encouragement from the Declaration of Independence, the great principles it contains, and the genius of American institutions, my spirit is also cheered by the obvious tendencies of the age. ❧

NOTES

10. **"The arm of the Lord is not shortened"** reference to the biblical passage Isaiah 59:1, assuring that God is able to hear and rescue those who call on him.

## Comprehension Check

**Complete the following items after you finish your first read.**

1. What kind of "easy and delightful" speech does Douglass wish he could present?

2. What is the "mournful wail" that gives Douglass the topic for his speech?

3. According to Douglass, how do laws in the South prove that slaves are human beings?

4. At the end of this excerpt, what encouraging signs does Douglass find?

5. **Notebook** Write a summary of this excerpt from "What to the Slave Is the Fourth of July?" to confirm your understanding of the speech.

### RESEARCH

**Research to Clarify** Choose at least one unfamiliar detail from the text. Briefly research that detail. In what way does the information you learned shed light on an aspect of the speech?

**Research to Explore** Choose something that interests you from the text, and formulate a research question about it.



DIGITAL PERSPECTIVES

## Comprehension Check

Possible responses:

1. Douglass wishes that he could speak about and express gratitude for the benefits of American independence.
2. The "mournful wail" is the sound of grieving Americans who are enslaved.
3. According to paragraph 5, the laws require a death penalty for African Americans for crimes that usually do not carry that punishment for white Americans. Some of the laws forbid teaching slaves to read or write. Douglass states that under some laws, animals are treated better than slaves.
4. He says, "There are forces in operation which must inevitably work the downfall of slavery," possibly referring to anti-slavery groups such as the one he is addressing. Because of this, he says, "the doom of slavery is certain."
5. Douglass acknowledges that the occasion normally would call for a speech that praises America's freedom. He uses the occasion, however, to point out that slaves have no freedom. He mentions ways in which slaves are viewed as less than human and argues vehemently against those who wish to see slavery continue. Douglass concludes by expressing certainty that slavery will end and hope that its end will come soon.

## Research

**Research to Clarify** If students cannot find a detail to research, you might point out that they can focus on one of these topics: abolition, human rights, the Declaration of Independence.

**Research to Explore** For students who cannot formulate a research question, guide them to use their findings from Research to Clarify as a starting point. For example, students who researched the Declaration of Independence might look into its authorship and signatories.

PERSONALIZE FOR LEARNING

### Challenge

**Research the Author** Have students reread paragraph 11 and research Frederick Douglass's life to learn more about this remarkable man. Topics to consider include:

- Douglass's life as a slave, especially how he learned to read
- His time in slavery and how he escaped to freedom
- His other published works, especially his 1845 autobiography, *Narrative of Frederick Douglass, an American Slave* and the country's reaction to it
- His travels overseas, focusing on his reasons for going to Ireland
- *The North Star,* his abolitionist newspaper
- His work with the suffragettes (he was the only African American to attend the Seneca Falls Convention)

TEACHING

## Jump Start

CLOSE READ Ask students, *What associations do the Fourth of July and Independence Day evoke?* Next, ask students how an enslaved person might have answered the same question in 1852, when Douglass delivered his speech on the Fourth of July. Guide students to explain the irony of Fourth of July celebrations to enslaved people.

## Close Read the Text

Walk students through the annotation model on the Student page. Encourage them to complete items 2 and 3 on their own. Review and discuss the sections students have marked. If needed, continue to model close reading by using the Annotation Highlights in the Interactive Teacher's Edition.

## Analyze the Text

Possible responses:

1. The reference lays a foundation for his discussion of freedom, the heart of his call for an end to slavery. (Paragraph 3) **DOK 2**
2. The allusions bring the power of the Bible and of Christianity to bear upon the issue. Douglass quotes the Bible by saying "may my right hand forget her my mouth." He also makes allusions to the Bible by using words such as *hallelujah and jubilee*. Responses will vary, but students should recognize the importance of the Bible and of Christian faith to Douglass's audience. (Paragraph 4) **DOK 2**
3. (a) His use of longer and more formal words is appropriate to a group of people who are presumably educated and used to being addressed formally. It also serves to show them that he is their equal. (b) A modern audience, more used to casual speech and a less intellectual vocabulary, might be put off by it. (Paragraph 5) **DOK 3**
4. He spoke harshly because he wanted to spur the audience to action. They already agreed with him about what change should occur, so Douglass had to motivate them to make the change happen. (Paragraph 10) **DOK 2**
5. Students' answers will vary. **DOK 3**

### FORMATIVE ASSESSMENT

### Analyze the Text

- **If** students fail to cite evidence, **then** remind them to support their ideas with specific information.
- **If** students struggle to identify the religious allusions in this speech, **then** have students research the references.

MAKING MEANING

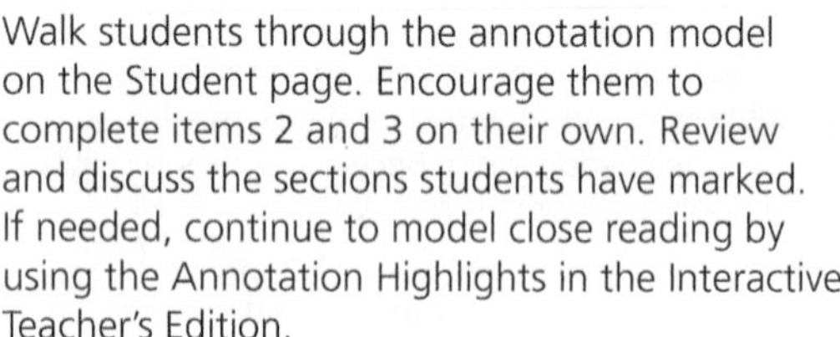

*from* WHAT TO THE SLAVE IS THE FOURTH OF JULY?

## Close Read the Text

1. This model, from paragraph 3 of the text, shows two sample annotations, along with questions and conclusions. Close read the passage, and find another detail to annotate. Then, write a question and your conclusion.

ANNOTATE • QUESTION • CONCLUDE — Close Read

ANNOTATE: These terms are similar.

QUESTION: What do these words show about Douglass's feelings toward American ideals?

CONCLUDE: They show his reverence. The legacy of freedom is both sacred ("blessings") and a part of every American's identity ("rich inheritance").

The blessings in which you, this day, rejoice are not enjoyed in common. The rich inheritance of justice, liberty, prosperity, and independence, bequeathed by your fathers, is shared by you, not by me. The sunlight that brought light and healing to you, has brought stripes and death to me. This Fourth of July is yours, not mine.

ANNOTATE: Here, Douglass is providing contrasts.

QUESTION: What point is Douglass making by this series of contrasts?

CONCLUDE: He is emphasizing the idea that enslaved Americans are denied freedom.

2. For more practice, go back into the text, and complete the close-read notes.
3. Revisit a section of the text you found important during your first read. Read this section closely, and **annotate** what you notice. Ask yourself **questions** such as "Why did the author make this choice?" What can you **conclude**?

**Tool Kit**
Close-Read Guide and Model Annotation

STANDARDS

**Reading Informational Text**
- Cite strong and thorough textual evidence to support analysis of what the text says explicitly as well as inferences drawn from the text, including determining where the text leaves matters uncertain.
- Analyze and evaluate the effectiveness of the structure an author uses in his or her exposition or argument, including whether the structure makes points clear, convincing, and engaging.
- Delineate and evaluate the reasoning in seminal U.S. texts, including the application of constitutional principles and use of legal reasoning and the premises, purposes, and arguments in works of public advocacy.

## Analyze the Text

CITE TEXTUAL EVIDENCE to support your answers.

Notebook Respond to these questions.

1. **Analyze** How does Douglass's opening reference to the Declaration of Independence reinforce his message?
2. **Interpret** Identify two biblical allusions Douglass makes, and then explain how each contributes to Douglass's overall argument.
3. (a) **Analyze** In what ways is Douglass's word choice suited to his audience? (b) **Evaluate** How effective would it be for a modern audience? Explain.
4. **Historical Perspectives** Douglass presented this speech to an antislavery society—an audience that was already on his side. Why, then, did Douglass speak as harshly as he did? Whom was he trying to reach?
5. **Essential Question:** *How does the struggle for freedom change with history?* What have you learned about the struggle for freedom from reading this speech?





PERSONALIZE FOR LEARNING

### English Language Support

**Sentence Starters** Provide sentence starters to help students organize their responses to the questions in the text analysis (paragraphs 3, 4, 5, and 10). For example, *Douglass's speech (would/would not) be effective for a modern audience because ____*. Pair students to complete the answers. Ask them to read their responses aloud help each other correct any errors.

## Analyze Craft and Structure

**Argumentative Structure** Frederick Douglass's famous speech "What to the Slave Is the Fourth of July?" is an **argument**, a discussion of a controversial or debatable issue. In an argument, a writer or speaker uses valid reasoning and evidence to support a **claim**—a particular belief, conclusion, or point of view. The person who presents the argument also may anticipate objections and challenges, or **counterclaims**, and then refute them.

In general, an argument addresses at least one of these purposes:

- to change the audience's mind about an issue
- to persuade the audience to accept an idea
- to motivate the audience to take a specific action

Douglass structures his speech to address all three purposes, either directly or by implication.

### Practice

**CITE TEXTUAL EVIDENCE** to support your answers.

**Notebook** Respond to these questions.

1. (a) What main claim shapes Douglass's speech? (b) How early in the speech does he introduce this claim?
2. In paragraph 10, Douglass states that "scorching irony, not convincing argument, is needed." Nevertheless, his speech does make an argument. (a) In one sentence, state Douglass's argument. (b) Up to that point, what evidence has he presented to support his claim?
3. (a) In paragraph 5, what does Douglass acknowledge as a counterclaim to his position? (b) How does he refute that counterclaim?
4. Reread the three purposes that most arguments address. (a) In the left-hand column of the chart, record those purposes in the order in which you think Douglass was effective in addressing them, from most successful to least successful. (b) Use the right-hand column to explain your choices.

| PURPOSE | EXPLANATION |
|---|---|
| addressed **most** effectively: | i. See possible responses in the Teacher's edition. |
| addressed **fairly** effectively: | ii. |
| addressed **least** effectively: | iii. |





## PERSONALIZE FOR LEARNING

### English Language Support

**Argumentative Structure** Ask students to write about Douglass's point of view in "What to the Slave Is the Fourth of July?" (paragraph 3) **EMERGING**

Ask students to write about the counter-argument in "What to the Slave Is the Fourth of July?" considering whether Douglass concedes that his opponents have a valid point (paragraphs 9 and 10). Have them explain. **BRIDGING**

**EXPANDING**

An expanded **English Language Support Lesson** on Argumentative Structure is available in the Interactive Teacher's Edition.

DIGITAL PERSPECTIVES 

## Analyze Craft and Structure

**Argumentative Structure** Discuss with students the arrangement of claim and counterclaim: authors and speakers often begin with the counterclaim and then present the claim. They do this to show the weakness of the counterclaim and the strength of the claim. For more support, see **Analyze Craft and Structure: Argumentative Structure.**

**MAKE IT INTERACTIVE**

Project the digital version of the excerpt from "What to the Slave Is the Fourth of July?" and read two or three sample paragraphs. Have student volunteers model how to locate the claim and counterclaim.

### Practice

Possible responses:

1. (a) Douglass's claim is that enslaved Americans must be granted their freedom. (b) He refers to "the chains of servitude" in paragraph 2. Perhaps the clearest statement of his claim appears in paragraph 4: " . . . to call in question and to denounce, with all the emphasis I can command, everything that serves to perpetuate slavery—the great sin and shame of America!"
2. (a) In the eyes of the law and of God, human beings should be free and slaves are human beings. (b) He identifies laws that treat slaves as human beings and gives examples of "human" work that African Americans do.
3. (a) Douglass acknowledges that some people oppose the tone and vehemence with which he and other abolitionists campaign for this reform. He even quotes an example of that counterclaim. (b) He asks questions and makes statements to indicate that the arguments against slavery already have been made and acknowledged, suggesting that more than reasoned argument is needed. He becomes more impassioned (the essence of the counterclaim) toward the end of paragraph 5, and his vehemence grows as he continues.
4. (i) Changing the audience's mind about an issue—primarily, to change from being complacent about the abolitionists' cause to taking it up with zeal. (ii) Persuading the audience to accept an idea is of secondary effectiveness; as Douglass himself points out, "The time for such argument is passed." (iii) Motivating the audience to take action, for he does not name a specific action. Instead, throughout the speech and especially in paragraph 10, he emphasizes that it is time for the call to end slavery to be proclaimed with greater energy than ever before.

### FORMATIVE ASSESSMENT

#### Analyze Craft and Structure

**If** students are unable to evaluate the effectiveness of Douglass's arguments, **then** have them start by skimming the selection to find and list the arguments. For Reteach and Practice, see **Analyze Craft and Structure: Argumentative Structure (RP).**

## Concept Vocabulary

**Why These Words?** Discuss with students the difference between saying *equivocate* and *lie*. How is the connotation, the emotional overtone, of the word *equivocate* different from that of the word *lie*?

**Possible responses:**

1. The words suggest that there clearly were two main positions on the issue and that each side was convinced of the correctness of its view.
2. Choices include *confess, eloquently, mock,* and *rebuke*.

### Practice

**Possible responses:**

1. You probably would not get them to agree with your point of view.
2. You probably would not want stolid friends: Friends enjoy having fun together, but stolid people do not show emotion.
3. Some students drive their cars to school, while other students can't afford a car.
4. People might write editorials or stage public protests.
5. You would ask people to give you the clear facts—the honest truth.
6. He probably accepted the other side's point of view instead of defending his own.

### Word Network

**Possible words:** *burden, fetters, inhuman, grievous, intolerable*

## Word Study

For more support, see **Concept Vocabulary and Word Study.**

**Possible responses:**

1. An *obstruction* is a structure or other object that is "against"—in other words, that hinders—movement.
2. *obfuscate* ("to make unclear") and *obviate* ("to anticipate and stop something or cause it to become unnecessary").

### FORMATIVE ASSESSMENT

#### Concept Vocabulary

**If** students fail to see the connection among the words, **then** have them use each word in a sentence and think about what is similar about the sentences.

#### Word Study

**If** students are unable to define the words, **then** have students focus on the meaning of the prefix *ob-*. For Reteach and Practice, see **Word Study: Latin Prefix *ob-* (RP).**



LANGUAGE DEVELOPMENT

from WHAT TO THE SLAVE IS THE FOURTH OF JULY?

## Concept Vocabulary

| obdurate | disparity | equivocate |
|---|---|---|
| stolid | denounce | conceded |

**Why These Words?** These concept vocabulary words help reveal the nature of the debate over slavery. For example, although many people *conceded* that slavery was profoundly wrong, few were willing to campaign against it. On the other hand, some Americans whose economic success depended on slave labor were *obdurate,* insisting that the institution continue. One word suggests an acknowledgement of another point of view, whereas the other suggests a rejection of it.

1. How does the concept vocabulary sharpen the reader's understanding of the debate over slavery?
2. What other words in the speech connect to this concept?

**WORD NETWORK**

Add words related to struggle from the text to your Word Network.

### Practice

**Notebook** Respond to these questions.

1. How would you expect *obdurate* people to respond to advertisements?
2. Would you want to have *stolid* friends? Why, or why not?
3. Give an example of a *disparity* that you have noticed between two groups of people.
4. How might a group of people *denounce* a government policy?
5. Suppose that you are trying to get information from people who *equivocate*. What would you ask them to do?
6. If someone *conceded* a point, did he or she continue to argue against it? Explain.

**STANDARDS**

**Language**

- Demonstrate command of the conventions of standard English grammar and usage when writing or speaking.
- Apply knowledge of language to understand how language functions in different contexts, to make effective choices for meaning or style, and to comprehend more fully when reading or listening.
- Consult general and specialized reference materials, both print and digital, to find the pronunciation of a word or determine or clarify its precise meaning, its part of speech, its etymology, or its standard usage.

## Word Study

**Notebook** **Latin Prefix: *ob-*** The Latin prefix *ob-* often means "against." It combines with the root *-dur-*, which means "hard," to form *obdurate*, which means "hardened against." The word suggests a lack of sympathy toward someone else's difficulty or need and is a good synonym for *hard-hearted*.

1. Write a definition of *obstruction* based on your understanding of the prefix *ob-*. Check your answer in a print or an online college-level dictionary.
2. Identify and define two other words in which the prefix *ob-* means "against." Use etymological information in a dictionary to verify your choices.





**AUTHOR'S PERSPECTIVE** Elfrieda Hiebert, Ph.D.

**Power of Word Choice** Draw students' attention to the fact that particular authors have distinct styles, and a key part of each writer's style is word choice. As evidenced by the concept vocabulary for "What to the Slave Is the Fourth of July?" the author's choice of words can help reveal the main idea of a text. (In this case, the words help highlight the debate over slavery). Remind students that the right words can make a text richer and add power to the author's message and style. One way to show this is to have students replace each concept vocabulary word in the text with a synonym to see how the power of the sentence changes and the author's style is affected.

## Conventions and Style

**Types of Phrases** A **noun phrase** consists of a noun and all of its modifiers. It functions just as a one-word noun does—as a subject, a direct or indirect object, a predicate nominative, an appositive, or the object of a preposition. A **verb phrase** consists of a main verb and all of its helping, or auxiliary, verbs.

Writers use noun phrases and verb phrases to add precision to their writing. A noun phrase can be quite specific and richly detailed. A verb phrase can indicate the exact tense, mood, and voice of the main verb.

This chart shows examples of noun phrases and verb phrases in the excerpt from "What to the Slave Is the Fourth of July?"

| TYPE OF PHRASE | COMPOSITION | EXAMPLES |
|---|---|---|
| noun phrase | a noun and its modifiers, including articles, adjectives, and adjective phrases | *I am not that man.* (predicate nominative)<br>*Your high independence only reveals the immeasurable distance between us.* (subject; direct object)<br>*To drag . . . into the grand illuminated temple of liberty . . .* (object of a preposition) |
| verb phrase | a main verb and its helping verbs, but not any interrupting adverbs, such as *not* | *. . . when the chains of servitude had been torn from his limbs?*<br>*In a case like that, the dumb might eloquently speak. . . .*<br>*. . . I do not despair of this country.* |

TIP

CLARIFICATION

Refer to the Grammar Handbook to learn more about verb tense, verb mood, and active and passive voice.

### Read It

1. Each of these sentences contains at least one noun phrase or verb phrase—or both. Mark and label those phrases.
   a. Douglass spoke to the Rochester Ladies Anti-Slavery Society.
   b. He felt that listeners had not supported abolitionism strongly enough, and that he could stir them into action.
   c. His powerful words and his urgent tone shocked many and are still resonating with readers today.
2. **Connect to Style** Reread paragraph 4 of the excerpt from "What to the Slave Is the Fourth of July?" Mark and label two noun phrases and two verb phrases. Explain how the use of the phrases you identified shapes Douglass's style—how the reader "hears" the speaker's voice.

### Write It

**Notebook** Replace each of these nouns with a noun phrase: *crowd, message, shame.* Replace each of these verbs with a verb phrase: *feel, participate, work.* Then, use each phrase in an original sentence that relates to Douglass's speech.





## PERSONALIZE FOR LEARNING

### English Language Support

**Word History** Direct students to the word *denounce* (paragraph 4). Explain that the word is very old, as it first appeared around A.D. 1250–1300. It comes from the Middle English *denouncen* and the Old French *denoncier*, which mean "to speak out." These words, in turn, derive from the Latin *dēnuntiāre*, which means "to threaten" (*dē-* + *nuntiāre* "to announce," derivative of *nuntius* "messenger"). Ask students to define *denounced* based on its history (to condemn, to make a formal accusation against).

DIGITAL  PERSPECTIVES 

## Conventions and Style

**Types of Phrases** Provide the following model to reinforce the difference between phrases and independent clauses.

**Noun phrase:** *the neighbor's cat*
**Verb phrase:** *must go*
**Independent clause:** *The neighbor's cat must go to the vet.*

For more support, see **Conventions and Style: Types of Phrases.**

### Read It

Possible responses:

1. (a) noun phrase: Rochester Ladies Anti-Slavery Society (b) verb phrases: had . . . supported; could stir (c) noun phrases: His powerful words; his urgent tone; verb phrase: are . . . resonating
2. Noun phrases include *your national, tumultuous joy; those bleeding children of sorrow; the popular theme;* and *the crushed and bleeding slave.* Verb phrases include *are rendered, do forget, would be,* and *will dare.*

   Possible response:

   Noun phrases contain modifiers, which help a writer draw a more complete picture for the reader. The verb phrases indicate the exact tense, underscoring the present problem and the potential for change.

### Write It

Possible responses:

The crowd at the meeting listened intently.
Douglass's message came through loud and clear.
We must end the shame of slavery.
The people must have felt lucky to hear Douglass speak.
African Americans could not participate in the nation's celebration.
They could work together to end slavery.

## FORMATIVE ASSESSMENT

### Conventions and Style

- **If** students cannot identify noun and verb phrases, **then** have them first identify the noun and the verb in each example. Then have students look at the surrounding words.
- **If** students cannot replace a noun with a noun phrase and a verb with a verb phrase, **then** have them look back at the examples for clarification. For Reteach and Practice, see **Conventions and Style: Types of Phrases (RP).**

# TEACHING

## Writing to Sources

Point out to students that when you present an argument to someone—when you try to convince someone of your opinion—you need to make sure that you both have the same facts at your disposal. For example, it would be harder to convince someone to wear sunscreen if that person didn't know that exposure to sunlight can cause cancer.

### Reflect on Your Writing

1. Students should suggest that refuting the misconceptions made their presentations clearer and more logical.
2. **Why These Words?** Have students list specific examples of words they chose that added power to their informative writing.

For more support, see **Writing to Sources: Informative Paragraph.**

### FORMATIVE ASSESSMENT

### Writing to Sources

**If** students are unable to make their writing interesting, **then** have them work in pairs to tell each other brief stories that illustrate the point they want to make in their writing. For Reteach and Practice, see **Writing to Sources: Informative Paragraph (RP).**

EFFECTIVE EXPRESSION

*from* WHAT TO THE SLAVE IS THE FOURTH OF JULY?

## Writing to Sources

As Douglass's speech demonstrates, you can strengthen an argument by addressing counterclaims. A similar technique can strengthen informative writing as well: By addressing misconceptions or disproven ideas, you can guide readers to a clearer understanding of the information that you present. For example, if you were writing to explain why explorer Christopher Columbus had difficulty gaining support for his first Atlantic voyage, you might correct the following misconception by stating the fact:

*Misconception*: People thought that the world was flat and that Columbus would sail off the edge.

*Fact*: People thought that Columbus had underestimated the distance and that the crew would die when supplies ran out.

**Assignment**

In this speech, Douglass mentions Southern laws that made it a criminal offense to teach a slave to read and write. Briefly research how some slaves, including Douglass himself, learned to read. Then, write an **informative paragraph** in which you draw connections between your research and Douglass's speech. Include these elements in your paragraph:

- a clear introduction to the topic
- a misconception that you correct with a fact
- a formal, objective tone

**Vocabulary and Conventions Connection** Consider using several of the concept vocabulary words. Also, remember to use noun phrases and verb phrases to make your sentences precise and informative.

| obdurate | disparity | equivocate |
|---|---|---|
| stolid | denounce | conceded |

### Reflect on Your Writing

After you have drafted your informative paragraph, answer the following questions.

1. How do you think that refuting a misconception strengthened your presentation?
2. **Why These Words?** The words you choose make a difference in your writing. Which words helped you convey information precisely?

STANDARDS

Writing

- Write informative/explanatory texts to examine and convey complex ideas, concepts, and information clearly and accurately through the effective selection, organization, and analysis of content.
- Establish and maintain a formal style and objective tone while attending to the norms and conventions of the discipline in which they are writing.

Speaking and Listening

Evaluate a speaker's point of view, reasoning, and use of evidence and rhetoric, assessing the stance, premises, links among ideas, word choice, points of emphasis, and tone used.





PERSONALIZE FOR LEARNING

### Strategic Support

**Research** If students are doing their research on the Internet, discuss the importance of search terms. What is the specific information they need to complete the assignment? For example, searching "misconception" will result in many interesting links, but will not help them find the specific information needed. Have students try more than one term in their search and evaluate the results.

## Speaking and Listening

**Assignment**
**Tone** is the attitude a speaker expresses toward the subject or audience. A speaker's tone may convey any emotion; for instance, it may be loving, angry, scornful, or amused. In this speech, Douglass changes his tone for a variety of reasons. With a partner, identify two passages from the excerpt that convey different tones. Then, take turns giving a **dramatic reading** of each example.

1. **Choose Examples** Together, look for examples of passages in which Douglass emphasizes each of these ideas.
   - He expresses confusion about his purpose for speaking at this occasion.
   - He seeks common ground with his audience.
   - He reaches a turning point.
   - He introduces a counterclaim.
   - He expresses outrage.
2. **Listen to Dramatic Readings** Before you present your dramatic readings, review your examples. Decide which example you will present and which one your partner will present. Then, follow these steps.
   - Practice reciting the passages. Try to convey the tone you feel Douglass wanted to express. Use your voice and body language to emphasize that tone.
   - Introduce each passage by stating the idea that Douglass wanted to present; then, deliver your dramatic reading.
   - After you have both recited, briefly summarize your thoughts about Douglass's use of tone in each passage.
3. **Evaluate the Examples** Use a presentation evaluation guide like the one shown to assess your classmates' readings. Then, as a class, discuss how Douglass's use of tone contributes to his argument.

**PRESENTATION EVALUATION GUIDE**

**Rate each statement on a scale of 1 (not demonstrated) to 5 (demonstrated).**

☐ The speaker clearly introduced the passage.

☐ The speaker communicated expressively.

☐ The speaker used body language, including gestures, to emphasize the tone of the passage.

☐ The speaker accurately interpreted the tone of the passage.

☐ The speaker showed a good understanding of the text.

**EVIDENCE LOG**

Before moving on to a new selection, go to your Evidence Log and record what you learned from "What to the Slave Is the Fourth of July?"





**DIGITAL PERSPECTIVES**

## Speaking and Listening

1. **Choose Examples** Given that they have read through the speech twice, students may have an idea where to find each of these points. If they don't, suggest they pick one of the points and keep it in mind as they read the text again until they find it. The points are listed in the order in which they occur, so students do not have to start reading from the beginning each time.
2. **Listen to Dramatic Readings** You may want to separate partners when they practice. Students will need to use voice and body language together to communicate a specific tone. Having privacy to practice without distraction will help the final presentation.
3. **Evaluate the Examples** Remind students that the Presentation Evaluation is for their use only; it does not affect their grade, so there is no motivation to score a friend more highly than is appropriate. Urge students to judge their partner's performance fairly and honestly.

For more support, see **Speaking and Listening: Dramatic Reading.**

**EVIDENCE LOG** Support students in completing their Evidence Log. Remind them to focus on the tone the speaker uses to interpret the reading. This paced activity will help prepare them for the Performance-Based Assessment at the end of the unit.

### FORMATIVE ASSESSMENT

### Speaking and Listening

**If** students are unable to speak in front of the class without significant distress, **then** have them deliver their recitation to a small group of students instead of the entire class. For Reteach and Practice, see **Speaking and Listening: Dramatic Reading (RP).**

### Selection Test

Administer the "What to the Slave Is the Fourth of July?" Selection Test, which is available in both print and digital formats online in Assessments.

# *from* Second Inaugural Address

**AUDIO SUMMARIES**
Audio summaries of the Second Inaugural Address by Abraham Lincoln are available in both English and Spanish and can be assigned to students in Pearson Realize™. Assigning these summaries prior to reading the selection may help students build additional background knowledge and set a context for their first read.

## Summary

Abraham Lincoln opens his Second Inaugural Address by announcing that it will be shorter than his first—a nation at war has no time to think about new policies. Four years ago it seemed that war could be avoided, but Lincoln says it was clear all along that the insurgents would rather destroy the Union than give up their slaves. Lincoln remarks that both sides pray to the same God but cites biblical authority as he suggests that this war could be God's punishment for the offense of slavery. He warns the insurgents that the slaughter may well continue until the accumulated debt for 250 years of unpaid labor has been paid in blood. Having issued this threat, Lincoln reminds his enemies that he wishes them no harm and urges the Union Army onward to victory.

### Insight

Asserting power is not always the best way to create change. Reading the Second Inaugural Address by Abraham Lincoln will help students understand the surprising strength of humility as a force for changing the way people think and feel. When those in power refuse to use it against those who have lost their power, a union between the two becomes possible.

ESSENTIAL QUESTION:
In what ways does the struggle for freedom change with history?

## Connection to Essential Question

The Second Inaugural Address by Abraham Lincoln provides a nuanced connection to the Essential Question, "In what ways does the struggle for freedom change with history?" Lincoln describes the circumstances that led to the Civil War and explains that the preservation of the Union was at stake. Now, four years later, he redefines the cause as slavery. The passing of time has changed the focus and put the fight to end slavery in the spotlight.

WHOLE-CLASS LEARNING PERFORMANCE TASK
Did the nation achieve the goals that Douglass and Lincoln desired?

UNIT PERFORMANCE-BASED ASSESSMENT
What motivates people to struggle for change?

## Connection to Performance Tasks

**Whole Class Learning Performance Task** In this Performance Task, students will research and report on whether the nation achieved the goals that Douglass and Lincoln desired. In his Second Inaugural Address, Lincoln states some of his goals for the nation, both when he was first elected and then when the end of the Civil War was in sight. Students will consider those goals as they work on their essays.

**Unit Performance-Based Assessment** This selection provides insight into the mind of someone who did not want change, who wanted the nation to remain united, but once it was divided, found that change was necessary.

DIGITAL PERSPECTIVES

 Audio  Video  Document  Annotation Highlights EL Highlights  Online Assessment

## LESSON RESOURCES

| | Making Meaning | Language Development | Effective Expression |
|---|---|---|---|
| Lesson | **First Read**<br>**Close Read**<br>**Concept Vocabulary**<br>**Analyze the Text**<br>**Analyze Craft and Structure** | **Concept Vocabulary**<br>**Word Study**<br>**Conventions and Style** | **Writing to Sources**<br>**Speaking and Listening** |
| Instructional Standards | **RI.10** By the end of grade 11, read and comprehend literary nonfiction . . .<br>**RI.2** Determine two or more central ideas of a text . . .<br>**RI.5** Analyze and evaluate the effectiveness of the structure an author uses . . .<br>**RI.6** Determine an author's point of view . . .<br>**RI.9** Analyze seventeenth-, eighteenth-, and nineteenth-century foundational U.S. documents . . . | **L.1** Demonstrate command of the conventions . . .<br>**L.3** Apply knowledge of language . . .<br>**L.5.b** Analyze nuances in the meanings of words . . .<br>**L.6** Acquire and use accurately general academic and domain-specific words and phrases . . . | **W.2** Write informative/explanatory texts . . .<br>**W.3** Write narratives . . .<br>**SL.3** Evaluate a speaker's point of view . . . |
| **STUDENT RESOURCES** | | | |
| Available online in the Interactive Student Edition or Unit Resources | Selection Audio<br>First-Read Guide: Nonfiction<br>Close-Read Guide: Nonfiction | Word Network | Evidence Log |
| **TEACHER RESOURCES** | | | |
| **Selection Resources**<br>Available online in the Interactive Teacher's Edition or Unit Resources | Audio Summaries<br>Annotation Highlights<br>EL Highlights<br>English Language Support Lesson: Eyewitness Accounts<br>Concept Vocabulary<br>Analyze Craft and Structure: Structure | Concept Vocabulary and Word Study<br>Word Study: Synonyms and Nuances<br>Conventions and Style: Types of Phrases | Writing to Sources: Informative Eyewitness Account<br>Speaking and Listening: Reading and Discussion |
| **Reteach / Practice**<br>Available online in the Interactive Teacher's Edition or Unit Resources | Analyze Craft and Structure: Structure (RP) | Word Study: Synonyms and Nuances (RP)<br>Conventions and Style: Types of Phrases (RP) | Writing to Sources: Informative Eyewitness Account (RP)<br>Speaking and Listening: Reading and Discussion (RP) |
| **Assessment**<br>Available online in Assessments | Selection Test | | |
| **My Resources** | A Unit 3 Answer Key is available online and in the Interactive Teacher's Edition. | | |

# Reading Support

| Text Complexity Rubric: Lincoln's Second Inaugural Address | |
|---|---|
| **Quantitative Measures** | |
| **Lexile:** 1490 **Text Length:** 697 words | |
| **Qualitative Measures** | |
| Knowledge Demands<br>①—②—**❸**—④—⑤ | Prior knowledge is needed of the Civil War, slavery, and Abraham Lincoln's presidency. |
| Structure<br>①—②—③—**❹**—⑤ | Structure is characteristic of an oral speech. Arguments are not presented in a predictable sequence and are interspersed with religious and philosophical speculations. |
| Language Conventionality and Clarity<br>①—②—③—④—**❺** | The speech has many very difficult sentences with archaic and unfamiliar syntax, multiple clauses, biblical references, and above-level vocabulary. |
| Levels of Meaning/Purpose<br>①—②—③—**❹**—⑤ | Multiple levels of meaning include Lincoln's opinions and persuasive arguments, as well as the philosophical and religious implications and beliefs that he expresses. |

DECIDE AND PLAN

## English Language Support

Provide English Learners with support for knowledge demands and language as they read the selection.

**Knowledge Demands** Before having students read the selection, write notes for them to copy of some of the background facts, stated in simple language. For example, *Lincoln gave two inaugural speeches. This is the second speech. At the time of the first speech, the Civil War was almost beginning. At the time of the second speech, the Civil War was almost ending.*

**Language/Clarity** Provide support by restating some of the very complex sentences and replacing some of the difficult vocabulary. For example, (second section) *At the first inaugural speech four years ago, people were thinking about the war. It was about to start. Everyone was trying to prevent it.*

## Strategic Support

Provide students with strategic support to ensure that they can successfully read the text.

**Knowledge Demands** Use the background information to review what students know about Abraham Lincoln's presidency, the Civil War, and slavery. Discuss the context of the speech: when he gave the first inaugural address, the country was on the brink of war. At the time of the second address, the Civil War had been fought and was drawing to a close.

**Language/Clarity** As students read, have them underline or copy some of the most complex and difficult sentences. Guide them to break down the ideas into smaller chunks in order to understand the meaning. Then have them reread the sentences.

## Challenge

Provide students who need to be challenged with ideas for how they can go beyond a simple interpretation of the text.

**Text Analysis** Ask students to distinguish between the ideas in the text that reflect Lincoln's religious viewpoint as opposed to statements that summarize events or popular sentiment. Ask them to write examples of each kind of statement.

**Written Response** Ask students to look up Lincoln's first inaugural address and to read it and copy lines from it. Have students memorize lines from each of the speeches and to take turns in pairs to deliver them as Lincoln. Then invite students to recite the speech for the whole class. Have the students who are listening write notes about the delivery of the speech in order to give comments to the speaker.

TEACH

## Read and Respond

Have students do their first read of the selection. Then, have them complete their close read. Finally, work with them on the Making Meaning, Language Development, and Effective Expression activities.

# Standards Support Through Teaching and Learning Cycle

## IDENTIFY NEEDS

Analyze results of the Beginning-of-Year Assessment, focusing on the items relating to Unit 3. Also take into consideration student performance to this point and your observations of where particular students struggle.

## DECIDE AND PLAN

- If students have performed poorly on items matching these standards, then provide selection scaffolds before assigning them the on-level lesson provided in the Student Edition.
- If students have done well on the Beginning-of-Year Assessment, then challenge them to keep progressing and learning by giving them opportunities to practice the skills in depth.
- Use the Selection Resources listed on the Planning pages for the Second Inaugural Address to help students continually improve their ability to master the standards.

| Instructional Standards: Second Inaugural Address | | | |
|---|---|---|---|
| | **Catching Up** | **This Year** | **Looking Forward** |
| **Reading** | You may wish to administer the **Analyze Craft and Structure: Structure (RP)** worksheet to help students understand that the framework for the speech is based on presenting events in time order. | **RI.5** Analyze and evaluate the effectiveness of the structure an author uses in his or her exposition or argument, including whether the structure makes points clear, convincing, and engaging. | Suggest that students look at another speech by Lincoln and compare the structure of that speech with the structure of the Second Inaugural Address. |
| **Writing** | You may wish to administer the **Writing to Sources: Informative Eyewitness Account (RP)** worksheet to help students understand how recorded personal experiences can bring historical events to life. | **W.3** Write narratives to develop real or imagined experiences or events using effective technique, well-chosen details, and well-structured event sequences. | Ask students to write a letter or journal entry on another speech presented in this unit, written as if they were in the audience when the speech was delivered. |
| **Speaking and Listening** | You may wish to administer the **Speaking and Listening: Reading and Discussion (RP)** worksheet to help students understand how to effectively deliver a speech. | **SL.3** Evaluate a speaker's point of view, reasoning, and use of evidence and rhetoric, assessing the stance, premises, links among ideas, word choice, points of emphasis, and tone used. | Challenge students to prepare and then orally deliver all or part of another speech by President Lincoln. |
| **Language** | You may wish to administer the **Conventions and Style: Types of Phrases (RP)** worksheet to help students identify the purpose of prepositional phrases and the words within a prepositional phrase.<br><br>Review the **Word Study: Synonyms and Nuances (RP)** worksheet with students to ensure that they understand the various shades of meaning conveyed by words that are synonyms. | **L.3** Apply knowledge of language to understand how language functions in different contexts, to make effective choices for meaning or style, and to comprehend more fully when reading or listening.<br><br>**L.5.b** Analyze nuances in the meanings of words with similar denotations. | Ask students to identify more examples of prepositional phrases from Lincoln's Second Inaugural Address. Have students choose five words in paragraph 2 of the Second Inaugural Address for which they can list several synonyms and suggest nuanced meanings. |

## ANALYZE AND REVISE

- Analyze student work for evidence of student learning.
- Identify whether students have met the expectations in the standards.
- Identify implications for future instruction.

## TEACH

Implement the planned lesson, and gather evidence of student learning.

## Jump Start

FIRST READ Before students undertake their first read, ask them the best way to get past a conflict with someone. Suppose that they won the conflict. Would it be a good idea to rub it in the face of the opponent and be vindictive? Why is it better to be gracious and forgiving?

### Second Inaugural Address 

Tell students that Lincoln is speaking at a time when it is clear the Union will win the war. What will he want to tell his audience? What will he say about those who started the war?

Model these and other questions readers might ask as they read Lincoln's Second Inaugural Address in order to connect students to the text and the Performance Task question. You can find selection audio and print capability for the selection in the Interactive Teacher's Edition.

### Concept Vocabulary

Circulate among students as they rank their words. Ask if they have encountered any of the words before. Remind them that each word will be defined in the side column so they can see each word in context.

### FIRST READ

The first time they go through the selection, students perform the steps of the first read:

NOTICE: Students should keep in mind the circumstances under which Lincoln is giving the speech.

ANNOTATE: Students may mark passages for several different reasons.

CONNECT: Students should connect their reading to other speeches or speakers they have heard.

RESPOND: Students will demonstrate their understanding of the text by answering questions and writing a summary.

Point out to students that while they will always complete the Respond step at the end of the first read, the other steps will probably happen somewhat concurrently. You may wish to print copies of the **First-Read Guide: Nonfiction** for students to use.

**Remind students not to answer the close-read questions during their first read.**

MAKING MEANING

About the Speaker

**Abraham Lincoln** (1809–1865) took office as president on March 4, 1861—just six weeks before the Civil War began. The war shaped his presidency, as he sought to reunify the nation. Lincoln took a keen interest in the operations of the war, appointing senior officers, following the war's progress through telegraph updates, and even visiting Union encampments. His belief that slavery was morally wrong drove him to issue a preliminary Emancipation Proclamation in 1862 and a final version on January 1, 1863. From that point on, the Civil War was viewed as a fight to end slavery, as well as to restore the Union.

**Tool Kit**
First-Read Guide and Model Annotation

STANDARDS
Reading Informational Text
• By the end of grade 11, read and comprehend literary nonfiction in the grades 11–CCR text complexity band proficiently, with scaffolding as needed at the high end of the range.

# Second Inaugural Address

## Concept Vocabulary

You will encounter the following words as you read Lincoln's second inaugural address. Before reading, note how familiar you are with each word. Then, rank the words in order from most familiar (1) to least familiar (6).

| WORD | YOUR RANKING |
|---|---|
| insurgent | |
| perish | |
| rend | |
| scourge | |
| unrequited | |
| malice | |

After completing the first read, come back to the concept vocabulary and review your rankings. Mark changes to your original rankings as needed.

### First Read NONFICTION

Apply these strategies as you conduct your first read. You will have an opportunity to complete the close-read notes after your first read.

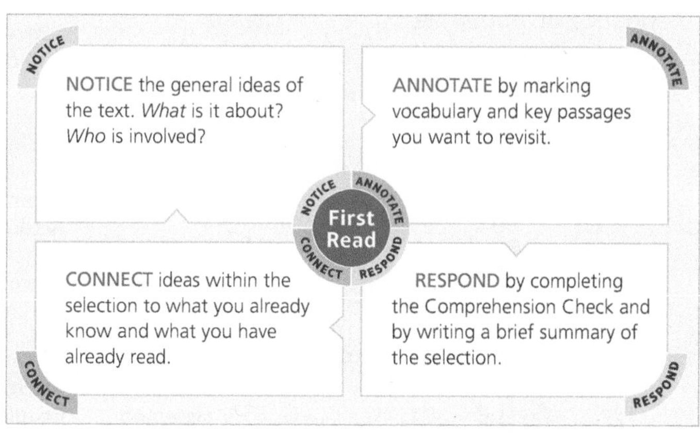
NOTICE the general ideas of the text. *What* is it about? *Who* is involved?
ANNOTATE by marking vocabulary and key passages you want to revisit.
CONNECT ideas within the selection to what you already know and what you have already read.
RESPOND by completing the Comprehension Check and by writing a brief summary of the selection.
First Read
NOTICE
ANNOTATE
CONNECT
RESPOND

## DIGITAL PERSPECTIVES

**Illuminating the Text** The day of Lincoln's second inauguration, March 4, 1865, was overcast and misty, the third day of rain. Because few streets in Washington, D.C., were paved in the mid-nineteenth century, everything was extremely muddy. Nonetheless, tens of thousands of people came for the inauguration, filling every bit of available space. (Refer to the background paragraph.) To help students visualize Lincoln's popularity and the grand scale of the event, have them go online to find photographs of the occasion. Invite students to suggest what views and angles they would have taken photos from, had they been present at the event.

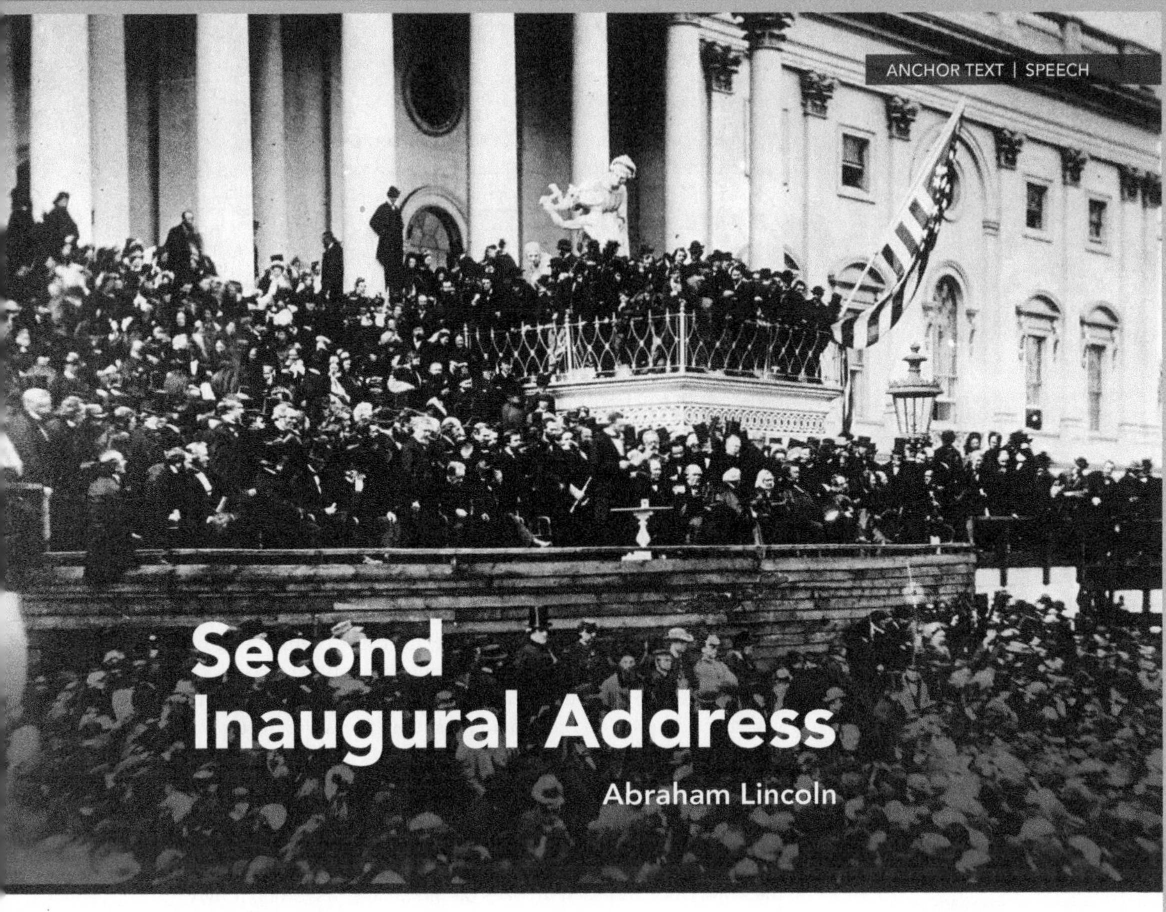


# Second Inaugural Address

Abraham Lincoln

DIGITAL PERSPECTIVES

BACKGROUND

On March 4, 1865, a crowd of perhaps as many as 40,000 people gathered on the muddy grounds of the United States Capitol to see Abraham Lincoln sworn in for his second term. Despite rain earlier in the morning, the sun broke through the clouds as Lincoln came forward. He gave the following speech to hopeful listeners, who (as one of his bodyguards later said) "seemed to hang on his words as though they were meat and drink." Indeed, Frederick Douglass told Lincoln that the speech had been "a sacred effort." Following the speech, Chief Justice Salmon P. Chase administered the oath of office. Ironically, Lincoln would die a little more than a month later at the hands of John Wilkes Booth, who stood in the crowd on the Capitol steps that day and listened to Lincoln give the speech.

SCAN FOR MULTIMEDIA 

NOTES

## Fellow-Countrymen:

1 At this second appearing to take the oath of the presidential office, there is less occasion for an extended address than there was at the first. Then a statement somewhat in detail of a course to be pursued seemed fitting and proper. Now, at the expiration of four years, during which public declarations have been constantly called



### PERSONALIZE FOR LEARNING

**English Language Support**

**Figures of speech** Review the Background information with students. Discuss the phrase in the Background information: *listeners seemed to hang on his words as though they were meat and drink.* Point out that this is an example of a figure of speech. Ask questions to help guide students to understand the meaning. For example, *Think about meat and drink. Why are they important?* (We can't live without them. We need them to survive.). *If his words were like meat and drink, what does that tell you about his words?* (His words tell us very important ideas that we need to know to sustain us.)

# TEACHING

## CLOSE READ

Point out that even now, with the war nearly over and the Union victorious, Lincoln takes the opportunity to persuade his listeners that the Union's cause was just. You may choose to model the idea this way:

**ANNOTATE:** As I read paragraph 3, I look for and mark the sentence that states the government's policy regarding the expansion of slavery.

**QUESTION:** It sets up a contrast between the government and the Confederacy.

**CONCLUDE:** It makes the Union seem reasonable and correct and the Confederacy seem rash and incorrect. Lincoln says the Confederacy was driven to destroy the Union, while the Union wanted to "do no more" than limit the expansion of slavery.

Additional **English Language Support** is available in the Digital Teacher's Edition.

NOTES

**insurgent** (ihn SUR juhnt) *adj.* rebellious or in revolt against a government in power

**perish** (PEH rish) *v.* die

**rend** (rehnd) *v.* tear apart with violent force

CLOSE READ

ANNOTATE: Mark the sentence in paragraph 3 that states the government's policy regarding the expansion of slavery.

QUESTION: Why does the president include this information?

CONCLUDE: What effect does this information have, particularly in shaping the audience's view of the Confederacy?

**scourge** (SKURJ) *n.* cause of serious trouble or suffering

**unrequited** (uhn rih KWY tihd) *adj.* not repaid or avenged

forth on every point and phase of the great contest which still absorbs the attention and engrosses the energies of the nation, little that is new could be presented. The progress of our arms, upon which all else chiefly depends, is as well known to the public as to myself, and it is, I trust, reasonably satisfactory and encouraging to all. With high hope for the future, no prediction in regard to it is ventured.

2 On the occasion corresponding to this four years ago, all thoughts were anxiously directed to an impending civil war. All dreaded it; all sought to avert it. While the inaugural address was being delivered from this place, devoted altogether to saving the Union without war, **insurgent** agents were in the city seeking to destroy it without war—seeking to dissolve the Union and divide effects by negotiation. Both parties deprecated war, but one of them would make war rather than let the nation survive, and the other would accept war rather than let it **perish**, and the war came.

3 One-eighth of the whole population were colored slaves, not distributed generally over the Union, but localized in the southern part of it. These slaves constituted a peculiar and powerful interest. All knew that this interest was somehow the cause of the war. To strengthen, perpetuate, and extend this interest was the object for which the insurgents would **rend** the Union even by war, while the government claimed no right to do more than to restrict the territorial enlargement of it. Neither party expected for the war the magnitude or the duration which it has already attained. Neither anticipated that the cause of the conflict might cease with or even before the conflict itself should cease. Each looked for an easier triumph, and a result less fundamental and astounding. Both read the same Bible and pray to the same God, and each invokes his aid against the other. It may seem strange that any men should dare to ask a just God's assistance in wringing their bread from the sweat of other men's faces, but "let us judge not, that we be not judged."[1] The prayers of both could not be answered. That of neither has been answered fully. The Almighty has his own purposes. "Woe unto the world because of offenses; for it must needs be that offenses come, but woe to that man by whom the offense cometh."[2] If we shall suppose that American slavery is one of those offenses which, in the providence of God, must needs come, but which, having continued through his appointed time, he now wills to remove, and that he gives to both North and South this terrible war as the woe due to those by whom the offense came, shall we discern therein any departure from those divine attributes which the believers in a living God always ascribe to him? Fondly do we hope, fervently do we pray, that this mighty **scourge** of war may speedily pass away. Yet, if God wills that it continue until all the wealth piled by the bondsman's two hundred and fifty years of **unrequited** toil

1. **"let us judge not, that we be not judged"** reference to the words of Jesus in the biblical passage Matthew 7:1.
2. **"Woe unto the world . . . the offense cometh."** reference to the biblical passage Matthew 18:7, in which Jesus warns about allowing sin into one's life.





## CROSS-CURRICULAR PERSPECTIVES

**Social Studies** Review paragraphs 1–3 with students and tell students that Abraham Lincoln's "Second Inaugural Address" is considered a masterpiece. *The London Spectator* reviewed the speech this way: "We cannot read it without a renewed conviction that it is the noblest political document known to history, and should have for the nation and the statesmen he left behind him something of a sacred and almost prophetic character." Have students review paragraphs 1–3 and consider what makes the speech a masterpiece. Have groups of students find other speeches that are considered masterpieces, such as Martin Luther King, Jr.'s "I Have a Dream," Franklin Roosevelt's "Day of Infamy," or William Faulkner's "Banquet Speech" upon receiving the Nobel Prize. Have students analyze the speech to identify the qualities that make it historic, and explain these qualities to the class. As a class, list the qualities that all great speeches share.

DIGITAL PERSPECTIVES

shall be sunk, and until every drop of blood drawn with the lash shall be paid by another drawn with the sword, as was said three thousand years ago, so still it must be said "the judgments of the Lord are true and righteous altogether."[3]

4 With **malice** toward none, with charity for all, with firmness in the right as God gives us to see the right, let us strive on to finish the work we are in, to bind up the nation's wounds, to care for him who shall have borne the battle and for his widow and his orphan, to do all which may achieve and cherish a just and lasting peace among ourselves and with all nations. ❧

NOTES

**malice** (MAL ihs) *n.* desire to harm or inflict injury

3. **"the judgments of the Lord are true and righteous altogether"** reference to the biblical Psalm 19:9, praising the rightness of God's ways.

## Comprehension Check

Complete the following items after you finish your first read.

1. To what event is Lincoln referring when he says, "On the occasion corresponding to this four years ago. . ."?
2. What was on people's minds at the time of the occasion you identified in item 1?
3. What is the "peculiar and powerful interest" that Lincoln says was "somehow the cause of the war?"
4. What does Lincoln intend to do to heal the nation, after the war?
5. **Notebook** Write a summary of Lincoln's second inaugural address to confirm your understanding of the speech.

### RESEARCH

**Research to Clarify** Choose at least one unfamiliar detail from the text. Briefly research that detail. In what way does the information you learned shed light on an aspect of the speech?

**Research to Explore** Choose something that interests you from the text, and formulate a research question about it.





## Comprehension Check

Possible responses:

1. Lincoln is referring to his first inaugural address.
2. People were preoccupied with thoughts that the nation might be headed for civil war.
3. The "interest" is slavery.
4. He intends to care for the wounded on both sides, as well as the widows and orphans of Union and Confederate soldiers.
5. Lincoln discusses the views of the Union and the Confederacy, with a special emphasis on the issue of slavery. He notes that the war has lasted longer than expected, finds it ironic that both sides should pray for victory, and speculates that the war is divine punishment for allowing slavery. Lincoln looks ahead to the end of war (and a Union victory) and a compassionate healing of the nation.

### Research to Clarify

If students struggle to come up with a detail to research, you may want to suggest that they focus on one of the following topics: the great loss of life in the Civil War, prevalent religious beliefs of the period, or the Confederacy.

### Research to Explore

If students have a hard time choosing a part of the text, ask questions such as, "What do you think was the most important thing Lincoln said?" or "What part do you think had the most beautiful use of language?"

## PERSONALIZE FOR LEARNING

### Challenge

**Historical Analysis** Ask students, "Is there a difference between doing the right thing and doing the most pragmatic thing?" Offer an example:

*Suppose you have two friends who are arguing, and you believe one of them is right, but you don't want to lose the other as a friend. What should you do?*

Explain that political leaders often face very difficult dilemmas. Tell students to review paragraph 4—specifically, Lincoln's use of the phrase "bind up the nation's wounds." Lincoln wanted to abolish slavery, but he also wanted to keep the nation whole. Ask partners to analyze the economic, political, and cultural divisions that forced Lincoln into a pragmatic position based on preserving the nation and re-shifting its wealth. Remind them to look back at the Historical Perspectives essay.

## Jump Start

CLOSE READ Present the following prompt to the class: *Imagine that your country has just won a war. You are addressing the nation. Would you speak of happiness or sadness? Why?* As students discuss in their groups, ask them to think about why winning could be an occasion for grief as well as joy.

## Close Read the Text

Walk students through the annotation model on the student page. Encourage them to complete items 2 and 3 on their own. Review and discuss the sections students have marked. If needed, continue to model close reading by using the Annotation Highlights in the Interactive Teacher's Edition.

## Analyze the Text

Possible responses:

1. (a) The future depends on how well the Union forces do on the battlefield. **DOK 2** (b) Lincoln is referring to the continued existence of the United States as one country. **DOK 1**
2. By citing the circumstances of his previous inaugural, he links past and present. **DOK 3**
3. (a) It appeared that the war would settle the question of slavery, but slavery was abolished and the war continued. **DOK 2** (b) Each side sees itself as right and asks God to help defeat the other. **DOK 2**
4. The speech points out that slavery was the cause of the war and points out the evil of the institution. **DOK 3**
5. The struggle may become more intense and destructive than originally imagined, but there is hope for reconciliation when the war ends. **DOK 3**

### FORMATIVE ASSESSMENT

### Analyze the Text

- **If** students fail to cite evidence, **then** remind them to support their ideas with specific information.
- **If** students struggle to explain what Lincoln means by "all else," **then** have them think about how the country might deal with the after effects of the Civil War.



MAKING MEANING

SECOND INAUGURAL ADDRESS

## Close Read the Text

1. This model, from paragraph 2 of the text, shows two sample annotations, along with questions and conclusions. Close read the passage, and find another detail to annotate. Then, write a question and your conclusion.

ANNOTATE: Lincoln is comparing and contrasting reasons the North and South went to war.

QUESTION: For what purpose might Lincoln do this?

CONCLUDE: By showing insight about the war's causes, Lincoln might be indicating his ability to reunite the nation.

Both parties deprecated war, but one of them would make war rather than let the nation survive, and the other would accept war rather than let it perish, and the war came.

ANNOTATE: The final words are very dramatic.

QUESTION: What is the effect of these words?

CONCLUDE: Appearing at the end of a long, complex sentence, the simple words emphasize the horror of war.

**Tool Kit**
Close-Read Guide and Model Annotation

2. For more practice, go back into the text, and complete the close-read notes.
3. Revisit a section of the text you found important during your first read. Read this section closely, and **annotate** what you notice. Ask yourself **questions** such as "Why did the author make this choice?" What can you **conclude**?

STANDARDS

**Reading Informational Text**
- Determine two or more central ideas of a text and analyze their development over the course of the text, including how they interact and build on one another to provide a complex analysis; provide an objective summary of the text.
- Analyze and evaluate the effectiveness of the structure an author uses in his or her exposition or argument, including whether the structure makes points clear, convincing, and engaging.
- Determine an author's point of view or purpose in a text in which the rhetoric is particularly effective, analyzing how style and content contribute to the power, persuasiveness, or beauty of the text.
- Analyze seventeenth-, eighteenth-, and nineteenth-century foundational U.S. documents of historical and literary significance for their themes, purposes, and rhetorical features.

## Analyze the Text

**CITE TEXTUAL EVIDENCE** to support your answers.

Notebook **Respond to these questions.**

1. (a) **Paraphrase**, or state in your own words, Lincoln's comment that "all else chiefly depends" upon "the progress of our arms." (b) **Interpret** To what is Lincoln referring with the words "all else"?
2. **Connect** How do Lincoln's statements in paragraph 2 connect to the rest of the speech?
3. (a) **Make Inferences** The term **irony** refers to a discrepancy between appearances and reality. Think about the irony in paragraph 3. In what way does Lincoln see irony in the abolition of slavery in the United States? (b) **Interpret** What does Lincoln find ironic about the prayers of both sides?
4. **Historical Perspectives** In what ways is this speech a commentary on the issue of slavery?
5. **Essential Question** *How does the struggle for freedom change with history?* What have you learned about the struggle for freedom from reading this speech?





### PERSONALIZE FOR LEARNING

**Strategic Support**
Students with learning challenges might have difficulty understanding and interpreting irony. Guide them through the literal interpretation of paragraph 3. Then ask if they think that this is really what Lincoln meant. Help them to think about what was happening in the nation at that time. Have them consider why Lincoln might have used irony to make his point.

## Analyze Craft and Structure

**Structure** Writers often use a **chronological structure,** or time order, as a framework for their ideas. You may be used to seeing chronological order in the plot of a novel or play, but this kind of structure is also effective in nonfiction. For example, listeners can more easily follow the logic of a speech when ideas are presented within a chronological structure.

- The speaker establishes the chronological structure by discussing the events or actions that led to the present situation—which is often the occasion for the speech.
- The present situation is examined. At this point, the audience understands the central idea of the speech and contemplates the author's reasoning.
- The chronological framework is completed by a discussion of the future. This part can be a persuasive call to action or an explanation of a final step. It is always a clear statement of the speaker's central idea.

In his second inaugural address, Lincoln recalls the past, discusses the present, and looks to the future.

### Practice

**CITE TEXTUAL EVIDENCE** to support your answers.

Notebook Respond to these questions.

1. (a) What does Lincoln say about the nature of the speech he made when he first took office, four years earlier? (b) How does he contrast that information with the speech that he is making in the present, at his second inauguration?
2. In this chart, briefly record the content of each part of the chronological framework of Lincoln's speech.

| LINCOLN'S SECOND INAUGURAL ADDRESS: CHRONOLOGICAL CONTENT | |
|---|---|
| Past | |
| Present | |
| Future | |

3. What does the content of the speech tell you about Lincoln's intended policy for his second term?
4. (a) What national issue does Lincoln discuss in paragraph 3? (b) What might have been the effect of the speech if Lincoln had developed it to discuss only this issue? Explain.
5. How does Lincoln's use of chronological structure contribute to the effectiveness of the speech? Explain.





## PERSONALIZE FOR LEARNING

### Strategic Support

**Chronological Order** If students have difficulty identifying the three chronological markers in Lincoln's speech, suggest they create a timeline and arrange textual details on it in the three categories: past, present, and future. Direct students to look for *past* information paragraph 2; *present* information in paragraph 3; and *future* information in paragraph 4.

DIGITAL PERSPECTIVES  

## Analyze Craft and Structure

**Structure** Discuss with students how authors help readers and listeners follow the chronological structure of their writing. Point out that writers use time-order transitions, such as "first" and "now," as well as dates, such as "four years ago." To help students follow the chronological structure of Lincoln's speech, have them look for the time-order transitions and dates that Lincoln uses.

For more support, see **Analyze Craft and Structure: Structure.**

**MAKE IT INTERACTIVE**

Project the digital version of the Second Inaugural Address and model finding a detail that relates to the past. This will help students understand how carefully Lincoln structured his address to trace the past, describe the present, and lay out his policy for the future.

### Practice

Possible responses:

1. (a) Lincoln says that the first speech was an extended address that detailed a future course of action. (b) In contrast, there will be no new information about the war, and he will make no predictions about the future.
2. Past: All dreaded war; the South wanted war but the North opposed it; war came. Present: The nation is still at war; war is divine punishment for slavery. Future: Heal the nation and take care of those in both North and South who were wounded or left in need.
3. He will work to heal the nation rather than to punish the South.
4. (a) Lincoln discusses the issue of slavery. (b) The speech probably would not have had a conciliatory tone.
5. Framing the past and present as he did made it easier for Lincoln to help his audience understand the reasons he was determined to act "with charity to all."

### FORMATIVE ASSESSMENT

### Analyze Craft and Structure

- **If** students are unable to determine what Lincoln says about the nature of the speech he made in the past, **then** have them reread the first paragraph of the speech.
- **If** students are having difficulty following the chronological structure of the beginning of the speech, **then** have them organize important notes into two columns: "Four Years Ago" and "Today." For Reteach and Practice, see **Analyze Craft and Structure: Structure (RP).**

TEACHING

## Concept Vocabulary

**Why These Words?**

Possible responses:

1. The vocabulary highlights the violent nature of the act of secession from the Union, and it evokes the brutality of the war.
2. Choices include *woe, lash, blood, wounds,* and *battle.*

### Practice

1. Responses will vary but should reflect accurately the meaning of each word.
2. Responses will vary, but most students will say that the sentences with the synonyms are less powerful, while the sentences with the original words are more negative.

### Word Network

**Possible words:** *offenses, wounds, conflict, toil, strive, triumph*

## Word Study

For more support, see **Concept Vocabulary and Word Study.**

1. Responses will vary but should reflect an understanding of the shades of meaning each use of *deprecate* shows in the sentence.
2. The synonym *blight* closely reflects Lincoln's use of the word *scourge* because a *blight*, like a war, is something that causes harm.

**FORMATIVE ASSESSMENT**

### Concept Vocabulary

**If** students fail to see the connection among the words, **then** have them use each word in a sentence and think about what is similar about the sentences.

### Word Study

**If** students have difficulty understanding shades of meaning in the words, **then** have them decide which word they would prefer to have applied to them, and why. For Reteach and Practice, see **Word Study: Synonyms and Nuances (RP).**

LANGUAGE DEVELOPMENT

SECOND INAUGURAL ADDRESS

## Concept Vocabulary

| insurgent | rend | unrequited |
|---|---|---|
| perish | scourge | malice |

**Why These Words?** These concept vocabulary words remind the audience of the terrible nature of the conflict that the nation was enduring at the moment. Lincoln says that the *insurgents* would *rend* the nation. He speaks of the *scourge* of war—and, indeed, the war took many American lives and destroyed much of the nation's property.

1. How does the concept vocabulary convey the nature of the conflict?

2. What other words in the speech connect to this concept?

### Practice

Notebook Complete these activities.

1. Use each concept vocabulary word in a sentence that demonstrates your understanding of the word's meaning.
2. In two of your sentences, replace the concept word with a synonym. What is the effect of your word change? For example, which sentence seems more powerful? Which one seems more positive or more negative?

WORD NETWORK

Add words related to struggle from the text to your Word Network.

## Word Study

**Synonyms and Nuances** In this speech, Lincoln refers to the "scourge" of war. *Scourge* is a very strong word, an example of charged language. Lincoln might have chosen another word with a similar denotation, such as *blight* or *curse*. These words are synonyms because they have similar general meanings. They are also all examples of charged, or emotionally laden language. However, each word has its own **nuance,** or shade of meaning. For example, *blight* suggests disease or withering, whereas *curse* suggests a supernatural source of suffering.

1. Write two sentences, using a synonym for *scourge* in each sentence. Make sure that each sentence demonstrates the shade of meaning of the synonym you choose.

2. Reread the second inaugural address. Which synonym for *scourge* most closely reflects Lincoln's use of the word? Explain.

STANDARDS

**Language**

- Demonstrate command of the conventions of standard English grammar and usage when writing or speaking.
- Apply knowledge of language to understand how language functions in different contexts, to make effective choices for meaning or style, and to comprehend more fully when reading or listening.
- Analyze nuances in the meaning of words with similar denotations.
- Acquire and use accurately general academic and domain-specific words and phrases, sufficient for reading, writing, speaking, and listening at the college and career readiness level; demonstrate independence in gathering vocabulary knowledge when considering a word or phrase important to comprehension or expression.





VOCABULARY DEVELOPMENT

**Graphic Organizers** Have students analyze the words *scourge* (paragraph 3) and *malice*, (paragraph 4) using a three-row organizer to show definition, characteristics, and examples. Then work with students to complete information about *deprecate* (paragraph 2) and *rend* (paragraph 3).

**scourge**

**Definition:** a lash, especially for the infliction of punishment; a person who administers punishment or severe criticism; a cause of affliction or calamity

**Characteristics:** cruel, painful, sore, aching, agonizing

**Examples:** whip, tormentor, plague, curse, torture

**malice**

**Definition:** desire to inflict injury, harm, or suffering on another due to meanness

**Characteristics:** spite, vindictiveness, ill will, retribution

**Examples:** hatred, malevolence, nastiness, wickedness, cruelty, evil

## Conventions and Style

**Types of Phrases** A **prepositional phrase** is a group of words that begins with a preposition. Some prepositions are listed here.

| | | | | |
|---|---|---|---|---|
| about | across | at | beneath | by |
| concerning | despite | except | for | from |
| in | into | near | of | on |
| regarding | than | to | toward | with |

A prepositional phrase also includes an object and any modifiers of that object. The object of the preposition may be a noun, a pronoun, a gerund (a verb form that acts as a noun), or, occasionally, a clause. Prepositional phrases function in sentences as either adverbs or adjectives. They help writers and speakers express their ideas with greater clarity and precision.

| TYPE OF PHRASE | DEFINITION | EXAMPLES |
|---|---|---|
| **adverb phrase** | a prepositional phrase that modifies a verb, an adjective, or another adverb, by telling *how, where, when,* or *to what degree* | Lincoln was assassinated at Ford's Theatre. (tells *where*)<br>John Wilkes Booth shot him during a play. (tells *when*) |
| **adjective phrase** | a prepositional phrase that modifies a noun or pronoun, by telling *what kind, how many,* or *which one* | The president from Illinois died soon after. (tells *which one*)<br>Crowds beyond number mourned his loss. (tells *how many*) |

### Read It

1. Mark the prepositional phrase in each sentence. Then, label each one as an adverb phrase or an adjective phrase.
   a. Lincoln delivered his address at the White House.
   b. The East Portico of the White House was a historic place.
   c. Lincoln spoke in a clear, strong voice.
2. **Connect to Style** Reread paragraph 3 of Lincoln's speech. Mark and then label two adjective phrases and two adverb phrases. Explain how the use of prepositional phrases contributes to Lincoln's style and helps clarify his ideas.

### Write It

**Notebook** Expand the numbered sentences by adding one or more adverb phrases or adjective phrases. Label each phrase in parentheses.

> EXAMPLE
> The sun began shining.
> The sun began shining ***through the clouds*** *(adverb phrase)* ***at the moment*** *(adverb phrase)* ***of Lincoln's speech*** *(adjective phrase).*

1. Lincoln spoke, and everyone paid rapt attention.
2. Most listeners applauded when the words touched their minds and hearts.





DIGITAL PERSPECTIVES 

## Conventions and Style

**Types of Phrases** As you review these examples with students, point out that there are many more prepositions, about 150 in all. Explain that students can determine whether a word is a preposition by using the following mnemonic: "The rabbit ran _____the hill." Any word that fits in the blank is a preposition. In addition to the words listed on this page, prepositions that work with this mnemonic include: *over, beneath, above, against, around, before, behind, besides, down, inside, onto, outside, past, underneath.* Note that there are some prepositions that do not fit the sentence, such as *despite.*

For more support, see **Conventions and Style: Types of Phrases.**

### Read It

1. a. at the White House; adverb phrase
   b. of the White House; adjective phrase
   c. in a clear, strong voice; adverb phrase
2. Adjective phrases include *of the whole population* and *from those divine attributes.* Adverb phrases include *by war* and *to the same God.* Lincoln uses prepositional phrases to add more information. In paragraph 4, the prepositional phrases *with malice toward none, with charity for all,* and *with firmness in the right* add rhythm and sophistication to the writing.

### Write It

Possible responses:
Added prepositional phrases are underlined.

1. Lincoln spoke to an eager crowd, and everyone in attendance paid rapt attention. (adverb phrase; adjective phrase)
2. Most listeners applauded with enthusiasm when the words of Lincoln's speech touched their minds and hearts. (adverb phrase; adjective phrase)

### FORMATIVE ASSESSMENT

### Conventions and Style

- **If** students are unable to distinguish between adjective and adverb phrases, **then** remind them that an adjective phrase tells *which kind? how many?* or *which one?* An adverb phrase tells *how? where? when?* or *to what degree?*
- **If** students have trouble identifying prepositions, **then** create a list of common prepositions and have students practice using them. For Reteach and Practice, see **Conventions and Style: Types of Phrases (RP).**

# TEACHING

## Writing to Sources

As students describe what Lincoln's inauguration was like, encourage them to use words that appeal to the five senses, vivid verbs, and specific nouns. Remind students who choose to write a letter to address it to a specific person, so they can tailor their writing to their audience's knowledge and needs.

Remind students that since the ceremony took place on March 4, 1865, people would have arrived by horse or horse and carriage, rather than by car, and that Lincoln would not have had a microphone. For more support, see **Writing to Sources: Informative Eyewitness Account.**

### Reflect on Your Writing

1. Paragraphs will vary, but students should have written as though they were indeed present at the inauguration, using the first-person point of view.
2. Paragraphs will vary, but students should have included details about what they heard, saw, and even smelled to make it seem as though they were actually present at the event.
3. **Why These Words?** Responses will vary. Have students list specific examples of words they chose that added power to their eyewitness account. Suggest peers review to comment or add to the writer's list of words.

### FORMATIVE ASSESSMENT

### Writing to Sources

**If** students are unable to make it seem that they were really at the inauguration, **then** have students sketch the scene and use details from the drawing in their writing. For Reteach and Practice, see **Writing to Sources: Informative Eyewitness Account (RP).**

EFFECTIVE EXPRESSION

SECOND INAUGURAL ADDRESS

## Writing to Sources

Eyewitness accounts are important sources of historical information. Historians look for as many such accounts as are available in order to compare what each eyewitness has recorded. In addition to each person's unique insights, historians look for corroboration of descriptions and sequences of events.

**Assignment**

Imagine that you had been present when Abraham Lincoln delivered this inaugural address. Write an **informative eyewitness account** in the form of a letter or journal entry. Include details such as these:

- personal details, such as where you were standing
- an estimate of how many people were present
- Lincoln's appearance and delivery
- the effect of the speech on the crowd
- your opinion of the speech

Report narrative details in an orderly sequence. You might want to remark, for example, on your difficulties as you looked for a place to stand and observe the occasion. Then, describe the scene from the vantage point you eventually found.

**Vocabulary and Conventions Connection** Consider including several of the concept vocabulary words. Also, remember to use prepositional phrases to add precision to your account.

| insurgent | rend | unrequited |
|---|---|---|
| perish | scourge | malice |

### Reflect on Your Writing

After you have drafted your informative eyewitness account, answer these questions.

1. Did you write as if you had been actually present?
2. What kinds of details did you add to make your account realistic?
3. **Why These Words?** The words you choose can greatly increase the effect of your writing. Which words do you think are most helpful in conveying the sense that "you had been there"?

**STANDARDS**

**Writing**

- Write informative/explanatory texts to examine and convey complex ideas, concepts, and information clearly and accurately through the effective selection, organization, and analysis of content.
- Write narratives to develop real or imagined experiences or events using effective technique, well-chosen details, and well-structured event sequences.

**Speaking and Listening**

Evaluate a speaker's point of view, reasoning, and use of evidence and rhetoric, assessing the stance, premises, links among ideas, word choice, points of emphasis, and tone used.





### PERSONALIZE FOR LEARNING

**English Language Support**

**Eyewitness Accounts** Ask students to fill out an organizer identifying a line from paragraph 4 of the speech and what kind of audience reaction that line might evoke. **EMERGING**

Ask students to fill out an organizer identifying a line from paragraph 4 and two different audience reactions that line might evoke. **EXPANDING**

Ask students to write a paragraph without an organizer identifying a line from paragraph 4 and two different reactions that line might evoke. **BRIDGING**

An expanded **English Language Support Lesson** on Eyewitness Accounts is available in the Interactive Teacher's Edition.

## Speaking and Listening

**Assignment**

With a partner, prepare a brief **reading and discussion** of key passages from Lincoln's speech.

1. **Choose the Passages** Work together to choose two passages that you feel express key ideas with particular force or clarity.
   - Read the sentences or passages aloud, pausing to restate, or paraphrase, Lincoln's words.
   - Work together to develop a clear statement about the reasons you chose the two passages: What qualities in the language or ideas make these two passages especially powerful?
2. **Prepare Your Delivery** Read through the passages, and note natural breaks. These may be indicated by punctuation marks, but you also can choose places where you will want to pause for emphasis.
3. **Deliver Your Reading and Analysis** Follow these tips as you read your passages aloud and discuss your choices.
   - Speak slowly so that listeners can follow any challenging language or ideas.
   - Use gestures and body language carefully to emphasize meaning without causing distraction. In addition, vary the volume of your voice and the speed with which you speak to accurately reflect the ideas you are expressing.
   - Remember that the language of Lincoln's speech is formal. In addition, some word choices are different from those in modern speech. Make sure your interpretation reflects the meanings of such words accurately.
   - Pause after you complete your readings of the passages. Then, present your interpretations of the passages in your own words.
4. **Evaluate Presentations** As your classmates deliver their presentations, listen attentively. Use the evaluation guide to analyze their presentations.

**PRESENTATION EVALUATION GUIDE**

**Rate each statement on a scale of 1 (not demonstrated) to 5 (demonstrated).**

- ☐ The speaker read the text with proper emphasis on meaning.
- ☐ The speaker used appropriate gestures and body language.
- ☐ The speaker's pace and volume were varied and appropriate for the thoughts and feelings expressed in the text.
- ☐ The speaker's interpretations and evaluations were accurate and well expressed.



**EVIDENCE LOG**

Before moving on to a new selection, go to your Evidence Log and record what you learned from Lincoln's second inaugural address.



**DIGITAL PERSPECTIVES**

## Speaking and Listening

### Assignment

If students have difficulty understanding the task, explain that they will not be reading the entire speech. Rather, they will be delivering sections of the speech to the class and then paraphrasing what they read to explain it to their classmates.

1. **Choose the Passages** Suggest students work together, reading aloud some passages to choose two suitable passages. Ask them to talk together about what the words mean and what is especially powerful. Remind students that much of the speech has theological and historical allusions, which they are likely going to want to explain.
2. **Prepare Your Delivery** As they mark their text to create scripts, remind students to also include marks for places they will add emphasis by speaking loudly or softly and raising or lowering their pitch. Also suggest that students mark places where they want to pause and make eye contact to emphasize a key point. Finally, students should mark any words they find difficult to pronounce and practice them—and the entire speech—until the presentation is fluent.
3. **Deliver Your Reading and Analysis** Remind students to stand up straight to reflect the formal occasion. Also encourage students to hold up their speech so their voice projects, rather than looking down and having their voice be muted.

For more support, see **Speaking and Listening: Reading and Discussion.**

### FORMATIVE ASSESSMENT

### Speaking and Listening

**If** students are unable to stand and speak in front of the class, **then** have students sit down at a desk as they deliver their lines. For Reteach and Practice, see **Speaking and Listening: Reading and Discussion (RP).**

### Selection Test

Administer the "Second Inaugural Address" Selection Test, which is available in both print and digital formats online in Assessments.

## PERSONALIZE FOR LEARNING

### English Language Support

**Text Chunking and Evaluating Speech** Help partners choose groups of sentences from paragraphs 1, 2, or 4 in the speech and read and mark them up, chunking sections by phrases, collocated words, and other parts that go together. Have them identify unfamiliar or hard-to-pronounce vocabulary and use context or a dictionary to help them. Then have them paraphrase the sentences to help them with meaning and fluency.

Next, have partners take turns reading aloud and evaluating each other, using the evaluation guide. Since rating can be challenging, have partners note reasons for their ratings (e.g., *I think you should have emphasized the first sentence more so I gave you a 3.*). Have partners use ratings to discuss ways each could improve, and read aloud again.

# Perspectives on Lincoln

**AUDIO SUMMARIES**
Audio summaries of "Perspectives on Lincoln" are available online in both English and Spanish in the Interactive Teacher's Edition or Unit Resources. Assigning these summaries prior to reviewing the selection may help students build additional background knowledge and set a context for their first review.

## Summary

Abraham Lincoln has not always been honored as an American icon. Image 1 and Image 2 show how the wartime president faced the mockery of political cartoonists and the smears of opponents as he campaigned for reelection. We see nobility in his gaunt stare, but his contemporaries mocked his homely features and lanky frame. To some admirers they made him likeable—the jokey familiarity of Image 3 is a surprise to Americans who only know the icon.

The Civil War ended on April 9, 1865. Six days later the national hero became a national martyr. News photographers, who were playing an increasingly important part in serious journalism, created a record of the greatest state funeral in American history. In Image 4 the camera witnesses history, but inept hand-finishing defeats the purpose of taking a photograph. Image 5 conveys the epic scale of the event in a composition of amazing depth and clarity. In Image 6, civil rights leaders honor the American icon.

### Insight

Viewing "Perspectives on Lincoln" will give students a point of view on Lincoln and his role in America's history that they may not have encountered before. In addition to the familiar reverential feelings toward Lincoln, some of the images present him in a negative light.

ESSENTIAL QUESTION
In what ways does the struggle for freedom change with history?

## Connection to Essential Question

"Perspectives on Lincoln" provides a visual approach to the Essential Question—*In what ways does the struggle for freedom change with history?* The images show the transition from a struggle for freedom that caused a war, resulting in hundreds and thousands of deaths, to a struggle that attempted to rise above violence while continuing the fight that Lincoln started. The images also show that the perceptions of Lincoln changed with time—from a divisive politician to a warmonger, from a great President to a martyr, and finally, to a symbol of the fight for freedom.

WHOLE-CLASS LEARNING PERFORMANCE
Did the nation achieve the goals that Douglass and Lincoln desired?

UNIT PERFORMANCE-BASED ASSESSMENT
What motivates people to struggle for change?

## Connection to Performance Tasks

**Whole-Class Learning Performance Task** In this Performance Task, students will research and report on whether the nation achieved the goals that Douglass and Lincoln desired. "Perspectives on Lincoln" includes images that provide insight into how Lincoln and his goals were viewed by others, both during and after his lifetime.

**Unit Performance-Based Assessment** This selection provides insight into the way that Lincoln was perceived as he worked tirelessly for change throughout his lifetime.

DIGITAL PERSPECTIVES

 Audio  Video  Document  Annotation Highlights  EL Highlights  Online Assessment

## LESSON RESOURCES

| | Making Meaning | Effective Expression |
|---|---|---|
| Lesson | **Media Vocabulary**<br>**First Review**<br>**Close Review**<br>**Analyze the Media** | **Speaking and Listening** |
| Instructional Standards | **RI.10** By the end of grade 11, read and comprehend literary nonfiction . . . | **RI.7** Integrate and evaluate multiple sources of information . . .<br>**SL.2** Integrate multiple sources of information . . .<br>**SL.5** Make strategic use of digital media . . . |
| **STUDENT RESOURCES** | | |
| Available online in the Interactive Student Edition or Unit Resources | Selection Audio<br>First-Review Guide: Media: Art and Photography<br>Close-Review Guide: Media: Art and Photography | Evidence Log |
| **TEACHER RESOURCES** | | |
| **Selection Resources** Available online in the Interactive Teacher's Edition or Unit Resources | Audio Summaries<br>Media Vocabulary | Speaking and Listening: Image Gallery |
| **My Resources** | A Unit 3 Answer Key is available online and in the Interactive Teacher's Edition | |

## Text Complexity Rubric: Perspectives on Lincoln

| Quantitative Measures | |
|---|---|
| **Format:** Caricatures and Photographs **Length:** Six images | |
| **Qualitative Measures** | |
| Knowledge Demands<br>① ② ❸ ④ ⑤ | Some knowledge of Abraham Lincoln and the issues and events surrounding the Civil War is needed. |
| Structure<br>❶ ② ③ ④ ⑤ | Structure is straightforward and easy to follow—a series of images that are explained by captions. |
| Language Conventionality and Clarity<br>① ❷ ③ ④ ⑤ | The language used in the captions is clear and direct. |
| Levels of Meaning/Purpose<br>① ② ❸ ④ ⑤ | The caricatures and cartoons contain deeper meanings, but these are explained by the captions. |

# TEACHING

## Jump Start

FIRST READ Ask students to consider the following prompt: *What other ways besides words do political commentators have for getting their message across?* Engage students in a discussion about the ways in which pictures, cartoons, or videos might be more effective than words in conveying a message. This can set the context for reading "Perspectives on Lincoln."

## Perspectives on Lincoln 

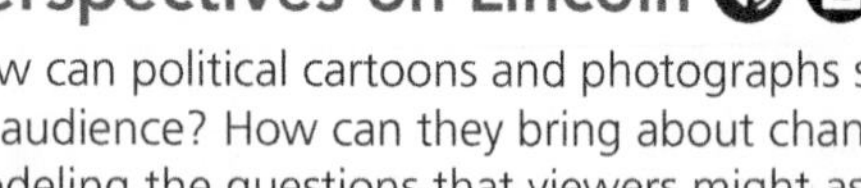

How can political cartoons and photographs sway an audience? How can they bring about change? Modeling the questions that viewers might ask as they review "Perspectives on Lincoln" brings the selection alive for students and connects it to the Whole-Class Performance Task question. Selection audio and print capability for the selection are available in the Interactive Teacher's Edition.

## Media Vocabulary

Encourage groups to discuss the three media vocabulary words. Have they seen the words in texts before? Do they use any of the words in their speech and writing?

Ask groups to brainstorm additional words used to discuss political cartoons and photographic journalism and share with the class. Students may offer *bias, sensationalism,* and *commentary*.

## FIRST REVIEW

As they review, students should perform the steps of the first review:

LOOK: Remind students to focus on the basic elements of the cartoons, photos, labels, and captions to ensure they understand what the art shows.

NOTE: Encourage students to mark any cartoons and photos they wish to revisit during their close review.

CONNECT: Encourage students to make connections between the political cartoons and photos here and other political cartoons, photos, campaigns, or related events.

RESPOND: Students will answer questions to demonstrate understanding.

Point out to students that while they will always complete the Respond step at the end of the first review, the other steps will probably happen somewhat concurrently. You may wish to print copies of the **First-Review Guide: Media: Art and Photography** for students to use.



MAKING MEANING

**About Political Cartoons and Photojournalism**

Many **political cartoons**, especially in the nineteenth century, were published anonymously; in fact, of the three cartoons in this gallery, only the pro-Lincoln caricature of the President's height is attributable (to Frank Billew). The others, expressing the dissatisfaction with Lincoln's leadership that seethed in the North among the Democrats and those Republicans unsatisfied with Lincoln's leadership in the war, were published anonymously in various newspapers.

**Photojournalism**—capturing news in photographs—emerged in the 1840s. The new technology of photography found a use in revealing events and preserving images for history, including battlefield photographs of the Civil War.

# Perspectives on Lincoln

## Media Vocabulary

The following words will be useful to you as you analyze, discuss, and write about political cartoons and photojournalism.

| | |
|---|---|
| Composition: arrangement of the parts of an image, whether drawn or recorded in some other visual format | • The composition may emphasize one part of an image more than another.<br>• The composition may offer clues to the political purpose of the image. |
| Caricature: exaggeration of details relating to people and events, often for humorous effect, in a cartoon or other created image | • In political cartoons, caricature often shows how the cartoonist (or the publication that hired the cartoonist) feels about a particular person, group, or situation.<br>• Sometimes, elements of a public figure's appearance become commonly caricatured, making that person easy to identify. |
| Labeling and Captions: written labels and other text that often accompany politically charged images to clarify their meanings | • In political cartoons, key details are often labeled to help readers recognize their meaning.<br>• Photographs are more likely to use captions or annotations that present the context in which the photograph was taken. |

## First Review MEDIA: ART AND PHOTOGRAPHY

Apply these strategies as you conduct your first review. You will have an opportunity to conduct a close review after your first review.

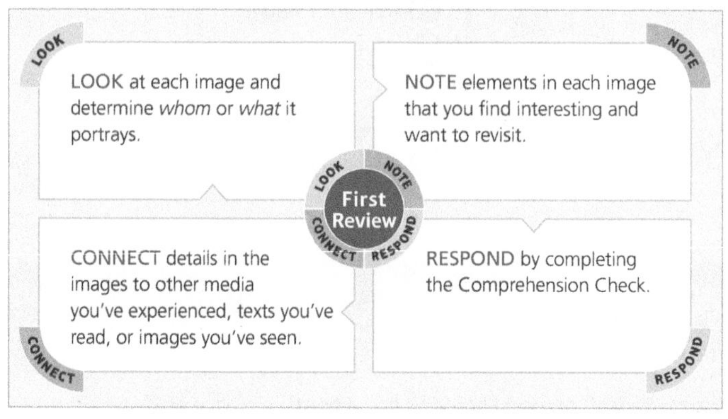

LOOK
LOOK at each image and determine *whom* or *what* it portrays.
NOTE
NOTE elements in each image that you find interesting and want to revisit.
First Review
CONNECT details in the images to other media you've experienced, texts you've read, or images you've seen.
RESPOND by completing the Comprehension Check.
CONNECT
RESPOND


STANDARDS

**Reading Informational Text**
By the end of grade 11, read and comprehend literary nonfiction in the grades 11–CCR text complexity band proficiently, with scaffolding as needed at the high end of the range.

MEDIA | IMAGE GALLERY

# Perspectives on Lincoln

BACKGROUND

As Lincoln's second election campaign approached, he was faced with a Republican party threatening to splinter, a bloody Civil War in its final stages, and a Democratic party ready to capitalize on his apparent vulnerability. However, Lincoln overcame these obstacles by combining the political heft of an impending Union victory, the support of the soldier vote, and political deals brokered within the Republican party. His campaign's slogan was "Don't change horses in the middle of a stream." As you study these images, ask yourself these questions: What opinions did people have of Lincoln in his own time? How is he thought of today?

SCAN FOR MULTIMEDIA 

**IMAGE 1: The Union Must Be Preserved at All Hazards** This 1864 cartoon depicts Democratic presidential candidate George Brinton McClellan trying to keep a map of the United States from being pulled apart by President Abraham Lincoln and the Confederate president Jefferson Davis. The cartoon depicts both Lincoln and Davis as short-sightedly putting their own political goals (abolition for Lincoln, secession for Davis) ahead of the country's well-being.

NOTES





CLOSER REVIEW

## Analyze Composition 

Students may have marked Image 1 during their first review. Use this image to help students analyze the effect **composition** has on the artist's message and the impact of the cartoon.

ANNOTATE: Have students mark elements in the cartoon that reveal its **composition.**

QUESTION: How are the figures arranged in this cartoon? Which part of the image is emphasized the most? Why?

**Possible response:** The figures are arranged in a triad, the center figure of McClellan balancing Lincoln on the left and Davis on the right. McClellan is the focus because he is keeping the other two figures apart, preventing them from tearing the Union in two.

CONCLUDE: What clues does the composition offer to the cartoon's political purpose? How does this composition help the artist convey his message?

**Possible response:** The composition suggests the deep division in the country and its leadership, a division that threatened to destroy the Union. Placing McClellan in the center allows the artist to show the importance of finding a way to resolve differences for the sake of the nation.

Remind students that the **composition** of an image, or the relationship among the objects, is important in helping to reinforce the message.

CLOSER REVIEW

## Examine Labeling and Captions

Students may have noted the labeling and caption on Image 2 during their first review. Use this cartoon to help students examine how the label and caption help clarify meaning by calling out key details.

**ANNOTATE:** Have students paraphrase the caption and the dialogue between Columbia and Lincoln.

**QUESTION:** What key details do the caption and dialogue reveal?

**Possible response:** The caption clarifies that the female figure represents America. The dialogue shows America's anger toward the war's high death toll and Lincoln's apparently nonchalant attitude toward it.

**CONCLUDE:** Why are the caption and dialogue important to your understanding of this cartoon?

**Possible response:** They make clear that the artist is bitterly attacking Lincoln's leadership because of the human toll of the Civil War. The caption and dialogue help the artist convey his lack of faith in Lincoln.

Remind students that **labels and captions** are the information that often accompany images in a presentation. This text can support viewer's understanding of the image.

**IMAGE 2: Columbia Demands Her Children!** "Columbia," a personification of America, is condemning Abraham Lincoln for the Union casualties of the Civil War. Lincoln's reply refers to a false report that Lincoln had told a joke on the battlefield of Antietam.

NOTES

**IMAGE 3: Long Abe a Little Longer** In this celebration of Lincoln's reelection, Lincoln is caricatured as being president "even longer"—a play on words regarding his height and his length of time in office, as well as a reference to his "stature," or importance, as president.

NOTES





PERSONALIZE FOR LEARNING

### English Language Support

**Literary Devices and Visual Cues** Review Image 1 and Image 2 with students. Guide students to realize that the goals of figurative language can be achieved in visuals as well as text. Help them notice the personification of the country as a woman, "Columbia" in Image 2. She is demanding Lincoln give her back her 500,000 casualties in the Civil War. Explain that the cartoon puts Lincoln in a bad light as he replies in a light-hearted way that her scolding reminds him of a story.

Point out how the visuals also develop the "play on words" in Image 3, which shows Lincoln after his successful reelection: *Long Abe a Little Longer.* Point out that the visual shows a Lincoln who is tall and "longer" in height to mean that he's grown in stature and importance. Explain that it also means that he'll be President longer because of his reelection.

**IMAGE 4: The Body of the Martyr President, Abraham Lincoln, Lying in State** Further increasing his stature in the eyes of the nation, Lincoln's assassination made him a martyr, as the North was united in grief. Many historians have called Lincoln's funeral the greatest in the history of the United States.

NOTES

**IMAGE 5: Funeral Procession in New York City** Millions turned out to see Lincoln's funeral train pass on its way to his burial in Springfield, Illinois—and, in some cities, to attend a ceremony in his honor. In this photograph of a funeral procession held during a stop in New York City, a young Theodore Roosevelt (later President Roosevelt) and his brother watch the scene from a window (in the upper left-hand corner of the image).

NOTES

DIGITAL PERSPECTIVES

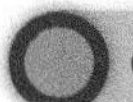

CLOSER REVIEW

## Understand Composition

Students may have marked Image 4 during their first review. Use this lithograph to help students analyze how the composition helps the artists convey the mood and message.

**ANNOTATE:** Guide groups to describe the **composition** of the figures and elements in the picture. Remind groups to consider how the composition can reveal what the artists want the audience to notice.

**QUESTION:** How are the elements arranged? What is the focal point, or the most important element, in this lithograph?

**Possible response:** The lithograph has classical balance, with groups of people on each side and the coffin in the center. The curve of the drapes, the bust on the top of the image, and the hanging cords all draw the reader's eye to the coffin.

**CONCLUDE:** What does the composition of this lithograph suggest about how the artists, Currier and Ives, felt about Lincoln and his death?

**Possible response:** The composition suggests their deep sorrow and their reverence for Lincoln. The echoes of neoclassicism suggests that Lincoln is a tragic hero of ancient Greek stature and that he "now belongs to the ages," as his friend Secretary of War Edwin M. Stanton supposedly said at Lincoln's deathbed on April 15, 1865.

Remind students that the composition of a photograph can be manipulated when the photographer chooses a specific place from which to take the picture. For example, in this photograph, the photographer chose to include the drapes in the shot, and that has an impact in the way the image is perceived.

## PERSONALIZE FOR LEARNING

### Strategic Support

**Composition** If any students struggle to comprehend how composition may stress one part of an image more than another, ask another student to help. Invite the student to conduct a think-aloud to investigate Image 4. The student should consider some of the strategies the artist has used to focus the viewer's attention on the subject of the picture. The student might notice that the drapes are like stage curtains, the raised platform between them resembles a stage, and the casket is placed at centerstage. Almost everyone in the picture—including the statues—is gazing at the casket and its occupant. The viewer's eyes follow the direction of everyone else's. Have other students suggest more ways in which the artist has used composition to focus attention on Lincoln as he lies in state.

# TEACHING

## CLOSER REVIEW

### Scrutinize Composition 

Students may have marked Image 6 during their first review. Use this photograph to help students analyze how the photographer uses composition to convey Lincoln's enduring importance.

**ANNOTATE:** Ask students to describe which part of the photograph is emphasized and why.

**QUESTION:** Which element is in the background? Which element is in the foreground? Why did the photographer arrange the composition in this way?

**Possible response:** The statue of Lincoln is in the background, but also above the others. The civil rights activists are in the foreground. This composition conveys Lincoln's lasting importance, as his legacy looms over the leaders and imbues them with his vision of equality for all people.

**CONCLUDE:** What do you think is the political purpose of this photograph, based on the composition?

**Possible response:** Placing the men in the foreground suggests how far America has come, as African American leaders, protesting for civil rights, have the power to bring about political and social change as significant as Lincoln's achievements a century ago. The twentieth-century activists may not have had the opportunity to lead without Lincoln's contributions in the nineteenth century.

**IMAGE 6: Civil Rights Activists at the Lincoln Memorial** Almost a century after Lincoln's death, leaders of the Civil Rights movement, including Dr. Martin Luther King, Jr., (seated, farthest right) gather in front of the Lincoln Memorial during the 1963 March on Washington. The Civil Rights movement often looked to Abraham Lincoln, "the Great Emancipator," for inspiration.

NOTES





## PERSONALIZE FOR LEARNING

### Strategic Support

Have students discuss and make notes on the meaning of the phrase "The Great Emancipator" as it related to the career and achievements of Abraham Lincoln. Explain that *to emanicipate* means "to free someone from slavery." Ask students why the men in Image 6 might have wished to be photographed in front of the Lincoln Memorial.

## Comprehension Check

Use the chart to note details about the subject of each image. Identify people and/or symbols, objects, the setting (if there is one), and activities or events depicted.

| IMAGE | PEOPLE AND/OR SYMBOLS | OBJECTS | SETTING | ACTIVITIES AND/OR EVENTS |
|---|---|---|---|---|
| IMAGE 1 | a. See possible responses in the Teacher's Edition. | b. | c. | d. |
| IMAGE 2 | e. | f. | g. | h. |
| IMAGE 3 | i. | j. | k. | l. |
| IMAGE 4 | m. | n. | o. | p. |
| IMAGE 5 | q. | r. | s. | t. |
| IMAGE 6 | u. | v. | w. | x. |

NOTES





## Comprehension Check

**Possible responses:**

a. President Lincoln, Democratic presidential candidate George Brinton McClellan, Confederate president Jefferson Davis, the possibility of the country being torn apart

b. map of the Union

c. the time of President Lincoln's reelection campaign

d. struggle between the Union and the Confederacy over abolition and secession

e. President Lincoln; "Columbia," a symbol representing America

f. handbill or flyer with the number of troops President Lincoln is asking to voluntarily enlist into the Union army

g. President Lincoln sitting in a kitchen during the Civil War

h. "Columbia" confronting President Lincoln over the number of dead soldiers

i. a stretched President Lincoln standing straight

j. a newspaper or bulletin announcing President Lincoln's reelection

k. none

l. President Lincoln is standing straight

m. a procession of mourners with black armbands

n. black curtains, black bunting, a bust of Lincoln, a coffin with President Lincoln's body

o. President Lincoln's wake

p. mourners paying their respects to an assassinated President Lincoln

q. a large crowd of onlookers, mounted escorts, soldiers and police officers, a boy looking out of the window (later identified as future president Teddy Roosevelt)

r. street lamps covered in black

s. New York City right after the end of the Civil War

t. a crowd watches a funeral procession move down a street

u. Reverend Dr. Martin Luther King, Jr., and other civil rights activists in front of a statue of President Lincoln

v. Political buttons, a statue of President Lincoln

w. Washington, D.C., during the civil rights era

x. Reverend Dr. Martin Luther King, Jr., and other civil rights activists pose in front of a statue of President Lincoln

## Jump Start

CLOSE REVIEW Ask students to consider the following quotation: "Outside of basic intelligence, there is nothing more important to a good political cartoonist than ill will." Explain that this quotation comes from Jules Feiffer, a famous political cartoonist. Engage students in a discussion about what "ill will" a cartoonist might have and how it relates to the theme of power, protest, and change.

## Close Review

Model close reviewing by using the Closer Review notes for the selection. Remind students to clarify anything they did not understand during their first review. You may wish to print the **Close-Review Guide: Media: Art and Photography** for students to use.

## Analyze the Media

1. Responses will vary. Remind students to close review in order to find details that support their assertions.
2. Responses will vary. Remind students to explain why they believe the cartoons and photographs are examples of art, journalism, or both.
3. Responses will vary, but should be supported with text details.

## Media Vocabulary

1. (a) Lincoln and Davis are on opposite sides of the frame, and McClellan is between them, pulling them both in. **DOK 1** (b) The artist uses this *composition* to convey the idea that Lincoln and Davis are on the fringe of public opinion, while McClellan, like most Americans, wants the country to remain intact. **DOK 2**
2. (a) The shield, sword, and tiara help create the identity, and the *caption* confirms her as Columbia. **DOK 2** (b) In this *caricature,* Lincoln's face and beard show who he is, and his great height is exaggerated for effect. **DOK 2**
3. (a) The *composition* of the photo helps convey the message that great men are carrying on the work that Lincoln started. **DOK 3** (b) Images 4 and 5 show the high regard Lincoln was held in at the time of his death. **DOK 3**

MAKING MEANING

PERSPECTIVES ON LINCOLN

## Close Review

Revisit the images and your first-review notes. Write down any new observations that seem important. What **questions** do you have? What can you **conclude?**

## Analyze the Media

Notebook Complete the activities.

1. **Present and Discuss** Choose the image you find most interesting or persuasive. Share your choice with the class, and discuss why you chose it. Explain what you noticed in the image, the questions it raised for you, and the conclusions you reached about it.
2. **Review and Synthesize** Review all the images. What perspectives do they present? What argument are they making? Are they examples of journalism, art, both, or neither? Explain.
3. **Essential Question:** ***In what ways does the struggle for freedom change with history?*** What have you learned about the struggle for freedom from these cartoons and photographs?

LANGUAGE DEVELOPMENT

## Media Vocabulary

composition caricature labeling and captions

Use these vocabulary words in your responses to the following questions.

1. (a) In Image 1, what are the positions of the three people in relation to one another? To the map of the United States? (b) What might the artist have intended to convey through this depiction?
2. (a) In Image 2, what visual details clarify the identity of the woman on the left? (b) On what visual details does Image 3 rely to convey its message?
3. (a) In what sense does Image 6 express a political idea? (b) How does that idea reflect the ideas expressed in Images 4 and 5?

STANDARDS

**Reading Informational Text**
Integrate and evaluate multiple sources of information presented in different media or formats as well as in words in order to address a question or solve a problem.

**Speaking and Listening**
- Integrate multiple sources of information presented in diverse formats and media in order to make informed decisions and solve problems, evaluating the credibility and accuracy of each source and noting any discrepancies among the data.
- Make strategic use of digital media in presentations to enhance understanding of findings, reasoning, and evidence and to add interest.





PERSONALIZE FOR LEARNING

### Strategic Support

**Reporting vs. Commentary** Students may struggle to comprehend the different roles of political cartoons and photographic journalism. Review the political images, describe the differences between reporting and commenting, and ask students to role-play these two journalistic roles so that they understand the different points of view. Explain that a publisher's opinions are expressed in editorials. A cartoonist's opinions are expressed in the form of political cartoons. On television and radio, commentators often provide their own opinions, but it is important that citizens understand the difference between objective reporting and commentary. Discuss the effect of these various roles in journalism.

EFFECTIVE EXPRESSION

## Speaking and Listening

**Assignment**

Create and present an **image gallery.** Choose a person about whom or an event about which Americans had or have varying perspectives. Conduct research, using print and online sources, to find relevant political cartoons and photographs. Create a slide show of your image gallery, and write an informative script to accompany your presentation.

**Plan the Project** To help you prepare your image gallery, consider these questions.

- Why is or was the person or event important? What are you trying to show your audience about the perspectives that people had or have of the person or event?
- What sources will you use to conduct your research?
- What technology will you need to present your image slide show?

When choosing photographs, consider how the images reflect attitudes, not just how they preserve a moment in time. When you have chosen your images, make a storyboard.

STORYBOARD TEMPLATE

**Prepare the Informative Script** Think about the relationships among the images. Consider how you might use the script to point out those relationships.

- Choose a logical sequence of images. Decide how to use transitions in your script to show that sequence.
- Decide how much time to spend on presenting each image. Tailor the length of each section of your script accordingly.
- Once you have written your script, practice reading it aloud.

**Present and Discuss** Present a slide show of your image gallery to the class, using your script to narrate each image as you show it. Afterward, discuss how well the various perspectives were captured in the images.

EVIDENCE LOG

Before moving on to a new selection, go to your Evidence Log and record what you learned from "Perspectives on Lincoln."





DIGITAL PERSPECTIVES

## Speaking and Listening

**Plan the Project** Have students research their subject in a variety of sources to make sure they can present a balanced viewpoint on the issues. Remind students that sources are biased, so they must weigh the opinions they find to form their own well-reasoned assessments.

Point out to students that a storyboard presents information in chronological order, so students should arrange their facts, details, opinions, and images the same way, from earlier to later in time.

**Prepare the Informative Script** Suggest that students allot the most time to the more authoritative and reliable images and facts. Less convincing information should receive proportionally less time and space in the presentation. Remind students that the informative script they create is an important part of the assignment. This can be thought of as a kind of narrative that shows how the person or event was perceived over time. The script should therefore include time-order words (such as *first, then,* and *last*) and specific dates.

**Present and Discuss** As students present the images, have them use the media vocabulary they learned in this lesson: *composition, caricature,* and *labeling* and *captions.* Remind students that using these subject-specific words will help them be precise when they analyze the images.

For more support, see **Speaking and Listening: Image Gallery.**

**Evidence Log** Support students in completing their Evidence Log. This paced activity will help prepare them for the Performance-Based Assessment at the end of the unit.

### FORMATIVE ASSESSMENT

### Speaking and Listening

**If** students are having trouble selecting a subject, **then** have them think of a well-known person or event about which people do not agree, and list the opposing viewpoints in two columns.

## PERSONALIZE FOR LEARNING

### English Language Support

**Storyboarding About Familiar Topics** To prepare students for the group work, arrange students in groups to create a storyboard of a current news event. Assign roles: discussion leader, partner researchers, partner image collectors, partner checkers/editors, and partner storyboard layout artists. Have the leader conduct a discussion to list ideas and then assign researchers to a news event. Once the research is completed, have researchers provide sources to image collectors, who will either download and label the images or write short descriptions of them. Have the checkers/editors check to be sure the images reveal a sequence and go together. Finally, have storyboard layout artists arrange the images on a storyboard.

Tell the discussion leader to engage the group in a review of the storyboards and choose the best one. Explain that students can use what they learned to create their group image galleries.

# TEACHING

## Jump Start

What goals did Frederick Douglass and Abraham Lincoln have regarding black Americans?

Have students review and discuss, by citing text evidence, "What to the Slave Is the Fourth of July?" and Second Inaugural Address in terms of goals explicitly stated or implied. They may be immediate or long-term goals.

## Write an Informative Text

In writing this informative essay, students will first need to determine and articulate what Douglass's and Lincoln's goals were in the first place (and how they were similar and different). The second part of their task will be to determine whether the nation achieved those goals. Remind students that additional material on this subject can be found online or in the library.

### Elements of an Informative Essay

Remind students that the body paragraphs of an informative essay should each have a central idea that is expressed in a topic sentence at the beginning of the paragraph. Each body paragraph should support the overarching central idea of the essay.

**MAKE IT INTERACTIVE**

Project "The Zigzag Road to Rights" from the Interactive Teacher's Edition, and invite students to provide specific examples of how arguments in the selection are built paragraph by paragraph.

## Academic Vocabulary

Consider asking students for examples of sentences they might use in their informative essays that incorporate academic vocabulary words.

PERFORMANCE TASK: WRITING FOCUS

WRITING TO SOURCES

- *from* WHAT TO THE SLAVE IS THE FOURTH OF JULY?
- SECOND INAUGURAL ADDRESS
- PERSPECTIVES ON LINCOLN

**Tool Kit**
Student Model of an Informative Essay

ACADEMIC VOCABULARY

As you write your essay, consider using some of the academic vocabulary you learned in the beginning of the unit.

informational
deduction
verbatim
inquire
specific

STANDARDS

**Writing**

- Write informative/explanatory texts to examine and convey complex ideas, concepts, and information clearly and accurately through the effective selection, organization, and analysis of content.
- Conduct short as well as more sustained research projects to answer a question or solve a problem; narrow or broaden the inquiry when appropriate; synthesize multiple sources on the subject, demonstrating understanding of the subject under investigation.
- Write routinely over extended time frames and shorter time frames for a range of tasks, purposes, and audiences.

# Write an Informative Essay

You've just read two important nineteenth-century speeches. In the first, Frederick Douglass looks forward to the liberation of people from slavery. In the second, Abraham Lincoln looks forward to the end of a war and to a just and lasting peace. You've also examined political cartoons and other images from the period that portray differing attitudes about Abraham Lincoln.

**Assignment**

Write an **informative essay** that looks at American history after the Civil War and that answers this question:

> Did the nation achieve the goals that Douglass and Lincoln desired?

Begin by doing some library or online research. Investigate the period following the Civil War by looking up "Reconstruction" and taking notes on your findings. Include facts, details, and definitions that clarify your response. Connect your findings to specific details from the selections in Whole-Class Learning.

### Elements of an Informative Essay

An **informative essay** uses facts, details, data, and other kinds of evidence to present information about a topic. Readers turn to informative texts when they wish to learn about a specific idea, concept, or subject area.

An effective informative essay contains these elements:

- a thesis statement that introduces the concept or subject
- relevant facts and concrete details that expand upon the topic
- extended definitions, quotations, and other examples that support the information presented
- use of varied sentence structures to clarify the relationships among ideas
- precise language and technical vocabulary where appropriate
- a formal style and an objective tone
- a conclusion that follows from and supports the information presented

**Model Informative Essay** For a model of a well-crafted informative essay, see the Launch Text, "The Zigzag Road to Rights." Review the Launch Text for examples of the elements described above. You will look more closely at these elements as you prepare to write your own informative essay.

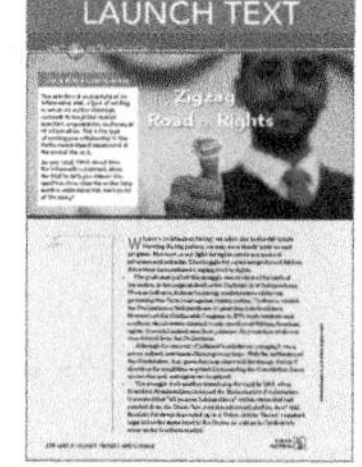






## PERSONALIZE FOR LEARNING

**Strategic Support**

If students struggle to identify any element in the list of "Elements of an Informative Essay," mark three words, phrases, or sentences in paragraphs 5–9 of "The Zigzag Road to Rights." One should be an example of the element in question; the other two should not. Ask students to pick the correct example from the three and explain why they chose it.

## Prewriting / Planning

**Write a Working Thesis** Reread the assignment. Based on the work you have done so far in this unit, think about what you want to say in response to the question that the assignment asks. Write a draft of your **thesis statement** (or **thesis**)—the sentence that presents the controlling idea of your text.

______________________________________________

______________________________________________.

**Compare and Contrast** Douglass and Lincoln had different goals, but some of their concerns were similar. Record some areas of comparison and contrast that you might use to support your thesis statement.

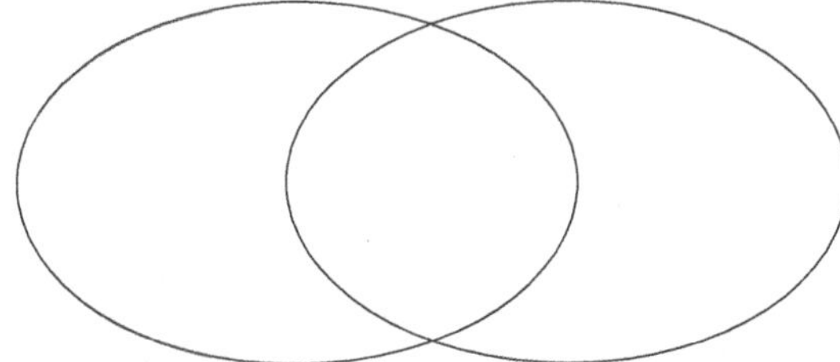

Douglass's Goals    Common Goals    Lincoln's Goals

**Gather Evidence** Several kinds of information support the thesis developed in the Launch Text. Think about ways in which you can effectively support your thesis. Consider these types of evidence:

- **facts:** relevant statements that can be proved true
- **statistics:** facts presented in the form of numerical data
- **definitions:** explanations of key terms that may be unfamiliar to readers
- **quotations:** statements from authoritative sources (such as historical documents)
- **examples:** specific circumstances that illustrate a general idea

Always confirm your evidence by using more than one source.

**Connect Across Texts** The prompt asks you to connect your findings to specific details from the speeches by Douglass and Lincoln. Also include details from the political cartoons and other images of Lincoln in your response. Return to those texts, and on note cards record **direct quotations** from the speeches that you might use to support your ideas. Look back at the Launch Text to see how the writer weaves direct quotations from court cases, proclamations, and amendments into the informative essay.

EVIDENCE LOG

Review your Evidence Log and identify key details you may want to cite in your informative essay.

STANDARDS

Writing

- Introduce a topic; organize complex ideas, concepts, and information so that each new element builds on that which precedes it to create a unified whole; include formatting, graphics, and multimedia when useful to aiding comprehension.
- Develop the topic thoroughly by selecting the most significant and relevant facts, extended definitions, concrete details, quotations, or other information and examples appropriate to the audience's knowledge of the topic.





DIGITAL PERSPECTIVES

## Prewriting/Planning

**Write a Working Thesis** Remind students that a working thesis can be changed once the organizational structure of the essay is more clearly fleshed out. Encourage students to briefly but specifically articulate the goals of Douglass and Lincoln, and then say why they did or did not achieve those goals. You can also remind students that a thesis statement may be longer than one sentence.

**Compare and Contrast** The compare/contrast exercise is meant to help students organize their thoughts about the goals of Douglass and Lincoln. Encourage students to draw a large Venn diagram on an 8 ½ x 11 sheet of paper to more easily see their ideas.

**Gather Evidence** Remind students that they can glean facts and statistics from any source, but if they use a source from the Internet, it's important to first evaluate the quality and validity of that source before using it in an informative essay. Encourage students to organize their evidence in a logical manner. The Venn diagram, along with the use of the compare/contrast strategy, should help them organize their material.

**Connect Across Texts** When using two or more texts to write one's own informative essay, it is especially important to attribute each piece of information to its source. Remind students to use signal phrases for exact quotations and paraphrased text. For example: "According to Douglass," "Lincoln notes that . . ." and "Both Douglass and Lincoln agree that . . ."

PERSONALIZE FOR LEARNING

### English Language Support

**Compare and Contrast Personal Goals** Share the background paragraph from the Second Inaugural Address. To help students prepare for comparing and contrasting the goals of Lincoln and Douglass, have them list some questions about their goals for today, a year from now, or ten years from now. Tell each student to list six questions and write his or her own answers. Then have students ask a partner those same questions and have the partner answer them. Have partners note their responses on a Venn diagram, writing any that are the same in the section where the circles overlap. Then have students compare and contrast their goals, using words such as *similarly, the same, both, on the other hand, however,* and *but.*

## Enriching Writing With Research

**Conducting Research** Many students turn first to the Internet when seeking information, so you may want to ask the librarian to show students how to access subscription databases.

Discuss with students their approach to research and their strategies for determining reliable resources.

**Assessing Strengths and Limitations of Information** As students check for reliable, current, and relevant material for their topics, alert them to note-taking strategies that help them document and track this information.

### Read It

Ask students to note relevant material that is quoted and supports the topic of the excerpt. Then ask them to show how the writer avoided plagiarism.

When students have completed this assignment, ask them to check their work against the steps provided here. Peer reviewers can also review these steps in their feedback.

PERFORMANCE TASK: WRITING FOCUS

## ENRICHING WRITING WITH RESEARCH

**Conducting Research** Most informative writing requires some research. Find relevant information from reputable sources, and then weave it into your essay.

**Assessing Strengths and Limitations of Information** Some information is reliable and useful, whereas other information may be suspect or simply not helpful. Evaluate the quality of the information you find by answering these questions:

- Will this information help me develop my topic or thesis?
- Will my audience understand this information, or will I need to provide more background or detail?
- Is this information current, or is it outdated?

### Read It

This excerpt from the Launch Text shows how the writer integrates details found through research. The researched information is underlined.

LAUNCH TEXT EXCERPT

The struggle took another crucial step forward in 1863, when President Abraham Lincoln issued the Emancipation Proclamation. It asserted that "all persons held as slaves" within states that had seceded from the Union "are, and henceforward, shall be free." Still, freedom for slaves depended upon a Union victory. Slavery remained legal in border states loyal to the Union, as well as in Confederate areas under Northern control.

The writer quotes directly from the researched text to illustrate one of the "zigzag" steps to rights for African Americans.

**Avoiding Plagiarism** *Plagiarism* means taking someone's ideas and words and passing them off as your own. Nobody expects you to be an expert in every subject. However, when you rely on other experts, you must credit them. Follow these steps to avoid plagiarism.

1. **Quote.** If the source uses wording that you find especially strong or apt, quote it directly. Make sure the reader can tell whom you are quoting.

   **Example:** *In his original draft of the Declaration of Independence, Thomas Jefferson included a strong condemnation of slavery, protesting this "cruel war against human nature."*

2. **Paraphrase.** When an author's ideas are important but the wording is less critical, restate the information in your own words.

   **Example:**

   **Original:** *The struggle took another crucial step forward in 1863, when President Abraham Lincoln issued the Emancipation Proclamation.*

   **Paraphrase:** Lincoln's Emancipation Proclamation of 1863 would prove to be a benchmark in the fight for civil rights.

3. **Cite.** Follow the format your teacher prefers to cite sources for any information you use that is not common public knowledge.

STANDARDS

Writing

Gather relevant information from multiple authoritative print and digital sources, using advanced searches effectively; assess the strengths and limitations of each source in terms of the task, purpose, and audience; integrate information into the text selectively to maintain the flow of ideas, avoiding plagiarism and overreliance on any one source and following a standard format for citation.

College and Career Readiness

### Write It

Organize your notes in a way that will best help you support your thesis statement.

**Taking and Organizing Notes** Develop a system for organizing your notes so that you know which are paraphrased and which are directly quoted. Try using this format for one of your notes to see whether it works well for you. Then, copy it or revise it to use for each of your sources.

TITLE: ______________________ PAGE ______

AUTHOR: ______________________

SUMMARY, QUOTATION, OR PARAPHASE? (Circle one)

NOTES:

**TIP**

CITATIONS

When citing sources, use a consistent style, such as the one established by the Modern Language Association (MLA):

- Sources are cited following the quotation or reference. The citation appears in parentheses with a page reference, as applicable.
- If the parenthetical citation appears at the end of a sentence, the period follows the final parenthesis.

**Evaluating Sources** Review your notes, and look for conflicting information. If you find substantial differences, consider the reliability and credibility of the sources: web sites ending with .edu or .gov generally provide more accurate information than sites ending with .com. When two sources conflict, look for a third source to confirm facts.

**Weaving Research Into Text** As you draft your essay, work to integrate quotations and other information from your sources. Clearly introduce each reference and note its relevance, as in this model.

INTEGRATING QUOTATIONS

Lincoln's proclamation was not guaranteed to have the effects he wanted. In his Lincoln Prize–winning book, *Lincoln's Emancipation Proclamation,* Gettysburg College professor Allen Guelzo called it "one of the biggest political gambles in American history" (7). It might easily have backfired.

The writer clearly introduces the quotation, identifying its author and integrating it with surrounding text, and then links it to a main point: *The proclamation might have made a situation worse instead of better.*





DIGITAL PERSPECTIVES

### Write It

Remind students how necessary taking and organizing notes are to writing research essays. Students, by this time in their school careers, should have established a pattern or routine for researching and writing papers, short essays, and reports.

Steps for such a routine may include:

- Copy citation information immediately and completely.
- Paraphrase notes and ideas that come from skimming resources.
- Distinguish "notes" from quotations—which should be copied, word for word, along with page or document number.
- Set up a format for the note cards, similar to this one, and use it consistently.

**Evaluating Sources** Elicit from students their methods for deciding which of two or more sources on the same topic are most authentic and relevant. Use .edu and .gov as the first way to evaluate authenticity of sources. Next, assess the journal, book, or author for further reliability as sources.

**Weaving Research Into Text** Review the model on the Student page in which a quotation and sources are integrated into the text. Discuss why this is an example of effective integration and how integrating quotations and citing sources properly adds to an essay.

# TEACHING

## Drafting

**Organize Your Essay** Help students see that, while the body of "The Zigzag Road to Rights" has a chronological structure, it is more than just a list of events in the order in which they occurred. The author characterizes each event as a victory or setback for equal rights, and points out—in the title, introduction, and conclusion—that the road to equality has not been a linear one.

Students will need to decide what structure the body of their own essays will have. For example, one possibility would be to describe Douglass's goals and examine whether they were achieved, then describe Lincoln's goals and examine whether they were achieved. Another possibility would be to describe both men's goals, examine whether the ones they had in common have been achieved, and then discuss the goals that one had that the other did not share.

There is no right or wrong structure. Students should devise a structure that allows them to convey the information most efficiently and clearly.

**Model** Have students create an outline to organize and structure their writing. Students should check their first draft against their outline to assure that all the main ideas and supporting details appear and that they appear in the intended order.

**Write a First Draft** If students generate a good outline, writing the first draft will not be difficult. Remind students that even though they may be using information from sources, they still have to provide their analysis or reflections on that material in the form of commentary. Their reflections or commentary may follow the evidence or precede it, or both.

PERFORMANCE TASK: WRITING FOCUS

## Drafting

**Organize Your Essay** Your essay should include an introduction, a body, and a conclusion. Each section of the essay should build on what has come before.

This outline shows the key sections of the Launch Text. In an informative essay, you have the option of adding headings to separate sections that belong together. Whether or not you use headings, each section of the text should have a specific purpose.

Consider the Launch Text outline as you organize information for your draft.

LAUNCH TEXT

**Model: "The Zigzag Road to Rights" Outline**

INTRODUCTION

Paragraph 1 states the thesis: *The struggle for equal recognition of African Americans demonstrates a zigzag road to rights.*

BODY

Paragraph 2 (failure): revisions to the Declaration of Independence

Paragraph 3 (improvement): Article V of the Constitution

Paragraph 4 (improvement): the Emancipation Proclamation

Paragraph 5 (improvement): the Thirteenth *Amendment*

Paragraph 6 (failure): *Plessy v. Ferguson*

Paragraph 7 (improvement): *Brown v. Board of Education*

Paragraph 8 (improvement): the Voting Rights Act of 1965

CONCLUSION

Paragraph 9 recalls the thesis: *History teaches us that rights gained can be lost, curtailed, or ignored—and perhaps gained once more.*

**Informative Essay Outline**

INTRODUCTION

BODY

CONCLUSION

STANDARDS

**Writing**

- Develop the topic thoroughly by selecting the most significant and relevant facts, extended definitions, concrete details, quotations, or other information and examples appropriate to the audience's knowledge of the topic.
- Provide a concluding statement or section that follows from and supports the information or explanation presented.

**Write a First Draft** Use your outline to write your first draft. Include a variety of evidence, and make clear connections among ideas. Be sure that each paragraph has a purpose and follows logically from the paragraphs that come before it. Keep your readers in mind as you craft your text. Consider what they might already know and what might be unfamiliar. Work at making your writing engaging and logical. Include headings if they might clarify things for your readers. Write a conclusion that follows from your thesis and supports the information you presented.





AUTHOR'S PERSPECTIVE **Jim Cummins, Ph.D.**

**The Importance of Frequent Writing** Students can benefit from frequent informal writing to build language production skills. Small assignments may be less overwhelming and they give students an incentive to write. These writing tasks also reinforce student knowledge of language and the way it works.

Teachers can build 5-minute writing tasks into lessons to allow students to write their thoughts on a particular topic. The writing does not need to be graded by the teacher. Instead, after students write, the teacher can use these ideas as the basis for a class or group discussion. Daily writing opportunities are critically important to the development of English writing and general academic skills.

LANGUAGE DEVELOPMENT: CONVENTIONS

## Syntax: Sentence Patterns

Sentences come in a variety of patterns. Some sentence patterns are best suited for simple ideas; some patterns better convey complex, related ideas.

### Read It

These sentences from the Launch Text demonstrate a variety of sentence patterns. Subjects are underlined once, and verbs are underlined twice.

- Simple Sentence (one independent clause): *In his original draft of the Declaration of Independence, Thomas Jefferson included a strong condemnation of slavery.*
- Inverted Sentence (verb precedes subject): *Powerful indeed was their pressure.*
- Compound Sentence (two or more independent clauses): *Laws can be changed, and rights can be gained.*
- Complex Sentence (one independent clause and one or more dependent clauses): *The struggle took another crucial step forward in 1863, when President Abraham Lincoln issued the Emancipation Proclamation.*
- Compound-Complex Sentence (two or more independent clauses and one or more dependent clauses): *While the path to progress is not smooth, one thing is certain: The zigzag will continue into the future.*

### Write It

As you draft, choose sentence patterns that best match the ideas you want to convey. Here are some strategies and examples.

| STRATEGY | EXAMPLES |
|---|---|
| To convey two closely related ideas, combine simple sentences to make compound sentences. | Today, all adult citizens can vote. Many hold higher office.<br>*Today, all adult citizens can vote, and many hold higher office.* |
| Invert simple sentences to add interest. | Voting rights are among an American's most important privileges.<br>*Among an American's most important privileges are voting rights.* |
| Add subordinate clauses to provide detail. | Eighteen-year-olds rarely vote.<br>*Eighteen-year-olds who are not informed rarely vote.*<br>*Even when the polls are nearby, eighteen-year-olds rarely vote.* |

TIP

PUNCTUATION

Punctuate compound and complex sentences correctly.

- Use a comma before the coordinating conjunction in a compound sentence.
- Use a semicolon between independent clauses in a compound sentence with no coordinating conjunction.
- Use a comma after a subordinate clause that begins a complex sentence.

STANDARDS

**Writing**

Use appropriate and varied transitions and syntax to link the major sections of the text, create cohesion, and clarify the relationships among complex ideas and concepts.

**Language**

Vary syntax for effect, consulting references for guidance as needed; apply an understanding of syntax to the study of complex texts when reading.





DIGITAL PERSPECTIVES

## Syntax: Sentence Patterns

### Read It

You may choose to have students go through their first drafts and identify the pattern of each sentence. It is certainly not required that an essay contain at least one example of each of the five patterns listed here. But if, for example, the inventory reveals that 95 percent of the sentences in the draft are simple sentences, a student should try to combine some of them into compound or complex sentences.

### Write It

Remind students to make sure that their combined and altered sentences are accurate and convey the same meaning that they had before.

**Example:** Anyone over the age of 18 can vote. Many eligible voters do not vote.
**Meaning changed:** Anyone over the age of 18 can vote, but they do not.
**Meaning preserved:** Anyone over the age of 18 can vote, but many of them do not.

**Example:** Voting is a fundamental right of all Americans.
**Inaccurate:** According to the Declaration of Independence, voting is a fundamental right of all Americans.
**Accurate:** With very few exceptions, such as incarcerated felons, voting is a fundamental right of all Americans.

## Revising

### Evaluating Your Draft

Encourage students to look beyond the checklist when evaluating their drafts.

### Revising for Focus and Organization

**Strong Conclusion** When writing a conclusion, students too often fall back on restating the thesis. Encourage students to write a summary of their ideas by rereading their essay with a fresh eye and thinking, "Now that we have come this far and have learned this much, we can conclude that . . . " Remind students that a conclusion should provide closure and leave the reader feeling satisfied that the topic has been covered in sufficient depth. A good researcher formulates a concluding question that provokes further research.

### Revising For Evidence and Elaboration

**Technical Vocabulary** Suggest that students make a list of words or terms in their essays that they had not been familiar with before they began doing their research. They should probably define those words and terms for readers.

## Revising

### Evaluating Your Draft

Use this checklist to evaluate the effectiveness of your first draft. Then, use your evaluation and the revising instructions on this page to guide your revision.

| FOCUS AND ORGANIZATION | EVIDENCE AND ELABORATION | CONVENTIONS |
|---|---|---|
| ☐ Provides an introduction that establishes the topic and thesis statement. | ☐ Develops the topic using relevant facts, definitions, details, quotations, examples, and/or other evidence. | ☐ Attends to the norms and conventions of the discipline, especially the correct use and punctuation of compound and complex sentences. |
| ☐ Presents main points in a logical order. | ☐ Uses vocabulary and word choices that are appropriate for the purpose and audience, including precise words and technical vocabulary where appropriate. | ☐ Uses appropriate and varied sentence structures to create cohesion and clarify relationships. |
| ☐ Uses words, phrases, and clauses to clarify relationships among ideas. | | |
| ☐ Provides a conclusion that follows logically from the preceding information. | | |

**WORD NETWORK**

Include interesting words from your Word Network in your informative essay.

### Revising for Focus and Organization

**Strong Conclusion** Your conclusion should reflect the information that precedes it, but it also should suggest the topic's importance or somehow connect the topic to a broader view. Notice how the Launch Text writer draws a conclusion about the topic's connection to the past and the future in the conclusion of "The Zigzag Road to Rights."

LAUNCH TEXT EXCERPT

> The history of African American rights features many crucial victories, from the Emancipation Proclamation through the Voting Rights Act. However, the record of the struggle also includes the difficult stumbling blocks that have had to be overcome. While the path to progress is not smooth, one thing is certain: The zigzag will continue into the future. History teaches us that rights gained can be lost, curtailed, or ignored—and perhaps gained once more.

### Revising for Evidence and Elaboration

**Technical Vocabulary** If you use topic-specific words, consider how you might define them for your audience. Be sure to spell and use those words correctly.

**STANDARDS**

**Writing**

- Use precise language, domain-specific vocabulary and techniques such as metaphor, simile, and analogy to manage the complexity of the topic.
- Provide a concluding statement or section that follows from and supports the information or explanation presented.

PEER REVIEW

Exchange essays with a classmate. Use the checklist to evaluate your classmate's essay and provide supportive feedback.

1. Is the thesis clear?
   - [ ] yes [ ] no If no, explain what confused you.
2. Are there sufficient examples and details to support the thesis?
   - [ ] yes [ ] no If no, tell what you think might be missing.
3. Does the text conclude in a logical, satisfying way?
   - [ ] yes [ ] no If no, indicate what you might change.
4. What is the strongest part of your classmate's essay? Why?

## Editing and Proofreading

**Edit for Conventions** Reread your draft for accuracy and consistency. Correct errors in grammar and word usage. Make sure that you have quoted your sources accurately and indicated your sources.

**Proofread for Accuracy** Read your draft carefully, looking for errors in spelling and punctuation. If you are including technical vocabulary, use a dictionary to check your spelling.

## Publishing and Presenting

Create a final version of your text. Pair up with a classmate (not your peer reviewer), and read each other's work. Discuss ways in which your two essays are alike and different. Are your thesis statements similar? Did you incorporate some of the same details? Even if the content is similar, do your styles differ? Share your findings with the class, and talk about what comparing the texts has taught you about developing a topic and supporting a thesis.

## Reflecting

Consider what you learned by writing your text. Was your research sufficient to respond to the prompt, or would you have preferred to spend more time researching the topic? Think about what you will do differently the next time you write an informative essay.

STANDARDS

**Writing**

Develop and strengthen writing as needed by planning, revising, editing, rewriting, or trying a new approach, focusing on addressing what is most significant for a specific purpose and audience.





DIGITAL PERSPECTIVES

## Peer Review

Make sure students understand that their responses are supposed to be supportive, but honest. If, for example, the thesis of the essay they are evaluating is not clear, they need to say so. Denying friends or classmates the opportunity to improve their work does not help them. They should be supportive by suggesting how a section or aspect of the essay can be improved but not by simply saying, "It's fine as it is."

## Publishing and Presenting

Suggest that students include maps, photos, and other other graphics that add information to their text, and remind them to cite the sources for all visual elements they may choose to include. If possible, suggest that students create podcasts or videos in which they present their completed informational texts.

HOW LANGUAGE WORKS

**Prepositional Phrases** If students struggle to comprehend the difference between an adverb phrase and an adjective phrase, assist them by giving examples of both kinds of prepositional phrase. Have students complete sentences like these with prepositional phrases, and identify them as adverb phrases or adjective phrases:

Abraham Lincoln was born (near Hodgenville, Kentucky; in 1809; in a log cabin). [adverb phrase]

Mr. Lincoln was a man (of great height; in a position of great authority) [adjective phrase], but he danced gracefully.

# OVERVIEW

## SMALL-GROUP LEARNING

### In what ways does the struggle for freedom change with history?

Remind students that the word *freedom* covers more than just physical freedom. During Small-Group Learning, students will read selections that deal with the freedom to achieve one's full potential. These selections show how people struggle to gain and maintain freedom in their choices.

### Small-Group Learning Strategies

Review the Learning Strategies with students and explain that as they work through Small-Group Learning, they will develop strategies to work in small-group environments.

- Have students watch the video on Small-Group Learning Strategies.
- A video on this topic is available online in the Professional Development Center.

You may wish to discuss some action items to add to the chart as a class before students complete it on their own. For example, for "Participate fully," you might solicit the following from students:

- Be sure to complete your share of the work.
- Offer your opinions, but do so respectfully.

### Block Scheduling

Each day in this Pacing Plan represents a 40–50 minute class period. Teachers using block scheduling may combine days to reflect their class schedule. In addition, teachers may revise pacing to differentiate and support core instruction by integrating components and resources as students require.

## OVERVIEW: SMALL-GROUP LEARNING

ESSENTIAL QUESTION:

# In what ways does the struggle for freedom change with history?

As you read these selections, work with your group to explore the various ways in which the struggle for freedom has changed over time.

**From Text to Topic** During the Civil War era, opponents of slavery argued that the nation had not fully lived up to its founding promise of liberty. In the selections in this section, others add their voices to the chorus, clamoring for liberty, justice, and equal rights. As you read, consider what the selections show about how the struggle for freedom has changed and grown over time.

## Small-Group Learning Strategies

Throughout your life, in school, in your community, and in your career, you will continue to develop strategies when you work in teams. Use these strategies during Small-Group Learning. Add ideas of your own for each step.

| STRATEGY | ACTION PLAN |
|---|---|
| Prepare | • Complete your assignments so that you are prepared for group work.<br>• Organize your thinking so you can contribute to your group's discussions.<br>• |
| Participate fully | • Make eye contact to signal that you are listening and taking in what is being said.<br>• Use text evidence when making a point.<br>• |
| Support others | • Build off ideas from others in your group.<br>• Invite others who have not yet spoken to join the discussion.<br>• |
| Clarify | • Paraphrase the ideas of others to ensure that your understanding is correct.<br>• Ask follow-up questions.<br>• |



SCAN FOR MULTIMEDIA 

### Pacing Plan

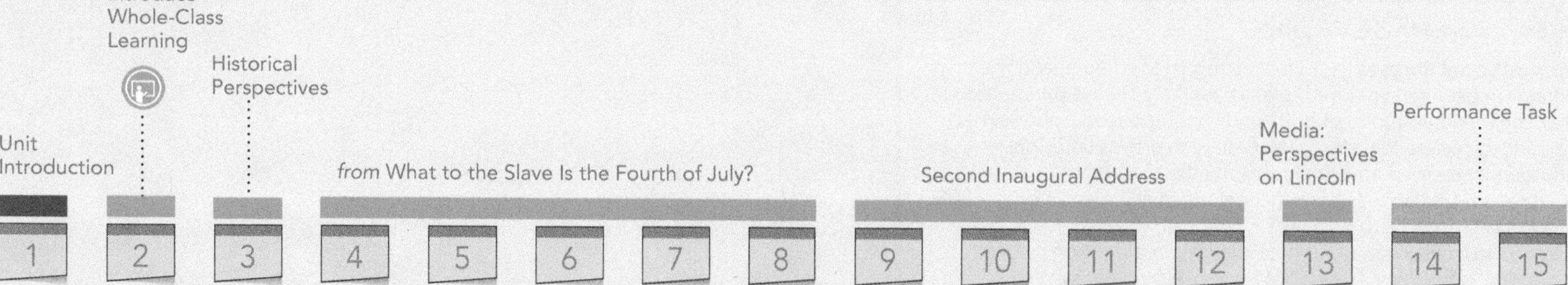

DIGITAL PERSPECTIVES

## CONTENTS







## Contents

**Selections** Monitor groups as they discuss the selections. If necessary, prompt students to discuss any knowledge they may already have about a selection or the work it is drawn from, or about any of the settings, situations, or objects shown in the photographs. You might also ask students which selection they think will provoke a lively discussion.

Remind students that throughout their lives—in school, in their community, in college, and in their careers—they will use the skill of communicating and collaborating in groups.

### Performance Task

**Present a Panel Discussion** Direct students' attention to the description of the Performance Task they will complete at the end of this section. Allow groups time to discuss the panel discussion they will present, and encourage them to think about the points of view they may want to present. Encourage them to keep these discussions in mind and jot down some notes as they read and discuss the selections.

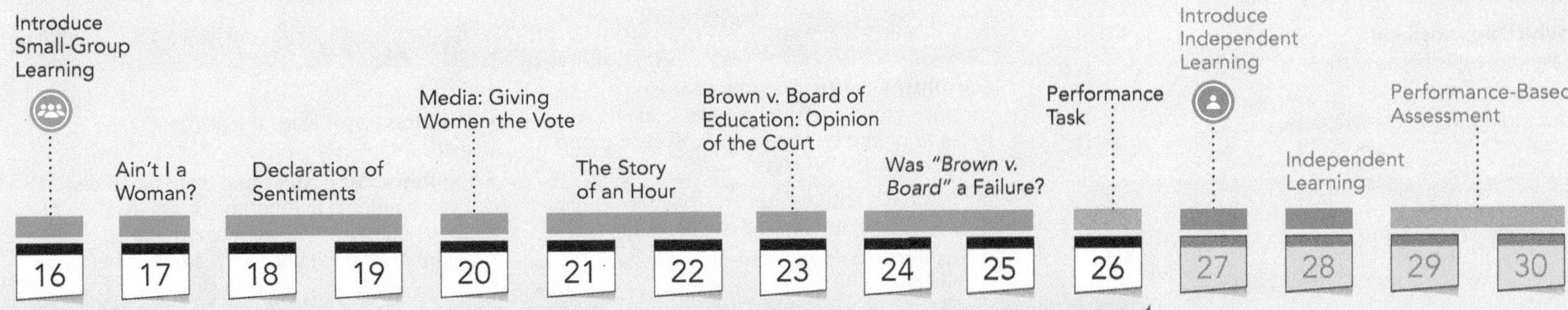

# OVERVIEW

## SMALL-GROUP LEARNING

### Working as a Team

1. **Take a Position** Make sure that all the members of each group get to share their responses. You may choose to set a time limit for the discussion.
2. **List Your Rules** You may wish to consolidate all the rules into a master list, which can be displayed in the classroom, allowing all the groups to follow all the rules.
3. **Apply the Rules** Circulate among the groups to ensure that the discussions stay on topic. You may choose to set a short time limit for the discussions.
4. **Name Your Group** Encourage students to be creative and have fun with this task.
5. **Create a Communication Plan** Groups should agree upon certain times during the day to share their ideas and a method for recording and saving their communications.

### Accountable Talk

Remind students that they are to communicate politely and respectfully during their group discussions. You may want to post these Accountable Talk suggestions and encourage students to extend the list.

**Remember to:**
Ask clarifying questions.

**Which sounds like:**
Can you give us an example?

What do you mean when you say _______?

I think you're saying _______. Am I understanding you correctly?

**Remember to:**
Explain your thinking.

**Which sounds like:**
The reason I believe this is _______.

**Remember to:**
Support your statements with evidence.

**Which sounds like:**
We know this because the author writes "_______."

According to the encyclopedia, _______.

## OVERVIEW: SMALL-GROUP LEARNING

### Working as a Team

1. **Take a Position** In your group, discuss the following question:

   **What issue today might persuade you to join a movement for social change?**

   As you take turns sharing your positions, be sure to provide reasons for your response. After all group members have shared, discuss some of the connections among the issues that were presented.

2. **List Your Rules** As a group, decide on the rules that you will follow as you work together. Two samples are provided. Add two more of your own. As you work together, you may add or revise rules based on your experience together.
   - People should respect each other's opinions.
   - No one should dominate the discussion.
   - _______________________________________________
   - _______________________________________________

3. **Apply the Rules** Share what you have learned about power, protest, and change. Make sure each person in the group contributes. Take notes on and be prepared to share with the class one thing that you heard from another member of your group.

4. **Name Your Group** Choose a name that reflects the unit topic.

   Our group's name: _______________________

5. **Create a Communication Plan** Decide how you want to communicate with one another. For example, you might use online platforms, collaboration apps, video conferencing, email, or group texts.

   Our group's decision: _______________________





### FACILITATING SMALL-GROUP LEARNING

**Forming Groups** Suggest a working model for small-group discussions. Have students work in teams of at least four, then have each group assign the following tasks:

- The **Coach** ensures that everyone has a chance to speak and encourages full participation.
- The **Recorder** takes notes on what each group member says.
- The **Moderator** leads the discussion and keeps it on track.
- The **Reframer** ensures that team members understand one another; he or she asks follow-up questions, as necessary, or paraphrases what another team member said.

## Making a Schedule

First, find out the due dates for the Small-Group activities. Then, preview the texts and activities with your group, and make a schedule for completing the tasks.

| SELECTION | ACTIVITIES | DUE DATE |
|---|---|---|
| Ain't I a Woman? | | |
| Declaration of Sentiments | | |
| Giving Women the Vote | | |
| The Story of an Hour | | |
| Brown v. Board of Education: Opinion of the Court | | |
| Was *Brown v. Board* a Failure? | | |

## Working on Group Projects

As your group works together, you'll find it more effective if each person has a specific role. Different projects require different roles. Before beginning a project, discuss the necessary roles, and choose one for each group member. Here are some possible roles; add your own ideas.

**Project Manager:** monitors the schedule and keeps everyone on task

**Researcher:** organizes research activities

**Recorder:** takes notes during group meetings

SCAN FOR MULTIMEDIA



DIGITAL PERSPECTIVES

## Making a Schedule

Have groups preview each reading selection and estimate how long each of the accompanying activities will take to complete. Point out that, while they must complete all of the tasks before the group Performance Task is due, the due date for any given task can be adjusted as needed.

Encourage groups to recheck their schedules each time they complete an activity and make sure they are on track to meet the final due date.

## Working on Group Projects

Tell students that the role assignments they settle on now can be changed later. Changes may be made based on an individual student's strengths, weaknesses, or time constraints.

That said, you may wish to review each group's assignments now and, if necessary, suggest changes based on your knowledge of individual students' strengths and weaknesses.

AUTHOR'S PERSPECTIVE **Ernest Morrell, Ph.D.**

**Pushing the Complacent Group** There are often groups who work through collaborative work without truly wrestling with the assignment. If a group has landed at consensus too easily, teachers can take the role of devil's advocate to help re-start the thinking. Ask students whether they have considered an opposing viewpoint; challenge them to see things from the other side; or take the opportunity to suggest to them an unpopular position. Once students begin to respond to this new angle, ask them to revisit their work to confirm their conclusions. Teachers may decide that assigning the role of devil's advocate in each group will improve student discussion, engagement, and deeper thinking.

# Ain't I a Woman?

**AUDIO SUMMARIES**
Audio summaries of "Ain't I a Woman?" are available online in both English and Spanish in the Interactive Teacher's Edition or Unit Resources. Assigning these summaries prior to reading the selection may help students build additional background knowledge and set a context for their first read.

## Summary

Sojourner Truth begins her speech "Ain't I a Woman?" by observing that when southern black men and northern white women protest their rights, white men are in trouble. She believes men are courteous to women because they think women are too weak to help themselves, and asks why she never receives such courtesy—*Ain't I a woman?* Truth repeats her question several times as she explains why she needs no help: farm labor has made her strong; she can work as hard, eat as much, and take a whipping as well as any man; and only Jesus helped her when her children were sold into slavery. When church ministers deny women the same rights as men because Christ wasn't a woman, Truth points out that His mother was. This leads her to some final thoughts—on Eve, the mother of us all.

### Insight

Reading "Ain't I a Woman?" will help students begin to reflect on the often personal nature of protest. The way a person is treated, how a person is perceived, the first-hand experience of being on the receiving end of discrimination—all of these can be fuel to light the fire of protest.

ESSENTIAL QUESTION:
In what ways does the struggle for freedom change with history?

## Connection to Essential Question

"Ain't I a Woman?" connects to the Essential Question by showing how one struggle for freedom and equality can pave the way for yet another fight for what is right. The struggle for women's rights would not lead to a war, but Sojourner Truth was one of its soldiers, and she was a veteran of the fight for freedom from slavery. That made her a powerful force in the fight for women's rights.

SMALL-GROUP LEARNING PERFORMANCE TASK
What were the goals of these reformers? Why did they want to achieve their goals?

UNIT PERFORMANCE-BASED ASSESSMENT
What motivates people to struggle for change?

## Connection to Performance Tasks

**Small-Group Learning Performance Task** In this Performance Task, students will focus on the goals and achievements of the reformers represented in the Small-Group Learning selections. "Ain't I a Woman?" provides a clearly stated goal. Students will consider to what extent that goal has been met.

**Unit Performance-Based Assessment** This selection provides stylistic examples of the techniques writers may use to affect an audience. Truth's rhetorical question works as a refrain and lends the speech a poetic air, while still projecting anger. Students reading this text can apply Truth's personal perspective on gender equality to the Performance-Based Assessment.

DIGITAL PERSPECTIVES

Audio

Video

Document

Annotation Highlights

EL Highlights

Online Assessment

## LESSON RESOURCES

| | Making Meaning | Language Development | Effective Expression |
|---|---|---|---|
| Lesson | **First Read**<br>**Close Read**<br>**Analyze the Text**<br>**Analyze Craft and Structure** | **Concept Vocabulary**<br>**Word Study**<br>**Author's Style** | **Writing to Sources** |
| Instructional Standards | **RI.10** By the end of grade 11, read and comprehend literary nonfiction . . .<br>**RI.2** Determine two or more central ideas of a text . . .<br>**RI.6** Determine an author's point of view . . .<br>**L.4.a** Use context as a clue . . .<br>**L.4.d** Verify the preliminary determination . . . | **L.1.a** Apply the understanding that usage is a matter of convention . . .<br>**L.3** Apply knowledge of language . . . | **W.2** Write informative/explanatory texts . . . |
| **STUDENT RESOURCES** | | | |
| Available online in the Interactive Student Edition or Unit Resources | Selection Audio<br>First-Read Guide: Nonfiction<br>Close-Read Guide: Nonfiction | Word Network | Evidence Log |
| **TEACHER RESOURCES** | | | |
| **Selection Resources** Available online in the Interactive Teacher's Edition or Unit Resources | Audio Summaries<br>Annotation Highlights<br>EL Highlights<br>English Language Support Lesson: Author's Style<br>Ain't I a Woman?: Text Questions<br>Analyze Craft and Structure: Effective Rhetoric | Concept Vocabulary and Word Study<br>Author's Style: Use of Words and Phrases | Writing to Sources: Informative Text |
| **Reteach/Practice (RP)** Available online in the Interactive Teacher's Edition or Unit Resources | Analyze Craft and Structure: Effective Rhetoric (RP) | Word Study: Latin Root *-lig-* (RP)<br>Author's Style: Use of Words and Phrases (RP) | Writing to Sources: Informative Text (RP) |
| **Assessment** Available online in Assessments | Selection Test | | |
| **My Resources** | A Unit 3 Answer Key is available online and in the Interactive Teacher's Edition. | | |

# Reading Support

| Text Complexity Rubric: Ain't I a Woman? | |
|---|---|
| **Quantitative Measures** | |
| **Lexile:** 750 **Text Length:** 355 words | |
| **Qualitative Measures** | |
| Knowledge Demands ①—②—③—❹—⑤ | To understand the speech, prior historical knowledge and basic background of these topics is needed: slavery, the abolitionist movement, the women's suffrage movement, and Bible references. |
| Structure ①—②—③—❹—⑤ | The ideas in the speech take multiple pathways rather than a chronological or sequential structure. Repetition of a rhetorical question helps to frame the structure. |
| Language Conventionality and Clarity ①—②—❸—④—⑤ | African American vernacular dialect and vocabulary are used, which may be unfamiliar; rhetorical questioning (*Ain't I a woman?*) is used repeatedly. |
| Levels of Meaning/Purpose ①—②—❸—④—⑤ | The central meaning of the speech, that women deserve equal rights, is never stated. The reader must recognize the ideas that imply this meaning throughout the speech. |

DECIDE AND PLAN

## English Language Support

Provide English Learners with support for meaning and language as they read the selection.

**Meaning/Purpose** Make sure students know the meaning of the word *rights* and the phrase *equal rights*. Read the following from paragraph 2: *If my cup won't hold but a pint, and yours holds a quart, wouldn't you be mean...* Discuss that the phrase is about *equality* or *equal rights*. Summarize the main concept: Women deserve equal rights.

**Language** Have students take turns reciting the first 7 lines of the second paragraph aloud as Sojourner Truth, with expression and feeling. Encourage them to point to the audience for *that man there* and to point to themselves with emphasis for *me* and *I* in the lines *Nobody ever helps me* and *Ain't I a woman?* Students may read, or for an added challenge, may memorize the lines.

## Strategic Support

Provide students with strategic support to ensure that they can successfully read the text.

**Knowledge Demands** Use the background information to discuss Sojourner Truth. Pair students and ask them to work together to write the facts they have learned about her. Then have them each read the facts to another pair.

**Meaning** Point out that the speech has a repeating rhetorical question, "Ain't I a Woman?" If students have trouble understanding the main concept, direct their attention to the second sentence about rights of negroes and women. Ask them to compare what the man says at the beginning of the second paragraph about how women should be treated (helped into carriages, lifted over ditches) and how Sojourner Truth was actually treated (ploughing, planting, losing children to slavery).

## Challenge

Provide students who need to be challenged with ideas for how they can go beyond a simple interpretation of the text.

**Text Analysis** Ask students to put in their own words the discrepancy between the view of how women should be treated and how women in slavery actually were treated.

**Written Response** Ask students what aspects of women's lives Sojourner Truth might find unfair in our modern society. For example, students may cite women's pay as compared with men's pay. Have them write a paragraph on the subject using a repeating rhetorical question—for example, *Don't men and women do the same kind of work?*

TEACH

## Read and Respond

Have students do their first read of the selection. Then, have them complete their close read. Finally, work with them on the Making Meaning, Language Development, and Effective Expression activities.

# Standards Support Through Teaching and Learning Cycle

## IDENTIFY NEEDS

Analyze results of the Beginning-of-Year Assessment, focusing on the items relating to Unit 3. Also take into consideration student performance to this point and your observations of where particular students struggle.

## DECIDE AND PLAN

- If students have performed poorly on items matching these standards, then provide selection scaffolds before assigning them the on-level lesson provided in the Student Edition.
- If students have done well on the Beginning-of-Year Assessment, then challenge them to keep progressing and learning by giving them opportunities to practice the skills in depth.
- Use the Selection Resources listed on the Planning pages for "Ain't I a Woman?" to help students continually improve their ability to master the standards.

**Instructional Standards: Ain't I a Woman?**

| | Catching Up | This Year | Looking Forward |
|---|---|---|---|
| Reading | You may wish to administer the **Analyze Craft and Structure: Effective Rhetoric (RP)** worksheet to help students understand the impact of rhetorical devices on what they read, say, or write.<br>Review the **Word Study: Latin Root *–lig–* (RP)** worksheet with students to ensure they understand that the meaning of a Latin root affects the meaning of the word in which it appears. | **RI.6** Determine an author's point of view or purpose in a text in which the rhetoric is particularly effective, analyzing how style and content contribute to the power, persuasiveness, or beauty of the text. | Challenge students to return to another speech in this unit and identify a rhetorical device that helped the writer build an argument or message.<br>Encourage students to find other words that contain the Latin root *–lig–*. Invite them to share the words, the parts of speech, and the meanings. |
| Writing | You may wish to administer the **Writing to Sources: Informative Text (RP)** worksheet to analyze this basic structure that may be used in developing arguments. | **W.2** Write informative/explanatory texts to examine and convey complex ideas, concepts, and information clearly and accurately through the effective selection, organization, and analysis of content. | Challenge students to return to another speech they have read in this unit and to identify examples of main points and/or supporting arguments presented with a cause-and-effect structure. |
| Language | You may wish to administer the **Author's Style: Use of Words and Phrases (RP)** worksheet to help students distinguish between these forms of diction and the effects of each form on ideas that are conveyed. | **L.3** Apply knowledge of language to understand how language functions in different contexts, to make effective choices for meaning or style, and to comprehend more fully when reading or listening.<br>**L.4.d** Verify the preliminary determination of the meaning of a word or phrase. | Challenge students to write a paragraph that explains why something they might write would have a positive impact due to the inclusion of colloquial diction. |

## ANALYZE AND REVISE

- Analyze student work for evidence of student learning.
- Identify whether or not students have met the expectations in the standards.
- Identify implications for future instruction.

## TEACH

Implement the planned lesson, and gather evidence of student learning.

# FACILITATING

## Jump Start

**FIRST READ** What is our responsibility to protect others? Before students undertake their first read, spend a few moments discussing the idea—prevalent in society until recently—that women need to be protected. Anti-suffrage arguments often hinged on women being too delicate for public affairs. Ask students whether protecting someone is ever a justification for limiting their rights or freedoms.

## Ain't I a Woman?

How does Truth describe society's attitude toward white women at the time? How does she compare it to the treatment of black women? Modeling the questions readers might ask as they read "Ain't I a Woman?" brings the text alive for students and connects it to the Small-Group Performance Task question. Selection audio and print capability for the selection are available in the Interactive Teacher's Edition.

## Concept Vocabulary

Ask groups to briefly discuss the three concept vocabulary words. Have they encountered any of the words before? Do they recognize the prefix, suffix, or base word of any of the concept vocabulary words?

Have groups consider the strategy of using context clues and discuss its advantages and disadvantages.

## FIRST READ

Have students perform the steps of the first read independently:

NOTICE: Students should determine what the point of Truth's speech is.

ANNOTATE: Students should mark any unfamiliar words or confusing sentences they will revisit during their close read.

CONNECT: Students should connect what they're reading to other works they have seen or read in order to gain insight and understanding.

RESPOND: Students will demonstrate their understanding of the text by answering questions and writing a summary.

Point out to students that while they will always complete the Respond step at the end of the first read, the other steps will probably happen somewhat concurrently. You may wish to print the **First-Read Guide: Nonfiction** for students to use.

MAKING MEANING

About the Author

**Sojourner Truth** (c. 1797–1883) was born into slavery in Swartekill, New York, as Isabella Baumfree. In 1826, when one of her owners refused to honor his promise to free her, Baumfree fled with Sophia, her infant daughter. In 1843, she changed her name to Sojourner Truth and began her career as an abolitionist. Her memoirs were published in 1850, and she toured the country to promote not only abolitionism but also equal civil rights for women.

# Ain't I a Woman?

## Concept Vocabulary

As you perform your first read of "Ain't I a Woman?" you will encounter these words.

racket fix obliged

**Context Clues** When you come across unfamiliar words in a text, you can often determine their meanings by using **context clues**—words and phrases Punishment was harsh; many were subjected to the lash, which tore the skin and caused lasting physical and emotional scars that appear in nearby text. There are various kinds of context clues. Some provide information from which you can draw inferences, or reasonable guesses, about a word's meaning.

**Example Sentence:** Punishment was harsh: Many were subjected to the **lash**, which tore the skin and caused deep physical and emotional scars.

**Inference:** Because it causes the skin to tear and leaves scars, a *lash* must be a whip or cane.

You can verify your preliminary definition by consulting a reliable print or online dictionary.

Apply your knowledge of context clues and other vocabulary strategies to determine the meanings of unfamiliar words you encounter during your first read.

## First Read NONFICTION

Apply these these strategies as you conduct your first read. You will have an opportunity to complete a close read after your first read.

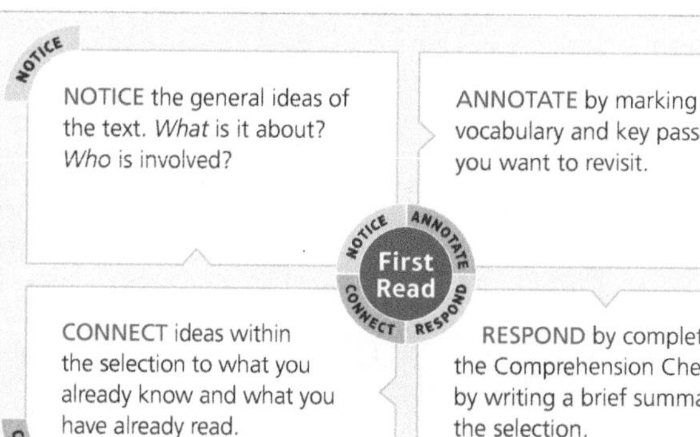
NOTICE
ANNOTATE
NOTICE the general ideas of the text. *What* is it about? *Who* is involved?
ANNOTATE by marking vocabulary and key passages you want to revisit.
First Read
CONNECT ideas within the selection to what you already know and what you have already read.
RESPOND by completing the Comprehension Check and by writing a brief summary of the selection.
CONNECT
RESPOND

STANDARDS

**Reading Informational Text**
By the end of grade 11, read and comprehend literary nonfiction in the grades 11–CCR Text complexity band proficiently, with scaffolding as needed at the high end of the range.

**Language**
- Use context as a clue to the meaning of a word or phrase.
- Verify the preliminary determination of the meaning of a word or phrase.

AUTHOR'S PERSPECTIVE **Jim Cummins, Ph.D.**

**Critical Literacies** Recent research shows that even early-stage English learners can use higher order thinking skills and engage with complex social issues with the appropriate instructional support. The following questions illustrate how teachers can support the development of critical thinking:

**Step 1: Textual Dimension** In order to help students read deeply to understand how the language and multimodal dimensions of the text construct meaning, ask, "When, where, and how did it happen?" and "Who did it? Why?"

**Step 2: Personal Dimension** Encourage students to reflect critically on the text in relation

# Ain't I a Woman?

Sojourner Truth

BACKGROUND

Sojourner Truth delivered this speech at the Women's Rights Convention in Akron, Ohio, in 1851. It was never transcribed or recorded, but a woman in attendance, Frances Gage, committed it to paper from memory many years later. The words may not be entirely accurate, but the power of Truth's speech remains intact.

SCAN FOR MULTIMEDIA 

1 Well, children, where there is so much racket there must be something out of kilter.[1] I think that 'twixt[2] the Negroes of the South and the women at the North, all talking about rights, the white men will be in a fix pretty soon. But what's all this here talking about?

2 That man over there says that women need to be helped into carriages, and lifted over ditches, and to have the best place everywhere. Nobody ever helps me into carriages, or over mudpuddles, or gives me any best place! And ain't I a woman? Look at me! Look at my arm! I have ploughed and planted, and gathered into barns, and no man could head me! And ain't I a woman? I could work as much and eat as much as a man—when I could get it—and bear the lash as well! And ain't I a woman? I have borne thirteen children, and seen them most all sold off to slavery, and when I cried

NOTES

Mark context clues or indicate another strategy you used that helped you determine meaning.

**racket** (RAK iht ) *n.*

MEANING:

**fix** (fihks) *n.*

MEANING:

1. **kilter** *n.* proper state or condition.
2. **'twixt** *prep.* between.





DIGITAL PERSPECTIVES

## Concept Vocabulary

**RACKET** If groups are struggling to define the word *racket* in paragraph 1, point out that the word has multiple meanings, so students need to use context clues to determine which meaning is intended by the author. Ask students if they think Truth uses *racket* here to mean "tennis racket." Then, point out that children are mentioned in the first part of the sentence, and children often make noise.

**Possible response:** In this context, the word *racket* must mean "a loud, confusing noise."

**FIX** If groups are struggling to define the word *fix* in paragraph 1, point out that this word has multiple meanings, so students must figure out what it means in the context of the selection. Truth isn't using the word to mean "repair," so we can guess that the word has something to do with how the white men view the situation.

**Possible response:** In this context, the word *fix* must mean "a difficult or problematic situation."

Additional **English Language Support** is available in the Digital Teacher's Edition.

to their experiences and emotions. Ask, "Have you ever seen, felt, or experienced something like this?" or "Have you ever wanted something similar?"

**Step 3: Critical Dimension** Engage students in critical analysis of issues in the text by asking questions such as: "Is what this person said valid? Always? Under what conditions? Are there any alternatives to this situation?"

**Step 4: Creative/Transformative Dimension** Engage students in creative, constructive actions that address the social realities discussed. Ask, "How can the problem or issues be resolved?" and "What role can we play in helping resolve the problem?" Projects can involve drama, role play, art, poetry, stories, and newsletter publication.

## Concept Vocabulary

**OBLIGED** If groups are struggling to define the word *obliged* in paragraph 3, point out that Truth uses this word at the beginning of the final sentence of her speech. Have them think about what someone might say to her audience at the end of a speech.

**Possible response:** *To be obliged* is to be glad for a favor or kindness performed.

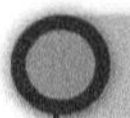

CLOSER LOOK

### Analyze Delivery

Circulate among groups as students conduct their close read. Suggest that groups close read paragraph 2. If needed, provide the following prompts:

**ANNOTATE:** In paragraph 2, mark the phrases and sentences that demonstrate that Truth is directly addressing the audience.

**QUESTION:** Why does Truth use so many questions in her speech?

**Possible response:** She wants her audience to respond to her and really consider her points, not just to listen passively.

**CONCLUDE:** How does Truth draw her audience into her speech? Cite evidence from the text to support your answer.

**Possible response:** She points out members of the audience such as "that man over there" and asks direct questions such as "Where did your Christ come from?" to elicit a response.

Remind students that **delivery** is a key part of the success of a speech. Point out that a speaker has an advantage over a writer, in that when the audience receives a speaker's words, the speaker is physically present. This gives the speaker many more tools for getting a message across, including tone of voice, body language, and, as shown here, addressing the audience directly.

NOTES

Mark context clues or indicate another strategy you used that helped you determine meaning.

**obliged** (uh BLYJD) *adj.*

MEANING:

out with my mother's grief, none but Jesus heard me! And ain't I a woman? Then they talk about this thing in the head; what's this they call it? [A member of the audience whispers, "Intellect."] That's it, honey. What's that got to do with women's rights or Negroes' rights? If my cup won't hold but a pint, and yours holds a quart, wouldn't you be mean not to let me have my little half measure full? Then that little man in black there, he says women can't have as much rights as men, 'cause Christ wasn't a woman! Where did your Christ come from? Where did your Christ come from? From God and a woman! Man had nothing to do with him.[3] If the first woman God ever made[4] was strong enough to turn the world upside down all alone, these women together ought to be able to turn it back, and get it right side up again! And now they is asking to do it, the men better let them.

3 **Obliged** to you for hearing me, and now old Sojourner ain't got nothing more to say. ❧

3. **Man had nothing to do with him** reference to the biblical teaching of the virgin birth of Jesus.

4. **the first woman God ever made** the biblical Eve.

FACILITATING SMALL-GROUP CLOSE READING

**CLOSE READ: Speech** Ask students why Sojourner Truth uses simple, homespun language. How does she appeal to natural human kindness, common sense, and shared belief in religion to support her case for women's rights and racial equality?

Have students consider how the phrase "Ain't I a Woman?" develops from an admission of humility into a triumphant assertion of female dignity.

## Comprehension Check

Complete the following items after you finish your first read. Review and clarify details with your group.

1. What two reform movements does Sojourner Truth connect?

2. According to Truth, what privileges do many people think women should enjoy?

3. Identify two hardships that Sojourner Truth says she has suffered.

4. What warning does Truth give just before concluding the speech?

5. **Notebook** Confirm your understanding of the text by writing a summary.

## RESEARCH

**Research to Clarify** Choose at least one unfamiliar detail from the text. Briefly research that detail. In what way does the information you learned shed light on an aspect of the speech?

**Research to Explore** This speech may spark your curiosity to learn more about the author, the era, or the topic. Briefly research a topic that interests you. You may want to share what you discover with your group.





## Comprehension Check

Possible responses:

1. Truth connects the "Negroes of the South" and the "women at the North."
2. Truth mentions that some men believe women need to be helped all the time—"into carriages… over ditches."
3. Truth ploughed and worked the farm and received "the lash," and she bore "thirteen children… and seen them sold into slavery…"
4. She warns that "the men better let" women get the world "right side up again" (by securing equal rights for women).
5. Truth counters the view that women cannot accomplish the same tasks as men can, noting her own ability to work as hard as any man and to survive all kinds of hardships. She believes that common sense, rather than intellect, is needed to achieve progress and that the history of women in the Bible proves that women have the power to achieve change. She indicates that the time for women to achieve a great change in American society has come.

## Research

**Research to Clarify** If students struggle to come up with a detail to research further, you may want to suggest that they choose a detail from the text that is related to social expectations of a woman in the nineteenth century.

**Research to Explore** If students struggle to come up with a research topic, you may want to suggest that they focus on one of the following topics: the history of women's rights in the United States or the history of African American rights in the United States.

## PERSONALIZE FOR LEARNING

### Challenge

**Comparative Analysis** Direct students to look online for an alternate version of "Ain't I a Woman?" Remind them that we don't know exactly what Sojourner Truth said, since her speech was written down by Frances Gage many years later. Some say Truth did not use informal dialect when she spoke. Ask students to compare two versions of her speech—one formal and one informal—and note the strengths and weaknesses of each. Suggest that they focus on the first several paragraphs. Ask students to comment on which version they find more engaging and explain why.

# FACILITATING

## Jump Start

**CLOSE READ** Present groups with the following prompt: *To bring about change most effectively, would you rather be a leader or a follower?* As students decide how they best contribute to social change, ask them to consider some of the personal attributes that both leaders and followers need in order to succeed.

## Close Read the Text

If needed, model close reading by using the Annotation Highlights in the Interactive Teacher's Edition.

Remind students to use Accountable Talk in their discussions and to support one another as they complete the close read.

## Analyze the Text

**Possible responses:**

1. Truth is saying that people who have much (the "pints") should share with those who have less (the "cups").
2. Answers will vary, but students should be able to support their passages.
3. At that time in American history, there was a struggle on two fronts: Both women and enslaved people were struggling for freedom.

## Concept Vocabulary

**Why These Words? Possible response:** The vocabulary words are all common words used in colloquial or conversational—even slangy—context.The informal tone affects the text, possibly by making it relevant to more listeners.

### Practice

**Possible responses:** The two roosters made a terrible ***racket*** as they fought in the chicken coop. George found himself in a ***fix*** when he got a flat tire ten miles from home. We were ***obliged*** to the police officer for giving us such good directions.

### Word Network

**Possible words:** *grief, rights*

## Word Study

For more support, see **Concept Vocabulary and Word Study.**

**Possible responses:**

*religion*: a group of people bound by faith and worship; *ligament*: tissue that binds bones together by connecting them; *ligature*: something that is used to tie or bind

MAKING MEANING

AIN'T I A WOMAN?

## Close Read the Text

With your group, revisit sections of the text you marked during your first read. **Annotate** details that you notice. What **questions** do you have? What can you **conclude**?

## Analyze the Text

**CITE TEXTUAL EVIDENCE** to support your answers.

**Complete the activities.**

1. **Review and Clarify** With your group, reread paragraph 2 of the selection. Discuss the figurative meanings of "pints" and "cups." What do they have to do with the overall argument in this speech?
2. **Present and Discuss** Now, work with your group to share the passages from the selection that you found especially important. Take turns presenting your passages. Discuss what you noticed in the selection, the questions you asked, and the conclusions you reached.
3. **Essential Question:** ***In what ways does the struggle for freedom change with history?*** What has this text taught you about power, protest, and change? Discuss with your group.

**TIP**

GROUP DISCUSSION

If you disagree with someone's opinion, allow the speaker to finish his or her point. Then, raise your objection tactfully—for example, you might say, "I see it a little differently." Make sure that you have textual evidence to support your idea.

LANGUAGE DEVELOPMENT

## Concept Vocabulary

racket fix obliged

**Why These Words?** The three concept vocabulary words are related. With your group, determine what the words have in common. How do these word choices enhance the impact of the text?

### Practice

**Notebook** Confirm your understanding of the concept vocabulary words by using them in sentences. Be sure to use context clues that hint at each word's meaning.

WORD NETWORK

Add words related to struggle from the text to your Word Network.

## Word Study

**Latin Root: *-lig-*** At the end of this speech, Sojourner Truth thanks her audience for listening by saying, "Obliged to you for hearing me. . . ." The English word *obliged* is built from the Latin root *-lig-,* which means "to bind." Find several other words that have this same root. Then, write the words and their meanings.

STANDARDS

**Reading Informational Text**

- Determine two or more central ideas of a text and analyze their development over the course of the text, including how they interact and build on one another to provide a complex analysis; provide an objective summary of the text.
- Determine an author's point of view or purpose in a text in which the rhetoric is particularly effective, analyzing how style and content contribute to the power, persuasiveness, or beauty of the text.

## FORMATIVE ASSESSMENT

### Analyze the Text

**If** students struggle to close read the text, **then** provide the **Ain't I a Woman?: Text Questions** available online in the Interactive Teacher's Edition or Unit Resources. Answers and DOK levels are also available.

### Concept Vocabulary

**If** students don't realize that all three words have multiple meanings, **then** have them define other words that also have colloquial meanings, such as "spell" and "nuts."

### Word Study

**If** students can't find other words with the same root, **then** have them use a search engine to locate a list of words that contain this Latin root.

For Reteach and Practice, see **Word Study: Latin Root *-lig-* (RP).**

## Analyze Craft and Structure

**Effective Rhetoric** "Ain't I a Woman?" is a speech that makes an **argument**; its message is meant to persuade an audience. Sojourner Truth connects her ideas and builds the argument to its climax by using a **refrain**, or repeated chorus. This refrain, "And ain't I a woman?" urgently restates Truth's main idea as she challenges listeners to rethink their ideas about equality.

### Practice

**CITE TEXTUAL EVIDENCE** to support your answers.

Work on your own to fill in the chart. Track the ways in which Sojourner Truth uses refrain to build her argument. Find each use of the repeated question, "Ain't I a woman?" Then, list the textual details that lead up to each repetition. Finally, consider how each set of details adds meaning to Truth's question. After you have completed the chart, share and discuss your responses with your group.

| TEXTUAL DETAILS THAT LEAD TO . . . | ADDED MEANING |
|---|---|
| first statement of the refrain: (Title) She asks a critical question. | Having the refrain as the title emphasizes the essential message of her speech. |
| first repetition of the refrain: (Paragraph 2) She is not put into carriages or carried over puddles. | She is not put on a pedestal as some other women are. |
| second repetition of the refrain: (Paragraph 2) Her body is strong and muscular. | She has worked as hard as a man. |
| third repetition of the refrain: (Paragraph 2) She has worked hard and survived the lash. | She has borne hardship as well as a man. |
| fourth repetition of the refrain: (Paragraph 2) She has borne many children with no help. | She has endured hardship beyond that of a man. |





### CROSS-CURRICULAR PERSPECTIVES

**Music** Point out to students that Sojourner Truth's speech is very rhythmic, as all effective speeches are, which makes it memorable as well as logical. Have students write a song based on "Ain't I a Woman?," conveying the same message and using as much of the original text as possible, especially the refrain. Ballads and folk songs are good models, as they use a refrain and convey a message, while rap and hip-hop songs have accentuated rhythms. Suggest that students model their songs on a ballad such as Harry Chapin's "Cat's in the Cradle." When students have finished composing their songs, have them share them with their group.

DIGITAL PERSPECTIVES  

## Analyze Craft and Structure

**Effective Rhetoric** Explain to students that the term *refrain* comes from a French word that means "to repeat." Point out that refrains are often used in poems, especially in ballads. Discuss with students how refrains contribute to the rhythm of a selection as well as emphasize an idea through repetition. Be sure students realize that prose and poetry have rhythm.

**MAKE IT INTERACTIVE**

Project the digital version of "Ain't I a Woman?" and model locating the refrain. This will help students appreciate Sojourner Truth's skill as a speaker, as she carefully placed the refrain to reinforce her main points.

For more support, see **Analyze Craft and Structure: Effective Rhetoric.**

See chart for possible responses.

### FORMATIVE ASSESSMENT

### Analyze Craft and Structure

**If** students are having difficulty understanding the significance of the refrains, **then** have them revisit the text, imagine the text without the refrains, and ask themselves if it would be as effective.

For Reteach and Practice, see **Analyze Craft and Structure: Effective Rhetoric (RP).**

# FACILITATING

## Author's Style

**Use of Words and Phrases** Remind students that it is important to match one's diction to the occasion and audience. Provide the following examples and have students identify the level of diction and probable audience:

> "You don't know about me without you have read a book by the name of *The Adventures of Tom Sawyer*; but that ain't no matter. That book was made by Mr. Mark Twain, and he told the truth, mainly. There was things which he stretched, but mainly he told the truth. That is nothing."

Discuss with students how this opening to *The Adventures of Huckleberry Finn* uses colloquial diction (such as "ain't") to appeal to its audience, young readers in the late nineteenth century, and to capture the flavor of the time and place.

> "Yesterday, December seventh, nineteen forty-one—a date which will live in infamy—the United States of America was suddenly and deliberately attacked by naval and air forces of the Empire of Japan."

Discuss how the opening of President Franklin Roosevelt's declaration of war uses formal diction (such as the word *infamy*) to convey the seriousness of the occasion and to inspire trust in his leadership.

For more support, see **Author's Style: Use of Words and Phrases.**

### Read It

Possible responses:

a. "Well, children, where there is so much racket there must be something out of kilter."

b. "If my cup won't hold but a pint, and yours holds a quart, wouldn't you be mean not to let me have my little half measure full?"

c. "And now they is asking to do it, the men better let them."

### Write It

Paragraphs will vary, but make sure students use colloquial diction in their writing.

### FORMATIVE ASSESSMENT

### Author's Style

**If** students are unable to identify colloquial diction, **then** have students read a brief excerpt from *The Adventures of Huckleberry Finn.*

For Reteach and Practice, see **Author's Style: Use of Words and Phrases (RP).**



LANGUAGE DEVELOPMENT

AIN'T I A WOMAN?

## Author's Style

**Use of Words and Phrases** A writer or speaker's **diction** is his or her choice of words and phrases. Diction is a key element of a speaker's style—his or her distinct way of using language.

- Diction may be formal, informal, elevated, simple, technical, poetic, or have many other qualities.
- Diction may change to reflect the **audience**—the listeners a speaker is attempting to reach.
- A speaker's diction reflects both the occasion and purpose of a speech.

This example from President Lincoln's second inaugural address fits the formality of the occasion.

**Formal Diction:** At this second appearing to take the oath of the presidential office, there is less occasion for an extended address than there was at the first.

Sojourner Truth was born into slavery and received no formal education. This example of her colloquial, or informal, diction reflects those circumstances.

**Colloquial Diction:** Obliged to you for hearing me, and now old Sojourner ain't got nothing more to say.

However, Truth's diction also demonstrates other aspects of her personality, as well as her purpose for speaking at the Women's Rights Convention.

STANDARDS

**Language**

- Apply the understanding that usage is a matter of convention, can change over time, and is sometimes contested.
- Apply knowledge of language to understand how language functions in different contexts, to make effective choices for meaning or style, and to comprehend more fully when reading or listening.

### Read It

Work individually. For each example of formal diction, find the colloquial original in "Ain't I a Woman?" When you have completed the chart, meet with your group to discuss how the colloquial diction may have helped Truth connect with her audience.

| FORMAL DICTION | ORIGINAL DICTION FROM "AIN'T I A WOMAN?" |
|---|---|
| *Ladies and gentlemen, where one hears such pandemonium, one suspects that something has gone awry.* | a. See possible responses in the Teacher's edition. |
| *If I have but a little, and you have a great deal, would it not be fair for you to share?* | b. |
| *Now that women are clamoring for change, it is incumbent on men to permit it.* | c. |

### Write It

**Notebook** Write a paragraph that suggests the impact that Sojourner Truth may have had on her audience in 1851. Try to use a mix of formal and colloquial diction in your paragraph.





## PERSONALIZE FOR LEARNING

### English Language Support

**Formal Diction and Colloquial Diction** Ask students to identify a section in paragraph 1 or 3 where the author uses colloquial diction. **EMERGING**

Ask students to identify a section in paragraph 1 or 3 where the author uses colloquial diction and the effect that this might have on her listener. **EXPANDING**

Ask students to identify a section in paragraph 1 or 3 where the author uses colloquial diction and compare it with the way this would be said in formal diction. **BRIDGING**

An expanded **English Language Support Lesson** on Formal Diction and Colloquial Diction is available in the Interactive Teacher's Edition.

EFFECTIVE EXPRESSION

## Writing to Sources

**Assignment**

With your group, prepare an **informative text** that presents facts about a topic. Choose from the following options:

- ☐ a **biographical sketch** about Sojourner Truth that expands upon the brief biography that accompanies this selection and that sheds light upon some of the references in "Ain't I a Woman?"
- ☐ an **extended definition** of *woman* as it would have been seen by many in Sojourner Truth's audience, focusing on the daily life of an ordinary woman in 1850s America
- ☐ a **cause-and-effect article** about the results of antislavery speeches by abolitionists in the 1850s

**Project Plan** Work with your group to divide the informative writing option that you chose into manageable sections or parts. Outline your ideas, and assign each member one part of the writing.

Working Title: ______________________________

| SECTION OR PART | ASSIGNED PERSON |
|---|---|
| Introduction | |
| Part I | |
| Part II | |
| Part III | |
| Part IV | |
| Part V | |
| Conclusion | |

**Tying It Together** Work together to draft an introduction that touches on all the sections or parts that you plan to write. Once everyone has written his or her part of the project, get together again to read the parts aloud, suggest revisions, and draft a conclusion that follows from those parts.

EVIDENCE LOG

Before moving on to a new selection, go to your Evidence Log and record what you learned from "Ain't I a Woman?"

STANDARDS

**Writing**

Write informative/explanatory texts to examine and convey complex ideas, concepts, and information clearly and accurately through the effective selection, organization, and analysis of content.





## DIGITAL PERSPECTIVES

**Illuminating the Standard** Have students search online for video clips from movies that have characters speaking in a local, informal dialect. Provide a few examples so they will understand what to look for: For example, pull up clips of Oprah Winfrey in *The Color Purple*. Remind students to stick to movies that have ratings of G or PG-13. Ask students to contrast two or more types of dialect and identify which parts of the country they come from. Invite students to examine metaphorical language or cadence and comment on the ability of informal language to carry meaning that is not found in formal or standard dialect.

DIGITAL PERSPECTIVES  

## Writing to Sources

**Assignment** Suggest that groups thoroughly discuss each of the three options to make sure they understand the requirements. For example, the biographical sketch has two parts: first, to provide additional information on Sojourner Truth; and second, to link her life to the events in the speech. This means that students should not repeat the biographical information in the text and that they must identify and explain how her life informed her work.

**Project Plan** Encourage students to first establish a clear and logical method of organization so the group's information is unified. Remind students of the two main ways to organize a cause-and-effect essay:

- all the causes first, then all the effects
- the causes and effects linked one by one, each cause to its effect

**Tying It Together** You may wish to have students create a "style sheet" before they start drafting to help produce a unified document. The style sheet should include information on font choice and size, margins, and heading format, for instance. Using a style sheet drastically reduces the time needed for editing and revising formatting issues. For more support, see **Writing to Sources: Informative Text.**

**Evidence Log** Support students in completing their Evidence Log. This paced activity will help prepare them for the Performance-Based Assessment at the end of the unit.

### FORMATIVE ASSESSMENT

**Writing**

**If** students aren't sure how to find reliable sources, **then** suggest that they consider websites that end in .edu or .gov and investigate an author's credentials. For Reteach and Practice, see **Writing to Sources: Informative Text (RP).**

**Selection Test**

Administer the "Ain't I a Woman?" Selection Test, which is available in both print and digital formats online in Assessments. 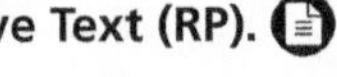

# Declaration of Sentiments

**AUDIO SUMMARIES**
Audio summaries of the "Declaration of Sentiments" are available online in both English and Spanish in the Interactive Teacher's Edition or Unit Resources. Assigning these summaries prior to reading the selection may help students build additional background knowledge and set a context for their first read.

## Summary

The "Declaration of Sentiments" echoes and extends the scope of the Declaration of Independence. Elizabeth Cady Stanton and her co-writers hold *this* truth above all to be self-evident: that all men and women are created equal. If any government denies that truth and creates laws designed to deprive certain citizens of their rights, it is the duty of those citizens to demand the overthrow of that government and to arrange to have it replaced by a government that respects the rights of all citizens. The "Declaration of Sentiments" makes a long list of laws that deprive women of their rights as citizens and demands that they be struck down and replaced by laws that respect those rights. Foremost among those rights must be the right to vote.

### Insight

Appropriating the language of the powers that be may give the powerless a voice that will be heard. Reading "Declaration of Sentiments" will help students understand the degree to which some people wield power over others. To lessen the disparity in power—a disparity sanctioned by law, no less—may require inventiveness rather than brute force.

ESSENTIAL QUESTION:
In what ways does the struggle for freedom change with history?

## Connection to Essential Question

"Declaration of Sentiments" provides a unique perspective on the Essential Question—*In what ways does the struggle for freedom change with history?* Elizabeth Cady Stanton uses the language, structure, and diction of the Declaration of Independence to make a case for women's rights. The freedom that the Revolutionaries won was freedom for an entire nation. Now, almost 75 years later, the struggle for freedom is smaller, but no less important.

SMALL-GROUP LEARNING PERFORMANCE TASK
What were the goals of these reformers? Why did they want to achieve their goals?

UNIT PERFORMANCE-BASED ASSESSMENT
What motivates people to struggle for change?

## Connection to Performance Tasks

**Small-Group Learning Performance Task** In this Performance Task, students will focus on the goals and achievements of the reformers represented in the selections in Small-Group Learning. "Declaration of Sentiments" provides a clearly stated goal. Students will consider to what extent that goal has been met.

**Unit Performance-Based Assessment** This selection provides stylistic examples of the techniques writers may use to affect an audience. Elizabeth Cady Stanton's allusion to the Declaration of Independence is a compelling foundation for her message.

## LESSON RESOURCES

| | Making Meaning | Language Development |
|---|---|---|
| Lesson | **First Read**<br>**Close Read**<br>**Analyze the Text**<br>**Analyze Craft and Structure** | **Concept Vocabulary**<br>**Word Study**<br>**Conventions and Style** |
| **Instructional Standards** | **RI.10** By the end of grade 11, read and comprehend literary nonfiction . . .<br>**L.4.d** Verify the preliminary determination . . .<br>**L.4.a** Use context as a clue . . .<br>**RI.9** Analyze seventeenth-, eighteenth-, and nineteenth-century foundational U.S. documents . . . | **L.4.c** Consult general and specialized reference materials . . .<br>**L.1** Demonstrate command of the conventions . . . |
| **STUDENT RESOURCES** | | |
| Available online in the Interactive Student Edition or Unit Resources | Selection Audio<br>First-Read Guide: Nonfiction<br>Close-Read Guide: Nonfiction | Word Network |
| **TEACHER RESOURCES** | | |
| **Selection Resources**<br>Available online in the Interactive Teacher's Edition or Unit Resources | Audio Summaries<br>Annotation Highlights<br>EL Highlights<br>Declaration of Sentiments: Text Questions<br>Analyze Craft and Structure: Author's Choices: Allusions | Concept Vocabulary and Word Study<br>Conventions and Style: Types of Clauses<br>English Language Support Lesson: Types of Clauses |
| **Reteach/Practice (RP)**<br>Available online in the Interactive Teacher's Edition or Unit Resources | Analyze Craft and Structure: Author's Choices: Allusions (RP) | Word Study: Latin Prefix: *sub-* (RP)<br>Conventions and Style: Types of Clauses (RP) |
| **Assessment**<br>Available online in Assessments | Selection Test | |
| **My Resources** | A Unit 3 Answer Key is available online and in the Interactive Teacher's Edition. | |

# Reading Support

| Text Complexity Rubric: Declaration of Sentiments | |
|---|---|
| **Quantitative Measures** | |
| **Lexile:** 1490 **Text Length:** 901 words | |
| **Quantitative Measures** | |
| Knowledge Demands<br>①—②—③—❹—⑤ | Understanding the selection requires knowledge of the Declaration of Independence and the specific language used in that document. |
| Structure<br>①—❷—③—④—⑤ | Clear structure with ideas arranged sequentially. Structure follows Declaration of Independence. Many paragraphs have repetitive beginnings (*He has...*). |
| Language Conventionality and Clarity<br>①—②—③—❹—⑤ | The language is modeled directly on the language from the Declaration of Independence. Contains syntax and vocabulary characteristic of legal documents. |
| Levels of Meaning/Purpose<br>①—②—❸—④—⑤ | Multiple levels of meaning. Deeper meaning of text can be understood when bringing prior knowledge of language from the Declaration of Independence. |

DECIDE AND PLAN

## English Language Support

Provide English Learners with support for language and knowledge demands as they read the selection.

**Language** Discuss the word *Declaration*, from the verb *to declare*. Ask students to look up the word *declaration* and find other words they know that define it, such as *statement* or *announcement*. Ask them to find the verbs that these nouns originate from, for example *state* or *announce*.

**Knowledge Demands** Write individual phrases from the Declaration of Independence and ask students to scan the "Declaration of Sentiments" for similar lines. Ask them to compare the lines they find word for word with the lines from which they are derived. Discuss the differences.

## Strategic Support

Provide students with strategic support to ensure that they can successfully read the text.

**Knowledge Demands** Use the background information to review that the document is based on the language from the Declaration of Independence. Discuss the purpose of that document and the reasons the women may have decided to use it as the basis for the "Declaration of Sentiments."

**Meaning/Purpose** As students read, point out language that is based on lines from the Declaration of Independence, for example *...that all men* ***and women*** *are created equal*. If students have trouble understanding the language, remind them of comparisons to the original language. Then have them reread the sentences with that meaning in mind.

## Challenge

Provide students who need to be challenged with ideas for how they can go beyond a simple interpretation of the text.

**Text Analysis** Ask students to read through the Declaration of Independence and compare it line by line with the "Declaration of Sentiments." Have them highlight the differences in the sentences or list them side by side to show the comparison.

Ask students to analyze certain phrases more deeply. For example, *What does it mean for a truth to be* self-evident?

**Written Response** Ask students to write a paragraph about the ways in which this document applies to people today. For example, are there any groups of people today who do not have equal rights in some way or who gained rights only recently?

TEACH

## Read and Respond

Have groups read the selection and complete the Making Meaning and Language Development activities.

# Standards Support Through Teaching and Learning Cycle

## IDENTIFY NEEDS

Analyze results of the Beginning-of-Year Assessment, focusing on the items relating to Unit 3. Also take into consideration student performance to this point and your observations of where particular students struggle.

## DECIDE AND PLAN

- If students have performed poorly on items matching these standards, then provide selection scaffolds before assigning them the on-level lesson provided in the Student Edition.
- If students have done well on the Beginning-of-Year Assessment, then challenge them to keep progressing and learning by giving them opportunities to practice the skills in depth.
- Use the Selection Resources listed on the Planning pages for "Declaration of Sentiments" to help students continually improve their ability to master the standards.

**Instructional Standards: Declaration of Sentiments**

| | Catching Up | This Year | Looking Forward |
|---|---|---|---|
| **Reading** | You may wish to administer the **Analyze Craft and Structure: Author's Choices: Allusions (RP)** worksheet to help students understand how allusions can add meaning to a text. | **RI.9** Analyze seventeenth-, eighteenth-, and nineteenth-century foundational U.S. documents of historical and literary significance for their themes, purposes, and rhetorical features. | Challenge students to create an argument for a modern-day cause by using one or more of the same allusions from the Declaration of Independence that Stanton used in her "Declaration of Sentiments." |
| **Language** | You may wish to administer the **Conventions and Style: Types of Clauses (RP)** worksheet to help students identify and understand subordinate clauses in sentences.<br>Review the Latin prefix *sub-* with students to ensure they understand that the meaning of the prefix contributes to the overall meaning of a word, as in the word *subordinate*. | **L.1** Demonstrate command of the conventions of standard English grammar and usage when writing or speaking.<br>**L.4.c** Consult general and specialized reference materials, both print and digital, to find the pronunciation of a word or determine or clarify its precise meaning, its part of speech, its etymology, or its standard usage. | Ask students to identify the subordinate clauses that appear in "Declaration of Sentiments."<br>Have students use a print or online dictionary to find other words that include the Latin prefix *sub-*. Invite students to share each word they found, along with its part of speech and meaning. |

## ANALYZE AND REVISE

- Analyze student work for evidence of student learning.
- Identify whether or not students have met the expectations in the standards.
- Identify implications for future instruction.

## TEACH

Implement the planned lesson, and gather evidence of student learning.

# FACILITATING

## Jump Start

**FIRST READ** At one time, only men could vote. Not so long ago, citizens had to be 21 to vote. Discuss how voting laws have changed over time. Then ask students if they think 15-year-olds should be able to vote. What does the right to vote represent?

## Declaration of Sentiments

We're all entitled to the same rights—or are we? What happens when half the population is denied those rights based solely on their gender? Modeling the questions readers might ask as they read "Declaration of Sentiments" brings the text alive for students and connects it to the Small-Group Performance Task question. Selection audio and print capability for the selection are available in the Interactive Teacher's Edition.

## Concept Vocabulary

Ask groups to briefly discuss the three concept vocabulary words. Have they encountered any of the words before? Do they recognize any word parts, such as a prefix or suffix?

Remind students of the context clue strategy and encourage them to work through the example and consider other types of context clues they might encounter while in a text.

## FIRST READ

Have students perform the steps of the first read independently:

NOTICE: Students should determine what the main argument of the essay is.

ANNOTATE: Students should mark details or passages that help the author make an argument.

CONNECT: Students should connect what they're reading to other works they have seen or read in order to gain insight and understanding.

RESPOND: Students will demonstrate their understanding of the text by answering questions and writing a summary.

Point out to students that while they will always complete the Respond step at the end of the first read, the other steps will probably happen somewhat concurrently. You may wish to print the **First-Read Guide: Nonfiction** for students to use.

MAKING MEANING

DECLARATION OF SENTIMENTS

## Comparing Text to Media

In this lesson, you will compare the Declaration of Sentiments, a public document related to the campaign for women's suffrage, and a podcast called "Giving Women the Vote." First, you will complete the first-read and close-read activities for the Declaration of Sentiments.

GIVING WOMEN THE VOTE

About the Author

**Elizabeth Cady Stanton** (1815–1902) became interested in reform movements through a cousin, who introduced her to Henry Brewster Stanton, an abolitionist. Cady and Stanton married in 1840—agreeing that the bride's promise to obey her husband would be omitted from their vows. Stanton was the primary writer of the Declaration of Sentiments, adopted at the 1848 Seneca Falls Convention. Later, Stanton and Susan B. Anthony founded the National Woman Suffrage Association.

# Declaration of Sentiments

## Concept Vocabulary

As you perform your first read, you will encounter these words.

degraded oppressed subordinate

**Context Clues** If these words are unfamiliar to you, try using **context clues**—other words and phrases that appear in a text—to help you determine their meanings. There are various kinds of context clues. Some provide details that help you infer the word's meaning. You can then use a dictionary to confirm your inference.

**Elaborating Details:** Even when the terrifying storm was at its worst, my cousin maintained her usual calm and cheerful **demeanor**.

**Inference:** *Calm* and *cheerful* relate to a person's behavior. *Demeanor* must mean "how someone behaves."

**Dictionary Meaning:** "outward behavior or bearing"

Apply your knowledge of context clues and other vocabulary strategies to determine the meanings of unfamiliar words you encounter during your first read.

## First Read NONFICTION

Apply these strategies as you conduct your first read. You will have an opportunity to complete a close read after your first read.

NOTICE the general ideas of the text. *What* is it about? *Who* is involved?

ANNOTATE by marking vocabulary and key passages you want to revisit.

CONNECT ideas within the selection to what you already know and what you have already read.

RESPOND by completing the Comprehension Check and by writing a brief summary of the selection.

First Read

STANDARDS

**Reading Informational Text**
By the end of grade 11, read and comprehend literary nonfiction in the grades 11–CCR text complexity band proficiently, with scaffolding as needed at the high end of the range.

**Language**
- Use context as a clue to the meaning of a word or phrase.
- Verify the preliminary determination of the meaning of a word or phrase.





338 UNIT 3 • POWER, PROTEST, AND CHANGE

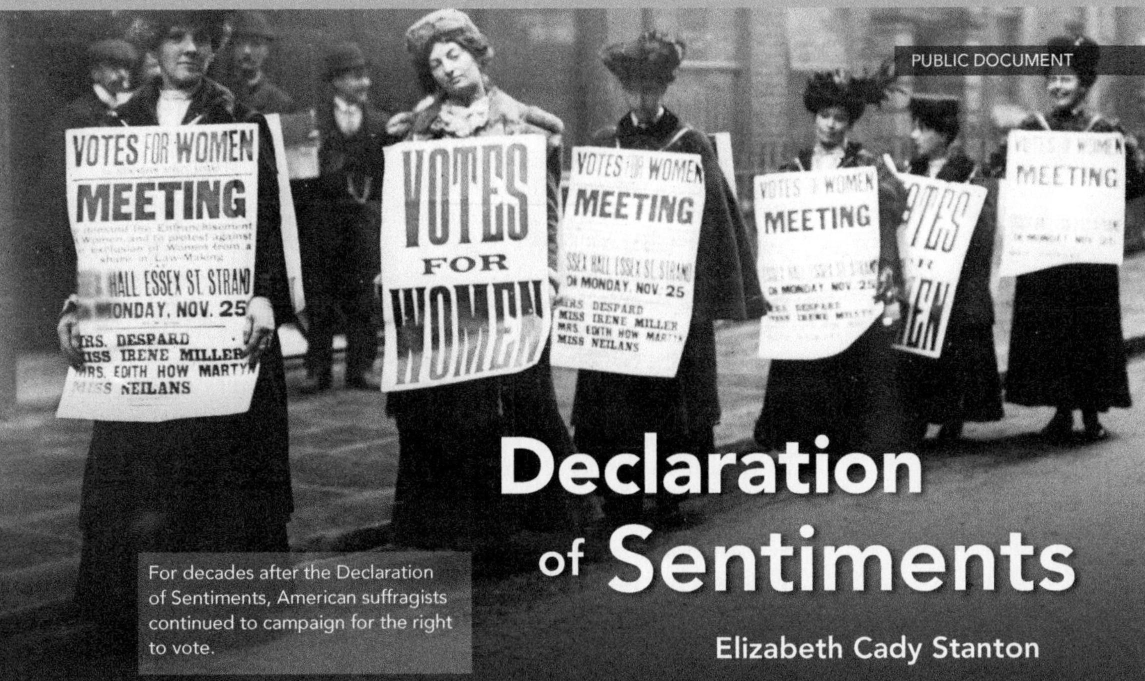


PUBLIC DOCUMENT

For decades after the Declaration of Sentiments, American suffragists continued to campaign for the right to vote.

# Declaration of Sentiments

Elizabeth Cady Stanton

DIGITAL  PERSPECTIVES

BACKGROUND

In 1848, Elizabeth Cady Stanton and Lucretia Mott convened the first women's rights conference to demand that women be given basic human rights, including the right to vote, to own property, and to have equal status under the law. Of those who attended the conference in Seneca Falls, New York, about a third—32 men and 68 women—signed the Declaration of Sentiments. The document was highly controversial. An article published shortly after the convention described it as "the most shocking and unnatural event ever recorded in the history of womanity."

SCAN FOR MULTIMEDIA 

1 When, in the course of human events, it becomes necessary for one portion of the family of man to assume among the people of the earth a position different from that which they have hitherto occupied, but one to which the laws of nature and of nature's God entitle them, a decent respect to the opinions of mankind requires that they should declare the causes that impel them to such a course.

2 We hold these truths to be self-evident: that all men and women are created equal; that they are endowed by their Creator with certain inalienable[1] rights; that among these are life, liberty, and the pursuit of happiness; that to secure these rights governments are instituted, deriving their just powers from the consent of the governed. Whenever any form of government becomes destructive of these ends, it is the right of those who suffer from it to refuse allegiance to it, and to insist upon the institution of a new government, laying its foundation on such principles, and organizing its powers in such

NOTES

1. **inalienable** (ihn AYL yuh nuh buhl) *adj.* absolute; not able to be taken or given away.





## CLOSER LOOK

### Analyze Author's Tone

Circulate among groups as students conduct their close read. Suggest that groups close read paragraph 1. If needed, provide the following prompts.

**ANNOTATE:** In paragraph 1, mark the phrases that convey the author's tone.

**QUESTION:** How would you describe Stanton's tone or attitude toward her audience? Why do you think she uses this tone?

**Possible response:** Stanton conveys a calm, businesslike tone. She uses this tone to show that women crusading for their rights are rational, not shrill or hysterical, as the negative stereotype portrayed them.

**CONCLUDE:** Why do you think Stanton deliberately used the same tone and phrasing of the Declaration of Independence?

**Possible response:** Stanton likens women's struggles for equality to America's fight for freedom from England to suggest that women have as strong a case as the colonies did.

Remind students that **tone** is the writer's attitude toward a subject. It is conveyed through word choice and style. Tell students that choosing a tone is very important when trying to convince people of something or spur them into action. Too much energy and emotion might turn people off; too little will bore them, or make them think you don't really care about the issue.

## PERSONALIZE FOR LEARNING

### English Language Support

**Complex Sentences** Have students re-read paragraph 1 of "Declaration of Sentiments," and call their attention to the fact that the paragraph is made up of just one sentence. Remind students that when they come across a long, complicated sentence in their reading, they can unpack the information by breaking down the sentence into simple sentences.

Work with students to unpack the information in paragraph 1. Possible answers: 1. At certain times, one part of the family of man has to take a different position among the people of the earth. 2. This happens at a particular time in human history. 3. It is a very different position from their place up until this time. 4. The laws of nature and of God entitle them to this new position. 5. They should explain to everyone the reasons for their present actions.

## Concept Vocabulary

**DEGRADED** If groups are struggling to define the word *degraded* in paragraph 5, point out that they can check their understanding of the word by looking at the context clues in the surrounding text. Students should note the words *most ignorant*. They should also note the use of the phrase "natives and foreigners," which may be used to emphasize the idea of the "most... degraded."

**Possible response:** In this context, the word *degraded* means "corrupted; reduced in quality; fallen below the standards of civilized society."

**OPPRESSED** If students have trouble defining the word *oppressed* in paragraph 6, have them look for context clues in the text. Students should note the word *deprived*.

**Possible response:** In this context, the word *oppressed* means "punished; maltreated; without rights."

Additional **English Language Support** is available in the Interactive Teacher's Edition.

NOTES

form, as to them shall seem most likely to effect their safety and happiness. Prudence, indeed, will dictate that governments long established should not be changed for light and transient[2] causes; and accordingly all experience hath shown that mankind are more disposed to suffer, while evils are sufferable, than to right themselves by abolishing the forms to which they are accustomed. But when a long train of abuses and usurpations[3] pursuing invariably the same object, evinces a design to reduce them under absolute despotism,[4] it is their duty to throw off such government, and to provide new guards for their future security. Such has been the patient sufferance of the women under this government, and such is now the necessity which constrains them to demand the equal station to which they are entitled. The history of mankind is a history of repeated injuries and usurpations on the part of man toward woman, having in direct object the establishment of an absolute tyranny over her. To prove this, let facts be submitted to a candid world.

3 He has never permitted her to exercise her inalienable right to the elective franchise.[5]

4 He has compelled her to submit to laws, in the formation of which she had no voice.

5 He has withheld from her rights which are given to the most ignorant and degraded men—both natives and foreigners.

6 Having deprived her of this first right of a citizen, the elective franchise, thereby leaving her without representation in the halls of legislation, he has oppressed her on all sides.

7 He has made her, if married, in the eye of the law, civilly dead.

8 He has taken from her all right in property, even to the wages she earns.

9 He has made her, morally, an irresponsible being, as she can commit many crimes with impunity,[6] provided they be done in the presence of her husband. In the covenant of marriage, she is compelled to promise obedience to her husband, he becoming, to all intents and purposes, her master—the law giving him power to deprive her of her liberty, and to administer chastisement.[7]

10 He has so framed the laws of divorce, as to what shall be the proper causes, and in case of separation, to whom the guardianship of the children shall be given, as to be wholly regardless of the happiness of women—the law, in all cases, going upon a false supposition of the supremacy of man, and giving all power into his hands.

11 After depriving her of all rights as a married woman, if single, and the owner of property, he has taxed her to support a government which recognizes her only when her property can be made profitable to it.

Mark context clues or indicate another strategy you used that helped you determine meaning.

**degraded** (dih GRAY dihd) *adj.*

MEANING:

**oppressed** (uh PREHST) *v.*

MEANING:

2. **transient** (TRAN see uhnt) *adj.* not lasting.
3. **usurpations** (yoo suhr PAY shuhnz) *n.* illegal seizures.
4. **evinces a design . . . despotism** shows an intent to submit women to a situation of total control.
5. **elective franchise** right to vote.
6. **impunity** (ihm PYOO nih tee) *n.* total freedom from punishment.
7. **chastisement** (CHAS tyz muhnt) *n.* strong, punishing criticism.





### FACILITATING SMALL-GROUP CLOSE READING

**CLOSE READ: Public Document** Direct students to work in groups to paraphrase the sixteen major grievances outlined by Stanton, beginning with "He has never permitted her . . ." in paragraph 3. To keep the task manageable, assign no more than four grievances to one group. Remind students to review the vocabulary that has been provided before they begin, and advise them to look up any additional words they may find difficult. Then ask students to share their paraphrases with the whole group, so that students can take notes on all the grievances in the text.

The demands of suffragist leaders aroused intense passions. In this artist's interpretation of a real event, suffragist Lucretia Mott is attacked by a mob when she appears in public.

NOTES

12 He has monopolized nearly all the profitable employments, and from those she is permitted to follow, she receives but a scanty remuneration. He closes against her all the avenues to wealth and distinction which he considers most honorable to himself. As a teacher of theology, medicine, or law, she is not known.

13 He has denied her the facilities for obtaining a thorough education, all colleges being closed against her.

14 He allows her in church, as well as state, but a **subordinate** position, claiming apostolic[8] authority for her exclusion from the ministry, and, with some exceptions, from any public participation in the affairs of the church.

15 He has created a false public sentiment by giving to the world a different code of morals for men and women, by which moral delinquencies which exclude women from society, are not only tolerated, but deemed of little account in man.

16 He has usurped the prerogative of Jehovah himself, claiming it as his right to assign for her a sphere of action, when that belongs to her conscience and to her God.

17 He has endeavored, in every way that he could, to destroy her confidence in her own powers, to lessen her self-respect, and to make her willing to lead a dependent and abject life.

Mark context clues or indicate another strategy you used that helped you determine meaning.

**subordinate** (suh BAWR duh niht) *adj.*

MEANING:

8. **apostolic** (ap uh STOL ihk) *adj.* derived from the Bible (specifically, from the apostles appointed by Jesus to spread the gospel).

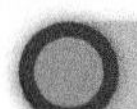

CLOSER LOOK

## Make an Inference 

Circulate among groups as students conduct their close read. Suggest that groups close read paragraph 12. If needed, provide the following prompts.

**ANNOTATE:** In paragraph 12, mark the phrases that show which careers are closed to women.

**QUESTION:** Which areas of "profitable employment" are completely closed to women? Why does Stanton believe women are not allowed to pursue careers in these fields?

**Possible response:** Women are not allowed to become teachers of theology (religion), medicine, or law. Stanton believes these careers are closed because they pay the most money and carry the most prestige.

**CONCLUDE:** What can you infer about the author's attitude regarding women working? Why do you think she feels this way?

**Possible response:** Stanton believes that women want to work and to work at prestigious, well-paying jobs.

Point out to students that this text gives them information but that **making inferences** will help them better understand the author's message. Working at a prestigious, high-paying job is not just a matter of equality or status. Help students see that when women were unable to make money on their own, they were completely reliant on their husbands for food, clothing, and shelter. Low-paying jobs—or no jobs—meant less freedom.

## Concept Vocabulary

**SUBORDINATE** If students have trouble defining the word *subordinate* in paragraph 14, have them look for context clues in the text. The words *exclusion* and *but* set up a contrast to the first part of the sentence by suggesting that a woman's place in church is not a full place.

**Possible response:** In this context, the word *subordinate* means "lower in rank; less important."

## DIGITAL PERSPECTIVES

**Illuminating the Text** Look online for a recording of the "Declaration of Sentiments." You might choose to search for one produced by The Iron Age Theatre, a theater company focusing on dramatic themes tied to social justice.

Have students follow along in their text, and then discuss the effect of hearing a dramatic reading. Ask them whether they understood the speech better after hearing it. You can also discuss the emotional impact and whether they were moved by hearing the catalogue of historical injustices against women. **(Research to Explore)**

# FACILITATING

## Comprehension Check

**Possible responses:**

1. The "self-evident" truths are that all men and women are created equal and that they have certain God-given, inalienable rights, including life, liberty, and the pursuit of happiness.
2. Women have a duty to throw off the government because they have been rendered powerless due to a long history of abuses and usurpations by men.
3. Without the ability to vote, women have no representation and continue to be oppressed on all sides.
4. The conclusion demands that women immediately receive all rights and privileges that male citizens have.
5. Summaries will vary, but should include the ideas that the text lists a number of grievances to prove that women have been oppressed and that the speaker requests that women be granted the rights to be treated as full citizens.

### Research to Explore

If students have trouble picking a research topic, you may want to suggest that they focus on one of the following topics: The Seneca Falls Convention, the women's suffragist movement, Elizabeth Cady Stanton.

NOTES

18 Now, in view of this entire disfranchisement of one-half the people of this country, their social and religious degradation—in view of the unjust laws above mentioned, and because women do feel themselves aggrieved, oppressed, and fraudulently deprived of their most sacred rights, we insist that they have immediate admission to all the rights and privileges which belong to them as citizens of the United States.

19 In entering upon the great work before us, we anticipate no small amount of misconception, misrepresentation, and ridicule; but we shall use every instrumentality within our power to effect our object. We shall employ agents, circulate tracts, petition the state and national legislatures, and endeavor to enlist the pulpit and the press in our behalf. We hope this convention will be followed by a series of conventions, embracing every part of the country.

20 Firmly relying upon the final triumph of the right and the true, we do this day affix our signatures to this declaration. ❧

## Comprehension Check

**Complete the following items after you finish your first read. Review and clarify details with your group.**

**1.** According to this document, which truths are self-evident?

**2.** According to Stanton, why do women have a duty to throw off the government?

**3.** What does Stanton say is the result of denying women the right to vote?

**4.** What governmental action does the Declaration of Sentiments demand?

**5.** **Notebook** Confirm your understanding of the text by writing a summary.

RESEARCH

**Research to Explore** This public document may spark your curiosity to learn more about this topic, author, or era. Briefly research a topic that interests you. You may wish to share what you discover with your group.





## PERSONALIZE FOR LEARNING

### Challenge

**Compare and Contrast** Have students note the phrase "deprived of their most sacred rights" in paragraph 18. Explain that phrases such as this are meant to call the Declaration of Independence to mind. Have students download and print a copy of the Declaration of Independence for the purpose of comparison to the "Declaration of Sentiments." Ask them to work with a partner to compare the two documents and generate a list of ten sentences—five explaining how the documents are similar and five pointing out how they are different. Ask students to make a summary statement on whether it made sense for Stanton to use the Declaration of Independence as the model for her own document, and have them explain their thinking.

DIGITAL PERSPECTIVES  

MAKING MEANING

## Close Read the Text

With your group, revisit sections of the text you marked during your first read. **Annotate** details that you notice. What **questions** do you have? What can you **conclude**?

## Analyze the Text

**CITE TEXTUAL EVIDENCE** to support your answers.

**Complete the activities.**

1. **Review and Clarify** With your group, discuss the "long train of abuses and usurpations" that are listed in the document. If you were to categorize them, what headings would you use? Explain.
2. **Present and Discuss** Now, work with your group to share the passages from the selection that you found especially important. Take turns presenting your passages. Discuss what you noticed in the selection, the questions you asked, and the conclusions you reached.
3. **Essential Question:** ***In what ways does the struggle for freedom change with history?*** What have you learned about the struggle for freedom from reading this text?

LANGUAGE DEVELOPMENT

## Concept Vocabulary

degraded    oppressed    subordinate

**Why These Words?** The three concept vocabulary words are related. With your group, discuss the words, and determine a concept that the words, have in common. How do these word choices enhance the text's impact?

### Practice

**Notebook** Confirm your understanding of the concept vocabulary words by using them in sentences. Be sure to use context clues that hint at each word's meaning.

## Word Study

**Latin Prefix: *sub-*** According to the Declaration of Sentiments, the document should tell the world that American women are in a *subordinate* position. The word *subordinate* begins with the Latin prefix *sub-*, which means "under." Find several other words that begin with this prefix. Use etymological information from the dictionary to verify your choices. Then, write the words and their meanings.



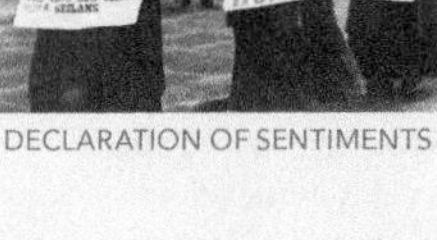


DECLARATION OF SENTIMENTS

TIP

GROUP DISCUSSION
Give everyone a chance to contribute to the discussion. If you notice that someone is not participating, encourage him or her to join in.

WORD NETWORK
Add words related to struggle from the text to your Word Network.

STANDARDS
**Language**
Consult general and specialized reference materials, both print and digital, to find the pronunciation of a word or determine or clarify its precise meaning, its part of speech, its etymology, or its standard usage.



## Jump Start

CLOSE READ: Present groups with the following prompt: *There are two powers in the world: one is the sword and the other is the pen. There is a great competition and rivalry between the two.* Have students debate which is mightier—the sword or the pen. Have students explain what each approach can accomplish and the strengths and weaknesses of each.

## Close Read the Text 

If needed, model close reading by using the Annotation Highlights in the Interactive Teacher's Edition.

Remind groups to use Accountable Talk in their discussions and to support one another as they complete the close read.

## Analyze the Text

**Possible responses:**

1. The "long train of abuses and usurpations" can use categories such as politics, economics, marriage, and education.
2. Important passages include paragraph 2, because it states the authors' thesis, and paragraph 20, because it reinforces the point.
3. This text suggests that people build upon strategies of others who have won their rights, that the struggle for freedom is difficult but worth the effort, and that people need to be assertive in securing their rights.

## Concept Vocabulary

**Why These Words? Possible response:** The words suggest a lowly position.

### Practice

**Possible responses:**

- After years of feeling *oppressed,* the workers finally rallied for the benefits they wanted.
- The road's *degraded* condition was blamed on overuse by heavy trucks.
- Most of the work was done by *subordinate* members of the research team.

### Word Network

**Possible words:** *impel, entitled, pursuit, usurped, abject*

## Word Study

For more support, see **Concept Vocabulary and Word Study.**

**Possible responses:**
*Submarine:*—a vehicle for underwater travel; *subside:*—to sink to a lower level; *subterranean:*—underground

## FORMATIVE ASSESSMENT

### Analyze the Text

**If** students struggle to close read the text, **then** provide the **Declaration of Sentiments: Text Questions** available online in the Interactive Teacher's Edition or Unit Resources. Answers and DOK levels are also available.

### Concept Vocabulary

**If** students can't determine how the words are related, **then** have them focus on the meaning of the prefixes *sub-* and *de-*.

### Word Study

**If** students can't find other words with the same root, **then** have them think of words such as "marine" and "division" that can be combined with the prefix *sub-*.

For Reteach and Practice, see **Word Study: Latin Prefix *sub-* (RP).**

# FACILITATING

## Analyze Craft and Structure

**Author's Choices: Allusions** Explain to students that allusions must be recognized by the audience to be effective. For instance, most people will understand that an allusion to an Achilles' heel is meant to evoke the idea of weakness, as Achilles was invulnerable except for his heel. Similarly, an allusion to Pygmalion evokes the idea of someone who tries to remake a person the way he or she wants the person to be.

Have students explain these famous allusions and their origins:

- Cinderella Story (the story of someone who achieves success after being mistreated
- Scrooge (a miser; from Charles Dickens's *A Christmas Carol*)
- Job (someone who suffers a great deal but retains his faith; from the Bible)

For more support, see **Analyze Craft and Structure: Author's Choices: Allusions.**

**MAKE IT INTERACTIVE**

Project the digital version of "Declaration of Sentiments" and model locating the allusions to the Declaration of Independence. This will help students as they complete the chart.

**Possible responses:**

a. The Declaration of Independence describes the "patient sufferance of the colonies"; the "Declaration of Sentiments" outlines the "patient sufferance of women under this government." Jefferson lists the colonists' grievances against King George.

b. The "Declaration of Sentiments" follows this same structure but uses "He" to address the men who are denying women their rights. By using the same structure and style, Stanton reinforces the fact that women are American citizens, just as men are.

c. Jefferson ends with a call for political freedom; Stanton ends with a call for marital and social freedom.

d. The argument in both documents builds to calling for action, not just agreement.

### FORMATIVE ASSESSMENT

### Analyze Craft and Structure

**If** students are unable to find the extended allusion, **then** have them underline unfamiliar parts of the text and compare them to the Declaration of Independence.

For Reteach and Practice, see **Analyze Craft and Structure: Author's Choices: Allusions (RP).**

MAKING MEANING

TIP

CLARIFICATION
An **extended allusion** may imitate or borrow the structure of the text after which it is modeled, the wording of that text, or both.

## Analyze Craft and Structure

**Author's Choices: Allusions** An **allusion** is an unexplained reference within a literary work to a well-known person, place, event, text, or work of art. An allusion adds meaning to a text by offering a point of similarity or comparison to the ideas the author is presenting. Authors assume that readers understand both the reference and the layer of meaning it adds.

Although most allusions are conveyed in a word or a phrase, some provide structure for an entire piece of writing. In the Declaration of Sentiments, Elizabeth Cady Stanton creates an extended allusion by modeling her argument after the Declaration of Independence.

**Practice**

**CITE TEXTUAL EVIDENCE** to support your answers.

Use this chart to analyze how the extended allusion to the Declaration of Independence helps introduce, develop, and conclude the argument made in the Declaration of Sentiments. A first example has been done for you. Gather your notes, and then share your responses with your group.

| DECLARATION OF SENTIMENTS | ALLUSION TO THE DECLARATION OF INDEPENDENCE | DEVELOPMENT OF IDEAS |
|---|---|---|
| Paragraphs 1–2 | The Declaration of Independence reads: "We hold these truths to be self-evident: that all men are created equal. . . . " Stanton revises this to read:". . . all men and women are created equal." | The allusion suggests that the Declaration of Sentiments is equal in importance to—and perhaps even goes beyond— the Declaration of Independence. |
| Paragraphs 3–17 | a. See possible responses in the Teacher's edition. | b. |
| Paragraphs 18–20 | c. | d. |





### CROSS-CURRICULAR PERSPECTIVES

**Art** Point out to students that the original "Declaration of Sentiments" did not have any art. Discuss with students the impact that a carefully chosen visual has on a written document. A picture in a brochure or advertisement, for example, can help convey an emotion. A map can help make driving directions much clearer, and a diagram can help people see how to assemble a piece of furniture. Have students prepare at least two illustrations for a published edition of "The Declaration of Sentiments." Their illustrations should be aimed at contemporary readers to help them understand the main ideas in the document.

## Conventions and Style

DECLARATION OF SENTIMENTS

**Types of Clauses** A **clause** is a group of words that has a subject and a predicate. An **independent clause** can stand on its own as a complete sentence. A **subordinate** (also called **dependent**) **clause** is unable to stand alone because it does not express a complete thought. Writers use a variety of subordinate clauses to add information, to clarify meaning, and to link related ideas.

| TYPE OF CLAUSE | COMPOSITION | EXAMPLES |
|---|---|---|
| Independent | subject, predicate; expresses a complete thought | *We hold these truths to be self-evident . . .* (paragraph 2)<br>*. . . it is their duty to throw off such government . . .* (paragraph 2) |
| Subordinate | subject, predicate; does not express a complete thought; begins with a word such as *which, who, that, since, when, if, as, although,* or *because* | *. . . that they should declare the causes . . .* (paragraph 1)<br>*. . . as she can commit many crimes with impunity . . .* (paragraph 9) |

### Read It

1. Each example contains one independent clause and one subordinate clause. Mark independent clauses once and subordinate clauses twice.
   a. Although some proponents of women's rights supported the Declaration of Sentiments, others considered it too radical.
   b. It was no secret that the work entailed danger and public censure.
   c. Because suffrage is such a precious right, Americans should vote in all elections.
2. **Connect to Style** Reread this excerpt from Declaration of Sentiments. Mark independent clauses once and subordinate clauses twice.

   We hold these truths to be self-evident: that all men and women are created equal; that they are endowed by their Creator with certain inalienable rights. . . .

**Notebook** Explain how the use of these clauses helps the writer show a main idea and the details that support it.

### Write It

**Notebook** Complete this paragraph by adding a clause to each sentence as directed.

If I had been working alongside Elizabeth Cady Stanton, [independent clause]. I also would have marched for female suffrage, [subordinate clause]. Many people fought against giving women the vote [subordinate clause]. The work was important, however, so [independent clause].



**EVIDENCE LOG**

Before moving on to a new selection, go to your Evidence Log and record what you learned from "Declaration of Sentiments."

**STANDARDS**

**Reading Informational Text**
Analyze seventeenth-, eighteenth-, and nineteenth-century foundational U.S. documents of historical and literary significance for their themes, purposes, and rhetorical features.

**Language**
Demonstrate command of the conventions of standard English grammar and usage when writing or speaking.



## PERSONALIZE FOR LEARNING

### English Language Support

**Types of Clauses** Ask students to write a one-paragraph summary of "Declaration of Sentiments" using at least one basic subordinate clause. **EMERGING**

Ask students to write a one-paragraph summary of "Declaration of Sentiments" using several basic subordinate clauses. **EXPANDING**

Ask students to write a two-paragraph summary of "Declaration of Sentiments" using a variety of subordinate clauses. **BRIDGING**

An expanded **English Language Support Lesson** on Types of Clauses is available in the Interactive Teacher's Edition.

DIGITAL PERSPECTIVES 

## Conventions and Style

**Types of Clauses** Point out that subordinate clauses often begin with subordinating conjunctions, such as: *that, as, after, because, when, since,* and *although*. Explain that identifying whether a clause begins with a subordinating conjunction can help identify the type of clause. Provide a model:

**Subordinate clause:** When the Declaration was presented at the Seneca Falls Convention
**Independent clause:** The Declaration was presented at the Seneca Falls Convention.

For more support, see **Conventions and Style: Types of Clauses.**

### Read It

Possible responses:

Independent clauses are underlined once; subordinate clauses are underlined twice.

1. a. Although some proponents of women's rights supported the "Declaration of Sentiments," others considered it too radical a statement.
   b. It was no secret that the work entailed danger and public censure.
   c. Because suffrage is such a precious right, Americans should vote in all elections.
2. **Connect to Style** We hold these truths to be self-evident: that all men and women are created equal; that they are endowed by their Creator with certain inalienable rights ... Whenever any form of Government becomes destructive of these ends, it is the right of those who suffer from it to refuse allegiance to it. (In the final sentence, the subordinate clause splits the independent clause.) The two subordinate clauses add information—they show what the "truths" in the independent clause are.

### Write It

Make sure students use independent and subordinate clauses in their writing.

**Evidence Log** Support students in completing their Evidence Logs. This paced activity will help prepare them for the Performance-Based Assessment at the end of the unit.

### FORMATIVE ASSESSMENT

### Conventions and Style

**If** If students cannot identify independent and subordinate clauses, **then** share examples.

For Reteach and Practice, see **Conventions and Style: Types of Clauses.**

### Selection Test

Administer the "Declaration of Sentiments" Selection Test, which is available in both print and digital formats online in Assessments.

# Giving Women the Vote

**AUDIO SUMMARIES**
Audio summaries of "Giving Women the Vote" are available online in both English and Spanish in the Interactive Teacher's Edition or Unit Resources. Assigning these summaries prior to reviewing the selection may help students build additional background knowledge and set a context for their first review.

## Summary

In her podcast "Giving Women the Vote," Sandra Sleight-Brennan tells the story of how the Nineteenth Amendment became law. In June 1919 the Nineteenth Amendment was sent to the states for ratification—it needed 36 votes to become law. By 1920 it had 35. Tennessee was the next state to vote on ratification. Suffragists and their opponents lobbied the State Legislature, and in August the first vote went against suffrage, 47/49. When a representative switched his allegiance the sides seemed tied—until 24-year-old Harry Burn, a confirmed anti-suffragist, amazed his colleagues at the roll call by voting "Aye." Burn had in his pocket a letter from his mother, telling him to "be a good boy" and vote for the amendment. "A mother's advice is always safest for a boy to follow," he explained.

### Insight

Listening to "Giving Women the Vote" will help students understand the bravery and integrity it takes to oppose the status quo and demand change. It will also make clear that those who already possess their freedom have a responsibility to defend that right for the oppressed.

ESSENTIAL QUESTION:
In what ways does the struggle for freedom change with history?

## Connection to Essential Question

"Giving Women the Vote" will help students answer the Essential Question—"In what ways does the struggle for freedom change with history?"—by demonstrating that the struggle for women's suffrage grew over time, gaining enough attention that it moved from being a concern of women only, to an issue that men recognized as important.

SMALL-GROUP LEARNING PERFORMANCE TASK
What were the goals of these reformers? Why did they want to achieve their goals?

UNIT PERFORMANCE-BASED ASSESSMENT
What motivates people to struggle for change?

## Connection to Performance Tasks

**Small-Group Learning Performance Task** In this Performance Task, students will focus on the goals and achievements of the reformers represented in this section's selections. "Giving Women the Vote" documents and dramatizes the fight for suffrage. Students will consider to what extent that goal has been met.

**Unit Performance-Based Assessment** This selection provides examples of the techniques media producers may use to affect an audience. Sandra Sleight-Brennan employs the use of authentic interviews and dramatizations to give listeners characters they can relate to as well as a narrative with a satisfying conclusion. She also uses music to heighten the drama and set the tone.

DIGITAL PERSPECTIVES

 Audio  Video  Document  Annotation Highlights  EL Highlights 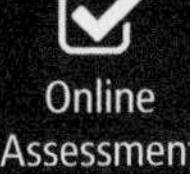 Online Assessment

## LESSON RESOURCES

| | Making Meaning | Effective Expression |
|---|---|---|
| Lesson | **First Review**<br>**Close Review**<br>**Analyze the Media**<br>**Media Vocabulary** | **Writing to Compare** |
| Instructional Standards | **RI.10** By the end of grade 11, read and comprehend literary nonfiction . . .<br>**SL.3** Evaluate a speaker's point of view . . . | **RI.5** Analyze and evaluate the effectiveness of the structure an author uses . . .<br>**RI.6** Determine an author's point of view . . .<br>**RI.7** Integrate and evaluate multiple sources of information . . . |
| **STUDENT RESOURCES** | | |
| Available online in the Interactive Student Edition or Unit Resources | Selection Video<br>First-Review Guide: Media-Audio<br>Close-Review Guide: Media-Audio | Evidence Log |
| **TEACHER RESOURCES** | | |
| **Selection Resources**<br>Available online in the Interactive Teacher's Edition or Unit Resources | Audio Summaries<br>Media Vocabulary<br>Giving Women the Vote: Media Questions | |
| **Assessment**<br>Available online in Assessments | Selection Test | |
| **My Resources** | A Unit 3 Answer Key is available online and in the Interactive Teacher's Edition. | |

## Text Complexity Rubric: Giving Women the Vote

| Quantitative Measures | |
|---|---|
| **Format and length:** 5:02 podcast | |
| **Qualitative Measures** | |
| Knowledge Demands<br>① ② ❸ ④ ⑤ | Some knowledge of the issue of women's suffrage and of the law-making process would be helpful to students. |
| Structure<br>① ❷ ③ ④ ⑤ | Clear structure and flow of ideas. Logical sequence and progression. |
| Language Conventionality and Clarity<br>① ② ❸ ④ ⑤ | Some of the language is conversational and easy to follow, but some terms are used that students may be unfamiliar with, such as *ratification*. |
| Levels of Meaning/Purpose<br>① ❷ ③ ④ ⑤ | Meaning is straightforward and purpose is to inform. On a deeper level, the amount of sacrifice and effort given to the movement is sometimes implied rather than stated directly. |

# FACILITATING

## Jump Start

FIRST REVIEW Ask groups to consider the following prompt: *Voting is the most precious right of every citizen.* If this is so, why do so many people choose not to vote? As students discuss in groups, ask them to consider how voting relates to the theme of power, protest, and change.

## Giving Women the Vote

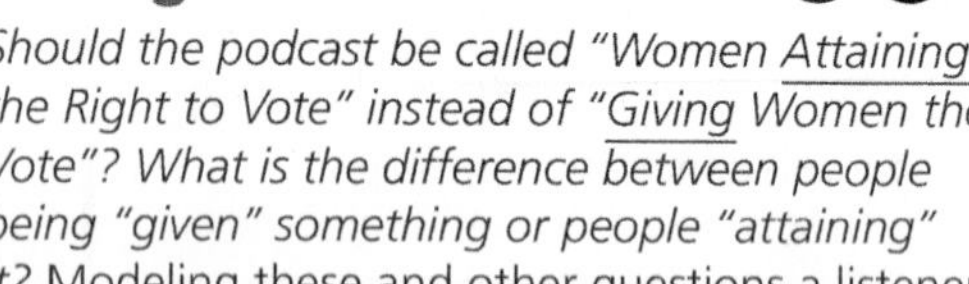

*Should the podcast be called "Women Attaining the Right to Vote" instead of "Giving Women the Vote"? What is the difference between people being "given" something or people "attaining" it?* Modeling these and other questions a listener might ask about how the podcast connects students to both the podcast and to the Small-Group Performance Task.

## Media Vocabulary

Encourage students to discuss the media vocabulary. Have they seen or used these words or concepts before? Do they use any of these words in their speech and writing?

### FIRST REVIEW

As they listen, students should perform the steps of the first review:

LISTEN: You may want to remind students to take notes as they listen to "Giving Women the Vote." Remind students to write down key points and details made during the podcast.

NOTE: Students should take notes about the most interesting people or most dramatic moments.

CONNECT: Encourage students to make connections beyond the podcast. If they have no connections in their lives, ask them if they know how laws are passed.

RESPOND: Students will answer questions to demonstrate understanding.

Point out to students that while they will always complete the Respond step at the end of the first review, the other steps will probably happen concurrently. You may wish to print copies of the **First-Review Guide: Media-Audio** for students to use.

MAKING MEANING

DECLARATION OF SENTIMENTS

### Comparing Text to Media

This podcast discusses the final steps that made women's suffrage a reality. After listening to it, you will compare how broadcast media can provide information in a way that differs from the way information is conveyed in a text.

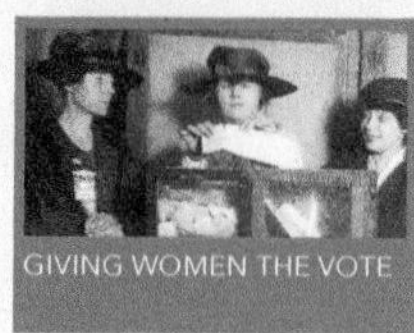

GIVING WOMEN THE VOTE

**About the Producer**

**Sandra Sleight-Brennan** (b. 1951) is an award-winning scriptwriter and media producer. She is the driving force behind many audio and video projects, Web-based documentaries, and a variety of multimedia efforts. Although she has covered a wide range of topics, she has a special interest in projects that show societal change and that reflect the struggles of minorities. Sleight-Brennan's work has been broadcast on radio stations across the country.

# Giving Women the Vote

## Media Vocabulary

These words or concepts will be useful to you as you analyze, discuss, and write about podcasts.

| | |
|---|---|
| **Frame:** main spoken narrative of a production | • A frame has a clear beginning, middle, and end.<br>• Usually, one narrator or host presents the frame. |
| **Special Elements:** features that provide points of emphasis in a production | • Sound effects can add realism. Background music can highlight the emotion connected with an event. Either element can set a mood.<br>• Interview segments can add information and insights. Dramatic reenactments can bring events to life. |
| **Tone:** production's attitude toward a subject or audience | • In a podcast, tone is created through the narrator or host's word choice and vocal qualities, as well as the use of special elements. |

### First Review MEDIA: AUDIO

Apply these strategies as you listen to the podcast.

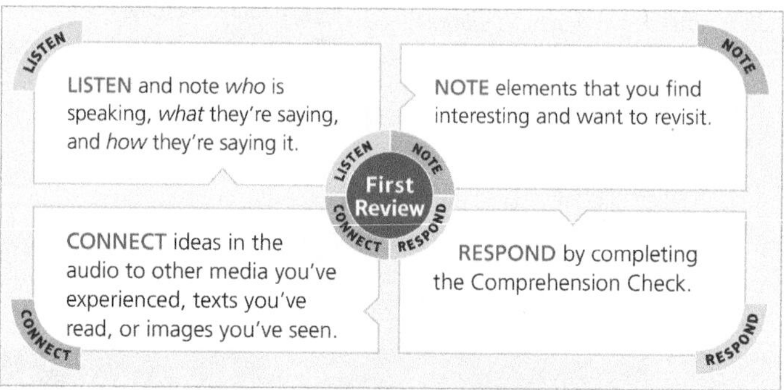

LISTEN
LISTEN and note *who* is speaking, *what* they're saying, and *how* they're saying it.
NOTE
NOTE elements that you find interesting and want to revisit.
First Review
CONNECT
CONNECT ideas in the audio to other media you've experienced, texts you've read, or images you've seen.
RESPOND
RESPOND by completing the Comprehension Check.


STANDARDS

**Reading Informational Text**
By the end of grade 11, read and comprehend literary nonfiction in the grades 11–CCR text complexity band proficiently, with scaffolding as needed at the high end of the range.

### Listening Strategy: Take Notes

**Notebook** As you listen, record your observations and questions, making sure to note time codes for later reference.



## PERSONALIZE FOR LEARNING

### Strategic Support

**Tone and Shades of Meaning** To help students confirm their understanding of how tone affects the meaning of texts that are read aloud, have group members write a sentence that, depending on how it is read, can have different meanings. Then, have groups members take turns reading the sentence aloud, using different tones and noting how altering the tone affects the meaning of the sentence. Encourage group members to refine their sentence to make its meaning even more dependent on the tone with which it is read aloud. Finally, ask a volunteer from each group to share the group's sentence with the class and to explain why tone plays an important role in understanding the intended meaning of the sentence.

MEDIA | PODCAST

# Giving Women the Vote

Sandra Sleight-Brennan

BACKGROUND

The campaign to give the vote to all American women faced many disappointments in the decades following the Seneca Falls Convention. Finally, however, in June 1919, Congress passed a women's suffrage amendment to the United States Constitution and sent it to the states for ratification. Nine months later, 35 states had ratified the amendment. Only one more state's ratification was needed, but the deadline for ratification was drawing near. "Giving Women the Vote," which Sandra Sleight-Brennan produced in 2010 to commemorate the ninetieth anniversary of the Nineteenth Amendment, tells the story of that final state's ratification—and the surprising way in which it happened.

SCAN FOR MULTIMEDIA

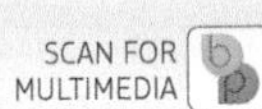



NOTES



DIGITAL PERSPECTIVES

CLOSER REVIEW

## Supporting Claims

During their first review, students may have noted the claim that "By the end of World War I, most people felt that women should be given the vote." This claim is presented at 2:48 in the podcast. Suggest that students revisit this part of the podcast. If needed, provide the following prompts.

**NOTE:** Have students note examples that show that the public was behind passing the right for women to vote.

**QUESTION:** What do these details show about how the public felt about giving women the right to vote?

**Possible response:** In 1920, women made extraordinary efforts to travel great distances to attend rallies and parades that supported the suffrage movement, often with the help of their families. Girls learned rhymes and songs supporting women's right to vote. When time came for the states to vote on ratifying the Nineteenth Amendment, thirty-six states were needed to ratify it, which happened within a year. There are also several examples of men who originally voted against ratification and changed their minds to support it.

**CONCLUDE:** How do these anecdotes support the producer's claim?

**Possible response:** Interviews of people that witnessed the movement and dramatizations of events provide evidence that many people supported the ratification of the Nineteenth Amendment.

Remind students that even when **claims,** or opinions are made orally, they should be supported by evidence.

PERSONALIZE FOR LEARNING

### Strategic Support

**Distinguish Voices** If students struggle with various voices on the podcast, help by pointing out that the recording is produced to be a combination of nonfiction story-telling and dramatic retelling. Point out that the narrator describes the history of the moment, but the additional voices help to bring the action in Tennessee to life. Ask students to consider these questions:

- Beginning at 1:33 of the podcast, how does hearing the experiences of women who remember the time help raise listener interest?
- How does hearing Burn's mother's words performed help listeners understand her perspective?

FACILITATING

## Comprehension Check

Possible responses:

1. Despite the suffragists' efforts, their work was taken for granted, and suffrage had not yet come.
2. Tennessee
3. Supporters of ratification wore yellow roses, and opponents wore red roses.
4. A letter from his mother urged Burn to vote for ratification, but Burn also expressed belief that suffrage was a right for all and his desire to "free seventeen million women from political slavery."
5. Possible response: Ratification by thirty-six states was needed to make the Nineteenth Amendment law, and Tennessee became the thirty-sixth state in August 1920. State legislators were tied (48–48) until Harry Burn changed his vote to the affirmative. Although pressured to oppose the amendment, Burn stood by his vote, and ratification was achieved.

## Research

**Research to Clarify** If students struggle to come up with an unfamiliar detail from the podcast to research, suggest that they focus on different people who speak during the podcast.

## Comprehension Check

**Complete the following items after you finish your first review. Review and clarify details with your group.**

1. According to the interview with the reporter from the Cleveland *Plain Dealer*, what was the result of the campaign for women's suffrage in the years just prior to 1920?

2. Which state became the final battleground for making the Nineteenth Amendment the law of the land?

3. What was the significance of the red or yellow roses worn by people on the scene?

4. According to the dramatic reenactment, why did Harry Burn change his vote?

5. **Notebook** Write a summary to confirm your understanding of the ratification of the Nineteenth Amendment, as presented in the podcast.

### RESEARCH

**Research to Clarify** Choose at least one unfamiliar detail from the podcast. Briefly research that detail. In what way does the information you learned shed light upon an aspect of the podcast? Share your findings with your group.





## PERSONALIZE FOR LEARNING

**English Language Support**

**Listening to Write a Summary** Explain that a summary is a brief explanation of a story or piece of writing. It needs to include only the main idea and the supporting facts. Guide your students though these steps as they prepare to write a summary of the podcast.

1. Listen to the podcast, noting key events.
2. Review your notes for your summary, identifying any gaps.
3. Ask questions after you listen to determine what you may need to hear again.
4. Listen a second time, noting additional important details.
5. Write one sentence that describes the main idea of the podcast. This is the first sentence of your summary.
6. Add details from your notes.
7. Write a conclusion.

## Close Review

With your group, review your notes. If necessary, listen to the podcast again. Record any new observations that seem important. What **questions** do you have? What can you **conclude**?

GIVING WOMEN THE VOTE

## Analyze the Media

CITE TEXTUAL EVIDENCE to support your answers.

Complete the activities.

1. **Present and Discuss** Choose the part of the podcast you find most interesting or powerful. Share your choice with your group, and discuss why you chose it. Explain what you noticed about that section, what questions it raised for you, and what conclusions you reached about it.
2. **Synthesize** With your group, review the entire podcast. Do the frame and the special elements work together to inform listeners? Are they examples of information, of entertainment, or of both? Explain.
3. **Essential Question:** *In what ways does the struggle for freedom change with history?* What have you learned about the struggle for freedom from listening to this podcast? Discuss with your group.

LANGUAGE DEVELOPMENT

## Media Vocabulary

frame    special elements    tone

Use these vocabulary words in your responses to the following questions.

1. **(a)** What do listeners learn from the narrator about the ratification process? **(b)** Why might Sleight-Brennan have wanted to include this information?
2. How do the comments dramatized by the characters of Harry Burn and his mother help to show the tensions surrounding this final vote for ratification?
3. This podcast was produced in recognition of the ninetieth anniversary of the Nineteenth Amendment. What attitude toward the event do you think it was meant to encourage in listeners? Explain.

STANDARDS

**Speaking and Listening**
Evaluate a speaker's point of view, reasoning, and use of evidence and rhetoric, assessing the stance, premises, links among ideas, word choice, points of emphasis, and tone used.





DIGITAL PERSPECTIVES 

## Close Review

Model close reviewing as needed by using the Close Review notes for the podcast. Remind groups to use Accountable Talk in their discussions and support one another as they complete the close review.

## Analyze the Media

**Possible responses:**

1. Responses will vary but should reflect especially dramatic or intriguing parts of the podcast.
2. Responses will vary, but students should cite specific examples of information from the podcast to support their assertions.
3. Students' responses will vary, but they should refer to specific parts of the podcast.

## Media Vocabulary

For more support, see **Media Vocabulary.**

**Possible responses:**

1. (a) In the narrator's frame, listeners learn about the passage of the amendment in Congress, the number of states needed to ratify it, the scene in the Tennessee legislature, how Harry Burn changed his vote, and the wording of the amendment. (b) She probably wanted listeners to have a well-rounded account.
2. The dramatization shows that supporters of the Nineteenth Amendment were pressured to denounce it. It also humanizes Harry Burn.
3. In addition to helping listeners become better informed about the ratification, the podcast encourages a greater appreciation of the suffragists' struggle and of the right to vote itself.

### FORMATIVE ASSESSMENT

### Analyze the Media

**If** students struggle to cite evidence to support their answers, **then** provide the **Giving Women the Vote: Media Questions** available online in the Interactive Teacher's Edition or Unit Resources. Answers and DOK levels are also available.

### Media Vocabulary

**If** students struggle to determine which qualities the suffragettes had in common, **then** remind students what obstacles the women faced and how they reacted to these road blocks.

## Writing to Compare

As students prepare to compare information they've gathered about the women's suffrage movement from a text and a podcast, they will consider the rhetorical elements of each medium.

### Prewriting

**Analyze the Texts** Ask students to provide examples of rhetoric from advertisements they have seen recently. Discuss why rhetorical elements are effective as persuasive devices. Then have groups complete the chart.

1. Responses will vary but should be supported by evidence.
   a. "He has never permitted her to exercise her inalienable right to the elective franchise."
   b. "We hold these truths to be self-evident: that all men and women are created equal . . ."
   c. "He has . . ." begins nine sentences.
   d. "He closes against her all the avenues to wealth and distinction . . ."
   e. The entire document is an allusion to the Declaration of Independence.
   f. "The history of mankind is a history of repeated injuries and usurpations on the part of man toward woman, . . ."
   g. "And here it was 1920, and they worked hard in the wartime activities, and that was taken for granted."
   h. A diagram of architectural columns shows the order in which the states ratified the Constitution.
   i. An illustration of a globe emphasizes how unusual it was to allow so many people to have a say in how their government is organized.
   j. "The suffragists and their supporters in the legislature wore yellow roses. The opposition wore red."
   k. "If Michigan goes wet, blame it on Pa" is an allusion to the repeal of Prohibition; Prohibition had ushered in a "dry" era of no alcohol.
   l. "I appreciated the fact that an opportunity such as seldom comes to a mortal man, to free seventeen million women from political slavery, was mine."
2. All elements can be found in both selections.
3. At first, the suffragists' strategy focused on written protests, but later, there were public protests in the streets and a campaign for a constitutional amendment.



EFFECTIVE EXPRESSION

DECLARATION OF SENTIMENTS

GIVING WOMEN THE VOTE

STANDARDS

**Reading Informational Text**
- Analyze and evaluate the effectiveness of the structure an author uses in his or her exposition or argument, including whether the structure makes points clear, convincing, and engaging.
- Determine an author's point of view or purpose in a text in which the rhetoric is particularly effective, analyzing how style and content contribute to the power, persuasiveness or beauty of the text.
- Integrate and evaluate multiple sources of information presented in different media or formats as well as in words in order to address a question or solve a problem.

## Writing to Compare

You have read a document that launched the women's suffrage movement—Elizabeth Cady Stanton's Declaration of Sentiments. You have also listened to a podcast about the ratification of the nineteenth amendment in 1920. Now, deepen your understanding of the issue of women's suffrage by comparing and contrasting elements of the two selections and putting your ideas in writing.

**Assignment**

Both the document and the podcast illustrate the methods suffragists and politicians used to convince people that granting women the vote was the right course of action. Write a **compare-and-contrast essay** in which you analyze how each selection shows persuasion at work. Focus on the arguments and rhetorical strategies used by the people involved in the campaign. How did they seek to communicate key ideas in powerful, convincing ways?

### Prewriting

**Analyze the Texts** **Persuasion** involves communicating a point of view and convincing others to adopt it. Persuasion is accomplished through effective **rhetoric,** or the use of stylistic elements to build meaning in a powerful way. The elements of rhetoric include:

- strong arguments—clearly stated claims supported by compelling evidence
- a lofty or passionate tone
- the repetition of words, phrases, or ideas
- the use of striking images
- allusions to established or respected ideas or texts
- the use of analogies, or comparisons.

**Notebook** Complete the activity, and answer the questions.

1. Analyze elements of rhetoric used by suffragists and their supporters in each selection. Assign each group member one element to look for in either one or both selections. Then, discuss and analyze your findings.

| Rhetorical Element | Declaration of Sentiments | Giving Women the Vote |
|---|---|---|
| Argument | a. See possible responses in Teacher's Edition. | g. |
| Tone | b. | h. |
| Repetition | c. | i. |
| Imagery | d. | j. |
| Allusion | e. | k. |
| Analogy | f. | l. |

2. Which elements of persuasion are showcased in both selections?
3. These two selections focus on events 70 years apart. How did the suffragists' arguments or strategies change over time?

## Drafting

**Draw Conclusions** As a group, review and discuss your Prewriting notes. Based on those notes, what can you conclude about the use of rhetoric in the suffrage movement, as illustrated by these two selections? Which elements carried the movement to its successful conclusion?

Thesis/central idea: ______________________________

______________________________

______________________________

**Develop a Project Plan** Work with your group to outline the body of your essay and divide the writing task into manageable parts. Use a chart like this one to assign parts. Write a description of each part in the left column, and the name of the person assigned to it in the right. Discuss and note key pieces of evidence to use in each section.

| SECTIONS OR PARTS | PERSON ASSIGNED |
|---|---|
| **Part I:**<br>Evidence: | |
| **Part II:**<br>Evidence: | |
| **Part III:**<br>Evidence: | |
| **Part IV:**<br>Evidence: | |
| **Part V:**<br>Evidence: | |

**Write a Draft** Work as a group to draft an introduction that includes your working thesis and touches on all the sections or parts the body of the essay will include. Then, work independently to draft the body sections. When everyone is finished, share your drafts aloud. Discuss revisions that will make each section stronger. Tie the parts of your essay together with effective transitions. Finally, draft a conclusion that follows logically from all sections of the essay.

## Reviewing, Revising, and Editing

Have each group member edit and proofread the text independently. Apply all your changes to the draft. Then, have one person read the finished essay aloud. What last small changes need to be made to finalize your work?

EVIDENCE LOG

Before moving on to a new selection, go to your Evidence Log and record what you've learned from the Declaration of Sentiments and "Giving Women the Vote."





DIGITAL PERSPECTIVES

## Drafting

**Draw Conclusions** Suggest that group members hold a discussion and come to a consensus about which rhetorical elements they thought were strongest and most effective. Groups can then gather text evidence to support their claims.

**Develop a Project Plan** Check in with groups to ensure that the workload is evenly distributed and that students have been assigned duties that they are capable of fulfilling. Group members should agree on the key pieces of evidence being used so that they will come together as a cohesive essay.

**Write a Draft** Remind group members that the body sections of the essay will need to come together as a whole. Therefore, after all of the sections have been written, students should spend time making sure that there are transitions between sections and that the essay as a whole flows smoothly.

## Review, Revise, and Edit

As groups revise, encourage them to review their draft for differences in writing styles in the various body sections; minor adjustments may be all that are needed to make the essay flow more smoothly. Ask them to review their word choice. Finally, remind students to check for grammar, usage, and mechanics.

For more support, see **Writing to Compare: Compare-and-Contrast Essay.**

**Evidence Log** Support students in completing their Evidence Log. This paced activity will help prepare them for the Performance-Based Assessment at the end of the unit.

**FORMATIVE ASSESSMENT**

### Writing to Compare

**If** students struggle to combine the individual parts of the essay into a whole, **then** have them use transition words and phrases to link the various body sections.

# The Story of an Hour

**AUDIO SUMMARIES**
Audio summaries of "The Story of an Hour" are available online in both English and Spanish in the Interactive Teacher's Edition or Unit Resources. Assigning these summaries prior to reading the selection may help students build additional background knowledge and set a context for their first read.


## Summary

At the beginning of "The Story of an Hour," by Kate Chopin, Mrs. Mallard learns that her husband has died in a train crash. She has heart trouble, so her sister breaks the news as gently as possible. As first Mrs. Mallard weeps, but when the initial storm of grief dies down, she goes alone to her room. As she looks out the window, she becomes aware of a feeling that shocks and confuses her. She tries to ignore it, but finally has to admit that the feeling is tremendous joy. She is free. She can at last live for herself and not in obedience to her husband. She hopes she will have a long life—only the day before she dreaded the thought. Mrs. Mallard finally leaves her room and walks triumphantly down the stairs. At the bottom of the stairs another surprise is waiting.


### Insight

Is to dream of freedom, only to have that dream quashed, worse than never having the dream? Reading "The Story of an Hour" will help students see that oppression can be insidious, especially when it hides behind societal norms. The oppressed may barely recognize that they have had their freedom and power stripped from them, until they get a glimpse of a life without oppression.

ESSENTIAL QUESTION:
In what ways does the struggle for freedom change with history?

## Connection to Essential Question

"The Story of an Hour" provides a unique perspective on the Essential Question—*In what ways does the struggle for freedom change with history?* Mrs. Mallard only becomes aware of her own struggle when she's faced with the absence of her oppressor. Hers is not a large-scale struggle to right social injustices; rather, her struggle is domestic and personal.

SMALL-GROUP LEARNING PERFORMANCE TASK
What were the goals of these reformers? Why did they want to achieve their goals?

UNIT PERFORMANCE-BASED ASSESSMENT
What motivates people to struggle for change?

## Connection to Performance Tasks

**Small-Group Learning Performance Task** In this Performance Task, students will focus on the goals and achievements of the reformers represented in these selections. "The Story of an Hour" uses literary techniques to suggest a goal, rather than stating it outright. Students will consider to what extent that goal has been met.

**Unit Performance-Based Assessment** This selection provides a stylistic example of the techniques writers may use to affect an audience. Kate Chopin skillfully uses irony to highlight the problem of women's oppression.

## LESSON RESOURCES

| | Making Meaning | Language Development | Effective Expression |
|---|---|---|---|
| Lesson | **First Read**<br>**Close Read**<br>**Analyze the Text**<br>**Analyze Craft and Structure** | **Concept Vocabulary**<br>**Word Study**<br>**Conventions and Style** | **Speaking and Listening** |
| Instructional Standards | **RL.10** By the end of grade 11, read and comprehend literature . . .<br>**L.4.b** Identify and correctly use patterns of word changes . . .<br>**RL.2** Determine two or more themes or central ideas of a text . . .<br>**RL.3** Analyze the impact of the author's choices . . . | **L.5.b** Analyze nuances in the meaning of words . . .<br>**RL.6** Analyze a case in which grasping point of view . . . | **SL.1.c** Propel conversations by posing and responding . . .<br>**SL.1.d** Respond thoughtfully to diverse perspectives; synthesize comments, claims, and evidence . . . |
| **STUDENT RESOURCES** | | | |
| Available online in the Interactive Student Edition or Unit Resources | Selection Audio<br>First-Read Guide: Fiction<br>Close-Read Guide: Fiction | Word Network | Evidence Log |
| **TEACHER RESOURCES** | | | |
| **Selection Resources**<br>Available online in the Interactive Teacher's Edition or Unit Resources | Audio Summaries<br>Annotation Highlights<br>EL Highlights<br>English Language Support Lesson: Classroom Discussion<br>The Story of an Hour: Text Questions<br>Analyze the Text Questions<br>Analyze Craft and Structure: Development of Theme | Concept Vocabulary and Word Study<br>Conventions and Style: Irony | Speaking and Listening: Group Discussion |
| **Reteach/Practice**<br>Available online in the Interactive Teacher's Edition or Unit Resources | Analyze Craft and Structure: Development of Theme (RP) | Word Study: Denotation and Connotation (RP)<br>Conventions and Style: Irony (RP) | Speaking and Listening: Group Discussion (RP) |
| **Assessment**<br>Available online in Assessments | Selection Test | | |
| **My Resources** | A Unit 3 Answer Key is available online and in the Interactive Teacher's Edition. | | |

# Reading Support

| Text Complexity Rubric: The Story of an Hour | |
|---|---|
| **Quantitative Measures** | |
| **Lexile:** 960 **Text Length:** 1,007 words | |
| **Qualitative Measures** | |
| Knowledge Demands ①—②—❸—④—⑤ | Contains content and experiences that will be unfamiliar to students (relationships of married women and their perspective and ideas). |
| Structure ①—❷—③—④—⑤ | A sequential short story with plot elements that are explained. Paragraphs are short, which makes structure easier to follow. |
| Language Conventionality and Clarity ①—②—❸—④—⑤ | Sentences are short, but sometimes contain difficult or unfamiliar syntax and vocabulary. |
| Levels of Meaning/Purpose ①—②—③—❹—⑤ | The reader must infer meaning on multiple levels beyond the plot itself (author's commentary on love, marriage, and independence of women); story has irony in both plot and message. |

DECIDE AND PLAN

## English Language Support

Provide English Learners with support for language and meaning as they read the selection.

**Language** Help students understand unfamiliar syntax by working with them to rephrase sentences. For example: (paragraph 2) *It was he who had been in the railroad office when news of the railroad disaster was received.* Begin a sentence and ask students to finish it: *Richards was in the railroad office when he heard ______ (about the railroad accident. / that the husband had died. / that there was a train wreck.)*

**Levels of Meaning** Help students clarify and express levels of meaning by modeling how to talk about ironic or surprising events. For example, *We thought Mrs. Mallard would be sad. We were surprised that she was also happy.*

## Strategic Support

Provide students with strategic support to ensure that they can successfully read the text.

**Knowledge Demands** Discuss that the story takes place in the late nineteenth century. Ask students to keep in mind that the independence and identity of women at that time was very different from what it is today.

**Meaning/Purpose** As students read, have them note sentences that give clues to the changing feeling of the woman throughout the story. Ask them to say or list the sentences, describing what is different about her feelings at each point. Then, have them reread the story keeping these changes in mind.

## Challenge

Provide students who need to be challenged with ideas for how they can go beyond a simple interpretation of the text.

**Text Analysis** Ask students to describe how the woman feels at key points in the story (finding out about the death, after her initial shock, then finding out that he is actually alive). Have them explain the reasons behind each of those feelings and how they changed.

**Written Response** Ask students to research and read more of Kate Chopin's writing about women in the late nineteenth century and their changing roles and relationships as mothers and wives. They may also read her biography to learn more about the events that influenced this short story. Ask them to write a short essay detailing what they learned.

TEACH

## Read and Respond

Have the groups read the selection and complete the Making Meaning, Language Development, and Effective Expression activities.

# Standards Support Through Teaching and Learning Cycle

## IDENTIFY NEEDS

Analyze results of the Beginning-of-Year Assessment, focusing on the items relating to Unit 3. Also take into consideration student performance to this point and your observations of where particular students struggle.

## DECIDE AND PLAN

- If students have performed poorly on items matching these standards, then provide selection scaffolds before assigning them the on-level lesson provided in the Student Edition.
- If students have done well on the Beginning-of-Year Assessment, then challenge them to keep progressing and learning by giving them opportunities to practice the skills in depth.
- Use the Selection Resources listed on the Planning pages for "The Story of an Hour" to help students continually improve their ability to master the standards.

**Instructional Standards: The Story of an Hour**

| | Catching Up | This Year | Looking Forward |
|---|---|---|---|
| **Reading** | You may wish to administer the **Analyze Craft and Structure: Development of Theme (RP)** worksheet to help students understand how internal monologues convey information about a character in a story. | **RL.2** Determine two or more themes or central ideas of a text and analyze their development over the course of the text, including how they interact and build on one another to produce a complex account; provide an objective summary of the text. | Encourage students to write a character analysis of Mrs. Mallard, based on the use of internal monologue and explicit dialogue and events in the story. |
| **Speaking and Listening** | You may wish to administer the **Speaking and Listening: Group Discussion (RP)** worksheet to help students understand how the ideas of an era may affect how different people of that era respond to a story. | **SL.1.c** Propel conversations by posing and responding to questions that probe reasoning and evidence; ensure a hearing for a full range of positions on a topic or issue; clarify, verify, or challenge ideas and conclusions; and promote divergent and creative perspectives. | Challenge students to imagine that they are a book reviewer from the year when "The Story of an Hour" was written. What would they convey to readers in their book review? How would the review differ from one they might write today? |
| **Language** | You may wish to administer the **Conventions and Style: Irony (RP)** worksheet to help students understand the various forms of irony.<br><br>You may wish to administer the **Word Study: Denotation and Connotation (RP)** worksheet to help students distinguish between literal meanings of words and connotative meanings of words. | **RL.6** Analyze a case in which grasping point of view requires distinguishing what is directly stated in a text from what is really meant.<br><br>**L.5.b** Analyze nuances in the meanings of words with similar denotations. | Have students find two examples of irony in "The Story of an Hour." Encourage them to explain why each example is ironic.<br><br>Challenge students to find and explain the denotative and connotative meanings of two to three words in the story. |

## ANALYZE AND REVISE

- Analyze student work for evidence of student learning.
- Identify whether or not students have met the expectations in the standards.
- Identify implications for future instruction.

## TEACH

Implement the planned lesson, and gather evidence of student learning.

# FACILITATING

## Jump Start

FIRST READ What does the bond of marriage mean for each partner in a couple? Engaging students in a discussion about the meaning of marriage and how it affects each partner sets the context for reading "The Story of an Hour." As students share their thoughts, have them focus on factors that influence their decision.

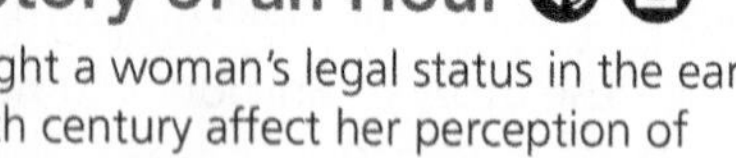

## The Story of an Hour

How might a woman's legal status in the early twentieth century affect her perception of marriage? In the past, what happened to married couples who were unhappy before divorce became common?

Modeling the questions readers might ask as they read "The Story of an Hour" brings the text alive for students and connects it to the Small-Group Performance Task question. Selection audio and print capability for the selection are available in the Interactive Teacher's Edition.

## Concept Vocabulary

Ask groups to discuss the concept vocabulary words and note if the words are similar in any way. Students should note that two of the words share the prefix *im-*. (paragraphs 15 and 18) Have students review the technique of considering all of the meanings of a prefix. Then, ask them to think of other words that contain the prefix *im-* and decide if the prefix has the same meaning in all of those words.

## FIRST READ

Have students perform the steps of the first read independently:

NOTICE: You might ask students to consider Mr. Mallard, who we see only through his wife's eyes.

ANNOTATE: Students may mark passages they find interesting as well as difficult.

CONNECT: Connecting the story to people and events they know, real or fictional, will help students understand the motivations of characters.

RESPOND: Students will demonstrate their understanding of the text by answering questions and writing a summary.

Point out to students that while they will always complete the Respond step at the end of the first read, the other steps will probably happen somewhat concurrently. You may wish to print the **First-Read Guide: Nonfiction** for students to use.

## MAKING MEANING

About the Author

**Kate Chopin** (1850–1904) was born Kate O'Flaherty in St. Louis, Missouri. At the age of 20, she married Louisiana cotton trader Oscar Chopin. The couple lived in New Orleans before moving to a rural Louisiana plantation. Chopin briefly ran the plantation after her husband's death but then returned to St. Louis with their six children. There, she began writing fiction. In the portraits of Louisiana that she created from that point forward, Chopin often addressed women's rights and racial prejudice.

# The Story of an Hour

### Concept Vocabulary

As you perform your first read of "The Story of an Hour," you will encounter these words.

persistence imploring importunities

**Familiar Word Parts** Separating a word into its parts can often help you identify its meaning. Those parts might include familiar prefixes.

Some prefixes, such as *im-*, have more than one meaning. When you come across an unfamiliar word, consider all the meanings of the prefix.

- For example, in the word *immobile, im-* means "not." Added to the base word *mobile,* which means "in motion," *im-* creates a new word that means "not mobile," or "still."
- In the word *immigrate, im-* means "into" or "toward." Added to the base word *migrate,* which means "move from one region to another," *im-* creates a new word that means "move into a new place."

When you read an unfamiliar word that has a prefix, think about other words with the same prefix. Consider which meaning makes the most sense with the base word. If a prefix has more than one meaning, try out both to determine the meaning of the unfamiliar word.

Apply your knowledge of familiar word parts and other vocabulary strategies to determine the meanings of unfamiliar words you encounter during your first read.

### First Read FICTION

Apply these strategies as you conduct your first read. You will have an opportunity to complete a close read after your first read.

NOTICE *whom* the story is about, *what* happened, *where* and *when* it happened, and *why* those involved reacted as they did.

ANNOTATE by marking vocabulary and key passages you want to revisit.

CONNECT ideas within the selection to what you already know and what you have already read.

RESPOND by completing the Comprehension Check and by writing a summary of the selection.

STANDARDS

Reading Literature
By the end of grade 11, read and comprehend literature, including stories, dramas, and poems, in the grades 11–CCR text complexity band proficiently, with scaffolding as needed at the high end of the range.

Language
Identify and correctly use patterns of word changes that indicate different meanings or parts of speech.





## FACILITATING SMALL-GROUP CLOSE READING

**CLOSE READ: Short Story** As groups perform the close read, circulate and offer support as needed.

- Remind groups that when they read a narrative, they should be sure to identify the main characters and plot.
- If a group is confused about why particular events are important, remind them to think about the time period and social norms reflected in the selection.
- Challenge groups to determine the theme of the text and the specific details that refine the theme.

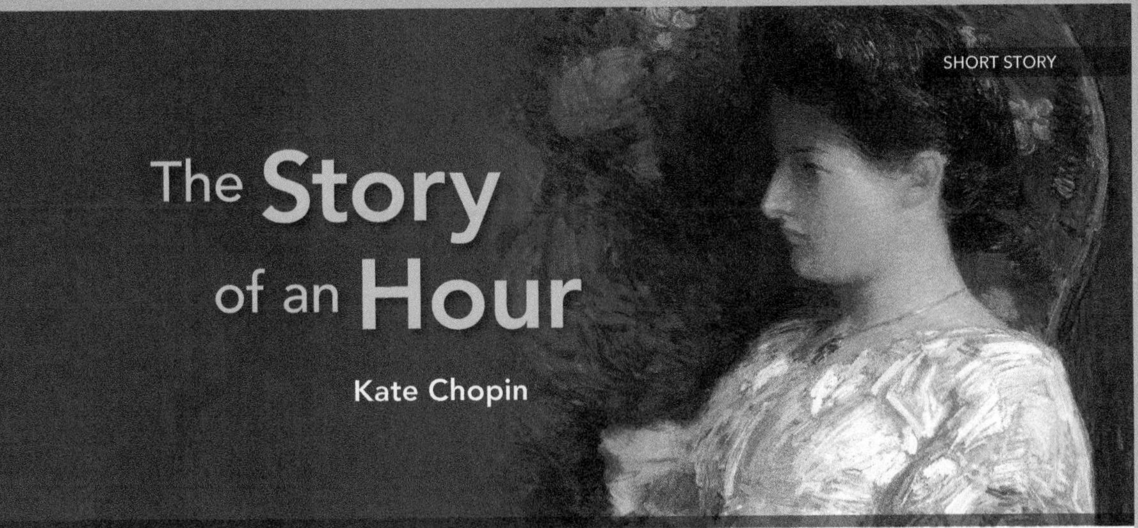


# The Story of an Hour

Kate Chopin



BACKGROUND

"The Story of an Hour" was considered daring in its time. The editors of at least two magazines refused the story, calling it immoral. They wanted Chopin to soften her female character and to make her less independent and less unhappy in her marriage. Undaunted, Chopin continued to deal with issues of women's growth and emancipation in her writing, advancing ideas that are widely accepted today.

SCAN FOR MULTIMEDIA 

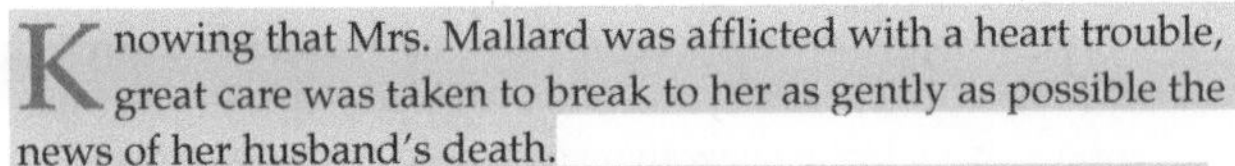

1 Knowing that Mrs. Mallard was afflicted with a heart trouble, great care was taken to break to her as gently as possible the news of her husband's death.

2 It was her sister Josephine who told her, in broken sentences; veiled hints that revealed in half concealing. Her husband's friend Richards was there, too, near her. It was he who had been in the newspaper office when intelligence of the railroad disaster was received, with Brently Mallard's name leading the list of "killed." He had only taken the time to assure himself of its truth by a second telegram, and had hastened to forestall any less careful, less tender friend in bearing the sad message.

3 She did not hear the story as many women have heard the same, with a paralyzed inability to accept its significance. She wept at once, with sudden, wild abandonment, in her sister's arms. When the storm of grief had spent itself she went away to her room alone. She would have no one follow her.

4 There stood, facing the open window, a comfortable, roomy armchair. Into this she sank, pressed down by a physical exhaustion that haunted her body and seemed to reach into her soul.

5 She could see in the open square before her house the tops of trees that were all aquiver with the new spring life. The delicious breath of rain was in the air. In the street below a peddler was crying his wares. The notes of a distant song which someone was singing reached her faintly, and countless sparrows were twittering in the eaves.

NOTES





## CLOSER LOOK

### Analyze Figurative Language

Circulate among groups as students conduct their close read. Have groups close read paragraph 3. If needed, provide the following prompts.

**ANNOTATE:** In paragraph 3, mark the metaphor that the author uses.

**QUESTION:** What is the "storm of grief" that is being referred to at this point in the story?

**Possible response:** The storm of grief is the intense emotion that Mrs. Mallard experiences when she learns of her husband's unexpected death.

**CONCLUDE:** What does the use of metaphor reveal about Mrs. Mallard? How does the metaphor help to set a tone for the story?

**Possible response:** Mrs. Mallard does not repress her ability to perceive or express emotions. "She did not hear the story as many women have heard the same, with a paralyzed inability to accept its significance." The metaphor of a storm helps create a tone for the story that matches the emotional intensity Mrs. Mallard feels.

Remind students that authors may use **figurative language**, vivid imaginative language that is not meant to be interpreted literally. **Metaphors** set two otherwise non-similar things equal to draw out a comparison. Figurative language can help set the tone or mood of a story, as well as characterize someone indirectly.

 Additional **English Language Support** is available in the Interactive Teacher's Edition.

## PERSONALIZE FOR LEARNING

### Challenge

**Modern Versus Archaic English** Review the style of language in paragraphs 1–5 with students. The English language has changed since 1894. Have students look through the first five paragraphs of the text to find words and expressions that have either changed their meaning or disappeared. Explain that the word *intelligence* in paragraph 2 means "news," or "information," and we no longer call street sellers *peddlers*. Nineteenth century authors were often less comfortable with "sensitive" material than we are—modern authors are usually more direct. In paragraph 2, the news of Brently Mallard's death is passed on to the reader with the same delicacy and unease as it is announced to Mrs. Mallard—in "veiled hints that revealed in half concealing." They also tended to use longer and more complex sentences than modern writers do. Have students rewrite the second paragraph of the story in modern English.

# FACILITATING

## Concept Vocabulary

**PERSISTENCE** If groups are struggling to define the word *persistence in paragraph 12,* remind them to look at word parts. Knowing that the suffix *–ence* changes verbs to nouns may help them to define the word. In this case, they should also consider the context in which the word is found. Students may know that to *persist* means "to continue for a long time."

**Possible response:** *Persistence* is a condition of existing beyond a longer than normal time.

**IMPLORING** If groups are struggling to define the word *imploring* in paragraph 15, point out that the prefix *im-* in this word does not have the negative meaning of *im-* in *impossible.* In *imploring,* it is an intensifier. Knowing that the root *-plorare-* means "to cry out" may help students to define the words.

**Possible response:** *Imploring* means "crying out intensely."

NOTES

6 There were patches of blue sky showing here and there through the clouds that had met and piled one above the other in the west facing her window.

7 She sat with her head thrown back upon the cushion of the chair, quite motionless, except when a sob came up into her throat and shook her, as a child who has cried itself to sleep continues to sob in its dreams.

8 She was young, with a fair, calm face, whose lines bespoke repression and even a certain strength. But now there was a dull stare in her eyes, whose gaze was fixed away off yonder on one of those patches of blue sky. It was not a glance of reflection, but rather indicated a suspension of intelligent thought.

9 There was something coming to her and she was waiting for it, fearfully. What was it? She did not know; it was too subtle and elusive to name. But she felt it, creeping out of the sky, reaching toward her through the sounds, the scents, the color that filled the air.

10 Now her bosom rose and fell tumultuously. She was beginning to recognize this thing that was approaching to possess her, and she was striving to beat it back with her will—as powerless as her two white slender hands would have been. When she abandoned herself a little whispered word escaped her slightly parted lips. She said it over and over under her breath: "free, free, free!" The vacant stare and the look of terror that had followed it went from her eyes. They stayed keen and bright. Her pulses beat fast, and the coursing blood warmed and relaxed every inch of her body.

11 She did not stop to ask if it were or were not a monstrous joy that held her. A clear and exalted perception enabled her to dismiss the suggestion as trivial. She knew that she would weep again when she saw the kind, tender hands folded in death; the face that had never looked save with love upon her, fixed and gray and dead. But she saw beyond that bitter moment a long procession of years to come that would belong to her absolutely. And she opened and spread her arms out to them in welcome.

Mark familiar word parts or indicate another strategy you used that helped you determine meaning.

**persistence** (puhr SIHS tuhns) *n.*

MEANING:

12 There would be no one to live for during those coming years; she would live for herself. There would be no powerful will bending hers in that blind **persistence** with which men and women believe they have a right to impose a private will upon a fellow creature. A kind intention or a cruel intention made the act seem no less a crime as she looked upon it in that brief moment of illumination.

13 And yet she had loved him—sometimes. Often she had not. What did it matter! What could love, the unsolved mystery, count for in the face of this possession of self-assertion which she suddenly recognized as the strongest impulse of her being!

14 "Free! Body and soul free!" she kept whispering.

**imploring** (ihm PLAWR ihng) *v.*

MEANING:

15 Josephine was kneeling before the closed door with her lips to the keyhole, **imploring** for admission. "Louise, open the door! I beg; open the door—you will make yourself ill. What are you doing, Louise? For heaven's sake open the door."





### VOCABULARY DEVELOPMENT

**Prefixes: *in-, im-, il-* and *ir-*** Ask students to further explore prefixes that mean "not." Remind them that *im-* is used in paragraphs 15 and 18. The prefixes *in-, il-, and ir-* also mean "not." Ask students to consider *illegible, illiterate, illicit,* and *illegitimate*, along with *irresponsible, irremediable, irreplaceable,* and *irregular*. Direct students to pair up to create two-column word charts for related word pairs and definitions. For example, students can list *legible* and *illegible,* meaning "able to be read" and "unreadable." Then invite students to work as a class to draw four word trees on chart paper, adding the words they learned that begin with these four prefixes.

DIGITAL PERSPECTIVES

16 "Go away. I am not making myself ill." No; she was drinking in a very elixir of life[1] through that open window.

17 Her fancy was running riot along those days ahead of her. Spring days, and summer days, and all sorts of days that would be her own. She breathed a quick prayer that life might be long. It was only yesterday she had thought with a shudder that life might be long.

18 She arose at length and opened the door to her sister's **importunities**. There was a feverish triumph in her eyes, and she carried herself unwittingly like a goddess of Victory. She clasped her sister's waist, and together they descended the stairs. Richards stood waiting for them at the bottom.

19 Someone was opening the front door with a latchkey. It was Brently Mallard who entered, a little travel-stained, composedly carrying his gripsack[2] and umbrella. He had been far from the scene of the accident, and did not even know there had been one. He stood amazed at Josephine's piercing cry; at Richards' quick motion to screen him from the view of his wife.

20 But Richards was too late.

21 When the doctors came they said she had died of heart disease—of the joy that kills. ❧

1. **elixir of life** mythical liquid believed to prolong a person's life indefinitely.
2. **gripsack** small bag for holding clothes; suitcase.

NOTES

Mark familiar word parts or indicate another strategy you used that helped you determine meaning.

**importunities** (ihm pawr TOO nuh teez) *n.*

MEANING:

## Comprehension Check

Complete the following items after you finish your first read. Review and clarify details with your group.

1. What medical problem afflicts Mrs. Mallard?

2. What news does Mrs. Mallard receive as the story opens?

3. As Mrs. Mallard sits alone in her room, what word does she keep whispering to herself?

4. What happens when Brently Mallard turns up, alive?

5. **Notebook** Write a summary of the story to confirm your understanding.

### RESEARCH

**Research to Explore** This story may spark your curiosity to learn more. Briefly research a relevant topic that interests you. You may want to share what you discover with your group.

The Story of an Hour **355**

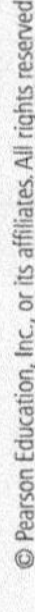


## Concept Vocabulary

If groups are struggling to define the word *importunities,* point out that the word contains the prefix *im-*, which has a negative meaning, and that the Latin root word is *importunus*. Knowing that the *importunities* is used as a noun and that the Latin root *importunus* means "troublesome" or "unfavorable" may help students to define the word.

**Possible response:** *Importunities* means "a troublesome request" or "a request that is not favored."

## Comprehension Check

Possible responses:

1. The narrator notes that Mrs. Mallard is afflicted with a "heart ailment."
2. Her sister informs her that her husband has been killed in a railway disaster.
3. Mrs. Mallard keeps whispering, "Free!"
4. Upon seeing that Mr. Mallard is alive, Mrs. Mallard dies of a heart attack.
5. Mrs. Mallard, who has a heart condition, learns that her husband has died, and she weeps. She retires to her room and stares out the window at the springtime scene. But a strange feeling swells within her, and she starts to recognize it as joy at her freedom. She begins to imagine her future—free from her husband's control. She returns downstairs with Josephine to join Richards. Mr. Mallard, however, returns home unhurt, and Mrs. Mallard suffers a heart attack and dies.

## Research

**Research to Explore** If students struggle to come up with a research topic, you may want to suggest that they focus on one of the following topics: the legal rights of married women at the turn of the twentieth century; well-known female American writers at the turn of the twentieth century; or book reviews and literary criticism on Kate Chopin from the time when her work was first published.

PERSONALIZE FOR LEARNING

### Challenge

**Text Analysis** Ask students to consider whether Mrs. Mallard loved her husband. Point out that the narrator says she would weep when she saw the "the kind, tender hands folded in death; the face that had never looked save with love upon her." (paragraph 11) Direct students to write about whether it is possible to love someone and at the same time feel stifled by them and wish to be free of them. Encourage students to include one or more examples, preferably from fiction. **Research to Explore**

# FACILITATING

## Jump Start

**CLOSE READ** Present groups with the following prompt: *What are the advantages and disadvantages of being married? Would you rather be married or single?* Have students discuss this prompt in their groups, considering the advantages and disadvantages of being part of a couple or being on their own.

## Close Read the Text 

If needed, model close reading by using the Annotation Highlights in the Interactive Teacher's Edition.

Remind students to use Accountable Talk in their discussions and to support one another as they complete the close read.

## Analyze the Text

**Possible responses:**

1. Students may suggest that although the physical reason for Mrs. Mallard's death is a heart attack (foreshadowed in the mention of her "affliction" in the story's first sentence), what triggers the attack is shock at realizing that she will not have a "free" future, after all.
2. Students may focus on details in paragraphs 9–18, in which Mrs. Mallard feels joy at thoughts of living for herself.
3. Married women at the time of this short story's writing were stuck in a life of servitude to their husbands, with no time for themselves.

## Concept Vocabulary

**Why These Words? Possible response:** The words all describe being pushy. They show strong emotion in the character of Mrs. Mallard.

### Practice

**Possible responses:**

- persistence: tirelessness, stubbornness
- imploring: begging, pleading
- importunities: demands, appeals
- Chopin's word choices are compelling and show strong feeling.

### Word Network

**Possible words:** *triumph, exhaustion, repression, tumultuously, self-assertion*

## Word Study

For more support, see **Concept Vocabulary and Word Study.**

**Possible responses:**
Students may rank *ask, request, nag, entreat, beseech, implore,* from least to most forceful.

MAKING MEANING

THE STORY OF AN HOUR

## Close Read the Text

With your group, revisit sections of the text you marked during your first read. **Annotate** details that you notice. What **questions** do you have? What can you **conclude**?

**TIP**

**GROUP DISCUSSION**
Listen carefully as others present their ideas so that you do not simply repeat their words when your turn comes. Try to add something new to the discussion.

## Analyze the Text

**CITE TEXTUAL EVIDENCE** to support your answers.

**Notebook** Complete the activities.

1. **Review and Clarify** With your group, discuss the ending of the story. Do you agree with the doctors' evaluation? Why, or why not?
2. **Present and Discuss** Now, work with your group to share the passages from the selection that you found especially important. Take turns presenting your passages. Discuss what you noticed in the selection, the questions you asked, and the conclusions you reached.
3. **Essential Question:** ***In what ways does the struggle for freedom change with history?*** What has this text taught you about the struggle for freedom? Discuss with your group.

LANGUAGE DEVELOPMENT

## Concept Vocabulary

| persistence | imploring | importunities |
|---|---|---|

**Why These Words?** The three concept vocabulary words from the text are related. With your group, discuss the words, and determine what the words have in common. How do these word choices enhance the text?

**WORD NETWORK**
Add words related to struggle from the text to your Word Network.

### Practice

**Notebook** Use a dictionary or thesaurus to find and record two synonyms for each of the concept vocabulary words. Then, write a sentence that explains how you think Chopin's word choices affect readers' understanding of the story. Share your sentences with your group.

## Word Study

**Notebook** **Denotation and Connotation** The **denotation** of a word is its dictionary meaning. **Connotation** refers to the shades of meaning a word conveys. As Mrs. Mallard sits in her room, she hears Josephine's *importunities* for her to open the door. The denotation of the word is "instances of persistent begging." The connotation, however, suggests that such begging is especially annoying. Use a thesaurus to find four other words that mean "to beg," and think about their connotations. Then, list the words in order—from least to most forceful, or from most negative to most positive.

**STANDARDS**
**Reading Literature**
- Determine two or more themes or central ideas of a text and analyze their development over the course of the text, including how they interact and build on one another to produce a complex account; provide an objective summary of the text.
- Analyze the impact of the author's choices regarding how to develop and relate elements of a story or drama.

**Language**
- Analyze nuances in the meaning of words with similar denotations.





## FORMATIVE ASSESSMENT

### Analyze the Text

**If** students struggle to close read the text, **then** provide the **The Story of an Hour: Text Questions** available on the Interactive Teacher's Edition.

### Concept Vocabulary

**If** students can't figure why the words have been grouped together, **then** have them find a synonym for each word and examine their relationship.

### Word Study

**If** students don't understand connotation, **then** have them explain the emotional overtones of these words that share the same denotation: *skinny, lean, slender, gaunt, emaciated, scrawny, undernourished.*

For Reteach and Practice, see **Word Study: Denotation and Connotation (RP).**

## Analyze Craft and Structure

**Development of Theme** In this story, the author develops a central idea, or **theme**, about the ways in which the society of her time constrains women. To develop that thematic insight, Chopin focuses on the contrast between Mrs. Mallard's **internal monologue**—her main character's thoughts and conversation with herself—and the external situation in which Mrs. Mallard finds herself.

### Practice

**CITE TEXTUAL EVIDENCE** to support your answers.

Use the chart to track Mrs. Mallard's actions and the emotional journey she undergoes. Then, explain how Mrs. Mallard's actions and feelings suggest Chopin's theme about the status of women in the society of her era. Note that there may be more than one theme. Complete this chart independently, and then share your responses with your group.

| PARAGRAPH | WHAT MRS. MALLARD DOES | WHAT MRS. MALLARD FEELS | THEMATIC MEANING |
|---|---|---|---|
| 3 | a. See possible responses in the Teacher's Edition. | b. | c. |
| 9 | d. | e. | f. |
| 10 | g. | h. | i. |
| 17 | j. | k. | l. |



## DIGITAL PERSPECTIVES

**Enriching the Text** To help students analyze how society constricted women and their roles, have them research photos and films of women in the 1890s, examining their clothing and considering how it reflected society's attitude toward women. Guide students to evaluate the fit of the clothing (especially at the waist), the length of the dresses, and the undergarments, as well. What generalizations can they draw about how clothing affected women's opportunities?

DIGITAL PERSPECTIVES  

## Analyze Craft and Structure

**Development of Theme** Point out that the first two sentences define how theme is developed in this story. The author reveals some of Mrs. Mallard's internal monologue through her dialogue, set off by quotation marks. In some of these instances, Mrs. Mallard is speaking to others, as when she says, "Go away. I am not making myself ill." Direct students to look at what Mrs. Mallard says as well as what she thinks and feels to identify the thematic meaning.

For more support, see **Analyze Craft and Structure: Development of Theme.**

**MAKE IT INTERACTIVE**

Project the digital version of "The Story of an Hour" and model locating an example of Mrs. Mallard's internal dialogue. This will help students as they complete the chart.

### Practice

Possible responses:

a. weeps "with sudden, wild abandonment"
b. shock, grief
c. Women should be completely dependent on their husbands.
d. sits in her chair and waits
e. fear, confusion
f. Women without men have no place in the society.
g. breathes hard and speaks the words "Free, free, free!"
h. recognition, excitement, acceptance
i. Women might have a different option.
j. imagines the future and prays that life will be long
k. joy, anticipation, relief
l. Women can live fulfilling lives on their own.

### FORMATIVE ASSESSMENT

### Analyze Craft and Structure

**If** students are unable to identify what Mrs. Mallard feels, **then** have them look for adjectives in the story that describe Mrs. Mallard's emotions.

For Reteach and Practice, see **Analyze Craft and Structure: Development of Theme (RP).**

## Conventions and Style

**Author's Choices: Irony** As you review these examples with students, point out that irony may be stated or implied. Consider providing the following models and have students identify and explain the type of irony in each one:

- In "The Gift of the Magi," by O. Henry, the husband sells his pocket watch to get enough money to buy his wife combs for her long hair; the wife cuts and sells her long hair to get the money to buy her husband a pocket watch chain. (situational irony)
- The shower scene in the movie *Psycho* starts out with the woman in the shower not hearing the killer because the water is running, but the audience knows he is there. (dramatic irony)
- "He enjoyed the movie as much as chewing on ground glass." (verbal irony)

Have students create their own examples of situational irony from everyday life, such as a fire station burning down or a window washer being afraid of heights.

For more support, see **Conventions and Style: Author's Choices: Irony.**

### Read It

Possible responses:

Paragraphs 5–6:

Situation: . . . the birds singing and the sun shining.

Why It's Ironic: We would expect her to see only dark, dreary things. The fact that she notices beauty and rebirth makes us doubt her grief.

Paragraphs 20–21:

Situation: . . . that her husband is alive, and that fact kills her.

Why It's Ironic: We would expect a wife to rejoice in finding that her husband has survived an accident. The fact that she doesn't celebrate shows how unhappy she was in her marriage.

### Write It

Students' new movie endings should be unexpected, opposite twists on familiar plots.

### FORMATIVE ASSESSMENT

### Conventions and Style

**If** students are unable to identify irony, **then** have them explain how the situation *should have* turned out in contrast to how *it did* turn out.

For Reteach and Practice, see **Conventions and Style: Author's Choices: Irony (RP).**

LANGUAGE DEVELOPMENT

THE STORY OF AN HOUR

## Conventions and Style

**Author's Choices: Irony** "The Story of an Hour" is an ironic tale. **Irony** is a contradiction between appearance and reality, between expectation and outcome, or between meaning and intention. In literature, readers frequently encounter three types of irony.

**Situational Irony:** Something happens that contradicts readers' expectations.
**Example:** In the story "The Necklace," a couple must replace a diamond necklace that the wife borrowed from a friend and lost. Years later, after falling into poverty in order to pay for the replacement necklace, the couple discover the original was a fake.

**Dramatic Irony:** Readers or viewers are aware of something that a character does not know.
**Example:** In *Romeo and Juliet*, characters believe that Juliet is dead, but the audience knows that she is simply in a drugged sleep.

**Verbal Irony:** Someone says something that deliberately contradicts what that person actually means.
**Example:** In *Julius Caesar*, Marc Antony refers to Brutus as "an honorable man" when he means to prove that Brutus, Caesar's killer, is extremely dishonorable.

### Read It

Work individually. Complete each situation below, and write your response to it based on the story. Then, reconvene with your group to compare and contrast your responses.

| PARAGRAPHS | SITUATION | WHY IS THIS IRONIC? |
|---|---|---|
| 5–6 | Mrs. Mallard has just learned about her husband's death, but now she notices . . . | |
| 20–21 | Mrs. Mallard has reconciled herself to her newfound freedom, but now she discovers . . . | |

### Write It

**Notebook** Choose a favorite movie with a classic, expected ending. Write a paragraph that changes the ending so that it becomes ironic. Explain how your new ending is an example of situational irony.

STANDARDS

**Reading Literature**
Analyze a case in which grasping point of view requires distinguishing what is directly stated in a text from what is really meant.

**Speaking and Listening**
- Propel conversations by posing and responding to questions that probe reasoning and evidence; ensure a hearing for a full range of positions on a topic or issue; clarify, verify, or challenge ideas and conclusions; and promote divergent and creative perspectives.
- Respond thoughtfully to diverse perspectives; synthesize comments, claims, and evidence made on all sides of an issue; resolve contradictions when possible; and determine what additional information or research is required to deepen the investigation or complete the task.





CROSS-CURRICULAR PERSPECTIVE

**Science** Mrs. Mallard dies of a heart attack because she experiences strong emotions. (paragraph 21) Is this possible? According to Dr. Daniel Brotman, a Johns Hopkins physician, strong emotion can indeed increase someone's risk of having a heart attack. Terror, sorrow, or being startled can cause a syndrome that doctors call a "stunned heart," and set off an abnormal heart beat. According to the Cleveland Clinic, extreme happiness can be as bad for your heart as extreme sorrow because sharp emotions set off a sudden increase in heart rate. The irony in Mrs. Mallard's death is that everyone assumes that she had a heart attack from a "broken heart" caused by grief, when actually too much joy caused her heart to stop. Have students research the topic, then role-play scenes in which they pretend to be doctors and explain this phenomenon to non-scientists.

EFFECTIVE EXPRESSION

## Speaking and Listening

**Assignment**

Hold a **group discussion** to consider how readers of Chopin's time might have responded to "The Story of an Hour." Use what you know about the history of the era. Choose one of these social groups as the focus for your discussion.

- ☐ How might women in various social roles have responded to the story?
- ☐ How might other writers or artists have responded to the story?
- ☐ How might social critics or activists have responded to the story?

**Preparing for the Discussion** Locate areas of the text that support your ideas about how the social group you selected might respond to the story. Record your best examples here. Then, join up with others who chose the same perspective, and compare notes as a group.

Perspective: ______________________

| SECTION OF TEXT | POSSIBLE RESPONSE / EXPLANATION |
|---|---|
| | |
| | |
| | |
| | |

**Holding the Discussion** Decide as a group whether you want to go through the story section by section and have each person respond from his or her chosen perspective, or whether you prefer to look at the whole text through one perspective at a time. Either way, make sure that everyone has a chance to speak and to express opinions that are supported with evidence from the text and knowledge about 1890s America. If questions emerge from your discussion, decide together how you will locate the answers.

**EVIDENCE LOG**

Before moving on to a new selection, go to your Evidence Log and record what you learned from "The Story of an Hour."





DIGITAL PERSPECTIVES

## Speaking and Listening

**Preparing for the Discussion** Before they add information to the chart, suggest that students tell the others in their group which of the three groups they will use to interpret passages.

**Holding the Discussion** Encourage students to include clear markers for each part of their presentation so their audience can follow their method of organization. These markers can be spoken, as in "Now we will present our first example of how this group might have responded to the story" or printed on paper and held up like scene divisions in a play.

For more support, see **Speaking and Listening: Group Discussion.**

**Evidence Log** Support students in completing their evidence log. This paced activity will help prepare them for the Performance-Based Assessment at the end of the unit.

### FORMATIVE ASSESSMENT

### Speaking and Listening

**If** students are unable to consider how readers in 1894 might have responded to the story, **then** have students consider what they learned about marriage and women's rights from Stanton's "Declaration of Sentiments."

### Selection Test

Administer the **"The Story of an Hour" Selection Test,** which is available in both print and digital formats online in Assessments.

## PERSONALIZE FOR LEARNING

### English Language Support

**Classroom Discussion** Ask pairs of students to choose whether students should be allowed to bring their cell phones to school. Have the pairs work together to write down a claim, a counterclaim, and two pieces of evidence that represent each point of view.

**EMERGING**

Ask pairs of students to choose whether students should be allowed to bring their cell phones to school. Since students are discussing opposing sides, tell them to be prepared with a claim, counterclaim, and evidence for their point of view.

**EXPANDING**

Have pairs of students debate whether students should be allowed to bring their cell phones to school. Tell them to be prepared with a claim, counterclaim, and evidence for their point of view. Have students make a video recording and discuss who had the stronger evidence.

**BRIDGING**

An expanded **English Language Support Lesson** on Classroom Discussion is available in the Interactive Teacher's Edition.

# Brown v. Board of Education

**AUDIO SUMMARIES**
Audio summaries of *Brown v. Board of Education* are available online in both English and Spanish in the Interactive Teacher's Edition or Unit Resources. Assigning these summaries prior to reading the selection may help students build additional background knowledge and set a context for their first read.

## Summary

In "Brown v. Board of Education: Opinion of the Court," Chief Justice Earl Warren explains the Supreme Court's unanimous ruling in favor of the Browns, an African American family of Topeka, Kansas, against their local board of education. The Browns complained that their daughter, a third grader, had to attend a school across town because the local school had refused her on account of her race. The board claimed it had acted in accord with the doctrine of "separate but equal" education established by the case of *Plessy* v. *Ferguson* in 1896. The Supreme Court, however, has decided to strike down *Plessy v. Ferguson* and declare that segregation in public schools violates the Equal Protection Clause of the Fourteenth Amendment and is therefore unconstitutional.

### Insight

Revolution is often found in the details. Reading "Brown v. Board of Education" will help students begin to reflect on the process by which change often occurs. The battle may not take place on the field of war but in the courtroom.

ESSENTIAL QUESTION:
In what ways does the struggle for freedom change with history?

## Connection to Essential Question

"Brown v. Board of Education" provides a legal perspective on the Essential Question—*In what ways does the struggle for freedom change with history?* The court decision to make segregation unconstitutional could only have happened after earlier legal cases set a precedent, and findings once deemed just were found to be irrelevant.

SMALL-GROUP LEARNING PERFORMANCE TASK
What were the goals of these reformers? Why did they want to achieve their goals?

UNIT PERFORMANCE-BASED ASSESSMENT
What motivates people to struggle for change?

## Connection to Performance Tasks

**Small-Group Learning Performance Task** In this Performance Task, students will focus on the goals and achievements of the reformers represented in the selections in Small-Group Learning. *Brown* v. *Board of Education* provides a clearly stated goal. Students will consider to what extent that goal has been met.

**Unit Performance-Based Assessment** This selection provides an example of the structural techniques writers may use to affect an audience. The opinion of the court is an example of a skillfully structured argument, including a counterclaim and rebuttal.

DIGITAL PERSPECTIVES

 Audio  Video Document  Annotation Highlights  EL Highlights 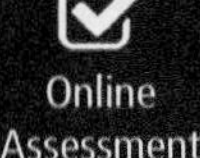 Online Assessment

## LESSON RESOURCES

| | Making Meaning | Language Development |
|---|---|---|
| Lesson | **First Read**<br>**Close Read**<br>**Analyze the Text**<br>**Analyze Craft and Structure** | **Concept Vocabulary**<br>**Word Study**<br>**Conventions and Style** |
| **Instructional Standards** | **RI.10** By the end of grade 11, read and comprehend literary nonfiction . . .<br>**L.4.b** Identify and correctly use patterns of word changes . . .<br>**RI.5** Analyze and evaluate the effectiveness of the structure an author uses . . . | **RI.4** Determine the meaning of words and phrases . . .<br>**L.6** Acquire and use accurately general academic and domain-specific words and phrases . . .<br>**L.1** Demonstrate command of the conventions . . .<br>**L.3** Apply knowledge of language . . . |
| **STUDENT RESOURCES** | | |
| Available online in the Interactive Student Edition or Unit Resources | Selection Audio<br>First-Read Guide: Nonfiction<br>Close-Read Guide: Nonfiction | Word Network |
| **TEACHER RESOURCES** | | |
| **Selection Resources**<br>Available online in the Interactive Teacher's Edition or Unit Resources | Audio Summaries<br>Annotation Highlights<br>Brown v. Board of Education: Opinion of the Court: Text Questions<br>EL Highlights<br>English Language Support Lesson: Conjunctions<br>Analyze Craft and Structure: Author's Choices: Structure | Concept Vocabulary and Word Study<br>Conventions and Style: Coordinating Conjunctions |
| **Reteach/Practice (RP)**<br>Available online in the Interactive Teacher's Edition or Unit Resources | Analyze Craft and Structure: Author's Choices: Structure (RP) | Word Study: Technical Words (RP)<br>Conventions and Style: Coordinating Conjunctions (RP) |
| **Assessment**<br>Available online in Assessments | Selection Test | |
| **My Resources** | A Unit 3 Answer Key is available online and in the Interactive Teacher's Edition. | |

# Reading Support

| Text Complexity Rubric: Brown v. Board of Education | |
|---|---|
| **Quantitative Measures** | |
| **Lexile:** 1370 **Text Length:** 2,105 words | |
| **Quantitative Measures** | |
| Knowledge Demands ①—②—❸—④—⑤ | Text contains unfamiliar content (segregation in schools), but it is mostly explained. Prior knowledge is helpful about the Supreme Court and about the history of racial segregation in the United States. |
| Structure ①—②—③—❹—⑤ | Explanations of court cases are mostly sequential, but text is dense so may be difficult to navigate. Summary at beginning of text is helpful. Facts and descriptions are interspersed with opinion. |
| Language Conventionality and Clarity ①—②—③—❹—⑤ | Complex sentences with multiple clauses. Syntax used is typical of formal legal language and may be unfamiliar. |
| Levels of Meaning/Purpose ①—❷—③—④—⑤ | Text has straightforward concept with one level of meaning. Main points and concepts are explicitly stated. |

DECIDE AND PLAN

## English Language Support

Provide English Learners with support for structure and language as they read the selection.

**Structure** Help students learn to scan through long passages to look for clues that highlight main points. Point out words for them to look for as they scan and then have them examine those sentences. For example: (paragraph 11) *The plaintiffs contend that* …. (paragraph 18) *We come then to the question*… (paragraph 22) *We conclude that*…

**Language Conventionality and Clarity** With students, examine difficult vocabulary or syntax, helping them to find alternative ways to state ideas, or alternate words to replace unfamiliar legal language. For example, replace *hence* with *therefore*, or use *because* and change the order of the sentence.

## Strategic Support

Provide students with strategic support to ensure that they can successfully read the text.

**Knowledge Demands** Use the background information to review what students know about the history of racial segregation in the United States. Discuss that *Brown* v. *Board of Education* was a critical step for the civil rights movement.

**Language and Structure** As students read, ask them to scan the beginnings of paragraphs to highlight phrases that help them navigate, for example, *Plaintiffs contend that . . . ; We come then to the questions presented; We conclude that . . .* If students have trouble following the text, point out these lines. Have them reread whole paragraphs after identifying these phrases.

## Challenge

Provide students who need to be challenged with ideas for how they can go beyond a simple interpretation of the text.

**Text Analysis** For students who are able to more easily understand the language and structure, ask them to restate the main concepts in their own words. Suggest that they summarize by writing the most important points.

**Written Response** Suggest that students research and read the decisions of the other court cases referenced in the text, for example *Plessy* v. *Ferguson*. Ask them to write an account of one of the cases. Have them include their ideas about what might have changed if the opposite decision had been made in the case.

TEACH

## Read and Respond

Have the groups read the selection and complete the Making Meaning and Language Development activities.

# Standards Support Through Teaching and Learning Cycle

## IDENTIFY NEEDS

Analyze results of the Beginning-of-Year Assessment, focusing on the items relating to Unit 3. Also take into consideration student performance to this point and your observations of where particular students struggle.

## DECIDE AND PLAN

- If students have performed poorly on items matching these standards, then provide selection scaffolds before assigning them the on-level lesson provided in the Student Edition.
- If students have done well on the Beginning-of-Year Assessment, then challenge them to keep progressing and learning by giving them opportunities to practice the skills in depth.
- Use the Selection Resources listed on the Planning pages for "Brown v. Board of Education" to help students continually improve their ability to master the standards.

**Instructional Standards: Brown v. Board of Education**

| | Catching Up | This Year | Looking Forward |
|---|---|---|---|
| **Reading** | You may wish to administer the **Analyze Craft and Structure: Author's Choice: Structure (RP)** worksheet to help students understand how an argument presents reasons and evidence to support a claim. | **RI.5** Analyze and evaluate the effectiveness of the structure an author uses in his or her exposition or argument, including whether the structure makes points clear, convincing, and engaging. | Ask students to state in their own words the decision of the Supreme Court in *Brown v. Board of Education*. Then have them summarize two or more supporting reasons with evidence that Justice Warren presented in his opinion. |
| **Language** | You may wish to administer the **Conventions and Style: Coordinating Conjunctions (RP)** worksheet to help students understand when and how coordinating conjunctions are used.<br><br>Review the **Word Study: Technical Words (RP)** worksheet with students to ensure they understand that each field uses technical words to explain things specific to that field. | **L.1** Demonstrate command of the conventions of standard English grammar and usage when writing or speaking.<br><br>**L.6** Acquire and use accurately general academic and domain-specific words and phrases, sufficient for reading, writing, speaking, and listening at the college and career readiness level; demonstrate independence in gathering vocabulary knowledge when considering a word or phrase important to comprehension or expression. | Ask students to find three examples of coordinating conjunctions in "Brown v. Board of Education," as well as three examples of coordinating conjunctions in other selections they have read in this unit.<br><br>Challenge students to work in groups to list as many technical words as they can find in "Brown v. Board of Education." Have groups compare their completed lists. |

## ANALYZE AND REVISE

- Analyze student work for evidence of student learning.
- Identify whether or not students have met the expectations in the standards.
- Identify implications for future instruction.

## TEACH

Implement the planned lesson, and gather evidence of student learning.

# FACILITATING

## Jump Start

**FIRST READ** *Why is equal access to education an important goal for society as a whole?*

Engage students in a discussion about the value of education that sets the context for reading "Brown v. Board of Education." As students share their thoughts, guide them to identify specific factors that affected their decisions.

### Brown v. Board of Education

What happens when students are treated separately in school? How do such students feel? How does separate treatment affect their learning and their sense of self?

Modeling the questions readers might ask as they read "Brown v. Board of Education: Opinion of the Court" brings the text alive for students and connects it to the Small-Group Performance Task question. Selection audio and print capability for the selection are available in the Interactive Teacher's Edition.

### Concept Vocabulary

Ask groups to briefly discuss the three concept vocabulary words. Have they encountered any of the words before? Do they recognize any word parts?

Ask students to think about using the technique of identifying familiar word parts and discuss how this vocabulary strategy can help clarify meaning.

### FIRST READ

Have students perform the steps of the first read independently:

NOTICE: Students should mark the facts and opinions that support the central idea.

ANNOTATE: Students should mark sections they deem important as well as those they find difficult.

CONNECT: Students may want to consider recent news stories that will help them relate to this text.

RESPOND: Students will demonstrate their understanding of the text by answering questions and writing a summary.

Point out to students that while they will always complete the Respond step at the end of the first read, the other steps will probably happen somewhat concurrently. You may wish to print copies of the **First-Read Guide: Nonfiction** for students to use.

## MAKING MEANING

BROWN v. BOARD OF EDUCATION: OPINION OF THE COURT

### Comparing Texts

In this lesson, you will read and compare the decision of the Supreme Court in the case *Brown v. Board of Education* and the magazine article "Was *Brown v. Board* a Failure?" First, you will complete the first-read and close-read activities for the Supreme Court decision. The work you do with your group on this title will help prepare you for your final comparison.

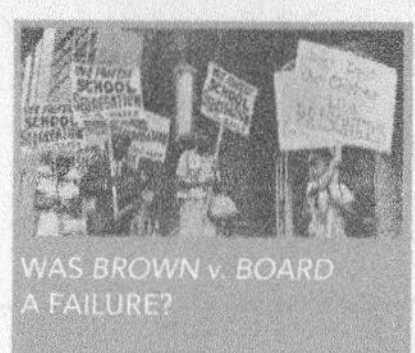
WAS BROWN v. BOARD A FAILURE?

**About the Author**

**Earl Warren** (1891–1974), a lawyer and three-time governor of California, served as the fourteenth Chief Justice of the United States, from 1953 to 1969. Warren's time on the Court was an active one, with landmark decisions in race relations, criminal procedure, and legislative apportionment. After the assassination of President John F. Kennedy in 1963, Warren headed a federal commission that investigated the murder.

# Brown v. Board of Education: Opinion of the Court

### Concept Vocabulary

As you read the Supreme Court's opinion in *Brown v. Board of Education*, you will encounter these words.

plaintiffs jurisdiction disposition

**Familiar Word Parts** In your reading, you may encounter words that are a bit unfamiliar but that seem to have word parts that you recognize. As this example shows, the word part that you recognize can help you determine the meaning of the unfamiliar word.

**Sentence:** A sense of possibilities can **embolden** children to learn.

**Familiar Word Part:** *bold,* which means "without fear" or "courageous"

**Conclusion:** Since *bold* involves a lack of fear, *embolden* must have something to do with instilling fearlessness in someone.

### First Read NONFICTION

Apply these strategies as you conduct your first read. You will have an opportunity to complete a close read after your first read.

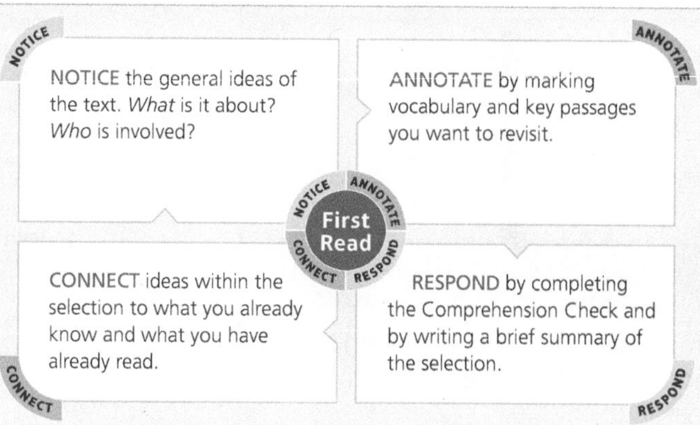

NOTICE the general ideas of the text. *What* is it about? *Who* is involved?
ANNOTATE by marking vocabulary and key passages you want to revisit.
CONNECT ideas within the selection to what you already know and what you have already read.
RESPOND by completing the Comprehension Check and by writing a brief summary of the selection.
First Read


**STANDARDS**

**Reading Informational Text**
By the end of grade 11, read and comprehend literary nonfiction in the grades 11–CCR text complexity band proficiently, with scaffolding as needed at the high end of the range.

**Language**
Identify and correctly use patterns of word changes that indicate different meanings or parts of speech.





### FACILITATING SMALL-GROUP CLOSE READING

**CLOSE READ: Legal Opinion** As groups perform the close read, circulate and offer support as needed.

- Tell students that the Syllabus is an unofficial summary of the opinion that follows. The opinion is the court's ruling and the reasoning behind it.
- To help students explore the relationship between the Syllabus and the opinion, ask groups to assign each member one of the sentences labeled a–f in the Syllabus. Have students look through the opinion and mark the related section. When they have finished, they can share their expertise with the others in their group.

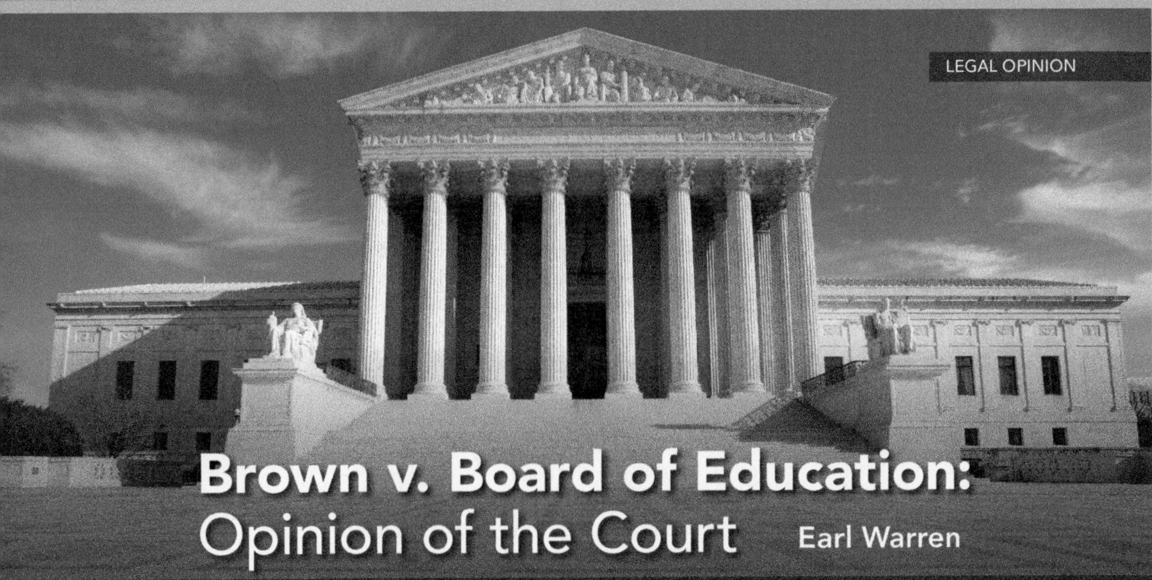


# Brown v. Board of Education: Opinion of the Court

Earl Warren

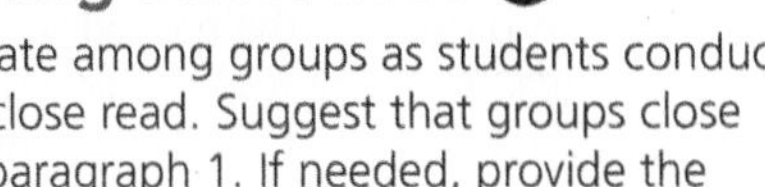


BACKGROUND

In 1951, when 17 states required schools to be segregated by race, 13 parents brought a lawsuit against the Board of Education of Topeka, Kansas. At the forefront of the case was the Brown family. Linda Brown, an African American third-grader, was not allowed to attend the elementary school seven blocks from her house. Instead, she was required to take a bus to a school across town. Since the United States Supreme Court decision in the 1896 case *Plessy v. Ferguson*, racial segregation of schools had been allowed so long as the schools were "separate but equal." In the landmark case of *Brown v. Board of Education*, the Supreme Court ruled unanimously (9–0) to overrule *Plessy*.

SCAN FOR MULTIMEDIA

SUPREME COURT OF THE UNITED STATES

Brown v. Board of Education,
347 U.S. 483 (1954) (USSC+)
347 U.S. 483
Argued December 9, 1952
Reargued December 8, 1953
Decided May 17, 1954

APPEAL FROM THE UNITED STATES DISTRICT COURT FOR THE DISTRICT OF KANSAS*

NOTES

## Syllabus

1 Segregation of white and Negro children in the public schools of a State solely on the basis of race, pursuant to[1] state laws permitting or requiring such segregation, denies to Negro children the equal protection of the laws guaranteed by the Fourteenth Amendment—even though the physical facilities and other "tangible" factors of white and Negro schools may be equal.

1. **pursuant to** in a way that agrees with or follows.





CLOSER LOOK

### Making Inferences

Circulate among groups as students conduct their close read. Suggest that groups close read paragraph 1. If needed, provide the following prompts:

**ANNOTATE:** In paragraph 1, mark the phrases that relate to state laws regarding segregation in schools.

**QUESTION:** What was the legal basis for school segregation across the United States at the time of *Brown v. Board of Education?*

**Possible response:** Some states required schools to be segregated, while other states allowed them to be segregated.

**CONCLUDE:** What was the national policy regarding school segregation in the United States in 1951?

**Possible response:** There was none. Each state did or did not set its own policy, and that policy varied within at least some of the states. This states' rights approach to the issue is the reason for the court case.

Remind students that there are federal laws, state laws, county laws and regulations, and often city or town laws. The Constitution says that when these laws conflict, the federal law is the one that applies. But if there is no federal law concerning an issue, the states are free to do whatever they want.

Explain that readers sometimes need to **infer** details that are not included in a text. Readers make inferences based on details in the text and their own knowledge and experience.

PERSONALIZE FOR LEARNING

### English Language Support

**Context Clues** Review context clues with students. Suggest that they look for the meaning of challenging words within the text. For example, have students find context clues for the word *segregation* in paragraph 1 (including "white and Negro children" and "white and Negro schools"), and explain that, in this context, the word *segregation* has to do with separating students into schools according to race.

# FACILITATING

## Concept Vocabulary

**PLAINTIFFS** If groups are struggling to define the word *plaintiffs* in paragraph 10, point out that the base, *plain*, is present in the related words *complaint* and *plaintive*. Context should also be helpful in decoding this word. Have students note the words and phrases in paragraph 10 that relate to the plaintiffs. Now have students write their definition.

**Possible response:** *Plaintiffs* are people who bring a lawsuit into a court of law.

**JURISDICTION** If students have difficulty defining the word *jurisdiction* in paragraph 11, point out the word parts they may know. *Diction* is related to words or speech, and *juris* is present in the words *jury* and *juror*, words related to law. Ask students to explain the role of a jury. After they identify other context clues in the paragraph, have students write a definition of *jurisdiction*.
**Possible response:** *Jurisdiction* is the right or responsibility to hear and decide a legal case

NOTES

2 (a) The history of the Fourteenth Amendment is inconclusive[2] as to its intended effect on public education.

3 (b) The question presented in these cases must be determined not on the basis of conditions existing when the Fourteenth Amendment was adopted, but in the light of the full development of public education and its present place in American life throughout the Nation.

4 (c) Where a State has undertaken to provide an opportunity for an education in its public schools, such an opportunity is a right which must be made available to all on equal terms.

5 (d) Segregation of children in public schools solely on the basis of race deprives children of the minority group of equal educational opportunities, even though the physical facilities and other "tangible" factors may be equal.

6 (e) The "separate but equal" doctrine adopted in *Plessy v. Ferguson,* 163 U.S. 537, has no place in the field of public education.

7 (f) The cases are restored to the docket[3] for further argument on specified questions relating to the forms of the decrees.

### Opinion

8 MR. CHIEF JUSTICE WARREN delivered the opinion of the Court.

9 These cases come to us from the States of Kansas, South Carolina, Virginia, and Delaware. They are premised on[4] different facts and different local conditions, but a common legal question justifies their consideration together in this consolidated opinion.

10 In each of the cases, minors of the Negro race, through their legal representatives, seek the aid of the courts in obtaining admission to the public schools of their community on a nonsegregated basis. In each instance, they had been denied admission to schools attended by white children under laws requiring or permitting segregation according to race. This segregation was alleged to deprive the **plaintiffs** of the equal protection of the laws under the Fourteenth Amendment. In each of the cases other than the Delaware case, a three-judge federal district court denied relief to the plaintiffs on the so-called "separate but equal" doctrine announced by this Court in *Plessy v. Fergson,* 163 U.S. 537. Under that doctrine, equality of treatment is accorded when the races are provided substantially equal facilities, even though these facilities be separate. In the Delaware case, the Supreme Court of Delaware adhered to that doctrine, but ordered that the plaintiffs be admitted to the white schools because of their superiority to the Negro schools.

11 The plaintiffs contend that segregated public schools are not "equal" and cannot be made "equal," and that hence they are deprived of the equal protection of the laws. Because of the obvious importance of the question presented, the Court took **jurisdiction**.

Mark familiar word parts or indicate another strategy you used that helped you determine meaning.

**plaintiffs** (PLAYN tihfs) *n.*

MEANING:

Mark familiar word parts or indicate another strategy you used that helped you determine meaning.

**jurisdiction** (jur ihs DIHK shuhn) *n.*

MEANING:

2. **inconclusive** *adj.* not fully resolving all doubts or questions.
3. **docket** *n.* list of the legal cases that will be tried in a court of law.
4. **premised on** based on.





## PERSONALIZE FOR LEARNING

### English Language Support

**Text Structure of a Legal Document** Review paragraphs 1–7 of the Opinion. Point out to students that this is a legal document and has the form of a legal document. English language learners may need help understanding the form and content. Explain that the items that are labeled (a) through (f) are the factors on which the Supreme Court Justices based their opinion in this case. These factors address the Fourteenth Amendment, a state's responsibilities, and the reasons why segregation and the concept of "separate but equal" schools are problematic. **(Research to Clarify)**

DIGITAL PERSPECTIVES

Argument was heard in the 1952 Term, and reargument was heard this Term on certain questions propounded[5] by the Court.

12 Reargument was largely devoted to the circumstances surrounding the adoption of the Fourteenth Amendment in 1868. It covered exhaustively consideration of the Amendment in Congress, ratification[6] by the states, then-existing practices in racial segregation, and the views of proponents and opponents of the Amendment. This discussion and our own investigation convince us that, although these sources cast some light, it is not enough to resolve the problem with which we are faced. At best, they are inconclusive. The most avid proponents of the post-War Amendments undoubtedly intended them to remove all legal distinctions among "all persons born or naturalized in the United States." Their opponents, just as certainly, were antagonistic to both the letter and the spirit of the Amendments and wished them to have the most limited effect. What others in Congress and the state legislatures had in mind cannot be determined with any degree of certainty.

13 An additional reason for the inconclusive nature of the Amendment's history with respect to segregated schools is the status of public education at that time. In the South, the movement toward free common schools, supported by general taxation, had not yet taken hold. Education of white children was largely in the hands of private groups. Education of Negroes was almost nonexistent, and practically all of the race were illiterate. In fact, any education of Negroes was forbidden by law in some states. Today, in contrast, many Negroes have achieved outstanding success in the arts and sciences, as well as in the business and professional world. It is true that public school education at the time of the Amendment had advanced further in the North, but the effect of the Amendment on Northern States was generally ignored in the congressional debates. Even in the North, the conditions of public education did not approximate those existing today. The curriculum was usually rudimentary; ungraded schools were common in rural areas; the school term was but three months a year in many states, and compulsory school attendance was virtually unknown. As a consequence, it is not surprising that there should be so little in the history of the Fourteenth Amendment relating to its intended effect on public education.

14 In the first cases in this Court construing the Fourteenth Amendment, decided shortly after its adoption, the Court interpreted it as proscribing all state-imposed discriminations against the Negro race. The doctrine of "separate but equal" did not make its appearance in this Court until 1896 in the case of *Plessy v. Ferguson*, supra,[7] involving not education but transportation. American courts have since labored with the doctrine for over half a century. In this

NOTES

5. **propounded** *v.* suggested for consideration.
6. **ratification** *n.* process of officially approving and accepting an agreement.
7. **supra** mentioned earlier in this writing.





CLOSER LOOK

## Infer Cultural Context

Circulate among groups as students conduct their close read. Suggest that groups close read paragraph 13. If needed, provide the following prompts:

**ANNOTATE:** In paragraph 13, mark the words that refer to the conditions of public education at the time the Fourteenth Amendment was passed.

**QUESTION:** What do these details tell you about the quality of education at that time?

**Possible response:** Education was much less rigorous than it is today, and students were not educated as well.

**CONCLUDE:** Why does Warren cite changes in school attendance to support his argument that the circumstances surrounding the ratification of the Fourteenth Amendment have little bearing on *Brown v. Board of Education?*

**Possible response:** Whether or not people at the time thought the Fourteenth Amendment would support or prohibit school segregation, they were in most cases dealing with schools that were a much less important part of a child's life then they are now.

Remind students that the cultural context is the set of values and beliefs that surround a culture at a given point in time. The court's work here address a complex issue which continues to be argued in politics and law, even today.

Should laws, including the Constitution, be interpreted to mean only what the people who wrote it intended? Or should the interpretation of laws be expanded to include circumstances that the original lawmakers could not have imagined? In this decision, the Court unanimously takes the latter position.

Additional **English Language Support** is available in the Interactive Teacher's Edition.

DIGITAL PERSPECTIVES

**Illuminating the Text** Review with students the meaning of "Jim Crow" and institutionalized segregation, which occurred after the Supreme Court handed down the court decision of *Plessy v. Ferguson* in 1896. Ask students to find images online of the public enforcement of segregation laws. Suggest that students search for "Freedom Riders," a documentary that appeared on public television. They may find short video clips of people discussing Jim Crow. Students can find additional video clips related to the Brown decision. Ask students to share how seeing these videos or images helps them understand the text. **(Research to Clarify)**

## CLOSER LOOK

### Comparing Text With Contemporary Experience

Circulate among groups as students conduct their close read. Have groups close read paragraph 17. If needed, provide the following prompts:

**ANNOTATE:** In paragraph 17, mark the phrases the author uses to emphasize the crucial importance of education in modern America.

**QUESTION:** How does education in modern America contrast with education at the time of the Fourteenth Amendment?

**Possible response:** Education today is more formal, more organized, more extensive, and more essential for success and for good citizenship.

**CONCLUDE:** Why would education be so important for citizenship?

**Possible response:** Education prepares people for citizenship by teaching them such skills as reading, critical thinking, and effective communication.

Remind students that good readers often **compare text with their own experiences.** Ask students to consider this description of education and one that they would write to describe's today's educational goals.

NOTES

Court, there have been six cases involving the "separate but equal" doctrine in the field of public education. In *Cumming v. County Board of Education,* 175 U.S. 528, and *Gong Lum v. Rice,* 275 U.S. 78, the validity of the doctrine itself was not challenged. In more recent cases, all on the graduate school level, inequality was found in that specific benefits enjoyed by white students were denied to Negro students of the same educational qualifications. *Missouri ex rel. Gaines v. Canada,* 305 U.S. 337; *Sipuel v. Oklahoma,* 332 U.S. 631; *Sweatt v. Painter,* 339 U.S. 629; *McLaurin v. Oklahoma State Regents,* 339 U.S. 637. In none of these cases was it necessary to reexamine the doctrine to grant relief to the Negro plaintiff. And in *Sweatt v. Painter*, supra, the Court expressly reserved decision on the question whether *Plessy v. Ferguson* should be held inapplicable to public education.

15 In the instant cases, that question is directly presented. Here, unlike *Sweatt v. Painter*, there are findings below that the Negro and white schools involved have been equalized, or are being equalized, with respect to buildings, curricula, qualifications and salaries of teachers, and other "tangible" factors. Our decision, therefore, cannot turn on merely a comparison of these tangible factors in the Negro and white schools involved in each of the cases. We must look instead to the effect of segregation itself on public education.

16 In approaching this problem, we cannot turn the clock back to 1868, when the Amendment was adopted, or even to 1896, when *Plessy v. Ferguson* was written. We must consider public education in the light of its full development and its present place in American life throughout the Nation. Only in this way can it be determined if segregation in public schools deprives these plaintiffs of the equal protection of the laws.

17 Today, education is perhaps the most important function of state and local governments. Compulsory school attendance laws and the great expenditures for education both demonstrate our recognition of the importance of education to our democratic society. It is required in the performance of our most basic public responsibilities, even service in the armed forces. It is the very foundation of good citizenship. Today it is a principal instrument in awakening the child to cultural values, in preparing him for later professional training, and in helping him to adjust normally to his environment. In these days, it is doubtful that any child may reasonably be expected to succeed in life if he is denied the opportunity of an education. Such an opportunity, where the state has undertaken to provide it, is a right which must be made available to all on equal terms.

18 We come then to the question presented: Does segregation of children in public schools solely on the basis of race, even though the physical facilities and other "tangible" factors may be equal, deprive the children of the minority group of equal educational opportunities? We believe that it does.

19 In *Sweatt v. Painter,* supra, in finding that a segregated law school for Negroes could not provide them equal educational opportunities,





364 UNIT 3 • POWER, PROTEST, AND CHANGE

this Court relied in large part on "those qualities which are incapable of objective measurement but which make for greatness in a law school." In *McLaurin v. Oklahoma State Regents*, supra, the Court, in requiring that a Negro admitted to a white graduate school be treated like all other students, again resorted to intangible considerations: ". . . his ability to study, to engage in discussions and exchange views with other students, and, in general, to learn his profession." Such considerations apply with added force to children in grade and high schools. To separate them from others of similar age and qualifications solely because of their race generates a feeling of inferiority as to their status in the community that may affect their hearts and minds in a way unlikely ever to be undone. The effect of this separation on their educational opportunities was well stated by a finding in the Kansas case by a court which nevertheless felt compelled to rule against the Negro plaintiffs:

> Segregation of white and colored children in public schools has a detrimental effect upon the colored children. The impact is greater when it has the sanction[8] of the law, for the policy of separating the races is usually interpreted as denoting the inferiority of the negro group. A sense of inferiority affects the motivation of a child to learn. Segregation with the sanction of law, therefore, has a tendency to [retard] the educational and mental development of negro children and to deprive them of some of the benefits they would receive in a racial[ly] integrated school system.

20 Whatever may have been the extent of psychological knowledge at the time of *Plessy v. Ferguson*, this finding is amply supported by modern authority. Any language in *Plessy v. Ferguson* contrary to this finding is rejected.

21 We conclude that, in the field of public education, the doctrine of "separate but equal" has no place. Separate educational facilities are inherently unequal. Therefore, we hold that the plaintiffs and others similarly situated for whom the actions have been brought are, by reason of the segregation complained of, deprived of the equal protection of the laws guaranteed by the Fourteenth Amendment. This **disposition** makes unnecessary any discussion whether such segregation also violates the Due Process Clause of the Fourteenth Amendment.

22 Because these are class actions, because of the wide applicability of this decision, and because of the great variety of local conditions, the formulation of decrees in these cases presents problems of considerable complexity. On reargument, the consideration of appropriate relief was necessarily subordinated to the primary question—the constitutionality of segregation in public education. We have now announced that such segregation is a denial of the equal

NOTES

Mark familiar word parts or indicate another strategy you used that helped you determine meaning.

**disposition** (dihs puh ZIHSH uhn) *n.*

MEANING:

8. **sanction** *n.* official permission or approval.





## Concept Vocabulary

**DISPOSITION** If groups are struggling to define the word *disposition* in paragraph 21, point out that the root word is *dispose*, which students will recognize as "throwing away."

The first three sentences in the paragraph set up the Court's opinion that the plaintiffs' case is valid. Therefore, the Court rules that there is no need to pursue the other question about segregation—the Due Process Clause.

**Possible response:** *Disposition*, as used in this text, means "final settlement or decision to end a discussion."

## CROSS-CURRICULAR PERSPECTIVES

**Social Studies** Explain that the *Brown* decision was one of the events that marked the beginning of the civil rights era. Direct students to research topics, such as the Montgomery bus boycott, desegregation of Little Rock High School and the University of Mississippi, the Freedom Rides, civil rights marches, and sit-ins. Many good online resources are available—especially clips from *Eyes on the Prize,* a series of documentaries on the civil rights movement that aired on public television. These videos can also be borrowed from many public libraries. **Research to Clarify**

FACILITATING

## Comprehension Check

Possible responses:

1. The plaintiffs are seeking the aid of the courts in obtaining admission to public schools on a non-segregated basis.
2. Educational treatment was considered "equal" if substantially equal facilities were provided to students of both races.
3. The fundamental conflict is that segregation denies to African American children "the equal protection of the laws guaranteed by the Fourteenth Amendment."
4. This document is the Supreme Court decision in the case of *Brown v. Board of Education.* The court says that the history of the Fourteenth Amendment is insufficient to decide the case because not enough is known about the intentions of the framers and about the application of the Amendment to public education. In the past, the "separate but equal" doctrine established by *Plessy* v. *Ferguson* (1896) has been applied. Considering the crucial importance of public education in American society, however, the Supreme Court decides to consider the findings of more modern psychology, which have determined that segregation has a detrimental effect on minority children. Therefore, to exclude children from schools on the basis of race conflicts directly with the Fourteenth Amendment guarantee of equal protection of the laws.

### Research to Clarify

If students struggle to come up with a research topic, you may want to suggest that they focus on one of the other court cases mentioned in the decision.

NOTES

protection of the laws. In order that we may have the full assistance of the parties in formulating decrees, the cases will be restored to the docket, and the parties are requested to present further argument on Questions 4 and 5 previously propounded by the Court for the reargument this Term. The Attorney General of the United States is again invited to participate. The Attorneys General of the states requiring or permitting segregation in public education will also be permitted to appear as amici curiae upon request to do so by September 15, 1954, and submission of briefs by October 1, 1954.

23 *It is so ordered.* ❧

## Comprehension Check

**Complete the following items after you finish your first read. Review and clarify details with your group.**

1. What change are the plaintiffs in this case seeking?

2. What standard had been set earlier by the *Plessy v. Ferguson* decision?

3. According to the opinion of the Court, what fundamental conflict exists between segregation and the Fourteenth Amendment?

4. **Notebook** Write a summary of *Brown v. Board of Education*.

RESEARCH

**Research to Clarify** Choose at least one unfamiliar detail from the text. Briefly research that detail. In what way does the information you learned shed light on an aspect of the Supreme Court's opinion? Share your findings with your group.





PERSONALIZE FOR LEARNING

### Challenge

**Research** Have students research the 1896 *Plessy v. Ferguson* case, in which the Supreme Court ruled that the state of Louisiana had a right to segregate railway cars by race as long as separate accommodations were "equal." Students should pay particular attention to what the court said about the "separate-but-equal" doctrine. Invite students to compare the Plessy and Brown decisions. Ask them to reflect on the role of the Supreme Court in interpreting the Constitution and how that interpretation can radically change with historical periods. Direct students to explore, in writing, why desegregation was an idea whose time had come in 1954.

MAKING MEANING

## Close Read the Text

With your group, revisit sections of the text you marked during your first read. **Annotate** details that you notice. What **questions** do you have? What can you **conclude?**

## Analyze the Text

**CITE TEXTUAL EVIDENCE** to support your answers.

Complete the activities.

1. **Review and Clarify** With your group, review paragraphs 15–19. Then, discuss the justices' argument about why "separate but equal" is inherently unequal.
2. **Present and Discuss** Share with your group the passages from the text that you found especially significant, taking turns with others. Discuss what you noticed in the text, what questions you asked, and what conclusions you reached.
3. **Essential Question:** *In what ways does the struggle for freedom change with history?* What has this text taught you about the struggle for freedom? Discuss with your group.

BROWN v. BOARD OF EDUCATION: OPINION OF THE COURT

TIP

GROUP DISCUSSION

If you do not fully understand a classmate's comment, ask for clarification. Using a respectful tone, state exactly what you don't understand.

WORD NETWORK

Add words related to struggle from the text to your Word Network.

LANGUAGE DEVELOPMENT

## Concept Vocabulary

plaintiffs jurisdiction disposition

**Why These Words?** The three concept vocabulary words from the text are related. With your group, discuss the words, and determine what the words have in common. How do these word choices enhance the text?

**Practice** Use each concept vocabulary word in a sentence. Make sure to include context clues that hint at the word's meaning.

## Word Study

**Technical Words** Most professions, including such fields as medicine and law, have their own technical language, often called **jargon**. In writing the Court's opinion in *Brown v. Board of Education*, Chief Justice Earl Warren uses technical legal words such as *plaintiffs*, *jurisdiction*, and *disposition*. Find four other words in the selection that could be classified as legal jargon. Write the words and their meanings.

STANDARDS

**Reading Informational Text**
Determine the meaning of words and phrases as they are used in a text, including figurative, connotative, and technical meanings; analyze how an author uses and refines the meaning of a key term or terms over the course of a text.

**Language**
Acquire and use accurately general academic and domain-specific words and phrases, sufficient for reading, writing, speaking, and listening at the college and career readiness level; demonstrate independence in gathering vocabulary knowledge when considering a word or phrase important to comprehension or expression.





DIGITAL PERSPECTIVES

## Jump Start

CLOSE READ Present groups with the following prompt: *When do you think Americans need to rely on the Supreme Court to bring about change? What other methods of gaining power should they try first—if any?* Invite groups to discuss this prompt and consider the use of the highest court in the land to achieve justice.

## Close Read the Text 

If needed, model close reading by using the Annotation Highlights in the Interactive Teacher's Edition.

Remind students to use Accountable Talk in their discussions and to support one another as they complete the close read.

## Analyze the Text

**Possible responses:**

1. Responses will vary by group. Suggest to groups that they go back into paragraphs 15–19 and discuss what they understand "separate but equal"to mean in education.
2. Passages will vary by group. Remind students to explain why they chose the passages they presented and to explain any conclusions they drew.
3. Responses will vary by group.

## Concept Vocabulary

**Why These Words? Possible response:** The words all refer to the activity of a court of law and therefore provide context.

### Practice

Possible responses:

- The *plaintiffs* sat quietly as their attorney presented their case to the judge and jury.
- Because the crime occurred in another country, this court has no *jurisdiction* to deliver a ruling.
- After the young teen confessed to the crime, her case went to juvenile court for its *disposition*.

### Word Network

Possible words: *segregation, proponents, movement*

## Word Study

For more support, see **Concept Vocabulary and Word Study.**

**Possible responses:**

*doctrine:* a set of beliefs or a policy; *proponents:* people who support a specific belief; *proscribing:* forbidding; *supra:* term used in legal writing, meaning "mentioned earlier"; *class actions:* lawsuits filed on behalf of a large group of people

**FORMATIVE ASSESSMENT**

### Analyze the Text

**If** students struggle to close read the text, **then** provide the ***Brown* v. *Board of Education*: Opinion of the Court: Text Questions** available online in the Interactive Teacher's Edition or Unit Resources. Answers and DOK levels are available.

### Concept Vocabulary

**If** students can't identify the uniting concept, **then** have them explain when they might expect to use these words.

### Word Study

**If** students can't find other examples of jargon, **then** have them look for any unfamiliar words, especially those that appear to be in Latin, and define them.

# FACILITATING

## Analyze Craft and Structure

**Author's Choices: Structure** Remind students that "analytical" contains the word "analyze," so an analytical argument uses critical thinking to examine an issue by methodically looking at its individual parts. In this type of logical reasoning, authors rely on facts rather than on emotions.

For more support, see **Analyze Craft and Structure: Author's Choices: Structure.**

**MAKE IT INTERACTIVE**

Project the digital version of "Brown v. Board of Education" and model locating a detail about the Fourteenth Amendment and the conclusion Judge Warren reached from this example. This will help students complete the chart.

### Practice

**Possible responses:**

a. intentions of framers are unclear; status of public education very different

b. history of the Amendment is inconclusive

c. transportation, not education; "separate but equal"

d. can "separate" really mean "equal"?

e. education the foundation of citizenship; no success in life without it

f. educational opportunity is a right

g. Fourteenth Amendment is not enough to solve the current problem. Intentions not clear. There have been many cases to challenge it.

h. basis for the case; court has to revisit the purpose of the amendment given its 1868 writing.

i. psychological studies and knowledge show that segregation generates feelings of inferiority

j. "separate but equal" must be rejected

MAKING MEANING

BROWN v. BOARD OF EDUCATION: OPINION OF THE COURT

## Analyze Craft and Structure

**Author's Choices: Structure** In *Brown v. Board of Education*, Chief Justice Earl Warren delivers the **opinion**, or legal judgment, of the Court. He defends the Court's position in the form of an analytical argument. In an **analytical argument**, a writer or speaker uses logical reasoning and persuasive evidence to examine an issue and to support a particular conclusion, called a **claim**. In legal opinions, the writer presenting the argument anticipates and considers objections and challenges, or **counterclaims.**

### Practice

**CITE TEXTUAL EVIDENCE** to support your answers.

Work with your group to analyze the structure of the Court's opinion. Review the text, and complete the chart. Notice the order of topics: Warren proceeds from historical to legal to social considerations before arriving at a conclusion. Identify specific details from each section of the opinion, and explain the main idea they develop. Then, explain how each section adds to the line of reasoning that results in the Court's decision.

| TOPIC | DETAILS IN THE TEXT | MAIN IDEA |
|---|---|---|
| Fourteenth Amendment (historical considerations) | a. See possible responses in the Teacher's Edition. | b. |
| *Plessy v. Ferguson* (legal considerations) | c. | d. |
| Importance of education (social considerations) | e. | f. |
| Conclusions reached by the Court | g.<br>i. | h.<br>j. |





## PERSONALIZE FOR LEARNING

### Strategic Support

**Choral Reading** To help students grasp the concepts in this selection, build fluency, increase vocabulary, and spark motivation, have groups conduct a choral reading of selected passages, such as paragraphs 20 and 22, from the text. You may wish to have the entire class read aloud in unison, or have groups take turns reading. Be sure that each student has a copy of the text so everyone can participate. You may wish to project the digital version of the text. Follow these steps:

- First, read the entire text aloud to model fluent reading for the class.
- Guide students to use their finger or a marker to follow along with you.
- Then have students read the passage together, again following the text with their finger or a marker.

## FORMATIVE ASSESSMENT

### Analyze Craft and Structure

**If** students are unable to locate details in the text that support each topic, **then** have them outline the text and jot down key ideas.

For Reteach and Practice, see **Analyze Craft and Structure: Author's Choices: Structure (RP).**

## Conventions and Style

**Coordinating Conjunctions** A **coordinating conjunction** connects words, phrases, or clauses of equal rank. You can improve your sentence variety by using coordinating conjunctions to combine short, simple sentences into compound sentences.

> **Original:** These cases are premised on different facts. A common legal question justifies their consideration together.
>
> **Revision:** These cases are premised on different facts, *but* a common legal question justifies their consideration together.

Coordinating conjunctions show different relationships between the words or ideas that they connect. Study this chart.

| COORDINATING CONJUNCTION | RELATIONSHIP |
|---|---|
| and | addition or similarity |
| but, yet | contrast |
| so | result or effect |
| for | reason or cause |
| or, nor | choice |

### Read It

In each item from or about the Supreme Court's opinion in *Brown v. Board of Education*, mark the coordinating conjunction and the words or groups of words that it connects.

1. Compulsory attendance laws and the great expenditures for education demonstrate our recognition of its importance.
2. Education is a principal instrument in awakening the child to cultural values, but success in life without the opportunity of an education is doubtful.
3. The state undertakes to make education available, yet it must be available to all on equal terms.
4. Education is a key function of government, for it is the very foundation of good citizenship.

### Write It

**Notebook** Use a coordinating conjunction to combine each pair of sentences. Write the new sentence.

1. According to the plaintiffs, public schools are not "equal." The schools cannot be made "equal."
2. Schools may have equal physical facilities. That doesn't guarantee equal educational opportunities.
3. Minority children in segregated schools may lack motivation to learn. By their very nature, such schools tend to instill a sense of inferiority.
4. The Court agreed. Segregation in public schools was struck down.

**TIP**

PUNCTUATION

If you use a coordinating conjunction to join two independent clauses, place a comma before the coordinating conjunction.

**EVIDENCE LOG**

Before moving on to a new selection, go to your Evidence Log and record what you learned from the Supreme Court's opinion in *Brown v. Board of Education*.

**STANDARDS**

**Reading Informational Text**
Analyze and evaluate the effectiveness of the structure an author uses in his or her exposition or argument, including whether the structure makes points clear, convincing, and engaging.

**Language**
- Demonstrate command of the conventions of standard English grammar and usage when writing or speaking.
- Apply knowledge of language to understand how language functions in different contexts, to make effective choices for meaning or style, and to comprehend more fully when reading or listening.





## PERSONALIZE FOR LEARNING

### English Language Support

**Conjunctions** Ask students to write a paragraph that compares the two sides of *Brown v. Board of Education* using conjunctions from the chart. **EMERGING**

Ask students to write a longer paragraph that discusses the two sides of *Brown v. Board of Education* using conjunctions without the aid of the chart. **EXPANDING**

Ask students to write a longer paragraph that discusses the two sides of *Brown v. Board of Education* using conjunctions without the aid of the chart. Ask each student to include how his/her opinion of "separate but equal" compares and contrasts with the two sides. **BRIDGING**

An expanded **English Language Support Lesson** on Conjunctions is available in the Interactive Teacher's Edition.

DIGITAL PERSPECTIVES

## Conventions and Style

**Coordinating Conjunctions** Have students combine the following pairs of sentences with the appropriate coordinating conjunction. Have students explain the relationship the conjunction establishes.

- The issue before the Court was not whether the schools were "equal." It was whether the doctrine of *separate* was constitutional.

  **Possible response:** *but;* the second independent clause shows a contrast to the first one

For more support, see **Conventions and Style: Coordinating Conjunctions.**

### Read It

**Possible responses:**

Connected words or groups of words are underlined; coordinating conjunctions are circled.

1. Compulsory attendance laws (and) the great expenditures for education demonstrate our recognition of its importance.
2. Education is a principal instrument in awakening the child to cultural values, (but) success in life without the opportunity of an education is doubtful.
3. The state undertakes to make education available, (yet) it must be available to all on equal terms.
4. Education is a key function of government, (for) it is the very foundation of good citizenship.

### Write It

**Possible responses:**

1. According to the plaintiffs, public schools are not "equal" and the schools cannot be made "equal."
2. Schools may have equal physical facilities, but that fact doesn't guarantee equal educational opportunities.
3. Minority children in segregated schools may lack motivation to learn, for by their very nature, such schools tend to instill a sense of inferiority.
4. The Court agreed, and segregation in public schools was struck down.

## FORMATIVE ASSESSMENT

### Conventions and Style

**If** students are unable to combine sentences using coordinating conjunctions, **then** have them first explain the relationship between the two independent clauses. For Reteach and Practice, see **Conventions and Style: Coordinating Conjunctions (RP).**

### Selection Test

Administer the **"Brown v. Board of Education: Opinion of the Court": Selection Test**, which is available in both print and digital formats online in Assessments.

# Was "Brown v. Board" a Failure?

**AUDIO SUMMARIES**
Audio summaries of "Was *'Brown v. Board'* a Failure?" are available online in both English and Spanish in the Interactive Teacher's Edition or Unit Resources. Assigning these summaries prior to reading the selection may help students build additional background knowledge and set a context for their first read.

## Summary

In her 2012 magazine article "Was *'Brown v. Board'* a Failure?" Sarah Garland reports that desegregation in public schools is winding down. School districts rarely receive, and even more rarely bother to obey, desegregation orders, and the decline in busing is leading to a return to racial isolation. The reliance on enforced busing has never taken account of the unpopularity and ill effects of long commutes, or of the poularity and good effects of going to school in one's own neighborhood—the destruction of neighborhood schools has caused widespread outrage. As commitment to desegregation has diminished, other initiatives have been put into effect. Their success or failure will be crucial to the future of our public schools.

### Insight

Reading "Was *'Brown v. Board'* a Failure?" will help students understand that affecting change can be a long, complicated procedure. Even well-intentioned changes can backfire and cause a whole new set of problems to arise.

ESSENTIAL QUESTION:
In what ways does the struggle for freedom change with history?

## Connection to Essential Question

"Was *'Brown v. Board'* a Failure?" has a somewhat academic connection to the Essential Question, "In what ways does the struggle for freedom change with history?" The struggle, in this case, is found in the numbers and statistics suggesting that the original fight may have won a civil victory, but left behind another obstacle to freedom. The passing of time reveals the weaknesses of *Brown* v. *Board of Education,* and shines a light on the current struggle.

SMALL-GROUP LEARNING PERFORMANCE TASK
What were the goals of these reformers? Why did they want to achieve their goals?

UNIT PERFORMANCE-BASED ASSESSMENT
What motivates people to struggle for change?

## Connection to Performance Tasks

**Small-Group Learning Performance Task** In this Performance Task, students will focus on the goals and achievements of the reformers represented in Small-Group Learning selections. "Was *'Brown v. Board'* a Failure?" questions the achievements of *Brown* v. *Board of Education,* and suggests that the current goal is to learn from past mistakes when it comes to education reform. Students will consider to what extent that goal has been met.

**Unit Performance-Based Assessment** This selection provides an example of the structural techniques writers may use to affect an audience. The report presents counterclaims as a way of strengthening the argument.

DIGITAL PERSPECTIVES

Audio

Video

Document

Annotation Highlights

EL Highlights

Online Assessment

## LESSON RESOURCES

| | Making Meaning | Language Development | Effective Expression |
|---|---|---|---|
| Lesson | **First Read**<br>**Close Read**<br>**Analyze the Text**<br>**Analyze Craft and Structure** | **Concept Vocabulary**<br>**Word Study**<br>**Conventions and Style** | **Writing to Compare** |
| Instructional Standards | **RI.10** By the end of grade 11, read and comprehend literary nonfiction . . .<br>**L.4.a** Use context as a clue . . .<br>**RI.5** Analyze and evaluate the effectiveness of the structure an author uses . . . | **L.4.c** Consult general and specialized reference materials . . .<br>**L.1** Demonstrate command of the conventions . . .<br>**L.3** Apply knowledge of language . . . | **RI.5** Analyze and evaluate the effectiveness of the structure an author uses . . .<br>**RI.8** Delineate and evaluate the reasoning in seminal U.S. texts . . .<br>**W.9.b** Apply *grades 11–12 reading standards* . . . |
| **STUDENT RESOURCES** | | | |
| **Available online in the Interactive Student Edition or Unit Resources** | Selection Audio<br>First-Read Guide: Nonfiction<br>Close-Read Guide: Nonfiction | Word Network | Evidence Log |
| **TEACHER RESOURCES** | | | |
| Selection Resources<br>**Available online in the Interactive Teacher's Edition or Unit Resources** | Audio Summaries<br>Annotation Highlights<br>EL Highlights<br>English Language Support Lesson: Using Historical References<br>Was "Brown v. Board" a Failure?: Text Questions<br>Analyze Craft and Structure: Author's Choices: Structure | Concept Vocabulary and Word Study<br>Conventions and Style: Subordinating Conjunctions | Writing to Compare: Informative Essay |
| Reteach/Practice (RP)<br>**Available online in the Interactive Teacher's Edition or Unit Resources** | Analyze Craft and Structure: Author's Choices: Structure (RP) | Word Study: Cognates (RP)<br>Conventions and Style: Subordinating Conjunctions (RP) | |
| Assessment<br>**Available online in Assessments** | Selection Test | | |
| My Resources | A Unit 3 Answer Key is available online and in the Interactive Teacher's Edition. | | |

# Reading Support

| Text Complexity Rubric: Was "*Brown v. Board*" a Failure? | |
|---|---|
| **Quantitative Measures** | |
| **Lexile:** 1340 **Text Length:** 1,070 words | |
| **Qualitative Measures** | |
| Knowledge Demands ①—②—❸—④—⑤ | Selection contains information that students will not be familiar with (policy decisions affecting racial desegregation), but most concepts are explained. |
| Structure ①—②—❸—④—⑤ | Selection follows a journalistic structure. Information is explained sequentially; long paragraphs contain multiple ideas and details. |
| Language Conventionality and Clarity ①—②—❸—④—⑤ | Vocabulary is on-level, but selection contains many long sentences with multiple clauses. |
| Levels of Meaning/Purpose ①—②—❸—④—⑤ | Main concepts and supporting details are straightforward and explicit, though sometimes difficult to pinpoint within lengthy text. |

DECIDE AND PLAN

## English Language Support

Provide English Learners with support for knowledge demands and language as they read the selection.

**Knowledge Demands** Have students look back to *Brown* v. *Board of Education.* Have groups list some of the facts they remember from that selection. Ask them to look at the date of that case (1954) and point out that this new selection was written more than 50 years later, looking back on that case.

**Language** Guide students to break down lengthy sentences into smaller chunks. Encourage them to write several short sentences with information they understand. For example, (paragraph 2): *This was the first study about court-ordered busing. The study was about Jim Crow in public education.*

## Strategic Support

Provide students with strategic support to ensure that they can successfully read the text.

**Knowledge Demands** Review what students learned and discussed from the previous selection, *Brown* v. *Board of Education.* Point out that the analysis they are about to read was written more than 50 years later.

**Meaning** As students read, encourage them to highlight lines in the text that indicate the main ideas. If students have trouble, encourage them to list several statements from each paragraph, for example, *In the 1990s, groups of parents fought desegregation. Main parties fighting were black. Court orders were unpopular.* Then have them reread the whole paragraph.

## Challenge

Provide students who need to be challenged with ideas for how they can go beyond a simple interpretation of the text.

**Text Analysis** Ask students to discuss the pros and cons of busing students to school for the purpose of desegregation. Then have pairs prepare a debate, defending each of the positions.

**Written Response** Have students research Michael Petrilli, author of *The Diverse Schools Dilemma* (cited in the selection), reading more about him, viewing his website, or reading segments of his book. Ask them to write several paragraphs detailing what they learn about him. Pair students and have them read aloud their written work.

TEACH

## Read and Respond

Have the groups read the selection and complete the Making Meaning, Language Development, and Effective Expression activities.

# Standards Support Through Teaching and Learning Cycle

## IDENTIFY NEEDS

Analyze results of the Beginning-of-Year Assessment, focusing on the items relating to Unit 3. Also take into consideration student performance to this point and your observations of where particular students struggle.

## DECIDE AND PLAN

- If students have performed poorly on items matching these standards, then provide selection scaffolds before assigning them the on-level lesson provided in the Student Edition.
- If students have done well on the Beginning-of-Year Assessment, then challenge them to keep progressing and learning by giving them opportunities to practice the skills in depth.
- Use the Selection Resources listed on the Planning pages for "Was '*Brown v. Board*' a Failure?" to help students continually improve their ability to master the standards.

**Instructional Standards: Was "*Brown v. Board*" a Failure?**

| | Catching Up | This Year | Looking Forward |
|---|---|---|---|
| **Reading** | You may wish to administer the **Analyze Craft and Structure: Author's Choices: Structure (RP)** worksheet to help students understand how an argument presents reasons and evidence to support a claim. | **RI.5** Analyze and evaluate the effectiveness of the structure an author uses in his or her exposition or argument, including whether the structure makes points clear, convincing, and engaging. | Ask students to identify a reason with evidence from "Was '*Brown v. Board*' a Failure?" that they felt best supported the author's claim, and explain why. |
| **Writing** | You may wish to administer the **Writing to Compare: Informative Essay** worksheet to help students understand how to connect research to an essay that informs or explains. | **W.9.b** Apply *grades 11–12 reading standards* to literary nonfiction. | Encourage students to develop a step-by-step checklist about how to write essays that inform. |
| **Language** | You may wish to administer the **Conventions and Style: Subordinating Conjunctions (RP)** worksheet to help students understand how to make one idea subordinate to another in a sentence and how to use a subordinating conjunction to connect those ideas.<br><br>Review the **Word Study: Cognates (RP)** worksheet with students to ensure they understand that cognates are words in different languages that come from the same source, with an original form in common. | **L.1** Demonstrate command of the conventions of standard English grammar and usage when writing or speaking.<br><br>**L.4.c** Consult general and specialized reference materials, both print and digital, to find the pronunciation of a word or determine or clarify its precise meaning, its part of speech, its etymology, or its standard usage. | Encourage students to find sentences that use subordinating conjunctions in both this selection and the previous selection of *Brown v. Board of Education*.<br><br>Ask students to look for one or more examples of cognates in the previous selection, *Brown v. Board of Education*. |

## ANALYZE AND REVISE

- Analyze student work for evidence of student learning.
- Identify whether or not students have met the expectations in the standards.
- Identify implications for future instruction.

## TEACH

Implement the planned lesson, and gather evidence of student learning.

# FACILITATING

## Jump Start

**FIRST READ** Pick a nearby town—or a neighborhood within your city—but not one adjacent to your community. Tell students that half of them will be going to school there, and half the students there will attend your school. Challenge them to devise a plan to accomplish this.

## Was "*Brown v. Board*" a Failure?

Linda Brown won the right to attend a school near her home. What if most or all of the students in her neighborhood, and therefore in that school, were African American? What could her community do to comply with *Brown v. Board of Education?*

Modeling the questions readers might ask as they read "Was *'Brown v. Board'* a Failure?" brings the text alive for students and connects it to the Small-Group Performance Task question. Selection audio and print capability for the selection are available in the Interactive Teacher's Edition.

## Concept Vocabulary

Ask groups to briefly discuss the three concept vocabulary words. Have they encountered any of the words before?

## FIRST READ

Have students perform the steps of the first read independently:

NOTICE: Ask students to distinguish the effects of desegregation from those of re-segregation.

ANNOTATE: Students may mark passages that promote desegregation or re-segregation

CONNECT: Connecting the article to real-life experiences or what students know from print and media will provide insight into the effects of court decisions on people's lives.

RESPOND: Students will demonstrate understanding by answering questions and writing a summary.

Point out to students that while they will always complete the Respond step at the end of the first read, the other steps will probably happen somewhat concurrently. You may wish to print copies of the **First-Read Guide: Nonfiction** for students to use.

MAKING MEANING

BROWN v. BOARD OF EDUCATION: OPINION OF THE COURT

### Comparing Texts

You will now read "Was *Brown v. Board* a Failure?" First, complete the first-read and close-read activities. Then, compare the structure of the analytical arguments in the Supreme Court's opinion in *Brown v. Board of Education* and "Was *Brown v. Board* a Failure?"

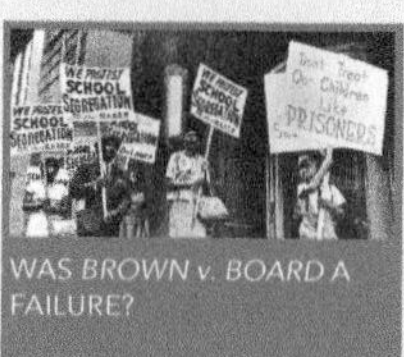

WAS BROWN v. BOARD A FAILURE?

About the Author

**Sarah Garland** (b. 1978) is a journalist who serves as both a writer and the executive editor for The Hechinger Report, a nonprofit news organization that focuses on education issues and the improvement of education. She has written newspaper and magazine articles about education, crime, and immigration. Garland also wrote the book *Divided We Fail: The Story of an African American Community That Ended the Era of School Desegregation.*

## Was *Brown v. Board* a Failure?

### Concept Vocabulary

As you read "Was *Brown v. Board* a Failure?" you will encounter these words.

legacy mission policy

**Context Clues** If these words are unfamiliar to you, you may be able to determine their meanings by using **context clues**, or words and phrases that appear in nearby text. In this example, details in the sentence suggest the meaning of the word *appease*. Someone is making efforts to soothe a crying child. *Appease* must mean "to calm or pacify."

**Example:** I tried everything I could think of to **appease** the crying child, but he continued to wail, refusing to calm down.

Apply your knowledge of context clues and other vocabulary strategies to determine the meanings of unfamiliar words you encounter during your first read.

### First Read NONFICTION

Apply these strategies as you conduct your first read. You will have an opportunity to complete a close read after your first read.

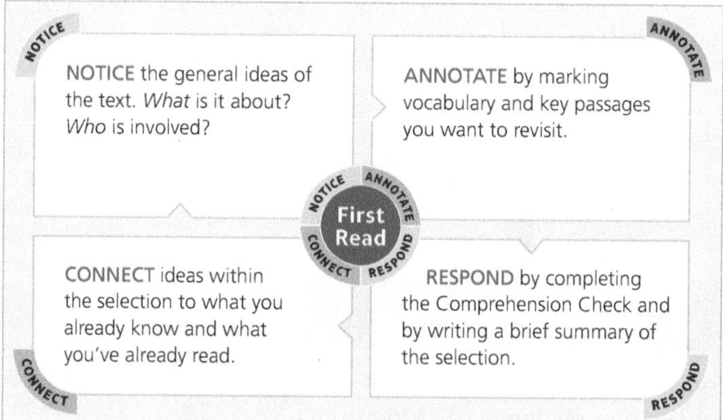

NOTICE
NOTICE the general ideas of the text. *What* is it about? *Who* is involved?
ANNOTATE
ANNOTATE by marking vocabulary and key passages you want to revisit.
First Read
CONNECT
CONNECT ideas within the selection to what you already know and what you've already read.
RESPOND
RESPOND by completing the Comprehension Check and by writing a brief summary of the selection.


STANDARDS

**Reading Informational Text**
By the end of grade 11, read and comprehend literary nonfiction in the grades 11–CCR text complexity band proficiently, with scaffolding as needed at the high end of the range.

**Language**
Use context as a clue to the meaning of a word or phrase.





## FACILITATING SMALL-GROUP CLOSE READING

### CLOSE READ: Magazine Article

Ask students to suggest why the title of the article takes the form of a question. Advise students that as they perform their close read they should look for evidence that might support an answer to the question. Circulate and offer support as needed. If any group members struggle to identify the kind of supporting evidence that validates the author's answer to her own question, demonstrate to them that the author first states the problem, and then takes the main body of the article to provide an answer—the supporting evidence appears throughout the article, as required by the context.

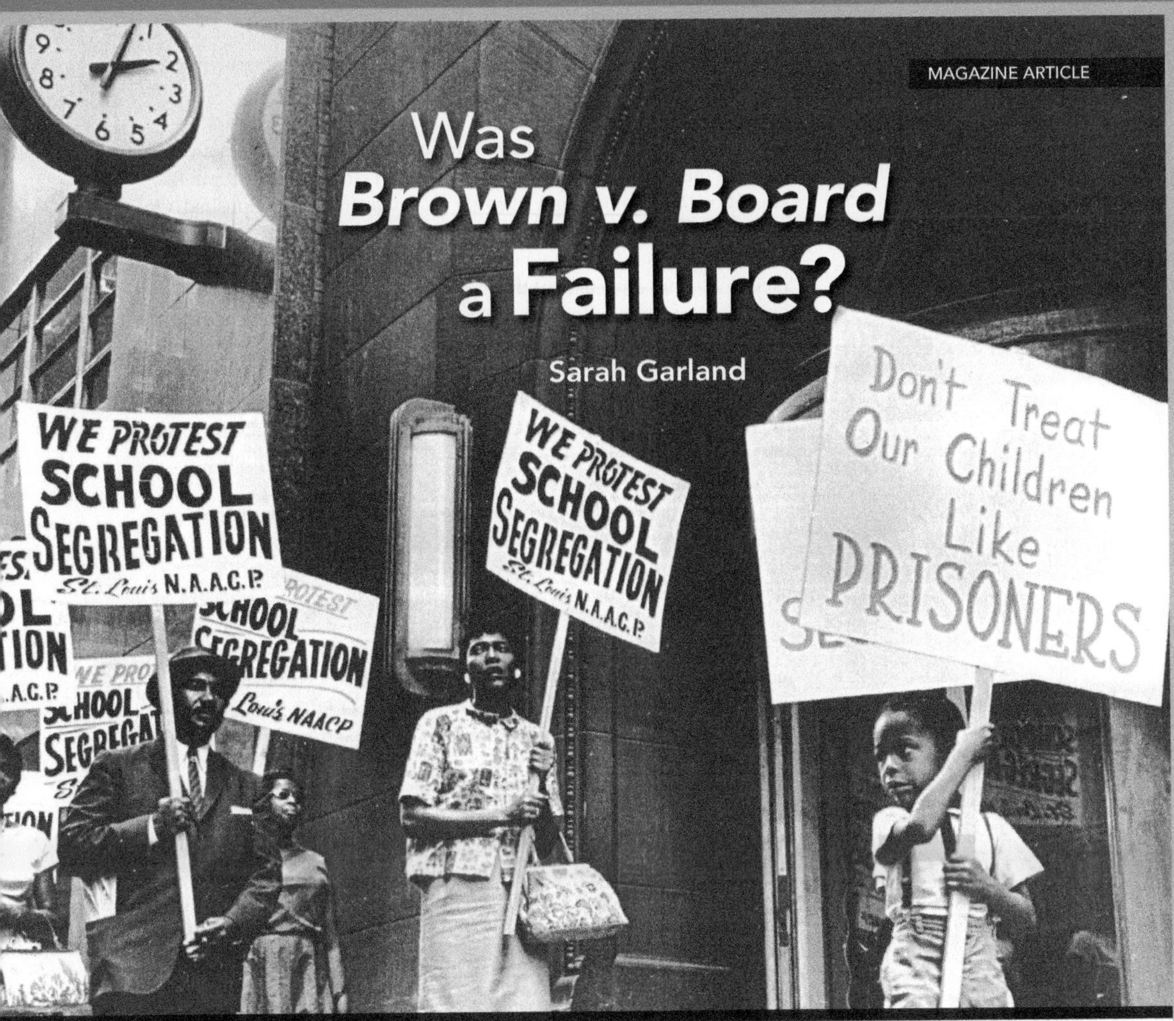


# Was *Brown v. Board* a Failure?

Sarah Garland

DIGITAL PERSPECTIVES   

BACKGROUND

This article is separated from the *Brown v. Board of Education* decision by exactly the same span of time—58 years—that separates *Brown v. Board of Education* from the case of *Plessy v. Ferguson*. Although social change seldom unfolds at an even (or even predictable) pace, it is reasonable to expect that race relations in America would have undergone many changes between 1954 and 2012. This article reports on a study regarding that expectation carried out at the Stanford University School of Education at the Center for Education Policy Analysis.

SCAN FOR MULTIMEDIA 

NOTES

1 After half a century, America's efforts to end segregation seem to be winding down. In the years after *Brown v. Board of Education*, 755 school districts were under desegregation orders. A new Stanford study reports that as of 2009, that number had dropped to as few as 268.





## CLOSER LOOK

### Interpret Historic Photographs

Circulate among groups as students conduct their close read. Suggest that groups focus on the historic photograph. If needed, provide the following prompts:

**ANNOTATE:** In the photograph, note what the signs say and who is carrying them. Also note where this protest is taking place.

**QUESTION:** Why would a child be carrying a sign like the one you see?

**Possible response:** The protest affects the lives of school children in St. Louis.

**CONCLUDE:** Why might the protesters feel that going to a segregated school is equivalent to being treated like a prisoner?

**Possible response:** Education is a basic right. Segregated schools take away children's rights, just as a prison takes away a prisoner's rights.

Remind students that **historic photographs** are photographs that show events as they happened. Often they can share information about an important event that text alone cannot.

## CROSS-CURRICULAR PERSPECTIVES

**Math** In paragraph 1 of the article, the author states that in 2009 the number of school districts under desegregation orders was 268. In 1954, after *Brown v. Board of Education*, that number was 755. Challenge students to write a math problem focusing on percentage using these numbers. One possible question is: *By what percentage did the number of school districts under desegregation orders drop in the 55 years between 1954 and 2009?* Tell students they must be able to answer whatever questions they write.

When they have finished, have students exchange questions with a partner and try to solve each other's problem.

## Concept Vocabulary

**LEGACY** If groups are struggling to define the word *legacy* in paragraph 2, have them look for clues that indicate when Jim Crow came to an end, including in the footnote for Jim Crow laws. Students should realize that if a 2009 study is looking at the legacy of something that ended in the 1960s, then a legacy must be something that lasts through time. Now ask students to use these clues to define the word.

**Possible response:** A *legacy* is "an object or idea handed down over generations."

**MISSION** If groups are struggling to define the word *mission* in paragraph 2, have them look for clues that indicate what the word might mean. The mission in question is ending the legacy of Jim Crow in public schools. Students learned from the footnote that the legacy of Jim Crow is segregation, so the mission is ending segregation in public schools. Then ask students to use these clues to define the word.

**Possible response:** A *mission* is "a strongly felt goal or purpose."

**POLICY** If groups are struggling to define the word *policy* in paragraph 3, have them look for clues in the next paragraph to understand that the policy of desegregation was a plan. Ask students to write their definition of the word.

**Possible response:** A *policy* is "a formal, often government-backed course of action."

Additional **English Language Support** is available in the Digital Teacher's Edition.

NOTES
Mark context clues or indicate another strategy you used that helped you determine meaning.

**legacy** (LEHG uh see) *n.*
MEANING:

**mission** (MIHSH uhn) *n.*
MEANING:

**policy** (POL uh see) *n.*
MEANING:

2 The study is the first to take a comprehensive look at whether court-ordered busing successfully ended the **legacy** of Jim Crow[1] in public education, and it suggests a **mission** that is far from accomplished. On average, those districts that stopped forcing schools to mix students by race have seen a gradual but steady—and significant—return of racial isolation, especially at the elementary level.

3 It's unclear what effect school "re-segregation" will have on minority achievement, though a large body of research suggests it certainly won't help efforts to improve test scores, graduation rates, and college entry levels for blacks and Hispanics, a growing share of the U.S. population. But the retreat from desegregation also suggests the **policy** had significant flaws—problems current education reformers should pay attention to.

4 The hope behind desegregation was that it would bring together white and black children to learn with, and from, each other, and end the disparities that blacks suffered under legal segregation—hand-me-down textbooks, decrepit buildings, lower-paid teachers, and, of course, lagging achievement. In the three decades following *Brown v. Board of Education,* courts ordered districts to create elaborate student assignment plans—often dependent on forced busing—to mix black, Hispanic, and white students together in the same schools. Most school boards complied reluctantly, and parents in places like Boston reacted violently.

5 A few educators and parents began to see substantial benefits that changed their minds. "It was really hard to do, but we all came together and over the years it has paid off," said Carol Haddad, a long-time school board member in Louisville, Kentucky, one of the few districts that has maintained desegregated schools voluntarily despite the lifting of its court order. "We can give equal opportunities to all kids."

6 Indeed, during the height of desegregation in the 1970s and '80s, the achievement gap between black and white students narrowed at the most rapid rate ever recorded in the history of the National Assessment of Education Progress (NAEP), the most reliable, long-term measure of student achievement in the U.S. Black graduation rates also rose at desegregated schools, research has found. War on Poverty programs and other efforts to improve life for black families were one factor. "There was a lot going on," said Sean Reardon, a Stanford sociologist and the study's lead author. "But clearly desegregation improved outcomes for blacks, and didn't harm them for whites."

7 Nevertheless, in most communities forced to try desegregation, the sacrifices weren't worth the benefits. Parents of all races complained about the hassle of busing and the loss of neighborhood schools, but for black families the burdens were often heavier: Their children tended to spend more time commuting, their own schools were

1. **Jim Crow** laws that enforced racial segregation in the American South following the Civil War and the abolition of slavery. These laws remained in effect until the Civil Rights movements of the 1960s.





### VOCABULARY DEVELOPMENT

**Analyzing Word Parts** Direct students' attention to the word *re-segregation* in quotation marks in paragraph 3. Tell students they can determine the meanings of this word and others like it by analyzing its parts. Explain that the base word *segregate* means "to separate or divide people, especially along racial lines," that the suffix *-tion* forms the noun and means "the act, state, or condition," and that the prefix *re-* means "again." Ask students to suggest meanings for *re-segregation*. Read the definition of *re-segregation*: "renewal of segregation after a period of desegregation." Have students suggest reasons why the author has hyphenated the word and used quotation marks. Explain that the word was created in 1988 specifically to describe this process, and that the author intends to emphasize its newness and unfamiliarity.

closed to make desegregation more convenient for whites (and prevent their flight to the suburbs or private schools), and their teachers were fired when white and black schools were merged.

NOTES

8 In the 1990s, a series of Supreme Court decisions made it much easier for school districts to get out from under court supervision. During that decade, school districts and groups of parents both went to court to fight desegregation orders. In a few cases, including in Louisville, the main parties fighting busing were black. "It's not surprising," said Michael Petrilli, author of *The Diverse Schools Dilemma* and executive vice president of the Thomas B. Fordham Institute, a think tank that advocates for school choice. "These court orders are by and large unpopular with parents, both white and black."

9 In the last decade, the speed of re-segregation has accelerated. The Bush administration took a proactive role in pushing for the end of desegregation in more than 200 districts, the Stanford study found. The districts were picked seemingly at random—on average, they still had levels of segregation in their schools that were about the same as the districts that remained under orders. "It wasn't like in some places desegregation had done a great job and that's why they were released and in other places there was still work to be done," Reardon said.

In the last decade, the speed of re-segregation has accelerated.

10 The strongest blow came in 2007, when the Supreme Court handed down a ruling restricting the use of race in school assignments in those districts not under court order. But by then, priorities had shifted. Both Democrats and Republicans embraced new ideas for closing the achievement gap, including No Child Left Behind's testing regimes, charter schools, and a push to make teachers more accountable for their performance. However, these new ideas have yet to show the same impact that desegregation seemed to have on minority student outcomes. Since 1990, when schools began re-segregating in large numbers, black gains on NAEP have slowed.

11 The next question Reardon plans to look at is whether re-segregation led to a widening of the achievement gap. Whatever he finds, it's unlikely that desegregation—at least in its forced-busing form—will ever experience a resurgence. A new generation of reformers has begun looking for ways to create voluntarily integrated schools in order to harness the benefits of racial and other kinds of diversity. "For the people who care about integration, we need a new set of strategies," Petrilli said.

12 Perhaps just as importantly, the demise of desegregation offers lessons about what *not* to do in order to improve outcomes for minority children. In black communities, desegregation lost support when thousands of teachers and principals lost jobs, schools were closed, and people felt that they lost power over their schools. For





DIGITAL PERSPECTIVES

## CLOSER LOOK

### Analyzing Sequence

Circulate among groups as students conduct their close read. Suggest that groups focus on the sequence of events described in paragraphs 8–10. If needed, provide the following prompts:

**ANNOTATE:** In paragraphs 8–10, mark the words and phrases that refer to a particular time period.

**QUESTION:** What sequence does the author follow in this section?

**Possible response:** She uses chronological order up until the end of paragraph 10. Each paragraph describes events or court decisions related to re-segregation that took place between the 1990s and 2007.

**CONCLUDE:** Why is chronological order an effective method of organization for this material?

**Possible response:** The author is examining changes in segregation from the busing era to the present. A series of events over that period affected the schools, and presenting those changes in the order in which they occurred makes the sequence much easier to understand.

Remind students that the **sequence**, or order of information, impacts the way readers understand a writer's main ideas. Remind students that authors may use more than one structure to convey information and present support and/or reasons and evidence for their main ideas or arguments. In this case, Garland presents events in chronological order as support for findings about problems people expressed about desegregation in their communities.

## DIGITAL PERSPECTIVES

**Illuminating the Text** Review paragraphs 7–13. Explain to students that *de facto* means "in reality," as opposed to *de jure,* "according to the law." It is illegal to deny someone housing based on their race. Theoretically, if that law is observed, all communities should be integrated. This is clearly not the case. De facto segregation occurs when people of a particular racial or ethnic group live in the same community because of social and economic circumstances, or simply because they choose to live among people who are like themselves.

Have students go online to find information on racial and ethnic diversity in neighborhoods in your city or in your state. Which are the most diverse? Which are the least? Discuss these questions as a class. **(Research to Clarify)**

FACILITATING

## Comprehension Check

Possible responses:

1. The Stanford study focused on whether court-ordered busing in the period 1954–2012 truly succeeded in ending school segregation.
2. Garland is referring to a return to a segregated education system, as in the pre-1954 period, before the Supreme Court struck down the doctrine of "separate but equal" as unconstitutional.
3. The height of desegregation occurred in the 1970s and 1980s.
4. Burdens for black families included increased commute time for children and the closing of their own schools to make desegregation more convenient for whites. In addition, minority teachers were fired when segregated schools were merged.
5. In "Was *'Brown v. Board'* a Failure?" Sarah Garland reports that a Stanford study has found a sharp decrease in the number of school districts nationwide that are under desegregation orders. The comprehensive study suggests that the mission of desegregation has not yet been accomplished. In fact, the trend over the past half century has amounted to "re-segregation," as the Supreme Court has made it steadily easier for school districts to get out from under court supervision.

## Research

**Research to Clarify** If students struggle to come up with a research topic, you may want to suggest that they focus on one of the following: the "No Child Left Behind" government initiative; the American experience with desegregation from the last half of the twentieth into the twenty-first century (for instance, related to housing or jobs); or the history and purpose of the NAEP (National Assessment of Education Progress).

NOTES

the same reasons, some of the intended beneficiaries[2] have not wholeheartedly embraced—and even protested—aspects of the current education reform movement.

13 As Fran Thomas, one black activist in Louisville, Kentucky, said of her decision to fight the district's desegregation system: "I can see why everybody was excited when the law came down that we were integrated. They thought this was utopia, and that everything was going to be all right. We got a new school. We got a swimming pool and trees. Everybody was happy and ecstatic. But they didn't know what the integration really meant—the harshness." Thomas says she stopped believing in the promises of desegregation when she saw "the destroying of schools under the name of education." ❧

2. **beneficiaries** (behn uh FIHSH ee ehr eez) *n.* people or organizations that are helped by something or someone.

## Comprehension Check

**Complete the following items after you finish your first read. Review and clarify details with your group.**

1. What was the focus of the Stanford study?
2. What does Garland mean by the term "school re-segregation"?
3. According to the article, when did the height of desegregation occur?
4. What were two burdens of desegregation for black families, according to Garland?
5. **Notebook** Write a summary of "Was *Brown v. Board* a Failure?"

## RESEARCH

**Research to Clarify** Choose at least one unfamiliar detail from the text. Briefly research that detail. In what way does the information you learned shed light on an aspect of the article?





PERSONALIZE FOR LEARNING

### Challenge

**Research** Ask students to research "No Child Left Behind" legislation (officially called the Elementary and Secondary Education Act), which was President George W. Bush's answer to continuing achievement disparities between whites and blacks and Hispanics. This legislation received bipartisan support in Congress when it was first passed. It has been recently updated and revised again and continues to cast a long shadow of influence on education. Ask students to look for information about the provisions of "No Child" and whether this legislation has had any success in closing the achievement gap for minority students. Invite students to take a stand on whether continued tweaks of the "No Child" legislation will be in the best interests of students and close the gaps in student achievement.

MAKING MEANING

## Close Read the Text

With your group, revisit sections of the text you marked during your first read. **Annotate** details that you notice. What **questions** do you have? What can you **conclude?**

## Analyze the Text

CITE TEXTUAL EVIDENCE to support your answers.

Complete the activities.

1. **Review and Clarify** With your group, review paragraphs 4–6. What were some of the hopes for desegregation and what gains were made in the early decades of the policy?
2. **Present and Discuss** Share with your group the passages from the text that you found especially significant, taking turns with others. Discuss what you noticed in the text, the questions you asked, and the conclusions you reached.
3. **Essential Question:** ***In what ways does the struggle for freedom change with history?*** What has this text taught you about the struggle for freedom? Discuss with your group.

WAS BROWN v. BOARD A FAILURE?

TIP

GROUP DISCUSSION

If a comment you wish to make pertains to a specific passage, event, or idea, mention a precise reference to help your classmates follow your train of thought.

LANGUAGE DEVELOPMENT

## Concept Vocabulary

legacy mission policy

**Why These Words?** With your group, determine what the concept vocabulary words have in common.

### Practice

Notebook Use each concept vocabulary word in a sentence. In each sentence, provide context clues that hint at the word's meaning.

## Word Study

Notebook **Cognates** Words in different languages that derive from the same source or a common original form are called **cognates**. For example, the English word *comprehend* has cognates in many languages with a basis in Latin: the Spanish *comprender*, the French *comprendre*, and the Italian *comprendere*. The concept vocabulary words for this selection have these cognates in Spanish: *legado (legacy), misión (mission)*, and *política (policy)*. Use an online bilingual dictionary or translation website to find English cognates of these words: *arte* (Spanish), *Bruder* (German), *féroce* (French), *magnifico* (Italian), *público* (Spanish), and *stazione* (Italian). Make a list of these cognates. Then, identify one more English word and its cognate in another language. Add the English word and its cognate to your list.

WORD NETWORK

Add words related to struggle from the text to your Word Network.

STANDARDS

**Language**

Consult general and specialized reference materials, both print and digital, to find the pronunciation of a word or determine or clarify its precise meaning, its part of speech, its etymology, or its standard usage.





DIGITAL PERSPECTIVES  

## Jump Start

**CLOSE REVIEW** Present groups with the following prompt: *How do you define success? How do you define failure?* Have students discuss this prompt in their groups, considering how people evaluate whether something is considered a "success."

## Close Read the Text

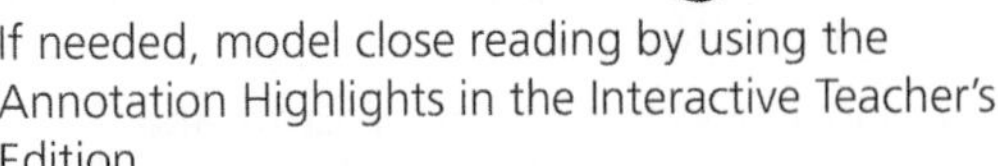

If needed, model close reading by using the Annotation Highlights in the Interactive Teacher's Edition.

Remind students to use Accountable Talk in their discussions and to support one another as they complete the close read.

## Analyze the Text

**Possible responses:**

1. There was great hope in the 1970s and 1980s and much effort toward people working together. Some cities succeeded, such as Louisville; others violently reacted to busing. The NAEP was a long-term success.
2. Ask students to justify choices with specific text.
3. Responses will vary by group.

## Concept Vocabulary

**Why These Words?**

**Possible response:** The words all suggest goals, past and present.

### Practice

**Possible responses:**

- Our grandparents left us a *legacy* of love and compassionate acts toward others.
- It was my sister's *mission* to plan a memorable surprise birthday party with a budget of $100.
- This school has a strict *policy* that says cellphones must be kept in students' lockers.

### Word Network

**Possible words:** *sacrifice, achievement, reformers, disparities, lagging, utopia*

## Word Study

For more support, see **Concept Vocabulary and Word Study.**

**Possible responses:**

*art, brother, ferocious, magnificent, public, station*

Students' cognate lists should include both a foreign word and and English one. For example, *major* (Spanish), *mayor* (English).

## FORMATIVE ASSESSMENT

### Analyze the Text

**If** students struggle to close read the text, **then** provide the **Was *"Brown v. Board"* a Failure?: Text Questions** available online in the Interactive Teacher's Edition or Unit Resources. Answers and DOK levels are also available.

### Concept Vocabulary

**If** students are unable to determine what the words have in common, **then** have them create dialogues using the words and study how they are used to find the commonality.

### Word Study

**If** students don't understand cognates, **then** have them examine some cognates for "night"— *nuit* (French), *nacht* (Dutch), *nicht* (Scot)—and explain how they can tell that all the words come from the same root.

For Reteach and Practice, see **Word Study: Cognates (RP).**

## Analyze Craft and Structure

**Author's Choices: Structure** Discuss with students the importance of structure to any piece of writing, but especially in an argument, when the author's purpose is to change the readers' minds about something or motivate them to act. Then point out how the quality of the evidence can make or break an argument, because weak evidence will not hold up under a reader's scrutiny. Direct students to evaluate the author's evidence as they complete the chart. Which facts, details, and examples did they find especially persuasive and why?

For more support, see **Analyze Craft and Structure: Author's Choices: Structure.**

**MAKE IT INTERACTIVE**

To help students complete the chart, project the digital version of "Was *'Brown v. Board'* a Failure?" and model locating a period detail in the text and a quoted conclusion.

### Practice

**Possible responses:**

a. rapid narrowing of student achievement gap between the races

b. "desegregation improved outcomes for blacks" (Sean Reardon)

c. easier for districts to get out from under court supervision

d. "court orders unpopular with parents, white and black" (Michael Petrilli)

e. resegregation has accelerated; 2007 decision

f. "destroying of schools under the name of education" (Fran Thomas)

### FORMATIVE ASSESSMENT

### Analyze Craft and Structure

**If** students are unable to identify period details in the text, **then** have them look for phrases that answer the questions *Who? What? When? Where? Why?* and *How?*

For Reteach and Practice, see **Analyze Craft and Structure: Author's Choices: Structure (RP).**

MAKING MEANING

WAS BROWN v. BOARD A FAILURE?

## Analyze Craft and Structure

**Author's Choices: Structure** "Was *Brown v. Board* a Failure?" is an **analytical argument,** a type of writing in which an author or speaker states a **claim**, or position, and defends it with valid reasoning and persuasive evidence. Like Earl Warren, Sarah Garland uses quotations to support her argument. In *Brown v. Board of Education*, the quotations are drawn from prior Supreme Court decisions. In contrast, Garland draws quotations from a variety of sources: a school board member, a Stanford University sociologist, an author in the field of education, and an activist. Notice another difference with *Brown v. Board of Education.* Warren structures his argument by topic, whereas Garland structures her argument chronologically, in time order.

### Practice

**CITE TEXTUAL EVIDENCE** to support your answers.

With your group, revisit the selection, and then fill out the chart. Identify details Garland presents in her discussion of each time period. Then, explain what key idea those details help develop.

| TIME PERIOD | DETAILS IN THE TEXT | KEY IDEAS |
|---|---|---|
| 1970s–1980s | a. See possible responses in Teacher's Edition. | b. |
| 1990s | c. | d. |
| 2000–2010 | e. | f. |





### PERSONALIZE FOR LEARNING

**Strategic Support**

**Review and Assess** Help students review the major points made in this article by providing them with a handout set up as a double-column entry worksheet titled, "Was *'Brown v. Board'* a Failure?" One column should be labeled, Failure and the other column labeled, Success. Direct students to find evidence in the text to list in both columns. On the bottom of the handout, invite them to summarize what they learned and state whether *Brown v. Board of Education* was a failure. Caution them to remember that the answer might be "yes and no" —it may have succeeded at some things but not at others.

LANGUAGE DEVELOPMENT

## Conventions and Style

**Subordinating Conjunctions** A **subordinating conjunction** connects ideas by making one idea subordinate to—that is, dependent on—the other. You can improve your sentence variety by using subordinating conjunctions to combine short, simple sentences into complex or compound-complex sentences that show relationships between ideas.

EXAMPLE

**Simple Sentences:** Parents of all races complained. They disliked the hassles of busing and the loss of neighborhood schools.

**Combined Sentence, Version 1:** Parents of all races complained ***because*** they disliked the hassles of busing and the loss of neighborhood schools.

**Combined Sentence, Version 2:** ***Because*** they disliked the hassles of busing and the loss of neighborhood schools, parents of all races complained.

Think about the relationships that these subordinating conjunctions suggest.

| after | as though | if | unless |
|---|---|---|---|
| although | because | since | until |
| as if | before | so that | when |
| as long as | even though | than | where |

### Read It

1. Identify the subordinating conjunction in each sentence.
   a. No one can predict the effects of "re-segregation" although research suggests a negative outcome for minorities.
   b. Because student assignment plans often depended on forced busing, most school boards complied reluctantly.
   c. Where forced busing has ended, racial isolation has gradually returned.
2. **Connect to Style** Identify a sentence in "Was *Brown v. Board* a Failure?" that includes a subordinating conjunction. Explain how the use of subordinating conjunctions helps the writer show relationships between ideas.

### Write It

**Notebook** Use a subordinating conjunction to combine each pair of sentences. Write the new sentence.

1. The 1990s arrived. The situation began to change.
2. School districts avoided court supervision. A series of Supreme Court decisions had made it easier to do so.
3. New efforts have been made to close the achievement gap. These measures have not yet shown much effect on minority student outcomes.

TIP

PUNCTUATION

If a subordinate clause begins a sentence, follow it with a comma. If the independent clause comes first, a comma generally is not needed.

STANDARDS

**Reading Informational Text**
Analyze and evaluate the effectiveness of the structure an author uses in his or her exposition or argument, including whether the structure makes points clear, convincing, and engaging.

**Language**
• Demonstrate command of the conventions of standard English grammar and usage when writing or speaking.
• Apply knowledge of language to understand how language functions in different contexts, to make effective choices for meaning or style, and to comprehend more fully when reading or listening.





PERSONALIZE FOR LEARNING

**Strategic Support**

**Using Subordinating Conjunctions** Some students may have difficulty combining sentences with subordinating conjunctions because they don't see the relationship each word conveys. If this is the case, have students make a chart showing the meaning and relationship of the most common subordinating conjunctions. For example:

| Subordinating Conjunction | Meaning | Conjunction | Meaning |
|---|---|---|---|
| after (paragraph 1) | later, subsequently | although | even if |
| if | doubt, stipulation | since | meanwhile, because |

Have students write model sentences for each subordinating conjunction.

DIGITAL PERSPECTIVES

## Conventions and Style

**Subordinating Conjunctions** Explain that a subordinate clause includes a subordinate conjunction followed by a subject and a verb. Point out that there are many more subordinating conjunctions, such as *as, whenever, whether, while, in case, in order, that, though, ever since,* and *so.* Explain that writers choose the conjunction that best expresses their idea. Share the following model and explain the relationship it expresses: (The subordinating conjunction is underlined.)

- People around the nation were shocked because the Supreme Court decision was unexpectedly unanimous. (*tells why people were shocked*)

For more support, see **Conventions and Style: Subordinating Conjunctions.**

### Read It

1. a. although
   b. because
   c. where
2. **Possible response:** In black communities, desegregation lost support when thousands of teachers and principals lost jobs, schools were closed, and people felt that they lost power over their schools. (paragraph 12) A subordinating conjunction shows that one clause is dependent on, occurred after, was caused by, or is in some other way subordinate to the other.

### Write It

Possible responses:

1. [When/After] the 1990s arrived, the situation began to change.
2. School districts avoided court supervision because a series of Supreme Court decisions made it easier to do so.
3. [Although/Even though] new efforts have been made to close the achievement gap, these measures have not yet shown much effect on minority student outcomes.

**FORMATIVE ASSESSMENT**

### Conventions and Style

**If** students are unable to identify the subordinating conjunctions, **then** have them find the two clauses in each sentence and the word that connects them.

For Reteach and Practice, see **Conventions and Style: Subordinating Conjunctions (RP).**

## Writing to Compare

As students prepare to compare information they've gathered about the two texts concerning the U.S. Supreme Court decision *Brown* v. *Board of Education*, they will consider the choices that writers make when presenting arguments.

### Prewriting

**Analyze the Texts** The first text, the court's decision, is lengthy and challenging. Encourage groups to assign members to different sections of that text to expedite the search process.

**Possible responses:**

a. "In each of the cases, minors of the Negro race, through their legal representatives, seek the aid of the courts in obtaining admission to the public schools of their community on a nonsegregated basis."

b. "Does segregation of children in public schools solely on the basis of race, even though the physical facilities and other 'tangible' factors may be equal, deprive the children of the minority group of equal educational opportunities? We believe that it does."

c. "The 'separate but equal' doctrine adopted in **Plessy v. Ferguson** . . . has no place in the field of public education."

d. "Perhaps just as importantly, the demise of desegregation offers lessons about what *not* to do in order to improve outcomes for minority children."

e. "After half a century, America's efforts to end segregation seem to be winding down."

f. "The study is the first to take a comprehensive look at whether court-ordered busing successfully ended the legacy of Jim Crow in public education, and it suggests a mission that is far from accomplished."

EFFECTIVE EXPRESSION

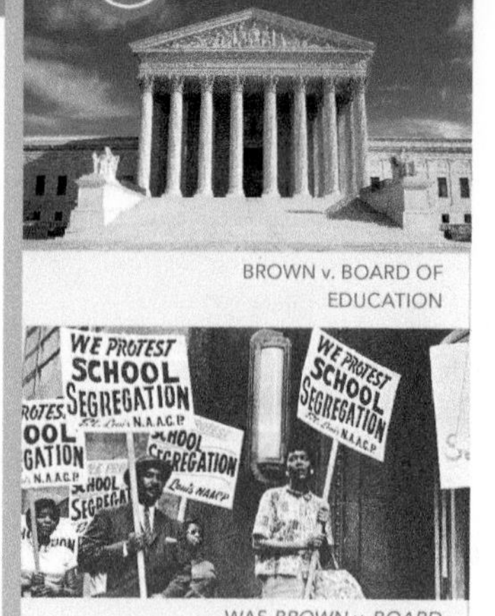


BROWN v. BOARD OF EDUCATION

WAS BROWN v. BOARD A FAILURE?

## Writing to Compare

You have read and analyzed two argumentative texts—the Supreme Court's opinion in *Brown v. Board of Education* and the magazine article "Was *Brown v. Board* a Failure?" Now, deepen your understanding of the texts by comparing and writing about them.

**Assignment**

Write a **comparison-and-contrast essay** in which you discuss how the following factors contribute to the choices these authors made in presenting and defending their arguments:

- awareness of purpose and audience
- understanding of the historical context
- sense of the historical importance of the text

Explain how these elements are reflected in the language, reasoning, and types of evidence each author uses. In your essay, use specific terms and vocabulary you studied as you analyzed the two selections separately, such as the following: *legal opinion, claim, counterclaim, plaintiffs, jurisdiction, disposition, legacy, mission,* and *policy.*

### Prewriting

**Analyze the Texts** With your group, choose passages from each selection that show each author's understanding of his or her purpose and audience, historical context, and legacy, or historical importance of the text. Look for specific examples of language, types of reasoning, and types of evidence. Work together to complete the chart.

| FACTOR | PASSAGES—BROWN V. BOARD OF EDUCATION | PASSAGES—WAS *BROWN V. BOARD* A FAILURE? |
|---|---|---|
| purpose and audience | a. See possible responses in the Teacher's edition. | d. |
| historical context | b. | e. |
| historical importance | c. | f. |

**STANDARDS**

**Reading Informational Text**

- Analyze and evaluate the effectiveness of a structure an author uses in his or her exposition or argument, including whether the structure makes points clear, convincing, and engaging.
- Delineate and evaluate the reasoning in seminal U.S. texts, including the application of constitutional principles and use of legal reasoning and the premises, purposes, and arguments in works of public advocacy.

**Writing**

Apply grades 11–12 reading standards to literary nonfiction.





378 UNIT 3 • POWER, PROTEST, AND CHANGE

## Drafting

**Frame Your Thesis** Review the notes from your group discussion. Then, write one sentence stating your central idea followed by three supporting ideas. Think of each supporting idea as a "because" statement. Record evidence from the texts you will use to illustrate each supporting idea.

Central Idea: ______________________________

Supporting Idea 1: ______________________________

Evidence: ______________________________

Supporting Idea 2: ______________________________

Evidence: ______________________________

Supporting Idea 3: ______________________________

Evidence: ______________________________

**Write a Draft** Use your essay frame to write a first draft that establishes a clear, logical sequence from the introduction, through your body paragraphs, to your conclusion. Remember to include evidence from both texts.

### Review, Revise, and Edit

Once you are done drafting, review your essay with the following questions in mind. Check the appropriate box for each question.

☐ Yes ☐ No Is your thesis specific and focused?

☐ Yes ☐ No Does each paragraph develop from your thesis?

☐ Yes ☐ No Is every idea supported with evidence?

☐ Yes ☐ No Does all the evidence clearly support your ideas?

☐ Yes ☐ No Do your ideas flow logically from the introduction to the body? Are they wrapped up elegantly in the conclusion?

If any of your answers to these questions is "no," make your thesis more specific, change or add evidence, or make other needed adjustments. Once you are comfortable with your content, work on the style. Consider using subordinating conjunctions to combine sentences, creating sentence variety and clarifying relationships among ideas. Then, review your draft for errors in spelling and punctuation, and make any necessary corrections.



EVIDENCE LOG

Before moving on to a new selection, go to your Evidence Log and record what you learned from the Supreme Court's opinion in *Brown v. Board of Education* and "Was *Brown v. Board* a Failure?"



DIGITAL PERSPECTIVES  

## Drafting

**Frame Your Thesis** Clarify for students that once they have completed the group prewriting activity, they will work individually to draft their essays. Also, encourage students to go beyond the quotations recorded during the prewriting activity to find additional evidence for their supporting ideas.

**Write a Draft** Note to students that the sentences they wrote in the Supporting Ideas section of the essay frame should work well as topic sentences for paragraphs in the body section of their essay.

## Review, Revise, and Edit

Consider making the checklist review a partner activity and remind students to be courteous when giving feedback to partners.

For more support, see **Writing to Compare: Comparison-and-Contrast Essay.** 

Evidence Log Support students in completing their Evidence Log. This paced activity will help prepare them for the Performance-Based Assessment at the end of the unit.

## FORMATIVE ASSESSMENT

### Writing to Compare

- **If** students struggle to come up with three supporting ideas for their essay frames, **then** have them reread the Assignment box on the previous page to see if they need additional supporting ideas to meet all of the requirements there.

### Selection Test

Administer the "Was Brown v. Board a Failure? (*with* Brown v. Board of Education: Opinion of the Court)" Selection Test, which is available in both print and digital formats online in Assessments.

## PERSONALIZE FOR LEARNING

### English Language Support

**Using Historical References** Ask students to compare two moments in the text where a historical reference to *Brown v. Board of Education* was made. (paragraphs 5 and 6) **EMERGING**

Ask students to contrast two moments in the text where a historical reference to *Brown v. Board of Education* was made for two different reasons. (paragraphs 5, 6, and 8-10) **EXPANDING**

Ask students to write a longer paragraph that discusses a variety of reasons that the historical references were included. (paragraphs 5, 6, and 8-10) **BRIDGING**

An expanded **English Language Support Lesson** on Using Historical References is available in the Interactive Teacher's Edition.

# FACILITATING

## Panel Discussion

Before groups begin work on their projects, have them clearly differentiate the role each group member will play. Remind groups to consult the schedule for Small-Group Learning to guide their work during the Performance Task.

Prior to beginning the Assessment, ask groups to discuss the issues that reformers address and ways that reformers can bring about social, political, and economic change.

## Plan With Your Group

**Analyze the Text** Groups should consult the primary texts and their notes as they complete the chart, making sure that they correctly identify each reformer's goals and reasons.

Remind groups that using specific details, quotes, facts, statistics, and examples from the texts will help them make their panel discussion interesting as well as accurate.

**Gather Evidence** Groups should consult authoritative sources, including more extensive biographies of the reformers and information from institutes and study centers dedicated to these topics and reformers.

Students should also consult other resources, especially:

- ways to structure informative text, available in Whole-Class Learning
- their Evidence Log
- their Word Network

PERFORMANCE TASK: SPEAKING AND LISTENING FOCUS

SOURCES

- AIN'T I A WOMAN?
- DECLARATION OF SENTIMENTS
- GIVING WOMEN THE VOTE
- THE STORY OF AN HOUR
- BROWN v. BOARD OF EDUCATION: OPINION OF THE COURT
- WAS *BROWN v. BOARD* A FAILURE?

# Panel Discussion

**Assignment**

You have read a variety of texts by people who sought to protest social ills and encourage change. Work with your group to hold an informative **panel discussion** that addresses these questions:

What were the goals of these reformers?

Why did they want to achieve those goals?

Make a video recording of your discussion to share with others.

## Plan With Your Group

**Analyze the Texts** There are five texts in the chart. If there are five members in your group, have each member choose one text as his or her area of expertise. If there are more than five members, form partnerships to choose texts. Use the chart headings to formulate key ideas about the particular text you or your partnership has chosen.

| TITLE | GOAL OF REFORMER | REASONS FOR GOAL |
|---|---|---|
| Ain't I a Woman? | | |
| Declaration of Sentiments | | |
| Giving Women the Vote | | |
| The Story of an Hour | | |
| Brown v. Board of Education: Opinion of the Court | | |
| Was *Brown v. Board* a Failure? | | |

**Gather Evidence** Find specific details from your text to support your ideas. Take notes or use note cards to list quotations from the text that support your understanding of the reformer's goal. If necessary, conduct research to locate evidence that supports your understanding of why that goal was important to the reformer.

STANDARDS

**Speaking and Listening**

Come to discussions prepared, having read and researched material under study; explicitly draw on that preparation by referring to evidence from texts and other research on the topic or issue to stimulate a thoughtful, well-reasoned exchange of ideas.





HOW LANGUAGE WORKS

**Levels of Usage** English is constantly changing: For instance, the contraction *ain't*, which Sojourner Truth uses in the title of her speech and in the refrain, is now considered substandard English, but from the 1600s-1800s, it was commonly used in educated speech and writing. Today, it is still commonplace, especially in the South and for emphasis, as in expressions such as "If it ain't broke, don't fix it."

Have students complete the following chart to replace substandard words with Standard Written English.

| Substandard | Standard |
|---|---|
| irregardless | regardless |
| being that | since, because |
| this here | this |
| hisself | himself |

**Organize Your Presentation** Choose a moderator to present the assignment questions, which each panel member will answer in turn. The moderator should also make sure that each speaker keeps to agreed-upon time limits and doesn't speak out of turn. Decide on the order in which presenters will speak. Ask a classmate from another group to make a video recording of your discussion.

## Rehearse With Your Group

**Practice With Your Group** Use this checklist to evaluate the effectiveness of your group's first run-through. Then, use your evaluation and these instructions to guide your revision.

| CONTENT | USE OF MEDIA | PRESENTATION TECHNIQUES |
|---|---|---|
| ☐ Each speaker clearly answers the questions asked.<br>☐ Each speaker supports ideas with evidence from the texts or additional research. | ☐ The equipment functions properly.<br>☐ The focus moves smoothly from speaker to speaker. | ☐ The speakers use formal language appropriately.<br>☐ The speakers make eye contact and speak clearly.<br>☐ Interactions between speakers and the moderator are civil and smooth. |

**Fine-Tune the Content** If necessary, find additional examples from your chosen text to support your ideas. Make sure that you have incorporated all of the outside research you did as you respond to the moderator's questions.

**Improve Your Use of Media** Watch a playback of your recording, and give feedback to your recorder. In particular, make sure that the sound is audible so that viewers can easily hear what is being asked and answered.

**Brush-Up on Your Presentation Techniques** Listen for places where you may revert to language that is more informal or less polished. Try to speak as though you are educating an audience that is eager to learn about these reformers.

## Present and Evaluate

As you record your final panel discussion, give all speakers equal time to share their ideas. As you watch the videos made by other groups, evaluate the presentations based on the evaluation checklist.

STANDARDS

**Speaking and Listening**

- Present information, findings, and supporting evidence, conveying a clear and distinct perspective, such that listeners can follow the line of reasoning, alternative or opposing perspectives are addressed, and the organization, development, substance, and style are appropriate to purpose, audience, and a range of formal and informal tasks.
- Adapt speech to a variety of contexts and tasks, demonstrating a command of formal English when indicated or appropriate.





AUTHOR'S PERSPECTIVE **Ernest Morrell, Ph.D.**

**The Art of Fielding Questions** Part of any successful presentation is the speaker's ability to answer questions with confidence and grace. Offer these tips for students:

- ***Prepare answers for likely questions in advance.*** Advise students to imagine what questions might come up and rehearse responses, especially for difficult questions.
- ***Repeat the question.*** By restating the question, a speaker can regain control of the room, gain some time before answering, and rephrase the question in a more positive way, if needed.
- ***Use a tone and stance that project authority.*** To avoid appearing defensive, students should be aware of their body language and the tone of their voice.

DIGITAL PERSPECTIVES

**Organize Your Presentation** The group should establish a set time for each speaker, such as three minutes. To help keep speakers to their allotted time, the moderator can hold up a sign that says "1 minute left" at that point in each presentation.

## Rehearse With Your Group

**Practice With Your Group** Remind students that each group member should practice his or her part ahead of time. Other group members should provide constructive feedback. Rehearsing can help with the timing and flow of the presentation, and can expose any equipment issues that may need to be resolved. You may wish to pair groups so that they can rehearse their presentations with each other.

**Fine-Tune the Content** As groups find additional content to include in their discussion, have them work together to trim extraneous information from their presentation so that they stay within the time allocation.

**Improve Your Use of Media** Groups may want to time themselves as they rehearse their panel discussion to ensure it doesn't run too long or isn't too brief.

**Brush Up Your Presentation Technique** Remind students to use the academic vocabulary from this unit to help to create the formal tone required in a panel discussion.

**MAKE IT INTERACTIVE**

Suggest that groups video record their rehearsal and watch together as a strategy for refining their presentation.

## Present and Evaluate

Before beginning the presentations, set the expectations for the audience. You may wish to have students consider these questions as groups present:

- What was the presenting group's claim?
- What were some of its supporting ideas?
- Which multimedia best illustrated its claim?
- What presentation strengths did the group demonstrate?

As students provide feedback to the presenting group, remind them that compliments are just as valuable as constructive criticism.

# OVERVIEW

## INDEPENDENT LEARNING

### In what ways does the struggle for freedom change with history?

Encourage students to think carefully about what they have already learned and what more they want to know about the unit topic of power, protest, and change.

This is a key first step to previewing and selecting the text they will read in Independent Learning.

### Independent Learning Strategies

Review the Learning Strategies with students and explain that as they work through Independent Learning, they will develop strategies to work on their own.

- Have students watch the video on Independent Learning Strategies.
- A video on this topic is available online in the Professional Development Center.

Students should include any favorite strategies that they might have devised on their own during the Whole-Class and Small-Group Learning. For example, for the strategy "Create a schedule," students might include:

- Review my plan at the end of each day.
- Remain flexible and make adjustments as needed.

**Block Scheduling**

Each day in this Pacing Plan represents a 40-50 minute class period. Teachers using block scheduling may combine days to reflect their class schedule. In addition, teachers may revise pacing to differentiate and support core instruction by integrating components and resources as students require.

## OVERVIEW: INDEPENDENT LEARNING

ESSENTIAL QUESTION:

# In what ways does the struggle for freedom change with history?

Freedom is a concept that means so many things, including the right to choose your path in life and to follow your ambitions wherever they may take you. In this section, you will complete your study of the struggle for freedom by exploring an additional selection related to the topic. You'll then share what you learn with classmates. To choose a text, follow these steps.

**Look Back** Think about the selections you have already studied. What more do you want to know about the topic of the struggle for freedom?

**Look Ahead** Preview the texts by reading the descriptions. Which one seems most interesting and appealing to you?

**Look Inside** Take a few minutes to scan the text you chose. Choose a different one if this text doesn't meet your needs.

## Independent Learning Strategies

Throughout your life, in school, in your community, and in your career, you will need to rely on yourself to learn and work on your own. Review these strategies and the actions you can take to practice them during Independent Learning. Add ideas of your own for each category.

| STRATEGY | ACTION PLAN |
|---|---|
| Create a schedule | • Understand your goals and deadlines.<br>• Make a plan for what to do each day.<br>• |
| Practice what you have learned | • Use first-read and close-read strategies to deepen your understanding.<br>• After you read, evaluate the usefulness of the evidence to help you understand the topic.<br>• After reading, consult reference sources for background information that can help you clarify meaning.<br>• |
| Take notes | • Record important ideas and information.<br>• Review your notes before preparing to share with a group.<br>• |



SCAN FOR MULTIMEDIA



### Pacing Plan

Unit Introduction — 1
Introduce Whole-Class Learning — 2
Historical Perspectives — 3
*from* What to the Slave Is the Fourth of July? — 4, 5, 6, 7, 8
Second Inaugural Address — 9, 10, 11, 12
Media: Perspectives on Lincoln — 13
Performance Task — 14, 15

DIGITAL PERSPECTIVES  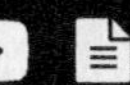

CONTENTS

Choose one selection. Selections are available online only.

SCAN FOR MULTIMEDIA





## Contents

**Selections** Encourage students to scan and preview the selections before choosing the one they would like to read. Suggest that they consider the genre and subject matter of each one before making their decision. You can use the information on the following planning pages to advise students in making their choice.

Remind students that the selections for Independent Learning are only available in the interactive edition of myPerspectives™. Allow students who do not have digital access at home to preview the digital selections using classroom or computer lab technology. Then either have students print the selection they choose or provide a printout for them.

## Performance-Based Assessment Prep

**Review Evidence for an Informative Essa y** Point out to students that collecting evidence during Independent Learning is the last step in completing their Evidence Log. After they finish their independent reading, they will synthesize all the evidence they have compiled in the unit. The evidence students collect will serve as their primary source of information they will use to complete the writing and audio recording for the Performance-Based Assessment at the end of the unit.

Introduce Small-Group Learning

16

Ain't I a Woman? 17

Declaration of Sentiments  18  19

Media: Giving Women the Vote  20

The Story of an Hour  21  22

Brown v. Board of Education: Opinion of the Court  23

Was "Brown v. Board" a Failure?  24 25

Performance Task 26

Introduce Independent Learning 27

Independent Learning 28

Performance-Based Assessment 29 30

INDEPENDENT LEARNING

# Poetry of Langston Hughes

## Summaries

The poem "I, Too" is Langston Hughes's response to Walt Whitman's "I Hear America Singing." Whitman's poem lists various American voices—but no black voice; no Langston Hughes. "I, Too" corrects the omission.

There are two ways to read the poem "Refugee in America." In the first, a foreign refugee celebrates America's proud tradition of hospitality. In the second, the refugee has always been in America. He is American, and not American—a refugee in his own country. In this reading, "Freedom" and "Liberty" have a tragic resonance.

In both stanzas of "Dream Variations," the speaker dances in the sun, rests under a tree at the end of the day, and welcomes the night. The second stanza, however, is shorter, faster, more urgent, and more passionate than the first.

In "The Negro Speaks of Rivers," the poet makes a connection between some of the world's major rivers and African American history.

## Insight

In his poetry, Langston Hughes celebrated the spirit of the African American community. Reading these four poems will illustrate for students the power of his eloquent expression of pride in his heritage as a black man, but also as an American. Hughes's poems protest the disenfranchisement of blacks in their own country, but the poems also maintain hope for change that will right the wrongs afflicting African Americans.

### SELECTION RESOURCES

- First-Read Guide: Poetry
- Close-Read Guide: Poetry
- Poetry Collection 1: Text Questions
- Audio Summaries
- Selection Audio
- Selection Test

ESSENTIAL QUESTION:
In what ways does the struggle for freedom change with history?

## Connection to Essential Question

When considering the Essential Question—*In what ways does the struggle for freedom change with history?*—in relation to these four poems, students may note the differences between Hughes's quiet eloquence and the bloody battles of the Civil War or the harsh rebuke of Frederick Douglass.

UNIT PERFORMANCE-BASED ASSESSMENT
What motivates people to struggle for change?

## Connection to Performance Task

**Unit Performance-Based Assessment** In these four poems, Langston Hughes uses imagery, repetition, and rhythm to present political and social issues in poetic forms.

### Text Complexity Rubric: Poetry of Langston Hughes

| **Quantitative Measures** | |
|---|---|
| **Lexile:** NP **Text Length:** 18 lines; 8 lines; 17 lines; 13 lines | |
| **Qualitative Measures** | |
| Knowledge Demands ①—❷—③—④—⑤ | Understanding of all four poems requires general knowledge of slavery, which students at this age will easily have. |
| Structure ①—❷—③—④—⑤ | The four poems follow conventional poetic structure. All four poems use repetition. "Refugee in America" and "Dream Variations" both use repetition and rhyme. |
| Language Conventionality and Clarity ①—❷—③—④—⑤ | Language in all four poems can be easily understood, with simple vocabulary. "The Negro Speaks of Rivers" and "Dream Variations" contain similes and metaphorical language. |
| Levels of Meaning/Purpose ①—②—❸—④—⑤ | Multiple levels of meaning; all contain symbolism. "The Negro Speaks of Rivers" and "Dream Variations" are the least explicit, requiring more understanding of symbolic language. Some meanings are ambiguous. (For example, "I, Too" could refer to slaves or servants.) |

DIGITAL PERSPECTIVES

Audio

Video

Document

Annotation Highlights

EL Highlights

Online Assessment

# Poems of Social Commentary

SELECTION RESOURCES

- First-Read Guide: Poetry
- Close-Read Guide: Poetry
- Poetry Collection 2: Text Questions
- Audio Summaries
- Selection Audio
- Selection Test

## Summaries

In Paul Laurence Dunbar's sonnet "Douglass," the speaker addresses Frederick Douglass, who had been dead for several years at the time of writing. Dunbar wishes Douglass would return, because his wisdom and authority are urgently required. Dunbar uses an elaborate form of poetic diction, intended to convey respect for his employer, friend, and hero.

In Sarah Browning's "The Fifth Fact," the speaker's seven-year-old son must put together five facts about Harriet Tubman. He only has four. The speaker tells him Tubman was a spy for the North during the Civil War, and it works like magic: he starts to write—and the poet starts to imagine. This is Washington. There are some serious old ghosts among the fast food joints and the liquor stores.

In Martin Espada's "Who Burns for the Perfection of Paper," the speaker remembers assembling legal pads for a printer after school. He was sixteen. He remembers the feel of the yellow paper and the pain when the glue gets into his paper-cuts.

## Insight

Reading these three poems will help students begin to reflect on the way the struggles and difficulties of the past reverberate in the present. Maintaining a connection with the past and those who worked for change—either large-scale or personal—reminds us of the efforts that went into creating the world we live in today, and points out the work still to be done.

ESSENTIAL QUESTION:
In what ways does the struggle for freedom change with history?

## Connection to Essential Question

These three poems of social commentary each provide a unique connection to the Essential Question. In all three, struggles from the past are compared with contemporary struggles. They discuss how some things have changed while others remain the same. "Who Burns for the Perfection of Paper" serves to remind us that the passing of time should not let us forget the struggles of the past.

UNIT PERFORMANCE-BASED ASSESSMENT
What motivates people to struggle for change?

## Connection to Performance Task

**Unit Performance-Based Assessment** These poems use a variety of techniques to affect an audience: emotional appeal, realism, allusion, and imagery.

### Text Complexity Rubric: Poems of Social Commentary

| **Quantitative Measures** | |
|---|---|
| **Lexile:** NP **Text Length:** 14 lines; 52 lines; 27 lines | |
| **Qualitative Measures** | |
| Knowledge Demands<br>① ② **❸** ④ ⑤ | "Douglass" requires awareness of Frederick Douglass's life and work; "The Fifth Fact" explains the subject matter within it (Harriet Tubman, Civil War, Lincoln); "Who Burns…" is about an unfamiliar subject (factory work), but details are described. |
| Structure<br>① **❷** ③ ④ ⑤ | "Douglass" follows a poetic structure using rhyme. "The Fifth Fact" and "Who Burns . . ." read more like prose, with full sentences within the structure of the poem. |
| Language Conventionality and Clarity<br>① ② **❸** ④ ⑤ | "Douglass" contains archaic language (*thee, thou, thy, didst*) that is uncommon in modern poetry and may be unfamiliar; "The Fifth Fact" has conventional language; "Who Burns…" has a lot of rich, descriptive language. |
| Levels of Meaning/Purpose<br>① ② ③ **❹** ⑤ | All poems have multiple levels of meaning. The reader needs to understand symbolism and figurative language in order to understand these meanings. Of the three poems, "Douglass" is least explicit in meaning. "The Fifth Fact" requires students to follow a stream of consciousness. |

# *from* The Warmth of Other Suns

## Summary

In this excerpt from "The Warmth of Other Suns," Isabel Wilkerson explains how the Civil War created in the South a vast population of sharecroppers to whom debt would always be a way of life. Reconstruction enabled the newly free to exercise their rights, but in the mid-1870s, sustained white hostility forced the North to withdraw its oversight of Reconstruction, and an elaborate race-based caste system began to evolve designed to create a permanent black underclass from which there could be no escape. This system was protected by local legislation that bypassed and violated federal law. Jim Crow developed fast. A white generation was emerging who had never known the old South. They wanted, in the words of the Governor of Alabama, "to wipe (the Negro) from the face of the earth." In 1916, almost unnoticed, black families began to take the train north.

### Insight

Sometimes surrender is a form of protest. Reading this excerpt from *The Warmth of Other Suns* offers students an opportunity to learn about an often-untold story of American history, when millions of African Americans gave up the fight against the cruel laws of the South and simply left the South behind.

### SELECTION RESOURCES

- First-Read Guide: Nonfiction
- Close-Read Guide: Nonfiction
- *from* The Warmth of Other Suns: Text Questions
- Audio Summaries
- Selection Audio
- Selection Test

ESSENTIAL QUESTION:
In what ways does the struggle for freedom change with history?

## Connection to Essential Question

When considering the Essential Question—*In what ways does the struggle for freedom change with history?*—in relation to the excerpt from *The Warmth of Other Suns,* students should recognize that the exodus of African Americans to the North was a direct reaction to the failed struggle against discrimination in the South.

UNIT PERFORMANCE-BASED ASSESSMENT
What motivates people to struggle for change?

## Connection to Performance Task

**Unit Performance-Based Assessment** *The Warmth of Other Suns* relies on vivid historical detail, blended seamlessly with a compelling narrative to affect readers. This text helps students see the motivation for equality and the ways that people make decisions about the way they want to live.

### Text Complexity Rubric: The Warmth of Other Suns

| **Quantitative Measures** | |
|---|---|
| **Lexile:** 1330 **Text Length:** 2,777 words | |
| **Qualitative Measures** | |
| Knowledge Demands ①—②—❸—④—⑤ | To understand the selection it is necessary to have some basic knowledge of the history of slavery, Reconstruction, and the Jim Crow laws. |
| Structure ①—②—❸—④—⑤ | Text has clear paragraph breaks and includes some quotations. Information is presented logically and is mostly sequential, but references to dates that support the analysis are sometimes out of chronological order. |
| Language Conventionality and Clarity ①—②—❸—④—⑤ | Many sentences in the selection are long and complex, with multiple clauses. Quotations from the early 1900s are included, some of which have unconventional syntax. |
| Levels of Meaning/Purpose ①—❷—③—④—⑤ | Concepts and meaning are straightforward and explicitly stated. |

DIGITAL PERSPECTIVES

Audio | Video | Document | Annotation Highlights | EL Highlights | Online Assessment

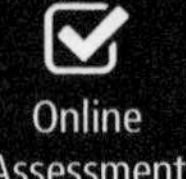

# What a Factory Can Teach a Housewife

## Summary

In her speech "What a Factory Can Teach a Housewife," Ida Tarbell informs American housewives that they exhibit the social and economic attitudes of eighteenth century aristocrats, and until they come to terms with the fact that they are living in a democratic society, they will never understand why they find it so difficult to hang on to good household staff. The fact is that good household staff would rather work in a factory than work for American housewives. A factory offers her regular hours, doesn't make her work on weekends, employs her to work at a single specified task without being constantly supervised and fussed over, and gives her the opportunity to live in a home and create her own domestic regime. If housewives wish to hang on to staff, they must offer similar terms, or better.

## Insight

Reading "What a Factory Can Teach a Housewife" will help students understand the limitations women faced when it came to work in the early part of the twentieth century. In the face of household work that demeaned women and made it impossible for them to have any independence, factory work was a much better option.

It may be necessary to point out that the improvement of factory work over household work was relative. Factory work has received its fair share of criticism since the time of Tarbell's writing, but at the time, her message was clearly about women's independence and dignity.

SELECTION RESOURCES

- First-Read Guide: Nonfiction
- Close-Read Guide: Nonfiction
- What a Factory Can Teach a Housewife: Text Questions
- Audio Summaries
- Selection Audio
- Selection Test

ESSENTIAL QUESTION:
In what ways does the struggle for freedom change with history?

## Connection to Essential Question

When considering the Essential Question—*In what ways does the struggle for freedom change with history?*—in relation to "What a Factory Can Teach a Housewife," students may consider the role of the advocate, or in this case, the role of a "muckraker" in calling attention to an issue that requires reform. Rather than uniting the workers to rally against their household employers, Tarbell uses her persuasive skills to educate housewives on how they can improve their own lot, while, of course, improving the lot of the workers.

UNIT PERFORMANCE-BASED ASSESSMENT
What motivates people to struggle for change?

## Connection to Performance Task

**Unit Performance-Based Assessment** "What a Factory Can Teach a Housewife" uses argumentative techniques to affect the audience. This text reinforces the ideals that drive a desire for equality.

### Text Complexity Rubric: What a Factory Can Teach a Housewife

| **Quantitative Measures** | |
|---|---|
| **Lexile:** 1210 **Text Length:** 963 words | |
| **Qualitative Measures** | |
| Knowledge Demands ①—②—❸—④—⑤ | Understanding the selection requires knowledge of women's roles at home and in the workforce during the early 1900s, some of which is explained. |
| Structure ①—②—③—❹—⑤ | Opinions and facts are logical, but there are few breaks to organize information; questions are posed but not followed by answers; flow of information can be hard to predict. |
| Language Conventionality and Clarity ①—②—③—❹—⑤ | As writing is from 1916, language does not follow modern style and tone. Syntax and vocabulary are nonconventional. |
| Levels of Meaning/Purpose ①—②—❸—④—⑤ | Main concepts are explicitly stated. Reader needs to distinguish between statements of facts and author's opinion to grasp meaning. |

# *from* Books as Bombs

## Summary

In this excerpt from his essay "Books as Bombs," Louis Menand discusses how Betty Friedan came to write *The Feminine Mystique*, and how it changed the world. Menand gives a detailed account of the author's life at the time she wrote it. A summa-cum-laude graduate of Smith, Friedan had been a freelance magazine writer for ten years when she began work on the book. She lived with her husband, Carl, an advertising executive, and their three children in an eleven room house overlooking the river in Grand View-on-Hudson. Readers at the time felt that Friedan had saved their lives, and referred to *The Feminine Mystique* as a survival manual. "This," Menand remarks, "is what it felt like to be an American housewife in 1963." This, Friedan says, is how it felt to be a woman trapped in the "comfortable concentration camp" of domestic life.

## Insight

Change may come from the unlikeliest of sources. Reading the excerpt from "Books as Bombs" will help students understand the power of the written word to effect change. Finding a language to express the issues of the day, and giving women the sense that they shared an experience, helped to start a revolution.

### SELECTION RESOURCES

- First-Read Guide: Nonfiction
- Close-Read Guide: Nonfiction
- *from* Books as Bombs: Text Questions
- Audio Summaries
- Selection Audio
- Selection Test

ESSENTIAL QUESTION:
In what ways does the struggle for freedom change with history?

## Connection to Essential Question

The relationship between the excerpt from "Books as Bombs" and the Essential Question—*In what ways does the struggle for freedom change with history?*—is fairly straightforward. At the time Friedan's book was written, women's struggle for freedom from unfair job practices and other social issues had become subsumed by the social norms of the day. It was a challenge to get women to realize that they were facing a struggle. The selection makes it clear, too, that books can have a strong effect on social change.

UNIT PERFORMANCE-BASED ASSESSMENT
What motivates people to struggle for change?

## Connection to Performance Task

**Unit Performance-Based Assessment** The excerpt from "Books as Bombs" uses relevant evidence and statistics to affect readers. This text is helpful in explaining the desire for women's rights and the power of language to help effect change.

### Text Complexity Rubric: *from* Books as Bombs

| **Quantitative Measures** | |
|---|---|
| **Lexile:** 1260 **Text Length:** 2,212 words | |
| **Qualitative Measures** | |
| Knowledge Demands<br>① ② ③ **❹** ⑤ | Knowledge of the feminist movement and the book *The Feminine Mystique* is required. Though it is the focus of the article, the main concepts of the book are not fully explained. |
| Structure<br>① ② **❸** ④ ⑤ | The text follows a journalistic structure, with concepts laid out in logical sequence but following multiple pathways, with a lot of information in each paragraph. |
| Language Conventionality and Clarity<br>① ② **❸** ④ ⑤ | Many sentences have multiple clauses, complex syntax, and some vocabulary or phrases that may be unfamiliar. |
| Levels of Meaning/Purpose<br>① ② ③ **❹** ⑤ | Ideas are clearly stated, but multiple viewpoints and a range of ideas are expressed, so the reader must tie many pieces together and interpret them in order to grasp overall meaning and concepts. |

DIGITAL PERSPECTIVES

Audio | Video | Document | Annotation Highlights | EL Highlights | Online Assessment

# A Balance Between Nature and Nurture


## Summary

"A Balance Between Nature and Nurture" is Gloria Steinem's contribution to the long-standing debate over whether nature or nurture has the greater influence over the development of the child and the formation of personality. She regards her own early childhood as a period free of nurture, and remembers when she discovered that she was a social being, subject to demands and expectations. She recognizes the political attitudes that play a necessary part in the taking of sides. She no longer subscribes to the "conservative" view that children are naturally selfish and destructive, and require "civilizing," or to the "liberal" view of children as blank slates on which anything may be written. Steinem commits herself to reason and investigation, rather than to a political loyalty, and to the glamour of conflict rather than to the dullness of compromise.


## Insight

A feminist foundation paves the way for a humanistic outlook. Listening to "A Balance Between Nature and Nurture" will help students see how questioning the status quo of a social issue, such as the position of women in society, can lead to new questions about the forces that constrain the lives of all human beings.

SELECTION RESOURCES

- First-Review Guide: Media Audio
- Close-Review Guide: Media Audio
- A Balance Between Nature and Nurture: Media Questions
- Audio Summaries
- Selection Audio

ESSENTIAL QUESTION:
In what ways does the struggle for freedom change with history?

## Connection to Essential Question

When considering the Essential Question—*In what ways does the struggle for freedom change with history?*—students may see that with the passing of time, the struggle for freedom has shifted—from fights between those with power and those without to challenging the ideas that constrain people from being their best selves. Gloria Steinem refutes the belief that our very natures are to blame for society's ills. She also refutes the belief that we are completely mutable and believes that it's possible to reprogram humans to eliminate those ills.

UNIT PERFORMANCE-BASED ASSESSMENT
What motivates people to struggle for change?

## Connection to Performance Task

**Unit Performance-Based Assessment** The speaker in "A Balance Between Nature and Nurture" employs the use of relevant personal anecdote, as well as logical reasoning, to effectively present her opinion on a controversial topic. This audio helps students see the fluid nature of the struggle for change. Here, the speaker is arguing for freedom of self, and that may be a much different fight than the other motivators in the unit.

### Media Complexity Rubric: A Balance Between Nature and Nurture

| Quantitative Measures | |
|---|---|
| **Format and Length:** audio of 6 minutes, 13 seconds | |
| **Qualitative Measures** | |
| Knowledge Demands<br>① ② ③ ❹ ⑤ | Previous knowledge is needed about the "nature vs nurture" debate, which is referenced but not fully explained. References to the movements of the 60s and 70s are also included without explanation. |
| Structure<br>① ② ❸ ④ ⑤ | Selection follows a structure of personal opinion narrative. Ideas flow with multiple pathways. |
| Language Conventionality and Clarity<br>① ② ❸ ④ ⑤ | Many sentences are complex and include multiple clauses, but language is conventional and colloquial, and syntax and vocabulary not overly difficult. |
| Levels of Meaning/Purpose<br>① ② ③ ❹ ⑤ | Selection has multiple levels of meaning, including facts, commentary, and ironic tone, which can make interpretation difficult. Some main points have unclear referents. (For example, it is ambiguous what *it* refers to in the first sentence.) |

# ADVISING

You may wish to direct students to use the generic **First-Read** and **Close-Read Guides** in the Print Student Edition. Alternatively, you may wish to print copies of the genre-specific **First-Read** and **Close-Read Guides** for students.

These are available online in the Interactive Student Edition or Unit Resources. 

## FIRST READ

Students should perform the steps of the first read independently:

NOTICE: Students should focus on the basic elements of the text to ensure they understand what is happening.

ANNOTATE: Students should mark any passages they wish to revisit during their close read.

CONNECT: Students should increase their understanding by connecting what they've read to other texts or personal experiences.

RESPOND: Students will write a summary to demonstrate their understanding.

Point out to students that while they will always complete the Respond step at the end of the first read, the other steps will probably happen somewhat concurrently. Remind students that they will revisit their first-read annotations during the close read.

After students have completed the First-Read Guide, you may wish to assign the Text questions for the selection that are available in the Interactive Teacher's Edition.

### Anchor Standards

In the first two sections of the unit, students worked with the whole class and in small groups to gain topical knowledge and greater understanding of the skills required by the anchor standards. In this section, they are asked to work independently, applying what they have learned and demonstrating increased readiness for college and career.

## INDEPENDENT LEARNING

### First-Read Guide

Tool Kit
First-Read Guide and Model Annotation

Use this page to record your first-read ideas.

Selection Title: ____________________

NOTICE

**NOTICE** new information or ideas you learn about the unit topic as you first read this text.

ANNOTATE

**ANNOTATE** by marking vocabulary and key passages you want to revisit.

**CONNECT** ideas within the selection to other knowledge and the selections you have read.

**RESPOND** by writing a brief summary of the selection.

CONNECT

RESPOND

STANDARD
**Reading** Read and comprehend complex literary and informational texts independently and proficiently.

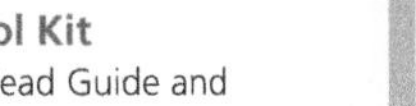


## Close-Read Guide

Tool Kit
Close-Read Guide and Model Annotation

Use this page to record your close-read ideas.

Selection Title: ____________________

### Close Read the Text

Revisit sections of the text you marked during your first read. Read these sections closely and **annotate** what you notice. Ask yourself **questions** about the text. What can you **conclude**? Write down your ideas.

### Analyze the Text

Think about the author's choices of patterns, structure, techniques, and ideas included in the text. Select one and record your thoughts about what this choice conveys.

### QuickWrite

Pick a paragraph from the text that grabbed your interest. Explain the power of this passage.

STANDARD
**Reading** Read and comprehend complex literary and informational texts independently and proficiently.





### CLOSE READ

Students should begin their close read by revisiting the sections they annotated during their first read. Next, they should analyze one of the author's choices regarding these elements:

- **patterns,** such as headings or a refrain
- **structure,** such as claim-and-counterclaim or chronological
- **techniques,** such as narrative details, allusions, or irony
- **ideas,** such as the main idea or the author's claim

You may wish to print copies of the Close-Read Guide for students to use.

**MAKE IT INTERACTIVE**
Group students according to the selection they have chosen. Then, have students meet to discuss the selection in-depth. Their discussions should be guided by their insights and questions.

# ADVISING

## Share Your Independent Learning

### Prepare to Share

Explain to students that sharing what they learned from their Independent Learning selection provides classmates who read a different selection with an opportunity to consider the text as a source of evidence during the Performance-Based Assessment. As students prepare to share, remind them to highlight how their selection contributed to their knowledge of the concept of power, protest, and change as well as how the selection connects to the question, *In what ways does the struggle for freedom change with history?*

### Learn From Your Classmates

As students discuss the Independent Learning selections, direct them to take particular note of how their classmates' chosen selections align with their current position on the Performance-Based Assessment question.

### Reflect

Students may want to add their reflection to their Evidence Log, particularly if their insight relates to a specific selection from the unit.

**Evidence Log** Support students in completing their Evidence Log. This paced activity will help prepare them for the Performance-Based Assessment at the end of the unit.

INDEPENDENT LEARNING

EVIDENCE LOG

Go to your Evidence Log and record what you learned from the text you read.

## Share Your Independent Learning

### Prepare to Share

In what ways does the struggle for freedom change with history?

Even when you read or learn something independently, your understanding continues to grow when you share what you have learned with others. Reflect on the text you explored independently, and write notes about its connection to the unit. In your notes, consider why this text belongs in this unit.

### Learn From Your Classmates

**Discuss It** Share your ideas about the text you explored on your own. As you talk with your classmates, jot down ideas that you learn from them.

### Reflect

Review your notes, and mark the most important insight you gained from these writing and discussion activities. Explain how this idea adds to your understanding of the meaning of freedom.

STANDARDS

**Speaking and Listening**

Initiate and participate effectively in a range of collaborative discussions with diverse partners on *grades 11–12 topics, texts, and issues,* building on others' ideas and expressing their own clearly and persuasively.





AUTHOR'S PERSPECTIVE **Ernest Morrell, Ph.D.**

**Discussing the Outcomes of Independent Learning** To increase the value of the **Share Your Independent Learning** activity, lead a class discussion. To support this critical college and career skill, teachers should remind students that they are responsible for learning from each other. Teachers can share the three key parts to learning from a discussion:

1. **Preparation** Encourage students to be ready to speak. Students who make self-facing notes will be better prepared to make meaningful contributions to class discussions.
2. **Note-Taking Show** Show students how to take notes based on their classmates' experiences and comments. Teachers can model effective ways to capture essential ideas.
3. **Reflection** Following the class discussion, student synthesis serves as an important closure point. Teachers can support this by assigning a quick writing activity that allows students to capture what they have learned from their classmates' contributions.

PERFORMANCE-BASED ASSESSMENT PREP

## Review Evidence for an Informative Essay

At the beginning of this unit, you took a position on the following question:

**What motivates people to struggle for change?**

EVIDENCE LOG

Review your Evidence Log and your QuickWrite from the beginning of the unit. Have your ideas changed?

| ☐ YES | ☐ NO |
|---|---|
| Identify at least three pieces of evidence that have caused you to reevaluate your ideas. | Identify at least three pieces of evidence that reinforced your original ideas. |
| 1. | 1. |
| 2. | 2. |
| 3. | 3. |

Develop your thoughts into a topic sentence: *One significant motivation that may inspire people to struggle for change is:* ______

______

______

Identify a historical example of the motivation you identified: ______

______

______

**Evaluate the Strength of Your Evidence** Which two texts that you read in this unit offer the strongest support for your topic sentence?

1. ______

2. ______

What are some other resources you might use to locate information about the topic?

1. ______ 2. ______

STANDARDS

**Writing**

Introduce a topic; organize complex ideas, concepts, and information so that each new element builds on that which precedes it to create a unified whole; include formatting, graphics, and multimedia when useful to aiding comprehension.





DIGITAL PERSPECTIVES

## Review Evidence for an Informative Essay

**Evidence Log** Make sure students understand that their opinions on an issue can change as they learn more about it and as they encounter other points of view. Remind students that their Evidence Log tracked the growth of their thinking during the unit. As they carefully consider what they've learned and the evidence they've found, the initial position they took on the question *"What motivates people to struggle for change?"* might continue to change.

### Evaluate the Strength of Your Evidence

Students have the choice of many different sources when looking for information about the topic, including:

- history textbooks
- mass-market history books
- biographies of individuals who struggled for change
- magazine articles
- websites about people or movements devoted to social justice, civil rights, or other kinds of societal change

Students need to judge not just the quantity of the evidence they gather about their topic, but also the reliability of that evidence. Discuss what might make evidence more credible, and suggest these questions:

- Did it come from a reliable source, such as governmental, educational, and professional organizations?
- Has it been reviewed by experts for accuracy?
- Does it include references to other sources?

## PERSONALIZE FOR LEARNING

### English Language Support

**Support the Task** Students may have difficulty with the vocabulary required to complete this task. Help students by simplifying the language in the direction lines. For example, instead of stating *"Identify at least three pieces of evidence that have caused you to reevaluate your ideas,"* support students' knowledge of the verb "identify," and restate the task. Ask students to *"List three reasons that have caused you to rethink your ideas."* Also, offer a new sentence frame for a topic sentence, *"One reason that might make someone want to work for change is: ______."* **ALL LEVELS**

## Writing to Sources: Informative Essay

Students should complete the Performance-Based Assessment independently, with little to no input or feedback during the process.

Prior to beginning the Assessment, ask students to think about the changes described in the unit selections and what might motivate people to struggle for such changes.

## Review the Elements of an Informative Essay

Students can review the work they did earlier in the unit as they complete the Performance-Based Assessment. They may also consult other resources such as:

- the elements of an informative essay, including language, tone, and grammar, as well as how to organize their text and enrich their writing with research, available in Whole-Class Learning
- their Evidence Logs
- their Word Networks

Although students will use evidence from the unit selections for their informative essay, they may need to collect additional evidence, including facts, statistics, anecdotes, quotations from authorities, or examples that support their topic sentence or thesis sentence.

PERFORMANCE-BASED ASSESSMENT

SOURCES

- WHOLE-CLASS SELECTIONS
- SMALL-GROUP SELECTIONS
- INDEPENDENT-LEARNING SELECTION

PART 1

## Writing to Sources: Informative Essay

In this unit, you read a variety of texts by reformers whose goal was to initiate change. Not all struggles were alike: The writers faced various obstacles in their quests for reform.

**Assignment**

Write an **informative essay** in which you explore this question:

**What motivates people to struggle for change?**

Begin by defining the various reasons people decide to fight for change. Identify two or three texts from this unit that you feel most clearly show the connections between motivation and action. Use specific examples from each text to support your analysis and deductions.

**Reread the Assignment** Review the assignment to be sure you fully understand it. The assignment may reference some of the academic words presented at the beginning of the unit. Be sure you understand each of the words given below in order to complete the assignment correctly.

**Academic Vocabulary**

| informational | verbatim | specific |
|---|---|---|
| inquire | deduction | |

WORD NETWORK

As you write and revise your text, use your Word Network to help vary your word choices.

**Review the Elements of an Informative Essay** Before you begin writing, read the Informative Text Rubric. Once you have completed your first draft, check it against the rubric. If one or more of the elements are missing or not as strong as they could be, revise your text to add or strengthen those components.

STANDARDS

Writing

- Write informative/explanatory texts to examine and convey complex ideas, concepts, and information clearly and accurately through the effective selection, organization, and analysis of content.
- Draw evidence from literary or informational texts to support analysis, reflection, and research.
- Write routinely over extended time frames and shorter time frames for a range of tasks, purposes, and audiences.





AUTHOR'S PERSPECTIVE **Kelly Gallagher, M.Ed.**

**Preparing for High-Stakes Tests** Writing is a gate-keeper to opportunity. Students constantly face on-demand writing in state assessments, college entrance exams, or even workplace writing samples.To improve performance, share the ABCD strategy:

- **Attack the prompt.** Show students how to read the prompt. Circle verbs like *discuss, share,* and *support*. Draw arrows to complete the direction: Discuss a *solution* or Support *with reasons*. Rewrite and number the circled words for a stepped-out prompt.
- **Brainstorm possible answers.** Before writing, students should list several suitable topics, addressing all steps of the prompt.
- **Choose the order of the response.** Using their ideas from the brainstorming task, show students how to map out a response before writing, noting what they will include and crossing out items that don't fit.
- **Detect Errors Before Turning Draft In.** Time taken to review writing before handing it in is time well spent. Even veteran writers will find mistakes they have made in timed writing situations.

## Informative Text Rubric

| | Focus and Organization | Evidence and Elaboration | Language Conventions |
|---|---|---|---|
| 4 | The introduction is engaging and reveals the topic in a way that appeals to a reader.<br>Facts, details, and examples progress logically, and transition words and phrases link and separate ideas.<br>The conclusion leaves a strong impression on the reader. | Ideas are supported with specific and relevant examples from research and the texts.<br>The style of the essay is formal, and the tone is objective.<br>Vocabulary is used strategically and appropriately for the audience and purpose. | The essay demonstrates a clear command of standard English conventions of usage and mechanics. |
| 3 | The introduction is engaging and clearly reveals the topic.<br>Facts, details, and examples progress logically, and transition words appear frequently.<br>The conclusion follows from the rest of the essay. | Ideas are supported with relevant examples from research and the texts.<br>The style of the essay is mostly formal, and the tone tends to be objective.<br>Vocabulary is generally appropriate for the audience and purpose. | The essay demonstrates accuracy in standard English conventions of usage and mechanics. |
| 2 | The introduction states the topic.<br>Facts, details and examples progress somewhat logically, and transition words may be used.<br>The conclusion restates the main ideas. | Many ideas are supported with examples from research and the texts.<br>The style of the essay is occasionally formal, and the tone is at times objective.<br>Vocabulary is somewhat appropriate for the audience and purpose. | The essay demonstrates some accuracy in standard English conventions of usage and mechanics. |
| 1 | The introduction does not clearly state the topic, or there is no introduction.<br>Facts, details, and examples do not progress logically, and sentences seem disconnected.<br>The conclusion does not follow from the essay, or there is no conclusion. | Ideas are not supported with examples from research and the texts, or examples are irrelevant.<br>The style of the essay is informal, and the tone frequently reveals biases.<br>Vocabulary is limited, ineffective, or inappropriate. | The essay contains mistakes in standard English conventions of usage and mechanics. |





DIGITAL PERSPECTIVES

## Informative Text Rubric

As you review the Informational Text Rubric with students, remind them that the rubric is a resource that can guide their revisions. Students should pay particular attention to the differences between an informational text that contains all of the required elements (a score of 3) and one that reveals the topic in a way that appeals to a reader and provides specific examples to support ideas (a score of 4).

## Speaking and Listening: Podcast

Students should annotate their informative essay in preparation for the oral presentation, marking the important elements (topic or thesis sentence, facts, details, and examples) as well as definitions, quotations, and/or graphics that support the information given.

Remind students that the effectiveness of a podcast relies on how well the speaker establishes credibility with his or her audience. If a speaker comes across as confident and authoritative, it will be easier for the audience to give credence to the information provided in the podcast.

**Review the Rubric** As you review the Podcast Rubric with students, remind them that it is a valuable tool that can help them plan a successful podcast. They should strive to achieve a score of 3. Draw their attention to some of the subtle differences between scores of 2 and 3.



PART 2

## Speaking and Listening: Podcast

**Assignment**

After completing the final draft of your informative essay, make a **podcast** or audio recording that could be uploaded for listeners. Then, share your recording, so that your classmates can listen to your work.

Follow these steps to make your podcast both informative and interesting.

- Give your podcast a title, and provide your name.
- Mark key examples in your informative essay that answer this question: *How does the motivator I analyzed encourage people to struggle for change?* These are the key points you will want to emphasize in your delivery.
- Practice your delivery, keeping in mind that you will be heard but not seen. You will need to vary your voice accordingly. Also, take care to eliminate distracting background noises.
- Deliver your podcast, being sure to maintain an even distance from the recording device. Focus on speaking clearly, and build in pauses so that listeners can follow and digest your ideas.

**Review the Rubric** The criteria by which your podcast will be evaluated appear in the rubric below. Review the criteria before recording to ensure that you are prepared.

| | Content | Use of Media | Presentation Technique |
|---|---|---|---|
| 3 | The podcast focuses on the question.<br>The flow of ideas is logical, clear, and easy to follow. | The voice on the recording is consistent and audible.<br>The podcast file has a title that clearly illustrates the focus. | The speaker's voice is consistently clear and appropriately loud for the recording.<br>The speaker varies tone and pace consistently and effectively. |
| 2 | The podcast mostly focuses on the question.<br>The flow of ideas is fairly logical and mostly easy to follow. | The voice on the recording may vary but is mostly audible.<br>The podcast file has a logical title. | The speaker's voice is mostly clear and sufficiently loud for the recording.<br>The speaker varies tone and pace to some extent. |
| 1 | The podcast has no clear focus.<br>The flow of ideas is illogical and difficult to follow. | The voice on the recording sometimes fades in and out.<br>The podcast file lacks a meaningful title. | The speaker mumbles or speaks too quickly or quietly.<br>The speaker does not vary tone and pace. |





DIGITAL PERSPECTIVES

**Illuminating the Standard** To help students understand what an effective media presentation sounds like, find examples on the Internet of informational podcasts. Play the examples for the class, and have students note the techniques that make each speaker successful. For example, point out pacing, tone, clarity in voice, and so on. Suggest that students listen to their podcasts prior to presenting them to the class so that they can incorporate some of the elements in the examples you have introduced.

## Reflect on the Unit

Now that you've completed the unit, take a few moments to reflect on your learning. Use the questions below to think about where you succeeded, what skills and strategies helped you, and where you can continue to grow in the future.

### Reflect on the Unit Goals

Look back at the goals at the beginning of the unit. Use a different colored pen to rate yourself again. Think about readings and activities that contributed the most to the growth of your understanding. Record your thoughts.

### Reflect on the Learning Strategies

**Discuss It** Write a reflection on whether you were able to improve your learning based on your Action Plans. Think about what worked, what didn't, and what you might do to keep working on these strategies. Record your ideas before a class discussion.

### Reflect on the Text

Choose a selection that you found challenging, and explain what made it difficult.

Explain something that surprised you about a text in the unit.

Which activity taught you the most about power, protest, and change? What did you learn?

SCAN FOR MULTIMEDIA



STANDARDS

**Speaking and Listening**
Come to discussions prepared, having read and researched material under study; explicitly draw on that preparation by referring to evidence from texts and other research on the topic or issue to stimulate a thoughtful, well-reasoned exchange of ideas.



DIGITAL PERSPECTIVES

## Reflect on the Unit

### Reflect on the Unit Goals

Students should reevaluate how well they met the unit goals now that they have completed the unit. You might ask them to provide a written commentary on the goal they made the most progress with as well as the goal they feel warrants continued focus.

### Reflect on the Learning Strategies

**Discuss It** If you want to make this a Discussion Board activity, create a discussion prompt. Go to Pearson Realize™, navigate to your Class, and click the Discuss tab. Then, create the activity. Type in the prompt from this student page, or create your own prompt. Assign the Discussion Board prompt. Alternatively, students can share their learning strategies reflection in a class discussion.

### Reflect on the Text

Consider having students share their text reflections with one another.

**MAKE IT INTERACTIVE**

Have students prepare one slide, using presentation software, that summarizes their reflection.

Collate student slides into a presentation that can be viewed by the class. Students should be prepared to give a thirty-second oral summary of their slide.

### Unit Assessment and Remediation

After students have completed the Performance-Based Assessment, administer the Unit Test. Based on students' performance on the test, assign the resources as indicated on the Interpretation Guide to remediate. Students who take the test online will be automatically assigned remediation, as warranted by test results.

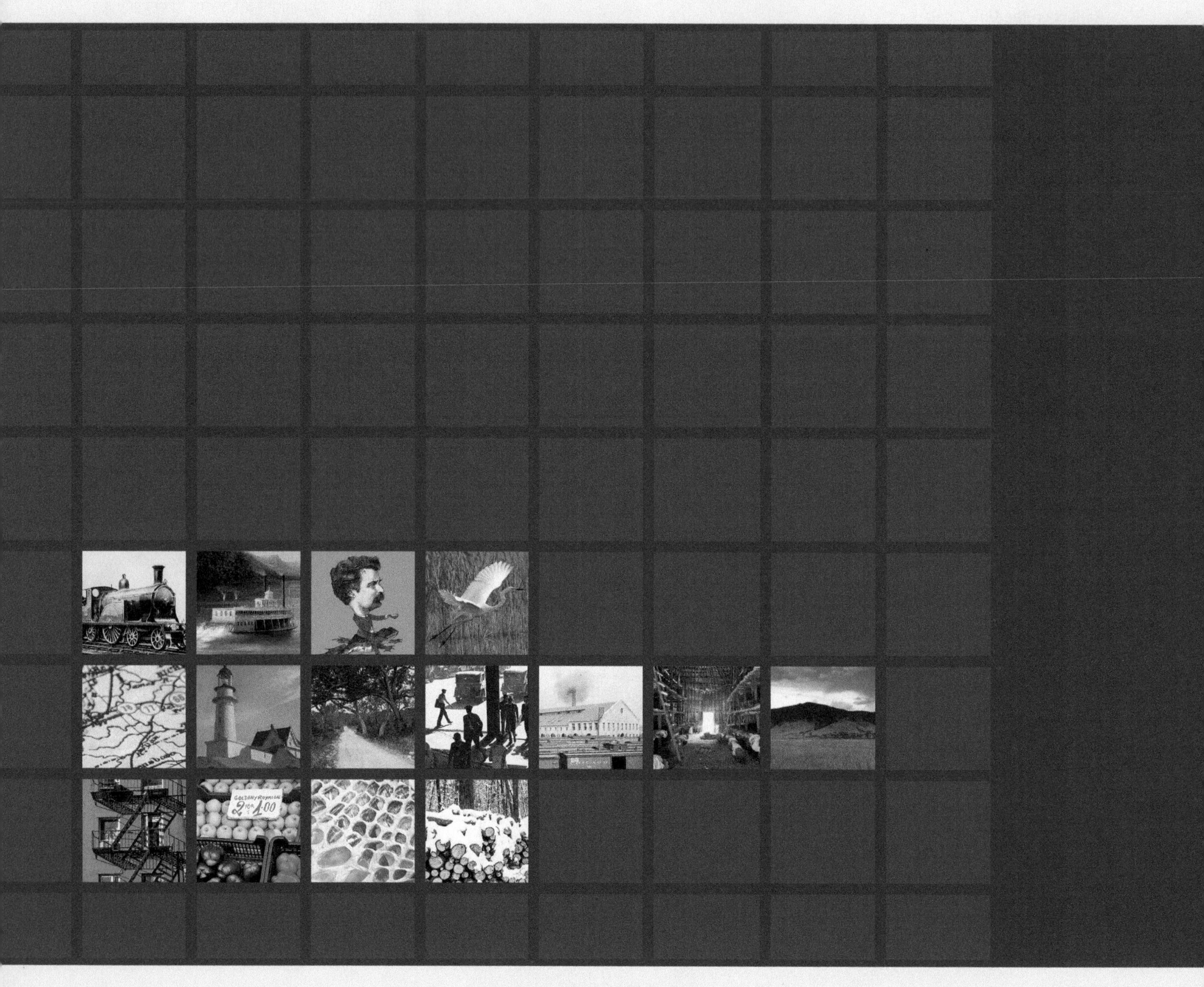

UNIT

# Grit and Grandeur

## The Importance of Place

# INTRODUCTION

## Jump Start

Ask students to imagine an uncut diamond that was formed by unbelievable pressure deep below the surface of the planet—it's rough and unimpressive, indistinguishable from a piece of clear beach glass. Then have them compare that diamond to a cut and polished stone, brilliant with flashing rainbows reflected off all its facets. One could say that a diamond possesses both grit and grandeur. Ask students to name other things that exemplify grit and grandeur.

## Grit and Grandeur

Ask students what the phrase ***grit*** and ***grandeur*** suggests to them. Point out that as they work through this unit, they will read many examples about places that can be described with the words grit and grandeur.

## Video

Project the introduction video in class, ask students to open the video in their interactive textbooks, or have students scan the BouncePage icon with their phones to access the video.

**Discuss It** If you want to make this a digital activity, go online and navigate to the Discussion Board. Alternatively, students can share their responses in a class discussion.

### Block Scheduling

Each day in this pacing calendar represents a 40–50 minute class period. Teachers using block scheduling may combine days to reflect their class schedule. In addition, teachers may revise pacing to differentiate and support core instruction by integrating components and resources as students require.

UNIT 4

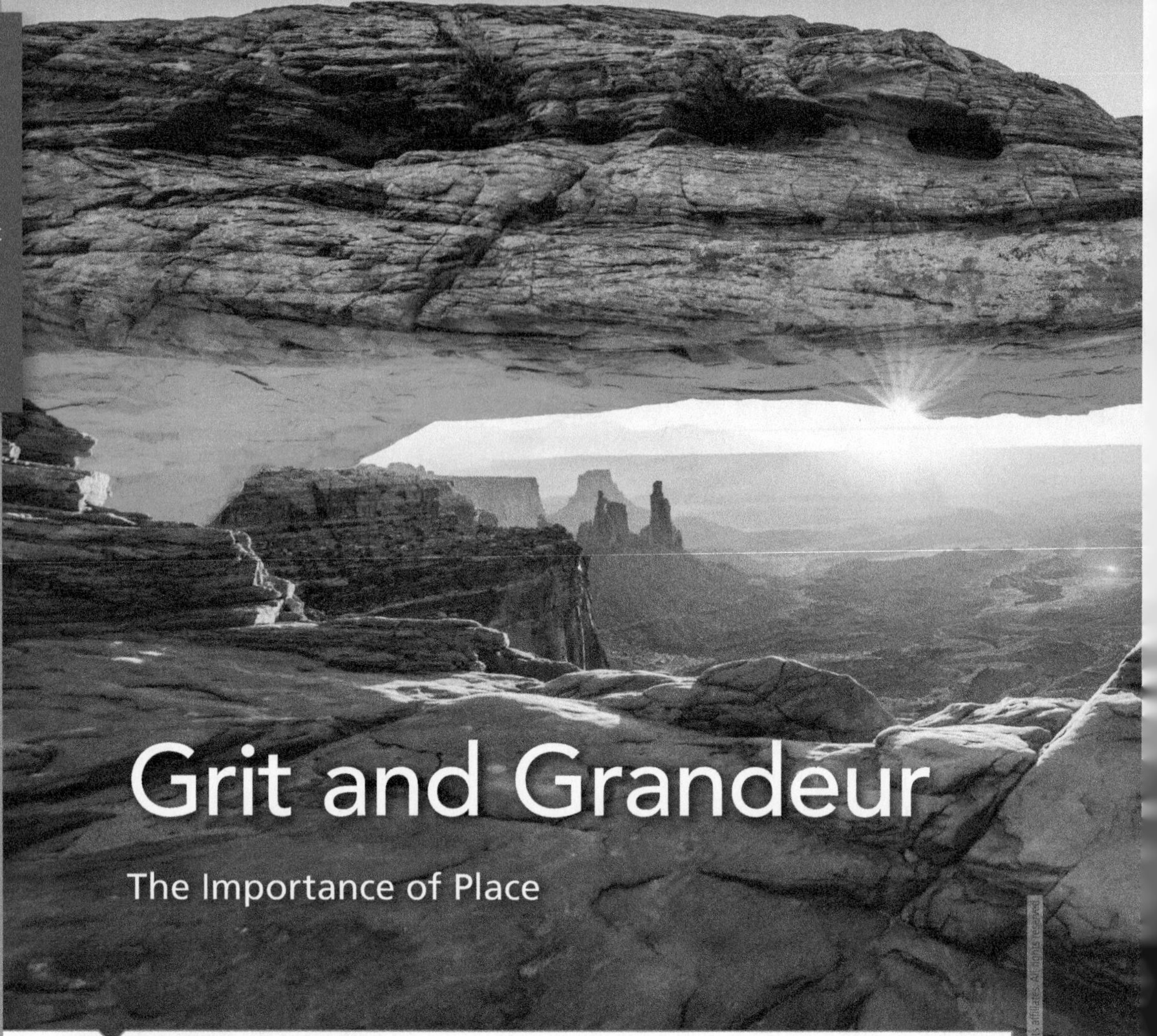

# Grit and Grandeur

## The Importance of Place

Ken Burns: Secrets of Yellowstone National Park

**Discuss It** Have you ever experienced a feeling of being changed by a place you visited? Describe what triggered the feeling.

Write your response before sharing your ideas.

SCAN FOR MULTIMEDIA



## Pacing Plan

| Day | Activity |
|---|---|
| 1 | Unit Introduction |
| 2 | Introduce Whole-Class Learning |
| 3 | Historical Perspectives |
| 4–6 | *from* Life on the Mississippi |
| 7–9 | The Notorious Jumping Frog of Calaveras County |
| 10–13 | A White Heron |
| 14–15 | Performance Task |

 Audio  Video  Document  Annotation Highlights  EL Highlights  Online Assessment

UNIT 4

**UNIT INTRODUCTION**

ESSENTIAL QUESTION: What is the relationship between literature and place?

LAUNCH TEXT
EXPLANATORY MODEL
Planning Your Trip to Gold Country

**WHOLE-CLASS LEARNING**

HISTORICAL PERSPECTIVES
*Focus Period: 1880–1920*
Bright Horizons, Challenging Realities

COMPARE

ANCHOR TEXT: MEMOIR
*from* Life on the Mississippi
*Mark Twain*
▸ MEDIA CONNECTION: Mark Twain and Tom Sawyer

ANCHOR TEXT: SHORT STORY
The Notorious Jumping Frog of Calaveras County
*Mark Twain*

ANCHOR TEXT: SHORT STORY
A White Heron
*Sarah Orne Jewett*

PERFORMANCE TASK
WRITING FOCUS:
Write an Explanatory Essay

**SMALL-GROUP LEARNING**

COMPARE

LITERARY CRITICISM
A Literature of Place
*Barry Lopez*

MEDIA: FINE ART GALLERY
American Regional Art

AUTOBIOGRAPHY
*from* Dust Tracks on a Road
*Zora Neale Hurston*

COMPARE

POETRY COLLECTION 1
Chicago
Wilderness
*Carl Sandburg*
▸ MEDIA CONNECTION: Carl Sandburg Reads "Wilderness"

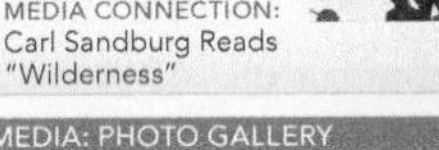

MEDIA: PHOTO GALLERY
Sandburg's Chicago

COMPARE

POETRY COLLECTION 2
In the Longhouse, Oneida Museum
*Roberta Hill*
Cloudy Day
*Jimmy Santiago Baca*

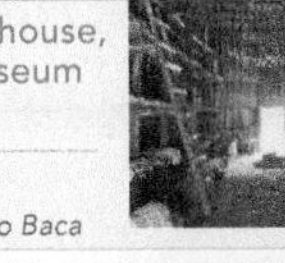

MEMOIR
Introduction *from* The Way to Rainy Mountain
*N. Scott Momaday*

PERFORMANCE TASK
SPEAKING AND LISTENING FOCUS:
Give an Explanatory Talk

**INDEPENDENT LEARNING**

SHORT STORY
The Rockpile
*James Baldwin*

POETRY
The Latin Deli: An Ars Poetica
*Judith Ortiz Cofer*

ESSAY
Untying the Knot
*Annie Dillard*

POETRY COLLECTION 3
The Wood-Pile
Birches
*Robert Frost*

PERFORMANCE-BASED ASSESSMENT PREP
Review Evidence for an Explanatory Essay

**PERFORMANCE-BASED ASSESSMENT**

Explanatory Text: Essay and Oral Presentation

PROMPT: What makes certain places live on in our memory?

393



## What is the relationship between literature and place?

Introduce the Essential Question and point out that students will respond to related prompts.

- **Whole-Class Learning** *How do American authors use regional details to make the events and themes of a narrative come to life for readers?*
- **Small-Group Learning** *Are the texts all inspired by a childhood sense of place, or are there other sources of inspiration, whether real or symbolic?*
- **Performance-Based Assessment** *What makes certain places live on in our memory?*

### Using Trade Books

Refer to the Teaching with Trade Books section in the Interactive Teacher's Edition for suggestions on how to incorporate the following thematically-related novels into this unit.

- *The Grapes of Wrath* by John Steinbeck
- *A Tale of Two Cities* by Charles Dickens
- *Dubliners* by James Joyce

### Current Perspectives

To increase student engagement, search online for stories about the importance of place, and invite students to recommend stories they find. Always preview content before sharing it with your class.

- **Interactive Map: "Mark Twain's America: Places Important In the Life of Samuel Langhorne Clemens," (Google MyMaps)** Explore the vast travels of Mark Twain.
- **Article: "A Historical Perspective of Robert Frost at the Derry, NH farm," (Robert Frost Farm)** Robert Frost's farm played a vital role in the poet's life.

Introduce Small-Group Learning

- 16: Introduce Small-Group Learning
- 17: A Literature of Place
- 18: Media: American Regional Art
- 19–20: *from* Dust Tracks on a Road
- 21: Poetry Collection 1
- 22: Media: Sandburg's Chicago
- 23–24: Poetry Collection 2
- 25: Introduction *from* The Way to Rainy Mountain
- 26: Performance Task
- 27: Introduce Independent Learning
- 28: Independent Learning
- 29–30: Performance-Based Assessment

# INTRODUCTION

## About the Unit Goals

These unit goals were backward designed from the Performance-Based Assessment at the end of the unit and the Whole-Class and Small-Group Performance Tasks. Students will practice and become proficient in many more standards over the course of this unit.

## Unit Goals

Review the goals with students and explain that as they read and discuss the selections in this unit, they will improve in reading, writing, research, language, and speaking and listening.

- Have students watch the video on Goal Setting.
- A video on this topic is available online in the Professional Development Center.

**Reading Goals** Tell students they will read and evaluate an explanatory essay. They will also read poetry, short stories, and a memoir to better understand the ways writers express ideas.

**Writing and Research Goals** Tell students that they will learn the elements of writing an explanatory text. They will also write their own explanatory text and include organizing and sharing ideas, reflecting on experiences, and gathering evidence. They will also conduct research.

**Language Goal** Tell students that they will develop a deeper understanding of effective style choices. They will then practice making choices regarding sentence variety, figurative language, and diction in their own writing.

**Speaking and Listening Goals** Explain to students that they will work together to build on ideas and communicate with one another. They will also learn to incorporate audio, visuals, and text in presentations.

### HOME Connection

A Home Connection letter to students' parents or guardians is available in the Interactive Teacher's Edition. The letter explains what students will be learning in this unit and how they will be assessed.



## Unit Goals

Throughout this unit, you will deepen your perspective on the importance of place by reading, writing, speaking, listening, and presenting. These goals will help you succeed on the Unit Performance-Based Assessment.

Rate how well you meet these goals right now. You will revisit your ratings later when you reflect on your growth during this unit.

SCALE: 1 NOT AT ALL WELL — 2 NOT VERY WELL — 3 SOMEWHAT WELL — 4 VERY WELL — 5 EXTREMELY WELL

| READING GOALS | 1 | 2 | 3 | 4 | 5 |
|---|---|---|---|---|---|
| • Read a variety of texts to gain the knowledge and insight needed to write about the importance of place. | O | O | O | O | O |
| • Expand your knowledge and use of academic and concept vocabulary. | O | O | O | O | O |
| **WRITING AND RESEARCH GOALS** | **1** | **2** | **3** | **4** | **5** |
| • Write an explanatory text that develops a topic thoroughly and includes evidence from research. | O | O | O | O | O |
| • Conduct research projects of various lengths to explore a topic and clarify meaning. | O | O | O | O | O |
| **LANGUAGE GOALS** | **1** | **2** | **3** | **4** | **5** |
| • Make effective style choices, including those regarding sentence variety, figurative language, and diction. | O | O | O | O | O |
| • Correctly use dashes and hyphens. | O | O | O | O | O |
| **SPEAKING AND LISTENING GOALS** | **1** | **2** | **3** | **4** | **5** |
| • Collaborate with your team to build on the ideas of others, develop consensus, and communicate. | O | O | O | O | O |
| • Integrate audio, visuals, and text to present information. | O | O | O | O | O |

**STANDARDS**

**Language**

Acquire and use accurately general academic and domain-specific words and phrases, sufficient for reading, writing, speaking, and listening at the college and career readiness level; demonstrate independence in gathering vocabulary knowledge when considering a word or phrase important to comprehension or expression.



SCAN FOR MULTIMEDIA 

**AUTHOR'S PERSPECTIVE** Ernest Morrell, Ph.D.

**Taking Responsibility for Learning** Teachers can talk to students about becoming motivated learners. Start by having students reflect on things they are good at outside of class, such as sports, music, and video games. Then have students think about how they take responsibility for their own achievement in these areas, such as having the discipline to practice. Help students further understand the value of becoming independent learners by providing tips on how to do so, such as these:

1. **Be self-motivated and persistent.** Don't be discouraged when faced with minor set-backs.
2. **Develop effective time management skills.** Track assignments and deadlines.
3. **Seek help when necessary.** Don't be afraid to get assistance when you need it.
4. **Set realistic goals.** Then plan ways to achieve your goals.
5. **Believe in yourself.** Visualize success. Recognize that you have the ability to soar.

DIGITAL PERSPECTIVES 

## Academic Vocabulary: Explanatory Text

Understanding and using academic terms can help you read, write, and speak with precision and clarity. Here are five academic words that will be useful in this unit as you analyze and write explanatory texts.

**Complete the chart.**

1. Review each word, its root, and the mentor sentences.
2. Use the information and your own knowledge to predict the meaning of each word.
3. For each word, list at least two related words.
4. Refer to a dictionary or other resources if needed.

TIP

FOLLOW THROUGH
Study the words in this chart, and mark them or their forms wherever they appear in the unit.

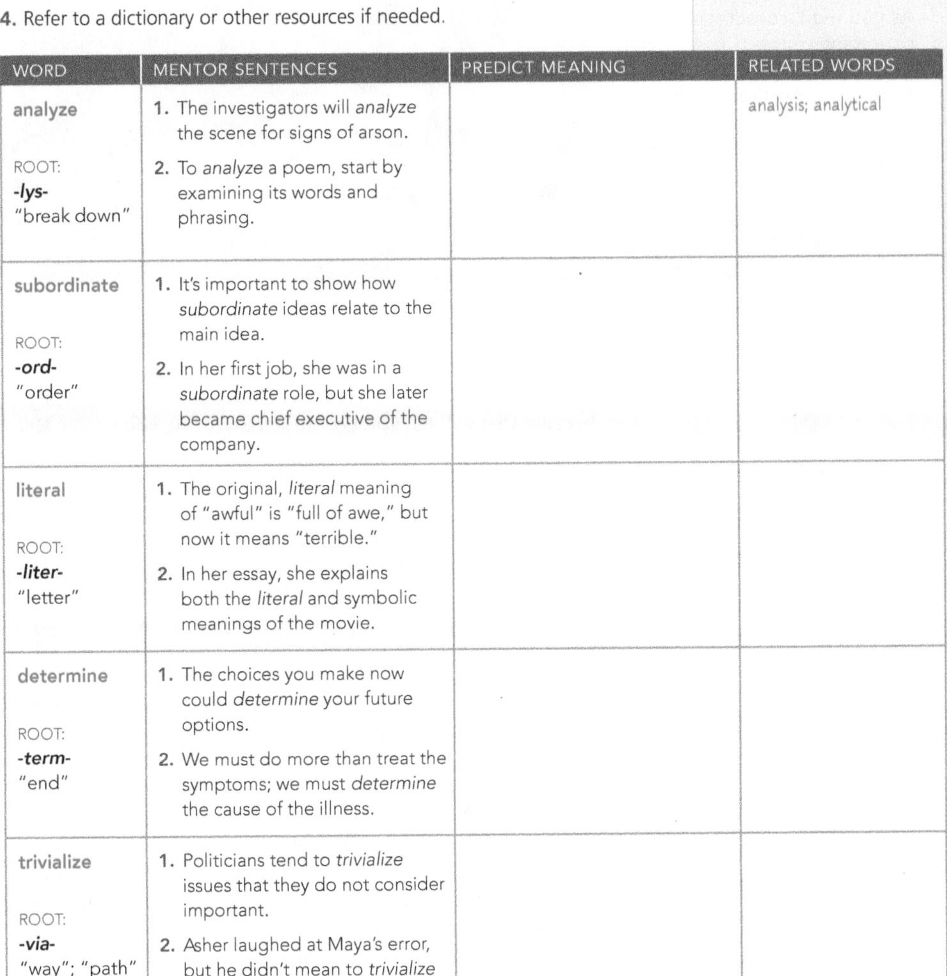

| WORD | MENTOR SENTENCES | PREDICT MEANING | RELATED WORDS |
|---|---|---|---|
| **analyze**<br>ROOT:<br>**-*lys*-**<br>"break down" | 1. The investigators will *analyze* the scene for signs of arson.<br>2. To *analyze* a poem, start by examining its words and phrasing. | | analysis; analytical |
| **subordinate**<br>ROOT:<br>**-*ord*-**<br>"order" | 1. It's important to show how *subordinate* ideas relate to the main idea.<br>2. In her first job, she was in a *subordinate* role, but she later became chief executive of the company. | | |
| **literal**<br>ROOT:<br>**-*liter*-**<br>"letter" | 1. The original, *literal* meaning of "awful" is "full of awe," but now it means "terrible."<br>2. In her essay, she explains both the *literal* and symbolic meanings of the movie. | | |
| **determine**<br>ROOT:<br>**-*term*-**<br>"end" | 1. The choices you make now could *determine* your future options.<br>2. We must do more than treat the symptoms; we must *determine* the cause of the illness. | | |
| **trivialize**<br>ROOT:<br>**-*via*-**<br>"way"; "path" | 1. Politicians tend to *trivialize* issues that they do not consider important.<br>2. Asher laughed at Maya's error, but he didn't mean to *trivialize* her struggle. | | |





## Academic Vocabulary: Explanatory Text

Introduce the blue academic vocabulary words in the chart on the student page. Point out that the root of each word provides a clue to its meaning. Discuss the mentor sentences to ensure students understand each word's usage. Students should also use the mentor sentences as context to help them predict the meaning of each word. Check that students are able to fill the chart in correctly. Complete pronunciations, parts of speech, and definitions are provided for you. Students are only expected to provide the definition.

**Possible responses:**

analyze *v.* (AN uh lyz)
**Meaning:** to examine carefully and in detail
**Related words:** analysis, analytica
**Additional words related to root *-lys-*:** analysis, dialysis

subordinate *adj.* (suh BAWR duh niht)
**Meaning:** having less importance
**Related words:** subordination; insubordinate
**Additional words related to root *-ord-*:** inordinate, ordinary

literal *adj.* (LIHT uhr uhl)
**Meaning:** true to fact; not exaggerated
**Related word:** literally
**Additional words related to root *-liter-*:** literary, illiterate

determine *v.* (dih TUR muhn)
**Meaning:** to decide; to find out the exact cause or reason
**Related word:** determined
**Additional words related to root *-term-*:** terminal, indeterminate

trivialize *v.* (TRIHV ee uh lyz)
**Meaning:** not important
**Related Words:** trivia, trival
**Additional words related to root *-via-*:** deviant; devious, obvious, voyage, viaduct

### PERSONALIZE FOR LEARNING

**English Language Support**
**Cognates** Many of the academic words have Spanish cognates. Use these cognates with students whose home language is Spanish.
**ALL LEVELS**

analyze – analizar
subordinate – subordinar
literal – literal
determine – determinar
trivialize – trivializar

## Purpose of the Launch Text

The Launch Text provides students with a common starting point to address the unit topic. After reading the Launch Text, all students will be able to participate in discussions about grit and grandeur.

**Lexile: 1220** The easier reading level of this selection makes it perfect to assign for homework. Students will need little or no support to understand it.

Additionally, Planning Your Trip to Gold Country provides a writing model for the Performance-Based Assessment students will complete at the end of the unit.

## Launch Text: Explanatory Text Model

Remind students to determine the main point of the explanatory text from the title and the introduction. They should note that the author uses the words *first* and *second* in the beginning of sentences describing key decisions. Then discuss the details that the author suggests could help make these key decisions. Students should mention maps and specific activities, such as museum visits and historical re-enactments.

You may choose to have students read this selection on their own. Encourage students to annotate unfamiliar words and sections of text they think are particularly important.

### AUDIO SUMMARIES

Audio summaries of "Planning Your Trip to Gold Country" are available online in both English and Spanish in the Interactive Teacher's Edition or Unit Resources. Assigning these summaries before students read the Launch Text may help them build additional background knowledge and set a context for their reading.



LAUNCH TEXT | EXPLANATORY TEXT

This selection is an example of an **explanatory text**, a type of writing in which the author explores the complexities of a topic, describes how to accomplish a task, or details how a process works. This is the type of writing you will develop in the Performance-Based Assessment at the end of the unit.

**As you read,** consider how each paragraph connects to the ideas presented in the introduction. Mark examples that the author provides to show the different types of trips a reader might undertake.

# Planning Your Trip to Gold Country

NOTES

1 Before you set off to explore California's Gold Country, you must make two key decisions: Choose the length of your trip, and determine the sort of explorer you are. First, decide the length of your trip, because that will tell you how much exploring you will be able to do. A map of the Sierra Nevada foothills will show you at a glance that Gold Country, the area where most of the California Gold Rush took place, extends from the Tahoe National Forest to the area around Lake Isabella, nearly 400 miles south. Second, decide what kind of explorer you are. Do you prefer museum-hopping and sightseeing, or do you want to get your hands dirty and find out what it was like to be a gold-seeker in the 1840s? Would you like to see history reenacted, or do you want to see the natural beauty of this special region?

2 If you have just a short time to spend in Gold Country, consider visiting the historic highlights. California's capital city, Sacramento, was founded in 1848 by John Sutter, Jr., a major Gold Rush figure. You may still visit the fort he built there and take a walking tour through streets lined with restored nineteenth-century buildings, departing on your tour from the excellent and informative Sacramento History Museum. From Sacramento, it's just an hour's drive north to Coloma, a tiny village along the sparkling American River. Coloma is home to Marshall Gold Discovery Park, which offers visitors dozens of activities that allow them to explore the history of the Gold Rush. Coloma is a must-see, because it is the very first place where gold was found in the Sierra Nevada foothills.





SCAN FOR MULTIMEDIA

## PERSONALIZE FOR LEARNING

### English Language Support

**Transitional Words** Tell students to keep a list of words and phrases that indicate a sequence of ideas. (paragraphs 1 and 2) Have them begin their lists with the words *first* and *second*. Then have students think of non-numerical words to add to their lists, such as *next*, *earlier*, and *afterward*. **BRIDGING**

3 If you have more time to spend and are eager for adventure, consider the trip my brother and I made last year. We drove from Coloma south to Jamestown along historic Highway 49. Stunned by the beautiful views, we enjoyed every mile. As we wound through hills and valleys dotted with wildflower meadows and piñon pines, we could imagine would-be miners on horses and in wagons making their way through the same landscape 165 years ago.

4 Jamestown boasts a number of businesses that allow you to take pans, trowels, and boots into the American River and test your ability to find gold. Sam and I found nothing but iron pyrite, the "fool's gold" that deceived many a Forty-Niner, but we had a thrilling time in the chilly water under a stark, blue sky. Searching Jamestown sites on the Internet will turn up a variety of tours and gold-prospecting adventures, and you can choose the one that best matches your needs.

5 Nature lovers should not pass up the opportunity to visit Yosemite, the world's first national park. The history of the region is a sad one; the spectacular Yosemite Valley was home to the native Ahwahnechee people before the influx of miners displaced them in the 1850s. Miners tore holes in the stately mountains and despoiled the clear water of the rivers until Abraham Lincoln signed a grant to preserve this territory for all time. Since that time, Yosemite's soaring cliffs and turbulent waterfalls have remained unique among American landscapes.

6 Start with a map and a schedule, and plan to spend at least a day at each major stop. Use the Internet to build your trip step by step, choosing the activities that suit your interests and fit into your timetable. There is plenty to do in Gold Country, no matter what kind of traveler you happen to be. Every acre of the region offers magnificent vistas and living tableaus of a significant era in American history.

NOTES

### WORD NETWORK FOR GRIT AND GRANDEUR

**Vocabulary** A word network is a collection of words related to a topic. As you read the unit selections, identify words related to *landscape*, and add them to your Word Network. For example, you might begin by adding words from the Launch Text, such as *foothills*. For each word you add, note a related word, such as a synonym or an antonym. Continue to add words as you complete this unit.

LANDSCAPE

foothills | peaks

**Tool Kit** Word Network Model





DIGITAL PERSPECTIVES

## Word Network for Grit and Grandeur

Tell students that they can fill in the Word Network as they read the texts in the unit, or they can jot down the words elsewhere and add them later. Point out to students that people may have personal associations with some words. A word that one student thinks is related to the concept of grit and grandeur might not be a word another student would pick. However, students should feel free to add any relevant words to their Word Network. Each person's Word Network will be unique. If you choose to print the Word Network, distribute it to students at this point so they can use it throughout the rest of the unit.

AUTHOR'S PERSPECTIVE **Elfrieda Hiebert, Ph.D.**

**Words in Complex Texts** Reassure students that complex texts will always have some words that they haven't encountered before. This point needs to be reviewed year after year because the texts always get harder, and with harder texts come more complex words. Share these ideas with students:

- Many words will be familiar, but they may be used in a different way with new topics and meanings.
- Authors choose the more complex words (the rare words) for deliberate effect—not serendipitously—to describe characters and contexts, to develop obstacles or problems, to show ways of solving problems.

Making and reviewing word networks helps students develop multiple words related to a concept and multiple meanings or concept applications for words. Also encourage students to study the words in context. Students may wish to use digital tools as they do so.

# INTRODUCTION

## Summary

Have students read the introductory paragraph. Provide them with tips for writing a summary:

- Write in the present tense.
- Make sure to include the title of the work.
- Be concise: a summary should not be equal in length to the original text.
- If you need to quote the words of the author, use quotation marks.
- Don't put your own opinions, ideas, or interpretations into the summary. The purpose of writing a summary is to accurately represent what the author says, not to provide a critique.

If necessary, students can refer to the Tool Kit for help in understanding the elements of a good summary.

**See possible summary on student page.**

## Launch Activity

Tell students that they will have many opportunities to discuss grit and grandeur as they work through this unit. Discuss with them the meaning of the words *grit* and *grandeur*, and have them locate examples from the launch text that relate to each of these terms. Examples include *beautiful views* that the author mentions as grandeur, and the history of mining as an example of grit.



## Summary

Write a summary of "Planning Your Trip to Gold Country." A **summary** is a concise, complete, and accurate overview of a text. It should not include a statement of your opinion or an analysis.

**Possible response:** In "Planning Your Trip to Gold Country," the author explains what must be done to explore locations where the Gold Rush took place in California. The author tells readers that they must first determine the length of their trip. Then they must decide on the type of trip they want to take—visiting historic highlights or experiencing the activities that Gold Rushers actually engaged in. The author describes sites in Sacramento, including the fort John Sutter built and the Sacramento History Museum. From Sacramento, the author encourages readers to drive north to Coloma, where gold was first discovered. For those more interested in hands-on activities, the author recommends taking a drive on Highway 49 and visiting Jamestown. Once there, explorers can panhandle for gold in the nearby American River. A visit to Yosemite is the final location on any visitor's trip to Gold Country.

## Launch Activity

**"How-to" Local Tourism** The Launch Text explains how to tour Gold Country in California. Work with 4–6 classmates to create a parallel explanation relating to a place of interest in your community.

- Imagine that someone who lives in a distant place is coming for a visit. Brainstorm for a list of attractions in your area that you think the visitor should see.
- Narrow the list to three "top stops." They can be connected by a theme (such as historical importance) or be varied (such as a sports venue, a restaurant, a farm, and a museum).
- Plan an itinerary for your visitor. Share ideas about the best way to get from each stop to the next. More important, share "how-to" ideas that will help the visitor get the most out of each stop.
- Meet with another group, and compare notes. Are any stops on both lists? If so, what "how-tos" do they share?





### PERSONALIZE FOR LEARNING

**Strategic Support**

**Vocabulary Development** Ask students to look up the definitions and two synonyms for the following vocabulary words that appear later in this unit: *picturesque* (paragraph 3), *vista* (paragraph 6), and *tableau* (paragraph 6). Ask if any of these words also appear in their word networks. Do any of their synonyms appear?

## QuickWrite

Consider class discussions, the video, and the Launch Text as you think about the prompt. Record your first thoughts here.

PROMPT: **What makes certain places live on in our memory?**

**Possible response:** The places that live on in our memory are the places that we associate with strong emotions. Emotions, both good and bad, make memories stronger.

In "Planning Your Trip to Gold Country," the author describes a road trip down Highway 49 and panning for gold in Jamestown. Because those events were so much fun, memories of those two locations are very strong.

When I was young, I was fishing with my grandfather. I fell off the pier and into the water. I wasn't in any real danger — I knew how to swim, and there were plenty of swimmers around me. Nonetheless, I was very scared. Now, 12 years later, I can recall every detail of the beach and the pier. The strong emotion I felt seared the place into my memory.

### EVIDENCE LOG FOR GRIT AND GRANDEUR

Review your QuickWrite. Summarize your thoughts in one sentence to record in your Evidence Log. Then, record evidence from "Planning Your Trip to Gold Country" that supports your thesis.

After each selection, you will continue to use your Evidence Log to record the evidence you gather and the connections you make. The graphic shows what your Evidence Log looks like.

**Tool Kit**
Evidence Log Model

Title of Text: ______ Date: ______

| CONNECTION TO PROMPT | TEXT EVIDENCE/DETAILS | ADDITIONAL NOTES/IDEAS |
| --- | --- | --- |
| | | |

How does this text change or add to my thinking? Date: ______

SCAN FOR MULTIMEDIA



DIGITAL PERSPECTIVES

## QuickWrite

In this QuickWrite, students should present their own answer to the question based on the material in the Unit Opener. This initial response will help inform their work when they complete the Performance-Based Assessment at the end of the unit. Students should make sure they clearly introduce a topic, develop it thoroughly by including relevant facts, examples, and definitions, and provide a concluding statement.

**See possible QuickWrite on student page.**

## Evidence Log for Grit and Grandeur

Students should record their initial ideas in their Evidence Logs. Then, they should record evidence from "Planning Your Trip to Gold Country" that supports their initial thinking.

If you choose to print the Evidence Log, distribute it to students at this point so they can use it throughout the rest of the unit.

### Performance-Based Assessment: Refining Your Thinking

- Have students watch the video on Refining Your Thinking.
- A video on this topic is available online in the Professional Development Center.

## PERSONALIZE FOR LEARNING

### English Language Support

**Understanding Context** Suggest that students research the California Gold Rush so they can understand related terms used in this text, such as pans and trowels, iron pyrite, and the practice of prospecting rivers for gold. (paragraph 4) Students may want to explore the impact of mining on the environment, or the relationship between the Gold Rush and state parks. Explain that understanding the context will help them visualize the setting that the author describes. **EMERGING**

# OVERVIEW

## WHOLE-CLASS LEARNING

### What is the relationship between literature and place?

The United States landscape features natural formations, such as the Grand Canyon, and human-made splendors such as the Hoover Dam. Engage students in a discussion about how both kinds of features demonstrate grit and grandeur. Ask students, "What are some memorable places you have seen?" During Whole-Class Learning, students will read selections about places of grit and of grandeur.

### Whole-Class Learning Strategies

Review the Learning Strategies with students and explain that as they work through Whole-Class Learning they will develop strategies to work in large-group environments.

- Have students watch the video on Whole-Class Learning Strategies.
- A video on this topic is available online in the Professional Development Center.

You may wish to discuss some action items to add to the chart as a class before students complete it on their own. For example, for "Monitor Understanding," suggest:

- Students, as a group, can take the time to research something that is unknown or unclear.
- Students can review all of their notes for more information.

**Block Scheduling**

Each day in this Pacing Plan represents a 40–50 minute class period. Teachers using block scheduling may combine days to reflect their class schedule. In addition, teachers may revise pacing to differentiate and support core instruction by integrating components and resources as students require.

## OVERVIEW: WHOLE-CLASS LEARNING

ESSENTIAL QUESTION:

# What is the relationship between literature and place?

As you read these selections, work with your whole class to explore the meaning and importance of the concept of "place."

**From Text to Topic** For Mark Twain, the majestic Mississippi River was a spiritual home that inspired his youthful daydreams of becoming a steamboat pilot. His writing celebrates the river's boats and bustling port towns—and the ambitions of all who were shaped by this busy place that linked America's East and West. For Sarah Orne Jewett, the Maine woods become the place where a lonely young girl learns what is most valuable to her. As you read, consider what the selections show about the importance of a sense of place in both literature and the lives of real-life Americans.

## Whole-Class Learning Strategies

Throughout your life, in school, in your community, and in your career, you will continue to learn and work in large-group environments.

Review these strategies and the actions you can take to practice them. Add ideas of your own for each step. Get ready to use these strategies during Whole-Class Learning.

| STRATEGY | ACTION PLAN |
|---|---|
| Listen actively | • Eliminate distractions. For example, put your cellphone away.<br>• Record brief notes on main ideas and points of confusion.<br>• |
| Clarify by asking questions | • If you're confused, other people probably are, too. Ask a question to help your whole class.<br>• Ask follow-up questions as needed—for example, if you do not understand the clarification or if you want to make an additional connection.<br>• |
| Monitor understanding | • Notice what information you already know, and be ready to build on it.<br>• Ask for help if you are struggling.<br>• |
| Interact and share ideas | • Share your ideas and offer answers, even if you are unsure.<br>• Build on the ideas of others by adding details or making a connection.<br>• |



SCAN FOR MULTIMEDIA



### Pacing Plan

| Day | Activity |
|---|---|
| 1 | Unit Introduction |
| 2 | Introduce Whole-Class Learning |
| 3 | Historical Perspectives |
| 4–6 | *from* Life on the Mississippi |
| 7–9 | The Notorious Jumping Frog of Calaveras County |
| 10–13 | A White Heron |
| 14–15 | Performance Task |

WHOLE-CLASS LEARNING

DIGITAL PERSPECTIVES

## CONTENTS

HISTORICAL PERSPECTIVES

Focus Period: 1880–1920

### Bright Horizons, Challenging Realities

The decades framing the turn of the century saw America expand across the continent and become an empire. Americans celebrated their country's strengths and looked for solutions to new problems.

COMPARE

ANCHOR TEXT: MEMOIR

### *from* Life on the Mississippi

*Mark Twain*

A boy who has grown up by the Mississippi River reveals his greatest wish.

▸ MEDIA CONNECTION: Mark Twain and Tom Sawyer

ANCHOR TEXT: SHORT STORY

### The Notorious Jumping Frog of Calaveras County

*Mark Twain*

Simon Wheeler tells a riotous tale—but is it true?

ANCHOR TEXT: SHORT STORY

### A White Heron

*Sarah Orne Jewett*

Torn between conflicting longings, a young girl instinctively protects the innocent.

PERFORMANCE TASK

WRITING FOCUS

### Write an Explanatory Essay

The Whole-Class readings celebrate some of the diverse landscapes that influence America's literature and sense of identity. After reading, you will create an explanatory text about the role that setting plays in these selections.





## Contents

**Anchor Texts** Preview the anchor texts with students to generate interest. Encourage students to discuss other texts they may have read or movies or television shows they may have seen that deal with the issues of the world's grit and grandeur.

You may wish to conduct a poll to determine which selection students think looks more interesting, and discuss the reasons for their preference. Students can return to this poll after they have read the selections to see if their preference changed.

## Performance Task

**Write an Explanatory Essay** Explain to students that after they have finished reading the selections, they will write an explanatory essay about influence of setting in the lives and work of American writers. To help them prepare, encourage students to think about the topic as they progress through the selections and as they participate in the Whole-Class Learning experience.

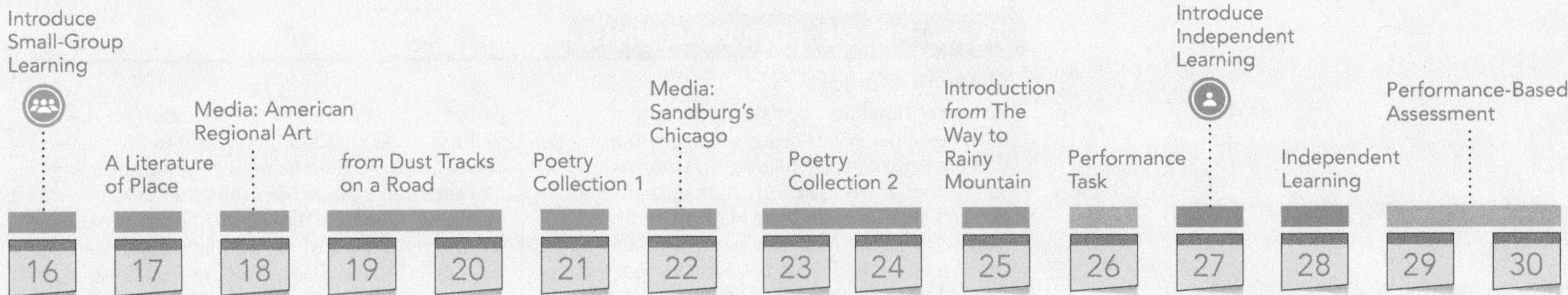

## HISTORICAL PERSPECTIVES

### Bright Horizons, Challenging Realities

This section analyzes the key events of the Focus Period: the disappearance of America's frontier, government regulation of railroads, movement of Native Americans onto reservations, electricity's effect on industry, the Gilded Age, Jim Crow laws, immigration policies, the transition from farm life to urbanization, American imperialism, and World War I. Have students connect these key events with the unit topic.

### Voices of the Period

You may wish to have individual students read these excerpts aloud, or have the group read them together. Ask students how each quotation relates to the sense of place expressed by someone of a different region or cultural background. Then have groups discuss this question: *How might a person's life experiences affect his or her reactions to change?*

### History of the Period

The movement of people was an important issue during the period 1880–1920. Some people moved from farms to cities, following the jobs that opened up with industrialization. Other people moved from their homelands to America, looking for new opportunities. Finally, some people were denied the right to move, or were moved against their wills. Ask students why they think the place where someone lives was and still is of such importance.



# Bright Horizons, Challenging Realities

## Voices of the Period

*"A wee child toddling in a wonder world, I prefer to their dogma my excursions into the natural gardens where the voice of the Great Spirit is heard in the twittering of birds, the rippling of mighty waters, and the sweet breathing of flowers."*

—Zitkala-Ša, author and Native American activist

*"The great city can teach something that no university by itself can altogether impart: a vivid sense of the largeness of human brotherhood; a vivid sense of man's increasing obligation to man; a vivid sense of our absolute dependence on one another."*

—Seth Low, educator and politician

*"A person may encircle the globe with mind open only to bodily comfort. Another may live his life on a sixty-foot lot and listen to the voices of the universe."*

—Bess Streeter Aldrich, author

## History of the Period

**The Frontier Disappears** Even as pioneers moved to the West, the vast plains at the center of the nation remained a frontier with huge unsettled tracts of land. By 1890, however, due in large part to the explosion of railroads carrying Americans across the continent, the Census Bureau declared the frontier officially gone. Replacing the open range were farms and small towns, plowed fields, grazing lands, and miles of fences. By 1900, what once had been frontier land had become 14 new states.

**Tracks Across the Nation** At the start of the twentieth century, almost 200,000 miles of train tracks crossed the continent, turning many small towns into cities. The federal government became involved, subsidizing railroad building and granting railroad companies western land to sell. As railroad networks increased and their wealthy owners grew in power, state governments and then the federal government tried to regulate the railroad monopolies. The federal government issued the Interstate Commerce Act of 1887, the first major government regulation of private business for the benefit of public interest.

**Enclosing Native Americans** As the frontier disappeared, the Native American peoples living there were displaced by settlers, fences, and towns. These new settlements often interfered with the ways in which the Native Americans had lived for centuries. The cultures clashed and the conflicts turned into battles, sometimes referred

### TIMELINE

1880

**1882:** Congress passes the first Chinese Exclusion Act (and later renews it).

**1883:** American railroads adopt standard time zones.

**1889: France** The Eiffel Tower is completed in Paris, becoming the world's tallest structure.

**1890:** Congress establishes Yosemite National Park.

**1890:** Federal troops and Native Americans fight their last major battle at Wounded Knee, South Dakota.





## PERSONALIZE FOR LEARNING

**Strategic Support**

**Historical Timelines** Remind students that timelines show events in sequence. Point out that timelines can also be used to compare and contrast what was going on in more than one person's life at a given time. Have three or four learners of different abilities work together to create a timeline of what happened to each of them at several given times. For example, each person might illustrate or list an important event in the year 2000, 2003, 2006, and to the present, or at age 10, 12, and so on. Let groups exchange timelines and analyze how the other group members' lives were alike and different. Discuss which events showed up on multiple timelines, such as birthdays, graduations, or vacations.

## Integration of Knowledge and Ideas

**Notebook** Overall, in which two census years was the immigrant population of these cities at its height? Review the events in the photographic timeline. Which event might account for the decline in the immigrant population of San Francisco?

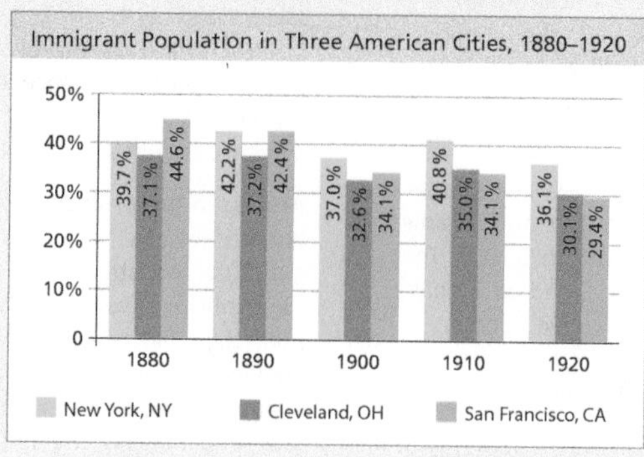


Source: U.S. Bureau of the Census

to as the Indian Wars. Against their will, whole Native American nations—totaling about 250,000 people—were moved to reservations, often far from their traditional homelands.

**The Second Industrial Revolution** The introduction of electricity in the 1880s launched a second Industrial Revolution. Americans began to enjoy electric lights, telephones, automobiles, motion pictures, and skyscrapers. Urban populations exploded as millions of immigrants arrived and people moved away from rural areas, providing cheap labor. Low wages, child labor, and disease were the norm for the working class.

**The Gilded Age** Along with the growth of industry came the accumulation of enormous fortunes in the hands of a few "robber barons"—men such as banker John Pierpont Morgan, oil magnate John D. Rockefeller, and steel titan Andrew Carnegie. Author Mark Twain coined the term "the Gilded Age," characterizing this era as having a golden and shiny surface that covered a base of corruption and greed. The energy of the nation led to change, however, as the power of monopolies inspired government regulation such as the Sherman Anti-Trust Act and political movements such as the Populist Party.



**1892:** Ellis Island opens as a receiving center for immigrants.

**1892:** A steelworkers' strike at Pennsylvania's Homestead steel mill is brutally suppressed.

**1895:** The first professional football game is played in Latrobe, Pennsylvania.

**1896:** *The Country of the Pointed Firs,* Sarah Orne Jewett's masterpiece, is published.

**1898:** France Marie and Pierre Curie discover radium and polonium.

1900



DIGITAL PERSPECTIVES

## Integration of Knowledge and Ideas

Have students analyze the data in each chart and draw conclusions to answer the two questions.

**Possible response:** The immigrant population of these cities was highest in the two census years 1880 and 1890. The immigrant population of San Francisco most likely declined after 1880 because of the Chinese Exclusion Act of 1882. The ruling prohibited Chinese citizens from relocating to America, and Congress continued to renew the law.

## Timeline

Have students examine the 1880–1920 Timeline and consider the key events. Encourage a discussion by asking students to notice major themes of growth and change that are highlighted. Use these questions to prompt a discussion: *Why might events featuring changes in technology and the rights of individuals be important? What geographic locations influenced change in America during the period?*

PERSONALIZE FOR LEARNING

### English Language Support

**Multiple-Meaning Words** Remind students that some words have more than one meaning. For example, the word *reservation* can mean "a plan to have a theater seat, hotel room, or dining table held for your use in the future," "a feeling of uncertainty or doubt about something," or "an area of land on which some Native Americans live." Direct students' attention to the word *reservations* in the paragraph labeled "Enclosing Native Americans." Have them tell which meaning is used in the sentence (*area of land*). Then ask volunteers to use *reservation* in a sentence to reflect one of the other meanings. Finally, have students find and explain the meanings of *coin(ed)*, and identify how it is used in paragraph 3. **ALL LEVELS**

# TEACHING

## History of the Period

Have students focus on the next-to-last paragraph of the text, "American Imperialism," and remind them that history is ongoing—events and attitudes from the past are connected to the present. Encourage a discussion by asking students: *How does America's continued development of new technology and economic expansion affect its relationship to the rest of the world?*

## HISTORICAL PERSPECTIVES • FOCUS PERIOD: 1880–1920

**Rise of Jim Crow** Reconstruction was meant to rebuild the South after the Civil War. However, instead of freedom and opportunity, African Americans in the South soon faced a wall of systematically enforced discrimination that came to be known as Jim Crow laws. Poll taxes and other restrictions prevented African Americans from voting, while schools and other public facilities were strictly segregated—a situation reinforced by a Supreme Court ruling that declared "separate but equal" facilities legal.

**Immigration—or Not** The "new immigrants" who arrived in America in the late 1800s came mainly from southern and eastern Europe. They flocked to New York, Chicago, and other major cities, where they congregated with others from their homelands. In general, their crowded communities were marked by harsh conditions, which some reformers sought to improve. At the same time, political bosses lobbied for immigrants' votes. A backlash of opinion grew because many native-born Americans felt threatened by the flood of cheap immigrant labor. By 1882, Congress began to pass legislation restricting the entrance of certain groups of immigrants, including a complete prohibition of immigrants from China.

**From Farm to City** By 1900, four out of ten Americans lived in urban environments. Inventions such as the elevator encouraged the building of skyscrapers, which made it possible for many more people to inhabit and work in the ever-growing metropolises of the East Coast and Midwest. Increasing urban density spawned slums, where disease and poverty were rampant. Reformers such as activist and Nobel Prize winner Jane Addams and photojournalist Jacob Riis worked to improve living conditions for the poor.

**Workers Unite** After the Civil War, American workers began to form labor unions. The new unions led workers in strikes to protest low salaries and harsh working conditions. The history of these strikes was full of setbacks and advances and outbreaks of violence. Many strikes were suppressed by the government or by business owners who hired private security firms.

**American Imperialism** As the twentieth century approached, the United States was growing as a result of industrialization and expansion across the continent. Governmental leaders, putting aside their reluctance to get involved in foreign conflicts, engaged in an international war with Spain in 1898, largely due to sympathy for an independence movement in nearby Cuba. The United States took control of the Philippines and Puerto Rico, freed Cuba from Spanish control, and annexed Hawaii. In 1901, a treaty that gave the United States the right to build a canal across the Isthmus of Panama was signed.

**The Great War** In 1914, the European Allies (the United Kingdom, France, and Russia) fought a war against the Central Powers (Germany and Austria-Hungary). Eventually Italy, Japan, the Ottoman Empire, and other nations were drawn into World War I, "the war to end all wars." The United States resisted involvement in the conflict until German attacks at sea precipitated a declaration of war in April 1917. By the war's end in November 1918, some 16 million people were dead, including more than 50,000 Americans.



### TIMELINE

1900

**1901: Italy** Guglielmo Marconi sends the first transatlantic radio telegraph message.

**1903:** The Wright brothers fly 852 feet in their airplane at Kitty Hawk, North Carolina.

**1905: Germany** Albert Einstein proposes his relativity theory.

**1906:** The Bureau of Immigration and Naturalization is established.

**1908:** The first Model T automobile is produced.

## PERSONALIZE FOR LEARNING

### English Language Support

**Connotation/Denotation** Remind students that **denotation** is the definition of a word; **connotation** is the feelings or images the word brings to mind. Connotations may be positive or negative. Provide this example: *I could describe someone by saying, "He's* tall.*" I could also say, "He's* statuesque.*" Someone else might say, "He's* gigantic.*"* The synonym *statuesque* has a positive connotation, but *gigantic* has a negative connotation.

Have students note the text labeled "American Imperialism." Explain that the denotation of *imperialism* is "the practice of stronger nations taking over weaker ones." Explain that the word's connotation is more negative—it may suggest invasions and loss of rights. Have students talk about the different meanings of *imperialism* and *colonization* and discuss which implies more negative or more positive connotations. **ALL LEVELS PI.8**

## Literature Selections

**Literature of the Focus Period** A number of the selections in this unit were written during the Focus Period and pertain to the sense of place expressed by Americans in different regions and of various cultural backgrounds:

from *Life on the Mississippi,* Mark Twain

"The Notorious Jumping Frog of Calaveras County," Mark Twain

"A White Heron," Sarah Orne Jewett

"Chicago," Carl Sandburg

"Wilderness," Carl Sandburg

"The Wood-Pile," Robert Frost

"Birches," Robert Frost

**Connections Across Time** A consideration of the importance of place both preceded and continued past the Focus Period. Indeed, it has influenced writers and commentators in many times and places.

"A Literature of Place," Barry Lopez

from *Dust Tracks on a Road*, Zora Neale Hurston

"In the Longhouse, Oneida Museum," Roberta Hill

"Cloudy Day," Jimmy Santiago Baca

Introduction from *The Way to Rainy Mountain*, N. Scott Momaday

"The Rockpile," James Baldwin

"Untying the Knot," Annie Dillard

"The Latin Deli: An Ars Poetica," Judith Ortiz Cofer

ADDITIONAL FOCUS PERIOD LITERATURE

**Student Edition**

UNIT 1
The Gettysburg Address, Abraham Lincoln

UNIT 2
The Writing of Walt Whitman

from "Nature," Ralph Waldo Emerson

from *Walden*, Henry David Thoreau

"The Love Song of J. Alfred Prufrock," T. S. Eliot

"A Wagner Matinée," Willa Cather

UNIT 3
The Poetry of Langston Hughes

from *The Warmth of Other Suns*, Isabel Wilkerson

UNIT 5
*The Crucible*, Arthur Miller

from *Farewell to Manzanar*, Jeanne Wakatsuki Houston and James D. Houston

"Antojos," Julia Alvarez

"Bears at Raspberry Time," Hayden Carruth

UNIT 6
"An Occurrence at Owl Creek Bridge," Ambrose Bierce

"The Man to Send Rain Clouds," Leslie Marmon Silko



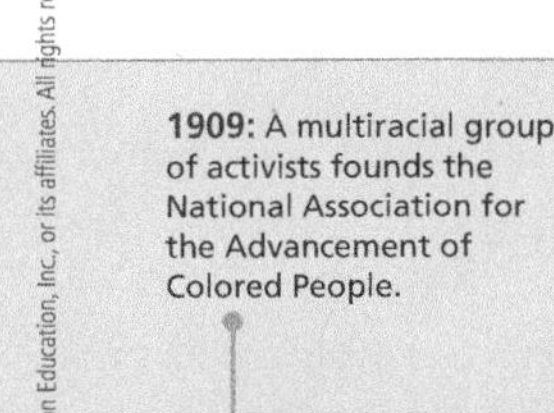

**1909:** A multiracial group of activists founds the National Association for the Advancement of Colored People.

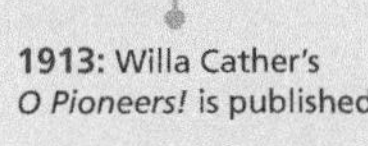

**1913:** Willa Cather's *O Pioneers!* is published.

**1914–1918:** World War I rages across Europe.

**1916:** Carl Sandburg's *Chicago Poems* is published.

**1917: Russia** Bolsheviks seize control of Russia in the October Revolution.

**1920:** The Nineteenth Amendment to the Constitution gives American women the right to vote.

1920



DIGITAL PERSPECTIVES

## Literature Selections

Have students discuss why and how place plays such an important role in literature. Guide the discussion to help students conclude that place, usually combined with events, allows authors to express their relationship to the world around them at a given moment. It speaks to the social setting and evokes an emotional response from the reader. This is true of "A White Heron," in which the author's telling of a young girl's story is wrapped in the time and place of an endangered species of bird. Point out that many titles listed on this page suggest the importance of place, telling readers in advance where things will happen and hopefully activating the mood. Have students compare and contrast the time and place revealed by the titles of different selections and discuss why these particular places might be pivotal in the focus period.

Have students review the selections in this unit organized under *Literature of the Focus Period* and *Connections Across Time*. Also point out the additional Focus Period Literature found in *myPerspectives*. Encourage them to utilize these selections for additional evidence as they complete this unit.

## Comprehension Check

Ask students to answer these questions independently and then to discuss them in a group.

1. How did the ever-increasing presence of railroads change life in the United States during the period of 1880–1920?

**Possible response:** Because of the railroads, many small towns turned into cities, bringing more people to an area. Railroad owners sold land beside the tracks that the federal government gave them, increasing their wealth and the number of settlers, fences, and towns. The land had been taken from Native Americans, who were moved onto reservations, often far from their homelands. As railroads and their owners grew in power, state and federal regulations were needed to protect citizens from business monopolies.

2. What was a result of overcrowding in cities as the populations grew very quickly during the period from 1880 to 1920?

**Possible response:** The overcrowding resulted in slum areas of dirty, run-down buildings where people suffered from widespread disease and poverty.

3. Why did many native-born Americans feel threatened by the immigration policies during the period of 1880–1920?

**Possible response:** Native-born Americans feared the abundance of immigrants who were willing to work for even less money, replacing them and leaving them unemployed.

4. What are three important events from the text or on the timeline that highlight women's achievements?

**Possible response:** Students may cite any of these events: France's Marie Curie and her husband discover radium; American activist Jane Addams works to improve living conditions for the poor; American novelist Sarah Orne Jewett's *The Country of the Pointed Firs* is published; American writer Willa Cather's *O Pioneers!* is published; The Nineteenth Amendment gives American women the right to vote.

# *from* Life on the Mississippi

**AUDIO SUMMARIES**
Audio summaries of this excerpt from *Life on the Mississippi* are available online in both English and Spanish in the Interactive Teacher's Edition or Unit Resources. Assigning these summaries prior to reading the selection may help students build additional background knowledge and set a context for their first read.

## Summary

In this excerpt from *Life on the Mississippi*, Mark Twain describes how as a youth he dreamed of being a steamboatman. He describes how his little sleepy town would come alive when a steamboat arrived. The townspeople would rush to the pier and observe the goods being removed from the ship, the sailors cleaning its floors and railings, and many other steamboat workers performing their tasks. Twain describes a young man from the town who was not highly regarded until he got a job as an apprentice engineer on a riverboat. He then became something of a legend whenever he would come back to town, especially after his boat blew up and he was injured. Other boys followed the young man's lead and sought jobs on the river, but no job was more respected than that of the pilot of a steamboat.

### Insight

The Mississippi River looms large in the history of the United States. More than 2,300 miles long and 7 miles across at its widest point, the mighty Mississippi River passes through ten states and, in combination with the Missouri River, forms the largest river system in the United States.

ESSENTIAL QUESTION:
What is the relationship between literature and place?

## Connection to Essential Question

While all literature is situated in some setting or place, in some literature, the sense of place is the story. That is the case in this excerpt from *Life on the Mississippi.* The river is so central to the memoir that it almost becomes a character or person.

WHOLE-CLASS LEARNING PERFORMANCE TASK
How do American authors use regional details to make the events and themes of a narrative come to life for readers?

UNIT PERFORMANCE-BASED ASSESSMENT
What makes certain places live on in our memory?

## Connection to Performance Tasks

**Whole-Class Learning Performance Task** Twain's memoir shows the importance of the Mississippi River and steamboats to the culture of this area of the United States. The river affected the daily lives and hopes of the people who lived near it.

**Unit Performance-Based Assessment** The riverboat itself creates a sense of place for the writer, creating memories that focus on the experience of growing up in a river town.

DIGITAL PERSPECTIVES

 Audio
 Video
 Document
 Annotation Highlights
 EL Highlights
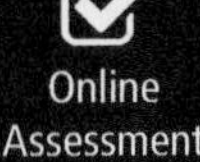 Online Assessment

## LESSON RESOURCES

| | Making Meaning | Language Development |
|---|---|---|
| **Lesson** | **First Read**<br>**Close Read**<br>**Analyze the Text**<br>**Analyze Craft and Structure** | **Concept Vocabulary**<br>**Word Study**<br>**Author's Style** |
| **Instructional Standards** | **RI.10** By the end of grade 11, read and comprehend literary nonfiction . . .<br>**RI.1** Cite strong and thorough textual evidence . . .<br>**RI.6** Determine an author's point of view . . . | **RI.4** Determine the meaning of words and phrases . . .<br>**L.4.b** Identify and correctly use patterns of word changes . . .<br>**L.4.d** Verify the preliminary determination . . . |
| **STUDENT RESOURCES** | | |
| Available online in the Interactive Student Edition or Unit Resources | Selection Audio<br>First-Read Guide: Nonfiction<br>Close-Read Guide: Nonfiction | Word Network |
| **TEACHER RESOURCES** | | |
| **Selection Resources**<br>Available online in the Interactive Teacher's Edition or Unit Resources | Audio Summaries<br>Annotation Highlights<br>EL Highlights<br>English Language Support Lesson: Suffixes<br>Analyze Craft and Structure: Author's Purpose | Concept Vocabulary and Word Study<br>Author's Style: Words and Phrases |
| **Reteach and Practice**<br>Available online in the Interactive Teacher's Edition or Unit Resources | Analyze Craft and Structure: Author's Purpose (RP) | Word Study: Suffix *-esque* (RP)<br>Author's Style: Words and Phrases (RP) |
| **Assessment**<br>Available online in Assessments | Selection Test | |
| **My Resources** | A Unit 4 Answer Key is available online and in the Interactive Teacher's Edition. | |

# Reading Support

| Text Complexity Rubric: *from* Life on the Mississippi | |
|---|---|
| **Quantitative Measures** | |
| **Lexile:** 1060 **Text Length:** 1,636 words | |
| **Qualitative Measures** | |
| Knowledge Demands ①—②—③—❹—⑤ | The experience central to the story (life on the Mississippi in the nineteenth century and ambition to be a steamboatman) will be unfamiliar to readers. |
| Structure ①—②—❸—④—⑤ | The text is dense with complex descriptions and details. Events are described chronologically. Ideas have logical connections and organization. |
| Language Conventionality and Clarity ①—②—③—❹—⑤ | The language is complex and descriptive, with syntax that may be archaic and unfamiliar (from the year 1883). Some sentences are very lengthy and complex, with multiple descriptions, difficult vocabulary, and jargon. |
| Levels of Meaning/Purpose ①—②—❸—④—⑤ | The meaning of this excerpt is accessible and clearly stated (about the ambition to become a steamboatman). Though descriptions are lengthy and complex, feelings of characters and relevance of events are clear. |

DECIDE AND PLAN

## English Language Support

Provide English Learners with support for knowledge demands and language as they read the selection.

**Knowledge Demands** Review some of the necessary information about the setting and characters. Remind students that the account is from the late 1800s. Have students find the Mississippi River on a map. Write the words *steamboat* and *steamboatman* (paragraph 1) and have students explain what they are by looking at the parts of those words. Discuss the meaning of the word *ambition*. (paragraph 1)

**Language** Show students how to approach long paragraphs and sentences by breaking large chunks of texts into smaller sections, stopping to discuss. For example, they may read 11 lines of paragraph 4 and discuss the different jobs the boy wanted.

## Strategic Support

Provide students with strategic support to ensure that they can successfully read the text.

**Language** If students will have difficulty with jargon, have them look at the definitions in the footnotes before they skim the excerpt. Then, have them reread the piece. Ask them to mark any phrases that they find difficult. Have them read aloud these parts. As a group, analyze the language, clarifying as necessary.

**Meaning** Ask questions to reinforce understanding of aspects of young Twain's ambition to become a steamboatman. First, ask what all the boys wanted to be. In paragraph 4, ask about the different jobs he wanted. Then in 5 and 6, ask how he felt when other boys worked on steamboats and what he did when his parents wouldn't let him get on the river.

## Challenge

Provide students who need to be challenged with ideas for how they can go beyond a simple interpretation of the text.

**Text Analysis** Ask one or more volunteers to read aloud from paragraph 4, about the boy who came back as an apprentice engineer. Discuss the feelings expressed in the passage.

**Written Response** Ask students to write an essay about ambition. Have them explain why they think readers respond to young Twain's ambition today, long after the era of steamboats. Have them write about a past or present ambition of their own or one of someone they know. They can describe the feelings of pursuing this dream or frustrations involved in trying to pursue it. Ask them to comment on similarities to the feelings expressed in the story.

TEACH

## Read and Respond

Have students do their first read of the selection. Then have them complete their close read. Finally, work with them on the Making Meaning and Language Development activities.

# Standards Support Through Teaching and Learning Cycle

## IDENTIFY NEEDS

Analyze results of the Beginning-of-Year Assessment, focusing on the items relating to Unit 4. Also take into consideration student performance to this point and your observations of where particular students struggle.

## DECIDE AND PLAN

- If students have performed poorly on items matching these standards, then provide selection scaffolds before assigning them the on-level lesson provided in the Student Edition.
- If students have done well on the Beginning-of-Year Assessment, then challenge them to keep progressing and learning by giving them opportunities to practice the skills in depth.
- Use the Selection Resources listed on the Planning pages for this excerpt from *Life On the Mississippi* to help students continually improve their ability to master the standards.

**Instructional Standards: *from* Life on the Mississippi**

| | Catching Up | This Year | Looking Forward |
|---|---|---|---|
| **Reading** | You may wish to administer the **Analyze Craft and Structure: Author's Purpose (RP)** worksheet to familiarize students with author's purpose.<br><br>You may wish to administer the **Author's Style: Words and Phrases (RP)** worksheet to help students better understand diction. | **RI.6** Determine an author's point of view or purpose in a text in which the rhetoric is particularly effective, analyzing how style and content contribute to the power, persuasiveness, or beauty of the text.<br><br>**RI.4** Determine the meaning of words and phrases as they are used in the text, including figurative, connotative, and technical meanings; analyze how an author uses and refines the meaning of a key term or terms over the course of a text. | Challenge students to write their own Twain-esque anecdotes with underlying social commentaries.<br><br>Have students identify other works they have read that have noteworthy mixes of styles of diction. |
| **Language** | Review the **Word Study: Suffix *-esque* (RP)** worksheet with students to better familiarize them with the suffix. | **L.4.b** Identify and correctly use patterns of word changes that indicate different meanings or parts of speech. | Have students create their own original words using the suffix *-esque*. |

## ANALYZE AND REVISE

- Analyze student work for evidence of student learning.
- Identify whether or not students have met the expectations in the standards.
- Identify implications for future instruction.

## TEACH

Implement the planned lesson, and gather evidence of student learning.

# TEACHING

## Jump Start

FIRST READ *How do dreams influence people's actions? Why do some people passionately follow their dreams, while others give up?* Engage students in a discussion about actions that people take to follow their dreams and why some people seem to be more persistent and determined than others.

## Concept Vocabulary

Circulate among students as they rank their words. Remind them that they will find the definitions of these words in the side column beside each word's location in the text.

### FIRST READ

The first time they go through the selection, students should perform the steps of the first read:

NOTICE: You may want to encourage students to notice the sensory details in the text.

ANNOTATE: Remind students to mark passages that create vivid images for the reader.

CONNECT: Have students compare Mark Twain's description of his village with their own hometown or community. Point out that they should consider the setting in terms of both place and time.

RESPOND: Students will demonstrate their understanding of the text by answering questions and writing a summary.

Point out to students that they will perform the first three steps concurrently as they are doing their first read. They will complete the Respond step after they have finished the first read. You may wish to print copies of the **First-Read Guide: Nonfiction** for students to use.

**Remind students that during their first read, they should not answer the close-read questions that appear in the selection.**

MAKING MEANING

from LIFE ON THE MISSISSIPPI

## Comparing Texts

You will read and compare an excerpt from Mark Twain's memoir with one of his short stories. First, you will complete the first-read and close-read activities for the excerpt from *Life on the Mississippi.* The work you do on this title will prepare you for the comparing task.

THE NOTORIOUS JUMPING FROG OF CALAVERAS COUNTY

# *from* Life on the Mississippi

## Concept Vocabulary

You will encounter the following words as you read this excerpt from *Life on the Mississippi.* Before reading, note how familiar you are with each word. Then, rank the words in order from most familiar (1) to least familiar (6).

| WORD | YOUR RANKING |
|---|---|
| gilded | |
| ornamented | |
| grandeur | |
| picturesquely | |
| exalted | |
| eminence | |

After completing your first read, come back to the concept vocabulary and review your rankings. Mark changes to your original rankings as needed.

### First Read NONFICTION

Apply these strategies as you conduct your first read. You will have an opportunity to complete the close-read notes after your first read.

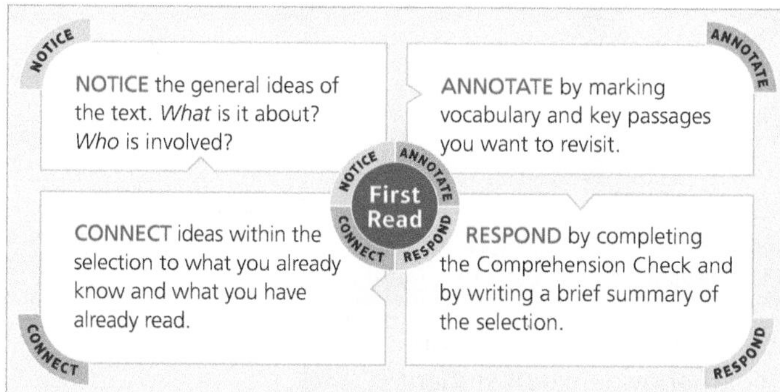
NOTICE the general ideas of the text. *What* is it about? *Who* is involved?
ANNOTATE by marking vocabulary and key passages you want to revisit.
First Read
CONNECT ideas within the selection to what you already know and what you have already read.
RESPOND by completing the Comprehension Check and by writing a brief summary of the selection.

**Tool Kit**
First-Read Guide and Model Annotation

**STANDARDS**
**Reading Informational Text**
By the end of grade 11, read and comprehend literary nonfiction in the grades 11–CCR text complexity band proficiently, with scaffolding as needed at the high end of the range.

AUTHOR'S PERSPECTIVE **Kelly Gallagher, M.Ed.**

**Deep Reading** *Deep reading* means taking the time to consider more than just what the text says by making inferences, seeing and thinking about information not literally on the page. Teachers can use the following techniques to model how to make inferences:

- **Study Photographs:** Have students study a photo and describe what might have happened in it. Discuss their responses, encouraging students to support their ideas.
- **Complete a Say/Doesn't Say Chart:** Draw a T-chart on the board. On the left, have students write what the passage says (literal comprehension). On the right, have them record what the passage doesn't say. This helps students get at the author's inference.
- **Use a Positive-Negative Chart:** Have students chart a character's good and bad behavior, positive and negative influence, or the highest and lowest point in a story. This technique is an excellent way to have students track specific literary elements in a novel or a play.
- **Play Literary Dominoes:** Start with the resolution of a narrative and have students work backwards, recording the events that to it. This creates a chain of key events.

## DIGITAL PERSPECTIVES

### from *Life on the Mississippi*

What characteristics make it more likely that people will follow their dreams? Are some dreams easier to pursue than others? Why do we like hearing stories about people who make their dreams come true? Modeling these and other questions readers might ask will bring *Life on the Mississippi* to life and connect it to the Performance Task question. Selection audio and print capability for the selection are available in the Interactive Teacher's Edition.

About the Author

# Mark Twain (1835–1910)

*At a time when most American writers were copying European novelists, Twain wrote about American themes.*

In the late 1800s, readers might have known him as Thomas Jefferson Snodgrass, W. Epaminondas Adrastus Blab, or simply Josh. Today we know Samuel Langhorne Clemens as Mark Twain, his most famous literary pseudonym. Whichever name he used, Twain pulled off a rare literary feat—he created stories, novels, and essays that were wildly popular in his own day and remain models of wit and skill more than a century later. Twain was so influential that fifty years after his death Ernest Hemingway said that "all modern American literature begins" with Twain's novel *The Adventures of Huckleberry Finn.*

**Life on the Mississippi** Born in 1835, Samuel Clemens grew up in the small river town of Hannibal, Missouri. Steamboat men, religious revivalists, circus performers, minstrel companies, showboat actors, and every other kind of traveler imaginable made appearances in Hannibal. As a boy, Clemens met many of the characters that he would later write about.

After his father's death in 1847, Clemens was forced to leave school and became a printer's apprentice. During the 1850s, he published a few stories and traveled the country. A boat trip down the Mississippi brought back childhood memories, and he decided to become a riverboat pilot. He served as a pilot until 1861, when the Civil War closed the Mississippi to boat traffic.

**"Mark Twain" Finds His Voice** In 1862, Clemens took a job as a reporter on a Virginia City, Nevada, newspaper, where he found his calling as a humorist under the byline Mark Twain. The new name, which is actually a signal yelled out by riverboat pilots, freed him to develop a new style. Before becoming "Twain," his work was typical of the low humor of the time, filled with bad puns and intentional misspellings. But in 1865, Twain published a short story entitled "The Notorious Jumping Frog of Calaveras County." The story won the author fame and financial success, and it marked the first appearance of his distinctive comic style.

**Ordinary American Speech** The targets of Twain's jokes were not new. He distrusted technology and railed against political figures, calling them swindlers and con men. What was new was Twain's feel for ordinary American people and their language. He wrote using the American English that people actually spoke. In that source, he found rich and comic poetry.

Twain's novels, such as *The Adventures of Tom Sawyer* and *The Adventures of Huckleberry Finn*, were unlike any books the world had ever seen. At a time when most American writers were copying European novelists, Twain wrote about American themes. His heroes were often poor and plain-spoken people, but in Twain's hands, their moral choices had as much drama as those of any tormented aristocrat in a European novel.

Not everyone appreciated Twain's humor. The author fled Virginia City when a rival journalist, offended by a story, challenged him to a pistol duel. He was chased out of San Francisco by policemen angered by critical articles. Even as his fame grew, some critics dismissed him as little more than a jokester. Yet the American public loved Twain. He made a fortune from his writings and eventually settled with his family into a Hartford, Connecticut, mansion that was decorated in cutting-edge style.

**The Old Man in a White Suit** In the late 1800s, Twain faced troubling challenges. He founded a publishing house that had moderate success but then went bankrupt. Other business ventures also failed. Although he presented a friendly face to the public, and despite the many awards that continued to come his way, Twain grew pessimistic. His mood darkened to bitterness and cynicism following the deaths of his wife and two of his daughters. Twain became reclusive—so much so that a newspaper reported he was dead. Twain immediately wired the editors, "Reports of my death have been greatly exaggerated." History has not exaggerated Twain's legacy. He was the first, and possibly the greatest, authentically American writer.





## CROSS-CURRICULAR PERSPECTIVES

**Math** Clemens borrowed his famous pseudonym, *Mark Twain*, from his beloved Mississippi River. The term *mark twain* means mark number two on the line that measured the depth of the river. The Mississippi River was measured in 6 foot increments, known as *fathoms*. Two marks or *fathoms*, also known as *mark twain*, was a safe depth for a steamboat to pass. Currently depth varies greatly in the Mississippi River. At its head waters it measures less than 3 feet deep. At its deepest, the river is 200 feet deep. Have students use this information to calculate in fathoms the river's depth at its most shallow and its deepest. (shallowest: ½ fathom; deepest 33.33 fathoms) Then encourage students to calculate the depth in fathoms of other bodies of water such as the Great Lakes, the Colorado River, and the Gulf of Mexico.

# TEACHING

## CLOSER LOOK

### Analyze Connotations

Students may have marked paragraph 2 during their first read. Use this paragraph to help students understand the connotation of Twain's word choice regarding *want* or *desire*. Encourage them to talk about the annotations that they marked. You may want to model a close read with the class based on the highlights shown in the text.

**ANNOTATE:** Have students mark words or phrases in the paragraph that are used to mean that the boys wanted or desired something, or have students participate while you highlight them.

**QUESTION:** Guide students to consider what these words or phrases connote. Ask what a reader can infer from the words Twain uses to describe the boys' desires, and accept student responses.

**Possible response:** "Burning" conveys a deep intensity of want. "Suffering" implies that the wanting is painful. "We had hope" is a bit more optimistic and" God would permit us" implies that their wants were seen as something they had to earn.

**CONCLUDE:** Help students to formulate conclusions about the connotations of Twain's word choices to convey the boys' wants in the text. Ask students why the author might have included these details.

**Possible response:** The word choice makes me think that the boys were desperate to do something admirable that would connect them with the outside world. Their want went very deep and was more like a yearning.

Explain to students that a **connotation** is an association or feeling that a word suggests. Although two words may mean the same thing in a dictionary or be listed as synonyms in a thesaurus, their connotations, or universally recognized meanings, can be quite different. For example, consider *wishing* and *longing*. *Wishing* can imply a casual or momentary desire, as in: *I am wishing for a day off from work.* However, the word *longing* conveys more of a serious want that would be difficult to fill: *I was longing to hear my grandfather's reassuring voice.*



ANCHOR TEXT | MEMOIR

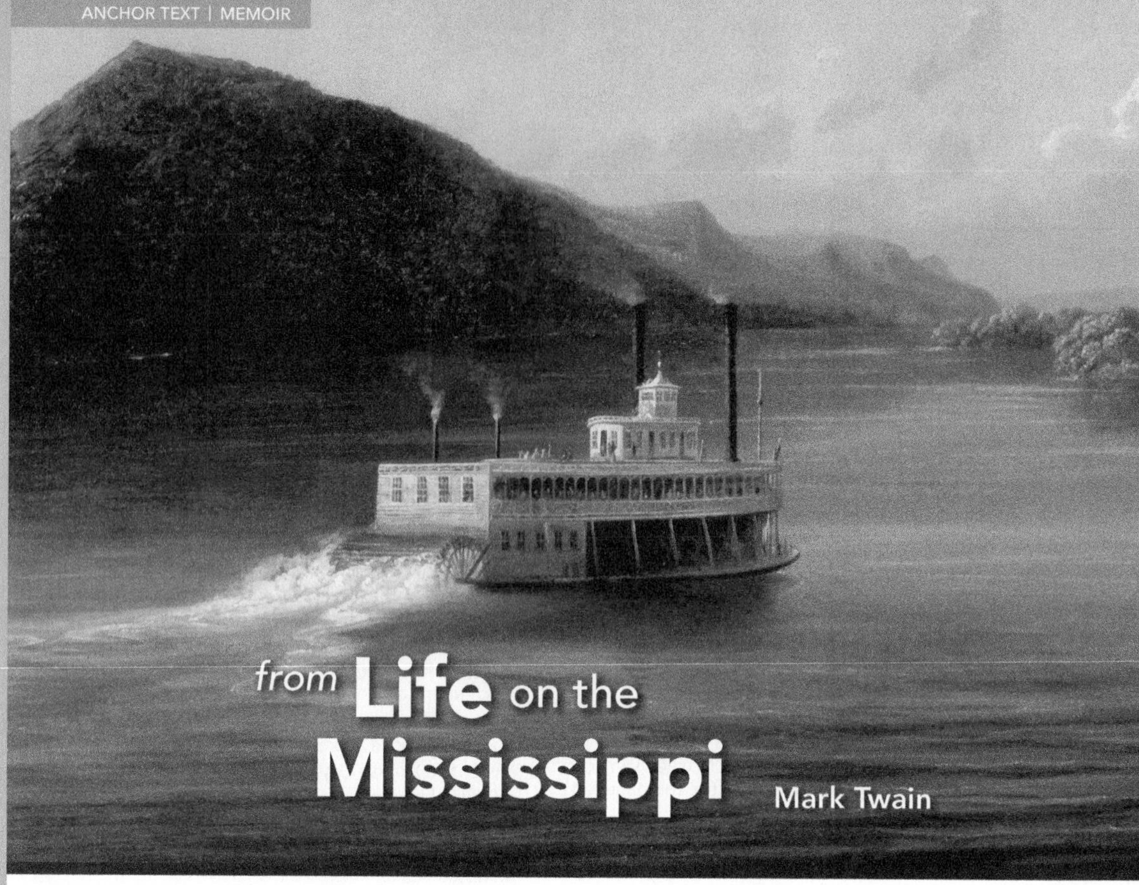

# from Life on the Mississippi

Mark Twain

SCAN FOR MULTIMEDIA

BACKGROUND

Mark Twain was an eyewitness to the nineteenth-century expansion of the western frontier. He traveled throughout the nation, working first on the Mississippi and then in the West, before settling in Connecticut. However, as this excerpt shows, the Mississippi River held a special place in his memory.

NOTES

## The Boy's Ambition

1 When I was a boy, there was but one permanent ambition among my comrades in our village[1] on the west bank of the Mississippi River. That was, to be a steamboatman. We had transient ambitions of other sorts, but they were only transient.

2 When a circus came and went, it left us all burning to become clowns; the first Negro minstrel show that came to our section left us all suffering to try that kind of life; now and then we had a hope

1. **our village** Hannibal, Missouri.





## DIGITAL PERSPECTIVES

**Illuminating the Text** Review paragraphs 1 and 2. Give students context for the text by explaining that in Twain's time, there was little ability for people who lived in a small town like Hannibal, Missouri, to connect to people in bigger, more glamorous cities. (background paragraph) The arrival of a steamboat brought with it a bit of the outside world. Likewise, the idea of working on a steamboat brought dreams of visiting faraway places. Have students conduct online research about the routes of steamboats along the Mississippi River and identify which stops would be considered "big cities" compared with Hannibal.

NOTES

that if we lived and were good, God would permit us to be pirates. These ambitions faded out, each in its turn; but the ambition to be a steamboatman always remained.

3 Once a day a cheap, gaudy packet[2] arrived upward from St. Louis, and another downward from Keokuk.[3] Before these events, the day was glorious with expectancy; after them, the day was a dead and empty thing. Not only the boys, but the whole village, felt this. After all these years I can picture that old time to myself now, just as it was then; the white town drowsing in the sunshine of a summer's morning; the streets empty, or pretty nearly so; one or two clerks sitting in front of the Water Street stores, with their splint-bottomed chairs tilted back against the wall, chins on breasts, hats slouched over their faces, asleep—with shingle shavings enough around to show what broke them down; a sow and a litter of pigs loafing along the sidewalk, doing a good business in watermelon rinds and seeds;

2. **packet** *n.* boat that travels a regular route, carrying passengers, freight, and mail.
3. **Keokuk** (KEE uh kuhk) town in southeastern Iowa.



**CLOSE READ**

**ANNOTATE:** In paragraph 3, mark descriptive details that suggest sleepiness or languor. Mark other descriptive details that refer to noise and activity.

**QUESTION:** Why does the author create the steamboat scene in this way?

**CONCLUDE:** What is the effect of these descriptive details?



DIGITAL PERSPECTIVES  

## CLOSE READ 

As students look for details about the sleepiness of the town in paragraph 3, remind them that they will be selecting details that describe the town both *before* the steamboat arrives and *after* the steamboat arrives. You may wish to model the Close Read using the following think-aloud format. Possible responses to questions on the Student page are included. You may also wish to print copies of the **Close-Read Guide: Nonfiction** for students to use. 

**ANNOTATE:** As I read paragraph 3, I notice and highlight the details that describe the "sleepy" and peaceful scene of the town and then I will need to identify contrasting details that show the town's liveliness once the steamboat has arrived.

**QUESTION:** When I look at these details, I see that Twain is contrasting the dreary and quiet life in the town to the excitement that occurs when a steamboat comes in. This helps me understand that in the context of the dreary town, the steamboat's arrival is a big event.

**CONCLUDE:** When I connect this observation to the central idea that Twain and the other boys want to work on a steamboat, I see that Twain's details about the dreary, sleepy life of the town help the reader relate to and better understand the boys' longing for the adventure of working on a steamboat.

## PERSONALIZE FOR LEARNING

### English Language Support

**Compare and Contrast** Review paragraph 3 with students. Students may struggle to explain differences in the town before and after the arrival of the steamboat. Have students work with a partner to create a two-column chart. On one side, have them write descriptive statements from the text about life in the town before the steamboat's arrival. On the other side, have them write descriptions from after the arrival of the boat. Then have partners take turns using these details to discuss the text. Suggest the following frames to guide their discussion:

*Before the steamboat arrives, _____. After the steamboat arrives, _____. The _____ before the steamboat arrives. The _____ after the steamboat arrives.* **ALL LEVELS**

| Before the Steamboat Arrives | After the Steamboat Arrives |
|---|---|
| *the streets are empty* | *the town drunkard stirs* |
| *clerks sit in front of Water Street store* | *the clerks wake up* |

CLOSER LOOK

## Identify Technical Terms 

Students may have marked paragraph 3 during their first read. Use this paragraph to help students understand the role of technical vocabulary in a nonfiction text. Encourage them to talk about the annotations that they marked. You may want to model a close read with the class based on the highlights shown in the text.

**ANNOTATE:** Have students mark details in this paragraph that show examples of technical terms.

**QUESTION:** Guide students to consider what these technical terms might tell them. Ask what a reader can infer from the author's use of so many technical terms.

**Possible response:** When I read this part, I feel as if Twain is an expert in the area of steamboats.

**CONCLUDE:** Help students to formulate conclusions about the importance of details. Ask why the author includes them.

**Possible response:** Using correct terminology makes Twain convincing as an authority on steamboats.

Explain to students that a **technical term** is specific to a particular line of work. Sometimes technical vocabulary is defined within a text or in a footnote. Other times, especially writing is geared toward people working in a field, the reader may need to look up *technical terms*.

Additional **English Language Support** is available in the Interactive Teacher's Edition.

NOTES

**gilded** (GIHLD ihd) *adj.* covered with a thin layer of gold

**ornamented** (AWR nuh mehnt ihd) *adj.* decorated; adorned

**grandeur** (GRAN juhr) *n.* state of being impressive; magnificence

**picturesquely** (pihk chuh REHSK lee) *adv.* in a way that resembles a picture; in a way that is striking or interesting

two or three lonely little freight piles scattered about the levee;[4] a pile of skids[5] on the slope of the stone-paved wharf, and the fragrant town drunkard asleep in the shadow of them; two or three wood flats[6] at the head of the wharf, but nobody to listen to the peaceful lapping of the wavelets against them; the great Mississippi, the majestic, the magnificent Mississippi, rolling its mile-wide tide a long, shining in the sun; the dense forest away on the other side; the point above the town, and the point below, bounding the river-glimpse and turning it into a sort of sea, and withal a very still and brilliant and lonely one. Presently a film of dark smoke appears above one of those remote points; instantly a Negro drayman,[7] famous for his quick eye and prodigious voice, lifts up the cry, "S-t-e-a-m-boat a-comin'!" and the scene changes! The town drunkard stirs, the clerks wake up, a furious clatter of drays follows, every house and store pours out a human contribution, and all in a twinkling the dead town is alive and moving. Drays, carts, men, boys, all go hurrying from many quarters to a common center, the wharf. Assembled there, the people fasten their eyes upon the coming boat as upon a wonder they are seeing for the first time. And the boat is rather a handsome sight, too. She is long and sharp and trim and pretty; she has two tall, fancy-topped chimneys, with a gilded device of some kind swung between them; a fanciful pilothouse, all glass and gingerbread,[8] perched on top of the texas deck[9] behind them; the paddleboxes are gorgeous with a picture or with gilded rays above the boat's name; the boiler deck, the hurricane deck, and the texas deck are fenced and ornamented with clean white railings; there is a flag gallantly flying from the jackstaff;[10] the furnace doors are open and the fires glaring bravely; the upper decks are black with passengers; the captain stands by the big bell, calm, imposing, the envy of all; great volumes of the blackest smoke are rolling and tumbling out of the chimneys—a husbanded grandeur created with a bit of pitch pine just before arriving at a town; the crew are grouped on the forecastle;[11] the broad stage is run far out over the port bow, and an envied deckhand stands picturesquely on the end of it with a coil of rope in his hand; the pent steam is screaming through the gauge cocks; the captain lifts his hand, a bell rings, the wheels stop; then they turn back, churning the water to foam, and the steamer is at rest. Then such a scramble as there is to get aboard, and to get ashore, and to take in freight and to discharge freight, all at one and the same time; and such a yelling and cursing as the mates facilitate it all with! Ten minutes later the steamer is under way again, with no flag on the jackstaff and no black

4. **levee** (LEHV ee) *n.* landing place along the bank of a river.
5. **skids** *n.* low, movable wooden platforms.
6. **flats** *n.* small, flat-bottomed boats.
7. **drayman** (DRAY muhn) *n.* driver of a dray, a low cart with detachable sides.
8. **gingerbread** *n.* showy ornamentation; fancy carving.
9. **texas deck** *n.* deck adjoining the officers' cabins, the largest cabins on the ship.
10. **jackstaff** *n.* small staff at the bow of a ship for flying flags.
11. **forecastle** (FOHK suhl) *n.* front part of the upper deck.





VOCABULARY DEVELOPMENT

**Using Context** Point students to the phrase "husbanded grandeur" (paragraph 3), an unusual expression they may not understand. Say to students: I see that the student book defines *grandeur* as the state of being impressive or magnificent. I use this definition as well as the context of the sentence to figure out what *husbanded grandeur* means. Twain uses the phrase to describe the thick black smoke rising from the steamboat's chimney. I know this effect is produced on purpose because Twain tells us that pitch pine is tossed into the boiler to fire just as the steamboat is coming into town. This tells me that the effect is probably designed to impress the townspeople. I think the phrase *husbanded grandeur* refers to a carefully managed grand effect.

smoke issuing from the chimneys. After ten more minutes the town is dead again, and the town drunkard asleep by the skids once more.

4 My father was a justice of the peace, and I supposed he possessed the power of life and death over all men and could hang anybody that offended him. This was distinction enough for me as a general thing; but the desire to be a steamboatman kept intruding, nevertheless. I first wanted to be a cabin boy, so that I could come out with a white apron on and shake a tablecloth over the side, where all my old comrades could see me; later I thought I would rather be the deckhand who stood on the end of the stage plank with the coil of rope in his hand, because he was particularly conspicuous. But these were only daydreams—they were too heavenly to be contemplated as real possibilities. By and by one of our boys went away. He was not heard of for a long time. At last he turned up as apprentice engineer or striker on a steamboat. This thing shook the bottom out of all my Sunday school teachings. That boy had been notoriously worldly, and I just the reverse; yet he was **exalted** to this **eminence**, and I left in obscurity and misery. There was nothing generous about this fellow in his greatness. He would always manage to have a rusty bolt to scrub while his boat tarried at our town, and he would sit on the inside guard and scrub it, where we could all see him and envy him and loathe him. And whenever his boat was laid up he would come home and swell around the town in his blackest and greasiest clothes, so that nobody could help remembering that he was a steamboatman; and he used all sorts of steamboat technicalities in his talk, as if he were so used to them that he forgot common people could not understand them. He would speak of the labboard[12] side of a horse in an easy, natural way that would make one wish he was dead. And he was always talking about "St. Looey" like an old citizen; he would refer casually to occasions when he "was coming down Fourth Street," or when he was "passing by the Planter's House," or when there was a fire and he took a turn on the brakes of "the old Big Missouri"; and then he would go on and lie about how many towns the size of ours were burned down there that day. Two or three of the boys had long been persons of consideration among us because they had been to St. Louis once and had a vague general knowledge of its wonders, but the day of their glory was over now. They lapsed into a humble silence, and learned to disappear when the ruthless cub engineer approached. This fellow had money, too, and hair oil. Also an ignorant silver watch and a showy brass watch chain. He wore a leather belt and used no suspenders. If ever a youth was cordially admired and hated by his comrades. this one was. No girl could withstand his charms. He cut out every boy in the village. When his boat blew up at last, it diffused a tranquil contentment among us such as we had not known for months. But when he came home the next week, alive, renowned, and appeared in church all

12. **labboard** (LAB uhrd) *n.* larboard; to the left of the ship.

NOTES

**CLOSE READ**

**ANNOTATE:** In the first few sentences of paragraph 4, mark the jobs that young Twain wanted to have someday.

**QUESTION:** Why does the author mention several jobs?

**CONCLUDE:** What is the effect of his including these details?

**exalted** (ehg ZAWLT ihd) *adj.* of high rank

**eminence** (EHM uh nuhns) *n.* position of great importance or superiority





DIGITAL PERSPECTIVES

## CLOSE READ 

As students mark jobs in the paragraph, point out that they should mark only the jobs the young Twain dreams of doing and not the other jobs mentioned in the paragraph. You may wish to model the close read using the following think-aloud format. Possible responses to questions on the Student page are included.

**ANNOTATE:** As I read paragraph 4, I notice and highlight the jobs that the young Twain wishes he could do someday. I also notice how he describes each job and focuses on how he could be noticed by others while he is doing them.

**QUESTION:** When I read this paragraph, I see that the young Twain keeps changing his mind. This gives me a glimpse into his youthful exuberance and how, to him, all these jobs are glamorous. I see that he focuses on aspects of each job that would make him noticeable. This tells me he is thinking less about the hard work associated with them and more about how they make him look to others.

**CONCLUDE:** When I read Twain fantasizing about each job, I gain insight into the young Twain's character and how he idealized all things related to the steamboat. I see that he is willing to do just about any job on a steamboat in order to be a part of the dream he so desperately wants to fulfill.

## PERSONALIZE FOR LEARNING

### Strategic Support

**Understand Regional Context** As students read paragraphs 3 and 4, ask them to note the towns and cities named. Encourage students to obtain and examine a map from the late 1800s showing the Mississippi River and the states of Missouri, Illinois, and Iowa. Help students locate the following towns, mentioned in the text: Hannibal, Keokuk, and St. Louis. Have them discuss the geography of these places. Then invite students to discuss how this region may have influenced Twain's ideas, dreams, and desires.

## CLOSE READ

As students read paragraph 5, remind them to focus on the part of the paragraph that describes the coveted pilot job. You may wish to model the close read using the following think-aloud format. Possible responses to questions on the Student page are included.

**ANNOTATE:** As I read paragraph 5, I am careful to identify only those adjectives that describe the pilot's salary and position. I notice the adjective *trivial*, but it is not describing the pilot's wage. It describes other wages of the time. I might want to remember this because it seems to be used as a way to contrast the words that do describe the pilot's salary.

**QUESTION:** I notice that Twain uses the word "princely" (paragraph 5), implying that the pilot is like royalty to him. These words show that to young Twain the job of a steamboat pilot was the most appealing he could imagine.

**CONCLUDE:** When I consider the effects of these adjectives, I see Twain's youthful enthusiasm and the extent to which he is enamored with life on a steamboat. I can sense the depth of his desire to make his dream a reality.

## Media Connection

Project the media connection video in class, ask students to open the video in their interactive textbooks, or have students scan the Bounce Page icon with their phones to access the video.

### Discuss It

**Possible responses:**

In both cases, Twain mixes everyday details with humor to create a picture of childhood in his hometown as a time of joy.

NOTES

**CLOSE READ**

**ANNOTATE:** In paragraph 5, mark the adjectives that describe the position and salary of a steamboat pilot.

**QUESTION:** Why does the author choose these adjectives to describe a pilot's status?

**CONCLUDE:** What is the effect of these adjectives?

battered up and bandaged, a shining hero, stared at and wondered over by everybody, it seemed to us that the partiality of Providence for an undeserving reptile had reached a point where it was open to criticism.

5 This creature's career could produce but one result, and it speedily followed. Boy after boy managed to get on the river. The minister's son became an engineer. The doctor's and the postmaster's sons became mud clerks; the wholesale liquor dealer's son became a barkeeper on a boat; four sons of the chief merchant, and two sons of the county judge, became pilots. Pilot was the grandest position of all. The pilot, even in those days of trivial wages, had a princely salary—from a hundred and fifty to two hundred and fifty dollars a month, and no board to pay. Two months of his wages would pay a preacher's salary for a year. Now some of us were left disconsolate. We could not get on the river—at least our parents would not let us.

6 So by and by I ran away. I said I never would come home again till I was a pilot and could come in glory. But somehow I could not manage it. I went meekly aboard a few of the boats that lay packed together like sardines at the long St. Louis wharf, and very humbly inquired for the pilots, but got only a cold shoulder and short words from mates and clerks. I had to make the best of this sort of treatment for the time being, but I had comforting daydreams of a future when I should be a great and honored pilot, with plenty of money, and could kill some of these mates and clerks and pay for them. ❧

MEDIA CONNECTION

Mark Twain and Tom Sawyer

**Discuss It** From what you see in this video, what connection can you make between the way that Mark Twain depicts his hometown in *The Adventures of Tom Sawyer* and the way that he depicts it in *Life on the Mississippi*?

**Write your response before sharing your ideas.**

SCAN FOR MULTIMEDIA





## PERSONALIZE FOR LEARNING

### English Language Support

**Expanding Noun Phrases** Review paragraphs 4–6 with students and call attention to Twain's practice of expanding noun phrases using adjectives. Have students consider the following noun phrases from the selection: *shining hero* (paragraph 4); *undeserving reptile* (paragraph 4); *four sons* (paragraph 5); *honored pilot* (paragraph 6). In each instance, have them identify the noun and the adjective. Then discuss what information the adjective adds to their understanding of the noun. Have students work with a partner to look back through the text and identify additional noun phrases. Then have them add adjectives to expand the following nouns into noun phrases: *river; steamboat; job; boy; stores; dreams.* Encourage them to then use the words in sentences and practice speaking the new sentences to each other. **EMERGING/EXPANDING**

DIGITAL PERSPECTIVES

## Comprehension Check

Complete the following items after you finish your first read.

1. What does Twain say is the one permanent ambition he and his boyhood friends shared?

2. According to Twain, how do the people of Hannibal respond to the arrival of the steamboat?

3. What kinds of activities impress young Twain during the steamboat's brief stop in Hannibal?

4. What happens when the boy who survived an explosion aboard a steamboat returns to town?

5. Under what condition does young Twain say he would return to Hannibal?

6. **Notebook** Write a summary of this excerpt from *Life on the Mississippi*.

### RESEARCH

**Research to Clarify** Choose at least one unfamiliar detail from the text. Briefly research that detail. In what way does the information you learned shed light on an aspect of the memoir?

**Research to Explore** Conduct research to find out why the Mississippi steamboats were essential to the economy of late-nineteenth-century America.





## Comprehension Check

Possible responses:

1. They all want to be steamboat men.
2. They hurry to greet the boat as it arrives and watch the boat's operations with fascination.
3. The flag flying from the ship's bow; the fires burning in the furnaces; the captain raising his arm; the ringing of a bell; the deckhand poised with a coil of rope
4. He becomes a town hero.
5. He will return when he becomes a pilot.
6. **Possible response:** The narrator recounts his boyhood dreams of becoming a steamboat man and working on one of the majestic boats on the river. He describes the contrast between the dullness of Hannibal, his small hometown, and the adventures that the river promises. He desires the opportunities and prestige the job affords, and he envies a boy who already has such a job.

## Research

**Research to Clarify** If students struggle to come up with a detail to research further, you may want to suggest that they focus on one of the following details to give context to the text: daily life in a small town in Twain's time; wages in the 1860s and 1870s for various professions; facts about the Mississippi River.

**Research to Explore** Students should discover that by the early nineteenth century, steamboats were regularly carrying cargo on the Mississippi and Ohio rivers and were essential to the economy of towns along these rivers, linking them to each other and to the rest of the world. Until the 1850s, when railroad development grew rapidly in the West, steamboats carried more freight than trains.

### PERSONALIZE FOR LEARNING

**Challenge**

**Creative Sketch** Have students do research to find out about daily life on great riverboats during Twain's time. Among other things, they can research routes, jobs, onboard entertainment, the size and speed of the boats, and the cargo they carried. Have students use their research to write a creative sketch of a day in the life of a steamboat worker or passenger.

## Jump Start

CLOSE READ Ask students to describe a detail in the classroom, using at least one set of synonyms in the description. Lead a discussion about why authors use synonyms in writing.

## Close Read the Text

Work with students on the annotation model, then have them complete items 2 and 3 on their own. When they have finished, review and discuss the sections students marked. If needed, continue to model close reading by using the Annotation Highlights in the Interactive Teacher's Edition.

## Analyze the Text

Possible responses:

1. (a) Being a steamboatman conveys worldliness, wealth, and attractiveness to girls. **DOK 1**

   (b) It suggests the same kind of spirit of adventure and heroism. **DOK 2**
2. (a) He has risen to a position they envy. **DOK 3** (b) They would probably be jealous of anyone, but they are especially jealous of him because he makes a great show of his new position. **DOK 3**
3. Yes, many people crave recognition for their success. The quest for lasting and widespread glory has motivated people through the ages. **DOK 3**
4. They wanted to be clowns, performers in a minstrel show, and pirates. These all came from their direct experience with those who travelled through Hannibal because this is all they knew of the outside world. **DOK 2**
5. Students should justify their answers by citing material from the text.

### FORMATIVE ASSESSMENT

### Analyze the Text

- **If** students fail to cite evidence, **then** remind them to support their ideas with specific information from the text.
- **If** students struggle to describe the syntax, **then** discuss different types of syntax, and illustrate with examples.



MAKING MEANING

*from* LIFE ON THE MISSISSIPPI

## Close Read the Text

1. This model, from paragraph 3 of the text, shows two sample annotations, along with questions and conclusions. Close read the passage, and find another detail to annotate. Then, write a question and your conclusion.

Close Read (ANNOTATE, QUESTION, CONCLUDE)

ANNOTATE: Twain uses many synonyms for *beautiful.*

QUESTION: Why does Twain describe the steamboat with these words?

CONCLUDE: Twain wants readers to understand the awe and admiration he felt.

She is long and sharp and trim and pretty; she has two tall, fancy-topped chimneys, with a gilded device of some kind swung between them; a fanciful pilothouse, all glass and gingerbread, perched on top of the texas deck behind them; the paddleboxes are gorgeous. . . .

ANNOTATE: Twain creates a long sentence with semicolons.

QUESTION: Why does Twain use this sentence structure?

CONCLUDE: The complex structure conveys how large the boat looms over the town and in his imagination.

2. For more practice, go back into the text, and complete the close-read notes.
3. Revisit a section of the text you found important during your first read. Read this section closely, and **annotate** what you notice. Ask yourself **questions** such as "Why did the author make this choice?" What can you **conclude?**

**Tool Kit**
Close-Read Guide and Model Annotation

## Analyze the Text

CITE TEXTUAL EVIDENCE to support your answers.

Notebook Respond to these questions.

1. (a) **Analyze** What does a job working on the steamboats represent to the boys of Twain's hometown? (b) **Connect** How does this childhood ambition reflect the American spirit that gave rise to the settlement of the frontier?
2. (a) **Analyze** Why do the boys feel as they do about the young apprentice engineer? (b) **Draw Conclusions** Would they feel the same if another boy from town found a position on a steamboat? Explain.
3. **Evaluate** Is the desire for glory a reasonable motivation in life? Explain.
4. **Historical Perspectives** What careers other than steamboat pilot did the boys in Hannibal consider? Explain where these ideas came from.
5. **Essential Question:** ***What is the relationship between literature and place?*** What have you learned about the relationship between literature and place by reading this memoir?

STANDARDS

Reading Informational Text

- Cite strong and thorough textual evidence to support analysis of what the text says explicitly as well as inferences drawn from the text, including determining where the text leaves matters uncertain.
- Determine an author's point of view or purpose in a text in which the rhetoric is particularly effective, analyzing how style and content contribute to the power, persuasiveness, or beauty of the text.





### PERSONALIZE FOR LEARNING

**Strategic Support**

**Using Conventions for Meaning** If students are overwhelmed by Twain's long sentences, explain that the semicolons provide an opportunity to pause and examine a shorter piece of the sentence. (paragraphs 5 and 6) Assign partners to select and approach one of Twain's long sentences by creating a T-chart.

On the left side, students write what the text describes. After they have completed a sentence, have students look back at their interpretations to better understand the sentence. Suggest students use this approach when encountering very long sentences in text.

## Analyze Craft and Structure

**Author's Purpose** Every author has a purpose—or multiple purposes—for writing. For example, an author may write to inform, to persuade, to describe, or to entertain. One of Twain's purposes for writing *Life on the Mississippi* is to entertain readers, which he does by using anecdotes and humorous descriptions.

- **Anecdotes** are brief stories about interesting, amusing, or strange events. Writers include anecdotes to entertain and to make a point. For example, Twain entertains readers by sharing an anecdote about how he ran away and tried to join a steamboat crew. He explains that he got only "a cold shoulder and short words from mates and clerks." At the same time, Twain is making a point about his burning ambition to become a steamboat man.
- **Humorous descriptions** present details that appeal to the senses even as they amuse readers. Humorous details in this example from paragraph 4 of the story appeal to the senses of sight and touch:

  *He would always manage to have a rusty bolt to scrub while his boat tarried at our town, and he would sit on the inside guard and scrub it, where we could all see him and envy him and loathe him.*

In addition to being funny, Twain's writing has an undercurrent of **social commentary**—that is, a discerning examination of society. Twain shares his keen observations of human weakness, which he usually describes with affection. In *Life on the Mississippi*, Twain looks back on his friends and neighbors fondly, but he also points out their flaws.

### Practice

**CITE TEXTUAL EVIDENCE** to support your answers.

Reread paragraphs 1–4 of *Life on the Mississippi.*

**Notebook** Respond to these questions.

1. (a) In paragraph 3, are the town and steamboat described using humorous or nonhumorous details, or a mixture of both? Explain. (b) What purpose or purposes does Twain address by presenting these details?
2. What social commentary about the values of the town's boys does Twain offer in paragraph 4?
3. (a) In paragraph 4, why does Twain call the apprentice "an undeserving reptile"? (b) What comment is Twain making about the boys by using this phrase?
4. In a chart like this one, record examples of humorous description from the text. Explain why each example is humorous. Then, explain what social comment Twain is making with the description.

| EXAMPLE OF HUMOROUS DESCRIPTION | EXPLANATION | SOCIAL COMMENTARY |
|---|---|---|
| We had transient ambitions of other sorts, but they were only transient. | The boys had passing interests of all sorts, but the desire to be transient was lasting. | The desire to leave the sleepy town for adventure was lasting and strong. |
| We had a hope that if we lived and were good, God would permit us to be pirates. | Pirates are considered bad, so becoming pirates with God's permission is humorous. | Being part of the steamboat world was more important than anything else. |
| After ten more minutes ... the town drunkard asleep by the skidsonce more. | The town quickly returns to its normal sleepy state. | The only exciting thing that happened in the town was the arrival of the steamboat. |
| | | |





## PERSONALIZE FOR LEARNING

### English Language Support

**Figurative Language** Have English learners explain how the choice of a particular word affects the reader. Point students to a word or phrase, such as "After ten more minutes the town is **dead** again. . ." (paragraph 3). Provide other words Twain could have chosen (sleepy, quiet, peaceful). Then, ask them to explain why they think Twain chose the word "dead." **EMERGING**

Point students to a word, such as "After ten more minutes the town is **dead** again. . ." Ask students what other words Twain could have chosen (sleepy, quiet, peaceful) Then, ask them to explain why they think Twain chose the word "dead." **EXPANDING**

Have students select a word or phrase that stands out to them. Ask them to list synonyms Twain could have used and then to explain the effect of the word he selected as opposed to the synonyms. **BRIDGING**

DIGITAL PERSPECTIVES  

## Analyze Craft and Structure

**Author's Purpose** Explain that Twain's humor in this selection is not laugh-out-loud funny, but, instead, contains a charming and amusing tone, which connects to social commentary. Explain that the humor softens Twain's social commentary, making it a nostalgic look at his past. For more support, see **Analyze Craft and Structure: Author's Purpose.**

**MAKE IT INTERACTIVE**

Ask students to reflect upon social commentary in contemporary life. Have volunteers recount their encounters with humorous social commentary such as those in films, books, comics, or on social media. Then discuss which societal critiques are underlying in these commentaries.

### Practice

Possible responses:

1. (a) Twain avoids humor to suggest the awe he felt about the steamboat. (b) The description is entertaining because it is very vivid, but not because it is humorous.
2. Twain offers social commentary on the human tendencies toward boasting and toward jealousy as he describes the pompousness of the apprentice engineer and the boys' feelings about him when he visits.
3. (a) Twain's humorous comment points out that he, unlike most of the townspeople, knew what the apprentice was really like. (b) The comment results from his disgust that the town would welcome the apprentice just for having survived an accident and that God would have allowed him to survive.
4. See possible responses in chart on Student page.

### FORMATIVE ASSESSMENT

### Analyze Craft and Structure

- **If** students struggle to locate or explain humorous descriptions, **then** have volunteers read humorous sections aloud and give opinions about why they are or are not humorous.
- **If** students fail to make the connection between the humor and social commentary, **then** select one example of a humorous excerpt and assign small groups to discuss what they learn about Hannibal from the excerpt.

For Reteach and Practice, see **Analyze Craft and Structure: Author's Purpose (RP).**

# TEACHING

## Concept Vocabulary

**Why These Words?**

Possible responses:

1. The words help readers understand Twain's admiration for the steamboat and convey the beauty that it holds for him and others.
2. Other words connected to this idea include *handsome* (paragraph 3), *pretty* (paragraph 3), *wonders* (paragraph 4), *silver (paragraph 4), charms* (paragraph 4), *and honored* (paragraph 6).

### Practice

Possible responses:

1. It might be decorated with features such as elegant window boxes, fancy shutters, different colors of paint, and gargoyles to make it fancy.
2. Gold paint or gold leaf would be used to make a gilded picture frame.
3. I would feel honored because an exalted person is revered.
4. The tourist probably would be impressed and would take many photographs.
5. A person of eminence should be addressed with respect and politeness.
6. Picturesque features might include a lake or river, a lovely dock, small boats, and seagulls.

### Word Network

**Possible words:** *drowsing, loafing, levee, skids, wharf, still, brilliant, lonely, remote*

## Word Study

Possible responses:

1. *Statuesque* means "majestic, like a statue."
2. Examples include *grotesque* (strange or unnatural in shape or character; fantastically ugly; bizarre) and *Lincolnesque* (having a character or style like that of Abraham Lincoln).

For more support, see **Concept Vocabulary and Word Study.**

### FORMATIVE ASSESSMENT

**Concept Vocabulary**

**If** students fail to see the connection between the words, **then** have them look back at the text and determine how each word is used in connection with Twain's experience on the steamboat.

**Word Study**

**If** students struggle to understand the suffix *-esque*, **then** help them understand that it means to be similar to, or like, whatever the root word is. For Reteach and Practice, see **Word Study: Suffix *-esque* (RP).**



LANGUAGE DEVELOPMENT

*from* LIFE ON THE MISSISSIPPI

## Concept Vocabulary

| gilded | grandeur | exalted |
|---|---|---|
| ornamented | picturesquely | eminence |

**Why These Words?** These concept vocabulary words are used to describe splendid objects or impressive people. For example, the *gilded* and *ornamented* devices on the steamboats added to their *grandeur*.

1. How does the concept vocabulary help readers understand how young Twain felt about the steamboat?
2. What other words in the selection connect to the idea of splendor?

### Practice

**Notebook** Respond to these questions.

1. How might a building be *ornamented*? Give examples.
2. What object might you expect to be *gilded*?
3. How would you feel if you met an *exalted* person? Why?
4. How might a tourist react to the *grandeur* of the Rocky Mountains?
5. What is the proper way to address a person of *eminence*?
6. Where might you pose *picturesquely* for a photo?

**WORD NETWORK**

Add words related to a sense of place from the text to your Word Network.

## Word Study

**Suffix: *-esque*** The suffix *-esque* is an adjective-forming suffix that means "having a certain style, manner, resemblance, or distinctive character." Thus, *picturesquely* means "in a way that resembles a picture."

The suffix has an interesting history. English borrowed it from French, which had previously borrowed it from Italian. It's ultimate source is unknown but was likely Germanic—that is, a language closely related to German and to English itself. Indeed, it is cognate with, or derives from the same source as, the English suffix *-ish* , and their meanings are still related.

1. Write a definition of *statuesque* based on your understanding of the suffix *-esque*. Check your answer in a print or digital college-level dictionary.
2. Identify and define two other words that end with the suffix *-esque*. Use a print or digital college-level dictionary to check your work.

**STANDARDS**

**Reading Informational Text**
Determine the meaning of words and phrases as they are used in a text, including figurative, connotative, and technical meanings; analyze how an author uses and refines the meaning of a key term or terms over the course of a text.

**Language**
- Identify and correctly use patterns of word changes that indicate different meanings or parts of speech.
- Verify the preliminary determination of the meaning of a word or phrase.



416 UNIT 4 • GRIT AND GRANDEUR

### PERSONALIZE FOR LEARNING

**English Language Support**

**Suffixes** Ask pairs of students to indicate the plural endings of the words *events, boys, years, streets.* **EMERGING**

Ask students to group the following words according to their endings as either plural nouns or past tenses: *lived, pirates, faded, remained, arrived, events, boys, streets, clerks.* **EXPANDING**

Ask students to reread the selection and identify what parts of speech these words are: *lived, faded, remained, arrived, tilted, slouched, scattered.* **BRIDGING**

An expanded **English Language Support Lesson** on Suffixes is available in the Interactive Teacher's Edition.

## Author's Style

**Words and Phrases** Two of the key elements of Twain's distinctive style are his **diction**, or choice of words and phrases, and his **tone,** or attitude toward his subject. This chart identifies the types of diction and tone Twain uses in *Life on the Mississippi.*

| TYPE OF DICTION OR TONE | DEFINITION | EXAMPLE |
|---|---|---|
| technical terms | words and phrases used in a specific technical or scientific field, such as nautical terms related to ships | *. . . the crew are grouped on the forecastle; the broad stage is run far out over the port bow. . . .* (paragraph 3) |
| colloquial language | informal words and phrases, including slang, that are used in speech but not in formal writing | *And he was always talking about "St. Looey" like an old citizen. . . .* (paragraph 4) |
| conversational tone | the effect created by the use of natural language spoken casually as in everyday life | *By and by one of our boys went away. He was not heard of for a long time.* (paragraph 4) |

Twain's use of both technical and colloquial diction in *Life on the Mississippi* creates a mixture of formality and informality in the memoir. As a result, readers get a multidimensional sense of the busy place, its people, and what they value.

### Read It

1. Mark the technical language in this passage from paragraph 3 of the excerpt from *Life on the Mississippi*. Then, explain how the diction helps establish a particular tone.

   *. . . the boiler deck, the hurricane deck, and the texas deck are fenced and ornamented with clean white railings; there is a flag gallantly flying from the jackstaff. . . .*

2. **Connect to Style** Mark two examples of colloquial language in paragraphs 4–6. Then, explain how Twain's diction helps create his humorous style.

3. **Notebook** Reread paragraph 6. How would you describe the diction in that paragraph? What tone does the diction help develop? Support your answer with textual evidence.

### Write It

**Notebook** Mimicking Twain's voice, write a paragraph about a minor argument between friends that uses the following examples of colloquial language. Create a relaxed, conversational tone.

| ornery | reckon | rile | ruckus |
|---|---|---|---|





DIGITAL PERSPECTIVES

## Author's Style

**Words and Phrases** Point out to students that diction and purpose are related. Explain that if Twain wrote about steamboats for strictly informational purposes, he would include technical terms but not colloquial language or conversational tone, both of which add to the entertainment purpose of the text. For more support, see **Author's Style: Words and Phrases.**

### Read It

Possible responses

1. The technical language is *boiler deck, hurricane deck, texas deck,* and *jackstaff.* The diction creates a formal tone.
2. Examples include *He cut out every boy in the village* (which creates humor because it conveys the childish pettiness the boys feel) and *the boats that lay packed together like sardines* (which helps Twain paint a descriptive picture of the time and place through its vivid sensory appeal).
3. Possible response: The diction is rather formal. That very formality creates humor through the contrast between the depth of the speaker's despair and his childish schemes.

### Write It

Have students use the Internet to define each of the terms before using them in writing. Encourage students to be creative in writing their paragraph.

### FORMATIVE ASSESSMENT

### Author's Style

**If** students struggle to write in Twain's colloquial language, **then** encourage them to reread the text aloud with a small group and work together to imitate the voice. For more Reteach and Practice, see **Author's Style: Words and Phrases (RP).**

### Selection Test

Administer the *Life on the Mississippi* Selection Test, which is available in both print and digital formats online in Assessments.

AUTHOR'S PERSPECTIVE **Elfrieda Hiebert, Ph.D.**

**Concept Vocabulary** Teachers can help students expand their word networks by using morphemes and cognates.

- **Morphemes** are the smallest grammatical units of a language that cannot be subdivided into further such elements. Tell students that morphemes can be words or parts of words, such as the words *as, the, write,* or the *-ed* in *stayed.* Many new words are members of morphological families of three to five words. For example, words that come from the Anglo-Saxon layer of English use inflected endings (such as *-s/-es, -ed, -ing*) and *-er* and *-est* for comparisons (such as *big, bigger, biggest*).
- **Cognates** are words that are descended from the same language, such as the English word *family,* the Spanish *familia,* the French *famille,* the Italian *famiglia,* and the German *familie.* Explain to students that knowing cognates can help build language by introducing multiple words and ways to decode unfamiliar words.

# The Notorious Jumping Frog of Calaveras County

**AUDIO SUMMARIES**
Audio summaries of "The Notorious Jumping Frog of Calaveras County" are available online in both English and Spanish in the Interactive Teacher's Edition or Unit Resources. Assigning these summaries prior to reading the selection may help students build additional background knowledge and set a context for their first read.

## Summary

In the short story "The Notorious Jumping Frog of Calaveras County" by Mark Twain, the narrator is asked by a friend to find out about Leonidas W. Smiley while visiting a Western mining camp. The narrator speaks with Simon Wheeler, who claims he does not know Leonidas. Wheeler tells the narrator stories about Jim Smiley, an inveterate gambler. One day a stranger meets Jim, who claims that he has trained a frog to jump higher than any other. The stranger says that he would bet against Jim's frog if he had one. Jim goes out to find another frog, leaving his own with the stranger, who fills it with buckshot. When Jim returns, the men get their frogs to jump and the stranger's frog jumps higher. Jim pays the stranger their $40 wager. Later, Jim realizes that he has been cheated. He chases the stranger, but he cannot find him. As the story ends, the narrator leaves to avoid hearing other stories by Wheeler.

### Insight

The Western mining town where the story is set is called Angel's Camp and is described as "decaying" and the bar as "dilapidated." However, these are the only two descriptive details of the setting provided. It is the dialect of Simon Wheeler that gives the reader a sense of the unique location of the story. Based on the events described and the language used by Wheeler, the reader has a sense that in the old town, there is little to keep people busy.

ESSENTIAL QUESTION:
What is the relationship between literature and place?

## Connection to the Essential Question

In "The Notorious Jumping Frog of Calaveras County," the setting is mainly shown by what the characters say and how they say it. Mark Twain uses dialect rather than description to give the reader a sense of place.

WHOLE CLASS LEARNING PERFORMANCE TASK
How do American authors use regional details to make the events and themes of a narrative come to life for readers?

UNIT PERFORMANCE-BASED ASSESSMENT
What makes certain places live on in our memory?

## Connection to Performance Tasks

**Whole-Class Learning Performance Task** Mark Twain uses the setting of the lonely mining town to make his characters come to life. The town is "decaying" so the reader gets the sense there there isn't much to do there other than talk and tell stories. The stories about Jim Smiley convey the themes of "The Notorious Jumping Frog of Calaveras County."

**Unit Performance-Based Assessment** This selection provides an interesting insight into the idea of "place" because it focuses mostly on an unremarkable event that forms the basis for a tall tale told by a local resident. Wheeler's speech and cadence reflect the boredom of the location. The story's dry, ironic quality is what makes it humorous.

DIGITAL PERSPECTIVES

 Audio
 Video
 Document
 Annotation Highlights
 EL Highlights
Online Assessment

## LESSON RESOURCES

| | Making Meaning | Language Development | Effective Expression |
|---|---|---|---|
| Lesson | **First Read**<br>**Close Read**<br>**Analyze the Text**<br>**Analyze Craft and Structure** | **Concept Vocabulary**<br>**Word Study**<br>**Author's Style** | **Writing to Compare** |
| **Instructional Standards** | **RL.10** By the end of grade 11, read and comprehend literature . . .<br>**RL.1** Cite strong and thorough textual evidence . . .<br>**RL.6** Analyze a case . . .<br>**L.5.a** Interpret figures of speech . . . | **RL.4** Determine the meaning of words and phrases . . .<br>**L.5** Demonstrate understanding of figurative language . . .<br>**L.5.b** Analyze nuances in the meanings of words . . . | **W.2** Write informative/explanatory texts . . .<br>**W.2.a** Introduce a topic . . .<br>**W.2.b** Develop the topic . . .<br>**W.5** Develop and strengthen writing as needed . . . |
| **STUDENT RESOURCES** | | | |
| Available online in the Interactive Teacher's Edition or Unit Resources | Selection Audio<br>First-Read Guide: Fiction<br>Close-Read Guide: Fiction | Word Network | Evidence Log |
| **TEACHER RESOURCES** | | | |
| **Selection Resources** Available online in the Interactive Teacher's Edition or Unit Resources | Audio Summaries<br>Annotation Highlights<br>EL Highlights<br>English Language Support Lesson: Denotation and Connotation<br>Analyze Craft and Structure: Point of View | Concept Vocabulary and Word Study<br>Author's Style: Impact of Word Choice | Writing to Compare: Explanatory Text |
| **Reteach/Practice (RP)** Available online in the Interactive Teacher's Edition or Unit Resources | Analyze Craft and Structure: Point of View (RP) | Word Study: Denotation and Connotation (RP)<br>Author's Style: Impact of Word Choice (RP) | |
| **Assessment** Available online in Assessments | Selection Test | | |
| **My Resources** | A Unit 4 Answer Key is available online and in the Interactive Teacher's Edition. | | |

# Reading Support

| Text Complexity Rubric: The Notorious Jumping Frog of Calaveras County | |
|---|---|
| **Quantitative Measures** | |
| **Lexile:** 1190 **Text Length:** 2,539 words | |
| **Qualitative Measures** | |
| Knowledge Demands ①—②—③—❹—⑤ | The situations and experiences will be unfamiliar to readers (story set in gold mining town in mid-1800s) and there are multiple themes (cunning and cleverness, honesty and deception, tall tales and exaggeration). |
| Structure ①—②—③—❹—⑤ | The story is a frame narrative—a story within a story. A narrator describes an encounter with a man who tells him a story. The beginning and end are spoken by the narrator, and the center of the text is the "inside story." |
| Language Conventionality and Clarity ①—②—③—❹—⑤ | The narrator speaks in educated diction that is formal and complex, with unfamiliar syntax and vocabulary. The storyteller speaks in uneducated vernacular, with regional dialect, slang, and run-on sentences. |
| Levels of Meaning/Purpose ①—②—❸—④—⑤ | The text employs multiple levels of meaning. The reader needs to follow the story within a story and infer meaning from the actions and words of the narrator and the content of the story he hears. |

DECIDE AND PLAN

## English Language Support

Provide English Learners with support for knowledge demands and structure as they read the selection.

**Structure** Make sure students understand the structure. If necessary, point out that in the first three paragraphs, the narrator is speaking. Ask them to notice the quotation marks at the beginnings of paragraphs 4–20 that indicate that Simon Wheeler is telling his story. From paragraph 21 to the end, it goes back to the original narrator telling the story about Simon Wheeler.

**Language** Point out that students will find two different styles of language. Read aloud examples, explaining that the narrator is educated and uses formal speech and difficult vocabulary. Simon Wheeler is uneducated and uses a regional dialect and slang.

## Strategic Support

Provide students with strategic support to ensure that they can successfully read the text.

**Language** Ask students to read aloud some examples of the speech of the narrator (from paragraphs 1–3 or the ending) and then some of the words of Simon Wheeler (from paragraphs 4–20). Ask them what they notice about how the two men speak. Point out that the author is showing that the narrator is an educated man, whereas Simon Wheeler is not.

**Meaning** Break the story into sections and discuss each one. For example, have students read the first three paragraphs, spoken by the narrator. Discuss how the narrator describes Wheeler, and how those descriptions tell us how he feels about him.

## Challenge

Provide students who need to be challenged with ideas for how they can go beyond a simple interpretation of the text.

**Text Analysis** Ask students to give an analysis of the narrator. Ask them how he feels about Wheeler and his tall tale, and how they know. Encourage them to cite examples of words and phrases the narrator uses to describe Wheeler and the experience of hearing his story.

**Written Response** Discuss that Wheeler's story is a "tall tale"—an exaggerated story. Ask students to write how they know if someone is exaggerating when telling a story. Are there times when it is humorous and appropriate? Times it feels boastful or dishonest? In what setting would it be okay to tell a tall tale? Encourage students to give real-life examples.

TEACH

## Read and Respond

Have students do their first read of the selection. Then have them complete their close read. Finally, work with them on the Making Meaning, Language Development, and Effective Expression activities.

# Standards Support Through Teaching and Learning Cycle

## IDENTIFY NEEDS

Analyze results of the Beginning-of-Year Assessment, focusing on the items relating to Unit 4. Also take into consideration student performance to this point and your observations of where particular students struggle.

## DECIDE AND PLAN

- If students have performed poorly on items matching these standards, then provide selection scaffolds before assigning them the on-level lesson provided in the Student Edition.
- If students have done well on the Beginning-of-Year Assessment, then challenge them to keep progressing and learning by giving them opportunities to practice the skills in depth.
- Use the Selection Resources listed on the Planning pages for from "The Notorious Jumping Frog of Calaveras County" to help students continually improve their ability to master the standards.

**Instructional Standards: The Notorious Jumping Frog of Calaveras County**

| | Catching Up | This Year | Looking Forward |
|---|---|---|---|
| Reading | You may wish to administer the **Analyze Craft and Structure: Point of View (RP)** worksheet to familiarize students with incongruity and hyperbole.<br><br>You may wish to administer the **Author's Style: Impact of Word Choice (RP)** worksheet to familiarize students dialect and idiomatic expressions. | **RL.6** Analyze a case in which grasping point of view requires distinguishing what is directly stated in a text from what is really meant.<br><br>**RL.4** Determine the meaning of words and phrases as they are used in the text, including figurative and connotative meanings; analyze the impact of specific word choices on meaning and tone, including words with multiple meanings or language that is particularly fresh, engaging, or beautiful. | Have students identify other works they have read that use incongruity and hyperbole.<br><br>Challenge students to list examples of local dialect and idioms. Then, invite them to try to create new ones. |
| Language | Review the **Word Study: Denotation and Connotation (RP)** worksheet with students to better familiarize them with connotation and denotation. | **L.5.b** Analyze nuances in the meaning of words with similar denotations. | Challenge students to speculate on how words develop connotations away from their original denotations. |

## ANALYZE AND REVISE

- Analyze student work for evidence of student learning.
- Identify whether or not students have met the expectations in the standards.
- Identify implications for future instruction.

## TEACH

Implement the planned lesson, and gather evidence of student learning.

## Jump Start

**FIRST READ** *What is the most boring story you have ever heard? What is the most interesting story you have ever heard?* Engage students in a discussion about what makes stories boring or interesting.

### The Notorious Jumping Frog of Calaveras County

Can a boring story be told in an interesting way? Modeling this and other questions readers might ask will bring "The Notorious Jumping Frog of Calaveras County" to life and connect it to the Performance Task question. Selection audio and print capability for the selection are available in the Interactive Teacher's Edition.

### Concept Vocabulary

Circulate among students as they rank their words. Remind them that they will find the definitions of these words in the side column beside each word's location in the text.

### FIRST READ

The first time they go through the selection, students should perform the steps of the first read:

NOTICE: You may want to encourage students to notice what makes them laugh or smile as they read.

ANNOTATE: Remind students to mark passages that contain humor.

CONNECT: Tell students that the narrator of the story believes that a friend played a trick on him to bore him to death. Ask students to think about a time that they were involved in an unexpected or amusing situation.

RESPOND: Students will demonstrate their understanding of the text by answering questions and writing a summary.

Point out to students that they will perform the first three steps concurrently as they are doing their first read. They will complete the Respond step after they have finished the first read. You may wish to print copies of the **First-Read Guide: Fiction** for students to use.

**Remind students that during their first read, they should not answer the close-read questions that appear in the selection.**

MAKING MEANING

from LIFE ON THE MISSISSIPPI

### Comparing Texts

Read "The Notorious Jumping Frog of Calaveras County," and complete the first-read and close-read activities. Then, compare Twain's approach to humor in this story with his approach in the excerpt from *Life on the Mississippi.*

THE NOTORIOUS JUMPING FROG OF CALAVERAS COUNTY

About the Author

When the Civil War closed traffic on the Mississippi, **Mark Twain** (1835–1910) went west to Nevada. There, he supported himself as a journalist and lecturer, developing the entertaining writing style that made him famous. In 1865, Twain published "The Notorious Jumping Frog of Calaveras County," his version of a tall tale he had heard in a mining camp in California while working as a gold prospector. The story launched Twain's career as a humorist widely regarded as one of the greatest of American writers.

# The Notorious Jumping Frog of Calaveras County

### Concept Vocabulary

You will encounter the following words in "The Notorious Jumping Frog of Calaveras County." Before reading, note how familiar you are with each word. Then, rank the words from most familiar (1) to least familiar (6).

| WORD | YOUR RANKING |
|---|---|
| garrulous | |
| exasperating | |
| tedious | |
| monotonous | |
| interminable | |
| buttonholed | |

After completing your first read, come back to the concept vocabulary and review your rankings. Mark changes to your original rankings as needed.

### First Read FICTION

Apply these strategies as you conduct your first read. You will have an opportunity to complete the close-read notes after your first read.

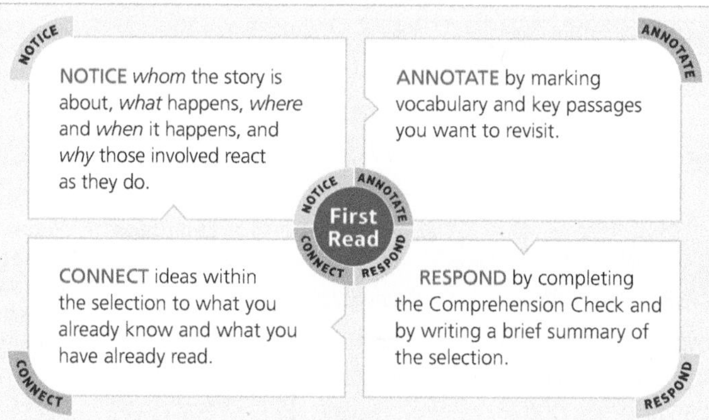
NOTICE
NOTICE *whom* the story is about, *what* happens, *where* and *when* it happens, and *why* those involved react as they do.
ANNOTATE
ANNOTATE by marking vocabulary and key passages you want to revisit.
First Read
CONNECT
CONNECT ideas within the selection to what you already know and what you have already read.
RESPOND
RESPOND by completing the Comprehension Check and by writing a brief summary of the selection.

STANDARDS

**Reading Literature**

By the end of grade 11, read and comprehend literature, including stories, dramas, and poems, in the grades 11–CCR text complexity band proficiently, with scaffolding as needed at the high end of the range.

418 UNIT 4 • GRIT AND GRANDEUR

### VOCABULARY DEVELOPMENT

**Concept Vocabulary** For additional practice with concept vocabulary, have students look up the words and record their meanings. Then, have students write a short paragraph, using at least four of the words. Have volunteers read their paragraphs aloud.

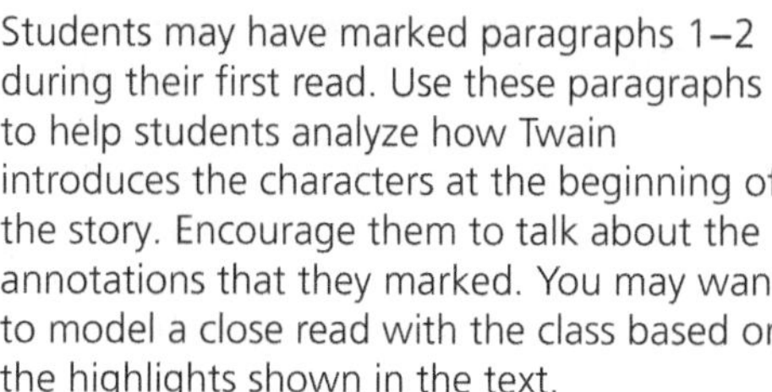


ANCHOR TEXT | SHORT STORY

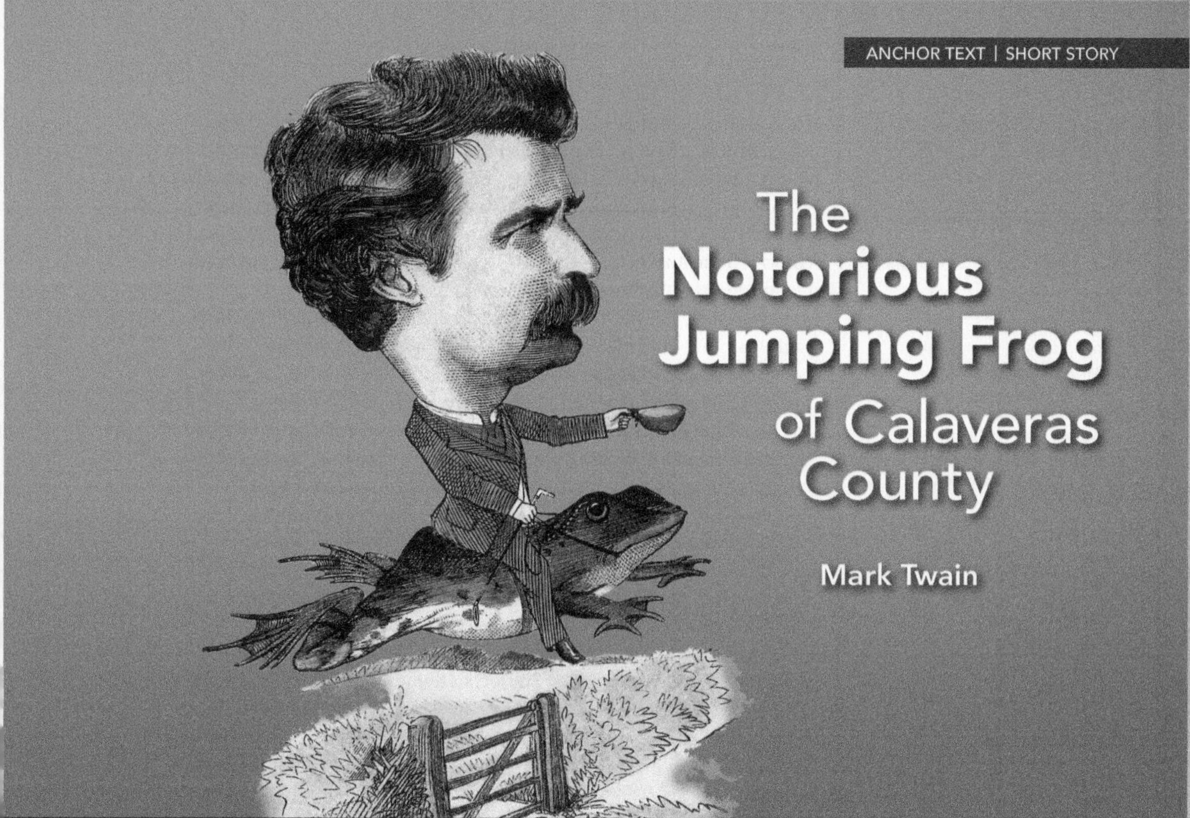

# The Notorious Jumping Frog of Calaveras County

Mark Twain

## CLOSER LOOK

### Analyze Direct Characterization

Students may have marked paragraphs 1–2 during their first read. Use these paragraphs to help students analyze how Twain introduces the characters at the beginning of the story. Encourage them to talk about the annotations that they marked. You may want to model a close read with the class based on the highlights shown in the text.

**ANNOTATE:** Have students mark details in these paragraphs that describe Simon Wheeler, or have students participate while you highlight them.

**QUESTION:** Guide students to consider what these details might tell them. Ask what a reader can infer from the words and phrases that describe Smiley, and accept student responses.

**Possible response:** Smiley is old, he talks a lot but he is good-natured and relaxed and means no harm.

**CONCLUDE:** Help students to formulate conclusions about the importance of these details in the text. Ask students why the author might have included these details.

**Possible response:** Many readers can relate to feeling trapped listening to a well-meaning person talk too much, when they would much rather be doing something else. In this introduction, Twain sets up a universal experience that his readers will relate to in a humorous way.

Remind students that **characterization** is the way a writer develops and reveals a character's personality and temperament. With **direct characterization,** a writer simply tells what a character is like. With **indirect characterization,** the writer shows a character's traits.

BACKGROUND

This story was Mark Twain's first successful fiction publication and exemplifies the author's sense of humor. It is framed as a story heard secondhand, and the narrator is himself a character. Published in 1865 under the title "Jim Smiley and His Jumping Frog," the story brought Twain national attention.

SCAN FOR MULTIMEDIA 

1 In compliance with the request of a friend of mine, who wrote me from the East, I called on good-natured, garrulous old Simon Wheeler, and inquired after my friend's friend, Leonidas W. Smiley, as requested to do, and I hereunto append the result. I have a lurking suspicion that *Leonidas W.* Smiley is a myth; that my friend never knew such a personage: and that he only conjectured that if I asked old Wheeler about him, it would remind him of his infamous *Jim* Smiley, and he would go to work and bore me to death with some exasperating reminiscence of him as long and as tedious as it should be useless to me. If that was the design, it succeeded.

2 I found Simon Wheeler dozing comfortably by the barroom stove of the dilapidated tavern in the decayed mining camp of Angel's, and I noticed that he was fat and baldheaded, and had an expression of winning gentleness and simplicity upon his tranquil countenance.

NOTES

**garrulous** (GAR uh luhs) *adj.* very talkative

**exasperating** (ehg ZAS puh rayt ihng) *adj.* annoying

**tedious** (TEE dee uhs) *adj.* boring; dull





## PERSONALIZE FOR LEARNING

### Strategic Support

**Comprehension** Review paragraph 1 to help students understand the premise of the story set forth in the opening. Point out that the narrator later realized that he might have been the target of his friend's prank. As needed, have students refer back to this opening passage when they have finished reading the story. As they read, have students locate moments in the story when the reader is given clues indicating that Simon Wheeler's garrulousness (paragraph 1) is intended to make the reader laugh and appreciate the narrator's plight all the more. Such moments include the extended description of Smiley's mare or the careful pause in which Wheeler makes sure the narrator knows the bulldog pup's name—Andrew Jackson—even though the information is completely irrelevant. Have students record these junctures in a chart.

CLOSER LOOK

## Understand Regional Dialect

Students may have marked paragraph 4 during their first read. Use this paragraph to help students identify and better understand Twain's use of regional dialect. Encourage them to talk about the annotations that they marked. You may want to model a close read with the class based on the highlights shown in the text.

**ANNOTATE:** Have students mark details in paragraph 4 that show examples of regional dialect, or have students participate while you highlight them.

**QUESTION:** Guide students to consider what these details might tell them. Ask what a reader can infer from the regional words and phrases that Twain includes, and accept student responses.

**Possible response:** Twain is using the slang of the time, and/or Smiley was not very educated.

**CONCLUDE:** Help students to formulate conclusions about the importance of these details in the text. Ask students why the author might have included these details.

**Possible response:** Having a character speak using slang terms and in a way that seems uneducated is a way of building a character and telling us more about Smiley.

Tell students that **dialect** is the form of a language spoken by people in a particular region or group. Different dialects often use unique grammar, syntax, vocabulary, and pronunciation. An author can reveal information about a character through the use of regional dialects. What characters choose to say; when characters speak or opt not to speak; and how characters express themselves can all provide a broader and more well-rounded picture of who they are.

NOTES

**monotonous** (muh NOT uh nuhs) *adj.* boring due to a lack of variety

**interminable** (ihn TUR muh nuh buhl) *adj.* seemingly unending

He roused up, and gave me good day. I told him a friend of mine had commissioned me to make some inquiries about a cherished companion of his boyhood named *Leonidas* W. Smiley—*Rev. Leonidas W.* Smiley, a young minister of the Gospel, who he had heard was at one time a resident of Angel's Camp. I added that if Mr. Wheeler could tell me anything about this Rev. Leonidas W. Smiley, I would feel under many obligations to him.

3 Simon Wheeler backed me into a corner and blockaded me there with his chair, and then sat down and reeled off the **monotonous** narrative which follows this paragraph. He never smiled, he never frowned, he never changed his voice from the gentle-flowing key to which he tuned his initial sentence, he never betrayed the slightest suspicion of enthusiasm; but all through the **interminable** narrative there ran a vein of impressive earnestness and sincerity, which showed me plainly that, so far from his imagining that there was anything ridiculous or funny about his story, he regarded it as a really important matter, and admired its two heroes as men of transcendent genius in *finesse*. I let him go on in his own way, and never interrupted him once.

4 "Rev. Leonidas W. H'm, Reverend Le—well, there was a feller here once by the name of *Jim* Smiley, in the winter of '49—or maybe it was the spring of '50—I don't recollect exactly, somehow, though what makes me think it was one or the other is because I remember the big flume[1] warn't finished when he first come to the camp; but anyway, he was the curiousest man about always betting on anything that turned up you ever see, if he could get anybody to bet on the other side; and if he couldn't he'd change sides. Any way that suited the other man would suit *him*—any way just so's he got a bet, *he* was satisfied. But still he was lucky, uncommon lucky; he most always come out winner. He was always ready and laying for a chance; there couldn't be no solit'ry thing mentioned but that feller'd offer to bet on it, and take any side you please, as I was just telling you. If there was a horse race, you'd find him flush or you'd find him busted at the end of it; if there was a dogfight, he'd bet on it; if there was a cat fight, he'd bet on it; if there was a chicken fight, he'd bet on it; why, if there was two birds setting on a fence, he would bet you which one would fly first; or if there was a camp meeting,[2] he would be there reg'lar to bet on Parson Walker, which he judged to be the best exhorter about here and so he was too, and a good man. If he even see a straddle bug[3] start to go anywheres, he would bet you how long it would take him to get to—to wherever he was going to, and if you took him up, he would foller that straddle bug to Mexico but what he would find out where he was bound for and how long he was on the road. Lots of the boys here has seen that Smiley, and can tell you about him. Why, it never made no difference to *him*—he'd bet on *any*

1. **flume** (floom) *n.* artificial channel for carrying water to provide power and transport objects.
2. **camp meeting** religious gathering at the mining camp.
3. **straddle bug** insect with long legs.





DIGITAL PERSPECTIVES

**Enriching the Text** Have students conduct online research about mining towns around the time period of 1860. Guide them to locate information, such as the gender ratio in the towns, what kind of ethnic diversity existed, what living conditions were like, how townspeople interacted with one another and what kinds of special problems existed in regard to providing basic goods, building shelters, and maintaining law and order. Then have students write a description of the setting of these mining towns. Provide time for students to share their research. Engage in a discussion of life during this time period and in this environment as a way to provide background for the text. **(Research to Explore)**

thing—the dangdest feller. Parson Walker's wife laid very sick once, for a good while, and it seemed as if they warn't going to save her; but one morning he come in, and Smiley up and asked him how she was, and he said she was considable better—thank the Lord for his inf'nite mercy—and coming on so smart that with the blessing of Prov'dence she'd get well yet; and Smiley, before he thought, says, 'Well, I'll resk two-and-a-half she don't anyway.'

NOTES

5 "Thish-yer Smiley had a mare—the boys called her the fifteen-minute nag, but that was only in fun, you know, because of course she was faster than that—and he used to win money on that horse, for all she was so slow and always had the asthma, or the distemper, or the consumption, or something of that kind. They used to give her two or three hundred yards start, and then pass her under way; but always at the fag end[4] of the race she'd get excited and desperate like, and come cavorting and straddling up, and scattering her legs around limber, sometimes in the air, and sometimes out to one side among the fences, and kicking up m-o-r-e dust and raising m-o-r-e racket with her coughing and sneezing and blowing her nose—and *always* fetch up at the stand just about a neck ahead, as near as you could cipher it down.

". . . kicking up m-o-r-e dust and raising m-o-r-e racket with her coughing and sneezing and blowing her nose—and *always* fetch up at the stand just about a neck ahead, . . ."

6 "And he had a little small bull-pup, that to look at him you'd think he warn't worth a cent but to set around and look ornery and lay for a chance to steal something. But as soon as money was up on him he was a different dog; his under-jaw'd begin to stick out like the fo'castle[5] of a steamboat, and his teeth would uncover and shine like the furnaces. And a dog might tackle him and bullyrag him, and bite him, and throw him over his shoulder two or three times, and Andrew Jackson—which was the name of the pup—Andrew Jackson would never let on but what *he* was satisfied, and hadn't expected nothing else—and the bets being doubled and doubled on the other side all the time, till the money was all up; and then all of a sudden he would grab that other dog jest by the j'int of his hind leg and freeze to it—not chaw, you understand, but only just grip and hang on till they throwed up the sponge, if it was a year. Smiley always come out winner on that pup, till he harnessed a dog once that didn't have no hind legs, because they'd been sawed off in a circular saw, and when the thing had gone along far enough, and the money was all up, and he come to make a snatch for his pet holt,[6] he see in a minute how he'd been imposed on, and how the other dog had him in the door, so to speak, and he 'peared surprised, and then he looked sorter discouraged-like, and

**CLOSE READ**

**ANNOTATE:** Mark details in paragraph 5 that describe the mare and the way that she acts.

**QUESTION:** Why does the narrator describe the mare in this way?

**CONCLUDE:** What is the effect of this description?

4. **fag end** last part.
5. **fo'castle** (FOHK suhl) *n.* forward part of the upper deck.
6. **holt** hold.





DIGITAL PERSPECTIVES  

 **CLOSE READ** 

As students look for details that describe the mare, remind them that they are reading dialogue and that it is the character, Wheeler, who is describing the mare in this way. You may wish to model the Close Read using the following think-aloud format. Possible responses to questions on the student page are included. You may also want to print copies of the **Close-Read Guide: Fiction** for students to use.

**ANNOTATE:** As I read paragraph 5, I notice and highlight the details that Wheeler uses to describe the mare and the way she acts. This tells me I will be looking for both adjectives and action words.

**QUESTION:** When I look back over these details, I see that they are exaggerated and that some are absurd, which makes them funny or lighthearted. For example, "scattering her legs around limber, sometimes in the air, and sometimes out to one side among the fences."

**CONCLUDE:** When I first read this paragraph, I had a moment of confusion about these details, but very soon, I realized that they were funny. These details make most readers want to continue reading because the story is funny.

## PERSONALIZE FOR LEARNING

### English Language Support

**Using Verbs and Verb Phrases** Call student attention to the description of the mare in paragraph 5. Students may benefit from more time exploring the many verbs and verb phrases in the description. Point out that the speaker uses more than one verb tense in this description. Explain that he begins by using the past tense to tell about an event that happened in the past, then switches to present progressive tense to describe the mare in action, as if she is in action now. Work with students to identify the verbs and verb phrases and identify their tense. Then have students list some of the more colorful verbs. Discuss their meanings to expand student vocabulary. Then challenge students to write their own description of the mare using some of the verbs. **ALL LEVELS**

## CLOSE READ

As students look for two things that Smiley teaches Dan'l Webster, remind them that Dan'l Webster is the name of the frog. You may wish to model the Close Read using the following think-aloud format. Possible responses to questions on the student page are included.

**ANNOTATE:** As I read paragraph 7, I notice and highlight the details that tell me what Smiley taught the frog. I will need to remember to read carefully because of Smiley's dialect.

**QUESTION:** I see that there is a lot of exaggeration and elaboration in this paragraph, so it takes some weeding through all the details to determine that Smiley taught the frog to jump and to catch flies. It makes me think that the author is using these details to build humor.

**CONCLUDE:** When I reflect upon these details, I realize that frogs do not need to be taught to jump or to catch flies—that is what they do naturally. These details are absurd and they make me laugh.

Additional **English Language Support** is available in the Interactive Teacher's Edition.

NOTES

**CLOSE READ**

**ANNOTATE:** In paragraph 7, mark the two skills that Smiley teaches Dan'l Webster.

**QUESTION:** Why might these details be important?

**CONCLUDE:** What is the effect of these details on readers?

didn't try no more to win the fight, and so he got shucked out bad. He give Smiley a look, as much as to say his heart was broke, and it was his fault, for putting up a dog that hadn't no hind legs for him to take holt of, which was his main dependence in a fight, and then he limped off a piece and laid down and died. It was a good pup, was that Andrew Jackson, and would have made a name for hisself if he'd lived, for the stuff was in him and he had genius—I know it, because he hadn't no opportunities to speak of, and it don't stand to reason that a dog could make such a fight as he could under them circumstances if he hadn't no talent. It always makes me feel sorry when I think of that last fight of his'n, and the way it turned out.

7 "Well, thish-yer Smiley had rat terriers,[7] and chicken cocks,[8] and tomcats and all them kind of things, till you couldn't rest, and you couldn't fetch nothing for him to bet on but he'd match you. He ketched a frog one day, and took him home, and said he cal'lated to educate him; and so he never done nothing for three months but set in his back yard and learn that frog to jump. And you bet you he *did* learn him, too. He'd give him a little punch behind, and the next minute you'd see that frog whirling in the air like a doughnut—see him turn one summerset, or maybe a couple, if he got a good start, and come down flatfooted and all right, like a cat. He got him up so in the matter of ketching flies, and kep' him in practice so constant, that he'd nail a fly every time as fur as he could see him. Smiley said all a frog wanted was education, and he could do 'most anything—and I believe him. Why, I've seen him set Dan'l Webster down here on this floor—Dan'l Webster was the name of the frog—and sing out, 'Flies, Dan'l, flies!' and quicker'n you could wink he'd spring straight up and snake a fly off'n the counter there, and flop down on the floor ag'in as solid as a gob of mud, and fall to scratching the side of his head with his hind foot as indifferent as if he hadn't no idea he'd been doin' any more'n any frog might do. You never see a frog so modest and straightfor'ard as he was, for all he was so gifted. And when it come to fair and square jumping on a dead level, he could get over more ground at one straddle than any animal of his breed you ever see. Jumping on a dead level was his strong suit, you understand; and when it come to that, Smiley would ante up money on him as long as he had a red.[9] Smiley was monstrous proud of his frog, and well he might be, for fellers that had traveled and been everywheres all said he laid over any frog that ever *they* see.

8 "Well, Smiley kep' the beast in a little lattice box, and he used to fetch him downtown sometimes and lay for a bet. One day a feller—a stranger in the camp, he was—come acrost him with his box, and says:

9 "'What might it be that you've got in the box?'

10 "And Smiley says, sorter indifferent-like, 'It might be a parrot, or it might be a canary, maybe, but it ain't—it's only just a frog.'

7. **rat terriers** dogs skilled in catching rats.
8. **chicken cocks** roosters trained to fight.
9. **a red** red cent; colloquial expression for "any money at all."





### HOW LANGUAGE WORKS

**Words and Phrases** Call student attention to the vocabulary level of paragraph 7. Teachers can help students refine their word networks by identifying adverbs in the text. Remind students that adverbs modify verbs and often end in *–ly.* Have students find adverbs in the text where Twain left off the *–ly* ending. For example, have students discuss the effect of words such as *constant, indifferent,* and *monstrous* in paragraph 7.

11 "And the feller took it, and looked at it careful, and turned it round this way and that, and says, 'H'm—so 'tis. Well, what's *he* good for?'

12 "'Well,' Smiley says, easy and careless, 'he's good enough for *one* thing, I should judge—he can outjump any frog in Calaveras county.'

13 "The feller took the box again, and took another long, particular look, and give it back to Smiley, and says, very deliberate, 'Well,' he says, 'I don't see no p'ints about that frog that's any better'n any other frog.'

14 "'Maybe you don't,' Smiley says. 'Maybe you understand frogs and maybe you don't understand 'em; maybe you've had experience, and maybe you ain't only a amature, as it were. Anyways, I've got *my* opinion, and I'll resk forty dollars that he can outjump any frog in Calaveras county.'

15 "And the feller studied a minute, and then says, kinder sad like, 'Well, I'm only a stranger here, and I ain't got no frog; but if I had a frog, I'd bet you.'

16 "And then Smiley says, 'That's all right—that's all right—if you'll hold my box a minute, I'll go and get you a frog.' And so the feller took the box, and put up his forty dollars along with Smiley's, and set down to wait.

17 "So he set there a good while thinking and thinking to hisself, and then he got the frog out and prized his mouth open and took a teaspoon and filled him full of quailshot[10]—filled him pretty near up to his chin—and set him on the floor. Smiley he went to the swamp and slopped around in the mud for a long time, and finally

NOTES

10. **quailshot** *n.* small lead pellets used for shooting quail, a small wild game bird.





DIGITAL PERSPECTIVES    

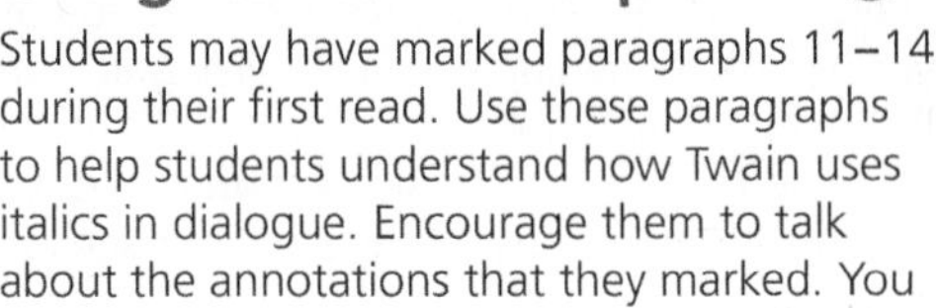

CLOSER LOOK

## Using Italics for Emphasis

Students may have marked paragraphs 11–14 during their first read. Use these paragraphs to help students understand how Twain uses italics in dialogue. Encourage them to talk about the annotations that they marked. You may want to model a close read with the class based on the highlights shown in the text.

**ANNOTATE:** Have students mark details in these paragraphs that show Twain's use of italics in dialogue, or have students participate while you highlight them.

**QUESTION:** Guide students to consider what this use of italics might tell them. Ask what a reader can infer from Twain's choice to italicize these words, and accept student responses.

**Possible response:** I look at the italicized words and it seems so me that Twain uses italics to show which words the speaker emphasizes.

**CONCLUDE:** Help students to formulate conclusions about the importance of these details in the text. Ask students why the author might have included these details.

**Possible response:** I see that Twain uses italics in dialogue. He was very concerned with conveying speech exactly as his characters said their words. He uses italics just as he uses regional dialect—to allow readers to "hear" how the characters sound.

Explain to students that although Twain uses **italics for emphasis,** today some experts frown upon such use and encourage writers to indicate emphasis by means of careful sentence construction and phrasing. Italics are commonly used for foreign words that are inserted into English texts.

## CROSS-CURRICULAR PERSPECTIVES

**Social Studies** Review Smiley's comments in paragraph 14. Explain that forty dollars—the amount of the bet placed on the frog's ability to jump—was a great deal of money at the time of the story, equal perhaps to a month's wages. Have students research to learn what basic necessities cost in America around the middle of the nineteenth century, as well as how much people were paid for various jobs. Students can then create a pie chart or other form of graphic organizer to show how far forty dollars would have taken a person toward the goal of paying for a month's worth of housing, food, clothing, and so on.

# TEACHING

## CLOSE READ

As students look for places in paragraph 20 where a dash (—) appears, remind them to notice which parts of the paragraph are dialogue within dialogue. You may wish to model the Close Read using the following think-aloud format. Possible responses to questions on the student page are included.

**ANNOTATE:** As I read paragraph 20, I notice and highlight three places where Twain uses a dash in the middle of the dialogue and one at the end of the paragraph. I am guessing that the different locations have some kind of different meaning or effect. I will read through the section again to see if I can determine what that might be.

**QUESTION:** As I read the dialogue, the dashes cause me to pause. The first three seem to indicate a pause for dramatic effect. The last one indicates that Simon was interrupted.

**CONCLUDE:** When I read this monologue that Simon is telling, I realize that the dashes add a sense of what he would sound like if I was actually hearing him speak. The dashes help me get a sense of Simon's storytelling style.

NOTES

he ketched a frog, and fetched him in, and give him to this feller, and says:

18 "'Now, if you're ready, set him alongside of Dan'l, with his forepaws just even with Dan'ls, and I'll give the word.' Then he says, 'One—two—three—*git*!' and him and the feller touched up the frogs from behind, and the new frog hopped off lively, but Dan'l give a heave, and hysted up his shoulders—so—like a Frenchman, but it warn't no use—he couldn't budge; he was planted as solid as a church, and he couldn't no more stir than if he was anchored out. Smiley was a good deal surprised, and he was disgusted too, but he didn't have no idea what the matter was, of course.

19 "The feller took the money and started away; and when he was going out at the door, he sorter jerked his thumb over his shoulder—so—at Dan'l, and says again, very deliberate, 'Well,' he says, 'I don't see no p'ints about that frog that's any better'n any other frog.'

20 "Smiley he stood scratching his head and looking down at Dan'l a long time, and at last he says, 'I do wonder what in the nation that frog throw'd off for—I wonder if there ain't something the matter with him—he 'pears to look mighty baggy, somehow.' And he ketched Dan'l by the nap of the neck, and hefted him, and says, 'Why blame my cats if he don't weigh five pound!' and turned him upside down and he belched out a double handful of shot. And then he see how it was, and he was the maddest man—he set the frog down and took out after that feller, but he never ketched him. And—"

**CLOSE READ**
**ANNOTATE:** Mark the places in paragraph 20 where a dash (—) appears.

**QUESTION:** Why does the author use dashes instead of more ordinary punctuation and sentence structure?

**CONCLUDE:** What is the effect of this punctuation?

21 Here Simon Wheeler heard his name called from the front yard, and got up to see what was wanted. And turning to me as he moved away, he said: "Just set where you are, stranger, and rest easy—I ain't going to be gone a second."

22 But, by your leave, I did not think that a continuation of the history of the enterprising vagabond *Jim* Smiley would be likely to afford me much information concerning the Rev. *Leonidas* W. Smiley, and so I started away.

23 At the door I met the sociable Wheeler returning, and he buttonholed me and recommenced:

**buttonholed** (BUHT uhn hohld) *v.* held in conversation

24 "Well, thish-yer Smiley had a yaller one-eyed cow that didn't have no tail, only just a short stump like a bannanner, and—"

25 However, lacking both time and inclination, I did not wait to hear about the afflicted cow, but took my leave.





## WriteNow Analyze and Interpret

**Dialect** Review paragraphs 21–25 and call student attention to the humor. Have students choose one paragraph from the story that they find particularly interesting and amusing. Have students rewrite the paragraph, using vernacular from their own location and any current generation. Tell students that for this paragraph, they can give whatever voice they choose to the character so long as it is consistent. They can choose to write the paragraph in the voice of a teacher, a parent, or a person their age. Encourage students to use slang if they choose and to keep their language appropriate for the classroom. Have volunteers read their paragraphs aloud.

DIGITAL PERSPECTIVES

## Comprehension Check

Complete the following items after you finish your first read.

1. What prompts Simon Wheeler to tell the story of Jim Smiley?

2. What is Simon Wheeler's manner as he tells the story of Jim Smiley?

3. According to Simon Wheeler, how does Jim Smiley react to any event?

4. How does Andrew Jackson, the dog, win fights?

5. What does Jim Smiley teach Dan'l Webster to do?

6. How does the stranger prevent Dan'l Webster from jumping?

7. **Notebook** Write a summary of "The Notorious Jumping Frog of Calaveras County."

### RESEARCH

**Research to Clarify** Choose at least one unfamiliar detail from the text. Briefly research that detail. In what way does the information you learned shed light on an aspect of the story?

**Research to Explore** Conduct research to learn more about life in the nineteenth-century mining camps of the American West.





## Comprehension Check

Possible responses:

1. The narrator's friend suggests that he ask Simon about someone who has the same last name.
2. Simon regards the story as "a really important matter" and embellishes with many details.
3. Smiley bets on the outcome.
4. The dog grabs the opposing dog by its hind leg and just hangs on until the other dog gives up.
5. Smiley teaches the frog to jump and catch flies.
6. He puts quailshot into his mouth to weigh him down.
7. Summaries will vary but should include most of the following events. The narrator calls on Simon Wheeler to ask if he is acquainted with Leonidas W. Smiley, a friend of a friend. Wheeler does not know Leonidas W. Smiley but then tells the narrator a long story about Jim Smiley, an inveterate gambler. Smiley bets on anything and everything, and he usually wins. Wheeler tells tales of Smiley's horse, dog, and frog. When Wheeler takes a break in the story, the narrator uses the opportunity to escape, to avoid having to listen to another long tale.

## Research

**Research to Clarify** If students struggle to focus their research, have them to come up with a detail to research further, you may want to suggest that they focus on one of the following details: where this story was first published and Twain's later successes and publications; horse races in Twain's time; frogs and whether they can be trained.

**Research to Explore** If students struggle to focus their research, have them apply what they know about the setting of the story where the narrator first comes across Simon Wheeler. Have students look for photos as well as descriptions of the camp and share their findings with the class.

### PERSONALIZE FOR LEARNING

**Challenge**

**Author Study** Tell students that many of Mark Twain's stories and essays are in the public domain, which means they belong to the public as a whole and therefore are no longer subject or protected by copyright laws. Suggest that students perform research to find a few other examples of works in the public domain. Have students find and read another selection by Twain online. Tell them to select a favorite paragraph from the selection and read it aloud to the class, explaining why they chose the paragraph and what they like about it.

## Jump Start

CLOSE READ Have students close read the title "The Notorious Jumping Frog of Calaveras County." Ask students to define the word *notorious,* and help them to understand that it means "publicly known in a disreputable way." Ask students to come up with examples of notorious figures in history, literature, or current events and to discuss what makes these examples notorious.

## Close Read the Text

Work with students on the annotation model, then have them complete items 2 and 3 on their own. Review and discuss the sections students marked. If needed, continue to model close reading by using the Annotation Highlights in the Interactive Teacher's Edition.

## Analyze the Text

Possible responses:

1. (a) The narrator's friend wants him to hear Wheeler's long-winded story of Jim Smiley, likely as a joke. **DOK 3** (b) Sentences 2–3, in paragraph 1, support this conclusion. **DOK 1**
2. (a) When the Parson says his wife is getting better, Smiley bets that she will die. **DOK 1** (b) He is obsessed with betting to the point of being inconsiderate. **DOK 3**
3. (a) It is absurd to think of a dog that wins fights by hanging on to the opponent's hind legs. **DOK 2** (b) The part about the dog without hind legs is in poor taste to use for humor, as it is about animal abuse. The text says the dog's legs "had been sawed off in a circular saw." However, keeping in mind the time during which Twain was writing, this example might have seemed more humorous than it does today, when we are more aware of mistreatment of animals. **DOK 3**
4. Insights will vary. **DOK 3**
5. Responses will vary. **DOK 3**

MAKING MEANING

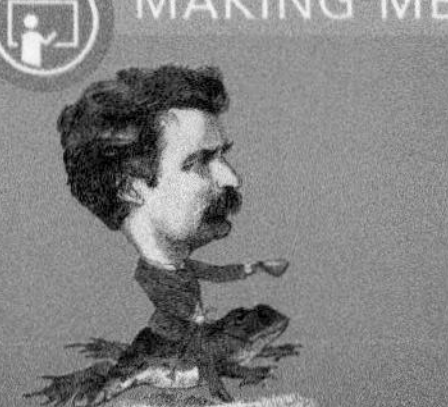

THE NOTORIOUS JUMPING FROG OF CALAVERAS COUNTY

## Close Read the Text

1. This model, from paragraph 4 of the text, shows two sample annotations, along with questions and conclusions. Close read the passage, and find another detail to annotate. Then, write a question and your conclusion.

ANNOTATE: Smiley bets on these things.

QUESTION: Why does Twain include so many examples of Smiley's bets?

CONCLUDE: Twain creates humor through repetition and exaggeration.

If there was a horse race, you'd find him flush or you'd find him busted at the end of it; if there was a dogfight, he'd bet on it; if there was a cat fight, he'd bet on it; if there was a chicken fight, he'd bet on it; . . . or if there was a camp meeting, he would be there reg'lar, to bet on Parson Walker. . . .

ANNOTATE: These words don't sound like standard English.

QUESTION: Why does Twain use this kind of language?

CONCLUDE: He wants to convey Wheeler's informal personality.

Tool Kit
Close-Read Guide and Model Annotation

2. For more practice, go back into the text, and complete the close-read notes.
3. Revisit a section of the text you found important during your first read. Read this section closely, and **annotate** what you notice. Ask yourself **questions** such as "Why did the author make this choice?" What can you **conclude**?

## Analyze the Text

CITE TEXTUAL EVIDENCE to support your answers.

Notebook Respond to these questions.

1. (a) **Draw Conclusions** Why does the narrator's friend suggest that the narrator ask Wheeler about Leonidas W. Smiley? (b) **Support** Which sentences support your conclusion?
2. (a) What punchline does Twain build to in paragraph 4? (b) **Analyze** What does this punchline reveal about Jim Smiley's character?
3. (a) **Analyze** What is humorous about the story of Andrew Jackson in paragraph 6? (b) **Evaluate** Do you find it amusing? Explain your position, citing textual evidence.
4. **Historical Perspectives** What insights do you gain about life in nineteenth-century miners' camps from the story?
5. **Essential Question:** *What is the relationship between literature and place?* What have you learned about the relationship between literature and place by reading this story?

STANDARDS

Reading Literature
- Cite strong and thorough textual evidence to support analysis of what the text says explicitly as well as inferences drawn from the text, including determining where the text leaves matters uncertain.
- Analyze a case in which grasping point of view requires distinguishing what is directly stated in a text from what is really meant.

Language
Interpret figures of speech in context and analyze their role in the text.





## FORMATIVE ASSESSMENT

### Analyze the Text

- **If** students fail to cite evidence, **then** remind them to support their ideas with specific information from the text.
- **If** students struggle to identify the role place plays in literature, **then** discuss the relationship between literature and place and illustrate with examples.

## PERSONALIZE FOR LEARNING

### English Language Support

**Close Read** Have English learners work in groups of two or three to complete the close read text annotations. Have them pay particular attention to how place is represented in this selection. Provide frames as needed to help students discuss these concepts and apply text evidence to support their arguments. *The author's use of ____ and ____ help me better understand ____. When* [character name] *says ____, it helps me understand that ____.* **ALL LEVELS**

## Analyze Craft and Structure

**Point of View** In literature, the term **point of view** can refer to the type of narrator an author uses to tell a story. For example, a story might use a first- or third-person narrative point of view. Point of view can also refer to the attitudes a narrator expresses. In some cases, the narrator may spell out those attitudes. In other cases, readers need to tease them out by analyzing story details. "The Notorious Jumping Frog of Calaveras County" is a **frame story,** or a story that brackets another story, so it has two narrators—the unnamed narrator of the frame, and Simon Wheeler, the long-winded narrator of the interior story. To appreciate the two narrators' very different points of view, consider Twain's use of incongruity and hyperbole.

- **Incongruity** occurs when two or more opposing or contradictory ideas are connected. For example, incongruity results when a speaker uses a serious tone to describe ridiculous events.
- **Hyperbole** is exaggeration for effect. For example, it would be hyperbolic if someone were to come inside from a thunderstorm and exclaim, "It's like the end of the world out there!"

### Practice

**CITE TEXTUAL EVIDENCE** to support your answers.

Notebook Respond to these questions.

1. In a chart like this one, record and explain four examples of hyperbole in "The Notorious Jumping Frog of Calaveras County."

| HYPERBOLE | WHAT IS EXAGGERATED | WHY IS IT HUMOROUS |
|---|---|---|
| If he even see a straddle-bug start to go anywhere ... he would foller that straddle-bug to Mexico... | It exaggerates the distance that Smiley would go. | Nobody would actually do that. |
| He was a different dog; his underjaw'd begin to stick out like the fo' castle of a steamboat... | The caricature-ish image of the dog with a jaw like a steamboat and teeth that shine like furnaces. | It makes the adorable little dog look monstrous. |
| And so he never done nothing for three months but set in his back yard and learn that frog to jump. | It exaggerates the time that Smiley spent. | It is ridiculous to do nothing but teaching a frog to jump for three whole months. |
| "Why, blame my cats if he don't weigh five pound!" | It exaggerates the amount the frog weighs. | The image of a gigantic frog is funny. |

2. (a) What happens at the beginning and the end of the frame story? (b) How does Twain use the frame story to create humor?
3. (a) What basic incongruity exists between the frame story's narrator and Simon Wheeler? (b) How does this incongruity emphasize each narrator's point of view? Explain.
4. (a) What is incongruous about Smiley's betting on the health of Parson Walker's wife? (b) Why is this incongruity humorous?





DIGITAL PERSPECTIVES 

## Analyze Craft and Structure

**Point of View** Point out to students that both incongruity and hyperbole play with the reader's expectations. These techniques both surprise the reader with a new and absurd way of looking at something, and, as a result, they make the reader laugh. For more support, see **Analyze Craft and Structure: Point of View.**

### Practice

Possible responses:

1. See possible responses in chart on student page.
2. (a) At the beginning, the narrator finds Wheeler dozing, and he observes that he is gentle and simple. He approaches him politely. At the end, the narrator runs away while Wheeler is mid-sentence. (b) The humor lies in the contrast between the narrator's approach of a sleeping man who seems harmless and gentle and his desperate escape at the end from the same person.
3. (a) The narrator is brisk and businesslike, while Wheeler is rambling. (b) Incongruity lies in the contrast between Wheeler's slang in paragraph 24, showing that he is very relaxed, and the narrator's elevated diction in paragraph 25, which shows his desire to distance himself from Wheeler.
4. (a) It is strange to bet on the outcome of someone's health. (b) The incongruity is humorous because no one person can control the health of another.

### FORMATIVE ASSESSMENT

### Analyze Craft and Structure

- **If** students have trouble identifying examples of hyperbole, **then** have them work in small groups and ask the question: *Which situations or events are highly exaggerated in this selection?*
- **If** students fail to recognize incongruities, **then** select and explain an example of incongruity.

For Reteach and Practice, see **Analyze Craft and Structure: Point of View (RP).**

## PERSONALIZE FOR LEARNING

### English Language Support

**Analyze Hyperbole** English learners may struggle with understanding hyperbole because their knowledge of vocabulary begins at the literal level. Since hyperbole necessitates a second level of understanding that goes beyond the literal, English learners may not understand the humor. To assist students with comprehension, select two or three examples of hyperbole from the text or other sources. Begin by explaining each at the literal level, then explain the humor in the second level of meaning. Check understanding by having students reiterate what they have heard and understood. Provide support and redirection as needed. **ALL LEVELS**

# TEACHING

## Concept Vocabulary

### Why These Words

**Possible responses:**

1. The words exaggerate how boring Wheeler is, and thus increase the humor in the story.
2. Other words connected to this concept include *blockaded, reeled off, earnestness, sincerity, sociable.*

### Practice

1. False; *tedious* (paragraph 1) means "tiresome; boring."
2. True; *buttonholed* (paragraph 23) means "caught in a situation/conversation."
3. False; *monotonous* (paragraph 3) means "dull due to a lack of variety."
4. False; *interminable* (paragraph 3) means "unending."
5. False; *exasperating* (paragraph 1) means "frustrating."
6. False; *garrulous* (paragraph 1) means "talkative."

### Word Network

**Possible words:** *dilapidated, decayed, flume, camp, tavern*

## Word Study

For more support, see **Concept Vocabulary and Word Study.**

**Possible responses:**

1. *Interminable* is the most intensely negative. It means "going on and on, unendingly," whereas *tedious* and *monotonous* have a milder meaning of "dull."
2. *Stale* would be a less intensely negative word than *tedious* or *monotonous; maddening* would be more intensely negative than *interminable.*

### FORMATIVE ASSESSMENT

**Concept Vocabulary**

**If** students fail to see the connection between the words, **then** have them write a short paragraph using at least four of the words.

**Word Study**

**If** students are having trouble understanding denotation and connotation, **then** have them use online resources to find examples of commonly used synonyms with different connotations.
For Reteach and Practice, see **Word Study: Denotation and Connotation (RP).**

LANGUAGE DEVELOPMENT

THE NOTORIOUS JUMPING FROG OF CALAVERAS COUNTY

## Concept Vocabulary

| garrulous | tedious | interminable |
|---|---|---|
| exasperating | monotonous | buttonholed |

**Why These Words?** These concept words are used to describe an experience with a boring, clueless person. For example, the *garrulous* Simon Wheeler tells the narrator a seemingly *interminable* story about Jim Smiley. At the end, the narrator is almost *buttonholed* by Wheeler for a second tale.

1. How does the concept vocabulary help readers understand how the narrator feels about Simon Wheeler?
2. What other words in the selection connect to this concept?

**WORD NETWORK**

Add words related to a sense of place from the text to your Word Network.

### Practice

**Notebook** Indicate whether each sentence is true or false. Explain your answers.

1. A *tedious* story is likely to fascinate an audience from start to finish.
2. If someone has been *buttonholed*, he or she is unable to get out of a conversation.
3. Listening to a *monotonous* speaker is a fun way to spend an evening.
4. An *interminable* wait goes by so quickly you hardly even notice that time has passed.
5. Most people enjoy *exasperating* tasks because they are filled with exciting surprises.
6. Someone who is naturally *garrulous* is likely to be very uncomfortable speaking in front of a crowd of attentive listeners.

## Word Study

**Denotation and Connotation** A word's **denotation** is its literal dictionary definition. Every word has at least one denotation. Many words also have **connotations**, subtle shades of meaning that a word evokes. A word's connotations may be neutral, negative, or positive. The concept vocabulary words *tedious, monotonous,* and *interminable* all have negative connotations.

1. Of the three words noted—*tedious, monotonous,* and *interminable*—which is the most intensely negative? Explain.
2. Add two words to that list. Choose one that is less intense in its negativity, and one that is more intense. Sort your five words on a scale from least to most negative.

**STANDARDS**

**Reading Literature**
Determine the meaning of words and phrases as they are used in the text, including figurative and connotative meanings; analyze the impact of specific word choices on meaning and tone, including words with multiple meanings or language that is particularly fresh, engaging, or beautiful.

**Language**
• Demonstrate understanding of figurative language, word relationships, and nuances in word meanings.
• Analyze nuances in the meaning of words with similar denotations.





### PERSONALIZE FOR LEARNING

**English Language Support**

**Denotation and Connotation** Ask pairs of students to write sentences stressing the similar denotation but different connotation of these words: *request, demand, oblige.* **EMERGING**

Ask students to write sentences, using in one of them the word *tedious*, and in the other the word *boring.* **EXPANDING**

Ask students to write four brief descriptions of either a person, place, or thing including in each one of the following words: *lifeless, tedious, uninteresting, soporific.* **BRIDGING**

An expanded **English Language Support Lesson** on Denotation and Connotation is available in the Interactive Teacher's Edition.

## Author's Style

**Word Choice** Mark Twain was among the first authors to use the American vernacular, or language as it is spoken by ordinary people. His diction includes both standard American English and variations that reflect a story's setting and characters' personalities. These variations include dialect and idiomatic expressions.

- **Dialect** is a way of speaking that is specific to a particular area or group of people. Twain spells passages of dialect as they would be pronounced.

  **Dialect:** *There couldn't be no solit'ry thing mentioned but that feller'd offer to bet on it, and take ary side you please. . . .*

  **Standard English:** You couldn't mention anything without having that fellow offer to bet on it, choosing either side.

- **Idiomatic expressions** are figures of speech that cannot be understood literally. For example, the idiom "it's raining cats and dogs" means that there is heavy rain, not that animals are falling from the sky.

  **Idiomatic Expression:** *If there was a horse race, you'd find him flush, or you'd find him busted at the end of it.*

  **Actual Meaning:** If there was a horse race, you would find him at the end either with plenty of money or none.

### Read It

1. Rewrite each example of dialect from Twain's story into standard English.

| DIALECT | STANDARD ENGLISH |
|---|---|
| I don't recollect exactly. | I don't remember exactly. |
| Thish-yer Smiley had a mare. | Smiley had a mare. |
| He would grab that other dog jest by the j'int of his hind leg. | He would grab that other dog by the joint of his hind leg. |
| He never done nothing for three months but set in his back yard and learn that frog to jump. | He didn't do anything for three months except sit in his backyard and teach that frog to jump. |

2. **Connect to Style** Reread paragraph 20 of the story. Identify an idiom in the paragraph, explain its literal meaning, and consider how it helps to develop Simon Wheeler's character.
3. **Notebook** Explain how Twain's use of dialect and idioms helps him portray his characters vividly and create humor.

### Write It

**Notebook** Use at least two of the following idioms in a paragraph. Use context clues to suggest their meaning.

| | |
|---|---|
| **a hot potato** | **worth writing home about** |
| **an arm and a leg** | **barking up the wrong tree** |





DIGITAL PERSPECTIVES

## Author's Style

**Word Choice** Discuss with students Twain's decision to use dialect and idiomatic expressions, asking for students' input on what their reading experience was like. Did they find it worthwhile to make the extra effort required to understand the dialect and idiomatic expressions in the story?

For more support, see **Author's Style: Impact of Word Choice.**

### Read It

Possible responses:

1. See chart on student page.
2. One example of an idiom is *blame my cats* (paragraph 20), which expresses Simon Wheeler's exasperation at having been tricked.
3. Dialect and idiomatic language help Twain recreate how people actually talked in the 1860s in California. These techniques enable Twain to make his characters and setting come to life.

### Write It

Possible response:

That movie cost me an arm and a leg—more than $20—and it sure wasn't worth writing home about. If you think I'm going to see another movie with those actors, you're barking up the wrong tree. The studio should drop those actors like a hot potato!

### FORMATIVE ASSESSMENT

#### Author's Style

**If** students don't understand the idiomatic expressions, **then** encourage them to use online resources for definitions and usage examples.

For Reteach and Practice, see **Author's Style: Impact of Word Choice (RP).**

### HOW LANGUAGE WORKS

**Impact of Word Choice** Have students examine the narrator's word choice when he is speaking in his own voice in "The Notorious Jumping Frog of Calaveras County." For example, point out the following word choice in paragraph 1: "In compliance," "Inquired after," "requested to do," "hereunto append the result." Ask students what these phrases reveal about the narrator. Have students find other places in the text where the narrator speaks in his own voice and analyze Twain's word choice. Have students discuss how the word choice Twain uses for the narrator makes the story all the more humorous.

# TEACHING

## Writing to Compare

Help students analyze the two works by exploring the humorous phrases used in each. Ask students to think about Twain's humor in relation to humorous works they have read by other authors.

### Assignment

Tell students that although they are being asked to write an explanatory text, they must also take a position about whether or not Twain follows his own rules in either or both of the selections. Thus, there will be an element of opinion and argument in their writing.

For more support, see **Writing to Compare: Explanatory Text.**

### Prewriting

**Analyze the Text** As students study the texts, ensure that they can paraphrase the prompt quotation well.

**Possible response:**

A funny story may be very, very long, taking as many detours as the author wishes and possibly not even having a point to it....it is told in all seriousness, with the narrator hiding his awareness of its humor.

See possible responses in chart on student page.

**Possible responses:**

1. "The Notorious Jumping Frog" seems to align more with Twain's definition because it's a story that doesn't seem to have a clear direction.
2. I prefer "Life on the Mississippi" because I can relate more to the situation he describes and find subtle humor in the relationships between the characters.

EFFECTIVE EXPRESSION

*from* LIFE ON THE MISSISSIPPI

THE NOTORIOUS JUMPING FROG OF CALAVERAS COUNTY

## Writing to Compare

You have read two works by Mark Twain—an excerpt from *Life on the Mississippi* and the short story "The Notorious Jumping Frog of Calaveras County." Now, deepen your understanding of Twain's humor by comparing the two works and expressing your ideas in writing.

**Assignment**

In an essay entitled "How to Tell a Story," Twain wrote: "The humorous story may be spun out to great length, and may wander around as much as it pleases, and arrive nowhere in particular. . . . it is told gravely; the teller does his best to conceal the fact that he even dimly suspects there is anything funny about it."

Write an **explanatory text** in which you explore whether Twain follows his own rules for telling a funny story in *Life on the Mississippi* and "The Notorious Jumping Frog of Calaveras County." Consider similarities and differences in the humor displayed in the two narratives.

### Prewriting

**Analyze the Texts** First, analyze the quotation from Twain's essay. Rephrase it in your own words to make sure you understand it.

Paraphrase: ______________________________

______________________________

Next, review the definitions of *diction, tone, dialect,* and *idiomatic expressions.* Then, choose several passages from both selections that are relevant to Twain's characterization of a humorous story. Use the chart to take notes.

| A HUMOROUS STORY . . . | LIFE ON THE MISSISSIPPI | THE NOTORIOUS JUMPING FROG . . . |
|---|---|---|
| "may be spun out to great length" | "he would go on and lie about how many towns the size of ours were burned down there that day." | "all through the interminable narrative there ran a vein of impressive earnestness and sincerity" |
| "may . . . arrive nowhere in particular" | "After ten more minutes the town is dead again, . . ." | "'he set the frog down and took out after that feller, but he never ketched him. And—' Here Simon Wheeler heard his name called from the front yard. . ." |
| "is told gravely" | "My father was a justice of the peace, . . . he possessed the power of life and death over all men" | "far from his imagining that there was anything ridiculous . . . , he regarded it as a really important matter" |
| conceals humor | "a litter of pigs loafing along the sidewalk, doing a good business in watermelon rinds" | "he would go to work and bore me to death with some exasperating reminiscence" |

**Notebook** Respond to these questions.

1. Which narrative most closely aligns with Twain's characterization of humorous writing?
2. Do you find that selection the funnier of the two? Why, or why not?

STANDARDS

**Writing**

- Write informative/explanatory texts to examine and convey complex ideas, concepts, and information clearly and accurately through the effective selection, organization, and analysis of content.
- Introduce a topic; organize complex ideas, concepts, and information so that each new element builds on that which precedes it to create a unified whole; include formatting, graphics, and multimedia when useful to aiding comprehension.
- Develop the topic thoroughly by selecting the most significant and relevant facts, extended definitions, concrete details, quotations, or other information and examples appropriate to the audience's knowledge of the topic.
- Develop and strengthen writing as needed by planning, revising, editing, rewriting, or trying a new approach, focusing on addressing what is most significant for a specific purpose and audience.





PERSONALIZE FOR LEARNING

**Strategic Support**

**Prepare to Write** If students struggle to compare the texts based on Twain's rules, have them choose one of the two texts as a basis for their writing. Support students by answering any questions they may have about gathering information to include in their writing. If students want additional support, allow them to work in pairs in order to gather ideas and note the information they want to include in their writing.

## Drafting

**Formulate Your Thesis, or Central Idea** In your essay, you will explain how the humor in the two narratives is similar and how it is different, with reference to the quotation from Twain. Clarify the focus of your essay by summarizing the similarities and differences you observe in the ways Twain makes each narrative funny. Then, write a working, or draft, thesis statement. You may always refine your thesis statement as you continue to work through your ideas.

I. **Main similarity:** ______

II. **Main difference:** ______

III. **Working Thesis Statement:** ______

**Draft Your Essay** Your essay should introduce and develop a unified, coherent set of ideas that you can trace from the introduction through the body paragraphs to the conclusion. As you draft your essay, follow these guidelines for each section:

**Introduction:**

- Identify which parts of Twain's quotation you will address.
- State your thesis or central idea.

**Body Paragraphs:**

- Develop your thesis with explanations and reasons.
- Include passages from both narratives to support your ideas. Introduce short passages with a comma. Introduce longer passages with a colon, and set them off by indenting them from both margins. Include a parenthetical page reference after each quotation.
- Explain how the passages you chose relate to Twain's quotation. Strengthen your analysis by including your own insights about how Twain builds humor.

**Conclusion:**

- Reintroduce Twain's quotation.
- Summarize or restate your thesis.
- End with a memorable statement, quotation, or insight.

## Review, Revise, and Edit

Once you are done drafting, reread and revise your essay. Review Twain's quotation to make sure you establish a connection between his rules for telling a humorous story and each passage you discuss. Edit for diction, choosing words and phrases that create a formal tone. Finalize your essay by proofreading it carefully.

**EVIDENCE LOG**

Before moving on to a new selection, go to your Evidence Log and record what you learned from *Life on the Mississippi* and "The Notorious Jumping Frog of Calaveras County."





## Drafting

Suggest that students write down several quotations from each selection, so they can choose the most apt quotations to support their comparison.

Remind students to double check their quotations to make sure they have used the author's exact words. Point out the irregular spelling may make that especially challenging, so they should pay extra attention.

**Evidence Log** Support students in completing their Evidence Log. This paced activity will help prepare them for the Performance-Based Assessment at the end of the unit.

## Review, Revise, and Edit

Tell students to take some time away from their draft before reviewing and revising so that they can view their work with "fresh eyes."

## PERSONALIZE FOR LEARNING

### English Language Support

**Explanatory Texts** Have English learners work with a partner and exchange and review each other's explanatory essays. Have students give each other positive feedback, singling out and explaining the effect of particular word choices. Encourage students to ask and answer questions to clarify points. Provide frames to support discussion. *I like the way you ____ because it helps me understand that ____. What did you mean by ____? I meant to explain that ____ when I included the details about ____.* **EXPANDING/BRIDGING**

## FORMATIVE ASSESSMENT

### Writing to Compare

**If** students struggle to determine whether Twain follows his own rules, **then** have them work in small groups and discuss ideas with each other.

### Selection Test

Administer the "The Notorious Jumping Frog of Calaveras County" Selection Test, which is available in both print and digital formats online in Assessments.

# A White Heron

**AUDIO SUMMARIES**
Audio summaries of "A White Heron" are available online in both English and Spanish in the Interactive Teacher's Edition or Unit Resources. Assigning these summaries prior to reading the selection may help students build additional background knowledge and set a context for their first read.


## Summary

In the short story "A White Heron" by Sarah Orne Jewett, shy nine-year-old Sylvia lives with her grandmother on a farm. Sylvia has come to love all of nature's creatures. One day, a friendly young man approaches her, looking for a white heron to shoot and add to his collection. The youthful hunter is invited to stay at the grandmother's house that evening. After dinner, he offers a reward to anyone who can lead him to the rare bird. The next day, Sylvia joins the young man in the woods looking for the heron, but they do not find it. The next morning Sylvia goes out looking for the heron's nesting site. She climbs a tall tree and spots the bird, but suddenly feels a deep connection with it and decides to keep its location secret. She says nothing to the hunter and he leaves. Years later, Sylvia wonders if she should have revealed the nesting spot. The narrator comments that the splendors of nature that Sylvia enjoys as an adult are what are truly valuable.


### Insight

The woodlands of Maine are among the most beautiful natural settings in the United States. For Sylvia, they are a wondrous source of deep connections with nature. The center of the woods near the pond vibrates with what seems like a magical energy, and it is there that Sylvia, who climbs the tallest tree, spots the rare white heron.

ESSENTIAL QUESTION:
What is the relationship between literature and place?

## Connection to Essential Question

The woodlands that Jewett so vividly describes are virtually a fourth main character in "A White Heron."

WHOLE CLASS LEARNING PERFORMANCE TASK
How do American authors use regional details to make the events and themes of a narrative come to life for readers?

UNIT PERFORMANCE-BASED ASSESSMENT
What makes certain places live on in our memory?

## Connection to Performance Tasks

**Whole-Class Learning Performance Task** The natural setting that Sylvia has come to love is, for all practical purposes, a character. The setting relates to one of the central themes of the story—personal growth often results from holding on to what one values most.

**Unit Performance-Based Assessment** This selection provides an interesting insight into the idea of conflict that may exist between two "places" in a story. Sylvia loves her new life in the country; she has come to appreciate the beauty of the natural setting. The young hunter, who is in search of a white heron, represents the viewpoint of a townsperson; he is someone trying to collect trophies of nature's beauty. Readers can identify with both types of nature lovers.

DIGITAL PERSPECTIVES

Audio

Video

Document

Annotation Highlights

EL Highlights

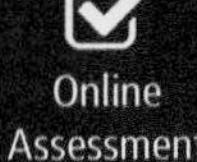
Online Assessment

## LESSON RESOURCES

| | Making Meaning | Language Development | Effective Expression |
|---|---|---|---|
| Lesson | **First Read**<br>**Close Read**<br>**Analyze the Text**<br>**Analyze Craft and Structure** | **Concept Vocabulary**<br>**Word Study**<br>**Conventions and Style** | **Writing to Sources**<br>**Speaking and Listening** |
| **Instructional Standards** | **RL.10** By the end of grade 11, read and comprehend literature . . .<br>**RL.1** Cite strong and thorough textual evidence . . .<br>**RL.2** Determine two or more themes or central ideas of a text . . . | **L.3** Apply knowledge of language . . .<br>**L.4.c** Consult general and specialized reference materials . . .<br>**L.4.d** Verify the preliminary determination . . . | **RL.5** Analyze how an author's choices . . .<br>**SL.1.c** Propel conversations . . . |
| **STUDENT RESOURCES** | | | |
| Available online in the Interactive Student Edition or Unit Resources | Selection Audio<br>First-Read Guide: Fiction<br>Close-Read Guide: Fiction | Word Network | Evidence Log |
| **TEACHER RESOURCES** | | | |
| **Selection Resources** Available online in the Interactive Teacher's Edition or Unit Resources | Audio Summaries<br>Annotation Highlights<br>EL Highlights<br>English Language Support Lesson: Multiple-Meaning Words<br>Analyze Craft and Structure: Thematic Development | Concept Vocabulary and Word Study<br>Conventions and Style: Sentence Variety | Writing to Sources: Critical Analysis<br>Speaking and Listening: Whole-Class Debate |
| **Reteach/Practice (RP)** Available online in the Interactive Teacher's Edition or Unit Resources | Analyze Craft and Structure: Thematic Development (RP) | Word Study: Latin Root Word: *hospes* (RP)<br>Conventions and Style: Sentence Variety (RP) | Writing to Sources: Critical Analysis (RP)<br>Speaking and Listening: Whole-Class Debate (RP) |
| **Assessment** Available online in Assessments | Selection Test | | |
| **My Resources** | A Unit 4 Answer Key is available online and in the Interactive Teacher's Edition. | | |

# Reading Support

| Text Complexity Rubric: A White Heron | |
|---|---|
| **Quantitative Measures** | |
| **Lexile** 1250 **Text Length** 4,274 words | |
| **Qualitative Measures** | |
| Knowledge Demands ①—②—❸—④—⑤ | Some readers may be unfamiliar with the rural setting and descriptions of nature, but not much prior knowledge is necessary to understand the descriptions. |
| Structure ①—②—❸—④—⑤ | The story is told chronologically, but with a lot of description of feelings and events, which makes it hard at times to discern plot events. |
| Language Conventionality and Clarity ①—②—③—❹—⑤ | The language is complex and highly descriptive, with a poetic tone; tense shifts from past to present; sentences are long and complex with multiple clauses. There is a lot of descriptive vocabulary. |
| Levels of Meaning/Purpose ①—②—③—❹—⑤ | There are multiple levels of meaning; selection uses symbolism and metaphors and the reader needs to infer meaning from feelings and actions of character and by understanding symbolic meaning. |

DECIDE AND PLAN

## English Language Support

Provide English Learners with support for structure and language as they read the selection.

**Language** As a group, analyze some of the descriptive language the author uses. Discuss some of the word choices the author made, the meanings of those words, and what other words she could have used. For example the word *horror-stricken* could be replaced with *scared*, but the author chose a stronger word.

**Structure** Point out that there are a lot of descriptions in every paragraph, and sometimes only a few actions happen in the plot. Have students take turns reading parts of paragraphs. Stop to discuss what new events happened and which parts of the paragraph were just describing the background.

## Strategic Support

Provide students with strategic support to ensure that they can successfully read the text.

**Language** Pair students. Ask them to copy words or phrases they don't understand. Encourage them to try to figure out the meaning from the context or by looking up words. If needed, help explain difficult words or phrases.

**Meaning** At different points in the story, stop to discuss the characters, events, and the deeper meaning of the story. For example, discuss Sylvia's connection to nature and to other people. At the end of the story, discuss the conflict she has between saving the heron or helping the hunter and therefore benefiting her family.

## Challenge

Provide students who need to be challenged with ideas for how they can go beyond a simple interpretation of the text.

**Text Analysis** Pair students and ask them to write a description of Sylvia and her connection to nature vs. her connection to people. Ask them to explain the conflict she has between taking the money or protecting the heron, and how she feels about the decision she made. Have pairs share their ideas. Then discuss the symbolism of the heron and the hunter as animal and human companions.

**Written Response** Ask students to write what they would do if they were in Sylvia's position. Encourage them to include the feelings they might have while making that kind of choice.

TEACH

## Read and Respond

Have students do their first read of the selection. Then have them complete their close read. Finally, work with them on the Making Meaning, Language Development, and Effective Expression activities.

# Standards Support Through Teaching and Learning Cycle

## IDENTIFY NEEDS

Analyze results of the Beginning-of-Year Assessment, focusing on the items relating to Unit 4. Also take into consideration student performance to this point and your observations of where particular students struggle.

## DECIDE AND PLAN

- If students have performed poorly on items matching these standards, then provide selection scaffolds before assigning them the on-level lesson provided in the Student Edition.
- If students have done well on the Beginning-of-Year Assessment, then challenge them to keep progressing and learning by giving them opportunities to practice the skills in depth.
- Use the Selection Resources listed on the Planning pages for "A White Heron" to help students continually improve their ability to master the standards.

**Instructional Standards: A White Heron**

| | Catching Up | This Year | Looking Forward |
|---|---|---|---|
| **Reading** | You may wish to administer the **Analyze Craft and Structure: Thematic Development (RP)** worksheet to familiarize students with imagery and symbols.<br>You may wish to administer the **Writing to Sources: Critical Analysis (RP)** worksheet for students to practice critical analysis. | **RL.2** Determine two or more themes or central ideas of a text and analyze their development over the course of the text . . .<br>**RL.5** Analyze how an author's choices concerning how to structure specific parts of a text . . . | Challenge students to investigate other works the themes of which are harder to pinpoint.<br>Challenge students to analyze the sentence variety (or lack thereof) from another work they have read. |
| **Speaking and Listening** | You may wish to administer the **Speaking and Listening: Whole-Class Debate (RP)** worksheet to help students prepare for their debate. | **SL.1.c** Propel conversations by posing and responding to questions that probe reasoning and evidence . . . | Have students take the debate to the next level by challenging another class in the area who are also reading "A White Heron." |
| **Language** | Review the **Word Study: Latin Root Word: *hospes* (RP)** worksheet with students to better familiarize them with the root word.<br>Review the **Conventions and Style: Sentence Variety (RP)** worksheet with students to better familiarize them with the four types of sentences. | **L.4.c** Consult general and specialized reference materials . . .<br>**L.3** Apply knowledge of language to understand how language functions in different contexts . . . | Have students select other words from the selection and look up their root words.<br>Challenge students to speculate how words develop connotations away from their original denotations. |

## ANALYZE AND REVISE

- Analyze student work for evidence of student learning.
- Identify whether or not students have met the expectations in the standards.
- Identify implications for future instruction.

## TEACH

Implement the planned lesson, and gather evidence of student learning.

## Jump Start

**FIRST READ** Prior to students' first read, invite them to share their ideas about the advantages of country life. Students may use personal experience or what they have learned from books, television, or movies.

### A White Heron

What was life like in an isolated rural area 150 years ago? What relationship did farmers have with wildlife? Modeling questions readers might ask will bring "A White Heron" to life and connect it to the Performance Task assignment. Selection audio and print capability for the selection are available in the Interactive Teacher's Edition.

### Concept Vocabulary

Circulate among students as they rank their words. Remind them that they will find the definitions of these words in the side column beside each word's location in the text.

### FIRST READ

As they read, students should perform the steps of the first read:

NOTICE: Encourage students to notice when the narrator provides general observations and descriptions or focuses on Sylvia, her grandmother, or the young hunter.

ANNOTATE: Ask students to mark passages that identify Sylvia's feelings about the natural world and consider how the passages affect what students think about Sylvia's conflict.

CONNECT: Invite students to go beyond the text to make personal connections to a hiking trip, a park visit, or a memorable television program or movie related to nature.

RESPOND: Students will answer questions and write a summary to demonstrate understanding.

Point out to students that while they will always complete the Respond step at the end of the first read, the other steps will happen somewhat concurrently. You may wish to print copies of the **First-Read Guide: Fiction** for students to use.

**Remind students that during their first read, they should not answer the close-read questions that appear in the selection.**

MAKING MEANING

About the Author

"A White Heron" is the most popular story **Sarah Orne Jewett** (1849–1909) wrote. As a young girl, she often accompanied her father, a physician, as he made house calls through rural Maine. Later, she would fold her keen recollections of the region's people and wildlife into her stories, novels, and poems. She sold her first story to the *Atlantic Monthly* when she was nineteen, and she soon became well-known for her precise descriptions and sharp observations of the women and men who lived near the Atlantic Ocean in southern Maine.

**Tool Kit**
First-Read Guide and Model Annotation

## A White Heron

### Concept Vocabulary

You will encounter the following words as you read "A White Heron." Before reading, note how familiar you are with each word. Then, rank the words in order from most familiar (1) to least familiar (6).

| WORD | YOUR RANKING |
|---|---|
| dilatory | |
| loitered | |
| hospitality | |
| squalor | |
| hermitage | |
| quaint | |

After completing your first read, come back to the concept vocabulary and review your ratings. Mark changes to your original rankings as needed.

### First Read FICTION

Apply these strategies as you conduct your first read. You will have an opportunity to complete the close-read notes after your first read.

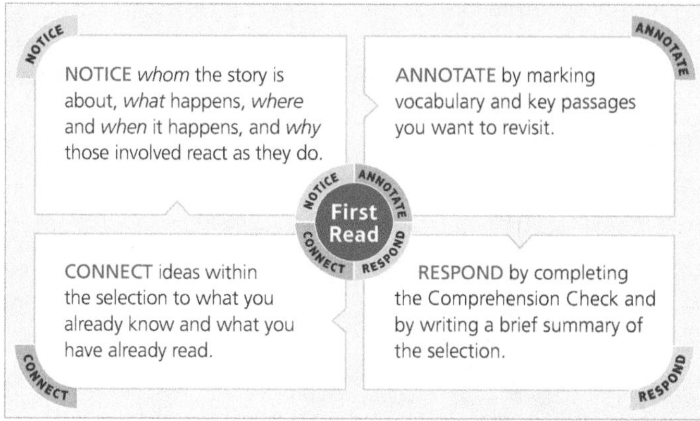
NOTICE
NOTICE *whom* the story is about, *what* happens, *where* and *when* it happens, and *why* those involved react as they do.
ANNOTATE
ANNOTATE by marking vocabulary and key passages you want to revisit.
First Read
CONNECT
CONNECT ideas within the selection to what you already know and what you have already read.
RESPOND
RESPOND by completing the Comprehension Check and by writing a brief summary of the selection.

STANDARDS
**Reading Literature**
By the end of grade 11, read and comprehend literature, including stories, dramas, and poems, in the grades 11–CCR text complexity band proficiently, with scaffolding as needed at the high end of the range.

### VOCABULARY DEVELOPMENT

**Concept Vocabulary Reinforcement** Help students define difficult vocabulary with strategies to connect to other words. At first glance, students might think the word *dilatory* (paragraph 1) (slow) relates to dilate. To remember *dilatory,* mentally connect it to *delay* and *dilly dally.* Similarly, *squalor* (paragraph 14) (filth, wretchedness) has nothing to do with a *squall* (a violent storm). Tell students *squalor* (paragraph 14) comes from the Latin *squālēre,* which means "to be filthy." The adjective form is *squalid.* Students might not know the word *hermitage* (paragraph 14) (a place of retreat). However, connecting it with the more familiar related word *hermit* (a person who retreats from society) might help them remember. Have students discuss with a partner their own strategies for remembering the meanings of concept vocabulary words.

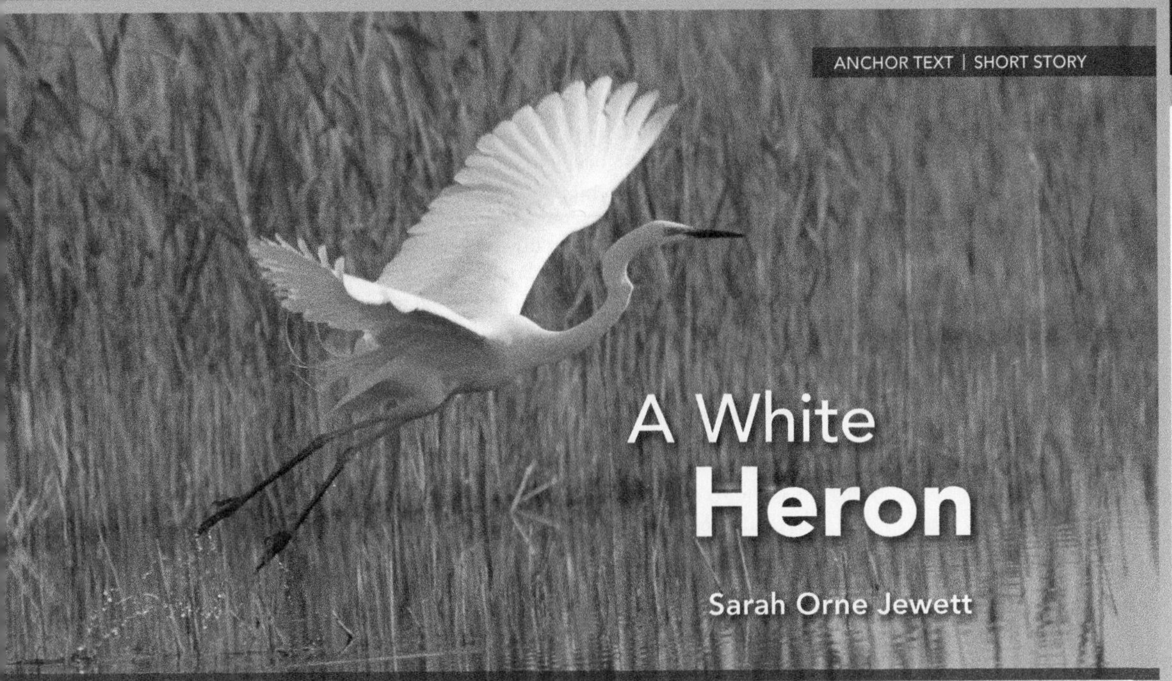

# A White Heron

Sarah Orne Jewett

BACKGROUND

The white heron in this story is another name for the snowy egret, a bird that nests near water and in swamps. At the time this story was written, the snowy egret was hunted for its feathers, and the species almost became extinct. However, the efforts of conservationists have since helped the snowy egret population to recover, and the bird is no longer considered endangered.

SCAN FOR MULTIMEDIA

## I.

1 The woods were already filled with shadows one June evening, just before eight o'clock, though a bright sunset still glimmered faintly among the trunks of the trees. A little girl was driving home her cow, a plodding, dilatory, provoking creature in her behavior, but a valued companion for all that. They were going away from whatever light there was, and striking deep into the woods, but their feet were familiar with the path, and it was no matter whether their eyes could see it or not.

2 There was hardly a night the summer through when the old cow could be found waiting at the pasture bars; on the contrary, it was her greatest pleasure to hide herself away among the huckleberry bushes, and though she wore a loud bell she had made the discovery that if one stood perfectly still it would not ring. So Sylvia had to hunt for her until she found her, and call Co'! Co'! with never an answering Moo, until her childish patience was quite spent. If the creature had not given good milk and plenty of it, the case would have seemed very different to her owners. Besides, Sylvia had all the time there

NOTES

**dilatory** (DIHL uh tawr ee) *adj.* inclined to delay; slow

CLOSE READ

ANNOTATE: In paragraph 1, mark four adjectives that describe the cow.

QUESTION: Why does the author use these adjectives?

CONCLUDE: What is the effect of this opening description?





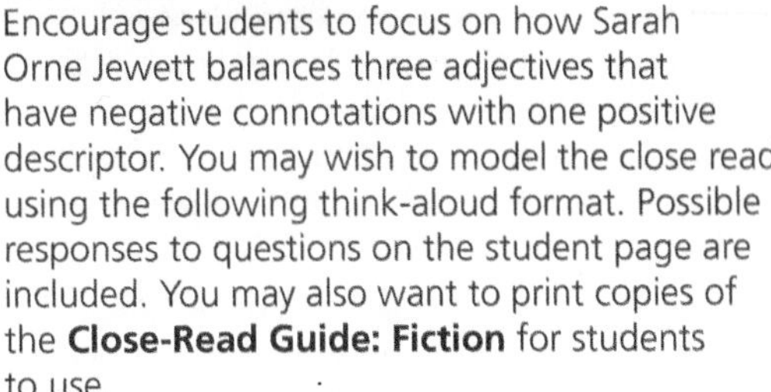

## CLOSE READ

Encourage students to focus on how Sarah Orne Jewett balances three adjectives that have negative connotations with one positive descriptor. You may wish to model the close read using the following think-aloud format. Possible responses to questions on the student page are included. You may also want to print copies of the **Close-Read Guide: Fiction** for students to use.

**ANNOTATE:** As I read the first paragraph, I notice and highlight three adjectives that have negative connotations: *plodding, dilatory,* and *provoking.* Then I observe the favorable phrase *valued companion* and highlight *valued.*

**QUESTION:** Even though the first three adjectives are negative, the fourth adjective, *valued,* eliminates the harshness that the three words alone would carry. The sentence suggests to me that the girl accepts the cow's annoying attributes, because she prizes the animal's company.

**CONCLUDE:** Cows are known to be poky and slow, a quality that many people would find annoying or *provoking.* The phrase *valued companion* is more surprising and has a greater impact on me and makes me wonder what the girl is like. I suspect that the girl may care about and connect easily with animals.

## WriteNow Analyze and Interpret

**Setting** Have students review paragraphs 1–2. The opening of "A White Heron" introduces a distinctive setting. Have students write a brief analysis of how Jewett establishes this setting in the opening 15 lines of the story. Have them consider these questions: What details does the author use to create the setting? What is Sylvia's connection to the setting? Is the setting likely to be integral to the story? Why or why not?

## CLOSE READ

Remind students to focus on descriptions involving shadows and shade in paragraph 4 on page 434. You may wish to model the close read using the following think-aloud format. Possible responses to questions on the student page are included.

**ANNOTATE:** As I read the first part of paragraph 4, I notice and highlight two details that refer to shade or shadows: *the shady wood-road* and *twilight moths*. The second example is less obvious; I know that *twilight* is the shadowy, almost-dark time of evening.

**QUESTION:** These details help me visualize an image of night beginning to fall. This image is reinforced by the sounds of birds "saying good-night to each other in sleepy twitters." These details give me the impression that the author wants to elicit a hint of fear about nightfall and the coming of darkness. The last sentence of the paragraph on page 435 shows that Sylvia's disquieting memory supports this impression.

**CONCLUDE:** I think this mix of details in the setting—the beauty of nightfall as well as the chill of night and darkness—reflects Sylvia's mixed feelings. She enjoys the experience of being outdoors on her own, but she also feels apprehensive and, likely, vulnerable at the same time.

NOTES

was, and very little use to make of it. Sometimes in pleasant weather it was a consolation to look upon the cow's pranks as an intelligent attempt to play hide and seek, and as the child had no playmates she lent herself to this amusement with a good deal of zest. Though this chase had been so long that the wary animal herself had given an unusual signal of her whereabouts, Sylvia had only laughed when she came upon Mistress Moolly at the swamp-side, and urged her affectionately homeward with a twig of birch leaves. The old cow was not inclined to wander farther, she even turned in the right direction for once as they left the pasture, and stepped along the road at a good pace. She was quite ready to be milked now, and seldom stopped to browse. Sylvia wondered what her grandmother would say because they were so late. It was a great while since she had left home at half-past five o'clock, but everybody knew the difficulty of making this errand a short one. Mrs. Tilley had chased the hornéd torment too many summer evenings herself to blame any one else for lingering, and was only thankful as she waited that she had Sylvia, nowadays, to give such valuable assistance. The good woman suspected that Sylvia loitered occasionally on her own account; there never was such a child for straying about out-of-doors since the world was made! Everybody said that it was a good change for a little maid who had tried to grow for eight years in a crowded manufacturing town, but, as for Sylvia herself, it seemed as if she never had been alive at all before she came to live at the farm. She thought often with wistful compassion of a wretched geranium that belonged to a town neighbor.

**loitered** (LOY tuhrd) *v.* lingered; moved slowly

3 "'Afraid of folks,'" old Mrs. Tilley said to herself, with a smile, after she had made the unlikely choice of Sylvia from her daughter's houseful of children, and was returning to the farm. "'Afraid of folks,' they said! I guess she won't be troubled no great with 'em up to the old place!" When they reached the door of the lonely house and stopped to unlock it, and the cat came to purr loudly, and rub against them, a deserted pussy, indeed, but fat with young robins, Sylvia whispered that this was a beautiful place to live in, and she never should wish to go home.

4 The companions followed the shady wood-road, the cow taking slow steps and the child very fast ones. The cow stopped long at the brook to drink, as if the pasture were not half a swamp, and Sylvia stood still and waited, letting her bare feet cool themselves in the shoal water, while the great twilight moths struck softly against her. She waded on through the brook as the cow moved away, and listened to the thrushes with a heart that beat fast with pleasure. There was a stirring in the great boughs overhead. They were full of little birds and beasts that seemed to be wide awake, and going about their world, or else saying good-night to each other in sleepy twitters. Sylvia herself felt sleepy as she walked along. However, it was not much farther to the house, and the air was soft and sweet. She was not often in the woods so late as this, and it made her feel as if she

**CLOSE READ**

**ANNOTATE:** In paragraph 4, mark two references to shade or shadows.

**QUESTION:** Why does the author include these details in an otherwise pleasant scene?

**CONCLUDE:** What purpose do these details serve?





## PERSONALIZE FOR LEARNING

### English Language Support

**Complex Syntax** Help students understand the next-to-last sentence in paragraph 2. Write the sentence on the board and underline the two independent clauses and conjunction *but* that connects them. *Everybody said that it was a good change for a little maid who had tried to grow for eight years in a crowded manufacturing town,* ***but,*** *as for Sylvia herself, it seemed as if she had never been alive at all before she came to live at the farm.*

Then have partners work together to answer these questions: To whom does "little maid" refer? (Sylvia) Why does everybody say coming to the farm was a "good change"? (Sylvia had been living for eight years in a crowded manufacturing town.) Guide students to see how the author uses a conjunction and a prepositional phrase to connect ideas. Invite students to write a compound or complex sentence of their own. **ALL LEVELS** were a part of the gray shadows and the moving leaves. She was just thinking how long it seemed since she first came to the farm a year ago, and wondering if everything went on in the noisy town just the same as when she was there; the thought of the great red-faced boy who used to chase and frighten her made her hurry along the path to escape from the shadow of the trees.

5 Suddenly this little woods-girl is horror-stricken to hear a clear whistle not very far away. Not a bird's-whistle, which would have a sort of friendliness, but a boy's whistle, determined, and somewhat aggressive. Sylvia left the cow to whatever sad fate might await her, and stepped discreetly aside into the bushes, but she was just too late. The enemy had discovered her, and called out in a very cheerful and persuasive tone, "Halloa, little girl, how far is it to the road?" And trembling Sylvia answered almost inaudibly, "A good ways."

6 She did not dare to look boldly at the tall young man, who carried a gun over his shoulder, but she came out of her bush and again followed the cow, while he walked alongside.

7 "I have been hunting for some birds," the stranger said kindly, "and I have lost my way, and need a friend very much. Don't be afraid," he added gallantly. "Speak up and tell me what your name is, and whether you think I can spend the night at your house, and go out gunning early in the morning."

8 Sylvia was more alarmed than before. Would not her grandmother consider her much to blame? But who could have foreseen such an accident as this? It did not seem to be her fault, and she hung her head as if the stem of it were broken, but managed to answer "Sylvy," with much effort when her companion again asked her name.

9 Mrs. Tilley was standing in the doorway when the trio came into view. The cow gave a loud moo by way of explanation.

10 "Yes, you'd better speak up for yourself, you old trial! Where'd she tucked herself away this time, Sylvy?" But Sylvia kept an awed silence; she knew by instinct that her grandmother did not comprehend the gravity of the situation. She must be mistaking the stranger for one of the farmer-lads of the region.

11 The young man stood his gun beside the door, and dropped a lumpy game-bag beside it; then he bade Mrs. Tilley good-evening, and repeated his wayfarer's story, and asked if be could have a night's lodging.

12 "Put me anywhere you like," he said. "I must be off early in the morning, before day; but I am very hungry, indeed. Yon can give me some milk at any rate, that's plain."

13 "Dear sakes, yes," responded the hostess, whose long slumbering **hospitality** seemed to be easily awakened. "You might fare better if you went out to the main road a mile or so, but you're welcome to what we've got. I'll milk right off, and you make yourself at home. You can sleep on husks[1] or feathers," she proffered graciously. "I

NOTES

**hospitality** (hos puh TAL uh tee) *n.* warm, welcoming attitude toward guests

1. **husks** *n.* corn husks, used to stuff a mattress.

Additional **English Language Support** is available in the Interactive Teacher's Edition.

## PERSONALIZE FOR LEARNING

### Strategic Support

**Reading Dialogue** Point out to students that all three characters meet for the first time in paragraphs 5 through 13. Have students break into groups of four and read those paragraphs together, with each student taking one part: Sylvia, the young man, Mrs. Tilley, and the narrator. After reading, instruct students to discuss what they learned about the characters and narrator in this section of the story. Have each group share their findings with the class.

# TEACHING

## CLOSE READ 

Encourage students to pay attention to Mrs. Tilley's down-to-earth language, idiomatic expressions, and slang. You may wish to model the close read using the following think-aloud format. Possible responses to questions on the student page are included.

**ANNOTATE:** As I read paragraph 16, I notice and highlight the first four details that reflect Mrs. Tilly's everyday way of speaking, such as "There aint a foot o' ground she don't know her way over"; wild creaturs counts her one o' themselves"; "Squer'ls she'll tame to come an' feed right out o' her hands and all sorts o' birds"; and "she got the jaybirds to bangeing here." I notice this colloquial language often includes interesting spellings, omissions of parts of the word, and slang forms of verbs.

**QUESTION:** I think that the author uses Mrs. Tilley's way of speaking to breathe life into her character. Mrs. Tilley's colorful language is full of examples that help her seem like a real person talking about the people and events in her life. This is an effective way of letting us learn about Mrs. Tilley without having the narrator tell us.

**CONCLUDE:** For me, Mrs. Tilley's way of speaking creates a positive impression of a decent, likeable person who is neither pretentious nor fake. I also feel sympathy for her because although her life has been difficult, she is still a generous, kind-hearted person.

NOTES

**squalor** (SKWOL uhr) *n.* filth; wretchedness

**hermitage** (HUR muh tihj) *n.* secluded retreat

**quaint** (kwaynt) *adj.* unusual; curious; singular

### CLOSE READ

**ANNOTATE:** Colloquial language is informal and may not observe the conventions of standard English. In paragraph 16, mark four examples of colloquial language in Mrs. Tilley's words.

**QUESTION:** Why does the author choose to have Mrs. Tilley speak in this way?

**CONCLUDE:** What effect does this use of colloquial language have?

raised them all myself. There's a good pasturing for geese just below here towards the ma'sh. Now step round and set a plate for the gentleman, Sylvy!" And Sylvia promptly stepped. She was glad to have something to do, and she was hungry herself.

14 It was a surprise to find as clean and comfortable a little dwelling in this New England wilderness. The young man had known the horrors of its most primitive housekeeping, and the dreary **squalor** of that level of society which does not rebel at the companionship of hens. This was the best thrift of an old-fashioned farmstead, though on such a small scale that it seemed like a **hermitage**. He listened eagerly to the old woman's **quaint** talk, he watched Sylvia's pale face and shining gray eyes with ever growing enthusiasm, and insisted that this was the best supper he had eaten for a month, and afterward the new-made friends sat down in the door-way together while the moon came up.

15 Soon it would be berry-time, and Sylvia was a great help at picking. The cow was a good milker, though a plaguy thing to keep track of, the hostess gossiped frankly, adding presently that she had buried four children, so Sylvia's mother, and a son (who might be dead) in California were all the children she had left. "Dan, my boy, was a great hand to go gunning," she explained sadly. "I never wanted for pa'tridges or gray squer'ls while he was to home. He's been a great wand'rer, I expect, and he's no hand to write letters. There, I don't blame him, I'd ha' seen the world myself if it had been so I could."

16 "Sylvy takes after him," the grandmother continued affectionately, after a minute's pause. "There ain't a foot o' ground she don't know her way over, and the wild creaturs counts her one o' themselves. Squer'ls she'll tame to come an' feed right out o' her hands, and all sorts o' birds. Last winter she got the jaybirds to bangeing[2] here, and I believe she'd a' scanted herself of her own meals to have plenty to throw out amongst 'em, if I hadn't kep' watch. Anything but crows, I tell her, I'm willin' to help support—though Dan he had a tamed one o' them that did seem to have reason same as folks. It was round here a good spell after he went away. Dan an' his father they didn't hitch,—but he never held up his head ag'in after Dan had dared him an' gone off."

17 The guest did not notice this hint of family sorrows in his eager interest in something else.

18 "So Sylvy knows all about birds, does she?" he exclaimed, as he looked round at the little girl who sat, very demure but increasingly sleepy, in the moonlight. "I am making a collection of birds myself. I have been at it ever since I was a boy." (Mrs. Tilley smiled.) "There are two or three very rare ones I have been hunting for these five years. I mean to get them on my own ground if they can be found."

2. **bangeing** lounging or hanging around.





## CROSS-CURRICULAR PERSPECTIVES

**Science** Review paragraph 16. Mrs. Tilly mentions a crow her son trained that seemed "to have reason same as folks." Tell students that scientists have investigated the intelligence of crows. A crow's brain is the size of a human thumb. Given the ratio of that size in comparison to the size of a crow's body, scientists believe the bird is on par with primates in its ability to solve complex problems. Invite students to consider the question: Are crows really smart? Ask students to research this topic on the Internet. Then have them write a short research report or create a poster on crow intelligence.

19 "Do you cage 'em up?" asked Mrs. Tilley doubtfully, in response to this enthusiastic announcement.

20 "Oh no, they're stuffed and preserved, dozens and dozens of them," said the ornithologist,[3] "and I have shot or snared every one myself. I caught a glimpse of a white heron a few miles from here on Saturday, and I have followed it in this direction. They have never been found in this district at all. The little white heron, it is," and he turned again to look at Sylvia with the hope of discovering that the rare bird was one of her acquaintances.

21 But Sylvia was watching a hop-toad in the narrow footpath.

22 "You would know the heron if you saw it," the stranger continued eagerly. "A queer tall white bird with soft feathers and long thin legs. And it would have a nest perhaps in the top of a high tree, made of sticks, something like a hawk's nest."

23 Sylvia's heart gave a wild beat; she knew that strange white bird, and had once stolen softly near where it stood in some bright green swamp grass, away over at the other side of the woods. There was an open place where the sunshine always seemed strangely yellow and hot, where tall, nodding rushes grew, and her grandmother had warned her that she might sink in the soft black mud underneath and never be heard of more. Not far beyond were the salt marshes just this side of the sea itself, which Sylvia wondered and dreamed much about, but never had seen, whose great voice could sometimes be heard above the noise of the woods on stormy nights.

24 "I can't think of anything I should like so much as to find that heron's nest," the handsome stranger was saying. "I would give ten dollars to anybody who could show it to me," he added desperately, "and I mean to spend my whole vacation hunting for it if need be. Perhaps it was only migrating, or had been chased out of its own region by some bird of prey."

25 Mrs. Tilley gave amazed attention to all this, but Sylvia still watched the toad, not divining, as she might have done at some calmer time, that the creature wished to get to its hole under the door-step, and was much hindered by the unusual spectators at that hour of the evening. No amount of thought, that night, could decide how many wished-for treasures the ten dollars, so lightly spoken of, would buy.

26 The next day the young sportsman hovered about the woods, and Sylvia kept him company, having lost her first fear of the friendly lad, who proved to be most kind and sympathetic. He told her many things about the birds and what they knew and where they lived and what they did with themselves. And he gave her a jack-knife, which she thought as great a treasure as if she were a desert-islander. All day long he did not once make her troubled or afraid except when he brought down some unsuspecting singing creature from its bough. Sylvia would have liked him vastly better without his gun; she could not understand why he killed the very birds he

NOTES

3. **ornithologist** (awr nih THOL uh jihst) *n.* one who practices the study of birds.





DIGITAL PERSPECTIVES

## DIGITAL PERSPECTIVES

**Enriching the Text** Encourage students to collect and write down Sylvia's meditations on nature and go online to find additional meditations. They might read and record these meditations in a grouping, such as a long prose poem. As an alternative, have class recitations in which students present their favorite excerpts. **(Research to Explore)**

## CLOSER LOOK

### Investigate Conflict 

Students may have marked paragraphs 23–25 during their first read. Use these paragraphs to help students understand the connection Sylvia feels with nature. Encourage students to talk about the annotations that they marked. You may want to model a close read with the class based on the highlights shown in the text.

**ANNOTATE:** Have students mark details in paragraphs 23–25 that show how Sylvia and the hunter each view nature.

**QUESTION:** Guide students to consider what these details might tell them. Ask what readers can infer from the depth of interest and attention Sylvia gives to the natural world, and accept student responses.

**Possible response:** Sylvia's bases her strong, vivid memory of the heron and its surroundings on intense study and attention. I also see that Sylvia "wondered and dreamed much about" these things. Later, Sylvia's similar observation of a toad distracts her from the adults who are speaking directly to her. By contrast, the hunter's main connection to the bird is his desire to hunt it, even being willing to pay to find its location.

**CONCLUDE:** Help students formulate conclusions about the importance of these details in the text. Ask students why the author might have included these details.

**Possible response:** I think the author is establishing a central conflict in the story. By alternating these almost poetic descriptions of Sylvia's close connection to nature with the hunter's materialistic attitude toward the bird, it seems that the author is setting up an internal conflict for Sylvia: Will she try to help the hunter find the bird and collect his ransom or not?

Remind students that **conflict** is a struggle between opposing forces. There are two kinds of conflicts: external and internal. In an **external conflict**, a character struggles against an outside force: another character, an element of nature, or some aspect of society. In an **internal conflict**, the conflict is within a single character who is struggling with opposing feelings, beliefs, needs, or desires. For example, a character's desire for independence might be at odds with her fear of growing up. Often a character experiences both an external and an internal conflict.

NOTES

seemed to like so much. But as the day waned, Sylvia still watched the young man with loving admiration. She had never seen anybody so charming and delightful; the woman's heart, asleep in the child, was vaguely thrilled by a dream of love. Some premonition of that great power stirred and swayed these young creatures who traversed the solemn woodlands with soft-footed silent care. They stopped to listen to a bird's song; they pressed forward again eagerly, parting the branches—speaking to each other rarely and in whispers; the young man going first and Sylvia following, fascinated, a few steps behind, with her gray eyes dark with excitement.

27 She grieved because the longed-for white heron was elusive, but she did not lead the guest, she only followed, and there was no such thing as speaking first. The sound of her own unquestioned voice would have terrified her—it was hard enough to answer yes or no when there was need of that. At last evening began to fall, and they drove the cow home together, and Sylvia smiled with pleasure when they came to the place where she heard the whistle and was afraid only the night before.

## II.

28 Half a mile from home, at the farther edge of the woods, where the land was highest, a great pine-tree stood, the last of its generation. Whether it was left for a boundary mark, or for what reason, no one could say; the woodchoppers who had felled its mates were dead and gone long ago, and a whole forest of sturdy trees, pines and oaks and maples, had grown again. But the stately head of this old pine towered above them all and made a landmark for sea and shore miles and miles away. Sylvia knew it well. She had always believed that whoever climbed to the top of it could see the ocean; and the little girl had often laid her hand on the great rough trunk and looked up wistfully at those dark boughs that the wind always stirred, no matter how hot and still the air might be below. Now she thought of the tree with a new excitement, for why, if one climbed it at break of day could not one see all the world, and easily discover from whence the white heron flew, and mark the place, and find the hidden nest?

29 What a spirit of adventure, what wild ambition! What fancied triumph and delight and glory for the later morning when she could make known the secret! It was almost too real and too great for the childish heart to bear.

30 All night the door of the little house stood open and the whippoorwills came and sang upon the very step. The young sportsman and his old hostess were sound asleep, but Sylvia's great design kept her broad awake and watching. She forgot to think of sleep. The short summer night seemed as long as the winter darkness, and at last when the whippoorwills ceased, and she was afraid the morning would after all come too soon, she stole out of the house and followed the pasture path through the woods, hastening





### WriteNow Express and Reflect

**Diary Entry** Review paragraph 26 and have students write a diary entry describing Sylvia's meeting with the young sportsman and her complex reaction to him. Encourage them to think about the following questions as they prepare to write the entry: *In what way were Sylvia's feelings toward the young man positive? Why? In what way were they negative or confused? Why? The author writes that: "the woman's heart, asleep in the child, was vaguely thrilled by a dream of love." What does this mean? How does it influence Sylvia's reaction? How does the jackknife influence in her reaction?*

DIGITAL PERSPECTIVES

toward the open ground beyond, listening with a sense of comfort and companionship to the drowsy twitter of a half-awakened bird, whose perch she had jarred in passing. Alas, if the great wave of human interest which flooded for the first time this dull little life should sweep away the satisfactions of an existence heart to heart with nature and the dumb life of the forest!

31 There was the huge tree asleep yet in the paling moonlight, and small and silly Sylvia began with utmost bravery to mount to the top of it, with tingling, eager blood coursing the channels of her whole frame, with her bare feet and fingers, that pinched and held like bird's claws to the monstrous ladder reaching up, up, almost to the sky itself. First she must mount the white oak tree that grew alongside, where she was almost lost among the dark branches and the green leaves heavy and wet with dew; a bird fluttered off its nest, and a red squirrel ran to and fro and scolded pettishly at the harmless housebreaker. Sylvia felt her way easily. She had often climbed there, and knew that higher still one of the oak's upper branches chafed against the pine trunk, just where its lowest boughs were set close together. There, when she made the dangerous pass from one tree to the other, the great enterprise would really begin.

NOTES

**CLOSE READ**

**ANNOTATE:** In the first sentence of paragraph 31, mark two adjectives that describe Sylvia and two adjectives that describe the pine tree.

**QUESTION:** Why does the author use these adjectives?

**CONCLUDE:** What is the effect of these word choices?





## CLOSE READ

Have students focus on the description of the pine tree at the start of the paragraph 31, when Sylvia begins her ascent. Encourage them to key in to how she feels in the presence of the great pine. You may wish to model the close read using the following think-aloud format. Possible responses to questions on the student page are included.

**ANNOTATE:** As I read paragraph 31, I notice and highlight the adjectives *small* and *silly* that describe Sylvia and *huge* and *monstrous* that describe the pine tree. These descriptive words give a strong sense of how Sylvia is experiencing her adventure. I agree with the author's description of Sylvia's undertaking as "utmost bravery"; it was extremely dangerous. No doubt her grandmother would have been horrified if she had found out about Sylvia's recklessness.

**QUESTION:** Reading about Sylvia climbing higher and higher, I get a sense of the immensity of the big old trees, and a feeling of awe. Her trip up the giant oak is difficult enough as she moves through a virtual forest of leaves and branches, and she still has to pass over to the gigantic pine and begin her final ascent. The adjectives describing Sylvia and the pine establish a wonderful contrast between her smallness and the tree's greatness.

**CONCLUDE:** I admire Sylvia's determination and courage. The contrast between Sylvia and her surroundings strengthens my admiration. The contrast also contributes to my suspense about whether Sylvia—and the heron—will survive.

## PERSONALIZE FOR LEARNING

**Strategic Support**

**Contrast** Discuss how the author uses contrast on several levels in paragraph 31, first to contrast Sylvia and her surroundings and then to set up a contrast between the oak tree and the pine tree. For example, the pine tree is much harder to climb. Ask students to find two additional examples in the paragraph that contrast the oak and the pine. ("monstrous ladder" versus "dark branches and green leaves"; "upper branches" versus "lowest boughs")

## CLOSER LOOK

### Explore Figurative Language

Students may have marked similes, metaphors, or personification in paragraphs 32–34 during their first read. Use these paragraphs to help students understand the author's use of imagery in this passage. Encourage them to talk about the annotations that they marked. You may want to model a close read with the class based on the highlights shown in the text.

**ANNOTATE:** Have students mark details in these paragraphs that use figurative language to create imagery.

**QUESTION:** Guide students to consider what these details might tell them. Ask what readers can infer from the similes, metaphors, and instances of personification that the author uses to describe both the tree and Sylvia, and accept student responses.

**Possible response:** The author gives the tree characteristics of a bird, a ship, and a human. First, the tree's limbs are compared to angry talons that scratch Sylvia's legs. Later the tree is compared to the main-mast of the ship, anchoring itself to the earth. In paragraph 33, the tree is described with human feelings and thoughts. Sylvia is described throughout with images of nature: her face like a pale star and her feeling that she could fly away among the clouds.

**CONCLUDE:** Help students formulate conclusions about the importance of these details in the text. Ask students why the author might have included these details.

**Possible response:** The author again grounds readers in the natural world as Sylvia is grounded in it. These details make readers look at the world a little differently. The author is trying to tell us to respect the natural world and all of the plants and creatures that share the world with us.

Review with students the terms *simile, metaphor,* and *personification,* using examples from the passage. A **metaphor** is a figure of speech that compares two apparently unlike things without using the words *like, as, than,* or *resembles.* Unlike a **simile,** a figure of speech that does use a connecting word, a metaphor speaks of one thing as if it were the other. **Personification** is a form of imagery that attributes human characteristics to animals or objects.

NOTES

32 She crept out along the swaying oak limb at last, and took the daring step across into the old pine-tree. The way was harder than she thought; she must reach far and hold fast, the sharp dry twigs caught and held her and scratched her like angry talons, the pitch made her thin little fingers clumsy and stiff as she went round and round the tree's great stem, higher and higher upward. The sparrows and robins in the woods below were beginning to wake and twitter to the dawn, yet it seemed much lighter there aloft in the pine-tree, and the child knew she must hurry if her project were to be of any use.

33 The tree seemed to lengthen itself out as she went up, and to reach farther and farther upward. It was like a great main-mast to the voyaging earth; it must truly have been amazed that morning through all its ponderous frame as it felt this determined spark of human spirit wending its way from higher branch to branch. Who knows how steadily the least twigs held themselves to advantage this light, weak creature on her way! The old pine must have loved his new dependent. More than all the hawks, and bats, and moths, and even the sweet voiced thrushes, was the brave, beating heart of the solitary gray-eyed child. And the tree stood still and frowned away the winds that June morning while the dawn grew bright in the east.

34 Sylvia's face was like a pale star, if one had seen it from the ground, when the last thorny bough was past, and she stood trembling and tired but wholly triumphant, high in the tree-top. Yes, there was the sea with the dawning sun making a golden dazzle over it, and toward that glorious east flew two hawks with slow-moving pinions. How low they looked in the air from that height when one had only seen them before far up, and dark against the blue sky. Their gray feathers were as soft as moths; they seemed only a little way from the tree, and Sylvia felt as if she too could go flying away among the clouds. Westward, the woodlands and farms reached miles and miles into the distance; here and there were church steeples, and white villages, truly it was a vast and awesome world!

35 The birds sang louder and louder. At last the sun came up bewilderingly bright. Sylvia could see the white sails of ships out at sea, and the clouds that were purple and rose-colored and yellow at first began to fade away. Where was the white heron's nest in the sea of green branches, and was this wonderful sight and pageant of the world the only reward for having climbed to such a giddy height? Now look down again, Sylvia, where the green marsh is set among the shining birches and dark hemlocks; there where you saw the white heron once you will see him again; look, look! a white spot of him like a single floating feather comes up from the dead hemlock and grows larger, and rises, and comes close at last, and goes by the landmark pine with steady sweep of wing and outstretched slender neck and crested head. And wait! wait! do not move a foot or a finger, little girl, do not send an arrow of light and consciousness from your two eager eyes, for the heron has perched on a pine bough not far





## PERSONALIZE FOR LEARNING

### English Language Support

**Figurative Language** Review paragraph 34. Focus on similes, beginning with this example: *High in the tree, Sylvia felt like a bird.* Make sure that students understand the idea that the subject (Sylvia) is being compared to something else (a bird) in this simile. Discuss the effect using such a comparison has on readers. Then offer other examples of similes, such as: *After exercising, I was as hungry as a lion. I walked through the was as hungry as a lion. I walked through the forest as quietly as a panther.* Read through *as a panther.* Read through the following frames with students. *The child danced as gracefully as ______. The classroom chattered as loudly as ______. The boy dashed like a ______. The pounding of their feet sounded like ______.* For each, discuss what the subject might be compared to. Then have students work with a partner to complete the frames to create similes of their own. **EXPANDING**

DIGITAL PERSPECTIVES

beyond yours, and cries back to his mate on the nest and plumes his feathers for the new day!

NOTES

36 The child gives a long sigh a minute later when a company of shouting cat-birds comes also to the tree, and vexed by their fluttering and lawlessness the solemn heron goes away. She knows his secret now, the wild, light, slender bird that floats and wavers, and goes back like an arrow presently to his home in the green world beneath. Then Sylvia, well satisfied, makes her perilous way down again, not daring to look far below the branch she stands on, ready to cry sometimes because her fingers ache and her lamed feet slip. Wondering over and over again what the stranger would say to her, and what he would think when she told him how to find his way straight to the heron's nest.

37 "Sylvy, Sylvy!" called the busy old grandmother again and again, but nobody answered, and the small husk bed was empty and Sylvia had disappeared.

38 The guest waked from a dream, and remembering his day's pleasure hurried to dress himself that might it sooner begin. He was sure from the way the shy little girl looked once or twice yesterday that she had at least seen the white heron, and now she must really be made to tell. Here she comes now, paler than ever, and her worn old frock is torn and tattered, and smeared with pine pitch. The grandmother and the sportsman stand in the door together and





PERSONALIZE FOR LEARNING

**Strategic Support**

**Point of View** Review paragraph 38. The story is told from the point of view of a third-person omniscient narrator who focuses mostly on Sylvia. This viewpoint shifts briefly to Mrs. Tilly and the young man, then back again to Sylvia. Ask students to identify where the narrator's viewpoint shifts in paragraphs 36–38. Encourage them to tell what the author suggests about the sportsman's motives during this shift. What is his "day's pleasure"? Why does he believe Sylvia is going to help him find the heron?

## CLOSE READ 

Remind students to focus on exclamatory sentences and questions and what their purpose might be. You may wish to model the close read using the following think-aloud format. Possible responses to questions on the student page are included.

**ANNOTATE:** As I read the beginning of paragraph 40, I am immediately struck by the imperative, exclamatory sentence that demands Sylvia not speak to the young sportsman. It's almost as if her conscience is ordering her. I notice this short sentence is followed by two questions.

**QUESTION:** I think the author uses an exclamation and two questions to suggest that Sylvia was in the midst of an internal conflict about whether to stay true to her love of nature or to earn her family money that they needed badly.

**CONCLUDE:** These three sentences catch my attention and make me pause, in part, because the two paragraphs before had neither an exclamation nor a question. In the story, the effect of these thoughts is similar. They stop the action that was in progress, when Sylvia was about to give away the secret of where to find the heron.

NOTES

**CLOSE READ**

**ANNOTATE:** Mark the exclamation and the questions in paragraph 40.

**QUESTION:** Why does the author choose to use an exclamation and questions rather than statements?

**CONCLUDE:** What is the effect of these sentence variations?

question her, and the splendid moment has come to speak of the dead hemlock tree by the green marsh.

39 But Sylvia does not speak after all, though the old grandmother fretfully rebukes her, and the young man's kind, appealing eyes are looking straight in her own. He can make them rich with money; he has promised it, and they are poor now. He is so well worth making happy, and he waits to hear the story she can tell.

40 No, she must keep silence! What is it that suddenly forbids her and makes her dumb? Has she been nine years growing and now, when the great world for the first time puts out a hand to her, must she thrust it aside for a bird's sake? The murmur of the pine's green branches is in her ears, she remembers how the white heron came flying through the golden air and how they watched the sea and the morning together, and Sylvia cannot speak; she cannot tell the heron's secret and give its life away.

41 Dear loyalty, that suffered a sharp pang as the guest went away disappointed later in the day, that could have served and followed him and loved him as a dog loves! Many a night Sylvia heard the echo of his whistle haunting the pasture path as she came home with the loitering cow. She forgot even her sorrow at the sharp report of his gun and the sight of thrushes and sparrows dropping silent to the ground, their songs hushed and their pretty feathers stained and wet with blood. Were the birds better friends than their hunter might have been,—who can tell? Whatever treasures were lost to her, woodlands and summer-time, remember! Bring your gifts and graces and tell your secrets to this lonely country child! ❧





## PERSONALIZE FOR LEARNING

### English Language Support

**Parts of Speech** Direct students' attention to the following sentence in paragraph 41: *She forgot even her sorrow at the sharp report of his gun and the sight of thrushes and sparrows dropping silent to the ground, their songs hushed and their pretty feathers stained and wet with blood.* Point out that this sentence contains a lengthy adverbial phrase that provides details about the action. Help students isolate the adverbial phrase (*at the sharp report of his gun and the sight of thrushes and sparrows dropping silent to the ground, their songs hushed and their pretty feathers stained and wet with blood*) and note the action it modifies (*forgot*). Now have students compare this sentence to one without the adverbial phrase: *She forgot even her sorrow.* Discuss the impact of the added details and have students explain why they think the author includes them. **ALL LEVELS**

## Comprehension Check

Complete the following items after you finish your first read.

1. Where had Sylvia lived before she came to stay at her grandmother's house?

2. What does the young stranger hope to find in the wilderness?

3. What does the stranger offer to give anyone who helps him achieve his goal?

4. Why does Sylvia climb the great pine tree?

5. What information does Sylvia refuse to share after her expedition to the pine tree?

6. **Notebook** Write a summary of "A White Heron" in order to confirm your understanding of the story.

### RESEARCH

**Research to Clarify** Choose at least one unfamiliar detail from the text. Briefly research that detail. In what way does the information you learned shed light on an aspect of the story?

**Research to Explore** Conduct research to learn more about Sarah Orne Jewett's life in the Maine woods.





### PERSONALIZE FOR LEARNING

**Challenge**

**Make Connections** Have students explore similarities and differences in the use of colloquial language between Jewett's "A White Heron" and Mark Twain's "The Notorious Jumping Frog of Calaveras County." They should consider these questions: *How important is colloquial language in each story? What function does it serve in each story? What insight does the use of everyday language shed on the characters, setting, and/or plot of each story?*

DIGITAL PERSPECTIVES

## Comprehension Check

Possible responses:

1. Sylvia had lived in a crowded manufacturing town.
2. He hopes to find birds, especially the nesting place of the white heron so that he can add the bird to his collection.
3. He offers a reward of ten dollars.
4. She believes that she may be able to spot the white heron from the treetop.
5. She refuses to betray the location of the heron's nest.
6. Sylvia lives with her grandmother deep in the woods. She responds deeply to nature and loves her surroundings. One day, a young bird hunter encounters Sylvia and then asks the grandmother if he can stay at their house. He is in search of a rare bird, the white heron, and wants to add it to his collection. Sylvia's feelings toward the sportsman quickly change from apprehension to admiration. He offers ten dollars for information about the bird's location, money badly needed by Sylvia and her grandmother. Early in the morning, Sylvia slips out of the house and climbs a great pine tree, believing that she will be able to spot the heron from the top. After much effort, she is successful. When she returns home, however, she silently refuses to reveal the bird's whereabouts.

## Research

**Research to Clarify** If students have difficulty choosing a detail for their research, suggest that they focus on one of the following: life in New England manufacturing towns in the mid-1800s; life on an old-fashioned farmstead in the mid-1800s; Vermont's early history; herons, sparrows, robins, or hawks.

**Research to Explore** If students find the topic too broad, suggest that they focus on one aspect of Jewett's childhood, such as the town of South Berwick, Maine, where she grew up or how her childhood rheumatoid arthritis affected her later in life.

## Jump Start

**CLOSE READ** Ask students whether they were surprised by Sylvia's decision not to reveal the heron's location. Did they find any clues throughout the story that suggested how she might respond in the end?

## Close Read the Text

Work with students on the annotation model on the student page, then have them complete items 2 and 3 on their own. Review and discuss the sections students marked. If needed, continue to model close reading by using the Annotation Highlights in the Interactive Teacher's Edition.

## Analyze the Text

Possible responses:

1. (a) She is frightened, as it brings to mind a large red-faced boy who used to chase her. (b) It foreshadows the young stranger's hunting trip and his bribe to get her help in finding and killing the white heron. **DOK 1, DOK 3**
2. (a) She is conflicted between his appeal and his killing of birds. (b) She is motivated by the reward and by her sense of adventure as well. **DOK 2, DOK 3**
3. Sylvia remains loyal to the heron and to herself and her own love of nature. **DOK 3**
4. The reward offers the possibility of help for Sylvia's grandmother, more food, some small luxuries, and perhaps a trip to the nearest town. This detail suggests that they live on an isolated farm where life is extremely simple and difficult. **DOK 2**
5. In "A White Heron," the story's setting on an isolated farm in the woods of New England is an essential element—fundamental to its plot, characterization, conflict, imagery, symbolism, and theme. **DOK 3**

### FORMATIVE ASSESSMENT

### Analyze the Text

- **If** students fail to cite evidence, **then** remind them to support their ideas with specific information from the text.
- **If** students struggle to analyze how Sylvia's initial fear of the stranger foreshadows future events, **then** discuss foreshadowing and illustrate with examples.



MAKING MEANING

A WHITE HERON

## Close Read the Text

1. This model, from paragraph 33 of the text, shows two sample annotations, along with questions and conclusions. Close read the passage and find another detail to annotate. Then, write a question and your conclusion.

ANNOTATE: Jewett uses contradictory terms to describe Sylvia.

QUESTION: What idea about Sylvia is Jewett expressing?

CONCLUDE: Sylvia's spirit is stronger than her small body reveals.

[The tree] must truly have been amazed that morning through all its ponderous frame as it felt this determined spark of human spirit wending its way from higher branch to branch. Who knows how steadily the least twigs held themselves to advantage this light, weak creature on her way! The old pine must have loved his new dependent.

ANNOTATE: The pine tree is given human emotions.

QUESTION: Why does Jewett personify the tree?

CONCLUDE: If the grand tree loves Sylvia, then she must truly be exceptional.

2. For more practice, go back into the text, and complete the close-read notes.
3. Revisit a section of the text you found important during your first read. Read this section closely, and **annotate** what you notice. Ask yourself **questions** such as "Why did the author make this choice?" What can you **conclude**?

**Tool Kit**
Close-Read Guide and Model Annotation

## Analyze the Text

CITE TEXTUAL EVIDENCE to support your answers.

**Notebook** Respond to these questions.

1. (a) What is Sylvia's reaction when she first hears the stranger's whistle? (b) **Analyze** What later events in the story does this reaction foreshadow, or predict?
2. (a) **Interpret** On the second day, how does Sylvia feel about the stranger? (b) **Evaluate** What motivates Sylvia to climb the pine tree?
3. **Synthesize** Jewett ends the story by invoking "Dear loyalty." To whom or what does Sylvia remain loyal by not telling the heron's secret? Explain your answer.
4. **Historical Perspectives** How would Sylvia's and her grandmother's lives have changed if they had the ten dollars from the stranger? What does that tell you about their time period and circumstances? Explain.
5. **Essential Question:** *What is the relationship between literature and place?* What have you learned about the relationship between literature and place by reading this story?

**STANDARDS**
**Reading Literature**
- Cite strong and thorough textual evidence to support analysis of what the text says explicitly as well as inferences drawn from the text, including determining where the text leaves matters uncertain.
- Determine two or more themes or central ideas of a text and analyze their development over the course of the text, including how they interact and build on one another to produce a complex account; provide an objective summary of the text.





## PERSONALIZE FOR LEARNING

### English Language Support

**Difficult Concepts** To help students understand foreshadowing, offer personal connections. Ask: *Did you ever see someone with a worried look and know that they were concerned something bad might happen?* Explain that the facial expression foreshadowed bad news. Remind students of the initial encounter with Sylvia and the hunter. (paragraphs 5-12) While Sylvia was focused on the wonders of nature, the hunter was excitedly sharing how his one desire was the hunt. Have students discuss with a partner how this scene could be viewed as an example of foreshadowing. (It foreshadows how Sylvia's love and connection with nature will overshadow her interest in the hunter and his desires.) **ALL LEVELS**

## Analyze Craft and Structure

**Thematic Development** The **theme** of a literary text is its central message or insight about human life or behavior. Sometimes, the theme is explicitly stated. More often, however, readers must piece together related ideas from the text to infer the theme. Theme should be expressed in a statement, not a single word. An author may develop more than one theme in a single work.

To help determine theme, readers can examine the imagery and symbolism in the text.

- **Imagery** is language that uses sensory details—words related to sight, hearing, touch, taste, or smell—to create word pictures in readers' minds. More broadly, imagery can include figurative language, or language that presents surprising comparisons to help readers understand ideas in a new way. "A White Heron" begins with vivid imagery that helps readers picture the rural Maine setting.
- A **symbol** is something—an object, a character, an animal, or a place—that represents something else. In "A White Heron," the great pine tree and the white heron are two powerful symbols that represent more than simply a tree and a bird. The deeper meanings of these symbols are clues to the larger ideas or themes of the story.

### Practice

CITE TEXTUAL EVIDENCE to support your answers.

**Notebook** Respond to these questions.

1. Reread the description of the great pine tree in paragraph 33. (a) What imagery does Jewett use in her description of the tree? (b) Based on these images, what might the pine tree represent?
2. (a) Trace Sylvia's attitude toward the stranger from the beginning of the story to the end. How do her feelings about him change? (b) Is the stranger a symbolic figure? Why, or why not?
3. (a) What does Sylvia have to gain by revealing the white heron's location? What does she gain by remaining silent? (b) What does the white heron represent?
4. Use a chart like this one to analyze imagery, symbols, and themes. For each topic listed in the left-hand column, record images, symbols, and other details from the story that help to reveal the author's central messages or insights. Then, write a theme statement for each topic.

| TOPIC | IMAGES, SYMBOLS, DETAILS | THEME STATEMENT |
|---|---|---|
| relationship of humans to nature and society | little woods-girl, great pine-tree, white heron | A price cannot be set on the value of nature. |
| self-discovery | Sylvia's flourishing in the wilderness, her conflicted feelings about the stranger | Self-discovery is thrilling, but also challenging. |
| loyalty | refusal to reveal the heron's location | Loyalty may involve sacrifice. |





DIGITAL PERSPECTIVES

## Analyze Craft and Structure

**Thematic Development** Remind students that all story elements connect to the story's themes. Through Sylvia, the author conveys messages about loyalty and self-discovery. Through the setting of the New England woods, the author conveys messages about the natural world's value. For more support, see **Analyze Craft and Structure: Thematic Development.**

### Practice

Possible responses:

1. (a) great main-mast; ponderous frame; least twigs held themselves to advantage; loved his new dependent (b) The personification of the tree suggests it is a sentient being with feelings and awareness.
2. (a) First, Sylvia feels frightened, but fear gives way to admiration. At the end of the story, she refuses to betray the heron and cause its death. (b) The stranger symbolizes a dominating view of nature, seen in his unemotional shooting of the birds, his stuffed collection, and his offer of ten dollars for the heron's location.
3. (a) By revealing the heron's location, Sylvia would gain needed money. By keeping silent, she maintains her close connection with nature and stays true to herself. (b) The white heron represents the beauty and the inherent value of the natural world.
4. See possible responses in chart on student page.

### FORMATIVE ASSESSMENT

### Analyze Craft and Structure

- **If** students have difficulty identifying a theme, **then** offer a theme and ask them to find story details to support it.
- **If** students have difficulty understanding symbols, **then** offer a concrete object such as a dining room table or a wedding ring and guide them in determining the symbolism behind it.

For Reteach and Practice, see **Analyze Craft and Structure: Thematic Development (RP).**

## PERSONALIZE FOR LEARNING

### Strategic Support

**Review Theme** If students are struggling to identify a theme in literature, remind them that all stories have a central theme, including those told in movies. Point out the themes of some popular movies. For example, the theme of *Jurassic Park* is that when technology misuses nature, obstacles (and monsters) are created. In the movie *Cast Away*, Tom Hanks shows man's ultimate desire to survive, even in the harshest of conditions.

Working in small groups, have students list two or three of their favorite movies. Then have them summarize the theme of each. Provide time for groups to share their ideas. Point out that a particular movie, or piece of literature, can have more than one theme. If students find others who express different themes for the same movie, challenge them to defend their ideas with details from the film.

## Concept Vocabulary

### Why These Words

Possible responses:

1. The concept vocabulary suggests that country life is slow-paced, plain, drab, and modest but worthy.
2. Other words connected to this concept include *lonely* (paragraph 41), *wayfarer's* (paragraph 11), *wilderness* (paragraph 14), *ornithologist* (paragraph 20), *thrift* (paragraph 14), *old-fashioned* (paragraph 14), and *woodlands* (paragraph 26).

### Practice

1. Responses will vary.
2. Responses will vary.

### Word Network

**Possible words:** *pasture, huckleberry, birch, twilight, shoal, boughs, waded, brook, woodlands, whippoorwills*

## Word Study

For more support, see **Concept Vocabulary and Word Study.**

Possible responses:

1. A *hospice* is a place of shelter for travelers or a facility for the gravely ill.
2. Examples include *host* (someone who entertains guests), *hostage* (someone taken prisoner by an enemy), *hospital* (an institution providing medical care), and *hostel* (an inn).

### FORMATIVE ASSESSMENT

#### Concept Vocabulary

**If** students fail to see the connection between the words, **then** have them write sentences connecting each of these word pairs: *hospitality* (paragraph 13) and *hermitage* (paragraph 14); *loitered* (paragraph 2) and *dilatory* (paragraph 1).

#### Word Study

**If** students have difficulty understanding the relationship among words derived from the root word *hospes*, **then** point out that a host (a meaning of *hospes*) is a person who welcomes guests/lodgers/visitors. Have them tie this meaning to other words in the word family. For Reteach and Practice, see **Word Study: Latin Root Word: *hospes* (RP).**

LANGUAGE DEVELOPMENT

A WHITE HERON

## Concept Vocabulary

| dilatory | hospitality | hermitage |
|---|---|---|
| loitered | squalor | quaint |

**Why These Words?** These concept vocabulary words help describe the pace and character of rural life. In contrast to life in a city, the pace of life in nineteenth-century rural Maine is unhurried. People often accept a *dilatory* speed, and it is not uncommon to *loiter*. The endurance of traditional values is evident in Mrs. Tilley's *hospitality* to the stranger.

1. How does the concept vocabulary clarify the reader's understanding of the story's setting?
2. What other words in the selection connect to this concept?

### Practice

**Notebook** The six concept words appear in "A White Heron."

1. Use each concept word in a sentence that demonstrates your understanding of the word's meaning.
2. In two of your sentences, replace the concept word with a synonym. How does the sentence change? For example, which word is stronger? Which one makes the sentence seem more positive or negative?

**WORD NETWORK**

Add words related to a sense of place from the text to your Word Network.

## Word Study

**Latin Root Word: *hospes*** The concept vocabulary word *hospitality* comes from the Latin root word *hospes*, meaning both "host" and "guest." Thus, *hospitality* means "a warm, welcoming attitude toward guests."

1. Write a definition of the word *hospice* based on your understanding of the Latin root word *hospes*. Check your answer in a print or online college-level dictionary.
2. Identify and define two other words that are derived from the Latin root word *hospes*. Use a specialized reference such as an etymological dictionary to verify your choices.

**STANDARDS**

Language

- Apply knowledge of language to understand how language functions in different contexts, to make effective choices for meaning or style, and to comprehend more fully when reading or listening.
- Consult general and specialized reference materials, both print and digital, to find the pronunciation of a word or determine or clarify its precise meaning, its part of speech, its etymology, or its standard usage.
- Verify the preliminary determination of the meaning of a word or phrase.





### PERSONALIZE FOR LEARNING

**Multiple-Meaning Words** Ask pairs of students to find cues to the meaning of *gallantly* (paragraph 7). "I have been hunting for some birds," the stranger said kindly, and I have lost my way... Don't be afraid," he added gallantly. **EMERGING**

Ask students to determine the meaning of the underlined multiple-meaning words. "You might fare (paragraph 13) better if you went out to the main road…" "I'll milk (paragraph 13) right off, and you make yourself at home." **EXPANDING**

Ask students to write sentences using the two meanings of fare and milk. **BRIDGING**

An expanded **English Language Support Lesson** on Multiple-Meaning Words is available in the Interactive Teacher's Edition.

## Conventions and Style

**Sentence Variety** There are four types of sentences: declarative, interrogative, exclamatory, and imperative. In "A White Heron," Jewett varies declarative sentences with occasional **interrogative sentences**, or questions, and **exclamations** to develop Sylvia's character—especially the way in which Sylvia processes her thoughts and feelings.

TIP

FOLLOW THROUGH
Refer to the Grammar Handbook to learn more about these terms.

| SENTENCE TYPE | FUNCTION | EXAMPLE |
|---|---|---|
| Declarative | makes a statement | *Besides, Sylvia had all the time there was, and very little use to make of it.* (paragraph 2) |
| Interrogative | asks a question | *What is it that suddenly forbids her and makes her dumb?* (paragraph 40) |
| Exclamatory | expresses strong feeling | *. . . there never was such a child for straying about out-of-doors since the world was made!* (paragraph 2) |
| Imperative | gives a command or makes a request | *Bring your gifts and graces and tell your secrets to this lonely country child!* (paragraph 41) |

### Read It

1. Reread paragraph 8 and identify the interrogative sentences. What do the questions reveal about Sylvia's feelings and state of mind?

2. Reread paragraphs 28 and 29. Mark the interrogative sentence and the exclamations. How does the progression of these sentences convey a steadily mounting sense of excitement in Sylvia?

3. **Connect to Style** Reread the last paragraph of "A White Heron." In a few sentences, explain how Jewett employs various types of sentences in this paragraph to create an effective conclusion to the story.

### Write It

**Notebook** Write a brief sketch, or descriptive paragraph, of Sylvia, Mrs. Tilley, or the stranger. Use at least one interrogative sentence and one exclamatory sentence in your paragraph.





DIGITAL PERSPECTIVES

## Conventions and Style

**Sentence Variety** Use variations on a declarative sentence to illustrate differences among the four types of sentences. You need a haircut. (declarative) Do you need a haircut? (interrogative) You need a haircut! (exclamatory) Get a haircut now. (imperative) For more support, see **Conventions and Style: Sentence Variety.**

### Read It

Possible responses:

1. Sentences 2 and 3. The questions reveal Sylvia's apprehension and alarm.
2. Last sentence of paragraph 28; sentences 1 and 2 of paragraph 29. The sentences follow Sylvia's excitement at the prospective discovery of the nest to her imagined delight at revealing the secret.
3. It begins with an exclamation focused on loyalty and continues with two declarative sentences rich with imagery. Jewett continues with a question about the story's central conflict and resolution. The paragraph concludes with two exclamations, both highly sympathetic to Sylvia.

### Write It

Responses will vary but might mention Sylvia's love of nature, her courage, and her loyalty; Mrs. Tilley's isolation, her hospitality, and her appreciation of Sylvia's love of nature; the stranger's worldliness, the paradox of his love for and killing of birds, and his kindness toward Sylvia. All paragraphs should use at least one interrogative sentence and one exclamatory sentence.

### HOW LANGUAGE WORKS

**Sentence Variety** Have students work with a partner to identify at least one example of each sentence type from the text. Then challenge pairs to rephrase their sentences into the other three forms. Have pairs discuss how the impact of the section of text might change with each revision. Do any of their revisions have greater impact than the original sentence? Encourage pairs to share their favorite text revisions with the class.

### FORMATIVE ASSESSMENT

### Conventions and Style

**If** students have difficulty writing an imperative sentence, **then** remind them that the subject of an imperative sentence is not stated directly. The subject of the command is understood to be the pronoun *you*. They might practice writing an order with the word *you* and then removing the pronoun in their final version.

**If** students have difficulty writing an exclamatory sentence, **then** remind them that exclamatory sentences show excitement (positive or negative). They might practice by beginning a declarative sentence with an interjection (wow, no, yes, sure), ending it with an exclamation point, and then removing the interjection in their final version.

For Reteach and Practice, see **Conventions and Style: Sentence Variety (RP).**

# TEACHING

## Writing to Sources

Remind students to keep in mind Sylvia's internal conflict as they analyze the story. Will Sylvia accept the young stranger's bribe or will she stay true to her love of nature? This conflict drives the events, dialogue, and descriptions of the story. It is at the heart of the story's suspense and readers' uncertainty about what Sylvia will decide. Students might consider these questions before they start writing: *Why is Sylvia's conflict so powerful for her? How do her changing feelings about the young stranger figure into this conflict? In what way does the conflict propel the story's suspense—and readers' uncertainty about what Sylvia will do in the end?* For more support, see **Writing to Sources: Critical Analysis.**

### Reflect on Your Writing

1. Responses will vary. If students need support, suggest that they first focus on one aspect of the question (plot, dialogue, or description).
2. Responses will vary. Suggest students use their answers to the first question to help them formulate their advice.
3. Responses will vary. Have students include specific words they used to convey aspects of the story.

### FORMATIVE ASSESSMENT

### Writing to Sources

**If** students struggle with the complexity of writing a critical analysis, **then** have them work through one bulleted element at a time. They could then work through plot, before continuing with dialogue or description. For Reteach and Practice, see **Writing to Sources: Critical Analysis (RP).**

EFFECTIVE EXPRESSION

A WHITE HERON

## Writing to Sources

In a critical analysis, you carefully examine the parts of a literary text. You identify the author's key techniques, and then evaluate their interaction and effectiveness. Your analysis should clarify important elements in the work and always be supported with textual evidence.

**Assignment**

Write a **critical analysis** of "A White Heron." Analyze the ways in which Jewett structures events and uses dialogue and description to keep readers uncertain about Sylvia's intentions until the end of the story. Include these elements in your writing:

- a clear discussion of Sylvia's character at the beginning and end of the story
- a commentary on the role that dialogue plays in the story
- an analysis of the effects of description and imagery
- an evaluation of the story's overall structure

**Vocabulary Connection** Consider including several of the concept vocabulary words in your critical analysis.

| dilatory | hospitality | hermitage |
|---|---|---|
| loitered | squalor | quaint |

### Reflect on Your Writing

After you have drafted your critical analysis, answer the following questions.

1. How do you think that analyzing the related elements of plot, dialogue, and description improves your understanding and appreciation of the story?
2. What advice would you give another student writing a critical analysis?
3. **Why These Words?** The words you choose make a difference in your writing. Which words helped you to convey important elements of Jewett's story?

STANDARDS

**Reading Literature**
Analyze how an author's choices concerning how to structure specific parts of a text contribute to its overall structure and meaning as well as its aesthetic impact.

**Speaking and Listening**
Propel conversations by posing and responding to questions that probe reasoning and evidence; ensure a hearing for a full range of positions on a topic or issue; clarify, verify, or challenge ideas and conclusions; and promote divergent and creative perspectives.





PERSONALIZE FOR LEARNING

**English Language Support**

**Background Knowledge** Review definitions of the elements covered in the assignment: plot, dialogue, and descriptive imagery. Work with students to find examples of dialogue and descriptive imagery in the text. Then have partners work together to write a plot summary. **EMERGING/EXPANDING**

## Speaking and Listening

**Assignment**

Form two teams and hold a **debate** about the question that Jewett poses in the final paragraph of "A White Heron":

*Were the birds better friends than their hunter might have been,—who can tell?*

Each team should adopt a clear point of view and formulate a claim to answer the question.

1. **Establish the Rules** Decide who will speak for each team. Assign roles to other team members—for example, note-taker, textual evidence finder, and argument evaluator. Discuss issues such as time limits and an alternating order of speakers, and then come to an agreement. Decide whether you will include time for rebuttals to refute the opposing side's arguments. Finally, determine who will judge the debate: your teacher or a student panel.
2. **Explore and Evaluate Claims** As you develop and assess a claim for your side of the issue, keep these factors in mind:
   - the characters' personalities
   - what Sylvia and the stranger know and don't know about each other
   - the characters' values, as revealed in the story
   - the characters' relationships to each other, as portrayed in the story

   Encourage everyone on your team to express opinions about these factors.
3. **Evaluate the Debate** As the other team presents their argument, listen attentively. Use an evaluation guide like the one shown to analyze their claims and evidence.

**EVALUATION GUIDE**

**Rank each statement on a scale of 1 (not demonstrated) to 5 (demonstrated).**

☐ Team members demonstrated that they were following orderly, practical rules.

☐ Team members explored and evaluated arguments on each side of the issue.

☐ Team members presented their arguments logically and effectively.

☐ Team members supported their arguments with relevant textual evidence from the story.



**EVIDENCE LOG**

Before moving on to a new selection, go to your Evidence Log and record what you learned from "A White Heron."



DIGITAL PERSPECTIVES

## Speaking and Listening

1. **Establish the Rules** Encourage students to vote on the issues referenced in this section of the lesson. Urge them not to get bogged down on deciding these issues.
2. **Explore and Evaluate Claims** Before students begin evaluating claims, they should discuss what the debate question means. Is it literal or figurative? In what way might the birds have been friends to Sylvia? In what way might the young hunter have been a friend? Also, to focus and strengthen their own claims, students should keep in mind arguments that the other team might use during the debate.
3. **Evaluate the Debate** Encourage students not to be too harsh in their evaluations of the other team.

For more support, see **Speaking and Listening: Whole-Class Debate.**

**Evidence Log** Support students in completing their Evidence Log. This paced activity will help prepare them for the Performance-Based Assessment at the end of the unit.

### FORMATIVE ASSESSMENT

### Speaking and Listening

- **If** students struggle to explore and evaluate claims, **then** encourage them to work methodically on one factor at a time.
- **If** have trouble working together effectively, **then** ask them to keep in mind their assigned roles.

For Reteach and Practice, see **Speaking and Listening: Whole-Class Debate (RP).**

### Selection Test

Administer the "A White Heron" Selection Test, which is available in both print and digital formats online in Assessments.

**PERSONALIZE FOR LEARNING**

### English Language Support

**Explain Ideas** Encourage students to take an active role in the debate and to offer claims. Have partners work together to practice using these frames:

The birds would be good friends to Sylvia because ________.
I think the stranger would be a good friend to Sylvia because ________. **EMERGING**

## Jump Start

Ask students to describe their favorite places and what makes those places special. You might guide them by asking "Where do you go in your free time, either in real life or in your imagination? Why?" As students share, guide a discussion about how the words we use to describe a place can make it "come alive" for others.

## Write an Explanatory Essay

Make sure students understand what they are being asked to do in the Assignment.

Students should complete the assignment using word processing software to take advantage of editing tools and features.

### Elements of an Explanatory Essay

Remind students that, in addition to the elements listed, an effective explanation is organized in a logical manner and uses examples to engage and concisely inform readers.

**MAKE IT INTERACTIVE**

Project "Planning Your Trip to Gold Country" from the Interactive Teacher's Edition and ask students to identify the elements of an explanatory essay.

## Academic Vocabulary

Ask volunteers to give examples of how they might use the vocabulary in an explanatory essay about a place. For example, *I don't wish to trivialize the importance of the meadow's glowing blooms by simply referring to them as flowers. metaphors to portray what it is like to cross a raging river may enable the reader to both imagine what it looks and feels like to be there.*

PERFORMANCE TASK: WRITING FOCUS

WRITING TO SOURCES

- *from* LIFE ON THE MISSISSIPPI
- THE NOTORIOUS JUMPING FROG OF CALAVERAS COUNTY
- A WHITE HERON

**Tool Kit**
Student Model of an Explanatory Text

# Write an Explanatory Essay

You have read an excerpt from a memoir and two short stories in which setting plays an essential role. In the memoir *Life on the Mississippi,* the location of Hannibal, Missouri, on the Mississippi River is the driving force behind all the events described, and in Twain's short story, the setting is important enough to appear in the title. "A White Heron" depends on setting for character development, plot, and conflict.

**Assignment**

Write a five-paragraph explanatory essay in which you address this question:

**How do American authors use regional details to make the events and themes of a narrative come to life for readers?**

Think about the role that specific geographic details play in the selections you have read. Use examples from each text to explain how authors use setting to create a desired impact on readers. In addition, briefly research American Regionalism, a literary movement that focused on the use of "local color" and celebrated the unique and varied landscapes of the country.

ACADEMIC VOCABULARY

As you craft your explanatory essay, consider using some of the academic vocabulary you learned in the beginning of the unit.

**analyze**
**subordinate**
**literal**
**determine**
**trivialize**

### Elements of an Explanatory Essay

An **explanatory essay** is a brief work of nonfiction in which the writer explains a topic. The explanation may focus on how to do a task, the reasons for a particular situation, or how something is put together or works in a certain way. The main purpose for explanatory texts is to instruct and inform the reader.

A well-written explanatory essay contains these elements:

- a clear thesis statement that presents the writer's main idea
- relevant facts, details, and examples that develop the topic
- accurate and relevant facts and details
- appropriate and accurate vocabulary, including definitions of unfamiliar terms
- a conclusion that supports and reaffirms the explanation

**Model Explanatory Text** For a model of a well-crafted explanatory text, see the Launch Text, "Planning Your Trip to Gold Country." Review the Launch Text for examples of the elements of an effective explanatory text. You will look more closely at these elements as you prepare to write your own explanatory essay.

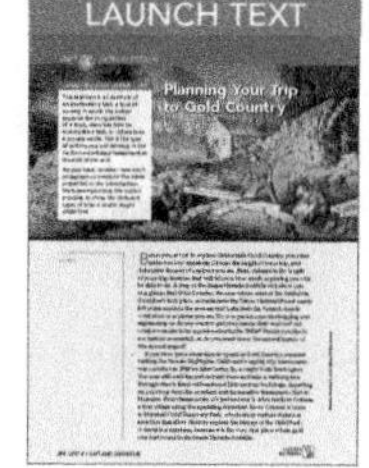


STANDARDS

Writing

- Write informative/explanatory texts to examine and convey complex ideas, concepts, and information clearly and accurately through the effective selection, organization, and analysis of content.
- Write routinely over extended time frames and shorter time frames for a range of tasks, purposes, and audiences.





AUTHOR'S PERSPECTIVE **Kelly Gallagher, M.Ed.**

**Purposeful Editing** Many students resist editing because they don't see its value. Explain that **editing,** the process of making things correct, adds power to writing. Teachers can model the process by using the Sentence of the Week (SoW) strategy. Before students enter the classroom each Monday, write three sentences with the same structural, grammatical, or style feature on the board. For example:

1. John, 14, is too young to drive.
2. My girlfriend, who is afraid of snakes, refuses to go to the zoo.
3. The player, exhausted from the long game, collapsed.

Students should copy the sentences. Below the sentences, write "What do I notice?" Students might write:

- All the sentences have interruptions.
- All have two commas.
- A comma goes before and after the interruption.
- If you take out the interruption, the sentences still make sense.

Teaching editing skills through sentence study helps students to generate the grammar rules organically.

## Prewriting / Planning

**Formulate a Thesis Statement** Go back and reread or skim the selections in Whole-Group Learning to answer questions 1 and 2. Then, use your answers to develop a thesis statement.

1. Which of the three regional settings sticks in your mind the most? Why? How does that setting help to develop the plot and theme(s) of the memoir or story?

2. What techniques do the authors use to depict the regions in which their narratives take place?

3. Write a thesis statement to respond to the prompt. You will defend this thesis using examples from the texts and research about American literary history.

**Notebook** **Gather Evidence** Your evidence for this essay should come from Twain's and Jewett's narratives. Return to the texts to find specific examples in which the regional setting helps make the events and themes of the narrative seem realistic. Consider literary elements that the authors employ, such as imagery, diction, and tone.

| TITLE | EXAMPLES |
|---|---|
| *from* Life on the Mississippi | |
| The Notorious Jumping Frog of Calaveras County | |
| A White Heron | |

**Evaluate Evidence** Use the following strategies to evaluate the evidence you collect:

- Mark details that provide the strongest support for your thesis so you will be sure to include them in your essay.
- Look for connections between ideas and techniques in order to build a unified explanation. For example, you might consider how imagery and figurative language work together to bring a setting to life.
- Identify details that might contradict your thesis. You can include them as counterexamples and explain why they do not invalidate your thesis.

EVIDENCE LOG

Review your Evidence Log and identify key details you may want to use in your essay.

STANDARDS

**Writing**

Introduce a topic; organize complex ideas, concepts, and information so that each new element builds on that which precedes it to create a unified whole; include formatting, graphics, and multimedia when useful to aiding comprehension.





DIGITAL PERSPECTIVES

## Prewriting/Planning

**Formulate a Thesis Statement** Remind students not to confuse the **topic** and the **thesis statement**: the topic is the subject matter; the thesis statement explains the topic. In this case, the topic is authors' choices about setting. Students should write a thesis statement that briefly summarizes their analysis of passages from the texts in this module. Stress that the thesis of an explanatory essay must never present an opinion or state an argument. It should be an informative statement that will be elaborated upon in the body of the essay.

**Gather Evidence** Allow ample time for students to return to the texts to look for examples. Encourage students to find at least three examples from each selection. Discuss why particular examples evoked visualization of the place. Did any arouse strong emotions, either positive or negative?

**Evaluate Evidence** Remind students to ensure that the evidence they have found supports their thesis and that they are able to refute any evidence that might undermine their thesis.

PERSONALIZE FOR LEARNING

### Strategic Support

**Imagery** Remind students that authors want readers to create pictures in their minds as they read. To do this, authors describe places and events with words that appeal to the five senses. Read the following two sentences to students:

- *People sit in the sun on the beach.*
- *Throngs of people stretch out like scattered litter on the beaches, soaking up the sun even as massive waves edge closer, crashing onto the hot, grainy sand.*

Ask: *Which sentence helps you better imagine the scene? Which makes you want to keep reading?* Point out that using a graphic organizer, such as a chart with columns for the five senses and sensory words listed for each sense, may be a good resource for creating sensory details. Suggest that students use words from the chart as they plan their essay anecdotes.

# TEACHING

**Gathering and Using Research** Have students brainstorm how using research to find additional resources can help them support thesis statements. Ask students to think of sources that can help provide definitions and explanations. Work with students to list literary, geologic, and geographic terms that might need definition, such as *verisimilitude, moraine,* and *archipelago.* Ask students to identify trustworthy print and online sources for supporting facts and details. Point out that state and city government sites may offer information about the history and significance of a place or region.

**Finding Information in Print and Digital Sources** Make sure that students are clear about the distinction between primary and secondary sources.

**Conducting Digital Searches** Remind students that not all websites are equally reliable and that they must be careful when they are performing internet searches.

**Using Research Effectively** Suggest that as students collect research, they organize it into categories. Evidence might be initially sorted as "definitely useful," "probably useful," and "not sure whether it's useful." Then, they can easily go back through the collection to find the evidence that best supports their thesis.

## PERFORMANCE TASK: WRITING FOCUS

### ENRICHING WRITING WITH RESEARCH

**Gathering and Using Research** Your goal in this essay is to inform your readers, but you are not expected to know everything about your subject. Thoughtful research can help you clarify or expand upon your ideas about the importance of setting in American literature.

**Finding Information in Print and Digital Sources** Look for information in sources that are reliable, using multiple resources to verify any details that are not common knowledge. Plan to consult the following resources:

- **Primary and Secondary Sources:** Primary sources—including news accounts, autobiographies, documentary footage, and journals—are texts created during the time period you are studying. In this case, you will use Twain's and Jewett's stories themselves as primary sources about regional writing. Secondary sources, such as textbooks or literary reviews, can help inform you about others' ideas. Be sure to credit ideas that are not your own.
- **Print and Digital Resources:** The Internet allows fast access to data, but print resources are often edited more carefully. Whenever possible, confirm information you find in one source by checking a second course.
- **Media Resources:** Documentaries, television programs, podcasts, and museum exhibitions are rich sources of information.

**Conducting Digital Searches** Careful strategies can help you locate reliable information on the Internet. In many search engines, using quotation marks can help you focus a search. Place a phrase in quotation marks to find pages that include exactly that phrase. To limit your search to .edu, .org, or .gov sites, which are generally more reliable than .com sites, use the search command "site:" followed by the extension. For example, enter "site:.edu" and "Lewis and Clark" and you will get a list of .edu (education) sites that include that exact phrase.

**Using Research Effectively** Thoughtful use of research can help you explain a subject to your readers. As you collect evidence, think about how each detail you find can support your thesis.

- **Precise Definitions:** Your readers may not recognize certain literary terms that you want to use. Researched information can help you define terms accurately.
- **Background and Context:** Your readers may need additional background information in order to understand elements of your analysis.
- **Additional Details:** You may need to go outside the texts or topic you are analyzing to add details that inform or engage your reader. Consider concepts in your writing that you might expand with interesting, relevant information you obtain from research.

**STANDARDS**

**Writing**

- Develop the topic thoroughly by selecting the most significant and relevant facts, extended definitions, concrete details, quotations, or other information and examples appropriate to the audience's knowledge of the topic.
- Gather relevant information from multiple authoritative print and digital sources, using advanced searches effectively; assess the strengths and limitations of each source in terms of the task, purpose, and audience; integrate information into the text selectively to maintain the flow of ideas, avoiding plagiarism and overreliance on any one source and following a standard format for citation.





## PERSONALIZE FOR LEARNING

### English Language Support

**Passive Voice** Remind students that in addition to verb types and tenses, sentences may be structured in the active voice, "The quarterback caught the ball," or the passive voice, "The ball was caught by the quarterback." Point out the passive voice in the last line of the Launch Text Excerpt (the place where gold was found), and clarify that passive voice focuses on the object of an action, rather than the person doing that action. Help students turn the following **passive-voice** sentences into active voice: "This cake was baked by Carlo." *(Carlo baked this cake.)* "The votes have been counted." *(They have counted the votes.)* "Our missing dog was found by my brother!" *(My brother found our missing dog!)* **EMERGING/EXPANDING/BRIDGING**

College and Career Readiness

### Read It

1. This excerpt shows how the Launch Text uses research to define a term.

LAUNCH TEXT EXCERPT

A map of the Sierra Nevada foothills will show you at a glance that Gold Country, the area where most of the California Gold Rush took place, extends from the Tahoe National Forest to the area named Lake Isabella, nearly 400 miles south.

The writer uses a resource to provide a detailed and thorough definition for the highlighted term.

2. Note two examples of information the Launch Text writer found through research. Explain how each detail provides necessary information.
3. Identify types of research sources the writer might have consulted.

### Write It

Review your thesis statement and the examples you found in each text. Then, consider your audience and what they already know about your topic. Will you need to define any literary terms? What specific information does the prompt ask you to include to provide context for your explanation? How can interesting details from research strengthen your writing?

Use the chart below to organize and complete your research.

| | WHERE COULD I FIND THIS INFORMATION? | INFORMATION FROM MY RESEARCH |
|---|---|---|
| **Terms to Define** (literary terms, unfamiliar terms from textual evidence or research) | | |
| **Background and Context** (information readers need to understand the analysis or ideas) | | |
| **Additional Details** (about settings, authors, history, and so on) | | |

TIP

CONVENTIONS
If you include a definition or explanation that is a restrictive appositive, set it off with a comma, as in these examples:

- He writes about the Mississippi, North America's largest drainage system.
- Huckleberries, dark blue berries that grow on low shrubs, are key to this passage.





DIGITAL PERSPECTIVES

### Read It

Discuss with students how adding details from the Launch Text explains what the Gold Country is and what it entails.

2. **Responses will vary** but should demonstrate that the intention of this text is to explain how to explore the Gold Country, the historical details add richness and give the reader a better sense of the place, or the setting, of this text.
3. **Responses will vary** but should include various sources, such as an almanac, history book, encyclopedia, or California state website that would contain such information.

### Write It

**Responses will vary** but should be based on reliable research.

If some students are struggling with completing the chart, suggest that they approach it as a reporter or detective, asking the 5 Ws and an H: *who, what, where, when, why,* and *how*. You may wish to allow students of diverse abilities to work together in pairs to facilitate the process. Remind students that if they are interested in definitions of certain terms or specific details about a place, their audience will likely be interested as well. Stress that research should aim to simplify information for the reader while revealing unknown or interesting facts that are relevant. Adding irrelevant information to an explanation can confuse a reader.

## PERSONALIZE FOR LEARNING

### English Language Support

**Adjectives to Describe** Remind students that we use adjectives–words that modify nouns–to describe locations. Adjectives can expand noun phrases with more information. Adjectives are often sensory words used to build images. In English, adjectives generally come before the noun (e.g. sandy beach, gigantic trees). Students whose native language is Hmong, Spanish, Vietnamese, Haitian Creole, or Vietnamese may place adjectives after the modified nouns. Provide support to help students place adjectives appropriately if added to their charts. If done incorrectly, read the phrase correctly and have the student repeat and rewrite it. **ALL LEVELS**

# TEACHING

**Organize Your Essay** Help students choose how to outline their material by giving them models of varying complexity. Provide an example of a formal outline using Roman numerals. Present an example of an informal outline using a simplified format. Show students how to use a simplified format, such as bullet points, to plan the parts of their essays. Demonstrate using a graphic organizer, such as a series of five boxes, to organize paragraph topic sentences in a logical order. Give students the option of making a storyboard, combining images or sketches with words and phrases to make a plan for writing.

## Drafting

**Write a First Draft** Encourage students to draft by writing all their ideas in the organization they have chosen. They will be able to return to revise later.

**Incorporate Anecdote** If students choose an anecdote to support their explanation, remind them that the story should relate closely to the ideas they are expressing.

PERFORMANCE TASK: WRITING FOCUS

**Organize Your Essay** Here is a basic five-paragraph outline commonly used for explanatory essays. Note than an introduction can be more than a single paragraph, as can a conclusion. This outline provides the most basic scaffolding for your ideas. Adapt it to suit your purposes.

| **Introduction** (1 paragraph)<br>Present and explain your thesis statement. |
|---|
| **Body** (3 paragraphs)<br>Support your thesis with facts, definitions, details, and examples. Each paragraph should have a specific topic, such as an author, a text, or a literary strategy. |
| **Conclusion** (1 paragraph)<br>Summarize and reaffirm your explanation. |

Review your evidence before you begin to draft. If, after gathering evidence, your original thesis no longer works well, revise it to better fit the details and examples you will use. Plan the order in which you will write about the way American authors use regional details. Decide where you will include information about American literary regionalism you found during research.

## Drafting

**Write a First Draft** Follow your outline to write your first draft. Start with your introduction and add examples from the three texts in a logical order. Well-developed body paragraphs put details and examples in context by using transitions and explaining how each example supports the thesis statement. Remember to add definitions and details from research that can help your readers understand your explanation. Include information about American literary regionalism, or local color, to provide context for your explanation. Finish with a conclusion that reaffirms your thesis.

**Incorporate Anecdote** You might choose to include a personal anecdote that strongly supports your explanation. Look closely at paragraph 4 of the Launch Text, "Planning Your Trip to Gold Country." It seamlessly combines an anecdote about the author's experience with facts and details related to planning a trip.

> *Jamestown boasts a number of businesses that allow you to take pans, trowels, and boots into the American River and test your ability to find gold. Sam and I found nothing but iron pyrite, the "fool's gold" that deceived many a Forty-Niner, but we had a thrilling time in the chilly water under a stark, blue sky. Searching Jamestown sites on the Internet will turn up a variety of tours and gold-prospecting adventures, and you can choose the one that best matches your needs.*

STANDARDS

Writing

- Introduce a topic; organize complex ideas, concepts, and information so that each new element builds on that which precedes it to create a unified whole; include formatting, graphics, and multimedia when useful to aiding comprehension.
- Provide a concluding statement or section that follows from and supports the information or explanation presented.





AUTHOR'S PERSPECTIVE **Jim Cummins, Ph.D.**

**Transfer of First Language** English learners' home languages are valuable cognitive tools that can be tapped to help them improve the quality of their first drafts. Having students write in their home language often produces higher quality writing than when students write only in English because it helps them capture, express, and organize their ideas. Translation software can be useful as a starting point to help students move from their home language draft to an English draft. Obviously, the machine-translated draft will require editing but this can be done collaboratively with help from the teacher and/or the students' classmates. After students have produced their initial drafts in English, teachers can work with them on the revision process, focusing on such key areas as organization, paragraph formation, and coherence. As students revise with teacher input, teachers should encourage them to pay special attention to cognates and genre rules.

LANGUAGE DEVELOPMENT: STYLE

## Add Variety: Vary Syntax

**Syntax** is the way in which words and phrases are arranged in sentences. Effective writers vary syntax to keep their writing lively.

### Read It

These examples from the Launch Text show some of the ways in which writers vary syntax.

| VARY SENTENCE LENGTHS | |
|---|---|
| short | *We drove from Coloma south to Jamestown along historic Highway 49.* |
| long | *As we wound through hills and valleys dotted with wildflower meadows and piñon pines, we could imagine would-be miners on horses and in wagons making their way through the same landscape 165 years ago.* |
| VARY SENTENCE TYPES | |
| declarative | *California's capital city, Sacramento, was founded in 1848 by John Sutter, Jr., a major Gold Rush figure.* |
| interrogative | *Would you like to see history re-enacted, or do you want to see the natural beauty of this special region?* |
| imperative | *Start with a map and a schedule, and plan to spend at least a day at each major stop.* |
| VARY SENTENCE STRUCTURE | |
| Begin with an adverbial phrase | ***Since that time,** Yosemite's soaring cliffs and turbulent waterfalls remain unique among American landscapes.* |
| Begin with a participial phrase | ***Stunned by the beautiful views,** we enjoyed every mile.* |
| Begin with a subordinate clause | ***If you have just a short time to spend in Gold Country,** consider visiting the historic highlights.* |

### Write It

As you write, consider using a reference resource for ideas on how to vary your sentences. Here are a few titles that you might find useful:

- *Spellbinding Sentences* by Barbara Baig
- *It Was the Best of Sentences, It Was the Worst of Sentences* by June Casagrande
- *How to Write a Sentence: and How to Read One* by Stanley Fish
- *Artful Sentences: Syntax as Style* by Virginia Tufte

TIP

PUNCTUATION
Punctuate introductory phrases and clauses correctly.

- Use a comma after a subordinate clause that begins a sentence.
- Use a comma after an introductory participial phrase.
- Use a comma after a series of introductory prepositional phrases.

STANDARDS

Writing
Use appropriate and varied transitions and syntax to link the major sections of the text, create cohesion, and clarify the relationships among complex ideas and concepts.

Language
Vary syntax for effect, consulting references for guidance as needed; apply an understanding of syntax to the study of complex texts when reading.





DIGITAL PERSPECTIVES

## Add Variety: Vary Syntax

Remind students that when we talk, we vary the length and structure of our sentences. By varying the arrangement of words, we capture the attention of our listeners. The same principle applies to writing. Readers are more apt to be engaged by sentences that vary in length and style than text that uses the same sentence type and structure over and over again. The use of variety also makes it easier for readers to understand our message and feelings we want to emphasize.

### Read It

Emphasize the importance of varying syntax to make sentences both interesting and more meaningful.

**MAKE IT INTERACTIVE**

Project "Planning Your Trip to Gold Country" from the Interactive Teacher's Edition and ask several volunteers to read aloud paragraphs 3–6 so students can listen to the rhythm created by the author's variable syntax.

Point out the importance of syntax variety by breaking down and reading aloud the first sentence in paragraph 4: "Jamestown has a number of businesses. They allow you to take pans, trowels, and boots into the American River. You can test your ability to find gold."

### Write It

As students write, they should try to use a variety of sentences. Consider reviewing additional examples of varying syntax. For example, read the following three sentences and invite volunteers to recast each one as a different length or sentence type, or begin each one with a phrase or clause. (The second two may also be made longer or shorter.)

- Five minutes from my house is the shoreline. (Make it longer or shorter.)
- There are sand dunes at the shore. (Make it a different sentence type.)
- Consider taking a trip to the shore. (Begin it with a phrase or clause.)

PERSONALIZE FOR LEARNING

### English Language Support

**Figures of Speech** Remind students that figurative language can also add interest to writing. Review some common forms.

**Simile:** compares two things, using *like* or *as*; "flowers as red as an apple . . ."

**Metaphor:** compares two things, not using like or as; "flowers are soldiers, guarding the meadow . . .'

**Personification:** gives human qualities to an object; "watch the Sun dancing across the meadow . . ."

**Hyperbole:** exaggeration used to make a point; "blue flowers that grow taller than the Empire State building!"

**Euphemism:** softens the reality of what is being said; "Overlooking the land where many are laid to rest . . ." (are buried)

Encourage students to discuss figures of speech that would enhance their writing. **ALL LEVELS**

## Revising

### Evaluating Your Draft

Remind students that when we evaluate something, we make a judgment about how well it meets certain standards. As students use the checklist to evaluate their draft, suggest they use sticky notes to mark each element in their essays. They can record on the sticky notes exactly what needs to be done as they move forward. Stress that recognizing that changes may be needed is an important learning experience. The next time students come across a similar problem, they will probably identify it earlier in the writing process.

### Revising for Focus and Organization

**Focus** Suggest that students check to ensure that their evidence relates to setting.

**Organization** Have students look back at the outlines they made before writing their first draft. The outline shows the path they intended to follow. Did they remember to include everything they intended to? Is there anything they now realize should be included to get their message across? Have students use sticky notes to add new comments.

### Revising for Evidence and Elaboration

**Tone** Remind students that tone is the writer's attitude toward the topic and the audience. The tone of a literary text may be serious, sarcastic, ironic, argumentative, solemn, apologetic, or something else. An explanatory essay should maintain an appropriate tone reflecting the writer's academic approach to the topic. Point out that although a writer may include a personal anecdote or other example containing casual speech, the overall tone of the essay should remain formal.

**Definitions** Encourage students to pay attention to providing context for difficult vocabulary words.

PERFORMANCE TASK: WRITING FOCUS

## Revising

### Evaluating Your Draft

Use this checklist to evaluate the effectiveness of your first draft. Then, use your evaluation and the instruction on this page to guide your revision.

| FOCUS AND ORGANIZATION | EVIDENCE AND ELABORATION | CONVENTIONS |
|---|---|---|
| ☐ Provides an introduction that establishes the topic and thesis statement.<br>☐ Presents main points in a logical order.<br>☐ Uses words, phrases, and clauses to clarify the relationships among ideas.<br>☐ Ends with a conclusion that follows logically from the preceding information. | ☐ Develops the topic using relevant facts, definitions, details, quotations, examples, and/or other evidence.<br>☐ Includes accurate and relevant information from research to support ideas.<br>☐ Uses vocabulary and word choices that are appropriate for the purpose and audience, including precise words and technical vocabulary where appropriate.<br>☐ Establishes and maintains a formal style and objective tone. | ☐ Attends to the norms and conventions of the discipline, especially in the use of phrases and clauses to vary sentences. |

WORD NETWORK

Include interesting words from your Word Network in your explanatory essay.

### Revising for Focus and Organization

**Focus** Does your thesis answer the question in the assignment? Reread your essay and make sure that all of your evidence clearly relates to the question of how writers use setting to bring a story to life.

**Organization** Review your essay to make sure you have clearly referred to each text you are analyzing. If your draft seems choppy, consider adding transition words, phrases, and clauses to clarify the connections you are making between texts and ideas.

### Revising for Evidence and Elaboration

**Tone** Although most of your explanation will be objective and formal, your tone may vary a bit if you include evidence from your own life—a personal anecdote that supports your explanation. Reread paragraphs 3 and 4 of the Launch Text to see how to blend anecdote with facts to keep your explanation seamless and consistent.

**Definitions** Make sure that you have defined any difficult vocabulary or special terms for your reader. You can define words without being too obvious about it if you use appositive phrases, as in these examples:

> The characters' patois, <u>or regional slang</u>, adds to the reader's sense of place.
>
> Small flats, <u>flat-bottomed wooden boats</u>, rock gently along the wharf.

STANDARDS

**Writing**
Establish and maintain a formal style and objective tone while attending to the norms and conventions of the discipline in which they are writing.





HOW LANGUAGE WORKS

**Vary Syntax** As students revise their explanatory essays, remind them that adding sentence variety can give their writing interest and rhythm. Too many sentences with the same length or structure become monotonous for readers. Varying sentence styles and structure can also be used to add emphasis. A long sentence can contain more information, but a short one calls attention to an essential idea. If necessary, review the differences between simple, complex, and compound sentences. Show examples of sentence diagrams to help students understand how sentence parts relate to each other. Finally, encourage students to consult references for guidance on how to analyze and rewrite sentences with effective syntax.

PEER REVIEW

Exchange essays with a classmate. Use the checklist to evaluate your classmate's explanatory essay and provide supportive feedback.

1. Is the topic of the essay clear?

☐ yes ☐ no If no, explain what confused you.

2. Did the writer use relevant examples from the texts?

☐ yes ☐ no If no, tell what you think might work better.

3. Did the essay include relevant and interesting information from research?

☐ yes ☐ no If no, identify one place where details from research would make the essay more effective.

4. Did the text conclude in a logical way?

☐ yes ☐ no If no, suggest what you might change.

5. What is the strongest part of your classmate's essay? Why?

## Editing and Proofreading

**Edit for Conventions** Reread your draft for accuracy and consistency. Correct errors in grammar and word usage. Make sure that you have used a variety of sentence lengths, types, and structures.

**Proofread for Accuracy** Read your draft carefully, looking for errors in spelling and punctuation. Use commas correctly with appositives and with introductory phrases and clauses.

## Publishing and Presenting

Meet with a group of three other students and share your work. Discuss which examples from texts you used and why, and compare your selections to those of your classmates. What did you learn about how American writers use regional settings in their writing?

## Reflecting

Reflect on what you learned by writing your explanatory essay. Was it difficult to find examples to support your thesis? How did researching American regional literature help you understand the texts and authors more deeply? Think about what you might do differently the next time you write an explanatory essay.

STANDARDS

**Writing**

Develop and strengthen writing as needed by planning, revising, editing, rewriting, or trying a new approach, focusing on addressing what is most significant for a specific purpose and audience.





DIGITAL PERSPECTIVES

## Peer Review

Remind students before they begin their peer review that they can learn from peer criticism. Explain that they should be brief as they do the reviewing, and keep comments positive. Add that although students should carefully reflect on the comments they receive, they should make a change only if they believe it will improve their writing.

## Editing and Proofreading

Remind students to look for common errors, such as incorrect noun-verb agreement, incorrect verb endings, incorrect pronoun-antecedent agreement, and misplaced commas as well as spelling mistakes. Stress that although word processing programs may catch many grammar and spelling mistakes, they are not failsafe. Students should also physically review the work.

## Publishing and Presenting

After incorporating peer feedback and the results of their own editing and proofreading passes, students should publish and present their work in class or online. Their final products may include multimedia such as photographs or illustrations of the settings discussed.

## Reflecting

Students should reflect not only on their essay and the process of writing it, but also on the comments received from their peers. Suggest that students ask themselves questions such as: *Which part of the writing process was easiest for me? Which was the hardest? What did I learn while writing this essay that can improve my writing skills?*

PERSONALIZE FOR LEARNING

### English Language Support

**Expand Vocabulary** Brainstorm with students a list of ELA-specific words that describe techniques an author uses to make events and places in a narrative come to life for readers (For example: *perspective*, *details*, *mood*, *senses*, etc.). List the words down the left side of a piece of chart paper. Ask volunteers to use each word in a sentence, then have students suggest at least one synonym and, if possible, one antonym for each word. Write those words down the right side of the chart. Keep the chart handy and urge students to use the words in their writings. **ALL LEVELS**

# OVERVIEW

## SMALL-GROUP LEARNING

### What is the relationship between literature and place?

Writers often use their immediate physical world as an inspiration for their stories. Whether they live in a cabin in the woods or a sprawling city can even determine the kind of story they write and who the characters are. During Small-Group Learning, students will read selections that are immersed in a particular locale or place. These places may evoke grit or grandeur.

### Small-Group Learning Strategies

Review the Learning Strategies with students and explain that they will develop strategies to work in small-group environments.

- Have students watch the video on Small-Group Learning Strategies.
- A video on this topic is available online in the Professional Development Center.

You may wish to discuss some action items to add to the chart as a class before students complete it on their own. For example, for "Support others" you might solicit the following from students:

- Students can encourage others in their group to elaborate on an idea.
- Students can invite others who have not yet spoken to join the discussion.

### Block Scheduling

Each day in this Pacing Plan represents a 40–50 minute class period. Teachers using block scheduling may combine days to reflect their class schedule. In addition, teachers may revise pacing to differentiate and support core instruction by integrating components and resources as students require.

OVERVIEW: SMALL-GROUP LEARNING

ESSENTIAL QUESTION:

## What is the relationship between literature and place?

As you read these selections, work with a small group to explore the meaning and importance of the concept of "place."

**From Text to Topic** From 1880 to 1920, the United States experienced drastic changes. The frontier was continually settled until it was no longer considered a frontier. At the same time, cities boomed as their businesses attracted both new generations of Americans and immigrants who hoped for a better life in the United States. As you read the selections in this section, consider how the authors bring to life urban settings as well as rural ones, and how they continue to reveal the influence of place.

## Small-Group Learning Strategies

Throughout your life, in school, in your community, and in your career, you will continue to develop strategies when you work in teams. Use these strategies during Small-Group Learning. Add ideas of your own for each step.

| STRATEGY | ACTION PLAN |
|---|---|
| Prepare | • Complete your assignments so that you are prepared for group work.<br>• Take notes on your reading so you can contribute to your group's discussions.<br>• |
| Participate fully | • Make eye contact to signal that you are listening and taking in what is being said.<br>• Use text evidence when making a point.<br>• |
| Support others | • Build off ideas from others in your group.<br>• State the relationship of your points to the points of others—whether you are supporting someone's point, refuting it, or taking the conversation in a new direction.<br>• |
| Clarify | • Paraphrase the ideas of others to ensure that your understanding is correct.<br>• Ask follow-up questions.<br>• |



SCAN FOR MULTIMEDIA



### Pacing Plan

Introduce Whole-Class Learning

Performance Task

| Unit Introduction | | Historical Perspectives | *from* Life on the Mississippi | | | The Notorious Jumping Frog of Calaveras County | | | A White Heron | | | | Performance Task | |
|---|---|---|---|---|---|---|---|---|---|---|---|---|---|---|
| 1 | 2 | 3 | 4 | 5 | 6 | 7 | 8 | 9 | 10 | 11 | 12 | 13 | 14 | 15 |

DIGITAL PERSPECTIVES

CONTENTS







## Contents

**Selections** Circulate among groups as they preview the selections. You might encourage groups to discuss any knowledge they already have about any of the selections or the situations and settings shown in the photographs. Students may wish to start a list of significant places students have been.

Remind students that communicating and collaborating in groups is an important skill that they will use throughout their lives—in school, in their careers, and in their community.

## Performance Task

**Give an Explanatory Talk** Give groups time to read about and briefly discuss the sense of place created by the authors in this section and the explanatory talk they will create after reading. Encourage students to do some preliminary thinking about the types of media they may want to use. This may help focus their subsequent reading and group discussion.

Introduce Small-Group Learning

A Literature of Place

Media: American Regional Art

*from* Dust Tracks on a Road

Poetry Collection 1

Media: Sandburg's Chicago

Poetry Collection 2

Introduction *from* The Way to Rainy Mountain

Performance Task

Introduce Independent Learning

Independent Learning

Performance-Based Assessment

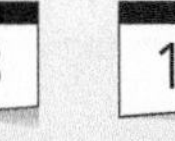

16 17 18 19 20 21 22 23 24 25 26 27 28 29 30

SMALL-GROUP LEARNING

# OVERVIEW

## SMALL-GROUP LEARNING

### Working as a Team

1. **Take a Position** Remind groups to let all members share their responses. You may wish to set a time limit for this discussion.
2. **List Your Rules** You may want to have groups share their lists of rules and consolidate them into a master list to be displayed and followed by all groups.
3. **Apply the Rules** As you circulate among the groups, ensure that students are staying on task. Consider a short time limit for this step.
4. **Name Your Group** This task can be creative and fun. If students have trouble coming up with a name, suggest that they think of something related to the unit topic. Encourage groups to share their names with the class.
5. **Create a Communication Plan** Encourage groups to include in their plans agreed-upon times during the day to share ideas. They should also devise a method for recording and saving their communications.

### Accountable Talk

Remind students that groups should communicate politely. You can post these Accountable Talk suggestions and encourage students to add their own. Students should:

**Remember to . . .**
Ask clarifying questions.

**Which sounds like . . .**
Can you please repeat what you said?

Would you give me an example?

I think you said _____. Did I understand you correctly?

**Remember to . . .**
Explain your thinking.

**Which sounds like . . .**
I believe _____ is true because _____.

**Remember to . . .**
Build on the ideas of others.

**Which sounds like . . .**
When _____ said _____, it made me think of _____.

## OVERVIEW: SMALL-GROUP LEARNING

### Working as a Team

1. **Take a Position** In your group, discuss the following question:

   **Which do you think is a better way to record a person's sense of place: a writing journal or a camera/video recorder? Explain.**

   As you take turns sharing your perceptions, be sure to provide reasons that support them. After all group members have shared, discuss connections among the ideas that were presented.

2. **List Your Rules** As a group, decide on the rules that you will follow as you work together. Two samples are provided. Add two more of your own. As you work together, you may add or revise rules based on your experience together.
   - Give everyone a chance to express and defend a position.
   - Allow group members to change their position if they feel that the evidence warrants it.
   - ______________________________
   - ______________________________

3. **Apply the Rules** Practice working as a group. Share what you have learned about place in American literature. Make sure each person in the group contributes. Take notes on and be prepared to share with the class one thing that you heard from another member of your group.

4. **Name Your Group** Choose a name that reflects the unit topic.

   Our group's name: ______________________________

5. **Create a Communication Plan** Decide how you want to communicate with one another. For example, you might meet as a group after school, hold a video conference, text, or use email.

   Our group's decision: ______________________________





### FACILITATING SMALL-GROUP LEARNING

**Forming Groups** You may wish to form groups for Small-Group Learning so that each consists of students with different learning abilities. Some students may be adept at organizing information whereas others may have strengths related to generating or synthesizing information. A good mix of abilities can make the experience of Small-Group Learning dynamic and productive.

## Making a Schedule

First, find out the due dates for the Small-Group activities. Then, preview the texts and activities with your group, and make a schedule for completing the activities.

| SELECTION | ACTIVITIES | DUE DATE |
|---|---|---|
| A Literature of Place | | |
| American Regional Art | | |
| *from* Dust Tracks on a Road | | |
| Chicago<br>Wilderness | | |
| Sandburg's Chicago | | |
| In the Longhouse, Oneida Museum<br>Cloudy Day | | |
| Introduction *from* The Way to Rainy Mountain | | |

## Working on Group Projects

As your group works together, you'll find it more effective if each person has a specific role. Different projects require different roles. Before beginning a project, discuss the necessary roles, and choose one for each group member. Some possible roles are listed here. Add your ideas to the list.

**Project Manager:** monitors the schedule and keeps everyone on task
**Researcher:** organizes research activities
**Recorder:** takes notes during group meetings

________________________________________

________________________________________

________________________________________

SCAN FOR MULTIMEDIA



DIGITAL PERSPECTIVES

## Making a Schedule

Encourage groups to preview the reading selections and to consider how long it will take them to complete the activities accompanying each selection. Point out that they can adjust the due dates for particular selections as needed as they work on their small-group projects. However, they must complete all assigned tasks before the group Performance Task is due. Encourage groups to review their schedules upon completing the activities for each selection to make sure they are on track to meet the final due date.

## Working on Group Projects

Point out to groups that the roles they assign can also be changed later. Students might have to make changes based on who is best at doing what. Try to make sure that there is no favoritism, cliquishness, or stereotyping by gender or other means in the assignment of roles.

Also, you should review the roles each group assigns to its members. Based on your understanding of students' individual strengths, you might find it necessary to suggest some changes.

AUTHOR'S PERSPECTIVE **Ernest Morrell, Ph.D.**

**Small Group Learning in Higher Education** College classrooms are becoming shared discussion spaces, marked by less lecturing and more small groups. That's because college professors increasingly realize that having students work in small groups helps develop higher-level learning and problem-solving skills, increases the success of computer-based instruction, and increases retention rates. As a result, more and more college professors now have small groups lead a portion of class by sharing/presenting what the group has learned. These professors focus on the importance of each group becoming expert at something that they must teach the class. Teachers can point out to students that the project-based small group learning in colleges is increasingly common in the workplace as well, as collective production is becoming a new norm. Teachers can encourage students to collaborate and develop rubrics to assess how well students are able to work together.

# A Literature of Place

**AUDIO SUMMARIES**
Audio summaries of "A Literature of Place" are available in both English and Spanish in the Interactive Teacher's Edition or Unit Resources. Assigning these summaries prior to reading the selection may help students build additional background knowledge and set a context for their first read.

## Summary

In the essay "A Literature of Place," Barry Lopez argues that nature writing is not new to American literature but rather one of the oldest threads in the nation's literary history. He notes that from Herman Melville and Henry David Thoreau to Willa Cather, John Steinbeck, and William Faulkner, many great American writers were, to some extent, nature writers. According to Lopez, what is unique to American nature writing is its hopefulness in the face of extreme problems created by technological progress. Lopez believes that writers must enjoy sensory experiences in order to gain intimacy with a place they wish to write about. The writer's job is to find a pattern that connects these sensory experiences to his or her understanding of place.

### Insight

The idea that writers must take time to reflect on the sensory experiences of the natural setting they find themselves within is one of the key ideas of Lopez's essay. This idea is also reflected in the fiction and poetry selections of this unit. In all instances, the reader can find references to specific interactions with nature that are communicated through the sensory language used by the writers.

ESSENTIAL QUESTION:
What is the relationship between literature and place?

## Connection to Essential Question

This essay, "A Literature of Place," connects to the Essential Question, "What is the relationship between literature and place?" and points out the strong connections between American writers and their appreciation for the geographic places they experienced in the lives.

SMALL-GROUP PERFORMANCE TASK
Explain the sense of place created by the authors and artists in this section.

UNIT PERFORMANCE-BASED ASSESSMENT
What makes certain places live on in our memory?

## Connection to Performance Tasks

**Small-Group Learning Performance Task** In this Performance Task, students will consider the question of whether or not all the selections in this unit are inspired by childhood experiences with a particular place. Students will note that one of Lopez's central points is that an artist's imagination is shaped by his or her youthful experiences.

**Unit Performance-Based Assessment** This selection provides an interesting insight into the idea of what makes certain places live on in our memories. Lopez seems to believe that our childhood memories create an artistic filter that we use in our adult experiences of place.

DIGITAL PERSPECTIVES

Audio

Video

Document

Annotation Highlights

EL Highlights

Online Assessment

## LESSON RESOURCES

| A Literature of Place | Making Meaning | Language Development |
|---|---|---|
| **Lesson** | **First Read**<br>**Close Read**<br>**Analyze the Text**<br>**Analyze Craft and Structure** | **Concept Vocabulary**<br>**Word Study**<br>**Conventions** |
| **Instructional Standards** | **RI.10** By the end of grade 11, read and comprehend literary nonfiction . . .<br>**RI.2** Determine two or more central ideas of a text . . .<br>**RI.3** Analyze a complex set of ideas . . .<br>**L.4** Determine or clarify the meaning of unknown and multiple-meaning words and phrases . . .<br>**L.4.a** Use context as a clue . . . | **L.4.b** Identify and correctly use patterns of word changes . . .<br>**L.2** Demonstrate command of the conventions . . .<br>**L.2.a** Observe hyphenation conventions . . . |
| **STUDENT RESOURCES** | | |
| Available online in the Interactive Student Edition or Unit Resources | Selection Audio<br>First-Read Guide: Nonfiction<br>Close-Read Guide: Nonfiction | Word Network |
| **TEACHER RESOURCES** | | |
| **Selection Resources** Available online in the Interactive Teacher's Edition or Unit Resources | Audio Summaries<br>Annotation Highlights<br>EL Highlights<br>English Language Support Lesson: Punctuation<br>A Literature of Place: Text Questions<br>Analyze Craft and Structure: Central Ideas and Voice | Concept Vocabulary and Word Study<br>Conventions and Style: Punctuation |
| **Reteach/Practice (RP)** Available online in the Interactive Teacher's Edition or Unit Resources | Analyze Craft and Structure: Central Ideas and Voice (RP) | Word Study: Latin Suffix *-al* (RP)<br>Conventions and Style: Punctuation (RP) |
| **Assessment** Available online in Assessments | Selection Test | |
| **My Resources** | A Unit 4 Answer Key is available online and in the Interactive Teacher's Edition. | |

# Reading Support

| Text Complexity Rubric: A Literature of Place | |
|---|---|
| **Quantitative Measures** | |
| **Lexile:** 1220 **Text Length:** 2,290 words | |
| **Qualitative Measures** | |
| Knowledge Demands ① ② ❸ ④ ⑤ | The selection contains many references to authors, events, and locations, some of which may be unfamiliar, though most are explained. It also addresses themes that are somewhat theoretical. |
| Structure ① ❷ ③ ④ ⑤ | Text is dense and covers a wide range of ideas, but organization of ideas is clear, explicit, and logical. |
| Language Conventionality and Clarity ① ② ❸ ④ ⑤ | Language is clear, explicit, highly descriptive, and at times abstract. Sentences are sometimes complex with multiple ideas and clauses. Vocabulary is descriptive and academic. |
| Levels of Meaning/Purpose ① ② ❸ ④ ⑤ | Concepts are expressed in a straightforward way and early in the selection, but some concepts are theoretical or abstract. |

DECIDE AND PLAN

## English Language Support

Provide English Learners with support for language and meaning as they read the selection.

**Language** For each paragraph, pull out key vocabulary and discuss words or phrases that students need to know in order to understand the meaning of the paragraph.

**Meaning** As students read, stop frequently to confirm their understanding of the meaning of each paragraph. Encourage students to summarize the main ideas by writing simple sentences. For example, for the first paragraph, they might write *There is a kind of writing called "nature writing" or "landscape writing." Many American authors have done this kind of writing.*

## Strategic Support

Provide students with strategic support to ensure that they can successfully read the text.

**Knowledge Demands** Before reading, list some of the names of authors that are referred to and find out which ones students know. Then discuss some of the concepts that students will see in the text – nature writing, and how geography affects people.

**Meaning** Work with students to go through the text paragraph by paragraph to summarize the key ideas. Ask students to write key phrases that help to identify main ideas, such as (paragraph 5) *geography as a shaping force* or (paragraph 7) *imagination is shaped by architecture.*

## Challenge

Provide students who need to be challenged with ideas for how they can go beyond a simple interpretation of the text.

**Text Analysis** Discuss with students why the author uses the term "Literature of Place." Ask them to reread paragraph 5 and to comment on why he finds the idea of geography important. Ask them to explain their interpretation of the last sentence of that paragraph—how a sense of place helps people develop morality or identity.

**Written Response** Ask students to write their ideas on how the environment they live in has influenced their lives. Ask them to include details about their feelings toward urban and rural landscapes and the effect that each of them have on their feelings, stress levels, or how they get inspired by their environment.

TEACH

## Read and Respond

Have students do their first read of the selection. Then have them complete their close read. Finally, work with them on the Making Meaning, Language Development, and Effective Expression activities.

# Standards Support Through Teaching and Learning Cycle

## IDENTIFY NEEDS

Analyze results of the Beginning-of-Year Assessment, focusing on the items relating to Unit 4. Also take into consideration student performance to this point and your observations of where particular students struggle.

## DECIDE AND PLAN

- If students have performed poorly on items matching these standards, then provide selection scaffolds before assigning them the on-level lesson provided in the Student Edition.
- If students have done well on the Beginning-of-Year Assessment, then challenge them to keep progressing and learning by giving them opportunities to practice the skills in depth.
- Use the Selection Resources listed on the Planning pages for from "A Literature of Place" to help students continually improve their ability to master the standards.

**Instructional Standards: "A Literature of Place"**

| | Catching Up | This Year | Looking Forward |
|---|---|---|---|
| **Reading** | You may wish to administer the **Analyze Craft and Structure: Central Ideas and Voice (RP)** worksheet to familiarize students with the techniques listed. | **RI.3** Analyze a complex set of ideas or sequence of events and explain how specific individuals, ideas, or events interact and develop over the course of the text. | Challenge students to break down the development of ideas of another nonfiction work they have read. |
| **Language** | Review the **Word Study: Latin Suffix *-al* (RP)** worksheet with students to better familiarize them with the suffix.<br>Review the **Conventions and Style: Punctuation (RP)** worksheet with students to better familiarize them with the four types of sentences. | **L.4.b** Identify and correctly use patterns of word changes that indicate different meanings or parts of speech.<br>**L.2.a** Observe hyphenation conventions. | Have students find other words from the selection that have Latin or Greek suffixes they recognize.<br>Take students to the next level by teaching them the difference between en and em dashes. |

## ANALYZE AND REVISE

- Analyze student work for evidence of student learning.
- Identify whether or not students have met the expectations in the standards.
- Identify implications for future instruction.

## TEACH

Implement the planned lesson, and gather evidence of student learning.

# FACILITATING

## Jump Start

FIRST READ *Do people today have the same relationship with nature as our ancestors?* Engage students in a conversation about how early humans needed to have a close relationship with nature because they lived off the land.

## A Literature of Place

How closely is nature related to the development of the human imagination? Model this and other questions to bring "A Literature of Place" to life. Selection audio and print capability for the selection are available in the Interactive Teacher's Edition.

## Concept Vocabulary

Have groups briefly discuss the three concept vocabulary words. Have they encountered any of the words before? Have groups consider the strategy of context clues and discuss its advantages and disadvantages.

## FIRST READ

Have students perform the steps of the first read independently:

NOTICE: You may want to encourage students to notice the general premise of the selection.

ANNOTATE: Remind students to mark passages that describe the author's and other people's relationship with the natural world.

CONNECT: Encourage students to ask: Does nature affect how they think or behave?

RESPOND: Students will demonstrate their understanding of the text by answering questions and writing a summary.

Point out to students that they will perform the first three steps concurrently as they are doing their first read. They will complete the Respond step after they have finished the first read. You may wish to print copies of the **First-Read Guide: Nonfiction** for students to use.

MAKING MEANING

A LITERATURE OF PLACE

## Comparing Texts

In this lesson, you will read and compare the essay "A Literature of Place" with a gallery of American regional art. First, you will complete the first-read and close-read activities for "A Literature of Place." The work you do with your group on this title will help prepare you for the comparing task.

AMERICAN REGIONAL ART

About the Author

**Barry Lopez** (b. 1945) was born in Port Chester, New York, grew up in Southern California and New York City, and attended college in the Midwest before moving to Oregon, where he has lived since 1968. Lopez's many honors include the 1986 National Book Award for his book, *Arctic Dreams*. Lopez is also the author of eight works of fiction and two collections of essays. His works appear in many leading journals, are widely translated, and have been included in dozens of anthologies.

# A Literature of Place

## Concept Vocabulary

As you perform your first read of "A Literature of Place," you will encounter these words.

| discern | temporal | spatial |
|---|---|---|

**Context Clues** If these words are unfamiliar to you, you may be able to determine their meanings by using **context clues**—words and phrases that appear in nearby text.

**Example:** This is a huge—therefore **unwieldy**—topic, and different writers approach it in vastly different ways.

**Conclusion:** When a topic is huge, it is difficult for writers to handle easily. *Unwieldy*, then, probably means something like "awkward" or "difficult to handle due to large size."

Apply your knowledge of context clues and other vocabulary strategies to determine the meanings of unfamiliar words you encounter during your first read.

## First Read NONFICTION

Apply these strategies as you conduct your first read. You will have an opportunity to complete a close read after your first read.

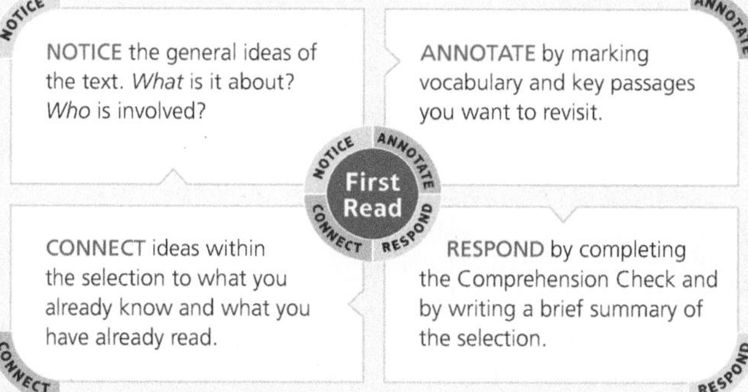
NOTICE the general ideas of the text. *What* is it about? *Who* is involved?
ANNOTATE by marking vocabulary and key passages you want to revisit.
CONNECT ideas within the selection to what you already know and what you have already read.
RESPOND by completing the Comprehension Check and by writing a brief summary of the selection.
First Read
NOTICE
ANNOTATE
CONNECT
RESPOND

STANDARDS

Reading Informational Text

By the end of grade 11, read and comprehend literary nonfiction in the grades 11–CCR text complexity band proficiently, with scaffolding as needed at the high end of the range.

Language

- Determine or clarify the meaning of unknown and multiple-meaning words and phrases based on *grades 11–12 reading and content*, choosing flexibly from a range of strategies.
- Use context as a clue to the meaning of a word or phrase.

AUTHOR'S PERSPECTIVE **Jim Cummins, Ph.D.**

**How Language Works** Briefly explaining the origins of the English language will help demystify the difference between conversational and academic language. Today's English is a hybrid language, formed from a merger of Anglo-Saxon spoken in Britain from about 400-1000 and French brought by the Norman invaders in 1066. Students can see this merger in synonyms of words derived from Anglo-Saxon and Latin/Greek sources: *meet/encounter, ask/inquire, come/arrive.* The Anglo-Saxon words were used by peasants who generally didn't have much education; in contrast, Greek/Latin vocabulary was used by more educated and high-status people and became the language of written text. Today, words with Anglo-Saxon roots are short and commonly used, while words with Greek/Latin roots tend to be low frequency and long. The most common Anglo-Saxon words in English are determiners *(the, a);* prepositions *(of, to, for, etc.);* pronouns *(he, she, I, etc.);* conjunctions *(and, but, etc.);* common verbs, nouns, and adjectives *(think, little, good, etc.).* Because these words are high frequency and are used daily, they are generally acquired quickly by English learners.

LITERARY CRITICISM

DIGITAL PERSPECTIVES 

# A Literature of Place

Barry Lopez

BACKGROUND

Nature writing, which Barry Lopez discusses in this essay, is literature written to describe the natural world and our relationship to it. This genre has a strong North American tradition. Possibly the most widely recognized American nature writer is Henry David Thoreau.

SCAN FOR MULTIMEDIA

NOTES

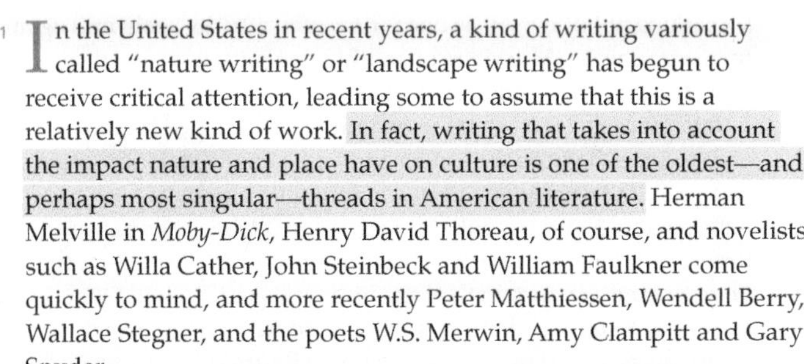

1 In the United States in recent years, a kind of writing variously called "nature writing" or "landscape writing" has begun to receive critical attention, leading some to assume that this is a relatively new kind of work. In fact, writing that takes into account the impact nature and place have on culture is one of the oldest—and perhaps most singular—threads in American literature. Herman Melville in *Moby-Dick*, Henry David Thoreau, of course, and novelists such as Willa Cather, John Steinbeck and William Faulkner come quickly to mind, and more recently Peter Matthiessen, Wendell Berry, Wallace Stegner, and the poets W.S. Merwin, Amy Clampitt and Gary Snyder.

2 If there is anything different in this area of North American writing—and I believe there is—it is the hopeful tone it frequently strikes in an era of cynical detachment, and its explicitly dubious view of technological progress, even of capitalism.

3 The real topic of nature writing, I think, is not nature but the evolving structure of communities from which nature has been removed, often as a consequence of modern economic development. (A recent conference at the Library of Congress in Washington, "Watershed: Writers, Nature and Community," focused on this kind of writing. It was the largest literary conference ever held at the Library. Sponsors, in addition to the Library, were U.S. Poet





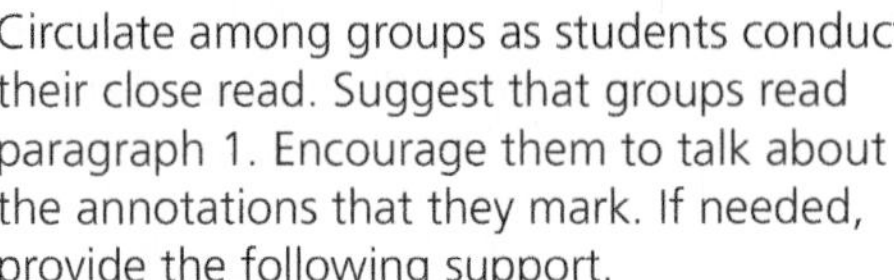

CLOSER LOOK

## Determine Key Ideas

Circulate among groups as students conduct their close read. Suggest that groups read paragraph 1. Encourage them to talk about the annotations that they mark. If needed, provide the following support.

**ANNOTATE:** Have students mark details in the paragraph that describe the author's definition of nature writing, or work with small groups to have students participate while you highlight them together.

**QUESTION:** Guide students to consider what these details might tell them. Ask what a reader can infer from the author's definition, and accept student responses.

**Possible response:** The author is saying that nature writing, which is about how culture is shaped by nature and surroundings, has been a part of American literature for a long time.

**CONCLUDE:** Help students formulate conclusions about the importance of these details in the text. Ask students why the author might have included these details.

**Possible response:** The author suggests that the beliefs, customs, and social behavior of people is shaped by nature and surroundings.

Remind students that when presenting an opinion or thesis, authors first present their **key ideas.** Encourage students to look for key ideas the author presents and the details that support them as they read through the text.

## FACILITATING SMALL-GROUP CLOSE READING

**CLOSE READ: Literary Criticism** As groups perform the close review, circulate and offer support as needed.

- Remind groups that when they read a work of nonfiction, they are concerned with analyzing, interpreting, and evaluating what the author is saying.
- If a group is confused about the author's meaning, remind them to think about the author's purpose and how the author uses key details to support his or her opinion.
- Challenge groups to determine the main ideas of the text and how those ideas might apply to their own lives.

FACILITATING

CLOSER LOOK

## Analyze Imagery

Circulate among groups as students conduct their close read. Suggest that groups read paragraphs 7 and 8. Encourage them to talk about the annotations that they mark. If needed, provide the following support.

**ANNOTATE:** Have students mark details in the paragraph that support the author's main ideas about nature writing and the details he uses to support his idea, or work with small groups to have students participate while you highlight them together.

**QUESTION:** Guide students to consider what these details might tell them. Ask them what the author means by "the architectures it encounters" and to give examples.

**Possible response:** By architectures, the author means the surrounding visual landscape. The author describes details of this landscape that shaped his imagination: *the way sunlight everywhere etches lines to accentuate forms and by streams or scent flowing faint and sharp in the larger oceans of air.*

**CONCLUDE:** Help students formulate conclusions about the importance of these details in the text. Ask students why the author might have included these details.

**Possible response:** The author believes that his imagination was formed by the visual landscape around him as he was growing up.

Remind students that **imagery,** such as the images in paragraphs 7 and 8, are words or phrases that appeal to the five senses. As students close read the paragraphs, have them describe how these images appeal to their sense of sight, sound, smell, touch, or taste.

Additional **English Language Support** is available in the Interactive Teacher's Edition.



NOTES

Laureate Robert Hass and The Orion Society of Great Barrington, Massachusetts.) It is writing concerned, further, with the biological and spiritual fate of those communities. It also assumes that the fate of humanity and nature are inseparable. Nature writing in the United States merges here, I think, with other types of post-colonial writing, particularly in Commonwealth[1] countries. In numerous essays it addresses the problem of spiritual collapse in the West, and like those literatures it is in search of a modern human identity that lies beyond nationalism and material wealth.

4 This is a huge—not to say unwieldy—topic, and different writers approach it in vastly different ways. The classic struggle of writers to separate truth and illusion, to distinguish between roads to heaven and detours to hell, knows only continuance, not ending or solution. But I sense collectively now in writing in the United States the emergence of a concern for the world outside the self. It is as if someone had opened the door to a stuffy and too-much-studied room and shown us a great horizon where once there had been only walls.

5 I want to concentrate on a single aspect of this phenomenon—geography—but in doing so I hope to hew to a larger line of truth. I want to talk about geography as a shaping force, not a subject. Another way critics describe nature writing is to call it "the literature of place." A specific and particular setting for human experience and endeavor is, indeed, central to the work of many nature writers. I would say a sense of place is also critical to the development of a sense of morality and of human identity.

6 After setting out a few thoughts about place, I'd like to say something about myself as one writer who returns again and again to geography, as the writers of another generation once returned repeatedly to Freud and psychoanalysis.[2]

7 It is my belief that a human imagination is shaped by the architectures it encounters at an early age. The visual landscape, of course, or the depth, elevation and hues of a cityscape play a part here, as does the way sunlight everywhere etches lines to accentuate forms. But the way we imagine is also affected by streams of scent flowing faint or sharp in the larger oceans of air: by what the composer John Luther Adams calls the sonic landscape; and, say, by an awareness of how temperature and humidity rise and fall in a place over a year.

8 My imagination was shaped by the exotic nature of water in a dry California valley; by the sound of wind in the crowns of eucalyptus trees, by the tactile sensation of sheened earth, turned in furrows by a gang plow; by banks of saffron, mahogany, and scarlet cloud piled above a field of alfalfa at dusk; by encountering the musk from

1. **Commonwealth** association of independent nations, mostly former parts of the British Empire, united for purposes of mutual assistance.
2. **Freud and psychoanalysis** Sigmund Freud (1856–1939), Austrian physician and neurologist, is known as the founder of psychoanalysis, a method of analyzing and attempting to treat psychological disorders.





CROSS-CURRICULAR PERSPECTIVES: Social Studies

**Commonwealth** Call students' attention to the reference to the Commonwealth in paragraph 3. The Commonwealth of Nations is a group of 53 states that were mostly part of the British Empire of the early 1900s. The Commonwealth strives to bring countries together and maintain unity through the values of democracy and human rights, as well as language, history, and culture. Countries join the Commonwealth voluntarily and must recognize England's Queen Elizabeth II as its head. Commonwealth countries include Canada, India, Australia and South Africa.

orange blossoms at the edge of an orchard; by the aftermath of a Pacific storm crashing a hot, flat beach.

9 Added to the nudge of these sensations were an awareness of the height and breadth of the sky, and of the geometry and force of the wind. Both perceptions grew directly out of my efforts to raise pigeons, and from the awe I felt before them as they maneuvered in the air. They gave me permanently a sense of the vertical component of life.

10 I became intimate with the elements of that particular universe. They fashioned me, and I return to them regularly in essays and stories in order to clarify or explain abstractions or to strike contrasts. I find the myriad relationships in that universe comforting, forming a "coherence" of which I once was a part.

11 If I were to try to explain the process of becoming a writer I could begin by saying that the comforting intimacy I knew in that California valley erected in me a kind of story I wanted to tell, a pattern I wanted to invoke—in countless ways. And I would add to this the two things that were most profoundly magical to me as a boy: animals and language. It's easy to see why animals might seem magical. Spiders and birds are bound differently than we are by gravity. Many wild creatures travel unerringly through the dark. And animals regularly respond to what we, even at our most attentive, cannot discern.

12 It's harder to say why language seemed magical, but I can be precise about this. The first book I read was *The Adventures of Tom Sawyer*. I still have the book. Underlined in it in pen are the first words I could recognize: *the, a, stop,* to *go,* to *see.* I can pick up the book today and recall my first feelings like a slow, silent detonation: words I heard people speak I was now able to perceive as marks on a page. I, myself, was learning to make these same marks on ruled paper. It seemed as glorious and mysterious as a swift flock of tumbler pigeons exploiting the invisible wind.

13 I can see my life prefigured in those two kinds of magic, the uncanny lives of creatures different from me (and, later, of cultures different from my own); and the twinned desires to go, to see. I became a writer who travels and one who focuses mostly, to be succinct, on what logical positivists sweep aside.

14 My travel is often to remote places—Antarctica, the Tanami Desert in central Australia, northern Kenya. In these places I depend on my own wits and resources, but heavily and just as often on the knowledge of interpreters—archaeologists, field scientists, anthropologists. Eminent among such helpers are indigenous[3] people, and I can quickly give you three reasons for my dependence on their insights. As a rule, indigenous people pay much closer attention to nuance in the physical world. They see more, and from a paucity of evidence, thoroughly observed, they can deduce more. Second, their

NOTES

Mark context clues or indicate another strategy you used that helped you determine meaning.

**discern** (dih SURN) *v.*

MEANING:

3. **indigenous** (ihn DIHJ uh nuhs) *adj.* native.





DIGITAL PERSPECTIVES

## Concept Vocabulary

**DISCERN** If groups are struggling to define the word *discern* in paragraph 11, point out that they can use the context clues within the sentence to determine its meaning. Draw students' attention to the words, *And animals regularly respond to what we.... cannot* and have them use context clues to define the word.

**Possible response:** *Discern* means "to perceive or recognize; to identify clearly."

DIGITAL PERSPECTIVES

**Enriching the Text** Have students choose one of the three locations mentioned in paragraph 14: Antarctica, the Tanami Desert in central Australia, or northern Kenya. Have students conduct online research about the location to write a description of life there, compared to life in the student's own community.

# FACILITATING

## Concept Vocabulary

**TEMPORAL** If groups are struggling to define the word *temporal* in paragraph 14, point out that students can use the context clues within the sentence and surrounding sentences to determine its meaning. Draw students' attention to the words *their history in a place; these histories;* and have them use context clues to define the word.

**Possible response:** *Temporal* means "having to do with time."

**SPATIAL** If groups are struggling to define the word *spatial* in paragraph 14, point out that students can use the context clues within the sentence to determine its meaning. Draw students' attention to the words *nuance in the physical world; history in a place; landscape, the landscape they sense; a storied relationship to place;* and have them use context clues to define the word.

**Possible response:** *Spatial* means "having to do with space or area."

NOTES

Mark context clues or indicate another strategy you used that helped you determine meaning.

**temporal** (TEHM puhr uhl) *adj.*

MEANING:

**spatial** (SPAY shuhl) *adj.*

MEANING:

history in a place, both tribal and personal, is typically deep. These histories create a **temporal** dimension in what is otherwise only a **spatial** landscape. Third, indigenous people tend to occupy the same moral universe as the landscape they sense.

15 Over time I have come to think of these three qualities—intimate attention; a *storied* relationship to place rather than a solely sensory awareness of it; and living in some sort of ethical unity with a place—I have come to think of these things as a fundamental human defense against loneliness. If you're intimate with a place, a place with whose history you're familiar, and you establish an ethical conversation with it, the implication that follows is this: the place knows you're there. It feels you. You will not be forgotten, cut off, abandoned.

16 As a writer I want to ask myself: How can you obtain this? How can you occupy a place and also have it occupy you? How can you find such a reciprocity?[4]

17 The key, I think, is to become vulnerable to a place. If you open yourself up you can build intimacy. Out of such intimacy will come a sense of belonging, a sense of not being isolated in the universe.

18 My question—how to secure this—is not idle. I want to be concrete about this, about how, actually, to enter a local geography. (We often daydream, I think, about entering childhood landscapes that dispel our anxiety. We court these feelings for a few moments in a park sometimes or during an afternoon in the woods.) Keeping this simple and practical, my first suggestion would be to be silent. Put aside the bird book, an analytic frame of mind, any compulsion to identify, and sit still. Concentrate instead on *feeling* a place, on using the sense of proprioception. Where in this volume of space are you situated? What is spread out behind you is as important as what you see before you. What lies beneath you is as relevant as what stands on the horizon. Actively use your ears to imagine the acoustical space you occupy. How does birdsong ramify[5] here? Through what air is it moving? Concentrate on smells in the belief that you *can* smell water and stone. Use your hands to get the heft and texture of a place—the tensile strength in a willow branch, the moisture in a pinch of soil, the different nap[6] of leaves. Open the vertical line of this place by consciously referring the color and form of the sky to what you see across the ground. Look *away* from what you want to scrutinize to gain a sense of its scale and proportion. Be wary of any obvious explanation for the existence of a color, a movement. Cultivate a sense of complexity, the sense that another landscape exists beyond the one you can subject to analysis.

19 The purpose of such attentiveness is to gain intimacy, to rid yourself of assumption. It should be like a conversation with someone you're attracted to, a person you don't want to send away by making too much of yourself. Such conversations, of course, can

4. **reciprocity** (rehs uh PROS uh tee) *n.* exchanging things with others for mutual benefit.
5. **ramify** (RAM uh fy) *v.* divide and spread.
6. **nap** *n.* soft, rough surface.





PERSONALIZE FOR LEARNING

### English Language Support

**Main Idea and Details** Have students reread paragraph 18. Then ask them to write a summary of the text, describing the author's main point and the details the author uses to support or defend his main point. Students may annotate the text, and then use their annotations to write their summaries. Remind students to write in complete sentences and use key words from their annotations. **BRIDGING**

take place simultaneously on several levels. And they may easily be driven by more than simple curiosity. The compelling desire, as in human conversation, may be for a sustaining or informing relationship.

20 A succinct way to describe the frame of mind one should bring to a landscape is to say it rests on the distinction between imposing and proposing one's views. With a sincere proposal you hope to achieve an intimate, reciprocal relationship that will feed you in some way. To impose your views from the start is to truncate such a possibility, to preclude understanding.

21 Many of us, I think, long to become the companion of a place, not its authority, not its owner. And this brings me to a closing point. Perhaps you wonder, as I do, why over the last few decades people in Western countries have become so anxious about the fate of undeveloped land, and concerned about losing the intelligence of people who've kept intimate relationships with those places. I don't know where your thinking has led you, but I believe this curiosity about good relations with a particular stretch of land is directly related to speculation that it may be more important to human survival now to be in love than to be in a position of power. It may be more important now to enter into an ethical and reciprocal relationship with everything around us than to continue to work toward the sort of control of the physical world that, until recently, we aspired to.

22 The simple issue of our biological plausibility, our chance for biological survival, has become so precarious, so basic a question, that finding a way out of the predicament—if one is to be had—is imperative. It calls on our collective imaginations with an urgency we've never known before. We are in need not just of another kind of logic, another way of knowing, but of a radically different philosophical sensibility.

23 When I was a boy, running through orange groves in southern California, watching wind swirl in a grove of blue gum, and

NOTES

 CLOSER LOOK

## Analyze Argument 

Circulate among groups as students conduct their close read. Suggest that groups read paragraph 21. Encourage them to talk about the annotations that they mark. If needed, provide the following support.

**ANNOTATE:** Have students mark details in the paragraph that support the author's main ideas about position of power and a reciprocal relationship, or work with small groups to have students participate while you highlight them together.

**QUESTION:** Guide students to consider what these details might tell them. Ask them what the author means by "the companion of a place, not its authority, not its owner."

**Possible response:** For both the land's survival and our own survival, there must be a relationship that is maintained that doesn't dominate the other but shares in a balanced relationship.

**CONCLUDE:** Help students formulate conclusions about the importance of these details in the text. Ask students why the author might have included these details.

**Possible response:** The author believes that by using the land without maintaining a balance may eventually lead to both of our extinctions.

Remind students that an **argument** must take a position or claim and support it with evidence. In this paragraph, the writer is building his argument, and presenting his final point.

PERSONALIZE FOR LEARNING

### Challenge

**Experience Nature** Review paragraph 18 and the suggestions Lopez offers. Invite students to pick a location near home or school—natural or built up—and, following Lopez's instructions, experience a place using their five senses. Encourage students to use descriptive language such as the author uses to describe his personal experiences with nature. Ask groups to share their writing by reading their work aloud.

# FACILITATING

## Comprehension Check

**Possible responses**

1. The fundamental topic of nature writing concerns our lack of connection to a sense of place and the natural world.
2. Lopez found language and animals magical.
3. Indigenous people see more and deduce more because they possess a deep personal history in a place. They also tend to occupy the same moral universe as the landscape they sense.
4. The author begins by noting the resurgence of American nature writing. The true subject of such writing, he declares, is the evolving structure of communities separated from nature. Lopez continues by discussing geography as a shaping force, and he illustrates this concept with an example from his own childhood in California. Two magical forces—animals and language—played a great part in the process of his becoming a writer. To gain intimacy and reciprocity with geography, Lopez recommends that we become vulnerable to a place. Partnership with the land, he believes, is a biological necessity for humanity.

**Research to Explore** Point out to the students that Lopez was raised in Southern California. Suggest students consult a map of California and pick out a specific area such as a national park or dry valley to research.

NOTES

swimming ecstatically in the foam of Pacific breakers, I had no such thoughts as these imperatives. I was content to watch a brace of pigeons fly across an azure sky, rotating on an axis that to this day I don't think I could draw. My comfort, my sense of inclusion in the small universe I inhabited, came from an appreciation of, a participation in, all that I saw, smelled, tasted and heard. That sense of inclusion not only assuaged my sense of loneliness as a child, it confirmed my imagination. And it is that single thing, the power of the human imagination to extrapolate from an odd handful of things—faint movement in a copse of trees, a wingbeat, the damp cold of field stones at night—to make from all this a pattern—the human ability to make a story, that fixed in me a sense of hope.

24 We keep each other alive with our stories. We need to share them as much as food. We also need good companions. One of the most extraordinary things about the land is that it knows this, and it compels language from some of us so that, as a community, we may actually speak of it. ❧

## Comprehension Check

**Complete the following items after you finish your first read. Review and clarify details with your group.**

1. According to Barry Lopez, what is the fundamental topic of nature writing?
2. What two things were magical to Lopez when he was a boy?
3. According to Lopez, why are indigenous people good guides to remote places?
4. **Notebook** Write a summary of "A Literature of Place" in order to confirm your understanding of the essay.

### RESEARCH

**Research to Explore** Conduct research to find one or two photos that show the Southern California landscapes that Barry Lopez describes. You may want to share what you discover with your group.





### PERSONALIZE FOR LEARNING

**Strategic Support**

**Five Senses** If group members struggle to describe their relationship with a specific place, have them create a chart of the five senses: sight, sound, taste, touch, and smell. For each, have students think of at least three things in their environment that would appeal to that sense. For example, sound might include birdsongs, airplanes, or train whistles. Encourage students to use the chart to create a cohesive paragraph.

## Close Read the Text

With your group, revisit sections of the text you marked during your first read. **Annotate** details that you notice. What **questions** do you have? What can you **conclude**?

A LITERATURE OF PLACE

## Analyze the Text

CITE TEXTUAL EVIDENCE support your answers.

Notebook Complete the activities.

1. **Review and Clarify** With your group, reread paragraph 5 of the essay. What is the author's main idea in this paragraph? How does the main idea of this paragraph support the central idea of the essay as a whole?
2. **Present and Discuss** Now, work with your group to share passages from the selection that you found especially important. Take turns presenting your passages. Discuss what you noticed in the text, what questions you asked, and what conclusions you reached.
3. **Essential Question:** ***What is the relationship between literature and place?*** What has this essay taught you about the way that geography influences writing? Discuss with your group.

LANGUAGE DEVELOPMENT

## Concept Vocabulary

discern temporal spatial

**Why These Words?** The three concept vocabulary words from the essay are related. With your group, determine what the words have in common. Write your ideas, and add another word that fits the category.

### Practice

Notebook Demonstrate your understanding of the concept vocabulary words by writing their meanings. Trade your definitions with a group member, and discuss any differences you notice.

## Word Study

**Latin Suffix: *-al*** The concept vocabulary words *temporal* and *spatial* both end with the Latin suffix *-al*, which forms adjectives and means "of," "like," or "related to." Write definitions of *spatial* and *temporal* in which you demonstrate your understanding of the suffix *-al*. Then, find two other adjectives that end with this suffix. Write the words and their definitions.

WORD NETWORK

Add words related to a sense of place from the text to your Word Network.

STANDARDS

Language
Identify and correctly use word patterns that indicate different meanings or parts of speech.





DIGITAL PERSPECTIVES

## Jump Start

CLOSE READ Ask students to consider the following prompt: *Would their imaginations have been very different if they had been born and raised in a very different environment than the one they live in now?* Have them consider the question from the points of view of a farmer or a city-dweller.

## Close Read the Text 

Model close reading as needed by using the Annotation Highlights in the Interactive Teacher's Edition. Remind groups to use Accountable Talk in their discussions and to support one another as they complete the close read.

## Analyze the Text

Possible responses

1. The main idea of paragraph 5 is that geography has more influence on an individual's perspective than a person's location. This concept connects to the central idea that place shapes the way people see the world.
2. Responses will vary.
3. Students may discuss that geography instills images in a writer's mind through the senses.

## Concept Vocabulary

**Why These Words? Possible response:** The words all describe perceptions of the world around us and relate to the senses, which connects geography and landscape writing.

### Practice

Students' responses will vary, but they should discuss differences with a group member.

### Word Network

**Possible words:** *landscape, evolving, geography, breadth, elevation, depth, hues, vertical, humidity, spatial, dimension*

## Word Study

For more support, see **Concept Vocabulary and Word Study.**

Possible responses:
Adjectives: regional, cynical, critical, magical
Nouns: proposal, recital, portal

### FORMATIVE ASSESSMENT

#### Analyze the Text

**If** students struggle to close read the text, **then** provide the **A Literature of Place: Text Questions** available online in the Interactive Teacher's Edition or Unit Resources. Answers and DOK levels are also available.

#### Concept Vocabulary

**If** students struggle to identify the concept, **then** have them use a thesaurus to find synonyms that will clarify word meaning.

#### Word Study

**If** students fail to identify words with *–al* suffixes, **then** suggest they work with a partner to consult a dictionary or online source. Have partners review each definition and check to see if the words are nouns or adjectives.
For Reteach and Practice, see **Word Study: Latin Suffix *-al* (RP).**

# FACILITATING

## Analyze Craft and Structure

**Central Ideas and Voice** Remind students that effective writers develop their ideas by using explicit examples rather than by imprecise generalities. The use of explicit, personal examples also strengthens the author's point of view and adds to the credibility of the essay. In order to develop a central set of ideas, an author must first state a position, or point of view. In "A Literature of Place," Lopez focuses on the importance of geography in the development of culture within society and a person's imagination.

For more support, see **Analyze Craft and Structure: Central Ideas and Voice.**

### Practice

See possible responses in chart on student page.

**Possible responses**

1. (a) In paragraphs 11–16, he mentions growing up in California, traveling, and being a writer. (b) By discussing animals and language, he makes his ideas more concrete for readers.
2. (a) Lopez's choices develop a connection because he is open about how his childhood experiences affected him. (b) If he were less personal, readers would be less able to identify with him and embrace his ideas.
3. Lopez's voice is personal, and his tone is frank and open. This openness allows readers to relate to him.

### FORMATIVE ASSESSMENT

### Analyze Craft and Structure

**If** students are unable to identify transitional expressions, **then** remind students that transitions connect ideas from one paragraph to the next. Have students skim the preceding paragraph to find a clue that will guide them in identifying transitions. For Reteach and Practice, see **Analyze Craft and Structure: Central Ideas and Voice (RP).**

MAKING MEANING

A LITERATURE OF PLACE

## Analyze Craft and Structure

**Author's Choices: Central Ideas and Voice** Students and other essay writers are often told to be objective and to avoid the use of personal statements in academic work. In "A Literature of Place," Lopez, who is a master writer and certainly knows this rule, ignores it. Instead, he injects himself directly into the essay, including many "I" statements and anecdotes from his own life. This create several effects:

- It creates an intimate **voice**, or sense of the writer's personality captured in words.
- It adds clarity to the development of Lopez's **central, or main, ideas.** Lopez is able to share his thought process in an open, obvious way, thus leading readers through his thinking.
- Even though Lopez uses elevated language, the personal quality of the essay creates a conversational **tone,** or attitude, toward the topic and reader.

### Practice

**CITE TEXTUAL EVIDENCE** to support your answers.

**Notebook** Work with your group to complete this reverse outline of Lopez's essay. Add notes about the central ideas and supporting details Lopez presents in each section. Then, answer the questions.

| SECTION | CENTRAL IDEA | SUPPORTING DETAILS |
|---|---|---|
| I. Introduction: American Landscape Writing | Landscape writing is actually an old concept. | This writing was used by Melville, Thoreau, Cather, Steinbeck, and Faulkner. |
| II. When and How People Develop a Sense of Geography | Place is critical to sense of identity. | Landscape plays a role in childhood development. |
| III. Indigenous Understanding of Place | Sense of place is shaped by where one lives. | Indigenous groups pay attention to their environment. |
| V. Proposing Views of New Landscapes Rather than Imposing Them | One should pursue a reciprocal relationship with place. | We must become vulnerable to a place. |
| IV. How to Enter a Local Geography | One should keep still, avoiding analysis. | By cultivating complexity, we gain intimacy with a place. |
| VI. Conclusion: Relationship Between Land and Community | Communing with the land can help avoid loneliness. | Place is a companion we can know rather than "own." |

1. (a) In which sections of the essay does Lopez include personal opinions and anecdotes? (b) How does his use of personal information help readers understand abstract ideas? Cite at least two specific examples.
2. (a) How do his choices develop a connection between the writer and his readers? (b) How would the essay be affected if Lopez remained objective and impersonal throughout? Explain.
3. Describe Lopez's voice and tone. Cite specific examples from the essay that support your descriptions.





PERSONALIZE FOR LEARNING

### English Language Support

**Transitional Words and Phrases** Have English Learners go back through the text and skim for examples of transitional words and phrases such as *in addition, in fact, as a rule, as well as* and *so on.* Have students explain how the words link ideas in the text.

**BRIDGING**

## LANGUAGE DEVELOPMENT

### Conventions and Style

**Punctuation** Punctuation is much more than simple mechanics. It is an important tool for helping readers gain a clear and subtle sense of a writer's meaning. Consider, for example, how Lopez uses two punctuation marks in "A Literature of Place": the **dash (—)** and the **hyphen (-)**.

- **Dashes**, either singly or in pairs, have a variety of purposes. Dashes may be used for emphasis:

  *If there is anything different in this area of North American writing—and I believe there is—it is the hopeful tone it frequently strikes. . . .* (paragraph 2)

  A dash or pair of dashes may be used to add clarification:

  *I want to concentrate on a single aspect of this phenomenon—geography—but in doing so I hope to hew to a larger line of truth.* (paragraph 5)

  Finally, dashes may set off additional information, such as examples that deepen the main idea of a sentence.

  *Use your hands to get the heft and texture of a place—the tensile strength in a willow branch. . . .* (paragraph 18)

- **Hyphens** are shorter in length than dashes. Their main function is to join words together. Hyphens are often used to form compound adjectives. Compound adjectives are made up of two or more words that present a single idea to modify a noun.

  | | |
  |---|---|
  | full-page photograph | dust-covered furniture |
  | first-aid kit | easy-to-follow directions |

  In "A Literature of Place," Lopez uses hyphens to create his own unique compound adjective.

  *It is as if someone had opened the door to a stuffy and too-much-studied room. . . .* (paragraph 4)

#### Read It

1. With your group, locate the compound adjective *too-much-studied* in paragraph 4. Discuss what this adjective means and why you think Lopez chose to create his own compound adjective instead of using a more common modifier.
2. Reread paragraph 22, and consider the author's use of dashes. With your group, discuss the effect of these dashes and what the author suggests with this aside.
3. **Connect to Style** How does Lopez's liberal use of dashes affect the tone and mood of his essay? Explain your answer.

#### Write It

**Notebook** In a paragraph, describe your own relationship to a specific place. As you discuss what this place is like and how it makes you feel, use dashes and hyphens to write precisely. Use a dash or pair of dashes to emphasize an idea, provide clarification, or give additional information. Use a hyphen or hyphens to create at least one compound adjective.

**TIP**

CLARIFICATION
Dashes are most effective when used sparingly. Too many dashes can be distracting or confusing. Dashes are best used to add a strong emphasis or when inserting a new sentence might interrupt the flow of ideas.

**EVIDENCE LOG**

Before moving on to a new selection, go to your Evidence Log and record what you've learned from "A Literature of Place."

**STANDARDS**

Language
- Demonstrate command of the conventions of standard English capitalization, punctuation, and spelling when writing.
- Observe hyphenation conventions.





## PERSONALIZE FOR LEARNING

### English Language Support

**Identifying Hyphens, En Dashes, and Em Dashes** Ask pairs of students to write three phrases using a hyphen, an en dash, and an em dash. **EMERGING**

Have students write a paragraph using a hyphen, and en dash, and an em dash. **EXPANDING**

Have students write a paragraph using a hyphen, an en dash, and an em dash, and then tell what keys they must type in their computers to insert each symbol. **BRIDGING**

An expanded **English Language Support Lesson** on Punctuation is available in the Interactive Teacher's Edition.

DIGITAL PERSPECTIVES  

### Conventions and Style

**Punctuation** Dashes and hyphens connect ideas in different ways. Provide the following model to explore the different effects of dashes:

*This is a huge—not to say unwieldy—topic, and different writers approach it in vastly different ways.* (paragraph 4) This example uses dashes to add another level of detail to the topic.

*Over time I have come to think of these three qualities—intimate attention; a storied relationship to place rather than a solely sensory awareness of it; and living in some sort of ethical unity with a place—I have come to think of these things as a fundamental human defense against loneliness.* (paragraph 15)

The hyphens here set off the three qualities at the beginning of the sentence and connect it to the ending. For more support, see **Conventions and Style: Punctuation.**

#### Read It

Possible responses

1. The adjective *too-much-studied* means "over examined." Lopez is trying to connote staleness and overuse.
2. The effect of the dashes in paragraph 22 is to create a pause in which a detail is elaborated upon.

**Connect to Style** Lopez's use of dashes expands the level of detail in his writing, even as it contributes to a conversational, relaxed tone.

#### Write It

**Notebook** Paragraphs will vary, but make sure students use at least one appropriate dash and one hyphenated modifier.

**Evidence Log** Support students in completing their Evidence Log. This paced activity will help prepare them for the Performance-Based Assessment at the end of the unit.

### FORMATIVE ASSESSMENT

#### Conventions and Style

**If** students are having difficulty adding hyphens and dashes to their paragraphs, **then** have them look for an idea in their writing they want to emphasize by adding a different phrase or describe something in more detail.

For Reteach and Practice, see **Conventions and Style: Punctuation (RP).**

#### Selection Test

Administer the "A Literature of Place" Selection Test, which is available in both print and digital formats online in Assessments.

# American Regional Art

**AUDIO SUMMARIES**
Audio summaries of "American Regional Art" are available online in both English and Spanish in the Interactive Teacher's Edition or Unit Resources. Assigning these summaries prior to reviewing the selection may help students build additional background knowledge and set a context for their first review.


## Summary

These works of art show different regions of the United States and reflect the connections between the artists and their local geography and culture. *The Lighthouse at Two Lights* by Edward Hopper shows a realistic landscape of a lighthouse set high on a bluff in Maine on a sunny day. In *Storm Lifting Over Wall Street*, Guy A. Wiggins paints an impressionistic landscape of Wall Street in New York City at the end of a snowfall. In *Among the Sierra Nevada, California*, Albert Bierstadt paints a romantic landscape of a western mountain range. *Deer's Skull with Pedernal* by Georgia O'Keeffe depicts a deer skull with a nearby New Mexico mountain in the background painted in a modernist style. In *Georgia Red Clay*, Nell Choate Jones paints a primitive-style rural scene of her native state. In *The Bronco Buster*, Frederick Remington creates a realistic sculpture of a western cowboy riding a bucking horse.


### Insight

Like writers, painters and sculptors use the places they experience as source materials in their creative processes. The art in this collection reflects the artists' personal experiences with geography and culture and is filtered through the artists' own aesthetic principles.

ESSENTIAL QUESTION:
What is the relationship between literature and place?

## Connection to the Essential Question

The collection "American Regional Art" connects to the Essential Question "What is the relationship between literature and place?" For this selection, students must evaluate the unique perspective the artist brings to his or her experience of the place or activity pictured.

SMALL-GROUP PERFORMANCE TASK
Explain the sense of place created by the authors and artists in this section.

UNIT PERFORMANCE-BASED ASSESSMENT
What makes certain places live on in our memory?

## Connection to Performance Tasks

**Small-Group Learning Performance Task** In this Performance Task, students will consider the question of whether or not all the selections in this unit are inspired by childhood experiences with a particular place. Students will note that adults created all the artwork in this collection, but some of their youthful experiences with nature likely informed the artistic viewpoints they used in creating the works.

**Unit Performance-Based Assessment** This selection provides an interesting insight into the idea of what makes certain places live on in our memory. Students should note that, although the artists may have personally experienced these place or activities, most of the works probably involve the artists' memories.

DIGITAL PERSPECTIVES

Audio

Video

Document

Annotation Highlights

EL Highlights

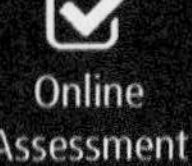
Online Assessment

## LESSON RESOURCES

| | Making Meaning | Language Development | Effective Expression |
|---|---|---|---|
| Lesson | **First Review**<br>**Close Review**<br>**Analyze the Media** | **Media Vocabulary** | **Writing to Compare** |
| Instructional Standards | **L.6** Acquire and use accurately general academic and domain-specific words and phrases . . . | **L.6** Acquire and use accurately general academic and domain-specific words and phrases . . . | **W.2** Write informative/explanatory texts . . .<br>**W.9** Draw evidence from literary or informational texts . . . |
| **STUDENT RESOURCES** | | | |
| Available online in the Interactive Student Edition or Unit Resources | Selection Audio<br>First-Review Guide: Media-Art and Photography<br>Close-Review Guide: Media Art and Photography | | Evidence Log |
| **TEACHER RESOURCES** | | | |
| **Selection Resources** Available online in the Interactive Teacher's Edition or Unit Resources | Audio Summaries<br>American Regional Art: Media Questions | Media Vocabulary | Writing to Compare: Interpretive Essay |
| **Assessment** Available online in Assessments | Selection Test | | |
| **My Resources** | A Unit 4 Answer Key is available online and in the Interactive Teacher's Edition. | | |

## Media Complexity Rubric: American Regional Art

| Quantitative Measures | |
|---|---|
| **Format and Length** 6 art images with captions | |
| **Qualitative Measures** | |
| Knowledge Demands<br>① ② ❸ ④ ⑤ | Examples of art cover a wide range of artists, years, and locations. Some of the backgrounds of the artists may be unfamiliar to students, but information is given in captions and the images are accessible. |
| Structure<br>❶ ② ③ ④ ⑤ | Captions correspond to each work of art, making it easy for students to focus on each one. |
| Language Conventionality and Clarity<br>① ❷ ③ ④ ⑤ | Captions are clear and explicit with information about content and labels for titles and dates. |
| Levels of Meaning/Purpose<br>① ② ❸ ④ ⑤ | Although captions give information about each artist, students need to be able to analyze and interpret the images. |

# FACILITATING

## Jump Start

**FIRST REVIEW** Engage students in a discussion about how art, like literature, can evoke sensations. *Do artists paint simply to reproduce a scene? Or does their art say more about landscape than what meets the eye?*

## American Regional Art  

What motivates artists to paint? How are artists affected by the landscape that surrounds them? Modeling these and other questions readers might ask will bring "American Regional Art" to life and connect it to the Performance Task question. Selection audio and print capability for the selection are available in the Interactive Teacher's Edition.

## Media Vocabulary

Have groups briefly discuss the media vocabulary. Have they encountered any of these terms before? Ask groups to look at the three groups of terms and describe what they have in common. What do they think of when they hear the terms realism, romanticism, and impressionism. Do these terms relate to literature? How so? How might they also relate to art?

### FIRST REVIEW

Have students perform the steps of the first review independently:

LOOK: Remind students to focus on the subject matter of each work of art, noting the artist and year the work was produced.

NOTE: Encourage students to write any questions they might have about the subject matter of each work.

CONNECT: Encourage students to make connections with the works of art they see here and other works of art with which they are familiar. Have them consider art they may have seen in museums.

RESPOND: Students will demonstrate their understanding by answering questions.

Point out to students that they will perform the first three steps concurrently as they are doing their first review. They will complete the Respond step after they have finished the first review. You may wish to print copies of the **First-Review Guide: Media: Art/ Photography** for students to use.

MAKING MEANING

A LITERATURE OF PLACE

## Comparing Text to Media

The works of art you are about to study are examples of American regional art. After completing the activities for this selection, you will compare how written and visual works communicate ideas.

AMERICAN REGIONAL ART

About the Artists

**Edward Hopper** (1882–1967)

**Guy A. Wiggins** (b. 1920)

**Albert Bierstadt** (1830–1902)

**Georgia O'Keeffe** (1887–1986)

**Nell Choate Jones** (1879–1981)

**Frederic Remington** (1861–1909)

# American Regional Art

## Media Vocabulary

These words will be useful to you as you analyze, discuss, and write about works of fine art.

| | |
|---|---|
| **Realism, Romanticism,** and **Impressionism:** painting styles | • In Realism, a scene is depicted exactly as it appears.<br>• In Romanticism, a scene is depicted with dramatic details, evoking an emotional response.<br>• In Impressionism, a scene is suggested through brush strokes, the use of color and light, and the depiction of movement. |
| **Palette:** range of colors used in a particular work | • An artist has nearly infinite variations of color options from which to choose.<br>• Color choices may help create an artwork's mood or atmosphere. For example, dark colors and shades of blue in a painting may suggest a somber or melancholy mood. |
| **Perspective:** method of giving a sense of depth on a flat or shallow surface | • Perspective indicates the vantage point from which a scene is viewed.<br>• The subject may seem very far away, at a middle distance, or very close to viewers. |

### First Review MEDIA: ART AND PHOTOGRAPHY

Apply these strategies as you complete your first review. You will have an opportunity to complete a close review after your first review.

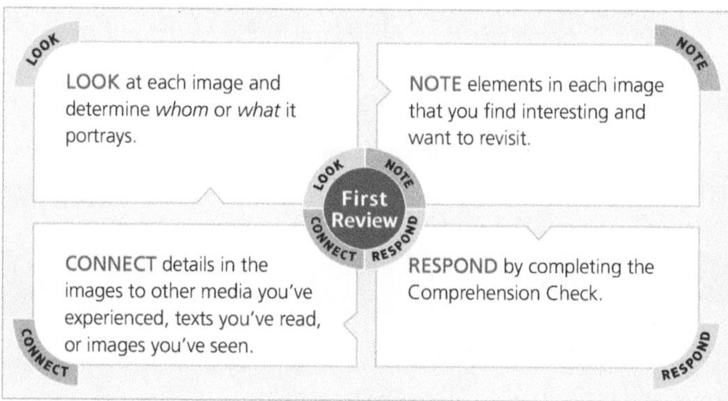

LOOK
LOOK at each image and determine *whom* or *what* it portrays.
NOTE
NOTE elements in each image that you find interesting and want to revisit.
First Review
CONNECT details in the images to other media you've experienced, texts you've read, or images you've seen.
RESPOND by completing the Comprehension Check.
CONNECT
RESPOND


STANDARDS

**Language**
Acquire and use accurately general academic and domain-specific words and phrases, sufficient for reading, writing, speaking, and listening at the college and career readiness level; demonstrate independence in gathering vocabulary knowledge when considering a word or phrase important to comprehension or expression.





### VOCABULARY DEVELOPMENT

**Multiple Meanings** Students should notice that the vocabulary terms have very specific meanings in the context of art. *Perspective* in art refers to the appearance of a distant object to a viewer. In conversational English, *perspective* may mean a person's evaluation or viewpoint of a particular situation. A *palette* may also refer to the board an artist uses to mix paints. It can also be used to describe tonal color in a musical piece.

# American Regional Art

BACKGROUND

Even though American art is influenced by the same developments in style that shape European art, it varies widely across the nation. Inspired by regional geography and culture, American painters and sculptors create works that depict an array of subjects in widely differing styles.

SCAN FOR MULTIMEDIA 

**IMAGE 1: *The Lighthouse at Two Lights*, Edward Hopper, Maine, 1929.** A painter of Realist landscapes and cityscapes throughout America, Hopper has been described as a "pure painter," interested primarily in form, color, and the division of space.

NOTES





DIGITAL PERSPECTIVES   

CLOSER REVIEW

## Analyze Perspective and Palette

Circulate among groups as students conduct their close review. Suggest that groups close review Image 1. Encourage them to talk about what they note. If needed, provide the following support.

**NOTE:** Have students note details in the image that relate to the colors in the image and the angle from which the viewer seems to view the scene. Or work with small groups to have students participate while you note them.
**Possible response:** The viewer is looking up at the lighthouse from below; the colors are muted greens, tans, and browns against a bright blue sky.

**QUESTION:** Guide students to consider what these details might tell them. Ask students how the perspective of the viewer and the colors of the scene add to the overall feeling, and accept student responses.
**Possible response:** These details contribute to a feeling of peaceful isolation.

**CONCLUDE:** Help students formulate conclusions about the importance of these details in the image. Ask students why the artist might have included these details.
**Possible response:** These details contribute to a feeling of peaceful isolation.
Remind students that **perspective** is the way an artist suggests distance and how the artist places a viewer in relationship to the objects in a painting. **Palette** is the range of colors an artist use. Each of these decisions impacts the way the art is received.

## FACILITATING SMALL-GROUP CLOSE REVIEWING

**CLOSE REVIEW: Fine Art Gallery** As students perform the close review, circulate and offer support as needed.

- Remind students that as they study art, they should consider the type of painting style that is represented: *realism, romanticism, or impressionism*. Have them explain why they classified each work as such.
- If a group is unclear as to why a particular painting is considered fine art, have them note facts about each artist and his or her particular style.

**IMAGE 2: *Storm Lifting Over Wall Street*, Guy A. Wiggins, New York, 2010.** A modern American artist who lives in New York City, Wiggins is a third-generation painter who inherited his Impressionist style from his father and grandfather.

NOTES

**IMAGE 3: *Among the Sierra Nevada, California*, Albert Bierstadt, California, 1868.** In creating his dramatic landscapes of the American West, Bierstadt used skills he gained through study in Germany and as a member of the Hudson River School in New York. He made many journeys west to gather material for his often enormous works.

NOTES





## DIGITAL PERSPECTIVES

**Enriching the Art** Review Image 3 with students. The Hudson River School was an American art movement that emerged in the mid–1850s by a group of landscape artists in New York City. It was an outgrowth of the Romantic movement of art and was characterized by picturesque scenes from the Catskill region of the Hudson Valley. Invite interested students to conduct online research to find paintings from various artists from this school. Students can prepare a slide presentation using software. Encourage students to write captions for the paintings and share with the class.

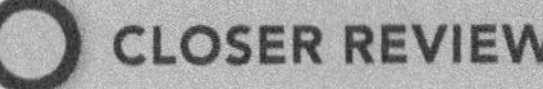

**IMAGE 4: *Deer's Skull With Pedernal,* Georgia O'Keeffe, New Mexico, 1936.** O'Keeffe is referred to as the "Mother of American Modernism," an experimental art movement that emerged primarily after World War I. She often painted the Pedernal, a mountain she could see from her New Mexico residence.

NOTES

**IMAGE 5: *Georgia Red Clay,* Nell Choate Jones, Georgia,1946.** In the 1920s, Jones was known for her European landscapes. After returning to the United States in 1936, she was inspired by the "picturesqueness" of her native rural Georgia. Her southern paintings are noted for their strong contours and use of color.

NOTES





CLOSER REVIEW

## Analyze Artistic Style 

Circulate among groups as students conduct their close review. Suggest that groups close review images 4 and 5. Encourage them to talk about what they note. If needed, provide the following support.

**NOTE:** Have students note details in the images that relate to the style of the painting, or work with small groups to have students participate while you note them.

**Possible response:** Image 4 shows an image of a skull set in the foreground against a stark background. Image 5 shows a sense of movement through the landscape with bold brushstrokes and bright colors.

**QUESTION:** Guide students to consider what these details might tell them. Ask students how the subject matter is presented in each of the paintings, and accept student responses.

**Possible response:** Image 4 seems stark and lifeless. Image 5 seems more welcoming.

**CONCLUDE:** Help students formulate conclusions about the importance of these details in the image. Ask students why the artist might have included these details.

**Possible response:** Both paintings depict landscapes, but neither is realistic nor romantic in style. The composition, brushstrokes, and color of image 5 show an impressionistic painting.

Remind students that **artistic style** includes several factors including subject, texture, color scheme, and mood. The decisions an artist makes help make each painter's work unique.

CROSS-CURRICULAR PERSPECTIVES

**Science** Georgia red clay is the name of a clay soil commonly found in Georgia. (image 5) The color of the clay is due to the properties of the soil, which contains iron oxide. The clay is hard and dense and contains little organic matter. Weathering in a warm, humid climate over a long period of time contributes to the formation of this red-colored clay.

# FACILITATING

## Comprehension Check

Possible responses

1. A lighthouse dominates Hopper's painting.
2. The painting depicts life in a city—that is, an urban setting. The specific setting is Wall Street, in New York City, on a stormy day.
3. The painting depicts a deer's skull.

## Research

**Research to Explore** Students may research one of the artists in the gallery, or they may choose to research a different artist. If students would like to research a different artist, suggest that they choose a genre of painting they like and then proceed to research an artist by using keywords in a search engine. Possible artists to research include:

- Realism: Edward Hopper, Gustave Courbet, Honore Daumier, Winslow Homer
- Romantics: Eugene Delacroix, John Constable, Thomas Cole, J.M.W. Turner
- Impressionists: Claude Monet, Pierre-Auguste Renoir, Mary Cassatt

**IMAGE 6: *The Bronco Buster,* Frederic Remington, American West, 1895.** Remington left his East Coast art school at the age of nineteen to travel to the West. His paintings and sculptures centered on horsemen and the landscapes of this frontier region.

NOTES

## Comprehension Check

**Complete the following items after you finish your first review. Review and clarify details with your group.**

**1.** What structure dominates Image 1, the painting by Edward Hopper?

**2.** What kind of American place is depicted in Image 2, the painting by Guy A. Wiggins?

**3.** What does Image 4, the painting by Georgia O'Keeffe, depict?

## RESEARCH

**Research to Explore** Chose an artist from this gallery who interests you, and formulate a research question about his or her life or work. Write your question here.



## PERSONALIZE FOR LEARNING

### Challenge

**Research** Invite students to research a painting or sculpture by two of the artists in the selection. Have students write a critical review of each painting, focusing on and comparing the styles, perspectives, and palettes of the works. Students should include a personal reaction to the art in their reviews. How did the art make them feel? What emotions, if any, do the works evoke? What about the work appeals to the senses? Encourage students to use sensory words in their reviews.

MAKING MEANING

## Close Review

With your group, revisit the artwork and your first-review notes. Record any new observations that seem important. What **questions** do you have? What can you **conclude**?

AMERICAN REGIONAL ART

## Analyze the Media

Complete the activities.

1. **Present and Discuss** Choose the artwork you find most interesting or powerful. Share your choice with the group, and discuss why you chose it. Explain what you noticed in the artwork, what questions it raised for you, and what conclusions you reached.
2. **Review and Synthesize** With your group, review all the works of art. Do they do more than simply portray different geographical locales or regions? Explain.
3. Notebook **Essential Question:** *What is the relationship between literature and place?* How do artists, like writers, establish connections to places? Support your response by identifying details from the works of art.

LANGUAGE DEVELOPMENT

### Media Vocabulary

| realism | impressionism | perspective |
|---|---|---|
| romanticism | palette | |

Use the vocabulary words in your responses to the questions.

1. **(a)** In your view, which of the works of art most closely resembles real life? Explain your choice. **(b)** Which image portrays a scene with the greatest drama or sense of emotional intensity? Explain.
2. **(a)** In your view, which painting most clearly exaggerates elements of the scene? **(b)** What is the effect of this exaggeration? Explain.
3. Which image most clearly or dramatically conveys a sense of movement or action? Explain your choice.

STANDARDS

**Language**

Acquire and use accurately general academic and domain-specific words and phrases, sufficient for reading, writing, speaking, and listening at the college and career readiness level; demonstrate independence in gathering vocabulary knowledge when considering a word or phrase important to comprehension or expression.





DIGITAL PERSPECTIVES

## Jump Start

CLOSE REVIEW Ask students to consider the following prompt: *What makes a person want to create art?* As students discuss the prompt in their groups, have them consider the importance of landscape and geography in the development of the artist's imagination.

## Close Review

Model close reviewing by using the Close Review note. Remind students to look for elements and details they did not observe during their first review. You may wish to print copies of the **Close-Review Guide: Media: Art/ Photography** for students to use.

## Analyze the Media

Possible responses:

1. **Responses will vary by group.** Remind students to discuss not only details from the artworks but also questions and conclusions inspired by those details.
2. **Responses will vary by group,** but make sure that students give examples from the artworks that support their ideas. In Image 4, students may suggest that O'Keeffe's work connects her imagination to the land she is living in, leading her to experiment with a style of emerging and dramatic modern art.
3. **Responses will vary by group.** Remind students to support their answers by identifying evidence from the artworks. For Image 2 or 6, students may suggest the art depicts a particular lifestyle, due to the motion and activity.

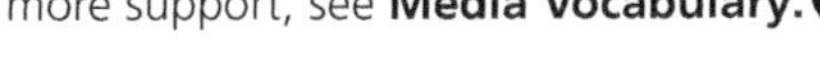

## Media Vocabulary

For more support, see **Media Vocabulary.**

Possible responses:

1. (a) Image 1 is a good example of realism, for the lighthouse scene looks just as you would expect it to look if you were standing in front of it. (b) Image 2 is also an example of realism, but the palette is much darker than Hopper's with dramatic contrast between light and dark and more well-defined details in the landscape.
2. (a) Answers may vary, but most students will likely identify Georgia O'Keeffe's painting as the painting that most clearly exaggerates elements of the scene. (b) O'Keeffe creates perspective by giving viewers a nearby, close-up view of a deer's skull but setting that against distant hills.
3. The palette is monochromatic, which emphasizes the three-dimensional perspective of the sculpture.

## FORMATIVE ASSESSMENT

### Analyze the Media

**If** students struggle to close review the art, **then** provide the **American Regional Art: Media Questions** available online in the Interactive Teacher's Edition or Unit Resources. Answers and DOK levels are also available.

### Media Vocabulary

**If** students struggle to identify the role perspective creates in the paintings and sculptures, **then** have them review the definition of *perspective* and encourage them to describe the different perspectives of each of the paintings.

## Writing to Compare

**Project Plan** In order to organize their writing, suggest students first make an outline. They should begin by stating their point of view about how Lopez's insights about place are connected with the artist's work. Then have students look for details in the works of art that reinforce the statement they have chosen. Students may focus individual paragraphs on subject matter, composition, palette, mood, or nuances of the works that support the statement. Remind students to include a paragraph that summarizes their ideas in a conclusion. For more support, see **Writing to Compare : Interpretive Essay.**

### Prewriting

Project the Interactive Teacher's Edition of Image 5 of Jones's *Georgia Red Clay* and paragraph 8 of "A Literature of Place" and model comparing them. Note that both works depict rich examples of the surrounding landscape. The painting uses bold strokes of color consisting of warm earth tones and rich shades of red and green, creating a vibrant, but welcoming mood. Lopez's description focuses on sound, scents, and colors of native plants and the surrounding landscape of sky, earth, and beach.

**See possible responses in chart on student page.**

Responses to both questions will vary but should clearly convey the rationale for the group's choice of image and a clear comparison between the essay and the artwork.

EFFECTIVE EXPRESSION

A LITERATURE OF PLACE

AMERICAN REGIONAL ART

## Writing to Compare

You have read the essay "A Literature of Place," by Barry Lopez, and viewed a gallery of American regional art. Now, deepen your understanding of both the text and the images by making connections between them and expressing your insights in writing.

**Assignment**

For Lopez, places give rise to stories. About his childhood, he writes: "The comforting intimacy of that California valley erected in me a kind of story I wanted to tell, a pattern I wanted to invoke—in countless ways."

- What "story" about place does Lopez tell in this essay? What kinds of details does he use to convey that story?
- What "story" about place do the artworks tell? What kinds of patterns and details do they use to "tell" those stories?

Write an **interpretive essay** in which you consider these questions. Think of the "story" as the main message or insight the work conveys. Work with your group to analyze the texts and complete the Prewriting activities. Then, write your own essay.

### Prewriting

**Analyze the Texts** With your group, identify key ideas, details, and images in Lopez's essay. Then, select and analyze an image from the gallery and do the same. Decide what the writer and the artist are saying, in different ways, about place and our connection to it.

| | KEY IDEAS, DETAILS, IMAGES, FEATURES | "STORY" BEING TOLD |
|---|---|---|
| Essay | Nature, animals, and people from a specific place | (Varies with image) Desert, city, short, horse and rider |
| Artwork | The visual landscape people encounter as children results in a sense of community; a sense of partnership and spiritual connection with the land | Reflects place where artist grew up |

**Notebook** Respond to these questions.

1. Why did your group choose the image you did?
2. How are the stories told by the image and the essay similar? How are they different?

**STANDARDS**

Writing

- Write informative/explanatory texts to examine and convey complex ideas, concepts, and information clearly and accurately through the effective selection, organization, and analysis of content.
- Draw evidence from literary or informational texts to support analysis, reflection, and research.





PERSONALIZE FOR LEARNING

**Strategic Support**

**Comparison** If group members have difficulty understanding how both selections can be compared and contrasted, have them go back and skim the text from "A Literature of Place" to look for and annotate text that describes details, atmosphere or mood, and how place inspires writing. Then have students go back and study each piece of art and the description of each artist, suggesting which piece or artist could be used to illustrate the text references they have selected. Have students discuss their choices.

### Drafting

**Tell Stories** Before writing your essay, gather with your group for a "storytelling" session. Use your Prewriting notes to summarize aloud the story each selection tells or suggests about place and our connection to it. Take turns identifying key ideas, elements, and details in each work. Finally, decide how the two works express similar ideas, and how they express different ones. Write your conclusions about the similarities and differences here:

| SIMILAR IDEAS | DIFFERENT IDEAS |
| --- | --- |
| | |

**Choose an Organizational Structure** Discuss various ways of organizing your essay.

- Will you first discuss Lopez's essay, then discuss the image, and then explain similarities and differences?
- Will you present a series of key ideas from the essay and show how the painting illustrates, extends, or departs from each one?
- Will you present the story told by the image, and support the different parts of the story with quotations from Lopez's essay?

After your group discusses possible ways of structuring the essay, choose one and draft your essay independently.

### Review, Revise and Edit

Exchange drafts of your essay with your group members. Use one color to mark parts of your peer's essay that address Lopez's writing, and a different color to mark parts of the essay that address the image. Offer suggestions for revising the essay to achieve greater balance. Then, use the feedback you receive to revise your essay. After you finalize your essay, read it aloud to the group. After the readings, discuss similarities and differences among your interpretations of the "stories" told by the works of art.

**EVIDENCE LOG**

Before moving on to a new selection, go to your Evidence Log and record what you learned from "A Literature of Place" and the gallery of American regional art.





**DIGITAL PERSPECTIVES**

## Drafting

Encourage students to use their groups as a brainstorming session for identifying key ideas and details from both works. Conclusions in the student chart will vary but should reflect similarities and differences.

## Review, Revise, and Edit

Remind students to provide feedback with a positive and constructive tone. Suggest that they make their feedback concrete and supportive.

**Evidence Log** Support students in completing the Evidence Log. This paced activity will help prepare them for the Performance-Based Assessment at the end of the unit.

### FORMATIVE ASSESSMENT

### Writing to Compare

**If** students are unable to make connections between the works of art and Lopez's insights, **then** have them skim "A Literature of Place" and compare the art works for ideas.

## PERSONALIZE FOR LEARNING

### English Language Support

**Noun Phrases** To help students in writing their compositions, give support that allows them to expand noun phrases in a variety of ways by adding adjectives and simple clauses. Present students with starter sentences such as:

*Storm Lifting Over Wall Street* is an impressionist painting.

*Georgia Red Clay* shows a landscape scene.

*The Bronco Buster* is a sculpture.

Have students expand the sentences by adding one or two adjectives and a simple clause to each. **ALL LEVELS**

# *from* Dust Tracks on a Road

**AUDIO SUMMARIES**
Audio summaries of "Dust Tracks on a Road" are available online in both English and Spanish in the Interactive Teacher's Edition or Unit Resources. Assigning these summaries prior to reading the selection may help students build additional background knowledge and set a context for their first read.

## Summary

In this excerpt from her memoir, *Dust Tracks on a Road,* Zora Neale Hurston describes growing up in central Florida. When two white women arrive unexpectedly at her school, her teacher, Mr. Calhoun, has several students, including Zora, read aloud a myth. Zora does the best job and is introduced to the women. The next day Zora is told to go to the hotel where the women are staying. They feed her some unusual treats, make her read, and send her away with a heavy cylinder tied with a ribbon, which she later discovers has 100 shiny pennies in it. The next day, several books from the two women arrive. Zora especially enjoys the rhythm of the words in some of the songs from a hymnbook. A month later, a box arrives from the women with more books and some fine used clothing. Zora loves the gifts, especially the book of Norse myths and the Bible.

### Insight

In this incident from her memoir, Hurston makes it clear that her drive to become a writer was awakened in her youth and her chance encounter with two white women, who, impressed by her at school, sent her books with stories that she came to love.

ESSENTIAL QUESTION:
What is the relationship between place and literature?

## Connection to the Essential Question

Students will note that Hurston's memoir describes her life as a child in central Florida and events that occurred there that shaped her future career as a writer.

SMALL-GROUP LEARNING PERFORMANCE TASK
Explain the sense of place created by the authors and artists in this section.

UNIT PERFORMANCE-BASED ASSESSMENT
What makes certain places live on in our memory?

## Connection to Performance Tasks

**Small-Group Learning Performance Task** In this Performance Task, students will consider the question of whether or not all the selections in this unit are inspired by childhood experiences with a particular place. Students will note that the central focus of this excerpt from Zora Neale Hurston's memoir is on her youth in central Florida and its formative role in her later career as a writer.

**Unit Performance-Based Assessment** This selection provides an interesting insight into the idea of what makes certain places live on in our memory. It is clear that Hurston values the experiences of her youth and believes that they are connected to her career as a writer.

DIGITAL PERSPECTIVES

 Audio
 Video
 Document
 Annotation Highlights
 EL Highlights
Online Assessment

## LESSON RESOURCES

| | Making Meaning | Language Development | Effective Expression |
|---|---|---|---|
| Lesson | **First Read**<br>**Close Read**<br>**Analyze the Text**<br>**Analyze Craft and Structure** | **Concept Vocabulary**<br>**Word Study**<br>**Author's Style** | **Speaking and Listening** |
| **Instructional Standards** | **RI.10** By the end of grade 11, read and comprehend literary nonfiction . . .<br>**RI.6** Determine an author's point of view . . .<br>**L.5** Demonstrate understanding of figurative language . . .<br>**L.4.b** Identify and correctly use patterns of word changes . . . | **L.4** Determine or clarify the meaning of unknown and multiple-meaning words and phrases . . .<br>**RI.4** Determine the meaning of words and phrases . . .<br>**RI.6** Determine an author's point of view . . .<br>**L.5.a** Interpret figures of speech . . . | **SL.6** Adapt speech to a variety of contexts and tasks . . . |
| **STUDENT RESOURCES** | | | |
| Available online in the Interactive Student Edition or Unit Resources | Selection Audio<br>First-Read Guide: Nonfiction<br>Close-Read Guide: Nonfiction | Word Network | Evidence Log |
| **TEACHER RESOURCES** | | | |
| **Selection Resources** Available online in the Interactive Teacher's Edition or Unit Resources | Audio Summaries<br>Annotation Highlights<br>EL Highlights<br>*from* Dust Tracks on a Road: Text Questions<br>English Language Support Lesson: Figurative Meanings<br>Analyze Craft and Structure: Literary Nonfiction | Concept Vocabulary and Word Study<br>Author's Style: Figurative Meanings | Speaking and Listening: Oral Presentation |
| **Reteach/Practice (RP)** Available online in the Interactive Teacher's Edition or Unit Resources | Analyze Craft and Structure: Literary Nonfiction (RP) | Word Study: Multiple-Meaning Words (RP)<br>Author's Style: Figurative Meanings (RP) | Speaking and Listening: Oral Presentation (RP) |
| **Assessment** Available online in Assessments | Selection Test | | |
| **My Resources** | A Unit 4 Answer Key is available online and in the Interactive Teacher's Edition. | | |

# Reading Support

| Text Complexity Rubric: *from* Dust Tracks on a Road | |
|---|---|
| **Quantitative Measures** | |
| **Lexile** 920 **Text Length** 2,739 words | |
| **Qualitative Measures** | |
| Knowledge Demands ①—②—❸—④—⑤ | The setting may be unfamiliar (Southern town in early 1900s in a racially segregated school), but little background is needed because all is clearly explained. |
| Structure ①—②—❸—④—⑤ | The organization is clear and chronological. At a few different points in the selection, the narrative switches to stories within the story as the character recounts stories she read. |
| Language Conventionality and Clarity ①—②—❸—④—⑤ | The story is told in first person with conversational, familiar tone. Sentences mostly have simple construction. Some dialect and regionalisms are used. |
| Levels of Meaning/Purpose ①—②—❸—④—⑤ | Meaning and purpose are straightforward and explicit. Events and feelings are conveyed in a way that is accessible. |

DECIDE AND PLAN

## English Language Support

Provide English Learners with support for structure and language as they read the selection.

**Structure** Help students identify places in which there is a "story within a story." Point out the clues that they will see that the narration is changing. For example, in paragraph 14, she says *So I read the story to the end....* and then begins describing the story of Persephone. In the next paragraph she is back to talking about her class. Other clues they can look for are the names of stories, as in paragraph 30.

**Language** Ask students to listen and read along as you read aloud examples of the grandmother's words: (paragraph 4) *Git down offa dat gate-post... don't stand in dat doorway...* Analyze the dialect together, for example *Git means Get, dat/that, dem/them.*

## Strategic Support

Provide students with strategic support to ensure that they can successfully read the text.

**Structure** Point out that there are places within the story when the author switches from recounting her own story to describing events in stories she has read. As students read, have them mark places where this occurs, noting where each "story within the story" begins and ends.

**Language** Ask volunteers to read aloud words that the author (narrator) says, for example in paragraph 1, and words her grandmother uses (paragraph 4). Ask students to compare the two ways of speaking and to tell you what they notice about these two dialects.

## Challenge

Provide students who need to be challenged with ideas for how they can go beyond a simple interpretation of the text.

**Text Analysis** Ask students to comment on the way in which Zora Neale Hurston uses characters to bring the reader into the atmosphere of the setting. For example, have them analyze how dialect serves to create voice and tone in the narrative. Then ask students why they think she chose to include full details and storylines from the stories she read. What does this tell us about how she feels about those stories or how important they are?

**Written Response** Have students read other selections by Zora Neale Hurston, or look up information about her life. Ask them to write an essay describing what they read. Have students share their writing with the class.

TEACH

## Read and Respond

Have groups do their first read of the selection. Then have them complete their close read. Finally, work with them on the Making Meaning, Language Development, and Effective Expression activities.

# Standards Support Through Teaching and Learning Cycle

## IDENTIFY NEEDS

Analyze results of the Beginning-of-Year Assessment, focusing on the items relating to Unit 4. Also take into consideration student performance to this point and your observations of where particular students struggle.

## DECIDE AND PLAN

- If students have performed poorly on items matching these standards, then provide selection scaffolds before assigning them the on-level lesson provided in the Student Edition.
- If students have done well on the Beginning-of-Year Assessment, then challenge them to keep progressing and learning by giving them opportunities to practice the skills in depth.
- Use the Selection Resources listed on the Planning pages for the excerpt from *Dust Tracks on a Road* to help students continually improve their ability to master the standards.

**Instructional Standards: *from* Dust Tracks on a Road**

| | Catching Up | This Year | Looking Forward |
|---|---|---|---|
| **Reading** | You may wish to administer the **Analyze Craft and Structure: Literary Nonfiction (RP)** worksheet to familiarize students with literary nonfiction. | **RI.6** Determine an author's point of view or purpose in a text in which the rhetoric is particularly effective, analyzing how style and content contribute to the power, persuasiveness, or beauty of the text. | Challenge students to define the difference between literary nonfiction and other forms of nonfiction. |
| **Speaking and Listening** | You may wish to administer the **Speaking and Listening: Oral Presentation (RP)** worksheet to help students prepare for their presentations. | **SL.6** Adapt speech to a variety of contexts and tasks, demonstrating a command of formal English when indicated or appropriate. | Challenge students to think of ways they can expand on their oral presentations after they have finished. |
| **Language** | Review the **Word Study: Multiple-Meaning Words (RP)** worksheet with students to remind them some words have multiple meanings.<br>Review the **Author's Style Style: Figurative Meanings (RP)** worksheet with students to better familiarize them with hyperbole and idioms. | **L.4** Determine or clarify the meaning of unknown and multiple-meaning words and phrases based on *grades 11–12 reading and content*, choosing flexibly from a range of strategies.<br>**L.5.a** Interpret figures of speech in context and analyze their role in the text. | Have students find other words from the selection that have multiple meanings.<br>Have students identify examples of hyperbole and idioms from other works they have read. |

## ANALYZE AND REVISE

- Analyze student work for evidence of student learning.
- Identify whether or not students have met the expectations in the standards.
- Identify implications for future instruction.

## TEACH

Implement the planned lesson, and gather evidence of student learning.

# FACILITATING

## Jump Start

**FIRST READ** *If you were to write an autobiography, what significant events would you write about?* Engage students in a conversation about how childhood experiences shape us in our adult lives.

## *from* Dust Tracks on a Road

Have attitudes, customs, or beliefs in our culture changed since you were a child? How so? Modeling these and other questions readers might ask will bring "Dust Tracks on a Road" to life and connect it to the Performance Task question. Selection audio and print capability for the selection are available in the Interactive Teacher's Edition.

## Concept Vocabulary

Have groups briefly discuss the three concept vocabulary words. Have they encountered any of the words before? Do they recognize the prefix, suffix, or base word of any of the concept vocabulary words?

Have groups consider the strategy for finding base words and discuss its advantages and disadvantages.

## FIRST READ

Have students perform the steps of the first read independently:

NOTICE: You may want to encourage students to notice the author's reaction to the two white women who come to visit their school.

ANNOTATE: Remind students to mark passages that describe the author's thoughts as she first sees and then meets the two women.

CONNECT: Encourage students to make connections in their own lives to the author's first experiences with reading books.

RESPOND: Students will demonstrate their understanding of the text by answering questions and writing a summary.

Point out to students that they will perform the first three steps concurrently as they are doing their first read. They will complete the Respond step after they have finished the first read. You may wish to print copies of the **First-Read Guide: Nonfiction** for students to use.

MAKING MEANING

About the Author

**Zora Neale Hurston** (1891–1960) grew up in Florida. In 1925, she moved to New York City, where she soon established herself as one of the bright new talents of the Harlem Renaissance. She returned to the South for six years to collect African American folk tales. In 1935, she published *Mules and Men*, the first volume of black American folklore compiled by an African American. Her work helped document the African American connection to the stories, songs, and myths of Africa. Hurston achieved critical and popular success with the novels *Jonah's Gourd Vine* (1934), *Their Eyes Were Watching God* (1937), *Moses, Man of the Mountain* (1939), and her prize-winning autobiography, *Dust Tracks on a Road* (1942).

## *from* Dust Tracks on a Road

### Concept Vocabulary

As you perform your first read of this excerpt from *Dust Tracks on a Road*, you will encounter these words.

self-assurance    forward    brazenness

**Base Words** Words that seem unfamiliar may actually contain words you know. Try looking for familiar base words within unfamiliar words. The word *irreplaceable*, for example, contains the base word *replace*, which means "to provide a substitute for." In this word, the prefix *ir-* means "not," and the suffix *-able* means "capable of being." *Irreplaceable*, then, means "not having the ability to be substituted for."

Note how the addition of prefixes or suffixes affects the meaning in these words.

| | |
|---|---|
| un**name**able | impossible to name |
| **wreck**age | pieces left after something is wrecked or destroyed |
| **humor**less | without a sense of humor |
| pre**exist**ing | existing at an earlier time |

Apply your knowledge of base words and other vocabulary strategies to determine the meanings of unfamiliar words you encounter during your first read.

### First Read NONFICTION

Apply these strategies as you conduct your first read. You will have an opportunity to complete a close read after your first read.

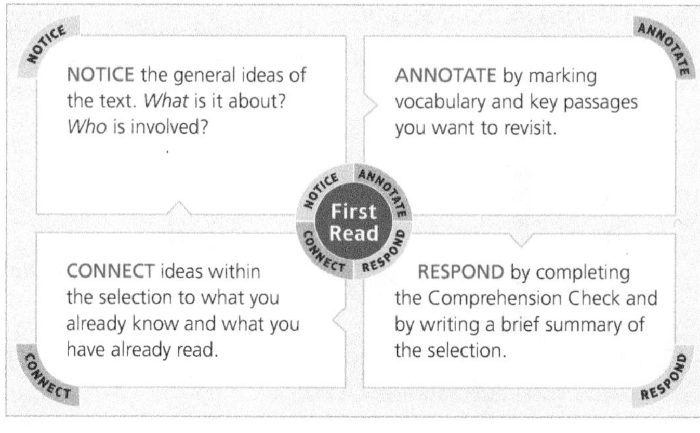
NOTICE the general ideas of the text. *What* is it about? *Who* is involved?
ANNOTATE by marking vocabulary and key passages you want to revisit.
CONNECT ideas within the selection to what you already know and what you have already read.
RESPOND by completing the Comprehension Check and by writing a brief summary of the selection.
First Read
NOTICE
ANNOTATE
CONNECT
RESPOND

STANDARDS

Reading Informational Text
By the end of grade 11, read and comprehend literary nonfiction in the grades 11–CCR text complexity band proficiently, with scaffolding as needed at the high end of the range.

Language
Identify and correctly use patterns of word changes that indicate different meanings or parts of speech.

### VOCABULARY DEVELOPMENT

**Word Forms** Expand students' vocabulary by helping them learn related forms of the base words. Encourage students to use the base words for *abash* and *length* to make word forms that include nouns, verbs, adjectives and adverbs. Have students label each word form.

| | |
|---|---|
| abash (verb) | abashment (noun), abashedly (adverb) |
| length (noun) | lengthy (adjective), lengthen (verb) |

# from *Dust Tracks on a Road*

Zora Neale Hurston

## Concept Vocabulary

**SELF-ASSURANCE** If groups are struggling to define the term *self-assurance* in paragraph 2, remind them to think about the base of the word, *assure*, which means to "make confident." *Self* refers to one's own self or one's innermost being. Taken together, these word parts mean "confidence in one's own abilities."

**Possible response:** *Self-assurance* means "confidence."

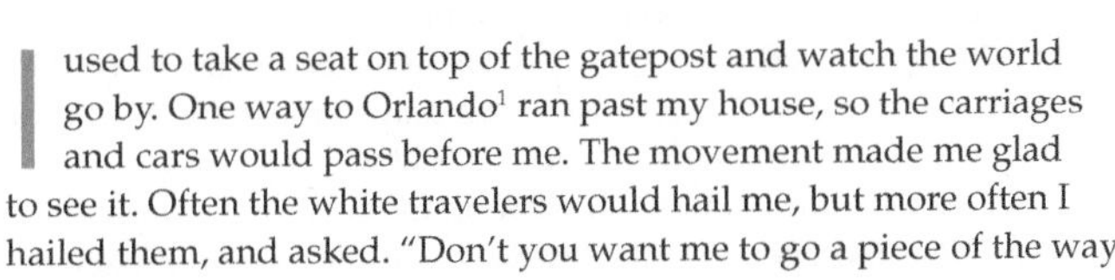

BACKGROUND

In this excerpt from Zora Neale Hurston's autobiography, the young Zora experiences an event that opens her eyes to the world of literature and sets the stage for her career as a writer.

SCAN FOR MULTIMEDIA 

1 I used to take a seat on top of the gatepost and watch the world go by. One way to Orlando[1] ran past my house, so the carriages and cars would pass before me. The movement made me glad to see it. Often the white travelers would hail me, but more often I hailed them, and asked. "Don't you want me to go a piece of the way with you?"

2 They always did. I know now that I must have caused a great deal of amusement among them, but my **self-assurance** must have carried the point, for I was always invited to come along. I'd ride up the road

NOTES

Mark base words or indicate another strategy you used that helped you determine meaning.

**self-assurance** (sehlf uh SHUR uhns) *n.*

MEANING:

1. **Orlando** (awr LAN doh) city in central Florida, about five miles from Eatonville, Hurston's hometown.



##  FACILITATING SMALL-GROUP CLOSE READING: Autobiography

**CLOSE READ: Autobiography** Monitor groups as they conduct their close read and offer support as needed.

- Remind students that an autobiography is a form of nonfiction in which a person tells all or part of his or her life story.
- Autobiographies are written in the first person. In an autobiography, the author traditionally focuses introspectively on his or her own life. Memoirs, on the other hand, traditionally focus on a writer's involvement in historically or culturally significant events—either as a participant or an eyewitness.
- Encourage students to look for instances in *Dust Tracks on a Road* in which Hurston gives introspective insight to her thoughts and feelings.

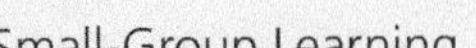

# FACILITATING

## Concept Vocabulary

**FORWARD** If groups are struggling to define the word *forward* in paragraph 3, remind them to think about the base of the word, *for(e). Fore* means "at front" and *-ward* is a suffix added to words to indicate direction, such as *eastward*. Students can infer meaning by noting the meaning of word parts and combining them. *Forward* can mean "to move ahead," but in this case students must look for context clues to further determine its meaning.

**Possible response:** *Forward* means "pushy," "bold," or "forthright."

**BRAZENNESS** If groups are struggling to define the word *brazenness* in paragraph 3, point out that the base word, *brazen,* means "brash or bold." The suffix *-ness* means "state or quality of being," so *brazenness* means "the quality of being bold."

**Possible response:** *Brazenness* means "boldness" or "impudence."

NOTES

Mark base words or indicate another strategy you used that helped you determine meaning.

**forward** (FAWR wuhrd) *adj.*

MEANING:

**brazenness** (BRAY zuhn nuhs) *n.*

MEANING:

for perhaps a half-mile, then walk back. I did not do this with the permission of my parents, nor with their foreknowledge.[2]

3 When they found out about it later, I usually got a whipping. My grandmother worried about my **forward** ways a great deal. She had known slavery and to her my **brazenness** was unthinkable.

4 "Git down offa dat gate-post! You li'l sow, you! Git down! Setting up dere looking dem white folks right in de face! They's gowine[3] to lynch you, yet. And don't stand in dat doorway gazing out at 'em neither. Youse too brazen to live long."[4]

5 Nevertheless. I kept right on gazing at them, and "going a piece of the way" whenever I could make it. The village seemed dull to me most of the time. If the village was singing a chorus, I must have missed the tune.

6 Perhaps a year before the old man[5] died, I came to know two other white people for myself. They were women.

7 It came about this way. The whites who came down from the North were often brought by their friends to visit the village school. A Negro school was something strange to them, and while they were always sympathetic and kind, curiosity must have been present, also. They came and went, came and went. Always, the room was hurriedly put in order, and we were threatened with a prompt and bloody death if we cut one caper while the visitors were present. We always sang a spiritual, led by Mr. Calhoun himself. Mrs. Calhoun always stood in the back, with a palmetto switch[6] in her hand as a squelcher. We were all little angels for the duration, because we'd better be. She would cut her eyes and give us a glare that meant trouble, then turn her face towards the visitors and beam as much as to say it was a great privilege and pleasure to teach lovely children like us. They couldn't see that palmetto hickory in her hand behind all those benches, but we knew where our angelic behavior was coming from.

8 Usually, the visitors gave warning a day ahead and we would be cautioned to put on shoes, comb our heads, and see to ears and fingernails. There was a close inspection of every one of us before we marched in that morning. Knotty heads, dirty ears and fingernails got hauled out of line, strapped and sent home to lick the calf over again.

9 This particular afternoon, the two young ladies just popped in. Mr. Calhoun was flustered, but he put on the best show he could. He dismissed the class that he was teaching up at the front of the room, then called the fifth grade in reading. That was my class.

10 So we took our readers and went up front. We stood up in the usual line, and opened to the lesson. It was the story of Pluto and

2. **foreknowledge** *n.* awareness of something before it happens or exists.
3. **gowine** "going."
4. **"Git down . . . live long"** Hurston's grandmother's fears reflect the fact of the times that it was often dangerous for African Americans to interact confidently with whites.
5. **the old man** white farmer who had developed a friendship with Hurston.
6. **palmetto** (pal MEHT oh) **switch** *n.* whip made from the fan-shaped leaves of the palmetto, a type of palm tree.





### HOW LANGUAGE WORKS

**Impact of Word Choice** Review the language in paragraph 4. Have students recall that an author's word choice contributes to the tone of a selection. In *Dust on the Tracks,* the author uses dialect, a regional variety of language, to add dimension to the speaker's voice. Have students examine the transliteration of dialect in paragraph 4 and then challenge them rewrite the sentences in standard English. For example, *Git down offa dat gate-post!* becomes *Get down off of that gate-post!*

Persephone. It was new and hard to the class in general, and Mr. Calhoun was very uncomfortable as the readers stumbled along, spelling out words with their lips, and in mumbling undertones before they exposed them experimentally to the teacher's ears.

11 Then it came to me. I was fifth or sixth down the line. The story was not new to me, because I had read my reader through from lid to lid, the first week that Papa had bought it for me.

12 That is how it was that my eyes were not in the book, working out the paragraph which I knew would be mine by counting the children ahead of me. I was observing our visitors, who held a book between them, following the lesson. They had shiny hair, mostly brownish. One had a looping gold chain around her neck. The other one was dressed all over in black and white with a pretty finger ring on her left hand. But the thing that held my eyes were their fingers. They were long and thin, and very white, except up near the tips. There they were baby pink. I had never seen such hands. It was a fascinating discovery for me. I wondered how they felt. I would have given those hands more attention, but the child before me was almost through. My turn next, so I got on my mark, bringing my eyes back to the book and made sure of my place. Some of the stories I had reread several times, and this Greco-Roman myth was one of my favorites. I was exalted by it and that is the way I read my paragraph.

13 "Yes, Jupiter had seen her (Persephone). He had seen the maiden picking flowers in the field. He had seen the chariot of the dark monarch pause by the maiden's side. He had seen him when he seized Persephone. He had seen the black horses leap down Mount Aetna's fiery throat. Persephone was now in Pluto's dark realm and he had made her his wife."

14 The two women looked at each other and then back to me. Mr. Calhoun broke out with a proud smile beneath his bristly moustache, and instead of the next child taking up where I had ended, he nodded to me to go on. So I read the story to the end, where flying Mercury, the messenger of the Gods, brought Persephone back to the sunlit earth and restored her to the arms of Dame Ceres, her mother, that the world might have springtime and summer flowers, autumn and harvest. But because she had bitten the pomegranate[7] while in Pluto's kingdom, she must return to him for three months of each year, and be his queen. Then the world had winter, until she returned to earth.

15 The class was dismissed, and the visitors smiled us away and went into a low-voiced conversation with Mr. Calhoun for a few minutes. They glanced my way once or twice and I began to worry. Not only was I barefooted, but my feet and legs were dusty. My hair was more uncombed than usual, and my nails were not shiny clean. Oh, I'm going to catch it now. Those ladies saw me, too. Mr. Calhoun is promising to 'tend to me. So I thought.

NOTES

7. **pomegranate** (POM uh gran iht) *n.* round, red-skinned fruit with many seeds.





DIGITAL PERSPECTIVES

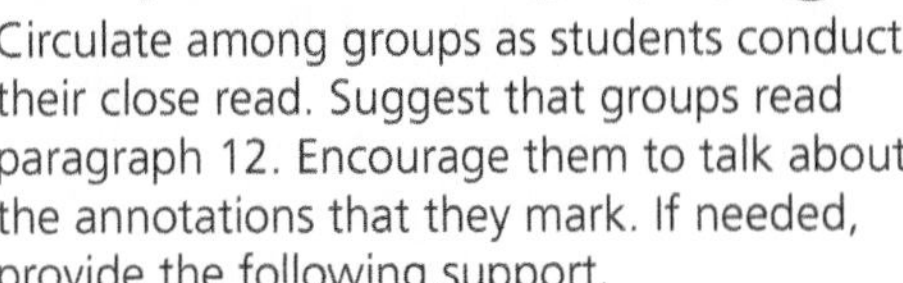

CLOSER LOOK

## Analyze Autobiography

Circulate among groups as students conduct their close read. Suggest that groups read paragraph 12. Encourage them to talk about the annotations that they mark. If needed, provide the following support.

**ANNOTATE:** Have students mark details in the paragraph that describe the author's impression of the two women who come to visit the school, or work with small groups to have students participate while you highlight them together.

**QUESTION:** Guide students to consider what these details might tell them. Ask what a reader can infer from why the author included this description of the two women, and accept student responses.

**Possible response:** The author has stated that she had met two white women earlier in the book. She is fascinated with the women and they way they look so she describes them in detail here.

**CONCLUDE:** Help students formulate conclusions about the importance of these details in the text. Ask students why the author might have included these details.

**Possible response:** The author has had very little contact with white women, as she views them from afar. Because this is probably her first experience with being up close to a white person, she wants to show insight as to what she was thinking at that time.

Remind students that in an **autobiography**, the author will not just write an account of events, but give insight to his or her thoughts and feelings about the events themselves. Here, the author lets the reader see what is going on inside her head as she prepares to read for the ladies.

CROSS-CURRICULAR PERSPECTIVES

**Humanities** Call students' attention to the myth detailed in paragraph 13 and 14. Pluto is the Roman god of the underworld. Hades is the Greek version of Pluto. Ceres is the Roman goddess of nature or agriculture, whose counterpart in Greek mythology is Demeter. Invite interested students to find a version of the Greco-Roman myth of Pluto and Persephone, a story explaining the changing seasons. Encourage students to retell the story of Pluto and Persephone in their own words.

CLOSER LOOK

## Analyze Word Choice

Circulate among groups as students conduct their close read. Suggest that groups read paragraphs 16 and 17. Encourage them to talk about the annotations that they mark. If needed, provide the following support.

**ANNOTATE:** Have students mark details in these paragraphs that show strong and interesting word choice, or work with small groups to have students participate while you highlight them together.

**QUESTION:** Guide students to consider what these details might tell them. Ask what a reader can infer from the author's choice of language in describing this scene, and accept student responses.

**Possible response:** The author uses language that helps set the scene in the classroom while also drawing readers into the time period. The phrase *get a whipping* help readers almost feel the possibility of the punishment. The word *snicker* helps the reader hear the low, almost hidden laughter of the classmates. Readers can envision the author's attitude to the laughter with the image of her switching her dress tail in response.

**CONCLUDE:** Help student formulate conclusions about the importance of these details in the text. Ask students why the author might have included these details.

**Possible response:** The author is using language that creates vivid images to help set the scene for the reader. She is trying to recreate the moment as she remembers it. The rich word choices help the reader experience the event along with the author.

Remind students that an author's **word choice** is an impact factor in the way ideas are conveyed.

Point out that the word *snicker* is an example of **onomatopoeia,** a word that sounds like what it means. Other words whose sound imitates their meaning are *buzz, hiss, murmur, thud, sizzle, whirr,* and *rustle.*

NOTES

16 Then Mr. Calhoun called me. I went up thinking how awful it was to get a whipping before company. Furthermore, I heard a snicker run over the room. Hennie Clark and Stell Brazzle did it out loud, so I would be sure to hear them. The smart-aleck was going to get it. I slipped one hand behind me and switched my dress tail at them, indicating scorn.

17 "Come here, Zora Neale," Mr. Calhoun cooed as I reached the desk. He put his hand on my shoulder and gave me little pats. The ladies smiled and held out those flower-looking fingers towards me. I seized the opportunity for a good look.

18 "Shake hands with the ladies, Zora Neale," Mr. Calhoun prompted and they took my hand one after the other and smiled. They asked if I loved school, and I lied that I did. There was *some* truth in it, because I liked geography and reading, and I liked to play at recess time. Who ever it was invented writing and arithmetic got no thanks from me. Neither did I like the arrangement where the teacher could sit up there with a palmetto stem and lick me whenever he saw fit. I hated things I couldn't do anything about. But I knew better than to bring that up right there, so I said yes, I *loved* school.

19 "I can tell you do," Brown Taffeta gleamed. She patted my head, and was lucky enough not to get sandspurs[8] in her hand. Children who roll and tumble in the grass in Florida are apt to get sandspurs in their hair. They shook hands with me again and I went back to my seat.

20 When school let out at three o'clock, Mr. Calhoun told me to wait. When everybody had gone, he told me I was to go to the Park House, that was the hotel in Maitland,[9] the next afternoon to call upon Mrs. Johnstone and Miss Hurd. I must tell Mama to see that I was clean

8. **sandspurs** *n.* spiny burrs that are the seeds of a grasslike weed.
9. **Maitland** (MAYT luhnd) city in Florida, close to Eatonville.

DIGITAL PERSPECTIVES

**Illuminating the Text** Review paragraphs 14–20 to discuss the way visitors may have felt about the school. Point out that this part of Hurston's autobiography takes place in the early 1900s. Call attention to the photo of school children at tables and ask students to describe some of the details. Have students conduct online research to find and share photos of African American students in the early 1900s. Have students discuss what they can infer from the photos about African-American schools during Hurston's time. Remind students that during this time in American history, most African-American students were separated from Caucasian students by sending them to separate schools.

DIGITAL PERSPECTIVES

NOTES

and brushed from head to feet, and I must wear shoes and stockings. The ladies liked me, he said, and I must be on my best behavior.

21 The next day I was let out of school an hour early, and went home to be stood up in a tub full of suds and be scrubbed and have my ears dug into. My sandy hair sported a red ribbon to match my red and white checked gingham dress, starched until it could stand alone. Mama saw to it that my shoes were on the right feet, since I was careless about left and right. Last thing, I was given a handkerchief to carry, warned again about my behavior, and sent off, with my big brother John to go as far as the hotel gate with me.

22 First thing, the ladies gave me strange things, like stuffed dates and preserved ginger, and encouraged me to eat all that I wanted. Then they showed me their Japanese dolls and just talked. I was then handed a copy of *Scribner's Magazine*,[10] and asked to read a place that was pointed out to me. After a paragraph or two, I was told with smiles, that that would do.

23 I was led out on the grounds and they took my picture under a palm tree. They handed me what was to me then a heavy cylinder done up in fancy paper, tied with a ribbon, and they told me goodbye, asking me not to open it until I got home.

24 My brother was waiting for me down by the lake, and we hurried home, eager to see what was in the thing. It was too heavy to be candy or anything like that. John insisted on toting it for me.

25 My mother made John give it back to me and let me open it. Perhaps, I shall never experience such joy again. The nearest thing to that moment was the telegram accepting my first book. One hundred goldy-new pennies rolled out of the cylinder. Their gleam lit up the world. It was not avarice[11] that moved me. It was the beauty of the thing. I stood on the mountain. Mama let me play with my pennies for a while, then put them away for me to keep.

26 That was only the beginning. The next day I received an Episcopal hymn-book bound in white leather with a golden cross stamped into the front cover, a copy of *The Swiss Family Robinson*, and a book of fairy tales.

27 I set about to commit the song words to memory. There was no music written there, just the words. But there was to my consciousness music in between them just the same. "When I Survey the Wondrous Cross" seemed the most beautiful to me, so I committed that to memory first of all. Some of them seemed dull and without life, and I pretended they were not there. If white people liked trashy singing like that, there must be something funny about them that I had not noticed before. I stuck to the pretty ones where the words marched to a throb I could feel.

28 A month or so after the young ladies returned to Minnesota, they sent me a huge box packed with clothes and books. The red coat with

10. ***Scribner's Magazine*** literary magazine, now no longer published.
11. **avarice** (AV uhr ihs) *n.* extreme desire for wealth; greed.

CLOSER LOOK

## Analyze Anecdotes

Circulate among groups as students conduct their close read. Suggest that groups read paragraph 25. Encourage them to talk about the annotations that they mark. If needed, provide the following support.

**ANNOTATE:** Have students mark details in the paragraph that describes how she felt about the coins, or work with small groups to have students participate while you highlight them together.

**QUESTION:** Guide students to consider what these details might tell them. Ask what a reader can infer from the author's reaction to the coins, and accept student responses.
**Possible response:** The author is joyful and thrilled with the beauty, not the value, of the coins.

**CONCLUDE:** Help students formulate conclusions about the importance of these details in the text. Ask students why the author might have included these details.
**Possible response:** The author probably never had anyone give her such a gift before. When she says she "stood on the mountain," she is describing how exhilarated she felt about receiving the coins. Using this anecdote evokes strong feelings in the reader. The author includes this story to help establish just how meaningful this event was in her life.

Remind students that autobiographies are filled with **anecdotes**, short personal accounts of real events. The anecdotes an author chooses to include can greatly influence the overall effect of the autobiography by evoking different emotions and responses in readers (e.g., sympathy, support, admiration, etc.).

Additional **English Language Support** is available in the Interactive Teacher's Edition.

PERSONALIZE FOR LEARNING

### English Language Support

**Summarize** Review paragraph 22 and have students write a brief summary of what happened when the author went to visit the women. Ask students to make inferences about how the author felt before, during, and after the visit based on what she says and what she did. Encourage students to use detailed sentences that contain a variety of verbs and adverbials (*seems that, indicates that, suggests, creates the impression that, and so on*). **ALL LEVELS**

NOTES

a wide circular collar and the red tam[12] pleased me more than any of the other things. My chums pretended not to like anything that I had, but even then I knew that they were jealous. Old Smarty had gotten by them again. The clothes were not new, but they were very good. I shone like the morning sun.

29 But the books gave me more pleasure than the clothes. I had never been too keen on dressing up. It called for hard scrubbings with Octagon soap suds getting in my eyes, and none too gentle fingers scrubbing my neck and gouging in my ears.

30 In that box were *Gulliver's Travels, Grimm's Fairy Tales, Dick Whittington, Greek and Roman Myths,* and best of all, *Norse Tales.* Why did the Norse tales strike so deeply into my soul? I do not know, but they did. I seemed to remember seeing Thor swing his mighty short-handled hammer as he sped across the sky in rumbling thunder, lightning flashing from the tread of his steeds and the wheels of his chariot. The great and good Odin, who went down to the well of knowledge to drink, and was told that the price of a drink from that fountain was an eye. Odin drank deeply, then plucked out one eye without a murmur and handed it to the grizzly keeper, and walked away. That held majesty for me.

31 Of the Greeks, Hercules moved me most. I followed him eagerly on his tasks. The story of the choice of Hercules as a boy when he met Pleasure and Duty, and put his hand in that of Duty and followed her steep way to the blue hills of fame and glory, which she pointed out at the end, moved me profoundly. I resolved to be like him. The tricks and turns of the other Gods and Goddesses left me cold. There were other thin books about this and that sweet and gentle little girl who gave up her heart to Christ and good works. Almost always they died from it, preaching as they passed. I was utterly indifferent to their deaths. In the first place I could not conceive of death, and in the next place they never had any funerals that amounted to a hill of beans, so I didn't care how soon they rolled up their big, soulful, blue eyes and kicked the bucket. They had no meat on their bones.

32 But I also met Hans Andersen and Robert Louis Stevenson. They seemed to know what I wanted to hear and said it in a way that tingled me. Just a little below these friends was Rudyard Kipling in his *Jungle Books.* I loved his talking snakes as much as I did the hero.

33 I came to start reading the Bible through my mother. She gave me a licking one afternoon for repeating something I had overheard a neighbor telling her. She locked me in her room after the whipping, and the Bible was the only thing in there for me to read. I happened to open to the place where David was doing some mighty smiting, and I got interested. David went here and he went there, and no matter where he went, he smote 'em hip and thigh. Then he sung songs to his harp awhile, and went out and smote some more. Not one time did David stop and preach about sins and other things. All

12. **tam** *n.* cap with a wide, round, flat top and sometimes a center pompom.





## PERSONALIZE FOR LEARNING

### Strategic Support

**Figurative Language** Call attention to the line at the end of paragraph 31, *They had no meat on their bones.* Tell students that here the meaning of this sentence is very different from its literal interpretation. The author is not talking about the actual amount of meat on the girls' bones, but is calling attention to the fact that the girls had no substance. Ask students to look for and annotate context clues in the paragraph that allow them to figure out the meaning of this sentence.

David wanted to know from God was who to kill and when. He took care of the other details himself. Never a quiet moment. I liked him a lot. So I read a great deal more in the Bible, hunting for some more active people like David. Except for the beautiful language of Luke and Paul, the New Testament still plays a poor second to the Old Testament for me. The Jews had a God who laid about Him when they needed Him. I could see no use waiting until Judgment Day to see a man who was just crying for a good killing, to be told to go and roast. My idea was to give him a good killing first, and then if he got roasted later on, so much the better. ❧

NOTES

## Comprehension Check

**Complete the following items after you finish your first read. Review and clarify details with your group.**

1. Why is young Zora Neale scolded by her grandmother?

2. At school, what detail in the visitors' physical appearance holds Zora's attention?

3. What is in the huge box that Mrs. Johnstone and Miss Hurd send Zora from Minnesota?

4. Which ancient Greek hero does Zora decide to emulate?

5. Why does Zora enjoy reading about David in the Bible?

6. **Notebook** Confirm your understanding of the text by writing a summary.

## RESEARCH

**Research to Clarify** Choose at least one unfamiliar detail from the text. Briefly research that detail. In what way does the information you learned shed light on an aspect of the autobiography?

**Research to Explore** Do research to learn how author Alice Walker brought the nearly forgotten writings of Zora Neale Hurston back into the mainstream of American literature. You may want to share what you discover with your group.





DIGITAL PERSPECTIVES

## Comprehension Check

**Possible responses**

1. Zora's grandmother scolds Zora for being too bold in greeting the white travelers who pass by the house.
2. The visitors' thin and whitish-pink hands hold Zora's attention.
3. Books of stories and used high-quality clothes fill the box.
4. She admires Hercules.
5. She admires the fact that David goes around "smiting" people as God commands him instead of preaching about sin.
6. Possible response: Zora recalls her childhood in a village in rural Florida in the early 1900s. A special memory focuses on the visit to her school by two white women from Minnesota. Impressed by Zora's reading aloud, the women invite her for a private meeting. A month after their departure, they send Zora a large box filled with clothes and books. Zora is thrilled to read Norse and Greek myths. She concludes her recollections with some impressions of reading the Bible, especially the Old Testament.

## Research

**Research to Clarify** If groups struggle to narrow their research topic, suggest they focus on one of the following aspects of the autobiography: Zora's description of school, the first encounter with the women from Minnesota, the private meeting with the women, the impression of books and myths she read.

**Research to Explore** Students should learn that Alice Walker was inspired by the writings of Zora Hurston. Walker visited Hurston's grave and fought to bring attention to her works, which were all but forgotten. Her novel, *The Color Purple*, picks up themes from Hurston's *Their Eyes Were Watching God.*

PERSONALIZE FOR LEARNING

### English Language Support

**Close Read** If group members struggle to comprehend the text during the first read, have them go back to the text and choose two or three paragraphs from *Dust Tracks on a Road*. Have students use a variety of detailed sentences to explain the ideas and insights in Hurston's autobiography, based on an additional close reading of the text. **BRIDGING**

## Jump Start

CLOSE READ Ask students to consider the following prompt: *Think about your early childhood. Do you think that the place where you grew up affected the way you think and act today?* As students discuss the prompt in their groups, have them consider the details of their childhood and how it might similar to and different from the childhood of the author.

## Close Read the Text

Model close reading as needed by using the Annotation Highlights in the Interactive Teacher's Edition.

Remind groups to use Accountable Talk in their discussions and to support one another as they complete the close read.

## Analyze the Text

**Possible responses:**

1. Paragraphs 1–5 suggest that Hurston grew up in a racially segregated society. Hurston's self-assurance leads her to disregard at least some of these expectations, causing her grandmother to become concerned.
2. Passages will vary by group.
3. Students may suggest that the social context in Hurston's recollections vividly evokes a past place and time.

## Concept Vocabulary

**Why These Words? Possible response:** The words relate to someone who is an extrovert.

### Practice

Possible responses:
Olivia was not shy and radiated *self-assurance.* Will hoped Sarah wouldn't think he was being *forward* when he offered her a ride home. The thieves' *brazenness* was hard to believe: When they robbed the bank in broad daylight, they left their business card on the branch manager's desk!

### Word Network

**Possible words:** *gatepost, village, North, Florida, lake*

## Word Study

For more support, see **Concept Vocabulary and Word Study.**

Possible responses:
*bank, track, station, label, level,* and *mission.*

MAKING MEANING

*from* DUST TRACKS ON A ROAD

## Close Read the Text

With your group, revisit sections of the text you marked during your first read. **Annotate** details that you notice. What **questions** do you have? What can you **conclude**?

TIP

GROUP DISCUSSION
Schedule enough time for each member of your group to actively participate without feeling rushed or pressured. Pauses and silences are a natural part of any discussion. These brief breaks allow people time to gather thoughts and evidence.

## Analyze the Text

CITE TEXTUAL EVIDENCE to support your answers.

Notebook Complete the activities.

1. **Review and Clarify** With your group, reread paragraphs 1–5. What do these paragraphs suggest about the place where Hurston grew up? How do these details reveal Hurston's purpose and point of view?
2. **Present and Discuss** Now, work with your group to share the passages from the selection that you found especially important. Take turns presenting your passages. Discuss what you noticed in the selection, what questions you asked, and what conclusions you reached.
3. **Essential Question:** ***What is the relationship between literature and place?*** What have you learned about literature and place from reading this autobiography? Discuss with your group.

LANGUAGE DEVELOPMENT

## Concept Vocabulary

self-assurance forward brazenness

**Why These Words?** The three concept vocabulary words from the text are related. With your group, determine what the words have in common. Write your ideas, and add another word that fits the category.

### Practice

Notebook Imagine a person who could be described using these words. Then, write sentences that explain how that person embodies the characteristics these words indicate.

WORD NETWORK
Add words related to a sense of place from the text to your Word Network.

STANDARDS
Reading Informational Text
Determine an author's point of view or purpose in a text in which the rhetoric is particularly effective, analyzing how style and content contribute to the power, persuasiveness, or beauty of the text.
Language
• Determine or clarify the meaning of unknown and multiple-meaning words and phrases based on *grades 11–12 reading and content*, choosing flexibly from a range of strategies.
• Demonstrate understanding of figurative language, word relationships, and nuances in word meanings.

## Word Study

**Multiple-Meaning Words** Many words in English have more than one meaning. For example, the word *forward* can mean "at or toward the front," or it can mean "progressive" or "advanced." In the excerpt from Hurston' autobiography, it has a different meaning altogether. Find at least one other word in the text that has more than one meaning. Write the definition of the word as it is used in the text and any alternate definitions. Use a dictionary to confirm the word's multiple meanings.





### FORMATIVE ASSESSMENT

### Analyze the Text

**If** students struggle to close read the text, **then** provide the ***from* Dust Tracks on a Road: Text Questions** available online in the Interactive Teacher's Edition or Unit Resources. Answers and DOK levels are also available.

### Concept Vocabulary

**If** students struggle to identify the concept, **then** have students use context clues in the text to clarify word meaning.

### Word Study

**If** students fail to identify words with multiple meanings, **then** supply students with a list of words and suggest they use a dictionary or thesaurus to check multiple meanings of these words. For Reteach and Practice, see **Word Study: Multiple-Meaning Words (RP).**

## Analyze Craft and Structure

**Literary Nonfiction Autobiography** is a nonfiction narrative account of a writer's life told in his or her own words. Because of their personal content, autobiographies often reveal **social context**—the attitudes, customs, and beliefs of the culture in which the writer lived. Hurston's autobiography provides a glimpse into the social context of her African American community in rural Florida during the early twentieth century. Hurston brings additional life to her narrative by using a variety of literary elements, notably dialogue and dialect:

- **Dialogue**: the conversations among people
- **Dialect**: the form of a language spoken by people of a particular region or group—usually, dialect does not follow the conventional rules of standard English grammar or pronunciation.

Hurston's use of dialogue allows the people who were part of her early life to speak for themselves. Her use of dialect allows them to speak with authenticity. Both dialogue and dialect add nuance and depth to the reader's understanding of Hurston's experience.

### Practice

**CITE TEXTUAL EVIDENCE** to support your answers.

Work with your group to analyze Hurston's use of literary elements in this excerpt. Use the chart to capture your analysis.

| PASSAGE | LITERARY ELEMENT | WHAT THE ELEMENT REVEALS |
|---|---|---|
| Paragraph 3 | Social context | Grandmother, a former slave, adheres to a strict code for social behavior of the races. |
| Paragraph 4 | Dialogue, dialect | Dialogue enlivens the scene; dialect places the grandmother in a specific social context (time and place). |
| Paragraph 8 | Social context | School officials wish to make the best possible impression on visitors; hospitality is valued in the community. |
| Paragraph 12 | Social context | The delicate, elegant hands of the ladies suggest that their background differs greatly from that of the hard-working residents of the village. |
| Paragraph 18 | Dialogue | The woman is fooled by Zora's lie about loving school. |
| Paragraph 22 | Social context | Zora's encounter with strange foods suggest she grew up with different customs than the elegant ladies. |





DIGITAL PERSPECTIVES  

## Analyze Craft and Structure

**Literary Nonfiction** Discuss with students that the autobiographical work of an author shows the complexity of the author's character in context of the time and place. Authors develop their autobiographies to show how they change and develop over the course of their lives. For more support, see **Analyze Craft and Structure: Literary Nonfiction.**

See possible responses in chart on student page.

### FORMATIVE ASSESSMENT

### Analyze Craft and Structure

**If** students struggle to determine what social contexts reveal about the author, **then** revisit the key passages, reminding students that social context pertains to events that take place during a particular time and place in history. For Reteach and Practice, see **Analyze Craft and Structure: Literary Nonfiction (RP).**

### PERSONALIZE FOR LEARNING

**English Language Support**

**Write a Memoir** Challenge students to write a brief memoir of a specific event in their childhood using at least one example of dialogue or dialect. Memoirs should describe the event in an entertaining manner. Encourage students to share their memoirs by reading them aloud in their groups. Provide frames for support, as needed. **EMERGING**

Have students focus on using chronological order to organize their memoirs. Remind them that this means to tell the events in the order in which they happen. Review common transitions that will aid in organization (*When I was younger, Later, then, at that time*). **EXPANDING/BRIDGING**

# FACILITATING

## Author's Style

**Figurative Meanings** Point out that if Hurston had not used overstatement and idioms, her recollections would have been drier and more abstract, lacking the vividness and humor that figurative meanings give to her narrative. Provide the following examples from the text to reinforce overstatement and idioms:

- **Overstatement** *utterly indifferent to their deaths*
- **Idioms** *amounted to a hill of beans; kicked the bucket; no meat on their bones*

For more support, see **Author's Style: Figurative Meanings.**

### Read It

Possible responses:

1. a. played any tricks or acted foolishly
   b. from cover to cover
   c. I will soon be punished
2. Overstatement: "utterly indifferent to their deaths"; Possible responses: Idioms: "amounted to a hill of beans"; "rolled up their big, soulful eyes"; "kicked the bucket"; "had no meat on their bones"; She overstates her feelings to be humorous and to emphasize that she saw the girls as having little substance.

### Write It

**Possible responses:** Paragraphs will vary, but make sure that students can recognize overstatement and idioms in their own writing and the writing of classmates. Suggest that students do an Internet search of common English idioms to help them in their writing.

### FORMATIVE ASSESSMENT

### Conventions and Style

**If** students are unable to restate the idioms in their own words, **then** have them look for context clues in the text that will help them interpret the meaning. For Reteach and Practice, see **Author's Style: Figurative Meanings (RP).**

LANGUAGE DEVELOPMENT

from DUST TRACKS ON A ROAD

## Author's Style

**Figurative Meanings** One notable aspect of Hurston's writing style is her strong and often comic use of two types of figurative, or imaginative, language: overstatement and idioms.

- **Overstatement**, sometimes called **hyperbole**, is deliberate exaggeration for effect. For instance, Hurston writes in paragraph 7 that the students were "threatened with a prompt and bloody death" if they misbehaved while visitors were present at school. The deliberately exaggerated punishment adds humor and a mischievous spark to Hurston's recollection.
- **Idioms** are expressions that are peculiar to a given language, region, community, or class of people and that cannot be understood literally. For example, when Zora asks the travelers in paragraph 1 whether they want her to go a "piece of the way" with them, she means "go a short distance." She is not speaking about a literal piece or chunk of the road.

### Read It

1. Work individually to locate each of these idioms in the excerpt. Use context clues to define each idiom. Then, restate each idiom in your own words.
   a. cut one caper (paragraph 7)
   b. from lid to lid (paragraph 11)
   c. I'm going to catch it now (paragraph 15)
2. **Connect to Style** Reread this passage from paragraph 31 of the excerpt. Mark one example of overstatement and two idioms. Then, with your group, discuss the ways these literary elements add to Hurston's portrayal of her younger self.

> *I was utterly indifferent to their deaths. In the first place I could not conceive of death, and in the next place they never had any funerals that amounted to a hill of beans, so I didn't care how soon they rolled up their big, soulful, blue eyes and kicked the bucket. They had no meat on their bones.*

### Write It

Write a paragraph describing a gift that you gave or received. In your paragraph, use at least one idiom and one example of overstatement.

TIP

CLARIFICATION

Like slang words and phrases, idioms often change over time. When you read texts from different eras, you may come across expressions that are seldom used today. Figure out the meanings of such unfamiliar expressions by analyzing context clues.

STANDARDS

**Reading Informational Text**

- Determine the meaning of words and phrases as they are used in a text, including figurative, connotative, and technical meanings; analyze how an author uses and refines the meaning of a key term or terms over the course of a text.
- Determine an author's point of view or purpose in a text in which the rhetoric is particularly effective, analyzing how style and content contribute to the power, persuasiveness, or beauty of the text.

**Language**

Interpret figures of speech in context and analyze their role in the text.





## PERSONALIZE FOR LEARNING

### English Language Support

**Understanding Figurative Meanings** Display the following two sentences: 1) That cellphone costs an arm and a leg. 2) I'm so hungry I could eat a horse.

Have students identify which one is an overstatement and which one is an idiom. (1. Overstatement; 2. Idiom) **EMERGING**

Have students explain the figurative meaning of each of the sentences. **EXPANDING**

Have students come up with their own examples for an overstatement and an idiom. Then ask them to share with the class the meaning of each. **BRIDGING**

An expanded **English Language Support Lesson** on Figurative Meanings is available in the Interactive Teacher's Edition.

EFFECTIVE EXPRESSION

## Speaking and Listening

**Assignment**

As a group, prepare and deliver an **oral presentation** based on events in the excerpt from Hurston's autobiography. Choose one of these three options.

- ☐ **Compare-and-Contrast Discussion** As a group, discuss the similarities and differences between the way young Zora sees herself and the way others (travelers, her family, the visitors, her classmates) see her.
- ☐ **Informative Talk** Present an informative speech about Hurston's childhood, summarizing and reenacting (if appropriate) the key events of the excerpt from her point of view.
- ☐ **Interview** Stage an interview between the adult Hurston and a journalist. One team member will play the reporter and ask questions about Hurston's childhood and influences. Another member will portray Hurston and use details from the excerpt to provide complete and accurate responses. Work together as a team to write questions and answers.

**Project Plan** Use the chart to assign tasks for each group member. For example, if you choose the compare-and-contrast discussion, choose a leader to moderate the discussion. Then, work together to compile a list of people in Hurston's text. Divide these people among group members, and take notes about their portrayals in the excerpt—how does Hurston believe each person perceived her?

Oral presentation option: ____________________

| TASK | WHO IS RESPONSIBLE | NOTES |
|---|---|---|
| | | |
| | | |
| | | |
| | | |
| | | |

EVIDENCE LOG

Before moving on to a new selection, go to your Evidence Log and record what you learned from the excerpt from *Dust Tracks on a Road.*

STANDARDS

Speaking and Listening

Adapt speech to a variety of contexts and tasks, demonstrating a command of formal English when indicated or appropriate.





DIGITAL PERSPECTIVES

## Speaking and Listening

Encourage students to choose an option that plays to their groups' strengths. Students who are analytical might enjoy a compare-and-contrast discussion. Students who enjoy drama may best be suited to reenact key events from the excerpt. Students who are good at role-play would be good at playing the roles of a reporter and the author during an interview.

**Project Plan** Ensure that all group members have a role during the group's discussion. Students who choose *Informative Talk* may benefit by doing research to find out more about Hurston's life. Students who choose *Interview* may want one or two students to create a list of questions, while other students take on the roles of reporter or the author. For more support, see **Speaking and Listening: Oral Presentation.**

**Evidence Log** Support students in completing the Evidence Log. This paced activity will help prepare them for the Performance-Based Assessment at the end of the unit.

### FORMATIVE ASSESSMENT

### Speaking and Listening

**If** students struggle to organize a meaningful presentation, **then** suggest the group reevaluate its mode of presentation. However, caution them to make such a change early in order to allow enough time to complete the assignment. For Reteach and Practice, see **Speaking and Listening: Oral Presentation (RP).**

### Selection Test

Administer the "*from* Dust Tracks on the Road" Selection Test, which is available in both print and digital formats online in Assessments.

### PERSONALIZE FOR LEARNING

**Strategic Support**

**Observe an Interviewer** If students choose **Interview** for their presentation, you may wish to show a video of a famous reporter conducting an interview to give students a sense of the kinds of questions a reporter might ask.

# Chicago • Wilderness

**AUDIO SUMMARIES**
Audio summaries of "Chicago" and "Wilderness" are available in both English and Spanish in the Interactive Teacher's Edition or Unit Resources. Assigning these summaries prior to reading the selection may help students build additional background knowledge and set a context for their first read.

## Summary

In the poem "Chicago," by Carl Sandburg, the speaker lists many of the activities associated with the city—hog-butcher, toolmaker, wheat stacker, and player with railroads. He also describes the qualities associated with these jobs. The speaker then addresses the criticisms often hurled against the city—"wicked," "cruel," and "brutal." He agrees with these criticisms and others but then counters them with the qualities of the city he loves—proud, strong, cunning, alive, and laughing. In "Wilderness," the speaker describes the characteristics he has inherited from wild animals—a wolf, a fox, a hog, a fish, a baboon, and finally an eagle and a mockingbird. He then mentions that he has gotten something else—a man-child heart and a woman-child heart, suggesting that while he possesses the traits of the wilderness, he also embodies the characteristics of humanity.

### Insight

In each poem, Carl Sandburg explores the meaning of a place that is important to him. In "Chicago," he deals with a physical place, a city he loved and lauded in his first major collection of poetry entitled *Chicago Poems*. In "Wilderness," Sandburg deals with an abstract place—the wilderness—that he carries within himself.

ESSENTIAL QUESTION:
What is the relationship between literature and place?

## Connection to the Essential Question

These poems connect to the Essential Question, "What is the relationship between place and literature?" Students will note that these paired poems offer two different notions of the idea of place—external and internal, the place we live in and experience and the influences of place that we carry within ourselves.

SMALL-GROUP PERFORMANCE LEARNING TASK
Explain the sense of place created by the authors and artists in this section.

UNIT PERFORMANCE-BASED ASSESSMENT
What makes certain places live on in our memory?

## Connection to Performance Tasks

**Small-Group Learning Performance Task** In this Performance Task, students will consider the question of whether or not all the selections in this unit are inspired by childhood experiences with a particular place. Students will note that in both poems the experience of place is tied to a long-term, if not youthful, experience with the evolution of the idea.

**Unit Performance-Based Assessment** Students may wish to use quotations from these poems or discuss their themes when writing their explanatory essays about what makes certain places live on in our memories.

DIGITAL PERSPECTIVES

 Audio  Video  Document  Annotation Highlights  EL Highlights  Online Assessment

## LESSON RESOURCES

| | Making Meaning | Language Development |
|---|---|---|
| Lesson | **First Read**<br>**Close Read**<br>**Analyze the Text**<br>**Analyze Craft and Structure** | **Concept Vocabulary**<br>**Word Study**<br>**Author's Style** |
| Instructional Standards | **RL.10** By the end of grade 11, read and comprehend literature . . .<br>**RL.4** Determine the meaning of words and phrases . . .<br>**L.5.a** Interpret figures of speech . . .<br>**L.4** Determine or clarify the meaning of unknown and multiple-meaning words and phrases . . .<br>**L.4.a** Use context as a clue . . . | **L.4.b** Identify and correctly use patterns of word changes . . .<br>**RL.5** Analyze how an author's choices . . . |
| **STUDENT RESOURCES** | | |
| Available online in the Interactive Student Edition or Unit Resources | Selection Audio<br>First-Read Guide: Poetry<br>Close-Read Guide: Poetry | Word Network<br>Evidence Log |
| **TEACHER RESOURCES** | | |
| **Selection Resources**<br>Available online in the Interactive Teacher's Edition or Unit Resources | Audio Summaries<br>Annotation Highlights<br>EL Highlights<br>English Language Support Lesson: Poetic Structures<br>Poetry Collection: Text Questions<br>Analyze Craft and Structure: Language and Meaning | Concept Vocabulary and Word Study<br>Author's Style: Poetic Structures |
| **Reteach/Practice (RP)**<br>Available online in the Interactive Teacher's Edition or Unit Resources | Analyze Craft and Structure: Language and Meaning (RP) | Word Study: Present Participles (RP)<br>Author's Style: Poetic Structures (RP) |
| **Assessment**<br>Available online in Assessments | Selection Test | |
| **My Resources** | A Unit 4 Answer Key is available online and in the Interactive Teacher's Edition. | |

# Reading Support

| Text Complexity Rubric: Chicago • Wilderness | |
|---|---|
| **Quantitative Measures** | |
| **Lexile** NP; NP **Text Length** 37 lines; 33 lines | |
| **Qualitative Measures** | |
| Knowledge Demands<br>① ② **❸** ④ ⑤ | Background information on Sandburg and the two poems is provided. Poems contain references that may be unfamiliar, but most of the imagery is still accessible to the reader. |
| Structure<br>① ② **❸** ④ ⑤ | Both poems are written in free verse. "Chicago" has some repetition of phrases throughout, and repeats beginning refrain at the end; "Wilderness" has a repeated phrase starting each stanza. |
| Language Conventionality and Clarity<br>① ② **❸** ④ ⑤ | Both poems use images to appeal to the senses and develop meaning. |
| Levels of Meaning/Purpose<br>① ② ③ **❹** ⑤ | Both poems have more than one level of meaning and require the interpretation of figurative language and symbolism to determine meaning. |

DECIDE AND PLAN

## English Language Support

Provide English Learners with support for structure and language as they read the selection.

**Structure** Have students identify some of the repetitive phrases used in "Chicago." For example, tell them to look at lines starting with *And they tell me you are...* (lines 8–10). Have students find the words from the beginning of the poem repeated at the end, and ask them what was added to those words *(proud to be)*. For "Wilderness" ask them to identify the repeated phrases (There is a/an ______ in me… / The wilderness will not let it go). (stanza 4)

**Language** Ask students to work in pairs to list the verbs that are used in the two poems and to help each other with the meanings of any that they don't know.

## Strategic Support

Provide students with strategic support to ensure that they can successfully read the text.

**Knowledge Demands** Have students read the background information and discuss what they learned about Sandburg and each of the poems. Discuss some of the references in the poems, for example the first few lines of "Chicago." Discuss what some of those phrases tell us about Chicago as a city.

**Meaning** Encourage students to read through each poem to get a sense of its meaning before analyzing individual lines. After they have read the poems, look at each one stanza by stanza, and discuss the impressions students have and the meanings of particular parts of the poems.

## Challenge

Provide students who need to be challenged with ideas for how they can go beyond a simple interpretation of the text.

**Text Analysis** Have students read the poems to themselves and write notes about their reactions, telling which lines of the poems they found the most moving, dramatic, or interesting. Have students share these lines with the class and give their interpretation of the meanings.

**Written Response** Have students read other poems by Carl Sandburg. Have them choose one of the poems to write about, telling why they liked the poem or what they think it means. Then ask them to do a dramatic reading of one of the poems for the class.

TEACH

## Read and Respond

Have groups do their first read of the selection. Then have them complete their close read. Finally, work with them on the Making Meaning and Language Development activities.

# Standards Support Through Teaching and Learning Cycle

## IDENTIFY NEEDS

Analyze results of the Beginning-of-Year Assessment, focusing on the items relating to Unit 4. Also take into consideration student performance to this point and your observations of where particular students struggle.

## DECIDE AND PLAN

- If students have performed poorly on items matching these standards, then provide selection scaffolds before assigning them the on-level lesson provided in the Student Edition.
- If students have done well on the Beginning-of-Year Assessment, then challenge them to keep progressing and learning by giving them opportunities to practice the skills in depth.
- Use the Selection Resources listed on the Planning pages for "Chicago" and "Wilderness" to help students continually improve their ability to master the standards.

**Instructional Standards: "Chicago" and "Wilderness"**

| | Catching Up | This Year | Looking Forward |
|---|---|---|---|
| **Reading** | You may wish to administer the **Analyze Craft and Structure: Language and Meaning (RP)** worksheet to help students better understand poetic devices.<br>Review the **Author's Style: Poetic Structures (RP)** worksheet with students to better familiarize them with structuring techniques. | **RL.4** Determine the meaning of words and phrases as they are used in the text, including figurative and connotative meanings; analyze the impact of specific word choices on meaning and tone, including words with multiple meanings or language that is particularly fresh, engaging, or beautiful.<br>**RL.5** Analyze how an author's choices concerning how to structure specific parts of a text contribute to its overall structure and meaning as well as its aesthetic impact. | Have students identify uses of these poetic devices in other works they have read.<br>Challenge students to consider other ways of structuring poems. |
| **Language** | Review the **Word Study: Present Participles (RP)** worksheet to review present participles. | **L.4.b** Identify and correctly use patterns of word changes that indicate different meanings or parts of speech. | Have students find a present participle that functions as an adjective by modifying a noun or pronoun. |

## TEACH

Implement the planned lesson, and gather evidence of student learning.

## ANALYZE AND REVISE

- Analyze student work for evidence of student learning.
- Identify whether or not students have met the expectations in the standards.
- Identify implications for future instruction.

# FACILITATING

## Jump Start

FIRST READ *Are poets public figures, or do they lead solitary, reclusive lives? Do they inhabit the world, or do they create their own worlds to live in? Is a poem a shared secret, or a public statement?* Discuss these questions with students as preparation for their reading of these two poems.

## Concept Vocabulary

Have groups briefly discuss the three concept vocabulary words. Have they encountered any of the words before? Do they recognize the prefix, suffix, or base word of any of the concept vocabulary words?
Have groups consider the strategy of context clues and discuss its advantages and disadvantages.

## FIRST READ

Have students perform the steps of the first read independently:

NOTICE: Have students notice how the speaker identifies himself in each poem.

ANNOTATE: Remind students to mark passages that they do not understand or that contain particularly interesting images or details.

CONNECT: Have students make connections between the poems and their own sense of belonging to a community, and their sense of affinity with the animal kingdom.

RESPOND: Students will demonstrate their understanding of the text by answering questions and writing a summary.

Point out to students that they will perform the first three steps concurrently as they are doing their first read. They will complete the Respond step after they have finished the first read. You may wish to print copies of the **First-Read Guide: Poetry** for students to use.

MAKING MEANING

POETRY COLLECTION 1

## Comparing Text to Media

In this lesson, you will read and compare poetry by Carl Sandburg with the photo gallery "Sandburg's Chicago." First, you will complete the first-read and close-read activities for the poems.

SANDBURG'S CHICAGO

POETRY COLLECTION 1

# Chicago
# Wilderness

## Concept Vocabulary

As you perform your first read of "Chicago" and "Wilderness," you will encounter these words.

brawling wanton cunning

**Context Clues** If these words are unfamiliar to you, try using **context clues** to determine their meanings. There are various types of context clues that may help you as you read.

**Definition:** The king regarded his chief minister with a **sneer**, his scorn clearly apparent in the curl in his upper lip.

**Contrast of Ideas:** The coach praised her players after the game, even though she had **admonished** them beforehand.

Apply your knowledge of context clues and other vocabulary strategies to determine the meanings of unfamiliar words you encounter during your first read.

## First Read POETRY

Apply these strategies as you conduct your first read. You will have an opportunity to complete a close read after your first read.

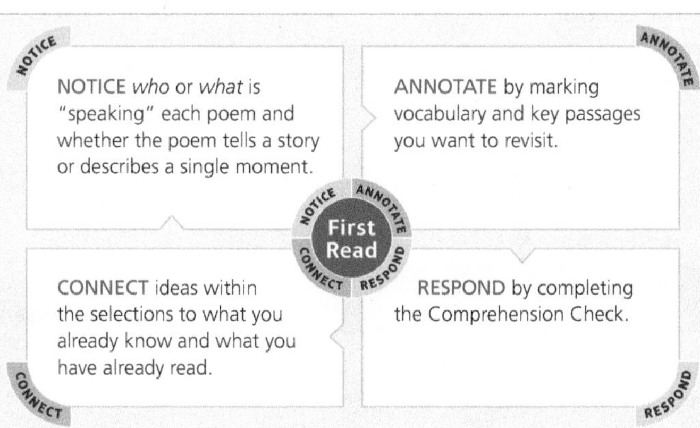

NOTICE
NOTICE *who* or *what* is "speaking" each poem and whether the poem tells a story or describes a single moment.
ANNOTATE
ANNOTATE by marking vocabulary and key passages you want to revisit.
First Read
CONNECT
CONNECT ideas within the selections to what you already know and what you have already read.
RESPOND
RESPOND by completing the Comprehension Check.


STANDARDS

**Reading Literature**
By the end of grade 11, read and comprehend literature, including stories, dramas, and poems, in the grades 11–CCR text complexity band proficiently, with scaffolding as needed at the high end of the range.

**Language**
- Determine or clarify the meaning of unknown and multiple-meaning words and phrases based on *grades 11–12 reading and content*, choosing flexibly from a range of strategies.
- Use context as a clue to the meaning of a word or phrase.





## VOCABULARY DEVELOPMENT

**Graphic Organizers** To explore prior knowledge and associations with the poems' two topics, have groups create two word webs with "Chicago" and "Wilderness" in the centers and record each group member's associations. Ask: *When you think of Chicago, what comes to mind? When you think of the word* wilderness, *what comes to mind?* Encourage students to include every image or idea that arises, both concrete and abstract, no matter how general or specific (e.g., Windy City, sports teams, Lake Michigan, pizza; forests, deserts, camping, hiking, national parks). Then have groups compare and contrast the results in their webs, discussing what themes are apparent in each grouping.

About the Poet

## Carl Sandburg

Carl Sandburg (1878–1967) was an optimist who believed in the power of ordinary people to fulfill their dreams. His poems were concrete and direct, capturing the energy and enthusiasm of industrial America. His vivid portraits of the working class made him one of the most popular poets of his day.

The son of Swedish immigrants, Sandburg left school after eighth grade to help support his family through work as a laborer. When he was nineteen, however, he set out to see the country, hitching rides on freight trains and taking odd jobs wherever he landed. He volunteered for military service during the Spanish-American War, though he did not fight. Later, he attended college for a brief period before hitting the road again.

**The Bard of Chicago** In 1912, Sandburg settled in the dynamic industrial city of Chicago. He worked as a newspaper reporter and began to publish his poetry in literary magazines. His first book, *Chicago Poems,* gained recognition for both Sandburg and Chicago. His second, *Cornhuskers,* won the Pulitzer Prize in 1918 and was followed by *Smoke and Steel* (1920) and *Slabs of the Sunburnt West* (1922).

While continuing to write poetry, Sandburg launched a career as a folksinger. His recitals included folk songs that he collected from cowboys, lumberjacks, factory workers, and hobos as he toured the country. His collection of this material, *The American Songbag,* appeared in 1927.

**Winning Awards** During his tours of the country, Sandburg also delivered lectures on Walt Whitman and Abraham Lincoln. His carefully researched, multivolume biography of Lincoln earned him a second Pulitzer Prize in 1940. In 1951, Sandburg received a third Pulitzer Prize for his *Complete Poems.* He was also awarded the United States Presidential Medal in 1964.

Sandburg offered a variety of definitions of poetry, among them these two: "Poetry is a search for syllables to shoot at the barriers of the unknown and the unknowable," and "Poetry is the opening and closing of a door, leaving those who look through to guess about what is seen during a moment."

## Backgrounds

### Chicago

This poem was published in *Poetry* magazine in 1914 and in book form in 1916. Sandburg described the poem as "a chant of defiance by Chicago" against other major cities in the United States and Europe.

### Wilderness

Sandburg's poem "Wilderness" is an example of a prose poem, a poetic work written in prose that uses poetic techniques, such as imagery and figurative language. Sandburg's poem is organized in seven stanzas, each of which develops a single main idea.





DIGITAL PERSPECTIVES 

## Chicago

## Wilderness

If you were to address the town or city you grew up in, what would you say? If you were to write a poem about the different parts of your own personality, how would you identify them? Modeling these and other questions readers might ask about poetry as self-expression will bring "Chicago" and "Wilderness" to life and connect them to the Performance Task question. Selection audio and print capability for the selection are available in the Interactive Teacher's Edition.

## FACILITATING SMALL-GROUP CLOSE READING: POETRY

**CLOSE READ: Comparing Poems by One Poet** Monitor groups as they conduct their close read. Offer support as needed.

- Remind readers that when they are presented with more than one poem by the same poet, they can practice their skills at interpreting a collection of poetry. Not only does each distinct text have meaning, but readers can also draw conclusions about the poet by finding similarities between or among the poems. Although "Chicago" and "Wilderness" look very different on their pages, Sandburg's speaker and voice are similar. Ask: *How are these two poems alike?*
- Suggest that students consider rhythm, voice, point of view, sound devices, diction, and themes. Based on their answers, invite students to make inferences about Sandburg as a poet.

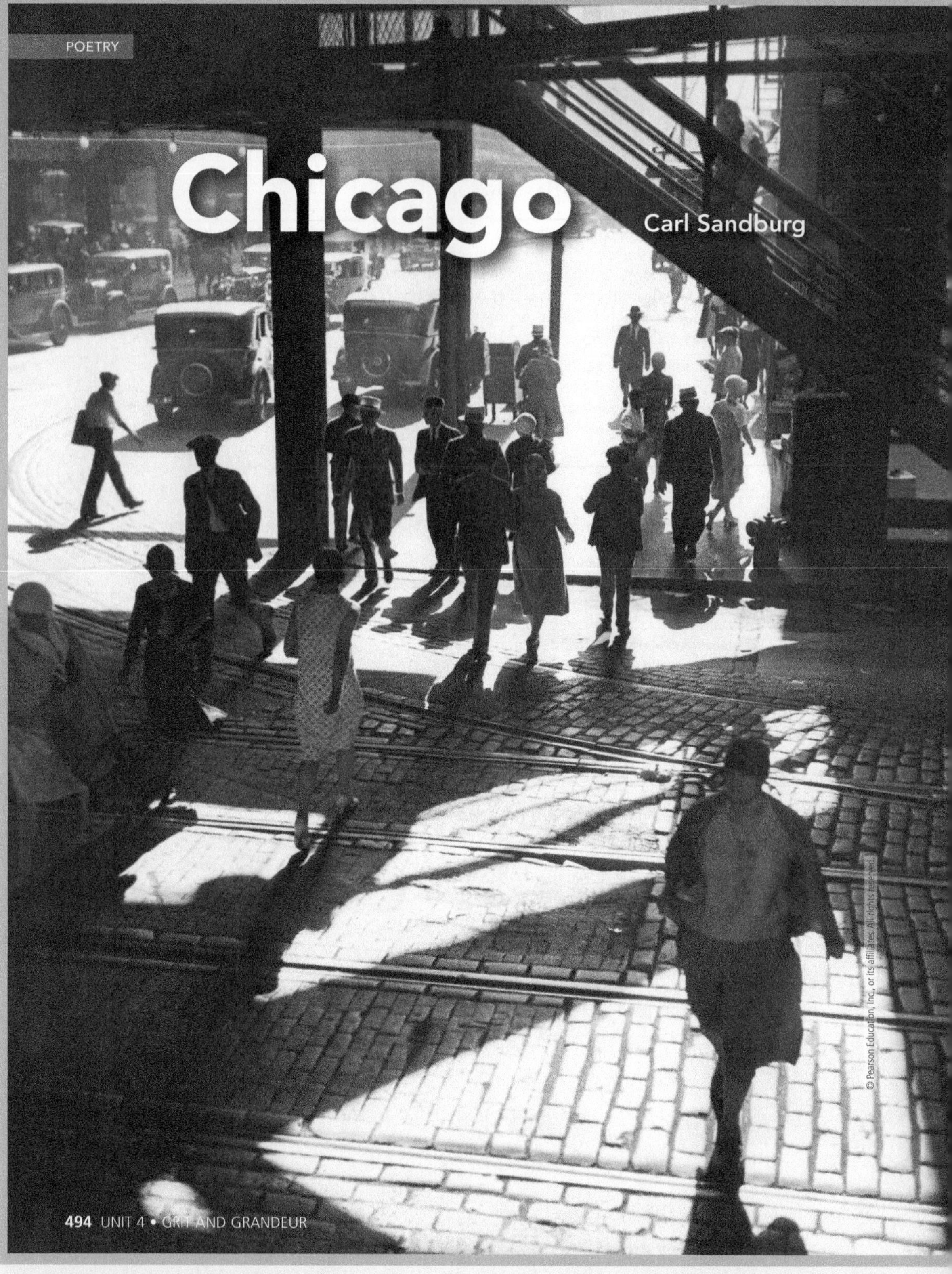


## WriteNow Express and Reflect

**Poems** Invite students to write poems about their own hometowns, cities, or neighborhoods, using "Chicago" as a model. Suggest that, like Sandburg, they should address the place as if it were a person and create a litany of names for it as he does in the first five lines. Encourage them to vary their line lengths and use capitalization liberally as Sandburg does. Offer opportunities for students to share their poems with each other, either in an open reading, an online class blog, or a printed anthology.

SCAN FOR MULTIMEDIA

Hog Butcher for the World,
Tool Maker, Stacker of Wheat,
Player with Railroads and the Nation's Freight Handler;
Stormy, husky, **brawling**,
City of the Big Shoulders:

They tell me you are wicked and I believe them, for I have seen
your painted women under the gas lamps luring the farm boys.
And they tell me you are crooked and I answer: Yes, it is true I
have seen the gunman kill and go free to kill again.
And they tell me you are brutal and my reply is: On the faces of
women and children I have seen the marks of **wanton** hunger.
And having answered so I turn once more to those who sneer at
this my city, and I give them back the sneer and say to them:
Come and show me another city with lifted head singing so proud
to be alive and coarse and strong and **cunning**.
Flinging magnetic curses amid the toil of piling job on job, here is
a tall bold slugger set vivid against the little soft cities;
Fierce as a dog with tongue lapping for action, cunning as a
savage pitted against the wilderness,
Bareheaded,
Shoveling,
Wrecking,
Planning,
Building, breaking, rebuilding,
Under the smoke, dust all over his mouth, laughing with
white teeth,
Under the terrible burden of destiny laughing as a young man
laughs,
Laughing even as an ignorant fighter laughs who has never lost
a battle,
Bragging and laughing that under his wrist is the pulse, and
under his ribs the heart of the people,
Laughing!
Laughing the stormy, husky, brawling laughter of Youth, half-
naked, sweating, proud to be a Hog Butcher, Tool Maker,
Stacker of Wheat, Player with Railroads and Freight Handler
to the Nation.

NOTES

Mark context clues or indicate another strategy you used that helped you determine meaning.

**brawling** (BRAWL ihng) *adj.*

MEANING:

**wanton** (WON tuhn) *adj.*

MEANING:

**cunning** (KUHN ihng) *adj.*

MEANING:





DIGITAL PERSPECTIVES

## Concept Vocabulary

**BRAWLING** If groups are struggling to define the word *brawling* as it is used in line 4, point out that "Stormy, husky" and "Big Shoulders" are context clues. Since the word is a present participle, they know that it describes the City by focusing on one of its many actions. Suggest that the first stanza depicts Chicago as a large man with many jobs, all of which demand physical labor and strength.

**Possible response:** *Brawling* means "quarreling or fighting noisily."

**WANTON** If groups are struggling to define the word *wanton* as it is used in line 8, point out that the context clue is the description of the look of hunger that the speaker sees on the faces of women and children in Chicago. It is also parallel to "brutal" in line 10, which is an additional context clue. Some students may know that *wanton* sometimes carries a sexual connotation, meaning "lascivious or promiscuous," (reflected in lines 6–7), but that is not its meaning here.

**Possible response:** *Wanton* means "unjust, undiscriminating, excessive, cruel"

**CUNNING** If groups are struggling to define the word *cunning* as it is used in line 10, point out that the clues are the other adjectives in the same line: *coarse* and *strong*. Another clue is the image of "lifted head singing so proud to be alive." The adjective clearly has a positive connotation, which is part of the speaker's defense of Chicago in answer to those who sneer at it in the previous stanza. Although cunning sometimes carries the negative meaning of "deceptive," that is not its meaning here.

**Possible response:** *Cunning* means "skilled, adept, intelligent."

Additional **English Language Support** is available in the Interactive Teacher's Edition.

CROSS-CURRICULAR PERSPECTIVES

**Art** Review lines 1–10 with students. Based on the myriad images in "Chicago," challenge students to create an illustration befitting the poem. Suggest that, like the poem, their illustration might use a ***collage*** technique that combines and assembles many different forms and images into one coherent whole. They can cut out photographs and images from magazines, newspapers, or online sources, and combine them with scraps or found objects to reflect lines, stanzas, and the whole expression. They may be interested to learn that the term *collage* was coined by Pablo Picasso in the beginning of the early 20th century, just about the same time Sandburg published this poem.

## CLOSER LOOK

### Analyzing Imagery

Circulate among groups as students begin their close read. Suggest that groups read the first two stanzas of the poem and mark the images that the poet uses. Encourage them to talk about the annotations that they mark. If needed, provide the following support.

**ANNOTATE:** Have students mark details in these first two stanzas that create images, or work with small groups to have students participate while you highlight them together. Remind them that images appeal to all five senses, not just sight.

**QUESTION:** Guide students to consider what these images might tell them. Ask what a reader can infer from what the speaker is saying about himself or herself through the use of these images, and accept student responses.

**Possible response:** The images in the first stanza are violent and aggressive, but also natural and wild. The images in the second stanza are also violent, but additionally they are cunning and deceptive.

**CONCLUDE:** Help students formulate conclusions about the importance of these images in the text. Ask students why the poet might have chosen to use this imagery.

**Possible response:** The poet wanted to begin his poem with drama and intensity. These images suggest the aggression of a wolf and the stealth of a fox.

Remind students that **imagery** is language that appeals to the senses: sight, hearing, touch, taste, or smell. In these two stanzas, Sandburg appeals to all five.

POETRY

# Wilderness

Carl Sandburg

SCAN FOR MULTIMEDIA

NOTES

1 There is a wolf in me . . . fangs pointed for tearing gashes . . . a red tongue for raw meat . . . and the hot lapping of blood—I keep this wolf because the wilderness gave it to me and the wilderness will not let it go.

2 There is a fox in me . . . a silver-gray fox . . . I sniff and guess . . . I pick things out of the wind and air . . . I nose in the dark night and take sleepers and eat them and hide the feathers . . . I circle and loop and double-cross.





## PERSONALIZE FOR LEARNING

### Strategic Support

**The Etymology of *Double-Cross*** Focus students' attention on the verb *double-cross* in line 8, which means "to cheat, betray, or deceive, especially by doing something different from what you say you will do." This is an idiom with a number of possible origins, each anecdotal. Challenge students to find at least two etymologies and share them with the group. (One is that a London bounty hunter kept a list of criminals; if they gave him useful information, he added a cross to their names; if they ceased to be of use, he added a second cross. Another is that it reflects the name of a British intelligence group in World War II who tricked German spies into defecting. A third is that it refers to the practice of swindling a horse race by first arranging for a horse to lose and then allowing the horse to win in a kind of double-dealing. Still another is that is refers to the expression "cross my heart" which means to tell the truth, so doing so twice may indicate a lie.)

DIGITAL PERSPECTIVES

NOTES

3 There is a hog in me . . . a snout and a belly . . . a machinery for eating and grunting . . . a machinery for sleeping satisfied in the sun—I got this too from the wilderness and the wilderness will not let it go.

4 There is a fish in me . . . I know I came from salt-blue water-gates . . . I scurried with shoals of herring . . . I blew waterspouts with porpoises . . . before land was . . . before the water went down . . . before Noah . . . before the first chapter of Genesis.[1]

5 There is a baboon in me . . . clambering-clawed . . . dog-faced . . . yawping a galoot's[2] hunger . . . hairy under the armpits . . . here are the hawk-eyed hankering men . . . here are the blonde and blue-eyed women . . . here they hide curled asleep waiting . . . ready to snarl and kill . . . ready to sing and give milk . . . waiting—I keep the baboon because the wilderness says so.

6 There is an eagle in me and a mockingbird . . . and the eagle flies among the Rocky Mountains of my dreams and fights among the Sierra crags of what I want . . . and the mockingbird warbles in the early forenoon before the dew is gone, warbles in the underbrush of my Chattanoogas of hope, gushes over the blue Ozark foothills of my wishes—And I got the eagle and the mockingbird from the wilderness.

7 O, I got a zoo, I got a menagerie, inside my ribs, under my bony head, under my red-valve heart—and I got something else: it is a man-child heart, a woman-child heart: it is a father and mother and lover: it came from God-Knows-Where: it is going to God-Knows-Where—For I am the keeper of the zoo: I say yes and no: I sing and kill and work: I am a pal of the world: I came from the wilderness.

1. **before Noah . . . Genesis** In Genesis, the first book of the Bible, Noah builds an ark to save himself, his family, and some of the world's animals from a terrible flood.
2. **galoot** *n.* uncivilized person.

MEDIA CONNECTION

Carl Sandburg Reads "Wilderness"

**Discuss It** How does hearing "Wilderness" read by its author affect your understanding of the poem? For example, does the reading seem to limit the ideas in the poem only to the person who wrote it, or does the reading add life to the poem?

Write your response before sharing your ideas.

SCAN FOR MULTIMEDIA 

## CLOSER LOOK

### Analyzing Repetition and Refrain

Circulate among groups as students begin their close read. Suggest that groups read stanzas 3 through 6 and mark the repetition. Encourage them to talk about the annotations that they mark. If needed, provide the following support.

**ANNOTATE:** Have students mark the repetition of words, phrases, or syntax in stanzas 3 through 6, or work with small groups to have students participate while you highlight them together.

**QUESTION:** Guide students to consider what this repetition might tell them. Ask what a reader can infer from the poet's use of repeated words, phrases, and constructions, and accept student responses.

**Possible response:** The various forms of repetition create rhythm as if the poem were the lyrics of a song that has a refrain. Repetition also serves to emphasize the most important images and ideas in the stanzas. It calls to mind the repetitive lives, actions and movements of the animals being described: hunting, eating, flying, swimming, waiting, singing.

**CONCLUDE:** Help students formulate conclusions about the importance of repetition in the poetry. Ask students why the poet might have chosen to use this technique.

**Possible response:** The poet wanted to reinforce the idea that life is cyclical, that we repeat actions day after day. He also wanted to make his poem sound like a song, or a machine that does the same thing again and again. He also wanted to question if we can keep our wild nature alive without—metaphorically—locking it up in a zoo.

Remind students that a **refrain** is a word, phrase, or line that is repeated at regular intervals throughout a poem or song. Reinforce the concept by showing students the lyrics of a song with an obvious refrain.

## PERSONALIZE FOR LEARNING

### English Language Support

**A Menagerie of Photographs** Review stanzas 1 and 2 and call attention to the structure of the poem. Each stanza identifies a different animal. Make sure that students know exactly what these eight animals look like by locating photographs online of each one in the habitat described in the poem: a wolf and fox in the woods, a hog on a farm, porpoises and herring in the sea, a baboon in a tree, an eagle and a mockingbird in flight. Also, make sure they understand the meaning of the word *menagerie* in line 28 ("a collection of many kind of animals kept for exhibition"). Ask: *Why is* menagerie *the perfect word to use in the last stanza?* Provide frames to support response. *Menagerie is the perfect word because _____. I think the poet uses the word menagerie because _____.* **ALL LEVELS**

FACILITATING

## Comprehension Check

Possible responses

Chicago

1. "They" tell the speaker that Chicago is a wicked, crooked, brutal city.
2. Chicago laughs like a person, "...dust all over his mouth, laughing with white teeth / Under the terrible burden of destiny laughing as a young man."
3. The city brags that the pulse of the people is under its wrist and that the heart of the people is under its ribs.

Wilderness

1. He got them from the wilderness.
2. The wilderness tells him to keep it.
3. He claims to be "a pal of the world" who "came from the wilderness."

## Research

**Research to Clarify If** groups struggle to come up with a research topic, **then** you may want to suggest that they focus on one of these topics from "Chicago": the Union Stockyards in Chicago, Chicago's history as a rail hub, or the Chicago Board of Trade. Suggest that they focus on one of these topics from "Wilderness": porpoises, Noah, Sierra crags, or the Ozark foothills.

**Research to Explore** If students want to explore a different avenue, then suggest that they can research facts about one of the animals named in "Wilderness," and the way it is personified in another famous work of literature.

## Comprehension Check

Complete the following items after you finish your first read. Review and clarify details with your group.

CHICAGO

**1.** In lines 6–8, what do "they" tell the speaker about Chicago?

**2.** According to the speaker, how does the city of Chicago laugh?

**3.** About what does the city of Chicago brag?

WILDERNESS

**1.** From where did the speaker get the wolf, the hog, the eagle, and the mockingbird?

**2.** Why does the speaker keep the baboon?

**3.** Who does the speaker claim to be in the last line of the poem?

## RESEARCH

**Research to Clarify** Choose at least one unfamiliar detail from one of the poems. Briefly research that detail. In what way does the information you learned shed light on an aspect of the poem?

**Research to Explore** Do research to find some facts about the city of Chicago in the early twentieth century. Be prepared to discuss how your findings reinforce what Sandburg expresses poetically. You also may want to use the information as you discuss "Sandburg's Chicago," the photo gallery in this lesson.





PERSONALIZE FOR LEARNING

### Strategic Support

**Jazz Fantasia** Challenge students to draw comparisons between these two poems and another famous poem by Sandburg titled "Jazz Fantasia," in which the poet explores the connection between the speaker and jazz musicians with a similar tone and theme. Like these poems, "Jazz Fantasia" is famous for its use of sound devices, rhythm, and repetition. Encourage students to find and listen to a recording of it online so that they can hear the devices used. Based on all three poems, invite students to write a sentence or two about how Sandburg is unique among American poets.

DIGITAL PERSPECTIVES

MAKING MEANING

## Close Read the Text

With your group, revisit sections of the text you marked during your first read. **Annotate** what you notice. What **questions** do you have? What can you **conclude**?

POETRY COLLECTION 1

## Analyze the Text

**CITE TEXTUAL EVIDENCE** to support your answers.

Notebook Complete the activities.

1. **Review and Clarify** With your group, reread lines 1–5 of "Chicago" and line 1 of "Wilderness." Compare and contrast the speakers in these poems, focusing on the images they use and on the values or characteristics suggested by these images.
2. **Present and Discuss** Now, work with your group to share passages from the poems that you found especially important. Take turns presenting your passages. Discuss what you noticed in the poems, what questions you asked, and what conclusions you reached.
3. **Essential Question:** ***What is the relationship between literature and place?*** What have you learned about literature and place from reading these poems?

TIP

GROUP DISCUSSION

The sounds of poetry often contribute to the meanings of lines and images. Read aloud striking or confusing passages before you begin to discuss them as a group.

LANGUAGE DEVELOPMENT

## Concept Vocabulary

brawling wanton cunning

**Why These Words?** The three concept vocabulary words from these texts are related. With your group, determine what the words have in common. Write your ideas, and add another word that fits the category.

**Practice**

Notebook Confirm your understanding of these words by writing synonyms and antonyms for them. Challenge yourself to come up with two synonyms and two antonyms for each. Then, trade lists with another group member. Discuss similarities and differences in your lists.

WORD NETWORK

Add words related to a sense of place from the text to your Word Network.

## Word Study

**Present Participle** A **present participle** is a verb form that ends in *-ing* and can function as an adjective, by modifying a noun or a pronoun. For instance, the speaker in "Chicago" uses the adjective *brawling*, the present participle of the verb *brawl*, to describe the city.

Find three other examples of present participles in lines 12–23 of "Chicago," and list them by line number. Then, form three present participles of your own from verbs of your choice.

STANDARDS

**Language**

Identify and correctly use patterns of word changes that indicate different meanings or parts of speech.





## Jump Start

FIRST READ Ask groups to consider the following prompts: *What is gritty about each of these poems by Carl Sandburg? What grandeur does each poem evoke?* As students discuss in their groups, ask them to cite specific examples of both grit and grandeur as evidence to support their general ideas.

### Close Read the Text

Model close reading as needed by using the Annotation Highlights in the Interactive Teacher's Edition.

Remind groups to use Accountable Talk in their discussions and to support one another as they complete the close read.

### Analyze the Text

**Possible responses:**

1. In "Chicago," the speaker uses graphic, vivid images that evoke strength and vigorously productive activity. In "Wilderness," the speaker's images evoke aggression, violence, predation, freedom from restraint, and instinctive behavior.
2. Passages will vary by group.
3. Responses will vary.

### Concept Vocabulary

**Why These Words? Possible response:** The words describe features or qualities of people or animals that also describe the city, and they make the city have a personality. Other possible words in this category: *thunderous, ostentatious, overfull, diverse, ambitious*

### Practice

Possible responses: *brawling* (paragraph 4): synonyms - wrangling, feuding, fighting; antonyms - agreeable, harmonious, peaceful. *wanton* (paragraph 11): synonyms - wayward, cruel, unkind; antonyms - kind, decent, pleasant. *cunning* (paragraph 14): synonyms - streetwise, sharp, intelligent; antonyms - ignorant, naive, dull

### Word Network

**Possible words:** *railroads, rebuilding, smoke, freight; wilderness, dew, underbrush, crags*

### Word Study

For more support, see **Concept Vocabulary and Word Study.**

**Possible responses:** flinging (16), lapping (18), shoveling (21), wrecking (22), planning (23), building (24), breaking (24), rebuilding (24), laughing (25, 27, 29, 31, 33, 34), bragging (31), sweating (35) Other adjectives: *gasping, swimming, coughing, smiling*

**FORMATIVE ASSESSMENT**

### Analyze the Text

**If** students struggle to close read the text, **then** provide the **Poetry Collection 1: Text Questions** available online in the Interactive Teacher's Edition or Unit Resources. Answers and DOK levels are also available.

### Concept Vocabulary

**If** students fail to see the connection among the words, **then** have them words in sentences and consider similarities.

### Word Study

**If** students struggle to to identify additional examples from the selection, **then** have them scan the text for words ending in *-ing.*

For Reteach and Practice, see **Word Study: Present Participles (RP).**

FACILITATING

## Analyze Craft and Structure

**Language and Meaning** Offer students examples of two more types of figurative language that Sandburg uses, both of which are sound devices:

- **Onomatopoeia** is the use of words that imitate sounds. Examples: *yawping* ("Wilderness," line 17), *snarl* ("Wilderness," line 20), *warbles* ("Wilderness," lines 24–25)
- **Alliteration** is the repetition of initial consonant sounds to achieve an effect. Example: sleeping satisfied in the sun ("Wilderness,"v line 10)

For more support, see **Analyze Craft and Structure: Language and Meaning.**

### Practice

Possible responses:

1. Vivid images in these lines include "silver-gray fox," "I sniff," "I pick things out of the wind," "I nose in the dark night," "hide the feathers," and "circle and loop and double-cross." The images are effective because they show powerful animalistic instincts.
2. (a) "And they tell me" repeats words used in the lines above. (b) The effect is to call for a powerful response on the speaker's part.
3. "You" stands for the city of Chicago. The speaker addresses the city's critics.
4. See possible responses in chart on student page.

### FORMATIVE ASSESSMENT

### Author's Style

**If** students are not able to understand the relationship between language and meaning in the poems, **then** have them listen as you read examples aloud, verbally exaggerating the devices used. For Reteach and Practice, see **Analyze Craft and Structure: Language and Meaning (RP).**

MAKING MEANING

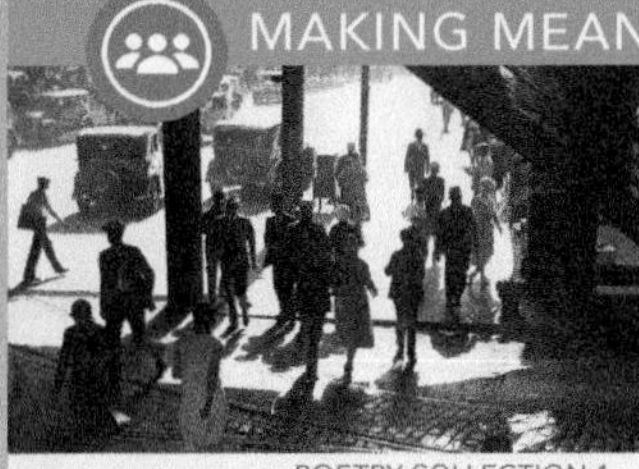

POETRY COLLECTION 1

## Analyze Craft and Structure

**Language and Meaning** Poets use figurative language and other devices to break through the usual ways of seeing and describing the world. In "Chicago" and "Wilderness," Sandburg's notable devices include imagery, repetition, and personification.

- **Imagery** is descriptive or figurative language that appeals to the senses of sight, hearing, touch, taste, or smell. For example, the line "white petals on a rain-wet branch" is a concrete visual image.
- **Repetition** of words and phrases emphasizes important ideas, adds emotional intensity, and creates a musical quality. In "Wilderness," six of the seven lines begin with "There is . . . in me."
- **Personification** is a figure of speech in which a nonhuman subject is given human qualities. In "Chicago," the city is personified as a strong young man. In "Wilderness," personification takes a different form. In a reversal of the usual pattern, human attributes and emotions are given animal qualities.

### Practice

CITE TEXTUAL EVIDENCE to support your answers.

**Notebook** Work individually to answer these questions. Then, share and discuss your responses with your group.

1. In stanza 2 of "Wilderness," what imagery makes the description of the fox especially vivid? Explain.
2. (a) Identify the repeated elements in lines 6–8 of "Chicago." (b) What is the effect of this repetition?
3. **Apostrophe** is a figure of speech in which a speaker directly addresses a thing, concept, or person who is dead or absent. (a) In "Chicago," who or what is meant by "you" in lines 6–8? (b) Whom does the speaker address in line 10?
4. Use this chart to analyze instances of imagery, repetition, and personification in Sandburg's poems. Record two examples of each. Then, discuss the effect of each example with your group.

| DEVICE | CHICAGO | WILDERNESS |
|---|---|---|
| Imagery | hog butcher, tool maker, wheat stacker, freight handler, big shoulders | fangs pointed for tearing gashes, red tongue for raw meat, a snout and a belly, salt-blue water-gates |
| Repetition | lines (1-5, 35-37); words and structures (6-11); parallel construction (18-19, 25-28) | words and structure (lines 1, 5, 9, 12, 16, 22); parallel construction (lines 5-8) |
| Personification | personification of Chicago in lines 1–5, 20–24, 25–30, and 31–37 | reverse personification in lines 1–27 |

STANDARDS

Reading Literature

- Determine the meaning of words and phrases as they are used in the text, including figurative and connotative meanings; analyze the impact of specific word choices on meaning and tone, including words with multiple meanings or language that is particularly fresh, engaging, or beautiful.
- Analyze how an author's choices concerning how to structure specific parts of a text contribute to its overall structure and meaning as well as its aesthetic impact.

Language

Interpret figures of speech in context and analyze their role in the text.





PERSONALIZE FOR LEARNING

### English Language Support

**Determine the Meaning of Words and Phrases** Ask pairs of students to indicate two denigrating or stereotyping expressions about Chicago in Sandburg's poem. **EMERGING**

Ask students to indicate the use of denigrating or stereotyping expressions in "Chicago" and their impact on the poem's general tone. **EXPANDING**

Ask students to write a paragraph explaining how the poet turns denigrating and stereotyping expressions about Chicago into a positive portrait of the city. **BRIDGING**

An expanded **English Language Support Lesson** on Poetic Structures is available in the Interactive Teacher's Edition.

LANGUAGE DEVELOPMENT

## Author's Style

**Poetic Structures** In "Chicago" and "Wilderness," Carl Sandburg uses two structures to create striking and powerful rhythms.

- **Line Lengths:** The individual lines of a poem may be long or short, and of the same or different lengths. They may be grouped into stanzas that look uniform and compact, or they may be strung out across the page. In "Chicago," Sandburg employs highly varied line lengths that are grouped in many different ways. Some lines contain a single word, whereas others include more than a dozen words. This dramatic variety reflects and reinforces the poet's portrayal of the city—Chicago is not a place that can be contained in the neat squares of equal line lengths and compact stanzas.
- **Ellipsis:** Ellipsis is the intentional omission of words or phrases signaled by a series of points ( . . . ). In line 1 of "Wilderness," for example, the first three images are set off by ellipses. The effect is to invite the reader to consider each surprising image and use his or her imagination to fill in the missing ideas.

### Read It

1. Reread lines 13–22 of "Chicago." With your group, discuss the effects Sandburg achieves by varying the line lengths in this passage.
2. In stanza 4 of "Wilderness," what does the speaker's use of ellipsis suggest about human identity, memory, and history? Discuss with your group.
3. **Connect to Style** What is the overall effect of Sandburg's use of varied line lengths and ellipses in these poems? Support your answer with examples from the texts.

### Write It

Write a short poem about a wild person, animal, or place. Vary your line lengths to create a specific tone or mood. Use at least one instance of ellipsis to draw attention to a particularly vivid detail or encourage your reader to consider missing information.

TIP

CLARIFICATION

Poets use line length to create a specific mood or feeling. A series of choppy or uneven lines may create a hectic or uneasy feeling. On the other hand, a series of equal lines can create a sense of stability and order.

EVIDENCE LOG

Before moving on to a new selection, go to your Evidence Log and record what you've learned from "The Poetry of Carl Sandburg."





HOW LANGUAGE WORKS

**Dependent Clauses** Call students' attention to two other poetic structures that Sandburg uses in these poems. In "Chicago," he capitalizes noun phrases that are not normally capitalized in lines 1–5, 20–24, and 35–37. In "Wilderness," he uses dashes before clauses that begin with "I" (sometimes with a conjunction) in lines 2, 10, 20, 27, 29, and 31. Ask: *What meaning or effect do these structures create?* **Possible responses:** In "Chicago," the capital letters further support the idea that the city is a person with a proper name, and in the middle of the poem, these actions are each their own line of poetry. In "Wilderness," the dashes signal a shift in the stanza from the animal to the speaker.

DIGITAL  PERSPECTIVES

## Author's Style

**Poetic Structures** Suggest that both poems also use another poetic structure called **enjambment,** that is, a technique in which the lines of poetry do not end with terminal punctuation or even with the end of a phrase or clause. The lines meet the right margin of the page and keep going without the usual line-end we associate with poetry. Ask: *What effect does enjambment have on both the meaning and the sound of the poem?* Encourage students to appreciate the momentum created by enjambment, a kind of breathless quality that reflects both subjects: a mechanized vibrant city that never stops moving and also the movement of the various animals in their habitats. For more support, see **Author's Style: Poetic Structures.**

### Read It

Possible responses:

1. By varying the line lengths, Sandburg creates an unpredictable, catchy rhythm in the passage—perhaps parallel to syncopated rhythm in jazz.
2. The use of ellipses suggests a sense of traveling through time—through history and even prehistory.
3. Sandburg's use of these devices piques readers' interest and keeps them off-balance, perhaps enhancing their receptiveness to the untraditional thematic messages of the poems.

### Write It

**Possible response:** Responses will vary by group, but make sure that students include at least one example each of a short and long line and one instance of ellipsis.

**Evidence Log** Support students in completing their Evidence Log. This paced activity will help prepare them for the Performance-Based Assessment at the end of the unit.

### FORMATIVE ASSESSMENT

### Author's Style

**If** students are not able to understand how poetic structures, such as line length and ellipses, enhance meaning, **then** have them imagine the poems without them. Ask them: *How would the meaning or effect of the poems change without these conventions?* For Reteach and Practice, see **Author's Style: Poetic Structures (RP).**

### Selection Test

Administer the "Chicago" and "Wilderness" Selection Tests, which are available in both print and digital formats online in Assessments.

# Photo Gallery: Sandburg's Chicago

**AUDIO SUMMARIES**
Audio Summaries of "Sandburg's Chicago" are available online in both English and Spanish in the Interactive Teacher's Edition or Unit Resources. Assigning these summaries prior to reviewing the selection may help students build additional background knowledge and set a context for their first review.

## Summary

This photo gallery, "Sandburg's Chicago," includes five photographs of the city from the early twentieth century. Images related to the Chicago that Sandburg praises include trains, the thriving downtown commercial district, the police holding two criminals, the grain exchange, and an Italian immigrant family.

### Insight

These black and white photographs present Chicago at a moment in its history when it had reached its pinnacle as the second largest city in the United States and as the most important city in the nation's Midwest. It is portrayed as a thriving center of industry, commerce, and artists transportation and as a home to new immigrant groups that were pouring into the nation at the beginning of the twentieth century.

ESSENTIAL QUESTION:
What is the relationship between literature and place?

## Connection to the Essential Question

These photographs connect to the Essential Question, "What is the relationship between literature and place?" For this gallery, students must evaluate the unique focus of the photographer's perspective as each seeks to capture the city's unique people and moments.

SMALL-GROUP PERFORMANCE TASK
Explain the sense of place created by the authors and artists in this section.

UNIT PERFORMANCE-BASED ASSESSMENT
What makes certain places live on in our memory?

## Connection to Performance Tasks

**Small-Group Learning Performance Task** In this Performance Task, students will consider the question of whether or not all the selections in this section reflect a sense of place. Students will note that these photographs are deeply grounded in the city. They depict places related to industry, commerce, and other adult activities.

**Unit Performance-Based Assessment** Students may wish to use these or similar photographs as a source of inspiration when writing their explanatory essay, or as a source of support for points they make in their writing.

DIGITAL PERSPECTIVES

Audio

Video

Document

Annotation Highlights

EL Highlights

Online Assessment

## LESSON RESOURCES

| (MEDIA) Sandburg's Chicago | Making Meaning | Language Development | Effective Expression |
|---|---|---|---|
| Lesson | **First Review**<br>**Close Review**<br>**Analyze the Media** | **Media Vocabulary** | **Writing to Compare** |
| Instructional Standards | **RI.10** By the end of grade 11, read and comprehend literary nonfiction . . .<br>**L.6** Acquire and use accurately general academic and domain-specific words and phrases . . . | **L.6** Acquire and use accurately general academic and domain-specific words and phrases . . . | **RI.7** Integrate and evaluate multiple sources of information . . .<br>**SL.5** Make strategic use of digital media . . . |
| **STUDENT RESOURCES** | | | |
| Available online in the Interactive Student Edition or Unit Resources | First-Review Guide: Media-Art and Photography<br>Close-Review Guide: Media-Art and Photography | | Evidence Log |
| **TEACHER RESOURCES** | | | |
| **Selection Resources** Available online in the Interactive Teacher's Edition or Unit Resources | Audio Summaries<br>Sandburg's Chicago: Media Questions | Media Vocabulary | Writing to Compare: Multimedia Account |
| **Assessment** Available online in Assessments | Selection Test | | |
| **My Resources** | A Unit 4 Answer Key is available online and in the Interactive Teacher's Edition. | | |

## Media Complexity Rubric: Sandburg's Chicago

| Quantitative Measures | |
|---|---|
| Format and Length | 5 photos with captions |
| **Qualitative Measures** | |
| Knowledge Demands ① **2** ③ ④ ⑤ | References are made in the background and captions to the Sandburg poems that students have read. Information in captions is clearly explained. |
| Structure **1** ② ③ ④ ⑤ | Each photograph is accompanied by a separate caption, making it very easy to locate information. |
| Language Conventionality and Clarity ① **2** ③ ④ ⑤ | Language used in the captions is explicit and straightforward, corresponding to the images shown . |
| Levels of Meaning/Purpose ① **2** ③ ④ ⑤ | Captions clearly explain the images shown in the photographs, with no additional interpretation needed. |

# FACILITATING

## Jump Start

**FIRST REVIEW** Use this prompt to encourage a discussion in groups: *How might a black and white photograph be more powerful or effective than a color photograph?* As students share their thoughts, guide them to identify specific factors that influence their ideas.

## Sandburg's Chicago

If you were to photograph your neighborhood, town, city, what subjects would you choose? How far away from your subject would you stand to take the photographs? Modeling this and other questions readers might ask will bring "Sandburg's Chicago" to life and connect them to the Performance Task question. Selection audio and print capability for the selection are available in the Interactive Teacher's Edition.

## Media Vocabulary

Have groups briefly discuss the media vocabulary. Have they encountered these terms before? Encourage volunteers to read the definitions and notes about each word aloud as others listen.

### FIRST REVIEW

Have students perform the steps of the first review independently:

LOOK: Remind students to focus their attention on the subject of each photograph and where exactly each photographer was standing when the photograph was taken.

NOTE: Encourage students to note the most important images in each photograph and to read the captions to determine when and where it was taken.

CONNECT: Encourage students to connect the subject of the photographs with images that they have seen in their own experience or in other forms of art.

RESPOND: Students will demonstrate their understanding by answering questions and writing a description.

Point out to students that they will perform the first three steps concurrently as they are doing their first review. They will complete the Respond step after they have finished the first review. You may wish to print copies of the **First-Review Guide: Media: Art/Photography** for students to use.

MAKING MEANING

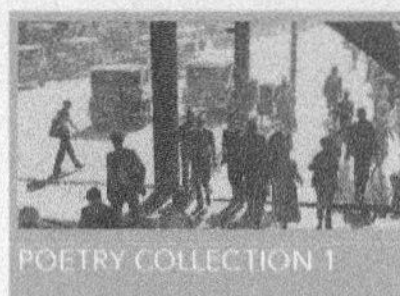
POETRY COLLECTION 1

### Comparing Text to Media

These photographs of Chicago were taken by various photographers. After studying the photo gallery, you will compare the ways in which poetry and photography can express ideas about the significance of place.

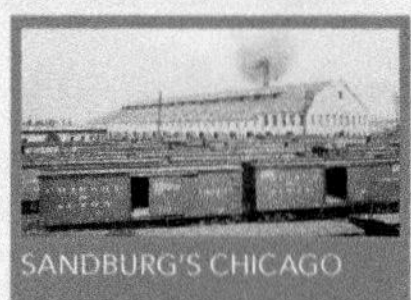
SANDBURG'S CHICAGO

## Sandburg's Chicago

### Media Vocabulary

These words will be useful to you as you analyze, discuss, and write about photography.

| | |
|---|---|
| **Focal Point:** center of activity or attention in a photograph | • The focal point of an image is typically linked to the photographer's main idea.<br>• The focal point is not necessarily in the middle of the image, or even in the foreground. |
| **Depth of Field:** distance between the closest and most distant objects that are in focus | • A very small area of focus is called a shallow depth of field; a very large one is called a deep depth of field.<br>• Analyzing the depth of field helps viewers understand what the subject of the photograph is and what the photographer wants to say about that subject. |
| **Foreground and Background:** closer objects are in the foreground, while more distant objects are in the background | • Foreground and background are usually determined by perspective, or a photographer's vantage point.<br>• Despite apparent differences in dimensions, foreground and background are often equally important in a photograph. |

### First Review MEDIA: ART AND PHOTOGRAPHY

Apply these strategies as you conduct your first review. You will have an opportunity to complete a close review after your first review.

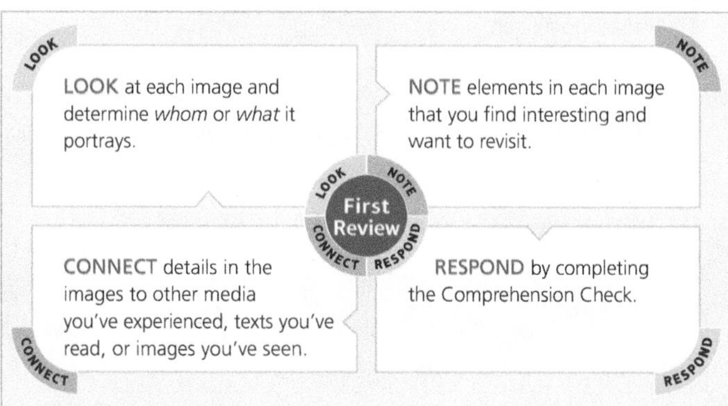

LOOK
NOTE
LOOK at each image and determine *whom* or *what* it portrays.
NOTE elements in each image that you find interesting and want to revisit.
First Review
CONNECT details in the images to other media you've experienced, texts you've read, or images you've seen.
RESPOND by completing the Comprehension Check.
CONNECT
RESPOND


**STANDARDS**

**Reading Informational Text**
By the end of grade 11, read and comprehend literary nonfiction in the grades 11–CCR text complexity band proficiently, with scaffolding as needed at the high end of the range.

**Language**
Acquire and use accurately general academic and domain-specific words and phrases, sufficient for reading, writing, speaking, and listening at the college and career readiness level; demonstrate independence in gathering vocabulary knowledge when considering a word or phrase important to comprehension or expression.





### VOCABULARY DEVELOPMENT

**Word Analysis** Remind students that the prefix *fore-*, as used in *foreground*, means "before," "front," or "superior to." Encourage them to create a word web with *fore-* in the center and list other words that include this prefix, such as *forehead, forecast, foretell, foreman, forefather, forearm, foreboding, foreclose, forefront, forego, foreknowledge, foremast, foreordain, foreplay, forerunner, foresee, foreshadow, foreshorten, foreside, foresight, forestall, foreskin, foreswear, foretell,* and *forethought.*

Have students choose three words that interest them, determine parts of speech and definitions, and write original sentences using the words.

# Sandburg's Chicago

BACKGROUND

As a hub for travel and trade, Chicago has been vital to America's culture and economy for more than a century. Between 1890 and 1982, Chicago was the second-largest city in the United States and came to be considered the prototypical American city.

SCAN FOR MULTIMEDIA 

**PHOTO 1: Chicago & Alton Railroad Shops at Bloomington, Illinois.** Circa 1904. As the primary rail hub of the United States, immense volumes of freight passed through Chicago from cities, such as Bloomington, all over the country. The third line of Sandburg's "Chicago"—"Player with Railroads and the Nation's Freight Handler"—echoes this fact.

NOTES





DIGITAL PERSPECTIVES  

CLOSER REVIEW

## Analyze Motifs in Photography Subject

Circulate among groups as students conduct their close review. Suggest that groups close review the Photo 1. Encourage them to talk about what they see. If needed, provide the following support.

**NOTE:** Have students note details in the photograph that repeat or appear more than once, or work with small groups to have students participate while you note them together.

**QUESTION:** Guide students to consider what these details might tell them. Ask what a viewer can infer from the repetition of images, and accept student responses.

**Possible response:** There is a lot of repetition in this photograph in both the foreground and the background: cars, labels, numbers, tracks, windows, openings, chimneys.

**CONCLUDE:** Help students to formulate conclusions about the importance of the repetition in the photograph. Ask students why the photographer might have included these details.

**Possible response:** The photographer may have wanted to show the immensity of volume of freight that passed through Chicago, how homogenous it was when it was shipped, and how the shipping happened endlessly, day after day. These motifs suggest that the same thing happens again and again in this place, many times over, day after day.

Remind students that a **motif** is a recurring element in a work of art. Motifs in a single work often appear as patterns or predictable arrangements.

## FACILITATING SMALL-GROUP CLOSE REVIEWING: Photo Gallery

**CLOSE REVIEW: Comparing and Contrasting Photographs** Support groups as they study these photographs. Share this information as needed.

- Suggest students consider each photograph in this collection singularly, noting details and using the media vocabulary as the basis for analysis and discussion.
- Encourage students to consider the five photographs as one "gallery," as if the photographs were all hanging in one physical space as a group. Students should look for the unifying subject that ties all the images together.
- When studying groups of photos, students should look for similarities and differences in the images. they should also look for the idea or message that the gallery conveys.

CLOSER REVIEW

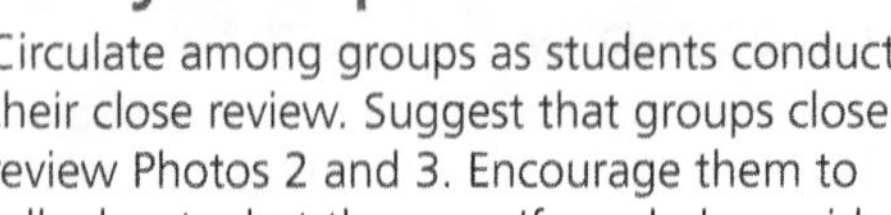

## Analyze Depth of Field

Circulate among groups as students conduct their close review. Suggest that groups close review Photos 2 and 3. Encourage them to talk about what they see. If needed, provide the following support.

**NOTE:** Have students note the difference in depth of field in the photographs, or work with small groups to have students participate while you note them together.

**QUESTION:** Guide students to consider what these details might tell them. Ask what a viewer can infer from the different depths of field in the two photographs, and accept student responses.

**Possible response:** Photo 2 has an extremely deep depth of field. There might be several blocks between what is in the foreground and what is in the background, and the city seems to vanish in a haze in the distance. Photo 3 has a shallower depth of field. There are only a few feet between the men in the foreground and the building in the background.

**CONCLUDE:** Help students to formulate conclusions about the importance of the depth of field in each photograph. Ask students why the photographer might have chosen each perspective.

**Possible response:** In Photo 2, the photographer may have wanted to show how busy and packed the streets were and how people, horses, trains, businesses, stores, and multi-storied buildings all functioned simultaneously, moving in all directions. In Photo 3, the photographer probably wanted to focus on an arrest and the small crowd of onlookers. It is a more intimate moment.

Remind students that **depth of field** allows the photographer to frame the image and may influence the message that that photography conveys.

**PHOTO 2: State St., Chicago, Illinois (N. from Adams): Noonday Crowds on a Thoroughfare 18 Miles Long.** Circa 1903. This picture shows bustling downtown Chicago at the turn of the twentieth century.

NOTES

**PHOTO 3: Police Holding Two Men Related to the Alexandro Murder Case.** Circa 1905. As Chicago's population grew, so did its reputation as a center for organized crime.

NOTES





## PERSONALIZE FOR LEARNING

### English Language Support

**Word Analysis** Focus students' attention on the word *thoroughfare* as it appears in the caption of Photo 1. Its denotation is "a passage or main road," but its connotation is that the road is very long, open, and busy. Explain that its meaning has nothing to do with the word *thorough* (meaning "complete and inclusive") but that the word came into usage before *thorough* had differentiated from *through*. Usually thoroughfares "go through" major urban areas, and we still use *fare* to mean "travel" or, as a noun, "the fee charged for public transportation." Invite students to write original sentences using the word *thoroughfare* and to add the word to their Word Network.
**ALL LEVELS**

**PHOTO 4: An Instantaneous Flash Picture of the Chicago Board of Trade in Session.** Circa 1900. The Chicago Board of Trade, organized in 1848, was the first grain futures exchange in the United States. A futures exchange is a contract to buy specific amounts of a commodity, such as grain or lumber, at a specific price for delivery at a future time.

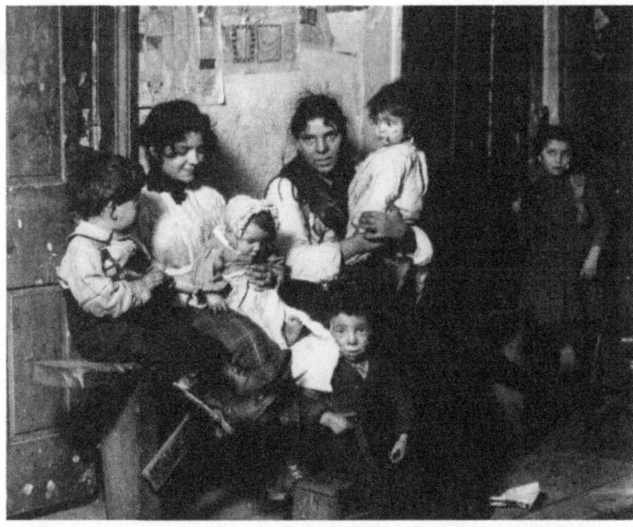

**PHOTO 5: Italian Family in Chicago Tenement.** Circa 1910. In the early twentieth century, Chicago became known for its large immigrant neighborhoods, many of which were densely packed and impoverished. The photographer, Lewis Wickes Hine, shot many photos of America's poor, and he is famous for his work to end child labor.

NOTES

DIGITAL PERSPECTIVES

CLOSE REVIEW

## Analyze Focal Points

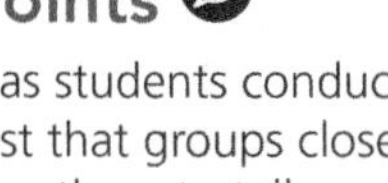

Circulate among groups as students conduct their close review. Suggest that groups close review Photo 5. Encourage them to talk about what they see. If needed, provide the following support.

**NOTE:** Have students note the center of attention in the photographs, acknowledging that different students may have differing ideas, or work with small groups to have students participate while you note them together.

**QUESTION:** Guide students to consider what these details might tell them. Ask what a viewer can infer from the choice of focal point of each photograph, and accept student responses.

**Possible response:** The focal point of Photo 5 may be the eyes of the father holding the child in the center of the frame. He seems to be looking straight at the viewer whereas everyone else is looking at someone else in the family.

**CONCLUDE:** Help students to formulate conclusions about the importance of these focal points in the photograph. Ask students why the photographer might have chosen them.

**Possible response:** In Photo 5, the photographer wants us to interact with one immigrant who is trying to provide for his family of seven.

Remind students that the focal point is the center of attention in a photograph.

Remind students that photographs can be cropped, or cut, to create **focal points.** Cropping involves not only choosing what a viewer will look at, but also choosing what a viewer will no longer see. The high resolution of digital photography allows photographers to crop closely, or zoom in on details, without sacrificing their definition.

## CROSS-CURRICULAR PERSPECTIVES

**Science and Art** Focus students' attention on the title of Photo 4 and the words "Instantaneous Flash Picture." Explain that early photography required long exposure times, so a scene like this one that involved much action would have been impossible to capture. The invention of the flash powder in the later 1800s allowed photographers to create artificial light that lasted in 2–3 seconds by burning magnesium. By the beginning of the twentieth century, flash technology was refined so that it was simpler, safer, and lasted for only 10 milliseconds. During the 1920s, the invention of flash bulbs made the process even safer. Encourage interested students to learn more about the history of flash photography and to analyze the lighting in the five photographs in this gallery.

# FACILITATING

## Comprehension Check

Possible responses

1. It shows the shipping by rail industry.
2. Buildings stand close together; people fill the sidewalks; and trolleys, horse-drawn carriages, and people crowd the street.
3. A crowd has gathered to watch a police action, perhaps an arrest.
4. The traders are in session on the floor of The Chicago Board of Trade. Wheat shares are being traded on a trading floor.
5. Photo 5 shows a family of Italian immigrants in Chicago. They live in a small space with five children with modest furnishings.
6. **Possible response**: These photographs give us a glimpse, or snapshot, of life in Chicago during the early twentieth century. They show that it was a center of business and transportation, but that it was also a place of crime and poverty.

## Comprehension Check

**Complete the following items after you finish your first review. Review and clarify details with your group.**

1. What type of business in the Chicago area does Photo 1 depict?

2. Which details in Photo 2 show that Chicago was a densely populated, busy place?

3. In Photo 3, what is happening? Why has a crowd gathered?

4. In Photo 4, what group is in session?

5. Who are the people in Photo 5, and what are their living conditions like?

6. **Notebook** Confirm your understanding of the photo gallery by writing a description of the settings, people, and events that the photographs portray.





### PERSONALIZE FOR LEARNING

**Challenge**

**Chicago Today** Challenge students to locate and share photographs of Chicago today that correspond to the five photographs in this gallery: trains, city streets, business, crime, and family. Have groups select five photographs that they consider the most dramatic or representative. Challenge students to choose photographs that use various depths of field and to write captions for each one. Give them an opportunity to display their "contemporary gallery" as a slideshow or on a print or digital bulletin board. Make sure they include titles, photographers' names, and dates in their captions.

MAKING MEANING

## Close Review

With your group, revisit the photographs and your first-review notes. Record any new observations that seem important. What **questions** do you have? What can you **conclude**?

SANDBURG'S CHICAGO

## Analyze the Media

CITE TEXTUAL EVIDENCE to support your answers.

**Complete the activities.**

1. **Present and Discuss** Choose the photograph you find most interesting or powerful. Share your choice with your group, and discuss why you chose it. Explain what you notice in the photograph, what questions it raises for you, and what conclusions you reach about it.
2. **Review and Synthesize** With your group, review all the photographs. Do they do more than simply present various aspects of a large American city? Explain.
3. Notebook **Essential Question:** ***What is the relationship between literature and place?*** Why might Carl Sandburg have felt that Chicago, with scenes like these, was a worthy topic for a poem? Refer to specific photographs in your response.

LANGUAGE DEVELOPMENT

## Media Vocabulary

focal point | depth of field | foreground and background

**Use the vocabulary words in your responses to the questions.**

1. In Photo 2, to what detail is your eye drawn first? Why? How does that detail influence the way you see the rest of the photograph?
2. On what area in Photo 4 does the photographer focus? What kind of mood or atmosphere does this focus create?
3. In Photo 5, how does the child on the far right affect your impressions of the photograph?

STANDARDS

**Language**

Acquire and use accurately general academic and domain-specific words and phrases, sufficient for reading, writing, speaking, and listening at the college and career readiness level; demonstrate independence in gathering vocabulary knowledge when considering a word or phrase important to comprehension or expression.





DIGITAL PERSPECTIVES

## Jump Start

CLOSE REVIEW Ask groups to consider the following questions: *What can a photograph show that a text cannot? What can a text provide that a photograph cannot?* As students discuss in their groups, have them cite specific examples from Sandburg's poem "Chicago" and the five photographs as evidence to support their ideas.

### Close Review

Model close reviewing by using the Close Review note. Remind students to look for elements and details they did not observe during their first review. You may wish to print copies of the **Close-Review Guide: Media Art/Photography** for students to use.

### Analyze the Media

**Possible responses:**

1. Responses will vary by group, but make sure that students include details that they notice, questions the photograph raises, and conclusions they reach about it.
2. Yes, the photographs do more than this. They may make viewers feel like they are in the city at a particular historical moment.
3. Carl Sandburg might have considered Chicago a worthy topic because it was like a huge animal: fierce, boisterous, busy, dramatic, dirty, gritty, grand, diverse, and wild. These photographs show these qualities. Students should refer to specific photographs to support their ideas.

### Media Vocabulary

For more support, see **Media Vocabulary.** 

**Possible responses:**

1. The focal point of the photograph may be the clock. Its prominence suggests that time is very important to people in the bustling city of Chicago. It makes me feel a sense of urgency that people in the photograph are rushing to get somewhere on time.
2. The distance between the photographer and the front half of the crowd makes up the photograph's depth of field. This focus helps create an atmosphere of noisy chatter that echoes in the large hall.
3. The child in the background of the photograph is looking at the group of people in the foreground. As a result, the viewer looks at the group through the child's eyes.

**FORMATIVE ASSESSMENT**

### Analyze the Media 

**If** students struggle to close review the photographs, **then** provide the **Sandburg's Chicago: Media Questions** available online in the Interactive Teacher's Edition or Unit Resources. Answers and DOK levels are also available.

### Media Vocabulary

**If** students struggle to apply the three terms to the historic photographs in this gallery, **then** have them practice using a contemporary photograph with which they are familiar.

# FACILITATING

## Writing to Compare

Remind students that each of these assignments will allow them the opportunity to combine objective facts with subjective opinions and emotional responses based on their reading and viewing. Encourage them to use additional outside resources such as historical essays, art and photographs, and personal writings and memoirs. Invite them to define their purpose, audience, and voice before beginning any of the three accounts. For more support, see **Writing to Compare: Multimedia Account.**

## Analyze the Texts

Explain that the key ideas should compare and contrast the two media and that the supporting details should support how the two are alike, and how they are different. For more support, see **Writing to Compare: Multimedia Account.**

**See possible responses in chart on student page.**

Students' responses to questions 1 and 2 will vary, but they should clearly delineate the differences in details that are revealed in each work.

EFFECTIVE EXPRESSION

POETRY COLLECTION 1

SANDBURG'S CHICAGO

STANDARDS

**Reading Informational Text**
Integrate and evaluate multiple sources of information presented in different media or formats as well as in words in order to address a question or solve a problem.

**Speaking and Listening**
Make strategic use of digital media in presentations to enhance understanding of findings, reasoning, and evidence and to add interest.

## Writing to Compare

Both "Chicago" by Carl Sandburg and the photo gallery "Sandburg's Chicago" provide information about early-twentieth-century Chicago. Now, analyze the texts and consider how the medium in which information is provided affects your understanding of the subject.

**Assignment**

Create a **multimedia presentation** about early-twentieth-century Chicago in which you weave together Sandburg's poem, images from the photo essay, and your own knowledge and ideas. Choose from these options:

- ☐ a **slide show** that presents the travel journal of someone visiting Chicago during the early twentieth century
- ☐ a plan for an informative **website** about early-twentieth-century Chicago
- ☐ a **museum exhibit guide** for a show featuring the photo essay

Either in your presentation or in a separate written text, explain how poetic words and photographic images bring early-twentieth-century Chicago to life for readers and viewers in different ways.

### Analyze the Texts

**Compare the Text and Photographs** With your group, identify ways in which the poem and the photo essay convey information. Use the chart to capture your observations.

| INFORMATION ABOUT CHICAGO | WHAT I LEARNED FROM "CHICAGO" | WHAT I LEARNED FROM "SANDBURG'S CHICAGO" | HOW TEXT COMPARES TO PHOTOGRAPHS |
|---|---|---|---|
| jobs and transportation | butchers, toolmakers, freight handlers, railroad workers | freight handers, railroad workers, businessmen, criminals, cops, | more white-collar jobs in photos, more poverty in photos |
| what the city is like | stormy, husky, brawling, wicked, crooked, fierce, laughing | bustling, full, impoverished, dusty | similar, text shows more dimensions |
| details about people | painted women, gunmen, workers, sluggers, fighters | travelers, police, criminals, businessmen, immigrants | similar, no white collar businessmen in poem |

**Notebook** Respond to these questions.

1. Do the photographs reveal dimensions of the city that the poem does not? Explain.
2. Does the poem conjure aspects of the city that the photographs do not? Explain.

## Planning and Prewriting

**Organize Tasks** Make a list of tasks you will need to complete in order to create your multimedia presentation. Assign the tasks to individual group members. You may add to or modify this list as needed.

**TASK LIST**

**Research and Choose Photographs:** Decide whether you need additional photos of Chicago. If you do, research and choose those images.

*Assigned to:* ______________________

**Research and Choose Texts:** Decide whether you need additional information about Chicago. If you do, research and select relevant information.

*Assigned to:* ______________________

**Write Text:** Identify all the parts of your presentation that need to be written. For example, you may need captions for photos, text for the different parts of the web site or museum guide, or travel journal entries.

*Assigned to:* ______________________

**Locate Other Media:** Find additional media—audio, video, or other visuals—to add interest and information. For example, you may want to include a map of Illinois or Chicago, recordings of portions of the poem, or voice-overs of travel journal entries.

*Assigned to:* ______________________

**Make a Rough Outline:** Set a sequence for your content as well as any special sections you want to include. You may always revise the sequence later as your project takes shape.

*Assigned to:* ______________________

## Drafting

**Inform Your Audience** As you assemble the pieces of your presentation, work to answer basic questions such as these:

- What was Chicago known for in the early twentieth century?
- Who lived there? Where did they come from? Why were they drawn to Chicago?
- What did they do there? How did they make a living?

**Include Comparisons of Texts to Photographs** Use your Prewriting notes to explain how poetic words and photographic images bring early-twentieth-century Chicago to life for readers and viewers in different ways. Do this in your presentation or in a short written text that accompanies it.

## Review, Revise, and Edit

Make sure all the images and other media you have chosen add value to the presentation. If necessary, cut content to make your presentation more focused and effective.

**EVIDENCE LOG**

Before moving on to a new selection, go to your Evidence Log and record what you learned from the poem "Chicago" and the photo graphic "Sandburg's Chicago."





**DIGITAL PERSPECTIVES**

### Planning and Prewriting

As students organize their groups, they may find that some tasks require more time than others. Encourage group members to be prepared to switch tasks as needed.

### Drafting

**Inform Your Audience** Suggest that students compile a list of facts about early twentieth-century Chicago that will supplement their audience's knowledge.

### Review, Revise, and Edit

Suggest that students focus images on those that are most striking and powerful.

**Evidence Log** Support students in completing their Evidence Log. This paced activity will help prepare them for the Performance-Based Assessment at the end of the unit.

### FORMATIVE ASSESSMENT

### Writing to Compare

**If** students are struggling to make comparisons, **then** have them use Venn diagrams to organize their thinking. Ask: *Which photograph(s) would most effectively illustrate the poem? Why?*

### Selection Test

Administer the "Sandburg's Chicago" Selection Test, which is available in both print and digital formats online in Assessments.

### CROSS-CURRICULAR PERSPECTIVES

**Music** Invite students to explore Chicago through yet another medium, music, by listening to Frank Sinatra's famous song "My Kind of Town," released in 1964, and finding the lyrics online. They will also likely be curious to learn more about Billy Sunday, the baseball player who became an evangelist in the early twentieth century, the mention of whom harkens to the time of Sandburg and the photographs. After students hear the song and study the lyrics, invite them to combine the three media (poem, photos, and music) into either an analytical paragraph that compares and contrasts or a new art form that creatively combines all three.

# In the Longhouse, Oneida Museum • Cloudy Day

**AUDIO SUMMARIES**
Audio Summaries of "In the Longhouse, Oneida Museum" and "Cloudy Day" are available online in both English and Spanish in the Interactive Teacher's Edition or Unit Resources. Assigning these summaries prior to reading the selection may help students build additional background knowledge and set a context for their first read.

## Summary

In Roberta Hill's poem "In the Longhouse, Oneida Museum," the speaker describes visiting an Iroquoian longhouse in a museum. She compares the peace and harmony she feels in the longhouse with the problems and poverty she felt in her childhood home. She became a wanderer, embracing her Native American heritage for strength.

The speaker in Jimmy Santiago Baca's poem "Cloudy Day" is in jail. He describes the fierce wind in the prison yard and the guard watching from the tower. The speaker then describes his arrest four years earlier and how his love for his beloved and himself sustains him.

### Insight

Both poets—Roberta Hill and Jimmy Santiago Baca—come from minority ethnic groups. Hill is a Native American and Baca is a Latino. Both poets express themselves as outsiders. In Hill's case, she views a historic break between her tribe, the Oneida people, from the larger Iroquois Confederacy, during the American Revolution. Although a member of the Latino community, in this poem Baca identifies himself as an outsider because of his prison experience.

ESSENTIAL QUESTION:
**What is the relationship between literature and place?**

## Connection to the Essential Question

These poems connect to the Essential Question, "What is the relationship between literature and place?" Both poets describe places that carry painful associations, but these places were important to their development as caring and creative people.

SMALL-GROUP PERFORMANCE TASK
**Explain the sense of place created by the authors and artists in this section.**

UNIT PERFORMANCE-BASED ASSESSMENT
**What makes certain places live on in our memory?**

## Connection to Performance Tasks

**Small-Group Learning Performance Task** In this Performance Task, students will consider the question of how the authors in this section created a sense of place. Students will note that in both these poems, the speakers are adults commenting on their sense of isolation. They use actual places to spark their reflections.

**Unit Performance-Based Assessment** Students may wish to use quotations from these poems or discuss their themes when writing explanatory essays about what makes certain places live on in our memories.

DIGITAL PERSPECTIVES

 Audio  Video  Document Annotation Highlights EL Highlights 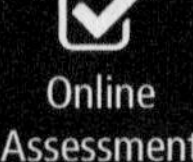 Online Assessment

## LESSON RESOURCES

| | Making Meaning | Language Development |
|---|---|---|
| Lesson | **First Read**<br>**Close Read**<br>**Analyze the Text**<br>**Analyze Craft and Structure** | **Concept Vocabulary**<br>**Word Study**<br>**Author's Style** |
| Instructional Standards | **RL.10** By the end of grade 11, read and comprehend literature . . .<br>**L.5** Demonstrate understanding of figurative language . . .<br>**L.4** Determine or clarify the meaning of unknown and multiple-meaning words and phrases . . .<br>**L.4.a** Use context as a clue . . . | **L.4.c** Consult general and specialized reference materials . . .<br>**RL.5** Analyze how an author's choices . . . |
| **STUDENT RESOURCES** | | |
| Available online in the Interactive Student Edition or Unit Resources | Selection Audio<br>First-Read Guide: Poetry<br>Close-Read Guide: Poetry | Word Network<br>Evidence Log |
| **TEACHER RESOURCES** | | |
| **Selection Resources** Available online in the Interactive Teacher's Edition or Unit Resources | Audio Summaries<br>Annotation Highlights<br>EL Highlights<br>English Language Support Lesson: Poetic Devices<br>Poetry Collection 2: Text Questions<br>Analyze Craft and Structure: Poetic Devices | Concept Vocabulary and Word Study<br>Author's Style: Poetic Conventions |
| **Reteach/Practice (RP)** Available online in the Interactive Teacher's Edition or Unit Resources | Analyze Craft and Structure: Poetic Devices (RP) | Word Study: Etymology (RP)<br>Author's Style: Poetic Conventions (RP) |
| **Assessment** Available online in Assessments | Selection Test | |
| **My Resources** | A Unit 4 Answer Key is available online and in the Interactive Teacher's Edition. | |

# Reading Support

| Text Complexity Rubric: Poems: In the Longhouse • Cloudy Day | |
|---|---|
| **Quantitative Measures** | |
| **Lexile:** NP; NP **Text Length:** 32 lines; 46 lines | |
| **Qualitative Measures** | |
| Knowledge Demands ①—②—③—❹—⑤ | Both poems are about situations and experiences that may be unfamiliar to readers. Prior knowledge is helpful about the Oneida ("Longhouse..") and about prison life ("Cloudy Day"). |
| Structure ①—②—❸—④—⑤ | "Longhouse…" is a poem in free verse with 8 stanzas of same length, but irregular meter; "Cloudy Day" is also in free verse, with no predictable meter and stanzas of varying length. |
| Language Conventionality and Clarity ①—②—③—❹—⑤ | "Longhouse.." has highly descriptive phrases and vocabulary and use of figurative language; "Cloudy Day" has a mix of concrete explicit language and also figurative phrases and descriptive vocabulary. |
| Levels of Meaning/Purpose ①—②—③—❹—⑤ | "Longhouse.." has multiple levels of meaning which are subtle and may be difficult to interpret; "Cloudy Day" has more concrete imagery that is easier to interpret. |

DECIDE AND PLAN

## English Language Support

Provide English Learners with support for knowledge demands and meaning as they read the selection.

**Knowledge Demands** Have students read the background information about the poets and the poems. Fill in any necessary information, for example, what a *longhouse* is or where the *Oneida* live.

**Meaning** Discuss the meaning of figurative phrases. Students may first need to understand what a phrase means literally in order to appreciate its figurative meaning. For example, in "Longhouse…", (lines 1–4) students may need to know that a furnace is a heater that sometimes makes rattling noises. The author is personifying the furnace by using *throat* and *wheezed*.

## Strategic Support

Provide students with strategic support to ensure that they can successfully read the text.

**Knowledge Demands** Before reading each of the poems, discuss the background information about the poet and the information about each poem. Discuss what students know about what a longhouse is and fill in information if needed. For "Cloudy Day," discuss that the poem deals with the author's experience in prison.

**Meaning** In a group, have volunteers take turns reading aloud stanzas of each poem. After reading the whole poem through once, have volunteers read it again. Discuss the impressions and feelings that students get from each part of the poem and what they think it means.

## Challenge

Provide students who need to be challenged with ideas for how they can go beyond a simple interpretation of the text.

**Text Analysis** Pair students and have each of them do a dramatic reading of one of the poems for their partner. Then have them discuss their impressions of each of the poems. After pairs practice the poems, invite volunteers to read the poem in front of a larger group. Ask them to share their interpretation of the poem.

**Written Response** Have students find and read other poems by the two authors. Ask them to write their impressions about one of the poems they read, describing what they liked about the poem and their interpretation of it.

TEACH

## Read and Respond

Have groups do their first read of the selection. Then have them complete their close read. Finally, work with them on the Making Meaning and Language Development activities.

# Standards Support Through Teaching and Learning Cycle

## IDENTIFY NEEDS

Analyze results of the Beginning-of-Year Assessment, focusing on the items relating to Unit 4. Also take into consideration student performance to this point and your observations of where particular students struggle.

## DECIDE AND PLAN

- If students have performed poorly on items matching these standards, then provide selection scaffolds before assigning them the on-level lesson provided in the Student Edition.
- If students have done well on the Beginning-of-Year Assessment, then challenge them to keep progressing and learning by giving them opportunities to practice the skills in depth.
- Use the Selection Resources listed on the Planning pages for "In the Longhouse, Oneida Museum" and "Cloudy Day" to help students continually improve their ability to master the standards.

**Instructional Standards: In the Longhouse, Oneida Museum • Cloudy Day**

| | Catching Up | This Year | Looking Forward |
|---|---|---|---|
| **Reading** | You may wish to administer the **Analyze Craft and Structure: Poetic Devices (RP)** worksheet to better familiarize students with these three techniques. | **RL.4** Demonstrate understanding of figurative language, word relationships, and nuances in word meanings. | Challenge students to identify uses of these poetic devices in works they have read in genres other than poetry. |
| **Language** | Review the **Author's Style: Poetic Conventions (RP)** worksheet to help students better understand traditional structural elements.<br><br>Review the **Word Study: Etymology (RP)** worksheet with students to further their understanding of etymology. | **RL.5** Analyze how an author's choices concerning how to structure specific parts of a text contribute to its overall structure and meaning as well as its aesthetic impact.<br><br>**L.4.c** Consult general and specialized reference materials, both print and digital, to find the pronunciation of a word or determine or clarify its precise meaning, its part of speech, its etymology, or its standard usage. | Challenge students to consider other ways of structuring poems.<br><br>Have students look up the etymologies of other words they are curious about. |

## ANALYZE AND REVISE

- Analyze student work for evidence of student learning.
- Identify whether or not students have met the expectations in the standards.
- Identify implications for future instruction.

## TEACH

Implement the planned lesson, and gather evidence of student learning.

# FACILITATING

## Jump Start

**FIRST READ** Ask: *Have you ever experienced a deep longing for someone or something you have lost? Have you ever felt isolated or alienated from others around you?* As students share their experiences, guide them to identify specific factors that influence their emotions.

## Concept Vocabulary

Have groups briefly discuss the three concept vocabulary words. Have they encountered any of the words before? Do they recognize the prefix, suffix, or base word of any of the concept vocabulary words?
Have groups consider the strategy of context clues and discuss its advantages and disadvantages.

## FIRST READ

Have students perform the steps of the first read independently:

NOTICE: Have students get a sense of the big idea of the poem.

ANNOTATE: Remind students to mark passages that they do not understand or that contain particularly poignant or intense images or details.

CONNECT: Have students compare the topics of each poem with other poems that they have read about longing and alienation.

RESPOND: Students will demonstrate their understanding of the text by answering questions.

Point out to students that they will perform the first three steps concurrently as they are doing their first read. They will complete the Respond step after they have finished the first read. You may wish to print copies of the **First-Read Guide: Poetry** for students to use.

MAKING MEANING

## Comparing Texts

In this lesson, you will compare two poems to an excerpt from a memoir. First, you will complete the first-read and close-read activities for the poems. The work you do with your group will help prepare you for the comparing task.

POETRY COLLECTION 2

# In the Longhouse, Oneida Museum

# Cloudy Day

### Concept Vocabulary

As you perform your first read, you will encounter these words.

strife    sinister    vigilant

**Context Clues** If these words are unfamiliar to you, try using **context clues**—words and phrases that appear nearby in the text—to help you determine their meanings.

**Example:** Luis is **gregarious**, unlike his shy and quiet brother.

**Conclusion:** The word *unlike* indicates that *shy* and *quiet* are in opposition to *gregarious*. *Gregarious* may mean "outgoing and talkative."

Apply your knowledge of context clues and other vocabulary strategies to determine the meanings of unfamiliar words you encounter during your first read.

### First Read POETRY

Apply these strategies as you conduct your first read. You will have an opportunity to complete a close read after your first read.

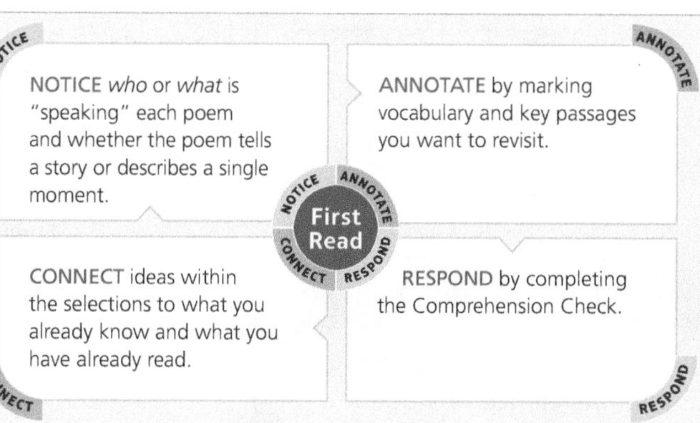

NOTICE *who* or *what* is "speaking" each poem and whether the poem tells a story or describes a single moment.
ANNOTATE by marking vocabulary and key passages you want to revisit.
CONNECT ideas within the selections to what you already know and what you have already read.
RESPOND by completing the Comprehension Check.
First Read
NOTICE
ANNOTATE
CONNECT
RESPOND


**STANDARDS**

**Reading Literature**
By the end of grade 11, read and comprehend literature, including stories, dramas, and poems, in the grades 11–CCR text complexity band proficiently, with scaffolding as needed at the high end of the range.

**Language**
- Determine or clarify the meaning of unknown and multiple-meaning words and phrases based on *grades 11–12 reading and content*, choosing flexibly from a range of strategies.
- Use context as a clue to the meaning of a word or phrase.

## About the Poets

**Roberta Hill** (b. 1947) was raised near Green Bay, Wisconsin, among the Oneida, one of the Iroquois nations. Her poetry often reflects feelings provoked by the legacy of forced migration and the dispossession of Oneida lands. The poems in her first collection, *Star Quilt* (1984), are organized according to six directions: north, south, east, west, skyward, and earthward.

In his poems, **Jimmy Santiago Baca** (b. 1952) celebrates the power of literature to change lives. Baca ran away from home at age 13 and then served a five-year prison sentence. While in jail, he learned to read and write, and discovered a deep passion for poetry. Following his literary heroes, the poets Pablo Neruda and Federico García Lorca, Baca devotes his life to writing and teaching. His workshops have helped many people improve their lives through writing and education.

## Backgrounds

### In the Longhouse, Oneida Museum

The Oneida Nation Museum in Green Bay, Wisconsin, presents displays and educational programming to help visitors understand Oneida and Iroquois history and culture. One of the museum's permanent exhibits shows a traditional Oneida longhouse, a large communal home constructed by covering a wooden frame with elm bark.

### Cloudy Day

Baca wrote this poem while serving time in a maximum-security prison. "Cloudy Day" was included in *Immigrants in Our Own Land* (1979), Baca's first collection of poetry, published the same year the poet was released from prison.





## In the Longhouse, Oneida Museum Cloudy Day

*Have you ever been in a place or a situation where you felt as if you did not belong? What did it feel like? What did you do?* Modeling these and other tough questions about alienation readers might ask will bring "In the Longhouse, Oneida Museum" and "Cloudy Day" to life and connect them to the Performance Task question. Selection audio and print capability for the selection are available in the Interactive Teacher's Edition.

## FACILITATING SMALL-GROUP LEARNING : Poetry

**CLOSE READ: Hearing the Poets' Voices**

- Monitor groups as they close read the poetry. Offer support as needed. The two poems students are about to read are intensely introspective and expressive. Invite volunteers to take turns reading aloud, stanza-by-stanza, so everyone can hear the words spoken. Hearing a variety of voices, both male and female, will lift these poems toward more universal meanings.
- Remind readers to read slowly so that listeners will hear every single syllable, and remind them to read through lines that do not end in punctuation.
- Either poem is suitable for choral reading. Encourage groups to read slowly, enunciate clearly, and savor every word.

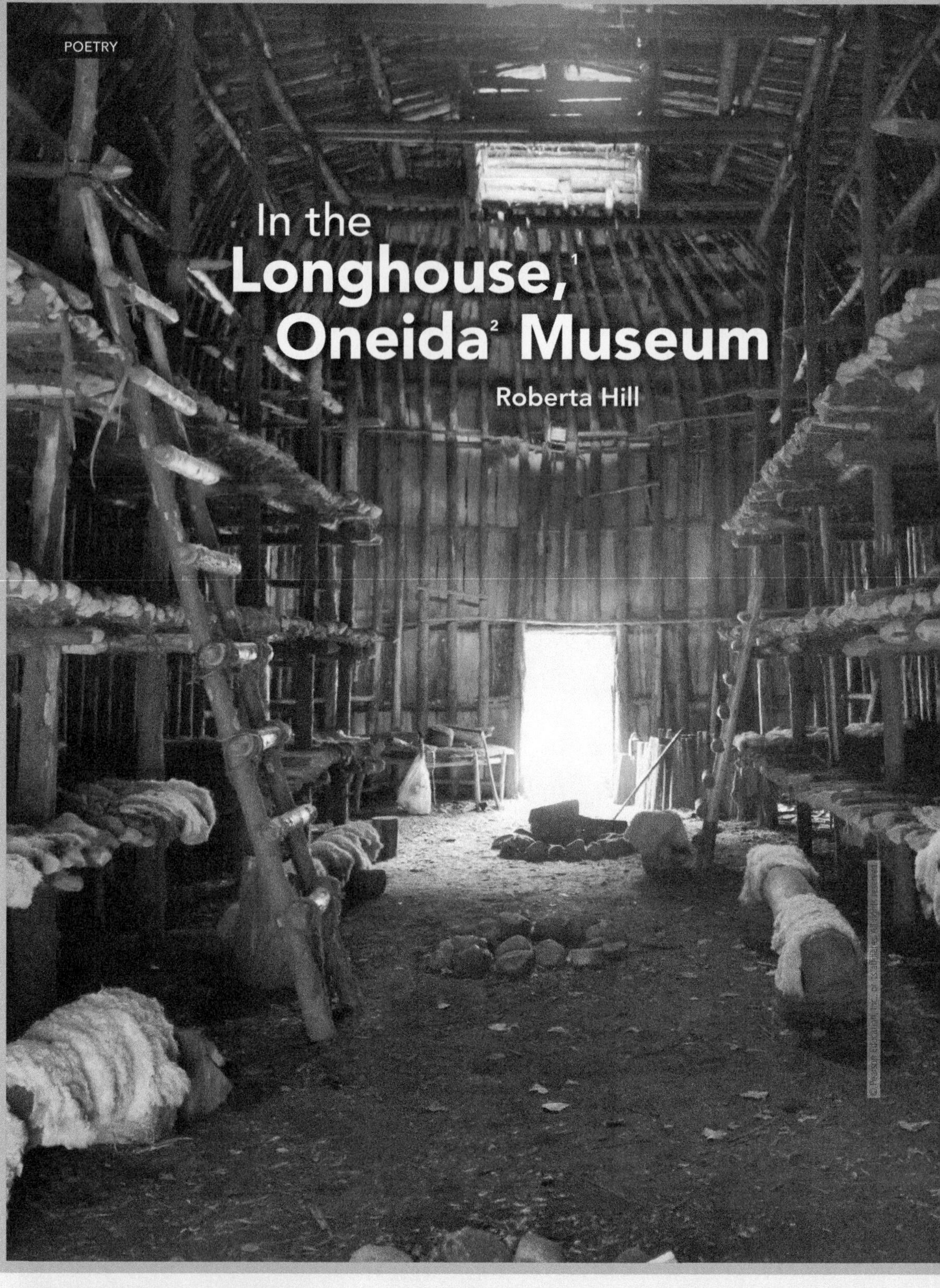


## DIGITAL PERSPECTIVES

**Illuminating the Text** Iroquois Longhouses are long, narrow, single-room homes that date to Neolithic times in Europe and have appeared in cultures all over the world. The Oneida people of the Iroquois Confederacy, located near the Great Lakes, build and use them in this poem. Their longhouses were made of wood boards and covered in bark. They provided communal shelter for several related families, and as this photograph shows, they often contained central fire pits for cooking and warmth. In fact, the Iroquois call themselves *Haudenosaunee*, which means "the people of the longhouses." Encourage students to conduct online research to locate and share other photographs and drawings of longhouses as they begin to consider why this poem uses the word *museum* in its title.

House of five fires, you never raised me.
Those nights when the throat of the furnace
wheezed and rattled its regular death,
I wanted your wide door,

your mottled air of bark and working sunlight,
wanted your smokehole with its stars,
and your roof curving its singing mouth above me.
Here are the tiers once filled with sleepers,

and their low laughter measured harmony or strife.
Here I could wake amazed at winter,
my breath in the draft a chain of violets.
The house I left as a child now seems

a shell of sobs. Each year I dream it sinister
and dig in my heels to keep out the intruder
banging at the back door. My eyes burn
from cat urine under the basement stairs

and the hall reveals a nameless hunger,
as if without a history, I should always walk
the cluttered streets of this hapless continent.
Thinking it best I be wanderer,

I rode whatever river, ignoring every zigzag,
every spin. I've been a fragment, less than my name,
shaking in a solitary landscape,
like the last burnt leaf on an oak.

What autumn wind told me you'd be waiting?
House of five fires, they take you for a tomb,
but I know better. When desolation comes,
I'll hide your ridgepole[3] in my spine

and melt into crow call, reminding my children
that spiders near your door
joined all the reddening blades of grass
without oil, hasp[4] or uranium.

1. **Longhouse** *n.* large, communal dwelling traditionally constructed by the Iroquois.
2. **Oneida** (oh NY duh) Native American people living originally near Oneida Lake in New York and now also in Wisconsin and Ontario.
3. **ridgepole** *n.* horizontal beam at the ridge of a roof, to which the upper ends of the rafters are attached.
4. **hasp** *n.* hinged metal fastening for a door.

NOTES

Mark context clues or indicate another strategy you used that helped you determine meaning.

**strife** (stryf) *n.*

MEANING:

**sinister** (SIHN uh stuhr) *adj.*

MEANING:





DIGITAL PERSPECTIVES

## Concept Vocabulary

**STRIFE** If groups are struggling to define the word *strife* in line 9, point out that "harmony" is a context clue because it is an antonym.
**Possible response:** *Strife* means "stress or disagreement between people."

**SINISTER** If groups are struggling to define the word *sinister* in line 13, point out that the context clue in the image "the intruder banging at the back door."
**Possible response:** *Sinister* means "appearing to be evil, harmful, or dangerous."

CLOSER LOOK

### Analyze Symbols

Circulate among groups as students begin their close read. Suggest that groups close read lines 28–32 of the poem. If needed, provide the following support.

**ANNOTATE:** Have students mark the three items that represent the culture that is not part of the longhouse.

**QUESTION** Ask: *Why did the poet choose these three images to represent the culture outside the longhouse?*
**Possible response:** The poet chose these symbols to represent a culture that is less natural.

**CONCLUDE:** Help students to formulate conclusions about the meaning in the last stanza.
**Possible response:** The poet longs for her culture, as represented by the longhouse.

Remind students that a **symbol** represents something larger than itself.

Additional **English Language Support** is available in the Interactive Teacher's Edition.

## WriteNow Analyze and Interpret

**Articulating a Theme** This poem is complex because of the density of its imagery, laden with symbols, and the many layers of experience described by the speaker. To articulate a theme, students will have to understand each line and each sentence to realize that the poet is contrasting her former life in the longhouse with "the cluttered streets of this hapless continent." (line 19)

As groups discuss the theme, invite them to complete a quickwrite that expresses it. Remind readers that the theme of a poem is rarely stated explicitly, but that it is an interpretation by the reader who must analyze a myriad of elements and synthesize many images and connotations.

# FACILITATING

## CLOSER LOOK

### Analyze Similes

Circulate among groups as students begin their close read. Suggest that groups close read the first four stanzas of the poem (lines 1-23), and note the similes. Encourage them to talk about the annotations that they mark. If needed, provide the following support.

**ANNOTATE:** Have students mark the three similes in the first four stanzas, or work with small groups to have students participate while you highlight them together. Ask them to note the two unlike elements being compared in each one.

**QUESTION:** Guide students to consider what these similes might tell them. Ask students to consider how these comparisons enhance or support the meaning and mood of the poem.

**Possible response:** In the first simile, the speaker compares the wind to a frightened cat, which reflects his or her own fear. In the second, the speaker compares the way he or she wishes she could snap the prison's main tower to the way a person can snap a cornstalk, which makes him or her feel powerful instead of powerless. In the third simile, the speaker compares the wind blowing to the sound of a flute, an ironically beautiful image in the midst of the violent images of barbwire and prison guards.

**CONCLUDE:** Help students to formulate conclusions about the importance of the similes in the text.

**Possible response:** The poet uses similes to compare the stark, harsh experience of the speaker with the softer, more beautiful images from his memory. They set up the tension between the two that is the foundation of the poem.

Remind students that **similes** are figures of speech that compare two unlike elements using *like* or *as* to make a point with an economy of language.

**VIGILANT** If groups are struggling to define the word *vigilant* in line 11 of "Cloudy Day," point out the context of the word. Explain that the nearby word *guard* can help them uncover the meaning of *vigilant*. Someone who guards something has to be alert and on the lookout. Based on this clue, have students infer the meaning of the word *vigilant*.

**Possible Response:** In this context, the word *vigilant* means "on the alert; watchful."



POETRY

# Cloudy Day

Jimmy Santiago Baca

SCAN FOR MULTIMEDIA

NOTES

It is windy today. A wall of wind crashes against,
windows clunk against, iron frames
as wind swings past broken glass
and seethes, like a frightened cat
in empty spaces of the cellblock.

In the exercise yard
we sat huddled in our prison jackets,
on our haunches against the fence,
and the wind carried our words
over the fences,
while the vigilant guard on the tower
held his cap at the sudden gust.

I could see the main tower from where I sat,
and the wind in my face
gave me the feeling I could grasp
the tower like a cornstalk,
and snap it from its roots of rock.

The wind plays it like a flute,
this hollow shoot of rock.
The brim girded with barbwire
with a guard sitting there also,
listening intently to the sounds
as clouds cover the sun.

Mark context clues or identify another strategy you used that helped you determine meaning.

**vigilant** (VIHJ uh luhnt) *adj.*

MEANING:





## PERSONALIZE FOR LEARNING

### English Language Support

**Multiple Meanings: *Shoot*** Focus students' attention on the phrase "this hollow shoot of rock" in line 19. Remind them that many English words have multiple meanings, and that shoot has dozens of meanings as a verb (both transitive and intransitive). It has many meanings as a noun, and it can even be an interjection, as in "Shoot! I missed the bus!" In this line, it is a noun that means "a new stem or branch on a plant" which may seem strange since it is naming the rock tower in a prison. However, naming the tower a shoot gives it life, and the wind plays it like a flute, suggesting that hollow reeds from plants were likely humans' first flutes. Have students make word webs with "shoot" in the center to explore its many meanings and to consult dictionaries to discover even more. **ALL LEVELS**

NOTES

I thought of the day I was coming to prison,
in the back seat of a police car,
hands and ankles chained, the policeman pointed,
"See that big water tank? The big
silver one out there, sticking up?
That's the prison."

And here I am, I cannot believe it.
Sometimes it is such a dream, a dream,
where I stand up in the face of the wind,
like now, it blows at my jacket,
and my eyelids flick a little bit,
while I stare disbelieving. . . .

The third day of spring,
and four years later, I can tell you,
how a man can endure, how a man
can become so cruel, how he can die
or become so cold. I can tell you this,
I have seen it every day, every day,
and still I am strong enough to love you,
love myself and feel good;
even as the earth shakes and trembles,
and I have not a thing to my name,
I feel as if I have everything, everything.

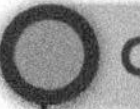

CLOSER LOOK

## Analyze Repetition

Circulate among groups as students begin their close read. Suggest that groups close read the lines 24–46 and mark the repetition. Encourage them to talk about the annotations that they mark. If needed, provide the following support.

**ANNOTATE:** Have students mark the repetition of words, phrases, or syntax in lines 24–46, or work with small groups to have students participate while you highlight them together.

**QUESTION:** Guide students to consider what these details might tell them. Ask what a reader can infer from a poet's repetition of so many words and phrases.

**Possible response:** The repetition of these words and phrases creates a kind of woeful echo in the poem. It is like the wind echoing through something hollow. The repetition also emphasizes some of the most important words and ideas: dreams, abilities, the passage of time and ultimately, everything that is held in the speaker's heart despite his literal poverty.

**CONCLUDE:** Help students to formulate conclusions about the importance of repetition in the text. Ask students why the poet might have chosen to use this technique.

**Possible response:** The poet may have wanted to reinforce the idea that the prisoner's life seems to be an endless cycle of days spent in the face of the wind, and the wind may represent his jailors and guards, constantly there, blowing in his face. It also suggests that he is "still strong enough" in the face of his situation: he endures.

Remind students that in poetry, **repetition** may suggest a **refrain**, a word, phrase, or line that is repeated at regular intervals throughout a poem or song.

PERSONALIZE FOR LEARNING

### Strategic Support

**Flashback** Review lines 24–29. Make sure that students understand the chronology of the poem. The fifth stanza occurs four years earlier when the speaker was first "coming to prison." He recalls not only being in the police car but also what the policeman said as they approached the prison. In this stanza, the poem becomes nearly narrative because the poet is using a narrative technique: flashback. Line 37 shows that the flashback happened four years prior to the lyric moment of the rest of the poem.

## Comprehension Check

In the Longhouse, Oneida Museum

Possible responses:

1. the roof, the smokehole, and the furnace
2. She "walked the cluttered streets of this hapless continent" as a wanderer, riding rivers, ignoring zigzags and spins.
3. Others see the longhouse as a "tomb."

Cloudy Day

Possible responses:

1. in prison
2. a memory of his initial arrival at the prison
3. The speaker is still strong enough "to love you,/love myself and feel good."

## Research

**Research to Clarify** If groups struggle to come up with a research topic, you may want to suggest that they focus on one of these topics from "In the Longhouse, Oneida Museum": longhouses, crows in Iroquois culture, or the Oneida tribe. Suggest that they focus on one of these topics from "Cloudy Day": prisons in the United States, cornstalks, barbwire, or earthquakes.

**Research to Explore** If students want a different avenue of exploration, suggest that they locate and learn about another poet of Native American heritage such as Louise Abeita, Natalie Diaz, Louise Erdrich, Red Haircrow, Simon J. Ortiz, Denise Sweet, or Gerald Vizenor.



## Comprehension Check

Complete the following items after you finish your first read. Review and clarify details with your group.

IN THE LONGHOUSE, ONEIDA MUSEUM

1. Name three parts of the longhouse that the speaker mentions in this poem.
2. What activity does the speaker's "nameless hunger" impel or motivate?
3. Near the end of the poem, what wrong understanding of the longhouse does the speaker say "they" hold?

CLOUDY DAY

1. Where is the speaker?
2. What memory does the speaker describe in the middle of the poem?
3. According to the final lines, what is the speaker still strong enough to do?

## RESEARCH

**Research to Clarify** Choose at least one unfamiliar detail from one of the poems. Briefly research that detail. In what way does the information you learned shed light on an aspect of the poem?

**Research to Explore** Research the life and work of either Roberta Hill or Jimmy Santiago Baca.



## PERSONALIZE FOR LEARNING

### Challenge

**Incarceration** The United States has the largest prison population of any country in the world and the second-largest per-capita incarceration rate behind the small country of Seychelles. Suggest that students who are interested in criminology learn more about one of these related topics: juvenile justice, recidivism, racial inequities, women in prison, the various levels of security in prisons, privatization, prison employees, costs, or the effects of imprisonment on prisoners, capital punishment, or parole. They may also want to learn more about the prison system in their state. Give students opportunities to share what they learn.

MAKING MEANING

## Close Read the Text

With your group, revisit sections of the poems you marked during your first read. **Annotate** what you notice. What **questions** do you have? What can you **conclude**?

## Analyze the Text

**CITE TEXTUAL EVIDENCE** to support your answers.

**Complete the activities.**

1. **Review and Clarify** With your group, reread lines 36–46 of "Cloudy Day." Identify and analyze one or more contrasts you find.
2. **Present and Discuss** Now, work with your group to share key passages from "In the Longhouse, Oneida Museum" and "Cloudy Day." Take turns presenting your passages. Discuss what you noticed in the poems, what questions you asked, and what conclusions you reached.
3. **Essential Question:** ***What is the relationship between literature and place?*** How do these poems link poetry and place? Discuss.

LANGUAGE DEVELOPMENT

## Concept Vocabulary

strife sinister vigilant

**Why These Words?** The three concept words from the poems are related. With your group, determine what the words have in common. How do these word choices add to the power of the poems?

**Practice**

Use the concept vocabulary words in a conversation with your group members. Each group member should use each word at least once.

## Word Study

Notebook **Etymology** A word's **etymology** is its history—including its language of origin and how its form and meaning have developed over time. Some words have a surprising etymology. For instance, the concept vocabulary word *sinister* comes from a Latin word meaning "left" or "on the left side." In the past, a number of cultures associated the left side with clumsiness, bad luck, or even evil.

Use a specialized reference, such as an etymological dictionary, to look up the etymology of the word *dexterity*. Write your findings, and discuss them with your group. Explain how the word's etymology is related to that of *sinister*.

POETRY COLLECTION 2

TIP

**GROUP DISCUSSION**

One group member can assume the role of note-taker and read notes to the group at the end of the discussion. This strategy can help all group members make sure they remember the same information.

WORD NETWORK

Add words related to a sense of place from the texts to your Word Network.

STANDARDS

**Language**

Consult general and specialized reference materials, both print and digital, to find the pronunciation of a word or determine or clarify its precise meaning, its part of speech, its etymology, or its standard usage.





DIGITAL PERSPECTIVES

## Jump Start

CLOSE READ Ask groups to consider the following prompts: *What is gritty about each of these poems? What grandeur does each poem evoke?* As students discuss in their groups, ask them to cite specific examples of both grit and grandeur as evidence to support their general ideas.

## Close Read the Text

Model close reading as needed by using the Annotation Highlights in the Interactive Teacher's Edition.

Remind groups to use Accountable Talk in their discussions and to support one another as they complete the close read.

## Analyze the Text

**Possible responses:**

1. The speaker has seen cruelty, death, and hard-heartedness in prison. Still, he feels that he has "everything" because he is still strong enough to love himself and his beloved.
2. **Passages will vary by group.** Remind students to explain why they chose the passage they presented to group members.
3. **Responses will vary by group.**

## Concept Vocabulary

**Why These Words? Possible response:**
The words all describe conflict. They enhance the impact of the texts by showing how the speakers struggle with their feelings or with their circumstances.

**Practice**

**Conversations will vary by group** but will likely be about difficult topics such as war, homelessness, or incarceration.

**Word Network**

**Possible words:** *furnace, smokehole, roof, tiers, basement, desolation, ridgepole, cellblock, barbwire*

## Word Study

For more support, see **Concept Vocabulary and Word Study.**
**Possible response:** *Dexterity* comes from the Latin root *dexter* ("on the right"). The word *dexterity* means "mental or physical skill" It is directionally related to "right," (perceived as desirable or good), and *sinister* is related to "left" (perceived as less desirable or bad).

**FORMATIVE ASSESSMENT**

### Analyze the Text

**If** students struggle to close read the text, **then** provide the **Poetry Collection 2: Text Questions** available online in the Interactive Teacher's Edition or Unit Resources.

### Concept Vocabulary

**If** students fail to see the connection between the words, **then** have them use each word in a sentence and think about what is similar about the sentences.

### Word Study

**If** students struggle to understand the concept of etymology, **then** point them to another example of a word with a rich and interesting history such as *museum, harmony,* or *police.*
For Reteach and Practice, see **Word Study: Etymology (RP).**

# FACILITATING

## Analyze Craft and Structure

**Poetic Devices** Remind students of two other examples of figurative language that these poets use:

**Onomatopoeia** is when words sound like their meanings. Examples: *wheezed* ("Longhouse," line 3), *snap* ("Cloudy Day," line 17)

**Alliteration** is the repetition of initial consonant sounds to achieve an effect. Example: five fires ("Longhouse," line 1 and 26), low laughter ("Longhouse," line 9), banging at the back door ("Longhouse," line 15)

For more support, see **Analyze Craft and Structure: Poetic Devices.**

### FORMATIVE ASSESSMENT

### Analyze Craft and Structure

**If** students are not able to understand the poetic devices in the poems, **then** have them listen as you read examples aloud, verbally exaggerating the devices used. For Reteach and Practice, see **Analyze Craft and Structure: Poetic Devices (RP).**

POETRY COLLECTION 2

**STANDARDS**

**Reading Literature**
• Analyze how an author's choices concerning how to structure specific parts of a text contribute to its overall structure and meaning as well as its aesthetic impact.

**Language**
Demonstrate understanding of figurative language, word relationships, and nuances in word meaning.

## Analyze Craft and Structure

**Poetic Devices** Poets often use **figurative language**, or language that is used imaginatively rather than literally and includes one or more **figures of speech**, devices for making unexpected comparisons. Three common figures of speech are personification, simile, and metaphor.

- **Personification:** A nonhuman subject is presented as if it had human qualities. For example, a writer might describe a bridge as "groaning under the weight of the traffic it bears."
- **Simile:** Two dissimilar things are compared using *like, as, seems, than, as if*, or a similar connecting word. For example, an author describing a raucous sports fan might write, "The fan roared like a wild animal."
- **Metaphor:** Two dissimilar things are compared without a connecting word such as *like* or *as*. For example, in "The Highwayman," the poet Alfred Noyes uses a ship metaphor when he writes, "The moon was a ghostly galleon tossed upon cloudy seas."

### Practice

**CITE TEXTUAL EVIDENCE** to support your answers.

**As a group, complete the chart with examples of figurative language from both poems. Then, discuss the insight or emotion each example helps to convey.**

| EXAMPLE PASSAGE | TYPE OF FIGURATIVE LANGUAGE | EFFECT |
|---|---|---|
| "furnace wheezed" (line 3) | personification | The house sounds as if it were alive. |
| "autumn wind told me" (line 25) | personification | The wind has wisdom. |
| "I've been a fragment" (line 22) | metaphor | The speaker feels broken. |
| "The wind plays like a flute" (line 18) | simile | The wind has a beautiful sound. |
| "roots of rock" (line 17) | metaphor | Like a tree, the tower rises high. |





## PERSONALIZE FOR LEARNING

### English Language Support

**Surrealism** Many of the images in "In the Longhouse, Oneida Museum" seem dreamlike and unearthly, and students may have a difficult time parsing the lines. For example, "My breath in the draft a chain of violets." (line 11) This kind of surreal language may elude non-native speakers. Assure them that it is enough to understand the sound and the suggestion made by the words, that it is not necessary to understand each phrase literally. Ask: *How can a breath be a chain of violets?* Let students brainstorm and free associate, but do not suggest that there is one correct answer to this kind of question. They may imagine a person breathing out violets, or the smell of violets, or chains of flowers that children make. All of these associations are valid and insightful. Then have students discuss what effect these words and phrases have on the reader of the poems. **ALL LEVELS**

## LANGUAGE DEVELOPMENT

## Author's Style

**Poetic Conventions** Traditional structural elements used in verse, or **poetic conventions,** include **repetition, end-stopped lines, enjambment,** and **stanza breaks**. These techniques focus and direct the reader's attention.

| POETIC CONVENTION | EXPLANATION | EXAMPLE |
|---|---|---|
| Repetition | Repetition reminds readers of an idea already expressed or emphasizes an important point. | *Sometimes it is such a dream, a dream …* (line 31, "Cloudy Day") |
| End-Stopped Lines | These are lines that complete a grammatical unit, usually with a punctuation mark at the end. End-stops highlight the structure of ideas. | *House of five fires, you never raised me.* (line 1, "In the Longhouse, Oneida Museum") |
| Enjambment | These are lines that do not end with a grammatical break and that do not make full sense without the line that follows. Enjambed lines create flow. Words at the ends of lines may receive a subtle emphasis. | *The house I left as a child now seems / a shell of sobs.* (lines 12–13, "In the Longhouse, Oneida Museum") |
| Stanza Breaks | The breaks in stanzas, or groups of lines, are similar to paragraphs in prose. They point to shifts in the speaker's thoughts and feelings. | *And here I am, I cannot believe it.* (line 30, "Cloudy Day") |

### Read It

1. Work individually. Identify the poetic conventions in each of these passages from the poems. Then, discuss with your group the effect the combination of conventions creates.
   a. lines 1–6 and 25–28, "In the Longhouse, Oneida Museum"
   b. lines 1–7, "Cloudy Day"
2. **Connect to Style** With your group, identify the poetic conventions in lines 40–43 of "Cloudy Day." Then, explain and evaluate their effect.

### Write It

**Notebook** Using the first nine lines of "In the Longhouse, Oneida Museum" as a model, write a short poem about a memory. Include at least three of the four poetic conventions: repetition, end-stopped lines, enjambment, and stanza breaks.



TIP

CLARIFICATION

A poet's style reflects choices about both language and structure. Word choices include imagery and figurative language. Structure choices include line and stanza breaks.

EVIDENCE LOG

Before moving on to a new selection, go to your Evidence Log and record what you've learned from the poems in "Poetry Collection 2."



## PERSONALIZE FOR LEARNING

### English Language Support

**Poetic Devices** Ask pairs of students to indicate who or what is the "you" in Hill's poem. (stanza 1) **EMERGING**

Ask students why they think the speaker in Hill's poem addresses her words to the longhouse. **EXPANDING**

Ask students to write a paragraph explaining the effect Roberta Hill attains by addressing her poem to the longhouse. **BRIDGING**

An expanded **English Language Support Lesson** on Poetic Devices is available in the Interactive Teacher's Edition. 

DIGITAL PERSPECTIVES

## Author's Style

**Poetic Conventions** Remind students of another poetic convention used in both of these poems: free verse. This open form of poetry uses no consistent meter or rhyme, therefore following the rhythms of natural speech. Suggest that this convention is itself a kind of metaphor. Both poets are breaking free of boundaries, discovering their own internal freedom, and following their own thoughts and hearts to new psychological places. Poets choose free verse to reflect their subjects and themes. For more support, see **Author's Style: Poetic Conventions.** 

### Read It

Possible responses

1. **a.** repetition: Emphasizes the size of the longhouse and its importance as a warm shelter
   **b.** enjambment: Encourages readers to pause to consider the meaning and effect of the complex statement
2. The poet uses repetition by repeating "every day" and "love." Because the poet end-stops the lines, he slows the reader down and creates a storytelling quality.

### Write It

Stanzas and analyses will vary, but make sure that students include examples of at least three of the four poetic conventions.

**Evidence Log** Support students in completing their Evidence Log. This paced activity will help prepare them for the Performance-Based Assessment at the end of the unit.

### FORMATIVE ASSESSMENT

### Conventions and Style

**If** students are not able to understand how poetic conventions such as repetition, end-stopped lines, enjambment, and stanza break enhance meaning, **then** have them imagine the poems without them.

For Reteach and Practice, see **Author's Style: Poetic Conventions (RP).**

### Selection Test

Administer the Selection Tests, which are available in both print and digital formats online in Assessments.

# Introduction *from* The Way to Rainy Mountain

**AUDIO SUMMARIES**
Audio summaries of "Introduction *from* The Way to Rainy Mountain" are available online in both English and Spanish in the Interactive Teacher's Edition or Unit Resources. Assigning these summaries prior to reading the selection may help students build additional background knowledge and set a context for their first read.

## Summary

In this excerpt from N. Scott Momaday's memoir "The Way to Rainy Mountain," the author describes a trip he takes to visit his grandmother's grave shortly after her death. She is buried near Rainy Mountain, which is a cultural landmark for the Kiowa tribe. The author explains the history and origin myth of the Kiowa, their arrival on the Plains and their eventual rise to dominance. He describes his grandmother's life as a witness to the "last great moments" of Kiowa history. As a child, she attended the last Sun Dance festival before her people were forcibly dispersed by American troops. He remembers times when he visited his grandmother's house as a child and she was an old woman still carrying on some of the tribal traditions. At the end, he finds his grandmother's grave and sees the mountain in the distance.

### Insight

In this excerpt, Momaday interweaves the chronicle of his journey to visit his grandmother's grave with the history of the demise of his tribal ancestors. It is through his grandmother that Momaday learns about painful events that changed the lives of these proud Native Americans who once ruled the Great Plains in Oklahoma.

ESSENTIAL QUESTION:
What is the relationship between literature and place?

## Connection to Essential Question

This memoir makes a deep connection to the Essential Question, "What is the relationship between literature and place?" The writer explores the central importance of Rainy Mountain and the area surrounding it to his own culture, to his grandmother's life, and to his own childhood experiences.

SMALL-GROUP PERFORMANCE TASK
Explain the sense of place created by the authors and artists in this section.

UNIT PERFORMANCE-BASED ASSESSMENT
What makes certain places live on in our memory?

## Connection to Performance Tasks

**Small-Group Learning Performance Task** In this Performance Task, students will consider how authors create a sense of place in their work. Students will note that in Momaday's memoir, the geography plays a significant role in the experiences that the author describes.

**Unit Performance-Based Assessment** This selection provides an interesting insight into the idea of what makes certain places live on in our memory. Important historical moments of the Kiowa people live on in the memories of Momaday's grandmother, even some events that she never actually experienced herself. Momaday makes it clear that those very memories, which he has come to appreciate through contact with his grandmother, now live on in him and motivate him to recount his journey to her grave.

DIGITAL PERSPECTIVES

 Audio  Video  Document  Annotation Highlights  EL Highlights 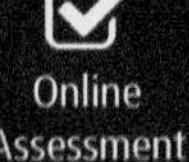 Online Assessment

## LESSON RESOURCES

| | Making Meaning | Language Development | Effective Expression |
|---|---|---|---|
| Lesson | **First Read**<br>**Close Read**<br>**Analyze the Text**<br>**Analyze Craft and Structure** | **Concept Vocabulary**<br>**Word Study**<br>**Author's Style** | **Writing to Compare** |
| Instructional Standards | **RI.10** By the end of grade 11, read and comprehend literary nonfiction . . .<br>**RI.6** Determine an author's point of view . . .<br>**L.4** Determine or clarify the meaning of unknown and multiple-meaning words and phrases . . .<br>**L.4.a** Use context as a clue . . . | **L.4.b** Identify and correctly use patterns of word changes . . .<br>**RI.4** Determine the meaning of words and phrases . . .<br>**L.5** Demonstrate understanding of figurative language . . . | **W.2** Write informative/explanatory texts . . .<br>**W.9** Draw evidence from literary or informational texts . . . |
| **STUDENT RESOURCES** | | | |
| Available online in the Interactive Student Edition or Unit Resources | Selection Audio<br>First-Read Guide: Nonfiction<br>Close-Read Guide: Nonfiction | Word Network | Evidence Log |
| **TEACHER RESOURCES** | | | |
| **Selection Resources** Available online in the Interactive Teacher's Edition or Unit Resources | Audio Summaries<br>Annotation Highlights<br>EL Highlights<br>Analyze Craft and Structure: Literary Nonfiction | Concept Vocabulary and Word Study<br>Author's Poetic Prose | Writing to Compare: Informative Essay |
| **Reteach/Practice (RP)** Available online in the Interactive Teacher's Edition or Unit Resources | Analyze Craft and Structure: Literary Nonfiction (RP) | Word Study: Latin Roots *-dei-* and *-cid-* (RP)<br>Author's Poetic Prose (RP) | |
| **Assessment** Available online in Assessments | Selection Test | | |
| **My Resources** | A Unit 4 Answer Key is available online and in the Interactive Teacher's Edition. | | |

# Reading Support

| Text Complexity Rubric: Introduction *from* The Way to Rainy Mountain | |
|---|---|
| **Quantitative Measures** | |
| **Lexile:** 1020 **Text Length:** 2,664 words | |
| **Qualitative Measures** | |
| Knowledge Demands ①—②—❸—④—⑤ | The selection contains detailed information about the Kiowas, both history and legends. Students may not have familiarity with the content, but it is explained clearly. |
| Structure ①—②—❸—④—⑤ | The selection alternates between description, historical events, recent events, and legends. |
| Language Conventionality and Clarity ①—②—❸—④—⑤ | There is descriptive poetic language; Sentence structure is a mix of some simple and some complex sentences, with a lot of descriptive vocabulary. |
| Levels of Meaning/Purpose ①—②—③—❹—⑤ | The selection covers a wide range of concepts and ideas, from historical information to legends that have symbolic meaning. |

DECIDE AND PLAN

## English Language Support

Provide English Learners with support for language and structure as they read the selection.

**Language** Help students to analyze some of the descriptive paragraphs and the ways in which the author chooses words to create vivid descriptions. For example, in paragraph 1, he describes the sound the grass makes under his feet. Have students take turns reading some descriptive paragraphs aloud. Help to clarify the meaning of unknown words or phrases.

**Structure** Point out to students that there are many kinds of information they will find in the text: descriptions of the land, historical events about the Kiowa, specific information about the grandmother and her life, and legends of the Kiowa.

## Strategic Support

Provide students with strategic support to ensure that they can successfully read the text.

**Language** Give examples of some of the descriptive language the author uses, for example in paragraph 1, he says *foliage seems almost to writhe in fire.* Ask students what is meant by the phrase and explain if necessary. Then ask students to work together in pairs to find other metaphors in the same paragraph and to explain their meaning.

**Meaning** Have students read to identify details about Kiowa history and the author's family. Encourage them to take notes on what they read. Then have them read sections describing the land and the legends of the people. Discuss the importance of the connection to nature that are apparent in all of these sections.

## Challenge

Provide students who need to be challenged with ideas for how they can go beyond a simple interpretation of the text.

**Text Analysis** Pair students. Ask them to read through the text to identify details that connect the author and the Kiowa family to nature. Then ask them to reread the legend in paragraphs 8 and 9. Ask them to comment on the ways in which animals and nature are used to explain phenomena such as stars in the sky.

**Written Response** Have students read more excerpts or the entire text of *The Way to Rainy Mountain*. Have them write their response to what they read, giving a summary and explaining what they found most interesting about the work.

TEACH

## Read and Respond

Have the groups do their first read of the selection. Then have them complete their close read. Finally, work with them on the Making Meaning, Language Development, and Effective Expression activities.

# Standards Support Through Teaching and Learning Cycle

## IDENTIFY NEEDS

Analyze results of the Beginning-of-Year Assessment, focusing on the items relating to Unit 4. Also take into consideration student performance to this point and your observations of where particular students struggle.

## ANALYZE AND REVISE

- Analyze student work for evidence of student learning.
- Identify whether or not students have met the expectations in the standards.
- Identify implications for future instruction.

## TEACH

Implement the planned lesson, and gather evidence of student learning.

## DECIDE AND PLAN

- If students have performed poorly on items matching these standards, then provide selection scaffolds before assigning them the on-level lesson provided in the Student Edition.
- If students have done well on the Beginning-of-Year Assessment, then challenge them to keep progressing and learning by giving them opportunities to practice the skills in depth.
- Use the Selection Resources listed on the Planning pages for "Introduction *from* The Way to Rainy Mountain" to help students continually improve their ability to master the standards.

**Instructional Standards: Introduction *from* The Way to Rainy Mountain**

| | Catching Up | This Year | Looking Forward |
|---|---|---|---|
| **Reading** | You may wish to administer the **Analyze Craft and Structure: Literary Nonfiction (RP)** worksheet to better familiarize students historical and reflective writing.<br><br>Review the **Conventions and Style: Poetic Prose (RP)** worksheet to help students explore poetic elements in prose writing. | **RI.6** Determine an author's point of view or purpose in a text in which the rhetoric is particularly effective, analyzing how style and content contribute to the power, persuasiveness, or beauty of the text.<br><br>**RI.4** Determine the meaning of words and phrases as they are used in a text, including figurative, connotative, and technical meanings; analyze how an author uses and refines the meaning of a key term or terms over the course of a text. | Challenge students to explore other forms of hybrid genres, such as literary nonfiction.<br><br>Challenge students to rewrite an essay or short story of theirs using poetic devices. |
| **Language** | Review the **Word Study: Latin Roots *-dei-* and *-cid-* (RP)** worksheet with students to ensure they understand the Latin root words. | **L.4.b** Identify and correctly use patterns of word changes that indicate different meanings or parts of speech. | Have students locate other Latin or Greek root words they may recognize in the selection. |

FACILITATING

## Jump Start

FIRST READ Ask: *Have you ever felt so connected to a place that it seemed like part of who you are? Have you ever read about or seen such a connection?* As students share prior experiences, guide them to identify specific factors that influence the emotions around place.

## Introduction *from* The Way to Rainy Mountain

*Have you ever returned to a place that you knew as a child and been surprised by how it had changed?* Modeling this and other questions that readers might ask will bring this excerpt from "The Way to Rainy Mountain" to life and connect them to the Performance Task question. Selection audio and print capability for the selection are available in the Interactive Teacher's Edition.

## Concept Vocabulary

Have groups briefly discuss the three concept vocabulary words. Have they encountered any of the words before? Do they recognize the prefix, suffix, or base word of any of the concept vocabulary words? Have groups consider the strategy of context clues and discuss its advantages and disadvantages.

### FIRST READ

Have students perform the steps of the first read independently:

NOTICE: You may want to encourage students to find the general idea of the selection in the first read.

ANNOTATE: Remind students to mark passages that they do not understand or that contain particularly interesting details.

CONNECT: Have students compare the text with other texts they have read about the history of Native Americans in North America.

RESPOND: Students will demonstrate their understanding of the text by answering questions and writing a summary.

Point out to students that they will perform the first three steps concurrently as they are doing their first read. They will complete the Respond step after they have finished the first read. You may wish to print copies of the **First-Read Guide: Nonfiction** for students to use.



MAKING MEANING

POETRY COLLECTION 2

## Comparing Texts

You will now read an excerpt from a memoir. Begin by completing the first-read and close-read activities. Then, compare the use of poetic elements in the Introduction from *The Way to Rainy Mountain* with the use of similar elements in the poems in Poetry Collection 2.

INTRODUCTION *from* THE WAY TO RAINY MOUNTAIN

About the Author

**N. Scott Momaday** (b. 1934) won the Pulitzer Prize for his first novel, *House Made of Dawn* (1969). A Native American from Oklahoma, much of his work draws on his Kiowa heritage, especially the Kiowa people's traditional tales and folklore. In addition to novels, Momaday has published poetry and nonfiction and painted his own illustrations for his work. He is the recipient of numerous awards and honors, including the National Medal of Arts in 2007.

# Introduction *from* The Way to Rainy Mountain

## Concept Vocabulary

As you perform your first read, you will encounter these words.

reverence    rites    deicide

**Context Clues** If these words are unfamiliar to you, try using **context clues** to help you determine their meanings.

**Example:** Fans were **elated** when the hometown team won the state championship.

**Conclusion:** The phrase "won the state championship" is a context clue. Winning an important game or an award is usually a happy occasion. *Elated*, then, must mean something like "very happy."

Apply your knowledge of context clues and other vocabulary strategies to determine the meanings of unfamiliar words you encounter during your first read.

## First Read NONFICTION

Apply these strategies as you conduct your first read. You will have an opportunity to complete a close read after your first read.

NOTICE the general ideas of the text. *What* is it about? *Who* is involved?

ANNOTATE by marking vocabulary and key passages you want to revisit.

First Read

CONNECT ideas within the selection to what you already know and what you have already read.

RESPOND by completing the Comprehension Check and by writing a brief summary of the selection.

STANDARDS

**Reading Informational Text**
By the end of grade 11, read and comprehend literary nonfiction in the grades 11–CCR text complexity band proficiently, with scaffolding as needed at the high end of the range.

**Language**
• Determine or clarify the meaning of unknown and multiple-meaning words and phrases based on *grades 11–12 reading and content*, choosing flexibly from a range of strategies.
• Use context as a clue to the meaning of a word or phrase.

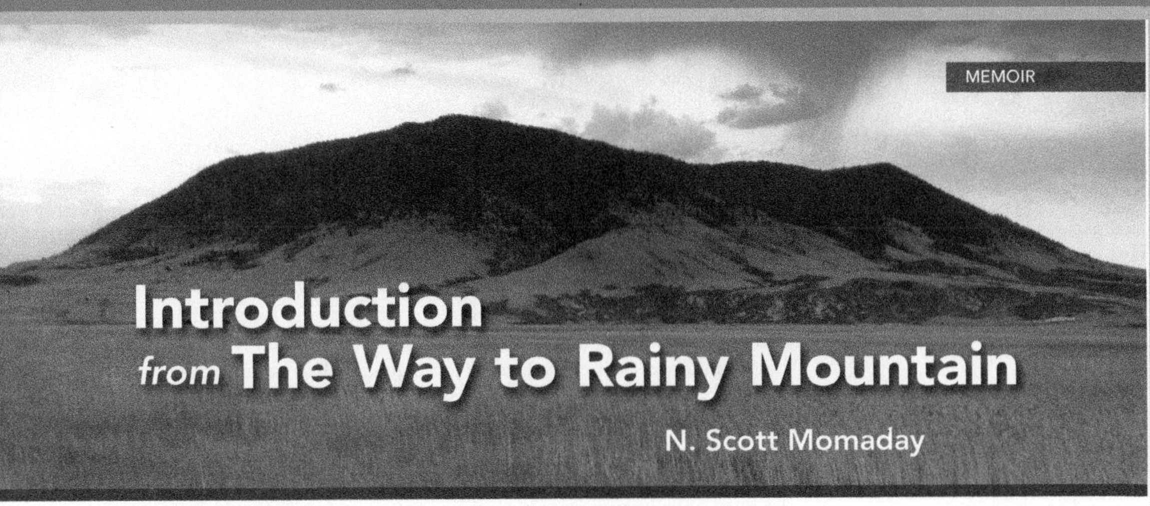

MEMOIR

# Introduction *from* The Way to Rainy Mountain

N. Scott Momaday

DIGITAL PERSPECTIVES

## CLOSER LOOK

### Examine Adjectives

Circulate among groups as students begin their close read. Suggest that groups close read paragraph 1. Encourage them to talk about the annotations that they mark. If needed, provide the following support.

**ANNOTATE:** Have students mark descriptive details in this paragraph, or work with small groups to have students participate while you highlight them together.

**QUESTION:** Have students review the adjectives they have marked. What effect do they create? Then focus student attention on the words *tornadic, linear,* and *isolate*.

**Possible response:** Students may say the adjectives describe both life and death. *Tornadic* means "like a tornado." *Linear* means "in straight lines." *Isolate* means "solitary, alone."

**CONCLUDE:** Help students to formulate conclusions about why Momaday chose these three adjectives.

**Possible response:** Students may say the adjectives describe both life and death.

Remind students that an **adjective** is used to describe or modify nouns or pronouns. Adjectives help authors express very specific ideas by adding nuance to their writing.

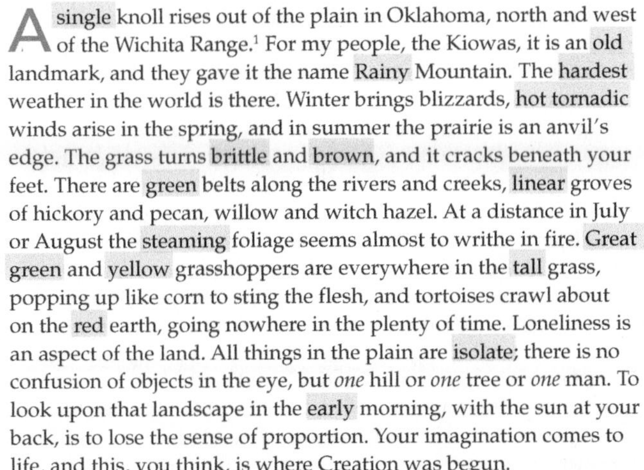

BACKGROUND

Throughout the nineteenth century, the United States expanded across the continent, and Native American nations were forced from their traditional lands onto reservations. In this introduction from his memoir, N. Scott Momaday describes both history of his Kiowa ancestors who were forcibly resettled and their relationship with the land.

SCAN FOR MULTIMEDIA

NOTES

1 A single knoll rises out of the plain in Oklahoma, north and west of the Wichita Range.[1] For my people, the Kiowas, it is an old landmark, and they gave it the name Rainy Mountain. The hardest weather in the world is there. Winter brings blizzards, hot tornadic winds arise in the spring, and in summer the prairie is an anvil's edge. The grass turns brittle and brown, and it cracks beneath your feet. There are green belts along the rivers and creeks, linear groves of hickory and pecan, willow and witch hazel. At a distance in July or August the steaming foliage seems almost to writhe in fire. Great green and yellow grasshoppers are everywhere in the tall grass, popping up like corn to sting the flesh, and tortoises crawl about on the red earth, going nowhere in the plenty of time. Loneliness is an aspect of the land. All things in the plain are isolate; there is no confusion of objects in the eye, but *one* hill or *one* tree or *one* man. To look upon that landscape in the early morning, with the sun at your back, is to lose the sense of proportion. Your imagination comes to life, and this, you think, is where Creation was begun.

2 I returned to Rainy Mountain in July. My grandmother had died in the spring, and I wanted to be at her grave. She had lived to be very old and at last infirm. Her only living daughter was with her when she died, and I was told that in death her face was that of a child.

3 I like to think of her as a child. When she was born, the Kiowas were living that last great moment of their history. For more than a hundred years they had controlled the open range from the Smoky Hill River to the Red, from the headwaters of the Canadian to the

1. **Wichita** (WIHCH uh taw) **Range** mountain range in southwestern Oklahoma.

## FACILITATING SMALL-GROUP CLOSE READING

**CLOSE READ: Memoir** As you facilitate student reading of this selection, you may want to offer this information to groups.

- Remind students that in a memoir, a writer describes and narrates moments and events that actually happened in his or her life.
- A memoir differs from an autobiography because it is more literary and subjective in nature and tone and more specific or narrow in subject and scope.
- Diaries and journals often feed memoirs as raw material, but memoirs are polished and stylized pieces of crafted writing.
- Some memoirs are essays; others are full-length books. Because memoirs are based on fact, they are nonfiction.

Ask students to make a list of memoirs that they have read or know about such as *A Moveable Feast* by Ernest Hemingway, *Growing Up* by Russell Baker, *Night* by Elie Wiesel, *American Childhood* by Annie Dillard, or *The Road from Coorain* by Jill Ker Conway.

## CLOSER LOOK

### Consider Abstract Nouns 

Circulate among groups as students begin their close read. Suggest that groups close read paragraph 4 and note the abstract nouns. Encourage them to talk about the annotations that they mark. If needed, provide the following support.

**ANNOTATE:** Have students mark the nouns that express ideas, or work with small groups to have students participate while you highlight them together. Note that there may be some disagreement about the classification of several of the words.

**QUESTION:** Guide students to consider what some of these abstract nouns might tell them. Ask what a reader can infer about what they words have in common, and accept student responses.

**Possible response:** These abstract nouns in the paragraph all describe big, important ideas. The words carry a kind of power that makes a reader feel the weight and importance of what the author is describing.

**CONCLUDE:** Help students to formulate conclusions about how Momaday uses abstract nouns in his memoir. Ask students why the author might have included these details.

**Possible response:** Momaday integrates these big ideas/abstract nouns with images that name concrete people and places. For him, the images are the ideas; they are equal and integrated, not subordinate or isolated.

Remind students that **nouns** can be classified as either concrete or abstract. Authors use nouns to name the topics and ideas at the heart of their writing.

Additional **English Language Support** is available in the Interactive Teacher's Edition.

NOTES

fork of the Arkansas and Cimarron.[2] In alliance with the Comanches,[3] they had ruled the whole of the southern Plains. War was their sacred business, and they were among the finest horsemen the world has ever known. But warfare for the Kiowas was preeminently a matter of disposition rather than of survival, and they never understood the grim, unrelenting advance of the U.S. Cavalry. When at last, divided and ill-provisioned, they were driven onto the Staked Plains in the cold rains of autumn, they fell into panic. In Palo Duro Canyon they abandoned their crucial stores to pillage and had nothing then but their lives. In order to save themselves, they surrendered to the soldiers at Fort Sill[4] and were imprisoned in the old stone corral that now stands as a military museum. My grandmother was spared the humiliation of those high gray walls by eight or ten years, but she must have known from birth the affliction of defeat, the dark brooding of old warriors.

4 Her name was Aho, and she belonged to the last culture to evolve in North America. Her forebears came down from the high country in western Montana nearly three centuries ago. They were a mountain people, a mysterious tribe of hunters whose language has never been positively classified in any major group. In the late seventeenth century they began a long migration to the south and east. It was a journey toward the dawn, and it led to a golden age. Along the way the Kiowas were befriended by the Crows,[5] who gave them the culture and religion of the Plains. They acquired horses, and their ancient nomadic spirit was suddenly free of the ground. They acquired Tai-me, the sacred Sun Dance doll, from that moment the object and symbol of their worship, and so shared in the divinity of the sun. Not least, they acquired the sense of destiny, therefore courage and pride. When they entered upon the southern Plains they had been transformed. No longer were they slaves to the simple necessity of survival; they were a lordly and dangerous society of fighters and thieves, hunters and priests of the sun. According to their origin myth, they entered the world through a hollow log. From one point of view, their migration was the fruit of an old prophecy, for indeed they emerged from a sunless world.

5 Although my grandmother lived out her long life in the shadow of Rainy Mountain, the immense landscape of the continental interior lay like memory in her blood. She could tell of the Crows, whom she had never seen, and of the Black Hills,[6] where she had never been. I wanted to see in reality what she had seen more perfectly

2. **Smoky Hill . . . Cimarron** (SIHM uh ron) rivers that run through or near Oklahoma. The area Momaday is defining stretches from central Kansas south through Oklahoma and from the Texas panhandle east to Tulsa, Oklahoma.
3. **Comanches** (kuh MAN cheez) Native American people of the southern Great Plains.
4. **Fort Sill** fort established by the United States government in 1869 as a base of operations during U.S. Army battles with Native Americans of the southern Plains.
5. **Crows** members of a Native American tribe of the northern Plains.
6. **Black Hills** mountain range running from southwestern South Dakota to northeastern Wyoming.





## DIGITAL PERSPECTIVES

**Enriching the Text** Go online to locate maps of western North America that include the places described in paragraph 3. Have students determine which area formerly belonged to the Kiowa and how its size compares to their own state or to another modern state in the U.S. Have them use online sources to locate specific places such as the Cimarron River and the Palo Duro Canyon and to share photographs that they find of these dramatic locations.

in the mind's eye, and traveled fifteen hundred miles to begin my pilgrimage.

NOTES

6 Yellowstone,[7] it seemed to me, was the top of the world, a region of deep lakes and dark timber, canyons and waterfalls. But, beautiful as it is, one might have the sense of confinement there. The skyline in all directions is close at hand, the high wall of the woods and deep cleavages of shade. There is a perfect freedom in the mountains, but it belongs to the eagle and the elk, the badger and the bear. The Kiowas reckoned their stature by the distance they could see, and they were bent and blind in the wilderness.

7 Descending eastward, the highland meadows are a stairway to the plain. In July the inland slope of the Rockies is luxuriant with flax and buckwheat, stonecrop and larkspur.[8] The earth unfolds and the limit of the land recedes. Clusters of trees, and animals growing far in the distance, cause the vision to reach away and wonder to build upon the mind. The sun follows a longer course in the day, and the sky is immense beyond all comparison. The great billowing clouds that sail upon it are shadows that move upon the grain like water, dividing light. Farther down, in the land of the Crows and Blackfeet,[9] the plain is yellow. Sweet clover takes hold of the hills and bends upon itself to cover and seal the soil. There the Kiowas paused on their way; they had come to the place where they must change their lives. The sun is at home on the plains. Precisely there does it have the certain character of a god. When the Kiowas came to the land of the Crows, they could see the dark lees of the hills at dawn across the Bighorn River, the profusion of light on the grain shelves, the oldest deity ranging after the solstices. Not yet would they veer southward to the caldron[10] of the land that lay below; they must wean their blood from the northern winter and hold the mountains a while longer in their view. They bore Tai-me in procession to the east.

8 A dark mist lay over the Black Hills, and the land was like iron. At the top of a ridge I caught sight of Devil's Tower upthrust against the gray sky as if in the birth of time the core of the earth had broken through its crust and the motion of the world was begun. There are things in nature that engender an awful quiet in the heart of man; Devil's Tower is one of them. Two centuries ago, because they could not do otherwise, the Kiowas made a legend at the base of the rock. My grandmother said:

9 Eight children were there at play, seven sisters and their brother. Suddenly the boy was struck dumb; he trembled and began to run upon his hands and feet. His fingers became claws, and his body was covered with fur. Directly there was a bear where the boy had been. The sisters were terrified; they ran, and the bear after them. They



7. **Yellowstone** Yellowstone National Park, located primarily in Wyoming but extending into southern Montana and eastern Idaho.
8. **flax . . . larkspur** various types of plants.
9. **Blackfeet** Native American people from the region that includes northern Montana and parts of southern Alberta, Canada.
10. **caldron** (KAWL druhn) *n.* pot for boiling liquids; large kettle.



## HOW LANGUAGE WORKS: Poetic Devices

**Similes and Metaphors** Review the language at play in paragraph 7. Have students recall what they learned in previous lessons about poetic devices, such as similes and metaphors. Note that many prose writers like Momaday borrow these tools for their own work. For example, *the highland meadows are a stairway to the plain* (paragraph 7) is a metaphor.

Have students work with a partner to identify other examples of similes and metaphors used by Momaday in this memoir. Ask them to make a two-column chart, listing the poetic device on the left and their understanding of each meaning on the right. Then have pairs compare charts. Note how different readers may interpret the meaning of the language differently. Point out that the subjective nature of such literary devices helps draw readers into the work by calling on them to add their own experiences and understandings.

## Concept Vocabulary

**REVERENCE** If groups are struggling to define *reverence* 11, as it is used in the context of paragraph, point out that the context clue is the synonymous phrase "a holy regard."
**Possible response:** In this context, *reverence* means "honor or respect.".

**RITES** (paragraph 11) If groups are struggling to define *rites* as it is used the context of paragraph, point 11, out that the context clue is in sentences before the word, in the references to Christianity and to the Sun Dances, and in the adjective "annual" which suggests that rites are recurring events.
**Possible response:** In this context, *rites* means "a ceremonial and repeated religious act, a ritual."

**DEICIDE** (paragraph 11) If groups are struggling to define *deicide* as it is used in the context of paragraph, point 11, out that the context clue is in the anecdote that culminates in "the animal sacrifice—to impale the head of a buffalo bull upon the medicine tree." If readers infer that the Kiowa worshiped the buffalo, they can also infer the meaning of *deicide*. Note that a knowledge of Knowledge of the root *dei*, meaning "god" and the suffix *–cide* meaning "the killing of" will also lead readers to infer the correct meaning.
**Possible response:** In this context, *deicide* means "the destruction of a divine being."

NOTES

came up to the stump of a great tree, and the tree spoke to them. It bade them climb upon it, and as they did so it began to rise into the air. The bear came to kill them, but they were just beyond its reach. It reared against the tree and scored the bark all around with its claws. The seven sisters were borne into the sky, and they became the stars of the Big Dipper.

10 From that moment, and so long as the legend lives, the Kiowas have kinsmen in the night sky. Whatever they were in the mountains, they could be no more. However tenuous their well-being, however much they had suffered and would suffer again, they had found a way out of the wilderness.

Mark context clues or indicate another strategy you used that helped you determine meaning.

**reverence** (REHV uhr uhns) *n.*
MEANING:

**rites** (ryts) *n.*
MEANING:

11 My grandmother had a **reverence** for the sun, a holy regard that now is all but gone out of mankind. There was a wariness in her, and an ancient awe. She was a Christian in her later years, but she had come a long way about, and she never forgot her birthright. As a child she had been to the Sun Dances; she had taken part in those annual **rites**, and by them she had learned the restoration of her people in the presence of Tai-me. She was about seven when the last Kiowa Sun Dance was held in 1887 on the Washita River above Rainy Mountain Creek. The buffalo were gone. In order to consummate the ancient sacrifice—to impale the head of a buffalo bull upon the medicine tree—a delegation of old men journeyed into Texas, there to beg and barter for an animal from the Goodnight herd. She was ten when the Kiowas came together for the last time as a living Sun Dance culture. They could find no buffalo; they had to hang an old hide from the sacred tree. Before the dance could begin, a company of soldiers rode out from Fort Sill under orders to disperse the tribe. Forbidden without cause the essential act of their faith, having seen the wild herds slaughtered and left to rot upon the ground, the Kiowas backed away forever from the medicine tree. That was July 20, 1890, at the great bend of the Washita. My grandmother was there. Without bitterness, and for as long as she lived, she bore a vision of **deicide**.

Mark context clues or indicate another strategy you used that helped you determine meaning.

**deicide** (DEE uh syd) *n.*
MEANING:

12 Now that I can have her only in memory, I see my grandmother in the several postures that were peculiar to her: standing at the wood stove on a winter morning and turning meat in a great iron skillet; sitting at the south window, bent above her beadwork, and afterwards, when her vision failed, looking down for a long time into the fold of her hands; going out upon a cane, very slowly as she did when the weight of age came upon her; praying. I remember her most often at prayer. She made long, rambling prayers out of suffering and hope, having seen many things. I was never sure that I had the right to hear, so exclusive were they of all mere custom and company. The last time I saw her she prayed standing by the side of her bed at night, naked to the waist, the light of a kerosene lamp moving upon her dark skin. Her long, black hair, always drawn and braided in the day, lay upon her shoulders and against her breasts like a shawl. I do not speak Kiowa, and I never understood her





### CROSS-CURRICULAR PERSPECTIVES

**Humanities** Encourage students to find and share myths from a variety of cultures that explain the seven stars of the Big Dipper. Guide them to explore not only Greco-Roman mythology but also stories from Micmac, Iroquois, Zuni, Basque, Chinese, Arabian, German, British, and Irish cultures. Ask: *What do these myths have in common? What makes each myth unique?* Interested students may want to create illustrations of the myths that include the northern constellation that they may know as the Big Dipper. Note that it is also known as Ursa Major, the Plough, the Great Wagon, Saptarishi, and the Saucepan. **Research to Explore**

prayers, but there was something inherently sad in the sound, some merest hesitation upon the syllables of sorrow. She began in a high and descending pitch, exhausting her breath to silence; then again and again—and always the same intensity of effort, of something that is, and is not, like urgency in the human voice. Transported so in the dancing light among the shadows of her room, she seemed beyond the reach of time. But that was illusion; I think I knew then that I should not see her again.

13 Houses are like sentinels in the plain, old keepers of the weather watch. There, in a very little while, wood takes on the appearance of great age. All colors wear soon away in the wind and rain, and then the wood is burned gray and the grain appears and the nails turn red with rust. The windowpanes are black and opaque; you imagine there is nothing within, and indeed there are many ghosts, bones given up to the land. They stand here and there against the sky, and you approach them for a longer time than you expect. They belong in the distance; it is their domain.

14 Once there was a lot of sound in my grandmother's house, a lot of coming and going, feasting and talk. The summers there were full of excitement and reunion. The Kiowas are a summer people; they abide the cold and keep to themselves, but when the season turns and the land becomes warm and vital they cannot hold still; an old love of going returns upon them. The aged visitors who came to my grandmother's house when I was a child were made of lean and leather, and they bore themselves upright. They wore great black hats and bright ample shirts that shook in the wind. They rubbed fat upon their hair and wound their braids with strips of colored cloth. Some of them painted their faces and carried the scars of old and cherished enmities. They were an old council of warlords, come to remind and be reminded of who they were. Their wives and daughters served them well. The women might indulge themselves; gossip was at once the mark and compensation of their servitude. They made loud and elaborate talk among themselves, full of jest and gesture, fright and false alarm. They went abroad in fringed and flowered shawls, bright beadwork and German silver. They were at home in the kitchen, and they prepared meals that were banquets.

15 There were frequent prayer meetings, and great nocturnal feasts. When I was a child I played with my cousins outside, where the lamplight fell upon the ground and the singing of the old people rose up around us and carried away into the darkness. There were a lot of good things to eat, a lot of laughter and surprise. And afterwards, when the quiet returned, I lay down with my grandmother and could hear the frogs away by the river and feel the motion of the air.

16 Now there is a funeral silence in the rooms, the endless wake of some final word. The walls have closed in upon my grandmother's house. When I returned to it in mourning, I saw for the first time in my life how small it was. It was late at night, and there was a white moon, nearly full. I sat for a long time on the stone steps by

NOTES





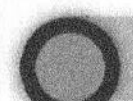

CLOSER LOOK

## Interpret Descriptive Details

Circulate among groups as students begin their close read. Suggest that as groups close read paragraph 14. Encourage them to talk about the annotations that they mark. If needed, provide the following support.

**ANNOTATE:** Have students mark details in this paragraph that describe the visitors to Momaday's grandmother's house, or work with small groups to have students participate while you highlight them together.

**QUESTION:** Guide students to consider what these details might tell them. Ask what a reader can infer from these descriptive, sensory details, and accept student responses.

**Possible response:** The details help me see what the men's clothing and faces look like. They are colorful and proud, but silent. The details help me picture the women as also bright and colorful, but I hear them too, with their gossiping voices "full of jest and gesture."

**CONCLUDE:** Help students to formulate conclusions about the importance of these details in the text. Ask students why the author might have included these details.

**Possible response:** These details help me imagine what it was like to be in Momaday's world, seeing the visitors, hearing their voices. The descriptive details are combined with Momaday's impressions of them and they support his ideas and opinions of them.

Remind students that **descriptive details** or **images** appeal to all five senses: sight, hearing, taste, smell, and touch. This selection has no dialogue and very little action, but the descriptive details help readers picture a vivid life.

PERSONALIZE FOR LEARNING

### English Language Support

**Explore a Simile** Focus students' attention on the simile, "Houses are like sentinels in the plain" that begins paragraph 13: First, make sure that students understand the denotation of *sentinel* ("a person, often a soldier, who guards a door or gate"). Use a graphic organizer such as a word web to explore all of the connotations of the simile. Begin by asking: *How are houses on the plains like sentinels?* Push students to think beyond the obvious, to explore, for example how the outside of the houses may resemble worn and dirty uniforms, or how a person might react when discovering one in the middle of a wide-open space. Ask: *What do the houses keep out? What do they keep in?* **ALL LEVELS**

FACILITATING

## Comprehension Check

Possible responses:

1. Momaday returns to visit his grandmother's grave.
2. It thrusts itself upward to the sky to symbolize the bear/tree/brother trying to grab his sisters, who became the stars of the Big Dipper. The legend represents the connection between the Kiowas and the sky.
3. Students may reference these activities: reunions, conversation, cooking for banquets, prayer meetings, feasts, playing with other children, singing
4. Momaday returns to Rainy Mountain to visit his grandmother's grave. He describes her childhood and the history of the Kiowa. He then describes the region and recounts the legend of the origin of the Big Dipper. He tells about the final Sun Dance and describes the final time he saw her. He recalls happy summers, her house joyous with family and friends. Now, however, the small house is quiet and empty. He visits her grave.

### Research

**Research to Explore** If students have difficulty choosing an interesting detail from the text, suggest they choose from the Wichita Range, the Cimarron River, the Crow nation, the Black Hills, Yellowstone National Park, or Devil's Tower.

NOTES

the kitchen door. From there I could see out across the land; I could see the long row of trees by the creek, the low light upon the rolling plains, and the stars of the Big Dipper. Once I looked at the moon and caught sight of a strange thing. A cricket had perched upon the handrail, only a few inches away from me. My line of vision was such that the creature filled the moon like a fossil. It had gone there, I thought, to live and die, for there, of all places, was its small definition made whole and eternal. A warm wind rose up and purled like the longing within me.

17 The next morning I awoke at dawn and went out on the dirt road to Rainy Mountain. It was already hot, and the grasshoppers began to fill the air. Still, it was early in the morning, and the birds sang out of the shadows. The long yellow grass on the mountain shone in the bright light, and a scissortail hied above the land. There, where it ought to be, at the end of a long and legendary way, was my grandmother's grave. Here and there on the dark stones were ancestral names. Looking back once, I saw the mountain and came away. ❧

## Comprehension Check

**Complete the following items after you finish your first read. Review and clarify details with your group.**

1. What reason does Momaday give for returning to Rainy Mountain in July?
2. What legend did the ancient Kiowas create about the origin of Devil's Tower?
3. Name three activities that Momaday recalls as he thinks about his grandmother's house.
4. **Notebook** Confirm your understanding by writing a summary of the selection.

### RESEARCH

**Research to Explore** Use online or library sources to find photographs of a place Momaday describes, such as Rainy Mountain or Devil's Tower.





PERSONALIZE FOR LEARNING

### Strategic Support

**Freezing a Moment** Guide students to stop and deeply imagine the moment that Momaday describes in paragraph 16 involving the cricket, the handrail, and the moon. Have students sketch or draw what they imagine as they read the sentences that begin "Once I looked . . ." Have them include what Momaday sees in the background (the land, the trees, and the Big Dipper) as well as what he sees in the foreground (the cricket that "filled the moon like a fossil"). Suggest that the meaning of the entire excerpt may be reflected in this single frozen moment, and let that suggestion fuel discussion.

MAKING MEANING

## Close Read the Text

With your group, revisit sections of the text you marked during your first read. **Annotate** what you notice. What **questions** do you have? What can you **conclude**?

INTRODUCTION *from* THE WAY TO RAINY MOUNTAIN

## Analyze the Text

**CITE TEXTUAL EVIDENCE** to support your answers.

Complete the activities.

1. **Review and Clarify** With your group, reread paragraph 3. Discuss how the lives of the Kiowa changed in the span of a century. How is North American geography important in light of the events that took place during that time?
2. **Present and Discuss** Now, work with your group to share passages from the selection that you found especially important. Take turns presenting your passages. Discuss what you noticed in the selection, what questions you asked, and what conclusions you reached.
3. **Essential Question:** ***What is the relationship between literature and place?*** What has this memoir taught you about the power of place in literature? Discuss with your group.

TIP

**GROUP DISCUSSION**
Beware of "groupthink," which occurs when people change their opinions or beliefs to agree with others and avoid conflict. If you disagree with the direction the group is taking, state your own opinion and the reasons behind it.

LANGUAGE DEVELOPMENT

## Concept Vocabulary

reverence  rites  deicide

**Why These Words?** The three concept vocabulary words are related. With your group, determine what the words have in common. How do these word choices enhance the impact of the memoir?

### Practice

**Notebook** Confirm your understanding of the concept vocabulary words by using them in a brief explanatory paragraph. Be sure to use context clues that hint at each word's meaning.

WORD NETWORK

Add words related to a sense of place from the text to your Word Network.

## Word Study

**Latin Roots: *-dei-* and *-cid-*** According to paragraph 11 of the Introduction from his memoir, Momaday's grandmother remembered the *deicide* that occurred when the soldiers disrupted the Sun Dance, an essential act of the Kiowa faith. The word *deicide* is formed from two Latin roots: *-dei-*, meaning "god," and *-cid-*, meaning "killing" or "cutting." Find and define another word with the root *-dei-* and another word with the root *-cid-*.

STANDARDS

**Language**
Identify and correctly use patterns of word changes that indicate different meanings or parts of speech.





DIGITAL PERSPECTIVES

## Jump Start

**CLOSE REVIEW** Ask groups to consider the following prompt: *Is this more of a happy or sad journey for the author?* As groups discuss this question, ask them to cite specific examples as evidence to support their ideas.

## Close Read the Text 

Model close reading as needed by using the Annotation Highlights in the Interactive Teacher's Edition.

Remind groups to use Accountable Talk in their discussions and to support one another as they complete the close read.

## Analyze the Text

**Possible responses:**

1. For more than a century, the tribe had controlled a vast swath of land, but the U.S. Cavalry drove them off their land, captured them, and imprisoned them.
2. Answers will vary.
3. Answers will vary.

## Concept Vocabulary

**Why These Words?**
Possible response: The words are related to religion. They reflect the devotion the Kiowa feel for the land.

### Practice

**Notebook** Possible response: The land was an object of <u>*reverence*</u> (paragraph 11) for the Kiowas, and they worshipped it every day. They practiced certain <u>*rites*</u> (paragraph 11) to celebrate the seasons. One of those rites included the ceremonial <u>*deicide*</u> (paragraph 11) of a buffalo, an animal they considered a symbol of their spirit.

### Word Network

**Possible words:** *knoll, landmark, foliage, proportion, migration, canyons, waterfall, confinement, meadows, soil*

## Word Study

For more support, see **Concept Vocabulary and Word Study.**

**Possible responses:**
*deify,* to treat someone or something as if it were a god or goddess
*deity,* a god or goddess
*insecticide,* a substance that kills insects
*fratricide,* murder of a sibling

### FORMATIVE ASSESSMENT

**Analyze the Text**

**If** students struggle to close read the text, then provide the **Introduction *from* The Way to Rainy Mountain: Text Questions** available online in the Interactive Teacher's Edition and Unit Resources. Answers and DOK levels are also available.

**Concept Vocabulary**

**If** students fail to see the connection between the words, **then** have them write a sentence for each word using either the word *holy* or *sacred*.

**Word Study**

**If** students struggle to understand the Latin parts *-dei-* and *-cide*, **then** offer *dieism* as another example ("a belief in a divine being"), or *algaecide* ("a chemical or organism that kills algae").
For Reteach and Practice, see **Word Study: Latin Roots *-dei-* and *-cid-* (RP).**

# FACILITATING

## Analyze Craft and Structure

**Literary Nonfiction** Suggest that students will never encounter a piece of literary nonfiction that is entirely objective. Simply by virtue of choosing some details and omitting others, a writer's language reveals personal bias and reflection. Emphasize that the categories of historical writing and reflective writing represent two ends of a spectrum, not an either/or classification. Memoirs, such as Momaday's, lie somewhere on the spectrum between objective and subjective, combining elements of each.

For more support, see **Analyze Craft and Structure: Literary Nonfiction.**

**See possible responses in chart on Student page.**

MAKING MEANING

INTRODUCTION *from* THE WAY TO RAINY MOUNTAIN

STANDARDS

**Reading Informational Text**

- Determine the meaning of words and phrases as they are used in a text, including figurative, connotative, and technical meanings; analyze how an author uses and refines the meaning of a key term or terms over the course of a text.
- Determine an author's point of view or purpose in a text in which the rhetoric is particularly effective, analyzing how style and content contribute to the power, persuasiveness, or beauty of the text.

## Analyze Craft and Structure

**Literary Nonfiction** Prose writing that relates the stories of real people, places, or events, and includes literary elements we usually associate with poetry or fiction is called **literary nonfiction.** A writer of literary nonfiction might use description or imagery. Likewise, he or she might tell a story from a highly subjective, or personal, perspective. The level of subjectivity and objectivity—subjectivity's opposite—varies depending on the type of literary nonfiction.

- **Historical writing** relates fact-based events from the past and usually has an objective tone. The author is often a historian who did not experience events firsthand.
- **Reflective writing** explores a topic or event from the writer's life. Reflective writing, by definition, includes the writer's personal thoughts and emotions.

In his memoir, N. Scott Momaday combines these two genres. He weaves Kiowa history and descriptions of the natural world into a personal account of the death of his grandmother and his trip to her grave.

### Practice

CITE TEXTUAL EVIDENCE to support your answers.

Work independently to analyze how Momaday combines historical and reflective writing. Use the chart to record your observations. Then, share and discuss your responses with your group. An example has been done for you.

| PARAGRAPH | HISTORICAL DETAIL | PERSONAL REFLECTION | INTERPRETATION |
|---|---|---|---|
| 3 | *In order to save themselves, they surrendered to the soldiers at Fort Sill and were imprisoned in the old stone corral. . . .* | *My grandmother was spared the humiliation of those high gray walls . . . but she must have known from birth the affliction of defeat. . . .* | Momaday feels his tribe's defeat and humiliation, even though he never experienced it. |
| 8 | "At the top of the ridge, I caught sight of Devil's Tower . . ." | "as if in the birth of time the core of the earth had broken through..." | Momaday imagines Devil's Tower was part of a creation story. |
| 12 | His grandmother made "long rambling prayers." | "something inherently sad in the sound" | Momaday felt the grief of his ancestors even though he could not understand the language. |





### FORMATIVE ASSESSMENT

### Analyze Craft and Structure

**If** students are not able to understand the poetic devices in the poems, **then** have them listen as you read examples aloud, verbally emphasizing the devices used.

For Reteach and Practice, see **Analyze Craft and Structure: Literary Nonfiction (RP).**

### PERSONALIZE FOR LEARNING

**English Language Support**

**Reflection** The abstract idea of reflection can be challenging for some students. Show students a mirror and explain that what they see in the mirror is a reflection. It is not their real selves. Likewise, when something happens in real time, it is an event. If a person remembers that event and describes it later, he or she will always put a personal "spin" on what happened. He or she will recall it in a unique way, so it is no longer real. Like the mirror, the reflector takes something real and changes it, even if those changes are slight and subtle. Reflectors add their own judgments, emotions, and opinions as they recall. Prompt a discussion by asking: *Is Momaday reporting, recalling, reflecting, or all three?* Then have students work with a partner to cite examples in the text where the author uses reflection. Provide frames like this one to support discussion: *The section that states _______ is an example of reflection because _______.* **ALL LEVELS**

LANGUAGE DEVELOPMENT

## Author's Style

**Poetic Prose** The Introduction from *The Way to Rainy Mountain* is prose, yet Momaday's style includes many strong poetic elements, such as **figurative language** and **imagery**. For example, he uses a vivid simile in paragraph 16 to describe a cricket perching on a handrail: "My line of vision was such that the creature filled the moon like a fossil."

| POETIC ELEMENT | DEFINITION | EXAMPLES |
|---|---|---|
| figurative language | language that is used imaginatively rather than literally | Simile: *the steaming foliage seems almost to writhe in fire*<br>Metaphor: *and in summer the prairie is an anvil's edge*<br>Personification: *Sweet clover takes hold of the hills* |
| imagery | words and phrases that appeal to the senses and create word pictures in readers' minds | The grass turns brittle and brown, and it cracks beneath your feet.<br><br>It reared against the tree and scored the bark all around with its claws. |

### Read It

1. Work individually to mark the figurative language or imagery in each line. With your group, discuss reasons Momaday uses each poetic element.
   a. Great green and yellow grasshoppers are everywhere in the tall grass, popping up like corn to sting the flesh. . . .
   b. In July the inland slope of the Rockies is luxuriant with flax and buckwheat, stonecrop and larkspur.
   c. From one point of view, their migration was the fruit of an old prophecy, for indeed they emerged from a sunless world.
   d. His fingers became claws, and his body was covered in fur.
2. **Connect to Style** Reread this sentence from paragraph 7 of the text. Identify the poetic elements that Momaday uses.

   *The great billowing clouds that sail upon it are shadows that move upon the grain like water, dividing light.*
3. **Notebook** How do poetic elements contribute to the power or beauty of the memoir?

### Write It

Write a brief description of an outdoor scene. Include figurative language and imagery to create a poetic impact with your prose.

STANDARDS

**Language**
Demonstrate understanding of figurative language, word relationships, and nuances in word meanings.





## PERSONALIZE FOR LEARNING

### English Language Support

**Conveying Meaning Explicitly and Implicitly** Ask pairs of students to indicate what the author implies by saying: "Directly there was a bear where the boy had been." (paragraph 9)

Ask students what they think the narrator implies by saying that his grandmother "had a reverence for the sun." (paragraph 11)

Ask students to indicate four sentences in the selection where the author implies that his grandmother was deeply connected to the Kiowa culture.

An expanded **English Language Support Lesson** on Poetic Prose is available in the Interactive Teacher's Edition.

DIGITAL PERSPECTIVES

## Author's Style

**Poetic Prose** Remind students that poetry and prose represent a spectrum of discourse, not either/or categories. Just as there can be poetic prose, there can also be prosaic poetry. As examples, cite "Chicago" and "Wilderness" by Carl Sandburg, two poems that use free verse and informal language to mirror the rhythms of natural speech.

For more support, see **Author's Style: Poetic Prose.**

### Read It

Possible responses:

1. a. By comparing the grasshoppers to popping corn, Momaday conveys the suddenness of their appearance.
   b. The descriptive details of the four types of plants create the effect of seeing the landscape closely enough to identify species.
   c. By comparing their migration to fruit and prophecy, the metaphor expresses the link them, suggesting that the migration is like a birth.
   d. The image of the boy becoming a bear helps readers see and feel the effect of the old legend.
2. **Connect to Style** Momaday uses figurative language and imagery to compare the clouds to a ship and the grain to the ocean.

   Possible response: The figurative language and imagery create a feeling of grandeur, majesty, and size, so readers imagine the prairie as a vast ocean. The poetic elements are very effective because they reinforce Momaday's main idea about the tribe's dignity and grandness, and as a force of nature.
3. Answers will vary.

### Write It

Descriptions will vary, but make sure that students describe an outdoor scene and include at least two of the three poetic elements.

### FORMATIVE ASSESSMENT

### Conventions and Style

**If** students are not able to understand how prose can be poetic, **then** have them imagine Momaday's memoir without the poetic elements. Ask them: *How would the meaning or effect change without these devices?*

For Reteach and Practice, see **Author's Style: Poetic Prose (RP).**

FACILITATING

## Writing to Compare

Although this assignment asks students to focus on literary analysis, students will likely want to consider the Native American roots of the three writers: Oneida, Apache/Chicano, and Kiowa, especially as these cultures and histories are reflected in the imagery the writers offer, the cadence of their voices, and the poetic forms they choose. They will be asked to incorporate an awareness of these ethnicities into their final products.

Explain to students that the words *devices, conventions,* **and** *techniques* can be used interchangeably.

### Prewriting

**See possible responses in chart on student page.**

Responses to questions 1 and 2 will vary but should be supported by details from the works.

EFFECTIVE EXPRESSION

POETRY COLLECTION 2

INTRODUCTION *from* THE WAY TO RAINY MOUNTAIN

## Writing to Compare

You have read and analyzed the poems "In the Longhouse, Oneida Museum" and "Cloudy Day," as well as the Introduction from *The Way to Rainy Mountain.* Now, deepen your understanding of these works by analyzing and comparing how the writers use poetic language.

**Assignment**

Poetic language is rich in imagery and detail. It conveys meaning through words, rhythms, and sounds that stir the emotions. In a single image, it can communicate a range of insights. Write an **informative essay** in which you examine the role and effects of poetic language in the two poems and the memoir excerpt. Consider the use of figurative language, imagery, and descriptive details in each work. In particular, explain how the writers use poetic language to develop a sense of place and a portrait of the people who have lived there. Work together to analyze the texts, but work on your own to write your essay.

### Prewriting

**Analyze the Texts** As a group, choose passages from each selection that are especially evocative, or that offer insights into a place or its people. Identify within those passages details, images, comparisons, sounds, or other elements that stir the emotions or communicate important information. Use the chart to capture your notes.

| LITERARY WORK | PASSAGE | ELEMENTS OF POETIC LANGUAGE | EFFECTS |
|---|---|---|---|
| In the Longhouse . . . | "House of five fires, you never raised me. . . . when the throats of the furnace wheezed and rattled its regular death" | metaphor, personification | provides a haunting tone of longing and grief |
| Cloudy Day | "wind swings past broken glass and seethes, like a frightened cat in empty spaces of the cellblock" | metaphor, simile, personification | provides a feeling of cold and fear |
| Introduction *from* The Way to Rainy Mountain | "...the immense landscape of the continental interior lay like memory in her blood." | personification, simile, imagery | provides a connection to one's ancestors and their history |

**Notebook** Respond to these questions.

1. Which portrait of a place and its people do you find most powerful? Why?
2. How is the poetic language of the poems different from the poetic language of the memoir?





PERSONALIZE FOR LEARNING

**English Language Support**

**Weaving** Focus attention on the question "How does he [Momaday] weave together historical writing and reflective writing . . . ,"and especially on the figurative use of *weave*.

Discuss the literal act of weaving, a common craft. Then have students discuss how this concept could be applied to the act of writing. Ask: *How is writing a poem, a memoir, or an informative essay like weaving a piece of cloth or a blanket?* List all responses and encourage students to continue to explore this metaphor as they draft their essays. **ALL LEVELS**

## Drafting

**Identify Key Components** Use your discussion and Prewriting notes to decide what you want to say in your essay. In a sentence or two, share your main idea with your group. Ask for feedback. Then, record a draft of your thesis here.

**Thesis:** ______________________________

______________________________

______________________________

**Choose a Structure** Next, decide how you want to structure your essay. Will you discuss each text one by one, or will you address one point of comparison at a time—for example, how the poems create a sense of place, how the poems shed light on a people, or how the poems evoke deep emotion? Lay out your ideas using a simple organizer like this one.

| Introduction | Thesis: |
|---|---|
| Body Section 1 | Main Idea: |
| Body Section 2 | Main Idea: |
| Body Section 3 | Main Idea: |
| Conclusion | Closing Thought: |

**Choose Passages** Decide which passages from each text best support your main ideas. Add them to your chart. Then, as you draft, integrate the quotations, following punctuation conventions. Make sure to use quotation marks to indicate where a quoted word or phrase begins and ends, and cite line or page numbers in parentheses after the close quotation marks.

> **Example:** In "Cloudy Day," Baca describes the prison tower as a "cornstalk" (16) and as a "hollow shoot of rock" (19). Both of these images create a dry, brittle, and desolate feeling.

**Review, Revise, and Edit**
When you are done drafting your essay, review and revise it. Make sure every body paragraph helps develop your thesis. If necessary, add quotations or other evidence to support your ideas. Once you are satisfied with the content of your essay, edit for word choice, sentence structure, and tone. Finally, proofread to eliminate errors in grammar, usage, spelling, and punctuation.

**EVIDENCE LOG**

Before moving on to a new selection, go to your Evidence Log and record what you learned from "In the Longhouse, Oneida Museum," "Cloudy Day," and the Introduction from *The Way to Rainy Mountain.*

**STANDARDS**

**Writing**
- Write informative/explanatory texts to examine and convey complex ideas, concepts, and information clearly and accurately through the effective selection, organization, and analysis of content.
- Draw evidence from literary or informational texts to support analysis, reflection, and research.





**DIGITAL PERSPECTIVES**  

## Drafting

Remind students that point-by-point organization means that each paragraph contains a general idea supported by evidence from all three texts. On the other hand, block organization means that the body of their essay will contain three paragraphs in which each paragraph is about one of the three texts.

## Review, Revise, and Edit

Remind students that reading a draft aloud to oneself or to others is an excellent way to catch errors and smooth and polish awkward sentences.

For more support, see **Writing to Compare: Informative Essay.**

**Evidence Log** Support students in completing their Evidence Log. This paced activity will help prepare them for the Performance-Based Assessment at the end of the unit.

### FORMATIVE ASSESSMENT

### Writing to Compare

**If** students are not able to understand how to draw comparisons across the three texts, **then** suggest that they reread each passage with this assignment in mind.

### Selection Test

Administer the "Introduction *from* The Way to Rainy Mountain" Selection Test, which is available in both print and digital formats online in Assessments.

## PERSONALIZE FOR LEARNING

### Strategic Support

**Integrating Quotations** Suggest that quotations should never stand alone as independent sentences. Good writers integrate quotations into their own sentences in four ways. Encourage students to experiment with all four, and suggest that the strategies increase in sophistication:

1. Introduce the quotation with a complete sentence and a colon. **Example:** Hill uses metaphors to express her truth: "I'll hide your ridgepole in my spine." (stanza 25)
2. Use an introductory or explanatory phrase, separated from the quotation with a comma. **Example:** Hill proposes, "I'll hide your ridgepole in my spine."
3. Make the quotation part of the sentence without any separating punctuation. **Example:** Hill suggests that she will "hide your ridgepole in my spine."
4. Use short quotations of only a few words as part of the sentence. **Example:** Hill claims that she will bodily enclose her history "in my spine."

# FACILITATING

## Give an Explanatory Talk

Before groups begin work on their projects, have them clearly differentiate the role each group member will play. Remind groups to consult the schedule for Small-Group Learning to guide their work during the Performance Task.

Students should complete the assignment using presentation software to take advantage of text, graphics, and sound features.

## Plan with Your Group

**Analyze the Prompt** Suggest that as groups review each selection they jot down a few notes about how the texts connect to the prompt. When they have made notes for all the texts, the group can look over the notes to see what patterns emerge that might help them articulate the thesis.

**Analyze the Text** Suggest students review the notes they made while analyzing the prompt in order to help them make decisions about placement of titles on the graphic organizer. If group members do not immediately agree about which texts most closely relate to Lopez's point, have individuals explain their thinking. If disagreements still exist, make tentative placements, with the understanding that after gathering evidence, group members will reconvene to decide if changes are needed.

**Gather Evidence** Provide time for students to analyze their assigned text(s) in detail before bringing the group together again to complete the graphic organizer. At that point if it seems the organizer—and so the presentation—is not organized in the way that best suits the textual evidence, guide groups in making the necessary revisions.

PERFORMANCE TASK: SPEAKING AND LISTENING FOCUS

SOURCES

- A LITERATURE OF PLACE
- AMERICAN REGIONAL ART
- *from* DUST TRACKS ON A ROAD
- CHICAGO
- WILDERNESS
- SANDBURG'S CHICAGO
- IN THE LONGHOUSE, ONEIDA MUSEUM
- CLOUDY DAY
- INTRODUCTION *from* THE WAY TO RAINY MOUNTAIN

## Give an Explanatory Talk

**Assignment**

In "A Literature of Place," Barry Lopez writes:

> **It is my belief that a human imagination is shaped by the architectures it encounters at an early age.**

Consider how Lopez's point applies to the texts in Small-Group Learning. Are they all inspired by a childhood sense of place, or are there other sources of inspiration? Work with your group to create and deliver an **oral presentation** in which you explain your understanding of the sense of place demonstrated in each of the texts in this section.

### Plan With Your Group

**Analyze the Prompt** With your group, discuss the prompt. Begin by analyzing Lopez's quotation. What does he mean by "architectures"? Paraphrase the quotation to be sure your group shares a complete understanding of Lopez's point. Then, read the rest of the prompt, and discuss the outcome and requirements of the assignment.

**Analyze the Texts** As a group, develop a preliminary thesis that can incorporate evidence from each source text. Then, decide how to label the graphic organizer. On the bottom row, write the title of the text that you think most strongly illustrates Lopez's point. In the row above that, write the title that has the next-strongest connection and so on.

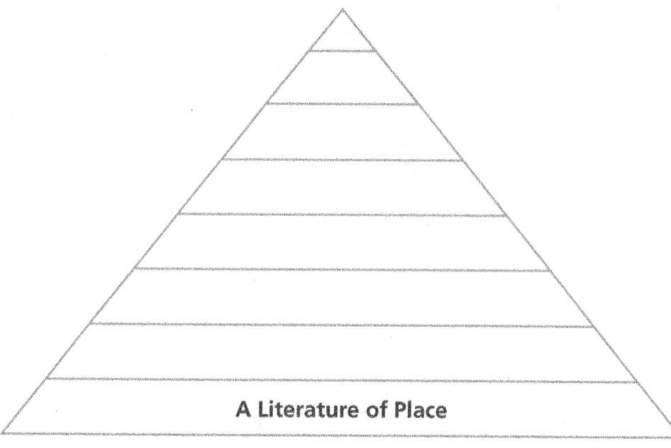


**Gather Evidence** Have each group member select one or more texts to analyze in detail. Then, discuss the texts as a group, noting evidence you might include in your oral presentation. One group member should be the note-taker, but all should offer suggestions.

STANDARDS

**Speaking and Listening**
Work with peers to promote civil, democratic discussions and decision-making, set clear goals and deadlines, and establish individual roles as needed.





AUTHOR'S PERSPECTIVE **Ernest Morrell, Ph.D.**

**Active Classroom Listening** Teachers can help students participate in class more effectively by discussing how to ask critical questions in classroom conversations. Teachers can guide students to determine which questions are most important and will yield good answers by modeling questions that synthesize multiple viewpoints and tap critical thinking skills. Here are some samples to use:

- What are the implications of…?
- What is the difference between … and …?
- What is the counterargument for …?
- What are the strengths and weakness of…?
- What is another way to look at…?

Remind students to avoid yes/no questions because they cut off discussion. Teachers can also teach students to use *critical listening*—weighing what has been said to decide if they agree with it or not. Critical listening can help students identify the salient parts of each question and integrate these parts to formulate an idea or an opinion.

**Organize Your Presentation** Review your group's notes. Determine the order in which you will discuss the source texts. You might begin by discussing the texts that provide your strongest evidence. Alternatively, you might decide to hold one strong piece of evidence until the end of the presentation.

## Rehearse With Your Group

**Practice With Your Group** Do a run-through of your talk, and use this checklist to evaluate your rehearsal and guide your revisions.

| CONTENT | PRESENTATION TECHNIQUES |
|---|---|
| ☐ Speakers respond to the prompt specifically and completely.<br>☐ Examples from the text clearly support each speaker's explanation. | ☐ Speakers use formal language.<br>☐ Speakers maintain eye contact and speak clearly.<br>☐ Speakers stay connected with the audience, even when referring to notes.<br>☐ No single speaker dominates the presentation. |

**Fine-Tune the Content** Check that your presentation includes a clear thesis statement that responds to Lopez's quotation. Also, ensure that all of the textual evidence clearly relates to the prompt.

Use academic vocabulary or domain-specific words as needed. For example, literary terms can help you name specific techniques and text structures authors use to create a strong sense of place. You might need geographic or architectural terminology to describe specific places. Consult reference materials to be sure your presentation uses technical terms correctly.

**Polish Your Presentation** Look for ways to improve your presentation by making it smoother, clearer, or more interesting. Prepare note cards with source quotations, and practice reading from notes while presenting. Consider adding music or sound effects to set a tone or emphasize key points.

## Present and Evaluate

When your group presents your explanation, listen respectfully to the members of your group, and be ready to take your turn. As you listen to other groups, notice how their talks differ from yours, both in content and in presentation techniques.



STANDARDS

**Speaking and Listening**
Present information, findings, and supporting evidence, conveying a clear and distinct perspective and a logical argument, such that listeners can follow the line of reasoning, alternative or opposing perspectives are addressed, and the organization, development, substance, and style are appropriate to purpose, audience, and a range of formal and informal tasks.

**Language**
Acquire and use accurately general academic and domain-specific words and phrases, sufficient for reading, writing, speaking, and listening at the college and career readiness level; demonstrate independence in gathering vocabulary knowledge when considering a word or phrase important to comprehension or expression.



DIGITAL PERSPECTIVES

**Organize Your Presentation** Urge groups to organize their presentations to build an argument. The evidence supporting their thesis should get stronger as they go along, with the strongest evidence going last.

## Rehearse With Your Group

**Practice With Your Group** Remind students to practice their part of the presentation alone before the group practices together. By the time the group meets to practice, group members should be very comfortable presenting their parts.

**Brush Up on Your Presentation Techniques** One way to help listeners understand quotations is to present them in writing as you speak them. Students may want to make slides or charts with significant and/or lengthy quotations on them. Doing so helps visual learners get more from the presentation than they might otherwise.

MAKE IT INTERACTIVE

Suggest groups video record their rehearsal and watch together as a strategy for refining their presentation.

## Present and Evaluate

Before beginning the presentations, set the expectations for the audience. You may wish to have students consider these questions as groups present.

- What was the presenting group's thesis?
- What evidence from the texts did the group use to support its thesis?
- What was most effective in the group's presentation?
- What might the group have done to make their presentation stronger?

PERSONALIZE FOR LEARNING

### English Language Support

**Exchanging Ideas** Working in groups can be challenging for English Language Learners, but doing so provides an excellent opportunity for them to practice their listening and comprehension skills. Urge students in each group to pause after they present an idea and give other students a chance to ask clarifying questions.

Suggest that students incorporate the following step into their group discussions: After a student speaks, have another student repeat back in their own words what the speaker said to be certain that they have understood correctly. The student might say, "I understood you to say.... Is that correct?" **ALL LEVELS**

# OVERVIEW

## INDEPENDENT LEARNING

### What is the relationship between literature and place?

Encourage students to think carefully about what they have already learned and what more they want to know about the unit topic of the grit and grandeur of places. This is a key first step to previewing and selecting the text they will read in Independent Learning.

### Independent Learning Strategies

Review the Learning Strategies with students and explain that as they work through Independent Learning they will develop strategies to work on their own.

- Have students watch the video on Independent Learning Strategies.
- A video on this topic is available online in the Professional Development Center.

Students should include any favorite strategies that they might have devised on their own during Whole-Class and Small-Group Learning. For example, for the strategy "Take notes," students might include:

- Students should have a folder, notebook or binder where they keep all of their notes together.
- Students might find a way to use color or highlight important notes.

### Block Scheduling

Each day in this Pacing Plan represents a 40–50 minute class period. Teachers using block scheduling may combine days to reflect their class schedule. In addition, teachers may revise pacing to differentiate and support core instruction by integrating components and resources as students require.

OVERVIEW: INDEPENDENT LEARNING

ESSENTIAL QUESTION:

## What is the relationship between literature and place?

The ways in which an author may be influenced by a particular place are as varied as literature itself. The physical setting, the events that took place there, the people who were involved, the author's view of the world—all of these elements affect how an author sees and writes about a landscape. In this section, you will complete your study of the importance of place in American literature by exploring an additional selection related to the topic. Then, you will share what you learn with classmates. To choose a text, follow these steps.

**Look Back** Think about the selections you have already studied. Which aspects of the concept of place do you wish to explore further? Which time period interests you the most?

**Look Ahead** Preview the texts by reading the descriptions. Which one seems most interesting and appealing to you?

**Look Inside** Take a few minutes to scan the text you chose. Choose a different one if this text doesn't meet your needs.

## Independent Learning Strategies

Throughout your life, in school, in your community, and in your career, you will need to rely on yourself to learn and work on your own. Review these strategies and the actions you can take to practice them during Independent Learning. Add ideas of your own for each category.

| STRATEGY | ACTION PLAN |
|---|---|
| Create a schedule | • Understand your goals and deadlines.<br>• Make a plan for what to do each day.<br>• |
| Practice what you have learned | • Use first-read and close-read strategies to deepen your understanding.<br>• After you read, evaluate the usefulness of the evidence to help you understand the topic.<br>• Consult reference sources for additional information that can help you clarify meaning.<br>• |
| Take notes | • Record important ideas and information.<br>• Review your notes before preparing to share with a group.<br>• |



SCAN FOR MULTIMEDIA



### Pacing Plan

| Unit Introduction | Introduce Whole-Class Learning | Historical Perspectives | *from* Life on the Mississippi | | | The Notorious Jumping Frog of Calaveras County | | | A White Heron | | | | Performance Task | |
|---|---|---|---|---|---|---|---|---|---|---|---|---|---|---|
| 1 | 2 | 3 | 4 | 5 | 6 | 7 | 8 | 9 | 10 | 11 | 12 | 13 | 14 | 15 |

Choose one selection. Selections are available online only.

## CONTENTS

SHORT STORY

### The Rockpile

*James Baldwin*

A mysterious and dangerous place becomes a source of conflict for a boy and his family.

POETRY

### The Latin Deli: An Ars Poetica

*Judith Ortiz Cofer*

For some Americans, heritage creates a "home away from home."

ESSAY

### Untying the Knot

*Annie Dillard*

The discovery of a snake's molted skin inspires thoughts of the meaning of life.

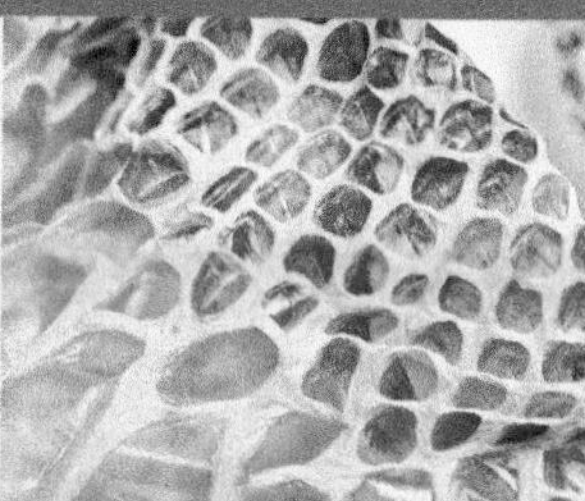

POETRY COLLECTION 3

### The Wood-Pile

### Birches

*Robert Frost*

Country scenes inspire speculation, memory, and reflection.

PERFORMANCE-BASED ASSESSMENT PREP

### Review Evidence for an Explanatory Essay

Complete your Evidence Log for the unit by evaluating what you have learned and synthesizing the information you have recorded.

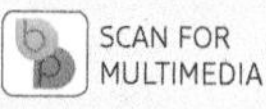
SCAN FOR MULTIMEDIA





DIGITAL PERSPECTIVES

## Contents

**Selections** Encourage students to scan and preview the selections before choosing the one they would like to read. Suggest that they consider the genre and subject matter of each one before making their decision. You can use the information on the following Planning pages to advise students in making their choice.

Remind students that the selections for Independent Learning are only available in the Interactive Student Edition. Allow students who do not have digital access at home to preview the selections using classroom or computer lab technology. Then either have students print the selection they choose or provide a printout for them.

## Performance Based-Assessment Prep

**Review Evidence for an Explanatory Essay** Point out to students that collecting evidence during Independent Learning is the last step in completing their Evidence Log. After they finish their independent reading, they will synthesize all the evidence they have compiled in the unit.

The evidence students collect will serve as the primary source of information they will use to complete the writing and oral presentation for the Performance-Based Assessment at the end of the unit.

Introduce Small-Group Learning

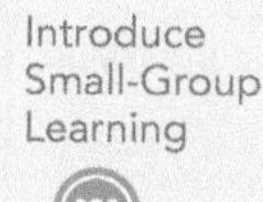

A Literature of Place

Media: American Regional Art

*from* Dust Tracks on a Road

Poetry Collection 1

Media: Sandburg's Chicago

Poetry Collection 2

Introduction *from* The Way to Rainy Mountain

Performance Task

Introduce Independent Learning

Independent Learning

Performance-Based Assessment

16 17 18 19 20 21 22 23 24 25 26 27 28 29 30

INDEPENDENT LEARNING

SELECTION RESOURCES

- First-Read Guide: Fiction
- Close-Read Guide: Fiction
- The Rockpile: Text Questions
- Audio Summaries
- Selection Audio
- Selection Test

# The Rockpile

## Summary

As the short story "The Rockpile" by James Baldwin begins, the narrator describes two young half-brothers sitting on a fire escape, overlooking a block in Harlem. The boys are looking across the street at a pile of stones that sticks up in an empty lot between two buildings. The boys' mother has forbidden them to play there for fear that they will be hurt. The younger brother, Roy, decides to join some neighborhood bad boys anyway. The older brother, John, tries to stop him, but Roy goes anyway. While playing, Roy is injured when a thrown can cuts his face. A friend of Roy's mother cleans the wound and bandages it. When the boy's father returns, there is a confrontation over who is responsible for the boy's injury. Meanwhile, the mother asks John why he let Roy go when they were told not to.

## Insight

Reading "The Rockpile" will help students realize that the places where we live and the places we treat as special are often used to explore personal themes in literature.

## Connection to the Essential Question

"The Rockpile" connects to the Essential Question, "What is the relationship between literature and place?" The story is set in the African-American community in New York City's Harlem neighborhood. It reveals how this place may affect events in young people's lives.

## Connection to Performance-Based Assessment

This selection connects to the question posed in the Performance-Based Assessment, "What makes certain places live on in our memory?" Students should consider the importance of the rockpile to the children in this story.

### Text Complexity Rubric: The Rockpile

| Quantitative Measures | |
|---|---|
| **Lexile:** 820 **Text Length:** 3,247 words | |
| **Qualitative Measures** | |
| Knowledge Demands ①—②—❸—④—⑤ | The selection relies on everyday experiences, but it is important for readers to be aware of the context and setting of Harlem during the Depression. Several themes are addressed that are sophisticated and complex. |
| Structure ①—❷—③—④—⑤ | The story is told clearly and sequentially, with narration, description and a lot of dialogue that breaks up the text and makes it easier to follow. |
| Language Conventionality and Clarity ①—②—❸—④—⑤ | The selection uses conversational and descriptive language. Dialogue uses vernacular and some slang; vocabulary is descriptive and mostly familiar. Some of the sentences are complex. |
| Levels of Meaning/Purpose ①—②—❸—④—⑤ | There are multiple levels of meaning. Plot events are simple and easy to follow, but several themes are implicit and complex including community violence, race relations, good versus evil, and family dynamics. |

DIGITAL PERSPECTIVES

 Audio  Video  Document Annotation Highlights EL Highlights  Online Assessment

SELECTION RESOURCES

- First-Read Guide: Poetry
- Close-Read Guide: Poetry
- The Latin Deli: An Ars Poetica: Text Questions
- Audio Summaries
- Selection Audio
- Selection Test

# The Latin Deli: An Ars Poetica


## Summary

In the poem "The Latin Deli: An Ars Poetica" by Judith Ortiz Cofer, the speaker describes a delicatessen where Latinos from all over shop for foods and brands that they used to buy in the homelands. These people come to the deli not just to buy food from their homelands but also to speak in, and listen to, Spanish and to find comfort from the difficulties of living as an immigrant in America.


## Insight

Reading "The Latin Deli: An Ars Poetica" will help students realize that immigrant newcomers to our country usually miss their homelands and may seek others who share their language or cultural heritage as a means of keeping them alive in their memories and their lives.

## Connection to the Essential Question

"The Latin Deli: An Ars Poetica" connects to the Essential Question, "What is the relationship between literature and place?" The final lines show a way for the poet to help Latinos maintain their cultural heritage and ethnic identity.

## Connection to Performance-Based Assessment

This selection connects to the question posed in the Performance-Based Assessment, "What makes certain places live on in our memory?" Students may see that the deli holds the memories of the customers' native land and language.

## Text Complexity Rubric: The Latin Deli: An Ars Poetica

| Quantitative Measures | |
|---|---|
| **Lexile:** NP **Text Length:** 38 lines | |
| **Qualitative Measures** | |
| Knowledge Demands ①—②—❸—④—⑤ | The poem is contemporary and familiar in style, but relies on understanding of references to Puerto Rican and other Latin American cultures that may be unfamiliar to some readers. |
| Structure ①—②—❸—④—⑤ | The poem is written in free verse with no regular or predictable pattern, stanzas, or meter. Multiple images and ideas are included in phrases and lines. |
| Language Conventionality and Clarity ①—②—❸—④—⑤ | The poem has figurative language; poetic syntax is used; the vocabulary includes many Spanish words. |
| Levels of Meaning/Purpose ①—②—❸—④—⑤ | The poem contains multiple levels of meaning that may be hard to interpret and has several themes, some of which are sophisticated, including identity, individuality, homesickness, and nostalgia. |

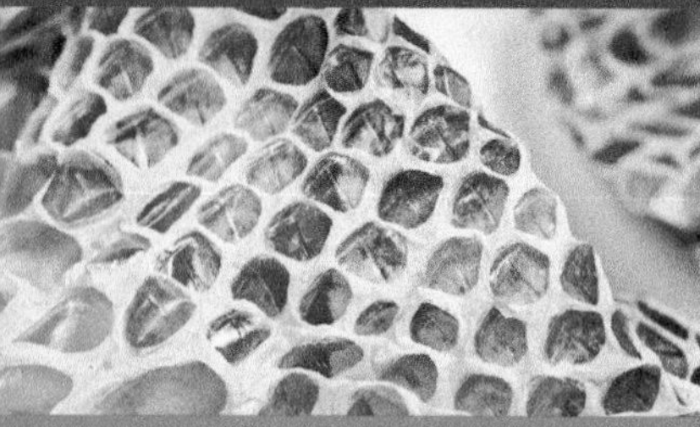

# Untying the Knot

## Summary

In Annie's Dillard's essay "Untying the Knot," the author is out walking in the woods trying "to catch" spring, the very moment when winter is over and spring is here. On her walk, she discovers a large discarded snakeskin that appears to be tied in a knot. She brings the snakeskin home and tries to untie it, only to be surprised at how it appears to be a perfect loop without beginning or end and impossible to untie. Dillard draws a comparison between the knot and the change of seasons. She eventually realizes that looking for the exact moment when one season turns into another is also impossible. Every season carries part of some other season in it. She wonders how long it would have taken the first person on Earth to determine that the seasons recur each year. Dillard concludes that, like the snakeskin, time and the seasons are continuous loops.

### Insight

Reading "Untying the Knot" will help students realize that concrete experiences, particularly those that occur in nature, often lead writers to reflect on abstract ideas such as time and place.

### SELECTION RESOURCES

- First-Read Guide: Nonfiction
- Close-Read Guide: Nonfiction
- Untying the Knot: Text Questions
- Audio Summaries
- Selection Audio
- Selection Test

## Connection to the Essential Question

"Untying the Knot" connects to the Essential Question, "What is the relationship between literature and place?" As the writer explores the woods, she realizes that nature offers observers experiences that are continuous.

## Connection to Performance-Based Assessment

This selection connects to the question posed in the Performance-Based Assessment, "What makes certain places live on in our memory?" Students should note how Dillard uses thought experiments to analyze her own experience of nature, place, and time.

### Text Complexity Rubric: Untying the Knot

| **Quantitative Measures** | |
|---|---|
| **Lexile:** 1170 **Text Length:** 1,522 words | |
| **Qualitative Measures** | |
| Knowledge Demands ①—②—③—❹—⑤ | Situations and experiences are based in nature; selection centers around multiple sophisticated themes including contemplation of life, nature, time, and seasons. |
| Structure ①—②—❸—④—⑤ | Multiple ideas are included and organization is not necessarily predictable, as the author describes events and contemplations about them. |
| Language Conventionality and Clarity ①—②—❸—④—⑤ | As it is a first person narrative, the language sounds conversational but is also complex with symbolic meaning. Many sentences have complex construction and multiple clauses. The vocabulary is descriptive. |
| Levels of Meaning/Purpose ①—②—③—❹—⑤ | The selection is centered around multiple themes. Although the author is explicit about the concepts she is contemplating, the themes of time, life, nature and seasons are sophisticated and theoretical. |

# Poetry Collection 2

SELECTION RESOURCES

- First-Read Guide: Poetry
- Close-Read Guide: Poetry
- Poetry Collection 2: Text Questions
- Audio Summaries
- Selection Audio
- Selection Test

## Summary

In the poem "The Wood-Pile" by Robert Frost, the speaker is walking through a frozen swamp. He thinks about turning back but instead continues walking. A small bird flies near, keeping a cautious distance between itself and the speaker. When the speaker is distracted by a pile of cut wood, the bird flies off. The speaker notices that the wood is several years old. He wonders what kind of person would have put so much effort into chopping wood, only to leave it to rot in the frozen swamp.

In Frost's poem "Birches," the speaker encounters some young birch trees that are bent over from the weight of snow and ice. The speaker prefers to think the trees are bent because some boys have been "swinging" on them, much as he had done as a boy. The speaker longs for those days of boyhood when he could escape life's troubles simply by climbing "toward heaven" until the tree bent and "set me down again."

## Insight

Reading "The Wood-Pile" and "Birches" will help students realize that often just being in a familiar landscape can bring back memories of a childhood experience or make a person reflect on something encountered in nature that relates to his or her own life.

## Connection to the Essential Question

"The Wood-Pile" and "Birches" connect to the Essential Question, "What is the relationship between literature and place?" Both poems are set in the cold New England landscape. In both poems, it is something that the speaker sees that affects him and prompts reflection.

## Connection to Performance-Based Assessment

This selection connects to the question posed in the Performance-Based Assessment, "What makes certain places live on in our memory?" Students should consider how the speaker in both poems is brought back to childhood memories. It is something unusual in the landscape that captures the speaker's interest.

### Text Complexity Rubric: Poetry Collection 2

| Quantitative Measures | |
|---|---|
| **Lexile:** NP **Text Length:** 40 lines; 59 lines | |
| **Qualitative Measures** | |
| Knowledge Demands<br>①—❷—③—④—⑤ | Imagery in both poems is of a country environment including woodpiles, trees, fireplaces, and frozen swamps). The images are accessible but some familiarity with country setting is helpful. |
| Structure<br>①—②—❸—④—⑤ | The poems do not have regular rhyme schemes and mostly follow the pattern of blank verse. |
| Language Conventionality and Clarity<br>①—②—❸—④—⑤ | The poems contain a mix of sentences and phrases with poetic syntax; the language is descriptive and figurative; the vocabulary is mostly familiar, with some unfamiliar usage of words. |
| Levels of Meaning/Purpose<br>①—②—❸—④—⑤ | The poems have multiple levels of meaning. Images are described in a straightforward clear way but have symbolic meaning that needs to be interpreted. |

MY NOTES

MY NOTES

# ADVISING

You may wish to direct students to use the generic **First-Read** and **Close-Read Guides** in the Print Student Edition. Alternatively, you may wish to print copies of the genre-specific **First-Read** and **Close-Read Guides** for students. These are available online in the Interactive Student Edition or Unit Resources.

## FIRST READ

Students should perform the steps of the first read independently.

NOTICE: Students should focus on the basic elements of the text to ensure they understand what is happening.

ANNOTATE: Students should mark any passages they wish to revisit during their close read.

CONNECT: Students should increase their understanding by connecting what they've read to other texts or personal experiences.

RESPOND: Students will write a summary to demonstrate their understanding.

Point out to students that while they will always complete the Respond step at the end of the first read, the other steps will probably happen somewhat concurrently. Remind students that they will revisit their first-read annotations during the close read. You may wish to print copies of the First-Read Guide for students to use.

After students have completed the First-Read Guide, you may wish to assign Text Questions for the selection that are available in the Interactive Teacher's Edition.

### Anchor Standards

In the first two sections of the unit, students worked with the whole class and in small groups to gain topical knowledge and greater understanding of the skills required by the anchor standards. In this section, they are asked to work independently, applying what they have learned and demonstrating increased readiness for college and career.

INDEPENDENT LEARNING

## First-Read Guide

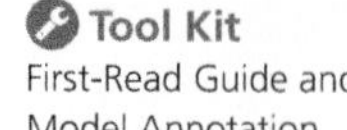

**Tool Kit**
First-Read Guide and Model Annotation

Use this page to record your first-read ideas.

Selection Title: ____________________

**NOTICE** new information or ideas you learned about the unit topic as you first read this text.

**ANNOTATE** by marking vocabulary and key passages you want to revisit.

**CONNECT** ideas within the selection to other knowledge, the Essential Question, and the selections you have read. Use reliable reference material to clarify historical context.

**RESPOND** by writing a brief summary of the selection.

STANDARD

**Reading** Read and comprehend complex literary and informational texts independently and proficiently.





## PERSONALIZE FOR LEARNING

### Strategic Support

**Text Connections** Help struggling students broaden their awareness of connections to the text. Point out that passages in a text may remind students of memories from their own lives, past reading or media experiences, or general observations they have made about the world. These connections build on what students already know, making a text more accessible to them. As students complete the First-Read Guide, ask them to identify the types of connections they make. Students can indicate these types:

- TS, or "text-to-self," reminds students of a personal memory.
- TTM, or "text-to-text/media," reminds students what they know from earlier reading or media experiences.
- TW, or "text-to-world," represents connections with general ideas they have about people and the world at large.

These codes can help students expand their ability to make connections to texts.

## Close-Read Guide

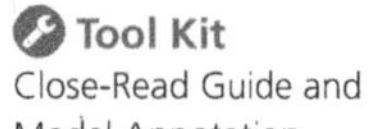

**Tool Kit**
Close-Read Guide and Model Annotation

Use this page to record your close-read ideas.

Selection Title: ______________________________

### Close Read the Text

Revisit sections of the text you marked during your first read. Read these sections closely and **annotate** what you notice. Ask yourself **questions** about the text. What can you **conclude**? Write down your ideas.

### Analyze the Text

Think about the author's choices of patterns, structure, techniques, and ideas included in the text. Select one and record your thoughts about what this choice conveys.

### QuickWrite

Pick a paragraph from the text that grabbed your interest. Explain the power of this passage.



STANDARD
**Reading** Read and comprehend complex literary and informational texts independently and proficiently.

### CLOSE READ

Students should begin their close read by revisiting the annotations they made during their first read. Then, students should analyze one of the author's choices regarding the following elements:

- **punctuation,** such as dashes or ellipses
- **word choices,** such as dialect or idiomatic expressions
- **literary devices,** such as personification or repetition
- **structure,** such as chronological, descriptive, or order of importance

**MAKE IT INTERACTIVE**
Group students according to the selection they have chosen. Then, have students meet to discuss the selection in depth. Their discussions should be guided by their insights and questions.

## Share Your Independent Learning

### Prepare to Share

Explain to students that sharing what they learned from their Independent Learning selection provides classmates who read a different selection with an opportunity to consider the text as a source of evidence during the Performance-Based Assessment. As students prepare to share, remind them to highlight how their selection connects to the question *What is the relationship between literature and place?*

### Learn From Your Classmates

As students discuss the Independent Learning selections, direct them to take particular note of how their classmates' chosen selections align with their current position on the Performance-Based Assessment question.

### Reflect

Students may want to add their reflection to their Evidence Log, particularly if their insight relates to a specific selection from the unit.

**MAKE IT INTERACTIVE**

Have students read aloud the ideas they learned from their classmates. Ask the student who generated each idea whether they think their classmate summed it up accurately, and why they think the idea is important.

**Evidence Log** Support students in completing their Evidence Log. This paced activity will help prepare them for the Performance-Based Assessment at the end of the unit.

INDEPENDENT LEARNING

EVIDENCE LOG

Go to your Evidence Log and record what you learned from the text you read.

## Share Your Independent Learning

**Prepare to Share**

**What is the relationship between literature and place?**

Even when you read or learn something independently, you can continue to grow by sharing what you have learned with others. Reflect on the text you explored independently, and write notes about its connection to the unit. In your notes, consider why this text belongs in this unit.

**Learn From Your Classmates**

**Discuss It** Share your ideas about the text you explored on your own. As you talk with your classmates, jot down ideas that you learn from them.

**Reflect**

Review your notes, and mark the most important insight you gained from these writing and discussion activities. Explain how this idea adds to your understanding of the importance of place in literature.

STANDARDS

**Speaking and Listening**

Initiate and participate effectively in a range of collaborative discussions with diverse partners on *grades 11–12 topics, texts, and issues,* building on others' ideas and expressing their own clearly and persuasively.





AUTHOR'S PERSPECTIVE **Ernest Morrell, Ph.D.**

**Self-facing Notes** Some students may not believe that they need to take notes because they'll remember what the teacher and their classmates said. However, taking notes can provide more than a memory jog. To reinforce the importance of taking good notes, teachers should remind students that they will need notes to learn effectively from their peers. In addition, self-facing notes may help students in discussion because these notes will help them prepare the key points they want to share. Point out that the Share Your Independent Learning activity will help students in these ways:

- **Provide Feedback:** Making self-facing notes will help students give classmates useful comments about their independent reading, which will result in deeper learning.
- **Share Key Ideas:** Model how to jot down information that is essential to understanding. Focus on identifying the main ideas and critical details. Students can use these notes to help them make valuable discussion contributions.
- **Expand on Other's Ideas:** Explain to students that effective notes help them cut to the heart of the matter and so provide a scaffolding for what others may have noticed in the reading.

## Review Evidence for an Explanatory Essay

At the beginning of this unit, you took a position on the following question:

What makes certain places live on in our memory?

EVIDENCE LOG

Review your Evidence Log and your QuickWrite from the beginning of the unit. Have your ideas or thesis changed?

| ☐ YES | ☐ NO |
|---|---|
| Identify at least three pieces of text evidence that convinced you to change your thesis. | Identify at least three pieces of evidence that reinforced your initial response. |
| 1. | 1. |
| 2. | 2. |
| 3. | 3. |

State your thesis now: ______

Identify a possible alternate viewpoint: ______

**Evaluate the Strength of Your Evidence** Consider your explanation. Do you have enough evidence to support your thesis? Do you have enough evidence to show that your thesis is stronger than an alternate viewpoint? If not, make a plan.

- ☐ Do some research.
- ☐ Talk with my classmates
- ☐ Reread a selection.
- ☐ Speak with an expert.
- ☐ Other: ______

STANDARDS

Writing

Introduce a topic; organize complex ideas, concepts, and information so that each new element builds on that which precedes it to create a unified whole; include formatting, graphics, and multimedia when useful to aiding comprehension.





DIGITAL PERSPECTIVES

## Review Evidence for an Explanatory Essay

**Evidence Log** Make sure students understand that their answer to a question can change as they learn more about it and as they encounter other points of view. Remind students that their Evidence Log tracked the growth of their thinking during the unit. As they carefully consider what they've learned and the evidence they've found, the initial answer they had for the question *What makes certain places live on in our memory?* might continue to change.

### Evaluate the Strength of Your Evidence

Students have the choice of many different sources when looking for information about the topic, including:

- memoirs
- articles about how memory works
- essays in which the author reminisces about a place
- books about writing memoirs

Students need to judge, not just the quantity of the evidence they gather about their topic, but also the reliability of that evidence. Discuss what might make evidence more credible, and suggest these questions:

- Did it come from a reliable source, such as governmental, educational, and professional organizations?
- Has it been reviewed by experts for accuracy?
- Does it include references to other sources?

ASSESSING

## Writing to Sources: Explanatory Essay

Students should complete the Performance-Based Assessment independently, with little to no input or feedback during the process. Students should use word processing software to take advantage of editing tools and features.

**Review the Elements of Effective Explanatory Essays** Students can review the work they did earlier in the unit as they complete the Performance-Based Assessment. They may also consult other resources such as:

- the elements of an effective explanatory essay including a clear thesis, textual evidence, logical organization, technical vocabulary where needed, and a strong conclusion, available in Whole-Class Learning.
- their Evidence Log.
- their Word Network.

Although students will use evidence from unit selections for their explanatory essay, they may need to collect additional evidence, including details about place, direct quotes, and anecdotes.

PERFORMANCE-BASED ASSESSMENT

SOURCES

- WHOLE-CLASS SELECTIONS
- SMALL-GROUP SELECTIONS
- INDEPENDENT-LEARNING SELECTION

PART 1

## Writing to Sources: Explanatory Essay

In this unit, you read a variety of texts in which setting plays a critical role. In some cases, setting provides a framework for events. In others, setting points to the theme of the text.

**Assignment**

**Write an explanatory essay in which you use examples from the texts in this unit and from your own life to answer this question:**

**What makes certain places live on in our memory?**

Analyze at least three texts from the unit to show how their authors address the question. Determine how and why a setting becomes essential rather than trivial to the meaning of a literary work. Cite examples from your chosen texts. Then, integrate one or more anecdotes from your own life into the essay. Show how and why certain places have especially affected you. Make the transition between examples from texts and anecdotes clear and smooth. Conclude with a section that ties your ideas together.

**Reread the Assignment** Review the assignment to be sure you fully understand it. The task may reference some of the academic words presented at the beginning of the unit. Be sure you understand each of the words given below in order to complete the assignment correctly.

**Academic Vocabulary**

| analyze | literal | trivialize |
|---|---|---|
| subordinate | determine | |

**Review the Elements of an Explanatory Essay** Before you begin writing, read the Explanatory Essay Rubric. Once you have completed your first draft, check it against the rubric. If one or more of the elements are missing or not as strong as they could be, revise your essay to add or strengthen those components.

WORD NETWORK

As you write and revise your explanatory essay, use your Word Network to help vary your word choices.

STANDARDS

Writing

- Write informative/explanatory texts to examine and convey complex ideas, concepts, and information clearly and accurately through the effective selection, organization, and analysis of content.
- Write routinely over extended time frames and shorter time frames for a range of tasks, purposes, and audiences.





PERSONALIZE FOR LEARNING

**English Language Support**

**Revising** Explain to students that hearing one's own writing read aloud helps a writer notice errors or awkward transitions. Have the students find a partner and read each other's explanatory essays aloud, then edit any errors they hear. Have pairs pay particular attention to the language choices made in the writing. Remind students that when writing an essay, they need to use language that is more formal than the language they use when speaking to a friend. **ALL LEVELS**

## Explanatory Essay Rubric

| | Focus and Organization | Evidence and Elaboration | Language Conventions |
|---|---|---|---|
| 4 | The introduction is engaging and reveals the topic in a way that appeals to a reader.<br>Examples progress logically, linked by transitional words and phrases.<br>The conclusion leaves a strong impression on the reader. | Ideas are supported with specific and relevant textual evidence and anecdotes.<br>The tone of the essay is formal and objective.<br>Vocabulary is strategic and appropriate for the audience and purpose. | The essay effectively demonstrates standard English conventions of usage and mechanics. |
| 3 | The introduction is engaging and clearly reveals the topic.<br>Examples progress logically, with frequent use of transitional words and phrases.<br>The conclusion follows from the rest of the text. | Ideas are supported with specific textual evidence and anecdotes.<br>The tone of the essay is mostly formal and objective.<br>Vocabulary is mostly strategic and appropriate for the audience and purpose. | The essay demonstrates fluency in standard English conventions of usage and mechanics. |
| 2 | The introduction states the topic.<br>Examples progress somewhat logically, with some use of transitional words and phrases.<br>The conclusion restates the main ideas. | Many ideas are supported with textual evidence or anecdotes.<br>The tone of the essay is occasionally formal and objective.<br>Vocabulary is somewhat appropriate for the audience and purpose. | The essay demonstrates some grasp of standard English conventions of usage and mechanics. |
| 1 | The introduction does not clearly state the topic, or it is missing altogether.<br>Examples do not progress logically. Sentences may seem disconnected.<br>The conclusion does not follow from the ideas and analysis or it is missing altogether. | Most ideas are not supported with textual evidence or anecdotes or the examples are irrelevant or contradict the thesis.<br>The tone of the essay is informal.<br>Vocabulary is limited or ineffective. | The essay contains mistakes in standard English conventions of usage and mechanics. |





DIGITAL PERSPECTIVES

## Explanatory Essay Rubric

As you review the Explanatory Essay Rubric with students, remind them that the rubric is a resource that can guide their revisions. Students should pay particular attention to the differences between an explanatory essay that contains all of the required elements (a score of 3) and one that is comprehensive, engaging, and progresses in a logical and thoughtful manner (a score of 4).

PERSONALIZE FOR LEARNING

### Strategic Support

**Make Connections** If students struggle to identify memorable settings in their own lives, it may be helpful for the student to list important events or accomplishments. Did they win an important sports competition? Overcome their fear to achieve a personal feat? Go on a trip or an adventure with friends? Where? After students have brainstormed a list of important events, have them use this resource to select the event that fits best with the essay.

## Speaking and Listening: Oral Presentation

Students should annotate their written explanatory essay in preparation for the oral presentation, marking the important elements (clear thesis, textual evidence, logical organization, technical vocabulary where needed, and a conclusion) as well as details about place, anecdotes, and direct quotes.

Remind students that the effectiveness of an oral presentation relies on how the speaker establishes credibility with his or her audience. If a speaker comes across as confident and authoritative, it will be easier for the audience to give credence to the speaker's presentation.

**Review the Rubric** As you review the Oral Presentation Rubric with students, remind them that it is a valuable tool that can help them plan their presentation. They should strive to include all of the criteria required to achieve a score of 3. Draw their attention to some of the subtle differences between scores of 2 and 3.

PERFORMANCE-BASED ASSESSMENT

PART 2

## Speaking and Listening: Oral Presentation

**Assignment**
After completing the final draft of your explanatory essay, use it as the foundation for a three-to-five-minute **oral presentation**.

Do not simply read your text aloud. Instead, take the following steps to make your presentation lively and engaging.

- Go back to your text, and mark your thesis statement. Then, annotate the most important ideas and supporting details from each part of your essay.
- Emphasize the connections between your ideas and your textual evidence so that listeners can easily follow your line of thinking.
- Practice reading with expression any quotations from the texts that you have chosen, as well as any anecdotes that you have included.
- Refer to your annotated text to guide your presentation, keep it focused, and hold the audience's attention.
- Deliver your presentation with a formal but sincere tone.

STANDARDS
**Speaking and Listening**
Present information, findings, and supporting evidence, conveying a clear and distinct perspective, such that listeners can follow the line of reasoning, alternative or opposing perspectives are addressed, and the organization, development, substance, and style are appropriate to purpose, audience, and a range of formal and informal tasks.

**Review the Rubric** The criteria by which your presentation will be evaluated appear in this rubric. Review the criteria before presenting to ensure that you are prepared.

| | Content | Presentation Techniques |
|---|---|---|
| 3 | The presentation is specifically geared to the target audience.<br>Key ideas are presented logically.<br>Examples from the chosen texts are introduced clearly and cited correctly. | The speaker enunciates clearly and uses an appropriate volume.<br>The speaker uses a formal but sincere tone overall, varying tone and pace to maintain the audience's interest.<br>The speaker maintains effective eye contact. |
| 2 | The presentation is mostly geared to the target audience.<br>Key ideas follow in a generally understandable way.<br>Examples from the chosen texts are introduced but may not be cited specifically. | The speaker enunciates clearly most of the time and usually uses an appropriate volume.<br>The speaker may be inconsistent in maintaining a formal but sincere tone overall or in varying tone and pace to maintain the audience's interest.<br>The speaker makes occasional eye contact. |
| 1 | The presentation is not clearly geared to the target audience.<br>Key ideas are hard to identify.<br>Examples from the chosen texts may not be appropriate or useful for the audience. | The speaker mumbles occasionally, speaks too quickly, or does not speak loudly enough.<br>The speaker fails to vary tone or varies it in inappropriate ways.<br>The speaker rarely or never makes eye contact. |





DIGITAL PERSPECTIVES

**Preparing For the Assignment** As students prepare their presentations, have them think about their gestures and mannerisms. Explain that gestures are physical expressions of an inner feeling or thought. Point out that it is important to avoid repetitive use of the same gesture. Have students also avoid jerky or exceedingly rapid movements, as these can be distracting. Instruct them to find examples on the Internet that demonstrate a speaker's use of gestures and mannerisms. Suggest students record themselves presenting their explanations prior to the class presentation so they can practice incorporating some of the gestures.

## Reflect on the Unit

Now that you've completed the unit, take a few moments to reflect on your learning. Use the questions below to think about where you succeeded, what skills and strategies helped you, and where you can continue to grow in the future.

### Reflect on the Unit Goals

Look back at the goals at the beginning of the unit. Use a different colored pen to rate yourself again. Think about readings and activities that contributed the most to the growth of your understanding. Record your thoughts.

### Reflect on the Learning Strategies

**Discuss It** Write a reflection on whether you were able to improve your learning based on your Action Plans. Think about what worked, what didn't, and what you might do to keep working on these strategies. Record your ideas before a class discussion.

### Reflect on the Text

Choose a selection that you found challenging, and explain what made it difficult.

Describe something that surprised you about a text in the unit.

Which activity taught you the most about the relationship between literature and place? What did you learn?

SCAN FOR MULTIMEDIA

STANDARDS

**Speaking and Listening**
Present information, findings, and supporting evidence, conveying a clear and distinct perspective, such that listeners can follow the line of reasoning, alternative or opposing perspectives are addressed, and the organization, development, substance, and style are appropriate to purpose, audience, and a range of formal and informal tasks.





DIGITAL PERSPECTIVES

## Reflect on the Unit

- Have students watch the video on Reflecting on Your Learning.
- A video on this topic is available online in the Professional Development Center.

### Reflect on the Unit Goals

Students should re-evaluate how well they met the Unit Goals now that they have completed the unit. You might ask them to provide a written commentary on the goal they made the most progress with as well as the goal they feel warrants continued focus.

### Reflect on the Learning Strategies

**Discuss It** If you want to make this a digital activity, go online and navigate to the Discussion Board. Alternatively, students can share their learning strategies reflections in a class discussion.

### Reflect on the Text

Consider having students share their text reflections with one another.

**MAKE IT INTERACTIVE**

Have students prepare one- or two-sentence summaries advertising their talks. The summaries should highlight the most important element of the presentation.

Record students reading their promotional summaries aloud. Play them prior to the presentations as a way to engage and prepare the audience.

### Unit Test and Remediation

After students have completed the Performance-Based Assessment, administer the Unit Test. Based on students' performance on the test, assign the resources as indicated on the Interpretation Guide to remediate. Students who take the test online will be automatically assigned remediation, as warranted by test results.

PERSONALIZE FOR LEARNING

**English Language Support**

**Develop Fluency** If students are having trouble with a fluent presentation, instruct them to capitalize words on notecards that require emphasis, speak slowly, and supply extra examples to make their points clear. **ALL LEVELS**

RISK
AHEAD

UNIT

# Facing Our Fears

## Victims and Victors

INTRODUCTION

## Jump Start

Ask students to name some "scary" costumes children are likely to wear on the holiday of Halloween. Then have students discuss whether the costumes can actually induce fear in other children, or whether pretending to be "scary" serves another purpose for the children dressing up. If you wish, extend the discussion to "scary" movies: ask why students think people find it entertaining to be frightened.

### Facing Our Fears

Ask students what the phrase *facing our fears* suggests to them. Point out that as they work through this unit, they will encounter many examples of people facing their fears.

### Video

Project the introduction video in class, ask students to open the video in their interactive textbooks, or have students scan the BouncePage icon with their phones to access the video.

**Discuss It** If you want to make this a digital activity, go online and navigate to the Discussion Board. Alternatively, students can share their responses in a class discussion.

### Block Scheduling

Each day in this pacing calendar represents a 40–50 minute class period. Teachers using block scheduling may combine days to reflect their class schedule. In addition, teachers may revise pacing to differentiate and support core instruction by integrating components and resources as students require.

UNIT 5

# Facing Our Fears

## Victims and Victors

The Hollywood Blacklist

**Discuss It** How should we respond to those who hold different political views or values than we do?

Write your response before sharing your ideas.

544

SCAN FOR MULTIMEDIA

### Pacing Plan

Introduce Whole-Class Learning

| Unit Introduction | Historical Perspectives | The Crucible, Act I | | The Crucible, Act II | | The Crucible, Act III | | The Crucible, Act IV | | Media: The Crucible | | Performance Task | |
|---|---|---|---|---|---|---|---|---|---|---|---|---|---|
| 1 | 2 | 3 | 4 | 5 | 6 | 7 | 8 | 9 | 10 | 11 | 12 | 13 | 14 | 15 |

DIGITAL PERSPECTIVES

 Audio  Video  Document  Annotation Highlights  EL Highlights  Online Assessment

UNIT 5

UNIT INTRODUCTION

ESSENTIAL QUESTION: How do we respond when challenged by fear?

LAUNCH TEXT ARGUMENT MODEL
Is It Foolish to Fear?

WHOLE-CLASS LEARNING

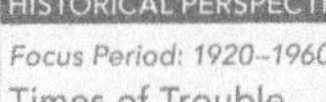

HISTORICAL PERSPECTIVES
*Focus Period: 1920–1960*
Times of Trouble

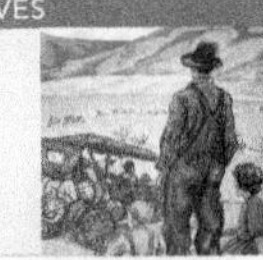

COMPARE

ANCHOR TEXT: DRAMA
The Crucible
*Arthur Miller*
Act I
Act II
Act III
Act IV

MEDIA: AUDIO PERFORMANCE
The Crucible
*L.A. Theatre Works*

PERFORMANCE TASK
WRITING FOCUS:
Write an Argument

SMALL-GROUP LEARNING

COMPARE

AUTOBIOGRAPHY
*from* Farewell to Manzanar
*Jeanne Wakatsuki Houston and James D. Houston*

MEDIA: VIDEO
Interview With George Takei
*Archive of American Television*

SHORT STORY
Antojos
*Julia Alvarez*

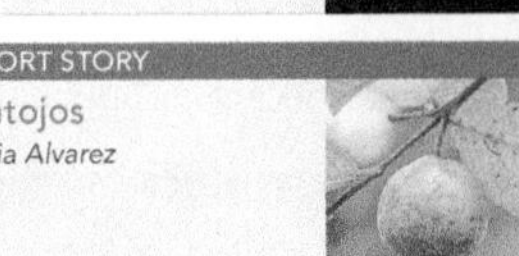

PERFORMANCE TASK
SPEAKING AND LISTENING FOCUS:
Present an Argument

INDEPENDENT LEARNING

MAGAZINE ARTICLE
What You Don't Know Can Kill You
*Jason Daley*

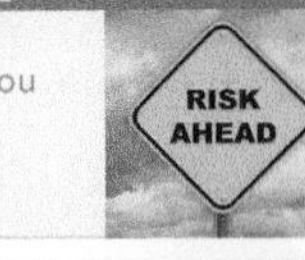


POETRY
Runagate Runagate
*Robert Hayden*

POETRY COLLECTION
1-800-FEAR
*Jody Gladding*

Bears at Raspberry Time
*Hayden Carruth*

For Black Women Who Are Afraid
*Toi Derricotte*

ESSAY
What Are You So Afraid Of?
*Akiko Busch*

PERFORMANCE-BASED ASSESSMENT PREP
Review Evidence for an Argument

PERFORMANCE-BASED ASSESSMENT

Argument: Essay and Speech

PROMPT:
Is fear always a harmful emotion?

545

## How do we respond when challenged by fear?

Introduce the Essential Question and point out that students will respond to related prompts.

- **Whole-Class Learning** *Could any of the characters in* The Crucible *have done more to end the hysteria in Salem?*
- **Small-Group Learning** *Do people usually learn from their fear?*
- **Performance-Based Assessment** *Is fear always a harmful emotion?*

### Using Trade Books

Refer to the Teaching with Trade Books section in this book or online in the Interactive Teacher's Edition for suggestions on how to incorporate these novels into this unit.

- *The Red Badge of Courage* by Stephen Crane
- *The Devil in The White City* by Erik Larson
- *Heart of Darkness* and *The Secret Sharer* by Joseph Conrad

### Current Perspectives

To increase student engagement, search online for stories about the effect of fear on the human brain. Always preview content.

- **News Story: "Why We NEVER Forget Gunshots." (DailyMail.com)** How our brains respond to fear influences future reactions.
- **Blog: "Outsmart Your Brain: Use the Science of Fear to Tackle Your Biggest Challenge." (HuffingtonPost.com)** We can use scientific understanding of the brain to tackle our challenges.

Introduce Small-Group Learning

16 | *from* Farewell to Manzanar: 17, 18, 19 | Media: Interview with George Takei: 20, 21 | Antojos: 22, 23, 24, 25 | Performance Task: 26

Introduce Independent Learning

27 | Independent Learning: 28 | Performance-Based Assessment: 29, 30

## About the Unit Goals

These unit goals were backward designed from the Performance-Based Assessment at the end of the unit and the Whole-Class and Small-Group Performance Tasks. Students will practice and become proficient in many more standards over the course of this unit.

## Unit Goals

Review the goals with students and explain that as they read selections in this unit, they will improve their skills in reading, writing, research, language, and speaking and listening.

- Have students watch the video on Goal Setting.
- A video on this topic is available online in the Professional Development Center.

**Reading Goals** Tell students they will read and evaluate an argumentative essay. They will also read fiction, nonfiction, and poetry to better understand the ways writers express ideas.

**Writing and Research Goals** Tell students that they will learn the elements of writing an argumentative essay. They will also write their own argumentative essay. Students will write for a number of reasons and will conduct research to clarify and explore ideas.

**Language Goal** Tell students that they will develop a deeper understanding of the correct use of pronouns and the use of irony in their writing. They will then practice adding meaning to their writing through irony.

**Speaking and Listening Goals** Explain to students that they will work to build on one another's ideas, and communicate with one another. They will also learn to incorporate audio, visuals, and text in presentations.

### HOME Connection

A Home Connection letter to students' parents or guardians is available in the Interactive Teacher's Edition. The letter explains what students will be learning in this unit and how they will be assessed.



## Unit Goals

Throughout this unit, you will deepen your perspective on the concept of fear by reading, writing, speaking, listening, and presenting. These goals will help you succeed on the Unit Performance-Based Assessment.

Rate how well you meet these goals right now. You will revisit your ratings later when you reflect on your growth during this unit.

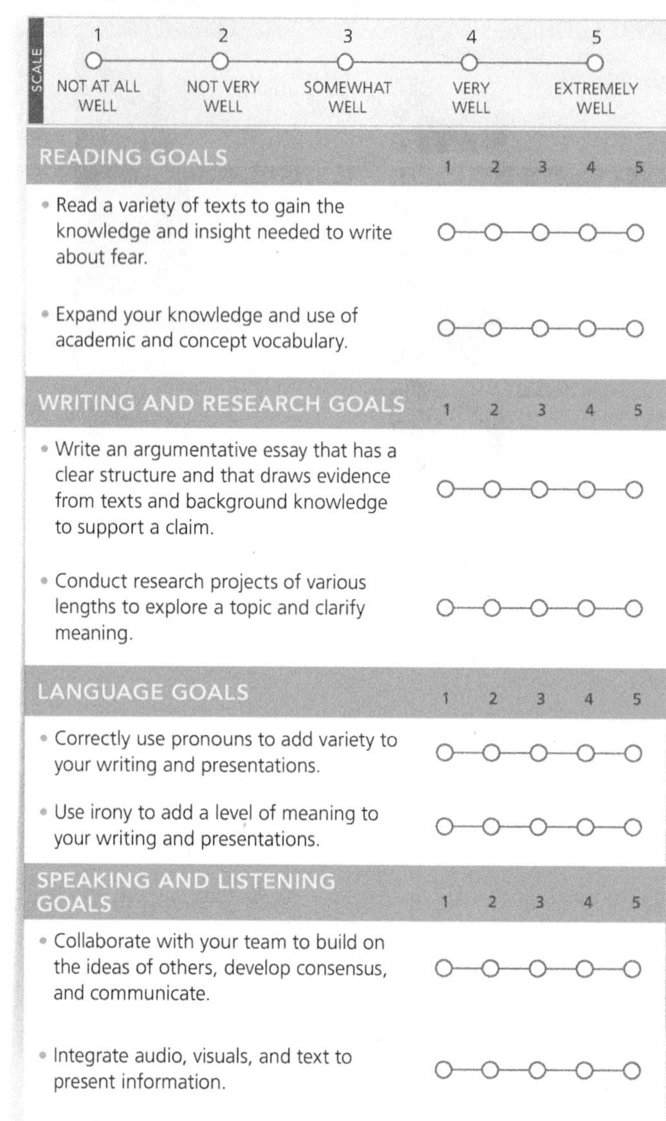

| SCALE | 1 | 2 | 3 | 4 | 5 |
|---|---|---|---|---|---|
| | NOT AT ALL WELL | NOT VERY WELL | SOMEWHAT WELL | VERY WELL | EXTREMELY WELL |

| READING GOALS | 1 | 2 | 3 | 4 | 5 |
|---|---|---|---|---|---|
| • Read a variety of texts to gain the knowledge and insight needed to write about fear. | O | O | O | O | O |
| • Expand your knowledge and use of academic and concept vocabulary. | O | O | O | O | O |

| WRITING AND RESEARCH GOALS | 1 | 2 | 3 | 4 | 5 |
|---|---|---|---|---|---|
| • Write an argumentative essay that has a clear structure and that draws evidence from texts and background knowledge to support a claim. | O | O | O | O | O |
| • Conduct research projects of various lengths to explore a topic and clarify meaning. | O | O | O | O | O |

| LANGUAGE GOALS | 1 | 2 | 3 | 4 | 5 |
|---|---|---|---|---|---|
| • Correctly use pronouns to add variety to your writing and presentations. | O | O | O | O | O |
| • Use irony to add a level of meaning to your writing and presentations. | O | O | O | O | O |

| SPEAKING AND LISTENING GOALS | 1 | 2 | 3 | 4 | 5 |
|---|---|---|---|---|---|
| • Collaborate with your team to build on the ideas of others, develop consensus, and communicate. | O | O | O | O | O |
| • Integrate audio, visuals, and text to present information. | O | O | O | O | O |

**STANDARDS**

**Language**

Acquire and use accurately general academic and domain-specific words and phrases, sufficient for reading, writing, speaking, and listening at the college and career readiness level; demonstrate independence in gathering vocabulary knowledge when considering a word or phrase important to comprehension or expression.



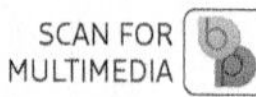




### AUTHOR'S PERSPECTIVE Ernest Morrell, Ph.D.

**How to Support Kids When They Have Trouble** When setting goals with students, have them consider these questions:

1. What are the opportunities open to me if I achieve this goal?
2. What are the biggest challenges that I will face in attempting to achieve this goal?
3. What support will I need from others in order to achieve this goal and how will I ensure that I get that support?

The first question helps students see that setting goals helps them take control of their life and focus on the issues that matter to them. As a result, they are likely to make good decisions.

The second question helps students understand that achieving goals takes hard work, resilience, and determination. The third question reassures students that help is available and shows them the importance of seeking and accepting help when necessary.

## Academic Vocabulary: Argument

Understanding and using academic terms can help you read, write, and speak with precision and clarity. Here are five academic words that will be useful to you in this unit as you analyze and write arguments.

**Complete the chart.**

1. Review each word, its root, and the mentor sentences.
2. Use the information and your own knowledge to predict the meaning of each word.
3. For each word, list at least two related words.
4. Refer to a dictionary or other resources if needed.

TIP

**FOLLOW THROUGH**
Study the words in this chart, and mark them or their forms wherever they appear in the unit.

| WORD | MENTOR SENTENCES | PREDICT MEANING | RELATED WORDS |
|---|---|---|---|
| **assert**<br><br>ROOT:<br>***-ser-***<br>"join" | 1. You cannot simply *assert* a position; you must support it with convincing evidence.<br>2. In the debate, my opponent was too timid and did not *assert* his ideas clearly. | | assertion; assertively |
| **relevant**<br><br>ROOT:<br>***-lev-***<br>"raise" | 1. That old-fashioned show is not *relevant* to most young viewers.<br>2. Chapter three may be *relevant* to your fascination with architecture. | | |
| **certify**<br><br>ROOT:<br>***-cert-***<br>"sure" | 1. After an election, an outside party may be brought in to *certify* the results.<br>2. Before you quote an expert, you should *certify* her credentials. | | |
| **immutable**<br><br>ROOT:<br>***-mut-***<br>"move" | 1. Some ideas are simply *immutable* and unchanging.<br>2. Shakespeare's characters are not *immutable*, because they can be interpreted in so many different ways. | | |
| **definitive**<br><br>ROOT:<br>***-fin-***<br>"end" | 1. In my opinion, that is the *definitive* biography of Arthur Miller.<br>2. It is too early to reach any *definitive* conclusions about the issue. | | |





DIGITAL PERSPECTIVES 

## Academic Vocabulary: Argument

Introduce the blue academic vocabulary words in the chart on the student page. Point out that the root of each word provides a clue to its meaning. Discuss the mentor sentences to ensure students understand each word's usage. Students should also use the mentor sentences as context to help them predict the meaning of each word. Check that students are able to fill the chart in correctly. Complete pronunciations, parts of speech, and definitions are provided for you. Students are only expected to provide the definition and two related words.

Possible responses

**assert** *v.* (uh SURT)
**Meaning:** to declare firmly; to insist
**Related words:** assertion, assertively
**Additional words related to root *-ser-*:** assertive, reassertion, series

**relevant** *adj.* (REHL uh vuhnt)
**Meaning:** purposeful; meaningful
**Related words:** relevance, nonrelevant
**Additional words related to root *-lev-*:** lever, levitate, relieve, alleviate

**certify** *v.* (SUR tuh fy)
**Meaning:** to declare something is true
**Related words:** certifier, precertify
**Additional words related to root *-cert-*:** certain, certificate, certifiable

**immutable** *adj.* (ih MYOO tuh buhl)
**Meaning:** never changing; not changeable
**Related words:** immutability, immutableness
**Additional words related to root *-mut-*:** mutable, permutation, mutation

**definitive** *adj.* (dih FIHN uh tihv)
**Meaning:** that decides or settles a question; final
**Related words:** definitively, nondefinitive
**Additional words related to root *-fin-*:** finish, infinite, final, definite

### PERSONALIZE FOR LEARNING

**English Language Support**
**Cognates** Many of the academic words have Spanish cognates. Use these cognates with students whose home language is Spanish.
**ALL LEVELS**

certify – certificar
immutable – inmutable
definitive – definitivo

### Purpose of the Launch Text

The Launch Text provides students with a common starting point to address the unit topic. After reading the Launch Text, all students will be able to participate in discussions about facing our fears.

**Lexile: 1000** The easier reading level of this selection makes it perfect to assign for homework. Students will need little or no support to understand it.

Additionally, "Is It Foolish to Fear?" provides a writing model for the Performance-Based Assessment students will complete at the end of the unit.

## Launch Text: Argument Model

Remind students that the author's position is usually apparent in the first few paragraphs of a text. Point out that if the title of a text contains a question, readers should be able to quickly determine the author's answer to the question. This answer represents the author's position, or claim. ("It is not foolish to fear–it is a matter of survival.") Guide students to identify an alternate or opposing claim presented in the text. ("We may feel foolish…") Finally, ask students to distinguish the relationships between the claim and reasons, and between reasons and evidence.

Encourage students to read this text on their own and annotate unfamiliar words and sections of text they think are particularly important.

### AUDIO SUMMARIES

Audio summaries of "Is It Foolish to Fear?" are available online in both English and Spanish in the Interactive Teacher's Edition or Unit Resources. Assigning these summaries before students read the Launch Text may help them build additional background knowledge and set a context for their reading.

LAUNCH TEXT | ARGUMENT MODEL

This selection is an example of an **argumentative text**, a type of writing in which the author presents a claim and organizes evidence and reasons to support that claim. This is the type of writing you will develop in the Performance-Based Assessment at the end of the unit.

**As you read,** notice how the writer uses relevant evidence to develop the claim. Mark the text to answer this question: What is the writer's position, and what evidence supports it?

# Is It Foolish to Fear?

NOTES

1 Fear of falling, fear of flying, fear of snakes and spiders—sometimes it seems that we humans are controlled by our fears. Some of us may seek professional help to rid ourselves of fears. However, fear plays an important role in life. It is not foolish to fear—it is a matter of survival.

2 Fear may feel negative, because it is an emotion that can be painful. The physical responses we have to objects or situations that we fear are often grouped together and characterized as a "fight or flight" instinct. Something alarms you, and instantly your brain causes a number of chemicals to be released into your bloodstream. Those chemicals race through the body, causing your heart to race, your muscles to tense, and your breathing to quicken. Your pupils dilate, so bright light hurts, but you can see more clearly. Your surface veins constrict, making your skin feel cold.

3 Long ago, such responses made it easier for early humans to escape from predators. Dilated pupils meant that they could see better in dim light. Quick breathing and tense muscles allowed them to run faster or leap higher than they normally could. Their skin grew cold as blood flowed to the major muscles, letting arms and legs move more rapidly. The entire body became an instrument focused





SCAN FOR MULTIMEDIA 

## PERSONALIZE FOR LEARNING

### English Language Support

**Clarifying Terms** Some English learners may struggle with terms associated with argumentative text, especially if they have not had much practice applying the terms to relatable examples. Have students work in pairs to review the definitions of *argument*, *claim*, and *evidence*. Then ask each pair to write a claim related to the text topic. For example, "Spiders are scary" or "Spiders are not scary." Next ask students to connect ideas by listing one or two reasons for their claim. ("Spiders are scary because they can bite you.") Finally, ask students to list evidence, or descriptions of evidence. For example, "Scientists verify that there are some groups of spiders that do bite humans." Or, for the counterclaim, "Spiders do not pose a threat to people. Scientists who study spiders show that spider bites in humans are rare." **EMERGING/ EXPANDING**

on surviving danger. If flight was possible, the person would run. If it was not, he or she would fight. Either way, fear stimulated the brain and primed the body for a response.

4 This response to fear was good for everyone who displayed it. The humans who felt and responded to fear most strongly were likely to be the ones who survived, whether the fear stimulus was a tiger, an earthquake, or a violent storm.

5 Today, our fear stimulus might be a dark alley, a swaying rope bridge, or a barking dog. We sense danger, and our bodies react. We may feel foolish when the alley proves to be empty, the bridge safe, and the dog friendly. Nevertheless, that initial rush of fear serves as our protector and should never be ignored.

6 Today, modern psychotherapies may include conditioning—a stimulus-response learning process—that helps people rid themselves of fears. After just a few sessions, nearly anyone can stop being afraid of speaking in public or driving through a tunnel. So why shouldn't we all condition ourselves to become braver?

7 First, there is a difference between fear and phobia. A phobia is an unnecessary fear of something that is unlikely to cause harm. For example, some people are afraid of clowns, but the odds of a clown's being harmful are small. Second, without fear, one would be in constant danger. It is important to be afraid of an oncoming car, a flying brick, or the rattling tail at the end of an unfamiliar snake. In such cases, fear is a matter of self-preservation.

8 Few of us enjoy being afraid. It is physically and mentally uncomfortable, and once any danger has passed, we may feel that our fears were unwarranted. It is worth remembering, however, that ever since you were a small child perched at the top of a staircase or toddling near a hot stove, a logical, sensible, inbred fear has protected you from harm. ❧

NOTES

WORD NETWORK FOR FACING OUR FEARS

**Vocabulary** A Word Network is a collection of words related to a topic. As you read the unit selections, identify interesting words related to the idea of fear, and add them to your Word Network. For example, you might begin by adding words from the Launch Text, such as *alarms*. For each word you add, note a related word, such as a synonym or an antonym. Continue to add words as you complete this unit.

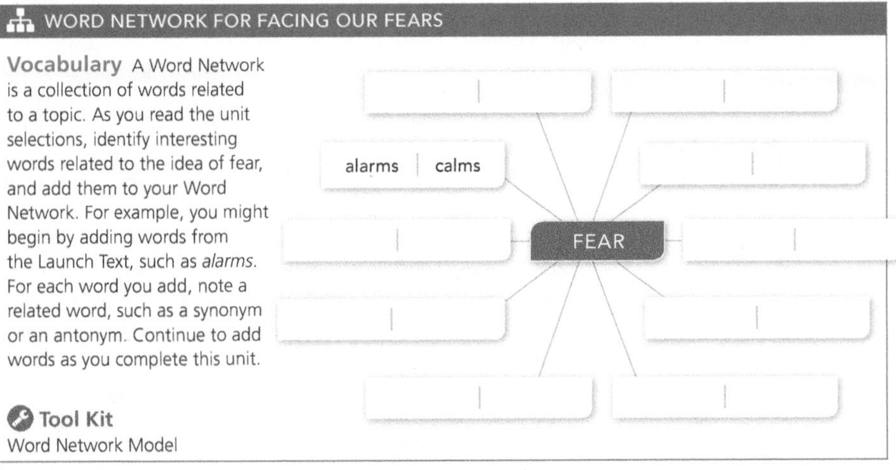


**Tool Kit**
Word Network Model

DIGITAL PERSPECTIVES

## Word Network for Facing Our Fears

Tell students that they can fill in the Word Network as they read the texts in the unit, or they can jot down the words elsewhere and add them later. Point out to students that people may have personal associations with some words. A word that one student thinks is related to the concept of facing our fears might not be a word another student would pick. However, students should feel free to add any relevant words to their Word Network. Each person's Word Network will be unique. If you choose to print the Word Network, distribute it to students at this point so they can use it throughout the rest of the unit.

AUTHOR'S PERSPECTIVE **Elfrieda Hiebert, Ph.D.**

**Rare Words** Increasing reading comprehension relies on a connection between fluency and vocabulary. **Rare words** are less frequently used words that represent what might be a common idea. Instead of calling a character *nervous*, an author might use *disconcerted*, or *flustered*. In reading/language arts, where many rare unknown words pertain to known concepts, teachers should emphasize semantic connections across words. This can be achieved effectively with concept maps or word networks that help students understand the essential characteristics of a word's meaning. Here's an example for *sluggish*:

heavy blah indolent
inactive comatose inert off sullen

Digital tools, including online dictionaries, often have features to help demonstrate the increasing complexity of the spectrum of these words by filtering out levels of complexity.

# INTRODUCTION

## Summary

Have students read the introductory paragraph. Provide them with tips for writing a summary:

- Write in the present tense.
- Make sure to include the title of the work.
- Be concise: a summary should not be equal in length to the original text.
- If you need to quote the words of the author, use quotation marks.
- Don't put your own opinions, ideas, or interpretations into the summary. The purpose of writing a summary is to accurately represent what the author says, not to provide a critique.

If necessary, students can refer to the Tool Kit for help in understanding the elements of a good summary.

**See possible Summary on student page.**

## Launch Activity

Tell students that they will have many opportunities to discuss facing our fears as they work their way through this unit. Remind students that brainstorming as a class is a collaborative process whereby people take turns sharing thoughts that come to mind. Reiterate that the fears for the list are those that are commonly expressed in print and media. Students do not need to share or identify their personal fears. Ensure that there are enough sticky notes and that every student has three. Once the class has reached a conclusion and written a claim, ask students what they would do next if they were to build on this claim. Students should volunteer that they would need to support the claim with reasons and relevant evidence and anticipate and address possible counterclaims.



## Summary

Write a summary of "Is It Foolish to Fear?" A **summary** is a concise, complete, and accurate overview of a text. It should not include a statement of your opinion or an analysis.

Possible response: "Is It Foolish to Fear?" opens with a description of the "fight or flight" response. When we become frightened, our brains produce chemicals that help our bodies prepare for the sudden exertion necessary to run away from or to fight a threat. Early humans who displayed this response were more likely to survive than those who did not. Today we sometimes react fearfully to things that turn out not to be a threat, and that might make us feel foolish. But there are actual threats in the world, too, and responding to them appropriately can keep us from getting hurt.

## Launch Activity

**Record "Popular" Fears** As a class, brainstorm for a list of fears that you have read about or seen portrayed in movies or television shows. Have a volunteer write each fear along the bottom of the chalkboard, another display area in your classroom, or a large piece of paper. Try to develop a row of ten to twelve fears.

- Now, work together to construct a bar graph. Take three sticky notes, and write your name on each one.
- Take turns going to the board (or other display location). Place one note each above a fear that you think actually afflicts many people. Make sure to place your notes above any that are already there so that you build columns.
- When you have all finished placing your notes, stand back and look at the graph you have constructed.
- Based on the graph, draw a conclusion about the fears that are commonly portrayed in books and entertainment media. Do these fears accurately represent those of regular people in real life? Discuss these questions, and come to a consensus. Write your consensus at the top of your bar graph.





### PERSONALIZE FOR LEARNING

**Strategic Support**

**The Media and Fears** Pose this question to students: *Do the fears portrayed in television programs and films reflect popular fears or help to reinforce, or even create them?* Allow students to volunteer their opinions, and then ask them to rephrase their opinion in writing as a claim for an argumentative text. If students have difficulty with the broad nature of the question, cite one of the fears on the class list (preferably one that is not too evocative or controversial) and ask them to write a claim to address the example. Have students work with a partner who shares a similar view (*Popular fears are reflected in television and film*). Student pairs should write an informal outline for their argument, consisting of initial ideas only.

## QuickWrite

Consider class discussions, the video, and the Launch Text as you think about the prompt. Record your first thoughts here.

PROMPT: **Is fear always a harmful emotion?**

Possible response: Fear can be a harmful emotion. For one thing, it can hold us back. Fear of looking foolish might prevent someone from asking a question in class, and so he or she gets a lower grade than he or she might have otherwise. If you like someone but are afraid to ask him or her out, you might be missing out on a wonderful, long-term relationship.

But the question is whether fear is always a harmful emotion, and the answer is obviously no. For example, being afraid to skateboard down a steep hill might prevent you from breaking your leg. Fear of walking down a dark street alone could keep you from getting mugged. There are definitely times when fear is valuable, not harmful.

### EVIDENCE LOG FOR FACING OUR FEARS

Review your QuickWrite. Summarize your thoughts in one sentence to record in your Evidence Log. Then, record textual details or evidence from "Is It Foolish to Fear?" that supports your initial position.

Prepare for the Performance-Based Assessment at the end of the unit by completing the Evidence Log after each selection.

**Tool Kit**
Evidence Log Model

Title of Text: ______ Date: ______

| CONNECTION TO PROMPT | TEXT EVIDENCE/DETAILS | ADDITIONAL NOTES/IDEAS |
|---|---|---|
| | | |

How does this text change or add to my thinking? Date: ______

SCAN FOR MULTIMEDIA



DIGITAL PERSPECTIVES

## QuickWrite

Students should use the material they have read and viewed in the Unit Overview to develop and present their own answer to the prompt. They should present their position clearly and support it with accurately cited details and logical reasoning.

This initial response will help inform their work when they complete the Performance-Based Assessment at the end of the unit. Suggest to students that they consider all the material and discussions addressed thus far in the unit, as well as their own thoughts, to come up with an initial position. Remind students that even in this QuickWrite they will want to draw on the model for argument—that is, they should respond to the prompt with a position statement that represents an agreement or disagreement and then elaborate with reasons, examples, and evidence.

**See possible QuickWrite on student page.**

## Evidence Log for Is It Foolish to Fear?

Students should record their initial position and include evidence from "Is It Foolish to Fear?" that supports it.

If you choose to print the Evidence Log, distribute it to students at this point so they can use it throughout the rest of the unit.

### Performance-Based Assessment: Refining Your Thinking

- Have students watch the video on Refining Your Thinking.
- A video on this topic is available online in the Professional Development Center.

## PERSONALIZE FOR LEARNING

### English Language Support

**Supporting Opinions** Some English learners may struggle with expressing their ideas in writing and may be better able to support their opinion orally. Give these students the option of responding to the QuickWrite through a discussion with a partner. Have each partner present a statement regarding the value of fear. If student pairs do not have opposing views, ask one of them to take the opposing position, as it is helpful practice for constructing an argument. Remind students that their goal is to persuade their partner. Therefore, each of them needs to back up their position with details, reasons, and possible evidence. Using a graphic organizer for argument as a guide, have partners assist each other in recording the results of their discussion. **EMERGING/EXPANDING**

# OVERVIEW

## WHOLE-CLASS LEARNING

### How do we respond when challenged by fear?

Engage students in a discussion of opposing reactions to fear, such as "flight" or "fight." Guide them to observe that feeling fear may cause us to act, as when we run from danger; it may cause us to freeze, as if hunted by a dangerous animal; or it may cause us to lash out in self-defense. During Whole-Class Learning, students will read selections about individuals facing their own fears as well as one another's.

### Whole-Class Learning Strategies

Review the Learning Strategies with students and explain that as they work through Whole-Class Learning they will develop strategies to work in large-group environments.

- Have students watch the video on Whole-Class Learning Strategies.
- A video on this topic is available online in the Professional Development Center.

You may wish to discuss some action items to add to the chart as a class before students complete it on their own. For example, for "Listen actively," you might solicit the following action from students:

- Make eye contact with the speaker.
- Nod or smile to encourage a tentative speaker.

**Block Scheduling**

Each day in this Pacing Plan represents a 40–50 minute class period. Teachers using block scheduling may combine days to reflect their class schedule. In addition, teachers may revise pacing to differentiate and support core instruction by integrating components and resources as students require.

## OVERVIEW: WHOLE-CLASS LEARNING

ESSENTIAL QUESTION:

# How do we respond when challenged by fear?

As you read these selections, work with your whole class to explore the meaning and power of fear.

**From Text to Topic** One person's unreasonable fears can make his or her life very difficult. What might happen, then, when a shared fear afflicts a family, a whole town, or an entire country? Arthur Miller explores this prospect in *The Crucible,* one of his most famous plays. Using a carefully researched case of mass hysteria from America's colonial past, Miller draws attention to fears haunting American culture in the 1950s. The story that he presents is powerful in its own right, but it also encourages audiences to consider how unrestrained, unreasonable fear can damage a society. As you read *The Crucible,* consider what the narrative shows about the far-reaching influence of fear.

## Whole-Class Learning Strategies

Throughout your life, in school, in your community, and in your career, you will continue to learn and work in large-group environments.

Review these strategies and the actions you can take to practice them as you work with your whole class. Add ideas of your own for each step. Get ready to use these strategies during Whole-Class Learning.

| STRATEGY | ACTION PLAN |
|---|---|
| Listen actively | • Eliminate distractions. For example, put your cellphone away.<br>• Record brief notes on main ideas and points of confusion.<br>• |
| Clarify by asking questions | • If you're confused, other people probably are, too. Ask a question to help your whole class.<br>• Ask follow-up questions as needed—for example, if you do not understand the clarification, or if you want to make an additional connection.<br>• |
| Monitor understanding | • Notice what information you already know and be ready to build on it.<br>• Ask for help if you are struggling.<br>• |
| Interact and share ideas | • Share your ideas and answer questions, even if you are unsure.<br>• Build on the ideas of others by adding details or making a connection.<br>• |





SCAN FOR MULTIMEDIA

### Pacing Plan

Introduce Whole-Class Learning

| Unit Introduction | Historical Perspectives | The Crucible, Act I | | The Crucible, Act II | | The Crucible, Act III | | The Crucible, Act IV | | Media: The Crucible | | Performance Task | |
|---|---|---|---|---|---|---|---|---|---|---|---|---|---|
| 1 | 2 | 3 | 4 | 5 | 6 | 7 | 8 | 9 | 10 | 11 | 12 | 13 | 14 | 15 |

WHOLE-CLASS LEARNING

552 UNIT 5 • FACING OUR FEARS

DIGITAL PERSPECTIVES

## CONTENTS

HISTORICAL PERSPECTIVES

Focus Period: 1920–1960

### Times of Trouble

As Americans moved into the middle of the twentieth century, they faced new difficulties. The Jazz Age quickly gave way to fears over the economic hardships that the Great Depression imposed. World War II brought a new set of fears, but it also inspired a new determination among Americans. After the war, however, anxiety over the spread of Communism kept many Americans in the grip of fear.

COMPARE

ANCHOR TEXT: DRAMA

### The Crucible *Arthur Miller*

Act I

A town in colonial Massachusetts is gripped by fears of witchcraft—but is the fear justified?

Act II

Act III

Act IV

MEDIA: AUDIO PERFORMANCE

### The Crucible

*L.A. Theatre Works*

A cast of some of Hollywood's best-known actors brings Arthur Miller's play to life.

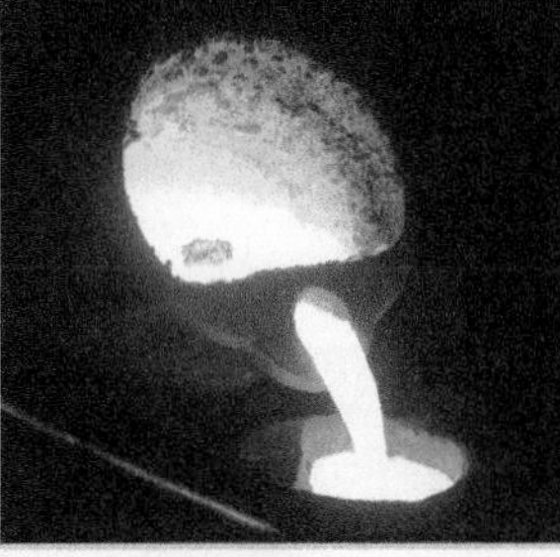

PERFORMANCE TASK

WRITING FOCUS

### Write an Argument

The Whole-Class reading dramatizes an actual case of mass hysteria in an American community. After reading, you will write an argument about the ways in which specific characters might have stopped the spread of fear rather than stand by and let it run wild.





## Contents

**Anchor Texts** Preview the anchor texts and audio performance with students to generate interest. Encourage students to discuss other texts they may have read or movies or television shows they may have seen that deal with the issue of people facing their fears.

You may wish to have students use an online or print thesaurus to find synonyms for *crucible*. Have them list the synonyms. Students can return to this list after they have read the selections to decide which synonyms are most appropriate for Arthur Miller's play.

## Performance Task

**Write an Argument** Explain to students that after they have finished the selections, they will write an argument about whether specific characters might have stopped the spread of fear in Salem. To help them prepare, encourage students to think about the topic as they progress through the selections and as they participate in the Whole-Class Learning experience.

Introduce Small-Group Learning

*from* Farewell to Manzanar | Media: Interview with George Takei | Antojos | Performance Task | Introduce Independent Learning | Independent Learning | Performance-Based Assessment

16 17 18 19 20 21 22 23 24 25 26 27 28 29 30

TEACHING

## HISTORICAL PERSPECTIVES

### Times of Trouble

This section analyzes the key events of the Focus Period: the Roaring Twenties, the Great Depression, Franklin Roosevelt's New Deal, World War II, the Cold War, the age of television, and the beginning of the civil rights movement. Have students connect these key events with the unit topic.

### Voices of the Period

Invite different volunteers to read each of the voices from the Focus Period. Ask students to paraphrase each quotation. Ask students what they think Franklin Roosevelt meant when he said, "The only thing we have to fear is fear itself." This statement was part of his first inaugural address, which took place in 1933 during the depths of the Great Depression. Use these prompts for discussion: *Do you agree with this statement? Is it still relevant? How much does fear affect our nation as we face today's challenges?*

### History of the Period

Tell students that this time period was marked by extremes, from an economic boom after World War I to economic disaster, followed by a struggle to recover both financially and psychologically. Then another costly world war was followed by another period of economic prosperity. Ask students what these swings tell them about our nation during this period. What did we need to learn? How well do they think we learned it?

HISTORICAL PERSPECTIVES • FOCUS PERIOD: 1920–1960

# Times of Trouble

## Voices of the Period

"*The only thing we have to fear is fear itself.*"

—Franklin Delano Roosevelt, 32nd president of the United States

"*I have learned over the years that when one's mind is made up, this diminishes fear; knowing what must be done does away with fear.*"

—Rosa Parks, political activist sometimes referred to as "the first lady of civil rights"

"*If you're not frightened that you might fail, you'll never do the job. If you're frightened, you'll work like crazy.*"

—César Chávez, political activist and co-founder of the National Farm Workers Association

"*Neither a wise man nor a brave man lies down on the tracks of history to wait for the train of the future to run over him.*"

—Dwight D. Eisenhower, 34th president of the United States

## History of the Period

**The Roaring Twenties** World War I ended in 1918, and in the decade that followed, the nation seemed to go on a binge of building, consumption, and speculation. The economy boomed, and skyscrapers rose. Prohibition made the sale of liquor illegal, which led to bootlegging and the rise of organized crime. Radio, jazz, and movies helped shape American culture. As people let go of prewar values, they let the "roar" of the Roaring Twenties drown out the sounds of war and the horror of death.

**The Great Depression** The boom, of course, could not last, and in October 1929 the stock market crashed, spurring what is known as the Great Depression. By mid-1932, about 12 million Americans—one-quarter of the country's workforce—were unemployed. Hungry and panicked people waited for food in bread lines and at soup kitchens. The government seemed unable to turn the economy around. Depression became more than an economic fact—it became a national state of mind.

**The New Deal** When elected president in 1932, Franklin Delano Roosevelt took action immediately, initiating a package of major economic reforms that came to be known as the New Deal. Many Americans soon found work on huge public projects, including building dams and bridges; conserving land; and recording the past and present in photographs, artwork, and writing. Roosevelt's leadership and policies helped end the Depression

TIMELINE

1920

1922: **Egypt** The tomb of King Tutankhamun is discovered.

1925: F. Scott Fitzgerald's *The Great Gatsby* is published.

1925: Louis Armstrong and his Hot Five become a headlining act on the radio.

1927: Charles Lindbergh flies solo and nonstop from New York to Paris.

PERSONALIZE FOR LEARNING

**English Language Support**

**Vocabulary Knowledge** Encourage students to point out vocabulary that can be confusing, such as the use of the word *roaring* to describe a time period or *boom* to describe economic prosperity. They might mention the use of *depression* to label both an economy and a state of mind and the use of *deal* to describe a package of economic reforms.

After students have suggested a number of these words, assign each word to a pair or small group. Ask students to define the word as it is used in this historical context and to write their own sentences that demonstrate that meaning. **ALL LEVELS**

## Integration of Knowledge and Ideas

**Notebook** What does the information in the graphs help you understand about the differences between World War I and World War II in terms of military deaths? What factors likely affected the increase of military deaths in World War II?

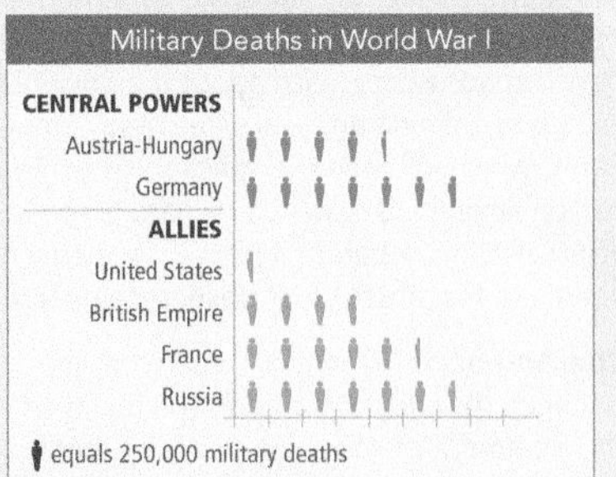


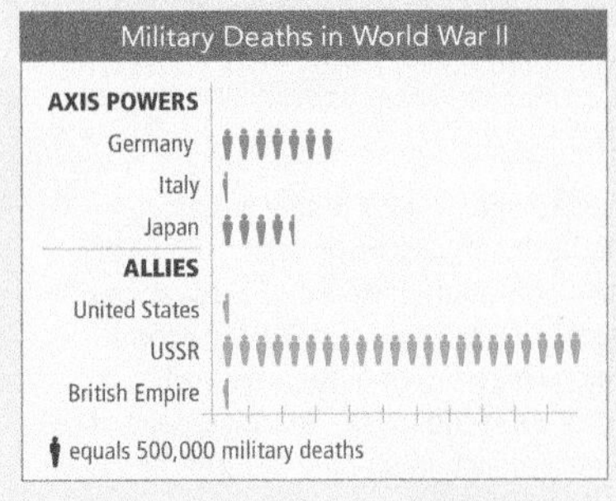


and earned him an unprecedented three reelections: in 1936, 1940, and 1944.

**World War II** Just twenty years after the end of World War I, Germany, under the rule of Adolf Hitler, ignited the Second World War with its invasion of neighboring countries. The dominant mood in the United States, however, was one of isolationism, with most Americans preferring to stay out of the conflict. This attitude changed dramatically when Japanese forces attacked the naval base at Pearl Harbor, Hawaii, on December 7, 1941. With more than 3,000 American casualties and the destruction of much of the American battleship fleet, neutrality and isolationism came to a swift end. The United States quickly declared war on the Axis Powers: Germany, Japan, and Italy. It took years of bitter fighting in Europe, North Africa, and the Pacific before the Allies—the United States, Great Britain, France, and the Soviet Union—defeated Italy, Germany, and then Japan. Japan surrendered only after the United States dropped an atomic bomb on the cities of Hiroshima and then Nagasaki. Peace—and the Atomic Age—had arrived.

**Face-Off With Communism** The threat of Communist infiltration and influence became a fixation in the United States after World War II.



**1928: China** Chiang Kai-shek becomes the leader of China's Nationalist government.

BROOKLYN DAILY EAGLE
WALL ST. IN PANIC AS STOCKS CRASH
Attempt Made to Kill Italy's Crown Prince

**1929:** The stock market crashes in October, followed by the Great Depression of the 1930s.

**1933: Germany** Adolf Hitler becomes Chancellor of Germany.

**1933:** President Franklin D. Roosevelt closes banks; Congress passes New Deal laws.

**1937:** Zora Neale Hurston's *Their Eyes Were Watching God* is published.

**1939: Poland** An invasion by German forces sets off World War II, which will extend across Europe and into Asia and North Africa.

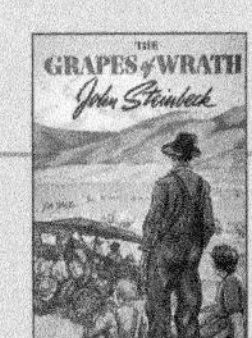


**1939:** John Steinbeck's *The Grapes of Wrath* is published.

1940



## Integration of Knowledge and Ideas

Have students analyze the data in the chart. Make sure they realize that one person on the World War I chart equals 250,000 deaths, but one person on the World War II chart equals 500,000 deaths. Ask students to draw conclusions from the data and answer the questions.

**Possible response:** There was a great increase in the number of deaths in World War II, probably caused by more powerful weapons and maybe by an increase in the number of soldiers involved.

## Timeline

Tell students to examine the 1920–1960 Timeline and reflect on the key events.

Ask how they think these events were chosen for the timeline. Which events do students think are the most important during this time period? Would they add any? Which of these events affected only the United States? Help students recognize that events that occur only in our nation often have far-reaching effects.

## PERSONALIZE FOR LEARNING

### Strategic Support

**Making Connections** Help students connect these events and periods with today's challenges. Use these questions to spark discussion:

- How was the Great Depression similar to our nation's recent "Great Recession"? Franklin Roosevelt used the New Deal to help end the Depression, but what actions did our government take to pull us out of the recession?
- How have the "allies" changed since World War II? Is the Soviet Union, now Russia, still our partner? What is our relationship to Japan? Which nation—or group of people—seems to be our nation's biggest threat today?

# TEACHING

## History of the Period (cont'd)

**Postwar Boom** What were the signs of prosperity after World War II? Discuss what it means to be "middle class." Do students think that sixty percent of our population would now be considered middle class? If not, what has changed since this postwar boom?

**The Television Age** Ask students why they think that television had such a powerful effect on the United States. Was its effect greater than that of the Internet? Urge students to provide specific evidence for their opinions.

**The American Dilemma** Encourage students to offer comments about the current state of race relations in our nation, but remind them to be respectful of others' feelings and opinions.

## HISTORICAL PERSPECTIVES • FOCUS PERIOD: 1920–1960

The United States battled against Communist China in Korea from 1950 to 1953. With the rise of the Soviet Union, the Cold War—competition between Eastern Bloc countries and the West—became intense. Fear of unchecked Soviet aggression marked the period. Espionage, economic sanctions, treaties, defense measures, and diplomatic conflicts were constantly in the news. By the mid-1950s, the country faced another Communist threat as conflict began in Vietnam.

Meanwhile, a "Red Scare," led by Senator Joseph McCarthy of Wisconsin, spread fear of Communist infiltration at home. Cold War anxiety was intensified by the existence of the atomic bomb, which created global fears as well as a new urgency surrounding the management of international conflict. In some ways, the postwar period could be characterized as an Age of Anxiety, as Americans seemed unable to stop thinking about terrible things that could or might happen. Schools regularly held air-raid drills, and Communists were hunted everywhere.

**Postwar Boom** The United States emerged from World War II as the most powerful nation on Earth. In the 1950s, despite the pressures of the Cold War, the nation enjoyed widespread prosperity, its suburbs expanded, and its consumer society flourished. Americans' incomes almost doubled in the 1950s, transforming American lives. By the mid-1950s, sixty percent of Americans were defined as being in the "middle class."

**The Television Age** The influence of television became especially powerful in the postwar era. In 1946, the nation had six TV stations; ten years later, there were more than 400 stations; by 1960, there was a television in almost every American home.

Television spearheaded revolutions in consumerism and mass communication. Millions of Americans saw the same advertisements and the same entertainment. Many watched television news broadcasts to learn about the Soviet Union's launch of the first artificial satellite to orbit the Earth, which initiated the space race. Some 70 million Americans watched Richard Nixon lose the 1960 election debates to John F. Kennedy, forever changing the structure of political campaigns.

**The American Dilemma** Deep conflicts between American ideals and the reality of the treatment of African Americans continued into the postwar decades. However, the 1950s saw the foundations of significant change in desegregating American society, beginning with the 1954 landmark Supreme Court decision in *Brown* v. *Board of Education of Topeka, Kansas*, which overturned the earlier decision that "separate but equal" facilities were legal. From that moment on, a Civil Rights movement began to build force under the leadership of people such as Martin Luther King, Jr., and the participation of a growing number of protestors, from students in Arkansas to bus riders in Alabama.

### TIMELINE

1940

**1941:** Japanese forces bomb Pearl Harbor, bringing the United States into World War II.

**1945:** World War II ends; the United Nations charter is signed.

**1947:** The Cold War between the United States and the Soviet Union begins.

**1949:** Arthur Miller's *Death of a Salesman* is produced.

**1950–1953: Korea** The Korean War is fought.





### PERSONALIZE FOR LEARNING

**Strategic Support**

**Identify Critical Details** Ask students to name factors mentioned in this Historical Perspectives content that helped shape their lives today.

- Did their great-grandparents live through the Great Depression? How might that have influenced their grandparents' lives and their parents' lives?
- Did any family members fight in any of the wars mentioned?
- Do their grandparents or great-grandparents ever talk about life before television?
- How have race relations affected them? Encourage a lively discussion as students connect with the details in the selection.

## Literature Selections

**Literature of the Focus Period** A key selection in this unit was written during the Focus Period and pertains to fear and its effects:

*The Crucible,* Arthur Miller

**Connections Across Time** A consideration of fear preceded and followed the Focus Period. Indeed, the theme has shaped the work of writers and commentators in various time periods and locations.

from *Farewell to Manzanar,* Jeanne Wakatsuki Houston and James D. Houston

"Antojos," Julia Alvarez

"What You Don't Know Can Kill You," Jason Daley

"Runagate Runagate," Robert Hayden

"1-800-FEAR," Jody Gladding

"Bears at Raspberry Time," Hayden Carruth

"For Black Women Who Are Afraid," Toi Derricotte

"What Are You So Afraid Of?" Akiko Busch

ADDITIONAL FOCUS PERIOD LITERATURE

**Student Edition**

UNIT 1
"The Pedestrian," Ray Bradbury

UNIT 3
*Brown v. Board of Education:* Opinion of the Court, Earl Warren

The Poetry of Langston Hughes

UNIT 4
"The Rockpile," James Baldwin

UNIT 6
"The Jilting of Granny Weatherall," Katherine Anne Porter



**1950:** Thousands are falsely accused of treason following Senator McCarthy's claims of Communist infiltration in the government.

**1954:** The Supreme Court rules public school segregation unconstitutional in *Brown v. Board of Education.*

**1955:** Rosa Parks is arrested, triggering the Montgomery Bus Boycott.

**1957: USSR** The Soviet Union launches *Sputnik I,* the first space satellite.

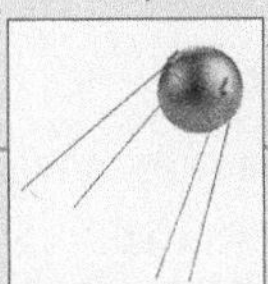

**1959:** Alaska and Hawaii are admitted to the Union as the 49th and 50th states.

**1959:** Lorraine Hansberry's *A Raisin in the Sun* is produced.

1960



PERSONALIZE FOR LEARNING

**Challenge**

**Find Out More** Encourage students (or pairs of students) to choose a topic covered in this selection and research some aspect of it. For example, how did Prohibition lead to the rise of organized crime? How did the Great Depression affect your state or community? Were any of the public projects initiated by the New Deal built in your region? How did that happen, and what were the effects? What was the "Red Scare," and how did it affect Hollywood? Provide time for students to share what they learn with the class through oral or written reports.

DIGITAL PERSPECTIVES

## Literature Selections

Have students review the selections in this unit listed under *Literature of the Focus Period* and *Connections Across Time.* Also point out the *Additional Focus Period Literature* found in *myPerspectives.* Encourage students to utilize these selections for additional evidence as they complete this unit.

## Comprehension Check

Ask students to answer these questions independently and then discuss them with the whole class or a group.

1. Why is this period labeled "Times of Trouble"?

**Possible response:** During this period, the United States recovered from World War I, but then slipped into the Great Depression and struggled to recover from it. World War II cost many lives and was followed by the scare of Communism. Race relations continued to be problematic.

2. How did our nation's economy change during this period?

**Possible response:** The nation experienced prosperity during the 1920s and great poverty during the 1930s. The New Deal got the nation back on its feet by creating huge public projects. After World War II, prosperity returned. The invention of the television greatly increased consumerism.

3. Based on this historical background, what can you infer about the relationship between war and the economy?

**Possible response:** The period after a war seems to be marked by an increase in spending and economic growth.

4. How did television change the United States?

**Possible response:** It increased communication: people knew much more about what was happening across the nation and around the world. People saw thousands of commercials and were encouraged to buy more products. They watched political debates and chose their leaders based on their performance during these debates.

5. Which problems described in this selection persist today?

**Possible response:** Our nation is still at war, but fewer people worry about Communism now. Our economy still has significant ups and downs. The effects of television have probably been surpassed by the Internet.

# *The Crucible*, Act I

**AUDIO SUMMARIES**
Audio summaries of Act I of *The Crucible* are available online in both English and Spanish in the Interactive Teacher's Edition or Unit Resources. Assigning these summaries prior to reading the selection may help students build additional background knowledge and set a context for their first read.

## Summary

As Act I of Arthur Miller's drama *The Crucible* begins, the Rev. Parris is praying for his sick daughter Betty. He had seen her and his niece Abigail in the woods the night before with his slave, Tituba, engaged in some kind of ritual. Word has already spread throughout Salem that there may be witchcraft involved. The Putnams, who feel bitter toward many in Salem, announce that their daughter is also very sick. Abigail tells the other girls who were in the forest what they should say. While they talk, Betty responds, showing she is not as sick as she pretends. When the married farmer John Proctor arrives, Abigail confronts him about their relationship, but John states that the affair they had is over. Parris asks the Rev. Hale, a noted expert on demonic possession, to determine whether or not sorcery is involved in Betty's illness.

### Insight

This first act sets up the plot and many of the themes of the play, including fear of societal disapproval and the loss of reputation and social status. The act also introduces a sense of fear of unknown evil.

ESSENTIAL QUESTION:
How do we respond when challenged by fear?

## Connection to the Essential Question

Act I of *The Crucible* demonstrates a growing sense of hysteria in the community as rumors of witchcraft begin to spread. The community is intent on verifying these rumors even at the cost of believing in events and causes that do not exist and ruining lives and reputations in the process.

WHOLE-CLASS LEARNING PERFORMANCE TASK
Could any of the characters in *The Crucible* have done more to end the hysteria in Salem?

UNIT PERFORMANCE-BASED ASSESSMENT
Is fear always a harmful emotion?

## Connection to Performance Tasks

**Whole-Class Learning Performance Task** Tituba may have prevented some of the hysteria had she told the truth about what she and the girls were doing in the woods, but if she had told the truth, her life would have been in danger. Similarly, Betty, Mary, and especially Abigail could have prevented the hysteria from escalating by telling the truth.

**Unit Performance-Based Assessment** Act I of *The Crucible* makes it clear some members of a society can manipulate the emotions of others through rumors and lies until fear dominates the community. Fear of what others can do can be a powerful motivation in an individual's life.

DIGITAL PERSPECTIVES

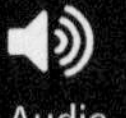 Audio  Video  Document  Annotation Highlights  EL Highlights 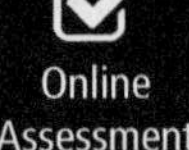 Online Assessment

## LESSON RESOURCES

| | Making Meaning | Language Development |
|---|---|---|
| Lesson | **First Read**<br>**Close Read**<br>**Analyze the Text**<br>**Analyze Craft and Structure** | **Concept Vocabulary**<br>**Word Study**<br>**Conventions and Style** |
| Instructional Standards | **RL.10** By the end of grade 11, read and comprehend literature . . .<br>**RL.3** Analyze the impact of the author's choices . . .<br>**RL.5** Analyze how an author's choices . . . | **L.5** Demonstrate understanding of figurative language . . .<br>**L.1** Demonstrate command of the conventions . . .<br>**L.1.a** Apply the understanding that usage is a matter of convention . . .<br>**L.3** Apply knowledge of language . . . |
| **STUDENT RESOURCES** | | |
| Available online in the Interactive Student Edition or Unit Resources | Audio Selection<br>First-Read Guide: Fiction<br>Close-Read Guide: Fiction | Word Network<br>Evidence Log |
| **TEACHER RESOURCES** | | |
| **Selection Resources** Available online in the Interactive Teacher's Edition or Unit Resources | Audio Summaries<br>Annotation Highlights<br>EL Highlights<br>English Language Support Lesson: Structural Elements of Drama<br>Analyze Craft and Structure: Structural Elements of Drama | Concept Vocabulary and Word Study<br>Conventions and Style: Personal Pronouns |
| **Reteach/Practice (RP)** Available online in the Interactive Teacher's Edition or Unit Resources | Analyze Craft and Structure: Structural Elements of Drama (RP) | Word Study: Latin Root *-fama-* (RP)<br>Conventions and Style: Personal Pronouns (RP) |
| **Assessment** Available online in Assessments | Selection Test | |
| **My Resources** | A Unit 5 Answer Key is available online and in the Interactive Teacher's Edition. | |

# Reading Support

| Text Complexity Rubric: *The Crucible*, Act I | |
|---|---|
| **Quantitative Measures** | |
| Lexile: NP Text Length: 12,961 words | |
| **Qualitative Measures** | |
| Knowledge Demands<br>①—②—③—❹—⑤ | Students will probably not be familiar with the situation that is central to the selection. Many, but not all, of the unfamiliar elements are made clear in dialogue, stage directions, and exposition by the playwright. |
| Structure<br>①—②—❸—④—⑤ | Organization of the narrative is mostly sequential, but important incidents occurred before the narrative begins and are only gradually revealed. |
| Language Conventionality and Clarity<br>①—②—③—❹—⑤ | Considerable above-level vocabulary and some archaic usages complicate the language, although most of the dialogue reflects ordinary speech. |
| Levels of Meaning/Purpose<br>①—②—③—❹—⑤ | One level of meaning is straightforward and compellingly presented. As a political allegory, the play operates on another level that requires more background knowledge to grasp. |

DECIDE AND PLAN

## English Language Support

Provide English Learners with support for knowledge demands and language as they read the selection.

**Knowledge Demands** Before reading the text, review the background information with students. Use a cause-and effect graphic organizer to show how clashing cultures led to a belief in witchcraft. When the action of the play is interrupted by exposition by the playwright, have someone read the text aloud, and ask students to summarize it.

**Language** Students will probably have difficulty with the above-level vocabulary and deviations from Standard English. Explain to students that it is not necessary for them to understand every word, so long as they have a basic understanding of the dialogue.

## Strategic Support

Provide students with strategic support to ensure that they can successfully read the text.

**Knowledge Demands** After reading the background information, make sure students understand that a colonial town was a fairly isolated unit where government and the church were closely intertwined. Ask students to consider how these conditions could lead to the domination of a community by a few people.

**Language** For students who have difficulty with nonstandard English, especially with the nonstandard use of the verbs *was* and *were*, encourage them to change the forms to standard forms, and then reread the sentences or lines of dialogue.

## Challenge

Provide students who need to be challenged with ideas for how they can go beyond a simple interpretation of the text.

**Text Analysis** Pair students and have them discuss how conditions of extreme hardship could lead a community to assign blame to forces beyond themselves. Have them summarize the conditions in Europe and Massachusetts that led to the belief in and persecution of those believed to be witches.

**Written Response** Have pairs of students rewrite a short passage of dialogue between two characters in language that might be used in the current time. Have them take roles and read their rewrites aloud.

TEACH

## Read and Respond

Have the class do their first read of the selection. Then have them complete their close read. Finally, work with them on the Making Meaning and Language Development activities.

# Standards Support Through Teaching and Learning Cycle

## IDENTIFY NEEDS

Analyze results of the Beginning-of-Year Assessment, focusing on the items relating to Unit 5. Also take into consideration student performance to this point and your observations of where particular students struggle.

## DECIDE AND PLAN

- If students have performed poorly on items matching these standards, then provide selection scaffolds before assigning them the on-level lesson provided in the Student Edition.
- If students have done well on the Beginning-of-Year Assessment, then challenge them to keep progressing and learning by giving them opportunities to practice the skills in depth.
- Use the Selection Resources listed on the Planning pages for *The Crucible,* Act 1, to help students continually improve their ability to master the standards.

**Instructional Standards: *The Crucible,* Act 1**

| | Catching Up | This Year | Looking Forward |
|---|---|---|---|
| **Reading** | You may wish to administer the **Analyze Craft and Structure: Structural Elements of Drama (RP)** worksheet to help students better understand exposition. | **RL.3** Analyze the impact of the author's choices regarding how to develop and relate elements of a story or drama. | Discuss with students how exposition may differ between stage and film. |
| **Language** | Review the **Word Study: Latin Root *-fama-* (RP)** worksheet with students to better familiarize them with the root word.<br><br>Review the **Conventions and Style: Personal Pronouns (RP)** worksheet with students to better familiarize them personal pronouns. | **L.5** Demonstrate understanding of figurative language, word relationships, and nuances in word meaning.<br><br>**L.1** Demonstrate command of the conventions of standard English grammar and usage when writing or speaking. | Have students identify other words in the text with Latin or Greek roots.<br><br>Challenge students to discuss Miller's choice to use modern usage of pronouns. What are the pros and cons of this? |

## ANALYZE AND REVISE

- Analyze student work for evidence of student learning.
- Identify whether or not students have met the expectations in the standards.
- Identify implications for future instruction.

## TEACH

Implement the planned lesson, and gather evidence of student learning.

## How to Read Drama

Remind students that a drama, or play, presents action mainly through dialogue, the conversations and speech of the characters. When a play is presented, the audience also sees the actors and their actions, as well as the setting. When you read a play, your imagination must fill in all those elements of the play. Most plays tell their stories over the course of a series of acts. Acts are further subdivided into scenes. Acts or scenes may shift in time or place.

Review the content in this feature and discuss student experiences in both watching performances and reading plays. You may choose to share this additional information with students.

- **Keep Characters in Mind** As students read through a play, point out that a character's feelings, thoughts, and emotions are revealed through dialogue. One important aspect of dialogue is the *aside*, when a character speaks directly to the audience. This dialogue is presumed to be inaudible to the other characters on stage. Characters may also deliver **soliloquies** when they are onstage alone. These speeches reveal their innermost thoughts.
- **Pay Attention to the Stage Directions** Emphasize the importance of stage directions. Point out that while plays are intended to be performed by actors, a good reader can derive helpful information from the script. Stage directions help readers visualize what would be taking place in an actual performance.

For much of the twentieth century, the theater was the center of American intellectual life. Great plays offered thrilling stories, crackling dialogue, and philosophical truth. As Arthur Miller wrote:

*"Great drama is great questions or it is nothing but technique. I could not imagine a theater worth my time that did not want to change the world."*

Dramatic literature shares many elements with prose, fiction, and poetry, but is written to be acted out on a stage before an audience rather than read quietly on your own. In a sense, when you read a play, you are not experiencing the work as it was meant to be experienced. You are reading a script, which is only part of the piece. However, you can help bring the drama to life and create the performance in your own imagination by applying the following strategies.

**Picture the Action** Reading a play without envisioning the action is like watching a movie with your eyes shut. Use the stage directions and other details to create the scene in your mind. Consider the situation, characters' motivations and feelings, and how staging or performance choices might convey those elements.

**Refer to the Cast of Characters** The details of characters' relationships are usually conveyed through dialogue, gestures, body language, and action rather than through direct statements. In addition, some plays feature numerous characters whose relationships to one another are complex. One way to keep things clear is to refer to the Cast of Characters list whenever a character joins—or re-joins—the action.

**Summarize the Action** Most plays are broken into smaller units called acts. Some plays are then broken into even smaller sections called scenes. These breaks give you an opportunity to review the action. Take the opportunities afforded by these separations to consider various questions: What conflicts are developing or intensifying? What decisions are characters making? Toward what outcome does the story seem to be heading?

**Be an Actor** Consider studying with a group and acting out scenes that you find difficult. When you inject appropriate emotion into the text, the meaning and nuances will often become clearer. You may also make connections among language, imagery, and character that you otherwise might not have noticed.

DIGITAL PERSPECTIVES

## Close Read the Text

Annotating the text as you read can help you tackle the challenges of reading a play rather than watching it in performance. Here are two sample annotations of an excerpt from *The Crucible,* Act I. The setting is home of Reverend Samuel Parris, the minister of the church in the Puritan colony of Salem, Massachusetts, in 1692. Betty, Parris's young daughter, is suffering a mysterious ailment. Parris and Abigail Williams, Betty's cousin, are in the sick room when Susanna Walcott arrives with a message from the doctor.

ANNOTATE: This stage direction is very specific.

QUESTION: What does this stage direction suggest about the situation?

CONCLUDE: Susanna seems to regard Betty as an object of curiosity. Parris seems to be trying to protect Betty by physically blocking Susanna's view.

SUSANNA WALCOTT, *a little younger than Abigail, a nervous, hurried girl enters.*

**Parris,** *eagerly*: What does the doctor say, child?

**Susanna,** *craning around* PARRIS *to get a look at* BETTY: He bid me come and tell you, reverend sir, that he cannot discover no medicine for it in his books.

**Parris:** Then he must search on.

**Susanna:** Aye, sir, he have been searchin' his books since he left you, sir. But he bid me tell you, that you might look to unnatural things for the cause of it.

**Parris,** *his eyes going wide*: No—no. There be no unnatural cause here. Tell him I have sent for Reverend Hale of Beverly, and Mr. Hale will surely confirm that. Let him look to medicine and put out all thought of unnatural causes here. There be none.

**Susanna:** Aye, sir. He bid me tell you. *She turns to go.*

**Abigail:** Speak nothin' of it in the village, Susanna.

**Parris:** Go directly home and speak nothing of unnatural causes.

**Susanna:** Aye, sir. I pray for her. *She goes out.*

ANNOTATE: When Susanna mentions "unnatural things," Parris reacts physically and then repeats the phrase "unnatural causes" three times.

QUESTION: Why does the playwright present Parris's reaction in this way?

CONCLUDE: To the Puritans of Salem, "unnatural causes" means the presence of dark, supernatural forces. Parris is terrified for his daughter's health, but he may be even more afraid of gossip and accusations.





AUTHOR'S PERSPECTIVE **Kelly Gallagher, M.Ed.**

**Reading Reasons** Students often ask "Why should I read?" Increasingly, teachers see students who often give up easily when confronted with challenging reading material, such as a biology textbook or a state-mandated exam. They are unable, or unwilling, to tackle difficult text. How do teachers turn around this apathy? How do teachers shelter fragile adolescent readers and help them grow into people for whom reading matters? Building reading motivation is complex, as there isn't a single correct motivational tool, but together, many of these techniques send the message that reading is rewarding.

- Give students access to high-interest reading material, which is provided in this program.
- Give students a time and place to read.
- Model the value of reading. Read with students, so they see you enjoying reading. Start a student book club in school.
- Provide structure to the reading program by logging the number of words, pages, and time that students read.

## Jump Start

**FIRST READ** Engage students in a discussion about witch hunts. *Witch hunts took place in the seventeenth century in Massachusetts, but do "witch hunts" take place in our modern society? Explain.* This discussion can set the context for reading *The Crucible*, Act I.

### Concept Vocabulary

Support students as they rank the words. Ask if they've ever heard, read, or used them. Reassure them that the definitions for these words are listed in the selection.

**FIRST READ**

As they read, students should perform the steps of the first read:

NOTICE: You may want to encourage students to notice where the characters are in each scene and the action that is taking place.

ANNOTATE: Remind students to mark passages that may confuse them or any words they do not understand.

CONNECT: Encourage students to think about the historical background of *The Crucible*. What do they already know about the seventeenth-century Salem witch trials? Does the hysteria that occurred about witchcraft during that time have any relevance to current events?

RESPOND: Students will answer questions to demonstrate understanding.

Point out to students that while they will always complete the Respond step at the end of the first read, the other steps will probably happen somewhat concurrently. You may wish to print copies of the **First-Read Guide: Fiction** for students to use.

**Remind students that during their first read, they should not answer the close-read questions that appear in the selection.**

MAKING MEANING

# The Crucible, Act I

## Concept Vocabulary

You will encounter the following words as you read Act I of *The Crucible*. Before reading, note how familiar you are with each word. Then, rank the words in order from most familiar (1) to least familiar (3).

| WORD | YOUR RANKING |
|---|---|
| vindictive | |
| calumny | |
| defamation | |

After completing the first read, come back to the concept vocabulary and review your rankings. Mark changes to your original rankings as needed.

## First Read DRAMA

Apply these strategies as you conduct your first read. You will have an opportunity to complete the close-read notes after your first read.

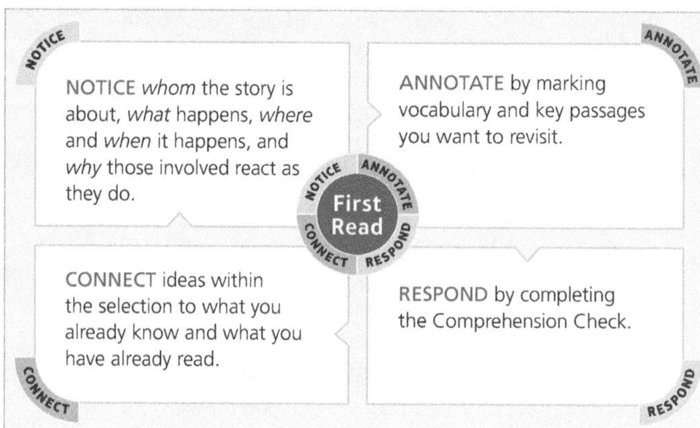

NOTICE
ANNOTATE
CONNECT
RESPOND
NOTICE *whom* the story is about, *what* happens, *where* and *when* it happens, and *why* those involved react as they do.
ANNOTATE by marking vocabulary and key passages you want to revisit.
First Read
CONNECT ideas within the selection to what you already know and what you have already read.
RESPOND by completing the Comprehension Check.


**Tool Kit**
First-Read Guide and Model Annotation

**STANDARDS**
**Reading Literature**
By the end of grade 11, read and comprehend literature, including stories, dramas, and poems, in the grades 11–CCR text complexity band proficiently, with scaffolding as needed at the high end of the range.





### VOCABULARY DEVELOPMENT

**Concept Vocabulary Reinforcement** Reinforce students' understanding of concept vocabulary by providing practice in the form of show-you-know sentences. The first part of the sentence uses the vocabulary word in its context. The second part of the sentence—the show-you-know part—clarifies meanings. For example:

There is no evidence to support the calumny, although the reporter ________.

**Possible response:** *defended the lies he wrote*

She was suing the newspaper for defamation of character because ________.

**Possible response:** *of the terrible lies written about her*

The vindictive character in the novel was ________.

**Possible response:** *obsessed by his desire for revenge*

About the Playwright

## Arthur Miller (1915–2005)

**Arthur Miller** was born in New York City and grew up during the Great Depression. By the time he graduated from high school in 1932, his father's family business had gone bankrupt, and Miller was forced to take odd jobs to raise money for college tuition.

**Major Talent** Miller began writing plays during his college years at the University of Michigan. In 1947, his play *All My Sons* was performed on Broadway to immediate acclaim, establishing Miller as a bright new talent. Two years later, *Death of a Salesman* opened on Broadway, earning Miller a Pulitzer Prize and elevating him to the status of a premier American playwright. His next play, *The Crucible*, opened to mixed reviews in 1953, largely because of its controversial political content. *The Crucible* was clearly a comment on the "witch hunts" for Communists that were being carried out at the time by Wisconsin Senator Joseph McCarthy and by the House Un-American Activities Committee (HUAC).

**In the Shadow of McCarthyism** Miller's experience with the HUAC hearings parallels the situation he portrayed in *The Crucible*. Called before the committee in 1956, Miller, like his *Crucible* character John Proctor, admitted to his own socialist leanings but refused to "name names" about fellow celebrities in the theater and in Hollywood.

At the time of his House testimony, Miller was firmly established as a major literary figure and celebrity, a status that soon skyrocketed when he married Marilyn Monroe, the most famous Hollywood star of the 1950s. Miller's celebrity did not protect him from the committee, however, and the "Red Scare" period continued to haunt him for the rest of his life. "It was as though the whole country had been born anew," he wrote, "without a memory even of certain elemental decencies which a year or two earlier no one would have imagined could be altered, let alone forgotten." The very personal terror Miller felt as a result of his dealings with HUAC he claimed underlay "every word in *The Crucible*."

**Voice of Conscience** Today, Miller is regarded as one of the true giants of the American theater. His *Death of a Salesman* is often discussed as the greatest American play ever written. Playwright Edward Albee said of Miller, "Arthur never compromised. He never sold out." Miller was able to use art to make enormously important social and political points that still resonate today.



Background for

## *The Crucible*

In 1692, the British colony of Massachusetts was convulsed by a witchcraft hysteria that resulted in the execution of 20 people and the jailing of more than 100 others. The incident, though unprecedented for New England, was not unique. During the sixteenth and seventeenth centuries, witch hunts swept through Europe, resulting in tens of thousands of executions.

For the New England colonies, the witchcraft episode was perhaps inevitable. Enduring harsh conditions and punishing hardship from day to day, many colonists attributed their misfortunes to the power of evil. In the small parish of Salem Village, many were quick to blame witchcraft when the minister's daughter and several other girls were afflicted by seizures and lapsed into unconsciousness.

A hunt to identify witches spread until some of the colony's most prominent citizens stood accused. Many historians have seen a pattern of social and economic animosity behind the accusations, but most scholars feel that mass hysteria—a strong, irrational fear that quickly spreads—was also a strong contributing factor.

A *crucible* is a heat-resistant container in which metals are melted or fused at very high temperatures. The word is used symbolically to suggest a severe trial or test. When *The Crucible* was first published, Arthur Miller added a note about the play's historical accuracy. He pointed out that he had fused many historical characters into one dramatic character, that he had raised Abigail's age, and that the characters of Hathorne and Danforth represented a composite of several historical judges. Miller then explained, "The fate of each character is exactly that of his historical model, and there is no one in the drama who did not play a similar—and in some cases exactly the same—role in history."



DIGITAL PERSPECTIVES

### *The Crucible*

Why do you think Miller chose to set his play in seventeenth-century Massachusetts and not during the time of the Senate hearings? How might the anticommunist hearings be considered modern-day "witch hunts"? Modeling these and other questions readers might ask will bring *The Crucible*, Act I, to life and connect it to the Performance Task assignment. Selection audio and print capability for the selection are available in the Interactive Teacher's Edition.

# The Crucible
## Act I

**Arthur Miller**

CHARACTERS

Reverend Parris
Betty Parris
Tituba
Abigail Williams
Susanna Walcott
Mrs. Ann Putnam
Thomas Putnam
Mercy Lewis
Mary Warren
John Proctor
Rebecca Nurse
Martha Corey
Reverend John Hale
Elizabeth Proctor
Francis Nurse
Ezekiel Cheever
Marshal Herrick
Judge Hathorne
Deputy Governor Danforth
Sarah Good
Hopkins
Giles Corey

(An Overture)

NOTES

1 *A small upper bedroom in the home of* REVEREND SAMUEL PARRIS, *Salem, Massachusetts, in the spring of the year 1692.*

2 *There is a narrow window at the left. Through its leaded panes the morning sunlight streams. A candle still burns near the bed, which is at the right. A chest, a chair, and a small table are the other furnishings. At the back a door opens on the landing of the stairway to the ground floor. The room gives off an air of clean spareness. The roof rafters are exposed, and the wood colors are raw and unmellowed.*

3 *As the curtain rises,* REVEREND PARRIS *is discovered kneeling beside the bed, evidently in prayer. His daughter,* BETTY PARRIS, *aged ten, is lying on the bed, inert.*

⌘ ⌘ ⌘

4 At the time of these events Parris was in his middle forties. In history he cut a villainous path, and there is very little good to be said for him. He believed he was being persecuted wherever he went, despite his best efforts to win people and God to his side. In meeting, he felt insulted if someone rose to shut the door without first asking his permission. He was a widower with no interest in children, or talent with them. He regarded them as young adults, and until this strange crisis he, like the rest of Salem, never conceived that the children were anything but thankful for being permitted to walk straight, eyes slightly lowered, arms at the sides, and mouths shut until bidden to speak.

5 His house stood in the "town"—but we today would hardly call it a village. The meeting house was nearby, and from this point outward—toward the bay or inland—there were a few small-windowed, dark houses snuggling against the raw Massachusetts winter. Salem had been established hardly forty years before. To the European world the whole province was a barbaric frontier inhabited by a sect of fanatics who, nevertheless, were shipping out products of slowly increasing quantity and value.

6 No one can really know what their lives were like. They had no novelists—and would not have permitted anyone to read a novel if one were handy. Their creed forbade anything resembling a theater or "vain enjoyment." They did not celebrate Christmas, and a holiday from work meant only that they must concentrate even more upon prayer.





CLOSER LOOK

## Interpret Stage Directions 

Students may have marked paragraph 3 during their first read. Use this paragraph to help students understand the importance of the Overture and the stage directions. Encourage them to talk about the annotations that they marked. You may want to model a close read with the class based on the highlights shown in the text.

**ANNOTATE:** Have students mark details in the paragraph that reveal important information, or have students participate while you highlight them.

**QUESTION:** Guide students to consider what these details might tell them. Ask what a reader can infer from these stage directions, and accept student responses.

**Possible response:** The stage directions identify the two people on stage and their relationship.

**CONCLUDE:** Help students to formulate conclusions about the importance of these details in the text. Ask students why the author might have included these details.

**Possible response:** The author is setting the scene for the events to come. Reverend Parris is praying and Betty is lying inert. Her illness must be a key factor in the plot in the upcoming act.

Remind students that **stage directions** can give readers insight to the action of the play. Here, we know the Reverend is praying and his daughter has some type of illness, yet no dialogue has yet been spoken.

DIGITAL PERSPECTIVES

### Illuminating the Text

**History Repeats Itself** Tell students that *The Crucible* was written in the early 1950s when fear of Communism swept America. This fear sprung from the fact that eastern Europe and China had recently fallen to Communism. In Congress, Republican senator Joseph McCarthy leapt into the limelight when he claimed to have "a list of 205 that were known to the Secretary of State as being members of the Communist Party and are … shaping the policy of the State Department." Leading a Senate investigation, McCarthy repeatedly charged that those who opposed his hearings were themselves Communists. No such list was ever produced and McCarthy was eventually discredited. The parallels between events in Salem, as Miller depicts them, and the ongoing events in Congress at the time Miller wrote the play are clear and deliberate. Find and display a short video or audio clip of one of McCarthy's speeches before the Senate on the subject of Communism. Remember to preview the video before showing it to students. **(Research to Clarify)**

## CLOSE READ 

Remind students that they are reading the Overture to the play. Point out that an overture is an introductory piece of music played before the curtain goes up in an opera or musical play. Here, Miller is making an introduction to the play and setting its context. You may wish to model the Close Read using the following think-aloud format. Possible responses to questions on the student page are included. You may also want to print copies of the **Close-Read Guide: Fiction** for students to use.

ANNOTATE: As I read paragraph 8, I notice and highlight the details that describe an informal twist on a familiar saying about not involving yourself in other people's lives.

QUESTION: Here, Miller is saying that people have a predilection, or liking, for minding other people's business; that it is actually time-honored, like a tradition. The time-honored saying is that people should mind their *own* business.

CONCLUDE: Miller's purpose in using this saying is to indicate that the mindset of the Puritans—minding other people's business—was instrumental in creating the suspicions which were to feed the coming madness. When he alludes to the madness, he is suggesting what is going to happen in the play.

NOTES

1. **shovelboard** *n.* game in which a coin or other disk is driven with the hand along a highly polished board, floor, or table marked with transverse lines.

CLOSE READ

ANNOTATE: In paragraph 8, mark the phrase that is an informal twist on a familiar saying about not involving yourself in other people's personal lives.

QUESTION: Why does Miller use this casual phrase?

CONCLUDE: What is the effect of this language, especially when applied to a discussion of Puritans?

7 Which is not to say that nothing broke into this strict and somber way of life. When a new farmhouse was built, friends assembled to "raise the roof," and there would be special foods cooked and probably some potent cider passed around. There was a good supply of ne'er-do-wells in Salem, who dallied at the shovelboard[1] in Bridget Bishop's tavern. Probably more than the creed, hard work kept the morals of the place from spoiling, for the people were forced to fight the land like heroes for every grain of corn, and no man had very much time for fooling around.

8 That there were some jokers, however, is indicated by the practice of appointing a two-man patrol whose duty was to "walk forth in the time of God's worship to take notice of such as either lye about the meeting house, without attending to the word and ordinances, or that lye at home or in the fields without giving good account thereof, and to take the names of such persons, and to present them to the magistrates, whereby they may be accordingly proceeded against." This predilection for minding other people's business was time-honored among the people of Salem, and it undoubtedly created many of the suspicions which were to feed the coming madness. It was also, in my opinion, one of the things that a John Proctor would rebel against, for the time of the armed camp had almost passed, and since the country was reasonably—although not wholly—safe, the old disciplines were beginning to rankle. But, as in all such matters, the issue was not clear-cut, for danger was still a possibility, and in unity still lay the best promise of safety.

9 The edge of the wilderness was close by. The American continent stretched endlessly west, and it was full of mystery for them. It stood, dark and threatening, over their shoulders night and day, for out of it Indian tribes marauded from time to time, and Reverend Parris had parishioners who had lost relatives to these heathen.

10 The parochial snobbery of these people was partly responsible for their failure to convert the Indians. Probably they also preferred to take land from heathens rather than from fellow Christians. At any rate, very few Indians were converted, and the Salem folk believed that the virgin forest was the Devil's last preserve, his home base and the citadel of his final stand. To the best of their knowledge the American forest was the last place on earth that was not paying homage to God.

11 For these reasons, among others, they carried about an air of innate resistance, even of persecution. Their fathers had, of course, been persecuted in England. So now they and their church found it necessary to deny any other sect its freedom, lest their New Jerusalem[2] be defiled and corrupted by wrong ways and deceitful ideas.

2. **New Jerusalem** in the Bible, the holy city of heaven.





## CROSS-CURRICULAR PERSPECTIVES

**Social Studies** Review paragraph 6. Tell students that among the Puritans, the fear that grew from living in harsh conditions on the edge of the wilderness was compounded by several factors. The Salem witch trials grew out of a climate of unrest and fear in which the Puritans saw enemies and dangers on all sides. For example, in 1643, preacher Roger Williams, whose open-minded views angered the Puritans, fled south and established the colony of Rhode Island, where religious groups were welcomed on the principles of religious freedom. In England, King Charles I revoked the charters guaranteeing the American colonies self-government, alarming the Puritans on economic and religious grounds. In addition, they lived in constant fear of Native Americans trying to reclaim their land.

12 They believed, in short, that they held in their steady hands the candle that would light the world. We have inherited this belief, and it has helped and hurt us. It helped them with the discipline it gave them. They were a dedicated folk, by and large, and they had to be to survive the life they had chosen or been born into in this country.

13 The proof of their belief's value to them may be taken from the opposite character of the first Jamestown settlement, farther south, in Virginia. The Englishmen who landed there were motivated mainly by a hunt for profit. They had thought to pick off the wealth of the new country and then return rich to England. They were a band of individualists, and a much more ingratiating group than the Massachusetts men. But Virginia destroyed them. Massachusetts tried to kill off the Puritans, but they combined; they set up a communal society which, in the beginning, was little more than an armed camp with an autocratic and very devoted leadership. It was, however, an autocracy by consent, for they were united from top to bottom by a commonly held ideology whose perpetuation was the reason and justification for all their sufferings. So their self-denial, their purposefulness, their suspicion of all vain pursuits, their hard-handed justice, were altogether perfect instruments for the conquest of this space so antagonistic to man.

14 But the people of Salem in 1692 were not quite the dedicated folk that arrived on the *Mayflower*. A vast differentiation had taken place, and in their own time a revolution had unseated the royal government and substituted a junta[3] which was at this moment in power. The times, to their eyes, must have been out of joint, and to the common folk must have seemed as insoluble and complicated as do ours today. It is not hard to see how easily many could have been led to believe that the time of confusion had been brought upon them by deep and darkling forces. No hint of such speculation appears on the court record, but social disorder in any age breeds such mystical suspicions, and when, as in Salem, wonders are brought forth from below the social surface, it is too much to expect people to hold back very long from laying on the victims with all the force of their frustrations.

15 The Salem tragedy, which is about to begin in these pages, developed from a paradox. It is a paradox in whose grip we still live, and there is no prospect yet that we will discover its resolution. Simply, it was this: for good purposes, even high purposes, the people of Salem developed a theocracy, a combine of state and religious power whose function was to keep the community together, and to prevent any kind of disunity that might open it to destruction by material or ideological enemies. It was forged for a necessary purpose and accomplished that

NOTES

3. **junta** (HOON tuh) *n.* assembly or council.

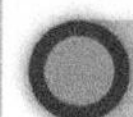
CLOSER LOOK

## Infer Key Ideas

Students may have marked paragraph 14 during their first read. Encourage students to talk about the annotations that they marked. You may want to model a close read with the class based on the highlights shown in the text.

**ANNOTATE:** Have students mark details in the lines that reveal information about the mindset of the Puritans, or have students participate while you highlight them.

**QUESTION:** Guide students to consider what these details might tell them. Ask what a reader can infer from Miller's description of the Puritans and why they thought the way they did, and accept student responses.

**Possible response:** Miller explains how the situation of the Puritans had changed since their arrival on the *Mayflower*. He describes how a different ruling council was in power and how easy it was for the Puritans to be confused.

**CONCLUDE:** Help students to formulate conclusions about the importance of these details in the text. Ask students why the author might have included these details.

**Possible response:** The author is setting the scene for the events to come. One key idea is that the factors of the time led the Puritans to believe that dark, or evil forces were at work, and these forces affected the way they acted.

Remind students that authors make certain claims, leaving it to the reader to infer **key ideas**. By giving details and examples, the author allows readers to fill in the gaps. Here, the author is describing the Puritans and how their mindset may have led to certain actions.

Additional **English Language Support** is available in the Interactive Teacher's Edition.

## CLOSER LOOK

### Analyze Background

Students may have marked paragraph 15 during their first read. Use these lines to help students understand the state of affairs in New England that set the witch hunt into motion. Encourage them to talk about the annotations that they marked. You may want to model a close read with the class based on the highlights shown in the text.

**ANNOTATE:** Have students mark details in the paragraph that reveal information about Puritan society, the type of government they set up, and how it led to the witch hunt, or have students participate while you highlight them.

**QUESTION:** Guide students to consider what these details might tell them. Ask what a reader can infer from Miller's description of Puritan society, and accept student responses.

**Possible response:** The Puritans set up a theocracy, or kind of government formed by religious leaders according to the principles of their religion.

**CONCLUDE:** Help students to formulate conclusions about the importance of these details in the text. Ask students why the author might have included these details.

**Possible response:** The author is describing how order and unity in Puritan society were needed in order for their society to survive. Nonconformists were seen as a threat to the community.

Remind students that authors must clarify characters' motives. By including this **background** in the exposition, Miller clarifies the motives behind the characters' behavior and helps the reader understand the historical and personal roots of the conflict.

NOTES

purpose. But all organization is and must be grounded on the idea of exclusion and prohibition, just as two objects cannot occupy the same space. Evidently the time came in New England when the repressions of order were heavier than seemed warranted by the dangers against which the order was organized. The witch-hunt was a perverse manifestation of the panic which set in among all classes when the balance began to turn toward greater individual freedom.

16 When one rises above the individual villainy displayed, one can only pity them all, just as we shall be pitied someday. It is still impossible for man to organize his social life without repressions, and the balance has yet to be struck between order and freedom.

17 The witch-hunt was not, however, a mere repression. It was also, and as importantly, a long overdue opportunity for everyone so inclined to express publicly his guilt and sins, under the cover of accusations against the victims. It suddenly became possible—and patriotic and holy—for a man to say that Martha Corey had come into his bedroom at night, and that, while his wife was sleeping at his side, Martha laid herself down on his chest and "nearly suffocated him." Of course it was her spirit only, but his satisfaction at confessing himself was no lighter than if it had been Martha herself. One could not ordinarily speak such things in public.

18 Long-held hatreds of neighbors could now be openly expressed, and vengeance taken, despite the Bible's charitable injunctions. Land-lust which had been expressed before by constant bickering over boundaries and deeds, could now be elevated to the arena of morality; one could cry witch against one's neighbor and feel perfectly justified in the bargain. Old scores could be settled on a plane of heavenly combat between Lucifer[4] and the Lord; suspicions and the envy of the miserable toward the happy could and did burst out in the general revenge.

4. **Lucifer** (LOO suh fuhr) the Devil.

19 REVEREND PARRIS *is praying now, and, though we cannot hear his words, a sense of his confusion hangs about him. He mumbles, then seems about to weep; then he weeps, then prays again; but his daughter does not stir on the bed.*

20 *The door opens, and his Negro slave enters.* TITUBA *is in her forties.* PARRIS *brought her with him from Barbados, where he spent some years as a merchant before entering the ministry. She enters as one does who can no longer bear to be barred from the sight of her beloved, but she is also very frightened because her slave sense has warned her that, as always, trouble in this house eventually lands on her back.*

21 **Tituba,** *already taking a step backward*: My Betty be hearty soon?

22 **Parris:** Out of here!





## PERSONALIZE FOR LEARNING

### English Language Learners

**Exchanging Ideas** As students read the play, provide opportunities for them to ask and answer questions as they interpret what they read. Begin by having students write what they think might happen next after they have read paragraph 18. Then as students read, have them go back to their prediction, and then write a brief statement explaining why these events have taken place. Allow students time to discuss their ideas and ask questions to clarify what they have read. **EXPANDING**

23 **Tituba,** *backing to the door:* My Betty not goin' die . . .

24 **Parris,** *scrambling to his feet in a fury:* Out of my sight! *She is gone.* Out of my—*He is overcome with sobs. He clamps his teeth against them and closes the door and leans against it, exhausted.* Oh, my God! God help me! *Quaking with fear, mumbling to himself through his sobs, he goes to the bed and gently takes* BETTY'S *hand.* Betty. Child. Dear child. Will you wake, will you open up your eyes! Betty, little one . . .

25 *He is bending to kneel again when his niece,* ABIGAIL WILLIAMS, *seventeen, enters—a strikingly beautiful girl, an orphan, with an endless capacity for dissembling. Now she is all worry and apprehension and propriety.*

26 **Abigail:** Uncle? *He looks to her.* Susanna Walcott's here from Doctor Griggs.

27 **Parris:** Oh? Let her come, let her come.

28 **Abigail,** *leaning out the door to call to Susanna, who is down the hall a few steps:* Come in, Susanna.

29 SUSANNA WALCOTT, *a little younger than Abigail, a nervous, hurried girl enters.*

30 **Parris,** *eagerly:* What does the doctor say, child?

31 **Susanna,** *craning around* PARRIS *to get a look at* BETTY: He bid me come and tell you, reverend sir, that he cannot discover no medicine for it in his books.

32 **Parris:** Then he must search on.

33 **Susanna:** Aye, sir, he have been searchin' his books since he left you, sir. But he bid me tell you, that you might look to unnatural things for the cause of it.

34 **Parris,** *his eyes going wide:* No—no. There be no unnatural cause here. Tell him I have sent for Reverend Hale of Beverly, and Mr. Hale will surely confirm that. Let him look to medicine and put out all thought of unnatural causes here. There be none.

35 **Susanna:** Aye, sir. He bid me tell you. *She turns to go.*

36 **Abigail:** Speak nothin' of it in the village, Susanna.

37 **Parris:** Go directly home and speak nothing of unnatural causes.

38 **Susanna:** Aye, sir. I pray for her. *She goes out.*

39 **Abigail:** Uncle, the rumor of witchcraft is all about; I think you'd best go down and deny it yourself. The parlor's packed with people, sir. I'll sit with her.

40 **Parris,** *pressed, turns on her:* And what shall I say to them? That my daughter and my niece I discovered dancing like heathen in the forest?

41 **Abigail:** Uncle, we did dance; let you tell them I confessed it—and I'll be whipped if I must be. But they're speakin' of witchcraft. Betty's not witched.

NOTES

**CLOSE READ**

**ANNOTATE:** In the stage directions in paragraph 24, mark details that suggest Parris's extreme emotions.

**QUESTION:** Why does Miller include these details?

**CONCLUDE:** How would these details affect the audience's perceptions of Parris in a performance?

As students close read, remind them to look for stage directions that show how a character should behave and how he or she should deliver lines during a performance. You may wish to model the Close Read using the following think-aloud format. Possible responses to questions on the student page are included.

**ANNOTATE:** As I read paragraph 24, I notice and mark details in the stage directions that suggest Parris's emotions.

**QUESTION:** Miller includes these details in the stage directions so that actors will know how to perform Parris's role in the play. These stage directions show the actions the actor should take as well as the way he should deliver his lines during this part of the play.

**CONCLUDE:** The details suggest that the actor playing the role of Parris must deliver a performance that vividly conveys Parris's acute emotional distress. The stage directions suggest that both Parris's words and actions should demonstrate his emotions of terror and fury. If the stage directions are properly executed, the audience will be able to fully appreciate Parris's extreme emotional state and the drama that it creates.

## CLOSER LOOK

### Analyze Character 

Students may have marked paragraphs 46 through 50 during their first read. Use these lines to help students understand why Parris is fearful. Encourage them to talk about the annotations that they marked. You may want to model a close read with the class based on the highlights shown in the text.

**ANNOTATE:** Have students mark details in these lines that describe Parris's concern over the discovery of Abigail and Betty's activities in the forest, or have students participate while you highlight them.

**QUESTION:** Guide students to consider what these details might tell them. Ask what a reader can infer from Parris's fears, and accept student responses.

**Possible response:** Parris is concerned that his enemies will ruin him and prevent him from preaching.

**CONCLUDE:** Help students to formulate conclusions about the importance of these details in the text. Ask students why the author might have included these details.

**Possible response:** Parris is afraid of what may happen if his enemies find out his daughter and niece participated in activities in the forest that may have involved witchcraft.

Remind students that **character** is one of the three major elements of a drama, the other two being plot and setting. A playwright establishes a character largely through dialogue and actions. However, in *The Crucible,* Miller also included long descriptions of the background and motivation of certain characters, such as Parris.

NOTES

42 **Parris:** Abigail, I cannot go before the congregation when I know you have not opened with me. What did you do with her in the forest?

43 **Abigail:** We did dance, uncle, and when you leaped out of the bush so suddenly, Betty was frightened and then she fainted. And there's the whole of it.

44 **Parris:** Child. Sit you down.

45 **Abigail,** *quavering, as she sits*: I would never hurt Betty. I love her dearly.

46 **Parris:** Now look you, child, your punishment will come in its time. But if you trafficked with spirits in the forest I must know it now, for surely my enemies will, and they will ruin me with it.

47 **Abigail:** But we never conjured spirits.

48 **Parris:** Then why can she not move herself since midnight? This child is desperate! *Abigail lowers her eyes.* It must come out—my enemies will bring it out. Let me know what you done there. Abigail, do you understand that I have many enemies?

49 **Abigail:** I have heard of it, uncle.

50 **Parris:** There is a faction that is sworn to drive me from my pulpit. Do you understand that?

51 **Abigail:** I think so, sir.

52 **Parris:** Now then, in the midst of such disruption, my own household is discovered to be the very center of some obscene practice. Abominations are done in the forest—

53 **Abigail:** It were sport, uncle!

54 **Parris,** *pointing at* BETTY: You call this sport? *She lowers her eyes. He pleads*: Abigail, if you know something that may help the doctor, for God's sake tell it to me. *She is silent.* I saw Tituba waving her arms over the fire when I came on you. Why was she doing that? And I heard a screeching and gibberish coming from her mouth. She were swaying like a dumb beast over that fire!

55 **Abigail:** She always sings her Barbados songs, and we dance.

56 **Parris:** I cannot blink what I saw, Abigail, for my enemies will not blink it. I saw a dress lying on the grass.

57 **Abigail,** *innocently*: A dress?

58 **Parris**—*it is very hard to say*: Aye, a dress. And I thought I saw—someone naked running through the trees!

59 **Abigail,** *in terror*: No one was naked! You mistake yourself, uncle!

60 **Parris,** *with anger*: I saw it! *He moves from her. Then, resolved*: Now tell me true, Abigail. And I pray you feel the weight of truth upon you, for now my ministry's at stake, my ministry and perhaps your cousin's life. Whatever abomination you have

done, give me all of it now, for I dare not be taken unaware when I go before them down there.

61 **Abigail:** There is nothin' more. I swear it, uncle.

62 **Parris,** *studies her, then nods, half convinced*: Abigail, I have fought here three long years to bend these stiff-necked people to me, and now, just now when some good respect is rising for me in the parish, you compromise my very character. I have given you a home, child. I have put clothes upon your back—now give me upright answer. Your name in the town—it is entirely white, is it not?

63 **Abigail,** *with an edge of resentment*: Why, I am sure it is, sir. There be no blush about my name.

64 **Parris,** *to the point*: Abigail, is there any other cause than you have told me, for your being discharged from Goody[5] Proctor's service? I have heard it said, and I tell you as I heard it, that she

NOTES

5. **Goody** title used for a married woman; short for Goodwife.

In the 1996 film version of *The Crucible*, Winona Ryder portrays Abigail Williams.





## PERSONALIZE FOR LEARNING

### Challenge

**Puritan Children** Review paragraph 62. Have students research to find out more about how children and adolescents in early Puritan America were treated. Were their high spirits indulged or repressed? Were they viewed as little adults? How did the treatment of males and females differ? Have students address these and other questions in oral reports that help the class understand the context in which the girls of Salem began accusing adults of witchcraft.

## CLOSE READ 

As students close read, remind them that descriptive words give them insight to a character's personality, thoughts, or feelings. You may wish to model the Close Read using the following think-aloud format. Possible responses to questions on the student page are included.

**ANNOTATE:** As I read paragraphs 65–69, I can find evidence that Abigail's reputation in Salem is questionable, since she was dismissed by one woman and was not hired by any other.

**QUESTION:** Miller includes these details because he wants the audience to be aware that other women may not trust Abigail.

**CONCLUDE:** The details suggest that some conflicts may result from jealousy among the women or concern about a spouse's infidelity.

NOTES

**CLOSE READ**

**ANNOTATE:** In the dialogue between Parris and Abigail, paragraphs 65–69, mark details that suggest Abigail's reputation in Salem may be questionable.

**QUESTION:** Why does Miller include these details about Abigail at this point in the play?

**CONCLUDE:** What conflicts do these clues suggest are at work in Salem?

comes so rarely to the church this year for she will not sit so close to something soiled. What signified that remark?

65 **Abigail:** She hates me, uncle, she must, for I would not be her slave. It's a bitter woman, a lying, cold, sniveling woman, and I will not work for such a woman!

66 **Parris:** She may be. And yet it has troubled me that you are now seven month out of their house, and in all this time no other family has ever called for your service.

67 **Abigail:** They want slaves, not such as I. Let them send to Barbados for that. I will not black my face for any of them! *With ill-concealed resentment at him*: Do you begrudge my bed, uncle?

68 **Parris:** No—no.

69 **Abigail,** *in a temper*: My name is good in the village! I will not have it said my name is soiled! Goody Proctor is a gossiping liar!

70 *Enter* MRS. ANN PUTNAM. *She is a twisted soul of forty-five, a death-ridden woman, haunted by dreams.*

71 **Parris,** *as soon as the door begins to open*: No—no. I cannot have anyone. *He sees her, and a certain deference springs into him, although his worry remains.* Why, Goody Putnam, come in.

72 **Mrs. Putnam,** *full of breath, shiny-eyed*: It is a marvel. It is surely a stroke of hell upon you.

73 **Parris:** No, Goody Putnam. It is—

74 **Mrs. Putnam,** *glancing at* BETTY: How high did she fly, how high?

75 **Parris:** No, no, she never flew—

76 **Mrs. Putnam,** *very pleased with it*: Why, it's sure she did. Mr. Collins saw her goin' over Ingersoll's barn, and come down light as bird, he says!

77 **Parris:** Now, look you, Goody Putnam, she never— *Enter* THOMAS PUTNAM, *a well-to-do, hard-handed landowner, near fifty.* Oh, good morning, Mr. Putnam.

78 **Putnam:** It is a providence the thing is out now! It is a providence. *He goes directly to the bed.*

79 **Parris:** What's out, sir, what's—?

80 MRS. PUTNAM *goes to the bed.*

81 **Putnam,** *looking down at* BETTY: Why, *her eyes* is closed! Look you, Ann.

82 **Mrs. Putnam:** Why, that's strange. *To* PARRIS: Ours is open.

83 **Parris,** *shocked*: Your Ruth is sick?

84 **Mrs. Putnam,** *with vicious certainty*: I'd not call it sick; the Devil's touch is heavier than sick. It's death, y'know, it's death drivin' into them, forked and hoofed.

85 **Parris:** Oh, pray not! Why, how does Ruth ail?

86 **Mrs. Putnam:** She ails as she must—she never waked this morning, but her eyes open and she walks, and hears naught, sees naught, and cannot eat. Her soul is taken, surely.

87 PARRIS *is struck.*

88 **Putnam,** *as though for further details*: They say you've sent for Reverend Hale of Beverly?

89 **Parris,** *with dwindling conviction now*: A precaution only. He has much experience in all demonic arts, and I—

90 **Mrs. Putnam:** He has indeed; and found a witch in Beverly last year, and let you remember that.

91 **Parris:** Now, Goody Ann, they only thought that were a witch, and I am certain there be no element of witchcraft here.

92 **Putnam:** No witchcraft! Now look you, Mr. Parris—

93 **Parris:** Thomas, Thomas, I pray you, leap not to witchcraft. I know that you—you least of all. Thomas, would ever wish so disastrous a charge laid upon me. We cannot leap to witchcraft. They will howl me out of Salem for such corruption in my house.

94 A word about Thomas Putnam. He was a man with many grievances, at least one of which appears justified. Some time before, his wife's brother-in-law, James Bayley, had been turned down as minister at Salem. Bayley had all the qualifications, and a two-thirds vote into the bargain, but a faction stopped his acceptance, for reasons that are not clear.

95 Thomas Putnam was the eldest son of the richest man in the village. He had fought the Indians at Narragansett, and was deeply interested in parish affairs. He undoubtedly felt it poor payment that the village should so blatantly disregard his candidate for one of its more important offices, especially since he regarded himself as the intellectual superior of most of the people around him.

96 His **vindictive** nature was demonstrated long before the witchcraft began. Another former Salem minister, George Burroughs, had had to borrow money to pay for his wife's funeral, and, since the parish was remiss in his salary, he was soon bankrupt. Thomas and his brother John had Burroughs jailed for debts the man did not owe. The incident is important only in that Burroughs succeeded in becoming minister where Bayley, Thomas Putnam's brother-in-law, had been rejected; the motif of resentment is clear here. Thomas Putnam felt that his own name and the honor of his family had been smirched by the village, and he meant to right matters however he could.

97 Another reason to believe him a deeply embittered man was his attempt to break his father's will, which left a disproportionate amount to a stepbrother. As with every other public cause in which he tried to force his way, he failed in this.

NOTES

**vindictve** (vihn DIHK tihv) *adj.* characterized by an intense, unreasoning desire for revenge





DIGITAL PERSPECTIVES

## CLOSER LOOK

### Analyze Plot

Students may have marked paragraphs 86–93 during their first read. Use these lines to help students understand how Goody Putnam's arrival affects events. Encourage them to talk about the annotations that they marked. You may want to model a close read with the class based on the highlights shown in the text.

**ANNOTATE:** Have students mark details in these paragraphs that describe how Goody Putnam's and Parris's dialogue affects the action, or have students participate while you highlight them.

**QUESTION:** Guide students to consider what these details might tell them. Ask what a reader can infer from Goody Putnam's suspicions and Parris's reaction, and accept student responses.

**Possible response:** Goody Putnam's daughter Ruth is also ill and she attributes the illness to the devil. Parris implores her and Thomas not to leap to conclusions about witchcraft.

**CONCLUDE:** Help students to formulate conclusions about the importance of these details in the text. Ask students why the author might have included these details.

**Possible response:** Parris is trying to avoid having his daughter and niece accused of witchcraft—an accusation that would be ruinous to him because is he a minister.

Remind students that a narrative's **plot** is usually divided into five parts: the exposition; the rising action; the climax; the falling action; and the resolution, or denouement. The exposition introduces the setting, the characters, and the basic situation. It is followed by the rising action, which usually contains an inciting incident that introduces the central conflict. During the rising action, the conflict increases in intensity until it reaches the climax. Here, the rising action includes the growing suspicions that Betty and other girls have been involved in witch craft activities, which will lead to the major conflict of the play.

## CROSS-CURRICULAR PERSPECTIVES

**Social Studies** Review paragraph 96. In colonial times, it was a customary practice to imprison a debtor until he paid off the debt. It was assumed that other family members would pay off the debt while the person was incarcerated. This was an unfair practice, since a debtor could hardly work off a debt while being held in jail. The debtor was also responsible to pay for his food and lodgings while in jail. In 1833, the federal government outlawed the jailing of debtors who owed money to Federal courts. Soon afterwards, states abolished debtors' prisons altogether.

## CLOSE READ

As students read, remind them that dialogue reveals character relationships and develops conflict. You may wish to model the Close Read using the following think-aloud format. Possible responses to questions on the student page are included.

**ANNOTATE:** As I read paragraph 101, I mark the details that relate to unexplainable things.

**QUESTION:** The details suggest that Mrs. Putnam believes supernatural forces are responsible for her children's deaths and illness.

**CONCLUDE:** These details add to the tension because they show that Mrs. Putnam's actions were the result of her belief that her children were taken from her by the devil.

NOTES

So it is not surprising to find that so many accusations against people are in the handwriting of Thomas Putnam, or that his name is so often found as a witness corroborating the supernatural testimony, or that his daughter led the crying-out at the most opportune junctures of the trials, especially when— But we'll speak of that when we come to it.

98 **Putnam**—*at the moment he is intent upon getting* PARRIS, *for whom he has only contempt, to move toward the abyss:*[6] Mr. Parris, I have taken your part in all contention here, and I would continue; but I cannot if you hold back in this. There are hurtful, vengeful spirits layin' hands on these children.

99 **Parris:** But, Thomas, you cannot—

100 **Putnam:** Ann! Tell Mr. Parris what you have done.

101 **Mrs. Putnam:** Reverend Parris, I have laid seven babies unbaptized in the earth. Believe me, sir, you never saw more hearty babies born. And yet, each would wither in my arms the very night of their birth. I have spoke nothin', but my heart has clamored intimations. And now, this year, my Ruth, my only—I see her turning strange. A secret child she has become this year, and shrivels like a sucking mouth were pullin' on her life too. And so I thought to send her to your Tituba—

102 **Parris:** To Tituba! What may Tituba—?

103 **Mrs. Putnam:** Tituba knows how to speak to the dead, Mr. Parris.

104 **Parris:** Goody Ann, it is a formidable sin to conjure up the dead!

105 **Mrs. Putnam:** I take it on my soul, but who else may surely tell us what person murdered my babies?

106 **Parris,** *horrified*: Woman!

107 **Mrs. Putnam:** They were murdered, Mr. Parris! And mark this proof! Mark it! Last night my Ruth were ever so close to their little spirits; I know it, sir. For how else is she struck dumb now except some power of darkness would stop her mouth? It is a marvelous sign, Mr. Parris!

108 **Putnam:** Don't you understand it, sir? There is a murdering witch among us, bound to keep herself in the dark. PARRIS *turns to* BETTY, *a frantic terror rising in him.* Let your enemies make of it what they will, you cannot blink it more.

109 **Parris,** *to* ABIGAIL: Then you were conjuring spirits last night.

110 **Abigail,** *whispering*: Not I, sir—Tituba and Ruth.

111 **Parris** *turns now, with new fear, and goes to* BETTY, *looks down at her, and then, gazing off*: Oh, Abigail, what proper payment for my charity! Now I am undone.

112 **Putnam:** You are not undone! Let you take hold here. Wait for no one to charge you—declare it yourself. You have discovered witchcraft—

6. **abyss** (uh BIHS) *n.* deep crack in the earth.

**CLOSE READ**

**ANNOTATE:** Mark details in Mrs. Putnam's speech in paragraph 101 that relate to things that are unexplainable or secret.

**QUESTION:** What do these details suggest about the ways in which Mrs. Putnam understands the world?

**CONCLUDE:** How do these details add to the growing sense of tension in the scene?





## CROSS-CURRICULAR PERSPECTIVES

**Humanities** Review paragraphs 103–104. Explain that, as a Puritan minister, Parris considers Tituba's claim and practice to speak to the dead scandalous. In many African religions, however, communication with the dead is central to the faith, for the dead are honored and deemed able to provide wisdom and advice to the living. Point out that Tituba is from Barbados in the West Indies which are islands in the Caribbean Sea. Note that when Europeans colonized these islands, they brought large numbers of African slaves to work on sugar plantations. People of African descent became the dominant culture, and their beliefs and customs mixed with those of the Europeans. Tituba practices Vodoun, or voodoo, a folk religion from the West Indies that mixed Roman Catholic beliefs with African religious practices.

**DIGITAL PERSPECTIVES**

113 **Parris:** In my house? In my house, Thomas? They will topple me with this! They will make of it a—

114 *Enter* MERCY LEWIS, *the Putnams' servant, a fat, sly, merciless girl of eighteen.*

115 **Mercy:** Your pardons. I only thought to see how Betty is.

116 **Putnam:** Why aren't you home? Who's with Ruth?

117 **Mercy:** Her grandma come. She's improved a little, I think—she give a powerful sneeze before.

118 **Mrs. Putnam:** Ah, there's a sign of life!

119 **Mercy:** I'd fear no more, Goody Putnam. It were a grand sneeze; another like it will shake her wits together, I'm sure. *She goes to the bed to look.*

120 **Parris:** Will you leave me now, Thomas? I would pray a while alone.

121 **Abigail:** Uncle, you've prayed since midnight. Why do you not go down and—

122 **Parris:** No—no. *To* PUTNAM: I have no answer for that crowd. I'll wait till Mr. Hale arrives. *To get* MRS. PUTNAM *to leave*: If you will, Goody Ann . . .

123 **Putnam:** Now look you, sir. Let you strike out against the Devil, and the village will bless you for it! Come down, speak to them—pray with them. They're thirsting for your word, Mister! Surely you'll pray with them.

124 **Parris,** *swayed*: I'll lead them in a psalm, but let you say nothing of witchcraft yet. I will not discuss it. The cause is yet unknown. I have had enough contention since I came; I want no more.

125 **Mrs. Putnam:** Mercy, you go home to Ruth, d'y'hear?

126 **Mercy:** Aye, mum.

127 MRS. PUTNAM *goes out.*

128 **Parris,** *to* ABIGAIL: If she starts for the window, cry for me at once.

129 **Abigail:** I will, uncle.

130 **Parris,** *to* PUTNAM: There is a terrible power in her arms today. *He goes out with* PUTNAM.

131 **Abigail,** *with hushed trepidation*: How is Ruth sick?

132 **Mercy:** It's weirdish. I know not—she seems to walk like a dead one since last night.

133 **Abigail,** *turns at once and goes to* BETTY, *and now, with fear in her voice*: Betty? BETTY *doesn't move. She shakes her.* Now stop this! Betty! Sit up now!

134 BETTY *doesn't stir.* MERCY *comes over.*

NOTES





**CLOSER LOOK**

## Explore Diction

Students may have marked paragraphs 115–123 during their first read. Use these lines to help students understand how Miller uses dialogue that sounds like the speech of the New England Puritans. Encourage them to talk about the annotations that they marked. You may want to model a close read with the class based on the highlights shown in the text.

**ANNOTATE:** Have students mark details in these lines that show archaic expressions or speech patterns, or have students participate while you highlight them.

**QUESTION:** Guide students to consider what these details might tell them. Ask what the effect is of the speech patterns of the characters in the play.

**Possible response:** Students may say that the character's speech patterns help the audience perceive the characters as being from a particular time and place.

**CONCLUDE:** Help students to formulate conclusions about the importance of these details in the text. Ask students why the author might have included these details.

**Possible response:** The author is trying to find language in the form of dialogue that relates to the nature of the characters. The language should spring naturally from the characters and their backgrounds.

Remind students that **diction** is the choice of words and phrases used in a piece of writing. In this play, the diction includes speech patterns and archaic language of the Puritans. Many of these expressions are no longer used in modern English.

CLOSER LOOK

## Analyze Character

Students may have marked paragraphs 135–145 during their first read. Use these lines to help students understand character development. Encourage them to talk about the annotations that they marked. You may want to model a close read with the class based on the highlights shown in the text.

**ANNOTATE:** Have students mark details in these lines that show what the girls know about witchcraft and the events in the forest, or have students participate while you highlight them.

**QUESTION:** Guide students to consider what these details might tell them. Ask what Mercy's suggestion about beating reveals about her view of Betty's bewitchment.

**Possible response:** It shows that she does not think Betty is bewitched and believes Betty's condition is fake.

**CONCLUDE:** Help students to formulate conclusions about the importance of these details in the text. Ask students why the author might have included these details.

**Possible response:** Mercy's reaction to Betty's unconsciousness and Mary Warren's remark about being called witches and having to tell the truth indicates that there was in fact no witchcraft. Some of the characters seem to understand the dangerous situation they are in.

Remind students that the development of **character** drives the plot. The dialogue between characters allows the reader to begin to understand their motives, unique personalities, thoughts, and feelings. Here, the girls' fear of being accused of witchcraft contributes to the rising action of the play.

NOTES

135 **Mercy:** Have you tried beatin' her? I gave Ruth a good one and it waked her for a minute. Here, let me have her.

136 **Abigail,** *holding* MERCY *back*: No, he'll be comin' up. Listen, now: if they be questioning us, tell them we danced—I told him as much already.

137 **Mercy:** Aye. And what more?

138 **Abigail:** He knows Tituba conjured Ruth's sisters to come out of the grave.

139 **Mercy:** And what more?

140 **Abigail:** He saw you naked.

141 **Mercy:** *clapping her hands together with a frightened laugh*: Oh, Jesus!

142 *Enter* MARY WARREN, *breathless. She is seventeen, a subservient, naive, lonely girl.*

143 **Mary Warren:** What'll we do? The village is out! I just come from the farm; the whole country's talkin' witchcraft! They'll be callin' us witches, Abby!

144 **Mercy,** *pointing and looking at* MARY WARREN: She means to tell. I know it.

145 **Mary Warren:** Abby, we've got to tell. Witchery's a hangin' error, a hangin' like they done in Boston two year ago! We must

In this still from the 1996 film version of *The Crucible*, the other girls hold Betty Parris back as she attempts to fly.

tell the truth, Abby! You'll only be whipped for dancin', and the other things!

146 **Abigail:** Oh, *we'll* be whipped!

147 **Mary Warren:** I never done none of it, Abby. I only looked!

148 **Mercy,** *moving menacingly toward* Mary: Oh, you're a great one for lookin', aren't you, Mary Warren? What a grand peeping courage you have!

149 Betty, *on the bed, whimpers.* Abigail *turns to her at once.*

150 **Abigail:** Betty? *She goes to* Betty. Now, Betty, dear, wake up now. It's Abigail. *She sits* Betty *up and furiously shakes her.* I'll beat you, Betty! Betty *whimpers.* My, you seem improving. I talked to your papa and I told him everything. So there's nothing to—

151 **Betty,** *darts off the bed, frightened of* Abigail, *and flattens herself against the wall*: I want my mama!

152 **Abigail,** *with alarm, as she cautiously approaches* Betty: What ails you, Betty? Your mama's dead and buried.

153 **Betty:** I'll fly to Mama. Let me fly! *She raises her arms as though to fly, and streaks for the window, gets one leg out.*

154 **Abigail,** *pulling her away from the window*: I told him everything, he knows now, he knows everything we—

155 **Betty:** You drank blood, Abby! You didn't tell him that!

156 **Abigail:** Betty, you never say that again! You will never—

157 **Betty:** You did, you did! You drank a charm to kill John Proctor's wife! You drank a charm to kill Goody Proctor!

158 **Abigail,** *smashes her across the face*: Shut it! Now shut it!

159 **Betty:** *collapsing on the bed*: Mama. Mama! *She dissolves into sobs.*

160 **Abigail:** Now look you. All of you. We danced. And Tituba conjured Ruth Putnam's dead sisters. And that is all. And mark this. Let either of you breathe a word, or the edge of a word, about the other things, and I will come to you in the black of some terrible night and I will bring a pointy reckoning that will shudder you. And you know I can do it; I saw Indians smash my dear parents' heads on the pillow next to mine, and I have seen some reddish work done at night, and I can make you wish you had never seen the sun go down! *She goes to* Betty *and roughly sits her up.* Now, you—sit up and stop this!

161 *But* Betty *collapses in her hands and lies inert on the bed.*

162 **Mary Warren,** *with hysterical fright*: What's got her? Abigail *stares in fright at* Betty. Abby, she's going to die! It's a sin to conjure, and we—

163 **Abigail,** *starting for* Mary: I say shut it, Mary Warren!

164 *Enter* John Proctor. *On seeing him,* Mary Warren *leaps in fright.*

NOTES

**CLOSE READ**

**ANNOTATE:** In Abigail's speech in paragraph 160, mark the short sentences.

**QUESTION:** Why does Miller mix short and long sentences in this speech?

**CONCLUDE:** How do these short sentences add to the emotional intensity of Abigail's speech?

Remind students that dialogue and the way it is written reflects a character's emotions. You may wish to model the Close Read using the following think-aloud format. Possible responses to questions on the student page are included.

**ANNOTATE:** As I read paragraph 160, I notice and highlight the short sentences in Abigail's speech.

**QUESTION:** As I read these words, I think that the author mixes up the use of short sentences and longer sentences to emphasize Abigail's emotions. I know that she is immoral and will do anything to get what she wants. I think the short sentences reveal that she is bossy and mean to the other girls.

**CONCLUDE:** I think that the audience and the girls would react to Abigail's speech in a similar manner. Both the audience and girls may be shocked at the drama and tension of the dialogue and action as Abigail threatens the girls.

## CROSS-CURRICULAR PERSPECTIVES

**Social Studies** Review paragraph 160. Point out that Abigail's memory of Indians "smashing my dear parents' heads on the pillows next to mine" is evidence of the increased tensions between the English settlers and Native Americans, as the settlers took over more and more of the Native American land. The reference reinforces the historical roots of the Puritan fears. On February 10, 1676, the Narragansett people attacked the tiny village of Lancaster, Massachusetts. They set fire to every building and killed most of the settlers, except a few whom they carried away and held for ransom. Invite interested students to research Mary Rowlandson, captured in the raid, who wrote an account of her experience. Students may also find and read other "captivity" narratives popular in colonial times.

CLOSER LOOK

### Interpret Stage Directions 

Students may have marked paragraphs 172–179. Encourage them to talk about the annotations that they marked. You may want to model a close read with the class based on the highlights shown in the text.

ANNOTATE: Have students mark details in these lines that show stage directions for Proctor and Abigail, or have students participate while you highlight them.

QUESTION: Guide students to consider what these details might tell them. Ask what important information a reader can infer from Abigail's behavior that is conveyed through stage directions in this scene.

**Possible response:** Abigail is "absorbing" Proctor's presence. She is "wide-eyed" and winningly coming "a little closer" to him and "grasping his hand." As Proctor attempts to leave, she "springs into his path." He looks at her with a "knowing smile" but her "concentrated desire destroys his smile."

CONCLUDE: Help students to formulate conclusions about the importance of these details in the text. Ask students why the author might have included these details.

**Possible response:** The stage directions suggest that Abigail has a romantic attachment and passionate feelings for Proctor. He is no longer interested in her as he attempts to leave, but she will not let him go. His "knowing smile" suggests that they have had an affair. The fact that she "destroys his smile" suggests that Proctor has ended the affair and is firm about not resuming it. He resists her advances.

Remind students that **stage directions** not only tell where actors are on stage, they can also give detailed descriptions of the action of the actors. These might include facial expressions, movement, tone of voice, and how they interact with each other. In this scene, the body language and gestures between Abigail and Proctor suggest more than the dialogue is telling.

NOTES

**calumny** (KAL uhm nee) *n.* the making of false statements with the intent to harm

165 Proctor was a farmer in his middle thirties. He need not have been a partisan of any faction in the town, but there is evidence to suggest that he had a sharp and biting way with hypocrites. He was the kind of man—powerful of body, even-tempered, and not easily led—who cannot refuse support to partisans without drawing their deepest resentment. In Proctor's presence a fool felt his foolishness instantly—and a Proctor is always marked for calumny therefore.

166 But as we shall see, the steady manner he displays does not spring from an untroubled soul. He is a sinner, a sinner not only against the moral fashion of the time, but against his own vision of decent conduct. These people had no ritual for the washing away of sins. It is another trait we inherited from them, and it has helped to discipline us as well as to breed hypocrisy among us. Proctor, respected and even feared in Salem, has come to regard himself as a kind of fraud. But no hint of this has yet appeared on the surface, and as he enters from the crowded parlor below it is a man in his prime we see, with a quiet confidence and an unexpressed, hidden force. Mary Warren, his servant, can barely speak for embarrassment and fear.

167 **Mary Warren:** Oh! I'm just going home, Mr. Proctor.

168 **Proctor:** Be you foolish, Mary Warren? Be you deaf? I forbid you leave the house, did I not? Why shall I pay you? I am looking for you more often than my cows!

169 **Mary Warren:** I only come to see the great doings in the world.

170 **Proctor:** I'll show you a great doin' on your arse one of these days. Now get you home; my wife is waitin' with your work! *Trying to retain a shred of dignity, she goes slowly out.*

171 **Mercy Lewis,** *both afraid of him and strangely titillated*: I'd best be off. I have my Ruth to watch. Good morning, Mr. Proctor.

172 Mercy *sidles out. Since* PROCTOR's *entrance,* ABIGAIL *has stood as though on tiptoe, absorbing his presence, wide-eyed. He glances at her, then goes to* BETTY *on the bed.*

173 **Abigail:** Gah! I'd almost forgot how strong you are, John Proctor!

174 **Proctor,** *looking at* ABIGAIL *now, the faintest suggestion of a knowing smile on his face*: What's this mischief here?

175 **Abigail,** *with a nervous laugh*: Oh, she's only gone silly somehow.

176 **Proctor:** The road past my house is a pilgrimage to Salem all morning. The town's mumbling witchcraft.

177 **Abigail:** Oh, posh! *Winningly she comes a little closer, with a confidential, wicked air.* We were dancin' in the woods last night, and my uncle leaped in on us. She took fright, is all.

178 **Proctor,** *his smile widening*: Ah, you're wicked yet, aren't y'! *A trill of expectant laughter escapes her, and she dares come closer, feverishly*





576 UNIT 5 • FACING OUR FEARS

*looking into his eyes*. You'll be clapped in the stocks before you're twenty. *He takes a step to go, and she springs into his path.*

179 **Abigail:** Give me a word, John. A soft word. *Her concentrated desire destroys his smile.*

180 **Proctor:** No, no, Abby. That's done with.

181 **Abigail,** *tauntingly*: You come five mile to see a silly girl fly? I know you better.

182 **Proctor,** *setting her firmly out of his path*: I come to see what mischief your uncle's brewin' now. *With final emphasis*: Put it out of mind, Abby.

183 **Abigail,** *grasping his hand before he can release her*: John—I am waitin' for you every night.

184 **Proctor:** Abby, I never give you hope to wait for me.

185 **Abigail,** *now beginning to anger—she can't believe it*: I have something better than hope, I think!

186 **Proctor:** Abby, you'll put it out of mind. I'll not be comin' for you more.

187 **Abigail:** You're surely sportin' with me.

188 **Proctor:** You know me better.

NOTES

In the 1996 film version of *The Crucible*, Daniel Day-Lewis portrays John Proctor. Here, Abigail, played by Winona Ryder, pleads with Proctor.

CLOSE READ

Remind students to consider what they already know about Proctor and Abigail's past relationship and what they are like as individuals. You may wish to model the Close Read using the following think-aloud format. Possible responses to questions on the student page are included.

**ANNOTATE:** As I read paragraphs 190–191, I notice and highlight the word that is repeated in Abigail's and Proctor's speeches.

**QUESTION:** I think Miller has both characters use the word to emphasize that Proctor and Abigail have had a difficult time constraining their emotions toward each other.

**CONCLUDE:** As I read these lines, I think that the author intended for the audience to view Abigail and Proctor as two people who are untamed, and give in to passion, even if it is considered sinful.

NOTES

**CLOSE READ**

**ANNOTATE:** In paragraphs 190–191, mark the repeated word that appears in both Proctor's and Abigail's lines.

**QUESTION:** Why does Miller have both characters use this word?

**CONCLUDE:** How does this word affect the way in which the audience views Abigail and Proctor?

189 **Abigail:** I know how you clutched my back behind your house and sweated like a stallion whenever I come near! Or did I dream that? It's she put me out, you cannot pretend it were you. I saw your face when she put me out, and you loved me then and you do now!

190 **Proctor:** Abby, that's a wild thing to say—

191 **Abigail:** A wild thing may say wild things. But not so wild, I think. I have seen you since she put me out; I have seen you nights.

192 **Proctor:** I have hardly stepped off my farm this seven month.

193 **Abigail:** I have a sense for heat, John, and yours has drawn me to my window, and I have seen you looking up, burning in your loneliness. Do you tell me you've never looked up at my window?

194 **Proctor:** I may have looked up.

195 **Abigail,** *now softening*: And you must. You are no wintry man. I know you, John. I *know* you. *She is weeping*. I cannot sleep for dreamin'; I cannot dream but I wake and walk about the house as though I'd find you comin' through some door. *She clutches him desperately*.

196 **Proctor,** *gently pressing her from him, with great sympathy but firmly*: Child—

197 **Abigail,** *with a flash of anger*: How do you call me child!

198 **Proctor:** Abby, I may think of you softly from time to time. But I will cut off my hand before I'll ever reach for you again. Wipe it out of mind. We never touched, Abby.

199 **Abigail:** Aye, but we did.

200 **Proctor:** Aye, but we did not.

201 **Abigail,** *with a bitter anger*: Oh, I marvel how such a strong man may let such a sickly wife be—

202 **Proctor,** *angered—at himself as well*: You'll speak nothin' of Elizabeth!

203 **Abigail:** She is blackening my name in the village! She is telling lies about me! She is a cold, sniveling woman, and you bend to her! Let her turn you like a—

204 **Proctor,** *shaking her*: Do you look for whippin'?

205 *A psalm is heard being sung below.*

206 **Abigail,** *in tears*: I look for John Proctor that took me from my sleep and put knowledge in my heart! I never knew what pretense Salem was, I never knew the lying lessons I was taught by all these Christian women and their covenanted men! And now you bid me tear the light out of my eyes? I will not, I cannot! You loved me, John Proctor, and whatever sin it is, you





578 UNIT 5 • FACING OUR FEARS

NOTES

love me yet! *He turns abruptly to go out. She rushes to him.* John, pity me, pity me!

207 *The words "going up to Jesus" are heard in the psalm. and* BETTY *claps her ears suddenly and whines loudly.*

208 **Abigail:** Betty? *She hurries to* BETTY, *who is now sitting up and screaming.* PROCTOR *goes to* BETTY *as* ABIGAIL *is trying to pull her hands down, calling "Betty!"*

209 **Proctor,** *growing unnerved*: What's she doing? Girl, what ails you? Stop that wailing!

210 *The singing has stopped in the midst of this, and now* PARRIS *rushes in.*

211 **Parris:** What happened? What are you doing to her? Betty! *He rushes to the bed, crying,* "Betty, Betty!" MRS. PUTNAM *enters, feverish with curiosity, and with her* THOMAS PUTNAM *and* MERCY LEWIS. PARRIS, *at the bed, keeps lightly slapping* BETTY'*s face, while she moans and tries to get up.*

212 **Abigail:** She heard you singin' and suddenly she's up and screamin'.

213 **Mrs. Putnam:** The psalm! The psalm! She cannot bear to hear the Lord's name!

214 **Parris:** No. God forbid. Mercy, run to the doctor! Tell him what's happened here! MERCY LEWIS *rushes out.*

215 **Mrs. Putnam:** Mark it for a sign, mark it!

216 REBECCA NURSE, *seventy-two, enters. She is white-haired, leaning upon her walking-stick.*

217 **Putnam,** *pointing at the whimpering* BETTY: That is a notorious sign of witchcraft afoot, Goody Nurse, a prodigious sign!

218 **Mrs. Putnam:** My mother told me that! When they cannot bear to hear the name of—

219 **Parris,** *trembling*: Rebecca, Rebecca, go to her, we're lost. She suddenly cannot bear to hear the Lord's—

220 GILES COREY, *eighty-three, enters. He is knotted with muscle, canny, inquisitive, and still powerful.*

221 **Rebecca:** There is hard sickness here, Giles Corey, so please to keep the quiet.

222 **Giles:** I've not said a word. No one here can testify I've said a word. Is she going to fly again? I hear she flies.

223 **Putnam:** Man, be quiet now!

224 *Everything is quiet.* REBECCA *walks across the room to the bed. Gentleness exudes from her.* BETTY *is quietly whimpering, eyes shut.* REBECCA *simply stands over the child, who gradually quiets.*

225 And while they are so absorbed, we may put a word in for Rebecca. Rebecca was the wife of Francis Nurse, who, from all

## PERSONALIZE FOR LEARNING

### Strategic Support

**Text Features** Some students may be confused by which words are dialogue and which are stage directions. Review paragraph 208. Point out that the stage directions are printed in italics and give information about how characters should move or speak. Another clue is that some stage directions, such as "She hurries to Betty," refer to the character in the third person. A character who is speaking would not refer to herself in the third person. Suggest that before students read they annotate the italicized stage directions.

NOTES

accounts, was one of those men for whom both sides of the argument had to have respect. He was called upon to arbitrate disputes as though he were an unofficial judge, and Rebecca also enjoyed the high opinion most people had for him. By the time of the delusion, they had three hundred acres, and their children were settled in separate homesteads within the same estate. However, Francis had originally rented the land, and one theory has it that, as he gradually paid for it and raised his social status, there were those who resented his rise.

226 Another suggestion to explain the systematic campaign against Rebecca, and inferentially against Francis, is the land war he fought with his neighbors, one of whom was a Putnam. This squabble grew to the proportions of a battle in the woods between partisans of both sides, and it is said to have lasted for two days. As for Rebecca herself, the general opinion of her character was so high that to explain how anyone dared cry her out for a witch—and more, how adults could bring themselves to lay hands on her—we must look to the fields and boundaries of that time.

227 As we have seen. Thomas Putnam's man for the Salem ministry was Bayley. The Nurse clan had been in the faction that prevented Bayley's taking office. In addition, certain families allied to the Nurses by blood or friendship, and whose farms were contiguous with the Nurse farm or close to it, combined to break away from the Salem town authority and set up Topsfield, a new and independent entity whose existence was resented by old Salemites.

228 That the guiding hand behind the outcry was Putnam's is indicated by the fact that, as soon as it began, this Topsfield-Nurse faction absented themselves from church in protest and disbelief. It was Edward and Jonathan Putnam who signed the first complaint against Rebecca; and Thomas Putnam's little daughter was the one who fell into a fit at the hearing and pointed to Rebecca as her attacker. To top it all, Mrs. Putnam—who is now staring at the bewitched child on the bed—soon accused Rebecca's spirit of "tempting her to iniquity," a charge that had more truth in it than Mrs. Putnam could know.

229 **Mrs. Putnam,** *astonished*: What have you done?

230 REBECCA, *in thought, now leaves the bedside and sits.*

231 **Parris,** *wondrous and relieved*: What do you make of it. Rebecca?

232 **Putnam,** *eagerly*: Goody Nurse, will you go to my Ruth and see if you can wake her?

233 **Rebecca,** *sitting*: I think she'll wake in time. Pray calm yourselves. I have eleven children, and I am twenty-six times a grandma, and I have seen them all through their silly seasons, and when it come on them they will run the Devil bowlegged





## PERSONALIZE FOR LEARNING

### Challenge

**Act It Out** Call students' attention to paragraphs 229–233. Miller's dialogue was meant to be heard rather than read silently. Invite students who enjoy dramatic speaking and oral interpretation of literature to form a group in which they read the dialogue aloud together. Begin with paragraphs 229–233. Readers can maintain the same roles or alternate so that everyone has a chance to read both major and minor characters. Students may also take turns reading paragraphs of the exposition aloud. Have students discuss how hearing the language enriches their experience of the play.

keeping up with their mischief. I think she'll wake when she tires of it. A child's spirit is like a child, you can never catch it by running after it; you must stand still, and, for love, it will soon itself come back.

234 **Proctor:** Aye, that's the truth of it, Rebecca.

235 **Mrs. Putnam:** This is no silly season, Rebecca. My Ruth is bewildered, Rebecca; she cannot eat.

236 **Rebecca:** Perhaps she is not hungered yet. *To* PARRIS: I hope you are not decided to go in search of loose spirits, Mr. Parris. I've heard promise of that outside.

237 **Parris:** A wide opinion's running in the parish that the Devil may be among us, and I would satisfy them that they are wrong.

238 **Proctor:** Then let you come out and call them wrong. Did you consult the wardens before you called this minister to look for devils?

239 **Parris:** He is not coming to look for devils!

240 **Proctor:** Then what's he coming for?

241 **Putnam:** There be children dyin' in the village, Mister!

242 **Proctor:** I seen none dyin'. This society will not be a bag to swing around your head, Mr. Putnam. *To* PARRIS: Did you call a meeting before you—?

243 **Putnam:** I am sick of meetings; cannot the man turn his head without he have a meeting?

244 **Proctor:** He may turn his head, but not to Hell!

245 **Rebecca:** Pray, John, be calm. *Pause. He defers to her*. Mr. Parris, I think you'd best send Reverend Hale back as soon as he come. This will set us all to arguin' again in the society, and we thought to have peace this year. I think we ought rely on the doctor now, and good prayer.

246 **Mrs. Putnam:** Rebecca, the doctor's baffled!

247 **Rebecca:** If so he is, then let us go to God for the cause of it. There is prodigious danger in the seeking of loose spirits. I fear it, I fear it. Let us rather blame ourselves and—

248 **Putnam:** How may we blame ourselves? I am one of nine sons; the Putnam seed have peopled this province. And yet I have but one child left of eight—and now she shrivels!

249 **Rebecca:** I cannot fathom that.

250 **Mrs. Putnam,** *with a growing edge of sarcasm*: But I must! You think it God's work you should never lose a child, nor grandchild either, and I bury all but one? There are wheels within wheels in this village, and fires within fires!

251 **Putnam,** *to* PARRIS: When Reverend Hale comes, you will proceed to look for signs of witchcraft here.

NOTES

CLOSER LOOK

## Analyze Conflict

Students may have marked paragraphs 237–244 during their first read. Use these lines to help students understand how the action of the play drives the plot. Encourage them to talk about the annotations that they marked. You may want to model a close read with the class based on the highlights shown in the text.

**ANNOTATE:** Have students mark details in these lines that describe how the characters create an atmosphere in which accusations of witchcraft can flourish, or have students participate while you highlight them.

**QUESTION:** Guide students to consider what these details might tell them. Ask what important information a reader can infer from the conversation among Parris, Proctor, and Putnam.

**Possible response:** Parris suggests that the people of Salem have the opinion that the Devil, or witchcraft may be among them. Putnam and Proctor argue over whether or not children are dying in the village; Proctor points out that none are dying and that there is no reason for Hale to come.

**CONCLUDE:** Help students to formulate conclusions about the importance of these details in the text. Ask students why the author might have included these details.

**Possible response:** Parris and Putnam's attitudes have helped create an atmosphere of excessive fear where accusations of witchcraft can flourish.

Remind students that **conflict** is the struggle between opposing forces. Conflict can be **external**, or between two or more characters, as in this section of the drama. Conflict can also be **internal**, existing within a single character who is struggling with his or her beliefs, feelings, desires, and so on.

## CLOSE READ

Remind students that there is growing evidence in the dialogue that Parris and Proctor are at odds with each other. You may wish to model the Close Read using the following think-aloud format. Possible responses to questions on the student page are included.

**ANNOTATE:** As I read paragraphs 261–271, I mark details related to business matters.

**QUESTION:** I think Miller includes these details to show that Parris is unhappy with the way the villagers are treating him, and men of the village think he is asking too much.

**CONCLUDE:** The effect of the details is that the audience understands there are grievances between the characters, and that characters are apt to claim the devil is at work when they are not happy with others.

NOTES

252 **Proctor,** *to* PUTNAM: You cannot command Mr. Parris. We vote by name in this society, not by acreage.

253 **Putnam:** I never heard you worried so on this society, Mr. Proctor. I do not think I saw you at Sabbath meeting since snow flew.

254 **Proctor:** I have trouble enough without I come five mile to hear him preach only hellfire and bloody damnation. Take it to heart, Mr. Parris. There are many others who stay away from church these days because you hardly ever mention God any more.

255 **Parris,** *now aroused*: Why, that's a drastic charge!

256 **Rebecca:** It's somewhat true; there are many that quail to bring their children—

257 **Parris:** I do not preach for children, Rebecca. It is not the children who are unmindful of their obligations toward this ministry.

258 **Rebecca:** Are there really those unmindful?

259 **Parris:** I should say the better half of Salem village—

260 **Putnam:** And more than that!

CLOSE READ

ANNOTATE: In paragraphs 261–271, mark details related to property, salaries, and other business matters.

QUESTION: Why does Miller include details about the business relationships among the characters?

CONCLUDE: What is the effect of these details, particularly in suggesting simmering conflicts?

261 **Parris:** Where is my wood? My contract provides I be supplied with all my firewood. I am waiting since November for a stick, and even in November I had to show my frostbitten hands like some London beggar!

262 **Giles:** You are allowed six pound a year to buy your wood, Mr. Parris.

263 **Parris:** I regard that six pound as part of my salary. I am paid little enough without I spend six pound on firewood.

264 **Proctor:** Sixty, plus six for firewood—

265 **Parris:** The salary is sixty-six pound, Mr. Proctor! I am not some preaching farmer with a book under my arm; I am a graduate of Harvard College.

266 **Giles:** Aye, and well instructed in arithmetic!

267 **Parris:** Mr. Corey, you will look far for a man of my kind at sixty pound a year! I am not used to this poverty; I left a thrifty business in the Barbados to serve the Lord. I do not fathom it, why am I persecuted here? I cannot offer one proposition but there be a howling riot of argument. I have often wondered if the Devil be in it somewhere; I cannot understand you people otherwise.

268 **Proctor:** Mr. Parris, you are the first minister ever did demand the deed to this house—

269 **Parris:** Man! Don't a minister deserve a house to live in?

270 **Proctor:** To live in, yes. But to ask ownership is like you shall own the meeting house itself; the last meeting I were at you

DIGITAL PERSPECTIVES

spoke so long on deeds and mortgages I thought it were an auction.

271 **Parris:** I want a mark of confidence, is all! I am your third preacher in seven years. I do not wish to be put out like the cat whenever some majority feels the whim. You people seem not to comprehend that a minister is the Lord's man in the parish; a minister is not to be so lightly crossed and contradicted—

272 **Putnam:** Aye!

273 **Parris:** There is either obedience or the church will burn like Hell is burning!

274 **Proctor:** Can you speak one minute without we land in Hell again? I am sick of Hell!

275 **Parris:** It is not for you to say what is good for you to hear!

276 **Proctor:** I may speak my heart, I think!

277 **Parris,** *in a fury*: What, are we Quakers?[7] We are not Quakers here yet, Mr. Proctor. And you may tell that to your followers!

278 **Proctor:** My followers!

279 **Parris—***now he's out with it*: There is a party in this church. I am not blind; there is a faction and a party.

280 **Proctor:** Against you?

281 **Putnam:** Against him and all authority!

282 **Proctor:** Why, then I must find it and join it.

283 *There is shock among the others.*

284 **Rebecca:** He does not mean that.

285 **Putnam:** He confessed it now!

286 **Proctor:** I mean it solemnly, Rebecca; I like not the smell of this "authority."

287 **Rebecca:** No, you cannot break charity with your minister. You are another kind, John. Clasp his hand, make your peace.

288 **Proctor:** I have a crop to sow and lumber to drag home. *He goes angrily to the door and turns to* COREY *with a smile.* What say you, Giles, let's find the party. He says there's a party.

289 **Giles:** I've changed my opinion of this man, John. Mr. Parris, I beg your pardon. I never thought you had so much iron in you.

290 **Parris,** *surprised*: Why, thank you, Giles!

291 **Giles:** It suggests to the mind what the trouble be among us all these years. *To all*: Think on it. Wherefore is everybody suing everybody else? Think on it now, it's a deep thing, and dark as a pit. I have been six time in court this year—

292 **Proctor,** *familiarly, with warmth, although he knows he is approaching the edge of Giles's tolerance with this*: Is it the Devil's fault that a man cannot say you good morning without you clap

NOTES

7. **Quakers** members of the Society of Friends, a Christian religious sect that was founded in the mid-seventeenth century and that has no formal creed, rites, or priesthood. Unlike the Quakers, the Puritans had a rigid code of conduct and were expected to heed to the words of their ministers.





## DIGITAL PERSPECTIVES

**Enriching the Text** Discuss with students how Proctor and Rebecca both express some distaste for Parris's preaching "hellfire and bloody damnation." Go online to refer students to Jonathan Edwards' sermon "Sinners in the Hands of an Angry God." Have students read the sermon in light of what they have read so far in *The Crucible.* Tell them to put themselves in the place of the congregation and imagine how they would have felt at hearing such sermons week after week, especially from a man like Reverend Parris. Ask students to consider how Parris's style of preaching might have alienated "the better half of Salem village." Then ask students what evidence they can find that Parris's attitude has helped to create an atmosphere of fear which will lead to accusations of witchcraft. **(Research to Clarify)**

NOTES

**defamation** (dehf uh MAY shuhn) *n.* unjust injury to someone's good reputation through the making of false statements

him for **defamation**? You're old, Giles, and you're not hearin' so well as you did.

293 **Giles**—*he cannot be crossed*: John Proctor, I have only last month collected four pound damages for you publicly sayin' I burned the roof off your house, and I—

294 **Proctor,** *laughing*: I never said no such thing, but I've paid you for it, so I hope I can call you deaf without charge. Now come along, Giles, and help me drag my lumber home.

295 **Putnam:** A moment, Mr. Proctor. What lumber is that you're draggin', if I may ask you?

296 **Proctor:** My lumber. From out my forest by the riverside.

297 **Putnam:** Why, we are surely gone wild this year. What anarchy is this? That tract is in my bounds, it's in my bounds, Mr. Proctor.

298 **Proctor:** In your bounds! *Indicating* REBECCA: I bought that tract from Goody Nurse's husband five months ago.

299 **Putnam:** He had no right to sell it. It stands clear in my grandfather's will that all the land between the river and—

300 **Proctor:** Your grandfather had a habit of willing land that never belonged to him, if I may say it plain.

301 **Giles:** That's God's truth; he nearly willed away my north pasture but he knew I'd break his fingers before he'd set his name to it. Let's get your lumber home, John. I feel a sudden will to work coming on.

302 **Putnam:** You load one oak of mine and you'll fight to drag it home!

303 **Giles:** Aye, and we'll win too, Putnam—this fool and I. Come on! *He turns to* PROCTOR and *starts out.*

304 **Putnam:** I'll have my men on you, Corey! I'll clap a writ on you!

305 *Enter* REVEREND JOHN HALE *of Beverly.*

306 Mr. Hale is nearing forty, a tight-skinned, eager-eyed intellectual. This is a beloved errand for him; on being called here to ascertain witchcraft he felt the pride of the specialist whose unique knowledge has at last been publicly called for. Like almost all men of learning, he spent a good deal of time pondering the invisible world, especially since he had himself encountered a witch in his parish not long before. That woman, however, turned into a mere pest under his searching scrutiny, and the child she had allegedly been afflicting recovered her normal behavior after Hale had given her his kindness and a few days of rest in his own house. However, that experience never raised a doubt in his mind as to the reality of the underworld or the existence of Lucifer's many-faced lieutenants. And his belief is not to his discredit. Better minds than Hale's





PERSONALIZE FOR LEARNING

**Strategic Support**

**Sentence Starters** Review paragraphs 294–304. Point out that the disagreement between Proctor and Putnam adds to the conflict at the center of the plot. Have students close read the text and then complete the following starter sentences with inferences and conclusions drawn from the text:

*I know that Putnam does not like Proctor because* ________. (**Possible response:** Putnam has criticized Proctor for not attending church and for being against authority)

*I know that the Putnam and Nurse clans have been in conflict over land. Now I learn that*

*Proctor has* ________. (**Possible response:** become part of that land dispute, supporting the Nurse clan and criticizing Putnam)

*Salem has become divided into two factions whose conflict may explain* ________. (**Possible response:** the witchcraft trials and accusations)

were—and still are—convinced that there is a society of spirits beyond our ken. One cannot help noting that one of his lines has never yet raised a laugh in any audience that has seen this play: it is his assurance that "We cannot look to superstition in this. The Devil is precise." Evidently we are not quite certain even now whether diabolism is holy and not to be scoffed at. And it is no accident that we should be so bemused.

307 Like Reverend Hale and the others on this stage, we conceive the Devil as a necessary part of a respectable view of cosmology. Ours is a divided empire in which certain ideas and emotions and actions are of God, and their opposites are of Lucifer. It is as impossible for most men to conceive of a morality without sin as of an earth without "sky." Since 1692 a great but superficial change has wiped out God's beard and the Devil's horns, but the world is still gripped between two diametrically opposed absolutes. The concept of unity, in which positive and negative are attributes of the same force, in which good and evil are relative, ever-changing, and always joined to the same phenomenon—such a concept is still reserved to the physical sciences and to the few who have grasped the history of ideas. When it is recalled that until the Christian era the underworld was never regarded as a hostile area, that all gods were useful and essentially friendly to man despite occasional lapses; when we see the steady and methodical inculcation into humanity of the idea of man's worthlessness—until redeemed—the necessity of the Devil may become evident as a weapon, a weapon designed and used time and time again in every age to whip men into a surrender to a particular church or church-state.

308 Our difficulty in believing the—for want of a better word—political inspiration of the Devil is due in great part to the fact that he is called up and damned not only by our social antagonists but by our own side, whatever it may be. The Catholic Church, through its Inquisition, is famous for cultivating Lucifer as the arch-fiend, but the Church's enemies relied no less upon the Old Boy to keep the human mind enthralled. Luther[8] was himself accused of alliance with Hell, and he in turn accused his enemies. To complicate matters further, he believed that he had had contact with the Devil and had argued theology with him. I am not surprised at this, for at my own university a professor of history—a Lutheran,[9] by the way—used to assemble his graduate students, draw the shades, and commune in the classroom with Erasmus.[10] He was never, to my knowledge, officially scoffed at for this, the reason being that the university officials, like most of us, are the children of a history which still sucks at the Devil's teats. At this writing, only England has held back before the temptations of contemporary diabolism. In the countries of the Communist ideology, all resistance of any import is linked to the totally malign capitalist

NOTES

8. **Luther** Martin Luther (1483–1546), German theologian who led the Protestant Reformation.

9. **Lutheran** member of the Protestant denomination founded by Martin Luther.

10. **Erasmus** Desiderius Erasmus (1466?–1536), Dutch humanist, scholar, and theologian.

CLOSER LOOK

## Analyze Background 

Students may have marked paragraph 307 during their first read. Use these lines to help students understand Miller's view of the world. Encourage them to talk about the annotations that they marked. You may want to model a close read with the class based on the highlights shown in the text.

**ANNOTATE:** Have students mark details in these lines that identify the two ways Miller views the world, or have students participate while you highlight them.

**QUESTION:** Guide students to consider what these details might tell them. Ask what important information a reader can infer from the concepts that Miller proposes in this section of the dramatic exposition.

**Possible response:** Miller discusses two viewpoints: one viewpoint stresses the unity of the world; the other sees good and evil as opposing forces.

**CONCLUDE:** Help students to formulate conclusions about the importance of these details in the text. Ask students why the author might have included these details.

**Possible response:** The author most likely included these viewpoints to propose that the world is too much in the grip of the notion of good versus evil and the idea that humanity is sinful in its natural state.

Point out that in this part of the historical **background** through which the author provides context for the story, Miller states viewpoints that are reflected in the characters he creates. Here, Proctor and Rebecca Nurse reflect Miller's viewpoints through their skepticism toward authority and their distaste for the preaching of Parris.

CLOSER LOOK

## Identify Claims

Students may have marked paragraph 310 during their first read. Use this paragraph to help students understand Miller's arguments. Encourage them to talk about the annotations that they marked. You may want to model a close read with the class based on the highlights shown in the text.

**ANNOTATE:** Have students mark details in these lines that identify Miller's arguments about the Devil in Salem's society and in modern society, or have students participate while you highlight them.

**QUESTION:** Guide students to consider what these details might tell them. Ask what important information a reader can infer from Miller's arguments that compare the Puritans' beliefs about the devil with beliefs of the modern world.

**Possible response:** In the same way that Puritans blamed negative events on the influence of the devil, modern people attribute the ills of the world to capitalists, communists, or others whom they consider evil or misguided.

**CONCLUDE:** Help students to formulate conclusions about the importance of these details in the text. Ask students why the author might have included these details.

**Possible response:** Miller makes a parallel between the Puritans and today's society—just as modern groups find it politically advantageous to accuse their enemies (such as communists) of immoral behavior, so too do the characters in the play advance their desires and pay back old scores by falsely accusing people of witchcraft.

Point out that in this part of the dramatic exposition, Miller makes the **claim**, or point in his argument, that the witch hunts in Salem are no different from the McCarthy-Era witch hunts. He does make the distinction that during the time of the Salem witch trials, witches did not actually exist, but in modern times, communists and capitalists do exist.

NOTES

**11. succubi** (SUHK yuh by) *n.* female demons thought to lie on sleeping men.

**12. abrogation** (ab ruh GAY shuhn) *n.* abolishment.

**13. congerie** (KON juh ree) *n.* heap; pile.

**14. klatches** *n.* informal gatherings.

**15. fetishes** *n.* objects believed to have magical power.

**16. Dionysiac** (dy uh NIHS ee ak) *adj.* characteristic of Dionysus, add part of speech Greek god of wine and revelry; thus, wild, frenzied, sensuous.

succubi,[11] and in America any man who is not reactionary in his views is open to the charge of alliance with the Red hell. Political opposition, thereby, is given an inhumane overlay which then justifies the abrogation[12] of all normally applied customs of civilized intercourse. A political policy is equated with moral right, and opposition to it with diabolical malevolence. Once such an equation is effectively made, society becomes a congerie[13] of plots and counterplots, and the main role of government changes from that of the arbiter to that of the scourge of God.

309 The results of this process are no different now from what they ever were, except sometimes in the degree of cruelty inflicted, and not always even in that department. Normally, the actions and deeds of a man were all that society felt comfortable in judging. The secret intent of an action was left to the ministers, priests, and rabbis to deal with. When diabolism rises, however, actions are the least important manifests of the true nature of a man. The Devil, as Reverend Hale said, is a wily one, and, until an hour before he fell, even God thought him beautiful in Heaven.

310 The analogy, however, seems to falter when one considers that, while there were no witches then, there are Communists and capitalists now, and in each camp there is certain proof that spies of each side are at work undermining the other. But this is a snobbish objection and not at all warranted by the facts. I have no doubt that people *were* communing with, and even worshiping, the Devil in Salem, and if the whole truth could be known in this case, as it is in others, we should discover a regular and conventionalized propitiation of the dark spirit. One certain evidence of this is the confession of Tituba, the slave of Reverend Parris, and another is the behavior of the children who were known to have indulged in sorceries with her.

311 There are accounts of similar *klatches*[14] in Europe, where the daughters of the towns would assemble at night and, sometimes with fetishes,[15] sometimes with a selected young man, give themselves to love, with some bastardly results. The Church, sharp-eyed as it must be when gods long dead are brought to life, condemned these orgies as witchcraft and interpreted them, rightly, as a resurgence of the Dionysiac[16] forces it had crushed long before. Sex, sin, and the Devil were early linked, and so they continued to be in Salem, and are today. From all accounts there are no more puritanical mores in the world than those enforced by the Communists in Russia, where women's fashions, for instance, are as prudent and all-covering as any American Baptist would desire. The divorce laws lay a tremendous responsibility on the father for the care of his children. Even the laxity of divorce regulations in the early years

DIGITAL PERSPECTIVES

of the revolution was undoubtedly a revulsion from the nineteenth-century Victorian[17] immobility of marriage and the consequent hypocrisy that developed from it. If for no other reasons, a state so powerful, so jealous of the uniformity of its citizens, cannot long tolerate the atomization of the family. And yet, in American eyes at least, there remains the conviction that the Russian attitude toward women is lascivious. It is the Devil working again, just as he is working within the Slav who is shocked at the very idea of a woman's disrobing herself in a burlesque show. Our opposites are always robed in sexual sin, and it is from this unconscious conviction that demonology gains both its attractive sensuality and its capacity to infuriate and frighten.

312 Coming into Salem now, Reverend Hale conceives of himself much as a young doctor on his first call. His painfully acquired armory of symptoms, catchwords, and diagnostic procedures are now to be put to use at last. The road from Beverly is unusually busy this morning, and he has passed a hundred rumors that make him smile at the ignorance of the yeomanry in this most precise science. He feels himself allied with the best minds of Europe—kings, philosophers, scientists, and ecclesiasts of all churches. His goal is light, goodness and its preservation, and he knows the exaltation of the blessed whose intelligence, sharpened by minute examinations of enormous tracts, is finally called upon to face what may be a bloody fight with the Fiend himself.

313 *He appears loaded down with half a dozen heavy books.*

314 **Hale:** Pray you, someone take these!

315 **Parris,** *delighted*: Mr. Hale! Oh! it's good to see you again! *Taking some books*: My, they're heavy!

316 **Hale,** *setting down his books*: They must be; they are weighted with authority.

317 **Parris,** *a little scared*: Well, you do come prepared!

318 **Hale:** We shall need hard study if it comes to tracking down the Old Boy. *Noticing* REBECCA: You cannot be Rebecca Nurse?

319 **Rebecca:** I am, sir. Do you know me?

320 **Hale:** It's strange how I knew you, but I suppose you look as such a good soul should. We have all heard of your great charities in Beverly.

321 **Parris:** Do you know this gentleman? Mr. Thomas Putnam. And his good wife Ann.

322 **Hale:** Putnam! I had not expected such distinguished company, sir.

323 **Putnam,** *pleased*: It does not seem to help us today, Mr. Hale. We look to you to come to our house and save our child.

324 **Hale:** Your child ails too?

NOTES

**17. Victorian** characteristic of the time when Victoria was queen of England (1837–1901), an era associated with respectability, prudery, and hypocrisy.

**CLOSE READ**

ANNOTATE: Mark details in paragraph 312 that are reflected in the dialogue and action of paragraphs 313–318.

QUESTION: Why does Miller include these details?

CONCLUDE: What impression does Hale make on other characters, and on the audience or readers?

**CLOSE READ** 

Point out that this is the first time readers are introduced to Reverend Hale, even though other characters have already mentioned his name. You may wish to model the Close Read using the following think-aloud format. Possible responses to questions on the student page are included.

**ANNOTATE:** As I read paragraphs 312–318, I notice and highlight the details that reveal Hale's character.

**QUESTION:** I think that Miller includes these details about Hale's sense of his own expertise to emphasize that Hale is eager to use his education to fight evil. Perhaps the books symbolize Hale himself.

**CONCLUDE:** When I read that Hale says the "books are weighted with authority" I think he is actually speaking about himself. The impression on the audience is that Hale thinks very highly of himself.

**PERSONALIZE FOR LEARNING**

**Strategic Support**

**Break It Down** Review paragraphs 312–323. The dramatic exposition that Miller presents is dense and complex, both in its language and arguments. Have students break it down into sections of speeches or lines, find the main idea and key supporting details in each section, and use these notes to summarize Miller's arguments. Encourage students to paraphrase the ideas in their own words. Students can then gather for a discussion of their reactions to Miller's ideas.

## CLOSE READ

Remind students that Reverend Hale has been called in because he is supposedly an expert in fighting demonic possession. You may wish to model the Close Read using the following think-aloud format. Possible responses to questions on the student page are included.

**ANNOTATE:** As I read paragraphs 339–344, I notice and highlight the punctuation that reveals how characters respond to Hale.

**QUESTION:** I think Miller included this punctuation in paragraph 340 to create dramatic pauses that increase the tension of the drama. A comma would have create a little pause, but a dash makes it seem as if Parris does not really know what to say.

**CONCLUDE:** When a dash is used within one character's lines, it seems to indicate an extra beat. When it is placed at the end of a character's lines, it indicates that another character is interrupting that line.

NOTES

325 **Mrs. Putnam:** Her soul, her soul seems flown away. She sleeps and yet she walks . . .

326 **Putnam:** She cannot eat.

327 **Hale:** Cannot eat! *Thinks on it. Then, to* PROCTOR *and* GILES COREY: Do you men have afflicted children?

328 **Parris:** No, no, these are farmers. John Proctor—

329 **Giles Corey:** He don't believe in witches.

330 **Proctor,** *to* HALE: I never spoke on witches one way or the other. Will you come, Giles?

331 **Giles:** No—no, John, I think not. I have some few queer questions of my own to ask this fellow.

332 **Proctor:** I've heard you to be a sensible man, Mr. Hale. I hope you'll leave some of it in Salem.

333 PROCTOR *goes.* HALE *stands embarrassed for an instant.*

334 **Parris,** *quickly:* Will you look at my daughter, sir? *Leads* HALE *to the bed.* She has tried to leap out the window; we discovered her this morning on the highroad, waving her arms as though she'd fly.

335 **Hale,** *narrowing his eyes:* Tries to fly.

336 **Putnam:** She cannot bear to hear the Lord's name, Mr. Hale; that's a sure sign of witchcraft afloat.

337 **Hale,** *holding up his hands:* No, no. Now let me instruct you. We cannot look to superstition in this. The Devil is precise; the marks of his presence are definite as stone, and I must tell you all that I shall not proceed unless you are prepared to believe me if I should find no bruise of hell upon her.

**CLOSE READ**

**ANNOTATE:** In paragraphs 339–344, mark punctuation that reveals how characters respond to Hale.

**QUESTION:** Why does Miller use this punctuation?

**CONCLUDE:** How does this punctuation suggest the ways in which these lines should be delivered and the emotions they should convey?

338 **Parris:** It is agreed, sir—it is agreed—we will abide by your judgment.

339 **Hale:** Good then. *He goes to the bed, looks down at* BETTY. *To* PARRIS: Now, sir, what were your first warning of this strangeness?

340 **Parris:** Why, sir—I discovered her—*indicating* ABIGAIL—and my niece and ten or twelve of the other girls, dancing in the forest last night.

341 **Hale,** *surprised:* You permit dancing?

342 **Parris:** No, no, it were secret—

343 **Mrs. Putnam,** *unable to wait:* Mr. Parris's slave has knowledge of conjurin', sir.

344 **Parris,** *to* MRS. PUTNAM: We cannot be sure of that, Goody Ann—

345 **Mrs. Putnam,** *frightened, very softly:* I know it, sir. I sent my child—she should learn from Tituba who murdered her sisters.

346 **Rebecca,** *horrified:* Goody Ann! You sent a child to conjure up the dead?





### CROSS-CURRICULAR PERSPECTIVES

**Science** Review paragraph 345. Infant mortality was high in Puritan New England. The simple explanation for Mrs. Putnam's losses was not witchcraft but lack of medical care, good sanitation, and other environmental factors. The Puritans' houses were heated only by open fires and could get bitterly cold in winter. In hot weather, flies and mosquitoes spread disease. If crops failed, families could starve. Doctors were not always available, and medical science was somewhat primitive.

347 **Mrs. Putnam:** Let God blame me, not you, not you. Rebecca! I'll not have you judging me any more! *To* HALE: Is it a natural work to lose seven children before they live a day?

348 **Parris:** Sssh!

349 REBECCA, *with great pain, turns her face away. There is a pause.*

350 **Hale:** Seven dead in childbirth.

351 **Mrs. Putnam,** *softly*: Aye. *Her voice breaks: she looks up at him. Silence.* HALE *is impressed.* PARRIS *looks to him. He goes to his books, opens one, turns pages, then reads. All wait, avidly.*

352 **Parris,** *hushed*: What book is that?

353 **Mrs. Putnam:** What's there, sir?

354 **Hale,** *with a tasty love of intellectual pursuit*: Here is all the invisible world, caught, defined, and calculated. In these books the Devil stands stripped of all his brute disguises. Here are all your familiar spirits—your incubi[18] and succubi, your witches that go by land, by air, and by sea; your wizards of the night and of the day. Have no fear now—we shall find him out if he has come among us, and I mean to crush him utterly if he has shown his face! *He starts for the bed.*

355 **Rebecca:** Will it hurt the child, sir?

356 **Hale:** I cannot tell. If she is truly in the Devil's grip we may have to rip and tear to get her free.

357 **Rebecca:** I think I'll go, then. I am too old for this. *She rises.*

358 **Parris,** *striving for conviction*: Why, Rebecca, we may open up the boil of all our troubles today!

359 **Rebecca:** Let us hope for that. I go to God for you, sir.

360 **Parris,** *with trepidation—and resentment*: I hope you do not mean we go to Satan here! *Slight pause.*

361 **Rebecca:** I wish I knew. *She goes out; they feel resentful of her note of moral superiority.*

362 **Putnam,** *abruptly*: Come, Mr. Hale, let's get on. Sit you here.

363 **Giles:** Mr. Hale, I have always wanted to ask a learned man—what signifies the readin' of strange books?

364 **Hale:** What books?

365 **Giles:** I cannot tell; she hides them.

366 **Hale:** Who does this?

367 **Giles:** Martha, my wife. I have waked at night many a time and found her in a corner, readin' of a book. Now what do you make of that?

368 **Hale:** Why, that's not necessarily—

NOTES

**18. incubi** (IHN kyuh by) *n.* spirits or demons thought to lie on sleeping women.





DIGITAL PERSPECTIVES

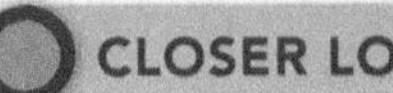

CLOSER LOOK

## Analyze Plot

Students may have marked paragraphs 345–351 during their first read. Encourage them to talk about the annotations that they marked. You may want to model a close read with the class based on the highlights shown in the text.

**ANNOTATE:** Have students mark details in these lines that describe how the characters' dialogue contributes to the rising action of the plot, or have students participate while you highlight them.

**QUESTION:** Guide students to consider what these details might tell them. Ask what a reader can infer from Mrs. Putnam's confession, and accept student responses.

**Possible response:** Her confession provides Hale with the evidence that Hale is looking for, that there is witchcraft in Salem.

**CONCLUDE:** Help students to formulate conclusions about the importance of these details in the text. Ask students why the author might have included these details.

**Possible response:** This opens the door for more accusations and further divides the characters in their conflict. Rebecca is portrayed as good and kind, while Mrs. Putnam is portrayed in a negative light, trying to escape the consequences of her actions and instead blames others.

Remind students that the **plot** of a play is its main story. Point out that as plot events contribute to the rising action of the play, the tension increases, building to a climax. Ask students to speculate about what may happen to each of the characters. Which characters will make accusations of witchcraft and which characters will be accused?

CLOSER LOOK

## Examine Character 

Students may have paragraphs 369–376 during their first read. Use these lines to help students understand Giles Corey. Encourage them to talk about the annotations that they marked. You may want to model a close read with the class based on the highlights shown in the text.

**ANNOTATE:** Have students mark details in these lines that describe how Giles Corey may fit into the conflict that has been set up or have students participate while you highlight them.

**QUESTION:** Guide students to consider what these details might tell them. Ask what a reader can infer from Giles's remarks about his wife and her books, and accept student responses.

**Possible response:** His remarks relate to the growing conflict at the center of the plot. The reader also gets a sense of the desperation the people feel. Giles Corey is willing to subject his own wife to unknown punishment.

**CONCLUDE:** Help students to formulate conclusions about the importance of these details in the text. Ask students why the author might have included these details.

**Possible response:** Giles's remarks about forgetting how to say his prayers will most likely cause people to suspect Martha of witchcraft. He believes that his wife's reading made him unable to pray, giving Hale more reason to suspect witchcraft.

Point out that the dramatic exposition of Giles Corey is yet another exposition that provides background about a **character** that is not revealed through dialogue. Miller cleverly marries dialogue and exposition to paint a picture of his characters and what it is about them that contributes to the rising action of the conflict.

NOTES

369 **Giles:** It discomfits me! Last night—mark this—I tried and tried and could not say my prayers. And then she close her book and walks out of the house, and suddenly—mark this—I could pray again!

370 Old Giles must be spoken for, if only because his fate was to be so remarkable and so different from that of all the others. He was in his early eighties at this time, and was the most comical hero in the history. No man has ever been blamed for so much. If a cow was missed, the first thought was to look for her around Corey's house; a fire blazing up at night brought suspicion of arson to his door. He didn't give a hoot for public opinion, and only in his last years—after he had married Martha—did he bother much with the church. That she stopped his prayer is very probable, but he forgot to say that he'd only recently learned any prayers and it didn't take much to make him stumble over them. He was a crank and a nuisance, but withal a deeply innocent and brave man. In court, once, he was asked if it were true that he had been frightened by the strange behavior of a hog and had then said he knew it to be the Devil in an animal's shape. "What frighted you?" he was asked. He forgot everything but the word "frighted," and instantly replied, "I do not know that I ever spoke that word in my life."

371 **Hale:** Ah! The stoppage of prayer—that is strange. I'll speak further on that with you.

372 **Giles:** I'm not sayin' she's touched the Devil, now, but I'd admire to know what books she reads and why she hides them. She'll not answer me, y' see.

373 **Hale:** Aye, we'll discuss it. *To all*: Now mark me, if the Devil is in her you will witness some frightful wonders in this room, so please to keep your wits about you. Mr. Putnam, stand close in case she flies. Now, Betty, dear, will you sit up? *PUTNAM comes in closer, ready-handed. HALE sits BETTY up, but she hangs limp in his hands.* Hmmm. *He observes her carefully. The others watch breathlessly.* Can you hear me? I am John Hale, minister of Beverly. I have come to help you, dear. Do you remember my two little girls in Beverly? *She does not stir in his hands.*

374 **Parris,** *in fright*: How can it be the Devil? Why would he choose my house to strike? We have all manner of licentious people in the village!

375 **Hale:** What victory would the Devil have to win a soul already bad? It is the best the Devil wants, and who is better than the minister?

376 **Giles:** That's deep, Mr. Parris, deep, deep!

377 **Parris,** *with resolution now*: Betty! Answer Mr. Hale! Betty!

378 **Hale:** Does someone afflict you, child? It need not be a woman, mind you, or a man. Perhaps some bird invisible to others

DIGITAL PERSPECTIVES

comes to you—perhaps a pig, a mouse, or any beast at all. Is there some figure bids you fly? *The child remains limp in his hands. In silence he lays her back on the pillow. Now, holding out his hands toward her, he intones:* In nomine Domini Sabaoth sui filiique ite ad infernos.[19] *She does not stir. He turns to* ABIGAIL, *his eyes narrowing.* Abigail, what sort of dancing were you doing with her in the forest?

379 **Abigail:** Why—common dancing is all.

380 **Parris:** I think I ought to say that I—I saw a kettle in the grass where they were dancing.

381 **Abigail:** That were only soup.

382 **Hale:** What sort of soup were in this kettle, Abigail?

383 **Abigail:** Why, it were beans—and lentils, I think, and—

384 **Hale:** Mr. Parris, you did not notice, did you, any living thing in the kettle? A mouse, perhaps, a spider, a frog—?

385 **Parris,** *fearfully:* I—do believe there were some movement—in the soup.

386 **Abigail:** That jumped in, we never put it in!

387 **Hale,** *quickly:* What jumped in?

388 **Abigail:** Why, a very little frog jumped—

389 **Parris:** A frog, Abby!

390 **Hale,** *grasping* ABIGAIL: Abigail, it may be your cousin is dying. Did you call the Devil last night?

391 **Abigail:** I never called him! Tituba, Tituba . . .

392 **Parris,** *blanched:* She called the Devil?

393 **Hale:** I should like to speak with Tituba.

394 **Parris:** Goody Ann, will you bring her up? MRS. PUTNAM *exits.*

395 **Hale:** How did she call him?

396 **Abigail:** I know not—she spoke Barbados.

397 **Hale:** Did you feel any strangeness when she called him? A sudden cold wind, perhaps? A trembling below the ground?

398 **Abigail:** I didn't see no Devil! *Shaking* BETTY: Betty, wake up. Betty! Betty!

399 **Hale:** You cannot evade me, Abigail. Did your cousin drink any of the brew in that kettle?

400 **Abigail:** She never drank it!

401 **Hale:** Did you drink it?

402 **Abigail:** No, sir!

403 **Hale:** Did Tituba ask you to drink it?

404 **Abigail:** She tried, but I refused.

405 **Hale:** Why are you concealing? Have you sold yourself to Lucifer?

NOTES

19. **In nomine Domini Sabaoth sui filiique ite ad infernos** (ihn NOH mee nay DOH mee nee SAB ay oth SOO ee FEE lee ee kway EE tay ahd ihn FUR nohs) "In the name of the Lord of Hosts and his son, get thee to the lower world" (Latin).





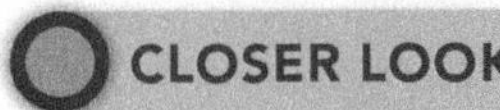

CLOSER LOOK

## Examine Conflict 

Students may have marked paragraph 378 during their first read. Encourage them to talk about the annotations that they marked. You may want to model a close read with the class based on the highlights shown in the text.

**ANNOTATE:** Have students mark details in these lines that describe how Hale's questioning adds to the conflict in the play or have students participate while you highlight them.

**QUESTION:** Guide students to consider what these details might tell them. Ask what a reader can infer from Hale's questioning of Betty and Abigail, and accept student responses.

**Possible response:** Hale offers details about what might have happened instead of waiting for Betty and Abigail to provide them.

**CONCLUDE:** Help students to formulate conclusions about the importance of these details in the text. Ask students why the author might have included these details.

**Possible response:** Instead of trying to find out the truth of what actually happened, Hale is leading Betty and Abigail, putting words into their mouths and showing them the direction he wants or expects their answers to take.

Remind students that **conflict** is the struggle between two opposing forces. Point out to students that this line of questioning in the dialogue was used in the play's opening exchanges to create conflict when Parris suggests to Abigail that she and the others were conjuring spirits; he does not just ask what they were doing, but leads her in a method of questioning.

PERSONALIZE FOR LEARNING

### Challenge

**Salem Witch Trials** Tell students that many of the characters in *The Crucible* actually lived and were involved in the Salem witch trials of 1692. Invite interested students to research a person of the Salem witch trials, such as John Proctor, Rebecca Nurse, Tituba, or Samuel Parris, and write a brief exposition describing that person and his or her role in the actual trial. **(Research to Clarify)**

## CLOSER LOOK

### Understand Character Motivation

Students may have marked paragraphs 408–423 during their first read. Use these lines to help students understand why Abigail behaves as she does. Encourage them to talk about the annotations that they marked. You may want to model a close read with the class based on the highlights shown in the text.

**ANNOTATE:** Have students mark details in these lines that illustrate Abigail's exchange with Hale or have students participate while you highlight them.

**QUESTION:** Guide students to consider what these details might tell them. Ask what a reader can infer from Abigail's exchange with Hale, and accept student responses.

**Possible response:** Abigail is accusing Tituba of witchcraft. She accuses Tituba of influencing her to do things she does not want to do.

**CONCLUDE:** Help students to formulate conclusions about the importance of these details in the text. Ask students why the author might have included these details.

**Possible response:** It appears that Hale is about to accuse Abigail of witchcraft, so she looks for someone else to blame. She turns Hale's attention to Tituba to deflect attention from herself. Because Tituba is a woman who is enslaved from Barbados, Abigail knows that her word will likely be believed over Tituba's.

Remind students that one of the ways authors create round, believable characters is by making us understand the complex medley of needs, desires, and circumstances that motivate their behavior. **Motivation** is the reason or reasons for a character's actions. This motivation may come from internal causes like fear, or from external causes like danger. Most character's motives are a combination of internal and external factors. Here, Abigail's motivations are expressed as fear in response to danger. She feels threatened by Hale and reacts to protect herself from accusation.

NOTES

406 **Abigail:** I never sold myself! I'm a good girl! I'm a proper girl!

407 MRS. PUTNAM *enters with* TITUBA, *and instantly* ABIGAIL *points at* TITUBA.

408 **Abigail:** She made me do it! She made Betty do it!

409 **Tituba,** *shocked and angry*: Abby!

410 **Abigail:** She makes me drink blood!

411 **Parris:** Blood!!

412 **Mrs. Putnam:** My baby's blood?

413 **Tituba:** No, no, chicken blood. I give she chicken blood!

414 **Hale:** Woman, have you enlisted these children for the Devil?

415 **Tituba:** No, no, sir, I don't truck with no Devil!

416 **Hale:** Why can she not wake? Are you silencing this child?

417 **Tituba:** I love me Betty!

418 **Hale:** You have sent your spirit out upon this child, have you not? Are you gathering souls for the Devil?

419 **Abigail:** She sends her spirit on me in church: she makes me laugh at prayer!

420 **Parris:** She have often laughed at prayer!

421 **Abigail:** She comes to me every night to go and drink blood!

422 **Tituba:** You beg *me* to conjure! She beg *me* make charm—

423 **Abigail:** Don't lie! *To* HALE: She comes to me while I sleep: she's always making me dream corruptions!

424 **Tituba:** Why you say that, Abby?

425 **Abigail:** Sometimes I wake and find myself standing in the open doorway and not a stitch on my body! I always hear her laughing in my sleep. I hear her singing her Barbados songs and tempting me with—

426 **Tituba:** Mister Reverend. I never—

427 **Hale,** *resolved now*: Tituba, I want you to wake this child.

428 **Tituba:** I have no power on this child, sir.

429 **Hale:** You most certainly do, and you will free her from it now! When did you compact with the Devil?

430 **Tituba:** I don't compact with no Devil!

431 **Parris:** You will confess yourself or I will take you out and whip you to your death, Tituba!

432 **Putnam:** This woman must be hanged! She must be taken and hanged!

433 **Tituba,** *terrified, falls to her knees*: No, no, don't hang Tituba! I tell him I don't desire to work for him, sir.

434 **Parris:** The Devil?





## PERSONALIZE FOR LEARNING

### Strategic Support

**Character Motivations** Review paragraphs 406–434. To help students understand the complex set of motives that drives the plot, have students work together in groups with proficient readers. Direct them to prepare a three-column list. In the first column, list the character's name. In the second column, identify dialogue and expository passages from the text that reveal each character's motivations. In the third column, have students write a statement that summarizes the character's motivations based on the dialogue and expository passages they noted.

592 UNIT 5 • FACING OUR FEARS

DIGITAL PERSPECTIVES

NOTES

435 **Hale:** Then you saw him! TITUBA *weeps*. Now Tituba, I know that when we bind ourselves to Hell it is very hard to break with it. We are going to help you tear yourself free—

436 **Tituba,** *frightened by the coming process*: Mister Reverend, I do believe somebody else be witchin' these children.

437 **Hale:** Who?

438 **Tituba:** I don't know, sir, but the Devil got him numerous witches.

439 **Hale:** Does he! *It is a clue*. Tituba, look into my eyes. Come, look into me. *She raises her eyes to his fearfully*. You would be a good Christian woman, would you not, Tituba?

440 **Tituba:** Aye, sir, a good Christian woman.

441 **Hale:** And you love these little children?

442 **Tituba:** Oh, yes, sir, I don't desire to hurt little children.

443 **Hale:** And you love God, Tituba?

444 **Tituba:** I love God with all my bein'.

445 **Hale:** Now, in God's holy name—

446 **Tituba:** Bless Him. Bless Him. *She is rocking on her knees, sobbing in terror*.

Arthur Miller wrote the screenplay for the 1996 film version of *The Crucible* and was pleased at the film's ability to "open wide enough to contain a whole society and move in close enough to see into a girl's heart." One way in which the film "opened wide" was to show this scene of the girls dancing in the forest, which is merely described in dialogue in the play.

CLOSER LOOK

## Analyze Cause and Effect

Students may have marked paragraphs 455–461 and 469–473 during their first read. Use these lines to help students understand relationships among characters. Encourage them to talk about the annotations that they marked. You may want to model a close read with the class based on the highlights shown in the text.

**ANNOTATE:** Have students mark details in these lines that illustrate Tituba's confessions or have students participate while you highlight them.

**QUESTION:** Guide students to consider what these details might tell them. Ask what a reader can infer from Tituba's confessions and Hale's and Parris's questioning. Guide students to consider whether Tituba believes her own statements, and accept student responses.

**Possible response:** Tituba is confessing to things she does not believe. She repeats the questions that she is asked, giving herself time to think of an answer. The questioning makes her give vague answers and she is unwilling to commit herself to too much detail.

**CONCLUDE:** Help students to formulate conclusions about the importance of these details in the text. Ask students why the author might have included these details.

**Possible response:** Hale and Parris manipulate her with questions. In fear of her own life, she is saying anything she can think of that Parris and Hale want to hear.

Remind students that **cause-and-effect** chains appear throughout the play beginning with Parris's first questions to Abigail through the accusations of witchcraft at the end of the first act. Characters react to other characters' actions and questions, resulting in actions that drive the conflicts of the plot.

NOTES

447 **Hale:** And to His glory—

448 **Tituba:** Eternal glory. Bless Him—bless God . . .

449 **Hale:** Open yourself, Tituba—open yourself and let God's holy light shine on you.

450 **Tituba:** Oh, bless the Lord.

451 **Hale:** When the Devil come to you does he ever come—with another person? *She stares up into his face.* Perhaps another person in the village? Someone you know.

452 **Parris:** Who came with him?

453 **Putnam:** Sarah Good? Did you ever see Sarah Good with him? Or Osburn?

454 **Parris:** Was it man or woman came with him?

455 **Tituba:** Man or woman. Was—was woman.

456 **Parris:** What woman? A woman, you said. What woman?

457 **Tituba:** It was black dark, and I—

458 **Parris:** You could see him, why could you not see her?

459 **Tituba:** Well, they was always talking; they was always runnin' round and carryin' on—

460 **Parris:** You mean out of Salem? Salem witches?

461 **Tituba:** I believe so, yes, sir.

462 *Now* HALE *takes her hand. She is surprised.*

463 **Hale:** Tituba. You must have no fear to tell us who they are, do you understand? We will protect you. The Devil can never overcome a minister. You know that, do you not?

464 **Tituba,** *kisses* HALE*'s hand: Aye,* sir, oh, I do.

465 **Hale:** You have confessed yourself to witchcraft, and that speaks a wish to come to Heaven's side. And we will bless you, Tituba.

466 **Tituba,** *deeply relieved*: Oh, God bless you, Mr. Hale!

467 **Hale,** *with rising exaltation*: You are God's instrument put in our hands to discover the Devil's agent among us. You are selected, Tituba, you are chosen to help us cleanse our village. So speak utterly, Tituba, turn your back on him and face God—face God, Tituba, and God will protect you.

468 **Tituba,** *joining with him*: Oh, God, protect Tituba!

469 **Hale,** *kindly*: Who came to you with the Devil? Two? Three? Four? How many?

470 TITUBA *pants, and begins rocking back and forth again, staring ahead.*

471 **Tituba:** There was four. There was four.

472 **Parris,** *pressing in on her*: Who? Who? Their names, their names!

473 **Tituba,** *suddenly bursting out*: Oh, how many times he bid me kill you, Mr. Parris!

474 **Parris:** Kill me!

475 **Tituba,** *in a fury*: He say Mr. Parris must be kill! Mr. Parris no goodly man. Mr. Parris mean man and no gentle man, and he bid me rise out of my bed and cut your throat! *They gasp*. But I tell him "No! I don't hate that man. I don't want kill that man." But he say, "You work for me, Tituba, and I make you free! I give you pretty dress to wear, and put you way high up in the air, and you gone fly back to Barbados!" And I say, "You lie, Devil, you lie!" And then he come one stormy night to me, and he say, "Look! I have *white* people belong to me." And I look—and there was Goody Good.

476 **Parris:** Sarah Good!

477 **Tituba,** *rocking and weeping*: Aye, sir, and Goody Osburn.

478 **Mrs. Putnam:** I knew it! Goody Osburn were midwife to me three times. I begged you, Thomas, did I not? I begged him not to call Osburn because I feared her. My babies always shriveled in her hands!

479 **Hale:** Take courage, you must give us all their names. How can you bear to see this child suffering? Look at her, Tituba. *He is indicating* BETTY *on the bed*. Look at her God-given innocence; her soul is so tender; we must protect her, Tituba: the Devil is out and preying on her like a beast upon the flesh of the pure lamb. God will bless you for your help.

480 ABIGAIL *rises, staring as though inspired, and cries out*.

481 **Abigail:** I want to open myself! *They turn to her, startled. She is enraptured, as though in a pearly light*. I want the light of God. I want the sweet love of Jesus! I danced for the Devil; I saw him: I wrote in his book; I go back to Jesus; I kiss His hand. I saw Sarah Good with the Devil! I saw Goody Osburn with the Devil! I saw Bridget Bishop with the Devil!

482 *As she is speaking,* BETTY *is rising from the bed, a fever in her eyes, and picks up the chant*.

483 **Betty,** *staring too*: I saw George Jacobs with the Devil! I saw Goody Howe with the Devil!

484 **Parris:** She speaks! *He rushes to embrace* BETTY. She speaks!

485 **Hale:** Glory to God! It is broken, they are free!

486 **Betty,** *calling out hysterically and with great relief*: I saw Martha Bellows with the Devil!

487 **Abigail:** I saw Goody Sibber with the Devil! *It is rising to a great glee*.

488 **Putnam:** The marshal, I'll call the marshal!

489 PARRIS *is shouting a prayer of thanksgiving*.

490 **Betty:** I saw Alice Barrow with the Devil!

491 *The curtain begins to fall*.

NOTES

**CLOSE READ**

**ANNOTATE:** In paragraphs 481–489, mark details that suggest the escalating emotional frenzy.

**QUESTION:** Why does Miller use this language?

**CONCLUDE:** What is the effect of this heightened language at the end of Act I?

## CLOSE READ

Remind students that the rising action of the play leads to the play's climax, the high point of tension or suspense in the plot. You may wish to model the Close Read using the following think-aloud format. Possible responses to questions on the student page are included.

**ANNOTATE:** As I read paragraphs 481–489, I notice and highlight the words and phrases in the stage directions and Abigail's speech that suggest the escalating emotional frenzy.

**QUESTION:** I think that Miller uses this kind of language to close Act I because the play has reached its climax. The tension has been building and building. Now the atmosphere on stage is tense and dramatic as the girls fall into a religious frenzy.

**CONCLUDE:** I think the language in this final part of Act I would have a great impact on the audience. The audience might be shocked at the accusations of names that are not familiar. The audience may have expected the girls to accuse characters such as Rebecca Nurse, whom the Puritans and others resent, or Martha Corey, to whose suspicious behavior her husband inadvertently calls to her, or John Proctor, whom the Putnams and Parris dislike and who has made an enemy of Abigail. The heightened language would shock the audience because it shows the extremes to which the girls are willing to go to save themselves, even if it means harming others.

TEACHING

## Comprehension Check

**Possible responses**

1. Parris sends for Reverend Hale because he is a pastor who is reputed to be an expert on demonic possession.
2. Mrs. Putnam believes that her babies died because of witchcraft.
3. Abigail and John Proctor had an affair. Abigail believes they are romantically involved, while Proctor does not. She does not want to let go. He wants nothing to do with her anymore. She is angry at his rejection.
4. They are in disagreement over ownership of land.
5. Tituba confesses to witchcraft and gives names of others who have practiced witchcraft.
6. **Possible response:** (1) The town girls gather in the forest in secret to dance and do other forbidden things. Abigail Williams attempts to perform a spell aimed at killing Elizabeth Proctor. (2) Reverend Parris catches the girls in the woods as they dance and chant. He also thinks he sees someone running naked through the trees. (3) Two of the girls, including Parris's daughter Betty, become ill—they go into a catatonic state. (4) The girls' illness prompts rumors of witchcraft, which begin circulating through Salem. (5) Prompted by the rumors and their own concerns, members of the community visit the Parris household. (6) Parris tells them he has called for Reverend Hale, an expert in witchcraft. (7) Parris confronts his niece, Abigail, who admits that the girls danced in the forest but denies all allegations of witchcraft. Parris also questions Abigail's virtue and whether her reputation in the town is "untarnished." (8) When Abigail is alone in the room with two of the other girls, Betty Parris suddenly cries out for her long-dead mother. (9) Abigail threatens the other girls with murder if they reveal that she performed a spell or did anything more than dance.

## Research

**Research to Clarify** If students are having difficulty choosing an unfamiliar detail, suggest they focus on Puritan history, the real story of the Salem witch trials, or the "Red Scare" of the 1950s.

---

NOTES

492 **Hale,** *as* PUTNAM *goes out*: Let the marshal bring irons!

493 **Abigail:** I saw Goody Hawkins with the Devil!

494 **Betty:** I saw Goody Bibber with the Devil!

495 **Abigail:** I saw Goody Booth with the Devil!

496 *On their ecstatic cries—*

THE CURTAIN FALLS

## Comprehension Check

**Complete the following items after you finish your first read.**

1. Why does Parris send for Reverend Hale?
2. What does Mrs. Putnam believe happened to her babies?
3. What conflict exists between Abigail and Proctor?
4. What is a source of disagreement between Proctor and Putnam?
5. To what does Tituba confess?
6. **Notebook** Write a timeline of the key events in Act I of *The Crucible*. Include important events mentioned in the text that occur before the action of the play begins.

## RESEARCH

**Research to Clarify** Choose at least one unfamiliar detail from the text. Briefly research that detail. In what way does the information you learned shed light on an aspect of Act I?





PERSONALIZE FOR LEARNING

### Challenge

**Perform** Through oral interpretation of literature, students can better grasp the emotional upheaval of the events that lead up to the end of Act I. Encourage volunteers to play the roles of Hale, Parris, Abigail, Tituba, and Putnam, with dialogue starting from Parris's line "How can it be the Devil?" (paragraph 374) through the act's end. Ask students what emotions and conflicts most strongly motivate the characters, and tell them to capture these emotions in their performances. Allow time for students to rehearse and then perform their roles for the rest of the class.

**596** UNIT 5 • FACING OUR FEARS

MAKING MEANING

## Close Read the Text

Reread paragraphs 165–166 in which Miller introduces readers to John Proctor. Mark details that describe Proctor's character. How do Proctor's actions in the following scene with Abigail reflect key points made in this description?

THE CRUCIBLE, ACT I

## Analyze the Text

**CITE TEXTUAL EVIDENCE** to support your answers.

**Notebook** Respond to these questions.

1. (a) What is Betty's condition when the play opens? (b) What does Abigail say she and Betty were doing in the forest? (c) **Make Inferences** What seems to be the main reason for Reverend Parris's concern about the girls' behavior in the forest? Explain.
2. (a) What do Abigail, Betty, Mercy, and Mary discuss after Parris leaves his daughter's room? (b) **Predict** What events does this scene suggest may occur later in the play?
3. (a) Who is Reverend Hale? (b) **Evaluate** Do you think he is fair and impartial in his actions so far? Explain.
4. (a) **Connect** What evidence suggests that sharp divisions exist among the people of Salem? (b) **Apply** Name two other characters who may be accused of witchcraft by the end of the play. Explain your choices.

**Tool Kit**
Close-Read Guide and Model Annotation

LANGUAGE DEVELOPMENT

## Concept Vocabulary

vindictive    calumny    defamation

**Why These Words?** The three concept vocabulary words are all used to describe speech or actions intended to harm others, particularly their reputations. What other words in Act I relate to this concept?

### Practice

**Notebook** Use each concept vocabulary word in a sentence that demonstrates its meaning.

**WORD NETWORK**
Add words related to fear from the text to your Word Network.

## Word Study

**Notebook** **Latin Root: *-fama-*** The Latin root *-fama-*, meaning "reputation," is found in many words that relate to the idea of public opinion. For example, *defamation* involves discrediting someone's reputation through untruthful statements. That idea is at the very heart of the action of *The Crucible*.

1. Use library or online resources to find the legal definition of "defamation of character." Explain how this meaning relates to the Latin root *-fama-*.
2. Explain how the root *-fama-* helps you determine the meanings of the words *famously, infamy,* and *euphemism*. Use a college-level dictionary to check your definitions.

**STANDARDS**
**Language**
Demonstrate understanding of figurative language, word relationships, and nuances in word meanings.





AUTHOR'S PERSPECTIVE **Elfrieda Hiebert, Ph.D.**

**Digital Tools** As students develop and expand their word networks, remind them of the digital tools available and of their value. Explain what digital tools offer—pronunciation; audio; word families; definitions; links to synonyms and antonyms; interactive levels of complexity of synonyms and antonyms; words in context sentences. Using digital tools to access word families is especially helpful in a cross-cultural context. A word family for science, for instance, might include the words *botanist, chemist, geneticist, neurologist, nutritionist, physicist, zoologist,* as they all end with the suffix *–ist*. Help students understand that digital tools also have drawbacks. For instance, the word family feature doesn't show how the words are related in meaning, only in sound.

DIGITAL PERSPECTIVES 

## Jump Start

CLOSE READ Ask: *When can public opinion be a good thing? When can it be a bad thing?* As students discuss, ask them to consider how public opinion affects their own lives.

## Close Read the Text 

Discuss sections students marked. If needed, continue to model close reading by using the Annotation Highlights in the Interactive Teacher's Edition.

## Analyze the Text

Possible responses

1. (a) She is in deep sleep. (b) dancing; (c) He is afraid this discovery will affect his standing. **DOK 2**
2. (a) The story they will tell. (b) They will lie if asked. **DOK 2**
3. (a) A pastor from Beverly. (b) Students may say that he is not fair because he presumes guilt rather than innocence and leads the girls with questions. **DOK 3**
4. (a) Parris mentions enemies who want him removed from the pulpit; the Putnams mention factions; Rebecca mentions town strife. (b) Putnam and Rebecca, as others resent them. **DOK 3**

## Concept Vocabulary

**Why These Words?** Possible responses: *liar, soils*

**Practice** Responses will vary.

**Word Network Possible words:** *barbaric, suspicions, madness, threatening, vengeance*

## Word Study

For more support, see **Concept Vocabulary and Word Study.**

Possible responses:

1. any intentionally false statement harmful to a reputation
2. *Famously* means "in a well-known way"; *infamy* means "disgrace due to bad behavior"; euphemism means "term less harsh in effect."

**FORMATIVE ASSESSMENT**

### Analyze the Text

**If** students struggle to make inferences, **then** discuss what motivates Parris.

### Word Study

**If** students are not able to relate word meaning to the Latin root *-fama-,* **then** remind them to look for the word that discredits a person's honor. For Reteach and Practice, see **Word Study: Latin Root *-fama-* (RP).** 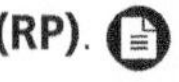

TEACHING

## Analyze Craft and Structure

**Structural Elements of Drama** Explain to students that the exposition is as much a part of the plot as the dialogue between the characters. Exposition contributes to the rising action of the play. For more support, see **Analyze Craft and Structure: Structural Elements of Drama.**

**MAKE IT INTERACTIVE**

Project the exposition of Reverend Hale from paragraph 312 and read it aloud. Then read it aloud again, pausing to discuss what the exposition reveals about Hale's character.

### Practice

Possible responses:

1. In the exchange between Abigail and Proctor, stage directions tell us more about how Abigail presses on and how Proctor refuses her advances. At the end of the act, stage directions add to the tension and drama of the girls' hysteria as they make accusations.
2. See possible responses in chart on student page.
3. (a) Villagers regarded the wilderness as a dark and threatening mystery. (b) These feelings contribute to the girls' uninhibited behavior in the woods and to Parris's shocked incredulity at what he sees there.
4. Mrs. Putnam is jealous of Rebecca's ability to bear children, as becomes clear in the stage directions and dialogue (paragraph 250); the Putnam and Nurse clans quarrel over land, as described in dramatic exposition (paragraph 226); Parris had been appointed to the Salem church after Putnam's brother-in-law had been denied, which is described in dramatic exposition (paragraphs 94–95).

**FORMATIVE ASSESSMENT**

### Analyze Craft and Structure

**If** students are unable to identify examples of Miller's dramatic exposition, **then** have students scan the play looking for long paragraphs of text that are not assigned to a specific character. For Reteach and Practice, see **Analyze Craft and Structure: Structural Elements of Drama (RP).**



MAKING MEANING

THE CRUCIBLE, ACT I

**STANDARDS**

**Reading Literature**

- Analyze the impact of the author's choices regarding how to develop and relate elements of a story or drama.
- Analyze how an author's choices concerning how to structure specific parts of a text contribute to its overall structure and meaning as well as its aesthetic impact.

## Analyze Craft and Structure

**Structural Elements of Drama** Most plays are written to be performed, not read. When reading drama, it is important to identify the text structures that provide information about the setting, characters, and conflicts. Dramatic text structures include the following.

- **Dialogue** is the words actors speak—their lines.
- **Stage directions** are notes included in a play to indicate how the work is meant to be performed or staged. Stage directions may describe sets, costumes, lighting, sound, props, and—in some cases—the ways in which actors should move and deliver their lines. These instructions may be printed in italics, set in brackets, or otherwise visually differentiated from the dialogue. Reading stage directions can help you picture the action and imagine how characters might look and sound in performance.
- **Dramatic exposition** refers to the prose commentaries, or brief essays, inserted by the playwright to provide information about the characters or situation. Dramatic exposition is a common element in twentieth-century American drama.

### Practice

CITE TEXTUAL EVIDENCE to support your answers.

**Notebook** Respond to these questions.

1. Give two examples of stage directions that are essential to understanding the action in Act I. Explain each choice.
2. Use the chart to examine how two specific events or characters described in the play's opening dramatic exposition are carried into the action of Act I.

| EVENT/CHARACTER | | DESCRIPTION | | ACTION |
|---|---|---|---|---|
| Parris | → | At the time of these events, Parris was in his middle forties. In history, he cut a villainous path, and there is very little good to be said for him. He believed he was being persecuted wherever he went, despite his best efforts to win people and God to his side. | → | This description of Parris leads to the action of his villainous ways as he manipulates the characters in the play. |
| People minding other people's business | → | This predilection for minding other people's business was time-honored among the people of Salem, and it undoubtedly created many of the suspicions which were to feed the coming madness. | → | This leads to the action in which characters argue over land ownership and people spend too much time wondering what the girls were doing in the forest. |

3. (a) According to the opening dramatic exposition, how did most of the members of Salem feel about the vast forest that surrounded them? (b) How might these attitudes have affected the girls' actions in the forest as well as Parris's reaction to what he saw there?
4. In Act I, what seeds of conflict exist between Rebecca Nurse, Reverend Parris, and the Putnams? Explain, citing details from all three text structures—dialogue, stage directions, and dramatic exposition—that support your response.





PERSONALIZE FOR LEARNING

### English Language Support

**Text Structure** Ask pairs of students in what way the beginning of Act I of *The Crucible* is unusual. **EMERGING**

Ask students to explain why they think the author felt the need to include such a long "Overture" at the beginning of the play. **EXPANDING**

Ask students to explain in what ways the "Overture" contributes to the plot and the characterization of the main characters in the play. **BRIDGING**

An expanded **English Language Support Lesson** on Structural Elements of Drama is available in the Interactive Teacher's Edition. 

LANGUAGE DEVELOPMENT

## Conventions and Style

**Personal Pronouns** A **pronoun** is a word that substitutes for a noun or noun phrase. **Personal pronouns** are those that reflect "person" in the grammatical sense of first person, second person, and so on. Such personal pronouns take different forms depending on gender, number, and **case,** or the word's function in a sentence.

- **Nominative Case:** The pronoun is the subject of the sentence.
- **Objective Case:** The pronoun is the object of a verb or preposition.
- **Possessive Case:** The pronoun expresses ownership.

The chart provides examples of personal pronouns according to case.

| | NOMINATIVE | OBJECTIVE | POSSESSIVE |
|---|---|---|---|
| **First-person pronouns** refer to the person speaking. | I, we | me, us | mine, ours |
| **Second-person pronouns** refer to the person spoken to. | you | you | your, yours |
| **Third-person pronouns** refer to a person spoken about. | he, she, it, they | him, her, it, them | his, hers, its, theirs |

*The Crucible* is set in 1692, when people commonly used pronoun forms such as *thee* and *thou* that are now archaic. However, Miller makes the stylistic choice to use modern personal pronouns. He also chooses to use nonstandard pronouns in Tituba's dialogue.

### Read It

1. Mark the pronouns in each excerpt from the play. Label the case and person of each pronoun.
   a. **Parris:** Now look you, child, your punishment will come in its time. But if you trafficked with spirits in the forest I must know it now, for surely my enemies will, and they will ruin me with it.
   b. **Putnam,** *pleased:* It does not seem to help us today, Mr. Hale. We look to you to come to our house and save our child.
2. **Connect to Style** Reread the dialogue between Tituba and Hale in paragraphs 413–417. Identify and classify each pronoun. Note whether each example reflects standard usage.

### Write It

**Notebook** Rewrite each line of dialogue to sound more realistic by replacing repeated nouns with personal pronouns. Decide whether or not to reflect standard usage, and explain the reasons for your choices.

1. **Proctor** *to Abigail:* Abigail must change Abigail's behavior if Abigail hopes to regain Proctor's respect.
2. **Tituba:** Tituba loves Betty. Betty has always treated Tituba kindly.
3. **Hale:** The people of Salem must confess what the people of Salem have done if the people of Salem hope to receive the people of Salem's rightful forgiveness.

EVIDENCE LOG

Before moving on to Act II, go to your Evidence Log and record what you learned from Act I of *The Crucible.*

STANDARDS

**Language**

- Demonstrate command of the conventions of standard English grammar and usage when writing or speaking.
- Apply the understanding that usage is a matter of convention, can change over time, and is sometimes contested.
- Apply knowledge of language to understand how language functions in different contexts, to make effective choices for meaning or style, and to comprehend more fully when reading or listening.





HOW LANGUAGE WORKS

**Personal Pronouns** Give students more practice with personal pronouns. Have students go back to the text and reread Tituba's lines in paragraphs 431–473. Have them use the chart to identify the personal pronouns and tell whether they reflect standard usage. If not, have students rewrite the dialogue using the standard form.

DIGITAL PERSPECTIVES

## Conventions and Style

**Personal Pronouns** Many students whose native language is not English have personal pronouns that are either masculine or feminine and must agree with the gender of the noun. Point out that in English, some personal pronouns also have gender. Encourage students to use each of the personal pronouns in the chart in a sentence. For more support, see **Conventions and Style: Personal Pronouns.**

### Read It

Possible responses

1. a. you (nominative, second person); your (possessive, second person); its (possessive, third person); you (objective, second person); I (nominative, first person); it (objective, third person); my (possessive, first person); they (nominative, third person); me (objective, first person); it (objective, third person) b. It (nominative, third person); us (objective, first person); We (nominative, first person); you (objective, second person); our (possessive, first person); our (possessive, first person)
2. Tituba and Hale use the following pronouns:
   I (nominative, standard);
   she (used as objective, nonstandard);
   you (nominative, standard);
   I (nominative, standard);
   she (nominative, standard);
   you (nominative, standard);
   I (nominative, standard);
   me (used as possessive, nonstandard)

### Write It

Possible responses

1. Abigail must change her behavior if she hopes to regain Proctor's (or his) respect.
2. I love Betty. Betty has always treated me kindly.
3. The people of Salem must confess what they have done if they hope to receive their rightful forgiveness.

**Evidence Log** Support students in completing their Evidence Log. This paced activity will help prepare them for the Performance-Based Assessment at the end of the unit.

### FORMATIVE ASSESSMENT

### Conventions and Style

**If** students struggle to replace the nouns with personal pronouns, **then** ask them to refer to the chart.

For Reteach and Practice, see **Conventions and Style: Personal Pronouns (RP).**

### Selection Test

Administer the "The Crucible, Act I" Selection Test, which is available in both print and digital formats online in Assessments.

# *The Crucible*, Act II

**AUDIO SUMMARIES**
Audio summaries of Act II of *The Crucible* are available online in both English and Spanish in the Interactive Teacher's Edition or Unit Resources. Assigning these summaries prior to reading the selection may help students build additional background knowledge and set a context for their first read.

## Summary

Act II of Arthur Miller's drama *The Crucible* opens with John and Elizabeth Proctor at home, discussing their farm and arguing about John's past affair with Abigail. Elizabeth is concerned about the witch trials and the fact that their servant, Mary Warren, is now an official at the trial. When Mary returns home, she gives Elizabeth a poppet, or doll, she made while in court. Thirty-nine women are now accused of witchcraft, and some have been given a death sentence. Rev. Hale arrives and John tells him that the children's sickness has nothing to do with witchcraft. Hale is concerned about whether or not the Proctors are good Christians, as Elizabeth has been mentioned as someone who might be a witch. Tension rises as others arrive at the Proctors, and Mary's gift to Elizabeth proves to be very unlucky for her.

### Insight

This second act reveals how rumor, once set in motion, produces rising paranoia and hysteria among members of the community. Fear, especially of a nonexistent threat, appears to have a life of its own.

ESSENTIAL QUESTION:
How do we respond when challenged by fear?

## Connection to the Essential Question

Act II of *The Crucible* connects to the Essential Question, "How do we respond when challenged by fear?" The social structure, represented by the courtroom trials and judges—magnifies the sense of fear and creates a new fear—being tried as a witch, being found guilty, and receiving punishment, especially a death sentence.

WHOLE CLASS LEARNING PERFORMANCE TASK
Could any of the characters in *The Crucible* have done more to end the hysteria in Salem?

UNIT PERFORMANCE-BASED ASSESSMENT
Is fear always a harmful emotion?

## Connection to Performance Tasks

**Whole-Class Learning Performance Task** In this Performance Task, students will consider the question "Could any of the characters in *The Crucible* have done more to end the hysteria in Salem?" Students will observe that Mary Warren has a number of opportunities to reduce, if not stop, further hysteria by revealing the truth. Students may note that Abigail, rather than telling the truth, continues to lie in the courtroom and raise the level of hysteria among the townspeople.

**Unit Performance-Based Assessment** Act II of *The Crucible* continues to support the idea that fear is a harmful emotion. Students should observe that by moving the fear of witchcraft into the courtroom, the play heightens the fear because of the possible consequences of jail, whipping, and even hanging.

DIGITAL PERSPECTIVES

Audio

Video

Document

Annotation Highlights

EL Highlights

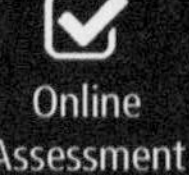
Online Assessment

## LESSON RESOURCES

| | Making Meaning | Language Development | Effective Expression |
|---|---|---|---|
| Lesson | **First Read**<br>**Close Read**<br>**Analyze the Text**<br>**Analyze Craft and Structure** | **Concept Vocabulary**<br>**Word Study** | **Speaking and Listening** |
| **Instructional Standards** | **RL.10** By the end of grade 11, read and comprehend literature . . .<br>**RL.3** Analyze the impact of the author's choices . . .<br>**RL.5** Analyze how an author's choices . . . | **L.4.c** Consult general and specialized reference materials . . .<br>**L.6** Acquire and use accurately general academic and domain-specific words and phrases . . . | **SL.1.a** Come to discussions prepared . . . |
| **STUDENT RESOURCES** | | | |
| Available online in the Interactive Student Edition or Unit Resources | Selection Audio<br>First-Read Guide: Fiction<br>Close-Read Guide: Fiction | Word Network | Evidence Log |
| **TEACHER RESOURCES** | | | |
| **Selection Resources** Available online in the Interactive Teacher's Edition or Unit Resources | Audio Summaries<br>Annotation Highlights<br>EL Highlights<br>English Language Support Lesson: Technical Words<br>Analyze Craft and Structure: Literary Elements in Drama | Concept Vocabulary and Word Study | Speaking and Listening: Whole-Class Discussion |
| **Reteach/Practice (RP)** Available online in the Interactive Teacher's Edition or Unit Resources | Analyze Craft and Structure: Literary Elements in Drama (RP) | Word Study: Technical Words (RP) | Speaking and Listening: Whole-Class Discussion (RP) |
| **Assessment** Available online in Assessments | Selection Test | | |
| **My Resources** | A Unit 5 Answer Key is available online and in the Interactive Teacher's Edition. | | |

# Reading Support

| Text Complexity Rubric: *The Crucible,* Act II | |
|---|---|
| **Quantitative Measures** | |
| **Lexile:** NP **Text Length:** 8,061 words | |
| **Qualitative Measures** | |
| Knowledge Demands ①—②—③—❹—⑤ | Students will probably not be familiar with the situation that is central to the selection. Many, but not all, of the unfamiliar elements are made clear in dialogue, stage directions, and exposition by the playwright. |
| Structure ①—②—❸—④—⑤ | Organization of the narrative is mostly sequential, but important incidents occurred before the narrative begins and are only gradually revealed. |
| Language Conventionality and Clarity ①—②—③—❹—⑤ | Considerable above-level vocabulary and some archaic usages complicate the language, although most of the dialogue reflects ordinary speech. |
| Levels of Meaning/Purpose ①—②—③—❹—⑤ | One level of meaning is straightforward and compellingly presented. As a political allegory, the play operates on another level that requires more background knowledge to grasp. |

DECIDE AND PLAN

## English Language Support

Provide English learners with support for knowledge demands and language as they read the selection.

**Knowledge Demands** Before reading the text, review the background information with students. Have students complete sentences such as, *At this point in their marriage, Elizabeth's trust in John _____. John is feeling that Elizabeth is _____.*

**Language** Students will probably have difficulty with the above-level vocabulary and deviations from standard English. Explain to students that it is not necessary for them to understand every word, so long as they have a basic understanding of the dialogue.

## Strategic Support

Provide students with strategic support to ensure that they can successfully read the text.

**Knowledge Demands** After reading the background information, have a discussion about forgiveness and trust. Ask, *If you forgive someone, do you automatically trust them again? Can old wounds heal without trust? Can trust grow before old wounds heal?*

**Language/Clarity** For students who have difficulty with the archaic constructions, such as "a minister may pray to God without he have golden candlesticks," encourage them to change the forms to more familiar ones and then reread the sentences or lines of dialogue.

## Challenge

Provide students who need to be challenged with ideas for how they can go beyond a simple interpretation of the text.

**Text Analysis** Pair students and have them choose one of the longer speeches in the act and go through it line by line, looking at the unconventional language, biblical allusions, and any other challenging elements.

**Written Response** Ask students to research the Salem witch trials and write a short paper on those trials.

TEACH

## Read and Respond

Have the class do their first read of the selection. Then have them complete their close read. Finally, work with them on the Making Meaning and Effective Expression activities.

# Standards Support Through Teaching and Learning Cycle

## IDENTIFY NEEDS

Analyze results of the Beginning-of-Year Assessment, focusing on the items relating to Unit 5. Also take into consideration student performance to this point and your observations of where particular students struggle.

## DECIDE AND PLAN

- If students have performed poorly on items matching these standards, then provide selection scaffolds before assigning them the on-level lesson provided in the Student Edition.
- If students have done well on the Beginning-of-Year Assessment, then challenge them to keep progressing and learning by giving them opportunities to practice the skills in depth.
- Use the Selection Resources listed on the Planning pages for *The Crucible,* Act II to help students continually improve their ability to master the standards.

**Instructional Standards: *The Crucible* Act II**

| | Catching Up | This Year | Looking Forward |
|---|---|---|---|
| Reading | You may wish to administer the **Analyze Craft and Structure: Literary Elements in Drama (RP)** worksheet to familiarize students with conflict. | **RL.5** Analyze how an author's choices concerning how to structure specific parts of a text contribute to its overall structure and meaning as well as its aesthetic impact. | Challenge students to identify works they have read in which there is no conflict, or the conflict is left uncertain. |
| Speaking and Listening | You may wish to administer the **Speaking and Listening: Whole-Class Discussion (RP)** worksheet to help students prepare for their discussion. | **SL.1.a** Come to discussions prepared, having read and researched material under study; explicitly draw on that preparation by referring to evidence from texts and other research on the topic or issue to stimulate a thoughtful, well-reasoned exchange of ideas. | Challenge students to find clues within the text that *foreshadow* what the outcome will be. |
| Language | Review the **Word Study: Technical Words (RP)** worksheet with students to better familiarize them with legalese. | **L.6** Acquire and use accurately general academic and domain-specific words and phrases, sufficient for reading, writing, speaking, and listening at the college and career readiness level; demonstrate independence in gathering vocabulary knowledge when considering a word or phrase important to comprehension or expression. | Challenge students to consider the effect the use of technical terms has on the play. What if Miller had left them out? |

## ANALYZE AND REVISE

- Analyze student work for evidence of student learning.
- Identify whether or not students have met the expectations in the standards.
- Identify implications for future instruction.

## TEACH

Implement the planned lesson, and gather evidence of student learning.

## Jump Start

FIRST READ Why do you think it is easy to get people to follow a fad or join a cult? Why is doing what's right often the hardest thing? Do you think our fears about terrorism have created modern "witch hunts"? Allow time for students to respond and discuss.

### *The Crucible,* Act II

Why do you think John Proctor is thought by many to epitomize the tragic American hero? Modeling this and other questions readers might ask will bring *The Crucible,* Act II to life and connect it to the Performance Task question. Selection audio and print capability for the selection are available in the Interactive Teacher's Edition.

### Concept Vocabulary

Circulate among students as they rank their words. Remind them that they will find the definitions of these words in the side column beside each word's location in the text.

### FIRST READ

The first time they go through the selection, students should perform the steps of the first read:

NOTICE: You may want to encourage students to notice the different conflicts and who is involved.

ANNOTATE: Remind students to mark actions by the characters that surprise them, confuse them, or shine a light on a character's true personality.

CONNECT: Encourage students to go beyond the selection to make self-to-world connections between the characters in the play and people living today. What traits do the girls have that some groups or cliques have today? Why is it important not to just "follow" every suggestion put to you?

RESPOND: Students will demonstrate their understanding of the text by answering questions and writing a summary.

Point out to students that they will perform the first three steps concurrently as they are doing their first read. They will complete the Respond step after they have finished the first read. You may wish to print copies of the **First-Read Guide: Fiction** for students to use.

**Remind students that during their first read, they should not answer the close-read questions that appear in the selection.**

Playwright

Arthur Miller

# The Crucible, Act II

## Concept Vocabulary

You will encounter the following words as you read Act II of *The Crucible.* Before reading, note how familiar you are with each word. Then, rank the words in order from most familiar (1) to least familiar (3).

| WORD | YOUR RANKING |
|---|---|
| condemnation | |
| magistrates | |
| proceedings | |

After completing the first read, come back to the concept vocabulary and review your rankings. Mark changes to your original rankings as needed.

## First Read DRAMA

Apply these strategies as you conduct your first read. You will have an opportunity to complete the close-read notes after your first read.

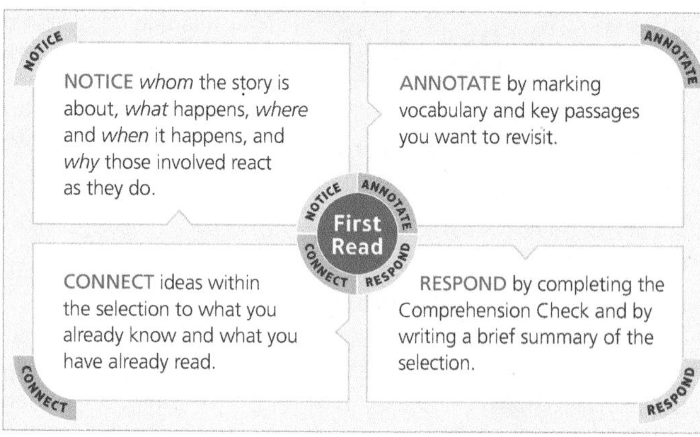
NOTICE
NOTICE *whom* the story is about, *what* happens, *where* and *when* it happens, and *why* those involved react as they do.
ANNOTATE
ANNOTATE by marking vocabulary and key passages you want to revisit.
First Read
CONNECT
CONNECT ideas within the selection to what you already know and what you have already read.
RESPOND
RESPOND by completing the Comprehension Check and by writing a brief summary of the selection.

STANDARDS
**Reading Literature**
By the end of grade 11, read and comprehend literature, including stories, dramas, and poems, in the grades 11–CCR text complexity band proficiently, with scaffolding as needed at the high end of the range.

### VOCABULARY DEVELOPMENT

**Concept Vocabulary Reinforcement** Students will benefit from added practice with inferring word meaning from context clues. Direct students' attention to the word *magistrates* in Elizabeth's speech in paragraph 49 of the play. Use the following "think aloud" to model the skill. Say, I *may not know the meaning of the word* magistrates *when I read this dialogue; however, I can look for clues to its meaning in nearby text. I realize that Elizabeth is using "weighty magistrates" for what she previously called "judges out of Boston." She goes on to say that these magistrates are "of the General Court," so I think* magistrates *are judges of some kind.*

DIGITAL PERSPECTIVES

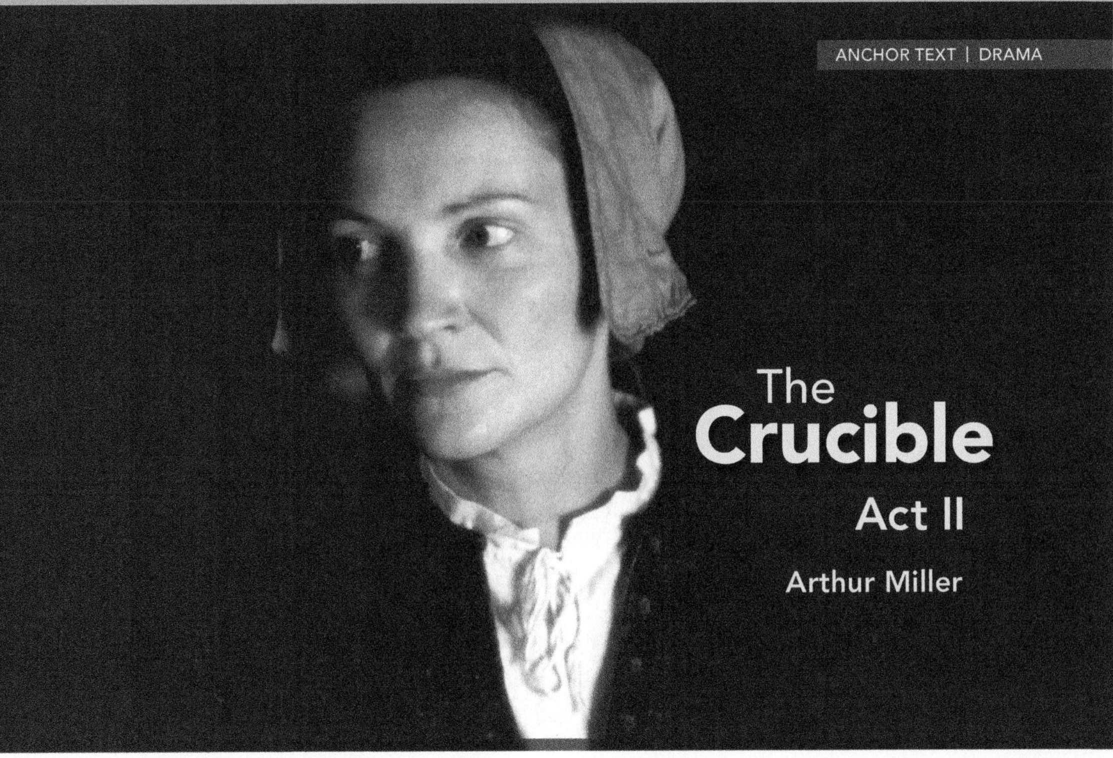

ANCHOR TEXT | DRAMA

# The Crucible

## Act II

**Arthur Miller**

### REVIEW AND ANTICIPATE

As Act I draws to a close, Salem is in the grip of mounting hysteria. What had begun as concern over the strange behavior of Betty—a reaction that may have stemmed from guilty feelings about her activities in the woods the night before—had swelled by the act's end to a mass hysteria, in which accusations of witchcraft were being made and accepted against a growing number of Salem's citizens. As you read, pay close attention to the nature of the accusations and the growing numbers of the accused.

SCAN FOR MULTIMEDIA

1 *The common room of* PROCTOR'S *house, eight days later.*

2 *At the right is a door opening on the fields outside.*

3 *A fireplace is at the left, and behind it a stairway leading upstairs. It is the low, dark, and rather long living room of the time. As the curtain rises, the room is empty. From above,* ELIZABETH *is heard softly singing to the children. Presently the door opens and* JOHN PROCTOR *enters, carrying his gun. He glances about the room as he comes toward the fireplace, then halts for an instant as he hears her singing. He continues on to the fireplace, leans the gun against the wall as he swings a pot out of the fire and smells it. Then he lifts out the ladle and tastes. He is not quite pleased. He reaches to a cupboard, takes a pinch of salt, and drops it into the pot. As he is tasting again, her footsteps*

NOTES



## PERSONALIZE FOR LEARNING

**Strategic Support**

**Sequencing** Review the "Review and Anticipate" paragraph at the beginning of Act II. To help students follow events of the eight days since Act 1 ended, have them create a K-W-L chart listing main events and speculating about what will happen next.

| | |
|---|---|
| **What I Know** | The girls told lies about people being witches.<br>People had to confess or be killed.<br>Many people believe the girls are bewitched. |
| **What I Want To Know** | Will the girls' lies be found out?<br>Will the girls name more people?<br>Will the Proctors split up? |
| **What I Learned** | |

## CLOSER LOOK

### Interpreting Conflict

Students may have marked paragraphs 23 through 28 during their first read. Use these lines to help students understand how to interpret struggle between characters. Encourage them to talk about the annotations that they marked. You may want to model a close read with the class based on the highlights shown in the text.

**ANNOTATE:** Have students mark details in these lines that show the ongoing conflict between Elizabeth and her husband, or have students participate while you highlight them.

**QUESTION:** Guide students to consider what these details might tell them. Ask what a reader can infer from what was annotated, and accept student responses.

**Possible response:** Proctor and his wife are being very cautious with one another.

**CONCLUDE:** Help students to formulate conclusions about the importance of these details in the text. Ask students why the author might have included these details.

**Possible response:** The author most likely wanted readers to know that because Proctor was unfaithful, his conflict with Elizabeth continues and she is polite, but not forgiving.

Remind students that **conflict** is the basis for narratives, because without conflict there could be no story. **Conflict** is a struggle between opposing forces. It may be as simple as someone fighting to get a door open to whole groups of people fighting, as in a war. Sometimes the conflict is just between two people, as it is with Proctor and his wife. They are at odds: he feels guilty about the affair and wonders why she won't forgive him; she doesn't trust him because he cheated. Big or small, the conflict is the thing that moves a story's plot along.

NOTES

*are heard on the stair. He swings the pot into the fireplace and goes to a basin and washes his hands and face.* ELIZABETH *enters.*

4 **Elizabeth:** What keeps you so late? It's almost dark.

5 **Proctor:** I were planting far out to the forest edge.

6 **Elizabeth:** Oh, you're done then.

7 **Proctor:** Aye, the farm is seeded. The boys asleep?

8 **Elizabeth:** They will be soon. *And she goes to the fireplace, proceeds to ladle up stew in a dish.*

9 **Proctor:** Pray now for a fair summer.

10 **Elizabeth:** Aye.

11 **Proctor:** Are you well today?

12 **Elizabeth:** I am. *She brings the plate to the table, and, indicating the food*: It is a rabbit.

13 **Proctor,** *going to the table*: Oh, is it! In Jonathan's trap?

14 **Elizabeth:** No, she walked into the house this afternoon; I found her sittin' in the corner like she come to visit.

15 **Proctor:** Oh, that's a good sign walkin' in.

16 **Elizabeth:** Pray God. It hurt my heart to strip her, poor rabbit. *She sits and watches him taste it.*

17 **Proctor:** It's well seasoned.

18 **Elizabeth,** *blushing with pleasure*: I took great care. She's tender?

19 **Proctor:** Aye. *He eats. She watches him.* I think we'll see green fields soon. It's warm as blood beneath the clods.

20 **Elizabeth:** That's well.

21 PROCTOR *eats, then looks up.*

22 **Proctor:** If the crop is good I'll buy George Jacob's heifer. How would that please you?

23 **Elizabeth:** Aye, it would.

24 **Proctor,** *with a grin*: I mean to please you, Elizabeth.

25 **Elizabeth**—*it is hard to say*: I know it, John.

26 *He gets up, goes to her, kisses her. She receives it. With a certain disappointment, he returns to the table.*

27 **Proctor,** *as gently as he can*: Cider?

28 **Elizabeth,** *with a sense of reprimanding herself for having forgot*: Aye! *She gets up and goes and pours a glass for him. He now arches his back.*

29 **Proctor:** This farm's a continent when you go foot by foot droppin' seeds in it.

30 **Elizabeth,** *coming with the cider*: It must be.





## PERSONALIZE FOR LEARNING

### English Language Support

**Apostrophes** Students may have difficulty with Miller's use of apostrophes in dialogue to show characters' pronunciation. To show that some characters turn the final /ng/ sound to an /n/ sound, Miller uses an apostrophe for the missing letter: *nothin'* for *nothing*, for example. Remind students that apostrophes also signal missing letters in regular contractions, such as *can't/cannot.* Write the following on the board, then have students supply the missing letters for each underlined word:

"It's almost dark." (paragraph 4)
"Oh, you're done then." (paragraph 6)
"Oh, that's a good sign walkin' in." (paragraph 15)
"I think we'll see green fields soon." (paragraph 19)
"This farm's a continent when you go foot by foot droppin' seeds in it." (paragraph 29)

**Answers:** It is, you are, that is, walking, we will, farm is, dropping. **ALL LEVELS**

DIGITAL PERSPECTIVES

31 **Proctor,** *drinks a long draught, then, putting the glass down*: You ought to bring some flowers in the house.

32 **Elizabeth:** Oh! I forgot! I will tomorrow.

33 **Proctor:** It's winter in here yet. On Sunday let you come with me, and we'll walk the farm together; I never see such a load of flowers on the earth. *With good feeling he goes and looks up at the sky through the open doorway.* Lilacs have a purple smell. Lilac is the smell of nightfall, I think. Massachusetts is a beauty in the spring!

34 **Elizabeth:** Aye, it is.

35 *There is a pause. She is watching him from the table as he stands there absorbing the night. It is as though she would speak but cannot. Instead, now, she takes up his plate and glass and fork and goes with them to the basin. Her back is turned to him. He turns to her and watches her. A sense of their separation rises.*

36 **Proctor:** I think you're sad again. Are you?

37 **Elizabeth**—*she doesn't want friction, and yet she must*: You come so late I thought you'd gone to Salem this afternoon.

38 **Proctor:** Why? I have no business in Salem.

39 **Elizabeth:** You did speak of going, earlier this week.

40 **Proctor**—*he knows what she means*: I thought better of it since.

41 **Elizabeth:** Mary Warren's there today.

42 **Proctor:** Why'd you let her? You heard me forbid her go to Salem any more!

43 **Elizabeth:** I couldn't stop her.

44 **Proctor,** *holding back a full* **condemnation** *of her*: It is a fault, it is a fault, Elizabeth—you're the mistress here, not Mary Warren.

45 **Elizabeth:** She frightened all my strength away.

46 **Proctor:** How may that mouse frighten you, Elizabeth? You—

47 **Elizabeth:** It is a mouse no more. I forbid her go, and she raises up her chin like the daughter of a prince and says to me, "I must go to Salem, Goody Proctor; I am an official of the court!"

48 **Proctor:** Court! What court?

49 **Elizabeth:** Aye, it is a proper court they have now. They've sent four judges out of Boston, she says, weighty **magistrates** of the General Court, and at the head sits the Deputy Governor of the Province.

50 **Proctor,** *astonished*: Why, she's mad.

51 **Elizabeth:** I would to God she were. There be fourteen people in the jail now, she says. PROCTOR *simply looks at her, unable to grasp it.* And they'll be tried, and the court have power to hang them too, she says.

NOTES

**condemnation** (kon dehm NAY shuhn) *n.* very strong disapproval

**magistrates** (MAJ uh strayts) *n.* officials who have some of the powers of a judge

## CLOSE READE

Remind students that it is important to note not only what a character says, but how he or she says it. The tone of a speaker can tell you how he or she feels and thinks. You may wish to model the Close Read using the following think-aloud format. Possible responses to questions on the student page are included. You may also want to print copies of the **Close-Read Guide: Fiction** for students to use.

**ANNOTATE:** As I read paragraphs 55–66, I notice details that relate to thoughts and beliefs about what has happened and what should be done about it. I think I'll highlight those details.

**QUESTION:** I think Miller uses repetition in this conversation to show the increasing tension between Proctor and his wife.

**CONCLUDE:** I think the audience will respond to this repetition by thinking that the conflict between these two will be difficult to resolve because of their different beliefs about what should be done.



NOTES

1. **part like . . . Israel** In the Bible, God commanded Moses, the leader of the Israelites, to part the Red Sea to enable the Israelites to escape from the Egyptians into Canaan.

### CLOSE READ

**ANNOTATE:** In paragraphs 55 through 66, mark details that relate to thought, belief, or conviction.

**QUESTION:** Why does Miller repeat these sorts of references?

**CONCLUDE:** What do these details suggest about the struggle the Proctors are experiencing?

52 **Proctor,** *scoffing but without conviction*: Ah, they'd never hang—

53 **Elizabeth:** The Deputy Governor promise hangin' if they'll not confess, John. The town's gone wild, I think. She speak of Abigail, and I thought she were a saint, to hear her. Abigail brings the other girls into the court, and where she walks the crowd will part like the sea for Israel.[1] And folks are brought before them, and if they scream and howl and fall to the floor—the person's clapped in the jail for bewitchin' them.

54 **Proctor,** *wide-eyed*: Oh, it is a black mischief.

55 **Elizabeth:** I think you must go to Salem, John. *He turns to her.* I think so. You must tell them it is a fraud.

56 **Proctor,** *thinking beyond this*: Aye, it is, it is surely.

57 **Elizabeth:** Let you go to Ezekiel Cheever—he knows you well. And tell him what she said to you last week in her uncle's house. She said it had naught to do with witchcraft, did she not?

58 **Proctor,** *in thought*: Aye, she did, she did. *Now, a pause.*

59 **Elizabeth,** *quietly, fearing to anger him by prodding*: God forbid you keep that from the court, John. I think they must be told.

60 **Proctor,** *quietly, struggling with his thought*: Aye, they must, they must. It is a wonder they do believe her.

61 **Elizabeth:** I would go to Salem now, John—let you go tonight.

62 **Proctor:** I'll think on it.

63 **Elizabeth,** *with her courage now*: You cannot keep it, John.

64 **Proctor,** *angering*: I know I cannot keep it. I say I will think on it!

65 **Elizabeth,** *hurt, and very coldly*: Good, then, let you think on it. *She stands and starts to walk out of the room.*

66 **Proctor:** I am only wondering how I may prove what she told me, Elizabeth. If the girl's a saint now, I think it is not easy to prove she's fraud, and the town gone so silly. She told it to me in a room alone—I have no proof for it.

67 **Elizabeth:** You were alone with her?

68 **Proctor,** *stubbornly*: For a moment alone, aye.

69 **Elizabeth:** Why, then, it is not as you told me.

70 **Proctor,** *his anger rising*: For a moment, I say. The others come in soon after.

71 **Elizabeth,** *quietly—she has suddenly lost all faith in him*: Do as you wish, then. *She starts to turn.*

72 **Proctor:** Woman. *She turns to him.* I'll not have your suspicion any more.

73 **Elizabeth,** *a little loftily*: I have no—

74 **Proctor:** I'll not have it!

NOTES

75 **Elizabeth:** Then let you not earn it.

76 **Proctor,** *with a violent undertone*: You doubt me yet?

77 **Elizabeth,** *with a smile, to keep her dignity*: John, if it were not Abigail that you must go to hurt, would you falter now? I think not.

78 **Proctor:** Now look you—

79 **Elizabeth:** I see what I see, John.

80 **Proctor,** *with solemn warning*: You will not judge me more, Elizabeth. I have good reason to think before I charge fraud on Abigail, and I will think on it. Let you look to your own improvement before you go to judge your husband any more. I have forgot Abigail, and—

81 **Elizabeth:** And I.

82 **Proctor:** Spare me! You forget nothin' and forgive nothin'. Learn charity, woman. I have gone tiptoe in this house all seven month since she is gone. I have not moved from there to there without I think to please you, and still an everlasting funeral marches round your heart. I cannot speak but I am doubted, every moment judged for lies, as though I come into a court when I come into this house!

83 **Elizabeth:** John, you are not open with me. You saw her with a crowd, you said. Now you—

84 **Proctor:** I'll plead my honesty no more, Elizabeth.

85 **Elizabeth**—*now she would justify herself*: John. I am only—

86 **Proctor:** No more! I should have roared you down when first you told me your suspicion. But I wilted, and, like a Christian, I confessed. Confessed! Some dream I had must have mistaken you for God that day. But you're not, you're not, and let you remember it! Let you look sometimes for the goodness in me, and judge me not.

87 **Elizabeth:** I do not judge you. The magistrate sits in your heart that judges you. I never thought you but a good man, John—*with a smile*—only somewhat bewildered.

88 **Proctor,** *laughing bitterly*: Oh. Elizabeth, your justice would freeze beer! *He turns suddenly toward a sound outside. He starts for the door as* MARY WARREN *enters. As soon as he sees her, he goes directly to her and grabs her by the cloak, furious.* How do you go to Salem when I forbid it? Do you mock me? *Shaking her.* I'll whip you if you dare leave this house again!

*Strangely, she doesn't resist him, but hangs limply by his grip.*

89 **Mary Warren:** I am sick, I am sick, Mr. Proctor. Pray, pray, hurt me not. *Her strangeness throws him off, and her evident pallor and weakness. He frees her.* My insides are all shuddery; I am in the proceedings all day, sir.

Additional **English Language Support** is available in the Interactive Teacher's Edition.



## PERSONALIZE FOR LEARNING

### Challenge

**Figurative Language** Review paragraphs 82 and 88. Use this point in the play to point out some of the many examples of figurative language that Miller's play contains:

"An everlasting funeral marches around your heart." (paragraph 82)

"Oh, Elizabeth, your justice would freeze beer!" (paragraph 88)

Ask students to note additional examples as they read. You may wish to suggest they mark them or attach a sticky note to each example. Then have students share their examples and discuss how the use of figurative language contributes to the portrayal of events and characters.

NOTES

**proceedings** (pruh SEE dihngz) *n.* events in a court of law

**2. poppet** *n.* doll.

90 **Proctor,** *with draining anger—his curiosity is draining it*: And what of these **proceedings** here? When will you proceed to keep this house, as you are paid nine pound a year to do—and my wife not wholly well?

91 *As though to compensate,* MARY WARREN *goes to* ELIZABETH *with a small rag doll.*

92 **Mary Warren:** I made a gift for you today, Goody Proctor. I had to sit long hours in a chair, and passed the time with sewing.

93 **Elizabeth,** *perplexed, looking at the doll*: Why, thank you, it's a fair poppet.[2]

94 **Mary Warren,** *with a trembling, decayed voice*: We must all love each other now, Goody Proctor.

95 **Elizabeth,** *amazed at her strangeness*: Aye, indeed we must.

96 **Mary Warren,** *glancing at the room*: I'll get up early in the morning and clean the house. I must sleep now. *She turns and starts off.*

97 **Proctor:** Mary. *She halts.* Is it true? There be fourteen women arrested?

98 **Mary Warren:** No, sir. There be thirty-nine now—*She suddenly breaks off and sobs and sits down, exhausted.*

99 **Elizabeth:** Why, she's weepin'! What ails you, child?

100 **Mary Warren:** Goody Osburn—will hang!

101 *There is a shocked pause, while she sobs.*

102 **Proctor:** Hang! *He calls into her face.* Hang, y'say?

103 **Mary Warren,** *through her weeping*: Aye.

104 **Proctor:** The Deputy Governor will permit it?

105 **Mary Warren:** He sentenced her. He must. To ameliorate it: But not Sarah Good. For Sarah Good confessed, y'see.

106 **Proctor:** Confessed! To what?

107 **Mary Warren:** That she—*in horror at the memory*—she sometimes made a compact with Lucifer, and wrote her name in his black book—with her blood—and bound herself to torment Christians till God's thrown down—and we all must worship Hell forevermore.

108 *Pause.*

109 **Proctor:** But—surely you know what a jabberer she is. Did you tell them that?

110 **Mary Warren:** Mr. Proctor, in open court she near to choked us all to death.

111 **Proctor:** How, choked you?

112 **Mary Warren:** She sent her spirit out.

113 **Elizabeth:** Oh, Mary, Mary, surely you—

114 **Mary Warren,** *with an indignant edge*: She tried to kill me many times, Goody Proctor!

115 **Elizabeth:** Why, I never heard you mention that before.

116 **Mary Warren:** I never knew it before. I never knew anything before. When she come into the court I say to myself, I must not accuse this woman, for she sleep in ditches, and so very old and poor. But then—then she sit there, denying and denying, and I feel a misty coldness climbin' up my back, and the skin on my skull begin to creep, and I feel a clamp around my neck and I cannot breathe air; and then—*entranced*—I hear a voice, a screamin' voice, and it were my voice—and all at once I remembered everything she done to me!

117 **Proctor:** Why? What did she do to you?

118 **Mary Warren,** *like one awakened to a marvelous secret insight*: So many time, Mr. Proctor, she come to this very door, beggin' bread and a cup of cider—and mark this: whenever I turned her away empty, she *mumbled*.

119 **Elizabeth:** Mumbled! She may mumble if she's hungry.

120 **Mary Warren:** But *what* does she mumble? You must remember, Goody Proctor. Last month—a Monday, I think—she walked away, and I thought my guts would burst for two days after. Do you remember it?

121 **Elizabeth:** Why—I do, I think, but—

122 **Mary Warren:** And so I told that to Judge Hathorne, and he asks her so. "Goody Osburn," says he, "what curse do you mumble that this girl must fall sick after turning you away?" And then she replies—*mimicking an old crone*—"Why, your excellence, no curse at all. I only say my commandments; I hope I may say my commandments," says she!

123 **Elizabeth:** And that's an upright answer.

124 **Mary Warren:** Aye, but then Judge Hathorne say, "Recite for us your commandments!"—*leaning avidly toward them*—and of all the ten she could not say a single one. She never knew no commandments, and they had her in a flat lie!

125 **Proctor:** And so condemned her?

126 **Mary Warren,** *now a little strained, seeing his stubborn doubt*: Why, they must when she condemned herself.



NOTES

**CLOSE READ**

**ANNOTATE:** In paragraphs 116–118, mark details that relate to new knowledge or awareness.

**QUESTION:** Why does Miller include these details?

**CONCLUDE:** What do these details suggest about the ways in which the characters and situation in Salem are changing?

DIGITAL PERSPECTIVES

## CLOSE READ

Remind students that in a play, as in a story, characters are shaped by what they believe and by what they are aware of. You may wish to model the Close Read using the following think-aloud format. Possible answers to the questions on the student page are included.

**ANNOTATE:** As I read paragraphs 116–118, I mark details that relate to new knowledge or awareness.

**QUESTION:** I believe Miller includes these details to show that what characters *believe*, or seem to believe, is being shaped by the hysterical atmosphere around them.

**CONCLUDE:** The details show that the situation is moving fast. Mary and the other girls may feel something towards someone, and others will take their word that the person is involved with evil.

## PERSONALIZE FOR LEARNING

### Challenge

**Courtroom Analysis** Review paragraphs 116 through 126. Students probably have a fairly good working knowledge of American courtroom procedure and rules, picked up from watching legal proceedings on TV or in movies. Ask students to evaluate Mary's tale of what happens in the Salem courtroom by modern standards they have observed. How would a modern judge treat the display of screaming such as Mary describes? How would modern lawyers react to the "hard proof" that Mary cites?

Encourage students to continue their comparisons thorough the play as they learn more about the courtroom proceedings in Salem. After finishing the play, students might role-play the Salem witchcraft trials as if they took place ina modern courtroom, taking on roles of judge, prosecutor, defense attorney, witnesses, and at least one accused. The rest of the class can serve as the jury to fairly decide if the evidence is "hard proof" enough to convict the defendant.

NOTES

127 **Proctor:** But the proof, the proof!

128 **Mary Warren,** *with greater impatience with him*: I told you the proof. It's hard proof, hard as rock, the judges said.

129 **Proctor,** *pauses an instant, then*: You will not go to court again, Mary Warren.

130 **Mary Warren:** I must tell you, sir, I will be gone every day now. I am amazed you do not see what weighty work we do.

131 **Proctor:** What work you do? It's strange work for a Christian girl to hang old women!

132 **Mary Warren:** But, Mr. Proctor, they will not hang them if they confess. Sarah Good will only sit in jail some time—*recalling*—and here's a wonder for you: think on this. Goody Good is pregnant!

133 **Elizabeth:** Pregnant! Are they mad? The woman's near to sixty!

134 **Mary Warren:** They had Doctor Griggs examine her, and she's full to the brim. And smokin' a pipe all these years, and no husband either! But she's safe, thank God, for they'll not hurt the innocent child. But be that not a marvel? You must see it, sir, it's God's work we do. So I'll be gone every day for some time. I'm—I am an official of the court, they say, and I—*She has been edging toward offstage.*

135 **Proctor:** I'll official you! *He strides to the mantel, takes down the whip hanging there.*

136 **Mary Warren,** *terrified, but coming erect, striving for her authority*: I'll not stand whipping any more!

137 **Elizabeth,** *hurriedly, as* PROCTOR *approaches*: Mary, promise now you'll stay at home—

138 **Mary Warren,** *backing from him, but keeping her erect posture, striving, striving for her way*: The Devil's loose in Salem, Mr. Proctor: we must discover where he's hiding!

139 **Proctor:** I'll whip the Devil out of you! *With whip raised he reaches out for her, and she streaks away and yells.*

140 **Mary Warren,** *pointing at* ELIZABETH: I saved her life today!

141 *Silence. His whip comes down.*

142 **Elizabeth,** *softly*: I am accused?

143 **Mary Warren,** *quaking*: Somewhat mentioned. But I said I never see no sign you ever sent your spirit out to hurt no one, and seeing I do live so closely with you, they dismissed it.

144 **Elizabeth:** Who accused me?

145 **Mary Warren:** I am bound by law, I cannot tell it. *To* PROCTOR: I only hope you'll not be so sarcastical no more. Four judges and

the King's deputy sat to dinner with us but an hour ago. I—I would have you speak civilly to me, from this out.

146 **Proctor,** *in horror, muttering in disgust at her*: Go to bed.

147 **Mary Warren,** *with a stamp of her foot*: I'll not be ordered to bed no more, Mr. Proctor! I am eighteen and a woman, however single!

148 **Proctor:** Do you wish to sit up? Then sit up.

149 **Mary Warren:** I wish to go to bed!

150 **Proctor,** *in anger*: Good night, then!

151 **Mary Warren:** Good night. *Dissatisfied, uncertain of herself, she goes out. Wide-eyed, both* PROCTOR *and* ELIZABETH *stand staring.*

152 **Elizabeth,** *quietly*: Oh, the noose, the noose is up!

153 **Proctor:** There'll be no noose.

154 **Elizabeth:** She wants me dead. I knew all week it would come to this!

155 **Proctor,** *without conviction*: They dismissed it. You heard her say—

156 **Elizabeth:** And what of tomorrow? She will cry me out until they take me!

157 **Proctor:** Sit you down.

158 **Elizabeth:** She wants me dead, John, you know it!

159 **Proctor:** I say sit down! *She sits, trembling. He speaks quietly, trying to keep his wits.* Now we must be wise, Elizabeth.

160 **Elizabeth,** *with sarcasm, and a sense of being lost*: Oh, indeed, indeed!

161 **Proctor:** Fear nothing. I'll find Ezekiel Cheever. I'll tell him she said it were all sport.

162 **Elizabeth:** John, with so many in the Jail, more than Cheever's help is needed now, I think. Would you favor me with this? Go to Abigail.

163 **Proctor,** *his soul hardening as he senses . . .* : What have I to say to Abigail?

164 **Elizabeth,** *delicately*: John—grant me this. You have a faulty understanding of young girls. There is a promise made in any bed—

165 **Proctor,** *striving against his anger*: What promise!

166 **Elizabeth:** Spoke or silent, a promise is surely made. And she may dote on it now—I am sure she does—and thinks to kill me, then to take my place.

167 PROCTOR'S *anger is rising; he cannot speak.*

NOTES

**CLOSE READ**

**ANNOTATE:** In paragraphs 146–151, mark details in both dialogue and stage directions that relate to childish behavior, and others that relate to mature behavior.

**QUESTION:** Why does Miller include these details?

**CONCLUDE:** What is the effect of these details, particularly in characterizing Mary Warren and her motivations?





**DIGITAL PERSPECTIVES**

## CLOSE READ

Remind students that in a play, as in real life, people's words and actions convey a lot about their character. In a play those actions may be spelled out in stage directions. You may wish to model the Close Read using the following think-aloud format. Possible answers to the questions on the student page are included.

**ANNOTATE:** In paragraphs 146–151, I see dialogue and stage directions that indicate childish behavior, along with more mature behavior. I will mark these details.

**QUESTION:** I believe Miller includes these details to show that Mary is in some ways still a child, even though she is eighteen.

**CONCLUDE:** These details make it easier for the audience to view Mary as being more easily influenced by peers, as an older child would be, and as being rebellious, as she is being here.

## PERSONALIZE FOR LEARNING

### Challenge

**Analyze a Scene** In paragraphs 162–186, Elizabeth urges John to speak privately to Abigail and persuade her to retract her accusations. Late in the original Broadway run of the play, Miller inserted a short scene to open Act III in which John fulfills this request. Have partners find the scene in a library text of the play and read or perform it for the class. Then have the entire class debate the value of the scene, discussing what, if anything, it adds to the play and why they think Miller chose to add it.

NOTES

168 **Elizabeth:** It is her dearest hope, John, I know it. There be a thousand names: why does she call mine? There be a certain danger in calling such a name—I am no Goody Good that sleeps in ditches, nor Osburn, drunk and half-witted. She'd dare not call out such a farmer's wife but there be monstrous profit in it. She thinks to take my place, John.

169 **Proctor:** She cannot think it! *He knows it is true.*

170 **Elizabeth,** *"reasonably"*: John, have you ever shown her somewhat of contempt? She cannot pass you in the church but you will blush—

171 **Proctor:** I may blush for my sin.

172 **Elizabeth:** I think she sees another meaning in that blush.

173 **Proctor:** And what see you? What see you, Elizabeth?

174 **Elizabeth,** *"conceding"*: I think you be somewhat ashamed, for I am there, and she so close.

175 **Proctor:** When will you know me, woman? Were I stone I would have cracked for shame this seven month!

176 **Elizabeth:** Then go and tell her she's a whore. Whatever promise she may sense—break it. John, break it.

177 **Proctor,** *between his teeth*: Good, then. I'll go. *He starts for his rifle.*

178 **Elizabeth,** *trembling, fearfully*: Oh, how unwillingly!

179 **Proctor,** *turning on her, rifle in hand*: I will curse her hotter than the oldest cinder in hell. But pray, begrudge me not my anger!

180 **Elizabeth:** Your anger! I only ask you—

181 **Proctor:** Woman, am I so base? Do you truly think me base?

182 **Elizabeth:** I never called you base.

183 **Proctor:** Then how do you charge me with such a promise? The promise that a stallion gives a mare I gave that girl!

184 **Elizabeth:** Then why do you anger with me when I bid you break it?

185 **Proctor:** Because it speaks deceit, and I am honest! But I'll plead no more! I see now your spirit twists around the single error of my life, and I will never tear it free!

186 **Elizabeth,** *crying out*: You'll tear it free—when you come to know that I will be your only wife, or no wife at all! She has an arrow in you yet, John Proctor, and you know it well!

187 *Quite suddenly, as though from the air, a figure appears in the doorway. They start slightly. It is* MR. HALE. *He is different now—drawn a little, and there is a quality of deference, even of guilt, about his manner now.*

188 **Hale:** Good evening.





## PERSONALIZE FOR LEARNING

### Strategic Support

**Character Development** Call students' attention to the stage directions in paragraph 187. Have students make a character web for Reverend Hale at the end of each act. Remind them that the words can be nouns, adjectives, verbs, or adverbs. Have students especially note changes in Hale's behavior and attitude from one act to the next. Then have them use the webs to write a short report tracing Hale's character development throughout the play.

189 **Proctor,** *still in his shock*: Why, Mr. Hale! Good evening to you, sir. Come in, come in.

190 **Hale,** *to* Elizabeth: I hope I do not startle you.

191 **Elizabeth:** No, no, it's only that I heard no horse—

192 **Hale:** You are Goodwife Proctor.

193 **Proctor:** Aye, Elizabeth.

194 **Hale,** *nods, then*: I hope you're not off to bed yet.

195 **Proctor,** *setting down his gun*: No, no. *HALE comes further into the room. And* PROCTOR, *to explain his nervousness*: We are not used to visitors after dark, but you're welcome here. Will you sit you down, sir?

196 **Hale:** I will. *He sits.* Let you sit, Goodwife Proctor.

197 *She does, never letting him out of her sight. There is a pause as* HALE *looks about the room.*

198 **Proctor**, *to break the silence*: Will you drink cider, Mr. Hale?

NOTES

In the 1996 film version of *The Crucible*, actor Rob Campbell portrays Reverend Hale.





DIGITAL PERSPECTIVES

CLOSER LOOK

## Explore Characterization 

Remind students that it is important to note how characters react to the actions or words of other characters. Students may have marked paragraphs 189 through 197 during their first read. Use these lines to help students understand how to analyze characters' reactions. Encourage them to talk about the annotations that they marked. You may want to model a close read with the class based on the highlights shown in the text.

**ANNOTATE:** Have students mark details in paragraphs 189 through 197 that show how the Proctors react to the appearance of Reverend Hale, and how he reacts to them, or have students participate while you highlight the lines.

**QUESTION:** Guide students to consider what these details might tell them. Ask what a reader can infer from the reactions of the characters, and accept student responses.

**Possible response:** I can infer that Proctor and his wife are surprised by Hale's appearance, and that Elizabeth is wary of Hale, who seems to be in a serious mood.

**CONCLUDE:** Help students to formulate conclusions about the importance of these details in the text. Ask students why the author might have included these details.

**Possible response:** I think Miller wants readers to see the tension building by having Hale show up late at night without invitation and having him talk mainly to Elizabeth, who is very wary of him and his reasons for coming.

Point out to students that **characterization** is the way a writer develops and reveals a character's personality and temperament. Characters in plays reveal themselves to readers through their actions and reactions, as well as the dialogue. Sometimes a reaction allows one character to take charge, such as Hale, and lead other characters in the direction he or she wants them to go. How another character reacts helps readers know more about what is important to each character.

NOTES

199 **Hale:** No, it rebels my stomach; I have some further traveling yet tonight. Sit you down, sir. PROCTOR *sits.* I will not keep you long, but I have some business with you.

200 **Proctor:** Business of the court?

201 **Hale:** No—no, I come of my own, without the court's authority. Hear me. *He wets his lips.* I know not if you are aware, but your wife's name is—mentioned in the court.

202 **Proctor:** We know it, sir. Our Mary Warren told us. We are entirely amazed.

203 **Hale:** I am a stranger here, as you know. And in my ignorance I find it hard to draw a clear opinion of them that come accused before the court. And so this afternoon, and now tonight, I go from house to house—I come now from Rebecca Nurse's house and—

204 **Elizabeth,** *shocked*: Rebecca's charged!

205 **Hale:** God forbid such a one be charged. She is, however—mentioned somewhat.

206 **Elizabeth,** *with an attempt at a laugh*: You will never believe, I hope, that Rebecca trafficked with the Devil.

207 **Hale:** Woman, it is possible.

208 **Proctor,** *taken aback*: Surely you cannot think so.

209 **Hale:** This is a strange time, Mister. No man may longer doubt the powers of the dark are gathered in monstrous attack upon this village. There is too much evidence now to deny it. You will agree, sir?

210 **Proctor,** *evading*: I—have no knowledge in that line. But it's hard to think so pious a woman be secretly a Devil's bitch after seventy year of such good prayer.

211 **Hale:** Aye. But the Devil is a wily one, you cannot deny it. However, she is far from accused, and I know she will not be. *Pause.* I thought, sir, to put some questions as to the Christian character of this house, if you'll permit me.

212 **Proctor,** *coldly, resentful*: Why, we—have no fear of questions, sir.

213 **Hale:** Good, then. *He makes himself more comfortable.* In the book of record that Mr. Parris keeps, I note that you are rarely in the church on Sabbath Day.

214 **Proctor:** No, sir, you are mistaken.

215 **Hale:** Twenty-six time in seventeen month, sir. I must call that rare. Will you tell me why you are so absent?

216 **Proctor:** Mr. Hale, I never knew I must account to that man for I come to church or stay at home. My wife were sick this winter.

217 **Hale:** So I am told. But you, Mister, why could you not come alone?





## CROSS-CURRICULAR PERSPECTIVES

**Math** Direct students' attention to paragraphs 213 through 215 and read the text aloud. Then say, *Reverend Hale says that Proctor is "rarely in the church on Sabbath Day," adding "Twenty-six time in seventeen month."* Is that really rare? Figure it out and decide. (Answer: 4 Sabbaths in a month × 17 months = 68 Sabbaths, or 26/68 which = 0.38 or 38%). Most students will agree that this does not qualify as "rare," but allow those who disagree to explain their thinking.

DIGITAL PERSPECTIVES 

218 **Proctor:** I surely did come when I could, and when I could not I prayed in this house.

219 **Hale:** Mr. Proctor, your house is not a church: your theology must tell you that.

220 **Proctor:** It does, sir, it does; and it tells me that a minister may pray to God without he have golden candlesticks upon the altar.

221 **Hale:** What golden candlesticks?

222 **Proctor:** Since we built the church there were pewter candlesticks upon the altar; Francis Nurse made them y'know, and a sweeter hand never touched the metal. But Parris came, and for twenty week he preach nothin' but golden candlesticks until he had them. I labor the earth from dawn of day to blink of night, and I tell you true, when I look to heaven and see my money glaring at his elbows—it hurt my prayer, sir, it hurt my prayer. I think, sometimes, the man dreams cathedrals, not clapboard meetin' houses.

223 **Hale,** *thinks, then*: And yet, Mister, a Christian on Sabbath Day must be in church. *Pause.* Tell me—you have three children?

224 **Proctor:** Aye. Boys.

225 **Hale:** How comes it that only two are baptized?

226 **Proctor,** *starts to speak, then stops, then, as though unable to restrain this*: I like it not that Mr. Parris should lay his hand upon my baby. I see no light of God in that man. I'll not conceal it.

227 **Hale:** I must say it, Mr. Proctor; that is not for you to decide. The man's ordained, therefore the light of God is in him.

228 **Proctor,** *flushed with resentment but trying to smile*: What's your suspicion, Mr. Hale?

229 **Hale:** No, no, I have no—

230 **Proctor:** I nailed the roof upon the church, I hung the door—

231 **Hale:** Oh, did you! That's a good sign, then.

232 **Proctor:** It may be I have been too quick to bring the man to book, but you cannot think we ever desired the destruction of religion. I think that's in your mind, is it not?

233 **Hale,** *not altogether giving way*: I—have—there is a softness in your record, sir, a softness.

234 **Elizabeth:** I think, maybe, we have been too hard with Mr. Parris. I think so. But sure we never loved the Devil here.

235 **Hale,** *nods, deliberating this. Then, with the voice of one administering a secret test*: Do you know your Commandments, Elizabeth?

236 **Elizabeth,** *without hesitation, even eagerly*: I surely do. There be no mark of blame upon my life, Mr. Hale. I am a covenanted Christian woman.

NOTES

**CLOSE READ**

**ANNOTATE:** In paragraphs 220–222, mark the name of the item that appears several times in the conversation between Hale and Proctor.

**QUESTION:** Why is this item important?

**CONCLUDE:** How do you think the audience feels about Parris after hearing this exchange?





## CLOSE READ

Remind students that symbols play an important role in many literary genres. The symbol may be an object, person, animal, place, or image that has its own meaning but also stands for something larger than itself, usually an abstract idea. You may wish to model the Close Read using the following think-aloud format. Possible responses to questions on the student page are included.

**ANNOTATE:** As I read paragraphs 220 through 222 I notice and highlight an object that appears several times in the conversation between Hale and Proctor.

**QUESTION:** I think these candlesticks must have special meaning to Proctor.

**CONCLUDE:** I think the audience will feel that Parris is more concerned with material possessions than in ministering to the people who come to worship at his church.

## PERSONALIZE FOR LEARNING

### English Language Support

**Pronunciation of Digraph *th*** Students may have trouble pronouncing the /th/ sound in *theology* (paragraph 219). Note that the sound, found in English and Greek but few other languages, often changes to a /t/ or /d/ sound when used by speakers of a native language where it is not found. The Greek root *theo–*, meaning "god," is related to the Spanish *dios* and French *dieu,* for example. Help students pronounce /th/ by offering simpler words in which it appears, such as *thick* and *thin*. Note that the spelling *th–* actually has two sounds in English, the unvoiced /th/ in *thick* and *thin* and the voiced /th/ in *the* and *this*. Pronounce each word and have students repeat it. Ask them to look for other words in the play that have the /th/ sound. **ALL LEVELS**

NOTES

237 **Hale:** And you, Mister?

238 **Proctor,** *a trifle unsteadily*: I—am sure I do, sir.

239 **Hale,** *glances at her open face, then at* JOHN, *then*: Let you repeat them, if you will.

240 **Proctor:** The Commandments.

241 **Hale:** Aye.

242 **Proctor,** *looking off, beginning to sweat*: Thou shalt not kill.

243 **Hale:** Aye.

244 **Proctor,** *counting on his fingers*: Thou shalt not steal. Thou shalt not covet thy neighbor's goods, nor make unto thee any graven image. Thou shalt not take the name of the Lord in vain; thou shalt have no other gods before me. *With some hesitation*: Thou shalt remember the Sabbath Day and keep it holy. *Pause. Then*: Thou shalt honor thy father and mother. Thou shalt not bear false witness. *He is stuck. He counts back on his fingers, knowing one is missing.* Thou shalt not make unto thee any graven image.

245 **Hale:** You have said that twice, sir.

246 **Proctor,** *lost*: Aye. *He is flailing for it.*

247 **Elizabeth,** *delicately*: Adultery, John.

248 **Proctor,** *as though a secret arrow had pained his heart*: Aye. *Trying to grin it away—to* HALE: You see, sir, between the two of us we do know them all. HALE *only looks at* PROCTOR, *deep in his attempt to define this man.* PROCTOR *grows more uneasy.* I think it be a small fault.

249 **Hale:** Theology, sir, is a fortress; no crack in a fortress may be accounted small. *He rises; he seems worried now. He paces a little, in deep thought.*

250 **Proctor:** There be no love for Satan in this house, Mister.

251 **Hale:** I pray it, I pray it dearly. *He looks to both of them, an attempt at a smile on his face, but his misgivings are clear.* Well, then—I'll bid you good night.

252 **Elizabeth,** *unable to restrain herself*: Mr. Hale. *He turns.* I do think you are suspecting me somewhat? Are you not?

253 **Hale,** *obviously disturbed—and evasive*: Goody Proctor, I do not judge you. My duty is to add what I may to the godly wisdom of the court. I pray you both good health and good fortune. *To* JOHN: Good night, sir. *He starts out.*

254 **Elizabeth,** *with a note of desperation*: I think you must tell him, John.

255 **Hale:** What's that?

256 **Elizabeth**, *restraining a call*: Will you tell him?

257 *Slight pause.* HALE *looks questioningly at* JOHN.





614 UNIT 5 • FACING OUR FEARS

258 **Proctor,** *with difficulty*: I—I have no witness and cannot prove it, except my word be taken. But I know the children's sickness had naught to do with witchcraft.

259 **Hale,** *stopped, struck*: Naught to do—?

260 **Proctor:** Mr. Parris discovered them sportin' in the woods. They were startled and took sick.

261 *Pause.*

262 **Hale:** Who told you this?

263 **Proctor,** *hesitates, then*: Abigail Williams.

264 **Hale:** Abigail.

265 **Proctor:** Aye.

266 **Hale,** *his eyes wide*: Abigail Williams told you it had naught to do with witchcraft!

267 **Proctor:** She told me the day you came, sir.

268 **Hale,** *suspiciously*: Why—why did you keep this?

269 **Proctor:** I never knew until tonight that the world is gone daft with this nonsense.

270 **Hale:** Nonsense! Mister, I have myself examined Tituba, Sarah Good, and numerous others that have confessed to dealing with the Devil. They have *confessed* it.

271 **Proctor:** And why not, if they must hang for denyin' it? There are them that will swear to anything before they'll hang; have you never thought of that?

272 **Hale:** I have. I—I have indeed. *It is his own suspicion, but he resists it. He glances at* ELIZABETH, *then at* JOHN. And you—would you testify to this in court?

273 **Proctor:** I—had not reckoned with goin' into court. But if I must I will.

274 **Hale:** Do you falter here?

275 **Proctor:** I falter nothing, but I may wonder if my story will be credited in such a court. I do wonder on it, when such a steady-minded minister as you will suspicion such a woman that never lied, and cannot, and the world knows she cannot! I may falter somewhat, Mister; I am no fool.

276 **Hale,** *quietly—it has impressed him*: Proctor, let you open with me now, for I have a rumor that troubles me. It's said you hold no belief that there may even be witches in the world. Is that true, sir?

277 **Proctor**—*he knows this is critical, and is striving against his disgust with* HALE *and with himself for even answering*: I know not what I have said, I may have said it. I have wondered if there be witches in the world—although I cannot believe they come among us now.

NOTES

**CLOSE READ**

**ANNOTATE:** In paragraphs 268–274, mark questions and exclamations.

**QUESTION:** Why does Miller use exclamations and questions here?

**CONCLUDE:** What is the effect of these sentence types in this scene?





## CLOSE READ

Remind students that an author's style includes every feature of his or her use of language, including the variety of sentences used in a selection. You may wish to model the Close Read using the following think-aloud format. Possible responses to questions on the student page are included.

**ANNOTATE:** As I read paragraphs 268 through 274, I notice an exclamation and questions. I highlight the punctuation at the end of these sentences.

**QUESTION:** I note that Miller interspersed different types of sentences in this dialogue between Proctor and Hale.

**CONCLUDE:** I think Miller has Hale exclaim to show the strength of his feelings about the trial. The questions show the uncertainty about what is right.

CLOSER LOOK

## Analyzing Character

Students may have marked paragraphs 281 through 286 during their first read. Encourage them to talk about the annotations that they marked. You may want to model a close read with the class based on the highlights shown in the text.

**ANNOTATE:** Have students mark details in paragraphs 281 through 286 that show the strength of Elizabeth Proctor's character, or have students participate while you highlight them.

**QUESTION:** Guide students to consider what these details might tell them. Ask what a reader can infer from Elizabeth's answers, and accept student responses.

**Possible response:** Readers can infer that Elizabeth always speaks the truth; she won't lie even to appease Hale and her husband.

**CONCLUDE:** Help students to formulate conclusions about the importance of these details in the text. Ask students why the author might have included these details.

**Possible response:** I think Miller wants readers to know that Elizabeth is not the kind of person to give in and lie, even to save her life, and that her husband doesn't speak for her; she speaks her own mind.

Remind students that an author provides clues about a **character** by describing his or her actions and feelings. The attitude of a character, such as the brashness of Elizabeth to stand up to Reverend Hale, helps readers better understand her personality. Knowing this, readers can often predict what that character will do in future events.

NOTES

278 **Hale:** Then you do not believe—

279 **Proctor:** I have no knowledge of it; the Bible speaks of witches, and I will not deny them.

280 **Hale:** And you, woman?

281 **Elizabeth:** I—I cannot believe it.

282 **Hale,** *shocked*: You cannot!

283 **Proctor:** Elizabeth, you bewilder him!

284 **Elizabeth,** *to* HALE: I cannot think the Devil may own a woman's soul, Mr. Hale, when she keeps an upright way, as I have. I am a good woman, I know it; and if you believe I may do only good work in the world, and yet be secretly bound to Satan, then I must tell you, sir, I do not believe it.

285 **Hale:** But, woman, you do believe there are witches in—

286 **Elizabeth:** If you think that I am one, then I say there are none.

287 **Hale:** You surely do not fly against the Gospel, the Gospel—

288 **Proctor:** She believe in the Gospel, every word!

289 **Elizabeth:** Question Abigail Williams about the Gospel, not myself!

In the 1996 film adaptation of *The Crucible*, Joan Allen portrays Elizabeth Proctor.





616 UNIT 5 • FACING OUR FEARS

290 HALE *stares at her.*

291 **Proctor:** She do not mean to doubt the Gospel, sir, you cannot think it. This be a Christian house, sir, a Christian house.

292 **Hale:** God keep you both; let the third child be quickly baptized, and go you without fail each Sunday to Sabbath prayer; and keep a solemn, quiet way among you. I think—

293 GILES COREY *appears in doorway.*

294 **Giles:** John!

295 **Proctor:** Giles! What's the matter?

296 **Giles:** They take my wife.

297 FRANCIS NURSE *enters.*

298 **Giles:** And his Rebecca!

299 **Proctor,** *to* FRANCIS: Rebecca's in the *jail*!

300 **Francis:** Aye, Cheever come and take her in his wagon. We've only now come from the jail, and they'll not even let us in to see them.

301 **Elizabeth:** They've surely gone wild now, Mr. Hale!

302 **Francis,** *going to* HALE: Reverend Hale! Can you not speak to the Deputy Governor? I'm sure he mistakes these people—

303 **Hale:** Pray calm yourself, Mr. Nurse.

304 **Francis:** My wife is the very brick and mortar of the church. Mr. Hale—*indicating* GILES—and Martha Corey, there cannot be a woman closer yet to God than Martha.

305 **Hale:** How is Rebecca charged, Mr. Nurse?

306 **Francis,** *with a mocking, half-hearted laugh*: For murder, she's charged! *Mockingly quoting the warrant*: "For the marvelous and supernatural murder of Goody Putnam's babies." What am I to do, Mr. Hale?

307 **Hale,** *turns from* FRANCIS, *deeply troubled, then*: Believe me, Mr. Nurse, if Rebecca Nurse be tainted, then nothing's left to stop the whole green world from burning. Let you rest upon the justice of the court; the court will send her home. I know it.

308 **Francis:** You cannot mean she will be tried in court!

309 **Hale,** *pleading*: Nurse, though our hearts break, we cannot flinch: these are new times, sir. There is a misty plot afoot so subtle we should be criminal to cling to old respects and ancient friendships. I have seen too many frightful proofs in court—the Devil is alive in Salem, and we dare not quail to follow wherever the accusing finger points!

310 **Proctor,** *angered*: How may such a woman murder children?

311 **Hale,** *in great pain*: Man, remember, until an hour before the Devil fell, God thought him beautiful in Heaven.

NOTES





DIGITAL PERSPECTIVES

## CROSS-CURRICULAR PERSPECTIVES

**Humanities: American Drama** Since the early 1900s, the theater has been a center of American intellectual life. Great plays offered exciting stories, dynamic dialogue, and philosophical truth. The best American playwrights of the twentieth century, such as Thorton Wilder (*Our Town*), Arthur Miller (*Death of a Salesman*), Lorraine Hansberry (*Raisin in the Sun*), Edward Albee (*Who's Afraid of Virginia Woolf?*), Lillian Hellman (*The Children's Hour*), Eugene O'Neill (*Long Day's Journey into Night*), and Tennessee Williams (*The Glass Menagerie*), chronicled different aspects of the American experience. Invite students to research the work of one of these famous playwrights, including reviews of his or her shows by theater critics. Have students share their findings with the class. **(Research to Explore)**

NOTES

312 **Giles:** I never said my wife were a witch, Mr. Hale: I only said she were reading books!

313 **Hale:** Mr. Corey, exactly what complaint were made on your wife?

314 **Giles:** That bloody mongrel Walcott charge her. Y'see, he buy a pig of my wife four or five year ago, and the pig died soon after. So he come dancin' in for his money back. So my Martha, she says to him. "Walcott, if you haven't the wit to feed a pig properly, you'll not live to own many," she says. Now he goes to court and claims that from that day to this he cannot keep a pig alive for more than four weeks because my Martha bewitch them with her books!

315 *Enter* EZEKIEL CHEEVER. *A shocked silence.*

316 **Cheever:** Good evening to you, Proctor.

317 **Proctor:** Why, Mr. Cheever. Good evening.

318 **Cheever:** Good evening, all. Good evening, Mr. Hale.

319 **Proctor:** I hope you come not on business of the court.

320 **Cheever:** I do, Proctor, aye. I am clerk of the court now, y'know.

321 *Enter* MARSHAL HERRICK, *a man in his early thirties, who is somewhat shamefaced at the moment.*

322 **Giles:** It's a pity, Ezekiel, that an honest tailor might have gone to Heaven must burn in Hell. You'll burn for this, do you know it?

323 **Cheever:** You know yourself I must do as I'm told. You surely know that, Giles. And I'd as lief[3] you'd not be sending me to Hell. I like not the sound of it, I tell you: I like not the sound of it. *He fears* PROCTOR, *but starts to reach inside his coat.* Now believe me, Proctor, how heavy be the law, all its tonnage I do carry on my back tonight. *He takes out a warrant.* I have a warrant for your wife.

324 **Proctor,** *to* Hale: You said she were not charged!

325 **Hale:** I know nothin' of it. *To* CHEEVER: When were she charged?

326 **Cheever:** I am given sixteen warrant tonight, sir, and she is one.

327 **Proctor:** Who charged her?

328 **Cheever:** Why, Abigail Williams charge her.

329 **Proctor:** On what proof, what proof?

330 **Cheever,** *looking about the room:* Mr. Proctor, I have little time. The court bid me search your house, but I like not to search a house. So will you hand me any poppets that your wife may keep here?

331 **Proctor:** Poppets?

332 **Elizabeth:** I never kept no poppets, not since I were a girl.

**3. as lief** (leef) *adv.* rather.





## DIGITAL PERSPECTIVES

**Illuminating the Text** Call student attention to the introduction of a poppet in paragraph 330. A poppet is a small doll. Sometimes, poppets were made to represent a person on whom a magic spell would be cast. Most poppets are made out of cloth, like a rag doll, but they can also be made out of wax, clay, or other materials. Poppets have been used in an effort to control people for centuries. Practitioners of "magic" believe that if they make a poppet, anything they do to it will affect the person it represents. Poppets have also been used with healing spells. For example, believers say if someone suffers from backaches, they can stick a needle in a poppet's back, then slowly remove it to take away the real person's pain. Encourage interested students to go online to find out more about how poppets have been used through history, beginning with the ancient Egyptians and Greeks. **(Research to Explore)**

333 **Cheever,** *embarrassed, glancing toward the mantel where sits* MARY WARREN'S *poppet:* I spy a poppet, Goody Proctor.

334 **Elizabeth:** Oh! *Going for it:* Why, this is Mary's.

335 **Cheever,** *shyly:* Would you please to give it to me?

336 **Elizabeth,** *handing it to him, asks* HALE: Has the court discovered a text in poppets now?

337 **Cheever,** *carefully holding the poppet:* Do you keep any others in this house?

338 **Proctor:** No, nor this one either till tonight. What signifies a poppet?

339 **Cheever:** Why, a poppet—*he gingerly turns the poppet over*—a poppet may signify—Now, woman, will you please to come with me?

340 **Proctor:** She will not! *To* ELIZABETH: Fetch Mary here.

341 **Cheever,** *ineptly reaching toward* ELIZABETH: No, no, I am forbid to leave her from my sight.

342 **Proctor,** *pushing his arm away:* You'll leave her out of sight and out of mind, Mister. Fetch Mary, Elizabeth. ELIZABETH *goes upstairs.*

343 **Hale:** What signifies a poppet, Mr. Cheever?

344 **Cheever,** *turning the poppet over in his hands:* Why, they say it may signify that she—*he has lifted the poppet's skirt, and his eyes widen in astonished fear.* Why, this, this—

345 **Proctor,** *reaching for the poppet:* What's there?

346 **Cheever:** Why—*He draws out a long needle from the poppet*—it is a needle! Herrick, Herrick, it is a needle!

347 HERRICK *comes toward him.*

348 **Proctor,** *angrily, bewildered:* And what signifies a needle!

349 **Cheever,** *his hands shaking:* Why, this go hard with her, Proctor, this—I had my doubts, Proctor. I had my doubts, but here's calamity.

350 *To* HALE, *showing the needle:* You see it, sir, it is a needle!

351 **Hale:** Why? What meanin' has it?

352 **Cheever,** *wide-eyed, trembling:* The girl, the Williams girl, Abigail Williams, sir. She sat to dinner in Reverend Parris's house tonight, and without word nor warnin' she falls to the floor. Like a struck beast, he says, and screamed a scream that a bull would weep to hear. And he goes to save her, and, stuck two inches in the flesh of her belly, he draw a needle out. And demandin' of her how she come to be so stabbed, she—*to* PROCTOR *now*—testify it were your wife's familiar spirit pushed it in.

353 **Proctor:** Why, she done it herself! *To* HALE: I hope you're not takin' this for proof, Mister!

NOTES

**CLOSE READ**

**ANNOTATE:** In paragraph 352, mark details that add vividness and drama to Cheever's account of the dinner scene.

**QUESTION:** Why does Miller give Cheever these strong, descriptive lines?

**CONCLUDE:** What is the effect of this description?







## CLOSE READ

Remind students that an author chooses words that will have an impact on a reader. You may wish to model the Close Read using the following think-aloud format. Possible responses to questions on the Student page are included.

**ANNOTATE:** As I read paragraph 352, I notice and mark the details that add interest and drama to Cheever's account of the dinner scene.

**QUESTION:** I think Miller gives Cheever these strong, descriptive lines so that the audience immediately grasps the importance of the needle in the poppet and its connection to Abigail's accusation.

**CONCLUDE:** The effect is to bring the scene to life for the audience.

## CLOSER LOOK

### Analyzing Style

Students may have marked paragraphs 360 through 369 during their first read. Use these lines to help students understand the author's use of language. Encourage them to talk about the annotations that they marked. You may want to model a close read with the class based on the highlights shown in the text.

**ANNOTATE:** Have students mark details in paragraphs 360 through 369 where the author has used a dash (—), or have students participate while you highlight them.

**QUESTION:** Guide students to consider what these details might tell them. Ask what a reader can infer from the use of dashes in the lines, and accept student responses.

**Possible response:** I think a reader can infer that the character is unsure about what to say.

**CONCLUDE:** Help students to formulate conclusions about the importance of this style in the text. Ask students why the writer chose to use dashes. Could he have used commas or some other punctuation?

**Possible response:** The author might have used dashes rather than adding more stage directions to tell actors to pause before speaking as if they are flustered or unsure; the author might have used commas but a dash gives extra emphasis to the fact that the speaker is taking his or her time, and everything else in the story is moving so fast.

Remind students that an **author's style** includes every feature of a writer's use of language and that authors choose their words and punctuation very carefully to enable them to convey their precise meaning and tone. The use of dashes to indicate an interruption in thought can be useful not only in plays, but in prose. Using the dashes the author can picture a character as frightened, as in "I—I—I—just saw the monster!" or just hesitant to answer, as in "M—m—my homework, ma'am?" Dashes can add interest to your writing—as long as you don't overdo it.

NOTES

354 Hale, *struck by the proof, is silent.*

355 **Cheever:** 'Tis hard proof! *To* HALE: I find here a poppet Goody Proctor keeps. I have found it, sir. And in the belly of the poppet a needle's stuck. I tell you true, Proctor, I never warranted to see such proof of Hell, and I bid you obstruct me not, for I—

356 *Enter* ELIZABETH *with* MARY WARREN. PROCTOR, *seeing* MARY WARREN, *draws her by the arm to* HALE.

357 **Proctor:** Here now! Mary, how did this poppet come into my house?

358 **Mary Warren,** *frightened for herself, her voice very small*: What poppet's that, sir?

359 **Proctor,** *impatiently, points at the doll in* CHEEVER'S *hand*: This poppet, this poppet.

360 **Mary Warren,** *evasively, looking at it*: Why, I—I think it is mine.

361 **Proctor:** It is your poppet, is it not?

362 **Mary Warren,** *not understanding the direction of this*: It—is, sir.

363 **Proctor:** And how did it come into this house?

364 **Mary Warren,** *glancing about at the avid faces*: Why—I made it in the court, sir, and—give it to Goody Proctor tonight.

365 **Proctor,** *to* HALE: Now, sir—do you have it?

366 **Hale:** Mary Warren, a needle have been found inside this poppet.

367 **Mary Warren,** *bewildered*: Why, I meant no harm by it, sir.

368 **Proctor,** *quickly*: You stuck that needle in yourself?

369 **Mary Warren:** I—I believe I did, sir, I—

370 **Proctor,** *to* HALE: What say you now?

371 **Hale,** *watching* MARY WARREN *closely*: Child, you are certain this be your natural memory? May it be, perhaps that someone conjures you even now to say this?

372 **Mary Warren:** Conjures me? Why, no, sir, I am entirely myself, I think. Let you ask Susanna Walcott—she saw me sewin' it in court. *Or better still*: Ask Abby. Abby sat beside me when I made it.

373 **Proctor,** *to* HALE, *of* CHEEVER: Bid him begone. Your mind is surely settled now. Bid him out, Mr. Hale.

374 **Elizabeth:** What signifies a needle?

375 **Hale:** Mary—you charge a cold and cruel murder on Abigail.

376 **Mary Warren:** Murder! I charge no—

377 **Hale:** Abigail were stabbed tonight; a needle were found stuck into her belly—

378 **Elizabeth:** And she charges me?

379 **Hale:** Aye.

380 **Elizabeth,** *her breath knocked out*: Why—! The girl is murder! She must be ripped out of the world!

381 **Cheever,** *pointing at* ELIZABETH: You've heard that, sir! Ripped out of the world! Herrick, you heard it!

382 **Proctor,** *suddenly snatching the warrant out of* CHEEVER'S *hands*: Out with you.

383 **Cheever:** Proctor, you dare not touch the warrant.

384 **Proctor,** *ripping the warrant*: Out with you!

385 **Cheever:** You've ripped the Deputy Governor's warrant, man!

386 **Proctor:** Damn the Deputy Governor! Out of my house!

387 **Hale:** Now, Proctor, Proctor!

388 **Proctor:** Get y'gone with them! You are a broken minister.

389 **Hale:** Proctor, if she is innocent, the court—

390 **Proctor:** If *she* is innocent! Why do you never wonder if Parris be innocent, or Abigail? Is the accuser always holy now? Were they born this morning as clean as God's fingers? I'll tell you what's walking Salem—vengeance is walking Salem. We are what we always were in Salem, but now the little crazy children are jangling the keys of the kingdom, and common vengeance writes the law! This warrant's vengeance! I'll not give my wife to vengeance!

391 **Elizabeth:** I'll go, John—

392 **Proctor:** You will not go!

393 **Herrick:** I have nine men outside. You cannot keep her. The law binds me, John. I cannot budge.

394 **Proctor,** *to* HALE, *ready to break him*: Will you see her taken?

395 **Hale:** Proctor, the court is just—

396 **Proctor:** Pontius Pilate![4] God will not let you wash your hands of this!

397 **Elizabeth:** John—I think I must go with them. *He cannot bear to look at her*. Mary, there is bread enough for the morning; you will bake, in the afternoon. Help Mr. Proctor as you were his daughter—you owe me that, and much more. *She is fighting her weeping. To* PROCTOR: When the children wake, speak nothing of witchcraft—it will frighten them.

398 *She cannot go on.*

399 **Proctor:** I will bring you home. I will bring you soon.

400 **Elizabeth:** Oh, John, bring me soon!

401 **Proctor:** I will fall like an ocean on that court! Fear nothing, Elizabeth.

402 **Elizabeth,** *with great fear*: I will fear nothing. *She looks about the room, as though to fix it in her mind*. Tell the children I have gone to visit someone sick.

NOTES

4. **Pontius Pilate** Roman governor who condemned Jesus to be crucified. Pilate washed his hands before the crowd to show that he refused to take responsibility for Jesus' death.





## CROSS-CURRICULAR PERSPECTIVES

**Humanities** Review paragraph 396. Explain that Pontius Pilate knew Jesus had been unjustly convicted and offered the crowd a choice: crucify either Jesus or the robber Barabbas. When the people chose Jesus, Pilate literally washed his hands in front of the crowd to show that he was not responsible—becoming a symbol of false innocence. Ask students: *How is Proctor's allusion to Pontius Pilate an insult to Hale?* Help students conclude that it suggests that even though Hale denies responsibility, he will knowingly allow the fraud to go forward.

NOTES

403 *She walks out the door.* HERRICK *and* CHEEVER *behind her. For a moment,* PROCTOR *watches from the doorway. The clank of chain is heard.*

404 **Proctor:** Herrick! Herrick, don't chain her! *He rushes out the door. From outside*: Damn you, man, you will not chain her! Off with them! I'll not have it! I will not have her chained!

405 *There are other men's voices against his.* HALE, *in a fever of guilt and uncertainty, turns from the door to avoid the sight*: MARY WARREN *bursts into tears and sits weeping.* GILES COREY *calls to* HALE.

406 **Giles:** And yet silent, minister? It is fraud, you know it is fraud! What keeps you, man?

407 PROCTOR *is half braced, half pushed into the room by two deputies and* HERRICK.

408 **Proctor:** I'll pay you, Herrick. I will surely pay you!

409 **Herrick,** *panting*: In God's name, John, I cannot help myself. I must chain them all. Now let you keep inside this house till I am gone! *He goes out with his deputies.*

## PERSONALIZE FOR LEARNING

### English Language Support

**Complex Characters** Review John Proctor's actions, ending with paragraphs 404–408. Have English Learners describe what makes a character static or dynamic. Then ask: *Is John Proctor a static or a dynamic character in this play?* Have students use the word *static* or *dynamic* as they offer evidence that John Proctor is a dynamic character; remind them to include text evidence, such as quotations and paraphrases. You may wish each student to write an individual response, or list the group's ideas on the board. **ALL LEVELS**

DIGITAL PERSPECTIVES

410 PROCTOR *stands there, gulping air. Horses and a wagon creaking are heard.*

411 **Hale,** *in great uncertainty*: Mr. Proctor—

412 **Proctor:** Out of my sight!

413 **Hale:** Charity, Proctor, charity. What I have heard in her favor, I will not fear to testify in court. God help me. I cannot judge her guilty or innocent—I know not. Only this consider: the world goes mad, and it profit nothing you should lay the cause to the vengeance of a little girl.

414 **Proctor:** You are a coward! Though you be ordained in God's own tears, you are a coward now!

415 **Hale:** Proctor, I cannot think God be provoked so grandly by such a petty cause. The jails are packed—our greatest judges sit in Salem now—and hangin's promised. Man, we must look to cause proportionate. Were there murder done, perhaps, and never brought to light? Abomination? Some secret blasphemy that stinks to Heaven? Think on cause, man, and let you help me to discover it. For there's your way, believe it, there is your only way, when such confusion strikes upon the world. *He goes to* GILES *and* FRANCIS. Let you counsel among yourselves; think on your village and what may have drawn from heaven such thundering wrath upon you all. I shall pray God open up our eyes.

416 HALE *goes out.*

417 **Francis,** *struck by* HALE'S *mood*: I never heard no murder done in Salem.

418 **Proctor—***he has been reached by* HALE'S *words*: Leave me, Francis, leave me.

419 **Giles,** *shaken*: John—tell me, are we lost?

420 **Proctor:** Go home now, Giles. We'll speak on it tomorrow.

421 **Giles:** Let you think on it. We'll come early, eh?

422 **Proctor:** Aye. Go now, Giles.

423 **Giles:** Good night, then.

424 GILES COREY *goes out. After a moment*:

425 **Mary Warren,** *in a fearful squeak of a voice*: Mr. Proctor, very likely they'll let her come home once they're given proper evidence.

426 **Proctor:** You're coming to the court with me, Mary. You will tell it in the court.

427 **Mary Warren:** I cannot charge murder on Abigail.

428 **Proctor,** *moving menacingly toward her*: You will tell the court how that poppet come here and who stuck the needle in.

429 **Mary Warren:** She'll kill me for sayin' that! PROCTOR *continues toward her.* Abby'll charge lechery[5] on you, Mr. Proctor!

430 **Proctor,** *halting*: She's told you!

NOTES

**CLOSE READ**

**ANNOTATE:** In paragraph 415, mark words and phrases that relate to causes and effects.

**QUESTION:** Why does Miller include this speech with this seeming expression of logic?

**CONCLUDE:** What is the effect of this speech?

5. **lechery** (LEHCH uhr ee) *n.* lust; adultery—a charge almost as serious as witchcraft in this Puritan community.

## CLOSE READ

Remind students to focus on what a character says and how he or she says it. This will help you know what is most important to that character. You may wish to model the Close Read using the following think-aloud format. Possible responses to questions on the student page are included.

**ANNOTATE:** As I read paragraph 415, I notice and highlight words and phrases that point to causes and effects.

**QUESTION:** I think that Miller has Hale include this language that has to do with logic so that the audience will understand that Hale believes God would not bring such calamity to a town unless the town had evil secrets.

**CONCLUDE:** The effect of the speech is to make the audience realize that Proctor may feel responsible because of his own sin of adultery. The audience may also realize that, since Hale wants to blame an unknown evil instead of the lying girls for the town's troubles, it will not be easy to save the accused.

TEACHING

## Comprehension Check

**Possible responses**

1. Hale visits the Proctors to question them and find out if they are good Christians.
2. They confess to being witches.
3. Cheever finds a poppet with a needle stuck in the belly.
4. The Proctors discuss growing hysteria in Salem, and Elizabeth urges John to tell the court that Abigail is lying. As they argue over his infidelity, Reverend Hale arrives. He questions them about being good Christians. Some of their answers are unusual but Hale is impressed by their honesty. Nonetheless, Cheever and Herrick bring a warrant for Elizabeth's arrest. They find a doll with a needle in its stomach and say that Elizabeth used it to put a needle in Abigail's stomach. Even though Mary confesses that she gave Elizabeth the doll, they take Elizabeth away. Proctor threatens to expose Abigail unless Mary confesses that all the claims of witchcraft are lies.

## Research

**Research to Explore** If students struggle to come up with a detail to research, you may want to suggest that they focus on "habeas corpus." Have them explain this right, guaranteed by the Constitution, and how it might have influenced the proceedings at the Salem witch trials.

NOTES

431 **Mary Warren:** I have known it, sir. She'll ruin you with it. I know she will.

432 **Proctor,** *hesitating, and with deep hatred of himself*: Good. Then her saintliness is done with. MARY *backs from him.* We will slide together into our pit; you will tell the court what you know.

433 **Mary Warren,** *in terror*: I cannot, they'll turn on me—

434 PROCTOR *strides and catches her, and she is repeating, "I cannot. I cannot!"*

435 **Proctor:** My wife will never die for me! I will bring your guts into your mouth but that goodness will not die for me!

436 **Mary Warren,** *struggling to escape him*: I cannot do it. I cannot!

437 **Proctor,** *grasping her by the throat as though he would strangle her*: Make your peace with it! Now Hell and Heaven grapple on our backs, and all our old pretense is ripped away—make your peace! *He throws her to the floor, where she sobs. "I cannot. I cannot . . ." And now, half to himself, staring, and turning to the open door*: Peace. It is a providence, and no great change; we are only what we always were, but naked now. *He walks as though toward a great horror, facing the open sky.* Aye, naked! And the wind, God's icy wind, will blow!

438 *And she is over and over again sobbing, "I cannot, I cannot. I cannot" as*

THE CURTAIN FALLS

## Comprehension Check

**Complete the following items after you finish your first read.**

1. Why does Hale visit the Proctors' home?
2. What do some of the accused, such as Sarah Good, do to save themselves from hanging?
3. What evidence of Elizabeth's guilt does Cheever find?
4. **Notebook** Write a summary of Act II of *The Crucible*.

## RESEARCH

**Research to Explore** Conduct research on an aspect of the text you find interesting. For example, you may want to learn about the Court of Oyer and Terminer, established to try and convict Salem witches.

MAKING MEANING

## Close Read the Text

Reread paragraphs 334–339. Mark Cheever's answers to the question "What signifies a poppet?" What do his replies indicate about his knowledge of the significance of the poppet?

THE CRUCIBLE, ACT II

## Analyze the Text

**CITE TEXTUAL EVIDENCE** to support your answers.

Notebook **Respond to these questions.**

1. (a) **Interpret** How does news of the arrest of Rebecca Nurse affect the Proctors? (b) **Connect** What does this news suggest about Abigail Williams's changing status in Salem? Explain.
2. **Evaluate** Is Hale a good person? Why, or why not?
3. **Infer** Did Mary Warren know how the poppet she gave Elizabeth would be used? Explain.
4. **Predict** What does the dialogue of Cheever and Herrick suggest will happen to Elizabeth? What chance does she have to prove her innocence?

LANGUAGE DEVELOPMENT

## Concept Vocabulary

condemnation    magistrates    proceedings

**Why These Words?** The three concept vocabulary words are all related to courts of law. What other words in Act II relate to this concept?

**Practice**

Notebook Write a paragraph about a court case, real or imaginary, that uses all three concept vocabulary words. Make sure the context of the paragraph demonstrates each word's meaning.

## Word Study

Notebook **Technical Words** Most professions have specialized vocabulary—words that are particular to the field, or that have specific meanings when used in that context. In *The Crucible,* Arthur Miller uses legal terminology, such as *magistrates* and *proceedings. Magistrates* applies only to the field of law. However, *proceedings,* when used without the final *s,* has a general meaning in everyday speech. It is a form of the verb *proceed,* meaning "continue a course of action."

1. Find two more words in Act II that are examples of legal terminology. Write those words and their definitions.
2. Use a legal dictionary to locate three other words used in the field of law. Write those definitions. If any of the terms also have meanings in general speech, write those definitions as well.

**WORD NETWORK**

Add words related to fear from the text to your Word Network.

**STANDARDS**

Language

• Consult general and specialized reference materials, both print and digital, to find the pronunciation of a word or determine or clarify its precise meaning, its part of speech, its etymology, or its standard usage.

• Acquire and use accurately general academic and domain-specific words and phrases, sufficient for reading, writing, speaking, and listening at the college and career readiness level; demonstrate independence in gathering vocabulary knowledge when considering a word or phrase important to comprehension or expression.





### VOCABULARY DEVELOPMENT

**Graphic Organizer** Have students find and use other forms of the word *condemnation* on a chart and in sentences. When they finish, encourage them to do the same for the other two vocabulary words.

| Word | Part of Speech | Meaning |
|---|---|---|
| condemnation | noun | disapproval or blame |
| condemn | verb | convict or denounce |
| condemning | adjective | accusing or judging |

DIGITAL PERSPECTIVES

## Jump Start

CLOSE READ Remind students that an old saying is "One lie leads to another." *Has this ever happened to someone you know? Did the person finally tell the truth?*

### Close Read the Text 

Possible response:

He avoids answering the question. This signifies that he believes a poppet has to do with witchcraft.

### Analyze the Text

Possible responses:

1. (a) They are very upset. **DOK 1** (b) It suggests that Abigail Williams has more power than even the most respected citizens of Salem. **DOK 2**
2. Yes, because he is clearly well-intentioned. **DOK 3**
3. No, she didn't know what Abigail planned to do. **DOK 3**
4. Unless John makes Mary confess, Elizabeth will be found guilty. Her only chance is for John to force Mary to tell all and confess to his own sin. **DOK 3**

### Concept Vocabulary

**Why These Words?** Possible responses: *court, judges, fraud, jail, evidence, accused, testify, tried, charged, warrant*

**Practice**

Responses will vary but should reflect correct use of the vocabulary.

**Word Network**

Possible words: *concern, frightened, terrified, quaking, danger, uneasy, worried, shaken, terror*

### Word Study

For more support, see **Concept Vocabulary and Word Study.**

Possible responses

1. *court; trial*
2. *adjudication, affidavit, deposition*

**FORMATIVE ASSESSMENT**

**Analyze the Text**

**If** students fail to cite evidence, **then** remind them to support their ideas with specific information from the text.

**Concept Vocabulary**

**If** students fail to see the connection between the words, **then** have them read the definitions again.

**Word Study**

**If** students cannot find legal jargon, **then** suggest they use a search engine on the Internet.
For Reteach and Practice, see **Word Study: Technical Words (RP).**

## Analyze Craft and Structure

**Literary Elements in Drama** Remind students that without conflict, there is no plot. Miller has filled *The Crucible* with an abundance of external conflict between people and between people and society, their community and their religion, and inner conflict of people and their consciences. All the tension of the conflicts make Miller's play exciting. For more support, see **Analyze Craft and Structure: Literary Elements in Drama.**

### Practice

Possible responses

1. (a) The innocent people struggle against a society that calls them guilty. **DOK 3** (b) The internal conflict is that they must confess or be killed. **DOK 2**
2. (a) Elizabeth is angry with John for his affair and has trouble forgiving or trusting him; John feels guilty about the affair and is angry that Elizabeth won't trust him; they have different ideas about what's going on in Salem. **DOK 3** (b) Elizabeth's struggle to forgive and trust John, and John's struggle with guilt are internal; John's struggle to gain Elizabeth's forgiveness and trust and both of them fighting against Elizabeth's being accused by others of witchcraft are external. **DOK 3**
3. John hesitates because he has inner conflict over still feeling some attraction toward Abigail and feeling guilty for having an affair with a girl in his employ. He has external conflict because he fears her reprisal and he doesn't want his community to know about his infidelity. **DOK 3**
4. The conflict is the struggle of innocent people against accusers incited by revenge, newly found power, or childish hysteria. **DOK 3**

### FORMATIVE ASSESSMENT

### Analyze Craft and Structure

**If** students are unable to distinguish between internal and external conflict, **then** discuss the conflicts in another familiar drama and identify examples of both. For Reteach and Practice, see **Analyze Craft and Structure: Literary Elements in Drama (RP).**

THE CRUCIBLE, ACT II

## Analyze Craft and Structure

**Literary Elements in Drama** All narrative writing is driven by **conflict,** or a struggle between opposing forces. The conflict is introduced, developed, and resolved through the **plot,** or the story's sequence of related events. The plot unfolds over a series of stages, often referred to as the "dramatic arc." These stages include the rising action, climax, falling action, and resolution. There are two broad categories of conflict that are explored in literature. In a complex narrative like this play, there are often numerous conflicts, and most characters experience both types:

- **External conflict** occurs between a character and an outside force, such as another person, society as a whole, nature, or even fate.
- **Internal conflict** occurs within the mind of a character who is torn between conflicting values or desires.

In the rising action of a play, the central conflicts are introduced and begin to build. These conflicts then intensify, and they often lead to other conflicts. It is important to note that characters' internal conflicts can be just as crucial to the plot as the external conflicts.

### Practice

**CITE TEXTUAL EVIDENCE** to support your answers.

**Answer these questions.**

1. (a) What external conflict confronts the people who are charged with witchcraft? (b) Describe the internal conflict that the accused face.
2. (a) What conflicts do Elizabeth and John Proctor struggle with in their marriage? (b) Which of these conflicts are internal and which are external? Explain.
3. Proctor knows that Abigail Williams is a fraud. What conflicts cause him to hesitate about revealing this knowledge?
4. What profound conflict does Proctor note when he confronts Hale with these words?
"I'll tell you what's walking Salem—vengeance is walking Salem. We are what we always were ...but now the little crazy children are jangling the keys of the kingdom ..."

STANDARDS

**Reading Literature**

- Analyze the impact of the author's choices regarding how to develop and relate elements of a story or drama.
- Analyze how an author's choices concerning how to structure specific parts of a text contribute to its overall structure and meaning as well as its aesthetic impact.





### PERSONALIZE FOR LEARNING

**Strategic Support**

**Literary Analysis: Conflict** Have students consider how John Proctor's past relationship with Abigail contributes to the conflict he has with his society at large. Use the following think aloud to model the skill of examining conflict. Say: *I know that John had an affair with Abigail, resulting in inner conflict that has made him reluctant to expose her. His ending the affair and wanting nothing to do with her has alienated Abigail, adding to the external conflict with her because she will do anything to get him back. Now she has manipulated her society with false charges that endanger John's wife. So John's affair is at the root of many of his current problems with his society.* Encourage students to analyze the internal and external conflict for another character, such as Cheever or Hale. Have students share their findings.

EFFECTIVE EXPRESSION

## Speaking and Listening

**Assignment**

Participate in a **whole-class discussion** about whether Mary Warren will defend or condemn Elizabeth Proctor in court. Refresh your memory by reviewing Act II. Then, follow these steps to prepare for the discussion.

1. **Consider the Situation** Review your notes from Act II. Jot down your thoughts about the situation in Salem on the evening of Elizabeth's arrest. Think about how these circumstances might affect Mary.
2. **Analyze Mary Warren's Character** Scan Acts I and II to find details about Mary's character. Use the chart to note reasons she may lie in court and reasons she may tell the truth. For each reason you list, jot down reminders of textual evidence you might refer to during the discussion.

| REASONS MARY MAY LIE IN COURT | REASONS MARY MAY TELL THE TRUTH |
|---|---|
| She is afraid of the other girls.<br>She is afraid of what will happen to her if she refuses to testify. | She is a Christian and will not lie.<br>She is afraid of John Proctor.<br>She regrets what she has done. |

3. **Prepare for the Discussion** Review your notes. Decide which is stronger—the evidence that suggests Mary will tell the truth or the evidence that suggests she will lie. Make a prediction as to what she will do and why.
4. **Participate in the Discussion** During the discussion, listen carefully to your classmates. Remember you can change your viewpoint of Mary when presented with evidence you had not previously considered. Use the evaluation guide to consider the quality of the discussion.

**EVALUATION GUIDE**

Rate each statement on a scale of 1 (not demonstrated) to 5 (demonstrated).

- [ ] Students presented a clear prediction about Mary Warren.
- [ ] Students supported predictions with evidence from Acts I and II.
- [ ] Students spoke clearly and expressively.
- [ ] Students who were not speaking listened respectfully and responded with relevant information.

**EVIDENCE LOG**

Before moving on to Act III, go to your Evidence Log and record what you learned from Act II of *The Crucible*.

**STANDARDS**

**Speaking and Listening**

Come to discussions prepared, having read and researched material under study; explicitly draw on that preparation by referring to evidence from texts and other research on the topic or issue to stimulate a thoughtful, well-reasoned exchange of ideas.





DIGITAL PERSPECTIVES   

## Speaking and Listening

1. **Consider the Situation** Remind students that it is because of Mary that Elizabeth is in danger. Allow time for students to go over their notes.
2. **Analyze Mary Warren's Character** Remind students to find logical textual evidence about Mary in both acts. See possible responses in the chart on the student page.
3. **Prepare for the Discussion** Encourage students to carefully review the evidence before making a prediction. Remind them that when we know how someone has acted in the past, we have a better chance of predicting, or inferring, how he or she will deal with a problem in the future.
4. **Participate in the Discussion** Remind students that a discussion is a give-and-take situation. Only one person should talk at a time, and everyone should be allowed to voice his or her opinion.

For more support, see **Speaking and Listening: Whole-Class Discussion.**

**Evidence Log** Support students in completing their Evidence Log. This paced activity will help prepare them for the Performance-Based Assessment at the end of the unit.

## PERSONALIZE FOR LEARNING

### English Language Development

**Technical Words** Ask pairs of students to locate in the selection five words from the same domain, be it farming, the law, or religion. **EMERGING**

Ask students why they think so many uneducated people in the play are often using legal terms. **EXPANDING**

Ask students in what ways the use of words from law and religion adds to the cohesion of the play. **BRIDGING**

An expanded **English Language Support Lesson** on Technical Words is available in the Interactive Teacher's Edition.

## FORMATIVE ASSESSMENT

### Speaking and Listening

- **If** students fail to cite evidence, **then** remind them to support their ideas with specific information from the text.
- **If** students struggle to take part in the whole-class discussion, **then** have them discuss what Mary will most likely do in a smaller group before entering into a large discussion group.

For Reteach and Practice, see **Speaking and Listening: Whole-Class Discussion (RP).**

### Selection Test

Administer the "The Crucible, Act II" Selection Test, which is available in both print and digital formats online in Assessments.

# *The Crucible*, Act III

**AUDIO SUMMARIES**
Audio Summaries of Act III of *The Crucible* are available online in both English and Spanish in the Interactive Teacher's Edition or Unit Resources. Assigning these summaries prior to reading the selection may help students build additional background knowledge and set a context for their first read.

## Summary

In Act III of Arthur Miller's drama *The Crucible*, Mr. Corey and Mr. Nurse come to the courthouse to disrupt the trial by saying that the girls are lying about the witchcraft. Judge Danforth does not believe them. John Proctor and Mary Warren arrive and try to save Elizabeth by denying Abigail's claims. The judge talks to Mary, and Rev. Parris asks her to show how she and the other girls fainted. When Mary is unable do this, Abigail and the other girls accuse Mary. While Hale is now convinced that Abigail and the other girls are lying, the judge looks for more evidence by questioning Mary, Elizabeth, and Abigail.

### Insight

The third act reveals how some community members attempt to manipulate fear for personal gain and to settle scores. For example, Thomas Putnam is accused of having his daughter charge George Jacobs with witchcraft in order to get Jacobs's property. The courtroom—awash in lies, half-truths, and innuendo—has supreme authority. As Judge Danforth says, "[a] person is either with this court or he must be counted against it, there be no road between."

ESSENTIAL QUESTION:
How do we respond when challenged by fear?

## Connection to Essential Question

Once the charges of witchcraft have reached the courtroom, it becomes more difficult to sort out the truth from the rumors. The power of the court—a theocratic institution in this case—renders its decisions as virtually infallible, thereby adding more credibility to the rumors of witchcraft.

WHOLE CLASS LEARNING PERFORMANCE TASK
Could any of the characters in *The Crucible* have done more to end the hysteria in Salem?

UNIT PERFORMANCE-BASED ASSESSMENT
Is fear always a harmful emotion?

## Connection to Performance Tasks

**Whole-Class Learning Performance Task** Although Mary Warren attempts to tell the truth, she too becomes afraid of becoming a victim of the out-of-control rumors that have overtaken the community and the courtroom. Despite the attempts of others, including John Proctor, Mr. Correy, and Mr. Nurse, no one seems capable of ending the hysteria.

**Unit Performance-Based Assessment** Act III of *The Crucible* extends the idea that fear is a harmful emotion. Many of the characters' statements and actions in the courtroom are based on fear. Even those with status in the community and with a desire to end the community's hysteria are unable to do so.

DIGITAL PERSPECTIVES

Audio

Video

Document

Annotation Highlights

EL Highlights

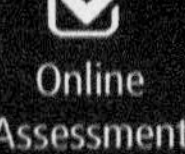
Online Assessment

## LESSON RESOURCES

| | Making Meaning | Language Development |
|---|---|---|
| Lesson | **First Read**<br>**Close Read**<br>**Analyze the Text**<br>**Analyze Craft and Structure** | **Concept Vocabulary**<br>**Word Study**<br>**Author's Style** |
| **Instructional Standards** | **RL.10** By the end of grade 11, read and comprehend literature . . .<br>**RL.3** Analyze the impact of the author's choices . . .<br>**RL.6** Analyze a case in which grasping point of view . . . | **L.5** Demonstrate understanding of figurative language . . .<br>**L.5.b** Analyze nuances in the meanings of words . . . |
| **STUDENT RESOURCES** | | |
| Available online in the Interactive Student Edition or Unit Resources | Selection Audio<br>First-Read Guide: Fiction<br>Close-Read Guide: Fiction | Word Network<br>Evidence Log |
| **TEACHER RESOURCES** | | |
| **Selection Resources** Available online in the Interactive Teacher's Edition or Unit Resources | Audio Summaries<br>Annotation Highlights<br>EL Highlights<br>English Language Support Lesson: Literary Devices<br>Analyze Craft and Structure: Character Development | Concept Vocabulary and Word Study<br>Author's Style: Literary Devices |
| **Reteach/Practice (RP)** Available online in the Interactive Teacher's Edition or Unit Resources | Analyze Craft and Structure: Character Development (RP) | Word Study: Connotation (RP)<br>Author's Style: Literary Devices (RP) |
| **Assessment** Available online in Assessments | Selection Test | |
| **My Resources** | A Unit 5 Answer Key is available online and in the Interactive Teacher's Edition. | |

# Reading Support

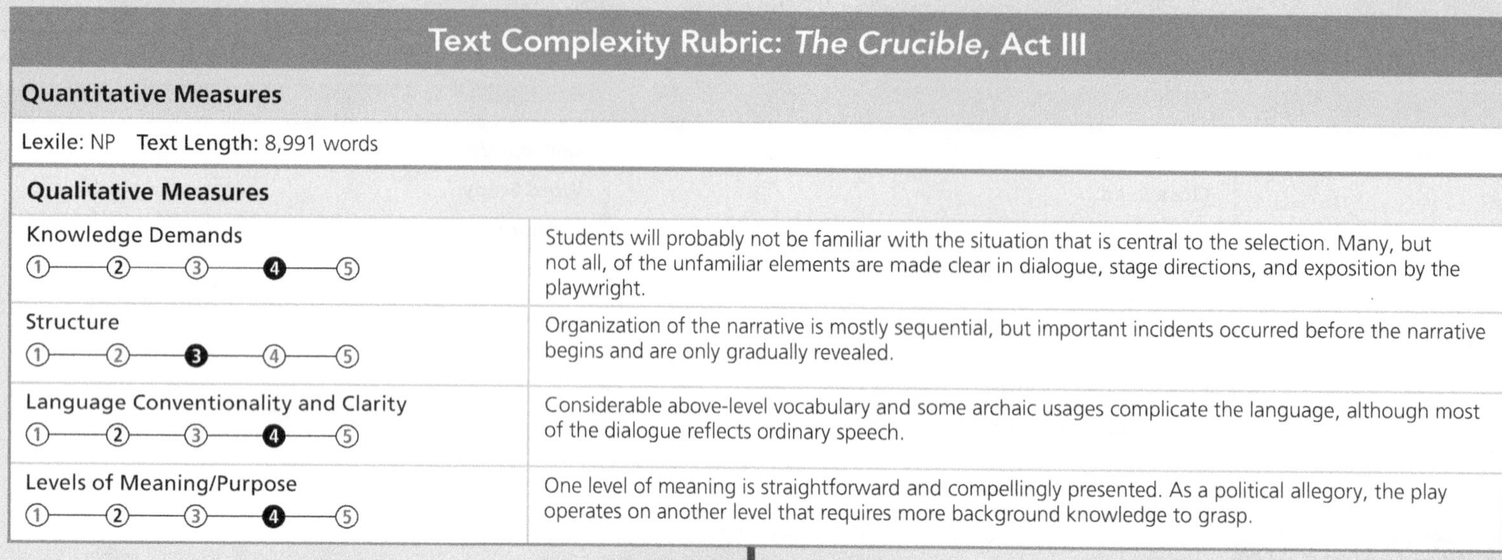

| Text Complexity Rubric: *The Crucible*, Act III | |
|---|---|
| **Quantitative Measures** | |
| **Lexile:** NP **Text Length:** 8,991 words | |
| **Qualitative Measures** | |
| Knowledge Demands ①—②—③—❹—⑤ | Students will probably not be familiar with the situation that is central to the selection. Many, but not all, of the unfamiliar elements are made clear in dialogue, stage directions, and exposition by the playwright. |
| Structure ①—②—❸—④—⑤ | Organization of the narrative is mostly sequential, but important incidents occurred before the narrative begins and are only gradually revealed. |
| Language Conventionality and Clarity ①—②—③—❹—⑤ | Considerable above-level vocabulary and some archaic usages complicate the language, although most of the dialogue reflects ordinary speech. |
| Levels of Meaning/Purpose ①—②—③—❹—⑤ | One level of meaning is straightforward and compellingly presented. As a political allegory, the play operates on another level that requires more background knowledge to grasp. |

DECIDE AND PLAN

## English Language Support

Provide English Learners with support for knowledge demands and language as they read the selection.

**Knowledge Demands** Before reading the text, review the background information with students. Have students complete sentence frames, such as *Giles Corey is trying to tell the judges _____. Judge Danforth believes that John Proctor is trying to* _____.

**Language** Students will probably have difficulty with the above-level vocabulary and deviations from Standard English. Explain to students that it is not necessary for them to understand every word, so long as they have a basic understanding of the dialogue.

## Strategic Support

Provide students with strategic support to ensure that they can successfully read the text.

**Knowledge Demands** After reading the background information, have students read again the section of the Historical Background information in which Arthur Miller explains his inspiration for the play.

**Language/Clarity** For students who have difficulty with the nonstandard English, especially with the misuse of verbs *was* and *were*, encourage them to change the forms to more standard ones and then reread the sentences or lines of dialogue.

## Challenge

Provide students who need to be challenged with ideas for how they can go beyond a simple interpretation of the text.

**Text Analysis** Pair students and have each pair choose one of the characters in this act. Ask them to go over any stage directions that describe this character, as well as the character's own words and actions, to determine what the character is like.

**Written Response** Have students write a brief character sketch of one of the characters in this act.

TEACH

## Read and Respond

Have students do their first read of the selection. Then have them complete their close read. Finally, work with them on the Making Meaning and Language Development activities.

# Standards Support Through Teaching and Learning Cycle

## IDENTIFY NEEDS

Analyze results of the Beginning-of-Year Assessment, focusing on the items relating to Unit 5. Also take into consideration student performance to this point and your observations of where particular students struggle.

## DECIDE AND PLAN

- If students have performed poorly on items matching these standards, then provide selection scaffolds before assigning them the on-level lesson provided in the Student Edition.
- If students have done well on the Beginning-of-Year Assessment, then challenge them to keep progressing and learning by giving them opportunities to practice the skills in depth.
- Use the Selection Resources listed on the Planning pages for *The Crucible,* Act III, to help students continually improve their ability to master the standards.

**Instructional Standards: The Crucible, Act III**

| | Catching Up | This Year | Looking Forward |
|---|---|---|---|
| **Reading** | You may wish to administer the **Analyze Craft and Structure: Character Development (RP)** worksheet to familiarize students with direct and indirect characterization.<br><br>Review the **Author's Style: Literary Devices (RP)** worksheet with students to better distinguish the types of irony. | **RL.3** Analyze the impact of the author's choices regarding how to develop and relate elements of a story or drama.<br><br>**RL.6** Analyze a case in which grasping point of view requires distinguishing what is directly stated in a text from what is really meant. | Challenge students to come up with examples of both types of characterizations from other works they are familiar with.<br><br>Have students identify popular examples of artists misusing the term "irony." |
| **Language** | Review the **Word Study: Connotation (RP)** worksheet with students to better familiarize them with connotation. | **L.5.b** Analyze nuances in the meanings of words with similar denotations. | Challenge students to consider how some words change connotation over time. |

## ANALYZE AND REVISE

- Analyze student work for evidence of student learning.
- Identify whether or not students have met the expectations in the standards.
- Identify implications for future instruction.

## TEACH

Implement the planned lesson, and gather evidence of student learning.

TEACHING

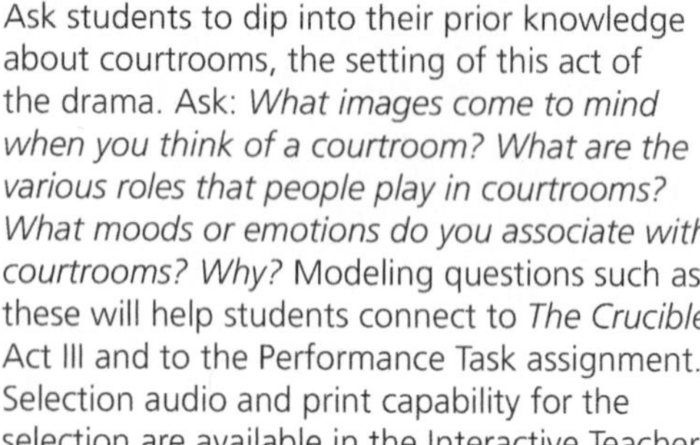

## Jump Start

FIRST READ Prior to students' first read, engage them in a discussion in which they predict what will happen next in the play. How will Elizabeth Proctor's arrest affect her? Her husband? John Hale? The community?

### *The Crucible*, Act III

Ask students to dip into their prior knowledge about courtrooms, the setting of this act of the drama. Ask: *What images come to mind when you think of a courtroom? What are the various roles that people play in courtrooms? What moods or emotions do you associate with courtrooms? Why?* Modeling questions such as these will help students connect to *The Crucible*, Act III and to the Performance Task assignment. Selection audio and print capability for the selection are available in the Interactive Teacher's Edition. Selection audio and print capability for the selection are available in the Interactive Teacher's Edition.

### Concept Vocabulary

Support students as they rank the words. Ask if they've ever heard, read, or used them. Reassure them that the definitions for these words are listed in the selection.

**FIRST READ**

As they read, students should perform the steps of the first read:

NOTICE: You may want to encourage students to notice how the change in setting heightens the tension among the characters in the play.

ANNOTATE: Remind students to mark lines of dialogue that seem especially important to the plot or theme of the play along with any words that are unfamiliar.

CONNECT: Encourage students to make connections with Acts I and II and also with any personal experience they have with courtrooms or trials.

RESPOND: Students will answer questions and write a summary to demonstrate understanding.

Point out to students that while they will always complete the Respond step at the end of the first read, the other steps will probably happen somewhat concurrently. You may wish to print copies of the **First-Read Guide: Fiction** for students to use.

**Remind students that during their first read, they should not answer the close-read questions that appear in the selection.**



MAKING MEANING

Playwright

**Arthur Miller**

# The Crucible, Act III

## Concept Vocabulary

You will encounter the following words as you read Act III of *The Crucible*. Before reading, note how familiar you are with each word. Then, rank the words in order from most familiar (1) to least familiar (3).

| WORD | YOUR RANKING |
|---|---|
| remorseless | |
| effrontery | |
| callously | |

After completing the first read, come back to the concept vocabulary and review your rankings. Mark changes to your original rankings as needed.

## First Read DRAMA

Apply these strategies as you conduct your first read. You will have an opportunity to complete the close-read notes after your first read.

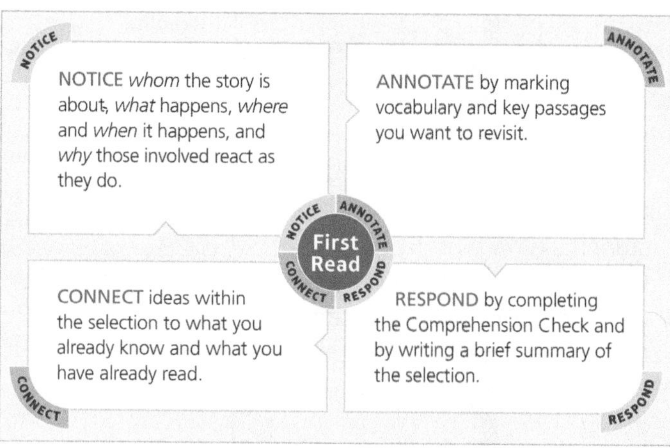

NOTICE *whom* the story is about, *what* happens, *where* and *when* it happens, and *why* those involved react as they do.
ANNOTATE by marking vocabulary and key passages you want to revisit.
CONNECT ideas within the selection to what you already know and what you have already read.
RESPOND by completing the Comprehension Check and by writing a brief summary of the selection.
First Read
NOTICE
ANNOTATE
CONNECT
RESPOND


STANDARDS

**Reading Literature**

By the end of grade 11, read and comprehend literature, including stories, dramas, and poems, in the grades 11–CCR text complexity band proficiently, with scaffolding as needed at the high end of the range.





## VOCABULARY DEVELOPMENT

**Concept Vocabulary Reinforcement** Students will benefit from additional examples and practice with the concept vocabulary. Reinforce their comprehension with "show you know" sentences. The first part of the sentence uses the vocabulary word in an appropriate context. The second part of the sentence—the "show-you-know" part—clarifies the first. Model the strategy with this example for *remorseless*: The child's *remorseless* attitude was shocking; after she made her little brother cry, she grinned.

Then, give students these first-part prompts, and ask them to create the clarification parts:

1. The candidate's *effrontery* was an insult to his opponents; ____.

**Possible response:** he claimed his victory was certain because of their incompetence.

2. The queen responded *callously* to her subjects' pleas for food; ____.

**Possible response:** she ignored them completely and ordered more cake.

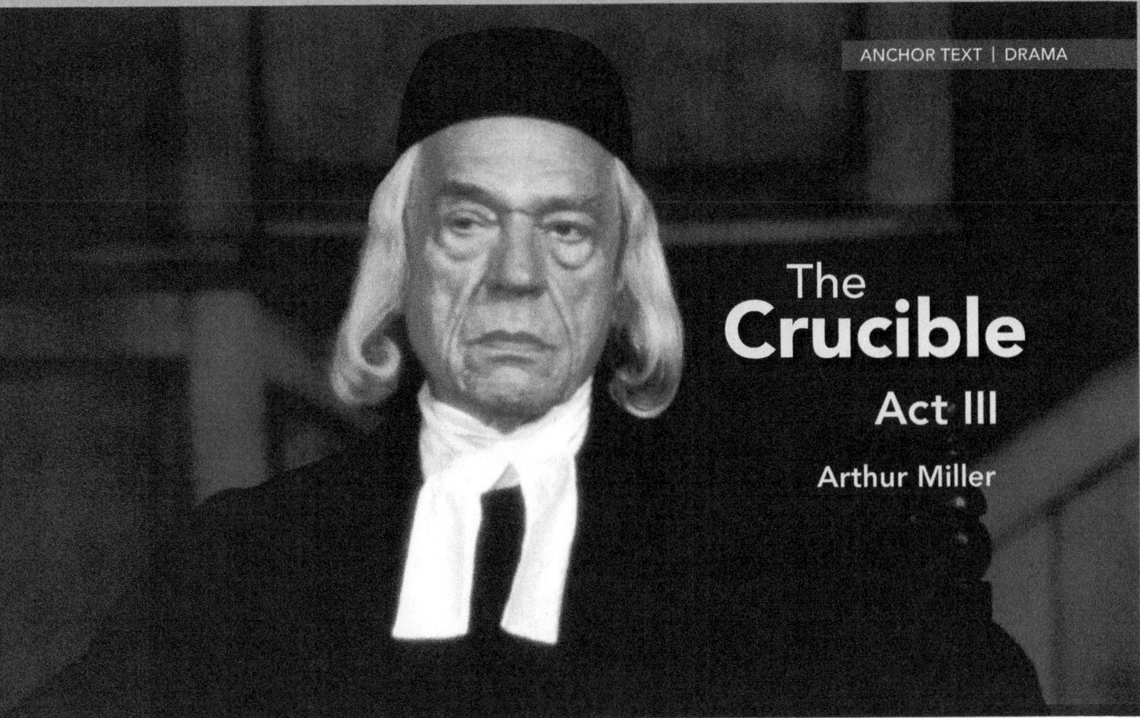


# The Crucible
## Act III
Arthur Miller

REVIEW AND ANTICIPATE

Act II ends as Elizabeth Proctor is accused of witchcraft and carted off to jail as a result of the scheming of Abigail Williams. John Proctor demands that Mary Warren tell the court the truth; Mary, though aware of Abigail's ploys, is terrified of exposing her. Find out how Mary handles this tricky and dangerous situation as you continue reading.

SCAN FOR MULTIMEDIA 

1 *The vestry room of the Salem meeting house, now serving as the anteroom of the General Court.*

2 *As the curtain rises, the room is empty, but for sunlight pouring through two high windows in the back wall. The room is solemn, even forbidding. Heavy beams jut out, boards of random widths make up the walls. At the right are two doors leading into the meeting house proper, where the court is being held. At the left another door leads outside.*

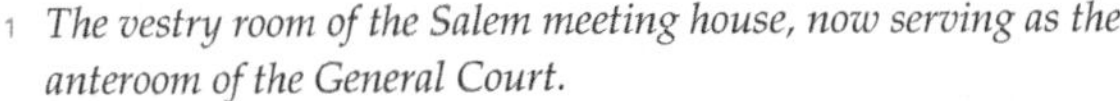

3 *There is a plain bench at the left, and another at the right. In the center a rather long meeting table, with stools and a considerable armchair snugged up to it.*

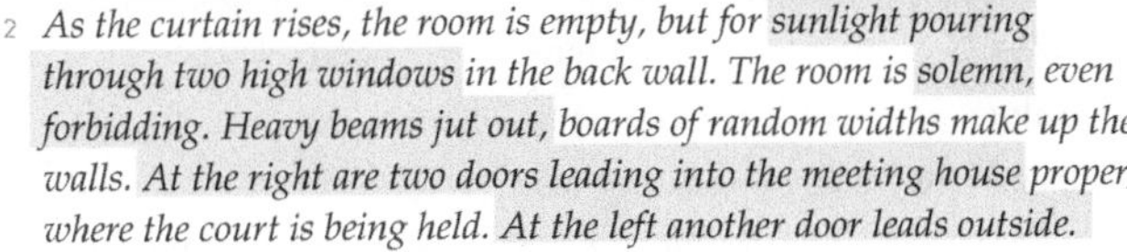

4 *Through the partitioning wall at the right we hear a prosecutor's voice,* JUDGE HATHORNE'S *, asking a question; then a woman's voice,* MARTHA COREY'S*, replying.*

NOTES





DIGITAL PERSPECTIVES   

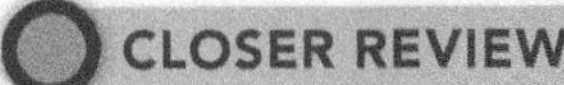
CLOSER REVIEW

### Interpret Symbols

Students may have noted paragraph 2 of the italicized stage directions during their first review. Use these directions to help students understand which details are important to note. Encourage them to talk about what they noted. You may want to model a close review with the class.

**ANNOTATE:** Have students note details in the stage directions that describe elements that might be symbols, or have students participate while you note them.

**QUESTION:** Guide students to consider what these details might tell them. Ask what a viewer can infer from the symbols, and accept student responses.

**Possible response:** The sunlight in the high windows may symbolize truth; the dark room with its heavy beams represents the opposite. The different doors might represent the two ways that these proceedings might go: right or wrong, enlightened or provincial, merciful or cruel.

**CONCLUDE:** Help students to formulate conclusions about the importance of these details in the text. Ask students why the author might have included these details.

**Possible response:** Miller uses details of setting to represent or foreshadow the action on the stage.

Remind students that a **symbol** is anything that stands for or represents something else. Explain to students that stage settings often have meaning and importance beyond simply reproducing the space in which the action takes place. Light or dark, bright colors or drab ones, cluttered or sparse, scattered or focused — details such as these comment on and help the audience understand the characters and actions they are going to see.

NOTES

5 **Hathorne's Voice:** Now, Martha Corey, there is abundant evidence in our hands to show that you have given yourself to the reading of fortunes. Do you deny it?

6 **Martha Corey's Voice:** I am innocent to a witch. I know not what a witch is.

7 **Hathorne's Voice:** How do you know, then, that you are not a witch?

8 **Martha Corey's Voice:** If I were, I would know it.

9 **Hathorne's Voice:** Why do you hurt these children?

10 **Martha Corey's Voice:** I do not hurt them. I scorn it!

11 **Giles's Voice,** *roaring*: I have evidence for the court!

12 *Voices of townspeople rise in excitement.*

13 **Danforth's Voice:** You will keep your seat!

14 **Giles's Voice:** Thomas Putnam is reaching out for land!

15 **Danforth's Voice:** Remove that man, Marshal!

16 **Giles's Voice:** You're hearing lies, lies!

17 *A roaring goes up from the people.*

18 **Hathorne's Voice:** Arrest him, excellency!

19 **Giles's Voice:** I have evidence. Why will you not hear my evidence?

20 *The door opens and* GILES *is half carried into the vestry room by* HERRICK.

21 **Giles:** Hands off, damn you, let me go!

22 **Herrick:** Giles, Giles!

23 **Giles:** Out of my way, Herrick! I bring evidence—

24 **Herrick:** You cannot go in there, Giles; it's a court!

25 *Enter* HALE *from the court.*

26 **Hale:** Pray be calm a moment.

27 **Giles:** You, Mr. Hale, go in there and demand I speak.

28 **Hale:** A moment, sir, a moment.

29 **Giles:** They'll be hangin' my wife!

**remorseless** (re MAWRS lihs) *adj.* relentless; cruel

30 JUDGE HATHORNE *enters. He is in his sixties, a bitter,* **remorseless** *Salem judge.*

31 **Hathorne:** How do you dare come roarin' into this court! Are you gone daft, Corey?

32 **Giles:** You're not a Boston judge yet, Hathorne. You'll not call me daft!

33 *Enter* DEPUTY GOVERNOR DANFORTH *and, behind him,* EZEKIEL CHEEVER *and* PARRIS. *On his appearance, silence falls.* DANFORTH *is a grave man in his sixties, of some humor and sophistication that does not, however,*





## PERSONALIZE FOR LEARNING

### Strategic Support

**Direct and Indirect Characterization** Review paragraph 30. Remind students that Miller uses both direct and indirect characterization throughout the play. With direct characterization, he explicitly tells us what a character is like. For example, the appositive phrase "a bitter, remorseless Salem judge" explicitly describes Hathorne. On the other hand, indirect characterization shows how a character acts, speaks, or appears. It can also reveal character by showing how other characters react, think, or respond to that character. For example, when Giles says, "You're not a Boston judge yet, Hathorne. You'll not call me daft!" to Hathorne, we can infer that Hathorne was acting too haughtily for his status as a provincial judge. With indirect characterization, the reader needs to make inferences about a character's personality. Ask: *Can you find another example of indirect characterization at this point in the play?*

*interfere with an exact loyalty to his position and his cause. He comes down to* GILES, *who awaits his wrath.*

34 **Danforth,** *looking directly at* GILES: Who is this man?

35 **Parris:** Giles Corey, sir, and a more contentious—

36 **Giles,** *to* PARRIS: I am asked the question, and I am old enough to answer it! *To* DANFORTH, *who impresses him and to whom he smiles through his strain*: My name is Corey, sir, Giles Corey. I have six hundred acres, and timber in addition. It is my wife you be condemning now. *He indicates the courtroom.*

37 **Danforth:** And how do you imagine to help her cause with such contemptuous riot? Now be gone. Your old age alone keeps you out of jail for this.

38 **Giles,** *beginning to plead*: They be tellin' lies about my wife, sir, I—

39 **Danforth:** Do you take it upon yourself to determine what this court shall believe and what it shall set aside?

40 **Giles:** Your Excellency, we mean no disrespect for—

41 **Danforth:** Disrespect indeed! It is disruption, Mister. This is the highest court of the supreme government of this province, do you know it?

42 **Giles,** *beginning to weep*: Your Excellency, I only said she were readin' books, sir, and they come and take her out of my house for—

43 **Danforth,** *mystified*: Books! What books?

44 **Giles,** *through helpless sobs*: It is my third wife, sir: I never had no wife that be so taken with books, and I thought to find the cause of it, d'y'see, but it were no witch I blamed her for. *He is openly weeping.* I have broke charity with the woman, I have broke charity with her. *He covers his face, ashamed.* DANFORTH *is respectfully silent.*

45 **Hale:** Excellency, he claims hard evidence for his wife's defense. I think that in all justice you must—

46 **Danforth:** Then let him submit his evidence in proper affidavit.[1] You are certainly aware of our procedure here, Mr. Hale. *To* HERRICK: Clear this room.

47 **Herrick:** Come now, Giles. *He gently pushes* COREY *out.*

48 **Francis:** We are desperate, sir; we come here three days now and cannot be heard.

49 **Danforth:** Who is this man?

50 **Francis:** Francis Nurse, Your Excellency.

51 **Hale:** His wife's Rebecca that were condemned this morning.

NOTES

CLOSE READ

**ANNOTATE:** In paragraphs 42–46, mark examples of nonstandard English.

**QUESTION:** Why does Miller use this type of language here?

**CONCLUDE:** What is the effect of this language, particularly on the audience's understanding of Giles Corey?

1. **affidavit** (af uh DAY viht) *n.* written statement made under oath.

## CLOSE READ

Remind students that apostrophes are often used to represent letters that are omitted in nonstandard English speech. Students will note that nonstandard English contains incorrect grammar as well. You may wish to model the Close Read using the following think-aloud format. Possible responses to questions on the student page are included. You may also want to print copies of the **Close-Read Guide: Fiction** for students to use.

**ANNOTATE:** As I read paragraphs 42–46, I notice and highlight the words *said she were readin'* and *d'y'see* and the words *they come and take* and *I never had no wife*. I notice the apostrophes that show how Giles pronounced these words and the ungrammatical verb tense and double negative.

**QUESTION:** I see that Giles is the character who uses nonstandard English. Miller is suggesting that Giles is less educated and less refined than the judges and some of other townspeople.

**CONCLUDE:** I can infer that Miller uses conventions of language as a form of indirect characterization. This nonstandard English shows that Giles is a common workingman. He is less concerned with abstract ideas and more concerned about saving his wife. His language reflects this aspect of his character.

CLOSER LOOK

## Analyze Character 

Students may have marked the details in paragraphs 60 through 65 during their first read. Use these lines to help students understand how details influence their impressions of Danforth. Encourage them to talk about the annotations that they marked. You may want to model a close read with the class based on the highlights shown in the text.

**ANNOTATE:** Have students mark details in these lines that give them important information about Danforth, or have students participate while you highlight them.

**QUESTION:** Guide students to consider what these details tell them. Ask what a reader can infer about Danforth, and accept student responses.

**Possible response:** Danforth is a strict, possibly cruel judge who jailed 400 people and condemned 72 to hanging. Francis says the judge is important, and he certainly seems to be. And while Francis also says Danforth is wise, he suggests the judge might be deceived.

**CONCLUDE:** Help students to formulate conclusions about the importance of these details in the text. Ask students why the author might have included these details.

**Possible response:** Miller included these facts to help the audience understand Danforth's character.

Point out that a playwright has three ways to convey information about a **character**: what the character says and does, how the character describes himself, and what other characters say about him. Of course, a character can be self-deluded, and other characters can have mistaken ideas about him. In these cases, dramatic irony arises. For example, a cruel tyrant saying, "I'm a gentle person" is ironic.

NOTES

52 **Danforth:** Indeed! I am amazed to find you in such uproar. I have only good report of your character, Mr. Nurse.

53 **Hathorne:** I think they must both be arrested in contempt, sir.

54 **Danforth,** *to* FRANCIS: Let you write your plea, and in due time I will—

55 **Francis:** Excellency, we have proof for your eyes: God forbid you shut them to it. The girls, sir, the girls are frauds.

56 **Danforth:** What's that?

57 **Francis:** We have proof of it, sir. They are all deceiving you.

58 DANFORTH *is shocked, but studying* FRANCIS.

59 **Hathorne:** This is contempt, sir, contempt!

60 **Danforth:** Peace, Judge Hathorne. Do you know who I am, Mr. Nurse?

61 **Francis:** I surely do, sir, and I think you must be a wise judge to be what you are.

62 **Danforth:** And do you know that near to four hundred are in the jails from Marblehead to Lynn, and upon my signature?

63 **Francis:** I—

64 **Danforth:** And seventy-two condemned to hang by that signature?

65 **Francis:** Excellency, I never thought to say it to such a weighty judge, but you are deceived.

66 *Enter* GILES COREY *from left. All turn to see as he beckons in* MARY WARREN with PROCTOR. MARY *is keeping her eyes to the ground;* PROCTOR *has her elbow as though she were near collapse.*

67 **Parris,** *on seeing her, in shock*: Mary Warren! *He goes directly to bend close to her face.* What are you about here?

68 **Proctor,** *pressing* PARRIS *away from her with a gentle but firm motion of protectiveness*: She would speak with the Deputy Governor.

69 **Danforth,** *shocked by this, turns to* HERRICK: Did you not tell me Mary Warren were sick in bed?

70 **Herrick:** She were, Your Honor. When I go to fetch her to the court last week, she said she were sick.

71 **Giles:** She has been strivin' with her soul all week. Your Honor; she comes now to tell the truth of this to you.

72 **Danforth:** Who is this?

73 **Proctor:** John Proctor, sir. Elizabeth Proctor is my wife.

74 **Parris:** Beware this man, Your Excellency, this man is mischief.

75 **Hale,** *excitedly*: I think you must hear the girl, sir, she—

DIGITAL PERSPECTIVES

NOTES

76 **Danforth,** *who has become very interested in* MARY WARREN *and only raises a hand toward* HALE: Peace. What would you tell us, Mary Warren?

77 Proctor *looks at her, but she cannot speak.*

78 **Proctor:** She never saw no spirits, sir.

79 **Danforth,** *with great alarm and surprise, to* MARY: Never saw no spirits!

80 **Giles,** *eagerly*: Never.

81 **Proctor,** *reaching into his jacket*: She has signed a deposition, sir—

82 **Danforth,** *instantly*: No, no. I accept no depositions. *He is rapidly calculating this; he turns from her to* PROCTOR. Tell me, Mr. Proctor, have you given out this story in the village?

83 **Proctor:** We have not.

84 **Parris:** They've come to overthrow the court, sir! This man is—

85 **Danforth:** I pray you, Mr. Parris. Do you know, Mr. Proctor, that the entire contention of the state in these trials is that the voice of Heaven is speaking through the children?

86 **Proctor:** I know that, sir.

87 **Danforth,** *thinks, staring at* PROCTOR, *then turns to* MARY WARREN: And you, Mary Warren, how come you to cry out people for sending their spirits, against you?

88 **Mary Warren:** It were pretense, sir.

89 **Danforth:** I cannot hear you.

90 **Proctor:** It were pretense, she says.

91 **Danforth:** Ah? And the other girls? Susanna Walcott, and—the others? They are also pretending?

92 **Mary Warren:** Aye, sir.

93 **Danforth,** *wide-eyed*: Indeed. *Pause. He is baffled by this. He turns to study* PROCTOR's *face.*

94 **Parris,** *in a sweat*: Excellency, you surely cannot think to let so vile a lie be spread in open court!

95 **Danforth:** Indeed not, but it strike hard upon me that she will dare come here with such a tale. Now, Mr. Proctor, before I decide whether I shall hear you or not, it is my duty to tell you this. We burn a hot fire here; it melts down all concealment.

96 **Proctor:** I know that, sir.

97 **Danforth:** Let me continue. I understand well, a husband's tenderness may drive him to extravagance in defense of a wife. Are you certain in your conscience, Mister, that your evidence is the truth?

98 **Proctor:** It is. And you will surely know it.





## WriteNow Analyze and Interpret

**Interpret a Title** Review paragraph 95. When Danforth warns John Proctor, "We burn a hot fire here; it melts down all concealment," he is invoking the image that serves as the title of the play. Ask questions such as these: *What exactly is a crucible? What is its function? Where does the word come from? What are its synonyms? Does it have both literal and figurative meanings? What connotations does it suggest?* Challenge students to use what they learned from the discussion as well as their own responses to the questions to write an analytical, interpretive paragraph in which they argue that the play's title is the perfect reflection of its plot, characters, and themes.

NOTES

99 **Danforth:** And you thought to declare this revelation in the open court before the public?

100 **Proctor:** I thought I would, aye—with your permission.

101 **Danforth,** *his eyes narrowing*: Now, sir, what is your purpose in so doing?

102 **Proctor:** Why, I—I would free my wife, sir.

103 **Danforth:** There lurks nowhere in your heart, nor hidden in your spirit, any desire to undermine this court?

104 **Proctor,** *with the faintest faltering*: Why, no, sir.

105 **Cheever,** *clears his throat, awakening*: I—Your Excellency.

106 **Danforth:** Mr. Cheever.

107 **Cheever:** I think it be my duty, sir—*Kindly, to* PROCTOR: You'll not deny it, John. *To* DANFORTH: When we come to take his wife, he damned the court and ripped your warrant.

108 **Parris:** Now you have it!

109 **Danforth:** He did that, Mr. Hale?

110 **Hale,** *takes a breath*: Aye, he did.

111 **Proctor:** It were a temper, sir. I knew not what I did.

112 **Danforth,** *studying him*: Mr. Proctor.

113 **Proctor:** Aye, sir.

114 **Danforth,** *straight into his eyes*: Have you ever seen the Devil?

115 **Proctor:** No, sir.

116 **Danforth:** You are in all respects a Gospel Christian?

117 **Proctor:** I am, sir.

118 **Parris:** Such a Christian that will not come to church but once in a month!

119 **Danforth,** *restrained—he is curious*: Not come to church?

120 **Proctor:** I—I have no love for Mr. Parris. It is no secret. But God I surely love.

121 **Cheever:** He plow on Sunday, sir.

122 **Danforth:** Plow on Sunday!

123 **Cheever,** *apologetically*: I think it be evidence, John. I am an official of the court, I cannot keep it.

124 **Proctor:** I—I have once or twice plowed on Sunday. I have three children, sir, and until last year my land give little.

125 **Giles:** You'll find other Christians that do plow on Sunday if the truth be known.

126 **Hale:** Your Honor, I cannot think you may judge the man on such evidence.





## DIGITAL PERSPECTIVES

**Enriching the Text: The Real Governor Danforth** Explain to students that the historical Thomas Danforth was a politician and magistrate in the Massachusetts Bay Colony. He served as Treasurer of Harvard, president of the province of Maine, and deputy governor of Massachusetts, but he never sat on the court of the Salem witch trials. Some critics claim that he is "inaccurately" portrayed in Miller's play, but remind readers that the play is creative fiction, based only loosely on historical events. Miller admitted that he collapsed characters and took liberties with others. In fact, Danforth's name appears only once in the Salem court records as part of a council that observed the proceedings. Danforth was openly critical of those proceedings and actually played a role in bringing them to an end. Encourage interested students to go online to find out more about the real Thomas Danforth and share what they learn with others. **(Research to Explore)**

DIGITAL PERSPECTIVES

127 **Danforth:** I judge nothing. *Pause. He keeps watching* PROCTOR, *who tries to meet his gaze.* I tell you straight, Mister—I have seen marvels in this court. I have seen people choked before my eyes by spirits; I have seen them stuck by pins and slashed by daggers. I have until this moment not the slightest reason to suspect that the children may be deceiving me. Do you understand my meaning?

128 **Proctor:** Excellency, does it not strike upon you that so many of these women have lived so long with such upright reputation, and—

129 **Parris:** Do you read the Gospel, Mr. Proctor?

130 **Proctor:** I read the Gospel.

131 **Parris:** I think not, or you should surely know that Cain were an upright man, and yet he did kill Abel.[2]

132 **Proctor:** Aye, God tells us that. *To* DANFORTH: But who tells us Rebecca Nurse murdered seven babies by sending out her spirit on them? It is the children only, and this one will swear she lied to you.

133 DANFORTH *considers, then beckons* HATHORNE *to him.* HATHORNE *leans in, and he speaks in his ear.* HATHORNE *nods.*

134 **Hathorne:** Aye, she's the one.

135 **Danforth:** Mr. Proctor, this morning, your wife send me a claim in which she states that she is pregnant now.

136 **Proctor:** My wife pregnant!

137 **Danforth:** There be no sign of it—we have examined her body.

138 **Proctor:** But if she say she is pregnant, then she must be! That woman will never lie, Mr. Danforth.

139 **Danforth:** She will not?

140 **Proctor:** Never, sir, never.

141 **Danforth:** We have thought it too convenient to be credited. However, if I should tell you now that I will let her be kept another month; and if she begin to show her natural signs, you shall have her living yet another year until she is delivered—what say you to that? JOHN PROCTOR *is struck silent.* Come now. You say your only purpose is to save your wife. Good, then, she is saved at least this year, and a year is long. What say you, sir? It is done now. *In conflict,* PROCTOR *glances at* FRANCIS *and* GILES. Will you drop this charge?

142 **Proctor:** I—I think I cannot.

143 **Danforth,** *now an almost imperceptible hardness in his voice:* Then your purpose is somewhat larger.

144 **Parris:** He's come to overthrow this court, Your Honor!

145 **Proctor:** These are my friends. Their wives are also accused—

NOTES

2. **Cain . . . Abel** In the Bible, Cain, the oldest son of Adam and Eve, killed his brother Abel.

**CLOSE READ**

**ANNOTATE:** In the stage directions in paragraph 143, mark the adverb and the adjective in the description of Danforth's voice.

**QUESTION:** Why does Miller use these modifiers?

**CONCLUDE:** How do these modifiers add to the portrayal of Danforth's character?

## CLOSE READ

Remind students that adjectives modify nouns and adverbs modify adjectives (or verbs or other adverbs). You may wish to model the Close Read using the following think-aloud format. Possible responses to questions on the student page are included.

**ANNOTATE:** As I read paragraph 143, I notice and highlight the words *imperceptible* and *almost*. *Imperceptible* is the adjective that modifies *hardness*. *Almost* is an adverb that modifies *imperceptible*.

**QUESTION:** I think Miller wants to suggest that Danforth, along with just about everyone else in the play, is hiding what he truly thinks. He is a hard man; but he doesn't let it show, or at least he tries to hide it. He might have used *nearly* or *practically* instead of *almost*. He might have used *inaudible* or *indistinguishable* instead of *imperceptible*.

**CONCLUDE:** I can infer that the delivery of this line with an "almost imperceptible" hardness might make the audience predict that things were going to turn for the worse for Proctor at this point. It's not as if Danforth was feeling pity or softness toward Proctor before this moment, but when Proctor says that he "cannot" drop the charge, Danforth feels even more strongly that Proctor is antagonistic toward the court.

NOTES

146 **Danforth,** *with a sudden briskness of manner*: I judge you not, sir. I am ready to hear your evidence.

147 **Proctor:** I come not to hurt the court: I only—

148 **Danforth,** *cutting him off*: Marshal, go into the court and bid Judge Stoughton and Judge Sewall declare recess for one hour. And let them go to the tavern, if they will. All witnesses and prisoners are to be kept in the building.

149 **Herrick:** Aye, sir. *Very deferentially*: If I may say it, sir. I know this man all my life. It is a good man, sir.

150 **Danforth**—*it is the reflection on himself he resents*: I am sure of it, Marshal. HERRICK *nods, then goes out.* Now, what deposition do you have for us, Mr. Proctor? And I beg you be clear, open as the sky, and honest.

151 **Proctor**, *as he takes out several papers*: I am no lawyer, so I'll—

152 **Danforth:** The pure in heart need no lawyers. Proceed as you will.

153 **Proctor,** *handing* DANFORTH *a paper*: Will you read this first, sir? It's a sort of testament. The people signing it declare their good opinion of Rebecca, and my wife, and Martha Corey.

154 DANFORTH *looks down at the paper.*

155 **Parris,** *to enlist* DANFORTH's *sarcasm*: Their good opinion! But DANFORTH *goes on reading, and* PROCTOR *is heartened.*

156 **Proctor:** These are all landholding farmers, members of the church. *Delicately, trying to point out a paragraph*: If you'll notice, sir—they've known the women many years and never saw no sign they had dealings with the Devil.

157 PARRIS *nervously moves over and reads over* DANFORTH's *shoulder.*

158 **Danforth,** *glancing down a long list*: How many names are here?

159 **Francis:** Ninety-one, Your Excellency.

160 **Parris,** *sweating*: These people should be summoned. DANFORTH *looks up at him questioningly*. For questioning.

161 **Francis,** *trembling with anger*: Mr. Danforth, I gave them all my word no harm would come to them for signing this.

162 **Parris:** This is a clear attack upon the court!

163 **Hale,** *to* PARRIS, *trying to contain himself*: Is every defense an attack upon the court? Can no one—?

164 **Parris:** All innocent and Christian people are happy for the courts in Salem! These people are gloomy for it. *To* DANFORTH *directly*: And I think you will want to know, from each and every one of them, what discontents them with you!

165 **Hathorne:** I think they ought to be examined, sir.

166 **Danforth:** It is not necessarily an attack, I think. Yet—





## PERSONALIZE FOR LEARNING

### Challenge

**Depositions** Review paragraph 150. A deposition is an out-of-court oral testimony by a witness, called a deponent, that is put in writing for later use in court. Like witnesses, deponents testify under oath. Their handling varies somewhat from state to state. Have students find out how depositions are handled in courtrooms in your state. When are such documents presented as evidence? How must the information be gathered? What is the difference between depositions and affidavits? Encourage interested students to interview lawyers or other legal professionals to find out more about depositions.

167 **Francis:** These are all covenanted Christians, sir.

168 **Danforth:** Then I am sure they may have nothing to fear. *Hands* CHEEVER *the paper*. Mr. Cheever, have warrants drawn for all of these—arrest for examination. *To* PROCTOR: Now, Mister, what other information do you have for us? FRANCIS *is still standing, horrified*. You may sit, Mr. Nurse.

169 **Francis:** I have brought trouble on these people; I have—

170 **Danforth:** No, old man, you have not hurt these people if they are of good conscience. But you must understand, sir, that a person is either with this court or he must be counted against it, there be no road between. This is a sharp time, now, a precise time—we live no longer in the dusky afternoon when evil mixed itself with good and befuddled the world. Now, by God's grace, the shining sun is up, and them that fear not light will surely praise it. I hope you will be one of those. MARY WARREN *suddenly sobs*. She's not hearty, I see.

171 **Proctor:** No, she's not, sir. *To* MARY, *bending to her, holding her hand, quietly*: Now remember what the angel Raphael said to the boy Tobias.[3] Remember it.

172 **Mary Warren,** *hardly audible*: Aye.

173 **Proctor:** "Do that which is good, and no harm shall come to thee."

174 **Mary Warren:** Aye.

175 **Danforth:** Come, man, we wait you.

176 MARSHAL HERRICK *returns, and takes his post at the door.*

177 **Giles:** John, my deposition, give him mine.

178 **Proctor:** Aye. *He hands* DANFORTH *another paper*. This is Mr. Corey's deposition.

179 **Danforth:** Oh? *He looks down at it. Now* HATHORNE *comes behind him and reads with him.*

180 **Hathorne,** *suspiciously*: What lawyer drew this, Corey?

181 **Giles:** You know I never hired a lawyer in my life, Hathorne.

182 **Danforth,** *finishing the reading*: It is very well phrased. My compliments. Mr. Parris, if Mr. Putnam is in the court, will you bring him in? HATHORNE *takes the deposition, and walks to the window with it.* PARRIS *goes into the court*. You have no legal training, Mr. Corey?

183 **Giles,** *very pleased*: I have the best, sir—I am thirty-three time in court in my life. And always plaintiff, too.

184 **Danforth:** Oh, then you're much put-upon.

185 **Giles:** I am never put-upon: I know my rights, sir, and I will have them. You know, your father tried a case of mine—might be thirty-five year ago, I think.

NOTES

3. **Raphael . . . Tobias** In the Bible, Tobias is guided by the archangel Raphael to save two people who have prayed to die. One of the two is Tobias's father, Tobit, who is despondent because he has lost his sight. The other is Sara, a woman who is afflicted by a demon that has killed each of her seven husbands on their wedding days. With Raphael's aid, Tobias exorcises the devil from Sara and cures his father of blindness.





DIGITAL PERSPECTIVES

CLOSER LOOK

## Analyze Metaphors 

Students may have marked paragraph 170 during their first read. Use these lines to help students understand how the language reflects the major themes of the play. Encourage them to talk about the annotations that they marked. You may want to model a close read with the class based on the highlights shown in the text.

**ANNOTATE:** Have students mark the metaphors in these lines, or have students participate while you highlight them.

**QUESTION:** Guide students to consider what these metaphors might tell them. Ask what a reader can infer about both Danforth as speaker and the idea of truth as Miller sees it, and accept student responses.

**Possible response:** Danforth compares the situation to two roads with no road in between and also to a place where the sun either shines or not; there is no "dusky afternoon" where the two mix. For him, it's a black-or-white, good-or-evil world: no gray, no ambiguity.

**CONCLUDE:** Help students to formulate conclusions about the importance of these metaphors in the text. Ask students why the author might have included these metaphors.

**Possible response:** Miller included these metaphors because they convey the problem of the play so well. The judges and the community are only seeing the extremes of good and evil, not the human condition, which is somewhere in between.

Students may think of **metaphors** and other figurative language as literary devices, which they are. But they are also often used in spoken language. The characters in the play use metaphors because they are literary creations, and also because people use metaphors in everyday speech. Some metaphors have even become reduced to clichés: Now you have to step up to the plate. She's going to either sink or swim.

Additional **English Language Support** is available in the Interactive Teacher's Edition.

NOTES

186 **Danforth:** Indeed.

187 **Giles:** He never spoke to you of it?

188 **Danforth:** No. I cannot recall it.

189 **Giles:** That's strange, he gave me nine pound damages. He were a fair judge, your father. Y'see, I had a white mare that time, and this fellow come to borrow the mare—*Enter* PARRIS *with* THOMAS PUTNAM. *When he sees* PUTNAM, GILES's *ease goes; he is hard*. Aye, there he is.

190 **Danforth:** Mr. Putnam, I have here an accusation by Mr. Corey against you. He states that you coldly prompted your daughter to cry witchery upon George Jacobs that is now in jail.

191 **Putnam:** It is a lie.

192 **Danforth,** *turning to* GILES: Mr. Putnam states your charge is a lie. What say you to that?

193 **Giles,** *furious, his fists clenched*: A fart on Thomas Putnam, that is what I say to that!

194 **Danforth:** What proof do you submit for your charge, sir?

195 **Giles:** My proof is there! *Pointing to the paper*. If Jacobs hangs for a witch he forfeit up his property—that's law! And there is none but Putnam with the coin to buy so great a piece. This man is killing his neighbors for their land!

196 **Danforth:** But proof, sir, proof.

197 **Giles,** *pointing at his deposition*: The proof is there! I have it from an honest man who heard Putnam say it! The day his daughter cried out on Jacobs, he said she'd given him a fair gift of land.

198 **Hathorne:** And the name of this man?

199 **Giles,** *taken aback*: What name?

200 **Hathorne:** The man that give you this information.

201 **Giles,** *hesitates, then*: Why, I—I cannot give you his name.

202 **Hathorne:** And why not?

203 **Giles,** *hesitates, then bursts out*: You know well why not! He'll lay in jail if I give his name!

204 **Hathorne:** This is contempt of the court, Mr. Danforth!

205 **Danforth,** *to avoid that*: You will surely tell us the name.

206 **Giles:** I will not give you no name. I mentioned my wife's name once and I'll burn in hell long enough for that. I stand mute.

207 **Danforth:** In that case, I have no choice but to arrest you for contempt of this court, do you know that?

208 **Giles:** This is a hearing; you cannot clap me for contempt of a hearing.





## DIGITAL PERSPECTIVES

**Enriching the Text: Hathorne and Hawthorne** One of the characters who has an actual historical counterpart is Judge Hathorne. Students may be interested to know that Hathorne had a famous descendant, Nathaniel Hawthorne, who lived in Salem during the nineteenth century. Hawthorne used the Puritan colonies of his ancestors as the settings for much of his fiction. For example, Hawthorne's best-known novel, *The Scarlet Letter*, examines the repressive side of Puritanism and the hypocrisy and pain that it produced. It, too, deals with adultery as a plot element, and ministers who lose credibility the way that the judges in *The Crucible* do.

Encourage students to go online to research how Hawthorne felt about Hathorne. Ask: *How might Hawthorne's feelings about Judge Hathorne have influenced his work?* **(Research to Explore)**

209 **Danforth:** Oh, it is a proper lawyer! Do you wish me to declare the court in full session here? Or will you give me good reply?

210 **Giles,** *faltering*: I cannot give you no name, sir, I cannot.

211 **Danforth:** You are a foolish old man. Mr. Cheever, begin the record. The court is now in session. I ask you, Mr. Corey—

212 **Proctor,** *breaking in*: Your Honor—he has the story in confidence, sir, and he—

213 **Parris:** The Devil lives on such confidences! *To* DANFORTH: Without confidences there could be no conspiracy, Your Honor!

214 **Hathorne:** I think it must be broken, sir.

215 **Danforth,** *to* GILES: Old man, if your informant tells the truth let him come here openly like a decent man. But if he hide in anonymity I must know why. Now sir, the government and central church demand of you the name of him who reported Mr. Thomas Putnam a common murderer.

216 **Hale:** Excellency—

217 **Danforth:** Mr. Hale.

218 **Hale:** We cannot blink it more. There is a prodigious fear of this court in the country—

219 **Danforth:** Then there is a prodigious guilt in the country. Are you afraid to be questioned here?

220 **Hale:** I may only fear the Lord, sir, but there is fear in the country nevertheless.

221 **Danforth,** *angered now*: Reproach me not with the fear in the country; there is fear in the country because there is a moving plot to topple Christ in the country!

222 **Hale:** But it does not follow that everyone accused is part of it.

223 **Danforth:** No uncorrupted man may fear this court. Mr. Hale! None! *To* GILES: You are under arrest in contempt of this court. Now sit you down and take counsel with yourself, or you will be set in the jail until you decide to answer all questions.

224 GILES COREY *makes a rush for* PUTNAM. PROCTOR *lunges and holds him.*

225 **Proctor:** No, Giles!

226 **Giles,** *over* PROCTOR*'s shoulder at* PUTNAM: I'll cut your throat, Putnam. I'll kill you yet!

227 **Proctor,** *forcing him into a chair*: Peace, Giles, peace. *Releasing him.* We'll prove ourselves. Now we will. *He starts to turn to* DANFORTH.

228 **Giles:** Say nothin' more, John. *Pointing at* DANFORTH: He's only playin' you! He means to hang us all!

229 MARY WARREN *bursts into sobs.*

NOTES

**CLOSE READ**

**ANNOTATE:** In paragraphs 218–222, mark references to fear.

**QUESTION:** Why does Miller repeat the word *fear* so many times?

**CONCLUDE:** How do Hale's and Danforth's reactions to this word capture their central disagreement?





**DIGITAL PERSPECTIVES**

## CLOSE READ

Remind students that writers use repetition to emphasize key ideas and to produce certain sound effects. You may wish to model the Close Read using the following think-aloud format. Possible responses to questions on the student page are included.

**ANNOTATE:** As I read paragraphs 218–222, I see that Miller repeats the word *fear* several times.

**QUESTION:** I think Miller includes this repetition because he is driving home a point in these lines, like pounding a drum. Fear is the enemy and it is *prodigious* (meaning "extraordinary, enormous, powerful").

**CONCLUDE:** I can infer that the repetition suggests the dissension between these two men. They both agree that fear is governing the community, but they disagree on what is being feared (the courts or the Lord). What the audience hears is "fear in the country, fear in the country, fear in the country," as if it were a refrain.

NOTES

**effrontery** (ih FRUHN tuh ree) *n.* shameless boldness

230 **Danforth:** This is a court of law, Mister. I'll have no effrontery here!

231 **Proctor:** Forgive him, sir, for his old age. Peace, Giles, we'll prove it all now. *He lifts up* MARY'S *chin.* You cannot weep, Mary. Remember the angel, what he say to the boy. Hold to it, now; there is your rock. MARY *quiets. He takes out a paper, and turns to* DANFORTH. This is Mary Warren's deposition. I—I would ask you remember, sir, while you read it, that until two week ago she were no different than the other children are today. *He is speaking reasonably, restraining all his fears, his anger, his anxiety.* You saw her scream, she howled, she swore familiar spirits choked her; she even testified that Satan, in the form of women now in jail, tried to win her soul away, and then when she refused—

232 **Danforth:** We know all this.

233 **Proctor:** Aye, sir. She swears now that she never saw Satan; nor any spirit, vague or clear, that Satan may have sent to hurt her. And she declares her friends are lying now.

234 PROCTOR *starts to hand* DANFORTH *the deposition, and* HALE *comes up to* DANFORTH *in a trembling state.*

235 **Hale:** Excellency, a moment. I think this goes to the heart of the matter.

236 **Danforth,** *with deep misgivings*: It surely does.

237 **Hale:** I cannot say he is an honest man; I know him little. But in all justice, sir, a claim so weighty cannot be argued by a farmer. In God's name, sir, stop here; send him home and let him come again with a lawyer—

238 **Danforth,** *patiently*: Now look you, Mr. Hale—

239 **Hale:** Excellency, I have signed seventy-two death warrants; I am a minister of the Lord, and I dare not take a life without there be a proof so immaculate no slightest qualm of conscience may doubt it.

240 **Danforth:** Mr. Hale, you surely do not doubt my justice.

241 **Hale:** I have this morning signed away the soul of Rebecca Nurse, Your Honor. I'll not conceal it, my hand shakes yet as with a wound! I pray you, sir, *this* argument let lawyers present to you.

242 **Danforth:** Mr. Hale, believe me: for a man of such terrible learning you are most bewildered—I hope you will forgive me. I have been thirty-two year at the bar, sir, and I should be confounded were I called upon to defend these people. Let you consider, now—*To* PROCTOR *and the others*: And I bid you all do likewise. In an ordinary crime, how does one defend the accused? One calls up witnesses to prove his innocence. But





## PERSONALIZE FOR LEARNING

### Challenge

**Mock Trial** Call attention to Hale's suggestion in paragraph 236. Invite students to hold their own imitation or mock trials in which they imagine that John Proctor has been permitted legal counsel to present his evidence, as Hale suggests. Suggest that students work as a team to prepare the legal argument for the acceptance of Mary's deposition and other evidence, pooling and writing their ideas and investigating some of the legal strategies they might use. Two or three members of the team should present the argument to the whole class, with backup assistance from the rest of the legal team. You may also want to share that there are mock trial programs in which students formally participate in pretend trials to learn about the legal system.

witchcraft is *ipso facto*,[4] on its face and by its nature, an invisible crime, is it not? Therefore, who may possibly be witness to it? The witch and the victim. None other. Now we cannot hope the witch will accuse herself: granted? Therefore, we must rely upon her victims—and they do testify, the children certainly do testify. As for the witches, none will deny that we are most eager for all their confessions. Therefore, what is left for a lawyer to bring out? I think I have made my point. Have I not?

243 **Hale:** But this child claims the girls are not truthful, and if they are not—

244 **Danforth:** That is precisely what I am about to consider, sir. What more may you ask of me? Unless you doubt my probity?[5]

245 **Hale,** *defeated*: I surely do not, sir. Let you consider it, then.

246 **Danforth:** And let you put your heart to rest. Her deposition, Mr. Proctor.

247 PROCTOR *hands it to him.* HATHORNE *rises, goes beside* DANFORTH *and starts reading.* PARRIS *comes to his other side.* DANFORTH *looks at* JOHN PROCTOR, *then proceeds to read.* HALE *gets up, finds position near the judge, reads too.* PROCTOR *glances at* GILES. FRANCIS *prays silently, hands pressed together.* CHEEVER *waits placidly, the sublime official,* dutiful. MARY WARREN *sobs once.* JOHN PROCTOR *touches her head reassuringly. Presently* DANFORTH *lifts his eyes, stands up, takes out a kerchief and blows his nose. The others stand aside as he moves in thought toward the window.*

248 **Parris,** *hardly able to contain his anger and fear*: I should like to question—

249 **Danforth**—*his first real outburst, in which his contempt for* PARRIS *is clear*: Mr. Parris, I bid you be silent! *He stands in silence, looking out the window. Now, having established that he will set the gait*: Mr. Cheever, will you go into the court and bring the children here? CHEEVER *gets up and goes out upstage.* DANFORTH *now turns to* MARY. Mary Warren, how came you to this turnabout? Has Mr. Proctor threatened you for this deposition?

250 **Mary Warren:** No, sir.

251 **Danforth:** Has he ever threatened you?

252 **Mary Warren,** *weaker*: No, sir.

253 **Danforth,** *sensing a weakening*: Has he threatened you?

254 **Mary Warren:** No, sir.

255 **Danforth:** Then you tell me that you sat in my court, callously lying, when you knew that people would hang by your evidence? *She does not answer.* Answer me!

256 **Mary Warren,** *almost inaudibly*: I did, sir.

NOTES

4. ***ipso facto*** (ihp soh FAK toh) "by that very fact"; "therefore" (Latin).

5. **probity** (PROH buh tee) *n.* complete honesty; integrity.

**callously** (KAL uhs lee) *adv.* without sympathy; coldly





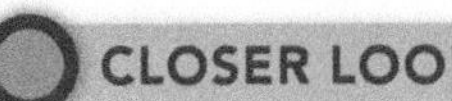

CLOSER LOOK

### Analyze Technique 

Students may have marked paragraph 247 during their first read. Use these lines to help students understand the stage directions. Encourage students to talk about the annotations that they marked. You may want to model a close read with the class based on the highlights shown in the text.

**ANNOTATE:** Have students mark details in these lines that occur between Proctor handing over the deposition and Parris speaking, or have students participate while you highlight them.

**QUESTION:** Guide students to consider what these details might tell them. Ask what a reader can infer from the stage directions, and accept student responses.

**Possible response:** There is a lot of movement, no words, and only two sounds: sobbing and nose blowing. There are looks, reading, glances, praying, and one touch. The details suggest that there is a lot of tension in the room.

**CONCLUDE:** Help students to formulate conclusions about the importance of these details in the text. Ask students why the author might have included these details.

**Possible response:** Miller included these stage directions so that the actors would slow down at this point. He wants there to be silence in the room except for two sounds: one by Mary that is submissive and the other by Danforth that is strangely physical and interruptive. The long stretch of near silence builds tension, as the audience must wait to find out what the reaction to the deposition will be.

Remind students that a writer's **technique**, or craft, can help set the pace of events. Explain to students that pace and timing are generally in the hands of the play's director. The director, working with the actors, decides when to speak and move quickly and when to slow down. But there are things the playwright can do to indicate his or her intentions. A director could have the actor playing Parris speak just a few moments after Proctor hands in the deposition. But a smart director will look at all the actions Miller put into the script and realize that the playwright wants a long stretch of silence here to build tension.

NOTES

257 **Danforth:** How were you instructed in your life? Do you not know that God damns all liars? *She cannot speak.* Or is it now that you lie?

258 **Mary Warren:** No, sir—I am with God now.

259 **Danforth:** You are with God now.

260 **Mary Warren:** Aye, sir.

261 **Danforth,** *containing himself*: I will tell you this—you are either lying now, or you were lying in the court, and in either case you have committed perjury and you will go to jail for it. You cannot lightly say you lied, Mary. Do you know that?

262 **Mary Warren:** I cannot lie no more. I am with God. I am with God.

263 *But she breaks into sobs at the thought of it, and the right door opens, and enter* SUSANNA WALCOTT, MERCY LEWIS, BETTY PARRIS, *and finally* ABIGAIL. CHEEVER *comes to* DANFORTH.

264 **Cheever:** Ruth Putnam's not in the court, sir, nor the other children.

265 **Danforth:** These will be sufficient. Sit you down, children. *Silently they sit.* Your friend, Mary Warren, has given us a deposition. In which she swears that she never saw familiar spirits, apparitions, nor any manifest of the Devil. She claims as well that none of you have seen these things either. *Slight pause.* Now, children, this is a court of law. The law, based upon the Bible, and the Bible, writ by Almighty God, forbid the practice of witchcraft, and describe death as the penalty thereof. But likewise, children, the law and Bible damn all bearers of false witness. *Slight pause.* Now then. It does not escape me that this deposition may be devised to blind us; it may well be that Mary Warren has been conquered by Satan, who sends her here to distract our sacred purpose. If so, her neck will break for it. But if she speak true, I bid you now drop your guile and confess your pretense, for a quick confession will go easier with you. *Pause.* Abigail Williams, rise. ABIGAIL *slowly rises.* Is there any truth in this?

266 **Abigail:** No, sir.

267 **Danforth,** *thinks, glances at* MARY *then back to* ABIGAIL: Children, a very augur bit[6] will now be turned into your souls until your honesty is proved. Will either of you change your positions now, or do you force me to hard questioning?

268 **Abigail:** I have naught to change, sir. She lies.

269 **Danforth,** *to* MARY: You would still go on with this?

270 **Mary Warren,** *faintly*: Aye, sir.

6. **augur (AW guhr) bit** sharp point of an augur, a tool used for boring holes.





## CROSS-CURRICULAR PERSPECTIVES

**Art: Set and Costume Design** Remind students that Puritans espoused "plainness," that is, a lack of ornament or pretense. This "plainness" translated to an emphasis on moderation, simplicity, and functionality in their clothing, buildings, furnishings, food, customs, and tools. This common belief and practice was a response to the "impure" practices of the Anglican Church, which they believed had been tainted by Catholic ceremony, excess, and ostentation. Ask students to design either a set or a costume for *The Crucible* that reflects this tendency, based on research of Puritan architecture or garments in the 1600s. They should create a full-color sketch accompanied by a verbal description and citation of their sources. Offer students the opportunity to share their sketches and descriptions on a classroom or digital bulletin board. **(Research to Explore)**

642 UNIT 5 • FACING OUR FEARS

271 **Danforth,** *turning to* ABIGAIL: A poppet were discovered in Mr. Proctor's house, stabbed by a needle. Mary Warren claims that you sat beside her in the court when she made it, and that you saw her make it and witnessed how she herself stuck her needle into it for safe-keeping. What say you to that?

272 **Abigail,** *with a slight note of indignation*: It is a lie, sir.

273 **Danforth,** *after a slight pause*: While you worked for Mr. Proctor, did you see poppets in that house?

274 **Abigail:** Goody Proctor always kept poppets.

275 **Proctor:** Your Honor, my wife never kept no poppets. Mary Warren confesses it was her poppet.

276 **Cheever:** Your Excellency.

277 **Danforth:** Mr. Cheever.

278 **Cheever:** When I spoke with Goody Proctor in that house, she said she never kept no poppets. But she said she did keep poppets when she were a girl.

279 **Proctor:** She has not been a girl these fifteen years, Your Honor.

280 **Hathorne:** But a poppet will keep fifteen years, will it not?

281 **Proctor:** It will keep if it is kept, but Mary Warren swears she never saw no poppets in my house, nor anyone else.

282 **Parris:** Why could there not have been poppets hid where no one ever saw them?

283 **Proctor,** *furious*: There might also be a dragon with five legs in my house, but no one has ever seen it.

284 **Parris:** We are here, Your Honor, precisely to discover what no one has ever seen.

285 **Proctor:** Mr. Danforth, what profit this girl to tum herself about? What may Mary Warren gain but hard questioning and worse?

286 **Danforth:** You are charging Abigail Williams with a marvelous cool plot to murder, do you understand that?

287 **Proctor:** I do, sir. I believe she means to murder.

288 **Danforth,** *pointing at* ABIGAIL, *incredulously*: This child would murder your wife?

289 **Proctor:** It is not a child. Now hear me, sir. In the sight of the congregation she were twice this year put out of this meetin' house for laughter during prayer.

290 **Danforth,** *shocked, turning to* ABIGAIL: What's this? Laughter during—!

291 **Parris:** Excellency, she were under Tituba's power at that time, but she is solemn now.

292 **Giles:** Aye, now she is solemn and goes to hang people!

NOTES

**CLOSE READ**

**ANNOTATE:** Mark the pronoun Proctor uses to refer to Abigail in the first sentence of paragraph 289.

**QUESTION:** Why does Miller have Proctor refer to Abigail in this way?

**CONCLUDE:** What is the effect of this use of language?

## CLOSE READ

Remind students that pronouns are words that are used in place of nouns—words such as *he, she, you, they, we,* and *it*. You may wish to model the Close Read using the following think-aloud format. Possible responses to questions on the student page are included.

**ANNOTATE:** As I read the first sentence of paragraph 289, I am surprised by the pronoun Proctor uses to replace Abigail Williams' name.

**QUESTION:** This is unusual because *it* is used to replace the name of an object, not a person. I think Miller is emphasizing Proctor's complete disdain for Abigail. He reduces her to being a thing, not a person.

**CONCLUDE:** I can infer that this language shows how John Proctor feels at this point in the play. He considers Abigail not even human, something to be reviled and scorned, not respected and heard.

## CLOSE READ

Remind students that dashes can replace commas, parentheses, colons, or ellipses and are usually used for emphasis or effect. You may wish to model the Close Read using the following think-aloud format. Possible responses to questions on the student page are included.

**ANNOTATE:** As I read paragraphs 297 through 304, I note that Miller uses a lot of dashes.

**QUESTION:** I think Miller uses these dashes to show that everyone is interrupting each other at this point in the play. Things are confused. Also, Mary is hesitant and looks to John Proctor for help. These lines should be read quickly, overlapping each other.

**CONCLUDE:** I can infer that this punctuation style creates a mood of confusion and turmoil in which many voices weave in and out and no one is able to complete his or her thoughts.

NOTES

**CLOSE READ**

**ANNOTATE:** In paragraphs 297 to 304, mark the punctuation that indicates characters are not fully stating their thoughts.

**QUESTION:** What does this punctuation suggest is happening in the scene?

**CONCLUDE:** What is the effect of these abbreviated bits of dialogue?

293 **Danforth:** Quiet, man.

294 **Hathorne:** Surely it have no bearing on the question, sir. He charges contemplation of murder.

295 **Danforth:** Aye. *He studies* ABIGAIL *for a moment, then*: Continue, Mr. Proctor.

296 **Proctor:** Mary. Now tell the Governor how you danced in the woods.

297 **Parris,** *instantly*: Excellency, since I come to Salem this man is blackening my name. He—

298 **Danforth:** In a moment, sir. *To* MARY WARREN, *sternly, and surprised*. What is this dancing?

299 **Mary Warren:** I—*She glances at* ABIGAIL, *who is staring down at her remorselessly. Then, appealing to* PROCTOR: Mr. Proctor—

300 **Proctor,** *taking it right up*: Abigail leads the girls to the woods. Your Honor, and they have danced there naked—

301 **Parris:** Your Honor, this—

302 **Proctor,** *at once*: Mr. Parris discovered them himself in the dead of night! There's the "child" she is!

303 **Danforth**—*it is growing into a nightmare, and he turns, astonished, to* PARRIS: Mr. Parris—

304 **Parris:** I can only say, sir, that I never found any of them naked, and this man is—

305 **Danforth:** But you discovered them dancing in the woods? *Eyes on* PARRIS, *he points at* ABIGAIL. Abigail?

306 **Hale:** Excellency, when I first arrived from Beverly, Mr. Parris told me that.

307 **Danforth:** Do you deny it, Mr. Parris?

308 **Parris:** I do not, sir, but I never saw any of them naked.

309 **Danforth:** But she have danced?

310 **Parris,** *unwillingly*: Aye, sir.

311 **Danforth,** *as though with new eyes, looks at* ABIGAIL.

312 **Hathorne:** Excellency, will you permit me? *He points at* MARY WARREN.

313 **Danforth,** *with great worry*: Pray, proceed.

314 **Hathorne:** You say you never saw no spirits, Mary, were never threatened or afflicted by any manifest of the Devil or the Devil's agents.

315 **Mary Warren,** *very faintly*: No, sir.

316 **Hathorne,** *with a gleam of victory*: And yet, when people accused of witchery confronted you in court, you would faint, saying their spirits came out of their bodies and choked you—





## DIGITAL PERSPECTIVES

**Enriching the Text: Dancing in the Woods/ The May-pole of Merry Mount** Although Puritans advocated a life devoid of leisure, their intolerance for dancing was not universal. For example, Nathaniel Hawthorne's short story "The May-pole of Merry Mount" fictionalizes a historical event that happened in a colonial town in which the villagers danced around a maypole to celebrate May Day. Encourage interested students to go online to locate and read Hawthorne's story. Ask them to compare its setting and characters with those in *The Crucible*. Ask: *How does the daily life in both villages compare and contrast*? Have students who read the story give an oral presentation to the rest of the class about Puritan attitudes toward dancing in the woods. **(Research to Explore)**

DIGITAL PERSPECTIVES

317 **Mary Warren**: That were pretense, sir.

318 **Danforth:** I cannot hear you.

319 **Mary Warren**: Pretense, sir.

320 **Parris:** But you did turn cold, did you not? I myself picked you up many times, and your skin were icy. Mr. Danforth, you—

321 **Danforth:** I saw that many times.

322 **Proctor:** She only pretended to faint, Your Excellency. They're all marvelous pretenders.

323 **Hathorne:** Then can she pretend to faint now?

324 **Proctor:** Now?

325 **Parris:** Why not? Now there are no spirits attacking her, for none in this room is accused of witchcraft. So let her turn herself cold now, let her pretend she is attacked now, let her faint. *He turns to* MARY WARREN. Faint!

326 **Mary Warren:** Faint?

327 **Parris:** Aye, faint. Prove to us how you pretended in the court so many times.

328 **Mary Warren,** *looking to* PROCTOR: I—cannot faint now, sir.

329 **Proctor,** *alarmed, quietly*: Can you not pretend it?

330 **Mary Warren:** I—*She looks about as though searching for the passion to faint*. I—have no sense of it now, I—

331 **Danforth:** Why? What is lacking now?

332 **Mary Warren:** I—cannot tell, sir, I—

333 **Danforth:** Might it be that here we have no afflicting spirit loose, but in the court there were some?

334 **Mary Warren:** I never saw no spirits.

335 **Parris:** Then see no spirits now, and prove to us that you can faint by your own will, as you claim.

336 **Mary Warren,** *stares, searching for the emotion of it, and then shakes her head*: I—cannot do it.

337 **Parris:** Then you will confess, will you not? It were attacking spirits made you faint!

338 **Mary Warren:** No, sir. I—

339 **Parris:** Your Excellency, this is a trick to blind the court!

340 **Mary Warren:** It's not a trick! *She stands*. I—I used to faint because I—I thought I saw spirits.

341 **Danforth:** *Thought* you saw them!

342 **Mary Warren:** But I did not, Your Honor.

343 **Hathorne:** How could you think you saw them unless you saw them?

NOTES





## CROSS-CURRICULAR PERSPECTIVES

**Science: Fainting** Review paragraphs 316 through 340. *Syncope*, also known as fainting, passing out, or swooning, is the medical term for a short loss of consciousness and muscle strength that has a fast onset, short duration (less than a couple of minutes), and a quick and complete recovery. Most often, it is caused by a decrease in blood flow to the brain. Although usually physically induced, fainting can also be caused by emotional distress, fear, or severe pain. Have students create a "What to Do if Someone Faints" poster or flyer to display in your classroom or school clinic.

CLOSER LOOK

## Explore Dialogue

Students may have marked parts of paragraph 344 during their first read. Use these lines to help students understand why the playwright punctuated the dialogue in this way. Encourage them to talk about the annotations that they marked. You may want to model a close read with the class based on the highlights shown in the text.

**ANNOTATE:** Have students mark the dashes in paragraph 344 and the words they separate, or have students participate while you highlight them.

**QUESTION:** Guide students to consider what the dashes might tell them. Ask what a reader can infer from the dashes, and accept student responses.

**Possible response:** In each case, Mary is starting to say something but stops, then starts again. In three cases she continues as before, but in one she changes what she was going to say.

**CONCLUDE:** Help students to formulate conclusions about the importance of these dashes in the text. Ask students why the author might have included these dashes.

**Possible response:** Mary is frightened and upset. People who are frightened and upset don't speak in clear, complete sentences. The punctuation reflects the way someone in that emotional state would speak.

Explain to students that the **dialogue** in a play must sound like actual spoken speech, but it cannot be actual spoken speech. Most people interrupt themselves and each other, leaving sentences unfinished and thoughts unconnected. In real life, we understand and expect this and don't even notice it most of the time. But dialogue generally has to be much closer to standard written English.

NOTES

344 **Mary Warren:** I—I cannot tell how, but I did. I—I heard the other girls screaming, and you, Your Honor, you seemed to believe them, and I—It were only sport in the beginning, sir, but then the whole world cried spirits, spirits, and I—I promise you, Mr. Danforth, I only thought I saw them but I did not.

345 DANFORTH *peers at her.*

346 **Parris,** *smiling, but nervous because* DANFORTH *seems to be struck by* MARY WARREN*'s story*: Surely Your Excellency is not taken by this simple lie.

347 **Danforth,** *turning worriedly to* ABIGAIL: Abigail. I bid you now search your heart and tell me this—and beware of it, child, to God every soul is precious and His vengeance is terrible on them that take life without cause. Is it possible, child, that the spirits you have seen are illusion only, some deception that may cross your mind when—

348 **Abigail:** Why, this—this—is a base question, sir.

349 **Danforth:** Child, I would have you consider it—

350 **Abigail:** I have been hurt, Mr. Danforth; I have seen my blood runnin' out! I have been near to murdered every day because I done my duty pointing out the Devil's people—and this is my reward? To be mistrusted, denied, questioned like a—

351 **Danforth,** *weakening*: Child, I do not mistrust you—

352 **Abigail,** *in an open threat*: Let *you* beware, Mr. Danforth. Think you to be so mighty that the power of Hell may not turn your wits? Beware of it! There is—*Suddenly from an accusatory attitude, her face turns, looking into the air above—it is truly frightened.*

353 **Danforth,** *apprehensively*: What is it, child?

354 **Abigail,** *looking about in the air, clasping her arms about her as though cold*: I—I know not. A wind, a cold wind, has come. *Her eyes fall on* MARY WARREN.

355 **Mary Warren,** *terrified, pleading*: Abby!

356 **Mercy Lewis,** *shivering*: Your Honor, I freeze!

357 **Proctor:** They're pretending!

358 **Hathorne,** *touching* ABIGAIL*'s hand*: She is cold, Your Honor, touch her!

359 **Mercy Lewis,** *through chattering teeth*: Mary, do you send this shadow on me?

360 **Mary Warren:** Lord, save me!

361 **Susanna Walcott:** I freeze, I freeze!

362 **Abigail,** *shivering, visibly*: It is a wind, a wind!

363 **Mary Warren:** Abby, don't do that!





646 UNIT 5 • FACING OUR FEARS

DIGITAL PERSPECTIVES

364 **Danforth,** *himself engaged and entered by* ABIGAIL: Mary Warren, do you witch her? I say to you, do you send your spirit out?

365 *With a hysterical cry* MARY WARREN *starts to run.* PROCTOR *catches her.*

366 **Mary Warren,** *almost collapsing*: Let me go, Mr. Proctor, I cannot, I cannot—

367 **Abigail,** *crying to Heaven*: Oh, Heavenly Father, take away this shadow!

368 *Without warning or hesitation,* PROCTOR *leaps at* ABIGAIL and, *grabbing her by the hair, pulls her to her feet. She screams in pain.* DANFORTH, *astonished, cries,* "What are you about?" *and* HATHORNE *and* PARRIS *call. "Take your hands off her!" and out of it all comes* PROCTOR'*s roaring voice.*

369 **Proctor:** How do you call Heaven! Whore! Whore!

370 HERRICK *breaks* PROCTOR *from her.*

371 **Herrick:** John!

NOTES

The girls react to a possible "bewitchment" by Mary Warren.

NOTES

372 **Danforth:** Man! Man, what do you—

373 **Proctor,** *breathless and in agony*: It is a whore!

374 **Danforth,** *dumfounded*: You charge—?

375 **Abigail:** Mr. Danforth, he is lying!

376 **Proctor:** Mark her! Now she'll suck a scream to stab me with, but—

377 **Danforth:** You will prove this! This will not pass!

378 **Proctor,** *trembling, his life collapsing about him*: I have known her, sir. I have known her.

379 **Danforth:** You—you are a lecher?

380 **Francis,** *horrified*: John, you cannot say such a—

381 **Proctor:** Oh. Francis, I wish you had some evil in you that you might know me! *To* DANFORTH: A man will not cast away his good name. You surely know that.

382 **Danforth,** *dumfounded*: In—in what time? In what place?

383 **Proctor,** *his voice about to break, and his shame great*: In the proper place—where my beasts are bedded. On the last night of my joy, some eight months past. She used to serve me in my house, sir. *He has to clamp his jaw to keep from weeping.* A man may think God sleeps, but God sees everything, I know it now. I beg you, sir, I beg you—see her what she is. My wife, my dear good wife, took this girl soon after, sir, and put her out on the highroad. And being what she is, a lump of vanity, sir—*He is being overcome.* Excellency, forgive me, forgive me. *Angrily against himself, he turns away from the* GOVERNOR *for a moment. Then, as though to cry out is his only means of speech left*: She thinks to dance with me on my wife's grave! And well she might, for I thought of her softly. God help me, I lusted, and there *is* a promise in such sweat. But it is a whore's vengeance, and you must see it; I set myself entirely in your hands. I know you must see it now.

384 **Danforth,** *blanched, in horror, turning to* ABIGAIL: You deny every scrap and tittle of this?

385 **Abigail:** If I must answer that, I will leave and I will not come back again!

386 DANFORTH *seems unsteady.*

387 **Proctor:** I have made a bell of my honor! I have rung the doom of my good name—you will believe me, Mr. Danforth! My wife is innocent, except she knew a whore when she saw one!

388 **Abigail,** *stepping up to* DANFORTH: What look do you give me? DANFORTH *cannot speak.* I'll not have such looks! *She turns and starts for the door.*





**648** UNIT 5 • FACING OUR FEARS

DIGITAL PERSPECTIVES

389 **Danforth:** You will remain where you are! HERRICK *steps into her path. She comes up short, fire in her eyes.* Mr. Parris, go into the court and bring Goodwife Proctor out.

390 **Parris,** *objecting*: Your Honor, this is all a—

391 **Danforth,** *sharply to* PARRIS: Bring her out! And tell her not one word of what's been spoken here. And let you knock before you enter. PARRIS *goes out.* Now we shall touch the bottom of this swamp. *To* PROCTOR: Your wife, you say, is an honest woman.

392 **Proctor:** In her life, sir, she have never lied. There are them that cannot sing, and them that cannot weep—my wife cannot lie. I have paid much to learn it, sir.

393 **Danforth:** And when she put this girl out of your house, she put her out for a harlot?

394 **Proctor:** Aye, sir.

395 **Danforth:** And knew her for a harlot?

396 **Proctor:** Aye, sir, she knew her for a harlot.

397 **Danforth:** Good then. *To* ABIGAIL: And if she tell me, child, it were for harlotry, may God spread His mercy on you! *There is a knock. He calls to the door.* Hold! *To* ABIGAIL: Turn your back. Turn your back. *To* PROCTOR: Do likewise. *Both turn their backs—*ABIGAIL *with indignant slowness.* Now let neither of you turn to face Goody Proctor. No one in this room is to speak one word, or raise a gesture aye or nay. *He turns toward the door, calls*: Enter! The door opens. ELIZABETH *enters with* PARRIS. PARRIS *leaves her. She stands alone, her eyes looking for* PROCTOR. Mr. Cheever, report this testimony in all exactness. Are you ready?

398 **Cheever:** Ready, sir.

399 **Danforth:** Come here, woman. ELIZABETH *comes to him, glancing at* PROCTOR'*s back.* Look at me only, not at your husband. In my eyes only.

400 **Elizabeth,** *faintly*: Good, sir.

401 **Danforth:** We are given to understand that at one time you dismissed your servant, Abigail Williams.

402 **Elizabeth:** That is true, sir.

403 **Danforth:** For what cause did you dismiss her? *Slight pause. Then* ELIZABETH *tries to glance at* PROCTOR. You will look in my eyes only and not at your husband. The answer is in your memory and you need no help to give it to me. Why did you dismiss Abigail Williams?

404 **Elizabeth,** *not knowing what to say, sensing a situation, wetting her lips to stall for time*: She—dissatisfied me. *Pause.* And my husband.

NOTES





## PERSONALIZE FOR LEARNING

### English Language Support

**Figurative Language** Focus students' attention on Danforth's claim in paragraph 391 that "Now we shall touch the bottom of this swamp." Ask: *What is being compared here?* **Possible response:** Miller is comparing the situation in Salem to a swamp. Ask: *What ideas does this comparison inspire?* Invite students to research swamps to learn more about them. Based on what they learn, initiate a discussion that pushes students to think beyond the obvious. For example, a swamp is a wetland on which a forest has grown, and the water levels in a swamp fluctuate. Ask: *How do these facts enhance the meaning of Danforth's comment and Miller's metaphor?* Finally, ask students if there are any swamps where they live, and if so, what they look like. **ALL LEVELS**

## CLOSER LOOK

### Recognize a Euphemism

Students may have marked the way Elizabeth describes her problem with her husband in paragraph 408 during their first read. Encourage them to talk about the annotations that they marked. You may want to model a close read with the class based on the highlights shown in the text.

**ANNOTATE:** Have students mark the way Elizabeth describes her problem with her husband in paragraph 408, or have students participate while you highlight it.

**QUESTION:** Guide students to consider what the way of speaking might tell them. Ask what a reader can infer from the euphemism, and accept student responses.

**Possible response:** Elizabeth uses the phrase "turning from me" to mean adultery or infidelity. Danforth repeats it in paragraph 413 and then escalates to the word "lechery" in paragraph 417.

**CONCLUDE:** Help students to formulate conclusions about the importance of the phrase in the text. Ask students why the author might have included these details.

**Possible response:** Elizabeth's diction reflects her character. She is a gentle woman who would probably not use words such as *cheat* or *unfaithful*, mild as they seem to us today.

Remind students that a **euphemism** is a mild word or expression used in place of a harsh or offensive word. Point out that a playwright might employ a euphemism for one or both of two reasons: to replace a word that the audience might find offensive, or to replace a word that the character would not be comfortable saying. The first reason doesn't come up very often today as audiences have become accustomed to all sorts of vulgarities in dialogue. But it was a concern through most of the 20th century.

Elizabeth Proctor is brought in for questioning.

NOTES

405 **Danforth:** In what way dissatisfied you?

406 **Elizabeth:** She were—*She glances at* PROCTOR *for a cue.*

407 **Danforth:** Woman, look at me? ELIZABETH *does.* Were she slovenly? Lazy? What disturbance did she cause?

408 **Elizabeth:** Your Honor, I—in that time I were sick. And I—My husband is a good and righteous man. He is never drunk as some are, nor wastin' his time at the shovelboard, but always at his work. But in my sickness—you see, sir, I were a long time sick after my last baby, and I thought I saw my husband somewhat turning from me. And this girl—*She turns to* ABIGAIL.

409 **Danforth:** Look at me.

410 **Elizabeth:** Aye, sir. Abigail Williams—*She breaks off.*

411 **Danforth:** What of Abigail Williams?

412 **Elizabeth:** I came to think he fancied her. And so one night I lost my wits. I think, and put her out on the highroad.

413 **Danforth:** Your husband—did he indeed turn from you?

414 **Elizabeth,** *in agony*: My husband—is a goodly man, sir.

415 **Danforth:** Then he did not turn from you.





650 UNIT 5 • FACING OUR FEARS

DIGITAL PERSPECTIVES

416 **Elizabeth,** *starting to glance at* PROCTOR: He—

417 **Danforth**, *reaches out and holds her face, then*: Look at me! To your own knowledge, has John Proctor ever committed the crime of lechery? *In a crisis of indecision she cannot speak.* Answer my question! Is your husband a lecher!

418 **Elizabeth,** *faintly*: No, sir.

419 **Danforth:** Remove her, Marshal.

420 **Proctor:** Elizabeth, tell the truth!

421 **Danforth:** She has spoken. Remove her!

422 **Proctor,** *crying out*: Elizabeth, I have confessed it!

423 **Elizabeth:** Oh, God! *The door closes behind her.*

424 **Proctor:** She only thought to save my name!

425 **Hale:** Excellency, it is a natural lie to tell; I beg you, stop now before another is condemned! I may shut my conscience to it no more—private vengeance is working through this testimony! From the beginning this man has struck me true. By my oath to Heaven, I believe him now, and I pray you call back his wife before we—

426 **Danforth:** She spoke nothing of lechery, and this man has lied!

427 **Hale:** I believe him! *Pointing at* ABIGAIL: This girl has always struck me false! She has—

428 ABIGAIL, *with a weird, wild, chilling cry, screams up to the ceiling.*

429 **Abigail:** You will not! Begone! Begone, I say!

430 **Danforth:** What is it, child? *But* ABIGAIL, *pointing with fear, is now raising up her frightened* eyes, *her awed face, toward the ceiling—the girls are doing the same—and now* HATHORNE, HALE, PUTNAM, CHEEVER, HERRICK, *and* DANFORTH *do the same.* What's there? *He lowers his eyes from the ceiling, and now he is frightened; there is real tension in his voice.* Child! *She is transfixed—with all the girls, she is whimpering, open-mouthed, agape at the ceiling.* Girls! Why do you—?

431 **Mercy Lewis,** *pointing*: It's on the beam! Behind the rafter!

432 **Danforth,** *looking up*: Where!

433 **Abigail:** Why—? *She gulps.* Why do you come, yellow bird?

434 **Proctor:** Where's a bird? I see no bird!

435 **Abigail**, *to the ceiling*: My face? My face?

436 **Proctor:** Mr. Hale—

437 **Danforth:** Be quiet!

438 **Proctor,** *to* HALE: Do you see a bird?

439 **Danforth:** Be quiet!

NOTES





## PERSONALIZE FOR LEARNING

### Challenge

**Act It Out** Call students' attention to the scene in paragraphs 389–424. Assign the roles of Danforth, Parris, John Proctor, and Elizabeth Proctor, and have students act out the scene. Encourage them to vary the pace, tone, rhythm, and volume of their voices as they try to capture the tension that is present during this "test" of Elizabeth and John's honesty. Encourage the whole group to discuss ways in which the live voices enhance the meaning. Ask: *What words and lines are the most important? What emotion does each character feel during these lines?* Based on the discussion, have the actors read the lines again, pushing the meaning and emotion even more. You might also let four different students try out their acting skills and encourage a discussion of how the effect changes with different voices.

NOTES

440 **Abigail,** *to the ceiling, in a genuine conversation with the "bird," as though trying to talk it out of attacking her*: But God made my face; you cannot want to tear my face. Envy is a deadly sin, Mary.

441 **Mary Warren,** *on her feet with a spring, and horrified, pleading*: Abby!

442 **Abigail,** *unperturbed, continuing to the "bird"*: Oh, Mary, this is a black art to change your shape. No, I cannot, I cannot stop my mouth; it's God's work I do.

443 **Mary Warren:** Abby, I'm *here!*

444 **Proctor,** *frantically*: They're pretending, Mr. Danforth!

445 **Abigail**—*now she takes a backward step, as though in fear the bird will swoop down momentarily*: Oh, please, Mary! Don't come down.

446 **Susanna Walcott:** Her claws, she's stretching her claws!

447 **Proctor:** Lies, lies.

448 **Abigail,** *backing further, eyes still fixed above*: Mary, please don't hurt me!

449 **Mary Warren,** *to* DANFORTH: I'm not hurting her!

450 **Danforth,** *to* MARY WARREN: Why does she see this vision?

451 **Mary Warren:** She sees nothin'!

452 **Abigail,** *now staring full front as though hypnotized, and mimicking the exact tone of* MARY WARREN*'s cry*: She sees nothin'!

453 **Mary Warren,** *pleading*: Abby, you mustn't!

454 **Abigail and All the Girls,** *all transfixed*: Abby, you mustn't!

455 **Mary Warren,** *to all the girls*: I'm here, I'm here!

456 **Girls:** I'm here, I'm here!

457 **Danforth,** *horrified*: Mary Warren! Draw back your spirit out of them!

458 **Mary Warren:** Mr. Danforth!

459 **Girls,** *cutting her off*: Mr. Danforth!

460 **Danforth:** Have you compacted with the Devil? Have you?

461 **Mary Warren:** Never, never!

462 **Girls:** Never, never!

463 **Danforth,** *growing hysterical*: Why can they only repeat you?

464 **Proctor:** Give me a whip—I'll stop it!

465 **Mary Warren:** They're sporting. They—!

466 **Girls:** They're sporting!

467 **Mary Warren,** *turning on them all hysterically and stamping her feet*: Abby, stop it!

468 **Girls,** *stamping their feet*: Abby, stop it!





## CROSS-CURRICULAR PERSPECTIVES

**Science: Medical Explanations** Researchers have suggested that some afflictions in Salem may have had a physical origin such as an illness like encephalitis. Another possible cause is ingestion of rye grain that has been infected by a fungus called ergot. Eating infested rye can cause stomach pain, itching sensations, burning extremities, hallucinations, and even convulsions. Ergot tends to appear on rye when the weather is damp. Rye was a staple in Salem and the weather had been rainy before the hysteria began. Have students investigate the credibility of some of these medical explanations for the Salem trials and publish their conclusions in the form of a newspaper article. **(Research to Explore)**

469 **Mary Warren:** Stop it!

470 **Girls:** Stop it!

471 **Mary Warren,** *screaming it out at the top of her lungs, and raising her fists:* Stop it!!

472 **Girls,** *raising their fists:* Stop it!!

473 MARY WARREN, *utterly confounded, and becoming overwhelmed by* ABIGAIL'S*—and the* GIRLS'*—utter conviction, starts to whimper, hands half raised, powerless, and all the girls begin whimpering exactly as she does.*

474 **Danforth:** A little while ago you were afflicted. Now it seems you afflict others; where did you find this power?

475 **Mary Warren,** *staring at* ABIGAIL: I—have no power.

476 **Girls:** I have no power.

477 **Proctor:** They're gulling[7] you, Mister!

478 **Danforth:** Why did you turn about this past two weeks? You have seen the Devil, have you not?

479 **Hale,** *indicating* ABIGAIL *and the* GIRLS: You cannot believe them!

480 **Mary Warren:** I—

481 **Proctor,** *sensing her weakening:* Mary, God damns all liars!

482 **Danforth,** *pounding it into her:* You have seen the Devil, you have made compact with Lucifer, have you not?

NOTES

**CLOSE READ**

**ANNOTATE:** In paragraphs 471–481, mark details in both stage directions and dialogue that relate to power and powerlessness.

**QUESTION:** Why does Miller highlight these concepts in this scene?

**CONCLUDE:** What change in the courtroom do these details emphasize?

**7. gulling** *v.* fooling.

Abigail "sees" the yellow bird she claims is Mary Warren's spirit.

DIGITAL PERSPECTIVES

## CLOSE READ

Remind students that playwrights can highlight important concepts in both dialogue and stage directions. You may wish to model the Close Read using the following think-aloud format. Possible responses to the questions on the student page are included.

**ANNOTATE:** As I read paragraphs 471 through 481, I notice that Miller includes words and actions that have to do with power and powerlessness.

**QUESTION:** I believe Miller highlights these concepts in the scene because the fate of the accused depends on who actually maintains power.

**CONCLUDE:** The details emphasize that Abigail and the other girls fight hard to maintain power, and that John Proctor loses power over Mary Warren as they regain influence over her.

NOTES

483 **Proctor:** God damns liars, Mary!

484 MARY *utters something unintelligible, staring at* ABIGAIL, *who keeps watching the* "bird" above.

485 **Danforth:** I cannot hear you. What do you say? MARY *utters again unintelligibly.* You will confess yourself or you will hang! *He turns her roughly to face him.* Do you know who I am? I say you will hang if you do not open with me!

486 **Proctor:** Mary, remember the angel Raphael—do that which is good and—

487 **Abigail,** *pointing upward*: The wings! Her wings are spreading! Mary, please, don't, don't—!

488 **Hale:** I see nothing, Your Honor!

489 **Danforth:** Do you confess this power! *He is an inch from her face.* Speak!

490 **Abigail:** She's going to come down! She's walking the beam!

491 **Danforth:** Will you speak!

492 **Mary Warren,** *staring in horror*: I cannot!

493 **Girls:** I cannot!

494 **Parris:** Cast the Devil out! Look him in the face! Trample him! We'll save you, Mary, only stand fast against him and—

495 **Abigail,** *looking up*: Look out! She's coming down!

496 *She and all the girls run to one wall, shielding their eyes. And now, as though cornered, they let out a gigantic scream, and* MARY, *as though infected, opens her mouth and screams with them. Gradually* ABIGAIL *and the girls leave off, until only* MARY *is left there, staring up at the "bird," screaming madly. All watch her, horrified by this evident fit.* PROCTOR *strides to her.*

497 **Proctor:** Mary, tell the Governor what they—*He has hardly got a word out, when, seeing him coming for her, she rushes out of his reach, screaming in horror.*

498 **Mary Warren:** Don't touch me—don't touch me! *At which the girls halt at the door.*

499 **Proctor,** *astonished*: Mary!

500 **Mary Warren,** *pointing at* PROCTOR: You're the Devil's man!

*He is stopped in his tracks.*

501 **Parris:** Praise God!

502 **Girls:** Praise God!

503 **Proctor,** *numbed*: Mary, how—?

504 **Mary Warren:** I'll not hang with you! I love God. I love God.

505 **Danforth,** *to* MARY: He bid you do the Devil's work?





## PERSONALIZE FOR LEARNING

### English Language Support

**Adverbs Ending in *–ly*** Ask students to locate and consider adverbs that end in *–ly*, used mostly in the stage directions. Here are a few examples: "Mary utters *unintelligibly*" and "He turns her *roughly* to face him," in paragraph 485. Abigail and the girls leave off "*gradually*" and Mary is "screaming *madly*" in paragraph 496. Proctor "has *hardly* got a word out" in paragraph 497.

Ask: *What does each adverb mean? What verb (or adjective or adverb) does each adverb describe or modify? How does each adverb enhance the meaning of the stage direction?* Ask students to write sentences about the action in Act III that use adverbs ending in *–ly*. Give them the opportunity to read their sentences aloud. **EMERGING**

506 **Mary Warren,** *hysterically, indicating* PROCTOR: He come at me by night and every day to sign, to sign, to—

507 **Danforth:** Sign what?

508 **Parris:** The Devil's book? He come with a book?

509 **Mary Warren,** *hysterically, pointing at* PROCTOR, *fearful of him*: My name, he want my name. "I'll murder you," he says, "if my wife hangs! We must go and overthrow the court," he says!

510 Danforth's *head jerks toward* PROCTOR, *shock and horror in his face.*

511 **Proctor,** *turning, appealing to* HALE: Mr. Hale!

512 **Mary Warren,** *her sobs beginning*: He wake me every night, his eyes were like coals and his fingers claw my neck, and I sign, I sign . . .

513 **Hale:** Excellency, this child's gone wild!

514 **Proctor,** *as* DANFORTH'*s wide eyes pour on him*: Mary, Mary!

515 **Mary Warren,** *screaming at him*: No, I love God; I go your way no more. I love God. I bless God. *Sobbing, she rushes to* ABIGAIL. Abby, Abby, I'll never hurt you more! *They all watch, as* ABIGAIL, *out of her infinite charity, reaches out and draws the sobbing* MARY *to her, and then looks up to* DANFORTH.

516 **Danforth,** *to* PROCTOR: What are you? PROCTOR *is beyond speech in his anger*. You are combined with anti-Christ,[8] are you not? I have seen your power; you will not deny it! What say you, Mister?

517 **Hale:** Excellency—

518 **Danforth:** I will have nothing from you, Mr. Hale! *To* PROCTOR: Will you confess yourself befouled with Hell, or do you keep that black allegiance yet? What say you?

519 **Proctor,** *his mind wild, breathless*: I say—I say—God is dead!

520 **Parris:** Hear it, hear it!

521 **Proctor,** *laughs insanely, then*: A fire, a fire is burning! I hear the boot of Lucifer. I see his filthy face! And it is my face, and yours, Danforth! For them that quail to bring men out of ignorance, as I have quailed, and as you quail now when you know in all your black hearts that this be fraud—God damns our kind especially, and we will burn, we will burn together.

522 **Danforth:** Marshal! Take him and Corey with him to the jail!

523 **Hale,** *staring across to the door*: I denounce these proceedings!

524 **Proctor:** You are pulling Heaven down and raising up a whore!

525 **Hale:** I denounce these proceedings, I quit this court! *He slams the door to the outside behind him.*

526 **Danforth,** *calling to him in a fury*: Mr. Hale! Mr. Hale!

THE CURTAIN FALLS

NOTES

**CLOSE READ**

**ANNOTATE:** Mark the repeated sentence in paragraphs 504 and 515.

**QUESTION:** Why does Miller repeat this sentence?

**CONCLUDE:** What is the effect of this repetition?

**8. anti-Christ** In the Bible, a spirit of opposition to Christianity, to be embodied someday in a person who will spread universal evil.





DIGITAL  PERSPECTIVES

## CLOSE READ

Remind students that repeated phrases and sentences are often used for emphasis. You may wish to model the Close Read using the following think-aloud format. Possible responses to questions on the student page are included.

**ANNOTATE:** As I read paragraphs 504 and 515, I notice that Miller repeats a sentence.

**QUESTION:** I think Miller repeats the sentence to emphasize the irony of Mary's words.

**CONCLUDE:** The effect is to highlight Mary's dishonesty and the dishonesty of all the girls who are claiming to be good Christians.

## Comprehension Check

Possible responses:

1. The action takes place in a courtroom in Salem, Massachusetts, in 1692.
2. Giles and Danforth provide Mary Warren as their "hard evidence." She is willing to state that she and the girls were pretending and that she never saw any spirits.
3. After they are accused of pretending, Abigail and the other girls "see" a bird with sharp claws above them on the ceiling. They claim that it is Mary Warren.
4. Elizabeth Proctor is brought before Danforth to corroborate her husband's testimony that he had sexual relations with Abigail, but she fails to do so.
5. In Act III, the accusations come to the courtroom. Giles asserts that Putnam is trying to make a land grab. Reverend Hale, Judge Hathorne, Deputy Governor Danforth, and Reverend Parris join Giles and Francis to discuss this matter. Some community members accuse and others defend themselves and their wives. Mary Warren states that she and the girls have been pretending and that they never saw any spirits. In order to reveal Abigail's sins and her possible motivation for lying, John Proctor admits he had an illicit relationship with Abigail. Danforth brings Elizabeth in to verify her husband's claim, but she does not, and Proctor appears to be a liar. Abigail and the girls "see" a bird on the rafter and claim it is Mary Warren. Their hysterics infect Mary and she turns against John Proctor. Hale quits the court when John Proctor, formerly the voice of reason, falls apart.

## Research

**Research to Explore** If students have difficulty choosing an interesting aspect of the text, then suggest they choose from colonial courts, poppets, or the idea of a "Devil's book."

## Comprehension Check

**Complete the following items after you finish your first read.**

1. Where does the action of Act III take place?

2. At the beginning of Act III, what "hard evidence" do Giles and Francis provide that the girls are frauds?

3. What appears to happen to Abigail and the others girls after they are accused by Mary Warren of pretending?

4. Why is Elizabeth Proctor brought into the Court?

5. **Notebook** Write a summary of Act III of *The Crucible.*

## RESEARCH

**Research to Explore** Conduct research on an aspect of the text you find interesting. For example, you may want to learn the possible medical reasons for the behavior of Abigail and the other accusers.





### PERSONALIZE FOR LEARNING

**Challenge**

**Two Films** Offer parts or all of two or more film productions of *The Crucible*, such as the 1996 film starring Daniel Day Lewis and Winona Ryder or the 1967 adaptation starring George C. Scott and Colleen Dewhurst. Discuss the similarities and differences between the two interpretations and presentations. Use these questions to guide discussion: *What does each version emphasize? How does each one present the setting? Do the actors effectively portray the characters? How does each version support the play's themes? Which film do you prefer? Why? Which is the most powerful performance? Why?* Ask a volunteer to act as note taker during discussion and then to write a summary of the group's ideas and opinions.

MAKING MEANING

## Close Read the Text

Reread paragraph 368, and mark the text in quotations. Why does Miller present the action in this way? What effect would this create for an audience?

THE CRUCIBLE, ACT III

## Analyze the Text

CITE TEXTUAL EVIDENCE to support your answers.

Notebook Respond to these questions.

1. (a) **Draw Conclusions** How does Danforth react to the news that Proctor has a deposition from Mary? (b) **Analyze** Why do you think Danforth asks whether Proctor has told the story to the village? Explain.
2. **Make Inferences** Why do you think Hale is so insistent that lawyers be brought in to argue Proctor's case?
3. (a) **Interpret** Why does Proctor confess to the affair with Abigail? (b) **Analyze** What does his confession reveal about his character?
4. (a) What term does Danforth use to describe Abigail and the girls? (b) **Analyze** What does his use of this term show about his views of the accusers?

LANGUAGE DEVELOPMENT

## Concept Vocabulary

remorseless effrontery callously

**Why These Words?** The concept vocabulary words refer to different kinds of disregard for others. What other words in Act III relate to this concept?

**Practice**

Notebook Use each concept vocabulary word in a sentence that demonstrates the word's meaning.

## Word Study

Notebook **Connotation** The **connotation** of a word refers to emotional connections that add meaning beyond its literal definition. Words can have similar connotations that vary mainly in degree, or intensity. For example, both *remorseless* and *callously* have similar negative connotations, but *remorseless* is a more extreme word. It suggests a harshness that goes beyond mere callousness. *Unfeeling*, on the other hand, has a less intense connotation.

1. Write two synonyms for each of these words: *denounce, eager, fraud, coldly.*
2. For each trio of words from item 1, indicate which has the most intense connotation and which has the least intense connotation.

WORD NETWORK

Add words related to fear from the text to your Word Network.

STANDARDS

Language

- Demonstrate understanding of figurative language, word relationships, and nuances in word meanings.
- Analyze nuances in the meaning of words with similar denotations.





DIGITAL PERSPECTIVES

## Jump Start

CLOSE READ *If you were acting in this play, would you like the stage directions? Why or why not?*

### Close Read the Text

**Possible response:** This presentation shows that all the characters are acting and reacting at once.

### Analyze the Text

**Possible responses:**

1. (a) Danforth says, "I accept no deposition." He wants to hear Mary's testimony in person. (b) Danforth doesn't want Proctor to undermine him in any way. **DOK 2**
2. Hale is beginning to side with John Proctor; he wants to protect his interests. **DOK 3**
3. (a) Proctor confesses to prove that Abigail is a fraud. (b) It reveals that he is willing to be honest to save his wife. **DOK 3**
4. (a) Danforth refers to them as children. (b) The term shows that he is focused on their seeming innocence. **DOK 3**

### Concept Vocabulary

**Why These Words? Possible responses:** *contempt, hardness, overthrow, sarcasm, resents, suspiciously, anger, anxiety, threat, accusatory, agony, horror*

**Practice**

Sentences will vary.

**Word Network**

**Possible words:** *grave, wrath, helpless*

### Word Study

For more support, see **Concept Vocabulary and Word Study.**

**Possible responses:**

1. Synonyms for *denounce: condemn* and *accuse;* synonyms for *eager: willing* and *keen;* synonyms for *fraud: fake* and *deception;* synonyms for *coldly: distantly* and *coolly.*
2. *Condemn* is most intense and *accuse* is least intense; *eager* is most intense and *willing* is least intense; *fraud* is most intense and *fake* is least intense; *coldly* is most intense and *distantly* is least intense.

## FORMATIVE ASSESSMENT

### Analyze the Text

- **If** students struggle to understand how Danforth reacts to the deposition, **then** ask them to reread paragraph 82.
- **If** students cannot identify the term Danforth uses to describe Abigail and the girls, **then** ask them to reread paragraph 85.

### Word Study

**If** students are completely unfamiliar with all the words, **then** direct them to a dictionary. For Reteach and Practice, see **Word Study: Connotation (RP).**

## Analyze Craft and Structure

**Character Development** A character may be *static* or *dynamic*. Static characters do not change in the course of a play. They fill necessary roles, but are the same at the end as they were at the beginning. Dynamic characters actively change for either the better or the worse.

For more support, see **Analyze Craft and Structure: Character Development.**

**MAKE IT INTERACTIVE**

Encourage pairs of students to describe the motivation of each character in *The Crucible*.

### Practice

Possible responses:

1. (a) Miller describes him as "ashamed" in the stage directions of paragraph 44 and explains that he "goes hard" in paragraph 189. (b) When Giles covers his face, it is an example of indirect characterization that supports "ashamed." When Giles clenches his fist in paragraph 193 and yells "A fart on Thomas Putnam," that shows he has gone hard.
2. (a) Mary fails to answer Danforth in paragraph 255; she sobs after saying she is "with God" in paragraphs 262 and 263; she almost collapses in paragraph 366. (b) The first example shows that she is afraid to tell the truth. The second shows how wrenching it is for her to tell the truth, and the third example shows how vulnerable she is to Abigail's suggestions.
3. (a) Elizabeth evades Danforth's questions because she does not want to tell the court about John's sexual relations with Abigail. (b) Her evasion suggests that she loves her husband and wants to protect his reputation but that she does not understand that the court is asking her to verify what he has already confessed.
4. (a) Hale realizes that the proceedings are being determined by Abigail's jealousy and vengeance. He has lost his faith is what she says. (b) In Act III, Hale changes from believing the accusations to disbelieving them.

### FORMATIVE ASSESSMENT

**Analyze Craft and Structure**

- **If** students have trouble understanding direct and indirect characterization, **then** make a chart that shows both as they apply to Elizabeth Proctor.
- **If** students struggle to describe characters' motivations, **then** ask, "What does this character want?"

For Reteach and Practice, see **Analyze Craft and Structure: Character Development (RP).**

MAKING MEANING

THE CRUCIBLE, ACT III

## Analyze Craft and Structure

**Character Development** The term **characterization** refers to the ways in which a writer reveals a character's personality. There are two types of characterization. In **direct characterization,** the author simply tells readers what a character is like. A playwright might use direct characterization in stage directions, but most dramatic literature requires **indirect characterization,** in which characters' traits are revealed through various types of details:

- the character's words, actions, and appearance
- other characters' comments
- other characters' reactions

Understanding characters through characterization is the key to unlocking their **motivations**—the reasons they feel, think, and behave as they do. Like people in real life, characters in plays are not always what they seem. Fear, greed, guilt, love, loyalty, pride, and revenge are some of the forces that drive human behavior, but they may be masked or hidden.

### Practice

**CITE TEXTUAL EVIDENCE** to support your answers.

**Notebook** Respond to these questions.

1. (a) Identify two examples of direct characterization of Giles Corey in stage directions. (b) Identify two examples of indirect characterization—in dialogue or in action—that amplify the examples of direct characterization. Explain your choices.
2. (a) Identify three examples of indirect characterization that reveal Mary Warren's personality. (b) For each example, explain what readers learn about her.
3. (a) What is Elizabeth's motivation for evading Danforth's questions about Abigail's dismissal from the Proctor household? (b) Considering Elizabeth's belief that lying is a sin, what does her evasion suggest about her character, her feelings for her husband, and her understanding of the court proceedings?
4. (a) What motivates Hale to denounce the proceedings and quit the court? (b) How does Hale's character change from the beginning to the end of Act III?

**STANDARDS**

**Reading Literature**

- Analyze the impact of the author's choices regarding how to develop and relate elements of a story or drama.
- Analyze a case in which grasping point of view requires distinguishing what is directly stated in a text from what is really meant.





### PERSONALIZE FOR LEARNING

**Strategic Support**

**What Drives Behavior?** Students may need help understanding the sentence "Fear, greed, guilt, love, loyalty, pride, and revenge are some of the forces that drive human behavior, but they may be masked or hidden." Explain that the sentence is somewhat figurative, since it personifies the forces, suggesting that they can "drive" behavior.

Invite discussion of personal examples of these forces driving behavior, examples from current events, popular culture, or other pieces of literature. Ask: *What forces drive you in your day-to-day life?* Encourage students to share their own thoughts and experiences.

## Author's Style

**Author's Choices: Literary Devices** Like characters, situations are also not always what they seem. When there is a contrast between expectation and reality, or between words and meaning, **irony** is at work. Playwrights often use irony to build suspense and create tension. Two types of irony are dramatic irony and verbal irony.

- **Dramatic irony** is the discrepancy between what a character believes or understands and what the audience knows to be true.

  EXAMPLE: In Shakespeare's *Romeo and Juliet*, the Capulets believe Juliet to be dead. The audience knows that she has taken a potion that mimics death, but that she is alive and will awaken.

- **Verbal irony** occurs when a character says one thing but means another.

  EXAMPLE: In Act III, Scene ii, of Shakespeare's *Julius Caesar*, Mark Antony refers to Brutus and the rest of Caesar's murderers as "honourable men." He does not really mean this.

### Read It

Complete this chart by recording two examples of dramatic irony and two examples of verbal irony in Act III. For examples of dramatic irony, describe what the audience understands or knows that the characters themselves do not. For examples of verbal irony, write what each speaker really means. For all examples, analyze the effect of the discrepancy.

| EXAMPLE | TYPE OF IRONY | ANALYSIS |
|---|---|---|
| I know you must see it now. | Dramatic | John thinks that his case against Abigail is now certain, but the audience knows that it is not. |
| My husband is—a goodly man, sir. | Dramatic | Elizabeth is protecting her husband, but the audience knows that he has already confessed. |
| There's the "child" she is! | Verbal | Proctor means that she is a grown woman capable of deceit and seduction. |
| I say—I say—God is dead! | Verbal | Proctor does not mean this literally; he means that justice is not being done here. |

### Write It

Notebook In what ways is Elizabeth Proctor's testimony ironic?

EVIDENCE LOG

Before moving on to Act IV, go to your Evidence Log and record what you learned from Act III of *The Crucible*.





DIGITAL PERSPECTIVES

## Author's Style

**Literary Devices** Most students will readily recognize the extreme form of verbal irony called *sarcasm* because they use it and hear it every day. Sarcasm is language that seems to be praise but is really critical. The word derives from the Greek *sarkazein* meaning "to tear flesh" or "grind teeth" suggesting that it means to speak bitterly or bitingly. Explain that sarcasm can be used to offend or it can be used for comic effect. Offer this famous example by Mark Twain: "I didn't attend the funeral, but I sent a nice letter saying I approved of it."

For more support, see **Author's Style: Literary Devices.**

### Read It

See possible responses in chart on Student page.

Evidence Log Support students in completing their Evidence Log. This paced activity will help prepare them for the Performance-Based Assessment at the end of the unit.

### Write It

**Possible response:**

Elizabeth Proctor's testimony is an example of dramatic irony because there is a discrepancy between what she knows and what the audience knows. The audience knows that John has confessed to adultery, but she does not know this. The effect on the audience is one of shock and regret for her: poor Elizabeth! She's lied to protect her husband, but she's doomed him instead. In paragraphs 420 through 424, John informs her and she realizes her ironic mistake.

### FORMATIVE ASSESSMENT

### Conventions and Style

**If** students have difficulty distinguishing between the two kinds of irony, **then** explain that dramatic irony always involves what the audience knows. Verbal irony does not.

For Reteach and Practice, see **Author's Style: Literary Devices (RP).**

### Selection Test

Administer the "The Crucible, Act III" Selection Test, which is available in both print and digital formats online in Assessments.

## PERSONALIZE FOR LEARNING

### English Language Development

**What Is Said and What Is Implied** Have students reread the scene in the court where a character cries, *"Thomas Putnam is reaching out for land."* (paragraph 14) Ask pairs of students to explain why in the middle of the court session a character may cry such a thing. **EMERGING**

Ask students to write a sentence explaining what Giles Corey implies when he cries that in court. **EXPANDING**

Ask students to write a paragraph explaining the relation between the main issues being treated by the court of Salem, and what Giles Corey says. **BRIDGING**

An expanded **English Language Support Lesson** on Literary Devices is available in the Interactive Teacher's Edition.

# *The Crucible*, Act IV

**AUDIO SUMMARIES**
Audio summaries of Act IV of *The Crucible* are available online in both English and Spanish in the Interactive Teacher's Edition or Unit Resources. Assigning these summaries prior to reading the selection may help students build additional background knowledge and set a context for their first read.

## Summary

In Act IV of Arthur Miller's drama *The Crucible*, Rebecca Nurse and John Proctor are in jail waiting to be hanged. Rev. Hale and Rev. Parris both try to get them to confess to witchcraft in order to save their lives. Meanwhile, Abigail has fled, having stolen money from Parris. Judge Danforth asks Elizabeth, still in jail, to talk to her husband in the hope of getting a confession from him. Elizabeth and John speak; they have not seen each other in months, and they both apologize for their mistakes. John struggles to decide whether or not to make a false confession.

### Insight

In the fourth act, we see the dire effects that fear of witchcraft has caused in Salem. A dozen have died unfairly and more than a hundred are accused. Judge Danforth's ultimate concern seems not to be genuine innocence or guilty but preserving his and the court's reputation.

ESSENTIAL QUESTION:
How do we respond when challenged by fear?

## Connection to Essential Question

In the fourth act of *The Crucible* John Proctor responds to fear by refusing to bend to it and by asserting the truth even though it results in his death.

WHOLE-CLASS LEARNING PERFORMANCE TASK
Could any of the characters in *The Crucible* have done more to end the hysteria in Salem?

UNIT PERFORMANCE-BASED ASSESSMENT
Is fear always a harmful emotion?

## Connection to Performance Tasks

**Whole-Class Learning Performance Task** Once set in motion, the witchcraft hysteria in Salem may have been impossible to end. However, if the actions of a few of the central characters (e.g., Abigail, Betty, Judge Danforth, and Tituba) had been different, the sad outcome of the story could have been prevented.

**Unit Performance-Based Assessment** In Act IV of *The Crucible*, John Proctor goes to his death with honor, and his wife, Elizabeth, whom he once betrayed with infidelity, calls him a good man. Fear of dishonor leads John to make the noble choice, which Elizabeth appreciates.

DIGITAL PERSPECTIVES

 Audio  Video  Document  Annotation Highlights  EL Highlights Online Assessment

## LESSON RESOURCES

| | Making Meaning | Language Development | Effective Expression |
|---|---|---|---|
| **Lesson** | **First Read**<br>**Close Read**<br>**Analyze the Text**<br>**Analyze Craft and Structure** | **Concept Vocabulary**<br>**Word Study**<br>**Author's Style** | **Writing to Sources**<br>**Speaking and Listening** |
| **Instructional Standards** | **RL.10** By the end of grade 11, read and comprehend literature . . .<br>**RL.2** Determine two or more themes or central ideas of a text . . .<br>**W.9** Draw evidence from literary or informational texts . . . | **L.4.c** Consult general and specialized reference materials . . .<br>**RL.4** Determine the meaning of words and phrases . . . | **W.1** Write arguments . . .<br>**W.9.a** Apply *grades 11–12 Reading standards* . . .<br>**SL.4** Present information, findings, and supporting evidence . . . |
| **STUDENT RESOURCES** | | | |
| Available online in the Interactive Student Edition or Unit Resources | Selection Audio<br>First-Read Guide: Fiction<br>Close-Read Guide: Fiction | Word Network | Evidence Log |
| **TEACHER RESOURCES** | | | |
| **Selection Resources** Available online in the Interactive Teacher's Edition or Unit Resources | Audio Summaries<br>Annotation Highlights<br>EL Highlights<br>English Language Support Lesson: Argument<br>Analyze Craft and Structure: Literary Forms<br>Analyze Craft and Structure: Biblical Allusions | Concept Vocabulary and Word Study<br>Author's Style: Realism | Writing to Sources: Argument<br>Speaking and Listening: Thematic Analysis |
| **Reteach/Practice (RP)** Available online in the Interactive Teacher's Edition or Unit Resources | Analyze Craft and Structure: Literary Forms (RP)<br>Analyze Craft and Structure: Biblical Allusions (RP) | Word Study: Etymology (RP)<br>Author's Style: Realism (RP) | Writing to Sources: Argument (RP)<br>Speaking and Listening: Thematic Analysis (RP) |
| **Assessment** Available online in Assessments | Selection Test | | |
| **My Resources** | A Unit 5 Answer Key is available online and in the Interactive Teacher's Edition. | | |

# Reading Support

| Text Complexity Rubric: *The Crucible*, Act IV | |
|---|---|
| **Quantitative Measures** | |
| **Lexile:** NP **Text Length:** 6,158 words | |
| **Qualitative Measures** | |
| Knowledge Demands ①—②—③—❹—⑤ | Students will probably not be familiar with the situation that is central to the selection. Many, but not all, of the unfamiliar elements are made clear in dialogue, stage directions, and exposition by the playwright. |
| Structure ①—②—❸—④—⑤ | Organization of the narrative is mostly sequential, but important incidents occurred before the narrative begins and are only gradually revealed. |
| Language Conventionality and Clarity ①—②—③—❹—⑤ | Considerable above-level vocabulary and some archaic usages complicate the language, although most of the dialogue reflects ordinary speech. |
| Levels of Meaning/Purpose ①—②—③—❹—⑤ | One level of meaning is straightforward and compellingly presented. As a political allegory, the play operates on another level that requires more background knowledge to grasp. |

DECIDE AND PLAN

## English Language Support

Provide English Learners with support for knowledge demands and language as they read the selection.

**Knowledge Demands** Before reading the text, review the background information with students. Remind students that the people in Salem believed that witches were real and walked among them. They believed that the devil could suddenly take possession of a good person and turn that person into a witch, who could then bewitch and kill others.

**Language** Students will probably have difficulty with the above-level vocabulary and deviations from standard English. Explain to students that it is not necessary for them to understand every word, so long as they have a basic understanding of the dialogue.

## Strategic Support

Provide students with strategic support to ensure that they can successfully read the text.

**Knowledge Demands** After reading the background information, have students discuss Danforth's statement, "A person is either with this court or he must be counted against it." What problems does this present for someone trying to prove his or her innocence?

**Language** For students who have difficulty with the nonstandard English, especially with the nonstandard use of verbs *has* and *have*, encourage them to change the forms to standard ones and then reread the sentences or lines of dialogue.

## Challenge

Provide students who need to be challenged with ideas for how they can go beyond a simple interpretation of the text.

**Text Analysis** Pair students and have them discuss what goodness means to different characters in the play. What does it mean to Elizabeth Proctor, to Judge Danforth, and to John Proctor?

**Written Response** Have students research the McCarthy hearings of the 1950s and write a short essay about the parallels they see between those hearings and the Salem witch trials as portrayed in *The Crucible*.

TEACH

## Read and Respond

Have students do their first read of the selection. Then have them complete their close read. Finally, work with them on the Making Meaning, Language Development, and Effective Expression activities.

# Standards Support Through Teaching and Learning Cycle

## IDENTIFY NEEDS

Analyze results of the Beginning-of-Year Assessment, focusing on the items relating to Unit 5. Also take into consideration student performance to this point and your observations of where particular students struggle.

## DECIDE AND PLAN

- If students have performed poorly on items matching these standards, then provide selection scaffolds before assigning them the on-level lesson provided in the Student Edition.
- If students have done well on the Beginning-of-Year Assessment, then challenge them to keep progressing and learning by giving them opportunities to practice the skills in depth.
- Use the Selection Resources listed on the Planning pages for *The Crucible,* Act IV, to help students continually improve their ability to master the standards.

**Instructional Standards: *The Crucible,* Act IV**

| | Catching Up | This Year | Looking Forward |
|---|---|---|---|
| Reading | Review the **Word Study: Etymology (RP)** worksheet with students to help them better understand word origins.<br><br>You may wish to administer the **Analyze Craft and Structure: Literary Forms (RP)** worksheet to familiarize students with literal and symbolic meanings.<br><br>You may wish to administer the **Analyze Craft and Structure: Biblical Allusions (RP)** worksheet to help students better understand allusions to religious texts. | **L.4.c** Consult general and specialized reference materials, both print and digital, to find the pronunciation of a word or determine or clarify its precise meaning, its part of speech, its etymology, or its standard usage.<br><br>**RL.2** Determine two or more themes or central ideas of a text and analyze their development over the course of the text, including how they interact and build on one another to produce a complex account; provide an objective summary of the text. | Have students locate the origins of other words in the text.<br><br>Challenge students to consider how allegories may be missed entirely by inattentive readers.<br><br>Challenge students to identify allusions to religious texts in other works they are familiar with. |
| Writing | You may wish to administer the **Writing to Sources: Argument (RP)** worksheet to better prepare students for their assignment. | **W.1** Write arguments to support claims in an analysis of substantive topics or texts, using valid reasoning and relevant and sufficient evidence. | Invite students to alternatively write an argumentative essay about why *The Crucible* is not relevant to today's world. |

## ANALYZE AND REVISE

- Analyze student work for evidence of student learning.
- Identify whether or not students have met the expectations in the standards.
- Identify implications for future instruction.

## TEACH

Implement the planned lesson, and gather evidence of student learning.

## Jump Start

FIRST READ Ask students to write a brief paragraph that answers these questions: *Does this play have villains? Who are they? Tell why you think so.* Have them read their paragraphs aloud. Lead a short discussion.

### *The Crucible,* Act IV  

Why does Parris want John Proctor and others to confess? Why does Hale want this, too? Why might Elizabeth want her husband to confess? Modeling these and other questions readers might ask will bring *The Crucible,* Act IV to life and connect it to the Performance Task assignment. Selection audio and print capability for the selection are available in the Interactive Teacher's Edition.

### Concept Vocabulary

Support students as they rank their words. Ask if they've ever heard, read or used them. Reassure them that the definitions for these words are listed in the selection.

### FIRST READ

As they read, students should perform the steps of the first read:

NOTICE: Remind students to notice which characters appear in Act IV (and which do not), what this act is mainly about, and why the characters react to one another as they do.

ANNOTATE: Remind students to mark unfamiliar words and phrases, parts of Act IV that surprise or confuse them, and details that they find especially revealing about the characters.

CONNECT: Encourage students to go beyond Act IV to make connections—Do the events make sense in terms of what's happened already in the play? Do the events remind them of events in other books they have read or movies they have seen?

RESPOND: Students will answer questions and write a summary to demonstrate understanding.

Point out to students that they will perform the first three steps concurrently as they are doing their first read. They will complete the Respond step after they have finished the first read. Print copies of the **First-Read Guide: Fiction** for students to use.

**Remind students that during their first read, they should not answer the close-read questions in the selection.**

Playwright

**Arthur Miller**

# The Crucible, Act IV

## Concept Vocabulary

You will encounter the following words as you read Act IV of *The Crucible*. Before reading, note how familiar you are with each word. Then, rank the words in order from most familiar (1) to least familiar (3).

| WORD | YOUR RANKING |
| --- | --- |
| conciliatory | |
| adamant | |
| disputation | |

After completing the first read, come back to the concept vocabulary and review your rankings. Mark changes to your original rankings as needed.

## First Read DRAMA

Apply these strategies as you conduct your first read. You will have an opportunity to complete the close-read notes after your first read.

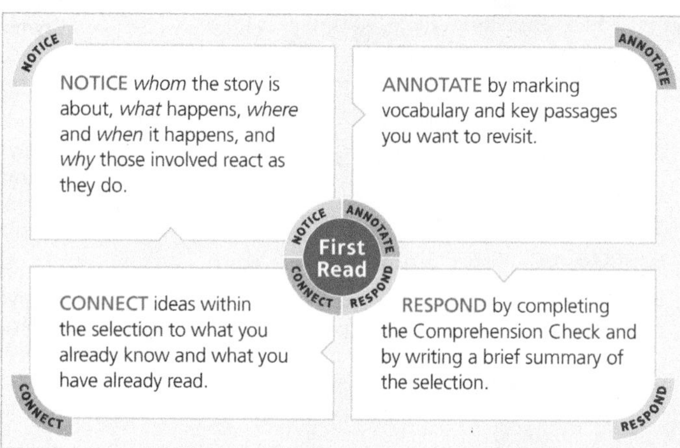
NOTICE
NOTICE *whom* the story is about, *what* happens, *where* and *when* it happens, and *why* those involved react as they do.
ANNOTATE
ANNOTATE by marking vocabulary and key passages you want to revisit.
First Read
CONNECT ideas within the selection to what you already know and what you have already read.
RESPOND by completing the Comprehension Check and by writing a brief summary of the selection.
CONNECT
RESPOND

**STANDARDS**
**Reading Literature**
By the end of grade 11, read and comprehend literature, including stories, dramas, and poems, in the grades 11–CCR text complexity band proficiently, with scaffolding as needed at the high end of the range.

DIGITAL PERSPECTIVES

# The Crucible
## Act IV
### Arthur Miller

REVIEW AND ANTICIPATE

"Is every defense an attack upon the court?" Hale asks in Act III. Danforth observes, "A person is either with this court or he must be counted against it." Such remarks stress the powerlessness of people like John Proctor and Giles Corey against the mounting injustices in Salem. In pursuing justice, their efforts backfire, and their own names join the list of those accused. What do you think the final outcome will be? Who will survive, and who will perish? Read the final act to see if your predictions are correct.

SCAN FOR MULTIMEDIA 

1 *A cell in Salem jail, that fall.*

2 *At the back is a high barred window; near it, a great, heavy door. Along the walls are two benches.*

3 *The place is in darkness but for the moonlight seeping through the bars. It appears empty. Presently footsteps are heard coming down a corridor beyond the wall, keys rattle, and the door swings open.* MARSHAL HERRICK *enters with a lantern.*

4 *He is nearly drunk, and heavy-footed. He goes to a bench and nudges a bundle of rags lying on it.*

5 **Herrick:** Sarah, wake up! Sarah Good! *He then crosses to the other benches.*

NOTES



## WriteNow Express and Reflect

**Interview Questions and Answers** Review paragraphs 1–3 and ask students to consider what will happen in Act IV. To prepare students for taking part in a mock interview, have them recall television interviews of famous people. Prompt students to consider the tone and content of the questions, the attitude and speech patterns of the interviewer, and the responses of the person being interviewed.

Have students work in a group to come up with useful questions and likely answers for a mock television interview with Arthur Miller. Then have two students conduct the interview, role-playing the interviewer and Miller. Questions and answers should be based on what students wrote beforehand, but role-players might ad-lib some parts of the interview to make it seem more authentic. After the interview, ask students to share any new insights they have into Miller's life, *The Crucible,* and Miller's other works.

## CLOSE READ

Remind students to focus on words and phrases that refer to the Devil. You may wish to model the close read using the following think-aloud format. Possible responses to questions on the student page are included. You may also want to print copies of the **Close-Read Guide: Fiction** for students to use.

**ANNOTATE:** As I read these dialogue lines in paragraphs 18 through 24, I notice and annotate words about the Devil. I can tell that Tituba's and Sarah's ideas about the Devil are completely different from those of the other characters in the play.

**QUESTION:** I think that the playwright has Tituba and Sarah refer to the Devil by names such as "that Old Boy" and "Majesty" to show that, to them, the Devil is a friendly, helpful leader rather than an evil monster.

**CONCLUDE:** Some audience members might laugh when they hear these references to the Devil.



NOTES

**CLOSE READ**

**ANNOTATE:** In paragraphs 18–24, mark each reference to the Devil.

**QUESTION:** Why does Miller have Sarah Good and Tituba refer to the Devil by various names?

**CONCLUDE:** What is the effect of these details?

6 **Sarah Good,** *rising in her rags*: Oh, Majesty! Comin', comin'! Tituba, he's here, His Majesty's come!

7 **Herrick:** Go to the north cell; this place is wanted now. *He hangs his lantern on the wall.* TITUBA *sits up.*

8 **Tituba:** That don't look to me like His Majesty; look to me like the marshal.

9 **Herrick,** *taking out a flask*: Get along with you now, clear this place. *He drinks, and* SARAH GOOD *comes and peers up into his face.*

10 **Sarah Good:** Oh, is it you, Marshal! I thought sure you be the devil comin' for us. Could I have a sip of cider for me goin' away?

11 **Herrick,** *handing her the flask*: And where are you off to, Sarah?

12 **Tituba,** *as* SARAH *drinks*: We goin' to Barbados, soon the Devil gits here with the feathers and the wings.

13 **Herrick:** Oh? A happy voyage to you.

14 **Sarah Good:** A pair of bluebirds wingin' southerly, the two of us! Oh, it be a grand transformation, Marshal. *She raises the flask to drink again.*

15 **Herrick,** *taking the flask from her lips*: You'd best give me that or you'll never rise off the ground. Come along now.

16 **Tituba:** I'll speak to him for you, if you desires to come along, Marshal.

17 **Herrick:** I'd not refuse it, Tituba; it's the proper morning to fly into Hell.

18 **Tituba:** Oh, it be no Hell in Barbados. Devil, him be pleasure man in Barbados, him be singin' and dancin' in Barbados. It's you folks—you riles him up 'round here; it be too cold 'round here for that Old Boy. He freeze his soul in Massachusetts, but in Barbados he just as sweet and—*A bellowing cow is heard, and* TITUBA *leaps up and calls to the window*: Aye, sir! That's him, Sarah!

19 **Sarah Good:** I'm here, Majesty! *They hurriedly pick up their rags as* HOPKINS, *a guard, enters.*

20 **Hopkins:** The Deputy Governor's arrived.

21 **Herrick,** *grabbing* TITUBA: Come along, come along.

22 **Tituba,** *resisting him*: No, he comin' for me. I goin' home!

23 **Herrick,** *pulling her to the door*: That's not Satan, just a poor old cow with a hatful of milk. Come along now, out with you!

24 **Tituba,** *calling to the window*: Take me home, Devil! Take me home!

25 **Sarah Good,** *following the shouting* TITUBA *out*: Tell him I'm goin', Tituba! Now you tell him Sarah Good is goin' too!

26 *In the corridor outside* TITUBA *calls on—"Take me home. Devil; Devil take me home!" and* HOPKINS'S *voice orders her to move on.* HERRICK *returns and begins to push old rags and straw into a corner. Hearing footsteps, he turns, and enter* DANFORTH *and* JUDGE HATHORNE. *They are in greatcoats and wear hats against the bitter cold. They are followed in by* CHEEVER, *who carries a dispatch case and a flat wooden box containing his writing materials.*

27 **Herrick:** Good morning, Excellency.

28 **Danforth:** Where is Mr. Parris?

29 **Herrick:** I'll fetch him. *He starts for the door.*

30 **Danforth:** Marshal. HERRICK *stops.* When did Reverend Hale arrive?

31 **Herrick:** It were toward midnight, I think.

32 **Danforth,** *suspiciously*: What is he about here?

33 **Herrick:** He goes among them that will hang, sir. And he prays with them. He sits with Goody Nurse now. And Mr. Parris with him.

34 **Danforth:** Indeed. That man have no authority to enter here, Marshal. Why have you let him in?

35 **Herrick:** Why, Mr. Parris command me, sir. I cannot deny him.

36 **Danforth:** Are you drunk, Marshal?

37 **Herrick:** No, sir; it is a bitter night, and I have no fire here.

38 **Danforth,** *containing his anger*: Fetch Mr. Parris.

39 **Herrick:** Aye, sir.

40 **Danforth:** There is a prodigious stench in this place.

41 **Herrick:** I have only now cleared the people out for you.

42 **Danforth:** Beware hard drink, Marshal.

43 **Herrick:** Aye, sir. *He waits an instant for further orders. But* DANFORTH, *in dissatisfaction, turns his back on him, and* HERRICK *goes out. There is a pause.* DANFORTH *stands in thought.*

44 **Hathorne:** Let you question Hale, Excellency; I should not be surprised he have been preaching in Andover[1] lately.

45 **Danforth:** We'll come to that; speak nothing of Andover. Parris prays with him. That's strange. *He blows on his hands, moves toward the window, and looks out.*

46 **Hathorne:** Excellency, I wonder if it be wise to let Mr. Parris so continuously with the prisoners. DANFORTH *turns to him, interested.* I think, sometimes, the man has a mad look these days.

47 **Danforth:** Mad?

NOTES

1. **Andover** During the height of the terror in Salem Village, a similar hysteria broke out in the nearby town of Andover. There, many respected people were accused of practicing witchcraft and confessed to escape death. However, the people of Andover soon began questioning the reality of the situation, and the hysteria quickly subsided.





DIGITAL PERSPECTIVES

CLOSER LOOK

## Identify Foreshadowing 

Students may have marked paragraphs 30 through 47 during their first read. Use these paragraphs to help students identify hints from the playwright about Reverend Hale and Reverend Parris. Encourage students to talk about the annotations they marked. You may want to model a close read with the class based on the highlights shown in the text.

**ANNOTATE:** Have students mark details in the lines that show Danforth's and Hathorne's suspicions about Hale and Parris, or have students participate while you highlight them.

**QUESTION:** Guide students to consider what these details (as well as earlier details about Hale and Parris) might tell them about Hale's and Parris's changing attitudes toward people who have been convicted of witchcraft.

**Possible response:** Both Hale and Parris now seem more sympathetic to the prisoners' plight and might be more on the prisoners' side than on Danforth's and Hathorne's.

**CONCLUDE:** Help students formulate conclusions about the importance of these details in the text. Ask what the playwright might be foreshadowing.

**Possible response:** Miller might be hinting that Hale and Parris are beginning to rebel against Danforth and Hathorne, and that Hale and Parris are hoping to save the prisoners' lives.

Remind students that when an author uses **foreshadowing**, he or she hints at events that are going to occur later in the story's plot. This technique helps an author to create **suspense,** the quality in a literary work that keeps readers wondering what will happen next. Writers who use foreshadowing skillfully are able to pique readers' curiosity without giving away the plot.

## DIGITAL PERSPECTIVES

**Enriching the Text** Inform students that the witchcraft hysteria in Salem briefly spread to nearby Andover, Massachusetts, when a few Andover residents invited Salem's "afflicted girls" to come and determine whether witches were causing people in Andover to become ill. Soon the authorities arrested scores of Andover residents as witches—even more than the Salem authorities accused. During the witchcraft hysteria, two Andover pastors were at odds with each other. Young Reverend Thomas Barnard promoted the witch hunt. A much older man, Reverend Francis Dane, would have nothing to do with the trials. Perhaps as a result, witch hunters accused Dane himself and many members of his family. Encourage interested students to go online to do additional research on witch trials in Andover and Salem. **(Research to Clarify)**

## CLOSE READ 

Remind students to find a word that Cheever repeats. You may wish to model the close read using the following think-aloud format. Possible responses to questions on the student page are included.

**ANNOTATE:** As I read paragraph 52, I notice and annotate the word *contention*. Cheever repeats this word three times. I also notice a synonym for *contention, disagreement*. It sounds as if the Salem witch trials are causing the town to fall completely apart.

**QUESTION:** I think Miller has Cheever repeat this word to emphasize the chaos that has descended in Salem. Miller may also want his audience to recall that disputes over land and property have prompted some Salem residents to accuse their neighbors of witchcraft. Synonyms Miller could have used instead of *contention* include *debate, argument, squabbling, wrangling,* and *bickering*.

**CONCLUDE:** Repeating the blocky-sounding three-syllable word *con-ten-tion* has the effect of putting up roadblocks in Cheever's dialogue. With Salem in such a chaotic, contentious state, it seems no wonder that Reverend Parris seems to be going slightly mad.

NOTES

**CLOSE READ**

**ANNOTATE:** In paragraph 52, mark the word that Cheever repeats as he describes a conflict that is going on in the community.

**QUESTION:** Why does Miller have Cheever repeat this word?

**CONCLUDE:** How does this repeated word add to the effect of this dialogue?

48 **Hathorne:** I met him yesterday coming out of his house, and I bid him good morning—and he wept and went his way. I think it is not well the village sees him so unsteady.

49 **Danforth:** Perhaps he have some sorrow.

50 **Cheever,** *stamping his feet against the cold*: I think it be the cows, sir.

51 **Danforth:** Cows?

52 **Cheever:** There be so many cows wanderin' the highroads, now their masters are in the jails, and much disagreement who they will belong to now. I know Mr. Parris be arguin' with farmers all yesterday—there is great contention, sir, about the cows. Contention make him weep, sir; it were always a man that weep for contention. *He turns, as do* HATHORNE *and* DANFORTH *hearing someone coming up the corridor.* DANFORTH *raises his head as* PARRIS *enters. He is gaunt, frightened, and sweating in his greatcoat.*

53 **Parris,** *to* DANFORTH, *instantly*: Oh, good morning, sir, thank you for coming. I beg your pardon wakin' you so early. Good morning, Judge Hathorne.

54 **Danforth:** Reverend Hale have no right to enter this—

55 **Parris:** Excellency, a moment. *He hurries back and shuts the door.*

56 **Hathorne:** Do you leave him alone with the prisoners?

57 **Danforth:** What's his business here?

58 **Parris,** *prayerfully holding up his hands*: Excellency, hear me. It is a providence. Reverend Hale has returned to bring Rebecca Nurse to God.

59 **Danforth,** *surprised*: He bids her confess?

60 **Parris,** *sitting*: Hear me. Rebecca have not given me a word this three month since she came. Now she sits with him, and her sister and Martha Corey and two or three others, and he pleads with them, confess their crimes and save their lives.

61 **Danforth:** Why—this is indeed a providence. And they soften, they soften?

62 **Parris:** Not yet, not yet. But I thought to summon you, sir, that we might think on whether it be not wise, to—*He dares not say it.* I had thought to put a question, sir, and I hope you will not—

63 **Danforth:** Mr. Parris, be plain, what troubles you?

64 **Parris:** There is news, sir, that the court—the court must reckon with. My niece, sir, my niece—I believe she has vanished.

65 **Danforth:** Vanished!

66 **Parris:** I had thought to advise you of it earlier in the week, but—

67 **Danforth:** Why? How long is she gone?





## PERSONALIZE FOR LEARNING

### English Language Support

**Antiquated Language** Note paragraph 48: "I bid him good morning—and he wept and went his way." Tell students that today's English speakers and writers rarely if ever use the word *bid* or the phrase "went his way" as Miller uses them here. Rephrase the sentence as follows: "I said 'good morning' to him, but he cried and continued walking in the same direction." Help students identify and "modernize" other antiquated language such as "it were always a man that weep for contention," "Excellency, hear me. It is a providence," "He bids her confess?" and "Rebecca have not given me a word this three month since she came." **EXPANDING/BRIDGING**

68 **Parris:** This be the third night. You see, sir, she told me she would stay a night with Mercy Lewis. And next day, when she does not return, I send to Mr. Lewis to inquire. Mercy told him she would sleep in *my* house for a night.

69 **Danforth:** They are both gone?!

70 **Parris,** *in fear of him*: They are, sir.

71 **Danforth**, *alarmed*: I will send a party for them. Where may they be?

72 **Parris:** Excellency. I think they be aboard a ship. DANFORTH *stands agape.* My daughter tells me how she heard them speaking of ships last week, and tonight I discover my—my strongbox is broke into. *He presses his fingers against his eyes to keep back tears.*

73 **Hathorne,** *astonished*: She have robbed you?

74 **Parris:** Thirty-one pound is gone. I am penniless. *He covers his face and sobs.*

75 **Danforth:** Mr. Parris, you are a brainless man! *He walks in thought, deeply worried.*

76 **Parris:** Excellency, it profit nothing you should blame me. I cannot think they would run off except they fear to keep in Salem any more. *He is pleading.* Mark it, sir. Abigail had close knowledge of the town, and since the news of Andover has broken here—

77 **Danforth:** Andover is remedied. The court returns there on Friday, and will resume examinations.

78 **Parris:** I am sure of it, sir. But the rumor here speaks rebellion in Andover, and it—

79 **Danforth:** There is no rebellion in Andover!

80 **Parris:** I tell you what is said here, sir. Andover have thrown out the court, they say, and will have no part of witchcraft. There be a faction here, feeding on that news, and I tell you true, sir, I fear there will be riot here.

81 **Hathorne:** Riot! Why at every execution I have seen naught but high satisfaction in the town.

82 **Parris:** Judge Hathorne—it were another sort that hanged till now. Rebecca Nurse is no Bridget that lived three year with Bishop before she married him. John Proctor is not Isaac Ward that drank his family to ruin. *To* DANFORTH: I would to God it were not so, Excellency, but these people have great weight yet in the town. Let Rebecca stand upon the gibbet[2] and send up some righteous prayer, and I fear she'll wake a vengeance on you.

NOTES

2. **gibbet** (JIHB iht) *n.* gallows.





CLOSER LOOK

## Identify Causes and Effects

Students may have marked paragraphs 73 through 82 during their first read. Use these lines to point out a cause-and-effect chain of events in the play. Encourage them to talk about the annotations that they marked. You may want to model a close read with the class based on the highlights shown in the text.

**ANNOTATE:** Have students mark events that cause other events to occur, and events that result from other events, or have students participate while you highlight them.

**QUESTION:** Guide students to consider what these cause-and-effect events might tell them. Ask what motivates Abigail to steal her uncle's money. Accept student responses.

**Possible response:** Because she has heard about the rebellion in Andover, Abigail is probably afraid that people in Salem will rebel, too, and will blame her for her actions that sparked the Salem witch hunt, trials, and executions. She steals her uncle's money so she can get on a ship and leave Salem forever.

**CONCLUDE:** Help students formulate conclusions about the effects that events in Andover have had on Salem residents' attitudes toward the witch trials.

**Possible response:** Apparently, people in Andover have stopped believing that the witch trials there are valid. They no longer believe that witchcraft is real or is a punishable offense. Word of the rebellion in Andover has spread to Salem, and some people in Salem have begun a similar revolt.

If necessary, remind students that a **cause-and-effect chain** is a linked series of **causes** (events that cause other events to happen) and **effects** (events that happen as a result of causes).

NOTES

83 **Hathorne**: Excellency, she is condemned a witch. The court have—

84 **Danforth,** *in deep concern, raising a hand to* HATHORNE: Pray you. *To* PARRIS: How do you propose, then?

85 **Parris:** Excellency, I would postpone these hangin's for a time.

86 **Danforth:** There will be no postponement.

87 **Parris:** Now Mr. Hale's returned, there is hope, I think—for if he bring even one of these to God, that confession surely damns the others in the public eye, and none may doubt more that they are all linked to Hell. This way, unconfessed and claiming innocence, doubts are multiplied, many honest people will weep for them, and our good purpose is lost in their tears.

88 **Danforth,** *after thinking a moment, then going to* CHEEVER: Give me the list.

89 CHEEVER *opens the dispatch case, searches.*

90 **Parris:** It cannot be forgot, sir, that when I summoned the congregation for John Proctor's excommunication there were hardly thirty people come to hear it. That speak a discontent, I think, and—

91 **Danforth,** *studying the list*: There will be no postponement.

**Parris:** Excellency—

92 **Danforth:** Now, sir—which of these in your opinion may be brought to God? I will myself strive with him till dawn. *He hands the list to* PARRIS, *who merely glances at it.*

93 **Parris:** There is not sufficient time till dawn.

94 **Danforth:** I shall do my utmost. Which of them do you have hope for?

95 **Parris,** *not even glancing at the list now, and in a quavering voice, quietly*: Excellency—a dagger—*He chokes up.*

96 **Danforth:** What do you say?

97 **Parris:** Tonight, when I open my door to leave my house—a dagger clattered to the ground. *Silence.* DANFORTH *absorbs this. Now* PARRIS *cries out*: You cannot hang this sort. There is danger for me. I dare not step outside at night!

98 REVEREND HALE *enters. They look at him for an instant in silence. He is steeped in sorrow, exhausted, and more direct than he ever was.*

99 **Danforth:** Accept my congratulations. Reverend Hale; we are gladdened to see you returned to your good work.

100 **Hale,** *coming to* DANFORTH *now*: You must pardon them. They will not budge.

HERRICK *enters, waits.*

101 **Danforth,** *conciliatory*: You misunderstand, sir; I cannot pardon these when twelve are already hanged for the same crime. It is not just.

**conciliatory** (kuhn SIHL ee uh tawr ee) *adj.* in a manner intended to make peace and bring about agreement





666 UNIT 5 • FACING OUR FEARS

DIGITAL PERSPECTIVES

102 **Parris,** *with failing heart*: Rebecca will not confess?

103 **Hale:** The sun will rise in a few minutes. Excellency, I must have more time.

104 **Danforth:** Now hear me, and beguile yourselves no more. I will not receive a single plea for pardon or postponement. Them that will not confess will hang. Twelve are already executed: the names of these seven are given out, and the village expects to see them die this morning. Postponement now speaks a floundering on my part; reprieve or pardon must cast doubt upon the guilt of them that died till now. While I speak God's law, I will not crack its voice with whimpering. If retaliation is your fear, know this—I should hang ten thousand that dared to rise against the law, and an ocean of salt tears could not melt the resolution of the statutes. Now draw yourselves up like men and help me, as you are bound by Heaven to do. Have you spoken with them all, Mr. Hale?

105 **Hale:** All but Proctor. He is in the dungeon.

106 **Danforth,** *to* HERRICK: What's Proctor's way now?

107 **Herrick:** He sits like some great bird: you'd not know he lived except he will take food from time to time.

108 **Danforth,** *after thinking a moment*: His wife—his wife must be well on with child now.

109 **Herrick:** She is, sir.

110 **Danforth:** What think you, Mr. Parris? You have closer knowledge of this man; might her presence soften him?

111 **Parris:** It is possible, sir. He have not laid eyes on her these three months. I should summon her.

112 **Danforth,** *to* HERRICK: Is he yet adamant? Has he struck at you again?

113 **Herrick:** He cannot, sir, he is chained to the wall now.

114 **Danforth,** *after thinking on it*: Fetch Goody Proctor to me. Then let you bring him up.

115 **Herrick:** Aye, sir. HERRICK *goes. There is silence.*

116 **Hale:** Excellency, if you postpone a week and publish to the town that you are striving for their confessions, that speak mercy on your part, not faltering.

117 **Danforth:** Mr. Hale, as God have not empowered me like Joshua to stop this sun from rising,[3] so I cannot withhold from them the perfection of their punishment.

118 **Hale,** *harder now*: If you think God wills you to raise rebellion, Mr. Danforth, you are mistaken!

119 **Danforth,** *instantly*: You have heard rebellion spoken in the town?

NOTES

CLOSE READ

ANNOTATE: In paragraph 104, mark words and phrases related to confusion or weakness. Mark other details related to strength or decisiveness.

QUESTION: What do these details show about Danforth's character?

CONCLUDE: What is the effect of this speech on Parris and Hale? On readers?

**adamant** (AD uh muhnt) *adj.* unrelenting; refusing to be persuaded

3. **Joshua . . . rising** In the Bible, Joshua, leader of the Israelites after the death of Moses, asks God to make the sun and the moon stand still during a battle, and his request is granted.

## CLOSE READ

Remind students to focus on details in paragraph 104 that relate to confusion or weakness and strength or decisiveness. You may wish to model the close read using the following think-aloud format. Possible responses to questions on the student page are included.

**ANNOTATE:** As I read paragraph 104, I notice and annotate details that have to do with weakness and strength.

**QUESTION:** I think Miller is characterizing Danforth as a merciless, inflexible person.

**CONCLUDE:** Hale and Parris are discouraged. The audience is probably on the prisoners' side, so Danforth's words might make audience members dislike the character even more. Also, Danforth's adamancy may signal to the audience that there is little hope for the play's heroes, John Proctor and Rebecca Nurse.

Additional **English Language Support** is available in the Interactive Teacher's Edition.

## CROSS-CURRICULAR PERSPECTIVES

**Humanities** Arthur Miller is only one of many authors and artists who focus on unfairness in the world. Inform students that playwright Wole Soyinka grew up in Nigeria, immersed in two cultures. His parents were English-speaking Christians, and his grandparents followed the local Yoruba religion. After attending college in Britain, Soyinka returned to Nigeria, organized a theater troupe, and wrote plays that combine elements of European drama with African folk culture. In 1960, Nigeria won its independence from Britain. Years of political violence followed, and a succession of dictators took control of the country. Soyinka wrote political satires that skewered the government, making him powerful enemies. During the 1960s, he was arrested twice and thrown in jail.

Although he has spent much of the last 40 years living in exile, Soyinka has continued writing about Africa. In 1984 he directed the world premiere of *A Play of Giants,* a dark satire about four African dictators visiting New York City. Two years later, Soyinka won the Nobel Prize for Literature. Point out that both Wole Soyinka and Arthur Miller are famous for using their artistic works to criticize injustice in their societies. **(Research to Explore)**

CLOSER LOOK

## Recognizing Voice and Identifying Tone

Students may have marked paragraphs 120 through 135 during their first read. Use these lines to help students recognize that Miller is speaking to his audience through Reverend Hale. Encourage students to talk about the annotations that they marked. You may want to model a close read with the class based on the highlights shown in the text.

ANNOTATE: Have students annotate details in these lines that help them identify what the playwright is telling his audience through Reverend Hale, or have students participate while you highlight them.

QUESTION: Guide students to consider what these details might tell them about Hale's beliefs and feelings. Accept student responses.

**Possible response:** Hale refers to his belief that, at first, he was wrong to help start the witchcraft hysteria. He now believes that the whole witch hunt has been wrong from the beginning.

CONCLUDE: Help students to formulate conclusions about Miller's reasons for including Hale's impassioned rhetoric at this point in the play—as the story comes to a climax.

**Possible response:** Miller feels the same way that Hale feels about the witch hunt in Salem: the hunt is based on hysteria, hatred, dogmatism, stubbornness, pride, malice, fear, and lies. Maybe Miller is also asking his audience to equate Danforth, Hathorne, and the witch trials to Senator Joseph McCarthy and to the House Un-American Activities Committee's activities during the 1950s.

Inform students that **voice** is a writer's distinctive way of "speaking" on the page. This voice may vary from work to work by the same writer, or it may represent a characteristic literary personality. Among other literary elements, voice is based on word choice and tone. An **author's tone** is the writer's attitude toward his or her audience and subject. This tone can often be described by a single adjective, such as *calm* or *anguished, sincere* or *sarcastic, sympathetic* or *scathing.*



NOTES

120 **Hale:** Excellency, there are orphans wandering from house to house; abandoned cattle bellow on the highroads, the stink of rotting crops hangs everywhere, and no man knows when the harlot's cry will end his life—and you wonder yet if rebellion's spoke? Better you should marvel how they do not burn your province!

121 **Danforth:** Mr. Hale, have you preached in Andover this month?

122 **Hale:** Thank God they have no need of me in Andover.

123 **Danforth:** You baffle me, sir. Why have you returned here?

124 **Hale:** Why, it is all simple. I come to do the Devil's work. I come to counsel Christians they should belie themselves. *His sarcasm collapses.* There is blood on my head! Can you not see the blood on my head!!

125 **Parris:** Hush! *For he has heard footsteps. They all face the door.* HERRICK *enters with* ELIZABETH. *Her wrists are linked by heavy chain, which* HERRICK *now removes. Her clothes are dirty; her face is pale and gaunt.* HERRICK *goes out.*

126 **Danforth,** *very politely*: Goody Proctor. *She is silent.* I hope you are hearty?

127 **Elizabeth,** *as a warning reminder*: I am yet six month before my time.

128 **Danforth:** Pray be at your ease, we come not for your life. We—*uncertain how to plead, for he is not accustomed to it.* Mr. Hale, will you speak with the woman?

129 **Hale:** Goody Proctor, your husband is marked to hang this morning. *Pause.*

130 **Elizabeth,** *quietly*: I have heard it.

131 **Hale:** You know, do you not, that I have no connection with the court? *She seems to doubt it.* I come of my own, Goody Proctor. I would save your husband's life, for if he is taken I count myself his murderer. Do you understand me?

132 **Elizabeth:** What do you want of me?

133 **Hale:** Goody Proctor, I have gone this three month like our Lord into the wilderness. I have sought a Christian way, for damnation's doubled on a minister who counsels men to lie.

134 **Hathorne:** It is no lie, you cannot speak of lies.

135 **Hale:** It is a lie! They are innocent!

136 **Danforth:** I'll hear no more of that!

137 **Hale,** *continuing to* ELIZABETH: Let you not mistake your duty as I mistook my own. I came into this village like a bridegroom to his beloved, bearing gifts of high religion; the very crowns of holy law I brought, and what I touched with my bright confidence, it died; and where I turned the eye of my great faith,



668 UNIT 5 • FACING OUR FEARS

blood flowed up. Beware, Goody Proctor—cleave to no faith when faith brings blood. It is mistaken law that leads you to sacrifice. Life, woman, life is God's most precious gift; no principle, however glorious, may justify the taking of it. I beg you, woman, prevail upon your husband to confess. Let him give his lie. Quail not before God's judgment in this, for it may well be God damns a liar less than he that throws his life away for pride. Will you plead with him? I cannot think he will listen to another.

138 **Elizabeth,** *quietly*: I think that be the Devil's argument.

139 **Hale,** *with a climactic desperation*: Woman, before the laws of God we are as swine! We cannot read His will!

140 **Elizabeth:** I cannot dispute with you, sir; I lack learning for it.

141 **Danforth,** *going to her*: Goody Proctor, you are not summoned here for disputation. Be there no wifely tenderness within you? He will die with the sunrise. Your husband. Do you understand it? *She only looks at him.* What say you? Will you contend with him? *She is silent.* Are you stone? I tell you true, woman, had I no other proof of your unnatural life, your dry eyes now would be sufficient evidence that you delivered up your soul to Hell! A very ape would weep at such calamity! Have the devil dried up any tear of pity in you? *She is silent.* Take her out. It profit nothing she should speak to him!

NOTES

**disputation** (dihs pyu TAY shuhn) *n.* debate or argument

142 **Elizabeth,** *quietly*: Let me speak with him, Excellency.

143 **Parris,** *with hope*: You'll strive with him? *She hesitates.*

144 **Danforth:** Will you plead for his confession or will you not?

145 **Elizabeth:** I promise nothing. Let me speak with him.

146 *A sound—the sibilance of dragging feet on stone. They turn. A pause.* HERRICK *enters with* JOHN PROCTOR. *His wrists are chained. He is another man, bearded, filthy, his eyes misty as though webs had overgrown them. He halts inside the doorway, his eyes caught by the sight of* ELIZABETH. *The emotion flowing between them prevents anyone from speaking for an instant. Now* HALE, *visibly affected, goes to* DANFORTH *and speaks quietly.*

147 **Hale:** Pray, leave them Excellency.

148 **Danforth,** *pressing* HALE *impatiently aside*: Mr. Proctor, you have been notified, have you not? PROCTOR *is silent, staring at* ELIZABETH. I see light in the sky, Mister; let you counsel with your wife, and may God help you turn your back on Hell. PROCTOR *is silent, staring at* ELIZABETH.

149 **Hale,** *quietly*: Excellency, let—

150 **Danforth** *brushes past* HALE *and walks out.* HALE *follows.* CHEEVER *stands and follows.* HATHORNE *behind.* HERRICK *goes.* PARRIS, *from a safe distance, offers*:





## CROSS-CURRICULAR PERSPECTIVES

**Humanities** Inform students that in his essay "The Crucible in History," Miller discusses the historical context of his own time and his reasons for writing the play. Have students locate and read this essay (available in Miller's essay anthology *Echoes Down the Corridor*) and hold a discussion in which they share their opinions about the content. Ask students to focus their discussion on two questions: *How does Miller's essay help us understand what happened during the Salem witch trials of the late 1600s? How does "The Crucible in History" help us understand what was happening in the United States when Miller wrote the play?* **(Research to Explore)**

## CLOSE READ

Remind students to look for actions that the actors playing John and Elizabeth Proctor are told to do. You may wish to model the close read using the following think-aloud format. Possible responses to questions on the student page are included.

**ANNOTATE:** In paragraph 152, I find and annotate phrases such as "Alone, Proctor walks to her, halts," "as he touches her, a strange soft sound, half laughter, half amazement, comes from his throat," and "She covers his hand with hers." Such details tell me that John and Elizabeth are amazed, grateful, and overwhelmed to see each other again.

**QUESTION:** Miller probably includes such a detailed description to show the actors exactly how he wants them to move and convey emotions in this scene.

**CONCLUDE:** The description helps actors to convey how tenderly John and Elizabeth behave as they reunite, and the love that exists between these two characters.

NOTES

**CLOSE READ**

**ANNOTATE:** In paragraph 152, mark each action that actors playing John and Elizabeth Proctor are told to do.

**QUESTION:** Why does Miller provide such a specific description of the characters' actions?

**CONCLUDE:** What is the effect of this description?

151 **Parris:** If you desire a cup of cider, Mr. Proctor, I am sure I— PROCTOR *turns an icy stare at him, and he breaks off.* PARRIS *raises his palms toward* PROCTOR. God lead you now. PARRIS *goes out.*

152 *Alone,* PROCTOR *walks to her, halts. It is as though they stood in a spinning world. It is beyond sorrow, above it. He reaches out his hand as though toward an embodiment not quite real, and as he touches her, a strange soft sound, half laughter, half amazement, comes from his throat. He pats her hand. She covers his hand with hers. And then, weak, he sits. Then she sits, facing him.*

153 **Proctor:** The child?

154 **Elizabeth:** It grows.

155 **Proctor:** There is no word of the boys?

156 **Elizabeth:** They're well. Rebecca's Samuel keeps them.

157 **Proctor:** You have not seen them?

158 **Elizabeth:** I have not. *She catches a weakening in herself and downs it.*

159 **Proctor:** You are a—marvel, Elizabeth.

160 **Elizabeth:** You—have been tortured?

161 **Proctor:** Aye. *Pause. She will not let herself be drowned in the sea that threatens her.* They come for my life now.

162 **Elizabeth:** I know it.

163 *Pause.*

164 **Proctor:** None—have yet confessed?

165 **Elizabeth:** There be many confessed.

166 **Proctor:** Who are they?

167 **Elizabeth:** There be a hundred or more, they say. Goody Ballard is one; Isaiah Goodkind is one. There be many.

168 **Proctor:** Rebecca?

169 **Elizabeth:** Not Rebecca. She is one foot in Heaven now; naught may hurt her more.

170 **Proctor:** And Giles?

171 **Elizabeth:** You have not heard of it?

172 **Proctor:** I hear nothin', where I am kept.

173 **Elizabeth:** Giles is dead.

174 *He looks at her incredulously.*

175 **Proctor:** When were he hanged?

176 **Elizabeth,** *quietly, factually:* He were not hanged. He would not answer aye or nay to his indictment; for if he denied the charge they'd hang him surely, and auction out his property. So he stand mute, and died Christian under the law. And so his sons

will have his farm. It is the law, for he could not be condemned a wizard without he answer the indictment, aye or nay.

NOTES

177 **Proctor:** Then how does he die?

178 **Elizabeth,** *gently*: They press him, John.

179 **Proctor:** Press?

180 **Elizabeth:** Great stones they lay upon his chest until he plead aye or nay. *With a tender smile for the old man*: They say he give them but two words. "More weight," he says. And died.

181 **Proctor,** *numbed—a thread to weave into his agony*: "More weight."

182 **Elizabeth:** Aye. It were a fearsome man, Giles Corey.

183 *Pause.*

184 **Proctor,** *with great force of will, but not quite looking at her*: I have been thinking I would confess to them, Elizabeth. *She shows nothing.* What say you? If I give them that?

185 **Elizabeth:** I cannot judge you, John.

186 *Pause.*

187 **Proctor,** *simply—a pure question*: What would you have me do?

188 **Elizabeth:** As you will, I would have it. *Slight pause*: I want you living, John. That's sure.

189 **Proctor,** *pauses, then with a flailing of hope*: Giles's wife? Have she confessed?

As the play reaches its climax, John and Elizabeth Proctor discuss whether he should confess to save his life.





## CROSS-CURRICULAR PERSPECTIVES

**Music** Review paragraphs 170 through 182. Point out that character Elizabeth Proctor's account is based on actual events: The real Giles Corey, over 80 years old, refused to make a plea even as rocks were lethally—and legally—piled on his chest. Witnesses reported that his last words were "More weight." His story inspired a long dramatic poem by Henry Wadsworth Longfellow and several ballads. One of the ballads is not at all sympathetic:

"More weight," now said this wretched Man,
"More weight," again he cryed,
And he did no Confession make,
But wickedly he died.

Ask students to use Internet sources to find and analyze songs and poems about Giles Corey.

TEACHING

## CLOSE READ

Remind students to focus on the adjective that modifies John Proctor's "longing." You may wish to model the close read using the following think-aloud format. Possible responses to questions on the student page are included.

**ANNOTATE:** In paragraph 199, I find the word *immortal*, which describes John Proctor's longing.

**QUESTION:** I think Miller uses this word to emphasize that Proctor is a Christian who believes in eternity and is struggling to decide on whether to lie to stay alive or stay honest and avoid eternal damnation.

**CONCLUDE:** The effect of the word *immortal* is to show the enormity of the decision. It should help guide the actor's acting choices by indicating that John Proctor is in a struggle to make a decision that may have eternal consequences.

NOTES

**CLOSE READ**

**ANNOTATE:** In paragraph 199, mark the adjective that modifies John Proctor's "longing."

**QUESTION:** Why does Miller use this word?

**CONCLUDE:** What is the effect of this word, and how might it guide the performance of an actor playing John Proctor?

190 **Elizabeth:** She will not.

191 *Pause.*

192 **Proctor:** It is a pretense, Elizabeth.

193 **Elizabeth:** What is?

194 **Proctor:** I cannot mount the gibbet like a saint. It is a fraud. I am not that man. *She is silent.* My honesty is broke, Elizabeth; I am no good man. Nothing's spoiled by giving them this lie that were not rotten long before.

195 **Elizabeth:** And yet you've not confessed till now. That speak goodness in you.

196 **Proctor:** Spite only keeps me silent. It is hard to give a lie to dogs. *Pause, for the first time he turns directly to her.* I would have your forgiveness, Elizabeth.

197 **Elizabeth:** It is not for me to give, John, I am—

198 **Proctor:** I'd have you see some honesty in it. Let them that never lied die now to keep their souls. It is pretense for me, a vanity that will not blind God nor keep my children out of the wind. *Pause.* What say you?

199 **Elizabeth,** *upon a heaving sob that always threatens*: John, it come to naught that I should forgive you, if you'll not forgive yourself. *Now he turns away a little, in great agony.* It is not my soul, John, it is yours. *He stands, as though in physical pain, slowly rising to his feet with a great immortal longing to find his answer. It is difficult to say, and she is on the verge of tears.* Only be sure of this, for I know it now: Whatever you will do, it is a good man does it. *He turns his doubting, searching gaze upon her.* I have read my heart this three month, John. *Pause.* I have sins of my own to count. It needs a cold wife to prompt lechery.

200 **Proctor,** *in great pain*: Enough, enough—

201 **Elizabeth,** *now pouring out her heart*: Better you should know me!

202 **Proctor:** I will not hear it! I know you!

203 **Elizabeth:** You take my sins upon you, John—

204 **Proctor,** *in agony*: No. I take my own, my own!

205 **Elizabeth:** John, I counted myself so plain, so poorly made, no honest love could come to me! Suspicion kissed you when I did; I never knew how I should say my love. It were a cold house I kept! *In fright, she swerves, as* HATHORNE *enters.*

206 **Hathorne:** What say you, Proctor? The sun is soon up.

207 **Proctor,** *his chest heaving, stares, turns to* ELIZABETH. *She comes to him as though to plead, her voice quaking.*

208 **Elizabeth:** Do what you will. But let none be your judge. There be no higher judge under Heaven than Proctor is! Forgive me,





## PERSONALIZE FOR LEARNING

### Strategic Support

**Using Graphic Organizers** As you help students interpret Elizabeth's comments in paragraph 199, point out that readers should consider the way the playwright seems to feel about his characters. Help students rank the characters who appear or are mentioned in Act IV on a scale of 1 to 10. Tell them that a character whom Miller totally disrespects and strongly dislikes should receive a 1, while one the playwright truly loves and fully respects should receive a 10. You might work with students to create a three-column chart with the following heads: Character, Ranking, Traits.

NOTES

forgive me, John—I never knew such goodness in the world! *She covers her face, weeping.*

209 PROCTOR *turns from her to* HATHORNE; *he is off the earth, his voice hollow.*

210 **Proctor:** I want my life.

211 **Hathorne** *electrified, surprised*: You'll confess yourself?

212 **Proctor:** I will have my life.

213 **Hathorne,** *with a mystical tone*: God be praised! It is a providence! *He rushes out the door, and his voice is heard calling down the corridor*: He will confess! Proctor will confess!

214 **Proctor,** *with a cry, as he strides to the door*: Why do you cry it? *In great pain he turns back to her.* It is evil, is it not? It is evil.

215 **Elizabeth,** in *terror, weeping*: I cannot judge you, John. I cannot!

216 **Proctor:** Then who will judge me? *Suddenly clasping his hands*: God in Heaven, what is John Proctor, what is John Proctor? *He moves as an animal, and a fury is riding in him, a tantalized search.* I think it is honest, I think so; I am no saint. *As though she had denied this he calls angrily at her*: Let Rebecca go like a saint; for me it is fraud! *Voices are heard in the hall, speaking together in suppressed excitement.*

217 **Elizabeth:** I am not your judge, I cannot be. *As though giving him release*: Do as you will, do as you will!

218 **Proctor:** Would you give them such a lie? Say it. Would you ever give them this? *She cannot answer.* You would not; if tongs of fire were singeing you you would not! It is evil. Good, then—it is evil, and I do it!

219 HATHORNE *enters with* DANFORTH, *and, with them,* CHEEVER, PARRIS, and HALE. *It is a businesslike, rapid entrance, as though the ice had been broken.*

220 **Danforth,** *with great relief and gratitude*: Praise to God, man, praise to God; you shall be blessed in Heaven for this. CHEEVER *has hurried to the bench with pen, ink, and paper.* PROCTOR *watches him.* Now then, let us have it. Are you ready, Mr. Cheever?

221 **Proctor,** *with a cold, cold horror at their efficiency*: Why must it be written?

222 **Danforth:** Why, for the good instruction of the village. Mister; this we shall post upon the church door! *To* PARRIS, *urgently*: Where is the marshal?

223 **Parris,** *runs to the door and calls down the corridor*: Marshal! Hurry!

224 **Danforth:** Now, then, Mister, will you speak slowly, and directly to the point, for Mr. Cheever's sake. *He is on record now, and is really dictating to* CHEEVER, *who writes.* Mr. Proctor, have you seen

## CLOSE READ

Remind students to focus on details that show what John Proctor does after Rebecca Nurse enters the room. You may wish to model the close read using the following think-aloud format. Possible responses to questions on the student page are included.

**ANNOTATE:** In paragraphs 231 through 240, I find and annotate stage directions for Proctor. These details show that Proctor is extremely uncomfortable about "confessing" when Rebecca is there to witness it.

**QUESTION:** Miller probably includes these stage directions to make it clear that Proctor hates "confessing" and is ashamed of doing so. Maybe the playwright also wants to use Rebecca's surprise to show that this is something Proctor would not ordinarily do.

**CONCLUDE:** Proctor is clearly the play's hero—with few exceptions, audience members are on his side, no matter what, at this point in the play. I think most of the audience members still sympathize deeply with Proctor, though a few may lose their respect for him when he confesses.

NOTES

**CLOSE READ**

**ANNOTATE:** In the stage directions in paragraphs 231–240, mark the actions that John Proctor takes after Rebecca Nurse enters the room.

**QUESTION:** Why does Miller include these stage directions?

**CONCLUDE:** What is the effect of these details?

the Devil in your life? PROCTOR'S *jaws lock.* Come, man, there is light in the sky; the town waits at the scaffold; I would give out this news. Did you see the Devil?

225 **Proctor:** I did.

226 **Parris:** Praise God!

227 **Danforth:** And when he come to you, what were his demand? PROCTOR *is silent.* DANFORTH *helps.* Did he bid you to do his work upon the earth?

228 **Proctor:** He did.

229 **Danforth:** And you bound yourself to his service? DANFORTH *turns, as* REBECCA NURSE *enters, with* HERRICK *helping to support her. She is barely able to walk.* Come in, come in, woman!

230 **Rebecca,** *brightening as she sees* PROCTOR: Ah, John! You are well, then, eh?

231 PROCTOR *turns his face to the wall.*

232 **Danforth:** Courage, man, courage—let her witness your good example that she may come to God herself. Now hear it, Goody Nurse! Say on, Mr. Proctor. Did you bind yourself to the Devil's service?

233 **Rebecca,** *astonished*: Why, John!

234 **Proctor,** *through his teeth, his face turned from* REBECCA: I did.

235 **Danforth:** Now, woman, you surely see it profit nothin' to keep this conspiracy any further. Will you confess yourself with him?

236 **Rebecca:** Oh, John—God send his mercy on you!

237 **Danforth:** I say, will you confess yourself. Goody Nurse?

238 **Rebecca:** Why, it is a lie, it is a lie; how may I damn myself? I cannot, I cannot.

239 **Danforth:** Mr. Proctor. When the Devil came to you did you see Rebecca Nurse in his company? PROCTOR *is silent.* Come, man, take courage—did you ever see her with the Devil?

240 **Proctor,** *almost inaudibly*: No.

241 DANFORTH, *now sensing trouble, glances at* JOHN *and goes to the table, and picks up a sheet—the list of condemned.*

242 **Danforth:** Did you ever see her sister, Mary Easty, with the Devil?

243 **Proctor:** No, I did not.

244 **Danforth,** *his eyes narrow on* PROCTOR: Did you ever see Martha Corey with the Devil?

245 **Proctor:** I did not.

246 **Danforth,** *realizing, slowly putting the sheet down*: Did you ever see anyone with the Devil?





674 UNIT 5 • FACING OUR FEARS

DIGITAL PERSPECTIVES

NOTES

247 **Proctor:** I did not.

248 **Danforth:** Proctor, you mistake me. I am not empowered to trade your life for a lie. You have most certainly seen some person with the Devil. PROCTOR *is silent.* Mr. Proctor, a score of people have already testified they saw this woman with the Devil.

249 **Proctor:** Then it is proved. Why must I say it?

250 **Danforth:** Why "must" you say it! Why, you should rejoice to say it if your soul is truly purged of any love for Hell!

251 **Proctor:** They think to go like saints. I like not to spoil their names.

252 **Danforth**, *inquiring, incredulous*: Mr. Proctor, do you think they go like saints?

253 **Proctor**, *evading*: This woman never thought she done the Devil's work.

254 **Danforth:** Look you, sir. I think you mistake your duty here. It matter nothing what she thought—she is convicted of the unnatural murder of children, and you for sending your spirit out upon Mary Warren. Your soul alone is the issue here, Mister, and you will prove its whiteness or you cannot live in a

John Proctor makes his final defense.





## CROSS-CURRICULAR PERSPECTIVES

**Music** Encourage interested students to select background music or compose their own theme music for a stage or film version of *The Crucible*. Students might submit sheet music, play recorded music in class, or give a live vocal and/or instrumental performance. Ask students to indicate which part(s) of *The Crucible* each musical piece is meant to accompany. Also have them explain what moods or ideas in the play they think their music expresses or emphasizes. **(Research to Explore)**

NOTES

Christian country. Will you tell me now what persons conspired with you in the Devil's company? PROCTOR *is silent.* To your knowledge was Rebecca Nurse ever—

255 **Proctor:** I speak my own sins: I cannot judge another. *Crying out, with hatred*: I have no tongue for it.

256 **Hale**, *quickly to* DANFORTH: Excellency. It is enough he confess himself. Let him sign it, let him sign it.

257 **Parris**, *feverishly*: It is a great service, sir. It is a weighty name; it will strike the village that Proctor confess. I beg you, let him sign it. The sun is up, Excellency!

258 **Danforth**, *considers; then with dissatisfaction*: Come, then, sign your testimony. *To* CHEEVER: Give it to him. CHEEVER *goes to* PROCTOR, *the confession and a pen in hand.* PROCTOR *does not look at it.* Come, man, sign it.

259 **Proctor**, *after glancing at the confession*: You have all witnessed it—it is enough.

260 **Danforth:** You will not sign it?

261 **Proctor:** You have all witnessed it; what more is needed?

262 **Danforth:** Do you sport with me? You will sign your name or it is no confession, Mister! *His breast heaving with agonized breathing,* PROCTOR *now lays the paper down and signs his name.*

263 **Parris:** Praise be to the Lord!

264 PROCTOR *has just finished signing when* DANFORTH *reaches for the paper. But* PROCTOR *snatches it up, and now a wild terror is rising in him, and a boundless anger.*

265 **Danforth**, *perplexed, but politely extending his hand*: If you please, sir.

266 **Proctor:** No.

267 **Danforth**, *as though* PROCTOR *did not understand*: Mr. Proctor, I must have—

268 **Proctor:** No, no. I have signed it. You have seen me. It is done! You have no need for this.

269 **Parris:** Proctor, the village must have proof that—

270 **Proctor:** Damn the village! I confess to God, and God has seen my name on this! It is enough!

271 **Danforth:** No, sir, it is—

272 **Proctor:** You came to save my soul, did you not? Here! I have confessed myself: it is enough!

273 **Danforth:** You have not con—

274 **Proctor:** I have confessed myself! Is there no good penitence but it be public? God does not need my name nailed upon the church! God sees my name; God knows how black my sins are! It is enough!





## PERSONALIZE FOR LEARNING

### English Language Support

**Antiquated Verb Usage** Call students' attention to paragraph 256. Characters in *The Crucible* use verbs in an antiquated manner that may confuse some students. For example, Hale says, "It is enough he confess himself." Point out that in modern English, Hale would say, "He confesses."

Tell students that at the time the play takes place, people spoke English this way. Work with them to find and convert to modern English similar examples of antiquated verb usage. **EXPANDING/BRIDGING**

275 **Danforth:** Mr. Proctor—

276 **Proctor:** You will not use me! I am no Sarah Good or Tituba. I am John Proctor! You will not use me! It is no part of salvation that you should use me!

277 **Danforth:** I do not wish to—

278 **Proctor:** I have three children—how may I teach them to walk like men in the world, and I sold my friends?

279 **Danforth:** You have not sold your friends—

280 **Proctor:** Beguile me not! I blacken all of them when this is nailed to the church the very day they hang for silence!

281 **Danforth:** Mr. Proctor, I must have good and legal proof that you—

282 **Proctor:** You are the high court, your word is good enough! Tell them I confessed myself; say Proctor broke his knees and wept like a woman; say what you will, but my name cannot—

283 **Danforth,** *with suspicion*: It is the same, is it not? If I report it or you sign to it?

284 **Proctor**—*he knows it is insane*: No, it is not the same! What others say and what I sign to is not the same!

285 **Danforth:** Why? Do you mean to deny this confession when you are free?

286 **Proctor:** I mean to deny nothing!

287 **Danforth:** Then explain to me. Mr. Proctor, why you will not let—

288 **Proctor**, *with a cry of his whole soul*: Because it is my name! Because I cannot have another in my life! Because I lie and sign myself to lies! Because I am not worth the dust on the feet of them that hang! How may I live without my name? I have given you my soul; leave me my name!

289 **Danforth**, *pointing at the confession in* PROCTOR'S *hand*: Is that document a lie? If it is a lie I will not accept it! What say you? I will not deal in lies, Mister! PROCTOR *is motionless.* You will give me your honest confession in my hand, or I cannot keep you from the rope. PROCTOR *does not reply.* What way do you go, Mister?

290 *His breast heaving, his eyes staring,* PROCTOR *tears the paper and crumples it, and he is weeping in fury, but erect.*

291 **Danforth:** Marshal!

292 **Parris**, *hysterically, as though the tearing paper were his life*: Proctor, Proctor!

293 **Hale:** Man, you will hang! You cannot!

294 **Proctor**, *his eyes full of tears*: I can. And there's your first marvel, that I can. You have made your magic now, for now I do think

NOTES

**CLOSE READ**

**ANNOTATE:** In paragraph 288, mark the repeated words.

**QUESTION:** Why do you think Miller has Proctor repeat these words?

**CONCLUDE:** What is the effect of this repetition?





**DIGITAL** 
**PERSPECTIVES**

 **CLOSE READ** 

Remind students to focus on words that John Proctor repeats. You may wish to model the close read using the following think-aloud format. Possible responses to questions on the student page are included.

**ANNOTATE:** In paragraph 288, I find and annotate Proctor's repeated words and phrases. These repeated words help me figure out why John Proctor feels ashamed of confessing.

**QUESTION:** I think Miller has the character repeat these words to show Proctor's anguish: Proctor is terribly ashamed that he lied. He doesn't want anyone else in the village to know he did a cowardly deed to save his own life.

**CONCLUDE:** When audience members hear Proctor wailing "Because" and "my name" over and over, they understand how tormented and ashamed the character feels. A few audience members might blame Proctor for confessing, but most feel sorry for him. He is in a dreadful position: if he is true to himself, he will die and leave his children fatherless. If he lies ("confesses"), it will make good, innocent people such as Rebecca Nurse look guilty—and help send them to their deaths.

Proctor and others are taken to their fate.

I see some shred of goodness in John Proctor. Not enough to weave a banner with, but white enough to keep it from such dogs. ELIZABETH, *in a burst of terror, rushes to him and weeps against his hand.* Give them no tear! Tears pleasure them! Show honor now, show a stony heart and sink them with it! *He has lifted her, and kisses her now with great passion.*

NOTES

295 **Rebecca:** Let you fear nothing! Another judgment waits us all!

296 **Danforth:** Hang them high over the town! Who weeps for these, weeps for corruption! *He sweeps out past them.* HERRICK *starts to lead* REBECCA, *who almost collapses, but* PROCTOR *catches her, and she glances up at him apologetically.*

297 **Rebecca:** I've had no breakfast.

298 **Herrick:** Come, man.

299 HERRICK *escorts them out,* HATHORNE *and* CHEEVER *behind them.* ELIZABETH *stands staring at the empty doorway.*

300 **Parris,** *in deadly fear, to* ELIZABETH: Go to him, Goody Proctor! There is yet time!

301 *From outside a drumroll strikes the air.* PARRIS *is startled.* ELIZABETH *jerks about toward the window.*

302 **Parris:** Go to him! *He rushes out the door, as though to hold back his fate.* Proctor! Proctor!

303 *Again, a short burst of drums.*

304 **Hale:** Woman, plead with him! *He starts to rush out the door, and then goes back to her.* Woman! It is pride, it is vanity. *She avoids his*





## PERSONALIZE FOR LEARNING

### Strategic Support

**Characters' Motivations** Review paragraphs 255 through 294. For students to fully appreciate the play's tragic, highly emotional ending, they need to understand why Proctor changes his mind. Lead a discussion about how the characters feel about Proctor's decision. Make sure students give evidence to support their positions.

*eyes, and moves to the window. He drops to his knees.* Be his helper!—What profit him to bleed? Shall the dust praise him? Shall the worms declare his truth? Go to him, take his shame away!

305 **Elizabeth**, *supporting herself against collapse, grips the bars of the window, and with a cry*: He have his goodness now. God forbid I take it from him!

306 *The final drumroll crashes, then heightens violently.* HALE *weeps in frantic prayer, and the new sun is pouring in upon her face, and the drums rattle like bones in the morning air.*

THE CURTAIN FALLS

NOTES

## Comprehension Check

Complete the following items after you finish your first read.

1. As Act IV opens, what is to take place at daybreak?

2. Why has Reverend Hale returned to Salem?

3. What does Parris say Abigail has recently done?

4. What does Danforth want John Proctor to do?

5. **Notebook** Write a summary of Act IV of *The Crucible*.

### RESEARCH

**Research to Clarify** Choose at least one unfamiliar detail from the text. Briefly research that detail. In what way does the information you learned shed light on an aspect of the play?

**Research to Explore** Conduct research on an aspect of the text you find interesting. For example, you may want to learn more about the play's reception during the McCarthy era.





DIGITAL PERSPECTIVES

## Comprehension Check

Possible responses:

1. Seven people, including John Proctor and Rebecca Nurse, are to be hanged.
2. Hale has tried to persuade the prisoners to confess—even though they are innocent. Confessing will keep them from being hanged.
3. Abigail has stolen her uncle's money and has run away from Salem on a ship.
4. Danforth wants John Proctor to confess, to implicate others, and to sign his confession.
5. Summaries will vary but should include the major events of Act IV.

## Research

**Research to Clarify** If students struggle to come up with an unfamiliar detail to research, suggest that they focus on one of the following: the Puritan religion in Salem and elsewhere; Cotton Mather, a minister who played an important role in the Salem witch trials; the "afflicted girls" of the Salem witch trials; or fact and fiction in *The Crucible*.

**Research to Explore** Encourage students to choose a topic such as: McCarthyism and the man it was named for, Senator Joseph McCarthy; the activities of the House Un-American Activities Committee (HUAC) during the 1950s and 1960s; the effects of HUAC's activities on Hollywood actors, writers, directors, and other moviemakers during the 1950s and 1960s; or Arthur Miller's own encounters with HUAC.

## PERSONALIZE FOR LEARNING

### English Language Support

**Latin Root *-rupt-*** Note Judge Danforth's exclamation in paragraph 296: "Hang them high over the town! Who weeps for these, weeps for corruption!" Tell students that, in this context, the word *corruption* means "lawlessness" or "lack of virtue or integrity." Ask a Spanish-speaking student to translate this English word into Spanish (*corrupción*). Point out that other languages with Latin components (such as French, Italian, and Portuguese) also have words similar to *corruption*. Inform students that the Latin root *-rupt-* means "to break." Help students list and define other words with the same root, such as *bankrupt, rupture, interrupt, erupt, disrupt,* and *abrupt*. **EXPANDING/BRIDGING**

## Jump Start

CLOSE READ Ask students to write a quick paragraph that answers the following questions: *If you were John Proctor, would you confess or not? Why?* Ask students to read aloud their answers. Hold a short discussion on these topics.

## Close Read the Text

**Possible response:** Probably Miller wants his audience to infer that the people who are about to die (such as Proctor and Rebecca Nurse) are highly respected in the village.

## Analyze the Text

**Possible responses:**

1. (a) Danforth refuses because none of the prisoners have confessed. **DOK 2** (b) Danforth's reasons for refusing show that he is dogmatic, inflexible, merciless, and afraid of losing face. **DOK 4**
2. (a) She says she thinks this is "the Devil's argument." **DOK 2** (b) She probably means that an argument that urges someone to lie to gain something is ungodly. **DOK 4**
3. John Proctor confesses so that he can live. He changes his mind because he realizes how horrified he is by the thought of others finding out that he confessed. **DOK 4**
4. Responses will vary. **DOK 4**

## Concept Vocabulary

### Why These Words?

**Possible words:** *disagreement, contention, dispute, desperation, plead, calamity, tortured*

### Practice

Paragraphs will vary.

### Word Network

**Possible words:** *quail, fearsome, frantic*

## Word Study

For more support, see **Concept Vocabulary and Word Study.**

**Possible responses:**

1. *unbreakable* or *unyielding*
2. In Greek mythology, *Tantalus* is condemned to spend eternity near food and drink that he cannot reach. The word *tantalize*, which means to torment, comes from this root. In Roman mythology, *Ceres* is a goddess of agriculture, including grain. The word *cereal*, which is a food made of grain, derives from *Ceres*.

MAKING MEANING

THE CRUCIBLE, ACT IV

## Close Read the Text

Reread Parris's remarks about the executions, beginning with paragraph 82. Mark references to the "sort" who were hanged previously. What does Miller want his audience to infer about the people who are about to die?

## Analyze the Text

**CITE TEXTUAL EVIDENCE** to support your answers.

Notebook **Respond to these questions.**

1. (a) When Hale urges Danforth to pardon the prisoners, why does Danforth refuse? (b) **Analyze** What does Danforth's attitude reveal about his sense of justice and the legitimacy of the executions?
2. (a) When urged by Hale to persuade her husband to confess, how does Elizabeth Proctor characterize Hale's argument? (b) **Interpret** What does Elizabeth mean by characterizing Hale's argument in this way?
3. **Interpret** Why does Proctor confess and then retract his confession?
4. **Essential Question:** ***How do we respond when challenged by fear?*** What have you learned about how people respond to fear from reading this play?

LANGUAGE DEVELOPMENT

## Concept Vocabulary

conciliatory adamant disputation

**Why These Words?** The concept vocabulary words relate to arguments and people's attitudes when engaged in them. What other words in Act IV relate to this concept?

**Practice**

Notebook Write a one-paragraph summary of Act IV that uses all three concept vocabulary words.

WORD NETWORK

Add words related to fear from the text to your Word Network.

## Word Study

Notebook **Etymology** The origin and development of a word is its **etymology**. The word *adamant* comes from the Greek word *adamas,* which refers to the hardest metal in the world. It is also the name of a character from Greek mythology. In contemporary English usage, *adamant* is most often used in a figurative sense.

1. Write a definition of *adamant* based on your understanding of its etymology. Check your answer in a college-level dictionary.
2. Use an etymological dictionary to research the Greek origins of the words *tantalize* and *cereal*. Explain your findings.

STANDARDS

**Reading Literature**
Determine two or more themes or central ideas of a text and analyze their development over the course of the text, including how they interact and build on one another to produce a complex account; provide an objective summary of the text.

**Language**
Consult general and specialized references, both print and digital, to find the pronunciation of a word or determine or clarify its precise meaning, its part of speech, its etymology, or its standard usage.





## FORMATIVE ASSESSMENT

### Concept Vocabulary

**If** students fail to see connections among the words, **then** have them use two of the words in a strong context sentence.

### Word Study

**If** students fail to define *adamant*, **then** have them use the word in sentences. For Reteach and Practice, see **Word Study: Etymology (RP).**

## Analyze Craft and Structure

**Author's Choices: Literary Forms** An **allegory** is a narrative that works on two levels of meaning: a literal meaning and one or more symbolic meanings.

- The **literal meaning** presents the characters and conflicts at face value. The literal story is complete and can be understood without reference to other stories or situations.
- The **symbolic meaning** interprets the characters and conflicts at a representative level—a deeper meaning that readers must infer. Characters may be symbols for real people, and the conflicts may focus readers on events or ideas that are not part of the literal narrative. Understanding an allegory's symbolic meaning can reveal the **theme**—the work's message or insight.

*The Crucible* is an allegory that Arthur Miller wrote to comment on the way that the 1950s "Red Scare" encouraged and preyed upon Americans' fears. At that time, Senator Joseph McCarthy and the separate House Un-American Activities Committee (HUAC) accused many Americans of being Communists, intent on overthrowing the United States government. Those targeted by HUAC investigation were often blacklisted and lost their jobs. After many life-ruining accusations, the public turned against the Communist hunts.

### Practice

**CITE TEXTUAL EVIDENCE** to support your answers.

**Notebook** Respond to these questions.

1. Use the chart to cite specific passages from the play and explain their importance to both the literal story and Miller's allegory. Begin with the twisted logic of Danforth's speech in paragraph 104 of Act IV.

| PASSAGE | LITERAL MEANING | ALLEGORICAL MEANING |
|---|---|---|
| Danforth's speech in Act IV, paragraph 104 | Danforth will not hear pleas for pardon. | The anti-Communist hearings were run by similarly inflexible people, and were similarly unjust. |
| Danforth's speech in Act IV, paragraph 117 | Danforth sees the punishments as inevitable because they are God's will. | Those in power may be self-righteous, even when they are wrong. |
| Proctor's speech in Act IV, paragraph 255 | Proctor is willing to make a false confession of his own sins but he does not want to name others. | In the McCarthy hearings, some refused to name names. Miller is showing his admiration for those people. |

2. (a) At the end of the play, John Proctor, Rebecca Nurse, and others make the noble decision. Is it the right decision? Explain. (b) What is Miller saying about those who stood fast against HUAC?
3. Miller has written about similarities between the Salem trials and the HUAC investigations: "Three hundred years apart, both prosecutors were alleging membership in a secret disloyal group; should the accused confess, his honesty could be proved only in precisely the same way—by naming former confederates." Explain how these ideas are developed in each act of *The Crucible*.





PERSONALIZE FOR LEARNING

**Strategic Support**

**Symbolic Meaning** Lead a classroom discussion about the symbolic meanings of well-known characters from folk tales and children's literature. For example, the two Little Pigs who build their homes from flimsy materials could be said to symbolize lazy people, while the Little Pig who builds a brick home symbolizes hardworking, diligent people.

DIGITAL PERSPECTIVES

## Analyze Craft and Structure

**Author's Choices: Literary Forms** If necessary, discuss the following with students:

- **Allegory** is not as common in modern literature as it was in the past. However, it still occasionally makes an appearance, as in George Orwell's novel *Animal Farm*.
- It may be difficult to differentiate between allegory and **symbolism**. The main distinction is that an allegory is a complete narrative work in which every story element has an equivalent symbolic meaning.
- Symbolism is part of what makes a narrative an allegory. However, symbolism can be present in works that are *not* full-scale allegories—in such works, certain story elements function as symbols, while others do not.
- For more support, see **Analyze Craft and Structure: Literary Forms.**

### Practice

Possible responses:

1. (a) See possible responses in chart on the student page.
2. (a) John decides not to confess publicly and Elizabeth decides not to try to convince him to confess. The decision is right because as respected people, their example is important. (b) Miller is saying that those who would not cooperate with the anti-Communist hearings were similarly noble.
3. In Act I, the girls who may be accused of witchcraft because they have been doing something secret in the woods begin to accuse others. In Act II, Elizabeth is framed for witchcraft by Abigail, who leads the girls. In Act III, Mary Warren testifies that she has lied, but the other girls pressure her to continue naming witches. She names John Proctor. In Act IV, Proctor at first is willing to confess, but he refuses to name others.

**FORMATIVE ASSESSMENT**

**Analyze Craft and Structure**

**If** students are unable to grasp the idea of allegory, **then** provide another example, such as Aesop's fables or George Orwell's *Animal Farm*.

For Reteach and Practice, see **Analyze Craft and Structure: Literary Forms (RP).**

# TEACHING

## Analyze Craft and Structure

**Biblical Allusions** If necessary, discuss the following with students:

- An **allusion** is a reference to a well-known person, event, place, literary work, or work of art.
- Writers often make allusions to the Bible, Greek and Roman mythology, Shakespeare's plays, famous poems, historical and current events, and popular culture—references they expect their readers (or at least some of them) to recognize.
- Allusions connect literary works to a larger cultural heritage. They are a kind of literary shorthand that allows writers to express complex ideas without being too literal.

For more support, see **Analyze Craft and Structure: Biblical Allusions.**

### Practice

See possible responses in chart on the student page.

### FORMATIVE ASSESSMENT

### Analyze Craft and Structure

- **If** students are unable to grasp the idea of Biblical allusion, **then** provide another example of an allusion, such as an allusion that a poet makes to a Greek myth.

For Reteach and Practice, see **Analyze Craft and Structure: Biblical Allusions (RP).**

MAKING MEANING

THE CRUCIBLE, ACT IV

**STANDARDS**

**Reading Literature**

Determine the meaning of words and phrases as they are used in the text, including figurative and connotative meanings; analyze the impact of specific word choices on meaning and tone, including words with multiple meanings or language that is particularly fresh, engaging, or beautiful.

**Writing**

Draw evidence from literary or informational texts to support analysis, reflection, and research.

## Analyze Craft and Structure

**Biblical Allusions** Some of the conflicts in *The Crucible* arise out of the religious worldview that dominates the Salem community. That worldview is revealed, in part, through the characters' actions and the descriptions of their way of life. It is also revealed through **Biblical allusions**—passing or unexplained references to people, places, or events from the Bible.

Biblical allusions remind characters—and the audience—of the religious beliefs on which the Puritan community is based. Allusions also help to portray individual characters. For example, in Act IV, paragraph 117, Danforth says, "Mr. Hale, as God have not empowered me like Joshua to stop this sun from rising, so I cannot withhold from them the perfection of their punishment." A note in the text identifies the source of this allusion, and the context makes its meaning clear: Just as Joshua could not delay the sun's movement, so Danforth cannot (or will not) delay his quest to obtain confessions from the condemned. The Biblical allusion reinforces the idea that Danforth sees his work as a mission from God.

### Practice

**CITE TEXTUAL EVIDENCE** to support your answers.

Some of the allusions Miller uses in *The Crucible* appear in the chart.
Determine what each allusion means. Then, explain what it reveals about the characters or situation.

| BIBLICAL ALLUSION | MEANING IN CONTEXT |
|---|---|
| Act II, paragraph 53: "Abigail brings the other girls into the court, and where she walks the crowd will part like the sea for Israel." (Source: Exodus 14:21–22) | Elizabeth Proctor means that people stupidly and blindly believe everything Abigail says. Abigail, Elizabeth (rightly) believes, has sparked the witchcraft hysteria in Salem. |
| Act II, paragraph 396: "Pontius Pilate! God will not let you wash your hands of this!" (Source: Matthew 27:22–26) | Proctor calls Hale Pontius Pilate to show that he, Proctor, thinks Hale is a coward who won't stand up for Hale's true opinion—that Elizabeth is innocent. |
| Act III, paragraph 131: "I think not, or you should surely know that Cain were an upright man, and yet he did kill Abel." (Source: Genesis 4:1–8) | Parris is saying that even a good woman like Rebecca could do something evil, as Cain did. |
| Act IV, paragraph 133: "Goody Proctor, I have gone this three month like our Lord into the wilderness." (Source: Luke 4:1) | Hale says this to Abigail. He means that, like Christ in the wilderness, Hale has been searching his soul for the right action to take. Hale has decided that the right action is to beg the prisoners to confess (lie) to save their lives. |





PERSONALIZE FOR LEARNING

### English Language Support

**Word Families** Display the words *allude, alluding, alluded,* and *allusion*. Work with students to define these related words, find synonyms for them, and use them in context sentences. **EXPANDING/ BRIDGING**

## Author's Style

**Realism** In visual art and literature, **Realism** is the presentation of the details of everyday life, showing them as they actually are (or were) seen and experienced. All the elements of a realistic drama—including the setting, plot, and dialogue—are presented in ways that mirror real life.

- The **setting**, or place and time in which the drama unfolds, is like a place in the real world. It may be an actual location or historical place and time. This setting may be represented on stage with historically accurate props, backdrops, and costumes that are recognizable as objects, places, and clothing from real life.
- The playwright bases the **plot**, or action of the play, on events that either did happen or could happen in real life. Characters' reactions to these events are authentic and plausible.
- The **dialogue**, or conversation between and among characters, reflects the ways in which people actually speak or did speak in a past era. Characters may use slang, regionalisms, dialect, or formal language. These choices reflect their circumstances and personalities.

### Read It

Review the opening scene of Act IV. Identify and describe one example of each dramatic element that is presented in a realistic way. Explain which textual details create or emphasize the realistic quality.

| ELEMENT | EXAMPLE | HOW MILLER MAKES IT SEEM REAL |
|---|---|---|
| Setting | *A cell in Salem jail, that fall. At the back is a high barred window; near it, a great, heavy door. Along the walls are two benches. The place is in darkness but for the moonlight seeping through the bars. It appears empty. Presently footsteps are heard coming down a corridor beyond the wall, keys rattle, and the door swings open.* (paragraphs 1–4) | Miller uses simple sensory language to make readers feel as if they can see "moonlight seeping through the bars," detect "footsteps...coming down a corridor," and hear "keys rattle" and a "door swing[ing] open." |
| Plot Event | *A sound—the sibilance of dragging feet on stone. They turn. A pause. Herrick enters with John Proctor. His wrists are chained. He is another man, bearded, filthy, his eyes misty as though webs had overgrown them. He halts inside the doorway, his eyes caught by the sight of Elizabeth. The emotion flowing between them prevents anyone from speaking for an instant.* (paragraph 146) | Miller creates a realistic but highly emotional scene by having John and Elizabeth meet on the morning when John is to hang. Miller shows us "bearded, filthy" John from his wife's point of view. The playwright also gives other characters' impressions of "the emotion flowing between" husband and wife. |
| Dialogue | Hale, *quietly:* Excellency, let— Danforth *brushes past Hale and walks out. Hale follows....* Parris, *from a safe distance, offers:* Parris: If you desire a cup of cider, Mr. Proctor, I am sure I— Proctor *turns an icy stare at him and he breaks off.* Parris *raises his palms toward* Proctor. God lead you now. (paragraphs 149–150) | Through dialogue and stage directions, Miller shows Hale's deep sympathy for the couple; Danforth's bullying insensitivity; Proctor's anguished, sorrowful love for his wife; Parris's ineffective attempt to ingratiate himself with Proctor; and Proctor's icy contempt for Parris. |

### Write It

**Notebook** In a paragraph, explain why you think Miller chose to tell the story of *The Crucible* in a realistic way. Why might realism be especially valuable in a play based on actual historical events?





DIGITAL PERSPECTIVES

## Author's Style

**Realism** You may wish to inform students that Realism with a capital *R* was a literary movement that flourished in the late 1800s and early 1900s. Realist writers aimed to portray life as faithfully and accurately as possible. Realist writers also renounced the elevated diction of poetry and poetic drama. Their novels and plays deal with grim social realities and controversial issues, presenting realistic portrayals of characters' psychological states.

Arthur Miller's work seems to fit into this category, even though he wrote his most famous plays during the mid-1900s. Miller may have been influenced by Realist playwrights such as George Bernard Shaw and Anton Chekhov, and by American Realist novelists such as Stephen Crane, Frank Norris, and Theodore Dreiser. For more support, see **Author's Style: Realism.**

### Read It

See possible responses in the chart on the student page.

### Write It

Responses will vary. Some students may say that it is easier to become emotionally caught up in a play that is very realistic. Some may say that it is especially valuable and appropriate to use realism to describe tragic events that really happened—and to draw parallels with contemporary events (as the "Red Scare" was happening when audiences first saw *The Crucible*).

### FORMATIVE ASSESSMENT

### Author's Style

**If** students struggle to connect Miller's writing style with realism, **then** show them specific examples from the play. For Reteach and Practice, see **Author's Style: Realism (RP).**

### PERSONALIZE FOR LEARNING

### Strategic Support

**Understanding Realism** Some students may have difficulty understanding the differences between writing styles such as Realism and Romanticism. Provide examples of both (for example, for Realism, *The Cherry Orchard* by Anton Chekhov and *Death of a Salesman* by Arthur Miller; for Romanticism, *Idylls of the King* by Alfred, Lord Tennyson and *The Sword in the Stone* by T. H. White). Lead a classroom discussion about both genres.

TEACHING

## Writing to Sources

Make sure students understand the meanings of the following academic terms:

| Term | Meaning |
|---|---|
| claim | in a written argument, a statement that clearly states the writer's opinion or viewpoint |
| theme | in a work of literature, an important idea that the author wants readers to discover, explore, and/or better understand |
| relevance | ways that a theme is applicable to today's world |
| evidence | excerpts from a text that support a writer's reasons for his or her opinion or claim |

For more support, see **Writing to Sources: Argument.**

## Reflect on Your Writing

Possible responses:

1. Reponses will vary.
2. Make sure students cite their most persuasive reasons and pieces of evidence.
3. **Why These Words?** Have students list specific examples of words and phrases they chose to clearly express their ideas and make their writing more persuasive.

### FORMATIVE ASSESSMENT

## Writing to Sources

**If** students are having difficulty finding a theme that they think is relevant to today's world, **then** ask them questions that will help them identify themes in *The Crucible.* Such questions might include: What observation does Miller make about weak people's behavior when they are afraid? What does he say about good, strong people's behavior when they are forced to make life-or-death decisions? What does the playwright say about dogmatic, inflexible religious beliefs? What does he say about authority and power? For Reteach and Practice, see **Writing to Sources: Argument (RP).**



EFFECTIVE EXPRESSION

THE CRUCIBLE, ACT IV

## Writing to Sources

When you write an argument, you take a position and then present reasons and evidence that develop and support it.

**Assignment**

Identify a theme from *The Crucible* that is relevant to today's world. Then, write an **argumentative essay** in which you make a claim as to why this theme still matters, or—perhaps—matters even more than it once did. Support your claim and your chosen theme with evidence from the text. Include these elements in your essay:

- a clear explanation of a theme expressed in *The Crucible*
- a clear claim about the relevance of the theme to today's world
- reasons that support the claim
- textual evidence from the play that supports your reasons

**Vocabulary Connection** In your essay, consider including some of the concept vocabulary words.

conciliatory adamant disputation

## Reflect on Your Writing

After you have written your argumentative essay, answer these questions.

1. In what ways did writing your essay increase your understanding and appreciation of *The Crucible?*
2. Which reasons and forms of evidence do you see as the most persuasive in your essay? How did these items help you build your argument?
3. **Why These Words?** The words you choose make a difference in your writing. Which words did you use to make your essay more persuasive?

STANDARDS

Writing
- Write arguments to support claims in an analysis of substantive topics or texts, using valid reasoning and relevant and sufficient evidence.
- Apply *grades 11–12 Reading standards* to literature.

Speaking and Listening
Present information, findings, and supporting evidence, conveying a clear and distinct perspective, such that listeners can follow the line of reasoning, alternative or opposing perspectives are addressed, and the organization, development, substance, and style are appropriate to purpose, audience, and a range of formal and informal tasks.



684 UNIT 5 • FACING OUR FEARS

PERSONALIZE FOR LEARNING

## English Language Development

**Supporting an Argument** Have students work in pairs to write down a claim and support it with one piece of evidence. **EMERGING**

Have students write a paragraph including a claim, an opposing point of view, and one piece of evidence to support their claim. **EXPANDING**

Have students write a short argumentative essay including a claim, an opposing point of view, and two or three pieces of evidence. **BRIDGING**

An expanded **English Language Development Lesson** on Argument is available in the Interactive Teacher's Edition.

## Speaking and Listening

**Assignment**
Prepare a **thematic analysis** in which you choose one theme from *The Crucible*, introduce it, and illustrate it with a dramatic reading of three sections of dialogue from the play. Follow these steps to complete the assignment.

1. **Identify a Theme** Review your notes on the play, and choose one theme that you think might be effectively illustrated with dialogue.
2. **Locate Examples** Once you have chosen a theme, scan the play to locate three pieces of dialogue that clearly illustrate that theme. Consider these questions:
   - Is it possible to find examples of dialogue from three different characters? The variety can strengthen your main idea and make your presentation more interesting.
   - Is it possible to find examples from three different sections or acts of the play? Connecting ideas across the whole play may help your listeners understand why the theme you chose is central to an understanding of Miller's text.
3. **Craft an Introduction** Decide how you will introduce the theme you chose, and how you will transition from your explanation to the dramatic readings.
4. **Prepare Your Delivery** Practice your presentation in front of a mirror or present it to a friend or family member. Keep these suggestions in mind:
   - Vary your intonation (tone and pitch) to reflect each character you portray. Speak naturally, but with attention to your enunciation and volume, when delivering your introduction.
   - Use facial expressions and gestures to help convey characters' emotions and meaning.
5. **Evaluate Analyses** As your classmates deliver their analyses, listen carefully. Use an evaluation guide like the one shown to assess their presentations.

EVALUATION GUIDE

**Rate each statement on a scale of 1 (not demonstrated) to 5 (demonstrated).**

☐ The speaker clearly introduced the theme.

☐ The speaker chose three examples from the play that illustrated the theme well.

☐ The speaker used a variety of vocal tones and pitches.

☐ The speaker used effective gestures and facial expressions.



EVIDENCE LOG

Before moving on to a new selection, go to your Evidence Log and record what you learned from *The Crucible*, Act IV.



DIGITAL PERSPECTIVES

## Speaking and Listening

1. **Identify a Theme** If students have difficulty choosing a theme to illustrate, suggest the following options:
- fear causes weaker people to "throw their friends and neighbors under the bus"
- moral strength allows some people to hold onto their humanity (kindness and selflessness), even when they are afraid for their lives
- power corrupts some people, turning them into worse people than they were
- remorse may lead to attempts to recompense others for your mistakes (as Hale tries to do)

2. **Locate Examples** Remind students to try to find examples of dialogue from three different characters and three different parts of the play. Also remind them to make sure that every one of their examples *strongly* illustrates the theme—if not, they should keep searching.
3. **Craft an Introduction** Tell students that in their introduction they should introduce the theme they picked, explain what the theme means or entails, and tell listeners why they chose that theme.
4. **Prepare Your Delivery** Make sure students understand the meanings of the following terms: *intonation, tone,* and *pitch*. If necessary, ask volunteers to give examples of each.
5. **Evaluate Analyses** If necessary, ask volunteers to explain in detail what it means to "clearly introduce a theme" and "choose examples that illustrate the theme well." Encourage students to take notes during classmates' analyses and use these as they complete the presentation evaluation guide.

For more support, see **Speaking and Listening: Thematic Analysis.**

Evidence Log Support students in completing their Evidence Log. This paced activity will help prepare them for the Performance-Based Assessment at the end of the unit.

### FORMATIVE ASSESSMENT

### Speaking and Listening

**If** students have difficulty choosing one theme for their analysis, **then** suggest that they choose their favorite speech from the play, choose a theme that that speech expresses, and then locate two more speeches that express the same theme. For more support, see **Speaking and Listening: Thematic Analysis (RP).**

### Selection Test

Administer the "The Crucible, Act IV" Selection Test, which is available in both print and digital formats online in Assessments.

# *The Crucible* (audio)

**AUDIO SUMMARIES**
Audio summaries of the L.A. Theatre Works' Production of *The Crucible*, Act I, are available online in both English and Spanish in the Interactive Teacher's Edition or Unit Resources. Assigning these summaries prior to reviewing the selection may help students build additional background knowledge and set a context for their first review.

## Summary

This radio production of Act I of *The Crucible* begins with the sound of young girls giggling in the woods. A rooster crows to indicate the time. Rev. Parris and his niece Abigail are engaged in a whispered dialogue about what happened there the night before. The Putnams arrive and Rev. Parris learns that they had engaged Tituba, Parris's black slave, to try to raise the spirits of their dead children. John Proctor and Rebecca Nurse believe that Betty is pretending to be ill. When Rev. Hale, a witch expert, arrives, Tituba confesses to devil worship and accuses other Salem women of witchcraft.

### Insight

This radio performance of Arthur Miller's *The Crucible* includes background sound effects such as thunder and rain and singing. Miller's prose descriptions of the characters' backgrounds and motivations have been left out of this production. The dialogue is sometimes changed to help listeners know to whom a particular character is talking.

ESSENTIAL QUESTION:
How do we respond when challenged by fear?

## Connection to Essential Question

This radio production of Act I of *The Crucible* connects to the Essential Question, "How do we respond when challenged by fear?" This act introduces the main characters in the play and lays the groundwork for future plot developments and themes including the spreading hysteria about witchcraft in the community.

WHOLE CLASS LEARNING PERFORMANCE TASK
Could any of the characters in *The Crucible* have done more to end the hysteria in Salem?

UNIT PERFORMANCE-BASED ASSESSMENT
Is fear always a harmful emotion?

## Connection to Performance Tasks

**Whole-Class Learning Performance Task** In this Performance Task, students will consider the question, "Could any of the characters in *The Crucible* have done more to end the hysteria in Salem?" Students may note that Tituba and Abigail could have prevented the hysteria from escalating by telling the truth. Similarly, Parris could have prevented the hysteria by not consulting the Reverend Hale.

**Unit Performance-Based Assessment** Students should note that Act I of *The Crucible* touches on how members of a society who choose to lie can manipulate the emotions and actions of others around them. Fear of what others can do is a powerful motivation to act irrationally.

DIGITAL PERSPECTIVES

 Audio  Video  Document  Annotation Highlights  EL Highlights 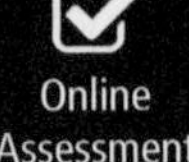 Online Assessment

## Media Complexity Rubric: *The Crucible* (audio)

| **Quantitative Measures** | |
|---|---|
| Format and Length | **L.A. Theatre Works** audio recording of Act I of *The Crucible* |
| **Qualitative Measures** | |
| Knowledge Demands ①—②—③—❹—⑤ | To fully understand the audio recording, prior knowledge is needed about the Salem witch trials. |
| Structure ①—②—❸—④—⑤ | The selection is an audio play with voice actors portraying each character from the play. The actors often speak quickly, which may be challenging. |
| Language Conventionality and Clarity ①—②—③—❹—⑤ | The dialogue in the audio play contains sophisticated language and challenging vocabulary with antiquated language. |
| Levels of Meaning/Purpose ①—②—❸—④—⑤ | The meaning is straightforward but may be difficult to grasp due to challenging language. |

## LESSON RESOURCES

| | Making Meaning | Language Development | Effective Expression |
|---|---|---|---|
| Lesson | **First Review**<br>**Close Review**<br>**Analyze the Media** | **Media Vocabulary** | **Writing to Compare** |
| Instructional Standards | **RL.10** By the end of grade 11, read and comprehend literature . . .<br>**RL.1** Cite strong and thorough textual evidence . . . | | **RL.7** Analyze multiple interpretations of a story, drama, or poem . . .<br>**W.9.a** Apply *grades 11–12 Reading standards . . .* |
| **STUDENT RESOURCES** | | | |
| Available online in the Interactive Student Edition or Unit Resources | Selection Audio<br>First-Review Guide: Media Audio<br>Close-Review Guide: Media Audio | | Evidence Log |
| **TEACHER RESOURCES** | | | |
| **Selection Resources** Available online in the Interactive Teacher's Edition or Unit Resources | Audio Summaries | Media Vocabulary | Writing to Compare: Critical Review |
| **My Resources** | A Unit 5 Answer Key is available online and in the Interactive Teacher's Edition. | | |

# TEACHING

## Jump Start

FIRST REVIEW Ask students if they've ever read a book and then seen a TV, movie, or theatrical adaptation of it. Discuss how the format affected their appreciation of the work.

### The Crucible (audio)

How do the interpretations and perceptions of actors affect an audience's experience with literary work? Modeling this and other questions readers might ask will bring the L.A Theatre Works production of *The Crucible* to life and connect it to the Performance Task question. Selection audio is available in the Interactive Teacher's Edition.

### Media Vocabulary

Encourage students to discuss the media vocabulary. Have they seen the terms in texts before? Do they use any of them in their speech and writing? For more support, see **Media Vocabulary.**

### FIRST REVIEW

The first time they go through the selection, students should perform the steps of the first review:

LISTEN: Remind students to pay attention to how the actors use expression and intonation in order to portray the characters.

NOTE: Encourage students to note what techniques the actors employ that they find particularly effective and how those techniques influence their experience of listening to the play.

CONNECT: Encourage students to make connections to movies they have watched or other plays they may have heard or seen performed.

RESPOND: Students will demonstrate their understanding by answering questions and writing a summary.

Point out to students that they will perform the first three steps concurrently as they are doing their first review. They will complete the Respond step after they have finished the first review. Print copies of the **First-Review Guide: Media Audio** for students to use.

MAKING MEANING

THE CRUCIBLE

## Comparing Text to Media

Now that you have read the text of *The Crucible*, listen to an audio performance of Act I. As you listen, consider the choices the actors make in their portrayals. You will then analyze the ways in which the theatrical production interprets the written text and compare the audio and written versions.

THE CRUCIBLE (audio)

**About the Theater Company**

**L.A. Theatre Works** is a nonprofit organization dedicated to recording live performances of classic and contemporary plays. Founded in 1974 in Los Angeles, California, the organization has more than 250 plays in its Audio Theatre Collection, featuring many of Hollywood's best-known actors. Those recordings can be downloaded, streamed, or borrowed from libraries across the country. LATW also airs performances in weekly public radio programs and presents live performances as well.

# The Crucible (audio)

## Media Vocabulary

These words will be useful to you as you analyze, discuss, and write about audio performances.

| | |
|---|---|
| **audio play:** theatrical performance of a drama produced for radio, podcast, or another non-visual and non-print recorded form | • Before the arrival of television, audio plays were popular on the radio.<br>• Audio plays may incorporate sound effects to add information, or music to suggest mood. |
| **inflection:** the rise and fall of pitch and tone in a person's voice | • The pitch of a voice is how high or low it is, and tone refers to the quality of the sound produced, such as a whisper or a growl.<br>• Inflection conveys emotion, and is part of an actor's interpretation of a character. |
| **expression:** tone of voice that indicates specific emotion | • The expression in a voice may hint at a character's unspoken thoughts or feelings. |

### First Review MEDIA: AUDIO

Apply these strategies as you listen to the audio performance of Act I of *The Crucible.*

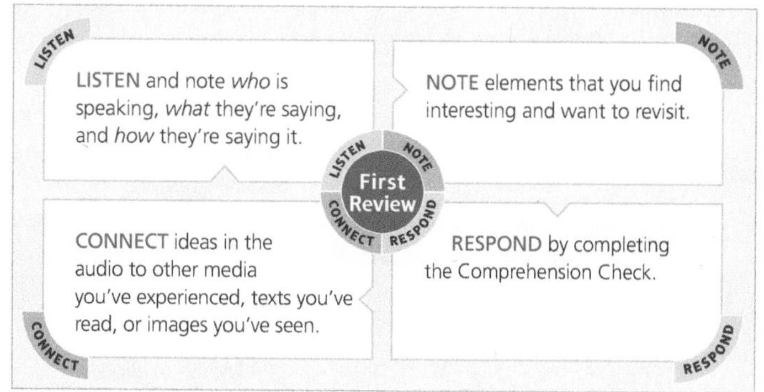

LISTEN
LISTEN and note *who* is speaking, *what* they're saying, and *how* they're saying it.
NOTE
NOTE elements that you find interesting and want to revisit.
First Review
CONNECT
CONNECT ideas in the audio to other media you've experienced, texts you've read, or images you've seen.
RESPOND
RESPOND by completing the Comprehension Check.


**STANDARDS**

**Reading Literature**

By the end of grade 11, read and comprehend literature, including stories, dramas, and poems, in the grades 11–CCR text complexity band proficiently, with scaffolding as needed at the high end of the range.





### VOCABULARY DEVELOPMENT

**Media Vocabulary Reinforcement** Reinforce students' comprehension of media vocabulary with "show-you-know" sentences. The first part of the sentence uses the vocabulary word in an appropriate context. The second part—the "show-you-know" part—clarifies the first. Give students these sentence prompts and coach them to create the clarification parts:

1. We listened to an audio play that ________.
   *(had actors reading the parts of Charles Dickens' classic* A Christmas Carol*)*
2. I was grateful the actors used inflection in their dialogue because ________.
   *(the rise and fall of their voices made it more interesting to listen to)*

# The Crucible

L.A. Theatre Works

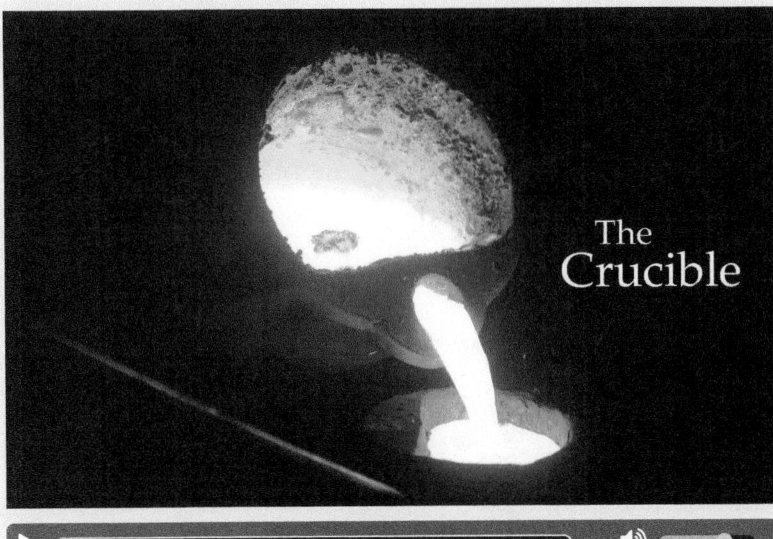


BACKGROUND

As part of the L.A. Theatre Works series, Martin Jenkins directed a radio play adaptation of *The Crucible* in 1988. You will listen to Act I. The cast features Richard Dreyfuss as Reverend Hale and Stacy Keach as John Proctor.

SCAN FOR MULTIMEDIA 

NOTES





## PERSONALIZE FOR LEARNING

### Strategic Support

**Active Listening** Students may struggle to keep up with the audio recording. Work with students in a small group setting and play the audio recording in shorter segments. After each three to five minute listening session, stop the recording and ask students to give a recap of what they heard. If students struggle to summarize a section, either replay it or provide the necessary content to help them maintain understanding of the plot line. **EMERGING/EXPANDING**

## CLOSER REVIEW

### Analyze Expression

Students may have noted 4:30 to 8:00 during their first review. Use this part of the audio recording to help students understand how performance choices add tension and emotion to the performance. Encourage them to talk about what they noted. You may want to model a close review with the class.

**NOTE:** Have students note details in the audio recording that create a sense of tension through the emotion of the characters, or have students participate while you note them.

**QUESTION:** Guide students to consider what these details might tell them. Ask what a listener can infer from the way the characters are speaking to one another, and accept student responses.

**Possible response:** First I notice that at the beginning of this section they seem to be trying very hard to whisper, or keep their voices in a hushed tone. I can infer they don't want the people downstairs to hear what they are saying. I also notice they are talking in a rushed manner. Reverend Parris, in particular, seems to be very upset. He pauses many times and seems to be trying to hold back anger. Then later when he asks Abigail if she had done something to dirty her reputation, he is deliberately slowing his pace of speech and pausing for longer breaks between words, as if he is trying to be patient but struggling to do so. Abigail's speech is also hushed and yet frantic. When her reputation is questioned, her voice rises and she sounds angry.

**CONCLUDE:** Help students to formulate conclusions about the importance of these details in the audio recording. Ask students why the actors may have made these choices in their performance.

**Possible response:** In an audio recording of a play, actors have no way of conveying their emotion except through their voice. When the actor playing Rev. Parris slows his pace, adds longer pauses, and uses inflection to hold back his words, the listener feels the tension building between the characters. When the actor playing Abigail raises her voice and responds in an angry tone, you can feel the situation escalate.

Remind students that **expression** is a tone of voice that indicates a specific emotion. Explain to students that the playwright will sometimes describe the tone or inflection she wants the actor to use for a certain piece of dialogue by writing something such as "**Mary:** (angrily)." Usually, though, the actor, working with the director, must decide how to read a given line.

## Comprehension Check

Possible Responses

1. Betty is unconscious after supposedly fainting in the woods.
2. Parris has called for Reverend Hale, an expert in witchcraft, to confirm the fact that no unnatural causes are the result of Betty's illness.
3. Abigail insists that the girls say only that they danced and that Tituba conjured Ruth Putnam's dead sisters.
4. At first, Tituba says, "I don't truck with no Devil." After being threatened, she says that she tells the Devil that she "don't desire to work for him" and that someone else is bewitching the children. After being questioned more, Tituba says that four people came to her with the Devil. Then she says that the Devil asked her to kill Mr. Parris. Finally, she says that Goody Good and Goody Osborn were with the Devil.
5. The excerpt ends with Abigail saying that she saw Sarah Good, Goody Osborn, and Bridget Bishop with the Devil. Betty joins in, saying that she saw George Jacobs, Goody Howe, and Martha Bellows with the Devil. The act ends as Abigail and Betty continue to name villagers that they claim they have seen with the Devil.

**Research to Clarify** If students are having difficulty choosing an unfamiliar detail, suggest they focus on domestic help in colonial households, Puritan attitudes toward trying to communicate with the dead, or Puritan attitudes toward music and dancing.

**Research to Explore** Encourage students to learn more about life expectancy, healthcare practices, and child mortality in Puritan settlements.

## Comprehension Check

Complete the following items after you finish your first review.

1. As the play opens, what is wrong with Reverend Parris's daughter Betty?

2. Why has Parris called for Reverend Hale?

3. What story does Abigail insist the other girls tell about their activities in the woods?

4. How does Tituba's story change as she is questioned?

5. What specific accusations end this excerpt of the audio performance?

**Research to Clarify** Choose at least one unfamiliar detail from the text. Briefly research that detail. In what way does the information you learned shed light on an aspect of the audio performance of *The Crucible?*

**Research to Explore** Conduct research on an aspect of the text you find interesting. For example, you may want to learn about the practice of midwifery, the profession of helping to deliver babies, as it was practiced in colonial America.





### PERSONALIZE FOR LEARNING

**Strategic Support**

**Review Plot** If students struggle to recall the plot points from Act I of the play, have them review the summaries they wrote when they read the text. Then invite pairs of students to retell the main plot points in Act I using their own words. If they forget any important details, have partners fill in the missing information.

MAKING MEANING

## Close Review

Listen to the audio performance again. Write down any new observations that seem important. What **questions** do you have? What can you **conclude**?

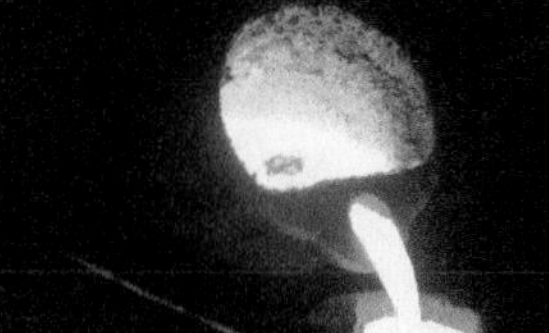

THE CRUCIBLE (audio)

## Analyze the Media

Notebook Respond to these questions.

1. (a) What does Abigail try to convince the other girls to say? (b) **Make Inferences** Why do the others seem willing to follow Abigail's wishes? Explain.
2. (a) What does Reverend Hale carry when he enters the scene? (b) **Analyze** How are the objects he carries symbols that help audiences understand his character and social position?
3. (a) What circumstances lead to Tituba's confession? (b) **Draw Conclusions** Is Tituba's confession likely to be trustworthy? Why or why not?
4. (a) **Interpret** What is each character in Act I afraid of? (b) **Evaluate** Which character feels the deepest fear? Explain the reasons for your choice.
5. **Essential Question:** ***How do we respond when challenged by fear?*** What have you learned about the nature of fear from listening to this audio performance?

LANGUAGE DEVELOPMENT

### Media Vocabulary

audio play inflection expression

1. (a) What are the first and last sounds the audience hears at the beginning and end of Act I of this radio play? (b) What theme is emphasized by the director's choice to highlight these sounds? Explain.
2. (a) What choices do the actors make that emphasize the emotional intensity of the situation in Act I? Cite specific examples. (b) What production techniques add to the intense atmosphere? Cite specific choices.
3. What acting choices do the performers make in this radio play to help audiences distinguish characters?



STANDARDS

**Reading Literature**
Cite strong and thorough textual evidence to support analysis of what the text says explicitly as well as inferences drawn from the text, including determining where the text leaves matters uncertain.



DIGITAL PERSPECTIVES

## Jump Start

CLOSE REVIEW Think about a time when you knew something was wrong with someone just by the tone of his or her voice. What gave away their emotions? What other feelings can you express simply by the way in which you speak? Engage students in a discussion of the power of expression through voice.

## Close Review the Media

Model close reviewing by using the Close Review note. Remind students to listen for details they did not observe during their first review. You may wish to print copies of the **Close-Review Guide: Media Audio** for students to use. 

## Analyze the Media

Possible responses:

1. (a) Abigail wants the other girls to say that they were dancing. **DOK 1** (b) Abigail threatens them. **DOK 2**
2. (a) Reverend Hale carries books. **DOK 1** (b) The books stand for Hale's education and show that he is seen as an expert on witchcraft. **DOK 2**
3. (a) Abigail accuses Tituba, who is questioned by Hale and Parris. When they threaten her, she confesses. **DOK 1** (b) Her testimony is not reliable because she changes her story after she is threatened. **DOK 2**
4. (a) Parris is afraid of scandal. Abigail is afraid of being accused of witchcraft. Proctor is afraid of Abigail's desire for him. Tituba is afraid of being hanged for witchcraft. **DOK 2** (b) Tituba may be the most afraid because, as an outsider, she may feel she has little power. **DOK 3**
5. Fear is contagious. When one person begins to express fear, it can soon affect others in the same group. Fear also makes people desperate and willing to do things that they know are wrong or hurtful. **DOK 3**

## FORMATIVE ASSESSMENT

### Analyze the Media

- **If** students fail to cite evidence, **then** remind them to support their ideas with specific information from the media.
- **If** students struggle to understand how fear is a factor in the story, **then** discuss how the emotions of the characters are expressed in the audio recording.

1. (a) The audience hears girls laughing at the beginning and end of Act I. (b) The girls' laughter emphasizes the theme that what seems like innocent child's play can have grave consequences.
2. (a) The actors cry, whisper, and adjust volume and inflection to convey emotional intensity. For example, Parris weeps at the start of Act 1. Abigail whispers quickly to Parris as they discuss what has happened. (b) Sound effects and background voices are audible as the characters talk. For example, thunder and voices in prayer add intensity to Abigail's conversation with the other girls.
3. Each actor uses a distinct way of speaking so that his or her character is easy to identify. For example, Rebecca Nurse speaks with a gruff voice and Tituba speaks with a distinct accent.

# TEACHING

## Writing to Compare

As students prepare to compare Act I of *The Crucible* with a video of a performance of Act I, they will evaluate the performance in a critical review.

### Prewriting

**Analyze the Texts** Encourage students to listen for sound effects and other background sounds in the audio that represent departures from or embellishments of the text.

a. The characters speak with a great deal of anxiety. The Rev. Parris weeps as he prays for Betty. Abigail shifts from a frightened tone with Rev. Parris to a threatening tone with the other girls to a beguiling tone with Proctor.

b. Sound effects of a storm are in the background. Most of the characters have New England accents.

c. The play opens with the sound of the girls laughing while dancing in the forest and fades into the sound of the Rev. Parris crying at the start of the first scene.

d. Some of the less important dialogue is skipped. As characters come and go, pronouns in the text are replaced with names in the audio.

e. The characters' anxious tone creates an emotionally charged atmosphere, which engages the audience. Abigail is highlighted as an antagonistic character with her willingness to lie and engage in dangerous behavior.

f. The storm creates an atmosphere of instability. The accents point to the setting of Massachusetts. On the whole, however, audio recordings cannot provide much information about setting.

g. The sound of the girls laughing is not in the text; including it in the audio adds an eerie mood that is effective.

h. The streamlining of the dialogue helps move along the action. The decreased use of pronouns makes it easier for the audience to follow the action in the audio.

**Possible responses:**

Answers will vary, but students should support their responses with evidence from the text.



EFFECTIVE EXPRESSION

THE CRUCIBLE

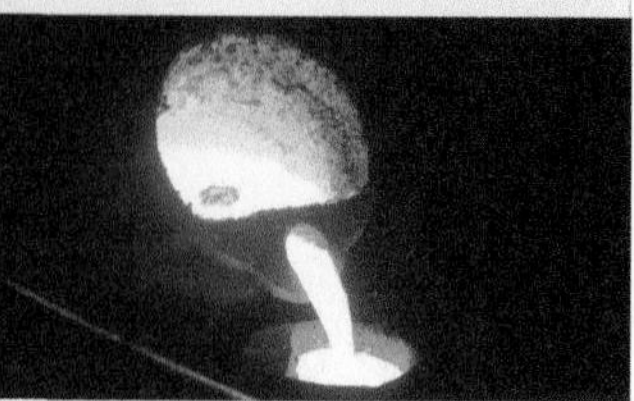
THE CRUCIBLE (audio)

## Writing to Compare

You have read *The Crucible*, and you have listened to a performance of Act I. The performance of a play is not simply a reading of the text. Instead, actors and directors make choices that reveal their interpretations. If you have read a play, you are in a good position to evaluate those choices.

**Assignment**

Write a **critical review** of the L.A. Theatre Works production of Act I of *The Crucible*. In your review, consider these questions.

- How does the performance present the setting, characters, and events? How does it establish a mood?
- Is the interpretation effective and insightful, or does it misinterpret the play?

In your conclusion, state whether you would or would not recommend the L.A. Theatre Works production to students studying the play or to general audiences.

STANDARDS

**Reading Literature**
Analyze multiple interpretations of a story, drama, or poem, evaluating how each version interprets the source text.

**Writing**
Apply grades 11–12 Reading standards to literature.

### Prewriting

**Analyze the Texts** To conduct a comparison of the text and the performance, follow these steps. Use the chart to capture your observations.

- Find portions of the audio performance that follow the text exactly.
- Find other portions that depart from the text. For example, dialogue may be cut or added. Consider reasons for these changes.
- Consider why the director or actors made certain choices and what each choice communicates.

| ELEMENT | NOTEWORTHY CHOICES | EFFECTIVENESS OF CHOICES |
|---|---|---|
| Portrayal of Characters | a. See answers in Teacher's Edition. | e. |
| Presentation of Setting | b. | f. |
| Creation of Mood | c. | g. |
| Portrayal of Action | d. | h. |

**Notebook** Does the performance bring out elements of the text that surprised you? If so, are these good surprises or disappointing ones?





PERSONALIZE FOR LEARNING

**Strategic Support**

**Finding Evidence** Students may struggle to narrow down specific examples for comparison. Suggest they begin by considering parts of the play that had the most impact on them. Have them make notes about scenes that are the most vivid in their memory. Then have students review the text version of *The Crucible* to locate that scene. After reviewing it and making notes about it in their chart, have them identify the same section in the audio version and make notes about that version. Encourage students to follow this procedure for at least two different scenes in Act I of the play.

## Drafting

**Develop Your Ideas** Before you begin writing, go over your Prewriting notes. Decide which of your insights are most compelling and can be best supported with evidence. Mark or highlight those notes, and then develop each one separately. To do so, express each note in a complete sentence. Then, record quotations, passages, or paraphrases that support it.

**Organize Ideas** Use the outline to organize your ideas and supporting evidence. Note that a critical review often begins with a summary of the work being reviewed as well as a brief statement of the reviewer's opinion.

**Outline for Critical Review**

| | |
|---|---|
| **Introduction:**<br>• State the title of the work and the production being reviewed.<br>• State the main idea—your opinion of the performance. | |
| **Body: Paragraph**<br>Develop main idea with supporting reason and evidence | |
| **Body: Paragraph**<br>Develop main idea with supporting reason and evidence | |
| **Body: Paragraph**<br>Develop main idea with supporting reason and evidence | |
| **Conclusion**<br>• Restate main idea<br>• End with a memorable image or insight | |

## Review, Revise, and Edit

When you have finished drafting, revise your work. Mark ideas that need more support, and then return to your notes, the original play, or the performance to find useful evidence. Check for logical transitions between paragraphs and major sections. Edit your work to eliminate errors in grammar, sentence structure, and word choice. Finally, proofread your review to correct any lingering spelling and punctuation errors.

**EVIDENCE LOG**

Before moving on to a new selection, go to your Evidence Log and record what you learned from the L.A. Theatre Works audio performance of Act I of *The Crucible.*





**DIGITAL PERSPECTIVES**  

## Drafting

**Develop Your Ideas** Students will likely need to review the audio multiple times to make their comparisons. Allow them to work individually on tablets or other devices if available, using headphones if possible.

**Organize Ideas** Before students begin filling out the outline chart, ask them to review the Assignment box on the previous page to note the various elements that need to be covered in the outline: setting, characters, events, mood. Encourage them to review additional elements that they find interesting.

## Review, Revise, and Edit

As students revise, encourage them to review their draft to be sure they have explained their thinking clearly. Ask them to review their word choice. Finally, remind students to check for grammar, usage, and mechanics.

For more support, see **Writing to Compare: Critical Review.**

**Evidence Log** Support students in completing their Evidence Log. This paced activity will help prepare them for the Performance-Based Assessment at the end of the unit.

## PERSONALIZE FOR LEARNING

### English Language Support

**Text Structure** Students may have difficulty organizing their writing using the compare and contrast text structure. Begin by reviewing that compare means to find ways the two texts are alike and contrast focuses on the differences between each. Provide key words that students can use when writing about each. For example, when discussing similarities students may choose to use words like *both, together, and, similar to,* and *compared to.* When discussing differences, students may use the words *unlike, instead of, as opposed to, in contrast to, but,* and *however.* Have students practice writing compare and contrast sentences about elements in the classroom. Guide them in construction and provide redirection and support as needed. **ALL LEVELS**

## FORMATIVE ASSESSMENT

### Writing to Compare

**If** students struggle to select a scene from the play to review, **then** suggest they choose the opening scene, paragraphs 1–69, since it introduces two main characters and the action is easier to follow.

# TEACHING

## Jump Start

Have students brainstorm ways people can check rumors to find out whether they are true or false. Then discuss which, if any, of the ways were available to the people in *The Crucible*.

## Write an Argument

Clarify that students are being asked to write about characters in the time and place the play is set. Remind students that the communal setting discouraged individual expression of freedom. What alternatives did the characters have?

Students should complete the assignment using word processing software to take advantage of editing tools and features.

### Elements of an Argument

Remind students to first establish a precise claim. Suggest they select a character they think could have acted differently and diffused the hysteria. Remind students that their reasoning must be logical and supported by relevant evidence from the play as well as from secondary sources.

**MAKE IT INTERACTIVE**

Project the Launch Text and have students identify the elements of an argument.

## Academic Vocabulary

Ask students how they might use the verbs *assert* and *certify* in stating the claim of an argumentative essay. Then ask them how they could use the adjectives *relevant, immutable,* and *definitive* in supporting their claims.

PERFORMANCE TASK: WRITING FOCUS

WRITING TO SOURCES

- THE CRUCIBLE
- THE CRUCIBLE (audio)

# Write an Argument

You have just read a play about mass hysteria and a community's response to it. You have also listened to an audio performance of Act I of that play, which brought the characters and their collective fears to life.

**Assignment**

In *The Crucible,* rumors spread across Salem and the result is mass hysteria in the community. Use your knowledge of *The Crucible* to write a brief **argumentative essay** in which you state and defend your position on this question:

**Could any of the characters in *The Crucible* have done more to end the hysteria in Salem?**

As you prepare to write your essay, first choose a position and state a claim. Then, develop and support that claim with quotations and examples from the text, as well as information about mass hysteria from secondary sources.

**Tool Kit**
Student Model of an Argument

### Elements of an Argument

An **argument** is a logical way of presenting a viewpoint, belief, or stand on an issue. One form of argument is the response to literature, a deep analysis of a text that leads to a conclusion or claim. This analysis may involve the text as a whole, an element of the text, or ideas that extend beyond the text to embrace other writings, human behavior, or world events. A well-written argumentative essay about literature may change readers' understanding of a text and its meaning or importance.

An effective argumentative essay contains these elements:

- a precise claim
- consideration of counterclaims, or opposing positions, and a discussion of their strengths and weaknesses
- logical organization that makes clear connections among claim, counterclaim, reasons, and evidence
- valid reasoning and relevant and sufficient evidence
- a concluding statement or section that logically completes the argument
- formal and objective language and tone
- error-free grammar, including correct use of indefinite pronouns

**ACADEMIC VOCABULARY**

As you craft your argument, consider using some of the academic vocabulary you learned in the beginning of the unit.

**assert**
**relevant**
**certify**
**immutable**
**definitive**

**Model Argument** For a model of a well-crafted argument, see the Launch Text, "Is It Foolish to Fear?" Challenge yourself to find all of the elements of an effective argument in the text. You will have an opportunity to review these elements as you prepare to write your own argument.

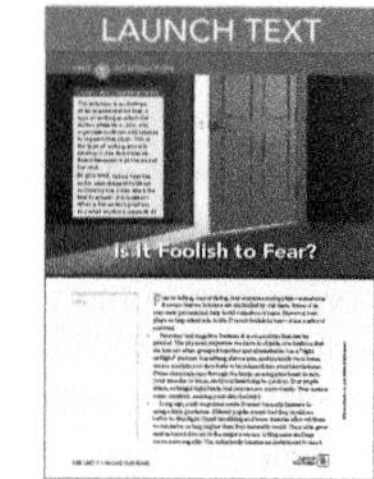


**STANDARDS**

Writing

- Write arguments to support claims in an analysis of substantive topics or texts, using valid reasoning and relevant and sufficient evidence.
- Write routinely over extended time frames and shorter time frames for a range of tasks, purposes, and audiences.





AUTHOR'S PERSPECTIVE **Kelly Gallagher, M.Ed.**

**Read, Analyze, Emulate** Teachers can use scaffolding to help students grow as writers by studying good writing with them. When students recognize the qualities of good writing, they begin producing it.

**Step 1: Read** Provide students with excellent narratives from the text and direct them to "read like a writer" by paying attention to ideas, style, voice, and organization. Encourage students to look for the moves the writer made to elicit a response in readers.

**Step 2: Analyze** Focus on the ideas by asking students questions such as "What is the writer's theme? How did the writer develop it?" Then turn to style and voice, asking, "How did the writer develop the characters?" "What effect did the dialogue have?" "What sensory details did the writer use?" and "Where do you hear the author's distinctive voice?" Finally, ask questions about organization, such as "How did the writer pace events?" and "What do you notice about the writer's paragraphing decisions?"

**Step 3: Emulate** Select one or two of the writer's moves to practice. Guide students to follow the models they studied as they write.

## Prewriting / Planning

**Ask Questions** One way to start writing an argument is to ask and answer questions about the topic. Your answers to the questions will help you focus your response. Use the following questions as a starting point for your own inquiry.

1. How might someone put an end to mass hysteria in a situation like the one that unfolds in *The Crucible*?

2. Which character or characters in *The Crucible* would be most capable of ending the hysteria? Why?

Now, write a **claim**, or the position you will argue in your essay, based on your answers to these questions.

**Gather Evidence** In an argument about a work of literature, most of your evidence will derive from the text itself. However, the prompt asks you to do some research on the topic to support your claim. In the Launch Text, the writer uses researched facts to underscore ideas about fear.

> *Something alarms you, and instantly your brain causes a number of chemicals to be released into your bloodstream. Those chemicals race through the body, causing your heart to race, your muscles to tense, and your breathing to quicken. Your pupils dilate, so bright light hurts, but you can see more clearly. Your surface veins constrict, making your skin feel cold.*
>
> —"Is It Foolish to Fear?"

Make a list of the types of sources you might use to find information about the topic of mass hysteria. Note your ideas here.

**EVIDENCE LOG**

Review your Evidence Log and identify key details you may want to cite in your argument.

**STANDARDS**

Writing

Introduce precise, knowledgeable claim(s), establish the significance of the claim(s), distinguish the claim(s) from alternate or opposing claims, and create an organization that logically sequences claim(s), counterclaims, reasons, and evidence.





**DIGITAL PERSPECTIVES**

## Prewriting/Planning

**Ask Questions** Possible responses:

1. Someone might have put an end to the mass hysteria by pointing out that confessions were unreliable since those who confessed were afraid of being condemned as witches.
2. Parris could have calmed the hysteria by addressing the issue at hand and not worrying about his own security. He had a position of authority but failed to exercise the necessary leadership in fear of losing his position.

Student claims will vary.

**Gather Evidence** Have students review their Evidence Log to find possible support for their claim. Remind them to go back and review the selections to identify evidence for their argument as well as support for the counterclaim they plan to address.

### PERSONALIZE FOR LEARNING

**English Language Support**

**Writing a Claim** Support students as they write a claim for their argument.

Have students review the definition of argument. Working with a partner, have each student write his or her claim in a short, complete sentence. Provide frames as needed. ________ *could have done more to end the hysteria in Salem by* ________. **EMERGING**

Have students review the definition of argument. Encourage them to write their claims in complete sentences, paying attention to how their ideas are organized. **EXPANDING**

Ask students to keep in mind that they are writing to argue in support of a claim. As students write their claims, have them list the evidence they have identified as support. **BRIDGING**

## Enriching Writing with Research

**Using Research** Have students look into the Salem witch trials on the Internet. Encourage them to compare their findings with information in the play. Ask the following question: *Does the playwright accurately portray the mood of the people in Salem in the spring of 1692?*

### Read It

**Evaluating Sources for Research** Tell students that "unreliable" sources may appear factual on first glance. Note that the appearance of professionalism on a website does not indicate reliability. Students must dig deeper to determine the sources of information before making final judgments.

PERFORMANCE TASK: WRITING FOCUS

## ENRICHING WRITING WITH RESEARCH

**Using Research** Argumentative or explanatory writing can almost always be strengthened by research. Use the library or credible online resources to locate specific information that supports your claim.

### Read It

This excerpt from the Launch Text provides an example of evidence found during research. In this case, the writer located an interesting fact about fear that could be used as part of a counterclaim—if there is a way to rid ourselves of fear, why shouldn't we use it?

LAUNCH TEXT EXCERPT

Today, modern psychotherapies may include conditioning—stimulus-response learning process—that helps people rid themselves of fears. After just a few sessions, nearly anyone can stop being afraid of speaking in public or driving through a tunnel. So why shouldn't we all condition ourselves to become braver?

Notice that the definition of *conditioning* and the description of its use are broad enough that the writer does not need to cite a particular source.

**Evaluating Sources for Research** As you locate sources of information, examine them carefully. Not every resource is trustworthy. Consider these questions before using a source.

- Is the author an expert in the field? Look up his or her name to find out. You may also look up the publication to ensure that it is a solid resource with a reputation for reliability and credibility.
- Is the article objective—neutral and unbiased—or does it represent one person's opinion? If it is a statement of opinion, is that opinion thoughtfully considered and supported?
- Is the article up to date? Check the date on all sources to make sure that they are current.
- Is information in the article supported by convincing facts and details?

If you are consulting a website, consider its domain. Domains such as .edu or .gov indicate sites that are affiliated with colleges or government agencies. You are likely to find reliable facts and figures on sites with those domains. Other websites may be affiliated with respected magazines and journals, and the information there is likely to be credible. Look for a date on the page to ensure that you are reading up-to-date information.

Always use more than one source as you research your topic. Doing so will allow you to cross-check information to be sure that you are using dependable evidence.

STANDARDS

**Writing**

- Develop claim(s) and counterclaims fairly and thoroughly, supplying the most relevant evidence for each while pointing out the strengths and limitations of both in a manner that anticipates the audience's knowledge level, concerns, values, and possible biases.
- Gather relevant information from multiple authoritative print and digital sources, using advanced searches effectively; assess the strengths and limitations of each source in terms of the task, purpose, and audience; integrate information into the text selectively to maintain the flow of ideas, avoiding plagiarism and overreliance on any one source and following a standard format for citation.





AUTHOR'S PERSPECTIVE **Jim Cummins, Ph.D.**

**Working in Pairs** There is an important sense in which the development of academic expertise on the part of English learners is a process of socialization rather than simply instruction. As a result, English writing development will be enhanced when students can work in pairs to create texts to share with others. That's because the process of collaboration and communication entails social interaction, which fosters language development.

- First, teachers can partner students to read, discuss, and react to a reading in the unit. Select a text, such as a nonfiction article, poem, or narrative.
- Have partners discuss the text, make notes about their ideas, and together write a response that highlights what they found important or responds to a prompt teachers provide. Encourage students to include specific details from the text in their drafts.
- Then, teachers can invite partners to share their writing with the whole class. Guide students to explain how working together helped them express their ideas more effectively than working alone.

College and Career Readiness

### Write It

Effective writers seamlessly integrate different kinds of information into an argument. Consider these sentences from the Launch Text.

LAUNCH TEXT EXCERPT

First, there is a difference between fear and phobia.

A phobia is an unnecessary fear of something that is unlikely to cause harm.

For example, some people are afraid of clowns, but the odds of a clown's being harmful are small.

The writer presents the first of two rebuttals of the counterargument.

The writer gives a definition from research.

The writer offers an example.

In this example, the first and last sentences state the writer's own reason and example, but the sentence in between is a researched definition. The sentences are sequenced to form a complete idea. When crafting your argument, work to sequence sentences logically, integrating your own ideas with researched evidence.

**Use Information From Sources** As you gather information from research, decide where it might fit into your writing. Ask yourself these questions:

- Is there a term that I should define for my reader?
- Can I introduce a fact from history that will help to support my claim?
- Did I find a fact or detail that addresses a possible counterclaim?

**Record Information** As you complete your research, use this chart to organize your findings.

| RESEARCH THAT DEFINES TERMS | RESEARCH THAT SUPPORTS MY CLAIM | RESEARCH THAT ADDRESSES A COUNTERCLAIM |
|---|---|---|
| | | |
| | | |

TIP

CONVENTIONS

Use punctuation correctly when citing sources.

- Underline or italicize the titles of books, newspapers, magazines, journals, or websites.
- Use quotation marks around titles of articles, chapters, or essays.





DIGITAL PERSPECTIVES

## Language Development: Conventions

### Write It

Remind students that definitions and examples from reliable sources will enhance support of their claims.

**Use Information from Sources** Remind students that good writers consider their audience first. When deciding what information to include, students should ask themselves *Will my reader need to know this to understand my point?*

Urge students to pay particular attention to information that supports or refutes the counterclaims they have chosen to address. Point out that the better they understand a counterclaim, the better they can argue against it, and effectively addressing a counterclaim will increase their credibility with readers.

PERSONALIZE FOR LEARNING

### Strategic Support

**Research** If students are doing research on the Internet, discuss search terms. What specific information will they need to complete the assignment? For example, searching "hysteria" will result in many intersecting links, but will not likely help them find specific information about mass hysteria during the 1600s. As students conduct research, have them try more than one term in their searches and evaluate the results.

PERFORMANCE TASK: WRITING FOCUS

## Drafting

**Present Your Reasoning** Have the students identify the type of reasoning that they plan to use to establish their claim. Are they starting with examples to inductively establish their claim, or are they starting with a claim that they will confirm through examples? As a practice they could try each approach to determine which approach fits better.

**Write a First Draft** Remind students of the following points about using a formal style with an objective tone:

- Consider using complex sentences to allow for explaining complex reasoning.
- Using an objective tone means avoiding emotive punctuation such as exclamation points.
- Students should avoid contractions and should spell out abbreviations at their first appearance.
- The third-person point of view should be used.

## Drafting

**Present Your Reasoning** You may use **deductive** or **inductive** reasoning to present a strong case for your claim.

| TYPE OF REASONING | DEFINITION | EXAMPLE |
|---|---|---|
| deductive reasoning | a general conclusion applied to a specific instance or situation | Helmet laws have been shown to reduce accidents. If we had a stronger helmet law, Alicia Martinez would not have been injured last month. |
| inductive reasoning | specific facts used to lead to a general conclusion | Bicycle injury rates in Oaktown decreased when a helmet law was passed. Therefore, a helmet law will help our community prevent bicycle injuries. |

In the Launch Text, the writer uses inductive reasoning to present a claim based on a series of facts. Facts about the human response to fear lead to and support a claim about the usefulness of fear for survival.

Use one of these patterns to draft your argument.

DEDUCTIVE

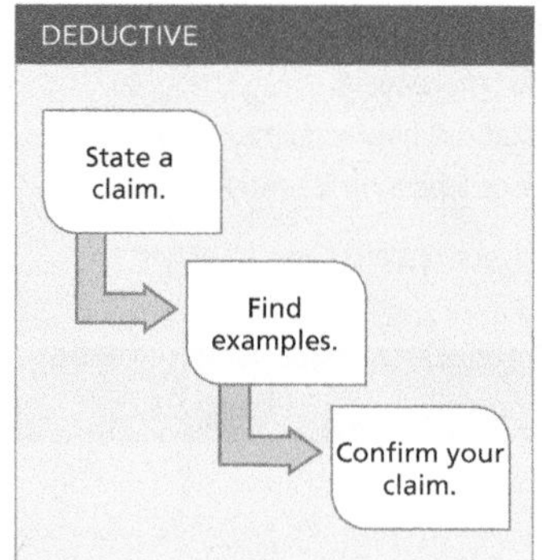


INDUCTIVE

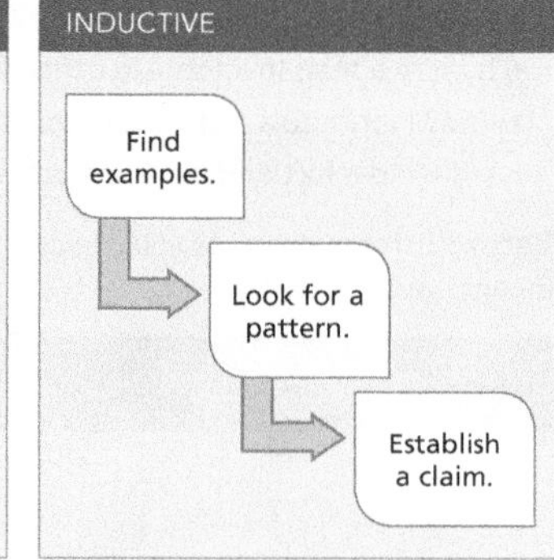


**Write a First Draft** Use inductive or deductive reasoning to write your first draft. Make sure to include a precise claim and to address counterclaims where possible. Use formal language and an objective tone to communicate your points clearly and effectively. Blend evidence from the text and audio performance of the play with evidence from your research on mass hysteria. Write a conclusion that follows logically from your argument, supports your claim, and adds interest to your writing.

STANDARDS

Writing

- Introduce precise, knowledgeable claim(s), establish the significance of the claim(s), distinguish the claim(s) from alternate or opposing claims, and create an organization that logically sequences claim(s), counterclaims, reasons, and evidence.
- Provide a concluding statement or section that follows from and supports the argument presented.





### HOW LANGUAGE WORKS

**Transitions** As students draft their arguments, remind them to use transitional words and phrases to connect and show relationships among ideas and create cohesion in their writing. Explain that using transitions is a key element in a logically organized argument. You may want to have students consider the following types of transitions as they revise their arguments:

| When... | Transition Type to Use |
|---|---|
| ...considering possible counterclaims | Contrast |
| ...providing reasons to support your reasons | List or add ideas; illustrate or show |
| ...using evidence to support your reasons | Show effect; compare |
| ...concluding your argument | Emphasize |

LANGUAGE DEVELOPMENT: CONVENTIONS

## Make Effective Choices: Indefinite Pronouns

An **indefinite pronoun,** like any pronoun, is a word that takes the place of a noun, a noun phrase, or another pronoun. However, an indefinite pronoun does not refer to a specific person, place, thing, or idea. Indefinite pronouns may be singular or plural.

### Read It

These sentences from the Launch Text use indefinite pronouns to refer to people or things that are unspecified, general, or universal.

- ***Some*** *of us may seek professional help to rid ourselves of fears.* **(an unspecified number)**
- ***Something*** *alarms you, and instantly your brain causes a number of chemicals to be released. . . .* **(an unspecified thing)**
- *This response to fear was good for* ***everyone*** *who displayed it.* **(all people)**
- *After just a few sessions, nearly* ***anyone*** *can stop being afraid of speaking in public. . . .* **(any unspecified person)**
- ***Few*** *of us enjoy* ***being afraid.*** **(an unspecified small number)**

### Write It

As you draft your argument, be sure to observe proper subject-verb agreement when you use indefinite pronouns.

| SINGULAR INDEFINITE PRONOUNS | PLURAL INDEFINITE PRONOUNS |
|---|---|
| another, other | both |
| anybody, anyone, anything | few |
| each | many |
| either, neither | others |
| everybody, everyone, everything | several |
| little, much | |
| nobody, no one, nothing | |
| one | |
| somebody, someone, something | |

A few indefinite pronouns may be singular or plural, depending on their **antecedents,** the words that they replace. These include *all, any, more, most, none,* and *some.*

TIP

USAGE

Certain indefinite pronouns may also be used as adjectives. Be sure you know which part of speech you are using. Study these examples.

- *Neither* plans to attend the party. (pronoun)
- *Neither* student plans to attend the party. (adjective)

STANDARDS

**Language**

Demonstrate command of the conventions of standard English grammar and usage when writing or speaking.





DIGITAL PERSPECTIVES

## Make Effective Choices: Indefinite Pronouns

### Read It

Have students identify the indefinite pronouns in the following sentences.

- The young girl thought no one would understand her. (no one)
- When asked to choose, he said, "Either will be fine." (either)

### Write It

Encourage students to check their work for subject-verb agreement. As practice, have students choose the correct verb for each sentence.

- Everybody (is/are) waiting. (is)
- Several (is/are) better than just one. (are)
- Many (have/has) tried, but few (succeed, succeeds). (have, succeed)

PERSONALIZE FOR LEARNING

### English Language Support

**Subject-Verb Agreement** English Learners often struggle with subject-verb agreement when writing. Rehearse with them some nouns they are likely to use in their arguments, such as *person, people, woman, women, man,* and *men*. Have them tell you whether each noun is singular or plural and choose a verb to go with it. **ALL LEVELS**

## Revising

### Evaluating Your Draft

Before students begin revising their writing, they should first evaluate their draft to make sure it contains all of the required elements, is organized in a logical manner, and adheres to the norms and conventions of writing an argument.

While using the checklist, if students come across an element that is not evident in their writing, have them make notes as to what is missing or needs correction, but continue on with their evaluation until they reach the end of their essay. At that point, have students make the necessary corrections and additions.

### Revising for Focus and Organization

**Clarifying Relationships** Suggest students read their writing aloud. If a particular section seems halting or choppy, have them review that area and consider adding a transitional word or phrase to improve the flow of ideas.

### Revising for Evidence and Elaboration

**Vocabulary and Tone** Have students review their use of domain specific language to make sure that each term is being used correctly.

**Use of Source Material** Suggest students read their drafts with a highlighter in hand and mark where they have specifically cited the text and other sources. Then have them see if they feel confident in the amount of evidence they have included to support their points.

PERFORMANCE TASK: WRITING FOCUS

## Revising

### Evaluating Your Draft

Use this checklist to evaluate the effectiveness of your first draft. Then, use your evaluation and the instruction on this page to guide your revision.

| FOCUS AND ORGANIZATION | EVIDENCE AND ELABORATION | CONVENTIONS |
|---|---|---|
| ☐ Provides an introduction that establishes a precise claim. | ☐ Develops the claim by using facts and details that provide relevant evidence and reasons. | ☐ Attends to the norms and conventions of the discipline, especially in the use of indefinite pronouns. |
| ☐ Distinguishes the claim from opposing claims. | ☐ Provides adequate examples for each major idea. | |
| ☐ Provides a conclusion that follows from the argument. | ☐ Uses vocabulary and word choices that are appropriate for the audience and purpose. | |
| ☐ Establishes a logical organization and develops a progression throughout the argument. | ☐ Establishes and maintains a formal style and objective tone. | |
| ☐ Uses words, phrases, and clauses to clarify the relationships between and among ideas. | | |

**WORD NETWORK**

Include interesting words from your Word Network in your argument.

### Revising for Focus and Organization

**Clarifying Relationships** Be sure to provide clear connections among claim, counterclaim, reasons, and evidence. Could you add transitional words or phrases like these to clarify the relationships between ideas?

| | | | |
|---|---|---|---|
| **for example** | **in addition** | **nevertheless** | **because** |
| **instead of** | **however** | **furthermore** | **consequently** |
| **similarly** | **for this reason** | **especially** | **meanwhile** |

### Revising for Evidence and Elaboration

**Vocabulary and Tone** When you write an argument about a literary text, consider using vocabulary specific to the study of literature. Words such as *character, setting, scene, conflict, dialogue, antagonist,* and so on may be appropriate to your task and may add to the formal tone of your essay.

**Use of Source Material** Reread your essay as though you were seeing it for the first time. Ask yourself these questions:

- Does every point that I make have supporting examples?
- Do I correctly cite examples from the play and other sources?
- Does my evidence from research blend well with my examples from the play?

**STANDARDS**

Writing

- Use words, phrases, and clauses as well as varied syntax to link the major sections of the text, create cohesion, and clarify the relationships between claim(s) and reasons, between reasons and evidence, and between claim(s) and counterclaims.
- Establish and maintain a formal style and objective tone while attending to the norms and conventions of the discipline in which they are writing.





## PERSONALIZE FOR LEARNING

### Strategic Support

**Transitions** Some students may require additional support in using transitions in their arguments. Pair students and have them identify places in each other's argument where transition words might clarify what the writer is trying to say or help the flow of the argument. Have them consider the specific relationships among the ideas. Finally, have students review the suggested transitions for the appropriate type of relationship and revise their argument.

PEER REVIEW

Exchange essays with a classmate. Use the checklist to evaluate your classmate's argument and provide supportive feedback.

1. Does the writer state a clear claim?
   ☐ yes ☐ no If no, explain what confused you.
2. Does the writer offer ample evidence from the play?
   ☐ yes ☐ no If no, tell what you think might be missing.
3. Are elements from research woven into the essay? Are the citations clear?
   ☐ yes ☐ no If no, suggest what your classmate might add.
4. What is the strongest part of your classmate's essay? Why?

## Editing and Proofreading

**Edit for Conventions** Reread your draft for accuracy and consistency. Correct errors in grammar and word usage. Look for correct use of indefinite pronouns.

**Proofread for Accuracy** Read your draft carefully, looking for errors in spelling and punctuation. Make sure to underline or italicize the name of the play and to capitalize and spell characters' names correctly as you cite examples.

## Publishing and Presenting

Create a final draft, print it, and place it in a folder in the classroom library. Attach an index card to the folder so that classmates can read your work and make constructive comments. Try to read and comment on at least three of your classmates' essays.

## Reflecting

Reflect on what you learned by writing your argumentative essay. Was it difficult to weave evidence from research into the evidence you found from the play? If you had to start this assignment over again, what might you do differently?

STANDARDS

**Writing**

Develop and strengthen writing as needed by planning, revising, editing, rewriting, or trying a new approach, focusing on addressing what is most significant for a specific purpose and audience.





DIGITAL PERSPECTIVES

## Peer Review

Remind students to review their classmate's work for clarity and completeness. They do not need to agree with the writer's stance on the prompt. However, they might suggest a counterclaim that could be addressed to strengthen their classmate's argument.

## Editing and Proofreading

Remind students that although many word processing programs catch grammar and spelling errors, they are not foolproof. Students should still review their work by reading it.

## Publishing and Presenting

Before students review their classmates' arguments, remind them to include positive comments. Encourage them to write any criticisms or disagreements respectfully and have them support their ideas with evidence.

## Reflecting

Students should consider not only their own feelings and opinions about their completed work, but also the process of giving and receiving feedback from peers.

PERSONALIZE FOR LEARNING

### English Language Support

**Development of Ideas** Have English learners analyze an argumentative essay for its claim, reasons, and supporting evidence.

Ask students to write a very brief summary of the essay, stating the claim and three specific reasons or pieces of supporting evidence using the connection word *because*. **EMERGING**

Ask students to write a summary of the essay, stating the claim and the writer's main arguments in support of the claim. **EXPANDING**

Ask students to write a summary of the essay, stating the claim, paraphrasing the writer's main argument in support of the claim, and identifying at least one counterclaim the writer addresses. **BRIDGING**

# OVERVIEW

## SMALL-GROUP LEARNING

### How do we respond when challenged by fear?

Fear may be a reasonable response to threatening conditions, but it can also be an emotion that limits our ability to act. During Small Group Learning, students will read selections about people who faced fears caused by other people's perceptions of them, or from their own imaginations.

### Small-Group Learning Strategies

Review the Learning Strategies with students and explain that as they work through Small-Group Learning they will develop strategies to work in small-group environments.

- Have students watch the video on Small-Group Learning Strategies.
- A video on this topic is available online in the Professional Development Center.

You may wish to discuss some action items to add to the chart as a class before students complete it on their own. For example, for "Clarify," you might solicit the following from students:

- Students should acknowledge how important it is to ask questions when something is unclear.
- Some students may learn better with spoken directives, while others learn better with written directives.

**Block Scheduling**

Each day in this Pacing Plan represents a 40–50 minute class period. Teachers using block scheduling may combine days to reflect their class schedule. In addition, teachers may revise pacing to differentiate and support core instruction by integrating components and resources as students require.

## OVERVIEW: SMALL-GROUP LEARNING

ESSENTIAL QUESTION:

# How do we respond when challenged by fear?

As you read these selections, work with your group to explore the meaning and power of fear.

**From Text to Topic** In the middle of the twentieth century, fear was a powerful force in America—fear of economic hardship, fear of war, fear of other forms of government, and even the fear of total annihilation. Still, fear was not, and is not, unique to a particular country and a particular time. As you read the selections in this section, consider what other ideas cause people to fear—and what people's reactions reveal about themselves and the times in which they live.

## Small-Group Learning Strategies

Throughout your life, in school, in your community, and in your career, you will continue to learn and work with others.

Review these strategies and the actions you can take to practice them as you work in teams. Add ideas of your own for each step. Use these strategies during Small-Group Learning.

| STRATEGY | ACTION PLAN |
|---|---|
| Prepare | • Complete your assignments so that you are prepared for group work.<br>• Organize your thinking so you can contribute to your group's discussions.<br>• |
| Participate fully | • Make eye contact to signal that you are listening and taking in what is being said.<br>• Use text evidence when making a point.<br>• |
| Support others | • Build on ideas from others in your group.<br>• Invite others who have not yet spoken to do so.<br>• |
| Clarify | • Paraphrase the ideas of others to ensure that your understanding is correct.<br>• Ask follow-up questions.<br>• |



SCAN FOR MULTIMEDIA

### Pacing Plan

Introduce Whole-Class Learning

| Unit Introduction | | Historical Perspectives | The Crucible, Act I | | The Crucible, Act II | | The Crucible, Act III | | The Crucible, Act IV | | Media: The Crucible | | Performance Task | |
|---|---|---|---|---|---|---|---|---|---|---|---|---|---|---|
| 1 | 2 | 3 | 4 | 5 | 6 | 7 | 8 | 9 | 10 | 11 | 12 | 13 | 14 | 15 |

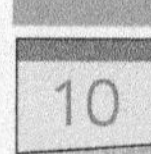

CONTENTS

COMPARE

AUTOBIOGRAPHY

## *from* Farewell to Manzanar

*Jeanne Wakatsuki Houston and James D. Houston*

In a time of war, how can fear suddenly turn neighbors into strangers, friends into enemies?

MEDIA: VIDEO

## Interview With George Takei

*Archive of American Television*

A child not yet old enough for kindergarten is imprisoned as a threat to America.

SHORT STORY

## Antojos

*Julia Alvarez*

What dangers—real or imagined—threaten a woman during a drive into the countryside?

PERFORMANCE TASK

SPEAKING AND LISTENING FOCUS

## Present an Argument

The Small-Group readings explore unreasonable fear from two different perspectives. In a story, a woman is swept away by her fear of others; in a real-life experience, a community—including its smallest children—becomes the focus of a nation's fears. After reading, your group will create and present a debate about what we can learn from fearful encounters.





DIGITAL PERSPECTIVES

## Contents

**Selections** Circulate among groups as they preview the selections. You might encourage groups to discuss any knowledge they already have about any of the selections or the situations and settings shown in the photographs. Students may wish to take a poll within their group to determine which selections look the most interesting.

Remind students that communicating and collaborating in groups is an important skill that they will use throughout their lives – in school, in their careers, and in their community.

### Performance Task

**Present an Argument** Give groups time to read about and briefly discuss the authors who explore unreasonable fear. The group will then prepare a multimedia presentation of their position on what we can learn from these encounters. Encourage students to do some preliminary thinking about the types of media they may want to use. This may help focus their subsequent reading and group discussion.

Introduce Small-Group Learning

*from* Farewell to Manzanar · Media: Interview with George Takei · Antojos · Performance Task

Introduce Independent Learning

Independent Learning

Performance-Based Assessment

16 17 18 19 20 21 22 23 24 25 26 27 28 29 30

SMALL-GROUP LEARNING

## SMALL-GROUP LEARNING

### Working as a Team

1. **Take a Position** Remind groups to let all members share their responses. You may wish to set a time limit for this discussion.
2. **List Your Rules** You may want to have groups share their lists of rules and consolidate them into a master list to be displayed and followed by all groups.
3. **Apply the Rules** As you circulate among the groups, ensure that students are staying on task. Consider a short time limit for this step.
4. **Name Your Group** This task can be creative and fun. If students have trouble coming up with a name, suggest that they think of something related to the unit topic. Encourage groups to share their names with the class.
5. **Create a Communication Plan** Encourage groups to include in their plans agreed-upon times during the day to share ideas. They should also devise a method for recording and saving their communications.

### Accountable Talk

Remind students that groups should communicate politely. You can post these Accountable Talk suggestions and encourage students to add their own. Students should:

**Remember to . . .**
Ask clarifying questions.

**Which sounds like . . .**
Can you please repeat what you said?

Would you give me an example?

I think you said _____. Did I understand you correctly?

**Remember to . . .**
Explain your thinking.

**Which sounds like . . .**
I believe _____ is true because _____.

**Remember to . . .**
Build on the ideas of others.

**Which sounds like . . .**
When _____ said _____, it made me think of _____.

## OVERVIEW: SMALL-GROUP LEARNING

### Working as a Team

1. **Take a Position** In your group, discuss the following question:

   **Which do you think creates the most frightening situation: a danger that you know about, a danger that you suspect may come to pass, or the feeling that danger is a possibility? Explain.**

   As you take turns sharing your positions, provide reasons for your choice. After all group members have shared, discuss some of the criteria by which you have evaluated these fears.

2. **List Your Rules** As a group, decide on the rules that you will follow as you work together. Samples are provided; add two more of your own. You may add or revise rules based on your experience together.
   - Encourage everyone to give examples in defense of his or her position.
   - Remind everyone to listen respectfully and offer helpful comments.
   - ______________________________
   - ______________________________

3. **Apply the Rules** Practice working as a group. Share what you have learned about fear. Make sure each person in the group contributes. Take notes on and be prepared to share with the class one thing that you heard from another member of your group.

4. **Name Your Group** Choose a name that reflects the unit topic.

   Our group's name: ______________________________

5. **Create a Communication Plan** Decide how you want to communicate with one another. For example, you might discuss the topic during lunch, use online collaboration tools, or schedule a set of video chats.

   Our group's decision: ______________________________





### FACILITATING SMALL-GROUP LEARNING

**Forming Groups** You may wish to form groups for Small-Group Learning so that each consists of students with different learning abilities. Some students may be adept at organizing information whereas others may have strengths related to generating or synthesizing information. A good mix of abilities can make the experience of Small-Group Learning dynamic and productive.

## Making a Schedule

First, find out the due dates for the small-group activities. Then, preview the texts and activities with your group, and make a schedule for completing the tasks.

| SELECTION | ACTIVITIES | DUE DATE |
|---|---|---|
| *from* Farewell to Manzanar | | |
| Interview With George Takei | | |
| Antojos | | |

## Working on Group Projects

As your group works together, you'll find it more effective if each person has a specific role. Different projects require different roles. Before beginning a project, discuss the necessary roles, and choose one for each group member. Here are some possible roles; add your own ideas.

**Project Manager:** monitors the schedule and keeps everyone on task

**Researcher:** organizes research activities

**Recorder:** takes notes during group meetings

SCAN FOR MULTIMEDIA



DIGITAL PERSPECTIVES

## Making a Schedule

Encourage groups to preview the reading selections and to consider how long it will take them to complete the activities accompanying each selection. Point out that they can adjust the due dates for particular selections as needed as they work on their small-group projects. However, they must complete all assigned tasks before the group Performance Task is due. Encourage groups to review their schedules upon completing the activities for each selection to make sure they are on track to meet the final due date.

## Working on Group Projects

Point out to groups that the roles they assign can also be changed later. Students might have to make changes based on who is best at doing what. Try to make sure that there is no favoritism, cliquishness, or stereotyping by gender or other means in the assignment of roles.

Also, you should review the roles each group assigns to its members. Based on your understanding of students' individual strengths, you might find it necessary to suggest some changes.

AUTHOR'S PERSPECTIVE **Kelly Gallagher, M.Ed.**

**Accountability in Group Work** The teacher's role during group work is to serve as the facilitator rather than as the leader. This means that the teacher should support the thinking and discussion, but not provide the answers or content direction. Problems can arise if a group is unfocused, if the task is not meaningful, or if there is no accountability. To help groups work together well, achieve their goals, and ensure accountability, teachers can follow these three steps:

1. First, define and clarify the task. Explain why it is valuable, and make sure students know what they are expect to do.
2. Let each group know that one student will be selected randomly to share the group's thinking. This builds accountability.
3. Pull the whole class back together to share back information and to check learning.

If groups struggle, teachers can prompt them with questions that support how they will get to the answer. For example, if they are unable to find the main point of the essay, ask them: *"In this type of text, where might a reader look to find the main idea?"*

# *from* Farewell to Manzanar

**AUDIO SUMMARIES**
Audio summaries of the selection from *Farewell to Manzanar* are available online in both English and Spanish in the Interactive Teacher's Edition or Unit Resources. Assigning these summaries prior to reading the selection may help students build additional background knowledge and set a context for their first read.


## Summary

In the selection from the memoir *Farewell to Manzanar*, which was co-authored by Jeanne Wakatsuki Houston and James D. Houston, Jeanne Wakatsuki Houston describes her family's time in a Japanese Wartime Relocation Agency camp called Manzanar. Jeanne's father had been a prisoner at Fort Lincoln, but he has been released to Manzanar, where his family is living. Her father is angry and frequently drunk. Jeanne learns that part of the problem is that he is thought to have been an *inu*, or an informant who has betrayed other Japanese civilians. When everyone is required to sign a loyalty oath to the American government, her father and many other Japanese men in the camp disagree about what to do. They are all angry about their treatment. Readers experience events through the eyes of an eight-year-old Jeanne, who is sometimes confused by what she sees.


### Insight

Rumor and innuendo are at the heart of the responses of many of the Japanese in Manzanar to Jeanne's father. He deals with this challenge by retreating from his family and others in the camp. Eventually, people's anger with and fear of government authorities sparks a response to their unfair treatment.

ESSENTIAL QUESTION:
How do we respond when challenged by fear?

## Connection to the Essential Question

This selection from *Farewell to Manzanar* connects to the Essential Question, "How do we respond when challenged by fear?" Jeanne's entire family along with others in the Japanese Wartime Relocation Agency camp respond to their fears about the loyalty act in a variety of ways. Some give in to their fears, others try to ignore them, and still others try to overcome them through positive action.

SMALL-GROUP PERFORMANCE TASK
Do people usually learn from their fear?

UNIT PERFORMANCE-BASED ASSESSMENT
Is fear always a harmful emotion?

## Connection to Performance Tasks

**Small-Group Learning Performance Task** In this Performance Task, students will respond to the question, "Do people usually learn from their fear?" Students will note that Jeanne's father and others in the camp try to learn from their fear when deciding the best way to respond to their unfair treatment.

**Unit Performance-Based Assessment** The fact that Jeanne's father meets with others about how best to respond to the unfair loyalty oath shows that fear can sometimes be a useful emotion in coping with and overcoming obstacles.

DIGITAL PERSPECTIVES

Audio

Video

Document

Annotation Highlights

EL Highlights

Online Assessment

## LESSON RESOURCES

| | Making Meaning | | Language Developement |
|---|---|---|---|
| **Lesson** | **First Read**<br>**Close Read** | **Analyze the Text**<br>**Analyze Craft and Structure** | **Concept Vocabulary**<br>**Word Study**<br>**Author's Style** |
| **Instructional Standards** | **RI.10** By the end of grade 11, read and comprehend literary nonfiction . . .<br>**L.4** Determine or clarify the meaning of unknown and multiple-meaning words and phrases . . .<br>**L.4.b** Identify and correctly use patterns of word changes . . .<br>**RI.1** Cite strong and thorough textual evidence . . .<br>**RI.3** Analyze a complex set of ideas or sequence of events . . . | | **L.4.b** Identify and correctly use patterns of word changes . . .<br>**L.4.d** Verify the preliminary determination . . .<br>**RI.6** Determine an author's point of view or purpose . . . |
| **STUDENT RESOURCES** | | | |
| Available online in the Interactive Student Edition or Unit Resources | Selection Audio<br>First-Read Guide: Nonfiction<br>Close-Read Guide: Nonfiction | | Word Network |
| **TEACHER RESOURCES** | | | |
| **Selection Resources**<br>Available online in the Interactive Teacher's Edition or Unit Resources | Audio Summaries<br>Annotation Highlights<br>EL Highlights<br>*from* Farewell to Manzanar: Text Questions<br>English Language Support Lesson: Author's Purpose and Point of View<br>Analyze Craft and Structure: Development of Complex Ideas | | Concept Vocabulary and Word Study<br>Author's Style: Author's Point of View |
| **Reteach/Practice (RP)**<br>Available online in the Interactive Teacher's Edition or Unit Resources | Analyze Craft and Structure: Development of Complex Ideas (RP) | | Word Study: Latin Suffix *-or* (RP)<br>Author's Style: Author's Point of View (RP) |
| **Assessment**<br>Available online in Assessments | Selection Test | | |
| **My Resources** | A Unit 5 Answer Key is available online and in the Interactive Teacher's Edition. | | |

# Reading Support

| Text Complexity Rubric: *from* Farewell to Manzanar | |
|---|---|
| **Quantitative Measures** | |
| **Lexile:** 1040 **Text Length** 2,864 words | |
| **Qualitative Measures** | |
| Knowledge Demands<br>① ② ③ ❹ ⑤ | Explores cultural and historical themes that will be unfamiliar to many readers, including the Japanese internment during World War II. |
| Structure<br>① ② ❸ ④ ⑤ | Story line is clear and mostly chronological, with references to past events but no actual flashback. |
| Language Conventionality and Clarity<br>① ② ❸ ④ ⑤ | Language is explicit, literal, and straightforward. Vocabulary is mostly on-level, contemporary, and familiar, with a few Japanese words that are clearly explained in the text. |
| Levels of Meaning/Purpose<br>① ② ❸ ④ ⑤ | Communicates multiple levels of meaning in a clear and understandable way. Themes—including prejudice, nationalism, loyalty, and fear—are developed over the entirety of the text. |

DECIDE AND PLAN

## English Language Support

Provide English Learners with support for knowledge demands and levels of meaning/purpose as they read the selection.

**Knowledge Demands** Clarify the situation of Japanese Americans during World War II by explaining that most of the people forced into the Wartime Relocation Agency camps were American citizens. Other were long-time residents forbidden by U. S. law to become citizens. They owned homes and businesses that they lost when they went into the camps.

**Levels of Meaning/Purpose** Help students outline plot events. Have them complete sentences. For example, *People in the camp suspected the father of* _____ and *The father drank because he felt* _____.

## Strategic Support

Provide students with strategic support to ensure that they can successfully read the text.

**Knowledge Demands** Find out what students know about past laws in the United States with regard to Asian immigration. Discuss the contradiction between the loyalty oath and the fact that no one born in Japan was allowed to become a U. S. citizen until 1952.

**Levels of Meaning** Ask about the conflicts in the story. For example, *Why did some people want to say "Yes, Yes" to the loyalty oath? Why did other people want to say "No, No"? Why did Woody want to fight in the U. S. military even though his family had been interned?*

## Challenge

Provide students who need to be challenged with ideas for how they can go beyond a simple interpretation of the text.

**Text Analysis** Discuss the family's reaction to the young woman who comes in to sing Japanese songs with the father. How does the music affect each of them?

**Written Response** Ask students to read more about the Japanese internment camps. Have them write short essays about life in the camps. Direct them to the photographs taken by Ansel Adams at Manzanar, which are available online at the Library of Congress, and suggest that they use these images to illustrate their essays.

TEACH

## Read and Respond

Have groups read the selection and complete the Making Meaning and Language Development activities.

# Standards Support Through Teaching and Learning Cycle

## IDENTIFY NEEDS

Analyze results of the Beginning-of-Year Assessment, focusing on the items relating to Unit 5. Also take into consideration student performance to this point and your observations of where particular students struggle.

## DECIDE AND PLAN

- If students have performed poorly on items matching these standards, then provide selection scaffolds before assigning them the on-level lesson provided in the Student Edition.
- If students have done well on the Beginning-of-Year Assessment, then challenge them to keep progressing and learning by giving them opportunities to practice the skills in depth.
- Use the Selection Resources listed on the Planning pages for "*from* Farewell to Manzanar" to help students continually improve their ability to master the standards.

**Instructional Standards: *from* Farewell to Manzanar**

| | Catching Up | This Year | Looking Forward |
|---|---|---|---|
| **Reading** | You may wish to administer the **Analyze Craft and Structure: Development of Complex Ideas (RP)** worksheet to help students better understand how writers develop characters.<br>You may wish to administer the **Author's Style: Author's Point of View** worksheet to help students better understand shifts in narrative perspective. | **RI.3** Analyze a complex set of ideas or sequence of events and explain how specific individuals, ideas, or events interact and develop over the course of the text.<br>**RI.6** Determine an author's point of view or purpose in a text in which the rhetoric is particularly effective, analyzing how style and content contribute to the power, persuasiveness, or beauty of the text. | Have students compare the character development in this selection to another work they are familiar with.<br>Challenge students to rewrite the selection using one single narrative perspective to show them why the author chose this method. |
| **Language** | Review the **Word Study: Latin Suffix *-or* (RP)** worksheet with students to better familiarize them with the suffix. | **L.4.d** Verify the preliminary determination of the meaning of a word or phrase. | Have students find one other Latin suffix from the selection and perform the same exercise in the Word Study. |

## ANALYZE AND REVISE

- Analyze student work for evidence of student learning.
- Identify whether or not students have met the expectations in the standards.
- Identify implications for future instruction.

## TEACH

Implement the planned lesson, and gather evidence of student learning.

# FACILITATING

## Jump Start

**FIRST READ** How do you think it would feel to be taken hundreds of miles from home and locked behind barbed wire? Engage students in a discussion about how it might have felt to be moved, locked up, and misunderstood. As students share their thoughts, explain that thousands of Japanese Americans found themselves in this situation during World War II.

## *from* Farewell to Manzanar

How do different people react to injustice and adversity? How do they deal with fear and uncertainty? Modeling these and other questions readers might ask will bring the excerpt from *Farewell to Manzanar* to life and connect it to the Performance Task question. Selection audio and print capability for the selection are available in the Interactive Teacher's Edition.

## Concept Vocabulary

Have groups briefly discuss the three concept vocabulary words. Do they recognize the prefix, suffix, or base word of any of the concept vocabulary words? Have groups consider the strategy of base words and discuss its advantages and disadvantages.

### FIRST READ

Have students perform the steps of the first read independently:

NOTICE: You may want to encourage students to notice how Jeanne Wakatsuki's family members interact with the other people in the camp.

ANNOTATE: Suggest passages that describe how people dealt with captivity.

CONNECT: Have students compare this account of the internment to what they learned in history classes.

RESPOND: Students will demonstrate their understanding of the text by answering questions.

Point out to students that they will perform the first three steps concurrently as they are doing their first read. They will complete the Respond step after they have finished the first read. You may wish to print copies of the **First-Read Guide: Nonfiction** for students to use.

MAKING MEANING

## Comparing Text to Media

In this lesson, you will compare an excerpt from the autobiography *Farewell to Manzanar* and a video interview with the actor George Takei. First, you will complete the first-read and close-read activities for the excerpt from *Farewell to Manzanar*. The work you do with your group on this title will help prepare you for the comparing task.

About the Authors

**Jeanne Wakatsuki Houston** (b. 1934) and **James D. Houston** (1933–2009) co-wrote not only this autobiography, but also a collection of related essays. Each author has also written several works independently.

# *from* Farewell to Manzanar

## Concept Vocabulary

As you perform your first read of the excerpt from *Farewell to Manzanar*, you will encounter these words.

collaborator  conspirators  espionage

**Base Words** If these words are unfamiliar to you, analyze each one to see whether it contains a base word you know. Then, use your knowledge of the "inside" word, along with context, to identify the meaning of the unfamiliar word. Study this example.

**Context:** By 1775, many American colonists considered the taxes and other burdensome restrictions imposed by the British to be **insupportable**.

**Familiar "Inside" Word:** *support*, meaning "bear" or "carry"

**Conclusion:** The taxes and restrictions are said to be burdensome, so *insupportable* might mean "unbearable" or "intolerable."

Apply your knowledge of base words and other vocabulary strategies to determine the meanings of unfamiliar words you encounter during your first read.

## First Read NONFICTION

Apply these strategies as you conduct your first read. You will have an opportunity to conduct a close read after your first read.

NOTICE the general ideas of the text. *What* is it about? *Who* is involved?

ANNOTATE by marking vocabulary and key passages you want to revisit.

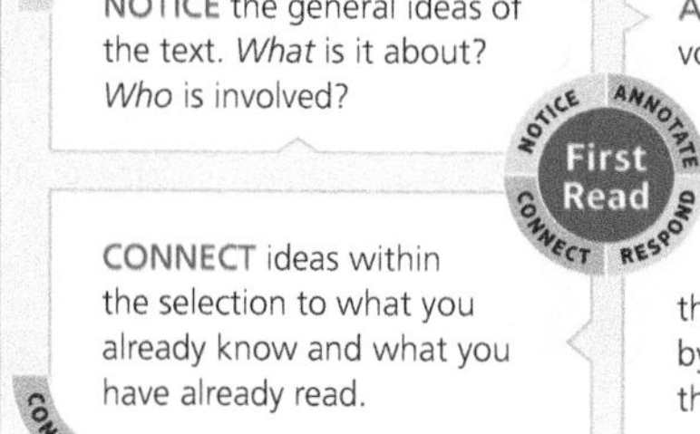


CONNECT ideas within the selection to what you already know and what you have already read.

RESPOND by completing the Comprehension Check and by writing a brief summary of the selection.

STANDARDS

**Reading Informational Text**
By the end of grade 11, read and comprehend literary nonfiction in the grades 11–CCR text complexity band proficiently, with scaffolding as needed at the high end of the range.

**Language**
- Determine or clarify the meaning of unknown and multiple-meaning words and phrases based on *grades 11–12 reading and content*, choosing flexibly from a range of strategies.
- Identify and correctly use patterns of word changes that indicate different meanings or parts of speech.





AUTHOR'S PERSPECTIVE **Jim Cummins, Ph.D.**

**Language Awareness** Vocabulary knowledge is an extremely robust predictor of students' reading comprehension. The Frayer model is an effective tool for enabling students to extend their vocabulary knowledge in a systematic way. The tool aims to deepen students' knowledge of words and concepts by focusing their attention not only on simple definitions but also on characteristics of the concept and examples and non-examples of it.

AUTOBIOGRAPHY

# *from* Farewell to Manzanar

Jeanne Wakatsuki Houston
and James D. Houston

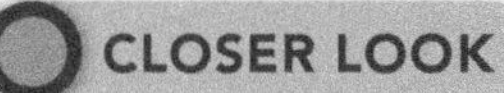

DIGITAL PERSPECTIVES

BACKGROUND

During World War II, the United States fought the Axis powers, which included Japan. Afraid of Japanese sympathizers, and driven by racial prejudices, the federal government ordered about 120,000 Japanese Americans to leave their homes and live in facilities known as internment camps. As this excerpt opens, Jeanne Wakatsuki's father arrives at Manzanar, one such internment camp, after his detention on false charges of having aided the enemy.

SCAN FOR MULTIMEDIA

## *Inu*

1 With Papa back our cubicle was filled to overflowing. Woody brought in another army bunk and tick mattress, up next to Mama's. But that was not what crowded the room. It was Papa himself, his dark, bitter, brooding presence. Once moved in, it seemed he didn't go outside for months. He sat in there, or paced, alone a great deal of the time, and Mama had to bring his meals from the mess hall.

2 He made her bring him extra portions of rice, or cans of the syrupy fruit they served. He would save this up and concoct brews in a homemade still he kept behind the door, brews that smelled so bad

NOTES





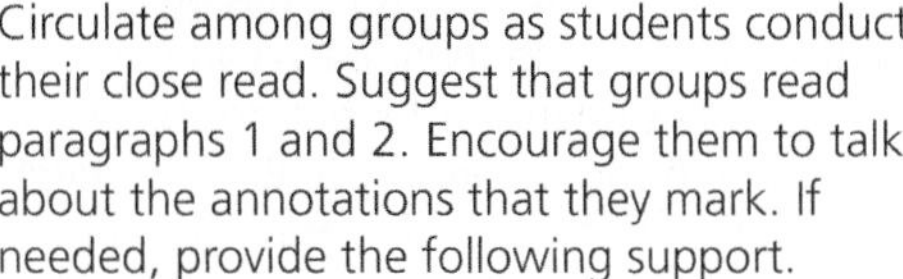

CLOSER LOOK

### Explore Verbs

Circulate among groups as students conduct their close read. Suggest that groups read paragraphs 1 and 2. Encourage them to talk about the annotations that they mark. If needed, provide the following support.

**ANNOTATE:** Have students mark details in these paragraphs that show what actions the author's father takes, or work with small groups to have students participate while you highlight them together.

**QUESTION:** Guide students to consider what these details might tell them. Ask what a reader can infer from the father's actions.

**Possible response:** The author uses strong action verbs to describe what the father does. By doing so, she warns the reader that the father is distressed and possibly dangerous.

**CONCLUDE:** Help students formulate conclusions about the importance of these details in the text. Ask students why the author might have included these details.

**Possible response:** By describing the father's actions, the author shows readers a great deal about him without having to write things such as, "My father was very upset about being at Manzanar." Rather than describe her father with adjectives (angry, upset, despairing) she shows readers what he does.

Explain to students that it has more impact on readers when an author shows readers his or her characters rather than telling readers about them. **Verbs** that describe a character's actions can reveal a great deal about the character, allowing readers to draw their own conclusions about what the character is like.

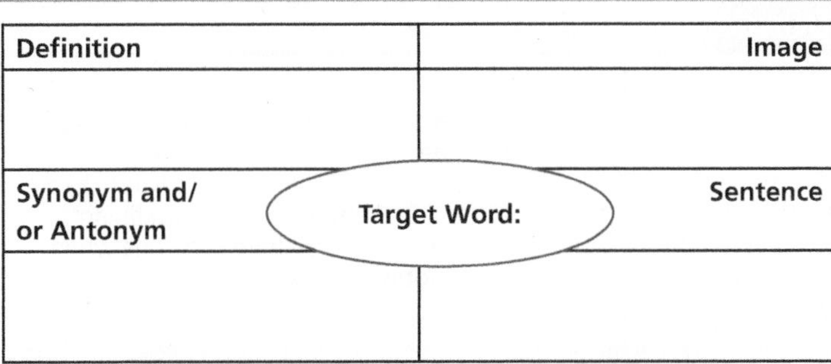


Create an electronic template and have students work in groups of "language detectives" to enter new and interesting words onto the group's template. If time allows, encourage students to complete two to five words each day. Where multiple home languages are represented in a group, students could take turns entering words in their home language, and all members of the group could learn that word. At the end of each week, the teacher could compile the words into a class quiz.

## Concept Vocabulary

**COLLABORATOR** If groups are struggling to define the word *collaborator* in paragraph 5, point out that they can look for a base word within the word to help them determine its meaning. Draw students' attention to the word *labor* within the vocabulary word. Remind them that the prefix *co–* means *with*. Have them use the base word and the prefix to define *collaborator*.

**Possible response:** A collaborator is "someone who works with others." In this instance it refers to someone who works with the enemy.

Additional **English Language Support** is available in the Interactive Teacher's Edition.

NOTES

Mama was ashamed to let in any visitors. Day after day he would sip his rice wine or his apricot brandy, sip till he was blind drunk and passed out. In the morning he would wake up groaning like the demon in a kabuki[1] drama; he would vomit and then start sipping again. He terrified all of us, lurching around the tiny room, cursing in Japanese and swinging his bottles wildly. No one could pacify him. Mama got nothing but threats and abuse for her attempts to comfort him.

3 I turned eight that fall. I remember telling myself that he never went out and never associated with others because he thought he was better than they were and was angry at being forced to live so close to them for the first time in his life. I told myself they whispered about him because he brewed his own foul-smelling wine in our barracks.

4 All of this was partly true. But there were deeper, uglier reasons for his isolation. I first sensed it one night when Mama and I went to the latrine together. By this time the stalls were partitioned. Two Terminal Island[2] women about Mama's age were leaving just as we walked in. They lingered by the doorway, and from inside my stall I could hear them whispering about Papa, deliberately, just loud enough for us to hear. They kept using the word "inu." I knew it meant "dog," and I thought at the time they were backbiting him because he never socialized.

5 Spoken Japanese is full of disrespectful insult words that can be much more cutting than mere vulgarity. They have to do with bad manners, or worse, breaches of faith and loyalty. Years later I learned that *inu* also meant collaborator or informer. Members of the Japanese American Citizens League were being called *inu* for having helped the army arrange a peaceful and orderly evacuation. Men who cooperated with camp authorities in any way could be labeled *inu*, as well as those genuine informers inside the camp who relayed information to the War Department and to the FBI.

Mark base words or indicate another strategy you used that helped you determine meaning.

**collaborator** (kuh LAB uh ray tuhr) *n.*

MEANING:

6 For the women in the late-night latrine Papa was an *inu* because he had been released from Fort Lincoln earlier than most of the Issei[3] men, many of whom had to remain up there separated from their families throughout the war. After investigating his record, the Justice Department found no reason to detain him any longer. But the rumor was that, as an interpreter, he had access to information from fellow Isseis that he later used to buy his release.

7 This whispered charge, added to the shame of everything that had happened to him, was simply more than he could bear. He did not yet have the strength to resist it. He exiled himself, like a leper,[4] and he drank.

* * *

1. **kabuki** (kuh BOO kee) *n.* stylized form of classical Japanese theater.
2. **Terminal Island** Japanese American community in Los Angeles that was entirely destroyed after the inhabitants were interned.
3. **Issei** (EE say) first-generation Japanese Americans, who have emigrated from Japan.
4. **like a leper** Historically, individuals with the disease leprosy were isolated from society, out of fear of contagion.





### PERSONALIZE FOR LEARNING

**English Language Support**

**Idioms** Explain to students that *backbiting* in paragraph 4 is an idiomatic expression. A one-word idiom (some idioms are phrases) is a word that is meant figuratively rather than literally. If students struggle to understand idioms, encourage them to think first about the literal meaning of the word, which can sometimes be quite revealing. Ask them what *backbiting* literally refers to—biting someone on the back. Then, have them think about what the word might represent when used figuratively. Guide them to see that backbiting means saying mean things about someone when that person is not present. **ALL LEVELS**

### Yes Yes No No

> **27.** Are you willing to serve in the Armed Forces of the United States on combat duty, wherever ordered?
>
> (yes) (no)
>
> **28.** Will you swear unqualified allegiance to the United States of America and faithfully defend the United States from any or all attack by foreign or domestic forces, and forswear any form of allegiance or obedience to the Japanese emperor, or any other foreign government, power, or organization?
>
> (yes) (no)
>
> —from the *War Relocation Authority Application for Leave Clearance, 1943*

8 Later in December the administration gave each family a Christmas tree hauled in from the Sierras. A new director had been appointed and this was his gesture of apology for all the difficulties that had led up to the riot, a promise of better treatment and better times to come.

9 It was an honest gesture, but it wasn't much of a Christmas that year. The presents were makeshift, the wind was roaring, Papa was drunk. Better times were a long way off, and the difficulties, it seemed, had just begun. Early in February the government's Loyalty Oath appeared. Everyone seventeen and over was required to fill it out. This soon became the most divisive issue of all. It cut deeper than the riot, because no one could avoid it. Not even Papa. After five months of self-imposed isolation, this debate was what finally forced him out of the barracks and into circulation again.

10 At the time, I was too young to understand the problem. I only knew there was no peace in our cubicle for weeks. Block organizers would come to talk to Papa and my brothers. They would huddle over the table awhile, muttering like conspirators, sipping tea or one of his concoctions. Their voices gradually would rise to shouts and threats. Mama would try to calm the men down. Papa would tell her to shut up, then Granny would interrupt and order him to quit disgracing Mama all the time. Once he just shoved Granny across the room, up against the far wall and back into her chair, and where she sat sniffling while the arguments went on.

11 If the organizers weren't there, Papa would argue with Woody. Or rather, Woody would listen to Papa lecture him on *true* loyalty, pacing from bunk to bunk, waving his cane.

12 "Listen to me, Woodrow. When a soldier goes into war he must go believing he is never coming back. This is why the Japanese are such courageous warriors. They are prepared to die. They expect nothing else. But to do that, you must *believe* in what you're fighting for. If you do not believe, you will not be willing to die. If you are not willing to die, you won't fight well. And if you don't fight well you will

NOTES

Mark base words or indicate another strategy you used that helped you determine meaning.

**conspirators** (kuhn SPIHR uh tuhrz) *n.*

MEANING:





DIGITAL PERSPECTIVES

## Concept Vocabulary

**CONSPIRATORS** If groups are struggling to define the word *conspirators* in paragraph 10, point out that they can look for base words within the word to help them determine its meaning. Draw students' attention to the word *conspire* within the vocabulary word, and point out that it is also the root of the word *conspiracy*. Ask students what a conspiracy is, and guide them to see that a conspiracy is a group effort to accomplish something illegal, wrong.

**Possible response:** *Conspirators* are "people who plot to do something illegal or wrong."

## FACILITATING SMALL-GROUP CLOSE READING: Autobiography

**CLOSE READ: Autobiography** Monitor groups as they conduct their close read and offer support as needed.

- Remind students that when they read an autobiography they should keep in mind that the story is being told by one person who lived through the experience being recounted. The author becomes a narrator of his or her own life.
- You might suggest that as readers, students look for clues about the writer. What factors influence his or her perceptions—Age? Historical moment? Relationships to other people in the story? Paying attention to these factors will help students determine the author's perspective and how it shapes the story.
- Suggest that as they read, they both focus on the author's point of view and think about how the situation the writer describes might look different had someone else been telling the tale.

## FACILITATING

### Concept Vocabulary

**ESPIONAGE** If groups are struggling to define the word *espionage* in paragraph 26, point out that they can look for a base word within the word to help them determine its meaning. In the case of *espionage*, the base word is spelled differently than it would be if it stood alone. Ask students what that base word is. Then ask them to define *espionage*.

**Possible response:** The base word is *spy*. *Espionage* means "spying," and an espionage agent is someone who spies.

NOTES

probably be killed stupidly, for the wrong reason, and unheroically. So tell me, how can you think of going off to fight?"

13 Woody always answered softly, respectfully, with a boyish and submissive smile.

14 "I will fight well, Papa."

15 "In this war? How is it possible?"

16 "I am an American citizen. America is at war."

17 "But look where they have put us!"

18 "The more of us who go into the army, the sooner the war will be over, the sooner you and Mama will be out of here."

19 "Do you think I would risk losing a son for that?"

20 "You want me to answer NO NO, Papa?"

21 "Do you think that is what I'm telling you? Of course you cannot answer NO NO. If you say NO NO; you will be shipped back to Japan with all those other *bakatare*!"

22 "But if I answer YES YES I will be drafted anyway, no matter how I feel about it. That is why they are giving us the oath to sign."

23 "No! That is not true! They are looking for volunteers. And only a fool would volunteer."

24 Papa stared hard at Woody, making this a challenge. Woody shrugged, still smiling his boyish smile, and did not argue. He knew that when the time came he would join the army, and he knew it was pointless to begin the argument again. It was a circle. His duty as a son was to sit and listen to Papa thrash his way around it and around it and around it.

25 A circle, or you might have called it a corral, like Manzanar itself, with no exit save via three narrow gates. The first led into the infantry, the second back across the Pacific. The third, called *relocation*, was just opening up: Interned citizens who could find a job and a sponsor somewhere inland, away from the west coast, were beginning to trickle out of camp. But the program was bogged down in paperwork. It was taking months to process applications and security clearances. A loyalty statement required of everyone, it was hoped, might save some time and a lot of red tape. This, together with the search for "loyal" soldiers, had given rise to the ill-fated "oath."

26 Two weeks before the December Riot, JACL[5] leaders met in Salt Lake City and passed a resolution pledging Nisei[6] to volunteer out of the camps for military service. In January the government announced its plan to form an all-Nisei combat regiment. While recruiting for this unit and speeding up the relocation program, the government figured it could simultaneously weed out the "disloyal" and thus get a clearer idea of exactly how many agents and Japanese sympathizers it actually had to deal with. This part of it would have been comical if

5. **JACL** Japanese American Citizens League.
6. **Nisei** (NEE say) second-generation Japanese Americans, who were born in the United States.





## PERSONALIZE FOR LEARNING

### Strategic Support

**Figurative Language** Remind students that authors sometimes use words imaginatively rather than literally. For example, in paragraph 25, the author says that there were three "narrow gates" that interned Japanese Americans could use to get out of Manzanar. At first students might think that there were three actual gates through which internees could exit the camp at Manzanar. But point out that as they read further, they can see that the author has used the term "narrow gates" figuratively, to refer to different methods that could be used to get out of the internment camp. Suggest that students use figurative language in their own writing to make it more vivid and lively.

708 UNIT 5 • FACING OUR FEARS

the results were not so grotesque. No self-respecting **espionage** agent would willingly admit he was disloyal. Yet the very idea of the oath itself—appearing at the end of that first chaotic year—became the final goad that prodded many once-loyal citizens to turn militantly anti-American.

27 From the beginning Papa knew his own answer would be YES YES. He agreed with Woody on this much, even though it meant swearing allegiance to the government that had sent him to Fort Lincoln and denying his connections with the one country in the world where he might still have the rights of a citizen. The alternative was worse. If he said NO NO, he could be sent to Tule Lake camp in northern California where all the "disloyal" were to be assembled for what most people believed would be eventual repatriation to Japan. Papa had no reason to return to Japan. He was too old to start over. He believed America would win the war, and he knew, even after all he'd endured, that if he had a future it still lay in this country. What's more, a move to Tule Lake could mean a further splitting up of our family.

28 This was a hard choice to make, and even harder to hold to. Anti-American feeling in camp ran stronger than ever. Pro-Japan forces were trying to organize a NO NO vote by blocks, in massive resistance. Others wanted to boycott the oath altogether in a show of noncooperation or through the mistaken fear that *anyone* who accepted the form would be shipped out of camp: the NO NOs back to Japan, the YES YESs into an American society full of wartime hostility and racial hate.

29 A meeting to debate the matter was called in our mess hall. Papa knew that merely showing his face would draw stares and muttered comments. YES YES was just what they expected of an *inu.* But he had to speak his mind before the NO NO contingent carried the block. Saying NO NO as an individual was one thing, bullying the entire camp into it was quite another. At the very least he didn't want to be sucked into such a decision without having his own opinion heard.

30 Woody wanted to go with him, but Papa said it was a meeting for "heads of households" only and he insisted on going alone. From the time he heard about it he purposely drank nothing stronger than tea. He shaved and trimmed his mustache and put on a silk tie. His limp was nearly gone now, but he carried his cane and went staggering off down the narrow walkway between the barracks, punching at the packed earth in front of him.

31 About four o'clock I was playing hopscotch in the firebreak with three other girls. It was winter, the sun had already dropped behind Mount Whitney. Now a wind was rising, the kind of biting, steady wind that could bring an ocean of sand into camp at any moment with almost no warning. I was hurrying back to the barracks when I heard a great commotion inside the mess hall, men shouting wildly, as if a fire had broken out. The loudest voice was Papa's, cursing.

32 *"Eta!* (trash) *Eta! Bakayaro! Bakayaro!"*

NOTES

Mark base words or indicate another strategy you used that helped you determine meaning.

**espionage** (EHS pee uh nozh) *n.*

MEANING:





DIGITAL PERSPECTIVES

CLOSER LOOK

## Recognize Topic Sentences

Circulate among groups as students conduct their close read. Suggest that groups read paragraphs 27 through 30. Encourage them to talk about the annotations that they mark. If needed, provide the following support.

**ANNOTATE:** Have students mark the topic sentences in these paragraphs, or work with small groups to have students participate while you highlight them together.

**QUESTION:** Guide students to consider what these details might tell them. Ask what a reader can infer from reading the topic sentences, and accept student responses.

**Possible response:** The topic sentences suggest that there is a great deal of controversy about how to complete the loyalty oath.

**CONCLUDE:** Help students formulate conclusions about the importance of these details in the text. Ask students why the author might have included these details.

**Possible response:** Reading the topic sentences in a segment of nonfiction like this one can provide a summary of the content of the paragraphs. In these paragraphs, the author is explaining her father's decision (paragraph 27), putting it in the context of other detainees' decisions (paragraph 28), describing how a decision would be made (paragraph 29), and watching her father prepare to go to the meeting (paragraph 30).

Remind students that **topic sentences** present the main idea of a paragraph. Point out that not all nonfiction is written such that each paragraph has a topic sentence. In cases where there are topic sentences, they will probably not appear in every single paragraph.

PERSONALIZE FOR LEARNING

### English Language Support

**Expanding Vocabulary** Review paragraph 27 and call student attention to the unfamiliar word *repatriation.* As they have been doing in this lesson, suggest that they look for a familiar word (or part of a word) within the larger word. If students struggle to find something they recognize, write *patriotic* on a line below the letters *–patria* in *repatriation*. Ask them what the word *patriotic* means, and how *patriot* might relate to it. Remind students that the prefix *re–* means *again*. Then guide students to see that *repatriation* means to be sent back to one's country of origin. **EMERGING/EXPANDING**

NOTES

33 The door of the mess hall flew open and a short, beefy man came tearing out. He jumped off the porch, running as his feet hit the ground. He didn't get far. Papa came through the doorway right behind him, in a flying leap, bellowing like a warrior, "Yaaaaaah!" He let go of his cane as he landed on the man's back, and they both tumbled into the dirt. The wind was rising. Half the sky was dark with a tide of sand pouring toward us. The dust billowed and spun as they kicked and pummeled and thrashed each other.

34 At the meeting, when Papa stood up to defend the YES YES position, murmurs of "*Inu, inu*" began to circulate around the mess hall. This man then jumped up at the speaker's table and made the charge aloud. Papa went for him. Now, outside in the dirt, Papa had him by the throat and would have strangled him, but some other men pulled them apart. I had never seen him so livid, yelling and out of his head with rage. While they pinned his arms, he kicked at the sand, sending windblown bursts of it toward the knot of men dragging his opponent out of reach.

Internees at Manzanar line up for lunch at a mess hall.





## HOW LANGUAGE WORKS

**Personal Pronouns** Use paragraphs 33–34 to provide a grammar review. A **personal pronoun** stands for a noun that refers to a person. Personal pronouns reflect the **gender**—masculine, feminine, or neuter—of the noun they replace. The **case** of a pronoun is the form it takes to show its use in a sentence.

| | Nominative Case | Objective Case | Possessive Case |
|---|---|---|---|
| First-person pronouns | I, we | me, us | mine, ours |
| Second-person pronouns | you | you | your, yours |
| Third-person pronouns | he, she, it, they | him, her, it, them | his, hers, its, theirs |

DIGITAL PERSPECTIVES

35 A few moments later the sandstorm hit. The sky turned black as night. Everyone ran for cover. Two men hustled Papa to our barracks. The fighting against the wind and sand to get there calmed him down some.

36 Back inside he sat by the stove holding his teacup and didn't speak for a long time. One cheekbone was raw where it had been mashed into the sand. Mama kept pouring him little trickles of tea. We listened to the wind howl. When the sand died down, the sky outside stayed black. The storm had knocked out the electricity all over the camp. It was a cold, lonely night, and we huddled around our oil stove while Mama and Woody and Chizu began to talk about the day.

37 A young woman came in, a friend of Chizu's, who lived across the way. She had studied in Japan for several years. About the time I went to bed she and Papa began to sing songs in Japanese, warming their hands on either side of the stove, facing each other in its glow. After a while Papa sang the first line of the Japanese national anthem, *Kimi ga yo*. Woody, Chizu, and Mama knew the tune, so they hummed along while Papa and the other woman sang the words. It can be a hearty or a plaintive tune, depending on your mood. From Papa, that night, it was a deep-throated lament. Almost invisible in the stove's small glow, tears began running down his face.

38 I had seen him cry a few times before. It only happened when he was singing or when someone else sang a song that moved him. He played the three-stringed *samisen*, which Kiyo and I called his "pinko-pinko." We would laugh together when we heard him plucking it and whining out old Japanese melodies. We would hold our ears and giggle. It was always a great joke between us, except for those rare times when Papa began to weep at the lyrics. Then we would just stare quietly—as I did that night—from some hidden corner of the room. This was always mysterious and incomprehensible.

39 The national anthem, I later learned, is what he had sung every morning as a schoolboy in Japan. They still sing it there, the way American kids pledge allegiance to the flag. It is not a martial song, or a victory song, the way many national anthems are. It is really a poem, whose words go back to the ninth century:

*Kimi ga yo wa chiyoni*
*yachiyoni sa-za-re i-shi no i-wa-o to*
*na-ri-te ko-ke no musu made.*

May thy peaceful reign last long.
May it last for thousands of years,
Until this tiny stone will grow
Into a massive rock, and the moss
Will cover it deep and thick.

NOTES





CLOSER LOOK

## Analyze Mood

Circulate among groups as students conduct their close read. Suggest that groups read paragraphs 36 and 37. Encourage them to talk about the annotations that they mark. If needed, provide the following support.

**ANNOTATE:** Have students mark details in these paragraphs that set the atmosphere of the scene, or work with small groups to have students participate while you highlight them together.

**QUESTION:** Guide students to consider what these details might tell them. Ask what a reader can infer from the details that the writer has included to describe the scene.

**Possible response:** The author describes a cold, dark place, the only light and warmth provided by a small stove. She describes the howling wind and her father's deep-throated lament.

**CONCLUDE:** Help students formulate conclusions about the importance of these details in the text. Ask students why the author might have included these details.

**Possible response:** The details create a haunted, lonely, sad mood.

Remind students that **mood** is the feeling created in the reader by a literary work or passage. Explain to students that sensory details are those that writers use to engage readers' five senses: sight, sound, touch, taste, and smell. When writers use sensory details, they not only describe the literal setting of the scene, they also build in the reader's mind an impression of the mood of the scene. When reading paragraphs 36 and 37 from the text, it is possible to imagine how it might feel to see one's father crying quietly by the light of a small stove.

### CROSS-CURRICULAR PERSPECTIVES

**Music** Review paragraphs 37–39 and discuss the author's description of the Japanese national anthem. He explains that "Kimigayo," can be sung in a hearty or plaintive tone. Suggest that students find several recordings of the song online, and listen to them. Groups of students might want to discuss the different ways the song is sung. What makes one presentation sound "hearty" and another sound "plaintive"? Urge students to bring in and share two recordings of another song, and explain what mood each version of the song creates and how it does so.

## Comprehension Check

Possible responses:

1. *Inu* means both "dog" and "collaborator."
2. The most divisive issue among the detainees is how to respond to the Loyalty Oath.
3. Woody's duty as a son is to listen to his father. Arguing is pointless.
4. Papa cries when a song moves him.
5. The narrator is eight years old and living with her family in a small room in an internment camp where they have been sent because it is World War II and they are Japanese American. Her father is brooding, drinking, and miserable, and never leaves the room. The narrator learns that other camp residents think he is a traitor. Internees argue about whether to sign a loyalty oath. The narrator's father will sign it because he believes doing so will keep his family together, but other detainees will see his signing as more proof that he is a collaborator. The narrator's father cries when he sings the Japanese national anthem.

## Research

**Research to Clarify** If groups struggle to identify a detail, you may want to suggest that they focus on one of the following: the living conditions in the Manzanar internment camp, the Japanese American Citizens League, or the Japanese Americans who served in the military during World War II.

It is a patriotic song that can also be read as a proverb, as a personal credo for endurance. The stone can be the kingdom or it can be a man's life. The moss is the greenery that, in time, will spring even from a rock. In Japan, before the turn of the century, outside my father's house there stood one of those stone lanterns, with four stubby legs and a small pagoda-like roof. Each morning someone in the household would pour a bucketful of water over his lantern, and after several years a skin of living vegetation began to show on the stone. As a boy he was taught that the last line of the anthem refers to a certain type of mossy lichen with exquisitely tiny white flowers sprinkled in amongst the green. ❧

## Comprehension Check

**Complete the following items after you finish your first read. Review and clarify details with your group.**

1. Identify two meanings for the Japanese word *inu*.

2. According to Jeanne Wakatsuki Houston, what is the most divisive issue among the internees?

3. Why doesn't Woody argue with Papa?

4. On what type of occasion does Papa cry, according to Jeanne Wakatsuki Houston?

5. **Notebook** Confirm your understanding of the text by writing a summary.

## RESEARCH

**Research to Clarify** Choose at least one unfamiliar detail from the text. Briefly research that detail. In what way does the information you learned shed light on an aspect of the text?





## PERSONALIZE FOR LEARNING

### Challenge

**Research** Numerous survivors of the Japanese American internment camps have written about their experiences. Have students extend their learning by reading another author's account of the experience. Suggest that each student choose a different account and then share what they have read with their classmates.

In addition to deepening their understanding of the internment, reading these accounts will provide an opportunity for students to see how a single topic is addressed in different genres, such as autobiography, fiction, memoir, and historical account.

## Close Read the Text

With your group, revisit sections of the text you marked during your first read. **Annotate** what you notice. What **questions** do you have? What can you **conclude?**

from FAREWELL TO MANZANAR

## Analyze the Text

CITE TEXTUAL EVIDENCE to support your answers.

Notebook Complete the activities.

1. **Review and Clarify** With your group, reread paragraphs 4 and 5 of the excerpt from *Farewell to Manzanar.* What do the authors suggest about the obstacles and challenges confronting Papa?
2. **Present and Discuss** Now, work with your group to share the passages from the text that you found especially important. Take turns presenting your passages. Discuss what you noticed in the selections, what questions you asked, and what conclusions you reached.
3. **Essential Question:** *How do we respond when challenged by fear?* What has this text taught you about people's responses to fear? Discuss with your group.

LANGUAGE DEVELOPMENT

## Concept Vocabulary

collaborator conspirators espionage

**Why These Words?** The three concept vocabulary words from the text are related. With your group, determine what the words have in common. Write your ideas, and add another word that fits the category.

**Practice**

Notebook Confirm your understanding of these words by looking up their definitions in a dictionary. Then, use the words to write a short narrative paragraph. Include context clues that hint at each word's meaning.

## Word Study

**Latin Suffix: *-or*** The suffix *-or* can be used to form nouns from verbs. For example, the words *collaborator* and *conspirators* are formed from *collaborate* and *conspire*, respectively. Reread paragraphs 2 and 8 of the selection. In each paragraph, find one noun formed from the suffix *-or*. Write the nouns and their meanings; then, list the verb used to form each noun.

**WORD NETWORK**

Add words related to fear from the text to your Word Network.

**STANDARDS**

Language
- Identify and correctly use patterns of word changes that indicate different meanings of parts or speech.
- Verify the preliminary determination of the meaning of a word or phrase.

DIGITAL PERSPECTIVES

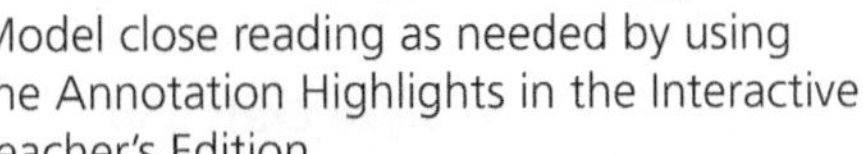

## Jump Start

CLOSE READ What conflicting feelings did the author's father have? How did he deal with the conflict? As students discuss in their groups, ask them to imagine how they might feel in the same situation.

## Close Read the Text

Model close reading as needed by using the Annotation Highlights in the Interactive Teacher's Edition.

Remind groups to use Accountable Talk in their discussions and to support one another as they complete the close read.

## Analyze the Text

**Possible responses:**

1. Papa had appeared to cooperate with the army, so many of the other interned people thought of him as a collaborator and traitor.
2. Passages will vary by group. Remind students to explain why they chose the passages they presented.
3. Responses will vary by group.

## Concept Vocabulary

**Why These Words?**
**Possible response:**
The words all refer to working secretly with the enemy. Another word that fits the category is *traitor*.

**Practice**

Possible responses:
During wartime, people take drastic action in order to win. **Espionage** is an important tool that **conspirators** use to gather information from the enemy to share with their allies. One way to gather such information is to appear to be a **collaborator**, to earn the respect of the enemy in order to gain access to top-secret data that could help win the war.

**Word Network**

**Possible words:** *exiled, threats, unheroically, lurching, chaotic*

## Word Study

For more support, see **Concept Vocabulary and Word Study.**

Possible responses
Noun: *visitor* - guest; Verb - *visit*
Noun: *director* - manager; Verb - *direct*

**FORMATIVE ASSESSMENT**

**Analyze the Text**

**If** students struggle to close read the text, **then** provide the ***from* Farewell to Manzanar: Text Questions** available online in the Interactive Teacher's Edition or Unit Resources. Answers and DOK levels are also available.

**Concept Vocabulary**

**If** students struggle to identify the concept, **then** have them brainstorm synonyms for each word and think about how the synonyms are related.

**Word Study**

**If** students fail to locate words with the Latin suffix *–or*, **then** suggest they identify verbs in the text and try making them into nouns by adding *or*. For Reteach and Practice, see **Word Study: Latin Suffix: *-or* (RP).**

FACILITATING

## Analyze Craft and Structure

**Development of Complex Ideas** In a first-person account, it is possible for readers to gain an understanding of the narrator's complexities by paying close attention to how he or she describes, responds to, and reacts to people or events. In paragraph 4 in the excerpt from *Farewell to Manzanar*, the author uses words, such as *lingered, deliberately*, and *just loud enough for us to hear*, that reveal her dislike for the women she and her mother encounter at the latrine.

For more support, see **Analyze Craft and Structure: Development of Complex Ideas.**

### Practice

Possible responses:

1. (a) The other people in the camp think Papa is an informant who traded information about fellow Japanese Americans in exchange for a release from Fort Lincoln. (b) Houston knows that her father is not an informant, so she sees her father as a victim of their mistreatment.
2. (a) Papa's willingness to answer YES YES suggests that he values his life and future more than any animosity he may feel. He believes Japan will lose the war, so it is in his best interests to declare his allegiance to the United States. (b) He believes America will win the war, and he knows, even after all he'd endured, that his future life will be in the United States.
3. See possible responses in chart on Student page.

### FORMATIVE ASSESSMENT

### Analyze Craft and Structure

**If** students struggle to make inferences about Papa's feelings, **then** ask them how they would be feeling if they did the things that he did in the story. For Reteach and Practice, see **Analyze Craft and Structure: Development of Complex Ideas (RP).**

MAKING MEANING

from FAREWELL TO MANZANAR

## Analyze Craft and Structure

**Development of Complex Ideas** Fiction writers use the tools of **characterization** to show what imaginary characters are like. Narrative nonfiction writers use the same tools to describe real people. There are two types of characterization: direct and indirect.

- With **direct characterization**, a writer explicitly states what a person is like—for example, "It was Papa himself, his dark, bitter, brooding presence." Here, Jeanne Wakatsuki Houston simply tells readers that her father was unhappy and sullen.
- With **indirect characterization**, writers provide details that allow readers to infer what people are like. A writer might describe a person's physical appearance and behavior, quote his or her statements, or report what other people say about him or her. For instance, when Houston recalls that other people called her father "inu," readers can infer that her father was neither liked nor respected.

To fully understand the people and their motivations in works of narrative nonfiction, compare and contrast descriptive details, statements, facts, and opinions presented in the text.

### Practice

CITE TEXTUAL EVIDENCE to support your answers.

**Notebook** Work independently to answer the questions and complete the chart. Then, share your responses with your group.

1. (a) Why do the other Japanese Americans in the camp view Papa as a traitor? (b) How do their opinions affect Houston's perceptions of her father?
2. (a) What does Papa's YES YES position reveal about him? (b) How does his stance on this issue give readers insight about his values and priorities?
3. Use the chart to record details about Papa's behavior during important episodes in the text. Then, use those details to make inferences about his feelings.

| EPISODE | PAPA'S BEHAVIOR | INFERENCE |
|---|---|---|
| Return to Manzanar (paragraphs 1–10) | stays inside, paces, makes alcoholic drinks, gets drunk, vomits, curses, swings bottles wildly | He felt alienated and angry; his behavior was out of control. |
| Meeting at the mess hall (paragraphs 29–35) | shaved and trimmed moustache, put on a silk tie, staggered, punched, cursed, leapt, bellowed, fought, almost strangled, kick the sand | He wanted to make a positive impression; he was enraged. |
| Papa singing songs (paragraphs 36–40) | sat by stove, sipped tea, sang, cried | He loved music and he loved and missed Japan. |





PERSONALIZE FOR LEARNING

### English Language Support

**Past Tenses** Remind students about the different ways to express the past tense. Share with them the table to help them clarify which form of the past tense to use in their writing. Have students identify different forms of the past tense in *Farewell to Manzanar*, and explain what each signifies. Then, have them write sentences that are examples of the different past tenses. **ALL LEVELS**

| Form of Past Tense | Example | Explained |
|---|---|---|
| Simple Past | The dog barked. | Actions at a specific time in the past |
| Past Continuous | The dog was barking incessantly. | Activities that took place in an ongoing way in the past |
| Past Perfect | The baby woke up because the dog had barked so loudly. | An action completed before another action in the past |
| Past Perfect Continuous | The dog had been barking for hours before we got home. | Actions in progress before some other actions |

LANGUAGE DEVELOPMENT

## Author's Style

**Author's Point of View** *Farewell to Manzanar* is an autobiographical account in which the author looks back on events she experienced as a young girl. The use of **first-person point of view**, signaled by pronouns such as *I*, *me*, and *my*, tells readers that the author is relating her own story. However, because the author is recalling these events years after they happened, the narrative unfolds on at least two levels. At times, Jeanne Wakatsuki Houston relates events from the perspective of a young child. At other times, she offers insights and reflections from an adult perspective. Sometimes, Houston signals a narrative shift with clues such as "at the time" and "years later I learned." At other points, though, the narrative shift is implied.

### Read It

1. Use this chart to compile your notes on shifting perspectives in the selection. Reread each passage identified in the left-hand column. Then, write a comment on the narrative perspective or shift in the right-hand column.

| PASSAGE | COMMENT(S) ON NARRATIVE PERSPECTIVE/SHIFT |
|---|---|
| paragraphs 9–10 | In paragraph 9, the author is looking back ("Better times were a long way off...") expressing something she could not have known at the time. In Paragraph 10, she returns to her perceptions as an eight-year-old ("At the time I was too young to understand the problem. I only knew..."). |
| paragraphs 28–29 | The author begins by describing the situation at the time, and then shifts to explaining her father's thinking, which she probably did not understand at the time. |
| paragraphs 39–40 | The author shifts at the start of paragraph 39, recounting what she "later learned." |

2. Notebook **Connect to Style** What is the overall effect of narrative shifts in the selection? Do such shifts clarify Houston's principal issues and conflicts? Explain your answer.

### Write It

Notebook Write a short narrative account of an event from your childhood. Use first-person point of view to tell your story, but shift perspectives to highlight the differences between how you experienced the event as a child and how you understand it now.

STANDARDS

**Reading Informational Text**

- Cite strong and thorough textual evidence to support analysis of what the text says explicitly as well as inferences drawn from the text, including determining where the text leaves matters uncertain.
- Analyze a complex set of ideas or sequence of events and explain how specific individuals, ideas, or events interact and develop over the course of the text.
- Determine an author's point of view or purpose in a text in which the rhetoric is particularly effective, analyzing how style and content contribute to the power, persuasiveness, or beauty of the text.





DIGITAL PERSPECTIVES

## Author's Style

**Author's Point of View** Remind students that in an autobiography, the story is always subjective, told as the author saw it. Urge students to look for clues that others might have told the story differently because their experience of it was different from the author's. Urge students to find an example in the text of the author's subjectivity and describe how another person in the scene might have told the story. For more support, see **Author's Style: Author's Point of View.**

### Read It

1. See possible responses in chart on Student page.
2. **Connect to Style** Possible response: The narrative shifts provide important insight for readers that help them understand the significance of what the author is describing. For example, learning about the national anthem in paragraphs 39 and 40 helps readers understand both Papa's reaction and the complexity of his situation.

### Write It

**Possible responses:**

Paragraphs will vary, but make sure that students shift perspectives to show the difference between their experiences as a child and their understanding of those experiences now.

### FORMATIVE ASSESSMENT

### Conventions and Style

**If** students are unable to shift perspectives, **then** suggest that they talk with a partner about the experience they are writing about, and work with the partner to distinguish past experience from current understanding. For Reteach and Practice, see **Author's Style: Author's Point of View (RP).**

### Selection Test

Administer the "*from* Farewell to Manzanar" Selection Test, which is available in both print and digital formats online in Assessments.

PERSONALIZE FOR LEARNING

### English Language Support

**Author's Purpose and Point of View**

Remind students that an author may have more than one purpose in mind to write a text.

Ask students to work in pairs to determine one purpose Jeanne Wakatsuki Houston and James D. Houston may have had to write this text. **EMERGING**

Ask students to write a paragraph describing the point of view from which this text is narrated. **EXPANDING**

Have students write an essay explaining how the point of view chosen by the authors contribute to the purpose they might have had when writing this text. **BRIDGING**

An expanded **English Language Support Lesson** on Author's Point of View is available in the Interactive Teacher's Edition.

# Interview With George Takei

**AUDIO SUMMARIES**
Audio summaries of "Interview With George Takei" are available online in both English and Spanish and can be assigned to students in the Interactive Teacher's Edition or Unit Resources. Assigning these summaries prior to reading the selection may help students build additional background knowledge and set a context for their first read.

## Summary

In this interview, actor George Takei discusses his family's experiences in an internment camp during World War II. The interview begins with Takei remembering the day when his family was taken from their home. His family was sent to Arkansas, but it was transferred to another camp in northern California after his parents refused to swear loyalty to the United States. Takei discusses the offensiveness of the loyalty oath, which involved a questionnaire that assumed Japanese Americans were loyal to the emperor of Japan.

### Insight

Takei's account and analysis of his internment reveals what many consider to be a disgraceful chapter in American history. It demonstrates how some act irrationally and others act bravely in the face of fear and uncertainty.

ESSENTIAL QUESTION:
How do we respond when challenged by fear?

## Connection to Essential Question

This selection, "Interview With George Takei," connects to the Essential Question, "How do we respond to fear?" Takei's family responds to their fears in ways that show the ability to cope in the face of harsh, unfair treatment by a fearful government.

SMALL-GROUP PERFORMANCE TASK
Do people usually learn from their fear?

UNIT PERFORMANCE-BASED ASSESSMENT
Is fear always a harmful emotion?

## Connection to Performance Tasks

**Small-Group Learning Performance Task** In this Performance Task, students will respond to the question, "Do people usually learn from their fear?" This selection, which describes both the treatment of Japanese Americans after the attack on Pearl Harbor and Japanese Americans' response to that treatment, provides evidence of what we learn about ourselves from our response to fear.

**Unit Performance-Based Assessment** In this interview, Takei discusses how the fears of one group, the U.S. government, harms another—Japanese Americans. It also demonstrates how facing fear might also strengthen our convictions.

DIGITAL PERSPECTIVES

 Audio  Video  Document  Annotation Highlights  EL Highlights  Online Assessment

## LESSON RESOURCES

| | Making Meaning | Language Development | Effective Expression |
|---|---|---|---|
| **Lesson** | **First Review**<br>**Close Review**<br>**Analyze the Media** | **Media Vocabulary** | **Writing to Compare** |
| **Instructional Standards** | **RI.10** By the end of grade 11, read and comprehend literary nonfiction . . .<br>**L.6** Acquire and use accurately general academic and domain-specific words and phrases . . . | **SL.3** Evaluate a speaker's point of view . . .<br>**L.6** Acquire and use accurately general academic and domain-specific words and phrases . . . | **RI.7** Integrate and evaluate multiple sources of information . . .<br>**W.2** Write informative/explanatory texts . . .<br>**W.9.b** Apply *grades 11–12 Reading standards* . . . |
| **STUDENT RESOURCES** | | | |
| Available online in the Interactive Student Edition or Unit Resources | Selection Audio<br>First-Review Guide: Media-Video | | Evidence Log |
| **TEACHER RESOURCES** | | | |
| **Selection Resources** Available online in the Interactive Teacher's Edition or Unit Resources | Audio Summaries<br>Interview With George Takei: Media Questions | Media Vocabulary | Writing to Compare: Compare-and-Contrast Essay |
| **My Resources** | A Unit 5 Answer Key is available online and in the Interactive Teacher's Edition. | | |

## Media Complexity Rubric: Interview With George Takei

| **Quantitative Measures** | |
|---|---|
| **Format and Length:** 7-minute video | |
| **Qualitative Measures** | |
| Knowledge Demands<br>① ② **❸** ④ ⑤ | The interview deals with Takei's experience in internment camps. Historical background will be needed. |
| Structure<br>① **❷** ③ ④ ⑤ | The selection is a straightforward interview in a question-and-answer format. |
| Language Conventionality and Clarity<br>① **❷** ③ ④ ⑤ | The language is conventional and clear. |
| Levels of Meaning/Purpose<br>① **❷** ③ ④ ⑤ | Meaning and concepts are clearly explained and easy to grasp. |

# FACILITATING

## Jump Start

**FIRST REVIEW** Now that you've read part of an autobiography written about an author's time in a Japanese American internment camp, you will watch an interview of another adult recalling a similar camp. How do you think the two might be alike? How might they be different?

## Interview With George Takei

How do people remember the hardships they faced? What might a person's account of an event reveal about his or her experience? Modeling questions such as these will help students connect to "Interview with George Takei" and to the Small-Group Performance Task assignment. Selection audio for the selection is available in the Interactive Teacher's Edition.

## Media Vocabulary

Encourage students to discuss the media vocabulary. Have they seen or used these terms before? Do they use any of them in their speech or writing? Urge groups to think of examples of each of the terms described by the media vocabulary.

### FIRST REVIEW

Have students perform the steps of the first review independently:

WATCH: Remind students to notice George Takei's expressions when he describes his experiences as a child in an internment camp.

NOTE: Encourage students to listen for Takei's description of his experiences, as well as his adult perspective on them.

CONNECT: Encourage students consider how Takei's comments are similar to and different from those in *Farewell to Manzanar*.

RESPOND: Students will answer questions to demonstrate understanding.

Point out to students that while they will always complete the Respond step at the end of the first review, the other steps will probably happen somewhat concurrently. You may wish to print copies of the **First-Review Guide: Media Video** for students to use.

MAKING MEANING

from FAREWELL TO MANZANAR

## Comparing Text to Media

This interview with George Takei, which focuses on the actor's internment experience during World War II, was drawn from the Archive of American Television. Watch and listen to the interview. Then, compare and contrast the points of view of two people who experienced similar hardships.

INTERVIEW WITH GEORGE TAKEI

About the Interviewee

**George Takei** (b. 1937) was born into a Japanese American family in Los Angeles. In college, he became interested in theater and made acting his career. Best known for portraying Hikaru Sulu in the original *Star Trek*, Takei has participated in dozens of films and television programs. He also has appeared in *Allegiance*, a musical inspired by his internment experience.

# Interview With George Takei

### Media Vocabulary

These words will be useful to you as you analyze, discuss, and write about video interviews.

| | |
|---|---|
| **Documentary:** program or film that provides a factual record or report of real events | • Documentaries may consist largely of interviews with people who are uniquely qualified to report on certain events or topics.<br>• Interviews may take place in a variety of formats and allow different types of interactions between the interviewer and the interviewee. |
| **Eyewitness Account:** description given by someone who was present at an event | • Eyewitness testimony is valuable for its immediacy and presumed credibility.<br>• Eyewitnesses, however, may be biased and only partially trustworthy. |
| **Framing:** composing a visual so that an enclosing border surrounds the image in the foreground | • Framing may offer a counterpoint or contrast between foreground and background images.<br>• Framing may alternate with close-up views, in which no background is visible. |

### First Review MEDIA: VIDEO

Apply these strategies as you perform your first review. You will have an opportunity to complete a close review after your first review.

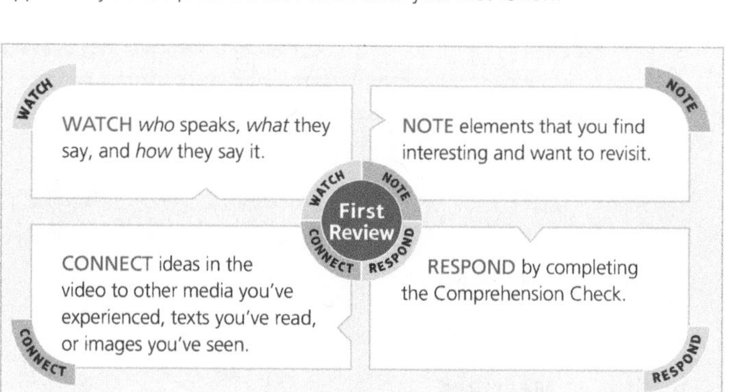

WATCH
WATCH *who* speaks, *what* they say, and *how* they say it.
NOTE
NOTE elements that you find interesting and want to revisit.
First Review
CONNECT
CONNECT ideas in the video to other media you've experienced, texts you've read, or images you've seen.
RESPOND
RESPOND by completing the Comprehension Check.


STANDARDS

**Reading Informational Text**
By the end of grade 11, read and comprehend literary nonfiction in the grades 11–CCR text complexity band proficiently, with scaffolding as needed at the high end of the range.

**Language**
Acquire and use accurately general academic and domain-specific words and phrases, sufficient for reading, writing, speaking, and listening at the college and career readiness level; demonstrate independence in gathering vocabulary knowledge when considering a word or phrase important to comprehension or expression.

716 UNIT 5 • FACING OUR FEARS



### PERSONALIZE FOR LEARNING

**English Language Support**
**Taking Notes** Urge students to take notes as they watch the video. Have groups view the video in short increments, pausing after each to jot down key ideas expressed during that segment of the video. Have group members compare their notes before they move on to the next segment. Doing so will help students clarify their understanding so that they can continue to follow what Takei says in the video. **ALL LEVELS**

MEDIA | VIDEO

# Interview With George Takei

BACKGROUND

The internment of Japanese Americans lasted from March 1942 to March 1946. However, Executive Order 9066, which established the policy of internment, was only officially repealed and apologized for in 1976. In this interview, George Takei describes how he and his family were forced from their home in Los Angeles and interned at two different camps—one in Arkansas and one in northern California—during World War II.

SCAN FOR MULTIMEDIA

NOTES





## CLOSER REVIEW

### Analyze the Setting

Circulate among groups as students conduct their close review. Suggest that groups focus on the setting of the interview. Encourage them to talk about what they note. If needed, provide the following support.

**NOTE:** Have students note what they see in the background, or work with small groups to have students participate while you note them together.

**QUESTION:** Guide students to consider what these details might tell them. Ask what a viewer can infer from what they see in the background, and accept student responses.

**Possible response:** George Takei looks like he is sitting in his living room.

**CONCLUDE:** Help students to formulate conclusions about the importance of these details in the video. Ask students why the interviewer might have shown Takei in this setting.

**Possible response:** The setting makes George Takei seem like an average American in his home. This emphasizes his similarity to other Americans as he recounts being treated as an other. This helps viewers feel more connected to Takei and sympathize with his experience.

Remind students that the **setting** of an interview is where it takes place. The setting provides part of the context of the message of the interview.

## FACILITATING SMALL-GROUP CLOSE REVIEW

**CLOSE REVIEW: Interview** Monitor students as the conduct their close review and offer support as needed.

- Students probably spend a great deal of their time watching videos, so they are accustomed to listening and watching at the same time, but may not be doing both purposefully. Encourage students to pay attention to how they watch the video, and to discuss their viewing process with members of their group.
- Some students probably focus more on what the person is saying than on what is presented visually. Other students may be particularly attuned to the visual elements. Encourage students to attend to both components of the video.
- Encourage students to take notes, especially tracking information that is new to them.

FACILITATING

## Comprehension Check

Possible responses:

1. Takei was four years old at the time of the attack on Pearl Harbor.
2. Soldiers armed with guns and bayonets came to Takei's home and ordered them to leave.
3. Takei marvels at how children can adapt to anything, since the camps felt normal to him.
4. Question 27 asked whether a person would bear arms to defend the United States. Question 28 asked whether a person would forswear loyalty to the emperor of Japan and swear loyalty to the United States.
5. Takei's parents answered "no" to both questions because they felt the questions were an affront to their dignity.
6. The Takei family was transferred to the camp in California because of how his parents answered Questions 27 and 28. They were deemed "disloyal."
7. The questions seemed ridiculous to ask. The first question was irrelevant to many of the people forced to answer it. The second question assumed that all Japanese Americans would feel some loyalty and connection to Japan simply because they were Japanese. It was also ironic that the government would seek an affirmation of loyalty from people it had incarcerated for a year.

## Comprehension Check

Complete the following items after you finish your first review. Review and clarify details with your group.

1. How old was Takei at the time of the attack on Pearl Harbor?
2. What does Takei remember about the day that he and his family were ordered out of their home?
3. As a young child, how did Takei feel about the internment camps?
4. What were the two key questions posed by the government's loyalty questionnaire?
5. How did Takei's parents respond to the key questions? What reasons did they give?
6. Why were Takei and his family transferred from a camp in Arkansas to Tule Lake in northern California?
7. **Notebook** Confirm your understanding of the interview by summarizing Takei's comments about the significance of the loyalty questionnaire.





PERSONALIZE FOR LEARNING

### Strategic Support

**Graphic Organizer** Explain to students that their work with the video interview does not end when the video ends. They must be certain that they fully understand the interview's content. Suggest that groups make a web to help them make sense of what George Takei said. In the center, they can write his name. In circles radiating out from the center, they can identify the topics he discusses. From each topic, they can add circles that provide additional information. Point out to students that they can easily transform the web into an outline of the key ideas in the interview.

## Close Review

With your group, revisit the video interview and your first-review notes. Record any new observations that seem important. What **questions** do you have? What can you **conclude**?

INTERVIEW WITH GEORGE TAKEI

## Analyze the Media

**Notebook** Complete the activities.

1. **Present and Discuss** Choose the interview segment you find most interesting or powerful. Share your choice with the group, and discuss why you chose it. Explain what you noticed in the segment, what questions it raised for you, and what conclusions you reached about it.
2. **Review and Synthesize** How does Takei reveal his perspective on the treatment of Japanese Americans during the war? Consider his tone of voice and facial expressions in addition to the details he shares.
3. **Essential Question:** ***How do we respond when challenged by fear?*** What have you learned about people's responses to fear from watching this interview?

LANGUAGE DEVELOPMENT

## Media Vocabulary

documentary eyewitness account framing

**Use the vocabulary words in your responses to the questions.**

1. Why is George Takei qualified to present a factual report on the internment camp experience?
2. **(a)** How does Takei's perspective offer a different way of seeing America's involvement in World War II? **(b)** What is the value of considering alternative perspectives on historic events?
3. What effect is created by having Takei talk in the foreground of a scene set in a comfortably furnished room?

STANDARDS

**Speaking and Listening**
Evaluate a speaker's point of view, reasoning, and use of evidence and rhetoric, assessing the stance, premises, links among ideas, word choice, points of emphasis, and tone used.

**Language**
Acquire and use accurately general academic and domain-specific words and phrases, sufficient for reading, writing, speaking, and listening at the college and career readiness level; demonstrate independence in gathering vocabulary knowledge when considering a word or phrase important to comprehension or expression.





DIGITAL PERSPECTIVES

## Jump Start

CLOSE REVIEW Ask students to consider this question: *How would you respond if you were placed in a situation like the one that George Takei and his family found themselves in after the bombing of Pearl Harbor?* Ask students to discuss their answers in their groups.

## Close Review

If needed, model close reviewing by using the Closer Review notes in the Interactive Teacher's Edition.

Remind groups to use Accountable Talk in their discussions and to support one another as they complete the close review.

## Analyze the Media

**Possible responses:**

1. **Responses will vary.** Remind students to cite details from the interview that led to their choice and to their questions.
2. Takei combines facts with his own memories. For instance, he calmly explains that Japanese Americans were taken to live in internment camps after the attack on Pearl Harbor, but he also recalls the fear he felt when soldiers came to his house to relocate his family.
3. Takei's explanation of how the U.S. government treated his family and other Japanese Americans suggests that sometimes people take drastic measures when fearful. His explanation of how his parents stood up for their convictions instead of responding "yes" to two questions on the loyalty questionnaire shows that bravery in the face of fear is not always rewarded. However, his clear admiration for his parents shows that there is value in taking a brave stance.

## Media Vocabulary

For more support, see **Media Vocabulary.**

**Possible responses:**

1. George Takei provides an **eyewitness account** of his experience at an internment camp.
2. (a) Takei's perspective in this **documentary** allows viewers to understand that the United States treated its Japanese citizens unfairly. (b) It is valuable to consider alternative perspectives on historic events so that we can get a fuller picture of what really happened.
3. **Framing** George Takei in a comfortable setting contrasts with the adverse conditions that he describes.

### FORMATIVE ASSESSMENT

### Analyze the Media

**If** students struggle to close review the video, **then** provide the **Interview with George Takei: Media Questions,** available online in the Interactive Teacher's Edition or Unit Resources. Answers and DOK levels are also available.

### Media Vocabulary

**If** students struggle to understand the concept of framing, **then** review the definition. Then show students a few short video clips and discuss the framing in each one.

# FACILITATING

## Writing to Compare

As students prepare to compare information they've gathered about the excerpt from *Farewell to Manzanar* and the George Takei interview, they will choose one of three prompts to respond to in a compare-and-contrast essay.

### Prewriting

**Analyze the Texts** Consider forming groups based on which question students choose to answer.

a. The father stopped drinking and started socializing with other adults again so he could discuss the oath. He became involved in heated arguments about whether to answer "yes" or "no." Both he and Woody answered "yes," but for different reasons. The father voted "yes" because he did not want to be sent back to Japan. Woody voted "yes" because he was ready to fight for the United States. During a camp-wide meeting about the oath, a fight broke out between the father and a man who accused the father of being a collaborator.

b. Takei's father did not want to answer "yes" because it would mean admitting prior loyalty to the Japanese emperor. His mother did not answer "yes" because it would have meant possible military service when she had small children to take care of. Those who answered "no" were moved to an internment camp that was even harsher.

c. People in the camps sometimes became very angry and turned on each other. The father dealt with his anger by turning to drinking. He was rumored to be a collaborator because he had been released from prison earlier than other men.

d. The Tule Lake internment camp had three levels of barbed-wire fences and tanks patrolling on the perimeter. Asian Americans who volunteered for military service were rejected on the basis of being "enemy non-aliens." Question 28 on the loyalty questionnaire was a two-part question that was impossible for many people to answer correctly.

**Possible responses:**

1. In the excerpt from *Farewell to Manzanar,* the speaker focuses on how internment caused conflict in her family and between different factions in the camp. George Takei focuses on how unjust the camps were and on conditions in the camp.
2. The two texts both suggest that conditions for Japanese Americans were very difficult during World War II.

EFFECTIVE EXPRESSION

*from* FAREWELL TO MANZANAR

INTERVIEW WITH GEORGE TAKEI

## Writing to Compare

Both the excerpt from *Farewell to Manzanar* and the interview with George Takei provide primary-source information about the experiences of interned Japanese Americans during World War II. Deepen your understanding of both sources by comparing the two accounts and the perspectives they express.

**Assignment**

Choose one of these three prompts, and respond to it in a **compare-and-contrast essay**.

- ☐ How are Papa's and Woody's understandings of the Loyalty Oath and its implications in *Farewell to Manzanar* similar to and different from Takei's parents' position on the same topic?
- ☐ Consider Houston's and Takei's reactions to their parents' decisions. How are they alike and different?
- ☐ What events do Houston and Takei emphasize in their respective accounts? How are their treatments of those events similar and different? Consider the details on which they focus, their word choices, and their tones.

### Prewriting

**Analyze the Texts** Before you choose a prompt to address, discuss the two texts with your group. Consider the following questions.

- How does each selection describe the Loyalty Oath and peoples' responses to it? What arguments are used to support both "yes" and "no" responses? What consequences follow each decision?
- What similar and different information and insights about the experiences of interned Japanese do the two texts present?

**Notebook** Record your ideas during the group discussion.

| FAREWELL TO MANZANAR | INTERVIEW WITH GEORGE TAKEI |
|---|---|
| a. See answers in Teacher's Edition. | b. |
| | |
| c. | d. |
| | |

**Notebook** **Respond to these questions.**

1. How do the points of view differ, in general?
2. What do these two texts suggest about the universal experience of Japanese Americans during World War II?

**STANDARDS**

**Reading Informational Text**
Integrate and evaluate multiple sources of information presented in different media or formats as well as in words in order to address a question or solve a problem.

**Writing**
- Apply *grades 11–12 Reading standards* to literary nonfiction.
- Write informative/explanatory texts to examine and convey complex ideas, concepts, and information clearly and accurately through the effective selection, organization, and analysis of content.





PERSONALIZE FOR LEARNING

**English Language Support**

**Preparing for Discussion** If students are uneasy about sharing their ideas with their group, suggest that they write down what they want to say before the group discusses the text and the video.
**ALL LEVELS**

## Drafting

**Choose a Question** Work independently to plan and write your essay. First, review your Prewriting notes.

- Which aspect of the autobiography or interview do you find most interesting or important?
- What strikes you as the most powerful difference between the two?

Your answers to these questions should help you choose a topic. Place a checkmark in the box next to your choice.

**Write a Thesis Statement** Your thesis statement should respond to your chosen prompt in one or two sentences. Write a first version of your thesis statement here. You may adjust or even change it altogether as you draft and refine your ideas.

**Thesis Statement:** ______________________________

______________________________

______________________________

**Select Evidence** Share your thesis statements other group members who are working from the same prompt. Then, work together to discuss and choose evidence from both the autobiography and the interview that will support each person's thesis. Use the chart to list the evidence you plan to use in your essay.

| EVIDENCE FROM AUTOBIOGRAPHY | EVIDENCE FROM INTERVIEW |
|---|---|
| | |

**Write a First Draft** Begin your essay with a thesis statement that offers a one- or two-sentence response to the prompt. Then, in the body of the essay, develop your thesis with details, quotations, or other support from the selections. Decide whether you will write about one selection first and then about the other one, or whether you will discuss the two texts' similarities and then their differences. Make a short outline to set up a structure to follow. Then, draft your essay.

### Review, Revise, and Edit

Read your draft aloud to your group. Ask for feedback, take notes, and then use your peers' suggestions and your own ideas to revise your draft. Make sure your treatment of the two selections is balanced. Then, check for logical transitions as you shift attention from one selection to the other. After revising, edit to improve grammar, word choice, and sentence structure. Proofread to eliminate errors in spelling and punctuation.

**EVIDENCE LOG**

Before moving on to a new selection, go to your Evidence Log and record what you've learned from the excerpt from *Farewell to Manzanar* and the interview with George Takei.





DIGITAL PERSPECTIVES 

## Drafting

**Choose a Question** Encourage students to use their prewriting chart to help them choose a question. The chart may provide more evidence for one of the questions than for the others.

**Write a Thesis Statement** Remind students a thesis statement must not be so specific that they cannot write a full essay about it; it also must not be too general.

**Select Evidence** Groups may divide up the task, with some looking for evidence in the memoir and others looking for evidence in the interview. If your classroom has computers and headphones, allow students to work individually on replaying the interview.

**Write a First Draft** Encourage students to return to the Assignment box after they have completed their draft. They should reread their question carefully to make sure they have answered it fully.

## Review, Revise, and Edit

As students revise, encourage them to review their draft to be sure they have explained their thinking clearly. Ask them to make sure they have included evidence for both the similarities and the differences between the two selections. Finally, remind students to check for grammar, usage, and mechanics.

For more support, see **Writing to Compare: Compare-and-Contrast Essay**.

**Evidence Log** Support students in completing their Evidence Log. This paced activity will help prepare them for the Performance-Based Assessment at the end of the unit.

### HOW LANGUAGE WORKS

**Author's Point of View** As students revise their writing, remind them that both the autobiography and the interview are first-person accounts. In *Farewell to Manzanar*, the author is writing on two different levels. On one level, she is writing from the point of view of a child; on another level, she is writing from the point of view of an adult looking back. Ask students to think about whether George Takei speaks on both of those levels in the interview. Urge them to think about how both the autobiography and the interview offer a fuller depiction of the writer's and interviewee's experiences.

### FORMATIVE ASSESSMENT

### Writing to Compare

**If** students struggle to find similarities between the memoir and the interview, **then** ask them to make a list of the main topics covered in each and see which topics the two have in common.

# Antojos

**AUDIO SUMMARIES**
Audio summaries of "Antojos" are available online in both English and Spanish in the Interactive Teacher's Edition or Unit Resources. Assigning these summaries prior to reading the selection may help students build additional background knowledge and set a context for their first read.

## Summary

In the short story "Antojos" by Julia Alvarez, a young woman named Yolanda drives north to find guavas during her visit to the Dominican Republic. Her aunts had warned her against traveling alone, but she dismissed their fears to pursue her *antojo*, a Spanish word for craving. Yolanda stops at a market to buy guavas, but instead local boys take her to pick some. At the end of their harvest, most of the boys disappear, leaving only Yolanda and a shy local boy. Her car gets a flat tire and the boy leaves to find help. While she is waiting, two men with machetes approach her. Yolanda's reaction and subsequent events help her understand her own relationship to her homeland.

### Insight

Ideas about craving and fear intertwine in this story. Yolanda's relatives ask about her *antojo,* but try to discourage her with fearful stories when she decides to satisfy her craving on her own. When Yolanda encounters the men with machetes, it seems that her aunts were right. Yolanda is paralyzed by fear, which turns out to be unnecessary. Later, Yolanda's interaction with the young boy suggests that other people hold on to their fear as well, since they assumed the boy was lying and trying to trick them.

ESSENTIAL QUESTION:
How do we respond when challenged by fear?

## Connection to the Essential Question

In "Antojos," Yolanda is warned about the dangers of traveling north and becomes extremely fearful when the men with machetes appear. She assumes they will harm her. Later, the shy boy's story further reveals that fear can cause people to become suspicious of others.

SMALL-GROUP PERFORMANCE TASK
Do people usually learn from their fear?

UNIT PERFORMANCE-BASED ASSESSMENT
Is fear always a harmful emotion?

## Connection to Performance Tasks

**Small-Group Learning Performance Task** In "Antojos," Yolanda learns that she can overcome her fear to accept help.

**Unit Performance-Based Assessment** In the text, Yolanda's fear prevents her from effectively communicating with the men who help her, but it does not harm her.

**DIGITAL PERSPECTIVES**

 Audio  Video  Document  Annotation Highlights  EL Highlights Online Assessment

## LESSON RESOURCES

| | Making Meaning | Language Development | Effective Expression |
|---|---|---|---|
| **Lesson** | **First Read**<br>**Close Read**<br>**Analyze the Text**<br>**Analyze Craft and Structure** | **Concept Vocabulary**<br>**Word Study**<br>**Conventions and Style** | **Research** |
| **Instructional Standards** | **RL.10** By the end of grade 11, read and comprehend literature . . .<br>**L.4** Determine or clarify the meaning of unknown and multiple-meaning words and phrases . . .<br>**L.4.a** Use context as a clue . . .<br>**RL.3** Analyze the impact of the author's choices . . .<br>**RL.5** Analyze how an author's choices . . . | **L.4.c** Consult general and specialized reference materials . . .<br>**L.1** Demonstrate command of the conventions . . . | **W.7** Conduct short as well as more sustained research projects . . . |
| **STUDENT RESOURCES** | | | |
| Available online in the Interactive Student Edition or Unit Resources | Selection Audio<br>First-Read Guide: Fiction<br>Close-Read Guide: Fiction | Word Network | Evidence Log |
| **TEACHER RESOURCES** | | | |
| **Selection Resources** Available online in the Interactive Teacher's Edition or Unit Resources | Audio Summaries<br>Annotation Highlights<br>EL Highlights<br>Antojos: Text Questions<br>English Language Support Lesson: Using Context as Clue to Meaning<br>Analyze Craft and Structure: Author's Choices: Narrative Structure | Concept Vocabulary and Word Study<br>Conventions and Style: Pronouns and Antecedents | Research: Research Project |
| **Reteach/Practice (RP)** Available online in the Interactive Teacher's Edition or Unit Resources | Analyze Craft and Structure: Author's Choices: Narrative Structure (RP) | Word Study: Loanwords (RP)<br>Conventions and Style: Pronouns and Antecedents (RP) | Research: Research Project (RP) |
| **Assessment** Available online in Assessments | Selection Test | | |
| **My Resources** | A Unit 5 Answer Key is available online and in the Interactive Teacher's Edition. | | |

# Reading Support

| Text Complexity Rubric: Antojos | |
|---|---|
| **Quantitative Measures** | |
| **Lexile:** 980 **Text Length:** 4,146 words | |
| **Qualitative Measures** | |
| Knowledge Demands ①—②—❸—④—⑤ | Some knowledge of the political and economic situation in the Dominican Republic is helpful for full comprehension of the themes and conflicts. |
| Structure ①—❷—③—④—⑤ | Organization of the narrative is mostly sequential, with references to previous events and one flashback. |
| Language Conventionality and Clarity ①—❷—③—④—⑤ | Language is largely explicit, literal, and straightforward. There is some above-level vocabulary and minimal Spanish language vocabulary. |
| Levels of Meaning/Purpose ①—②—❸—④—⑤ | The inner conflicts of the protagonist and the class divisions are somewhat complex and subtle. |

DECIDE AND PLAN

## English Language Support

Provide English Learners with support for knowledge demands and meaning as they read the selection.

**Knowledge Demands** Before reading the text, discuss with students specific words that can be used to describe class divisions and how those words convey the different experiences of people within cultures.

**Meaning** In order to help students describe the inner conflicts of the protagonist, Yolanda, have them note words that express the emotions she experiences in her encounters with other characters in the story. Have them complete sentences such as *When the bus filled with men passes her, Yolanda feels* _____.

## Strategic Support

Provide students with strategic support to ensure that they can successfully read the text.

**Knowledge Demands** After reading the background information, make sure that students understand something of the political and economic situation in the country Yolanda is visiting. Ask students to name some of the issues that might confront a young woman who has lived away from her home county in the United States for many years.

**Meaning** Ask questions about the basic plot elements of the story. For example, *Why don't the aunts want Yolanda to travel by herself in the country? Why does Yolanda think they finally agreed to lend her a car?*

## Challenge

Provide students who need to be challenged with ideas for how they can go beyond a simple interpretation of the text.

**Text Analysis** Ask students to discuss what elements affect Yolanda's response to the men with machetes who find her alone with her car. How much does her consciousness of class differences contribute to her fear? Why does she pretend not to speak Spanish?

**Written Response** Have students write a short essay about the title of the story. Have them use Yolanda's conversation with her aunts to define the word. Then have them discuss how the desire for a particular food, piece of music, or kind of clothing might be an expression of other feelings.

TEACH

## Read and Respond

Have groups read the selection and complete the Making Meaning, Language Development, and Effective Expression activities.

# Standards Support Through Teaching and Learning Cycle

## IDENTIFY NEEDS

Analyze results of the Beginning-of-Year Assessment, focusing on the items relating to Unit 5. Also take into consideration student performance to this point and your observations of where particular students struggle.

## DECIDE AND PLAN

- If students have performed poorly on items matching these standards, then provide selection scaffolds before assigning them the on-level lesson provided in the Student Edition.
- If students have done well on the Beginning-of-Year Assessment, then challenge them to keep progressing and learning by giving them opportunities to practice the skills in depth.
- Use the Selection Resources listed on the Planning pages for "Antojos" to help students continually improve their ability to master the standards.

**Instructional Standards: Antojos**

| | Catching Up | This Year | Looking Forward |
|---|---|---|---|
| **Reading** | You may wish to administer the **Analyze Craft and Structure: Author's Choices: Narrative Structure (RP)** worksheet to help students better understand these narrative techniques. | **RL.5** Analyze how an author's choices concerning how to structure specific parts of a text contribute to its overall structure and meaning as well as its aesthetic impact. | Challenge students to rewrite this selection using a different narrative structure. |
| **Writing** | You may wish to administer the **Research: Research Project (RP)** worksheet to help students prepare for their assignment. | **W.7** Conduct short as well as more sustained research projects to answer a question or solve a problem; narrow or broaden the inquiry when appropriate; synthesize multiple sources on the subject, demonstrating understanding of the subject under investigation. | Challenge students to find other works written about Rafael Trujillo for comparison, or find true stories about other dictators. |
| **Language** | Review the **Word Study: Loanwords (RP)** worksheet with students to better familiarize them with the word origins.<br>Review the **Conventions and Style: Pronouns and Antecedents (RP)** worksheet with students to better familiarize them with pronoun-antecedent agreement. | **L.4.c** Consult general and specialized reference materials, both print and digital, to find the pronunciation of a word or determine or clarify its precise meaning, its part of speech, its etymology, or its standard usage.<br>**L.1** Demonstrate command of the conventions of standard English grammar and usage when writing or speaking. | Challenge students to find new words that are not related to earlier languages.<br>Challenge students to look up pronouns in other languages and determine their similarities and differences. |

## ANALYZE AND REVISE

- Analyze student work for evidence of student learning.
- Identify whether or not students have met the expectations in the standards.
- Identify implications for future instruction.

## TEACH

Implement the planned lesson, and gather evidence of student learning.

## Jump Start

FIRST READ How might you feel traveling alone in a country far from where you now live? What types of problems might you encounter? What would you hope to find? Engage students in a discussion about the adventures and difficulties they might encounter traveling alone.

### Antojos

What are the dangers of traveling to countries in the midst of political or economic struggles? How does the ability to speak the language affect your travel to a foreign country? Modeling these and other questions readers might ask will bring "Antojos" to life and connect it to the Performance Task question. Selection audio and print capability for the selection are available in the Interactive Teacher's Edition.

### Concept Vocabulary

Have groups briefly discuss the three concept vocabulary words. Have they encountered any of the words before? Do they recognize the prefix, suffix, or base word of any of the concept vocabulary words? Have groups consider the strategy of context clues and discuss its advantages and disadvantages.

### FIRST READ

Have students perform the steps of the first read independently:

NOTICE: You may want to encourage students to notice the description of the setting and the main character's thoughts and feelings about the locations in the story.

ANNOTATE: Remind students to mark passages that describe the main character's reactions to the places she travels and the events she experiences.

CONNECT: Encourage students to make connections to their own travel experiences and stories they have heard from people who have traveled to other countries.

RESPOND: Students will demonstrate their understanding of the text by answering questions and writing a summary.

Point out to students that they will perform the first three steps concurrently as they are doing their first read. They will complete the Respond step after they have finished the first read. You may wish to print copies of the **First-Read Guide: Fiction** for students to use.



MAKING MEANING

About the Author

**Julia Alvarez** (b. 1950) was born in New York City but spent much of her childhood in the Dominican Republic. She and her family returned to the United States when her father's participation in a plot to overthrow the dictator Rafael Trujillo was discovered—a move that she considers foundational to her decision to be a writer. Calling writing "a way to understand yourself," Alvarez often draws upon her personal experiences and her Caribbean heritage for inspiration.

# Antojos

## Concept Vocabulary

As you perform your first read of "Antojos," you will encounter the following words.

cantina    cabana    machetes

**Context Clues** If these words are unfamiliar to you, try using **context clues**—other words and phrases that appear in the surrounding text—to help you determine their meanings. Here is an example of how to apply the strategy.

**Unfamiliar Word:** *replete*

**Context:** Although the story lacks action, it is replete with interesting characters.

**Conclusion:** The word *Although* indicates that the words *lacks action* are in contrast or opposition to the word *replete. Replete,* then, must mean something opposite to "lacking"—perhaps "filled."

Apply your knowledge of context clues and other vocabulary strategies to determine the meanings of unfamiliar words you encounter during your first read.

## First Read FICTION

Apply these strategies as you conduct your first read. You will have an opportunity to complete a close read after your first read.

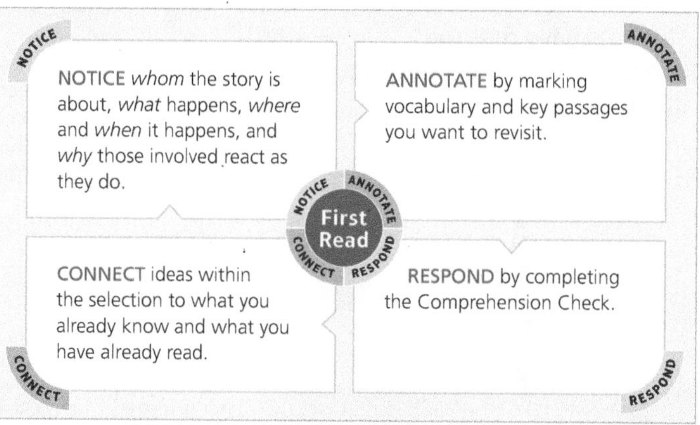

NOTICE
ANNOTATE
NOTICE *whom* the story is about, *what* happens, *where* and *when* it happens, and *why* those involved react as they do.
ANNOTATE by marking vocabulary and key passages you want to revisit.
First Read
CONNECT ideas within the selection to what you already know and what you have already read.
RESPOND by completing the Comprehension Check.
CONNECT
RESPOND


STANDARDS

**Reading Literature**
By the end of grade 11, read and comprehend literature, including stories, dramas, and poems, in the grades 11–CCR text complexity band proficiently, with scaffolding as needed at the high end of the range.

**Language**
- Determine or clarify the meaning of unknown and multiple-meaning words and phrases based on *grades 11–12 reading and content,* choosing flexibly from a range of strategies.
- Use context as a clue to the meaning of a word or phrase.





## VOCABULARY DEVELOPMENT

**Concept Vocabulary Reinforcement** Provide students with additional examples of and practice with the concept vocabulary. Reinforce comprehension by having students work with partners to complete "show-you-know" sentences. After students have completed the practice sentences, encourage them to write their own first-part prompts to share with other pairs.

1. The group of travelers stopped at the *cantina* ______.

**Possible response:** to relax and have something to drink

2. We reserved a *cabana* at the beach ______.

**Possible response:** so we would have shelter from the sun and heat

3. The workers used *machetes* ______.

**Possible response:** to cut their way through the thick vines

DIGITAL PERSPECTIVES

# Antojos

Julia Alvarez

BACKGROUND

Alvarez's homeland, the Dominican Republic, won independence in 1844 after a successful rebellion against Haitian rule. In the century that followed, however, the country suffered through several dictatorships and frequent foreign domination. One of the most ruthless dictators was Rafael Trujillo, who ruled the country with the support of the military and his secret police from 1930 until he was assassinated in 1961. Despite his death, the climate of fear created by Trujillo persisted into the 1980s, flavoring the setting of "Antojos."

SCAN FOR MULTIMEDIA

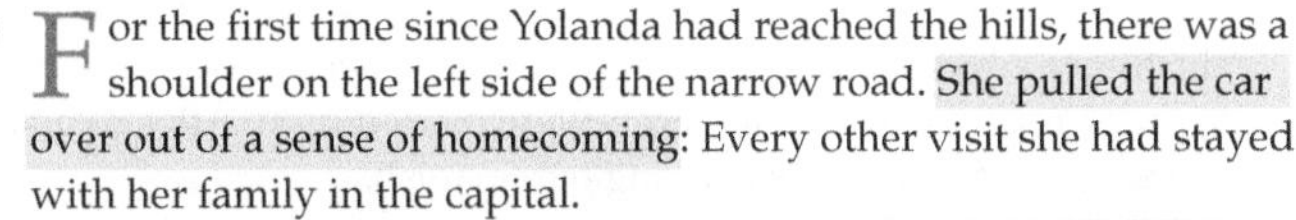

1 For the first time since Yolanda had reached the hills, there was a shoulder on the left side of the narrow road. She pulled the car over out of a sense of homecoming: Every other visit she had stayed with her family in the capital.

2 Once her own engine was off, she heard the sound of another motor, approaching, a pained roar as if the engine were falling apart. She made out an undertow of men's voices. Quickly, she got back into the car, locked the door, and pulled off the shoulder, hugging her right side of the road.

NOTES



## CLOSER LOOK

### Analyze Plot

Circulate among groups as students conduct their close read. Suggest that groups close read paragraphs 1 and 2. Encourage them to talk about the annotations that they mark. If needed, provide the following support.

**ANNOTATE:** Have students mark details in these paragraphs that describe the action in the story, or work with small groups to have students participate while you highlight them together.

**QUESTION:** Guide students to consider what these details might tell them. Ask what a reader can infer from how the story begins, and accept student responses.

**Possible response:** The story begins without any background information. It immediately shows a character in action. She seems to be driving in a dangerous area and is somewhat afraid.

**CONCLUDE:** Help students draw conclusions about the importance of these details in the text. Ask students why the author might have included these details.

**Possible response:** The author seems to want to start the story with something exciting happening. The description of the narrow road and the driver's nervousness about the oncoming car makes readers feel uneasy, but interested to know more.

Remind students that **plot** is the sequence of events in a literary work. Authors can use different techniques to make a story more exciting or immediate. Review the concept of ***in medias res***, which means "in the midst of things." Point out that this technique involves an author beginning the story in the middle of the action rather than providing a background or preamble to set up what is happening. Explain that this technique, often used in film, pulls readers in with action, emotion, and setting, making them want to know what will happen next.

## FACILITATING SMALL-GROUP CLOSE LEARNING

**CLOSE READ: Short Story** As groups perform the close read, circulate and offer support as needed. Suggest groups ask themselves a series of questions before, during, and after reading in order to deepen their understanding and analysis of the text. For example:

- What does the title tell about the story? Does it foreshadow an event or name a particular character? Does it reference something outside of the story?
- Where and when does the story take place? Is the setting an important part of the story? How does the setting contribute to the story's overall meaning?
- What does the main character want? What is standing in her way? From what point-of-view is this story told?
- What problem or problems does the main character encounter? How are the problems resolved?

CLOSER LOOK

## Recognize Flashback

Circulate among groups as students conduct their close read. Suggest that groups close read paragraph 6. Encourage them to talk about the annotations that they mark. If needed, provide the following support.

**ANNOTATE:** Have students mark details in the paragraph that give clues about a change in when and where the action is happening, or work with small groups to have students participate while you highlight them together.

**QUESTION:** Guide students to consider what these details might tell them. Ask what a reader can infer from the abrupt change in time and place, and accept student responses.

**Possible response:** It seems the author is telling about something that happened before Yolanda arrived at this current moment on the road. The phrase "in the capital" shows a change in place and the past perfect verb tense *had plied* shows that the event happened in the past.

**CONCLUDE:** Help students draw conclusions about the importance of these details in the text. Ask students why the author might have included these details.

**Possible response:** The author may have wanted to give some background information about the character and why she is traveling on the road. Now that the reader is interested in the story, the author can add in more details to explain her situation.

Point out that a **flashback** is a scene within a narrative that interrupts the sequence of events to relate an event that occurred in the past. Explain that writers use flashback to show what motivates a character or to reveal something about a character's past. Note that flashback has its roots in narratives that open *in medias res* and provide expository material to introduce the setting, characters, and basic situation after the reader is drawn into the story.

NOTES

3 —Just in time too. A bus came lurching around the curve, obscuring her view with a belching of exhaust, the driver saluting or warning with a series of blasts on his horn. It was an old army bus, the official name brushed over with paint that didn't quite match the regulation gray. The passengers saw her only at the last moment, and all up and down her side of the bus, men poked out of the windows, hooting and yelling, waving purple party flags, holding out bottles and beckoning to her. She speeded up and left them behind, the small compact climbing easily up the snakey highway, its well-oiled hum a gratifying sound after the hullabaloo of the bus.

4 She tried the radio again, but all she could tune to was static even here on the summit hills. She would have to wait until she got to the coast to hear news of the hunger march in the capital. Her family had been worried that trouble would break out, for the march had been scheduled on the anniversary of the failed revolution nineteen years ago today. A huge turnout was expected. She bet that bus she had just passed had been delayed by breakdowns on its way to the capital. In fact, earlier on the road when she had first set out, Yolanda had passed buses and truckloads of men, drinking and shouting slogans. It crossed her mind that her family had finally agreed to loan her a car because they knew she'd be far safer on the north coast than in the capital city where revolutions always broke out.

5 The hills began to plane out into a high plateau, the road widening. Left and right, roadside stands began appearing. Yolanda slowed down and kept an eye out for guavas, supposedly in season this far north. Piled high on wooden stands were fruits she hadn't seen in so many years: pinkish-yellow mangoes, and tamarind pods oozing their rich sap, and small cashew fruits strung on a rope to keep them from bruising each other. There were little brown packets of roasted cashews and bars of milk fudge wrapped in waxed paper and tied with a string, the color of which told what filling was inside the bar. Strips of meat, buzzing with flies, hung from the windows of butcher stalls. An occasional display of straw hats and baskets and hammocks told that tourists sometimes did pass by here. Looking at the stores spread before her, it was hard to believe the poverty the organizers of the march kept discussing on the radio. There seemed to be plenty here to eat—except for guavas.

6 In the capital, her aunts had plied her with what she most craved after so many years away. "Any little *antojo*,[1] you must tell us!" They wanted to spoil her, so she'd stay on in her nativeland before she forgot where she had come from. "What exactly does it mean, *antojo*?" Yolanda asked. Her aunts were proven right: After so many years away, their niece was losing her Spanish.

7 "An *antojo*—" The aunts exchanged quizzical looks. "How to put it? An *antojo* is like a craving for something you have to eat."

8 A cousin blew out her cheeks. "Calories."

1. ***antojo*** (ahn TOH hoh) "craving" (Spanish). The story explores additional connotations of the word.





DIGITAL PERSPECTIVES

**Enriching the Text** Call student attention to the reference to guavas in paragraph 5. Tell students that the guava is a fruit that grows on trees and shrubs in Central and South America. There are many species of guava: the common guava, the cattley, the *cás*, the *guisaro*, and the Brazilian guava. In the story, it is the common guava that Yolanda craves. Encourage students to select one of the fruits or other food items listed in paragraph 5 and go online to research it. Have them create an advertisement for the food item that describes it and explains the different ways it is enjoyed.

9 An *antojo*, one of the older aunts continued, was a very old Spanish word from before "your United States was thought of," she added tartly. In the countryside some *campesinos*[2] still used the word to mean possession by an island spirit demanding its due.

10 Her island spirit certainly was a patient soul, Yolanda joked. She hadn't had her favorite *antojo*, guavas, since her last trip seven years ago. Well, on this trip, her aunts promised, Yoyo could eat guavas to her heart's content. But when the gardener was summoned, he wasn't so sure. Guavas were no longer in season, at least not in the hotter lowlands of the south. Maybe up north, the chauffeur could pick her up some on his way back from some errand. Yolanda took this opportunity to inform her aunts of her plans: She could pick the guavas herself when she went up north in a few days.

11 —She was going up north? By herself? A woman alone on the road! "This is not the States." Her old aunts had tried to dissuade her. "Anything can happen." When Yolanda challenged them, "What?" they came up with boogeymen stories that made her feel as if she were talking to china dolls.[3] Haitian hougans[4] and Communist kidnappers. "And Martians?" Yolanda wanted to tease them. They had led such sheltered lives, riding from one safe place to another in their air-conditioned cars.

12 She had left the fruit stands behind her and was approaching a compound very much like her family's in the capital. The underbrush stopped abruptly at a high concrete wall, topped with broken bottle glass. Parked at the door was a chocolate-brown Mercedes. Perhaps the owners had come up to their country home for the weekend to avoid the troubles in the capital?

13 Just beyond the estate, Yolanda came upon a small village—ALTAMIRA in rippling letters on the corrugated tin roof of the first house. It was a little cluster of houses on either side of the road, a good place to stretch her legs before what she'd heard was a steep and slightly (her aunts had warned "very") dangerous descent to the coast. Yolanda pulled up at a cantina, the thatched roof held up by several posts. Instead of a menu, there was a yellowing, grimy poster for Palmolive soap tacked on one of the posts with a picture of a blonde woman under a spraying shower, her head thrown back in seeming ecstasy, her mouth opened in a wordless cry. ("Palmolive?" Yolanda wondered.) She felt even thirstier and grimier looking at this lathered beauty after her hot day on the road.

14 An old woman emerged at last from a shack behind the cabana, buttoning up a torn housedress, and followed closely by a little boy, who kept ducking behind her whenever Yolanda smiled at him. Asking him his name just drove him further into the folds of the old woman's skirt.

NOTES

Mark context clues or indicate another strategy you used that helped you determine meaning.

**cantina** (kan TEE nuh) *n.*

MEANING:

**cabana** (kuh BAN uh) *n.*

MEANING:

2. **campesinos** (kahm pay SEE nohs) "poor farmers; simple rural dwellers" (Spanish).
3. **china dolls** old-fashioned, delicate dolls made of fragile, high-quality porcelain or ceramic ware.
4. **Haitian hougans** (oo GAHNZ) voodoo priests or cult leaders.





DIGITAL PERSPECTIVES

## Concept Vocabulary

**CANTINA** If groups are struggling to define the word *cantina* in paragraph 13, suggest they use context clues to determine the word's meaning. Draw students' attention to the context clues *thatched roof held up by several posts, menu,* and *felt thirstier,* and have students use these context clues to define the word.

Possible responses: *Cantina* means "a bar or restaurant."

**CABANA** If groups are struggling to define the word *cabana* in paragraph 14, suggest they use context clues to determine the word's meaning. Draw students' attention to the context clues *emerged from* and *shack*, and have students use these context clues to define the word.

Possible response: Here a *cabana* seems to mean "a small structure, or hut."

Additional **English Language Support** is available in the Interactive Teacher's Edition.

PERSONALIZE FOR LEARNING

### Challenge

**Setting and Characters** Review paragraphs 10 through 14. Have students analyze the settings and characters introduced in these paragraphs. For each concrete detail the author provides, have students speculate about why the author included that detail and what conclusions readers can draw from it.

**CLOSER LOOK**

## Analyze Cultural Context

Circulate among groups as students conduct their close read. Suggest that groups close read paragraphs 15–17, and 23. Encourage them to talk about the annotations that they mark. If needed, provide the following support.

**ANNOTATE:** Have students mark details in these paragraphs that highlight details about the cultural, political, and social environment of the story's setting, or work with small groups while you highlight them together.

**QUESTION:** Guide students to consider what these details might tell them. Ask what a reader can infer about the setting from the children's behavior, the boy's name, and the way the older woman treats Yolanda, and accept student responses.

**Possible response:** The country has undergone a political transformation, and children are named after liberators. People are free, but live in poverty. There is an economic divide, and the boys don't see many cars. The older woman thinks Yolanda is from wealth and calls her *the doña* and asks how she can "serve" her.

**CONCLUDE:** Help students draw conclusions about the importance of these details in the text. Ask students why the author might have included these details.

**Possible response:** These details give information about the setting and show how it is different from the one Yolanda comes from. The description offers a contrast to the idyllic setting that Yolanda hopes to experience, and explains why her family worries about her traveling alone.

Explain that the **cultural context** of a literary work is the economic, social, and historical environment the characters inhabit. This includes the attitudes and customs of the culture's historical era. Point out that authors often include details unique to a geographic region.

NOTES

15 "You must excuse him, doña,"[5] she apologized. "He's not used to being among people." But Yolanda knew the old woman meant, not the people in the village, but the people with money who drove through Altamira to the beaches on the coast. "Your name," the old woman repeated, as if Yolanda hadn't asked him in Spanish. The little boy mumbled at the ground. "Speak up!" the old woman scolded, but her voice betrayed pride when she spoke up for him. "This little know-nothing is José Duarte Sánchez y Mella García."

16 Yolanda laughed. Not only were those a lot of names for such a little boy, but they certainly were momentous: the surnames of the three liberators of the country!

17 "Can I serve the doña in any way?" the woman asked. Yolanda gave the tree line beyond the woman's shack a glance. "You think you might have some guavas around?"

18 The old woman's face scrunched up. "Guavas?" she murmured and thought to herself a second. "Why, they're all around, doña. But I can't say as I've seen any."

19 "With your permission—" José Duarte had joined a group of little boys who had come out of nowhere and were milling around the car, boasting how many automobiles they had ridden in. At Yolanda's mention of guavas, he sprung forward, pointing across the road towards the summit of the western hills. "I know where there's a whole grove of them." Behind him, his little companions nodded.

20 "Go on, then!" His grandmother stamped her foot as if she were scatting a little animal. "Get the doña some."

21 A few boys dashed across the road and disappeared up a steep path on the hillside, but before José could follow, Yolanda called him back. She wanted to go along too. The little boy looked towards his grandmother, unsure of what to think. The old woman shook her head. The doña would get hot, her nice clothes would get all dirty. José would get the doña as many guavas as she was wanting.

22 "But they taste so much better when you've picked them yourself." Yolanda's voice had an edge, for suddenly, it was as if the woman had turned into the long arm of her family, keeping her away from seeing her country on her own.

23 The few boys who had stayed behind with José had congregated around the car. Each one claimed to be guarding it for the doña. It occurred to Yolanda that there was a way to make this a treat all the way around. "What do you say we take the car?"

24 "*Sí, Sí, Sí*,"[6] the boys screamed in a riot of excitement.

25 The old woman hushed them but agreed that was not a bad idea if the doña insisted on going. There was a dirt road up ahead she could follow a ways and then cross over onto the road that was paved all the way to the coffee barns. The woman pointed south in the direction of the big house. Many workers took that short cut to work.

5. **doña** (DOH nyah) "madam" (Spanish).
6. ***Sí, Sí, Sí*** (see) "Yes, Yes, Yes" (Spanish).





**PERSONALIZE FOR LEARNING**

**Strategic Support**

**Review Plot** Review paragraphs 1–25. Have students recall what has happened to this point in the short story. Invite them to write a short summary of the events that have happened.

Have students use past tense verb construction in their summaries and include simple transition words such as *first, next,* and *last* to show the sequence of events. **EMERGING**

Have students use past tense and past perfect tense to show the difference between events of the story and the flashback elements included by the author. Encourage students to include transition words such as *meanwhile, however,* and *on the other hand.* **EXPANDING**

Have students write their summaries using past and past perfect tense. Then have them add one or two sentences predicting what they think will happen next. Remind students to use future tense verbs for their predictions. **BRIDGING**

726 UNIT 5 • FACING OUR FEARS

DIGITAL PERSPECTIVES

26 They piled into the car, half a dozen boys in the back, and José as co-pilot in the passenger seat beside Yolanda. They turned onto a bumpy road off the highway, which got bumpier and bumpier, and climbed up into wilder, more desolate country. Branches scraped the sides and pebbles pelted the underside of the car. Yolanda wanted to turn back, but there was no room to maneuver the car around. Finally, with a great snapping of twigs and thrashing of branches across the windshield, as if the countryside were loath to release them, the car burst forth onto smooth pavement and the light of day. On either side of the road were groves of guava trees. Among them, the boys who had gone ahead on foot were already pulling down branches and shaking loose a rain of guavas. The fruit was definitely in season.

27 For the next hour or so, Yolanda and her crew scavenged the grove, the best of the pick going into the beach basket Yolanda had gotten out of the trunk, with the exception of the ones she ate right on the spot, relishing the slightly bumpy feel of the skin in her hand, devouring the crunchy, sweet white meat. The boys watched her, surprised by her odd hunger.

NOTES

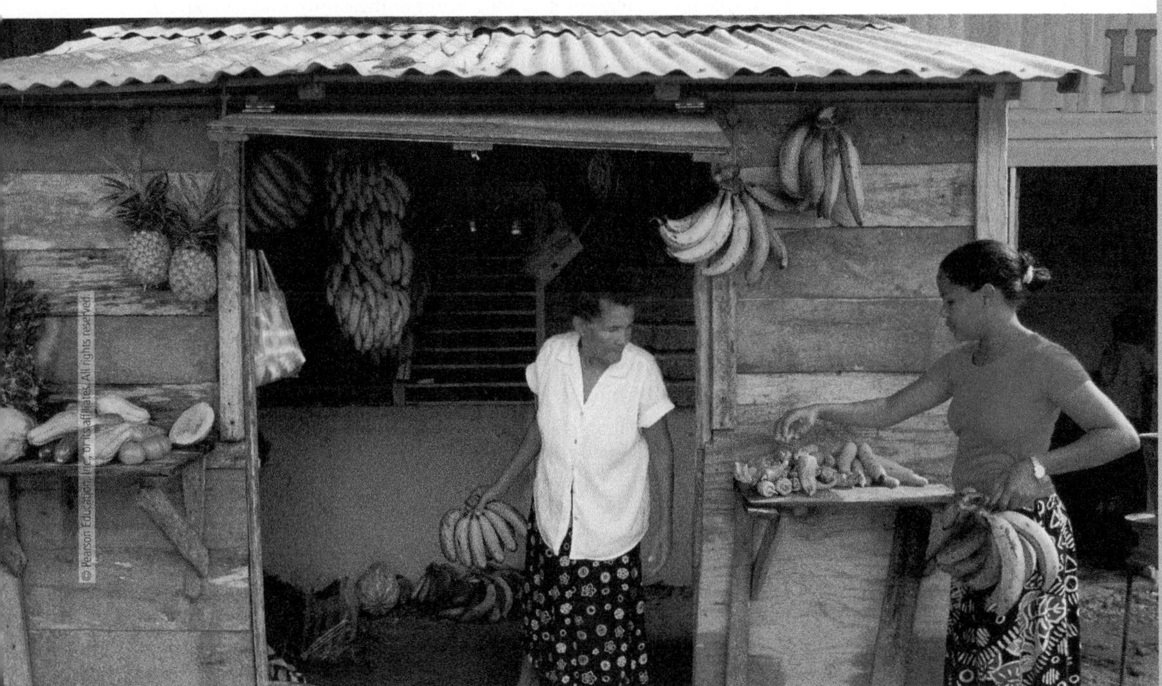




**WriteNow**

**Express and Reflect** Review paragraph 27. Have students choose a food that holds special significance for them as guavas do for Yolanda. Have students find out all they can about the food and then blend some of this information with their feelings. Then have them write an explanation about why they chose the food as their favorite. Challenge students to incorporate their research, their own feelings, and their personal experiences into their writing.

NOTES

28 Yolanda and José, partners, wandered far from the path that cut through the grove. Soon they were bent double to avoid getting entangled in the thick canopy of branches overhead. Each addition to the basket caused a spill from the stash already piled high above the brim. Finally, it was a case of abandoning the treasure in order to cart some of it home. With José hugging the basket to himself and Yolanda parting the wayward branches in front of them, they headed back toward the car.

29 When they cleared the thicket of guava branches, the sun was low on the western horizon. There was no sign of the other boys. "They must have gone to round up the goats," José observed.

30 Yolanda glanced at her watch: It was past six o'clock. She'd never make the north coast by nightfall, but at least she could get off the dangerous mountain roads while it was still light. She hurried José back to the car, where they found a heap of guavas the other boys had left behind on the shoulder of the road. Enough guavas to appease even the greediest island spirit for life!

31 They packed the guavas in the trunk quickly and climbed in, but the car had not gone a foot before it lurched forward with a horrible hobble. Yolanda closed her eyes and laid her head down on the wheel, then glanced over at José. The way his eyes were searching the inside of the car for a clue as to what could have happened, she could tell he didn't know how to change a flat tire either.

32 It was no use regretting having brought the car up that bad stretch of road. The thing to do now was to act quickly. Soon the sun would set and night would fall swiftly, no lingering dusk as in the States. She explained to José that they had a flat tire and had to hike back to town and send for help down the road to the big house. Whoever tended to the brown Mercedes would know how to change the tire on her car.

33 "With your permission," José offered meekly. He pointed down the paved road. "This goes directly to the big house." The doña could just wait in the car and he would be back in no time with someone from the Miranda place.

34 She did not like the idea of staying behind in the car, but José could probably go and come back much quicker without her. "All right," she said to the boy. "I'll tell you what." She pointed to her watch. It was almost six thirty. "If you're back by the time this hand is over here, I'll give you"—she held up one finger—"a dollar." The boy's mouth fell open. In no time, he had shot out of his side of the car and was headed at a run toward the Miranda place. Yolanda climbed out as well and walked down a pace, until the boy had disappeared in one of the turnings of the road.

35 Suddenly, the countryside was so very quiet. She looked up at the purple sky. A breeze was blowing through the grove, rustling the leaves, so they whispered like voices, something indistinct. Here and there a light flickered on the hills, a *campesino* living out his solitary life. This was what she had been missing without really knowing





## HOW LANGUAGE WORKS

**Personal Pronouns** Remind students that a pronoun is a word that takes the place of a noun, a group of words acting as a noun, or another pronoun. Point out that personal pronouns refer to a specific person or thing. These pronouns can be singular or plural. They can be first person, second person, or third person. They are male, female, or neutral in gender and can perform in the subject or object case of a sentence. Provide examples of various personal pronouns in different forms and have students identify the number, person, gender, and case in each sentence.

*She* likes to have coffee with *us*. (*she*: singular/female/third person/subject; *us*: plural/male or female, depending on the situation/first person/object)

*It* looks great on *you*! (*it*: singular/neuter/third person/subject; *you*: singular or plural, depending on the situation/male or female, depending on the situation/second person/object)

Then have students work in pairs to locate and identify personal pronouns in paragraph 34.

that she was missing it all these years. She had never felt at home in the States, never, though she knew she was lucky to have a job, so she could afford her own life and not be run by her family. But independence didn't have to be exile. She could come home, home to places like these very hills, and live here on her own terms.

36 Heading back to the car, Yolanda stopped. She had heard footsteps in the grove. Could José be back already? Branches were being thrust aside, twigs snapped. Suddenly, a short, dark man, and then a slender, light-skinned man emerged from a footpath on the opposite side of the grove from the one she and José had scavenged. They wore ragged work clothes stained with patches of sweat; their faces were drawn and tired. Yolanda's glance fell on the **machetes** that hung from their belts.

37 The men's faces snapped awake from their stupor at the sight of her. They looked beyond her at the car. "Yours?" the darker man spoke first. It struck her, even then, as an absurd question. Who else's would it be here in the middle of nowhere?

38 "Is there some problem?" the darker man spoke up again. The taller one was looking her up and down with interest. They were now both in front of her on the road, blocking her escape. Both—she had looked them up and down as well—were strong and quite capable of catching her if she made a run for the Mirandas'. Not that she could have moved, for her legs seemed suddenly to have been hammered into the ground beneath her. She thought of explaining that she was just out for a drive before dinner at the big house, so that these men would think someone knew where she was, someone would come looking for her if they tried to carry her off. But she found she could not speak. Her tongue felt as if it'd been stuffed in her mouth like a rag to keep her quiet.

They were now both in front of her on the road, blocking her escape.

39 The men exchanged a look—it seemed to Yolanda of collusion. Then the shorter, darker one spoke up again. "Señorita,[7] are you all right?" He peered at her. The darkness of his complexion in the growing darkness of the evening made it difficult to distinguish an expression. He was no taller than Yolanda, but he gave the impression of being quite large, for he was broad and solid, like something not yet completely carved out of a piece of wood. His companion was tall and of a rich honey-brown color that matched his honey-brown eyes. Anywhere else, Yolanda would have found him extremely attractive, but here on a lonely road, with the sky growing darker by seconds, his good looks seemed dangerous, a lure to catch her off her guard.

40 "Can we help you?" the shorter man repeated.

41 The handsome one smiled knowingly. Two long, deep dimples appeared like gashes on either side of his mouth. "*Americana*,"

7. **Señorita** (say nyoh REE tah) "Miss" (Spanish).

NOTES

Mark context clues or indicate another strategy you used that helped you determine meaning.

**machetes** (muh SHEHT eez) *n.*

MEANING:





DIGITAL PERSPECTIVES

## Concept Vocabulary

**MACHETES** If groups are struggling to define the word *machetes* in paragraph 36, suggest they use context clues to determine the word's meaning. Draw students' attention to the context clues *wore ragged work clothes* and *hung from their belts,* and have students use these context clues to define the word.

**Possible responses:** *Machetes* must be some kind of cutting tool or knife.

## PERSONALIZE FOR LEARNING

### Strategic Support

**Analyze Character** Review paragraphs 36 through 39. Have students chart the trajectory of Yolanda's emotions in her initial encounter with the men. Prompt the discussion by asking questions such as: *How does Yolanda feel as she walks outside the car? How do her feelings change when she sees the men? Why is Yolanda afraid of the men? Are her fears rational?*

Suggest students create a visual representation of these emotions and mark each rise and fall with a specific plot point.

## CLOSER LOOK

### Explore Point of View

Circulate among groups as students conduct their close read. Suggest that groups close read paragraphs 43–45. Encourage them to talk about the annotations that they mark. If needed, provide the following support.

**ANNOTATE:** Have students mark details in these paragraphs that show from what point of view the story is being told, or work with small groups to have students participate while you highlight them together.

**QUESTION:** Guide students to consider what these details might tell them. Ask what a reader can infer from what was annotated, and accept student responses.

**Possible response:** The story tells only what Yolanda is thinking and doing. It is not first-person point of view, but we do know what is going on inside her head because the text says, "She thought of something…" We also know how Yolanda is feeling when, for example, the text says, "it soothed her…"

**CONCLUDE:** Help students draw conclusions about the importance of these details in the text. Ask students why the author might have included these details.

**Possible response:** The author may have included these details because they add to the emotion of the scene. We can feel how Yolanda is feeling on this darkening road as two strange men approach her. It almost gives the reader the feeling of being inside her head and feeling the fear and anxiety with her.

Remind students that **point of view** is the perspective, or vantage point, from which a story is told. It is determined by what type of **narrator**, or voice, is telling the story. A story told from the **limited third-person point of view** is told by a narrator who sees the world through a single character's eyes and reveals only what that character is experiencing, thinking, or feeling. Not every narrative is told from a unified point of view. Sometimes a short story or novel includes different sections told by different narrators.

NOTES

he said to the other in Spanish, pointing to the car. "She doesn't understand."

42 The darker man narrowed his eyes and studied Yolanda a moment. "*Americana?*" he asked her as if not quite sure what to make of her.

43 She had been too frightened to carry out any strategy, but now a road was opening before her. She laid her hand on her chest—she could feel her pounding heart—and nodded. Then, as if the admission itself loosened her tongue, she explained in English how it came that she was on a back road by herself, her craving for guavas, her never having learned to change a flat. The two men stared at her, uncomprehendingly, rendered docile by her gibberish. Strangely enough, it soothed her to hear herself speaking something they could not understand. She thought of something her teacher used to say to her when as a young immigrant girl she was learning English, "Language is power." It was her only defense now.

44 Yolanda made the motions of pumping. The darker man looked at the other, who had shown better luck at understanding the foreign lady. But his companion shrugged, baffled as well. "I'll show you." Yolanda waved for them to follow her. And suddenly, as if after pulling and pulling at roots, she had finally managed to yank them free of the soil they had clung to, she found she could move her own feet forward to the car.

45 The small group stood staring at the sagging tire a moment, the two men kicking at it as if punishing it for having failed the señorita. They squatted by the passenger's side, conversing in low tones. Yolanda led them to the rear of the car, where the men lifted the spare out of its sunken nest—then set to work, fitting the interlocking pieces of the jack, unpacking the tools from the deeper hollows of the trunk. They laid their machetes down on the side of the road, out of the way. Yolanda turned on the headlights to help them see in the growing darkness. Above the small group, the sky was purple with twilight.

46 There was a problem with the jack. It squeaked and labored, but the car would not rise. The shorter man squirmed his way underneath and placed the mechanism deeper under the bowels of the car. There, he pumped vigorously, his friend bracing him by holding him down by the ankles. Slowly, the car rose until the wheel hung suspended. When the man came out from under the car, his hand was bloody where his knuckles had scraped against the pavement.

47 Yolanda pointed to the man's hand. She had been sure that if any blood were going to be spilled tonight, it would be hers. She offered him the towel she kept draped on her car seat to absorb her perspiration. But he waved it away and sucked his knuckles to make the bleeding stop.

48 Once the flat had been replaced with the spare, the two men lifted the deflated tire into the trunk and put away the tools. They handed Yolanda her keys. There was still no sign of José and the Mirandas. Yolanda was relieved. As she had waited, watching the two men hard





## CROSS-CURRICULAR PERSPECTIVES

**Science** Point out the description in paragraph 47 of the man sucking the blood from his scraped knuckles. Tell students that while this may seem like an unsanitary practice, scientists have researched the effectiveness of using saliva on minor abrasions and found it to be very helpful in the healing process. Have students work in pairs to research the protein histatin, found in saliva, and write a short report explaining why it works and what promises it might hold for the future of wound care.

at work, she had begun to dread the boy's return with help. The two men would realize she spoke Spanish. It was too late to admit that she had tricked them, to explain she had done so only because she thought her survival was on the line. The least she could do now was to try and repay them, handsomely, for their trouble.

NOTES

49 "I'd like to give you something." She began reaching for the purse she'd retrieved from the trunk. The English words sounded hollow on her tongue. She rolled up a couple of American bills and offered them to the men. The shorter man held up his hand. Yolanda could see where the blood had dried dark streaks on his palm. *"No, no, señorita. Nuestro placer."*[8] Our pleasure.

50 Yolanda turned to the other man, who had struck her as more pliant than his sterner companion. "Please," she urged the bills on him. But he too looked down at the ground with the bashfulness she had observed in José of country people not wanting to offend. She felt the poverty of her response and stuffed the bills quickly into his pocket.

51 The two men picked up their machetes and raised them to their shoulders like soldiers their guns. The tall man motioned towards the big house. *"Directo, directo."*[9] He enunciated the words carefully. Yolanda looked in the direction of his hand. In the faint light of what was left of day, she could barely make out the road ahead. It was as if the guava grove had overgrown into the road and woven its mat of branches so securely and tightly in all directions, she would not be able to escape.

52 But finally, she was off! While the two men waited a moment on the shoulder to see if the tire would hold, Yolanda drove a few yards, poking her head out the window before speeding up. *"Gracias!"*[10] she called, and they waved, appreciatively, at the foreign lady making an effort in their native tongue. When she looked for them in her rear-view mirror, they had disappeared into the darkness of the guava grove.

53 Just ahead, her lights described the figure of a small boy: José was walking alone, listlessly, as if he did not particularly want to get to where he was going.

54 Yolanda leaned over and opened the door for him. The small overhead light came on; she saw that the boy's face was streaked with tears.

55 "Why, what's wrong, José?"

56 The boy swallowed hard. "They would not come. They didn't believe me." He took little breaths between words to keep his tears at bay. He had lost his chance at a whole dollar. "And the guard, he said if I didn't stop telling stories, he was going to whip me."

57 "What did you tell him, José?"



8. ***Nuestro placer*** (noo AYS troh plah SAYR) "Our pleasure" (Spanish).
9. ***Directo, directo*** (dee REHK toh) "Straight, straight" (Spanish).
10. ***Gracias*** (GRAH see ahs) "Thank you" (Spanish).



## PERSONALIZE FOR LEARNING

### English Language Support

**Connecting Ideas** Review paragraphs 48 through 56. Have students demonstrate their understanding of the events that took place between Yolanda and the men by connecting ideas and showing how details are related. For example, the men fixed Yolanda's car, so she wanted to give them money as payment. Invite pairs to practice making sentences that show connections between events. Suggest they continue to discuss why José came back without help and why he reacted with tears when speaking to Yolanda. **EMERGING**

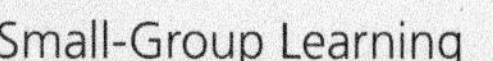

NOTES

58 "I told him you had broken your car and you needed help fixing it."

59 She should have gone along with José to the Mirandas'. Given all the trouble in the country, they would be suspicious of a boy coming to their door at nightfall with some story about a lady on a back road with a broken car. "Don't you worry, José." Yolanda patted the boy. She could feel the bony shoulder through the thin fabric of his worn shirt. "You can still have your dollar. You did your part."

60 But the shame of being suspected of lying seemed to have obscured any immediate pleasure he might feel in her offer. Yolanda tried to distract him by asking what he would buy with his money, what he most craved, thinking that on a subsequent trip, she might bring him his little *antojo*. But José Duarte Sánchez y Mella said nothing, except a bashful thank you when she left him off at the cantina with his promised dollar. In the glow of the headlights, Yolanda made out the figure of the old woman in the black square of her doorway, waving goodbye. Above the picnic table on a near post, the Palmolive woman's skin shone; her head was thrown back, her mouth opened as if she were calling someone over a great distance. ❧





## PERSONALIZE FOR LEARNING

### Strategic Support

**Clarify the Sentence** Review paragraph 60. Students may need help in understanding the lengthy sentence "Yolanda tried to distract him by asking what he would buy with his money, what he most craved, thinking that on a subsequent trip, she might bring him his little *antojo*." Point out that the commas set off Yolanda's different thoughts. Have students rewrite the sentence vertically, breaking each line at the comma. Then work with them to clarify each part of the sentence and how it contributes to the whole meaning.

| | |
|---|---|
| Yolanda tried to distract him by asking what he would buy with his money | *She was trying to make him feel better by talking about what he would buy with his money.* |
| what he most craved | *She wanted him to think about what he wanted most.* |
| thinking that on a subsequent trip | *She might come back to see him again.* |
| she might bring him his little *antojo*. | *If she did, she would bring the thing he wanted most.* |

## Comprehension Check

Complete these items after you finish your first read. Review and clarify details with your group.

1. What political event is taking place in the city as Yolanda drives into the hills?

2. Whom does Yolanda meet at a roadside cantina?

3. What are *antojos*?

4. As Yolanda and José start to leave the guava grove, what happens to the car?

5. What does Yolanda pretend when she is approached by the two men?

6. **Notebook** Confirm your understanding of the text by creating a storyboard of key events.

### RESEARCH

**Research to Clarify** Choose at least one unfamiliar detail from the text. Briefly research that detail. In what way does the information you learned shed light on an aspect of the story?

**Research to Explore** Conduct research on an aspect of the text you find interesting. For example, you may want to learn about the history and culture of the Dominican Republic.





DIGITAL PERSPECTIVES

## Comprehension Check

Possible responses:

1. People are going on a hunger march in the capital city as Yolanda is driving through the hills.
2. Yolanda meets an old woman and a little boy.
3. *Antojos* are cravings for certain foods.
4. The car lurches forward because of a flat tire.
5. She pretends that she is American and does not speak Spanish.
6. Responses will vary. Students should include key events such as: Yolanda drives through the hills and pulls off the road. She has an encounter with a bus of rowdy locals and recalls her aunts' warnings not to travel alone. She meets José and the older woman. José goes with her to find guavas. After picking fruit, they get a flat tire. José offers to go for help. Two men wander by. At first Yolanda is afraid, but the men help her. José returns saddened because he could not get help. Yolanda takes him home and tries unsuccessfully to cheer him up.

## Research

**Research to Clarify** If students are having difficulty choosing an unfamiliar detail, then suggest they select from the geography of the Dominican Republic, the political structure and climate of the Dominican Republic, the capital city Santo Domingo, or the agricultural practices of farmers in the Dominican Republic.

**Research to Explore** If students are struggling to choose which topic most interests them from the text, then suggest they research Juan Pablo Duarte, Matías Ramón Mella, Francisco del Rosario Sánchez, housing and building materials of the region, climate and weather conditions in the Dominican Republic, or games and sports popular with children of the area.

PERSONALIZE FOR LEARNING

### Challenge

**Research Cultures** People from many different cultures live in the Dominican Republic. Encourage students to research one of these cultures. Point out that students should consider the history of the Dominican Republic and how each cultural group arrived there. Have them create a multi-media presentation complete with images, and if possible, video and sound or music clips representing elements of the region.

# FACILITATING

## Jump Start

**CLOSE READ** Engage students in a discussion of how fear can be an obstacle to accomplishing one's dreams and goals.

## Close Read the Text 

Model close reading as needed by using the Annotation Highlights in the Interactive Teacher's Edition.

Remind groups to use Accountable Talk in their discussions and to support one another as they complete the close read.

## Analyze the Text

**Possible responses:**

1. The fact that there is a hunger march suggests that some of the country's citizens are unhappy with their leaders and their economic situation.
2. Passages will vary by group.
3. Responses will vary.

## Concept Vocabulary

**Why These Words?**

Possible response: The words all come directly from the Spanish language. They give the story an authentic and regional feel, making it easier for the reader to experience the cultural context.

### Practice

**Possible responses:** The **cantina** served local drinks and was popular with tourists.The flimsy walls and roof of the **cabana** shifted as the storm winds began to blow. The workers used **machetes** to cut the coconuts from the tops of the trees.

### Word Network

**Possible words:** *boogeyman, hougans, troubles, dangerous, frightened, desolate, survival, dread*

## Word Study

For more support, see **Concept Vocabulary and Word Study.**

**Possible responses:** *plateau* means "flat elevated land" and comes from French; *mango* means "a sweet tropical fruit" and comes from Portuguese; *hammock* means "a hanging bed made of net or cloth" and comes from Spanish.

MAKING MEANING

ANTOJOS

## Close Read the Text

With your group, revisit sections of the text you marked during your first read. **Annotate** what you notice. What **questions** do you have? What can you **conclude?**

## Analyze the Text

**CITE TEXTUAL EVIDENCE** to support your answers.

**Notebook** Complete the activities.

1. **Review and Clarify** With your group, reread paragraphs 1–4 of "Antojos." What do these paragraphs suggest about the country's political situation and the economic issues that shape the story?
2. **Present and Discuss** Now, work with your group to share the passages from the selection that you found especially important. Take turns presenting your passages. Discuss what you noticed in the selection, what questions you asked, and what conclusions you reached.
3. **Essential Question:** *How do we respond when challenged by fear?* What have you learned about people's responses to fear from reading this story? Discuss with your group.

LANGUAGE DEVELOPMENT

## Concept Vocabulary

cantina    cabana    machetes

**Why These Words?** The three concept vocabulary words are related. With your group, determine what the words have in common. How do these word choices enhance the impact of the text?

**Practice**

**Notebook** Confirm your understanding of the concept vocabulary words by using them in sentences. Include context clues that hint at each word's meaning.

## Word Study

**Notebook** **Loanwords** A **loanword** is a word that one language borrows from another language and makes its own. The English language is rich with loanwords; for instance, *cantina*, *cabana*, and *machetes* are all borrowed from Spanish. Use a dictionary to look up these loanwords from paragraph 5 of "Antojos": *plateau, mango, hammock*. For each word, write down its meaning and the language from which it is borrowed.

**WORD NETWORK**

Add words related to fear from the text to your Word Network.

**STANDARDS**

**Reading Literature**

- Analyze the impact of the author's choices regarding how to develop and relate elements of a story or drama.
- Analyze how an author's choices concerning how to structure specific parts of a text contribute to its overall structure and meaning as well as its aesthetic impact.

**Language**

Consult general and specialized reference materials, both print and digital, to find the pronunciation of a word or determine or clarify its precise meaning, its part of speech, its etymology, or its standard usage.





## FORMATIVE ASSESSMENT

### Analyze the Text

**If** students struggle to close read the text, then provide the **Antojos: Text Questions** available in the Interactive Teacher's Edition or Unit Resources. Answers and DOK levels are also available.

### Concept Vocabulary

**If** students struggle to identify the concept, **then** have them locate each word in context and think about how the Spanish word origin adds to their understanding of the sentences.

### Word Study

**If** students fail to find words borrowed from foreign languages, **then** suggest they begin by identifying words that are most unfamiliar to them and search these words in an online etymology dictionary. For Reteach and Practice, see **Word Study: Loanwords (RP).**

## Analyze Craft and Structure

**Author's Choices: Narrative Structure** Many stories begin at the start of a series of events and continue in a straightforward time sequence known as **chronological order**. However, some writers use a variety of different plot devices that play with the order of events, thus helping to build interest and suspense.

- ***In medias res:*** This term is Latin for "in the middle of things." When a story begins *in medias res*, the reader is dropped directly into the action. Introductory segments, or exposition, that tell the reader who characters are and what has already happened are omitted.
- **Flashback:** A flashback is a scene from the past that interrupts the present action of a story. A writer may present a flashback as a character's memory, a story told by a character, or a dream or daydream.
- **Foreshadowing:** Foreshadowing is the placing of textual clues to suggest events that have yet to occur. Foreshadowing often seeds details that contribute to a particular mood or atmosphere.

Alvarez uses all of these plot devices to provide background information, heighten suspense, and add interest and excitement to this story.

### Practice

CITE TEXTUAL EVIDENCE to support your answers.

Analyze Alvarez's use of plot devices in this story. Work together as a group to complete the chart.

| PASSAGE | PLOT DEVICE | SIGNIFICANT DETAILS | EFFECT |
|---|---|---|---|
| paragraphs 1–3 | in medias res | the narrow curving road; the bus filled with rowdy men; no radio signal | sets the scene for a dangerous and remote location |
| paragraphs 6–11 | flashback | loving, protective aunts who spoiled her; Yolanda is forgetting her Spanish; aunts warnings of danger | gives the impression that Yolanda has lost touch with the current condition of her native land; her aunts seem wise and protective |
| paragraph 26 | foreshadowing | bumpy road; desolate country; narrow path; closing in of branches | gives a foreboding of something dangerous and bad to come |





DIGITAL PERSPECTIVES

## Analyze Craft and Structure

**Author's Choices: Narrative Structure** Tell students that the term *in medias res* finds its roots in the wisdom of ancient writers. The Roman poet Horace advised aspiring writers to go straight to the heart of the story instead of beginning at the beginning. Homer likewise used this technique in the *Iliad* and the *Odyssey*. The *Iliad* begins with a dramatic battle between Achilles and Agamemnon during the Trojan War. Explain that though its roots are in ancient epic poems, *in medias res* is used today in both fiction and nonfiction. Note the technique is commonly employed by both film and television screenwriters. For more support, see **Analyze Craft and Structure: Author's Choices: Narrative Structure.**

See possible responses in chart on student page.

### FORMATIVE ASSESSMENT

### Analyze Craft and Structure

**If** students struggle to differentiate between the plot devices, **then** have them associate *flashback* with *past*, *in medias res* with *present*, and *foreshadowing* with *future*. For Reteach and Practice, see **Analyze Craft and Structure: Narrative Structure (RP)**.

## PERSONALIZE FOR LEARNING

### English Language Development

**Using Context as Clue to Meaning** Read paragraph 9 in the selection where one of the aunts says, "before 'your United States was thought of... '" Help students infer its meaning by considering the context and speakers involved.

Ask students to work in pairs to explain why they think the aunt used the word *your* before mentioning the United States. **EMERGING**

Ask students to write a paragraph about why the aunt might point at the States as a "new" country or culture, and in what ways the same idea is expressed in the selection. **EXPANDING**

Ask students to write a paragraph explaining in what ways this passage condenses ideas that are developed throughout the selection. **BRIDGING**

An expanded **English Language Development Lesson** on Using Context as Clue to Meaning is available in the Interactive Teacher's Edition.

# FACILITATING

## Conventions and Style

**Pronouns and Antecedents** Point out that some kinds of nouns and pronouns require special attention when looking at pronoun and antecedent agreement. When a collective noun refers to a group as a single unit, a singular pronoun is used.

The *team* decided *it* wanted to ride the bus.

If the collective noun refers to the group's members as individuals, then a plural pronoun is used.

The *team* wore *their* commemorative jerseys for the game.

Explain that students should use singular pronouns to refer to indefinite pronouns (such as *everybody, none, nobody, someone*) used as antecedents. *Everybody* at the game received *his* or *her* own souvenir t-shirt. *Each* of the boys chose *his* favorite color.

For more support, see **Conventions and Style: Pronouns and Antecedents.**

### Read It

Possible responses:

1. *They were now both looking her up and down with interest.* Antecedents: they-darker man/taller one, her-Yolanda; *...so that these men would think someone knew where she was, someone would come looking for her if they tried to carry her off.* Antecedents: she/her-Yolanda, they-these men
2. **Connect to Style** Paragraph 44: his-darker man; you-the men; them-the men; her/she-Yolanda; them/they-roots; she/her-Yolanda; Paragraph 45: it-sagging tire; They-the men; them-the men; its-spare tire; They/their-the men; them-the men; Paragraph 46: It-the jack; his-the shorter man; he-the shorter man; his/him-the shorter man. Possible response: Using pronouns effectively helps the reader understand what is happening with the action. It is easy to shift between the men's actions, the car, and Yolanda because the pronouns are clearly linked with their antecedents.

### Write It

Responses will vary.

---

**FORMATIVE ASSESSMENT**

### Conventions and Style

If students are having difficulty matching pronouns with their antecedents, then have them read the sentences aloud and consider: *Whom or what is being referred to? Whom or what is this pronoun acting in place of?* For Reteach and Practice, see **Conventions and Style: Pronouns and Antecedents (RP).**



LANGUAGE DEVELOPMENT

ANTOJOS

## Conventions and Style

**Pronouns and Antecedents** A **pronoun** is a word that stands for a noun, a noun phrase, or another pronoun—known as the pronoun's **antecedent**. A pronoun and its antecedent must agree in number (singular or plural), person (first, second, or third), and gender (feminine, masculine, or neuter).

Pronouns are useful because they allow speakers and writers to avoid the repetition of nouns and noun phrases, which may be awkward or cumbersome. However, a pronoun should be used only when its antecedent is clear to the listener or reader. Consider these sentences:

*Maya sent Gloria an email during* ***her*** *trip to Italy.*

*Kirk told Malik that* ***he*** *would be elected team captain.*

In each sentence, the antecedent of the pronoun is unclear. Who was traveling in Italy: Maya or Gloria? Who would be elected captain: Kirk or Malik?

When you notice an ambiguous pronoun in your writing, try restructuring the sentence so that the pronoun and antecedent are closer together. Alternatively, try repeating the antecedent for clarity. Notice that the antecedents are clear in these revised sentences:

*During Maya's trip to Italy,* ***she*** *sent Gloria an email.*

*Kirk told Malik that* ***he****, Kirk, would be elected team captain.*

### Read It

1. Reread paragraph 38 of "Antojos," and note the multiple switches of pronouns and antecedents. Mark three pronouns in the paragraph, and identify their antecedents.
2. **Connect to Style** Reread paragraphs 44–46. Mark the personal pronouns, and identify their antecedents. As a group, compare your annotations. Then, working individually, explain in a few sentences how the careful use of pronouns helps make the events of this story clear.

### Write It

Write a paragraph describing a trip or voyage you've taken with a friend or family member. Use at least five personal pronouns in your paragraph. Make sure that the antecedent for each pronoun is clear.

**STANDARDS**

**Language**
Demonstrate command of the conventions of standard English grammar and usage when writing or speaking.





HOW LANGUAGE WORKS

**Pronouns and Antecedents** Explain to students that pronouns usually refer to someone or something that was already mentioned in a sentence or in a previous sentence. However, in many sections of "Antojos," the singular pronoun *she* was repeated without direct connection to Yolanda. Point out that this is acceptable if there are no conflicting antecedents, such as multiple female characters in the scene. In general, it is best to closely connect pronouns with their antecedents so as to avoid confusion.

Have students write sentences with pronouns. Then have them draw an arrow from each pronoun to its antecedent. Have students exchange sentences with a partner and verify that the pronouns agree with the antecedents they identified.

# EFFECTIVE EXPRESSION

## Research

**Assignment**

Choose one of the following **research project** options.

- ☐ **Timeline** Create a timeline of the key events of the dictatorship of Rafael Trujillo in the Dominican Republic, covering the years 1930–1961. Events that you may want to include are the Parsley Massacre, Hurricane San Zenón, the Batista imprisonment, the Betancourt assassination attempt, and Trujillo's assassination.
- ☐ **Map** Create a map of the Dominican Republic indicating the route Yolanda may have traveled to get from Santo Domingo through the mountains to Altamira, together with a description of that route.
- ☐ **Field-Guide Entry** Create a field-guide entry for the guava plant, *Psidium guajava*, including facts and diagrams about how and where it grows.

In your report, include a section in which you explain how the information you researched contributes to your understanding of the characters, setting, and conflicts depicted in "Antojos" by Julia Alvarez.

**EVIDENCE LOG**

Before moving on to a new selection, go to your Evidence Log and record what you learned from "Antojos."

**STANDARDS**

Writing

Conduct short as well as more sustained research projects to answer a question or solve a problem; narrow or broaden the inquiry when appropriate; synthesize multiple sources on the subject, demonstrating understanding of the subject under investigation.

**Research Plan** Use the chart to record the tasks you will need to accomplish as your group progresses through the assignment. With your group, decide how you will divide up the research and writing tasks necessary to complete the work.

| INFORMATION NEEDED | IMAGES OR MEDIA NEEDED | SOURCES TO USE | WRITING TASKS TO COMPLETE |
|---|---|---|---|
| | | | |
| | | | |
| | | | |





## PERSONALIZE FOR LEARNING

### English Language Support

**Sharing Opinions** Students may struggle to express their opinions and persuade others when working in small groups. Suggest students take a few moments to gather their thoughts and ideas and make notes prior to beginning the group discussion and planning session. Then provide frames for support to enable students to engage in negotiation. For example: *Could you repeat that please? I believe _____ because _____. You make a valid point, but my view is _____. I see that you believe that _____, but I have a different idea. I think that _____.* **ALL LEVELS**

DIGITAL PERSPECTIVES 

## Research

Encourage groups to consider any special interests or talents they may have that would draw them toward one or the other of the assignment options. For example, those who feel most comfortable with linear, fact-focused projects may gravitate toward the timeline. Those who feel particularly drawn to artistic projects may select the map, and those who enjoy scientific research may select the field-guide entry. Remind students that everyone in the group need not exhibit the same strengths, but each person must contribute something to the final outcome.

**Research Plan** As students work to complete the planning chart, have them also divide the research work and determine who will be responsible for finding each identified element. Suggest they write the name of the person assigned to each task in the corresponding box of their planning chart.

For more support, see **Research: Research Project.**

**Evidence Log** Support students in completing their Evidence Log. This paced activity will help prepare them for the Performance-Based Assessment at the end of the unit.

### FORMATIVE ASSESSMENT

### Research

**If** students struggle to identify what research is needed for their project, **then** have them break apart the prompt and make a list of all the important technical and domain specific vocabulary. Suggest they use these words as a springboard for researching their topic. For Reteach and Practice, see **Research: Research Project (RP).**

### Selection Test

Administer the "Anotojos" Selection Test, which is available in both print and digital formats online in Assessments.

## Present an Argument

Before groups begin work on their projects, have them clearly differentiate the role each group member will play. Remind groups to consult the schedule for Small-Group Learning to guide their work during the Performance Task.

Students should complete the assignment using presentation software to take advantage of text, graphics, and sound features.

## Plan With Your Group

**Analyze the Prompt** Remind students that although some of the examples they identify in the texts support the opposing point of view, it is useful for them to know and understand them. Explain that it is useful in a debate to be able to see how someone might reach the opposite conclusion than the one you are supporting. When debaters know and appreciate the other side's arguments, they are in a stronger position to respond to and neutralize opposing viewpoints.

**Gather Evidence and Media Examples** Suggest that students think about and gather examples of how people deal with fear from their own experience as well as from movies, television, and current events. Connecting history and literature to personal and present-day situations makes it easier for people to understand and empathize with people from the past.

PERFORMANCE TASK: SPEAKING AND LISTENING FOCUS

SOURCES

- *from* FAREWELL TO MANZANAR
- INTERVIEW WITH GEORGE TAKEI
- ANTOJOS

# Present an Argument

**Assignment**

You have read an autobiography, watched an interview, and read a short story about people who are either affected by other people's fears or face their own. Work with your group to plan and present a **debate** on this question:

**Do people usually learn from their fear?**

Divide into teams on opposite sides of the argument. Find examples from the texts that you can cite to support your ideas. Then, conduct your debate for the class.

## Plan With Your Group

**Analyze the Prompt** Divide into two subgroups. One will support the "yes" response to the question, and the other will support the "no" response. With your subgroup, discuss how the people and characters in the selections respond to their fears. Consider both the actions of the people telling the stories and those of the people or characters they describe. Decide which details and examples from the texts provide the most relevant support for your side of the debate.

| TITLE | WHO EXPERIENCES FEAR? | HOW DO THEY RESPOND? |
|---|---|---|
| *from* Farewell to Manzanar | | |
| Interview With George Takei | | |
| Antojos | | |
| The most logical examples in support of our side are: | | |

STANDARDS

**Speaking and Listening**

Propel conversations by posing and responding to questions that probe reasoning and evidence; ensure a hearing for a full range of positions on a topic or issue; clarify, verify, or challenge ideas and conclusions; and promote divergent and creative perspectives.

**Gather Evidence and Media Examples** Find details from the texts and interview that you will cite in support of your side of the debate. Note that your personal opinion may not the be the same as the one you will argue. Choose the evidence that best supports your assigned position. If they are relevant and you are comfortable sharing, you may also refer to personal experiences or anecdotes from your own life. Make sure all members of your subgroup make suggestions and contribute to the discussion.





AUTHOR'S PERSPECTIVE **Ernest Morrell, Ph.D.**

**Digital Speech** Since "a picture is worth a thousand words," help students find and use effective images for oral presentations. Remind students to give full credit to visual sources, as they would for print ones. Teachers can guide students to create rhetorically powerful digital presentations such as slideshows, blogs, and online forums using these suggestions:

- *Keep it simple.* Choose one striking image rather than several smaller ones. Position the visual carefully, allowing "white space" to make the image stand out.
- *Go for quality.* Choose clear, high-quality images or take high-resolution photos.
- *Limit bullet points and text.* The most effective slideshows have limited text. Suggest that slides should have no more than six words across and six lines down of text.
- *Choose color and font carefully.* Cool colors (blues, greens) work best for backgrounds; warm colors (orange, red) work best for objects in the foreground. Use a simple, standard font such as Arial or Helvetica.

Last, teachers can help students create a rubric to assess presentations.

**Organize Your Debate** Work together to come up with a list of main points in support of your group's claim, as well as a list of details, examples, and other evidence to support each point. Divide these points and corresponding evidence evenly among group members. Brainstorm some counterarguments that the other side may use to refute your points. Decide how you might respond to each counterargument.

## Rehearse With Your Group

**Practice With Your Group** As you prepare to participate in the debate, use this checklist to evaluate the effectiveness of your group's practice sessions. Then, use your evaluation and the instructions here to guide improvements.

| CONTENT | EFFECTIVENESS | PRESENTATION TECHNIQUES |
|---|---|---|
| ☐ The speakers present and defend a claim.<br>☐ The main ideas are supported with evidence from the texts in Small-Group Learning. | ☐ The language used is well chosen and appropriate for the audience and purpose.<br>☐ The speakers acknowledge and refute counterarguments. | ☐ The speakers enunciate clearly and respond to one another respectfully.<br>☐ The speakers use vocal tone, eye contact, and body language to emphasize key points. |

**Fine-Tune the Content** Does each speaker from your side have sufficient evidence to support his or her claim? If not, work with your subgroup to locate more evidence.

**Improve Your Debate Form** Keep your language formal and objective as you debate the topic. Refute counterarguments clearly and respectfully. If needed, return to the texts and look for more details and examples to support your points.

**Brush Up on Your Presentation Techniques** A key part of a debate is responding to the opposition's ideas. Remember to listen carefully to what the other team says and respond thoughtfully.

## Present and Evaluate

As you present your debate, work as a group. Support your teammates and build on each other's points to support your claim and refute counterclaims. As you watch other groups debate, think about how well they meet the requirements on the checklist.

STANDARDS

**Speaking and Listening**
Present information, findings, and supporting evidence, conveying a clear and distinct perspective and a logical argument, such that listeners can follow the line of reasoning, alternative or opposing perspectives are addressed, and the organization, development, substance, and style are appropriate to purpose, audience, and a range of formal and informal tasks.





DIGITAL PERSPECTIVES

**Organize Your Debate** Remind groups that refuting the opposing team's argument and responding to their effort to refute yours are very important steps in preparing for a debate.

## Rehearse With Your Group

**Practice With Your Group** Remind students to have each group member practice his or her argument ahead of time. Other group members should provide constructive feedback so that all group members can improve their performance for the final debate. Rehearsing can also help students determine how much time their arguments take. They might find that they have much more content than they will have time to present. Knowing that ahead of time will give them an opportunity to rectify the situation.

**Fine-Tune the Content** Suggest that when students listen to their teammates present their portion of the debate, they listen as though they were on the other team looking for weak links in the argument. When they share their thinking with their teammates, they should remember that they are working together to make a stronger performance, so it is best to present their feedback in a constructive manner.

**Improve Your Debate Form** Remind students to focus their rebuttals on the content of the other team's argument and evidence rather than attacking the individuals who are presenting.

## Present and Evaluate

Before beginning the presentations, set the expectations for the audience. You may wish to have students consider these questions as groups present:

- What evidence did the presenting group present to support their claim?
- From which sources did the presenting group select its evidence?
- How effective was the evidence in supporting the claim?
- What were the group's strongest presentation skills?

PERSONALIZE FOR LEARNING

### Strategic Support

**Understanding Evidence** Be prepared to assist students in understanding how their evidence represents a response to fear. Model for students:

- *I think that the people who decided to place Japanese Americans in internment camps were responding to their fear, believing that locking up Japanese Americans would keep them safe. I think that listening to George Takei helps people learn that that is not a good way to respond to fear.*
- *In from* Farewell from Manzanar, *the women who gossiped about the author's father were probably afraid of what would happen to them, so they criticized and mocked their neighbor. In the part of the autobiography that we read, they did not learn to respond differently to their fear.*

# OVERVIEW

## INDEPENDENT LEARNING

### How do we respond when challenged by fear?

Encourage students to think carefully about what they have already learned and what more they want to know about the unit topic of facing our fears. This is a key first step to previewing and selecting the text or media they will read or review in Independent Learning.

### Independent Learning Strategies

Review the Learning Strategies with students and explain that as they work through Independent Learning they will develop strategies to work on their own.

- Have students watch the video on Independent Learning Strategies.
- A video on this topic is available online in the Professional Development Center.

Students should include any favorite strategies that they might have devised on their own during Whole-Class and Small-Group Learning. For example, for the strategy "Participate fully," students might include:

- Actively engage in the discussion, even if only by asking a question.
- Bring in a related article or story to share with the group.

### Block Scheduling

Each day in this Pacing Plan represents a 40–50 minute class period. Teachers using block scheduling may combine days to reflect their class schedule. In addition, teachers may revise pacing to differentiate and support core instruction by integrating components and resources as students require.

## OVERVIEW: INDEPENDENT LEARNING

ESSENTIAL QUESTION:

# How do we respond when challenged by fear?

Is the way in which we respond to fear an essential part of each of our identities as individuals? Is it a key part of a communal or national identity? In this section, you will complete your study of responses to fear by exploring an additional selection related to the topic. You'll then share what you learn with classmates. To choose a text, follow these steps.

**Look Back** Think about the selections you have already studied. What more do you want to know about the topic of fear?

**Look Ahead** Preview the texts by reading the descriptions. Which one seems most interesting and appealing to you?

**Look Inside** Take a few minutes to scan the text you chose. Choose a different one if this text doesn't meet your needs.

## Independent Learning Strategies

Throughout your life, in school, in your community, and in your career, you will need to rely on yourself to learn and work on your own. Review these strategies and the actions you can take to practice them during Independent Learning. Add ideas of your own to each category.

| STRATEGY | ACTION PLAN |
|---|---|
| Create a schedule | • Understand your goals and deadlines.<br>• Make a plan for what to do each day.<br>• |
| Practice what you have learned | • Use first-read and close-read strategies to deepen your understanding.<br>• After you read, evaluate the usefulness of the evidence to help you understand the topic.<br>• Consult reference sources for additional information that can help you clarify meaning.<br>• |
| Take notes | • Record important ideas and information.<br>• Review your notes before preparing to share with a group.<br>• |

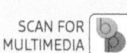



SCAN FOR MULTIMEDIA



## Pacing Plan

Introduce Whole-Class Learning

Unit Introduction — 1

Historical Perspectives — 3

The Crucible, Act I — 4, 5

The Crucible, Act II — 6, 7

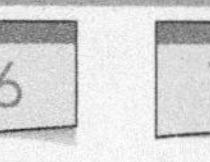

The Crucible, Act III — 8, 9

The Crucible, Act IV — 10, 11

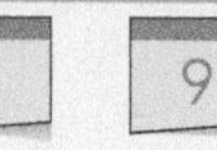

Media: The Crucible — 12, 13

Performance Task — 14, 15

1 2 3 4 5 6 7 8 9 10 11 12 13 14 15

## CONTENTS

Choose one selection. Selections are available online only.

MAGAZINE ARTICLE

### What You Don't Know Can Kill You

*Jason Daley*

Are we simply scared of the wrong things?

POETRY

### Runagate Runagate *Robert Hayden*

The hunger for freedom overrides the terror of capture among enslaved Africans fleeing to the North.

POETRY COLLECTION

### 1-800-FEAR *Jody Gladding*

### Bears at Raspberry Time *Hayden Carruth*

### For Black Women Who Are Afraid *Toi Derricotte*

These poems address fears of both real and imagined dangers.

ESSAY

### What Are You So Afraid Of?

*Akiko Busch*

What are the origins of fear, and are they pointing us in the wrong direction?

PERFORMANCE-BASED ASSESSMENT PREP

### Review Evidence for an Argument

Complete your Evidence Log for the unit by evaluating what you have learned and synthesizing the information you have recorded.

SCAN FOR MULTIMEDIA





DIGITAL PERSPECTIVES

## Contents

**Selections** Encourage students to scan and preview the selections before choosing the one they would like to read or review. Suggest that they consider the genre and subject matter of each one before making their decision. You can use the information on the following Planning pages to advise students in making their choice.

Remind students that the selections for Independent Learning are only available in the Interactive Student Edition. Allow students who do not have digital access at home to preview the selections using classroom or computer lab technology. Then either have students print the selection they choose or provide a printout for them.

## Performance Based-Assessment Prep

**Review Evidence for an Argument** Point out to students that collecting evidence during Independent Learning is the last step in completing their Evidence Log. After they finish their independent reading, they will synthesize all the evidence they have compiled in the unit.

The evidence students collect will serve as the primary source of information they will use to complete the writing and oral presentation for the Performance-Based Assessment at the end of the unit.

Introduce Small-Group Learning

*from* Farewell to Manzanar

Media: Interview with George Takei

Antojos

Performance Task

Introduce Independent Learning

Independent Learning

Performance-Based Assessment

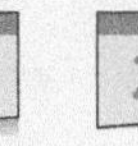

27 28 29 30

INDEPENDENT LEARNING

SELECTION RESOURCES

- First-Read Guide: Nonfiction
- Close-Read Guide: Nonfiction
- What You Don't Know Can Kill You: Text Questions
- Audio Summaries
- Selection Audio
- Selection Test

# What You Don't Know Can Kill You

## Summary

In the article "What You Don't Know Can Kill You," Jason Daley describes research about misperceptions people have about risk in their daily lives. The author begins by discussing the behavior of people after the Japanese earthquake and tsunami that destroyed a nuclear reactor. The author notes that, despite the fact that Americans were in no danger from the accident, many Californians bought iodide pills to stop possible physical illness from radiation. The author provides other examples such as threats from smoking, traffic accidents, and nanotechnology. Frequently, our idea of risk does not match reality. Illogical behavior in the face of little or no risk is common and, according to Daley, is hard-wired in our brains. Scientists have studied the way people make decisions. They have discovered that personal beliefs often get in the way of the truth. People are more afraid of things that are covered in the news, even though events like shark attacks and airplane accidents are very rare compared to more common dangers such as heart disease. Communicating actual facts about such risks does little to change irrational behavior and has little effect on public policies toward risk.

## Insight

Scientists study human mental strategies for determining what to fear. This article includes a list of causes of death which helps put risks in perspective.

## Connection to Essential Question

This selection, "What You Don't Know Can Kill You," may help students better understand the Essential Question—"How do we respond when challenged by fear?" According to the article, people often rate situations and events as more risky than they actually are based on preconceptions of what they fear.

## Connection to Performance-Based Assessment

This selection will help students respond to the question, "Is fear always a harmful emotion?" Students may note that the author clearly states that from an evolutionary viewpoint fear has provided a way to respond successfully to dangerous situations. Nonetheless, the author argues that we often over focus on illusionary threats at the expense of real ones.

### Text Complexity Rubric: What You Don't Know Can Kill You

| Quantitative Measures | |
|---|---|
| **Lexile:** 1390 **Text Length:** 3,815 words | |
| **Qualitative Measures** | |
| Knowledge Demands ①—②—③—❹—⑤ | The text deals with information from a number of fields of science. Although the ideas are clearly explained, a certain amount of previous knowledge is helpful. |
| Structure ①—②—③—❹—⑤ | The structure of the article is a series of virtually self-contained examples supporting the author's point. It is possible to lose sight of the author's point. |
| Language Conventionality and Clarity ①—②—③—❹—⑤ | Sentences often contain embedded clauses and/or long participial phrases that may require syntactical analysis, slowing comprehension. There is considerable above-level vocabulary |
| Levels of Meaning/Purpose ①—②—③—❹—⑤ | Meaning and purpose are straightforward—a explanation of why people are bad at calculating risks. |

DIGITAL PERSPECTIVES 

Audio | Video | Document | Annotation Highlights | EL Highlights | Online Assessment

SELECTION RESOURCES

- First-Read Guide: Poetry
- Close-Read Guide: Poetry
- Runagate Runagate: Text Questions
- Audio Summaries
- Selection Audio
- Selection Test

# Runagate Runagate

## Summary

In the poem "Runagate Runagate" by Robert Hayden, the poet employs a number of voices to describe the tense, desperate flight of runaway slaves trying to reach freedom in the North by means of the Underground Railroad. The first section opens with the escaping slaves running, falling, and stumbling in the darkness, following lanterns that lead the way to the "mythic North" and "star-shaped yonder Bible city." The second section focuses on Harriet Tubman, describing how she leads those escaping on the Underground Railroad physically and spiritually. Words from wanted posters call her "Stealer of Slaves," and the poet uses these and other voices to portray her forcefully. The poem ends with the musical lines: "Come ride-a my train / Mean mean mean to be free."

## Insight

The poet Robert Hayden uses rhythmic meters to suggest the frantic pace of the slaves as they escape. These same rhythms mimic the rumbling of a train, a reference to the idea of the Underground Railroad that Harriet Tubman ran.

## Connection to Essential Question

This selection, "Runagate Runagate," connects to the Essential Question, "How do we respond when challenged by fear?" According to the poem, runaway slaves experienced extreme fear on their paths to freedom in the north.

## Connection to Performance-Based Assessment

This selection will help students respond to the question, "Is fear always a harmful emotion?" Students may note that it is the fear runaway slaves experience that drives them as they run to freedom.

### Text Complexity Rubric: Runagate Runagate

| Quantitative Measures | |
|---|---|
| **Lexile:** NP **Text Length:** 73 lines | |
| **Qualitative Measures** | |
| Knowledge Demands (1 ❷ 3 4 5) | Comprehension depends on basic knowledge of slavery in the American South during the antebellum period. |
| Structure (1 2 3 ❹ 5) | The structure of the poem, while powerful, is not linear, as narrative blends with voice and comment. |
| Language Conventionality and Clarity (1 2 ❸ 4 5) | Much of the syntax is unconventional and, while most of the vocabulary is on-level, a few allusions and archaic words may be challenging. |
| Levels of Meaning/Purpose (1 ❷ 3 4 5) | The desperation of escaping slaves is compelling and unambiguous. |

# 1-800-FEAR • Bears at Raspberry Time • For Black Women Who Are Afraid

**SELECTION RESOURCES**

- First-Read Guide: Poetry
- Close-Read Guide: Poetry
- Poetry Collection: Text Questions
- Audio Summaries
- Selection Audio
- Selection Test

## Summary

Jody Gladding's poem "1-800-FEAR" describes a brief interaction between the speaker and a group of people who have come to talk about living in fear. The speaker turns them away and they ask whether there are others nearby who might be interested.

In the poem "Bears at Raspberry Time" by Hayden Carruth, the speaker sees a mother bear and three cubs looking for berries. The speaker is not afraid of the bears, but is afraid someone will shoot them. He also worries about unfinished work but enjoys a moment in the middle of the night when the bears seem to be in sight.

In the poem "For Black Women Who Are Afraid" by Toi Derricotte, the speaker talks with a black woman at a writing workshop. The woman is afraid to read her poem because it is about a white woman and she fears that the others might not understand. The speaker tells the woman to write a poem about being afraid to write.

## Insight

These poems show that there are a variety of fears that humans have. Many are personal and focused on their own experiences.

## Connection to Essential Question

These poems, "1-800-FEAR," "Bears at Raspberry Time," and "For Black Women Who Are Afraid" connect to the Essential Question, "How do we respond when challenged by fear?" Students should note that the speakers in each of all these poems recognize the cause of fear and deal with what is frightening without becoming paralyzed or overwhelmed.

## Connection to Performance-Based Assessment

This poetry collection will help students respond to the question, "Is fear always a harmful emotion?" Students may note that in these poems fear is used to help the speakers or people they are addressing to accomplish goals.

### Text Complexity Rubric: 1-800-FEAR • Bears at Raspberry Time • For Black Women Who Are Afraid

| Quantitative Measures | |
|---|---|
| **Lexile:** NP; NP; NP **Text Length:** 11 lines; 49 lines; 17 lines | |
| **Qualitative Measures** | |
| Knowledge Demands ①—②—❸—④—⑤ | Understanding some of these poems requires life experience or the literary knowledge of trying to do creative work and meeting deadlines. |
| Structure ①—②—❸—④—⑤ | The narrative structures include much that is implicit rather than explicit. "1-800-FEAR" is prose poetry. |
| Language Conventionality and Clarity ①—②—③—❹—⑤ | The language in these poems mixes the abstract and the concrete with a fairly sophisticated use of irony and figurative language. |
| Levels of Meaning/Purpose ①—②—❸—④—⑤ | The texts operate on multiple levels of complex meaning concerning the theme of fear. |

DIGITAL PERSPECTIVES — Audio | Video | Document | Annotation Highlights | EL Highlights | Online Assessment

# What Are You So Afraid Of?

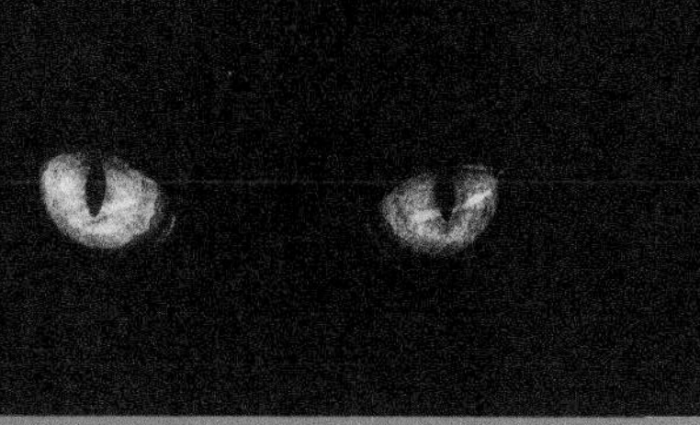

SELECTION RESOURCES

- First-Read Guide: Nonfiction
- Close-Read Guide: Nonfiction
- What Are You So Afraid Of?: Text Questions
- Audio Summaries
- Selection Audio
- Selection Test

## Summary

In the essay, "What Are You So Afraid Of?," Akiko Busch wonders if humans are afraid of the right things. She begins by questioning whether her fear of snakes results from her own childhood encounter with a dangerous snake or from humanity's thousands of years of such encounters. The author believes that the mix of our genetic-based fears and our personal experience is essential to our survival. However, she asserts that we often fear the wrong things in our lives. Many Americans were panicked by an Ebola virus outbreak even though they are much more likely to die from the flu. Atmospheric carbon and extreme weather are much more likely to harm us than insects, reptiles, and heights. The author cites E.O. Wilson who says that humans are not fearful of dangerous electricity, knives, and cars because humanity has not had enough time to become hard-wired with these fears. This means that people are not afraid of the things that should scare them—the current social, political, and environmental events around them.

## Insight

This essay provides a personal, not a scientific or quantitative, approach to the origins of fear. While asserting that our fears may be a combination of inherited traits and responses to actual dangers, the author stresses that people, nonetheless, often focus their fear or anxieties on situations and things that have a low probability of occurrence while ignoring others that present actual physical danger.

## Connection to Essential Question

This selection connects to the Essential Question, "How do we respond when challenged by fear?" According to the article, people often are fearful of things that are not real dangers. People's fears instead are based on genetic-predisposition to things that were dangerous during our evolution.

## Connection to Performance-Based Assessment

This selection will help students respond to the question, "Is fear always a harmful emotion?" Students may note that the author believes that evolution has provided people with instinctual fears of things that were commonly dangerous in the past but not commonly dangerous today.

### Text Complexity Rubric: What Are You So Afraid Of?

| Quantitative Measures | |
|---|---|
| **Lexile:** 1280 **Text Length:** 795 words | |
| **Qualitative Measures** | |
| Knowledge Demands: 3 (scale 1–5) | The text explores a single somewhat complex theme from a single perspective. The experiences portrayed are fairly common. |
| Structure: 2 (scale 1–5) | The text uses a straightforward organization of presenting a main idea and supporting it with anecdotes and information. |
| Language Conventionality and Clarity: 4 (scale 1–5) | Sentences sometimes contain embedded clauses and/or long participial phrases. There is some above-level vocabulary |
| Levels of Meaning/Purpose: 3 (scale 1–5) | The article operates on only one level of meaning, which has a certain complexity to it. |

MY NOTES

DIGITAL PERSPECTIVES

Audio

Video

Document

Annotation Highlights

EL Highlights

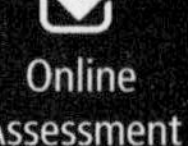
Online Assessment

MY NOTES

# ADVISING

You may wish to direct students to use the generic **First-Read** and **Close-Read Guides** in the Print Student Edition. Alternatively, you may wish to print copies of the genre-specific **First-Read** and **Close-Read Guides** for students. These are available online in the Interactive Student Edition or Unit Resources.

## FIRST READ

Students should perform the steps of the first read independently:

NOTICE: Students should focus on the basic elements of the text to ensure they understand what is happening.

ANNOTATE: Students should mark any passages they wish to revisit during their close read.

CONNECT: Students should increase their understanding by connecting what they've read to other texts or personal experiences.

RESPOND: Students will write a summary to demonstrate their understanding.

Point out to students that while they will always complete the Respond step at the end of the first read, the other steps will probably happen somewhat concurrently. Remind students that they will revisit their first-read annotations during the close read.

After students have completed the First-Read Guide, you may wish to assign the Text Questions for the selection that are available in the Interactive Teacher's Edition.

### Anchor Standards

In the first two sections of the unit, students worked with the whole class and in small groups to gain topical knowledge and greater understanding of the skills required by the anchor standards. In this section, they are asked to work independently, applying what they have learned and demonstrating increased readiness for college and career.

## INDEPENDENT LEARNING

### First-Read Guide

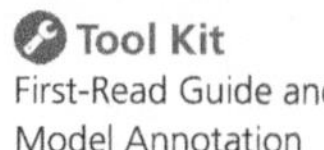


Use this page to record your first-read ideas.

Selection Title: ______________________

**NOTICE** new information or ideas you learned about the unit topic as you first read this text.

**ANNOTATE** by marking vocabulary and key passages you want to revisit.

**CONNECT** ideas within the selection to other knowledge and the selections you have read.

**RESPOND** by writing a brief summary of the selection.



STANDARD

**Reading** Read and comprehend complex literary and informational texts independently and proficiently.



## PERSONALIZE FOR LEARNING

### English Language Support

**Writing a Summary** Support students who struggle to write a text summary. Have them review their first-read coded annotations for key ideas ("*"). Give students these guidelines:

- Identify the text title and author then briefly paraphrase the author's ideas or plot.
- Present the main ideas for nonfiction texts and descriptions of important elements for literary texts (i.e., main character(s), setting, point of view).
- Use transitional words and phrases to signal the relationships among ideas such as order of events or order of importance.
- Have students work with partners to review their summaries for the main ideas and important details, as well as to make suggestions for the use of transitions. **ALL LEVELS**

DIGITAL PERSPECTIVES 

## Close-Read Guide

**Tool Kit**
Close-Read Guide and Model Annotation

Use this page to record your close-read ideas.

Selection Title: ______________________________

### Close Read the Text

Revisit sections of the text you marked during your first read. Read these sections closely and **annotate** what you notice. Ask yourself **questions** about the text. What can you **conclude?** Write down your ideas.

### Analyze the Text

Think about the author's choices of patterns, structure, techniques, and ideas included in the text. Select one and record your thoughts about what this choice conveys.

### QuickWrite

Pick a paragraph from the text that grabbed your interest. Explain the power of this passage.



STANDARD
**Reading** Read and comprehend complex literary and informational texts independently and proficiently.



### CLOSE READ

Students should begin their close read by revisiting the annotations they made during their first read. Then, students should analyze one of the author's choices regarding the following elements:

- **plot devices,** such as flashbacks or foreshadowing
- **structure,** such as chronological or *in media res*
- **devices,** such as dramatic irony or verbal irony
- **conflict,** whether internal conflict or external conflict

**MAKE IT INTERACTIVE**
Group students according to the selection they have chosen. Then, have students meet to discuss the selection in depth. Their discussion should be guided by their insights and questions.

### PERSONALIZE FOR LEARNING

**Challenge**
**Sharing in Pairs** Extend the independent reading experience for students who are ready. Have students work with partners who have selected a different independent reading text. Student pairs can take turns talking about the texts they read. Encourage students to reference their First-Read Guide summaries and their Close-Read Guide entries as they share their ideas. Ask students to discuss the annotations that helped them unlock text meaning. Once students have introduced each text, ask partners to compare and contrast their texts in terms of the topic or genre, main ideas and details, text structure, or author's craft. You may wish to have student pairs report their text comparisons to the rest of the class, inviting participation and additional ideas from other students.

# ADVISING

## Share Your Independent Learning

### Prepare to Share

Explain to students that sharing what they learned from their Independent Learning selection provides classmates who read a different selection with an opportunity to consider the text as a source of evidence during the Performance-Based Assessment. As students prepare to share, remind them to highlight how their selection contributed to their knowledge of the concept of facing our fears as well as how the selection connects to the question *Is fear always a harmful emotion?*

### Learn from Your Classmates

As students discuss the Independent Learning selections, direct them to take particular note of how their classmates' chosen selections align with their current position on the Performance-Based Assessment question.

### Reflect

Students may want to add their reflection to their Evidence Log, particularly if their insight relates to a specific selection from the unit.

**MAKE IT INTERACTIVE**

Group students in pairs, making sure that each half of the pair read a different selection. Have each student interview his or her partner about the selection the partner chose. Encourage them to focus on the connections between the text, the Essential Question, and the insights. You may choose to suggest topics for questions, such as what annotations, questions, or conclusions led up to the insight, why it resonates with the student, and how it might inform the student's approach to the Performance-Based Assessment.

**Evidence Log** Support students in completing their Evidence Log. This paced activity will help prepare them for the Performance-Based Assessment at the end of the unit.

# INDEPENDENT LEARNING

**EVIDENCE LOG**

Go to your Evidence Log and record what you learned from the text you read.

## Share Your Independent Learning

**Prepare to Share**

Is fear always a harmful emotion?

Even when you read something independently, your understanding continues to grow when you share what you have learned with others. Reflect on the text you explored independently, and write notes about its connection to the unit. In your notes, consider why this text belongs in this unit.

**Learn from Your Classmates**

**Discuss It** Share your ideas about the text you explored on your own. As you talk with your classmates, jot down ideas that you learn from them.

**Reflect**

Review your notes, and mark the most important insight you gained from these writing and discussion activities. Explain how this idea adds to your understanding of the topic of fear.

**STANDARDS**

**Speaking and Listening**

Initiate and participate effectively in a range of collaborative discussions with diverse partners on *grades 11–12 topics, texts, and issues,* building on others' ideas and expressing their own clearly and persuasively.





**AUTHOR'S PERSPECTIVE** Ernest Morrell, Ph.D.

**Powerful Speaking in Small Groups** Explain to students that learning how to speak with confidence, without over-compensating, will help them make and/or defend an argument and point of view in a small group. Point out that their goal is to be convincing, but not argumentative. To help build this skill, provide students with the following guidelines:

1. **Earn credibility.** Speakers who are prepared with evidence tailored to their audience's needs will sway their audience with the power of their proof. As a result, these speakers will have no need to try to harass or intimidate their listeners.
2. **Choose words carefully.** Effective speakers use the exact words they need, words that convey their precise meaning. Further, effective speakers avoid "loaded words" that attempt to sway an audience by appealing to stereotypes.
3. **Be audible, not loud.** Speakers who avoid shouting convey their point with greater confidence than those who do raise their voices.

## Review Evidence for an Argument

At the beginning of this unit, you took a position on the following question:

**Is fear always a harmful emotion?**

EVIDENCE LOG

Review your Evidence Log and your QuickWrite from the beginning of the unit. Has your position changed?

| ☐ YES | ☐ NO |
|---|---|
| Identify at least three pieces of evidence that convinced you to change your mind. | Identify at least three pieces of evidence that reinforced your original position. |
| 1. | 1. |
| 2. | 2. |
| 3. | 3. |

State your position now: ______________________

______________________

______________________

Identify a possible counterclaim: ______________________

______________________

______________________

**Evaluate the Strength of Your Evidence** Consider your argument. Do you have enough evidence to support your claim? Do you have enough evidence to refute a counterclaim? If not, make a plan.

☐ Do more research ☐ Talk with my classmates

☐ Reread a selection ☐ Ask an expert

☐ Other: ______________________

STANDARDS

**Writing**

Introduce precise, knowledgeable claim(s), establish the significance of the claim(s), distinguish the claim(s) from alternate or opposing claims, and create an organization that logically sequences claim(s), counterclaims, reasons, and evidence.





DIGITAL PERSPECTIVES

## Review Evidence for Argument

**Evidence Log** Students should understand that their position on an issue can evolve as they learn more about the subject and are exposed to additional points of view. Point out that just because they took an initial position on the question *Is fear always a harmful emotion?*, doesn't mean that they can't rethink their ideas after careful consideration of their learning and evidence.

### Evaluate the Strength of Your Evidence

Students have the choice of many different sources when doing additional research on the topic, including:

- memoirs
- mass-market psychology books
- psychology textbooks
- self-help books

Students need to judge, not just the quantity of the evidence they gather about their topic, but also the reliability of that evidence. Discuss what might make evidence more credible, and suggest these questions:

- Did it come from a reliable source, such as a governmental, educational, or professional organization?
- Has it been reviewed by experts for accuracy?
- Does it include references to other sources?

# ASSESSING

## Writing to Sources: Argument

Students should complete the Performance-Based Assessment independently, with little to no input or feedback during the process. Students should use word processing software to take advantage of editing tools and features.

Prior to beginning the Assessment, ask students to think about the ways that they have responded to fear and whether their responses were positive as well as negative.

**Review the Elements of Effective Argument** Students can review the work they did earlier in the unit as they complete the Performance-Based Assessment. They may also consult other resources such as:

- the elements of an effective argument, including making a claim and providing supporting evidence, available in Whole-Class Learning
- their Evidence Log
- their Word Network

Although students will use evidence from unit selections for their argument, they may need to collect additional evidence, including examples from literature, history, and personal experience.

PERFORMANCE-BASED ASSESSMENT

SOURCES

- WHOLE-CLASS SELECTIONS
- SMALL-GROUP SELECTIONS
- INDEPENDENT-LEARNING SELECTION

PART 1

## Writing to Sources: Argument

In this unit, you read about characters and real people who experience fear and react to it. In these texts, fear moves beyond a personal emotion, leading readers to question the role fear plays on a larger level in communities and between groups of people.

**Assignment**

Write an **argumentative essay** that responds to this question:

**Is fear always a harmful emotion?**

Begin by asserting a claim. Cite relevant evidence from at least three texts from this unit, as well as from your own experience, to support that claim. Organize your evidence in a logical way that helps you structure your argument clearly and definitively. Use formal language and an objective tone, and end your argument with a conclusion that flows naturally from your claim and the evidence you presented.

**Reread the Assignment** Review the assignment to be sure you fully understand it. The task may reference some of the academic words presented at the beginning of the unit. Be sure you understand each of the words here in order to complete the assignment correctly.

**Academic Vocabulary**

| assert | certify | definitive |
|---|---|---|
| relevant | immutable | |

WORD NETWORK

As you write and revise your essay, use your Word Network to help vary your word choices.

**Review the Elements of Effective Argument** Before you begin writing, read the Argument Rubric. Once you have completed your first draft, check it against the rubric. If one or more of the elements is missing or not as strong as it could be, revise your essay to add or strengthen that component.

STANDARDS

Writing

- Write arguments to support claims in an analysis of substantive topics or texts, using valid reasoning and relevant and sufficient evidence.
- Write routinely over extended time frames and shorter time frames for a range of tasks, purposes, and audiences.





PERSONALIZE FOR LEARNING

**English Language Support**

**Feedback and Revision** Help students write their claims in a single sentence. Then have small groups meet, with each student presenting his or her claim and receiving feedback from group members. Urge students to revise their claims by incorporating what their peers suggested.

Follow the same process with supporting evidence, focusing on topic sentences. Have students write a topic sentence for each paragraph of supporting evidence, present the sentences to the group, and revise based on useful feedback. Finally, suggest that students share their conclusions with group members and revise as necessary. **EXPANDING/BRIDGING**

## Argument Rubric

| | Focus and Organization | Evidence and Elaboration | Language Conventions |
|---|---|---|---|
| 4 | The introduction clearly and effectively states a precise, logical claim.<br>The essay clearly acknowledges counterclaims and uses sufficient reasons and evidence to refute them.<br>Writing always follows a logical organizational structure and makes clear connections among ideas.<br>The argument includes a conclusion that follows from and supports the claim. | Body paragraphs always use valid reasoning and include relevant and sufficient evidence.<br>The tone of the argument is always formal and objective.<br>The argument always uses language that is appropriate for the purpose and audience. | The argument consistently and accurately follows the conventions of standard English usage and mechanics.<br>Writing always uses indefinite pronouns correctly and effectively. |
| 3 | The introduction clearly states a precise claim.<br>The essay acknowledges counterclaims and uses reasons and evidence to refute them.<br>Writing mostly follows a logical organizational structure and makes clear connections among ideas.<br>The argument includes a conclusion that mostly follows from and supports the claim. | Body paragraphs mostly use valid reasoning and include relevant and sufficient evidence.<br>The tone of the argument is mostly formal and objective.<br>The argument mostly uses language that is appropriate for the purpose and audience. | The argument mostly follows the conventions of standard English usage and mechanics.<br>Writing mostly uses indefinite pronouns correctly. |
| 2 | The introduction states a claim.<br>The essay acknowledges counterclaims.<br>Writing follows a somewhat logical organizational structure and makes connections among ideas.<br>The argument includes a conclusion that somewhat follows from and supports the claim. | Body paragraphs sometimes use valid reasoning and relevant evidence.<br>The tone of the argument is sometimes formal and objective.<br>The argument occasionally uses language that is inappropriate for the purpose and audience. | The argument sometimes follows the conventions of standard English usage and mechanics.<br>Writing sometimes uses indefinite pronouns correctly. |
| 1 | The introduction does not state a claim.<br>The essay does not acknowledge counterclaims.<br>Writing does not follow a logical organizational structure or make clear connections among ideas.<br>The argument does not include a conclusion, or it includes a conclusion that does not follow from or support the claim. | Body paragraphs do not use valid reasoning or evidence to support claims.<br>The tone of the argument is informal or inappropriate.<br>The argument uses language that is not appropriate for the purpose and audience. | The argument does not follow the conventions of standard English usage and mechanics.<br>Writing does not use indefinite pronouns correctly. |





DIGITAL PERSPECTIVES

## Argument Rubric

As you review the Argument Rubric with students, remind them that the rubric is a resource that can guide their revisions. Students should pay particular attention to the differences between an argument that handles most of the required elements well (a score of 3) and one that is always logical and effective in presenting those elements (a score of 4).

## Speaking and Listening: Speech

Students should annotate their written argument to use as a script for the speech. Suggest that they think of themselves as actors whose job is to persuade an audience to agree.

Remind students that the effectiveness of a speech relies on how the speaker establishes credibility with his or her audience. If a speaker comes across as confident and authoritative, it will be easier for the audience to give credence to the speaker's argument.

**Review the Rubric** As you review the Oral Presentation Rubric with students, remind them that it is a valuable tool that can help them plan their presentation. They should strive to include all of the criteria required to achieve a score of 3. Draw their attention to some of the subtle differences between scores of 2 and 3.

PERFORMANCE-BASED ASSESSMENT

PART 2

## Speaking and Listening: Speech

**Assignment**

After completing a final draft of your essay, prepare a **speech** in which you present your argument. Use your voice, facial expressions, and gestures to effectively communicate your ideas to your audience.

Follow these steps to make your speech dynamic and interesting.

- Review your argument, and mark the ideas and evidence you want to emphasize.
- Practice reading your essay aloud several times. Consider revising wording to make your text more effective as a speech. For example, you may want to begin or end with more dramatic language. As you read, remember to look up from your paper occassionally. Making eye contact with your audience will help them feel more engaged.
- When you deliver your speech, use pauses effectively, speak slowly and clearly, and vary your volume to add drama.

STANDARDS

**Speaking and Listening**

Present information, findings, and supporting evidence, conveying a clear and distinct perspective, such that listeners can follow the line of reasoning, alternative or opposing perspectives are addressed, and the organization, development, substance, and style are appropriate to purpose, audience, and a range of formal and informal tasks.

**Review the Rubric** The criteria by which your speech will be evaluated appear in this rubric. Review these criteria before presenting to ensure that you are prepared.

| | Content | Effectiveness | Presentation Techniques |
|---|---|---|---|
| 3 | The speaker presents a clear and effective claim.<br>The speaker always uses well-chosen evidence to support his or her ideas. | Language is always appropriate for the audience and task.<br>The speaker emphasizes all of his or her key points. | The speaker always uses tone of voice and body language effectively.<br>The speaker maintains effective eye contact. |
| 2 | The speaker presents a claim.<br>The speaker uses some well-chosen evidence to support his or her ideas. | Language is mostly appropriate for the audience and task.<br>The speaker emphasizes most of his or her key points. | The speaker mostly uses tone of voice and body language effectively.<br>The speaker mostly maintains effective eye contact. |
| 1 | The speaker does not present a clear claim.<br>The speaker does not use well-chosen evidence to support his or her ideas. | Language is not appropriate for the audience and task.<br>The speaker does not emphasize his or her key points. | The speaker does not use tone of voice or body language effectively.<br>The speaker does not make eye contact with the audience. |





DIGITAL PERSPECTIVES

**Preparing for the Assignment** To help students prepare to give an effective dramatic reading, find examples on the Internet of people performing dramatic readings. Project the examples for the class, and have students note the techniques that make each reader successful (that is, body language, pace, tone of voice, appropriate language, and so on). Suggest that students record themselves doing their dramatic reading so that they can practice incorporating elements that they have seen in the examples.

## Reflect on the Unit

Now that you've completed the unit, take a few moments to reflect on your learning. Use the questions below to think about where you succeeded, what skills and strategies helped you, and where you can continue to grow in the future.

### Reflect on the Unit Goals

Look back at the goals at the beginning of the unit. Use a different colored pen to rate yourself again. Think about readings and activities that contributed the most to the growth of your understanding. Record your thoughts.

### Reflect on the Learning Strategies

**Discuss It** Write a reflection on whether you were able to improve your learning based on your Action Plans. Think about what worked, what didn't, and what you might do to keep working on these strategies. Record your ideas before joining a class discussion.

### Reflect on the Text

Choose a selection that you found challenging, and explain what made it difficult.

Explain something that surprised you about a text in the unit.

Which activity taught you the most about responding to fear? What did you learn?

**STANDARDS**

**Speaking and Listening**
Come to discussions prepared, having read and researched material under study; explicitly draw on that preparation by referring to evidence from texts and other research on the topic or issue to stimulate a thoughtful, well-reasoned exchange of ideas.

SCAN FOR MULTIMEDIA





DIGITAL PERSPECTIVES

## Reflect on the Unit

- Have students watch the video on Reflecting on Your Learning.
- A video on this topic is available online in the Professional Development Center.

### Reflect on the Unit Goals

Students should re-evaluate how well they met the unit goals now that they have completed the unit. You might ask them to provide a written commentary on the goal they made the most progress with as well as the goal they feel warrants continued focus.

### Reflect on the Learning Strategies

**Discuss It** If you want to make this a digital activity, go online and navigate to the Discussion Board. Alternatively, students can share their learning strategies reflections in a class discussion.

### Reflect on the Text

Consider having students share their text reflections with one another.

**MAKE IT INTERACTIVE**

Have students prepare one slide using presentation software that summarizes their reflection.

Have partners interview each other, using video if possible, to create one-sentence statements beginning "*The Crucible* taught me that ________."

Collate student responses into a presentation that can be viewed by the class. Students can discuss their responses to the presentation.

**Unit Test and Remediation** 

After students have completed the Performance-Based Assessment, administer the Unit Test. Based on students' performance on the test, assign the resources as indicated on the Interpretation Guide to remediate. Students who take the test online will be automatically assigned remediation, as warranted by test results.

## PERSONALIZE FOR LEARNING

### English Language Support

**Oral Presentations** Oral presentations provide an excellent opportunity for English language learners to practice speaking with preparation and without interruption. After students complete their dramatic readings, suggest that they turn their argument into a brief presentation using note cards, with a few words to remind them of salient examples. Then have them practice the presentation using just the cards so that they feel familiar with it, confident, and fluent. You may offer students a chance to practice speaking more spontaneously during a question and answer session after the formal presentation. **ALL LEVELS**

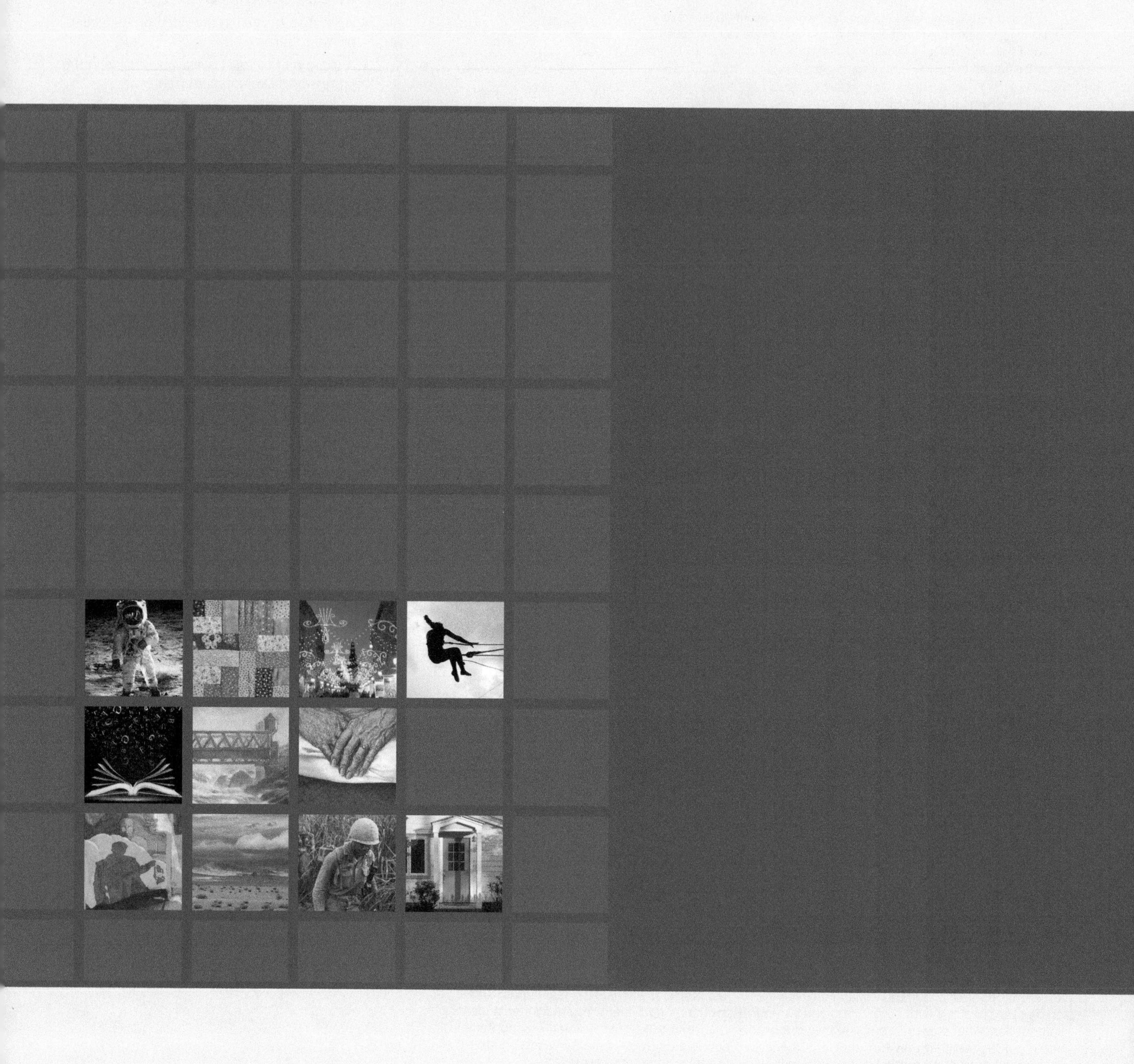

UNIT

# Ordinary Lives, Extraordinary Tales

## The American Short Story

# INTRODUCTION

## Jump Start

Ask: *Why do you think people read short stories? If you read them on your own, why do you do so?* Have students briefly discuss what they and others get out of reading stories.

## Ordinary Lives, Extraordinary Tales

Ask students what *Ordinary Lives, Extraordinary Tales* suggests to them. Point out that as they work through this unit, they will read many examples about the human condition.

## Video

Project the introduction video in class, ask students to open the video in their digital textbooks, or have students scan the BouncePage icon with their phones to access the video.

**Discuss It** If you want to make this a digital activity, go online and navigate to the Discussion Board. Alternatively, students can share their responses in a class discussion.

### Block Scheduling

Each day in this pacing calendar represents a 40–50 minute class period. Teachers using block scheduling may combine days to reflect their class schedule. In addition, teachers may revise pacing to differentiate and support core instruction by integrating components and resources as students require.

UNIT 6

# Ordinary Lives, Extraordinary Tales

The American Short Story

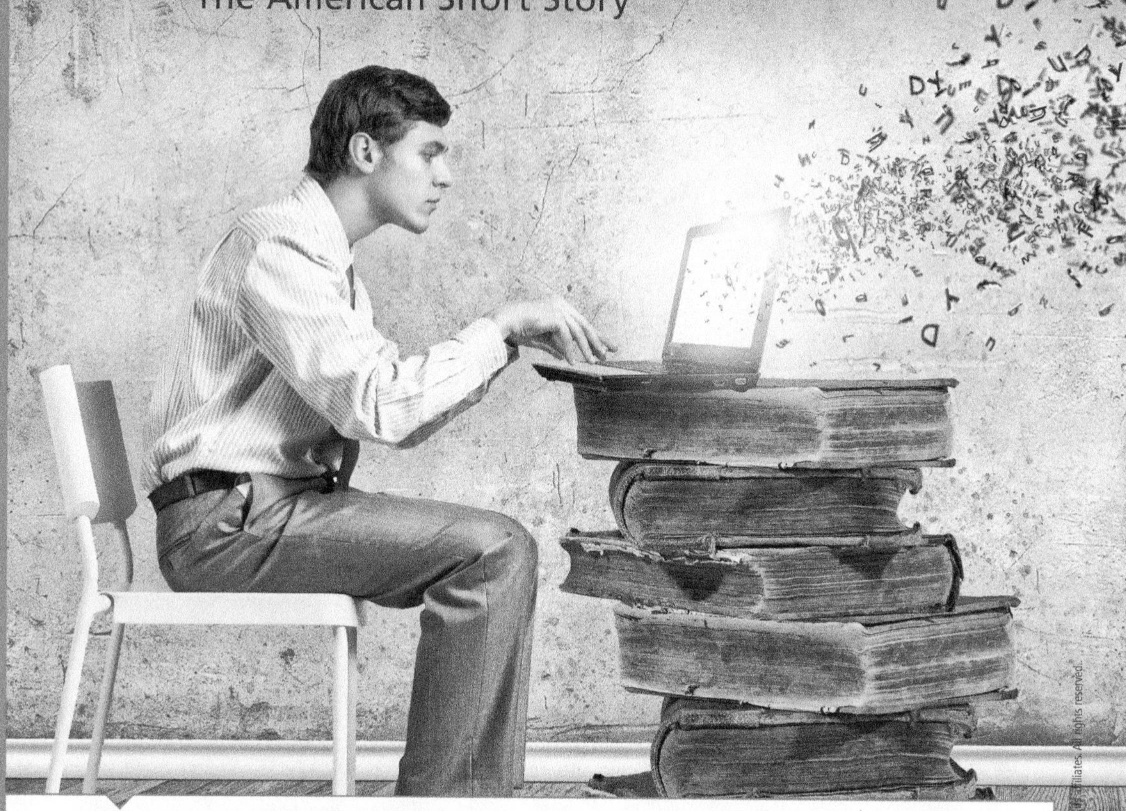

Why Do Stories Matter? That's Like Asking Why You Should Eat

**Discuss It** Which of the thoughts expressed in this video are most similar to your own thoughts about stories?

**Write your response before sharing your ideas.**

750

SCAN FOR MULTIMEDIA

Pacing Plan

Introduce Whole-Class Learning

| Day | Activity |
|---|---|
| 1 | Unit Introduction |
| 2 | Introduce Whole-Class Learning |
| 3 | Historical Perspectives |
| 4–6 | Everyday Use |
| 7–9 | Everything Stuck to Him |
| 10–13 | The Leap |
| 14–15 | Performance Task |

Audio

Video

Document

Annotation Highlights

EL Highlights

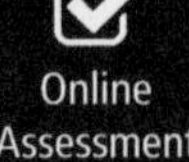
Online Assessment

UNIT 6

UNIT INTRODUCTION

ESSENTIAL QUESTION: What do stories reveal about the human condition?

LAUNCH TEXT NARRATIVE MODEL
Old Man at the Bridge
*Ernest Hemingway*

| WHOLE-CLASS LEARNING | SMALL-GROUP LEARNING | INDEPENDENT LEARNING |
|---|---|---|
| HISTORICAL PERSPECTIVES<br>*Focus Period: 1950–Present*<br>A Fast-Changing Society  | LITERARY HISTORY<br>A Brief History of the Short Story<br>*D. F. McCourt*  | SHORT STORY<br>The Tell-Tale Heart<br>*Edgar Allan Poe*  |
| ANCHOR TEXT: SHORT STORY<br>Everyday Use<br>*Alice Walker*<br>MEDIA CONNECTION: Alice Walker's "Everyday Use" 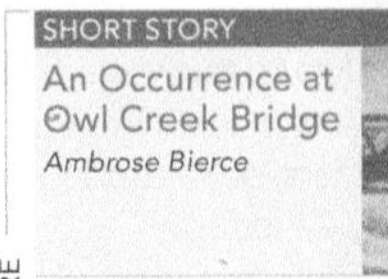 | COMPARE: SHORT STORY<br>An Occurrence at Owl Creek Bridge<br>*Ambrose Bierce* 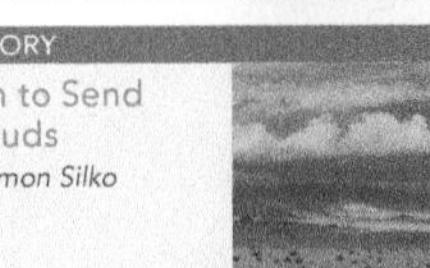 | SHORT STORY<br>The Man to Send Rain Clouds<br>*Leslie Marmon Silko* |
| ANCHOR TEXT: SHORT STORY<br>Everything Stuck to Him<br>*Raymond Carver* | COMPARE: SHORT STORY<br>The Jilting of Granny Weatherall<br>*Katherine Anne Porter* 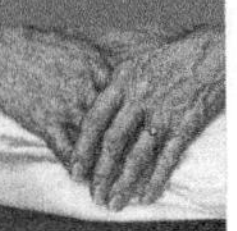 | SHORT STORY<br>Ambush<br>*Tim O'Brien*  |
| ANCHOR TEXT: SHORT STORY<br>The Leap<br>*Louise Erdrich*  | | SHORT STORY<br>Housepainting<br>*Lan Samantha Chang*  |
| PERFORMANCE TASK<br>WRITING FOCUS:<br>Write a Narrative | PERFORMANCE TASK<br>SPEAKING AND LISTENING FOCUS:<br>Present a Narrative | PERFORMANCE-BASED ASSESSMENT PREP<br>Review Notes for a Narrative |

PERFORMANCE-BASED ASSESSMENT

Narrative: Short Story and Storytelling Session

PROMPT:
How does a fictional character or characters respond to life-changing news?

751



## What do stories reveal about the human condition?

Introduce the Essential Question and point out that students will respond to related prompts.

- **Whole-Class Learning** *How do stressful situations often reveal the best and worst in people?*
- **Small-Group Learning** *Present a stream-of-conscious narrative based on this idea: The day felt as if it would never end.*
- **Performance-Based Assessment** *How does a fictional character or characters respond to life-changing news?*

### Using Trade Books

Refer to the Teaching with Trade Books section in this book or online in the Interactive Teacher's Edition for suggestions on how to incorporate the following thematically related novels into this unit.

- *The Help* by Kathryn Stockett
- *The Glass Castle* by Jeanette Walls
- *Of Mice and Men* by John Steinbeck

### Current Perspectives

To increase student engagement, search online for stories about ordinary lives: extraordinary tales, and invite your students to recommend stories they find. Always preview content before sharing it with your class.

- **News Story: Your Brain on Fiction *(The New York Times)*** Brain scans show that reading fiction stimulates brain activity and can alter the way we act.
- **Blog Post: "Reading Literary Fiction Improves Empathy" *(The Guardian)*** Can reading a good book help you connect with others?

Introduce Small-Group Learning

A Brief History of the Short Story

An Occurrence at Owl Creek Bridge

The Jilting of Granny Weatherall

Performance Task

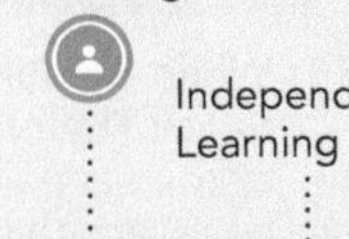

Introduce Independent Learning

Independent Learning

Performance-Based Assessment

16 17 18 19 20 21 22 23 24 25 26 27 28 29 30

# INTRODUCTION

### About the Unit Goals

These unit goals were backward designed from the Performance-Based Assessment at the end of the unit and the Whole-Class and Small-Group Performance Tasks. Students will practice and become proficient in many more standards over the course of this unit.

## Unit Goals

Review the goals with students and explain that as they read and discuss the selections in this unit, they will improve their skills in reading, writing, research, language, and speaking and listening.

- Have students watch the video on Goal Setting.
- A video on this topic is available online in the Professional Development Center.

**Reading Goals** Tell students they will read and evaluate narrative texts. They will read many short stories to better understand the various ways writers have for telling a story.

**Writing and Research Goals** Tell students that they will learn the elements of narrative as a writing mode. They will also write their own narrative. Students will write for a number of reasons, including organizing and sharing ideas, reflecting on experiences, and gathering evidence. They will conduct research to clarify and explore ideas.

**Language Goals** Tell students that they will develop a deeper understanding of style choices. They will then practice the elements of a story in their own writing.

**Speaking and Listening** Explain to students that they will work together to build on one another's ideas, develop consensus, and communicate with one another. They will also learn to incorporate audio, visuals, and text in presentations.

### HOME Connection

A Home Connection letter to students' parents or guardians is available in the Interactive Teacher's Edition. The letter explains what students will be learning in this unit and how they will be assessed.



## Unit Goals

Throughout this unit, you will deepen your perspective on how stories explore the human condition by reading, writing, speaking, listening, and presenting. These goals will help you succeed on the Unit Performance-Based Assessment.

Rate how well you meet these goals right now. You will revisit your ratings later when you reflect on your growth during this unit.

| SCALE | 1 | 2 | 3 | 4 | 5 |
|---|---|---|---|---|---|
| | NOT AT ALL WELL | NOT VERY WELL | SOMEWHAT WELL | VERY WELL | EXTREMELY WELL |

| READING GOALS | 1 | 2 | 3 | 4 | 5 |
|---|---|---|---|---|---|
| • Analyze narratives to understand how authors order the action, introduce and develop characters, and introduce and develop multiple themes. | O | O | O | O | O |
| • Expand your knowledge and use of academic and concept vocabulary. | O | O | O | O | O |

| WRITING AND RESEARCH GOALS | 1 | 2 | 3 | 4 | 5 |
|---|---|---|---|---|---|
| • Write a narrative text that uses effective narrative techniques to develop fictional experiences, events, and characters. | O | O | O | O | O |
| • Conduct research projects of various lengths to explore topics and clarify meaning. | O | O | O | O | O |

| LANGUAGE GOALS | 1 | 2 | 3 | 4 | 5 |
|---|---|---|---|---|---|
| • Make effective style choices regarding figurative language and dialect. | O | O | O | O | O |
| • Demonstrate an understanding of frequently confused words, passive voice, and sentence fragments. | O | O | O | O | O |

| SPEAKING AND LISTENING GOALS | 1 | 2 | 3 | 4 | 5 |
|---|---|---|---|---|---|
| • Collaborate with your team to build on the ideas of others, develop consensus, and communicate. | O | O | O | O | O |
| • Integrate audio, visuals, and text to present information. | O | O | O | O | O |

**STANDARDS**

**Language**
Acquire and use accurately general academic and domain-specific words and phrases, sufficient for reading, writing, speaking, and listening at the college and career readiness level; demonstrate independence in gathering vocabulary knowledge when considering a word or phrase important to comprehension or expression.





SCAN FOR MULTIMEDIA 

### AUTHOR'S PERSPECTIVE Ernest Morrell, Ph.D.

**When Students Feel They Can't Reach Their Goals** People often get discouraged when they can't reach their goals, and this feeling can be especially difficult for students. Teachers can help students overcome their pessimism about setting and meeting goals with these strategies:

- *Offer occasions for students to revisit and revise their goals.* Explain that this step in the process is common and important. Remind students that sometimes the goals we set are unrealistic and they will need to be revised.
- *Help break down the goals into smaller steps.* Building intermediate steps into goals may make them more manageable. For example, when students are setting long-term goals, have them identify a first step. Ask them what they can do immediately, over the next few days. Help students identify the steps they'll need to take to achieve a goal and encourage them to take them one at a time.

DIGITAL PERSPECTIVES  

## Academic Vocabulary: Narrative Text

Understanding and using academic terms can help you read, write, and speak with precision and clarity. Here are five academic words that will be useful to you in this unit as you analyze and write fictional narratives.

**Complete the chart.**

1. Review each word, its root, and the mentor sentences.
2. Use the information and your own knowledge to predict the meaning of each word.
3. For each word, list at least two related words.
4. Refer to a dictionary or other resources if needed.

TIP

FOLLOW THROUGH
Study the words in this chart, and mark them or their forms wherever they appear in the unit.

| WORD | MENTOR SENTENCES | PREDICT MEANING | RELATED WORDS |
|---|---|---|---|
| colloquial<br><br>ROOT:<br>***-loqu-***<br>"speak"; "say" | 1. When I was studying Spanish, I learned formal terms more easily than *colloquial* expressions.<br>2. I love how the poet combines cultured diction with *colloquial* language. | | colloquially; colloquialism |
| protagonist<br><br>ROOT:<br>***-agon-***<br>"contest" | 1. Is the *protagonist* of the story really a talking dog?<br>2. In this movie, the *protagonist* must defeat a politician who has a sinister goal. | | |
| tension<br><br>ROOT:<br>***-tens-***<br>"stretch" | 1. News of an important announcement increased the level of *tension* at school.<br>2. What *tension* I felt as my turn to speak drew close! | | |
| resolution<br><br>ROOT:<br>***-solv-***<br>"loosen" | 1. In the play's *resolution*, the thief is caught and taken to jail.<br>2. The two sides in the dispute reached a surprising and imaginative *resolution*. | | |
| epiphany<br><br>ROOT:<br>***-phan-/-phen-***<br>"show" | 1. That *epiphany* changed my life because it made my career choice clear.<br>2. At the end of the story, Julia has an *epiphany*, but we aren't sure if she will act on that insight. | | |





## Academic Vocabulary: Narrative

Introduce the blue academic vocabulary words in the chart on the student page. Point out that the root of each word provides a clue to its meaning. Discuss the mentor sentences to ensure students understand each word's usage. Students should also use the mentor sentences as context to help them predict the meaning of each word. Check that students are able to fill the chart in correctly. Complete pronunciations, parts of speech, and definitions are provided for you. Students are only expected to provide the definition.

Possible responses:

colloquial *adj.* (kuh LOH kwee uhl)
**Meaning:** informal language used in everyday conversation
**Related words:** colloquially, colloquialism
**Additional words related to root *-loqui-*:** loquacious, locution, eloquent

protagonist *n.* (proh TAG uh nihst)
**Meaning:** main character in a play, story, or novel
**Additional words related to root *-agon-*:** antagonist, antagonism, agony, antagonize

tension *n.* (TEHN shuhn)
**Meaning:** stress caused by pulling
**Related word:** tense
**Additional words related to root *-tens-*:** intensity, tensor, pretense

resolution *n.* (rehz uh LOO shuhn)
**Meaning:** the act of resolving or deciding; formal expression of opinion
**Related word:** resolute
**Additional words related to root *-solv-*:** solve, resolve, solvent

epiphany *n.* (ih PIHF uh nee)
**Meaning:** flash of insight and understanding
**Additional words related to root *-phan-/-phen-*:** phantasmagoria, phantom, cellophane, phenom, diaphanous

### PERSONALIZE FOR LEARNING

**English Language Support**
**Cognates** Many of the academic words have Spanish cognates. Use these cognates with students whose home language is Spanish. **ALL LEVELS**

colloquial — coloquial
protagonist — protagonista
tension — tensión
resolution — resolución
epiphany — epifanía

## Purpose of the Launch Text

The Launch Text provides a common introduction to the unit theme for all students. After they read the Launch Text, all students will be able to participate in discussions about how stories explore the human condition.

**Lexile: 700L** This selection's easier reading level means that it needs little or no support, so it can be assigned as homework. In addition, students can use "Old Man at the Bridge" as a model when they complete the Performance-Based Assessment at the end of the unit.

## Launch Text: Narrative Model

As you review the launch text with students, remind them that details and dialogue will give them insight into the characters and the situation. For example, point out the description of the old man in the first paragraph—"an old man with steel rimmed spectacles and very dusty clothes" who is "too tired to go any farther." Have students notice the contrast between the exhaustion of the old man and the movement of the other people described in paragraph 1. Explain that paragraph 1 sets the scene for the rest of the selection and that students should keep in mind what is happening around the characters as they have their conversational exchange.

You may choose to have students read this selection on their own. If so, encourage them to annotate elements such as words they don't know or sections they think are particularly important.

**AUDIO SUMMARIES**

Audio summaries of "Old Man at the Bridge" are available online in both English and Spanish in the Interactive Teacher's Edition or Unit Resources. Assigning these summaries before students read the Launch Text may help them build additional background knowledge and set a context for their reading.



LAUNCH TEXT | NARRATIVE MODEL

This selection is an example of a **narrative text.** It is a **fictional narrative** because it is narrated by a character and describes events that did not actually happen. This is the type of writing you will develop in the Performance-Based Assessment at the end of the unit.

**As you read,** look closely at the author's use of details and dialogue. Mark words and phrases that suggest the personalities of the narrator and the old man, as well as the tension of the situation in which they meet.

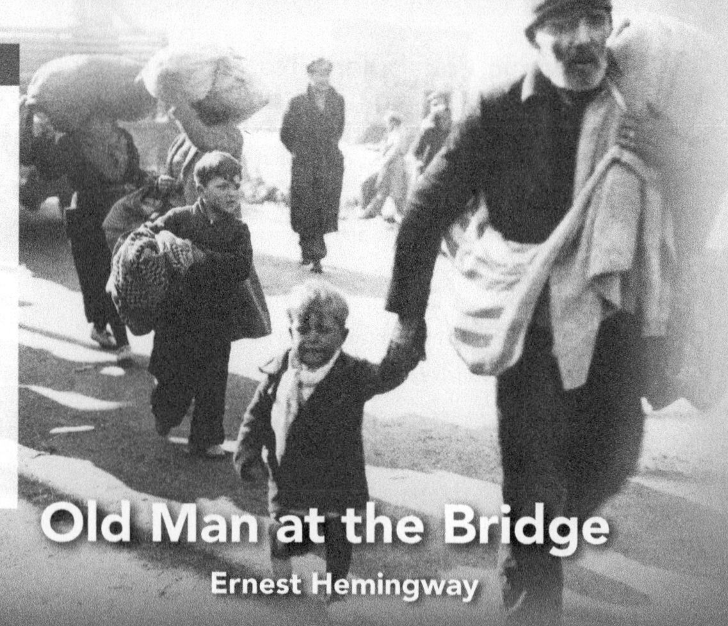

# Old Man at the Bridge

**Ernest Hemingway**

1 An old man with steel rimmed spectacles and very dusty clothes sat by the side of the road. There was a pontoon bridge across the river and carts, trucks, and men, women and children were crossing it. The mule-drawn carts staggered up the steep bank from the bridge with soldiers helping push against the spokes of the wheels. The trucks ground up and away heading out of it all and the peasants plodded along in the ankle deep dust. But the old man sat there without moving. He was too tired to go any farther.

2 It was my business to cross the bridge, explore the bridgehead beyond and find out to what point the enemy had advanced. I did this and returned over the bridge. There were not so many carts now and very few people on foot, but the old man was still there.

3 "Where do you come from?" I asked him.

4 "From San Carlos," he said, and smiled.

5 That was his native town and so it gave him pleasure to mention it and he smiled.

6 "I was taking care of animals," he explained.

7 "Oh," I said, not quite understanding.

8 "Yes," he said, "I stayed, you see, taking care of animals. I was the last one to leave the town of San Carlos."

9 He did not look like a shepherd nor a herdsman and I looked at his black dusty clothes and his gray dusty face and his steel rimmed spectacles and said, "What animals were they?"

10 "Various animals," he said, and shook his head. "I had to leave them."

11 I was watching the bridge and the African looking country of the Ebro Delta and wondering how long now it would be before we would see the enemy, and listening all the while for the first noises that would signal that ever mysterious event called contact, and the old man still sat there.

12 "What animals were they?" I asked.

13 "There were three animals altogether," he explained. "There were two goats and a cat and then there were four pairs of pigeons."

14 "And you had to leave them?" I asked.

15 "Yes. Because of the artillery. The captain told me to go because of the artillery."





SCAN FOR MULTIMEDIA 

## PERSONALIZE FOR LEARNING

### English Language Support

**Language Choices: Repetition** English learners may have trouble understanding how Hemingway's style contributes to the nuances of the text. Have students meet in small groups to review how Hemingway uses repetition in "Old Man at the Bridge." Have students work together to note instances of repetition. Then, have students explain their ideas about the effect of the repetition. Encourage students to come up with theories of how the repetition supports a theme related to the human condition. Have a group representative summarize the group's ideas. **ALL LEVELS**

16 "And you have no family?" I asked, watching the far end of the bridge where a few last carts were hurrying down the slope of the bank.

17 "No," he said, "only the animals I stated. The cat, of course, will be all right. A cat can look out for itself, but I cannot think what will become of the others."

18 "What politics have you?" I asked.

19 "I am without politics," he said. "I am seventy-six years old. I have come twelve kilometers now and I think now I can go no further."

20 "This is not a good place to stop," I said. "If you can make it, there are trucks up the road where it forks for Tortosa."

21 "I will wait a while," he said, "and then I will go. Where do the trucks go?"

22 "Towards Barcelona," I told him.

23 "I know no one in that direction," he said, "but thank you very much. Thank you again very much."

24 He looked at me very blankly and tiredly, then said, having to share his worry with some one, "The cat will be all right, I am sure. There is no need to be unquiet about the cat. But the others. Now what do you think about the others?"

25 "Why they'll probably come through it all right."

26 "You think so?"

27 "Why not," I said, watching the far bank where now there were no carts.

28 "But what will they do under the artillery when I was told to leave because of the artillery?"

29 "Did you leave the dove cage unlocked?" I asked.

30 "Yes."

31 "Then they'll fly."

32 "Yes, certainly they'll fly. But the others. It's better not to think about the others," he said.

33 "If you are rested I would go," I urged. "Get up and try to walk now."

34 "Thank you," he said and got to his feet, swayed from side to side and then sat down backwards in the dust.

35 "I was taking care of animals," he said dully, but no longer to me. "I was only taking care of animals."

36 There was nothing to do about him. It was Easter Sunday and the Fascists were advancing toward the Ebro. It was a gray overcast day with a low ceiling so their planes were not up. That and the fact that cats know how to look after themselves was all the good luck that old man would ever have. ❧

### WORD NETWORK FOR ORDINARY LIVES, EXTRAORDINARY TALES

**Vocabulary** A Word Network is a collection of words related to a topic. As you read the unit selections, identify words related to the human condition and add them to your Word Network. For example, you might begin by adding words from the Launch Text, such as *family*. For each word you add, add a related word, such as a synonym or an antonym. Continue to add words as you complete this unit.

family | relatives

THE HUMAN CONDITION

**Tool Kit**
Word Network Model





DIGITAL PERSPECTIVES

## Word Network for the Ordinary Lives, Extraordinary Tales

Students may fill in the Word Network as they read the selections in the unit, or they may choose to jot down words as they read and complete the Word Network when they are done.

Explain to students that many word associations are subjective; one student might think a word relates to the human condition, while another student does not. Tell students to fill in the Word Network with any words they think are relevant. Each student's Word Network will be unique. If you choose to print the Word Network, distribute it to students at this point so they can use it throughout the rest of the unit.

AUTHOR'S PERSPECTIVE **Elfrieda Hiebert, Ph.D.**

**Multiple-Meaning Words** A word can have different meanings across content groups. Therefore, the same word will appear in different content maps. It may appear in more than one concept group: some words with multiple meanings even appear in many concept groups.

For example, when the word *channel* is used as a noun in geology, it refers to the bed of a river or other waterway; a navigable route between two bodies of a wide strait; or the deeper part of a waterway. When used as a noun in the field of communication, it refers to the specific, official course or means of discourse. Further, when *channel* is used as a verb in biology ("channel your energy"), economics ("channel money into the program"), or geology ("channel water in the fields"), its meaning changes yet again. As a result, the word *channel* has a place in a variety of concept maps.

Work with students to increase their awareness of multiple-meaning words. Seeing words in their various contexts used across subject areas can help building their vocabulary knowledge.

## Summary

Have students read the introductory paragraph. Then ask students to suggest tips for writing a summary of a text. These should include:

- Start with the title of the text and the author's name.
- Use the present tense.
- Keep it short; a summary should be shorter than the original text.
- Accurately reflect the author's point of view.
- Do not inject your own opinions, ideas, or interpretations.
- If you must include some of the original text, put it in quotation marks.

You may choose to refer students to the Tool Kit for help in understanding the elements of a good summary.

**See possible summary on student page.**

## Launch Activity

Tell students that they will have many opportunities to discuss how stories explore the human condition as they work their way through this unit. Prepare students to brainstorm as a group by encouraging them to be open to all sincerely contributed ideas, no matter how absurd they may sound at first. Explain that in a brainstorming session, people use each other's ideas as a jumping-off point for new, related ideas. Encourage students to embrace this opportunity for creative group collaboration and to welcome and work with all ideas.



## Summary

Write a summary of "Old Man at the Bridge." Remember that a **summary** is a concise, complete, and accurate overview of a text. It should not include a statement of your opinion or an analysis.

Possible response:
The narrator of Ernest Hemingway's short story "Old Man at the Bridge" is a soldier who crosses a refugee-choked bridge, observes enemy positions, and then returns. On his first crossing, he sees an old man sitting on the side of the road. When the narrator returns, the old man is still there. The narrator tells him he must move on before enemy troops arrive. The old man says he is too tired to walk any farther. He worries about the welfare of several animals he had to abandon in his hometown. The narrator realizes there is nothing he can do to save the old man, and so he leaves.

## Launch Activity

**Create an Alternate Ending** Consider this statement by the narrator near the end of "Old Man at the Bridge": **There was nothing to be done for him.** Discuss how you might rewrite the story's ending so that something *could* be done for the old man.

- With a small group, brainstorm for ways in which the narrator might do something for the old man, after all. Record the two options that your group likes best.

  *Option 1:* ______________________

  *Option 2:* ______________________

- Choose the option that you think would better communicate a message about the human condition—about human nature or situations that are part of human experience.
- Frame your group's idea for an alternate ending: *We think that an ending in which* ______________________ *would show that* ______________________ *is part of the human condition.*





### PERSONALIZE FOR LEARNING

**English Language Support**

**Summary** If students struggle to write a summary of "Old Man at the Bridge," have them work with a partner. Have partners read the narrative aloud, each taking the role of one character. As they read, students should take notes of the important events and record any questions they may have. Assist students by answering their questions and, if needed, by helping them organize their notes into an outline to use for their summary. Then, have partners work together to create a written summary. **ALL LEVELS**

## QuickWrite

Consider class discussions, the video, and the Launch Text as you think about the prompt. Record your first thoughts here.

PROMPT: **How does a fictional character or characters respond to life-changing news?**

Possible response: I believe that fictional characters can respond to life-changing news in a variety of ways. Or, to be more precise, well-written fictional characters can teach us how to respond to life-changing news.

For example, Hemingway's short story "The Old Man at the Bridge" shows what it might be like to leave home during war. The man in this story is exhausted because he may have stayed in an area longer than other people have. He was caring for the animals and putting their safety over his own. Readers may wonder how they would react in a similar situation.

If a character is well written, he or she might act, think, and respond as a real person would. A fictional character can seem so real that we think of him or her as an actual person. Seeing a realistic character like this react to life-changing news, we can decide for ourselves whether the reaction was right or wrong, justified or overblown, helpful or not helpful. It's the same as learning from one of our friends. The difference is that, for most of us, there are many more fictional characters than friends receiving life-changing news.

### EVIDENCE LOG FOR THE HUMAN CONDITION

Review your QuickWrite. Summarize your initial idea in one sentence to record in your Evidence Log. Then, record details from "Old Man at the Bridge" that connect to your idea.

Prepare for the Performance-Based Assessment at the end of the unit by completing the Evidence Log after each selection.

**Tool Kit**
Evidence Log Model

Title of Text: ______ Date: ______

| CONNECTION TO PROMPT | TEXT EVIDENCE/DETAILS | ADDITIONAL NOTES/IDEAS |
|---|---|---|
| | | |

How does this text change or add to my thinking? Date: ______

SCAN FOR MULTIMEDIA



## DIGITAL PERSPECTIVES

## QuickWrite

Students should use the material they have read and viewed in the Unit Overview and Introduction to develop and present their own answer to the prompt. They should present their position clearly and support it with accurately cited details and logical reasoning.

Their responses here will come into play when they complete the Performance-Based Assessment at the end of the unit. Students should make sure their ideas are well considered and well supported with examples from "Old Man at the Bridge."

**See possible QuickWrite on student page.**

## Evidence Log for Ordinary Lives, Extraordinary Tales

Students should record their initial idea and include evidence from "Old Man at the Bridge" that supports it.

If you have decided to print the Evidence Log, distribute the copies now. Students will be able to use it throughout the unit.

### Performance-Based Assessment: Refining Your Thinking

- Have students watch the video on Refining Your Thinking
- A video on this topic is available online in the Professional Development Center.

## PERSONALIZE FOR LEARNING

### English Language Support

**Arguing** English learners may have trouble tempering their opinion statements with modal expressions. Clarify that the QuickWrite prompt asks students to express their opinions. Explain that modal expressions can help them to express their opinions more precisely.

Discuss the following modal expressions with students, and help them come up with examples of proper usage. Then, have students incorporate at least one modal expression into their QuickWrite.

*may, can* **EMERGING**

*possibly, likely, could, would* **EXPANDING**

*potentially, certainly, absolutely* **BRIDGING**

## OVERVIEW

### WHOLE-CLASS LEARNING

### What do stories reveal about the human condition?

Ask students: *Have you ever noticed the chill down your back or lump in your throat after hearing a good story? What makes stories do that?* During whole-class learning, talk about that question. Point out how the three short stories in this section weave together objects and words that may create chills, knowing smiles, and lessons for living life.

### Whole-Class Learning Strategies

Review the Learning Strategies with students and explain that as they work through Whole-Class Learning they will develop strategies to work in large-group environments.

- Have students watch the video on Whole-Class Learning Strategies.
- A video on this topic is available online in the Professional Development Center.

You may wish to discuss some action items to add to the chart as a class before students complete it on their own. For example for "Clarify by asking questions" you might solicit the following from students:

- As you read, point out words or phrases that are challenging to you and ask others for their ideas.
- Consider the characters and ask questions to explore their feelings.

**Block Scheduling**

Each day in this Pacing Plan represents a 40–50 minute class period. Teachers using block scheduling may combine days to reflect their class schedule. In addition, teachers may revise pacing to differentiate and support core instruction by integrating components and resources as students require.

OVERVIEW: WHOLE-CLASS LEARNING

ESSENTIAL QUESTION:

## What do stories reveal about the human condition?

As you read these selections, work with your whole class to explore how short stories provide insights into what it means to be human.

**From Text to Topic** For one family, conflict over an heirloom highlights individual strengths and weaknesses, and suggests different ways of valuing the past. For one father and daughter, a present moment opens a window to a poignant memory. For one woman, a series of anecdotes reveals her mother's extraordinary character. As you read these stories, consider the understanding of human nature that informs each one—how it reveals qualities that we equate with the human condition, regardless of time or place.

### Whole-Class Learning Strategies

Throughout your life, in school, in your community, and in your career, you will continue to learn and work in large-group environments.

Review these strategies and the actions you can take to practice them as you work with your whole class. Add ideas of your own for each step. Get ready to use these strategies during Whole-Class Learning.

| STRATEGY | ACTION PLAN |
|---|---|
| Listen actively | • Eliminate distractions. For example, put your cellphone away.<br>• Record brief notes on main ideas and points of confusion.<br>• |
| Clarify by asking questions | • If you're confused, other people probably are, too. Ask a question to help your whole class.<br>• Ask follow-up questions as needed.<br>• |
| Monitor understanding | • Notice what information you already know, and be ready to build on it.<br>• Ask for help if you are struggling.<br>• |
| Interact and share ideas | • Share your ideas and offer answers, even if you are unsure.<br>• Build on the ideas of others by adding details or making a connection.<br>• |





SCAN FOR MULTIMEDIA

### Pacing Plan

Unit Introduction: 1
Introduce Whole-Class Learning: 2
Historical Perspectives: 3
Everyday Use: 4, 5, 6
Everything Stuck to Him: 7, 8, 9
The Leap: 10, 11, 12, 13
Performance Task: 14, 15

WHOLE-CLASS LEARNING

CONTENTS







## Contents

**Anchor Texts** Preview the anchor texts with students to generate interest. Highlight the different points of view in "Everyday Use"; ask students to figure out the relationship between the frame stories in "Everything Stuck to Him"; and dare them not to feel suspense in "The Leap." Encourage students to discuss other texts they may have read or movies or television shows they may have seen that deal with the human condition and the issues that challenge people to take extraordinary measures.

You may wish to conduct a poll to determine which selection students think looks most interesting, and discuss the reasons for their preference. Students can return to this poll after they have read the selections to see if their preference changed.

## Performance Task

**Write a Narrative** Explain to students that after they have finished reading the selections, they will write a narrative that creates a meaningful tale told using stream-of-consciousness technique. To help them prepare, encourage students to think about the topic of how everyday people often do extraordinary things as they progress through the selections and participate in the Whole-Class Learning experience.

Introduce Small-Group Learning

16

A Brief History of the Short Story

17

An Occurrence at Owl Creek Bridge

18

19

20

21

The Jilting of Granny Weatherall

22

23

24

25

Performance Task

26

Introduce Independent Learning

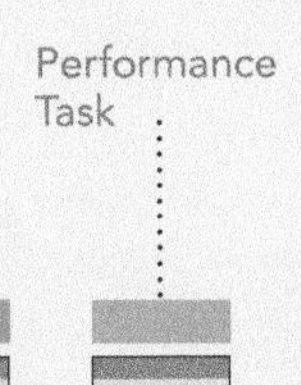

27

Independent Learning

28

Performance-Based Assessment

29

30

## HISTORICAL PERSPECTIVES

# A Fast-Changing Society

This section analyzes the key ideas and events of the Focus Period: the optimism of the "American dream" and the growth of suburban America; the controversy surrounding the Vietnam War; the struggles for racial, cultural, and gender equality; the threat of terrorism and the tragic events of September 11, 2001; an increasing societal awareness of environmental issues; and the rapid expansion of technology. Have students connect these key events with the unit topic.

## Voices of the Period

Point out to students that the Michio Kaku quotation embraces individualism as well as social responsibility. Have groups discuss these questions: *Is it possible to develop individual talents to the fullest at the same time as "trying to leave the world a better place?" Can the two goals be addressed simultaneously? How does one choose between them when there is a conflict?* Have students support their opinions with examples drawn from the events described in this section.

## History of the Period

This period in history is filled with conflict and destruction—the explosion of the first hydrogen bomb, the Vietnam War, Kennedy's assassination, the events of 9/11, and the controversial military action that followed. At the same time, there was great growth and progress during this period. Ask students to discuss the growth that occurred and what relationships they can find between destruction and growth.



# A Fast-Changing Society

## Voices of the Period

*"There is more recognition now that things are changing, but not because there is a political move to do it. It is simply a result of the information being there. Our survival won't depend on political or economic systems. It's going to depend on the courage of the individual to speak the truth, and to speak it lovingly and not destructively."*

—Buckminster Fuller, architect and inventor

*"[E]xperience has taught me that you cannot value dreams according to the odds of their coming true. Their real value is in stirring within us the will to aspire."*

—Sonia Sotomayor, Supreme Court Justice

*"Beyond work and love, I would add two other ingredients that give meaning to life. First, to fulfill whatever talents we are born with. However blessed we are by fate with different abilities and strengths, we should try to develop them to the fullest. . . . Second, we should try to leave the world a better place than when we entered it."*

—Michio Kaku, futurist, theoretical physicist, and author

## History of the Period

**Chasing the American Dream** By the 1950s, postwar America was "on top of the world" with pride and confidence in its position as a world power. The nation had a booming economy and a booming population. As a result of a strong job market and the availability of federal loans to returning soldiers and other service personnel, Americans purchased houses in record numbers. More than eighty percent of new homes were in suburbs, which became the new lifestyle norm—a change made possible by the rise of "car culture."

**The Age of Aquarius** Elected president in 1960, John F. Kennedy spearheaded new domestic and foreign programs, known collectively as the New Frontier. Among these initiatives was the goal of landing an American on the moon and the establishment of the Peace Corps, an overseas volunteer program. A national spirit of optimism turned to grief, however, when Kennedy was assassinated in 1963.

The escalating and increasingly unpopular war in Vietnam elicited waves of protest, with idealistic but strident demands for an end to the conflict, as well as changes in society. As the 1960s wore on, more and more Americans made strong assertions of their individuality. This new spirit of independence energized passions for justice and equality. Some Americans expressed idealistic values that called for an "Age of Aquarius"—an era of universal peace and love. At the same time, some Americans created a counterculture, seeking lifestyles that challenged the prevailing



### TIMELINE

1950

**1952:** The U.S. detonates the first hydrogen bomb.

**1957:** President Eisenhower sends troops to Little Rock, Arkansas, to enforce high school integration.

**1957:** Jack Kerouac's *On the Road* is published.

**1963:** President John F. Kennedy is assassinated.

**1965:** Congress passes the Voting Rights Act.



## PERSONALIZE FOR LEARNING

### Strategic Support

**Historic Context** Ask struggling students to locate their own years of birth on the timeline, as well as the years of birth of siblings, parents, and grandparents. Then, ask them to research a historic event that they believe is missing from the timeline. For example, point out that the first personal computer is listed on the timeline. Ask what other technological "firsts" they might be curious about. Have students research the invention of the first mobile phone, the spread of the Internet, or some other appropriate topic. Have students discuss their timeline research.

norms in music, art, literature, occupations, speech, and dress.

**Protest and Progress** Although there were times of crisis and confrontation, the 1960s also was an era of genuine progress, especially in the continuing struggle for civil rights and racial equality. Civil rights leaders and other Americans, both black and white, protested segregation and racism. Violence and unrest spread as protestors faced resistance in places such as Birmingham and Selma, Alabama. The nation made momentous progress when, under the leadership of President Lyndon B. Johnson, Congress passed key legislation in 1964 and 1965 to counter racism. A century after constitutional amendments guaranteed rights to African Americans, the struggle to claim them continued.

**Changing Roles** Throughout the 1960s, American women struggled for greater economic and social power, changing the workforce and the political landscape in the process. In 1970, thousands of women marched to honor the fiftieth anniversary of women's suffrage. The women's movement continued to gain strength in the 1970s, with various groups forming to protest gender discrimination.

Following the lead of the civil rights and women's movements, other groups from a variety of backgrounds, ranging from Native Americans to migrant workers to gays and lesbians, organized to demand their rights. Over time, most Americans have come to appreciate the variety of perspectives that diversity can bring. Today, virtually every societal group has entered into the mainstream of American political, business, and artistic life.

**Leadership and Conflict** Voters sent Ronald Reagan, the Republican governor of California, to the White House in 1980 and again in 1984. George H. W. Bush, Reagan's vice president, was elected president in 1988 and sought reelection in 1992, but was defeated by to Democrats Bill Clinton and his running mate, Al Gore—the youngest ticket in American history—who were reelected in 1996. In 2000, Vice President Al Gore lost his presidential bid to George Bush's son, George W. Bush. Bush was reelected in 2004. The contests of 2008 and 2012 resulted in historic victories, with the election and reelection of Barack Obama, the nation's first African American president.

**9/11: A World Transformed** The terrorist attacks of September 11, 2001, had an enormous impact on the American consciousness. In addition to the tragic loss of thousands of lives, the threat of terrorism brought profound changes to the sense of security and openness that Americans had long enjoyed. The 9/11 attacks also precipitated controversial military action in Afghanistan and later in Iraq. Today, the continued rise of global terrorism continues to challenge the world's safety.

**Planet Earth** In 1962, Rachel Carson's book *Silent Spring* exposed the sometimes catastrophic effect of human actions on the natural world. In 1972, American astronauts took a photograph of Earth that became famously known as "the big blue marble." Over the years, Americans have become increasingly aware of the importance of caring for the planet's health. In recent years, human-induced climate change—long a concern of scientists—has emerged as a significant issue in the public's consciousness and actions to slow its impact are widely discussed and argued about in the media and in government.



**1968:** Civil rights leader Martin Luther King, Jr., is assassinated.

**1969:** Astronaut Neil Armstrong becomes the first person to set foot on the moon.

**1972:** Congress passes the Equal Rights Amendment, but it fails to achieve ratification.

**1973:** The last U.S. combat troops leave Vietnam, where war has been waged since 1955.

**1974:** President Richard Nixon resigns after the Watergate crisis.

1980



DIGITAL PERSPECTIVES

## Timeline

Ask students to examine the 1950–Present Timeline and to reflect on the key events. Encourage a discussion by asking students how one event may be related to others. For example, ask students to discuss how the struggles and victories for equal rights may have influenced other events.

PERSONALIZE FOR LEARNING

### English Language Support

**Compound Sentences** Support English learners by reviewing how to connect their ideas using compound and complex sentences. Explain that a compound sentence has two independent clauses or complete sentences that are joined with a coordinating conjunction (such as *and, nor, but, or, yet, so*). Use this example from the text: *Congress passes the Equal Rights Amendment,* ***but*** *it fails to achieve ratification.* Ask students to practice writing compound sentences. **EMERGING**

Explain to students that a complex sentence contains an independent clause and one or more dependent clauses and uses a subordinating conjunction (such as: *although, as, before, if, since, whereas, while*). Use this example from the text:

***Although*** *there were times of crisis and confrontation, the 1960s also was an era of genuine progress, especially in the continuing struggle for civil rights and racial equality.* Help students practice writing complex sentences. **EXPANDING, BRIDGING**

## Integration of Knowledge and Ideas

Have students analyze the data in the graph and draw conclusions to answer the two questions.

Possible responses: According to this survey, 92 percent of students go online at least once a day. The information suggests that a vast majority of teenagers find entertainment in playing video games and in going online.

## History of the Period (cont.)

Have students focus on the sections labeled *Planet Earth*, *A Technological Revolution* and *The New Millennium*. Point out that concerns about the planet and the growth of technology are not generally viewed as related. Encourage a discussion by asking students the following question: *How can technology be used to encourage citizens to take care of the planet?*



### Integration of Knowledge and Ideas

**Notebook** According to this survey, what total percentage of teenagers go online at least once a day? What do the graph and table suggest about entertainment among today's teens?

**Teenagers Online, 2015**

- 56% Online several times/day
- 24% Online almost constantly
- 12% Online once/day
- 6% Online weekly
- 2% Online less than once/week

**Teenagers and Video Games, 2015**

| | Girls | Boys |
|---|---|---|
| Own or have access to a game console | 70% | 91% |
| Play video games online or on their phone | 59% | 84% |

Source: Pew Research Center's Teens Relationship Survey 2014, 2015

**A Technological Revolution** With the introduction of the microprocessor in the 1970s, life shifted dramatically. In a breathtakingly short time, computers—which began as military and business tools—transformed industry and became personal companions for many Americans. Ever smaller, faster, and easier to use, technology—via the Internet—can now electronically connect anyone with everyone, raising complex questions about privacy and personal relations.

**The New Millennium** Despite technological advances, traditional issues still dominate human affairs. How do—and how should—human beings relate to the natural world? How can people of different cultures live together peacefully? How can people build a better future? One thing is certain: Although the world will continue to change as the new millennium moves forward, Americans will continue to explore new aspects and applications of the principles of life, liberty, and the pursuit of happiness.

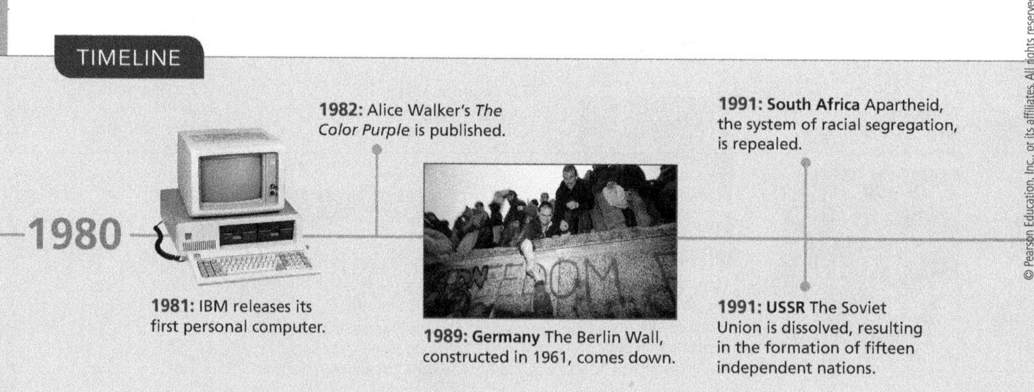

TIMELINE
1980
1981: IBM releases its first personal computer.
1982: Alice Walker's The Color Purple is published.
1989: Germany The Berlin Wall, constructed in 1961, comes down.
1991: South Africa Apartheid, the system of racial segregation, is repealed.
1991: USSR The Soviet Union is dissolved, resulting in the formation of fifteen independent nations.






### PERSONALIZE FOR LEARNING

**Strategic Support**

**Comprehension** Students may need support to better understand the events in the timeline. Have students identify events that interest them. Assign each student one to three events to research with the goal of getting brief clarification of the event's significance. Have students take notes and share their findings.

## Literature Selections

**Literature of the Focus Period** Some of the selections in this unit were written during the Focus Period and pertain to an exploration of the human condition:

"Everyday Use," Alice Walker

"Everything Stuck to Him," Raymond Carver

"The Leap," Louise Erdrich

"A Brief History of the Short Story," D. F. McCourt

"The Man to Send Rain Clouds," Leslie Marmon Silko

"Ambush," Tim O'Brien

"Housepainting," Lan Samantha Chang

**Connections Across Time** Literary works that consider aspects of the human condition are not confined to the Focus Period, of course. They have been a topic of interest in every era of literature in every culture since ancient times. These American short stories are from a period that precedes the Focus Period by several decades:

"An Occurrence at Owl Creek Bridge," Ambrose Bierce

"The Jilting of Granny Weatherall," Katherine Anne Porter

"The Tell-Tale Heart," Edgar Allan Poe

### ADDITIONAL FOCUS PERIOD LITERATURE

**Student Edition**

UNIT 1
"Speech to the Young Speech to the Progress-Toward," Gwendolyn Brooks

"The Pedestrian," Ray Bradbury

UNIT 2
"Sweet Land of . . . Conformity?" Claude Fischer

"Hamadi," Naomi Shihab Nye

UNIT 3
from *The Warmth of Other Suns*, Isabel Wilkerson

"Books as Bombs," Louis Menand

UNIT 4
"In the Longhouse, Oneida Museum," Roberta Hill

"Cloudy Day," Jimmy Santiago Baca

"The Rockpile," James Baldwin

UNIT 5
*The Crucible*, Arthur Miller

from *Farewell to Manzanar*, Jeanne Wakatsuki Houston and James D. Houston

"What You Don't Know Can Kill You," Jason Daley

"Runagate Runagate," Robert Hayden

"For Black Women Who Are Afraid," Toi Derricote

"What Are You So Afraid Of?" Akiko Busch

**1993:** Toni Morrison wins the Nobel Prize for Literature.

**1996: Scotland** "Dolly" the sheep becomes the first mammal to be cloned from an adult cell.

**2001:** Terrorists use commercial planes to attack the United States on 9/11, killing some 3,000 people.

**2008:** Barack Obama is elected the first African American president of the United States.

Present

**2010:** The population of the United States reaches 308.7 million.



## PERSONALIZE FOR LEARNING

### Challenge

**Multimedia Presentation** Ask students to select one event or concept mentioned in this section as their topic for a three-minute class presentation. If students struggle to pick an event, allow them to select one of the following: the first IBM personal computer; the publication of *Silent Spring*; the 1957 integration of a high school in Little Rock, AK; the "Age of Aquarius." Have students research their selected event or concept and create a presentation for the class about it. Set aside a class period for students to share their presentations.

DIGITAL PERSPECTIVES

## Literature Selections

Have students consider the human condition as a literary theme. Ask students to discuss the following questions: *What makes issues related to the human condition a universal theme? How is a universal theme, such as one related to the human condition, affected by the time period in which a story is set?*

Have students review the selections in this unit organized under *Literature of the Focus Period* and *Connections Across Time*. Also point out the additional Focus Period Literature found in *my*Perspectives. Encourage students to use these selections for additional evidence as they complete this unit.

## Comprehension Check

Ask students to answer these questions independently and to then discuss them in a group.

1. What were the moments of progress and setback related to equality and freedom during this period? **Possible responses:** Progress: school integration; the Voting Rights Act; first African American President. Setbacks: The need for troops to enforce school integration; assassinations of JFK and MLK; violence and protests.
2. What did the "Age of Aquarius" signify and how do its ideals fit with historical events of the time? **Possible responses:** The "Age of Aquarius" was a time when people expressed idealistic values of universal peace and love. These ideals fit with the war protests—people wanted peace, not war—and with the ideas of equality for all people and the protests against racism and segregation.
3. How did the events of September 11, 2001 transform the world? How might these events have affected the movement toward equality and freedom for all?
**Possible responses:** There was more fear among Americans. There was also military action in Afghanistan and Iraq. Suspicions about fellow citizens having terrorist ties as well as increased security could detract from equality and freedom.

# Everyday Use

**AUDIO SUMMARIES**
Audio summaries of "Everyday Use" are available online in both English and Spanish in the Interactive Teacher's Edition or Unit Resources. Assigning these summaries prior to reading the selection may help students build additional background knowledge and set a context for their first read.

## Summary

"Everyday Use" is a short story by Alice Walker. The narrator is a mother with two very different daughters, Maggie and Dee. Maggie, who lives with her mother, is painfully shy and embarrassed by burn scars she received in a terrible fire. Dee, by contrast, is educated and self assured. Sometimes the mother dreams of having a joyful reunion with her estranged daughter, Dee, but then realizes that kind of thing happens only on TV shows. Dee announces that she now uses the African name Wangero instead of her given name. Dee, who has always been disdainful of her mother's "backward" ways, now wants to take family heirlooms with her as part of her quest to celebrate her heritage.

### Insight

This short story demonstrates that book learning is no substitute for kindness and sensitivity. Dee, who has always had things handed to her, shows a lack of understanding of her mother's strength and her sister's daily struggles. In the end, the mother decides that just for once, Maggie is going to get what only Maggie can fully appreciate: the quilts.

ESSENTIAL QUESTION:
**What do stories reveal about the human condition?**

## Connection to Essential Question

The short story "Everyday Use" connects to the Essential Question in that it reveals much about the human condition. Students may notice the way Dee/Wangero does not seem to respect the way her family lives or the disdainful way she treats her weaker sister.

WHOLE-CLASS LEARNING PERFORMANCE TASK
**How do stressful situations often reveal the best and worst in people?**

UNIT PERFORMANCE-BASED ASSESSMENT
**How does a fictional character or characters respond to life-changing news?**

## Connection to Performance Tasks

**Whole-Class Learning Performance Task** In this Performance Task, students will consider the human response to stressful situations. Maggie's actions may provide content for their writing.

**Unit Performance-Based Assessment** The characters in this story offer their own techniques for interacting with others and managing life-changing news. Students may notice that Dee/Wangero has rejected her home and her name. She attacks her family's "ignorance" of its heritage. The story shows both the mother's pain and her strength in response to this abandonment.

## LESSON RESOURCES

| | Making Meaning | Language Development | Effective Expression |
|---|---|---|---|
| Lesson | **First Read**<br>**Close Read**<br>**Analyze the Text**<br>**Analyze Craft and Structure** | **Concept Vocabulary**<br>**Word Study**<br>**Conventions and Style** | **Writing to Sources**<br>**Speaking and Listening** |
| Instructional Standards | **RL.10** By the end of grade 11, read and comprehend literature . . .<br>**RL.1** Cite strong and thorough textual evidence . . .<br>**RL.3** Analyze the impact of the author's choices . . . | **L.1.a** Apply the understanding that usage is a matter of convention . . .<br>**L.1.b** Resolve issues of complex or contested usage . . .<br>**L.3.a** Vary syntax for effect . . . | **W.3.a–e** Write narratives . . .<br>**SL.1** Initiate and participate effectively in a range of collaborative discussions . . .<br>**SL.1.a** Come to discussions prepared . . . |
| **STUDENT RESOURCES** | | | |
| Available online in the Interactive Student Edition or Unit Resources | Selection Audio<br>First-Read Guide: Fiction<br>Close-Read Guide: Fiction | Word Network | Evidence Log |
| **TEACHER RESOURCES** | | | |
| **Selection Resources** Available online in the Interactive Teacher's Edition or Unit Resources | Audio Summaries<br>Annotation Highlights<br>EL Highlights<br>Analyze Craft and Structure: Character | Concept Vocabulary and Word Study<br>Conventions and Style: Dialect | Writing to Sources: Narrative<br>Speaking and Listening: Partner Discussion<br>English Language Support Lesson: Partner Discussion |
| **Reteach and Practice (RP)** Available online in the Interactive Teacher's Edition or Unit Resources | Analyze Craft and Structure: Character (RP) | Word Study: Exocentric Compounds (RP)<br>Conventions and Style: Dialect (RP) | Writing to Sources: Narrative (RP)<br>Speaking and Listening: Partner Discussion (RP) |
| **Assessment** Available online in Assessments | Selection Test | | |
| **My Resources** | A Unit 6 Answer Key is available online and in the Interactive Teacher's Edition. | | |

# Reading Support

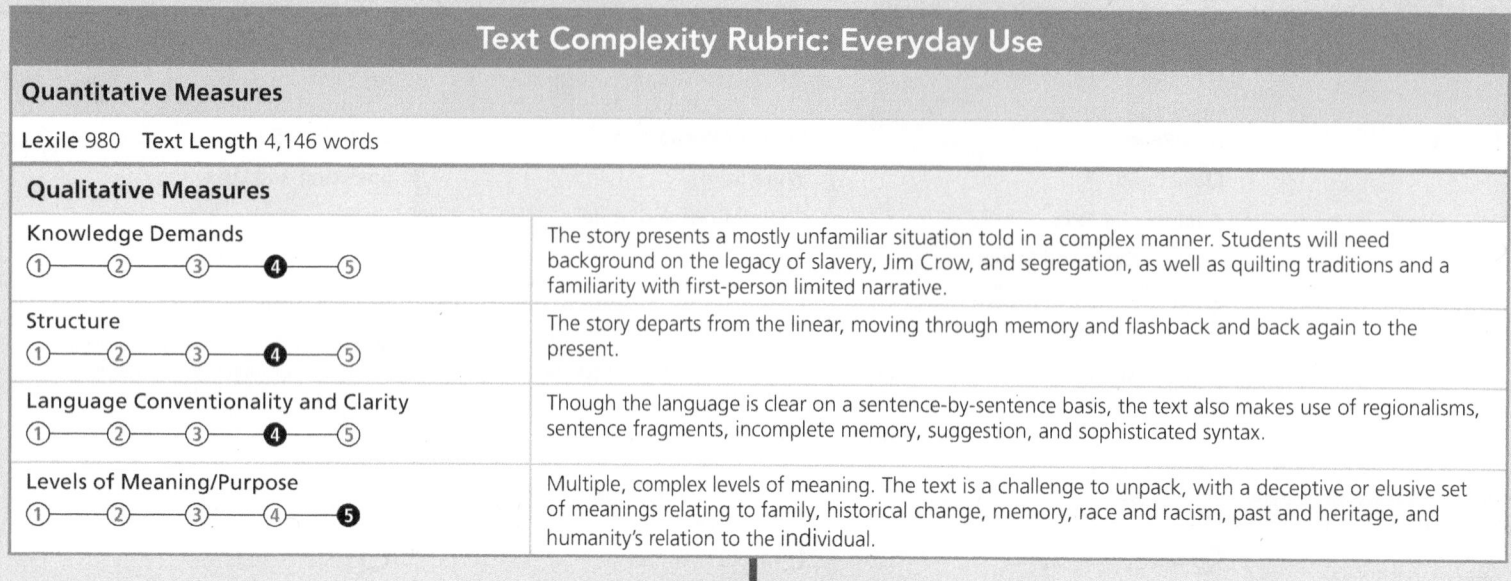

| Text Complexity Rubric: Everyday Use | |
|---|---|
| **Quantitative Measures** | |
| **Lexile** 980 **Text Length** 4,146 words | |
| **Qualitative Measures** | |
| Knowledge Demands ①—②—③—❹—⑤ | The story presents a mostly unfamiliar situation told in a complex manner. Students will need background on the legacy of slavery, Jim Crow, and segregation, as well as quilting traditions and a familiarity with first-person limited narrative. |
| Structure ①—②—③—❹—⑤ | The story departs from the linear, moving through memory and flashback and back again to the present. |
| Language Conventionality and Clarity ①—②—③—❹—⑤ | Though the language is clear on a sentence-by-sentence basis, the text also makes use of regionalisms, sentence fragments, incomplete memory, suggestion, and sophisticated syntax. |
| Levels of Meaning/Purpose ①—②—③—④—❺ | Multiple, complex levels of meaning. The text is a challenge to unpack, with a deceptive or elusive set of meanings relating to family, historical change, memory, race and racism, past and heritage, and humanity's relation to the individual. |

DECIDE AND PLAN

## English Language Support

Provide English Learners with support for language and meaning as they read the selection.

**Language** Students will need help understanding the story's first-person perspective. Ask students to notice which tenses (past, present, future) appear in the text, and tell them to consider why Walker might have shifted the time in this manner.

**Meaning** Discuss the idea of artifacts versus household items. The title of the story suggests that the quilt and the butter churn may be items meant for everyday use, but Dee/Wangero sees art in these items. Engage students in a discussion of this conflict.

## Strategic Support

Provide students with strategic support to ensure that they can successfully read the text.

**Language** Remind students that a story can be told from one of any number of perspectives. Give an example from the first paragraph of the text's use of perspective, and have them think about the significance of this. Ask them to look out for other changes such as the shift from future to present to past tense.

**Meaning** Help students understand the conflict between Dee/Wangero's new life and her family's life. Ask students to look for details in the text that describe the way the family lives and to look for Dee's opinion about these details.

## Challenge

Provide students who need to be challenged with ideas for how they can go beyond a simple interpretation of the text.

**Text Analysis** Ask students to look out for changes in perspective and to make a list of the different ones they notice. Students can do this in pairs, comparing the excerpts they culled from the text to discuss narrative use of tense.

**Written Response** Help students see that the narrator of the story provides her perspective and includes information about her daughters, but cannot share their thoughts or opinions. Ask students to write a section of this story from the perspective of Maggie or Dee.

TEACH

## Read and Respond

Have students complete a first read of the selection. Then, have them complete their close read. Finally, work with them on the Making Meaning, Language Development, and Effective Expression activities.

# Standards Support Through Teaching and Learning Cycle

## IDENTIFY NEEDS

Analyze results of the Beginning-of-Year Assessment, focusing on the items relating to Unit 6. Also take into consideration student performance to this point and your observations of where particular students struggle.

## DECIDE AND PLAN

- If students have performed poorly on items matching these standards, then provide selection scaffolds before assigning them the on-level lesson provided in the Student Edition.
- If students have done well on the Beginning-of-Year Assessment, then challenge them to keep progressing and learning by giving them opportunities to practice the skills in depth.
- Use the Selection Resources listed on the Planning pages for "Everyday Use" to help students continually improve their ability to master the standards.

**Instructional Standards: Everyday Use**

| | Catching Up | This Year | Looking Forward |
|---|---|---|---|
| **Reading** | Administer the **Analyze Craft and Structure: Character (RP)** worksheet to help students interpret character and perspectives. | **RL.3** Analyze the impact of the author's choices regarding how to develop and relate elements of a story or drama. | Ask students to chart the varied perspectives each daughter has on the items in the house and on the quilts. |
| **Writing** | Give students the **Writing to Sources: Narrative (RP)** worksheet to prepare for writing descriptively. | **W.3** Write narratives to develop real or imagined experiences or events using effective technique, well-chosen details, and well-structured event sequences. | Suggest that students peer review and assist one another in refining how they use narrative techniques. |
| **Speaking and Listening** | You may wish to administer the **Speaking and Listening: Partner Discussion (RP)** worksheet to prepare students for collaborating. | **SL.1** Initiate and participate effectively in a range of collaborative discussions with diverse partners on grades 11–12 topics, texts, and issues, building on others' ideas and expressing their own clearly and persuasively. | You may want to invite students to observe one pair that is working collaboratively on the concept of heritage. |
| **Language** | Suggest students work together on the **Conventions and Style: Dialect (RP)** worksheet so that they better grasp regionalism.<br><br>Review the **Word Study: Exocentric Compounds (RP)** worksheet with students to help them better understand how compound words are formed. | **L.3.a** Vary syntax for effect, consulting references for guidance as needed; apply an understanding of syntax to the study of complex texts when reading.<br><br>**L.1.a** Apply the understanding that usage is a matter of convention, can change over time, and is sometimes contested. | Suggest that students prepare a paragraph on some phrases they know that originate in the part of the country they are from.<br><br>Ask students to keep a running list of compound words that they find as they read newspapers, books, or magazines. Have them note which ones are exocentric compounds. |

## ANALYZE AND REVISE

- Analyze student work for evidence of student learning.
- Identify whether or not students have met the expectations in the standards.
- Identify implications for future instruction.

## TEACH

Implement the planned lesson, and gather evidence of student learning.

TEACHING

## Jump Start

**FIRST READ** Ask students what kinds of mementos represent their heritage. Are the objects tucked away in storage or do families use them regularly? Tell students that the story they are about to read questions whether family heirlooms should be in "everyday use."

## Everyday Use

How would you feel if a relative you had not seen for years came back to visit and you discovered that you didn't have a lot in common anymore? Modeling this and other questions readers might ask will bring "Everyday Use" to life and connect it to the Performance Task question. Selection audio and print capability for the selection are available in the Interactive Teacher's Edition.

## Concept Vocabulary

Circulate among students as they rank their words. Remind them that the definitions for these words are listed in the text.

### FIRST READ

The first time they go through the selection, students should perform the steps of the first read:

NOTICE: You may want to encourage students to notice details that help them understand the story's conflict.

ANNOTATE: Remind students to mark passages that surprise them, confuse them, or illuminate a character's true personality.

CONNECT: Encourage students to go beyond the text to make connections between how Alice Walker writes about family and heritage and how they usually think about these concepts.

RESPOND: Students will demonstrate their understanding of the text by answering questions and writing a summary.

Point out to students that they will perform the first three steps concurrently as they are doing their first read. They will complete the Respond step after they have finished the first read. You may wish to print copies of the **First-Read Guide: Fiction** for students to use.

**Remind students that during their first read, they should not answer the close-read questions that appear in the selection.**

MAKING MEANING

About the Author

When **Alice Walker** (b. 1944) was eight, she suffered an injury that blinded her in one eye and left her scarred. For comfort, she turned to reading and writing poetry. Later, she became a highly successful writer with many bestsellers—among them the novel *The Color Purple*, a 1983 Pulitzer Prize winner. Her writing is renowned for its keen observations about relationships and for its strong personal voice. Walker has also published numerous short-story collections and many volumes of poetry.

**Tool Kit**
First-Read Guide and Model Annotation

STANDARDS
**Reading Literature**
By the end of grade 11, read and comprehend literature, including stories, dramas, and poems, in the grades 11–CCR text complexity band proficiently, with scaffolding as needed at the high end of the range.

# Everyday Use

## Concept Vocabulary

You will encounter the following words as you read "Everyday Use." Before reading, note how familiar you are with each word. Then, rank the words in order from most familiar (1) to least familiar (6).

| WORD | YOUR RANKING |
|---|---|
| sidle | |
| shuffle | |
| furtive | |
| cowering | |
| awkward | |
| hangdog | |

After completing the first read, come back to the concept vocabulary and review your rankings. Mark changes to your original rankings as needed.

## First Read FICTION

Apply these strategies as you conduct your first read. You will have an opportunity to complete the close-read notes after your first read.

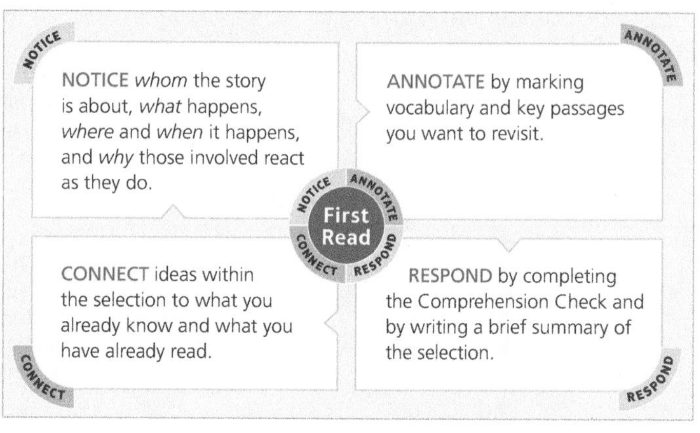

NOTICE
NOTICE *whom* the story is about, *what* happens, *where* and *when* it happens, and *why* those involved react as they do.
ANNOTATE
ANNOTATE by marking vocabulary and key passages you want to revisit.
First Read
CONNECT ideas within the selection to what you already know and what you have already read.
RESPOND by completing the Comprehension Check and by writing a brief summary of the selection.
CONNECT
RESPOND






AUTHOR'S PERSPECTIVE **Kelly Gallagher, M.Ed.**

**Ten Reasons to Read** Students often question why they should read; after all, so much information is now available in audio and video formats. Students are also likely to say that reading is dull and difficult, especially regarding canonical and traditional texts. Teachers can counter these claims by providing students with these ten reasons to read. Revisit these reasons throughout the year, asking students to discuss and write about them.

1. Reading is rewarding.
2. Reading builds a mature vocabulary, which fights "word poverty."
3. Reading makes you a better writer.
4. Reading is "hard" and "hard" is necessary.

# Everyday Use

Alice Walker

BACKGROUND

Quilts play an important part in this story. Quilting, in which layers of fabric and padding are sewn together, dates back to the Middle Ages and perhaps even to ancient Egypt. Today, quilts serve both practical and aesthetic purposes: keeping people warm, recycling old clothing, providing focal points for social gatherings, preserving precious bits of family history, and adding color and beauty to a home. Pay attention to how these purposes relate to the tension that arises among the characters you meet in this story.

SCAN FOR MULTIMEDIA 

1 I will wait for her in the yard that Maggie and I made so clean and wavy yesterday afternoon. A yard like this is more comfortable than most people know. It is not just a yard. It is like an extended living room. When the hard clay is swept clean as a floor and the fine sand around the edges lined with tiny, irregular grooves, anyone can come and sit and look up into the elm tree and wait for the breezes that never come inside the house.

2 Maggie will be nervous until after her sister goes: she will stand hopelessly in corners, homely and ashamed of the burn scars down her arms and legs, eyeing her sister with a mixture of envy and awe. She thinks her sister has held life always in the palm of one hand, that "no" is a word the world never learned to say to her.

NOTES

CLOSE READ

ANNOTATE: In paragraph 2, mark the adjectives that describe Maggie.

QUESTION: Why does the author choose these adjectives?

CONCLUDE: What portrait of Maggie do these adjectives help paint?

DIGITAL PERSPECTIVES

## CLOSE READ

Remind students that authors use adjectives to help readers visualize characters in literature. You may wish to model the close read using the following think-aloud format. Possible responses to questions on the student page are included. You may also want to print copies of the **Close-Read Guide: Fiction** for students to use.

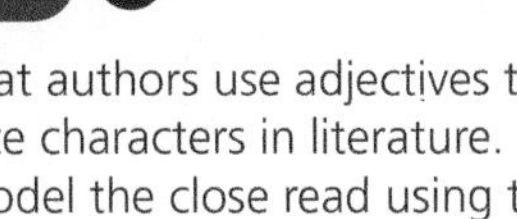

**ANNOTATE:** As I read paragraph 2, I notice and highlight details that describe the character Maggie.

**QUESTION:** I think the author chooses these words to help me visualize Maggie. They demonstrate that she is intimidated by her sister.

**CONCLUDE:** The adjectives paint a picture of a very lonely and shy girl who thinks her sister is better than she is.

Additional **English Language Support** is available in the Interactive Teacher's Edition.

5. Reading makes you smarter.
6. Reading prepares you for the world of work.
7. Reading is financially rewarding.
8. Reading opens doors to college and beyond.
9. Reading arms you against oppression.
10. Reading leads you to a deeper understanding of the world.

NOTES

3 You've no doubt seen those TV shows where the child who has "made it" is confronted, as a surprise, by her own mother and father, tottering in weakly from backstage. (A pleasant surprise, of course: What would they do if parent and child came on the show only to curse out and insult each other?) On TV mother and child embrace and smile into each other's faces. Sometimes the mother and father weep, the child wraps them in her arms and leans across the table to tell how she would not have made it without their help. I have seen these programs.

4 Sometimes I dream a dream in which Dee and I are suddenly brought together on a TV program of this sort. Out of a dark and soft-seated limousine I am ushered into a bright room filled with many people. There I meet a smiling, gray, sporty man like Johnny Carson who shakes my hand and tells me what a fine girl I have. Then we are on the stage and Dee is embracing me with tears in her eyes. She pins on my dress a large orchid, even though she has told me once that she thinks orchids are tacky flowers.

5 In real life I am a large, big-boned woman with rough, man-working hands. In the winter I wear flannel nightgowns to bed and overalls during the day. I can kill and clean a hog as mercilessly as a man. My fat keeps me hot in zero weather. I can work outside all day, breaking ice to get water for washing; I can eat pork liver cooked over the open fire minutes after it comes steaming from the hog. One winter I knocked a bull calf straight in the brain between the eyes with a sledge hammer and had the meat hung up to chill before nightfall. But of course all of this does not show on television. I am the way my daughter would want me to be: a hundred pounds lighter, my skin like an uncooked barley pancake. My hair glistens in the hot bright lights. Johnny Carson has much to do to keep up with my quick and witty tongue.

6 But that is a mistake. I know even before I wake up. Who ever knew a Johnson with a quick tongue? Who can even imagine me looking a strange white man in the eye? It seems to me I have talked to them always with one foot raised in flight, with my head turned in whichever way is farthest from them. Dee, though. She would always look anyone in the eye. Hesitation was no part of her nature.

7 "How do I look, Mama?" Maggie says, showing just enough of her thin body enveloped in pink skirt and red blouse for me to know she's there, almost hidden by the door.

8 "Come out into the yard," I say.

9 Have you ever seen a lame animal, perhaps a dog run over by some careless person rich enough to own a car, **sidle** up to someone who is ignorant enough to be kind to him? That is the way my Maggie walks. She has been like this, chin on chest, eyes on ground, feet in **shuffle**, ever since the fire that burned the other house to the ground.

**sidle** (SY duhl) *v.* move sideways, as in an unobtrusive, stealthy, or shy manner

**shuffle** (SHUHF uhl) *n.* dragging movement of the feet over the ground or floor without lifting them





## CROSS-CURRICULAR PERSPECTIVES

**Humanities: Investigating Popular Culture** Review paragraph 4 with students. The story's narrator alludes to television shows that were popular in the mid-twentieth century. *This Is Your Life*, a show with host Ralph Edwards that ran from 1952 to 1961, staged reunions between celebrities and people who had been influential in their lives on the way to stardom. Encourage interested students to seek out episodes or clips from *This Is Your Life* online. Have students compare that "reality TV" to similar shows that are produced today and share their findings with the class.

10 Dee is lighter than Maggie, with nicer hair and a fuller figure. She's a woman now, though sometimes I forget. How long ago was it that the other house burned? Ten, twelve years? Sometimes I can still hear the flames and feel Maggie's arms sticking to me, her hair smoking and her dress falling off her in little black papery flakes. Her eyes seemed stretched open, blazed open by the flames reflected in them. And Dee. I see her standing off under the sweet gum tree she used to dig gum out of; a look of concentration on her face as she watched the last dingy gray board of the house fall in toward the red-hot brick chimney. Why don't you do a dance around the ashes? I'd want to ask her. She had hated the house that much.

11 I used to think she hated Maggie, too. But that was before we raised the money, the church and me, to send her to Augusta to school. She used to read to us without pity; forcing words, lies, other folks' habits, whole lives upon us two, sitting trapped and ignorant underneath her voice. She washed us in a river of make-believe, burned us with a lot of knowledge we didn't necessarily need to know. Pressed us to her with the serious way she read, to shove us away at just the moment, like dimwits, we seemed about to understand.

12 Dee wanted nice things. A yellow organdy dress to wear to her graduation from high school; black pumps to match a green suit she'd made from an old suit somebody gave me. She was determined to stare down any disaster in her efforts. Her eyelids would not flicker for minutes at a time. Often I fought off the temptation to shake her. At sixteen she had a style of her own, and knew what style was.

13 I never had an education myself. After second grade the school was closed down. Don't ask me why: in 1927 colored asked fewer questions than they do now. Sometimes Maggie reads to me. She stumbles along good-naturedly but can't see well. She knows she is not bright. Like good looks and money, quickness passed her by. She will marry John Thomas (who has mossy teeth in an earnest face) and then I'll be free to sit here and I guess just sing church songs to myself. Although I never was a good singer. Never could carry a tune. I was always better at a man's job. I used to love to milk till I was hooved in the side in '49. Cows are soothing and slow and don't bother you, unless you try to milk them the wrong way.

14 I have deliberately turned my back on the house. It is three rooms, just like the one that burned, except the roof is tin; they don't make shingle roofs any more. There are no real windows, just some holes cut in the sides, like the portholes in a ship, but not round and not square, with rawhide holding the shutters up on the outside. This house is in a pasture, too, like the other one. No doubt when Dee sees it she will want to tear it down. She wrote me once that no matter where we "choose" to live, she will manage to come see us. But she will never bring her friends. Maggie and I thought about this and Maggie asked me, "Mama, when did Dee ever *have* any friends?"

NOTES

**CLOSE READ**

**ANNOTATE:** In paragraph 14, mark Maggie's response to Dee's declaration about never bringing friends to Mama's house.

**QUESTION:** What is surprising about this response?

**CONCLUDE:** What might this response signal to readers?





DIGITAL PERSPECTIVES

## CLOSE READ

Remind students that it is important to note how characters respond to the actions or words of other characters. You may wish to model the close read using the following think-aloud format. Possible responses to questions on the student page are included.

**ANNOTATE:** As I read paragraph 14, I notice and highlight what Maggie says about her sister bringing friends to their house.

**QUESTION:** Her response is something of a surprise because she has only spoken once before in the story.

**CONCLUDE:** Maggie's response shows that she is smart enough to see how little Dee knows about herself.

## WriteNow Analyze and Interpret

**Response** Encourage students to consider how the narrator feels about Dee based on what they read in paragraphs 11–14. Point out that the word *choose* in paragraph 14 is in quotation marks because it is used ironically—the narrator and Maggie cannot choose where they want to live. Ask students to write a brief response to this incident from Maggie's perspective.

## CLOSE READ 

Remind students that writers often use a variety of sentence structures to add interest and excitement as they narrate events or describe scenes and characters. You may wish to model the close read using the following think-aloud format. Possible responses to questions on the student page are included.

**ANNOTATE:** As I read paragraph 20, I mark the sentence fragments.

**QUESTION:** I think the author uses the fragments to show Mama's shock at the way Dee is dressed. This sentence structure also shows that the narrator is not formal.

**CONCLUDE:** The sentence fragments add to the drama and tension because Mama is both appalled and repelled by Dee's appearance. Her narrative style shows that she is not fancy. The sentence fragments seem to deliver the information without flowery language.

NOTES

**furtive** (FUHR tihv) *adj.* done or acting in a stealthy manner to avoid being noticed; secret

15 She had a few. **Furtive** boys in pink shirts hanging about on washday after school. Nervous girls who never laughed. Impressed with her they worshiped the well-turned phrase, the cute shape, the scalding humor that erupted like bubbles in lye.[1] She read to them.

16 When she was courting Jimmy T she didn't have much time to pay to us, but turned all her faultfinding power on him. He *flew* to marry a cheap city girl from a family of ignorant flashy people. She hardly had time to recompose herself.

17 When she comes I will meet—but there they are!

18 Maggie attempts to make a dash for the house, in her shuffling way, but I stay her with my hand. "Come back here," I say. And she stops and tries to dig a well in the sand with her toe.

19 It is hard to see them clearly through the strong sun. But even the first glimpse of leg out of the car tells me it is Dee. Her feet were always neat-looking, as if God himself had shaped them with a certain style. From the other side of the car comes a short, stocky man. Hair is all over his head a foot long and hanging from his chin like a kinky mule tail. I hear Maggie suck in her breath. "Uhnnnh," is what it sounds like. Like when you see the wriggling end of a snake just in front of your foot on the road. "Uhnnnh."

20 Dee next. A dress down to the ground, in this hot weather. A dress so loud it hurts my eyes. There are yellows and oranges enough to throw back the light of the sun. I feel my whole face warming from the heat waves it throws out. Earrings gold, too, and hanging down to her shoulders. Bracelets dangling and making noises when she moves her arm up to shake the folds of the dress out of her armpits. The dress is loose and flows, and as she walks closer, I like it. I hear Maggie go "Uhnnnh" again. It is her sister's hair. It stands straight up like the wool on a sheep. It is black as night and around the edges are two long pigtails that rope about like small lizards disappearing behind her ears.

**CLOSE READ**

**ANNOTATE:** In paragraph 20, mark sentence fragments—groups of words punctuated as sentences that do not contain both a subject and a verb.

**QUESTION:** Why does the author use fragments in this description?

**CONCLUDE:** How does the use of fragments add to the drama or tension of the moment?

21 "Wa-su-zo-Tean-o!"[2] she says, coming on in that gliding way the dress makes her move. The short stocky fellow with the hair to his navel is all grinning and he follows up with "Asalamalakim,[3] my mother and sister!" He moves to hug Maggie but she falls back, right up against the back of my chair. I feel her trembling there and when I look up I see the perspiration falling off her chin.

22 "Don't get up," says Dee. Since I am stout it takes something of a push. You can see me trying to move a second or two before I make it. She turns, showing white heels through her sandals, and goes back to the car. Out she peeks next with a Polaroid. She stoops down quickly and lines up picture after picture of me sitting there in front

1. **lye** (ly) *n.* strong alkaline solution used in cleaning and making soap.
2. **Wa-su-zo-Tean-o** (wah soo zoh TEEN oh) "Good morning" in Lugandan, a language spoken in the African country of Uganda.
3. **Asalamalakim** *Salaam aleikhim* (suh LAHM ah LY keem) Arabic greeting meaning "Peace be with you" that is commonly used by Muslims.





## PERSONALIZE FOR LEARNING

**Strategic Support**

**Chronological Order** Review paragraphs 15–18 with students, and point out the shift in time. Help students practice organizing events sequentially. Have pairs of students interview each other, asking questions about things that have happened so far in "Everyday Use." Encourage pairs to take turns being interviewer and interviewee. The interviewer takes notes as his or her partner answers questions about what happened first, next, and so on.

Remind students that this task might be tricky because Mama reminisces about things that happened years before. Finally, have partners use their notes to construct a timeline or flowchart to visually show the chronological order of events. Suggest pairs leave space to add to the timeline/flowchart as they read on.

DIGITAL PERSPECTIVES

of the house with Maggie cowering behind me. She never takes a shot without making sure the house is included. When a cow comes nibbling around the edge of the yard she snaps it and me and Maggie and the house. Then she puts the Polaroid in the back seat of the car, and comes up and kisses me on the forehead.

NOTES

**cowering** (KOW uhr ihng) *adj.* crouching or drawing back in fear or shame

23 Meanwhile Asalamalakim is going through motions with Maggie's hand. Maggie's hand is as limp as a fish, and probably as cold, despite the sweat, and she keeps trying to pull it back. It looks like Asalamalakim wants to shake hands but wants to do it fancy. Or maybe he don't know how people shake hands. Anyhow, he soon gives up on Maggie.

24 "Well," I say. "Dee."

25 "No, Mama," she says. "Not 'Dee,' Wangero Leewanika Kemanjo!"

26 "What happened to 'Dee'?" I wanted to know.

27 "She's dead." Wangero said. "I couldn't bear it any longer, being named after the people who oppress me."

28 "You know as well as me you was named after your aunt Dicie," I said. Dicie is my sister. She named Dee. We called her "Big Dee" after Dee was born.

"I couldn't bear it any longer, being named after the people who oppress me."

29 "But who was *she* named after?" asked Wangero.

30 "I guess after Grandma Dee," I said.

31 "And who was she named after?" asked Wangero.

32 "Her mother," I said, and saw Wangero was getting tired. "That's about as far back as I can trace it," I said. Though, in fact, I probably could have carried it back beyond the Civil War through the branches.

33 "Well," said Asalamalakim, "there you are."

34 "Uhnnnh," I heard Maggie say.

35 "There I was not," I said, "before 'Dicie' cropped up in our family, so why should I try to trace it that far back?"

36 He just stood there grinning, looking down on me like somebody inspecting a Model A car. Every once in a while he and Wangero sent eye signals over my head.

37 "How do you pronounce this name?" I asked.

38 "You don't have to call me by it if you don't want to," said Wangero.

39 "Why shouldn't I?" I asked. "If that's what you want us to call you, we'll call you."

40 "I know it might sound awkward at first," said Wangero.

**awkward** (AWK wuhrd) *adj.* not graceful or skillful in movement or shape; clumsy

41 "I'll get used to it," I said. "Ream it out again."

42 Well, soon we got the name out of the way. Asalamalakim had a name twice as long and three times as hard. After I tripped over it two or three times he told me to just call him Hakim-a-barber. I wanted to ask him was he a barber, but I didn't really think he was, so I didn't ask.

43 "You must belong to those beef-cattle people down the road," I said. They said "Asalamalakim" when they met you, too, but they didn't shake hands. Always too busy: feeding the cattle, fixing the fences,





## DIGITAL PERSPECTIVES

**Illuminating the Text** Review the dialogue in paragraphs 25–42. In the 1960s and early 1970s, some African Americans took African or Arabic names, rejecting the names acquired through their slave ancestry, and some converted to Islam. Muslims, or members of Islam, follow the teachings of Mohammed, established in the seventh century and expressed in the Koran. Malcolm Little, who joined Islam while in prison, changed his name to Malcolm X to signal his lost African heritage. He went on to lead many others to Islam. World-famous boxer Cassius Clay changed his name to Muhammad Ali. A group of African American Muslims called the Nation of Islam became familiar during the period because of its leader, Elijah Muhammad. Encourage interested students to go online to research more about the link between African Americans and Islam.

NOTES

putting up salt-lick shelters, throwing down hay. When the white folks poisoned some of the herd the men stayed up all night with rifles in their hands. I walked a mile and a half just to see the sight.

44 Hakim-a-barber said, "I accept some of their doctrines, but farming and raising cattle is not my style." (They didn't tell me, and I didn't ask, whether Wangero (Dee) had really gone and married him.)

45 We sat down to eat and right away he said he didn't eat collards[4] and pork was unclean. Wangero, though, went on through the chitlins[5] and corn bread, the greens and everything else. She talked a blue streak over the sweet potatoes. Everything delighted her. Even the fact that we still used the benches her daddy made for the table when we couldn't afford to buy chairs.

46 "Oh, Mama!" she cried. Then turned to Hakim-a-barber. "I never knew how lovely these benches are. You can feel the rump prints," she said, running her hands underneath her and along the bench. Then she gave a sigh and her hand closed over Grandma Dee's butter dish. "That's it!" she said. "I knew there was something I wanted to ask you if I could have." She jumped up from the table and went over in the corner where the churn stood, the milk in it clabber by now. She looked at the churn and looked at it.

47 "This churn top is what I need," she said. "Didn't Uncle Buddy whittle it out of a tree you all used to have?"

48 "Yes," I said.

49 "Uh huh," she said happily. "And I want the dasher, too."

50 "Uncle Buddy whittle that, too?" asked the barber.

51 Dee (Wangero) looked up at me.

52 "Aunt Dee's first husband whittled the dash," said Maggie so low you almost couldn't hear her. "His name was Henry, but they called him Stash."

53 "Maggie's brain is like an elephant's," Wangero said, laughing. "I can use the churn top as a centerpiece for the alcove table," she said, sliding a plate over the churn, "and I'll think of something artistic to do with the dasher."

54 When she finished wrapping the dasher the handle stuck out. I took it for a moment in my hands. You didn't even have to look close to see where hands pushing the dasher up and down to make butter had left a kind of sink in the wood. In fact, there were a lot of small sinks; you could see where thumbs and fingers had sunk into the wood. It was beautiful light yellow wood, from a tree that grew in the yard where Big Dee and Stash had lived.

55 After dinner Dee (Wangero) went to the trunk at the foot of my bed and started rifling through it. Maggie hung back in the kitchen over the dishpan. Out came Wangero with two quilts. They had been pieced by Grandma Dee and then Big Dee and me had hung them on the quilt frames on the front porch and quilted them. One was in the Lone Star pattern. The other was Walk Around the Mountain. In both of them

4. **collards** *n.* leaves of the collard plant, often referred to as "collard greens."
5. **chitlins** *n.* chitterlings, a pork dish popular among southern African Americans.

were scraps of dresses Grandma Dee had worn fifty and more years ago. Bits and pieces of Grandpa Jarrell's Paisley shirts. And one teeny faded blue piece, about the size of a penny matchbox, that was from Great Grandpa Ezra's uniform that he wore in the Civil War.

56 "Mama," Wangero said sweet as a bird. "Can I have these old quilts?"

57 I heard something fall in the kitchen, and a minute later the kitchen door slammed.

58 "Why don't you take one or two of the others?" I asked. "These old things was just done by me and Big Dee from some tops your grandma pieced before she died."

59 "No," said Wangero. "I don't want those. They are stitched around the borders by machine."

60 "That'll make them last better," I said.

61 "That's not the point," said Wangero. "These are all pieces of dresses Grandma used to wear. She did all this stitching by hand. Imagine!" She held the quilts securely in her arms, stroking them.

62 "Some of the pieces, like those lavender ones, come from old clothes her mother handed down to her," I said, moving up to touch the quilts. Dee (Wangero) moved back just enough so that I couldn't reach the quilts. They already belonged to her.

63 "Imagine!" she breathed again, clutching them closely to her bosom.

64 "The truth is," I said, "I promised to give them quilts to Maggie, for when she marries John Thomas."

65 She gasped like a bee had stung her.

66 "Maggie can't appreciate these quilts!" she said. "She'd probably be backward enough to put them to everyday use."

67 "I reckon she would," I said. "God knows I been saving 'em for long enough with nobody using 'em. I hope she will!" I didn't want to bring up how I had offered Dee (Wangero) a quilt when she went away to college. Then she had told me they were old-fashioned, out of style.

68 "But they're *priceless*!" she was saying now, furiously; for she has a temper. "Maggie would put them on the bed and in five years they'd be in rags. Less than that!"

69 "She can always make some more," I said. "Maggie knows how to quilt."

70 Dee (Wangero) looked at me with hatred. "You just will not understand. The point is these quilts, *these quilts*!"

71 "Well," I said, stumped. "What would *you* do with them?"

72 "Hang them," she said. As if that was the only thing you *could* do with quilts.

73 Maggie by now was standing in the door. I could almost hear the sound her feet made as they scraped over each other.

74 "She can have them, Mama," she said, like somebody used to never winning anything, or having anything reserved for her.

NOTES

**CLOSE READ**

**ANNOTATE:** In paragraph 55, mark details that describe the fabrics used in the quilts.

**QUESTION:** Why does the author include this information?

**CONCLUDE:** How does this information affect readers' sympathies?

Remind students to notice the details that the author includes to help readers visualize objects in the story. You may wish to model the close read using the following think-aloud format. Possible responses to questions on the student page are included.

**ANNOTATE:** As I read paragraph 55, I notice and mark details about what kinds of things were used to make the quilts.

**QUESTION:** I think the author includes this information so I can visualize the quilts and understand why Mama values them so much.

**CONCLUDE:** As the story unfolds, readers want Maggie, not Dee/Wangero, to have the quilts because Maggie learned to make quilts with Grandma Dee. She appreciates the quilts and the memories sewn into them more than her sister does.

## VOCABULARY DEVELOPMENT

**Multiple Meanings** Review the use of the word *backward* in paragraph 66. Remind students that some words have more than one meaning. For example, the word *backward* can mean "toward what is behind" or "not as advanced in learning and development as others." Direct students' attention to the word *backward* in paragraph 66. Have them decide which meaning is used in the sentence *(not as advanced in learning and development as others)*. Then ask volunteers to use *backward* in a sentence to reflect the other meaning, such as "I looked backward and saw the dog following me." Finally, have students research and explain the meanings of these other multiple-meaning words and identify how each is used in the selection: *last* (paragraph 60), *temper* (paragraph 68), *hit* (paragraph 77).

## CLOSE READ

Remind students that authors reveal a lot about a character through that character's thoughts and feelings. Readers can also learn a lot about a character by knowing what other characters believe he or she is feeling or thinking. You may wish to model the close read using the following think-aloud format. Possible responses to questions on the student page are included.

**ANNOTATE:** As I read paragraph 76, I notice and mark sentences in which Mama expresses Maggie's feelings and thoughts.

**QUESTION:** I think the author wants Mama to say how Maggie feels to show that she understands how her daughter thinks.

**CONCLUDE:** This emphasizes the difference in Mama's relationships with her daughters because she knows that Maggie is willing to do anything for family, whereas Dee/Wangero only cares about herself. The author's choice may also allow Maggie to be even more silent, but Mama's insights let readers understand Maggie's thinking.

## Media Connection

Project the media connection video in class, ask students to open the video in their interactive textbooks, or have students scan the Bounce Page icon with their phones to access the video.

**Discuss It** Possible Response: Hearing the sarcasm and ridicule in the voices of Dee and Hakim-a-barber make me realize even more that they are the ignorant ones, not Mama and Maggie.

NOTES

**hangdog** (HANG DAWG) *adj.* sad; ashamed; guilty

CLOSE READ

**ANNOTATE:** In paragraph 76, mark the sentences in which Mama expresses Maggie's feelings and thoughts.

**QUESTION:** Why does the author choose to have Mama express Maggie's feelings?

**CONCLUDE:** How does this choice emphasize differences in Mama's relationships with her two daughters?

75 "I can 'member Grandma Dee without the quilts."

76 I looked at her hard. She had filled her bottom lip with checkerberry snuff and it gave her face a kind of dopey, hangdog look. It was Grandma Dee and Big Dee who taught her how to quilt herself. She stood there with her scarred hands hidden in the folds of her skirt. She looked at her sister with something like fear but she wasn't mad at her. This was Maggie's portion. This was the way she knew God to work.

77 When I looked at her like that something hit me in the top of my head and ran down to the soles of my feet. Just like when I'm in church and the spirit of God touches me and I get happy and shout. I did something I never had done before: hugged Maggie to me, then dragged her on into the room, snatched the quilts out of Miss Wangero's hands and dumped them into Maggie's lap. Maggie just sat there on my bed with her mouth open.

78 "Take one or two of the others," I said to Dee.

79 But she turned without a word and went out to Hakim-a-barber.

80 "You just don't understand,'" she said, as Maggie and I came out to the car.

81 "What don't I understand?" I wanted to know.

82 "Your heritage," she said. And then she turned to Maggie, kissed her, and said, "You ought to try to make something of yourself, too, Maggie. It's really a new day for us. But from the way you and Mama still live you'd never know it."

83 She put on some sunglasses that hid everything above the tip of her nose and her chin.

84 Maggie smiled; maybe at the sunglasses. But a real smile, not scared. After we watched the car dust settle I asked Maggie to bring me a dip of snuff. And then the two of us sat there just enjoying, until it was time to go in the house and go to bed. ❧



MEDIA CONNECTION

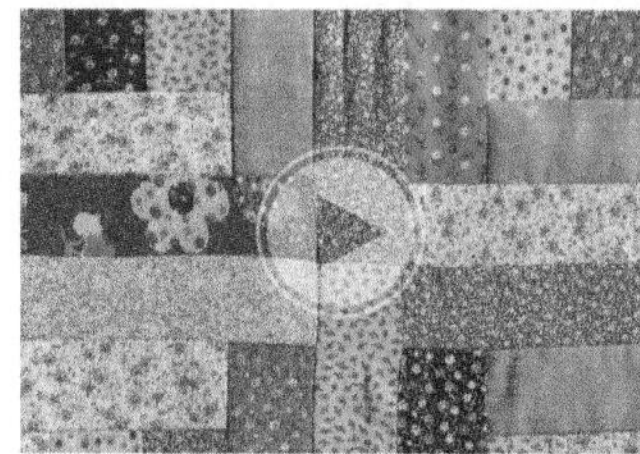

Alice Walker's "Everyday Use"

**Discuss It** How does listening to someone tell this story help you understand Mama and the tensions among the characters?

**Write your response before sharing your ideas.**

SCAN FOR MULTIMEDIA  

## PERSONALIZE FOR LEARNING

### English Language Support

**Comparing and Contrasting** Review paragraphs 78–84 pointing out the author's use of the word *but.* Remind students that words and phrases can signal when two things are being compared or contrasted. Write the following on the board or on a screen: *like, different from, similar to, also, on the other hand, as well as, however, but, as opposed to, in the same way.* Discuss whether each word or phrase indicates a comparison or a contrast. Ask students to use each in a sentence about two characters in "Everyday Use" that demonstrates either a likeness or a difference in the two. **ALL LEVELS**

## Comprehension Check

Complete the following items after you finish your first read.

1. Early in the story, how does Mama describe herself?

2. According to Mama, how did Dee treat her and Maggie when she came home from college?

3. Who arrives with Dee/Wangero on this visit?

4. Why has Dee changed her name to Wangero?

5. What household objects does Dee/Wangero want? Which ones does Mama give her?

6. **Notebook** To confirm your understanding, write a summary of "Everyday Use."

### RESEARCH

**Research to Clarify** Choose at least one unfamiliar detail from the text. Briefly research that detail. In what way does the information you learned shed light on an aspect of the story?

**Research to Explore** Conduct research on an aspect of the text you find interesting. For example, you may want to learn about the Black Power movement of the 1970s that led to the cultural nationalism Dee/Wangero and Asalamalakim find appealing.





PERSONALIZE FOR LEARNING

### Challenge

**The Art of Quilting** Invite students to research quilting techniques and designs. They may wish to focus on quilts made by African American women or those made by early American pioneers. Ask students to make presentations to the class in which they display photographs and their own drawings of quilt designs and, if possible, actual examples of quilts. Students may be able to find a local quilt maker who can visit the class for a talk, or possibly present a demonstration of the art.

## Comprehension Check

**Possible responses:**

1. Mama describes herself as a big, strong woman who can handle difficult farm tasks, such as slaughtering a hog or cow. These are jobs usually done by men.
2. She used to read to Mama and Maggie, making them feel dimwitted and ignorant about information they didn't understand.
3. Dee/Wangero brings with her a man named Asalamalakim (Hakim-a-barber) who might be just a friend, her boyfriend, or her husband.
4. Dee says she changed her name because she no longer wanted a name given to her by the oppressor.
5. Dee/Wangero wants the handle of a butter churn and her mother gives it to her. She also wants two special handmade quilts that are Mama's and Maggie's favorites. Mama gives her several other quilts, not the ones that have special meaning because they have distinctive parts of her ancestors' clothes.
6. The narrator (Mama) and her daughter, Maggie, wait in the yard for Dee, Maggie's older sister, who is coming to visit. Mama tells how the sisters are different—Dee is pretty and self-centered; Maggie is shy and scarred from a fire that burned down their old house. Finally Dee arrives with a male companion. They are dressed in African-influenced clothing, and Dee has changed her name to Wangero to reflect her African heritage. In her desire to show off her African heritage, she selfishly wants to take parts of the old family butter churn and handmade quilts, favorites of the narrator and Maggie, just to display them for her new friends. Mama stands up to Dee/Wangero, snatches the quilts, and gives them to Maggie. Dee/Wangero gets angry and leaves, and Maggie smiles.

## Research

**Research to Clarify** If students struggle to find a detail to research, you may want to suggest that they focus on Johnny Carson's show or the ways that people chose names to reflect an African heritage.

**Research to Explore** Encourage students to report their findings about the Black Power movement of the 1970s, or any other topic they chose, to the class.

EVERYDAY USE

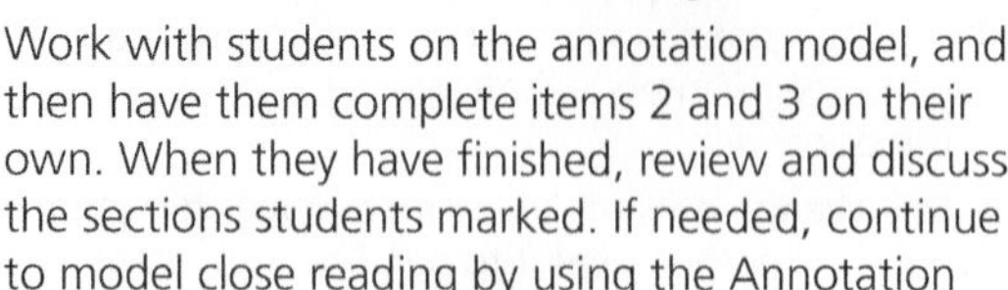

## Jump Start

CLOSE READ Have students read the title "Everyday Use." Ask them if they can think of objects they use every day that in the future might be treasured as collectible symbols of their heritage. Then ask whether and why students think this might be a good topic for other writers to explore.

## Close Read the Text

Work with students on the annotation model, and then have them complete items 2 and 3 on their own. When they have finished, review and discuss the sections students marked. If needed, continue to model close reading by using the Annotation Highlights in the Interactive Teacher's Edition.

## Analyze the Text

Possible responses:

1. It shows that she understands how her daughter Dee/Wangero sees her, and that the only way to please Dee/Wangero would be if she lost one hundred pounds, had lighter skin, and looked more fashionable; then her daughter could hug her and appear to be proud of her in front of a big audience. (paragraph 4) **DOK 3**
2. (a) The quilts symbolize the family's heritage and the relationship of the family to the generations before them. **DOK 2** (b) Dee/Wangero wants the quilts to show off her sense of "culture." Maggie wants them because she learned to make them from Grandma Dee. **DOK 2**
3. (a) Dee/Wangero plans to display the butter churn handle and to hang the quilts on her wall so people can admire them. **DOK 1** (b) It is ironic because she does not honor their role in her family's life. **DOK 3**
4. At that time many African Americans looked to their African roots in an effort to reconnect with their heritage. Many wore colorful dashikis or colorful flowing robes and sandals, as their ancestors did in Africa. **DOK 3**
5. Responses will vary.

### FORMATIVE ASSESSMENT

#### Analyze the Text

**If** students fail to cite evidence, **then** remind them to support their ideas with specific information from the text.



## Close Read the Text

1. This model, from paragraph 10 of the text, shows two sample annotations, along with questions and conclusions. Close read the passage, and find another detail to annotate. Then, write a question and your conclusion.

Close Read (ANNOTATE • QUESTION • CONCLUDE)

ANNOTATE: These details contrast the two daughters' reactions to the fire.

QUESTION: Why does the author include these details?

CONCLUDE: The details emphasize Maggie's involvement and Dee's distance.

Sometimes I can still . . . feel Maggie's arms sticking to me, her hair smoking and her dress falling off her in little black papery flakes. . . . And Dee. I see her standing off under the sweet gum tree. . . . Why don't you do a dance around the ashes? I'd want to ask her.

ANNOTATE: This question is sarcastic and funny.

QUESTION: What does this detail reveal about Mama?

CONCLUDE: Mama is not naive; she has good insight about her daughters.

**Tool Kit**
Close-Read Guide and Model Annotation

2. For more practice, go back into the text and complete the close-read notes.
3. Revisit a section of the text you found important during your first read. Read this section closely, and **annotate** what you notice. Ask yourself **questions** such as "Why did the author make this choice?" What can you **conclude**?

## Analyze the Text

CITE TEXTUAL EVIDENCE to support your answers.

**Notebook** Respond to these questions.

1. **Make Inferences** What does Mama's dream of being on Johnny Carson's show illustrate about her relationship to Dee/Wangero?
2. (a) **Interpret** What do the quilts symbolize, or represent? (b) **Compare and Contrast** In what ways do the quilts hold different meanings for Dee/Wangero and for Maggie?
3. (a) What does Dee/Wangero plan to do with the items that she requests? (b) **Evaluate** What is ironic about her request for these objects and her professed interest in her heritage?
4. **Historical Perspectives** How do Dee/Wangero's and her companion's clothing and overall appearances reflect a change in African American culture in the 1960s?
5. **Essential Question:** *What do stories reveal about the human condition?* What has reading this story taught you about family relationships?

STANDARDS
**Reading Literature**
• Cite strong and thorough textual evidence to support analysis of what the text says explicitly as well as inferences drawn from the text, including determining where the text leaves matters uncertain.
• Analyze the impact of the author's choices regarding how to develop and relate elements of a story or drama.





### PERSONALIZE FOR LEARNING

#### English Language Support

**Idioms** Review paragraph 2 of the text. Students may struggle with the idiom "held life always in the palm of one hand." Explain to students that this is an idiom—the words are not meant to be taken literally. Make sure students understand that this idiom means "can easily make people do or think what she wants." If students struggle to understand idioms, encourage them to look for context clues. In this instance, the clue is in the rest of the sentence: *that "no" is a word the world never learned to say to her*. Encourage students to look for more idioms in the story, such as *talked a blue streak* in paragraph 44, and determine its meaning together (It means "to say a lot very fast"; it refers to the blue streak in the sky from a jet plan going fast). **ALL LEVELS**

## Analyze Craft and Structure

**Literary Elements: Character** Writers reveal key messages or themes in stories through **characterization**—what characters say, what they do, and how they interact with other characters.

Short stories often feature a main character as a first-person narrator. It is through this character's eyes that readers learn about events and perceive the other characters. This first-person narrator serves as a guide through the world of the story, presenting his or her thoughts, feelings, observations, and perceptions. Inevitably, every narrator comes with biases, or leanings, so readers have to decide how much they trust the narrator's interpretation of events. The perspective the first-person narrator brings to the story is a key element that leads readers to the story's **themes,** or insights about life.

### Practice

**CITE TEXTUAL EVIDENCE** to support your answers.

Notebook Respond to these questions.

1. (a) Who is the narrator of "Everyday Use"? (b) Identify three thoughts and feelings that the narrator shares with readers. (c) Do you trust this narrator's account of people and events? Explain.
2. In the chart, record details about Mama and Dee/Wangero related to their appearances, life experiences, relationships, and values. Then, identify a possible theme that Walker develops by setting up contrasts between these two characters.

| MAMA | DEE (WANGERO) |
|---|---|
| See possible responses in Teacher's Edition. | |
| THEME: | |

3. Think about the words and actions of Hakim-a-barber. How does the inclusion of this character help develop other characters in the story?





## PERSONALIZE FOR LEARNING

### Strategic Support

**Character Interaction** Encourage small groups of students to examine Hakim-a-barber's behavior toward Maggie and her mother. Ask the groups to discuss the reasons that Maggie and her mother do not like him. Then have each group collaborate to write a letter to Hakim-a-barber, giving him advice about how to get along with people who are different from him. Allow time for groups to share their letters.

DIGITAL PERSPECTIVES 

## Analyze Craft and Structure

**Literary Elements: Character** Remind students that a writer reveals a character's personality by describing how he or she looks and what he or she says. Moreover, through *indirect characterization*, the writer also describes the character's behavior and how it affects other characters. How one character responds to another helps readers know more about both characters' personalities.

For more support, see **Analyze Craft and Structure: Character.**

**MAKE IT INTERACTIVE**

Ask students to think about family life in contemporary times. Some families describe themselves as "dysfunctional," with conflicts between family members. Have volunteers share their knowledge of this subject from TV, in films or books, or on social media.

### Practice

Possible responses:

1. (a) Mama is the narrator. (b) She appreciates the simple things in life. She thinks Maggie has deep feelings and can empathize with others. She thinks that Dee/Wangero is self-centered, and that Hakim-a-barber looks down on Maggie and her mother. (c) Students may say that they trust the narrator because they can understand the feelings she shares.
2. **MAMA:** little education; strong and able to support her family; understands correct grammar but speaks in a way that reflects her heritage; understands both Maggie and Dee

   **DEE/WANGERO:** highly educated; has new boyfriend or husband; confident; condescending; changed her name; new-found interest in heritage comes from academics, not life
   **THEME:** Even within a family, heirlooms may have different meanings to different people.
3. Hakim-a-barber and Dee seem to think alike and it almost appears that she is following his lead in her new life. He looks down on Mama and Maggie. His arrival points out what a kind person Mama is. She tries to pronounce his name correctly, and she treats him as a guest although he belittles her. His presence in the story reinforces Dee/Wangero's new life.

**FORMATIVE ASSESSMENT**

### Analyze Craft and Structure

**If** students struggle to analyze interactions between characters, **then** discuss indirect characterization, and illustrate with examples.

For Reteach and Practice, see **Analyze Craft and Structure: Character (RP).**

## Concept Vocabulary

**Why These Words?**

Possible responses:

1. The concept words help me see that Maggie is intimidated and frightened.
2. Other words include *nervous, hopelessly, homely, ashamed, stumble, envy, awe, lame, ignorant.*

### Practice

Possible responses:

1. Responses will vary.
2. **Antonyms**—*sidle/swagger, furtive/direct, awkward/relaxed, shuffle/run, cowering/challenging, hangdog/cheery.* If these words were used, Maggie would be stronger and able to stand up against her sister.

### Word Network

**Possible words**: *heritage, hated, knowledge, trapped, ignorant, temper, scarred*

## Word Study

For more support, see **Concept Vocabulary and Word Study.**

Possible responses:

1. *egghead, turncoat, highbrow, blue-collar, blockhead*
2. Responses will vary.

### FORMATIVE ASSESSMENT

### Concept Vocabulary

**If** students fail to see the connection between the words, **then** have them look back at the text and determine how each word is used in connection with the characters.

### Word Study

**If** students struggle to find examples of exocentric compounds, **then** encourage them to use an online search engine. For Reteach and Practice, see **Word Study: Exocentric Compounds (RP).**

LANGUAGE DEVELOPMENT

EVERYDAY USE

## Concept Vocabulary

| sidle | furtive | awkward |
|---|---|---|
| shuffle | cowering | hangdog |

**Why These Words?** These concept vocabulary words help reveal the tentative way Maggie acts in the story. Mama describes Maggie as *cowering* behind her and as moving her feet in a *shuffle*. These words describe a person who wants to be invisible.

1. How do the concept vocabulary words help you understand why Mama and Dee/Wangero have different attitudes toward Maggie?

2. What other words in the selection connect to this concept?

### Practice

**Notebook** The concept vocabulary words appear in "Everyday Use."

1. Write three sentences, using two of the concept words in each sentence, to demonstrate your understanding of the words' meanings.
2. Choose an antonym—a word with an opposite meaning—for each concept vocabulary word. How would the story be different if these words were used to describe Maggie?

## Word Study

**Exocentric Compounds** Most compound words contain at least one word part that connects directly to what is being named or described. For example, the compound word *sunflower* names a type of flower. Some compound words, however, connect two words of which neither names the thing or person described. These **exocentric compound** words are often used to name or describe people—for example, *tattletale*, *birdbrain*, and *pickpocket*. In "Everyday Use," the narrator describes Maggie as having "a dopey, hangdog look." *Hangdog* means "guilty" or "ashamed."

1. Use a dictionary to find five examples of exocentric compounds. Record them here.

2. Use each of your choices in a sentence. Be sure to include context clues that hint at each word's meaning.

**WORD NETWORK**

Add words related to the human condition from the text to your Word Network.

**STANDARDS**

Language

- Apply the understanding that usage is a matter of convention, can change over time, and is sometimes contested.
- Resolve issues of complex or contested usage, consulting references as needed.
- Vary syntax for effect, consulting references for guidance as needed; apply an understanding of syntax to the study of complex texts when reading.





**AUTHOR'S PERSPECTIVE** Elfrieda Hiebert, Ph.D.

**Collocation** Teachers can explain to students that many words often occur together, a process called *collocation*. Point out examples such as the words *stormy* and *weather* go together, as do *adverse weather conditions*—*adverse* is not used to describe other nouns such as *assignments*. Other examples of weather collocation include a *change in the weather* and *to weather the storm*.

Teachers can have students share and discuss the following examples. Focus on the fact that although the underlined words are synonyms, they are not interchangeable:

| warm greeting | but not | a hot greeting |
|---|---|---|
| tall people | but not | high people |

Guiding students to collect words that collocate can support them in becoming flexible in the use of language. Further, learning collocation provides a store of ready-made expressions, helping students express language concisely. Help students learn more about collocation by using the Academic Collocation List developed by Pearson, posted at http://pearsonpte.com/research/academic-collocation-list/.

## Conventions and Style

**Dialect** Writers may use dialect and regionalisms to add depth to characters and settings.

- **Dialect** is a way of using English that is specific to a certain area or group of people.
- **A regionalism** is an expression common to a specific place.

These nonstandard forms of language can make characters more realistic by reflecting culture, customs, and educational levels.

### Read It

1. Study the examples of dialogue in this chart. Then, use formal English to rewrite each sentence. One example has been done for you.

| FROM "EVERYDAY USE" | FORMAL ENGLISH |
|---|---|
| *"You know as well as me you was named after your aunt Dicie."* (paragraph 28) | "You know as well as I do that you were named after your aunt Dicie." |
| *"I'll get used to it. . . . Ream it out again."* (paragraph 41) | "I will be able to pronounce it, just say it again." |
| *"The truth is . . . I promised to give them quilts to Maggie, for when she marries John Thomas."* (paragraph 64) | "The truth is, I promised to give those quilts to Maggie when she marries John Thomas." |
| *"I reckon she would. . . . God knows I been saving 'em for long enough with nobody using 'em."* (paragraph 67) | "I guess she would. God knows I have been saving them for a long time without anyone using them." |

2. **Connect to Style** Find one other example of dialect or regionalism in "Everyday Use." Explain how the example develops a character or the setting.

### Write It

**Notebook** Use examples from "Everyday Use" to describe what would be lost if Alice Walker had chosen to write dialogue using the same style that she uses for description.





DIGITAL PERSPECTIVES 

## Conventions and Style

**Dialect** Explain to students that people from different communities have characteristic ways of talking. Some people mistakenly call it "an accent," such as "He has a southern accent." However, an accent is simply how words are pronounced. A dialect includes distinct grammar, vocabulary, syntax, and common, or colloquial, expressions. For example, a character from one community might say, "It don't make me never-no-mind," while a character from a different community might say, "IDC!" Both characters are saying, "I don't care."

For more support, see **Conventions and Style: Dialect.**

### Read It

**Possible responses:**

1. See possible responses in chart on student page.
2. "*I can 'member Grandma Dee without the quilts.*" (paragraph 75) This line helps to develop Maggie's character as she speaks up and doesn't give in to her sister.

### Write It

Students should note that Walker wrote the narration with correct grammar and standard English. Student responses should show dialogue without the dialect, making the story more formal and potentially less realistic.

### FORMATIVE ASSESSMENT

### Conventions and Style

- **If** students struggle to understand dialect, **then** encourage them to reread the text aloud to imitate the voice.
- **If** students struggle to rewrite dialect in Standard English, **then** provide an example of a simple sentence in any regional dialect, including your region, and have the group decipher it together.

For more Reteach and Practice, see **Conventions and Style: Dialect (RP).**

# TEACHING

## Writing to Sources

Explain to students that when they write a narrative from a different point of view, they should focus on the aspects of the text that allow them to say something meaningful. They should first choose a character and determine how he or she fits into the story. Next, they should decide what they need to tell to clarify the character's motivation and actions. Suggest students ask themselves: *What fresh take on the situation does this character offer? What language patterns would this character use: dialect, standard English, or both?*

For more support, see **Writing to Sources: Narrative.**

### Reflect on Your Writing

1. Responses will vary. If students need support, ask them to think about how their character observed things differently from Walker's narrator because of his or her role in the family.
2. Responses will vary. Remind students that learning a method of handling a challenging situation can help them avoid the same problem in the future.
3. **Why These Words?** Have students list specific examples of words they chose to add power to their narrative.

### FORMATIVE ASSESSMENT

### Writing to Sources

- **If** students struggle to identify a character to serve as narrator in their writing, **then** have them list all of the possible characters and choose the one whose actions they most nearly relate to.
- **If** students struggle to include specific details in their narratives, **then** ask them to review the text and jot down how that person feels about the situation.

For Reteach and Practice, see **Writing to Sources: Narrative (RP).**

## EFFECTIVE EXPRESSION

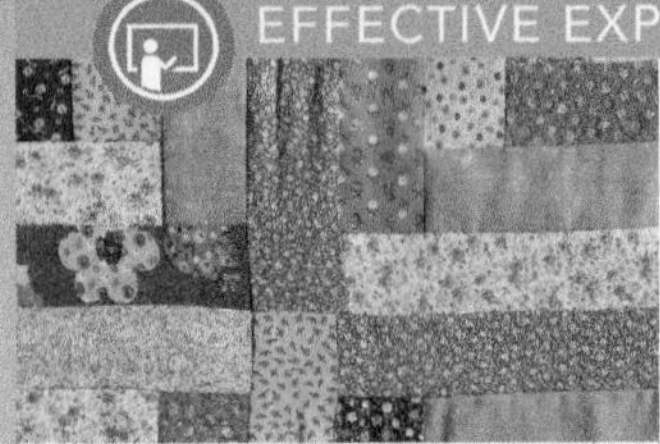

EVERYDAY USE

## Writing to Sources

Narrative writing would be dull if it only reported basic events. However, vivid descriptive details about setting and characters can bring a narrative to life and engage readers. For example, recall how the narrator in "Everyday Use" describes Maggie: "Have you ever seen a lame animal, perhaps a dog run over by some careless person rich enough to own a car, sidle up to someone who is ignorant enough to be kind to him?" This description helps readers picture precisely how Maggie moves and acts around other people.

**Assignment**

Write a short **narrative** of 500 words or less in which you retell an event from "Everyday Use" from the perspective of a character other than Mama. You may choose to describe Dee's visit or an event from the past. Make sure your narrative is consistent with the characters and setting created by Walker. Include descriptive details that illustrate the character's thoughts and engage the reader.

Include these elements in your narrative:

- a narrator other than Mama from "Everyday Use"
- a clear description of the event, including how the narrator feels about it
- dialect or regionalisms in dialogue or narration, as appropriate

**Vocabulary Connection** Consider including a few of the concept vocabulary words in your narrative.

| sidle | furtive | awkward |
|---|---|---|
| shuffle | cowering | hangdog |

### Reflect on Your Writing

After you have written your short narrative, answer these questions.

1. How did writing your narrative strengthen your understanding of Walker's story?
2. What part of writing this narrative was most challenging, and how did you handle it?
3. **Why These Words?** The words you choose make a difference in your writing. Which words did you choose to create vivid descriptive details?

**STANDARDS**

**Writing**
Write narratives to develop real or imagined experiences or events using effective technique, well-chosen details, and well-structured event sequences.

**Speaking and Listening**
- Initiate and participate effectively in a range of collaborative discussions with diverse partners on *grades 11–12 topics, texts, and issues,* building on others' ideas and expressing their own clearly and persuasively.
- Come to discussions prepared, having read and researched material under study; explicitly draw on that preparation by referring to evidence from texts and other research on the topic or issue to stimulate a thoughtful, well-reasoned exchange of ideas.





## VOCABULARY DEVELOPMENT

**Word Forms** Remind students that a good way to build vocabulary is to identify other forms of a word. For example, *quilt* as a noun describes a kind of blanket; *quilt* as a verb describes the action of putting together the parts of that blanket. Have partners choose a concept word and create a word web to show different tenses (verbs) or word forms.

For example, using the verb *shuffle*, the word web might include *shuffle* (center), past: *shuffled*, future: *will shuffle*, present perfect: *has shuffled*, past perfect: *had shuffled*, future perfect: *will have shuffled*. A word web for the adjective *furtive* might contain the following:

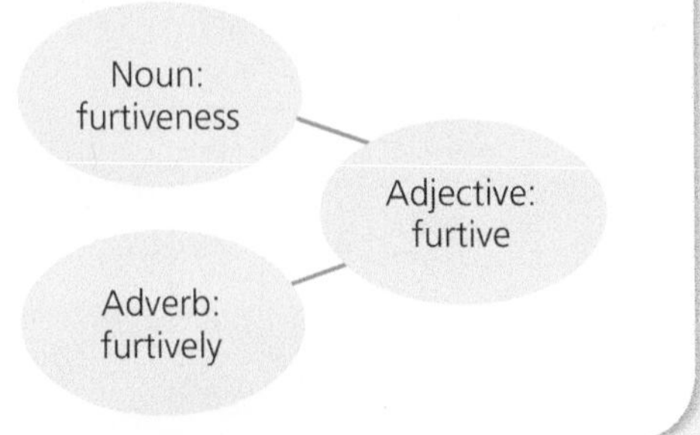

## Speaking and Listening

**Assignment**

Have a **partner discussion** about what factors lead a person to embrace, reject, or feel neutral about his or her heritage. Before working with your partner, think about the two daughters' perspectives on heritage, and take notes about how the text inspires your own thoughts on the subject. As you discuss, build on one another's ideas, asking respectful questions, listening politely, and adding your own insights. At the end of your discussion, create an extended definition of *heritage*. Follow these steps to complete the assignment.

1. **Focus on the Text** Choose examples from the story.
    - Consider ways the author indirectly describes characters.
    - Compare and contrast the three women's attitudes toward objects in the house.
    - Discuss what the story's resolution says about heritage.
2. **Share Personal Experiences** Share your own experiences with heritage and traditions in your family. Consider questions such as the following:
    - What are some objects in your home or family that are part of a heritage or tradition?
    - How and when are these objects used? Every day? Only on holidays?
    - Does everyone recognize the objects as special?
3. **Craft an Extended Definition** To create an extended definition of *heritage*, come to a consensus about the most important ideas to include.
    - Summarize your notes in three main points.
    - Summarize your personal experiences with heritage.
    - Draft and refine an extended definition that includes all of your most important thoughts.
4. **Evaluate the Activity** When you have finished, use the evaluation guide to analyze the way that you and your partner worked together to discuss a topic and create an extended definition.

**EVALUATION GUIDE**

**Rate each statement on a scale of 1 (not demonstrated) to 5 (demonstrated).**

☐ Both partners contributed equally to the discussion.

☐ Partners commented upon the text and also shared personal experiences.

☐ Partners were attentive to and respectful of the thoughts presented.

☐ Partners worked collaboratively to create an extended definition of *heritage*.

**EVIDENCE LOG**

Before moving on to a new selection, go to your Evidence Log and record what you learned from "Everyday Use."





**DIGITAL PERSPECTIVES**  

## Speaking and Listening

1. **Focus on the Text** Remind students to compare and contrast what heritage means to different characters in the story. Students should reference specific objects in their discussion.
2. **Share Personal Experiences** Remind partners to be respectful of one another's opinions: what is a special heirloom to one person may be a common, ordinary object to another.
3. **Craft an Extended Definition** As partners collaborate on their definition, remind them to include samples from both their reading and their and personal knowledge.
4. **Evaluate the Activity** Encourage students to be objective as they review their collaborative activity.

For more support, see **Speaking and Listening: Partner Discussion.**

**Evidence Log** Support students in completing their Evidence Log. This paced activity will help prepare them for the Performance-Based Assessment at the end of the unit.

### FORMATIVE ASSESSMENT

### Speaking and Listening

- **If** students struggle to work together without significant disagreement, **then** have them use sticky notes to mark the text and establish what each character thinks *heritage* means.
- **If** students are worried about presenting their definition, **then** suggest that they write it on a poster so the audience can read it.

For Reteach and Practice, see **Speaking and Listening: Partner Discussion (RP).** instead of the entire class.

### Selection Test

Administer the "Everyday Use" Selection Test, which is available in both print and digital formats online in Assessments.

## PERSONALIZE FOR LEARNING

### English Language Support

**Preparing for a Partner Discussion** Some students may struggle to list ideas for this discussion. Display a chart with three categories: Embrace, Reject, Neutral. Students can use this chart to direct their thinking. Ask students to put ideas in each column in advance of their discussion. **ALL LEVELS**

An expanded **English Language Support Lesson** on Partner Discussion is available in the Digital Teacher's Edition.

# Everything Stuck to Him

**AUDIO SUMMARIES**
Audio summaries of "Everything Stuck to Him" are available online in both English and Spanish in the Interactive Teacher's Edition or Unit Resources. Assigning these summaries prior to reading the selection may help students build additional background knowledge and set a context for their first read.

## Summary

Raymond Carver's short story "Everything Stuck to Him" explores the lives of two teenaged newlyweds and their baby daughter. They are very much in love with each other but in many ways are still young and immature. A conflict occurs between the couple over the young man's plans to go on a hunting trip. The baby cries for most of the night before the trip. The girl decides that she wants her husband to skip his hunting trip, stay home, and help her take care of the baby. The husband argues, explaining that his friend Carl is depending on him to keep his plans. The girl gives her husband an ultimatum: "You're going to have to choose," she tells him. "Carl or us."

### Insight

The story is set in a frame of many years, helping to add the perspective of time to the narrative. "Everything Stuck to Him" addresses issues of identity, commitment, maturity, and responsibility. Reading it will help students understand that commitment and maturity involve making choices. Faced with his wife's ultimatum, the father makes his choice and cancels his hunting trip, thus reinforcing the idea that fatherhood means taking responsibility.

ESSENTIAL QUESTION:
What do stories reveal about the human condition?

## Connection to Essential Question

The story "Everything Stuck to Him" shows that the responsibilities of parenting can be challenging. This story is a memory the father shares with his daughter, showing that experiences bond people over time.

WHOLE-CLASS LEARNING PERFORMANCE TASK
How do stressful situations often reveal the best and worst in people?

UNIT PERFORMANCE-BASED ASSESSMENT
How does a fictional character or characters respond to life-changing news?

## Connection to Performance Tasks

**Whole-Class Learning Performance Task** This story reveals a young couple working to navigate the stress of living with a newborn. The outcome of their struggle provides an answer to the performance task prompt.

**Unit Performance-Based Assessment** The selection examines a seemingly small event that poses a huge, potentially life-changing choice for the young father. Students may decide to use the experiences described in the story to address the prompt.

DIGITAL PERSPECTIVES

 Audio  Video  Document  Annotation Highlights  EL Highlights  Online Assessment

## LESSON RESOURCES

| | Making Meaning | Language Development | Effective Expression |
|---|---|---|---|
| **Lesson** | **First Read**<br>**Close Read**<br>**Analyze the Text**<br>**Analyze Craft and Structure** | **Concept Vocabulary**<br>**Word Study**<br>**Conventions and Style** | **Writing to Sources**<br>**Speaking and Listening** |
| **Instructional Standards** | **RL.10** By the end of grade 11, read and comprehend literature . . .<br>**RL.1** Cite strong and thorough textual evidence . . .<br>**RL.5** Analyze how an author's choices . . . | **L.1** Demonstrate command of the conventions . . .<br>**L.3** Apply knowledge of language . . . | **RL.3** Analyze the impact of the author's choices . . .<br>**W.3.a–e** Write narratives . . .<br>**SL.4** Present information, findings, and supporting evidence . . .<br>**SL.6** Adapt speech to a variety of contexts and tasks . . . |
| **STUDENT RESOURCES** | | | |
| Available online in the Interactive Student Edition or Unit Resources | Selection Audio<br>First-Read Guide: Fiction<br>Close-Read Guide: Fiction | Word Network | Evidence Log |
| **TEACHER RESOURCES** | | | |
| **Selection Resources** Available online in the Interactive Teacher's Edition or Unit Resources | Audio Summaries<br>Annotation Highlights<br>EL Highlights<br>English Language Support Lesson: Pronouns and Antecedents<br>Analyze Craft and Structure: Narrative Structure | Concept Vocabulary and Word Study<br>Conventions and Style: Pronouns and Antecedents | Writing to Sources: Narrative Scene<br>Speaking and Listening: Dialogue |
| **Reteach/Practice (RP)** Available online in the Interactive Teacher's Edition or Unit Resources | Analyze Craft and Structure: Narrative Structure (RP) | Word Study: Endocentric Compounds (RP)<br>Conventions and Style: Pronouns and Antecedents (RP) | Writing to Sources: Narrative Scene (RP)<br>Speaking and Listening: Dialogue (RP) |
| **Assessment** Available online in Assessments | Selection Test | | |
| **My Resources** | A Unit 6 Answer Key is available online and in the Interactive Teacher's Edition. | | |

# Reading Support

| Text Complexity Rubric: Everything Stuck to Him | |
|---|---|
| **Quantitative Measures** | |
| Lexile 460 **Text Length** 1,996 words | |
| **Qualitative Measures** | |
| Knowledge Demands<br>① ❷ ③ ④ ⑤ | The story explores a situation that may be familiar—the conflict of responsibility and personal enjoyment. |
| Structure<br>① ② ❸ ④ ⑤ | The narrative is simple and the language unadorned, though the story does demonstrate a simple example of frame narrative, a technique that some students may not know. |
| Language Conventionality and Clarity<br>❶ ② ③ ④ ⑤ | In the minimalist style, syntax and sentence structure are easy to understand. Vocabulary is on-level and descriptions are light. |
| Levels of Meaning/Purpose<br>① ② ③ ❹ ⑤ | There is much ambiguity in the conclusion, and students may struggle to determine the meaning of the story. Multiple readings may be required to examine concepts of memory, family, and human relationships. |

DECIDE AND PLAN

## English Language Support

Provide English Learners with support for structure and meaning as they read the selection.

**Structure** Though the language is straightforward, the structure of the short story is complicated by the use of narrative frame. Ask students to imagine the story as told without Carver's frame narrative, and to consider how the meaning of the text may or may not change in the absence of the encapsulating father-and-daughter framework.

**Meaning** Encourage students to try to understand how the frame gives the story itself meaning. Ask them to make a list of possible conclusions they can come to about the father, the daughter, their relationship, why they might have come to Milan, and whether the story the father tells is true.

## Strategic Support

Provide students with strategic support to ensure that they can successfully read the text.

**Structure** Discuss or provide examples of other frame narratives for students who would like further information on the topic. Talk about the different benefits of such a narrative technique in comparison to a more straightforward style. For example, a frame narrative allows for the passage of time or the additional level of complexity.

**Meaning** Ask the students to identify the two different narratives in the story. Then have them go through the text and underline every instance of the encapsulating father-daughter frame narrative. When they find that not all the references to the father and daughter in Milan are in one place, have them discuss why they think that is.

## Challenge

Provide students who need to be challenged with ideas for how they can go beyond a simple interpretation of the text.

**Text Analysis** Have students analyze the language used. Students should decide whether it is simple or complex, and why it might be that way. Then have them read the two narratives in the story separately, and think about whether the two stories have as much meaning on their own as they do together. Discuss how the minimalist style and complex structure complement each other.

**Written Response** Ask the students to compose their own short frame narrative. Have them discuss with each other the two different narratives they may use, and how they will use narrative strategies to move from the outer frame narrative to the other inner narrative.

TEACH

## Read and Respond

Have students do their first read of the selection. Then have them complete their close read. Finally, work with them on the Making Meaning, Language Development, and Effective Expression activities.

# Standards Support Through Teaching and Learning Cycle

## IDENTIFY NEEDS

Analyze results of the Beginning-of-Year Assessment, focusing on the items relating to Unit 6. Also take into consideration student performance to this point and your observations of where particular students struggle.

## DECIDE AND PLAN

- If students have performed poorly on items matching these standards, then provide selection scaffolds before assigning them the on-level lesson provided in the Student Edition.
- If students have done well on the Beginning-of-Year Assessment, then challenge them to keep progressing and learning by giving them opportunities to practice the skills in depth.
- Use the Selection Resources listed on the Planning pages for "Everything Stuck to Him" to help students continually improve their ability to master the standards.

**Instructional Standards: Everything Stuck to Him**

| | Catching Up | This Year | Looking Forward |
|---|---|---|---|
| **Reading** | Give students the **Analyze Craft and Structure: Narrative Structure (RP)** worksheet so they can see how a frame story works. | **RL.5** Analyze how an author's choices concerning how to structure specific parts of a text contribute to its overall structure and meaning as well as its aesthetic impact. | After writing a frame story, ask students to graphically show how the framing of the story works. |
| **Writing** | Give students the **Writing to Sources: Narrative Scene (RP)** worksheet to help them create a narrative scene. | **W.3** Write narratives to develop real or imagined experiences or events using effective technique, well-chosen details, and well-structured event sequences. | Pair students to start creating a frame story together and then assign each to develop one part of the frame. Invite students to discuss the issues this approach presents. |
| **Speaking and Listening** | Administer the **Speaking and Listening: Dialogue (RP)** worksheet to help students how dialogue adds to a story. | **SL.6** Adapt speech to a variety of contexts and tasks, demonstrating a command of formal English when indicated or appropriate. | To create a dialogue, choose a story both partners know and decide on a region for the story's setting. |
| **Language** | Administer the **Conventions and Style: Pronouns and Antecedents (RP)** worksheet. This worksheet gives students familiarity with problematic antecedents.<br><br>Review the **Word Study: Endocentric Compounds (RP)** worksheet with students to help them better understand how compound words are formed. | **L.3** Apply knowledge of language to understand how language functions in different contexts, to make effective choices for meaning or style, and to comprehend more fully when reading or listening.<br><br>**L.1** Demonstrate command of the conventions of standard English grammar and usage when writing or speaking. | Suggest that students work in pairs to find an example where Carver breaks a rule, but the meaning is clear.<br><br>Ask students to keep a running list of compound words that they find as they read newspapers, books, or magazines. Have them note which ones are endocentric compounds. |

## ANALYZE AND REVISE

- Analyze student work for evidence of student learning.
- Identify whether or not students have met the expectations in the standards.
- Identify implications for future instruction.

## TEACH

Implement the planned lesson, and gather evidence of student learning.

## Jump Start

FIRST READ Ask students to write a brief paragraph about their earliest memory. Ask them to answer the following questions: *Were any family members or friends there? Who were they? How old were they? How did they act? How do their older selves compare to the way they are in your memory?* Invite student volunteers to read aloud their paragraphs.

## Everything Stuck to Him  

How old do you think most parents are when they have their first baby? What might be scary about having a baby when you are only in your teens? Modeling these and other questions readers might ask will bring "Everything Stuck to Him" to life and connect it to the Performance Task question. Selection audio and print capability for the selection are available in the Interactive Teacher's Edition.

## Concept Vocabulary

Circulate among students as they rank their words. Remind them that the definitions for these words are listed in the selection.

### FIRST READ

The first time they go through the story, students should perform the steps of the first read:

NOTICE: During their first read, remind students to notice details that help them follow the events of the story.

ANNOTATE: Remind students to mark unfamiliar words and phrases as well as parts of the story that seem important.

CONNECT: Encourage students to connect to other stories they have read, experiences in their own lives, and family stories.

RESPOND: Students will demonstrate their understanding of "Everything Stuck to Him" by answering questions and writing a summary.

Point out to students that they will perform the first three steps concurrently as they are doing their first read. They will complete the Respond step after they have finished the first read. You may wish to print copies of the **First-Read Guide: Fiction** for students to use.

**Remind students that during their first read, they should not answer the close-read questions that appear in the selection.**





**About the Author**

Born in a small Oregon logging town to a mill worker and a waitress, **Raymond Carver** (1938–1988) drew heavily from his life in his stories about the hardships of the working poor. By age twenty, Carver had two children and was struggling to support his family, taking on a series of jobs as a janitor, a sawmill worker, and a gas-station attendant. In 1958, he took a creative writing class, and soon he began to work nights and study writing during the day. His earliest acclaim was for his 1967 story "Will You Please Be Quiet, Please?" In 1971, he began a decade-long partnership with the editor Gordon Lish, who encouraged a "less-is-more" writing approach. Carver's writing became lean and sparse, earning him a reputation as an expert minimalist and one of the greatest storytellers of his time.

# Everything Stuck to Him

## Concept Vocabulary

You will encounter the following words as you read "Everything Stuck to Him." Before reading, note how familiar you are with each word. Then, rank the words in order from most familiar (1) to least familiar (4).

| WORD | YOUR RANKING |
|---|---|
| waterfowl | |
| letterhead | |
| overcast | |
| shotgun | |

After completing the first read, come back to the concept vocabulary and review your rankings. Mark changes to your original rankings as needed.

## First Read FICTION

Apply these strategies as you conduct your first read. You will have an opportunity to complete the close-read notes after your first read.

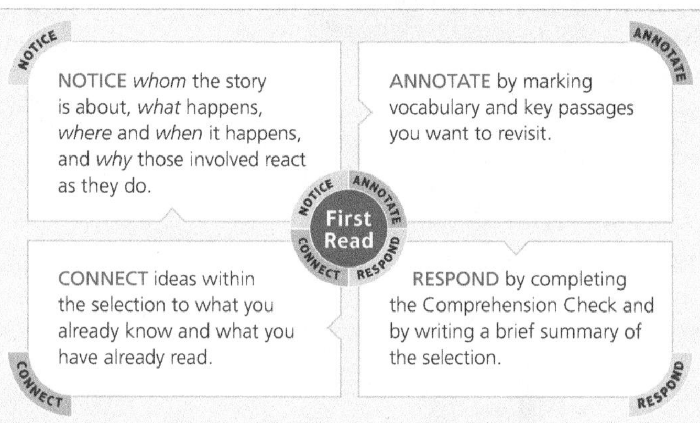

NOTICE *whom* the story is about, *what* happens, *where* and *when* it happens, and *why* those involved react as they do.
ANNOTATE by marking vocabulary and key passages you want to revisit.
CONNECT ideas within the selection to what you already know and what you have already read.
RESPOND by completing the Comprehension Check and by writing a brief summary of the selection.
First Read
NOTICE
ANNOTATE
CONNECT
RESPOND


**STANDARDS**
**Reading Literature**
By the end of grade 11, read and comprehend literature, including stories, dramas, and poems, in the grades 11–CCR text complexity band proficiently, with scaffolding as needed at the high end of the range.

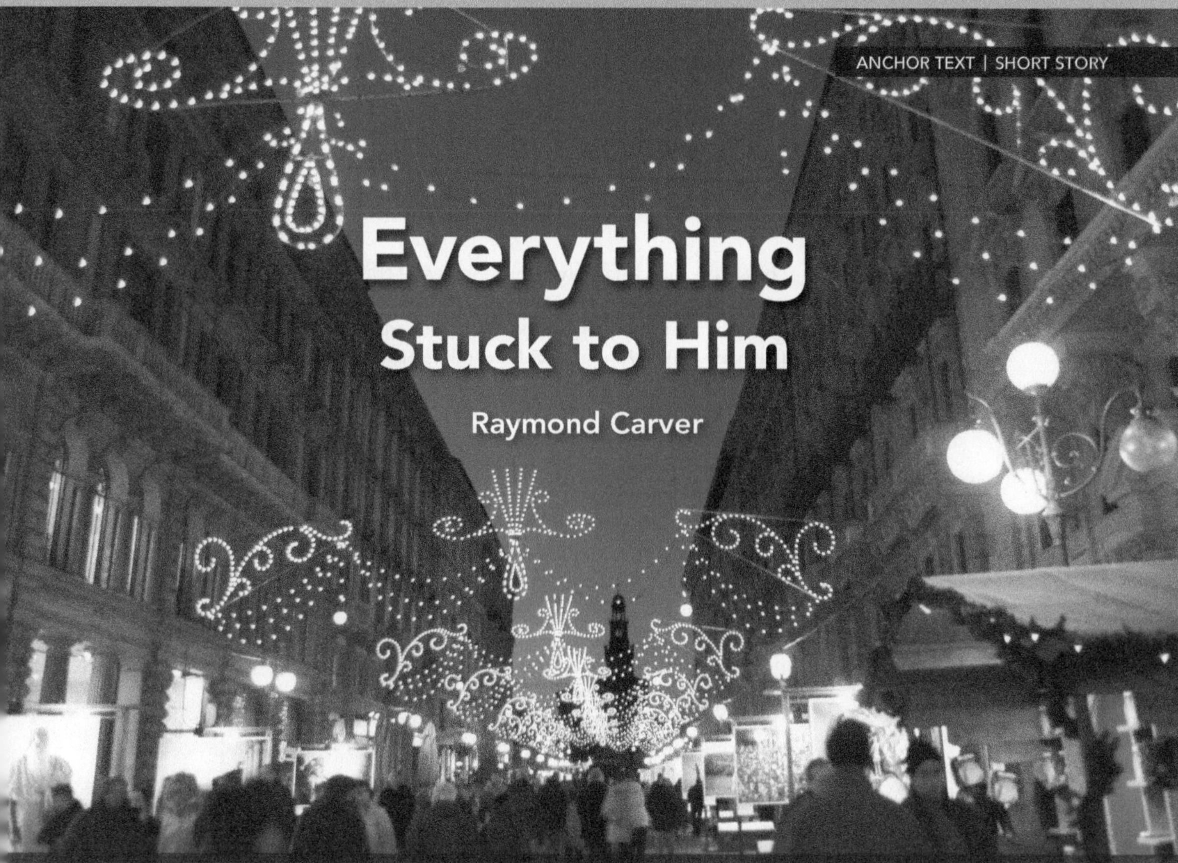


# Everything Stuck to Him

Raymond Carver

BACKGROUND
This is a frame story, or a story within a story. There are many frame narratives in world literature, including the *Arabian Nights* and *The Canterbury Tales*. "The Notorious Jumping Frog of Calaveras County," by Mark Twain (in Unit 4), is an American example. In frame narratives, the introductory story is typically of secondary importance to the internal one. Consider whether this is true of Carver's tale.

SCAN FOR MULTIMEDIA 

1 She's in Milan for Christmas and wants to know what it was like when she was a kid.

2 Tell me, she says. Tell me what it was like when I was a kid. She sips Strega,[1] waits, eyes him closely.

3 She is a cool, slim, attractive girl, a survivor from top to bottom.

4 That was a long time ago. That was twenty years ago, he says.

5 You can remember, she says. Go on.

6 What do you want to hear? he says. What else can I tell you? I could tell you about something that happened when you were a baby. It involves you, he says. But only in a minor way.

NOTES

1. **Strega** Italian herbal liqueur.



DIGITAL PERSPECTIVES  

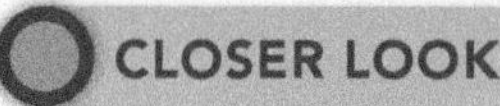

CLOSER LOOK

## Identify Foreshadowing

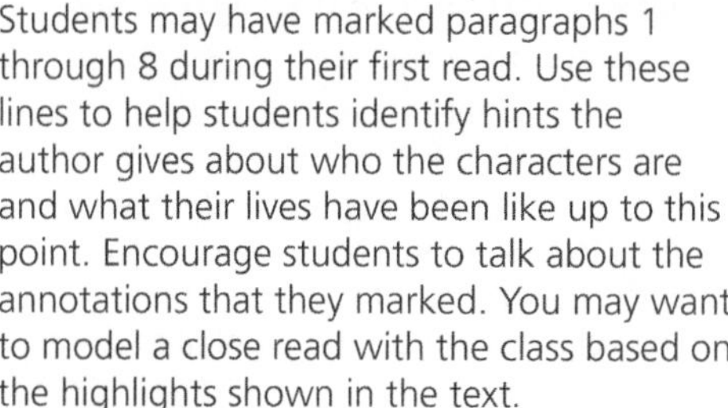

Students may have marked paragraphs 1 through 8 during their first read. Use these lines to help students identify hints the author gives about who the characters are and what their lives have been like up to this point. Encourage students to talk about the annotations that they marked. You may want to model a close read with the class based on the highlights shown in the text.

**ANNOTATE:** Have students mark details in these lines that hint at story events to be revealed later in the narrative, or have students participate while you highlight them.

**QUESTION:** Ask students to use the author's hints to predict what they will learn about this father and daughter.

**Possible response:** The father lives in Milan, and the daughter is visiting him for Christmas. The author does not mention the girl's mom. This omission must mean either that the mother is dead, or that the parents are divorced. Probably the girl has had to "survive" one of these unhappy events.

**CONCLUDE:** Help students to formulate conclusions about the importance of hints such as these in the text. Ask why the author might have included these details.

**Possible responses:** The author might have included these details to hint at what the characters' family situation is like now and what it was like in the past, when the girl was a baby.

Remind or inform students that **foreshadowing** is the use of clues hinting at events that will occur later in a story. This technique helps create suspense.

CLOSER LOOK

## Analyze Story Structure

Students may have marked paragraphs 11–16 during their first read. Use this section to help students track the way story events jump between past and present. Encourage students to talk about the annotations they marked. You may want to model a close read with the class based on the highlights shown in the text.

**ANNOTATE:** Have students mark details in these lines that show where the frame story briefly breaks in before the interior story resumes.

**QUESTION:** Guide students to consider why the author might have gone briefly back to the frame story after beginning the interior story. Accept student responses.

**Possible response:** Maybe the author wants to make sure that readers understand who is who—the man telling the story in Milan is "the boy" in the interior story.

**CONCLUDE:** Help students to formulate conclusions about the importance of these transitions in the text. Ask them whether they think the frame story leads naturally and smoothly into the interior story, and why.

**Possible response:** The frame story leads smoothly into the interior story when the adult daughter asks her father to tell what life was like when she was little.

Remind students that a **frame story** is a story that brackets—or frames—another story, thus creating a story-within-a-story narrative structure. Typically, the framing narrative appears at the beginning of the work to set up the situation of the storytelling within the frame. The narrative then shifts to another story or series of stories and usually returns to the frame story at the end.

Additional **English Language Support** is available in the Interactive Teacher's Edition.

NOTES

**waterfowl** (WAWT uhr fowl) *n.* birds that live in or near water

**letterhead** (LEHT uhr hehd) *n.* personalized stationery

7 Tell me, she says. But first fix us another so you won't have to stop in the middle.

8 He comes back from the kitchen with drinks, settles into his chair, begins.

9 They were kids themselves, but they were crazy in love, this eighteen-year-old boy and this seventeen-year-old girl when they married. Not all that long afterwards they had a daughter.

10 The baby came along in late November during a cold spell that just happened to coincide with the peak of the **waterfowl** season. The boy loved to hunt, you see. That's part of it.

11 The boy and girl, husband and wife, father and mother, they lived in a little apartment under a dentist's office. Each night they cleaned the dentist's place upstairs in exchange for rent and utilities. In summer they were expected to maintain the lawn and the flowers. In winter the boy shoveled snow and spread rock salt on the walks. Are you still with me? Are you getting the picture?

12 I am, she says.

13 That's good, he says. So one day the dentist finds out they were using his **letterhead** for their personal correspondence. But that's another story.

14 He gets up from his chair and looks out the window. He sees the tile rooftops and the snow that is falling steadily on them.

15 Tell the story, she says.

16 The two kids were very much in love. On top of this they had great ambitions. They were always talking about the things they were going to do and the places they were going to go.

DIGITAL PERSPECTIVES

17 Now the boy and girl slept in the bedroom, and the baby slept in the living room. Let's say the baby was about three months old and had only just begun to sleep through the night.

18 On this one Saturday night after finishing his work upstairs, the boy stayed in the dentist's office and called an old hunting friend of his father's.

19 Carl, he said when the man picked up the receiver, believe it or not, I'm a father.

20 Congratulations, Carl said. How is the wife?

21 She's fine, Carl. Everybody's fine.

22 That's good, Carl said, I'm glad to hear it. But if you called about going hunting, I'll tell you something. The geese are flying to beat the band. I don't think I've ever seen so many. Got five today. Going back in the morning, so come along if you want to.

23 I want to, the boy said.

24 The boy hung up the telephone and went downstairs to tell the girl. She watched while he laid out his things. Hunting coat, shell bag, boots, socks, hunting cap, long underwear, pump gun.

25 What time will you be back? the girl said.

26 Probably around noon, the boy said. But maybe as late as six o'clock. Would that be too late?

27 It's fine, she said. The baby and I will get along fine. You go and have some fun. When you get back, we'll dress the baby up and go visit Sally.

28 The boy said, Sounds like a good idea.

29 Sally was the girl's sister. She was striking. I don't know if you've seen pictures of her. The boy was a little in love with Sally, just as he

NOTES

**CLOSE READ**

**ANNOTATE:** In paragraphs 18–24, mark the phrases that the author uses to refer to the two protagonists of the remembered (internal) story.

**QUESTION:** Why does the author name Carl, a minor character, but leave the two protagonists unnamed?

**CONCLUDE:** What effect does this choice have on the way that readers perceive the characters?



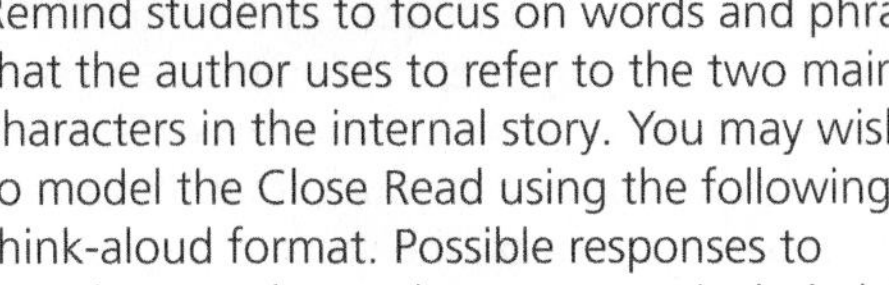

## CLOSE READ

Remind students to focus on words and phrases that the author uses to refer to the two main characters in the internal story. You may wish to model the Close Read using the following think-aloud format. Possible responses to questions on the student page are included. You may also want to print copies of the **Close-Read Guide: Fiction** for students to use.

**ANNOTATE:** As I read paragraphs 18 through 24, I annotate phrases, such as "the boy," "his father's," "the wife," and "the girl."

**QUESTION:** By leaving the two protagonists unnamed, the author may be suggesting that the story has a universal application. These characters could represent any number of young parents who find themselves in similar situations.

**CONCLUDE:** The author's choice to avoid naming the characters makes them more generic. It may also make it hard for readers to develop empathy.

## PERSONALIZE FOR LEARNING

### English Language Support

**Unfamiliar Terms** Point out to students the phrase *to beat the band* in paragraph 22. Tell students that this is an old-fashioned English idiom that means "unusually frequently or intensely." Help students identify and rephrase other idioms and unfamiliar terms in the text, such as *an old hunting friend of his father's*, [telephone] *receiver, shell bag, long underwear,* and [we] *will get along fine.* **ALL LEVELS**

## CLOSE READ

Remind students to note phrases and sentences that tell what the baby keeps doing over and over again. You may wish to model the Close Read using the following think-aloud format. Possible responses to questions on the student page are included.

**ANNOTATE:** As I read paragraphs 39–45, I notice and annotate the phrases and sentences that show that the baby cries. It seems that this is not the way the baby usually behaves.

**QUESTION:** The fact that the baby won't stop crying increases the tension between the boy and the girl. It also makes readers aware that the boy's hunting trip—something he is really looking forward to—may not happen.

**CONCLUDE:** The tension-producing cries help push the story to its climax. Readers want to know what will happen in the morning.

NOTES

**overcast** (OH vuhr kast) *adj.* covered with clouds, as a gray sky

**shotgun** (SHOT guhn) *n.* gun with a long, smooth barrel, that is often used to fire "shot," or small, pellet-like ammunition

**CLOSE READ**

**ANNOTATE:** In paragraphs 39–45, mark the repeated actions of the baby.

**QUESTION:** Why does the author repeat references to this action?

**CONCLUDE:** How does this repeated detail add to the effect of the remembered story?

was a little in love with Betsy, who was another sister the girl had. The boy used to say to the girl, If we weren't married, I could go for Sally.

30 What about Betsy? the girl used to say. I hate to admit it, but I truly feel she's better looking than Sally and me. What about Betsy?

31 Betsy too, the boy used to say.

32 After dinner he turned up the furnace and helped her bathe the baby. He marveled again at the infant who had half his features and half the girl's. He powdered the tiny body. He powdered between fingers and toes.

33 He emptied the bath into the sink and went upstairs to check the air. It was overcast and cold. The grass, what there was of it, looked like canvas, stiff and gray under the street light.

34 Snow lay in piles beside the walk. A car went by. He heard sand under the tires. He let himself imagine what it might be like tomorrow, geese beating the air over his head, shotgun plunging against his shoulder.

35 Then he locked the door and went downstairs.

36 In bed they tried to read. But both of them fell asleep, she first, letting the magazine sink to the quilt.

37 It was the baby's cries that woke him up.

38 The light was on out there, and the girl was standing next to the crib rocking the baby in her arms. She put the baby down, turned out the light, and came back to the bed.

39 He heard the baby cry. This time the girl stayed where she was. The baby cried fitfully and stopped. The boy listened, then dozed. But the baby's cries woke him again. The living room light was burning. He sat up and turned on the lamp.

40 I don't know what's wrong, the girl said, walking back and forth with the baby. I've changed her and fed her, but she keeps on crying. I'm so tired I'm afraid I might drop her.

41 You come back to bed, the boy said. I'll hold her for a while.

42 He got up and took the baby, and the girl went to lie down again.

43 Just rock her for a few minutes, the girl said from the bedroom. Maybe she'll go back to sleep.

44 The boy sat on the sofa and held the baby. He jiggled it in his lap until he got its eyes to close, his own eyes closing right along. He rose carefully and put the baby back in the crib.

45 It was a quarter to four, which gave him forty-five minutes. He crawled into bed and dropped off. But a few minutes later the baby was crying again, and this time they both got up.

46 The boy did a terrible thing. He swore.

47 For God's sake, what's the matter with you? the girl said to the boy. Maybe she's sick or something. Maybe we shouldn't have given her the bath.

48 The boy picked up the baby. The baby kicked its feet and smiled.





## WriteNow Express and Reflect

**Prediction Paragraph** Review and discuss paragraph 29. Have students write a paragraph that answers the following question: *The husband and wife recognize and even joke about the fact that the husband finds his two sisters-in-law attractive. Does this bode well or ill for their marriage?* **Possible responses:** Some students may predict that the husband will fall in love with one of his wife's sisters, divorce his wife, and marry the sister. Others may say that since the boy and girl joke about his attraction to her sisters, it means that neither the husband nor the wife takes this fact seriously or recognizes it as a threat to their marriage.

NOTES

49 Look, the boy said, I really don't think there's anything wrong with her.

50 How do you know that? the girl said. Here, let me have her. I know I ought to give her something, but I don't know what it's supposed to be.

51 The girl put the baby down again. The boy and the girl looked at the baby, and the baby began to cry.

52 The girl took the baby. Baby, baby, the girl said with tears in her eyes.

53 Probably it's something on her stomach, the boy said.

54 The girl didn't answer. She went on rocking the baby, paying no attention to the boy.

55 The boy waited. He went to the kitchen and put on water for coffee. He drew his woolen underwear on over his shorts and T-shirt, buttoned up, then got into his clothes.

56 What are you doing? the girl said.

57 Going hunting, the boy said.

58 I don't think you should, she said. I don't want to be left alone with her like this.

59 Carl's planning on me going, the boy said. We've planned it.

60 I don't care about what you and Carl planned, she said. And I don't care about Carl, either. I don't even know Carl.

61 You've met Carl before. You know him, the boy said. What do you mean you don't know him?

62 That's not the point and you know it, the girl said.

63 What is the point? the boy said. The point is we planned it.

64 The girl said, I'm your wife. This is your baby. She's sick or something. Look at her. Why else is she crying?

65 I know you're my wife, the boy said.

66 The girl began to cry. She put the baby back in the crib. But the baby started up again. The girl dried her eyes on the sleeve of her nightgown and picked the baby up.

67 The boy laced up his boots. He put on his shirt, his sweater, his coat. The kettle whistled on the stove in the kitchen.

68 You're going to have to choose, the girl said. Carl or us. I mean it.

69 What do you mean? the boy said.

70 You heard what I said, the girl said. If you want a family, you're going to have to choose.

If you want a family, you're going to have to choose.

71 They stared at each other. Then the boy took up his hunting gear and went outside. He started the car. He went around to the car windows and, making a job of it, scraped away the ice.

72 He turned off the motor and sat awhile. And then he got out and went back inside.

**CLOSE READ**

Remind students to mark only nouns, pronouns functioning as nouns, verbs, adverbs, and adjectives—no possessive pronouns, conjunctions, articles, interjections, or prepositions that are not acting as adverbs. You may wish to model the Close Read using the following think-aloud format. Possible responses to questions on the Student page are included.

**ANNOTATE:** In paragraphs 74 through 84, I find and annotate nouns such as *boy* and *boots*, verbs such as *took* and *sat*, adjectives such as *long* and *sorry*, and adverbs such as *out* (in "came out") and *all* (in "all right").

**QUESTION:** The author might omit most modifiers because he wants to focus on the action. His writing style is very simple and straightforward.

**CONCLUDE:** The author's simple, straightforward writing style makes this scene seem starkly realistic and poignant—full of understated emotion and simple beauty.

NOTES

**CLOSE READ**

**ANNOTATE:** In paragraphs 74–84, mark the main parts of speech—nouns, verbs, and any adjectives or adverbs.

**QUESTION:** Why does the author omit most modifiers?

**CONCLUDE:** What is the effect of the author's choice to limit the types of words used in this scene?

73 The living-room light was on. The girl was asleep on the bed. The baby was asleep beside her.

74 The boy took off his boots. Then he took off everything else. In his socks and his long underwear, he sat on the sofa and read the Sunday paper.

75 The girl and the baby slept on. After a while, the boy went to the kitchen and started frying bacon.

76 The girl came out in her robe and put her arms around the boy.

77 Hey, the boy said.

78 I'm sorry, the girl said.

79 It's all right, the boy said.

80 I didn't mean to snap like that.

81 It was my fault, he said.

82 You sit down, the girl said. How does a waffle sound with bacon?

83 Sounds great, the boy said.

84 She took the bacon out of the pan and made waffle batter. He sat at the table and watched her move around the kitchen.

85 She put a plate in front of him with bacon, a waffle. He spread butter and poured syrup. But when he started to cut, he turned the plate into his lap.

86 I don't believe it, he said, jumping up from the table.

87 If you could see yourself, the girl said.

88 The boy looked down at himself, at everything stuck to his underwear.

89 I was starved, he said, shaking his head.

90 You were starved, she said, laughing.

91 He peeled off the woolen underwear and threw it at the bathroom door. Then he opened his arms and the girl moved into them.

92 We won't fight anymore, she said.

93 The boy said, We won't.

94 He gets up from his chair and refills their glasses.

95 That's it, he says. End of story. I admit it's not much of a story.

96 I was interested, she says.

97 He shrugs and carries his drink over to the window. It's dark now but still snowing.

98 Things change, he says. I don't know how they do. But they do without your realizing it or wanting them to.

99 Yes, that's true, only—But she does not finish what she started.

100 She drops the subject. In the window's reflection he sees her study her nails. Then she raises her head. Speaking brightly, she asks if he is going to show her the city, after all.

101 He says, Put your boots on and let's go.

102 But he stays by the window, remembering. They had laughed. They had leaned on each other and laughed until the tears had come, while everything else—the cold, and where he'd go in it—was outside, for a while anyway. ❧





PERSONALIZE FOR LEARNING

**Challenge**

**Comparing Authors' Style** Inform students that another twentieth-century short-story writer from the United States, Ernest Hemingway, wrote in a style like Raymond Carver's. Hemingway's prose was similarly stark. Ask students to review the launch text and then read one of Hemingway's earlier short stories such as "Up in Michigan" or "The Doctor and the Doctor's Wife." Invite them to hold a discussion in which they compare and contrast Carver's and Hemingway's writing styles, subject matter, moods, and tones. **(Research to Explore)**

## Comprehension Check

Complete the following items after you finish your first read.

1. Where and at what time of year does the introductory story take place?

2. How old are the boy and girl in the internal story?

3. What does the boy want to do on Sunday?

4. What causes the quarrel between the young husband and wife?

5. What event at breakfast explains the story's title?

6. **Notebook** Write a summary of "Everything Stuck to Him" to confirm your understanding of the text.

## RESEARCH

**Research to Clarify** Choose at least one unfamiliar detail from the story. Briefly research that detail. In what way does the information you learned shed light on an aspect of the story?

**Research to Explore** Conduct research on an aspect of the text you find interesting. Think about ways in which your research helped deepen your understanding of the story.





DIGITAL PERSPECTIVES

## Comprehension Check

Possible responses:

1. The introductory story takes place in Milan, Italy, at Christmastime.
2. The boy (the husband) is eighteen, and the girl (the wife) is seventeen.
3. He wants to go hunting with Carl, one of his father's old friends.
4. The quarrel arises because the girl wants the boy to stay home to help take care of the baby.
5. At breakfast, a plate holding a syrup-covered waffle and bacon overturns in the boy's lap, and the syrup makes everything stick (as the story's title indicates) to his long underwear.
6. Over drinks in Milan, a father tells his adult daughter a story about a young couple and a baby. The young man wants to go hunting. His wife doesn't want him to go because the baby has been crying a lot and may be sick. He sets out to go hunting but returns soon and makes up with his wife. In Milan, the adult daughter understands that she is the baby in the story.

## Research

**Research to Clarify** If students struggle to come up with an unfamiliar detail to research, suggest that they focus on reasons that babies cry or how to sooth a crying baby.

**Research to Explore** If students struggle to find a topic, suggest that learn more about colic, the average ages of men and women for first marriage during different decades of the twentieth century, or divorce rates among couples who marry in their teens and twenties.

## PERSONALIZE FOR LEARNING

### English Language Support

**Dramatic Reading** Encourage students to choose roles and perform a dramatic reading of this text. Before students rehearse, they should each study their part and make sure they understand every word in it. Provide help as needed. As students rehearse, provide help with pronunciation, enunciation, pacing, cadence, and expressive reading. Since Carl has such a small part, students might swap roles and do a second reading. **EMERGING/EXPANDING**

MAKING MEANING

EVERYTHING STUCK TO HIM

## Jump Start

CLOSE READ Engage students in discussion with the following question: *What do you think the father who tells the story means by "Things change. I don't know how they do. But they do without your realizing it or wanting them to"?*

## Close Read the Text

Work with students on the annotation model, and then have them complete items 2 and 3 on their own. When they have finished, review and discuss the sections students marked. If needed, continue to model close reading by using the Annotation Highlights in the Interactive Teacher's Edition.

## Analyze the Text

Possible responses:

1. The request suggests that the young woman may not have a close relationship with her father. She seems not to know much about her family's situation when she was little. **DOK 2**
2. (a) The boy may want a break from the hard-working routine that he and his wife follow. **DOK 2** (b) The list of chores that the couple must do for the dentist, the fact that most teens don't have as many responsibilities as the boy and girl have, and the boy's conversation with Carl all support this interpretation. **DOK 3**
3. The girl's insistence is justified because she believes the baby is ill, and she is asking only that her husband assume his share of parental responsibility. **DOK 3**
4. Details such as the boy's car, the telephone receiver, the dentist's letterhead, electric lights, and the boy's long woolen underwear indicate that the interior story is anchored in the mid-twentieth century. However, the story conflict is timeless. **DOK 3**
5. Answers will vary. **DOK 4**

## Close Read the Text

1. This model, from paragraph 11 of the text, shows two sample annotations, along with questions and conclusions. Close read the passage, and find another detail to annotate. Then, write a question and your conclusion.

Close Read — ANNOTATE, QUESTION, CONCLUDE

ANNOTATE: The narrator uses third-person pronouns.

QUESTION: Why does the narrator use this point of view?

CONCLUDE: The narrator may be trying to distance himself from the person he was.

Each night they cleaned the dentist's place upstairs in exchange for rent and utilities. In summer they were expected to maintain the lawn and the flowers. In winter the boy shoveled snow and spread rock salt on the walks. Are you still with me? Are you getting the picture?

ANNOTATE: The narrator asks two questions.

QUESTION: Why do these questions appear here?

CONCLUDE: The narrator is pausing to check his daughter's understanding of the story thus far.

2. For more practice, go back into the text, and complete the close-read notes.
3. Revisit a section of the text you found important during your first read. Read this section closely, and **annotate** what you notice. Ask yourself **questions** such as "Why did the author make this choice?" What can you **conclude**?

**Tool Kit**
Close-Read Guide and Model Annotation

## Analyze the Text

CITE TEXTUAL EVIDENCE to support your answers.

Notebook Respond to these questions.

1. **Make Inferences** What does the daughter's request suggest about her relationship to her father?
2. (a) **Interpret** Why might the boy have been so eager to go hunting with Carl? (b) **Support** What details in the text support your interpretation?
3. **Make a Judgment** Was the girl right to insist that the boy stay home? Explain your answer.
4. **Historical Perspectives** Could this story have taken place in any historical period, or do you see evidence that the tale is specifically anchored in the mid-twentieth century? Explain.
5. **Essential Question: *What do stories reveal about the human condition?*** What have you learned about relationships and youth by reading this text?

STANDARDS

**Reading Literature**

- Cite strong and thorough textual evidence to support analysis of what the text says explicitly as well as inferences drawn from the text, including determining where the text leaves matters uncertain.
- Analyze how an author's choices concerning how to structure specific parts of a text contribute to its overall structure and meaning as well as its aesthetic impact.

788 UNIT 6 • ORDINARY LIVES, EXTRAORDINARY TALES



## FORMATIVE ASSESSMENT

### Analyze the Text

- **If** students fail to cite evidence, **then** remind them to support their ideas with specific information from the text.
- **If** students struggle to understand the concept of timeless conflicts in stories, **then** point out that even fairy tales and folk tales teach universal lessons. For example, "Goldilocks and the Three Bears" teaches not to enter someone else's home without an invitation.

DIGITAL PERSPECTIVES 

## Analyze Craft and Structure

**Narrative Structure** A **frame story** is a narrative that consists of two parts: an introductory story and an internal story. The narrative begins and ends with the **introductory story**, which frames the **internal story** like bookends.

- In this narrative structure, the internal story, or story-within-a-story, is typically the more important tale.
- The internal story usually takes place in another time and place.
- The narrator of the introductory story may or may not be a character in the internal story.

### Practice

**CITE TEXTUAL EVIDENCE** to support your answers.

Notebook Respond to these questions.

1. In which paragraph does the internal story begin? How do you know?
2. Use this chart to record notes about the internal story in "Everything Stuck to Him."

| ELEMENTS | DETAILS AND IMAGES |
|---|---|
| Setting | residence of a very young, hard-working couple: "a little apartment under a dentist's office" |
| Characters | 18-year-old husband, 17-year-old wife, baby daughter, and Carl "an old hunting friend" of the husband's dad |
| Conflict | The baby cries all the time, raising the possibility that she is sick. The boy wants to go hunting with Carl, but the girl wants him to stay home and help care for the baby. |
| Climax | The boy gets ready to go hunting, sits in his car for a while, but finally decides not to go. |
| Resolution | Reconciled, the boy and girl make breakfast. A funny incident occurs: the boy overturns his plate and a waffle and bacon end up stuck to his long underwear with sticky syrup. This makes the couple laugh hysterically and hug each other. |

3. Suppose that the internal story had a first-person narrator. How do you think the story's emotional impact would be different? Explain.
4. Reread paragraphs 93–99, when the narrative returns to the introductory story. (a) What do you think the father may mean when he says, "Things change"? (b) Why do you think the adult daughter "does not finish what she started"?





## Analyze Craft and Structure

**Narrative Structure** If necessary, review the following with students:

- A **frame story** is a story that brackets—or frames—another story, thus creating a **story-within-a-story narrative structure.**
- A story told within a frame story is called an **inner story**, an **interior story**, or a **story within a story.**
- Typically, the framing narrative appears at the beginning of the work to set up the situation of the storytelling within the frame. The narrative then shifts to the interior story and usually returns to the frame story after the interior one ends.
- Sometimes, a frame story brackets a whole series of interior stories rather than just one. This is true of *The Thousand and One Nights* and of Geoffrey's Chaucer's long poem *The Canterbury Tales.*

For more support, see **Analyze Craft and Structure: Narrative Structure Story.**

### Practice

**Possible responses:**

1. The internal story launches with paragraph 9, which begins "They were kids themselves, but they were crazy in love...." The author signals the transition by using the word *begins* at the end of paragraph 8 and by switching from present-tense verbs to past-tense verbs.
2. See possible responses in the chart on the student page.
3. Using a first-person narrator might make the internal story more specific to this one young family. A more specific story might make the themes seem less universal.
4. (a) The father may mean that his newly-married youth seems very long ago and/or that his circumstances are now very different. Maybe he and his wife divorced long ago, or maybe she died. (b) Perhaps the daughter does not finish her thought because she does not want to upset her father by accusing him of making mistakes that ruined the marriage.

## FORMATIVE ASSESSMENT

### Analyze Craft and Structure

- **If** students are unable to identify the transition from the frame story to the internal one, **then** point out the difference in tense between the verbs in paragraph 8 and paragraph 9.
- **If** students fail to understand how changing to a first-person narrator would change the internal story, **then** have them rewrite paragraph 9 as if the father were narrating it in the first person from his younger self's point of view.

For Reteach and Practice, see **Analyze Craft and Structure: Narrative Structure (RP).**

# TEACHING

## Concept Vocabulary

**Why These Words?** Remind students that a compound word's meaning combines the meanings of the shorter words that comprise the compound.

Possible responses

1. The words name or describe specific details. Some students may suggest that the compound words align with the starkness of the writer's style.
2. Other compound words in the story include *rooftops, downstairs, bathroom, bedroom.*

### Practice

Possible responses:

1. Answers may vary.
2. Answers may vary; some students may suggest that the synonyms add more color or description.

### Word Network

**Possible words:** *survivor, marveled, ambitions*

## Word Study

For more support, see **Concept Vocabulary and Word Study.**

Possible responses

1. Examples of endocentric compounds include *tablecloth, speedboat, toothpaste, paperback,* and *sunglasses.*
2. **tablecloth:** (base word) cloth, (modifier) table, (definition) cloth used to cover a tabletop: **speedboat:** (base word) boat, (modifier) speed, (definition) high-speed boat; **toothpaste:** (base word) paste, (modifier) tooth, (definition) paste for cleaning teeth; **paperback:** (base word) back, (modifier) paper, (definition) book with a soft, or paper, cover; **sunglasses:** (base word) glasses, (modifier) sun, (definition) glasses worn in the sun.

LANGUAGE DEVELOPMENT

EVERYTHING STUCK TO HIM

## Concept Vocabulary

| waterfowl | letterhead | overcast | shotgun |
|---|---|---|---|

**Why These Words?** The concept vocabulary words are all compound words. They help create a sense of the internal story's setting and action. For example, the sky was *overcast*, and the boy planned to hunt *waterfowl*.

1. How does the concept vocabulary clarify the reader's understanding of the internal story's setting and action?
2. What other compound words in the selection can you identify?

### Practice

**Notebook** The concept vocabulary words appear in "Everything Stuck to Him."

1. Use each word in a sentence that demonstrates your understanding of the word's meaning.
2. Challenge yourself to replace each concept vocabulary word in the sentences you wrote with one or two related words. How does each word change affect the meaning of your original sentence?

**WORD NETWORK**

Add words related to the human condition from the text to your Word Network.

## Word Study

**Endocentric Compounds** A compound word is made up of two or more individual words. An **endocentric compound** combines one word that conveys the basic meaning and a modifier that restricts or specifies the meaning of the word. For example, the compound word *waterfowl* combines the words *water* and *fowl*. The modifier *water* describes the type of fowl, or bird.

1. Find five examples of endocentric compounds, and record them.
2. For each word, note the base word and the modifier. Finally, provide a definition of each word.

**STANDARDS**

Language

• Demonstrate command of the conventions of standard English grammar and usage when writing or speaking.

• Apply knowledge of language to understand how language functions in different contexts, to make effective choices for meaning or style, and to comprehend more fully when reading or listening.

790 UNIT 6 • ORDINARY LIVES, EXTRAORDINARY TALES



### FORMATIVE ASSESSMENT

### Concept Vocabulary

**If** students fail to see connections among the words, **then** break each compound into two shorter words.

### Word Study

**If** students fail to understand what endocentric compounds are, **then** provide more examples, break words into base words and modifiers, and explain how each modifier modifies each base word.

For Reteach and Practice, see **Word Study: Endocentric Compounds (RP).**

## Conventions and Style

**Pronouns and Antecedents** An experienced writer may stretch or break the rules and conventions of standard English in order to achieve an effect, create a personal style, or capture the reader's attention.

Carver purposely breaks English conventions in "Everything Stuck to Him." For example, he does not enclose dialogue with quotation marks. He also leaves the subjects of some sentences deliberately ambiguous, or unclear. This is especially true when the subjects of his sentences are **pronouns,** words that stand for a person, place, or thing, without a clear **antecedent,** what the pronoun refers to.

EXAMPLE

**"She's** in Milan for Christmas and wants to know what it was like when she was a kid."

The pronoun *she* does not have a clear antecedent. Readers need to gather details over the next few paragraphs before concluding that "She" is the narrator's adult daughter.

TIP

FOLLOW THROUGH

Refer to the Grammar Handbook to learn more about these terms.

### Read It

1. Analyze examples of pronouns in Carver's story that lack a clear antecedent. In the right-hand column, rewrite the example so that the meaning is clear.

| PASSAGE | REWRITE |
|---|---|
| The boy loved to hunt, you see. That's part of it. (paragraph 10) | When he was younger, the narrator loved to hunt. His love of hunting will be an important part of the story. |
| He gets up from his chair and looks out the window. (paragraph 14) | The father gets up from his chair and looks out the window. |
| It's fine, she said. (paragraph 27) | "It's fine if you don't get home until six," his wife said. |
| That's not the point and you know it, the girl said. (paragraph 62) | "Whether or not I know Carl isn't the point and you know it," his wife said. |
| It was my fault, he said. (paragraph 81) | "It was my fault that we quarreled," the young husband said. |

2. **Connect to Style** Reread paragraphs 94–95 of "Everything Stuck to Him." Mark the pronouns, and identify their antecedents. Then, write a possible explanation of why Carver leaves pronoun-antecedent relationships unclear. What effect does this ambiguity have on readers?

### Write It

**Notebook** Choose a short passage from "Everything Stuck to Him" that contains unclear antecedents, and rewrite it to be unambiguous. Then, explain how the rewrite changes the impact of the passage.





## PERSONALIZE FOR LEARNING

### English Language Support

**Identifying Pronouns and Antecedents** Display these sentences: *Laura was cooking bacon. She made breakfast for him every day*. Have students identify the subject in both sentences. (Laura/She) Ask them what the antecedent is for "She" in the second sentence (Laura). **EMERGING**

Have students find an example of a subject pronoun and an antecedent in the text. (Possible response: "they"—The boy and the girl—in paragraph 11) **EXPANDING**

Ask students to write a sentence or two in which they use a subject and then a pronoun with an antecedent. **BRIDGING**

An expanded **English Language Support Lesson** on Pronouns and Antecedents is available in the Interactive Teacher's Edition.

DIGITAL PERSPECTIVES 

## Conventions and Style

**Pronouns and Antecedents** Discuss Carver's writing style with students. While it is spare, the text does leave ambiguities for readers.

For more support, see **Conventions and Style: Pronouns and Antecedents.**

### Read It

Possible responses:

1. See possible responses in the chart on the student page.
2. **Connect to Style** *He, his,* and *I* refer to the narrator (the father); *their* refers to the narrator and his adult daughter; and the word *it* in "That's it" and in "it's" both refer to the internal story that the narrator has just told.

Carver may have written in this ambiguous style to create a stark and bleak mood. He may also have chosen to create characters who seem like archetypes, or generic people struggling with relationships.

### Write It

Responses will vary. Students' rewritten passages should include no pronouns whose antecedents are unclear. For example, paragraph 90 originally reads as follows:

> You were starved, she said, laughing. He peeled off the woolen underwear and threw it at the bathroom door. Then he opened his arms and the girl moved into them.

Students might rewrite it as follows:

> "You were starved," the boy's wife said, laughing. The young husband peeled off the woolen underwear and threw it at the bathroom door. Then he opened his arms and his wife moved into them.

Some students may say that the rewritten version seems less stark and less understated.

### FORMATIVE ASSESSMENT

### Conventions and Style

**If** students struggle to figure out whether a pronoun's antecedent is clear or unclear, **then** show them more examples, such as the following:

Unclear Antecedents: I told him that my brother's coat would not fit him, and that he would be mad if he borrowed it without asking.

Clear Antecedents: I told my friend Leo that my brother Matt's coat would not fit him, and that Matt would be mad if Leo borrowed the coat without asking. For Reteach and Practice, see **Conventions and Style: Pronouns and Antecedents (RP).**

## Writing to Sources

Make sure students understand the meanings of the following academic terms:

- narrative writing: writing that tells a story.
- expository details: words in the text that explain information or ideas.
- background: information that explains why people in a story behave or think in a certain way. Background may or may not appear in the text.
- minimalist style: a writing style that limits sentences to their basic frame. For example, Carver's style leaves out people's names, adjectives, and even some antecedents for pronouns.

For more support, see **Writing to Sources: Narrative Scene.**

## Reflect on Your Writing

**Possible responses:**

1. Some students may say that trying to imitate Carver's style encouraged them to look more closely at his exact words and that reading closely helped them figure out more precisely what happens in the story.
2. Some students may have incorporated into their narrative the fact that colic is a common, but not life-threatening, condition among young babies. Knowing this fact would have been reassuring to the young couple, and the girl may have given her permission for the boy to go hunting while she stayed with the fussy baby.
3. **Why These Words?** Have students list specific examples of words and phrases they have chosen to clearly express their ideas and make their writing memorable to readers.

### FORMATIVE ASSESSMENT

**Writing to Sources**

**If** students are having difficulty imitating Carver's minimalist writing style, **then** review a passage from the story and point out the elements he leaves out of his prose, such as names and clear antecedents for pronouns. For Reteach and Practice, see **Writing to Sources: Narrative Scene (RP).**

EVERYTHING STUCK TO HIM

## Writing to Sources

Narrative writing often contains factual details that make the plot and setting seem realistic, even when the story is fictional.

**Assignment**

Colic is a condition in which an otherwise healthy baby cries for extended periods of time. Conduct research on colic and its effects on newborns and parents. Then, integrate the information you find into a realistic **narrative scene** that shows how the boy and the girl in "Everything Stuck to Him" might have reacted if they had known what colic is and whether or not their baby had it.

Your narrative should include:

- information about colic and its effects
- details from "Everything Stuck to Him," used as background to develop events and dialogue
- a minimalist style consistent with Carver's

**Vocabulary and Conventions Connection** In your narrative, consider including several of the concept vocabulary words. Consider whether ambiguous pronouns will help you create an effective narrative.

waterfowl letterhead overcast shotgun

### Reflect on Your Writing

After you have written your narrative, answer the following questions.

1. How did your effort to imitate Carver's style influence your understanding of his story and writing style?
2. What details about colic or characteristics of the boy and the girl characters did you use in your writing? How did they help support your narrative?
3. **Why These Words?** The words you choose make a difference in your writing. Which words helped you to convey important ideas precisely?

**STANDARDS**

**Reading Literature**
Analyze the impact of the author's choices regarding how to develop and relate elements of a story or drama.

**Writing**
Write narratives to develop real or imagined experiences or events using effective technique, well-chosen details, and well-structured event sequences.

**Speaking and Listening**
Adapt speech to a variety of contexts and tasks, demonstrating a command of formal English when indicated or appropriate.





### PERSONALIZE FOR LEARNING

**Strategic Support**

**Writing a Narrative** Students may need guidance as they incorporate facts about colic into their narrative. Give them examples of words and expressions they can use to introduce information, such as these: *experts say, it seems that, in most cases, generally, with few exceptions*.

## Speaking and Listening

**Assignment**

With a partner, improvise a **dialogue** between the father and his daughter that continues the conversation they were having at the end of "Everything Stuck to Him." Once you have polished and rehearsed your dialogue, present it to the class. After your presentation, lead a whole-class discussion about how the dialogue connected to the story and continued its themes. Follow these steps to complete the assignment.

1. **Analyze the Characters** With your partner, discuss the relationship between the father and his daughter. Decide what the daughter was starting to say at the end of the story before she changed the subject. Draw a conclusion about what happened to the mother. Make sure your decisions are consistent with information in the story.
2. **Plan Your Dialogue** As you develop your dialogue, focus on each character's motivations. Why is the daughter bringing this topic up now? Is there anything the father has been wanting to say to his daughter? Do the characters want to reach an understanding or resolution before their dialogue is over?
3. **Prepare Your Delivery** Practice your dialogue with your partner. Pay attention to nonverbal methods of communication, such as tone, pitch, volume, pacing, facial expressions, and body language.
4. **Evaluate Dialogues** As your classmates deliver their dialogues, listen carefully. Use an evaluation guide like the one shown to analyze their dialogues.

**EVALUATION GUIDE**

Rate each statement on a scale of 1 (not demonstrated) to 4 (demonstrated).

- ☐ Partners clearly enacted the characters and the situation.
- ☐ Partners crafted a dialogue consistent with the story.
- ☐ Partners communicated clearly and expressively.
- ☐ Partners used a variety of speaking tones and pitches.
- ☐ Partners used gestures and other body language effectively.

**EVIDENCE LOG**

Before moving on to a new selection, go to your Evidence Log and record what you learned from "Everything Stuck to Him."





DIGITAL PERSPECTIVES 

## Speaking and Listening

Pairs might begin by rereading and discussing the last nine paragraphs of the story.

1. **Analyze the Characters** Students will have to develop their own interpretations of some of the character's life experiences. Suggest that pairs work together to answer the following questions:
   - *When did the father and daughter last see each other before this Christmas in Milan?*
   - *If the parents divorced, how old was the daughter when they did?*
   - *Do the father and daughter feel comfortable with one another now? Why or why not?*
   - *What are the daughter's hopes for her relationship with her dad?*
   - *What are the father's hopes for his relationship with his daughter?*
2. **Plan Your Dialogue** Make sure students know that the term *motivations* means "reasons." Point out that sometimes people blurt things out without knowing their own motivations. Ask:
   - *If you were the man's daughter, what would you want to ask him about himself, your mother, and his feelings for you?*
   - *If you were the father, what would you want to ask or tell your daughter?*
3. **Prepare Your Delivery** Briefly go over with students the meanings of the terms *tone, pitch, volume, pacing, facial expressions,* and *body language.*
4. **Evaluate Dialogues** Encourage students to take notes during other pairs' presentations and use their notes to complete each presentation evaluation guide.

For more support, see **Speaking and Listening: Dialogue.**

**Evidence Log** Support students in completing their Evidence Log. This paced activity will help prepare them for the Performance-Based Assessment at the end of the unit.

### FORMATIVE ASSESSMENT

### Speaking and Listening

**If** students have difficulty planning their dialogues, **then** suggest that they reread parts of the story that contain dialogue.

For Reteach and Practice, see **Speaking and Listening: Dialogue (RP).**

### Selection Test

Administer the "Everything Stuck to Him" Selection Test, which is available in both print and digital formats online in Assessments.

# The Leap

**AUDIO SUMMARIES**
Audio summaries of "The Leap" are available online in both English and Spanish in the Interactive Teacher's Edition or Unit Resources. Assigning these summaries prior to reading the selection may help students build additional background knowledge and set a context for their first read.

## Summary

In Louise Erdrich's short story "The Leap" the narrator explores the life of her mother, Anna, who in her early life was part of a circus blindfold trapeze act. The story has three leaps, and each leap tells something essential about the narrator's mother. The first leap occurs when Anna saves her own life after lightning strikes the main pole in the circus tent. Her husband and unborn child do not survive. The second leap occurs while Anna is in the hospital. Here, Anna meets her future husband and the narrator's father. Anna is distraught over her losses, but she has the courage to open herself up to a new relationship. The final leap occurs when the narrator recalls a childhood memory of her family's house catching fire. In this last leap her mother saves the narrator's life.

### Insight

Reading this story will help students understand the remarkable courage some parents exhibit as they strive to protect their children.

ESSENTIAL QUESTION:
What do stories reveal about the human condition?

## Connection to Essential Question

The story "The Leap" connects to the Essential Question and to the human condition in its exploration of a child's growing understanding of a parent.

WHOLE-CLASS LEARNING PERFORMANCE TASK
How do stressful situations often reveal the best and worst in people?

UNIT PERFORMANCE-BASED ASSESSMENT
How does a fictional character or characters respond to life-changing news?

## Connection to Performance Tasks

**Whole-Class Learning Performance Task** In this Performance Task, students will consider the ways stress can bring out human strengths and weaknesses. This story provides students with the experiences of a strong woman who does not give in to terrifying circumstances.

**Unit Performance-Based Assessment** The selection examines three events that the narrator regards as life changing. Some students may find the story to be instructional as they learn how the mother reacts to difficult situations.

DIGITAL PERSPECTIVES

 Audio  Video  Document  Annotation Highlights  EL Highlights  Online Assessment

## LESSON RESOURCES

| | Making Meaning | Language Development | Effective Expression |
|---|---|---|---|
| **Lesson** | **First Read**<br>**Close Read**<br>**Analyze the Text**<br>**Analyze Craft and Structure** | **Concept Vocabulary**<br>**Word Study**<br>**Author's Style** | **Writing to Sources**<br>**Speaking and Listening** |
| **Instructional Standards** | **RL.10** By the end of grade 11, read and comprehend literature . . .<br>**RL.1** Cite strong and thorough textual evidence . . .<br>**RL.3** Analyze the impact of the author's choices . . . | **RL.4** Determine the meaning of words and phrases . . .<br>**L.4.b** Identify and correctly use patterns of word changes . . . | **W.3** Write narratives . . .<br>**SL.4** Present information, findings, and supporting evidence . . . |
| **STUDENT RESOURCES** | | | |
| Available online in the Interactive Student Edition or Unit Resources | Selection Audio<br>First-Read Guide: Fiction<br>Close-Read Guide: Fiction | Word Network | Evidence Log |
| **TEACHER RESOURCES** | | | |
| **Selection Resources** Available online in the Interactive Teacher's Edition or Unit Resources | Audio Summaries<br>Annotation Highlights<br>EL Highlights<br>English Language Support Lesson: Suspense<br>Analyze Craft and Structure: Narrative Structure | Concept Vocabulary and Word Study<br>Author's Style: Motif | Writing to Sources: Anecdote<br>Speaking and Listening: Response to Literature |
| **Reteach/Practice (RP)** Available online in the Interactive Teacher's Edition or Unit Resources | Analyze Craft and Structure: Narrative Structure (RP) | Word Study: Latin Root *-strict-* (RP)<br>Author's Style: Motif (RP) | Writing to Sources: Anecdote (RP)<br>Speaking and Listening: Response to Literature (RP) |
| **Assessment** Available online in Assessments | Selection Test | | |
| **My Resources** | A Unit 6 Answer Key is available online and in the Interactive Teacher's Edition. | | |

# Reading Support

| Text Complexity Rubric: The Leap | |
|---|---|
| **Quantitative Measures** | |
| **Lexile** 1250 **Text Length** 2,883 words | |
| **Qualitative Measures** | |
| Knowledge Demands<br>① ❷ ③ ④ ⑤ | The story may require some knowledge of circuses. Much of the rest of the text describes familiar situations. |
| Structure<br>① ② ❸ ④ ⑤ | "The Leap" is not totally conventional in structure. Using the narrator's multiple memories, and her mother's own stories, the narrator pieces together one full story. |
| Language Conventionality and Clarity<br>① ② ❸ ④ ⑤ | The language contains metaphors, foreshadowing, and many dense paragraphs. |
| Levels of Meaning/Purpose<br>① ② ③ ❹ ⑤ | Multiple levels of meaning. The story is told from the perspective of the narrator in a time when the heroic mother is blind and aging. The theme of "leaping" runs throughout the story, and, although the conclusion is not complicated, it does elicit awe at the mother's stunning life story. |

DECIDE AND PLAN

## English Language Support

Provide English Learners with support for structure and language as they read the selection.

**Structure** Erdrich makes use of the narrator's mother's memories to begin the story. She then moves into the narrator's own memories toward the conclusion. Ask the students to think about whether the mother's memories before the narrator's birth were needed for the story to seem complete, and what the reader might be left with if the mother's memories, as told by the narrator, were left out.

**Language** The language is dense but very clear. Have students think about how the use of specifics and details—the various references to the exotic circus acts, as well as the climate of the Midwest—give the narrative its strength and power. Talk about what kinds of feelings this story evokes, based just on its language.

## Strategic Support

Provide students with strategic support to ensure that they can successfully read the text.

**Structure** Ask students to review the text and mark the three times that the narrator's mother saved her life. Then have them comb the story for the mother's stories and the daughter's stories. Talk about how the combination helps to extend the story's meaning beyond present experience to comment on intergenerational relationships and memories.

**Language** In paragraph 2 of "The Leap," there is a stunning moment of foreshadowing when the room goes dark and the narrator feels fire in a sewing thread. After students read the full text, discuss what this "thread of fire" foreshadowed for the story, and how the delicate language used made this moment a powerful one.

## Challenge

Provide students who need to be challenged with ideas for how they can go beyond a simple interpretation of the text.

**Text Analysis** Have the students analyze the moment of foreshadowing in paragraph 2 and talk about what that brings to the narrative. Discuss how foreshadowing is used today in writing, and also in film and other media. Talk about why an author would employ such a technique when the story could be told without it.

**Written Response** Have students compose a one-page story in which they attempt to produce their own example of foreshadowing. Ask them to refine their story over time and to think about why it would be less useful in the beginning of the story to simply state what will happen in the end in lieu of foreshadowing. Talk about what this technique brings to their story.

TEACH

## Read and Respond

Have students do their first read of the selection. Then, have them complete their close read. Finally, work with them on the Making Meaning, Language Development, and Effective Expression activities.

# Standards Support Through Teaching and Learning Cycle

## IDENTIFY NEEDS

Analyze results of the Beginning-of-Year Assessment, focusing on the items relating to Unit 6. Also take into consideration student performance to this point and your observations of where particular students struggle.

## DECIDE AND PLAN

- If students have performed poorly on items matching these standards, then provide selection scaffolds before assigning them the on-level lesson provided in the Student Edition.
- If students have done well on the Beginning-of-Year Assessment, then challenge them to keep progressing and learning by giving them opportunities to practice the skills in depth.
- Use the Selection Resources listed on the Planning pages for "The Leap" to help students continually improve their ability to master the standards.

**Instructional Standards: The Leap**

| | Catching Up | This Year | Looking Forward |
|---|---|---|---|
| **Reading** | To build narrative techniques, give students the **Analyze Craft and Structure: Narrative Structure (RP)** worksheet. | **RL.3** Analyze the impact of the author's choices regarding how to develop and relate elements of a story or drama. | Challenge students to write one paragraph that builds suspense. |
| **Writing** | Administer the **Writing to Sources: Anecdote (RP)** worksheet so that students learn how to write anecdotes that are part of a coherent whole. | **W.3** Write narratives to develop real or imagined experiences or events using effective technique, well-chosen details, and well-structured event sequences. | Ask students to research how other writers use anecdotes in writing effectively and take notes to share with the class. |
| **Speaking and Listening** | Give students the **Speaking and Listening: Response to Literature (RP)** worksheet. | **SL.4** Present information, findings, and supporting evidence, conveying a clear and distinct perspective and a logical argument . . . | Make a poster of the themes students create for their response to literature. |
| **Language** | You may want to administer the **Author's Style: Motif (RP)** worksheet so that students can review the place of motif in a story.<br>Review the **Word Study: Latin Root *-strict-* (RP)** worksheet with students to better familiarize them with the meaning of the Latin root *-strict-*. | **RL.4** Determine the meaning of words and phrases as they are used in the text, including figurative and connotative meanings; analyze the impact of specific word choices on meaning and tone, including words with multiple meanings or language that is particularly fresh, engaging, or beautiful.<br>**L.4.b** Identify and correctly use patterns of word changes that indicate different meanings or parts of speech. | Challenge students to analyze the narrator's character based on the pattern of three leaps in the story.<br>Have students list other words they find that are formed from this Latin root. |

## ANALYZE AND REVISE

- Analyze student work for evidence of student learning.
- Identify whether or not students have met the expectations in the standards.
- Identify implications for future instruction.

## TEACH

Implement the planned lesson, and gather evidence of student learning.

## Jump Start

**FIRST READ** We often don't think of our parents in terms of their past pursuits and their lives before we were born. In this story, the narrator describes detailed events about her mother's past as a circus performer, and how her talents became of crucial importance to the narrator's own life. Ask student volunteers to share any unusual or extraordinary talents that exist among family or friends. What extraordinary or unusual talents exist in your family?

## The Leap

Who is the narrator? What is unusual about the character introduced in the beginning of the story? Modeling these and other questions readers might ask will bring "The Leap" to life and connect it to the Performance Task question. Selection audio and print capability for the selection are available in the Interactive Teacher's Edition.

## Concept Vocabulary

Circulate among students as they rank their words. Remind them that they will find the definitions of these words listed in the selection.

### FIRST READ

The first time they go through the selection, students should perform the steps of the first read:

NOTICE: You may want to encourage students to notice the main events described in the text.

ANNOTATE: Remind students to mark passages that indicate a shift in time—from present to past, and back again.

CONNECT: Encourage students to go beyond the text to think about how the story connects with their own experiences. Is there a family member to whom they owe a debt of gratitude?

RESPOND: Students will demonstrate their understanding of the text by answering questions and writing a summary.

Point out to students that they will perform the first three steps concurrently as they are doing their first read. They will complete the Respond step after they have finished the first read. You may wish to print copies of the **First-Read Guide: Fiction** for students to use.

**Remind students that during their first read, they should not answer the close-read questions that appear in the selection.**



MAKING MEANING

About the Author

Award-winning novelist, poet, and short-story writer **Louise Erdrich** (b.1954) was born to a German American father and a mother who was half Chippewa. In a popular series of interrelated novels, including *Love Medicine* (1984) and *The Beet Queen* (1986), Erdrich describes the lives of three families living in a fictional North Dakota town. Native American traditions and lore have greatly influenced Erdrich's writing, which often merges local history with current issues and employs multiple narrators to reflect a complex variety of perspectives. Her 2012 novel *The Round House* won the National Book Award.

# The Leap

## Concept Vocabulary

You will encounter the following words as you read "The Leap." Before reading, note how familiar you are with each word. Then, rank the words in order from most familiar (1) to least familiar (6).

| WORD | YOUR RANKING |
|---|---|
| encroaching | |
| instantaneously | |
| anticipation | |
| constricting | |
| perpetually | |
| superannuated | |

After completing the first read, come back to the concept vocabulary and review your rankings. Mark changes to your original rankings as needed.

## First Read FICTION

Apply these strategies as you conduct your first read. You will have an opportunity to complete the close-read notes after your first read.

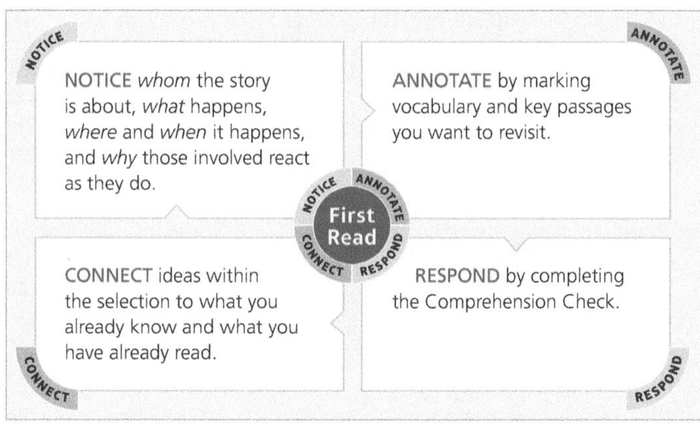

NOTICE *whom* the story is about, *what* happens, *where* and *when* it happens, and *why* those involved react as they do.
ANNOTATE by marking vocabulary and key passages you want to revisit.
CONNECT ideas within the selection to what you already know and what you have already read.
RESPOND by completing the Comprehension Check.
First Read
NOTICE
ANNOTATE
CONNECT
RESPOND


STANDARDS

**Reading Literature**

By the end of grade 11, read and comprehend literature, including stories, dramas, and poems, in the grades 11–CCR text complexity band proficiently, with scaffolding as needed at the high end of the range.





### VOCABULARY DEVELOPMENT

**Word Forms** Model usage of the vocabulary words in sentences. Then instruct students to find the verb forms of the concept words *encroaching, anticipation,* and *constricting,* and use each of them in a sentence.

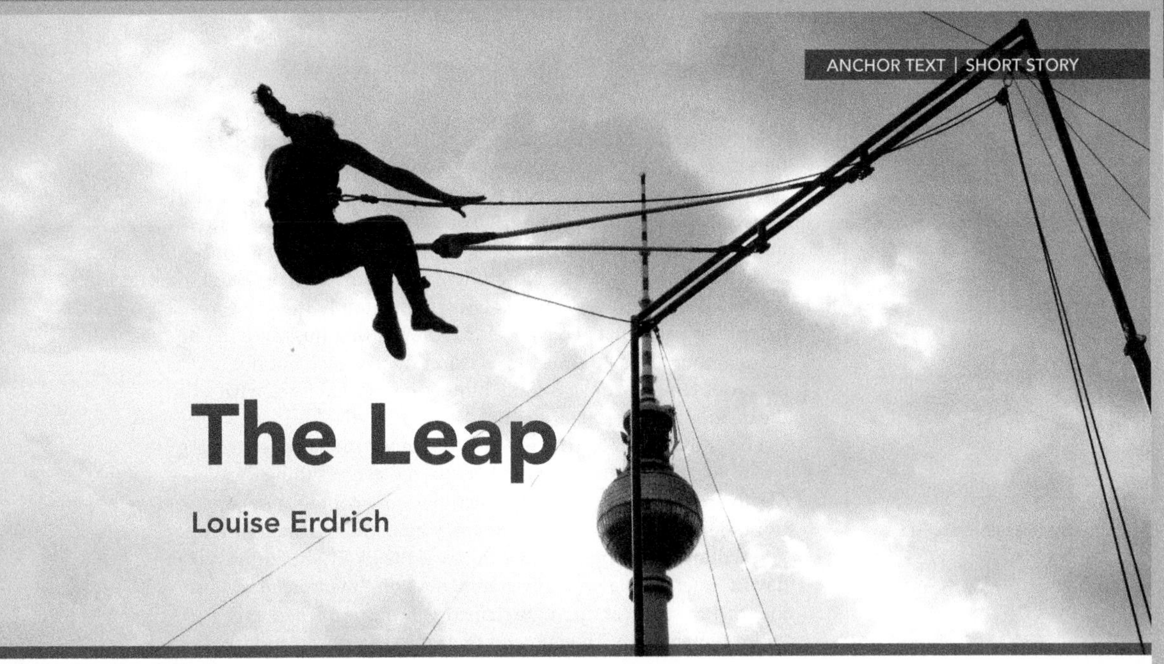


# The Leap

Louise Erdrich

## CLOSE READ 

Remind students to look for adjectives the author uses to describe the characters. You may wish to model the Close Read using the following think-aloud format. Possible responses to questions on the student page are included. You may also want to print copies of the **Close-Read Guide: Fiction** for students to use.

**ANNOTATE:** As I read paragraph 2, I notice and highlight the descriptive details in the last sentence.

**QUESTION:** The contrast in sentence length changes the rhythm of the writing. The last sentence demonstrates a deft use of language and suggests an almost acrobatic way of writing.

**CONCLUDE:** These words suggest danger and excitement but describe the very ordinary event of sewing. This type of language may push the reader to expect suspenseful language in the story that follows.

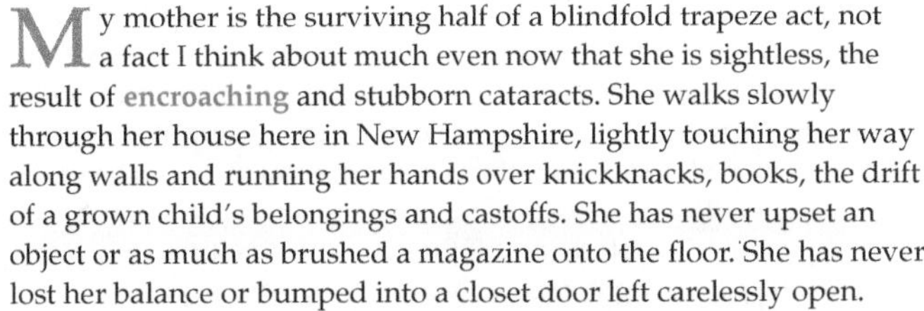

BACKGROUND

Traveling circuses first came to the United States from Great Britain in 1793 and quickly established themselves as a part of American popular culture. Showcasing a variety of performers—including clowns, animal trainers, and trapeze artists—circuses would draw and thrill crowds in large cities and small towns alike.

SCAN FOR MULTIMEDIA 

1 My mother is the surviving half of a blindfold trapeze act, not a fact I think about much even now that she is sightless, the result of encroaching and stubborn cataracts. She walks slowly through her house here in New Hampshire, lightly touching her way along walls and running her hands over knickknacks, books, the drift of a grown child's belongings and castoffs. She has never upset an object or as much as brushed a magazine onto the floor. She has never lost her balance or bumped into a closet door left carelessly open.

2 It has occurred to me that the catlike precision of her movements in old age might be the result of her early training, but she shows so little of the drama or flair one might expect from a performer that I tend to forget the Flying Avalons. She has kept no sequined costume, no photographs, no fliers or posters from that part of her youth. I would, in fact, tend to think that all memory of double somersaults and heart-stopping catches had left her arms and legs were it not for the fact that sometimes, as I sit sewing in the room of the rebuilt house in which I slept as a child, I hear the crackle, catch a whiff of smoke from the stove downstairs, and suddenly the room goes dark, the stitches burn beneath my fingers, and I am sewing with a needle of hot silver, a thread of fire.

NOTES

**encroaching** (ehn KROHCH ihng) *adj.* intruding; steadily advancing

CLOSE READ

**ANNOTATE:** In paragraph 2, mark descriptive words and phrases in the final sentence.

**QUESTION:** Why might the author have chosen to craft such a long, almost poetic, sentence to follow two ordinary sentences?

**CONCLUDE:** What overall effect does this sentence create?

## PERSONALIZE FOR LEARNING

### Strategic Support

**Foreshadowing** Have students make note of the last sentence of paragraph 2. Ask students if this sentence make sense to them. Encourage students to explain their responses. As part of a discussion, explain to them that this sentence is an example of direct foreshadowing because it hints at an upcoming event. Discuss with the class what they might guess the upcoming event to be. Encourage students to base their guesses on other clues in this paragraph.

CLOSER LOOK

## Analyze Simile

Students may have marked paragraph 5 during their first read. Encourage them to talk about the annotations that they marked. You may want to model a close read with the class based on the highlights shown in the text.

**ANNOTATE:** Have students mark details in the paragraph that use a comparison to describe the trapeze artists, or have students participate while you highlight them.

**QUESTION:** Guide students to consider what these details might tell them. Ask what a reader can infer from this comparison and accept student responses.

**Possible response:** I see that the two things that the simile compares are the trapeze artists and sparkling birds. I can infer from this simile that the trapeze artists appear to fly through the air gracefully, like birds, and that they are dressed in flashy costumes.

**CONCLUDE:** Help students to formulate conclusions about the importance of these details in the text. Ask students why the author might have included these details.

**Possible response:** The author may have included this simile to give readers the impression of the trapeze artists' ability to fly through the air with agility.

Remind students that a **simile** is a figure of speech that compares two apparently unlike things by using *like, as, than,* or *resembles*. A simile is different from a metaphor, a figure of speech that makes its comparison without using a connecting word, speaking of one thing as if it were the other. Writers use similes to present ideas in new and fresh ways.

NOTES

**instantaneously** (ihn stuhn TAY nee uhs lee) *adv.* immediately

**anticipation** (an tihs uh PAY shuhn) *n.* eager expectation

3 I owe her my existence three times. The first was when she saved herself. In the town square a replica tent pole, cracked and splintered, now stands cast in concrete. It commemorates the disaster that put our town smack on the front page of the Boston and New York tabloids. It is from those old newspapers, now historical records, that I get my information. Not from my mother, Anna of the Flying Avalons, nor from any of her in-laws, nor certainly from the other half of her particular act, Harold Avalon, her first husband. In one news account it says, "The day was mildly overcast, but nothing in the air or temperature gave any hint of the sudden force with which the deadly gale would strike."

4 I have lived in the West, where you can see the weather coming for miles, and it is true that out here we are at something of a disadvantage. When extremes of temperature collide, a hot and cold front, winds generate instantaneously behind a hill and crash upon you without warning. That, I think, was the likely situation on that day in June. People probably commented on the pleasant air, grateful that no hot sun beat upon the striped tent that stretched over the entire center green. They bought their tickets and surrendered them in anticipation. They sat. They ate caramelized popcorn and roasted peanuts. There was time, before the storm, for three acts. The White Arabians[1] of Ali-Khazar rose on their hind legs and waltzed. The Mysterious Bernie folded himself into a painted cracker tin, and the Lady of the Mists made herself appear and disappear in surprising places. As the clouds gathered outside, unnoticed, the ringmaster cracked his whip, shouted his introduction, and pointed to the ceiling of the tent, where the Flying Avalons were perched.

5 They loved to drop gracefully from nowhere, like two sparkling birds, and blow kisses as they threw off their plumed helmets and high-collared capes. They laughed and flirted openly as they beat their way up again on the trapeze bars. In the final vignette of their act, they actually would kiss in midair, pausing, almost hovering as they swooped past one another. On the ground, between bows, Harry Avalon would skip quickly to the front rows and point out the smear of my mother's lipstick, just off the edge of his mouth. They made a romantic pair all right, especially in the blindfold sequence.

6 That afternoon, as the anticipation increased, as Mr. and Mrs. Avalon tied sparkling strips of cloth onto each other's face and as they puckered their lips in mock kisses, lips destined "never again to meet," as one long breathless article put it, the wind rose, miles off, wrapped itself into a cone, and howled. There came a rumble of electrical energy, drowned out by the sudden roll of drums. One detail not mentioned by the press, perhaps unknown—Anna was pregnant at the time, seven months and hardly showing, her stomach muscles were that strong. It seems incredible that she would work high above the ground when any fall could be so dangerous, but the

1. **Arabians** horses of the Arabian breed.





DIGITAL PERSPECTIVES

**Enriching the Text** Paragraph 4 describes trapeze artists and their performance. Help students who do not have this background knowledge. Find a video online of trapeze artists and acrobats to show the class. Be sure to preview the video before playing it for the class. After viewing the video, ask students what other similes or metaphors they can think of to describe trapeze artists and acrobats. Instruct students to write a paragraph about these types of performers, using either a metaphor or a simile. Have volunteers share their writing with the class.

explanation—I know from watching her go blind—is that my mother lives comfortably in extreme elements. She is one with the constant dark now, just as the air was her home, familiar to her, safe, before the storm that afternoon.

7 From opposite ends of the tent they waved, blind and smiling, to the crowd below. The ringmaster removed his hat and called for silence, so that the two above could concentrate. They rubbed their hands in chalky powder, then Harry launched himself and swung, once, twice, in huge calibrated beats across space. He hung from his knees and on the third swing stretched wide his arms, held his hands out to receive his pregnant wife as she dove from her shining bar.

8 It was while the two were in midair, their hands about to meet, that lightning struck the main pole and sizzled down the guy wires, filling the air with a blue radiance that Harry Avalon must certainly have seen through the cloth of his blindfold as the tent buckled and the edifice[2] toppled him forward, the swing continuing and not returning in its sweep, and Harry going down, down into the crowd with his last thought, perhaps, just a prickle of surprise at his empty hands.

9 My mother once said that I'd be amazed at how many things a person can do within the act of falling. Perhaps, at the time, she was teaching me to dive off a board at the town pool, for I associate the idea with midair somersaults. But I also think she meant that even in that awful doomed second one could think, for she certainly did. When her hands did not meet her husband's, my mother tore her blindfold away. As he swept past her on the wrong side, she could have grasped his ankle, the toe-end of his tights, and gone down clutching him. Instead, she changed direction. Her body twisted toward a heavy wire and she managed to hang on to the braided metal, still hot from the lightning strike. Her palms were burned so terribly that once healed they bore no lines, only the blank scar tissue of a quieter future. She was lowered, gently, to the sawdust ring just underneath the dome of the canvas roof, which did not entirely settle but was held up on one end and jabbed through, torn, and still on fire in places from the giant spark, though rain and men's jackets soon put that out.

10 Three people died, but except for her hands my mother was not seriously harmed until an overeager rescuer broke her arm in extricating her and also, in the process, collapsed a portion of the tent bearing a huge buckle that knocked her unconscious. She was taken to the town hospital, and there she must have hemorrhaged,[3] for they kept her, confined to her bed, a month and a half before her baby was born without life.

11 Harry Avalon had wanted to be buried in the circus cemetery next to the original Avalon, his uncle, so she sent him back with his brothers. The child, however, is buried around the corner, beyond

2. **edifice** (EHD uh fihs) *n.* large structure or building.
3. **hemorrhaged** (HEHM uh rihjd) *v.* bled heavily.

NOTES

CLOSE READ

ANNOTATE: Mark the section of paragraph 9 that interrupts the story the narrator is telling about her mother's feat at the circus years earlier.

QUESTION: Why does the narrator interrupt her story?

CONCLUDE: How does this interruption affect the reader's understanding of both the mother and the narrator?

DIGITAL PERSPECTIVES

## CLOSE READ

Remind students that fiction uses many literary techniques to enrich a story, such as interrupting the flow of the story to build suspense. You may wish to model the Close Read using the following think-aloud format. Possible responses to questions on the student page are included.

**ANNOTATE:** As I read paragraph 9, I notice and highlight the details that indicate an interruption in the story that the narrator is telling about her mother's past.

**QUESTION:** I think about how the break makes me pause from immediately learning the outcome of the story. It builds the suspense for me. The author may want to delay the main action in order to offer a reflection or to increase the curiosity of the readers.

**CONCLUDE:** The interruption shows readers that the mother has been sharing advice during the narrator's life and that the narrator has been listening. The intention of the break may vary from its actual affect. Readers may appreciate the personal insight, or they may grow impatient for the story to continue. Either way, it has a positive effect of getting the readers to want to read more and to prepare them for the details that follow.

Additional **English Language Support** is available in the Interactive Teacher's Edition.

## HOW LANGUAGE WORKS

**Subjects and Antecedents** Review paragraph 7, and ask students to identify pronouns and their antecedents. Remind students that an antecedent is a subject—a word, phrase, or clause—that is later replaced with a pronoun. Point out to students that there are pronouns in paragraph 7 that do not have antecedents. Have a student read the first sentence of paragraph 7 aloud, and ask students to whom the pronouns are referring. Discuss with the class why the author may have written this scene without antecedents. Guide the discussion to include indentifying the people in this scene as the narrator's mother, Anna, and her first husband, Harry. Point out possible reasons for the author not giving the characters' names initially may be to show that this was not the mother she knew, or that this was from her mother's life before her and thus, a stranger to her. Alternatively, the author could be simply repeating the facts as her source, a newspaper article, described them.

## CLOSE READ

Remind students that in a novel or short story, a particular character or even the whole setting might function as a symbol, representing an important theme or motif. You may wish to model the Close Read using the following think-aloud format. Possible responses to questions on the Student page are included.

**ANNOTATE:** As I read paragraph 12, I notice and highlight the details that describe increasing size or clarity.

**QUESTION:** The narrator sees the lamb statue, the horizon, the edge of the wood, and things at a distance becoming more clearly defined.

**CONCLUDE:** The narrator seems to be seeing more clearly, and it is likely that she is also getting a better view and understanding of her mother's past.

NOTES

**CLOSE READ**

**ANNOTATE:** In paragraph 12, mark words and phrases that describe increasing size or clarity.

**QUESTION:** For the narrator, what types of things are becoming larger or more clearly defined?

**CONCLUDE:** What does this passage suggest about the narrator's perspective on life?

this house and just down the highway. Sometimes I used to walk there just to sit. She was a girl, but I rarely thought of her as a sister or even as a separate person really. I suppose you could call it the egocentrism[4] of a child, of all young children, but I considered her a less finished version of myself.

12 When the snow falls, throwing shadows among the stones, I can easily pick hers out from the road, for it is bigger than the others and in the shape of a lamb at rest, its legs curled beneath. The carved lamb looms larger as the years pass, though it is probably only my eyes, the vision shifting, as what is close to me blurs and distances sharpen. In odd moments, I think it is the edge drawing near, the edge of everything, the unseen horizon we do not really speak of in the eastern woods. And it also seems to me, although this is probably an idle fantasy, that the statue is growing more sharply etched, as if, instead of weathering itself into a porous mass, it is hardening on the hillside with each snowfall, perfecting itself.

13 It was during her confinement in the hospital that my mother met my father. He was called in to look at the set of her arm, which was complicated. He stayed, sitting at her bedside, for he was something of an armchair traveler and had spent his war quietly, at an air force training grounds, where he became a specialist in arms and legs broken during parachute training exercises. Anna Avalon had been to many of the places he longed to visit—Venice, Rome, Mexico, all through France and Spain. She had no family of her own and was taken in by the Avalons, trained to perform from a very young age. They toured Europe before the war, then based themselves in New York. She was illiterate.

14 It was in the hospital that she finally learned to read and write, as a way of overcoming the boredom and depression of those weeks, and it was my father who insisted on teaching her. In return for stories of her adventures, he graded her first exercises. He bought her her first book, and over her bold letters, which the pale guides of the penmanship pads could not contain, they fell in love.

15 I wonder if my father calculated the exchange he offered: one form of flight for another. For after that, and for as long as I can remember, my mother has never been without a book. Until now, that is, and it remains the greatest difficulty of her blindness. Since my father's recent death, there is no one to read to her, which is why I returned, in fact, from my failed life where the land is flat. I came home to read to my mother, to read out loud, to read long into the dark if I must, to read all night.

16 Once my father and mother married, they moved onto the old farm he had inherited but didn't care much for. Though he'd been thinking of moving to a larger city, he settled down and broadened his practice in this valley. It still seems odd to me, when they could have gone anywhere else, that they chose to stay in the town where

4. **egocentrism** (ee goh SEHN trihz uhm) *n.* self-centeredness; inability to distinguish one's own needs and interests from those of others.





## PERSONALIZE FOR LEARNING

**English Language Support**

**Writing** Have students re-read paragraph 14 and write a paragraph to summarize the action. Ask students to consider what the mother exchanges for reading and writing lessons. Next, ask students to consider how paragraph 14 helps them understand the phrase "exchanging one form of flight for another" which appears in paragraph 15. **ALL LEVELS**

NOTES

the disaster had occurred, and which my father in the first place had found so **constricting**. It was my mother who insisted upon it, after her child did not survive. And then, too, she loved the sagging farmhouse with its scrap of what was left of a vast acreage of woods and hidden hay fields that stretched to the game park.

**constricting** (kuhn STRIHKT ihng) *adj.* limiting; tightening

17 I owe my existence, the second time then, to the two of them and the hospital that brought them together. That is the debt we take for granted since none of us asks for life. It is only once we have it that we hang on so dearly.

18 I was seven the year the house caught fire, probably from standing ash. It can rekindle, and my father, forgetful around the house and **perpetually** exhausted from night hours on call, often emptied what he thought were ashes from cold stoves into wooden or cardboard containers. The fire could have started from a flaming box, or perhaps a buildup of creosote inside the chimney was the culprit. It started right around the stove, and the heart of the house was gutted. The baby-sitter, fallen asleep in my father's den on the first floor, woke to find the stairway to my upstairs room cut off by flames. She used the phone, then ran outside to stand beneath my window.

**perpetually** (puhr PEHCH oo uhl lee) *adv.* happening all the time

19 When my parents arrived, the town volunteers had drawn water from the fire pond and were spraying the outside of the house, preparing to go inside after me, not knowing at the time that there was only one staircase and that it was lost. On the other side of the house, the **superannuated** extension ladder broke in half. Perhaps the clatter of it falling against the walls woke me, for I'd been asleep up to that point.

**superannuated** (soo puhr AN yu ayt ihd) *adj.* too old to be usable; obsolete

20 As soon as I awakened, in the small room that I now use for sewing, I smelled the smoke. I followed things by the letter then, was good at memorizing instructions, and so I did exactly what was taught in the second-grade home fire drill. I got up. I touched the back of my door before opening it. Finding it hot, I left it closed and





DIGITAL PERSPECTIVES

## CLOSER LOOK

### Analyze Characterization

Students may have marked paragraph 18 during their first read. Use this paragraph to help students understand the narrator's father. Encourage them to talk about the annotations that they marked. You may want to model a close read with the class based on the highlights shown in the text.

**ANNOTATE:** Have students mark details in the paragraph that describe the narrator's father, or have students participate while you highlight them.

**QUESTION:** Guide students to consider what these details might tell them. Ask what overall impression the narrator creates by describing her father's behaviors.

**Possible response:** The details tell us her father was a bit absent-minded. He was a hard worker who was well meaning even though he was not very cautious.

**CONCLUDE:** Help students to formulate conclusions about the importance of these details in the text. Ask students why the author might have included these details.

**Possible response:** Her father accidentally almost killed her, although he clearly loved his family and worked hard for it. He was a well-meaning person, but the narrator's mother once again had to be the one to save herself or others.

Remind students that **characterization** is the literary technique that allows writers to develop characters in fiction. Writers can describe characters through their actions, their own words, or the words others use to describe them. Note that in this passage, the father does not speak, but the way the narrator describes his actions tells a great deal about him.

## CLOSE READ

You may wish to model the Close Read using the following think-aloud format. Possible responses to questions on the student page are included.

**ANNOTATE:** As I read paragraph 24, I notice and highlight the details that describe the mother's manner as she rescues her daughter.

**QUESTION:** These words emphasize the mother's ease with danger. The mother is an extraordinary person who leaped for a living, so to her, her actions felt ordinary. The mother was doing something she had been trained to do and had done many times before in a different situation.

**CONCLUDE:** The contrast between the mother's extraordinary act and her ordinary response makes it clear she is extraordinary. This contrast makes the mother appear more heroic and creates even greater amazement at the mother's courage.

NOTES

stuffed my rolled-up rug beneath the crack. I did not hide under my bed or crawl into my closet. I put on my flannel robe, and then I sat down to wait.

21 Outside, my mother stood below my dark window and saw clearly that there was no rescue. Flames had pierced one side wall, and the glare of the fire lighted the massive limbs and trunk of the vigorous old elm that had probably been planted the year the house was built, a hundred years ago at least. No leaf touched the wall, and just one thin branch scraped the roof. From below, it looked as though even a squirrel would have had trouble jumping from the tree onto the house, for the breadth of that small branch was no bigger than my mother's wrist.

22 Standing there, beside Father, who was preparing to rush back around to the front of the house, my mother asked him to unzip her dress. When he wouldn't be bothered, she made him understand. He couldn't make his hands work, so she finally tore it off and stood there in her pearls and stockings. She directed one of the men to lean the broken half of the extension ladder up against the trunk of the tree. In surprise, he complied. She ascended. She vanished. Then she could be seen among the leafless branches of late November as she made her way up and, along her stomach, inched the length of a bough that curved above the branch that brushed the roof.

23 Once there, swaying, she stood and balanced. There were plenty of people in the crowd and many who still remember, or think they do, my mother's leap through the ice-dark air toward that thinnest extension, and how she broke the branch falling so that it cracked in her hands, cracked louder than the flames as she vaulted with it toward the edge of the roof, and how it hurtled down end over end without her, and their eyes went up, again, to see where she had flown.

**CLOSE READ**

**ANNOTATE:** In paragraph 24, mark words and phrases that describe the mother's manner as she rescues her daughter.

**QUESTION:** What aspect of the mother's character does the author emphasize with these details?

**CONCLUDE:** What is the effect of the contrast between the mother's actions and her attitude?

24 I didn't see her leap through air, only heard the sudden thump and looked out my window. She was hanging by the backs of her heels from the new gutter we had put in that year, and she was smiling. I was not surprised to see her, she was so matter-of-fact. She tapped on the window. I remember how she did it, too. It was the friendliest tap, a bit tentative, as if she was afraid she had arrived too early at a friend's house. Then she gestured at the latch, and when I opened the window she told me to raise it wider and prop it up with the stick so it wouldn't crush her fingers. She swung down, caught the ledge, and crawled through the opening. Once she was in my room, I realized she had on only underclothing, a bra of the heavy stitched cotton women used to wear and step-in, lace-trimmed drawers. I remember feeling light-headed, of course, terribly relieved, and then embarrassed for her to be seen by the crowd undressed.

25 I was still embarrassed as we flew out the window, toward earth, me in her lap, her toes pointed as we skimmed toward the painted target of the fire fighter's net.

26 I know that she's right. I knew it even then. As you fall there is time to think. Curled as I was, against her stomach, I was not startled by the cries of the crowd or the looming faces. The wind roared and beat its hot breath at our back, the flames whistled. I slowly wondered what would happen if we missed the circle or bounced out of it. Then I wrapped my hands around my mother's hands. I felt the brush of her lips and heard the beat of her heart in my ears, loud as thunder, long as the roll of drums. ❧

NOTES

## Comprehension Check

Complete the following items after you finish your first read.

1. What happened when lightning hit the circus tent while the Avalons were performing?

2. What did Anna's second husband teach Anna to do?

3. Why has the narrator returned from the West to live with her mother?

4. How did Anna Avalon save the narrator when the narrator was seven years old?

5. **Notebook** To confirm your understanding, create a timeline of key events in "The Leap."

### RESEARCH

**Research to Clarify** Choose at least one unfamiliar detail from the text. Briefly research that detail. In what way does the information you learned shed light on an aspect of the story?

## Comprehension Check

Possible responses:

1. Harold Avalon plunges to his death, and his wife saves herself by grabbing a wire.
2. He taught her to read and write.
3. She has returned to live with her mother who has gone blind. She reads aloud to her.
4. Anna rescued the narrator from the family's burning house by climbing a tree, entering her daughter's room from the roof, and leaping with the child to a safety net below.
5. Responses will vary but should focus on three key story events: the accident that leaves Anna a widow; meeting her second husband and learning to read; and the fire from which Anna rescues her daughter.

## Research

**Research to Clarify** If students struggle to choose a detail to research, suggest that they scan the story as well as their notes for unfamiliar words. Students may want to learn more about circuses, acrobats, trapezes, extreme weather, or home fires.

### PERSONALIZE FOR LEARNING

**English Language Support**

**Literary Analysis** Read paragraph 26 aloud to students, and discuss how it describes a moment when the narrator finally experiences something from her mother's prior life firsthand. Then ask them to write 2 to 3 paragraphs comparing and contrasting this scene to her mother's experience as a trapeze artist. Suggest students review the story and their notes for details to support their writing. **BRIDGING**

## Jump Start

CLOSE READ As the students close read, ask them to think about the title and the many "leaps" described in the story. Ask students to decide which leap is referenced in the title.

## Close Read the Text

Work with students on the annotation model, and then have them complete items 2 and 3 on their own. When they have finished, review and discuss the sections students marked. If needed, continue to model close reading by using the Annotation Highlights in the Interactive Teacher's Edition.

## Analyze the Text

**Possible responses:**

1. (a) The narrator learns of the tent pole disaster from the national newspapers. (b) It suggests that the memories of the disaster may have been too painful to share. **DOK 2**
2. She is coming home because reading made her mother happy, but now her mother is blind so she is coming home to read to her. This suggests that her mother's happiness is important enough to move home for, and she will read all night to her. The structure of the story develops the three ways she feels indebted to her mother for her life. **DOK 3**
3. Anna had been raised at a time when children did not necessarily go to school, and orphaned children could be taken in by families and raised by them. After the war, Anna was exceptional in that she was illiterate. **DOK 3**
4. Student responses will vary but should reflect the understanding that love can produce remarkable courage when disaster threatens. **DOK 4**



THE LEAP

## Close Read the Text

1. This model, from paragraph 9 of the text, shows two sample annotations, along with questions and conclusions. Close read the passage, and find another detail to annotate. Then, write a question and your conclusion.

ANNOTATE QUESTION Close Read CONCLUDE

ANNOTATE: This sentence describes Anna's actions as she falls.

QUESTION: What do these actions suggest about Anna?

CONCLUDE: She is brave and quick thinking.

Her body twisted toward a heavy wire and she managed to hang on to the braided metal, still hot from the lightning strike. Her palms were burned so terribly that once healed they bore no lines, only the blank scar tissue of a quieter future.

ANNOTATE: This phrase seems to have a deeper meaning for Anna's future.

QUESTION: What later decision does this phrase suggest?

CONCLUDE: Anna will leave her circus life behind.

2. For more practice, go back into the text and complete the close-read notes.
3. Revisit a section of the text you found important during your first read. Read this section closely and **annotate** what you notice. Ask yourself **questions** such as "Why did the author make this choice?" What can you **conclude**?

**Tool Kit**
Close-Read Guide and Model Annotation

## Analyze the Text

**CITE TEXTUAL EVIDENCE** to support your answers.

**Notebook** Respond to these questions.

1. (a) What is the source for the narrator's account of the tent pole disaster? (b) **Interpret** What does this explanation suggest about the impact of the disaster on Anna? Explain.
2. **Analyze** What does the narrator's return from the West to her mother's house suggest about her feelings toward her mother? Does she feel obligated, or does she feel something deeper?
3. **Historical Perspectives** What connections can you make between Anna's life changes and the United States before and after World War II?
4. **Essential Question Connection:** *What do stories reveal about the human condition?* What have you learned about human bravery and sacrifice by reading this story?

**STANDARDS**
**Reading Literature**
• Cite strong and thorough textual evidence to support analysis of what the text says explicitly as well as inferences drawn from the text, including determining where the text leaves matters uncertain.
• Analyze the impact of the author's choices regarding how to develop and relate elements of a story or drama.





### FORMATIVE ASSESSMENT

### Analyze the Text

- **If** students fail to cite evidence, **then** remind them to support their ideas with specific information from the text.
- **If** students struggle to analyze why the narrator's return hints at a sense of obligation, **then** discuss analysis and illustrate with examples.

### PERSONALIZE FOR LEARNING

**English Language Support**

**Vocabulary** Students may decide that the leap in the title is not a literal one but a figurative one—when Anna makes the leap to live a life of danger, or takes the leap to marry her second husband. Have students write a paragraph describing the difference between the terms *literal* and *figurative*, and give examples of both. **BRIDGING**

## Analyze Craft and Structure

**Narrative Structure** In literary works, **suspense** is the feeling of growing curiosity, tension, or anxiety the reader feels about the outcome of events. Writers create suspense by raising questions in the minds of their readers. Suspense reaches its peak at the climax of a plot. In "The Leap," Erdrich skillfully uses two techniques to build suspense.

- **Foreshadowing** is the use of clues to suggest events that have not yet happened. For example, at the end of paragraph 2, details such as "I hear the crackle," "the stitches burn," and "a thread of fire" hint at the impact of the powerful fire that the narrator will describe in the climax of the short story.
- **Pacing** is the speed or rhythm of writing. Writers may deliberately speed up or slow down pacing in order to create suspense. For example, in paragraph 4, the narrator delays her account of the tent pole disaster by describing the setting and the circus acts. These digressions increase readers' feelings of tension and anticipation.

### Practice

**CITE TEXTUAL EVIDENCE** to support your answers.

**Notebook** Respond to these questions.

1. Reread paragraph 7 and identify three details that contribute to suspense.
2. Reread paragraphs 18–19. Describe how the story is paced in these paragraphs. What effect does this pacing create?
3. Use this chart to record notes about Erdrich's use of suspense, foreshadowing, and pacing.

| PARAGRAPH(S) | NOTES ON SUSPENSE, FORESHADOWING, OR PACING |
|---|---|
| 3 | The narrator mentions the disaster, then goes into details about how she learned about it, then hints at a terrible gale storm, foreshadowing the event. |
| 6–9 | The narrator describes the act and the happy appearances of the Flying Avalons to build suspense and make the readers care about the characters. |
| 15 | The narrator builds suspense by implying that she came home because she owes her mother something. |
| 24 | The narrator slows the pace with memories and details, despite the urgency of the situation. |

4. Describe the overall effect of pacing and foreshadowing in the story. How do these elements affect the reader's understanding of events, characters, and themes?





DIGITAL PERSPECTIVES  

## Analyze Craft and Structure

**Narrative Structure** Remind students that telling a story effectively is an art form. Authors have a variety of techniques available to them to move plot events along in a text, including flashback, foreshadowing, and changes in pacing. When action is paused with a flashback or interrupted by description or reflection, the writer may be working to build suspense. For more support, see **Analyze Craft and Structure: Narrative Structure.**

### Practice

**Possible responses:**

1. The writer describes minute details, puts commas between details that act as pauses in between these details to slow down events even though the reader has been alerted to the fact that something dramatic is about to happen. She writes, "once, twice," to describe each swing of the trapeze, and ends the paragraph in literal suspense, of Harry in the air, waiting to feel his wife's hands meet his.
2. The narrator starts paragraph 18 with a definitive statement of an emergency: "I was seven the year the house caught fire." Before describing the events, the narrator discusses how the fire could have started. It isn't until the end of paragraph 19 that the narrator herself comes into the story. The details are related calmly, though the lost staircase and broken ladder make escape seem impossible. The pacing and description seem to mute the emergency.
3. See possible responses in the chart on the student page.
4. These literary techniques make the story seem a deep reflection, taking situations that seem to be dire and de-emphasizing them so that the author can make the bigger point about the mother's extraordinary life.

## PERSONALIZE FOR LEARNING

### English Language Support

**Narrative Structure: Analyze Suspense** To support students' understanding of suspense and the pacing of a story, explain that readers are often eager to hear how story events resolve. Have students provide an example of foreshadowing from the story. **EMERGING**

Have students find an example in the story in which the pacing helps create suspense. Ask students to identify which details control the pacing. **EXPANDING**

Ask students to think of a suspenseful plot in a story or a movie. Have them write a short paragraph to list the elements that made the plot suspenseful. **BRIDGING**

An expanded **English Language Support Lesson** on Suspense is available in the Interactive Teacher's Edition.

### FORMATIVE ASSESSMENT

### Analyze Craft and Structure

**If** students fail to identify suspense, **then** have them look for clues that indicate foreshadowing and pacing. For Reteach and Practice, see **Analyze Craft and Structure: Narrative Structure (RP).**

# TEACHING

## Concept Vocabulary

**Why These Words?**

Possible responses:

1. The vocabulary words relate to time either expanding or contracting. They can be linked to the element of suspense in the story, which relates in turn to pacing in the narration of events.
2. Other words include *precision, swooped, calibrated, hurtled, sudden,* and *flew.*

## Practice

Possible responses:

1. Although the rangers patrolled the national park conscientiously, poachers were *encroaching* with steadily more damaging results. When they received the accident report, police and fire officers responded *instantaneously*. On the morning of their first visit to a circus, the children could hardly contain their *anticipation*. For a native of a big city, life in a small town can sometimes feel *constricting* and dull. Jenna disliked her accounting job, which seemed to immerse her *perpetually* in constant wrangling with her boss, as well as with the firm's clients. Pay phone booths have become *superannuated* due to inexpensive cell phone service.
2. Synonyms will vary, but student responses should comment on the effect of the change.

## Word Network

Possible words: *blindness, cataracts, grateful, egocentrism, failed, embarrassed*

## Word Study

For more support, see **Concept Vocabulary and Word Study.**

Possible responses:

1. *restrict, (medical) stricture, strictly*
2. *restrict*—verb—limit
   *restriction*—noun—limitation
   *strictly*— adverb— rigidly
   *stricture*—noun—critique

### FORMATIVE ASSESSMENT

**Concept Vocabulary**

**If** students fail to see the connection between the words, **then** have them research synonyms in a thesaurus.

**Word Study**

**If** students fail to create accurate sentences, **then** have them find examples online. For Reteach and Practice, see **Word Study: Latin Root *-strict-* (RP).**

THE LEAP

## Concept Vocabulary

| encroaching | anticipation | perpetually |
|---|---|---|
| instantaneously | constricting | superannuated |

**Why These Words?** These concept vocabulary words all suggest distance or closeness, especially in relation to time. For example, *instantaneously* means "in an instant," or "immediately." Something that happens *perpetually* is continuous or endless. A *superannuated* tool or object is so old-fashioned or worn out that it is no longer useful.

1. How does the concept vocabulary clarify the reader's understanding of the story?
2. What other words in the selection connect to this concept?

### Practice

Notebook Respond to these questions.

1. Use each concept vocabulary word in a sentence that demonstrates your understanding of the word's meaning.
2. Challenge yourself to replace each concept vocabulary word in your sentences with a synonym. How does changing the words affect the meanings of your sentences? Which word choices are more effective?

**WORD NETWORK**

Add words related to the human condition from the text to your Word Network.

## Word Study

**Latin Root: *-strict-*** The Latin root *-strict-* means "to bind" or "to compress." In paragraph 16, the narrator's father finds his hometown *constricting,* or limiting. The word *constrict* also has a medical meaning. It is used to describe a part of the body that narrows, closes, or compresses. For example, when you step out in bright sunlight, your pupils *constrict*, or get smaller, to take in less light.

1. Find four words that contain the root *-strict-*. Challenge yourself to come up with one word that has a medical meaning.
2. For each word you choose, record the word, its part of speech, and its meaning. Use a print or online college-level dictionary as needed.

**STANDARDS**

**Reading Literature**
Determine the meaning of words and phrases as they are used in the text, including figurative and connotative meanings; analyze the impact of specific word choices on meaning and tone, including words with multiple meanings or language that is particularly fresh, engaging, or beautiful.

**Language**
Identify and correctly use patterns of word changes that indicate different meanings or parts of speech.

## Author's Style

**Motif** A **motif** is an important recurring, or repeating, element in literature, mythology, or other type of artistic expression. In "The Leap," Erdrich uses recurring motifs to highlight symbols and develop themes.

- A **symbol** is a person, place, object, or idea that represents not only itself but also something beyond or outside itself.
- A **theme** in a work is an underlying central insight about human life or behavior.

The first step in interpreting motifs is to recognize when they are present. While reading, be alert to repetition in events, imagery, description, or dialogue. For example, you might notice the repetition of Anna's three "leaps." Once you have identified a possible motif, consider what this repetition may represent and how it connects to the story's themes.

### Read It

1. Use the chart to analyze motifs in "The Leap." Consider how the meanings and associations of each motif change with each appearance.

| MOTIF | WHERE IT APPEARS | ANALYSIS |
|---|---|---|
| "roll of drums" | paragraph 6 | See possible responses in Teacher's Edition. |
| | paragraph 26 | b. |
| arms/limbs | paragraph 10 | c. |
| | paragraph 13 | d. |
| | paragraph 21 | e. |

2. Explain how Anna's three leaps are both literal and symbolic.

3. **Connect to Style** How does Erdrich use recurring images to develop the story's most important themes?



### Write It

**Notebook** Another motif in the story is the idea of the narrator's debt to her mother for her existence. This motif first occurs in paragraph 3: "I owe her my existence three times." In a paragraph, explain what this motif contributes to the story. What would be lost if this motif were omitted?



DIGITAL PERSPECTIVES

## Author's Style

**Motif** Tell students motifs occur in fairy tales, film, and television, too. Some common motifs are evil stepmothers, a dangerous path through the forest, and a full moon. For more support, see **Author's Style: Motif.**

### Read It

Possible responses:

1. a. The roll of drums is part of a performance. It grabs audience attention and builds suspense.
   b. The roll of drums is part of a simile. It compares this live-saving leap to the circus performance.
   c. Anna's arms are broken after she survives the fall in the circus tent.
   d. The doctor is an arm and leg specialist who comes to help Anna's recovery.
   e. The tree is compared to an arm. The tree is critical to the narrator's rescue.
2. Explain how Anna's three leaps are both literal and symbolic. Anna's first leap is literal as she works as on a trapeze. It is symbolic because she trusts her husband to catch her. Anna's second leap is mostly symbolic as she trusts her second husband to share a life. The third leap is literal in that she jumps to save the narrator. It is symbolic because she takes brave action that no one else would.
3. Erdrich uses the motifs in the chart to help suggest and reinforce the important ideas in the story.

### Write It

Responses will vary. Student responses should point out that the story is bound together by the narrator's gratitude to her mother and the narrator's need to show her gratitude by returning to her mother when the mother's sight fails.

### FORMATIVE ASSESSMENT

### Conventions and Style

**If** students can't identify motifs, **then** remind them to look for any recurrent ideas, actions, or objects.

For Reteach and Practice, see **Author's Style: Motif (RP).**

PERSONALIZE FOR LEARNING

**English Language Support**

**Point of View** "The Leap" is written from the daughter's perspective. Have students write a paragraph from the mother's point of view. They can choose to retell the story of the fire, or write about something different, such as her daughter's return.

**ALL LEVELS**

## Writing to Sources

Tell students that anecdotes should be used to illustrate an idea. Support students in selecting an anecdote. Encourage them to think about a lesson they have learned, and then ask them to think about the event that taught them the lesson. This event may be a good subject for the anecdote. For more support, see **Writing to Sources: Anecdote.**

### Reflect on Your Writing

1. Responses will vary. Students may say that writing their own anecdote helped them see the way the author used several events to support a larger idea.
2. Encourage students to share their anecdote with a classmate and get feedback to answer this question if they are having difficulty on their own.
3. Responses will vary. Have students list specific examples of words they have chosen that bring the anecdote to life.

### FORMATIVE ASSESSMENT

### Writing to Sources

**If** students struggle to write an anecdote, **then** suggest they create a concept map to develop ideas. For example, students might list a key word such as "trust," "responsibility," or "bravery" at the center of a page and then jot down examples of events and experiences that support the idea. Students can select an anecdote after this brainstorming activity. For Reteach and Practice, see **Writing to Sources: Anecdote (RP).**

EFFECTIVE EXPRESSION

THE LEAP

## Writing to Sources

An anecdote is a brief story about an interesting, amusing, or strange event. An anecdote is told to entertain or to make a point. The person telling an anecdote may include a brief opinion or argument to underscore a moral or lesson. For example, in paragraph 17 of "The Leap" the narrator provides this commentary:

> I owe my existence, the second time then, to the two of them and the hospital that brought them together. That is the debt we take for granted since none of us asks for life. It is once we have it that we hang on so dearly.

**Assignment**
Write a short, entertaining **anecdote** about an event in your or your family's past. Tell about a time when a parent, teacher, or coach intervened in a situation in a way that made you feel grateful. Include an opinion that highlights an important lesson. Conclude your anecdote with a paragraph that explains how your experience compares to that of the narrator in "The Leap."

**Vocabulary and Conventions Connection** You may want to use some of the concept vocabulary words in your anecdote. Consider varying your pacing or adding foreshadowing to increase suspense.

| encroaching | anticipation | perpetually |
|---|---|---|
| instantaneously | constricting | superannuated |

### Reflect on Your Writing

After completing your anecdote, answer the following questions.

1. How did writing an anecdote improve your understanding of Erdrich's style?
2. What literary elements did you use to make your anecdote more entertaining or effective? Were they successful? Explain.
3. **Why These Words?** The words you choose make a difference in your writing. Which words helped you convey important details or ideas?

STANDARDS

**Writing**
Write narratives to develop real or imagined experiences or events using effective technique, well-chosen details, and well-structured event sequences.

**Speaking and Listening**
Present information, findings, and supporting evidence, conveying a clear and distinct perspective, such that listeners can follow the line of reasoning, alternative or opposing perspectives are addressed, and the organization, development, substance, and style are appropriate to purpose, audience, and a range of formal and informal tasks.





PERSONALIZE FOR LEARNING

### Challenge

**History** The story mentions that the circus Anna was a part of traveled throughout Europe before World War II but moved to America when the war began. It mentions Venice, Rome, France, and Spain. Choose one of these cities or countries and research what it was like before and after World War II. Ask students to share information about the effects of the war on the area they chose.

## Speaking and Listening

**Assignment**

Choose one of the following quotations, and explain in a brief **oral response to literature** how it connects to the plot and themes of "The Leap." Present your response to the class, and lead the class in a discussion of your ideas.

- Love is the chain whereby to bind a child to its parents.
  — Abraham Lincoln
- Courage is grace under pressure.
  — Ernest Hemingway
- What do we owe to those we love?
  — Ellen McLaughlin

1. **Analyze the Quotations** Carefully consider each quotation—both its meaning and its associations. Paraphrase each quotation and think about its purpose. Lincoln's statement, for example, focuses on children, parents, and love; Hemingway provides a concise definition of courage. Choose the quotation that you think is the best match with "The Leap."
2. **Connect to Plot and Theme** Review the major plot events in the story. Check that you understand the chronology of events, as well as their causes and effects. Then, state one important theme the events bring out, and explain how that theme relates to the quotation you selected.
3. **Prepare Your Delivery** As you practice, be sure to pay attention to nonverbal methods of communication, such as volume, tone, pitch, pacing, posture, gestures, eye contact, and facial expressions.
4. **Evaluate Responses** As your classmates deliver their oral responses, listen carefully. Use an evaluation guide like the one shown to analyze their responses.

EVALUATION GUIDE

**Rate each statement on a scale of 1 (not demonstrated) to 4 (demonstrated).**

☐ The speaker clearly identified the quotation being discussed.

☐ The speaker identified specific and persuasive links between the meaning of the quotation and the story's plot and theme.

☐ The speaker used a variety of inflections and tones when speaking.

☐ The speaker used appropriate pacing, posture, gestures, and facial expressions.



EVIDENCE LOG

Before moving on to a new selection, go to your Evidence Log and record what you learned from "The Leap."



PERSONALIZE FOR LEARNING

### English Language Support

**Reading Fiction Aloud** Remind students that reading fiction aloud requires a different register, or range of voice, than a factual or persuasive presentation. Find online videos of storytellers to illustrate for students. Be sure to preview the videos first. Then, have students share their anecdotes from the Writing to Sources with the class, paying close attention to matching their register with the tone. **BRIDGING**

DIGITAL PERSPECTIVES  

## Speaking and Listening

Point out to students that stories illustrate an important theme or message about life. The quotations provided here each address possible themes of Erdrich's story. Ask students to consider each quotation as they prepare their oral responses. For more support, see **Speaking and Listening: Response to Literature.**

1. **Analyze the Quotations** Encourage students to give themselves time to understand each quotation and what it means in the story.
2. **Connect to Plot and Theme** Support students as they explore the connections between the story and the quotations they have selected. Encourage students to make notes that will help them share their ideas with others.
3. **Prepare Your Delivery** Once students have their ideas collected, provide them with time to practice their oral responses. You may choose to pair students to allow each one to give a partner feedback.
4. **Evaluate Responses** Review the evaluation guide to remind students about the criteria for successful oral presentations.

Evidence Log Support students in completing their Evidence Log. This paced activity will help prepare them for the Performance-Based Assessment at the end of the unit.

### FORMATIVE ASSESSMENT

### Speaking and Listening

- **If** students have difficulty connecting the quote to the plot, **then** have them write a summary of the plot first.
- **If** students have difficulty connecting the quote to the theme, **then** suggest they connect the quote to the characters they refer to first.

For Reteach and Practice, see **Speaking and Listening: Response to Literature (RP).**

### Selection Test

Administer the "The Leap" Selection Test, which is available in both print and digital formats online in Assessments.

## Jump Start

Encourage students to brainstorm a list of possible reactions to stress. They may suggest feeling panic, worry, or anxiety; rising to the challenge; asking for help; taking the opportunity to learn something new; trying to escape; getting angry; or other reactions. Ask students to categorize these responses to stress as positive or negative.

## Write a Narrative

Point out to students that the purpose of a narrative is to tell a story. Ask students to identify types of fictional narrative texts. They may name myths, folktales, adventure stories, short stories, etc. Remind students that they will be writing a realistic short story.

Students should complete the assignment using word processing software to take advantage of editing tools and features.

### Elements of a Fictional Narrative

Students can use the bulleted list to develop an initial story plan by brainstorming ideas for each bullet. Later, they can use the bulleted list as a checklist, making sure they have included each element in their story.

**MAKE IT INTERACTIVE**

Project "Old Man at the Bridge" from the Interactive Teacher's Edition and have students identify the elements of a narrative text.

PERFORMANCE TASK: WRITING FOCUS

WRITING TO SOURCES

- EVERYDAY USE
- EVERYTHING STUCK TO HIM
- THE LEAP

# Write a Narrative

You have read three short stories that employ flashbacks or framing devices to tell stories. Now you will use your understanding of those texts to create a narrative that explores a question related to the human condition in a fresh way.

**Assignment**

Write a **fictional narrative** addressing this question:

**How do stressful situations often reveal the best and worst in people?**

Begin by creating a fictional scenario that is dramatic and stressful enough to trigger widely different responses from characters. Then, think about how you might develop characters whose reactions will give readers insight into the issues raised by the prompt. Finally, reflect on the structure of the stories you read in this unit. Use plot devices similar to the ones in those texts, such as frame stories or flashbacks, to add interest to your narrative and provide additional insight into characters and events.

**Tool Kit**
Student Model of a Fictional Narrative

### Elements of a Fictional Narrative

A **fictional narrative** is a story about an imagined experience. The elements of such narratives are invented by their authors. A fictional narrative may feature a narrator who is part of the story or a narrator who is a detached observer of the action.

A well-written fictional narrative usually contains these elements:

- a clear and consistent point of view
- well-developed characters
- a smooth sequence of events or experiences, which may include flashbacks, subplots, or frame stories
- effective use of dialogue, description, and/or reflection to develop the story
- sensory language and precise, descriptive details to clarify experiences
- a conclusion that brings the story to a satisfying close

**Model Narrative Text** For a model of a well-crafted fictional narrative, see the Launch Text, "Old Man at the Bridge."

Challenge yourself to find all of the elements of an effective fictional narrative in the text. You will have an opportunity to review these elements as you prepare to write your own fictional narrative.

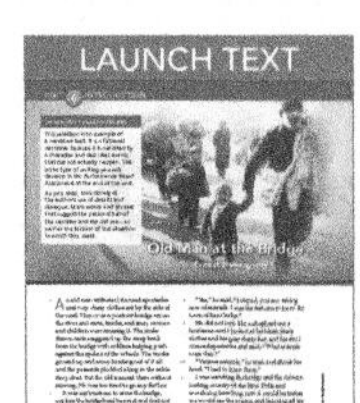


**STANDARDS**

**Writing**

- Write narratives to develop real or imagined experiences or events using effective technique, well-chosen details, and well-structured event sequences.
- Write routinely over extended time frames and shorter time frames for a range of tasks, purposes, and audiences.





AUTHOR'S PERSPECTIVE **Kelly Gallagher, M.Ed.**

**Drafting** Like reading, writing is not a "one and done" activity. Teachers can use a surfing metaphor to reinforce the importance of drafting, of evaluating ideas to find the best ones. Explain that ideas come in sets of waves. Remind students that a surfer can sit in the water for ten minutes or longer, waiting for a new set of waves to come in. When a wave finally comes in, an inexperienced surfer might catch it immediately, but a more experienced surfer recognizes that waves come in sets. The second wave in the set is usually larger than the first one, the third wave may be even larger, and so on.

As tempting as that first wave may be, the experienced surfer looks for the best wave in the set, just as a skilled writer sifts ideas and evaluates drafts, looking for the best ones. Encourage students to draft and then consider additional ideas that can improve their writing.

## Prewriting / Planning

**Focus on a Conflict** The stories that you, like all writers, tell are influenced by your own life. Make a list of conflicts you have experienced, witnessed, or studied. Choose a conflict from your list, and think about ways you can turn that conflict into a fictional story that reveals characters at their best and worst.

EVIDENCE LOG

Review your Evidence Log and identify key details you may want to use in your narrative.

**Create a Story Chart** Make a story chart, like the one shown, to plan the stages of your narrative. Events from "Old Man at the Bridge" have been filled in so that you can trace the narrative arc in the Launch Text.

STORY CHART

| **Exposition:** Establish the setting and characters, and set up the conflict. | **Rising Action:** Describe the events that increase the conflict and tension. | **Climax:** Identify the point of greatest tension. | **Resolution:** Tell how the conflict is or is not resolved. |
|---|---|---|---|
| *During the Spanish Civil War, an old man sits by a bridge while others evacuate. The narrator stops to talk to him.* | *The narrator wants to get the old man out of danger, but the old man is too tired to move.* | *The old man tries to get up and move, but he sits back down. He can't get up. He is worried about animals he left behind.* | *The conflict doesn't resolve: The old man gives up; the narrator leaves him to face the advancing enemy alone.* |

**Develop Your Characters** Once you have selected the characters who will appear in your narrative, start to develop them using a chart like this one.

| | MAIN CHARACTER |
|---|---|
| **Appearance** | |
| **Attitude/Personal Characteristics** | |
| **Motivations** | |

**Connect to Texts** After you have identified the basic plot events and characters, decide how you can use *plot devices* to add interest to your story. Review the use of the *frame story* in "Everything Stuck to Him" and "The Leap." Determine if a similar framing device might work for your story. Also, consider Erdrich's use of *foreshadowing* in "The Leap." Just as she dropped hints about the fire, you could hint at later events in your story.

One final device to consider is the **flashback,** in which the action suddenly reverts back to a past event that was important to the main character's development or to the present action of the story.

STANDARDS

Writing

• Engage and orient the reader by setting out a problem, situation, or observation and its significance, establishing one or multiple point(s) of view, and introducing a narrator and/or characters; create a smooth progression of experiences or events.

• Use a variety of techniques to sequence events so that they build on one another to create a coherent whole and build toward a particular tone and outcome.





DIGITAL PERSPECTIVES

## Prewriting/Planning

**Focus on a Conflict** Students may benefit from working in pairs to list several ideas about conflict, or they may work independently to jot down ideas about experiences or events that might be stressful.

**Create a Story Chart** While some students may prefer to write without a plan, encourage them to take the time to plan out the stages of the story. This will help them write with better focus, allowing them to devote more time to developing their characters and the conflict.

**Develop Your Characters** Remind students about the importance of conflict in a story. Students should gather details to help them to differentiate their characters. The details that students list here will help them bring their characters to life in their narratives.

**Connect Across Texts** Encourage students to develop a setting that makes sense with the characters. Point out that setting should connect with the story's theme, as well.

**Evidence Log** Students' evidence logs may remind them of the characters in unit stories they have already read and the way those characters managed conflict.

PERSONALIZE FOR LEARNING

### English Language Support

**Developing Characters** Point out that the best way to get to know a person is by asking him or her questions. Brainstorm with students a list of "getting to know you" questions that they might ask their characters. Have students answer each question as their character might answer. **ALL LEVELS**

## Drafting

**Establish a Point of View** Review student options for their narrator, pointing out the point of view that the anchor selections have modeled. Work with students to discuss the positive and negative features of each type of narrator.

**Begin the Story Memorably** Encourage students to think about innovative ways to start their narratives. Students may decide to try a few options before choosing the one they think works best.

**Highlight the Conflict** As students write, suggest that they build the tension level by adding details and phrases that emphasize the conflict or stress in the narrative.

**End in a Satisfying Way** Students may decide to end their narratives with a conclusion that clearly states the lesson that the story illustrates. Alternatively, they may present an ending that is more subtle, showing what the character learned from the experience without dramatically labeling a message.

PERFORMANCE TASK: WRITING FOCUS

## Drafting

**Establish a Point of View** The point of view you choose helps set the tone for your story. Are you going to be a neutral observer, reporting on events rather than participating in them? Then, you will use a third-person narrator. Are you going to interpret events directly through the eyes of a narrator who participates in the events of the story? Then, you will write using a first-person point of view. Notice how the choice of point of view affects the examples in this chart.

| NARRATOR | DESCRIPTION | EXAMPLE |
|---|---|---|
| First-person | The narrator is a character in the story. | *I knew what I had to do. I had to tell Shana the truth.* |
| Third-person omniscient | The narrator is outside the story and knows everything that happens. | *Julia was finally ready to tell Shana the truth, but Shana didn't want to hear it.* |
| Third-person limited | The narrator is outside the story and knows only what one character does and thinks. | *Julia was finally ready to tell Shana the truth. But would Shana listen?* |

**Begin the Story Memorably** You can draw from a variety of strategies to engage your readers right from the start. Remember to select a strategy that sets a proper tone for your story, whether you intend your story to be serious or humorous, thoughtful or lighthearted. Here are a few ideas to grab the attention of your audience:

- *Start off with a simple declarative statement:* It was not my most heroic moment.
- *Start off with a question:* What makes us do the right thing in the worst possible situations?
- *Start in the middle of the action:* As I looked down at the 200-foot drop I said to myself, "What am I doing here?"

**Highlight the Conflict** When you are setting up the exposition, rising action, and climax of the story, be sure to emphasize the main conflict. The prompt asks you to explore how people react in times of stress. This lends itself naturally to describing characters and their responses to events in a way that builds tension throughout the story until the climax.

**End in a Satisfying Way** Make sure that your ending flows naturally from the events of the story. Above all, though, end it in a way that will be satisfying and memorable, and that reinforces the main point of the story—people under stress behave both their best and their worst. Keep in mind that it can be just as effective to end a story with some elements unresolved as it is to tie all the loose ends up neatly.

STANDARDS

**Writing**

- Engage and orient the reader by setting out a problem, situation, or observation and its significance, establishing one or multiple point(s) of view, and introducing a narrator and/or characters; create a smooth progression of experiences or events.
- Use a variety of techniques to sequence events so that they build on one another to create a coherent whole and build toward a particular tone and outcome.
- Provide a conclusion that follows from and reflects on what is experienced, observed, or resolved over the course of the narrative.





AUTHOR'S PERSPECTIVE **Jim Cummins, Ph.D.**

**Writing Vibrant Sentences** Having students focus on writing expressive sentences encourages them to pay attention to how ideas are conveyed in the texts they read. Students will develop an enhanced awareness of how to control rich descriptive language when teachers draw their attention to vivid descriptions in the texts they are reading. Teachers can point to "strong sentences" in these passages in order to sensitize students to ways in which meanings can be expressed powerfully and imaginatively.

**Step 1:** Select an expressive sentence from the text to use as a model.

**Step 2:** Draw students' attention to the range of adjectives, adverbs, nouns, and verbs in the sentence that enabled the author to create lively images of what is being described.

**Step 3:** Show students how to expand simple nouns into noun phrases that provide additional information about what is being described.

LANGUAGE DEVELOPMENT: STYLE

## Add Variety: Dialogue

**Dialogue** The conversations between and among people in a story are called **dialogue**. This narrative technique can serve several purposes:

- exposing conflict between characters
- revealing personality traits
- providing explanation or advancing the plot
- showing what characters think and value
- indicating what characters understand and how they communicate

### Read It

These sentences from the Launch Text use dialogue to establish a connection between the two characters and to reveal their feelings and traits.

- *"Where do you come from?" I asked him.* (The narrator expresses his interest mainly through questions directed to the old man.)
- *"I am without politics," he said. "I am seventy-six years old. I have come twelve kilometers now and I think now I can go no further."* (The old man states his problem and reveals his innocence in his own words.)
- *"Why not," I said, watching the far bank where now there were no carts.* (The narrator's curt response suggests that the old man's problems are not his main concern.)
- *"I was taking care of animals," he said dully, but no longer to me. "I was only taking care of animals."* (The old man talks to himself, expressing his confusion and sorrow.)

TIP

PUNCTUATION

Punctuate dialogue correctly.

- Use quotation marks before and after a character's spoken words.
- Use a comma to set off the speaker's tag from the speaker's words.
- Use quotation marks around each part of a divided quotation.
- If end punctuation, such as a question mark or an exclamation point, is part of the quotation, keep it inside the quotation marks.

### Write It

As you draft your narrative, look for ways to incorporate dialogue. Start a new paragraph each time the speaker changes. There are a variety of ways in which to write dialogue. Notice in these examples how the words being spoken are set apart from their tags, such as *he said* or *I urged.*

| PLACEMENT OF DIALOGUE | EXAMPLE |
|---|---|
| **before a tag** | *"Where do you come from?" I asked him.* |
| **after a tag** | *. . . I looked at his black dusty clothes and his gray dusty face and his steel rimmed spectacles and said, "What animals were they?"* |
| **splitting a single sentence** | *"I know no one in that direction," he said, "but thank you very much."* |
| **splitting multiple sentences** | *"If you are rested I would go," I urged. "Get up and try to walk now."* |

STANDARDS

**Writing**
Use narrative techniques, such as dialogue, pacing, description, reflection, and multiple plot lines, to develop experiences, events, and/or characters.

**Language**
Demonstrate command of the conventions of standard English capitalization, punctuation, and spelling when writing.





DIGITAL PERSPECTIVES

## Add Variety: Dialogue

**Dialogue** Engage students in a discussion about short stories that include dialogue and those that don't. Students may say that dialogue in a text helps to move the plot along and helps readers to imagine each character's personality.

### Read It

Many factors determine the way people speak and the kind of language they use. Encourage students to keep in mind important influences on their characters. They should be able to answer these questions about their characters: *What life events affected them most deeply? How did these events affect them? Who affected them most deeply? How did these people affect them? What ambitions do they have? What problems do they face?*

### Write It

Point out to students that they should beware of writing extremely long speeches. Generally, people do not speak in lengthy, uninterrupted monologues. If students write a long speech, they should make sure that it fits the situation and the character. If not, they might look for ways to redirect the speaker: for example, by incorporating the reactions of another character or introducing dialogue with another character.

PERSONALIZE FOR LEARNING

### English Language Support

**Tagging Dialogue** Help students to understand the different ways of writing dialogue with the appropriate punctuation and language to indicate who is speaking. Begin with one quotation and illustrate several ways of tagging dialogue.

**Start With the Quotation** "Your kid brother is really getting on my nerves," Ginny told Liz.

**Split the Sentence** "Your kid brother," Ginny told Liz, "is really getting on my nerves.

**Start with the Tag** After Tom had interrupted her several times, Ginny told Liz, "Your kid brother is really getting on my nerves."

**Tag Between Sentences** "Your kid brother is really getting on my nerves," Ginny told Liz. "Please speak with him."

Then have students practice with this example: "This football game is going to be awesome," Max said. **ALL LEVELS**

# TEACHING

## Making Writing Sophisticated

**Integrating Sensory Language** Give students practice finding the most precise word possible for a given situation. For every word in the chart, ask students to find one vivid synonym. Ask students to share their findings and explain how each new selection differs from the word in the chart.

### Read It

Review the launch text to help students study setting.

Remind students that setting is the place and time in which the events of a story takes place.

Encourage students to add details to their writing to build a sense of place in their narratives.

PERFORMANCE TASK: WRITING FOCUS

## MAKING WRITING SOPHISTICATED

**Integrating Sensory Language** Vivid, detailed description makes characters and settings come alive for readers. An important part of such description is **sensory language**, which features details that appeal to one of the five senses. Writers use sensory language to describe how things look, sound, taste, feel, or smell. Vivid sensory adjectives, adverbs, and verbs can combine to create an overall impression of a scene or event. Notice how each of these examples affects you as you read it.

| | ADJECTIVE | ADVERB | VERB |
|---|---|---|---|
| **Sight** | scarlet | garishly | soar |
| **Hearing (Sound)** | piercing | softly | creak |
| **Taste** | bitter | juicily | savor |
| **Touch** | slippery | roughly | tap |
| **Smell** | rancid | fragrantly | reek |

### Read It

These examples from the Launch Text show how the writer uses sensory language to establish a sense of place

LAUNCH TEXT EXCERPT

An old man with steel rimmed spectacles and very dusty clothes sat by the side of the road. There was a pontoon bridge across the river and carts, trucks, and men, women and children were crossing it. The mule-drawn carts staggered up the steep bank from the bridge with soldiers helping push against the spokes of the wheels. The trucks ground up and away heading out of it all and the peasants plodded along in the ankle deep dust. But the old man sat there without moving. He was too tired to go any farther.

The initial description sets the scene. Readers can envision the old man and can both "see" and "hear" the peasants, carts, and trucks.

...

I was watching the bridge and the African looking country of the Ebro Delta and wondering how long now it would be before we would see the enemy, and listening all the while for the first noises that would signal that ever mysterious event called contact, and the old man still sat there.

The comparison in this paragraph shows the dryness of the Spanish countryside and points to the silence and the strain on the narrator as he listens for the enemy's approach.





## PERSONALIZE FOR LEARNING

### Challenge

**Give It Your Spin** Ask students to replace underlined examples of sensory language with vague language. Ask students to share the results and discuss which version of the text is more appealing or precise. Guide students to understand how sensory language appeals to one or more of the senses and recreates sensory experiences with words.

College and Career Readiness

## Write It

Think of sensory words and phrases that can clarify a reader's impression of your characters and the situations in which you place them. Start by completing this chart with specific details. Then, go back to your draft to determine how to incorporate those details into your narrative.

| SENSE | CHARACTER 1 | CHARACTER 2 | SETTING |
|---|---|---|---|
| **Sight** | | | |
| **Hearing (Sound)** | | | |
| **Taste** | | | |
| **Touch** | | | |
| **Smell** | | | |

**Use a Thesaurus to Find Precise Words** Even the most experienced writers sometimes refer to a thesaurus to find the words that best express what they want to say. A thesaurus can be a valuable resource when it comes to finding sensory language that fits your needs. Here are thesaurus lists of synonyms for the first three examples from the chart of sensory words. Note that not every synonym is appropriate in every case; you must choose the word that works best in context.

SCARLET *syn*. crimson, red, ruby, cherry, garnet

GARISHLY *syn*. brashly, gaudily, brightly, vulgarly, flamboyantly

SOAR *syn*. fly, ascend, rocket, circle, arise, climb

STANDARDS

**Writing**
Use precise words and phrases, telling details, and sensory language to convey a vivid picture of the experiences, events, setting, and/or characters.

**Language**
Consult general and specialized reference materials, both print and digital, to find the pronunciation of a word or determine or clarify its precise meaning, its part of speech, its etymology, or its standard usage.





DIGITAL PERSPECTIVES

## Write It

Explain to students that most good writers create unique characters who are differentiated from the others. The more information students can gather about their characters the easier it may be to write about them as they draft.

**Use a Thesaurus to Find Precise Words** As students prepare to write their narratives, encourage them to think about the words they will use. Remind students to use dictionary resources to find words that are precise, but to avoid using words that are unfamiliar. Very often unique words in a synonym map have specific uses, and students risk choosing the wrong word and making their writing awkward.

PERSONALIZE FOR LEARNING

### Strategic Support

**Word Connotations** The concept of connotations is difficult to master. Give students these synonym groups: smart, brilliant, intelligent, bright; bitter, astringent, tart, acidic. Have students practice ranking synonyms in each group from most neutral to most negative (or positive) in connotation, by placing each synonym on a line graph similar to the one shown. Then encourage students to be aware of the connotations of the words they use in their writing.

most neutral | somewhat neutral | somewhat negative/positive | most negative/positive

## Revising

### Evaluating Your Draft

Suggest that students conduct their reviews in stages. Students may first review their drafts according to the criteria in the Purpose and Organization column. First carry out the review in the column under PURPOSE AND ORGANIZATION. Doing so will help them to avoid having to redo part of their work. The last two columns suggest a more detailed level of review that should come *after* students make any changes to the introduction, sequence of events, or resolution of their story.

### Revising for Focus and Organization

**Sequence of Events** Point out to students that having a ready arsenal of sequence words and phrases can be helpful. Invite partners to work together to develop a list of additional sequence phrases, such as *after a few days, in an instant, in the meantime, just then,* and *lastly*. Ask students to share their findings with the class.



## Revising

### Evaluating Your Draft

Use the following checklist to evaluate the effectiveness of your first draft. Then, use your evaluation and the instruction on this page to guide your revision.

| FOCUS AND ORGANIZATION | EVIDENCE AND ELABORATION | CONVENTIONS |
|---|---|---|
| ☐ Provides an introduction that sets the scene and introduces characters and conflict.<br>☐ Establishes a sequence of events that unfolds smoothly and logically.<br>☐ Incorporates plot devices, such as foreshadowing, flashback, and frame stories, to add interest to the story.<br>☐ Provides a conclusion that resolves the narrative in a satisfying way. | ☐ Uses techniques such as dialogue, description, and reflection to develop the experience being narrated.<br>☐ Uses sensory language and precise details to clarify events for the reader.<br>☐ Uses vocabulary and word choices that are appropriate for the audience and purpose. | ☐ Attends to the norms and conventions of the discipline, especially the correct punctuation of dialogue. |

**WORD NETWORK**

Include interesting words from your Word Network in your narrative.

### Revising for Focus and Organization

**Sequence of Events** Maintaining a consistent point of view will help you present a realistic perspective on setting, characters, and events. Would a reader be puzzled about what happened first, next, and last in your narrative? Consider adding time words and phrases that clarify the sequence. Some examples are given here.

| after a while | at that point | before | by then |
|---|---|---|---|
| eventually | initially | just then | later |
| meanwhile | previously | soon afterward | ultimately |

**Conclusion** Remember that your conclusion should settle or resolve the conflict and provide a satisfying ending for the reader. Is your conclusion too abrupt? Should you add more detail to the falling action in the plot to make your conclusion seem more plausible?

### Revising for Evidence and Elaboration

**Dialogue** The effectiveness of your narrative depends on how well you establish a believable conversation between the characters. Have you captured the "sound" of each character? Would each character be likely to say the words you have given him or her? If not, make some changes to your dialogue to improve its authenticity.

**STANDARDS**

Writing

- Use narrative techniques, such as dialogue, pacing, description, reflection, and multiple plot lines, to develop experiences, events, and/or characters.
- Provide a conclusion that follows from and reflects on what is experienced, observed, or resolved over the course of the narrative.

PEER REVIEW

Exchange drafts with a classmate. Use the checklist to evaluate your classmate's narrative, and provide supportive feedback.

1. Does the dialogue advance the plot or serve some other important purpose, such as building tension?

☐ yes ☐ no If no, suggest what you might change.

2. Does the introduction clearly set a scene and introduce the conflict?

☐ yes ☐ no If no, tell what you think should be added.

3. Is the ending satisfying, believable, and understandable?

☐ yes ☐ no If no, tell what you found confusing.

4. What is the strongest part of your classmate's narrative? Why?

## Editing and Proofreading

**Edit for Conventions** Reread your draft for accuracy and consistency. Correct errors in grammar and word usage. Make sure that you have used sensory language correctly in context.

**Proofread for Accuracy** Read your draft carefully, correcting errors in spelling and punctuation. Punctuate dialogue correctly, using quotation marks and commas or end marks as needed.

## Publishing and Presenting

Work with a partner to present your narrative as a dramatic dialogue. Each of you should take the part of one of your characters and read the dialogue as though you were actors in a play. If you wish, one of you may read the narration as well. Practice together and then present your dialogue to the class.

## Reflecting

Reflect on what you learned by writing your narrative. Are you happy with the characters you chose? Were you able to incorporate them into a unified narrative? What was difficult about incorporating a narrative technique, such as flashback or foreshadowing, into your narrative?

STANDARDS

**Writing**

Develop and strengthen writing as needed by planning, revising, editing, rewriting, or trying a new approach, focusing on addressing what is most significant for a specific purpose and audience.





DIGITAL PERSPECTIVES

## Peer Review

Point out to students that even professional writers need editors and critics to make their writing stronger. While professional critics are sometimes harsh, the role of student peer reviewers is to be helpful, and never hurtful. The peer review checklist is designed to focus student comment.

## Editing and Proofreading

Offer students a proofreading checklist, such as the following.

Check for errors in:

- capitalization
- end marks
- use of commas, colons, semicolons
- use of quotation marks
- use of apostrophes
- spelling

## Reflecting

Remind students that they might use the peer review form to help them objectively evaluate their work. However, they should keep in mind that each of us can be our own harshest critics.

PERSONALIZE FOR LEARNING

### English Language Support

**Pay Attention to Punctuation** Work with students to expand on the proofreading checklist and focus on punctuation. Guide them to understand that punctuation tells readers when to pause and also indicates relationships between words. With students, review the different types of punctuation on a chart like the one shown. **ALL LEVELS**

| Punctuation Mark | Meaning |
|---|---|
| comma | brief pause |
| period | pause at the end of a thought |
| exclamation point | pause that indicates emphasis |
| semicolon | pause between related but distinct thoughts |
| colon | pause before giving explanation or examples |

# OVERVIEW

## SMALL-GROUP LEARNING

### What do stories reveal about the human condition?

Students continue their study of the unit topic—this time through riveting stories about how people deal with death. During Small-Group Learning, students will read selections about what goes through people's minds as they are dying.

### Small-Group Learning Strategies

Review the Learning Strategies with students and explain that as they work through Small-Group Learning they will develop strategies to work in small-group environments.

- Have students watch the video on Small-Group Learning Strategies.
- A video on this topic is available online in the Professional Development Center.

You may wish to discuss some action items to add to the chart as a class before students complete it on their own. For example, for "Support others," you might solicit the following from students:

- Ask follow-up questions about others' reactions to the stories.
- When you can, provide additional detail to support another group member's idea.

**Block Scheduling**

Each day in this Pacing Plan represents a 40–50 minute class period. Teachers using block scheduling may combine days to reflect their class schedule. In addition, teachers may revise pacing to differentiate and support core instruction by integrating components and resources as students require.

## OVERVIEW: SMALL-GROUP LEARNING

ESSENTIAL QUESTION:

# What do stories reveal about the human condition?

As you read these selections, work with your group to explore how short stories allow us to see life from vastly different perspectives.

**From Text to Topic** Perhaps the word *change* best characterizes the past few decades of American life. In a time of rapid change, Americans have embraced new technologies, new social rules, and new ways of interacting with the rest of the world. As you read the selections in this section, consider how they address enduring human traits and what it means to live in a civil society.

## Small-Group Learning Strategies

Throughout your life, in school, in your community, and in your career, you will continue to develop strategies when you work in teams. Use these strategies during Small-Group Learning. Add ideas of your own at each step.

| STRATEGY | ACTION PLAN |
|---|---|
| Prepare | • Complete your assignments so that you are prepared for group work.<br>• Organize your thinking so you can contribute to your group's discussions.<br>• |
| Participate fully | • Make eye contact to signal that you are listening and taking in what is being said.<br>• Use text evidence when making a point.<br>• |
| Support others | • Build on ideas from others in your group.<br>• Invite others who have not yet spoken to join the discussion.<br>• |
| Clarify | • Paraphrase the ideas of others to ensure that your understanding is correct.<br>• Ask follow-up questions.<br>• |





SCAN FOR MULTIMEDIA

**Pacing Plan**

Introduce Whole-Class Learning

Unit Introduction | Historical Perspectives | Everyday Use | Everything Stuck to Him | The Leap | Performance Task

1 2 3 4 5 6 7 8 9 10 11 12 13 14 15

DIGITAL PERSPECTIVES

CONTENTS

LITERARY HISTORY

## A Brief History of the Short Story

*D. F. McCourt*

The short story, as a genre, is passing away—or is it?

COMPARE

SHORT STORY

## An Occurrence at Owl Creek Bridge

*Ambrose Bierce*

What thoughts go through the mind of a man who is about to be executed?

SHORT STORY

## The Jilting of Granny Weatherall

*Katherine Anne Porter*

A dying woman wrestles with memories of the past and realities of the present.

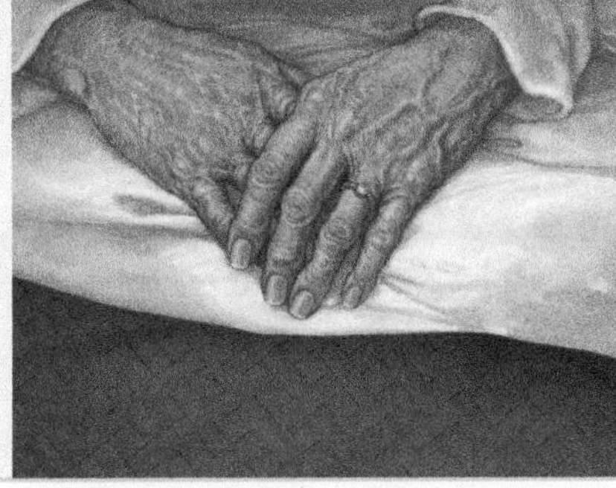

PERFORMANCE TASK

SPEAKING AND LISTENING FOCUS

## Present a Narrative

The Small-Group readings focus on "last moments"—of characters' lives and possibly even for short stories as a genre. After reading, your group will write and present a narrative.





## Contents

**Selections** Circulate among groups as they preview the selections. You might encourage groups to discuss any knowledge they already have about any of the selections or the situations and settings shown in the photographs. Students may wish to take a poll within their group to determine which selections look the most interesting.

Remind students that communicating and collaborating in groups is an important skill that they will use throughout their lives—in school, in their careers, and in their community.

### Performance Task

**Present a Narrative** After their reading, give groups time to briefly discuss developing a narrative. It will focus on the tension between the protagonist and another character from a third-person point of view. Encourage students to do some preliminary thinking about different techniques they may want to use. This may help focus their subsequent reading and group discussion.

Introduce Small-Group Learning

| 16 | 17 | 18 | 19 | 20 | 21 | 22 | 23 | 24 | 25 | 26 | 27 | 28 | 29 | 30 |
|---|---|---|---|---|---|---|---|---|---|---|---|---|---|---|
| Introduce Small-Group Learning | A Brief History of the Short Story | An Occurrence at Owl Creek Bridge | | | | The Jilting of Granny Weatherall | | | | Performance Task | Introduce Independent Learning | Independent Learning | Performance-Based Assessment | |

SMALL-GROUP LEARNING

# OVERVIEW

## SMALL-GROUP LEARNING

### Working as a Team

1. **Take a Position** Present the question for group discussion. Remind groups to let all members share their responses. You may wish to set a time limit for this discussion. Ask students to use examples from their reading, if possible, as a way to support their position.
2. **List Your Rules** You may want to have groups share their lists of rules and consolidate them into a master list to be displayed and followed by all groups. Suggest students reflect as a group on how the list has helped them through these units.
3. **Apply the Rules** As you circulate among the groups, ensure that students are staying on task. Consider a short time limit for this step.
4. **Name Your Group** This task can be creative and fun. If students have trouble coming up with a name, suggest that they see themselves as today's storytellers. Encourage groups to share their names with the class.
5. **Create a Communication Plan** Encourage groups to include in their plans agreed-upon times during the day to share ideas. They should also devise a method for recording and saving their communications.

### Accountable Talk

Remind students that groups should communicate politely. You can post these Accountable Talk suggestions and encourage students to add their own. Students should:

**Remember to . . .**
Ask clarifying questions.

**Which sound like . . .**
Can you please repeat what you said?

Would you give me an example?

I think you said _____. Did I understand you correctly?

**Remember to . . .**
Explain your thinking.

**Which sounds like . . .**
I believe _____ is true because _____.

**Remember to . . .**
Build on the ideas of others.

**Which sounds like . . .**
When _____ said _____, it made me think of _____.

## OVERVIEW: SMALL-GROUP LEARNING

### Working as a Team

1. **Take a Position** In your group, discuss the following question:

   **What life experiences or situations are universal—true for all people in all times and places?**

   As you take turns sharing your positions, be sure to provide reasons for your response. After all group members have shared, discuss how people deal with these experiences or situations differently and what their responses reveal about their personalities.

2. **List Your Rules** As a group, decide on the rules that you will follow as you work together. Two samples are provided. Add two more of your own. As you work together, you may add or revise rules based on your experience together.
   - Encourage a variety of ideas before you look for common features.
   - Give group members the chance to comment further on their ideas as discussion continues.
   - ______________________________
   - ______________________________

3. **Apply the Rules** Practice working as a group. Share what you have learned about the ways in which stories reveal truths about the human condition. Make sure each person in the group contributes. Take notes on and be prepared to share with the class one insight that you heard from another member of your group.

4. **Name Your Group** Choose a name that reflects the unit topic.

   Our group's name: ______________________________

5. **Create a Communication Plan** Decide how you want to communicate with one another. For example, you might use online collaboration tools, email, or instant messaging.

   Our group's decision: ______________________________





### FACILITATING SMALL-GROUP LEARNING

**Forming Groups** You may wish to form groups for Small-Group Learning so that each consists of students with different learning abilities. Some students may be adept at organizing information whereas other may have strengths related to generating or synthesizing information. A good mix of abilities can make the experience of Small-Group Learning dynamic and productive.

## Making a Schedule

First, find out the due dates for the small-group activities. Then, preview the texts and activities with your group, and make a schedule for completing the tasks.

| SELECTION | ACTIVITIES | DUE DATE |
|---|---|---|
| A Brief History of the Short Story | | |
| An Occurrence at Owl Creek Bridge | | |
| The Jilting of Granny Weatherall | | |

## Working on Group Projects

As your group works together, you'll find it more effective if each person has a specific role. Different projects require different roles. Before beginning a project, discuss the necessary roles, and choose one for each group member. Some possible roles are listed here. Add your ideas to the list.

**Project Manager:** monitors the schedule and keeps everyone on task
**Researcher:** organizes research activities
**Recorder:** takes notes during group meetings

SCAN FOR MULTIMEDIA



DIGITAL PERSPECTIVES

## Making a Schedule

Encourage groups to preview the reading selections and to consider how long it will take them to complete the activities accompanying each selection. Point out that they can adjust the due dates for particular selections as needed as they work on their small-group projects; however, they must complete all assigned tasks before the group Performance Task is due. Encourage groups to review their schedules upon completing the activities for each selection to make sure they are on track to meet the final due date.

## Working on Group Projects

Point out to groups that the roles they assign can also be changed later. Students might have to make changes based on who is best at doing what. Try to make sure that there is no favoritism, cliquishness, or stereotyping by gender or other means in the assignment of roles.

Also, you should review the roles each group assigns to its members. Based on your understanding of students' individual strengths, you might find it necessary to suggest some changes.

AUTHOR'S PERSPECTIVE **Ernest Morrell, Ph.D.**

**Supporting Groups** As student work in groups, they may need some help to resolve issues and move ahead. Teachers can use these suggestions:

- If groups get stuck on a trivial point or a bone of contention, encourage members to move on so that they will get their work done. Intense discussions are fine, but they shouldn't be a substitute for getting work done.
- If the group has not realized that the issue has more than one side and that all sides deserve consideration, teachers might step in and play devil's advocate by arguing an unpopular position so that students can take it into consideration.
- If the group has come too easily to a consensus and not thoughtfully weighed all aspects of the issue, teachers can push groups who need a challenge.

As facilitators in the room, teachers can encourage students to move beyond their comfort zone and work to exceed expectations and do their best thinking.

# A Brief History of the Short Story

**AUDIO SUMMARIES**
Audio summaries of "A Brief History of the Short Story" are available online in both English and Spanish in the Interactive Teacher's Edition or Unit Resources. Assigning these summaries prior to reading the selection may help students build additional background knowledge and set a context for their first read.

## Summary

D. F. McCourt's "A Brief History of the Short Story" chronicles the history of the short story from its beginnings in the 1820s to its current state today. The popularity of "gift books" in the 1820s created the need for short pieces of prose and, in time, led to the development of literary and popular magazines. Horror stories, detective stories, and science fiction stories all had their start in magazines. But in the 1950s the short story came close to dying out. It was during this period that television became an integral part of American life. In the decades that followed, the circulation of magazines featuring short fiction saw a steady decline. Then in 2007 e-books were introduced and saved the short story format. Since 2007, the Internet has firmly replaced the dominance of television. Increasingly, people are reading on a computer or e-book screen. A story that can be read in one sitting works best for reading on a screen. This is the very definition of the short story. Thus, the short story has come back to life.

### Insight

The article not only chronicles the history of the short story but also teaches how change and innovation can radically affect human endeavors, such as writing and reading short stories.

ESSENTIAL QUESTION:
What do stories reveal about the human condition?

## Connection to Essential Question

This essay addresses the business of fiction and provides an interesting angle on the Essential Question. The success of the short story form and its challenges during the rise of television and other media reveal some interesting ideas about the human need for distraction, entertainment, or intellectual stimulation.

SMALL-GROUP LEARNING PERFORMANCE TASK
Present a stream-of-conscious narrative based on this idea: *The day felt as if it would never end.*

UNIT PERFORMANCE-BASED ASSESSMENT
How does a fictional character or characters respond to life-changing news?

## Connection to Performance Tasks

**Small-Group Learning Task** Understanding the history and evolution of the short story will help students understand and appreciate the many ways there are to tell a story. This text discusses high-brow and low-brow literature, science-fiction, and detective stories, which students might consider as they approach the task.

**Unit Performance-Based Assessment** This essay provides background on the development of the short story, and may help students as they consider the Performance-Based Assessment prompt.

DIGITAL PERSPECTIVES

 Audio  Video  Document  Annotation Highlights  EL Highlights 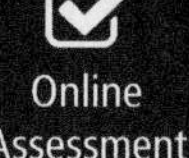 Online Assessment

## LESSON RESOURCES

| | Making Meaning | Language Development | Effective Expression |
|---|---|---|---|
| **Lesson** | **First Read**<br>**Close Read**<br>**Analyze the Text**<br>**Analyze Craft and Structure** | **Concept Vocabulary**<br>**Word Study**<br>**Conventions and Style** | **Research** |
| **Instructional Standards** | **RI.10** By the end of grade 11, read and comprehend literary nonfiction . . .<br>**L.4.a** Use context as a clue . . .<br>**RI.3** Analyze a complex set of ideas . . .<br>**RI.5** Analyze and evaluate the effectiveness of the structure an author uses . . . | **L.4.b** Identify and correctly use patterns of word changes . . .<br>**L.1.a** Apply the understanding that usage is a matter of convention . . . | **W.7** Conduct short as well as more sustained research projects . . . |
| **STUDENT RESOURCES** | | | |
| Available online in the Interactive Student Edition or Unit Resources | Selection Audio<br>First-Read Guide: Nonfiction<br>Close-Read Guide: Nonfiction | Word Network | Evidence Log |
| **TEACHER RESOURCES** | | | |
| **Selection Resources** Available online in the Interactive Teacher's Edition or Unit Resources | Audio Summaries<br>Annotation Highlights<br>EL Highlights<br>A Brief History of the Short Story: Text Questions<br>Analyze Craft and Structure: Sequence of Events | Concept Vocabulary and Word Study<br>Conventions and Style: Active and Passive Voice<br>English Language Support Lesson: Active and Passive Voice | Research: Research Report |
| **Reteach/Practice (RP)** Available online in the Interactive Teacher's Edition or Unit Resources | Analyze Craft and Structure: Sequence of Events (RP) | Word Study: Latin Root *-scend-* (RP)<br>Conventions and Style: Active and Passive Voice (RP) | Research: Research Report (RP) |
| **Assessment** Available online in Assessments | Selection Test | | |
| **My Resources** | A Unit 6 Answer Key is available online and in the Interactive Teacher's Edition. | | |

# Reading Support

| Text Complexity Rubric: A Brief History of the Short Story | |
|---|---|
| **Quantitative Measures** | |
| **Lexile:** 1270 **Text Length:** 988 words | |
| **Quantitative Measures** | |
| Knowledge Demands<br>①—❷—③—④—⑤ | Students will probably be familiar with the short story, but they might benefit from further information on Margaret Atwood, genre fiction, and literary journals, among other topics. |
| Structure<br>①—❷—③—④—⑤ | The piece is a short magazine article and is structured conventionally. |
| Language Conventionality and Clarity<br>①—②—❸—④—⑤ | The author refers to historical and cultural events, making use of figurative language, metaphors, and quotes from or references to other writers. |
| Levels of Meaning/Purpose<br>①—❷—③—④—⑤ | The text has one purpose and level of meaning. The informational purpose of the article is clear and straightforward, with an easily grasped main concept. |

DECIDE AND PLAN

## English Language Support

Provide English Learners with support for knowledge and language as they read the selection.

**Knowledge** Students may not have deep familiarity with genre fiction and could benefit from a discussion of these distinctions as commercial categories. Talk to them about different science fiction, horror, and mystery-thriller writers and about the wealth of literary history these genre authors draw on.

**Language** Have the students point out the differences between narrative fiction and journalism, and how the two different kinds of writing employ different voices and methods. You may draw comparisons to different styles of movies or television programs to support student understanding.

## Strategic Support

Provide students with strategic support to ensure that they can successfully read the text.

**Knowledge** Ask students to use the Internet to look up any topics, ideas, or authors they don't recognize from McCourt's piece. Students can make a research log of the different subjects referenced and can even use their work to choose a genre writer to read and explore on their own.

**Language** Ask students to think about whether the straightforward, informational style of the article helps McCourt's thesis or main idea. Have them write a brief summary of the text. Next, discuss points in the text where the author's language becomes less formal and ask students to respond to those style choices.

## Challenge

Provide students who need to be challenged with ideas for how they can go beyond a simple interpretation of the text.

**Text Analysis** Ask students to analyze the text for all its resource and background information. Have them think about where the author could have located this information, whether the Internet, libraries, or the use of a primary resources like an interview.

**Written Response** Ask students to consider a topic they would like to explore as journalists. Asks students to consider topics that interest them and to determine how they might gather information. Ask students to produce a topic, a research question, and several proposed research sources.

TEACH

## Read and Respond

Have groups do their first read of the selection. Then have them complete their close read. Finally, work with them on the Making Meaning, Language Development, and Effective Expression activities.

# Standards Support Through Teaching and Learning Cycle

## IDENTIFY NEEDS

Analyze results of the Beginning-of-Year Assessment, focusing on the items relating to Unit 6. Also take into consideration student performance to this point and your observations of where particular students struggle.

## DECIDE AND PLAN

- If students have performed poorly on items matching these standards, then provide selection scaffolds before assigning them the on-level lesson provided in the Student Edition.
- If students have done well on the Beginning-of-Year Assessment, then challenge them to keep progressing and learning by giving them opportunities to practice the skills in depth.
- Use the Selection Resources listed on the Planning pages for "A Brief History of the Short Story" to help students continually improve their ability to master the standards.

**Instructional Standards: A Brief History of the Short Story**

| | Catching Up | This Year | Looking Forward |
|---|---|---|---|
| **Reading** | You may wish to administer the **Analyze Craft and Structure: Sequence of Events (RP)** worksheet to help students better understand chronological order. | **RL.3** Analyze a complex set of ideas or sequence of events and explain how specific individuals, ideas, or events interact and develop over the course of the text. | Challenge students to consider why writers might create nonfiction that includes a non-chronological presentation of events. |
| **Writing** | You may wish to administer the **Research: Research Report (RP)** worksheet to help students better prepare for their research. | **W.7** Conduct short as well as more sustained research projects to answer a question or solve a problem; narrow or broaden the inquiry when appropriate; synthesize multiple sources on the subject, demonstrating understanding of the subject under investigation. | Challenge students to review the research ideas presented in the Student Edition and suggest an additional option for presenting their research reports. |
| **Language** | Review the **Word Study: Latin Root *-scend-* (RP)** worksheet with students to better familiarize them with the root word.<br><br>Review the **Conventions and Style: Active and Passive Voice (RP)** worksheet with students to better familiarize them with these types of voices. | **L.4.b** Identify and correctly use patterns of word changes that indicate different meanings or parts of speech.<br><br>**L.1.a** Apply the understanding that usage is a matter of convention, can change over time, and is sometimes contested. | Have students locate other root words they recognize in the text.<br><br>Challenge students to go about their days paying attention to when they normally use active versus passive voices. |

## ANALYZE AND REVISE

- Analyze student work for evidence of student learning.
- Identify whether or not students have met the expectations in the standards.
- Identify implications for future instruction.

## TEACH

Implement the planned lesson, and gather evidence of student learning.

# FACILITATING

## Jump Start

FIRST READ Engage students in a discussion to set the context for reading "A Brief History of the Short Story." Use these questions: *Do you like reading short stories? Is there a specific author or style you enjoy?*

## A Brief History of the Short Story

What might people have read before there were short stories? Modeling questions will bring "A Brief History of the Short Story" to life and connect it to the Performance Task question. Selection audio and print capability for the selection are available in the Interactive Teacher's Edition.

## Concept Vocabulary

Have groups consider the advantages of using context clues to help determine the meanings of concept vocabulary words.

### FIRST READ

Have students perform the first read independently:

NOTICE: Have students notice main events in the history of the short story.

ANNOTATE: Remind students to mark passages that they find particularly important to the main idea.

CONNECT: Encourage students to connect the ups and downs in the history of the short story to the ups and downs of other media forms.

RESPOND: Students will demonstrate their understanding of the text by answering questions and writing a summary.

Students will perform the first three steps concurrently as they do their first read. They will complete the Respond step last. You may wish to print copies of the **First-Read Guide: Nonfiction** for students.

MAKING MEANING

About the Author

As a child, **D. F. ("Duff") McCourt,** a freelance writer and the co-founder and editor of *AE—The Canadian Science Fiction Review*, developed a great love for books and magazines. That passion continued into his adult life. A writer of published short stories and novellas himself, he is interested in the history of both forms. He believes firmly that the strength of magazines as a medium is essential to the continued vitality of science fiction and other genres.

# A Brief History of the Short Story

## Concept Vocabulary

As you perform your first read of "A Brief History of the Short Story," you will encounter these words.

supplanted ascendant renaissance

**Context Clues** If these words are unfamiliar to you, try using **context clues**—words and phrases that appear in nearby text—to help you determine their meanings. There are various types of context clues that you may encounter as you read.

**Restatement, or Synonyms:** That **diminutive** child is so tiny that she can't reach the first step.

**Definition:** Studies show that the vocabulary children learn when they are very young is **formative**, or fundamental to their development.

**Contrast of Ideas:** That social movement could have **soldiered on**. Instead, it died out.

Apply your knowledge of context clues and other vocabulary strategies to determine the meanings of unfamiliar words you encounter during your first read.

## First Read NONFICTION

Apply these strategies as you conduct your first read. You will have an opportunity to complete a close read after your first read.

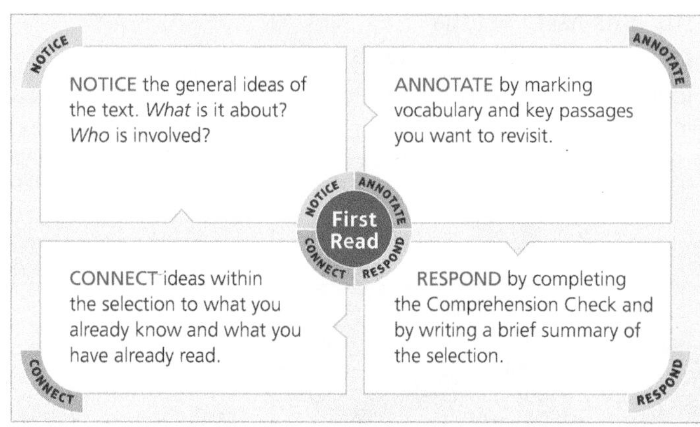

NOTICE
NOTICE the general ideas of the text. *What* is it about? *Who* is involved?
ANNOTATE
ANNOTATE by marking vocabulary and key passages you want to revisit.
First Read
CONNECT ideas within the selection to what you already know and what you have already read.
CONNECT
RESPOND by completing the Comprehension Check and by writing a brief summary of the selection.
RESPOND


STANDARDS

**Reading Informational Text**
By the end of grade 11, read and comprehend literary nonfiction in the grades 11–CCR text complexity band proficiently, with scaffolding as needed at the high end of the range.

**Language**
Use context as a clue to the meaning of a word or phrase.





AUTHOR'S PERSPECTIVE **Jim Cummins, Ph.D.**

**Language Tasks** Teachers can reinforce students' grasp of how academic language works by explicitly identifying the functions that language serves in different kinds of texts. Possibilities include *describing, comparing, contrasting, sequencing, choosing, classifying*, and *evaluating*. Teachers can scaffold students' understanding of these language functions by using graphic organizers. Here is a sample:

| Language Tasks | Related Key Visuals/ Graphic Organizers |
|---|---|
| Identifying | Tables |
| Describing | Diagrams |
| Comparing | T-charts |
| Contrasting | Pictures, plans |

These language demands can be applied across the curriculum. Teachers might provide an example for biology ("Compare the structure and function of plant and animal cells") and one for social studies ("Analyze similarities and differences in social values and aspects of life between present-day city dwellers and those who lived in cities between 1900–1950.") Following this process helps students see what steps they need to take and helps them achieve greater reading success.

LITERARY HISTORY

# A Brief History of the Short Story

D. F. McCourt

BACKGROUND

Electronic books, or e-books, are digital files that can display on various devices, such as computers and cellphones, in a way similar to printed books. Though e-books first emerged in the late 1990s, they failed to gain popularity until the mid-2000s, when dedicated electronic reading devices improved the quality of the reading experience. This new medium has allowed more writers to publish a wider variety of work, including short stories. It has also lowered the costs that writers and publishers previously faced when bringing new work to appreciative audiences.

SCAN FOR MULTIMEDIA

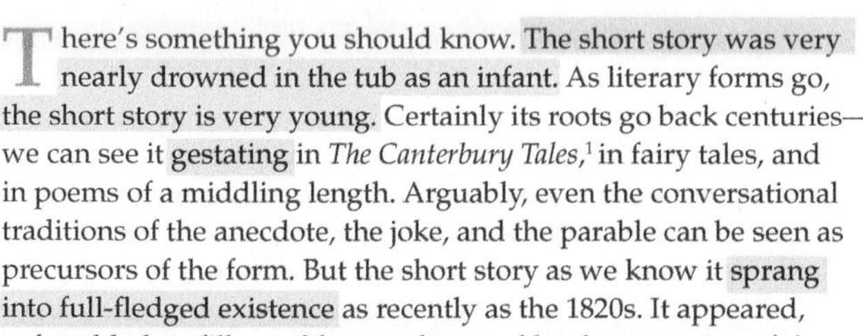

1 There's something you should know. The short story was very nearly drowned in the tub as an infant. As literary forms go, the short story is very young. Certainly its roots go back centuries—we can see it gestating in *The Canterbury Tales*,[1] in fairy tales, and in poems of a middling length. Arguably, even the conversational traditions of the anecdote, the joke, and the parable can be seen as precursors of the form. But the short story as we know it sprang into full-fledged existence as recently as the 1820s. It appeared, unheralded, to fill a sudden need created by the invention of the "gift book."

2 Gift books were annual collections of poems, artwork, and literary criticism, aimed primarily at an audience of upper-class women in England and North America. Seeking additional ways to fill the pages of these popular publications, editors began soliciting submissions of short pieces of prose to accompany artwork already purchased (rather the opposite of the way it is usually done these days). In so doing, they created the first paying market for short fiction. All modern literary magazines can trace their pedigree back to these gift books. In 1837, Nathaniel Hawthorne collected a number of stories that he had written for the gift book market and published them to great critical acclaim as *Twice Told Tales*. And with that, short stories had arrived.

NOTES

1. ***The Canterbury Tales*** collection of stories written by Geoffrey Chaucer in the fourteenth century.





DIGITAL PERSPECTIVES

## CLOSER LOOK

### Identify Extended Metaphor

Circulate among groups as students conduct their close read. Suggest that groups close read paragraphs 1 and 2. Encourage them to talk about the annotations that they mark. If needed, provide the following support.

**ANNOTATE:** Have students mark details in these paragraphs where the author talks about the short story genre as though it were a living thing, or work with small groups to have students participate while you highlight these details together.

**QUESTION:** Guide students to consider what these details might tell them. Ask what a reader can infer from the author's use of these phrases. Accept student responses.

**Possible response:** The author wants to make the topic more interesting by implying that the short story, like a person, was born.

**CONCLUDE:** Help students to formulate conclusions about the importance of these details in the text. Ask why the author might have included these details.

**Possible response:** By describing the short story as though it were a living thing that was born and nearly died, the author conveys that literary forms are not static. They change over time, and some that we take for granted have not always existed.

Remind students that a **metaphor** is a figure of speech that compares two apparently unlike things without using the words *like*, *as*, or *resembles*. A metaphor uses language imaginatively rather than literally. An **extended metaphor**, such as the one in these two paragraphs, is a metaphor that is sustained and developed.

Additional **English Language Support** is available in the Interactive Teacher's Edition.

## FACILITATING SMALL-GROUP CLOSE READING

**CLOSE READ: Literary History** Monitor groups as they conduct a close read of the text. Offer support as needed.

- Explain to students that this text is nonfiction about literature. It analyzes the popularity of the short story genre over time.
- Remind students to look for the main idea that the text conveys. Explain that history is the study of continuity and change over time, so they should look for what the author is saying changed and/or stayed the same.
- Point out that many histories are written chronologically. Even those that are written thematically generally tell a story about continuity and change over time. Locating the time markers will help students understand the author's message.

CLOSER LOOK

## Identify Causality

Circulate among groups as students conduct their close read. Suggest that groups close read paragraphs 3 and 5, in particular. Encourage them to talk about the annotations that they mark. If needed, provide the following support.

**ANNOTATE:** Have students mark details in paragraphs 3 and 5 that explain that something caused something else to happen, or work with small groups to have students participate while you highlight causes and effects together.

**QUESTION:** Guide students to consider what these details might tell them. Ask what a reader can infer from the author's use of phrases that demonstrate causality—the notion that one thing caused another. Accept student responses.

**Possible response:** The author is guiding readers through a chronological account of the ups and downs of the short story genre by presenting a string of causes and effects.

**CONCLUDE:** Help students to formulate conclusions about the importance of these relationships in the text. Ask why the author might have included these details.

**Possible response:** The author presents an historical account in which various factors interacted to give rise to the short story, to threaten its existence, and then to save it.

Explain to students that **cause-and-effect** relationships help show the connection among events. Share with students that historians try to identify what might have happened to cause a specific effect. However, remind students that time order does not prove cause and effect. For example, radio was invented before World War I, but it did not cause World War I.

## Concept Vocabulary

**SUPPLANTED** If groups are struggling to define the word *supplanted* in paragraph 6, urge them to look at the sentence in which the word appears. The first part of the sentence says that television was "still clinging" to its role in the culture. The second part of the sentence begins with *but*, which suggests that the clinging changed or ended, a change or ending brought about by the Internet.

**Possible response:** *Supplanted* means "replaced."

NOTES

3 Two hundred years may seem quite a long time, but consider that the novel dates back to at least 1605 (the year Miguel de Cervantes's *Don Quixote* was published) and you get a better idea of the short story's relative youth. Over its entire lifetime, the fate of the form has been inextricably tied to that of magazines. In the early twentieth century, literacy in the United States and Canada became near universal for the first time and, as a direct result, magazine sales boomed. On the erudite[2] front, there were publications like *The English Review* and *The Southwest Review*, but there were also the decidedly lower brow *Argosy* and *Adventure*. This was the era of the pulp magazine and it brought with it the birth of genre literature.

4 Horror stories, detective stories, and most especially science fiction evolved in short stories, cut their teeth in the magazines. It is no surprise that the beginning of the Golden Age of Science Fiction is identified most strongly not with a novel but with the publication of a magazine (the July 1939 issue of *Astounding Science Fiction*, to be precise). Most of the formative novels of early- and mid-twentieth-century science fiction were more like grown-up short stories in form than like other contemporary novels. In fact, some of the most famous science fiction novels—including Isaac Asimov's *Foundation*, A. E. Van Vogt's *The Silkie*, Robert A. Heinlein's *Orphans of the Sky*, and Ray Bradbury's *The Martian Chronicles*—were fix-ups (a term for a novel created by stitching a series of previously published short stories together). It wasn't until quite recently, around the 1984 publication of William Gibson's *Neuromancer* and the 1985 publication of Margaret Atwood's *The Handmaid's Tale*, that the two parallel traditions of the science fiction novel and the modern literary novel began to collide.

5 And yet, despite the fact that in its brief history the short story had brought into existence entire genres and traditions of literature, it came perilously close to death. In the 1950s, owning a television suddenly became within reach of the average North American family. The half-an-hour-less-commercials format of shows like *I Love Lucy*, *Dragnet*, and *The Honeymooners* targeted the same entertainment niche as the magazine. Over the decades that followed, the circulation numbers of almost all magazines that ran short fiction saw a steady decline. The novel soldiered on, but the state of the short story became so dire that in 2007 Stephen King[3] opened his piece "What Ails the Short Story" for the *New York Times Book Review* thus:

> *The American short story is alive and well. Do you like the sound of that? Me too. I only wish it were actually true.*

6 So much can happen in four years. 2007 was the year that e-book readers burst onto the scene and, while the rise of the online magazine was already underway, it has stepped up considerably in the years since. More importantly, in 2007 television was still clinging to its cultural sovereignty, but it has since been firmly **supplanted**

Mark context clues or indicate another strategy you used that helped you determine meaning.

**supplanted** (suh PLANT ihd) *v.*

MEANING:

2. **erudite** (EHR oo dyt) *adj.* characterized by great knowledge; learned or scholarly.
3. **Stephen King** (b. 1947) American author of horror novels and short stories.





### CROSS-CURRICULAR PERSPECTIVES

**Literature** Review the genres discussed in paragraph 4. Explain that science fiction is a genre that imagines scientific or technological advances and explores how they might affect people and society. It came into being after industrialization when writers began to explore the possible benefits and dangers of technology. Many literary historians consider Jules Verne and H.G. Wells to be the first science fiction writers. Others, however, cite Mary Shelley's *Frankenstein*, published in 1818. Shelley's novel imagined what might happen if a scientist were able to create human life. Point out to students that all of these prominent science fiction authors wrote well before the advent of the science-fiction magazine.

by the Internet. At the turn of the millennium, there was much ink spilled over the decline in the amount of reading people were doing, but the truth is that many of us are reading more than ever, we just aren't doing it on paper. When reading on a screen rather than the page, there are new considerations. A narrative of a few thousand words can be easily read, enjoyed, and digested while sitting before a monitor; a novella, far less so. This is an environment practically designed for the literary form Edgar Allan Poe defined as a tale that "can be read in one sitting." Further, e-book readers are allowing publishers to easily make shorter works available at a reasonable price, without having to worry that a book's spine be thick enough to hold its own on a bookstore shelf.

7 Video, of course, is quite at home online, but the real meat of the Internet has always been text. Preferably text that limits itself to a screen or two in length. As long as the Internet holds its throne as the defining medium of our time, the short story will be **ascendant**. It is true however that the form is undoubtedly being influenced and changed by the demands of its new homes. Personally, I'm thrilled to be taking part in that continued evolution, thrilled just to be present for the **renaissance** of the form that shaped science fiction, thrilled to be able to say unequivocally: "The short story is alive and well." ❧

NOTES

Mark context clues or indicate another strategy you used that helped you determine meaning.

**ascendant** (uh SEHN duhnt) *adj.*

MEANING:

**renaissance** (REHN uh sons) *n.*

MEANING:

## Comprehension Check

**Complete the following items after you finish your first read. Review and clarify details with your group.**

1. According to the author, what significant event happened in 1837?

2. According to the author, what three genres owe their origins to the short story?

3. Why did the short story nearly die in the 1950s? What developments made it strong again?

4. **Notebook** Confirm your understanding of the text by writing a summary.

### RESEARCH

**Research to Explore** Conduct research on an aspect of the text you find interesting. For example, you may want to learn more about one of the short-story magazines the author mentions: *The English Review, The Southwest Review, Argosy, Adventure,* or *Astounding Science Fiction.* Share your discoveries with your group.





## PERSONALIZE FOR LEARNING

### Challenge

**Researching Literary Forms** Encourage students to research the history of another literary form, such as the sonnet, epic poem, or graphic novel. Suggest that they use "A Brief History of the Short Story" as a model. For example, point out that the author identifies factors that contributed to the short story's invention and development. Some of those factors were social (such as increased literacy), and some were technological (such as the development of television and the Internet). Remind students to look for the factors that influenced the origin and development of the form they choose to research.

DIGITAL PERSPECTIVES

## Concept Vocabulary

**ASCENDANT** If groups are struggling to define the word *ascendant* in paragraph 8, point out that the rest of the paragraph can help. The paragraph suggests that the future of the short story is bright.

**Possible response:** *Ascendant* means "rising in power or influence."

**RENAISSANCE** If groups are struggling to define the word *renaissance* in paragraph 8, have them focus on the word "evolution" and the context of the last sentence: "The short story is alive and well." Guide them to think about what has been said about threats to the short story and what has happened for it to be "alive and well."

**Possible response:** *Renaissance* means "rebirth" or "revival."

## Comprehension Check

Possible responses:

1. In 1837, Nathaniel Hawthorne collected a number of stories that he had written for the gift book market and published them as *Twice Told Tales*. This was important for the rise of the short story.
2. Horror stories, detective stories, and science fiction all originated with the short story.
3. TV sets became affordable in the 1950s, almost causing the short story to die. The growing popularity of eBooks and the Internet brought the short story back to life.
4. The roots of the short story go back centuries, but the form we know dates to the "gift books" of the 1820s. The short story became widely popular after Nathaniel Hawthorne published a book of short stories in 1837. From the early to the mid-20th century, short stories thrived in magazines, which benefited from widespread literacy. The genres of horror stories, detective stories, and science fiction also were established. Then, in the 1950s, television caused a decline in recreational reading. The short story has been revived in more recent decades, however, because of the eBook reader and the Internet.

## Research

**Research to Explore** If groups struggle to define a research topic, suggest that they consider learning more about one of the genres identified in the text: science fiction, horror stories, or detective stories.

# FACILITATING

## Jump Start

CLOSE READ Engage student groups in a brief discussion using this prompt: *Do you think that the Internet will be supplanted by another medium? What would happen to the short story?*

## Close Read the Text

Model close reading as needed by using the Annotation Highlights in the Interactive Teacher's Edition. Remind students to use accountable talk in their group discussions.

## Analyze the Text

**Possible responses:** 1. The gift book was an annual collection of poems, artwork, and literary criticism. Short stories were solicited to fill them, giving rise to both the short story and the literary magazine.
2. Passages will vary by group. 3. Responses will vary. Some students may say that the short story meets the need for entertainment or intellectual stimulation.

## Concept Vocabulary

**Why These Words?** Possible response: The words relate to change and status.

### Practice

**Possible responses:** During World War II, women *supplanted* men in many factories. Romance books are on the decline, whereas dystopian novels are *ascendant*. Old comedies have enjoyed a *renaissance* in recent years.

### Word Network

**Possible words:** *infant, existence, lifetime*

## Word Study

For more support, see **Concept Vocabulary and Word Study.**

**Possible responses:** *descend, crescendo*

### FORMATIVE ASSESSMENT

### Analyze the Text

**If** students struggle to close read the text, **then** provide **A Brief History of the Short Story: Text Questions** available online in the Interactive Teacher's Edition or Unit Resources. Answers and DOK levels are also available.

### Concept Vocabulary

**If** students struggle to identify the concept, **then** suggest that they find the words in a thesaurus to find words with similar meanings.

### Word Study

**If** students fail to find words with the root *-scend-*, **then** suggest they find a website that lists Latin roots and see what words the site lists.

For Reteach and Practice, see **Word Study: Latin Root *-scend-* (RP).**

A BRIEF HISTORY OF THE SHORT STORY

## Close Read the Text

With your group, revisit sections of the text you marked during your first read. **Annotate** details that you notice. What **questions** do you have? What can you **conclude**?

## Analyze the Text

**CITE TEXTUAL EVIDENCE** to support your answers.

Complete the activities.

1. **Review and Clarify** With your group, reread paragraphs 1–2. How did the gift book give rise to the short story and to literary magazines?
2. **Present and Discuss** Now, work with your group to share the passages from the selection that you found especially important. Take turns presenting your passages. Discuss what you noticed in the selection, what questions you asked, and what conclusions you reached.
3. **Essential Question:** ***What do stories reveal about the human condition?*** How does this literary history shed light on the short story's ability to address the human condition? Discuss with your group.

**TIP**

GROUP DISCUSSION
Almost everyone has personal preferences regarding short fiction. Encourage group members to relate the author's information and insights to their own reading experiences.

LANGUAGE DEVELOPMENT

## Concept Vocabulary

| supplanted | ascendant | renaissance |
|---|---|---|

**Why These Words?** The three concept vocabulary words from the text are related. With your group, determine what the words have in common. Write your ideas and add another word that fits the category.

**WORD NETWORK**
Add words related to the human condition from the text to your Word Network.

### Practice

**Notebook** Confirm your understanding of these words from the text by using them in sentences. Be sure to use context clues that hint at each word's meaning.

## Word Study

**Latin Root: *-scend-*** Many words in English use the Latin root *-scend-*, which means "climb." For example, *ascendant* is an adjective that combines the root *-scend-* with the prefix *ad-*, meaning "to" or "toward." *Ascendant*, then, means "climbing toward" or "rising." Find several other words that have this same root. Use a reliable print or digital dictionary to verify your choices. Record the words and their meanings.

**STANDARDS**

**Reading Informational Text**
- Analyze a complex set of ideas or sequence of events and explain how specific individuals, ideas, or events interact and develop over the course of the text.
- Analyze and evaluate the effectiveness of the structure an author uses in his or her exposition or argument, including whether the structure makes points clear, convincing, and engaging.

**Language**
Identify and correctly use patterns of word changes that indicate different meanings or parts of speech.

## Analyze Craft and Structure

**Sequence of Events** Authors often use **chronological order**, or the order in which things happened, to structure nonfiction pieces that describe historical events or explain a change over time. When you read a text that describes a sequence of events, look at how specific people, ideas, or events are connected. Consider the details the author chooses to include about each time period and why those details might be significant or important.

TIP

GROUP DISCUSSION

As members of your group discuss their charts, you may find it helpful to plot out key events on a timeline.

CITE TEXTUAL EVIDENCE to support your answers.

### Practice

Use the chart below to analyze how McCourt structures events in "A Brief History of the Short Story." Then, share your chart with your group, and discuss how McCourt uses this organization to emphasize his main ideas about the short story.

| PARAGRAPH | TIME FRAME | EVENT | SIGNIFICANCE |
|---|---|---|---|
| 1 | • 14th century<br>• 1820s | • *Canterbury Tales* published<br>• "gift books" invented | • first use of short story form<br>• created need for short stories |
| 2 | • 1820s<br>• 1837 | • Gift books introduced<br>• *Twice Told Tales* | • made short stories popular<br>• first collection of short stories |
| 3 | • early 20th century | • increased literacy<br>• magazine sales boomed | • more people sought reading material<br>• genre stories become widespread |
| 4 | • early and mid-20th century<br>• 1984–1985 | • magazines, fix-ups became popular<br>• science-fiction novel and literary novel converge | • science fiction became very popular<br>• birth of science fiction novel |
| 5–6 | • 1950s<br>• late 20th century | • television supplanted reading<br>• Stephen King wrote of stories' decline | • short story nearly died<br>• recognized the near demise of short story |
| 7–8 | • 2007–today | • eBook readers introduced<br>• Internet brings stories back to life | • more people reading<br>• perfect medium for short stories |





DIGITAL PERSPECTIVES

## Analyze Craft and Structure

**Sequence of Events** Point out to students that writers often use words that help their readers follow the chronology that they are presenting. They might, for example, use words such as *first, second,* and *third* to guide readers through events that take place in a certain order. They might also use words such as *before, after,* and *in the meantime* to show readers how the events are connected to each other in time. Urge students to look for such words when they are reading so that they can follow the sequence the author is presenting.

See possible responses in chart on student page.

For more support, see **Analyze Craft and Structure: Sequence of Events.**

### FORMATIVE ASSESSMENT

### Analyze Craft and Structure

**If** students struggle to identify the significance of the events they listed in the Event column, **then** suggest that they write the main idea of "A Brief History of the Short Story" and ask how each event they identified relates to that idea.

For Reteach and Practice, see **Analyze Craft and Structure: Sequence of Events (RP).**

FACILITATING

## Conventions and Style

**Active and Passive Voice** Explain to students that news headlines are often written in the active voice to grab attention and save space. Review several headlines to help students make this connection. For example, *Mayor Gives Speech, Team Wins Pennant,* or *Economy Improves*. Ask students to rewrite these headlines to see and discuss the difference. *Speech Is Given by Mayor, Pennant Is Won by Team,* or *Economy Is Improved*.

For more support, see **Conventions and Style: Active and Passive Voice.**

### Read It

1. a. passive
   b. active
   c. active
   d. passive

Student discussions will vary, but students should see that active voice give power to the subjects in sentences, suggestion that they take control, instead of receiving the action, or having the action happen to them.

### Write It

Possible responses:

Paragraphs will vary, but make sure that students can recognize and use both the active and the passive voice appropriately in their writing.

### FORMATIVE ASSESSMENT

### Conventions and Style

**If** students struggle to distinguish between active and passive voice, **then** have them identify the subject of several sentences and determine whether the subject is performing the action or receiving it.

For Reteach and Practice, see **Conventions and Style: Active and Passive Voice (RP).**

LANGUAGE DEVELOPMENT

A BRIEF HISTORY OF THE SHORT STORY

TIP

CLARIFICATION

Some grammar handbooks or style guides may advise against using passive voice. However, it is a stylistic choice that may give clarity or provide emphasis. For example, "The reactor was shut down" emphasizes the event, whereas "The head engineer shut the reactor down" gives more emphasis to the person performing the action.

## Conventions and Style

**Active and Passive Voice** In grammar, **voice** reveals the relationship between the subject of a sentence and the action described in that sentence. Voice may be either active or passive.

- In active voice, the subject of the sentence *performs* the action.

  Isabel reads science fiction novels.

  A high-speed elevator carried passengers to the Observation Deck.

- In **passive voice,** the subject of the sentence *receives* the action. Passive voice often uses or implies a form of the verb "be," such as *am, is, are, was,* or *were.*

  Science fiction novels are read by Isabel.

  The passengers were carried to the Observation Deck by a high-speed elevator.

Active voice helps the writer create strong, clear writing. Active voice also keeps writing concise because it uses fewer words than passive voice does to describe an action. However, the passive voice may be useful in scientific writing or other explanations because it removes names or pronouns and instead focuses on describing facts or concepts. Passive voice can also be useful when the writer does not know—or does not want to name—the person or thing performing the action, or when that person or thing is unimportant.

The lost toddler was found in the mall's food court.

The rumors that are being spread have no basis in fact.

### Read It

**1.** Label each of these sentences from the text as active or passive.

a. The short story was very nearly drowned in the tub as an infant.

b. All modern literary magazines can trace their pedigree back to these gift books.

c. But the short story . . . sprang into full-fledged existence as recently as the 1820s.

d. A narrative of a few thousand words can be easily read, enjoyed, and digested while sitting before a monitor. . . .

**Connect to Style** With your group, discuss why the author's use of the active voice is effective, as well as why he uses the passive voice when he does.

### Write It

**Notebook** Write a paragraph to express your thoughts about a short story you found particularly exciting or moving. Experiment with using both the active and the passive voice in your writing.

STANDARDS

**Writing**
Conduct short as well as more sustained research projects to answer a question or solve a problem; narrow or broaden the inquiry when appropriate; synthesize multiple sources on the subject, demonstrating understanding of the subject under investigation.

**Language**
Apply the understanding that usage is a matter of convention, can change over time, and is sometimes contested.





PERSONALIZE FOR LEARNING

### English Language Support

**Using Active and Passive Voice** Display the following sentence: *The kids at that school wore uniforms.* Have students rewrite the sentence in passive voice. (Possible response: *Uniforms were worn by the students at that school.*) **EMERGING**

Have students find an example of a sentence in passive voice in the selection. Then ask them to rewrite it in active voice. **EXPANDING**

Ask students to write a sentence in active voice and then to rewrite it in passive voice. Have a volunteer explain to the class how the change from active to passive was accomplished. **EXPANDING**

An expanded **English Language Support Lesson** on Active and Passive Voice is available in the Interactive Teacher's Edition.

## Research

**Assignment**

As a group, create a **research report** that relates to "A Brief History of the Short Story" to share with the class. Choose one of these options:

- ☐ an **extended definition** of the term *short story* that shows how its meaning has developed over time
- ☐ a **graph** that shows how e-book sales compare with print book sales over time, along with a summary of what you learned about publishing trends and people's reading habits
- ☐ an **analytical paper** that presents and compares what a variety of famous American authors have said about the short story genre

**Project Plan** Have each group member review "A Brief History of the Short Story" and do some general reading about the subject you have chosen, to get an idea of the information you need. Then, as a group, list these kinds of information. Assign individual group members to research different aspects of the topic. Finally, determine how you will present the text and what images will accompany it.

**Conduct Research** Use this chart to keep track of the types of information you are researching and the group member assigned to each type. Also, record the sources each person consults and the details needed for proper citation.

| KIND OF INFORMATION | WHO IS RESPONSIBLE | SOURCE INFORMATION FOR CITATION |
| --- | --- | --- |
| | | |
| | | |
| | | |
| | | |
| | | |

**EVIDENCE LOG**

Before moving on to a new selection, go to your Evidence Log and record what you learned from "A Brief History of the Short Story."





DIGITAL PERSPECTIVES  

## Research

**Project Plan** Encourage groups to brainstorm for the types of information they will want to locate. For example, the graph assignment will require quantitative data, while the analytical paper will require that they conduct qualitative research to find out what various authors have said about short stories.

**Conduct Research** After students fill in a table like the one shown, suggest that they talk about the benefits and drawbacks of each type of information. For example, ask students to consider what statistics can show that literary criticism cannot. Remind students to evaluate the credibility of their sources.

For more support, see **Research: Research Report.**

**Evidence Log** Support students in completing their Evidence Log. This paced activity will help prepare them for the Performance-Based Assessment at the end of the unit.

### FORMATIVE ASSESSMENT

#### Research

**If** If students have difficulty deciding what information to use in their report, **then** suggest that they reread the assignment and evaluate each piece of information to be sure it is closely related to the assignment.

For Reteach and Practice, see **Research: Research Report (RP).**

#### Selection Test

Administer the "A Brief History of the Short Story" Selection Test, which is available in both print and digital formats online in Assessments.

### PERSONALIZE FOR LEARNING

**English Language Support**

**Extended Definitions** Remind students that the definitions they find in a dictionary are a kind of shorthand. They provide readers with a basic definition, but no more than that. Explain that brief dictionary definitions cannot express the subtleties, depth, or expansiveness of a more thorough definition. If students write an extended definition of a term like *short story,* they can include examples that show readers what the term means. They can also include quotations from writers who have studied short stories and have a deep understanding of the form. Encourage students to write paragraph-length definitions of words like *courage, friendship,* and *happy*. Then, suggest that the class discuss what they have learned from writing longer definitions. **BRIDGING**

# An Occurrence at Owl Creek Bridge

**AUDIO SUMMARIES**
Audio summaries of "An Occurrence at Owl Creek Bridge" are available online in both English and Spanish in the Interactive Teacher's Edition or Unit Resources. Assigning these summaries prior to reading the selection may help students build additional background knowledge and set a context for their first read.

## Summary

Ambrose Bierce's short story "An Occurrence at Owl Creek Bridge" opens at the scene of a Civil War execution. A group of people have gathered at a railroad bridge for a military hanging. Peyton Farquhar, the prisoner, is a wealthy plantation owner who supports the Confederate cause. He has been accused of tampering with the railroad bridges Union soldiers were trying to fix. As he awaits his execution, he looks at the water and imagines his escape. At the moment of his hanging, Farquhar falls through the bridge and sees himself freeing his hands, removing the noose, and escaping. He swims to the opposite shore. He hurries home, anxious to see his wife, but as he moves to embrace her he feels a powerful blow against the back of his neck.

### Insight

The story dramatically illustrates the human instinct to survive and to hope against hope that others survive as well. Just as Farquhar cannot take in the thought that he is about to die, readers participate in his fantasy of escape.

ESSENTIAL QUESTION:
What do stories reveal about the human condition?

## Connection to Essential Question

The story reveals something essential and universal about the human condition: the instinct for survival.

SMALL-GROUP LEARNING PERFORMANCE TASK
Present a stream-of-consciousness narrative based on this idea: *The day felt as if it would never end.*

UNIT PERFORMANCE-BASED ASSESSMENT
How does a fictional character or characters respond to life-changing news?

## Connection to Performance Tasks

**Small-Group Learning Task** Because the story is largely set in Farquhar's imagination, it presents a dramatic example of stream-of-consciousness technique. This story will help students as they create their stream-of-consciousness narrative.

**Unit Performance-Based Assessment** The events recounted in the story show a human being reacting to a traumatic and life-changing event. In this case, the character imagines an escape despite the fact that an escape is impossible. This story models the way that fiction give readers the chance to imagine themselves in experiences they otherwise would not likely face.

DIGITAL PERSPECTIVES

 Audio  Video  Document  Annotation Highlights  EL Highlights Online Assessment

## LESSON RESOURCES

| | Making Meaning | Language Development |
|---|---|---|
| Lesson | **First Read**<br>**Close Read**<br>**Analyze the Text**<br>**Analyze Craft and Structure** | **Concept Vocabulary**<br>**Word Study**<br>**Conventions and Style** |
| Instructional Standards | **RL.10** By the end of grade 11, read and comprehend literature . . .<br>**L.4.a** Use context as a clue . . .<br>**RL.5** Analyze how an author's choices . . . | **L.4** Determine or clarify the meaning of unknown and multiple-meaning words and phrases . . .<br>**L.4.b** Identify and correctly use patterns of word changes . . .<br>**L.1.a** Apply the understanding that usage is a matter of convention . . .<br>**L.3.a** Vary syntax for effect . . . |
| **STUDENT RESOURCES** | | |
| Available online in the Interactive Student Edition or Unit Resources | Selection Audio<br>First-Read Guide: Fiction<br>Close-Read Guide: Fiction | Word Network<br>Evidence Log |
| **TEACHER RESOURCES** | | |
| **Selection Resources** Available online in the Interactive Teacher's Edition or Unit Resources | Audio Summaries<br>Annotation Highlights<br>EL Highlights<br>An Occurrence at Owl Creek Bridge: Text Questions<br>English Language Support Lesson: Patterns of Organization<br>Analyze Craft and Structure: Structure | Concept Vocabulary and Word Study<br>Conventions and Style: Varying Syntax for Effect |
| **Reteach/Practice (RP)** Available online in the Interactive Teacher's Edition or Unit Resources | Analyze Craft and Structure: Structure (RP) | Word Study: Latin Suffix *-um* (RP)<br>Conventions and Style: Varying Syntax for Effect (RP) |
| **Assessment** Available online in Assessments | Selection Test | |
| **My Resources** | A Unit 6 Answer Key is available online and in the Interactive Teacher's Edition. | |

# Reading Support

| Text Complexity Rubric: An Occurrence at Owl Creek Bridge | |
|---|---|
| **Quantitative Measures** | |
| **Lexile** 1000 **Text Length** 3,723 words | |
| **Qualitative Measures** | |
| Knowledge Demands ①—②—❸—④—⑤ | Some knowledge of the Civil War and American history will help students understand the story. Students may also benefit from knowledge of different methods of capital punishment during wartime. |
| Structure ①—②—③—❹—⑤ | The story structure departs from the traditional narrative with a flashback that helps explain why Farquhar is being executed. |
| Language Conventionality and Clarity ①—②—③—❹—⑤ | The language is archaic with complex sentence structure and above-level vocabulary. The text has a lot of description, little dialogue, and the conclusion is unexpected. |
| Levels of Meaning/Purpose ①—②—③—❹—⑤ | Although the horrific details of Farquhar's execution elicit sympathy, the reader is also privy to his support of the "Southern cause" of slavery. His death represents a complex moral ambiguity. |

DECIDE AND PLAN

## English Language Support

Provide English Learners with support for language and meaning as they read the selection.

**Language** Ambrose Bierce's stylistic register and portrayal of events will be a challenge for students, so help them parse the story. Discuss how the heavily detailed descriptions add layers to the experience of reading, and ask students whether they believe a simpler, minimalist style might have been as powerful a method for this tale.

**Meaning** Provide some background on the Civil War and then encourage students to consider whether they think Bierce was a supporter of the Northern or Southern cause. You may choose to engage students in a discussion about capital punishment of civilians during wartime.

## Strategic Support

Provide students with strategic support to ensure that they can successfully read the text.

**Language** Inform students that Bierce was writing in an era when the familiar first-person narrative was not so predominant and when literature was much more formalized. Have them mark passages they find to be particularly interesting, and make lists of words they find challenging. Assist them in doing this, and in defining any unknown words.

**Meaning** Ask students to guess at Bierce's intention or purpose in writing "An Occurrence at Owl Creek Bridge." There is much ambiguity throughout the story. Ask students to consider what the author thought about the execution, and to look for evidence in the text that might suggest that he was for or against Farquhar's killing. Ask students to think about how they might feel about capital punishment if they had to be the executioner.

## Challenge

Provide students who need to be challenged with ideas for how they can go beyond a simple interpretation of the text.

**Text Analysis** Help students analyze the center portion of the text, Part II. Talk about why the brief bit about Farquhar's background appeared there and not in the beginning, and what Bierce may have been getting at by including it at all. From reading just that portion, encourage students to come to some conclusion about Farquhar's character.

**Written Response** Ask students to write their own thoughts on how enemies of war should be treated; then have them interview other classmates to get a sense of popular opinions about capital punishment. If the majority of the class believes that Farquhar should be executed, ask them how they'd feel if they learned that Bierce was against it.

TEACH

## Read and Respond

Have groups read the selection and complete the Making Meaning and Language Development activities.

# Standards Support Through Teaching and Learning Cycle

## IDENTIFY NEEDS

Analyze results of the Beginning-of-Year Assessment, focusing on the items relating to Unit 6. Also take into consideration student performance to this point and your observations of where particular students struggle.

## DECIDE AND PLAN

- If students have performed poorly on items matching these standards, then provide selection scaffolds before assigning them the on-level lesson provided in the Student Edition.
- If students have done well on the Beginning-of-Year Assessment, then challenge them to keep progressing and learning by giving them opportunities to practice the skills in depth.
- Use the Selection Resources listed on the Planning pages for "An Occurrence at Owl Creek Bridge" to help students continually improve their ability to master the standards.

**Instructional Standards: An Occurrence at Owl Creek Bridge**

| | Catching Up | This Year | Looking Forward |
|---|---|---|---|
| **Reading** | You may wish to administer the **Analyze Craft and Structure: Structure (RP)** worksheet to have a clearer understanding of chronological order. | **RL.5** Analyze how an author's choices concerning how to structure specific parts of a text contribute to its overall structure and meaning as well as its aesthetic impact. | Have students find another fictional narrative and identify how the narrative is organized. |
| **Language** | You may wish to administer the **Conventions and Style: Run-ons and Fragments (RP)** worksheet to practice language conventions.<br><br>Review: the **Word Study: Latin Suffix *-um* (RP)** worksheet with students to better familiarize them with how the suffix is used to form the singular of many Latin nouns. | **L.1.a** Apply the understanding that usage is a matter of convention, can change over time, and is sometimes contested.<br><br>**L.4.b** Identify and correctly use patterns of word changes that indicate different meanings or parts of speech. | Have students work in pairs to create and correct run-on and fragment sentences.<br><br>Have students locate other Greek, Latin, and Anglo-Saxon suffixes they recognize in the text. |

## ANALYZE AND REVISE

- Analyze student work for evidence of student learning.
- Identify whether or not students have met the expectations in the standards.
- Identify implications for future instruction.

## TEACH

Implement the planned lesson, and gather evidence of student learning.

# FACILITATING

## Jump Start

**FIRST READ** Engage groups in a conversation about death during wartime. Ask: *What might be the last thoughts of a person who is condemned to die? How might a person who has committed treason feel about his or her decision to do so? Engage students in a discussion of last thoughts during wartime.*

## An Occurrence at Owl Creek Bridge

What happens to traitors in times of war? Modeling this and other questions readers might ask will bring "An Occurrence at Owl Creek Bridge" to life and connect it to the Performance Task question. Selection audio and print capability for the selection are available in the Interactive Teacher's Edition.

## Concept Vocabulary

Have groups briefly discuss the three concept vocabulary words. Have they encountered any of the words before? Do they recognize the prefix, suffix, or base word of any of the concept vocabulary words?

Have groups consider the strategy of context clues, particularly in relation to elaborating details, and synonyms and antonyms, and discuss its advantages and disadvantages.

## FIRST READ

Have students perform the steps of the first read independently:

NOTICE: You may want to encourage students to notice the three-part structure of the story.

ANNOTATE: Remind students to mark passages that help them differentiate among the different parts of the story.

CONNECT: Encourage students to think of other stories that build suspense for readers.

RESPOND: Students will demonstrate their understanding of the text by answering questions and writing a summary.

Point out to students that they will perform the first three steps concurrently as they are doing their first read. They will complete the Respond step after they have finished the first read. You may wish to print copies of the **First-Read Guide: Fiction** for students to use.

MAKING MEANING

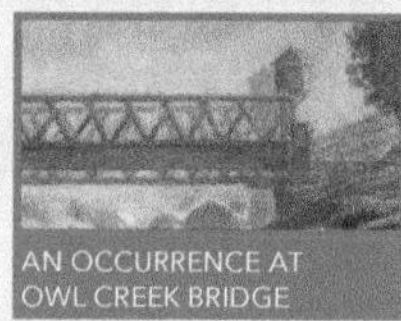
AN OCCURRENCE AT OWL CREEK BRIDGE

## Comparing Texts

In this lesson, you will read and compare "An Occurrence at Owl Creek Bridge" and "The Jilting of Granny Weatherall." The work you do with your group on "An Occurrence at Owl Creek Bridge" will help prepare you for the comparing task.

THE JILTING OF GRANNY WEATHERALL

About the Author

**Ambrose Bierce** (1842–1914?) was born in Ohio and raised on a farm in Indiana. The poverty in which he was raised helped foster Bierce's unsentimental outlook. His writing and worldview were further shaped by his career as a Union officer in the Civil War. The brutality he saw during the war cemented his cynicism. Bierce explored themes of cruelty and death in his writing, earning himself the nickname "Bitter Bierce."

STANDARDS

**Reading Literature**
By the end of grade 11, read and comprehend literature, including stories, dramas, and poems, in the grades 11–CCR text complexity band proficiently, with scaffolding as needed at the high end of the range.

**Language**
Use context as a clue to the meaning of a word or phrase.

# An Occurrence at Owl Creek Bridge

## Concept Vocabulary

As you perform your first read of "An Occurrence at Owl Creek Bridge," you will encounter these words.

etiquette    deference    dictum

**Context Clues** If these words are unfamiliar to you, try using **context clues** such as these to help you determine their meanings.

**Elaborating Details:** The former officer was **abject** when he was reduced in rank from captain to corporal.

**Restatement, or Synonyms:** The general was a **paragon** of leadership, the standard against which other officers were judged.

Apply your knowledge of context clues and other vocabulary strategies to determine the meanings of unfamiliar words you encounter during your first read.

## First Read FICTION

Apply these strategies as you conduct your first read. You will have an opportunity to complete a close read after your first read.

NOTICE *whom* the story is about, *what* happens, *where* and *when* it happens, and *why* those involved react as they do.

ANNOTATE by marking vocabulary and key passages you want to revisit.

CONNECT ideas within the selection to what you already know and what you have already read.

RESPOND by completing the Comprehension Check and by writing a brief summary of the selection.

First Read





PERSONALIZE FOR LEARNING

### Strategic Support

**First Read Support** If group members struggle to comprehend the text during the first read, have another group member conduct a think-aloud to explain the thought process as he or she works through the NOTICE, ANNOTATE, CONNECT, and RESPOND steps.

For example, students might notice that the story opens *in medias res* ("in the middle of things"). The student might annotate "A rope closely encircled his neck" in paragraph 1 to revisit in the close read to see when and how the author explains why this man is being hanged.

DIGITAL PERSPECTIVES

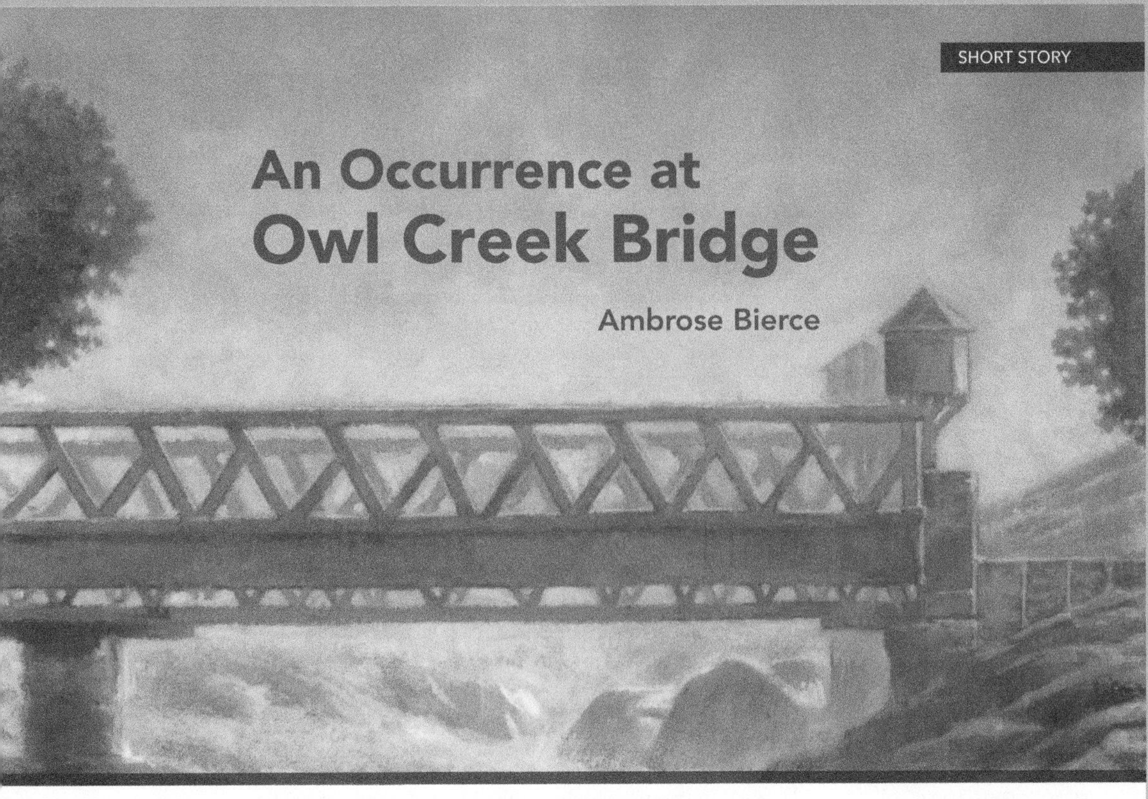


# An Occurrence at Owl Creek Bridge

Ambrose Bierce

## BACKGROUND

The senseless violence, death, and destruction Ambrose Bierce witnessed during the American Civil War (1861–1865) convinced him that war was terrible and futile. He set much of his best fiction, including this story, against the backdrop of this divisive war, in which the agricultural South, whose economy was based on slavery, battled the more industrialized North. Fought mostly in the South, the war caused hundreds of thousands of casualties on both sides.

SCAN FOR MULTIMEDIA 

## I

1 A man stood upon a railroad bridge in northern Alabama, looking down into the swift water twenty feet below. The man's hands were behind his back, the wrists bound with a cord. A rope closely encircled his neck. It was attached to a stout cross timber above his head and the slack fell to the level of his knees. Some loose boards laid upon the sleepers supporting the metals of the railway supplied a footing for him and his executioners—two private soldiers of the Federal army, directed by a sergeant who in civil life may have been a deputy sheriff. At a short remove upon the same temporary platform was an officer in the uniform of his rank, armed. He was a captain. A sentinel at each end of the bridge stood with his rifle in

NOTES



## FACILITATING SMALL-GROUP CLOSE READING

**CLOSE READ: Short Stories** As groups perform the close read, circulate and offer support as needed.

- Remind groups that when they read a short story, they should identify the main characters and the plot.
- If a group is confused about why particular events are important, remind them to think about how the events are related to the story's conflict.
- Challenge groups to determine the theme or message of the text and the specific details that develop and refine the theme.

# FACILITATING

## Concept Vocabulary

**ETIQUETTE** If groups are struggling to define the word *etiquette* in paragraph 2, suggest that they use context clues to determine the word's meaning. Draw students' attention to the context clues "code," "fixity," and "forms," and have students use these context clues to define the word.

**Possible response:** *Etiquette* means a "code for proper behavior."

**DEFERENCE** If groups are struggling to define the word *deference* in paragraph 2, suggest that they use context clues to determine the word's meaning. Draw students' attention to the context clues, "silence" and "respect," and have students use these clues to define the word.

**Possible response:** *Deference* means "respectful behavior."

Additional **English Language Support** is available in the Interactive Teacher's Edition.

NOTES

Mark context clues or indicate another strategy you used that helped you determine meaning.

**etiquette** (EHT ih kiht) *n.*

MEANING:

**deference** (DEHF uhr uhns) *n.*

MEANING:

the position known as "support," that is to say, vertical in front of the left shoulder, the hammer resting on the forearm thrown straight across the chest—a formal and unnatural position, enforcing an erect carriage of the body. It did not appear to be the duty of these two men to know what was occurring at the center of the bridge; they merely blockaded the two ends of the foot planking that traversed it.

2 Beyond one of the sentinels nobody was in sight: the railroad ran straight away into a forest for a hundred yards, then, curving, was lost to view. Doubtless there was an out-post farther along. The other bank of the stream was open ground—a gentle acclivity[1] topped with a stockade of vertical tree trunks, loopholed for rifles, with a single embrasure through which protruded the muzzle of a brass cannon commanding the bridge. Midway of the slope between bridge and fort were the spectators—a single company of infantry in line, at "parade rest," the butts of the rifles on the ground, the barrels inclining slightly backward against the right shoulder, the hands crossed upon the stock. A lieutenant stood at the right of the line, the point of his sword upon the ground, his left hand resting upon his right. Excepting the group of four at the center of the bridge, not a man moved. The company faced the bridge, staring stonily, motionless. The sentinels, facing the banks of the stream, might have been statues to adorn the bridge. The captain stood with folded arms, silent, observing the work of his subordinates, but making no sign. Death is a dignitary who when he comes announced is to be received with formal manifestations of respect, even by those most familiar with him. In the code of military **etiquette** silence and fixity are forms of **deference**.

3 The man who was engaged in being hanged was apparently about thirty-five years of age. He was a civilian, if one might judge from his habit, which was that of a planter. His features were good—a straight nose, firm mouth, broad forehead, from which his long, dark hair was combed straight back, falling behind his ears to the collar of his well-fitting frock coat. He wore a mustache and pointed beard, but no whiskers; his eyes were large and dark gray, and had a kindly expression which one would hardly have expected in one whose neck was in the hemp. Evidently this was no vulgar assassin. The liberal military code makes provision for hanging many kinds of persons, and gentlemen are not excluded.

4 The preparations being complete, the two private soldiers stepped aside and each drew away the plank upon which he had been standing. The sergeant turned to the captain, saluted and placed himself immediately behind that officer, who in turn moved apart one pace. These movements left the condemned man and the sergeant standing on the two ends of the same plank, which spanned three of the crossties of the bridge. The end upon which the civilian stood almost, but not quite, reached a fourth. This plank had been held in place by the weight of the captain; it was now held by that of

1. **acclivity** (uh KLIHV uh tee) *n.* upward slope.





## PERSONALIZE FOR LEARNING

### English Language Support

**Descriptive Language** English learners may struggle with the high-level, formal vocabulary in this text. Direct students' attention to paragraph 2. Point out the author's use of descriptive language to paint a scene for the reader. You may want to select a few examples to demonstrate this point. For example, *a gentile acclivity, topped with a stockade of vertical tree trunks, loopholed for rifles, with a single bridge, embrasure through which protruded a muzzle of brass cannon commanding the . . .*

Have students read through the paragraph sentence by sentence. After each sentence, have them explain what the author is describing and how each sentence adds to the scene as a whole. You might ask students to draw a picture of the scene, based on the descriptive sentences. Then have students discuss how the use of descriptive language adds to the reader's understanding of the scene. **ALL LEVELS** the sergeant. At a signal from the former the latter would step aside, the plank would tilt and the condemned man go down between two ties. The arrangement commended itself to his judgment as simple and effective. His face had not been covered nor his eyes bandaged. He looked a moment at his "unsteadfast footing," then let his gaze wander to the swirling water of the stream racing madly beneath his feet. A piece of dancing driftwood caught his attention and his eyes followed it down the current. How slowly it appeared to move! What a sluggish stream!

5 He closed his eyes in order to fix his last thoughts upon his wife and children. The water, touched to gold by the early sun, the brooding mists under the banks at some distance down the stream, the fort, the soldiers, the piece of drift—all had distracted him. And now he became conscious of a new disturbance. Striking through the thought of his dear ones was a sound which he could neither ignore nor understand, a sharp, distinct, metallic percussion like the stroke of a blacksmith's hammer upon the anvil; it had the same ringing quality. He wondered what it was, and whether immeasurably distant or near by—it seemed both. Its recurrence was regular, but as slow as the tolling of a death knell. He awaited each stroke with impatience and—he knew not why—apprehension. The intervals of silence grew progressively longer; the delays became maddening. With their greater infrequency the sounds increased in strength and sharpness. They hurt his ear like the thrust of a knife; he feared he would shriek. What he heard was the ticking of his watch.

6 He unclosed his eyes and saw again the water below him. "If I could free my hands," he thought, "I might throw off the noose and spring into the stream. By diving I could evade the bullets and, swimming vigorously, reach the bank, take to the woods and get away home. My home, thank God, is as yet outside their lines; my wife and little ones are still beyond the invader's farthest advance."

7 As these thoughts, which have here to be set down in words, were flashed into the doomed man's brain rather than evolved from it the captain nodded to the sergeant. The sergeant stepped aside.

## II

8 Peyton Farquhar was a well-to-do planter, of an old and highly respected Alabama family. Being a slave owner and like other slave owners a politician he was naturally an original secessionist and ardently devoted to the Southern cause. Circumstances of an imperious nature, which it is unnecessary to relate here, had prevented him from taking service with the gallant army that had fought the disastrous campaigns ending with the fall of Corinth,[2] and he chafed under the inglorious restraint, longing for the release of his energies, the larger life of the soldier, the opportunity for distinction.

NOTES

2. **Corinth** Mississippi town that was the site of an 1862 Civil War battle.





DIGITAL PERSPECTIVES

CLOSER LOOK

### Recognize Suspense

Circulate among groups as students conduct their close read. Suggest that groups close read paragraph 7. Encourage them to talk about the annotations that they mark. If needed, provide the following support.

**ANNOTATE:** Have students mark details in this paragraph that hint at the story's conclusion, or work with small groups to have students participate while you highlight them together.

**QUESTION:** Guide students to consider what these details might tell them. Ask what a reader can infer from the last sentence of the paragraph, and accept student responses.

**Possible response:** As the sergeant steps aside, readers should infer that the man was hanged.

**CONCLUDE:** Help students to formulate conclusions about the importance of these details in the text. Ask students why the author might have included these details. Encourage students to notice other examples of foreshadowing as the story progresses.

**Possible response:** Beginning the story with a man's death makes readers wonder what the rest of the story will explore. It may make the reader think that a hanging or the action that led to the hanging might play a role in something else that happens in this story.

Remind students that **suspense** is a narrative technique that slows down the action to build interest, excitement, and anxiety about the outcome of actions.

VOCABULARY DEVELOPMENT

**Graphic Organizers** To build student vocabulary fluency, have students fill out a word map for the word *imperious* (paragraph 8).

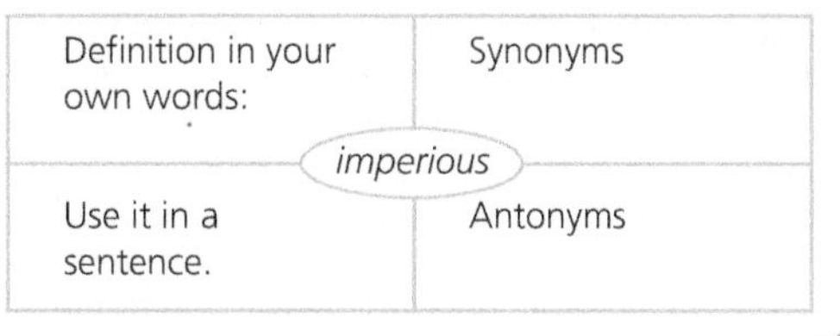

Definition in your own words:
Synonyms
imperious
Use it in a sentence.
Antonyms

# FACILITATING

## Concept Vocabulary

**DICTUM** If groups are struggling to define the word *dictum* in paragraph 8, point out context clues that can help students with the word. Draw students' attention to the context clue "all is fair in love and war," and have students use this context clue to determine the word's meaning.

**Possible response:** *Dictum* must mean "a well-known saying."

NOTES

Mark context clues or indicate another strategy you used that helped you determine meaning.

**dictum** (DIHK tuhm) *n.*

MEANING:

That opportunity, he felt, would come, as it comes to all in war time. Meanwhile he did what he could. No service was too humble for him to perform in aid of the South, no adventure too perilous for him to undertake if consistent with the character of a civilian who was at heart a soldier, and who in good faith and without too much qualification assented to at least a part of the frankly villainous **dictum** that all is fair in love and war.

9 One evening while Farquhar and his wife were sitting on a rustic bench near the entrance to his grounds, a gray-clad soldier rode up to the gate and asked for a drink of water. Mrs. Farquhar was only too happy to serve him with her own white hands. While she was fetching the water her husband approached the dusty horseman and inquired eagerly for news from the front.

10 "The Yanks are repairing the railroads," said the man, "and are getting ready for another advance. They have reached the Owl Creek bridge, put it in order and built a stockade on the north bank. The commandant has issued an order, which is posted everywhere, declaring that any civilian caught interfering with the railroad, its bridges, tunnels or trains will be summarily hanged. I saw the order."

11 "How far is it to the Owl Creek bridge?" Farquhar asked.

12 "About thirty miles."

13 "Is there no force on this side the creek?"

14 "Only a picket post[3] half a mile out, on the railroad, and a single sentinel at this end of the bridge."

15 "Suppose a man—a civilian and student of hanging—should elude the picket post and perhaps get the better of the sentinel," said Farquhar, smiling, "what could he accomplish?"

16 The soldier reflected. "I was there a month ago," he replied. "I observed that the flood of last winter had lodged a great quantity of

3. **picket post** troops sent ahead with news of a surprise attack.





## CROSS-CURRICULAR PERSPECTIVES

**Social Studies** Direct students' attention to the phrase "a gray-clad soldier" in paragraph 9. Remind students that in the Civil War, the Union, or northern, soldiers wore blue, and the Confederates, or southern soldiers wore gray. Explain that at the beginning of the war, uniforms were not "uniform" at all. During the Battle of Bull Run (or Manassas, as it was called by the Confederates) in 1861, some southern companies wore blue—a fact that was partially responsible for the Confederate victory. Have students describe a hypothetical instance when, in contrast to Bull Run, wearing the enemy's colors would be a disadvantage. Have them explain the value of uniform colors for each side during a conflict.

NOTES

driftwood against the wooden pier at this end of the bridge. It is now dry and would burn like tow."[4]

17 The lady had now brought the water, which the soldier drank. He thanked her ceremoniously, bowed to her husband and rode away. An hour later, after nightfall, he repassed the plantation, going northward in the direction from which he had come. He was a Federal scout.

## III

18 As Peyton Farquhar fell straight downward through the bridge he lost consciousness and was as one already dead. From this state he was awakened—ages later, it seemed to him—by the pain of a sharp pressure upon his throat, followed by a sense of suffocation. Keen, poignant agonies seemed to shoot from his neck downward through every fiber of his body and limbs. These pains appeared to flash along well-defined lines of ramification[5] and to beat with an inconceivably rapid periodicity. They seemed like streams of pulsating fire heating him to an intolerable temperature. As to his head, he was conscious of nothing but a feeling of fullness—of congestion. These sensations were unaccompanied by thought. The intellectual part of his nature was already effaced: he had power only to feel, and feeling was torment. He was conscious of motion. Encompassed in a luminous cloud, of which he was now merely the fiery heart, without material substance, he swung through unthinkable arcs of oscillation, like a vast pendulum. Then all at once, with terrible suddenness, the light about him shot upward with the noise of a loud plash; a frightful roaring was in his ears, and all was cold and dark. The power of thought was restored; he knew that the rope had broken and he had fallen into the stream. There was no additional strangulation; the noose about his neck was already suffocating him and kept the water from his lungs. To die of hanging at the bottom of a river!—the idea seemed to him ludicrous. He opened his eyes in the darkness and saw above him a gleam of light, but how distant, how inaccessible! He was still sinking, for the light became fainter and fainter until it was a mere glimmer. Then it began to grow and brighten, and he knew that he was rising toward the surface—knew it with reluctance, for he was now very comfortable. "To be hanged and drowned," he thought, "that is not so bad; but I do not wish to be shot. No; I will not be shot; that is not fair."

19 He was not conscious of an effort, but a sharp pain in his wrist apprised him that he was trying to free his hands. He gave the struggle his attention, as an idler might observe the feat of a juggler, without interest in the outcome. What splendid effort!— what magnificent, what superhuman strength! Ah, that was a fine endeavor!

4. **tow** (toh) *n.* coarse, broken fibers of hemp or flax before spinning.
5. **flash along well-defined lines of ramification** spread out quickly along branches from a central point.





**WriteNow** Express and Reflect

**Argument** At the end of paragraph 17, the reader finds out that the "gray-clad soldier" was actually a Union, or northern, scout who deliberately lured Farquhar into a trap. Have students consider whether this was solid military strategy or underhanded, unethical behavior. Have them choose a point of view and write a paragraph defending or attacking the action. You may want to have students consider the behavior in light of the dictum "all is fair in love and war," which appeared earlier in the story.

## CLOSER LOOK

### Determine Point of View

Circulate among groups as students conduct their close read. Suggest that groups close read paragraphs 20, 21, and 22 to determine the point of view from which the story is being told. Encourage them to talk about the annotations that they mark. If needed, provide the following support.

**ANNOTATE:** Have students mark details in these paragraphs that indicate the point of view from which this part of the story is being told, or work with small groups to have students participate while you highlight them together.

**QUESTION:** Guide students to consider what these details might tell them. Who is the narrator at this point of the story? How did the point of view change from earlier in the story? Ask what a reader can infer from who the narrator is at this point in the story and how that point of view changed from earlier in the story, and accept student responses.

**Possible response:** Farquhar is the narrator at this point of the story. The perspective has shifted to third-person limited point of view. We now can only know what Farquhar is feeling and thinking. The beginning of the story, in contrast, was told from the omniscient point of view.

**CONCLUDE:** Help students to formulate conclusions about the importance of these details in the text. Ask students why the author might have included these details.

**Possible response:** The change in the point of view builds the suspense of the story as readers have insight into his direct thoughts.

Remind students that **point of view** is the perspective, or vantage point, from which a story is told. Point of view is determined by what type of narrator, or voice, is telling the story. There are two types of third-person points of view. A story told from the **omniscient point of view** is told by an all-knowing observer who can describe everything that happens and reveal the thoughts and feelings of all the characters. A story told from the **limited third-person point of view** is told by a narrator who sees the world through a single character's eyes and reveals only what that character is experiencing, thinking, and feeling.

NOTES

Bravo! The cord fell away; his arms parted and floated upward, the hands dimly seen on each side in the growing light. He watched them with a new interest as first one and then the other pounced upon the noose at his neck. They tore it away and thrust it fiercely aside, its undulations resembling those of a water-snake. "Put it back, put it back!" He thought he shouted these words to his hands, for the undoing of the noose had been succeeded by the direst pang that he had yet experienced. His neck ached horribly; his brain was on fire; his heart, which had been fluttering faintly, gave a great leap, trying to force itself out at his mouth. His whole body was racked and wrenched with an insupportable anguish! But his disobedient hands gave no heed to the command. They beat the water vigorously with quick, downward strokes, forcing him to the surface. He felt his head emerge: his eyes were blinded by the sunlight; his chest expanded convulsively, and with a supreme and crowning agony his lungs engulfed a great draft of air, which instantly he expelled in a shriek!

20 He was now in full possession of his physical senses. They were, indeed, preternaturally[6] keen and alert. Something in the awful disturbance of his organic system had so exalted and refined them that they made record of things never before perceived. He felt the ripples upon his face and heard their separate sounds as they struck. He looked at the forest on the bank of the stream, saw the individual trees, the leaves and the veining of each leaf—saw the very insects upon them: the locusts, the brilliant-bodied flies, the gray spiders stretching their webs from twig to twig. He noted the prismatic colors in all the dewdrops upon a million blades of grass. The humming of the gnats that danced above the eddies of the stream, the beating of the dragonflies' wings, the strokes of the water spiders' legs, like oars which had lifted their boat—all these made audible music. A fish slid along beneath his eyes and he heard the rush of its body parting the water.

21 He had come to the surface facing down the stream: in a moment the visible world seemed to wheel slowly round, himself the pivotal point, and he saw the bridge, the fort, the soldiers upon the bridge, the captain, the sergeant, the two privates, his executioners. They were in silhouette against the blue sky. They shouted and gesticulated, pointing at him. The captain had drawn his pistol, but did not fire; the others were unarmed. Their movements were grotesque and horrible, their forms gigantic.

22 Suddenly he heard a sharp report and something struck the water smartly within a few inches of his head, spattering his face with spray. He heard a second report, and saw one of the sentinels with his rifle at his shoulder, a light cloud of blue smoke rising from the muzzle. The man in the water saw the eye of the man on the bridge gazing into his own through the sights of the rifle. He observed that it was a gray eye and remembered having read that gray eyes were keenest, and that all famous marksmen had them. Nevertheless, this one had missed.

6. **preternaturally** (pree tuhr NACH uhr uh lee) *adv.* abnormally; extraordinarily.





## PERSONALIZE FOR LEARNING

### Strategic Support

**Reality and Illusion** Review paragraph 22 and ask students to consider Farquhar's thoughts and feelings. Point out to students that the limited point of view of Part III, coupled with the detailed sensory narrative, leads the reader to believe that this is really happening to Farquhar. Yet the reader may also wonder how a doomed man could have escaped. Have students consider the blurring between reality and illusion that Bierce conveys in this story. Ask students to write a paragraph explaining how the shifting point of view helps achieve the author's purpose.

23 A counterswirl had caught Farquhar and turned him half round; he was again looking into the forest on the bank opposite the fort. The sound of a clear, high voice in a monotonous singsong now rang out behind him and came across the water with a distinctness that pierced and subdued all other sounds, even the beating of the ripples in his ears. Although no soldier, he had frequented camps enough to know the dread significance of that deliberate, drawling, aspirated chant; the lieutenant on shore was taking a part in the morning's work. How coldly and pitilessly—with what an even, calm intonation, presaging,[7] and enforcing tranquility in the men—with what accurately measured intervals fell those cruel words:

24 "Attention, company! . . . Shoulder arms! . . . Ready! . . . Aim! . . . Fire!"

25 Farquhar dived—dived as deeply as he could. The water roared in his ears like the voice of Niagara, yet he heard the dulled thunder of the volley and, rising again toward the surface, met shining bits of metal, singularly flattened, oscillating slowly downward. Some of them touched him on the face and hands, then fell away, continuing their descent. One lodged between his collar and neck; it was uncomfortably warm and he snatched it out.

26 As he rose to the surface, gasping for breath, he saw that he had been a long time under water; he was perceptibly farther down stream—nearer to safety. The soldiers had almost finished reloading; the metal ramrods flashed all at once in the sunshine as they were drawn from the barrels, turned in the air, and thrust

7. **presaging** (prih SAY jihng) *v.* predicting; warning.

NOTES

## DIGITAL PERSPECTIVES

**Illuminating the Text** Review paragraph 24. To help students grasp what it took to fire a Civil War-era rifle, find videos of people demonstrating this multi-stepped process. Firing such a rifle required holding the gun with one hand while tearing the cartridge with the other, pouring the powder from the cartridge into the barrel, inserting the bullet, ramming it down, then ramming the cartridge into the base of the barrel. An experienced soldier could fire approximately three times in a minute.

Discuss whether or not it would be significantly easier to escape from a group of soldiers firing weapons like these than from a group of soldiers firing modern automatic weapons. Preview any video before sharing it with students.

NOTES

into their sockets. The two sentinels fired again, independently and ineffectually.

27 The hunted man saw all this over his shoulder; he was now swimming vigorously with the current. His brain was as energetic as his arms and legs: he thought with the rapidity of lightning.

28 "The officer," he reasoned, "will not make that martinet's[8] error a second time. It is as easy to dodge a volley as a single shot. He has probably already given the command to fire at will. God help me, I cannot dodge them all!"

29 An appalling plash within two yards of him was followed by a loud, rushing sound, *diminuendo*,[9] which seemed to travel back through the air to the fort and died in an explosion which stirred the very river to its deeps! A rising sheet of water curved over him, fell down upon him, blinded him, strangled him! The cannon had taken a hand in the game. As he shook his head free from the commotion of the smitten water he heard the deflected shot humming through the air ahead, and in an instant it was cracking and smashing the branches in the forest beyond.

30 "They will not do that again," he thought; "the next time they will use a charge of grape.[10] I must keep my eye upon the gun; the smoke will apprise me—the report arrives too late; it lags behind the missile. That is a good gun."

31 Suddenly he felt himself whirled round and round—spinning like a top. The water, the banks, the forests, the now distant bridge, fort and men—all were commingled and blurred. Objects were represented by their colors only; circular horizontal streaks of color—that was all he saw. He had been caught in a vortex and was being whirled on with a velocity of advance and gyration that made him giddy and sick. In a few moments he was flung upon the gravel at the foot of the left bank of the stream—the southern bank—and behind a projecting point which concealed him from his enemies. The sudden arrest of his motion, the abrasion of one of his hands on the gravel, restored him, and he wept with delight. He dug his fingers into the sand, threw it over himself in handfuls and audibly blessed it. It looked like diamonds, rubies, emeralds; he could think of nothing beautiful which it did not resemble. The trees upon the bank were giant garden plants; he noted a definite order in their arrangement, inhaled the fragrance of their blooms. A strange, roseate[11] light shone through the spaces among their trunks and the wind made in their branches the music of aeolian harps.[12] He had no wish to perfect his escape—was content to remain in that enchanting spot until retaken.

8. **martinet** (mahr tuh NEHT) *n.* strict military disciplinarian.
9. **diminuendo** (duh mihn yoo EHN doh) musical term used to describe a gradual reduction in volume.
10. **charge of grape** cluster of small iron balls—"grape shot"—that disperse once fired from a cannon.
11. **roseate** (ROH zee iht) *adj.* rose-colored.
12. **aeolian** (ee OH lee uhn) **harps** stringed instruments that produce music when played by the wind. In Greek mythology, Aeolus is the god of the winds.





PERSONALIZE FOR LEARNING

### Challenge

**Research** Direct students' attention to these phrases in paragraph 28: "dodge a volley" and "fire at will." Have students do research to find out how a volley differed from firing at will. Students may write a paragraph describing these differences, or they might draw images that illustrate the two offensive military strategies.

DIGITAL PERSPECTIVES

32 A whiz and rattle of grapeshot among the branches high above his head roused him from his dream. The baffled cannoneer had fired him a random farewell. He sprang to his feet, rushed up the sloping bank, and plunged into the forest.

33 All that day he traveled, laying his course by the rounding sun. The forest seemed interminable; nowhere did he discover a break in it, not even a woodman's road. He had not known that he lived in so wild a region. There was something uncanny in the revelation.

34 By night fall he was fatigued, footsore, famishing. The thought of his wife and children urged him on. At last he found a road which led him in what he knew to be the right direction. It was as wide and straight as a city street, yet it seemed untraveled. No fields bordered it, no dwelling anywhere. Not so much as the barking of a dog suggested human habitation. The black bodies of the trees formed a straight wall on both sides, terminating on the horizon in a point, like a diagram in a lesson in perspective. Overhead, as he looked up through this rift in the wood, shone great golden stars looking unfamiliar and grouped in strange constellations. He was sure they were arranged in some order which had a secret and malign significance. The wood on either side was full of singular noises, among which—once, twice, and again, he distinctly heard whispers in an unknown tongue.

35 His neck was in pain and lifting his hand to it he found it horribly swollen. He knew that it had a circle of black where the rope had bruised it. His eyes felt congested: he could no longer close them. His tongue was swollen with thirst; he relieved its fever by thrusting it forward from between his teeth into the cold air. How softly the turf had carpeted the untraveled avenue—he could no longer feel the roadway beneath his feet!

36 Doubtless, despite his suffering, he had fallen asleep while walking, for now he sees another scene—perhaps he has merely recovered from a delirium. He stands at the gate of his own home. All is as he left it, and all bright and beautiful in the morning sunshine. He must have traveled the entire night. As he pushes open the gate and passes up the wide white walk, he sees a flutter of female garments; his wife, looking fresh and cool and sweet, steps down from the veranda to meet him. At the bottom of the steps she stands waiting, with a smile of ineffable joy, an attitude of matchless grace and dignity. Ah, how beautiful she is! He springs forward with extended arms. As he is about to clasp her he feels a stunning blow upon the back of the neck; a blinding white light blazes all about him with a sound like the shock of a cannon—then all is darkness and silence!

37 Peyton Farquhar was dead; his body, with a broken neck, swung gently from side to side beneath the timbers of the Owl Creek bridge. ❧

NOTES





CLOSER LOOK

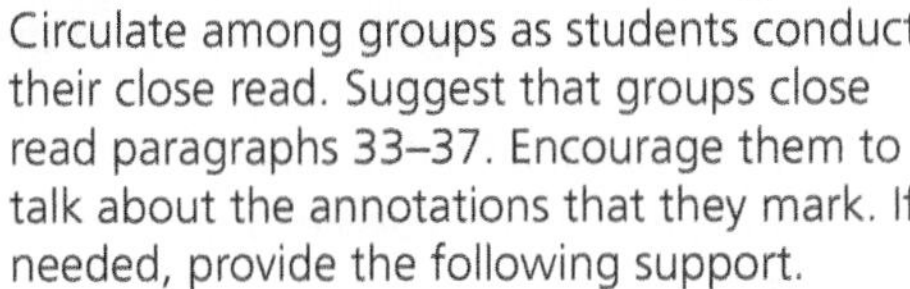

## Analyze Story Ending

Circulate among groups as students conduct their close read. Suggest that groups close read paragraphs 33–37. Encourage them to talk about the annotations that they mark. If needed, provide the following support.

**ANNOTATE:** Have students mark details in these paragraphs that show the passage of time or are critical to the plot line, or work with small groups to have students participate while you highlight them together.

**QUESTION:** Guide students to consider what these details might tell them. Ask what a reader can infer from the way Bierce structured the ending, and accept student responses.

**Possible response:** Bierce builds an almost heavenly scene where Farquhar finally makes it home to his wife. But then, in the last paragraph, readers learn that he is dead. He has not escaped the hanging and he has not traveled at all.

**CONCLUDE:** Help students to formulate conclusions about the importance of these details in the text. Ask students to consider why the surprise ending in this story is so effective.

**Possible response:** The details Bierce provides are so descriptive, and by the end of the story, the reader is almost rooting for Farquhar to escape. The escape details reach a crescendo when Farquhar seems to unite with his wife. And that is when the fantasy of escape falls apart. The reader is drawn into the story with this hopeful image and then abruptly and painfully pulled back into the brutal reality of Farquhar's death.

Explain to students that a **surprise ending** is an ending that violates the expectations of the reader in a way that is both logical and believable. Readers may be startled but should find on reflection that the ending makes sense. When a story includes a surprise ending, a skillful writer has usually planted clues to help the reader predict the final twist.

PERSONALIZE FOR LEARNING

### Strategic Support

**Connecting to Literature** Ask students to respond to paragraph 37. Have students think of other stories they have read that have surprise endings. Two classics are Guy de Maupassant's "The Necklace" and O. Henry's "The Gift of the Magi." Have students write a brief comparison of one of these stories to "An Occurrence at Owl Creek Bridge." Then have students explain why many readers enjoy surprise endings.

# FACILITATING

## Comprehension Check

Possible responses:

1. A man is about to be hanged by members of the Federal army.
2. Farquhar supports the Confederacy.
3. Farquhar has been found guilty of attempted sabotage.
4. The rope apparently breaks, and Farquhar falls into the water.
5. The soldiers shoot at Farquhar and fire a cannon at him.
6. A Civil War planter, Peyton Farquhar, is being hanged for attempted sabotage. While he is being hanged, the rope seems to break, and he seems to escape and return home to his wife. In the end, it is revealed that he has indeed died by hanging and only imagined his escape as he was dying.

## Research

**Research to Clarify** Students may be unfamiliar with many details in the story. If they have trouble deciding what to focus on, you may wish to suggest the following details: a hanging out in the open at the spot of the attempted treason, the importance of Owl Creek during the Civil War, or battles in Alabama during the war.

**Research to Explore** Students may struggle to choose which aspect of the story they find most interesting. You may want to suggest the following topics for possible research: northern Alabama during the Civil War, the importance of the railroads to military strategy of that time, the governing of territory won back from the Confederates by the Federal armies.

## Comprehension Check

**Complete the following items after you finish your first read. Review and clarify details with your group.**

1. As the story begins, what event is about to take place on the bridge?

2. In the war that divides the nation, which side does Farquhar support?

3. Why has Farquhar been sentenced to die?

4. What surprising event happens after Farquhar first loses consciousness?

5. How do the soldiers try to stop Farquhar after he drops into the water?

6. **Notebook** Confirm your understanding of the story by writing a summary.

### RESEARCH

**Research to Clarify** Choose at least one unfamiliar detail from the story. Briefly research that detail. In what way does the information you learned shed light on an aspect of the story?

**Research to Explore** Conduct research on an aspect of the story you find interesting. For example, you may want to learn about the Battle of Shiloh, which took place in part along Owl Creek.





## PERSONALIZE FOR LEARNING

### English Language Support

**Determining Main Ideas** Point out to students that titles or subtitles often express the main idea of the text that follows. Have students look back at the three parts in which the story is organized. Have them decide what would be a good subtitle for each story segment. Support students in determining these subtitles, and encourage them to share their subtitles with their groups. **ALL LEVELS**

MAKING MEANING

## Close Read the Text

With your group, revisit sections of the text you marked during your first read. **Annotate** details that you notice. What **questions** do you have? What can you **conclude**?

AN OCCURRENCE AT OWL CREEK BRIDGE

## Analyze the Text

**CITE TEXTUAL EVIDENCE** to support your answers.

Complete the activities.

1. **Review and Clarify** With your group, reread paragraphs 36–37 of the selection. Do the details in the story prepare readers for that ending, or does it come as a complete surprise? What does the ending suggest about the nature of reality?
2. **Present and Discuss** Now, work with your group to share the passages from the text that you found especially important. Take turns presenting your passages. Discuss what you noticed in the selection, what questions you asked, and what conclusions you reached.
3. **Essential Question:** ***What do stories reveal about the human condition?*** What has this narrative taught you about the human condition? Discuss with your group.

LANGUAGE DEVELOPMENT

## Concept Vocabulary

etiquette deference dictum

**Why These Words?** The concept vocabulary words from the text are related. With your group, determine what the words have in common. Write your ideas, and add another word that fits the category.

**WORD NETWORK**

Add words related to the human condition from the text to your Word Network.

### Practice

**Notebook** Confirm your understanding of these words from the text by using them in a short narrative paragraph. Then, trade papers with another group member and challenge him or her to underline the context clues that reveal the meaning of each word.

## Word Study

**Latin Suffix: *-um*** In "An Occurrence at Owl Creek Bridge," the author uses the word *dictum*, which is the singular form of the Latin noun *dicta*. The Latin suffix *-um* is used to form the singular of many Latin nouns, including *bacteria*, *curricula*, and *media*. Use a dictionary or online source to find three other words that feature this suffix. Record the words and their meanings.

**STANDARDS**

Language

- Determine or clarify the meaning of unknown and multiple-meaning words and phrases based on *grades 11–12 reading and content*, choosing flexibly from a range of strategies.
- Identify and correctly use patterns of word changes that indicate different meanings or parts of speech.





DIGITAL PERSPECTIVES

## Jump Start

**CLOSE READ** *Why do you think Bierce structured his story the way he did? What effect does the surprise ending have?*

## Close Read the Text

Model close reading as needed by using the Annotation Highlights in the Interactive Teacher's Edition. Remind groups to use Accountable Talk in their discussions and to support one another as they complete the close read.

## Analyze the Text

**Possible responses:**

1. Students may express surprise or confusion over the story's ending. Some students may marvel at the human mind creating an extended fantasy within a few seconds of real time.
2. Passages will vary by group. Remind students to explain why they chose the passage they present to group members.
3. Students may suggest that reading the story—especially as it is relayed through Farquhar's thoughts—presents a powerful image of the human desire to survive.

## Concept Vocabulary

**Why These Words? Possible response:** The words relate to formalities. They enhance the impact of the text by highlighting the strict military code that governs Farquhar's execution. Another word that fits this category is *protocol*.

### Practice

**Possible response:**

I have always believed in the *dictum* that I should treat others the way I wish to be treated. It is because of this belief that I make a point of following strict *etiquette* when meeting someone new. For example, I show *deference* to my elders by calling them "ma'am" or "sir."

### Word Network

Possible words: *dignitary, gallant, revelation, malign, ineffable*

## Word Study

For more support, see **Concept Vocabulary and Word Study.**

**Possible response:** *datum:* a single piece of information, such as a fact or statistic; *spectrum:* a single array, series, or range; *addendum:* an addition

**FORMATIVE ASSESSMENT**

### Analyze the Text

**If** students struggle to close read the text, **then** provide the **An Occurrence at Owl Creek Bridge: Text Questions** available online in the Interactive Teacher's Edition or Unit Resources. Answers and DOK levels are also available.

### Concept Vocabulary

**If** students struggle to identify the connection between the words, **then** have them use each word in a sentence and think about what is similar in the sentences.

### Word Study

**If** students fail to find other words with the suffix *–um*, **then** suggest they do an Internet search using the key words "words with the suffix *–um*."

For Reteach and Practice, see **Word Study: Latin Suffix: *–um* (RP).**

# FACILITATING

## Analyze Craft and Structure

**Author's Choices: Structure** Discuss this story's unique power to convey information in a way that both captures readers' interest and surprises them. Part of the art of this story is the author's decision to use a shift in the point of view. For more support see **Analyze Craft and Structure: Structure.**

### Practice

Possible responses:

1. a. OMNISCIENT: The man who was engaged in being hanged was apparently about thirty-five years of age. (paragraph 3)
   b. Narrative seems objective and unbiased.
   c. LIMITED: From this state he was awakened—ages later, it seemed to him—by a pain of a sharp pressure upon his throat. (paragraph 18)
   d. Narrative is very intimate; readers imagine pain only the man could know.
2. **(a)** Farquhar is loyal to the South. As a civilian, he was willing to take on risks and tasks that would support the Confederacy. **(b)** He is being hanged for his actions related to the war.
3. **(a)** Section III is from a third-person limited point of view. **(b)** This point of view builds empathy. Readers root for Farquhar. **(c)** The last paragraph is shocking as the point of view changes and readers realize that Farquhar has not made a dramatic escape but is dead.
4. **(a)** Details presented in stream-of-consciousness style are related to Farquhar's reaction to his escape. **(b)** The sharp pain is his body's reaction to the hanging. **(c)** This passage is not linear and focused. Instead, several ideas compete for attention.

### FORMATIVE ASSESSMENT

### Analyze Craft and Structure

**If** students are unable to determine the shifts in point of view in the text, **then** have them reread each part and ask themselves, *Who would have knowledge of this kind of information?*

For Reteach and Practice, see **Analyze Craft and Structure: Structure.**

MAKING MEANING

AN OCCURRENCE AT OWL CREEK BRIDGE

## Analyze Craft and Structure

**Author's Choices: Structure** Ambrose Bierce chose to structure this story in three sections, each representing a shift in time and perspective. The shift in perspective is amplified by Bierce's choice of point of view, which affects every aspect of the story. Different points of view convey different types of information to the reader.

- In stories told from an **omnisicient third-person point of view,** the narrator is an observer who can describe everything that happens, as well as the private thoughts and feelings of all the characters.
- In stories told from a **limited third-person point of view,** readers' information is limited to what a single character feels, thinks, and observes.

The point of view in this story shifts. As it shifts, so do the emotional tone and sense of time. To emphasize this change, Bierce introduces yet another narrative approach. He uses **stream of consciousness,** a technique in which a character's thoughts are presented as the mind experiences them—in short bursts without obvious logic.

TIP

COLLABORATION

You may want to have individual group members complete the activity and questions first, and then work as a group to share and agree on responses.

### Practice

CITE TEXTUAL EVIDENCE to support your answers.

**Notebook** Complete the activity and questions.

1. Working with your group, reread the story to find examples of the two different points of view Bierce uses. Then, use a chart like this one to analyze the effect of these choices.

| THIRD-PERSON POINT OF VIEW | |
|---|---|
| Limited or Omniscient? | Effect |
| a.See possible responses in Teacher's Edition. | b. |
| c. | d. |
| | |

2. **(a)** What do you learn in Section II about the main character's home life, political loyalties, and motivations? **(b)** How does this detailed information shed light on the scene described in Section I?
3. **(a)** What point of view does Bierce use in Section III? **(b)** Explain why this choice of point of view is essential to the story's overall impact. **(c)** What is the effect of the shift in point of view in the last paragraph of the story?
4. **(a)** Which details in the second paragraph of Section III are revealed through the use of stream of consciousness? **(b)** What is the "sharp pain" that sparks Farquhar's thoughts? **(c)** In what way does this passage mimic the natural, jumbled flow of thought?

STANDARDS

**Reading Literature**

Analyze how an author's choices concerning how to structure specific parts of a text contribute to its overall structure and meaning as well as its aesthetic impact.





## PERSONALIZE FOR LEARNING

### English Language Support

**Understanding Patterns of Organization** Have students give an example of a non-linear story. Ask them to explain what makes the organization of the story non-linear. **EMERGING**

Ask students to write a short paragraph explaining where Little Red Riding Hood might begin if told as an "in medias res" story. **EXPANDING**

Ask students to write a short paragraph in stream-of-consciousness style. **BRIDGING**

An expanded **English Language Support Lesson** on Patterns of Organization is available in the Interactive Teacher's Edition.

## Conventions and Style

**Varying Syntax for Effect** Writers often vary their **syntax**, or the structures of their sentences, to achieve particular effects. In doing so, they may even choose to deviate from the conventions of standard English grammar. Ambrose Bierce, for example, employs a device known as **asyndeton**—the omission of a coordinating conjunction, such as *and* or *or*, where one would normally appear—to reinforce the stream-of-consciousness feel of Section III of "An Occurrence at Owl Creek Bridge."

Consider this excerpt from the story:

> *He looked at the forest on the bank of the stream, saw the individual trees, the leaves and the veining of each leaf—saw the very insects upon them: the locusts, the brilliant-bodied flies, the gray spiders stretching their webs from twig to twig.* (paragraph 20)

Typically, the coordinating conjunction *and* would precede the underlined word. Bierce's choice to employ asyndeton, however, speeds up the rhythm of the passage. The reader gets the sense that the narrator is listing each creature just as it catches Farquhar's eye—that the reader is experiencing Farquhar's world at the very moment that he is.

### Read It

1. Work individually. Read these examples of Bierce's use of asyndeton in "An Occurrence at Owl Creek Bridge." In each sentence, mark where Bierce has chosen to omit a coordinating conjunction.

   a. The humming of the gnats that danced above the eddies of the stream, the beating of the dragonflies' wings, the strokes of the water spiders' legs, like oars which had lifted their boat—all these made audible music.

   b. A rising sheet of water curved over him, fell down upon him, blinded him, strangled him!

   c. It looked like diamonds, rubies, emeralds; he could think of nothing beautiful which it did not resemble.

   d. The trees upon the bank were giant garden plants; he noted a definite order in their arrangement, inhaled the fragrance of their blooms.

2. **Connect to Style** Reread paragraph 21 of "An Occurrence at Owl Creek Bridge," and identify the sentence in which Bierce employs asyndeton. Then, discuss with your group how the syntax of this sentence contributes to Bierce's stream-of-consciousness narration.

### Write It

**Notebook** Write a one-paragraph stream-of-consciousness narrative. Use asyndeton in at least one of your sentences. Indicate where you have omitted any coordinating conjunctions.



STANDARDS

**Language**

- Apply the understanding that usage is a matter of convention, can change over time, and is sometimes contested.
- Vary syntax for effect, consulting references for guidance as needed; apply an understanding of syntax to the study of complex texts when reading.



DIGITAL PERSPECTIVES

## Conventions and Style

**Varying Syntax for Effect** Tell students that some writers, such as Bierce, achieve powerful effects by using unusual syntax that sounds more like natural speech.

For more support, see **Conventions and Style: Varying Syntax for Effect**

### Read It

1. **a.** Bierce has omitted the conjunction "and" before the phrase "the strokes of the water spiders' legs."

   **b.** Bierce has omitted the conjunction "and" before the phrase "strangled him."

   **c.** Bierce has omitted the conjunction "and" before the word "emeralds."

   **d.** Bierce has omitted the conjunction "and" before the phrase "inhaled their blooms."

2. Students should discuss the first sentence of the paragraph.

### Write It

Responses will vary by group. Make sure that the action in the narratives is clear, regardless of the style chosen. Confirm that students have correctly used asyndeton.

### FORMATIVE ASSESSMENT

#### Conventions and Style

**If** students are struggling to identify the omission of coordinating conjunctions, **then** practice with simpler sentences that follow this pattern.

For Reteach and Practice, see **Conventions and Style: Varying Syntax for Effect (RP).**

#### Selection Test

Administer the "An Occurrence at Owl Creek Bridge" Selection Test, which is available in both print and digital formats online in Assessments.

# The Jilting of Granny Weatherall

**AUDIO SUMMARIES**
Audio summaries of "The Jilting of Granny Weatherall" are available online in both English and Spanish in the Interactive Teacher's Edition or Unit Resources. Assigning these summaries prior to reading the selection may help students build additional background knowledge and set a context for their first read.

## Summary

In Katherine Anne Porter's short story, "The Jilting of Granny Weatherall," eighty-year old Granny is dying, although she is unaware of how sick she is. She is tough and independent and resents the doctor's condescending tone. She wishes her daughter Cornelia would leave her alone. The old woman thinks about the next day's work. She thinks about death and she remembers the time she was jilted by a man she was supposed to marry. Many family members surround her at her bedside. The doctor returns and Father Connolly arrives, too. Granny starts to have trouble hearing and no one can understand what she's saying. She wants to see George, the man who jilted her. She would want to tell him that in spite of his cruelty she has lived a wonderful life. Granny finally realizes that she is dying. She looks for a sign from God, but gets none. She thinks about being jilted once more and then, she takes her last breath.

### Insight

The story illustrates the cost of building up walls to protect ourselves from pain. Granny Weatherall is strong, but she is also resentful and angry and dies that way.

ESSENTIAL QUESTION:
What do stories reveal about the human condition?

## Connection to Essential Question

The story reveals something true about the human condition: that while walls may protect us from pain, they also make it impossible to feel joy.

SMALL-GROUP LEARNING PERFORMANCE TASK
Present a stream-of-consciousness narrative based on this idea: *The day felt as if it would never end.*

UNIT PERFORMANCE-BASED ASSESSMENT
How does a fictional character or characters respond to life-changing news?

## Connection to Performance Tasks

**Small-Group Learning Task** The story is in part a stream-of-consciousness narrative, which may help students prepare for the task. The reader hears all of the intimate thoughts of a dying and confused old woman.

**Unit Performance-Based Assessment** The central experience recounted in the story—the jilting—shows a character reacting to a life-changing event. Granny lives her life with the reminder of this painful event.

DIGITAL PERSPECTIVES

 Audio  Video  Document  Annotation Highlights  EL Highlights 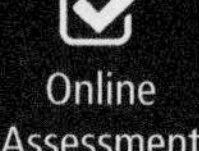 Online Assessment

## LESSON RESOURCES

| | Making Meaning | Language Development | Effective Expression |
|---|---|---|---|
| **Lesson** | **First Read**<br>**Close Read**<br>**Analyze the Text**<br>**Analyze Craft and Structure** | **Concept Vocabulary**<br>**Word Study**<br>**Author's Style** | **Writing to Compare** |
| **Instructional Standards** | **RL.10** By the end of grade 11, read and comprehend literature . . .<br>**L.4.b** Identify and correctly use patterns of word changes . . .<br>**RL.5** Analyze how an author's choices . . . | **L.4.b** Identify and correctly use patterns of word changes . . .<br>**RL.4** Determine the meaning of words and phrases . . .<br>**L.5** Demonstrate understanding of figurative language . . . | **W.2** Write informative/explanatory texts . . .<br>**RL.5** Analyze how an author's choices . . .<br>**SL.6** Adapt speech to a variety of contexts and tasks . . . |
| **STUDENT RESOURCES** | | | |
| Available online in the Interactive Student Edition or Unit Resources | Selection Audio<br>First-Read Guide: Fiction<br>Close-Read Guide: Fiction | Word Network | Evidence Log |
| **TEACHER RESOURCES** | | | |
| **Selection Resources** Available online in the Interactive Teacher's Edition or Unit Resources | Audio Summaries<br>Annotation Highlights<br>EL Highlights<br>The Jilting of Granny Weatherall: Text Questions<br>English Language Support Lesson: Similes and Metaphors<br>Analyze Craft and Structure: Narrative Structure | Concept Vocabulary and Word Study<br>Author's Style: Figurative Language | Writing to Compare: Oral Presentation |
| **Reteach/Practice (RP)** Available online in the Interactive Teacher's Edition or Unit Resources | Analyze Craft and Structure: Narrative Structure (RP) | Word Study: Greek Prefix *dys-* (RP)<br>Author's Style: Figurative Language (RP) | |
| **Assessment** Available online in Assessments | Selection Test | | |
| **My Resources** | A Unit 6 Answer Key is available online and in the Interactive Teacher's Edition. | | |

# Reading Support

| Text Complexity Rubric: The Jilting of Granny Weatherall | |
|---|---|
| **Quantitative Measures** | |
| **Lexile** 780 **Text Length** 3,861 words | |
| **Qualitative Measures** | |
| Knowledge Demands ①—❷—③—④—⑤ | The story focuses on the last hours of a woman's life, including her memories of many years. |
| Structure ①—②—③—❹—⑤ | The story is presented from the dying woman's perspective and the events are clouded by her confusion and exhaustion. |
| Language Conventionality and Clarity ①—②—❸—④—⑤ | The third-person narrative complicates the texture of the story. Though the vocabulary is not difficult, some words are above-level, and sentences are somewhat ornate with a lot of figurative language. |
| Levels of Meaning/Purpose ①—②—③—❹—⑤ | Multiple levels of meaning. The story describes an aging woman who, after having lived with hurt feelings all her life, nears death and still cannot let go of her pain. The text touches on aging, time, memory, the volatility of human emotion, and death. |

DECIDE AND PLAN

## English Language Support

Provide English Learners with support for language and meaning as they read the selection.

**Language** Encourage the students to consider what makes Granny Weatherall's language and voice unique. Discuss the method of the author's writing style and how she moves among voices to show Granny Weatherall's volatile emotional and mental state.

**Meaning** Ask the students to think about the action at the end of the story, and to discuss what evidence they may find in the text that supports their opinions. Then have them talk about which is more frightening to Granny, death or suffering. Discuss whether she is afraid to die or just afraid to suffer.

## Strategic Support

Provide students with strategic support to ensure that they can successfully read the text.

**Language** Work with students to locate where the text demonstrates true third-person perspective, and then help them point out where the text slips, for brief periods, into first-person. Talk about how Porter's method helps to portray Granny Weatherall's desperation; ask students to think about other ways you could portray such a person's deteriorating mental state.

**Meaning** Talk to the students about the title, and what evidence the title of the story may hold for the story's ultimate meaning. Granny Weatherall seems very unhappy, but finding out what she is most upset about will bring clarity to the story's ultimate goal. Ask students to determine who jilted Granny Weatherall, and why she could not get over it.

## Challenge

Provide students who need to be challenged with ideas for how they can go beyond a simple interpretation of the text.

**Text Analysis** Ask students to analyze the activities of Cornelia and the doctor. Find different examples of confusion in the text and explore them with students. In paragraph 31, Cornelia puts her head on the pillow and then makes "strange shapes" with her mouth. Ask students why the author may have chosen not to directly say that Granny is deaf in one ear.

**Written Response** Ask students to think about someone they may know who is old and dealing with infirmity and the idea of mortality. Ask if they think a story like this could help other people deal with losing grandparents. Have students write a response to the story based on their own ideas of aging and caring for the sick.

TEACH

## Read and Respond

Have groups read the selection and complete the Making Meaning, Language Development, and Effective Expression activities.

# Standards Support Through Teaching and Learning Cycle

## IDENTIFY NEEDS

Analyze results of the Beginning-of-Year Assessment, focusing on the items relating to Unit 6. Also take into consideration student performance to this point and your observations of where particular students struggle.

## DECIDE AND PLAN

- If students have performed poorly on items matching these standards, then provide selection scaffolds before assigning them the on-level lesson provided in the Student Edition.
- If students have done well on the Beginning-of-Year Assessment, then challenge them to keep progressing and learning by giving them opportunities to practice the skills in depth.
- Use the Selection Resources listed on the Planning pages for "The Jilting of Granny Weatherall" to help students continually improve their ability to master the standards.

**Instructional Standards: The Jilting of Granny Weatherall**

| | Catching Up | This Year | Looking Forward |
|---|---|---|---|
| **Reading** | You may wish to administer the **Analyze Craft and Structure: Narrative Structure (RP)** worksheet to help student understand this narrative technique. | **RL.5** Analyze how an author's choices concerning how to structure specific parts of a text contribute to its overall structure and meaning as well as its aesthetic impact. | Challenge pairs to analyze the stream of consciousness in paragraph 26. Define what the technique is and share your definitions with the class. |
| **Language** | You may wish to administer the **Author's Style: Figurative Language (RP)** worksheet to review types of figurative devices with students.<br>Review the **Word Study: Greek Prefix *dys-* (RP)** worksheet to familiarize students with this prefix. | **L.5** Demonstrate understanding of figurative language, word relationships, and nuances in word meaning.<br>**L.4.b** Identify and correctly use patterns of word changes that indicate different meanings or parts of speech. | Challenge students to find and explain figurative language in other fiction.<br>Have students locate other Greek, Latin, and Anglo-Saxon suffixes they recognize in the text. |

## ANALYZE AND REVISE

- Analyze student work for evidence of student learning.
- Identify whether or not students have met the expectations in the standards.
- Identify implications for future instruction.

## TEACH

Implement the planned lesson, and gather evidence of student learning.

# FACILITATING

## Jump Start

**FIRST READ** Engage groups in a discussion using these prompts: *If you knew you were dying, what would you think about? Would you review your life to decide if it had been a good one? Would you have regrets, and if so, about what?* This discussion about mortality sets the context for reading "The Jilting of Granny Weatherall."

## The Jilting of Granny Weatherall

How did Granny Weatherall approach death? What issues made her unwilling to leave her life? Modeling these and other questions readers might ask will bring "The Jilting of Granny Weatherall" to life and connect it to the Performance Task question. Selection audio and print capability for the selection are available in the Interactive Teacher's Edition.

## Concept Vocabulary

Have groups briefly discuss the three concept vocabulary words. Have they encountered any of the words before? Do they recognize the prefix, suffix, or base word of any of the concept vocabulary words?

Have groups consider the strategy of identifying familiar word parts and discuss its advantages and disadvantages.

## FIRST READ

Have students perform the steps of the first read independently:

NOTICE: You may want to encourage students to notice what is happening in the story and to whom it is happening.

ANNOTATE: Remind students to mark passages that shed light on Granny's concerns as she lies in bed.

CONNECT: Encourage students to compare Granny's concerns with those of other elderly people they know.

RESPOND: Students will demonstrate their understanding of the text by answering questions and writing a summary.

Point out to students that they will perform the first three steps concurrently as they are doing their first read. They will complete the Respond step after they have finished the first read. You may wish to print copies of the **First-Read Guide: Fiction** for students to use.

MAKING MEANING

### Comparing Texts

AN OCCURRENCE AT OWL CREEK BRIDGE

You will now read "The Jilting of Granny Weatherall." First, complete the first-read and close-read activities. Then, compare the narrative structures in "The Jilting of Granny Weatherall" and "An Occurrence at Owl Creek Bridge."

THE JILTING OF GRANNY WEATHERALL

**About the Author**

The life of **Katherine Anne Porter** (1890–1980) spanned World War I, the Great Depression, World War II, and the rise of the nuclear age. For Porter, her fiction was an "effort to grasp the meaning of those threats, to trace them to their sources, and to understand the logic of this majestic and terrible failure of the life of man in the Western world." Her stories often feature characters at pivotal moments, who face dramatic change, the constricting bonds of family, and the weight of the past.

# The Jilting of Granny Weatherall

### Concept Vocabulary

As you perform your first read of "The Jilting of Granny Weatherall," you will encounter these words.

clammy hypodermic dyspepsia

**Familiar Word Parts** Separating an unfamiliar word into its parts—roots, prefixes, or suffixes—can often help you determine its meaning.

**Example:** The root *-circ-* means "ring" or "circle." Thus, something that is *circular* has a ringlike shape, and something that *circulates* moves in a ringlike path. When you come across an unfamiliar word that contains the root *-circ-*, such as *circuitous,* you know that it has properties that relate to a circle. Even if you cannot identify a word's exact definition, you can approximate the meaning well enough to keep reading. *Circuitous* is an adjective that means "roundabout; indirect."

Apply your knowledge of familiar word parts and other vocabulary strategies to determine the meanings of unfamiliar words you encounter during your first read.

### First Read FICTION

Apply these strategies as you conduct your first read. You will have an opportunity to complete a close read after your first read.

NOTICE *whom* the story is about, *what* happens, *where* and *when* it happens, and why those involved react as they do.

ANNOTATE by marking vocabulary and key passages you want to revisit

CONNECT ideas within the selection to what you already know and what you have already read.

RESPOND by completing the Comprehension Check and by writing a brief summary of the selection.

**STANDARDS**

**Reading Literature**
By the end of grade 11, read and comprehend literature, including stories, dramas, and poems, nonfiction in the grades 11–CCR text complexity band proficiently, with scaffolding as needed at the high end of the range.

**Language**
Identify and correctly use patterns of word changes that indicate different meanings or parts of speech.





## VOCABULARY DEVELOPMENT

**Word Analysis** Point out to students that a story's title often gives the reader insight into the story's theme. Have them scrutinize the title of the story. Make sure students understand the meaning of *jilting*. The have them look at Granny's last name. Have students identify the words that make up this compound word. Have them suggest what Granny's last name might imply about her.

Finally, have students return to the title as a whole. What is strange or unusual about it? Help students understand how odd it is to think of an older woman—a granny—being jilted.

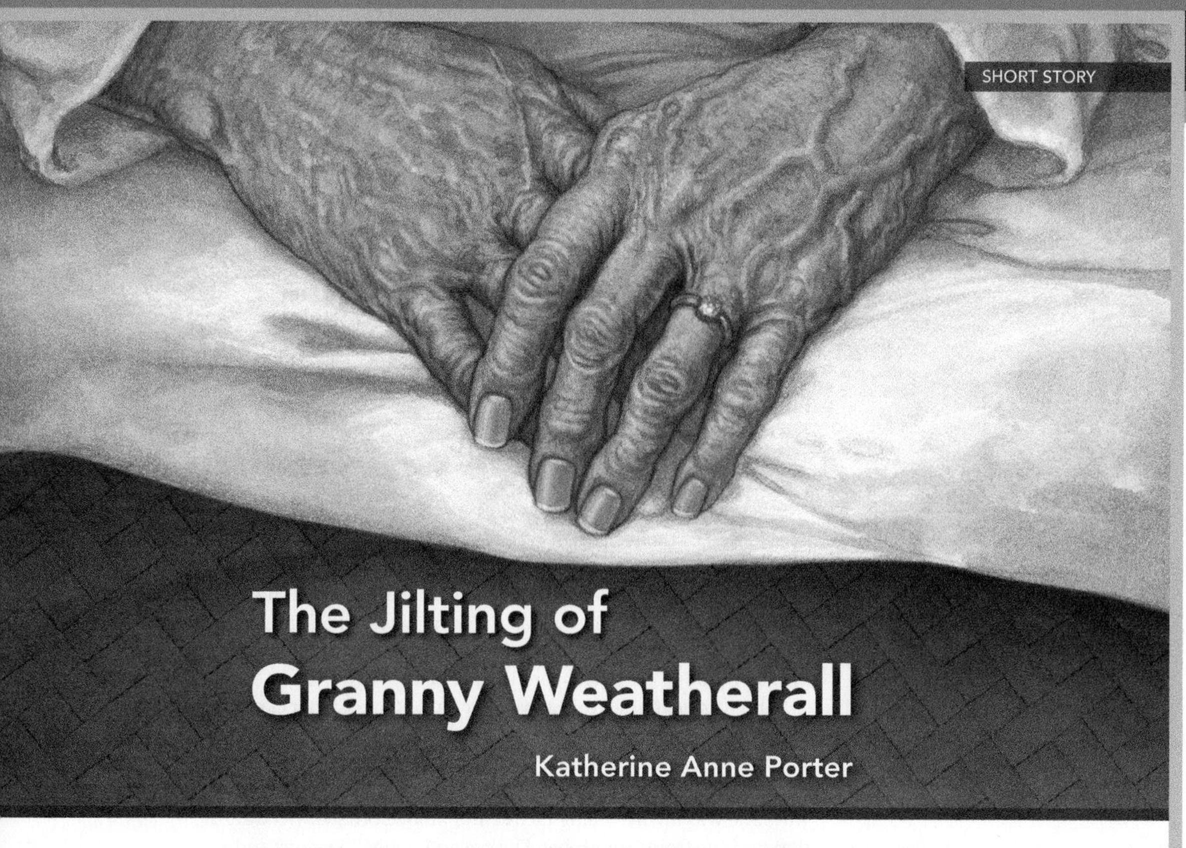


# The Jilting of Granny Weatherall

Katherine Anne Porter

DIGITAL PERSPECTIVES

## BACKGROUND

Katherine Anne Porter's view of life and the fiction she wrote were shaped by a sense of disillusionment resulting from World War I, the despair of the Great Depression, and the World War II horrors of Nazism and nuclear warfare. Sometimes, as in the novel *Ship of Fools*, Porter focuses on political issues such as Nazism. In contrast, works such as "The Jilting of Granny Weatherall" pinpoint the dissolving families and communities of the modern age.

SCAN FOR MULTIMEDIA

1 She flicked her wrist neatly out of Doctor Harry's pudgy careful fingers and pulled the sheet up to her chin. The brat ought to be in knee breeches. Doctoring around the country with spectacles on his nose! "Get along now, take your schoolbooks and go. There's nothing wrong with me."

2 Doctor Harry spread a warm paw like a cushion on her forehead where the forked green vein danced and made her eyelids twitch. "Now, now, be a good girl, and we'll have you up in no time."

3 "That's no way to speak to a woman nearly eighty years old just because she's down. I'd have you respect your elders, young man."

4 "Well, Missy, excuse me," Doctor Harry patted her cheek. "But I've got to warn you, haven't I? You're a marvel, but you must be careful or you're going to be good and sorry."

NOTES



## FACILITATING SMALL-GROUP CLOSE READING

**CLOSE READ: Short Story** As groups perform the close read, circulate and offer support as needed.

- Remind students that when they read a short story, they should identify the main characters. The plot of some stories is not as important as the characters within the story.
- If a group is confused about why particular thoughts or events are important, remind them to think about the time period and social norms reflected in the selection.
- Challenge groups to determine the theme of the text and the specific details that develop and refine the theme.

CLOSER LOOK

## Analyze Character

Circulate among groups as students conduct their close read. Suggest that groups close read paragraphs 7–17. Encourage them to talk about the annotations that they mark. If needed, provide the following support.

**ANNOTATE:** Have students mark details in these paragraphs that reveal aspects of Granny Weatherall's character, or work with small groups to have students participate while you highlight them together.

**QUESTION:** Guide students to consider what these details might tell them. Ask what a reader can infer from Granny's response to Doctor Harry, her opinion of Cornelia, and her ideas about order, and accept student responses.

**Possible:** response: Granny argues with Doctor Harry, she has a low opinion of Cornelia, and she appreciates order in the household.

**CONCLUDE:** Help students to formulate conclusions about the importance of these details in the text. Ask students why the author might have included these details.

**Possible response:** These details about Granny Weatherall reveal that she is a feisty, independent old woman. She is annoyed by Cornelia's solicitousness, and she likes order in the house.

Remind students that **characterization** is the way a writer develops and reveals a character's personality and temperament. With **direct characterization**, a writer simply tells us what a character is like. With **indirect characterization**, the writer shows us a character's traits, using some or all of the following methods:

- showing a character's actions and behavior
- presenting a character's words and thoughts
- describing a character's physical appearance
- revealing what other characters say or think about a character
- showing how a character affects other people

NOTES

5 "Don't tell me what I'm going to be. I'm on my feet now, morally speaking. It's Cornelia. I had to go to bed to get rid of her."

6 Her bones felt loose, and floated around in her skin, and Doctor Harry floated like a balloon around the foot of the bed. He floated and pulled down his waistcoat and swung his glasses on a cord. "Well, stay where you are, it certainly can't hurt you."

7 "Get along and doctor your sick," said Granny Weatherall. "Leave a well woman alone. I'll call for you when I want you . . . Where were you forty years ago when I pulled through milk leg[1] and double pneumonia? You weren't even born. Don't let Cornelia lead you on," she shouted, because Doctor Harry appeared to float up to the ceiling and out. "I pay my own bills, and I don't throw my money away on nonsense!"

8 She meant to wave good-bye, but it was too much trouble. Her eyes closed of themselves, it was like a dark curtain drawn around the bed. The pillow rose and floated under her, pleasant as a hammock in a light wind. She listened to the leaves rustling outside the window. No, somebody was swishing newspapers: no, Cornelia and Doctor Harry were whispering together. She leaped broad awake, thinking they whispered in her ear.

9 "She was never like this, never like this!" "Well, what can we expect?" "Yes, eighty years old. . . ."

10 Well, and what if she was? She still had ears. It was like Cornelia to whisper around doors. She always kept things secret in such a public way. She was always being tactful and kind. Cornelia was dutiful; that was the trouble with her. Dutiful and good: "So good and dutiful," said Granny, "that I'd like to spank her." She saw herself spanking Cornelia and making a fine job of it.

11 "What'd you say, Mother?"

12 Granny felt her face tying up in hard knots.

13 "Can't a body think, I'd like to know?"

14 "I thought you might want something."

15 "I do. I want a lot of things. First off, go away and don't whisper."

16 She lay and drowsed, hoping in her sleep that the children would keep out and let her rest a minute. It had been a long day. Not that she was tired. It was always pleasant to snatch a minute now and then. There was always so much to be done, let me see: tomorrow.

17 Tomorrow was far away and there was nothing to trouble about. Things were finished somehow when the time came; thank God there was always a little margin over for peace: then a person could spread out the plan of life and tuck in the edges orderly. It was good to have everything clean and folded away, with the hair brushes and tonic bottles sitting straight on the white embroidered linen: the day started without fuss and the pantry shelves laid out with rows of jelly glasses and brown jugs and white stone-china jars with blue whirligigs and words painted on them: coffee, tea, sugar, ginger,

1. **milk leg** painful swelling of the leg.





DIGITAL PERSPECTIVES

**Illuminating the Text** Review paragraph 3. Tell students that in 1930, when this story was written, life expectancy was much lower than it is today. Have students research on the Internet to find out the life expectancies of Americans in 1930 and in the present. Ask students to discuss whether an elderly person in Granny Weatherall's state of mind would be considered normal today. Students may want to propose pros and cons for this argument.

DIGITAL PERSPECTIVES 

cinnamon, allspice: and the bronze clock with the lion on top nicely dusted off. The dust that lion could collect in twenty-four hours! The box in the attic with all those letters tied up, well, she'd have to go through that tomorrow. All those letters—George's letters and John's letters and her letters to them both—lying around for the children to find afterwards made her uneasy. Yes, that would be tomorrow's business. No use to let them know how silly she had been once.

18 While she was rummaging around she found death in her mind and it felt clammy and unfamiliar. She had spent so much time preparing for death there was no need for bringing it up again. Let it take care of itself now. When she was sixty she had felt very old, finished, and went around making farewell trips to see her children and grandchildren, with a secret in her mind: This is the very last of your mother, children! Then she made her will and came down with a long fever. That was all just a notion like a lot of other things, but it was lucky too, for she had once for all got over the idea of dying for a long time. Now she couldn't be worried. She hoped she had better sense now. Her father had lived to be one hundred and two years old and had drunk a noggin of strong hot toddy on his last birthday. He told the reporters it was his daily habit, and he owed his long life to that. He had made quite a scandal and was very pleased about it. She believed she'd just plague Cornelia a little.

19 "Cornelia! Cornelia!" No footsteps, but a sudden hand on her cheek. "Bless you, where have you been?"

20 "Here, mother."

21 "Well, Cornelia, I want a noggin of hot toddy."

22 "Are you cold, darling?"

23 "I'm chilly, Cornelia. Lying in bed stops the circulation. I must have told you that a thousand times."

24 Well, she could just hear Cornelia telling her husband that Mother was getting a little childish and they'd have to humor her. The thing that most annoyed her was that Cornelia thought she was deaf, dumb, and blind. Little hasty glances and tiny gestures tossed around her and over her head saying, "Don't cross her, let her have her way, she's eighty years old," and she sitting there as if she lived in a thin glass cage. Sometimes Granny almost made up her mind to pack up and move back to her own house where nobody could remind her every minute that she was old. Wait, wait, Cornelia, till your own children whisper behind your back!

25 In her day she had kept a better house and had got more work done. She wasn't too old yet for Lydia to be driving eighty miles for advice when one of the children jumped the track, and Jimmy still dropped in and talked things over: "Now, Mammy, you've a good business head, I want to know what you think of this? . . ." Old. Cornelia couldn't change the furniture around without asking. Little things, little things! They had been so sweet when they were little. Granny wished the old days were back again with the children young and everything to be done over. It had been a hard pull, but not too

NOTES

Mark familiar word parts or indicate another strategy you used that helped you determine meaning.

**clammy** (KLAM ee) *adj.*

MEANING:





## Concept Vocabulary

**CLAMMY** If groups are struggling to define the word *clammy* in paragraph 18, point out the familiar word part, *clam*. Most students know that a clam is moist and soft.

**Possible response:** *Clammy* means "moist, soft." It is generally used to describe something negative and uncomfortable.

## PERSONALIZE FOR LANGUAGE

### Strategic Support

**Critical Details** Direct students' attention to the last part of paragraph 17, beginning with "The box in the attic . . . " Ask students to identify which letter made Granny uneasy. Ask them to suggest who George and John might be. Then have students discuss the meaning and impact of the paragraph's last line.

NOTES

much for her. When she thought of all the food she had cooked, and all the clothes she had cut and sewed, and all the gardens she had made—well, the children showed it. There they were, made out of her, and they couldn't get away from that. Sometimes she wanted to see John again and point to them and say, Well, I didn't do so badly, did I? But that would have to wait. That was for tomorrow. She used to think of him as a man, but now all the children were older than their father, and he would be a child beside her if she saw him now. It seemed strange and there was something wrong in the idea. Why, he couldn't possibly recognize her. She had fenced in a hundred acres once, digging the post holes herself and clamping the wires with just a negro boy to help. That changed a woman. John would be looking for a young woman with the peaked Spanish comb in her hair and the painted fan. Digging post holes changed a woman. Riding country roads in the winter when women had their babies was another thing: sitting up nights with sick horses and sick children and hardly ever losing one. John, I hardly ever lost one of them! John would see that in a minute, that would be something he could understand, she wouldn't have to explain anything!

26 It made her feel like rolling up her sleeves and putting the whole place to rights again. No matter if Cornelia was determined to be everywhere at once, there were a great many things left undone on this place. She would start tomorrow and do them. It was good to be strong enough for everything, even if all you made melted and changed and slipped under your hands, so that by the time you finished you almost forgot what you were working for. What was it I set out to do? she asked herself intently, but she could not remember. A fog rose over the valley, she saw it marching across the creek swallowing the trees and moving up the hill like an army of ghosts. Soon it would be at the near edge of the orchard, and then it was time to go in and light the lamps. Come in, children, don't stay out in the night air.

27 Lighting the lamps had been beautiful. The children huddled up to her and breathed like little calves waiting at the bars in the twilight. Their eyes followed the match and watched the flame rise and settle in a blue curve, then they moved away from her. The lamp was lit, they didn't have to be scared and hang on to mother any more. Never, never, never more. God, for all my life I thank Thee. Without Thee, my God, I could never have done it. Hail Mary, full of grace.

28 I want you to pick all the fruit this year and see that nothing is wasted. There's always someone who can use it. Don't let good things rot for want of using. You waste life when you waste good food. Don't let things get lost. It's bitter to lose things. Now, don't let me get to thinking, not when I am tired and taking a little nap before supper. . . .

29 The pillow rose about her shoulders and pressed against her heart and the memory was being squeezed out of it: oh, push down the pillow, somebody: it would smother her if she tried to hold it. Such a





Additional **English Language Support** is available in the Interactive Teacher's Edition.

## CROSS-CURRICULAR PERSPECTIVES

**Science** Review paragraphs 26 and 27 and point out to students that Granny's thought process seems confused. Tell students that dementia is a medical illness that causes a person to be unable to think clearly. The person often cannot understand what is real and what is not. Dementia is more common among older people.

Have students conduct research to find out more specific symptoms of dementia. Then have them discuss whether they believe that Granny Weatherall suffered from dementia, or if her illness just mimicked the signs of dementia.

fresh breeze blowing and such a green day with no threats in it. But he had not come, just the same. What does a woman do when she has put on the white veil and set out the white cake for a man and he doesn't come? She tried to remember. No, I swear he never harmed me but in that. He never harmed me but in that . . . and what if he did? There was the day, the day, but a whirl of dark smoke rose and covered it, crept up and over into the bright field where everything was planted so carefully in orderly rows. That was hell, she knew hell when she saw it. For sixty years she had prayed against remembering him and against losing her soul in the deep pit of hell, and now the two things were mingled in one and the thought of him was a smoky cloud from hell that moved and crept in her head when she had just got rid of Doctor Harry and was trying to rest a minute. Wounded vanity, Ellen, said a sharp voice in the top of her mind. Don't let your wounded vanity get the upper hand of you. Plenty of girls get jilted. You were jilted, weren't you? Then stand up to it. Her eyelids wavered and let in streamers of blue-gray light like tissue paper over

NOTES

DIGITAL PERSPECTIVES

CLOSER LOOK

## Infer Key Ideas

Circulate among groups as students conduct their close read. Suggest that groups close read paragraph 29. Encourage them to talk about the annotations that they mark. If needed, provide the following support.

**ANNOTATE:** Have students mark details in the paragraph that show how Granny Weatherall felt about her jilting sixty years ago, or work with small groups to have students participate while you highlight them together.

**QUESTION:** Guide students to consider what these details might tell them. Ask what a reader can infer from Granny's recollections, and accept student responses.

**Possible response:** Granny Weatherall is still suffering deeply from this jilting.

**CONCLUDE:** Help students to formulate conclusions about the importance of these details in the text. Ask students why the author might have included these details.

**Possible response:** The jilting is a key idea in the story. It destroyed the order that was essential to Granny. It made her feel that she had lost her soul, and maybe her faith as well.

Remind students that authors often require that readers infer **key ideas.** By adding details that are not explained directly, the author makes the reader fill in the gaps that the text leaves out.

PERSONALIZE FOR LEARNING

### English Language Support

**Text Analysis** Point out to students that much of paragraph 29 takes place in Granny Weatherall's mind. Have small groups of students examine the paragraph, sentence by sentence. Have them describe what is happening in each sentence. For example, in sentence 1, Granny feels that her pillow is pressing against her heart, so hard that a long-kept memory is forced out. In addition to describing each sentence, have students note whether the action is outside or within Granny Weatherall's mind. **ALL LEVELS**

## Concept Vocabulary

**HYPODERMIC** If groups are struggling to define the word *hypodermic* in paragraph 40, point out the familiar word parts *hypo* which means "under," and *derm*, which means "skin."

**Possible response:** A *hypodermic* is "something to be inserted under the skin." This is often used to describe a needle.

NOTES

her eyes. She must get up and pull the shades down or she'd never sleep. She was in bed again and the shades were not down. How could that happen? Better turn over, hide from the light, sleeping in the light gave you nightmares. "Mother, how do you feel now?" and a stinging wetness on her forehead. But I don't like having my face washed in cold water!

30 Hapsy? George? Lydia? Jimmy? No, Cornelia, and her features were swollen and full of little puddles. "They're coming, darling, they'll all be here soon." Go wash your face, child, you look funny.

31 Instead of obeying, Cornelia knelt down and put her head on the pillow. She seemed to be talking but there was no sound. "Well, are you tongue-tied? Whose birthday is it? Are you going to give a party?"

32 Cornelia's mouth moved urgently in strange shapes. "Don't do that, you bother me, daughter."

33 "Oh, no, Mother. Oh, no. . . ."

34 Nonsense. It was strange about children. They disputed your every word. "No what, Cornelia?"

35 "Here's Doctor Harry."

36 "I won't see that boy again. He just left five minutes ago."

37 "That was this morning, Mother. It's night now. Here's the nurse."

38 "This is Doctor Harry, Mrs. Weatherall. I never saw you look so young and happy!"

39 "Ah, I'll never be young again—but I'd be happy if they'd let me lie in peace and get rested."

40 She thought she spoke up loudly, but no one answered. A warm weight on her forehead, a warm bracelet on her wrist, and a breeze went on whispering, trying to tell her something. A shuffle of leaves in the everlasting hand of God, He blew on them and they danced and rattled. "Mother, don't mind, we're going to give you a little **hypodermic**." "Look here, daughter, how do ants get in this bed? I saw sugar ants yesterday." Did you send for Hapsy too?

Mark familiar word parts or indicate another strategy you used that helped you determine meaning.

**hypodermic** (hy puh DUR mihk) *n.*

MEANING:

41 It was Hapsy she really wanted. She had to go a long way back through a great many rooms to find Hapsy standing with a baby on her arm. She seemed to herself to be Hapsy also, and the baby on Hapsy's arm was Hapsy and himself and herself, all at once, and there was no surprise in the meeting. Then Hapsy melted from within and turned flimsy as gray gauze and the baby was a gauzy shadow, and Hapsy came up close and said, "I thought you'd never come," and looked at her very searchingly and said, "You haven't changed a bit!" They leaned forward to kiss, when Cornelia began whispering from a long way off, "Oh, is there anything you want to tell me? Is there anything I can do for you?"

42 Yes, she had changed her mind after sixty years and she would like to see George. I want you to find George. Find him and be sure to tell him I forgot him. I want him to know I had my husband just the same and my children and my house like any other woman. A good house too and a good husband that I loved and fine children out of him.





## WriteNow Analyze and Interpret

**Explanation** Direct students' attention to the second sentence in paragraph 40: "A warm weight on her forehead, a warm bracelet on her wrist, and a breeze went on whispering, trying to tell her something." Point out that the author describes what Granny Weatherall is sensing—but what is really happening in this sentence? Remind students that the author may be trying to convey Granny's confusion. Have students write a brief paragraph explaining what an observer in the room would be seeing and hearing.

DIGITAL PERSPECTIVES

NOTES

Better than I hoped for even. Tell him I was given back everything he took away and more. Oh, no, oh, God, no, there was something else besides the house and the man and the children. Oh, surely they were not all? What was it? Something not given back. . . . Her breath crowded down under her ribs and grew into a monstrous frightening shape with cutting edges; it bored up into her head, and the agony was unbelievable: Yes, John, get the Doctor now, no more talk, my time has come.

43 When this one was born it should be the last. The last. It should have been born first, for it was the one she had truly wanted. Everything came in good time. Nothing left out, left over. She was strong, in three days she would be as well as ever. Better. A woman needed milk in her to have her full health.

44 "Mother, do you hear me?"

45 "I've been telling you—"

46 "Mother, Father Connolly's here."

47 "I went to Holy Communion only last week. Tell him I'm not so sinful as all that."

48 "Father just wants to speak to you."

49 He could speak as much as he pleased. It was like him to drop in and inquire about her soul as if it were a teething baby, and then stay on for a cup of tea and a round of cards and gossip. He always had a funny story of some sort, usually about an Irishman who made his little mistakes and confessed them, and the point lay in some absurd thing he would blurt out in the confessional showing his struggles between native piety and original sin. Granny felt easy about her soul. Cornelia, where are your manners? Give Father Connolly a chair. She had her secret comfortable understanding with a few favorite saints who cleared a straight road to God for her. All as surely signed and sealed as the papers for the new Forty Acres. Forever . . . heirs and assigns[2] forever. Since the day the wedding cake was not cut, but thrown out and wasted. The whole bottom dropped out of the world, and there she was blind and sweating with nothing under her feet and the walls falling away. His hand had caught her under the breast, she had not fallen, there was the freshly polished floor with the green rug on it, just as before. He had cursed like a sailor's parrot and said, "I'll kill him for you." Don't lay a hand on him, for my sake leave something to God. "Now, Ellen, you must believe what I tell you. . . ."

50 So there was nothing, nothing to worry about any more, except sometimes in the night one of the children screamed in a nightmare, and they both hustled out shaking and hunting for the matches and calling, "There, wait a minute, here we are!" John, get the doctor now, Hapsy's time has come. But there was Hapsy standing by the bed in a white cap. "Cornelia, tell Hapsy to take off her cap. I can't see her plain."

2. **assigns** *n.* people to whom property is transferred.





## CROSS-CURRICULAR PERSPECTIVES

**Humanities** Explain to students that Granny Weatherall is probably a member of the Catholic Church, as suggested by the references to Father Connolly and Holy Communion in paragraphs 46 and 47. Make sure that students understand that Father Connolly has come to administer the Anointing of the Sick to Granny Weatherall.

The Anointing of the Sick is one of the Seven Sacraments of the Catholic Church. Have students share what they know about this ritual or ask them to do research to find out more about the Seven Sacraments. Have them explain what each sacrament is, what the Anointing of the Sick used to be called, and why Granny Weatherall is ready to receive this sacrament.

NOTES

51 Her eyes opened very wide and the room stood out like a picture she had seen somewhere. Dark colors with the shadows rising towards the ceiling in long angles. The tall black dresser gleamed with nothing on it but John's picture, enlarged from a little one, with John's eyes very black when they should have been blue. You never saw him, so how do you know how he looked? But the man insisted the copy was perfect, it was very rich and handsome. For a picture, yes, but it's not my husband. The table by the bed had a linen cover and a candle and a crucifix. The light was blue from Cornelia's silk lampshades. No sort of light at all, just frippery. You had to live forty years with kerosene lamps to appreciate honest electricity. She felt very strong and she saw Doctor Harry with a rosy nimbus around him.

52 "You look like a saint, Doctor Harry, and I vow that's as near as you'll ever come to it."

53 "She's saying something."

54 "I heard you, Cornelia. What's all this carrying on?"

55 "Father Connolly's saying—"

56 Cornelia's voice staggered and bumped like a cart in a bad road. It rounded corners and turned back again and arrived nowhere. Granny stepped up in the cart very lightly and reached for the reins, but a man sat beside her and she knew him by his hands, driving

DIGITAL PERSPECTIVES

the cart. She did not look in his face, for she knew without seeing, but looked instead down the road where the trees leaned over and bowed to each other and a thousand birds were singing a Mass. She felt like singing too, but she put her hand in the bosom of her dress and pulled out a rosary, and Father Connolly murmured Latin in a very solemn voice and tickled her feet.[3] My God, will you stop that nonsense? I'm a married woman. What if he did run away and leave me to face the priest by myself? I found another a whole world better. I wouldn't have exchanged my husband for anybody except St. Michael[4] himself, and you may tell him that for me with a thank you in the bargain.

57 Light flashed on her closed eyelids, and a deep roaring shook her. Cornelia, is that lightning? I hear thunder. There's going to be a storm. Close all the windows. Call the children in. . . . "Mother, here we are, all of us." "Is that you, Hapsy?" "Oh, no. I'm Lydia. We drove as fast as we could." Their faces drifted above her, drifted away. The rosary fell out of her hands and Lydia put it back. Jimmy tried to help, their hands fumbled together, and Granny closed two fingers around Jimmy's thumb. Beads wouldn't do, it must be something alive. She was so amazed her thoughts ran round and round. So, my dear Lord, this is my death and I wasn't even thinking about it. My children have come to see me die. But I can't, it's not time. Oh, I always hated surprises. I wanted to give Cornelia the amethyst set—Cornelia, you're to have the amethyst set, but Hapsy's to wear it when she wants, and, Doctor Harry, do shut up. Nobody sent for you. Oh, my dear Lord, do wait a minute. I meant to do something about the Forty Acres, Jimmy doesn't need it and Lydia will later on, with that worthless husband of hers. I meant to finish the altar cloth and send six bottles of wine to Sister Borgia for her **dyspepsia**. I want to send six bottles of wine to Sister Borgia, Father Connolly, now don't let me forget.

58 Cornelia's voice made short turns and tilted over and crashed. "Oh, Mother, oh, Mother, oh Mother. . . ."

59 "I'm not going, Cornelia. I'm taken by surprise. I can't go."

60 You'll see Hapsy again. What about her? "I thought you'd never come." Granny made a long journey outward, looking for Hapsy. What if I don't find her? What then? Her heart sank down and down, there was no bottom to death, she couldn't come to the end of it. The blue light from Cornelia's lampshade drew into a tiny point in the center of her brain, it flickered and winked like an eye, quietly it fluttered and dwindled. Granny lay curled down within herself, amazed and watchful, staring at the point of light that was herself; her body was now only a deeper mass of shadow in an endless darkness and this darkness would curl around the light and swallow it up. God, give a sign!

NOTES

Mark familiar word parts or indicate another strategy you used that helped you determine meaning.

**dyspepsia** (dihs PEHP see uh) *n.*

MEANING:

3. **murmured . . . feet** administered the last rites of the Catholic Church.
4. **St. Michael** one of the archangels.





## Concept Vocabulary

**DYSPEPSIA** If groups are struggling to define the word *dyspepsia* in paragraph 57, point out the familiar word parts *dys-*, meaning "bad," and *-peps-*, meaning "stomach."

**Possible response:** *Dyspepsia* must mean "indigestion."

CLOSER LOOK

## Interpreting a Symbol 

Circulate among groups as students conduct their close read. Suggest that groups close read paragraph 60. Encourage them to talk about the annotations that they mark. If needed, provide the following support.

**ANNOTATE:** Have students mark details in the paragraph that have to do with light and darkness, or work with small groups to have students participate while you highlight them together.

**QUESTION:** Guide students to consider what these details might tell them. Ask what a reader can infer from Porter's use of light, particularly blue light, and accept student responses.

**Possible response:** The blue light becomes a light in Granny's mind.

**CONCLUDE:** Help students to formulate conclusions about the importance of these details in the text. What does the blue light symbolize in the text?

**Possible response:** The blue light symbolizes life. Granny watches as that light dims in her mind. The light is contrasted with "endless darkness," which symbolizes death or the end of existence.

Remind students that **symbols** are objects that have their own meaning, but they also stand for something larger than themselves, usually an abstract idea. Some symbols are widely known; for example, the American flag symbolizes the United States. Authors also may create their own personal symbols by emphasizing a certain element in a literary work. The use of symbolism adds complex layers of meaning to a literary work.

PERSONALIZE FOR LEARNING

### Strategic Support

**Theme** Have students look at the last sentence of paragraph 60: "God, give a sign!" Have students discuss what Granny wanted God to give a sign about. Was Granny's wish granted? Have groups of students propose how faith in God relates to the theme in "The Jilting of Granny Weatherall."

# FACILITATING

## Comprehension Check

Possible responses:

1. Granny Weatherall is in her bed.
2. Granny's daughter, Cornelia, is taking care of her.
3. Because she thought that she was dying, Granny made farewell trips to each of her children.
4. George, her husband-to-be, jilted her at the altar.
5. Granny wants George to know she did just fine without him.
6. Granny Weatherall is sick and dying in bed. As she lies there, she reflects on her life, her family, and the fact that she was jilted on her wedding day. Once she realizes that she is dying, she asks God for a sign but does not receive one. Once again, she has been jilted.

## Research

**Research to Clarify** If students struggle to identify an unfamiliar detail, you may want to suggest the following topics: doctors making house calls, tonic bottles and jelly glasses, or lighting kerosene lamps. Some students may also be unfamiliar with an elderly person dying.

**Research to Explore** If students struggle to identify an aspect of the text to research, you may want to point out that the story has a rural setting. Many fewer Americans live in rural areas today than when Porter wrote this story. Students may want to research the changing demographics of American society between 1930 and the present.

NOTES

61 For the second time there was no sign. Again no bridegroom and the priest in the house. She could not remember any other sorrow because this grief wiped them all away. Oh, no, there's nothing more cruel than this—I'll never forgive it. She stretched herself with a deep breath and blew out the light. ❧

## Comprehension Check

**Complete the following items after you finish your first read. Review and clarify details with your group.**

**1.** Where is Granny Weatherall as she speaks to the doctor?

**2.** Who is taking care of Granny Weatherall as she is dying?

**3.** What journey did Granny Weatherall take when she was sixty years old?

**4.** What happened to Granny Weatherall sixty years earlier?

**5.** What does Granny Weatherall want George to know?

**6.** **Notebook** Confirm your understanding of the text by writing a summary.

## RESEARCH

**Research to Clarify** Choose at least one unfamiliar detail from the text. Briefly research that detail. In what way does the information you learned shed light on an aspect of the story?

**Research to Explore** Conduct research on an aspect of the text you find interesting. For example, you may want to learn about doctors' house calls—why they once were a widespread practice, why they are less common today, and whether they might again become popular. Share your findings with your group.





## PERSONALIZE FOR LEARNING

### Challenge

**Writing an Obituary** Remind students that an obituary is a notice of a person's death, usually including a brief biographical account. Have students consider Granny Weatherall's life and personality. Have them write an obituary about her for the local newspaper. Ask students to consider whether to include her jilting in the obituary. If students are unclear as to the contents or structure of an obituary, have them do research to examine several examples.

MAKING MEANING

## Close Read the Text

With your group, revisit sections of the text you marked during your first read. **Annotate** details that you notice. What **questions** do you have? What can you **conclude**?

THE JILTING OF GRANNY WEATHERALL

## Analyze the Text

**CITE TEXTUAL EVIDENCE** to support your answers.

**Complete the activities.**

1. **Review and Clarify** With your group, reread the sections of the story that describe Hapsy (paragraphs 41, 50, and 57–60). Discuss her role in Granny Weatherall's thoughts. Why do you think Hapsy is such an important figure for Granny Weatherall?
2. **Present and Discuss** Now, work with your group to share the passages from the selection that you found especially important. Take turns presenting your passages. Discuss what you noticed in the story, what questions you asked, and what conclusions you reached.
3. **Essential Question: *What do stories reveal about the human condition?*** What has this story taught you about life and loss? Discuss with your group.

**TIP**

**GROUP DISCUSSION**
Granny Weatherall's jumbled thoughts concern the past and the present. As you discuss the story, cite textual evidence to support your interpretation of when the events are taking place.

LANGUAGE DEVELOPMENT

## Concept Vocabulary

hypodermic clammy dyspepsia

**Why These Words?** The three concept vocabulary words from the text are related. With your group, determine what the words have in common. Write your ideas, and add another word that fits the category.

### Practice

Confirm your understanding of the concept vocabulary words by using them in a short conversation with your group members. If you are unsure about the exact meaning of a word, look it up in a print or online college-level dictionary before you begin.

**WORD NETWORK**
Add words related to the human condition from the text to your Word Network.

## Word Study

**Greek Prefix: *dys-*** In "The Jilting of Granny Weatherall," Granny Weatherall thinks about Sister Borgia's *dyspepsia*. This word includes the Greek prefix *dys-*, meaning "bad" or "difficult." This prefix often appears in scientific terms involving medical or psychological diagnoses. Use a dictionary or online resource to identify three other words that have this prefix. Write the words and their meanings. Explain how the meaning of the prefix contributes to the meaning of each word.

**STANDARDS**
**Language**
Identify and correctly use patterns of word changes that indicate different meanings or parts of speech.





DIGITAL PERSPECTIVES

## Jump Start

CLOSE READ Engage groups in a brief discussion based on this prompt: *An old woman is on her death bed: how can that make for an interesting story?*

## Close Read the Text 

Model close reading as needed by using the Annotation Highlights in the Interactive Teacher's Edition.

Remind groups to use Accountable Talk in their discussions and to support one another as they complete the close read.

## Analyze the Text

**Possible responses:**

1. **Responses will vary by group,** but make sure that students cite details from the text to support their interpretations.
2. **Passages will vary by group.** Remind students to explain why they chose the passage that they present to group members.
3. Students may suggest that the deathbed thoughts of Granny Weatherall reveal the way humans reflect on their choices and regrets and try to find meaning at the end of their lives.

## Concept Vocabulary

**Why These Words? Possible response:**
These medical words relate to someone who is in poor health. They enhance the impact of the text by highlighting Granny Weatherall's deteriorating condition.

### Practice

Conversations will vary.

### Word Network

Possible words: *secret, dutiful, tactful, kind, habit, childish*

## Word Study

For more support, see **Concept Vocabulary and Word Study.**

Possible responses: *dysfunctional* (behaving in an impaired or abnormal manner); *dyslexia* (a disturbance of the ability to read); and *dystopia* (an imaginary place that is terrible)

### FORMATIVE ASSESSMENT

#### Analyze the Text

**If** students struggle to close read the text, **then** provide **The Jilting of Granny Weatherall: Text Questions** available online in the Interactive Teacher's Edition or Unit Resources. Answers and DOK levels are also available.

#### Concept Vocabulary

**If** students struggle to identify the concept, **then** discuss the words in more detail, emphasizing the qualities of things that can be described by the words.

#### Word Study

**If** students fail to identify words beginning with the prefix *dys–*, **then** suggest they consult a dictionary and list words that they recognize from the words they find.

For Reteach and Practice, see **Word Study: Greek Prefix: *dys–* (RP).**

FACILITATING

## Analyze Craft and Structure

**Author's Choices: Narrative Structure** Ask students to consider the way their minds provide constant narratives as they go through their days. Help students to see that internal voices are often interrupted by new thoughts about actions in the present or by memories. Ask students to think about how their minds make unexpected connections, and to consider how difficult it is at times for them to stay focused. Stream-of-consciousness technique plays off this challenge. For more support, see **Analyze Craft and Structure: Narrative Structure.**

### Practice

1. a. Cornelia was always tactful and kind. Cornelia was dutiful.
   b. Cornelia whispering. (paragraph 10)
   c. Granny would like to spank her.
   d. Children don't need to be frightened.
   e. The children were gathered around her. (paragraph 27)
   f. I have had a full life. Hail Mary, full of grace.
2. **(a)** Granny sees a fog coming in. **(b)** In the flashback, she is protecting the children and they huddle around her. They are gathered around her now.
3. **(a)** *Flashback 1:* Paragraph 18 presents a memory of her farewell trip. *Flashback 2:* Paragraph 29 presents a memory of the day Granny was jilted. **(b)** *Flashback 1:* Readers learn that she thought she would die at 60. *Flashback 2:* Readers learn that she is still hurt by the jilting.
4. **(a)** The stream-of-consciousness technique allows the writer to convey Granny's state of mind. **(b)** Responses will vary, but students may agree that this is a good choice because is expresses Granny's confusion and inability to focus.

### FORMATIVE ASSESSMENT

### Analyze Craft and Structure

**If** students are unable to track the connections within the stream of consciousness, **then** have them focus on one paragraph to follow the ideas.

For Reteach and Practice, see **Analyze Craft and Structure: Narrative Structure (RP).**

MAKING MEANING

THE JILTING OF GRANNY WEATHERALL

## Analyze Craft and Structure

**Author's Choices: Narrative Structure** People's thoughts do not flow in neat patterns. Instead, they move unpredictably among perceptions, memories, and ideas. During the early 1900s, some writers began using a literary device called **stream of consciousness** to try to re-create a sense of the disjointed, natural flow of thought. Stream-of-consciousness narratives feature the following qualities:

- They present sequences of thought as if they were coming directly from a character's mind. The thoughts may or may not be complete or relate to one another.
- They tend to omit punctuation and transitions that appear in more traditional prose.

Stream-of-consciousness narratives often involve the use of **flashback,** a scene from the past that interrupts the present action of a story. A flashback may take the form of a memory, a story, a dream or daydream, or a switch by the narrator to a time in the past. Stream-of-consciousness stories may also involve shifts in the **narrative point of view,** or the perspective from which events are told. In this story, Porter's third-person narrator essentially disappears into Granny Weatherall's first-person narration.

### Practice

**Notebook** Work with your group to answer the questions.

1. Use the chart to identify two points at which Granny's thoughts shift from one subject to another without an obvious transition. What associations might connect her thoughts in each of these examples?

| THOUGHT OR MEMORY | TRIGGERING DETAIL | NEXT THOUGHT OR MEMORY |
|---|---|---|
| a. See possible responses in Teacher's Edition. | b. | c. |
| d. | e. | f. |

2. **(a)** What details trigger Granny's flashback to lighting the lamps when the children were young? **(b)** What is the connection between the flashback and her experience in the present?
3. Analyze two other flashbacks in the story. **(a)** Identify the form the flashback takes (i.e., dream, memory, etc.). **(b)** Explain what you learn from each flashback about Granny's life.
4. **(a)** What qualities does the use of stream-of-consciousness narration, flashback, and shifting narrative point of view lend to the story? **(b)** Overall, do you think these techniques are effective for the telling of this particular tale? Explain.

STANDARDS

**Reading Literature**

Analyze how an author's choices concerning how to structure specific parts of a text contribute to its overall structure and meaning as well as its aesthetic impact.





PERSONALIZE FOR LEARNING

### English Language Support

**Point of View** Provide English Learners with practice in identifying shifting points of view. First, direct them to paragraphs 1 through 5 in the story. Help students see that these paragraphs are narrated in the third person, as if someone were in the room reporting the conversation between Doctor Harry and Granny Weatherall.

Then have students look at paragraph 6. The first sentence is told from Granny's point of view: readers know that Doctor Harry wasn't really floating like a balloon. The dialogue at the end of the paragraph, however, reverts to third-person point of view: Doctor Harry said these words.

Direct students' attention to paragraph 56. Have them work in small groups to determine and explain when the author is using the third-person point of view and when the narrative shifts to first person. Point out how the monologue also moves between the present and the past.
**ALL LEVELS**

## Author's Style

**Author's Choices: Figurative Language** Literary works almost always contain two broad types of language—literal and figurative. Literal language means what it says, conveying information, ideas, and feelings in a direct way. **Figurative language,** by contrast, is language that is used imaginatively and expresses more than its literal meanings. Two common types of figurative language are metaphors and similes.

- A **metaphor** is a direct comparison between two apparently unlike things.

  **Example:** *Doctor Harry spread a warm* paw . . . on *her forehead. . . .* (paragraph 2)

- A **simile** is a comparison between two apparently unlike things made using an explicit comparison word such as *like, as, than,* or *resembles.*

  **Example:** *The pillow rose and floated under her, pleasant as a hammock in a light wind.* (paragraph 8)

Porter uses these devices to show how Granny Weatherall makes connections in her mind as she begins to lose her connection to reality.

### Read It

1. Work individually. Use this chart to identify the simile or metaphor in each passage from "The Jilting of Granny Weatherall."

| PASSAGE | METAPHOR OR SIMILE | EFFECT |
|---|---|---|
| *Her bones felt loose, and floated around in her skin, and Doctor Harry floated like a balloon around the foot of the bed.* (paragraph 6) | Doctor Harry floated like a balloon around the foot of the bed (simile) | Text tells readers that Granny is not perceiving her surroundings clearly and may be hallucinating |
| *Cornelia's voice staggered and bumped like a cart in a bad road.* (paragraph 56) | Cornelia's voice staggered and bumped like a cart in a bad road (simile) | Text tells readers that Cornelia's voice irritates Granny and that Granny struggled to hear her. |
| *Things were finished somehow when the time came; thank God there was always a little margin over for peace: then a person could spread out the plan of life and tuck in the edges orderly.* (paragraph 17) | a person could spread out the plan of life and tuck in the edges orderly (metaphor) | Text tells readers that Granny is trying to make sense of her life as she is dying |

2. **Connect to Style** With your group, discuss how the author's use of simile and metaphor affects what you envision as you read each of the passages in the chart.

### Write It

**Notebook** Write a paragraph in which you describe what you learned about the human condition from "The Jilting of Granny Weatherall." Use at least one simile and one metaphor to make your language more vivid and interesting.

**STANDARDS**

**Reading Literature**
Determine the meaning of words and phrases as they are used in the text, including figurative and connotative meanings; analyze the impact of specific word choices on meaning and tone, including words with multiple meanings or language that is particularly fresh, engaging, or beautiful.

**Language**
Demonstrate understanding of figurative language, word relationships, and nuances in word meanings.





DIGITAL PERSPECTIVES

## Author's Style

**Author's Choices: Figurative Language** Some students may not understand or appreciate the value of using figurative language. They may think that it is confusing to compare unlike things or say that one thing is something else. Help students to see that comparisons can lead readers to consider things in new ways, and they may help them to understand ideas more deeply.

For more support, see **Author's Style: Figurative Language**

### Read It

See possible responses in chart on student page.

### Write It

Paragraphs will vary, but make sure that students can recognize similes and metaphors in their own writing and the writing of classmates.

**FORMATIVE ASSESSMENT**

### Conventions and Style

**If** students are struggling to identify the effect of figurative language, **then** provide additional examples of similes and metaphors and have students explore the connections between the objects being compared.

For Reteach and Practice, see **Author's Style: Figurative Language (RP).**

**PERSONALIZE FOR LEARNING**

### English Language Support

**Identifying Similes and Metaphors** Write these sentences on the board:

1. *His face resembled the surface of the moon.*
2. *The student's mouth was a garbage can of insults.* Have students identify which one is a simile and which one is a metaphor. (1) Simile (2) Metaphor. Work with students to analyze each example. **EMERGING**

Have students find an example of one simile and one metaphor in the selection. (Possible responses: *simile –He had cursed like a sailor's parrot; metaphor: a warm bracelet on her wrist.)* Work with students to discuss the value of each example. **EMERGING**

Have students write an example of a simile and a metaphor and explain what each example compares. **BRIDGING**

An expanded **English Language Support Lesson** on Similes and Metaphors is available in the Interactive Teacher's Edition.

# FACILITATING

## Writing to Compare

As students prepare to compare the short story by Ambrose Bierce with the short story by Katherine Anne Porter, they will consider the authors' use of the stream-of-consciousness technique.

### Planning

**Analyze the Texts** Groups' definitions of "stream-of-consciousness" should be compatible with the explanation given on page 840 of the student text.

As students prepare to gather information individually for the chart, remind them that they should keep in mind their group's definition of "stream-of-consciousness" when they select passages.

**Possible responses:**

a. paragraph 19

b. Farquhar imagines being free of the rope, setting into motion a narration that misleads the reader.

c. paragraph 36

d. ends the imaginary sequence and brings the reader back to the harsh reality of Farquhar's death

e. paragraph 17

f. shows Granny thinks that most of her life is in order and that any tasks that need to be done are small and can be put off until "tomorrow"

g. paragraph 57

h. Granny feels death approaching and tries to resist; her thoughts have become delirious.

EFFECTIVE EXPRESSION

AN OCCURRENCE AT OWL CREEK BRIDGE

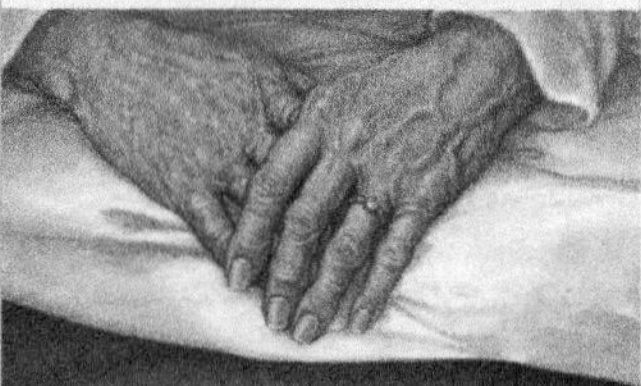

THE JILTING OF GRANNY WEATHERALL

## Writing to Compare

You have read two classic American stories that employ nonlinear narrative techniques: "An Occurrence at Owl Creek Bridge" and "The Jilting of Granny Weatherall." Now, deepen your understanding of both stories by comparing them and sharing your analysis in a group presentation.

**Assignment**

Prepare and deliver an **oral presentation** in which you compare and contrast how stream-of-consciousness narration works in the two stories you have studied. During your presentation, include dramatic readings of relevant passages to highlight important features of the stream-of-consciousness technique. End your presentation by drawing conclusions about the strengths and limitations of this literary device. Then, hold a brief question-and-answer session with your audience.

### Planning

**Define the Term** Work with your group to craft a definition of stream of consciousness. Complete this sentence.

**Stream of consciousness is** ____________________

____________________

____________________.

**Analyze the Texts** Review the stories individually, looking for passages that illustrate specific features of stream-of-consciousness narration. Use the chart to gather your ideas. Then, work together as a group to select examples that best reveal similarities and differences between the two stories. Aim to include at least two passages from each story.

| | PROPOSED PASSAGE | QUALITY OR EFFECT IT SHOWS |
|---|---|---|
| An Occurrence at Owl Creek Bridge | a. See answers in Teacher's Edition. | b. |
| | c. | d. |
| The Jilting of Granny Weatherall | e. | f. |
| | g. | h. |

STANDARDS

**Reading Literature**
Analyze how an author's choices concerning how to structure specific parts of a text contribute to its overall structure and meaning as well as its aesthetic impact.

**Writing**
Write informative/explanatory texts to examine and convey complex ideas, concepts, and information clearly and accurately through the effective selection, organization, and analysis of content.

**Speaking and Listening**
Adapt speech to a variety of contexts and tasks, demonstrating a command of formal English when indicated or appropriate.





PERSONALIZE FOR LEARNING

**Strategic Support**

**Contrasts** Group members may have difficulty distinguishing among the three narrative techniques of nonlinear narrative, interior monologue, and stream of consciousness. These techniques may occur simultaneously in narrative works, further compounding possible confusion.

Provide students with practice in pairing the names of the techniques with examples. Have students read passages from both selections and decide which technique each most clearly exemplifies.

## Organize the Presentation

**Outline the Content** Your presentation should include these elements:

- a formal introduction in which you define stream of consciousness
- explanations of at least two effects of stream-of-consciousness narration
- dramatic readings from the stories that provide strong examples of each effect and reveal similarities and differences between the two works
- a memorable conclusion
- a lively question-and-answer session

With your group, follow this outline frame to plan an effective sequence. Decide how you will transition from explanations to examples.

**EVIDENCE LOG**

Before moving on to a new selection, go to your Evidence Log and record what you learned from "An Occurrence at Owl Creek Bridge" and "The Jilting of Granny Weatherall."

**Outline Frame**

1. **Introduction:** Define stream-of-consciousness narration.
2. **Present Point 1:** Explain one effect of stream-of-consciousness narration. *Deliver readings:* Read passages from each story that show similarities and differences in how this quality appears in the two stories.
3. **Present Point 2:** Explain a second effect of stream-of-consciousness narration. *Deliver readings:* Read passages from each story that show similarities and differences in how this quality appears in the two stories.
4. **Conclusion:** Explain what makes stream-of-consciousness narration effective in the two stories under discussion.
5. **Question & Answer Session**

**Assign Tasks and Write** Some of the sections of your presentation need to be written ahead of time, whereas others simply need preparation. Decide whether you will work together to draft or prepare for each section, or whether you will assign the different tasks to individual group members.

**Annotate Passages and Rehearse** An annotated reading script will help you deliver dramatic readings with power and expression. Copy the passages exactly and practice reading them aloud several times, trying different approaches. The following annotations can help you remember the best choices.

| | |
|---|---|
| / = brief pause | // = longer pause |
| underscore = emphasis | double underscore = strong emphasis |
| !!! = speed up | XXX = slow down |

### Deliver the Presentation

Keep the following points in mind as you give your oral presentation:

- Do not keep your eyes glued to the page during the dramatic readings. Instead, look up to make a connection with your audience.
- Speak clearly and avoid either rushing or speaking too slowly.

During the final question-and-answer session, share the responsibility of answering. If your audience is reluctant to speak, pose and answer questions that they might find interesting.





DIGITAL PERSPECTIVES

## Organize the Presentation

**Outline the Contents** Clarify for students that, while they completed the chart on the previous page individually, they should now rejoin their groups for the remainder of the assignment. Suggest they draw on their charts to provide example passages in their outlines.

**Assign Tasks and Write** If any students experience deep anxiety when making oral presentations, assign them partners who can share their tasks and help provide support during the presentation. Also, remind students that the assignment requires them to draw conclusions about both the strengths and the limitations of the stream-of-consciousness technique.

**Annotate Passages and Rehearse** Encourage students to create their own emoticons if any of the ones shown in the student text are difficult to remember. They may also create their own emoticons for additional effective speaking techniques, such as making eye contact with the audience and using gestures to emphasize key points.

## Deliver the Presentation

Explain that making eye contact and not speaking too quickly are two of the most challenging aspects of oral presentations for students. Tell students to resist the temptation to "just get it over with" and instead focus on making sure the audience understands the information.

For more support, see **Writing to Compare: Oral Presentation.**

**Evidence Log** Support students in completing their Evidence Log. This paced activity will help prepare them for the Performance-Based Assessment at the end of the unit.

**FORMATIVE ASSESSMENT**

### Writing to Compare

**If** groups have difficulty assigning tasks for the presentation, **then** have them use their outlines to assign members specific passages to present.

**PERSONALIZE FOR LEARNING**

### English Language Support

**Organizing an Essay** Provide a prompt for English Learners to help them focus their thesis statements: What narrative structures do the authors of "An Occurrence at Owl Creek Bridge" and "The Jilting of Granny Weatherall" use?

Have students state their thesis and describe the structure of their essay to a partner before they begin to write. Have them explain why they chose either the point-by-point or the block organization for their essay. **ALL LEVELS**

## Present a Narrative

Before groups begin work on their projects, have them clearly differentiate the role each group member will play. Remind groups to consult the schedule for Small-Group Learning to guide their work during the Performance Task.

Students should complete the assignment using presentation software to take advantage of text, graphics, and sound features.

## Plan With Your Group

**Analyze the Text** Remind students that analyzing a text means that they examine it closely. In this assignment, their analysis involves looking for examples of stream of consciousness. Encourage students to revisit the texts to study them from a writer's perspective.

**Draft Your Narrative** Remind students that stream-of-consciousness narration is only a style of writing. Encourage students to be certain of the plot structure which will be central to their narrative. Once students map out plot events, they can begin to plan ways to include stream-of-consciousness into their writing.

PERFORMANCE TASK: SPEAKING AND LISTENING FOCUS

SOURCES

- A BRIEF HISTORY OF THE SHORT STORY
- AN OCCURRENCE AT OWL CREEK BRIDGE
- THE JILTING OF GRANNY WEATHERALL

# Present a Narrative

**Assignment**

You have read a history of the short story, and you have read and compared two short stories that feature stream-of-consciousness narration. Review how the technique is used in short stories. Then, work with your group to plan, present, and video-record a **stream-of-consciousness narrative** that responds to this statement:

**The day felt as if it would never end.**

Form teams and work together to find examples from the texts to help you write. Then, present your video narrative for the class.

## Plan With Your Group

**Analyze the Text** Divide into two subgroups. One will analyze stream-of-consciousness techniques within one of the selections; the other group will analyze the other selection. Decide which techniques your group will use in your narrative.

| TITLE | WHICH CHARACTERS ARE REVEALED THROUGH STREAM OF CONSCIOUSNESS? HOW? |
|---|---|
| An Occurrence at Owl Creek Bridge | |
| The Jilting of Granny Weatherall | |
| The best examples of the techniques are: | |

**Draft Your Narrative** With your group, plan your narrative, roughing out the plot and characters. Identify the main conflict, and decide how it will be resolved. Then, work on incorporating stream-of-consciousness techniques into the story.

**Plan Use of Media** Consider how to make the best use of the digital media available to you. With your group, discuss graphics, audio, or visual elements you will use to help viewers better understand your stream-of-consciousness video.

STANDARDS

**Speaking and Listening**
Propel conversations by posing and responding to questions that probe reasoning and evidence; ensure a hearing for a full range of positions on a topic or issue; clarify, verify, or challenge ideas and conclusions; and promote divergent and creative perspectives.





AUTHOR'S PERSPECTIVE **Ernest Morrell, Ph.D.**

**Fielding Questions** When students give presentations that have question and answer portions, they should be prepared to field questions confidently and to defend their positions without being defensive. Teachers can share the following techniques with students for answering difficult questions.

- Speakers should show that they understand the questioner's point of view by restating the question before offering an answer.
- Speakers should not make up answers. If they don't know the answer, they should say so and say, "Let me get back to you." Teachers should emphasize that it is critical that speakers do indeed return with an answer, as this establishes trust and credibility.
- Keep answers simple without adding too much technical language. If the question might take the speaker away from the central topic, the speaker can provide a brief answer and offer to talk to the questioner after the presentation.

**Organize Your Presentation** Decide how your group will convert your story into a script and then a video. Create a detailed storyboard. Make sure that your stream-of-consciousness techniques are visually represented. Make a plan for presenting your narrative by answering questions such as these: How many different characters are in your video? How will you divide the technical tasks? Use this chart to organize tasks.

## Rehearse With Your Group

**Practice With Your Group** As you act out your narrative, use this checklist to evaluate the effectiveness of your group's first run-through. Then, use your evaluation and the instructions here to guide your revision.

| CONTENT | USE OF MEDIA | PRESENTATION TECHNIQUES |
|---|---|---|
| ☐ The narrative relates to the prompt.<br>☐ Stream-of-consciousness techniques are used in the narrative. | ☐ Digital media is used effectively to aid understanding and create interest. | ☐ Actors speak clearly, with appropriate emotion.<br>☐ Actors seem well prepared. |

**Film the Narrative** When you are satisfied with your narrative, find a quiet place to film it using a recorder or smart phone. Depending on your equipment, you may want to film several versions before deciding on the one you want to share. If desired, you may want to use digital effects to enhance the presentation.

### Present and Evaluate

Present your video to the class, and invite feedback. As you watch other groups' videos, evaluate how well they meet the requirements on the checklist.



STANDARDS

Writing

- Write narratives to develop real or imagined experiences or events using well-chosen details, and well-structured event sequences.
- Use narrative techniques, such as dialogue, pacing, description, reflection, and multiple plot lines, to develop experiences, events, and/or characters.



DIGITAL PERSPECTIVES

**Organize Your Presentation** Explain to students that a storyboard is a graphic organizer that will help them create a visual product. If their product were written, they might make an outline. A storyboard will enable them to plot out both the story they are telling and the visual images they will use to tell it.

## Rehearse With Your Group

**Practice With Your Group** Remind students to provide constructive feedback to group members so that everyone can make their part of the presentation stronger.

**Film the Narrative** Remind groups that being familiar with their lines will improve their presentation because they won't sound as if they are reading. Speaking, as opposed to reading, lines will make the presentation more fluid and interesting for the audience.

## Present and Evaluate

Before beginning the presentations, set the expectations for the audience. You may wish to have students consider these questions as groups present.

- What story did the presentation tell?
- How did the group use stream of consciousness in their presentation?
- How did the visual element of the presentation contribute to the story?

As students provide feedback to the presenting group, remind them that compliments are as valuable as constructive criticism.

- If the question is difficult and if the speaker feels it is intended to attack, the speaker should answer calmly and move on to the next question as quickly as possible. If the question might take the speaker away from the central topic, the speaker can provide a brief answer and offer to talk to the questioner after the presentation.

# OVERVIEW

## INDEPENDENT LEARNING

### What do stories reveal about the human condition?

Encourage students to think carefully about what they have already learned and what more they want to know about the unit topic of how ordinary people have extraordinary tales to tell. This is a key first step to previewing and selecting the text they will read in Independent Learning.

### Independent Learning Strategies

Review the Learning Strategies with students and explain that as they work through Independent Learning they will develop strategies to work on their own.

- Have students watch the video on Independent Learning Strategies.
- A video on this topic is available online in the Professional Development Center.

Students should include any favorite strategies that they might have devised on their own during Whole-Class and Small-Group Learning. For example, for the strategy "Practice what you have learned," students might include:

- Review the unit to confirm key points you have studied, such as narrative techniques, narrative structure, and author's style.
- Apply these concepts to the new texts you read.

**Block Scheduling**

Each day in this Pacing Plan represents a 40–50 minute class period. Teachers using block scheduling may combine days to reflect their class schedule. In addition, teachers may revise pacing to differentiate and support core instruction by integrating components and resources as students require.

OVERVIEW: INDEPENDENT LEARNING

ESSENTIAL QUESTION:

## What do stories reveal about the human condition?

Some situations are shaped by changes in society, but many aspects of human life are timeless. In this section, you will complete your study of short stories and the human condition by exploring an additional selection related to the topic. You'll then share what you learn with classmates. To choose a text, follow these steps.

**Look Back** Think about the selections you have already studied. What more do you want to know about short stories and the insights they provide?

**Look Ahead** Preview the texts by reading the descriptions. Which one seems most interesting and appealing to you?

**Look Inside** Take a few minutes to scan the text you chose. Choose a different one if this text doesn't meet your needs.

### Independent Learning Strategies

Throughout your life, in school, in your community, and in your career, you will need to rely on yourself to learn and work on your own. Review these strategies and the actions you can take to practice them during Independent Learning. Add ideas of your own for each category.

| STRATEGY | ACTION PLAN |
|---|---|
| Create a schedule | • Understand your goals and deadlines.<br>• Make a plan for what to do each day.<br>• |
| Practice what you have learned | • Use first-read and close-read strategies to deepen your understanding.<br>• After you read, evaluate the usefulness of the evidence to help you understand the topic.<br>• Consider the quality and reliability of the source.<br>• |
| Take notes | • Record important ideas and information.<br>• Review your notes before preparing to share with a group.<br>• |





SCAN FOR MULTIMEDIA

### Pacing Plan

| Unit Introduction | Introduce Whole-Class Learning | Historical Perspectives | Everyday Use | | | Everything Stuck to Him | | | The Leap | | | | Performance Task | |
|---|---|---|---|---|---|---|---|---|---|---|---|---|---|---|
| 1 | 2 | 3 | 4 | 5 | 6 | 7 | 8 | 9 | 10 | 11 | 12 | 13 | 14 | 15 |

DIGITAL PERSPECTIVES

CONTENTS

Choose one selection. Selections are available online only.

SHORT STORY

## The Tell-Tale Heart

*Edgar Allan Poe*

Violence, revenge, and madness converge in this classic short story.

SHORT STORY

## The Man to Send Rain Clouds

*Leslie Marmon Silko*

Initially at odds, two ancient traditions come together in a tribute to a beloved grandfather.

SHORT STORY

## Ambush

*Tim O'Brien*

For one Vietnam War veteran, a child's question evokes vivid memories from a distant battlefield.

SHORT STORY

## Housepainting

*Lan Samantha Chang*

Why would a seemingly simple task spark tensions within a family?

PERFORMANCE-BASED ASSESSMENT PREP

## Review Notes for a Narrative

Complete your Evidence Log for the unit by evaluating what you have learned and synthesizing the information you have recorded.

SCAN FOR MULTIMEDIA





## Contents

**Selections** Encourage students to scan and preview the selections before choosing the one they would like to read. Suggest that they consider the genre and subject matter of each one before making their decision. You can use the information on the following planning pages to advise students in making their choice.

Remind students that the selections for Independent Learning are only available in the Interactive Student Edition. Allow students who do not have digital access at home to preview the selections using classroom or computer lab technology. Then either have students print the selection they choose or provide a printout for them.

## Performance-Based Assessment Prep

**Review Evidence for a Narrative** Point out to students that collecting evidence during Independent Learning is the last step in completing their Evidence Log. Explain that the "evidence" one needs for writing a narrative usually comes from checking how accurately and carefully they have described the action and characters. After they finish their independent reading, they will synthesize all the evidence they have compiled in the unit.

The evidence students collect will serve as the primary source of support they will use to complete the writing and oral presentation for the Performance-Based Assessment at the end of the unit.

Introduce Small-Group Learning

A Brief History of the Short Story

An Occurrence at Owl Creek Bridge

The Jilting of Granny Weatherall

Performance Task

Introduce Independent Learning

Independent Learning

Performance-Based Assessment

16 17 18 19 20 21 22 23 24 25 26 27 28 29 30

INDEPENDENT LEARNING

SELECTION RESOURCES

- First-Read Guide: Fiction
- Close-Read Guide: Fiction
- The Tell-Tale Heart: Text Questions
- Audio Summaries
- Selection Audio
- Selection Test

# The Tell-Tale Heart

## Summary

In the short story "The Tell-Tale Heart," Edgar Allan Poe creates a nameless narrator to share a frightening experience. From the beginning, the narrator describes himself as extremely nervous, but nonetheless insists he is sane. The narrator talks about an old man whom he says he loved. However, he was annoyed and bothered by the old man's eye, which he said resembled the eye of a vulture. The eye obsesses him, and eventually the narrator kills the old man. The narrator then drags the old man's body off the bed and pulls the bed on top of the body. Because the narrator thinks he can hear the old man's heart beating, he cuts him up and hides the remains under the floor. When a neighbor calls the police about hearing screams, three officers arrive to investigate. The narrator convinces the police that the old man often screamed in his sleep, then sits down to chat with them. The narrator hears the sound of a beating heart and, driven to madness by the sound, admits his guilt.

## Insight

Often credited as the inventor of detective and crime stories, Poe was intrigued by dark themes, crime, and death. Some students may find Poe's description of cutting up the old man's body parts disturbing.

## Connection to Essential Question

The story explores some of the darker facets of the Essential Question: What do stories reveal about the human condition? Poe's story reveals some of the sinister aspects of the human condition.

## Connection to Performance-Based Assessment

The Performance-Based Assessment asks students to consider how fictional characters respond to life-changing situations. Students may be able to use Poe's insightful analysis of the mind of a deeply disturbed person for ideas as they complete their work.

### Text Complexity Rubric: The Tell-Tale Heart

| **Quantitative Measures** | |
|---|---|
| **Lexile** 860 **Text Length** 2,076 words | |
| **Qualitative Measures** | |
| Knowledge Demands ①–**❷**–③–④–⑤ | Poe's story presents a familiar horror-story scenario. Some knowledge of the horror genre, gothic, and first-person narrative will be needed. |
| Structure **❶**–②–③–④–⑤ | The piece is a straightforward short story in a conventional first-person format. |
| Language Conventionality and Clarity ①–②–③–**❹**–⑤ | Some archaic language and high-level vocabulary may challenge some students. |
| Levels of Meaning/Purpose ①–②–**❸**–④–⑤ | This text raises the quesiton of the reliability of the narrator. Poe's approach to conveying the narrator's state of mind adds a level of meaning to the story. |

DIGITAL PERSPECTIVES

Audio | Video | Document | Annotation Highlights | EL Highlights | Online Assessment

SELECTION RESOURCES

- First-Read Guide: Fiction
- Close-Read Guide: Fiction
- The Man to Send Rain Clouds: Text Questions
- Audio Summaries
- Selection Audio
- Selection Test

# The Man to Send Rain Clouds


## Summary

In the story "The Man to Send Rain Clouds," Leslie Marmon Silko describes the death and burial of an elderly Native American in Laguna, New Mexico. Teofilo has died peacefully while tending sheep at the sheep camp away from the village. Leon and his brother-in-law Ken find him and notice that his sheep have wandered away. After corralling the sheep, the two men prepare Teofilo for burial. They paint his face, tie a grey feather in his hair, and wrap him in a red blanket. On the way back to their home, they meet the local priest, Father Paul, but do not tell him about Teofilo's death because they wish to avoid a Roman Catholic funeral. Instead, their medicine men perform their traditional funeral. The only thing they asked of the priest was that he sprinkle water on Teofilo's body so that the old man would have plenty of water. Leon feels good about having the water sprinkled over Teofilo because he knows that the old man will send big thunderclouds.


## Insight

This story explores the way that many Native Americans in New Mexico blended Catholic rituals with their own traditional rituals. The tension between maintaining traditional Pueblo practices and guarding outside influences is a theme that Silko often explores in her work.

## Connection to Essential Question

This story confronts a challenge in modern society, addressing the Essential Question: What do stories reveal about the human condition? Silko's story explores a common human tension between maintaining traditional ideals and yielding to outside influences.

## Connection to Performance-Based Assessment

The Performance-Based Assessment asks students to consider the ways fictional characters respond to life-changing situations. Students will find a useful example of fictional characters responding to life-changing news in Silko's masterful rendering of a simple story.

## Text Complexity Rubric: The Man to Send Rain Clouds

| Quantitative Measures | |
|---|---|
| **Lexile** 910 **Text Length** 1,736 words | |
| **Qualitative Measures** | |
| Knowledge Demands (1–2–**3**–4–5) | Concepts of Catholicism, Native American belief and tradition, colonialism, cultural tension, and American Christian evangelism will be required for students to get a clear picture of the significance of the burial. |
| Structure (1–**2**–3–4–5) | The story's pacing and structure is traditional. |
| Language Conventionality and Clarity (1–**2**–3–4–5) | The language is simple. Some explanation of significant regional or cultural words, "arroyo," "cassock," will be needed. |
| Levels of Meaning/Purpose (1–2–3–**4**–5) | The story has many levels of meaning. The sense of religious or cultural tension is subtle, and Leon's simplistic interpretation of the Father's Catholic rites betrays a flawed understanding of his own cultural trauma and the real ambitions of Christian evangelism in the Southwest. The story also touches on the ongoing conflict between voluntary cultural exchange and cultural assimilation, as well as the contemporary consequences of the colonial era. |

SELECTION RESOURCES

- First-Read Guide: Fiction
- Close-Read Guide: Fiction
- Ambush: Text Questions
- Audio Summaries
- Selection Audio
- Selection Test

# Ambush

## Summary

In the short story "Ambush" by Tim O'Brien, the narrator's nine-year-old daughter, aware that her father is always writing war stories, asks him if he ever killed someone. He tells her that he hadn't, but he knows that is not true. This reflection leads him to write about an incident that continues to haunt him. It happened during the Vietnam War, in the trail outside of My Khe. At night, soldiers worked in two-man teams so one man could sleep and the other stay awake. While on watch, the narrator sees a young man come out of the fog. Out of instinct and fear, he pulls the pin in a grenade and throws it at the young man. In retrospect, the narrator understands that the young man probably posed no real danger. His partner tries to reassure him that the young man would probably have been killed by someone else, even if the narrator had not thrown the grenade. It does no good. Years later, the narrator continues to relive the episode, imagining a version of it in which he hadn't thrown the grenade.

## Insight

This story explores the effect of war on the soldiers who fight it. Years after a war time incident, a soldier still reflects on it.

## Connection to Essential Question

This text helps readers address the Essential Question: What do stories reveal about the human condition? Students may see that war is fought among people, not governments; that soldiers often act out of fear; and that war experiences live on in human memory long past the battle.

## Connection to Performance-Based Assessment

Students will consider the ways fictional characters respond to life-changing news. O'Brien's story provides vivid detail about how a character reacted in such a situation.

## Text Complexity Rubric: Ambush

| Quantitative Measures | |
|---|---|
| **Lexile** 950 **Text Length** 1,002 words | |
| **Qualitative Measures** | |
| Knowledge Demands ①—❷—③—④—⑤ | Although most students will find a combat story to be unfamiliar, the text is very accessible. It is told from the perspective of a retired American soldier, who speaks to his daughter about his past. Some knowledge of the Vietnam War will be required. |
| Structure ①—②—❸—④—⑤ | The story departs from linear narrative, using a flashback to describe the circumstances of the killing of a young enemy soldier in Vietnam. |
| Language Conventionality and Clarity ①—❷—③—④—⑤ | The piece contains on-level vocabulary and simple sentences without a lot of dialogue. The conclusion is ambiguous and allows the reader to ponder the significance of the event in this soldier's life, as well as the impact of the story on his daughter. |
| Levels of Meaning/Purpose ①—②—③—❹—⑤ | The story addresses multiple levels of meaning. The story touches on grief, memory, morality, and humankind's responsibility to future generations. |

DIGITAL PERSPECTIVES

Audio

Video

Document

Annotation Highlights

EL Highlights

Online Assessment

SELECTION RESOURCES

- First-Read Guide: Fiction
- Close-Read Guide: Fiction
- Housepainting: Text Questions
- Audio Summaries
- Selection Audio
- Selection Test

# Housepainting

## Summary

When the story "Housepainting" by Lan Samantha Chang opens, the Chinese parents of Frances are awaiting a visit from her and her boyfriend, Wei. Although the family is thoroughly Americanized, the parents try to maintain and instill in their children traditional Chinese values. Wei wants Frances to marry him, but she is undecided. Frances's parents love Wei, especially the father, who appreciates his constant help with household tasks. Finally, the mother asks Frances why she hasn't decided to marry Wei. This question is very upsetting to Frances, who feels that her parents have never understood her. Wei, in the meantime, is helping out by painting the entire house yellow. When the parents leave for a four-hour drive to Chicago, Frances lashes out at Wei, accusing him of being the traditional Chinese son, bowing to her parents' every wish. Frances decides to repaint the house blue. Eventually, however, she backs down and together she and Wei finish painting the house yellow. And she tells Wei she will marry him.

## Insight

Chang's story explores the conflict one young woman experiences between her own wishes and the wants and needs of her parents. The story may help students understand the often conflicting wants and needs between family members.

## Connection to Essential Question

By developing a common intergenerational conflict, this story helps students address the Essential Question: What do stories reveal about the human condition?

## Connection to Performance-Based Assessment

As students work to respond to the Performance-Based Assessment prompt, they will consider how fictional characters respond to life-changing news. This realistic short story shows characters who struggle to navigate the changes that occur as they grow up and take more responsibility for their lives and happiness. Students may find this story presents characters and their approach to stressful situations.

## Text Complexity Rubric: Housepainting

| Quantitative Measures | |
|---|---|
| **Lexile** 650 **Text Length** 3,589 words | |
| **Qualitative Measures** | |
| Knowledge Demands ① ❷ ③ ④ ⑤ | Some knowledge of Chinese immigrant culture in America and intergenerational tension is needed. The text is a first-person narrative about an elder sister returning home from college with her boyfriend for a brief holiday. |
| Structure ① ❷ ③ ④ ⑤ | A straightforward and conventional short story told from the perspective of the somewhat innocent younger daughter. |
| Language Conventionality and Clarity ① ❷ ③ ④ ⑤ | Text includes on-level vocabulary with some figurative language and a lot of dialogue. Language reflects a realistic, contemporary setting. |
| Levels of Meaning/Purpose ① ② ③ ❹ ⑤ | The main idea, concerning the pressure felt by second-generation immigrants from the elder generation's cultural expectations, is subtly rendered. Concepts of family, marriage, Chinese-American culture, and contemporary cultural shifts are explored. |

MY NOTES

DIGITAL PERSPECTIVES

Audio

Video

Document

Annotation Highlights

EL Highlights

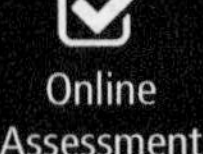
Online Assessment

MY NOTES

# ADVISING

You may wish to direct students to use the generic **First-Read** and **Close-Read Guides** in the Print Student Edition. Alternatively, you may wish to print copies of the genre-specific **First-Read** and **Close-Read Guides** for students. These are available online in the Interactive Student Edition or Unit Resources.

## FIRST READ

Students should perform the steps of the first read independently.

NOTICE: In order to understand what is happening in the selection, students should focus on the basic elements of the text.

ANNOTATE: Students should mark any passage they want to revisit during their close read.

CONNECT: Connecting what they're reading to other texts and to personal experiences will increase students' comprehension of the text.

RESPOND: Students will demonstrate their understanding of the text by writing a summary of it.

Point out to students that while they will always complete the Respond step at the end of the first read, the other steps will probably happen somewhat concurrently. Remind students that they will revisit their first-read annotations during the close read.

After students have completed the First-Read Guide, you may wish to assign the Text Questions for the selection that are available in the Interactive Teacher's Edition.

### Anchor Standards

In the first two sections of the unit, students worked with the whole class and in small groups to gain topical knowledge and greater understanding of the skills required by the anchor standards. In this section, they are asked to work independently, applying what they have learned and demonstrating increased readiness for college and career.

## INDEPENDENT LEARNING

### First-Read Guide

**Tool Kit**
First-Read Guide and Model Annotation

Use this page to record your first-read ideas.

Selection Title: ____________________

NOTICE

**NOTICE** new information or ideas you learn about the unit topic as you first read this text.

ANNOTATE

**ANNOTATE** by marking vocabulary and key passages you want to revisit.

NOTICE ANNOTATE First Read CONNECT RESPOND

**CONNECT** ideas within the selection to other knowledge and the selections you have read.

**RESPOND** by writing a brief summary of the selection.

CONNECT

RESPOND



STANDARD
**Reading** Read and comprehend complex literary and informational texts independently and proficiently.



## PERSONALIZE FOR LEARNING

### Challenge

**Additional Questions** To help students reflect on their first read and prepare for the close read, encourage them to think about what more they would like to know about a text. Ask students to write two to three questions they have about the text. Then, students can meet in small groups with others who have read the same text. Each group can share First-Read Guides and their additional questions before proceeding to the Close Read.

DIGITAL PERSPECTIVES

## Close-Read Guide

**Tool Kit**
Close-Read Guide and Model Annotation

Use this page to record your close-read ideas.

Selection Title: 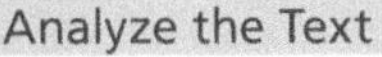

### Close Read the Text

Revisit sections of the text you marked during your first read. Read these sections closely and **annotate** what you notice. Ask yourself **questions** about the text. What can you **conclude**? Write down your ideas.

ANNOTATE · QUESTION · Close Read · CONCLUDE

### Analyze the Text

Think about the author's choices of patterns, structure, techniques, and ideas included in the text. Select one and record your thoughts about what this choice conveys.

### QuickWrite

Pick a paragraph from the text that grabbed your interest. Explain the power of this passage.

STANDARD
**Reading** Read and comprehend complex literary and informational texts independently and proficiently.





### CLOSE READ

Students should begin their close read by revisiting the annotations they made during their first read. Then, students should analyze one of the author's choices regarding the following elements:

- **point of view,** such as first-person or third-person
- **organization,** such as chronological or *in media res*—in the middle of things
- **techniques,** such as foreshadowing or pacing
- **structure,** such as frame story or stream of consciousness

**MAKE IT INTERACTIVE**
Group students by the selection they read, and have groups discuss the selection in depth. Participants should be guided by their insights and their questions.

### PERSONALIZE FOR LEARNING

**Challenge**
**Research** Those students who seek a challenge based on their selected text may want to develop a question about the text or the author that they can answer by conducting brief research. Allow time for students to conduct research. Students should take notes on their findings, list the sources they used, and cite the sources in their work. Provide some class time for students to present their findings in an informal oral report. In a follow-up class discussion, ask presenters how further research related to the text or author helped them better understand the text or appreciate writing choices made by the author.

ADVISING

## Share Your Independent Learning

### Prepare to Share

Explain to students that sharing what they learned from their Independent Learning selection provides classmates who read a different selection with an opportunity to consider the text as a source of evidence during the Performance-Based Assessment. As students prepare to share, remind them to highlight how their selection contributed to their knowledge of the concept of survival as well as how the selection connects to the question *What do stories reveal about the human condition?*

### Learn from Your Classmates

As students discuss the Independent Learning selections, direct them to take particular note of how their classmates' chosen selections align with their current position on the Performance-Based Assessment question.

### Reflect

Students may want to add their reflection to their Evidence Log, particularly if their insight relates to a specific selection from the unit.

**MAKE IT INTERACTIVE**

Group students by the text they selected. Have each student choose two or three passages that were especially meaningful to them. Within each group, students can discuss the passages of their choice.

**Evidence Log** Support students in completing their Evidence Log. This paced activity will help prepare them for the Performance-Based Assessment at the end of the unit.

INDEPENDENT LEARNING

EVIDENCE LOG

Go to your Evidence Log and record what you learned from the text you read.

## Share Your Independent Learning

**Prepare to Share**

What do stories reveal about the human condition?

Even when you read something independently, you can continue to grow by sharing what you have learned with others. Reflect on the text you explored independently, and write notes about its connection to the unit. In your notes, consider why this text belongs in this unit.

**Learn From Your Classmates**

**Discuss It** Share your ideas about the text you explored on your own. As you talk with your classmates, jot down ideas that you learn from them.

**Reflect**

Review your notes, and mark the most important insight you gained from these writing and discussion activities. Explain how this idea adds to your understanding of the importance of stories as they reveal the human condition.

STANDARDS

**Speaking and Listening**

Initiate and participate effectively in a range of collaborative discussions with diverse partners on grades 11–12 topics, texts, and issues, building on others' ideas and expressing their own clearly and persuasively.





AUTHOR'S PERSPECTIVE Ernest Morrell, Ph.D.

**Asking Good Questions** Students may not know how to ask effective questions, a critical component in learning from others. To teach this skill, teachers can explain that effective questioners always show respect, clarify the goals of the discussion, and solicit everyone's ideas. In addition, effective questions are open ended rather than yes/no requests, so they allow group members to express more extensive and complex responses and solicit follow-up responses. Teachers can use these models of effective questions to model the skill:

- **Ask to clarify:** Sample questions include: "Can you give an example?" "Where in the text do you see that?" and "How did you reach this conclusion?"
- **Ask to start a discussion:** Sample techniques include taking the opposite opinion and setting up a "What If?" situation.
- **Push for the larger idea:** Sample questions include: "Is it always this way?" "Why do we believe this?" and "How has this changed our thinking?"

PERFORMANCE-BASED ASSESSMENT PREP

## Review Notes for a Narrative

At the beginning of this unit, you expressed a point of view about the following question:

**How does a fictional character or characters respond to life-changing news?**

EVIDENCE LOG

Review your Evidence Log and your QuickWrite from the beginning of the unit. Have your ideas changed?

| ☐ YES | ☐ NO |
|---|---|
| Identify at least three textual details that caused you to alter your ideas. | Identify at least three textual details that reinforced your original ideas. |
| 1. | 1. |
| 2. | 2. |
| 3. | 3. |

Give one example of life-changing news that might affect someone strongly:

______________________________

______________________________

Give one example of a way in which someone might react to that news:

______________________________

______________________________

**Evaluate the Strength of Your Content** Do you have enough content to write your narrative? Do you have enough details to develop multiple characters? If not, make a plan.

☐ Do research about short stories ☐ Talk with my classmates

☐ Reread a selection ☐ Ask a fiction writer

☐ Other: ______________________________





DIGITAL PERSPECTIVES

## Review Notes for a Narrative

**Evidence Log** Make sure students understand that their answer to a question can change as they learn more and as they encounter other points of view. Remind students that their Evidence Log tracked the growth of their thinking during the unit. As they carefully consider what they've learned and the evidence they've found, the initial answer they had for the question *Can fictional characters teach us how to respond to life changing news?* might continue to change.

### Evaluate the Strength of Your Content

Students have the choice of many different sources when looking for information about the topic, including:

- short stories
- novels
- graphic novels
- movies and television shows
- authors' blogs
- books on how to write fiction

Students need to judge not just the quantity of the evidence they gather about their topic, but also the applicability of that evidence. Discuss what might make evidence more credible, and suggest these questions:

- Did the character seem realistic?
- Was the news the character received actually life changing?
- Did the character's reaction seem realistic?

## Writing to Sources: Narrative Text

Students should complete the Performance-Based Assessment independently, with little to no input or feedback during the process. Students should use word processing software to take advantage of editing tools and features.

Prior to beginning the assessment, ask students to think about these questions: *What constitutes life-changing news? What do we, as humans in a developed country, expect when we wake up each morning? What do expectations have to do with life-changing news?*

### Review the Elements of Effective Narrative

Students can review the work they did earlier in the unit as they complete the Performance-Based Assessment. They may also consult other resources such as:

- the elements of an effective narrative text including engaging character(s); realistic dialogue; precise sensory details; tension and conflict; a smooth, logical sequence of events; a satisfying resolution of the conflict and conclusion, available in Whole-Class Learning
- their Evidence Log
- their Word Network

Although students will use evidence from unit selections for their narrative text, they may need to collect additional evidence, including research about the time period, setting, or particular conflict they choose to write about.

PERFORMANCE-BASED ASSESSMENT

SOURCES

- WHOLE-CLASS SELECTIONS
- SMALL-GROUP SELECTIONS
- INDEPENDENT-LEARNING SELECTION

PART 1

## Writing to Sources: Narrative

In this unit, you read a variety of texts in which ordinary lives prove to contain extraordinary moments. You met characters who encounter stressful, unexpected, or life-changing situations. In each case, characters' responses reveal their strengths and weaknesses, as well as their hopes and fears. By reading stories about fictional characters, you may have learned something useful about what it means to be human.

**Assignment**

Write a **short story** in which you introduce and develop a protagonist, and set up a problem or conflict the character must face. Use the third-person point of view. Before you write, think about your answer to this question:

**How does a fictional character or characters respond to life-changing news?**

As your character faces conflicts, how does he or she respond? Will your character's response be instructive to readers? If so, how? If not, why not? What will your character learn, and in what ways will he or she change? Bring your character's story to a resolution or epiphany that demonstrates a truth about the human condition.

**WORD NETWORK**

As you write and revise your narrative, use your Word Network to help vary your word choices.

**Reread the Assignment** Review the assignment to be sure you fully understand it. The task may reference some of the academic words presented at the beginning of the unit. Be sure you understand each of the words given below in order to complete the assignment correctly.

**Academic Vocabulary**

| colloquial | tension | epiphany |
|---|---|---|
| protagonist | resolution | |

**Review the Elements of a Narrative** Before you begin writing, read the Narrative Rubric. Once you have completed your first draft, check it against the rubric. If one or more of the elements is missing or not as strong as it could be, revise your narrative to add or strengthen that component.

**STANDARDS**

**Writing**

- Write narratives to develop real or imagined experiences or events using effective technique, well-chosen details, and well-structured event sequences.
- Write routinely over extended time frames and shorter time frames for a range of tasks, purposes, and audiences.





PERSONALIZE FOR LEARNING

### English Language Support

**Literary Terms** English learners may need support to understand a number of literary terms, including some terms from the prompt. Check for student understanding of the following terms, encouraging discussion to facilitate a full understanding of each term. Once all of the terms are understood, have volunteers discuss what the prompt requires. **ALL LEVELS**

| protagonist | traits |
|---|---|
| outside force | resolution |
| third-person point of view | epiphany |
| life-changing news | tension |

## Narrative Rubric

| | Focus and Organization | Technique and Development | Language Conventions |
|---|---|---|---|
| 4 | The introduction engages the reader and introduces original characters and conflict.<br>The narrative establishes an engrossing sequence of events that unfolds smoothly and logically.<br>The conclusion follows from and resolves the narrative in a satisfying way. | The narrative adeptly incorporates dialogue and description.<br>Precise details and sensory language give the reader a clear picture of events. | The narrative consistently uses conventions of standard English usage and mechanics. |
| 3 | The introduction is somewhat engaging and introduces characters and conflict.<br>The narrative establishes a sequence of events that unfolds smoothly and logically.<br>The conclusion follows from and resolves the narrative. | Dialogue and description move the narrative forward.<br>Some precise details and sensory language give the reader a picture of events. | The narrative demonstrates accuracy in conventions of standard English usage and mechanics. |
| 2 | The introduction introduces characters and conflict.<br>Events are mostly in sequence, but some events may not belong or may be omitted.<br>The conclusion follows from the narrative. | Some dialogue or description may appear.<br>Some details give the reader a general picture of events. | The narrative demonstrates some accuracy in conventions of standard English usage and mechanics. |
| 1 | The introduction fails to introduce characters and conflict, or there is no introduction.<br>Events are not in a clear sequence, and some events may be omitted.<br>The conclusion does not follow from the narrative, or there is no conclusion. | Dialogue and description do not appear or are minimal and seem to appear as afterthoughts.<br>Few details are included, or details fail to give the reader a picture of events. | The narrative contains mistakes in conventions of standard English usage and mechanics. |





DIGITAL PERSPECTIVES

## Narrative Rubric

As you review the Narrative Rubric with students, remind them that the rubric is a resource that can guide their revisions. Students should pay particular attention to the differences between a narrative that contains all of the required elements (a score of 3) and one that is comprehensive, engaging, and progresses in a logical and thoughtful manner (a score of 4).

PERSONALIZE FOR LEARNING

### Strategic Support

**Rubric** If students struggle with the conceptual nature of the rubric, use the rubric to rate the response to narrative model "Old Man at the Bridge." Discuss with students specific examples and whether they fulfill each requirement for a score of "4" in the narrative rubric. Answer student questions about rubric requirements.

## Speaking and Listening: Storytelling Session

Students should annotate their written writing mode in preparation for the oral presentation, marking the important elements: key plot points, character descriptions, and most important lines of dialogue.

Remind students that effective storytelling relies on how the speaker establishes credibility with his or her audience. If a speaker comes across as confident and authoritative, it will be easier for the audience to give credence to the speaker's presentation.

**Review the Rubric** As you review the Oral Presentation Rubric with students, remind them that it is a valuable tool that can help them plan their presentation. They should strive to include all of the criteria required to achieve a score of 3. Draw their attention to some of the subtle differences between scores of 2 and 3.

PERFORMANCE-BASED ASSESSMENT

PART 2

## Speaking and Listening: Storytelling Session

**Assignment**

After completing your narrative, conduct a **storytelling session** for your class. Memorize the key plot points, character descriptions, and most important lines of dialogue from your story. You may refer to some notes as you tell your story, but do not read aloud. When you address your audience, remember to use appropriate eye contact, adequate volume, and clear pronunciation.

Select digital audio to add interest and enhance the mood of your story. Consider using sound effects, background music, or an instrumental musical score to accompany your story.

STANDARDS

**Speaking and Listening**
Make strategic use of digital media in presentations to enhance understanding of findings, reasoning, and evidence and to add interest.

To be an effective storyteller, consider the following:

- Keep it simple. What can you cut from your written narrative while retaining the gist of the story?
- Pump up the emotion. How can music and sound cues affect your audience and improve their listening experience?

**Review the Rubric** Before you tell your story, check your plans against this rubric. If one or more of the elements is missing or not as strong as it could be, revise your presentation.

| | Content | Use of Media | Presentation Techniques |
|---|---|---|---|
| 3 | The storyteller engages the audience by describing original characters, conflict, and resolution. | Included media have a positive impact on listener experience. | The speaker's word choice, volume, pitch, and eye contact reflect the story's content and are appropriate to the audience. |
| 2 | The storyteller describes characters, conflict, and resolution. | Included media neither improve nor detract from listener experience. | The speaker's word choice, volume, pitch, and eye contact somewhat reflect the story's content and are appropriate to the audience. |
| 1 | The storyteller's presentation is flat and dull, or the sequence of events is hard to follow. | Included media are distracting or otherwise detract from listener experience. | The speaker's word choice, volume, pitch, and eye contact do not reflect the story's content and are not appropriate to the audience. |





DIGITAL PERSPECTIVES

**Preparing for the Assignment** To help inspire students to tell their stories to the class, find examples of fiction read on podcasts. Be sure to preview the podcasts before playing them for students. After listening to the examples, have students discuss what elements made the reading engaging and/or less engaging. To help students integrate this information and prepare for their own presentation, have them rate the podcast they heard using the Oral Presentation rubric and discuss their ratings as well as the reasons for their ratings with the class.

## Reflect on the Unit

Now that you've completed the unit, take a few moments to reflect on your learning. Use the questions below to think about where you succeeded, what skills and strategies helped you, and where you can continue to grow in the future.

### Reflect on the Unit Goals

Look back at the goals at the beginning of the unit. Use a different colored pen to rate yourself again. Think about readings and activities that contributed the most to the growth of your understanding. Record your thoughts.

### Reflect on the Learning Strategies

**Discuss It** Write a reflection on whether you were able to improve your learning based on your Action Plans. Think about what worked, what didn't, and what you might do to keep working on these strategies. Record your ideas before joining a class discussion.

### Reflect on the Text

Choose a selection that you found challenging, and explain what made it difficult.

Explain something that surprised you about a text in the unit.

Which activity taught you the most about how stories reveal the human condition? What did you learn?

SCAN FOR MULTIMEDIA



**STANDARDS**

**Speaking and Listening**
Come to discussions prepared, having read and researched material under study; explicitly draw on that preparation by referring to evidence from texts and other research on the topic or issue to stimulate a thoughtful, well-reasoned exchange of ideas.



**DIGITAL PERSPECTIVES**

## Reflect on the Unit

- Have students watch the video on Reflecting on Your Learning.
- You may choose to watch the video on this topic that is available online in the Professional Development Center.

### Reflect on the Unit Goals

Students should re-evaluate how well they met the Unit Goals now that they have completed the unit. You might ask them to provide a written commentary on the goal they made the most progress with as well as the goal they feel warrants continued focus.

### Reflect on the Learning Strategies

**Discuss It** If you want to make this a digital activity, go online and navigate to the Discussion Board. Alternatively, students can share their learning strategies reflections in a class discussion.

### Reflect on the Text

Consider having students share their text reflections with one another.

**MAKE IT INTERACTIVE**

Have students write one or two sentences that sum up a "truth" they learned about the human condition based on one or more selections in this unit. Set aside a class period and have students read their "truths" aloud. After each, allow an opportunity for classmates' comments and questions.

**Unit Test and Remediation** 

After students have completed the Performance-Based Assessment, administer the Unit Test. Based on students' performance on the test, assign the resources as indicated on the Interpretation Guide to remediate. Students who take the test online will be automatically assigned remediation, as warranted by test results.

## PERSONALIZE FOR LEARNING

### English Language Support

**Support Opinions** English learners may have trouble supporting their positions and/or persuading others of their opinions. Have partners work together to complete the activities outlined in "Reflect on the Text." Tell students to tell their partners their opinions and support the opinions with reasons and examples from the texts.

Instruct students to ask for clarification or repetition where needed, using the sentence: *Could you repeat that?* or *Could you explain that?* **EMERGING**

Encourage students to present counterarguments using the sentence: *I see your point, but I prefer. . . :* or *I agree with you and I would like to add. . .* **EXPANDING**

Inspire students to express opinions by elaborating on a partner's comments, finding areas of agreement and disagreement. **BRIDGING**

# RESOURCES

## CONTENTS

### TOOL KIT



### GLOSSARY



### INDEXES



### ACKNOWLEDGMENTS

## Marking the Text: Strategies and Tips for Annotation

When you close read a text, you read for comprehension and then reread to unlock layers of meaning and to analyze a writer's style and techniques. Marking a text as you read it enables you to participate more fully in the close-reading process.

Following are some strategies for text mark-ups, along with samples of how the strategies can be applied. These mark-ups are suggestions; you and your teacher may want to use other mark-up strategies.

| | |
|---|---|
| * | Key Idea |
| ! | I love it! |
| ? | I have questions |
| ◯ | Unfamiliar or important word |
| ---- | Context Clues |

### Suggested Mark-Up Notations

| WHAT I NOTICE | HOW TO MARK UP | QUESTIONS TO ASK |
|---|---|---|
| Key Ideas and Details | • Highlight key ideas or claims.<br>• Underline supporting details or evidence. | • What does the text say? What does it leave unsaid?<br>• What inferences do you need to make?<br>• What details lead you to make your inferences? |
| Word Choice | • Circle unfamiliar words.<br>• Put a dotted line under context clues, if any exist.<br>• Put an exclamation point beside especially rich or poetic passages. | • What inferences about word meaning can you make?<br>• What tone and mood are created by word choice?<br>• What alternate word choices might the author have made? |
| Text Structure | • Highlight passages that show key details supporting the main idea.<br>• Use arrows to indicate how sentences and paragraphs work together to build ideas.<br>• Use a right-facing arrow to indicate foreshadowing.<br>• Use a left-facing arrow to indicate flashback. | • Is the text logically structured?<br>• What emotional impact do the structural choices create? |
| Author's Craft | • Circle or highlight instances of repetition, either of words, phrases, consonants, or vowel sounds.<br>• Mark rhythmic beats in poetry using checkmarks and slashes.<br>• Underline instances of symbolism or figurative language. | • Does the author's style enrich or detract from the reading experience?<br>• What levels of meaning are created by the author's techniques? |

# CLOSE READING

* Key Idea
! I love it!
? I have questions
○ Unfamiliar or important word
---- Context Clues

NOTES

In a first read, work to get a sense of the main idea of a text. Look for key details and ideas that help you understand what the author conveys to you. Mark passages which prompt a strong response from you.

Here is how one reader marked up this text.

MODEL

INFORMATIONAL TEXT

## *from* Classifying the Stars

**Cecilia H. Payne**

1 Sunlight and starlight are composed of waves of various lengths, which the eye, even aided by a telescope, is unable to separate. We must use more than a telescope. In order to sort out the component colors, the light must be dispersed by a prism, or split up by some other means. For instance, sunbeams passing through rain drops, are transformed into the myriad-tinted rainbow. The familiar rainbow spanning the sky is Nature's most glorious demonstration that light is composed of many colors.

2 The very beginning of our knowledge of the nature of a star dates back to 1672, when Isaac Newton gave to the world the results of his experiments on passing sunlight through a prism. To describe the beautiful band of rainbow tints, produced when sunlight was dispersed by his three-cornered piece of glass, he took from the Latin the word *spectrum*, meaning an appearance. The rainbow is the spectrum of the Sun. . . .

3 In 1814, more than a century after Newton, the spectrum of the Sun was obtained in such purity that an amazing detail was seen and studied by the German optician, Fraunhofer. He saw that the multiple spectral tints, ranging from delicate violet to deep red, were crossed by hundreds of fine dark lines. In other words, there were narrow gaps in the spectrum where certain shades were wholly blotted out. We must remember that the word spectrum is applied not only to sunlight, but also to the light of any glowing substance when its rays are sorted out by a prism or a grating.

MODEL

## First-Read Guide

You may want to use a guide like this to organize your thoughts after you read. Here is how a reader completed a First-Read Guide.

Use this page to record your first-read ideas.

Selection Title: Classifying the Stars

NOTICE

**NOTICE** new information or ideas you learned about the unit topic as you first read this text.

Light = different waves of colors. (Spectrum)

Newton - the first person to observe these waves using a prism.

Faunhofer saw gaps in the spectrum.

ANNOTATE

**ANNOTATE** by marking vocabulary and key passages you want to revisit.

Vocabulary
- myriad
- grating
- component colors

Different light types = different lengths

Isaac Newton also worked theories of gravity.

Multiple spectral tints? "colors of various appearance"

Key Passage:
Paragraph 3 shows that Fraunhofer discovered more about the nature of light spectrums: he saw the spaces in between the tints.

NOTICE ANNOTATE First Read CONNECT RESPOND

CONNECT

**CONNECT** ideas within the selection to other knowledge and the selections you have read.

I remember learning about prisms in science class.

Double rainbows! My favorite. How are they made?

RESPOND

**RESPOND** by writing a brief summary of the selection.

Science allows us to see things not visible to the naked eye. What we see as sunlight is really a spectrum of colors. By using tools, such as prisms, we can see the components of sunlight and other light. They appear as single colors or as multiple colors separated by gaps of no color. White light contains a rainbow of colors.

# CLOSE READING

* Key Idea
! I love it!
? I have questions
◯ Unfamiliar or important word
---- Context Clues

In a close read, go back into the text to study it in greater detail. Take the time to analyze not only the author's ideas but the way that those ideas are conveyed. Consider the genre of the text, the author's word choice, the writer's unique style, and the message of the text.

Here is how one reader close read this text.

MODEL

INFORMATIONAL TEXT

## *from* Classifying the Stars

**Cecilia H. Payne**

NOTES

explanation of sunlight and starlight

What is light and where do the colors come from?

1 Sunlight and starlight are composed of waves of various lengths, which the eye, even aided by a telescope, is unable to separate. We must use more than a telescope. In order to sort out the component colors, the light must be dispersed by a prism, or split up by some other means. For instance, sunbeams passing through rain drops, are transformed into the myriad-tinted rainbow. The familiar rainbow spanning the sky is Nature's most glorious demonstration that light is composed of many colors.

This paragraph is about Newton and the prism.

What discoveries helped us understand light?

2 The very beginning of our knowledge of the nature of a star dates back to 1672, when Isaac Newton gave to the world the results of his experiments on passing sunlight through a prism. To describe the beautiful band of rainbow tints, produced when sunlight was dispersed by his three-cornered piece of glass, he took from the Latin the word *spectrum*, meaning an appearance. The rainbow is the spectrum of the Sun. . . .

Fraunhofer and gaps in spectrum

3 In 1814, more than a century after Newton, the spectrum of the Sun was obtained in such purity that an amazing detail was seen and studied by the German optician, Fraunhofer. He saw that the multiple spectral tints, ranging from delicate violet to deep red, were crossed by hundreds of fine dark lines. In other words, there were narrow gaps in the spectrum where certain shades were wholly blotted out. We must remember that the word spectrum is applied not only to sunlight, but also to the light of any glowing substance when its rays are sorted out by a prism or a grating.

MODEL

# Close-Read Guide

You can use the Close-Read Guide to help you dig deeper into the text. Here is how a reader completed a Close-Read Guide.

**Use this page to record your close-read ideas.**

**Selection Title:** Classifying the Stars

## Close Read the Text

Revisit sections of the text you marked during your first read. Read these sections closely and **annotate** what you notice. Ask yourself **questions** about the text. What can you **conclude?** Write down your ideas.

Paragraph 3: Light is composed of waves of various lengths. Prisms let us see different colors in light. This is called the spectrum. Fraunhofer proved that there are gaps in the spectrum, where certain shades are blotted out.

More than one researcher studied this and each built off the ideas that were already discovered.

ANNOTATE · QUESTION · CONCLUDE · Close Read

## Analyze the Text

Think about the author's choices of patterns, structure, techniques, and ideas included in the text. Select one, and record your thoughts about what this choice conveys.

The author showed the development of human knowledge of the spectrum chronologically. Helped me see how ideas were built upon earlier understandings. Used dates and "more than a century after Newton" to show time.

## QuickWrite

Pick a paragraph from the text that grabbed your interest. Explain the power of this passage.

The first paragraph grabbed my attention, specifically the sentence "The familiar rainbow spanning the sky is Nature's most glorious demonstration that light is composed of many colors." The paragraph began as a straightforward scientific explanation. When I read the word "glorious," I had to stop and deeply consider what was being said. It is a word loaded with personal feelings. With that one word, the author let the reader know what was important to her.

Close Read
ANNOTATE QUESTION CONCLUDE

## Analyzing Legal Meanings and Reasoning

Reading historical and legal texts requires careful analysis of both the vocabulary and the logical flow of ideas that support a conclusion.

NOTES

### Understanding Legal Meanings

The language of historical and legal documents is formal, precise, and technical. Many words in these texts have specific meanings that you need to understand in order to follow the flow of ideas. For example, the second amendment to the U.S. Constitution states that "A well regulated Militia being necessary to the security of a free State, the right of the people to keep and bear Arms shall not be infringed." To understand this amendment, it is important to know that in this context *militia* means "armed forces," *bear* means "carry," and *infringed* means "denied." To understand legal meanings:

- Use your knowledge of word roots to help you understand unfamiliar words. Many legal terms use familiar Greek or Latin roots, prefixes, or suffixes.
- Do not assume that you know a word's legal meaning: Use a dictionary to check the meanings of key words to be certain that you are applying the correct meaning.
- Paraphrase the text to aid comprehension. Replace difficult words with synonyms to make sure you follow the logic of the argument.

### Delineating Legal Reasoning

Works of public advocacy, such as court decisions, political proclamations, proposed laws, or constitutional amendments, use careful reasoning to support conclusions. These strategies can help you understand the legal reasoning in an argument:

- State the **purpose** of the document in your own words to help you focus on the writer's primary goal.
- Look for the line of reasoning that supports the **arguments** presented. To be valid and persuasive, key arguments should be backed up by clearly stated logical analysis. Be aware of persuasive techniques, such as citing facts and statistics, referring to expert testimonials, and using emotional language with strong connotations.
- Identify the **premises,** or evidence, upon which a decision rests. In legal texts, premises often include **precedents,** which are earlier examples that must be followed or specifically overturned. Legal reasoning is usually based on the decisions of earlier trials. Be sure you understand precedents in order to identify how the court arrived at the current decision.

MODEL

Note the strategies used to evaluate legal meanings and reasoning in this Supreme Court decision from 1954 regarding the legality of segregated, "separate but equal" schools for students of different races.

LEGAL TEXT

## from *Brown v. Board of Education of Topeka*, Opinion of the Supreme Court by Chief Justice Earl Warren

We come then to the question presented: Does segregation of children in public schools solely on the basis of race, even though the physical facilities and other "tangible" factors may be equal, deprive the children of the minority group of equal educational opportunities? We believe that it does.

In *Sweatt v. Painter*, in finding that a segregated law school for Negroes could not provide them equal educational opportunities, this Court relied in large part on "those qualities which are incapable of objective measurement but which make for greatness in a law school." In *McLaurin v. Oklahoma State Regents*, the Court, in requiring that a Negro admitted to a white graduate school be treated like all other students, again resorted to intangible considerations: ". . . his ability to study, to engage in discussions and exchange views with other students, and, in general, to learn his profession." Such considerations apply with added force to children in grade and high schools. To separate them from others of similar age and qualifications solely because of their race generates a feeling of inferiority as to their status in the community that may affect their hearts and minds in a way unlikely ever to be undone. The effect of this separation on their educational opportunities was well stated by a finding in the Kansas case by a court which nevertheless felt compelled to rule against the Negro plaintiffs: Segregation of white and colored children in public schools has a detrimental effect upon the colored children. The impact is greater when it has the sanction of the law, for the policy of separating the races is usually interpreted as denoting the inferiority of the negro group. A sense of inferiority affects the motivation of a child to learn. Segregation with the sanction of law, therefore, has a tendency to [retard] the educational and mental development of negro children and to deprive them of some of the benefits they would receive in a racially integrated school system. Whatever may have been the extent of psychological knowledge at the time of *Plessy v. Ferguson*, this finding is amply supported by modern authority. Any language in *Plessy v. Ferguson* contrary to this finding is rejected.

We conclude that, in the field of public education, the doctrine of "separate but equal" has no place. Separate educational facilities are inherently unequal.

**Use Word Roots** The word *tangible* comes from the Latin root meaning "to touch." In this decision, the court contrasts tangible, measurable features with intangible features that are difficult to measure.

**Identify the Premises** The court cites two precedents: earlier cases relating to unequal education opportunities for black students.

**Paraphrase the Text** Here's one way you might break down the ideas in this sentence when you paraphrase: Segregating students just because of their race makes them feel as if they are less valued by our society. This separation can have a permanent negative influence on their character.

**Line of Reasoning** The conclusion makes the **purpose** of the decision clear: to overturn the precedent established by *Plessy v.* Ferguson. The **argument** describes the reasons the Court no longer considers the reasoning in that earlier case to be valid.

## Argument

When you think of the word *argument*, you might think of a disagreement between two people, but an argument is more than that. An argument is a logical way of presenting a belief, conclusion, or stance. A good argument is supported with reasoning and evidence.

Argument writing can be used for many purposes, such as to change a reader's point of view or opinion or to bring about an action or a response from a reader.

### Elements of an Argumentative Text

An **argument** is a logical way of presenting a viewpoint, belief, or stand on an issue. A well-written argument may convince the reader, change the reader's mind, or motivate the reader to take a certain action.

An effective argument contains these elements:

- a precise claim
- consideration of counterclaims, or opposing positions, and a discussion of their strengths and weaknesses
- logical organization that makes clear connections among claim, counterclaim, reasons, and evidence
- valid reasoning and evidence
- a concluding statement or section that logically completes the argument
- formal and objective language and tone
- error-free grammar, including accurate use of transitions

MODEL

ARGUMENT: SCORE 1

## Community Service Should be a Requirement for High School Graduation

Volunteering is a great idea for high school students. Those who don't volunteer are missing out.

The claim is not clearly stated in the introduction.

You can learn a lot at your volunteer job. It might not seem like a big deal at the time, but the things you learn and do can be useful. You might volunteer somewhere with a spreadsheet. Everyone needs to know how to use a spreadsheet! That's going to be a useful again really soon.

Their lots of reasons to get involved. One of them is to become a better student in school. Also, to feel better about yourself and not act out so much.

The argument contains mistakes in standard English conventions of usage and mechanics.

So, volunteering helps you learn and get better at lots of things, not just what you are doing at your volunteer job. It's good not just to learn reading and writing and math and science all the time—the usual stuff we study in school. That's how volunteering can help you out.

The vocabulary used is limited and ineffective, and the tone is informal.

Students today are really busy and they can't add anything more to they're busy schedules. But I think they can add a little more if it doesn't take too much time. Especially if it is important like volunteering.

The writer does not acknowledge counterclaims.

High school students who volunteer get involved with the real world outside school, and that means a lot. They have a chance to do something that can make a difference in the world. This helps them learn things that maybe they can't learn in school, like, how to be kind and jenerous and care about making the world a better place.

Volunteering in high school is a great idea. Everybody should do it. There are lots of different ways to volunteer. You can even do it on weekends with your friends.







**R9**

# WRITING

MODEL

ARGUMENT: SCORE 2

## Community Service Should be a Requirement for High School Graduation

High school students should have to volunteer before they can graduate. It makes sense because it is helpful to them and others. Some students would volunteer anyway even if it wasn't required, but some wouldn't. If they have to do it for graduation then they won't miss out.

The introduction establishes the claim.

Their lots of reasons to get involved. One is to be a better student in school. Researchers have done studies to see the connection between community service and doing well in school. One study showed that most schools with programs said grades went up most of the time for kids that volunteered. Another study said elementary and middle school kids got better at problem-solving and were more interested in school. One study said students showed more responsibility. Another researcher discovered that kids who been volunteering have better self-esteem. They also have fewer problems.

The tone of the argument is occasionally formal and objective.

Volunteering helps you learn and improve at lots of things, not just what you are doing at your volunteer job. One thing you might get better at is being a nicer person, like having more patience and listening well to others. Because you might need those skills when you are volunteering at a senior center or a preschool.

Some people say that volunteering in high school should NOT be required for graduation. They say students already have too much to do and they can't add anything more to they're schedules. But they can add a little more if it doesn't take too much time. Especially if it is important like volunteering.

The writer briefly acknowledges and refutes counterclaims.

Why should students be forced to do something, even if it is good? Well, that's just the way it is. When you force students to do something that is good, you are doing them a favor. Like forcing them to eat their vegetables or do their homework. The kids might not like it at first but what do you want to bet they are happy about it later on. That's the point.

The writers relies too much on weak anecdotal evidence.

Volunteering should be required for all high school students before they graduate. That's not just because they can do a lot of good in the world, but also because doing community service will help them in lots of ways.

The conclusion offers some insight into the claim and restates some information.

MODEL

ARGUMENT: SCORE 3

## Community Service Should be a Requirement for High School Graduation

Requiring community service for high school graduation is an excellent idea that offers benefits not only to the community but to the student as well. Making it a requirement ensures that all students will be able to get in on the act.

> The claim is established in the introduction but is not as clear as it could be.

Volunteering is a great way to build skills. It might not seem like a big deal at the time, but the experience you gain is very likely to be useful in the future. For example, while tracking, sorting, and distributing donations at an afterschool program, a volunteer might learn how to use a spreadsheet. That's going to come in handy very quickly, both in and out of school.

Participating in service learning can help you do better in school. ("Service learning" is when community service is part of a class curriculum.) For example, one study found that most schools with service learning programs reported grade point averages of participating students improved 76 percent of the time. Another study showed improved problem-solving skills and increased interest in academics among elementary and middle school students.

> The tone of the argument is mostly formal and objective.

A study showed that middle and high school students who participated in quality service learning projects showed more personal and social responsibility. Another study found that students were more likely to help each other and be kind to each other, and care about doing their best. Studies also show better self-esteem and fewer behavioral problems in students who have been involved with service learning.

> The writer does not transition very well into new topics.

Despite all this, many people say that volunteering in high school should NOT be a requirement for graduation. They point out that students today are already over-stressed and over-scheduled. There simply isn't room for anything more.

> The writer uses some transitional phrases.

> The writer gives a reason for the counterclaim, but does not provide firm examples.

True! But community service doesn't have to take up a lot of time. It might be possible for a group of time-stressed students to use class-time to organize a fundraiser, or to squeeze their service into a single "marathon" weekend. It's all a question of priorities.

In short, volunteering is a great way for students to help others, and reap benefits for themselves as well. Making it a requirement ensures that all students have the chance to grow through involvement with their communities. Volunteering opens doors and offers life-long benefits, and high school is the perfect time to get started!

> The conclusion restates the claim and provides additional detail.

TOOL KIT: WRITING

MODEL

ARGUMENT: SCORE 4

## Community Service Should be a Requirement for High School Graduation

Every high school student should be required to do community service in order to graduate. Volunteering offers life-long benefits that will prepare all students for adulthood.

First and foremost, studies show that participating in service learning —when community service is part of a class curriculum—often helps students do better in school. For example, a study conducted by Leeward County found that 83 percent of schools with service learning programs reported grade point averages of participating students improved 76 percent of the time. Another study, conducted by Hilliard Research, showed improved problem-solving skills and increased interest in academics among elementary and middle school students who participated in service learning.

But it's not just academic performance that can improve through volunteering: There are social and psychological benefits as well. For example, a student survey showed that students who participated in quality service learning projects showed more personal and social responsibility. Another survey found that students involved in service learning were more likely to be kind to each other, and care about doing their best. Studies also show better self-esteem and fewer behavioral problems in students who have been involved with service learning.

Despite all this, there are still many who say that volunteering in high school should NOT be a requirement for graduation. They point out that students today are already over-stressed and over-scheduled. What's more, requiring community service for graduation would be particularly hard on athletes and low-income students who work after school to help their families make ends meet.

Good points, but community service does not have to take up vast quantities of time. It might be possible for a group of time-stressed students to use class-time to organize a fundraiser, or to compress their service into a single "marathon" weekend. Showing students that helping others is something to make time for is an important lesson.

In short, volunteering encourages engagement: It shows students that their actions matter, and that they have the power—and responsibility—to make the world a better place. What could be a more important lesson than that?

The introduction establishes the writer's claim in a clear and compelling way.

The writer uses a variety of sentence transitions.

Sources of evidence are comprehensive and contain relevant information.

Counterclaims are clearly acknowledged and refuted.

The conclusion offers fresh insight into the claim.

## Argument Rubric

| | Focus and Organization | Evidence and Elaboration | Conventions |
|---|---|---|---|
| 4 | The introduction engages the reader and establishes a claim in a compelling way.<br>The argument includes valid reasons and evidence that address and support the claim while clearly acknowledging counterclaims.<br>The ideas progress logically, and transitions make connections among ideas clear.<br>The conclusion offers fresh insight into the claim. | The sources of evidence are comprehensive and specific and contain relevant information.<br>The tone of the argument is always formal and objective.<br>The vocabulary is always appropriate for the audience and purpose. | The argument intentionally uses standard English conventions of usage and mechanics. |
| 3 | The introduction engages the reader and establishes the claim.<br>The argument includes reasons and evidence that address and support my claim while acknowledging counterclaims.<br>The ideas progress logically, and some transitions are used to help make connections among ideas clear.<br>The conclusion restates the claim and important information. | The sources of evidence contain relevant information.<br>The tone of the argument is mostly formal and objective.<br>The vocabulary is generally appropriate for the audience and purpose. | The argument demonstrates general accuracy in standard English conventions of usage and mechanics. |
| 2 | The introduction establishes a claim.<br>The argument includes some reasons and evidence that address and support the claim while briefly acknowledging counterclaims.<br>The ideas progress somewhat logically. A few sentence transitions are used that connect readers to the argument.<br>The conclusion offers some insight into the claim and restates information. | The sources of evidence contain some relevant information.<br>The tone of the argument is occasionally formal and objective.<br>The vocabulary is somewhat appropriate for the audience and purpose. | The argument demonstrates some accuracy in standard English conventions of usage and mechanics. |
| 1 | The introduction does not clearly state the claim.<br>The argument does not include reasons or evidence for the claim. No counterclaims are acknowledged.<br>The ideas do not progress logically. Transitions are not included to connect ideas.<br>The conclusion does not restate any information that is important. | Reliable and relevant evidence is not included.<br>The vocabulary used is limited or ineffective.<br>The tone of the argument is not objective or formal. | The argument contains mistakes in standard English conventions of usage and mechanics. |







R13

# WRITING

## Informative/Explanatory Texts

Informative and explanatory writing should rely on facts to inform or explain. Informative writing serves several purposes: to increase readers' knowledge of a subject, to help readers better understand a procedure or process, or to provide readers with an enhanced comprehension of a concept. It should also feature a clear introduction, body, and conclusion.

### Elements of Informative/Explanatory Texts

**Informative/explanatory texts** present facts, details, data, and other kinds of evidence to give information about a topic. Readers turn to informational and explanatory texts when they wish to learn about a specific idea, concept, or subject area, or if they want to learn how to do something.

An effective informative/explanatory text contains these elements:

- a topic sentence or thesis statement that introduces the concept or subject
- relevant facts, examples, and details that expand upon a topic
- definitions, quotations, and/or graphics that support the information given
- headings (if desired) to separate sections of the essay
- a structure that presents information in a direct, clear manner
- clear transitions that link sections of the essay
- precise words and technical vocabulary where appropriate
- formal and object language and tone
- a conclusion that supports the information given and provides fresh insights

MODEL

INFORMATIVE: SCORE 1

## How Technology is Changing the Way We Work

Lot's of people work on computers. So, technology is everywhere. If you feel comfortable using computers and all kinds of other technology, your going to be a head at work, for sure.

They're new Devices and Apps out there every day. Each different job has its own gadgets and programs and apps that you have to learn. Every day their more new apps and devices, they can do all kinds of things.

In the past, people only worked at the office. They didn't get to work at home. Now, if you have a smart phone, you can check your email wherever. You can work at home on a computer. You can work in cafés or wherever. Also on a tablet. If you wanted to, you can be working all the time. But that will be a drag!

Technology is now an important part of almost every job. You also have to have a website. You have to have a social media page. Maybe if your business is doing really well you could afford to hire someone to take care of all that stuff—but it would be better if you knew how to do it yourself.

Technology brings people together and helps them work. It could be someone next to you or someone even on the other side of the world. You can connect with them using email. You can send a text. You could have a conference or video call.

Working from home is cheaper for the worker and boss. They can get stuff done during the day like going to the post office or the library, or picking up their kids at school. This is all thanks to technology.

Lots of jobs today are in technology. Way more than before! That's why it's a good idea to take classes and learn about something in technology, because then you will be able to find a job.

There are apps to find houses for sale, find restaurants, learn new recipes, keep track of how much you exercise, and all kinds of other things, like playing games and tuning your guitar. And there are apps to help you work. It's hard to imagine how people would manage to work now without this kind of technology to help them.

The writer's opening statement does not adequately introduce the thesis, and there are numerous spelling mistakes.

The writer's word choice often does not support the proper tone the essay ought to have.

The essay's sentences are often not purposeful, varied, or well-controlled.

The writer does not include a concluding statement.

MODEL

INFORMATIVE: SCORE 2

## How Technology is Changing the Way We Work

Technology affects the way we work, in every kind of job and industry. Each different job has its own gadgets and programs and apps that you have to learn. Every day there are more new apps and devices that can do all kinds of things.

The writer's opening does not clearly introduce the thesis.

In the past, people went to the office to work. That's not always true today. Now if you have a smart phone, you can check your email wherever you are. You can work at home on a desktop computer. You can work on a laptop in a café or wherever. Or a tablet. Technology makes it so people can work all the time.

It doesn't matter whether the person is on the other side of the world—technology brings you together. Theirs email. Theirs text messaging. You have conference calls. You've got video calling. All these things let people work together wherever they are. And don't forget, today people can access files from the cloud. That helps them work from whatever device they want. More than one person can work on the same file.

The essay is somewhat lacking in organizational structure.

Different kinds of work places and schedules are becoming more common and normal. Working from home has benefits businesses. It means cost savings. It means higher productivity. It means higher job satisfaction. They can get stuff done during the day like going to the post office or the bank, or picking up their kids at school. That is very convenient.

The essay has many interesting details, but some do not relate specifically to the topic.

It's also true that lots and lots of jobs today are in technology, or related to technology in some way. Way more than before! That's why it's a good idea to get a degree or take classes and learn about something in technology, because it seems like that's where all the new jobs are. Software designers make a really good salary, and so do other tech-related jobs.

The writer's word choice is overly informal.

Technology is now an important part of almost every job. It's no longer enough to be just a photographer or whatever. You have to get a social media page. You have to be able to use the latest tech gadgets. You can't just take pictures.

The writer's sentences are disjointed and ineffective.

In todays world, technology is changing how we work. You have to be able to feel comfortable with technology in order to survive at work. Even if you really don't like technology, you don't really have a choice. So, get used to it!

The conclusion follows logically but is not mature and is overly informal.

MODEL

INFORMATIVE: SCORE 3

## How Technology Is Changing the Way We Work

Technology has been changing how we work for a long time, but the pace of change has gotten dramatically faster. No industry or job is exempt. Powerful computing technology and Internet connectivity affects all sectors of the economy. It doesn't matter what job you're talking about: Technology is transforming the way people work. It's an exciting time to be entering the workforce!

### The Office Is Everywhere

Technology is rapidly changing not just *how* but *where, when,* and *with whom* we work. It used to be that work was something that happened only at the office. All kinds of different work places and schedules are becoming much more common and normal. According to a study, telecommuting (working from home) rose 79 percent between 2005 and 2012. Working from home has benefits for both the employee and employer. It means cost savings for both, increased productivity, and higher job satisfaction.

### The Cloud

Cloud and other data storage and sharing options mean that workers have access to information whenever they want, wherever they are. Whether it's one person who wants the convenience of being able to work on a file from several devices (and locations), or several people who are working on something together, the ability to store data in the cloud and access it from anywhere is a huge change in the way we work. It's almost like all being in the same office, working on the same computer.

### Tech Industries and Jobs

Technology is changing the way we work in part by making technology itself such an important element in almost every profession. Therefore, you can see it's no longer good enough to be just a photographer or contractor. You have to know something about technology to do your job, market yourself, and track your performance. No matter what jobs someone does they have to be tech-savvy to be able to use their devices to connect and interact with each other across the globe.

### Conclusion

In todays world, technology is quickly and continuously changing how we work, what we do, where and when we do it. In order to do well and thrive, everyone has to be a little bit of a tech geek. So, get used to technology being a part of your work life. And get used to change. Because, in a constantly changing technological world, change is going to be one of the few things that stays the same!

The thesis is introduced but is buried in the introduction.

The writer uses headings to help make the organization of ideas clear.

Statistics support the writer's claim.

The writer uses some transitions and sentence connections, but more would be helpful.

There are a few errors in spelling and punctuation but they do not detract from the effectiveness of the essay.

The conclusion sums up the main ideas of the essay and links to the opening statements.

MODEL

INFORMATIVE: SCORE 4

## How Technology Is Changing the Way We Work

While advances in technology have been changing how we work for hundreds of years, the pace of change has accelerated dramatically in the past two decades. With powerful computing technology and Internet connectivity affecting all sectors of the economy, no industry or profession is exempt. It doesn't matter whether you're talking about financial advisors, architects, or farmers: Technology is transforming the way people work.

### The Office Is Everywhere

Technology is rapidly revolutionizing not just *how* but *where, when,* and *with whom* we work. It used to be that work was something that happened strictly at the office. In fact, non-traditional work places are becoming much more common. According to one study, telecommuting rose 79 percent between 2005 and 2012. Working from home has proven benefits for both the employee and employer, including cost savings for both, increased productivity, and job satisfaction.

### Working with the Cloud

Another important technological advancement that is impacting how we work is the development of cloud computing. Whether it's one person who wants the convenience of being able to work from several devices, or several people who are working together from different locations, the ability to store data in the cloud and access it from anywhere is a huge change in the way we work. Over long distances, coworkers can not only *communicate* with each other, they can *collaborate*, in real time, by sharing and accessing files through the. Only five years ago, this kind of instant access was impossible.

### Tech Industries and Jobs

Technology is changing the way we work is by making technology itself an important element in almost every job. It's no longer good enough to be just a photographer or contractor: you have to know something about technology to perform, market, and track your work. No matter what job someone is doing, he or she has to be tech-savvy to be able to use their devices to connect and interact.

### Conclusion

In today's world, technology is quickly and continuously changing what work we do, and how, where, when, and with whom we do it. Comfort with new technology—and with rapid technological change—is a prerequisite for success, no matter where your interests lie, or what kind of job you are looking to find. It's a brave new technological world of work, and it's changing every day!

The opening paragraph ends with a thesis, which is strong and clear.

The writer makes an effort to be thoughtful and engage the reader.

Headings help ensure that the organizing structure of the essay is clear and effective.

The sentences in the essay are purposeful and varied.

The progression of ideas in the essay is logical and well-controlled.

The writer's word choice contributes to the clarity of the essay and shows awareness of the essay's purpose and tone.

## Informative/Explanatory Rubric

| | Focus and Organization | Evidence and Elaboration | Conventions |
|---|---|---|---|
| 4 | The introduction engages the reader and states a thesis in a compelling way.<br>The essay includes a clear introduction, body, and conclusion.<br>The conclusion summarizes ideas and offers fresh insight into the thesis. | The essay includes specific reasons, details, facts, and quotations from selections and outside resources to support thesis.<br>The tone of the essay is always formal and objective.<br>The language is always precise and appropriate for the audience and purpose. | The essay uses standard English conventions of usage and mechanics.<br>The essay contains no spelling errors. |
| 3 | The introduction engages the reader and sets forth the thesis.<br>The essay includes an introduction, body, and conclusion.<br>The conclusion summarizes ideas and supports the thesis. | The research includes some specific reasons, details, facts, and quotations from selections and outside resources to support the thesis.<br>The tone of the research is mostly formal and objective.<br>The language is generally precise and appropriate for the audience and purpose. | The essay demonstrates general accuracy in standard English conventions of usage and mechanics.<br>The essay contains few spelling errors. |
| 2 | The introduction sets forth the thesis.<br>The essay includes an introduction, body, and conclusion, but one or more parts is weak.<br>The conclusion partially summarizes ideas but may not provide strong support of the thesis. | The research includes a few reasons, details, facts, and quotations from selections and outside resources to support the thesis.<br>The tone of the research is occasionally formal and objective.<br>The language is somewhat precise and appropriate for the audience and purpose. | The presentations demonstrates some accuracy in standard English conventions of usage and mechanics.<br>The essay contains some spelling errors. |
| 1 | The introduction does not state the thesis clearly.<br>The essay does not include an introduction, body, and conclusion.<br>The conclusion does not summarize ideas and may not relate to the thesis. | Reliable and relevant evidence is not included.<br>The tone of the essay is not objective or formal.<br>The language used is imprecise and not appropriate for the audience and purpose. | The essay contains mistakes in standard English conventions of usage and mechanics.<br>The essay contains many spelling errors. |

## Narration

Narrative writing conveys experience, either real or imaginary, and uses time to provide structure. It can be used to inform, instruct, persuade, or entertain. Whenever writers tell a story, they are using narrative writing. Most types of narrative writing share certain elements, such as characters, setting, a sequence of events, and, often, a theme.

### Elements of a Narrative Text

A **narrative** is any type of writing that tells a story, whether it is fiction, nonfiction, poetry, or drama.

An effective nonfiction narrative usually contains these elements:

- an engaging beginning in which characters and setting are established
- characters who participate in the story events
- a well-structured, logical sequence of events
- details that show time and place
- effective story elements such as dialogue, description, and reflection
- the narrator's thoughts, feelings, or views about the significance of events
- use of language that brings the characters and setting to life

An effective fictional narrative usually contains these elements:

- an engaging beginning in which characters, setting, or a main conflict is introduced
- a main character and supporting characters who participate in the story events
- a narrator who relates the events of the plot from a particular point of view
- details that show time and place
- conflict that is resolved in the course of the narrative
- narrative techniques such as dialogue, description, and suspense
- use of language that vividly brings to life characters and events

MODEL

NARRATIVE: SCORE 1

## Getting Away With It

That night, Luanne made two mistakes.

She ran in the house.

The McTweedys were rich and had a huge place and there was an expensive rug.

She was sad in her room remembering what happened:

She was carrying a tray of glasses back to the kitchen and spilled on the carpet. She tried to put furniture over it. Then she ran in the rain.

Luanne should have come clean. She would of said I'm sorry, Mrs. Mc Tweedy, I spilled punch on ur carpet.

She knew getting away with it felt crummy for some reason. it was wrong and she also didn't want to get in trouble.

The phone rings.

"Oh, hello?"

"It's Mrs. Tweedy's!" said her mom. "You forgot to get paid!"

Luanne felt relieve. She was going to do the right thing.

The introduction is interesting but is not built upon.

The chronology and situation are unclear.

The narrative contains mistakes in standard English conventions of usage and mechanics.

The name of the character does not remain consistent.

The conclusion reveals what will happen but is not interesting.

TOOL KIT: WRITING

# WRITING

MODEL

NARRATIVE: SCORE 2

## Getting Away With It

That night, Luanne made two fatal mistakes: ruining a rug, and thinking she could get away with it.

She ran in the house.

The McTweedys hired her to be a waiter at their party. They were rich and had a huge place and there was an expensive rug.

She was sad in her room remembering what happened:

Luanne was wearing black pants and a white shirt. She was carrying a tray of glasses back to the kitchen. One spilled on the carpet. She tried to put furniture to cover up the stain. She ran away in the rain.

Luanne should have come clean right away. But what would she have said? I'm sorry, Mrs. McTweedy, but I spilled punch all over your expensive carpet.

Luanne imagined getting away with it. But getting away with it felt crummy for some reason. She knew it was wrong somehow, but she also didn't want to get in trouble.

The phone rang.

"Oh, hello, how was the party?"

Luanne felt like throwing up.

"Mrs. McTweedy's on the phone!" her mom sang out. "She said you forgot your check!"

Luanne felt relieved. But she already made up her mind to do the right thing.

The introduction establishes a clear context.

The writer has made some mistakes in spelling, grammar, and punctuation.

The chronology is sometimes unclear.

Narrative techniques, such as the use of dialogue, are used at times.

The conclusion tells what will happen but is not interesting.







R22

MODEL

NARRATIVE: SCORE 3

## Getting Away With It

That night, Luanne made two fatal mistakes: (1) ruining a priceless Persian rug, and (2) thinking she could get away with it.

She bursted in the front door breathless.

"How was it?" called her mom.

The McTweedys had hired her to serve drinks at their fundraiser. Henry and Estelle McTweedy loved having parties. They were rich and had a huge apartment filled with rare books, art, and tapestries from all over the world.

"Luanne? Are you alright?"

"Just tired, Mom."

Actually she was face-planted on her bed, replaying the scene over and over just in case she could change it.

It was like a movie: A girl in black trousers and a crisp white shirt carrying a tray of empty glasses back to the kitchen. Then the girl's horrified expression as she realizes that one of the glasses was not quite as empty as she'd thought and was dripping onto the carpet. The girl frantically moving furniture to cover up the stain. The girl running out of the apartment into the hard rain.

Luanne kicked herself. She should have come clean right away. But what would she have said? I'm sorry, Mrs. McTweedy, but I spilled punch all over your expensive carpet.

Luanne imagined getting away with it. But getting away with it felt crummy for some reason. She knew it was wrong somehow, but she also didn't want to get in trouble.

The phone was ringing. Luanne froze.

"Oh, hello there, Mrs. McTweedy! How was the party?"

Luanne felt felt like throwing up.

"Mrs. McTweedy's on the phone!" her mom sang out. "She said you forgot your check!"

Luanne felt relief. It was nothing at all! Although she'd already made up her mind to come clean. Because she had to do the right thing.

She walked into the kitchen. And then she explained the whole thing to both her mom and Mrs. McTweedy.

The story's introduction establishes a clear context and point of view.

Descriptive details, sensory language, and precise words and phrases help to bring the narrative to life.

The writer mostly attends to the norms and conventions of usage and punctuation, but sometimes makes mistakes.

The writer has effectively used dialogue in her story.

The conclusion follows logically but is not memorable.

# WRITING

MODEL

NARRATIVE: SCORE 4

## Getting Away With It

That night, Luanne made two fatal mistakes: (1) ruining a priceless Persian rug, and (2) thinking she could get away with it.

She'd burst in the front door breathless.

"How was it?" called her mother from the kitchen.

The McTweedys had hired Luanne to serve drinks at their fundraiser. Henry and Estelle McTweedy loved entertaining. They loved traveling, and the opera, and the finer things in life. They had a huge apartment filled with rare books, art, and tapestries from all over the world.

"Luanne? Are you alright?"

"Just tired, Mom."

Actually she was face-down on her bed, replaying the humiliating scene over and over just in case she could make it come out differently.

It was like a movie: A girl in black trousers and a crisp white shirt carrying a tray of empty glasses back to the kitchen. Cut to the girl's horrified expression as she realizes that one of the glasses —not quite as empty as she'd thought—was dripping its lurid contents onto the carpet. Close in on the girl's frantic attempts to move furniture over the stain. Montage of images showing the girl running out of the apartment into the pounding rain. Fade to Black.

Luanne could kick herself. She should have come clean right away. But what would she have said? *I'm sorry, Mrs. McTweedy, but I spilled punch all over your irreplaceable carpet.*

Luanne imagined getting away with it. If she got away with it, she'd be a person who got away with things. For the rest of her life, no matter what, she'd be a person who got away with things. And if something good happened to her, she'd feel like she didn't deserve it.

Somewhere in the house, a phone was ringing. Luanne froze and listened in.

"Oh, hello there, Estelle! How was the party?"

Luanne felt cold, then hot. Her skin prickled. She was sweating. She felt like throwing up.

"Mrs. McTweedy's on the phone!" Luanne's mother sang out. "She wants to tell you that you forgot your check!"

Luanne felt a surge a relief wash over her—it was nothing, nothing at all!—but she'd already made up her mind to come clean. Not because owning up to it was so Right, but because getting away with it was so wrong. Which made it right.

Luanne padded into the kitchen. "Don't hang up," she told her mother.

The writer provides an introduction that establishes a clear context and point of view.

The writer has used descriptive details, sensory language, and precise words and phrases.

The writer's use of movie terminology is clever and memorable.

The narrative presents a clear chronological sequence of events.

The writer effectively uses narrative techniques, such as dialogue.

The story's conclusion is abrupt but fitting. It reveals a critical decision that resolves the conflict.

## Narrative Rubric

| | Focus and Organization | Development of Ideas/ Elaboration | Conventions |
|---|---|---|---|
| 4 | The introduction establishes a clear context and point of view.<br>Events are presented in a clear sequence, building to a climax, then moving towards the conclusion.<br>The conclusion follows from and reflects on the events and experiences in the narrative. | Narrative techniques such as dialogue, pacing, and description are used effectively to develop characters, events, and strengths.<br>Descriptive details, sensory language, and precise words and phrases are used to convey the experiences in the narrative and to help the reader imagine the characters and setting.<br>Voice is established through word choice, sentence structure, and one. | The narrative uses standard English conventions of usage and mechanics; deviations from standard English are intentional and serve the purpose of the narrative.<br>Rules of spelling and punctuation are followed. |
| 3 | The introduction gives the reader some context and sets the point of view.<br>Events are presented logically, though there are some jumps in time.<br>The conclusion logically ends the story, but provides only some reflection on the experiences related in the story. | Narrative techniques such as dialogue, pacing, and description are used occasionally.<br>Description details, sensory language, and precise words and phrases are used occasionally.<br>Voice is established through word choice, sentence structure, and tone occasionally, though not evenly. | The narrative mostly uses standard English conventions of usage and mechanics, though there are some errors.<br>There are few errors in spelling and punctuation. |
| 2 | The introduction provides some description of a place. The point of view can be unclear at times.<br>Transitions between events are occasionally unclear.<br>The conclusion comes abruptly and provides only a small amount of reflection on the experiences related in the narrative. | Narrative techniques such as dialogue, pacing, and description are used sparingly.<br>The story contains few examples of descriptive details and sensory language.<br>Voice is not established for characters, so that it becomes difficult to determine who is speaking. | The narrative contains some errors in standard English conventions of usage and mechanics.<br>There are many errors in spelling and punctuation. |
| 1 | The introduction fails to set a scene or is omitted altogether. The point of view is not always clear.<br>The events are not in a clear sequence, and events that would clarify the narrative may not appear.<br>The conclusion does not follow from the narrative or is omitted altogether. | Appropriate narrative techniques such as dialogue, pacing, or reflection, are not used.<br>Details are vague or missing. No sensory language is included.<br>Voice has not been developed. | The text contains mistakes in standard English conventions of usage and mechanics.<br>Rules of spelling and punctuation have not been followed. |

## Conducting Research

We are lucky to live in an age when information is accessible and plentiful. However, not all information is equally useful, or even accurate. Strong research skills will help you locate and evaluate information.

### Narrowing or Broadening a Topic

The first step of any research project is determining your topic. Consider the scope of your project and choose a topic that is narrow enough to address completely and effectively. If you can name your topic in just one or two words, it is probably too broad. Topics such as Shakespeare, jazz, or science fiction are too broad to cover in a single report. Narrow a broad topic into smaller subcategories.

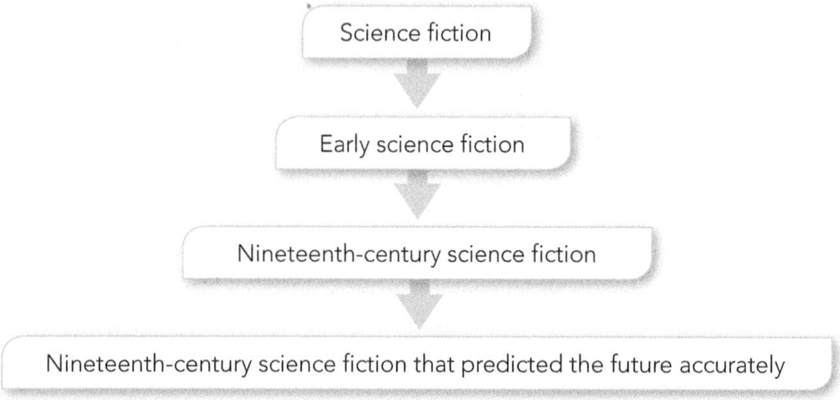

Science fiction

↓

Early science fiction

↓

Nineteenth-century science fiction

↓

Nineteenth-century science fiction that predicted the future accurately

When you begin to research a topic, pay attention to the amount of information available. If you feel overwhelmed by the number of relevant sources, you may need to narrow your topic further.

If there isn't enough information available as your research, you might need to broaden your topic. A topic is too narrow when it can be thoroughly presented in less space than the required size of your assignment. It might also be too narrow if you can find little or no information in library and media sources, so consider broadening your topic to include other related ideas.

### Generating Research Questions

Use research questions to focus your research. Specific questions can help you avoid time-wasting digressions. For example, instead of simply hunting for information about Mark Twain, you might ask, "What jobs did Mark Twain have, other than being a writer?" or "Which of Twain's books was most popular during his lifetime?"

In a research report, your research question often becomes your thesis statement, or may lead up to it. The question will also help you focus your research into a comprehensive but flexible search plan, as well as prevent you from gathering unnecessary details. As your research teaches you more about your topic, you may find it necessary to refocus your original question.

## Consulting Print and Digital Sources

Effective research combines information from several sources, and does not rely too heavily on a single source. The creativity and originality of your research depends on how you combine ideas from multiple sources. Plan to consult a variety of resources, such as the following:

- **Primary and Secondary Sources:** To get a thorough view of your topic, use primary sources (firsthand or original accounts, such as interview transcripts, eyewitness reports, and newspaper articles) and secondary sources (accounts, created after an event occurred, such as encyclopedia entries).
- **Print and Digital Resources:** The Internet allows fast access to data, but print resources are often edited more carefully. Use both print and digital resources in order to guarantee the accuracy of your findings.
- **Media Resources:** You can find valuable information in media resources such as documentaries, television programs, podcasts, and museum exhibitions. Consider attending public lectures given by experts to gain an even more in-depth view of your topic.
- **Original Research:** Depending on your topic, you may wish to conduct original research to include among your sources. For example, you might interview experts or eyewitnesses, or conduct a survey of people in your community.

**Using Online Encyclopedias**

Online encyclopedias are often written by anonymous contributors who are not required to fact-check information. These sites can be very useful as a launching point for research, but should not be considered accurate. Look for footnotes, endnotes, or hyperlinks that support facts with reliable sources that have been carefully checked by editors.

**Evaluating Sources** It is important to evaluate the credibility, validity, and accuracy of any information you find, as well as its appropriateness for your purpose and audience. You may find the information you need to answer your research question in specialized and authoritative sources, such as almanacs (for social, cultural, and natural statistics), government publications (for law, government programs, and subjects such as agriculture), and information services. Also, consider consumer, workplace, and public documents.

Ask yourself questions such as these to evaluate these additional sources:

- **Authority:** Is the author well known? What are the author's credentials? Does the source include references to other reliable sources? Does the author's tone win your confidence? Why or why not?
- **Bias:** Does the author have any obvious biases? What is the author's purpose for writing? Who is the target audience?
- **Currency:** When was the work created? Has it been revised? Is there more current information available?







R27

# RESEARCH

## Using Search Terms

Finding information on the Internet can be both easy and challenging. Type a word or phrase into a general search engine and you will probably get hundreds—or thousands—of results. However, those results are not guaranteed to be relevant or accurate.

These strategies can help you find information from the Internet:

- Create a list of keywords that apply to your topic before you begin using a search engine. Consult a thesaurus to expand your list.
- Enter six to eight keywords.
- Choose precise nouns. Most search engines ignore articles and prepositions. Verbs may be used in multiple contexts, leading to sources that are not relevant. Use modifiers, such as adjectives, when necessary to specify a category.
- Use quotation marks to focus a search. Place a phrase in quotation marks to find pages that include exactly that phrase. Add several phrases in quotation marks to narrow your results.
- Spell carefully. Many search engines autocorrect spelling, but they cannot produce accurate results for all spelling errors.
- Scan search results before you click them. The first result isn't always the most relevant. Read the text and consider the domain before make a choice.
- Utilize more than one search engine.



### Evaluating Internet Domains

Not everything you read on the Internet is true, so you have to evaluate sources carefully. The last three letters of an Internet URL identify the Website's domain, which can help you evaluate the information of the site.

- **.gov**—Government sites are sponsored by a branch of the United States federal government, such as the Census Bureau, Supreme Court, or Congress. These sites are considered reliable.
- **.edu**—Education domains include schools from kindergartens to universities. Information from an educational research center or department is likely to be carefully checked. However, education domains can also include student pages that are not edited or monitored.
- **.org**—Organizations are nonprofit groups and usually maintain a high level of credibility. Keep in mind that some organizations may express strong biases.
- **.com** and **.net**—Commercial sites exist to make a profit. Information may be biased to show a product or service in a good light. The company may be providing information to encourage sales or promote a positive image.

## Taking Notes

Take notes as you locate and connect useful information from multiple sources, and keep a reference list of every source you use. This will help you make distinctions between the relative value and significance of specific data, facts, and ideas.

For long-term research projects, create source cards and notecards to keep track of information gathered from multiple resources.

### Source Cards

Create a card that identifies each source.

- For print materials, list the author, title, publisher, date of publication, and relevant page numbers.
- For Internet sources, record the name and Web address of the site, and the date you accessed the information.
- For media sources, list the title, person, or group credited with creating the media, and the year of production.

### Notecards

Create a separate notecard for each item of information.

- Include the fact or idea, the letter of the related source card, and the specific page(s) on which the fact or idea appears.
- Use quotation marks around words and phrases taken directly from print or media resources.
- Mark particularly useful or relevant details using your own annotation method, such as stars, underlining, or colored highlighting.

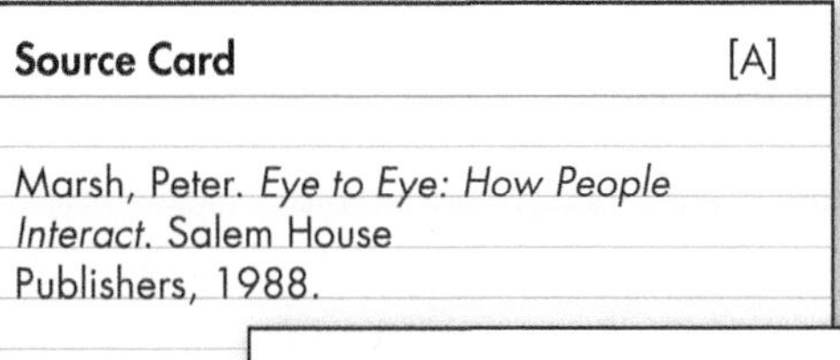

**Source Card** [A]

Marsh, Peter. *Eye to Eye: How People Interact.* Salem House Publishers, 1988.

**Notecard**

Gestures vary from culture to culture. The American "OK" symbol (thumb and forefinger) is considered insulting in Greece and Turkey.

Source Card: A, p. 54.

**Quote Accurately** Responsible research begins with the first note you take. Be sure to quote and paraphrase your sources accurately so you can identify these sources later. In your notes, circle all quotations and paraphrases to distinguish them from your own comments. When photocopying from a source, include the copyright information. When printing out information from an online source, include the Web address.

# RESEARCH

## Reviewing Research Findings

While conducting research, you will need to review your findings, checking that you have collected enough accurate and appropriate information.

### Considering Audience and Purpose

Always keep your audience in mind as you gather information, since different audiences may have very different needs. For example, if you are writing an in-depth analysis of a text that your entire class has read together and you are writing for your audience, you will not need to gather background information that has been thoroughly discussed in class. However, if you are writing the same analysis for a national student magazine, you cannot assume that all of your readers have the same background information. You will need to provide facts from reliable sources to help orient these readers to your subject. When considering whether or not your research will satisfy your audience, ask yourself:

- Who am I writing for?
- Have I collected enough information to explain my topic to this audience?
- Are there details in my research that I can omit because they are already familiar to my audience?

Your purpose for writing will also influence your review of research. If you are researching a question to satisfy your own curiosity, you can stop researching when you feel you understand the answer completely. If you are writing a research report that will be graded, you need to consider the criteria of the assignment. When considering whether or not you have enough information, ask yourself:

- What is my purpose for writing?
- Will the information I have gathered be enough to achieve my purpose?
- If I need more information, where might I find it?

### Synthesizing Sources

Effective research writing does not merely present facts and details; it synthesizes—gathers, orders, and interprets—them. These strategies will help you synthesize information effectively:

- Review your notes and look for connections and patterns among the details you have collected.
- Arrange notes or notecards in different ways to help you decide how to best combine related details and present them in a logical way.
- Pay close attention to details that support one other, emphasizing the same main idea.
- Also look for details that challenge each other, highlighting ideas about which there is no single, or consensus, opinion. You might decide to conduct additional research to help you decide which side of the issue has more support.

## Types of Evidence

When reviewing your research, also consider the kinds of evidence you have collected. The strongest writing contains a variety of evidence effectively. This chart describes three of the most common types of evidence: statistical, testimonial, and anecdotal.

| TYPE OF EVIDENCE | DESCRIPTION | EXAMPLE |
|---|---|---|
| Statistical evidence includes facts and other numerical data used to support a claim or explain a topic. | Examples of statistical evidence include historical dates and information, quantitative analyses, poll results, and quantitative descriptions. | "Although it went on to become a hugely popular novel, the first edition of William Goldman's book sold fewer than 3,000 copies." |
| Testimonial evidence includes any ideas or opinions presented by others, especially experts in a field. | Firsthand testimonies present ideas from eyewitnesses to events or subjects being discussed. | "The ground rose and fell like an ocean at ebb tide."<br>—Fred J. Hewitt, eyewitness to the 1906 San Francisco earthquake |
| | Secondary testimonies include commentaries on events by people who were not involved. You might quote a well-known literary critic when discussing a writer's most famous novel, or a prominent historian when discussing the effects of an important event | Gladys Hansen insists that "there was plenty of water in hydrants throughout [San Francisco] . . . The problem was this fire got away." |
| Anecdotal evidence presents one person's view of the world, often by describing specific events or incidents. | Compelling research should not rely solely on this form of evidence, but it can be very useful for adding personal insights and refuting inaccurate generalizations. An individual's experience can be used with other forms of evidence to present complete and persuasive support. | Although many critics claim the novel is universally beloved, at least one reader "threw the book against a wall because it made me so angry." |

## Incorporating Research Into Writing

### Avoiding Plagiarism

Plagiarism is the unethical presentation of someone else's ideas as your own. You must cite sources for direct quotations, paraphrased information, or facts that are specific to a single source. When you are drafting and revising, circle any words or ideas that are not your own. Follow the instructions on pages R34 and R35 to correctly cite those passages.

**Review for Plagiarism** Always take time to review your writing for unintentional plagiarism. Read what you have written and take note of any phrases or sentences that do not have your personal writing voice. Compare those passages with your resource materials. You might have copied them without remembering the exact source. Add a correct citation to give credit to the original author. If you cannot find the questionable phrase in your notes, revise it to ensure that your final report reflects your own thinking and not someone else's work.

### Quoting and Paraphrasing

When including ideas from research into your writing, you will decide to quote directly or paraphrase.

**Direct Quotation** Use the author's exact words when they are interesting or persuasive. You might decide to include direct quotations for these reasons:

- to share an especially clear and relevant statement
- to reference a historically significant passage
- to show that an expert agrees with your position
- to present an argument that you will counter in your writing.

Include complete quotations, without deleting or changing words. If you need to omit words for space or clarity, use ellipsis points to indicate the omission. Enclose direct quotations in quotation marks and indicate the author's name.

**Paraphrase** A paraphrase restates an author's ideas in your own words. Be careful to paraphrase accurately. Beware of making sweeping generalizations in a paraphrase that were not made by the original author. You may use some words from the original source, but a legitimate paraphrase does more than simply rearrange an author's phrases, or replace a few words with synonyms.

| | |
|---|---|
| **Original Text** | "*The Tempest* was written as a farewell to art and the artist's life, just before the completion of his forty-ninth year, and everything in the play bespeaks the touch of autumn." Brandes, Georg. "Analogies Between *The Tempest* and *A Midsummer Night's Dream*." *The Tempest*, by William Shakespeare, William Heinemann, 1904, p. 668. |
| **Patchwork Plagiarism**<br>phrases from the original are rearranged, but too closely follows the original text. | A farewell to art, Shakespeare's play, *The Tempest*, was finished just before the completion of his forty-ninth year. The artist's life was to end within three years. The touch of autumn is apparent in nearly everything in the play. |
| **Good Paraphrase** | Images of autumn occur throughout *The Tempest*, which Shakespeare wrote as a way of saying goodbye to both his craft and his own life. |

## Maintaining the Flow of Ideas

Effective research writing is much more that just a list of facts. Be sure to maintain the flow of ideas by connecting research information to your own ideas. Instead of simply stating a piece of evidence, use transition words and phrases to explain the connection between information you found from outside resources and your own ideas and purpose for writing. The following transitions can be used to introduce, compare, contrast, and clarify.

## Useful Transitions

**When providing examples:**

for example    for instance    to illustrate    in [name of resource], [author]

**When comparing and contrasting ideas or information:**

in the same way    similarly    however    on the other hand

**When clarifying ideas or opinions:**

in other words    that is    to explain    to put it another way

Choosing an effective organizational structure for your writing will help you create a logical flow of ideas. Once you have established a clear organizational structure, insert facts and details from your research in appropriate places to provide evidence and support for your writing.

| ORGANIZATIONAL STRUCTURE | USES |
|---|---|
| **Chronological order** presents information in the sequence in which it happens. | historical topics; science experiments; analysis of narratives |
| **Part-to-whole order** examines how several categories affect a larger subject. | analysis of social issues; historical topics |
| **Order of importance** presents information in order of increasing or decreasing importance. | persuasive arguments; supporting a bold or challenging thesis |
| **Comparison-and-contrast organization** outlines the similarities and differences of a given topic. | addressing two or more subjects |

# RESEARCH

## Formats for Citing Sources

In research writing, cite your sources. In the body of your paper, provide a footnote, an endnote, or a parenthetical citation, identifying the sources of facts, opinions, or quotations. At the end of your paper, provide a bibliography or a Works Cited list, a list of all the sources referred to in your research. Follow an established format, such as Modern Language Association (MLA) style.

**Parenthetical Citations (MLA Style)** A parenthetical citation briefly identifies the source from which you have taken a specific quotation, factual claim, or opinion. It refers readers to one of the entries on your Works Cited list. A parenthetical citation has the following features:

- It appears in parentheses.
- It identifies the source by the last name of the author, editor, or translator, or by the title (for a lengthy title, list the first word only).
- It provides a page reference, the page(s) of the source on which the information cited can be found.

A parenthetical citation generally falls outside a closing quotation mark but within the final punctuation of a clause or sentence. For a long quotation set off from the rest of your text, place the citation at the end of the excerpt without any punctuation following.

**Sample Parenthetical Citations**

It makes sense that baleen whales such as the blue whale, the bowhead whale, the humpback whale, and the sei whale (to name just a few) grow to immense sizes (Carwardine et al. 19–21). The blue whale has grooves running from under its chin to partway along the length of its underbelly. As in some other whales, these grooves expand and allow even more food and water to be taken in (Ellis 18–21).

Authors' last names

Page numbers where information can be found

**Works Cited List (MLA Style)** A Works Cited list must contain accurate information to enable a reader to locate each source you cite. The basic components of an entry are as follows:

- name of the author, editor, translator, and/or group responsible for the work
- title of the work
- publisher
- date of publication

For print materials, the information for a citation generally appears on the copyright and title pages. For the format of a Works Cited list, consult the examples on this page and in the MLA Style for Listing Sources chart.

**Sample Works Cited List (MLA 8th Edition)**

Carwardine, Mark, et al. *The Nature Company Guides: Whales, Dolphins, and Porpoises.* Time-Life, 1998.

"Discovering Whales." *Whales on the Net.* Whales in Danger, 1998, www.whales.org.au/discover/index.html. Accessed 11 Apr. 2017.

Neruda, Pablo. "Ode to Spring." *Odes to Opposites*, translated by Ken Krabbenhoft, edited and illustrated by Ferris Cook, Little, 1995, p. 16.

*The Saga of the Volsungs*. Translated by Jesse L. Byock, Penguin, 1990.

List an anonymous work by title.

List both the title of the work and the collection in which it is found.

**Works Cited List or Bibliography?**

A Works Cited list includes only those sources you paraphrased or quoted directly in your research paper. By contrast, a bibliography lists all the sources you consulted during research—even those you did not cite.

## MLA (8th Edition) Style for Listing Sources

| | |
|---|---|
| **Book with one author** | Pyles, Thomas. *The Origins and Development of the English Language.* 2nd ed., Harcourt Brace Jovanovich, 1971.<br>[Indicate the edition or version number when relevant.] |
| **Book with two authors** | Pyles, Thomas, and John Algeo. *The Origins and Development of the English Language.* 5th ed., Cengage Learning, 2004. |
| **Book with three or more authors** | Donald, Robert B., et al. *Writing Clear Essays.* Prentice Hall, 1983. |
| **Book with an editor** | Truth, Sojourner. *Narrative of Sojourner Truth.* Edited by Margaret Washington, Vintage Books, 1993. |
| **Introduction to a work in a published edition** | Washington, Margaret. Introduction. *Narrative of Sojourner Truth,* by Sojourner Truth, edited by Washington, Vintage Books, 1993, pp. v–xi. |
| **Single work in an anthology** | Hawthorne, Nathaniel. "Young Goodman Brown." *Literature: An Introduction to Reading and Writing,* edited by Edgar V. Roberts and Henry E. Jacobs, 5th ed., Prentice Hall, 1998, pp. 376–385.<br>[Indicate pages for the entire selection.] |
| **Signed article from an encyclopedia** | Askeland, Donald R. "Welding." *World Book Encyclopedia,* vol. 21, World Book, 1991, p. 58. |
| **Signed article in a weekly magazine** | Wallace, Charles. "A Vodacious Deal." *Time,* 14 Feb. 2000, p. 63. |
| **Signed article in a monthly magazine** | Gustaitis, Joseph. "The Sticky History of Chewing Gum." *American History,* Oct. 1998, pp. 30–38. |
| **Newspaper article** | Thurow, Roger. "South Africans Who Fought for Sanctions Now Scrap for Investors." *Wall Street Journal,* 11 Feb. 2000, pp. A1+.<br>[For a multipage article that does not appear on consecutive pages, write only the first page number on which it appears, followed by the plus sign.] |
| **Unsigned editorial or story** | "Selective Silence." Editorial. *Wall Street Journal,* 11 Feb. 2000, p. A14.<br>[If the editorial or story is signed, begin with the author's name.] |
| **Signed pamphlet or brochure** | [Treat the pamphlet as though it were a book.] |
| **Work from a library subscription service** | Ertman, Earl L. "Nefertiti's Eyes." *Archaeology,* Mar.–Apr. 2008, pp. 28–32. *Kids Search,* EBSCO, New York Public Library. Accessed 7 Jan. 2017.<br>[Indicating the date you accessed the information is optional but recommended.] |
| **Filmstrips, slide programs, videocassettes, DVDs, and other audiovisual media** | *The Diary of Anne Frank.* 1959. Directed by George Stevens, performances by Millie Perkins, Shelley Winters, Joseph Schildkraut, Lou Jacobi, and Richard Beymer, Twentieth Century Fox, 2004.<br>[Indicating the original release date after the title is optional but recommended.] |
| **CD-ROM (with multiple publishers)** | Simms, James, editor. *Romeo and Juliet.* By William Shakespeare, Attica Cybernetics / BBC Education / Harper, 1995. |
| **Radio or television program transcript** | "Washington's Crossing of the Delaware." *Weekend Edition Sunday,* National Public Radio, 23 Dec. 2013. Transcript. |
| **Web page** | "Fun Facts About Gum." ICGA, 2005–2017, www.gumassociation.org/index.cfm/facts-figures/fun-facts-about-gum. Accessed 19 Feb. 2017.<br>[Indicating the date you accessed the information is optional but recommended.] |
| **Personal interview** | Smith, Jane. Personal interview, 10 Feb. 2017. |

All examples follow the style given in the MLA Handbook, 8th edition, published in 2016.

MODEL

## Evidence Log

Unit Title: Discovery

Perfomance-Based Assessment Prompt:
Do all discoveries benefit humanity?

My initial thoughts:
Yes - all knowledge moves us forward.

As you read multiple texts about a topic, your thinking may change. Use an Evidence Log like this one to record your thoughts, to track details you might use in later writing or discussion, and to make further connections.

Here is a sample to show how one reader's ideas deepened as she read two texts.

Title of Text: Classifying the Stars    Date: Sept. 17

| CONNECTION TO THE PROMPT | TEXT EVIDENCE/DETAILS | ADDITIONAL NOTES/IDEAS |
|---|---|---|
| Newton shared his discoveries and then other scientists built on his discoveries. | Paragraph 2: "Isaac Newton gave to the world the results of his experiments on passing sunlight through a prism." Paragraph 3: "In 1814 . . . the German optician, Fraunhofer . . . saw that the multiple spectral tints . . . were crossed by hundreds of fine dark lines." | It's not always clear how a discovery might benefit humanity in the future. |

How does this text change or add to my thinking? This confirms what I think.    Date: Sept. 20

Title of Text: Cell Phone Mania    Date: Sept. 21

| CONNECTION TO THE PROMPT | TEXT EVIDENCE/DETAILS | ADDITIONAL NOTES/IDEAS |
|---|---|---|
| Cell phones have made some forms of communication easier, but people don't talk to each other as much as they did in the past. | Paragraph 7: "Over 80% of young adults state that texting is their primary method of communicating with friends. This contrasts with older adults who state that they prefer a phone call." | Is it good that we don't talk to each other as much?<br><br>Look for article about social media to learn more about this question. |

How does this text change or add to my thinking?    Date: Sept. 25
Maybe there are some downsides to discoveries. I still think that knowledge moves us forward, but there are sometimes unintended negative effects.

MODEL

## Word Network

A word network is a collection of words related to a topic. As you read the selections in a unit, identify interesting theme-related words and build your vocabulary by adding them to your Word Network.

Use your Word Network as a resource for your discussions and writings. Here is an example:

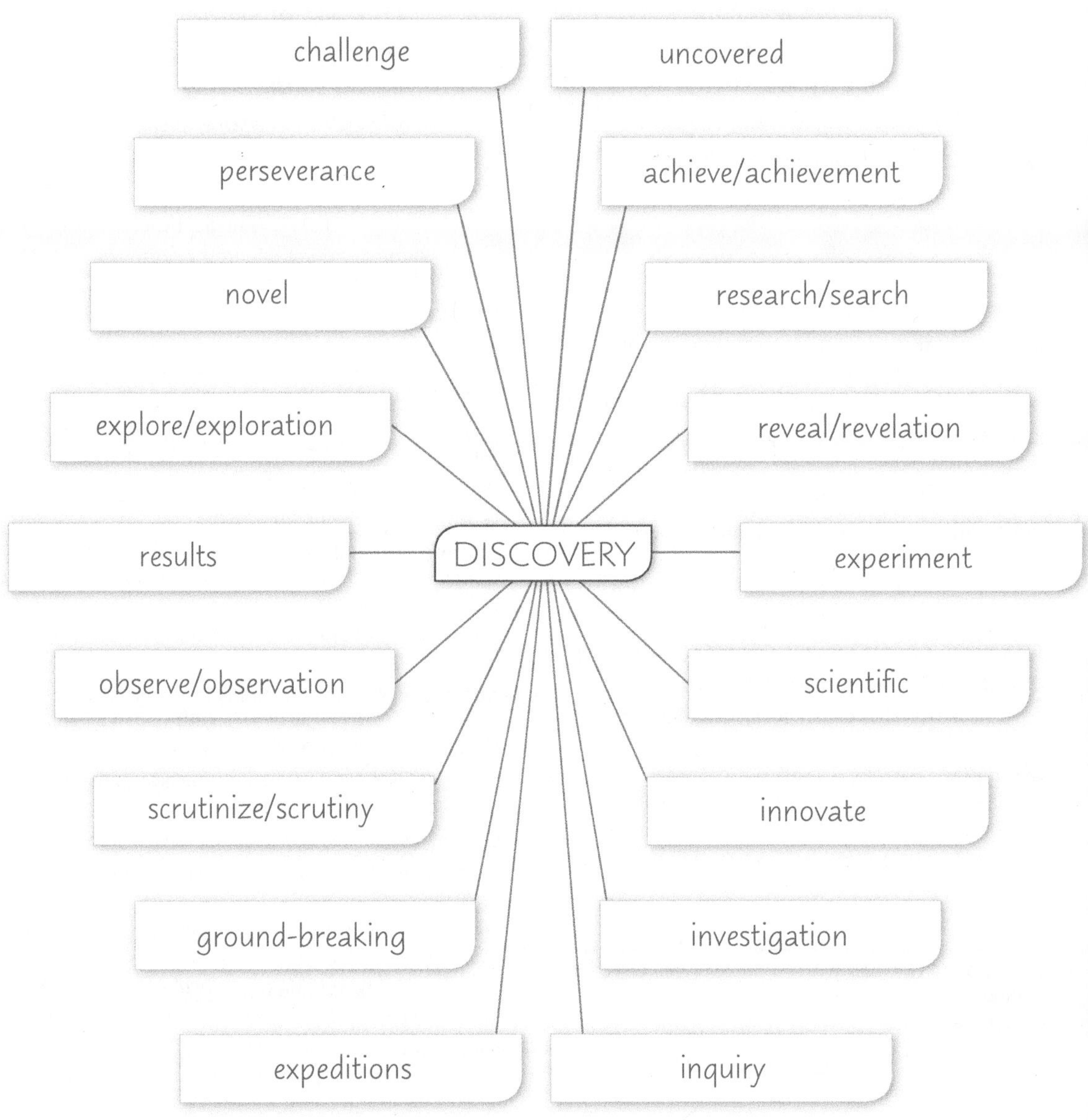

# ACADEMIC / CONCEPT VOCABULARY

Academic vocabulary appears in **blue type**.

## Pronunciation Key

| Symbol | Sample Words | Symbol | Sample Words |
|---|---|---|---|
| a | ***at, catapult, Alabama*** | oo | ***boot, soup, crucial*** |
| ah | ***father, charms, argue*** | ow | ***now, stout, flounder*** |
| ai | ***care, various, hair*** | oy | ***boy, toil, oyster*** |
| aw | ***law, maraud, caution*** | s | ***say, nice, press*** |
| awr | ***pour, organism, forewarn*** | sh | ***she, abolition, motion*** |
| ay | ***ape, sails, implication*** | u | ***full, put, book*** |
| ee | ***even, teeth, really*** | uh | ***ago, focus, contemplation*** |
| eh | ***ten, repel, elephant*** | ur | ***bird, urgent. perforation*** |
| ehr | ***merry, verify, terribly*** | y | ***by, delight, identify*** |
| ih | ***it, pin, hymn*** | yoo | ***music, confuse, few*** |
| o | ***shot, hopscotch, condo*** | zh | ***pleasure, treasure, vision*** |
| oh | ***own, parole, rowboat*** | | |

## A

**abridging** (uh BRIHJ ihng) *adj.* limiting

**acquiesce** (ak wee EHS) *v.* accept something reluctantly but without protest

**adamant** (AD uh muhnt) *adj.* unrelenting; refusing to be persuaded

**ampler** (AM pluhr) *adj.* more abundant

**analyze** (AN uh lyz) *v.* examine carefully and in detail

**anticipation** (an tihs uh PAY shuhn) *n.* eager expectation

**appeal** (uh PEEL) *n.* ability to attract and engage an audience's mind or emotions

**ascendant** (uh SEHN duhnt) *adj.* moving upward; rising

**assent** (uh SEHNT) *n.* approval or agreement

**assert** (uh SURT) *v.* declare firmly; insist upon; claim to be true

**audio play** (AW dee oh) (play) *n.* theatrical performance of a drama produced for radio, podcast, or another non-visual and non-print recorded form

**awkward** (AWK wuhrd) *adj.* not graceful or skillful in movement or shape; clumsy

## B

**background** (BAK grownd) *n.* more distant objects in a photograph

**brawling** (BRAWL ihng) *adj.* fighting noisily

**brazenness** (BRAY zuhn nuhs) *n.* act of being shameless; boldness

**breadth** (brehdth) *n.* wide range; expansive extent

**buttonholed** (BUHT uhn hohld) *v.* held in conversation

## C

**cabana** (kuh BAN uh) *n.* small tent or cabin

**callously** (KAL uhs lee) *adv.* without sympathy; coldly

**calumny** (KAL uhm nee) *n.* the making of false statements with the intent to harm

**cantina** (kan TEE nuh) *n.* tavern

**caption** (KAP shuhn) *n.* in graphic novels, separate text that presents information that cannot be expressed quickly and easily in dialogue

**captivity** (kap TIHV ih tee) *n.* condition of being held prisoner

**caricature** (KAIR ih kuh chuhr) *n.* exaggeration of details relating to people or events, often for humorous effect, in a cartoon or other created image

**certify** (SUR tuh fy) *v.* declare something is true; verify that something is true

**clammy** (KLAM ee) *adj.* cold and damp

**collaborator** (kuh LAB uh ray tuhr) *n.* person who helps the enemy

**colloquial** (kuh LOH kwee uhl) *adj.* written or spoken in informal language used in everyday conversation

**commentary** (KOM uhn tehr ee) *n.* remarks that illustrate a point, prompt a realization, or explain something

**composition** (kom puh ZIH shuhn) *n.* arrangement of the parts of an image, whether drawn or recorded in some other visual format

**conceded** (kuhn SEED ihd) *v.* admitted

**conciliatory** (kuhn SIHL ee uh tawr ee) *adj.* in a manner intended to make peace and bring about agreement

**conclave** (KON klayv) *n.* private meeting

**condemnation** (kon dehm NAY shuhn) *n.* very strong disapproval

**confirm** (kuhn FURM) *v.* prove the truth of; verify

**consecrate** (KON sih krayt) *v.* set apart as holy; dedicate

**conspirators** (kuhn SPIHR uh tuhrz) *n.* people who join in a secret plan

**constrains** (kuhn STRAYNZ) *v.* requires or forces

**constricting** (kuhn STRIHKT ihng) *adj.* limiting; tightening

**conviction** (kuhn VIHK shuhn) *n.* strong belief; certainty

**corrupted** (kuh RUHPT ihd) *adj.* dishonest

**cowering** (KOW uhr ihng) *adj.* crouching or drawing back in fear or shame

**cross-section** (KRAWS sehk shuhn) *n.* view of a three-dimensional object that shows the interior as if a cut has been made across the object

**cunning** (KUHN ihng) *adj.* done with skill or cleverness

## D

**dedicated** (DEHD uh kayt ihd) *adj.* committed; devoted

**deduction** (dih DUHK shuhn) *n.* the process of using reason or logic to come to a conclusion or form an opinion

**defamation** (dehf uh MAY shuhn) *n.* unjust injury to someone's good reputation through the making of false statements

**deference** (DEHF uhr uhns) *n.* great respect

**definitive** (dih FIHN uh tihv) *adj.* deciding or settling a question; final

**degraded** (dih GRAYD ihd) *adj.* reduced in respectablility; disgraced

**deicide** (DEE uh syd) *n.* killing of a god

**dejected** (dee JEHK tihd) *adj.* depressed; sad

**demonstrate** (DEHM uhn strayt) *v.* show how to do something

**denounce** (dih NOWNS) *v.* criticize harshly

**depth of field** (dehpth) (uhv) (feeld) n. distance between the closest and most distant objects that are in focus

**despotism** (DEHS puh tihz uhm) *n.* absolute rule; tyranny

**determine** (dih TUR muhn) *v.* decide; find out, as the exact cause or reason

**dictum** (DIHK tuhm) *n.* short statement that expresses a general truth; saying or proverb

**digress** (dih GREHS) *v.* go off topic in speaking or writing

**dilatory** (dihl uh TAWR ee) *adj.* inclined to delay; slow

**discern** (dih SURN) *v.* recognize as different

**disparity** (dihs PAR uh tee) *n.* great difference or inequality

**disposition** (DIHS puh ZIHSH uhn) *n.* act of settling a case or argument; decision

**disputation** (dihs pyu TAY shuhn) *n.* debate or argument

**dissented** (dih SENT ihd) *v.* rejected an official opinion; disagreed

**documentary** (dok yuh MEHN tuhr ee) *n.* program or film that provides a factual record or report of real events

**dyspepsia** (dihs PEHP see uh) *n.* indigestion

## E

**effrontery** (ih FRUHN tuh ree) *n.* shameless boldness

**eminence** (EHM uh nuhns) *n.* position of great importance or superiority

**eminent** (EHM uh nuhnt) *adj.* distinguished; famous; noteworthy

**emperor** (EHM puhr uhr) *n.* ruler of highest rank and authority, especially of an empire

**encroaching** (ehn KROHCH ihng) *adj.* intruding; steadily advancing

**epiphany** (ih PIHF uh nee) *n.* flash of insight and understanding

**equivocate** (ih KWIHV uh kayt) *v.* use unclear language to avoid committing oneself to something

**espionage** (EHS pee uh nozh) *n.* use of spies to obtain secret information

**establish** (ehs TAB lihsh) *v.* set up; prove; demonstrate

**etiquette** (EHT uh kiht) *n.* proper manners

**exalted** (ehg ZAWLT ihd) *adj.* of high rank

**exasperating** (ehg ZAS puh rayt ihng) *adj.* annoying

**exercise** (EHK suhr syz) *n.* implementation; state of putting something into action

**expression** (ehk SPREHSH uhn) *n.* tone of voice that indicates specific emotion

**eyewitness account** (Y WIHT nihs) (uh KOWNT) n. description given by someone who was present at an event

## F

**figure** (FIHG yuhr) *n.* one of a set of drawings or illustrations

**fix** (fihks) *n.* difficult or awkward situation

**focal point** (FOH kuhl) (poynt) *n.* center of activity or attention in a photograph

**foment** (foh MEHNT) *v.* stir up; agitate

**foreground** (FAWR grownd) *n.* nearer or closer objects in a photograph

**forward** (FAWR wuhrd) *adj.* bold; brazen; shameless

**frame** (fraym) *n.* main spoken narrative of a production

**framing** (FRAYM ihng) *n.* composing a visual so that an enclosing border surrounds the image in the foreground

**furtive** (FUR tihv) *adj.* done or acting in a stealthy way to avoid being noticed; secret

## G

**garrulous** (GAR uh luhs) *adj.* very talkative

**gilded** (GIHLD ihd) *adj.* covered with a thin layer of gold

**grandeur** (GRAN juhr) *n.* state of being impressive; magnificence

## H

**hallow** (HAL oh) *v.* make sacred; consecrate

**hangdog** (HANG dawg) *adj.* sad; ashamed; guilty

**hermitage** (HUR muh tihj) *n.* secluded retreat

**hospitality** (hos puh TAL uh tee) *n.* warm, welcoming attitude toward guests

**host** (hohst) *n.* master of ceremonies, moderator, or interviewer on a broadcast

**hypodermic** (hy puh DUR mihk) *n.* injection of medicine

## I

**immutable** (ih MYOO tuh buhl) *adj.* never changing; not changeable

**impact** (IHM pakt) *n.* collision; powerful or lasting effect

**imperial** (ihm PEER ee uhl) *adj.* like something associated with an empire; magnificent or majestic

**imploring** (ihm PLAWR ihng) *v.* asking or begging someone for something

**importunities** (ihm pawr TOO nuh teez) *n.* annoyingly urgent requests

**impressionism** (ihm PREHSH uh nihz uhm) *n.* style of art where mood, color, and light matter more than details

**incident** (IHN suh duhnt) *n.* event; occurrence

**indecisions** (ihn dih SIHZH uhnz) *n.* things not decided or finalized

**infallibility** (ihn fal uh BIHL uh tee) *n.* inability to be in error

**inflection** (ihn FLEHK shuhn) *n.* rise and fall of pitch and tone in a person's voice

**informational** (ihn fuhr MAY shuh nuhl) *adj.* giving knowledge and facts

**infringed** (ihn FRIHNJD) *v.* violated

**inquire** (ihn KWYR) *v.* ask for information

**instantaneously** (ihn stuhn TAY nee uhs lee) *adv.* immediately

**insurgent** (ihn SUR juhnt) *adj.* rebellious or in revolt against a government in power

**integrity** (in TEHG rih tee) *n.* virtue of following moral or ethical principles

**interminable** (ihn TUR muh nuh buhl) *adj.* seemingly unending

**interview** (IHN tuhr vyoo) *n.* conversation in which a host asks questions of one or more guests

## J

**jurisdiction** (juhr ihs DIHK shuhn) *n.* legal power to hear and decide cases

## L

**labeling** and **captions** (LAY buhl ihng) (KAP shuhnz) *n.* written labels and other text that often accompany politically charged images to clarify their meanings

**layout** (LAY owt) *n.* overall design and look of a graphic presentation

**legacy** (LEHG uh see) *n.* anything handed down from someone

**letterhead** (LEHT uhr hehd) *n.* personalized stationery

**literal** (LIHT uhr uhl) *adj.* true to fact; not exaggerated

**loathsome** (LOHTH suhm) *adj.* causing disgust

**loitered** (LOY tuhrd) *v.* lingered; moved slowly

## M

**machetes** (muh SHEHT eez) *n.* knives

**magistrates** (MAJ uh strayts) *n.* officials who have some of the powers of a judge

**malice** (MAL ihs) *n.* desire to harm or inflict injury

**mission** (MIHSH uhn) *n.* goal or ambition

**monotonous** (muh NOT uh nuhs) *adj.* boring due to a lack of variety

**motifs** (moh TEEFS) *n.* major themes, features, or elements

**multitudes** (MUHL tuh toodz) *n.* large number of people or things; masses

## O

**obdurate** (OB duhr iht) *adj.* resistant to persuasion

**obliged** (uh BLYJD) *adj.* grateful

**oppressed** (uh PREHST) *v.* deprived of rights or power

**ornamented** (AWR nuh mehnt ihd) *adj.* decorated; adorned

**overcast** (OH vuhr kast) *adj.* covered with clouds, as a gray sky

**overture** (OH vuhr chuhr) *n.* musical introduction to an opera or symphony

## P

**palette** (PAL iht) *n.* range of colors used in a particular work

**perish** (PEH rihsh) *v.* die

**perpetually** (puhr PEHCH oo uh lee) *adv.* happening all the time

**persistence** (puhr SIHS tuhns) *n.* act of not giving up

**perspective** (puhr SPEHK tihv) *n.* method of giving a sense of depth on a flat or shallow surface

**petition** (puh TIHSH uhn) *v.* formally request; seek help from

**picturesquely** (pihk chuh REHSK lee) *adv.* in a way that resembles a picture; in a way that is striking or interesting

**plaintiffs** (PLAYN tihfs) *n.* people who bring a lawsuit to court

**policy** (POL uh see) *n.* particular course of action by a person, government, organization

**populist** (POP yuh lihst) *adj.* related to serving the needs of common people

**prejudices** (PREHJ uh dihs ihz) *n.* unfavorable opinions or feelings formed beforehand or without factual support

**prelude** (PRAY lood) *n.* introduction to a musical work; overture

**prescribed** (prih SKRYBD) *v.* stated in writing; set down as a rule

**proceedings** (pruh SEE dihngz) *n.* events in a court of law

**prolific** (pruh LIHF ihk) *adj.* fruitful; abundant

**propaganda** (prop uh GAN duh) *n.* information, ideas, or rumors spread widely and deliberately to help or harm a person, group, movement, cause, or nation

**protagonist** (proh TAG uh nihst) *n.* main character in a play, story, or novel

## Q

**quaint** (kwaynt) *adj.* unusual; curious; singular

## R

**racket** (RAK iht) *n.* noisy confusion; uproar

**realism** (REE uh lihz uhm) *n.* style of art closely resembling reality

**rectitude** (REHK tuh tood) *n.* morally correct behavior or thinking; uprightness

**redeemers** (rih DEE muhrz) *n.* people who pay for the wrongdoing of others

**redress** (rih DREHS) *n.* correction; setting right of some wrong

**relevant** (REHL uh vuhnt) *adj.* puposeful; meaningful

**remorseless** (rih MAWRS lihs) *adj.* relentless; cruel

**renaissance** (REHN uh sons) *n.* revival; period of cultural importance

**rend** (rehnd) *v.* tear apart with violent force

**resolution** (rehz uh LOO shuhn) *n.* act of coming to a decision; the part of a story in which the plot is made clear

**reverence** (REHV uhr uhns) *n.* feeling of deep respect

**rites** (ryts) *n.* ceremonies

**romanticism** (roh MAN tuh sihz uhm) *n.* style of art evoking emotion by idealizing subjects



## S

**salutary** (SAL yuh tehr ee) *adj.* beneficial; promoting a positive purpose

**sanctity** (SANGK tuh tee) *n.* fact of being sacred; holiness

**scourge** (skurj) *n.* cause of serious trouble or suffering

**self-assurance** (sehlf uh SHUR uhns) *n.* self-confidence

**sequence** (SEE kwuhns) *n.* particular order

**shotgun** (SHOT guhn) *n.* gun with a long, smooth barrel, that is often used to fire "shot," or small, pellet-like ammunition

**shuffle** (SHUHF uhl) *n.* dragging movement of the feet over the ground or floor without lifting them

**sidle** (SY duhl) *v.* move sideways, as in an unobtrusive, stealthy, or shy manner

**significant** (sihg NIHF uh kuhnt) *adj.* full of meaning; important

**sinister** (SIHN uh stuhr) *adj.* evil; threatening

**sovereign** (SOV ruhn) *n.* monarch or ruler

**spatial** (SPAY shuhl) *adj.* existing in space

**special elements** (SPEHSH uhl) (EHL uh muhnts) *n.* features that provide points of emphasis in a production

**specific** (spih SIHF ihk) *adj.* definite; precise; particular

**specifications** (spehs uh fuh KAY shuhnz) *n.* section of a patent application in which the inventor fully describes the invention

**speech balloon** (speech) (buh LOON) *n.* shape used in graphic novels and comic books to show what a character says

**squalor** (SKWOL uhr) *n.* filth; wretchedness

**stolid** (STOL ihd) *adj.* feeling little or no emotion

**strife** (stryf) *n.* act of fighting

**subordinate** (suh BAWR duh niht) *adj.* having less importance

**sufficed** (suh FYST) *v.* was adequate

**superannuated** (soo puhr AN yu ayt uhd) *adj.* too old to be usable; obsolete

**superfluous** (suh PUR floo uhs) *adj.* more than is needed or wanted; unnecessary

**supplanted** (suh PLANT ihd) *v.* took the place of; removed

**supplement** (SUHP luh muhnt) *n.* something added; *v.* add to

**symbolism** (SIHM buh lihz uhm) *n.* use of images or objects to represent ideas or qualities

## T

**tedious** (TEE dee uhs) *adj.* boring; dull

**teeming** (TEE mihng) *adj.* full

**temporal** (TEHM puhr uhl) *adj.* not eternal; limited by time

**tension** (TEHN shuhn) *n.* mental or nervous stress; uneasiness; state of strained relations

**tone** (tohn) *n.* production's attitude toward a subject or audience

**transcendent** (tran SEHN duhnt) *adj.* beyond the limits of possible experience

**treason** (TREE zuhn) *n.* betrayal of trust or faith, especially against one's country

**trivialize** (TRIHV ee uhl yz) *v.* treat as not important; make trivial

**tyranny** (TIHR uh nee) *n.* oppressive power

## U

**unalienable** (un AYL yuh nuh buhl) *adj.* impossible to take away or give up

**unique** (yoo NEEK) *adj.* being the only one of its kind

**unrequited** (uhn rih KWY tihd) *adj.* not repaid or avenged

## V

**vassals** (VAS uhlz) *n.* subjects of a kingdom; servants

**vast** (vast) *adj.* very great in size

**verbatim** (vuhr BAY tihm) *adv.* in exactly the same words; *adj.* repeating the original word for word

**vigilant** (VIHJ uh luhnt) *adj.* on the alert; watchful

**vindictive** (vihn DIHK tihv) *adj.* characterized by an intense, unreasoning desire for revenge

**vital** (VY tuhl) *adj.* necessary or important

## W

**wanton** (WON tuhn) *adj.* unrestrained; wild

**waterfowl** (WAWT uhr fowl) *n.* birds that live in or near water

**wretched** (REHCH ihd) *adj.* very unhappy; miserable

# VOCABULARIO ACADÉMICO/ VOCABULARIO DE CONCEPTOS

**abridging: abreviar** *v.* limitar

**acquiesce: consentir** *v.* aceptar algo con pocas ganas pero sin protestar

**adamant: terco/a** *adj.* que no se deja convencer; inflexible

**ampler: más copioso/a** *adj.* más abundante

**analyze: analizar** *v.* examinar detalladamente y en profundidad

**anticipation: anticipación** *s.* expectación; espera ansiosa

**appeal: cautivar** *v.* capacidad de atraer e involucrar al público, sus pensamientos o emociones

**ascendant: ascendente** *adj.* que se mueve hacia arriba; que se eleva

**assent: consentimiento** *s.* aprobación o acuerdo

**assert: aseverar** *v.* afirmar; insistir

**audio play: radioteatro** *s.* obra de teatro producida para la radio, para un *podcast* o para otro tipo de grabación no visual ni impresa

**awkward: torpe** *adj.* desmañado/a; sin gracia, patoso

## B

**backdrop: fondo** *s.* escena o decorado detrás de fotografías y retratos

**background: fondo** *s.* objetos lejanos en una fotografía

**brawling: pendenciero/a** *adj.* que se pelea ruidosamente; alborotador/a

**brazenness: descaro** *s.* no tener vergüenza; atrevimiento

**breadth: anchura** *s.* amplitud

**buttonholed: acorraló** *v.* detuvo a alguien en una conversación

## C

**cabana: cabaña** *s.* tienda pequeña, choza

**callously: despiadadamente** *adv.* sin compasión; fríamente

**calumny: calumnia** *s.* afirmación falsa que intenta herir o dañar

**cantina: cantina** *s.* taberna

**caption: leyenda** *s.* en las novelas gráficas, texto en un recuadro que presenta información que no puede expresarse rápida y fácilmente en el diálogo

**captivity: cautividad** *s.* estado de privación de libertad; ser prisionero

**caricature: caricatura** *s.* exageración, generalmente con efecto humorístico, de detalles relacionados con personas o sucesos en una tira cómica u otra imagen creada

**certify: certificar** *v.* declarar que algo es cierto

**clammy: sudado/a** *adj.* frío y húmedo

**collaborator: colaboracionista** *s.* persona que colabora con o ayuda al enemigo

**colloquial: coloquial** *adj.* lenguaje informal que se usa en las conversaciones diarias

**commentary: comentario** *s.* observación o ejemplo que ilustra una idea, una opinión o explica algo

**composition: composición** *s.* disposición de las partes de una imagen, ya sea de un dibujo o de cualquier otro formato visual

**conceded: concedió** *v.* admitió

**conciliatory: conciliador/a** *adj.* que tiene la intención de hacer las paces y llegar a un acuerdo

**conclave: cónclave** *s.* reunión privada

**condemnation: condena** *s.* fuerte desaprobación; repulsa

**confirm: confirmar** *v.* probar la certeza de algo; verificar

**consecrate: consagrar** *v.* declarar algo como sagrado; dedicar

**conspirators: conspiradores** *s.* personas que se unen a un plan secreto

**constrains: constriñe** *v.* requiere, obliga

**constricting: estrecho/a** *adj.* limitado/a

**conviction: condena** *s.* acto de dar a alguien un veredicto de culpabilidad

**conviction: convicción** *s.* creencia firme

**correlate: correlacionar** *v.* mostrar la conexión entre dos elementos

**corrupted: corrupto/a** *adj.* deshonesto/a

**cowering: achicarse** *v.* encogerse de miedo

**cross-section: sección transversal** *s.* imagen de un objeto tridimensional que muestra su interior como si se hubiera hecho un corte transversal del objeto

**cunning: astuto/a** *adj.* con ingenio y astucia

## D

**dedicate: dedicar** *v.* apartar para un objetivo especial

**deduction: deducción** *s.* el proceso de usar la razón o la lógica para llegar a una conclusión o formar una opinion

**defamation: difamación** *s.* dañar la reputación de alguien injustamente mediante afirmaciones falsas

**deference: deferencia** *s.* gran respeto

**defining: definir** *v.* aclarar el significado; explicar

**definitive: definitivo** *adj.* que decide y resuelve una cuestión

**degraded: degradado** *adj.* con respetabilidad reducida; desgraciado

**deicide: deicidio** *s.* matar a un dios

**dejected: abatido/a** *adj.* deprimido/a; triste

**demonstrate: demostrar** *v.* enseñar cómo hacer algo

**denounce: denunciar** *v.* criticar duramente

**depth of field: profundidad de campo** *s.* la distancia entre los objetos más cercanos y los más lejanos que enfoca una cámara

**despotism: despotismo** *s.* ejercicio de autoridad absoluta

**determine: determinar** *v.* decidir; buscar la causa o la razón exacta

**dictum: dicho** *s.* un enunciado corto que expresa una verdad general; un refrán o proverbio

**digress: divagar** *v.* desviarse del tema al hablar o escribir

**dilatory: dilatorio/a** *adj.* inclinado a retrasarse; lento/a

**discern: discernir** *v.* reconocer como diferente

**disparity: disparidad** *s.* gran diferencia o desigualdad

**disposition: disposición** *s.* el acto de llegar a un acuerdo en un caso o discusión; predisposición

**disputation: disputa** *s.* debate o discusión

**dissented: disintió** *v.* rechazó una opinion oficial; estuvo en desacuerdo

**documentary: documental** *s.* programa o película que ofrece datos o un informe sobre hechos reales

**dyspepsia: dispepsia** *s.* indigestión

## E

**effrontery: desfachatez** *s.* descaro; desvergüenza

**eminence: eminencia** *s.* persona con un cargo de gran importancia o superioridad

**eminent: eminente** *adj.* distinguido; famoso; notorio

**emperor: emperador** *s.* gobernante supremo de un imperio

**encroaching: traspasar** *v.* infringir; meterse; avanzar continuamente

**epiphany: epifanía** *s.* sensación súbita de comprensión o entendimiento

**equivocate: usar equívocos** *v.* usar un lenguaje ambiguo para evitar comprometerse a algo

**espionage: espionaje** *s.* uso de espías para obtener información secreta

**establish: establecer** *v.* instituir, crear, montar

**etiquette: etiqueta** *s.* buenos modales

**exalted: elevado/a** *adj.* de alto rango

**exasperating: exasperante** *adj.* molesto

**exercise: ejercicio** *s.* implementación; puesta en práctica

**expression: expresión** *s.* tono de voz que indica una emoción específica

**eyewitness account: declaración de un testigo** *s.* descripción hecha por alguien que estuvo presente en un suceso

## F

**faultfinder: criticón/a** *adj.* persona que critica con frecuencia; un quejica

**figure: figura** *s.* grupo de dibujos o ilustraciones

**fix: momento difícil** *s.* una situación complicada

**focal point: punto de enfoque** *s.* el centro de actividad o de atención de una fotografía

**foment: fomentar** *v.* suscitar, promover; agitar

**foreground: primer plano** *s.* objetos más cercanos en una fotografía

**forward: atrevido/a** *adj.* audaz; descarado/a

**frame: prototipo** *s.* la narrativa oral principal de una producción

**framing: composición** *s.* creación visual de forma que el marco rodee la imagen del primer plano

**furtive: furtivo/a** *adj.* hecho de forma sigilosa, a escondidas, para evitar ser descubierto: secreto/a

## G

**garrulous: charlatán/a** *adj.* que habla mucho; parlanchín/a

**gilded: bañado en oro** *adj.* cubierto con una capa fina de oro

**grandeur: esplendor** *s.* magnificencia; grandeza; majestuosidad

## H

**hallow: santificar** *v.* hacer sagrado; consagrar

**hangdog: abatido/a** *adj.* avergonzado/a; triste; culpable

**heedless: ignorando** *adj.* sin escuchar el consejo; imprudente

**hermitage: retiro** *s.* lugar apartado, solitario

**hospitality: hospitalidad** *s.* actitud cálida de bienvenida hacia los invitados

**host: anfitrión** *s.* maestro de ceremonia, moderador o presentador de un programa

**hypodermic: inyección hipodérmica** *s.* inyección de un medicamento

## I

**immutable: inmutable** *adj.* que no cambia nunca

**impact: colisión** *s.* choque; *v.* colisionar, chocar

**imperial: imperial** *adj.* de calidad superior

**imploring: implorar** *v.* pedir algo a alguien o suplicar

**importunities: importunidades** *s.* peticiones urgentes molestas

**impressionism: impresionismo** *s.* estilo artístico en el que el estado de ánimo, el color y la luz importan más que los detalles

**incident: incidente** *s.* suceso

**indecisions: indecisiones** *s.* cosas que no están decididas o finalizadas

**infallibility: infalibilidad** *s.* imposibilidad de equivocarse

**inflection: inflexión** *s.* subidas y bajadas en el tono de voz de una persona

**informational: informativo/a** *adj.* que proporciona conocimientos y hechos

**infringed: infringió** *v.* violó la ley

**instantaneously: instantáneamente** *adv.* inmediatamente

**insurgent: insurgente** *adj.* rebelde o que se rebela contra el gobierno en el poder

**integrity: integridad** *s.* la virtud de seguir principios morales o éticos

**interminable: interminable** *adj.* que parece que no tiene fin

**interview: entrevista** *s.* conversación en la que un presentador hace preguntas a uno o más invitados

**inquire: inquirir** *v.* solicitar información; indagar

**investigate: investigar** *v.* indagar a fondo

## J

**jurisdiction: jurisdicción** *s.* poder legal para escuchar una causa y dictar sentencia

## L

**labeling** and **captions: rótulos** y **leyendas** *s.* etiquetas y texto que suelen acompañar las imágenes de contenido político para clarificar su significado

**layout: diseño** *s.* la disposición gráfica de una presentación

**legacy: legado** *s.* algo heredado, que se traspasa

**letterhead: membrete** *s.* papelería personalizada

**literal: literal** *adj.* acorde a los hechos; sin exagerar

**loathsome: repugnante** *adj.* que causa gran desagrado

**loitered: deambuló** *v.* holgazaneó; que se movió despacio

## M

**machetes: machetes** *s.* cuchillos

**magistrates: magistrados** *s.* cargos públicos que tienen el poder de un juez

**majority: mayoría** *s.* más de la mitad

**malice: malicia** *s.* deseo de herir a alguien

**mission: misión** *s.* objetivo o ambición

**monotonous: monótono/a** *adj.* aburrido/a debido a la falta de variación

**motifs: motivos** *s.* temas, características o elementos principales

**multitudes: multitudes** *s.* gran número de personas

## O

**obdurate: obstinado/a** *adj.* resistente a la persuasión

**obliged: agradecido/a** *adj.* que da las gracias

**oppressed: oprimidos/as** *s.* personas cuyo derechos son pisoteados por otros

**ornamented: ornamentado** *adj.* decorado; adornado

**overcast: nublado** *adj.* cubierto de nubes

**overture: obertura** *s.* introducción musical de un ópera o sinfonía

## P

**palette: paleta** *s.* rango de colores usados en una obra determinada

**perish: perecer** *v.* morir; ser matado

**perpetually: perpetuamente** *adv.* que sucede todo el tiempo

**persistence: persistencia** *s.* acción de no darse por vencido

**perspective: perspectiva** *s.* método mediante el cual se le da sentido de profundidad a una superficie plana

**petition: petición** *s.* hacer una solicitud formal; buscar la ayuda de alguien

**picturesquely: de modo pintoresco** *adv.* de manera que parece un cuadro; de manera sorprendente o interesante

**plaintiffs: demandantes** *s.* las personas que interponen una demanda en un juicio

**policy: política** *s.* acciones específicas de una persona, gobierno u organización

**populist: populista** *adj.* persona que cree servir las necesidades del pueblo

**prejudices: prejuicios** *s.* sentimientos u opiniones desfavorables formados con anterioridad o sin apoyarse en los hechos

**prelude: preludio** *s.* introducción de una obra musical; obertura

**prescribed: prescrito** *v.* manifestado por escrito; mandado

**proceedings: pleito** *s.* proceso judicial, los sucesos de un juzgado

**prolific: prolífico** *adj.* fructífero

**propaganda: propaganda** *s.* información, ideas o rumores que se divulgan amplia y deliberadamente para hacerle daño a una persona, grupo, movimiento, causa o nación

**protagonist: protagonista** *s.* el personaje principal de una obra de teatro, cuento o novela

## Q

**quaint: singular** *adj.* inusual; curioso

## R

**racket: barullo** *s.* confusión ruidosa; jaleo

**realism: realismo** *s.* estilo artístico que se parece mucho a la realidad

**rectitude: rectitud** *s.* comportamiento o pensamiento moralmente correcto; integridad

**redeemers: redentores** *s.* personas que pagan por las malas acciones de otros

**redress: rectificación** *s.* corrección reparación de un daño

**relevant: relevante** *adj.* pertinente

**remorseless: despiadado/a** *adj.* que no tiene remordimientos; cruel

**renaissance: renacimiento** *s.* resurgimiento; periodo de importancia cultural

**rend: rasgar** *v.* hacer pedazos con fuerza

**resolution: resolución** *s.* acción de resolver o decidir; expresión formal de una opinión

**reverence: reverencia** *s.* sentimiento de profundo respeto

**rites: ritos** *s.* ceremonias

**romanticism: romanticismo** *s.* estilo artístico que evoca la emoción idealizando los sujetos

## S

**salutary: saludable** *adj.* beneficioso/a

**sanctity: santidad** *s.* hecho de ser sagrado

**scourge: azote** *s.* causa de serios problemas o sufrimiento

**self-assurance: autoconfianza** *s.* seguridad en uno mismo

**sequence: secuencia** *s.* en un orden particular; *v.* (secuenciar) poner en orden

**sequence photography: secuencia fotográfica** *n.* una serie de imágenes en las que se ve el sujeto en instantes sucesivos

**shotgun: escopeta** *s.* arma de cañón largo, con frecuencia usada para disparar perdigones

**shuffle: arrastrar los pies** *v.* caminar sin levantar los pies

**sidle: caminar de lado** *v.* moverse de costado furtiva o tímidamente

**significant: significativo/a** *adj.* lleno/a de significado; importante

**sinister: siniestro** *adj.* malvado; amenazador

**sovereign: soberano** *s.* un monarca o gobernante

**spatial: espacial** *adj.* que existe en el espacio

**special elements: elementos especiales** *s.* características que dan puntos de énfasis en una producción

**specific: específico/a** *adj.* definido/a; preciso/a; particular

**specifications: especificaciones** *s.* apartado de una patente en que el inventor describe con detalle el invento

**speech balloon: bocadillo** *s.* el modo en que se representa lo que dice cada personaje en las novelas gráficas

**squalor: mugre** *s.* suciedad; estado lamentable

**stolid: impasible** *adj.* imperturbable; que no siente emoción alguna

**strife: lucha** *s.* acción de luchar; conflicto

**subordinate: subordinado/a** *adj.* que tiene menos importancia

**subordinate: subordinado/a** *s.* una persona de menor rango o clase

**superannuated: viejo/a** *adj.* demasiado viejo/a para usarse; obsoleto/a

**superfluous: superfluo/a** *adj.* más de lo necesario o deseado; innecesario/a

**supplanted: suplantó** *v.* tomó el lugar de; quitó a

**supplement: suplemento** *s.* algo añadido

**surrealism: surrealismo** *s.* uso intencional de detalles imaginativos y hasta extraños en el arte

**symbolism: simbolismo** *s.* uso de imágenes u objetos para representar ideas o cualidades

## T

**tedious: tedioso/a** *adj.* aburrido/a, soso/a

**teeming: repleto/a** *adj.* lleno/a

**temporal: temporal** *adj.* no eterno, limitado por el tiempo

**tension: tensión** *s.* estrés causado al tirar

**tone: tono** *s.* la actitud de una producción hacia un tema o el público

**transcendent: trascendente** *adj.* más allá de los límites de la experiencia posible

**treason: traición** *s.* deslealtad hacia la confianza o la fe

**trivialize: trivializar** *v.* quitar importancia; hacer trivial

**tyranny: tiranía** *s.* poder opresivo

## U

**unalienable: inalienable** *adj.* imposible de quitar o de abandonar

**unique: único/a** *adj.* que es el único de su especie o tipo

**unrequited: no correspondido** *adj.* que no se ha liquidado o vengado

## V

**vassals: vasallos** *s.* sujetos de un reino; siervos

**vast: vasto/a** *adj.* de gran tamaño

**verbatim: textualmente** *adv.* palabra por palabra

**vigilant: vigilante** *adj.* en alerta, atento/a

**vindictive: vengativo/a** *adj.* lleno/a de un deseo intenso e irracional de venganza

## W

**wanton: excesivo/a** *adj.* descontrolado/a; sin ley

**waterfowl: ave acuática** *s.* relativo a las aves acuáticas

**wretched: desdichado/a** *adj.* muy infeliz; desgraciado/a







R46

**ALLEGORY** An ***allegory*** is a story or tale with two or more levels of meaning—a literal level and one or more symbolic levels. The events, setting, and characters in an allegory are symbols for ideas and qualities.

**ALLUSION** An ***allusion*** is a reference to a well-known person, place, event, literary work, or work of art. Writers often make allusions to stories from the Bible, to Greek and Roman myths, to plays by Shakespeare, to political and historical events, and to other materials with which they can expect their readers to be familiar.

**ANALOGY** An ***analogy*** is an extended comparison of relationships. It is based on the idea that the relationship between one pair of things is like the relationship between another pair. Unlike a metaphor, an analogy involves an explicit comparison, often using the words *like* or *as*.

**ANAPHORA** **Anaphora** is a type of parallel structure in which a word or phrase is repeated at the beginning of successive clauses for emphasis.

**ANECDOTE** An ***anecdote*** is a brief story about an interesting, amusing, or strange event. An anecdote is told to entertain or to make a point.

**APPEAL** An ***appeal*** is a rhetorical device used in argumentative writing to persuade an audience.

An appeal to ethics (Ethos) shows that an argument is just or fair.

An appeal to logic (Logos) shows that an argument is well reasoned.

An appeal to authority shows that a higher power supports the ideas.

An appeal to emotion (Pathos) is designed to influence readers' feelings.

**ARGUMENT** An ***argument*** is writing or speech that attempts to convince a reader to think or act in a particular way. An argument is a logical way of presenting a belief, conclusion, or stance. A good argument is supported with reasoning and evidence.

**AUTOBIOGRAPHY** An ***autobiography*** is a form of nonfiction in which a person tells his or her own life story. *Memoirs*, first-person accounts of personally or historically significant events in which the writer was a participant or an eyewitness, are a form of autobiographical writing.

**BIOGRAPHY** A ***biography*** is a form of nonfiction in which a writer tells the life story of another person.

**CATALOGUE** A ***catalogue*** in poetry is a list of people, objects, or situations, used to evoke a range of experience and/or emotion.

**CHARACTER** A ***character*** is a person or an animal that takes part in the action of a literary work. The following are some terms used to describe various types of characters:

The ***main character*** in a literary work is the one on whom the work focuses. ***Major characters*** in a literary work include the main character and any other characters who play significant roles. A ***minor character*** is one who does not play a significant role. A ***round character*** is one who is complex and multifaceted, like a real person. A ***flat character*** is one who is one-dimensional. A ***dynamic character*** is one who changes in the course of a work. A ***static character*** is one who does not change in the course of a work.

**CHARACTERIZATION** ***Characterization*** is the act of creating and developing a character. In **direct characterization,** a writer simply states a character's traits. In ***indirect characterization,*** character is revealed through one of the following means:

1. words, thoughts, or actions of the character
2. descriptions of the character's appearance or background
3. what other characters say about the character
4. the ways in which other characters react to the character

**CLAIM** A ***claim*** is a particular belief, conclusion, or point of view that a writer presents in an ***argument.***

**CONCESSION** ***Concession*** is a rhetorical device that acknowledges the opposition's arguments.

**CONFLICT** A ***conflict*** is a struggle between opposing forces. Sometimes this struggle is internal, or within a character. At other times, this struggle is external, or between a character and an outside force. Conflict is one of the primary elements of narrative literature because most plots develop from conflicts.

**CONNOTATION** The ***connotation*** is an association that a word calls to mind in addition to the dictionary meaning of the word. Many words that are similar in their dictionary meanings, or denotations, are quite different in their connotations. Poets and other writers choose their words carefully so that the connotations of those words will be appropriate.

**COUNTERCLAIM** A ***counterclaim*** is an objection or challange to the ***claim***—or particular belief, conclusion, or point of view—that a writer presents in an ***argument.*** Counterclaims are often brought up by the writer of the argument in anticipation of challenges.

**DENOTATION** The ***denotation*** of a word is its objective meaning, independent of other associations that the word brings to mind.

**DESCRIPTION** A ***description*** is a portrayal, in words, of something that can be perceived by the senses. Writers create descriptions by using images.

**DIALECT** A ***dialect*** is the form of a language spoken by people in a particular region or group. Writers often use dialect to make their characters seem realistic and to create local color.

**DIALOGUE** A ***dialogue*** is a conversation between characters. Writers use dialogue to reveal character, to present events, to add variety to narratives, and to arouse their readers' interest.

**DICTION** ***Diction*** is a writer's or speaker's word choice. Diction is part of a writer's style and may be described as formal or informal, plain or ornate, common or technical, abstract or concrete.

**DRAMA** A ***drama*** is a story written to be performed by actors. The playwright supplies dialogue for the characters to speak, as well as ***stage directions*** that give information about costumes, lighting, scenery, properties, the setting, and the characters' movements and ways of speaking. Dramatic conventions include soliloquies, asides, or the passage of time between acts or scenes. ***Dramatic exposition*** is a brief essay, or prose commentary, inserted by the writer to help readers and producers understand the characters and past conflicts. ***Background knowledge*** includes information about the period during which the action takes place.

**DRAMATIC MONOLOGUE** A ***dramatic monologue*** is a poem or speech in which an imaginary character speaks to a silent listener.

**DRAMATIC POEM** A ***dramatic poem*** is one that makes use of the conventions of drama. Such poems may be monologues or dialogues or may present the speech of many characters. Robert Frost's "The Death of the Hired Man" is a famous example of a dramatic poem.

See also ***Dramatic Monologue.***

**EPIC THEME** An ***epic theme*** is an underlying message that all people of all times are connected by their shared experiences.

**EDITORIAL** An ***editorial*** is a form of persuasive writing or argument. Editorials must have a clear position, be supported by reasons, and include an appeal to ethics, logic, authority, and/or emotion.

**ELLIPTICAL PHRASING** ***Elliptical phrasing*** is a style of poetry in which the poet omits words that are expected to be understood by the reader.

**ENUMERATION** ***Enumeration*** is a document style in which the major ideas are listed in numerical order.

**ESSAY** An ***essay*** is a short nonfiction work about a particular subject. Essays can be classified as ***formal*** or ***informal, personal,*** or ***impersonal***. They can also be classified according to purpose, such as ***cause-and-effect, satirical,*** or ***reflective.*** Modes of discourse, such as ***expository***, ***descriptive, persuasive,*** or ***narrative,*** are other means of classifying essays.

**EXPLANATORY ESSAY** An ***explanatory essay*** describes and summarizes information gathered from a number of sources on a concept.

**FICTION** ***Fiction*** is prose writing that tells about imaginary characters and events. Short stories and novels are works of fiction.

**FIGURATIVE LANGUAGE** ***Figurative language*** is writing or speech not meant to be taken literally. Writers use figurative language to express ideas in vivid and imaginative ways.

**FIGURE OF SPEECH** A ***figure of speech*** is an expression or a word used imaginatively rather than literally.

**FLASHBACK** A ***flashback*** is a section of a literary work that interrupts the chronological presentation of events to relate an event from an earlier time. A writer may present a flashback as a character's memory or recollection, as part of an account or story told by a character, as a dream or a daydream, or simply by having the narrator switch to a time in the past.

**FORESHADOWING** ***Foreshadowing*** in a literary work is the use of clues to suggest events that have yet to occur.

**FRAME STORY** A ***frame story*** is a story that brackets—or frames—another story or group of stories. This device creates a story-within-a-story narrative structure.

**FREE VERSE** ***Free verse*** is poetry that lacks a regular rhythmical pattern, or meter. A writer of free verse is at liberty to use any rhythms that are appropriate to what he or she is saying.

**GENRE** A ***genre*** is a division, or type, of literature. Literature is commonly divided into three major genres: poetry, prose, and drama. Each major genre can in turn be divided into smaller genres. Poetry can be divided into lyric, concrete, dramatic, narrative, and epic poetry. Prose can be divided into fiction and nonfiction. Drama can be divided into serious drama, tragedy, comic drama, melodrama, and farce.

**HUMOR** ***Humor***, used in an argument, can be an effective rhetorical device. Humorous language and details make characters and situations seem funny.

**HYPERBOLE** A ***hyperbole*** is a deliberate exaggeration or overstatement, often used for comic effect.

**IDIOMATIC EXPRESSION** ***Idiomatic expressions*** are figures of speech that cannot be understood literally. For example, a rainstorm might be described as "raining cats and dogs."

**IN MEDIA RES** ***In media res***, which is Latin for "in the middle of things," is a plot device writers use to grab reader's attention.

**IMAGE** An ***image*** is a word or phrase that appeals to one or more of the five senses—sight, hearing, touch, taste, or smell.

**IMAGERY** ***Imagery*** is the descriptive or figurative language used in literature to create word pictures for the reader. These pictures, or images, are created by details of sight, sound, taste, touch, smell, or movement.

**INCONGRUITY** ***Incongruity*** is a technique writers use to create humor and occurs when two or more ideas relate to one another in a way that is contrary to the readers' expectations.

**IRONY** ***Irony*** is a contrast between what is stated and what is meant, or between what is expected to happen and what actually happens. In ***verbal irony***, a word or a phrase is used to suggest the opposite of its usual meaning. In ***dramatic irony***, there is a contradiction between what a character thinks and what the reader or audience knows. In ***irony of situation***, an event occurs that contradicts the expectations of the characters, of the reader, or of the audience.

**LETTER** A ***letter*** is a written message or communication addressed to a reader or readers and is generally sent by mail. Letters may be ***private*** or ***public***, depending on their intended audience. A public letter, also called a ***literary letter*** or ***epistle***, is a work of literature written in the form of a personal letter but created for publication.

**MEMOIR** A ***memoir*** is a type of nonfiction autobiographical writing that tells about a person's own life, usually focusing on the writer's involvement in historically or culturally significant events—either as a participant or an eyewitness.

**METAPHOR** A ***metaphor*** is a figure of speech in which one thing is spoken of as though it were something else. The identification suggests a comparison between the two things that are identified, as in "death is a long sleep."

A ***mixed metaphor*** occurs when two metaphors are jumbled together. For example, thorns and rain are illogically mixed in "the thorns of life rained down on him." A ***dead metaphor*** is one that has been overused and has become a common expression, such as "the arm of the chair" or "nightfall."

**MONOLOGUE** A ***monologue*** is a speech delivered entirely by one person or character.

**MOTIF** A ***motif*** is a recurrent, or repeated, object or idea in a literary work.

**NARRATION** ***Narration*** is writing that tells a story. The act of telling a story is also called ***narration***. The ***narrative,*** or story, is told by a storyteller called the ***narrator.*** A story is usually told chronologically, in the order in which events take place in time, though it may include flashbacks and foreshadowing. Narratives may be true or fictional. Narration is one of the forms of discourse and is used in novels, short stories, plays, narrative poems, anecdotes, autobiographies, biographies, and reports.

**NARRATIVE** A ***narrative*** is a story told in fiction, nonfiction, poetry, or drama. Narratives are often classified by their content or purpose. An ***exploration narrative*** is a firsthand account of an explorer's travels in a new land. "The Interesting Narrative of the Life of Olaudah Equiano" is a ***slave narrative***, an account of the experiences of an enslaved person. A ***historical narrative*** is a narrative account of significant historical events.

A ***personal narrative*** is a first-person story about a real-life experience. In a ***reflective narrative*** the author describes describes his or her feelings about a scene, incident, memory, or event. A ***nonlinear narrative*** does not follow chronological order. It may contain flashbacks, dream sequences, or other devices that interrupt the chronological order of events.

**NARRATOR** A ***narrator*** is a speaker or character who tells a story. A story or novel may be narrated by a main character, by a minor character, or by someone uninvolved in the story. The narrator may speak in the first person or in the third person. An ***omniscient narrator*** is all-knowing, while a limited narrator knows only what one character does.

**NONFICTION** ***Nonfiction*** is prose writing that presents and explains ideas or that tells about real people, places, objects, or events. Two of the main types of literary nonfiction are historical writing and reflective writing. Essays, biographies, autobiographies, journals, and reports are all examples of nonfiction.

**NOVEL** A ***novel*** is a long work of fiction. A novel often has a complicated plot, many major and minor characters, a significant theme, and several varied settings. Novels can be classified in many ways, based on the historical periods in which they are written, the subjects and themes that they treat, the techniques that are used in them, and the literary movements that inspired them. A ***novella*** is not as long as a novel but is longer than a short story.

**ONOMATOPOEIA** ***Onomatopoeia*** is the use of words that imitate sounds. Examples of such words are *buzz, hiss, murmur,* and *rustle*.

**ORATORY** ***Oratory*** is public speaking that is formal, persuasive, and emotionally appealing. Patrick Henry's "Speech in the Virginia Convention" (p. 100) is an example of oratory.

**OXYMORON** An ***oxymoron*** is a figure of speech that combines two opposing or contradictory ideas. An oxymoron, such as "freezing fire," suggests a paradox in just a few words.

**PACING** ***Pacing*** is the speed or rhythm of writing. Writers use different paces to achieve different effects, such as suspense.

**PARADOX** A ***paradox*** is a statement that seems to be contradictory but that actually presents a truth.

**PARALLELISM** ***Parallelism*** is the presentation of similar ideas, in sequence, using the same grammatical structure.

**PARALLEL STRUCTURE** In a list, each item should use ***parallel structure*** in which the part of speech and grammatical phrasing is the same for all items.

**PERSONIFICATION** ***Personification*** is a form of figurative language in which a nonhuman subject is given human characteristics. Effective personification of things or ideas makes them seem vital and alive, as if they were human.

**PHILOSOPHICAL ASSUMPTIONS** Beliefs that are taken for granted are ***philosophical assumptions***. Some assumptions are ***explicit***, or directly stated. Other assumptions are ***implicit***, meaning the reader must make inferences to understand.

**PLOT** ***Plot*** is the sequence of events in a literary work. In most fiction, the plot involves both characters and a central conflict. The plot usually begins with an ***exposition*** that introduces the setting, the characters, and the basic situation. This is followed by the ***inciting incident,*** which introduces the central conflict. The conflict then increases during the ***development*** until it reaches a high point of interest or suspense, the ***climax***. The climax is followed by the end, or resolution, of the central conflict. Any events that occur after the ***resolution*** make up the ***denouement***. The events that lead up to the climax make up the ***rising action***. The events that follow the climax make up the ***falling action***.

**POETRY** ***Poetry*** is one of the three major types of literature. In poetry, form and content are closely connected, like the two faces of a single coin. Poems are often divided into lines and stanzas and often employ regular rhythmical patterns, or meters. Most poems use highly concise, musical, and emotionally charged language. Many also make use of imagery, figurative language, and special devices such as rhyme.

**POETIC STRUCTURE** The basic structures of poetry are lines and stanzas. A ***line*** is a group of words arranged in a row. A line of poetry may break, or end, in different ways. Varied ***line lengths*** can create unpredictable rhythms.

An ***end-stopped line*** is one in which both the grammatical structure and sense are complete at the end of the line.

A ***run-on, or enjambed***, line is one in which both the grammatical structure and sense continue past the end of the line.

**POINT OF VIEW** ***Point of view*** is the perspective, or vantage point, from which a story is told. Three commonly used points of view are first person, omniscient third person, and limited third person.

In the ***first-person point of view***, the narrator is a character in the story and refers to himself or herself with the first-person pronoun "I."

The two kinds of third-person point of view, limited and omniscient, are called "third person" because the narrator uses third-person pronouns such as "he" and "she" to refer to the characters. There is no "I" telling the story.

In stories told from the omniscient third-person point of view, the narrator knows and tells about what each character feels and thinks.

In stories told from the ***limited third-person point of view,*** the narrator relates the inner thoughts and feelings of only one character, and everything is viewed from this character's perspective.

**PREAMBLE** A ***preamble*** is a statement that explains who is issuing the document and for what purpose.

**PRIMARY SOURCE** A ***primary source*** is one created by someone who directly participated in or observed the event being described.

**PROSE** ***Prose*** is the ordinary form of written language. Most writing that is not poetry, drama, or song is considered prose. Prose is one of the major genres of literature. It occurs in two forms: fiction and nonfiction.

**PROTAGONIST** The protagonist is the main character in a literary work.

**REFRAIN** A ***refrain*** is a repeated line or group of lines in a poem or song. Most refrains end stanzas. Although some refrains are nonsense lines, many increase suspense or emphasize character and theme.

**REGIONALISM** ***Regionalism*** in literature is the tendency among certain authors to write about specific geographical areas. Regional writers present the distinct culture of an area, including its speech, customs, beliefs, and history.

**RHETORICAL DEVICES** Rhetorical devices are special patterns of words and ideas that create emphasis and stir emotion, especially in speeches or other oral presentations. ***Parallelism***, for example, is the repetition of a grammatical structure in order to create a rhythm and make words more memorable. Other common rhetorical devices include: ***analogy,*** *drawing comparisons between two unlike things;* ***charged language,*** words that appeal to the emotions; ***concession***, an acknowledgement of the opposition's argument; ***humor***, using language and details that make characters or situations funny; ***paradox,*** statements that seem to contradict but present a truth ***restatement,*** expressing the same idea in different words,

***rhetorical questions,*** questions with obvious answers, ***tone, the author's attitude toward the audience***

**RHYME** ***Rhyme*** is the repetition of sounds at the ends of words. Rhyming words have identical vowel sounds in their final accented syllables. The consonants before the vowels may be different, but any consonants occurring after these vowels are the same, as in *frog* and *bog* or *willow* and *pillow*. ***End rhyme*** occurs when rhyming words are repeated at the ends of lines. ***Internal rhyme*** occurs when rhyming words fall within a line. ***Approximate,*** or ***slant, rhyme*** occurs when the rhyming sounds are similar, but not exact, as in *prove* and *glove*.

**REPETITION** ***Repetition*** of words and phrases is a literary device used in prose and poetry to emphasize important ideas.

**RHYTHM** ***Rhythm*** is the pattern of beats, or stresses, in spoken or written language. Prose and free verse are written in the irregular rhythmical patterns of everyday speech.

**RHETORICAL QUESTIONS** Rhetorical questions call attention to an issue by implying obvious answers.

**ROMANTICISM** ***Romanticism*** was a literary and artistic movement of the nineteenth century that arose in reaction to eighteenth-century Neoclassicism and placed a premium on imagination, emotion, nature, individuality, and exotica. Romanticism is particularly evident in the works of the Transcendentalists.

**SECONDARY SOURCE** A ***secondary source*** is one created by someone with indirect knowledge of the event being described. Secondary sources rely on ***primary sources,*** or firsthand descriptions.

**SENSORY LANGUAGE** ***Sensory language*** is writing or speech that appeals to one or more of the five senses.

**SEQUENCE OF EVENTS** Authors often use ***sequence of events***, or the order in which things happened, to structure nonfiction pieces that describe historical events or explain a change over time. Authors frequently describe important events in ***chronological order,*** or time order.

**SETTING** The ***setting*** of a literary work is the time and place of the action. A setting may serve any of a number of functions. It may provide a background for the action. It may be a crucial element in the plot or central conflict. It may also create a certain emotional atmosphere, or mood.

**SHORT STORY** A ***short story*** is a brief work of fiction. The short story resembles the novel but generally has a simpler plot and setting. In addition, the short story tends to reveal character at a crucial moment rather than developing it through many incidents. For example, Thomas Wolfe's "The Far and the Near" concentrates on what happens to a train engineer when he visits people who had waved to him every day.

**SERIAL COMMA** A ***serial comma*** is a comma placed after each item in a list except for the final item.

**SIMILE** A ***simile*** is a figure of speech that makes a direct comparison between two subjects, using either *like* or as.

**SLANT RHYME** In ***slant rhyme,*** the final sounds in two lines of a poem are similar, but not identical.

**SOCIAL COMMENTARY** In works of ***social commentary,*** an author seeks to highlight, usually in a critical way, an aspect of society.

**SPEAKER** The ***speaker*** is the voice of a poem. Although the speaker is often the poet, the speaker may also be a fictional character or even an inanimate object or another type of nonhuman entity. Interpreting a poem often depends upon recognizing who the speaker is, whom the speaker is addressing, and what the speaker's attitude, or tone, is.

**STANZA** A ***stanza*** is a group of lines in a poem that are considered to be a unit. Many poems are divided into stanzas that are separated by spaces. Stanzas often function just like paragraphs in prose. Each stanza states and develops a single main idea.

Stanzas are commonly named according to the number of lines found in them, as follows:

1. Couplet: a two-line stanza
2. Tercet: a three-line stanza
3. Quatrain: a four-line stanza
4. Cinquain: a five-line stanza
5. Sestet: a six-line stanza
6. Heptastich: a seven-line stanza
7. Octave: an eight-line stanza

**STREAM OF CONSCIOUSNESS** ***Stream of consciousness*** is a narrative technique that presents thoughts as if they were coming directly from a character's mind. Instead of being arranged in chronological order, the events are presented from the character's point of view, mixed in with the character's thoughts just as they might spontaneously occur.

**STYLE** A writer's ***style*** includes word choice, tone, degree of formality, figurative language, rhythm, grammatical structure, sentence length, organization—in short, every feature of a writer's use of language.

**SUSPENSE** ***Suspense*** is a feeling of growing uncertainty about the outcome of events. Writers create suspense by raising questions in the minds of their readers. Suspense builds until the climax of the plot, at which point the suspense reaches its peak.

**SYMBOL** A ***symbol*** is anything that stands for or represents something else. A ***conventional symbol*** is one that is widely known and accepted, such as a voyage symbolizing life or a skull symbolizing death. A ***personal***

***symbol*** is one developed for a particular work by a particular author.

**SYMBOLISM** ***Symbolism*** refers to an author's use of people, places, or objects to represent abstract qualities or ideas.

**SYNTAX** ***Syntax*** is the structure of sentences.

**THEME** A ***theme*** is a central message or insight into life revealed by a literary work. In most works of fiction, the theme is only indirectly stated: A story, poem, or play most often has an ***implied theme***.

**TONE** The tone of a literary work is the writer's attitude toward his or her subject, characters, or audience. A writer's tone may be formal or informal, friendly or distant, personal or pompous. The tone of a work can also be described as technical, conversational, or colloquial.

**TRANSCENDENTALISM** ***Transcendentalism*** was an American literary and philosophical movement of the nineteenth century. The Transcendentalists, who were based in New England, believed that intuition and the individual conscience "transcend" experience and thus are better guides to truth than the senses and logical reason. Influenced by Romanticism, the Transcendentalists respected the individual spirit and the natural world, believing that divinity was present everywhere, in nature and in each person.

**USAGE** ***Usage*** is the way in which a word or phrase is used. The meaning, pronunciation, and spelling of some words have changed over time.

**VOICE** A writer's voice is the way in which the writer's personality is revealed in his or her writing. Elements that influence a writer's style are diction, the types of words used, syntax, the types of sentences used, and tone, the writer's attitude toward the topic or audience.

**ALLEGORY / ALEGORÍA** Una ***alegoría*** es un relato o cuento con dos niveles de significado: un nivel literal y uno o más niveles simbólicos. Los hechos, ambientación y personajes de una alegoría son símbolos de ideas o cualidades.

**ALLUSION / ALUSIÓN** Una ***alusión*** es una referencia a una persona, lugar, hecho, obra literaria u obra de arte muy conocida. Los escritores a menudo hacen alusiones a relatos de la Biblia, a los mitos griegos y romanos, a las obras de Shakespeare, a hechos políticos e históricos y a otros materiales con los que suponen que sus lectores estén familiarizados.

**ANALOGY / ANALOGÍA** Una ***analogía*** establece una comparación extensa de relaciones. Se basa en la idea de que la relación entre un par de cosas es como la relación entre otro par. A diferencia de la metáfora, una analogía requiere una comparación explícita, a menudo usando las palabras *como* o *semejante*.

**ANAPHORA / ANÁFORA** Una ***anáfora*** es un tipo de estructura paralela en la que una palabra o frase se repite al principio de cláusulas consecutivas para dar énfasis.

**ANECDOTE / ANÉCDOTA** Una ***anécdota*** es un relato breve sobre un hecho interesante, divertido o extraño, que se narra con el fin de entretener o decir algo importante.

**APPEAL / APELACIÓN** Una ***apelación*** es un recurso retórico que se usa en los escritos de argumentación para persuadir al público.

Una apelación a la ética (Ethos) muestra que un argumento es justo.

Una apelación a la lógica (Logos) muestra que un argumento está bien razonado.

Una apelación a la autoridad muestra que alguien importante respalda las ideas.

Una apelación a las emociones (Pathos) tiene como fin influenciar los sentimientos de los lectores.

**ARGUMENT / ARGUMENTO** Un ***argumento*** es un escrito o discurso que trata de convencer al lector para que siga una acción o adopte una opinión en particular. Un argumento es una manera lógica de presentar una creencia, una conclusión o una postura. Un buen argumento se respalda con razonamientos y pruebas.

**AUTOBIOGRAPHY / AUTOBIOGRAFÍA** Una ***autobiografía*** es una forma de no-ficción en la que una persona narra su propia vida. Las *memorias* son relatos en primera persona de hechos personal o históricamente significativos en los que el escritor participó o de los cuales fue testigo directo. Las memorias son una forma de escrito autobiográfico.

**BIOGRAPHY / BIOGRAFÍA** Una ***biografía*** es una forma de no-ficción en la que un escritor cuenta la vida de otra persona.

**CATALOGUE / CATÁLOGO** Un ***catálogo*** en poesía es una lista de gente, objetos o situaciones que se usan para evocar un abanico de experiencias o emociones.

**CHARACTER / PERSONAJE** Un ***personaje*** es una persona o animal que participa de la acción en una obra literaria. A continuación hay algunos términos que se usan para describir varios tipos de personajes:

El ***protagonista***, o ***personaje principal***, en una obra literaria es aquel en el que se centra la obra. Los ***personajes importantes*** en una obra literaria incluyen el personaje principal y otros personajes que tienen papeles significativos. Un ***personaje menor*** es aquel que no tiene un papel importante. Un ***personaje complejo*** es aquel que muestra muchos rasgos diferentes. Un ***personaje plano*** muestra solo un rasgo. Un ***personaje dinámico*** se desarrolla y crece en el curso del relato. Un ***personaje estático*** no cambia a lo largo de la obra.

**CHARACTERIZATION / CARACTERIZACIÓN** La ***caracterización*** es el acto de crear y desarrollar un personaje. En una ***caracterización directa***, el autor expresa explícitamente los rasgos de un personaje. En una ***caracterización indirecta***, el personaje se revela a partir de una de estas maneras:

1. palabras, pensamientos o acciones del personaje
2. descripciones de la apariencia física del personaje o de su procedencia
3. lo que otros personajes dicen sobre el personaje
4. la forma en la que otros personajes reaccionan al personaje

**CLAIM / AFIRMACIÓN** Una ***afirmación*** es una opinión, conclusión o punto de vista determinado que el escritor presenta mediante un ***argumento***.

**CONCESSION / CONCESIÓN** La ***concesión*** es un recurso retórico que reconoce los argumentos de la oposición.

**CONFLICT / CONFLICTO** Un ***conflicto*** es una lucha entre fuerzas opuestas. A veces la lucha es interna, o dentro de un personaje. Otras veces la lucha es externa, o entre un personaje y una fuerza exterior. El conflicto es uno de los elementos principales de la literatura narrativa porque la mayoría de tramas se desarrollan a partir de conflictos.

**CONNOTATION / CONNOTACIÓN** La ***connotación*** es la asociación que una palabra trae a la mente, además de su definición del diccionario. Muchas palabras que son similares en sus significados del diccionario, o denotaciones, son muy diferentes en sus connotaciones. Los poetas y otros escritores escogen sus palabras cuidadosamente para que las connotaciones de esas palabras sean apropiadas.







R53

**COUNTERCLAIM / CONTRAARGUMENTO** Un ***contraargumento*** es una objeción o desafío a la ***afirmación***—u opinión, conclusión o punto de vista determinado—que el escritor presenta en un ***argumento***. El escritor suele incluir contraargumentos para anticiparse a los desafíos.

**DENOTATION / DENOTACIÓN** La ***denotación*** de una palabra es su significado objetivo, independientemente de otras asociaciones que esa palabra traiga a la mente.

**DESCRIPTION / DESCRIPCIÓN** Una ***descripción*** es un retrato en palabras de algo que se puede percibir con los sentidos. Los escritores crean descripciones usando imágenes.

**DIALECT / DIALECTO** El ***dialecto*** es la forma de un lenguaje hablado por la gente en una región o grupo particular. Los escritores a menudo usan dialecto para hacer que sus personajes parezcan más reales y para reflejar el habla de una zona determinada.

**DIALOGUE / DIÁLOGO** Un ***diálogo*** es una conversación entre personajes. Los escritores usan el diálogo para revelar personajes, para presentar hechos, para añadir variedad a la narración o para despertar el interés de los lectores.

**DICTION / DICCIÓN** La ***dicción*** comprende la elección de palabras que hace un autor o hablante. La dicción es parte del estilo de un escritor y se puede describir como formal o informal, sencilla u ornamentada, común o técnica, abstracta o concreta.

**DRAMA / DRAMA** Un ***drama*** es una historia escrita para ser representada por actores. El guión de un drama proporciona el diálogo para que los personajes hablen, así como las ***acotaciones*** que dan información sobre el vestuario, la iluminación, la ambientación, los objetos y la manera en la que los personajes se mueven o hablan. Las convenciones dramáticas incluyen soliloquios, apartes, o el paso del tiempo entre actos o escenas. La ***exposición dramática*** es un ensayo breve o comentario en prosa del escritor y que tiene como objetivo que los lectores y productores entiendan a los personajes y sus conflictos. El ***conocimiento previo*** incluye información sobre el período en el cual tiene lugar la acción.

**DRAMATIC MONOLOGUE / MONÓLOGO DRAMÁTICO** Un ***monólogo dramático*** es un poema o discurso en el que un personaje imaginario le habla a un oyente silencioso.

**DRAMATIC POEM / POEMA DRAMÁTICO** Un **poema dramático** es aquel que usa las reglas del drama. Estos poemas pueden ser monólogos o diálogos o pueden presentar el parlamento de varios personajes. "The Death of the Hired Man" de Robert Frost es un ejemplo muy famoso de poema dramático.

Ver también ***monólogo dramático***.

**EPIC THEME / TEMA ÉPICO** Un ***tema épico*** es el mensaje subyacente de que todas las personas de todas las épocas están conectadas por experiencias compartidas.

**EDITORIAL / EDITORIAL** Un ***editorial*** es una forma de escritura persuasiva o argumento. Los editoriales deben tener una postura clara, respaldarse con razonamientos e incluir una apelación a la ética, a la lógica, a la autoridad o a la emoción.

**ELLIPTICAL PHRASING / FRASEO ELÍPTICO** El ***fraseo elíptico*** es un estilo de poesía en el que el poeta omite palabras que se espera que sean comprendidas por el lector.

**ENUMERATION / ENUMERACIÓN** Una ***enumeración*** es un estilo de documento en el que las ideas principales se listan en orden numérico.

**ESSAY / ENSAYO** Un ***ensayo*** es una obra breve de no-ficción sobre un tema en particular. Los ensayos pueden clasificarse como ***formal*** o ***informal***, ***personal*** o ***impersonal***. También se pueden clasificar de acuerdo a su propósito, como por ejemplo ***de causa y efecto***, ***satírico*** o ***reflexivo***. Otras maneras de clasificar ensayos es por el modo de discurso, como por ejemplo ***expositivo, descriptivo, persuasivo*** o ***narrativo***.

**EXPLANATORY ESSAY / ENSAYO EXPLICATIVO** Un ***ensayo explicativo*** describe y resume información sobre un concepto recogida a partir de varias fuentes.

**FICTION / FICCIÓN** La ***ficción*** es un escrito en prosa que cuenta algo sobre personajes y hechos imaginarios. Los cuentos y las novelas son obras de ficción.

**FIGURATIVE LANGUAGE / LENGUAJE FIGURADO** El ***lenguaje figurado*** es un escrito o discurso que no se debe interpretar literalmente. Los escritores usan lenguaje figurado para expresar ideas de forma vívida e imaginativa.

**FIGURE OF SPEECH / FIGURA RETÓRICA** Una ***figura retória*** es una expresión o palabra usada de forma imaginativa en vez de literal.

**FLASHBACK / FLASHBACK** Un ***flashback*** o ***escena retrospectiva*** es una sección de una obra literaria que interrumple la presentación cronológica de los hechos para relatar un hecho de un tiempo anterior. Un escritor puede presentar un flashback como el recuerdo de un personaje, como parte de lo que cuenta un personaje, como un sueño o simplemente haciendo que el narrador cambie a un tiempo en el pasado.

**FORESHADOWING / PREFIGURACIÓN** La ***prefiguración*** es el uso, en una obra literaria, de claves que sugieren hechos que van a suceder.

**FRAME STORY / CUENTO DE ENMARQUE** Un ***cuento de enmarque*** es un relato dentro del cual se incluye otro relato o relatos. Este recurso permite crear una estructura narrativa del tipo "cuento dentro del cuento".

**FREE VERSE / VERSO LIBRE** El ***verso libre*** es una forma poética en la que no se sigue un patrón regular de metro ni de rima. Un escritor de verso libre tiene la libertad de usar cualquier ritmo que sea apropiado a lo que está diciendo.

**GENRE / GÉNERO** Un ***género*** es una categoría o tipo de literatura. La literatura se divide por lo general en tres géneros principales: poesía, prosa y drama. Cada uno de estos géneros principales se dividen a su vez en géneros más pequeños. La poesía se puede dividir en lírica, concreta, dramática, narrativa y épica. La prosa se puede dividir en ficción y no ficción. El drama se puede dividir en drama serio, tragedia, drama cómico, melodrama y farsa.

**HUMOR / HUMOR** El ***humor***, usado en un argumento, puede ser un recurso retórico efectivo. El lenguaje y los detalles humorísticos pueden hacer que los personajes y las situaciones parezcan divertidos.

**HYPERBOLE / HIPÉRBOLE** Una ***hipérbole*** es una exageración o magnificación deliberada que a menudo se usa para producir un efecto cómico.

**IDIOMATIC EXPRESSION / EXPRESIÓN IDIOMÁTICA** Las ***expresiones idiomáticas*** son figuras retóricas que no se pueden entender literalmente. Por ejemplo, una tormenta se puede describir como "llover a cántaros".

**IMAGE / IMAGEN** Una ***imagen*** es una palabra o frase que apela a uno o más de los cinco sentidos: la vista, el oído, el tacto, el gusto o el olfato.

**IMAGERY / IMÁGENES** Las ***imágenes*** son el lenguaje figurado o descriptivo que se usa en la literatura para crear una descripción verbal para los lectores. Estas descripciones verbales, o imágenes, se crean incluyendo detalles visuales, auditivos, gustativos, táctiles, olfativos o de movimiento.

**IN MEDIA RES / IN MEDIA RES** ***In media res***, que quiere decir "en el medio de las cosas" en latín, es un resuso que usan los escritores para captar la atención del lector.

**INCONGRUITY / INCONGRUENCIA** La ***incongruencia*** es una técnica que usan los escritores para crear humor y ocurre cuando dos o más ideas se relacionan entre sí de una manera que no es de la esperada por el lector.

**IRONY / IRONÍA** ***Ironía*** es un contraste entre lo que se dice y lo que se quiere decir, o entre lo que se espera que ocurra y lo que pasa en realidad. En una ***ironía verbal***, las palabras se usan para sugerir lo opuesto a lo que se dice. En la ***ironía dramática*** hay una contradicción entre lo que el personaje piensa y lo que el lector o la audiencia sabe que es verdad. En una ***ironía situacional***, ocurre un suceso que contradice directamente las expectativas de los personajes, del lector o de la audiencia.

**LETTER / CARTA** Una ***carta*** es un mensaje escrito dirigido a un lector o lectores y generalmente se envía por correo. Las cartas pueden ser ***privadas*** o ***públicas***, dependiendo de la audiencia a la que van dirigidas. Una ***carta pública***, también llamada ***carta literaria*** o ***epístola***, es una obra literara escrita en forma de carta personal pero creada para ser publicada.

**MEMOIR / MEMORIAS** Unas **memorias** son un tipo de escrito de no ficción autobiográfica en el que el autor cuenta algo de su propia vida, generalmente centrándose en la participación del autor en hechos significativos históricos o culturales, ya sea como participante directo o como testigo.

**METAPHOR / METÁFORA** Una **metáfora** es una figura literaria en la que algo se describe como si fuera otra cosa. La identificación sugiere una comparación entre las dos cosas que se identifican, como "la muerte es un largo sueño".

Una ***metáfora mixta*** ocurre cuando dos metáforas se unen. Por ejemplo, las espinas y la lluvia se mezclan ilógicamente en "le llovieron encima las espinas de la vida". Una ***metáfora muerta*** es aquella que se ha sobreutilizado mucho y se ha convertido en una expresión común, como "el brazo del sillón" o "la noche que cae".

**MONOLOGUE / MONÓLOGO** Un ***monólogo*** es un discurso narrado por completo por una sola persona o personaje.

**MOTIF / MOTIVO** El ***motivo*** es un objeto o idea que se repite de forma recurrente en una obra literaria.

**NARRATION / NARRACIÓN** Una ***narración*** es un escrito que cuenta una historia. El acto de contar una historia de forma oral también se llama ***narración***. La ***narrativa,*** o relato, la cuenta el ***narrador.*** Un relato generalmente se cuenta en orden cronológico, en el orden en el que suceden los hechos, aunque puede incluir flashbacks y prefiguración. Las narrativas pueden ser verdaderas o inventadas. La narración es una de las muchas formas de discurso que existen y se usa en novelas, cuentos, obras de teatro, poemas narrativos, anécdotas, autobiografías, biografías e informes.

**NARRATIVE / RELATO** Se llama ***relato*** a la historia que se narra en una obra de ficción, de no-ficción, en un poema o en un drama. Los relatos a menudo se clasifican por su contenido o propósito. Un ***relato de exploración*** es una narración en primera persona de los viajes de un explorador en una tierra desconocida. "The Interesting Narrative of the Life of Olaudah Equiano" es un ***relato de esclavos***, la narración de las experiencias de una persona esclavizada. Un ***relato histórico*** es la narración de hechos históricos significativos. Un ***relato personal*** es una narración en primera persona sobre una experiencia real. En un ***relato de reflexión*** el autor describe sus sentimientos sobre una escena, incidente, recuerdo o hecho. Un ***relato no lineal*** no sigue el orden cronológico. Puede contener flashbacks, secuencias de sueño u otros recursos que interrumpen el orden cronológico de los hechos.

**NARRATOR / NARRADOR** Un ***narrador*** es el hablante o el personaje que cuenta una historia. El cuento o novela lo puede narrar un personaje principal, un personaje menor o alguien que no está involucrado en la trama. El narrador puede hablar en primera persona o en tercera persona. Un ***narrador omnisciente*** lo sabe todo, mientras que un ***narrador limitado*** sólo sabe lo que hace un personaje.

**NONFICTION / NO-FICCIÓN** La ***no-ficción*** es un escrito en prosa que presenta y explica ideas o cuenta algo acerca de personas, lugares, ideas o hechos reales. Dos de los tipos principales de literatura de no-ficción son los escritos históricos y los escritos de reflexión. Los ensayos, las biografías, las autobiografías, los diarios y los reportajes son todos ejemplos de no-ficción.

**NOVEL / NOVELA** Una ***novela*** es una obra extensa de ficción. A menudo tiene una trama complicada, con personajes principales y secundarios, con un tema significativo y una ambientación variada. Las novelas pueden clasificarse de muchas maneras, basadas en los periodos históricos en los que se escribieron, en los temas que tratan, en las técnicas que se usan en ellas y en los movimientos literarios que las inspiraron. Una ***novela corta*** no es tan extensa como una novela, pero es más larga que un cuento.

**ONOMATOPOEIA / ONOMATOPEYA** La ***onomatopeya*** es el uso de palabras que imitan sonidos, tales como *zum*, *pío-pío, tic-tac* o *susurro*.

**ORATORY / ORATORIA** La ***oratoria*** es hablar en público de manera formal, persuasiva y emocionalmente atractiva. El "Discurso en la Convención de Virginia" es un ejemplo de oratoria.

**OXYMORON / OXÍMORON** Un ***oxímoron*** es una figura literaria que combina dos ideas opuestas o contradictorias. Un oxímoron, como "fuego helado", sugiere una paradoja en solo unas palabras.

**PACING / RITMO LITERARIO** El ***ritmo literario*** es la velocidad o el paso de la escritura. Los escritores usan diferentes ritmos literarios para lograr distintos efectos, como el suspenso.

**PARADOX / PARADOJA** Una ***paradoja*** es un enunciado que parece contradictorio pero que sin embargo presenta una verdad.

**PARALLELISM / PARALELISMO** El ***paralelismo*** es la presentación de ideas similares, en secuencia, usando la misma estructura gramatical.

**PARALLEL STRUCTURE / ESTRUCTURA PARALELA** En una lista, cada objeto listado debe usar ***estructura paralela*** en la cual la morfología y frase gramatical sea igual para todos los objetos.

**PERSONIFICATION / PERSONIFICACIÓN** La ***personificación*** es una forma de lenguaje figurado en la que se da rasgos y actitudes humanas a un sujeto no humano. La personificación efectiva de cosas o ideas hace que se vean llenas de vida, como si fueran humanas.

**PHILOSOPHICAL ASSUMPTIONS / SUPOSICIONES FILOSÓFICAS** Las creencias que se dan por sentadas son ***suposiciones filosóficas***. Algunas suposiciones son ***explícitas***, o enunciadas directamente. Otras suposiciones son ***implícitas***, que quiere decir que el lector debe hacer inferencias para comprenderlas.

**PLOT / TRAMA o ARGUMENTO** La ***trama*** o ***argumento*** es la secuencia de los eventos que suceden en una obra literaria. En la mayoría de las obras de ficción, la trama implica tanto a los personajes como al conflicto central. La trama por lo general empieza con una ***exposición*** que introduce la ambientación, los personajes y la situación básica. A ello le sigue el ***suceso desencadenante***, que introduce el conflicto central. Este conflicto aumenta durante el ***desarrollo*** hasta que alcanza el punto más alto de interés o suspenso, llamado ***clímax***. Al clímax le sigue el final o resolución del conflicto central. Todos los hechos que ocurren después de la ***resolución***, forman el ***desenlace***. Todos los sucesos que conducen al clímax constituyen la ***acción dramática creciente***. Los sucesos que siguen al clímax forman la ***acción dramática decreciente***.

**POETIC STRUCTURE / ESTRUCTURA POÉTICA** Las ***estructuras poéticas*** básicas son los versos y las estrofas. Un ***verso*** es un grupo de palabras ordenadas en un mismo renglón. Un verso puede terminar, o cortarse, de distintas maneras. La variedad en la ***extensión de los versos*** crea ritmos inesperados.

En un ***verso no encabalgado*** la estructura gramatical y el sentido se completan al final de esa línea.

En un ***verso encabalgado*** tanto la estructura gramatical como el sentido de una línea continúa en el verso que sigue.

**POETRY / POESÍA** La ***poesía*** es uno de los tres géneros literarios más importantes. En poesía, la forma y el contenido están íntimamente relacionados, como dos caras de la misma moneda. Los poemas a menudo se dividen en versos y estrofas y emplean patrones rítmicos regulares, llamados metros. La mayoría de los poemas están escritos en un lenguaje altamente conciso, musical y emocionalmente rico. Muchos también hacen uso de imágenes, de figuras retóricas y de sonoros, tales como la rima.

**POINT OF VIEW / PUNTO DE VISTA** El ***punto de vista*** es la perspectiva desde la cual se narran o describen los hechos de un relato. Tres puntos de vista que se usan frecuentemente son: primera persona, tercera persona omnisciente y tercera persona limitada.

En el ***punto de vista de primera persona***, el narrador es un personaje del relato y se refiere a sí mismo con el pronombre de primera persona "yo".

Los dos tipos de punto de vista de tercera persona, limitado y omnisciente, se llaman "tercera persona" porque el narrador usa pronombres de tercera persona como "él o "ella" para referirse a los personajes. No hay "yo" que narre la historia.

En los relatos contados desde el ***punto de vista de tercera persona omnisciente***, el narrador conoce y cuenta cosas sobre lo que cada personaje piensa y siente.

En los relatos contados desde el ***punto de vista de tercera persona limitada***, el narrador relata los pensamientos internos y sentimientos de sólo un personaje y todo se ve desde el punto de vista de ese personaje.

**PREAMBLE / PREÁMBULO** El ***preámbulo*** es un enunciado que explica quién expide un documento y con qué propósito.

**PRIMARY SOURCE / FUENTE PRIMARIA** Una ***fuente primaria*** es la que ha sido creada por alguien que participó u observó directamente el suceso que se describe.

**PROSE / PROSA** La ***prosa*** es la forma común del lenguaje escrito. La mayoría de los escritos que no son poesía, ni drama, ni canciones, se consideran prosa. La prosa es uno de los géneros literarios más importantes y puede ser de dos formas: de ficción y de no-ficción.

**PROTAGONIST / PROTAGONISTA** El o la ***protagonista*** es el personaje principal de una obra literaria.

**REFRAIN / REFRÁN** Un ***refrán*** es un verso o grupo de versos que se repite en un poema o canción. Muchos refranes terminan estrofas. Si bien es cierto que algunos refranes no tienen sentido, la mayoría sirve para aumentar el suspenso o para realzar un personaje o enfatizar un tema.

**REGIONALISM / REGIONALISMO** El ***regionalismo*** en literatura es la tendencia entre ciertos autores a escribir sobre áreas geográficas específicas. Los escritores regionales presentan la cultura específica de un área, incluyendo su dialecto, costumbres, creencias e historia.

**REPETITION / REPETICIÓN** La ***repetición*** de palabras y frases es un recurso literario que se usa en prosa y poesía para dar énfasis a ideas importantes.

**RHETORICAL DEVICES / FIGURAS RETÓRICAS** Las ***figuras retóricas*** son patrones especiales de palabras e ideas que dan énfasis y producen emoción, especialmente en discursos y otras presentaciones orales. El ***paralelismo***, por ejemplo, es la repetición de una estructura gramatical con el propósito de crear un ritmo y hacer que las palabras resulten más memorables.

Otras figuras retóricas muy frecuentes son: la ***analogía***, que establece una comparación entre dos cosas diferentes; el ***lenguaje emocionalmente cargado***, en el que las palabras apelan a las emociones; la ***concesión***, mediante la que se acepta el argumento del oponente; el ***humor***, que usa el lenguaje y los detalles para hacer que los personajes o las situaciones resulten cómicas; la ***paradoja***, enunciados que parecen contradecirse pero que presentan una verdad; la ***reafirmación***, en la que se expresa la misma idea con distintas palabras; las ***preguntas retóricas***, que son interrogaciones cuyas respuestas son obvias; el ***tono***, la actitud del autor hacia la audiencia.

**RHETORICAL QUESTIONS / PREGUNTAS RETÓRICAS** Las ***preguntas retóricas*** llaman la atención a un hecho al insinuar respuestas obvias.

**RIMA** La ***rima*** es la repetición de los sonidos finales de las palabras. Las palabras que riman tienen sonidos vocálicos iguales en las sílabas finales acentuadas. Las consonantes que están antes de esas vocales acentuadas pueden ser diferentes, pero las consonantes que estén después de esas vocales deben ser iguales, como en *frog* y *bog* o en *willow* y *pillow*. La ***rima de final de verso*** tiene lugar cuando se repiten las palabras que riman al final de dos o más versos. La ***rima interna*** se produce cuando las palabras que riman están en el mismo verso. La ***rima aproximada*** tiene lugar cuando los sonidos son parecidos pero no exactos, como en *prove* y *glove*.

**RITMO** El ***ritmo*** es el patrón de cadencia o acentuación en la lengua hablada o escrita. La prosa y el verso libre se escriben en los patrones rítmicos irregulares del lenguaje hablado cotidiano.

**ROMANTICISM / ROMANTICISMO** El ***romanticismo*** fue un movimiento literario y artístico del siglo. XIX que surgió como reacción contra el neoclasicismo del siglo. XVII y que daba énfasis a la imaginación, la emoción, la naturaleza, la individualidad y lo extótico. El romanticismo es particularmente evidente en las obras de los transcendentalistas.

**SECONDARY SOURCE / FUENTE SECUNDARIA** Una ***fuente secundaria*** es la que ha sido creada por alguien con información indirecta del suceso que se describe. Las fuentes secundarias dependen de las ***fuentes primarias***, o descripciones de primera mano.

**SENSORY LANGUAGE / LENGUAJE SENSORIAL** El ***lenguaje sensorial*** es un escrito o discurso que incluye detalles que apelan a uno o más de los sentidos.

**SEQUENCE OF EVENTS / SECUENCIA DE SUCESOS** Los autores a menudo usan la ***secuencia de sucesos***, o el orden en que sucenden las cosas, para estructurar piezas de no ficción que describen hechos históricos o que explican cambios a lo largo del tiempo. Los autores frecuentemente describen hechos importantes en ***orden cronológico,*** u orden de tiempo.

**SETTING / AMBIENTACIÓN** La ***ambientación*** de una obra literaria es la época y el lugar en el que se desarrolla la acción. La ambientación puede servir varias funciones. Puede proporcionar el telón de fondo para la acción. Puede ser un elemento crucial en la trama o conflicto central. También puede crear una atmósfera emotiva.

**SHORT STORY / CUENTO** Un ***cuento*** es una obra breve de ficción. El cuento se parece a la novela, pero suele tener una trama y ambientación más sencillas. Además, el cuento tiende a revelar el carácter de los personajes en un momento particular en lugar de irlo desarrollando a lo largo de numerosos acontecimientos. Por ejemplo, el cuento "The Far and the Near" de Thomas Wolfe se centra en lo que le sucede a un maquinista cuando visita a la gente que lo ha saludado diariamente.

**SERIAL COMMA / COMA EN SERIE** En inglés, se pone una ***coma en serie*** después de cada objeto en una lista, excepto en el objeto final.

**SIMILE / SÍMIL** Un ***símil*** es una figura retórica en la que se usa la palabra *como* para establecer una comparación directa entre dos cosas.

**SLANT RHYME / RIMA ASONANTE** En una ***rima asonante*** los sonidos finales de dos versos del poema son similares, pero no idénticos.

**SOCIAL COMMENTARY / COMENTARIO SOCIAL** En obras de ***comentario social,*** el autor tiene como objetivo resaltar, de forma crítica, un aspecto de la sociedad.

**SPEAKER / HABLANTE** El ***hablante*** es la voz de un poema. Aunque a menudo el hablante es el poeta, el hablante puede ser también un personaje imaginario o incluso un objeto inanimado o cualquier otro tipo de sujeto no humano. Interpretar un poema a menudo depende de reconocer quién es el hablante, a quién se dirige el hablante y cuál es la actitud o tono del hablante.

**STANZA / ESTROFA** Una ***estrofa*** es un grupo de versos en un poema que se consideran una unidad. Muchos poemas se dividen en estrofas que están separadas por espacios. Las estrofas a menudo funcionan como los párrafos en la prosa. Cada estrofa enuncia y desarrolla una sola idea principal.

Las estrofas a menudo reciben su nombre del número de versos que las componen, como siguen:

1. Pareado o dístico: estrofa de dos versos
2. terceta: estrofa de tres versos
3. cuarteta: estrofa de cuatro versos
4. quintilla: estrofa de cinco versos
5. sextilla: estrofa de seis versos
6. septeto: estrofa de siete versos
7. octavilla: estrofa de ocho versos

**STREAM OF CONSCIOUSNESS / MONÓLOGO INTERIOR** El ***monólogo interior*** es una técnica narrativa que presenta los pensamientos como si vinieran directamente de la mente de un personaje. En vez de ordenarse cronológicamente, los hechos se presentan desde el punto de vista del personaje, mezclados con los pensamientos como si ocurrieran espontáneamente.

**STYLE / ESTILO** El ***estilo*** de un escritor incluye su dicción, tono, grado de formalidad, lenguaje figurado, ritmo, estructura gramatical, tamaño de las oraciones, organización, etc. En resumen, cada rasgo del uso del lenguaje de un escritor.

**SUSPENSE / SUSPENSO** El ***suspenso*** es la sensación creciente de incertidumbre sobre el resultado de los hechos. Los escritores crean suspenso poniendo preguntas en la mente de sus lectores. El suspenso crece hasta el clímax de la trama, punto en el que alcanza su momento álgido.

**SYMBOL / SÍMBOLO** Un ***símbolo*** es algo que representa otra cosa. Un ***símbolo convencional*** es uno ampliamente conocido y aceptado, como un viaje como símbolo de la vida o una calavera como símbolo de la muerte. Un ***símbolo personal*** es el que desarrolla un autor en concreto para una obra en particular.

**SYMBOLISM / SIMBOLISMO** El ***simbolismo*** hace referencia al uso de personas, lugares u objetos que usa un autor para representar cualidades o ideas abstractas.

**SYNTAX / SINTAXIS** La ***sintaxis*** es la estructura de las oraciones.

**THEME / TEMA** Un ***tema*** es el mensaje central o la concepción de la vida que revela una obra literaria. El tema de un ensayo a menudo se menciona directamente en la tesis. En la mayoría de obras de ficción el tema se enuncia sólo indirectamente: un cuento, poema u obra de teatro a menudo tienen un ***tema implícito***.

**TONE / TONO** El ***tono*** de una obra literaria es la actitud del escritor hacia su tema, sus personajes o su audiencia. El tono de un escritor puede ser formal o informal, amistoso o distante, personal o pretencioso. El tono de una obra también se puede describir como técnico, conversacional o coloquial.

**TRANSCENDENTALISM /TRANSCENDENTALISMO** El ***transcendentalismo*** fue un movimiento estadounidense literario y filosófico del siglo. XIX. Los transcendentalistas, que estaban radicados en Nueva Inglaterra, creían que la intuición y consciencia individual "transcendían" la experiencia y por tanto eran mejores guías a la verdad que los sentidos y la razón lógica. Influidos por el Romanticismo, los transcendentalistas respetaban el espíritu individual y el mundo natural, creyendo que lo divino estaba presente en todas partes, en la naturaleza y en cada persona.

**USAGE / USO** El ***uso*** es la manera en la que una palabra o frase se usa. El significado, pronunciación y ortografía de algunas de las palabras ha cambiado con el tiempo.

**VOICE / VOZ** La ***voz*** es el "sonido" distintivo de un escritor, o la manera en que "habla" en la página. Se relaciona a elementos tales como la dicción, los tipos de palabras, la sintaxis, el tipo de oraciones empleadas y el tono, que es la actitud del autor hacia el tema o la audiencia.

## PARTS OF SPEECH

Every English word, depending on its meaning and its use in a sentence, can be identified as one of the eight parts of speech. These are nouns, pronouns, verbs, adjectives, adverbs, prepositions, conjunctions, and interjections. Understanding the parts of speech will help you learn the rules of English grammar and usage.

**Nouns** A **noun** names a person, place, or thing. A **common noun** names any one of a class of persons, places, or things. A **proper noun** names a specific person, place, or thing.

| Common Noun | Proper Noun |
|---|---|
| writer, country, novel | Charles Dickens, Great Britain, *Hard Times* |

**Pronouns** A **pronoun** is a word that stands for one or more nouns. The word to which a pronoun refers (whose place it takes) is the **antecedent** of the pronoun.

A **personal pronoun** refers to the person speaking (first person); the person spoken to (second person); or the person, place, or thing spoken about (third person).

| | Singular | Plural |
|---|---|---|
| **First Person** | I, me, my, mine | we, us, our, ours |
| **Second Person** | you, your, yours | you, your, yours |
| **Third Person** | he, him, his, she, her, hers, it, its | they, them, their, theirs |

A **reflexive pronoun** reflects the action of a verb back on its subject. It indicates that the person or thing performing the action also is receiving the action.

I keep *myself* fit by taking a walk every day.

An **intensive pronoun** adds emphasis to a noun or pronoun.

It took the work of the president *himself* to pass the law.

A **demonstrative** pronoun points out a specific person(s), place(s), or thing(s).

this, that, these, those

A **relative pronoun** begins a subordinate clause and connects it to another idea in the sentence.

that, which, who, whom, whose

An **interrogative pronoun** begins a question.

what, which, who, whom, whose

An **indefinite pronoun** refers to a person, place, or thing that may or may not be specifically named.

all, another, any, both, each, everyone, few, most, none, no one, somebody

**Verbs** A **verb** expresses action or the existence of a state or condition.

An **action verb** tells what action someone or something is performing.

gather, read, work, jump, imagine, analyze, conclude

A **linking verb** connects the subject with another word that identifies or describes the subject. The most common linking verb is *be*.

appear, be, become, feel, look, remain, seem, smell, sound, stay, taste

A **helping verb,** or **auxiliary verb,** is added to a main verb to make a verb phrase.

be, do, have, should, can, could, may, might, must, will, would

**Adjectives** An **adjective** modifies a noun or pronoun by describing it or giving it a more specific meaning. An adjective answers the questions:

| | |
|---|---|
| What kind? | *purple* hat, *happy* face, *loud* sound |
| Which one? | *this* bowl |
| How many? | *three* cars |
| How much? | *enough* food |

The articles *the, a,* and *an* are adjectives.

A **proper adjective** is an adjective derived from a proper noun.

French, Shakespearean

**Adverbs** An **adverb** modifies a verb, an adjective, or another adverb by telling *where, when, how,* or *to what extent.*

will answer *soon, extremely* sad, calls *more* often

**Prepositions** A **preposition** relates a noun or pronoun that appears with it to another word in the sentence.

Dad made a meal *for* us. We talked *till* dusk. Bo missed school *because of* his illness.

**Conjunctions** A **conjunction** connects words or groups of words. A **coordinating conjunction** joins words or groups of words of equal rank.

bread *and* cheese, brief *but* powerful

**Correlative conjunctions** are used in pairs to connect words or groups of words of equal importance.

*both* Luis *and* Rosa, *neither* you *nor I*

**Subordinating conjunctions** indicate the connection between two ideas by placing one below the other in rank or importance. A subordinating conjunction introduces a subordinate, or dependent, clause.

We will miss her *if* she leaves. Hank shrieked *when* he slipped on the ice.

### Interjections

An **interjection** expresses feeling or emotion. It is not related to other words in the sentence.

ah, hey, ouch, well, yippee

## PHRASES AND CLAUSES

### Phrases

A **phrase** is a group of words that does not have both a subject and a verb and that functions as one part of speech. A phrase expresses an idea but cannot stand alone.

### Prepositional Phrases

A **prepositional phrase** is a group of words that begins with a preposition and ends with a noun or pronoun that is the **object of the preposition.**

before dawn     as a result of the rain

An **adjective phrase** is a prepositional phrase that modifies a noun or pronoun.

Eliza appreciates the beauty **of a well-crafted poem.**

An **adverb phrase** is a prepositional phrase that modifies a verb, an adjective, or an adverb.

She reads Spenser's sonnets **with great pleasure.**

### Appositive Phrases

An **appositive** is a noun or pronoun placed next to another noun or pronoun to add information about it. An **appositive phrase** consists of an appositive and its modifiers.

Mr. Roth, **my music teacher**, is sick.

### Verbal Phrases

A **verbal** is a verb form that functions as a different part of speech (not as a verb) in a sentence. **Participles, gerunds,** and **infinitives** are verbals.

A **verbal phrase** includes a verbal and any modifiers or complements it may have. Verbal phrases may function as nouns, as adjectives, or as adverbs.

A **participle** is a verb form that can act as an adjective. Present participles end in *-ing;* past participles of regular verbs end in *-ed.*

A **participial phrase** consists of a participle and its modifiers or complements. The entire phrase acts as an adjective.

Jenna's backpack, **loaded with equipment,** was heavy.

**Barking incessantly,** the dogs chased the squirrels out of sight.

A **gerund** is a verb form that ends in *-ing* and is used as a noun.

A **gerund phrase** consists of a gerund with any modifiers or complements, all acting together as a noun.

**Taking photographs of wildlife** is her main hobby. [acts as subject]

We always enjoy **listening to live music.** [acts as object]

An **infinitive** is a verb form, usually preceded by *to,* that can act as a noun, an adjective, or an adverb.

An **infinitive phrase** consists of an infinitive and its modifiers or complements, and sometimes its subject, all acting together as a single part of speech.

She tries **to get out into the wilderness often.** [acts as a noun; direct object of *tries*]

The Tigers are the team **to beat.** [acts as an adjective; describes *team*]

I drove twenty miles **to witness the event.** [acts as an adverb; tells why I drove]

### Clauses

A **clause** is a group of words with its own subject and verb.

### Independent Clauses

An independent clause can stand by itself as a complete sentence.

George Orwell wrote with extraordinary insight.

### Subordinate Clauses

A subordinate clause cannot stand by itself as a complete sentence. Subordinate clauses always appear connected in some way with one or more independent clauses.

George Orwell, **who wrote with extraordinary insight,** produced many politically relevant works.

An **adjective clause** is a subordinate clause that acts as an adjective. It modifies a noun or a pronoun by telling *what kind* or *which one.* Also called relative clauses, adjective clauses usually begin with a **relative pronoun:** *who, which, that, whom, or whose.*

"The Lamb" is the poem **that I memorized for class.**

An **adverb clause** is a subordinate clause that, like an adverb, modifies a verb, an adjective, or an adverb. An adverb clause tells *where, when, in what way, to what extent, under what condition,* or *why.*

The students will read another poetry collection **if their schedule allows.**
**When I recited the poem,** Mr. Lopez was impressed.

A **noun clause** is a subordinate clause that acts as a noun.

William Blake survived on **whatever he made as an engraver.**

## SENTENCE STRUCTURE

### Subject and Predicate

A **sentence** is a group of words that expresses a complete thought. A sentence has two main parts: a *subject* and a *predicate*.

A **fragment** is a group of words that does not express a complete thought. It lacks an independent clause.

The **subject** tells *whom* or *what* the sentence is about. The **predicate** tells what the subject of the sentence does or is.

A subject or a predicate can consist of a single word or of many words. All the words in the subject make up the **complete subject.** All the words in the predicate make up the **complete predicate.**

**Complete Subject** **Complete Predicate**
Both of those girls | have already read *Macbeth*.

The **simple subject** is the essential noun, pronoun, or group of words acting as a noun that cannot be left out of the complete subject. The **simple predicate** is the essential verb or verb phrase that cannot be left out of the complete predicate.

**Both** of those girls | **have** already **read** *Macbeth*.
[Simple subject: *Both;* simple predicate: *have read*]

A **compound subject** is two or more subjects that have the same verb and are joined by a conjunction.

**Neither the horse nor the driver** looked tired.

A **compound predicate** is two or more verbs that have the same subject and are joined by a conjunction.

She **sneezed and coughed** throughout the trip.

### Complements

A **complement** is a word or word group that completes the meaning of the subject or verb in a sentence. There are four kinds of complements: *direct objects, indirect objects, objective complements,* and *subject complements.*

A **direct object** is a noun, a pronoun, or a group of words acting as a noun that receives the action of a transitive verb.

We watched the **liftoff**.
She drove **Zach** to the launch site.

An **indirect object** is a noun or pronoun that appears with a direct object and names the person or thing to which or for which something is done.

He sold the **family** a mirror. [The direct object is *mirror.*]

An **objective complement** is an adjective or noun that appears with a direct object and describes or renames it.

The decision made her **unhappy**.
[The direct object is *her.*]
Many consider Shakespeare the greatest **playwright.** [The direct object is *Shakespeare.*]

A **subject complement** follows a linking verb and tells something about the subject. There are two kinds: *predicate nominatives* and *predicate adjectives.*

A **predicate nominative** is a noun or pronoun that follows a linking verb and identifies or renames the subject.

"A Modest Proposal" is a **pamphlet.**

A **predicate adjective** is an adjective that follows a linking verb and describes the subject of the sentence.

"A Modest Proposal" is **satirical.**

### Classifying Sentences by Structure

Sentences can be classified according to the kind and number of clauses they contain. The four basic sentence structures are *simple, compound, complex,* and *compound-complex.*

A **simple sentence** consists of one independent clause.

Terrence enjoys modern British literature.

A **compound sentence** consists of two or more independent clauses. The clauses are joined by a conjunction or a semicolon.

Terrence enjoys modern British literature, but his brother prefers the classics.

A **complex sentence** consists of one independent clause and one or more subordinate clauses.

Terrence, who reads voraciously, enjoys modern British literature.

A **compound-complex sentence** consists of two or more independent clauses and one or more subordinate clauses.

Terrence, who reads voraciously, enjoys modern British literature, but his brother prefers the classics.

### Classifying Sentences by Function

Sentences can be classified according to their function or purpose. The four types are *declarative, interrogative, imperative,* and *exclamatory.*

## SENTENCE STRUCTURE continued

A **declarative sentence** states an idea and ends with a period.

An **interrogative sentence** asks a question and ends with a question mark.

An **imperative sentence** gives an order or a direction and ends with either a period or an exclamation mark.

An **exclamatory sentence** conveys a strong emotion and ends with an exclamation mark.

## PARAGRAPH STRUCTURE

An effective paragraph is organized around one **main idea,** which is often stated in a **topic sentence.** The other sentences support the main idea. To give the paragraph **unity,** make sure the connection between each sentence and the main idea is clear.

### Unnecessary Shift in Person

Do not change needlessly from one grammatical person to another. Keep the person consistent in your sentences.

**Max** went to the bakery, but **you** can't buy mints there. [shift from third person to second person]

**Max** went to the bakery, but **he** can't buy mints there. [consistent]

### Unnecessary Shift in Voice

Do not change needlessly from active voice to passive voice in your use of verbs.

Elena and I **searched** the trail for evidence, but no clues **were found.** [shift from active voice to passive voice]

Elena and I **searched** the trail for evidence, but we **found** no clues. [consistent]

## AGREEMENT

### Subject and Verb Agreement

A singular subject must have a singular verb. A plural subject must have a plural verb.

**Dr. Boone uses** a telescope to view the night sky.

The **students use** a telescope to view the night sky.

A verb always agrees with its subject, not its object.

*Incorrect:* The best part of the show were the jugglers.

*Correct:* The best part of the show was the jugglers.

A phrase or clause that comes between a subject and verb does not affect subject-verb agreement.

His **theory**, as well as his claims, **lacks** support.

Two subjects joined by *and* usually take a plural verb.

The **dog** and the **cat are** healthy.

Two singular subjects joined by *or* or *nor* take a singular verb.

The **dog** or the **cat is** hiding.

Two plural subjects joined by *or* or *nor* take a plural verb.

The **dogs** or the **cats are** coming home with us.

When a singular and a plural subject are joined by *or* or *nor,* the verb agrees with the closer subject.

Either the **dogs** or the **cat is** behind the door.

Either the **cat** or the **dogs are** behind the door.

### Pronoun and Antecedent Agreement

Pronouns must agree with their antecedents in number and gender. Use singular pronouns with singular antecedents and plural pronouns with plural antecedents.

**Doris Lessing** uses **her** writing to challenge ideas about women's roles.

**Writers** often use **their** skills to promote social change.

Use a singular pronoun when the antecedent is a singular indefinite pronoun such as *anybody, each, either, everybody, neither, no one, one, or someone.*

Judge **each** of the articles on **its** merits.

Use a plural pronoun when the antecedent is a plural indefinite pronoun such as *both, few, many,* or *several.*

**Both** of the articles have **their** flaws.

The indefinite pronouns *all, any, more, most, none,* and *some* can be singular or plural depending on the number of the word to which they refer.

**Most** of the *books* are in **their** proper places.

**Most** of the *book* has been torn from **its** binding.

## USING VERBS

### Principal Parts of Regular and Irregular Verbs

A verb has four principal parts:

| Present | Present Participle | Past | Past Participle |
|---|---|---|---|
| learn | learning | learned | learned |
| discuss | discussing | discussed | discussed |
| stand | standing | stood | stood |
| begin | beginning | began | begun |

**Regular verbs** such as *learn* and *discuss* form the past and past participle by adding *-ed* to the present form. **Irregular verbs** such as *stand* and *begin* form the past and past participle in other ways. If you are in doubt about the principal parts of an irregular verb, check a dictionary.

### The Tenses of Verbs

The different tenses of verbs indicate the time an action or condition occurs.

The **present tense** expresses an action that happens regularly or states a current condition or a general truth.

Tourists **flock** to the site yearly.

Daily exercise **is** good for your heallth.

The **past tense** expresses a completed action or a condition that is no longer true.

The squirrel **dropped** the nut and **ran** up the tree.

I **was** very tired last night by 9:00.

The **future tense** indicates an action that will happen in the future or a condition that will be true.

The Glazers **will visit** us tomorrow.

They **will be** glad to arrive from their long journey.

The **present perfect tense** expresses an action that happened at an indefinite time in the past or an action that began in the past and continues into the present.

Someone **has cleaned** the trash from the park.

The puppy **has been** under the bed all day.

The **past perfect tense** shows an action that was completed before another action in the past.

Gerard **had revised** his essay before he turned it in.

The **future perfect tense** indicates an action that will have been completed before another action takes place.

Mimi **will have painted** the kitchen by the time we finish the shutters.

## USING MODIFIERS

### Degrees of Comparison

Adjectives and adverbs take different forms to show the three degrees of comparison: the *positive*, the *comparative*, and the *superlative*.

| Positive | Comparative | Superlative |
|---|---|---|
| fast | faster | fastest |
| crafty | craftier | craftiest |
| abruptly | more abruptly | most abruptly |
| badly | worse | worst |

### Using Comparative and Superlative Adjectives and Adverbs

Use comparative adjectives and adverbs to compare two things. Use superlative adjectives and adverbs to compare three or more things.

This season's weather was **drier** than last year's.

This season has been one of the **driest** on record.

Jake practices **more often** than Jamal.

Of everyone in the band, Jake practices **most often.**

## USING PRONOUNS

### Pronoun Case

The **case** of a pronoun is the form it takes to show its function in a sentence. There are three pronoun cases: *nominative, objective,* and *possessive*.

| Nominative | Objective | Possessive |
|---|---|---|
| I, you, he, she, it, we, you, they | me, you, him, her, it, us, you, them | my, your, yours, his, her, hers, its, our, ours, their, theirs |

Use the **nominative case** when a pronoun functions as a *subject* or as a *predicate nominative.*

**They** are going to the movies. [subject]

The biggest movie fan is **she.** [predicate nominative]

Use the **objective case** for a pronoun acting as a *direct object*, an *indirect object,* or the *object of a preposition.*

The ending of the play surprised **me**. [direct object]

Mary gave **us** two tickets to the play. [indirect object]

The audience cheered for **him.** [object of preposition]

Use the **possessive case** to show ownership.

The red suitcase is **hers.**







R63

## COMMONLY CONFUSED WORDS

**Diction** The words you choose contribute to the overall effectiveness of your writing. **Diction** refers to word choice and to the clearness and correctness of those words. You can improve one aspect of your diction by choosing carefully between commonly confused words, such as the pairs listed below.

**accept, except**

*Accept* is a verb that means "to receive" or "to agree to." *Except* is a preposition that means "other than" or "leaving out."

Please **accept** my offer to buy you lunch this weekend.

He is busy every day **except** the weekends.

**affect, effect**

*Affect* is normally a verb meaning "to influence" or "to bring about a change in." *Effect* is usually a noun meaning "result."

The distractions outside **affect** Steven's ability to concentrate.

The teacher's remedies had a positive **effect** on Steven's ability to concentrate.

**among, between**

*Among* is usually used with three or more items, and it emphasizes collective relationships or indicates distribution. *Between* is generally used with only two items, but it can be used with more than two if the emphasis is on individual (one-to-one) relationships within the group.

I had to choose a snack **among** the various vegetables.

He handed out the booklets **among** the conference participants.

Our school is **between** a park and an old barn.

The tournament included matches **between** France, Spain, Mexico, and the United States.

**amount, number**

*Amount* refers to overall quantity and is mainly used with mass nouns (those that can't be counted). *Number* refers to individual items that can be counted.

The **amount** of attention that great writers have paid to Shakespeare is remarkable.

A **number** of important English writers have been fascinated by the legend of King Arthur.

**assure, ensure, insure**

*Assure* means "to convince [someone of something]; to guarantee." *Ensure* means "to make certain [that something happens]." *Insure* means "to arrange for payment in case of loss."

The attorney **assured** us we'd win the case.

The rules **ensure** that no one gets treated unfairly.

Many professional musicians **insure** their valuable instruments.

**bad, badly**

Use the adjective *bad* before a noun or after linking verbs such as *feel, look,* and *seem*. Use *badly* whenever an adverb is required.

The situation may seem **bad**, but it will improve over time.

Though our team played **badly** today, we will focus on practicing for the next match.

**beside, besides**

*Beside* means "at the side of" or "close to." *Besides* means "in addition to."

The stapler sits **beside** the pencil sharpener in our classroom.

**Besides** being very clean, the classroom is also very organized.

**can, may**

The helping verb *can* generally refers to the ability to do something. The helping verb *may* generally refers to permission to do something.

I **can** run one mile in six minutes.

**May** we have a race during recess?

**complement, compliment**

The verb *complement* means "to enhance"; the verb *compliment* means "to praise."

Online exercises **complement** the textbook lessons.

Ms. Lewis **complimented** our team on our excellent debate.

**compose, comprise**

*Compose* means "to make up; constitute." *Comprise* means "to include or contain." Remember that the whole comprises its parts or is composed of its parts, and the parts compose the whole.

The assignment **comprises** three different tasks.

The assignment is **composed** of three different tasks.

Three different tasks **compose** the assignment.

**different from, different than**

*Different from* is generally preferred over *different than,* but *different than* can be used before a clause. Always use *different from* before a noun or pronoun.

Your point of view is so **different from** mine.

His idea was so **different from** [or **different than**] what we had expected.

**farther, further**

Use *farther* to refer to distance. Use *further* to mean "to a greater degree or extent" or "additional."

Chiang has traveled **farther** than anybody else in the class.

If I want **further** details about his travels, I can read his blog.







R64

**fewer, less**

Use *fewer* for things that can be counted. Use *less* for amounts or quantities that cannot be counted. *Fewer* must be followed by a plural noun.

Fewer students drive to school since the weather improved.

There is **less** noise outside in the mornings.

**good, well**

Use the adjective *good* before a noun or after a linking verb. Use *well* whenever an adverb is required, such as when modifying a verb.

I feel **good** after sleeping for eight hours.

I did **well** on my test, and my soccer team played **well** in that afternoon's game. It was a **good** day!

**its, it's**

The word *its* with no apostrophe is a possessive pronoun. The word *it's* is a contraction of "it is."

Angelica will try to fix the computer and **its** keyboard.

**It's** a difficult job, but she can do it.

**lay, lie**

*Lay* is a transitive verb meaning "to set or put something down." Its principal parts are *lay, laying, laid, laid. Lie* is an intransitive verb meaning "to recline" or "to exist in a certain place." Its principal parts are *lie, lying, lay, lain.*

Please **lay** that box down and help me with the sofa.

When we are done moving, I am going to **lie** down.

My hometown **lies** sixty miles north of here.

**like, as**

*Like* is a preposition that usually means "similar to" and precedes a noun or pronoun. The conjunction *as* means "in the way that" and usually precedes a clause.

**Like** the other students, I was prepared for a quiz.

**As** I said yesterday, we expect to finish before noon.

Use **such as,** not **like,** before a series of examples.

Foods **such as** apples, nuts, and pretzels make good snacks.

**of, have**

Do not use *of* in place of *have* after auxiliary verbs such as *would, could, should, may, might,* or *must.* The contraction of *have* is formed by adding *-ve* after these verbs.

I **would have** stayed after school today, but I had to help cook at home.

Mom **must've** called while I was still in the gym.

**principal, principle**

*Principal* can be an adjective meaning "main; most important." It can also be a noun meaning "chief officer of a school." *Principle* is a noun meaning "moral rule" or "fundamental truth."

His strange behavior was the **principal** reason for our concern.

Democratic **principles** form the basis of our country's laws.

**raise, rise**

*Raise* is a transitive verb that usually takes a direct object. *Rise* is intransitive and never takes a direct object.

Iliana and Josef **raise** the flag every morning.

They **rise** from their seats and volunteer immediately whenever help is needed.

**than, then**

The conjunction *than* is used to connect the two parts of a comparison. The adverb *then* usually refers to time.

My backpack is heavier **than** hers.

I will finish my homework and **then** meet my friends at the park.

**that, which, who**

Use the relative pronoun *that* to refer to things or people. Use *which* only for things and *who* only for people.

*That* introduces a restrictive phrase or clause, that is, one that is essential to the meaning of the sentence. *Which* introduces a nonrestrictive phrase or clause—one that adds information but could be deleted from the sentence—and is preceded by a comma.

Ben ran to the park **that** just reopened.

The park, **which** just reopened, has many attractions.

The man **who** built the park loves to see people smiling.

**when, where, why**

Do not use *when, where,* or *why* directly after a linking verb, such as *is*. Reword the sentence.

*Incorrect:* The morning is when he left for the beach.

*Correct:* He left for the beach in the morning.

**who, whom**

In formal writing, use *who* only as a subject in clauses and sentences. Use *whom* only as the object of a verb or of a preposition.

**Who** paid for the tickets?

**Whom** should I pay for the tickets?

I can't recall to **whom** I gave the money for the tickets.

**your, you're**

*Your* is a possessive pronoun expressing ownership. *You're* is the contraction of "you are."

Have you finished writing **your** informative essay?

**You're** supposed to turn it in tomorrow. If **you're** late, **your** grade will be affected.

## Capitalization

### First Words

Capitalize the first word of a sentence.

**S**tories about knights and their deeds interest me.

Capitalize the first word of direct speech.

**S**haron asked, "**D**o you like stories about knights?"

Capitalize the first word of a quotation that is a complete sentence.

**E**instein said, "**A**nyone who has never made a mistake has never tried anything new."

### Proper Nouns and Proper Adjectives

Capitalize all proper nouns, including geographical names, historical events and periods, and names of organizations.

**T**hames **R**iver    **J**ohn **K**eats    the **R**enaissance
**U**nited **N**ations    **W**orld **W**ar II    **S**ierra **N**evada

Capitalize all proper adjectives.

**S**hakespearean play    **B**ritish invaision
**A**merican citizen    **L**atin **A**merican literature

### Academic Course Names

Capitalize course names only if they are language courses, are followed by a number, or are preceded by a proper noun or adjective.

**S**panish    **H**onors **C**hemistry    **H**istory 101
**g**eology    **a**lgebra    **s**ocial **s**tudies

### Titles

Capitalize personal titles when followed by the person's name.

**M**s. Hughes    **D**r. Perez    **K**ing George

Capitalize titles showing family relationships when they are followed by a specific person's name, unless they are preceded by a possessive noun or pronoun.

**U**ncle Oscar    Mangan's **s**ister    his **a**unt Tessa

Capitalize the first word and all other key words in the titles of books, stories, songs, and other works of art.

*Frankenstein*    "**S**hooting an **E**lephant"

## Punctuation

### End Marks

Use a **period** to end a declarative sentence or an imperative sentence.

We are studying the structure of sonnets.
Read the biography of Mary Shelley.

Use periods with initials and abbreviations.

D. H. Lawrence    Mrs. Browning
Mt. Everest    Maple St.

Use a **question mark** to end an interrogative sentence.

What is Macbeth's fatal flaw?

Use an **exclamation mark** after an exclamatory sentence or a forceful imperative sentence.

That's a beautiful painting!    Let me go now!

### Commas

Use a **comma** before a coordinating conjunction to separate two independent clauses in a compound sentence.

The game was very close, but we were victorious.

Use commas to separate three or more words, phrases, or clauses in a series.

William Blake was a writer, artist, and printer.

Use commas to separate coordinate adjectives.

It was a witty, amusing novel.

Use a comma after an introductory word, phrase, or clause.

When the novelist finished his book, he celebrated with his family.

Use commas to set off nonessential expressions.

Old English, of course, requires translation.

Use commas with places and dates.

Coventry, England    September 1, 1939

### Semicolons

Use a **semicolon** to join closely related independent clauses that are not already joined by a conjunction.

Tanya likes to write poetry; Heather prefers prose.

Use semicolons to avoid confusion when items in a series contain commas.

They traveled to London, England; Madrid, Spain; and Rome, Italy.

### Colons

Use a **colon** before a list of items following an independent clause.

Notable Victorian poets include the following: Tennyson, Arnold, Housman, and Hopkins.

Use a colon to introduce information that summarizes or explains the independent clause before it.

She just wanted to do one thing: rest.
Malcolm loves volunteering: He reads to sick children every Saturday afternoon.

### Quotation Marks

Use **quotation marks** to enclose a direct quotation.

"Short stories," Ms. Hildebrand said, "should have rich, well-developed characters."

An **indirect quotation** does not require quotation marks.

Ms. Hildebrand said that short stories should have well-developed characters.

Use quotation marks around the titles of short written works, episodes in a series, songs, and works mentioned as parts of collections.

"The Lagoon"    "Boswell Meets Johnson"

### Italics

Italicize the titles of long written works, movies, television and radio shows, lengthy works of music, paintings, and sculptures.

*Howards End* *60 Minutes* *Guernica*

For handwritten material, you can use underlining instead of italics.

The Princess Bride Mona Lisa

### Dashes

Use **dashes** to indicate an abrupt change of thought, a dramatic interrupting idea, or a summary statement.

I read the entire first act of *Macbeth*—you won't believe what happens next.

The director—what's her name again?—attended the movie premiere.

### Hyphens

Use a **hyphen** with certain numbers, after certain prefixes, with two or more words used as one word, and with a compound modifier that comes before a noun.

seventy-two
self-esteem
president-elect
five-year contract

### Parentheses

Use **parentheses** to set off asides and explanations when the material is not essential or when it consists of one or more sentences. When the sentence in parentheses interrupts the larger sentence, it does not have a capital letter or a period.

He listened intently (it was too dark to see who was speaking) to try to identify the voices.

When a sentence in parentheses falls between two other complete sentences, it should start with a capital letter and end with a period.

The quarterback threw three touchdown passes. (We knew he could do it.) Our team won the game by two points.

### Apostrophes

Add an **apostrophe** and an *s* to show the possessive case of most singular nouns and of plural nouns that do not end in *-s* or *-es*.

Blake's poems the mice's whiskers

Names ending in *s* form their possessives in the same way, except for classical and biblical names, which add only an apostrophe to form the possessive.

Dickens's Hercules'

Add an apostrophe to show the possessive case of plural nouns ending in *-s* and *-es*.

the girls' songs the Ortizes' car

Use an apostrophe in a contraction to indicate the position of the missing letter or letters.

She's never read a Coleridge poem she didn't like.

### Brackets

Use **brackets** to enclose clarifying information inserted within a quotation.

Columbus's journal entry from October 21, 1492, begins as follows: "At 10 o'clock, we arrived at a cape of the island [San Salvador], and anchored, the other vessels in company."

### Ellipses

Use three ellipsis points, also known as an **ellipsis,** to indicate where you have omitted words from quoted material.

Wollestonecraft wrote, "The education of women has of late been more attended to than formerly; yet they are still . . . ridiculed or pitied. . . ."

In the example above, the four dots at the end of the sentence are the three ellipsis points plus the period from the original sentence.

Use an ellipsis to indicate a pause or interruption in speech.

"When he told me the news," said the coach, "I was . . . I was shocked . . . completely shocked."

## Spelling

### Spelling Rules

Learning the rules of English spelling will help you make **generalizations** about how to spell words.

### Word Parts

The three word parts that can combine to form a word are roots, prefixes, and suffixes. Many of these word parts come from the Greek, Latin, and Anglo-Saxon languages.

The **root word** carries a word's basic meaning.

| Root and Origin | Meaning | Examples |
|---|---|---|
| -leg- (-log-) [Gr.] | to say, speak | *legal, logic* |
| -pon- (-pos-) [L.] | to put, place | *postpone, deposit* |

A **prefix** is one or more syllables added to the beginning of a word that alter the meaning of the root.

| Prefix and Origin | Meaning | Example |
|---|---|---|
| anti- [Gr.] | against | *antipathy* |
| inter- [L.] | between | *international* |
| mis- [A.S.] | wrong | *misplace* |

A **suffix** is a letter or group of letters added to the end of a root word that changes the word's meaning or part of speech.

| Suffix and Origin | Meaning and Example | Part of Speech |
|---|---|---|
| -ful [A.S.] | full of: *scornful* | adjective |
| -ity [L.] | state of being: *adversity* | noun |
| -ize (-ise) [Gr.] | to make: *idolize* | verb |
| -ly [A.S.] | in a manner: *calmly* | adverb |

### Rules for Adding Suffixes to Root Words

When adding a suffix to a root word ending in *y* preceded by a consonant, change *y* to *i* unless the suffix begins with *i*.

ply + -able = pliable  happy + -ness = happiness
defy + -ing = defying  cry + -ing = crying

For a root word ending in *e*, drop the *e* when adding a suffix beginning with a vowel.

drive + -ing = driving  move + -able = movable
SOME EXCEPTIONS: traceable, seeing, dyeing

For root words ending with a consonant + vowel + consonant in a stressed syllable, double the final consonant when adding a suffix that begins with a vowel.

mud + -y = muddy  submit + -ed = submitted
SOME EXCEPTIONS: mixing, fixed

### Rules for Adding Prefixes to Root Words

When a prefix is added to a root word, the spelling of the root remains the same.

un- + certain = uncertain  mis- + spell = misspell

With some prefixes, the spelling of the prefix changes when joined to the root to make the pronunciation easier.

in- + mortal = immortal  ad- + vert = avert

### Orthographic Patterns

Certain letter combinations in English make certain sounds. For instance, *ph* sounds like *f*, *eigh* usually makes a long *a* sound, and the *k* before an *n* is often silent.

**ph**armacy  n**eigh**bor  **k**nowledge

Understanding **orthographic patterns** such as these can help you improve your spelling.

### Forming Plurals

The plural form of most nouns is formed by adding *-s* to the singular.

computers  gadgets  Washingtons

For words ending in *s, ss, x, z, sh,* or *ch,* add *-es*.

circus**es**  tax**es**  wish**es**  bench**es**

For words ending in *y* or *o* preceded by a vowel, add *-s*.

key**s**  patio**s**

For words ending in *y* preceded by a consonant, change the *y* to an *i* and add *-es*.

cit**ies**  enem**ies**  troph**ies**

For most words ending in *o* preceded by a consonant, add *-es*.

echo**es**  tomato**es**

Some words form the plural in irregular ways.

women  oxen  children  teeth  deer

### Foreign Words Used in English

Some words used in English are actually foreign words that have been adopted. Learning to spell these words requires memorization. When in doubt, check a dictionary.

sushi  enchilada  au pair  fiancé
laissez faire  croissant

# INDEX OF SKILLS

## Analyzing Text









R69

INDEX OF SKILLS

## Assessment

## Language Conventions



## Research

## Speaking and Listening



## Vocabulary

R74

## Writing, 190, 625

R77

# INDEX OF AUTHORS AND TITLES

The following authors and titles appear in the print and online versions of Pearson Literature.

# ADDITIONAL SELECTIONS: AUTHOR AND TITLE INDEX

The following authors and titles appear in the Online Literature Library.

## Acknowledgments

The following selections appear in Grade 11 of *my*Perspectives. Some selections appear online only.

**Arte Publico Press.** "The Latin Deli" from *America's Review* by Judith Ortiz Cofer (©1992 Arte Publico Press—University of Houston).

**Audible Inc.** "How to Tell a True War Story" from *The Things They Carried* by Tim O'Brien. Copyright ©1990 by Tim O'Brien.

**BBC Worldwide Americas, Inc.** Boston Tea Party ©BBC Worldwide Learning; The U. S. Constitution ©BBC Worldwide Learning; Great Lives: Emily Dickinson—BBC Worldwide Learning; Civil Rights Marches ©BBC Worldwide Learning; CBS Sunday Morning segment "Mark Twain and Tom Sawyer" ©BBC Worldwide Learning.

**Bloomsbury Publishing Plc.** "Antojos," Copyright ©1991 by Julia Alvarez. Later published in slightly different form in *How the Garcia Girls Lost Their Accents*. Used with permission of Bloomsbury Publishing Plc.

**Brooks Permissions.** "Speech to the Young, Speech to the Progress-Toward," reprinted By Consent of Brooks Permissions.

**Browning, Sarah.** "The Fifth Fact," from *Whisky in the Garden of Eden* (The Word Words, Washington, DC, 2007). Used with permission.

**Chopin, Kate.** "The Story of An Hour" by Kate Chopin, originally appeared in *Vogue*, 1894.

**CNN.** The Hollywood Blacklist: 1947–1960 ©CNN.

**Contently.** Why Do Stories Matter? That's Like Asking Why You Should Eat ©Contently 2015

**Copper Canyon Press.** Hayden Carruth, "Bears at Raspberry Time" from *Collected Shorter Poems* 1946–1991. Copyright ©1983 by Hayden Carruth. Reprinted with the permission of The Permissions Company, Inc., on behalf of Copper Canyon Press, www.coppercanyonpress.org.

**Daily Signal.** "Rugged Individualism Fades from National Character" by Marion Smith, from *Daily Signal,* June 11, 2012; http://dailysignal.com/print/?post_id=99695. Used with permission.

**Don Congdon Associates.** "The Pedestrian," reprinted by permission of Don Congdon Associates, Inc. Copyright ©1951 by the Fortnightly Publishing Company, renewed 1979 by Ray Bradbury.

**Douglass, Frederick.** "What to the Slave is the 4th of July?" by Frederick Douglass (1818–1895).

**Dunbar, Paul Laurence.** "Douglass" by Paul Laurence Dunbar (1872–1906).

**Espada, Martin.** "Who Burns for the Perfection of Paper," from *city of coughing and dead radiators* by Martin Espada. Copyright ©1993 by Martin Espada. Used by permission of the author.

**Estate of Galway Kinnell.** "Reckless Genius" by Galway Kinnell, from Salon.com. Used with permission of the Estate of Galway Kinnell.

**Faber & Faber, Ltd. (UK).** "The Love Song of J. Alfred Prufrock" from *Collected Poems*, 1909–1062 by T.S. Eliot. Reprinted by permission of the publisher, Faber and Faber, Ltd.

**Farrar, Straus and Giroux.** Jacket design and excerpts from *The United States Constitution: A Graphic Adaptation* by Jonathan Hennessey, artwork by Aaron McConnell. Text copyright ©2008 by Jonathan Hennessey. Artwork Copyright ©2008 by Aaron McConnell. Reprinted by permission of Hill and Wang, a division of Farrar, Straus and Giroux, LLC.; "The Fish" from *The Complete Poems* 1927–1979 by Elizabeth Bishop. Copyright ©1979, 1983 by Alice Helen Methfessel. Reprinted by permission of Farrar, Straus and Giroux, LLC.

**Fischer, Claude.** "Sweet Land of...Conformity?," *Boston Globe,* June 6, 2010, as adapted from the blog, Made in America.

**Garland, Sarah.** "Was 'Brown v Board' a Failure?" by Sarah Garland, from the *Hechinger Report*, http://hechingerreport.org/was-brown-v-the-board-a-failure/. Reprinted by permission.

**Harold Ober Associates.** "Dream Variations," reprinted by permission of Harold Ober Associates Incorporated. Copyright ©1994 by The Estate Of Langston Hughes; "I, Too," reprinted by permission of Harold Ober Associates Incorporated. Copyright ©1994 by The Estate Of Langston Hughes; "The Negro Speaks of Rivers," reprinted by permission of Harold Ober Associates Incorporated. Copyright ©1994 by The Estate Of Langston Hughes; "Refugee in America," reprinted by permission of Harold Ober Associates Incorporated. Copyright ©1994 by The Estate Of Langston Hughes.

**Harper's Magazine.** "The Leap," Copyright ©1990 Harper's Magazine. All rights reserved. Reproduced from the March issue by special permission.

**HarperCollins Publishers.** Pages 33–40 from *Dust Tracks on a Road* by Zora Neale Hurston. Copyright 1942 by Zora Neale Hurston; renewed ©1970 by John C. Hurston. Reprinted by permission of HarperCollins Publishers; "Untying the Knot" from *Pilgrim at Tinker Creek* by Annie Dillard. Copyright ©1974 by Annie Dillard. Reprinted by permission of HarperCollins Publishers.

**HarperCollins Publishers Ltd. (UK).** "Storyteller," "How to Tell a True War Story" from *The Things They Carried* by Tim O'Brien. Copyright ©1990 by Tim O'Brien. Reprinted by permission of HarperCollins Publishers Ltd.

**Harvard Law Review.** "Reflections on the Bicentennial of the United States Constitution," republished with permission of *Harvard Law Review,* from Harvard Law Review, 101, November 1987; permission conveyed through Copyright Clearance Center, Inc.

**Harvard University Press.** "They shut me up in Prose," *The Poems of Emily Dickinson: Reading Edition,* edited by Ralph W. Franklin, Cambridge, Mass.: The Belknap Press of Harvard University Press, Copyright ©1998, 1999 by the President and Fellows of Harvard College. Copyright ©1951, 1955 by the President and Fellows of Harvard College. Copyright © renewed 1979, 1983 by the President and Fellows of Harvard College. Copyright ©1914, 1918, 1919, 1924, 1929, 1930, 1932, 1935, 1937, 1942 by Martha Dickinson Bianchi. Copyright ©1952, 1957, 1958, 1963, 1965 by Mary L. Hampson; "I'm Nobody," *The Poems of Emily Dickinson,* edited by Thomas H. Johnson, Cambridge, Mass.: The Belknap Press of Harvard University Press, Copyright ©1951, 1955 by the President and Fellows of Harvard College. Copyright ©renewed 1979, 1983 by the President and Fellows of Harvard College. Copyright ©1914, 1918, 1919, 1924, 1929, 1930, 1932, 1935, 1937, 1942 by Martha Dickinson Bianchi. Copyright ©1952, 1957, 1958, 1963, 1965 by Mary L. Hampson.

**Henry Holt & Co.** "A Balance Between Nature and Nurture" by Gloria Steinem. Copyright ©2005 by Gloria Steinem. From the audio book collection THIS I BELIEVE: The Personal Philosophies of

Remarkable Men and Women edited by Jay Allison and Dan Gedimen. Copyright ©2006 by This I Believe, Inc. Used by permission of Henry Holt and Company, LLC. All rights reserved; "A Balance Between Nature and Nurture" by Gloria Steinem. Copyright © 2005 by Gloria Steinem. From the book *This I Believe: The Personal Philosophies of Remarkable Men and Women* edited by Jay Allison and Dan Gediman. Copyright ©2006 by This I Believe, Inc. Used by permission of Henry Holt and Company, LLC. All rights reserved.

**Holy Cow! Press.** Roberta Hill Whiteman, "In the Longhouse, Oneida Museum" from *Star Quilt.* Copyright ©1984, 2001 Roberta Hill Whiteman. Reprinted with the permission of The Permissions Company, Inc., on behalf of Holy Cow! Press, www.holycowpress.org.

**Houghton Mifflin Harcourt.** "Wilderness" from *The Complete Poems of Carl Sandburg. Revised and Expanded Edition.* Copyright ©1970, 1969 by Lilian Steichen Sandburg, Trustee. Reprinted by permission of Houghton Mifflin Harcourt Publishing Company. All rights reserved; "How to Tell a True War Story" from *The Things They Carried* by Tim O'Brien. Copyright ©1990 by Tim O'Brien. Reprinted by permission of Houghton Mifflin Harcourt Publishing Company. All rights reserved.

**Houghton Mifflin Harcourt Publishing Co.** Excerpts from *Farewell to Manzanar* by Jeanne W. Houston and James D. Houston. Copyright ©1973 by James D. Houston, renewed 2001 by Jeanne Wakatsuki Houston and James D. Houston. Reprinted by permission of Houghton Mifflin Harcourt Publishing Company. All rights reserved; "Everyday Use" from *In Love & Trouble: Stories of Black Women* by Alice Walker. Copyright ©1973, and renewed 2001 by Alice Walker. Reprinted by permission of Houghton Mifflin Harcourt Publishing Company. All rights reserved; "The Jilting of Granny Weatherall" from *Flowering Judas and Other Stories* by Katherine Anne Porter. Copyright ©1930 by Katherine Anne Porter. Copyright © Renewed1958 by Katherine Anne Porter. Reprinted by permission of Houghton Mifflin Harcourt Publishing Company. All rights reserved.

**James Baldwin Estate.** "The Rockpile," ©1965 by James Baldwin. Copyright renewed. Collected in *Going to the Man*, published by Vintage Books. Reprinted by arrangement with the James Baldwin Estate.

**John F. Kennedy Presidential Library.** Senator Kennedy Reads The Declaration of Independence -1957 - John F. Kennedy Presidential Library and Museum.

**Joy Harris Literary Agency, Inc.** "Everyday Use" from *In Love & Trouble: Stories of Black Women* by Alice Walker. Copyright ©1973, and renewed 2001 by Alice Walker. Reprinted by permission of The Joy Harris Literary Agency, Inc.; "Everyday Use" from IN LOVE & TROUBLE: Stories of Black Women by Alice Walker. Copyright ©1973, and renewed 2001 by Alice Walker. Reprinted by permission of The Joy Harris Literary Agency, Inc.

**Katherine Anne Porter Literary Trust.** "The Jilting of Granny Weatherall" from *Flowering Judas and Other Stories*. Used with permission of The Katherine Anne Porter Literary Trust c/o The Permissions Company, Inc., www.permissionscompany.com.

**LA Theatre Works.** Audio of *The Crucible* production by LA Theatre Works.

**Lincoln, Abraham.** President Abraham Lincoln's Second Inaugural Address, 16th President of the United States (1861–1865).

**Lippincott Massie McQuilkin Literary Agents.** "Dear Abigail: The Intimate Lives and Revolutionary Ideas of Abigail Adams and Her Two Remarkable Sisters," reprinted by permission of Lippincott Massie McQuilkin as agents for the author. Copyright ©2014 by Diane Jacobs.

**Little, Brown and Co. (UK).** From *Dust Tracks on a Road* by Zora Neale Hurston. Used by permission of Little, Brown Book Group Ltd.

**Liveright Publishing Corporation.** "Runagate Runagate." Copyright ©1966 by Robert Hayden, from *Collected Poems of Robert Hayden*, edited by Frederick Glaysher. Used with permission of Liveright Publishing Corporation.

**Milkweed Editions.** "1-800-FEAR" from *Translations* from Bark Beetle by Jody Gladding (Minneapolis: Milkweed Editions, 2014). Copyright ©2014 by Jody Gladding. Reprinted with permission from Milkweed Editions. www.milkweed.org.

**New Directions Publishing Corp.** "Cloudy Day," by Jimmy Santiago Baca, from *Immigrants in Our Own Land*, copyright ©1979 by Jimmy Santiago Baca. Reprinted by permission of New Directions Publishing Corp.

**PARS International Corporation.** "What You Don't Know Can Kill You," from *Discover*, October 3, 2011 ©2011 Discover Media. All rights reserved. Used by permission and protected by the Copyright Laws of the United States. The printing, copying, redistribution, or retransmission of this Content without express written permission is prohibited; "What Are You So Afraid Of?," from *The New York Times*, October 26, 2014 ©2014 The New York Times. All rights reserved. Used by permission and protected by the Copyright Laws of the United States. The printing, copying, redistribution, or retransmission of this Content without express written permission is prohibited; USA Today Ken Burns: Secrets of Yellowstone National Park from USA Today - Education, 2016 ©2014 Gannett-USA Today Education Resources. All rights reserved. Used by permission and protected by the Copyright Laws of the United States. The printing, copying, redistribution, or retransmission of this Content without express written permission is prohibited.

**Penguin Group.** *The Crucible* by Arthur Miller, copyright 1952, 1953, 1954, renewed ©1980, 1981, 1982 by Arthur Miller. Used by permission of Viking Books, an imprint of Penguin Publishing Group, a division of Penguin Random House LLC.

**Penguin Publishing Group.** "The Man to Send Rain Clouds," *Storyteller* by Leslie Marmon Silko, copyright ©1981, 2012 by Leslie Marmon Silko. Used by permission of Viking Books, an imprint of Penguin Publishing Group, a division of Penguin Random House LLC.

**Princeton University Press.** From *Walden* by Henry David Thoreau. Copyright ©1971 by Princeton University Press, 1999 renewed PUP, 1989 paperback edition.

**Random House Group Ltd., Permissions Department.** "The Fish," from *Poems* by Elizabeth Bishop. Published by Chatto & Windus. Reprinted by permission of The Random House Group Limited; "Everything Stuck to Him," from *What We Talk About When We Talk About Love* by Raymond Carver. Published by Harvill Press. Reprinted by permission of The Random House Group Limited.

**Random House UK Limited.** "Old Man at the Bridge," from *The First Forty-Nine Stories* by Ernest Hemingway. Published by Jonathan Cape. Reprinted by permission of The Random House Group Limited.

**Random House, Inc.** "Chapter 1: In the Beginning" from *America's Constitution: A Biography* by Akhil Reed Amar, copyright ©2005 by Akhil Reed Amar. Used by permission of Random House, an imprint and division of Penguin Random House LLC. All rights reserved. Any third party use of this material, outside of this publication, is prohibited. Interested parties must apply directly to Penguin Random House LLC for permission; Excerpt(s) from *Dear Abigail: The Intimate Lives and Revolutionary Ideas of Abigail Adams Her Two Remarkable Sisters* by Diane Jacobs, copyright ©2014 by Diane Jacobs. Used by permission of Ballantine Books, an imprint of Random House, a division of Penguin Random House LLC. All rights reserved. Any third party use of this material, outside of this publication, is prohibited. Interested parties must apply directly to Penguin Random House LLC for permission; "The Stirrings of Discontent," Excerpt(s) from *The*

*Warmth of Other Suns: The Epic Story of America's Great Migration* by Isabel Wilkerson, copyright ©2010 by Isabel Wilkerson. Used by permission of Random House, an imprint and division of Penguin Random House LLC. All rights reserved. Any third party use of this material, outside of this publication, is prohibited. Interested parties must apply directly to Penguin Random House LLC for permission; "Mother to Son," "Dream Variation," "I, Too," "The Negro Speaks of Rivers," and "Refugee in America" from *The Collected Poems of Langston Hughes* by Langston Hughes, edited by Arnold Rampersad with David Roessel, Associate Editor, copyright ©1994 by the Estate of Langston Hughes. Used by permission of Alfred A. Knopf, an imprint of the Knopf Doubleday Publishing Group, a division of Penguin Random House LLC. All rights reserved. Any third party use of this material, outside of this publication, is prohibited. Interested parties must apply directly to Penguin Random House LLC for permission.

**Recorded Books, LLC.** Excerpts from *Farewell to Manzanar* by Jeanne W. Houston and James D. Houston. Copyright ©1973 by James D. Houston, renewed 2001 by Jeanne Wakatsuki Houston and James D. Houston. Used with permission of Recorded Books.

**Russell & Volkening, Inc.** "Untying the Knot," reprinted by the permission of Russell & Volkening as agents for the author. Copyright ©1974 by Annie Dillard, renewed in 2002 by Annie Dillard.

**Seymour Agency LLC.** "A Brief History of the Short Story" by D. F. McCourt, from AE Sci Fi, http://aescifi.ca/index.php/non-fiction/37-editorials/792-a-brief-history-of-the-short-story?tmpl=component&print=1&layout=default&page=. Used with permission of the author and Seymour Agency.

**Shihab Nye, Naomi.** "Hamadi," by permission of the author, Naomi Shihab Nye, 2015. First appeared in *America Street*.

**Simon & Schuster, Inc.** "Old Man at the Bridge," reprinted with the permission of Scribner, a division of Simon & Schuster, Inc. from *The Short Stories of Earnest Hemingway* by Ernest Hemingway. Copyright ©1938 by Ernest Hemingway. Copyright renewed 1966 by Mary Hemingway. All rights reserved.

**Skyhorse Publishing.** Excerpted from *Democracy is Not a Spectator Sport* by Arthur Blaustein with the permission of Skyhorse Publishing, Inc.

**Sleight Brennan, Sandra.** Giving Women the Vote by Sandra Sleight-Brennan ©Sandra Sleight-Brennan.

**Sterling Lord Literistic, Inc.** "A Literature of Place," reprinted by permission of SLL/Sterling Lord Literistic, Inc. Copyright by Barry Holstun Lopez.

**Susan Bergholz Literary Services.** "Antojos," Copyright ©1991 by Julia Alvarez. Later published in slightly different form in *How the Garcia Girls Lost Their Accents* by Algonquin Books of Chapel Hill. By permission of Susan Bergholz Literary Services, New York, NY and Lamy, NM. All rights reserved.

**Symphony Space.** "Everyday Use" by Alice Walker, as performed by Carmen de Lavallade at Symphony Space on January 19, 1994. Courtesy of Symphony Space.

**Syracuse University Press.** *Arthur C. Parker on the Iroquois: Iroquois Uses of Maize and Other Food Plants, The Code of Handsome Lake; The Seneca Prophet, The Constitution of the Five Nations* by Arthur Parker. Copyright ©1981. Used with permission of Syracuse University Press.

**Tarbell, Ida.** "What a Factory Can Teach a Housewife" by Ida Tarbell, *The Association Monthly*, Volume X (February 1916–February 1917).

**Television Academy Foundation.** George Takei on the Japanese internment camps during WWII ©Television Academy Foundation.

**The White House Photo Office.** Richard Blanco reading 2013 inaugural poem courtesy of The White House.

**U.S. Supreme Court.** "Supreme Court Decision / Chief Justice Earl Warren's opinion, Brown v. Board of Education, 347 U.S. 483 (1954).

**University of New Mexico Press (Rights).** From *The Way to Rainy Mountain* by N. Scott Momaday. Copyright ©1969 University of New Mexico Press, 1969.

**University of Pittsburgh Press.** "For Black Women Who Are Afraid" from *Tender*, by Toi Derricotte, ©1997. Reprinted by permission of the University of Pittsburgh Press.

**Venture Literary.** From *The United States Constitution: A Graphic Adaptation* by Jonathan Hennessey, illustrated by Aaron McConnell. Copyright 2008. Used with permission of Venture Literary, Inc.

**W. W. Norton & Co.** "Who Burns for the Perfection of Paper," from *city of coughing and dead radiators* by Martin Espada. Copyright ©1993 by Martin Espada. Used by permission of W. W. Norton & Company, Inc.

**Writers' Representatives, Inc.** From *America's Constitution: A Biography* by Akhil Amar. Copyright ©2005. Used by permission of Akhil Amar c/o Writers Representatives LLC, New York, NY 10011. All rights reserved.

**Wylie Agency.** Excerpt from "Books as Bombs: Why the women's movement needed 'The Feminine Mystique'" by Louis Menand, originally published in *The New Yorker*. Copyright ©2011 by Louis Menand, used by permission of The Wylie Agency LLC.; *The Crucible* by Arthur Miller. Copyright ©1952, 1953, 1954 by Arthur Miller, copyright renewed © 1980, 1981, 1982 by Arthur Miller, used by permission of The Wylie Agency LLC.; "Everything Stuck to Him" by Raymond Carver, collected in *What We Talk About When We Talk About Love*. Copyright ©1974, 1976, 1977, 1978, 1980, 1981 by Raymond Carver; 1989 by Tess Gallagher, used by her permission; "The Man to Send Rain Clouds" from *Storyteller* by Leslie Marmon Silko. Copyright ©1981, 2012 by Leslie Marmon Silko, used by permission of The Wylie Agency LLC.; "Housepainting" by Lan Samantha Chang. Copyright ©1995 by Lan Samantha Chang, used by permission of The Wylie Agency LLC.

## Credits

**Photo locators denoted as follows Top (T), Center (C), Bottom (B), Left (L), Right (R), Background (Bkgd)**

**Cover** ©niroworld/Fotolia, (Bkgd) Brandon Bourdages/ 123RF GB Ltd.

**vi** (C) David Smart/Shutterstock, (Bkgd) Ja-images/Shutterstock; **viii** Hidesy/Shutterstock; **x** Corbis; **xii** Spaces Images/Blend Images/Getty Images; **xiv** Fred de Noyelle/Godong/Corbis; **xvi** Sergey Nivens/Fotolia; **2** (C) David Smart/Shutterstock, (Bkgd) Ja-images/Shutterstock; **3** (B) Ken Schulze/Shutterstock, (BCL) Fine Art Premium/Corbis, (BCR) Zack Frank/Shutterstock, (BL) Prints & Photographs Division, Library of Congress, LC-USZC4-5315.,(BR) Louis S. Glanzman/National Geographic/Getty Images, (C) DEA/G. Dagli Orti/Getty Images, (CBR) Ramn Cami/EyeEm/Getty Images, (CL) 2/Craig Brewer/Ocean/Corbis, (CR) Jacek Chabraszewski/Shuterstock, (CT) Sergign/Shutterstock, (T) LDDesign/Shutterstock, (TCL) GL Archive/Alamy, (TCR) J. Helgason/ Shutterstock, (TL) SuperStock/Glow Images, (TR) Rawpixel/Shutterstock; **6** LDDesign/Shutterstock; **11** (B) Prints & Photographs Division, Library of Congress, LC-USZC4-5315., (BR) Fine Art Premium/Corbis, (C) 2/Craig Brewer/Ocean/Corbis, (T) SuperStock/Glow Images, (TR) GL Archive/ Alamy; **12** (L) World History Archive/Alamy, (R) SuperStock/Glow Images; **13** (C) Lvy Close Images/Alamy, (L) The Gallery Collection/ Corbis, (R) Larryhw/123RF; **14** North Wind Picture Archives/Alamy; **15** (C) People and Politics/Alamy, (L) Bettmann/Corbis, (R) Dbimages/Alamy; **16, 18, 24, 26, 28** GL Archive/Alamy; **17** Painting/Alamy; **21** Susan Law Cain/Shutterstock; **23** Hank Walker/The LIFE Picture Collection/Getty Images; **30** (B) People and Politics/Alamy, (T) Everett Historical/ Shutterstock; **31, 34, 36, 38** 2/Craig Brewer/Ocean/Corbis; **40, 42, 46, 48, 50** Fine Art Premium/Corbis; **41** Akademie/Alamy; **50** Fine Art Premium/Corbis; **53** Prints & Photographs Division, Library of Congress, LC-USZC4-5315.; **54** North Wind Picture Archives/Alamy; **55** Prints and Photographs Division, Library of Congress, cph.3a13536.; **56** (B) Fotosearch/Stringer/Getty,(T) Universal Images Group Limited/Alamy; **57** (BL) Universal Images Group Limited/Alamy, (C) Prints and Photographs Division, Library of Congress, cph.3a13536.; **57** (T) Prints & Photographs Division, Library of Congress, LC-USZC4-5315.; (TL) North Wind Picture Archives/Alamy; **58** Prints & Photographs Division, Library of Congress, LC-USZC4-5315.; **60** LDDesign/Shutterstock; **69** (B) Ken Schulze/ Shutterstock, (C) DEA/G. Dagli Orti/Getty Images, (T) Sergign/ Shutterstock; **72** (BL) Akhil Reed Amar,(TL) Sergign/Shutterstock; **73, 79, 80** Sergign/Shutterstock; **82** (BL) David Shoenfelt, (TL) Sergign/ Shutterstock; **90** Sergign/Shutterstock; **92** World History Archive/Alamy; **93, 98** DEA/G. Dagli Orti/Getty Images; **95** ClassicStock/Alamy; **103, 119** Everett Historical/Shutterstock; **110** Glasshouse Images/Alamy; **118, 120, 122, 124** Ken Schulze/Shutterstock; **129** (T): Rawpixel/ Shutterstock, (TC): J. Helgason/Shutterstock, (B): Louis S. Glanzman/ National Geographic/Getty Images, (BC): Zack Frank/Shutterstock, (C): Jacek Chabraszewski/Shuterstock, (CB): Ramn Cami/EyeEm/Getty Images; **138** Hidesy/Shutterstock; **139** (BC) Nebraska State Historical Society, [Digital ID, e.g., nbhips 12036], (BCR) Babayuka/Shutterstock, (BR) Denis Belitsky/Shutterstock, (C) Mansell/The LIFE Picture Collection/ Getty Images, (BC) Eugene Ivanov/Shutterstock, (B(CL)) Atomic/Alamy, (BCR) adoc-photos/Corbis, (CL) Win Nondakowit/123RF, (CR) Pictorial Press Ltd/Alamy, (TC) Zack Frank/Shutterstock, (T) Everett Historical/ Shutterstock, (TC) Richard Cavalleri/Shutterstock, (CL) Solarseven/ Shutterstock, (TL) Ralf Hettler/Getty Images, (TR) Pogonici/Shutterstock; **142** Everett Historical/Shutterstock; **147** (B) Atomic/Alamy, (BL) Win Nondakowit/123RF, (T) Ralf Hettler/Getty Images, (TL) Solarseven/ Shutterstock; **148** (L) Gianni Dagli Orti/The Art Archive at Art Resource, New York, (R) Bettmann/Corbis; **149** (L) Bettmann/Corbis, (R) Ralf Hettler/Getty Images; **150** (L) Everett Historical/Shutterstock, (R) De Agostini Picture Library/Getty Images; **151** Joe_Potato/Getty Images; 152,154,164,166,168 Solarseven/Shutterstock; 153 History Archives/ Alamy; **156** (B) Pictorial Press Ltd/Alamy, (T) Ase/Shutterstock; **160** Strelka/Shutterstock; **161** Sarun T/Shutterstock; **162** Alex Pix/ Shutterstock; **170, 172, 180, 182, 184** Win Nondakowit/123RF; **171** Atomic/Alamy; **173** Victor Tongdee/Shutterstock; **174** Liveshot/ Shutterstock; **176** Poprotskiy Alexey/Shutterstock; **177** Edward Bruns/ Shutterstock; **178** GlebStock/Shutterstock; **186** (TL) Win Nondakowit/123RF, (TR) Atomic/Alamy; **187** Atomic/Alamy; **189** (B) Atomic/Alamy, (T) Win Nondakowit/123RF; **190** (B) Atomic/Alamy, (T) Win Nondakowit/123RF; **192** Everett Historical/Shutterstock; **201** (B) Solomon D. Butcher/Nebraska State Historical Society, (BR) Eugene Ivanov/Shutterstock, (C) Mansell/The LIFE Picture Collection/Getty Images, (T) Richard Cavalleri/Shutterstock, (TR) Zack Frank/Shutterstock; **204** Everett Historical/Shutterstock; **205 ,201 ,212** Richard Cavalleri/ Shutterstock; **207** W2 Photography/Corbis; **214** Everett Collection/ Alamy; **215, 226, 228** Zack Frank/Shutterstock; **220** Nelson Sirlin/ Shutterstock; **223** Nobeastsofierce/Shutterstock; **231** Mansell/The LIFE Picture Collection/Getty Images; **232** The National Archives Records of the Patent and Trademark Office, 1836–1978; **234** Mansell/The LIFE Picture Collection/Getty Images; **236, 238, 244, 246** Eugene Ivanov/ Shutterstock; **237** Lebrecht Music and Arts Photo Library/Alamy; **248** E.O. Hoppe/Corbis; **249, 258, 260** Solomon D. Butcher/Nebraska State Historical Society; **254** Erich Lessing/Art Resource, New York; **265** (T): Pogonici/Shutterstock, (B): Denis Belitsky/Shutterstock, (BR): Babayuka/ Shutterstock, (C): adoc-photos/Corbis, (TR): Pictorial Press Ltd/Alamy; **274** (C) Corbis, (Bkgd) BBC Worldwide Learning; **275** (B) National Archives/Getty Images, (BC) fstockfoto/Shutterstock, (BCR) Harold M. Lambert/Lambert/Getty Images, (BL) National Photo Company Collection/Library of Congress, (BR) Bettmann/Corbis, (C) Library of Congress Prints and Photographs Division [LC-USZ62-75334], (BC) Heritage Image Partnership Ltd/Alamy, (CBL) Corbis, (CBR) Three Lions/ Getty Images, (CT) GL Archive/Alamy, (CTR) Jack Delano Farm Security Administration/Office of War Information Black-and-White Negatives collection, Prints & Photographs Division, Library of Congress, LC-USF34-040837-D, (T) Hill Street Studios/Getty Images, (TC) Corbis, (TCL) Kutay Tanir/Digital Vision/Getty Images, (TCR) Bettmann/Corbis, (TL) Everett Historical/Shutterstock, (TR) Herber W. Pelton/Corbis; **278** Hill Street Studios/Getty Images; **283** (B) Corbis, (BC) National Photo Company Collection/Library of Congress, (T) Everett Historical/ Shutterstock, (TC) Kutay Tanir/Digital Vision/Getty Images; **284** Everett Historical/Shutterstock; **285** (L) Bob Pardue-SC/Alamy, (R) Randy Raszler/ Fotolia; **286** (C) World History Archive/Alamy, (L, R) Everett Historical/ Shutterstock; **287** (L) Everett Historical/Shutterstock, (R) Jorisvo/ Shutterstock; **288** Library of Congress Prints and Photographs Division [LC-3a18122u]; 289,294,296,298 Kutay Tanir/Digital Vision/Getty Images; 300 Library of Congress Prints and Photographs Division [LC-3a32145u]; **301, 304, 306, 308** National Photo Company Collection/Library of Congress; **311, 312, 314, 316** Corbis; **313** (B) Corbis, (T) Everett Collection/AGE Fotostock; **315** Corbis, (BC) Everett Collection/AGE Fotostock; **327** (B) National Archives/Getty Images, (BC) fstockfoto/Shutterstock, (C) Library of Congress Prints and Photographs Division [LC-USZ62-75334]; **327** (BC) Heritage Image Partnership Ltd/ Alamy, (T) Corbis, (TC) GL Archive/Alamy; 330 Library of Congress Prints and Photographs Division [LC-3c19343u]; **331, 334, 336** Corbis; **338** (CL) Everett Collection Historical/Alamy, (TL) GL Archive/Alamy; **338** (TR) Library of Congress Prints and Photographs Division [LC-USZ62-75334]; **339, 343, 345** GL Archive/Alamy; **346** (CL) Sandra Sleight Brennan; **346, 350** (TL) GL Archive/Alamy; **346** (TR), **347, 349, 350** (CL) Library of Congress Prints and Photographs Division [LC-USZ62-75334]; **352** Missouri History Museum, St. Louis.; **353, 356, 358** Heritage Image Partnership Ltd/Alamy; **360** (CL) New York Times Co/Getty Images, (TL) fstockfoto/Shutterstock, (TR) National Archives/Getty Images; **361, 367, 369** fstockfoto/Shutterstock; **370** (CL) Jackie Mader/The Hechinger Report, (TL) fstockfoto/Shutterstock, (TR) National Archives/Getty Images; **371, 375, 376** National Archives/Getty Images; **378** (B) National Archives/Getty Images, (T) fstockfoto/Shutterstock; **383** (T) Herber W. Pelton/Corbis; **383** (B) Bettmann/Corbis; 383 (BC) Harold M. Lambert/ Lambert/Getty Images; **383** (C): Jack Delano Farm Security Administration/Office of War Information Black-and-White Negatives collection, Prints & Photographs Division, Library of Congress, LC-USF34-040837-D, (BC): Three Lions/Getty Images, (TC): Bettmann/ Corbis; **392** Spaces Images/Blend Images/Getty Images; **393** (B) George Burba/123RF, (BC) Marilyn Angel Wynn/Nativestock/Getty Images, (BCL) Pictorial Press Ltd/Alamy, (BCR) Ekaterina Fribus/Fotolia, (BL) Herbert Kratky/123RF, (BR) Anna Baburkina/Shutterstock, (T) Library of Congress, (C) Lake County Museum/Corbis, (BC) Underwood & Underwood/ Corbis, (CR) Joserpizarro/Fotolia; (TC) The Metropolitan Museum of Art./





R84

Art Resource, New York; (CTR) Alan Collins/123RF; (TC) Scott Rothstein/123RF; (TCL) Minnesota Historical Society/Corbis; (TL) FromOldBooks.org/Alamy; (TR) Everett Historical/Shutterstock; **396** Everett Historical/Shutterstock; **401** (B) Herbert Kratky/123RF, (BC) Pictorial Press Ltd/Alamy; (T) FromOldBooks.org/Alamy; 401 (TC) Minnesota Historical Society/Corbis; **402** (L) FromOldBooks.org/Alamy, (R) World History Archive/Alamy; (C) ClassicStock/Alamy; **403** (L) Everett Historical/Shutterstock, (R) Pictorial Press Ltd/Alamy; **404** (C) AF archive/Alamy, (L) Everett Historical/Shutterstock, (R) Everett Collection/Alamy; **405** (C) Kletr/Shutterstock, (L) Mary Evans Picture Library/Alamy, (R) Bettmann/Corbis; **406** (L) Minnesota Historical Society/Corbis, (R) Pictorial Press Ltd/Alamy; **407** Everett Historical/Shutterstock; **408, 414, 416** Minnesota Historical Society/Corbis; **418** (CL) Everett Historical/Shutterstock, (TL) Minnesota Historical Society/Corbis, (TR) Pictorial Press Ltd/Alamy; **419** Pictorial Press Ltd/Alamy; **423** Lebrecht; **426, 428** Pictorial Press Ltd/Alamy; **430** (B) Pictorial Press Ltd/Alamy, (T) Minnesota Historical Society/Corbis; **432** Bettmann/Corbis; **433, 444, 446, 448** Herbert Kratky/123RF; **439** Maor Winetrob/Shutterstock; **441** Andrei Orlov/123RF; **450** Everett Historical/Shutterstock; **459** (B) George Burba/123RF, (BC) Marilyn Angel Wynn/Nativestock/Getty Images; **459** (BCR) Library of Congress, (C) Lake County Museum/Corbis, (BC) Underwood & Underwood/Corbis; **459** (T) Scott Rothstein/123RF, (TC) The Metropolitan Museum of Art./Art Resource, New York; **462** (B) Ulf Andersen/Getty Images, (TL) Scott Rothstein/123RF, (TR) The Metropolitan Museum of Art./Art Resource, New York; **463, 469, 470** Scott Rothstein/123RF; **467** EdgeOfReason/Shutterstock; **472** (L) Scott Rothstein/123RF, (R) The Metropolitan Museum of Art./Art Resource, New York; **473** The Metropolitan Museum of Art./Art Resource, New York; **474** Reprinted with Permission of the Artist; **475** (B) Georgia Red Clay, 1946 (oil on canvas), Jones, Nell Choate (1879–1981)/Morris Museum of Art, Augusta, Georgia, USA/Morris Museum of Art, Augusta, Georgia/Bridgeman Art Library; **476** The Broncho Buster, 1895 (bronze with brown patina), Remington, Frederic (1861–1909)/Private Collection/Bridgeman Art Library; **477** The Metropolitan Museum of Art./Art Resource, New York; **478** (B) Scott Rothstein/123RF, (T) The Metropolitan Museum of Art./Art Resource, New York; **480** Historical/Corbis; **481** Lake County Museum/Corbis; **484** Hulton Archive/Getty Images; **488, 490** Lake County Museum/Corbis; **492** (L) Underwood & Underwood/Corbis, (R) Library of Congress; **493** AP Images; **494, 499, 500** Underwood & Underwood/Corbis; **496** Andamanec/Shutterstock; **497** AP Images; **502** (L) Underwood & Underwood/Corbis, (R) Library of Congress; **503** Library of Congress; **504** (B) Courtesy of the Chicago Historical Society, (T) Library of Congress, (B) Lewis Hine, photographer; **505** Lawrence, Geo. R/Library of Congress; **507** Library of Congress; **508** (B) Library of Congress, (T) Underwood & Underwood/Corbis; **510** (L) Marilyn Angel Wynn/Nativestock/Getty Images, (R) George Burba/123RF; **511** (B) Christopher Felver/Corbis, (T) Chris Felver/Getty Images; **512, 517, 519** Marilyn Angel Wynn/Nativestock/Getty Images; **514, 515** Maxriesgo/Shutterstock; **520** (B) Chris Felver/Archive Photos/Getty Images; **520** (R) George Burba/123RF, (TL) Marilyn Angel Wynn/Nativestock/Getty Images; **521, 527, 528** George Burba/123RF; **530** (B) George Burba/123RF, (T) Marilyn Angel Wynn/Nativestock/Getty Images; **535** (T): Alan Collins/123RF; (TC): Joserpizarro/Fotolia (B): Anna Baburkina/Shutterstock, (BC): Ekaterina Fribus/Fotolia; **544** Fred de Noyelle/Godong/Corbis; **545** (B) Patricia Verbruggen/123RF, (BC) Nuwatphoto/Shutterstock, (BL) Safakcakir/Shutterstock, (BR) Frederick Bass/fStop Images GmbH/Alamy, (CL) 20th Century-Fox Film Corp/Everett Collection, (CR) Jerry Pinkney/National Geographic Image Collection/Alamy, (T) William Fehr/123RF, (TC) Library of Congress Prints and Photographs Division [LC-DIG-ppprs-00286], (TL) Granger, NYC/Lebrecht Music & Arts, (TR) Lurin/Shutterstock; **548** William Fehr/123RF; **553** (BCL),( CR), (TL) 20th Century Fox Film Corp/Everett Collection, (BL) AF Archive/Alamy, (BR) Safakcakir/Shutterstock, (TR) Granger, NYC/Lebrecht Music & Arts, (CTL) 20th Century Fox Film Corp/Everett Collection; **554** (C) Jan Persson/JazzSign/Lebrecht Music & Arts, (L) Christopher Dodge/Fotolia, (R) JT Vintage/Glasshouse Images/Alamy; **555** (C) Historic Florida/Alamy, (L) Underwood Archives/The Image Works, (R) Granger, NYC/Lebrecht Music & Arts; **556** Imagemore Co., Ltd; **557** (CL) Underwood Archives/UIG Universal Images Group/Newscom, (CR) 3drenderings/Fotolia, (L) Al Muto/Bettmann/Corbis, (R) Everett Collection/Everett Collection Historical/Alamy; **558** Blend Images/Alamy; **560** AFP/Getty Images; **561** AFP/Getty Images; **562, 597, 601, 625, 626, 629, 647, 657 ,675 ,678, 680, 682, 684** 20th Century-Fox Film Corp/Everett Collection; **569, 574, 611, 616, 650, 653, 671** Twentieth Century Fox Film Corporation/Photofest; **577, 593** AF Archive/Alamy; **600** AFP/Getty Images; **607** Pocumtuck Valley Memorial Association, Deerfield MA. All rights reserved; **622, 660, 661** AF archive/Alamy; **686** (R), **690** (B) Safakcakir/Shutterstock, **686** (L), **690** (T) 20th Century-Fox Film Corp/Everett Collection; **687, 689** Safakcakir/Shutterstock; **692** William Fehr/123RF; **701** (B) Nuwatphoto/Shutterstock, (C) Television Academy Foundation; **701, 704, 705, 710, 713, 715, 720** (T) Library of Congress Prints and Photographs Division [LC-DIG-ppprs-00286]; **716** (BL) Bruce Glikas/FilmMagic/Getty Images, (L) Library of Congress Prints and Photographs Division [LC-DIG-ppprs-00286], (R) Television Academy Foundation; **717, 719, 720** (B) Television Academy Foundation; **723, 734, 736** Nuwatphoto/Shutterstock; **727** Catherine Karnow/Corbis; **741** (T): Lurin/Shutterstock, (BC): Frederick Bass/fStop Images GmbH/Alamy, (CT): Jerry Pinkney/National Geographic Image Collection/Alamy, (B): Patricia Verbruggen/123RF; **750** Sergey Nivens/Fotolia; **751** (BCL) World Pictures/Alamy, (BCR) Historical/Corbis, (BL) Classic Collection/Shotshop GmbH/Alamy, (BR) Joseph Shields/Getty Images, (CR) Galyna Andrushko/Shutterstock, (T) Hulton-Deutsch Collection/Historical/Corbis, (TC) Ximagination/123RF, (TCL) jam4travel/123RF, (TL) NASA; **754** Hulton-Deutsch Collection/Historical/Corbis; **759** (B) Classic Collection/Shotshop GmbH/Alamy, (BC) World Pictures/Alamy; **759** (T) NASA, (TC) jam4travel/123RF; **760** (C) Bettmann/Corbis, (L) H. Armstrong Roberts/ClassicStock/Alamy, (R) Everett Collection Historical/Alamy; **761** (C) NASA, (L) Bettmann/Corbis, (R) Wally McNamee/Historical/Corbis; **762** (L) Interfoto/History/Alamy, (R) Robert Maass/Corbis; **763** (CL) Jeremy Sutton Hibbert/REX/Newscom, (CR) PCN Photography/Alamy, (L) AP Images, (R) Library of Congress; **764** Brad Barket/Getty Images; **765, 772, 774, 776, 778** jam4travel/123RF; **771** Gabe Palmer/Alamy; **780** Sophie Bassouls/Sygma/Corbis; **781** World Pictures/Alamy; **782** Gordo25/Fotolia; **788, 790, 792** World Pictures/Alamy; 794 Ulf Andersen/Getty Images; **795, 802, 804, 806** Classic Collection/Shotshop GmbH/Alamy; **799** John Hanley/Shutterstock; **808** Hulton-Deutsch Collection/Historical/Corbis; **817, 821, 824, 826** Ximagination/123RF; **820** Max Meyer; **828** Bettmann/Corbis; **842** Bernard Gotfryd/Getty Images; **861** (TC): Galyna Andrushko/Shutterstock, (BC): Historical/Corbis, (B): Joseph Shields/Getty Images.

**Credits for Images in Interactive Student Edition Only**

**Unit 1**

Arthur Blaustein; B Christopher/Alamy; Bettmann/Corbis; De Agostini Picture Library/Getty Images; Everett Collection Historical/Alamy; Everett Collection Inc/Alamy; Nelosa/Shutterstock; Svetara /Shutterstock; Svetara/Shutterstock; © Helen Matatov

**Unit 2**

Arthur Mones/Brooklyn Museum/Corbis; Courtesy C-Span; Handout/KRT/Newscom; Jane Scherr; Lebrecht Music and Arts Photo Library/Alamy; Volodymyr Baleha/Shutterstock

**Unit 3**

Daily Hampshire Gazette, Kevin Gutting/AP Images; Hulton Archive/Getty Images; Konstantin Mironov/Shutterstock; Library of Congress Prints and Photographs Division [LC-3a10453u]; Library of Congress Prints and Photographs Division [LC-3c17943r]; Louis Menand; Melissa Tuckey; Mike Flippo/Shutterstock; Rob Kim/Getty Images for Hearst; Tetra Images/Corbis; ZUMA Press, Inc./Alamy; 2/Frank Krahmer/Ocean/Corbis

**Unit 4**

Anthony Barboza/Getty Images; Elena Akimova/123RF; Eric Schaal/The LIFE Picture Collection/Getty Images; Peter Turnley/Corbis; Richard Howard/The LIFE Images Collection/Getty Images; Scott McDermott/Corbis; Tanya Cofer

**Unit 5**

Akiko Busch; Beowulf Sheehan/ZUMA Press/Newscom; Keith Levit/Design Pics/Getty Images; Oscar White/Pach Brothers/Corbis; Wrangler/Shutterstock; © Craig Line

**Unit 6**

Chris Felver/Getty Images; Elise Amendola/AP Images; Everett Historical/Shutterstock; Peter Power/Getty Images.